ARTE CHICANO

ARTE CHICANO

A Comprehensive Annotated Bibliography
of Chicano Art, 1965-1981

Compiled by

Shifra M. Goldman

and

Tomás Ybarra-Frausto

with an introduction
by the compilers

679169

Chicano Studies Library Publications Unit
University of California, Berkeley
1985

CHICANO STUDIES LIBRARY PUBLICATIONS SERIES, NO. 11

Additional bibliographic citations contributed by the
Chicano Periodical Indexing Project.
Project Director and Manager of Chicano Database: Lillian Castillo-Speed

Published by
Chicano Studies Library Publications Unit
3404 Dwinelle Hall
University of California, Berkeley
Berkeley, CA 94720

Editor-in-Chief: Francisco García-Ayvens

Managing Editor: Lillian Castillo-Speed

Production Manager: Carolyn Soto

Cover Design: Rupert Garcia

Library of Congress Cataloging-in-Publication Data

Goldman, Shifra M., 1926-
    Arte Chicano.

    (Chicano Studies Library publications series ;
no. 11)
    Includes indexes.
    Mexican American arts--Bibliography.
2. Ethnic arts--United States--Bibliography.
I. Ybarra-Frausto, Tomás, 1938-   II. Title.
III. Series.
Z5961.U5G64 1985   016.704'036872073   85-29156
[NX512.3M4]
ISBN 0-918520-09-6 (pbk.)

ACKNOWLEDGEMENTS

The people and groups who have helped us over the years are too many to acknowledge here. We hope the unmentioned will accept our grateful thanks. However, we do wish to acknowledge persons and institutions who have contributed substantially to our efforts.

First and foremost we wish to thank Francisco García-Ayvens, former coordinator of the Chicano Studies Library, University of California, Berkeley; Lillian Castillo-Speed, the present coordinator of the Chicano Studies Library; and members of her staff, Carolyn Soto, Joseph Anthony Gonzales, Kyung-Hee Choi, and Vivian Thomas, for the dedication, untiring effort, and encouragement which made this bibliography possible. Also of great help were Richard Chabran, Chicano Studies Research Center Library, UCLA; Christine Marin, Chicano Studies Collection, Arizona State University, Tempe; Laura Gutierrez-Witt, Director of the Nettie Lee Benson Latin American Collection, University of Texas at Austin; Elvira Chavaria, former librarian of the Mexican-American Studies Collection, University of Texas at Austin; Orlando Romero, History Department Librarian, Museum of New Mexico, Santa Fe; Robert Trujillo, Curator of Chicano Collections, Stanford University; Evelyn Escatiola and Linda Chavez of the Chicano Resource Center, East Los Angeles Library; and finally, the Chicano Resource Center at California State University, Fullerton.

Organizations and groups (by state) who put their archives at our disposal include: (ARIZONA) Louis LeRoy, former National Endowment for the Arts Regional Representative, Movimiento Artistico del Rio Salado (MARS) of Phoenix (Roberto Buitron, former Director); (CALIFORNIA) Galeria de la Raza, San Francisco (Maria Vita Pinedo, Archivist), The Mexican Museum, San Francisco (Peter Rodriguez, former Director), Centro Cultural de la Raza, San Diego (Veronica Enrique, Executive Director), Casa de la Raza, Santa Barbara (Manuel Unzueta and Armando Vallejo), Self-Help Graphics and Art, Inc., Los Angeles (Sister Karen Boccalero), the Royal Chicano Air Force (RCAF), Sacramento, La Brocha del Valle, Fresno (Ernesto Palomino), Artistas Latinos de Orange County, Los Four, Los Angeles (Gilbert Sanchez Lujan), ASCO, Los Angeles (Harry Gamboa, Jr.); (MICHIGAN) Nuestras Artes de Michigan (with special thanks to Nora Mendoza, Jose Narezo, and Jesse Gonzales), the former Raza Art and Media Collective, Ann Arbor (Ana Cardona); (NEW MEXICO) Museum of Fine Arts, Santa Fe, Santa Fe Council for the Arts (Suzanne Jamison), La Cofradia de Artes y Artesanos Hispanicos (Frederico Vigil and Pola Lopez de Jaramillo), Santuario de Guadalupe of Santa Fe (Virginia Castellano, Director); (TEXAS) the League of United Chicano Artists (LUCHA), Austin, the former Ladrones de la Luz, San Antonio (David Cardenas and Kathy Vargas), the Witte Memorial Museum, San Antonio, Xochil Art Institute, Mission (Xavier Gorena and Enrique C. Flores), Nuevo Santander Museum, Laredo (with special thanks to Marilyn de King); (WASHINGTON) Evergreen Galleries, The Evergreen State College of Olympia (Sid White and Pat Matheny-White).

Individuals who provided regional archival materials include Jose Gonzalez (Chicago), Cecilio Garcia-Camarillo (Albuquerque), Jesus Salvador Treviño (Los Angeles), Ray Atilano of the former Mechicano Art Center (Los Angeles), Santa Barraza (Austin), Salvador Roberto Torres (San Diego), Carlos Santistevan (Denver), Mary Meadows (Denver), Manuel Martinez (Morrison, CO), Rupert Garcia (Oakland, CA), Leo Tanguma (formerly of Houston), and Mel Casas (San Antonio). We must mention that many individual artists provided us with materials about their own work, and, although their names may not be included above, we express here our appreciation.

Finally, we wish to thank the following persons who provided valuable criticism of the draft for the introduction "Revelando la imagen/Revealing the Image": Mario Barrera, Richard Griswold del Castillo, Keith McElroy, Renato Rosaldo, Victor Sorell, and Jesus Salvador Treviño.

PREFACE

There are many compelling reasons for the creation of a reference work such as *ARTE CHICANO*. The compilers, in the course of creating chronologies, writing critical or historical articles, preparing lectures, and guiding research in the field of Chicano Art, have found an increasing need for an organized reference tool in this area. Such a tool would indicate how and where to locate materials on the broad questions of Chicano art, and on specific material like dates, places, artists, techniques, exhibits, etc. Though we both have extensive personal archives, which are reflected in this bibliography, the materials were not systematically organized or cross-referenced. Our first beneficiaries, we concluded, would be ourselves! However, we also realized that this largely unresearched area could be tremendously expanded, and, in so doing, a national community of researchers in many disciplines would be served.

This bibliography is not exhaustive, however it includes as much material as we could discover (working since 1978 as independent researchers, without funding, institutional support, or much clerical help) about the major states in the United States in which enclaves of artists have created work. Beginning, therefore, with our own archives, we compiled citations from Chicano libraries, museum libraries and archives, gallery and organizational archives, and, finally, collections of individual artists. We undertook to examine and annotate books, theses, newspapers, magazines, journals, newsletters, catalogs, unpublished materials, invitations to exhibitions, and other ephemeral documentation. We also felt that, for the visual arts, knowledge of the published reproduction of portfolios or single works of art, not necessarily accompanied by text, would also be an indispensable resource, and we have noted where such reproductions can be found.

We found that the sheer quantity of material, frequently printed in alternative and little-known publications (which were not and may still not be indexed) and in local and regional newspapers; the dearth of books on the subject under investigation; and the disinterest of academic libraries (with the exception of Chicano Studies libraries) in collecting alternative magazines and newspapers, or art catalogs when such were produced, has made for a bibliography which required an extraordinary amount of travel and examination of archives often indifferently organized. Thus the research and annotation have not always been as systematic or as complete as the compilers would have liked. Nevertheless, as the only such bibliography in existence, it is, by default, the most complete, and the compilers view it as an important first step toward filling an enormous vacuum. Furthermore, we anticipate and welcome not only corrections in the data, but all substantive additions which might be incorporated into the database annually. Moreover, obedient to the necessity of terminating at some arbitrary date in order to complete the task, we have included writings only through the year 1981.

CONTENTS
INTRODUCTION

CONTENTS
BIBLIOGRAPHY OF CHICANO ART, 1965-1981

Introduction

I. REVELANDO LA IMAGEN/REVEALING THE IMAGE

The making of a work of art is one historical process among many other acts, events and structures - it is a series of actions in but also on history.

T.J. Clark[1]

Correctly viewed, the arts should be considered a means of communication and emotional engagement, as well as aesthetic satisfaction, or, more accurately stated, as an effective means of communication precisely *because* they engage the recipient on the levels of emotion and aesthetic appeal, levels often missing in the conveyance of information by journalism and the social sciences. This fact has been widely recognized by organizations and groups struggling for liberation in Third World countries, and by the governments of those nations that have emerged victorious in these struggles. Post-revolutionary nations stress not only universal literacy but also the arts, understanding the important role played by culture with the simultaneous advancement of economic programs and the structuring of political power. Liberation is achieved not only militarily and politically, but also intellectually and psychologically. Thereby culture - which includes in its broadest definitions "behavior, lifestyles, habits, collective representations, beliefs and values[2] which are projected and reflected in the arts and in mass media - is understood to express and affect consciousness. Consciousness, in its turn, shapes the actions and vision of human beings who undertake to determine their own destiny.

As is well known, the Chicano political movement of the 1960s generated a groundswell of artistic production: literature, theatre, film, dance, music, song, and the visual arts. With the exception of literature, however, this production has been inadequately documented and analyzed. One "litmus test" can be applied by surveying the number of existing cultural bibliographies, or bibliographic entries in general compilations, that make reference to the performing and visual arts. It quickly becomes apparent that only one such publication exists: Jorge Huerta's *A Bibliography of Chicano and Mexican Dance, Drama and Music,* published in 1972 and now outdated by more than a decade.[3] No comparable compilation exists for the visual arts, a vacuum which we hope to fill with the present volume. Parenthetically, it should be noted that the whole field of counter-culture in the United States during the 1960s and 1970s has been inadequately documented though the area of "engaged art" from the social art produced under the New Deal to the present is a growing field of interest.

Bibliographies, Resources, Methodologies

In discussing compilations of Chicano materials, Ray Padilla in "Apuntes para la documentación de la cultura chicana"[4] suggests that bibliographies appearing in the middle and late sixties treated themes that were important in that decade: education; the "minorities melting pot" theory; and Chicano reaction to distortions of all kinds by scholars subscribing

[1] T.J. Clark, *Image of the People: Gustave Courbet and the Second French Republic 1848-1851.* Greenwich, CT: New York Graphic Society Ltd., 1973, p. 13.

[2] Maurice Duverger quoted in Armand Mattelart, *Transnationals and the Third World: The Struggle for Culture,* translated by David Buxton. South Hadley, MA: Bergin & Garvey, 1983, p. 9.

[3] Jorge Huerta, *A Bibliography of Chicano and Mexican Dance, Drama and Music.* Oxnard, CA: Colegio Quetzalcoatl, 1972.

[4] Ray Padilla, "Apuntes para la documentación de la cultura chicana," *El Grito: A Journal of Contemporary Mexican-American Thought,* Vol. 5, no. 2 (Winter 1971-72), p. 26-27.

to views of the Chicano held by the dominant society. With the rise of the Chicano movement, which challenged previous assumptions and stereotypes, more Chicano-oriented bibliographies were produced in three or four years, says Padilla, than in the previous three or four decades. Generally speaking, most Chicano bibliographies were dedicated to history and the social sciences, with cultural citations oriented toward education and bilingualism. As the cultural expression of the Chicano movement came into focus in the 1970s, the fine arts began to be included as part of what Padilla calls a "complex pattern" of interests.

Literature was the first area to "break out" of general listings into special interest bibliographies. Because of its ready availability in published form, literature has been the most consistently tracked and compiled in bibliographies of various sorts. By the same token, literary (and theoretical) criticism has been more available than criticism of other forms, since the writers themselves often undertook critical roles.

Concerning entries on the visual arts in general bibliographies, the only area of extensive inclusion over a lengthy period of time has been that pertaining to the colonial and modern production of what has variously been called "Hispanic crafts" or the "popular arts and folklore" of the "Spanish" Southwest. Many articles and books that have appeared from the 1920s to the present document secular and mission architecture and religious and domestic handicrafts. Almost unknown, however, until the 1973 appearance of Jacinto Quirarte's book *Mexican American Artists,*[5] has been the artistic production of fine artists working in the 20th century. Information about popular or commercial artists such as caricaturists, cartoonists, illustrators, studio and newspaper photographers, theatrical and filmic scene painters, sign painters, muralists and decorators of stores, restaurants, saloons and bars, and graphic designers - some of whom also worked in the area of fine arts - is almost totally lacking. The history of women artists must also be retrieved from oblivion; only the most rudimentary research has been carried out. Preliminary investigations reveal that important nuggets of artistic history concerning the fine, popular, and commercial arts exist in many places: local and regional libraries and museums; in the archives of historical societies; in the New Deal archives located in Washington, D.C., and in numbers of catalogs, books and unpublished theses on the New Deal period. Books, catalogs, bibliographies and dictionaries of Western art have yet to be mined for Spanish-surnamed artists of Mexican descent, and followed back to original sources in local periodicals and documentary depositories. Spanish language periodicals must be systematically scanned for artistic production within their pages, as well as for announcements of exhibits. The heroic task of excavating this information has barely begun. Nevertheless, we cannot say that the history of Mexican American and Chicano art has been definitively articulated until these sources have been explored and added to the existing information about the colonial and post-colonial art production of the Southwest.

The Chicano Time Frame

Chicano art, seen within the context of Mexican and Mexican-descent peoples of the southwest United States, is simply the most contemporaneous expression of a long cultural history. Definitions of the term "Chicano," and a suggested periodization for the consideration of Mexican American and Chicano culture, follow below. Suffice it to indicate here that this bibliography deals primarily with the most recent phase of that culture, and with its visual expression in the arts and in film. This phase is characterized by three exceptional facts: (1) that the economic, political and social movement was paralleled by an artistic movement that can truly be called national in scope, not only geographically, but often through conceptual, thematic and stylistic cohesiveness, (2) that the Chicano movement coincided in time with reform and liberation movements of many peoples within and without the United States which forced recognition of its existence by publications which previously had tended to ignore or disparage the movements (3) that the Chicano movement was born at a time when the importance of communication as an international shaper of ideology and events was

---

[5] Jacinto Quirarte, *Mexican American Artists.* Austin, TX: University of Texas Press, 1973.

coming to the forefront of consciousness. As a result, the movement itself, both political and artistic, early recognized the imperative of establishing press and publication houses. Thus it could write its own history and disseminate its own culture in contrast, or in opposition to the press and publications of the dominant society. The newspapers, magazines, and journals that emerged were a richly nurturing medium in which fledgling writers and artists of the new national movement could try their wings, and maturing artists and writers could be recognized much before their acceptance by the dominant cultural institutions. These interlocking facts led to a further fact: as alternative organizations and collectives developed within the Chicano movement, the importance of receiving public recognition in the dominant press, and the importance of maintaining archives of published materials of all sorts were emphasized. The power of communication in the age of universal television and the global transmission of information and visual imagery via satellite might not have been perceived consciously by all groups that accumulated archives of material, but they were part of the *zeitgeist* of the 1960s and 1970s, a kind of subliminal "archival consciousness," so to speak, with one eye on the media and the other on history. Commenting on the role media has played in the last half century and the changed perception of media by social organizations, Todd Gitlin had the following to say in his book *The Whole World is Watching:*

> Since the advent of radio broadcasting half a century ago, social movements have organized, campaigned, and formed their social identities on a floodlit social terrain. The economic concentration of the media and their speed and efficiency in spreading news and telling stories have combined to produce a new situation for movements seeking to change the order of society.
>
> ...In a floodlit society, it becomes extremely difficult, perhaps unimaginable, for an opposition movement *to define itself and its world view, to build up an infrastructure of self-generated cultural institutions, outside the dominant culture* (emphasis ours).[6]

If the Chicano political/economic movement sought media attention for boycotts and demonstrations, the artistic world looked to newspapers and magazines (reporters, art critics, and art historians) for media attention. This was particularly true at that point in time when artists began to move away from public art (the street mural and the store window or telephone-pole-mounted poster serving as community "newspapers" for the dissemination of meanings) toward private gallery/museum/collector art. Media assured public attention, attendance at artistic events, possible sales, validation, and (historical) fame. The paradox for the Chicano movement, as for other oppositional movements, is the dependence on dominant institutions like the media for making public statements of meaning about their activities when, as Gitlin points out, they "have no voice in what the media make of what they say or do, or in the context within which the media frame their activity."[7]

The most institutional expression of the "archival consciousness" was the struggle to create Chicano Studies libraries in major universities and in colleges. The "oasis" nature of these libraries, for published materials and for ephemera, is strikingly demonstrated when a search for Chicano-related materials has to be made in any traditional academic library.

Pioneering Publications

One of the earliest historical publications on Mexican American art of the 19th and 20th centuries was Jacinto Quirarte's article "The Art of Mexican-America," published by the Humble Oil & Refining Company of Houston, Texas.[8] This article set up the schema for his

---

[6] Todd Gitlin, *The Whole World is Watching: Mass Media in the Making and Unmaking of the New Left.* Berkeley, CA: University of California Press, 1980, p. 1,3.

[7] *Ibid.*

[8] Jacinto Quirarte, "The Art of Mexican-America," *Humble Oil and Refining Co. [Houston, TX], Second Quarter,* Vol. 9, no. 2 (1970), p. 2-9.

1973 book *Mexican American Artists,* which remains, as of this writing, the only historical book on the subject. Its importance lies in the fact that it identified a body of work from the Southwest that had never been integrated into the story of U.S. art. Quirarte's history begins with the continuing northerly expansion of the Spanish empire in the New World into an area that conflicted with, and was eventually absorbed (as a result of the Mexican American War) into a westward expansionist thrust of the Anglo United States. The ongoing influence of Mexican art in this region is pointed out and artists are presented in generational groupings. The Quirarte book is essentially pre-Chicano, although some of the artists mentioned in the more recent time frame identified themselves with the Chicano movement.

The unfolding of the rich panorama known as Chicano art does not begin until the mid-1960s, and becomes an identifiable national movement with shared concepts and iconography in the decade of the 1970s. Possibly the earliest comprehensive compilation recognizing and documenting this phenomenon is *Chicano Art of the Southwest,* a color slide library with accompanying documentation, essays, and artist biographies. Photographed by San Antonio artist Cesar Augusto Martinez, who had traveled the southwestern United States for two years meeting with Chicano artists, the original slide collection comprised over a thousand works, of which 220 were divided into five categories for dissemination: La Familia, Folklore, Social Commentary, Religion, and Images of the Barrio. It was initiated by the Instituto Chicano de Artes y Artesanias, the cultural component of the Texas Institute for Educational Development, San Antonio, and was for sale to public schools, universities, libraries and other institutions in 1975. Though *Chicano Art of the Southwest* was preceded by the inclusion of Mexican American art works in the 1972 slide collection of the Ethnic American Art Slide Library of the University of South Alabama in Mobile, the latter collection was not only much smaller and without educational materials, but, more importantly, it lacked the sense of a *movement* which infused the Texas collection. "Chicano art," says the brochure issued by the Instituto Chicano, "emerged from the Chicano movement which gained visibility during the middle sixties and continues today. Chicano art touches upon all aspects of Chicano life. It is a means for exploring and defining Chicano culture and raising the consciousness of the people."

A third, and much less-widely circulated compilation, was Patricia Rodriguez's *Selected Readings on Chicano Art,* a 1977 photocopied production of published articles by the Chicano Studies Program at the University of California, Berkeley. This still unpublished compilation remains the most comprehensive reader available on Chicano art; its updating and publication with a lengthy introductory essay and preliminary remarks for each of its divisions would be a highly desirable undertaking for an interested publishing house. The Reader is divided into nine categories: 1) Mexican Muralists in the U.S., 2) Views on Chicano Art, 3) Chicano Artists, 4) Pinto (prisoner) Art, 5) Raza Murals and Muralists, 6) Plaqueasos (graffiti), 7) Chicana Artists, 8) Art Politics and the Community, 9) Two Historical Examples: Cuba and Chile. The information is national in scope, and the organization of the readings establish the influences, social concerns, and variety of ideas within the movement.

The establishment of Chicano libraries brought an important new resource: the publication of the *Chicano Periodical Index (ChPI)*[9] which accessed alternative publications to scholars. It is in the pages of *ChPI* that the first substantial references to the Chicano visual arts became available. However, even *ChPI* was limited in its scope by the parameters of its own sources: materials published by and for Chicanos. We are happy to note that the third edition of *ChPI* is being expanded to include citations from mainstream as well as Chicano journals.

---

[9] *Chicano Periodical Index (ChPI).* Boston, MA: G.K. Hall & Co., 1981 and 1983.

II. OUTLINE OF A THEORETICAL MODEL
FOR THE STUDY OF CHICANO ART

THEORIES AND DEFINITIONS

...the striving for an inward pattern of a culture is the projection in a social group of the strivings for security and identity of the individuals who compose it....What maintains a culture is access to an environment adequate to its survival and subsistence and shelter, and freedom from outside constraints on its own forms of value, ritual, art belief, feelings and institutional behavior.

Ernesto Galarza[10]

Theories

Ernesto Galarza, highly respected scholar, poet, lecturer, and teacher, has provided an excellent, if pessimistic, paradigm within which to view the emergence of the Chicano movement as a recent phase of Mexican American history. Galarza argues that since the 1800s throughout the American Southwest, to which he sardonically refers as the "Mexican Northwest,"[11] the institutions of Mexican colonialism such as pueblos, presidios, missions, and ranchos, were destroyed or reduced to relics by the second conquest of Mesoamerican history, that of the United States over the Mexican borderlands. This destruction stripped the early settlers (and conquerors of the Indians) of their lands. As a result, says Galarza, Mexican people of the Southwest have no land base as part of their system of identification and, since they have no base, they have not been able to prevent slow erosion of the inward process of culture. The immigrants who headed north from 1910 to 1940 came at a time when agribusiness was laying its foundations, and the basis of small-family farming (which immigrant Mexicans could afford), was gradually yielding to agribusiness. Mexicans, therefore, settled in rural *colonias* where they formed the proletariat for large Anglo ranching and agricultural enterprises and, after 1940, they joined the general exodus to the cities where they settled in urban *barrios*. Both *colonias* and *barrios* developed in marginal and undesirable areas, and formed "cores of poverty" in which Mexican culture had its polarization and configuration.

According to Galarza, Mexicans of the Southwest are located in the five states of California, Arizona, New Mexico, Colorado, and Texas. Within these states there are seven fairly discernable regional groupings: San Francisco Bay basin, metropolitan Los Angeles, the Central Valley of California, the Salt River Valley of Arizona, the upper Rio Grande Valley of New Mexico and Colorado, and a less-defined area centering in Denver and Texas. The eighth area, which affects all the others, is the Border Belt. Cities that form the pivots of seven of these areas are San Jose, Fresno, Phoenix, Denver, Albuquerque, and San Antonio. The Border Belt has no center: it is a narrow stretch of desert some 1800 miles long between Brownsville and Tijuana - on both sides of an imaginary line called the "frontier" - as "drawn by treaty, ignored by nature, transgressed by men [sic]."[12] To this demography, pertinent in the early 1970s, must now be added the growing clusters of Mexican population in the Midwest, particularly Illinois, Indiana, and Michigan; and the Pacific Northwest, with a center in Seattle. In cultural terms, all the areas mentioned, and many more cities, have

---

[10] Ernesto Galarza, "Mexicans in the Southwest: A Culture in Process," in *Plural Society in the Southwest*, edited by Edward H. Spicer and Raymond H. Thompson. New York: Interbook, Inc., 1972, p. 264-265.

[11] *Ibid.*, p. 271.

[12] *Ibid.*, p. 266-267.

developed centers or galleries, as a perusal of our prefatory acknowledgements will quickly verify. Since 1981, even the Border Belt has been under intense international scholarly scrutiny conducted by the University of California Consortium on Mexico and the United States (known as UC MEXUS) in collaboration with the Consortium of Research Programs for Mexico. This has led to annual publication of the *International Inventory of Current Mexico-Related Research*.[13] In addition, the University of Texas at El Paso has established the Center for Interamerican and Border Studies. Increasingly, artists and writers are developing a more acute "border consciousness," and promoting cultural interchanges, particularly in the border cities of San Diego/Tijuana and El Paso/Juarez. Beyond this, descendents of Mexicans as well as new arrivals have fanned out to most of the industrial and farming states of the East in more thinly populated configurations. The new Chicano professional and artistic middle class can also be found in cities like New York and Washington, D.C. where opportunities for individual advancement and employment in their respective disciplines are seen as more favorable than in the West.

The colonias and barrios in which Mexicans settled, have been physically marked out for destruction, says Galarza, by the constant pressure of Anglo "progress, political requirements, suburbanism, planning, and primitivism in sociological perception" - in other words, by the destructive power of the dominant society. Galarza, from his vantage point in the early 1970s, despaired that the relics of Mexican culture allowed to survive by the dominant society can continue to do so in the face of disintegrating pressures. With the destruction of communities where these cultural processes found a base, he felt these residues would yield to acculturation. His only feeling of (qualified) hope was in what he called "the cultural reactivity of Mexicans" which was beginning to act in response to the containment being practiced by the dominant society. The search for identity, which is a prime factor of this reaction, is most dramatically heard among the "young avant garde," that is, by the Chicanos. Through combatting stereotypes, reinterpreting history, challenging the dominant media with alternative publications and demanding Chicano presence in dominant institutions; through education, political and economic action, and, finally, through cultural manifestations, there is hope that Mexican culture - certainly transformed and transfigured by intercultural exchange both nationally and internationally - can continue to have a vital life in the United States. It is possible that Galarza's view of culture is too static. Any diminution of attributes directly derived from Mexico of the early 20th century is considered deterioration, though he recognizes that the Mexico of that era has passed into history. Young Chicanos, he says, "want to go home again" to regain the humanism and cultural identity they feel they have lost, "but if they do, they will find that Mexico, too, is on the way to becoming a land of precision, profit, and conformity," the very characteristics to which *chicanismo* stood in opposition. Today Mexico is far along the path to dependent industrial capitalism; its middle and upper classes look to the United States for living standards, consumerism, and life styles at the same time that U.S. "materialism" is rhetorically disdained. The young "avant garde" of Mexico has assumed a critical stance vis-a-vis the failed promises of the Mexican Revolution, and its members were astonished in the late 1970s to realize that the Chicano avant garde was nostalgically glorifying aspects of Mexican culture which the Mexicans themselves had long since brought under questioning scrutiny.[14]

---

[13] Wayne A. Cornelius and Ricardo Anzaldua (eds.), *International Inventory of Current Mexico-Related Research*. San Diego, CA: University of California Consortium on Mexico and the United States (UC MEXUS), and the Consortium of U.S. Research Programs for Mexico (PROFMEX). The first volume appeared in Spring 1982.

[14] This point was made by Mexican artist Felipe Ehrenberg in 1983 at a round table discussion accompanying the Mexican-sponsored art exhibit *A traves de la frontera* organized by the Centro de Estudios Economicos y Sociales del Tercer Mundo. Galarza himself points out in "Mexicans in the Southwest," p. 288, that "the worship of Zapata [by Chicanos] has become more the end of a pilgrimage than the beginning of a search for the historical forces that lie behind such tragic symbols like his."

It is true that Mexicans living in the United States begin to lose their national/cultural identities within one or two generations, beginning with the Spanish language. This has resulted from a triple process: the extreme pressures exerted on language and culture by the dominant society; the assimilation accompanying the shift from rural colonias to barrios in big cities and the move out of cohesive barrios forced by Anglo destruction; and finally, by upward social mobility which has been on the rise since the 1970s for a selected group.

Dominant society pressures on culture have included the prohibition of Spanish language usage on school campuses, the Eurocentricity of education, the anglicizing of given names, and a host of other signals suggesting to children at an early age the inferiority of the Mexican culture. The move to big cities has meant the loss of community (marginal though it was in the colonias) and support structures in the forced commingling with a broad spectrum of non-Mexican, often prejudiced, neighbors. The romantic idealizing of the Pachuco by the Chicano movement, symbolically recognizes this double process: cultural loss of the Mexican, acquisition of the North American, with full integration and acceptance by neither. It is no accident that the Pachuco phenomenon occurred in the early 1940s, the transitional period between rural and urban existence for Mexican families moving from Mexico to the United States, from one part of the Southwest to another, or out of the Southwest entirely. The image of the Pachuco remains the metaphor for the loss of one identity and the formation of another and, correspondingly, is being deeply explored by contemporary Chicano artists and writers for its multilevels of significance.

An increased pace of upward social mobility for a small, youthful, talented segment of the Mexican American community resulted from the militancy of the political movement in the 1960s, and the temporary acquiescence of the dominant society faced by obvious fractures in the democratic facade. The brief burst of extraordinary activity on the political and economic fronts, within the context of the general upheavals of dissident "minorities" (Blacks, youth, women, Chicanos, Native Americans, gays) that marked the decade, forced a number of concessions from the establishment - many of which were eroded in the late 1970s and 1980s. Following a dynamic which seems to be peculiarly North American, the Chicano cultural movement began with a working class thrust, and has "graduated" to a middle class orientation directed toward success with mainstream publishing houses, commercial film, mainstream museums, private galleries, and private collectors, with understandable loss of social protest content.

To re-engage once more Galarza's despair about the vanishing relics of Mexican culture within the U.S. paradigm, the late sixties and the decade of the seventies have proved that ethnic identity and its cultural manifestations are more resistant than this despair predicted. The search for identity, a primordial imperative in the struggle for self-determination, began with the already mentioned challenge by Chicano scholarship to the distortions and stereotypes held by the dominant society. In a recent study, Stanford University anthropologist Renato Rosaldo sets up a history of the initial assault and subsequent critiques and corrections made by Chicano social scientists concerning such stereotypes.[15] Rosaldo points out that in a series of papers from 1968 to 1970, anthropologist Octavio Romano-V and sociologist Nick C. Vaca, editors of the Chicano journal *El Grito,* stridently attacked previous writings by Anglo anthropologists for negative stereotyping: an attack which influenced a generation of graduate students and set up new terms of debate for Chicano Studies in the coming decade. The thrust of Romano's criticism was that the victims were blamed for their own victimization both by former victims who had raised themselves out of poverty and by society in general. Social scientific notions about Chicanos, said Romano and Vaca, reflected institutional racism and forms of domination prevailing in society. In 1978 anthropologist Americo Paredes, in a reasoned and modulated posture that was ultimately "more devastating [but also] more constructive" according to Rosaldo, pointed out that Anglo ethnographers "erred

---

[15] Renato Rosaldo, "Chicano Studies, 1970-1984," *Annual Review of Anthropology,* Vol. 14 (1985), p. 405-427.

less in overt prejudice than in the more subtle (and therefore more pernicious) unconscious perpetration of stereotypes."[16] Paredes suggested that such ethnographers need to hone their grasp of the Spanish language, arrive at a finer understanding of social relations, develop a richer sense of social context, and consider their own ethnicity and class affiliation (the dominant ones) when dealing with a subordinate culture. In other words, Paredes links cultural performance with power relations. Going beyond critique, Paredes establishes a theory of culture eschewing crude idealist and materialist theories which, on one hand, remove cultural formations from the political and economic factors that condition them or, on the other hand, reduce all interests to socioeconomic factors. In Paredes' analysis, culture neither determines all human behavior nor dissolves into the economic base. In recent anthropology, says Rosaldo, the critical stance faces in two directions: looking inward at the discipline which had developed through colonizing traditions and looking outward toward Anglo American society for analysis and critique of dominant perspectives and institutions. For the future, argues Rosaldo, the studies of Jose E. Limon which fruitfully combine symbolic anthropology and Marxian analysis, are especially creative. In this scholar's view, each aspect of folklore should be examined in its own social/cultural context, within the social circumstances of a given period.

Why so much concern with anthropology in an art historical model? We think the inclusion is justifiable. Just as it has been argued that pre-Columbian art history would benefit from closer alignment with social sciences in the same field,[17] so we would argue that contemporary art history, especially that of the Chicano, can learn much from, as well as adding important dimensions to, closer alignment with modern social science. The cultural theories of Paredes, Limon, and others can be broadly and beneficially applied to the study of the visual arts. At the same time, we can look afield for theoretical models established by scholars treating culture among other Latino groups. For example, in summarizing the Puerto Rican experience in the United States, Felix Cortes, Angel Falcon, and Juan Flores[18] address the relationship between "the culture of the subject classes" and that of the dominant culture. They argue that the migrant Puerto Rican population, in New York specifically, has changed its situation from a national setting and a movement of national independence, to one in which the subject class is composed of a variety of nationalities, causing the context of Puerto Rican cultural experience to change accordingly. "In the United States," they say, "the cultural life of Puerto Ricans is defined increasingly with other national sections of the working class." From a primarily national perspective, mixing Puerto Rican culture with strains of other national traditions must invariably be considered a degradation and betrayal of the national ideal. However, from the vantage point of the working class, the blending of Puerto Rican culture with other cultural traditions is an "appropriate expression of social reality."[19] Indeed, they argue, within the complex of interacting elements of existing cultures, the cultural expression of Puerto Ricans migrating to the United States represents an unfolding expansion and enrichment of what has been known historically as the culture of Puerto Rico. The authors warn against both a defensive "fear of assimilation," on the one hand, and cultural nostalgia, on the other.

In references to the latter point, it should be pointed out that in the Chicano experience, cultural nostalgia - which was expressed as separatist cultural nationalism in the early years of the movement - has tended to lead in the arts to the dead end of ethnic exotica. Chicanos, like Puerto Ricans, also subsist in what Edward H. Spicer has called a "plural society,"[20] and

16 *Ibid.*

17 Cecelia F. Klein, "Arte precolombino y ciencias sociales," *Plural,* Segunda epoca, 9-4, no. 124 (Jan. 1982), p. 40-48.

18 Felix Cortes, Angel Falcon, and Juan Flores, "The Cultural Expression of Puerto Ricans in New York: A Theoretical Perspective and Critical Review," *Latin American Perspectives,* Issue 10, Vol. 3, no. 3 (Summer 1976), p. 117-152.

19 *Ibid.,* p. 121.

20 Spicer and Thompson (eds.), *Plural Society in the Southwest.*

Rosaldo warns us that this concept stands as a reminder that Chicanos cannot be understood in isolation. Even further, it has been amply clear that Chicano artists, particularly muralists, have always worked within multiethnic and multicultural contexts, and have networked with numerous groupings throughout the years. The clearest confirmation of this collaboration and interchange is documented in the pages of *Community Murals Magazine* which covers, among other things, the national conferences that have taken place since the mid-1970s, and in the new lengthy publication by Alan Barnett, *Community Murals: The People's Art,* as well as the older pioneering book *Toward a People's Art.*[21]

At the same time that Chicano artists have created internal infrastructures to support and disseminate the expressions of their own culture, they have worked with, formed alliances with, and learned from other groups: Latin Americans from many countries, Blacks, Asians, and progressive whites. This has been most pronounced in cosmopolitan areas like the San Francisco Bay cities, and in Chicago, though national and international networking has been a growing phenomenon since the late 1970s. The "fear of assimilation," raised as a problem by Galarza, can be seen today in a different light. It is not a question of assimilation, pure and simple, that offers the great threat, but of assimilation with *what* and with *whom* and toward what end. The dominant "national culture" of the North American bourgeoisie, say Cortez, Falcon, and Flores,

> includes an entire wardrobe specially tailored for its local Puerto Rican clientele....
> In fact, an indispensable device of imperialist control constitutes precisely cultural
> amalgamation, that is, enforced subordination and assimilation of the colonial cul-
> ture to the modes and standards of that more 'civilized' culture of the oppressing
> nation.[22]

To the degree that Chicano artists resisted imperialist control by charting a course in opposition to the cultural "norms" of the dominant society, they resisted assimilation within the dominant culture. While maintaining the most positive elements of Mexican national culture, they freely borrowed and adapted cultural input from many sources. This amalgam, as elaborated in the 1970s, has been in a healthy process of evolution. It has produced new vigorous and valid forms of culture.

---

[21] Alan W. Barnet, *Community Murals: The People's Art.* Philadelphia, PA: The Art Alliance Press, 1984; Eva Cockcroft, John Weber, and Jim Cockcroft, *Toward a People's Art: The Contemporary Mural Movement.* New York: E.P. Dutton & Co., 1977.

[22] Felix Cortes et al., "The Cultural Expressions of Puerto Ricans in New York," p. 121.

Definitions

In order to discuss a model for a social history of Chicano art, it is, perhaps, best to begin by defining the term "Chicano" and the term "art history," not etymologically but historically and socially. "Chicano" is one of a long series of designations which peoples of Mexican descent living within the present boundaries of the United States have chosen for themselves, as distinguished from numbers of appelations (sometimes pejorative) they have been assigned by the dominant culture. Tino Villanueva has written a very complete exploration of the term in the prologue of *Chicanos: Antologia historica y literaria.*[23] In his explanation, the original use of the word "Chicano" referred to a newly arrived undocumented Mexican worker, while the word "pocho" referred to a Mexican born in the United States or of long established residence in the country and therefore more "assimilated" to the English language and U.S. customs. The "Chicano" was classified into an inferior category because he was a migratory worker who had to move from job to job in order to stay alive. In his autobiographical book *Barrio Boy,* Ernesto Galarza uses the term "Chicano" in this sense, adding that it was a term of sympathy and identity among persons of this class.[24] Obviously, by the 1960s, the term had been variously used in different contexts, but it still retained negative and working class connotations among Mexican Americans, many of whom considered "Chicanos" to be "low class."

The term was consciously assumed and aggressively popularized in the mid-1960s by young people articulating their frustration at what they considered traditional style politics in the Mexican American community. It was given a militant political and Indian-oriented connotation (associating it with the word "Aztlan," which situated the mythical home of the Aztecs in the U.S. Southwest) as a title of pride and new consciousness. The militant significance of the term "Chicano" was perhaps most cogently expressed in brief form by Texas artist and curator Santos Martinez, Jr: "Chicano - a Mexican American involved in a socio-political struggle to create a relevant, contemporary and revolutionary consciousness as a means of accelerating social change and actualizing an autonomous cultural reality among other Americans of Mexican descent. To call oneself Chicano is an overt political act."[25] Like many of the artistic and cultural icons and symbols developed during the height of *chicanismo* (the mid-sixties through the mid-seventies), the word "Chicano" served to unify the movement nationally. It was also used interchangeably with "La Raza" - literally "the race" but meaning "our people" - which was used on a social level to indicate solidarity between all peoples of Spanish and Portuguese America.

Parenthetically, the validity and vitality of the term "Chicano" may not endure beyond the generation that adopted it, and some of its younger followers. Contemporary observers are noting (so far, impressionistically) that younger generations are reverting back to "Mexican" or "Mexican American" as a self-designation or, under institutional pressure from the dominant society, to the homogenizing term "Hispanic" which has become a convenient handle by which government and corporations refer to all people of Latin American descent living in the United States, particularly the largest groupings of Mexicans, Puerto Ricans, and Cubans. According to historian Rodolfo Acuña, the Nixon administration consolidated Latin Americans into a national minority called "Hispanic" in order to manage them more easily.[26]

---

[23] Tino Villanueva, *Chicanos: Antologia historica y literaria.* Mexico: Fondo de Cultura Economica, 1980.

[24] Ernesto Galarza, *Barrio Boy.* New York: Ballantine Books, 1971, p. 265.

[25] Contemporary Arts Museum, Houston, Texas, *Dale Gas/Give It Gas: The Continued Acceleration of Chicano Art.* Houston, TX: Contemporary Arts Museum, 1977.

[26] Rodolfo F. Acuña, *A Community Under Siege: A Chronicle of Chicanos East of the Los Angeles River, 1945-1975.* Los Angeles, CA: Chicano Studies Research Center Publications, University of California, Los Angeles, p. 180.

Certainly the term "Hispanic" has none of the warmth and comradeship implied in the word "raza;" not only does it leave out the Indian and Black presence in the Americas, but it is an imposed rather than a self-designation. The term "Latino" used by many Chicanos as an English equivalent of "raza" may not be wholly satisfactory but it has the virtue of being self-chosen.

In its pristine condition, the discipline of "art history" for much of the 20th century has been formalist in nature - the manner in which it has been and is yet taught in educational establishments. In other words, art history has been concerned largely with questions of "style" and the linear inheritance of Euro-American vanguardism as the norm of excellence and importance for the international world of art. The formalist ideology, established as a paradigm for "modernism" by the writings of English critics Roger Fry and Clive Bell in the early 20th century and canonized in the United States in the post World War II period by critic Clement Greenberg (among others), effectively downgraded representational art and meaning in the work of art as matters for practice, discussion or interest. Because of this emphasis, modern Mexican art (so influential in the United States during the 1930s and 1940s), regionalist art, and social realist art influenced by the Mexicans, were essentially written out of art history. But the blackout was not a matter solely determined by internal art practices. The depoliticalization of intellectuals as early as 1939, the onset of the Cold War and the U.S. search for world economic and cultural hegemony in the late 1940s, and the rabid anti-communism of McCarthyism in the 1950s, made any art of social comment, criticism, or progressive advocacy suspect and open to attack as "literary," "anecdotal," or "propagandistic" - in other words, art not to be taken seriously.[27] Pioneer Chicano artists attending art schools in the 1950s and 1960s found themselves confronted and discouraged by the formalist concerns of their teachers which seemed so irrelevant to their experiences and aspirations.[28]

Beyond the question of discouragement, however, was the almost absolute absence of any information on the formidable contributions to modern art of the revolutionary Mexican School: its forerunners like Jose Guadalupe Posada who has been of primary importance to the Chicano art movement; its progenitors, Diego Rivera, Jose Clemente Orozco, and David Alfaro Siqueiros, all of whom painted in the United States during the 1930s; and its successor, the Taller de Grafica Popular (Popular Graphic Art Workshop) which formed the print component of Mexican public art forms. As a result, Mexican art was largely unknown to the generations born after 1940, and had to be rediscovered in the Chicano period. Even the history of pre-Columbian art arrived late on the scene and was relegated to second class citizenship. Until the late sixties the visual objects of ancient Mesoamerica were primarily taught at the university level by anthropologists and archeologists; art historians trained in this area did not begin to appear in any numbers until the late 1960s.[29] Even so, the field of Mesoamerican antiquities was the stepchild of antiquities studies in general. For example, as of 1978, the prestigious art history journal *The Art Bulletin* had published only two articles on pre-Columbian art in the previous twenty years. Compounding the problem was the designation of pre-Columbian art in the category of "primitive" despite the fact that much of the art had

[27] For the most complete examination of this process, see Serge Guilbaut, *How New York Stole the Idea of Modern Art: Abstract Expressionism, Freedom, and the Cold War,* translated by Arthur Goldhammer. Chicago, IL: The University of Chicago Press, 1983; Max Kozloff, "American Painting During the Cold War," *Artforum,* Vol. 11, no. 9 (May 1973), p. 43-54. For the U.S. search for cultural hegemony in Latin America, see Eva Cockcroft, "Abstract Expressionism, Weapon of the Cold War," *Artforum,* Vol. 12, no. 10 (June 1974), p. 39-41; and Shifra M. Goldman, *Contemporary Mexican Painting in a Time of Change.* Austin, TX: University of Texas Press, 1983, p. 29-35.

[28] For example, Chicano artists in the San Francisco Bay Area attended the San Francisco Art Institute (then the California School of Fine Arts) which was dominated from 1946 to 1950 by abstract expressionists, and whose director covered over the Diego Rivera mural painted in 1931 (it has since been uncovered) as incompatible with the new vangardism. Abstraction dominated the Bay Area to the late fifties. See Peter Plagens, *Sunshine Muse: Contemporary Art on the West Coast.* New York: Praeger, 1974, p. 31-45.

[29] Cecelia Klein argues that the necessity for Pre-Columbian art historians arose when a significant market arose for the artifacts in the United States. See Klein, "Arte precolombino y ciencias sociales," p. 45.

been produced by high civilizations which developed their own systems of astronomy, mathematics, and hieroglyphics; had an advanced calendrical system; complex religious, social, and class structures; and a sophisticated urban development. The category "primitive," with its implicit suggestions of "crude," "unsophisticated," and "inferior," has been used to establish a hierarchy of antiquities that is European biased. Art of Old World societies like Egypt and Mesopotamia are considered "civilized" and "historical" according to the linear history developed in art textbooks which show a developmental sequence from the Near East, Rome, and Western Europe, while new World antiquities (as well as those of Black Africa) are designated "primitive." Egypt influenced Greece; Rome learned from the Greeks; and the West took its standards from the Greco-Roman. Within this paradigm, the Indian cultures of the New World - lumping together the tribal society with those of the city-state - have occupied a secondary order of importance and, as a result, the implication that theirs was a culture and art of lesser quality. One can understand the effect of this hierarchization and its implications for Chicano artists bent on the recovery of their non-European origins.

Actually, the recognition and reevaluation of pre-Columbian culture is intimately tied to the emergence of the Mexican School of art in the early 20th century. While the discovery and excavation of isolated Mesoamerican sites predate this century, it was the Mexican Revolution of 1910 and its cultural-nationalist renaissance that generated the revised evaluation of pre-Columbian art and artifacts, including the village folk arts that had survived (with numerous adaptations) from the pre-conquest period.[30] Mexican cultural nationalism sought to bring all sections of the community (including the isolated Indian villagers) into national life. The elite, including the artists, sought, in the indigenous peoples and in folk culture, the values they had previously accepted from Europe.[31] When the Chicano movement projected its own neo-indigenism, in the 1960s, it signified equally a rejection of European (i.e. U.S. Anglo) values. Chicanos were speaking as *mestizos,* not just of Spanish-Mesoamerican Indian mingling, but of a *mestizaje* between Mexicans and North American Indian peoples, expressed in New Mexico today as Indo-Hispano. As a consequence of the foregoing, any treatment of Chicano art history during the last fifteen years would have to take into consideration the conjunction of historical patterns attendant not only upon the emergence of the Chicano political movement, but of the ideological differences and conflicts within the realm of art history itself which affected aesthetic and conceptual formulations for hundreds of aspiring and maturing Chicano artists. In other words, choices had to be made by the artists. These concerned not only the needs of various political and social organizations which they served or organized, but the thematic emphasis, the style, and the artistic techniques which were to express a Chicano world view, a Chicano ethic, and a Chicano aesthetic, if such existed. Should Chicano art be realistic or abstract? Should Chicano artists study the regulation European and North American art history, or should they erase these influences from their consciousness? Should they look to Latin American prototypes? Should all Chicano art be political and didactic, or could it also deal with personal concerns and with poetic evocations? Should Chicano artists deal only with Chicano subject matter? How should color be used? How line, texture, design? Were there materials specifically Chicano that could be incorporated into art as signs of identity - materials like tortillas, menudo bones, feathers, chiles, parts of low-rider cars as sculpture, *papel picado* (cut paper), etc.? Should works be

---

30 Romantic glorifications of indigenism existed prior to the 1910 Mexican Revolution--during the late eighteenth century and through the 1810-1820 independence period by a creole elite which saw its best interests in separation from Spain, and looked for American models as symbols. See John Leddy Phelan, "Neo-Aztecism in the Eighteenth Century and the Genesis of Mexican Nationalism," in Stanley Diamond (ed.), *Culture in History: Essays in Honor of Paul Radin.* New York: Columbia University Press, 1960, p. 760-777. (We are indebted to Cecelia Klein for bringing this article to our attention). During the late decadent phase of the Porfiriato, the Diaz regime assigned funds for archeological research and publications, as long as scholars did not discuss the plight of living Indians. See Benjamin Keen, *The Aztec Image in Western Thought.* New Brunswick, NJ: Rutgers University Press, 1971, p. 417.

31 Jean Franco, *The Modern Culture of Latin America: Society and the Artist,* (revised edition). Harmondsworth, England: Penguin Books, 1970, p. 84-85.

expressionistic and dramatic like that of the Mexicans, or could other emotional modes be used? Should filmmakers use the Hollywood aesthetic systems or should other styles and visual languages be sought? At later stages, discussions raged about symbols that had become cliches, or symbols that were not pertinent to Chicano reality but were uncritically borrowed from Mexico. Should Chicanos go on painting cactus, eagles, pyramids, Virgins of Guadalupe, Zapatas, and brown fists? Perhaps the motifs were a valid and important aspect of the Mexican ethnic experience, but could they be varied, presented in new configurations, expanded in meaning, linked with new precepts? What should be the relation of the Chicano artist to the dominant society? To the mainstream art world? Even to mainstream art practices and styles? Should filmmakers continue to use the existing channels of film and TV dissemination or should they create independent structures that would permit more artistic and philosophical freedom? As women artists became an important presence in the later 1970s, new questions arose. What were the unique qualities of a woman's expression? Can women paint murals? (Some were doing just that in the early 1970s.) Or is theirs a more intimate art? Who would be their role model? It is in the second half of the 1970s that Mexican painter Frida Kahlo became an important symbol for both the feminist art movement in the United States and for Chicano artists. For Chicanas, Frida Kahlo was not only an inspiration and a role model to whom they paid homage, but an example that gave validity to the possibility of rendering a woman's most intimate and domestic concerns in the language of visual art. The same art history that had excluded Mexican artists had also excluded women, and therefore required renovation. Chicanas reconsidered the domestic arts and crafts of their female ancestors: the collection and utilization of bric-a-brac, the making and adornment of altars, the production of weavings and other handicrafts (especially in New Mexico), and so forth.

Defining "Chicano art" meant redefining contemporary art history and criticism. The task was carried out by the artists themselves in manifestos and discussions; by writers active in literature who turned their talents on occasion toward art criticism; and by a small number of trained art historians and critics who saw the importance of the Chicano art movement and undertook to record and analyze it, sometimes in local, sometimes in national, and sometimes in international perspective.

CHRONOLOGY

In presenting the chronological portion of this theoretical outline, we wish to emphasize that the periodization and the possible subdivisions suggested here are tentative. In fact we feel that the present state of research precludes setting up a definitive structure, since any art historical structure must be closely tied to historical facts, social formations, movements of peoples, realities and mythologies (of the dominant and the domineered society), clash of cultures and ideologies, and so forth, and the art forms which arise in these specific contexts. Lacking this research, our outline leans heavily on models created by Chicano historians. However, cultural formations respond to different rhythms, being part of ideological and communicative structures which can change either more rapidly or more slowly than social events, and take shorter or longer periods of time both to develop and be superceded. The periodization that we have adopted, therefore, reflects the divisions found useful by historians, tempered by what the present state of research reveals about artistic developments. In addition, since the focus of the bibliography is Chicano art, a relatively contemporary phenomenon, we have weighted our model in the direction of modern art. As will readily be seen, the periods from 1598 to 1821 and 1821-1910 are of extreme brevity. Our focus is the 20th century, the era of modern art, with an emphasis on the contemporary, or Chicano period. There was a conscious decision in the compilation of the bibliographical materials to restrict ourselves to citations concerning artists and art activities functioning in the contemporary period, beginning approximately 1965. However, we felt it necessary to set forth, at least in a schematic way, earlier history that establishes the framework for the modern period. Our periodization, as it is presently outlined, consists of the following:

1598 to 1821 - The First Conquest: Settlement and Colonization

1821 to 1910 - Mexican Independence, the Second Conquest,
                  Mexican American Resistance

1910 to 1965 - The Mexican American Period

1965 to 1981 - The Chicano Period

1598 - 1821
The First Conquest: Settlement and Colonization

From 1521 to 1821, New Spain (Mexico) was under Spanish rule. Cortes' quick defeat of the Aztecs created an illusion of superiority over the Indians. This subjugation proved to be the prelude of a far longer military struggle against the Indian peoples of the northern area (called the Chichimeca) which lasted from 1550 to 1590.[32] During the course of this conquest, exploratory parties were sent into what is now the U.S. West, particularly New Mexico, Texas, and California. However, actual settlement did not occur until 1598 with the Juan de Oñate expedition which, poaching on the Indians, set up a series of settlements and missions in New Mexico. These were extinguished during the 1680 Pueblo Revolt, in which the Pan-Indian group engineering the revolt was joined by mestizo (mixed blood) rebels and drove the Spaniards out of Santa Fe.[33] Twelve years later the settlements were reestablished. As E. Boyd points out, present knowledge of domestic architecture and artifacts can only be based on 18th century production, since those of the 17th century were destroyed by the revolt. However, New Mexicans continued to repeat 16th century forms, as has been ascertained through archeological excavations.[34]

The major institutional forms that appeared in the 1598 to 1821 time frame were the *entrada* or military expedition, the *presidio* or military outpost, the missions, which combined religion and ideological dissemination, and the *pueblos* or civilian settlements. During the three hundred years of expansion and colonization, these institutions underwent many changes. They existed until the end of the colonial era, and some persisted in modified form during the early post independence period.[35]

The most significant aesthetic achievement was the construction of the mission complexes and civic architecture in the northern borderlands, utilizing Indian labor. Nevertheless, despite the benign view we have of the missions and the missionaries in the romanticized visions of North American art, they were actually used as a vehicle for deculturalization, Hispanization, and exploitation of Indian labor, through peonage and slavery. Cruelty was integral to their policy.[36] Indians were the laborers and the artisans, and formed the basis of mission wealth, which later passed to the ranches established by land grants after the secularization of the missions by the newly independent Mexican nation in the 19th century.

Ecclesiastical, civic, and domestic architecture were based on Spanish prototypes fused with elements from native building traditions. The result was a functional organic architecture. An example of the fusion between European and Indian means and materials in New Mexico was the use by the settlers of the Indian adobe techniques, which were changed from the native puddling (pouring in layers) to that of making mud and straw bricks in wooden frames. At the same time the Indians also learned measurements, the construction of windows and doors, and the use of European iron tools.

Spanish city planning also provided the prototype for pueblo layout. The city of Santa Fe, New Mexico, begun in 1609, was based on detailed plans sent from Spain. There was to be a large central plaza, with a palace-fort on one side and the church on an adjacent side.

---

[32] Philip Wayne Powell, *Soldiers, Indians, & Silver: North America's First Frontier War.* Tempe, AZ: Arizona State University, 1975, p. vii.

[33] Jack D. Forbes, "Analco: The Birthplace of the Chicano," in Jack D. Forbes (ed.), *Aztecas del Norte: The Chicanos of Aztlan.* Greenwich, CT: Fawcett Publications, Inc., 1973, p. 72-76.

[34] Hall, Elizabeth Boyd (White), *Popular Arts of Spanish New Mexico.* Santa Fe, NM: Museum of New Mexico Press, 1974, p. 2-3.

[35] Juan Gomez Quiñones, *Development of the Mexican Working Class North of the Rio Bravo: Work and Culture Among Laborers and Artisans, 1600-1900.* Los Angeles, CA: Chicano Studies Research Center Publications, University of California, Los Angeles, 1982, p. 7.

[36] *Ibid.,* p. 11.

Thus the three aspects of Spanish rule - civilian administration, the military, and the church - were linked spatially as well as politically. Private houses were also constructed on the Spanish plan. Built around the central patio were the few rooms used by the family. They were made of adobe, the walls finished with a smooth coating of adobe mud inside and out. Room sizes and spaces were dictated by the length of the vigas, or logs, placed at regularly spaced intervals to form roofs. Wood was used for doors, windows, and frames, and occasionally floors were covered with thin stone slabs. With the exception of the house layout, the Spaniards limited themselves to simply improving on the logical Indian practices.[37]

As the mestizo population in the borderlands established more permanent communities, fusions of Indo-Hispanic elements, especially in the upper Rio Grande, defined much of the craft production. During the 18th century the metal tools and weapons, the horses, the fruit and crops introduced by the Spaniards, wrought profound changes in what was known of New Mexican Indian Pueblo life. At the same time the settlers learned from the Indians to live with the earth and use its materials for artistic production: clays, earth colors for paint, dyes, etc. (This closeness and interchange persist to this day, and are being revived in contemporary consciousness by the descendents of both groups, not only in New Mexico, but in other states of the Southwest with a large Indian presence.)

By 1692, the Camino Real, a network of roads stretching from Mexico City to the borderlands, had been established. There was a northward though insufficient flow of ecclesiastical and domestic goods, tools, and artifacts which, for a period of time, served to set standards in the settlements. By the 17th century as well, a system of trade fairs dispersed goods from the New Mexico colonies southward.[38] Local artisans, finding inspiration in the artifacts from the Mexican interior, produced their own, circumscribed by local materials and their own skills. Thus developed the famous production in New Mexico of *santos* (images of saints and other holy personages): the *retablos,* or painted altarscreens, and the *bultos,* or carved images. The earliest *retablo* identified was painted about 1625[39] and the legend persists of a statue of Our Lady taken to El Paso del Norte by the refugees from the Pueblo Revolt in 1680. In the area of textiles, the Spaniards were impressed by the skills with which the Pueblo Indian weavers made cotton clothing. Cotton was eventually discontinued in favor of wool from the sheep brought in by the Spaniards, and by 1776, colonial clothing was made of dyed woolen homespun using Indian spinning methods, Spanish looms, and Indian and Spanish dyes. Saintmaking and weaving, however, reached their peak in New Mexico after 1830, and will be considered in more detail in the next section.

---

[37] Trent Elwood Sanford, *The Architecture of the Southwest: Indian, Spanish, American.* Westport, CT: Greenwood Press, 1971, p. 91-93.

[38] Santa Barbara Museum of Art (California), *The Saltillo Sarape.* 1978, p. 23.

[39] Boyd, *Popular Arts of Spanish New Mexico,* p. 327.

1821 marks the establishment of the independent Mexican nation, after which the peripheral territories suffer (benign?) neglect by the central authorities in Mexico City. This led to secessionist ideas (which actually took place in 1836 in Texas) and also to the invigoration of local artistic and artesanal production in the borderlands to compensate for the dwindling flow of goods from the center. Mexico's capitalist policies opened the door for the borderlands to trade with other countries, especially the United States.[40] Forced to be self-reliant, interprovincial trade routes emerged. In 1829 the Old Spanish Trail linked Los Angeles with Santa Fe. After Mexican independence, the Santa Fe Trail (established 1822) led to markets in the eastern United States.

In New Mexico, artisanry established during the colonial period, flourished. There the church had been a source of initial employment and inspiration; Spanish priests established the models for the first santos, and retablos were first produced for the church and later for private use. The *santeros* who made the religious objects (retablos and bultos) were specialists of status.[41] After the arrival of the French-born Bishop John Lamy in 1851, who frowned upon the local santero production and had plaster religious images imported, the flagellant order of Los Hermanos Penitentes (the Penitent Brothers) - which had been verbally condemned by the Church as early as 1833 and now suffered new repression - became a major patron for traditional religious artifacts which they used for the *moradas* (chapter houses), as well as a haven for Hispano culture in the face of official Catholic disapproval. The development of New Mexico/southern Colorado production of religious and domestic artifacts reaches an apex between 1821 and 1860. After that there is an influx of Anglo industrially produced products with the extension of the railroad into what, after the Mexican American War and the 1848 Treaty of Guadalupe Hidalgo, would then comprise the Southwest United States. By the 1890s, this artesanal production was in decline due to decreasing demand, until it was rediscovered in the 1920s by a new wave of Anglo artists moving into northern New Mexico who "revived" the older colonial arts.[42]

In southern California, where the secularization of the missions in 1833 opened up their large prosperous lands, which had been worked with Indian labor, to ownership by the upper class through land grants, ranch-oriented artisanship became important. The social structure of the *Californios* resembled that of the Deep South: the upper class was the plantation owners, Indians were the slaves, and the Mexicans were the artisans, *vaqueros* (cowboys) and majordomos of the ranches, and the craftsmen of the small towns.[43] Saddlery and leatherwork were well known craft products until the 1860s, when the industries passed into the hands of Anglo entrepreneurs who profited from Mexican skills.[44] In addition, the wealthy Californios - including not only ranchers but merchants and government officials - must have given employment to artisans not only in leather, but in silver which trimmed the horse equipage and the male costume, as well as to dressmakers for the imported silks and laces of the women.[45] The mythology of the *charro,* the elegantly and expensively festooned horseman

[40] E.A. Mares, "Hispanic Humanities Resources of New Mexico," in *Hispanics and the Humanities in the Southwest: A Directory of Resources,* edited by F. Arturo Rosales and David William Foster. Tempe, AZ: Center for Latin American Studies, Arizona State University, 1983, p. 178.

[41] Gomez-Quiñones, *Development of the Mexican Working Class,* p. 28.

[42] Charles L. Briggs, *The Wood Carvers of Cordova, New Mexico: Social Dimensions of an Artistic "Revival".* Knoxville, TN: The University of Tennessee Press, 1980, p. 44-53.

[43] Carey McWilliams, *North From Mexico: The Spanish-Speaking People of the United States.* New York: Greenwood Press, 1968, p. 90.

[44] Gomez-Quiñones, *Development of the Mexican Working Class,* p. 30.

[45] Arthur L. Campa, *Hispanic Culture in the Southwest.* Norman, OK: University of Oklahoma Press, 1979, p. 96.

who is the prototype for the contemporary charro groups of middle and upper class elements of Mexican American and Anglo society, should be contrasted with the working vaquero, who was much less elaborately attired. (Whether a similar ranch artisanship arose in Texas cattle country, and to what extent, is a question still to be explored.) If New Mexico, southern Colorado, and California seem to predominate in art, artisanship, and architecture, this is based on the pattern of Spanish settlement in the borderlands which consisted of a firmly rooted colony in New Mexico, an easily held and fairly prosperous chain of missions in coastal California, and a number of feebly garrisoned, constantly imperiled settlements in eastern and central Texas and in Arizona.[46]

The situation, however, was far different along the southern Texas border, in the area known as Nuevo Santander. After Mexican independence, large land grants were parceled out to government favorites, and increasing Mexican migration continued throughout the period of Texas independence (1836-1846) and U.S. occupation, up to 1910. In the Lower Rio Grande Valley, a way of life developed similar to what had prevailed in early California: large Mexican landholdings based on a system of Mexican-Indian peonage. The landowners and vaqueros were mestizo. Landowners built square, flat-roofed homes, usually of stone, furnished with luxury items imported from Mexico.

From the 1860s, the rapid growth of towns in southern, central and western Texas brought a need for skilled artisans: stone masons, furniture repairers, silversmiths, tinsmiths, and blacksmiths who made both ornamental and utilitarian ironwork. Many were construction workers, building Spanish-style town and ranch homes for affluent southern and western Texans. As Arnoldo De Leon has pointed out, much more study into the role these craftsmen played in the civilization of southern and western Texas remains to be done.[47] Another area that needs investigation is the development, from the 1850s to the 1890s, of various types of fiestas, and the *artesania* (crafts) necessary to carry on these activities. Patriotic Mexican holidays as well as U.S. holidays were celebrated. The artesania included richly trimmed clothing and horse furniture, decorated floats with costumed historical personages, and all kinds of souvenirs like ceramics, needlework, and skins. One lesser holiday commemorated June 24, 1520 when Hernando Cortes reentered the Aztec capital Tenochtitlan. "Attired in gaudy costumes redolent of the times, the characters acted out Aztec roles of authority. Finally they circled the national pyramid, a pole artistically decorated with ribbons of three colors."[48]

By the 1820s there was massive Anglo immigration into borderland territories, encouraged by central Mexican policy, eventually transforming the Mexican majority in some areas into a minority. In Texas and in post Civil War Arizona the Anglo population came primarily from the Deep South, and brought with it a rooted racism against all dark-skinned peoples. Arizona was made into a "white buffer state" between Anglos and the Spanish-speaking people of New Mexico and Sonora, Mexico. Thus until the industrialization of Arizona attracted many Mexican immigrants in later years, Indians were a more important cultural influence than the Spanish-speaking.[49] Anglo racism in Texas, which started much earlier and accompanied Black slavery in Texas, is a prejudice that persisted, and caused Texas to be considered one of the most discriminatory against Mexicans of all the southwestern states.

---

[46] McWilliams, *North From Mexico*, p. 261.

[47] Arnoldo De Leon, *The Tejano Community, 1836-1900.* Albuquerque, NM: University of New Mexico Press, 1982.

[48] *Ibid.*, p. 178-182 passim.

[49] McWilliams, *North From Mexico*, p. 83.

The Second Conquest: The Land and the Railroads

Affecting all the Southwest economically, politically, and culturally, was the passage of the 1851 Land Act, hard on the heels of the 1848 northern California Gold Rush, which immediately followed the signing of the Treaty of Guadalupe Hidalgo. The Land Act effectively stripped the Californios of their land grants and the Gold Rush brought thousands of migrants into northern California. By the 1870s the coming of the transcontinental railroad into southern California brought a land boom and another population explosion, and by the 1880s, Anglos had numerical dominance in the south. The Hispanic impact on culture became increasingly marginal.[50] The impoverishment of the California Mexicans brought women into the labor market.

The railroad affected Mexican culture in other areas of the Southwest. Between 1870 and the early 1900s, rail lines extended throughout Texas and caused an economic transformation in New Mexico where the importation of mass-produced statues and of imported lithographs and chromoliths had, since the 1850s, displaced the local manufacture of wooden figures and painted altarscreens. The arrival of the railroad in the last decades of the 19th century virtually amounted to a *coup de grace*.[51]

The Culture of Resistance

As dismal as the prospects seemed, however, Mexican culture in the Southwest was far from being dislodged by Anglo penetration. The culture of a conquered people is very persistent, though it undergoes permutation. Both upper class culture and village colonial culture declined in the domain of the visual arts. These are the hardest art forms to maintain in face of conquest and physical displacement of their users compared to, for example, language, song, dance, story telling, and even theatre, which are more portable. Thereafter, more personal types of folk culture remained active. As ready mentioned, fiestas continued to utilize crafts. Various aspects of folk Catholicism called forth visual artifacts for the decoration of public and home altars (a rich domain for women which persists into the present and has strongly influenced Chicano artists of both sexes). Funerary processions and grave decoration required visual materials.[52] Finally, the cult of the *curandero* (folk healer) Don Pedrito Jaramillo in southern Texas (c. 1880-1905) gave rise to numbers of plaster statues for home altars quite outside the province of the institutional church. Both *curanderismo* and Don Pedrito have had important resonances in Texan Chicano art.

---

[50] Carlos E. Cortes, "Hispanics and the Humanities in California," in *Hispanics and the Humanities in the Southwest*, p. 70-71.

[51] Briggs, *The Wood Carvers of Cordova, New Mexico*, p. 29.

[52] Photographs of grave decorations in Texas were included in the exhibit *Un encuentro sin palabras*, organized by MAS (Mujeres Artistas del Suroeste) and held at the Doughtery Cultural Arts Center in Austin, 1980.

Displaced by the military phase of the Mexican Revolution (1910-1917) and continuing up to 1930, millions of Mexicans migrated north, many settling in the marginal *colonias* of the Southwest. The "north from Mexico" immigration produced a xenophobic nativism among Anglo-Americans during a period which witnessed one of the largest mass movements of people in history.[53] The movement occurred in a period which included World War I, the expansion of mining and railroads, the demise of small farmers and the growth of agribusiness, and a series of recessions and depressions culminating in the "Great Depression" of the 1930s. Mexicans comprised a large army of reserve labor for Anglo employers who wanted low wage workers who would return to their native land when they finished their work. Working not only in agriculture in the Southwest and Pacific Northwest, but supplying a need for industrial labor during the shortage of labor caused by World War I, Mexicans were persuaded to enter the United States through the easing of U.S. immigration laws. Many reached midwestern cities like Chicago, Kansas City, and Gary, Indiana. However, during periods of economic depression, thousands were deported. This form of labor exploitation becomes a recurring social pattern.

In the exodus of Mexicans during and after the revolution were artists and photographers as well as many skilled artisans such as weavers, ironworkers, and furniture makers. The new arrivals reinforced folk cultural practices such as altar making, the creation of Christmas *nacimientos* (creches), the elaboration of costumes and masks for *pastorelas* (nativity mystery plays), and the traditional clothing and ensembles for communal rituals like the *Conchero* and *Matachin* dances. The latter derive from syncretic historical and religious customs in which the dancers see themselves as the "soldiers of Christ and the Conquest" *(Concheros)* deriving from a miraculous conversion of Chichimec Indians in 1531, and appear in extremely elaborate costumes and headdress using feathers, mirrors, beadwork, embroidery, and leatherwork. The *Matachines* appear as "soldiers of the Virgin" in white shirts with red ribbons, crowns with colored flowers, lined capes, and masks. The *Conchero* dancers originated in central Mexico; the *Matachines* among the Yaqui, Mayo and Tarahumara Indians of Sonora. Both groups participate in religious festivals in different areas of the U.S. Southwest, as well as Mexico. Chicano artist Rogelio Ruiz Valdovin of Tucson has continued the tradition in the 1970s with a feathered and painted version of a costume dedicated to the Aztec emperor Cuauhtemoc which resembles the brilliant assemblages presently in use by the Mexican *Concheros.*[54]

Other aspects of Mexican popular arts were similarly adapted to the local conditions of the *colonias* and *barrios.* A certain number of illustrators and caricaturists found employment with Spanish-language newspapers like *La Prensa* of San Antonio and *La Opinion* of Los Angeles in which *chistes* (jokes) and caricatures dealt with predominantly political issues from the conservative viewpoint of the publisher.[55] Artists decorated local restaurants and *cantinas* (bars) using motifs and styles related to the early 20th century *pulqueria* murals of Mexico which had been painted by self-taught artists in working class *pulque* bars; and with the romanticized interpretations of Mexican myth and history deriving from *almanaques*

---

[53] Rodolfo Acuña, *Occupied America: A History of Chicanos* (2nd edition). New York: Harper & Row, 1981, p. 123.

[54] For details about the *Conchero* and *Matachin* groups in Mexico see Frances Toor, *A Treasury of Mexican Folkways.* New York: Crown Publishers, 1947, 1979, p. 323-330 and 336-337. Also see *The Laredo Times,* (December 9, 1980), front page, for a photograph of contemporary *Matachines* in procession. Ruiz Valdovin's costume appears in *Raices antiguas/Visiones nuevas: Ancient Roots/New Visions,* Tucson, AZ: Tucson Museum of Art, 1977-78, p. 28.

[55] Mario T. Garcia, "Chistes and Caricatures in the Mexican American Press, Los Angeles 1926-1927," *Studies in Latin American Popular Culture,* Vol. 1 (1982), p. 74-90.

(calendars) which were freely distributed to the customers of small *colonia* and *barrio* shops.[56]
These calendars were assembled by local printers using imported chromolith reproductions
designed for this trade in Mexico, and were saved and displayed in households like the later
Chicano posters. Many Chicano murals of the 1970s similarly show the influence of the
mythologized subjects and glamourized styles of these calendars which are still ubiquitous in
Mexican American communities.

The 1920s and the "Fantasy Heritage"

> Colonialism is not satisfied merely with holding a people in its grip and emptying
> the native's brain of all form and content. By a kind of perverted logic, it turns to
> the past of the oppressed people, and distorts, disfigures, and destroys it.[57]

Opposition to Mexican immigration crystallized in the 1920s when U.S. nativists oppos-
ing entry not only to Mexicans, but to Asians, and Europeans from southern and eastern
Europe (the "racially inferior" areas), caused passage of the Immigration Act of 1921. The act
started a battle between the nativists who wanted to keep the country "Anglo American" and
the capitalists who needed low cost workers and wanted a free flow of Mexican labor.[58] Paradoxically, this is the same period which saw the emergence in many Southwest communities
of what Carey McWilliams has dubbed "the fantasy heritage," the Hispanization of Southwest
history and culture which so deeply permeated the social and cultural life of the borderlands
that it began to assume the proportions of a "schizophrenic mania."[59] "Spanish" fiestas blossomed in Los Angeles, Santa Barbara, Tucson, and other cities, featuring parades with dash-
ing *caballeros* on richly caparisoned horses, *senoritas* in Hollywoodesque versions of aristo-
cratic Spanish attire, "Spanish" food and drink (suspiciously Mexican), *flamenco* guitars, and
the rhythm of castanets - a fantasy heritage indeed! The periodic trotting out of Mexican
names to participate with civic committees served a dual purpose: the appearance of a Latin
American presence; and the knowledge that the Spanish-surnamed person will act in the same
manner as the Anglos who really determine policy. "Thus the dichotomy which exists in the
borderlands between what is 'Spanish' and what is 'Mexican' is a functional, not an ornamental arrangement. Its function is to deprive the Mexicans of their heritage and to keep them in
their place."[60]

Anglo entrepreneurs were not long in seeing the lucrative prospects of the fantasy heritage. In the sunbelt cities (Tucson, Los Angeles, Santa Fe, San Antonio) the traditional Mexican populations as well as the Indian populations served as picturesque props for the tourist
businesses, promoted by the transportation industries and local Chambers of Commerce. In
visual images, the Indians remained Indians of the "noble savage" variety, or the dashing-
horseman-on-the-pony variety. They corresponded to a romanticized vision out of the past,
with little resemblance to the real reservation Indians living meagerly in pastoral or agricultural pursuits, or the disenfranchised alienated Indians of the cities.

The Myth of Olvera Street

Anglo patrons, stimulated by the potential tourist trade, as well as more altruistic goals
of cultural perservation permeated with 20th century nostalgia for "primitive" and "simple"
life, organized to restore crumbling adobes and original pueblos such as Olvera Street in Los
Angeles and La Villita in San Antonio. The mythification of Olvera Street, officially known
today as El Pueblo de Los Angeles State Historic Park, is sufficiently interesting to outline

---

[56] (Marshall) Rupert Garcia, "La Raza Murals of California, 1963 to 1970: A Period of Social Change
and Protest." Master's Thesis, University of California, Berkeley, 1981, p. 25-26.

[57] Frantz Fanon, *The Wretched of the Earth,* translated by Constance Farrington. New York: Grove
Press, 1963, p. 210.

[58] Acuña, *Occupied America,* p. 130, 131.

[59] McWilliams, *North From Mexico,* p. 36.

[60] *Ibid.,* p. 39.

some of the details, with the recommendation that an understanding of this process would be well served by a continuing in-depth investigation of the gestation and transformation of El Pueblo that has been started by the Society of Architectural Historians, Southern California Chapter.[61] El Pueblo, established in 1781, is the original site of the city of Los Angeles. Carey McWilliams lists the names of the "Spaniards" who were the first settlers: including the wives, two were Spaniards (married to Indian women), one was mestizo, two were Blacks, eight were mulattoes, and nine were Indians, including the first mayor.[62] El Pueblo ceased to be a pueblo by the 1830s when, with the growth of the cattle industry and trade due to the secularization of the California missions, a gentry of wealthy ranchers grouped their houses in or near the Plaza, which was already a shopping and trading center of the city.

The myth of Olvera Street was begun in 1928 through the efforts of San Francisco-born Christine Sterling who was fascinated by the Spanish-Mexican history of Los Angeles. In conjunction with Harry Chandler *(Los Angeles Times)* and other business people, "El Paseo de Los Angeles" was incorporated and opened in 1930. (Ironically, it was just a year later, during the Great Depression, that the U.S. government began a program of deportations resulting in the "repatriation" of between 300,000 and 500,000 Mexicans, many of them U.S.-born.)[63] Its rejuvenation transformed Olvera Street into what promotional literature called "an enchanting Mexican village thoroughfare," even though its purpose was commercial and diplomatic: to convert Olvera Street into a social and commercial Latin American center.[64] To accomplish this, all signs of the thriving (but disliked) Chinese commercial community in the Plaza, the nearby Black community (regrettably known as "Nigger Alley"), the presence of French and Italian interests and buildings, were removed or glossed over. The late 19th century industrial Simpson building was redesigned with Spanish colonial arches and Mexican tile to become a Mexican-style bank complete with Spanish-speaking personnel (now a branch of the Bank of America). Some authentic Californio buildings have been preserved, notably the Avila Adobe (c. 1818), and the Pico House, built for the former governor in 1869-1870. The earlier Pio Pico Town House (c. 1840) was destroyed in 1897,[65] and had been a symbol of the Californio ruling class during the Mexican period of California. The very term "Californio" adopted by the second generation denoted disassociation with things Mexican, particularly the lower class immigrants coming into the area.[66] The Californios were "Spaniards," the working class "Mexicans."

Paradoxically, Olvera Street with its numerous vendors under colorful awnings and its "Spanish" dancers, was the gateway to what was known since the 1850s as "Sonora Town" because so many of its residents were from northern Mexico. In 1932, two years after the completion of Olvera Street in its new identity, Mexican muralist David Alfaro Siqueiros painted his large critical mural *Tropical America* on a second story wall. So distasteful to Christine Sterling was the mural's exposure of the true status of Mexicans in southern California and the United States that, in 1934, it was completely whitewashed.[67]

---

[61] "El Pueblo: Myths and Realities," *Review,* Society of Architectural Historians, Southern California Chapter, Vol. 1, no. 1 (Fall 1981).

[62] McWilliams, *North From Mexico,* p. 36.

[63] Acuña, *Occupied America,* p. 138.

[64] "El Pueblo: Myths and Realities," p. 3.

[65] Richard Griswold del Castillo in *The Los Angeles Barrio, 1850-1890: A Social History,* Berkeley, CA: University of California, 1979, p. 128, erroneously speaks of these two buildings as one. The existence of two separate buildings of which the later Pico House remains today, was confirmed for the authors by Jean Bruce Poole, Senior Curator for El Pueblo de Los Angeles State Historic Park.

[66] Leonard Pitt, *The Decline of the Californios: A Social History of the Spanish-Speaking Californians, 1846-1890.* Berkeley, CA: University of California Press, 1966, p. 6-7.

[67] See Shifra M. Goldman, "Siqueiros and Three Early Murals in Los Angeles," *Art Journal,* Vol. 33, no. 4 (Summer 1974), p. 321-327. Also see Jesus Salvador Treviño's film *America Tropical,* produced for Channel 28, NET/PBS (Los Angeles, CA) in 1971.

Spanish Revival Architecture

By the mid-1920s, Mission or Spanish Revival became the preferred architectural style both for baronial estates in Florida and California and for thousands of domestic tract dwellings for the new arrivals in California, New Mexico, and Arizona. The Mission style was first introduced with the California Building at the 1893 Columbian Exposition in Chicago. This structure, which romanticized California Spanish mission culture, served as a catalyst for the spread of the style, particularly through a series of railroad stations and hotels. From 1894 through 1904, the Santa Fe Railroad brought the style, employing light-colored stucco walls, red tile roofs, arcaded porches, parapets, and towers, to New Mexico.[68] San Diego's 1915 Panama-California exposition had its California Building designed in the Spanish Churrigueresque style - an ornamental style that replaced the austere Mission-Revival, and was perpetuated along the central museum route of Balboa Park. Thereafter, Spanish Churrigueresque became the official style from San Antonio to Santa Barbara. In 1925, the Spanish Renaissance in California was a brief bubble that produced a plethora of poorly designed Spanish-style houses. Santa Barbara is the city that has most maintained this Spanish character with well-designed structures. (It is also the site of the most persistent of annual fantasy heritage parades.) Throughout the Southwest, the old missions have been restored as historical symbols and as tourist attractions. In San Antonio, the restoration of the Governor's Palace set an example of architecture, as did the missions. However, as Trent Sanford has pointed out, when twin mission bells are used on the facade of a railway station, things have gone too far.[69] Arizona is a very young state, therefore its architecture is North American and International. However, the Phoenix Post Office and the Veteran's Hospital in Tucson go back to Mexico and Spain for their inspiration.

New Mexico's Spanish Revival began in 1904 at the Louisiana Purchase Centennial Exposition in St. Louis. The New Mexico Building borrowed the California Mission style. However, tourism to New Mexico prompted the development of a pseudo-Pueblo adobe house construction, and the construction of the Museum of New Mexico in 1909 brought this style to maturity.[70] The Spanish-Pueblo style is a regional variation of the Spanish Revival; it draws eclectically on Indian mission architecture. Both the Museum and the reconstructed Governor's Palace in Santa Fe gave rise to an explosion of architecture in adobe and mock-adobe (with or without vigas, or roof logs) throughout the state and spreading to Arizona and California. Interestingly enough, the so-called "Santa Fe" style of architecture had, as a major contributor to its development, California-born Carlos Vierra, an artist of Portuguese descent who built his own home and studio near Santa Fe in this style in the first decade of the 20th century.[71] The other type of house that took root in modern California and Texas is the popular large rambling ranch house of the land grant days, one story in height with a sloping roof.

Santos and Santeros: The New Mexico Colonial "Revival"

The Roaring Twenties, after World War I, also saw an influx in New Mexico, especially Taos and Santa Fe, of East Coast Anglo artists (many following Mabel Dodge Luhan) who came for their health, for local color, and "as a relief from the sporty, unhinged, car-oriented world of post-war America."[72] Following the advent of African-influenced cubism in Europe and its introduction to the avant garde at New York's Armoury show, neo-primitivism

[68] Christopher Wilson, "The Spanish Pueblo Revival Defined, 1904-1921," *New Mexico Studies in the Fine Arts,* Vol. 7 (1982), p. 24-30. We are indebted to Keith McElroy who called this article to our attention.

[69] Sanford, *The Architecture of the Southwest,* p. 251.

[70] Wilson, "The Spanish Pueblo Revival Defined," p. 28.

[71] Edna Robertson and Sarah Nestor, *Artists of the Canyons and Caminos: Santa Fe, the Early Years.* Salt Lake City, UT: Gibbs M. Smith, 1982, p. 24-26.

[72] Sanford Schwartz, "When New York Went to New Mexico," *Art in America,* Vol. 64, no. 4 (July-August 1976), p. 93.

became a fashionable stance among artists and writers in the United States, and the nearest "primitives" on hand were the Pueblo Indians and the Hispano-Mexicans, both living in traditional ways (albeit with great hardship) within a strikingly beautiful landscape. The picturesqueness of northern New Mexico derived from the presence of 19th century Anglo artists, and their near-illustrator successors who maintained the cowboy-Indian motifs of the West, and the galleries which by the mid-twenties made Santa Fe and Taos leading art colonies. Though using picturesque motifs, the artists themselves regarded the local populations "at best with kindly superiority."[73] As for the new arrivals, they were described in salty language by Edmund Wilson in 1930 as "an extraordinary population of rich people, writers and artists who pose as Indians, cowboys, prospectors, desperados, Mexicans and other nearly extinct species."[74] Needless to say, Indians and Mexicans were far from extinct, though the other types might be!

Out of the Santa Fe writers and artists community emerged a "revivalist" patronage movement to preserve and foster Spanish colonial arts and crafts, with a goal of isolating the purely traditional, colonial, or Spanish crafts from syncretic innovations. The definition of "traditional" was determined by the patrons' own historical assessment and aesthetic judgement, rather than the artists' understanding of their heritage. As part of the revival, craftspeople were encouraged to not only copy old designs, but to create new ones in the same spirit. To market these new productions, the Santa Fe Fiesta took place in 1919, and the Spanish Colonial Arts Society was established in 1925, complementing the annual Spanish Market of the Fiesta. In 1929 the Spanish Arts Shop (later the Native Market) was established, and the structure for forming Hispano aesthetics along Anglo requirements was in place.[75] In all fairness it should be noted that at a time when overt Anglo racism against Hispanos and Indians was marked, the Anglo members of this movement were among the more sensitive and well-intentioned of the newcomers. Nevertheless, the "revival" involved a classically patronizing formula - "the appropriation of control over an ethnic resource primarily by members of a superordinate society."[76] In the 1930s the Federal Arts Project of the Works Project Administration employed a number of artists, like woodcarver Patrocinio Barela, as they did with other impoverished artists throughout the nation during the Depression. Governmental support not only allowed the artists to survive, but gave a boost to the industry. The important question that arises, amply explored by Charles L. Briggs in his groundbreaking study, is the turning of an internally oriented religious and domestic art production toward an external production for collectors, with corresponding loss of meaning. As we shall see, in the 1970s Hispano-Chicano artists recaptured the aesthetic (if not the commercial) initiative, which appears to be returning partially to its original internal focus. This is true not only for woodcarving, painting, and crafts, but for architecture as well.

Mexican Americans in the Fine Arts

Outside of New Mexico, various Mexican American painters, sculptors, and printmakers were also producing work. Jacinto Quirarte's book *Mexican American Artists* has amply charted this territory, at least in terms of accepted norms of the "fine arts." Before giving representative examples of some of this production, however, it is worth repeating the comments of writer Philip D. Ortego. Although there were Mexican American artists at various times since 1848, he says, these artists did not reflect any significant thrust by Mexican Americans into artistic endeavors; they represented only individual successes.[77] Ortego's point is

---

[73] Robertson and Nestor, *Artists of the Canyons and Caminos,* p. 105.

[74] Edmund Wilson quoted in Schwartz, "When New York Went to New Mexico," p. 93.

[75] Briggs, *The Wood Carvers of Cordova, New Mexico,* p. 46-48.

[76] *Ibid.,* p. 50.

[77] Philip D. Ortego y Gasca, "The Chicano Renaissance," reprinted without attribution or dating in Richard A. Garcia (ed.) *The Chicanos in America, 1540-1974: A Chronology and Fact Book,* Dobbs Ferry, NY: Oceana Publications, 1977, p. 191-204.

meant to underline the difference between the isolated condition of Mexican American artists prior to 1965 in contrast to the sense of a *movement* in the Chicano era, and we would add to that the sense of a *national* movement with shared precepts and iconography. As for the "fine arts," we would consider it important to also trace the history of Mexican American visual producers in the area of popular, commercial, graphic, and photographic arts, as well as the self-taught artists. It is equally necessary to trace the artistic production of women, in both fine and applied arts. As the biographies of Chicano artists are increasingly compiled, it becomes apparent that some artists come from families where fathers, mothers, and other family members practiced the arts (whether recognized publicly or not), and were often teachers as well as supporters of an incipient artist. Two cases in point will suffice: one is that of El Paso sculptor Luis Jimenez whose father was a very creative and successful maker of neon signs and in whose workshop Jimenez learned a great deal about plastics that perhaps disposed him to the Pop style in which he eventually excelled. The other is Arizona sculptor and muralist Zarco Guerrero whose father was trained in fine arts and ran a sign company in the Phoenix area. Many such older generation artists and artisans need to be rediscovered and their histories recorded, including those who taught in the educational system.

Five examples of artists producing fine arts during the 1910-1965 period include the Corpus Christi painter Antonio Garcia (b. 1910); the Texas photographer Jesus Murillo (1895-1971); and three California painters: Xavier Martinez (1869-1943), Hernando Gonzallo Villa (1881-1952), and Manuel Valencia (1856-1935). Garcia is a muralist and easel painter as well as a teacher. His painting *Aztec Advance* (1929) features an Aztec warrior theme which prefigures later Chicano interest in pre-Columbian Indians. Garcia studied in Chicago from 1927 to 1930, and it is worth noting for the record that Mexicans in the Chicago area, in response to color prejudice, had to some extent developed a pride in being of the Aztec "race." The *Correo Mexicano* of September 6, 1926 stated that "we do not forget that we are descended from a progressive and cultured race, as were our ancestors, the Aztec."[78] We don't, of course, know for certain that Garcia was aware of this stance during his Chicago stay when he executed this work, but it is tempting to make the correlation. What is certain is that in Mexico itself during the 1920s, indigenism in painting, music, and literature was in full swing, and probably was the source of this conception among Mexican Americans. In 1939 Garcia tackled another ethnic theme: he depicted an important Black community celebration in his painting *Juneteenth Revue.* The celebration marks the Emancipation Proclamation of 1863, and was first observed by Black farmers in Texas beginning in 1939, and has since spread to many other cities of the Southwest.[79] Considering the racism in white society at the time, and the divisions engendered by the dominant society between different ethnic and racial peoples, Garcia treats the subject with sympathy and devoid of stereotype. (Both paintings are illustrated in the Quirarte book, pages 42 and 44.)

Facts about photographer Jesus Murillo have recently come to light thanks to the Houston Metropolitan Research Center of the Houston Public Library which is documenting the colonia's history from the 19th century to the present. Several important Mexican professional photographers have been discovered, including Murillo who worked in Houston from 1916-1930 taking studio portraits of the Mexican American community and painting and sketching. He also documented local cultural life. Tom Kreneck of the Research Center validly urges the need for archivist-historians to locate, acquire, preserve, and make available for scholarship the work of other such photographers across the United States. In developing collections, he suggests contact with Mexican American families who, more than other groups, have taken and preserved photographs.[80] It should be mentioned parenthetically that a number of Chicano artists have already discovered and used this rich source for paintings and

---

[78] Forbes, *Aztecas del Norte,* p. 157.

[79] Texas has since made this date into a state holiday.

[80] Tom Kreneck, "With the Eye of An Artist: Jesus Murillo's Houston, 1927-1933," *Revista Chicano-Riqueña,* Vol. 8, no. 3 (Summer 1980), p. 104.

drawings of their own and other families, rediscovering their past by this method.

San Francisco-based Xavier (Tizoc) Martinez was academically trained and as a boy apprenticed to the artists of his family in Guadalajara where he was born. His style is essentially that of 19th century post-Impressionist European art, combined with some Mexican influence, and the style of Western landscape and figure painters of the early 20th century. He taught at the California School of Arts and Crafts from 1908 to 1942 - a school which became one of the training grounds for San Francisco Chicano artists three decades after he left. In the Bay Area, Martinez moved in a circle of bohemian artists and writers, but though he was unalterably cosmopolitan after study in Europe, he struggled to reconcile his Mexican cultural heritage with the upper class milieu in which he functioned - thus the "Tizoc" which he added to his name in recognition of his Indian heritage.[81]

Hernando Gonzallo Villa and Manuel Valencia were both born in California, the former in Los Angeles of an immigrated family, the latter of a wealthy land grant family that came north with the De Anza expedition that settled in San Francisco and apparently lost its land by the 20th century. Villa was a muralist, an easel painter of Mexican and California landscape, of romanticized Indian and cowboy themes, and of picturesque Mexican dancers, guitarists, and *fiestas*. His view of both Mexicans and Indians was that of the dominant society, with whom his work was very successful. He focused on utopian aspects of Indian life, occasionally colored by his forty year artistic association with the Santa Fe Railroad for whom he painted, and for whom he designed the Indian head logo for the train known as "The Chief."[82] Valencia was a self-taught artist who worked as a commercial designer and a landscapist for wealthy patrons in order to support his large family. He taught his son to be a painter.[83]

The record, though not replete, does offer fascinating glimpses of Mexican American artistic life that have not yet been explored, with the few exceptions mentioned above and those contained in the Quirarte book. For example, one wants to know more about Mexican-born Jose Aceves (1909-1968) who painted New Deal murals in Texas; Mexican-born Southwest illustrator Jose Cisneros (b. 1910) living in El Paso as of 1974; Mexican-born Mario Ruben Cooper (b. 1905), raised in Los Angeles and educated at Otis Art Institute and Chouinard School of Art, who was a decorative painter of Aztec and Maya designs; Francisco Cornejo, active in Los Angeles from 1913 on; Mexican-born painter Marco Antonio Gomez (1910-1972), son of a portait painter who brought him to Arizona in 1918, and who also studied at Chouinard and the Art Center in Los Angeles; California Western painter Pete Martinez (b. 1894), living in Tucson as of 1968; Mexican-born Raoul Murillo who came to Los Angeles in 1927 and did caricature portraits in Olvera Street; the brothers Leandro and Tony Reveles who worked as scenic painters in the Hollywood film industry and one of whom (Tony) worked with Siqueiros on the *Tropical America* mural in 1932; and many more whose names will surface with patient searching of the resources available. One would like to know how many and which artists exhibited with the organization "Mexican Painters and Photographers of California," which held its first exhibition in Los Angeles in May 1921 (concurrent with a Cinco de Mayo celebration?). We know one was Leopoldo Quijano, but have no further information about him.

---

[81] Over the years, Martinez changed his name from Javier Timoteo Martinez y Orozco to Xavier Tizoc Martinez Suarez which he used when signing his Spanish newspaper column and his poetry. See the Oakland Museum catalog, *Xavier Martinez (1869-1943)*, 1974, p. 58, note 8.

[82] See the Sotheby Parke Bernet (Los Angeles, CA) auction catalogs *American Indian Art and a Collection of Western Paintings by Hernando Villa*, October [1972], and *A Collection of Paintings by Hernando Villa Including Indian, Mexican, Cowboy and California Subjects*, May 1973.

[83] See the Laguna Beach Museum of Art catalog *Southern California Artists, 1890-1940*, 1979, which includes biographies of Manuel Valencia and Hernando Gonzallo Villa.

Mexican Artists in the United States

There is no question that the U.S.-Mexico border was just as fluid for artists and art influences as it was for other aspects of Mexican/ Mexican American social and cultural life, with the exception that it was harder for *persons* to cross the frontier into the United States than for their *influences*. This became even more difficult as the Russian Revolution of 1917 influenced many creators in the direction of Socialism and Communism. The U.S. government hardened its attitudes on politically "tainted" artists like Diego Rivera and David Alfaro Siqueiros, the latter of whom, for example, could not enter the U.S. for many years due to the McCarran Act of 1950. Nevertheless, many artists did enter over the years, and a number lived, worked, exhibited and taught in the U.S. for extended periods of time. In addition to the *Tres Grandes* (Orozco, Rivera, Siqueiros), there were also Alfredo Ramos Martinez, Miguel Covarrubias, Luis Arenal, Jean Charlot, Jorge Juan Crespo de la Serna, Frida Kahlo, Gerardo Murillo (Dr. Atl), to mention just a few. And, of course, Rufino Tamayo who, from 1928 on, regularly lived in the United States (or Europe) for portions of many years. Though the impact of the Mexican mural movement on the New Deal period is known, it has never been given the complete historical treatment that it deserves, though at this writing one scholar is working on the presence of the Tres Grandes in the United States during the thirties.[84] Even less researched is the impact of the Taller de Grafica Popular (Popular Graphic Arts Workshop) of Mexico on U.S. artists, though there certainly were similar workshops established in various cities. Needless to say, there exists no study of the Mexican influence on Mexican American artists. The degree to which Mexican American graphics (especially the wood and linoleum cut) owed a debt to the Taller is still an area to be explored. We can chart the impact of both the murals and graphics of Mexico in the post-1965 period, but not before. In the area of motion pictures more study needs to be devoted to the impact Mexican actors such as Ramon Novarro, Gilbert Roland, Antonio Moreno, Lupe Velez, Dolores del Rio, and others had on the Hollywood film industry.

Finally, knowledge about Mexican art was provided in metropolitan centers like San Antonio and Chicago (and doubtless other cities) through periodic traveling exhibitions often sponsored by a Mexican consulate. For example, the Art Institute of Chicago was the first to present exhibits of Leopoldo Mendez and Jose Guadalupe Posada in the 1930s.[85] Newsreels from Mexico showing in Spanish language movie houses provided coverage and commentary on the artistic production and social antics of the Mexican muralists, and the Spanish language press gave sustained coverage to Rivera, Orozco, and Siqueiros as they traveled and worked in New York, Detroit, Los Angeles, and San Francisco in the early 1930s.

The Pachuco: Fact and Myth

By the mid-1940s, the social process of urbanization was transforming the Mexican American community. Some entered the skilled labor market, but a large majority was kept poor through discrimination, exploitation, and limited geographic mobility. With a mounting sense of marginalization and alienation in the cities was created the Pachuco subculture.

Treating the Pachuco phenomenon of the early 1940s is not as simple as the title of this section suggests. The facts can be summed up as follows: Pachucos were young urban working class people of Mexican descent whose parents maintained and imposed cultural standards viable in Mexico but unworkable in the United States, according to their children who rejected these standards. They were young people who were themselves rejected by the dominant society which they wished to enter on equal terms. As a result they withdrew into their own formations which, in the 1940s - during the World War II years - included sartorial, linguistic, and social behavior and codes which were considered acceptable neither by the Mexican community nor by the dominant Anglo community. This behavior worried and

---

[84] Laurence Hurlburt of Wisconsin.

[85] Information provided by Victor Sorell of Chicago, IL.

shamed the former and was attacked by the latter. The most famous (or infamous) attack was that known as the "Zoot Suit Riots" of 1943 during which hordes of servicemen invaded the barrios and the downtown areas of Los Angeles, urged on by the Hearst press, to strip and beat the zootsuiters in the name of "Americanism." (This was the same period in which Japanese Americans were herded into concentration camps.) However, Pachucos were attacked in many other ways, more concentrated perhaps, but not much different from those practiced against persons of Mexican descent since the 19th century: poor education, lack of job training and skills, poor housing, segregation, discrimination, and police brutality, to mention just a few. It was the combination of rejection on both sides that probably caused the Pachuco configuration, but it must essentially be seen in terms of urban congestion and nativist Anglo hostility.

It must be stressed, however, that *pachuquismo* was not a self-conscious rebellious existentialism, as was urged by Octavio Paz in his influential book *The Labyrinth of Solitude: Life and Thought in Mexico*,[86] nor was it simply a subculture of nihilism which produced primarily criminal violence, as some of the more extreme social scientists have claimed.[87] In fact, it was the result of compression in cities with different sets of values, the fragmentation of the extended family, the stereotyping of all things Mexican by the dominant society through readily available mass media, the violent racism of dominant authority figures particularly in the school, on the streets, and in areas of possible employment. And, in the final analysis, it was the perceived impossibility of attaining the so-called "American Dream" (shown on every silver screen), or even a decent modicum of that Dream, that opened up a generation gap and forced teenagers into gangs and often into juvenile delinquency. The Southwest had its own "Harlems" where rage and desperation among the young produced a subculture of personal protest, a subculture often of self-destruction. Members of the subculture wore zoot suits (very likely adopted from the Harlem costume made popular by Cab Calloway, with a female variation among Pachucas); spoke *caló* (a type of slang which mixed English and Spanish and had the advantage of being understood neither by parents nor Anglo authority); danced to the boogie, a Black musical form which had passed into white mass culture; drove hot rod cars (the forerunner of the lowrider) when money was available; tattooed their hands and graffitied the walls with *plaqueasos (or placas),* both signs of personal identity and group affiliation created by powerless groups with no other way of "making their mark." The placas used stylized calligraphy that was painstakingly developed by each individual; the tattoos on the hands were done with India ink, and body tattoos drew on Catholic imagery as well as sexual imagery within the lexicon of the tattoo parlors. The personal stance was to be "hip" or "cool," in other words tough and controlled, and not to show one's wounds in public. The gang was a self-defensive as well as aggressive instrument, turning its rage against other gangs, since it was kept by police violence from confronting the Anglo establishment, and did not have the political understanding or methods to supercede personal aggrievement and anger to struggle against the basic source of its oppression.

The Pachuco myth began with Octavio Paz whom the Chicano movement discovered in the 1960s and welcomed uncritically, at first, simply because a great Mexican writer had recognized and written about a youth culture which was part of Chicano history and had not been treated either sympathetically or poetically before. Paz's existential position, popular in the late 1940s when his book was written, passed into Chicano perception in the form of the Pachuco myth: the Pachuco as a dandy, a lonely rebel flaunting society which would not accept him, sustained simply by his will-to-be or, conversely, courting death with his flamboyant costume and style. (The masculine gender appears in the original; neither Paz, nor many Chicanos, recognized the Pachuca except as an auxiliary.) Many Chicanos had either been

[86] Octavio Paz, *The Labyrinth of Solitude: Life and Thought in Mexico,* translated by Lysander Kemp. New York: Grove Press, 1961.

[87] See, for example, Richard A. Garcia, "Do Zoot Suiters Deserve Hoorays?", *Los Angeles Times,* (August 27, 1978), p. V-6.

Pachucos themselves or had relatives who were. The root of the problem, racism and economic exploitation, escaped Paz and the myth, though it is found in the still mythic presentation of Luis Valdez's drama and film *Zoot Suit* in the late 1970s and early 1980s.

We have spent so much time with this topic because the Pachuco(a) and the successors to *pachuquismo,* --the *cholos* and *cholas* --have been absorbed into Chicano art. The cholo costumes have variously included army surplus khakis and oversized white t-shirts and (after the farmworkers' unionization campaigns in the 1960s) the colorful flowered cotton sweat kerchiefs worn across the brow and eyes. Young women are known for extravagant makeup, jewelry, jeans, and sleeveless t-shirts. Both men and women use identifying tattoos. The customized lowrider (an older car, creatively painted and upholstered), often with hydraulics that permit it to bounce to incredible heights like a bucking bronco, has taken the place of the hot-rod. It is a processional vehicle ("cruising" slowly along the street and attracting attention) and a sexual symbol for courting. The ornamental charro's horse has been replaced with a mechanical one from Detroit, both decorated at considerable expense. The traditions of the tattoo and graffiti have continued, often learned from older family members.

In Chicano art, Pachucos have been rendered in murals, easel paintings, and prints. The most famous image is that designed for the play *Zoot Suit* by Los Angeles illustrator Ignacio Gomez, modeled on the defiant and mythic role created by actor Edward James Olmos. The younger cholos(as) have been the special preserve of photographer and painter John Valadez of Los Angeles. However, the most respected and influential reviver of the Pachuco image has been veteran artist and poet Jose Montoya of the Royal Chicano Air Force in Sacramento, California. Known for his sensitive line drawings and prints of Pachucos, Montoya supported a traveling historical exhibit on the "Zoot Suit Riots." He revived the zoot suit as a nostalgic costume. Through his anguished poetry celebrating the *elan* and the destruction of a Pachuco, Montoya has elaborated the myth without losing the sense of the tragic original, which he links with contemporary reality. Lowriders have become sculptural forms; graffiti has been integrated into murals and used as creative calligraphy on book and magazine covers; photographers have recorded and painters reproduced the elaborate tattooing that often covers a young man's arms and torso; the graffito symbol "*con safos,*" or "C/S" (roughly translated as "the same to you") has become the name of a magazine *(Con Safos,* in Los Angeles), and an artistic group (Con Safo, in San Antonio), and is often used, with the artist's or group's name, to sign a work of art.

1965 - 1981
The Chicano Period

The Chicano political movement grew out of an alliance formed in the 1960s by exploited farmworkers struggling to establish unions against the powerful agribusiness and ranching interests of California and Texas, the disenfranchised and dispossessed land grant owners of New Mexico, the urban working classes of the Southwest and Midwest, and the growing student movement. All these were essential participants in the Chicano movement, although not all embraced the term "Chicano."

Although great economic struggles, supported by national boycotts, took place in the rural areas - and were the unifying symbol of the Chicano movement - many of the political and cultural activities of the 1960s and 1970s were centered in the cities where the greatest number of Mexican Americans and Chicanos live today. Issues in the cities included police brutality, violations of civil rights, low-paid employment, inadequate housing and social services, gang warfare, drug abuse, inadequate and irrelevant education, and lack of political power. (The formation of La Raza Unida party in 1970 was one response to the need for political power.) The Vietnam War was a crucial issue, and antiwar sentiment was growing. From the mid-sixties on, students were the shock troops of the urban movement.

The Chicano art movement - and it must be viewed in this period as a movement rather than simply as a collection of individuals - arose toward the end of the 1960s. The history of the movement can be divided into two periods: from 1968 to 1975 and from 1975 to 1981 and beyond. The first period was marked by a totally noncommercial community-oriented character in the attitudes and expectations of the art groups, the purposes they served, the audiences they addressed, the facilities that were established to promote the arts, and the collectives that flourished. The second period is witnessing the changing dynamic of an art movement subject to the fluctuations of the political movement and to the imperatives of the dominant society to which that art was opposed. Crucial to this second period is the changing perception of the Chicano role in the United States and in the international arena - a perception that brought an end to separatism for most Chicanos and a closer alignment with the Third World, especially Latin American struggles. At the same time, other segments of the Chicano community became more assimilationist in relation to the dominant society and its values, and more commercial in the content and dissemination of their art. This point is further discussed below.

A high sense of idealism was intrinsic to the 1968-1975 period. It explains the emphasis on community-oriented and public art forms like postermaking and muralism and on the development of artistic collectives, as well as an insistence on political and ethnic themes. Art was part of a whole movement to recapture a people's history and culture, albeit at times romantically, as part of the struggle for self-determination.

A cultural nationalist philosophy, separatist in nature, was also developed in the early period by the youth and students of the movement, and expressed most influentially in the utopian "El Plan Espiritual de Aztlan" (The Spiritual Plan of Aztlan) adopted in March 1969 at a huge Chicano Youth Conference in Denver. Key points were a call for reclamation and control of lands stolen from Mexico (the U.S. Southwest), anti-Europeanism, an insistence on the importance and glory of the brown-skinned Indian heritage, and an emphasis on humanistic and nonmaterialistic culture and education. "Aztlan" (the Southwest from which, presumably, the Aztecs came), it proclaimed, "belongs to those who plant the seeds, water the fields, and gather the crops, and not to foreign Europeans.... We are a Bronze People with a Bronze culture." The Plan committed all levels of Chicano society to the Cause: "We must insure that our writers, poets, musicians and artists produce literature and art that is appealing to our people and relates to our revolutionary cause. Our cultural values of life, family, and home will serve as a powerful weapon to defeat the gringo dollar value system and encourage the process of love and brotherhood."[88] Thus, in a few pages of text, were established not only the

---

[88] Luis Valdez and Stan Steiner (eds.), *Aztlan: An Anthology of Mexican American Literature.* New York: Vintage Books, 1972, p. 402-406.

ideals but also the themes of Chicano art and letters: the life, history, and heritage of a working class, Indian, spiritual, and revolutionary people.[89]

ISSUES AND IMAGES[90]

Civil Rights

In the seamless fabric of human history, events are not easily contained within neatly pigeonholed time periods. Thus, the turbulent sixties which saw the genesis of that phase of the Mexican American struggle known as the Chicano period actually can be said to have begun with consciousness of the Black Civil Rights Movement that swept the South for ten years, beginning in 1956 after Mrs. Rosa Parks refused to obey the Montgomery, Alabama, law providing for segregation on city buses, and the Supreme Court outlawed that segregation. Two years earlier, the Supreme Court had struck down the segregation of schoolchildren through the "separate but equal" doctrine.

Many Chicano artists now past age thirty-five have testified to the fact that they were impacted by the Black Civil Rights Movement. However, spoken or written testimony is not the only kind; the images appear in works of art. One of the earliest manifestations is that of the mural in Del Rey, California, by Antonio Bernal, discussed below in the section on labor. Other artists have dealt with related issues in images of George Jackson and the Soledad (California) case, and of Angela Davis. The civil rights movement led by Martin Luther King, Jr. generally followed a non-violent philosophy; however there were Black resisters who preached self-defense against violence, with guns if necessary.[91] Malcolm X and the Black Panthers took a more militant stance to reflect the real anger in the Black community. In the Chicano movement the Brown Berets and the Comancheros del Norte represented the self-defensive posture. And it was the Black Panthers who initiated a social and cultural movement to complement the political-economic one, with breakfast programs, cultural activities, and art. There is no clear connection between this aspect of the Black movement and that of the Chicano movement, but it is known that Black Panther graphic artist Emory Douglas was widely known and respected in the San Francisco Bay Area. Similarly, Black artist and muralist William Walker was very influential in Chicago. In both Chicago and San Francisco, civil rights and Third World movements of the late sixties included a spectrum of Black, Latino, Asian, and white artists working in concert.

The Cuban Revolution

Ushering in the decade of the sixties was the Cuban Revolution of 1959, which had tremendous repercussions in all of Latin America and among Latinos in the United States. It was especially significant for Mexicans, who in 1910 had launched the first revolution of the 20th century in the Americas - a revolution that had become truncated over the years, but was still an important symbol for the Mexican communities of the Southwest.

Almost from the beginning, the Cuban government had supported culture and the arts, and Cuba generated an outstanding production in the area of posters, billboards, and films. By 1970, knowledge of the Cuban posters became widespread in the United States through

[89] This introduction has been excerpted from Shifra M. Goldman, "A Public Voice: Fifteen Years of Chicano Posters," *Art Journal*, Vol. 44, no. 1 (Spring 1984), p. 50-57.

[90] Three publications were basic sources for the historical information in this section: Rodolfo Acuña, *Occupied America* (second edition); Juan Gomez-Quiñones, *Mexican Students por La Raza: The Chicano Student Movement in Southern California, 1967-1977*, Santa Barbara, CA: Editorial La Causa, 1978; and Howard Zinn, *A People's History of the United States*, New York: Harper & Row, 1980. With some exceptions, they will not be cited again. Information on the arts, except as otherwise noted, derives from the personal research of the compilers.

[91] Robert Williams of Monroe, North Carolina, whose followers fought off the Ku Klux Klan, as did a North Carolina Indian Community. Zinn, *A People's History of the United States*, p. 443-444.

publication of the oversize picture book *The Art of Revolution: Castro's Cuba, 1959-1970,*[92] while in San Francisco, the Chicano-run Galeria de la Raza mounted an exhibit of photographs of Cuba and silkscreen posters by Cuban artist Rene Mederos. This was in 1970; by 1974 Chicano artist Juan Fuentes organized a Cuban poster exhibit at San Francisco's Palace of the Legion of Honor. Exposure to Cuban posters was very important for the burgeoning Chicano poster movement of northern California, one of the strongest in the country.[93]

Labor: The Farmworkers Movement

Labor conflict, particularly in the large factory-farms of California where Mexicans and other racial and ethnic peoples were employed under wretched conditions, was nothing new. Vigilantes and repressive laws repeatedly crushed strikes, followed by deportations. Almost without exception every strike in which Mexicans participated in the 1930s and after was broken by the use of violence and deportations. The chief difference in the 1960s with Cesar Chavez and the United Farm Workers (UFW) is that the "green giants" were challenged, and the union succeeded. In addition, because of its creative organizing methods, the UFW brought the labor struggle to the attention of the nation and the world. In the organizing process, two strong visual symbols emerged, used in every procession and manifestation, which became central to Chicano visual artists: the Virgin of Guadalupe and the red, black, and white thunderbird flag. In addition, from 1964 on the union began publishing the bilingual twice-monthly newspaper *El Malcriado: The Voice of the Farmworker* in which graphics and photography played a major role. Andy Zermeno was the staff cartoonist for many years producing extremely effective caricatures on issues affecting the farmworkers, from the boycott of grapes to the activities of Richard Nixon. Zermeno invented a folksy character whom he called "Don Sotaco" (the underdog), who is constantly the butt of outrageous behavior by the "*patroncito*" (the boss) and "*Don Coyote*" (the labor contractor). *El Malcriado* used for its covers the prints of 19th century Mexican engraver Jose Guadalupe Posada, whose famous *calaveras* (animated skeletons) swept the Chicano art movement; and prints by the Taller de Grafica Popular (TGP; Popular Graphics Art Workshop) of Mexico, thus familiarizing Chicano artists with Mexican social protest art. In the 1970s one image in particular struck the imagination of Chicano activists, as it had earlier struck the 1968 student demonstrators in Mexico: a linoleum cut of a man's head with its mouth gagged by a large chain and lock. Incorrectly attributed as an anonymous student movement poster, it is actually the work of TGP artist Adolfo Mexiac who, as a teacher at the San Carlos Art Academy during the student strikes, was instrumental in the art students' immense quantity of graphic production during 1968.

The entire Chicano movement was energized by the farmworkers, particularly the grape and lettuce boycotts which were carried out nationally and engaged the participation of thousands of city dwellers. The first cultural expression was that of the Teatro Campesino, created in 1965 in Delano, California, to teach and organize Chicano farm workers, and headed by Luis Valdez. After performing in the Southwest, the company toured the country to publicize the strike, then established El Centro Cultural, an independent farmworkers' cultural center in Del Rey, California where the theatre developed "History Happenings," with puppets and music, and artists gave music and art classes to the community.[94] Antonio Bernal's 1968 two-panel mural at El Centro Cultural is one of the earliest Chicano murals we have been able to date in California. Its significance lies in its double theme: one panel depicts pre-Columbian personages in linear arrangement headed by a woman and reminiscent of the Bonampak murals, and the other panel headed by La Adelita of the Mexican Revolution pictures Mexican, Mexican American and Chicano leaders and terminates with images of a

---

[92] Dugald Stermer, *The Art of Revolution: Castro's Cuba, 1959-1970,* with an introductory essay by Susan Sontag. New York: McGraw-Hill Book Co., 1970.

[93] See Goldman, "A Public Voice: Fifteen Years of Chicano Posters," p. 52.

[94] Valdez and Stein (eds.), *Aztlan,* p. 360-361.

Black Panther and Martin Luther King, Jr. Thus, iconographically, are intertwined themes and allegiances that were later spelled out in thousands of Chicano murals across the country in multiple ways and combinations. Unusual was the prominent and active role given women in this mural, and the homage to the Black leaders, placed on an equal level with the Mexican.

So important to the Chicano art movement was the UFW struggle and its counterparts in the Midwest and Texas, that the fact can only be recorded here. Salvador Roberto "Queso" Torres of San Diego did a series of easel paintings called "La Huelga" (The Strike) on variations of the UFW eagle. Painter Carlos Almaraz of Los Angeles worked several years fulltime for the UFW, made banners for the union's convention, and in 1974, with a group of young people in East Los Angeles, painted an enormous (now vanished) mural with the slogan "Don't Buy Gallo Wine." Amado M. Pena of Austin made a silkscreen print, with a bleeding head of lettuce, urging viewers not to buy non-union lettuce. More than once Pena helped the Texas farmworkers with posters designed for them.

Among the many things lacking in historical research on Chicano art are iconographical studies which could reveal the extent, variety, and significance of ways in which the unionizing struggles of farmworkers were expressed by Chicano artists.

Education: The Student and Youth Movements

1968 was a year of international student protest. The student movement could trace its history back to the Free Speech Movement launched in 1964 at the University of California, Berkeley, in which students confronted the administration with their right to use the traditional free speech zone at the campus to articulate the many political issues fermenting at the time. Chicano students were particularly responsive to student demonstrations in Mexico during the 1968 Olympic games, in the graphics of that movement, and in the Tlatelolco massacre of protesters on October 2nd that brought these events to world attention.[95] The rise of student movements north and south of the border coincided, though the student movement in Mexico was much more advanced ideologically and structurally and its action dwarfed anything in the U.S. Nevertheless, in an overwhelmingly working class community like the Mexican American, the impact of students was particularly great, since the middle and upper class sectors were small. Most of the students themselves were only a step away from the working class, often the first in a family to attend college.

Chicanismo, says Juan Gomez-Quiñones, evolved from the student movement. Chicanismo involved a radicalization of politics. It engaged and made attractive the issues of national identity, dignity, self-worth, pride, uniqueness, and a sense of cultural rebirth. Thus it could cut across class, regional, and occasionally generational lines, though it was primarily a youth phenomenon. The mystiques of nationalism and indigenism contained within the concept of chicanismo were unifying factors in a very heterogeneous movement; they provided the cement for a national network of students and youth which began to come together in the second half of the 1960s.

An early set of events which led to a large cultural expression was the East Los Angeles high school "blowouts," when students left school demanding relevant education and an end to racist teachers. In May 1969 the committee organized around these educational demands put on the Fiesta de los Barrios in Lincoln High School which featured music, dance, literature, art, and food, and attracted about 10,000 people in four days of activities.

The Chicano student and youth movement was the fertile soil for Chicano artists. From the late sixties to 1975 there were a number of Chicano art teachers in various parts of the United States, though it should be noted here that research to determine the full range of

---

[95] For the impact of the Mexican student movement and the Tlatelolco massacre on young Mexican artists of the 1970s, see Shifra M. Goldman, "Elite Artists and Popular Audiences: Can They Mix? The Mexican Front of Cultural Workers," *Studies in Latin American Popular Culture*, Vol. 4 (1985) p. 139-154.

teachers (both Chicano and non-Chicano) for the Chicano generation remains a task for the future. Artists do not spring out of a void, either socio-political or cultural, and while many Chicano art students were forced through institutional disinterest or hostility into a process of research and self-education regarding their roots and heritage and the development of an artistic language of protest and self-identification, there undoubtedly were influential teachers in many schools. In Los Angeles a number of Chicano students (like their Mexican American predecessors) passed through the Otis Art Institute whose legacy had long been that of figurative humanism based on the teachings of Rico Lebrun (d. 1964) and Black artist Charles White (d. 1979). The University of California, Los Angeles, also served as a training ground for artists: in the early sixties Eduardo Carrillo (whose father and brothers were also artists), Louis Lunetta, and Roberto Chavez were enrolled; at the end of the 1960s, Ramses Noriega attended; in the early seventies, Theresa Herrera Verdine; and in the mid-1970s, Barbara Carrasco. In Texas various universities and colleges provided training for Chicano artists. Chicano-controlled Jacinto Trevino College was established in 1970 and accredited by the Antioch Graduate School of Education. It later gave birth to Juarez-Lincoln University in Austin, with branches in other cities. Art and cultural activities were part of the curriculum. At Texas A & I University in Kingsville in the late 1960s, art professor Pedro Rodriguez played a seminal role in promoting consciousness of Chicano art and muralism. In the early seventies, Rodriguez moved to Highlands University, Las Vegas, New Mexico, where a mural program developed under his direction; and in 1973 he began teaching at Washington State University, Pullman. Melesio (Mel) Casas has been teaching at San Antonio College since the early sixties and has been an important influence on younger Chicano artists. During the 1970s Roberto Chavez and Louis Lunetta taught at East Los Angeles College, and Eduardo Carrillo at the University of California, Santa Cruz. In Sacramento Jose Montoya and Esteban Villa organized the Royal Chicano Air Force with a core of their students from Sacramento State College/now University. Malaquias Montoya has taught graphics at the University of California, Berkeley and presently teaches at Oakland's California College of Arts and Crafts. Rupert Garcia has taught at San Francisco State University and the University of California, Berkeley, as have Patricia Rodriguez, Ray Patlan, and Yolanda Lopez. In the mid-1970s Mario Castillo taught at the University of Illinois, Champaign-Urbana, and photographer Louis Carlos Bernal has been teaching at Pima College in Tucson for many years. Art historian Victor Sorell has been a committed teacher for many years at Chicago State University. These are just some of the earliest and most influential; many Chicano artists (male and female) have since taught art and Mexican/Chicano art history for longer and shorter periods at educational institutions throughout the United States. This list does not begin to explore the teachers at the high school level like David Ramirez who, until his retirement, taught at Garfield High School (one of the "blowout" schools) where many contemporary Chicano artists passed through his classes. He also taught at Los Angeles City College, and actively participated in exhibits by the Mechicano Art Center in the early 1970s. Jose Maria Lozano taught at Martin High School in Laredo, Texas; he was Amado Pena's teacher and had been giving classes in commercial art since 1953.

The other equally important structure for artistic education and dissemination has been the network of alternative centers and galleries. Artists functioning as teachers for the local community, as muralists and mural art directors, and as exhibiting artists, coalesced in centers and galleries that provided an outlet for didactic and aesthetic energies. Numerous lectures, conferences, and round tables were sponsored or held on the temporary or permanent premises of these centers. In the Midwest these have included Casa Aztlan (Chicago) and the Movimiento Artistico Chicano (MARCH), as well as the multiethnic Chicago Mural Group and the Public Art Workshop. In Arizona, the Movimiento Artistico del Rio Salado (MARS, Phoenix), and the El Rio Neighborhood Center (Tucson) offered a base for artists. In Denver the Crusade for Justice Building housed, from 1968 to 1972, El Grito de Aztlan Art Gallery and a mural program, as well as the Escuela y Colegio Tlatelolco. More recently, the Chicano Humanities and Arts Council (CHAC) was established with display space, artists' studios, and an office, in Denver. In New Mexico, Casa Armijo has housed the Taller Media

(Media Workshop) and lent its walls to murals (Albuquerque); La Galeria de Colores, established by Pola Lopez de Jaramillo, is in Las Vegas, and the Santuario de Guadalupe offers exhibits in Santa Fe. Texas has had the Centro Cultural Aztlan, the Instituto Cultural sponsored by the Universidad Nacional Autonoma de Mexico, and the newly established Guadalupe Cultural Arts Center (all in San Antonio), the League of United Chicano Artists (LUCHA) housed at the Centro Cultural (Austin), and the Xochil Art Institute (formerly Estudio Rio, Mission). California has (or has had) the Centro Cultural de la Raza (San Diego), the Mechicano Art Center (now defunct), the Plaza de la Raza, the Goez Gallery, Self-Help Graphics & Art, and the Social and Public Art Resource Center, or SPARC (all in Los Angeles); the Casa de la Raza (Santa Barbara); the former Casa Hispana de Bellas Artes, Galeria de la Raza/Studio 24, the Mexican Museum, La Raza Graphic Center, Inc. (all in San Francisco); and the Centro de Artistas Chicanos (Sacramento). Seattle's Centro de la Raza served as the site for murals, poster making and cultural activities, and Oregon has the Colegio Cesar Chavez (Mount Angel), an independent Chicano institution which has been the base for posters and murals.

Finally, it should be noted that Chicano studies and research libraries, academic departments, and student organizations like the United Mexican American Students (UMAS) and related groups such as the Mexican American Youth Organization (MAYO), which later became the Movimiento Estudiantil Chicano de Aztlan (MEChA), were instrumental in getting commissions for murals on college and university campuses, publishing student newspapers and magazines which included works of art, pressuring campus art galleries for Chicano art exhibits, and establishing archives of Chicano culture and occasionally of Chicano film. In the late 1960s and early 1970s Semanas de la Raza were popular on college campuses, generally around the 5th of May or the 16th of September, and these included visual arts and other cultural forms during the week of activities.

The Anti-Vietnam War Movement

From 1964 to 1972, the United States was involved in a maximum military effort in Vietnam that eventually spread to Cambodia and Laos. In the course of this conflict there developed in the United States the greatest antiwar movement the nation had ever experienced - a movement that played a critical part in bringing the war to an end. By early 1968, the war began touching the conscience of many Americans. There was the question of 50,000 American dead, 250,000 wounded, untold numbers of Vietnamese casualties, documented stories of U.S. brutalities like the My Lai massacre, and no end in sight. Early opposition to the war came from the civil rights movement, and from other peoples of color in the United States who felt that too many of their own were dying in Vietnam in what many considered a "white man's war" while their own peoples lived with poverty and racism in the United States.

As early as 1967 Rodolfo "Corky" Gonzalez of Denver's Crusade for Justice and Reies Lopez Tijerina of New Mexico's La Alianza Federal de Mercedes (the Federal Alliance of Land Grants) spoke at an East Los Angeles antiwar rally. In 1969, as one event in a nationwide series of moratoria, the newly formed National Chicano Moratorium Committee held its first demonstration in Los Angeles, followed by hundreds of local Chicano moratoria in other cities. These actions culminated in the National Moratorium in East Los Angeles on August 29, 1970 attended by between 20,000 and 30,000 participants.[96] The demonstration was attacked by deputy sheriffs and police, and resulted in the death of *Los Angeles Times* newsman Ruben Salazar, killed by a tear gas projectile while sitting in the Silver Dollar Cafe. It was the same year that four protesting students were killed at Kent State University, which received far wider news coverage than the Salazar death.

Chicano artists were strongly moved by these events which were commemorated in murals, posters, paintings, and documentary films. Images from the march, the attack of the

---

[96] Acuña, *Occupied America*, p. 367.

police, the officers gathered outside the Silver Dollar, and portraits of Ruben Salazar as a martyr made their appearance during succeeding years in many works of art.

The American Indian Movement and Chicano Neo-Indigenism

In the first half of the 1960s, Indian communities and nations which had been fighting battles against genocide and land expropriation long before the 20th century, again began to raise the embarrassing topic of treaties violated by the United States government. "Fish-ins" were held in Washington state; a Pan-Indian group occupied Alcatraz Island in 1969; Navajos and Hopi of New Mexico protested strip mining at Black Mesa; Pit River Indians of northern California occupied their former lands, etc. However, the most widely publicized and dramatic event was the 1973 occupation by the Oglala Sioux of Wounded Knee village at the Pine River Reservation in South Dakota, the site of an 1890 massacre by the U.S. Cavalry. The occupation was a symbol of the demand for Indian land and rights, and the Oglala Sioux were joined by outside friends, including Chicano activists.

It is an irony of history that the Indians of the Southwest were first conquered (either controlled, placed in peonage, or enslaved) by the Spanish and mestizo invaders and colonizers of the 17th century. However, by the 19th century, both Indians and Mexicans were subjugated under variations of the ideology of "manifest destiny," and the process of Anglo usurpation of lands affected both groups. Mexicans and Mexican Americans in the borderlands, especially in the Rio Grande Valley from El Paso to Taos, had long made common cause with sedentary Indian communities against the nomadic and warlike Comanche and Apache raiders of the Southwest who never accepted Spanish political domination.[97] In the 1960s the surge of Indian protest on behalf of land rights paralleled that of the newly organized Chicano movement. Reies Lopez Tijerina organized the land rights movement in New Mexico, laying claim to millions of acres originally owned by Hispano-Mexican communities, in precisely the same time period that Indians had unsuccessfully occupied Alcatraz to establish an Indian University. Two years later the "Indians of all Tribes" occupied it again. That Chicanos and Indians should continue to make common cause was for the benefit of both groups, combatting what was seen as a common oppressor. In California, that common cause was culturally expressed through the creation of D-Q University which, from 1970 to 1978, was a joint Indian-Chicano educational institution whose name derived from Deganawidah, the founder of the Iroquois Confederacy, and Quetzalcoatl, Toltec leader, statesman, and deity from central Mexico.[98]

Chicano-Indian unity was expressed by the Chicano artistic movement in a number of ways, the primary of which are encompassed by what can be called two Indian "time lines" - that of the pre-Columbian Indian civilizations of Middle America, and the other of the modern Indian cultures in both Mexico and the United States. So pervasive has been the focus on pre-Columbian imagery in Chicano art from its earliest years to the present, that we can designate this consciousness as neo-indigenist, comparing it to the great wave of indigenism prevalent in Latin America in the 1920s and 1930s, most strongly in Mexico, and most thoroughly in the work of Diego Rivera.[99]

It has been pointed out that Indianist culture in Latin America had two distinct functions: one, a direct social purpose to arouse an awareness of the plight of submerged sections of the population; the other, to set up values of Indian culture and civilization as an

---

[97] Edward H. Spicer, *Cycles of Conquest: The Impact of Spain, Mexico, and the United States on the Indians of the Southwest, 1533-1960.* Tucson, AZ: The University of Arizona Press, 1981, p. 241.

[98] See Jennifer Kerr, "Indian School Survives Battle. School Appeared Doomed Only Year Ago," *The Los Angeles Times* (September 21, 1980), p. I-3.

[99] For a comparison of Mexican indigenism and Chicano neo-indigenism in the visual arts, see Shifra M. Goldman, "Mexican Muralism: Its Social-Educative Roles in Latin America and the United States," *Aztlán: International Journal of Chicano Studies Research,* Vol. 13, nos. 1 and 2 (Spring-Fall 1982), p. 113-117 and 129-130.

alternative to European values.[100] In both the Mexican and Chicano cases, indigenism had similar functions, though under far different historical circumstances. Equally in both cases indigenism was of an archaisizing and romantic character. In the search for roots, for an affirmation of heritage in the extinguished past, the urge toward the creation of heroic mythology was strong. Thus in Chicano culture we encounter the concept of Aztlan, which is a speculative bit of history, itself derived from Aztec myth, not verified (or verifiable?) by archeology. We further encounter the notion, widely disseminated in visual and literary forms, of Chicanos as descendents of the elite rulers of the Aztec and the Maya. The hundreds, perhaps thousands of pyramids, Aztec or Maya princes, princesses, warriors, elitist religious symbols, adaptations of monumental sculptures and temple paintings, and similar material that permeate Chicano visual arts in all media and techniques, is sufficient testimony to this preoccupation.

Nevertheless, mythologizing is not necessarily a negative process for a modern political and cultural community systematically deprived of its history and ethnicity. Starting from a materialist point of view, the Russian writer Maxim Gorky speaking in 1934 gives us what can be considered a profound understanding of the relationship between mythical creation and reality. He said:

> Any myth is a piece of imagining. Imagining means abstracting the fundamental idea underlying the sum of a given reality, and embodying it in an image; that gives us realism. But if the meaning of what has been abstracted from reality is amplified through the addition of the desired and the possible - if we supplement it through the logic of hypothesis...then we have the kind of romanticism which underlies the myth, and is most beneficial in promoting a revolutionary attitude toward reality, an attitude that in practice refashions the world.[101]

A similar thought is expressed in the following statement: "the linkage of indigenous thought to contemporary reality gave the Chicano movement mythic and psychic energies that could be directed toward its political and economic goals."[102] For our present purposes, we can consider the mythologizing of pre-Columbian cultures by the Mexican School and by Chicano artists, as poetic symbols for contemporary struggles. The utopian function can merge with an exemplary function so that mythic heroes (and heroines) serve as models for emulation, as ways to freedom, as signposts to victory over hostile forces.[103] This process functioned in modern Mexico through the idealizing of the Aztec emperor Cuauhtemoc and the Toltec deified ruler Quetzalcoatl. The process also appplied to the colonial Virgin of Guadalupe. And it occurred with the heroicizing of Father Hidalgo from the Independence period, and the revolutionary leaders Emiliano Zapata and Francisco "Pancho" Villa, the former of whom became almost sanctified in post-Zapata artmaking among contemporary Chicanos as among Mexicans in earlier periods.[104]

Nevertheless, in spite of this argument for the special historical and social circumstances within which myth-making is a positive and life-enhancing aspect of "refashioning the world," a critical - not to say skeptical - eye must always be directed at mythologizing. When it becomes fixed, ossified, dogmatic, and unthinking, it passes into ideology (or in art, empty decoration) which can seriously lag behind reality and be detrimental to understanding. (The

---

[100] Franco, *The Modern Culture of Latin America*, p. 120.

[101] Maxim Gorky reprinted in Maynard Solomon (ed.), *Marxism and Art: Essays Classic and Contemporary*. New York: Random House, 1974, p. 244.

[102] Tomás Ybarra-Frausto, "Alurista's Poetics: The Oral, the Bilingual, the Pre-Columbian," in Joseph Sommers and Tomás Ybarra-Frausto (eds.), *Modern Chicano Writers: A Collection of Critical Essays*. Englewood Cliffs, NJ: Prentice-Hall, 1979, p. 119.

[103] Solomon (ed.), *Marxism and Art*, p. 242.

[104] See the catalog *Exposición homenaje nacional a Emiliano Zapata en el centenario de su nacimiento (1879-1979)*. Mexico City: Instituto Nacional de Bellas Artes/SEP, 1979-1980. Two hundred eighty-four works of art and historical documents were on exhibit.

same can be said for nationalism: its application can be progressive and liberating; but it can also be reactionary and obfuscating.) To the degree that pre-Columbian motifs in Chicano art served to establish pride and a sense of historical identity for the artists and the communities they addressed, to the degree that such motifs were an antidote to modern anti-Indian racism which considered all Indians and mestizos inferior peoples with a long list of negative and undesirable traits, neo-indigenism served a positive function. It permitted Chicanos to trace their history not only in Middle American Indian sources, but their more recent mestizaje with modern Indians - from the 1680 Pueblo Revolt in New Mexico to the commingling that has continued to take place among Mexicans and Indians in the borderlands (both personally and culturally) - a fact of history that had been obscured in the Southwest by emphasis on the fantasy of the "Spanish" heritage.

The contemporary Chicano-Indian alliance, born from a sense of shared oppression and racism, has found expression in Chicano art with images of Indian leaders of the past and of the present. At this stage of U.S. history, with Indians of all tribes, nations and communities considered subjugated, and with Apache and Comanche raids a thing of the past,[105] Chicano artists have rendered homage to such Apache leaders as Geronimo whose consistent posture of resistance to the U.S. government and consequent imprisonments in the last quarter of the 19th century serve as a symbol for contemporary resistance.[106] From present Indian resistance comes an image such as that of Leonard Peltier, an important leader within the American Indian Movement which spearheaded the Wounded Knee occupation. On the national defense committee formed when Peltier was indicted on criminal charges, is Texas Chicano poet Raul Salinas who strongly identifies with Indian issues not only in the United States, but in Latin America. Salinas, like others (including Chicago artist/poet Carlos Cortez) has carried this identification into the sartorial, assuming certain Indian articles of clothing, as well as braided hair, jewelry, and religious symbols. Some have assumed North American Indian names which complement the pre-Columbian names adopted in the early seventies. In addition, many Chicano student newspapers have reproduced graphics and stories from Native American publications. In 1977 the Movimiento Artistico Chicano (MARCH) of Chicago joined with the Chicago Indian Artists' Guild for a series of cultural events and an art exhibit under the title of "Anisinabe Waki-Aztlan." Its statement of purpose is worth quoting in some detail since it illuminates the theoretical point being raised here, and makes more emphatic on a cultural level the updating of Indianism from the ancient era to the modern:

> ANISINABE WAKI-AZTLAN...a strange powerful concept, this coming together of native peoples....How did it happen that these two peoples - Chicanos and Native Americans - who do not often act in concert, decided at this time and in this place to attempt the potent magic of a coming together?

> The setting was about a year ago, when members of MARCH and of the American Indian Artists' Guild discovered each other's existence and began a series of informal discussions in an effort to find the extent of their mutual interests and a common bond. The talks were sometimes difficult, as cross-cultural contact can be, but the clear existence of a shared experience of conquest and cultural alienation made both groups want to carry on.[107]

A similar process took place in 1980 when the group Academia de la Nueva Raza composed of writers, academics, and artists from Albuquerque and the Upper Rio Grande Valley of New Mexico joined with the Tri-Centennial Commission of the All-Indian Pueblo Council

---

[105] Though it should be noted that as late as the 1930s and 1940s, Southwest communities objected to New Deal murals depicting these Indian peoples because the memory of the raids was still strong.

[106] Victor Ochoa's image of Geronimo on the exterior of the Centro Cultural de la Raza in San Diego, CA is one such example. North American Indians have been depicted by Carlos Rosas of Texas and Adolfo "Zarco" Guerrero of Arizona, among others.

[107] Program for *Anisinabe Waki-Aztlan* exhibit and activities, Truman College, Chicano, IL, 1977.

to celebrate the 300 year legacy of the 1680 Pueblo Indian Revolt. In the publication that resulted from this celebration, Rudolfo Anaya, co-editor with Indian writer Simon Ortiz, wrote the following:

> Active revolt against oppressive government is not a new notion to the native people of the Americas....In that year of 1680 the land and the survival of a native culture were at stake, and those who would oppress sought to use these elements to turn the people against each other. But in spite of these tyrants [the Spanish rulers]...they learned to live together and to share the precious earth and water of the Rio Grande Valley and the mountains of the Sangre de Cristo. These people were...the common people of the land.[108]

Like the Chicago collaboration, *Ceremony of Brotherhood* is illustrated by works of art from Native American and Chicano artists from many parts of the Southwest. Chicano artists and writers in New Mexico have questioned the New Mexican version of the "fantasy heritage" which insists on the appelation "Hispanic" or "Spanish" (and sometimes "pure-blooded" Spanish) maintained largely by the Spanish-speaking middle and upper class. They prefer to use the more accurate term "Indo-Hispano/ic." In the arts the unique cultural heritage of the Upper Rio Grande (New Mexico/Southern Colorado) has been taken up by Chicanos challenging the archaistic attitudes established by the "revivalist" Spanish Colonial Arts Society and continued by local arts planners and tourist-oriented merchants. While rooting themselves in the traditional arts of adobe house construction and hand plastering (not the jerry-built concrete imitations of motel owners and land speculators), spinning and weaving, carving, ceramic pottery, and domestic crafts, Chicano artists insist on their right and duty to combine these traditions with modern innovations so as to create a *living* art. Further, they openly and proudly acknowledge the infusion of Indian Pueblo architecture and craft methods and ideas in the work they do.[109]

One further example can be mentioned in connection with this question: the fifth Kanto al Pueblo[110] which took place in 1982 in Chicago was held "In the Spirit of Sitting Bull." This national multi-disciplinary cultural event, one of a series held since 1977, was hosted at its fourth convocation by the Fort McDowell Yavapai Indian Reservation near Phoenix (1980). The sixth event is planned to include active participation from various indigenous communities from Canada, the United States, Central and South America.

We have dealt above with the political aspects of Chicano neo-indigenism. However, there has been, since the beginning, a strong religious component - spiritual or mystical, depending on how one wishes to define this phenomenon - which is apparent in Chicano literature, theatre, and visual arts. Chicanos were very impressed with Carlos Castaneda's *The Teachings of Don Juan: A Yaqui Way of Knowledge,* published in 1968 and purportedly based on interviews with a Mexican *brujo,* or shaman, while Castaneda was an anthropology student at the University of California, Los Angeles. In the drug-oriented culture of the sixties, this book had immediate general success, as did Castaneda's subsequent volumes, being compared favorably with Aldous Huxley's *Doors of Perception.* Its Southwest orientation, as well as the Latino nationality of the author made it especially attractive to Chicanos who were certainly not immune to the hippyism and drug culture attitudes of the sixties. If North American middle class hippies expressed their revolt and romantic nostalgia by reverting to pioneer and Indian dress (buckskin, beads, "granny" dresses, Benjamin Franklin eyeglasses, long or braided hair, etc.); a return to communal living and the land; and an immersion in Hindu mysticism; working class Chicano artists and writers looked to the sacred texts, social

---

[108] Rudolfo A. Anaya and Simon J. Ortiz (eds.), *1680-1980: A Ceremony of Brotherhood.* Albuquerque, NM: Academia, 1981, p. 2-3.

[109] Interviews with *enjarradora/* contractor Anita Rodriguez, El Prado, NM (June 10, 1984) and weaver Teresa Archuleta-Sagel, Española, NM (June 9, 1984).

[110] The substitution of the "K" for the "C" in the four preceding Canto al Pueblo events was specifically assumed to conform to usages in indigenous languages, according to the promoters.

customs, and artistic forms of the ancient Maya, Aztec, and Toltec, and to modern Indian spiritual beliefs in the later years. Chicanos felt, with reason, that they had a more legitimate claim to Amerindian culture than the hippies, and that they were indigenous to and had a claim to the land by virtue of their history (not excluding the fact that many came from rural or migrant labor families and knew about farming and picking crops in a brutal, first hand way).

Furthermore, Chicano indigenist religiosity was syncretic, combining ancient Indian deities with Catholic ones - a combination with many Mexican folk and fine art predecessors, including the earlier-mentioned Conchero and Matachin dancers of the borderlands. Quetzalcoatl, the feathered serpent (certainly one of the most ubiquitous images in Chicano art) fuses with, or replaces, Christ "as our own god." Serpents and pyramids are routinely combined with Christian crosses, sacred hearts, and other Catholic symbols in Chicano art. In recent years, as Chicana women have increasingly forefronted in the artistic scene, the image of Coatlicue, dread Aztec goddess of the snake heads and skirts, has been compared with the Virgin of Guadalupe as common mothers of the "race."

Though the spiritual aspect of neo-indigenism is concurrent with the political aspect, it would appear that when the Chicano art/cultural movement lost its political base in the mid-1970s, neo-indigenism increasingly focused on mystical elements from contemporary Indian life on both sides of the border. In the poetry of Alurista, in the early theatre of Luis Valdez and the Teatro Campesino, the mythic of both pre-Columbian and Catholic was fused with social protest, with ideas of reform and even nationhood. In the later years, neo-indigenism has become more exclusively cultural, magical, or mystical.

Feminism and the Chicana Artist[111]

There is no question that Chicana women were influenced by the feminist movement whose modern reincarnation was almost simultaneous with that of the Chicano movement: both products of the sixties. Though women played a prominent role in the Chicano movement, they felt the need for a clearer articulation of their own role in society. The movement called for an end to oppression - discrimination, racism, and poverty - goals which Chicanas supported unequivocally; but it did not propose basic changes in male-female relations or the status of women. Chicanas began to sense their power and speak out on their own behalf. They established organizations like the Mexican American Women's Organization, the Comision Femenil Mexicana, the Mexican American Business and Professional Women, the Hijas de Cuauhtemoc, and the Concilio Mujeres. In Texas, the art group Mujeres Artistas del Suroeste (MAS; Southwestern Women Artists) organized exhibits for Chicana and Latina women. In San Francisco the Mujeres Muralistas painted murals as a collective. Publications like *Encuentro Femenil, Popo Femenil,* and *La Razon Mestiza* appeared.

For women, simply becoming artists frequently involved breaking stereotypes within the patriarchial family (or the working class family that conceived no economic advantage to be derived from entering the arts); persisting within the educational system, especially in opposition to its insistence on "mainstream" culture and art forms; juggling duties as lovers, wives, mothers, and workers with the time for creative work; and finally, being sufficiently self-confident and assertive to obtain exhibition space or commissions.

If information is sparse about Mexican American male artists before 1965, the information about women is even more sparse. Quirarte's book *Mexican American Artists* mentions only two women, both born in the early years of this century.[112] However there is little doubt that Mexican American women exercised their creativity in a multitude of ways within their

---

[111] The section on feminism and the Chicana artist has been excerpted from text of the catalog by Shifra M. Goldman, *Chicana Voices & Visions: A National Exhibit of Women Artists,* Venice, CA: Social and Public Art Resource Center, 1983.

[112] Consuelo Gonzalez Amezcua and Margaret Herrera Chavez.

own homes. Extrapolating from the evidence that is slowly coming in, women decorated their homes, crocheted, embroidered, knitted, made lace, and painted on a variety of surfaces. New Mexican women have a long history as artisans and *enjarradoras* (plasterers of adobe houses).

After 1965, the public phase of Chicana art - street murals and posters - which reached its production nadir in the mid-seventies, was not conducive to much female participation. The problems of working outdoors on a large scale, of being subject to the comments of the passing public, and the strenuous nature of the work in light of how women are socialized for physical effort, militated against their participation. Among the dedicated women muralists, Judith Baca, then director of the Mural Resource Center in Los Angeles, early recognized this problem and, in addition to her regular mural manual for art directors and neighborhood teams, photocopied an illustrated *Woman's Manual: How to Assemble Scaffolding.*

The great surge of women artists corresponded with the "privatization" of Chicano art in the late seventies - which itself corresponded to a diminution of the intense activism of earlier years. As the Chicano gallery structure expanded in many states of the Southwest, and community and feminist galleries became aware of Chicanas, the possibilities for exhibitions of smaller, more intimate work also expanded. Women's art (overwhelmingly representational) has engaged many new themes and interpretations that reflect different realities and perceptions. From the beginning, positive images of active women began to appear. One of the most ubiquitous images in male art (derived from Mexican calendars) has been the sexy, often semi-nude figure of the Aztec princess from the Ixtaccihuatl/Popocatepetl legend, carried "Jane/Tarzan" fashion by a gloriously arrayed prince. This rendition epitomizes the notion of the passive woman protected by the active man. In its place, Chicana artists substituted the heroines from the Mexican Revolution (particularly those culled from the photographic archives of Agustin Victor Casasola), labor leaders, women associated with alternative schools and clinics, working women, women in protest. In other words, *active* women who shape their lives and environments.

These were extroverted images. The life and art of Mexican painter Frida Kahlo provided an introverted model: woman focused on her interior life, on the cycles of birth and death, on pain and fortitude, on the sublimation of the self in art. The whole feminist art movement was fascinated by Kahlo; but for Chicana artists she provided a needed role model. Not only was her art of great interest and beauty, but her whole life, lived as a work of art, was intriguing. Kahlo's brilliant color, minute detail, exuberant use of plant forms, fusion of the pre-Columbian and the modern, and use of the self-portrait as a mode began to appear in many Chicana works.

Another source of female imagery and inspiration (not only for women, but for men as well) was the vernacular art of the Southwest, particularly home altars which are created and tended by women. Reinforced by Mexican altars for the Dia de los Muertos (Day of the Dead), the altar, as a cumulative sculptural object, passed into Chicano(a) art in numerous variations.

Pintas and Pintos (Prisons and Prisoners)

One can hardly talk about poverty and racism without raising the issue of prisons and their inmates. It has long been known that the numbers of Black and Chicano prisoners far exceed their relative proportion in the population. In addition to "economic" prisoners, we can talk about "social" prisoners, those in jail because the system which kept them in poverty, without hope, without dignity and a sense of self-worth, finally caused an explosion of wrath, or a continuous state of wrath.

To economic and social prisoners must be added, in the 1960s and 1970s, the number of political prisoners. These are people who went to jail in great numbers on behalf of political principles and active social protest, or who, being in jail, developed political consciousness as a means of understanding their plight in the context of the world outside, and of alleviating it. In the sixties and seventies, prison rebellions multiplied and took on an unprecedented political character.

Prisons and prisoners figure in Chicano literature, from the imprisonment of Pachucos in *Zoot Suit,* to the poetry of writers who are former *pintos.* Pintos not only wrote poetry, but published newspapers with illustrations, and painted murals within the jails when they were able and in the community when released. The Chicano movement gave hope and pride to the incarcerated, and painters in prison, largely self-taught, began to use the motifs of the Chicano movement in their art. The only study on this subject of which we are aware is a student paper (June 1979) by Angelina Veyna, done for a pre-Columbian art history class at the University of California, Los Angeles. It is titled "Pre-Columbian Motifs Displayed in Pinto Art." Veyna takes her information from two pinto newspapers, *El Grito de Aztlan* and *El Alambre,* and discusses the purely Indian motifs and those in which contemporary motifs (like the United Farm Workers flag) are combined with the Indian. At least one Chicano artist, Leonard Castellanos of the Mechicano Art Center, spent considerable time teaching art in a California penal institution.

Imprisonment in the barrio is related to imprisonment in jail, and the cultural manifestations of either "jail" is a subject to be studied for anyone interested in the social history of Chicano art. An excellent beginning would be a survey of Chicano murals in U.S. prisons.

Hollywood: Making and Breaking the Stereotypes

The history of Chicano filmmaking has been made very much more accessible by the recent (1985) appearance of *Chicano Cinema: Research, Reviews, and Resources,* edited by Gary D. Keller,[113] with a splendid essay by the editor, an extensive filmography, including names and addresses of distributors, of Chicano/Latino films, and a number of excellent critical and historical articles on this most public of Chicano art forms.

Chicano Cinema is the third book to appear that deals with the image of Mexicans/Chicanos in film; it is the first that focuses completely on films made *by* Chicanos. The other two (Allen L. Woll, *The Latin Image in American Film,* and Arthur G. Pettit, *Images of the Mexican American in Fiction and Film)*[114] document the stereotypes perpetuated within the film genre emanating from Hollywood, from the early part of the 20th century through their respective dates of publication. All three books agree that Hollywood has shown male Mexicans as "greasers," bandidos, buffoons, gay lovers, and gangsters, and as "violent, dirty, thieving, rapacious, and stupid,"[115] and women as "Mexican spitfires" or dark ladies - sexy, seductive, fickle, or suffering mother or wife. The Mexican is one "to be killed, mocked, punished, seduced, or redeemed by Anglo protagonists."[116] The woman can get her man only if she is not confronted with competition from a blonde Anglo; in that case, she is automatically out of the running.

At certain politic moments (like the socially oriented 1930s and the period prior to World War II when the United States wished better relations with potential Latin American allies) the Hollywood formula improved somewhat. However, as late as the 1980s, Hollywood responded to its own perceived interests and a changing market by following the "Blaxploitation" (Black exploitation) films, often made by Black directors and actors, with "Mexploitation" films like *Boulevard Nights* (1979) and *Walk Proud* (1981) in which Chicano actors appeared.

---

113 Gary D. Keller (ed.), *Chicano Cinema: Research, Reviews, and Resources.* Binghamton, NY: Bilingual Review/Press, 1985.

114 Allen L. Woll, *The Latin Image in American Film,* Los Angeles, CA: Latin American Center Publications, University of California, Los Angeles, 1977 and 1980 [revised edition]. Arthur G. Pettit, *Images of the Mexican American in Fiction and Film.* College Station, TX: Texas A & M University Press, 1980.

115 Sylvia Morales, "Chicano-Produced Celluloid Mujeres," in Keller (ed.), *Chicano Cinema,* p. 89.

116 Gary D. Keller, "The Image of the Chicano in Mexican, United States, and Chicano Cinema: An Overview," in Keller (ed.), *Chicano Cinema,* p. 30.

If the Hollywood blacklist of the 1950s can be said to have had any positive aspect, it surely would be the production of the first film to effectively and seriously deal with Mexican Americans as people and as workers, including a strong role for women: the film *Salt of the Earth,* directed by Herbert Biberman from a screenplay by Michael Wilson. Since then, there have been sensitive filmmakers who are not Chicano who have made exemplary films, like Les Blank's *Chulas Fronteras,* and Robert Young's *Alambrista.*

However, overwhelmingly, it was obvious that if the image of Mexicans in the United States was to be presented without stereotypes and with veracity, the job had to be done by Chicano filmmakers themselves, and in the late 1960s such filmmakers appeared. The earliest to make a film was the Teatro Campesino (1967), followed several years later by Chicanos working in television to produce documentaries, particularly Jesus Salvador Trevino, Moctezuma Esparza, Sylvia Morales, Susan Racho, Jose Luis Ruiz, Ricardo Soto, Esperanza Vasquez, and others. A younger generation is ably represented by Mexican-born Isaac Artenstein of San Diego-based Cinewest, and Gregory Nava, also of San Diego, producer of *El Norte.* That Chicanos got their start, and continued to produce primarily documentary rather than feature films (including films on Chicano art) throughout the seventies, had less to do with preference than with available funding. However, a number of important films were produced which received circulation on educational and occasionally commercial television, and through Chicano studies programs in academic institutions. In addition, filmmakers, like artists and writers, were faced with problems of dissemination, and created alternative structures to show Chicano films, and, on occasion, networked with a broad spectrum of independent filmmakers across the United States.[117] The San Antonio Cinefestival, originally sponsored by Oblate College since 1975, and in recent years by the Guadalupe Cultural Arts Center, has had two functions: to create a forum for Chicano and Latino films *not* widely distributed through mainstream television and the film industry, and to provide a wider audience for all Chicano-made film. A few years later, in July 1977, the Chicano Cinema Caucus was established in Los Angeles, publishing its first *Newsletter* in December 1978. The stated purpose of the "forty independent producers and filmmakers" was to advance the "development, production, distribution, promotion and exhibition of a body of film and video productions which meaningfully address the social, economic, political and cultural needs and concerns of the Latino people in the United States." The group met regularly through 1979 to discuss the "aesthetics, ideology, production and distribution of Chicano and related cinema and to view and critique films of all kinds." The Coalition included both professionals and postgraduate film students.[118] Through the leadership of Jesus Trevino and the steering group, the Coalition established ties with other independent filmmakers and with Latin American filmmakers, particularly with those of Mexico, Puerto Rico, Cuba, and Chile (those in exile). In late 1983, a Hollywood-based membership group of media professionals calling itself HAMAS (Hispanic Academy of Media Arts and Sciences) was established to promote "equitable employment opportunities for qualified Hispanics" and to combat negative portrayals in the arts and in the media.[119]

The San Antonio Cinefestival was followed in 1981 and 1982 by the "Cine Sin Fronteras" (Cinema Without Borders) festival of Chicano and Mexican films organized by film students at the University of California, Los Angeles; the 1982 and 1983 "Chicano Film Festival" in Detroit, sponsored by Eastern Michigan University and the Bilingual Review/Press; and the 1985 film conference "New Film, New Frontiers: Contemporary Mexican and

---

[117] The U.S. Conference for an Alternative Cinema held at Bard College, New York (June 12-17), 1979. A critique of the conference from the Black perspective and a position paper of the Third World Caucus at the Conference can be found in *Chamba Notes: A Film Newsletter,* Hollywood, CA, (Summer 1979), p. 6-8. See also *Jump Cut,* no. 21 (November 1979) for a full report.

[118] "Chicano Cinema Coalition," unpublished manuscript, September 1, 1979.

[119] Brochure for the Hispanic Academy of Media Arts and Sciences (HAMAS), Hollywood Chapter, n.d. See also Luis Jimenez, "Cambia la imagen del Latino en Hollywood," *La Opinion,* (June 9, 1985), *La Comunidad* supplement, p. 14-15.

Chicano Film" at the University of California, Irvine.

It is evident that the 1970s was a period in which the absolute hegemony of the Hollywood film industry was under challenge, not only by independent filmmakers in the United States but by the growing film production in nations that had long been considered peripheral: Australia, Latin American and Caribbean countries - particularly those involved in New Cinema (Brazil, Chile, Argentina, Cuba, etc.) and Mexico during the Echeverria regime, - African countries, China, etc. This is not to suggest that these films were readily available to broad audiences; they required viewing at special festivals like Los Angeles' Filmex (an annual international film festival that began in 1971) from which they passed to commercial viewing at the "art" houses which catered to special, generally middle class intellectual audiences. PBS, the Public Broadcasting System (National Educational Television/NET circuit) also offered airing, on occasion, to non-European and independent films. In fact, PBS, under pressure in the Southwest, was the earliest to present Chicano documentary programming and give employment to filmmakers. The Hollywood film industry, however, by and large did not open its gates to Chicano filmmakers, with the notable exception of *Zoot Suit*. Thus there was the need for alternative methods of production and dissemination. As of this writing, Chicano film still remains a very marginal operation. What the future holds in the direction of cable television (in which several filmmakers are already involved commercially), and the notion of narrow target audiences rather than the "lowest common denominator" philosophy which seems to dominate television presently, remains to be seen.

Any consideration of film and television, however, must always take into account that these mass media forms, and the profitable apparatus set up for their dissemination and marketing, are not only the most expensive art forms in existence but the most totally under control of corporate interests. They are the main ideological apparatus of the capitalist system - not only in the United States, but throughout the world where U.S. film and television (via satellite) are dominant - and are part of a larger structure of mass communication. For the reader interested in exploring this structure, we recommend Herbert I. Schiller's two books *Mass Communications and American Empire* and *The Mind Managers,* and Armand Mattelart's *Transnationals and the Third World,* especially sections in the latter which discuss the culture, knowledge, and consciousness industries and the film and television industries.[120] The point to be made here is that Chicano filmmakers, of all Chicano artists, function under the most difficult economic and ideological conditions. Even independent films can cost upwards of a half million dollars, must depend on governmental (fast diminishing) or private funding, and be shown in movie houses posited on the profit motive, or on television which even in the "public sector" (PBS) has increasingly come to be dominated over the last ten or more years by giant corporate interests like Mobil Oil, Exxon, and others.

Architecture

The place to begin considering Chicano involvement in architecture is New Mexico, though we have seen in the earlier segments of the chronology that Mexican American artisans played a role in building and ornamenting houses in several areas of the Southwest. What we are concerned with here, however, is the *designing* as well as the construction, and until we have more evidence about states like Texas and California in the period before 1965, we must conclude that only in New Mexico (and southern Colorado which was originally part of New Mexican territory) did Mexican Americans take an active role in constructing and designing their own buildings as part of a long tradition dating back to the 17th century.

During the 1960s, as *chicanismo* penetrated many areas of the Southwest, a very regional variation of that consciousness occurred in New Mexico. Among young intellectuals and artists a new kind of revivalism occurred, one that was conscious of the rapidly vanishing character of Indo-Hispano culture under the impact of land loss and continuing

---

120 Herbert I. Schiller, *Mass Communications and American Empire.* Boston, MA: Beacon Press, 1969. Herbert I. Schiller, *The Mind Managers.* Boston, MA: Beacon Press, 1973. Mattelart book, see note 2.

impoverishment of New Mexican peoples of the Upper Rio Grande, long the stronghold of this culture. This revivalism took two forms: one was to document as much of this vanishing culture as possible in the form of photographs, paintings, and written material; the other was to update and bring into contemporary usage the traditional cultural forms of the past without the intervention of outside "patronage" such as characterized the 1920s. One manifestation of this revival was the building of contemporary adobe homes. Traditional materials and techniques were employed, but combined with contemporary design and conveniences. (Ironically, the parents of some adobe house builders were only too glad to move out of their "old fashioned" houses, as economics permitted, as were siblings with no connection to the idealist revival concepts.)

The personality that emerges in northern New Mexico is Anita Rodriguez, who terms herself an "enjarradora" or plasterer, a role assigned wholly to women in the Pueblo Indian villages, and in the Indo-Hispano communities as well. Rodriguez, however, is more than a plasterer. With an all-female crew and a contractor's license, she designs and builds adobe fireplaces, built-in benches, waxed mud floors, and entire rooms. The fireplaces, for example, have the most up-to-date flues, though they conform to the older fireplaces in form. Her work is very sculptural in feeling, and well-suited to the climate.

Two other centers of Chicano architecture have arisen in the San Francisco Bay Area and in Los Angeles. In Spring 1972, architecture students at the University of California, Berkeley, produced an unpublished manifesto called "Tonitines Chicano Architecture por Chicanos in Architecture." The word *Tonitines* is a reference to Tonatiuh, the sun god occupying the central position in the Aztec Calendar Stone. The manifesto called upon Chicano architecture students to shape an alternative education for themselves so they could enter the barrio after graduation and construct buildings reflecting the "values and concerns of the poor and oppressed." They also saw "professionalism as one of the threats to the real progress of Chicanos in Aztlan," a not uncommon notion among artists in the early seventies. "Professionalism" could connote European values, Anglo efficiency and the profit motive, and other concepts of the dominant society that Chicanos rejected in favor of greater humanism. Organized in 1971 as the Chicano Architectural Students Association, or CASA (house), the students were approached by the Richmond Architectural Commission to design a cultural center and market. The unbuilt design that eventually evolved for the market was a sloped, presumably Maya, pyramid with four ramps surrounded by four courtyards raised on stilts, all within a walled complex with ramps and tunnels. Suggested as ideas toward a Chicano aesthetic were the following: the use of flags and banners, the use of the traditional Spanish colonial sense of space, painted walls, signs in Spanish, and a human scale. Suggested materials for decoration were pottery reliefs, mobile pottery stools, mosaic, flowers and trees. The goal of the students was to design architecture in the barrio in an atmosphere free from money, from profit, from machinery - where clients were not mere clients, and service not mere money.

These obviously utopian and high-spirited ideals were very much in keeping with the euphoria of the Chicano movement at the time, and were no more realizable in architecture than they would have been in film, since both are high-priced art forms subject to the patronage of governments or corporations. Nevertheless the students networked and shared ideas with others from Arizona State University, Colorado State University, the University of Colorado, Denver, Harvard University, the University of California, Los Angeles, and Laney College in Oakland. CASA continues to exist, and in 1983 published a collection of essays in a book, *Our Barrios: Past, Present and Future.*[121] Leafing through its pages, the finished buildings and designs for buildings illustrated demonstrate that Chicano architects have not abandoned some of the ideas projected over ten years earlier: pyramid-like shapes, Spanish colonial elements, and external ornamentation combine with contemporary house and building

---

[121] *Our Barrios: Past, Present and Future. A Look at Raza/Latinos and the Built Environment.* Berkeley, CA: Chicano Architectural Students Association, University of California, Berkeley, 1983.

forms in the International Style. It should be noted that the only woman architect included, Sandra Aguilar (a graduate student at Berkeley), is from New Mexico, and her plan reverts to the Spanish-Pueblo style.

In Los Angeles, four architects have banded together in a private company known as Barrio Planners, Inc., whose activities are not only in East Los Angeles, but in other parts of California, including participation in building homes at the self-run community known as Cabrillo Village.[122]

Finally, mention should be made of Roland V. Rodriguez of San Antonio whose *Urban Design Primer*[123] comes full circle to the first pueblos and city planning of the Spanish colonizers. Rodriguez conveyed to his architecture students at San Antonio College, that the buildings and spatial use in San Antonio resonate with European influence - particularly that of Italy. In other words, Rodriguez is projecting the Mediterranean influence which the Spaniards brought to the New World, in its Texas variety.

---

[122] See Tony Fernandez, "Barrio Planners, Inc.," *La Opinion*, (March 20, 1983), *La Comunidad* supplement, p. 6-7+.

[123] *Urban Design Primer: Comparative Analyses of San Antonio Urbanscapes. San Antonio, TX: Roland V. Rodriguez, n.d. [c. 1979].*

SUMMARY AND CONCLUSIONS

We have seen, schematically, in the foregoing periodization, the development of changing political and economic relationships during a three hundred year period that have set the context for cultural expression. The pioneering culture of the Spanish colonial period reflects the development of frontier handicrafts for religious and domestic use in a peripheral area of the Spanish empire which, superficially, might be compared to the frontier culture of the U.S Anglo expansion in North America. However, though similarly exploitive of Indian lands and labor, Spanish racial attitudes toward the Indians contrasted with those of the Anglos, therefore marriage and the intermingling of Indian-Spanish material culture were more common. The Spaniards were determined to dominate economically and ideologically, and introduced a semi-feudal, semi-mercantile capitalist structure accompanied by the mission system for indoctrination and pacification of the Indian population. The mercantile capitalist aspect of Spanish empire is expressed in the search for precious metals which marked the Spanish conquest from its beginnings, and was satisfied by the rich silver mines of New Spain. Oñate, the earliest colonizer in New Mexico, was a very rich owner of silver mines in Zacatecas, Mexico. It should be noted that the mining skills the Forty-Niners learned from Mexicans in the Southwest were those acquired under Spanish domination. Likewise the cowboy skills acquired from Mexican vaqueros derived from the *hacienda* system (large land grants for agriculture and ranching) that developed with the 19th century secularization of the missions under the new Mexican nation.

The Mexican war for independence from Spain in 1810 had objectives similar to that of the U.S. Revolution against England in 1776: the desire of the upper and middle class colonists to control their own economic and political destiny, and to enrich themselves instead of their European imperial rulers. The fact that the U.S. Revolution, and the growth of the U.S. nation preceded that of Mexico's first revolution by some thirty-four years had fateful consequences for Mexico and the rest of Latin America in that United States expansionism clashed with Spanish expansionism, and took advantage of the inability of Mexico to keep a firm grip on its peripheral lands. Thus, in 1848, less than thirty years after Mexico consolidated its independence, the Second Conquest of the northern Mexican borderlands occurred, and its population passed under the domination of the United States. Racially and ethnically, this borderland population was very different from the Anglo conquerors, and this difference became the excuse for the discriminatory, even genocidal, patterns (if we consider genocide to extend to a people's psychological and cultural, as well as physical, existence) that marked the encounter of the two groups, and which Anglo society had already practiced against the Indian peoples of North America. On the class level, the new conquerors intermarried to some degree with upper class Mexican landholding families, but the general pattern was one of proletarianization of the Mexican and Indian inhabitants of the Southwest through the expropriation (by fair means and foul) of the land. The final step of the process, and one that is still continuing, was the encouragement of *controlled* immigration of Mexican labor into the Southwest to provide low paid labor for the large ranching, farming, and mining interests, and later for industrial plants and service industries.

Simultaneously - and this is the aspect in which culture and the arts play a major role - the conquered population did not submit as easily as our school history textbooks would have us believe. What we have outlined in the foregoing is the culture of *resistance,* which was established with folklore like songs and jests, according to Americo Paredes and his successors, at the time of the 1848 conquest; the culture of *maintenance* to which Ernesto Galarza referred; and the culture of new *affirmation* of which the Chicano manifestation is part. The culture of affirmation was able to arise in the particular configuration of social, economic, and political forms that it took because the sixties was a period of worldwide rebellion, particularly among youth but also among oppressed segments of many nations in the capitalist orbit concurring with active revolution in many parts of the Third World. The rebellions, which it can be argued were essentially for reform rather than revolution despite sloganeering, have been amply documented. However, almost universally, these documentations do not include the history of the Mexican peoples in the United States. This derives largely from the efforts of Chicano social scientists and lays the the basis of this present work. To return therefore to the Chicano period, we wish before closing to examine several issues which have not been explored in our chronological outline: that of the renewed Mexican influence on Mexican American art in the contemporary period; a discussion of Chicano art in its two main trends of public art and non-public art (gallery/museum art); the unique use made by Chicano artists of various avant garde tendencies of Euro-American art during the last two decades; and, finally, a brief consideration of Mexican-descent artists who, for various reasons, were not part of the Chicano movement or consciousness. The future direction of Chicano art will also be considered briefly.

Mexican Influence and Interchange in the Chicano Period

As has been stated, the art of the Mexican School, most influential from the 1920s to the 1940s outside of Mexico, was written out of art history during the Cold War years following World War II. The same was true for U.S. social realism which flourished, with influence from Mexico, during the 1930s and 1940s, especially during the New Deal period. However the decade of the sixties encouraged younger generations of artists to explore, once again, the possibilities of social protest art. With the formation of the Chicano movement, particularly its student component which was dedicated to relevant curriculum on high school and college campuses, Mexican art was again brought into focus. Books were sought out, classes were organized, and Chicano artists made trips to Mexico to study the murals and occasionally to meet the living muralists of the Mexican School. The most revered Mexican artist for the Chicano movement was David Alfaro Siqueiros (d. 1974) whose sustained political militancy (he served his last jail sentence as a political prisoner between 1960 and 1964) was inspiring, and whose energetic, dramatically foreshortened and sculptural painting style can be seen in hundreds of murals across the United States. After his death, the Taller Siqueiros (Siqueiros Workshop) continued under the direction of his brother-in-law Luis Arenal, and provided information and training to U.S. muralists, including Chicanos. Los Angeles muralist and founder of the Social and Public Art Resource Center, Judith Baca, studied there in 1977, and the impact of this training is readily visible in the later segments of her team-painted, half-mile-long mural, the *Great Wall of Los Angeles.*

Jose Guadalupe Posada has also had an enormous impact on Chicano artists who have employed his *calaveras* (animated skeletons) in numerous works of art, exhibited his prints, and evolved theatre costumes based on the skeletons. The adoption of the Mexican folk tradition celebrating the *Dia de los Muertos* (Day of the Dead), with roots in pre-Columbian and Spanish Catholic practices, has resulted not only in skeletal images, but construction of traditional and innovative altars, with all the crafts production revolving around altar installations: ceramics, *papel picado* (cut paper), flowers, etc. Altar making is also linked with artistic interest in the home altars maintained by Mexican American women of the Southwest, probably earliest articulated by Texas-born artist Carmen Lomas Garza. Dia de los Muertos celebrations have been on the increase since the late seventies, as militant artistic expression has declined. There has also been a noticeable institutionalization of the celebration by mainstream museums, galleries, and schools. Ironically, as Mexico industrializes and increasing numbers of rural peoples move into Mexico City seeking employment, Dia de los Muertos celebrations are decreasing in Mexico and, where they continue to be practiced, are increasingly commercialized for the tourist industry.[124]

---

[124] *See the section "70,000 turistas crearon en Janitzio una cultura fotogenica" in Nestor Garcia Canclini, Las culturas populares en capitalismo.* Mexico City: Editorial Nueva Imagen, 1982, p. 178-181, reprinted in "Fiestas populares o espectaculos para turistas?" *Plural,* Segunda Epoca, 11-6, no. 126 (March 1982), p. 48. For a general survey of the situation of artisanship in contemporary Mexico, see Victoria Novelo, *Artesanias y capitalismo en Mexico.* Mexico City: Centro de Investigaciones Superiores, Instituto Nacional de Antropologia e Historia, 1976.

The Mexican photographer Agustin Victor Casasola, best known for his documentation of the Mexican Revolution, has been receiving considerable attention among Chicano artists who have circulated exhibits of his work and, like the Mexican artists before them, incorporated his images into paintings.[125] Frida Kahlo, outstanding painter and wife of Diego Rivera, has had a tremendous revival in the United States and has been of particular importance to the Chicano movement, particularly to women who find her an admirable role model. The influence of her style and subject matter can be found in many paintings and prints, as well as altars which include her image.

In a more contemporary vein, Mexican draftsman/printmaker Jose Luis Cuevas, and Mexican muralist Arnold Belkin (both born in the 1930s) have impacted Chicano artists, though to a much slighter degree than the Mexican School. Even more recently, ties have been established with the flowering Mexican (and Latin American) photography movement through the invitation of Chicano photographers to the three colloquia and exhibits of Latin American photography in 1978 and 1981 (in Mexico City), and 1984 (in Havana). The work of contemporary Mexican photographers is increasingly becoming available in the United States through exhibits and catalogs, the most notable of which were the exhibits of Manuel Alvarez Bravo and four younger artists working in his vein during the year-long "Mexico Today" symposium in 1978, organized and circulated through official institutions in Washington, D.C.[126] The most recent Mexican-organized Mexican/Chicano contact was the large exhibit *A traves de la frontera* circulated for four months in Mexico City (1983) and in border towns of Baja California (1984).[127] The contact with Mexican vanguard artist Felipe Ehrenberg that resulted from the photography colloquia and the *Frontera* exhibit has now been enlarged by a number of invitations to English-speaking Ehrenberg to visit or teach in various cities (Los Angeles, Tijuana/San Diego, Chicago, San Francisco).

Finally, the Chicano film movement has been recognized in Mexico, with invitations and the showing of films (including the commercial distribution of *Zoot Suit);* the invitation to Jesus Trevino to make the first (and only) feature film by a Chicano in Mexico *(Raices de Sangre);* and the Mexican/Chicano film festivals in the United States mentioned above. In general, Chicano artists have been consolidating ties with Latin America and Caribbean countries.

Chicano Art and the U.S. Mainstream

As succinctly expressed by a 1979 publication of the La Raza Silkscreen Center of San Francisco, "La Raza culture is not isolated from the 'mainstream' or dominant North American culture, but in fact is 'influenced' by and affects the dominant society."[128] The first half of that statement should come as no surprise since we are aware that U.S. culture has been promoted internationally since the end of World War II by the most efficient public relations machinery available. Abstract Expressionism, as so promoted, originated in the United States and became an international style. It is obvious that Chicanos living within the United States and attending its art schools should be aware of and utilize most of the mainstream tendencies. What is interesting in this context is that many utilize these tendencies in their own ways; that is, they do not simply *enter* the mainstream, but expropriate it to their own ends. Thus we find trends like photorealism, pop art, performance, installation, and video art

---

[125] See Victor Sorell, "The Photograph as a Source for Visual Artists: Images From the Archivo Casasola in the Works of Mexican and Chicano Artists," in *The World of Agustin Victor Casasola: Mexico: 1900-1938.* Washington, DC: Fondo del Sol Visual Arts and Media Center, 1984. Our thanks to Victor Sorell for sending us this catalog.

[126] See Shifra M. Goldman, "Rewriting the History of Mexican Art: The Politics and Economics of Contemporary Culture," in *Contemporary Mexico: Crisis and Change.* El Paso, TX: Texas Western Press, University of Texas, El Paso, [in press].

[127] See the catalog *A traves de la frontera.* Mexico City: Centro de Estudios Economicos y Sociales del Tercer Mundo and the Instituto de Investigaciones Esteticas, UNAM, 1983.

[128] See the catalog *La Raza Silkscreen Center, "Images of a Community":* An Exhibit of Silkscreen Posters and Graphic Works from 1971 to 1979. San Francisco, CA: Galeria de la Raza, 1979.

adopted and altered for Chicano needs and subjects. Any extensive overview of Chicano art nationally would encounter these expressions as well as the more traditional social realism of the Mexican School. The impact on the dominant society is less well known, and can perhaps be indicated by one cogent example: the spread of altar making as an aspect of installation art. The most notable (as well as most deplorable) borrowing has been the Ken Price exhibit "Happy's Curios," shown by the Los Angeles County Museum of Art in 1978, and since circulated in other areas. Price had moved from Los Angeles to Taos, New Mexico, and his patronizing depiction of the most stereotypical images on the painted ceramics that adorn his altars, and the use of the word *curios* (scornfully referred to by Siqueiros many years earlier to indicate tourist visions of Mexican art), seem to echo, almost sixty years later, the incursion of primitivizing Anglo artists into New Mexico, and their well-meant but controlled "revival" of colonial folk arts. Price did not borrow directly from the contemporary Chicano movement (his altar making dates back to 1972), however he was drawing on the Mexican tradition maintained not only in Mexico, but in the Southwest, and trivializing it. As one critic pointed out, his work remains a "display piece - whimsical...slick, obsessive," never achieving any kind of primal power. "Its decorative precision cannot evoke, except superficially, the sense of tradition and history from which it has been derived."[129] By a reverse irony, artist Rene Yanez borrowed the picket fences which Price installed in front of many altars, and reintegrated this innovation into Chicano art by using them in front of his altars which are an homage to the Mexican/Chicano experience. In Yanez's context, they become allusions to the picket fences which surround so many small frame houses in the barrio.

Mexican American Artists in the Chicano Period

We revert here to our definition of the term "Chicano" as one expressing a militant political and Indian-oriented consciousness assumed, primarily, by young people in the mid-sixties. It was not necessarily accepted by large numbers of the population who preferred designating themselves as Mexican, Mexican American, Spanish American, and numerous other terms determined by history and personal preference. By the same token, there were also artists who did not participate in Chicano affiliation or consciousness. Some artists predated the movement and had formed their visual language before its onset; others opted for mainstream directions though they were contemporary with the movement; still others rejected the political and ethnic direction of the Chicano art movement, etc. This disaffiliation with the art movement and its vocabulary and/or aesthetic did not prevent some of these artists from exhibiting in Chicano shows, or sympathizing with the goals of the movement. Others, particularly in New Mexico, wore two hats: they continued with the traditional arts of their families or region, fusing these on occasion with more contemporary design; but they also painted murals or identified themselves with *chicanismo* as a philosophy. Others utilized elements from the Chicano plastic vocabulary as *form* alone (colors, shapes, Indian references, etc.) without involvement in the political dimension. The spectrum is broad and varied. No history of Chicano art should omit detailing and discussing this spectrum, and exploring its relationship to the movement. There is little question that the Chicano political and social struggle opened doors for artists of Mexican descent to receive schooling, develop as fine artists (rather than earlier choices as artisans or commercial artists, regardless of talent), and find (still limited) places to exhibit, or receive commissions. In the 1980s, there have been, and continue to be as of this writing, an increasing number of Chicano art shows, but more typically, a number of Latin American shows or "Hispanic" shows that include Chicanos without necessarily identifying them as such. These generally exclude the more militant expressions still being produced, as they are often patronized by government institutions or corporations.

---

[129] Hedy Weiss, "Ken Price," *New Art Examiner* (Chicago, IL), Vol. 8, no. 8 (March 1981), p. 17. See also the catalog *Ken Price: Happy's Curios.* Los Angeles, CA: Los Angeles County Museum of Art, 1978.

Public Arts and Gallery Arts

From the late sixties on, public arts were the most visible form of Chicano art. Public arts included murals, posters, film, and street processions and performances - using "performance" in its most avant garde neo-dada visual arts sense, that is, a type of "theatre" that depends for communication on the use of visual objects (including the body of the performer) used in certain configurations rather than being based on a written text with a plot which is orally performed. Sound is not precluded in performance by any means, and often gives content, but the principal vehicle of communication is visual. In the early years very few Chicanos employed vanguard technques like performance and art video. The only exception, to our knowledge, was the Los Angeles group ASCO (nausea) which has been growing and acquiring new adherents since the late seventies though it was organized in 1972. ASCO was a performance presence at outdoor demonstrations in East Los Angeles, and has done many of its pieces in outdoor locations, thus its presentations can be considered public art forms. Processions include events like the *Dia de los Muertos* masked parades and ceremonies at an East Los Angeles cemetery that were held annually by Self Help Graphics and Art.

Muralism has been such an important, widespread, and publicized part of Chicano art (the bibliographical section on muralism is one of the largest of the compilation) that it warrants additional explication. Chicano muralism began as a massive grassroots artistic explosion - the regional expression of a national phenomenon - that swept great numbers of trained and untrained people into artistic activity. California leads the Southwest in sheer quantity. Considering murals that adorn buildings inside and out in dozens of cities large and small, there must be upwards of 2,000 murals in the state, and more are being painted. Texas has murals in Crystal City, San Antonio, Houston, Austin, El Paso, and Dallas. New Mexico has murals in Albuquerque, Las Vegas, and Santa Fe. Colorado has murals in Denver and Boulder. Many murals have been painted in Chicago, and in Michigan cities. Arizona has also found the mural an appropriate vehicle of public expression, particularly in the early militant era when artists gave visual form to the struggles, needs, aspirations, cultural identity, and anger of an oppressed people. Visual influences were eclectic, however the dramatic work of Mexican muralist David Alfaro Siqueiros has been primary.

From the great groundswell of the mid-seventies, which has now subsided, emerged wall painters of talent and persistence who developed mural painting as a professional category for the first time since the New Deal forties. Such was the case of Los Angeles' Willie Herron, Gilberto Guzman of Santa Fe, Graciela Carrillo of San Francisco, Raul Valdez of Austin, Rudy Trevino of San Antonio, Manuel Martinez of Colorado, and Leo Tanguma, formerly of Houston and now in Denver. Tanguma is experimenting with complex Siqueiros-inspired three-dimensional mural constructions. Ray Patlan (originally from Chicago) is Siqueiros- and Orozco-influenced and has studied in Mexico with Arnold Belkin. As part of a team, Patlan worked with Osha Neumann, Anna de Leon, and O'Brian Thiele to create the spectacular three-dimensional mural in Berkeley called *Song of Unity,* painted on billboard-influenced shaped wooden panels. The team combined paint with acrylic-impregnated papier mache to model the head and hands of assassinated Chilean songwriter Victor Jara which dominate the mural. An eagle and condor of glazed ceramic are bolted to the surface.

Murals have been characterized by the "team" approach, i.e. an art director working with a group of artists and/or community residents. Mural artists have also solicited community input as a guide to relevance of a given theme and its articulation. The notion of an artistic team collaborating on a public mural can be found in the early writings of Siqueiros, however the inclusion of (often untrained) community participants as painters appears to be unique to the U.S. street mural movement of the 1970s. Subscribing to a collectivist philosophy at the point of *production* counterparts a similar philosophy in regard to dissemination. Briefly summarized, public artists work as a team and address their work to a community which, hopefully, will understand and subscribe to its message. This stance negates the individualism and elitism common to mainstream fine arts.

"Gallery arts," for lack of a more definitive name, include all those artistic expressions which are better shown indoors due to scale, intimacy of viewing, fragility, costliness, and portability. A public work of art must either be non-portable (a mural painted on a wall or a large sculpture), inexpensive (a poster produced in multiple runs), ephemeral (processions and performances), or available to such mass audiences that they are public expressions (film and documentary videos). The other concommitant of public art is that it is not purchased at great cost to the individual who continues to experience it. (Obviously "cost" is a relative question when it comes to mass media for which we all pay through product purchases, or museums which we pay for through taxes.) Gallery art includes drawings, easel painting, graphics (both printmaking and design), sculpture, crafts, photography, some performance, many installation pieces, and video art (closed circuit). All these forms can be reproduced in books, but remain within the gallery structure for viewing of originals. The two forms of art are also funded differently. Except for performance, the public arts require large financial outlays which are obtained *in advance* of production; the gallery arts are considered to be for sale to an individual (or a museum) after production.

It is in the realm of public art that Chicano artists achieved a national character and cohesiveness that justifies the word "movement." Certain motifs and symbols, certain stylistic characteristics deriving from the Mexican influence and Southwest concentration and history, and certain preferred techniques can be said to be nationally disseminated, appearing from El Paso to Chicago, from Seattle to Los Angeles. In the area of gallery arts, there are similar unifying images and symbols, but the gamut of themes, styles and techniques is much more heterogenous. The range runs from completely abstract (both organic and geometric) to photorealist; from traditional techniques to the most experimental. There is in both types, public and non-public, a sizeable input from the vernacular: from graffiti lettering incorporated into the work to the use of lowrider parts as sculpture, to the installation of traditional altars.

Changing Directions: The Future of Chicano Art

By 1975, or even earlier, the Chicano political movement was changing course, and rifts opened in the alliance among students, urban workers, and farmworkers. The fraternal, unified community of the early period began to fragment as more Chicanos entered the middle class, attained professional or business status, and established a stake in the status quo. Simultaneously, a schism opened between artists who chose to continue serving the still largely working class Mexican population and those who were beginning to enter the mainstream art world of elitist museums, private galleries, and collectors. In 1980 artist Malaquias Montoya sounded an admonishing note about the cooptation of Chicano art and the transformation of its focus from "liberation" to "validation."[130] The schism was not unique to the visual arts; similar tendencies have been noted by observers in other areas of Chicano culture. The term that has surfaced is "commercialization," whether within the private art (and film) market, or within the public and corporate funding sectors. For several years up to and including the time of this writing, the National Endowment for the Arts has promoted seminars for artists on marketing strategies with the aim of developing a "small business" mentality among artists and artists' groups. Simultaneously, funding sources have been drying up, or have increasingly been directed toward "establishment" cultural institutions. The most devastating funding cut was that of CETA (the Comprehensive Employment and Training Act) which at its peak provided over 200 million dollars to support arts groups through public service employment. This cut affected mural programs and other community-oriented arts services by cutting staffs. The pressure on both Chicano art groups like galleries and centers, and individual artists, is to move toward increased corporate funding, when it can be obtained,[131] or into the private highly-competitive art market. Obviously the work of artists

---

130 Malaquías Montoya and Lezlie Salkowitz-Montoya, "A Critical Perspective on the State of Chicano Art," *Metamorfosis,* Vol. 3, no. 1 (Spring/Summer 1980), p. 3-7.

131 See "Coping With Cuts: Neighborhood Arts Carry On," *Cultural Democracy* (Baltimore, MD), no. 22 (March 1982).

who continue to make social protest the subject of their art is not very marketable, and tendencies toward self-censorship develop.

It is difficult to predict the future of Chicano art. There is no question that it still exists as a movement, with all the networking and shared concerns implicit in the word "movement." However it is in a process of change, accelerated by the entry of younger generations with different experiences and historical perspectives. One thing appears certain: the Chicano period opened the gates to artists of Mexican descent across the nation, and never again will Mexican Americans be an "invisible minority," artistically or socially.

INDEX TO INTRODUCTION

Bibliography of Chicano Art, 1965-1981

HOW TO USE THIS BIBLIOGRAPHY

To make effective use of the bibliography, the reader should have some understanding of the innovative nature of the present work. *Arte Chicano* is unique in that it represents a blending of two traditional reference book approaches: the classified bibliography and the subject index to a specialized body of literature. This dual approach enhances the value of this work for research purposes by providing the best of both approaches. The essence of our approach is that by using the new technology available, we can offer a more detailed breakdown of subjects (as in the typical subject index), and at the same time list in one place all material classified under any one specific category.

Because many citations included were identified by the Chicano Periodical Indexing Project and extracted from Berkeley's *Chicano Database,* the bibliography conforms to the format established by prior issues of the *Chicano Periodical Index* [ChPI], (Boston, MA: G.K. Hall & Co., 1981 and 1983). The reader is referred in particular to the 1983 edition of the *Chicano Periodical Index* [ChPI] for additional information regarding its use-- information which applies equally to the use of this bibliography. The reader will also find in the 1983 edition of *ChPI* a complete copy of the third edition of the *Chicano Thesaurus.*

The *ARTE CHICANO* bibliography is arranged by detailed subject matter. The subject headings which make up the classification scheme were taken from the third edition of the *Chicano Thesaurus.* On the average, each of the approximately 2500 citations included here has been assigned four distinct subject headings. The citation and corresponding annotation are then repeated in their entirety under each heading. In this way we eliminate the frustration of typical subject index entries which refer the user to numerous references to another part of the book. As a result, it is now possible to scan the bibliography under an appropriate heading and find in one place complete listings and annotations for all items in the bibliography related to that heading.

In the subject section the user will locate pertinent information *about* specific topics, issues, trends, forms of art, groups, and individuals. Under the specific heading (whether a topic or personal name) appears a complete list of citations which contain information about that particular heading. The citations provide complete bibliographic data: author(s), editor(s), or compiler(s); title; journal source or book imprint; date of publication; and pages. In addition, each entry includes a brief descriptive annotation. The only exceptions are entries for reproductions of individual works of art. These are properly identified within the citation and listed without annotations.

SAMPLE SUBJECT ENTRY

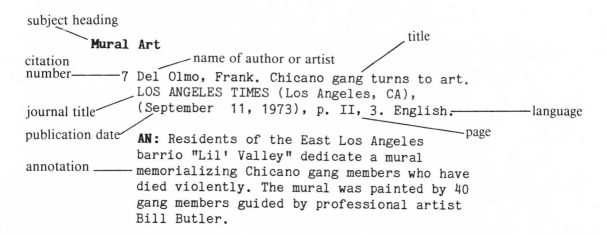

63

Supplementing the coverage of the main subject section are separate author/artist and title indexes. The "Author/Artist" index is an alphabetical listing of persons or corporate entities with primary authorship responsibility for written works or for creative works of art. A researcher interested, for example, in identifying works of art history or criticism *written* by Rupert Garcia would look under his name in the "Author/Artist" index. Similarly, if a researcher wanted to locate published reproductions of artworks *by* Rupert Garcia, these would also be listed under his name in the "Author/Artist" index. [A researcher interested in writings *about* Rupert Garcia would look under "Garcia, Rupert" as a subject term.]

SAMPLE AUTHOR/ARTIST ENTRY

```
        Garcia, Rupert
              Community art-murals: an exhibition of
                 original drawings, sketches, and designs,
                 1795.
 title———— The politics of popular art, 4050.——————— citation number
              Portfolio [drawings], 2834.
              [Untitled drawing], 2835.
```

The title index lists in alphabetic order the titles of all works listed in the bibliography whether written or graphic.

SAMPLE TITLE ENTRIES

```
     title                                         citation number
                                                  /
           The great wall of Los Angeles, 901.
           Gronk and Herron, 1078.
           Group showing of Southern California artists, 97.
```

ABBREVIATIONS

The following abbreviations are used throughout the bibliography in the citation entries:

Bk cover	Back cover
Ft cover	Front cover
In BkCover	Inside back cover
In FtCover	Inside front cover

Periodical names may also be slightly abbreviated throughout the bibliography.
See Appendix B: Periodicals Cited in Bibliography.

Subject Index

La Academia de la Nueva Raza, Dixon, NM

1 Anaya, Rudolfo A. and Ortiz, Simon J.
1680-1980: a ceremony of brotherhood.
Albuquerque, NM: Academic, 1981. English.

AN: A cooperative publication by members
of the former La Academia de la Nueva Raza
(1969-1976) formed of writers and artists,
and the Tri-Centennial Commission of the
All-Indian Pueblo Council. Includes writings
and artworks by Chicanos and Indians from
New Mexico, California, Texas, and Arizona.
Chicano artists works included are by Ellen
Arellano, Juan Estevan Arellano, Alberto
Baros, Jose Antonio Burciaga, Juan Reyes
Cervantes, Rudy Cuellar, Ricardo Favela, El
Zarco Guerrero, Luis Jimenez, Jr., Carlos
Quinto Kemm, Alejandro Lopez, Floyd Lujan,
Jose Montoya, Juanishi Orozco, Leo Romero,
Secundino Sandoval, Jaime Valdez, Maria
Varela, Esteban Villa.

2 Centro de artistas, Sacra: recuerdo ...
descubrimiento ... voluntad. CHISMEARTE,
Vol. 1, no. 1 (Fall 1976), p. 6-7.
English.

AN: Summary of activities of the Centro
de Artistas Chicanos, made up of artists
from the Royal Chicano Air Force and other
groups. The Centro makes posters, T-shirts,
decals, murals and puts on a number of
cultural and social events. Report on a
"mass migration" July 1976 to the Academia
de la Nueva Raza in Dixon, NM for two weeks
of communion.

ACCION CHICANO [film]

3 Gamboa, Harry, Jr. Film, television, and
Trevino. LA LUZ, Vol. 6, no. 10 (October
1977), p. 7-8. English.

AN: Jesus Salvador Trevino has been an
active proponent and participant in
transforming cultural inaccuracy about
Chicanos in the media to accurate mass media
models. A biography of Trevino follows,
including discussion of some of his films:
THE SALAZAR INQUEST, CHICANO MORATORIUM
AFTERMATH, SOLEDAD, AMERICA TROPICAL, YO SOY
CHICANO, RAICES DE SANGRE, as well as
television series like ACCION CHICANO,
AHORA, and INFINITY FACTORY.

Aceves, Jose

4 Valdez, Salvador. A forgotten artist's work
lives on. NOSOTROS, Vol. 2, no. 6. English.

AN: Narrative of the life and times of
Jose Aceves, a self taught El Paso artist
(1909-1968), noted for his desert
landscapes.

Acosta, Joe Frank

5 Con safo to hold Lutheran college exhibition
at Texas. CHICANO TIMES, Vol. 7, no. 89
(March 26, 1976), p. [15]. English.

AN: Discusses the aims of "Con Safos"
group: to interpret their environment and
react to it; to act as spokespeople and give
visual reality to the Chicano vision; to
destroy stereotypes and demolish visual
cliches. The participating artists include
Rudy R. Trevino, Mel Casas, Lucas Hinojosa,
Kathy Vargas, Joe Frank Acosta, Emilio
Aguirre and Homero Ureste.

Acosta, John

6 Community Programs in the Arts and Sciences
(COMPAS). Artists in the city: a report on
C.E.T.A. artists in St. Paul. St. Paul, MN:
COMPAS, 1978. English.

AN: Includes data on Chicano muralists
John Acosta, Thomas Acosta, Paul Basquez,
Armando Estrella, and photographer Raphael
Romo.

7 Flanagan, Barbara. Murals warm up west St.
Paul. MINNEAPOLIS STAR, (December 20,
1977). English.

AN: Discussion of mural activity in West
St. Paul, Minnesota by Armando Estrella,
Paul Basquez and John Acosta. The subject of
most murals in Minnesota is either
political, religious or historic. Of the
three artists involved, Paul Basquez grew up
in the barrio of West St. Paul. He tells how
mural activity in the region is related to
the Chicano art movement. About a half-dozen
murals have been painted in St. Paul.

Acosta, Manuel

8 Acosta, a man and his art. NOSOTROS, Vol. 2,
no. 6. English.

AN: Biographical information and
thematic analysis of the work of El Paso
artist Manuel Acosta. He is especially
noted for genre paintings of humble people
reflecting social life and cultural
traditions.

9 Manuel Acosta. LA LUZ, Vol. 3, no. 10-11
(January, February, 1975), p. 30. English.

AN: Biographical and exhibition data
focusing on Acosta's ability to paint
Mexican American types from the border area.

Acosta, Thomas

10 Community Programs in the Arts and Sciences
(COMPAS). Artists in the city: a report on
C.E.T.A. artists in St. Paul. St. Paul, MN:
COMPAS, 1978. English.

AN: Includes data on Chicano muralists
John Acosta, Thomas Acosta, Paul Basquez,
Armando Estrella, and photographer Raphael
Romo.

Actors
USE: Artists

Actresses
USE: Artists

Adame, Esteban

11 Trevino, Rudy. San Antonio murals a self
portrait. PICANTE, Vol. 1, no. 3, p. 60-61.
English.

AN: Commentary on the San Antonio Mural
Project assisted by the CETA program and the
Barrio Betterment and Development
Corporation (BBDC). Goals and information on
the light murals in progress in the Casiano
Housing Project. Participating artists: Juan
Hernandez, Esteban Adame, Andrew Gutierrez,
Bob Tate, and Roberto de La Fuente.

La Adelita

> 12 Vasquez y Sanchez, Ramon. La Adelita.
>   CARACOL, Vol. 1, no. 9 (May 1975), p. 1.

Admonty
>   USE: Montemayor, Alice Dickerson "Admonty"

Adobe Houses

> 13 Bendau, Clifford P. Preserving an ancient
>   craft. MS.MAGAZINE, Vol. 9, no. 11 (May
>   1981), p. 26. English.
>
>   **AN:** 40-year-old native Taos, NM resident
>   Anita Otilia Rodriguez travels the Southwest
>   as a professional enjarradora building homes
>   and fireplaces from earth and straw. Article
>   discusses the history of adobe construction,
>   Rodriguez's innovations with the ancient
>   technique. Illustrated.

> 14 Rodriguez, Anita. Las enjarradoras: women of
>   the earth. NEW MEXICO, (February 1980), p.
>   46-47+. English.
>
>   **AN:** History of adobe construction in New
>   Mexico, its decline and its present revival
>   in Arizona and New Mexico. Written by a
>   professional adobe architect and feminist
>   who defines the traditional terms and
>   techniques of this woman's craft.
>   Illustrated.

> 15 Rodriguez, Anita. Tradiciones de adobe en
>   Nuevo Mejico norteno = adobe traditions in
>   Northern New Mexico. ADOBE NEWS, no. 15
>   (1977). Bilingual.
>
>   **AN:** History of adobe construction in New
>   Mexico, from primarily Indian sources with
>   Spanish input. For 400 years, women were
>   builders and architects of the Southwest;
>   today they are "enjarradoras" (plasterers).
>   Written by a professional enjarradora from
>   New Mexico. Illustrated.

> 16 Simpson, Claudette. An adobe fireplace:
>   Anita Rodriguez has built many - each one
>   different. PRESCOTT COURIER-WEEKLY FEATURE,
>   (December 1, 1978). English.
>
>   **AN:** Anita Rodriguez is an enjarradora--a
>   professional specializing in adobe
>   architecture--in New Mexico. She builds
>   fireplaces, lays mud floors, builds hornos
>   (outdoor ovens) and does interior and
>   exterior plastering. Well illustrated.

> 17 Southwick, Marcia. Build with adobe.
>   Chicago, IL: Swallow, 1965. English.
>
>   **AN:** Modern building techniques for
>   construction of adobe homes with information
>   on traditional building practices.

> 18 Stedman, Myrtle and Stedman, Wilfred. Adobe
>   architecture. Santa Fe, NM: Sunstone Press,
>   1973. English.
>
>   **AN:** The technology and aesthetics of
>   adobe homes. An illustrated manual of house
>   plans and building techniques. Includes
>   drawings of Southwestern "colonial"
>   furniture.

Adolescents
>   USE: Youth

Advertising

> 19 Garcia, Rupert. Pulqueria art--defiant art
>   of the barrios [Part I]. EL TECOLOTE, Vol.
>   8, no. 4 (December 1977), p. 7. Bilingual.

>   **AN:** In contrast to billboards that
>   function as calculated visual corporate
>   advertisements, Chicano-Latino communities
>   have evolved a form of colorful wall
>   paintings that draw attention to goods
>   available in the neighborhood. Related to
>   the "Pulqueria" paintings of Mexico, these
>   wall paintings are validated as a true
>   people's art. In the best examples,
>   pulqueria art functions to provide images of
>   a positive and innovative nature.

> 20 Garcia, Rupert. Pulqueria art--defiant art
>   of the barrios [Part II]. EL TECOLOTE, Vol.
>   8, no. 5 (February 1978), p. 8. Bilingual.
>
>   **AN:** In the Mission District of San
>   Francisco, various artists like Irene Perez,
>   Esther Fernandez, Chuy Campusano, Graciela
>   Carrillo de Lopez, Consuelo Mendez Castillo,
>   and Mike Rios have embellished business
>   sites with wall decorations similar in
>   spirit to the "Pulqueria" art of Mexico.
>   Illustrated with three "Pulqueria"-type wall
>   paintings: ATARDECER DE UN IMPERIO by Oscar
>   Carveo at the Azteca Restaurant (Mission and
>   20th Sts.), El Buen Boricano Restaurant
>   facade (24th and Harrison Sts.) and
>   Fruitlandia facade (24th and Treat Sts.).

Africa

> 21 Goll, Dave. More than handball on this
>   court. MENLO-ATHERTON RECORDER, (May 23,
>   1978), p. 15. English.
>
>   **AN:** Emmanuel Montoya is painting a mural
>   on African and Chicano unity at the handball
>   court of Fair Oaks Community Center in
>   Redwood City, CA. Montoya is working because
>   of CETA (Comprehensive Employment Training
>   Act) funds. Illustrated.

> 22 In the middle of something good.
>   MENLO-ATHERTON RECORDER, (September 19,
>   1978), p. 16. English.
>
>   **AN:** Illustration of Emmanuel Montoya's
>   African-Mexican unity mural at the Redwood
>   City Fair Oaks Community Center handball
>   courts.

African National Congress

> 23 De Lappe, Pele. Saga of Rupert Garcia's
>   poster: from pen to UN. PEOPLE'S WORLD, Vol.
>   44, no. 28 (July 11, 1981), p. 10. English.
>
>   **AN:** Desiring to produce a poster on
>   Nelson Mandela and South African political
>   prisoners, San Francisco artist Rupert
>   Garcia, appealed for support to the African
>   National Congress, and the Liberation
>   Support Movement. The United Nations Center
>   Against Apartheid provided a grant for
>   production, indicating it should be
>   distributed free. Illustrated.

Afro-Americans
>   USE: Blacks

Aged
>   USE: Ancianos

Agricultural Laborers

> 24 Baca, Walter R. Campesino [mural]. DE
>   COLORES, Vol. 1, no. 2 (Spring 1974), p. 64.
>   Spanish.

Agricultural Laborers (cont.)

25 Mural depicts la lucha campesina del
   mexicano. EL HISPANO, Vol. 8, no. 12
   (September 9, 1975). English.

   AN: Photograph and commentary on the
   mural by J. Orozco for the Sacramento
   Farmworker's Migrant Program on F. Street.
   Centered by the Virgin of Guadalupe, the
   mural is divided into four sections: The
   Farmworker in the Fields, The Tree of Life,
   Violence Against the Farmworkers, and the
   Racist System.

26 OMICA Housing Corp., Inc., Homestead
   (Miami), FL. Dedication of heritage village.
   Brochure, 1977. English.

   AN: Brochure of non-profit housing
   corporation which built, with Housing and
   Urban Development (HUD) funds, public
   homeownership housing for farmworkers and
   low-income rural residents of South Dade
   County. Illustrated with a mural by Roberto
   Rios of San Antonio, one of three done in
   Florida.

27 Zermeno, Andy. Don Sotaco: caricaturas de la
   huelga de Delano. Delano, CA: Farmworkers
   Press, 1966. English.

   AN: Short vignettes depicting the
   farmworkers' struggle and how Don Sotaco
   comes to understand his role in that social
   movement. Illustrated with caricatures of
   the various personages in the struggle;
   patrones, coyotes, esquiroles, campesinos
   and huelguistas. Centerfold and back cover
   photographs by Jon Lewis.

Agricultural Workers
   USE: Agricultural Laborers

Aguayo, Emilio

28 Aguayo, Emilio. Chicano art: a new art-style
   of the future. (Unpublished Study Project
   for Prof. Brauman, Art Dept., Univ. of
   Washington, Seattle), June 6, 1972. English.

   AN: Autobiographical account and
   self-analysis of artist's work. Beginning in
   1965 the artist has created 40,000 small ink
   drawings in a contour line technique.
   Situating himself within the Chicano Arts
   Movement, Aguayo describes his dominant
   themes, symbols, and stylistic
   preoccupations.

29 And/Or Gallery, Seattle, WA. Artistas de
   Aztlan. Exhibition announcement, 1975.
   English.

   AN: Exhibition announcement for an
   important exhibit of Northwest Chicano art.
   Co-sponsored by MEChA and the Chicano
   Studies Program at the University of
   Washington, the exhibit presented works by
   Emilio Aguayo, Danny Desiga, Ricardo
   Aguirre, Ramiro Benavidez, Elma Herada,
   Pedro Rodriguez and others. A selection of
   posters by Armando Cid of the R.C.A.F. group
   from Sacramento, California was also
   presented. Concurrently, at the Heny Gallery
   of the University of Washington, Esteban
   Villa presented a one-man show.

Aguilar, Cruz

30 Corazon del norte: wood carving. GRITO DEL
   NORTE, Vol. 2, no. 5 (March 28, 1969), p.
   11. English.

   AN: Focus on the Aguilar family, folk
   artists from Los Ojos (Parkview), northern
   New Mexico. Sr. Cruz Aguilar is a sculptor
   and furniture maker, his 80-year-old mother
   Dona Cresanta Cruz is a quilter. Illustrated
   with photographs of the Aguilars and
   examples of their work.

Aguilar, Porfirio

31 Consejo Mexicano de Fotografia, A.C., Mexico
   City. Hecho en latinoamerica: segundo
   coloquio latinoamericano de fotografia.
   Exhibition catalog, 1982. Spanish.

   AN: Catalog/book of the second
   colloquium and exhibit of Latin American
   photography. Among the Chicano artists whose
   work is reproduced are Louis Carlos Bernal,
   Robert C. Buitron, David Cardenas, Isabel
   Castro, Harry Gamboa, Jr., Luis Garza,
   Roberto Gil de Montes, John M. Valadez,
   Kathy Vargas. In the exhibit were also
   Porfirio Aguilar, Elsa Marie Flores, Ricardo
   Valverde. Great number of illustrations. In
   Spanish.

Aguilera, Manuel

32 Galeria de arte de Aztlan. AZTLAN (U.S.
   Penitentiary, Leavenworth, KA), Vol. 1, no.
   2. English.

   AN: Pictorial supplement with
   reproductions of pinto art by Manuel
   Aguilera, Jessie Hernandez, Ruben Estrella,
   Tomas Torres and Jose D. Marin. Many of
   these works were reproduced in other Chicano
   newspapers demonstrating the solidarity that
   existed in the Chicano movement inside and
   outside the prison walls.

33 Rodriguez, Pedro. Chicano art arising. PAPEL
   CHICANO, Vol. 1, no. 9 (December 21, 1971),
   p. 5. English.

   AN: A concise formulation on the nature
   of Chicano Art. It arises from a new
   cultural formation influenced by Mexican and
   Anglo American cultural forms yet distinct
   from either. In visual terms, artists are
   reflecting and affirming this new cultural
   synthesis. Illustrated with reproductions of
   three oil paintings: GRITO DE LIBERTAD by
   Jose D. Marin, WOMAN IN BLUE by Manuel
   Aguilera, and ALEGORIA MEXICANA by Tomas
   Torres. All three are pinto artists from
   Leavenworth Penitentiary.

Aguirre, Emilio

34 Con safo to hold Lutheran college exhibition
   at Texas. CHICANO TIMES, Vol. 7, no. 89
   (March 26, 1976), p. [15]. English.

   AN: Discusses the aims of "Con Safos"
   group: to interpret their environment and
   react to it; to act as spokespeople and give
   visual reality to the Chicano vision; to
   destroy stereotypes and demolish visual
   cliches. The participating artists include
   Rudy R. Trevino, Mel Casas, Lucas Hinojosa,
   Kathy Vargas, Joe Frank Acosta, Emilio
   Aguirre and Homero Ureste.

Aguirre, Emilio (cont.)

35 The Mexican Museum, San Francisco, CA and
Quirarte, Jacinto. 17 artists:
Hispano/Mexican-American/Chicano. Exhibition
catalog, 1977. English.

AN: Catalog of an exhibit for artists
Emilio Aguirre, Consuelo Gonzalez Amezcua,
Al Barela, Pedro Cervantez, Edward Chavez,
Antonio Garcia, Louis Gutierrez, Harry
Louie, Vincent Perez, Michael Ponce de Leon,
Eugenio Quesada, Gustavo Rivera, Peter
Rodriguez, Alex Sanchez, Darryl Sapien, Rudy
Trevino, Manuel Villamor. Illustrated.

Aguirre, Lupe

36 De Marroquin, Moron. Denver Harbor artists.
LA PRENSA, (June 2, 1978). Spanish.

AN: Commentary on two exhibitions. THE
DENVER HARBOR ARTISTS includes information
on paintings by Lupe Aguirre, Josie Mendoza
and Abel Gonzalez--all from Houston. The
solo show MAGIC BLANCA featured the work of
Brownsville, Texas artist Jorge Truan.
Truan's work is mystical and visionary.

Aguirre, Ricardo

37 And/Or Gallery, Seattle, WA. Artistas de
Aztlan. Exhibition announcement, 1975.
English.

AN: Exhibition announcement for an
important exhibit of Northwest Chicano art.
Co-sponsored by MEChA and the Chicano
Studies Program at the University of
Washington, the exhibit presented works by
Emilio Aguayo, Danny Desiga, Ricardo
Aguirre, Ramiro Benavidez, Elma Herada,
Pedro Rodriguez and others. A selection of
posters by Armando Cid of the R.C.A.F. group
from Sacramento, California was also
presented. Concurrently, at the Heny Gallery
of the University of Washington, Esteban
Villa presented a one-man show.

Aguirre, Tito

38 Guggenheim Gallery, Chapman College, Orange,
CA. Hexagono: paintings, sculpture,
drawings, prints. Exhibit invitation, 1977.
English.

AN: Invitation to an exhibit for artists
Tito Aguirre, Isabel Castro, Rick Martinez,
Esau Quiroz, Linda Vallejo, Emigdio Vasquez,
Barrows, and Shanahan, sponsored by MEChA.
Profiles and pictures of the artists.

AHORA! [television series]

39 Gamboa, Harry, Jr. Film, television, and
Trevino. LA LUZ, Vol. 6, no. 10 (October
1977), p. 7-8. English.

AN: Jesus Salvador Trevino has been an
active proponent and participant in
transforming cultural inaccuracy about
Chicanos in the media to accurate mass media
models. A biography of Trevino follows,
including discussion of some of his films:
THE SALAZAR INQUEST, CHICANO MORATORIUM
AFTERMATH, SOLEDAD, AMERICA TROPICAL, YO SOY
CHICANO, RAICES DE SANGRE, as well as
television series like ACCION CHICANO,
AHORA, and INFINITY FACTORY.

40 Knapp, Dan. KCET's show for Chicano viewers.
LOS ANGELES TIMES, (April 3, 1970), p. IV,
18. English.

AN: Story on the television series
AHORA! started September 1969 on KCET, Los
Angeles' National Educational Television.
Edward Moreno is program director and host;
Victor Millan is producer-director; Claudio
Fenner-Lopez, senior producer, has staff
including set-designer David Villasenor,
production manager James Val, and alternate
host-narrator Jesus Trevino. The program has
shown exhibits of artists Gilberto Lujan and
Daniel Ramirez.

Al Frente Communications

41 Romero, Raul V. Chicanarte, a major
exposition of California arts. NEWORLD,
(Fall 1975). English.

AN: CHICANARTE at the Los Angeles
Municipal Gallery, Barnsdall Park from Sept.
14 -Oct. 12, 1975 remains the most
comprehensive statewide exposition of
Chicano arts in California. This article
details the production apparatus and history
of the exposition. In particular, the
contributions of Al Frente Communications,
Inc., the Chicano Arts Council of U.C.L.A.
and the Comite Chicanarte. Illustrated.

Alambristas
USE: Undocumented Workers

The Alamo, San Antonio, TX

42 Vasquez y Sanchez, Ramon. Documentacion del
ejercito mexicano en la campana del Alamo
[drawings]. CARACOL, Vol. 1, no. 9 (May
1975), p. 12-13.

Alaniz, Ricardo

43 Valdez, Armando. El calendario chicano 1977.
Hayward, CA: Southwest Network, 1977.
English.

AN: Fifth in a series of historical
calendars produced in 1972, 1974, 1975, 1976
by La Causa Publications and Southwest
Network. Artists whose work is reproduced
are Malaquias Montoya, Amado Maurilio Pena,
Ramori Zamora, Glugio J.L. Nicandro [Gronk],
Etta Delgado, Ricardo Alaniz, Diane Gamboa,
Elisa Marina Coleman, Margarita Calderon,
Jose Antonio Burciaga, Cesar Augusto
Martinez, Maria Ochoa y Valtierra, Juan
Renteria Fuentes, from California, New
Mexico, and Texas.

ALBA [art group], Chicago, IL

44 Garza, Alex. Entrevista con Alex Garza.
ABRAZO, Vol. 1, no. 2 (Summer 1979), p.
27-29. English.

AN: Brief article exploring Alex Garza's
technique, philosophy, and setting for his
sculptural work. The artist expresses his
desire to see artists break with tradition
and not allow the political rhetoric of the
early Chicano Movement to promote
stagnation. His connection to the art
organization ALBA is also briefly mentioned.

Alberro, Malu
USE: Ortega, Malu

Albert, Margo

45 Baciu, Joyce A. and Diaz, Katherine A. Margo
Albert: a woman who gets things done = una
mujer que realiza lo que desea. CAMINOS,
Vol. 2, no. 5 (September 1981), p. 44-46.
Bilingual.

AN: Mexican-born Margo Albert is a
well-known Los Angeles, CA artist, dancer,
and actress who has been most active on
behalf of the Plaza de la Raza in East Los
Angeles. This article describes her
activities as Co-chairperson of the Los
Angeles Bicentennial Committee. For Margo,
the highlights of the celebration marking
the 200th anniversary of the founding of Los
Angeles, included a day-long Fiesta del
Bicentenario; groundbreaking ceremonies for
the Ruben Salazar Bicentennial Building; and
the reception for an official delegation of
charros, sponsored as a gift to the people
of Los Angeles by the Mexican government.

Albuquerque Arthritis Foundation

46 'Festival of arts' planned by Arthritis
Foundation. SANTA FE NEW MEXICAN, (October
11, 1972), p. B6. English.

AN: The Albuquerque Arthritis Foundation
has invited professional artists and
craftsmen from New Mexico to display their
paintings, watercolors, sculpture, prints,
lithographs, jewelry. Joel Ramirez's
painting THE WEAVERS is selected for full
color art prints. Illustrated.

Albuquerque Museum, Albuquerque, NM

47 Sanchez, Arley. Santeros. ALBUQUERQUE JRNL,
(August 21, 1977), p. C, 1. English.

AN: Review of THE SANTERO EXPERIENCE, an
exhibition of contemporary folk art by
eleven New Mexican santeros, most in their
30s, at the Albuquerque Museum. The carvers
include Juan Lucero, Ben Lopez, Luisito
Lujan, Horacio Valdez, C. Garcia, George
Lopez. A revival of the art has been taking
place within last several years due to
cultural awareness being experienced by
Hispanos. Contemporary santeros still donate
some pieces to the church, but most are
marketed to private collectors, displayed in
museums, or kept.

Albuquerque, NM

48 Diaz, Katherine A. Murals of New Mexico.
CAMINOS, Vol. 2, no. 5 (October 1981), p.
9-10. English.

AN: Illustrations of murals in Santa Fe
and Albuquerque by Gilberto Guzman,
Francisco Le Fevere[sic; Lefebre], Manuel
Unzueta, and Fernando Penalosa.

49 Tijerina lauds Chicano Congress results.
SANTA FE NEW MEXICAN, (October 24, 1972),
p. A3. English.

AN: At the First National Chicano
Congress for Land and Cultural Reform in
Albuquerque, it was pointed out that younger
delegates are just coming to the realization
of being Chicano but are behind in knowledge
about the relationships between Spaniards,
Mexicans and Indians. This was the reason
for unveiling the mural BIRTH OF THE
INDO-HISPANO [called elsewhere REBIRTH OF
THE CHICANO] at the Alianza headquarters
October 19, 1972.

Allende, Salvador, Pres. of Chile

50 De la Torre, Susana. [Untitled drawing of
Salvador Allende and Fidel Castro]. CARACOL,
Vol. 3, no. 11 (July 1977), p. 23.

Almaguer, Miguel

51 Temko, Allan. Ole! It's already a triumph.
REVIEW [supplement to SAN FRANCISCO SUNDAY
EXAMINER], (December 28, 1980), p. 13-14.
English.

AN: A glowing report on the Mexican
Museum as it celebrates its fifth
anniversary. Provides details about
programs, financing and goals. Brief
analysis of the work of sculptor Manuel Neri
and painters Manuel Villamor, Gustavo
Rivera, Alfredo Arreguin and Miguel
Almaguer. Informative profile on Peter
Rodriguez, founder and Executive Director of
the Museum.

Almanza, Felix

52 Galeria Tonantzin, Centro Cultural de LUCHA,
Austin, TX. Young Chicano photographers from
throughout Texas. Exhibition brochure, n.d.
English.

AN: This exhibition is the collection of
the winners of the contest (by the same
name) sponsored by the Extension Cultural
SRE-UNAM in San Antonio. Photographers
represented were: Grace Alvarez, David
Cardenas, Hector Cardenas, Stephen Casanova,
Ronald Cortez, Raul Espinosa, Felix Almanza,
Carolina Flores, David Garza Perez, Xavier
Garza, Conrad Guerra, Melinda Hasbrook, Juan
Jose de Hoyes, Beverly Kennon, Art Moreno,
David Perez, Isabelle Purden, Patricia
Santell, Nancy de los Santos, Jose Soria,
Richard Tichich, Kathy Vargas, Vivian Yaten,
and Johnny Zamarria.

Almaraz, Carlos D.

53 Adrienne Simard Gallery, Los Angeles, CA.
Presenting Carlos Almaraz: pastel drawings,
1969-1981. Exhibition invitation, 1981.
English.

AN: Invitation to exhibit of Los Angeles
painter Carlos Almaraz. includes color
illustration.

54 Almaraz, Carlos. The artist as a
revolutionary. CHISMEARTE, no. 1 (Fall
1976), p. 47-55. English.

AN: Los Angeles painter Carlos D.
Almaraz gives a detailed history of a
cartoon-banner he made for the first
constitutional convention of the United Farm
Workers of America while he was an
illustrator for EL MALCRIADO, and a mural he
did for the UFWA administration building in
La Paz. He also elucidates his philosophy
about politics, the role of the
revolutionary artist in our time, and the
artist's relation to the bourgeois art
market.

Almaraz, Carlos D.(cont.)

55 Almaraz, Carlos. Introduccion: vida urbana y artistas chicanos. COMUNIDAD, Vol. 55, no. 22 (May 3, 1981), p. 2. Spanish.

AN: In the controversial period of the early 1980s, Chicano advances are being attacked. In this political climate, some Los Angeles artists are interested in beauty and artistic creation: Carlos Almaraz, best-known of the Los Four group; Yreina Cervantez; Elsa Flores; John Valadez, presently working on a mural; and musicians Louie Perez and Tito Rodriguez Larriva.

56 Andrews, Colman. Art of the state: California. NEW WEST MAGAZINE, (January 1981), p. 54-59. English.

AN: Short text on California artists who are presumably influenced by the state's light, color, space, etc. Works of 16 artists reproduced in full color, including one by Carlos Almaraz of Los Angeles. Statements by each artist.

57 Art Gallery, University of California, Irvine and Los Angeles County Museum of Art, Los Angeles, CA. Los Four: Almaraz, de la Rocha, Lujan, Romero. Exhibition brochure, 1973-74. English.

AN: Photographs and biographies of Carlos Almaraz, Roberto de la Rocha, Gilbert S. Lujan, Frank Romero.

58 Arte chicano y el pueblo. COMUNIDAD, no. 41 (May 3, 1981), p. 1-15. Spanish.

AN: The whole issue of the Sunday Supplement deals with Los Angeles Chicano art and music. Works by painter Carlos Almaraz, photographer Elsa Flores, painter Yreina Cervantez, muralist and draftsman John Valadez, and a performance piece by Elsa Flores and Louie Perez are featured. Biographical information, and statements by the artists.

59 California. State College. Los Angeles. Art Department. Fifth California small images exhibition. Exhibition catalog, [1972]. English.

AN: Catalog for an exhibit including the work of Charles D. Almaraz, Mary Lynn Dominguez, Gilbert Sanchez Lujan (who won Purchase Awards), Stephen Anaya, Martha Villegas. Illustrated.

60 Chicano art. ARTES VISUALES, no. 29 (1981). English.

AN: Issue on Chicano art, introduced by Los Angeles artist Roberto Gil de Montes. Includes works and statements by: Pedro Lujan (Texas); Raul M. Guerrero (Calif.); Sylvia Salazar Simpson (New Mexico/Calif.); Carlos Almaraz (Calif.); Rene Yanez (Calif.); Jack Vargas (Calif.); Ray Bravo (Calif.); John Valadez (Calif.); Gloria Maya (Calif.); Elsa Flores (Calif.); Willie Herron (Calif.); Gilbert "Magu" Lujan (Calif.); Kay Torres, Jerry Lucas, and Louis Perez (Calif.).

61 Cultura chicana: Los Angeles. COMUNIDAD, no. 11 (July 13, 1980), p. 1-15. Spanish.

AN: The whole issue of the Cultural Supplement concerns Chicano art and music. Captioned photographs deal with visual artists Carlos Almaraz, Jerry Dreva [not Chicano], Glugio Gronk, Willie Herron, John Valadez, Patssi Valdez, with examples of their work. With the exception of Dreva, all the artists are members of Los Four or Asco. Asco member Harry Gamboa, Jr. sums up the 1960s and 1970s and activities of artists in his essay "Seis imaginaciones: Artistas chicanos en Los Angeles." Well illustrated.

62 Davis, Alonzo, ed. Los Angeles street graphics. Los Angeles, CA: Brockman Gallery Productions, [ca. 1975]. English.

AN: Portfolio of art in public places. Includes Charles Felix (murals), Leo Limon (mural), Charles Almaraz (billboard mural), Johnny Alvarez (mural), Mexican artist Gonzalo Duran, and graffiti.

63 Exploratorium, Student Union, California State University, Los Angeles. An exhibit of published prints of Aztlan Multiples. Exhibition catalog, 1981. English.

AN: The published silkscreen prints of Aztlan Multiples, a small business run by Richard Duardo of Los Angeles, features works by Duardo, John Valadez, and Carlos Almaraz, among others. Illustrations.

64 Los Four [art group]. Tales from the barrio by Los Four and friends. Los Angeles, CA: Los Four, Liberty Hill Foundation, United Steel Workers, [1977]. English.

AN: Comic book designed with drawings, comic strips, and calligraphy by Frank Romero, George Yepes, Carlos D. Almaraz, Leo Limon, Judithe Hernandez.

65 Los Four exhibit in Union Gallery. UNIVERSITY TIMES, (November 6, 1975), p. 4. English.

AN: "Los Four," a group of four Chicano artists - Frank Romero, Roberto "Beto" de la Rocha, Gilbert Lujan, and Carlos Almaraz, with newcomer Judithe Hernandez - work with political cartoons, Catholic symbols, works of sardonic humor. They also paint street murals: several have been done recently in Los Angeles, La Puente, and Long Beach. Illustrated.

66 Gamboa, Harry, Jr. Los murales de Aztlan. COMUNIDAD, (June 28, 1981), p. 8-9+. Spanish.

AN: Review of the exhibit at the Craft and Folk Art Museum of Los Angeles of MURALS OF AZTLAN: THE STREET PAINTERS OF EAST LOS in which Carlos Almaraz, Gronk, Judithe Hernandez, Willie Herron, Frank Romero, John Valadez and the East Los Streetscapers (David Botello, Wayne Healy, George Yepes) painted portable murals in the gallery. The murals are described and illustrated.

Almaraz, Carlos D.(cont.)

67 Gamboa, Harry, Jr. Seis imaginaciones: artistas chicanos en Los Angeles. COMUNIDAD, (July 13, 1980), p. 10. Spanish.

AN: A limited flow of media information about Los Angeles Chicanos has produced a "ghost" culture. Only sensational events are published. Alternative magazines like LA RAZA, CON SAFOS, and REGENERACION have disseminated Chicano ideas of the 1970s. The Chicano imagination has appeared in murals by Willie Herron, Gronk, Carlos Almaraz, John Valadez; in pieces like "walking" and "instant" murals by the group ASCO; by the group Los Four; by group exhibits like "Chicanismo en el arte," and "Chicanarte." Patssi Valdez showed Photobooth Piece at the "Chicanismo" show. Gronk and Jerry Dreva exhibited their mail art at "Punk Meets Art." In Spanish.

68 Goldman, Shifra M. Thorns and roses. ARTWEEK, Vol. 11, no. 30 (September 20, 1980), p. 1. English.

AN: Report on four Chicano artists exhibiting at L.A.C.E. Gallery, Los Angeles: Carlos Almaraz, Teddy Sandoval, John Valadez, and Linda Vallejo. Illustrated.

69 Kim, Howard. Chicano art: is it an art form? Or simply art by Chicanos. NEWORLD, Vol. 6, no. 4 (1980), p. 26-30. English.

AN: An attempt to define Chicano art through interviews with Carlos Almaraz, John Valadez, (Los Four), Robert Delgado, Sister Karen Boccalero (Self-Help Graphics), Harry Gamboa, Jr. (ASCO), Ricardo Duardo, Ignacio Gomez, and others. Well illustrated.

70 L.A.C.E. (Los Angeles Contemporary Exhibitions), Los Angeles, CA. Espina (Thorn): Carlos Almaraz, Elsa Flores, Louie Perez, Teddy Sandoval, John Valadez, Linda Vallejo. Exhibition announcement, 1980. English.

AN: Announcement of an exhibition and a performance piece by six Los Angeles artists.

71 Mascorro, Julie. Mechicano Art Center exhibit to grace Price gallery walls. CAMPUS NEWS, (November 24, 1971). English.

AN: Brief history of Mechicano Art Center activities from its establishment in 1969 to 1971. Exhibiting are Charles Almaraz, Roberto Amaral, Raymond Atilano, William Bejarano, Armando Cabrera, Edward Carbajal, Leonard Castellanos, Henry de Vega, Antonio Esparza, Bob Gomez, Lucila V. Grijalva, Jesus Gutierrez, Santos Lira, Frank Martinez, Ernest Palomino, Louis Quijada, Richard Raya, Frank Romero. Illustrated.

72 Mechicano Art Center, Los Angeles, CA. Paper pieces by C.D.A. [Carlos D. Almaraz]. Exhibition invitation, [1973]. English.

AN: Invitation to a gallery exhibit by the artist, with his manifesto, "Notes on an Aesthetic Alternative".

73 MEXICAN MUSEUM NEWSLETTER. Vol. 6, no. 1 (Winter 1980, 1981). English.

AN: Regular report on the activities, finances, membership, and other information about the Museum. Announces several upcoming

shows: Rupert Garcia, six Mexican geometric artists, paintings and prints by Mexican American and Mexican women artists, Mexican Leonel Maciel and Chicano Carlos Almaraz, Mexican folk art, Manuel Neri sculpture, and Mexican Luis Jaso.

74 The Mexican Museum, San Francisco, CA. Recent works of Leonel Maciel and Carlos Almaraz. Exhibition invitation, 1981. English.

AN: Invitation to an exhibit of works by Mexican artist Maciel and Chicano painter Almaraz.

75 Monteverde, Mildred. Contemporary Chicano art. AZTLAN, Vol. 2, no. 2 (Fall 1971), p. 51-61. English.

AN: An historical survey of trends and influences on contemporary Chicano art. Discusses San Diego's Toltecas en Aztlan and the projected Centro Cultural de la Raza; Los Angeles' Mechicano Art Center, Goez Gallery and Plaza de la Raza; pinto (prison) art; New Mexican art. Many artists are mentioned.

76 Moreno, Eduardo. Los Four. Half-hour 16mm film. English.

AN: Film about the Los Angeles group of artists known as Los Four (originally Carlos Almaraz, Gilbert Sanchez Lujan, Roberto de la Rocha, Frank Romero), at the time of their exhibit at the Los Angeles County Museum of Art - the first time Chicano art was shown at the Museum.

77 Muchnic, Suzanne. Damaged goods in the big city. LOS ANGELES TIMES, (July 23, 1979), p. IV-11. English.

AN: Review of the exhibit at Otis Art Institute of Parsons School of Design of L.A. PARKS AND WRECKS, featuring Carlos Almaraz, John Valadez, and Black artist John Woods. Almaraz paints auto wrecks, and landscapes of Echo Park. Valadez does pencil portraits of young Chicanos. Illustrated.

78 Oakland Museum, Oakland, CA and Laney College, Oakland, CA. In search of Aztlan. Exhibition brochure, 1974. English.

AN: Brochure for exhibit featuring Los Four: Carlos Almaraz, Gilbert Lujan, Roberto de la Rocha, Frank Romero, Judithe Hernandez.

79 Oakland Museum, Oakland, CA. In search of Aztlan. Exhibition invitation, 1974. English.

AN: Invitation to an exhibit by Los Four, a Chicano art group started about 1973 in Los Angeles. On exhibit are the original members, Carlos Almaraz, Gilbert Lujan, Roberto de la Rocha, Frank Romero, and new member Judithe Hernandez.

Almaraz, Carlos D.(cont.)

80 Oakland Museum presents 5 L.A. Chicano artists. EL MUNDO (Hayward, CA), (August 1974). English.

AN: Report on the exhibit THE SEARCH FOR AZTLAN, featuring paintings, murals, tortilla art, folk and religious symbols and totems by Carlos Almaraz, Roberto de la Rocha, Gilbert Lujan, Frank Romero and Judithe Hernandez. Included in the more than 100 works are a wall mural, a folk art pyramid, and part of a primed '51 Chevy lowrider. Illustrated.

81 Otis/Parsons Gallery, Los Angeles, CA; Nieto, Margarita; and Price, Aimee Brown. L.A. parks & wrecks: a reflection of urban life/parques y choques: un reflejo de la vida urbana. Exhibition catalog, [1979]. Bilingual.

AN: Catalog poster discussing the works of the three artists on exhibit: Carlos Almaraz, John Valadez and John Woods who concentrate on urban images. Detailed descriptions of each artist's work accompany the many illustrations. Essays in English and Spanish.

82 Plagens, Peter. Los Four (Roberto de la Rocha, Carlos Almaraz, Gilbert Lujan and Frank Romero) at LACMA. ARTFORUM, (September 1974), p. 87-88. English.

AN: Review of Los Four exhibit at Los Angeles County Museum of Art which calls it a "sociological bazaar" in which Chicanos have been "corrupted" by art schools and "museumized".

83 EL PLAYANO (Loyola University, Los Angeles). (Spring 1973).

AN: Illustrations by Simon Gonzales, Gronk, Harry Gamboa, Jr., Willie Herron, Charles Almaraz, Sister Teresa Munoz, Patsy Valdez, Diane Gamboa.

84 The Point Gallery, Santa Monica, CA. ASCO (Gronk, Patssi, Gamboa, Herron), Los Four (Almaraz, de la Rocha, Judithe Hernandez, Gloriamalia Flores, Mauricio Ramirez, John Valadez. Exhibition invitation, [1975]. English.

AN: Illustrated invitation to an exhibit of Los Angeles artists.

85 Polack, Clark. A question of style - Los Four and the Los Angeles County Museum of Art. SOUTHWEST ART, (July, August, 1974). English.

AN: A double-edged assessment of the "Los Four" exhibit. The exhibition is at once lauded for being provocative and stimulating while at the same time failing artistically. Author feels that special treatment given Carlos Almaraz, Gilbert Lujan, Roberto de la Rocha and Frank Romero by the L.A. County Art Museum has not been extended to other young Los Angeles artists.

86 Rand, Steve. Carlos David Almaraz. LOS ANGELES FREE PRESS, Vol. 11, no. 10 (March 8, 1974), p. 14. English.

AN: Brief biographical sketch on Mexican-born, Los Angeles artist Carlos Almaraz on the occasion of the Los Four exhibit at the Los Angeles County Museum of Art, artists who are, the author says

inaccurately, largely self-taught. Almaraz studied at Garfield High School with David Ramirez, and at Otis Art Institute. One illustration.

87 San Francisco Museum of Modern Art, San Francisco, CA and Pearlstein, Howard. Aesthetics of graffiti. Exhibition catalog, 1978. English.

AN: Graffiti are defined as any coherently-intended presence written, scratched, painted, engraved, printed, pasted or otherwise impressed in a public place. Graffiti have been incorporated into works by artists. In this catalog, works by Chicano artists Carlos Almaraz, Wilfred Castano, Judithe Hernandez, Gilbert Lujan, Gustavo Rivera, Frank Romero, John M. Valadez, Victor M. Valle, Xavier Viramontes - as well as many Latino and non-Latino artist, appear.

88 Santa Ana College, Santa Ana, CA and Goldman, Shifra M. Chicano art. Exhibition catalog, 1974. English.

AN: Thirteen California artists are presented in a short essay defining Chicano as a double mestizaje of Mexican mestizo and U.S. influences that exists in a state of "reconciled conflict." Its aim is communication. Artists included are Malaquias Montoya, Rupert Garcia, Manuel Hernandez, Esteban Villa, Robert Gomez, Harvey Tarango, Mary Helen Castro, Eduardo Carrillo, Graciela Carrillo, and "Los Four": Carlos Almaraz, Robert de la Rocha, Judithe Hernandez, Gilbert Lujan and Frank Romero.

89 Sol Art Gallery, San Diego, CA. Group showing of Southern California artists. Exhibition brochure, 1980. English.

AN: First exhibit of new Chicano art gallery showing Los Angeles artists Carlos Almaraz, Judithe Hernandez, John Valadez, Linda Vallejo, Ricardo Duardo, Barbara Carrasco.

90 William Grant Still Community Arts Center, Los Angeles, CA. Latin American artists exhibition. Exhibition brochure, 1978. English.

AN: Exhibit curated by Linda Vallejo including Carlos Almaraz, Michael M. Amescua, Ray Bravo, Isabel Castro, Yreina Cervantez, Luis Serrano-Cordero, Cynthia Honesto, Judith Miranda, Teddy Sandoval, John Taboada, Emigdio Vasquez. Illustrated.

91 Wilson, William. 30 works from the grass roots. LOS ANGELES TIMES, (June 4, 1973), p. IV,2. English.

AN: Review of a show at the Junior Arts Center in Barnsdall Park by 15 members of the Mechicano Art Center. The critic feels contemporary groups that aim for change today (unlike past groups) are unable to articulate their spirit in a cohesive style. The top talent in this show is Charles Almaraz; also on exhibit are paintings by Jose Cervantes, Guillermo Martinez, Ray Atilano, sculpture by Manuel Cruz, and photography by (Oscar) R. Castillo.

Almazan, Jesse

92 Con Safo. San Antonio, TX: Pintores Chicanos
de San Antonio, [ca. 1975]. English.

AN: Illustrated pamphlet issued by the
San Antonio artists' group Con Safo.
Includes a self-definition and a brief
history of the group under the names El
Grupo, Los Pintores de Aztlan, Los Pintores
de la Nueva Raza, Con Safo (from 1967 on).
Members include Jesse A. Almazan, Mel Casas,
Jose P. Garza, Cesar Augusto
Martinez, Santos Martinez, Felipe Reyes,
Roberto Rios, Jesus C. Trevino, and Vicente
Velasquez.

93 Corpus Christy State University for the Arts
and Weil Gallery Center for the Arts, Corpus
Christi State University. Southwest artists
invitational: an exhibition of contemporary
art by seven Texas artists of Hispanic
American descent. Ehxibition brochure, 1980.
English.

AN: Artists Jesse Almazan, Luis Jimenez,
Cesar Martinez, Lydia Martinez, Manuel
Mauricio, Guillermo Pulido, and Jesse
Trevino show a variety of techniques and
styles. Text by Roberto Tomas Esparza.
Statements by and about the artists.
Illustrated.

Almeida, Al

94 Art Gallery, California State University,
Long Beach and Lujan, Gilbert Sanchez
"Magu". El arte del pocho. Exhibit brochure,
October 1968. English.

AN: Information about Southern
California artists John Deheras, Marcus
Villagran, Roberto de la Rocha, Santos
Zuniga, Crispin Gonzales, Richard Martinez,
Jesus Gutierrez, Ed Oropeza, Pete Mendez,
David Ramirez, Gilbert Sanchez Lujan, Willie
Hernandez, Art Ponce, Carmen Tostado, Al
Almeida, David Ceja, Robert E. Chavez,
Thomas A. Ferriera. All art students,
graduates, or faculty.

Almendarez, Johnny

95 La Raza art festival. PAPEL CHICANO, Vol. 1,
no. 6 (May 21, 1971), p. 8-9. English.

AN: Two-page centerfold of photographs
by Johnny Almendarez of the LA RAZA ART
FESTIVAL held at Ripley House in Segundo
Barrio of Houston, Texas, May 5-9, 1971.
Includes installation view of the exhibit,
two photos of artists in action and a cover
photograph of artist Pedro Rodriguez
conducting a silkscreen workshop.

Alonzo, Ricardo

96 MARCH: Movimiento artistico Chicano
(Mexican-American Art Movement). QUARTERLY,
(Spring 1976), p. 10. English.

AN: Brief history of MARCH.
Illustrations of murals by Ricarco Alonzo,
Jose Gonzalez, Vicente Mendoza. Ray Patlan.

Altars

97 Altars as folk art. ARRIBA, Vol. 1, no. 1
(July 1980, 194), p. 4. English.

AN: Focusing on the home altar of
Josefina De Leon from Cuero, Texas, the
article describes this folk expression on
two levels: first as a subjective religious

intermediator and secondly as a masterpiece
of collected objects. Contains interesting
information on the form, function and
meaning of altars. Illustrated with
photographs.

98 Lomas Garza, Carmen. Altares: arte
espiritual del hogar. HOJAS, (1976).
English.

AN: Commentary and five photographs from
the author's visual documentation of home
altars in Kingsville, Texas. Brief analysis
of the form, meaning and function of home
altars in Chicano daily life.

99 Navar, M. Margarita. La vela prendida: home
altars. ARRIBA, Vol. 1, no. 5 (February
1980), p. 12. English.

AN: Brief commentary on the exhibit LA
VELA PRENDIDA: MEXICAN AMERICAN WOMEN'S HOME
ALTARS at the Texas Memorial Museum during
December 1980. Aside from altars, the
exhibit focused on nichos, grutas and
lapidas.

100 Texas Memorial Museum, University of Texas,
Austin, TX. La vela prendida:
Mexican-American women's home altars.
Exhibition catalog, 1980. Bilingual.

AN: Bilingual illustrated
brochure-catalog of exhibit. Includes home
altars and graveyard headstones.

Alternative Cinema Conference, N.Y., 1979

101 CHICANO CINEMA NEWSLETTER. Vol. 1, no. 6
(August 1979). English.

AN: Announcements of the San Antonio
Chicano Film Festival, a seminar on the
business of art, the receipt of a report of
the Task Force on Minorities in Public
Broadcasting, a critical report on the
Alternative Cinema Conference in New York,
which was attended by eleven members of the
Chicano Cinema Coalition, and a report and
critique of the report by the Task Force.

102 CHICANO CINEMA NEWSLETTER. Vol. 1, no. 4
(June 1979). English.

AN: Report and cautionary note on the
upcoming Alternative Cinema Conference;
announcement of ONLY ONCE IN A LIFETIME and
CHICANA film releases; other new films and
TV programs; a Chicano cinema bibliography;
a list of Chicano production companies and
distributors; a theoretical article on the
nature (proposed) of Chicano cinema as an
alternative cinema; statement of purpose of
the Los Angeles Chicano Cinema Coalition.

103 CHICANO CINEMA NEWSLETTER. Vol. 1, no. 3
(May 1979). English.

AN: Announcements for the U.S.
Conference for an Alternative Cinema (N.Y.),
a "Nosotros" banquet, application dates for
the Film Fund, deadlines for the National
Endowment for the Humanities, and criticism
of the Hollywood feature film BOULEVARD
NIGHTS.

Alurista

104 Murphy, Patricia Lee. Artists renew Toltecas crafts heritage. LOS ANGELES TIMES, (May 23, 1971), p. E, 10. English.

AN: The Toltecas en Aztlan, creative arm of the Chicano Federation of San Diego County, Inc., will shortly move into their new Centro Cultural de la Raza in Balboa Park, San Diego. The group includes Mario Acevedo (Peruvian), Guillermo Aranda, Tomas Castaneda, Victor Ochoa and Salvador Torres (visual artists) and poet Alurista.

Alvarez Bravo, Manuel

105 Bravo, Antonio. Manuel Alvarez Bravo at the San Francisco Art Institute. CHISMEARTE, Vol. 2, no. 1 (Summer 1978), p. 37. English.

AN: Presentation of the Mexican photographer's work in relation to a visiting exhibit in the United States. Illustrated.

Alvarez, Felix

106 Concilio de arte popular. CHISMEARTE, Vol. 1, no. 2 (Winter, Spring, 1977), p. 54. English.

AN: Report of a meeting February 12, 1977 by the Concilio de Arte Popular (CAP) which published CHISMEARTE. Introduces members of the Board and summarizes discussions of problems of the organization and their publication.

Alvarez, Grace

107 Galeria Tonantzin, Centro Cultural de LUCHA, Austin, TX. Young Chicano photographers from throughout Texas. Exhibition brochure, n.d. English.

AN: This exhibition is the collection of the winners of the contest (by the same name) sponsored by the Extension Cultural SRE-UNAM in San Antonio. Photographers represented were: Grace Alvarez, David Cardenas, Hector Cardenas, Stephen Casanova, Ronald Cortez, Raul Espinosa, Felix Almanza, Carolina Flores, David Garza Perez, Xavier Garza, Conrad Guerra, Melinda Hasbrook, Juan Jose de Hoyes, Beverly Kennon, Art Moreno, David Perez, Isabelle Purden, Patricia Santell, Nancy de los Santos, Jose Soria, Richard Tichich, Kathy Vargas, Vivian Yaten, and Johnny Zamarria.

Alvarez, Johnny

108 Davis, Alonzo, ed. Los Angeles street graphics. Los Angeles, CA: Brockman Gallery Productions, [ca. 1975]. English.

AN: Portfolio of art in public places. Includes Charles Felix (murals), Leo Limon (mural), Charles Almaraz (billboard mural), Johnny Alvarez (mural), Mexican artist Gonzalo Duran, and graffiti.

109 Sommer, Robert. Street art. New York: Quick Fox, 1975. English.

AN: Introductory essay covering the history of the new mural movement, forms of street art, politics, street sculpture, how to locate and photograph street art. Chicano murals include Charles Felix and others at Estrada Courts (L.A.), RCAF murals in Sacramento, Jose Montoya and others (Broderick, Ca.) Marcos Raya (Chicago), Mike

Rios (Neighborhood Legal Aid, S.F.) Mechicano Art Center (L.A.) Johnny Alvarez (L.A.), New Mexico State Employment Bldg., Albuquerque mural, Lorena Street School (L.A.), two murals, Casa de la Raza Alternative School (Berkeley), Santa Fe, New Mexico mural, Francisco Hernandez (L.A.), Artes Guadalupanos de Aztlan (N. Mexico), Willie Herron (L.A.). Better documentation would have been welcome.

Alvarez, Tina

110 Hernandez, Manuel de Jesus. Zapata murals depict Chicano struggle. LA HONDA, Vol. 5, no. 3 (March, April, 1979). English.

AN: Critical vignettes on the content of Chicano murals at Casa Zapata, a Chicano theme dorm at Stanford University. The muralists include Zarco Guerrero, Esteban Chavez, Hector Chacon, and Tina Alvarez.

Amaral, Roberto

111 Mascorro, Julie. Mechicano Art Center exhibit to grace Price gallery walls. CAMPUS NEWS, (November 24, 1971). English.

AN: Brief history of Mechicano Art Center activities from its establishment in 1969 to 1971. Exhibiting are Charles Almaraz, Roberto Amaral, Raymond Atilano, William Bejarano, Armando Cabrera, Edward Carbajal, Leonard Castellanos, Henry de Vega, Antonio Esparza, Bob Gomez, Lucila V. Grijalva, Jesus Gutierrez, Santos Lira, Frank Martinez, Ernest Palomino, Louis Quijada, Richard Raya, Frank Romero. Illustrated.

Ambriz

112 El Centro Cultural de La Raza, San Diego, CA. Espejo del barrio-art exposition. Exhibition brochure, June 1975. English.

AN: Illustrated brochure announcement for a cultural exposition of Chicano music, art and drama. Includes some biographical information and one reproduction of painter Manuel Unzueta, woodworker Ambriz, muralist Victor Orozco Ochoa and designer/illustrator J. Armando Nunez.

AMERICA EN LA MIRA [exhibit]

113 Lucas, Jerry. Testimonios de Latinoamerica. CHISMEARTE, no. 6 (February 1980), p. 6-9. English.

AN: Review of the exhibits TESTIMONIOS DE LATINOAMERICA and AMERICA EN LA MIRA, brought to Los Angeles Contemporary Exhibitions Gallery by Chicano curator Roberto Gil de Montes, as part of a cultural exchange between the Mexican Cultural Workers Front and Felipe Ehrenberg of the Grupo Proceso Pentagono of Mexico, and Chicano artists and photographers from the Council of Latino Photography/USA in Los Angeles. Well illustrated.

AMERICA TROPICAL [film]

114 Gamboa, Harry, Jr. Film, television, and
Trevino. LA LUZ, Vol. 6, no. 10 (October
1977), p. 7-8. English.

AN: Jesus Salvador Trevino has been an
active proponent and participant in
transforming cultural inaccuracy about
Chicanos in the media to accurate mass media
models. A biography of Trevino follows,
including discussion of some of his films:
THE SALAZAR INQUEST, CHICANO MORATORIUM
AFTERMATH, SOLEDAD, AMERICA TROPICAL, YO SOY
CHICANO, RAICES DE SANGRE, as well as
television series like ACCION CHICANO,
AHORA, and INFINITY FACTORY.

115 Smith, Cecil. YO SOY captures the Chicano
soul. LOS ANGELES TIMES, (August 17, 1972),
p. IV, 20. English.

AN: Trevino's films YO SOY CHICANO and
AMERICA TROPICAL shown on KCET.

116 Trevino, Jesus Salvador. America tropical.
(1971). English.

AN: Half-hour 16mm color film produced
and written by Jesus Salvador Trevino and
directed by Barry Nye about the painting and
whitewashing in 1932-34 of Mexican muralist
David Alfaro Siqueiros' mural AMERICA
TROPICAL in Olvera Street, Los Angeles.
Traces the attempts at restoration of the
mural starting in the late 1960s and
continuing in the 1970s. History of the
mural set within social/political context of
Mexican Americans in the 1930s, and
counterpart struggles of Chicanos in the
1970s.

117 Zheutlin, Barbara and Talbot, David. Jesus
Salvador Trevino. In: CREATIVE DIFFERENCES:
PROFILES OF HOLLYWOOD DISSIDENTS. Boston,
MS: South End Press, 1978, p. 345-352.
English.

AN: Within the context of New Left
alternative filmmakers who chose to work
within Hollywood, Trevino sets forth his
standards and goals. His films and TV
productions include SOLEDAD (1971), AMERICA
TROPICAL (1971), YO SOY CHICANO (1972),
RAICES DE SANGRE (1977) and INFINITY FACTORY
(1975-1976).

AMERICA TROPICAL [mural]

118 Barrera, Manuel. "Maestro" Siqueiros. LA
RAZA, Vol. 2, no. 2 (1974), p. 40-41.
English.

119 Garcia, Rupert. Echos de la Mision - Alfaro
Siqueiros (1896-1974). EL TECOLOTE, Vol. 4,
no. 3 (February 22, 1974), p. 11. English.

AN: Biographical and artistic trajectory
of Mexican artist David Alfaro Siqueiros.
Artist painted three murals in Southern
California in 1932 (MEETING IN THE STREET
and TROPICAL AMERICA were done in Los
Angeles on the walls of the Chouinard School
of Art and the Plaza Art Center, Olvera
Street area respectively. The third mural
PORTRAIT OF MEXICO was privately
commissioned in Santa Monica). The three
California murals deal with themes of
censorship, racism, colonialism, capitalism,
and imperialism. Article suggests that Raza
artists are much influenced by the ideas and
work of Siqueiros. Illustrated with Rupert
Garcia's silkscreen poster SIQUEIROS.

120 Goldman, Shifra M. Las creaturas de la
America tropical: Siqueiros y los murales
chicanos en Los Angeles. REVISTA DE BELLAS
ARTES, no. 25 (January, February, 1976), p.
38-46. Spanish.

AN: Treats the influence of Siqueiros'
1932 outdoor mural in Los Angeles on the
Chicano street mural movement of the 1970s.

121 M.E.C.H.A. cultura y evolucion mexicana. EL
CLARIN, (May 2, 1974), p. 3. Spanish.

AN: Report on the mural designed and
painted under the direction of Mexican-born
designer Sergio O'Cadiz at Santa Ana
College, Santa Ana, Calif. Collaborators
were instructor Shifra Goldman and gallery
director Mike Davis, with members of the
MEChA Club and other students. The mural
concerns the history of Mexico and of the
Chicano and includes a tribute to David
Alfaro Siqueiros' Los Angeles mural AMERICA
TROPICAL, painted and white-washed in the
1930s. Illustrated.

122 Rowe, Richard. On Olvera Street: one vision
realized, another white washed. REVIEW
(Society of Architectural Historians,
Pasadena, CA), Vol. 1, no. 1 (Fall 1981),
p. 7. English.

AN: Documentation about AMERICA
TROPICAL, 1932 mural by David Alfaro
Siqueiros. The mural, commissioned by F.K.
Ferenz of the Plaza Art Center on Olvera
Street in Los Angeles, was a 16' by 80'
painting on the second-story wall of the old
Italian Hall. From 1968 on, art historian
Shifra M. Goldman, working with a small
committee, has been actively involved in the
attempt to restore the mural. Article
details the travails of restoration and
underscores the mural's importance.
Illustrated.

123 Viva Siqueiros. CON SAFOS, no. 7 (Winter
1971), p. 26-27. English.

AN: Brief recapitulation of the
controversy surrounding David Alfaro
Siqueiros' visit to Los Angeles, CA in 1932.
It was during this visit that he painted the
only public Siqueiros mural in the U.S.
which still remains, albeit covered over
with whitewash. The details of the visit are
explained by Siqueiros in his book: MI
RESPUESTA. The article is illustrated with
two black and white details of the mural.

American Film Institute

124 CHICANO CINEMA NEWSLETTER. Vol. 1, no. 1
(December 1978). English.

AN: Reports on activities of Chicano
filmmakers in producing films, meeting with
organizations like the American Film
Institute, the Hispanic Task Force of the
National Endowment for the Arts, the WNET
Independent Documentary Film Fund.
International film news also included.

American Indians
USE: Native Americans

Amescua, Michael M.

125 Una galeria de artistas = A gallery of
artists. CAMINOS, Vol. 1, no. 6 (October
1980), p. 20-26. Bilingual.

AN: Features California artists Domingo
O. Ulloa (Imperial Valley images), Gloria
Chacon, photographer Maria Pinedo (San
Francisco), Willie Herron (Los Angeles),
Joaquin Patino (Delano), Pedro Pelayo (Long
Beach), sculptor Rudi Sigala (San Diego),
Mario Torero (San Diego), sculptor Michael
M. Amescua (Los Angeles), and the East Los
Streetscapers. Illustrated.

126 William Grant Still Community Arts Center,
Los Angeles, CA. Latin American artists
exhibition. Exhibition brochure, 1978.
English.

AN: Exhibit curated by Linda Vallejo
including Carlos Almaraz, Michael M.
Amescua, Ray Bravo, Isabel Castro, Yreina
Cervantez, Luis Serrano-Cordero, Cynthia
Honesto, Judith Miranda, Teddy Sandoval,
John Taboada, Emigdio Vasquez. Illustrated.

Amezcua, Consuelo Gonzalez "Chelo"

127 Cox, Sue. Female psychology: the emerging
self. New York: St. Martin's Press, 2nd ed.,
1981, p. 138+. English.

AN: Reproductions of works by Carmen
Lomas Garza, Graciela Carrillo, Consuelo
Gonzalez Amezcua.

128 Galerias Paco, New York, NY. Consuelo
Gonzalez Amezcua - filigree art. Exhibition
announcement, n.d. English.

AN: Two-page exhibition announcement
illustrated with two examples of the Texas
artist's "filigree art" and a sample of her
poetry.

129 Marion Koogler McNay Art Institute, San
Antonio, TX and Lee, Amy Freeman. Filigree
drawings by Consuelo Gonzalez Amezcua.
Exhibition catalog, 1968. English.

AN: Illustrated catalog for an
exhibition of 42 filigree drawings by Texas
artist "Chelo" Amezcua. Apart from
biographical and historical information, the
text evokes the ambiance of magic and
mysticism surrounding the artist.

130 The Mexican Museum, San Francisco, CA and
Quirarte, Jacinto. 17 artists:
Hispano/Mexican-American/Chicano. Exhibition
catalog, 1977. English.

AN: Catalog of an exhibit for artists
Emilio Aguirre, Consuelo Gonzalez Amezcua,
Al Barela, Pedro Cervantez, Edward Chavez,
Antonio Garcia, Louis Gutierrez, Harry
Louie, Vincent Perez, Michael Ponce de Leon,
Eugenio Quesada, Gustavo Rivera, Peter
Rodriguez, Alex Sanchez, Darryl Sapien, Rudy
Trevino, Manuel Villamor. Illustrated.

131 Petersen, Karen and Wilson, J.J. Women
artists: Third World. New York, NY: Harper &
Row, 1975. English.

AN: Catalog of slides with accompanying
notes. Slides of Chicana artists available:
Margaret Herrera (Chavez), Consuelo (Chelo)
Gonzalez Amezcua, Santa Barraza, Mujeres
Muralistas, El Grupo de Santa Ana, Carmen
Lomas Garza, Carolina Flores.

132 Quirarte, Jacinto. Chelo Gonzalez Amezcua.
QUETZAL, Vol. 1, no. 2 (Winter 1970, 1971),
p. 33-36.

AN: Biographical information based on a
taped interview with the Del Rio, Texas
artist. As a self-taught artist, Chelo
Gonzalez Amezcua developed a drawing style
using colored ball point pens which she
calls "Filigree Art", a new Texas culture.
Poorly illustrated.

133 Quirarte, Jacinto. Image and text (poetry)
in the work of Consuelo (Chelo) Gonzalez
Amezcua, a Texas artist (1903-1975).
RESEARCH CENTER FOR THE ARTS REVIEW, Vol. 5,
no. 1 (January 1982), p. 1-3. English.

AN: The use of images and poetry in the
work of self-taught Del Rio, Texas artist
Chelo Gonzalez Amezcua is demonstrated by
focusing on her drawing EL MOSAICO DE LAS
AVES of 1972, in which her use of both sides
of the paper is contrasted with similar uses
in Aztec sculpture. Illustrated.

134 University of Texas. San Antonio. Medical
School and Lee, Amy Freeman. Consuelo
Gonzales Amezcua. Exhibition catalog, n.d.
English.

AN: Exhibition catalog with a text by
Amy Freeman Lee. This major exhibit
presented 110 of the artist's works. Price
list included.

Anaya, Stephen

135 California. State College. Los Angeles. Art
Department. Fifth California small images
exhibition. Exhibition catalog, [1972].
English.

AN: Catalog for an exhibit including the
work of Charles D. Almaraz, Mary Lynn
Dominguez, Gilbert Sanchez Lujan (who won
Purchase Awards), Stephen Anaya, Martha
Villegas. Illustrated.

Anchorage, AK

136 Haines, Bruce J. Gonzales' works are
controlled and full of detail. ANCHORAGE
DAILY NEWS, (May 23, 1980). English.

AN: Positive review of an exhibit titled
THE HEAD TASTES BEST by Mariano Gonzales.
Born in El Paso, Texas but reared in Alaska,
Gonzales' works in various media from
drawings and paintings to metals, ivory,
enamel and plastics. The critic praises the
artist for his "volatile intricacy" and his
fusion of materials "always with craft and
finesse". Includes reproductions of two
paintings.

137 McCullom, Pat. Gonzales: his paintings are
like hieroglyphs. ANCHORAGE TIMES, (June
25, 1978), p. I, 3. English.

AN: Mariano Gonzales born in El Paso
Texas, reared in Anchorage and trained at
the Rhode Island School of Design has a
developing reputation as an artist from the
far north. This positive review is for an
exhibit of paintings, jewelry and metal work
pieces. Gonzales' paintings are heavily
saturated with subconscious symbolism and
his sculptures generally feature mechanical,
movable parts.

Ancianos

138 Seniors mural to be dedicated at RC Center.
REDWOOD CITY TRIBUNE, (December 31, 1977),
p. 3. English.

AN: A portable mural depicting the birth
of the senior citizen hot meal program in
San Mateo County will be dedicated at the
Senior Citizens Drop-In Center. The 12x18-ft
mural was painted by Emmanuel Montoya of
Menlo Park, CA. Illustrated.

ANCIENT ROOTS/NEW VISIONS [exhibit]
USE: RAICES ANTIGUAS/VISIONES NUEVAS
[exhibit]

Andrade, Bruno, Jr.

139 Galeria de la Raza, San Antonio, TX.
Celebration seventy-four. Exhibition
catalog, [ca. 1974]. English.

AN: Catalog of extensive exhibition
including European, Mexican, and the
following Texan Chicano artists: Rolando
Garces, Cesar Martinez, Ray Chavez, Vicente
Rodriguez, Jorge Garza, Alfred Rodriguez,
Luis Guerra, Carmen Lomas Garza, Bruno
Andrade, Jr., Amado M. Pena Jr., Roberto
Rios, Jose Trevino, Rudy Trevino, Luis
Santoyo, Tati Rubio, Eduardo C. Garza,
Arthur de la Fuente, and Jesus Campos
Trevino.

140 The Mexican Museum, San Francisco, CA. Bruno
Andrade (from Missouri) and Antonio Lopez
Saenz (from Mexico). Exhibition
announcement, 1978. English.

AN: Flyer announcing an exhibit at the
Mexican Museum of Texas-born Andrade who is
exhibiting large abstract landscapes.
Andrade teaches in Columbia, Missouri; this
is his first California exhibit.

Anguiano, Mary Ann

141 Xochil Art and Culture Center, Mission, TX.
Besame mucho. Exhibition invitation, 1979.
English.

AN: Invitation to exhibit of Texas
artists from Mujeres Artistas del Suroeste
(MAS): Mary Ann Anguiano, Alicia Arredondo,
Santa Barraza, Nora Gonzales-Dodson, Maria
Flores, Carolina Flores, Mary Ann Ambray
Gonzales, Sylvia Orozco, Nancy de los
Santos, Modesta Barbina Trevino.
Illustrated.

Antioch Juarez-Lincoln Graduate School

142 Valdez, Raul. Hombre de bronce [mural].
VILLAGER, no. 48 (April 9, 1976), p. 9.
English.

AN: Illustration and description of Raul
Valdez's indoor mural HOMBRE DE BRONCE at
Antioch Juarez-Lincoln College (Centro
Cultural de LUCHA).

Anton, Don

143 Conversation on photography in the Los
Angeles Latino community. OBSCURA, Vol. 2,
no. 2 (December, February, 1981, 1982), p.
22-32. English.

AN: Interview on the nature and
distinguishing characteristics of Chicano
photography with Chicano photographers
Isabel Castro (Council for Latino
Photography), Lorenzo Hernandez (Director of

Cityscape Gallery, publisher PHOTOSHOW
magazine), Joseph G. Uribe (California State
University, Los Angeles, Center for the
Visual Arts, Director of West Colorado
Gallery), Patssi Valdez, Becky Villasenor,
and sculptor, curator, and Art Director for
Academia Quinto Sol, Inc., Linda Vallejo,
Portfolio of photography by Chicanos Don
Anton, Louis Carlos Bernal, Sean Carrillo,
Patssi Valdez, Ricardo Valverde, and by
Morrie Camhi and Elizabeth Sisco on Chicano
subjects.

144 Los Angeles Municipal Art Gallery, Los
Angeles, CA. Multicultural focus: a
photography exhibition for the Los Angeles
Bicentennial. Exhibition catalog, 1981.
English.

AN: Catalog of an exhibit demonstrating
the multi-ethnic character of Los Angeles.
Chicano photographers include Don Anton, Ron
Bernal, Daniel Martinez, Rick Tejada-Flores.
Illustrated.

Anzaldua, Mario

145 Imagenes de la Chicana. Menlo Park, CA:
Nowels Publications (Stanford University
Chicano Press), [ca 1975]. English.

AN: Collections of writings by Chicanas;
illustrated by unsigned drawings, and
photographs by Lena Bugarin, Martina Puente,
Francisco Camplis, Mario Anzaldua.

Apodaca, Ricardo

146 Garcia, Rupert. Laminas de la Raza. San
Francisco: Garcia Litho and Printing
Service, 1975. English.

AN: Portfolio of drawings and prints by
Patricia Rodriguez, Ricardo Apodaca,
Xochitl, Domingo Rivera, Francisco Camplis,
Rafael Maradiaga, Tom Rios, Juan Fuentes,
Ricardo Diaz, Jose Romero, Consuelo Mendez,
Jose Antonio Burciaga, Irene Perez, Ricardo
Rios, Mike Rios, Graciela Carrillo, Rene
Yanez, Luis Talamantez, Guillermo Bermudez,
all from Northern California.

Aponte, Cynthia Reyes
USE: Reyes Aponte, Cynthia

Aragon, Rafael

147 Santos of New Mexico, art of our people.
GRITO DEL NORTE, Vol. 3, no. 1 (January 17,
1970), p. 8-9. English.

AN: Historical trajectory of santero
tradition in New Mexico. Distinguished
santeros like Rafael Aragon of Cordova,
Miguel Herrera of Arroyo Hondo, Juan Ramon
Velasquez of Conjilon, Jose Benito Ortega of
La Cueva all created art wedded to the
environment of the Southwest. Illustrated
with a portfolio of santos and retablos from
the Folk Art Museum of Santa Fe, NM.

Aranda, Guillermo

148 Art directors, take note. INTERRACIAL BOOKS
FOR CHILDREN, Vol. 5, no. 7-8 (1975), p. 19.
English.

AN: Focus on the work of three Chicano
illustrators: Salvador Barajas V., Arturo
Roman, and Guillermo Aranda. Includes
representative examples of their work.

Aranda, Guillermo (cont.)

149 Murphy, Patricia Lee. Artists renew Toltecas crafts heritage. LOS ANGELES TIMES, (May 23, 1971), p. E, 10. English.

AN: The Toltecas en Aztlan, creative arm of the Chicano Federation of San Diego County, Inc., will shortly move into their new Centro Cultural de la Raza in Balboa Park, San Diego. The group includes Mario Acevedo (Peruvian), Guillermo Aranda, Tomas Castaneda, Victor Ochoa and Salvador Torres (visual artists) and poet Alurista.

150 NATIONAL MURALS NETWORK COMMUNITY NEWSLETTER. (Spring 1981). English.

AN: Reports, or illustrations, of murals by Guillermo Aranda (Calif.), Francisco Lefebre (New Mexico); Marcos Raya's section of Chicago's anti-war mural; Gilberto Guzman's mural (New Mexico); vandalism on a Michael Schnorr mural at Chicano Park, San Diego, Calif.

Arau, Alfonso

151 Vasquez, Richard. Mojado power: a boost for illegal aliens. CALENDAR, (February 22, 1981), p. 41. English.

AN: An uncritical review of the commercial film made by Mexican film star and comedian Alfonso Arau in the United States primarily for the "American-Hispanic" market on a low-cost budget. Arau planned to distribute in Mexico, Latin America and Spain. The film is a light-weight comedy about a "wetback" who launches a campaign for "mojado power" but falls victim to dope smugglers and is sent to jail.

Arce, Josefina

152 Amor sin fronteras. Los Angeles, CA: Colectivo El Ojo, n.d.. English.

AN: Fotonovela with Josefina Arce, Eduardo Dominguez and Mike Jauregui produced by the Colectivo: Eduardo Dominguez, Roberto Gil de Montes, Jerry Lucas, Kay Torres, students at California State University, Los Angeles.

Architecture

153 Adams, Robert. The architecture and art of early Hispanic Colorado. Boulder, CO: Colorado Associated University Press in cooperation with the State Historical Society of Colorado, 1974. English.

AN: Robert Adams is a photographer and writer from Longmont, CO who has evocatively captured scenes in the San Luis and Purgatory Valleys of Southern Colorado. The text and photographs focus on "Hispano" village life, customs and traditions.

154 Ahlborn, Richard E. The Penitente Moradas of Abiquiu. Washington, D.C.: Smithsonian Institution Press, 1968 (Contributions from the Museum of History and Technology, Paper 63). English.

AN: The history and organization of the Penitente Brotherhood. Detailed analysis of the architecture of Penitente moradas and the artifacts within them. Illustrated with many ethnographic photographs.

155 Fine Arts Society of San Diego, CA. The cross and the sword. Exhibition catalog, 1976. Bilingual.

AN: Bi-lingual exhibition catalog of Southwestern art forms; santero art, vernacular architecture and traditional folk art. Important essays by experts in each field. Contains an iconographical summary of santos and a good bibliography. Profusely illustrated.

156 Rodriguez, Anita. Las enjarradoras: women of the earth. NEW MEXICO, (February 1980), p. 46-47+. English.

AN: History of adobe construction in New Mexico, its decline and its present revival in Arizona and New Mexico. Written by a professional adobe architect and feminist who defines the traditional terms and techniques of this woman's craft. Illustrated.

157 Rodriguez, Anita. Tradiciones de adobe en Nuevo Mejico norteno = adobe traditions in Northern New Mexico. ADOBE NEWS, no. 15 (1977). Bilingual.

AN: History of adobe construction in New Mexico, from primarily Indian sources with Spanish input. For 400 years, women were builders and architects of the Southwest; today they are "enjarradoras" (plasterers). Written by a professional enjarradora from New Mexico. Illustrated.

158 Rodriguez, Roland V. Urban design primer: comparative analyses of San Antonio urbanscapes. [s.l.: s.n., ca. 1979]. English.

AN: Proposal for a study to compare six sites in San Antonio with models of European townscapes. The purpose is to educate the public to enjoy its city and make future city planners sensitive to urban design. Also useful for architectural students.

159 Southwick, Marcia. Build with adobe. Chicago, IL: Swallow, 1965. English.

AN: Modern building techniques for construction of adobe homes with information on traditional building practices.

160 Stedman, Myrtle and Stedman, Wilfred. Adobe architecture. Santa Fe, NM: Sunstone Press, 1973. English.

AN: The technology and aesthetics of adobe homes. An illustrated manual of house plans and building techniques. Includes drawings of Southwestern "colonial" furniture.

161 Tonitines: Chicano architecture por Chicanos in architecture. Unpublished manuscript, Spring 1972. English.

AN: Manuscript deposited at Chicano Library, University of California, Berkeley. Aspirations for service; esthetics; interface between architecture and economics politics for group of students in Department of Architecture, University of California, Berkeley.

Archuleta, Eppie

162 Nelson, Kathryn J. Excerpts from los
    testamentos: Hispanic women folk artists of
    the San Luis Valley, Colorado. FRONTIERS,
    Vol. 5, no. 3 (Fall 1980), p. 34-43.
    English.

    AN: Eppie Archuleta, weaver from the San
    Luis Valley in Southern Colorado talks
    about her life philosophy, Hispanic cultural
    traditions and her role as a community
    artist. First person account amply
    illustrated with photographs.

Archuleta, Felipe

163 Barrett, Marjorie. Carving out a living - a
    primitive process. ROCKY MOUNTAIN NEWS,
    (December 15, 1979), p. 90. English.

    AN: In the village of Teseque outside
    Santa Fe, NM, Felipe Archuleta, a
    69-year-old folk carver has emerged as an
    international art celebrity, famous for his
    naive animal carvings. His work expecially
    life-sized renditions of animals, is
    represented in many distinguished
    collections and is prized for its wit and
    lack of predictability. Illustrated with
    photograph of carver and one of his
    creations.

164 Elaine Horwitch Galleries, Santa Fe, NM. New
    Mexico woodcarving. Exhibition catalog,
    1980. English.

    AN: Invitation to an exhibit at the
    Horwitch galleries of Scottsdale, Arizona,
    and Santa Fe, NM of sculptors Felipe
    Archuleta, Leroy Archuleta, Frank Brito,
    Alonso Jimenez, Horatio Valdez, and others.
    Illustration.

Archuleta, Leroy

165 Elaine Horwitch Galleries, Santa Fe, NM. New
    Mexico woodcarving. Exhibition catalog,
    1980. English.

    AN: Invitation to an exhibit at the
    Horwitch galleries of Scottsdale, Arizona,
    and Santa Fe, NM of sculptors Felipe
    Archuleta, Leroy Archuleta, Frank Brito,
    Alonso Jimenez, Horatio Valdez, and others.
    Illustration.

Archuleta, Robert

166 Wilson, Anne. Chicanos show off talents in
    Magna SOCIO projects. SALT LAKE CITY
    TRIBUNE, (July 9, 1979), p. C-1. English.

    AN: In the rural Utah community of
    Magna, SOCIO (Spanish Speaking Organization
    for Community Integrity and Opportunity)
    established various art projects. Three
    murals were painted by community youth under
    the guidance of Robert Archuleta and Becky
    Berru. One of the murals depicts "man and
    labor." Illustrated with photographs of
    project directors, maquette of the mural and
    a mural painting "brigade".

Arellano, Estevan

167 Anaya, Rudolfo A. and Ortiz, Simon J.
    1680-1980: a ceremony of brotherhood.
    Albuquerque, NM: Academic, 1981. English.

    AN: A cooperative publication by members
    of the former La Academia de la Nueva Raza
    (1969-1976) formed of writers and artists,
    and the Tri-Centennial Commission of the
    All-Indian Pueblo Council. Includes writings
    and artworks by Chicanos and Indians from
    New Mexico, California, Texas, and Arizona.
    Chicano artists works included are by Ellen
    Arellano, Juan Estevan Arellano, Alberto
    Baros, Jose Antonio Burciaga, Juan Reyes
    Cervantes, Rudy Cuellar, Ricardo Favela, El
    Zarco Guerrero, Luis Jimenez, Jr., Carlos
    Quinto Kemm, Alejandro Lopez, Floyd Lujan,
    Jose Montoya, Juanishi Orozco, Leo Romero,
    Secundino Sandoval, Jaime Valdez, Maria
    Varela, Esteban Villa.

168 Artist registry financed. RIO GRANDE SUN,
    (January 17, 1980). English.

    AN: A $15,000 grant received from the
    National Endowment for the Arts to begin a
    New Mexico Hispanic Arts Community Outreach
    project, which will include a central
    registry of New Mexico Hispanic artists with
    current resume, documentation of work, and
    other information. In charge will be
    artists Estevan Arellano, Albert Baros, and
    Susan Jamison of the Santa Fe Council for
    the Arts.

Arenal, Luis

169 Notes on 2nd National Community Muralists'
    Network Conference, Chicago, Ill. April
    20-23, 1978. San Francisco, CA, 1978.
    English.

    AN: Rupert Garcia, Raul Martinez,
    Patricia Rodriguez, Ray Patlan (San
    Francisco Bay Area) and Jaime Valadez (San
    Jose), among others, attended the conference
    in Chicago. Reports were heard from many
    parts of the United States on mural
    activities, including that of Aurelio Diaz
    of Chicago, representing MARCH (Movimiento
    Artistico Chicano). A workshop presentation
    was made by Luis Arenal and others from the
    Taller Siqueiros of Cuernavaca, Mexico. An
    experimental mural to try Siqueiros'
    techniques was created. Illustrated.

Arenas, Rosa Maria

170 El calendario hispano de Michigan, 1981.
    Stanton, MI: Montcalm Intermediate School
    District and Nuestras Artes de Michigan,
    1981. English.

    AN: Months of historical calendar
    illustrated with art works by George Vargas,
    Nora Chapa Mendoza, Jesse Gonzalez, Julio
    Perazza(Puerto Rican), Hector Valdez, Pamela
    M. Gonzalez, Isabell Escojico (7-year-old
    child), Jose Narezo, Martin Moreno, Laurie
    Mendoza Psarianos, Rosa Maria Arenas.

Arenivar, Roberto

171 Nevarez, Joe R. Chicano art blooms in barrio
    warehouse. LOS ANGELES TIMES, (December 26,
    1974), p. I, 32. English.

    AN: Former meat packing warehouse
    transformed into Goez Art Studios by Joe and
    John Gonzalez. Exhibiting David Negron,
    Eddie Martinez, David Lopez (Hollywood
    scenic artists) and Roberto Arenivar. Lists
    activities of the gallery: exhibits, murals,
    restoration.

Arizona

172 Arizona Commission on the Arts and
Humanities. Humanizarte: the art of Zarco
Guerrero. Exhibition brochure, 1978.
English.

AN: Illustrated brochure of ceramic
masks and bronze sculptures by Zarco
Guerrero. The exhibit traveled throughout
Arizona.

173 Arizona Commission on the Arts and
Humanities. Humanizarte: the art of Zarco
Guerrero. Announcement, n.d. English.

AN: Poster announcement for an
exhibition of bronze sculptures and ceramic
masks by Zarco Guerrero.

174 Armas, Jose and Buitron, Robert. Issues.
ARIZTLAN NEWSLETTER, (August 1981).
English.

AN: Thoughts and definitions of Chicano
art by Dr. Jose Armas, founder of Pajarito
Publications, and by photographer and MARS
member Robert Buitron.

175 Barnett, Alan. Southern journey. NATIONAL
MURALS NETWORK COMMUNITY NEWSLETTER, (Fall
1980), p. 22-32. English.

AN: Rather gossipy account of murals
seen in a swing of the southern United
States. Includes the work of dozens of
artists and arts groups from California,
Arizona, New Mexico, Texas, and Colorado.

176 Bernal, Luis Carlos. A luminous view of a
simple lifestyle. NUESTRO, Vol. 2, no. 7
(July 1978), p. 26-27. English.

AN: Color photographic essay with notes
by the photographer Luis Carlos Bernal.
Documenting Arizona Chicanos, Bernal focuses
on the objects and environments that help
define their lifestyle.

177 Chu, Amy. Focus on cultural heritage.
READER: SAN DIEGO WEEKLY, (September 17,
1981). English.

AN: Review of exhibit FIVE
PHOTOGRAPHERS: CONTEMPORARY VIEWS OF MEXICAN
AND MEXICAN-AMERICAN CULTURE which includes
two Chicano photographers from Arizona:
Louis Carlos Bernal (Tucson), and Robert C.
Buitron (Tempe). Details some of Bernal's
work between 1973 and 1980; Buitron's more
personal work (1978-1981) is from his FAMILY
AND PHOTOGRAPHY book-in-progress.

178 Donaghy, Kathleen. Two Arizona firsts:
Chicano gallery and Spanish theatre. ARIZONA
ARTS AND LIFESTYLE, (1981). English.

AN: The MARS (Movimiento Artistico del
Rio Salado) Gallery has opened in downtown
Phoenix, run by MARS founder Jim
Covarrubias. Louis Leroy, expansion arts
coordinator for the Arizona Commission on
the Arts, says it is the only arts-oriented
space that caters to Chicanos in Arizona.

179 Donnell-Kotrozo, Carol. Containment and
discovery. ARTWEEK, Vol. 11, no. 41
(December 6, 1980), p. 12. English.

AN: Review of an exhibit at Scottsdale,
Arizona gallery, C.G. Rein by Rudy
Fernandez. Discussed in detail is one of his
altar-like boxes of mixed media which
contain personal symbolisms. Illustrated.

180 The First Unitarian Universalist Church,
Paradise Valley, AZ. Five Chicano artists.
Exhibition brochure, 1971. English.

AN: Exhibit organized by L. Eugene
Grigsby, Jr., Art Department of Arizona
State University, Tempe, AZ. 21 works by
Eugene Quesada, David Nunez, Fernando
Navarro, Luis Baiz (of Arizona) and Saul
Solache (of Los Angeles). Brief biographies
of the artists.

181 Five views on Mexican culture. LA JOLLA
LIGHT, (September 10, 1981), p. B-6.
English.

AN: Review of a show at the University
of California, San Diego's Mandeville Art
Gallery called FIVE PHOTOGRAPHERS:
CONTEMPORARY VIEWS OF MEXICAN AND
MEXICAN-AMERICAN CULTURE and featuring
Arizona photographers Louis Carlos Bernal,
Robert C. Buitron, and three others.

182 Grigsby, J. Eugene, Jr. Art & ethnics:
background for teaching youth in a
pluralistic society. Dubuque, IO: Wm.C.
Brown Co. Publishers, 1977. English.

AN: Grigsby teaches in the Art
Department of Arizona State University,
Tempe. His book contains illustrations of
Arizona artists Eugenio Quedada, David
Nunez, and Luis Baiz, and a chapter called
"The Spanish-Speaking Ethnics:
Chicano/Mexican-American/Puerto
Rican/Cuban/South American artists".

183 MARS: Movimiento Artistico del Rio Salado.
Phoenix, AZ: Mars Studio/Gallery, 1978.
English.

AN: History and manifesto of MARS, 13
member group of Arizona painters, sculptors,
designers, and photographers: Jose Andres
Giron, Jose Jimenez Rodriguez, Antonio
Tocora (Colombian-born), Ramon Delgadillo,
Francisco Zuniga, Jim Covarrubias, Ed Diaz,
David Martinez, Roberto Buitron, Juan
Rodriguez, Eddie Lopez, Zarco Guerrero, Joe
Sanchez.

184 Miller, Marlan. Heard speaks Spanish through
art. PHOENIX GAZETTE, (September 23, 1978).
English.

AN: Four new exhibits at the Heard
Museum of Phoenix include "Hispanic crafts
of the Southwest", and "Southwest Chicano
Art Invitational". The former focuses on New
Mexico and Colorado crafts, organized by the
Taylor Museum if the Colorado Springs Fine
Arts Center; the latter includes Rupert
Garcia and Xavier Miramontes of San
Francisco, Rudy Fernandez of Salt Lake City
(now in Scottsdale, AZ), and Antonio Pazos
of Tucson.

Arizona Commission on the Arts

185 Thwaites, Lynette. Art on the border.
COMMUNITY ARTS NEWSLETTER, Vol. 3, no. 3
(July 1981). English.

AN: The Centro Cultural de la Raza has
been a pioneer of intercultural activity
between Mexico and the United States in the
San Diego area. The Arizona Commission on
the Arts has promoted numerous exchanges and
publishes a bilingual quarterly bulletin. In
Mission, Texas, Xavier Gorena of the Xochil
Art Center is forging ties with Mexico City.

Arizona Mara Gang, Los Angeles, CA

186 Greenberg, David; Smith, Kathryn; and
Teacher, Stuart. Megamurals & supergraphics:
big art. Philadelphia, PN: Running Press,
1977. English.

AN: A full-color picture book of murals
throughout the United States. Chicano murals
include Michael Rios (San Francisco),
Mujeres Muralistas (San Francisco), Leonard
Castellanos and Tomas Gonzales with others
(Los Angeles), Los Artes Guadalupanos de
Aztlan (New Mexico), Willie Herron (Los
Angeles), Toltecas en Aztlan (San Diego),
David Botello (Los Angeles), David Lopez and
Arizona Mara Gang (Los Angeles), Vatos de
Maravilla (Los Angeles), Carlito Gaegos (Los
Angeles), Gil Hernandez (Los Angeles), Wayne
[Alaniz] Healy (Los Angeles).

Armory for the Arts Gallery, Santa Fe, NM

187 Eichstaedt, Peter. Hispanic festival
cultural showcase. NEW MEXICAN WEEKEND,
(May 25, 1979), p. 3. English.

AN: Announcement of the week-long
HISPANIC HERITAGE FESTIVAL/EL FESTIVAL
HISPANICO co-sponsored by La Cofradia de
Artes y Artesanos Hispanicos and the Santa
Fe Council fo the Arts at the Armory for the
Arts in Santa Fe. Outlines the cultural
activities, including a visual arts exhibit.
La Cofradia is a recently formed
organization which has assembled regional
shows at the Santuario de Guadalupe which
gave opportunities to local artists to show
their work. Festival artists are primarily
from the upper Rio Grande but also include
artists from the State Penitentiary, as well
as Albuquerque and Las Cruces. Illustration
of painting by Sam Leyba.

Arpa, Jose

188 Goddarth, Ruth. Porfirio Salinas. Austin,
TX: Rock House Press, 1975. English.

AN: Born on Nov. 6, 1910 on a farm near
Bastrop, Texas, Porfirio Salinas studied art
with Spanish artist Jose Arpa in San Antonio
and gradually became a regional landscapist
of wide renown. Salinas died April 18, 1973
at the age of 62. The book is lavishly
illustrated.

Arredondo, Alicia

189 Goldman, Shifra M. Chicana artists at work.
ARRIBA, [n.d.], p. 3+. English.

AN: Excerpt of a longer article on the
Texas women's group Mujeres Artistas del
Suroeste (MAS). Integral to the group are
artists Santa Barraza, Nora Gonzalez-Dodson,
Alicia Arredondo, Maria Flores, Sylvia
Orozco, and Modesta Trevino.

190 Goldman, Shifra M. Women artists of Texas:
MAS = More + Artists + Women = MAS.
CHISMEARTE, no. 7 (January 1981), p. 21-22.
English.

AN: History of Texas Chicana women
artists' organization, Mujeres Artistas del
Suroeste (MAS), co-founded in 1977 by Santa
Barraza and Nora Gonzalez-Dodson in the
framework of the burgeoning feminist art
movement, particularly Women and Their Work
of Texas. Brief history of Chicano politics
and the corresponding art movement of
southern and central Texas. In addition to
Barraza and Gonzalez-Dodson, Alicia

Arredondo, Modesta Trevino, and Maria Flores
are considered. Illustrated.

191 Women artists: forming a Texas network.
Brochure, 1979. English.

AN: Biographic and bibliographic
information on women artists groups from
Austin, Dallas, Houston and San Antonio.
Includes brief history of MAS (Mujeres
Artistas del Suroeste), a list of members,
and biographies of Alicia Arredondo, Santa
Barraza, Mary Ann Ambray Gonzalez, and
Sylvia Orozco.

192 Xochil Art and Culture Center, Mission, TX.
Besame mucho. Exhibition invitation, 1979.
English.

AN: Invitation to exhibit of Texas
artists from Mujeres Artistas del Suroeste
(MAS): Mary Ann Anguiano, Alicia Arredondo,
Santa Barraza, Nora Gonzales-Dodson, Maria
Flores, Carolina Flores, Mary Ann Ambray
Gonzales, Sylvia Orozco, Nancy de los
Santos, Modesta Barbina Trevino.
Illustrated.

Arreguin, Alfredo

193 Bellevue Art Museum, Bellevue, WA. Alfredo
Arreguin. s.n.:s.l., n.d. English.

AN: Profusely illustrated exhibition
catalog for a one-man retrospective of
paintings by Alfredo Arreguin. Exploring the
possibilities of pattern painting, the
intent of his art is to be visionary. His
paintings have affinity with Pre-Columbian
and Colonial Mexican designs and is related
to decorative emotional images of various
cultures. Includes photograph of artist and
a selected bibliography.

194 Cardona, Patricia. Gana adeptos de Museo
Mexicano de San Francisco: Pedro Rodriguez.
UNO MAS UNO, (February 6, 1978), p. 18.
Spanish.

AN: Report and brief history of the
Mexican Museum which opened in 1975 with a
collection of colonial santos. The museum
offers a vista of Mexican culture to people
in the United States. Director Peter
Rodriguez says that Chicano artists Roberto
Gonzalez, Felipe Reyes, Alfredo Arreguin,
Gustavo Rivera, and Carmen Lomas Garza are
some of the best. Illustrated.

195 Contreras, Carlos. Nuestra cultura. LA VOZ:
Concilio for the Spanish Speaking of King
Co., Seattle, no. 7 (August 1979).

AN: Information of Washington state
murals painted by members of La Extension
Cultural; Armando Lara's autobiographical
mural titled "El Rio" is installed at the
Concilio offices, 107 Cherry St. Suite 210.
Arturo Artorez completed a wall painting
using the image of Quetzalcoatl at El Centro
de la Raza with funding from the Seattle
Arts Commission. Francisco Siqueiros used
the themes of ecology and Mexican mythology
for two murals at Seattle Community College.
Commentary on Alfredo Arreguin's painting
exhibition at the Kiku Gallery and his wall
painting at the Childrens Orthopedic
Hospital in Seattle.

Arreguin, Alfredo (cont.)

196 The new logo. LA VOZ: Concilio for the
    Spanish Speaking of King Co., Seattle, no. 5
    (June 1979). English.

    AN: Biographical information on artist
    Alfredo Arreguin. Born in Uruapan, Michoacan
    Mexico and residing in Seattle for eighteen
    years, Arrequin is active in La Extension
    Cultural, an agency formed to meet the
    cultural needs of "Hispanics" in the Pacific
    Northwest. In his logo for the "Concilio,"
    Arreguin employs symbols representing
    history, beauty, unity, ethnicity and
    communication.

197 Segade, Gustavo V. Alfredo Arreguin.
    CITYBENDER, Vol. 2, no. 9 (1978). English.

    AN: Brief profile of Mexican-born
    painter Arreguin who lives in the state of
    Washington. Three illustrations.

198 Temko, Allan. Ole! It's already a triumph.
    REVIEW [supplement to SAN FRANCISCO SUNDAY
    EXAMINER], (December 28, 1980), p. 13-14.
    English.

    AN: A glowing report on the Mexican
    Museum as it celebrates its fifth
    anniversary. Provides details about
    programs, financing and goals. Brief
    analysis of the work of sculptor Manuel Neri
    and painters Manuel Villamor, Gustavo
    Rivera, Alfredo Arreguin and Miguel
    Almaguer. Informative profile on Peter
    Rodriguez, founder and Executive Director of
    the Museum.

199 Thorne, Judy. Alfredo Arreguin - painting in
    patterns. SEATTLE TIMES, (June 15, 1980),
    p. 18-19. English.

    AN: Biographical information on
    Mexican-born Seattle painter Alfredo
    Arreguin. Includes mention of his selection
    as a city art commissioner in Seattle.
    Discussion of artist's distinctive style
    based on use of intricate patterns. Well
    illustrated with four color reproductions of
    artist's work.

200 Tsutakaua, Mayumi. Despite hostilities,
    Arreguin is transcending. SEATTLE TIMES,
    (September 2, 1979). English.

    AN: Biographical sketch of Northwest
    Chicano painter and ceramicist Alfredo
    Arreguin. Artistic chronology and negative
    relationship with local mainstream art
    institutions.

201 Winn Galleries, Seattle, WA. Alfredo
    Arreguin. Exhibition catalog, 1981. English.

    AN: Catalog of an exhibit by
    Mexican-born Washington painter. Many
    reproductions, some in color.

202 XIe festival international de la peinture.
    Exhibition catalog, 1980. English.

    AN: Catalog of an international
    exposition in Cagnes-Sur-Mer, France. The
    United States exhibit included the work of
    Seattle artist Alfredo Mendoza Arreguin.
    Biographical information and reproduction of
    Arreguin's oil painting URUAPAN.

203 Yarbro-Bejarano, Yvonne. La forma del sueno:
    arte y pensamiento de Alfredo Arreguin.
    METAMORFOSIS, Vol. 3, no. 2 (1980, 1981), p.
    10-24. Spanish.

    AN: Interview and portfolio of
    Mexican-born painter who has been living in
    Seattle for more than 20 years. Contains
    biographical data and the artist's view on
    the role of the Chicano artist. Ten
    illustrations.

Arrola, Gustavo Montano

204 De Lappe, Pele. Gordo plus folk art.
    PEOPLE'S WORLD, Vol. 42, no. 41 (October 13,
    1979), p. 10. English.

    AN: Announcement of an exhibit at the
    Mexican Museum of Gus Arriola's syndicated
    comic strip "Gordo." Arizona-born Arriola
    was an animator for Columbia and MGM
    cartoons until he created "Gordo" in 1941.
    Illustrated.

205 Morch, Albert. Mexican art through a
    cartoonist's eyes. SAN FRANCISCO EXAMINER,
    (September 24, 1979), p. 28. English.

    AN: Review of "GORDO'S WORLD" and the
    paintings of Alexander Maldonado, an
    exhibition at the Mexican Museum.
    Biographical information on Gustavo Montano
    Arriola, creator of the Gordo cartoon in
    1941. The exhibit conceived and designed by
    the San Diego Museum of Art, had
    representative blow-ups of the strip along
    with artifacts. Maldonado, a self-taught
    artist started painting at age 60. His
    canvases embrace a fascination with towers,
    unique buildings, underground cities and
    skylines from an imagined urban environment.

Arroyo, Romero

206 Hale, David. Exhibit backers hope for
    Chicano cultural center plan. FRESNO BEE,
    (July 14, 1974), p. K5. English.

    AN: Review of a Chicano art exhibition
    in the Sarah McCardle Room of the downtown
    Fresno County Public Library. According to
    artist-organizer Ernie Palomino, the exhibit
    is a trial balloon to see if enough Chicano
    artists can surface and cooperate in the
    establishment of a Chicano Cultural Center
    in Southeast Fresno. Illustrated with
    reproduction of a portrait by Romero Arroyo
    of Mendota, California and a painting by
    Victor Hernandez from Visalia, California.

Art Conferences

208 Chicano art conference kicks off. AUSTIN
    AMERICAN STATESMAN, (September 14, 1979).
    English.

    AN: Announcement of upcoming CONFERENCIA
    PLASTICA CHICANA to be held in Austin, TX.

209 Concilio de arte popular. CHISMEARTE, Vol.
    1, no. 2 (Winter, Spring, 1977), p. 54.
    English.

    AN: Report of a meeting February 12,
    1977 by the Concilio de Arte Popular (CAP)
    which published CHISMEARTE. Introduces
    members of the Board and summarizes
    discussions of problems of the organization
    and their publication.

Art Conferences (cont.)

210 Conferencia plastica chicana. Conference brochure, 1979. English.

   AN: Schedule of proceedings at internationally attended conference on Chicano and Mexican art and photography sponsored by the Centro Cultural de LUCHA (League of United Chicano Artistas) and MAS (Mujeres Artistas del Suroeste). Brief biographies of presentors. Illustrated.

Art Documentation   n Art

211 Artist registry financed. RIO GRANDE SUN, (January 17, 1980). English.

   AN: A $15,000 grant received from the National Endowment for the Arts to begin a New Mexico Hispanic Arts Community Outreach project, which will include a central registry of New Mexico Hispanic artists with current resume, documentation of work, and other information. In charge will be artists Estevan Arellano, Albert Baros, and Susan Jamison of the Santa Fe Council for the Arts.

Art Galleries

212 Alarcon, Francisco X. El Museo Mexicano, quinto aniversario. EL TECOLOTE LITERARY MAGAZINE, (December 10, 1981). Spanish.

   AN: Goals of the Mexican Museum in San Francisco are contextualized within the social nexus of the Chicano Art Movement of the 1960s. Explains functional difference between Mexican Museum and community art galleries.

213 Ariav, Al. Hispanics' work ignored, artist says. ARIZONA DAILY STAR, (June 3, 1978). English.

   AN: Hispanic-Americans in Tucson have no gallery, little access to museums, and no recognition for their work, says Roberto Borboa, artist and cultural organizer. He welcomes the National Task Force of Hispanic American art which visited Tucson.

214 Armando Cid art works on display at Barrio Gallery. EL HISPANO, Vol. 5, no. 44 (April 24, 1973). English.

   AN: Description of Armando Cid's M.A. thesis exhibition. The dominant impulse in the paintings is an attempt to define and reflect a Chicano style.

215 Art Gallery, California State University, Long Beach and Lujan, Gilbert Sanchez "Magu". El arte del pocho. Exhibit brochure, October 1968. English.

   AN: Information about Southern California artists John Deheras, Marcus Villagran, Roberto de la Rocha, Santos Zuniga, Crispin Gonzales, Richard Martinez, Jesus Gutierrez, Ed Oropeza, Pete Mendez, David Ramirez, Gilbert Sanchez Lujan, Willie Hernandez, Art Ponce, Carmen Tostado, Al Almeida, David Ceja, Robert E. Chavez, Thomas A. Ferriera. All art students, graduates, or faculty.

216 Art Gallery, University of California, Irvine and Los Angeles County Museum of Art, Los Angeles, CA. Los Four: Almaraz, de la Rocha, Lujan, Romero. Exhibition brochure, 1973-74. English.

   AN: Photographs and biographies of Carlos Almaraz, Roberto de la Rocha, Gilbert S. Lujan, Frank Romero.

217 Chicano artists exhibit at USC. CALENDAR, (September 23, 1973), p. 61. English.

   AN: Announcement of an exhibit of paintings, drawings, sculpture and graphics by artists from the Mechicano Art Center of Los Angeles at the University of Southern California Art Galleries. Slide presentations of murals and supergraphics.

218 Valadez, Kathy L. Ten hints in buying Chicano and Mexican art/10 ideas para la compra de obras de arte. CAMINOS, Vol. 1, no. 6 (October 1980), p. 15-17. Bilingual.

   AN: An interior design/investment approach to Mexican and Chicano art. Some of the characterizations of both types of art are unfortunate and uninformed. Seems to be an article to boost sales for Joe Gonzales' Goez Gallery, but lists a number of other locations in California to purchase art. Illustrated.

Art History

219 Galeria de la Raza/Studio 24. Mimeograph, [1980]. English.

   AN: Mimeographed history of the Galeria de la Raza/Studio 24 which opened in 1970 as a showcase for Chicano/Latino artists. Its programs include exhibitions, murals and billboads, beautification of the community, education. Along with public grants, the Galeria strives to be self-sustaining through Studio 24 with retail sales and printing services.

220 Galeria de la Raza/Studio 24, San Francisco, CA and Garcia, Rupert. La Raza Silkscreen Center: "Images of a community", an exhibit of silkscreen posters and graphic works from 1971 to 1979. Exhibition catalog, 1979. English.

   AN: First large scale retrospective exhibit of the La Raza Silkscreen Center's eight years of postermaking. Includes list of 90 artists.

221 Gamboa, Harry, Jr. and Gronk. Gronk: off-the-wall artist. NEWORLD, Vol. 6, no. 4 (1980), p. 33-43. English.

   AN: Interview with Gronk about his No Movies, by Harry Gamboa, Jr., both members (with Willie Herron and Patssi Valdez) of ASCO. The interview itself can be seen as an "art piece" with photographs by Gamboa; it contains valuable information about the ideas and activities of the group.

222 Garcia, Rupert. Raza murals & muralists: an historical perspective. San Francisco, CA: Rupert Garcia, n.d.. English.

   AN: Basic assumptions are that socio-economic, political and cultural relationships exist between the Raza of Mexico and those of Aztlan (the Southwest United States) Half the text deals with Mexican murals, the other half sets Raza murals in social context, and focuses on murals in San Francisco's Mission District, in four locations. 19 illustrations; 9 of Raza murals. Mural map of the Mission district.

Art History (cont.)

223 Garcia, Rupert. La Raza murals of
California, 1963 to 1970: a period of social
change and protest. Master's thesis, UC
Berkeley, 1981. English.

AN: Important introduction to a selected
group of murals from Northern and Southern
California. Garcia deals with murals of
"accommodation" from 1960 to 1965; the
Chicano protest movement, 1965 and 1970; and
Chicano protest murals from 1968 to 1970.
Murals are discussed within historical,
political and cultural contexts.
Illustrated.

224 Goldman, Shifra M. Chicana artists at work.
ARRIBA, [n.d.], p. 3+. English.

AN: Excerpt of a longer article on the
Texas women's group Mujeres Artistas del
Suroeste (MAS). Integral to the group are
artists Santa Barraza, Nora Gonzalez-Dodson,
Alicia Arredondo, Maria Flores, Sylvia
Orozco, and Modesta Trevino.

225 Goldman, Shifra M. Chicano art alive and
well in Texas: a 1981 update. REVISTA
CHICANO-RIQUENA, Vol. 9, no. 1 (Winter
1981), p. 34-40. English.

AN: Reprint of article published as
"Supervivencia y prosperidad del arte
chicano en Texas: nueva revision" in
COMUNIDAD (Los Angeles, CA) [Sunday
Supplement to LA OPINION], September 21,
1980, p. 3, 15+.

226 Goldman, Shifra M. Las creaturas de la
America tropical: Siqueiros y los murales
chicanos en Los Angeles. REVISTA DE BELLAS
ARTES, no. 25 (January, February, 1976), p.
38-46. Spanish.

AN: Treats the influence of Siqueiros'
1932 outdoor mural in Los Angeles on the
Chicano street mural movement of the 1970s.

227 Goldman, Shifra M. Les muraux chicanos aux
Etats-Unis: un double language. In L'ART
PUBLIC. Paris: Jacques Damase Editeur, 1981,
p. 20-32. Other.

AN: Updating of new artistic and social
developments surrounding Chicano mural
production. Illustrated.

228 Goldman, Shifra M. Resistance and identity:
street murals of occupied Aztlan. LATIN
AMERICAN LITERARY REVIEW, Vol. 5, no. 10
(Spring, Summer, 1977), p. 124-128. English.

AN: Two periods of Mexican muralism's
influence in the U.S.: 1930s and 1960s.
Differences between Mexican and Chicano
murals nationally. Comparison of the
respective iconographies and funding
sources. This article was reprinted as
"Resistencia e Identidad: Los Murales
Callejeros de Aztlan, La Ciudad (sic)
Ocupada," in ARTES VISUALES (Mexico, D.F.),
no. 16, Fall-Winter, 1977, p. 22-25.

229 Goldman, Shifra M. Resistencia e identidad:
los murales callejeros de Aztlan, la ciudad
(sic) ocupada. ARTES VISUALES, no. 16 (Fall,
Winter, 1977), p. 22-25. Spanish.

AN: Reprint of article published as
"Resistance and identity: street murals of
occupied Aztlan" in LATIN AMERICAN LITERARY
REVIEW, Vol. 5, no. 10, Spring-Summer 1977,
p. 124-128.

230 Goldman, Shifra M. Supervivencia y
prosperidad del arte chicano en Texas: nueva
revision. COMUNIDAD, Vol. 55, no. 5
(September 21, 1980), p. 3,15+. Spanish.

AN: Focuses on six Chicano artists from
Austin, Houston, San Antonio, and
Kingsville: Mel Casas, Cesar Martinez, Amado
M. Pena, Leo Tanguma, Carmen Lomas Garza,
and Santa Barraza. Well illustrated. This
article was reprinted as "Chicano Art Alive
and Well in Texas: A 1981 Update," in
REVISTA CHICANO-RIQUENA (Houston), Vol. 9,
no. 1, Winter 1981, p. 34-40.

231 Mechicano Art Center. Brochure, [1975].
English.

AN: Illustrated brochure detailing the
history, community programs (drawing,
painting, silkscreen, sculpture and mural
classes), gallery exhibits, travelling
exhibits, murals and supergraphics, and
financial status of the Whittier Blvd.
Center.

232 Monteverde, Mildred. Contemporary Chicano
art. AZTLAN, Vol. 2, no. 2 (Fall 1971), p.
51-61. Bibliography. English.

AN: An historical survey of trends and
influences on contemporary Chicano art.
Discusses San Diego's Toltecas en Aztlan and
the projected Centro Cultural de la Raza;
Los Angeles' Mechicano Art Center, Goez
Gallery and Plaza de la Raza; pinto (prison)
art; New Mexican art. Many artists are
mentioned.

233 Montoya, Jose E. and Carrillo, John M.
Posada: the man and his art. A comparative
analysis of Jose Guadalupe Posada and the
current Chicano art movement as they apply
toward social and cultural change: a visual
resource unit for Chicano education.
Unpublished thesis, 1975. English.

AN: Includes a historical background of
19th century Mexican engraver Posada, the
significance of his work, a background of
Chicano art, and the influence of Posada and
the "calavera" on Chicano art. The unit
includes 227 slides of Posada and other
Mexican artists; and slides of Chicano
artists using the calavera theme.

234 Pimentel, Ricardo. Graffiti: expression or
scourge? FRESNO BEE, (February 23, 1981),
p. Metro, B1+. English.

AN: A rapid review of graffiti symbols,
their meaning and social context. Commentary
by various young people explaining the
value, style and meanings of plaqueasos
(spray painted graffiti). Some Chicano
artists like Bob Cruz, director of La Brocha
del Valle, see mural painting as a positive
alternative to graffiti art forms. Article
also provides views of local businessmen to
the graffiti phenomenon.

235 Quirarte, Jacinto. The art of Mexican
America. HUMBLE WAY, Vol. 9, no. 2 (1970),
p. 2-9. English.

AN: One of the earliest surveys of
Mexican American/Chicano artists. Provided
the framework for Quirarte's book, Mexican
American Artists.

Art History (cont.)

236 Quirarte, Jacinto. Mexican-American artists.
Austin, TX: University of Texas Press, 1973.
English.

AN: First comprehensive historical text
on artists of Mexican descent in the United
States. Sets up the antecedents from
settlement to the visits of Mexican
muralists Rivera, Siqueiros, Orozco and
Tamayo in the U.S., though only Orozco and
Tamayo are considered at length. Mexican
American artists are divided by decades of
birth, from 1901 to 1946. Twenty-seven
artists (two women) are discussed. The
epilogue is a discussion on the terms
"Mexican American" and "Chicano," the latter
articulated by Esteban Villa, who is not in
the text.

237 R.C.A.F. artistas precursores del arte
chicano. EL HISPANO, Vol. 8, no. 35
(February 17, 1976), p. 1. English.

AN: Information on the R.C.A.F.
organization. Includes group photograph of
R.C.A.F. members, Jose Montoya, Esteban
Villa, John Carrillo, Ricardo Fabela, Rudy
Cuellar, Juanishi Orozco and Frank Godena.

238 Rodriguez, Pedro. Arte como expresion del
pueblo. METAMORFOSIS, Vol. 3, no. 2 (1980,
1981), p. 59-62. English.

AN: Texas-born artist and teacher traces
the history of the Chicano art movement from
early struggles to limited recognition,
takes a critical position toward artistic
cooptation and the anti-political stance of
many artists, and suggests a direction for
the future.

239 Rodriguez, Pedro. Chicano art arising. PAPEL
CHICANO, Vol. 1, no. 9 (December 21, 1971),
p. 5. English.

AN: A concise formulation on the nature
of Chicano Art. It arises from a new
cultural formation influenced by Mexican and
Anglo American cultural forms yet distinct
from either. In visual terms, artists are
reflecting and affirming this new cultural
synthesis. Illustrated with reproductions of
three oil paintings: GRITO DE LIBERTAD by
Jose D. Marin, WOMAN IN BLUE by Manuel
Aguilera, and ALEGORIA MEXICANA by Tomas
Torres. All three are pinto artists from
Leavenworth Penitentiary.

240 S.A. site for National Symposium on Mexican
American Art. CHICANO TIMES, Vol. 4, no. 30
(November 9, 1973), p. 5. English.

AN: Held at Trinity University, the
Symposium discussed such issues as, creative
evolution, art education, artistic
relationships to Mexico and the evolution of
Mexican American art in the California
barrios. Participating artists included Rudy
Trevino, Mel Casas, Octavio Medellin,
Antonio Garcia, Carmen Garza, Esteban Villa,
Jose Montoya, Ernesto Palomino, Michael
Ponce de Leon, Luis Jimenez and Eugenio
Quesada.

241 Santos of New Mexico, art of our people.
GRITO DEL NORTE, Vol. 3, no. 1 (January 17,
1970), p. 8-9. English.

AN: Historical trajectory of santero
tradition in New Mexico. Distinguished
santeros like Rafael Aragon of Cordova,
Miguel Herrera of Arroyo Hondo, Juan Ramon

Velasquez of Conjilon, Jose Benito Ortega of
La Cueva all created art wedded to the
environment of the Southwest. Illustrated
with a portfolio of santos and retablos from
the Folk Art Museum of Santa Fe, NM.

242 Southern Colorado State College, Pueblo, CO
and Monteverde, Mildred. Chicanos graficos
[sic]...California. Exhibition brochure,
[1974]. Spanish.

AN: Brief background of California art
movement and 13 artists from San Francisco,
Los Angeles, Sacramento, Fresno. Important
factual information despite numerous errors
with names and Spanish terms. 16
illustrations of silkscreens, lithograph,
etching.

243 Stellweg, Carla. De como el arte chicano es
tan indocumentado como los
indocumentados/the way in which Chicano art
is as undocumented as the 'undocumented'.
ARTES VISUALES, no. 29 (June 1981), p.
23-32. Bilingual.

AN: An overview of Chicano art from its
beginnings to the present. Suggestion that
present art is improved by abandoning the
nationalist, derivative and folkloric phase.
Statements and biographies of artists. Some
non-Chicanos included as Chicanos. Many
illustrations. Bilingual.

244 Venegas, Sybil. Conditions for producing
Chicana art. CHISMEARTE, Vol. 1, no. 4 (Fall,
Winter, 1977, 1978), p. 2, 4. English.

AN: Chicana artists face more obstacles
than white women or Chicano counterparts in
the arts. Mexican life style has portrayed
the ideal of a submissive woman, but the
values have changed. Chicana artists are
concerned with women and their struggles.
Muralists include Patricia Rodriguez, Irene
Perez, Consuelo Mendez de Castillo, Susan
Cervantes, Ester Hernandez, Miriam Olivo,
Ruth Rodriguez, of the Mujeres Muralistas
(San Francisco). Other artists are Etta
Delgado and Barbara Carrasco.

245 Wilson, William. A bit of the barrio at
County Museum. LOS ANGELES TIMES, (February
27, 1974), p. IV, 1+. English.

AN: Review of the Los Four exhibit at
the Los Angeles County Museum of Art. Quotes
from artists, history of group's formation
in 1973.

246 Ybarra-Frausto, Tomas. A history of Chicano
art. EL TECOLOTE LITERARY MAGAZINE, Vol. 2,
no. 4 (December 1980), p. 3+. English.

AN: Brief survey of the origins and
influences affecting the arts (popular and
fine) of Mexican-descended peoples in the
United States from the colonizing period to
the present.

ART IN PUBLIC PLACES [project]

247 Fabricant, Don. Show reveals Hispanic art. NEW MEXICAN WEEKEND, (June 1, 1979). English.

AN: Review of two exhibits in Santa Fe: EL FESTIVAL HISPANICO, mounted by La Cofradia de Artes y Artesanos Hispanicos and Gilberto Guzman at the Black Kachina Gallery. The reviewer feels the traditional-style woodcarving done by contemporaries is the strongest part of the show; works that break with these forms seem weaker, less skillful and cliche-ridden. Crafts are excellent. Muralist Guzman has blossomed in murals and easel paintings since he was employed by the 1978 Art in Public Places project. His work is intense and expressive, sometimes erotic. Illustration of work by sculptor Ruben Montoya.

Art Industries

248 Exploratorium, Student Union, California State University, Los Angeles. An exhibit of published prints of Aztlan Multiples. Exhibition catalog, 1981. English.

AN: The published silkscreen prints of Aztlan Multiples, a small business run by Richard Duardo of Los Angeles, features works by Duardo, John Valadez, and Carlos Almaraz, among others. Illustrations.

249 Galeria de la Raza/Studio 24. Mimeograph, [1980]. English.

AN: Mimeographed history of the Galeria de la Raza/Studio 24 which opened in 1970 as a showcase for Chicano/Latino artists. Its programs include exhibitions, murals and billboads, beautification of the community, education. Along with public grants, the Galeria strives to be self-sustaining through Studio 24 with retail sales and printing services.

250 Galeria de la Raza/Studio 24, San Francisco, CA. Published prints of Hecho en Aztlan Multiples. Exhibition announcement, 1980. English.

AN: Announcement of exhibit of the published silkscreen prints of Hecho en Aztlan Multiples; a small business run by Richard Duardo of Los Angeles.

251 Geyer, Anne; Hernandez, Lorenzo; and Valverde, Ricardo. Latino photographers of U.S. still seeking identity. THE NEWS, (September 5, 1981), p. 17. English.

AN: Interview with Lorenzo Hernandez, photo dealer and owner of Cityscape Foto Gallery, Pasadena, Calif. in which he compares Mexican with U.S. Latino photography. Interview with Ricardo Valverde, Chicano photographer and co-chair of the Council of Latino Photography/USA, discussing his work. Illustrated.

252 Herbeck, Ray, Jr. Regional report, The arts: the many credits of Ruben Lopez. NUESTRO, Vol. 1, no. 4 (July 1977), p. 13-14. English.

AN: Brief biographical article about Ruben Orozco Lopez, a Chicano artist who is widely recognized for his court-room sketching and commercial art work for the Hollywood film industry. For the past few years, Lopez has been working with the Chicano News Media Association to recruit barrio youths into the news artist profession.

253 SPARC (Social and Public Arts Resource Center), Venice, CA and Los Angeles. Ceta VI, Venice, CA. Hecho en Aztlan multiples: screen printed works. Exhibition invitation, 1980. English.

AN: Invitation to an exhibit of silkscreen prints by Hecho en Aztlan Multiples, a small business run by Richard Duardo. At the Social and Public Art Resource Center, Venice, Calif.

Art Merchandising & Investment

254 Art directors, take note. INTERRACIAL BOOKS FOR CHILDREN, Vol. 5, no. 7-8 (1975), p. 19. English.

AN: Focus on the work of three Chicano illustrators: Salvador Barajas V., Arturo Roman, and Guillermo Aranda. Includes representative examples of their work.

255 Association for Resources and Technical Services, Inc. (ARTS); Tejano Artists, Inc.; and Performing Artists Nucleus, Inc. (PAN). Tejano arts workshop. Brochure, 1981. English.

AN: Call to a two-day arts workshop in San Antonio designed to inform participants on organizational development, networking, fundraising, touring, marketing, public relations, and audience development. Southwest in scope, with input and organization from Washington, D.C. and New York.

256 Briggs, Charles L. The wood carvers of Cordova, New Mexico: social dimensions of an artistic "revival". Knoxville, TN: University of Tennessee Press, 1980. English.

AN: One of the few books that deals with the traditional and contemporary-traditional religious art of New Mexico within social context. The author explores the influence of Anglo patronage and tourism on the meaning, aesthetics and distribution of the santos, and non-religious carving of the town of Cordoba.

257 Chicano cinema coalition. Mimeographed copy, September 1, 1979. English.

AN: An informational bulletin about the Coalition founded July 1978 in Los Angeles of forty independent producers and filmmakers who joined together for "the development, production, distribution, promotion and exhibition...of film and video productions which meaningfully address...needs and concerns of the Latino people in the United States." Professionals with their own companies (Amanecer Films, Bilingual Educational Services, Luis Ruiz Productions), television producers, and post-graduate film students make up the group. The Coalition published the CHICANO CINEMA NEWSLETTER. Ties are promoted with Latin American cinema people.

Art Merchandising & Investment (cont.)

258 CHICANO CINEMA NEWSLETTER. Vol. 1, no. 6
(August 1979). English.

AN: Announcements of the San Antonio
Chicano Film Festival, a seminar on the
business of art, the receipt of a report of
the Task Force on Minorities in Public
Broadcasting, a critical report on the
Alternative Cinema Conference in New York,
which was attended by eleven members of the
Chicano Cinema Coalition, and a report and
critique of the report by the Task Force.

259 Dean, Nancy. Denver artist dues are paid in
full. ROCKY MOUNTAIN NEWS, (April 5, 1981),
p. 6. English.

AN: Profile of artist Ramon Kelley
focusing on his successful career and
detailing his rise on the art market.
Includes photograph of the artist.

260 Diaz, Katherine A. Art is business: an
interview with Joe L. Gonzalez. CAMINOS,
Vol. 2, no. 5 (October 1981), p. 21-22.
English.

AN: Business advice to the artist and to
the collector from the owner of the two Goez
art galleries in Los Angeles. How to
merchandise or buy art as a good investment.

261 New co-op in San Cristobal. GRITO DEL NORTE,
Vol. 3, no. 8 (July 5, 1970), p. 13.
English.

AN: Details formation of the San
Cristobal Valley Arts Inc., a community
corporation formed to train people in a
silkscreen business venture. Aiming to use
expressive forms as a source of economic
development, the corporation published and
distributed a line of Chicano silkscreen
posters. Illustrated by three posters, WE
SHALL ENDURE, SOMOS AZTLAN, and TAOS PUEBLO.

262 Parr, June. Amado Maurilio Pena, Jr.: a
talented and dedicated artist. ARRIBA,
(October 1980), p. 1. English.

AN: Pena is represented in forty-two
galleries internationally. Recently, Pena
opened his studio and gallery, El Taller, in
Austin. His latest works focus on the Indian
heritage and are based on trips to New
Mexico. Illustrated.

263 Pena, Amado Maurilio, Jr. Amado Maurilio
Pena, Jr. Brochure [1980]. English.

AN: Promotional brochure including a
biographical profile of the artist, a list
of representing galleries throughout the
United States, and eight good quality
reproductions of serigraphs and mixed media
drawings, six in color, on the theme of New
Mexican Pueblo Indians.

264 Pino, Thomas E. Ramon Kelley: the business
of art. LA LUZ, Vol. 7, no. 5 (May 1978), p.
24-26. English.

AN: Biographical information on Colorado
artist Ramon Kelley. Business aspects of
art: marketing, selling, art as investment.

265 Posters by Ignacio Gomez: in full color
suitable for framing. CAMINOS, (May 1981),
p. 49. English.

AN: Six full-color posters on Latino
subjects by illustrator Gomez advertised for

sale. The best-known is Gomez's poster for
ZOOT SUIT, a play by Luis Valdez.

266 Sanchez, Arley. Santeros. ALBUQUERQUE JRNL,
(August 21, 1977), p. C, 1. English.

AN: Review of THE SANTERO EXPERIENCE, an
exhibition of contemporary folk art by
eleven New Mexican santeros, most in their
30s, at the Albuquerque Museum. The carvers
include Juan Lucero, Ben Lopez, Luisito
Lujan, Horacio Valdez, C. Garcia, George
Lopez. A revival of the art has been taking
place within last several years due to
cultural awareness being experienced by
Hispanos. Contemporary santeros still donate
some pieces to the church, but most are
marketed to private collectors, displayed in
museums, or kept.

267 Spurgin, Judy. Amado Maurilio Pena, Jr.
ULTRA MAGAZINE, Vol. 1, no. 1 (September
1981). English.

AN: Succinct treatment of Pena's
artistic trajectory and a superficial
analysis of his work. Information on his
patrons and supporters.

268 Valadez, Kathy L. Ten hints in buying
Chicano and Mexican art/10 ideas para la
compra de obras de arte. CAMINOS, Vol. 1,
no. 6 (October 1980), p. 15-17. Bilingual.

AN: An interior design/investment
approach to Mexican and Chicano art. Some of
the characterizations of both types of art
are unfortunate and uninformed. Seems to be
an article to boost sales for Joe Gonzales'
Goez Gallery, but lists a number of other
locations in California to purchase art.
Illustrated.

269 White, Ron. Bluebonnet the flower of South
Texas painting. SAN ANTONIO EXPRESS-NEWS,
(December 14, 1975), p. 7-H. English.

AN: The South Texas landscape paintings
by Porfirio Salinas are immensely popular
and command high prices. This analysis of
the career and the production of the late
artist (died April 18, 1973), concludes that
Salinas was "a mediocre artist with mediocre
skills and a poor sense of imagination".

Art Organizations & Groups

270 Acosta, Dan. Paintings reflect life
experiences. THE ECCENTRIC, (June 26,
1980). English.

AN: Review of one-woman show by Nora
Chapa Mendoza at the Heritage Art Gallery,
Ypsilanti, MI. Mendoza works in abstract
impressionist style with wet streams of
colors that express energy. Her subjects are
landscapes, moods, nudes, and Hispanic
themes. She is active in the Detroit Latino
Artist Association, Nuestras Artes de
Michigan, and the New Detroit Art Council.

271 Adams Hotel, Phoenix, AZ. Chicano and Indian
art exhibit. Exhibit invitation, 1979.
English.

AN: Invitation to an exhibit of 16
artists. Brief history of the organization
MARS (Moviemiento Artistico del Rio Salado)
of Phoenix, AZ, formed in Summer 1978 after
a Floricanto Culture Week. 98% of MARS
members are Chicano or Indian. Their purpose
is to build the Salt River Valley as a
cultural center of the Southwest.

Art Organizations & Groups (cont.)

272 Alarcon, Francisco X. El Museo Mexicano, quinto aniversario. EL TECOLOTE LITERARY MAGAZINE, (December 10, 1981). Spanish.

AN: Goals of the Mexican Museum in San Francisco are contextualized within the social nexus of the Chicano Art Movement of the 1960s. Explains functional difference between Mexican Museum and community art galleries.

273 Albright, Thomas. Pre-Columbian art: New Galeria de la Raza. SAN FRANCISCO CHRONICLE, (July 15, 1970), p. 49. English.

AN: A new gallery is launched at 425 14th St. in San Francisco with an exhibit by Sacramento State College teacher Esteban Villa, with bold angular abstractions of roosters, comments on the Frito Bandito, and expressionist pen and pencil drawings. Other exhibits are also on display. The Galeria is sponsored by Casa Hispana de Bellas Artes.

274 Albright, Thomas. Three remarkable Latin murals. SAN FRANCISCO CHRONICLE, (June 7, 1974), p. 48. English.

AN: The myth of the melting pot is vanishing: we recognize a variety of "publics" today. This is shown in three remarkable murals in the San Francisco Mission District. The Mission branch of the Bank of America has a 90 foot mural designed by Jesus Campusano, assisted by Luis Cortazar and Michael Rios, with technical advice from Emmy Lou Packard. Another mural is by the Mujeres Muralistas (Graciela Carrillo, Consuelo Mendez, Irene Perez, Patricia Rodriguez); the third by Michael Rios on the 24th St. mini-park.

275 Almaraz, Carlos. Introduccion: vida urbana y artistas chicanos. COMUNIDAD, Vol. 55, no. 22 (May 3, 1981), p. 2. Spanish.

AN: In the controversial period of the early 1980s, Chicano advances are being attacked. In this political climate, some Los Angeles artists are interested in beauty and artistic creation: Carlos Almaraz, best-known of the Los Four group; Yreina Cervantez; Elsa Flores; John Valadez, presently working on a mural; and musicians Louie Perez and Tito Rodriguez Larriva.

276 Amor sin fronteras. Los Angeles, CA: Colectivo El Ojo, n.d.. English.

AN: Fotonovela with Josefina Arce, Eduardo Dominguez and Mike Jauregui produced by the Colectivo: Eduardo Dominguez, Roberto Gil de Montes, Jerry Lucas, Kay Torres, students at California State University, Los Angeles.

277 Ariav, Al. Hispanics' work ignored, artist says. ARIZONA DAILY STAR, (June 3, 1978). English.

AN: Hispanic-Americans in Tucson have no gallery, little access to museums, and no recognition for their work, says Roberto Borboa, artist and cultural organizer. He welcomes the National Task Force of Hispanic American art which visited Tucson.

278 Armas, Jose and Buitron, Robert. Issues. ARIZTLAN NEWSLETTER, (August 1981). English.

AN: Thoughts and definitions of Chicano art by Dr. Jose Armas, founder of Pajarito Publications, and by photographer and MARS member Robert Buitron.

279 Around the Bay. METAMORFOSIS, Vol. 3, no. 2 (1980), p. 101-108. English.

AN: Cultural review of activities in the Bay Area, northern California, and Sacramento. Includes history of the Galeria de la Raza/Studio 24 (San Francisco), the Centro de Artistas Chicanos/RCAF, Royal Chicano Air Force (Sacramento), and a review of Rupert Garcia's pastel portraits exhibit at the Mexican Museum (S.F.) in 1981. Illustrated. Continued in Vol. 4, no. 1, 1981.

280 Art wall for Plaza de la Raza March 28. EASTSIDE JRNL, (March 11, 1971), p. 1. English.

AN: On March 28, 1971, the art dealers of Los Angeles sponsored an"art walk" on "Gallery Row" on Melrose Place and La Cienega Blvds as a benefit for Plaza de la Raza, Mexican American cultural Center at Lincoln Park. Art dealers financed a limited edition lithograph by Mexican muralist David Alfaro Siqueiros. The print shows Ruben Salazar, slain Mexican American journalist and community leader with the famous figure from Siqueiros' mural "New Democracy" below it. Illustrated.

281 Artes 6 Gallery, San Francisco, CA. Mixed media. Exhibition announcement, [ca. 1969-70]. English.

AN: Announcement of exhibit including Jim Cortez, Luis Cervantez, Vicente Rascon, Rene Yanes, Graciela Carrillo, Lorenza Camplis. The Artes 6 artists eventually formed the Galeria de la Raza of San Francisco.

282 Artist registry financed. RIO GRANDE SUN, (January 17, 1980). English.

AN: A $15,000 grant received from the National Endowment for the Arts to begin a New Mexico Hispanic Arts Community Outreach project, which will include a central registry of New Mexico Hispanic artists with current resume, documentation of work, and other information. In charge will be artists Estevan Arellano, Albert Baros, and Susan Jamison of the Santa Fe Council for the Arts.

283 Arts Council Center for the Arts of Greater Lansing, Lansing, MI. Raza fine arts festival. Festival program, 1978. English.

AN: This festival program mentions Jose Narezo's mural at the Holland National Guard Armory, Grand Rapids; includes a statement of the Raza Art/Media Collective, Inc.; the philosophy of artists Zaragosa Vargas and S. Kaneta Kosiba-Vargas; and profiles of exhibiting artists George Vargas, Martin Moreno, Hector Perez, Michael L. Selley, Jesse Gonzales, Nora Chapa Mendoza, Jesse Soriano, Jose Luis Narezo.

Art Organizations & Groups (cont.)

284 Avalos, David. A pure Mexican accent: the popular engravings of Jose Guadalupe Posada. PROCEEDINGS OF THE PACIFIC COAST COUNCIL ON LATIN AMER STUDIES, Vol. 7, (1980, 1981), p. 123-138. English.

AN: As a documentor of injustice and oppression, Posada, 19th century Mexican engraver, is a master who inspires Chicano artists. Appreciation for his art has been expressed by Sacramento artist Jose E. Montoya. Arsacio Vanegas Arroyo, grandson of Posada's publisher, has made his private collection available to Chicano cultural centers, including El Centro Cultural de la Raza, San Diego. Illustrated.

285 Baca, Judith F. Judith F. Baca. In: SOCIAL WORKS: AN EXHIBITION OF ART CONCERNED WITH SOCIAL CHANGE. Los Angeles, CA: Institute of Contemporary Art, 1979, p. 44. English.

AN: Statement of purpose and history of the Tujunga Wash Mural (San Fernando Valley, CA) in process from 1976 on, by muralist and founder of Social and Public Art Resource Center (SPARC), Judith Baca. Illustrated.

286 Barnes, Peter. Fringe benefits of a depression: bringing back the WPA. NEW REPUBLIC, Vol. 172, no. 11 (March 15, 1975), p. 19-21. English.

AN: A well-researched and comprehensive analysis of the CETA (Comprehensive Employment and Training Act) impact on public art in San Francisco. Material on Chicano-Latino murals in the Mission district. Includes viewpoints by artist-activists Patricia Rodriguez, Mike Rios, and writer Roberto Vargas. Important compendium on funding sources of various neighborhood art programs stressing their value as community assets.

287 Barnett, Alan. Southern journey. NATIONAL MURALS NETWORK COMMUNITY NEWSLETTER, (Fall 1980), p. 22-32. English.

AN: Rather gossipy account of murals seen in a swing of the southern United States. Includes the work of dozens of artists and arts groups from California, Arizona, New Mexico, Texas, and Colorado.

288 Blaine, John and Baker, Decia. Finding community through the arts: spotlight on cultural pluralism in Los Angeles. ARTS IN SOCIETY, Vol. 10, no. 1 (Spring, Summer, 1973), p. 125-138. English.

AN: Community arts expression by ethnic minorities is burgeoning everywhere, especially in Los Angeles. Various Black, Asian, and Chicano art administrators are interviewed, including Frank Lopez of Plaza de la Raza and Leonard Castellanos of Mechicano Art Center. Illustrated.

289 Bright, John; Bright, Mura; and Castellanos, Leonard. L.A. Chicano street art. Venice, CA: Environmental Communications, 1974. English.

AN: Annotated slide catalog of Chicano murals in East Los Angeles compiled by staff of Mechicano Art Center. Also includes article reprints on painted bus benches by Mechicano artists (SUNSET Magazine, n.d.), murals of East Los Angeles (LOS ANGELES TIMES, 12/3/73, and SUNSET Magazine, April 1973). Well illustrated.

290 Briseno, Rodolfo. Interview with a muralist. ARRIBA, Vol. 1, no. 1 (July 1980), p. 5+. English.

AN: Raul Valdez, muralist from Del Rio, Texas has been painting murals in Austin and was a founding member of LUCHA (League of United Chicano Artists) in 1976. Having studied with Siqueiros in Mexico, Valdez sees strong affinities in content and form between Chicano and Mexican muralism. Illustrated with two photographs of Valdez's Juarez-Lincoln mural.

291 Bruce Novoa, Juan. [Interview with Jose Montoya]. IN CHICANO AUTHORS: INQUIRY BY INTERVIEW. Austin, TX: University of Texas Press, 1980, p. 115-136. English.

AN: Biography of Sacramento, CA artist and poet Jose Montoya. Emphasizes the close relationship between art and poetry in his life and in that of the Royal Chicano Air Force, which he co-founded.

292 Calendar 1977. CHISMEARTE, no. 2 (Winter, Spring, 1977), p. 26-27. English.

AN: Reproduction of one month of the 1977 silkscreen calendar produced in limited edition by the Galeria de la Raza of San Francisco and the Royal Chicano Air Force of Sacramento, California. Displayed is Rene Yanez's screen HISTORICAL PHOTO-SILKSCREENMOVIE.

293 Callum, Diane. Regional report, The arts: walls of passion. NUESTRO, Vol. 3, no. 11 (December 1979), p. 16, 51. English.

AN: Focusing on muralist Gilberto Guzman, one of the founders of Artes Guadalupanos in Santa Fe, the article details his efforts in the promotion and preservation of Chicano murals in New Mexico.

294 Campesino Business and Joint Enterprise Building, Fresno, CA. Sabor a Fresno. Arte chicano: los Four and la Brocha. Exhibition invitation [1976]. English.

AN: Invitation to an exhibit of works by Los Four of Los Angeles and members of La Brocha del Valle of Fresno: Arturo Roman, Sal Garcia, John Sierra, Juan Truner, Sapo de Aztlan, Fernando Hernandez, Alberto Reyes, Ernesto Palomino, Lee Orona, Francisco Barrios, Juan Ybarra, Bobby Reyes, Alberto Hernandez. Brocha was started by Palomino (California State University, Fresno professor) to pool talents of Central Valley artists.

295 Canavier, Elena Karina. Los Four. ARTWEEK, Vol. 5, no. 10 (March 9, 1974), p. 1, 16. English.

AN: Illustrated review, with detailed description of work of the Los Four exhibit at the Los Angeles County Museum of Art.

Art Organizations & Groups (cont.)

296 Cantu, Jesus "Chista". Entrevista: Jesus
Maria Cantu, 'El Chista'. MAGAZIN, Vol. 1,
no. 4 (April 1972), p. 52-65. Spanish.

AN: Discusses his life in San Antonio;
his apprenticeship since childhood to his
uncle Miguel Angel Tellez who taught him to
paint billboards, wall signs and church
decorations; his membership in the group
Artistas de la Nueva Raza; his artistic and
political philosophy. In Spanish.

297 Capitol Art Gallery, Lansing, MI. Arte de
Nora Mendoza, Hector Perez, George Vargas,
Martin Moreno. Exhibition invitation [1979].
English.

AN: Invitation to an art exhibit
organized by Nuestras Artes de Michigan.

298 Cardona, Patricia. El museo mexicano de San
Francisco. EL DIA, (July 6, 1977), p. 10.
Spanish.

AN: Report on the Mexican Museum giving
a brief overview of its programs. The
Mexican Museum opened Nov. 20, 1975 and has
been a vital force in the cultural life of
San Francisco, showing the work of one
Mexican and one Chicano artist every two
months.

299 Case study: Centro de Artistas Chicanos,
Sacramento, California. Washington, D.C.:
Neighborhood Art Program National Organizing
Committee, n.d. English.

AN: In various regions of the Southwest,
local artists have started Centros
Culturales "whose primary purpose is the
proliferation and safeguarding of Chicano
art and culture." This case study presents
pertinent information on the Centro de
Artistas Chicanos founded in 1972 in
Sacramento, California. It spells out the
philosophy, goals, programs, components and
management structure of the R.C.A.F. (Royal
Chicano Air Force) and Centro de Artistas. A
useful and important document. Illustrated.

300 Castellanos, Leonard. Chicano centros,
murals, and art. ARTS IN SOCIETY, Vol. 12,
no. 1 (Spring, Summer, 1975), p. 38-43.
English.

AN: One of the organizers of the
Mechicano Art Center in Los Angeles talks
about the history of the Center, the
artist's relationship to the mainstream; the
importance of the street mural movement; the
economic problems of the muralists and their
dedication to the community; the need for
alternative centers like the "centros." An
excerpt of this article appeared in
CHISMEARTE, no. 1 (Fall 1976), p. 26-27.

301 La Causa Publications, Oakland, CA. New
symbols for la Nueva Raza. Exhibition
announcement, [ca. 1969]. English.

AN: Announcement for exhibition of the
four founding artists of the Mexican
American Liberation Art Front (MALAF):
Esteban Villa, Rene Yanez, Manuel Hernandez,
Malaquias Montoya. Collage of portraits by
the artists.

302 El Centro Cultural de La Raza, San Diego,
CA. Espejo del barrio-art exposition.
Exhibition brochure, June 1975. English.

AN: Illustrated brochure announcement

for a cultural exposition of Chicano music,
art and drama. Includes some biographical
information and one reproduction of painter
Manuel Unzueta, woodworker Ambriz, muralist
Victor Orozco Ochoa and designer/illustrator
J. Armando Nunez.

303 El Centro Cultural de La Raza, San Diego,
CA. One hundred year anniversary: Jose
Guadalupe Posada, Antonio Vanegas Arroyo.
Exhibition invitation, 1980. English.

AN: Invitation to an exhibition of
Mexican engravers Posada and Manuel Manilla
and an homage to their publisher. Also, a
"Chicano Tribute to Jose Guadalupe Posada,"
with contemporary works influenced by
Posada. At the Centro, and at Southwestern
College in Chula Vista.

304 El Centro Cultural de La Raza, San Diego, CA
and Enrique, Veronica. Tenth anniversary
celebration, July 11, 1981. San Diego, CA:
El Centro Cultural de la Raza, 1981.
English.

AN: Anniversary brochure of the Centro,
founded in 1970 by the Toltecas en Aztlan
artistic collective and established at its
Balboa Park location in 1971. Briefly
reviews the history and activities of the
Centro, including the establishment of
Chicano Park in 1970 and the painting of
murals at the Park and at the Centro. Well
illustrated.

305 El centro cultural y museo del barrio,
history and activities. Taos, NM: El Centro
Cultural y Museo del Barrio, n.d.. English.

AN: Photo-copied history of the New
Mexico organization which is a centro and
museo "without walls" begun in 1973. Founded
by Juan and Patricia Navarrete, it
collaborates with established museums for
community art events.

306 Centro de artistas chicanos. EL HISPANO,
Vol. 6, no. 39 (March 19, 1974). English.

AN: Description of goals and community
oriented programs of the Centro. Illustrated
with an R.C.A.F. poster announcing Teatro
Campesino production of "LA CARPA DE LOS
RASQUACHIS".

307 Centro de Artistas Chicanos, Sacramento, CA.
La arte cosmica [sic] de Esteban Villa:
Chicano art exposition. Sacramento, CA:
Centro de Artistas Chicanos, 1973. English.

AN: Invitation to an exhibition of works
by Esteban Villa at the RCAF's center.

308 Centro de artistas, Sacra: recuerdo ...
descubrimiento ... voluntad. CHISMEARTE,
Vol. 1, no. 1 (Fall 1976), p. 6-7.
English.

AN: Summary of activities of the Centro
de Artistas Chicanos, made up of artists
from the Royal Chicano Air Force and other
groups. The Centro makes posters, T-shirts,
decals, murals and puts on a number of
cultural and social events. Report on a
"mass migration" July 1976 to the Academia
de la Nueva Raza in Dixon, NM for two weeks
of communion.

Art Organizations & Groups (cont.)

309 Centro mural recipient of orchid award. LA
    PRENSA SAN DIEGO, (November 20, 1981), p.
    5. English.

    AN: The American Institute of
    Architects, the American Society of Interior
    Designers, the American Planning Association
    and the American Society of Landscape
    Architects award the Centro Cultural de la
    Raza of Balboa Park, San Diego, CA for
    Victor Ochoa's mural on its walls.
    Illustrated.

310 Chavez, Jaime and Vallecillo, Ana Maria. A
    political, historical, philosophical
    perspective of muralist art in the
    Southwest. RAYAS, Vol. 1, no. 3 (May, June,
    1978), p. 6. English.

    AN: Relates Chicano mural art to main
    issues of the Chicano movement. The
    Mechicano Art Center in Los Angeles and
    Artes Guadalupanos de Aztlan in Santa Fe are
    seen as examples of groups creating a new
    people's art; art forms where esthetics are
    allied to politics.

311 Chicano art of the Southwest. San Antonio,
    TX: Instituto Chicano de Artes y Artesanias
    of the Texas Institute for Educational
    Development, 1975. English.

    AN: Collection of 220 slides
    supplemented by slide annotation and
    artists' biographies researched and
    photographed by Texas artist Cesar A.
    Martinez over two years. Biographies cover
    20 Texas, 6 New Mexico, and 15 northern
    California artists. Slides include, in
    addition, murals from Los Angeles and San
    Diego.

312 A Chicano artist: Emigdio Vasquez. CANNERY
    WORKER, Vol. 1, no. 4 (February 1977), p. 5.
    Bilingual.

    AN: Story on an exhibit by Esteban Villa
    in the Galeria Barrios of Sacramento,
    California, which is dedicated to the
    Cannery Workers Committee on its eighth
    anniversary. Five works by Villa are
    illustrated, and a group photograph of the
    Centro de Artistas Chicanos is included.

313 Chicano artists exhibit at USC. CALENDAR,
    (September 23, 1973), p. 61. English.

    AN: Announcement of an exhibit of
    paintings, drawings, sculpture and graphics
    by artists from the Mechicano Art Center of
    Los Angeles at the University of Southern
    California Art Galleries. Slide
    presentations of murals and supergraphics.

314 Chicano cinema coalition. Mimeographed copy,
    September 1, 1979. English.

    AN: An informational bulletin about the
    Coalition founded July 1978 in Los Angeles
    of forty independent producers and
    filmmakers who joined together for "the
    development, production, distribution,
    promotion and exhibition...of film and video
    productions which meaningfully
    address...needs and concerns of the Latino
    people in the United States." Professionals
    with their own companies (Amanecer Films,
    Bilingual Educational Services, Luis Ruiz
    Productions), television producers, and
    post-graduate film students make up the
    group. The Coalition published the CHICANO
    CINEMA NEWSLETTER. Ties are promoted with

Latin American cinema people.

315 CHICANO CINEMA NEWSLETTER. Vol. 1, no. 4
    (June 1979). English.

    AN: Report and cautionary note on the
    upcoming Alternative Cinema Conference;
    announcement of ONLY ONCE IN A LIFETIME and
    CHICANA film releases; other new films and
    TV programs; a Chicano cinema bibliography;
    a list of Chicano production companies and
    distributors; a theoretical article on the
    nature (proposed) of Chicano cinema as an
    alternative cinema; statement of purpose of
    the Los Angeles Chicano Cinema Coalition.

316 Chicano exhibit set. SANTA FE NEW MEXICAN,
    (September 22, 1972), p. A4. English.

    AN: A Chicano art show organized by El
    Instituto Chicano de Artes y Artesanias of
    San Antonio, TX is scheduled for Highlands
    University Gallery, Las Vegas, NM.

317 Clark, Yoko and Hama, Chizu. California
    murals. Berkeley, CA: Lancaster-Miller,
    1979. English.

    AN: Picture book of Bay Area and Los
    Angeles murals with brief descriptions.
    Chicano artists included: Daniel Galvez,
    Irene Perez, Patricia Rodriguez, Graciela
    Carrillo (Mujeres Muralistas), Ray Patlan.

318 The class of '79. SA: THE MAGAZINE OF SAN
    ANTONIO, Vol. 3, no. 4 (June 1979). English.

    AN: Well-illustrated article on students
    of James Newberry, photography teacher at
    the University of Texas, San Antonio.
    Includes photos of top prizewinners and
    members of Ladrones de la Luz, David
    Cardenas and Kathy Vargas.

319 CODEX NEWSLETTER (Galeria de la Raza, San
    Francisco, CA). Vol. 1, no. 2 (September
    1973). English.

    AN: An in-house bulletin of upcoming
    events: EL SOL NUNCA MUERE,
    photography/poster exhibit, Rolando Garces,
    and Peruvian posters; Mujeres de Aztlan,
    women artists' collective exhibit;
    Filipino/Samoan art exhibit; Galeria
    Christmas art sale; Galeria pavilion at S.F.
    annual art festival; Rockefeller scholarship
    for Galeria curator Luis Santana; Galeria
    coloring book; Balmy Alley mural project;
    Diego Rivera exhibit; first installment of
    Rupert Garcia's RAZA MURALS AND MURALISTS:
    AN HISTORICAL VIEW.

320 La Cofradia de Artes y Artesanos Hispanicos
    and Santa Fe Council for the Arts. El
    festival hispanico. Festival program, [ca.
    1979]. English.

    AN: Program for the festival which
    included over 70 visual artists from
    northern New Mexico selected and hung by the
    Cofradia at the Armory for the Arts gallery
    in Santa Fe. The poster for the festival,
    reproduced on the program cover, is taken
    from a painting by Gilberto Guzman. The
    festival also featured music, cuentos,
    dance, slide show, poetry, films.

Art Organizations & Groups (cont.)

321 COMMUNITY MURALS (San Francisco, CA). (Fall 1981). English.

AN: Citywide Murals Group of Denver, Colorado assisted the Chilean-oriented Brigada Orlando Letelier with a mural in their city; Carlos Sandoval of Denver doing mural in Guerrero, Mexico; Ray Patlan of Berkeley, California assisting with mural in Mexico painted by Arnold Belkin's class at the Academy of San Carlos; report on the exhibit MURALS OF AZTLAN: THE STREET PAINTERS OF EAST LOS with a reprint of debate on the event by Shifra M. Goldman, Judithe Elena Hernandez de Neikrug, and comments by John Pitman Weber and Tim Drescher; report on DAR LUZ mural directed by Santa Barraza in Austin, Texas, and a new mural in Hayward, California directed by Enrique Romero; a mural sponsored by the Chicano Youth Center of Fresno, California showing the influence of Mexican calendars; a new mural, OAKLAND'S PORTRAIT by Daniel Galvez in Oakland, California; pro-and-con discussion of social function of graffiti in response to letter from Belgian source; reprint of story on spray paint crime bill (anti-graffiti) sponsored by California Assemblyman Richard Alatorre. Entire issue illustrated.

322 Con Safo. San Antonio, TX: Pintores Chicanos de San Antonio, [ca. 1975]. English.

AN: Illustrated pamphlet issued by the San Antonio artists' group Con Safo. Includes a self-definition and a brief history of the group under the names El Grupo, Los Pintores de Aztlan, Los Pintores de la Nueva Raza, Con Safo (from 1967 on). Members include Jesse A. Almazan, Mel Casas, Jose Esquivel, Jose P. Garza, Cesar Augusto Martinez, Santos Martinez, Felipe Reyes, Roberto Rios, Jesus C. Trevino, and Vicente Velasquez.

323 Con safo to hold Lutheran college exhibition at Texas. CHICANO TIMES, Vol. 7, no. 89 (March 26, 1976), p. [15]. English.

AN: Discusses the aims of "Con Safos" group: to interpret their environment and react to it; to act as spokespeople and give visual reality to the Chicano vision; to destroy stereotypes and demolish visual cliches. The participating artists include Rudy R. Trevino, Mel Casas, Lucas Hinojosa, Kathy Vargas, Joe Frank Acosta, Emilio Aguirre and Homero Ureste.

324 Concilio de arte popular. CHISMEARTE, Vol. 1, no. 2 (Winter, Spring, 1977), p. 54. English.

AN: Report of a meeting February 12, 1977 by the Concilio de Arte Popular (CAP) which published CHISMEARTE. Introduces members of the Board and summarizes discussions of problems of the organization and their publication.

325 Conferencia plastica chicana. Conference brochure, 1979. English.

AN: Schedule of proceedings at internationally attended conference on Chicano and Mexican art and photography sponsored by the Centro Cultural de LUCHA (League of United Chicano Artistas) and MAS (Mujeres Artistas del Suroeste). Brief biographies of presenters. Illustrated.

326 Congreso de Artistas Chicanos en Aztlan, San Diego, CA. Diego Rivera, David Alfaro Siqueiros, Jose Clemente Orozco: exhibit of local artists, La Logan [San Diego]. Exhibition brochure, n.d. [c.1974]. English.

AN: Announcement of a traveling exhibit organized by Galeria de la Raza, San Francisco, from the collection of the San Francisco Museum of Art. Illustrated with a San Diego mural.

327 Contemporary Arts Museum, Houston, TX and Martinez, Santos G., Jr. Mexican movie posters. Exhibition invitation, 1979. English.

AN: Invitation to an exhibit of posters primarily from the collecttion of Enrique Flores and Xavier Gorena of Xochil Art Center, Mission, Texas. Martinez considers the posters monumental, with expressive qualities that have influenced Chicano poster makers like the Royal Chicano Air Force, and Rupert Garcia, and Texas artists like Luis Jimenez, Jesse Trevino and Cesar Martinez. One illustration. Introduction by guest curator Santos G. Martinez, Jr. (See Rupert Garcia's essay in the exhibition catalog: POSTERS FROM THE GOLDEN AGE OF MEXICAN CINEMA, for another point of view).

328 Contreras, Carlos. Nuestra cultura. LA VOZ: Concilio for the Spanish Speaking of King Co., Seattle, no. 7 (August 1979).

AN: Information of Washington state murals painted by members of La Extension Cultural; Armando Lara's autobiographical mural titled "El Rio" is installed at the Concilio offices, 107 Cherry St. Suite 210. Arturo Artorez completed a wall painting using the image of Quetzalcoatl at El Centro de la Raza with funding from the Seattle Arts Commission. Francisco Siqueiros used the themes of ecology and Mexican mythology for two murals at Seattle Community College. Commentary on Alfredo Arreguin's painting exhibition at the Kiku Gallery and his wall painting at the Childrens Orthopedic Hospital in Seattle.

329 Conversation on photography in the Los Angeles Latino community. OBSCURA, Vol. 2, no. 2 (December, February, 1981, 1982), p. 22-32. English.

AN: Interview on the nature and distinguishing characteristics of Chicano photography with Chicano photographers Isabel Castro (Council for Latino Photography), Lorenzo Hernandez (Director of Cityscape Gallery, publisher PHOTOSHOW magazine), Joseph G. Uribe (California State University, Los Angeles, Center for the Visual Arts, Director of West Colorado Gallery), Patssi Valdez, Becky Villasenor, and sculptor, curator, and Art Director for Academia Quinto Sol, Inc., Linda Vallejo, Portfolio of photography by Chicanos Don Anton, Louis Carlos Bernal, Sean Carrillo, Patssi Valdez, Ricardo Valverde, and by Morrie Camhi and Elizabeth Sisco on Chicano subjects.

Art Organizations & Groups (cont.)

330 Corneil, Paul. Militant barrio murals of
Santa Fe. Venice, CA: Environmental
Communications, n.d. English.

AN: Annotated slide catalog with
introductory text about the mural group Los
Artes Guadalupanos de Aztlan of Santa Fe.
Gilberto Guzman is mentioned as one of the
group.

331 COUNCIL OF LATINO PHOTOGRAPHY/USA
NEWSLETTER. no. 1 (January 1979). English.

AN: First number of photocopied
newsletter produced by the Council of Latino
Photography/USA announcing the formation of
the organization and its affiliation with
the Consejo Latinoamericano de Fotografia
established in Mexico City in May 1978.
Organizers of CLP/USA were photographers
Isabel Castro, Harry Gamboa, Jr., Adam
Avila, Luis Garza, and art historian Shifra
Goldman.

332 COUNCIL OF LATINO PHOTOGRAPHY/USA
NEWSLETTER. no. 2 (January 1980). English.

AN: Photocopied newsletter reporting on
the "First Communication" meeting of the
organization, the opening of a Council
gallery and darkroom in Pasadena, news from
San Francisco/Berkeley group, news of the
activities of the Consejo Mexicano de
Fotografia, Mexico, and an announcement of
the II COLLOQUIUM OF LATIN AMERICAN
PHOTOGRAPHY for 1981.

333 Cuellar, Rodolfo. Esteban Villa-maximo
exponente del arte indigena mexicano. EL
HISPANO, Vol. 8, no. 23 (January 27, 1976),
p. 3. Spanish.

AN: Biographical data on the artist
focusing on his activism in the formation of
the Centro de Artistas Chicanos in
Sacramento and the coalition of Centros
Chicanos in California. Illustrated with
photographs of the artist, one of his murals
and a special emblem for the "Esteban Villa
Fan Club" designed by the R.C.A.F.

334 Cultura chicana: Los Angeles. COMUNIDAD, no.
11 (July 13, 1980), p. 1-15. Spanish.

AN: The whole issue of the Cultural
Supplement concerns Chicano art and music.
Captioned photographs deal with visual
artists Carlos Almaraz, Jerry Dreva [not
Chicano], Glugio Gronk, Willie Herron, John
Valadez, Patssi Valdez, with examples of
their work. With the exception of Dreva, all
the artists are members of Los Four or Asco.
Asco member Harry Gamboa, Jr. sums up the
1960s and 1970s and activities of artists in
his essay "Seis imaginaciones: Artistas
chicanos en Los Angeles." Well illustrated.

335 Daigh, Janice. Old church alive with art.
TAOS NEWS BULLETIN, (January 25, 1979), p.
B, 1. English.

AN: Commentary on the formation of the
Cofradia de Artes y Artesanos Hispanicos.
The organization projects an ambitious
program including the expansion of artistic
endeavors by contemporary crafts people and
artists, the restoration of historic
buildings and the education of Hispanic
children in their artistic heritage as well
as providing information to the general
public.

336 De colores mural team. Brochure, [ca. 1975].
English.

AN: Brochure giving brief history of the
De Colores Mural Team established in 1972 as
part of the Horizons Unlimited program with
Chuy Campusano as coordinator. The team
participated in murals at the Jamestown
Center, Balmy Alley, Redding Elementary
School, Mission Childcare Center, Mission
Branch Bank of America and Horizons
Unlimited from 1972 to 1975.

337 Diaz, Jean; Dominguez, Edward; and Torres,
Kay. Bi-Lingual blues [fotonovela]. SOMOS,
Vol. 1, no. 1 (April, May, 1978), p. 33-36.
English.

AN: Reproduction of a "fotonovela",
BI-LINGUAL BLUES by Ojo Productions, a group
of students connected with the Latin
American Studies Department of California
State University, Los Angeles.

338 Documentary to include work by Cuate Santos.
LAREDO NEWS, (July 17, 1980). English.

AN: Photography by Laredo News
photographer Cuate Santos included in
exhibit "Un encuentro sin palabras," a
documentary show on Mexican American life in
Texas sponsored by Mujeres Artistas del
Suroeste (MAS). The state-wide show was
juried by Los Angeles photographer Isabel
Castro. Illustrated.

339 Donaghy, Kathleen. Two Arizona firsts:
Chicano gallery and Spanish theatre. ARIZONA
ARTS AND LIFESTYLE, (1981). English.

AN: The MARS (Movimiento Artistico del
Rio Salado) Gallery has opened in downtown
Phoenix, run by MARS founder Jim
Covarrubias. Louis Leroy, expansion arts
coordinator for the Arizona Commission on
the Arts, says it is the only arts-oriented
space that caters to Chicanos in Arizona.

340 Dunsmore de Carrillo, Patricia. On Rene
Yanez of the Galeria de la Raza. CHISMEARTE,
Vol. 1, no. 1 (Fall 1976), p. 8-9.
English.

AN: Report on Yanez's negotiations with
the Foster Kleiser Company to take over a
billboard located outside the Galeria in San
Fancisco which has been painted by Michael
Rios, the Centro de Cambio and TIN TAN
magazine, Zaiver (Xavier) Viramontes, and
others.

341 Editorial - Mexican Museum. SAN FRANCISCO
CHRONICLE, (November 2, 1981), p. 38.
English.

AN: Editorial statement lauding the
Mexican Museum as an important cultural
asset for the city of San Francisco. As the
Museum relocates to Ft. Mason from its old
headquarters in The Mission District, it
expands its exhibitions, cultural and
educational programs.

Art Organizations & Groups (cont.)

342 Eichstaedt, Peter. Hispanic festival
cultural showcase. NEW MEXICAN WEEKEND,
(May 25, 1979), p. 3. English.

   AN: Announcement of the week-long
   HISPANIC HERITAGE FESTIVAL/EL FESTIVAL
   HISPANICO co-sponsored by La Cofradia de
   Artes y Artesanos Hispanicos and the Santa
   Fe Council fo the Arts at the Armory for the
   Arts in Santa Fe. Outlines the cultural
   activities, including a visual arts exhibit.
   La Cofradia is a recently formed
   organization which has assembled regional
   shows at the Santuario de Guadalupe which
   gave opportunities to local artists to show
   their work. Festival artists are primarily
   from the upper Rio Grande but also include
   artists from the State Penitentiary, as well
   as Albuquerque and Las Cruces. Illustration
   of painting by Sam Leyba.

343 Encanto Pavilion, Encanto Park, Phoenix, AZ.
Exposicion de arte para la raza: Arizona
Chicano art show. Exhibition catalog, [ca.
1978]. English.

   AN: Catalog for an exhibit organized by
   MARS (Movimiento Artistico del Rio Salado).
   Colombian-born Antonio L. Tocora, Jim
   Covarrubias, Ed Dias, Robert C. Buitron,
   Armando Leon Hernandez, Guillermo Galindo,
   Richard Luna Cisneros, Jose Andres Giron,
   Robert L. Matta included.

344 'Fashion Moda' at Galeria de la Raza.
PEOPLE'S WORLD, Vol. 44, no. 48 (November
29, 1981), p. 10. English.

   AN: A joint exhibit, FASHION MODA AT
   GALERIA DE LA RAZA, focuses on people
   interested in cross-cultural interaction. 50
   artists from the San Francisco Bay Area, the
   South Bronx, Los Angeles, and New York City
   were shown. Fashion Moda is located in the
   South Bronx, an area of severe urban
   devastation. Illustrated.

345 Fitch, Bob. Los artes: a story the people
live as well as paint. YOUTH MAGAZINE, Vol.
26, no. 3 (March 1975), p. 2-11. English.

   AN: Illustrated story on the formation
   and early murals of Los Artes Guadalupanos
   de Aztlan of Santa Fe.

346 Forest Home Library, Milwaukee, WI. Arte
chicano de Carlos Rosas, Chicano muralist.
Exhibition invitation, 1978. English.

   AN: Invitation to an exhibit by Carlos
   Rosas [originally from El Paso, TX] who has
   created murals with Chicano themes in many
   parts of the United States. Sponsored by El
   Taller Obrero Cultural de Milwaukee.

347 Los Four exhibit in Union Gallery.
UNIVERSITY TIMES, (November 6, 1975), p. 4.
English.

   AN: "Los Four," a group of four Chicano
   artists - Frank Romero, Roberto "Beto" de la
   Rocha, Gilbert Lujan, and Carlos Almaraz,
   with newcomer Judithe Hernandez - work with
   political cartoons, Catholic symbols, works
   of sardonic humor. They also paint street
   murals: several have been done recently in
   Los Angeles, La Puente, and Long Beach.
   Illustrated.

348 Frankenstein, Alfred. An artistic taste of
Mexico in the city. SAN FRANCISCO CHRONICLE,
(November 29, 1975), p. 29. English.

   AN: A very favorable review of the
   inaugural exhibit at the Mexican Museum. The
   opening show was a panoramic view of Mexican
   art including pre-Hispanic, colonial, folk
   art and fine art. Among the Mexican American
   artists presented were Roberto Gonzalez,
   Raul Mora and Gustavo Rivera.

349 Galeria de la Raza/Studio 24, San Francisco,
CA and Garcia, Rupert. La Raza Silkscreen
Center: "Images of a community", an exhibit
of silkscreen posters and graphic works from
1971 to 1979. Exhibition catalog, 1979.
English.

   AN: First large scale retrospective
   exhibit of the La Raza Silkscreen Center's
   eight years of postermaking. Includes list
   of 90 artists.

350 Galeria de la Raza/Studio 24, San Francisco,
CA. Royal Chicano Air Force presents
"Chicanos del Valle Tortilla Opening".
Exhibition invitation, 1971. English.

351 Galeria Museo, Mission Cultural Center, San
Francisco, CA and Rodriguez, Patricia.
Patricia Rodriguez: simbolos y fantasias
culturales. Exhibition catalog, 1981.
English.

   AN: Catalog of an exhibition of
   sculpture and painting. Autobiographical
   information about the Texas-born artist who
   lives in San Francisco and was a co-founder
   of Mujeres Muralistas. She explains her
   techniques in making portrait masks of
   Chicano/a artists in plaster and mixed
   media. Well illustrated.

352 Gamboa, Harry, Jr. and Gronk. Gronk:
off-the-wall artist. NEWORLD, Vol. 6, no. 4
(1980), p. 33-43. English.

   AN: Interview with Gronk about his No
   Movies, by Harry Gamboa, Jr., both members
   (with Willie Herron and Patssi Valdez) of
   ASCO. The interview itself can be seen as an
   "art piece" with photographs by Gamboa; it
   contains valuable information about the
   ideas and activities of the group.

353 Garcia, Rupert. 'Fifth Sun' Raza art show at
UC Berkeley Museum. EL TECOLOTE, Vol. 8, no.
3 (November 1977), p. 8+. English.

   AN: Review of THE FIFTH SUN:
   CONTEMPORARY TRADITIONAL CHICANO AND LATINO
   ART, co-sponsored by University of
   California, Berkeley Chicano Studies and
   Arte Popular, and curated by artist Ralph
   Maradiaga, co-director of Galeria de la
   Raza, showing at the UC Berkeley Museum. It
   will travel to the University of California,
   Santa Barbara's Art Museum. Illustrated.

354 Garcia, Sol. Vato Loco y Chata La Gata
[comic strip]. CHISMEARTE, no. 2 (Winter,
Spring, 1977), p. Bk cover. Calo.

   AN: Comic strip format utilized to
   invite all interested persons to meeting of
   the Concilio de Arte Popular. The artist is
   a member of the Brocha del Valle group from
   Fresno, CA.

Art Organizations & Groups (cont.)

355 Garcia's art. Gallery brochure, n.d. English.

AN: Brochure of a non-profit center featuring an art gallery and other cultural activities to promote knowledge and education about Chicano and Mexican arts. [Headed by Ralph Garcia who in 1981 is director of PAN, Performance Artists Nucleus.].

356 Gardiner, Henry G. Painted exterior walls of Southern California. CURRANT ART MAGAZINE, Vol. 1, no. 2 (June, July, 1975), p. 16-23+. English.

AN: Good survey of street muralism, primarily in Los Angeles and San Diego, which started in 1968. Divided into eight "schools," including Chicano and non-Chicano muralists. Most Chicano murals associated with Goez Brothers Art Gallery and Mechicano Art Center in Los Angeles, the Coronado Bay Bridge group [Chicano Park] and Balboa Park group [Centro Cultural de la Raza]. Mural discussed in detail. Well illustrated.

357 Geyer, Anne; Hernandez, Lorenzo; and Valverde, Ricardo. Latino photographers of U.S. still seeking identity. THE NEWS, (September 5, 1981), p. 17. English.

AN: Interview with Lorenzo Hernandez, photo dealer and owner of Cityscape Foto Gallery, Pasadena, Calif. in which he compares Mexican with U.S. Latino photography. Interview with Ricardo Valverde, Chicano photographer and co-chair of the Council of Latino Photography/USA, discussing his work. Illustrated.

358 Gilroy's public art form. THE VALLEY WORLD, (July 19, 1978). English.

AN: Article cites activities of "The Tortuga Patrol" a Chicano muralist group from the Watsonville California area.

359 Goldman, Shifra M. Chicana artists at work. ARRIBA, [n.d.], p. 3+. English.

AN: Excerpt of a longer article on the Texas women's group Mujeres Artistas del Suroeste (MAS). Integral to the group are artists Santa Barraza, Nora Gonzalez-Dodson, Alicia Arredondo, Maria Flores, Sylvia Orozco, and Modesta Trevino.

360 Goldman, Shifra M. Women artists of Texas: MAS = More + Artists + Women = MAS. CHISMEARTE, no. 7 (January 1981), p. 21-22. English.

AN: History of Texas Chicana women artists' organization, Mujeres Artistas del Suroeste (MAS), co-founded in 1977 by Santa Barraza and Nora Gonzalez-Dodson in the framework of the burgeoning feminist art movement, particularly Women and Their Work of Texas. Brief history of Chicano politics and the corresponding art movement of southern and central Texas. In addition to Barraza and Gonzalez-Dodson, Alicia Arredondo, Modesta Trevino, and Maria Flores are considered. Illustrated.

361 Gonzales, Juan. Galeria de la Raza: "our people deserve the best". EL TECOLOTE, Vol. 7, no. 11 (July 1977), p. 14. English.

AN: "We are not here to sell our art, but to sell the idea of art." This could well be the motto of Galeria de la Raza who under co-directors Rene Yanez and Ralph Maradiaga has become a key cultural institution in the Mission District of San Francisco. The two directors have a broad definition of art that encompasses everything from cartoons to craftwork. The article details past exhibits and future goals. A half-page photograph of the exterior of Galeria de la Raza by Pilar Mejia illustrates the article. Reprint of article entitled "Our people deserve the best" which appeared in NUESTRO, Vol. 1, no. 2 (May, 1977), p. 56-57.

362 Gonzalez, Ellen. U.S. art project: Chicanas painting 'future history'. LOS ANGELES TIMES, (March 16, 1978), p. II, 4. English.

AN: Women muralists from the murals workshop of the Chicana Service Action Center working on murals at City Terrace and Humphrey Avenue elementary schools in East Los Angeles. Illustrated.

363 Gonzalez, Hector. El arte de Esteban Villa. EL HISPANO, Vol. 6, no. 20 (November 6, 1973). Spanish.

AN: Commenting on Esteban Villa's one man show at the Centro de Artistas Chicanos that presented sixty-five pieces of art ranging from acrylics, watercolors, woodcuts, to pen and ink drawings. Villa fuses Indian symbols, mythology, folklore and customs to create a new "cosmic" dimension for the Chicano experience.

364 Gonzalez, Jose Carlos. Consejo mexicano de fotografia: foto latino en el suroeste de los Estado Unidos. ARTES VISUALES, Vol. 29, no. 29 (June 1981), p. 55-56. Spanish.

AN: Review of a photography show in Mexico City organized by Lorenzo Hernandez, Cityscape Photo Gallery of Pasadena, and the Council of Latino Photography/USA. The show featured Latinos of the Southwest and Latino themes by non-Latino photographers.

365 Gonzalez, Victoria. Chair in the sky: Ernesto Palomino. HERE AND NOW, Vol. 2, no. 2 (Fall 1981). English.

AN: An important article tracing the artistic career of Ernie Palomino, professor of art at California State University, Fresno. Includes biographical information, formation of La Brocha Del Valle (Chicano Arts Organization), information about Palomino's film MY TRIP IN A '52 FORD and commentary on Palomino's music and artistic philosophy. Well illustrated.

366 Greenberg, David; Smith, Kathryn; and Teacher, Stuart. Megamurals & supergraphics: big art. Philadelphia, PN: Running Press, 1977. English.

AN: A full-color picture book of murals throughout the United States. Chicano murals include Michael Rios (San Francisco), Mujeres Muralistas (San Francisco), Leonard Castellanos and Tomas Gonzales with others (Los Angeles), Los Artes Guadalupanos de Aztlan (New Mexico), Willie Herron (Los Angeles), Toltecas en Aztlan (San Diego), David Botello (Los Angeles), David Lopez and Arizona Mara Gang (Los Angeles), Vatos de Maravilla (Los Angeles), Carlito Gaegos (Los Angeles), Gil Hernandez (Los Angeles), Wayne [Alaniz] Healy (Los Angeles).

Art Organizations & Groups (cont.)

367 Grimke, Angelina. Chicano art finds home in Mission galeria. PEOPLE'S WORLD, Vol. 33, no. 32 (August 8, 1970), p. 11. English.

AN: Commentary on the exhibition CHICANOS, CUBA Y LOS 10 MILLONES held at the original Galeria de la Raza at 425 14th Street in San Francisco. The show presented photographs by Jay Ojeda and Roberto Perez-Diaz, drawings by Gloria Ozuna together with paintings and photographs by Cuban artist Mederos. Provides information about the goals of the Galeria as the visual arts department of Casa Hispana de Bellas Artes. Exhibition curator was Rolando Castellon.

368 Guadalupe Historic Foundation, Santa Fe, NM. Cofradia de artes y artesanos hispanicos. Mimeograph, 1979. Spanish.

AN: Mimeographed call to join and support the Cofradia, an organization begun by and sustained by artists and craftsmen to help support each other. Stated aims: "to encourage the revival, continuation, and growth of traditional and contemporary Hispanic arts and crafts, to serve as a source of public information for these crafts and their producers, and to promote the general social, cultural, and economic welfare of the Hispanic arts and crafts".

369 Hale, David. La Brocha del Valle artists deal with Chicano reality. FRESNO BEE, (October 1, 1978), p. G, 5. English.

AN: Positive critique of a collective exhibition by members of La Brocha del Valle Group held at Fresno State University's Phebe Conley Art Building Gallery. With divergent attitudes, styles and ideas, the group is united by their focus on subject matter that deals with the diverse realities of being Chicano. Illustrated with photograph of Juan Ybarra's bronze sculpture, ONLY ONE TIME.

370 Hale, David. Exhibit backers hope for Chicano cultural center plan. FRESNO BEE, (July 14, 1974), p. K5. English.

AN: Review of a Chicano art exhibition in the Sarah McCardle Room of the downtown Fresno County Public Library. According to artist-organizer Ernie Palomino, the exhibit is a trial balloon to see if enough Chicano artists can surface and cooperate in the establishment of a Chicano Cultural Center in Southeast Fresno. Illustrated with reproduction of a portrait by Romero Arroyo of Mendota, California and a painting by Victor Hernandez from Visalia, California.

371 Hebert, Ray. $10 million Latin cultural center: Lincoln Park to get new life. LOS ANGELES TIMES, (March 19, 1972), p. B-7. English.

AN: Report on the start of East Los Angeles cultural center Plaza de la Raza, intended as a showcase for Model Cities agency funding.

372 Herrera, Barbara. Chicano park expansion sought: barrio idealists face strong barriers. EVENING TRIBUNE, (August 10, 1974), p. A-10. English.

AN: Last of a three part series on Chicano Park. Barrio activists of the Chicano Park Steering Committee plan to extend the Chicano Park under the Coronado bridge from 5.8 acres to the bay, painting all the pillars with murals, and ending with a small marina. They are facing opposition from government officials, but are hopeful of success.

373 Hillinger, Charles. 'Chicano Air Force' flies high. LOS ANGELES TIMES, (July 22, 1979), p. I, 3+. English.

AN: Illustrated review of the personnel and purpose of the Royal Chicano Air Force.

374 La historia de California, 1977. San Francisco, CA: Galeria de la Raza, 1977. English.

AN: Handprinted silkscreen calendar of history seen from a Mexican point of view. Twelve sheets and a cover. Artists are: Ralph Maradiaga, Irene Perez, Louie "The Foot" Gonzalez, Max Garcia, Patricia Rodriguez, Jose Romero, Esteban Villa, Juanishi Orozco, Rodolfo Cuellar, Jose Montoya, Xavier Viramontes, Rene Yanez, Ricardo Favela, associated with the Galeria de la Raza, or the Royal Chicano Air Force of Sacramento.

375 La historia de Mechicano. LA GENTE DE AZTLAN, Vol. 8, no. 1 (November 2, 1977), p. 14. English.

AN: Excellent and complete account of the formation and development of Mechicano Art Center from 1968 to 1977. Explains goals, activities and participating artists.

376 Houston Chicanismo. LA PRENSA, Vol. 1, no. 2 (March 31, 1978). English.

AN: In Houston, Texas, the AMA Gallery (Association for the Advancement of Mexican Americans) was opened in February 1976 to showcase Chicano art. Noel Rodriguez, gallery director, informs about the goals and objectives of the gallery. A current exhibit presents paintings by Josie Mendoza and Atanacio Davila, ceramics by Jesse Sifuentes and mixed-media works by Joe Ramirez. Illustrated with two pieces from exhibit, THANKSGIVING, an acrylic painting by Josie Mendoza and BIRDS, a ceramic piece.

377 Incorporated Artes Monumentales/Inc., Denver, CO. IAM: art exhibit. Exhibition brochure, n.d. English.

AN: Large format, well illustrated brochure with information on muralists Roberto Lucero, Al Sanchez, Andrew Manning, Ricardo Barrera and Bob Reyes. Includes some biographical information situating these artists within the dynamic artistic traditions of the Mexican and the Chicano mural movements.

378 Institute of American Indian Arts Museum, Santa Fe, NM. Native American/Hispanic festival, contemporary & historic visions. Santa Fe, NM: Institute of American Indian Arts Museum, 1981. English.

AN: Catalog for exhibit co-sponsored by La Cofradia de Artes y Artesanos Hispanicos, the Institute of American Indian Arts, and the Santa Fe Council for the Arts. Exhibit stresses the inter-relationship between the Indian and Hispano peoples of New Mexico. 31 contemporary Hispano artists included. Illustrated.

Art Organizations & Groups (cont.)

379 Instituto Chicano de Artes y Artesanias
(Texas Instit. Educational Development)
and Instituto Cultural Mexicano (SER/UNAM), San
Antonio, TX. Artistas chicanos: Los
Quemados. San Antonio, TX: Instituto
Chicano, Texas Institute for Educational
Development, 1975. English.

AN: Invitation to an exhibit and
manifesto of 1975 Austin-San Antonio
artists' group, Los Quemados. Included Santa
Barraza, Carolina Flores, Carmen Lomas
Garza, Luis Guerra, Cesar Augusto Martinez,
Santos Martinez, Amado Maurilio Pena, Jr.,
Jose Rivera, Vicente Rodriguez, Jose
Trevino.

380 Kagawa, Paul and Rilkin, Scott. La Raza
Silkscreen Center, in step with the Mission.
ARTS BIWEEKLY, no. 44 (March 15, 1977).
English.

AN: Concise history and goals of the
Silkscreen Center: the Center's values are
reflected in the collective process that
produces the posters, as well as in the
collective style of the art; in the emphasis
upon education. The Center trains
apprentices, educates the student community
about the silkscreen process and Raza
history and produces posters that have an
information impact. The Silkscreen Center is
part of a coalition of La Raza Information
Center, Tutorial Center, and Centro Legal
which evolved from La Raza En Accion Social
founded in 1970.

381 Kelley sparks Chicano growth. ROCKY MOUNTAIN
NEWS, (February 18, 1973), p. Festival,7.
English.

AN: Denver artist John Flores speaks
about his work and provides details about
the small but strong Chicano art colony in
Denver. Flores credits Ramon Kelley, an
established Chicano artist, with providing
much leadership and encouragement in the
development of Chicano art in Colorado.

382 Kleinhaus, Chuck; Seiter, Ellen; and Steven,
Peter. Conference report: struggling for
unity. JUMP CUT, no. 21 (November 1979), p.
35-37. English.

AN: Report and critique of the U.S.
Conference for an Alternative Cinema held in
mid-June 1979 at Bard College in New York
state to chart a course for independent
filmmakers. Chicano, Black, Asian and Puerto
Rican film people attended, including Jesus
Salvador Trevino and Sylvia Morales from the
Chicano Cinema Coalition of Los Angeles.

383 Kroll, Eric. Folk art in the barrios.
NATURAL HISTORY, Vol. 82, no. 5 (May 1973),
p. 56-65. English.

AN: Well-illustrated informative report
on Santa Fe, New Mexico murals by Los Artes
Guadalupanos de Aztlan. Author's somewhat
condescending attitude rectified in the
ARTFORUM reprint which drops the term "folk
art". [See Murals in New Mexico].

384 L.A.C.E. (Los Angeles Contemporary
Exhibitions), Los Angeles, CA. Gronk/Dreva,
1968-1978: ten years of art/life. Exhibition
brochure, 1978. English.

AN: Exhibit and other acitivities by
Gronk of the group ASCO and Jerry Dreva.

385 League of United Chicano Artists, Austin,
TX. La cultura es el derecho del pueblo.
Brochure-poster, [ca. 1970]. Bilingual.

AN: Bilingual brochure-color poster
describing activities of the Centro Cultural
de LUCHA: an umbrella organization of the
arts in Austin which also published the
magazine TEJIDOS.

386 Loniak, Walter. The true New Mexico
contemporary style. SANTA FE REPORTER, (May
31, 1979). English.

AN: Review of three exhibits in Santa
Fe, EL FESTIVAL HISPANICO co-sponsored by
the Cofradia de Artes y Artesanos Hispanicos
and the Santa Fe Council for the Arts; a
wood carving exhibit at Elaine Horwitch
Gallery, and easel paintings by muralist
Gilberto Guzman at the Black Kachina
Gallery. Concerning the Festival exhibit,
the critic states that the sculptural pieces
are the strongest; two dimensional work is
inconsistent or unimpressive, weaving is not
well represented (though usually the
strongest medium), and there are few
photographs or prints. Illustration.

387 Lopez, Gerard. Estrada murals. LA LUZ, Vol.
4, no. 3 (June 1975), p. 21. English.

AN: Describes goals and procedures of a
barrio mural project under the guidance of
"Los Ninos del Mundo", a group of Chicano
artists, musicians and social workers.

388 Lucas, Jerry. Testimonios de Latinoamerica.
CHISMEARTE, no. 6 (February 1980), p. 6-9.
English.

AN: Review of the exhibits TESTIMONIOS
DE LATINOAMERICA and AMERICA EN LA MIRA,
brought to Los Angeles Contemporary
Exhibitions Gallery by Chicano curator
Roberto Gil de Montes, as part of a cultural
exchange between the Mexican Cultural
Workers Front and Felipe Ehrenberg of the
Grupo Proceso Pentagono of Mexico, and
Chicano artists and photographers from the
Council of Latino Photography/USA in Los
Angeles. Well illustrated.

389 Lyle, Cindy. Chicano mural art: a mixture of
the barrio's rage and pride. NEW YORK TIMES,
(August 17, 1975), p. Sec.2, 21. English.

AN: Brief history of San Diego's Chicano
Park, why and how it was established, and
the establishment of the Centro Cultural de
la Raza in Balboa Park. Iconography of
several murals is examined, and the
longevity of outdoor murals discussed.
Illustrated.

390 MacLatchie, Sharon. Art in the barrios: one
man's commitment. LA LUZ, Vol. 3, no. 9
(December 1974), p. 17-18. English.

AN: Describes the Centro de Artistas
Chicanos in Sacramento, California.
Highlights the program for art in the Barrio
and focuses on the work and personality of
Jose Montoya.

391 Manley, Paula. If walls could speak, a
festival of murals. DAILY TEXAN, (August 4,
1980). English.

AN: Commentary on community murals in
Austin, including murals painted by LUCHA
(The League of United Chicano Artists).

Art Organizations & Groups (cont.)

392 MARCH: Movimiento artistico Chicano
(Mexican-American Art Movement). QUARTERLY,
(Spring 1976), p. 10. English.

AN: Brief history of MARCH.
Illustrations of murals by Ricarco Alonzo,
Jose Gonzalez, Vicente Mendoza. Ray Patlan.

393 MARS: Movimiento Artistico del Rio Salado.
Phoenix, AZ: Mars Studio/Gallery, 1978.
English.

AN: History and manifesto of MARS, 13
member group of Arizona painters, sculptors,
designers, and photographers: Jose Andres
Giron, Jose Jimenez Rodriguez, Antonio
Tocora (Colombian-born), Ramon Delgadillo,
Francisco Zuniga, Jim Covarrubias, Ed Diaz,
David Martinez, Roberto Buitron, Juan
Rodriguez, Eddie Lopez, Zarco Guerrero, Joe
Sanchez.

394 MARS: Movimiento Artistico del Rio Salado.
Exhibition brochure, [1981]. English.

AN: Illustrated brochure for the MARS
organization and its studio-gallery.
Includes a brief history, list of
exhibitions from 1978 to 1981, news about
its studio-workshop for the community, and
its goals.

395 MARS: Movimiento Artistico del Rio Salado.
Phoenix, AZ: [MARS], n.d. English.

AN: Illustrated brochure for the MARS
organization and its studio-gallery.
Includes a brief history, list of
exhibitions from 1978 to 1981, news about
its studio-workshop for the community, and
its goals.

396 Martinez, Anita. Raza! Arte! Raza! Arte!
EL TECOLOTE, Vol. 1, no. 2 (September 7,
1970), p. 3. Bilingual.

AN: Galeria de la Raza opened on July,
1970 at 425 14th St. San Francisco. It was
an outgrowth of the Arte Seis organization
(an art effort established in the Mission
District in 1967 by Francisco Camplis,
Rupert Garcia, Ralph McNeil, Jay Ojeda and
Jack Ruiz). These and other artists brought
together by the Neighborhood Arts Program
have coalesced in the new Galeria de la
Raza. Article gives goals, organizational
scheme and plans for the Galeria. It's first
exhibit was a one man show by Esteban Villa
together with a photo and sketch exhibit on
Cuba by Jay Ojeda, Roberto Diaz Perez and
Gloria Ozuna. Illustrated with installation
view of new Galeria.

397 Mascorro, Julie. Mechicano Art Center
exhibit to grace Price gallery walls. CAMPUS
NEWS, (November 24, 1971). English.

AN: Brief history of Mechicano Art
Center activities from its establishment in
1969 to 1971. Exhibiting are Charles
Almaraz, Roberto Amaral, Raymond Atilano,
William Bejarano, Armando Cabrera, Edward
Carbajal, Leonard Castellanos, Henry de
Vega, Antonio Esparza, Bob Gomez, Lucila V.
Grijalva, Jesus Gutierrez, Santos Lira,
Frank Martinez, Ernest Palomino, Louis
Quijada, Richard Raya, Frank Romero.
Illustrated.

398 Mechicano Art Center. Brochure, [1975].
English.

AN: Illustrated brochure detailing the
history, community programs (drawing,
painting, silkscreen, sculpture and mural
classes), gallery exhibits, travelling
exhibits, murals and supergraphics, and
financial status of the Whittier Blvd.
Center.

399 Mechicano Art Center attracts community
artists. EL HISPANO, Vol. 5, no. 2 (June 10,
1972). English.

AN: Commentary by Leonard Castellanos,
Director of Mechicano Art Center, who
explains funding sources and programs of the
Centro.

400 Metro Denver Urban Coalition, Denver, CO.
City walls. Brochure, 1979. English.

AN: Brochure/poster giving history of
City Walls Project and biographies of seven
artists: Jon Howe, Jerry Jaramillo, Steve
Lucero, Jowinnie Moore, Al Sanchez, Fred
Sanchez, Carlos M. Sandoval. Illustrated.

401 Mexican American liberation art front: la
Raza Nueva, Rene Yanez, Esteban Villa,
Malaquias Montoya, Manuel Hernandez. BRONCE,
Vol. 1, no. 3 (March 1969), p. 6-7. English.

AN: Manifesto of MALAF, a germinal
Chicano art group in northern California.
Compares revolutionary Chicanos of 1968 with
the Mexicans of 1910; equally Chicano
artists reject European-influenced art.
Announces the exhibit NEW SYMBOLS FOR LA
RAZA NUEVA, at La Causa in Oakland, March 22
to April 5, 1969. Puts forth the group's
philosophy and goals, particularly exhibits
and art services to the "barrio".
Illustrated.

402 MEXICAN MUSEUM NEWSLETTER. Vol. 6, no. 1
(Winter 1980, 1981). English.

AN: Regular report on the activities,
finances, membership, and other information
about the Museum. Announces several upcoming
shows: Rupert Garcia, six Mexican geometric
artists, paintings and prints by Mexican
American and Mexican women artists, Mexican
Leonel Maciel and Chicano Carlos Almaraz,
Mexican folk art, Manuel Neri sculpture, and
Mexican Luis Jaso.

403 Mills House Visual Arts Complex, Garden
Grove, CA. Menudo: artistas latinos de
Orange County. Exhibit invitation, 1980.
English.

AN: Invitation to an exhibit organized
for the first anniversary of Artistas
Latinos de Orange County including Delores
Grajeda, William Hernandez, Marylee Montano,
Patricia Murillo, Irene Ramos, Juan Ramos,
Ricardo Serrato, Miguel Shanahan, Arthur
Valenzuela, Benjamin Valenzuela, Jack
Vargas, Alonzo Whitney, Emigdio Vasquez,
Susana Zaccagnino, and Mexican artist
Artemio Sepulveda.

Art Organizations & Groups (cont.)

404 Minutaglio, Bill. S.A. aims at becoming Hispanic art center. SAN ANTONIO EXPRESS-NEWS, (January 18, 1981), p. 3-M+. English.

AN: Rick Reyna is director of the fledging San Antonio Consortium for Hispanic Arts (SACHA), a city-funded umbrella organization covering seven art groups, three of which - Centro Cultural del Pueblo (instruction for young people), Community Cultural Arts Program (murals), and Performance Artists Nucleus (displays and exhibits) - concern the visual arts. Rudy Garcia, Anastacio "Tache" Torres, and Ralph Garcia (formerly of Garcia's Art Gallery) head the three groups respectively.

405 Miranda, Keta. Refunding battle for mural project. PEOPLE'S WORLD, Vol. 39, no. 20 (May 15, 1976), p. 5+. English.

AN: History of the Mural Arts and Resource Center (Los Angeles Citywide Mural Project) from 1974 to its imminent demise in 1976. Joe Bravo mural illustrated.

406 Mitchell, Raye Bemis. March to an aesthetic of revolution. NEW ART EXAMINER, (February 1977). English.

AN: Interesting article that defines Chicano social-realism as a compelling aesthetic in opposition to avant-garde formalism. Exhibit by members of Chicago's MARCH group. Illustrated.

407 Monroe, Julie T. A splash of art from Idaho's Mexican-Americans. IDAHO STATESMAN, (March 11, 1977), p. 4D. English.

AN: As a Bicentennial tribute to all people of Latin American heritage, Illinois Bell Telephone Company organized a national exhiibit of 17 Mexican-American/Chicano artists. In Idaho, the touring exhibition was augmented by a local presentation, MEXICAN-AMERICAN: IDAHO, shown at the Boise Gallery of Art under sponsorship of Boise Cascade. Jose Rodriguez, local artist presents his views on the meanings of the word "Chicano" and "Chicano Art." Illustrated with a photograph of Jose Rodriguez and a reproduction of one of his oil paintings entitled THE HOE.

408 Montoya, Jose E. Pachuco art: a historical update. Sacramento, CA: Royal Chicano Air Force, 1977. English.

AN: Booklet outlining the history of the Zoot Suit Riots of 1943 and the making of the Pachuco myth, written by Montoya and illustrated with his pen-and-ink drawings of Pachucos and Pachucas.

409 Moody Hall, St. Edwards University, Austin, TX. Las companeras. Exhibition invitation, 1980. English.

AN: Invitation to an exhibition of Chicana/Latina artists sponsored by Mujeres Muralistas del Suroeste (MAS). Illustrated.

410 Morch, Albert. He put down his brushes for a dream. SAN FRANCISCO SUNDAY EXAMINER AND CHRONICLE, (October 2, 1977), p. Scene, 3. English.

AN: Brief profile of painter Peter Rodriguez, founder and director of the Mexican Museum in San Francisco which opened in 1975. On exhibit are the works of San Francisco artist Jerry Concha. Illustrated.

411 Moreno, Eduardo. Los Four. Half-hour 16mm film. English.

AN: Film about the Los Angeles group of artists known as Los Four (originally Carlos Almaraz, Gilbert Sanchez Lujan, Roberto de la Rocha, Frank Romero), at the time of their exhibit at the Los Angeles County Museum of Art - the first time Chicano art was shown at the Museum.

412 Moser, Charlotte. Arte chicano de Texas/Texas Chicano art. ARTES VISUALES, no. 29 (June 1981), p. 57-63. Bilingual.

AN: History of Chicano art and art organizations in Texas. A younger generation of artists is complying with a mainstream European esthetic rather than a regional Chicano one. Statements and biographies of artists. Many illustrations.

413 LA MOVIDA CON SAFO. no. 2 (February 1976). English.

AN: Mimeographed newsletter issued by Mel Casas about the San Antonio artists' group Con Safo. Reports on the exhibits, symposium, festival, TV appearance, film, and other activities of the group or its individual members. Illustrated.

414 LA MOVIDA CON SAFO. no. 1 (Fall 1975). English.

AN: Mimeographed newletter issued by Mel Casas about the San Antonio artists' group Con Safo. Includes history of the group and its activities.

415 Mujeres de Aztlan. EL TECOLOTE, Vol. 4, no. 1 (October 10, 1973), p. 3. English.

AN: A collective of Third World women artists plan an art show at Galeria de la Raza in San Francisco. Stressing the need for art forms that bring awareness and present the true nature of women's living conditions, this call for submission of art work reflects some feminist concerns of the period.

416 Las muralistas del barrio. CHISMEARTE, no. 2 (Winter, Spring, 1977), p. 48-49. English.

AN: Brief announcement about a Chicana artists' organization formed in Fresno, California which started work on a billboard-like mural, 60x8 feet on the theme of women. The mural received funding through Fresno's La Brocha del Valle. About fifteen women are involved, including Helen Gonzalez and Cecelia Risco.

417 Murals around the U.S.A. TEJANO ARTISTS INC. NEWSLETTER, Vol. 2, no. 2 (January, February, 1981). English.

AN: Mimeographed newsletter published by Tejano Artists, Inc. of Houston. Survey of U.S. mural events and publications; report on murals in Texas: El Paso, San Antonio, Austin, Crystal City, San Juan, Corpus Christi, Houston.

Art Organizations & Groups (cont.)

418 Murphy, Patricia Lee. Artists renew Toltecas crafts heritage. LOS ANGELES TIMES, (May 23, 1971), p. E, 10. English.

AN: The Toltecas en Aztlan, creative arm of the Chicano Federation of San Diego County, Inc., will shortly move into their new Centro Cultural de la Raza in Balboa Park, San Diego. The group includes Mario Acevedo (Peruvian), Guillermo Aranda, Tomas Castaneda, Victor Ochoa and Salvador Torres (visual artists) and poet Alurista.

419 Museum of Fine Arts, Santa Fe, NM. Luis Jimenez, sculpture, drawings and prints: La Cofradia de Artes y Artesanos Hispanicos, selected works. Exhibition invitation, 1979. English.

AN: Invitation to an exhibit of Texas sculptor and printmaker Luis Jimenez, and New Mexican artists and artisans.

420 NATIONAL MURALS NETWORK COMMUNITY NEWSLETTER. (Spring 1980). English.

AN: Reports on the Sept. 1979 conference of Chicano visual arts held at UT Austin, organized by the Mujeres Artistas del Suroeste, and the Liga Unida de Chicanos Artistas, which brought together participants from the U.S. and Mexico City; on Manuel Martinez's five murals (1976-78); murals by Roberto Lucero, Al Sanchez, and Jerry Jaramillo; as well as by the Chilean group Orlando Letelier Brigade, all in Denver, Colorado; murals by Leo Tanguma in Houston; the story about the "forbidden" Chicano mural in Blue Island, Illinois. Illustrated.

421 NATIONAL MURALS NETWORK COMMUNITY NEWSLETTER. (Fall 1979). English.

AN: Reports on mural projects by Fermin Coronado working with students in Houston; Galeria de la Raza's billboard used as a mural surface for changing images; murals under the Flor en la Comunidad program of El Centro Cultural de la Gente in San Jose, California and led by artist Jaime Valadez; murals in Grand Rapids and other cities of western Michigan; murals by Jose Guerrero and others from the Chicago Mural Group; a survey of Chicano murals in the Pilsen area of Chicago guided by Jose Gonzalez.

422 NATIONAL MURALS NETWORK COMMUNITY NEWSLETTER. (1978). English.

AN: This issue features reports from muralists. Includes information about murals at: La Pena Cultural Center in Berkeley, CA; the Social and Public Art Resource Center's Tujunga Wash Mural in Venice, CA; the Citywide Mural Project in Los Angeles, CA; activities at Chicano Park, and of the Congress of American Cosmic Artists (CACA), both in San Diego, CA; murals in San Mateo County, CA; the Task Force on Hispanic American Arts headed by Jacinto Quirarte of San Antonio; the 1978 Canto Al Pueblo in Corpus Christi, TX; murals in Chicago; and other works by non-Chicano artists.

423 New co-op in San Cristobal. GRITO DEL NORTE, Vol. 3, no. 8 (July 5, 1970), p. 13. English.

AN: Details formation of the San Cristobal Valley Arts Inc., a community corporation formed to train people in a silkscreen business venture. Aiming to use expressive forms as a source of economic development, the corporation published and distributed a line of Chicano silkscreen posters. Illustrated by three posters, WE SHALL ENDURE, SOMOS AZTLAN, and TAOS PUEBLO.

424 A new cultural center for Houston. AGENDA, Vol. 7, no. 2 (March, April, 1977), p. 17-18. English.

AN: Goals and programs of a proposed Mexican American cultural center for Houston, Texas. Since August of 1976, the center has been operating from a temporary location and has sponsored various art exhibits. Expected to be in full operation by 1980, the Houston Bellas Artes will sponsor workshops, symposia, performances and exhibits related to Mexican American culture. Illustrated with two photographs of the cultural activities of the Houston Bellas Artes Center.

425 New Galeria de la Raza. EL HISPANO, (July 28, 1970), p. 9. English.

AN: Review of the first exhibit at the Galeria de la Raza at 425 14th St. in San Francisco. The inaugural exhibition featured Esteban Villa, Luis Gutierrez and Luis Cervantes. The new Galeria is sponsored by Casa Hispana de Bellas Artes assisted by San Francisco Art Commission through its Neighborhood Arts Program.

426 New mural on Mission Street. EL HISPANO, Vol. 7, no. 13 (September 19, 1974), p. 5. English.

AN: Description of mural at the corner of 24th Street and South Van Ness in San Francisco. Painted by Mujeres Muralistas--Consuelo Mendez, Graciela Carrillo, Susan Cervantes and Miriam Olivo, the 30-foot mural depicts people in a tropical, Latin American setting.

427 Nora Mendoza: pintora de ascendencia mexicana triunfa en los EE. UU. BUENHOGAR, (May 1979), p. 7. Spanish.

AN: Profile of Texas-born Nora Mendoza of Michigan, a painter of abstractions in acrylic. She is an active member of many Detroit and Michigan organizations, including Nuestras Artes de Michigan which she co-founded with Jorge Vargas, Martin Moreno and Jessie Gonzalez.

428 Notes on 2nd National Community Muralists' Network Conference, Chicago, Ill. April 20-23, 1978. San Francisco, CA, 1978. English.

AN: Rupert Garcia, Raul Martinez, Patricia Rodriguez, Ray Patlan (San Francisco Bay Area) and Jaime Valadez (San Jose), among others, attended the conference in Chicago. Reports were heard from many parts of the United States on mural activities, including that of Aurelio Diaz of Chicago, representing MARCH (Movimiento Artistico Chicano). A workshop presentation was made by Luis Arenal and others from the Taller Siqueiros of Cuernavaca, Mexico. An experimental mural to try Siqueiros' techniques was created. Illustrated.

Art Organizations & Groups (cont.)

429 Oakland Museum, Oakland, CA and Laney
College, Oakland, CA. In search of Aztlan.
Exhibition brochure, 1974. English.

AN: Brochure for exhibit featuring Los
Four: Carlos Almaraz, Gilbert Lujan, Roberto
de la Rocha, Frank Romero, Judithe
Hernandez.

430 Oakland Museum, Oakland, CA. In search of
Aztlan. Exhibition invitation, 1974.
English.

AN: Invitation to an exhibit by Los
Four, a Chicano art group started about 1973
in Los Angeles. On exhibit are the original
members, Carlos Almaraz, Gilbert Lujan,
Roberto de la Rocha, Frank Romero, and new
member Judithe Hernandez.

431 Ojeda, Jay. Galeria de la Raza--art for the
community. SAN FRANCISCO PROGRESS, (March
24, 1972). English.

AN: Analysis of group exhibition by
thirty-four Raza artists. Commentary on the
work of Latin American artists Consuelo
Mendez, Rolando Castellon, and Chicano
artists Rupert Garcia, Chuy Campusano and
Peter Rodriguez.

432 Orange Co. Library. El Modena Branch. The
Hispanic Artist Association of Orange County
presents "Empanada," a tasty Mexican group
art exhibit filled with a variety of
digestible treats. Exhibition invitation,
1979. English.

AN: Poster/invitation to an exhibit of
artists (See "Empanada").

433 Orozco, Sylvia. Las mujeres - Chicana
artists come into their own. MOVING ON, Vol.
2, no. 3 (May 1978), p. 14-16. English.

AN: Illustrated feature prepared by
artist Sylvia Orozco on the founding of
Mujeres Artistas del Suroeste in Austin,
September 1977. Artworks and statements by
Nora Gonzalez Dodson, Maria Flores, Modesta
Trevino, Santa Barraza, as well as musicians
and singers.

434 Orth, Maureen. The soaring spirit of Chicano
arts. NEW WEST MAGAZINE, Vol. 3, no. 19
(September 11, 1978), p. 41-46. English.

AN: Overview of California Chicano
culture. Color illustrations of works by
Mexican muralist David Alfaro Siqueiros,
Rupert Garcia, Mujeres Muralistas, Willie
Herron, Rene Yanez, Rudy Martinez, San
Diego's Chicano Park, ASCO, Jose Montoya.

435 Parachini, Allan. Tujunga wash mural stands
up to storm. LOS ANGELES TIMES, (March 13,
1980), p. V, 1. English.

AN: Information about the mural project
near Los Angeles Valley College in Van Nuys,
Calif. sponsored by SPARC (Social and Public
Art Resource Center) of Venice, Calif. and
coordinated by Judy Baca. Illustrated.

436 Pepe and Pepito. SANTA FE NEW MEXICAN,
(August 16, 1972), p. A2. English.

AN: Among the barrio groups receiving
funding from the COPAS Cultural Awareness
Program of the Model Cities program are Los
Artesanos and Los Artes Guadalupanos.

437 Petraitis, Louise. Student union murals:
walls with tongues. PHOENIX MAGAZINE,
(April 21, 1977), p. 12. English.

AN: San Francisco State University
instructor Ray Patlan and his La Raza Mural
Workshop are painting murals in the Student
Union basement. The relationship of a mural
to architecture, the process of transferring
a sketch to the wall, the underpainting, and
the finishing painting processes are
explained. A videotape of the mural is being
made. Illustrated.

438 Pinedo, Maria Vita. Galeria de la Raza. KPFA
FOLIO, Vol. 28, no. 2 (February 1977).
English.

AN: Brief history of San Francisco's
Galeria de la Raza.

439 Plagens, Peter. Los Four (Roberto de la
Rocha, Carlos Almaraz, Gilbert Lujan and
Frank Romero) at LACMA. ARTFORUM,
(September 1974), p. 87-88. English.

AN: Review of Los Four exhibit at Los
Angeles County Museum of Art which calls it
a "sociological bazaar" in which Chicanos
have been "corrupted" by art schools and
"museumized".

440 Plaza de la Raza: place of the people.
Brochure, n.d. English.

AN: Glossy promotional brochure for
Plaza de la Raza, a cultural center in East
Los Angeles. Brief history of the Plaza and
photographs of its activities with children.

441 The Point Gallery, Santa Monica, CA. ASCO
(Gronk, Patssi, Gamboa, Herron), Los Four
(Almaraz, de la Rocha, Judithe Hernandez,
Gloriamalia Flores, Mauricio Ramirez, John
Valadez. Exhibition invitation, [1975].
English.

AN: Illustrated invitation to an exhibit
of Los Angeles artists.

442 Polack, Clark. A question of style - Los
Four and the Los Angeles County Museum of
Art. SOUTHWEST ART, (July, August, 1974).
English.

AN: A double-edged assessment of the
"Los Four" exhibit. The exhibition is at
once lauded for being provocative and
stimulating while at the same time failing
artistically. Author feels that special
treatment given Carlos Almaraz, Gilbert
Lujan, Roberto de la Rocha and Frank Romero
by the L.A. County Art Museum has not been
extended to other young Los Angeles artists.

443 Preuss, Karen. The new Mission murals. SAN
FRANCISCO BAY GUARDIAN, (June 28, 1975), p.
14-15. English.

AN: Mural art in San Francisco's Mission
District has covered nearly every wall and
alley on lower 24th Street. Murals by Mike
Rios, the Mujeres Muralistas (Patricia
Rodriguez, Graciela Carrillo, Consuelo
Mendez, Miriam Olivo, Irene Perez, Susan
Cervantes) appear in the area. Others have
been painted by artists associated with the
Galeria de la Raza. Illustrations.

Art Organizations & Groups (cont.)

444 Quintero, Victoria. Mujeres muralistas. LA RAZON MESTIZA, Vol. 11, (Summer 1975).

AN: Goals and artistic procedures of the Mujeres Muralistas Collective. Article emphasizes the solidarity of Latin American women and Chicanas and how their joint artistic production reflects a woman's viewpoint in aesthetic terms.

445 Quintero, Victoria. A mural is a painting on a wall done by human hands. EL TECOLOTE, Vol. 5, no. 1 (September 13, 1974), p. 6+. English.

AN: The women's collective, Mujeres Muralistas, exists within the strong San Francisco mural movement. Originally the group included Graciela Carrillo, Consuelo Mendez, Irene Perez, and Patricia Rodriguez. The group has expanded to include Susan Cervantes, Ester Hernandez, and Miriam Olivo. The two murals completed have been criticized for not being political; the women answer that they want the atmosphere to be surrounded with life, with colors. Illustrated.

446 Rand, Steve. Carlos David Almaraz. LOS ANGELES FREE PRESS, Vol. 11, no. 10 (March 8, 1974), p. 14. English.

AN: Brief biographical sketch on Mexican-born, Los Angeles artist Carlos Almaraz on the occasion of the Los Four exhibit at the Los Angeles County Museum of Art, artists who are, the author says inaccurately, largely self-taught. Almaraz studied at Garfield High School with David Ramirez, and at Otis Art Institute. One illustration.

447 Rangel, Jesus. Heirs of Jose Posada: revolution lives in Chicano art. SAN DIEGO UNION, (February 24, 1980), p. D6. English.

AN: 19th century Mexican engraver Jose Guadalupe Posada has been an inspiration to Chicano artists. Along with two exhibits of his work, the Centro Cultural de la Raza is also showing calavera (skeleton) images by Chicano artists: skull-masks from the Teatro Campesino, a print by Amalia Mesa-Baines of Frida Kahlo, and a collaged box by Jose Antonio Burciaga. Illustration: Salvador Roberto Torres work.

448 La Raza art festival. PAPEL CHICANO, Vol. 1, no. 6 (May 21, 1971), p. 8-9. English.

AN: Two-page centerfold of photographs by Johnny Almendarez of the LA RAZA ART FESTIVAL held at Ripley House in Segundo Barrio of Houston, Texas, May 5-9, 1971. Includes installation view of the exhibit, two photos of artists in action and a cover photograph of artist Pedro Rodriguez conducting a silkscreen workshop.

449 La Raza Silk Screen Center. TRA, no. 4 (1973), p. 18-25. English.

AN: Manifesto and portfolio of four posters by the San Francisco Center.

450 R.C.A.F. artistas precursores del arte chicano. EL HISPANO, Vol. 8, no. 35 (February 17, 1976), p. 1. English.

AN: Information on the R.C.A.F. organization. Includes group photograph of R.C.A.F. members, Jose Montoya, Esteban Villa, John Carrillo, Ricardo Fabela, Rudy Cuellar, Juanishi Orozco and Frank Godena.

451 Reaves, John. Santa Barbara. NEWORLD, Vol. 6, no. 2 (March, April, 1980), p. 7+. English.

AN: Report on the activities of Casa de la Raza in Santa Barbara within social context. Erroneous attribution of murals, not all of which are by Vallejo.

452 Rickey, Carrie. The writing on the wall. ART IN AMERICA, Vol. 69, no. 5 (May 1981), p. 54-57. English.

AN: Detailed article on the career of Judy Baca, director of SPARC (Social and Public Arts Resource Center) in Venice, Calif., and of the Great Wall of Los Angeles, a five year mural project at the Tujunga Wash. Well illustrated in black and white and color.

453 Rios, Sam. Chicano muralist: Toltecotl in Aztlan. Unpublished paper, 1980. English.

AN: History of pre-Columbian, Mexican, and Chicano wall paintings. Describes in detail murals by Jose Montoya, Juanishi Orozco, Esteban Villa, Stan Padilla, Juan Cervantes, Lorraine Garcia of the Centro de Artistas Chicanos, Royal Chicano Air Force, painted in 1977 at Southside Park, Sacramento, Calif. Symbolism is explained.

454 Roberts, Tim. For art's sake, for the community, for the working class. ORANGE CITY NEWS, Vol. 10, (March 14, 1979), p. 1,8-9. English.

AN: Illustrated article on Orange County, Calif. realist painter Emigdio Vasquez. Focuses on his community murals, and his attitudes toward his art. Also announces the first exhibit, "Empanada" of the newly formed Hispanic Artists Association of Orange County. 13 participants including Vasquez.

455 Rodriguez, Luis. A Center for Cultural Preservation and Human Resources. SOMOS, Vol. 1, no. 4 (September 1978), p. 26-29. English.

AN: Report on the founding, purposes, and continuing social and cultural activities of the Casa de La Raza. Illustrated.

456 Romero, Raul V. Chicanarte, a major exposition of California arts. NEWORLD, (Fall 1975). English.

AN: CHICANARTE at the Los Angeles Municipal Gallery, Barnsdall Park from Sept. 14 -Oct. 12, 1975 remains the most comprehensive statewide exposition of Chicano arts in California. This article details the production apparatus and history of the exposition. In particular, the contributions of Al Frente Communications, Inc., the Chicano Arts Council of U.C.L.A. and the Comite Chicanarte. Illustrated.

Art Organizations & Groups (cont.)

457 Ruiz, Elvia. Whitewashed mural.
SENTIMIENTOS, Vol. 1, no. 2 (May 1978), p.
7-10. English.

AN: Illustrated article about Las
Mujeres Muralistas del Valle. Their mural
titled, "History of the Chicanos From a
Woman's Perspective" was vandalized. Members
of the mural group recall its creation and
comment on its destruction.

458 San Francisco. ART NEWS MAGAZINE, Vol. 69,
no. 6 (October 1970), p. 83. English.

AN: Review of Esteban Villa's show, the
first held by the newly constituted Galeria
de la Raza in San Francisco. Illustrated.

459 San Francisco's neighborhood arts program.
San Francisco, CA: San Francisco Art
Commission, [1971]. English.

AN: Booklet in pictures describing the
activities underwritten by the city and
county of San Francisco, the National
Endowment for the Arts, the San Francisco
Foundation, and the Zellerbach Family Fund.
The interracial, interethnic staff includes
Rene Yanez. Organizations listed are Galeria
de la Raza, Galeria de la Comunidad, Galeria
de las Bellas Artes, Galeria de las
Pinturas, Galeria de la Musica, Galeria de
la Poesia, Galeria de la Instruccion.

460 San Jose Museum of Art. Cinco de Mayo: el
arte chicano de hoy, the works of Mexican
American artists. Exhibition catalog, 1974.
English.

AN: Bilingual, illustrated, small
exhibition catalogue. Includes collective
work by Centro de la Gente of San Jose and
the Royal Chicano Air Force (R.C.A.F.) of
Sacramento, California. Also lists more than
twenty other exhibiting artists.

461 Santa Ana College, Santa Ana, CA and
Goldman, Shifra M. Chicano art. Exhibition
catalog, 1974. English.

AN: Thirteen California artists are
presented in a short essay defining Chicano
as a double mestizaje of Mexican mestizo and
U.S. influences that exists in a state of
"reconciled conflict." Its aim is
communication. Artists included are
Malaquias Montoya, Rupert Garcia, Manuel
Hernandez, Esteban Villa, Robert Gomez,
Harvey Tarango, Mary Helen Castro, Eduardo
Carrillo, Graciela Carrillo, and "Los Four":
Carlos Almaraz, Robert de la Rocha, Judithe
Hernandez, Gilbert Lujan and Frank Romero.

462 Santuario de N.S. [Nuestra Senora] de
Guadalupe, Santa Fe, NM. Artes Guadalupanos
de Aztlan: Samuel Leyba, Gilberto Guzman,
Geronimo Garduno, Carlos Leyba, Pancho
Hunter. Exhibition invitation, 1979.
English.

463 SF muralists display paintings. VIVA,
(October 8, 1972), p. 19. English.

AN: Paintings, and photos of murals
taken by Gilberto Romero, on display at the
New Mexico Arts Commission. Artists Sammy,
Carlos and Albert Leyba (the original
members), Gilberto Guzman and Geronimo
Garduno, part of the Artes Guadalupanos de
Aztlan, finished a mural at Tot Lot in 1971
and are team-painting La Clinica de la
Gente. They have also painted a mural for
West Las Vegas High School.

464 Sinisi, J. Sebastian J. Following footsteps
of Diego Rivera. CONTEMPORARY, (January 13,
1980), p. 28-30. English.

AN: Story on West Denver murals,
particularly by Manuel Martinez and Carlos
Sandoval at the La Alma Recreation Center,
Summer 1979. Murals done through the Denver
City Walls Project by artists belonging to
Incorporated Artes Monumentales.
Illustrated.

465 Social and public art resource center.
Brochure, [1977]. English.

AN: Brochure including the history,
philosophy, and resources of SPARC, an
outgrowth of the Los Angeles Citywide Mural
Project/Mural Resource Center headed by Judy
Baca. Illustrated.

466 Sommer, Robert. Street art. New York: Quick
Fox, 1975. English.

AN: Introductory essay covering the
history of the new mural movement, forms of
street art, politics, street sculpture, how
to locate and photograph street art. Chicano
murals include Charles Felix and others at
Estrada Courts (L.A.), RCAF murals in
Sacramento, Jose Montoya and others
(Broderick, Ca.) Marcos Raya (Chicago), Mike
Rios (Neighborhood Legal Aid, S.F.)
Mechicano Art Center (L.A.) Johnny Alvarez
(L.A.), New Mexico State Employment Bldg.,
Albuquerque mural, Lorena Street School
(L.A.), two murals, Casa de la Raza
Alternative School (Berkeley), Santa Fe, New
Mexico mural, Francisco Hernandez (L.A.),
Artes Guadalupanos de Aztlan (N. Mexico),
Willie Herron (L.A.). Better documentation
would have been welcome.

467 Sorell, Victor A. Barrio murals in Chicago:
painting the Hispanic-American experience on
"our community" walls. REVISTA
CHICANO-RIQUENA, Vol. 4, no. 4 (Fall
1976), p. 51-72. English.

AN: Important survey of Chicago's Latino
murals, with key works considered in detail.
Among the Chicano art organizations and
muralists mentioned are MARCH (Movimiento
Artistico Chicano), and Yolanda Galvan,
Juanita Jaramillo, Jose Nario, Raymond
Patlan, Vicente Mendoza, Marcos Raya,
Ricardo Alonzo, Jose G. Gonzalez and Mario
Castillo, author of the earliest Latino
mural in Chicago (1968). Puerto Rican and
non-Latino muralists and mural groups are
also discussed. Well illustrated.

468 SPARC (Social and Public Arts Resource
Center), Venice, CA and Los Angeles. Ceta
VI, Venice, CA. Hecho en Aztlan multiples:
screen printed works. Exhibition invitation,
1980. English.

AN: Invitation to an exhibit of
silkscreen prints by Hecho en Aztlan
Multiples, a small business run by Richard
Duardo. At the Social and Public Art
Resource Center, Venice, Calif.

Art Organizations & Groups (cont.)

469 Symposium on the politics of the arts:
    minorities and the arts. ARTS IN SOCIETY,
    Vol. 10, no. 3 (Fall , Winter, 1973), p.
    66-73. English.

    AN: One panel from the Colloquium
    "Politics of the Arts" presented by the UCLA
    Management in the Arts Program, Graduate
    School of Management, 1972, included, among
    others, Leonard Castellanos of Mechicano Art
    Center, and James Woods of Studio Watts
    Workshop, both in Los Angeles. A major topic
    was how minorities dealing with the
    corporate capitalist structure can keep
    control of their art programs.

470 [Tapia exhibit invitation]. Exhibition
    invitation. Santa Fe, NM: Santuario de
    Nuestra Senora de Guadalupe, 1979. English.

    AN: Invitation to an exhibit of works by
    Luis and Star Tapia.

471 Tapia, Ludy. Montoya and the art of
    survival. LA VOZ DEL PUEBLO, Vol. 3, no. 5
    (June 1972), p. 6. English.

    AN: Profile of San Francisco Bay area
    poster maker and artist Malaquias Montoya,
    who first became involved in the Chicano
    movement in San Jose working with MASC and
    EL MACHETE paper. In Berkeley (1968), he met
    Esteban Villa and, with others, formed the
    Mexican American Liberation Art Front
    (MALAF). Montoya is against elitism
    influencing Chicano art, and is concerned
    with commercialization of Chicano art and
    artists. Illustrated.

472 Testimonios de Latinoamerica. LA PRENSA SAN
    DIEGO, (October 26, 1979), p. 3. Spanish.

    AN: Announcement of an exhibit at the
    Centro Cultural de la Raza, San Diego,
    "Testimonios de Latino America" and "America
    en la mira," political graphics organized by
    Mexican artist Felipe Ehrenberg and also
    shown at the Los Angeles Contemporary
    Exhibitions gallery (LACE).

473 Thwaites, Lynette. Art on the border.
    COMMUNITY ARTS NEWSLETTER, Vol. 3, no. 3
    (July 1981). English.

    AN: The Centro Cultural de la Raza has
    been a pioneer of intercultural activity
    between Mexico and the United States in the
    San Diego area. The Arizona Commission on
    the Arts has promoted numerous exchanges and
    publishes a bilingual quarterly bulletin. In
    Mission, Texas, Xavier Gorena of the Xochil
    Art Center is forging ties with Mexico City.

474 Townsend, Dorothy and Driscoll, John. Fiesta
    honors expansion of Latino center. LOS
    ANGELES TIMES, (June 28, 1981), p. I, 3.
    English.

    AN: Ground is broken for the Ruben
    Salazar Bicertennial Building in Plaza de la
    Raza's Lincoln Park location.

475 Troelstrup, Glenn. Former delinquent paints
    his way out of corner. DENVER POST, (April
    23, 1977), p. 2. English.

    AN: Manuel Martinez started sketching at
    13; at 29, after studying with Siqueiros
    (1967-68), he painted a number of murals in
    Denver and Albuquerque. In 1977 he organized
    Incorporated Artists Monumentales. Color
    illustration.

476 Tully, Robert. City walls. LA VOZ (Denver,
    CO), (August 3, 1979), p. 7. English.

    AN: In a project managed by Metro Denver
    Urban Coalition, several Chicano artists
    were hired to work consistently in creating
    murals for the inner city. Article focuses
    on the goals, procedures, and activities of
    the muralists. Grouped as Incorporated Artes
    Monumentales, the group included Jerry
    Jaramillo, Steve Lucero, Al Sanchez, Fred
    Sanchez, and Carlos Sandoval. Illustrated by
    a group photograph of artists and a
    photograph of a wall painting by the
    Chilean-led Brigada Orlando Letelier in
    Denver.

477 Unique $1000 art competition beautifies East
    L.A.: community votes for favorite bus bench
    paintings. PACEMAKER, (February 1972).
    English.

    AN: Mechicano Art Center contest to
    beautify the community by painting bus
    benches for maximum public exposure. Eight
    of 29 benches illustrated.

478 University Art Museum, Berkeley, CA. The
    Fifth Sun: Contemporary/Traditional Chicano
    & Latino Art. Exhibition catalog, 1977.
    English.

    AN: Catalog of exhibit including 45
    artists of northern California. Texts deal
    with Mexican muralists, Mujeres Muralistas &
    other muralists, posters, the Chicano art
    movement, altars, La Raza Silkscreen Center,
    Galeria de la Raza, the Mexican Museum, the
    Sacramento Centro de Artistas Chicanos/RCAF.
    Mural maps of S.F. Bay Area and Sacramento.
    Many illustrations.

479 Unzueta, Manuel and La Casa de la Raza
    Gallery, Santa Barbara, CA. Murals art
    murals art: featuring the murals of la Casa
    de la Raza, Santa Barbara, California.
    Exhibition brochure, n.d. English.

    AN: Illustrated booklet of Unzueta's
    murals and easel paintings.

480 Valdez, Armando. El calendario chicano 1975.
    Hayward, CA: Southwest Network, 1975.
    English.

    AN: Third in a series of historical
    calendars produced in 1972 and 1974 by La
    Causa Publications and Southwest Network.
    Artists included for each month are Carmen
    Lomas Garza, Sergio Hernandez, Malaquias
    Montoya, Mujeres Muralistas (Graciela
    Carrillo, Venezuelan Consuelo Mendez, Irene
    Perez, Patricia Rodriguez), Ramses Noriega,
    Ernie Palomino, Amado Maurilio Pena, Martin
    Perez. All but Texan Pena are California
    artists.

481 Valencia, Manuel. Store front academy for
    Chicano artists. SACRAMENTO UNION, (January
    17, 1973). English.

    AN: Article includes comments by Armando
    Cid, Ricardo Fabela and Jose Montoya in a
    free-wheeling discussion of the goals and
    underlying philosophy of the Centro de
    Artistas Chicanos in Sacramento. More than
    simply exposing the people to art, the
    artists explain that they are looking for an
    alternative art expression and method of
    instruction never offered in traditional art
    schools or university departments of art.

Art Organizations & Groups (cont.)

482 Venegas, Sybil. Conditions for producing Chicana art. CHISMEARTE, Vol. 1, no. 4 (Fall, Winter, 1977, 1978), p. 2, 4. English.

AN: Chicana artists face more obstacles than white women or Chicano counterparts in the arts. Mexican life style has portrayed the ideal of a submissive woman, but the values have changed. Chicana artists are concerned with women and their struggles. Muralists include Patricia Rodriguez, Irene Perez, Consuelo Mendez de Castillo, Susan Cervantes, Ester Hernandez, Miriam Olivo, Ruth Rodriguez, of the Mujeres Muralistas (San Francisco). Other artists are Etta Delgado and Barbara Carrasco.

483 Venegas, Sybil. Dia de los muertos. SOMOS, Vol. 1, no. 5 (October 1978), p. 42-47. English.

AN: Brief history of Dia de los muertos ceremonies. While the custom is dying in Mexico (except for tourists), Chicano organizations like Galeria de la Raza (S.F.), El Centro de Artistas Chicanos (Sacramento, Ca.) celebrate the event annually, as does [Self-Help Graphics and Art, Inc.] in East Los Angeles. Well illustrated with photographs by Guillermo Bejarano and Daniel Duran.

484 Wasserman, Isabelle. Photos on exhibit capture Mexican revolution. SAN DIEGO UNION, (November 26, 1981), p. D10. English.

AN: Report on the photographic exhibition of Mexican revolutionary photographer Agustin V. Casasola at the Centro Cultural de la Raza in San Diego. Illustrated.

485 Werley, Lenora. Murals give young artists community pride, sculptor says. YUMA DAILY SUN, (February 4, 1981). English.

AN: Mesa, Arizona sculptor Adolfo "Zarco" Guerrero feels murals give young people pride in their community. Guerrero is part of the Xicanindio Artist Coalition that is CETA-contracted to run summer art programs for high school students. Illustrated.

486 West Colorado Gallery, Pasadena, CA. Gronk/Patssi. Exhibition brochure, 1979. English.

AN: Works on exhibit by ASCO members Gronk and Patssi Valdez. Photo of artists.

487 Wilson, Anne. Chicanos show off talents in Magna SOCIO projects. SALT LAKE CITY TRIBUNE, (July 9, 1979), p. C-1. English.

AN: In the rural Utah community of Magna, SOCIO (Spanish Speaking Organization for Community Integrity and Opportunity) established various art projects. Three murals were painted by community youth under the guidance of Robert Archuleta and Becky Berru. One of the murals depicts "man and labor." Illustrated with photographs of project directors, maquette of the mural and a mural painting "brigade".

488 Wilson, William. 30 works from the grass roots. LOS ANGELES TIMES, (June 4, 1973), p. IV,2. English.

AN: Review of a show at the Junior Arts Center in Barnsdall Park by 15 members of the Mechicano Art Center. The critic feels contemporary groups that aim for change today (unlike past groups) are unable to articulate their spirit in a cohesive style. The top talent in this show is Charles Almaraz; also on exhibit are paintings by Jose Cervantes, Guillermo Martinez, Ray Atilano, sculpture by Manuel Cruz, and photography by (Oscar) R. Castillo.

489 Wilson, William. Art of barrios in East L.A. LOS ANGELES TIMES, (July 27, 1970), p. IV,1+. English.

AN: Rather personalized view of ARTE DE LOS BARRIOS traveling exhibit organized by Casa Hispana de Bellas Artes with Artistas Latinos Americanos, San Francisco, and featuring "100 Chicano paintings, photographs, and other works of art".

490 Wilson, William. A bit of the barrio at County Museum. LOS ANGELES TIMES, (February 27, 1974), p. IV, 1+. English.

AN: Review of the Los Four exhibit at the Los Angeles County Museum of Art. Quotes from artists, history of group's formation in 1973.

491 Wilson, William. Chicana artists still seeking identification. LOS ANGELES TIMES, (June 23, 1975), p. VI, 5. English.

AN: Ten Chicana artists are exhibiting their work in the Boathouse Gallery of Plaza de la Raza in Lincoln Park: Judithe Hernandez, Patssi Valdez, Judy Baca, Josefina Quesada, Victoria del Castillo-Leon, Olga Muniz, Gloria Flores, Sylvia Morales, Isabel Castro and Celia Tejadak. The work is still tentative and may develop.

492 Wilson, William. 'Los Four' a statement of Chicano spirit. CALENDAR, (March 10, 1974), p. 64+. English.

AN: Lengthy critical review of Los Four exhibit at Los Angeles County Museum of Art. Illustrated.

493 Woodblock and linoleum prints by Carlos Cortez, member of the Chicago mural group. TIN TAN, Vol. 2, no. 6 (December 1, 1977). English.

AN: Seven works reproduced from prints by Cortez, also an active member of the Movimiento Artistico Chicano of Chicago, dating from 1971 to 1976.

494 Xochil Art and Culture Center, Mission, TX. Besame mucho. Exhibition invitation, 1979. English.

AN: Invitation to exhibit of Texas artists from Mujeres Artistas del Suroeste (MAS): Mary Ann Anguiano, Alicia Arredondo, Santa Barraza, Nora Gonzales-Dodson, Maria Flores, Carolina Flores, Mary Ann Ambray Gonzales, Sylvia Orozco, Nancy de los Santos, Modesta Barbina Trevino. Illustrated.

Art Organizations & Groups (cont.)

495 Xochitiotzin, Antonia. Que viva el arte de la Raza! GRITO DEL NORTE, Vol. 5, no. 4 (June 27, 1972), p. 1. English.

AN: Front page article on "Los Artes Guadalupanos de Aztlan," a mural group in Santa Fe, NM. Focus on aims and function of organization. Illustrated with photographs of four murals painted by group.

Art Patronage

496 Celebrate!: the story of the Museum of International Folk Art. Santa Fe, NM: Museum of New Mexico Press, 1979. English.

AN: History of the Museum; its founding in 1953 by Chicago philanthropist Florence Dibell Bartlett; its patronage of New Mexico Hispanic crafts as well as international crafts.

Art Philosophy
USE: Philosophy of Art

Arte Chicanesca

497 Blum, Walter. The vision behind the mirror. CALIFORNIA LIVING, (November 26, 1978), p. 40-44. English.

AN: Illustrated article with background information on the non-Chicano photographers (Roger Minick, Morrie Camhi, and Abigail Heyman) who spent a year documenting the Chicano community. Their work was issued as a portfolio, "Espejo: Reflections of the Mexican American," by the Mexican-American Legal Defense and Educational Fund (MALDEF). It is one of the most extensive photographic records made of the Chicano experience.

498 California. University. Los Angeles. Instructional Media Library. 1975-76 film catalog. Film catalog, 1976, p. 30-31. English.

AN: List of films available from the Chicano Film Collection. 34 films on Chicano and Mexican subjects by Chicano and non-Chicano film makers.

499 Conversation on photography in the Los Angeles Latino community. OBSCURA, Vol. 2, no. 2 (December, February, 1981, 1982), p. 22-32. English.

AN: Interview on the nature and distinguishing characteristics of Chicano photography with Chicano photographers Isabel Castro (Council for Latino Photography), Lorenzo Hernandez (Director of Cityscape Gallery, publisher PHOTOSHOW magazine), Joseph G. Uribe (California State University, Los Angeles, Center for the Visual Arts, Director of West Colorado Gallery), Patssi Valdez, Becky Villasenor, and sculptor, curator, and Art Director for Academia Quinto Sol, Inc., Linda Vallejo, Portfolio of photography by Chicanos Don Anton, Louis Carlos Bernal, Sean Carrillo, Patssi Valdez, Ricardo Valverde, and by Morrie Camhi and Elizabeth Sisco on Chicano subjects.

500 Del Olmo, Frank. Chicano gang turns to art. LOS ANGELES TIMES, (September 11, 1973), p. II, 3. English.

AN: Residents of the East Los Angeles barrio "Lil' Valley" dedicate a mural memorializing Chicano gang members who have died violently. The mural was painted by 40 gang members guided by professional artist Bill Butler.

501 Espejo: reflections of the Mexican American: Louis Carlos Bernal, Morrie Camhi, Abigail Heyman, Roger Minick, Neal Slavin. SOMOS, Vol. 2, no. 1 (February 1978), p. 26-35. English.

AN: Announcement of the ESPEJO photographic exhibit to be held at Goez Gallery in East Los Angeles. Statements by the four artists and a portfolio of their works: Abigail Heyman, Roger Minick, Morrie Camhi, and Arizona Chicano photographer Louis Carlos Bernal. Includes color photographs by Bernal on cover. This 1979 issue is erroneously dated 1978.

502 Fischer, Hal. Espejo: reflections of the Mexican American: Louis Carlos Bernal, Morrie Camhi, Abigail Heyman, Roger Minick, Neal Slavin. PICTURE MAGAZINE, no. 9 (1978). English.

AN: Oversize portfolio of photographs recording contemporary Mexican American life commissioned by the Mexican American Legal Defense and Education Fund. Three photographers, Louis Carlos Bernal (from Arizona), Morrie Camhi and Abagail Heyman focus on the family and the home; the fourth, Roger Minick, juxtaposes the Mexican American against "barrio" murals. Only Bernal is Chicano. 24 photographs, six of which (Bernal's) are in color.

503 Four and four: Mexican and Latino photography, April 25 through June 14 on the balcony. CALENDAR: SANTA BARBARA MUSEUM OF ART, (April 1981). English.

AN: Announcement of exhibit organized by Lorenzo Hernandez of the Cityscape Foto Gallery, Pasadena, Calif. Sought to present "the observable differences between the 'classic' vision of the Mexican National and the 'realistic' vision of the re-rooted Mexican/American." The latter included Louis Bernal (Tucson) and Ricardo Valverde (Los Angeles) as well as two Spanish Sephardics of Los Angeles, Camhi and Sisco.

504 Gonzalez, Jose Carlos. Consejo mexicano de fotografia: foto latino en el suroeste de los Estado Unidos. ARTES VISUALES, Vol. 29, no. 29 (June 1981), p. 55-56. Spanish.

AN: Review of a photography show in Mexico City organized by Lorenzo Hernandez, Cityscape Photo Gallery of Pasadena, and the Council of Latino Photography/USA. The show featured Latinos of the Southwest and Latino themes by non-Latino photographers.

505 Lucas, Jerry and Gil de Montes, Roberto, et al. CHOQUE DE AMOR: fotonovela by Lamp. Los Angeles, CA: Colectivo El Ojo, Latin American Studies Dept., CSULA, 1979. English.

AN: "Fotonovela" featuring Elsa Flores, Rosa Marin, and Jerry Lucas produced by the collective work of Lucas, Roberto Gil de Montes, Mario Massinelli, Luis Soto, and Kay Torres.

Arte Chicanesca (cont.)

506 NATIONAL MURALS NETWORK COMMUNITY
NEWSLETTER. (Fall 1980). English.

AN: Reports on murals in San Francisco,
CA, by the Chicano Moratorium Coalition; in
Chicago about the Anti-War Preparations
mural; in Houston by a student at the
Association for Advancement of Mexican
Americans; on Michael Schorr's mural in
Chicanok, San Diego, CA; on a segment being
painted at the Tujunga Wash mural in Los
Angeles under Judy Baca; on south San Diego
murals being painted out; Alan Barnett's
survey of Southwest murals. Illustrated.

507 Oakland Museum, Oakland, CA. Espejo:
reflections of the Mexican American: Louis
Carlos Bernal, Morrie Camhi, Abigail Heyman,
Roger Minick, Neal Slavin. Exhibit brochure,
1978. English.

AN: Twenty-five photographs from the
documentary series commissioned by the
Mexican American Legal Defense and Education
Fund. Only Bernal is Chicano.

508 Pettit, Arthur G. Images of the Mexican
American in fiction and film. College
Station, TX: Texas A & M Univ. Press, 1980.
English.

AN: A study on Anglo-American attitudes
toward Mexican people in the Southwest as
reflected in the sterotypes of popular
literature and film. Most of the book is
historical. The afterword (by Dennis
Showalter) argues that these patterns have
not improved, citing television series such
as CHICO AND THE MAN and CHIPS.

509 Rivera, Humberto R. Film notes. CHISMEARTE,
Vol. 1, no. 2 (Winter, Spring, 1977), p.
20-24. English.

AN: Summary of films produced by and/or
about Chicanos for cinema and television.
Includes REALIDADES (TV) by David Sandoval,
Rudy Vargas, Luis Torres, Jose Luis Ruiz,
Antonio Reyes; A POLITICAL RENAISSANCE from
the LA RAZA series (TV) by Moctezuma
Esparza; CHILDREN OF THE STATE by Andres
Markovits, Richard Trubo, Frank Christopher
(film); LA RAZA UNIDA (released as RAICES DE
SANGRE) by Jesus Salvador Trevino (Mexican
film by a Chicano); CHULAS FRONTERAS (film)
by Les Blank; THE MURALS OF EAST LOS
ANGELES, A MUSEUM WITHOUT WALLS by Humberto
R. Rivera and Heather R. Howell.
Announcement for the National Latino Media
Coalition.

510 Varda, Agnes. Mur murs/mural murals on the
wall ... Film, Cine Tamaris, Paris, 1980.
English.

AN: Full length documentary film
produced for French television; also
available with English subtitles. Deals
impressionistically with the murals and
muralists of Los Angeles. Included are Wayne
Alaniz Healy, David Botello, Willie Herron,
Manuel Cruz, Judy Baca, the murals in
Venice, CA, graffiti - among others. Color.

511 Wilson, Michael and Biberman, Herbert. Salt
of the earth [film]. 16mm, 94 min., b&w.
English.

AN: The first feature film made in the
U.S. of, by and for labor, it deals with a
real strike of Mexican American miners in
New Mexico in which women played a key role

in the men's victory and their own demands.
Mexican actress Rosaura Revueltas starred
with labor leader Juan Chacon. One of the
best films on the subject.

512 Wilson, William. Photography - the state of
the art. CALENDAR, (January 28, 1979), p.
87. English.

AN: Includes review of ESPEJO:
REFLECTIONS OF THE MEXICAN-AMERICAN exhibit:
four photographers--Louis Carlos Bernal,
Abigail Heyman, Morrie Camhi, and Roger
Minick--who worked independently for a year
to record facets of Chicano life.

ARTE DE LOS BARRIOS [exhibit]

513 Wilson, William. Art of barrios in East L.A.
LOS ANGELES TIMES, (July 27, 1970), p.
IV,1+. English.

AN: Rather personalized view of ARTE DE
LOS BARRIOS traveling exhibit organized by
Casa Hispana de Bellas Artes with Artistas
Latinos Americanos, San Francisco, and
featuring "100 Chicano paintings,
photographs, and other works of art".

Arte Popular

514 Garcia, Rupert. 'Fifth Sun' Raza art show at
UC Berkeley Museum. EL TECOLOTE, Vol. 8, no.
3 (November 1977), p. 8+. English.

AN: Review of THE FIFTH SUN:
CONTEMPORARY TRADITIONAL CHICANO AND LATINO
ART, co-sponsored by University of
California, Berkeley Chicano Studies and
Arte Popular, and curated by artist Ralph
Maradiaga, co-director of Galeria de la
Raza, showing at the UC Berkeley Museum. It
will travel to the University of California,
Santa Barbara's Art Museum. Illustrated.

Arte Seis [art organization]

515 Martinez, Anita. Raza! Arte! Raza! Arte!
EL TECOLOTE, Vol. 1, no. 2 (September 7,
1970), p. 3. Bilingual.

AN: Galeria de la Raza opened on July,
1970 at 425 14th St. San Francisco. It was
an outgrowth of the Arte Seis organization
(an art effort established in the Mission
District in 1967 by Francisco Camplis,
Rupert Garcia, Ralph McNeil, Jay Ojeda and
Jack Ruiz). These and other artists brought
together by the Neighborhood Arts Program
have coalesced in the new Galeria de la
Raza. Article gives goals, organizational
scheme and plans for the Galeria. It's first
exhibit was a one man show by Esteban Villa
together with a photo and sketch exhibit on
Cuba by Jay Ojeda, Roberto Diaz Perez and
Gloria Ozuna. Illustrated with installation
view of new Galeria.

Artes 6 Gallery, San Francisco, CA

516 Artes 6 Gallery, San Francisco, CA. Mixed
media. Exhibition announcement, [ca.
1969-70]. English.

AN: Announcement of exhibit including
Jim Cortez, Luis Cervantez, Vicente Rascon,
Rene Yanes, Graciela Carrillo, Lorenza
Camplis. The Artes 6 artists eventually
formed the Galeria de la Raza of San
Francisco.

Artes Antigua Society

517 Benson, Nancy C. Preserving an early
Hispanic art. EMPIRE MAGAZINE, (June 8,
1980), p. 50. English.

AN: 84-year-old colcha-stitchery artist
Maria Theofila Lujan is a founding member of
a stitchery group of the 1930s, now called
Artes Antigua Society. Her work is in museum
collections.

ARTES DE LA RAZA [exhibit]

518 Albright, Thomas. Oakland Museum: a wide
range in Latin art. SAN FRANCISCO CHRONICLE,
(September 12, 1970), p. 33. English.

AN: A large show called ARTES DE LA RAZA
at the Oakland Museum includes Mercedes
Gutierrez-McDermid, Louis Gutierrez, Luis
Cervantez, Calvin Tondre, Manuel Villamor,
Rene Yanez, Jose Ramirez, Jorge Lerma,
Rolando Castellon, Esteban Villa, Rupert
Garcia, and Gustavo Rivera who is also
having an exhibit at the Galeria de la Raza.

Los Artes Guadalupanos de Aztlan, Santa Fe, NM

519 Bartak, Bonnie. Murals make walls political
forum. ARIZONA REPUBLIC, (April 21, 1975),
p. A-12. English.

AN: Tempe, AZ murals located at the
Valle del Sol Institute (South 1st St.), the
Tempe Escalante Center (East Orange), and
the Barrio Youth Project (South 1st St.).
Illustrated.

520 Callum, Diane. Regional report, The arts:
walls of passion. NUESTRO, Vol. 3, no. 11
(December 1979), p. 16, 51. English.

AN: Focusing on muralist Gilberto
Guzman, one of the founders of Artes
Guadalupanos in Santa Fe, the article
details his efforts in the promotion and
preservation of Chicano murals in New
Mexico.

521 Chavez, Jaime and Vallecillo, Ana Maria. A
political, historical, philosophical
perspective of muralist art in the
Southwest. RAYAS, Vol. 1, no. 3 (May, June,
1978), p. 6. English.

AN: Relates Chicano mural art to main
issues of the Chicano movement. The
Mechicano Art Center in Los Angeles and
Artes Guadalupanos de Aztlan in Santa Fe are
seen as examples of groups creating a new
people's art; art forms where esthetics are
allied to politics.

522 Cockcroft, Eva; Weber, John; and Cockcroft,
James D. Towards a people's art: the
contemporary mural movement. New York: E.P.
Dutton, 1977. English.

AN: A survey of the street mural
movement in the United States, from about
1967 on. Several chapters are written by the
artists themselves: John Weber on the
Chicago mural group; Susan Shapiro-Kiok on
Cityarts Workshop of New York; Eva Cockcroft
on People's painters of New Jersey; Geronimo
Garduno on Artes Guadalupanos de Aztlan of
New Mexico. Chicano murals illustrated
include those of Mujeres Muralistas, Ray
Patlan, William F. Herron, Hoyo-Mara Gang,
Artes Guadalupanos de Aztlan, Vicente
Mendoza and Jose Nario (with Patlan) Mario
Castillo, Michael Rios, Toltecas en Aztlan,

Roberto Chavez, Ernie Palomino, Chuy
Campusano and Luis Cortazar (with Rios).

523 Corneil, Paul. Militant barrio murals of
Santa Fe. Venice, CA: Environmental
Communications, n.d. English.

AN: Annotated slide catalog with
introductory text about the mural group Los
Artes Guadalupanos de Aztlan of Santa Fe.
Gilberto Guzman is mentioned as one of the
group.

524 Fitch, Bob. Los artes: a story the people
live as well as paint. YOUTH MAGAZINE, Vol.
26, no. 3 (March 1975), p. 2-11. English.

AN: Illustrated story on the formation
and early murals of Los Artes Guadalupanos
de Aztlan of Santa Fe.

525 Greenberg, David; Smith, Kathryn; and
Teacher, Stuart. Megamurals & supergraphics:
big art. Philadelphia, PN: Running Press,
1977. English.

AN: A full-color picture book of murals
throughout the United States. Chicano murals
include Michael Rios (San Francisco),
Mujeres Muralistas (San Francisco), Leonard
Castellanos and Tomas Gonzales with others
(Los Angeles), Los Artes Guadalupanos de
Aztlan (New Mexico), Willie Herron (Los
Angeles), Toltecas en Aztlan (San Diego),
David Botello (Los Angeles), David Lopez and
Arizona Mara Gang (Los Angeles), Vatos de
Maravilla (Los Angeles), Carlito Gaegos (Los
Angeles), Gil Hernandez (Los Angeles), Wayne
[Alaniz] Healy (Los Angeles).

526 Kroll, Eric. Folk art in the barrios.
NATURAL HISTORY, Vol. 82, no. 5 (May 1973),
p. 56-65. English.

AN: Well-illustrated informative report
on Santa Fe, New Mexico murals by Los Artes
Guadalupanos de Aztlan. Author's somewhat
condescending attitude rectified in the
ARTFORUM reprint which drops the term "folk
art".

527 Pepe and Pepito. SANTA FE NEW MEXICAN,
(August 16, 1972), p. A2. English.

AN: Among the barrio groups receiving
funding from the COPAS Cultural Awareness
Program of the Model Cities program are Los
Artesanos and Los Artes Guadalupanos.

528 Santuario de N.S. [Nuestra Senora] de
Guadalupe, Santa Fe, NM. Artes Guadalupanos
de Aztlan: Samuel Leyba, Gilberto Guzman,
Geronimo Garduno, Carlos Leyba, Pancho
Hunter. Exhibition invitation, 1979.
English.

529 SF muralists display paintings. VIVA,
(October 8, 1972), p. 19. English.

AN: Paintings, and photos of murals
taken by Gilberto Romero, on display at the
New Mexico Arts Commission. Artists Sammy,
Carlos and Albert Leyba (the original
members), Gilberto Guzman and Geronimo
Garduno, part of the Artes Guadalupanos de
Aztlan, finished a mural at Tot Lot in 1971
and are team-painting La Clinica de la
Gente. They have also painted a mural for
West Las Vegas High School.

Los Artes Guadalupanos de Aztlan, Santa Fe, NM
(cont.)

530 Sommer, Robert. Street art. New York: Quick
Fox, 1975. English.

AN: Introductory essay covering the
history of the new mural movement, forms of
street art, politics, street sculpture, how
to locate and photograph street art. Chicano
murals include Charles Felix and others at
Estrada Courts (L.A.), RCAF murals in
Sacramento, Jose Montoya and others
(Broderick, Ca.) Marcos Raya (Chicago), Mike
Rios (Neighborhood Legal Aid, S.F.)
Mechicano Art Center (L.A.) Johnny Alvarez
(L.A.), New Mexico State Employment Bldg.,
Albuquerque mural, Lorena Street School
(L.A.), two murals, Casa de la Raza
Alternative School (Berkeley), Santa Fe, New
Mexico mural, Francisco Hernandez (L.A.),
Artes Guadalupanos de Aztlan (N. Mexico),
Willie Herron (L.A.). Better documentation
would have been welcome.

531 Xochitiotzin, Antonia. Que viva el arte de
la Raza! GRITO DEL NORTE, Vol. 5, no. 4
(June 27, 1972), p. 1. English.

AN: Front page article on "Los Artes
Guadalupanos de Aztlan," a mural group in
Santa Fe, NM. Focus on aims and function of
organization. Illustrated with photographs
of four murals painted by group.

Los Artesanos [art group], Santa Fe, NM

532 Pepe and Pepito. SANTA FE NEW MEXICAN,
(August 16, 1972), p. A2. English.

AN: Among the barrio groups receiving
funding from the COPAS Cultural Awareness
Program of the Model Cities program are Los
Artesanos and Los Artes Guadalupanos.

Artistas de Aztlan [art group], Tempe, AZ

533 Bartak, Bonnie. Murals make walls political
forum. ARIZONA REPUBLIC, (April 21, 1975),
p. A-12. English.

AN: Tempe, AZ murals located at the
Valle del Sol Institute (South 1st St.), the
Tempe Escalante Center (East Orange), and
the Barrio Youth Project (South 1st St.).
Illustrated.

**Artistas de la Nueva Raza [art group], San
Antonio, TX**

534 Cantu, Jesus "Chista". Entrevista: Jesus
Maria Cantu, 'El Chista'. MAGAZIN, Vol. 1,
no. 4 (April 1972), p. 52-65. Spanish.

AN: Discusses his life in San Antonio;
his apprenticeship since childhood to his
uncle Miguel Angel Tellez who taught him to
paint billboards, wall signs and church
decorations; his membership in the group
Artistas de la Nueva Raza; his artistic and
political philosophy. In Spanish.

Los Artistas de los Barrios (San Diego, CA)

535 Monteverde, Mildred. Contemporary Chicano
art. AZTLAN, Vol. 2, no. 2 (Fall   1971), p.
51-61. Bibliography. English.

AN: An historical survey of trends and
influences on contemporary Chicano art.
Discusses San Diego's Toltecas en Aztlan and
the projected Centro Cultural de la Raza;
Los Angeles' Mechicano Art Center, Goez
Gallery and Plaza de la Raza; pinto (prison)

art; New Mexican art. Many artists are
mentioned.

**Artistas Latinos Americanos [art group], San
Francisco, CA**

536 Wilson, William. Art of barrios in East L.A.
LOS ANGELES TIMES, (July 27, 1970), p.
IV,1+. English.

AN: Rather personalized view of ARTE DE
LOS BARRIOS traveling exhibit organized by
Casa Hispana de Bellas Artes with Artistas
Latinos Americanos, San Francisco, and
featuring "100 Chicano paintings,
photographs, and other works of art".

Artistas Latinos de Orange County, CA

537 Mills House Visual Arts Complex, Garden
Grove, CA. Menudo: artistas latinos de
Orange County. Exhibit invitation, 1980.
English.

AN: Invitation to an exhibit organized
for the first anniversary of Artistas
Latinos de Orange County including Delores
Grajeda, William Hernandez, Marylee Montano,
Patricia Murillo, Irene Ramos, Juan Ramos,
Ricardo Serrato, Miguel Shanahan, Arthur
Valenzuela, Benjamin Valenzuela, Jack
Vargas, Alonzo Whitney, Emigdio Vasquez,
Susana Zaccagnino, and Mexican artist
Artemio Sepulveda.

Artists

538 59th Street Gallery, St. Louis, MO. Midwest
Mexican-American art exhibit: Mexico and its
artists. Exhibition brochure, 1981. English.

AN: Sponsored by the Sociedad Mexicana
"Benito Juarez" and the international
Institute of St. Louis, this three-part
exhibit includes 1) MEXICO AS SEEN BY HER
CHILDREN, a bilingual exhibit from Mexico
traveling under Smithsonian Institution
auspices, 2) MEXICAN CHILDREN IN THE U.S.A.,
3) MEXICAN AMERICAN ARTISTS. In the latter
are included Stephen Capiz (Roseville,
Minn.), Jose Gonzalez (Chicago), Cesar A.
Martinez (San Antonio), Ada Medina (Des
Moines), Nora Chapa Mendoza (West
Bloomfield, Mich.), Rene David
Michel-Trapaga (St. Louis), David Munoz
(Kansas City, Mo.), Jose Luis Narezo (Grand
Rapids, Mich.), Benny Ordonez, Roman
Villarreal (Chicago), Alejandro Romero
(Chicago), Aurelio Diaz "Tekpankalli"
(Chicago), Simon Ybarra (St. Louis).

539 Acosta, a man and his art. NOSOTROS, Vol. 2,
no. 6. English.

AN: Biographical information and
thematic analysis of the work of El Paso
artist Manuel Acosta. He is especially
noted for genre paintings of humble people
reflecting social life and cultural
traditions.

Artists (cont.)

540 Acosta, Dan. Paintings reflect life experiences. THE ECCENTRIC, (June 26, 1980). English.

AN: Review of one-woman show by Nora Chapa Mendoza at the Heritage Art Gallery, Ypsilanti, MI. Mendoza works in abstract impressionist style with wet streams of colors that express energy. Her subjects are landscapes, moods, nudes, and Hispanic themes. She is active in the Detroit Latino Artist Association, Nuestras Artes de Michigan, and the New Detroit Art Council.

541 Adrienne Simard Gallery, Los Angeles, CA. Presenting Carlos Almaraz: pastel drawings, 1969-1981. Exhibition invitation, 1981. English.

AN: Invitation to exhibit of Los Angeles painter Carlos Almaraz. includes color illustration.

542 Aguayo, Emilio. Chicano art: a new art-style of the future. (Unpublished Study Project for Prof. Brauman, Art Dept., Univ. of Washington, Seattle), June 6, 1972. English.

AN: Autobiographical account and self-analysis of artist's work. Beginning in 1965 the artist has created 40,000 small ink drawings in a contour line technique. Situating himself within the Chicano Arts Movement, Aguayo describes his dominant themes, symbols, and stylistic preoccupations.

543 Aguila, Pancho. 11 poems. MANGO, (1977). English.

AN: Art works by Northern California artists Emmanuel Montoya and Jose Antonio Burciaga.

544 Aguirre, Tito. Interview with artist Jose Trevino. ARRIBA, Vol. 2, no. 2 (1981). English.

AN: Biographical information and artistic trajectory of Austin artist Jose Trevino. Illustrated with photo of artist and three of his portraits.

545 Alba-King Kong Studios, Chicago, IL. Latina Art Expo '77. Chicago, IL: ALBA-King Kong Studios, 1977. English.

AN: An exhibit by 16 Chicana, Mexican, Puerto Rican and other Latina artists. Brief biographies of the artists.

546 Alex Maldonado, primitive painter. SAN FRANCISCO FOCUS MAGAZINE, (1973). English.

AN: Biographical information on 72 year old Alexander Maldonado who started painting upon his retirement. His "naif" work has gained wide critical acclaim and he has had more than 200 exhibitions throughout the United States. Illustrated with reproduction of one of Maldonado's paintings.

547 Almaraz, Carlos. The artist as a revolutionary. CHISMEARTE, no. 1 (Fall 1976), p. 47-55. English.

AN: Los Angeles painter Carlos D. Almaraz gives a detailed history of a cartoon-banner he made for the first constitutional convention of the United Farm Workers of America while he was an illustrator for EL MALCRIADO, and a mural he did for the UFWA administration building in La Paz. He also elucidates his philosophy about politics, the role of the revolutionary artist in our time, and the artist's relation to the bourgeois art market.

548 Altars as folk art. ARRIBA, Vol. 1, no. 1 (July 1980), p. 4. English.

AN: Focusing on the home altar of Josefina De Leon from Cuero, Texas, the article describes this folk expression on two levels: first as a subjective religious intermediator and secondly as a masterpiece of collected objects. Contains interesting information on the form, function and meaning of altars. Illustrated with photographs.

549 Amor sin fronteras. Los Angeles, CA: Colectivo El Ojo, n.d.. English.

AN: Fotonovela with Josefina Arce, Eduardo Dominguez and Mike Jauregui produced by the Colectivo: Eduardo Dominguez, Roberto Gil de Montes, Jerry Lucas, Kay Torres, students at California State University, Los Angeles.

550 Anderson, Howard J.; Young, Robert S.; and Kilgore, Andrew. Amado Maurilio Pena, Jr. Albuquerque, NM: Robert Stephan Young Publishing Co., 1981. English.

AN: Coffee-table type of art book about the Laredo-born painter and printmaker. The text includes impressionistic writing about Pena's life, interlaced with statements by the artist about his life and work. Though including a few plates from his early (1974-1978) political and family silkscreens, over 50 color plates reproduce his "Santa Fe Indian" works from 1978 to the present.

551 Andrews, Colman. Art of the state: California. NEW WEST MAGAZINE, (January 1981), p. 54-59. English.

AN: Short text on California artists who are presumably influenced by the state's light, color, space, etc. Works of 16 artists reproduced in full color, including one by Carlos Almaraz of Los Angeles. Statements by each artist.

552 Andrews, Rena. The fine arts. ROUNDUP, (March 15, 1970), p. 16+. English.

AN: Biographical information on Chicano artist Ramon Kelley. Described as an impressionist, his work has affinity with Monet and Manet.

553 Andrews, Rena. The fine arts. ROUNDUP, (November 25, 1973), p. 22. English.

AN: Article places work of Ramon Kelley within the impressionist mode. At the De Colores Gallery in his hometown of Denver, Kelley's exhibit titled, "Faces of the Southwest" included drawings, water color and pastel painting, oils and acrylics.

Artists (cont.)

554 Art Gallery, California State University,
Long Beach and Lujan, Gilbert Sanchez
"Magu". El arte del pocho. Exhibit brochure,
October 1968. English.

AN: Information about Southern
California artists John Deheras, Marcus
Villagran, Roberto de la Rocha, Santos
Zuniga, Crispin Gonzales, Richard Martinez,
Jesus Gutierrez, Ed Oropeza, Pete Mendez,
David Ramirez, Gilbert Sanchez Lujan, Willie
Hernandez, Art Ponce, Carmen Tostado, Al
Almeida, David Ceja, Robert E. Chavez,
Thomas A. Ferriera. All art students,
graduates, or faculty.

555 Art Gallery, University of California,
Irvine and Los Angeles County Museum of Art,
Los Angeles, CA. Los Four: Almaraz, de la
Rocha, Lujan, Romero. Exhibition brochure,
1973-74. English.

AN: Photographs and biographies of
Carlos Almaraz, Roberto de la Rocha, Gilbert
S. Lujan, Frank Romero.

556 The art of Rodolfo Leal. TIN TAN, Vol. 2,
no. 6 (December 1, 1977), p. 15-18. English.

AN: Two calligraphic ink drawings and a
serigraph by Texas-born Leal who lives in
San Francisco.

557 Artist registry financed. RIO GRANDE SUN,
(January 17, 1980). English.

AN: A $15,000 grant received from the
National Endowment for the Arts to begin a
New Mexico Hispanic Arts Community Outreach
project, which will include a central
registry of New Mexico Hispanic artists with
current resume, documentation of work, and
other information. In charge will be
artists Estevan Arellano, Albert Baros, and
Susan Jamison of the Santa Fe Council for
the Arts.

558 Artista de Aztlan. EL DIARIO DE LA GENTE,
Vol. 4, no. 8 (April 1976), p. 7. Spanish.

AN: Interview with Mike Garcia, staff
artist for the DIARIO. Born in Alamosa,
Colorado, the artist defines his work as
"mestizo art because it expresses our Indian
heritage, using motifs of the revolutionary
struggles to reflect the possibilities of
the future." Well illustrated.

559 Ashford, Gerald. Artistic styles have no
ethnic bonds. SUNDAY ONE, (October 18,
1970), p. [18]. English.

AN: Biographical information on
Spanish-surnamed artists living and working
in San Antonio. Includes commentary on
Porfirio Salinas Jr. and Mel Casas.

560 Avalos, David. A pure Mexican accent: the
popular engravings of Jose Guadalupe Posada.
PROCEEDINGS OF THE PACIFIC COAST COUNCIL ON
LATIN AMER STUDIES, Vol. 7, (1980, 1981),
p. 123-138. English.

AN: As a documentor of injustice and
oppression, Posada, 19th century Mexican
engraver, is a master who inspires Chicano
artists. Appreciation for his art has been
expressed by Sacramento artist Jose E.
Montoya. Arsacio Vanegas Arroyo, grandson of
Posada's publisher, has made his private
collection available to Chicano cultural
centers, including El Centro Cultural de la
Raza, San Diego. Illustrated.

561 Barnstone, Gertrude and Tanguma, Leo. The
big picture: 'I want to indict the system
that has condemned us!'. HOUSTON
BREAKTHROUGH, (March 1980), p. 16-19.
English.

AN: Houston muralist Leo Tanguma studied
with John Biggers at Texas Southern
University who encouraged him and other
Chicanos to study Mexican murals. The
article is an interview with Tanguma which
details his strong political orientation and
ideals, and the problems he has encountered
as a result. Three illustrations.

562 Barrett, Marjorie. Carving out a living - a
primitive process. ROCKY MOUNTAIN NEWS,
(December 15, 1979), p. 90. English.

AN: In the village of Teseque outside
Santa Fe, NM, Felipe Archuleta, a
69-year-old folk carver has emerged as an
international art celebrity, famous for his
naive animal carvings. His work expecially
life-sized renditions of animals, is
represented in many distinguished
collections and is prized for its wit and
lack of predictability. Illustrated with
photograph of carver and one of his
creations.

563 Barrett, Marjorie. Experimental art of a
realist. ROCKY MOUNTAIN NEWS, (August 2,
1970), p. 74. English.

AN: Recognized as one of the area's top
realist painters, Ramon Kelley is a
diligent, hard-working artist. Current work
includes experiments with abstraction,
strong facial studies and landscapes.
Includes photograph of artist and three
examples of his work.

564 Baxter Art Gallery, California Institute of
Technology and Rosenstone, Robert A. In
search of...four women/four cultures.
Exhibition catalog, 1976. English.

AN: Catalog of an exhibit including
Donna Nakao, Cheri Pann, Betye Saar, and Los
Angeles Chicana artist Judithe E. Hernandez.
One work of each artist illustrated.

565 A beautiful book just published...: book
review of MEXICAN AMERICAN ARTISTS. LA LUZ,
Vol. 2, no. 4 (August 1973), p. 26. English.

566 Bejarano, William. Utah Chicano forum.
CHISMEARTE, Vol. 1, no. 1 (Fall 1976), p.
9-10. English.

AN: Report on the CULTURE, ARTE Y MEDIOS
DE COMUNICACION workshop at the Third
National Chicano Forum at the University of
Utah, Salt Lake City. The panel, moderated
by artist Carmen Lomas Garza, set up a plan
of action for the visual, literary,
performing arts and the mass media which
included planning a national conference to
discuss cultural work, financial support,
recognition and moral support, among other
issues.

Artists (cont.)

567 Bendau, Clifford P. Preserving an ancient
craft. MS.MAGAZINE, Vol. 9, no. 11 (May
1981), p. 26. English.

AN: 40-year-old native Taos, NM resident
Anita Otilia Rodriguez travels the Southwest
as a professional enjarradora building homes
and fireplaces from earth and straw. Article
discusses the history of adobe construction,
Rodriguez's innovations with the ancient
technique. Illustrated.

568 Beronius, George. The murals of East Los
Angeles. HOME MAGAZINE, (April 11, 1976),
p. 10-11+. English.

AN: Well-illustrated historical article
focusing on murals at Estrada Courts and
those produced through Goez Gallery and
Judith Baca in East Los Angeles.

569 Blue Sky Productions. Los santeros. Color
film, 29 min., 1979. English.

AN: A 29 minute color film produced with
funding assistance from New Mexico Highlands
University and the National Endowment for
the Arts. Features santeros Luis Tapia,
Orlando Romero, Horacio Valdez.

570 Bruce Novoa, Juan. [Interview with Jose
Montoya]. In CHICANO AUTHORS: INQUIRY BY
INTERVIEW. Austin, TX: University of Texas
Press, 1980, p. 115-136. English.

AN: Biography of Sacramento, CA artist
and poet Jose Montoya. Emphasizes the close
relationship between art and poetry in his
life and in that of the Royal Chicano Air
Force, which he co-founded.

571 Burkhardt, Dorothy. Chicano pride and anger
mix at 'Califas'. THE TAB, (April 12,
1981), p. 34. English.

AN: CALIFAS: AN EXHIBITION OF CHICANO
ARTISTS IN CALIFORNIA represents a
cross-section of artists exhibiting work for
at least ten years: Rupert Garcia, Ernie
Palomino, Eduardo Carrillo, Judy Baca, Rene
Yanez, Carmen Lomas Garza, Salvador Roberto
Torres, Roberto Chavez, Willie Herron, Ralph
Maradiaga, Sue Martinez, Jose Montoya,
Malaquias Montoya, Ramses Noriega and
Esteban Villa. Illustrated.

572 Calendario de March: 1977. Chicago, IL:
MARCH, Inc., 1976. English.

AN: Historical calendar with photos and
biographies of artists. Illustrations of
artwork by Ray Patlan, Jose Nario, Frank J.
Sanchez, Salvador Dominguez, Salvador Vega,
Marguerite Ortega, Aurelio Diaz, Carlos
Cortez, Mario E. Castillo, Francisco Blasco,
Rey Vasquez, and Efrain Martinez. History of
MARCH (Movimiento Artistico Chicano).

573 California. State College. Los Angeles. Art
Gallery. Twelve Chicano artists. Exhibition
invitation, n.d. English.

AN: Invitation to an exhibit: Jose
Montoya, Gilbert Sanchez Lujan, Esteban
Villa, Rene Yanez, Joe Moran, Armando Cid,
Leonard Castellas, Juanishi Orozco, Rudy
Cuellar, Beltran, Lopez and Cabrera.

574 Cantu, Jesus "Chista". Entrevista: Jesus
Maria Cantu, 'El Chista'. MAGAZIN, Vol. 1,
no. 4 (April 1972), p. 52-65. Spanish.

AN: Discusses his life in San Antonio;
his apprenticeship since childhood to his
uncle Miguel Angel Tellez who taught him to
paint billboards, wall signs and church
decorations; his membership in the group
Artistas de la Nueva Raza; his artistic and
political philosophy. In Spanish.

575 Capitol Art Gallery, Lansing, MI. Arte de
Nora Mendoza, Hector Perez, George Vargas,
Martin Moreno. Exhibition invitation [1979].
English.

AN: Invitation to an art exhibit
organized by Nuestras Artes de Michigan.

576 Carlos Sandoval to complete mural in
Zihuatanejo, Mexico. TIERRA Y LIBERTAD, Vol.
2, no. 4 (July 1980), p. 3, 10. English.

AN: Biographical information on Colorado
artist Carlos Sandoval. The Municipal
Library in the city of Zihuatanejo in the
state of Guerrero is the site of Sandoval's
mural which visually and symbolically
projects the cultural and historical unity
between Mejicanos and Chicanos.

577 Carraro, Francine. Refined rhythmic
references: Amado Pena, Jr. SOUTHWEST ART,
Vol. 9, no. 6 (November 1979), p. 70-75.
English.

AN: Well-illustrated (including 4 color)
story on Austin silkscreen artist Amado M.
Pena. Features his recent stylized work
based on New Mexican indian motifs.

578 La Casa de la Raza Gallery, Santa Barbara,
CA. Judithe Hernandez: virgen, madre, mujer;
imagenes de la mujer chicana. Exhibition
invitation [1979]. English.

AN: Invitation to an exhibit with a list
of projects, murals, and exhibitions.
Illustrated.

579 Castellanos, Leonard. Chicano centros,
murals, and art. CHISMEARTE, Vol. 1, no. 1
(Fall 1976), p. 26-27. English.

AN: Excerpt of an article originally
published under the same title in ARTS IN
SOCIETY (Spring-Summer 1975).

580 Castro, Mike. Climb from barrio is tough:
artist finds life a waiting game. LOS
ANGELES TIMES [Central Section], (November
2, 1973), p. IV, 1+. English.

AN: Edward Carbajal, graduate of
Chouinard Institute of the Arts in Valencia,
has a hard time making a living. He
approached the Los Angeles County Museum of
Art about exhibits for Chicano artists, with
no result, though the Museum says it is
still interested. Illustrated.

581 La Causa Publications, Oakland, CA. New
symbols for la Nueva Raza. Exhibition
announcement, [ca. 1969]. English.

AN: Announcement for exhibition of the
four founding artists of the Mexican
American Liberation Art Front (MALAF):
Esteban Villa, Rene Yanez, Manuel Hernandez,
Malaquias Montoya. Collage of portraits by
the artists.

Artists (cont.)

582 Celebracion Chican-india. CAMINOS, Vol. 1, no. 3 (May 1980), p. 38-39+. English.

AN: Portfolio of works exhibited at the Galeria Capistrano in southern California: Zarco Guerrero, Domingo Ulloa, Mario Torero, Guillermo Acevedo. Judithe Hernandez, who also exhibited, is not included in the portfolio.

583 Center for the Visual Arts, Oakland, CA. Fujioka, Herman, Rivera and Rodriguez. ARTSLETTER, Vol. 6, no. 3 (May, June, 1980). English.

AN: Article unites Gustavo Rivera and Peter Rodriguez as artists who share a commitment to expressionist techniques. Illustrated with one black and white photograph of each artist's work.

584 Cesar Martinez. ARTES VISUALES, no. 29 (June 1981), p. 63. Bilingual.

AN: Two illustrations by the San Antonio, Texas artist, a brief biography, and the reprint of a letter published in the catalog CUATRO CAMINOS, Southwest Texas State University, San Marcos.

585 Champlin, Chuck, Jr. Working for more than peanuts. LOS ANGELES TIMES, (June 21, 1980), p. II, 8, 10. English.

AN: Bill Melendez has been an animator 21 years for Charles Schulz's Charlie Brown and Peanuts comic strips, TV specials, and feature films. Melendez began his career with Walt Disney Productions in 1938.

586 Chavez, Jaime. Rayaprofiles: Manuel Unzueta. RAYAS, Vol. 2, no. 3 (May, June, 1979), p. 5. Spanish.

AN: Brief biography of Mexican-born Chicano artist and muralist from Santa Barbara, California. Manuel Unzueta is active with La Casa de la Raza and its publication XALMAN. Unzueta is invited to paint a mural in Albuquerque. A Santa Barbara mural is illustrated.

587 Chavez, Lucy. A Chicano muralist. REVISTA MARYKNOLL, (July 1981). English.

AN: Denver artist Carlotta Espinosa decided early in life that she was going to be an artist. Espinosa has painted murals in Arizona, Texas and the San Luis Valley in Colorado. Illustrated with photographs of artist and details from her murals.

588 Chicago. Public Library Cultural Center, Chicago, IL. La mujer: a visual dialogue. Exhibition invitation, 1978. English.

AN: Invitation to an exhibit spotlighting women artists from Mexico and the United States. Organized by the Movimiento Artistico Chicano (MARCH) of Chicago. 40 paintings by women artists included, and 50 works based on the theme of women. Poetry readings, music, dance, film, theatre, and panels of men and women artists included. Illustrated by work by Linda Vallejo.

589 Chicano art. ARTES VISUALES, no. 29 (1981). English.

AN: Issue on Chicano art, introduced by Los Angeles artist Roberto Gil de Montes.

Includes works and statements by: Pedro Lujan (Texas); Raul M. Guerrero (Calif.); Sylvia Salazar Simpson (New Mexico/Calif.); Carlos Almaraz (Calif.); Rene Yanez (Calif.); Jack Vargas (Calif.); Ray Bravo (Calif.); John Valadez (Calif.); Gloria Maya (Calif.); Elsa Flores (Calif.); Willie Herron (Calif.); Gilbert "Magu" Lujan (Calif.); Kay Torres, Jerry Lucas, and Louis Perez (Calif.).

590 Chicano art of the Southwest. San Antonio, TX: Instituto Chicano de Artes y Artesanias of the Texas Institute for Educational Development, 1975. English.

AN: Collection of 220 slides supplemented by slide annotation and artists' biographies researched and photographed by Texas artist Cesar A. Martinez over two years. Biographies cover 20 Texas, 6 New Mexico, and 15 northern California artists. Slides include, in addition, murals from Los Angeles and San Diego.

591 CJL. Artist profile-Amado Pena. FOUR WINDS, Vol. 1, no. 4 (1980), p. 10. English.

AN: Amado Pena works within the expectations of an American Indian artist, but also within the context of the Mexican American culture. The article treats Pena's artistic trajectory and provides biographical information. Illustrated with photograph of the artist and reproductions of one lithograph and one mixed-media drawing.

592 Cockcroft, Eva. Women in the community mural movement. HERESIES, no. 1 (January 1977), p. 14-22. English.

AN: Women's role in the community mural movement is much greater than generally recognized. Among the many women muralists discussed are included the Mujeres Muralistas (Patricia Rodriguez, Irene Perez, Graciela Carrillo de Lopez, and Venezuelan Consuelo Mendez Castillo) of San Franisoc, and Judy Baca of Los Angeles. Illustrated.

593 Coe, Kathryn. Heritage plus science yields art. SCOTTSDALE DAILY PROGRESS, (August 28, 1981), p. 27. English.

AN: Biography of Colorado-born Rudy Fernandez who bases many of his paintings and mixed media boxes on the religious imagery of Colorado. He studied geology; travelled to Spain and Mexico to know his heritage. All these factors influence his art, in which he uses symbols personally.

594 Contemporary Arts Museum, Houston, TX. Dale gas: give it gas. The continued acceleration of Chicano art. Exhibition catalog, 1977. English.

AN: A comprehensive catalog including 28 works of art exhibited by 13 Texas artists: Melesio (Mel) Casas, Jose Esquivel, Francisco (Frank) Fajardo, Carmen Lomas Garza, Luis Jimenez, Cesar Augusto Martinez, Santos G. Martinez, Jr., Amado Pena, Roberto Rios, Jose Rivera, Joe B. Rodriguez, Jesus (Jesse) Trevino, and George Truan. Many illustrations, some in color. Introduction by James Harithas. Essay by Santos Martinez, Jr. Poetry, literature and essays by Chicano writers.

Artists (cont.)

595 Contemporary Arts Museum, Houston, TX. Fire!
An exhibition of 100 Texas artists.
Exhibition brochure, 1979. English.

AN: Includes eleven Chicano artists.
Unfortunately, not illustrated, though a
checklist of works is included. Mel Casas,
Carmen Lomas Garza, Xavier Gorena, Luis
Jimenez, Cesar Martinez, Guillermo Z.
Pulido, Philip Renteria, Jose L. Rivera, Joe
Rodriguez, George Truan, Juan B. Vela.
Introduction by James Surls. Statements by
the artists.

596 Corazon del norte: Jose Alfredo Maestas.
GRITO DEL NORTE, Vol. 2, no. 7 (May 19,
1969), p. 13. English.

AN: Jose Alfredo Maestas, born in San
Juan Pueblo is a folk carver imbued with the
mythical and spiritual Indo-Hispano
tradition. His carved figurines made from
cotton wood roots, balsam and driftwood are
in many museums and private collections.
Illustrated with photographs of artist at
work and two photographs of his sculpture.

597 Cox, Sue. Female psychology: the emerging
self. New York: St. Martin's Press, 2nd ed.,
1981, p. 138+. English.

AN: Reproductions of works by Carmen
Lomas Garza, Graciela Carrillo, Consuelo
Gonzalez Amezcua.

598 Cox, Vic. Beauty in the barrio. WESTWAYS,
Vol. 67, no. 2 (February 1975), p. 50-53.
English.

AN: "Tooner Flats" is another name for
the barrio of East Los Angeles. These
streets are the home and inspiration to
Frank Hernandez who illustrates the article
with pen and ink sketches of buildings.

599 Crossley, Mimi. Tejano artists. HOUSTON
POST, (August 19, 1976). English.

AN: Exhibition of 19 Texas artists
organized by Joe Rodriguez of the AAMA
(Association for the Advancement of Mexican
Americans) Art Center in Houston, Texas.
Working within a wide range of styles and a
great scope of subject matter. Includes
brief commentary on the work of Amado Pena,
Carmen Lomas Garza, Cesar Martinez, Enrique
Campos, Carolina Flores, Jesus Trevino and a
host of others.

600 Cuellar, Rodolfo. Esteban Villa-maximo
exponente del arte indigena mexicano. EL
HISPANO, Vol. 8, no. 23 (January 27, 1976),
p. 3. Spanish.

AN: Biographical data on the artist
focusing on his activism in the formation of
the Centro de Artistas Chicanos in
Sacramento and the coalition of Centros
Chicanos in California. Illustrated with
photographs of the artist, one of his murals
and a special emblem for the "Esteban Villa
Fan Club" designed by the R.C.A.F.

601 Cultura chicana: Los Angeles. COMUNIDAD, no.
11 (July 13, 1980), p. 1-15. Spanish.

AN: The whole issue of the Cultural
Supplement concerns Chicano art and music.
Captioned photographs deal with visual
artists Carlos Almaraz, Jerry Dreva [not
Chicano], Glugio Gronk, Willie Herron, John
Valadez, Patssi Valdez, with examples of

their work. With the exception of Dreva, all
the artists are members of Los Four or Asco.
Asco member Harry Gamboa, Jr. sums up the
1960s and 1970s and activities of artists in
his essay "Seis imaginaciones: Artistas
chicanos en Los Angeles." Well illustrated.

602 Day, Orman. Hispanic life mirrored by ethnic
artists. THE REGISTER, (July 5, 1981), p.
B1+. English.

AN: Story on artists Manuel Hernandez
Trujillo and Emigdio Vasquez whose work
opened the new Galeria in Santa Ana, and
poet Manuel Gomez. Color illustrations.

603 De la Torre, Alfredo and Tellez, Miguel
Angel. Entrevista con Don Miguel Angel
Tellez=Interview with Don Miguel Angel
Tellez. CARACOL, Vol. 5, no. 11-12 (July,
August, 1979), p. 16-22. Bilingual.

AN: Tellez, born in San Antonio about
1915, son and grandson of painters who
taught him the trade, tells about his life
as commercial artist and his more symbolic
work started in 1962. Illustrated.

604 De Marroquin, Moron. Denver Harbor artists.
LA PRENSA, (June 2, 1978). Spanish.

AN: Commentary on two exhibitions. THE
DENVER HARBOR ARTISTS includes information
on paintings by Lupe Aguirre, Josie Mendoza
and Abel Gonzalez--all from Houston. The
solo show MAGIC BLANCA featured the work of
Brownsville, Texas artist Jorge Truan.
Truan's work is mystical and visionary.

605 Dean, Nancy. Denver artist dues are paid in
full. ROCKY MOUNTAIN NEWS, (April 5, 1981),
p. 6. English.

AN: Profile of artist Ramon Kelley
focusing on his successful career and
detailing his rise on the art market.
Includes photograph of the artist.

606 Delgado, Sylvia. My people never smile: a
profile of a young Chicano artist.
REGENERACION, Vol. 2, no. 1 (1971), p. 23.
English.

AN: Very brief biographical sketch of
Willie Herron.

607 Dickson, Joanne. Manuel Neri. El Cajon, CA:
Grossmont College Gallery, 1980. English.

AN: Essay documents Neri's career and
situates him within the Bay Area figurative
style. As a sculptor, the artist has worked
in plaster or bronze, cast paper, fiberglass
and more recently in marble.

608 Dietmeier, R. C. City artist finds his
inspiration where he lives. ORANGE CITY
NEWS, (December 23, 1981), p. 2. English.

AN: Illustrated story on Emigdio
Vasquez's ten year retrospective of
realistic paintings taken from photographs,
held at the Galeria in Santa Ana, Calif.
Vasquez records his environment and events
from the 1940s and 1950s as an artistic and
documentary statement.

Artists (cont.)

609 Directo, Cyril. Leo Guzman:
woodcarver/tallador in madera. ENTRELINEAS,
Vol. 1, no. 2 (February, March, 1968), p. 8.
English.

AN: Biographical facts and commentary on
artist's work. Illustrated with photographs
of artist and examples of his work.

610 Documentary to include work by Cuate Santos.
LAREDO NEWS, (July 17, 1980). English.

AN: Photography by Laredo News
photographer Cuate Santos included in
exhibit "Un encuentro sin palabras," a
documentary show on Mexican American life in
Texas sponsored by Mujeres Artistas del
Suroeste (MAS). The state-wide show was
juried by Los Angeles photographer Isabel
Castro. Illustrated.

611 Donnell-Kotrozo, Carol and Perlman, Barbara.
Male passages: a secular santero of the '80s
interprets machismo. ARIZONA ARTS AND
LIFESTYLE, Vol. 4, no. 1 (1982), p. 32-39.
English.

AN: Rudy Fernandez moves freely between
two- and three-dimensional forms using
personal symbols such as cacti, roosters,
flying hearts, trout, in paintings or
lead-covered shelves of boxes reminiscent of
retablos. Colorado-born Fernandez has lived
in Arizona, Utah, New Mexico, and
Washington. His art is not religious, but is
influenced by a strong Catholic background.
Many color illustrations, including the
cover.

612 Donnell-Kotrozo, Carol. Rudy Fernandez.
SOUTHWESTERN CONTEMPORARY ARTS QUARTERLY,
(Fall 1981). English.

AN: Well-illustrated article on the
mixed media creations of Rudy Fernandez who
lives in Scottsdale, AZ.

613 Donnell-Kotrozo, Carol. Rudy Fernandez.
ARTSPACE, Vol. 5, no. 4 (Fall 1981), p.
18-23. English.

AN: Scottsdale, Arizona resident Rudy
Fernandez converts cultural symbols into a
private system language that revolves around
love, family, manhood and self-identity. His
mixed media altar-like forms are based on
interest in Southwest santos, their format
and presentation. Fernandez does paintings,
and assembled wood pieces. Handsomely
illustrated, with color.

614 Dougherty Arts Center, Austin, TX. From the
fringe: artists choose artists. Exhibition
catalog, 1981. English.

AN: Catalog of an exhibit featuring
eight women artists, including Santa Barraza
of Austin. Barraza also designed the
catalog.

615 Drescher, Tim and Garcia, Rupert. Recent
Raza murals in the U.S. RADICAL AMERICA,
Vol. 12, no. 2 (March, April, 1978), p.
14-31. English.

AN: Like the cultural revolution of
Mexico in the 1920s, La Raza of Aztlan
emphasizes the Native American and mestizo
heritage as well as the Mexican
revolutionary heritage. Within a social
context, the authors discuss Chicano and
Latino murals nationally. Iconography and

its relation to Chicano experience is
explored, as well as images by and about
women. Illustrations.

616 Edward Chavez: sculptor-painter. LA LUZ,
Vol. 2, no. 2 (May 1973), p. 28-31. English.

AN: Lavishly illustrated biographical
account of Edward Chavez. Born in Ocate, New
Mexico in 1917, Chavez has a distinguished
career as a painter and sculptor. During the
1940's he executed a number of murals under
sponsorship of various government art
projects. These murals were placed in public
buildings in Nebraska, Colorado and Wyoming.
Although living and working in New York most
of his adult life, the work of Edward Chavez
has always been influenced by the Southwest.

617 Edwards, Jim. The folk art tradition.
ARTWEEK, Vol. 6, no. 18 (May 3, 1975), p. 7.
English.

AN: Includes commentary on painter
Alexander Maldonado who is placed within the
surrealist mode. His imagination sees a dual
world of earthly landscapes filled with
strange architecture and celestial visions
in which the moon, stars and comets prevail.

618 Elaine Horwitch Galleries, Santa Fe, NM. New
Mexico woodcarving. Exhibition catalog,
1980. English.

AN: Invitation to an exhibit at the
Horwitch galleries of Scottsdale, Arizona,
and Santa Fe, NM of sculptors Felipe
Archuleta, Leroy Archuleta, Frank Brito,
Alonso Jimenez, Horatio Valdez, and others.
Illustration.

619 Encuentro artistico femenil. Austin, TX:
Juarez-Lincoln Institute, Centro Cultural de
LUCHA, 1977. English.

AN: Program of music, literature and
visual art. Lists works by 12 Latina artists
and brief biographies. Part of "Women &
Their Work" festival.

620 ENCUENTRO FEMENIL (San Fernando, CA). Vol.
1, no. 1 (Spring 1973), p. 1+. English.

AN: Publication sponsored by Hijas de
Cuauhtemoc, a Chicana femenist group. Black
and white drawings on cover by Pat Portera
Crary. Art work by Vicki Thrall, Adelaida
del Castillo, and Maria Hortencia Garcia.
Photography by Cindy Honesto and David
Lazarin.

621 Espinoza. EMPIRE MAGAZINE, (October 22,
1972), p. 28. English.

AN: Biographical information and
artistic trajectory of Ray Espinoza from
Colorado's San Luis Valley. Focus on
Espinoza as a community artist who expresses
aspects of Southwestern culture. Illustrated
with photographs of three wax sculptures by
Ray Espinoza.

Artists (cont.)

622 Exhibit at UCSD: Chicana artist to show works. LOS ANGELES TIMES [San Diego County edition], (December 6, 1978), p. II, 8. English.

AN: Artist and activist from San Diego, Yolanda Lopez, will be showing sketches and paintings at the Mandeville Center, University of California, San Diego, from which she was the first Chicana to graduate with a Master's degree in visual arts. Her show is based on her family, and the icon of the Virgin of Guadalupe. Illustrated.

623 Exxon Company, Houston, TX and Quirarte, Jacinto. Chicano art of the barrio. Exhibition brochure, n.d. [c.1976]. English.

AN: Brochure for a traveling exhibit of photographically-reproduced Chicano murals: Leo Limon, Lucila Villasenor Grijalva, Antonio Esparza, Susan Saenz, Charles Felix, Hoyo-Mara gang, David A. Lopez and team, Roberto Chavez and team (Los Angeles); Jerry Concha, Ruben Guzman, Chuy Campusano (San Francisco); Manuel Unzueta (Santa Barbara). Ernie Palomino and Leo Esequiel Ozona (Fresno). Leo Tanguma (Houston), Roberto Lucero, Manuel Martinez and Al Sanchez (Denver).

624 The First Unitarian Universalist Church, Paradise Valley, AZ. Five Chicano artists. Exhibition brochure, 1971. English.

AN: Exhibit organized by L. Eugene Grigsby, Jr., Art Department of Arizona State University, Tempe, AZ. 21 works by Eugene Quesada, David Nunez, Fernando Navarro, Luis Baiz (of Arizona) and Saul Solache (of Los Angeles). Brief biographies of the artists.

625 Focus: Yolanda Lopez. CITYBENDER, Vol. 2, no. 5 (1978). English.

AN: Brief biography and illustrations of drawings by San Diego/San Francisco artist Yolanda Lopez titled THREE GENERATIONS: TRES MUJERES.

626 Fowler, Carol. A study on contrasts at valley art. SUNDAY MAGAZINE [Supplement to CONTRA COSTA COUNTY TIMES, CA], (October 9, 1980). English.

AN: David Gallegos' unpeopled landscapes are composed of large color patches which portray the industrial fringes of San Francisco Bay. He works within a luminist tradition, stressing light. Illustrated.

627 Frankenstein, Alfred. At the museum: when politics and art do mix. SAN FRANCISCO CHRONICLE, (March 15, 1978), p. 54. English.

AN: Glowing review of exhibit at the San Francisco Museum of Modern Art by Rupert Garcia who, the critic says, has a genius for saying the essential thing without a line, a gesture or a touch of color more than necessary. Illustrated.

628 Frankenstein, Alfred. Prison's artist in residence. SAN FRANCISCO CHRONICLE, (May 5, 1978), p. 60. English.

AN: Review of the exhibition MUNDOS PERDIDOS, curated at the Galeria de la Raza by Leonard Castellanos. Show consisted of work by Castellanos and inmates at Lompoc

Federal Correctional Institution near Santa Barbara. Documents a prison mural, tattoos and silkscreen prints with socially critical themes.

629 La Galeria de Colores, Las Vegas, NM. La galeria de colores. Gallery brochure, [1980]. English.

AN: Brochure for a gallery/studio run by painter Pola Lopez de Jaramillo since 1980.

630 Galeria de la Raza/Studio 24, San Francisco, CA. 2001: a group exhibit of mixed media. Exhibit invitation, n.d. English.

AN: Invitation to an exhibit featuring the work of 40 artists.

631 Galeria de la Raza/Studio 24, San Francisco, CA. Blanca Flor Gutierrez - oil pastels. Exhibition announcement, 1981.

AN: Color xeroxed announcement for a window display of oil pastels by Gutierrez.

632 Galeria de la Raza/Studio 24, San Francisco, CA. Canto a Cuba. Exhibition invitation, [1974]. English.

AN: Invitation to an exhibit of prints, posters, paintings and drawings by two Cuban artists.

633 Galeria de la Raza/Studio 24, San Francisco, CA and Milkie, Anne. Carnaval '80. Exhibition catalog, 1980. English.

AN: Catalog of an exhibit of photographs and other media recording San Francisco's multi-ethnic CARNAVAL, organized in 1978 by Panamanian-born dancer. Included in the exhibit were the photographs of Chicana Maria V. Pinedo, who also designed the catalog.

634 Galeria de la Raza/Studio 24, San Francisco, CA and Lomas Garza, Carmen. Self-portraits by Chicano and Latino artists. Exhibition catalog, 1980. English.

AN: Catalog of a national exhibition by 66 artists. Gives names, residence, date of birth, and information on the work shown for each of the artists. 45 are from California, and 3 each from Puerto Rico, Arizona, New York, 9 from Texas, 2 from Washington, 1 from Virginia. 9 are women.

635 Galeria de la Raza/Studio 24, San Francisco, CA. Third world women arts exhibit: literary, performing & visual arts. Exhibition invitation [1971]. English.

AN: Invitation to an exhibit.

636 Galeria Museo - new art gallery opens in the Mission. EL TECOLOTE, Vol. 8, no. 1 (September 1977), p. 8. Bilingual.

AN: Brief article on the inauguration of the Art Gallery at the Mission Cultural Center. The opening Exhibit (August 13, 1977) was entitled SIXTY-THREE SHOW and included work in various media by Sixty three Bay Area Latino artists. Gilberto Osorio was designated as the first artist-in-residence. Information on future plans for the Galeria-Museo.

Artists (cont.)

637 Galeria Museo, Mission Cultural Center, San Francisco, CA and Rodriguez, Patricia. Patricia Rodriguez: simbolos y fantasias culturales. Exhibition catalog, 1981. English.

AN: Catalog of an exhibition of sculpture and painting. Autobiographical information about the Texas-born artist who lives in San Francisco and was a co-founder of Mujeres Muralistas. She explains her techniques in making portrait masks of Chicano/a artists in plaster and mixed media. Well illustrated.

638 Galeria Otra Vez, Los Angeles, CA. Rosemary Quesada-Weiner, Mary McNally: a photographic exhibition. Exhibition invitation, [1981]. English.

AN: Invitation to an exhibition including Chicana photographer Quesada-Weiner. Illustrated.

639 Galeria Tonantzin, Centro Cultural de LUCHA, Austin, TX. Visiones Chicanas: images and demonstrations by Chicana and Latina visual artists. Exhibition invitation, 1979. English.

AN: Invitational poster for an exhibit and a series of workshops organized by Mujeres Artistas del Suroeste (MAS), affiliated with LUCHA, League of United Chicano Artists of Austin, TX.

640 Gamboa, Harry, Jr. and Gronk. Gronk: off-the-wall artist. NEWORLD, Vol. 6, no. 4 (1980), p. 33-43. English.

AN: Interview with Gronk about his No Movies, by Harry Gamboa, Jr., both members (with Willie Herron and Patssi Valdez) of ASCO. The interview itself can be seen as an "art piece" with photographs by Gamboa; it contains valuable information about the ideas and activities of the group.

641 Gamboa, Harry, Jr. Los murales de Aztlan. COMUNIDAD, (June 28, 1981), p. 8-9+. Spanish.

AN: Review of the exhibit at the Craft and Folk Art Museum of Los Angeles of MURALS OF AZTLAN: THE STREET PAINTERS OF EAST LOS in which Carlos Almaraz, Gronk, Judithe Hernandez, Willie Herron, Frank Romero, John Valadez and the East Los Streetscapers (David Botello, Wayne Healy, George Yepes) painted portable murals in the gallery. The murals are described and illustrated.

642 Gamboa, Harry, Jr. Seis imaginaciones: artistas chicanos en Los Angeles. COMUNIDAD, (July 13, 1980), p. 10. Spanish.

AN: A limited flow of media information about Los Angeles Chicanos has produced a "ghost" culture. Only sensational events are published. Alternative magazines like LA RAZA, CON SAFOS, and REGENERACION have disseminated Chicano ideas of the 1970s. The Chicano imagination has appeared in murals by Willie Herron, Gronk, Carlos Almaraz, John Valadez; in pieces like "walking" and "instant" murals by the group ASCO; by the group Los Four; by group exhibits like "Chicanismo en el arte," and "Chicanarte." Patssi Valdez showed Photobooth Piece at the "Chicanismo" show. Gronk and Jerry Dreva exhibited their mail art at "Punk Meets Art." In Spanish.

643 Garcia, Rupert. Echos de la Mision - Alfaro Siqueiros (1896-1974). EL TECOLOTE, Vol. 4, no. 3 (February 22, 1974), p. 11. English.

AN: Biographical and artistic trajectory of Mexican artist David Alfaro Siqueiros. Artist painted three murals in Southern California in 1932 (MEETING IN THE STREET and TROPICAL AMERICA were done in Los Angeles on the walls of the Chouinard School of Art and the Plaza Art Center, Olvera Street area respectively. The third mural PORTRAIT OF MEXICO was privately commissioned in Santa Monica). The three California murals deal with themes of censorship, racism, colonialism, capitalism, and imperialism. Article suggests that Raza artists are much influenced by the ideas and work of Siqueiros. Illustrated with Rupert Garcia's silkscreen poster SIQUEIROS.

644 Garcia, Ruperto. Las companeras art exhibit. ARRIBA, Vol. 1, no. 4 (October 1980), p. 9. English.

AN: Illustrated story on an art show featuring Texas Latinas organized by MAS (Mujeres Artistas del Suroeste) in Austin. More than 18 women were represented.

645 Goddarth, Ruth. Porfirio Salinas. Austin, TX: Rock House Press, 1975. English.

AN: Born on Nov. 6, 1910 on a farm near Bastrop, Texas, Porfirio Salinas studied art with Spanish artist Jose Arpa in San Antonio and gradually became a regional landscapist of wide renown. Salinas died April 18, 1973 at the age of 62. The book is lavishly illustrated.

646 Goez proudly presents. Exhibit brochure, n.d. [1970]. English.

AN: Brochure produced by the Goez Gallery of Los Angeles for an inaugural exhibit showing the work of 76 artists.

647 Goldman, Shifra M. Artistas en accion: conferencia de las mujeres chicanas. COMUNIDAD, (August 10, 1980), p. 15. Spanish.

AN: In Chicano Studies programs, the fine arts have had second class status to social sciences and literature. Similarly a Chicano Issues Conference overlooked artists until a special effort was made. A round table, which included visual artists Gloriamalia Flores and Carmen Lomas Garza, discussed the social functions of art, woman as an image maker, problems of the Chicana as creator and cultural worker, and professionalism in the arts.

648 Goldman, Shifra M. Chicana artists at work. ARRIBA, [n.d.], p. 3+. English.

AN: Excerpt of a longer article on the Texas women's group Mujeres Artistas del Suroeste (MAS). Integral to the group are artists Santa Barraza, Nora Gonzalez-Dodson, Alicia Arredondo, Maria Flores, Sylvia Orozco, and Modesta Trevino.

Artists (cont.)

649 Goldman, Shifra M. Chicano art alive and
    well in Texas: a 1981 update. REVISTA
    CHICANO-RIQUENA, Vol. 9, no. 1 (Winter
    1981), p. 34-40. English.

    AN: Reprint of article published as
    "Supervivencia y prosperidad del arte
    chicano en Texas: nueva revision" in
    COMUNIDAD (Los Angeles, CA) [Sunday
    Supplement to LA OPINION], September 21,
    1980, p. 3, 15+.

650 Goldman, Shifra M. The intense realism of
    Frida Kahlo. CHISMEARTE, Vol. 1, no. 4 (Fall,
    Winter, 1977), p. 8-11. English.

    AN: A brief, one-page biographical
    sketch of Frida Kahlo's life and work. This
    is accompanied by black and white
    reproductions of her paintings: AUTORRETRATO
    COMO TEHUANA (1943), AUTORRETRATO (1946),
    RAICES (1943), LA VENADITA (1946), and LA
    NOVIA QUE SE ESPANTA DE VER LA VIDA ABIERTA
    (n.d.).

651 Goldman, Shifra M. Supervivencia y
    prosperidad del arte chicano en Texas: nueva
    revision. COMUNIDAD, Vol. 55, no. 5
    (September 21, 1980), p. 3,15+. Spanish.

    AN: Focuses on six Chicano artists from
    Austin, Houston, San Antonio, and
    Kingsville: Mel Casas, Cesar Martinez, Amado
    M. Pena, Leo Tanguma, Carmen Lomas Garza,
    and Santa Barraza. Well illustrated. This
    article was reprinted as "Chicano Art Alive
    and Well in Texas: A 1981 Update," in
    REVISTA CHICANO-RIQUENA (Houston), Vol. 9,
    no. 1, Winter 1981, p. 34-40.

652 Gonzales, Juan. Regional report, The arts:
    "Our people deserve the best". NUESTRO, Vol.
    1, no. 2 (May 1977), p. 56-57. English.

    AN: Activities of San Francisco's
    Galeria de la Raza; interviews with its
    directors, Rene Yanez and Ralph Maradiaga.
    Reprinted as "Galeria de la Raza: our people
    deserve the best" in EL TECOLOTE (San
    Francisco, CA), Vol. 7, no. 11 (July, 1977),
    p. 14.

653 Gonzalez, Ellen. U.S. art project: Chicanas
    painting 'future history'. LOS ANGELES
    TIMES, (March 16, 1978), p. II, 4. English.

    AN: Women muralists from the murals
    workshop of the Chicana Service Action
    Center working on murals at City Terrace and
    Humphrey Avenue elementary schools in East
    Los Angeles. Illustrated.

654 Gonzalez, Hector and Cid, Armando. An
    interview with Armando Cid. EL HISPANO, Vol.
    5, no. 32 (January 23, 1973). English.

    AN: Biographical information and
    commentary on Cid's career and his art style
    which is described as containing
    pre-Columbian motifs and mannerisms of the
    people in the barrio.

655 Gonzalez, Victoria. Chair in the sky:
    Ernesto Palomino. HERE AND NOW, Vol. 2, no.
    2 (Fall   1981). English.

    AN: An important article tracing the
    artistic career of Ernie Palomino, professor
    of art at California State University,
    Fresno. Includes biographical information,
    formation of La Brocha Del Valle (Chicano
    Arts Organization), information about

Palomino's film MY TRIP IN A '52 FORD and
commentary on Palomino's music and artistic
philosophy. Well illustrated.

656 Graham Gallery, New York, NY and Perreault,
    John. Luis Jimenez. Exhibition catalog,
    1970. English.

    AN: Well-illustrated catalog of an
    exhibit by El Paso-born sculptor. Some
    biographical material.

657 The Green Line Gallery, San Pedro, CA.
    Lithographs and woodcuts by Muriel Olguin.
    Exhibit invitation, 1980. English.

    AN: Invitation to an exhibit.
    Illustrated.

658 Grigsby, J. Eugene, Jr. Art & ethnics:
    background for teaching youth in a
    pluralistic society. Dubuque, IO: Wm.C.
    Brown Co. Publishers, 1977. English.

    AN: Grigsby teaches in the Art
    Department of Arizona State University,
    Tempe. His book contains illustrations of
    Arizona artists Eugenio Quedada, David
    Nunez, and Luis Baiz, and a chapter called
    "The Spanish-Speaking Ethnics:
    Chicano/Mexican-American/Puerto
    Rican/Cuban/South American artists".

659 Guerrero, Adolfo "El Zarco". The new vision
    of Xicanindio art. RAYAS, Vol. 2, no. 1
    (January, February, 1979), p. 3. Bilingual.

    AN: Zarco Guerrero explains his personal
    artistic philosophy that unites Amerindian
    concepts of art to contemporary art forms,
    especially in sculpture. For Guerrero, "the
    Chicano artist is making a monumental effort
    to arrive at a new universal language and to
    create a new meaning of community through
    art.

660 Hagen, Carol. Mission murals. ARTWEEK, Vol.
    5, no. 30 (September 14, 1974), p. 6.
    English.

    AN: Report on two recently completed
    murals in San Francisco's Mission District:
    Jesus Campusano's 90x10-ft mural in the Bank
    of America branch, and the Mujeres
    Muralistas' mural adjacent to the Mission
    Model Cities building. Illustrated.

661 Hale, David. Fresnan gets grant to create
    five story high mural. FRESNO BEE, (April
    16, 1978), p. Forum, C4. English.

    AN: Details on the awarding of a grant
    to John Sierra, Fresno artist, for the
    creation of what will be the largest piece
    of public art in that city. The artwork is a
    6000 square foot mural titled THE PLANTING
    OF THE CULTURES. Article contains
    biographical information on the artist and
    presents goals of his mural project.

662 Harbor Area Community Art Center, San Pedro,
    CA. Mi arte, mi raza: an exhibition of
    current work by Judithe Hernandez.
    Exhibition invitation, 1979. English.

    AN: Invitation to an exhibit.

Artists (cont.)

663 Heard Museum, Phoenix, AZ. Second Southwest Chicano Art Invitational. Exhibit catalog, 1978. English.

AN: Exhibit by eight artists: Antonio Pazos (Tucson), Rudy Fernandez (Salt Lake City), Harry Gamboa (Los Angeles), Rupert Garcia and Xavier Viramontes (San Francisco), Roberto Rios (San Antonio), Roberto Espinoza (Yuma), and Roberto Borboa (Tucson). Brief biographies of all but Rios. 29 illustrations.

664 Helen Euphrat Gallery, De Anza College, Cupertino, CA. Staying visible: the importance of archives. Art and "saved stuff" of eleven 20th century California artists. Cupertino, CA: Helen Euphrat Gallery, De Anza College, 1981. English.

AN: Catalog issued in conjunction with an exhibit held in the gallery Sept. 22 to October 23, 1981 which included documentation on Chicana artists Patricia Rodriguez and Carmen Lomas Garza. Each artist explains her method of saving, storing and using cultural material in her creations. Includes biographical sketch, photograph of the artist and reproduction of artwork.

665 HEMBRA: HERMANAS EN MOVIMIENTO BROTANDO RAICES DE AZTLAN (University of Texas, Austin). (Spring 1976).

AN: Raul Valdez, drawing, p. 3; Carolina Flores, drawing, p. 5; Maria Flores, photograph, pp. 7, 11, 30; M.E. Secrest-Ramirez, drawing, p. 12; Amacio Zarate, drawing, p. 15; Santa Barraza, drawings, pp. 16, 17, 18, 26, 32; Nora Gonzales-Dodson, painting, p. 19; Gilberto Cardenas, photograph, pp. 22, 28; Nanci de los Santos, photograph, p. 23, 29; Amado Maurilio Pena, Jr. p. 31.

666 Herbeck, Ray, Jr. Regional report, The arts: the many credits of Ruben Lopez. NUESTRO, Vol. 1, no. 4 (July 1977), p. 13-14. English.

AN: Brief biographical article about Ruben Orozco Lopez, a Chicano artist who is widely recognized for his court-room sketching and commercial art work for the Hollywood film industry. For the past few years, Lopez has been working with the Chicano News Media Association to recruit barrio youths into the news artist profession.

667 Hernandez, Judithe Elena and Goldman, Shifra M. Readers' forum. ARTWEEK, Vol. 12, no. 25 (August 1, 1981), p. 16. English.

AN: Critical interchange between artist Judithe Elena Hernandez de Neikrug and critic Shifra M. Goldman concerning the latter's review of MURALS OF AZTLAN exhibit.

668 Hertzog, Carl. Tribute to Jose Cisneros. THE PASSWORD, Vol. 19, no. 4 (Winter 1974). English.

AN: Tribute to artist-illustrator Jose Cisneros, who has "enhanced the appearance of programs, exhibition catalogs, newspaper articles, magazines and special stationery. He has designed emblems such as the seal of the University of Texas at El Paso, the seal of the city of Juarez, Mexico, and the emblem of the Western History Association".

669 Hispanic American artist - Secundino Sandoval. LA LUZ, Vol. 7, no. 9 (September 1978), p. 51. English.

AN: Biographical data and analysis of "Sec", Sandoval's technique as a realist watercolorist.

670 Hispanic artists' [sic] mural unveiled. SOUTHFIELD ECCENTRIC, Exhibition catalog, 1980. English.

AN: A mural titled SYNERGY by Michigan artist Nora Mendoza is unveiled at the R.J. Sullivan Funeral Home. Mendoza has exhibited at numerous one-person shows.

671 Holliday-Abbott, Anne. Suitcase is 2nd home for arts liaison. ARIZONA DAILY STAR, (June 18, 1981), p. H-3. English.

AN: Arizona artist Louis LeRoy who paints, makes prints, and does assemblage is also a regional representative for the National Endowment for the Arts in Arizona, New Mexico, Colorado, Utah, and Wyoming. LeRoy has always been an "advocate of people being proud of their ethnic backgrounds." He feels artists can be self-supporting without commercializing.

672 Hunt, Annette and McNally, Mary. Community art centers in Los Angeles. SPINNING OFF, Vol. 2, no. 19 (January 1980), p. 1. English.

AN: Article includes an interview with Linda Vallejo on the community artistic work of Self-Help Graphics and Art, Inc.

673 Imagenes de la Chicana. Menlo Park, CA: Nowels Publications (Stanford University Chicano Press), [ca 1975]. English.

AN: Collections of writings by Chicanas; illustrated by unsigned drawings, and photographs by Lena Bugarin, Martina Puente, Francisco Camplis, Mario Anzaldua.

674 Inner City Mural Program. Glendale, CA: Los Angeles County Dept. of Parks and Recreation, [ca. 1974]. English.

AN: Brief history and philosophy of the Inner City Mural Program from June 1, 1973 to May 31, 1974, when it was sponsored by the Cultural Arts Section of the Los Angeles County Department of Parks and Recreation, and coordinated by Lukman Glasgow. Artists Judithe Hernandez and Frank Romero included. 20 illustrations, some in color.

675 Instituto Chicano de Artes y Artesanias (Texas Instit. Educational Development). Chicano art of the Southwest. San Antonio, TX: Texas Institute for Educational Development, [ca. 1975]. English.

AN: Illustrated brochure announcing a color slide library on Chicano art supplemented by slide annotation and artists biographies available to institutions. Statement of purpose by Executive Director of program, Cesar Augusto Martinez.

676 Jesus Gutierrez Gallery, San Pedro, CA. "Two of a kind" prints by Linda Vallejo, Muriel Olguin. Exhibition invitation [1978]. English.

AN: Invitation to an exhibit.

Artists (cont.)

677 Jose Montoya: poeta, pintor, profesor, humanista, padre, abuelo. EL HISPANO, Vol. 8, no. 27 (December 23, 1975), p. 5. Spanish.

AN: Biographical data on the Sacramento artist, his contributions to the Chicano Movement and his life as an artist-activist. Photographs of his family and reproduction of one drawing.

678 Joslyn Art Center. Multi-media art exhibit: Muriel Olguin (printmaking), Myrna Shiras (mixed media), Linda Vallejo (painting). Exhibition invitation, 1979. English.

AN: Invitation to an exhibit.

679 Kantar, Chris and Villa, Esteban. An interview with Esteban Villa. Unpublished paper, 1978. English.

AN: A detailed and informative interview with Esteban Villa, prominent Chicano artist. Focus on Villa's philosophy of art, life, and the Chicano art movement. A good primary source. (The unpublished manuscript is deposited in the archives of the R.C.A.F. in Scaramento.)

680 Karam, Bruce G. The murals of Tucson. NUESTRO, Vol. 5, no. 8 (November 1981), p. 58-60. English.

AN: Themes of ethnic pride, cultural unity and cooperation define the murals of Tucson. Brief commentary on the relationship of artists and the community. Illustrated with color photographs.

681 Kelley sparks Chicano growth. EMPIRE MAGAZINE, (December 19, 1971), p. 32. English.

AN: Ramon Kelley, successful and well known Denver artist is credited with fomenting and developing a small but strong Chicano art colony in Denver. As owner of the De Colores Gallery, Kelley has sponsored exhibits and personally encouraged many Chicano artists. John Flores, one of Kelley's proteges talks about his artistic development within the Chicano art and political milieu in Denver. Artist provides information on his daily life and work habits on the occasion of an exhibit of his work at the De Colores Gallery. Flores is a member of the Denver Arts and Humanities Commission. Illustrated with a reproduction of a pastel drawing by John Flores.

682 Knapp, Dan. KCET's show for Chicano viewers. LOS ANGELES TIMES, (April 3, 1970), p. IV, 18. English.

AN: Story on the television series AHORA! started September 1969 on KCET, Los Angeles' National Educational Television. Edward Moreno is program director and host; Victor Millan is producer-director; Claudio Fenner-Lopez, senior producer, has staff including set-designer David Villasenor, production manager James Val, and alternate host-narrator Jesus Trevino. The program has shown exhibits of artists Gilberto Lujan and Daniel Ramirez.

683 L.A.C.E. (Los Angeles Contemporary Exhibitions), Los Angeles, CA. Espina (Thorn): Carlos Almaraz, Elsa Flores, Louie Perez, Teddy Sandoval, John Valadez, Linda Vallejo. Exhibition announcement, 1980.

English.

AN: Announcement of an exhibition and a performance piece by six Los Angeles artists.

684 Laguna Gloria Art Museum, Austin, TX. Tierra, familia sociedad, Amado Pena's themes. Exhibition catalog, 1980. Bilingual.

AN: Illustrated exhibition catalog with artist's biography and chronology of exhibitions. The bi-lingual text by Santos G. Martinez, Jr. situates the artist's work within a dual phased trajectory. First a period (1971-1975) in which the artist creates images armed with a social-political focus and (1975-present), a period starting with the PEOPLESCAPE series in which the artist enters a more lyrical introspective phase.

685 Lomas Garza, Carmen. Altares: arte espiritual del hogar. HOJAS, (1976). English.

AN: Commentary and five photographs from the author's visual documentation of home altars in Kingsville, Texas. Brief analysis of the form, meaning and function of home altars in Chicano daily life.

686 Lomas Garza, Carmen; Montoya, Jose E.; and Pinedo, Maria Vita. What we are...now. Exhibition catalog, n.d. English.

AN: Drawings by Sacramento women artists: Lorraine Garcia, Eva C. Garcia, Kathryn E. Garcia, Celia Rodriguez, Patricia Carrillo.

687 Lopez, Yolanda M. Portrait of my grandmother. CONNEXIONS, no. 2 (Fall 1981). English.

AN: Four mixed-media images representing different ages in the life of the artist's grandmother. A hand written text by the artist provides biographical and social commentary.

688 Lucero, Linda. Compositions from my kitchen/composiciones de mi cocina: an international cookbook. San Francisco, CA: La Raza Graphic Center, 1981. English.

AN: International recipes illustrated with drawings and a poster by Linda Lucero, as well as other artists.

689 Lujan, Pedro and Morton, Carlos. Una platica entre Carlos Morton y Pedro Lujan. CARACOL, Vol. 3, no. 4 (December 1976), p. 10-12. Bilingual.

AN: Carlos Morton interviews Pedro Lujan, a Chicano sculptor who spends six months a year in New York and six months traveling throughout the Southwest. Lujan discusses his preference for creating works from available materials such as scraps of wood, wire, and rope.

690 Manuel Acosta. LA LUZ, Vol. 3, no. 10-11 (January, February, 1975), p. 30. English.

AN: Biographical and exhibition data focusing on Acosta's ability to paint Mexican American types from the border area.

Artists (cont.)

691 Mario Falcon. CHISMEARTE, Vol. 2, no. 1 (Summer 1978), p. 29. Spanish.

AN: Mexican muralist Mario Falcon, who has painted murals in Long Beach and Wilmington (Los Angeles, County), is a political exile in the U. S. Support is asked to prevent his return to Mexico. Illustrated.

692 Marion Koogler McNay Art Institute, San Antonio, TX and Lee, Amy Freeman. Filigree drawings by Consuelo Gonzalez Amezcua. Exhibition catalog, 1968. English.

AN: Illustrated catalog for an exhibition of 42 filigree drawings by Texas artist "Chelo" Amezcua. Apart from biographical and historical information, the text evokes the ambiance of magic and mysticism surrounding the artist.

693 Marquez, Rosa Maria. Artistas chicanas together at C.S.A.C., an interview by Rosa Maria Marquez. CHISMEARTE, Vol. 1, no. 4 (Fall , Winter, 1977), p. 39. English.

AN: An interview with several women doing murals as part of the East Los Angeles Senior Citizens Housing and Mural Beautification Program under the sponsorship of the Chicana Service Action Center. Funding for the project through CETA (Comprehensive Employment Training Act).

694 Martinez, Manuel. Promotional brochure. Brochure, n.d. English.

AN: Biographical information on Chicano muralist who was a pupil of David Alfaro Siqueiros. Illustrated with photographs of two acrylic murals and a photo of the artist.

695 Mechicano Art Center, Los Angeles, CA. Lucila [V. Grijalva] reception. Exhibition announcement [1976]. English.

AN: Flyer announcing an exhibit for the Los Angeles painter and muralist.

696 Memorial Union Display Cases, Arizona State University, Tempe, AZ. The material culture of the Cabezas Redondas, reconstructed by Liz Lerma Bowerman. Exhibition invitation, 1977. English.

AN: Invitation to an exhibit of pottery helmets and other artifacts of an imaginary Bronze Age people, conceived and created by Liz Lerma Bowerman from Mesa, AZ.

697 Mencion Don Quijote: Atanasio P. Davila. LA VOZ DE HOUSTON, (June 5, 1980). English.

AN: Illustrated biography of 70-year-old Mexican-born Texas painter who returned to art after his retirement and had just completed a mural for Houston's Ripley House medical clinic.

698 Mendiville, Miguel and Saavedra-Vela, Pilar. A time for less talk and more action. AGENDA, Vol. 7, no. 5 (September, October, 1977), p. 33-34. English.

AN: The exhibit RAICES Y VISIONES, funded by the National Endowment for the Arts, was composed of more than 100 artworks by Chicano and Latino artists and toured the United States in 1977. The exposition was organized in four sections; artists whose work is influenced or related to Pre-Columbian art, art that explores social and political realities, and works that are more personal and introspective. Gives itinerary and listing of participating artists. Illustrated by photographs of the work of Rudy Trevino, Cesar Martinez, Luis Jimenez from Texas and Larry Fuente from California.

699 Merritt College, Oakland, CA. The role of the Chicano artist and the involvement of the barrio: integrity and tokenism. RASCA TRIPAS, Vol. 2, no. 1 (October 12, 1970). English.

AN: First of an important three-part statement on the form and content of Chicano art and the social role of the Chicano artist. Essential reading for understanding the evolving polemic in the early stages of the Chicano art movement. Part II, entitled "Chicano Art Style," was published in vol. 2, no. 2 (Dec. 1970); and part III, "The Chicano Artist and the Involvement of the Community: Point of View of the Chicano Artist," is in vol. 3, no. 1 (Jan. 1971).

700 Mesa-Bains, Amalia. Homage to Frida Kahlo opens Nov. 2, at Galeria de la Raza. EL TECOLOTE, Vol. 9, no. 1 (September 1978), p. 7. English.

AN: Announcement and call for artwork to Galeria de la Raza's exhibition honoring Frida Kahlo on Nov. 2, 1978. The proposed "Homage to Frida Kahlo" will encompass four major areas; artists' work, documentation/publication, related art productions, and educational activities. The Galeria educated participating artists to the life and art of Frida Kahlo through slide presentations and written material. The exhibition became a milestone in the Galeria de la Raza history.

701 Metro Denver Urban Coalition, Denver, CO. City walls. Brochure, 1979. English.

AN: Brochure/poster giving history of City Walls Project and biographies of seven artists: Jon Howe, Jerry Jaramillo, Steve Lucero, Jowinnie Moore, Al Sanchez, Fred Sanchez, Carlos M. Sandoval. Illustrated.

702 Mexican American Community Service Organization, San Jose, CA. Exhibition of contemporary art. Exhibition brochure, 1968. English.

AN: Biographical and exhibition data for Al Barela, Bert Hermosillo, Octavio Romano, Luis Valdez, Vincent P. Rascon, John Soares and Al Espinoza.

703 The Mexican Museum, San Francisco, CA. Alexander Maldonado. Exhibition brochure, 1979. English.

AN: One page autobiographical statement by Alexander Maldonado. Includes sources of his imagery.

704 The Mexican Museum, San Francisco, CA. Los primeros cinco anos: fifth anniversary exhibit. Exhibition brochure, 1980-81. English.

AN: 65 Mexican, Chicano, and Latino artists exhibited for the fifth anniversary of the Mexican Museum, directed by artist Peter Rodriguez. Cover is drawing by Carmen Lomas Garza.

Artists (cont.)

705 The Mexican Museum, San Francisco, CA.
    Rupert Garcia: portraits/retratos.
    Exhibition brochure, 1981. English.

    AN: Exhibition brochure with
    biographical information and exhibition
    chronology for Rupert Garcia.

706 The Mexican Museum, San Francisco, CA.
    Virginia Jaramillo. Exhibition brochure,
    1980. English.

    AN: Exhibition brochure with
    biographical information, exhibition
    chronology and an artist's statement.

707 Mexican-American Institute of Cultural
    Exchange, San Antonio, TX and Alvarez
    Acosta, Miguel. Mel Casas paintings.
    Exhibition brochure, 1963. Bilingual.

    AN: Exhibition brochure with
    biographical and exhibition chronology for
    El Paso born painter, Meliseo Casas. He is
    the first non-Mexican born artist invited to
    exhibit at the art gallery sponsored by the
    International Organization of Cultural
    Promotion for Foreign Relations in San
    Antonio.

708 Mexico. Secretaria de Relaciones Exteriores.
    Direccion General de Asuntos.. Exposicion:
    estampas y remembranzas; Admonty y Geomonte.
    Exhibition catalog, 1979. Bilingual.

    AN: Catalog of an exhibit by Alice
    Dickerson Montemayor (Admonty). Born in
    Laredo, Texas in 1902, she began painting in
    1976. Her nephew, George A. Montemayor, who
    resides in Houston, is the Coordinator for
    the La Porte Independent School District.

709 Michigan State University, East Lansing, MI.
    Voces del norte. Brochure, 1978. English.

    AN: Photos and graphics by 11 Chicanos
    residing in Michigan.

710 Mills, Kay. The great wall of Los Angeles.
    MS.MAGAZINE, (October 1981), p. 66-69+.
    English.

    AN: THE GREAT WALL OF LOS ANGELES in the
    Tujunga flood control channel in the San
    Fernando Valley, was started as a
    Bicentennial project in 1976. Artistic
    director Judy Baca of the Social and Public
    Art Resource Center, works with crews of
    young people painting aspects of Los Angeles
    history that is not generally found in
    textbooks. Well illustrated.

711 Montini, Ed. Masks reflect the spirit of an
    artist. ARIZONA REPUBLIC, (May 31, 1981),
    p. G-1,G-3. English.

    AN: The paper and ceramic masks of Zarco
    Guerrero reflect many different emotions.
    Masking has long been a tradition in Mexico,
    where Guerrero got his inspiration. Guerrero
    uses his masks for theatre and as an
    educational tool. Illustrated.

712 Montoya, Jose E. Rupert Garcia and the SF
    Museum of Modern Art. RAYAS, Vol. 2, no. 2
    (March, April, 1979), p. 5,11. English.

    AN: Commentary apropos an exhibit of
    pastel drawings by Rupert Garcia at the San
    Francisco Museum of Modern Art. Author
    gives a capsule history of the relationship
    between Raza artists and mainstream cultural

institutions. Rupert Garcia is seen as
belonging to a stalwart group of Chicano
artists.

713 Moody Hall, St. Edwards University, Austin,
    TX. Las companeras. Exhibition invitation,
    1980. English.

    AN: Invitation to an exhibition of
    Chicana/Latina artists sponsored by Mujeres
    Muralistas del Suroeste (MAS). Illustrated.

714 Morales, Sylvia. Chicana. 20 min., 16 mm,
    color, 1979. English.

    AN: Color film tracing the history of
    the Chicana back to pre-Columbian women's
    history. Utilizes images of pre-Columbian
    and modern Mexican murals, as well as
    filming of contemporary Chicanas and their
    activities. Based on a slide show by Anna
    Nieto-Gomez, adapted for the screen by
    Morales.

715 Moser, Charlotte; Renteria, Phil; and Wray,
    Dick. Phil Renteria and Dick Wray. ART IN
    AMERICA, Vol. 64, no. 4 (July, August,
    1976), p. 82-83. English.

    AN: Interview with Laredo-born Houston
    artist Renteria, and Wray, both of whom
    teach at the Museum of Fine Arts. Renteria
    gives much biographical information and his
    philosophy of art. Illustrated in color.

716 Muchnic, Suzanne. LAICA looks at social
    works. CALENDAR, (October 7, 1979), p. 93.
    English.

    AN: Review of the exhibit SOCIAL WORKS
    at the Los Angeles Institute of Contemporary
    Art. Illustration and discussion of Judith
    F. Baca's mural UPRISING OF THE MUJERES, a
    four-part portable canvas mural in the style
    of Siqueiros.

717 Las mujeres muralistas. Exhibition
    invitation, 1974. English.

    AN: Invitation to the inauguration of
    the mural PARA EL MERCADO at Paco's Tacos in
    San Francisco's Mission District by the
    Mujeres Muralistas, Sept. 15, 1974.
    Illustrated by Venezuelan artist Consuelo
    Mendez.

718 Mujeres muralistas de San Diego. CITYBENDER,
    Vol. 2, no. 7 (1978). English.

    AN: Photographic essay on four women
    working on their mural at Chicano Park, San
    Diego.

719 Mural Resource Center, Los Angeles, CA.
    Woman's manual: how to assemble scaffolding.
    Mimeographed booklet, n.d. English.

    AN: Publication to service increasing
    number of women participating in muralism.

720 Las muralistas: Patricia Rodriguez, Consuelo
    Mendez, Graciela Carrillo, Irene Perez.
    Exhibition invitation, 1974. English.

    AN: Invitation to the inauguration of
    the mural LATINO AMERICA by the Mujeres
    Muralistas at the Mission Neighborhood Model
    Cities in San Francisco's Mission District,
    May 31, 1974.

Artists (cont.)

721 Musica hispana en nuestras vidas/Hispanic
music in our lives: almanaque 1982/calendar.
Milwaukee, WI: Miller Brewing Co., 1981.
English.

AN: Twelve Latino artists were
commissioned to illustrate a calendar with
paintings on Hispanic music. The Chicano
artists include Frederico Vigil (New
Mexico), Joe Bastida Rodriguez
(Texas/Washington, D.C.), Manuel Martinez
(Colorado), Jose Antonio Burciaga
(California), Ignacio Gomez (California),
Carolina Flores (Texas), Frank Martinez
(California). Color.

722 Navar, M. Margarita. La vela prendida: home
altars. ARRIBA, Vol. 1, no. 5 (February
1980), p. 12. English.

AN: Brief commentary on the exhibit LA
VELA PRENDIDA: MEXICAN AMERICAN WOMEN'S HOME
ALTARS at the Texas Memorial Museum during
December 1980. Aside from altars, the
exhibit focused on nichos, grutas and
lapidas.

723 Nelson, Kathryn J. Excerpts from los
testamentos: Hispanic women folk artists of
the San Luis Valley, Colorado. FRONTIERS,
Vol. 5, no. 3 (Fall 1980), p. 34-43.
English.

AN: Eppie Archuleta, weaver from the San
Luis Valley in Southern Colorado talks
about her life philosophy, Hispanic cultural
traditions and her role as a community
artist. First person account amply
illustrated with photographs.

724 Neumeier, Marty. Ignacio Gomez.
COMMUNICATION ARTS MAGAZINE, Vol. 21, no. 6
(January, February, 1980), p. 78-87.
English.

AN: Story on commercial designer and
illustrator Ignacio Gomez of Los Angeles
which describes his background, education
and life style. 17 full-color illustrations
of his art work, including the ZOOT SUIT
poster for the Mark Taper Forum play.

725 The new logo. LA VOZ: Concilio for the
Spanish Speaking of King Co., Seattle, no. 5
(June 1979). English.

AN: Biographical information on artist
Alfredo Arreguin. Born in Uruapan, Michoacan
Mexico and residing in Seattle for eighteen
years, Arrequin is active in La Extension
Cultural, an agency formed to meet the
cultural needs of "Hispanics" in the Pacific
Northwest. In his logo for the "Concilio,"
Arreguin employs symbols representing
history, beauty, unity, ethnicity and
communication.

726 New mural on Mission Street. EL HISPANO,
Vol. 7, no. 13 (September 19, 1974), p. 5.
English.

AN: Description of mural at the corner
of 24th Street and South Van Ness in San
Francisco. Painted by Mujeres
Muralistas--Consuelo Mendez, Graciela
Carrillo, Susan Cervantes and Miriam Olivo,
the 30-foot mural depicts people in a
tropical, Latin American setting.

727 Newport Harbor Art Museum, Newport Beach,
CA. Our own artists: art in Orange County.
Exhibition catalog, 1979. English.

AN: Includes Patricia Murillo and
Emigdio Vasquez with illustrations of one
work each. Biographies of the artists.

728 Nora Mendoza: pintora de ascendencia
mexicana triunfa en los EE. UU. BUENHOGAR,
(May 1979), p. 7. Spanish.

AN: Profile of Texas-born Nora Mendoza
of Michigan, a painter of abstractions in
acrylic. She is an active member of many
Detroit and Michigan organizations,
including Nuestras Artes de Michigan which
she co-founded with Jorge Vargas, Martin
Moreno and Jessie Gonzalez.

729 Oakland County Cultural Affairs, MI. Nora
Mendoza: an exhibition of
abstract/impressionism. Exhibition brochure,
[1981]. English.

AN: Exhibit brochure for Texas-born Nora
Chapa Mendoza who studied
abstract-impressionism with Michigan artist
Ljubo Biro. She is a leader in the artistic
and Hispanic communities and runs galleries
in Clarkston and Detroit.

730 La onda artistica de Carmen Lomas Garza.
MAGAZIN, Vol. 1, no. 2 (November 1971), p.
29-37. Spanish.

AN: Short biographical sketch of artist
and reproduction of seven early drawings.
The art of Carmen Lomas Garza is situated
within important events of the Chicano
Movement in Texas: the student walkouts in
Kingsville, and the formation of Colegio
Jacinto Trevino.

731 Orange Co. Library. El Modena Branch.
Empanada: a tasty Mexican group art exhibit
filled with a variety of digestable treats.
Exhibition catalog, [1979]. English.

AN: Catalog of an exhibit by 15 artists:
Dolores Grajeda, William Hernandez-M.,
Marylee Montano, Patricia Murillo, Eduardo
Navarro, Susana A. Zaccagnino, Esau Quiroz,
Juan Elias Ramos, Ricardo M. Serrato,
Benjamin Valenzuela, Emigdio C. Vasquez,
Arthur Valenzuela, Jack Vargas, Alonso
Whitney, and Mexican artist Artemio
Sepulveda living in Orange County. Brief
profiles of the artists.

732 Orange Co. Library. El Modena Branch. The
Hispanic Artist Association of Orange County
presents "Empanada," a tasty Mexican group
art exhibit filled with a variety of
digestible treats. Exhibition invitation,
1979. English.

AN: Poster/invitation to an exhibit of
artists (See "Empanada").

733 Orozco, Irma. Women & their work. PARA LA
GENTE, Vol. 1, no. 4 (October 1977), p. 12.
English.

AN: Illustrated story about "Women &
Their Work" festival in Austin, Texas,
Oct-Dec 1977. Photographers Maria Flores and
Teresina Guerra, Santa Barraza, Nora
Gonzalez Dodson, Sylvia Orozco, and Modesta
Trevino exhibited.

Artists (cont.)

734 Orozco, Sylvia. Las mujeres - Chicana
    artists come into their own. MOVING ON, Vol.
    2, no. 3 (May 1978), p. 14-16. English.

    AN: Illustrated feature prepared by
    artist Sylvia Orozco on the founding of
    Mujeres Artistas del Suroeste in Austin,
    September 1977. Artworks and statements by
    Nora Gonzalez Dodson, Maria Flores, Modesta
    Trevino, Santa Barraza, as well as musicians
    and singers.

735 Orozco, Sylvia and Trevino, Jose. Trevino's
    arte interprets el mundo Chicano. PARA LA
    GENTE, Vol. 1, no. 10 (May 1978), p. 7-9.
    English.

    AN: Interview with Jose Trevino of
    Austin and his artist wife, Modesta.
    Reproduction and discussion of four works.
    Centerspread reproduction of a Trevino
    poster, part of a set of 10 designed for
    bilingual classrooms.

736 Painting changes woman's life at age when
    most ready to retire. LAREDO NEWS,
    (November 4, 1979), p. 1-C. English.

    AN: Interview with 77 year old Alice D.
    Montemayor "Admonty" on the occasion of her
    San Antonio exhibit with her nephew George
    "Geomonte" Montemayor.

737 Palomino, Ernesto ("Ernie"). In black and
    white: evolution of an artist. Fresno, CA:
    Academy Library Guild, 1956. English.

    AN: Illustrations of Palomino's work
    between 1945 and 1955 when he was a student
    in Fresno's Edison High and Adult Schools
    with art teacher Elizabeth Daniels Baldwin,
    who promoted the publication of the book.
    Drawings show extraordinary power and the
    social commentary of a young, essentially
    self-taught artist.

738 Parachini, Allan. Tujunga wash mural stands
    up to storm. LOS ANGELES TIMES, (March 13,
    1980), p. V, 1. English.

    AN: Information about the mural project
    near Los Angeles Valley College in Van Nuys,
    Calif. sponsored by SPARC (Social and Public
    Art Resource Center) of Venice, Calif. and
    coordinated by Judy Baca. Illustrated.

739 Parr, June. Amado Maurilio Pena, Jr.: a
    talented and dedicated artist. ARRIBA,
    (October 1980), p. 1. English.

    AN: Pena is represented in forty-two
    galleries internationally. Recently, Pena
    opened his studio and gallery, El Taller, in
    Austin. His latest works focus on the Indian
    heritage and are based on trips to New
    Mexico. Illustrated.

740 Pena, Amado Maurilio, Jr. Amado Maurilio
    Pena, Jr. Brochure [1980]. English.

    AN: Promotional brochure including a
    biographical profile of the artist, a list
    of representing galleries throughout the
    United States, and eight good quality
    reproductions of serigraphs and mixed media
    drawings, six in color, on the theme of New
    Mexican Pueblo Indians.

741 Perales Leven, Humberto. Marcos Raya -
    Mexican painter. IMAGENES, Vol. 1, no. 1
    (July 1976). Bilingual.

    AN: Mexican born Chicago muralist Marcos
    Raya painted a mural titled HOMAGE TO RIVERA
    in the Pilsen barrio of Chicago at the
    corner of 18th Street and May. Raya
    articulates the role of the muralist and his
    function within the working class community.
    Also in this issue is an article on the
    formation of MARCH (Movimiento Artistico
    Chicano) in 1972 in East Chicago Indiana.
    Portfolio of drawings by Marcos Raya and
    photographs by Mario Castillo. Bilingual
    text.

742 Perez, Demetrio. Mel Casas - humanscapes.
    Houston, TX: Contemporary Arts Museum, 1976.
    English.

    AN: Catalog for Mel Casas exhibition
    Oct. 22-Nov. 23, 1976. Artist calls his
    paintings "visual conundrums which play with
    our cultural concepts, with our cultural
    vision." Includes biographical information
    and exhibition chronology. Well illustrated
    with nine reproductions of artists work and
    two photos of the artist.

743 Petersen, Karen and Wilson, J.J. Women
    artists: Third World. New York, NY: Harper &
    Row, 1975. English.

    AN: Catalog of slides with accompanying
    notes. Slides of Chicana artists available:
    Margaret Herrera (Chavez), Consuelo (Chelo)
    Gonzalez Amezcua, Santa Barraza, Mujeres
    Muralistas, El Grupo de Santa Ana, Carmen
    Lomas Garza, Carolina Flores.

744 Plagens, Peter. Sunshine muse: contemporary
    art on the West Coast. New York: Praeger,
    1974. English.

    AN: Despite his rather "chic" art
    critical prose and mainstream orientation,
    Plagen's book is an important compendium of
    arts and cultural activities on the West
    Coast, primarily California. Gives the
    history of important artists, movements, and
    art schools. These set the institutional
    framework for the education of Chicano
    artists from the 1950s on. Manuel Neri
    discussed (p. 89, 94, 99) and illustrated
    (p. 92).

745 Portraying Latino women in the Mission. SAN
    FRANCISCO EXAMINER, (September 10, 1974),
    p. 26. English.

    AN: Three muralists of the Mission
    District, Irene Perez, Patricia Rodriguez,
    and Venezuelan Consuelo Mendez, are
    preparing a six-paneled
    painting-construction, the RHOMBOIDAL
    PARALLELOGRAM, for the 28th annual San
    Francisco Art Festival. It will illustrate
    the life of women in the Mission.
    Illustrated.

746 Preuss, Karen. The new Mission murals. SAN
    FRANCISCO BAY GUARDIAN, (June 28, 1975), p.
    14-15. English.

    AN: Mural art in San Francisco's Mission
    District has covered nearly every wall and
    alley on lower 24th Street. Murals by Mike
    Rios, the Mujeres Muralistas (Patricia
    Rodriguez, Graciela Carrillo, Consuelo
    Mendez, Miriam Olivo, Irene Perez, Susan
    Cervantes) appear in the area. Others have
    been painted by artists associated with the
    Galeria de la Raza. Illustrations.

Artists (cont.)

747 Quesada-Weiner, Rosemary. Las mujeres: 1977 National Women's Conference. Los Angeles, CA: Rosemary Quesada-Weiner, 1978. English.

AN: Portfolio (with captions) of photographs taken by Quesada-Weiner.

748 Quinonez, Naomi H. In her own backyard = En su propio traspatio. CAMINOS, Vol. 2, no. 2 (March 1981), p. 34-36,62. Bilingual.

AN: Describes the establishment of the Centro de Arte in Long Beach, CA by Chicana artist Lola de la Riva and her family. The Centro, which is in de la Riva's Long Beach home, is designed to give members of her barrio a chance to develop and display their artistic talents. Frequent workshops in mask making, clay sculpture, painting, and graphics are held at the Centro, and the works of local artists are usually on display in her backyard.

749 Quintero, Victoria. Mujeres muralistas. LA RAZON MESTIZA, Vol. 11, (Summer 1975).

AN: Goals and artistic procedures of the Mujeres Muralistas Collective. Article emphasizes the solidarity of Latin American women and Chicanas and how their joint artistic production reflects a woman's viewpoint in aesthetic terms.

750 Quintero, Victoria. A mural is a painting on a wall done by human hands. EL TECOLOTE, Vol. 5, no. 1 (September 13, 1974), p. 6+. English.

AN: The women's collective, Mujeres Muralistas, exists within the strong San Francisco mural movement. Originally the group included Graciela Carrillo, Consuelo Mendez, Irene Perez, and Patricia Rodriguez. The group has expanded to include Susan Cervantes, Ester Hernandez, and Miriam Olivo. The two murals completed have been criticized for not being political; the women answer that they want the atmosphere to be surrounded with life, with colors. Illustrated.

751 Quirarte, Jacinto. Chelo Gonzalez Amezcua. QUETZAL, Vol. 1, no. 2 (Winter 1970, 1971), p. 33-36.

AN: Biographical information based on a taped interview with the Del Rio, Texas artist. As a self-taught artist, Chelo Gonzalez Amezcua developed a drawing style using colored ball point pens which she calls "Filigree Art", a new Texas culture. Poorly illustrated.

752 Quirarte, Jacinto. Image and text (poetry) in the work of Consuelo (Chelo) Gonzalez Amezcua, a Texas artist (1903-1975). RESEARCH CENTER FOR THE ARTS REVIEW, Vol. 5, no. 1 (January 1982), p. 1-3. English.

AN: The use of images and poetry in the work of self-taught Del Rio, Texas artist Chelo Gonzalez Amezcua is demonstrated by focusing on her drawing EL MOSAICO DE LAS AVES of 1972, in which her use of both sides of the paper is contrasted with similar uses in Aztec sculpture. Illustrated.

753 Ramon Kelley. ARTISTS OF THE ROCKIES, Vol. 1, no. 1 (Spring 1974), p. 6-11. English.

AN: Biographical information on Ramon Kelley and a listing of his invitational shows. Illustrated with a photograph of the artist and a portfolio of ten works (three in color).

754 Rand, Steve. Carlos David Almaraz. LOS ANGELES FREE PRESS, Vol. 11, no. 10 (March 8, 1974), p. 14. English.

AN: Brief biographical sketch on Mexican-born, Los Angeles artist Carlos Almaraz on the occasion of the Los Four exhibit at the Los Angeles County Museum of Art, artists who are, the author says inaccurately, largely self-taught. Almaraz studied at Garfield High School with David Ramirez, and at Otis Art Institute. One illustration.

755 Raoul Mora. ESENCIA, Vol. 1, no. 3 (March, April, 1982).

AN: Brief article on Stockton-born landscape painter and lithographer who records the beauties of Northern California in flat patterns and strong color. Illustrated.

756 Rayaprofile: Carlos Cortez. RAYAS, Vol. 1, no. 6 (November, December, 1978), p. 3. English.

AN: Biographical profile of Chicago artist Carlos Cortez.

757 Reser, Phil. Rene Yanez: state-of-the-xerox art. CITY ARTS, Vol. 3, no. 8 (August 1981). English.

AN: Five years ago when Xerox came out with a color copier, Yanez started experimenting with the machine's color buttons, which he uses like a musical instrument or a paint brush. Yanez's work is showing at the Electro-Arts Gallery in San Francisco. Brief profile of the artist, whose father and grandfather were both artists.

758 Richard Henkin, Inc., Beverly Hills, CA. Veloy Vigil. Exhibition brochure, n.d. English.

AN: Full color brochure about the Denver-born artist who has exhibited in many galleries and museums in the United States. His paintings deal with western subjects.

759 Rickey, Carrie. The writing on the wall. ART IN AMERICA, Vol. 69, no. 5 (May 1981), p. 54-57. English.

AN: Detailed article on the career of Judy Baca, director of SPARC (Social and Public Arts Resource Center) in Venice, Calif., and of the Great Wall of Los Angeles, a five year mural project at the Tujunga Wash. Well illustrated in black and white and color.

760 Rivera, Humberto R. and Howell, Heather R. The murals of East Los Angeles. Film. English.

AN: Puerto Rican filmmaker Rivera deals with Chicano murals and their makers. Views of the murals and interviews with the artists make up the bulk of the film. Unfortunately Rivera focuses the camera on the artists and the streets and seldom gives the viewer a detailed look at the mural under discussion.

Artists (cont.)

761 Rodriguez, Anita. Las enjarradoras: women of the earth. NEW MEXICO, (February 1980), p. 46-47+. English.

AN: History of adobe construction in New Mexico, its decline and its present revival in Arizona and New Mexico. Written by a professional adobe architect and feminist who defines the traditional terms and techniques of this woman's craft. Illustrated.

762 Rodriguez, Anita. Tradiciones de adobe en Nuevo Mejico norteno = adobe traditions in Northern New Mexico. ADOBE NEWS, no. 15 (1977). Bilingual.

AN: History of adobe construction in New Mexico, from primarily Indian sources with Spanish input. For 400 years, women were builders and architects of the Southwest; today they are "enjarradoras" (plasterers). Written by a professional enjarradora from New Mexico. Illustrated.

763 Rodriguez, Patricia. Portfolio: Patricia Rodriguez; the visual interview. METAMORFOSIS, Vol. 3, no. 1-2 (1980, 1981), p. 38-45. English.

AN: Statement by the artist reprinted from her exhibit "The Visual Interview" at the Mission Cultural Center, San Francisco. Discusses her fifteen mask-box-sculptures of Chicano artists from northern California. Illustrated with photographs of the artist at work and five of her sculptures. This issue of METAMORFOSIS combines volumes 3 and 4.

764 Rodriguez, Pedro. Chicano art arising. PAPEL CHICANO, Vol. 1, no. 9 (December 21, 1971), p. 5. English.

AN: A concise formulation on the nature of Chicano Art. It arises from a new cultural formation influenced by Mexican and Anglo American cultural forms yet distinct from either. In visual terms, artists are reflecting and affirming this new cultural synthesis. Illustrated with reproductions of three oil paintings: GRITO DE LIBERTAD by Jose D. Marin, WOMAN IN BLUE by Manuel Aguilera, and ALEGORIA MEXICANA by Tomas Torres. All three are pinto artists from Leavenworth Penitentiary.

765 Rodriguez, Pedro. Chicano artist's paintings on display at WWC. UNION BULLETIN, (February 19, 1981). English.

AN: Commentary by artist Pedro Rodriguez stressing the social context of Chicano art and the role and function of the Chicano artist. Illustrated with a photograph of the artist and reproductions of two oil paintings: EL OBRERO and CIUDAD LIBERTAD.

766 Romotsky, Jerry and Romotsky, Sally R. Placas and murals. ARTS IN SOCIETY, Vol. 2, no. 1 (Summer, Fall , 1974), p. 286-299. English.

AN: Details how Chicano muralists have recognized the aesthetics of graffiti and incorporated them into their murals. Among the earliest to do so were Lucille Grijalva and Willie Herron. Illustrated.

767 Ruben Salazar Library, Sonoma State University, Sonoma, CA. Patricia Rodriguez: Chicano sculpture and masks. Exhibition invitation, 1981. English.

AN: Invitation to an exhibit.

768 Ruiz, Elizabeth. Fiesta artist. THE RANGER, (April 23, 1981). English.

AN: Biographical information on San Antonio painter Jesus Trevino. Artist describes his work as "realism" with "a focus on Mexican American and Chicano culture, the people and their lives".

769 Ruiz, Elvia. Whitewashed mural. SENTIMIENTOS, Vol. 1, no. 2 (May 1978), p. 7-10. English.

AN: Illustrated article about Las Mujeres Muralistas del Valle. Their mural titled, "History of the Chicanos From a Woman's Perspective" was vandalized. Members of the mural group recall its creation and comment on its destruction.

770 Salazar, Veronica. Aspiration comes true. SAN ANTONIO EXPRESS-NEWS, (October 28, 1979), p. 8-H. English.

AN: History of Alice Dickerson Montemayor of Laredo, Texas (known as "Admonty") who started to paint at 74 on the occasion of her second exhibit at the Mexican government's Instituto Cultural.

771 Salazar, Veronica. Prominent Mexican-Americans-Porfirio Salinas. SAN ANTONIO EXPRESS-NEWS, (April 1, 1973), p. I-4. English.

AN: Biographical information and artistic chronology of Porfirio Salinas. This self-taught artist is the most prominent painter of Texas landscapes, especially with bluebonnets. Former president Lyndon B. Johnson was an ardent fan and patron.

772 Salinas, Porfirio. Porfirio Salinas: blue bonnets and cactus; an album of Southwestern paintings. Austin, TX: Pemberton Press, 1967. English.

AN: A lavishly illustrated edition of five short stories interspersed with reproductions of Porfirio Salinas landscapes. Salinas is considered an important Southwestern landscapist.

773 Salinas, Raul. Nueva estrella en el horizonte. LA RAZA, Vol. 1, no. 2 (1970), p. 79. Spanish.

AN: Brief introduction to the work of painter Ruben Estrella, a native of San Antonio, who at the time was serving out his penalty at Leavenworth State Prison.

774 Salinas, Raul. Portrait of an artist. ENTRELINEAS, Vol. 1, no. 5-6 (October, December, 1971), p. 3-5. English.

AN: Biographical and artistic information on Ruben Estrella who developed as a "pinto" artist within Leavenworth Penitentiary.

Artists (cont.)

775 Samuels, Peggy and Samuels, Harold.
    Cisneros, Jose. In: THE ILLUSTRATED
    BIOGRAPHICAL ENCYCLOPEDIA OF ARTISTS OF THE
    AMERICAN WEST. Garden City, NY: Doubleday,
    1976, p. 95. English.

    AN: Brief biography on book illustrator,
    Jose Cisneros, who is a leading authority on
    the costume, weapons, and trappings of
    Mexican border horsemen.

776 Samuels, Peggy and Samuels, Harold. Grandee,
    Joe Ruiz. In: THE ILLUSTRATED BIOGRAPHICAL
    ENCYCLOPEDIA OF ARTISTS OF THE AMERICAN
    WEST. NY: Doubleday, 1976, p. 193. English.

    AN: Brief biography of third generation
    Texan, Western painter of history, military,
    portrait subjects and illustrator living in
    Arlington, TX where his collection of
    Western artifacts is at the "Joe Grandee
    Gallery and Museum of the Old West." 1974
    one person retrospective in Washington, DC.

777 Samuels, Peggy and Samuels, Harold. Salinas,
    Porfirio. In THE ILLUSTRATED BIBLIOGRAPHICAL
    ENCYCLOPEDIA OF THE AMERICAN WEST. Garden
    City, NY: Doubleday, 1976, p. 415. English.

    AN: Brief biography of Texas "bluebonnet
    painter" (b. 1910). Only teachers were Jose
    Arpa and Robert Wood of San Antonio. (See
    also Jacinto Quirarte's book: MEXICAN
    AMERICAN ARTISTS).

778 San Antonio Museum Association, San Antonio,
    TX. Real, really real, super real.
    Exhibition brochure, 1981. English.

    AN: Exhibit surveying modern and
    contemporary realism in the U.S. Includes a
    brief biography, personal statement, and
    color illustration of work by Jesse C.
    Trevino, San Antonio, Texas photorealist
    painter and muralist, (pp. 146-147).

779 San Francisco Museum of Modern Art, San
    Francisco, CA and Pearlstein, Howard.
    Aesthetics of graffiti. Exhibition catalog,
    1978. English.

    AN: Graffiti are defined as any
    coherently-intended presence written,
    scratched, painted, engraved, printed,
    pasted or otherwise impressed in a public
    place. Graffiti have been incorporated into
    works by artists. In this catalog, works by
    Chicano artists Carlos Almaraz, Wilfred
    Castano, Judithe Hernandez, Gilbert Lujan,
    Gustavo Rivera, Frank Romero, John M.
    Valadez, Victor M. Valle, Xavier Viramontes
    - as well as many Latino and non-Latino
    artist, appear.

780 San Francisco Museum of Modern Art, San
    Francisco, CA; Chavez, Ray; and Gordon,
    Allan M. Carmen Lomas Garza/prints and
    gouaches: Margo Humphrey/monotypes.
    Exhibition catalog, 1980. English.

    AN: Carmen Lomas Garza, though working
    in a "naive" style is technically adept and
    academically trained, though she draws
    motifs from folk production of her native
    Texas. Her themes in this exhibit are
    memories of her childhood. Well illustrated.

781 San Pedro Municipal Art Gallery, San Pedro,
    CA. Celebration: Muriel Olguin and Linda
    Vallejo. San Pedro, CA: San Pedro Municipal
    Art Gallery, [1978]. English.

    AN: Invitation to an exhibit.
    Illustrated.

782 Santa Ana College, Santa Ana, CA and
    Goldman, Shifra M. Chicano art. Exhibition
    catalog, 1974. English.

    AN: Thirteen California artists are
    presented in a short essay defining Chicano
    as a double mestizaje of Mexican mestizo and
    U.S. influences that exists in a state of
    "reconciled conflict." Its aim is
    communication. Artists included are
    Malaquias Montoya, Rupert Garcia, Manuel
    Hernandez, Esteban Villa, Robert Gomez,
    Harvey Tarango, Mary Helen Castro, Eduardo
    Carrillo, Graciela Carrillo, and "Los Four":
    Carlos Almaraz, Robert de la Rocha, Judithe
    Hernandez, Gilbert Lujan and Frank Romero.

783 Santa Ana Public Library, Newhope Branch,
    Santa Ana, CA. Artistas latinos de Orange
    County. Exhibition brochure, 1979. English.

    AN: Exhibit of six artists: Dolores
    Grajeda, Eduardo Navarro, Arthur Valenzuela,
    Benjamin Valenzuela, Emigdio Vasquez, Susana
    A. Zaccagnino.

784 Segade, Gustavo V. Alfredo Arreguin.
    CITYBENDER, Vol. 2, no. 9 (1978). English.

    AN: Brief profile of Mexican-born
    painter Arreguin who lives in the state of
    Washington. Three illustrations.

785 Shakti Gallery, Long Beach, CA. "Fire in the
    lodge," paper sculptures by Linda Vallejo.
    Exhibit invitation, 1981. English.

    AN: Invitation to an exhibit by Long
    Beach, CA artist Linda Vallejo. Illustrated.

786 Sharing a bit of magic with John Mendoza.
    ARTISTS OF THE ROCKIES, Vol. 1, no. 2
    (Spring 1974), p. 14-17. English.

    AN: Growing up in the St. Charles Mesa
    east of Pueblo Colorado, John Mendoza has
    sought to capture the essence of nature in
    that part of the country in his paintings.
    Blending realism and abstraction, Mendoza
    has evolved a distinctive personal idiom.
    Illustrated with reproductions of two
    watercolors and six drawings. Includes two
    photos of the artist and his pupils.

787 Simon, Joan. Report from New Mexico. ART IN
    AMERICA, Vol. 68, no. 6 (Summer 1980), p.
    33-41. English.

    AN: Luis Jimenez worked four years as
    artist-in-residence at the Roswell Museum
    and Art Center, Roswell, NM, which enabled
    him to produce his PROGRESS series and other
    monumental sculpture.

788 Simpson, Claudette. An adobe fireplace:
    Anita Rodriguez has built many - each one
    different. PRESCOTT COURIER-WEEKLY FEATURE,
    (December 1, 1978). English.

    AN: Anita Rodriguez is an enjarradora--a
    professional specializing in adobe
    architecture--in New Mexico. She builds
    fireplaces, lays mud floors, builds hornos
    (outdoor ovens) and does interior and
    exterior plastering. Well illustrated.

Artists (cont.)

789 Social and public art resource center.
Brochure, [1977]. English.

   AN: Brochure including the history,
   philosophy, and resources of SPARC, an
   outgrowth of the Los Angeles Citywide Mural
   Project/Mural Resource Center headed by Judy
   Baca. Illustrated.

790 Southern Colorado State College, Pueblo, CO
and Monteverde, Mildred. Chicanos graficos
[sic]...California. Exhibition brochure,
[1974]. Spanish.

   AN: Brief background of California art
   movement and 13 artists from San Francisco,
   Los Angeles, Sacramento, Fresno. Important
   factual information despite numerous errors
   with names and Spanish terms. 16
   illustrations of silkscreens, lithograph,
   etching.

791 Spurgin, Judy. Amado Maurilio Pena, Jr.
ULTRA MAGAZINE, Vol. 1, no. 1 (September
1981). English.

   AN: Succinct treatment of Pena's
   artistic trajectory and a superficial
   analysis of his work. Information on his
   patrons and supporters.

792 Stamper, Frances. Fluid washes of ink and
acrylic. TEXAS HOMES MAGAZINE, Vol. 4, no. 1
(January, February, 1980), p. 104-112.
English.

   AN: Well illustrated article with color
   reproductions of the work of Philip
   Renteria. Provides biographical information
   and focuses on the consumate craftsmanship
   of his drawings and paintings.

793 Stellweg, Carla. De como el arte chicano es
tan indocumentado como los
indocumentados/the way in which Chicano art
is as undocumented as the 'undocumented'.
ARTES VISUALES, no. 29 (June 1981), p.
23-32. Bilingual.

   AN: An overview of Chicano art from its
   beginnings to the present. Suggestion that
   present art is improved by abandoning the
   nationalist, derivative and folkloric phase.
   Statements and biographies of artists. Some
   non-Chicanos included as Chicanos. Many
   illustrations. Bilingual.

794 Tapia, Ludy. Montoya and the art of
survival. LA VOZ DEL PUEBLO, Vol. 3, no. 5
(June 1972), p. 6. English.

   AN: Profile of San Francisco Bay area
   poster maker and artist Malaquias Montoya,
   who first became involved in the Chicano
   movement in San Jose working with MASC and
   EL MACHETE paper. In Berkeley (1968), he met
   Esteban Villa and, with others, formed the
   Mexican American Liberation Art Front
   (MALAF). Montoya is against elitism
   influencing Chicano art, and is concerned
   with commercialization of Chicano art and
   artists. Illustrated.

795 Texas Memorial Museum, University of Texas,
Austin, TX. La vela prendida:
Mexican-American women's home altars.
Exhibition catalog, 1980. Bilingual.

   AN: Bilingual illustrated
   brochure-catalog of exhibit. Includes home
   altars and graveyard headstones.

796 Through the eyes of Joe Giron. NUESTRO, Vol.
5, no. 9 (December 1981), p. 34-40. English.

   AN: A 9-photo collection of the work of
   Las Cruces, NM photographer, Joe Giron.
   Typical scenes in Texas, NM, and Ohio.

797 Tone Briones, artist of Aztlan. PAPEL
CHICANO, Vol. 2, no. 11 (December 20, 1972),
p. 4. English.

   AN: Biographical information on
   caricaturist and cartoonist Tony Briones
   from Laredo, TX, who is staff artist for
   PAPEL CHICANO. Illustrated with one
   editorial caricature, "Be a Good Chicano,
   Join the Army," and a two-panel cartoon.

798 Torres, Louis R. A Profile of an Hispano
Artist: Charlie "Clavos" Felix. LA LUZ, Vol.
4, no. 6-7 (September, October, 1975), p.
3-4. English.

   AN: Biographical data on artist and his
   unique nail relief sculpture.

799 Trafford, Al. The giant painted photo album:
Jesse Trevino. SOUTHWEST ART, (April 1979).
English.

   AN: Well illustrated story on San
   Antonio photorealist painter Jesse Trevino.
   Includes biographical material, description
   of his working methods for murals and easel
   paintings, and self-characterization of his
   work as "cultural documentary painting".

800 Trujillo, Marcella. The dilemma of the
modern Chicana artist and critic. HERESIES,
Vol. 2, no. 4 (1979), p. 5-10. English.

   AN: Recommended for its application to
   the visual arts in its discussion of
   iconography common to literature and art,
   and symbols popular with Chicana artists: La
   Malinche, the Virgin of Guadalupe,
   Tonantzin, Mother Earth, etc.

801 Tsutakaua, Mayumi. Artist paints from
heritage. SEATTLE TIMES, (September 15,
1980). English.

   AN: Biographical information on Armond
   Lara, Northwest Chicano-Navajo artist. He is
   coordinating the restoration of a mural done
   in Seattle by Mexican artist Pablo
   O'Higgins. In his own work Lara is
   experimenting with paper making and the use
   of natural pigments.

802 Tsutakaua, Mayumi. Despite hostilities,
Arreguin is transcending. SEATTLE TIMES,
(September 2, 1979). English.

   AN: Biographical sketch of Northwest
   Chicano painter and ceramicist Alfredo
   Arreguin. Artistic chronology and negative
   relationship with local mainstream art
   institutions.

803 Turner, Mark. Muralist uses walls to break
barriers between people. ARIZONA DAILY STAR,
(July 23, 1981). English.

   AN: Luis Gustavo Mena works on his
   latest mural, an image of Benito Juarez with
   the Mexican and "Latin Empire" flags, and a
   scale of justice. Information about the
   artist, son of an artistic family, and
   recent high school graduate.

Artists (cont.)

804 University of Texas. El Paso. Chicano
     Studies Program. "Chicanotations": paintings
     and drawings by Manuel Unzueta. Exhibition
     brochure, 1979. English.

     AN: Exhibition handout includes
     biographical data and a listing of the 20
     works exhibited by Unzueta.

805 University of Texas. San Antonio. Medical
     School and Lee, Amy Freeman. Consuelo
     Gonzales Amezcua. Exhibition catalog, n.d.
     English.

     AN: Exhibition catalog with a text by
     Amy Freeman Lee. This major exhibit
     presented 110 of the artist's works. Price
     list included.

806 Unzueta, Manuel. Iconography: strictly
     Chicano. XALMAN, Vol. 1, no. 4 (Spring
     1977), p. 17-18. English.

     AN: Only a Chicano artist can portray
     the unique experience of being Chicano
     through visual images of despair and self
     pride: opinion of painter Unzueta.

807 Unzueta, Manuel. Social commentary on
     Chicano art: a painter's critical brush.
     XALMAN, Vol. 1, no. 5 (Fall   1977), p.
     63-68. English.

     AN: Personal manifesto of painter
     Unzueta. Description of popular Chicano
     iconography and esthetics.

808 Valdez, Armando. El calendario chicano 1975.
     Hayward, CA: Southwest Network, 1975.
     English.

     AN: Third in a series of historical
     calendars produced in 1972 and 1974 by La
     Causa Publications and Southwest Network.
     Artists included for each month are Carmen
     Lomas Garza, Sergio Hernandez, Malaquias
     Montoya, Mujeres Muralistas (Graciela
     Carrillo, Venezuelan Consuelo Mendez, Irene
     Perez, Patricia Rodriguez), Ramses Noriega,
     Ernie Palomino, Amado Maurilio Pena, Martin
     Perez. All but Texan Pena are California
     artists.

809 Valdez, Armando. El calendario chicano 1977.
     Hayward, CA: Southwest Network, 1977.
     English.

     AN: Fifth in a series of historical
     calendars produced in 1972, 1974, 1975, 1976
     by La Causa Publications and Southwest
     Network. Artists whose work is reproduced
     are Malaquias Montoya, Amado Maurilio Pena,
     Ramori Zamora, Glugio J.L. Nicandro [Gronk],
     Etta Delgado, Ricardo Alaniz, Diane Gamboa,
     Elisa Marina Coleman, Margarita Calderon,
     Jose Antonio Burciaga, Cesar Augusto
     Martinez, Maria Ochoa y Valtierra, Juan
     Renteria Fuentes, from California, New
     Mexico, and Texas.

810 Valdez, Salvador. A forgotten artist's work
     lives on. NOSOTROS, Vol. 2, no. 6. English.

     AN: Narrative of the life and times of
     Jose Aceves, a self taught El Paso artist
     (1909-1968), noted for his desert
     landscapes.

811 Valenzuela-Crocker, Elvira. Tanguma: a man
     and his murals. AGENDA, no. 5 (Summer 1974),
     p. 14-17. English.

     AN: Illustrated report on Houston
     muralist Leo Tanguma's 1973 work REBIRTH OF
     OUR NATIONALITY as well as other murals in
     progress. Tanguma's social views and his
     debt to Mexican muralist David Alfaro
     Siqueiros are detailed.

812 Valle, Victor Manuel and Vasquez, Emigdio.
     Emigdio Vasquez Interview. SOMOS,
     (December, January, 1978, 1979), p. 42-43.
     English.

     AN: Article on Arizona-born painter, son
     of a miner, living in Orange County,
     California. Discusses his realistic style
     (from photographs), technique, humanism,
     interest in murals, and loan of work for
     Alejandro Grattan's film ONLY ONCE IN A
     LIFETIME. Illustrated.

813 Vallejo, Linda. I am...Linda Vallejo.
     CHISMEARTE, Vol. 1, no. 4 (Fall   , Winter,
     1977, 1978), p. 27-30.

     AN: Brief autobiographical sketch
     illustrated with three drawings.

814 Varda, Agnes. Mur murs/mural murals on the
     wall ... Film, Cine Tamaris, Paris, 1980.
     English.

     AN: Full length documentary film
     produced for French television; also
     available with English subtitles. Deals
     impressionistically with the murals and
     muralists of Los Angeles. Included are Wayne
     Alaniz Healy, David Botello, Willie Herron,
     Manuel Cruz, Judy Baca, the murals in
     Venice, CA, graffiti - among others. Color.

815 Vasquez, Emigdio. The Cypress Street Barrio
     and my art: a statement of intent.
     Unpublished manuscript, 1978. English.

     AN: The Arizona-born artist whose family
     moved to Orange, Calif. in 1941 describes
     his working class barrio and the perspective
     it gave him of "life, people and society."
     He turned to this subject matter as a young
     artist and has continued to paint the
     barrio. Description of sources and methods
     of work.

816 Vasquez, Emigdio and Goldman, Shifra M.
     Painter: Emigdio Vasquez. Brochure, [1981].
     English.

     AN: Brochure including a brief biography
     and illustrations of eight paintings.

817 Vasquez, Esperanza and Esparza, Moctezuma.
     Agueda Martinez. 16 mm. color film. English.

     AN: Sixteen-minute film directed by
     Esperanza Vasquez and produced by Moctezuma
     Esparza concerning the life and weaving of
     an elderly New Mexican woman. Martinez
     carries on the tradition of floor loom
     weaving, as well as farming.

818 Venegas, Sybil. The artists and their
     work--the role of the Chicana artist.
     CHISMEARTE, Vol. 1, no. 4 (Fall   , Winter,
     1977), p. 3, 5. English.

Artists (cont.)

819 Vergara, Dora Maria. New artist del barrio
Canta Ranas. REVISTA RIO BRAVO, Vol. 1, no.
1 (Winter 1981), p. 2. English.

AN: Biography of self-taught artist
Pedro Martinez who lives in and records the
life and people of the westide barrio
"Cantaranas" in Laredo, Texas. Five drawings
reproduced in this issue.

820 Vigil, Rita. Veloy Vigil: artist capturing
ethereal horizons and the Indian spirit.
SOUTHWEST ART COLLECTOR, Vol. 1, no. 3
(March, April, 1980), p. 2. English.

AN: Denver-born artist who changed from
commercial to fine art in 1972 when he was
40 years old, though he "sidelined" in fine
art from the early 1960s. Resides in Taos
and Southern California.

821 Vincent, Kathy Ariana. Monty Montemayor:
portrait of an artist. ARRIBA, Vol. 1, no. 7
(1980). English.

AN: Born in Laredo, TX, in 1902, "Monty"
Montemayor paints in the naif tradition. As
an older artist, she has been a role model
for younger Chicana artists. Brief profile
of the self-taught artist. Illustrated.

822 Wagner Gallery presents paintings by Manuel
Garza. SOUTHWEST ART COLLECTOR, Vol. 1, no.
3 (March, April, 1980), p. 3. English.

AN: Story on Texas landscape and
blue-bonnet painter influenced by Porfirio
Salinas.

823 Walking tour and guide to the Great Wall at
Tujunga Wash. Venice, CA: Social and Public
Art Resource Center, [1981]. English.

AN: History and symbolism of the GREAT
WALL, directed by Judy Baca, and created by
teams of young people working on the mural
since 1976. Illustrated.

824 Weil Gallery Center for the Arts, Corpus
Christi State University. Caras y mascaras:
the art of El Zarco Guerrero. Exhibition
invitation, 1981. English.

AN: Invitation to exhibit of Arizona
artist. Color illustration.

825 White, Ron. Bluebonnet the flower of South
Texas painting. SAN ANTONIO EXPRESS-NEWS,
(December 14, 1975), p. 7-H. English.

AN: The South Texas landscape paintings
by Porfirio Salinas are immensely popular
and command high prices. This analysis of
the career and the production of the late
artist (died April 18, 1973), concludes that
Salinas was "a mediocre artist with mediocre
skills and a poor sense of imagination".

826 Wilks, Flo. Joseph A. Chavez. ART VOICES
SOUTH, Vol. 3, no. 1 (January, February,
1980), p. 30. English.

AN: Brief resume on art and life of
Albuquerque sculptor. Illustrated.

827 William Grant Still Community Arts Center,
Los Angeles, CA. Latin American artists
exhibition. Exhibition brochure, 1978.
English.

AN: Exhibit curated by Linda Vallejo
including Carlos Almaraz, Michael M.

Amescua, Ray Bravo, Isabel Castro, Yreina
Cervantez, Luis Serrano-Cordero, Cynthia
Honesto, Judith Miranda, Teddy Sandoval,
John Taboada, Emigdio Vasquez. Illustrated.

828 Wilson, William. Chicana artists still
seeking identification. LOS ANGELES TIMES,
(June 23, 1975), p. VI, 5. English.

AN: Ten Chicana artists are exhibiting
their work in the Boathouse Gallery of Plaza
de la Raza in Lincoln Park: Judithe
Hernandez, Patssi Valdez, Judy Baca,
Josefina Quesada, Victoria del
Castillo-Leon, Olga Muniz, Gloria Flores,
Sylvia Morales, Isabel Castro and Celia
Tejadak. The work is still tentative and may
develop.

829 Wine and cheese: foto fun. Berkeley, CA:
Exhibition invitation, 1979. English.

AN: Invitation to an evening of
photographic slides and prints and
discussion by photographers Jose Romero and
Maria Pinedo.

830 Woman who began at 73 is shaping Chicano
art. SAN ANTONIO EXPRESS-NEWS, (August 18,
1978), p. 6-W. English.

AN: 76-year-old Laredoan Alicia
Dickerson Montemayor who began painting on
guajes (gourds) from her garden three years
ago, now paints on canvas stories from her
life in the Valley, nature, and people. An
exhibit of her work, referred to by Chicano
art critics as "el arte de la inocencia"
opens at Gallery of El Centro Cultural de
LUCHA, in Austin, TX.

831 Woman's Building, Los Angeles, CA.
Crosspollination: a blending of traditional
and contemporary art by Asian, Black and
Chicana women. Los Angeles, CA: Woman's
Building, 1979. English.

AN: Invitation to an exhibit in which
are included Patricia Murillo and Linda
Vallejo.

832 Women artists: forming a Texas network.
Brochure, 1979. English.

AN: Biographic and bibliographic
information on women artists groups from
Austin, Dallas, Houston and San Antonio.
Includes brief history of MAS (Mujeres
Artistas del Suroeste), a list of members,
and biographies of Alicia Arredondo, Santa
Barraza, Mary Ann Ambray Gonzalez, and
Sylvia Orozco.

833 Xochil Art and Culture Center, Mission, TX.
Besame mucho. Exhibition invitation, 1979.
English.

AN: Invitation to exhibit of Texas
artists from Mujeres Artistas del Suroeste
(MAS): Mary Ann Anguiano, Alicia Arredondo,
Santa Barraza, Nora Gonzales-Dodson, Maria
Flores, Carolina Flores, Mary Ann Ambray
Gonzales, Sylvia Orozco, Nancy de los
Santos, Modesta Barbina Trevino.
Illustrated.

Artists (cont.)

834 Yarbro-Bejarano, Yvonne. La forma del sueno: arte y pensamiento de Alfredo Arreguin. METAMORFOSIS, Vol. 3, no. 2 (1980, 1981), p. 10-24. Spanish.

AN: Interview and portfolio of Mexican-born painter who has been living in Seattle for more than 20 years. Contains biographical data and the artist's view on the role of the Chicano artist. Ten illustrations.

Artorez, Arturo

835 Contreras, Carlos. Nuestra cultura. LA VOZ: Concilio for the Spanish Speaking of King Co., Seattle, no. 7 (August 1979).

AN: Information of Washington state murals painted by members of La Extension Cultural; Armando Lara's autobiographical mural titled "El Rio" is installed at the Concilio offices, 107 Cherry St. Suite 210. Arturo Artorez completed a wall painting using the image of Quetzalcoatl at El Centro de la Raza with funding from the Seattle Arts Commission. Francisco Siqueiros used the themes of ecology and Mexican mythology for two murals at Seattle Community College. Commentary on Alfredo Arreguin's painting exhibition at the Kiku Gallery and his wall painting at the Childrens Orthopedic Hospital in Seattle.

836 Cultural department. RECOBRANDO, Vol. 1, no. 15. Spanish.

AN: The development of "Raza" culture in the Northwest and the role played by the Centro de la Raza. Mentions the "talleres de arte" set up by Carlos Contreras and Arturo Artorez, artists from Mexico who moved to Seattle in 1978. Details cultural events sponsored by the Centro in the fields of art, music, dance, and theater.

Arts and Crafts

837 Aguilar, George. Raul Rodriguez, parade artist extraordinaire. NUESTRO, Vol. 6, no. 10 (December 1982), p. 11-14. English.

AN: Raul Rodriguez, a Mexican American float designer is considered a top artist in his field and one of the most successful in the country. Many of his floats have won prizes in the Tournament of Roses. In addition, Rodriguez designs facades for hotels on the Las Vegas Strip, most notably the facades of the Flamingo Hotel, the Dunes, and the Oasis.

838 Arredondo, Alicia. Bolsillo [weaving]. TEJIDOS, Vol. 5, no. 1 (1978), p. 23. Spanish.

839 Celebrate!: the story of the Museum of International Folk Art. Santa Fe, NM: Museum of New Mexico Press, 1979. English.

AN: History of the Museum; its founding in 1953 by Chicago philanthropist Florence Dibell Bartlett; its patronage of New Mexico Hispanic crafts as well as international crafts.

840 Directo, Cyril. Leo Guzman: woodcarver/tallador in madera. ENTRELINEAS, Vol. 1, no. 2 (February, March, 1968), p. 8. English.

AN: Biographical facts and commentary on artist's work. Illustrated with photographs of artist and examples of his work.

841 Ditmar, Joanne. A new industry, done the old way. EMPIRE MAGAZINE, (September 26, 1976), p. 22-25. English.

AN: The Virginia Blue Resource Center for Colorado Women is embarked on a project to revive handicrafts and skills among Hispano women in the San Luis Valley. Igniting interest in traditional crafts like embroideries, tin work, straw mosaic and filigree jewelry, the Center hopes to revive or maintain these traditions. Detailed information on a project to create a group of embroidered wall hangings depicting San Luis Valley life past and present. Illustrated with examples of the completed wall hangings.

842 Fabricant, Don. Show reveals Hispanic art. NEW MEXICAN WEEKEND, (June 1, 1979). English.

AN: Review of two exhibits in Santa Fe: EL FESTIVAL HISPANICO, mounted by La Cofradia de Artes y Artesanos Hispanicos and Gilberto Guzman at the Black Kachina Gallery. The reviewer feels the traditional-style woodcarving done by contemporaries is the strongest part of the show; works that break with these forms seem weaker, less skillful and cliche-ridden. Crafts are excellent. Muralist Guzman has blossomed in murals and easel paintings since he was employed by the 1978 Art in Public Places project. His work is intense and expressive, sometimes erotic. Illustration of work by sculptor Ruben Montoya.

843 'Festival of arts' planned by Arthritis Foundation. SANTA FE NEW MEXICAN, (October 11, 1972), p. B6. English.

AN: The Albuquerque Arthritis Foundation has invited professional artists and craftsmen from New Mexico to display their paintings, watercolors, sculpture, prints, lithographs, jewelry. Joel Ramirez's painting THE WEAVERS is selected for full color art prints. Illustrated.

844 Galeria de la Raza/Studio 24, San Francisco, CA. Ajo, granadas y tres flores. Exhibition announcement, 1981.

AN: Announcement for an exhibition featuring Ruben Trejo, sculpture (Spokane, Washington), Cesar A. Martinez, paintings (San Antonio, Texas), Xavier Gorena, paper cut-outs (Mission, Texas).

845 Galeria de la Raza/Studio 24, San Francisco, CA. Images of the Southwest. Exhibition catalog, 1977. English.

AN: Invitation/catalog for an exhibit including Rudy M. Fernandez(Utah), Enrique Flores(Texas), Xavier Gorena(Texas), C.A.[Cesar] Martinez(Texas), Santos Martinez, Jr.(Texas), Pedro Rodriguez(Texas), Arnold Trujillo(New Mexico). Block prints, paper cut-outs, drawings, photographs, copper enamels, and sculpture were shown. Five illustrations.

846 Gaytan, Ray. [[Untitled art work]. TEJIDOS, Vol. 3, no. 1 (Spring 1976), p. 4. English.

Arts and Crafts (cont.)

847 Guadalupe Historic Foundation, Santa Fe, NM.
Artes en la primavera. (1981). English.

AN: Catalog of exhibit by four New
Mexico artists: Manuel Lopez, sculptor from
Chili; Andres Martinez, painter from Santa
Cruz; Victoria Lopez, colcha embroiderer
from San Pedro; Sam Quintana, jeweler from
La Mesilla.

848 Guadalupe Historic Foundation, Santa Fe, NM.
Cofradia de artes y artesanos hispanicos.
Mimeograph, 1979. Spanish.

AN: Mimeographed call to join and
support the Cofradia, an organization begun
by and sustained by artists and craftsmen to
help support each other. Stated aims: "to
encourage the revival, continuation, and
growth of traditional and contemporary
Hispanic arts and crafts, to serve as a
source of public information for these
crafts and their producers, and to promote
the general social, cultural, and economic
welfare of the Hispanic arts and crafts".

849 Guerra, Victor, ed. El camino de la cruz.
Austin, TX: Tejidos Publications, 1981.
Spanish.

AN: Carlos Andres Guerra, portfolio;
painting (in color), sculpture, drawing,
jewelry. Luis Guerra drawing on cover.

850 Guerrero, Yolanda Eligia. Weaving [artwork].
TEJIDOS, Vol. 5, no. 1 (1978), p. 24.
Bilingual.

851 Hansen, Barbara. Food for the soul: an
earthly delight. HOME MAGAZINE, (October
22, 1978), p. 53-54. English.

AN: Story on El Dia de los Muertos.
Color illustrations of annual celebration by
Self-Help Graphics and Art, Inc. with
costumes, masks, floats.

852 Johnston, Jerry. A man with a message: let's
build strength, pride. DESERET NEWS, (June
28, 1980), p. S3. English.

AN: Story on Nephtali De Leon,
playwright, poet, and illustrator of
children's literature. In addition to I WILL
CATCH THE SUN and I COLOR MY GARDEN
children's books, he works with oil
painting, stained glass and woodcuts.

853 Le Page, David. He was pioneer in permanent
Indian sand paintings: artist found his
niche by returning to his roots. LOS ANGELES
TIMES [San Gabriel Valley edition], (April
26, 1981), p. IX,1,11. English.

AN: David Villasenor learned crafts from
Indian students at school he attended in
Sonora, after his family moved to the U.S.
in 1929. He was brought to Santa Fe, New
Mexico at 16 to teach boyscouts
wood-carving. He perfected a method for
gluing Indian-influenced sand paintings to a
surface, and has made many for museums. Well
illustrated.

854 Loniak, Walter. The true New Mexico
contemporary style. SANTA FE REPORTER, (May
31, 1979). English.

AN: Review of three exhibits in Santa
Fe, EL FESTIVAL HISPANICO co-sponsored by
the Cofradia de Artes y Artesanos Hispanicos
and the Santa Fe Council for the Arts; a
wood carving exhibit at Elaine Horwitch
Gallery, and easel paintings by muralist
Gilberto Guzman at the Black Kachina
Gallery. Concerning the Festival exhibit,
the critic states that the sculptural pieces
are the strongest; two dimensional work is
inconsistent or unimpressive, weaving is not
well represented (though usually the
strongest medium), and there are few
photographs or prints. Illustration.

855 Mexican-American Advisory Committee of the
Museum of Science and Industry. Second
annual Mexican-American art fiesta.
Exhibition brochure, 1975. English.

AN: Exhibit of paintings, sculpture,
crafts, and photography by 49 artists from
Illinois, Indiana, and Mexico. Includes many
of the most important Chicano artists of the
Chicago area.

856 Museum of Fine Arts, Santa Fe, NM. Luis
Jimenez, sculpture, drawings and prints: La
Cofradia de Artes y Artesanos Hispanicos,
selected works. Exhibition invitation, 1979.
English.

AN: Invitation to an exhibit of Texas
sculptor and printmaker Luis Jimenez, and
New Mexican artists and artisans.

857 Rios, Esther. Spotted leopard [sculpture].
TEJIDOS, Vol. 4, no. 3 (Fall 1977), p. 26.
English.

858 Sagel, Jaime. Art of brothers taps New
Mexico heritage. JOURNAL NORTH, (December
16, 1981). English.

AN: Three brothers, graphics artist,
painter, photographer, potter and poet
Alejandro Lopez and his older self-taught
brothers Felix and Manuel, are working with
traditional New Mexican art forms (bultos,
straw inlay crosses) and with newer
innovative forms - reflecting the fusion of
traditional-experimental art developing in
New Mexico among young artists.

859 Stedman, Myrtle and Stedman, Wilfred. Adobe
architecture. Santa Fe, NM: Sunstone Press,
1973. English.

AN: The technology and aesthetics of
adobe homes. An illustrated manual of house
plans and building techniques. Includes
drawings of Southwestern "colonial"
furniture.

860 Taylor Museum of the Colorado Springs Fine
Arts Center, Colorado Springs, CO. Hispanic
crafts of the Southwest. Catalog, 1977.
English.

AN: An excellent and profusely
illustrated catalog covering weaving,
embroidery, furniture making, woodcarving,
jewelry making, tinwork and straw inlay,
both past and present. Historical background
of crafts production, techniques, and
biographies of the artists are provided.

861 Vasquez, Esperanza and Esparza, Moctezuma.
Agueda Martinez. 16 mm. color film. English.

AN: Sixteen-minute film directed by
Esperanza Vasquez and produced by Moctezuma
Esparza concerning the life and weaving of
an elderly New Mexican woman. Martinez
carries on the tradition of floor loom
weaving, as well as farming.

Arts and Crafts (cont.)

862 Villasenor, David and Villasenor, Jean. How
to do permanent sand painting. Glendora, CA:
David and Jean Villasenor, 1972. English.

AN: A how-to book with techniques,
examples, and explanations of Indian motifs
by David Villasenor who has made a career of
producing sand paintings for museums and
other clients. Color and black and white
illustrations.

863 Woman who began at 73 is shaping Chicano
art. SAN ANTONIO EXPRESS-NEWS, (August 18,
1978), p. 6-W. English.

AN: 76-year-old Laredoan Alicia
Dickerson Montemayor who began painting on
guajes (gourds) from her garden three years
ago, now paints on canvas stories from her
life in the Valley, nature, and people. An
exhibit of her work, referred to by Chicano
art critics as "el arte de la inocencia"
opens at Gallery of El Centro Cultural de
LUCHA, in Austin, TX.

ASCO [art group], Los Angeles, CA

864 Cultura chicana: Los Angeles. COMUNIDAD, no.
11 (July 13, 1980), p. 1-15. Spanish.

AN: The whole issue of the Cultural
Supplement concerns Chicano art and music.
Captioned photographs deal with visual
artists Carlos Almaraz, Jerry Dreva [not
Chicano], Glugio Gronk, Willie Herron, John
Valadez, Patssi Valdez, with examples of
their work. With the exception of Dreva, all
the artists are members of Los Four or Asco.
Asco member Harry Gamboa, Jr. sums up the
1960s and 1970s and activities of artists in
his essay "Seis imaginaciones: Artistas
chicanos en Los Angeles." Well illustrated.

865 Dreva & Gronk exhibit at L.A.C.E.: Gronkart
live; Bonbon returns. Exhibition invitation,
1978. English.

AN: Illustrated invitation/poster to
exhibit of Asco's Gronk, and Jerry Dreva, a
collaborative show featuring ten years of
work:photos, correspondence, documents,
ephemera and other art.

866 Exploratorium, Student Union, California
State University, Los Angeles. Herron/Gronk
in ILLEGAL LANDSCAPE. Exhibition catalog,
1980. English.

AN: Invitation to a "performance" piece
NO MOVIE by Willie Herron and Gronk, two
members of ASCO. Illustrated.

867 Flaco, Eduardo. Chicanismo en el arte.
ARTWEEK, Vol. 6, no. 20 (May 17, 1975), p.
3. English.

AN: Review of competitive exhibition
composed of Chicano artists between
seventeen and twenty-six from Los Angeles
colleges, universities and art schools.
Focuses on work of ASCO, the only noteworthy
art in the show, according to the critic.

868 Gamboa, Harry, Jr. ASCO: no phantoms. HIGH
PERFORMANCE, Vol. 4, no. 2 (Summer 1981), p.
15. English.

AN: "The media's hit and run attitude
has generally relegated the influence by
Chicanos on Los Angeles to that of a phantom
culture," says Gamboa's introduction to an
ASCO No Movie event, NO PHANTOMS: "various

overt acts of communal alienation."
Illustrated.

869 Gamboa, Harry, Jr. Cafe en blanco y negro.
COMUNIDAD, (April 26, 1981), p. 3-5.
Spanish.

AN: An essay on how to take black and
white photographs in the barrio as works of
art, as visual propaganda, and as visual
history by ASCO photographer Harry Gamboa.
Illustrated with five of his photographs.

870 Gamboa, Harry, Jr.

Fadein. CHISMEARTE, Vol. 1, no. 2 (Winter,
Spring, 1977), p. 38. English.

AN: A conceptual art piece by Harry
Gamboa, Jr. of ASCO. The piece consists of
drawings and text.

871 Gamboa, Harry, Jr.; Gronk; and Herron,
Willie. Gronk and Herron. NEWORLD, Vol. 2,
no. 3 (Spring 1976), p. 28-30. English.

AN: An interview with ASCO members Gronk
and Willie Herron by a third member, Gamboa.
Brief historical introduction (1970 on). The
witty tongue-in-cheek interview can be
considered an artwork by this performance
art group. Illustrated.

872 Gamboa, Harry, Jr. and Gronk. Gronk:
off-the-wall artist. NEWORLD, Vol. 6, no. 4
(1980), p. 33-43. English.

AN: Interview with Gronk about his No
Movies, by Harry Gamboa, Jr., both members
(with Willie Herron and Patssi Valdez) of
ASCO. The interview itself can be seen as an
"art piece" with photographs by Gamboa; it
contains valuable information about the
ideas and activities of the group.

873 Gamboa, Harry, Jr. Pistol whippersnapper.
R.A.M. COLLECTIVE, Vol. 2, no. 1 (June 1,
1977), p. 10-11. English.

AN: Photography and poetry by Harry
Gamboa, Jr., member of ASCO, Los Angeles.

874 Gamboa, Harry, Jr. Seis imaginaciones:
artistas chicanos en Los Angeles. COMUNIDAD,
(July 13, 1980), p. 10. Spanish.

AN: A limited flow of media information
about Los Angeles Chicanos has produced a
"ghost" culture. Only sensational events are
published. Alternative magazines like LA
RAZA, CON SAFOS, and REGENERACION have
disseminated Chicano ideas of the 1970s. The
Chicano imagination has appeared in murals
by Willie Herron, Gronk, Carlos Almaraz,
John Valadez; in pieces like "walking" and
"instant" murals by the group ASCO; by the
group Los Four; by group exhibits like
"Chicanismo en el arte," and "Chicanarte."
Patssi Valdez showed Photobooth Piece at the
"Chicanismo" show. Gronk and Jerry Dreva
exhibited their mail art at "Punk Meets
Art." In Spanish.

ASCO [art group], Los Angeles, CA (cont.)

875 Geyer, Anne and Gamboa, Harry, Jr. Artists'
exhibits are street performances. THE NEWS,
(September 11, 1981), p. 18. English.

AN: Illustrated interview with
photographer/writer Harry Gamboa, Jr.,
member and documenter of the performance art
group ASCO. Description of the NO MOVIE, NO
PHANTOM, walking and instant murals of the
group, and other performance street art
which Gamboa considers as Chicano
self-documentation and expression.

876 Gronk and Gamboa, Harry, Jr. Interview:
Gronk and Gamboa. CHISMEARTE, Vol. 1, no. 1
(Fall 1976), p. 31-33. English.

AN: Interview with two members of the
group Asco concerning their NO MOVIE series.
Questions and answers were probably written
by the artists themselves as a performance
art piece. Includes a description of the
group and their 1972 ACTION PROJECT PIE IN
DEFACE: L.A. COUNTY MUSEUM OF ART.
Illustrations.

877 Kim, Howard. Chicano art: is it an art form?
Or simply art by Chicanos. NEWORLD, Vol. 6,
no. 4 (1980), p. 26-30. English.

AN: An attempt to define Chicano art
through interviews with Carlos Almaraz, John
Valadez, (Los Four), Robert Delgado, Sister
Karen Boccalero (Self-Help Graphics), Harry
Gamboa, Jr. (ASCO), Ricardo Duardo, Ignacio
Gomez, and others. Well illustrated.

878 L.A.C.E. (Los Angeles Contemporary
Exhibitions), Los Angeles, CA. Gronk/Dreva,
1968-1978: ten years of art/life. Exhibition
brochure, 1978. English.

AN: Exhibit and other acitivities by
Gronk of the group ASCO and Jerry Dreva.

879 L.A.C.E. (Los Angeles Contemporary
Exhibitions), Los Angeles, CA. No Movie: Gil
de Montes, Teddy, Glugio [Gronk], Patssi,
Gamboa. Exhibition invitation, 1978.
English.

AN: Invitation to "performance" piece by
Roberto Gil de Montes, Teddy Sandoval,
Gronk, Patssi Valdez and Harry Gamboa, Jr.,
the latter three of the ASCO group.
Illustrated.

880 Literally live movie at NO MOVIE exhibit.
CIVIC CENTER NEWS, Vol. 7, no. 17 (April 25,
1978), p. 1. English.

AN: Story on the ASCO "performance" NO
MOVIE, described by "Glugio" Gronk as
"movies without celluloid" to be held at
LACE Gallery. Illustrated.

881 Los Angeles City College. Latinos de tres
mundos. Exhibition invitation, 1980.
English.

AN: Invitation to an exhibit featuring
the work of ASCO members Harry Gamboa, Jr.,
Gronk, Willie Herron; painters Xavier Mendez
and Olivia Sanchez; and photographer Ricardo
Valverde.

882 Mechicano Art Center, Los Angeles, CA.
Schizophrenibeneficial. Exhibition
invitation, 1977. English.

AN: Invitation to an ASCO "performance"
work: "Projecting of Visual and/or Verbal

Personality Disorders Onto Person or Persons
Unknown." Glugio (Gronk), Teddy (Sandoval),
(Roberto) Gil de Montes, Patssi (Valdez),
(Harry) Gamboa.

883 Orth, Maureen. The soaring spirit of Chicano
arts. NEW WEST MAGAZINE, Vol. 3, no. 19
(September 11, 1978), p. 41-46. English.

AN: Overview of California Chicano
culture. Color illustrations of works by
Mexican muralist David Alfaro Siqueiros,
Rupert Garcia, Mujeres Muralistas, Willie
Herron, Rene Yanez, Rudy Martinez, San
Diego's Chicano Park, ASCO, Jose Montoya.

884 The Point Gallery, Santa Monica, CA. ASCO
(Gronk, Patssi, Gamboa, Herron), Los Four
(Almaraz, de la Rocha, Judithe Hernandez,
Gloriamalia Flores, Mauricio Ramirez, John
Valadez. Exhibition invitation, [1975].
English.

AN: Illustrated invitation to an exhibit
of Los Angeles artists.

885 West Colorado Gallery, Pasadena, CA.
Gronk/Patssi. Exhibition brochure, 1979.
English.

AN: Works on exhibit by ASCO members
Gronk and Patssi Valdez. Photo of artists.

Asociacion Chicana de Cineastas

886 Cine chicano: primer acercamiento.
COMUNIDAD, no. 20 (November 16, 1980), p.
1-15. Spanish.

AN: The entire cultural supplement of LA
OPINION is dedicated to Chicano film.
Includes articles by Jason Johansen, Jeff
Penichet, Harry Gamboa, Jr., Jesus Salvador
Trevino, Carlos Penichet, Sylvia Morales,
Julio Moran, and Jose Luis Borau. Also
includes a declaration of purpose by the
Asociacion Chicana de Cineastas, and a
filmography of Chicano cinema compiled by
Trevino.

**Association for the Advancement of Mexican
Americans (AMA) Gallery, Houston, TX**

887 Crossley, Mimi. Tejano artists. HOUSTON
POST, (August 19, 1976). English.

AN: Exhibition of 19 Texas artists
organized by Joe Rodriguez of the AAMA
(Association for the Advancement of Mexican
Americans) Art Center in Houston, Texas.
Working within a wide range of styles and a
great scope of subject matter. Includes
brief commentary on the work of Amado Pena,
Carmen Lomas Garza, Cesar Martinez, Enrique
Campos, Carolina Flores, Jesus Trevino and a
host of others.

888 Houston Chicanismo. LA PRENSA, Vol. 1, no. 2
(March 31, 1978). English.

AN: In Houston, Texas, the AMA Gallery
(Association for the Advancement of Mexican
Americans) was opened in February 1976 to
showcase Chicano art. Noel Rodriguez,
gallery director, informs about the goals
and objectives of the gallery. A current
exhibit presents paintings by Josie Mendoza
and Atanacio Davila, ceramics by Jesse
Sifuentes and mixed-media works by Joe
Ramirez. Illustrated with two pieces from
exhibit, THANKSGIVING, an acrylic painting
by Josie Mendoza and BIRDS, a ceramic piece.

Association of the Latin Brotherhood of Artists (ALBA)

889 Alba-King Kong Studios, Chicago, IL. Latina Art Expo '77. Chicago, IL: ALBA-King Kong Studios, 1977. English.

AN: An exhibit by 16 Chicana, Mexican, Puerto Rican and other Latina artists. Brief biographies of the artists.

Astorga, Jerry

890 Oakes College, University of California, Santa Cruz, CA and Carrillo, Eduardo. Corazon de Aztlan: a Chicano arts show. Exhibition catalog, 1981. English.

AN: Catalog of exhibit including works by Eduardo Carrillo, Juana Franklin, Cruz Zamarron, Jerry Astorga, Jaime Valadez, Ernesto Palomino, Sal Garcia, Roger Sierra, Jose Montoya, Esteban Villa, Juanishi Orozco, from Santa Cruz, San Jose, Fresno and Sacramento. Presentations of films and by the Teatro de la Tierra Morena of Santa Cruz County.

Atilano, Raymond

891 Images of Aztlan at Mechicano. CHISMEARTE, Vol. 1, no. 1 (Fall 1976), p. 3-4. English.

AN: History of Mechicano Art Center from its opening in West Los Angeles in 1969 through its 1976 location during which it decided to become a center serving its own community in East Los Angeles. Led by Leonard Castellanos, Victor Franco and Ray Atilano, the Center developed programs in supergraphics, silkscreen, and mural painting, as well as an "open-wall" art gallery for artists not allowed in establishment galleries.

892 Mascorro, Julie. Mechicano Art Center exhibit to grace Price gallery walls. CAMPUS NEWS, (November 24, 1971). English.

AN: Brief history of Mechicano Art Center activities from its establishment in 1969 to 1971. Exhibiting are Charles Almaraz, Roberto Amaral, Raymond Atilano, William Bejarano, Armando Cabrera, Edward Carbajal, Leonard Castellanos, Henry de Vega, Antonio Esparza, Bob Gomez, Lucila V. Grijalva, Jesus Gutierrez, Santos Lira, Frank Martinez, Ernest Palomino, Louis Quijada, Richard Raya, Frank Romero. Illustrated.

893 Mechicano Art Center. Los Angeles, CA: Mechicano Art Center, 1971. English.

AN: Announcement of an exhibit by painters Ramon Atilano, Xavier Lopez Ortega, and Frank A. Martinez. Martinez and Lopez Ortega are also muralists. Brief profiles of the artists. Illustrated.

894 Wilson, William. 30 works from the grass roots. LOS ANGELES TIMES, (June 4, 1973), p. IV,2. English.

AN: Review of a show at the Junior Arts Center in Barnsdall Park by 15 members of the Mechicano Art Center. The critic feels contemporary groups that aim for change today (unlike past groups) are unable to articulate their spirit in a cohesive style. The top talent in this show is Charles Almaraz; also on exhibit are paintings by Jose Cervantes, Guillermo Martinez, Ray

Atilano, sculpture by Manuel Cruz, and photography by (Oscar) R. Castillo.

Audiovisual Instruction

895 Additions to Ethnic Art Slide Catalog. Supplement to the Afro American, Mexican American, Native American Art Slide Catalog. Mobile, AL: Ethnic American Art Slide Library, The College of Arts & Sciences, University of South Alabama, 1976. English.

AN: Since 1973-74, the slide library has included Mexican American and Native American slides in their collection for sale. Six Chicano artists' slides are available in the supplement, in addition to those already listed in 1973-74, and 1974-75.

896 Afro American, Mexican American, Native American art slide catalog, 1973-74. Mobile, AL: Ethnic American Art Slide Library, The College of Arts & Sciences, Univ. of South Alabama, 1973-74. English.

AN: Preceded by the 1971-72 Ethnic American Art Catalog which dealt with Afro-American artists only, the Slide Library issues the present catalog of slides for sale. Slides are available for eighteen Chicano artists from the Southwest.

897 Afro American, Mexican American, Native American art slide catalog, 1974-75. Mobile, AL: Ethnic American Art Slide Library, The College of Arts & Sciences, Univ. of South Alabama, 1974-75. English.

AN: Preceded by the 1971-72 Ethnic American Art Catalog which dealt with Afro American artists only, the Slide Library has issued a 1973-74 catalog including Mexican American and Native American slides for sale, followed by the present catalog. Slides are available for twenty-three Chicano artists from the Southwest.

898 Bright, John; Bright, Mura; and Castellanos, Leonard. L.A. Chicano street art. Venice, CA: Environmental Communications, 1974. English.

AN: Annotated slide catalog of Chicano murals in East Los Angeles compiled by staff of Mechicano Art Center. Also includes article reprints on painted bus benches by Mechicano artists (SUNSET Magazine, n.d.), murals of East Los Angeles (LOS ANGELES TIMES, 12/3/73, and SUNSET Magazine, April 1973). Well illustrated.

899 Bright, John; Bright, Mura; and Castellanos, Leonard. "Placas": graffiti and the environment. Venice, CA: Environmental Communications, 1974. English.

AN: Annotated slide catalog of Chicano graffiti on walls, murals, and tattoos, compiled by staff of Mechicano Art Center.

Audiovisual Instruction (cont.)

900 Chicano art of the Southwest. San Antonio, TX: Instituto Chicano de Artes y Artesanias of the Texas Institute for Educational Development, 1975. English.

AN: Collection of 220 slides supplemented by slide annotation and artists' biographies researched and photographed by Texas artist Cesar A. Martinez over two years. Biographies cover 20 Texas, 6 New Mexico, and 15 northern California artists. Slides include, in addition, murals from Los Angeles and San Diego.

901 Films for the inner city. Los Angeles, CA: Los Angeles Public Library Federal Project, 1971. English.

AN: Annotated catalog of 16mm films and filmstrips, educational and documentary. Those concerning Mexican heritage include CHICANO FROM THE SOUTHWEST (1970), HENRY...BOY OF THE BARRIO (1969); HOW'S SCHOOL, ENRIQUE (1970), I AM JOAQUIN (1970), THE MEXICAN AMERICAN: HERITAGE AND DESTINY (1970), A MEXICAN AMERICAN FAMILY (1970), MEXICAN AMERICANS: QUEST FOR EQUALITY (1968), MEXICAN OR AMERICAN (1970), SIQUEIROS: "EL MAESTRO" (THE MARCH OF HUMANITY IN LATIN AMERICA) (1969). Filmstrips include THE AWAKENING (LA RAZA) - Part IV, CONFLICT OF CULTURES (LA RAZA) - Part III, MASTERWORKS OF MEXICAN ART, OUT OF THE MAINSTREAM, PILGRIMAGE (GRAPE STRIKERS). Also listed are films and filmstrips for children.

902 Instituto Chicano de Artes y Artesanias (Texas Instit. Educational Development). Chicano art of the Southwest. San Antonio, TX: Texas Institute for Educational Development, [ca. 1975]. English.

AN: Illustrated brochure announcing a color slide library on Chicano art supplemented by slide annotation and artists biographies available to institutions. Statement of purpose by Executive Director of program, Cesar Augusto Martinez.

903 Petersen, Karen and Wilson, J.J. Women artists: Third World. New York, NY: Harper & Row, 1975. English.

AN: Catalog of slides with accompanying notes. Slides of Chicana artists available: Margaret Herrera (Chavez), Consuelo (Chelo) Gonzalez Amezcua, Santa Barraza, Mujeres Muralistas, El Grupo de Santa Ana, Carmen Lomas Garza, Carolina Flores.

Austin, TX

904 Barrios, Greg. Big art comes of age. RIVER CITY SUN, (July 21, 1978), p. 9. English.

AN: Report on the meeting of Mexican and Chicano muralists at a mural conference in Austin. Includes a "Guide to Mural Art in East Austin," most of whose murals were done by Raul Valdez. Illustrated.

905 Bolger, Kathryn McKenna. Amado Pena's art. AUSTIN AMERICAN STATESMAN, (March 29, 1980), p. 10-11. English.

AN: A review of Pena's show of silkscreens, watercolors, and drawings at the Laguna Gloria Art Museum in Austin, Texas, March-May, 1980. Suggests that the artist has turned from a confrontational to an assimilationist stance. At present he visually documents the peaceful amalgamation of the cultural heritage on both sides of the Rio Grande.

906 Carraro, Francine. Refined rhythmic references: Amado Pena, Jr. SOUTHWEST ART, Vol. 9, no. 6 (November 1979), p. 70-75. English.

AN: Well-illustrated (including 4 color) story on Austin silkscreen artist Amado M. Pena. Features his recent stylized work based on New Mexican indian motifs.

907 Conferencia plastica chicana. Conference brochure, 1979. English.

AN: Schedule of proceedings at internationally attended conference on Chicano and Mexican art and photography sponsored by the Centro Cultural de LUCHA (League of United Chicano Artistas) and MAS (Mujeres Artistas del Suroeste). Brief biographies of presentors. Illustrated.

908 Dougherty Arts Center, Austin, TX. From the fringe: artists choose artists. Exhibition catalog, 1981. English.

AN: Catalog of an exhibit featuring eight women artists, including Santa Barraza of Austin. Barraza also designed the catalog.

909 Flores, Jose. Peregrino [drawing]. In MESQUI + TIERRA. Albuquerque, NM: Pajarito Publications, 1977. English.

AN: Drawings by Jose F. Trevino of Austin, Texas.

910 Garcia, Guillermo. Wall-to-wall art for the people. AUSTIN AMERICAN STATESMAN, (January 22, 1978), p. E-1. English.

AN: Illustrated story on Raul Valdez's mural (in progress) The Oral Tradition. Valdez discusses his methods and art philosophy when creating community murals.

911 Hennessey, Kathy. Amado Pena, Chicano artist. REVISTA RIO BRAVO, no. 1 (Fall 1980), p. 2+. English.

AN: Review of the life and art of Laredo-born artist Pena whose early work in the 1960s was abstracted figures in bright colors; in the 1970s his work became political commentary for the Chicano movement; most recently he is doing paintings and silkscreens about New Mexican Indian life. As a teacher he influenced many students, especially in Anderson High School (Austin). Illustrations throughout the issue.

912 League of United Chicano Artists, Austin, TX. La cultura es el derecho del pueblo. Brochure-poster, [ca. 1970]. Bilingual.

AN: Bilingual brochure-color poster describing activities of the Centro Cultural de LUCHA: an umbrella organization of the arts in Austin which also published the magazine TEJIDOS.

Austin, TX (cont.)

913 Manley, Paula. If walls could speak, a
festival of murals. DAILY TEXAN, (August 4,
1980). English.

AN: Commentary on community murals in
Austin, including murals painted by LUCHA
(The League of United Chicano Artists).

914 Moody Hall, St. Edwards University, Austin,
TX. Las companeras. Exhibition invitation,
1980. English.

AN: Invitation to an exhibition of
Chicana/Latina artists sponsored by Mujeres
Muralistas del Suroeste (MAS). Illustrated.

915 Murales - 'expresan nuestra realidad'.
AYUDA, Vol. 1, no. 6 (September 1977).
English.

AN: Brief illustrated article on Raul
Valdez's 1977 mural LOS ELEMENTOS on the
outside wall of Antioch's Juarez-Lincoln
College (Centro Cultural de LUCHA). Explains
the iconography of the mural. Includes brief
biography of the artist.

916 Orozco, Irma. Women & their work. PARA LA
GENTE, Vol. 1, no. 4 (October 1977), p. 12.
English.

AN: Illustrated story about "Women &
Their Work" festival in Austin, Texas,
Oct-Dec 1977. Photographers Maria Flores and
Teresina Guerra, Santa Barraza, Nora
Gonzalez Dodson, Sylvia Orozco, and Modesta
Trevino exhibited.

917 Orozco, Sylvia and Trevino, Jose. Trevino's
arte interprets el mundo Chicano. PARA LA
GENTE, Vol. 1, no. 10 (May 1978), p. 7-9.
English.

AN: Interview with Jose Trevino of
Austin and his artist wife, Modesta.
Reproduction and discussion of four works.
Centerspread reproduction of a Trevino
poster, part of a set of 10 designed for
bilingual classrooms.

918 Rodriguez, Alfred. A historical survey of
Chicano murals in the Southwest: an
interdisciplinary teaching unit. Unpublished
paper, 1980. English.

AN: Lists murals by title, artist and
date (when known), location and subject. Los
Angeles, San Francisco, San Diego, Fresno,
San Antonio, Austin, Corpus Christi, Santa
Fe, New Mexico murals are included.
Circulated by the Institute of Latin
American Studies, University of Austin,
Texas.

919 Zuniga, R. and Gonzalez, M. Entrevista con
los muralistas de East Austin. TEJIDOS, Vol.
5, no. 2-4 (1978), p. 128-130. Spanish.

AN: Extremely brief interview with two
Austin, TX, muralists. Includes 5 black and
white photographs of different murals.

Authors

920 Trujillo, Marcella. The dilemma of the
modern Chicana artist and critic. HERESIES,
Vol. 2, no. 4 (1979), p. 5-10. English.

AN: Recommended for its application to
the visual arts in its discussion of
iconography common to literature and art,
and symbols popular with Chicana artists: La

Malinche, the Virgin of Guadalupe,
Tonantzin, Mother Earth, etc.

AUTOBIOGRAPHY OF A BROWN BUFFALO

921 Hernandez, Sergio. [Brown Buffalo
(painting)]. CON SAFOS, no. 7 (Winter 1971),
p. COVER.

922 Lujan, Gilbert Sanchez "Magu". [Untitled
drawing]. CON SAFOS, no. 7 (Winter 1971), p.
36.

923 Lujan, Gilbert Sanchez "Magu". [Untitled
drawings]. CON SAFOS, no. 7 (Winter 1971),
p. 43.

924 Lujan, Gilbert Sanchez "Magu". [Untitled
drawings]. CON SAFOS, no. 7 (Winter 1971),
p. 41.

925 Lujan, Gilbert Sanchez "Magu". [Untitled
drawings]. CON SAFOS, no. 7 (Winter 1971),
p. 39.

Avila, Adam

926 COUNCIL OF LATINO PHOTOGRAPHY/USA
NEWSLETTER. no. 1 (January 1979). English.

AN: First number of photocopied
newsletter produced by the Council of Latino
Photography/USA announcing the formation of
the organization and its affiliation with
the Consejo Latinoamericano de Fotografia
established in Mexico City in May 1978.
Organizers of CLP/USA were photographers
Isabel Castro, Harry Gamboa, Jr., Adam
Avila, Luis Garza, and art historian Shifra
Goldman.

Avila, Justina

927 Teatro de la Tierra Morena, Santa Cruz, CA.
Fuego en Aztlan: a Chicano arts show.
Exhibition brochure, 1980. English.

AN: Folder of information on the
exhibition curated by Cruz Zamarron and
Eduardo Carrillo. Exhibiting artists were:
Justina Avila, Terry Benitez, Eduardo
Carrillo, Hernando Chavez, Bob Cruz, Juanita
Estrada, Juana Franklin, Sal Garcia, Leticia
Hernandez, David "Sir Loco" Jimenez, Raoul
Mendez, Vicente Mendez, Maria V. Pinedo,
Gonzalo Placencia, Ramon Rodriguez, Roberto
Salas, George Silva and Cruz Zamarron. A
special feature was a live tattoo
demonstration entitled "Walking Art".

Avilez, Tomas "Sapo"

928 Campesino Business and Joint Enterprise
Building, Fresno, CA. Sabor a Fresno. Arte
chicano: los Four and la Brocha. Exhibition
invitation [1976]. English.

AN: Invitation to an exhibit of works by
Los Four of Los Angeles and members of La
Brocha del Valle of Fresno: Arturo Roman,
Sal Garcia, John Sierra, Juan Truner, Sapo
de Aztlan, Fernando Hernandez, Alberto
Reyes, Ernesto Palomino, Lee Orona,
Francisco Barrios, Juan Ybarra, Bobby Reyes,
Alberto Hernandez. Brocha was started by
Palomino (California State University,
Fresno professor) to pool talents of Central
Valley artists.

THE AWAKENING (LA RAZA - PART IV) [film]

929 Films for the inner city. Los Angeles, CA: Los Angeles Public Library Federal Project, 1971. English.

AN: Annotated catalog of 16mm films and filmstrips, educational and documentary. Those concerning Mexican heritage include CHICANO FROM THE SOUTHWEST (1970), HENRY...BOY OF THE BARRIO (1969); HOW'S SCHOOL, ENRIQUE (1970), I AM JOAQUIN (1970), THE MEXICAN AMERICAN: HERITAGE AND DESTINY (1970), A MEXICAN AMERICAN FAMILY (1970), MEXICAN AMERICANS: QUEST FOR EQUALITY (1968), MEXICAN OR AMERICAN (1970), SIQUEIROS: "EL MAESTRO" (THE MARCH OF HUMANITY IN LATIN AMERICA) (1969). Filmstrips include THE AWAKENING (LA RAZA) - Part IV, CONFLICT OF CULTURES (LA RAZA) - Part III, MASTERWORKS OF MEXICAN ART, OUT OF THE MAINSTREAM, PILGRIMAGE (GRAPE STRIKERS). Also listed are films and filmstrips for children.

Awards

930 Scottsdale resident wins art fellowship. SCOTTSDALE DAILY PROGRESS, (April 10, 1981), p. 29. English.

AN: Rudy M. Fernandez, Jr. awarded the 1981 Visual Arts Fellowship in painting by the Arizona Commission on the arts. Fernandez holds an M.F.A. from Washington State University, and is affiliated with the Elaine Horwitch Gallery in Scottsdale and the Galeria de la Raza in San Francisco.

Aztlan

931 Garcia, Rupert. Raza murals & muralists: an historical perspective. San Francisco, CA: Rupert Garcia, n.d.. English.

AN: Basic assumptions are that socio-economic, political and cultural relationships exist between the Raza of Mexico and those of Aztlan (the Southwest United States) Half the text deals with Mexican murals, the other half sets Raza murals in social context, and focuses on murals in San Francisco's Mission District, in four locations. 19 illustrations; 9 of Raza murals. Mural map of the Mission district.

Aztlan Multiples [art group]

932 Exploratorium, Student Union, California State University, Los Angeles. An exhibit of published prints of Aztlan Multiples. Exhibition catalog, 1981. English.

AN: The published silkscreen prints of Aztlan Multiples, a small business run by Richard Duardo of Los Angeles, features works by Duardo, John Valadez, and Carlos Almaraz, among others. Illustrations.

933 Galeria de la Raza/Studio 24, San Francisco, CA. Published prints of Hecho en Aztlan Multiples. Exhibition announcement, 1980. English.

AN: Announcement of exhibit of the published silkscreen prints of Hecho en Aztlan Multiples; a small business run by Richard Duardo of Los Angeles.

AZTLAN [painting]

934 Rosas, Carlos. Aztlan [painting]. REVISTA CHICANO-RIQUENA, Vol. 6, no. 1 (Winter 1977), p. 28. Spanish.

Baca, Judith F.

935 Baca, Judith F. Judith F. Baca. In: SOCIAL WORKS: AN EXHIBITION OF ART CONCERNED WITH SOCIAL CHANGE. Los Angeles, CA: Institute of Contemporary Art, 1979, p. 44. English.

AN: Statement of purpose and history of the Tujunga Wash Mural (San Fernando Valley, CA) in process from 1976 on, by muralist and founder of Social and Public Art Resource Center (SPARC), Judith Baca. Illustrated.

936 Beronius, George. The murals of East Los Angeles. HOME MAGAZINE, (April 11, 1976), p. 10-11+. English.

AN: Well-illustrated historical article focusing on murals at Estrada Courts and those produced through Goez Gallery and Judith Baca in East Los Angeles.

937 Burkhardt, Dorothy. Chicano pride and anger mix at 'Califas'. THE TAB, (April 12, 1981), p. 34. English.

AN: CALIFAS: AN EXHIBITION OF CHICANO ARTISTS IN CALIFORNIA represents a cross-section of artists exhibiting work for at least ten years: Rupert Garcia, Ernie Palomino, Eduardo Carrillo, Judy Baca, Rene Yanez, Carmen Lomas Garza, Salvador Roberto Torres, Roberto Chavez, Willie Herron, Ralph Maradiaga, Sue Martinez, Jose Montoya, Malaquias Montoya, Ramses Noriega and Esteban Villa. Illustrated.

938 Cockcroft, Eva. Women in the community mural movement. HERESIES, no. 1 (January 1977), p. 14-22. English.

AN: Women's role in the community mural movement is much greater than generally recognized. Among the many women muralists discussed are included the Mujeres Muralistas (Patricia Rodriguez, Irene Perez, Graciela Carrillo de Lopez, and Venezuelan Consuelo Mendez Castillo) of San Francisoc, and Judy Baca of Los Angeles. Illustrated.

939 Lugavere, Joel P. Artists to add '40s to Great Wall mural. LOS ANGELES TIMES [Glendale/Burbank edition], (September 20, 1981), p. 1. English.

AN: Brief illustrated story on 1981 extension of the Tujunga Wash mural, THE GREAT WALL OF LOS ANGELES, directed by Judy Baca of SPARC, (Social and Public Arts Resource Center in Venice California).

940 Mills, Kay. The great wall of Los Angeles. MS.MAGAZINE, (October 1981), p. 66-69+. English.

AN: THE GREAT WALL OF LOS ANGELES in the Tujunga flood control channel in the San Fernando Valley, was started as a Bicentennial project in 1976. Artistic director Judy Baca of the Social and Public Art Resource Center, works with crews of young people painting aspects of Los Angeles history that is not generally found in textbooks. Well illustrated.

Baca, Judith F.(cont.)

941 Mitchell, John L. History restarted with mural grant. LOS ANGELES TIMES [Valley edition], (February 3, 1980), p. XI,1,4. English.

AN: Interview with Judith Baca on the goals and purposes of the "Great Wall of Los Angeles" mural project. The central aim is to provide work, educational experience and skills for 40 ethnically-mixed unemployed youngsters between the ages of 14-21. Article details evolution of the project and funding sources. Illustrated.

942 Muchnic, Suzanne. LAICA looks at social works. CALENDAR, (October 7, 1979), p. 93. English.

AN: Review of the exhibit SOCIAL WORKS at the Los Angeles Institute of Contemporary Art. Illustration and discussion of Judith F. Baca's mural UPRISING OF THE MUJERES, a four-part portable canvas mural in the style of Siqueiros.

943 NATIONAL MURALS NETWORK COMMUNITY NEWSLETTER. (Fall 1980). English.

AN: Reports on murals in San Francisco, CA, by the Chicano Moratorium Coalition; in Chicago about the Anti-War Preparations mural; in Houston by a student at the Association for Advancement of Mexican Americans; on Michael Schorr's mural in Chicanok, San Diego, CA; on a segment being painted at the Tujunga Wash mural in Los Angeles under Judy Baca; on south San Diego murals being painted out; Alan Barnett's survey of Southwest murals. Illustrated.

944 Parachini, Allan. Tujunga wash mural stands up to storm. LOS ANGELES TIMES, (March 13, 1980), p. V, 1. English.

AN: Information about the mural project near Los Angeles Valley College in Van Nuys, Calif. sponsored by SPARC (Social and Public Art Resource Center) of Venice, Calif. and coordinated by Judy Baca. Illustrated.

945 Rickey, Carrie. The passion of Ana. VILLAGE VOICE, Vol. 25, no. 37 (September 10, 1980), p. 75. English.

AN: Review of the exhibition DIALECTICS OF ISOLATION, AN EXHIBITION OF THIRD WORLD WOMEN ARTISTS OF THE UNITED STATES at the A.I.R Gallery in New York, September 1980. Includes a capsule analysis of Judith Baca's colossal mural in Tujunga Wash in Los Angeles. The mural "proposes to restore to public consciousness the ethnic and cultural history of the city's minorities." Details work procedures, content and political aims of the project. Eleven blue prints of mural cartoons detailing highlights of the mural's visual narrative were displayed in the exhibit.

946 Rickey, Carrie. The writing on the wall. ART IN AMERICA, Vol. 69, no. 5 (May 1981), p. 54-57. English.

AN: Detailed article on the career of Judy Baca, director of SPARC (Social and Public Arts Resource Center) in Venice, Calif., and of the Great Wall of Los Angeles, a five year mural project at the Tujunga Wash. Well illustrated in black and white and color.

947 Social and public art resource center. Brochure, [1977]. English.

AN: Brochure including the history, philosophy, and resources of SPARC, an outgrowth of the Los Angeles Citywide Mural Project/Mural Resource Center headed by Judy Baca. Illustrated.

948 Street, Sharon. Califas - a celebration of Chicano culture and art. CITY ON A HILL, (April 16, 1981). English.

AN: Review of an exhibit at College V's Sesnon Gallery featuring 15 California artists: Ramses Noriega, Judy Baca, Salvador Roberto Torres, Malaquias Montoya, Rene Yanez, Ralph Maradiaga, Jose Montoya, Esteban Villa, Carmen Lomas Garza, Robert Chavez, among others. Illustrated.

949 Varda, Agnes. Mur murs/mural murals on the wall ... Film, Cine Tamaris, Paris, 1980. English.

AN: Full length documentary film produced for French television; also available with English subtitles. Deals impressionistically with the murals and muralists of Los Angeles. Included are Wayne Alaniz Healy, David Botello, Willie Herron, Manuel Cruz, Judy Baca, the murals in Venice, CA, graffiti - among others. Color.

950 Walking tour and guide to the Great Wall at Tujunga Wash. Venice, CA: Social and Public Art Resource Center, [1981]. English.

AN: History and symbolism of the GREAT WALL, directed by Judy Baca, and created by teams of young people working on the mural since 1976. Illustrated.

951 Wilson, William. Chicana artists still seeking identification. LOS ANGELES TIMES, (June 23, 1975), p. VI, 5. English.

AN: Ten Chicana artists are exhibiting their work in the Boathouse Gallery of Plaza de la Raza in Lincoln Park: Judithe Hernandez, Patssi Valdez, Judy Baca, Josefina Quesada, Victoria del Castillo-Leon, Olga Muniz, Gloria Flores, Sylvia Morales, Isabel Castro and Celia Tejadak. The work is still tentative and may develop.

952 Wu, Ying Ying. Mural, mural on the Great Wall. LOS ANGELES TIMES, (September 16, 1980), p. VI,4. English.

AN: Information on a video project directed by John Rier to document work on the 1700-ft. mural THE GREAT WALL OF LOS ANGELES which depicts California history with an emphasis on the role that minorities had in forging that history. Three teen-agers were trained in video production while assisting with taping the mural project. Simultaneously, 40 other youngsters hired from the Summer Program for the Employment of Disadvantaged Youth painted a 400-ft. section of the mural in 1980. Article describes the various skills mathematical, social and artistic developed by youth involved in the project. The mural was started as a Bicentennial Project in 1976 by Judy Baca for the Social and Public Art Resources Center in Venice, California. Illustrated with 3 photographs of various aspects of the Project.

Baiz, Luis

953 The First Unitarian Universalist Church,
Paradise Valley, AZ. Five Chicano artists.
Exhibition brochure, 1971. English.

AN: Exhibit organized by L. Eugene
Grigsby, Jr., Art Department of Arizona
State University, Tempe, AZ. 21 works by
Eugene Quesada, David Nunez, Fernando
Navarro, Luis Baiz (of Arizona) and Saul
Solache (of Los Angeles). Brief biographies
of the artists.

954 Grigsby, J. Eugene, Jr. Art & ethnics:
background for teaching youth in a
pluralistic society. Dubuque, IO: Wm.C.
Brown Co. Publishers, 1977. English.

AN: Grigsby teaches in the Art
Department of Arizona State University,
Tempe. His book contains illustrations of
Arizona artists Eugenio Quedada, David
Nunez, and Luis Baiz, and a chapter called
"The Spanish-Speaking Ethnics:
Chicano/Mexican-American/Puerto
Rican/Cuban/South American artists".

Bank of America

955 Bank of America, Mission-23rd St. Branch,
San Francisco, CA. A community mural
dedicated by the artists to Mexican muralist
David Alfaro Siqueiros. 1974. English.

AN: Brochure about the Bank of America
mural in the Mission District of San
Francisco designed by Jesus Campusano and
Luis J. Cortazar, assisted by Michael Rios,
Jaime Carrillo, Candice Ho, Julio Lopez,
Anthony Machado, Jack Nevarez. Technical
advisor, Emmy Lou Packard. Well illustrated.

956 Barrio heritage reflected in bank mural. EL
CHICANO, Vol. 8, no. 50 (May 30, 1974), p.
8-9. English.

AN: Jesus Campusano and Luis J. Cortazar
were artist-designers of a monumental mural
painted inside the Mission Branch of the
Bank of America. Michael Rios was color
coordinator and five young artists worked
collectively on the project for four months.
Realistic scenes of everyday life in the
Mission barrio are contrasted to heroic
personalities from Latin America. Folk art
imagery, Indian and Spanish cultural symbols
and historical personages form a pageant of
Latin American history. Mural was
inaugurated on June 4, 1974.

957 Garcia, Rupert. "This mural is not for the
bankers. It's for the people". EL TECOLOTE,
Vol. 4, no. 6 (June 10, 1974), p. 11+.
English.

AN: On June 4, 1974, a mural by eight
Mission District artists was unveiled inside
the Bank of America on 23rd and Mission Sts.
in San Francisco. Roberto Vargas, Bay Area
poet was prevented from reading his poetry
during the mural inauguration. Finally
allowed to read, Vargas compared this event
to one in the 1930s when Diego Rivera
painted a mural for the Pacific Stock
Exchange Building in San Francisco. Includes
commentary by community activists about
incident. Illustrated by photograph of
Roberto Vargas reading in front of the
controversial mural.

BANNERS AND PAPER [exhibit]

958 [Untitled photograph]. CHISMEARTE, no. 2

(Winter, Spring, 1977), p. 34.

AN: Reproduction of the invitation to a
Los Four exhibit at Mount San Antonio
College Art Gallery, BANNERS AND PAPER,
April 12 - May 6, 1977.

Barajas, Salvador

959 Art directors, take note. INTERRACIAL BOOKS
FOR CHILDREN, Vol. 5, no. 7-8 (1975), p. 19.
English.

AN: Focus on the work of three Chicano
illustrators: Salvador Barajas V., Arturo
Roman, and Guillermo Aranda. Includes
representative examples of their work.

Barela, Al

960 Bloomfield, Arthur. Zesty show at Mexican
museum. SAN FRANCISCO EXAMINER, (February
1, 1977), p. 24. English.

AN: Review of an exhibit of Mexican and
Mexican American artists from the Southwest
and the San Francisco area. Commentary and
analysis on artists Vincent Perez and
Gustavo Rivera, Rudy Trevino and Al Barela.
The work selected focused on aesthetic
quality rather than the ethnic
identification of the artist.

961 Mexican American Community Service
Organization, San Jose, CA. Exhibition of
contemporary art. Exhibition brochure, 1968.
English.

AN: Biographical and exhibition data for
Al Barela, Bert Hermosillo, Octavio Romano,
Luis Valdez, Vincent P. Rascon, John Soares
and Al Espinoza.

962 The Mexican Museum, San Francisco, CA and
Quirarte, Jacinto. 17 artists:
Hispano/Mexican-American/Chicano. Exhibition
catalog, 1977. English.

AN: Catalog of an exhibit for artists
Emilio Aguirre, Consuelo Gonzalez Amezcua,
Al Barela, Pedro Cervantez, Edward Chavez,
Antonio Garcia, Louis Gutierrez, Harry
Louie, Vincent Perez, Michael Ponce de Leon,
Eugenio Quesada, Gustavo Rivera, Peter
Rodriguez, Alex Sanchez, Darryl Sapien, Rudy
Trevino, Manuel Villamor. Illustrated.

Barela, Casimiro

963 Martinez, O.W. "Bill". Here comes la gente
fragmented and fused [paintings]. LA LUZ,
Vol. 1, no. 1 (April 1972), p. 56-57.
English.

Barela, Patrocinio

964 Crews, Mildred T. Saint-maker from Taos.
AMERICAS, Vol. 21, no. 3 (March 1969).
English.

AN: An in-depth study of woodcarver
Patrocino Barela (died 1964). Barela's work
is an evolvement of the "santero" tradition
filtered through an intensely personal
style. His work was widely collected by
institutions like The Museum of Modern Art,
New York, The San Francisco Museum of Art
and The New Mexico Fine Arts Museum.
Well-illustrated with photographs of the
artist and example of his work.

Barnett, Alan

965 NATIONAL MURALS NETWORK COMMUNITY
NEWSLETTER. (Fall 1980). English.

AN: Reports on murals in San Francisco,
CA, by the Chicano Moratorium Coalition; in
Chicago about the Anti-War Preparations
mural; in Houston by a student at the
Association for Advancement of Mexican
Americans; on Michael Schorr's mural in
Chicanok, San Diego, CA; on a segment being
painted at the Tujunga Wash mural in Los
Angeles under Judy Baca; on south San Diego
murals being painted out; Alan Barnett's
survey of Southwest murals. Illustrated.

Baros, Albert

966 Artist registry financed. RIO GRANDE SUN,
(January 17, 1980). English.

AN: A $15,000 grant received from the
National Endowment for the Arts to begin a
New Mexico Hispanic Arts Community Outreach
project, which will include a central
registry of New Mexico Hispanic artists with
current resume, documentation of work, and
other information. In charge will be
artists Estevan Arellano, Albert Baros, and
Susan Jamison of the Santa Fe Council for
the Arts.

967 La Sociedad Historica de Nuestra Senora de
Guadalupe, Santa Fe, NM. Meditacion.
Exhibition invitation, 1980. English.

AN: Invitation to an exhibit by four
artists: Filomeno Martinez (graphic artist,
Albuquerque), Ruben Montoya (santero, Santa
Fe), Santiago Chavez (painter, Santa Rosa),
Jose Alberto Baros (sculptor, Espanola).

Barraza, Santa

968 Cardenas de Dwyer, Carlota, ed. Chicano
voices. Boston, MS: Houghton Mifflin, 1975.
English.

AN: Includes artwork by: Peter
Rodriguez, Arturo Anselmo Roman, Carmen
Lomas Garza, Santa Barraza, and Cesar
Augusto Martinez.

969 COMMUNITY MURALS (San Francisco, CA). (Fall
1981). English.

AN: Citywide Murals Group of Denver,
Colorado assisted the Chilean-oriented
Brigada Orlando Letelier with a mural in
their city; Carlos Sandoval of Denver doing
mural in Guerrero, Mexico; Ray Patlan of
Berkeley, California assisting with mural in
Mexico painted by Arnold Belkin's class at
the Academy of San Carlos; report on the
exhibit MURALS OF AZTLAN: THE STREET
PAINTERS OF EAST LOS with a reprint of
debate on the event by Shifra M. Goldman,
Judithe Elena Hernandez de Neikrug, and
comments by John Pitman Weber and Tim
Drescher; report on DAR LUZ mural directed
by Santa Barraza in Austin, Texas, and a new
mural in Hayward, California directed by
Enrique Romero; a mural sponsored by the
Chicano Youth Center of Fresno, California
showing the influence of Mexican calendars;
a new mural, OAKLAND'S PORTRAIT by Daniel
Galvez in Oakland, California; pro-and-con
discussion of social function of graffiti in
response to letter from Belgian source;
reprint of story on spray paint crime bill
(anti-graffiti) sponsored by California
Assemblyman Richard Alatorre. Entire issue
illustrated.

970 Diseno Studios, Austin, TX. Diseno Studios
Gallery. Brochure, 1981. English.

971 Dougherty Arts Center, Austin, TX. From the
fringe: artists choose artists. Exhibition
catalog, 1981. English.

AN: Catalog of an exhibit featuring
eight women artists, including Santa Barraza
of Austin. Barraza also designed the
catalog.

972 Goldman, Shifra M. Chicana artists at work.
ARRIBA, , p. 3+. English.

AN: Excerpt of a longer article on the
Texas women's group Mujeres Artistas del
Suroeste (MAS). Integral to the group are
artists Santa Barraza, Nora Gonzalez-Dodson,
Alicia Arredondo, Maria Flores, Sylvia
Orozco, and Modesta Trevino.

973 Goldman, Shifra M. Chicano art alive and
well in Texas: a 1981 update. REVISTA
CHICANO-RIQUENA, Vol. 9, no. 1 (Winter
1981), p. 34-40. English.

AN: Reprint of article published as
"Supervivencia y prosperidad del arte
chicano en Texas: nueva revision" in
COMUNIDAD (Los Angeles, CA) [Sunday
Supplement to LA OPINION], September 21,
1980, p. 3, 15+.

974 Goldman, Shifra M. Supervivencia y
prosperidad del arte chicano en Texas: nueva
revision. COMUNIDAD, Vol. 55, no. 5
(September 21, 1980), p. 3,15+. Spanish.

AN: Focuses on six Chicano artists from
Austin, Houston, San Antonio, and
Kingsville: Mel Casas, Cesar Martinez, Amado
M. Pena, Leo Tanguma, Carmen Lomas Garza,
and Santa Barraza. Well illustrated. This
article was reprinted as "Chicano Art Alive
and Well in Texas: A 1981 Update," in
REVISTA CHICANO-RIQUENA (Houston), Vol. 9,
no. 1, Winter 1981, p. 34-40.

975 Goldman, Shifra M. Women artists of Texas:
MAS = More + Artists + Women = MAS.
CHISMEARTE, no. 7 (January 1981), p. 21-22.
English.

AN: History of Texas Chicana women
artists' organization, Mujeres Artistas del
Suroeste (MAS), co-founded in 1977 by Santa
Barraza and Nora Gonzalez-Dodson in the
framework of the burgeoning feminist art
movement, particularly Women and Their Work
of Texas. Brief history of Chicano politics
and the corresponding art movement of
southern and central Texas. In addition to
Barraza and Gonzalez-Dodson, Alicia
Arredondo, Modesta Trevino, and Maria Flores
are considered. Illustrated.

976 HEMBRA: HERMANAS EN MOVIMIENTO BROTANDO
RAICES DE AZTLAN (University of Texas,
Austin). (Spring 1976).

AN: Raul Valdez, drawing, p. 3; Carolina
Flores, drawing, p. 5; Maria Flores,
photograph, pp. 7, 11, 30; M.E.
Secrest-Ramirez, drawing, p. 12; Amacio
Zarate, drawing, p. 15; Santa Barraza,
drawings, pp. 16, 17, 18, 26, 32; Nora
Gonzales-Dodson, painting, p. 19; Gilberto
Cardenas, photograph, pp. 22, 28; Nanci de
los Santos, photograph, p. 23, 29; Amado
Maurilio Pena, Jr. p. 31.

Barraza, Santa (cont.)

977 Instituto Chicano de Artes y Artesanias
(Texas Instit. Educational Development) and
Instituto Cultural Mexicano (SER/UNAM), San
Antonio, TX. Artistas chicanos: Los
Quemados. San Antonio, TX: Instituto
Chicano, Texas Institute for Educational
Development, 1975. English.

AN: Invitation to an exhibit and
manifesto of 1975 Austin-San Antonio
artists' group, Los Quemados. Included Santa
Barraza, Carolina Flores, Carmen Lomas
Garza, Luis Guerra, Cesar Augusto Martinez,
Santos Martinez, Amado Maurilio Pena, Jr.,
Jose Rivera, Vicente Rodriguez, Jose
Trevino.

978 Orozco, Irma. Women & their work. PARA LA
GENTE, Vol. 1, no. 4 (October 1977), p. 12.
English.

AN: Illustrated story about "Women &
Their Work" festival in Austin, Texas,
Oct-Dec 1977. Photographers Maria Flores and
Teresina Guerra, Santa Barraza, Nora
Gonzalez Dodson, Sylvia Orozco, and Modesta
Trevino exhibited.

979 Orozco, Sylvia. Las mujeres - Chicana
artists come into their own. MOVING ON, Vol.
2, no. 3 (May 1978), p. 14-16. English.

AN: Illustrated feature prepared by
artist Sylvia Orozco on the founding of
Mujeres Artistas del Suroeste in Austin,
September 1977. Artworks and statements by
Nora Gonzalez Dodson, Maria Flores, Modesta
Trevino, Santa Barraza, as well as musicians
and singers.

980 Petersen, Karen and Wilson, J.J. Women
artists: Third World. New York, NY: Harper &
Row, 1975. English.

AN: Catalog of slides with accompanying
notes. Slides of Chicana artists available:
Margaret Herrera (Chavez), Consuelo (Chelo)
Gonzalez Amezcua, Santa Barraza, Mujeres
Muralistas, El Grupo de Santa Ana, Carmen
Lomas Garza, Carolina Flores.

981 Romero, Ernestina. Chicano culture to be
explored at conference. DAILY TEXAN,
(September 10, 1979). English.

AN: Announcement of the internationally
attended CONFERENCIA PLASTICA CHICANA.
Statements by organizers Santa Barraza and
Pedro Rodriguez.

982 Women artists: forming a Texas network.
Brochure, 1979. English.

AN: Biographic and bibliographic
information on women artists groups from
Austin, Dallas, Houston and San Antonio.
Includes brief history of MAS (Mujeres
Artistas del Suroeste), a list of members,
and biographies of Alicia Arredondo, Santa
Barraza, Mary Ann Ambray Gonzalez, and
Sylvia Orozco.

983 Xochil Art and Culture Center, Mission, TX.
Besame mucho. Exhibition invitation, 1979.
English.

AN: Invitation to exhibit of Texas
artists from Mujeres Artistas del Suroeste
(MAS): Mary Ann Anguiano, Alicia Arredondo,
Santa Barraza, Nora Gonzales-Dodson, Maria
Flores, Carolina Flores, Mary Ann Ambray
Gonzales, Sylvia Orozco, Nancy de los

Santos, Modesta Barbina Trevino.
Illustrated.

Barrera, Jesus

984 Phelon, Craig. Sculptor survives on the edge
of a concrete canyon. EL PASO TIMES, (July
11, 1980). English.

AN: 84 year old Jesus Barrera sculpted
and painted hundreds of religious plaster
statues until forced to abandon sculpture in
1962 because lead-based paint ruined his
health.

Barrera, Ricardo

985 Incorporated Artes Monumentales/Inc.,
Denver, CO. IAM: art exhibit. Exhibition
brochure, n.d. English.

AN: Large format, well illustrated
brochure with information on muralists
Roberto Lucero, Al Sanchez, Andrew Manning,
Ricardo Barrera and Bob Reyes. Includes some
biographical information situating these
artists within the dynamic artistic
traditions of the Mexican and the Chicano
mural movements.

986 Manning, Andrew. Damaged mural inspires
community restoration project. CHISMEARTE,
Vol. 2, no. 1 (Summer 1978), p. 28. English.

AN: Describes the damage caused to a
Willie Herron mural by inclement weather
conditions and the community drive to fund a
restoration project. The project is being
directed by Ricardo Barrera.

**Barrio Betterment and Development Corporation
(BBDC), San Antonio, TX**

987 Trevino, Rudy. San Antonio murals a self
portrait. PICANTE, Vol. 1, no. 3, p. 60-61.
English.

AN: Commentary on the San Antonio Mural
Project assisted by the CETA program and the
Barrio Betterment and Development
Corporation (BBDC). Goals and information on
the light murals in progress in the Casiano
Housing Project. Participating artists: Juan
Hernandez, Esteban Adame, Andrew Gutierrez,
Bob Tate, and Roberto de La Fuente.

Barrio, Raymond

988 Barrio, Raymond. Mexico's art & Chicano
artists. Sunnyvale, CA: Ventura Press, 1975.
English.

AN: A personal resume with commentaries
by the author on Mexican and Chicano art.

Barrios

989 The affectionate realism of Jesse Trevino.
SA: THE MAGAZINE OF SAN ANTONIO, Vol. 3, no.
10 (December 1979), p. 70-73. English.

AN: Brief story about, and personal
statement by San Antonio photorealist
painter and muralist. Trevino focuses on
portraits of people and sites in the
Westside barrio. Color illustrations.

Barrios (cont.)

990 Arte del varrio. San Jose: A.T.M Communications, Inc., Nos. 1-3, 1979-81.. English.

AN: Large format color illustrated albums of "Varrio art." Includes examples of tattoo art, placasos (graffiti) and barrio murals.

991 Chicano art: East Los Angeles graffiti. LA GENTE DE AZTLAN, Vol. 6, no. 5 (May 1976), p. 5. English.

AN: The particular forms and styles of Chicano graffiti are affirmed as stemming from the social conditions of the barrio circa 1930. Gangs and their social world are examined as contributors to the creation of graffiti, tattoos and "calo," a dialect of Chicano Spanish.

992 Cox, Vic. Beauty in the barrio. WESTWAYS, Vol. 67, no. 2 (February 1975), p. 50-53. English.

AN: "Tooner Flats" is another name for the barrio of East Los Angeles. These streets are the home and inspiration to Frank Hernandez who illustrates the article with pen and ink sketches of buildings.

993 De Leon, Hector. Barrio art--the community's reflection of itself. AGENDA, Vol. 9, no. 4 (July, August, 1979), p. 7, 38. English.

AN: Barrio art is communal, its forms such as posters, pamphlets, graffiti, and murals have an educative function. Its style is eclectic and its content is stark and direct. Through various forms of graphic representation, people in the barrio have reappropriated art forms to give meaning to their daily experiences. Includes nine illustrations of barrio art.

994 Del Olmo, Frank. Chicano gang turns to art. LOS ANGELES TIMES, (September 11, 1973), p. II, 3. English.

AN: Residents of the East Los Angeles barrio "Lil' Valley" dedicate a mural memorializing Chicano gang members who have died violently. The mural was painted by 40 gang members guided by professional artist Bill Butler.

995 Gamboa, Harry, Jr. Cafe en blanco y negro. COMUNIDAD, (April 26, 1981), p. 3-5. Spanish.

AN: An essay on how to take black and white photographs in the barrio as works of art, as visual propaganda, and as visual history by ASCO photographer Harry Gamboa. Illustrated with five of his photographs.

996 Johnston, Tracy. La vida loca. NEW WEST MAGAZINE, (January 29, 1979), p. 38-46. English.

AN: A journalistic account of barrio lifestyles composed from conversations with young Cholos in Los Angeles. Amid poverty, unemployment, drug abuse and familial disintegration, codes of group solidarity and rituals of connection occur. Information on urban Chicano forms of self expression such as mascaras (chola make up), tattoos and graffiti. Well illustrated with photographs.

997 Lopez, Gerard. Estrada murals. LA LUZ, Vol.

4, no. 3 (June 1975), p. 21. English.

AN: Describes goals and procedures of a barrio mural project under the guidance of "Los Ninos del Mundo", a group of Chicano artists, musicians and social workers.

998 Ortega, Gil. The 50's and other assorted Chicano graffiti. La Habra, CA: s.n., 1981. English.

AN: Album of caricatures of barrio types; black and white drawings in six categories: The Parties and Dances, Schooldays, Oldtime Lowriders, Refine, Los Veteranos, Los Vatos. Some drawings accompanied by commentary.

999 Riches of the barrios. ARIZONA [supplement to ARIZONA REPUBLIC], (September 11, 1977), p. 50. English.

AN: Louis Carlos Bernal of Tucson shows his collection of photographic portratis of the barrios at the Heard Museum in Phoenix. Well illustrated.

1000 Romotsky, Jerry and Romotsky, Sally R. Los Angeles barrio calligraphy. Los Angeles, CA: Dawson's Book Shop, 1976. English.

AN: Deals with visual quality, styles, and meanings of Los Angeles "placas," or graffiti. Well illustrated.

1001 S.A. site for National Symposium on Mexican American Art. CHICANO TIMES, Vol. 4, no. 30 (November 9, 1973), p. 5. English.

AN: Held at Trinity University, the Symposium discussed such issues as, creative evolution, art education, artistic relationships to Mexico and the evolution of Mexican American art in the California barrios. Participating artists included Rudy Trevino, Mel Casas, Octavio Medellin, Antonio Garcia, Carmen Garza, Esteban Villa, Jose Montoya, Ernesto Palomino, Michael Ponce de Leon, Luis Jimenez and Eugenio Quesada.

Barrios, Francisco

1002 Campesino Business and Joint Enterprise Building, Fresno, CA. Sabor a Fresno. Arte chicano: los Four and la Brocha. Exhibition invitation [1976]. English.

AN: Invitation to an exhibit of works by Los Four of Los Angeles and members of La Brocha del Valle of Fresno: Arturo Roman, Sal Garcia, John Sierra, Juan Truner, Sapo de Aztlan, Fernando Hernandez, Alberto Reyes, Ernesto Palomino, Lee Orona, Francisco Barrios, Juan Ybarra, Bobby Reyes, Alberto Hernandez. Brocha was started by Palomino (California State University, Fresno professor) to pool talents of Central Valley artists.

Bartlett, Florence Dibell

1003 Celebrate!: the story of the Museum of International Folk Art. Santa Fe, NM: Museum of New Mexico Press, 1979. English.

AN: History of the Museum; its founding in 1953 by Chicago philanthropist Florence Dibell Bartlett; its patronage of New Mexico Hispanic crafts as well as international crafts.

Basquez, Paul

1004 Carlson, Scott. Artist's mural puts a little
     beauty in prison cellblock. ST. PAUL
     DISPATCH, (December 5, 1978), p. East,1,3.
     English.

     AN: Biographical information on Chicano
     artist Paul Basquez and his eleven mural
     projects at Stillwater State Prison.

1005 Community Programs in the Arts and Sciences
     (COMPAS). Artists in the city: a report on
     C.E.T.A. artists in St. Paul. St. Paul, MN:
     COMPAS, 1978. English.

     AN: Includes data on Chicano muralists
     John Acosta, Thomas Acosta, Paul Basquez,
     Armando Estrella, and photographer Raphael
     Romo.

1006 Flanagan, Barbara. Murals warm up west St.
     Paul. MINNEAPOLIS STAR, (December 20,
     1977). English.

     AN: Discussion of mural activity in West
     St. Paul, Minnesota by Armando Estrella,
     Paul Basquez and John Acosta. The subject of
     most murals in Minnesota is either
     political, religious or historic. Of the
     three artists involved, Paul Basquez grew up
     in the barrio of West St. Paul. He tells how
     mural activity in the region is related to
     the Chicano art movement. About a half-dozen
     murals have been painted in St. Paul.

1007 Knapp, Martha. West side is part of mural
     art renaissance. WEST SAINT PAUL VOICE, Vol.
     5, no. 19 (November 21, 1977). English.

     AN: Pre-Columbian symbology in the mural
     program painted by Paul Basquez and Armando
     Estrella in the Chicano barrio; information
     and data on the mural renaissance in
     Minnesota.

Batos Locos

1008 Johnston, Tracy. La vida loca. NEW WEST
     MAGAZINE, (January 29, 1979), p. 38-46.
     English.

     AN: A journalistic account of barrio
     lifestyles composed from conversations with
     young Cholos in Los Angeles. Amid poverty,
     unemployment, drug abuse and familial
     disintegration, codes of group solidarity
     and rituals of connection occur. Information
     on urban Chicano forms of self expression
     such as mascaras (chola make up), tattoos
     and graffiti. Well illustrated with
     photographs.

1009 Lujan, Gilbert Sanchez "Magu". El arte del
     Chicano - "The Spirit of the Experience".
     CON SAFOS, no. 7 (Winter 1971), p. 11-13.
     English.

     AN: Definition of Chicano Art by artist
     Lujan as the expression of an unique
     experience that is neither Mexican nor U.S.
     Anglo, that has its own vitality and
     dynamics. Chicanos can draw upon common
     cultural elements and transform them into
     images and art forms such as sculptured
     menudo bones, tortilla drawings, vato loco
     portraits, etc. Four woodcuts by Roberto de
     la Rocha are shown as examples.

Bay Area, CA

1010 Albright, Thomas. 'Unspoiled' Bay Area art.
     SAN FRANCISCO CHRONICLE, (August 29, 1974),
     p. 40. English.

     AN: Review of an exhibit titled ART NAIF
     curated by Rolando Castellon. The show
     featured 15 Bay Area painters who are
     basically self-taught and share a personal
     expression unhampered by prevailing art
     conventions and trends. Includes material on
     Alexander Maldonado, 72-year-old "primitive"
     painter from San Francisco. Some of
     Maldonado's work includes references to his
     childhood and youth in Mexico.

1011 Clark, Yoko and Hama, Chizu. California
     murals. Berkeley, CA: Lancaster-Miller,
     1979. English.

     AN: Picture book of Bay Area and Los
     Angeles murals with brief descriptions.
     Chicano artists included: Daniel Galvez,
     Irene Perez, Patricia Rodriguez, Graciela
     Carrillo (Mujeres Muralistas), Ray Patlan.

1012 Dickson, Joanne. Manuel Neri. El Cajon, CA:
     Grossmont College Gallery, 1980. English.

     AN: Essay documents Neri's career and
     situates him within the Bay Area figurative
     style. As a sculptor, the artist has worked
     in plaster or bronze, cast paper, fiberglass
     and more recently in marble.

1013 Drescher, Tim and Goldman, Ruth. A survey of
     East Bay murals of the 1970s. San Francisco,
     CA: Murals, 1980. English.

     AN: Compendium of murals including
     title, location, size, artists,dates,
     funding, materials, content, and comments on
     each mural.

1014 Galeria Museo - new art gallery opens in the
     Mission. EL TECOLOTE, Vol. 8, no. 1
     (September 1977), p. 8. Bilingual.

     AN: Brief article on the inauguration of
     the Art Gallery at the Mission Cultural
     Center. The opening Exhibit (August 13,
     1977) was entitled SIXTY-THREE SHOW and
     included work in various media by Sixty
     three Bay Area Latino artists. Gilberto
     Osorio was designated as the first
     artist-in-residence. Information on future
     plans for the Galeria-Museo.

1015 Hartnell College Studio Gallery, Salinas,
     CA. Paintings, drawings, prints by San
     Francisco Bay Area Chicano artists. Exhibit
     brochure, 1971. English.

     AN: Brochure for exhibit featuring
     Francisco Camplis, Graciela Carrillo, Sal
     Castaneda, Priscilla Dominguez, J. Duarte,
     Rupert Garcia, Carlos Loarca, Irene Perez,
     Vincent Rascon, Michael Rios, Peter
     Rodriguez, Luis Valsoto, Esteban Villa, Rene
     Yanez, Zala. Illustrated by Rupert Carcia
     print.

1016 Los Medanos College Gallery, [CA].
     Cinco/five: an exhibit of five Bay Area
     artists. Exhibition brochure, n.d. English.

     AN: Artists Gerry Concha, Gustavo
     Rivera, Raoul Mora, Manuel Villamor and
     Peter Rodriguez included in the show.
     Illustrated by Peter Rodriguez's portraits
     of the five.

Bay Area, CA (cont.)

1017 San Francisco Museum of Modern Art, San Francisco, CA and Castellon, Rolando. Posters and society. Exhibition catalog, 1975. English.

AN: 26 artists exhibiting public announcement and social political commentary posters. Includes 14 Bay Area and Sacramento, Calif. Latino artists.

Bejarano, William

1018 Mascorro, Julie. Mechicano Art Center exhibit to grace Price gallery walls. CAMPUS NEWS, (November 24, 1971). English.

AN: Brief history of Mechicano Art Center activities from its establishment in 1969 to 1971. Exhibiting are Charles Almaraz, Roberto Amaral, Raymond Atilano, William Bejarano, Armando Cabrera, Edward Carbajal, Leonard Castellanos, Henry de Vega, Antonio Esparza, Bob Gomez, Lucila V. Grijalva, Jesus Gutierrez, Santos Lira, Frank Martinez, Ernest Palomino, Louis Quijada, Richard Raya, Frank Romero. Illustrated.

1019 EL PLAYANO (Loyola University, Los Angeles). (Spring 1972).

AN: Illustrations by Willie Herron, Harry Gamboa, Jr., Gronk, Diane Gamboa, William A. Bejarano, Eddie Garcia.

1020 Street art explosion in Los Angeles. SUNSET, (April 1973), p. 110-113. English.

AN: Illustrated article on Los Angeles street murals including those by Roberto Chavez, Willie Herron, Frank Romero, Richard Jimenez, William Bejarano, Gilbert Lujan, Armando Cabrera, Frank Martinez, Charles Felix, and others.

1021 Venegas, Sybil. Dia de los muertos. SOMOS, Vol. 1, no. 5 (October 1978), p. 42-47. English.

AN: Brief history of Dia de los muertos ceremonies. While the custom is dying in Mexico (except for tourists), Chicano organizations like Galeria de la Raza (S.F.), El Centro de Artistas Chicanos (Sacramento, Ca.) celebrate the event annually, as does [Self-Help Graphics and Art, Inc.] in East Los Angeles. Well illustrated with photographs by Guillermo Bejarano and Daniel Duran.

Benavides, Edmon

1022 San Antonio Public Library. Art in the little world. News release, n.d. English.

AN: This news release includes a statement by the San Antonio born artist Edmon H. Benavides. Expressing himself through the medium of water color, Benavides paints Texas wildlife and nature scenes in a realistic style.

Benavidez, Ramiro

1023 And/Or Gallery, Seattle, WA. Artistas de Aztlan. Exhibition announcement, 1975. English.

AN: Exhibition announcement for an important exhibit of Northwest Chicano art. Co-sponsored by MEChA and the Chicano Studies Program at the University of Washington, the exhibit presented works by Emilio Aguayo, Danny Desiga, Ricardo Aguirre, Ramiro Benavidez, Elma Herada, Pedro Rodriguez and others. A selection of posters by Armando Cid of the R.C.A.F. group from Sacramento, California was also presented. Concurrently, at the Heny Gallery of the University of Washington, Esteban Villa presented a one-man show.

Benitez, Terry

1024 Teatro de la Tierra Morena, Santa Cruz, CA. Fuego en Aztlan: a Chicano arts show. Exhibition brochure, 1980. English.

AN: Folder of information on the exhibition curated by Cruz Zamarron and Eduardo Carrillo. Exhibiting artists were: Justina Avila, Terry Benitez, Eduardo Carrillo, Hernando Chavez, Bob Cruz, Juanita Estrada, Juana Franklin, Sal Garcia, Leticia Hernandez, David "Sir Loco" Jimenez, Raoul Mendez, Vicente Mendez, Maria V. Pinedo, Gonzalo Placencia, Ramon Rodriguez, Roberto Salas, George Silva and Cruz Zamarron. A special feature was a live tattoo demonstration entitled "Walking Art".

Benito Juarez High School

1025 Elitzik, Paul. Mural magic. AMERICAS, (June, July, 1981). English.

AN: Brief illustrated account of murals in the Pilsen barrio of Chicago. Mentions work by Aurelio Diaz, Marcos Raya, and Salvador Vega. Focuses on the controversial mural at Benito Juarez High School painted by Jaime Longoria and Malu Ortega.

Berkeley, CA

1026 Erickson, Barbara. La Pena's new face. NORTH EAST BAY INDEPENDENT, no. 4 (September 5, 1978), p. 11. English.

AN: Illustrated story on the relief mural SONG OF UNITY by Ray Patlan, O'Brien Thiele, Osha Neumann, and Anna de Leon on the facade of La Pena cultural center in Berkeley, California. Chilean songwriter Victor Jara and the music of North and South America are the motifs.

1027 Mural. ARTE, no. 1 (1977). English.

AN: Describes a section of the mural A PEOPLE'S HISTORY OF TELEGRAPH AVENUE painted by Daniel Galvez and Brian Thiele. The mural represents the work of dozens of additional artists.

1028 Mural celebration. GRASSROOTS, (September 6, 1978), p. 8. English.

AN: Illustrated story on the new mural of plywood, papier mache and ceramic painted and modeled by artists from Commonarts for la Pena Cultural Center. The mural depicts peoples of the Americas coming together, singing and playing musical instruments, with Chilean musician Victor Jara as the major symbol.

Berkeley, CA (cont.)

1029 New radical wall art. PEOPLE'S WORLD, Vol. 41, no. 37 (September 16, 1978), p. 10. English.

AN: Illustrated story and explanation of the imagery on the new mural resulting from a collaboration of Commonarts and La Pena Cultural Center. The artists are Ray Patlan, O'Brien Thiele, Osha Neumann, and Anna de Leon.

Bernal, Louis Carlos

1030 Arizona. ARIZONA REPUBLIC, (September 11, 1977), p. 50. English.

AN: Exhibit of photographs by Louis Carlos Bernal from Tucson in the Heard Museum in Phoenix, Arizona. Includes 6 illustrations.

1031 Bernal, Luis Carlos. La fotografia como reflejo de las estructuras sociales. In HECHO EN LATINOAMERICA: SEGUNDO COLOQUIO LATINOAMERICANO DE FOTOGRAFIA, MEXICO CITY, 1982, p. 92-94. Spanish.

AN: Presentation made by Tucson, AZ photographer Louis Carlos Bernal at the Second Latin American Colloquium of Photography and exhibit in 1981.

1032 Bernal, Luis Carlos. A luminous view of a simple lifestyle. NUESTRO, Vol. 2, no. 7 (July 1978), p. 26-27. English.

AN: Color photographic essay with notes by the photographer Luis Carlos Bernal. Documenting Arizona Chicanos, Bernal focuses on the objects and environments that help define their lifestyle.

1033 Chu, Amy. Focus on cultural heritage. READER: SAN DIEGO WEEKLY, (September 17, 1981). English.

AN: Review of exhibit FIVE PHOTOGRAPHERS: CONTEMPORARY VIEWS OF MEXICAN AND MEXICAN-AMERICAN CULTURE which includes two Chicano photographers from Arizona: Louis Carlos Bernal (Tucson), and Robert C. Buitron (Tempe). Details some of Bernal's work between 1973 and 1980; Buitron's more personal work (1978-1981) is from his FAMILY AND PHOTOGRAPHY book-in-progress.

1034 Consejo Mexicano de Fotografia, A.C., Mexico City and Tibol, Raquel. Hecho en Latinoamerica: primera muestra de la fotografia latinoamericana contemporanea. Exhibition catalog, 1978. Spanish.

AN: Catalog/book of the first colloquium and exhibit of Latin American photography. Among the Chicano artists in the exhibit were Francisco X. Camplis, Louis Carlos Bernal, Harry Gamboa, Jose P. Romero, Harvey J. Tarango, Isabel Castro. Statements by some of the artists. Great number of illustrations.

1035 Conversation on photography in the Los Angeles Latino community. OBSCURA, Vol. 2, no. 2 (December, February, 1981, 1982), p. 22-32. English.

AN: Interview on the nature and distinguishing characteristics of Chicano photography with Chicano photographers Isabel Castro (Council for Latino Photography), Lorenzo Hernandez (Director of Cityscape Gallery, publisher PHOTOSHOW magazine), Joseph G. Uribe (California State University, Los Angeles, Center for the Visual Arts, Director of West Colorado Gallery), Patssi Valdez, Becky Villasenor, and sculptor, curator, and Art Director for Academia Quinto Sol, Inc., Linda Vallejo, Portfolio of photography by Chicanos Don Anton, Louis Carlos Bernal, Sean Carrillo, Patssi Valdez, Ricardo Valverde, and by Morrie Camhi and Elizabeth Sisco on Chicano subjects.

1036 Espejo: reflections of the Mexican American: Louis Carlos Bernal, Morrie Camhi, Abigail Heyman, Roger Minick, Neal Slavin. SOMOS, Vol. 2, no. 1 (February 1978), p. 26-35. English.

AN: Announcement of the ESPEJO photographic exhibit to be held at Goez Gallery in East Los Angeles. Statements by the four artists and a portfolio of their works: Abigail Heyman, Roger Minick, Morrie Camhi, and Arizona Chicano photographer Louis Carlos Bernal. Includes color photographs by Bernal on cover. This 1979 issue is erroneously dated 1978.

1037 Fischer, Hal. Espejo: reflections of the Mexican American: Louis Carlos Bernal, Morrie Camhi, Abigail Heyman, Roger Minick, Neal Slavin. PICTURE MAGAZINE, no. 9 (1978). English.

AN: Oversize portfolio of photographs recording contemporary Mexican American life commissioned by the Mexican American Legal Defense and Education Fund. Three photographers, Louis Carlos Bernal (from Arizona), Morrie Camhi and Abagail Heyman focus on the family and the home; the fourth, Roger Minick, juxtaposes the Mexican American against "barrio" murals. Only Bernal is Chicano. 24 photographs, six of which (Bernal's) are in color.

1038 Five views on Mexican culture. LA JOLLA LIGHT, (September 10, 1981), p. B-6. English.

AN: Review of a show at the University of California, San Diego's Mandeville Art Gallery called FIVE PHOTOGRAPHERS: CONTEMPORARY VIEWS OF MEXICAN AND MEXICAN-AMERICAN CULTURE and featuring Arizona photographers Louis Carlos Bernal, Robert C. Buitron, and three others.

1039 Four and four: Mexican and Latino photography, April 25 through June 14 on the balcony. CALENDAR: SANTA BARBARA MUSEUM OF ART, (April 1981). English.

AN: Announcement of exhibit organized by Lorenzo Hernandez of the Cityscape Foto Gallery, Pasadena, Calif. Sought to present "the observable differences between the 'classic' vision of the Mexican National and the 'realistic' vision of the re-rooted Mexican/American." The latter included Louis Bernal (Tucson) and Ricardo Valverde (Los Angeles) as well as two Spanish Sephardics of Los Angeles, Camhi and Sisco.

Bernal, Louis Carlos (cont.)

1040 Mandeville Art Gallery, University of
California, San Diego. Five photographers:
contemporary views of Mexican and
Mexican-American culture. Exhibition
catalog, 1981. English.

AN: Catalog of exhibit including Louis
Carlos Bernal, Robert C. Buitron, Alberto
Lau, Richard Tichich, and Meridel
Rubenstein. Illustrated.

1041 Oakland Museum, Oakland, CA. Espejo:
reflections of the Mexican American: Louis
Carlos Bernal, Morrie Camhi, Abigail Heyman,
Roger Minick, Neal Slavin. Exhibit brochure,
1978. English.

AN: Twenty-five photographs from the
documentary series commissioned by the
Mexican American Legal Defense and Education
Fund. Only Bernal is Chicano.

1042 Raices y visiones [portfolio]. REVISTA
CHICANO-RIQUENA, Vol. 7, no. 2 (Spring
1979), p. 29-44.

AN: Portfolio of works from the exhibit
RAICES ANTIGUAS/VISIONES NUEVAS: ANCIENT
ROOTS/NEW VISIONS. Artists included are
Patssi Valdez (Los Angeles), Eloisa
Castellanos-Sanchez (New York), Benjamin
Serrano, Jr. (Tijuana, Mexico), Alex Garza
(Chicago), Martin Y. Moreno (Michigan), Luis
A. Jimenez (New Mexico), Rene Castro
(Oakland, CA), Sita Gomez de Kanelba (New
York), Susana Lasta (Tucson, AZ), Domingo
Garcia (New York), Consuelo Mendez Castillo
(Caracas, Venezuela), Naomi Castillo
Simonetti (New Jersey), Louis Carlos Bernal,
and Eddie Comptis.

1043 Riches of the barrios. ARIZONA [supplement
to ARIZONA REPUBLIC], (September 11, 1977),
p. 50. English.

AN: Louis Carlos Bernal of Tucson shows
his collection of photographic portratis of
the barrios at the Heard Museum in Phoenix.
Well illustrated.

1044 Wilson, William. Photography - the state of
the art. CALENDAR, (January 28, 1979), p.
87. English.

AN: Includes review of ESPEJO:
REFLECTIONS OF THE MEXICAN-AMERICAN exhibit:
four photographers--Louis Carlos Bernal,
Abigail Heyman, Morrie Camhi, and Roger
Minick--who worked independently for a year
to record facets of Chicano life.

Berru, Becky

1045 Wilson, Anne. Chicanos show off talents in
Magna SOCIO projects. SALT LAKE CITY
TRIBUNE, (July 9, 1979), p. C-1. English.

AN: In the rural Utah community of
Magna, SOCIO (Spanish Speaking Organization
for Community Integrity and Opportunity)
established various art projects. Three
murals were painted by community youth under
the guidance of Robert Archuleta and Becky
Berru. One of the murals depicts "man and
labor." Illustrated with photographs of
project directors, maquette of the mural and
a mural painting "brigade".

Bibliography

1046 Garcia, Rupert. A source for mural art
education: an annotated bibliography of

three Chicano newspapers. Unpublished paper,
1974 (Chicano Studies Library, Univ. of
California, Berkeley). English.

AN: A research project showing how
Chicano newspapers reported and educated
their readers to mural activity by Raza
artists during the period 1968-1978. The
newspapers analized are EL GALLO (Denver,
CO), EL CHICANO (San Bernardino, CA), and EL
TECOLOTE (San Francisco, CA). Author draws
eight conclusions about the form, meaning
and significance of mural activity in
Chicano barrios and the importance of
community newspapers as a fruitful and
meaningful source for art education.

1047 Rodriguez, Patricia. Bibliografia sobre el
arte chicano. ARTES VISUALES, no. 29 (June
1981), p. 32. Bilingual.

AN: Brief bibliography on Chicano art.
Bilingual.

Bicultural Education
USE: Bilingual Bicultural Education

Biggers, John

1048 Barnstone, Gertrude and Tanguma, Leo. The
big picture: 'I want to indict the system
that has condemned us!'. HOUSTON
BREAKTHROUGH, (March 1980), p. 16-19.
English.

AN: Houston muralist Leo Tanguma studied
with John Biggers at Texas Southern
University who encouraged him and other
Chicanos to study Mexican murals. The
article is an interview with Tanguma which
details his strong political orientation and
ideals, and the problems he has encountered
as a result. Three illustrations.

Bilingual Bicultural Education

1049 Diaz, Jean; Dominguez, Edward; and Torres,
Kay. Bi-Lingual blues [fotonovela]. SOMOS,
Vol. 1, no. 1 (April, May, 1978), p. 33-36.
English.

AN: Reproduction of a "fotonovela",
BI-LINGUAL BLUES by Ojo Productions, a group
of students connected with the Latin
American Studies Department of California
State University, Los Angeles.

1050 Hernandez, Greg. Bilingual education
[painting]. SOMOS, Vol. 1, no. 3 (August
1978), p. 21. English.

Bilingualism

1051 Reyes, Luis. Seguin: traidor o heroe.
COMUNIDAD, (April 12, 1981), p. 8-9.
Spanish.

AN: Report on the pilot film for an
eight-part series called LA HISTORIA made by
Jesus Trevino for the Public Broadcasting
Service. The pilot treats the life of an
"anti-hero," Juan Seguin, during the Texas
war for independence from Mexico, and
relates the little-known history of the
Mexican defenders of the Alamo. Trevino
chose this controversial subject because it
exemplified an early case of the dual nature
of bilingualism and biculturalism.
Description of the research and filming of
the pilot. Illustrated.

Biography

1052 Acosta, a man and his art. NOSOTROS, Vol. 2, no. 6. English.

AN: Biographical information and thematic analysis of the work of El Paso artist Manuel Acosta. He is especially noted for genre paintings of humble people reflecting social life and cultural traditions.

1053 Aguayo, Emilio. Chicano art: a new art-style of the future. (Unpublished Study Project for Prof. Brauman, Art Dept., Univ. of Washington, Seattle), June 6, 1972. English.

AN: Autobiographical account and self-analysis of artist's work. Beginning in 1965 the artist has created 40,000 small ink drawings in a contour line technique. Situating himself within the Chicano Arts Movement, Aguayo describes his dominant themes, symbols, and stylistic preoccupations.

1054 Aguilar, George. Raul Rodriguez, parade artist extraordinaire. NUESTRO, Vol. 6, no. 10 (December 1982), p. 11-14. English.

AN: Raul Rodriguez, a Mexican American float designer is considered a top artist in his field and one of the most successful in the country. Many of his floats have won prizes in the Tournament of Roses. In addition, Rodriguez designs facades for hotels on the Las Vegas Strip, most notably the facades of the Flamingo Hotel, the Dunes, and the Oasis.

1055 Aguirre, Tito. Interview with artist Jose Trevino. ARRIBA, Vol. 2, no. 2 (1981). English.

AN: Biographical information and artistic trajectory of Austin artist Jose Trevino. Illustrated with photo of artist and three of his portraits.

1056 Albright, Thomas. Manuel Neri's survivors: sculpture for the age of anxiety. ART NEWS MAGAZINE, Vol. 80, no. 1 (January 1981), p. 54-59. English.

AN: Critical evaluation of Neri's development as a sculptor in the figurative tradition. Biographical information and placement of artist within California art and international tendencies.

1057 Alex Maldonado, primitive painter. SAN FRANCISCO FOCUS MAGAZINE, (1973). English.

AN: Biographical information on 72 year old Alexander Maldonado who started painting upon his retirement. His "naif" work has gained wide critical acclaim and he has had more than 200 exhibitions throughout the United States. Illustrated with reproduction of one of Maldonado's paintings.

1058 Anderson, Howard J.; Young, Robert S.; and Kilgore, Andrew. Amado Maurilio Pena, Jr. Albuquerque, NM: Robert Stephan Young Publishing Co., 1981. English.

AN: Coffee-table type of art book about the Laredo-born painter and printmaker. The text includes impressionistic writing about Pena's life, interlaced with statements by the artist about his life and work. Though including a few plates from his early (1974-1978) political and family silkscreens, over 50 color plates reproduce

his "Santa Fe Indian" works from 1978 to the present.

1059 Andrews, Rena. The fine arts. ROUNDUP, (March 15, 1970), p. 16+. English.

AN: Biographical information on Chicano artist Ramon Kelley. Described as an impressionist, his work has affinity with Monet and Manet.

1060 Art Gallery, California State University, Long Beach and Lujan, Gilbert Sanchez "Magu". El arte del pocho. Exhibit brochure, October 1968. English.

AN: Information about Southern California artists John Deheras, Marcus Villagran, Roberto de la Rocha, Santos Zuniga, Crispin Gonzales, Richard Martinez, Jesus Gutierrez, Ed Oropeza, Pete Mendez, David Ramirez, Gilbert Sanchez Lujan, Willie Hernandez, Art Ponce, Carmen Tostado, Al Almeida, David Ceja, Robert E. Chavez, Thomas A. Ferriera. All art students, graduates, or faculty.

1061 Art Gallery, University of California, Irvine and Los Angeles County Museum of Art, Los Angeles, CA. Los Four: Almaraz, de la Rocha, Lujan, Romero. Exhibition brochure, 1973-74. English.

AN: Photographs and biographies of Carlos Almaraz, Roberto de la Rocha, Gilbert S. Lujan, Frank Romero.

1062 Arte chicano y el pueblo. COMUNIDAD, no. 41 (May 3, 1981), p. 1-15. Spanish.

AN: The whole issue of the Sunday Supplement deals with Los Angeles Chicano art and music. Works by painter Carlos Almaraz, photographer Elsa Flores, painter Yreina Cervantez, muralist and draftsman John Valadez, and a performance piece by Elsa Flores and Louie Perez are featured. Biographical information, and statements by the artists.

1063 Artista de Aztlan. EL DIARIO DE LA GENTE, Vol. 4, no. 8 (April 1976), p. 7. Spanish.

AN: Interview with Mike Garcia, staff artist for the DIARIO. Born in Alamosa, Colorado, the artist defines his work as "mestizo art because it expresses our Indian heritage, using motifs of the revolutionary struggles to reflect the possibilities of the future." Well illustrated.

1064 Ashford, Gerald. Artistic styles have no ethnic bonds. SUNDAY ONE, (October 18, 1970), p. [18]. English.

AN: Biographical information on Spanish-surnamed artists living and working in San Antonio. Includes commentary on Porfirio Salinas Jr. and Mel Casas.

1065 Baciu, Joyce A. Hispanic artists: combining energy and emotion. CAMINOS, Vol. 2, no. 5 (October 1981), p. 14-17. English.

AN: Brief profiles of Mario Uribe, Ernest De Soto, Peter Rodriguez, Margarita Jauregui Weiner, Virginia Jaramillo, Luis Urrea, Ramses Noriega, Jose Lopez, Olivia Sanchez.

--   --
Biography (cont.)

1066 Baciu, Joyce A. and Diaz, Katherine A. Margo
     Albert: a woman who gets things done = una
     mujer que realiza lo que desea. CAMINOS,
     Vol. 2, no. 5 (September 1981), p. 44-46.
     Bilingual.

     AN: Mexican-born Margo Albert is a
     well-known Los Angeles, CA artist, dancer,
     and actress who has been most active on
     behalf of the Plaza de la Raza in East Los
     Angeles. This article describes her
     activities as Co-chairperson of the Los
     Angeles Bicentennial Committee. For Margo,
     the highlights of the celebration marking
     the 200th anniversary of the founding of Los
     Angeles, included a day-long Fiesta del
     Bicentenario; groundbreaking ceremonies for
     the Ruben Salazar Bicentennial Building; and
     the reception for an official delegation of
     charros, sponsored as a gift to the people
     of Los Angeles by the Mexican government.

1067 Barnstone, Gertrude and Tanguma, Leo. The
     big picture: 'I want to indict the system
     that has condemned us!'. HOUSTON
     BREAKTHROUGH, (March 1980), p. 16-19.
     English.

     AN: Houston muralist Leo Tanguma studied
     with John Biggers at Texas Southern
     University who encouraged him and other
     Chicanos to study Mexican murals. The
     article is an interview with Tanguma which
     details his strong political orientation and
     ideals, and the problems he has encountered
     as a result. Three illustrations.

1068 Barrett, Marjorie. Carving out a living - a
     primitive process. ROCKY MOUNTAIN NEWS,
     (December 15, 1979), p. 90. English.

     AN: In the village of Teseque outside
     Santa Fe, NM, Felipe Archuleta, a
     69-year-old folk carver has emerged as an
     international art celebrity, famous for his
     naive animal carvings. His work expecially
     life-sized renditions of animals, is
     represented in many distinguished
     collections and is prized for its wit and
     lack of predictability. Illustrated with
     photograph of carver and one of his
     creations.

1069 Barrett, Marjorie and Flores, John. Flores:
     artist's gamble paid off. ROCKY MOUNTAIN
     NEWS, (May 18, 1980), p. 27. English.

     AN: In less than a decade, John Flores
     has gone from being a part-time painter
     working in a meat packing plant to a
     prolific fulltime artist. This interview on
     the occasion of Flores' one person show at
     the De Colores Gallery reviews his artistic
     trajectory. The 30 odd paintings in the
     exhibit include still lifes, pastel
     portraits, street scenes and landscapes in
     oil. Experimenting with vivid color, Flores
     is turning to his own cultural roots.

1070 Barrett, Marjorie. Ray Espinoza: versatile
     artist. ROCKY MOUNTAIN NEWS, (February 12,
     1973), p. 44. English.

     AN: Ray Espinoza whose family spans six
     generations in the San Luis Valley of
     Colorado is steeped in Southwestern art
     traditions. Drawing from his ancestral
     heritage, he has become a prominent sculptor
     working in wax. Illustrated with photograph
     of artist and two of his sculptures.

1071 Barrio, Raymond. Mexico's art & Chicano

artists. Sunnyvale, CA: Ventura Press, 1975.
English.

     AN: A personal resume with commentaries
     by the author on Mexican and Chicano art.

1072 Bayview Federal Savings, San Francisco, CA.
     Peter Rodriguez. [S.n.: s.l.], 1974.
     English.

     AN: Well-illustrated brochure includes
     photograph of San Francisco artist Peter
     Rodriguez and four of his paintings. Also
     provides biographical information,
     exhibition chronology and critical excerpts
     from reviews of several shows. Artist's
     basic style is lyrical abstractionism
     centered on organic forms derived from
     nature.

1073 Berges, Marshall. Sister Karen Boccalero:
     dedicated to the community, she helps others
     find strength in art. HOME MAGAZINE,
     (December 17, 1978), p. 42-45. English.

     AN: History of the Franciscan nun who
     studied with Sister Mary Corita at
     Immaculate Heart College. Details the
     founding and concepts of Self-Help Graphics
     in East Los Angeles, a year-round program to
     "help Chicanos rediscover their cultural
     heritage".

1074 Boettner, Jack. Youths help in fight against
     graffiti: muralist fights spray cans with
     brushes. LOS ANGELES TIMES [Orange County
     edition], (May 26, 1979), p. II, 12-13.
     English.

     AN: Illustrated and descriptive story
     about Orange County painter Emigdio Vasquez
     working on a series of murals with youth.
     Locations of murals by the group,
     biographical information about Vasquez, and
     his statement about art are given.
     Illustrated.

1075 Botello, David Rivas and Healy, Wayne
     Alaniz. Los Dos Streetscapers. SOMOS, Vol.
     1, no. 3 (August 1978), p. 12-17. English.

     AN: Autobiographical material by Los
     Angeles street muralists Botello and Healy.
     Illustrated.

1076 Bruce Novoa, Juan. [Interview with Jose
     Montoya]. In CHICANO AUTHORS: INQUIRY BY
     INTERVIEW. Austin, TX: University of Texas
     Press, 1980, p. 115-136. English.

     AN: Biography of Sacramento, CA artist
     and poet Jose Montoya. Emphasizes the close
     relationship between art and poetry in his
     life and in that of the Royal Chicano Air
     Force, which he co-founded.

1077 Calendario de March: 1977. Chicago, IL:
     MARCH, Inc., 1976. English.

     AN: Historical calendar with photos and
     biographies of artists. Illustrations of
     artwork by Ray Patlan, Jose Nario, Frank J.
     Sanchez, Salvador Dominguez, Salvador Vega,
     Marguerite Ortega, Aurelio Diaz, Carlos
     Cortez, Mario E. Castillo, Francisco Blasco,
     Rey Vasquez, and Efrain Martinez. History of
     MARCH (Movimiento Artistico Chicano).

Biography (cont.)

1078 Cantu, Jesus "Chista". Entrevista: Jesus
     Maria Cantu, 'El Chista'. MAGAZIN, Vol. 1,
     no. 4 (April 1972), p. 52-65. Spanish.

     AN: Discusses his life in San Antonio;
     his apprenticeship since childhood to his
     uncle Miguel Angel Tellez who taught him to
     paint billboards, wall signs and church
     decorations; his membership in the group
     Artistas de la Nueva Raza; his artistic and
     political philosophy. In Spanish.

1079 Carlos Sandoval to complete mural in
     Zihuatanejo, Mexico. TIERRA Y LIBERTAD, Vol.
     2, no. 4 (July 1980), p. 3, 10. English.

     AN: Biographical information on Colorado
     artist Carlos Sandoval. The Municipal
     Library in the city of Zihuatanejo in the
     state of Guerrero is the site of Sandoval's
     mural which visually and symbolically
     projects the cultural and historical unity
     between Mejicanos and Chicanos.

1080 Carraro, Francine. Refined rhythmic
     references: Amado Pena, Jr. SOUTHWEST ART,
     Vol. 9, no. 6 (November 1979), p. 70-75.
     English.

     AN: Well-illustrated (including 4 color)
     story on Austin silkscreen artist Amado M.
     Pena. Features his recent stylized work
     based on New Mexican indian motifs.

1081 El Centro Cultural de La Raza, San Diego,
     CA. Espejo del barrio-art exposition.
     Exhibition brochure, June 1975. English.

     AN: Illustrated brochure announcement
     for a cultural exposition of Chicano music,
     art and drama. Includes some biographical
     information and one reproduction of painter
     Manuel Unzueta, woodworker Ambriz, muralist
     Victor Orozco Ochoa and designer/illustrator
     J. Armando Nunez.

1082 Cesar Martinez. ARTES VISUALES, no. 29 (June
     1981), p. 63. Bilingual.

     AN: Two illustrations by the San
     Antonio, Texas artist, a brief biography,
     and the reprint of a letter published in the
     catalog CUATRO CAMINOS, Southwest Texas
     State University, San Marcos.

1083 Champlin, Chuck, Jr. Working for more than
     peanuts. LOS ANGELES TIMES, (June 21,
     1980), p. II, 8, 10. English.

     AN: Bill Melendez has been an animator
     21 years for Charles Schulz's Charlie Brown
     and Peanuts comic strips, TV specials, and
     feature films. Melendez began his career
     with Walt Disney Productions in 1938.

1084 Chavez, Jaime. Rayaprofiles: Manuel Unzueta.
     RAYAS, Vol. 2, no. 3 (May, June, 1979), p.
     5. Spanish.

     AN: Brief biography of Mexican-born
     Chicano artist and muralist from Santa
     Barbara, California. Manuel Unzueta is
     active with La Casa de la Raza and its
     publication XALMAN. Unzueta is invited to
     paint a mural in Albuquerque. A Santa
     Barbara mural is illustrated.

1085 Chavez, Lucy. A Chicano muralist. REVISTA
     MARYKNOLL, (July 1981). English.

     AN: Denver artist Carlotta Espinosa
     decided early in life that she was going to
     be an artist. Espinosa has painted murals in
     Arizona, Texas and the San Luis Valley in
     Colorado. Illustrated with photographs of
     artist and details from her murals.

1086 Chicano art of the Southwest. San Antonio,
     TX: Instituto Chicano de Artes y Artesanias
     of the Texas Institute for Educational
     Development, 1975. English.

     AN: Collection of 220 slides
     supplemented by slide annotation and
     artists' biographies researched and
     photographed by Texas artist Cesar A.
     Martinez over two years. Biographies cover
     20 Texas, 6 New Mexico, and 15 northern
     California artists. Slides include, in
     addition, murals from Los Angeles and San
     Diego.

1087 CJL. Artist profile-Amado Pena. FOUR WINDS,
     Vol. 1, no. 4 (1980), p. 10. English.

     AN: Amado Pena works within the
     expectations of an American Indian artist,
     but also within the context of the Mexican
     American culture. The article treats Pena's
     artistic trajectory and provides
     biographical information. Illustrated with
     photograph of the artist and reproductions
     of one lithograph and one mixed-media
     drawing.

1088 Coe, Kathryn. Heritage plus science yields
     art. SCOTTSDALE DAILY PROGRESS, (August 28,
     1981), p. 27. English.

     AN: Biography of Colorado-born Rudy
     Fernandez who bases many of his paintings
     and mixed media boxes on the religious
     imagery of Colorado. He studied geology;
     travelled to Spain and Mexico to know his
     heritage. All these factors influence his
     art, in which he uses symbols personally.

1089 Coffman Gallery I, The University of
     Minnesota, Minneapolis, MN. Ruben Trejo:
     visiting Chicano artist. Exhibition
     brochure, 1981. English.

     AN: Exhibition brochure of a sculpture
     show by Ruben Trejo presented from April 25
     to May 6. Trejo's sculptures are created
     from laminated wood, metal and plastic.
     Dominant motifs in this exhibit were the
     skull, the pepper and the heart. Brochure
     includes biographical information, checklist
     of the 28 works exhibited and one black and
     white photograph.

1090 Conferencia plastica chicana. Conference
     brochure, 1979. English.

     AN: Schedule of proceedings at
     internationally attended conference on
     Chicano and Mexican art and photography
     sponsored by the Centro Cultural de LUCHA
     (League of United Chicano Artistas) and MAS
     (Mujeres Artistas del Suroeste). Brief
     biographies of presentors. Illustrated.

1091 Corazon del norte: Jose Alfredo Maestas.
     GRITO DEL NORTE, Vol. 2, no. 7 (May 19,
     1969), p. 13. English.

     AN: Jose Alfredo Maestas, born in San
     Juan Pueblo is a folk carver imbued with the
     mythical and spiritual Indo-Hispano
     tradition. His carved figurines made from
     cotton wood roots, balsam and driftwood are
     in many museums and private collections.
     Illustrated with photographs of artist at
     work and two photographs of his sculpture.

Biography (cont.)

1092 Cuellar, Rodolfo. Esteban Villa-maximo exponente del arte indigena mexicano. EL HISPANO, Vol. 8, no. 23 (January 27, 1976), p. 3. Spanish.

AN: Biographical data on the artist focusing on his activism in the formation of the Centro de Artistas Chicanos in Sacramento and the coalition of Centros Chicanos in California. Illustrated with photographs of the artist, one of his murals and a special emblem for the "Esteban Villa Fan Club" designed by the R.C.A.F.

1093 Day, Orman. Hispanic life mirrored by ethnic artists. THE REGISTER, (July 5, 1981), p. B1+. English.

AN: Story on artists Manuel Hernandez Trujillo and Emigdio Vasquez whose work opened the new Galeria in Santa Ana, and poet Manuel Gomez. Color illustrations.

1094 De la Torre, Alfredo and Tellez, Miguel Angel. Entrevista con Don Miguel Angel Tellez=Interview with Don Miguel Angel Tellez. CARACOL, Vol. 5, no. 11-12 (July, August, 1979), p. 16-22. Bilingual.

AN: Tellez, born in San Antonio about 1915, son and grandson of painters who taught him the trade, tells about his life as commercial artist and his more symbolic work started in 1962. Illustrated.

1095 Dean, Nancy. Denver artist dues are paid in full. ROCKY MOUNTAIN NEWS, (April 5, 1981), p. 6. English.

AN: Profile of artist Ramon Kelley focusing on his successful career and detailing his rise on the art market. Includes photograph of the artist.

1096 Delgado, Sylvia. My people never smile: a profile of a young Chicano artist. REGENERACION, Vol. 2, no. 1 (1971), p. 23. English.

AN: Very brief biographical sketch of Willie Herron.

1097 Dickson, Joanne. Manuel Neri. El Cajon, CA: Grossmont College Gallery, 1980. English.

AN: Essay documents Neri's career and situates him within the Bay Area figurative style. As a sculptor, the artist has worked in plaster or bronze, cast paper, fiberglass and more recently in marble.

1098 Dietmeier, R. C. City artist finds his inspiration where he lives. ORANGE CITY NEWS, (December 23, 1981), p. 2. English.

AN: Illustrated story on Emigdio Vasquez's ten year retrospective of realistic paintings taken from photographs, held at the Galeria in Santa Ana, Calif. Vasquez records his environment and events from the 1940s and 1950s as an artistic and documentary statement.

1099 Directo, Cyril. Leo Guzman: woodcarver/tallador in madera. ENTRELINEAS, Vol. 1, no. 2 (February, March, 1968), p. 8. English.

AN: Biographical facts and commentary on artist's work. Illustrated with photographs of artist and examples of his work.

1100 Donnell-Kotrozo, Carol and Perlman, Barbara. Male passages: a secular santero of the '80s interprets machismo. ARIZONA ARTS AND LIFESTYLE, Vol. 4, no. 1 (1982), p. 32-39. English.

AN: Rudy Fernandez moves freely between two- and three-dimensional forms using personal symbols such as cacti, roosters, flying hearts, trout, in paintings or lead-covered shelves of boxes reminiscent of retablos. Colorado-born Fernandez has lived in Arizona, Utah, New Mexico, and Washington. His art is not religious, but is influenced by a strong Catholic background. Many color illustrations, including the cover.

1101 Donnell-Kotrozo, Carol. Rudy Fernandez. ARTSPACE, Vol. 5, no. 4 (Fall 1981), p. 18-23. English.

AN: Scottsdale, Arizona resident Rudy Fernandez converts cultural symbols into a private system language that revolves around love, family, manhood and self-identity. His mixed media altar-like forms are based on interest in Southwest santos, their format and presentation. Fernandez does paintings, and assembled wood pieces. Handsomely illustrated, with color.

1102 Edward Chavez: sculptor-painter. LA LUZ, Vol. 2, no. 2 (May 1973), p. 28-31. English.

AN: Lavishly illustrated biographical account of Edward Chavez. Born in Ocate, New Mexico in 1917, Chavez has a distinguished career as a painter and sculptor. During the 1940's he executed a number of murals under sponsorship of various government art projects. These murals were placed in public buildings in Nebraska, Colorado and Wyoming. Although living and working in New York most of his adult life, the work of Edward Chavez has always been influenced by the Southwest.

1103 Encuentro artistico femenil. Austin, TX: Juarez-Lincoln Institute, Centro Cultural de LUCHA, 1977. English.

AN: Program of music, literature and visual art. Lists works by 12 Latina artists and brief biographies. Part of "Women & Their Work" festival.

1104 Espinoza. EMPIRE MAGAZINE, (October 22, 1972), p. 28. English.

AN: Biographical information and artistic trajectory of Ray Espinoza from Colorado's San Luis Valley. Focus on Espinoza as a community artist who expresses aspects of Southwestern culture. Illustrated with photographs of three wax sculptures by Ray Espinoza.

1105 The First Unitarian Universalist Church, Paradise Valley, AZ. Five Chicano artists. Exhibition brochure, 1971. English.

AN: Exhibit organized by L. Eugene Grigsby, Jr., Art Department of Arizona State University, Tempe, AZ. 21 works by Eugene Quesada, David Nunez, Fernando Navarro, Luis Baiz (of Arizona) and Saul Solache (of Los Angeles). Brief biographies of the artists.

Biography (cont.)

1106 Focus: Yolanda Lopez. CITYBENDER, Vol. 2, no. 5 (1978). English.

AN: Brief biography and illustrations of drawings by San Diego/San Francisco artist Yolanda Lopez titled THREE GENERATIONS: TRES MUJERES.

1107 Una galeria de artistas = A gallery of artists. CAMINOS, Vol. 1, no. 6 (October 1980), p. 20-26. Bilingual.

AN: Features California artists Domingo O. Ulloa (Imperial Valley images), Gloria Chacon, photographer Maria Pinedo (San Francisco), Willie Herron (Los Angeles), Joaquin Patino (Delano), Pedro Pelayo (Long Beach), sculptor Rudi Sigala (San Diego), Mario Torero (San Diego), sculptor Michael M. Amescua (Los Angeles), and the East Los Streetscapers. Illustrated.

1108 Galeria de la Raza/Studio 24, San Francisco, CA and Lomas Garza, Carmen. Self-portraits by Chicano and Latino artists. Exhibition catalog, 1980. English.

AN: Catalog of a national exhibition by 66 artists. Gives names, residence, date of birth, and information on the work shown for each of the artists. 45 are from California, and 3 each from Puerto Rico, Arizona, New York, 9 from Texas, 2 from Washington, 1 from Virginia. 9 are women.

1109 Gamboa, Harry, Jr. Film, television, and Trevino. LA LUZ, Vol. 6, no. 10 (October 1977), p. 7-8. English.

AN: Jesus Salvador Trevino has been an active proponent and participant in transforming cultural inaccuracy about Chicanos in the media to accurate mass media models. A biography of Trevino follows, including discussion of some of his films: THE SALAZAR INQUEST, CHICANO MORATORIUM AFTERMATH, SOLEDAD, AMERICA TROPICAL, YO SOY CHICANO, RAICES DE SANGRE, as well as television series like ACCION CHICANO, AHORA, and INFINITY FACTORY.

1110 Gamboa, Harry, Jr.; Gronk; and Herron, Willie. Gronk and Herron. NEWORLD, Vol. 2, no. 3 (Spring 1976), p. 28-30. English.

AN: An interview with ASCO members Gronk and Willie Herron by a third member, Gamboa. Brief historical introduction (1970 on). The witty tongue-in-cheek interview can be considered an artwork by this performance art group. Illustrated.

1111 Garcia, Rupert. Echos de la Mision - Alfaro Siqueiros (1896-1974). EL TECOLOTE, Vol. 4, no. 3 (February 22, 1974), p. 11. English.

AN: Biographical and artistic trajectory of Mexican artist David Alfaro Siqueiros. Artist painted three murals in Southern California in 1932 (MEETING IN THE STREET and TROPICAL AMERICA were done in Los Angeles on the walls of the Chouinard School of Art and the Plaza Art Center, Olvera Street area respectively. The third mural PORTRAIT OF MEXICO was privately commissioned in Santa Monica). The three California murals deal with themes of censorship, racism, colonialism, capitalism, and imperialism. Article suggests that Raza artists are much influenced by the ideas and work of Siqueiros. Illustrated with Rupert Garcia's silkscreen poster SIQUEIROS.

1112 Garcia-Camarillo, Cecilio and Rosas, Carlos. Platicando con Carlos Rosas. RAYAS, Vol. 1, no. 6 (November, December, 1978), p. 12, 11. Spanish.

AN: Muralist Carlos Rosas painted murals in Boulder and Denver, Colorado; Milwaukee, Wisconsin, and El Paso, Texas. Commentary on cross ethnic murals, views on art in socialist countries, influence of Mexican murals and information on his personal preocupation as a politically engaged artist.

1113 Garcia-Camarillo, Cecilio and Martinez, Dennis. Platicando con Dennis Martinez. RAYAS, Vol. 1, no. 5 (September, October, 1978), p. 12, 11. Bilingual.

AN: Interview with Dennis Martinez, illustrator of BLESS ME ULTIMA, NAMBE: YEAR ONE, and MI ABUELA FUMABA PUROS. The books share New Mexican setting and their illustrator seeks to capture the essence of the landscape in that region. In his drawings Dennis Martinez hopes to evoke history in relation to landscape and culture. Illustrated.

1114 Goddarth, Ruth. Porfirio Salinas. Austin, TX: Rock House Press, 1975. English.

AN: Born on Nov. 6, 1910 on a farm near Bastrop, Texas, Porfirio Salinas studied art with Spanish artist Jose Arpa in San Antonio and gradually became a regional landscapist of wide renown. Salinas died April 18, 1973 at the age of 62. The book is lavishly illustrated.

1115 Goldman, Shifra M. The intense realism of Frida Kahlo. CHISMEARTE, Vol. 1, no. 4 (Fall, Winter, 1977), p. 8-11. English.

AN: A brief, one-page biographical sketch of Frida Kahlo's life and work. This is accompanied by black and white reproductions of her paintings: AUTORRETRATO COMO TEHUANA (1943), AUTORRETRATO (1946), RAICES (1943), LA VENADITA (1946), and LA NOVIA QUE SE ESPANTA DE VER LA VIDA ABIERTA (n.d.).

1116 Gonzalez, Hector and Cid, Armando. An interview with Armando Cid. EL HISPANO, Vol. 5, no. 32 (January 23, 1973). English.

AN: Biographical information and commentary on Cid's career and his art style which is described as containing pre-Columbian motifs and mannerisms of the people in the barrio.

1117 Gonzalez, Victoria. Chair in the sky: Ernesto Palomino. HERE AND NOW, Vol. 2, no. 2 (Fall 1981). English.

AN: An important article tracing the artistic career of Ernie Palomino, professor of art at California State University, Fresno. Includes biographical information, formation of La Brocha Del Valle (Chicano Arts Organization), information about Palomino's film MY TRIP IN A '52 FORD and commentary on Palomino's music and artistic philosophy. Well illustrated.

Biography (cont.)

1118 Graham Gallery, New York, NY and Amaya,
     Mario. Luis Jimenez. Exhibition catalog,
     1969. English.

     AN: Well-illustrated catalog of an
     exhibit by El Paso-born sculptor. Some
     biographical material.

1119 Graham Gallery, New York, NY and Perreault,
     John. Luis Jimenez. Exhibition catalog,
     1970. English.

     AN: Well-illustrated catalog of an
     exhibit by El Paso-born sculptor. Some
     biographical material.

1120 Hale, David. Fresnan gets grant to create
     five story high mural. FRESNO BEE, (April
     16, 1978), p. Forum, C4. English.

     AN: Details on the awarding of a grant
     to John Sierra, Fresno artist, for the
     creation of what will be the largest piece
     of public art in that city. The artwork is a
     6000 square foot mural titled THE PLANTING
     OF THE CULTURES. Article contains
     biographical information on the artist and
     presents goals of his mural project.

1121 Hancock de Sandoval, Judith. Regional
     report, The arts: the workaholic. NUESTRO,
     Vol. 2, no. 10 (October 1978), p. 14.
     English.

     AN: Biographical sketch of Jacinto
     Quirarte, author and educator, currently
     Dean of the College of Fine and Applied Arts
     at the University of Texas, San Antonio.

1122 Heard Museum, Phoenix, AZ. Second Southwest
     Chicano Art Invitational. Exhibit catalog,
     1978. English.

     AN: Exhibit by eight artists: Antonio
     Pazos (Tucson), Rudy Fernandez (Salt Lake
     City), Harry Gamboa (Los Angeles), Rupert
     Garcia and Xavier Viramontes (San
     Francisco), Roberto Rios (San Antonio),
     Roberto Espinoza (Yuma), and Roberto Borboa
     (Tucson). Brief biographies of all but Rios.
     29 illustrations.

1123 Helen Euphrat Gallery, De Anza College,
     Cupertino, CA. Staying visible: the
     importance of archives. Art and "saved
     stuff" of eleven 20th century California
     artists. Cupertino, CA: Helen Euphrat
     Gallery, De Anza College, 1981. English.

     AN: Catalog issued in conjunction with
     an exhibit held in the gallery Sept. 22 to
     October 23, 1981 which included
     documentation on Chicana artists Patricia
     Rodriguez and Carmen Lomas Garza. Each
     artist explains her method of saving,
     storing and using cultural material in her
     creations. Includes biographical sketch,
     photograph of the artist and reproduction of
     artwork.

1124 Herrera, Estela. La mujer en el mundo: una
     chicana en las artes. LA OPINION, (March
     25, 1982), p. III,6. Spanish.

     AN: Illustrated interview with Judith
     Elena Hernandez de Niekrug including
     biographical information and discussion of
     her attitudes toward her murals, paintings,
     and graphics.

1125 Herrera, Juan Felipe and Paramo, Bobby.
     Cerco Blanco, the balloon man and fighting

City Hall: on being a Chicano filmmaker.
METAMORFOSIS, Vol. 3, no. 2 (1980, 1981), p.
77-82. English.

     AN: Autobiographical article about his
     life and his introduction and immersion in
     filmmaking by Bobby Paramo. His experiences
     with documentary films, television, the Los
     Angeles Chicano film movement, are recorded.

1126 Hispanic American artist - Secundino
     Sandoval. LA LUZ, Vol. 7, no. 9 (September
     1978), p. 51. English.

     AN: Biographical data and analysis of
     "Sec", Sandoval's technique as a realist
     watercolorist.

1127 Hollister, Kelly. Linda Vallejo. CAMINOS,
     Vol. 1, no. 6 (October 1980), p. 19.
     Bilingual.

     AN: Story on Long Beach, California
     artist Linda Vallejo who also works with
     Self-Help Graphics in Los Angeles and has
     curated a number of exhibits. Vallejo
     describes her work as containing
     "archetypal, mythological or dream-world
     imagery" combined with the "modern idea of
     self-knowledge." Illustrated on p. 17.

1128 Incorporated Artes Monumentales/Inc.,
     Denver, CO. IAM: art exhibit. Exhibition
     brochure, n.d. English.

     AN: Large format, well illustrated
     brochure with information on muralists
     Roberto Lucero, Al Sanchez, Andrew Manning,
     Ricardo Barrera and Bob Reyes. Includes some
     biographical information situating these
     artists within the dynamic artistic
     traditions of the Mexican and the Chicano
     mural movements.

1129 Instituto Chicano de Artes y Artesanias
     (Texas Instit. Educational Development).
     Chicano art of the Southwest. San Antonio,
     TX: Texas Institute for Educational
     Development, [ca. 1975]. English.

     AN: Illustrated brochure announcing a
     color slide library on Chicano art
     supplemented by slide annotation and artists
     biographies available to institutions.
     Statement of purpose by Executive Director
     of program, Cesar Augusto Martinez.

1130 Jose Montoya: poeta, pintor, profesor,
     humanista, padre, abuelo. EL HISPANO, Vol.
     8, no. 27 (December 23, 1975), p. 5.
     Spanish.

     AN: Biographical data on the Sacramento
     artist, his contributions to the Chicano
     Movement and his life as an artist-activist.
     Photographs of his family and reproduction
     of one drawing.

1131 Kantar, Chris and Villa, Esteban. An
     interview with Esteban Villa. Unpublished
     paper, 1978. English.

     AN: A detailed and informative interview
     with Esteban Villa, prominent Chicano
     artist. Focus on Villa's philosophy of art,
     life, and the Chicano art movement. A good
     primary source. (The unpublished manuscript
     is deposited in the archives of the R.C.A.F.
     in Scaramento).

Biography (cont.)

1132 Kim, Howard. Judithe Hernandez and a glimpse at the Chicana artist. SOMOS, (October, November, 1979), p. 6-11. English.

AN: Biographical information on Chicana artist Judithe Hernandez. Commentary on her contributions to Plaza de la Raza, Los Angeles Citywide Mural Project and her work as designer consultant to AZTLAN: INTERNATIONAL JOURNAL OF CHICANO RESEARCH. The article focuses on her mural activity, particularly two murals: EL MUNDO DE BARRIO SOTEL and LA CHICANA DE AZTLAN. Her personal art philosophy is presented in relation to Third World Art.

1133 Kreneck, Tom. With the eye of an artist: Jesus Murillo's Houston, 1927-1933. REVISTA CHICANO-RIQUENA, Vol. 8, no. 3 (Summer 1980), p. 104-105. English.

AN: Biographical sketch of Mexican-born commercial and portrait photographer who worked professionally in Texas from 1916 until his death in 1971. The illustrations concern his Houston stay.

1134 Laguna Gloria Art Museum, Austin, TX. Tierra, familia sociedad, Amado Pena's themes. Exhibition catalog, 1980. Bilingual.

AN: Illustrated exhibition catalog with artist's biography and chronology of exhibitions. The bi-lingual text by Santos G. Martinez, Jr. situates the artist's work within a dual phased trajectory. First a period (1971-1975) in which the artist creates images armed with a social-political focus and (1975-present), a period starting with the PEOPLESCAPE series in which the artist enters a more lyrical introspective phase.

1135 Lopez, Yolanda M. Portrait of my grandmother. CONNEXIONS, no. 2 (Fall 1981). English.

AN: Four mixed-media images representing different ages in the life of the artist's grandmother. A hand written text by the artist provides biographical and social commentary.

1136 Lujan, Pedro and Morton, Carlos. Una platica entre Carlos Morton y Pedro Lujan. CARACOL, Vol. 3, no. 4 (December 1976), p. 10-12. Bilingual.

AN: Carlos Morton interviews Pedro Lujan, a Chicano sculptor who spends six months a year in New York and six months traveling throughout the Southwest. Lujan discusses his preference for creating works from available materials such as scraps of wood, wire, and rope.

1137 Manuel Acosta. LA LUZ, Vol. 3, no. 10-11 (January, February, 1975), p. 30. English.

AN: Biographical and exhibition data focusing on Acosta's ability to paint Mexican American types from the border area.

1138 Marion Koogler McNay Art Institute, San Antonio, TX and Lee, Amy Freeman. Filigree drawings by Consuelo Gonzalez Amezcua. Exhibition catalog, 1968. English.

AN: Illustrated catalog for an exhibition of 42 filigree drawings by Texas artist "Chelo" Amezcua. Apart from biographical and historical information, the text evokes the ambiance of magic and mysticism surrounding the artist.

1139 Martinez, Anita. Villa - "arte por toda la Raza". EL TECOLOTE, Vol. 1, no. 5 (October 19, 1970), p. 2. English.

AN: Biographical information and artistic trajectory of Esteban Villa, artist from Sacramento. Villa says that to be a Chicano is to have developed a cultural independence. He posits his ideas on the nature of Chicano art, its forms, functions, and educative role. Villa describes the evolving Chicano Art Movement with its goals based on moral principles. Illustrated with one of Villa's works, "Chicano Rebirth".

1140 Martinez, Manuel. Promotional brochure. Brochure, n.d. English.

AN: Biographical information on Chicano muralist who was a pupil of David Alfaro Siqueiros. Illustrated with photographs of two acrylic murals and a photo of the artist.

1141 McCullom, Pat. Gonzales: his paintings are like hieroglyphs. ANCHORAGE TIMES, (June 25, 1978), p. I, 3. English.

AN: Mariano Gonzales born in El Paso Texas, reared in Anchorage and trained at the Rhode Island School of Design has a developing reputation as an artist from the far north. This positive review is for an exhibit of paintings, jewelry and metal work pieces. Gonzales' paintings are heavily saturated with subconscious symbolism and his sculptures generally feature mechanical, movable parts.

1142 Mechicano Art Center. Los Angeles, CA: Mechicano Art Center, 1971. English.

AN: Announcement of an exhibit by painters Ramon Atilano, Xavier Lopez Ortega, and Frank A. Martinez. Martinez and Lopez Ortega are also muralists. Brief profiles of the artists. Illustrated.

1143 Mencion Don Quijote: Atanasio P. Davila. LA VOZ DE HOUSTON, (June 5, 1980). English.

AN: Illustrated biography of 70-year-old Mexican-born Texas painter who returned to art after his retirement and had just completed a mural for Houston's Ripley House medical clinic.

1144 Metro Denver Urban Coalition, Denver, CO. City walls. Brochure, 1979. English.

AN: Brochure/poster giving history of City Walls Project and biographies of seven artists: Jon Howe, Jerry Jaramillo, Steve Lucero, Jowinnie Moore, Al Sanchez, Fred Sanchez, Carlos M. Sandoval. Illustrated.

1145 Mexican American Community Service Organization, San Jose, CA. Exhibition of contemporary art. Exhibition brochure, 1968. English.

AN: Biographical and exhibition data for Al Barela, Bert Hermosillo, Octavio Romano, Luis Valdez, Vincent P. Rascon, John Soares and Al Espinoza.

Biography (cont.)

1146 The Mexican Museum, San Francisco, CA.
Alexander Maldonado. Exhibition brochure,
1979. English.

AN: One page autobiographical statement
by Alexander Maldonado. Includes sources of
his imagery.

1147 The Mexican Museum, San Francisco, CA.
Rupert Garcia: portraits/retratos.
Exhibition brochure, 1981. English.

AN: Exhibition brochure with
biographical information and exhibition
chronology for Rupert Garcia.

1148 Mexican-American Institute of Cultural
Exchange, San Antonio, TX and Alvarez
Acosta, Miguel. Mel Casas paintings.
Exhibition brochure, 1963. Bilingual.

AN: Exhibition brochure with
biographical and exhibition chronology for
El Paso born painter, Meliseo Casas. He is
the first non-Mexican born artist invited to
exhibit at the art gallery sponsored by the
International Organization of Cultural
Promotion for Foreign Relations in San
Antonio.

1149 Montini, Ed. Masks reflect the spirit of an
artist. ARIZONA REPUBLIC, (May 31, 1981),
p. G-1,G-3. English.

AN: The paper and ceramic masks of Zarco
Guerrero reflect many different emotions.
Masking has long been a tradition in Mexico,
where Guerrero got his inspiration. Guerrero
uses his masks for theatre and as an
educational tool. Illustrated.

1150 Moser, Charlotte. Arte chicano de
Texas/Texas Chicano art. ARTES VISUALES, no.
29 (June 1981), p. 57-63. Bilingual.

AN: History of Chicano art and art
organizations in Texas. A younger generation
of artists is complying with a mainstream
European esthetic rather than a regional
Chicano one. Statements and biographies of
artists. Many illustrations.

1151 Moser, Charlotte; Renteria, Phil; and Wray,
Dick. Phil Renteria and Dick Wray. ART IN
AMERICA, Vol. 64, no. 4 (July, August,
1976), p. 82-83. English.

AN: Interview with Laredo-born Houston
artist Renteria, and Wray, both of whom
teach at the Museum of Fine Arts. Renteria
gives much biographical information and his
philosophy of art. Illustrated in color.

1152 Murales - 'expresan nuestra realidad'.
AYUDA, Vol. 1, no. 6 (September 1977).
English.

AN: Brief illustrated article on Raul
Valdez's 1977 mural LOS ELEMENTOS on the
outside wall of Antioch's Juarez-Lincoln
College (Centro Cultural de LUCHA). Explains
the iconography of the mural. Includes brief
biography of the artist.

1153 Nelson, Kathryn J. Excerpts from los
testamentos: Hispanic women folk artists of
the San Luis Valley, Colorado. FRONTIERS,
Vol. 5, no. 3 (Fall 1980), p. 34-43.
English.

AN: Eppie Archuleta, weaver from the San
Luis Valley in Southern Colorado talks
about her life philosophy, Hispanic cultural
traditions and her role as a community
artist. First person account amply
illustrated with photographs.

1154 Neumeier, Marty. Ignacio Gomez.
COMMUNICATION ARTS MAGAZINE, Vol. 21, no. 6
(January, February, 1980), p. 78-87.
English.

AN: Story on commercial designer and
illustrator Ignacio Gomez of Los Angeles
which describes his background, education
and life style. 17 full-color illustrations
of his art work, including the ZOOT SUIT
poster for the Mark Taper Forum play.

1155 The new logo. LA VOZ: Concilio for the
Spanish Speaking of King Co., Seattle, no. 5
(June 1979). English.

AN: Biographical information on artist
Alfredo Arreguin. Born in Uruapan, Michoacan
Mexico and residing in Seattle for eighteen
years, Arrequin is active in La Extension
Cultural, an agency formed to meet the
cultural needs of "Hispanics" in the Pacific
Northwest. In his logo for the "Concilio,"
Arreguin employs symbols representing
history, beauty, unity, ethnicity and
communication.

1156 Newport Harbor Art Museum, Newport Beach,
CA. Our own artists: art in Orange County.
Exhibition catalog, 1979. English.

AN: Includes Patricia Murillo and
Emigdio Vasquez with illustrations of one
work each. Biographies of the artists.

1157 Nora Mendoza: pintora de ascendencia
mexicana triunfa en los EE. UU. BUENHOGAR,
(May 1979), p. 7. Spanish.

AN: Profile of Texas-born Nora Mendoza
of Michigan, a painter of abstractions in
acrylic. She is an active member of many
Detroit and Michigan organizations,
including Nuestras Artes de Michigan which
she co-founded with Jorge Vargas, Martin
Moreno and Jessie Gonzalez.

1158 La onda artistica de Carmen Lomas Garza.
MAGAZIN, Vol. 1, no. 2 (November 1971), p.
29-37. Spanish.

AN: Short biographical sketch of artist
and reproduction of seven early drawings.
The art of Carmen Lomas Garza is situated
within important events of the Chicano
Movement in Texas: the student walkouts in
Kingsville, and the formation of Colegio
Jacinto Trevino.

1159 Parr, June. Amado Maurilio Pena, Jr.: a
talented and dedicated artist. ARRIBA,
(October 1980), p. 1. English.

AN: Pena is represented in forty-two
galleries internationally. Recently, Pena
opened his studio and gallery, El Taller, in
Austin. His latest works focus on the Indian
heritage and are based on trips to New
Mexico. Illustrated.

Biography (cont.)

1160 Pena, Amado Maurilio, Jr. Amado Maurilio Pena, Jr. Brochure [1980]. English.

AN: Promotional brochure including a biographical profile of the artist, a list of representing galleries throughout the United States, and eight good quality reproductions of serigraphs and mixed media drawings, six in color, on the theme of New Mexican Pueblo Indians.

1161 Pena, Ruben R. Mel Casas - people in the arts. BUSINESS AND THE ARTS, (September, October, 1979), p. 15. English.

AN: Probing analysis of the work and life of San Antonio artist Mel Casas. Article is divided into five sections in which the artist gives his views on culture, art, society, the Southwest and himself. Contains biographical information and artistic trajectory.

1162 Perez, Demetrio. Mel Casas - humanscapes. Houston, TX: Contemporary Arts Museum, 1976. English.

AN: Catalog for Mel Casas exhibition Oct. 22-Nov. 23, 1976. Artist calls his paintings "visual conundrums which play with our cultural concepts, with our cultural vision." Includes biographical information and exhibition chronology. Well illustrated with nine reproductions of artists work and two photos of the artist.

1163 Pino, Thomas E. Ramon Kelley: the business of art. LA LUZ, Vol. 7, no. 5 (May 1978), p. 24-26. English.

AN: Biographical information on Colorado artist Ramon Kelley. Business aspects of art: marketing, selling, art as investment.

1164 Pollock, Duncan. He sallied forth to paint. ROCKY MOUNTAIN NEWS, (February 7, 1971), p. 1. English.

AN: Biographical information about Martin Saldana, an eccentric personality labeled as Denver's answer to Grandma Moses. Saldana died in 1965 leaving behind a cache of "primitive" paintings that soon became much sought after by collectors. His work portrayed the rural pageant of Mexican life. Illustrated with self-portrait.

1165 Pollock, Duncan. Recognition arrives for Martin Saldana. ROCKY MOUNTAIN NEWS, (January 13, 1972), p. 55. English.

AN: After a long career as a vegetable cook at the venerable Brown Palace Hotel in Denver, Martin Saldana started art classes at the Denver Art Museum. His work was fresh, imaginative and totally naive. After the artist's death in 1965 at age 90, his paintings started to receive critical acclaim. Article details Saldana's rise to prominence and compares his artwork to that of Henry Rousseau. Illustrated with photograph of Martin Saldana.

1166 Quinonez, Naomi H. In her own backyard = En su propio traspatio. CAMINOS, Vol. 2, no. 2 (March 1981), p. 34-36,62. Bilingual.

AN: Describes the establishment of the Centro de Arte in Long Beach, CA by Chicana artist Lola de la Riva and her family. The Centro, which is in de la Riva's Long Beach home, is designed to give members of her barrio a chance to develop and display their artistic talents. Frequent workshops in mask making, clay sculpture, painting, and graphics are held at the Centro, and the works of local artists are usually on display in her backyard.

1167 Quirarte, Jacinto. Chelo Gonzalez Amezcua. QUETZAL, Vol. 1, no. 2 (Winter 1970, 1971), p. 33-36.

AN: Biographical information based on a taped interview with the Del Rio, Texas artist. As a self-taught artist, Chelo Gonzalez Amezcua developed a drawing style using colored ball point pens which she calls "Filigree Art", a new Texas culture. Poorly illustrated.

1168 Ramon Kelley. ARTISTS OF THE ROCKIES, Vol. 1, no. 1 (Spring 1974), p. 6-11. English.

AN: Biographical information on Ramon Kelley and a listing of his invitational shows. Illustrated with a photograph of the artist and a portfolio of ten works (three in color).

1169 Rand, Steve. Carlos David Almaraz. LOS ANGELES FREE PRESS, Vol. 11, no. 10 (March 8, 1974), p. 14. English.

AN: Brief biographical sketch on Mexican-born, Los Angeles artist Carlos Almaraz on the occasion of the Los Four exhibit at the Los Angeles County Museum of Art, artists who are, the author says inaccurately, largely self-taught. Almaraz studied at Garfield High School with David Ramirez, and at Otis Art Institute. One illustration.

1170 Rayaprofile: Carlos Cortez. RAYAS, Vol. 1, no. 6 (November, December, 1978), p. 3. English.

AN: Biographical profile of Chicago artist Carlos Cortez.

1171 Reser, Phil. Rene Yanez: state-of-the-xerox art. CITY ARTS, Vol. 3, no. 8 (August 1981). English.

AN: Five years ago when Xerox came out with a color copier, Yanez started experimenting with the machine's color buttons, which he uses like a musical instrument or a paint brush. Yanez's work is showing at the Electro-Arts Gallery in San Francisco. Brief profile of the artist, whose father and grandfather were both artists.

1172 Richard Henkin, Inc., Beverly Hills, CA. Veloy Vigil. Exhibition Catalog, n.d.. English.

AN: Full color catalog of graphics by Denver-born painter who lives in Taos and Southern California. Biographical information, but lacks dates.

1173 Ruiz, Elizabeth. Fiesta artist. THE RANGER, (April 23, 1981). English.

AN: Biographical information on San Antonio painter Jesus Trevino. Artist describes his work as "realism" with "a focus on Mexican American and Chicano culture, the people and their lives".

Biography (cont.)

1174 Rupert Garcia. SAN FRANCISCO BAY GUARDIAN, (October 3, 1975), p. 22-23. English.

AN: Informative piece focusing on the artist's work procedures; his techniques of image selection, transformation and manipulation. Presents Garcia's political and aesthetic credo and situates him as a community activist and artist. Illustrated with reproduction of Garcia's BICENTENNIAL POSTER.

1175 Salazar, Veronica. Artist doesn't starve now. SAN ANTONIO EXPRESS-NEWS, (June 13, 1976), p. 18-A. English.

AN: Raul Gutierrez, water colorist from Laredo, Texas, has emerged as a nationally recognized master painter of western and wildlife themes. His work is avidly collected and exhibited. Article details his artistic trajectory and provides biographical information.

1176 Salazar, Veronica. Mel Casas sees things brown. SAN ANTONIO EXPRESS-NEWS, (December 23, 1973). English.

AN: Searching for "visual congruity," Mel Casas has slowly moved toward figurative art. Article traces aspects of his artistic trajectory and the philosophic basis of his aesthetic vision. Includes photograph of artist.

1177 Salazar, Veronica. Prominent Mexican-Americans-Porfirio Salinas. SAN ANTONIO EXPRESS-NEWS, (April 1, 1973), p. I-4. English.

AN: Biographical information and artistic chronology of Porfirio Salinas. This self-taught artist is the most prominent painter of Texas landscapes, especially with bluebonnets. Former president Lyndon B. Johnson was an ardent fan and patron.

1178 Salinas, Raul. Portrait of an artist. ENTRELINEAS, Vol. 1, no. 5-6 (October, December, 1971), p. 3-5. English.

AN: Biographical and artistic information on Ruben Estrella who developed as a "pinto" artist within Leavenworth Penitentiary.

1179 Samuels, Peggy and Samuels, Harold. Cisneros, Jose. In: THE ILLUSTRATED BIOGRAPHICAL ENCYCLOPEDIA OF ARTISTS OF THE AMERICAN WEST. Garden City, NY: Doubleday, 1976, p. 95. English.

AN: Brief biography on book illustrator, Jose Cisneros, who is a leading authority on the costume, weapons, and trappings of Mexican border horsemen.

1180 Samuels, Peggy and Samuels, Harold. Grandee, Joe Ruiz. In: THE ILLUSTRATED BIOGRAPHICAL ENCYCLOPEDIA OF ARTISTS OF THE AMERICAN WEST. NY: Doubleday, 1976, p. 193. English.

AN: Brief biography of third generation Texan, Western painter of history, military, portrait subjects and illustrator living in Arlington, TX where his collection of Western artifacts is at the "Joe Grandee Gallery and Museum of the Old West." 1974 one person retrospective in Washington, DC.

1181 San Antonio Museum Association, San Antonio,

TX. Real, really real, super real. Exhibition brochure, 1981. English.

AN: Exhibit surveying modern and contemporary realism in the U.S. Includes a brief biography, personal statement, and color illustration of work by Jesse C. Trevino, San Antonio, Texas photorealist painter and muralist, (pp. 146-147).

1182 San Antonio Museum of Modern Art. Paperwork: an exhibition of Texas artists. San Antonio, TX: San Antonio Museum of Modern Art, 1979. English.

AN: Includes Roberto Munguia, Mexican American artist from Kingsville, Texas. Working with shaped paper, the artist describes his material and methods of creation. Includes biography of artist together with an exhibition list. Illustrated with photographs of five paper constructions by Roberto Munguia.

1183 San Francisco Art Commission Gallery. Rolando Castellon, Gustavo Rivera, Jerry Concha. Exhibition brochure, 1971. English.

AN: Brochure for exhibit by Sacramento-born Jerry Concha, Mexican-born Gustavo Rivera, and Nicaraguan-born Rolando Castellon titled CAPRICORN ASUNDER. Brief biographies of the artists.

1184 Seattle Art Museum, Seattle, WA and Dickson, Joanne. Manuel Neri, sculpture and drawings. Exhibition catalog, 1981. English.

AN: Beautifully illustrated catalog. Text by Joanne Dickson from Oakland California, biography and very complete chronology of Neri exhibitions.

1185 Segade, Gustavo V. Alfredo Arreguin. CITYBENDER, Vol. 2, no. 9 (1978). English.

AN: Brief profile of Mexican-born painter Arreguin who lives in the state of Washington. Three illustrations.

1186 Sharing a bit of magic with John Mendoza. ARTISTS OF THE ROCKIES, Vol. 1, no. 2 (Spring 1974), p. 14-17. English.

AN: Growing up in the St. Charles Mesa east of Pueblo Colorado, John Mendoza has sought to capture the essence of nature in that part of the country in his paintings. Blending realism and abstraction, Mendoza has evolved a distinctive personal idiom. Illustrated with reproductions of two watercolors and six drawings. Includes two photos of the artist and his pupils.

1187 Stamper, Frances. Fluid washes of ink and acrylic. TEXAS HOMES MAGAZINE, Vol. 4, no. 1 (January, February, 1980), p. 104-112. English.

AN: Well illustrated article with color reproductions of the work of Philip Renteria. Provides biographical information and focuses on the consumate craftsmanship of his drawings and paintings.

Biography (cont.)

1188 Stellweg, Carla. De como el arte chicano es
tan indocumentado como los
indocumentados/the way in which Chicano art
is as undocumented as the 'undocumented'.
ARTES VISUALES, no. 29 (June 1981), p.
23-32. Bilingual.

AN: An overview of Chicano art from its
beginnings to the present. Suggestion that
present art is improved by abandoning the
nationalist, derivative and folkloric phase.
Statements and biographies of artists. Some
non-Chicanos included as Chicanos. Many
illustrations. Bilingual.

1189 Tapia, Ludy. Montoya and the art of
survival. LA VOZ DEL PUEBLO, Vol. 3, no. 5
(June 1972), p. 6. English.

AN: Profile of San Francisco Bay area
poster maker and artist Malaquias Montoya,
who first became involved in the Chicano
movement in San Jose working with MASC and
EL MACHETE paper. In Berkeley (1968), he met
Esteban Villa and, with others, formed the
Mexican American Liberation Art Front
(MALAF). Montoya is against elitism
influencing Chicano art, and is concerned
with commercialization of Chicano art and
artists. Illustrated.

1190 Thorne, Judy. Alfredo Arreguin - painting in
patterns. SEATTLE TIMES, (June 15, 1980),
p. 18-19. English.

AN: Biographical information on
Mexican-born Seattle painter Alfredo
Arreguin. Includes mention of his selection
as a city art commissioner in Seattle.
Discussion of artist's distinctive style
based on use of intricate patterns. Well
illustrated with four color reproductions of
artist's work.

1191 Tone Briones, artist of Aztlan. PAPEL
CHICANO, Vol. 2, no. 11 (December 20, 1972),
p. 4. English.

AN: Biographical information on
caricaturist and cartoonist Tony Briones
from Laredo, TX, who is staff artist for
PAPEL CHICANO. Illustrated with one
editorial caricature, "Be a Good Chicano,
Join the Army," and a two-panel cartoon.

1192 Torres, Louis R. A Profile of an Hispano
Artist: Charlie "Clavos" Felix. LA LUZ, Vol.
4, no. 6-7 (September, October, 1975), p.
3-4. English.

AN: Biographical data on artist and his
unique nail relief sculpture.

1193 Trafford, Al. The giant painted photo album:
Jesse Trevino. SOUTHWEST ART, (April 1979).
English.

AN: Well illustrated story on San
Antonio photorealist painter Jesse Trevino.
Includes biographical material, description
of his working methods for murals and easel
paintings, and self-characterization of his
work as "cultural documentary painting".

1194 Trejo, Frank. S.A. mission doors inspired
wood carver. SAN ANTONIO LIGHT, (January
10, 1971), p. 18. English.

AN: Biographical and exhibition
information on San Antonio woodcarver Jesse
V. Garcia. Illustrated by photograph of
artist.

1195 Tsutakaua, Mayumi. Artist paints from
heritage. SEATTLE TIMES, (September 15,
1980). English.

AN: Biographical information on Armond
Lara, Northwest Chicano-Navajo artist. He is
coordinating the restoration of a mural done
in Seattle by Mexican artist Pablo
O'Higgins. In his own work Lara is
experimenting with paper making and the use
of natural pigments.

1196 Tsutakaua, Mayumi. Despite hostilities,
Arreguin is transcending. SEATTLE TIMES,
Exhibition brochure, n.d. English.

AN: Biographical sketch of Northwest
Chicano painter and ceramicist Alfredo
Arreguin. Artistic chronology and negative
relationship with local mainstream art
institutions.

1197 Turner, Mark. Muralist uses walls to break
barriers between people. ARIZONA DAILY STAR,
(July 23, 1981). English.

AN: Luis Gustavo Mena works on his
latest mural, an image of Benito Juarez with
the Mexican and "Latin Empire" flags, and a
scale of justice. Information about the
artist, son of an artistic family, and
recent high school graduate.

1198 University of Texas. El Paso. Chicano
Studies Program. "Chicanotations": paintings
and drawings by Manuel Unzueta. Exhibition
brochure, 1979. English.

AN: Exhibition handout includes
biographical data and a listing of the 20
works exhibited by Unzueta.

1199 Valadez, Kathy L. and Valadez, Kathy L.
Living in the understanding of success/el
endendimiento [sic] del exito. CAMINOS, Vol.
1, no. 6 (October 1980), p. 12-14, 40.
Bilingual.

AN: Story about financially successful
Los Angeles illustrator Ignacio Gomez who
produced the illustration for the play ZOOT
SUIT and designs posters, catalogs, magazine
covers and layouts. Also see front cover and
inside of front cover for illustrations.

1200 Valdez, Salvador. A forgotten artist's work
lives on. NOSOTROS, Vol. 2, no. 6. English.

AN: Narrative of the life and times of
Jose Aceves, a self taught El Paso artist
(1909-1968), noted for his desert
landscapes.

1201 Valle, Victor Manuel and Vasquez, Emigdio.
Emigdio Vasquez Interview. SOMOS,
(December, January, 1978, 1979), p. 42-43.
English.

AN: Article on Arizona-born painter, son
of a miner, living in Orange County,
California. Discusses his realistic style
(from photographs), technique, humanism,
interest in murals, and loan of work for
Alejandro Grattan's film ONLY ONCE IN A
LIFETIME. Illustrated.

1202 Vallejo, Linda. I am...Linda Vallejo.
CHISMEARTE, Vol. 1, no. 4 (Fall , Winter,
1977, 1978), p. 27-30.

AN: Brief autobiographical sketch
illustrated with three drawings.

Biography (cont.)

1203 Vasquez, Emigdio. The Cypress Street Barrio
and my art: a statement of intent.
Unpublished manuscript, 1978. English.

AN: The Arizona-born artist whose family
moved to Orange, Calif. in 1941 describes
his working class barrio and the perspective
it gave him of "life, people and society."
He turned to this subject matter as a young
artist and has continued to paint the
barrio. Description of sources and methods
of work.

1204 Vasquez, Emigdio and Goldman, Shifra M.
Painter: Emigdio Vasquez. Brochure, [1981].
English.

AN: Brochure including a brief biography
and illustrations of eight paintings.

1205 Vasquez, Emigdio. La vida through the eyes
of Emigdio Vasquez. Q-VO, (April 1979), p.
36. English.

AN: Interview with Orange County,
California, realist and documentary painter
Emigdio Vasquez who focuses on barrio life
he knew in the 1940s and 1950s. Vasquez
works from his own photographs and those of
others. Includes biographical information
and illustrations.

1206 Vergara, Dora Maria. New artist del barrio
Canta Ranas. REVISTA RIO BRAVO, Vol. 1, no.
1 (Winter 1981), p. 2. English.

AN: Biography of self-taught artist
Pedro Martinez who lives in and records the
life and people of the westide barrio
"Cantaranas" in Laredo, Texas. Five drawings
reproduced in this issue.

1207 Vigil, Rita. Veloy Vigil: artist capturing
ethereal horizons and the Indian spirit.
SOUTHWEST ART COLLECTOR, Vol. 1, no. 3
(March, April, 1980), p. 2. English.

AN: Denver-born artist who changed from
commercial to fine art in 1972 when he was
40 years old, though he "sidelined" in fine
art from the early 1960s. Resides in Taos
and Southern California.

1208 White, Ron. Bluebonnet the flower of South
Texas painting. SAN ANTONIO EXPRESS-NEWS,
(December 14, 1975), p. 7-H. English.

AN: The South Texas landscape paintings
by Porfirio Salinas are immensely popular
and command high prices. This analysis of
the career and the production of the late
artist (died April 18, 1973), concludes that
Salinas was "a mediocre artist with mediocre
skills and a poor sense of imagination".

1209 Wilks, Flo. Joseph A. Chavez. ART VOICES
SOUTH, Vol. 3, no. 1 (January, February,
1980), p. 30. English.

AN: Brief resume on art and life of
Albuquerque sculptor. Illustrated.

1210 Work of Southwest artist sings to soul,
heart. NUESTRO, Vol. 5, no. 7 (October
1981), p. 57-61. English.

AN: Brief profile of Laredo-born Texas
artist Amado Pena who designed the first
conmemorative poster for the Congressional
Hispanic Caucus' observance of National
Hispanic Heritage Week. The poster is
reproduced on the cover. The article

includes full-color illustrations.

1211 Yarbro-Bejarano, Yvonne. La forma del sueno:
arte y pensamiento de Alfredo Arreguin.
METAMORFOSIS, Vol. 3, no. 2 (1980, 1981), p.
10-24. Spanish.

AN: Interview and portfolio of
Mexican-born painter who has been living in
Seattle for more than 20 years. Contains
biographical data and the artist's view on
the role of the Chicano artist. Ten
illustrations.

1212 Zheutlin, Barbara and Talbot, David. Jesus
Salvador Trevino. In: CREATIVE DIFFERENCES:
PROFILES OF HOLLYWOOD DISSIDENTS. Boston,
MS: South End Press, 1978, p. 345-352.
English.

AN: Within the context of New Left
alternative filmmakers who chose to work
within Hollywood, Trevino sets forth his
standards and goals. His films and TV
productions include SOLEDAD (1971), AMERICA
TROPICAL (1971), YO SOY CHICANO (1972),
RAICES DE SANGRE (1977) and INFINITY FACTORY
(1975-1976).

BIRTH, DEATH AND RESURRECTION [mural]

1213 Rodebaugh, Dale. Graffiti replaces popular
mural in Santa Cruz arcade. SAN JOSE
MERCURY, (April 13, 1979), p. B, [1].
English.

AN: The efforts of Eduardo Carrillo to
restore his mural, "Birth Death and
Resurrection in a downtown arcade. The
artist comments on the intention and
significance of the mural and the political
reasons for its obliteration.

BIRTH OF MOSES [painting]

1214 Kahlo, Frida and Del Solar, Daniel. Frida
Kahlo's THE BIRTH OF MOSES. TIN TAN, Vol. 1,
no. 2 (September 1975), p. 2-6. Bilingual.

AN: Mexican painter Frida Kahlo's
explanation of her painting THE BIRTH OF
MOSES in Spanish, with an error-ridden
translation to English. Source of the
original text not given. Illustrated.

BIRTH OF THE INDO-HISPANO [mural]

1215 Pepe and Pepito. SANTA FE NEW MEXICAN,
(October 11, 1972), p. A7. English.

AN: The unveiling of a mural entitled
"Rebirth of the Chicano" will take places on
the eve (Oct., 19) of the First Chicano
National Congress for Land and Cultural
Reform held in Albuquerque Oct., 20-22. (See
"Chicano Congress Set for Albuquerque" SFNM
6/21/72).

1216 Tijerina lauds Chicano Congress results.
SANTA FE NEW MEXICAN, (October 24, 1972),
p. A3. English.

AN: At the First National Chicano
Congress for Land and Cultural Reform in
Albuquerque, it was pointed out that younger
delegates are just coming to the realization
of being Chicano but are behind in knowledge
about the relationships between Spaniards,
Mexicans and Indians. This was the reason
for unveiling the mural BIRTH OF THE
INDO-HISPANO [called elsewhere REBIRTH OF
THE CHICANO] at the Alianza headquarters
October 19, 1972.

Black Coral [film] Award

1217 CHICANO CINEMA NEWSLETTER. Vol. 2, no. 1 (January 1, 1980). English.

AN: 17 Chicano filmmakers from Los Angeles, Albuquerque, Sacramento, San Francisco and Boston attended the First Annual International Festival of New Latin American Cinema in Cuba. Chicano cinema received the "Black Coral" award for a retrospective screened as part of the festival. Includes reports on coming events.

Black Kachina Gallery, Santa Fe, NM

1218 Fabricant, Don. Show reveals Hispanic art. NEW MEXICAN WEEKEND, (June 1, 1979). English.

AN: Review of two exhibits in Santa Fe: EL FESTIVAL HISPANICO, mounted by La Cofradia de Artes y Artesanos Hispanicos and Gilberto Guzman at the Black Kachina Gallery. The reviewer feels the traditional-style woodcarving done by contemporaries is the strongest part of the show; works that break with these forms seem weaker, less skillful and cliche-ridden. Crafts are excellent. Muralist Guzman has blossomed in murals and easel paintings since he was employed by the 1978 Art in Public Places project. His work is intense and expressive, sometimes erotic. Illustration of work by sculptor Ruben Montoya.

1219 Loniak, Walter. The true New Mexico contemporary style. SANTA FE REPORTER, (May 31, 1979). English.

AN: Review of three exhibits in Santa Fe, EL FESTIVAL HISPANICO co-sponsored by the Cofradia de Artes y Artesanos Hispanicos and the Santa Fe Council for the Arts; a wood carving exhibit at Elaine Horwitch Gallery, and easel paintings by muralist Gilberto Guzman at the Black Kachina Gallery. Concerning the Festival exhibit, the critic states that the sculptural pieces are the strongest; two dimensional work is inconsistent or unimpressive, weaving is not well represented (though usually the strongest medium), and there are few photographs or prints. Illustration.

Blacks

1220 Amalgamated Meat Cutters and Butcher Workmen of North America. Cry for justice. 1972. English.

AN: Well-illustrated catalog of Chicago street murals by Black, Chicano, White and Puerto Rican artists.

1221 Blaine, John and Baker, Decia. Finding community through the arts: spotlight on cultural pluralism in Los Angeles. ARTS IN SOCIETY, Vol. 10, no. 1 (Spring, Summer, 1973), p. 125-138. English.

AN: Community arts expression by ethnic minorities is burgeoning everywhere, especially in Los Angeles. Various Black, Asian, and Chicano art administrators are interviewed, including Frank Lopez of Plaza de la Raza and Leonard Castellanos of Mechicano Art Center. Illustrated.

Blasco, Francisco

1222 Calendario de March: 1977. Chicago, IL: MARCH, Inc., 1976. English.

AN: Historical calendar with photos and biographies of artists. Illustrations of artwork by Ray Patlan, Jose Nario, Frank J. Sanchez, Salvador Dominguez, Salvador Vega, Marguerite Ortega, Aurelio Diaz, Carlos Cortez, Mario E. Castillo, Francisco Blasco, Rey Vasquez, and Efrain Martinez. History of MARCH (Movimiento Artistico Chicano).

Blow-outs

1223 Fiesta de los barrios observes Cinco de Mayo. EASTSIDE SUN, (May 1, 1969). English.

AN: The Fiesta de los Barrios is a cultural festival organized by the committee pressuring the Los Angeles Board of Education for better and more relevant education after the East Los Angeles high school "blowouts." The Fiesta features art, music, dance and literature.

Blue Island, IL

1224 NATIONAL MURALS NETWORK COMMUNITY NEWSLETTER. (Spring 1980). English.

AN: Reports on the Sept. 1979 conference of Chicano visual arts held at UT Austin, organized by the Mujeres Artistas del Suroeste, and the Liga Unida de Chicanos Artistas, which brought together participants from the U.S. and Mexico City; on Manuel Martinez's five murals (1976-78); murals by Roberto Lucero, Al Sanchez, and Jerry Jaramillo; as well as by the Chilean group Orlando Letelier Brigade, all in Denver, Colorado; murals by Leo Tanguma in Houston; the story about the "forbidden" Chicano mural in Blue Island, Illinois. Illustrated.

Boalt Hall, University of California, Berkeley

1225 Gonzalez, Hector. Rivera paints Boalt Hall mural. EL HISPANO, Vol. 5, no. 29 (January 2, 1973). English.

AN: Brief commentary on Sacramento artist Edward Rivera and his design for a mural to be installed in Boalt Hall at the University of California's Berkeley campus.

Boccalero, Sister Karen

1226 Berges, Marshall. Sister Karen Boccalero: dedicated to the community, she helps others find strength in art. HOME MAGAZINE, (December 17, 1978), p. 42-45. English.

AN: History of the Franciscan nun who studied with Sister Mary Corita at Immaculate Heart College. Details the founding and concepts of Self-Help Graphics in East Los Angeles, a year-round program to "help Chicanos rediscover their cultural heritage".

Boise Gallery of Art

1227 Monroe, Julie T. A splash of art from
     Idaho's Mexican-Americans. IDAHO STATESMAN,
     (March 11, 1977), p. 4D. English.

     AN: As a Bicentennial tribute to all
     people of Latin American heritage, Illinois
     Bell Telephone Company organized a national
     exhiibit of 17 Mexican-American/Chicano
     artists. In Idaho, the touring exhibition
     was augmented by a local presentation,
     MEXICAN-AMERICAN: IDAHO, shown at the Boise
     Gallery of Art under sponsorship of Boise
     Cascade. Jose Rodriguez, local artist
     presents his views on the meanings of the
     word "Chicano" and "Chicano Art."
     Illustrated with a photograph of Jose
     Rodriguez and a reproduction of one of his
     oil paintings entitled THE HOE.

Boise, Idaho

1228 Boise Gallery of Art, Idaho Migrant Council
     and Boise Cascade Corp. 17 artists:
     Hispano/Mexican-American/Chicano. Boise, ID:
     1977. English.

     AN: Announcement of a national
     exhibition organized and toured by Illinois
     Bell Telephone. In Idaho, the exhibit (March
     12 to April 10, 1977) also included local
     Chicano artists.

Bonilla, Roberto

1229 Gonzalez, Tobias and Gonzalez, Sandra.
     Perspectives on Chicano education. Stanford,
     CA: Stanford University, 1975. English.

     AN: Reproductions of artworks by Ralph
     Maradiaga, Patricia Rodriguez, Roberto
     Bonilla, Francisco Camplis, Graciela
     Carrillo-Lopez, Juan Fuentes, Irene Perez,
     Roger Reyes, Carlos Loarca, Xavier
     Viramontes, Ralph McNeill, Rupert Garcia,
     Jose Romero.

Book Reviews

1230 A beautiful book just published...: book
     review of MEXICAN AMERICAN ARTISTS. LA LUZ,
     Vol. 2, no. 4 (August 1973), p. 26. English.

1231 Martinez, Santos G., Jr. Review of: MEXICAN
     AMERICAN ARTISTS. DE COLORES, Vol. 2, no. 2
     (1975), p. 47-51. English.

     AN: A review essay by a noted Chicano
     artist. The basic shortcoming of Quirarte's
     book is "the author's failure to recognize
     the distinction between the terms Mexican
     American and Chicano. Consequently, Dr.
     Quirarte has failed to establish what
     exactly a Chicano is and in turn has failed
     to fully recognize the existence of Chicano
     art; an art by Chicanos about Chicanos and
     their culture." Reprinted in CARACOL, vol.
     2, no. 3, 1975 and in TEJIDOS, vol. 3, no.
     3, 1976.

Books and Reading for Children
     USE: Children's Literature

Borboa, Roberto

1232 Ariav, Al. Hispanics' work ignored, artist
     says. ARIZONA DAILY STAR, (June 3, 1978).
     English.

     AN: Hispanic-Americans in Tucson have no
     gallery, little access to museums, and no
     recognition for their work, says Roberto
     Borboa, artist and cultural organizer. He

welcomes the National Task Force of Hispanic
American art which visited Tucson.

1233 Heard Museum, Phoenix, AZ. Second Southwest
     Chicano Art Invitational. Exhibit catalog,
     1978. English.

     AN: Exhibit by eight artists: Antonio
     Pazos (Tucson), Rudy Fernandez (Salt Lake
     City), Harry Gamboa (Los Angeles), Rupert
     Garcia and Xavier Viramontes (San
     Francisco), Roberto Rios (San Antonio),
     Roberto Espinoza (Yuma), and Roberto Borboa
     (Tucson). Brief biographies of all but Rios.
     29 illustrations.

1234 Huge mural displayed at El Con Shopping
     Center. ARIZONA DAILY STAR, (January 31,
     1979). English.

     AN: A 15 x 50 foot mural called The
     Creation of Cultures, a latex-enamel on
     panels, was painted by Tucson muralist
     Roberto Borboa. Its final site has not been
     determined. Illustrated.

1235 New name, new face. TUCSON CITIZEN, OLD
     PUEBLO SECTION, (December 6, 1979), p. 6.
     English.

     AN: Tucson muralist Roberto Borboa works
     on a mural EDUCATION at the Edward L.
     Lindsay Adult learning Center. Illustrated.

1236 Tucson Public Library; Sonoran Heritage; and
     De la Cruz, Frank. Mexican American mural
     art: the power of cultural identity.
     Brochure, 1980. English.

     AN: Brochure on Tucson murals painted by
     Antonio Pazos, David Tineo, Danny Garza,
     Cynthia Reyes, Darlene Marcos, Roberto
     Borboa, and others.

1237 Vigil, Maria. Hello, walls: Tucson's murals.
     WEEKENDER MAGAZINE, (March 29, 1980), p.
     14-16. English.

     AN: Article on muralism, from the
     Mexican to those of Chicanos. Focuses on
     Tucson murals by Roberto Borboa, Antonio
     Pazos, David Tineo and Fred Monreal. Color
     illustrations.

Border Patrol

1238 Rodriguez, Pedro. Fronteras falsas
     [painting]. REVISTA CHICANO-RIQUENA, Vol. 8,
     no. 3 (Summer 1980), p. 73. Bilingual.

Border Region

1239 Cisneros, Jose. Riders of the border. El
     Paso, TX: Texas Western Press, 1971.
     English.

     AN: Jose Cisneros, El Paso artist has
     illustrated (in total or in part) over forty
     books, most of which deal with the
     Southwest. This collection ia a picture book
     rendering the picturesqueness and pagentry
     of the various riders along the border.
     Illustrated with 30 black and white drawings
     and text by the artist.

1240 Manuel Acosta. LA LUZ, Vol. 3, no. 10-11
     (January, February, 1975), p. 30. English.

     AN: Biographical and exhibition data
     focusing on Acosta's ability to paint
     Mexican American types from the border area.

Border Region (cont.)

1241 Samuels, Peggy and Samuels, Harold. Cisneros, Jose. In: THE ILLUSTRATED BIOGRAPHICAL ENCYCLOPEDIA OF ARTISTS OF THE AMERICAN WEST. Garden City, NY: Doubleday, 1976, p. 95. English.

AN: Brief biography on book illustrator, Jose Cisneros, who is a leading authority on the costume, weapons, and trappings of Mexican border horsemen.

Botello, David

1242 Botello, David Rivas and Healy, Wayne Alaniz. Los Dos Streetscapers. SOMOS, Vol. 1, no. 3 (August 1978), p. 12-17. English.

AN: Autobiographical material by Los Angeles street muralists Botello and Healy. Illustrated.

1243 Del Olmo, Frank. Murals changing face of East L.A. LOS ANGELES TIMES, (December 3, 1973), p. II, 1+. English.

AN: First Los Angeles Times report on burgeoning Los Angeles mural movement with a map of 15 mural sites. Mentioned are C.W. Felix (originator of Estrada Courts project), Willie Herron, David Botello, Armando Campero, Edward Carbajal. (Chicano Art Committee).

1244 Los Dos Streetscapers. Los Dos Streetscapers, mural detail. NATIONAL GEOGRAPHIC, Vol. 155, no. 1 (January 1979), p. 38-39. English.

AN: One panel of Los Angeles mural by Wayne Alaniz Healey and David Botello, CHICANO TIME TRIP.

1245 Una galeria de artistas = A gallery of artists. CAMINOS, Vol. 1, no. 6 (October 1980), p. 20-26. Bilingual.

AN: Features California artists Domingo O. Ulloa (Imperial Valley images), Gloria Chacon, photographer Maria Pinedo (San Francisco), Willie Herron (Los Angeles), Joaquin Patino (Delano), Pedro Pelayo (Long Beach), sculptor Rudi Sigala (San Diego), Mario Torero (San Diego), sculptor Michael M. Amescua (Los Angeles), and the East Los Streetscapers. Illustrated.

1246 Gamboa, Harry, Jr. Los murales de Aztlan. COMUNIDAD, (June 28, 1981), p. 8-9+. Spanish.

AN: Review of the exhibit at the Craft and Folk Art Museum of Los Angeles of MURALS OF AZTLAN: THE STREET PAINTERS OF EAST LOS in which Carlos Almaraz, Gronk, Judithe Hernandez, Willie Herron, Frank Romero, John Valadez and the East Los Streetscapers (David Botello, Wayne Healy, George Yepes) painted portable murals in the gallery. The murals are described and illustrated.

1247 Greenberg, David; Smith, Kathryn; and Teacher, Stuart. Megamurals & supergraphics: big art. Philadelphia, PN: Running Press, 1977. English.

AN: A full-color picture book of murals throughout the United States. Chicano murals include Michael Rios (San Francisco), Mujeres Muralistas (San Francisco), Leonard Castellanos and Tomas Gonzales with others (Los Angeles), Los Artes Guadalupanos de Aztlan (New Mexico), Willie Herron (Los

Angeles), Toltecas en Aztlan (San Diego), David Botello (Los Angeles), David Lopez and Arizona Mara Gang (Los Angeles), Vatos de Maravilla (Los Angeles), Carlito Gaegos (Los Angeles), Gil Hernandez (Los Angeles), Wayne [Alaniz] Healy (Los Angeles).

1248 Kushner, Sam. It was a meat market in East L.A. LOS ANGELES FREE PRESS, Vol. 11, no. 34 (August 23, 1974), p. 17. English.

AN: Data on the formation of Goez Gallery by John Gonzalez and David Botello in 1970. Created in what once was a meat market in the East Los Angeles barrio, Goez became an important showcase for Chicano art.

1249 Varda, Agnes. Mur murs/mural murals on the wall ... Film, Cine Tamaris, Paris, 1980. English.

AN: Full length documentary film produced for French television; also available with English subtitles. Deals impressionistically with the murals and muralists of Los Angeles. Included are Wayne Alaniz Healy, David Botello, Willie Herron, Manuel Cruz, Judy Baca, the murals in Venice, CA, graffiti - among others. Color.

Boulder, CO

1250 Artista de Aztlan. EL DIARIO DE LA GENTE, Vol. 4, no. 8 (April 1976), p. 7. Spanish.

AN: Interview with Mike Garcia, staff artist for the DIARIO. Born in Alamosa, Colorado, the artist defines his work as "mestizo art because it expresses our Indian heritage, using motifs of the revolutionary struggles to reflect the possibilities of the future." Well illustrated.

BOULEVARD NIGHTS [film]

1251 CHICANO CINEMA NEWSLETTER. Vol. 1, no. 3 (May 1979). English.

AN: Announcements for the U.S. Conference for an Alternative Cinema (N.Y.), a "Nosotros" banquet, application dates for the Film Fund, deadlines for the National Endowment for the Humanities, and criticism of the Hollywood feature film BOULEVARD NIGHTS.

Bova, Joe

1252 Estudios Rio: gallery of contemporary arts and crafts. Exhibition catalog, 1976. English.

AN: Catalog including identification, portraits and works of participating artists: Joe Bova, Enrique Flores, Carmen Lomas Garza, Xavier Gorena, Erik Gronborg, Lucas Hinojosa, Ben Holland, Kris Hotvedt, William Kaars-Sijpesteijn, Cesar Martinez, Chris Mende, Roberto Mungia, Steve Reynolds, Vicente Rodriguez, William Wilhelmi.

Bowerman, Liz Lerma
USE: Lerma Bowerman, Liz

Boycotts

1253 Torres, Salvador Roberto. Arte de la Raza
[portfolio]. DE COLORES, Vol. 1, no. 1
(Winter 1973), p. 34-43. Bilingual.

AN: A portfolio consisting of four
drawings representing the "progression" of
the symbol of the banner adopted by the
United Farm Workers (UFW). Included are four
out of six drawings, each with its own
explication in English and Spanish, and
brief biographical data about the artist.

1254 Zermeno, Andy. Don Sotaco: caricaturas de la
huelga de Delano. Delano, CA: Farmworkers
Press, 1966. English.

AN: Short vignettes depicting the
farmworkers' struggle and how Don Sotaco
comes to understand his role in that social
movement. Illustrated with caricatures of
the various personages in the struggle;
patrones, coyotes, esquiroles, campesinos
and huelguistas. Centerfold and back cover
photographs by Jon Lewis.

Bravo, Joe

1255 Miranda, Keta. Refunding battle for mural
project. PEOPLE'S WORLD, Vol. 39, no. 20
(May 15, 1976), p. 5+. English.

AN: History of the Mural Arts and
Resource Center (Los Angeles Citywide Mural
Project) from 1974 to its imminent demise in
1976. Joe Bravo mural illustrated.

1256 [Untitled photograph]. CALENDAR, (April 30,
1978), p. 102. English.

AN: Illustration of Joe Bravo mural in
progress, Venice, California.

1257 Zahn, Debbie. Citywide murals: outlook bleak
for funding of art work by Chicanos.
FORTY-NINER, (May 4, 1976). English.

AN: The Los Angeles City Council decides
to terminate the 1974 program, Citywide
Murals, which provided funds for Chicano
artists. Description of Joe Bravo's 2000 sq
ft mural at the Wilmington Recreation
Center, painted with a team, which makes a
positive statement against gang warfare.
Illustrated.

Bravo, Ray

1258 Chicano art. ARTES VISUALES, no. 29 (1981).
English.

AN: Issue on Chicano art, introduced by
Los Angeles artist Roberto Gil de Montes.
Includes works and statements by: Pedro
Lujan (Texas); Raul M. Guerrero (Calif.);
Sylvia Salazar Simpson (New Mexico/Calif.);
Carlos Almaraz (Calif.); Rene Yanez
(Calif.); Jack Vargas (Calif.); Ray Bravo
(Calif.); John Valadez (Calif.); Gloria Maya
(Calif.); Elsa Flores (Calif.); Willie
Herron (Calif.); Gilbert "Magu" Lujan
(Calif.); Kay Torres, Jerry Lucas, and Louis
Perez (Calif.).

1259 William Grant Still Community Arts Center,
Los Angeles, CA. Latin American artists
exhibition. Exhibition brochure, 1978.
English.

AN: Exhibit curated by Linda Vallejo
including Carlos Almaraz, Michael M.
Amescua, Ray Bravo, Isabel Castro, Yreina
Cervantez, Luis Serrano-Cordero, Cynthia

Honesto, Judith Miranda, Teddy Sandoval,
John Taboada, Emigdio Vasquez. Illustrated.

Brigada Orlando Letelier (Chile)

1260 COMMUNITY MURALS (San Francisco, CA). (Fall
1981). English.

AN: Citywide Murals Group of Denver,
Colorado assisted the Chilean-oriented
Brigada Orlando Letelier with a mural in
their city; Carlos Sandoval of Denver doing
mural in Guerrero, Mexico; Ray Patlan of
Berkeley, California assisting with mural in
Mexico painted by Arnold Belkin's class at
the Academy of San Carlos; report on the
exhibit MURALS OF AZTLAN: THE STREET
PAINTERS OF EAST LOS with a reprint of
debate on the event by Shifra M. Goldman,
Judithe Elena Hernandez de Neikrug, and
comments by John Pitman Weber and Tim
Drescher; report on DAR LUZ mural directed
by Santa Barraza in Austin, Texas, and a new
mural in Hayward, California directed by
Enrique Romero; a mural sponsored by the
Chicano Youth Center of Fresno, California
showing the influence of Mexican calendars;
a new mural, OAKLAND'S PORTRAIT by Daniel
Galvez in Oakland, California; pro-and-con
discussion of social function of graffiti in
response to letter from Belgian source;
reprint of story on spray paint crime bill
(anti-graffiti) sponsored by California
Assemblyman Richard Alatorre. Entire issue
illustrated.

Briones, Tone

1261 NEW ERA (U.S. Penitentiary, Leavenworth,
KA). (Fall , Winter, 1970). English.

AN: Under the art direction of Ruben
Estrella from San Antonio, Texas, NEW ERA, a
prison cultural magazine also featured the
caricatures and cartoons of Tone Briones
from Laredo, Texas. Raul Salinas, poet from
Austin, Texas was Associate Editor for both
issues.

1262 Tone Briones, artist of Aztlan. PAPEL
CHICANO, Vol. 2, no. 11 (December 20, 1972),
p. 4. English.

AN: Biographical information on
caricaturist and cartoonist Tone Briones
from Laredo, TX, who is staff artist for
PAPEL CHICANO. Illustrated with one
editorial caricature, "Be a Good Chicano,
Join the Army," and a two-panel cartoon.

Brito, Frank

1263 Elaine Horwitch Galleries, Santa Fe, NM. New
Mexico woodcarving. Exhibition catalog,
1980. English.

AN: Invitation to an exhibit at the
Horwitch galleries of Scottsdale, Arizona,
and Santa Fe, NM of sculptors Felipe
Archuleta, Leroy Archuleta, Frank Brito,
Alonso Jimenez, Horatio Valdez, and others.
Illustration.

Broadcast Media

1264 CHICANO CINEMA NEWSLETTER. Vol. 1, no. 6 (August 1979). English.

AN: Announcements of the San Antonio Chicano Film Festival, a seminar on the business of art, the receipt of a report of the Task Force on Minorities in Public Broadcasting, a critical report on the Alternative Cinema Conference in New York, which was attended by eleven members of the Chicano Cinema Coalition, and a report and critique of the report by the Task Force.

La Brocha Del Valle [Chicano Arts Organization], Fresno, CA

1265 Campesino Business and Joint Enterprise Building, Fresno, CA. Sabor a Fresno. Arte chicano: los Four and la Brocha. Exhibition invitation [1976]. English.

AN: Invitation to an exhibit of works by Los Four of Los Angeles and members of La Brocha del Valle of Fresno: Arturo Roman, Sal Garcia, John Sierra, Juan Truner, Sapo de Aztlan, Fernando Hernandez, Alberto Reyes, Ernesto Palomino, Lee Orona, Francisco Barrios, Juan Ybarra, Bobby Reyes, Alberto Hernandez. Brocha was started by Palomino (California State University, Fresno professor) to pool talents of Central Valley artists.

1266 Garcia, Sol. Vato Loco y Chata La Gata [comic strip]. CHISMEARTE, no. 2 (Winter, Spring, 1977), p. Bk cover. Calo.

AN: Comic strip format utilized to invite all interested persons to meeting of the Concilio de Arte Popular. The artist is a member of the Brocha del Valle group from Fresno, CA.

1267 Gonzalez, Victoria. Chair in the sky: Ernesto Palomino. HERE AND NOW, Vol. 2, no. 2 (Fall 1981). English.

AN: An important article tracing the artistic career of Ernie Palomino, professor of art at California State University, Fresno. Includes biographical information, formation of La Brocha Del Valle (Chicano Arts Organization), information about Palomino's film MY TRIP IN A '52 FORD and commentary on Palomino's music and artistic philosophy. Well illustrated.

1268 Hale, David. La Brocha del Valle artists deal with Chicano reality. FRESNO BEE, (October 1, 1978), p. G, 5. English.

AN: Positive critique of a collective exhibition by members of La Brocha del Valle Group held at Fresno State University's Phebe Conley Art Building Gallery. With divergent attitudes, styles and ideas, the group is united by their focus on subject matter that deals with the diverse realities of being Chicano. Illustrated with photograph of Juan Ybarra's bronze sculpture, ONLY ONE TIME.

1269 Las muralistas del barrio. CHISMEARTE, no. 2 (Winter, Spring, 1977), p. 48-49. English.

AN: Brief announcement about a Chicana artists' organization formed in Fresno, California which started work on a billboard-like mural, 60x8 feet on the theme of women. The mural received funding through Fresno's La Brocha del Valle. About fifteen women are involved, including Helen Gonzalez

and Cecelia Risco.

Brothers of Light
USE: Hermanos Penitentes

Bugarin, Lena

1270 Imagenes de la Chicana. Menlo Park, CA: Nowels Publications (Stanford University Chicano Press), [ca 1975]. English.

AN: Collections of writings by Chicanas; illustrated by unsigned drawings, and photographs by Lena Bugarin, Martina Puente, Francisco Camplis, Mario Anzaldua.

Building
USE: Architecture

Buitron, Robert C.

1271 Armas, Jose and Buitron, Robert. Issues. ARIZTLAN NEWSLETTER, (August 1981). English.

AN: Thoughts and definitions of Chicano art by Dr. Jose Armas, founder of Pajarito Publications, and by photographer and MARS member Robert Buitron.

1272 Chu, Amy. Focus on cultural heritage. READER: SAN DIEGO WEEKLY, (September 17, 1981). English.

AN: Review of exhibit FIVE PHOTOGRAPHERS: CONTEMPORARY VIEWS OF MEXICAN AND MEXICAN-AMERICAN CULTURE which includes two Chicano photographers from Arizona: Louis Carlos Bernal (Tucson), and Robert C. Buitron (Tempe). Details some of Bernal's work between 1973 and 1980; Buitron's more personal work (1978-1981) is from his FAMILY AND PHOTOGRAPHY book-in-progress.

1273 Consejo Mexicano de Fotografia, A.C., Mexico City. Hecho en latinoamerica: segundo coloquio latinoamericano de fotografia. Exhibition catalog, 1982. Spanish.

AN: Catalog/book of the second colloquium and exhibit of Latin American photography. Among the Chicano artists whose work is reproduced are Louis Carlos Bernal, Robert C. Buitron, David Cardenas, Isabel Castro, Harry Gamboa, Jr., Luis Garza, Roberto Gil de Montes, John M. Valadez, Kathy Vargas. In the exhibit were also Porfirio Aguilar, Elsa Marie Flores, Ricardo Valverde. Great number of illustrations. In Spanish.

1274 Encanto Pavilion, Encanto Park, Phoenix, AZ. Exposicion de arte para la raza: Arizona Chicano art show. Exhibition catalog, [ca. 1978]. English.

AN: Catalog for an exhibit organized by MARS (Movimiento Artistico del Rio Salado). Colombian-born Antonio L. Tocora, Jim Covarrubias, Ed Dias, Robert C. Buitron, Armando Leon Hernandez, Guillermo Galindo, Richard Luna Cisneros, Jose Andres Giron, Robert L. Matta included.

Buitron, Robert C (cont.)

1275 Five views on Mexican culture. LA JOLLA
LIGHT, (September 10, 1981), p. B-6.
English.

AN: Review of a show at the University
of California, San Diego's Mandeville Art
Gallery called FIVE PHOTOGRAPHERS:
CONTEMPORARY VIEWS OF MEXICAN AND
MEXICAN-AMERICAN CULTURE and featuring
Arizona photographers Louis Carlos Bernal,
Robert C. Buitron, and three others.

1276 Mandeville Art Gallery, University of
California, San Diego. Five photographers:
contemporary views of Mexican and
Mexican-American culture. Exhibition
catalog, 1981. English.

AN: Catalog of exhibit including Louis
Carlos Bernal, Robert C. Buitron, Alberto
Lau, Richard Tichich, and Meridel
Rubenstein. Illustrated.

Burciaga, Jose Antonio

1277 Aguila, Pancho. 11 poems. MANGO, (1977).
English.

AN: Art works by Northern California
artists Emmanuel Montoya and Jose Antonio
Burciaga.

1278 Anaya, Rudolfo A. and Ortiz, Simon J.
1680-1980: a ceremony of brotherhood.
Albuquerque, NM: Academic, 1981. English.

AN: A cooperative publication by members
of the former La Academia de la Nueva Raza
(1969-1976) formed of writers and artists,
and the Tri-Centennial Commission of the
All-Indian Pueblo Council. Includes writings
and artworks by Chicanos and Indians from
New Mexico, California, Texas, and Arizona.
Chicano artists works included are by Ellen
Arellano, Juan Estevan Arellano, Alberto
Baros, Jose Antonio Burciaga, Juan Reyes
Cervantes, Rudy Cuellar, Ricardo Favela, El
Zarco Guerrero, Luis Jimenez, Jr., Carlos
Quinto Kemm, Alejandro Lopez, Floyd Lujan,
Jose Montoya, Juanishi Orozco, Leo Romero,
Secundino Sandoval, Jaime Valdez, Maria
Varela, Esteban Villa.

1279 Bauer, Bernard. Angry artists deface own
mural. BERKELEY BARB, (March 1978), p. 7.
English.

AN: Chicano artists Jose Antonio
Burciaga and Gilberto Romero Rodriguez
recall a few struggles to sensitize local
arts organizations to Raza art. Financial
and political aspects of their painting a
patriotic mural, "Danzas mexicanas" in
Redwood City. Artists explain why they
defaced their own mural as an act of
protest.

1280 Burciaga, Jose Antonio. Mural protest.
CHISMEARTE, Vol. 2, no. 1 (Summer 1978), p.
27-28. English.

AN: Mexican muralist Gilberto Romero
Rodriguez and Chicano poet and artist
Burciaga splatter their own mural at
dedication ceremonies to protest their
exploitation as artists and the opportunism
and insensitivity of the commissioning
organization, The Multicultural Arts Council
of San Mateo County, CA. The mural was
painted in Redwood City, CA. Illustrated.

1281 Burciaga, Jose Antonio and Zamora, Bernice.

Restless serpents. Menlo Park, CA: Disenos
Literarios, 1976. English.

AN: Includes numerous drawings by
northern California artist and poet Jose
Antonio Burciaga.

1282 Danzas mexicanas. Flyer, 1978. English.

AN: Illustrated flyer about a mural
designed and painted by Chicano artist and
poet Jose Antonio Burciaga and Mexican
muralist Gilberto Romero Rodriguez. Detail
of the 147 x 22 feet mural in Redwood City,
California is reproduced.

1283 Frankenstein, Alfred. One artist's
self-defense. SAN FRANCISCO CHRONICLE,
(March 9, 1978), p. 44. English.

AN: Art critic Frankenstein opens his
columns to Jose Antonio Burciaga to explain
why he, and fellow muralist Gilberto Romero
Rodriguez, splattered red, white and blue
paint on their completed mural at the
dedication ceremony. They were protesting
the exploitation, use and abuse of artists,
particularly by arts councils.

1284 Garcia, Rupert. Laminas de la Raza. San
Francisco: Garcia Litho and Printing
Service, 1975. English.

AN: Portfolio of drawings and prints by
Patricia Rodriguez, Ricardo Apodaca,
Xochitl, Domingo Rivera, Francisco Camplis,
Rafael Maradiaga, Tom Rios, Juan Fuentes,
Ricardo Diaz, Jose Romero, Consuelo Mendez,
Jose Antonio Burciaga, Irene Perez, Ricardo
Rios, Mike Rios, Graciela Carrillo, Rene
Yanez, Luis Talamantez, Guillermo Bermudez,
all from Northern California.

1285 Largest mural in San Mateo County becomes
official Saturday. REDWOOD CITY TRIBUNE,
(February 23, 1978), p. 12. English.

AN: Mural DANZAS MEXICANAS by Chicano
artist and poet Jose Antonio Burciaga and
Mexican muralist Gilberto Romero Rodriguez
was commissioned by the Multi-cultural Arts
Council of San Mateo County. Color
illustration.

1286 Martinez, Sue. New mural unveiled in Redwood
City. EL TECOLOTE, Vol. 8, no. 7 (April
1978), p. 7. English.

AN: Commentary on the 147x22-ft. mural,
DANZAS MEXICANAS, painted by Chicano artist
Jose Antonio Burciaga and Mexican artist
Gilberto Romero at the Redwood City Civic
Center. The mural depicts dance rituals from
various Mexican regions and the flora and
fauna of Mexico. The mural became a subject
of controversy when its creators splattered
paint on it during its unveiling as a form
of protest against the San Mateo Arts
Council for its exploitation of Third World
artists. Detail of mural showing "La Danza
De Los Viejitos".

1287 Mission to honor Frida Kahlo: famous Mexican
artist. EL TECOLOTE, Vol. 9, no. 3 (November
1978), p. 1. Bilingual.

AN: Announcement of an homage to Mexican
painter Frida Kahlo at the Galeria de la
Raza's annual celebration of Dia de los
Muertos. Works reproduced with the article
include those of Emmanuel C. Montoya, Yreina
Cervantez, Jose Antonio Burciaga, Nina
Serrano and Lisa Kokin. Bilingual.

Burciaga, Jose Antonio (cont.)

1288 Montoya, Emmanuel; Rodriguez, Patricia; and
Acevedo, Mario (Torero). Canto al pueblo
'78. NATIONAL MURALS NETWORK COMMUNITY
NEWSLETTER, (1978). English.

AN: The second annual Canto al Pueblo
took place in Corpus Christi, Texas, where
more than six murals were painted: "Wall of
Cultural Education" by 13 artists headed by
Roel Montealva; Carlota Espinoza, with
children; Gilberto Romero, Jose Antonio
Burciaga and Patricia Rodriguez,
"Incomprehension al arte"; "Madre Tierra" by
Manuel Martinez of Denver with Amador
Hinojosa (Corpus Christi) and Enriquette
Vasquez (New Mexico); Mario Torero; Salvador
Vega of Chicago whose mural some Canto
participants considered "insulting".

1289 Musica hispana en nuestras vidas/Hispanic
music in our lives: almanaque 1982/calendar.
Milwaukee, WI: Miller Brewing Co., 1981.
English.

AN: Twelve Latino artists were
commissioned to illustrate a calendar with
paintings on Hispanic music. The Chicano
artists include Frederico Vigil (New
Mexico), Joe Bastida Rodriguez
(Texas/Washington, D.C.), Manuel Martinez
(Colorado), Jose Antonio Burciaga
(California), Ignacio Gomez (California),
Carolina Flores (Texas), Frank Martinez
(California). Color.

1290 Rangel, Jesus. Heirs of Jose Posada:
revolution lives in Chicano art. SAN DIEGO
UNION, (February 24, 1980), p. D6. English.

AN: 19th century Mexican engraver Jose
Guadalupe Posada has been an inspiration to
Chicano artists. Along with two exhibits of
his work, the Centro Cultural de la Raza is
also showing calavera (skeleton) images by
Chicano artists: skull-masks from the Teatro
Campesino, a print by Amalia Mesa-Baines of
Frida Kahlo, and a collaged box by Jose
Antonio Burciaga. Illustration: Salvador
Roberto Torres work.

1291 Valdez, Armando. El calendario chicano 1977.
Hayward, CA: Southwest Network, 1977.
English.

AN: Fifth in a series of historical
calendars produced in 1972, 1974, 1975, 1976
by La Causa Publications and Southwest
Network. Artists whose work is reproduced
are Malaquias Montoya, Amado Maurilio Pena,
Ramori Zamora, Glugio J.L. Nicandro [Gronk],
Etta Delgado, Ricardo Alaniz, Diane Gamboa,
Elisa Marina Coleman, Margarita Calderon,
Jose Antonio Burciaga, Cesar Augusto
Martinez, Maria Ochoa y Valtierra, Juan
Renteria Fuentes, from California, New
Mexico, and Texas.

Burrow, Walter

1292 Valade, Carole. Mural depicts artist's
heritage. ADRIAN DAILY TELEGRAM, (September
15, 1978). English.

AN: Detailed description of Vibrations
of a New Awakening, mural at Community
Action Art Center by Martin Moreno with
assistants Hector Perez and Walter Burrow.

Butler, Bill

1293 Del Olmo, Frank. Chicano gang turns to art.
LOS ANGELES TIMES, (September 11, 1973), p.

II, 3. English.

AN: Residents of the East Los Angeles
barrio "Lil' Valley" dedicate a mural
memorializing Chicano gang members who have
died violently. The mural was painted by 40
gang members guided by professional artist
Bill Butler.

Cabarga, Leslie

1294 An.i.ma.tion: the arts, techniques, and
processes involved in giving apparent life
and movement to inanimate objects by means
of cinematography. San Francisco, CA:
Galeria de la Raza, n.d. English.

AN: Illustrated booklet on animation.
Reproductions and sequences illustrated by
Leslie Cabarga, Xavier Viramontes and Ralph
Maradiaga.

Cabrera, Armando

1295 Mascorro, Julie. Mechicano Art Center
exhibit to grace Price gallery walls. CAMPUS
NEWS, (November 24, 1971). English.

AN: Brief history of Mechicano Art
Center activities from its establishment in
1969 to 1971. Exhibiting are Charles
Almaraz, Roberto Amaral, Raymond Atilano,
William Bejarano, Armando Cabrera, Edward
Carbajal, Leonard Castellanos, Henry de
Vega, Antonio Esparza, Bob Gomez, Lucila V.
Grijalva, Jesus Gutierrez, Santos Lira,
Frank Martinez, Ernest Palomino, Louis
Quijada, Richard Raya, Frank Romero.
Illustrated.

1296 Mechicano Art Center, Los Angeles, CA.
Recent works of Armando Cabrera, Ed
Carbajal, Joe Cervantes. Exhibition
invitation, 1971. English.

AN: Invitation to an exhibit.

1297 Street art explosion in Los Angeles. SUNSET,
(April 1973), p. 110-113. English.

AN: Illustrated article on Los Angeles
street murals including those by Roberto
Chavez, Willie Herron, Frank Romero, Richard
Jimenez, William Bejarano, Gilbert Lujan,
Armando Cabrera, Frank Martinez, Charles
Felix, and others.

Calaveras

1298 Montoya, Jose E. and Carrillo, John M.
Posada: the man and his art. A comparative
analysis of Jose Guadalupe Posada and the
current Chicano art movement as they apply
toward social and cultural change: a visual
resource unit for Chicano education.
Unpublished thesis, 1975. English.

AN: Includes a historical background of
19th century Mexican engraver Posada, the
significance of his work, a background of
Chicano art, and the influence of Posada and
the "calavera" on Chicano art. The unit
includes 227 slides of Posada and other
Mexican artists; and slides of Chicano
artists using the calavera theme.

1299 The Tortuga paints a new mural. CHISMEARTE,
Vol. 2, no. 1 (Summer 1978), p. 12-13.
English.

AN: Black and white details of new
indoor mural painted at the Gilroy's
Recreation Center.

Calderon, Margarita

1300 Valdez, Armando. El calendario chicano 1977. Hayward, CA: Southwest Network, 1977. English.

   AN: Fifth in a series of historical calendars produced in 1972, 1974, 1975, 1976 by La Causa Publications and Southwest Network. Artists whose work is reproduced are Malaquias Montoya, Amado Maurilio Pena, Ramori Zamora, Glugio J.L. Nicandro [Gronk], Etta Delgado, Ricardo Alaniz, Diane Gamboa, Elisa Marina Coleman, Margarita Calderon, Jose Antonio Burciaga, Cesar Augusto Martinez, Maria Ochoa y Valtierra, Juan Renteria Fuentes, from California, New Mexico, and Texas.

EL CALENDARIO CHICANO, 1975

1301 Chicano pride reflected in '75 calendar. LOS ANGELES TIMES, (December 2, 1974), p. I, 34. English.

   AN: The 1975 edition of EL CALENDARIO CHICANO, developed for the Southwest Network of Hayward, focuses on Chicano history and dates that are significant to Mexican Americans.

Calendars

1302 Art Space - Open Ring Gallery, Sacramento, CA. El Pachuco art de Jose Montoya: a historical update. Exhibition invitation, 1977. English.

   AN: Invitation to an exhibit. Illustrated with a reproduction of a 1977 silkscreen calendar page in color by Montoya.

1303 Calendar 1977. CHISMEARTE, no. 2 (Winter, Spring, 1977), p. 26-27. English.

   AN: Reproduction of one month of the 1977 silkscreen calendar produced in limited edition by the Galeria de la Raza of San Francisco and the Royal Chicano Air Force of Sacramento, California. Displayed is Rene Yanez's screen HISTORICAL PHOTO-SILKSCREENMOVIE.

1304 Calendario 1973. San Francisco, CA: Galeria de la Raza, 1973. English.

   AN: Handprinted silkscreen calendar by artists of the Galeria de la Raza.

1305 Calendario de comida 1976. San Francisco, CA: Galeria de la Raza, 1976. English.

   AN: Handprinted silkscreen calendar consisting of twelve sheets and a cover. The work of the following artists is included: Ralph Maradiaga, Juanishi Orozco, Francisco Camplis, Ruben Guzman, Rodolfo Cuellar, Xavier Viramontes, Jose Montoya, Esteban Villa, Rene Yanez, Max Garcia and Louis "The Foot" Gonzalez, Patricia Rodriguez, and Ricardo Favela. All of the above are associated with the Galeria de la Raza, or the Royal Chicano Air Force of Sacramento, CA.

1306 Calendario de March: 1977. Chicago, IL: MARCH, Inc., 1976. English.

   AN: Historical calendar with photos and biographies of artists. Illustrations of artwork by Ray Patlan, Jose Nario, Frank J. Sanchez, Salvador Dominguez, Salvador Vega, Marguerite Ortega, Aurelio Diaz, Carlos Cortez, Mario E. Castillo, Francisco Blasco, Rey Vasquez, and Efrain Martinez. History of MARCH (Movimiento Artistico Chicano).

1307 El calendario hispano de Michigan, 1981. Stanton, MI: Montcalm Intermediate School District and Nuestras Artes de Michigan, 1981. English.

   AN: Months of historical calendar illustrated with art works by George Vargas, Nora Chapa Mendoza, Jesse Gonzalez, Julio Perazza(Puerto Rican), Hector Valdez, Pamela M. Gonzalez, Isabell Escojico (7-year-old child), Jose Narezo, Martin Moreno, Laurie Mendoza Psarianos, Rosa Maria Arenas.

1308 Chicano pride reflected in '75 calendar. LOS ANGELES TIMES, (December 2, 1974), p. I, 34. English.

   AN: The 1975 edition of EL CALENDARIO CHICANO, developed for the Southwest Network of Hayward, focuses on Chicano history and dates that are significant to Mexican Americans.

1309 La historia de California, 1977. San Francisco, CA: Galeria de la Raza, 1977. English.

   AN: Handprinted silkscreen calendar of history seen from a Mexican point of view. Twelve sheets and a cover. Artists are: Ralph Maradiaga, Irene Perez, Louie "The Foot" Gonzalez, Max Garcia, Patricia Rodriguez, Jose Romero, Esteban Villa, Juanishi Orozco, Rodolfo Cuellar, Jose Montoya, Xavier Viramontes, Rene Yanez, Ricardo Favela, associated with the Galeria de la Raza, or the Royal Chicano Air Force of Sacramento.

1310 Musica hispana en nuestras vidas/Hispanic music in our lives: almanaque 1982/calendar. Milwaukee, WI: Miller Brewing Co., 1981. English.

   AN: Twelve Latino artists were commissioned to illustrate a calendar with paintings on Hispanic music. The Chicano artists include Frederico Vigil (New Mexico), Joe Bastida Rodriguez (Texas/Washington, D.C.), Manuel Martinez (Colorado), Jose Antonio Burciaga (California), Ignacio Gomez (California), Carolina Flores (Texas), Frank Martinez (California). Color.

1311 Valdez, Armando. El calendario chicano 1975. Hayward, CA: Southwest Network, 1975. English.

   AN: Third in a series of historical calendars produced in 1972 and 1974 by La Causa Publications and Southwest Network. Artists included for each month are Carmen Lomas Garza, Sergio Hernandez, Malaquias Montoya, Mujeres Muralistas (Graciela Carrillo, Venezuelan Consuelo Mendez, Irene Perez, Patricia Rodriguez), Ramses Noriega, Ernie Palomino, Amado Maurilio Pena, Martin Perez. All but Texan Pena are California artists.

Calendars (cont.)

1312 Valdez, Armando. El calendario chicano 1977. Hayward, CA: Southwest Network, 1977. English.

AN: Fifth in a series of historical calendars produced in 1972, 1974, 1975, 1976 by La Causa Publications and Southwest Network. Artists whose work is reproduced are Malaquias Montoya, Amado Maurilio Pena, Ramori Zamora, Glugio J.L. Nicandro [Gronk], Etta Delgado, Ricardo Alaniz, Diane Gamboa, Elisa Marina Coleman, Margarita Calderon, Jose Antonio Burciaga, Cesar Augusto Martinez, Maria Ochoa y Valtierra, Juan Renteria Fuentes, from California, New Mexico, and Texas.

CALIFAS [art exhibit], Santa Cruz, CA

1313 Burkhardt, Dorothy. Chicano pride and anger mix at 'Califas'. THE TAB, (April 12, 1981), p. 34. English.

AN: CALIFAS: AN EXHIBITION OF CHICANO ARTISTS IN CALIFORNIA represents a cross-section of artists exhibiting work for at least ten years: Rupert Garcia, Ernie Palomino, Eduardo Carrillo, Judy Baca, Rene Yanez, Carmen Lomas Garza, Salvador Roberto Torres, Roberto Chavez, Willie Herron, Ralph Maradiaga, Sue Martinez, Jose Montoya, Malaquias Montoya, Ramses Noriega and Esteban Villa. Illustrated.

1314 Carrillo, Eduardo. Califas, is Chicano art safe in Santa Cruz? ARTS AT SANTA CRUZ, Vol. 1, no. 1 (1981). English.

AN: Illustrated essay surveying Chicano art in Santa Cruz with details about the planning and presentation of the CALIFAS exhibit at the Mary Porter Seanon Gallery. This exhibition presented the work of fifteen Chicano(a) artists united and defined by a shared vision: a conscious identification with Mexican/Chicano culture and an alliance with art circuits outside the mainstream.

1315 Goldman, Shifra M. Chicano art - looking backward. ARTWEEK, Vol. 12, no. 22 (June 20, 1981), p. 3-4. English.

AN: Review of Chicano art shows in Santa Cruz (CALIFAS) and Los Angeles (MURALS OF AZTLAN: THE STREET PAINTERS OF EAST LOS) featuring a total of 24 artists and how the shows reflect the critical crossroad at which Chicano artists presently find themselves.

1316 Street, Sharon. Califas - a celebration of Chicano culture and art. CITY ON A HILL, (April 16, 1981). English.

AN: Review of an exhibit at College V's Sesnon Gallery featuring 15 California artists: Ramses Noriega, Judy Baca, Salvador Roberto Torres, Malaquias Montoya, Rene Yanez, Ralph Maradiaga, Jose Montoya, Esteban Villa, Carmen Lomas Garza, Robert Chavez, among others. Illustrated.

California

1317 Albright, Thomas. Manuel Neri's survivors: sculpture for the age of anxiety. ART NEWS MAGAZINE, Vol. 80, no. 1 (January 1981), p. 54-59. English.

AN: Critical evaluation of Neri's development as a sculptor in the figurative tradition. Biographical information and placement of artist within California art and international tendencies.

1318 Allen, Jane and Guthrie, Derek. La mujer: a visual dialogue. NEW ART EXAMINER, Vol. 5, no. 10 (July 1978), p. 14. English.

AN: Review of international show by MARCH of Chicago on women's themes. Criticizes male Chicano artistic stereotypes of women compared to women's art on women from California.

1319 Andrews, Colman. Art of the state: California. NEW WEST MAGAZINE, (January 1981), p. 54-59. English.

AN: Short text on California artists who are presumably influenced by the state's light, color, space, etc. Works of 16 artists reproduced in full color, including one by Carlos Almaraz of Los Angeles. Statements by each artist.

1320 Around the Bay. METAMORFOSIS, Vol. 3, no. 2 (1980), p. 101-108. English.

AN: Cultural review of activities in the Bay Area, northern California, and Sacramento. Includes history of the Galeria de la Raza/Studio 24 (San Francisco), the Centro de Artistas Chicanos/RCAF, Royal Chicano Air Force (Sacramento), and a review of Rupert Garcia's pastel portraits exhibit at the Mexican Museum (S.F.) in 1981. Illustrated. Continued in Vol. 4, no. 1, 1981.

1321 Barnett, Alan. Southern journey. NATIONAL MURALS NETWORK COMMUNITY NEWSLETTER, (Fall 1980), p. 22-32. English.

AN: Rather gossipy account of murals seen in a swing of the southern United States. Includes the work of dozens of artists and arts groups from California, Arizona, New Mexico, Texas, and Colorado.

1322 El Centro Cultural de La Raza, San Diego, CA. Reflexions: a Chicano-Latin art exhibit. San Diego, CA: El Centro Cultural de la Raza, 1978. English.

AN: Statewide art exhibit of 126 works by 46 artists from all parts of CA.

1323 Clark, Yoko and Hama, Chizu. California murals. Berkeley, CA: Lancaster-Miller, 1979. English.

AN: Picture book of Bay Area and Los Angeles murals with brief descriptions. Chicano artists included: Daniel Galvez, Irene Perez, Patricia Rodriguez, Graciela Carrillo (Mujeres Muralistas), Ray Patlan.

1324 Comite Chicanarte and Los Angeles Municipal Art Gallery, Los Angeles, CA. Chicanarte. Exhibition catalog, 1975. English.

AN: Catalog of an exhibit of 102 California artists. 86 illustrations of works of art.

California (cont.)

1325 Fine Arts Gallery, California State University, Los Angeles and Goldberg, Aron. Edward Carrillo: selected works, 1960-1975. Exhibition catalog, 1975. English.

AN: Catalog of exhibit covering fifteen years of this California figurative painter's work. Eight illustrations, including one in color. (A printing error reproduced the same illustrations twice.).

1326 Una galeria de artistas = A gallery of artists. CAMINOS, Vol. 1, no. 6 (October 1980), p. 20-26. Bilingual.

AN: Features California artists Domingo O. Ulloa (Imperial Valley images), Gloria Chacon, photographer Maria Pinedo (San Francisco), Willie Herron (Los Angeles), Joaquin Patino (Delano), Pedro Pelayo (Long Beach), sculptor Rudi Sigala (San Diego), Mario Torero (San Diego), sculptor Michael M. Amescua (Los Angeles), and the East Los Streetscapers. Illustrated.

1327 Garcia, Rupert. La Raza murals of California, 1963 to 1970: a period of social change and protest. Master's thesis, UC Berkeley, 1981. English.

AN: Important introduction to a selected group of murals from Northern and Southern California. Garcia deals with murals of "accommodation" from 1960 to 1965; the Chicano protest movement, 1965 and 1970; and Chicano protest murals from 1968 to 1970. Murals are discussed within historical, political and cultural contexts. Illustrated.

1328 La historia de California, 1977. San Francisco, CA: Galeria de la Raza, 1977. English.

AN: Handprinted silkscreen calendar of history seen from a Mexican point of view. Twelve sheets and a cover. Artists are: Ralph Maradiaga, Irene Perez, Louie "The Foot" Gonzalez, Max Garcia, Patricia Rodriguez, Jose Romero, Esteban Villa, Juanishi Orozco, Rodolfo Cuellar, Jose Montoya, Xavier Viramontes, Rene Yanez, Ricardo Favela, associated with the Galeria de la Raza, or the Royal Chicano Air Force of Sacramento.

1329 Miller, Marlan. Heard speaks Spanish through art. PHOENIX GAZETTE, (September 23, 1978). English.

AN: Four new exhibits at the Heard Museum of Phoenix include "Hispanic crafts of the Southwest", and "Southwest Chicano Art Invitational". The former focuses on New Mexico and Colorado crafts, organized by the Taylor Museum if the Colorado Springs Fine Arts Center; the latter includes Rupert Garcia and Xavier Miramontes of San Francisco, Rudy Fernandez of Salt Lake City (now in Scottsdale, AZ), and Antonio Pazos of Tucson.

1330 Orth, Maureen. The soaring spirit of Chicano arts. NEW WEST MAGAZINE, Vol. 3, no. 19 (September 11, 1978), p. 41-46. English.

AN: Overview of California Chicano culture. Color illustrations of works by Mexican muralist David Alfaro Siqueiros, Rupert Garcia, Mujeres Muralistas, Willie Herron, Rene Yanez, Rudy Martinez, San Diego's Chicano Park, ASCO, Jose Montoya.

1331 Plagens, Peter. Sunshine muse: contemporary art on the West Coast. New York: Praeger, 1974. English.

AN: Despite his rather "chic" art critical prose and mainstream orientation, Plagen's book is an important compendium of arts and cultural activities on the West Coast, primarily California. Gives the history of important artists, movements, and art schools. These set the institutional framework for the education of Chicano artists from the 1950s on. Manuel Neri discussed (p. 89, 94, 99) and illustrated (p. 92).

1332 Quirarte, Jacinto. The murals of el barrio. EXXON USA, (February 1974), p. 2-9. English.

AN: Well illustrated article on California murals from Santa Barbara, San Diego, Los Angeles, Fresno, and San Francisco.

1333 Ripley, Deborah. A sticky business. NEW WEST MAGAZINE, (July 28, 1980). English.

AN: Essay on California artists who take discarded objects and upgrade them into art works. Includes photographs of Larry Fuentes and three of his creations.

1334 Ross, Bob and Lyndon, George. The case of three California muralists: Roberto Chavez, Eduardo Carrillo, John Chamberlin. ARTS AND ENTERTAINMENT, (July 1981). English.

AN: Well documented reports on the destruction of the Carrillo, Chavez and Chamberlin murals. Focus is on the legal implications of mural effacement in relation to present California law.

1335 S.A. site for National Symposium on Mexican American Art. CHICANO TIMES, Vol. 4, no. 30 (November 9, 1973), p. 5. English.

AN: Held at Trinity University, the Symposium discussed such issues as, creative evolution, art education, artistic relationships to Mexico and the evolution of Mexican American art in the California barrios. Participating artists included Rudy Trevino, Mel Casas, Octavio Medellin, Antonio Garcia, Carmen Garza, Esteban Villa, Jose Montoya, Ernesto Palomino, Michael Ponce de Leon, Luis Jimenez and Eugenio Quesada.

1336 Southern Colorado State College, Pueblo, CO and Monteverde, Mildred. Chicanos graficos [sic]...California. Exhibition brochure, [1974]. Spanish.

AN: Brief background of California art movement and 13 artists from San Francisco, Los Angeles, Sacramento, Fresno. Important factual information despite numerous errors with names and Spanish terms. 16 illustrations of silkscreens, lithograph, etching.

California (cont.)

1337 Valdez, Armando. El calendario chicano 1975.
Hayward, CA: Southwest Network, 1975.
English.

AN: Third in a series of historical
calendars produced in 1972 and 1974 by La
Causa Publications and Southwest Network.
Artists included for each month are Carmen
Lomas Garza, Sergio Hernandez, Malaquias
Montoya, Mujeres Muralistas (Graciela
Carrillo, Venezuelan Consuelo Mendez, Irene
Perez, Patricia Rodriguez), Ramses Noriega,
Ernie Palomino, Amado Maurilio Pena, Martin
Perez. All but Texan Pena are California
artists.

1338 Valdez, Armando. El calendario chicano 1977.
Hayward, CA: Southwest Network, 1977.
English.

AN: Fifth in a series of historical
calendars produced in 1972, 1974, 1975, 1976
by La Causa Publications and Southwest
Network. Artists whose work is reproduced
are Malaquias Montoya, Amado Maurilio Pena,
Ramori Zamora, Glugio J.L. Nicandro [Gronk],
Etta Delgado, Ricardo Alaniz, Diane Gamboa,
Elisa Marina Coleman, Margarita Calderon,
Jose Antonio Burciaga, Cesar Augusto
Martinez, Maria Ochoa y Valtierra, Juan
Renteria Fuentes, from California, New
Mexico, and Texas.

1339 Yarbro-Bejarano, Yvonne. Resena de revistas
chicanas: problemas y tendencias, Part I. LA
PALABRA, Vol. 2, no. 1 (Spring 1980), p.
76-85. Spanish.

AN: Review of five Chicano magazines of
California discussing their contents, both
literary and artistic, taking a critical
attitude toward both. The five are FUEGO DE
AZTLAN, VORTICE, PRISMA, MAIZE, and MANGO.

California State University, San Francisco

1340 Petraitis, Louise. Student union murals:
walls with tongues. PHOENIX MAGAZINE,
(April 21, 1977), p. 12. English.

AN: San Francisco State University
instructor Ray Patlan and his La Raza Mural
Workshop are painting murals in the Student
Union basement. The relationship of a mural
to architecture, the process of transferring
a sketch to the wall, the underpainting, and
the finishing painting processes are
explained. A videotape of the mural is being
made. Illustrated.

California State University, Sacramento

1341 Joseph Chowning Gallery; Laguna Beach Museum
of Art; and Fitzgibbon, John. California
connections: Sacramento State College, the
early 1970s. Exhibit brochure, 1982.
English.

AN: Works by 35 artists, teachers and
students at Sacramento State College. Color
plate by Eduardo Carrillo and anecdotal
material about Carrillo in text. Time frame
is important for Jose Montoya and Esteban
Villa, co-founders of the Royal Chicano Air
Force in Sacramento.

Camacho, Jose

1342 Camplis, Francisco X. Towards the
development of a Raza cinema. TIN TAN, Vol.
2, no. 5 (June 1, 1977), p. 5-7. English.

AN: Chicanos and other minorities remain
invisible to white America, an expression of
neo-colonialism. Camplis defines "Chicano"
and "Raza" as terms, and states there are
few, if any, full-length feature films
available. Without role models, Chicano/Raza
filmmakers can learn from contemporary
revolutionary Latin American filmmakers, be
familiar with European and Hollywood films,
though the latter are alien models. Camplis
suggests directions for Chicano films, and
reviews films by Jesus Trevino, Jose
Camacho, and Luis Valdez.

Camhi, Morrie

1343 Blum, Walter. The vision behind the mirror.
CALIFORNIA LIVING, (November 26, 1978), p.
40-44. English.

AN: Illustrated article with background
information on the non-Chicano photographers
(Roger Minick, Morrie Camhi, and Abigail
Heyman) who spent a year documenting the
Chicano community. Their work was issued as
a portfolio, "Espejo: Reflections of the
Mexican American," by the Mexican-American
Legal Defense and Educational Fund (MALDEF).
It is one of the most extensive photographic
records made of the Chicano experience.

1344 Espejo: reflections of the Mexican American:
Louis Carlos Bernal, Morrie Camhi, Abigail
Heyman, Roger Minick, Neal Slavin. SOMOS,
Vol. 2, no. 1 (February 1978), p. 26-35.
English.

AN: Announcement of the ESPEJO
photographic exhibit to be held at Goez
Gallery in East Los Angeles. Statements by
the four artists and a portfolio of their
works: Abigail Heyman, Roger Minick, Morrie
Camhi, and Arizona Chicano photographer
Louis Carlos Bernal. Includes color
photographs by Bernal on cover. This 1979
issue is erroneously dated 1978.

1345 Fischer, Hal. Espejo: reflections of the
Mexican American: Louis Carlos Bernal,
Morrie Camhi, Abigail Heyman, Roger Minick,
Neal Slavin. PICTURE MAGAZINE, no. 9 (1978).
English.

AN: Oversize portfolio of photographs
recording contemporary Mexican American life
commissioned by the Mexican American Legal
Defense and Education Fund. Three
photographers, Louis Carlos Bernal (from
Arizona), Morrie Camhi and Abagail Heyman
focus on the family and the home; the
fourth, Roger Minick, juxtaposes the Mexican
American against "barrio" murals. Only
Bernal is Chicano. 24 photographs, six of
which (Bernal's) are in color.

Campero, Armando

1346 Del Olmo, Frank. Murals changing face of
East L.A. LOS ANGELES TIMES, (December 3,
1973), p. II, 1+. English.

AN: First Los Angeles Times report on
burgeoning Los Angeles mural movement with a
map of 15 mural sites. Mentioned are C.W.
Felix (originator of Estrada Courts
project), Willie Herron, David Botello,
Armando Campero, Edward Carbajal. (Chicano
Art Committee).

Campero, Armando (cont.)

1347 Mexican-American lawyers' club donates
Kennedy mural to the people of Mexico.
EASTSIDE SUN, (November 28, 1968). English.

AN: East Los Angeles artist Armando
Campero commissioned to paint mural for
"Unidad de Kennedy" housing development in
Mexico City.

1348 Muralist Campero shows works. EASTSIDE JRNL,
(June 3, 1971), p. 6. English.

AN: Photograph of artist Armando Campero
with samples of his graphic work. The artist
was completing a 3,000 square foot mural,
JOHN KENNEDY SAGA NUMBER 2 for installation
at the City Terrace Social Hall.

Campesinos
USE: Agricultural Laborers

Camplis, Francisco X.

1349 Calendario de comida 1976. San Francisco,
CA: Galeria de la Raza, 1976. English.

AN: Handprinted silkscreen calendar
consisting of twelve sheets and a cover. The
work of the following artists is included:
Ralph Maradiaga, Juanishi Orozco, Francisco
Camplis, Ruben Guzman, Rodolfo Cuellar,
Xavier Viramontes, Jose Montoya, Esteban
Villa, Rene Yanez, Max Garcia and Louis "The
Foot" Gonzalez, Patricia Rodriguez, and
Ricardo Favela. All of the above are
associated with the Galeria de la Raza, or
the Royal Chicano Air Force of Sacramento,
CA.

1350 Consejo Mexicano de Fotografia, A.C., Mexico
City and Tibol, Raquel. Hecho en
Latinoamerica: primera muestra de la
fotografia latinoamericana contemporanea.
Exhibition catalog, 1978. Spanish.

AN: Catalog/book of the first colloquium
and exhibit of Latin American photography.
Among the Chicano artists in the exhibit
were Francisco X. Camplis, Louis Carlos
Bernal, Harry Gamboa, Jose P. Romero, Harvey
J. Tarango, Isabel Castro. Statements by
some of the artists. Great number of
illustrations.

1351 Garcia, Rupert. Laminas de la Raza. San
Francisco: Garcia Litho and Printing
Service, 1975. English.

AN: Portfolio of drawings and prints by
Patricia Rodriguez, Ricardo Apodaca,
Xochitl, Domingo Rivera, Francisco Camplis,
Rafael Maradiaga, Tom Rios, Juan Fuentes,
Ricardo Diaz, Jose Romero, Consuelo Mendez,
Jose Antonio Burciaga, Irene Perez, Ricardo
Rios, Mike Rios, Graciela Carrillo, Rene
Yanez, Luis Talamantez, Guillermo Bermudez,
all from Northern California.

1352 Gonzalez, Tobias and Gonzalez, Sandra.
Perspectives on Chicano education. Stanford,
CA: Stanford University, 1975. English.

AN: Reproductions of artworks by Ralph
Maradiaga, Patricia Rodriguez, Roberto
Bonilla, Francisco Camplis, Graciela
Carrillo-Lopez, Juan Fuentes, Irene Perez,
Roger Reyes, Carlos Loarca, Xavier
Viramontes, Ralph McNeill, Rupert Garcia,
Jose Romero.

1353 Hartnell College Studio Gallery, Salinas,
CA. Paintings, drawings, prints by San

Francisco Bay Area Chicano artists. Exhibit
brochure, 1971. English.

AN: Brochure for exhibit featuring
Francisco Camplis, Graciela Carrillo, Sal
Castaneda, Priscilla Dominguez, J. Duarte,
Rupert Garcia, Carlos Loarca, Irene Perez,
Vincent Rascon, Michael Rios, Peter
Rodriguez, Luis Valsoto, Esteban Villa, Rene
Yanez, Zala. Illustrated by Rupert Garcia
print.

1354 Imagenes de la Chicana. Menlo Park, CA:
Nowels Publications (Stanford University
Chicano Press), [ca 1975]. English.

AN: Collections of writings by Chicanas;
illustrated by unsigned drawings, and
photographs by Lena Bugarin, Martina Puente,
Francisco Camplis, Mario Anzaldua.

1355 Martinez, Anita. Raza! Arte! Raza! Arte!
EL TECOLOTE, Vol. 1, no. 2 (September 7,
1970), p. 3. Bilingual.

AN: Galeria de la Raza opened on July,
1970 at 425 14th St. San Francisco. It was
an outgrowth of the Arte Seis organization
(an art effort established in the Mission
District in 1967 by Francisco Camplis,
Rupert Garcia, Ralph McNeil, Jay Ojeda and
Jack Ruiz). These and other artists brought
together by the Neighborhood Arts Program
have coalesced in the new Galeria de la
Raza. Article gives goals, organizational
scheme and plans for the Galeria. It's first
exhibit was a one man show by Esteban Villa
together with a photo and sketch exhibit on
Cuba by Jay Ojeda, Roberto Diaz Perez and
Gloria Ozuna. Illustrated with installation
view of new Galeria.

1356 Martinez, Anita. Raza art. EL TECOLOTE, Vol.
1, no. 8 (November 30, 1970), p. 1. English.

AN: Jay Ojeda, newly selected director
of Galeria de la Raza, describes the
memorial exhibition dedicated to Ruben
Salazar installed at the Galeria on Dec. 12,
1970. Salazar symbolized and synthesized
many of the goals subscribed to by artist
members of La Galeria. The exhibit included
work by Chicano and Latino artists Francisco
Camplis, Jay Ojeda, Jose Romero, Rolando
Castellon, Rene Yanez, Luis Valsoto, Mike
Ruiz, Carlos Perez, Gustavo Rivera, Peter
Rodriguez, Carlos Loarca and Ralph
Maradiaga.

Camplis, Lorenza

1357 Artes 6 Gallery, San Francisco, CA. Mixed
media. Exhibition announcement, [ca.
1969-70]. English.

AN: Announcement of exhibit including
Jim Cortez, Luis Cervantez, Vicente Rascon,
Rene Yanes, Graciela Carrillo, Lorenza
Camplis. The Artes 6 artists eventually
formed the Galeria de la Raza of San
Francisco.

Campos, Enrique

1358 Crossley, Mimi. Tejano artists. HOUSTON POST, (August 19, 1976). English.

AN: Exhibition of 19 Texas artists organized by Joe Rodriguez of the AAMA (Association for the Advancement of Mexican Americans) Art Center in Houston, Texas. Working within a wide range of styles and a great scope of subject matter. Includes brief commentary on the work of Amado Pena, Carmen Lomas Garza, Cesar Martinez, Enrique Campos, Carolina Flores, Jesus Trevino and a host of others.

Campusano, Jesus "Chuy"

1359 Albright, Thomas. Three remarkable Latin murals. SAN FRANCISCO CHRONICLE, (June 7, 1974), p. 48. English.

AN: The myth of the melting pot is vanishing: we recognize a variety of "publics" today. This is shown in three remarkable murals in the San Francisco Mission District. The Mission branch of the Bank of America has a 90 foot mural designed by Jesus Campusano, assisted by Luis Cortazar and Michael Rios, with technical advice from Emmy Lou Packard. Another mural is by the Mujeres Muralistas (Graciela Carrillo, Consuelo Mendez, Irene Perez, Patricia Rodriguez); the third by Michael Rios on the 24th St. mini-park.

1360 Bank of America, Mission-23rd St. Branch, San Francisco, CA. A community mural dedicated by the artists to Mexican muralist David Alfaro Siqueiros. 1974. English.

AN: Brochure about the Bank of America mural in the Mission District of San Francisco designed by Jesus Campusano and Luis J. Cortazar, assisted by Michael Rios, Jaime Carrillo, Candice Ho, Julio Lopez, Anthony Machado, Jack Nevarez. Technical advisor, Emmy Lou Packard. Well illustrated.

1361 Barrio heritage reflected in bank mural. EL CHICANO, Vol. 8, no. 50 (May 30, 1974), p. 8-9. English.

AN: Jesus Campusano and Luis J. Cortazar were artist-designers of a monumental mural painted inside the Mission Branch of the Bank of America. Michael Rios was color coordinator and five young artists worked collectively on the project for four months. Realistic scenes of everyday life in the Mission barrio are contrasted to heroic personalities from Latin America. Folk art imagery, Indian and Spanish cultural symbols and historical personages form a pageant of Latin American history. Mural was inaugurated on June 4, 1974.

1362 De colores mural team. Brochure, [ca. 1975]. English.

AN: Brochure giving brief history of the De Colores Mural Team established in 1972 as part of the Horizons Unlimited program with Chuy Campusano as coordinator. The team participated in murals at the Jamestown Center, Balmy Alley, Redding Elementary School, Mission Childcare Center, Mission Branch Bank of America and Horizons Unlimited from 1972 to 1975.

1363 Exxon Company, Houston, TX and Quirarte, Jacinto. Chicano art of the barrio. Exhibition brochure, n.d. [c.1976]. English.

AN: Brochure for a traveling exhibit of photographically-reproduced Chicano murals: Leo Limon, Lucila Villasenor Grijalva, Antonio Esparza, Susan Saenz, Charles Felix, Hoyo-Mara gang, David A. Lopez and team, Roberto Chavez and team (Los Angeles); Jerry Concha, Ruben Guzman, Chuy Campusano (San Francisco); Manuel Unzueta (Santa Barbara). Ernie Palomino and Leo Esequiel Ozona (Fresno). Leo Tanguma (Houston), Roberto Lucero, Manuel Martinez and Al Sanchez (Denver).

1364 Garcia, Rupert. Pulqueria art--defiant art of the barrios [Part II]. EL TECOLOTE, Vol. 8, no. 5 (February 1978), p. 8. Bilingual.

AN: In the Mission District of San Francisco, various artists like Irene Perez, Esther Fernandez, Chuy Campusano, Graciela Carrillo de Lopez, Consuelo Mendez Castillo, and Mike Rios have embellished business sites with wall decorations similar in spirit to the "Pulqueria" art of Mexico. Illustrated with three "Pulqueria"-type wall paintings: ATARDECER DE UN IMPERIO by Oscar Carveo at the Azteca Restaurant (Mission and 20th Sts.), El Buen Boricano Restaurant facade (24th and Harrison Sts.) and Fruitlandia facade (24th and Treat Sts.).

1365 Hagen, Carol. Mission murals. ARTWEEK, Vol. 5, no. 30 (September 14, 1974), p. 6. English.

AN: Report on two recently completed murals in San Francisco's Mission District: Jesus Campusano's 90x10-ft mural in the Bank of America branch, and the Mujeres Muralistas' mural adjacent to the Mission Model Cities building. Illustrated.

1366 Kamin, Ira. Come on in, bring your paint. PACIFIC SUN, (May 30, 1974), p. 11-12. English.

AN: Chatty report on murals and art exhibit in San Francisco's Mission District: murals by Chuy Campusano, Michael Rios, Richard Montez, Trish (Patricia) Rodriguez, Graciela Carrillo, Consuelo Mendez and Irene Perez. Illustrated.

1367 Mexican artists paint mural for Bank of America. EL HISPANO, Vol. 6, no. 49. English.

AN: Commentary by Jesus Campusano and Michael Rios about the 90-ft. mural they painted inside the Bank of America on Mission and 23rd Streets in San Francisco. They describe the mural as "...a montage of symbols and images depicting the heritage, day-to-day experiences and hopes of the people in the area.

1368 Ojeda, Jay. Galeria de la Raza--art for the community. SAN FRANCISCO PROGRESS, (March 24, 1972). English.

AN: Analysis of group exhibition by thirty-four Raza artists. Commentary on the work of Latin American artists Consuelo Mendez, Rolando Castellon, and Chicano artists Rupert Garcia, Chuy Campusano and Peter Rodriguez.

Campusano, Jesus "Chuy" (cont.)

1369 Opton, Suzanne. Short strokes. SAN FRANCISCO FAULT, (December 29, 1971), p. 9-10. English.

AN: The currently homeless Galeria de la Raza has begun a series of wall painting projects. Artist "Spain" did a Horizons mural; Puerto Rican photograper Adal Maldonado did photographic murals; Jerry Concha, Tom Rios, did rooms in the Center for Change drug program building, Chuy Campusano, working with cartoonist R. Crumb, and the Mission Rebel Kids did a cartoon mural. Model Cities day care centers are next to be painted.

Cannery and Agricultural Worker's Industrial Union

1370 Goldman, Shifra M. Resistencia e identidad: los murales callejeros de Aztlan, la ciudad (sic) ocupada. ARTES VISUALES, no. 16 (Fall, Winter, 1977), p. 22-25. Spanish.

AN: Reprint of article published as "Resistance and identity: street murals of occupied Aztlan" in LATIN AMERICAN LITERARY REVIEW, Vol. 5, no. 10, Spring-Summer 1977, p. 124-128.

Cannery Workers Committee (CWC)

1371 A Chicano artist: Emigdio Vasquez. CANNERY WORKER, Vol. 1, no. 4 (February 1977), p. 5. Bilingual.

AN: Story on an exhibit by Esteban Villa in the Galeria Barrios of Sacramento, California, which is dedicated to the Cannery Workers Committee on its eighth anniversary. Five works by Villa are illustrated, and a group photograph of the Centro de Artistas Chicanos is included.

CANTO AL PUEBLO I

1372 Guernica, Antonio Jose and Saavedra-Vela, Pilar. El Midwest Canto al pueblo: "Otra Vez, C/S". AGENDA, Vol. 7, no. 3 (May, June, 1977), p. 4-13. Bilingual.

AN: A thorough report on the various phases and events of the Midwest Canto al Pueblo in Milwaukee, Wisconsin on April 28 to May 8, 1977. The festival brought together artists, poets, musicians, and cultural workers to reaffirm, share, and celebrate the identity of La Raza with El Pueblo. Includes a thematic and iconographic overview of Chicano murals in California by Jose Montoya, and an analysis of his sculpture by Zarco Guerrero from Meza, Arizona. Well illustrated. Includes a photograph of the collective mural painted at 5th St. and National Avenue in Milwaukee, Wisconsin during the course of the conference.

CANTO AL PUEBLO II, Corpus Christi, TX, June 2-9, 1978

1373 Canto al Pueblo Steering Committee. Canto al Pueblo [poster]. CARACOL, Vol. 4, no. 9 (May 1978), p. 23.

1374 Montoya, Emmanuel; Rodriguez, Patricia; and Acevedo, Mario (Torero). Canto al pueblo '78. NATIONAL MURALS NETWORK COMMUNITY NEWSLETTER, (1978). English.

AN: The second annual Canto al Pueblo took place in Corpus Christi, Texas, where more than six murals were painted: "Wall of Cultural Education" by 13 artists headed by Roel Montealva; Carlota Espinoza, with children; Gilberto Romero, Jose Antonio Burciaga and Patricia Rodriguez, "Incomprehension al arte"; "Madre Tierra" by Manuel Martinez of Denver with Amador Hinojosa (Corpus Christi) and Enriquette Vasquez (New Mexico); Mario Torero; Salvador Vega of Chicago whose mural some Canto participants considered "insulting".

1375 NATIONAL MURALS NETWORK COMMUNITY NEWSLETTER. (1978). English.

AN: This issue features reports from muralists. Includes information about murals at: La Pena Cultural Center in Berkeley, CA; the Social and Public Art Resource Center's Tujunga Wash Mural in Venice, CA; the Citywide Mural Project in Los Angeles, CA; activities at Chicano Park, and of the Congress of American Cosmic Artists (CACA), both in San Diego, CA; murals in San Mateo County, CA; the Task Force on Hispanic American Arts headed by Jacinto Quirarte of San Antonio; the 1978 Canto Al Pueblo in Corpus Christi, TX; murals in Chicago; and other works by non-Chicano artists.

1376 Romero, Orlando and Cumpian, Carlos. A Canto al Pueblo artist at the second "Canto" en 1978, Corpus Christi, Tex Aztlan, enjoying the fruits of the struggle on to the third ... Canto al Pueblo!!! CARACOL, Vol. 5, no. 1 (September 1978), p. 19.

Cantu, Jesus "El Chista"

1377 Cantu, Jesus "Chista". Entrevista con "Chista" Cantu. SIN FRONTERAS, Vol. 1, no. 12 (November 15, 1974), p. 16. Spanish.

AN: Conversation in which Cantu speaks about his art which is based on the essential duality of all things. Includes photograph of design for an album cover CANTOS SIN FRONTERAS and a photograph of one of his murals representing the "cosmic unity of things as seen by people of the corn culture".

1378 Cantu, Jesus "Chista". Entrevista: Jesus Maria Cantu, 'El Chista'. MAGAZIN, Vol. 1, no. 4 (April 1972), p. 52-65. Spanish.

AN: Discusses his life in San Antonio; his apprenticeship since childhood to his uncle Miguel Angel Tellez who taught him to paint billboards, wall signs and church decorations; his membership in the group Artistas de la Nueva Raza; his artistic and political philosophy. In Spanish.

1379 Stephens, Martha. Murals introduce Carlos Castaneda to Neil Armstrong. SAN ANTONIO EXPRESS-NEWS, (January 11, 1981), p. M, 1, 3. English.

AN: Survey of commissioned murals in San Antonio including Mexican artist Juan O'Gorman's mosaic at the Theatre for Performing Arts; Carlos Merida's and Fred Samuelson's at the Convention Center; Howard Cook's New Deal mural in the downtown post-office; Peter Hurd's, and James Sicner's (in progress) mural at Trinity University; Jesse "Chista" Cantu's at Mario's Restaurant; and Jesse Trevino's mural at Our Lady of the Lake University. Illustrated.

Capitalism

1380 Herron, Willie. [The foundation of capitalism (drawing)]. REGENERACION, Vol. 2, no. 1 (1971), p. 8.

Capiz, Stephen

1381 59th Street Gallery, St. Louis, MO. Midwest Mexican-American art exhibit: Mexico and its artists. Exhibition brochure, 1981. English.

AN: Sponsored by the Sociedad Mexicana "Benito Juarez" and the international Institute of St. Louis, this three-part exhibit includes 1) MEXICO AS SEEN BY HER CHILDREN, a bilingual exhibit from Mexico traveling under Smithsonian Institution auspices, 2) MEXICAN CHILDREN IN THE U.S.A., 3) MEXICAN AMERICAN ARTISTS. In the latter are included Stephen Capiz (Roseville, Minn.), Jose Gonzalez (Chicago), Cesar A. Martinez (San Antonio), Ada Medina (Des Moines), Nora Chapa Mendoza (West Bloomfield, Mich.), Rene David Michel-Trapaga (St. Louis), David Munoz (Kansas City, Mo.), Jose Luis Narezo (Grand Rapids, Mich.), Benny Ordonez, Roman Villarreal (Chicago), Alejandro Romero (Chicago), Aurelio Diaz "Tekpankalli" (Chicago), Simon Ybarra (St. Louis).

Caravana Internacional Chicana del Tratado de Guadalupe Hidalgo

1382 Martinez, Cesar Augusto. Caravana Internacional Chicano del Tratado de Guadalupe Hidalgo [drawing]. CARACOL, Vol. 2, no. 10 (June 1976), p. 1.

Carbajal, Edward

1383 Castro, Mike. Climb from barrio is tough: artist finds life a waiting game. LOS ANGELES TIMES [Central Section], (November 2, 1973), p. IV, 1+. English.

AN: Edward Carbajal, graduate of Chouinard Institute of the Arts in Valencia, has a hard time making a living. He approached the Los Angeles County Museum of Art about exhibits for Chicano artists, with no result, though the Museum says it is still interested. Illustrated.

1384 Del Olmo, Frank. Murals changing face of East L.A. LOS ANGELES TIMES, (December 3, 1973), p. II, 1+. English.

AN: First Los Angeles Times report on burgeoning Los Angeles mural movement with a map of 15 mural sites. Mentioned are C.W. Felix (originator of Estrada Courts project), Willie Herron, David Botello, Armando Campero, Edward Carbajal. (Chicano Art Committee).

1385 Mascorro, Julie. Mechicano Art Center exhibit to grace Price gallery walls. CAMPUS NEWS, (November 24, 1971). English.

AN: Brief history of Mechicano Art Center activities from its establishment in 1969 to 1971. Exhibiting are Charles Almaraz, Roberto Amaral, Raymond Atilano, William Bejarano, Armando Cabrera, Edward Carbajal, Leonard Castellanos, Henry de Vega, Antonio Esparza, Bob Gomez, Lucila V. Grijalva, Jesus Gutierrez, Santos Lira, Frank Martinez, Ernest Palomino, Louis Quijada, Richard Raya, Frank Romero. Illustrated.

1386 Mechicano Art Center, Los Angeles, CA.

Recent works of Armando Cabrera, Ed Carbajal, Joe Cervantes. Exhibition invitation, 1971. English.

AN: Invitation to an exhibit.

Cardenas, David

1387 The class of '79. SA: THE MAGAZINE OF SAN ANTONIO, Vol. 3, no. 4 (June 1979). English.

AN: Well-illustrated article on students of James Newberry, photography teacher at the University of Texas, San Antonio. Includes photos of top prizewinners and members of Ladrones de la Luz, David Cardenas and Kathy Vargas.

1388 Consejo Mexicano de Fotografia, A.C., Mexico City. Hecho en latinoamerica: segundo coloquio latinoamericano de fotografia. Exhibition catalog, 1982. Spanish.

AN: Catalog/book of the second colloquium and exhibit of Latin American photography. Among the Chicano artists whose work is reproduced are Louis Carlos Bernal, Robert C. Buitron, David Cardenas, Isabel Castro, Harry Gamboa, Jr., Luis Garza, Roberto Gil de Montes, John M. Valadez, Kathy Vargas. In the exhibit were also Porfirio Aguilar, Elsa Marie Flores, Ricardo Valverde. Great number of illustrations. In Spanish.

1389 Galeria Tonantzin, Centro Cultural de LUCHA, Austin, TX. Young Chicano photographers from throughout Texas. Exhibition brochure, n.d. English.

AN: This exhibition is the collection of the winners of the contest (by the same name) sponsored by the Extension Cultural SRE-UNAM in San Antonio. Photographers represented were: Grace Alvarez, David Cardenas, Hector Cardenas, Stephen Casanova, Ronald Cortez, Raul Espinosa, Felix Almanza, Carolina Flores, David Garza Perez, Xavier Garza, Conrad Guerra, Melinda Hasbrook, Juan Jose de Hoyes, Beverly Kennon, Art Moreno, David Perez, Isabelle Purden, Patricia Santell, Nancy de los Santos, Jose Soria, Richard Tichich, Kathy Vargas, Vivian Yaten, and Johnny Zamarria.

1390 San Antonio Museum of Modern Art. Zarzamora: inaugural exhibition of Ladrones de la Luz. Exhibition invitation, 1979. English.

AN: Illustrated invitation to photographic exhibition including Norman Avila, David Cardenas, Franco Cernero, Enrique Hernandez, Robert Maxham, James Newberry, Isaac Rodriguez, Daryl Studebaker, Richard Tichich, Beverly Ulmer, Kathy Vargas.

Cardenas, Gilbert

1391 HEMBRA: HERMANAS EN MOVIMIENTO BROTANDO RAICES DE AZTLAN (University of Texas, Austin). (Spring 1976).

AN: Raul Valdez, drawing, p. 3; Carolina Flores, drawing, p. 5; Maria Flores, photograph, pp. 7, 11, 30; M.E. Secrest-Ramirez, drawing, p. 12; Amacio Zarate, drawing, p. 15; Santa Barraza, drawings, pp. 16, 17, 18, 26, 32; Nora Gonzales-Dodson, painting, p. 19; Gilberto Cardenas, photograph, pp. 22, 28; Nanci de los Santos, photograph, p. 23, 29; Amado Maurilio Pena, Jr. p. 31.

Cardenas, Hector

1392 Galeria Tonantzin, Centro Cultural de LUCHA, Austin, TX. Young Chicano photographers from throughout Texas. Exhibition brochure, n.d. English.

AN: This exhibition is the collection of the winners of the contest (by the same name) sponsored by the Extension Cultural SRE-UNAM in San Antonio. Photographers represented were: Grace Alvarez, David Cardenas, Hector Cardenas, Stephen Casanova, Ronald Cortez, Raul Espinosa, Felix Almanza, Carolina Flores, David Garza Perez, Xavier Garza, Conrad Guerra, Melinda Hasbrook, Juan Jose de Hoyes, Beverly Kennon, Art Moreno, David Perez, Isabelle Purden, Patricia Santell, Nancy de los Santos, Jose Soria, Richard Tichich, Kathy Vargas, Vivian Yaten, and Johnny Zamarria.

Cardenas, Rogelio

1393 Rogelio Cardenas--making murals. EL MUNDO (San Francisco, CA), (September 14, 1978). English.

AN: Rogelio Cardenas' fourth mural, LA MUJER, on the La Mexicana Tortilleria in Hayward, California. Interview with the artist who explains the mural's symbolism and his future plans. Illustrated.

Caricature

1394 450 anos del pueblo chicano/450 years of Chicano history in pictures. Albuquerque, NM: Chicano Communications Center, 1976. English.

AN: A pictorial history of Mexico, Mexican Americans and Chicanos through photographs and art works. P. 138 is dedicated to murals, graphics, cartoons and photographs from Chicago and the Southwest, but other murals, graphics, cartoons and photographs by Chicanos and non-Chicanos are scattered throughout. In addition, 450 ANOS has been a rich source book of imagery for Chicano artists, especially historical works of art.

1395 Almaraz, Carlos. The artist as a revolutionary. CHISMEARTE, no. 1 (Fall 1976), p. 47-55. English.

AN: Los Angeles painter Carlos D. Almaraz gives a detailed history of a cartoon-banner he made for the first constitutional convention of the United Farm Workers of America while he was an illustrator for EL MALCRIADO, and a mural he did for the UFWA administration building in La Paz. He also elucidates his philosophy about politics, the role of the revolutionary artist in our time, and the artist's relation to the bourgeois art market.

1396 Amor sin fronteras. Los Angeles, CA: Colectivo El Ojo, n.d.. English.

AN: Fotonovela with Josefina Arce, Eduardo Dominguez and Mike Jauregui produced by the Colectivo: Eduardo Dominguez, Roberto Gil de Montes, Jerry Lucas, Kay Torres, students at California State University, Los Angeles.

1397 Chairez, Bob. Bob's Chicano chronicles: The Latino athlete, then and now. CAMINOS, Vol. 1, no. 4 (July, August, 1980), p. 46. Bilingual.

1398 Chairez, Bob. Bob's Chicano chronicles: the Chicano in art [drawing]. CAMINOS, Vol. 1, no. 6 (October 1980), p. 40. Bilingual.

1399 Champlin, Chuck, Jr. Working for more than peanuts. LOS ANGELES TIMES, (June 21, 1980), p. II, 8, 10. English.

AN: Bill Melendez has been an animator 21 years for Charles Schulz's Charlie Brown and Peanuts comic strips, TV specials, and feature films. Melendez began his career with Walt Disney Productions in 1938.

1400 Colectivo El Ojo. CHOQUE DE AMOR: fotonovela by Lamp. CHISMEARTE, Vol. 1, no. 4 (Fall , Winter, 1977), p. 35-37. Bilingual.

AN: Several students with the help of the Latin American Media Project (LAMP) and the Latin American Studies Department of California State University, Los Angeles produced the fotonovela CHOQUE DE AMOR, a variation on the typical "fotonovela" romance. This one encourages readers to reevaluate traditional female roles. The group also includes Kay Torres. Six frames of the fotonovela are reproduced.

1401 De Lappe, Pele. Gordo plus folk art. PEOPLE'S WORLD, Vol. 42, no. 41 (October 13, 1979), p. 10. English.

AN: Announcement of an exhibit at the Mexican Museum of Gus Arriola's syndicated comic strip "Gordo." Arizona-born Arriola was an animator for Columbia and MGM cartoons until he created "Gordo" in 1941. Illustrated.

1402 Diaz, Jean; Dominguez, Edward; and Torres, Kay. Bi-Lingual blues [fotonovela]. SOMOS, Vol. 1, no. 1 (April, May, 1978), p. 33-36. English.

AN: Reproduction of a "fotonovela", BI-LINGUAL BLUES by Ojo Productions, a group of students connected with the Latin American Studies Department of California State University, Los Angeles.

1403 Los Four [art group]. Tales from the barrio by Los Four and friends. Los Angeles, CA: Los Four, Liberty Hill Foundation, United Steel Workers, [1977]. English.

AN: Comic book designed with drawings, comic strips, and calligraphy by Frank Romero, George Yepes, Carlos D. Almaraz, Leo Limon, Judithe Hernandez.

1404 Los Four exhibit in Union Gallery. UNIVERSITY TIMES, (November 6, 1975), p. 4. English.

AN: "Los Four," a group of four Chicano artists - Frank Romero, Roberto "Beto" de la Rocha, Gilbert Lujan, and Carlos Almaraz, with newcomer Judithe Hernandez - work with political cartoons, Catholic symbols, works of sardonic humor. They also paint street murals: several have been done recently in Los Angeles, La Puente, and Long Beach. Illustrated.

1405 Gamboa, Harry, Jr. Mexican Murder Comix presents Genocide Patrol [drawing]. REGENERACION, Vol. 2, no. 1 (1971), p. 12-13. English.

Caricature (cont.)

1406 Garcia, Ruben A. Chicano comics [comic strip]. XALMAN, Vol. 1, no. 5 (Fall 1977), p. 71.

1407 Garcia, Sol. Vato Loco y Chata La Gata [comic strip]. CHISMEARTE, no. 2 (Winter, Spring, 1977), p. Bk cover. Calo.

AN: Comic strip format utilized to invite all interested persons to meeting of the Concilio de Arte Popular. The artist is a member of the Brocha del Valle group from Fresno, CA.

1408 Garcia-Camarillo, Cecilio. Zaz y Cuas. CARACOL, Vol. 1, no. 12 (August 1975), p. 8. Spanish.

1409 Gonzalez, Jose Gamaliel. Boycott [drawing]. REVISTA CHICANO-RIQUENA, Vol. 5, no. 1 (Winter 1977), p. 9. English.

1410 Hernandez, Sergio. Justicia. REGENERACION, Vol. 1, no. 8 (1970), p. FRNT COVER.

1411 Limon, Leo. Christopher's movement. CHISMEARTE, Vol. 1, no. 2 (Winter, Spring, 1977), p. 28-29. English.

AN: Caricatures illustrating a poem written by Olivia Sanchez. The poem makes allusion to Christopher Columbus as the originator of the "Wetback Problem" by bringing his European compatriots across the sea to the American continent.

1412 Limon, Leo and Guerrero, Lalo. No way Jose [comic strip]. CHISMEARTE, Vol. 2, no. 1 (1978), p. [42].

1413 Lucas, Costa Ben. Chato [comic strip]. ABRAZO, Vol. 1, no. 2 (Summer 1979), p. 16-17. English.

AN: One installment of CHATO, the cartoon strip created by Costa Ben Lucas. Also provides a brief explanation of how the character was created and his principal characteristics.

1414 Lucas, Jerry and Gil de Montes, Roberto, et al. CHOQUE DE AMOR: fotonovela by Lamp. Los Angeles, CA: Colectivo El Ojo, Latin American Studies Dept., CSULA, 1979. English.

AN: "Fotonovela" featuring Elsa Flores, Rosa Marin, and Jerry Lucas produced by the collective work of Lucas, Roberto Gil de Montes, Mario Massinelli, Luis Soto, and Kay Torres.

1415 Morch, Albert. Mexican art through a cartoonist's eyes. SAN FRANCISCO EXAMINER, (September 24, 1979), p. 28. English.

AN: Review of "GORDO'S WORLD" and the paintings of Alexander Maldonado, an exhibition at the Mexican Museum. Biographical information on Gustavo Montano Arriola, creator of the Gordo cartoon in 1941. The exhibit conceived and designed by the San Diego Museum of Art, had representative blow-ups of the strip along with artifacts. Maldonado, a self-taught artist started painting at age 60. His canvases embrace a fascination with towers, unique buildings, underground cities and skylines from an imagined urban environment.

1416 NEW ERA (U.S. Penitentiary, Leavenworth, KA). (Fall , Winter, 1970). English.

AN: Under the art direction of Ruben Estrella from San Antonio, Texas, NEW ERA, a prison cultural magazine also featured the caricatures and cartoons of Tone Briones from Laredo, Texas. Raul Salinas, poet from Austin, Texas was Associate Editor for both issues.

1417 La Nopalera. Hace un chingo de anos ... (drawing)]. MAIZE, Vol. 1, no. 2 (Winter 1978), p. 18. Spanish.

1418 Ortega, Gil. The 50's and other assorted Chicano graffiti. La Habra, CA: s.n., 1981. English.

AN: Album of caricatures of barrio types; black and white drawings in six categories: The Parties and Dances, Schooldays, Oldtime Lowriders, Refine, Los Veteranos, Los Vatos. Some drawings accompanied by commentary.

1419 Posada, Jose Guadalupe. Calavera huertista [graphic]. REGENERACION, Vol. 1, no. 7 (1970), p. COVER.

1420 Ramirez de Robe, Jose "Controll". [Cartoon]. CARACOL, Vol. 1, no. 10 (June 1975), p. 7. Spanish.

1421 Ramirez de Robe, Jose "Controll". [Pensamientos de... (drawing)]. CARACOL, Vol. 1, no. 3 (November 1974), p. 3. Bilingual.

1422 Ramirez de Robe, Jose "Controll". [Which way to the revolution, ese? (caricature)]. CARACOL, Vol. 1, no. 7 (March 1975), p. 2. Bilingual.

1423 Sanchez, Al. Murals destroyed. EL DIARIO DE LA GENTE, Vol. 4, no. 14 (August 13, 1976), p. 7. English.

AN: Open letter from Al Sanchez, originator of the cartoon "The Tortilla Kid" and graphics contributor to EL DIARIO. Letter details events which led to painting over of six "cultural" paintings at the Denver Community Development Corporation Building (4142 Tejon, Denver, CO). Artist wants due compensation, specifically monies for "the replacement of artwork to be done by a community artist on portable murals".

1424 Tone Briones, artist of Aztlan. PAPEL CHICANO, Vol. 2, no. 11 (December 20, 1972), p. 4. English.

AN: Biographical information on caricaturist and cartoonist Tony Briones from Laredo, TX, who is staff artist for PAPEL CHICANO. Illustrated with one editorial caricature, "Be a Good Chicano, Join the Army," and a two-panel cartoon.

1425 Vincent, Stephen. Omens from the flight of the birds: the first 101 days of Jimmy Carter: a collective journal of writers & artists. San Francisco, CA: Momos Press, 1977. English.

AN: Rene Yanez, performance piece on El Santero, and two comic strips.

1426 Yanez, Rene. The Tin-Tan I know [comic strip]. TIN TAN, Vol. 1, no. 2 (September 1975), p. 13.

---   ---

Caricature (cont.)

1427 Zermeno, Andy. Don Sotaco: caricaturas de la
     huelga de Delano. Delano, CA: Farmworkers
     Press, 1966. English.

     AN: Short vignettes depicting the
     farmworkers' struggle and how Don Sotaco
     comes to understand his role in that social
     movement. Illustrated with caricatures of
     the various personages in the struggle;
     patrones, coyotes, esquiroles, campesinos
     and huelguistas. Centerfold and back cover
     photographs by Jon Lewis.

Carrasco, Barbara

1428 Sol Art Gallery, San Diego, CA. Group
     showing of Southern California artists.
     Exhibition brochure, 1980. English.

     AN: First exhibit of new Chicano art
     gallery showing Los Angeles artists Carlos
     Almaraz, Judithe Hernandez, John Valadez,
     Linda Vallejo, Ricardo Duardo, Barbara
     Carrasco.

1429 Venegas, Sybil. The artists and their
     work--the role of the Chicana artist.
     CHISMEARTE, Vol. 1, no. 4 (Fall , Winter,
     1977), p. 3, 5. English.

1430 Venegas, Sybil. Conditions for producing
     Chicana art. CHISMEARTE, Vol. 1, no. 4 (Fall,
     Winter, 1977, 1978), p. 2, 4. English.

     AN: Chicana artists face more obstacles
     than white women or Chicano counterparts in
     the arts. Mexican life style has portrayed
     the ideal of a submissive woman, but the
     values have changed. Chicana artists are
     concerned with women and their struggles.
     Muralists include Patricia Rodriguez, Irene
     Perez, Consuelo Mendez de Castillo, Susan
     Cervantes, Ester Hernandez, Miriam Olivo,
     Ruth Rodriguez, of the Mujeres Muralistas
     (San Francisco). Other artists are Etta
     Delgado and Barbara Carrasco.

Carrillo, Eduardo

1431 Burkhardt, Dorothy. Chicano pride and anger
     mix at 'Califas'. THE TAB, (April 12,
     1981), p. 34. English.

     AN: CALIFAS: AN EXHIBITION OF CHICANO
     ARTISTS IN CALIFORNIA represents a
     cross-section of artists exhibiting work for
     at least ten years: Rupert Garcia, Ernie
     Palomino, Eduardo Carrillo, Judy Baca, Rene
     Yanez, Carmen Lomas Garza, Salvador Roberto
     Torres, Roberto Chavez, Willie Herron, Ralph
     Maradiaga, Sue Martinez, Jose Montoya,
     Malaquias Montoya, Ramses Noriega and
     Esteban Villa. Illustrated.

1432 California. University. Santa Cruz. College
     Eight Gallery. Four artists: Edward
     Carrillo, Consuelo Mendez Castillo, Louis
     Gutierrez, Jose Montoya. Exhibition catalog,
     n.d. English.

     AN: Exhibit of three Chicano artists and
     Venezuelan-born artist Consuelo Mendez de
     Castillo.

1433 Depicts Chicano attitudes: library receives
     new mural. DAILY BRUIN, (September 29,
     1970), p. 6. English.

     AN: Illustrated story of mural painted
     in UCLA's Mexican American Library by
     Eduardo Carrillo, Ramses Noriega, Sergio
     Hernandez, Saul Solache.

1434 Fine Arts Gallery, California State
     University, Los Angeles and Goldberg, Aron.
     Edward Carrillo: selected works, 1960-1975.
     Exhibition catalog, 1975. English.

     AN: Catalog of exhibit covering fifteen
     years of this California figurative
     painter's work. Eight illustrations,
     including one in color. (A printing error
     reproduced the same illustrations twice.).

1435 Joseph Chowning Gallery; Laguna Beach Museum
     of Art; and Fitzgibbon, John. California
     connections: Sacramento State College, the
     early 1970s. Exhibit brochure, 1982.
     English.

     AN: Works by 35 artists, teachers and
     students at Sacramento State College. Color
     plate by Eduardo Carrillo and anecdotal
     material about Carrillo in text. Time frame
     is important for Jose Montoya and Esteban
     Villa, co-founders of the Royal Chicano Air
     Force in Sacramento.

1436 McAlister, John. Carrillo paintings on view
     in art gallery. UNIVERSITY TIMES, (April 2,
     1975), p. 7. English.

     AN: Review of 25 works by California
     painter Eduardo Carrillo. Illustrated.

1437 Oakes College, University of California,
     Santa Cruz, CA and Carrillo, Eduardo.
     Corazon de Aztlan: a Chicano arts show.
     Exhibition catalog, 1981. English.

     AN: Catalog of exhibit including works
     by Eduardo Carrillo, Juana Franklin, Cruz
     Zamarron, Jerry Astorga, Jaime Valadez,
     Ernesto Palomino, Sal Garcia, Roger Sierra,
     Jose Montoya, Esteban Villa, Juanishi
     Orozco, from Santa Cruz, San Jose, Fresno
     and Sacramento. Presentations of films and
     by the Teatro de la Tierra Morena of Santa
     Cruz County.

1438 Rodebaugh, Dale. Graffiti replaces popular
     mural in Santa Cruz arcade. SAN JOSE
     MERCURY, (April 13, 1979), p. B, [1].
     English.

     AN: The efforts of Eduardo Carrillo to
     restore his mural, "Birth Death and
     Resurrection in a downtown arcade. The
     artist comments on the intention and
     significance of the mural and the political
     reasons for its obliteration.

1439 Ross, Bob and Lyndon, George. The case of
     three California muralists: Roberto Chavez,
     Eduardo Carrillo, John Chamberlin. ARTS AND
     ENTERTAINMENT, (July 1981). English.

     AN: Well documented reports on the
     destruction of the Carrillo, Chavez and
     Chamberlin murals. Focus is on the legal
     implications of mural effacement in relation
     to present California law.

Carrillo, Eduardo (cont.)

1440 Santa Ana College, Santa Ana, CA and
     Goldman, Shifra M. Chicano art. Exhibition
     catalog, 1974. English.

     AN: Thirteen California artists are
     presented in a short essay defining Chicano
     as a double mestizaje of Mexican mestizo and
     U.S. influences that exists in a state of
     "reconciled conflict." Its aim is
     communication. Artists included are
     Malaquias Montoya, Rupert Garcia, Manuel
     Hernandez, Esteban Villa, Robert Gomez,
     Harvey Tarango, Mary Helen Castro, Eduardo
     Carrillo, Graciela Carrillo, and "Los Four":
     Carlos Almaraz, Robert de la Rocha, Judithe
     Hernandez, Gilbert Lujan and Frank Romero.

1441 Teatro de la Tierra Morena, Santa Cruz, CA.
     Fuego en Aztlan: a Chicano arts show.
     Exhibition brochure, 1980. English.

     AN: Folder of information on the
     exhibition curated by Cruz Zamarron and
     Eduardo Carrillo. Exhibiting artists were:
     Justina Avila, Terry Benitez, Eduardo
     Carrillo, Hernando Chavez, Bob Cruz, Juanita
     Estrada, Juana Franklin, Sal Garcia, Leticia
     Hernandez, David "Sir Loco" Jimenez, Raoul
     Mendez, Vicente Mendez, Maria V. Pinedo,
     Gonzalo Placencia, Ramon Rodriguez, Roberto
     Salas, George Silva and Cruz Zamarron. A
     special feature was a live tattoo
     demonstration entitled "Walking Art".

Carrillo, Graciela

1442 Albright, Thomas. Three remarkable Latin
     murals. SAN FRANCISCO CHRONICLE, (June 7,
     1974), p. 48. English.

     AN: The myth of the melting pot is
     vanishing: we recognize a variety of
     "publics" today. This is shown in three
     remarkable murals in the San Francisco
     Mission District. The Mission branch of the
     Bank of America has a 90 foot mural designed
     by Jesus Campusano, assisted by Luis
     Cortazar and Michael Rios, with technical
     advice from Emmy Lou Packard. Another mural
     is by the Mujeres Muralistas (Graciela
     Carrillo, Consuelo Mendez, Irene Perez,
     Patricia Rodriguez); the third by Michael
     Rios on the 24th St. mini-park.

1443 Art in public places. Program statement,
     1977-78. English.

     AN: Documents an eleven-month program
     funded by CETA for 21 artists to produce
     murals, prints and weavings as public art.
     Includes murals by Gilberto Guzman and
     Graciela Carrillo-Lopez in Santa Fe.
     Statements by the artists. Illustrated.

1444 Artes 6 Gallery, San Francisco, CA. Mixed
     media. Exhibition announcement, [ca.
     1969-70]. English.

     AN: Announcement of exhibit including
     Jim Cortez, Luis Cervantez, Vicente Rascon,
     Rene Yanes, Graciela Carrillo, Lorenza
     Camplis. The Artes 6 artists eventually
     formed the Galeria de la Raza of San
     Francisco.

1445 Clark, Yoko and Hama, Chizu. California
     murals. Berkeley, CA: Lancaster-Miller,
     1979. English.

     AN: Picture book of Bay Area and Los
     Angeles murals with brief descriptions.
     Chicano artists included: Daniel Galvez,

Irene Perez, Patricia Rodriguez, Graciela
Carrillo (Mujeres Muralistas), Ray Patlan.

1446 Cockcroft, Eva. Women in the community mural
     movement. HERESIES, no. 1 (January 1977), p.
     14-22. English.

     AN: Women's role in the community mural
     movement is much greater than generally
     recognized. Among the many women muralists
     discussed are included the Mujeres
     Muralistas (Patricia Rodriguez, Irene Perez,
     Graciela Carrillo de Lopez, and Venezuelan
     Consuelo Mendez Castillo) of San Francisoc,
     and Judy Baca of Los Angeles. Illustrated.

1447 Cox, Sue. Female psychology: the emerging
     self. New York: St. Martin's Press, 2nd ed.,
     1981, p. 138+. English.

     AN: Reproductions of works by Carmen
     Lomas Garza, Graciela Carrillo, Consuelo
     Gonzalez Amezcua.

1448 Galeria Museo, Mission Cultural Center, San
     Francisco, CA. La sirena y el nopal:
     Graciela Carrillo - Juan R. Fuentes. An
     exhibition of paintings, drawings, and
     graphics. Exhibition catalog, 1981. English.

     AN: Invitation/catalog for an exhibit.
     Includes reproductions and statements by the
     two San Francisco artists. Well illustrated.

1449 Garcia, Rupert. Pulqueria art--defiant art
     of the barrios [Part II]. EL TECOLOTE, Vol.
     8, no. 5 (February 1978), p. 8. Bilingual.

     AN: In the Mission District of San
     Francisco, various artists like Irene Perez,
     Esther Fernandez, Chuy Campusano, Graciela
     Carrillo de Lopez, Consuelo Mendez Castillo,
     and Mike Rios have embellished business
     sites with wall decorations similar in
     spirit to the "Pulqueria" art of Mexico.
     Illustrated with three "Pulqueria"-type wall
     paintings: ATARDECER DE UN IMPERIO by Oscar
     Carveo at the Azteca Restaurant (Mission and
     20th Sts.), El Buen Boricano Restaurant
     facade (24th and Harrison Sts.) and
     Fruitlandia facade (24th and Treat Sts.).

1450 Gonzalez, Tobias and Gonzalez, Sandra.
     Perspectives on Chicano education. Stanford,
     CA: Stanford University, 1975. English.

     AN: Reproductions of artworks by Ralph
     Maradiaga, Patricia Rodriguez, Roberto
     Bonilla, Francisco Camplis, Graciela
     Carrillo-Lopez, Juan Fuentes, Irene Perez,
     Roger Reyes, Carlos Loarca, Xavier
     Viramontes, Ralph McNeill, Rupert Garcia,
     Jose Romero.

1451 Hartnell College Studio Gallery, Salinas,
     CA. Paintings, drawings, prints by San
     Francisco Bay Area Chicano artists. Exhibit
     brochure, 1971. English.

     AN: Brochure for exhibit featuring
     Francisco Camplis, Graciela Carrillo, Sal
     Castaneda, Priscilla Dominguez, J. Duarte,
     Rupert Garcia, Carlos Loarca, Irene Perez,
     Vincent Rascon, Michael Rios, Peter
     Rodriguez, Luis Valsoto, Esteban Villa, Rene
     Yanez, Zala. Illustrated by Rupert Carcia
     print.

Carrillo, Graciela (cont.)

1452 How we came to the Fifth World = Como vinimos al quinto mundo. San Francisco, CA: Children's Book Press/Imprenta de Libros Infantiles, 1976. Bilingual.

AN: Children's book illustrated by Graciela Carrillo de Lopez. Color.

1453 Kamin, Ira. Come on in, bring your paint. PACIFIC SUN, (May 30, 1974), p. 11-12. English.

AN: Chatty report on murals and art exhibit in San Francisco's Mission District: murals by Chuy Campusano, Michael Rios, Richard Montez, Trish (Patricia) Rodriguez, Graciela Carrillo, Consuelo Mendez and Irene Perez. Illustrated.

1454 Las muralistas: Patricia Rodriguez, Consuelo Mendez, Graciela Carrillo, Irene Perez. Exhibition invitation, 1974. English.

AN: Invitation to the inauguration of the mural LATINO AMERICA by the Mujeres Muralistas at the Mission Neighborhood Model Cities in San Francisco's Mission District, May 31, 1974.

1455 New Mexico Arts Division, Santa Fe, NM. Art in public places. Catalog, 1977-78, p. 9, 11. English.

AN: Catalog of CETA-funded project. Illustrated murals by Graciela Carrillo of San Francisco, and Gilbert Guzman of Santa Fe.

1456 New mural on Mission Street. EL HISPANO, Vol. 7, no. 13 (September 19, 1974), p. 5. English.

AN: Description of mural at the corner of 24th Street and South Van Ness in San Francisco. Painted by Mujeres Muralistas--Consuelo Mendez, Graciela Carrillo, Susan Cervantes and Miriam Olivo, the 30-foot mural depicts people in a tropical, Latin American setting.

1457 Preuss, Karen. The new Mission murals. SAN FRANCISCO BAY GUARDIAN, (June 28, 1975), p. 14-15. English.

AN: Mural art in San Francisco's Mission District has covered nearly every wall and alley on lower 24th Street. Murals by Mike Rios, the Mujeres Muralistas (Patricia Rodriguez, Graciela Carrillo, Consuelo Mendez, Miriam Olivo, Irene Perez, Susan Cervantes) appear in the area. Others have been painted by artists associated with the Galeria de la Raza. Illustrations.

1458 Quintero, Victoria. A mural is a painting on a wall done by human hands. EL TECOLOTE, Vol. 5, no. 1 (September 13, 1974), p. 6+. English.

AN: The women's collective, Mujeres Muralistas, exists within the strong San Francisco mural movement. Originally the group included Graciela Carrillo, Consuelo Mendez, Irene Perez, and Patricia Rodriguez. The group has expanded to include Susan Cervantes, Ester Hernandez, and Miriam Olivo. The two murals completed have been criticized for not being political; the women answer that they want the atmosphere to be surrounded with life, with colors. Illustrated.

1459 San Francisco Museum of Modern Art, San Francisco, CA and Castellon, Rolando. People's murals: some events in American history. Exhibition catalog, 1976. English.

AN: Eight portable murals by San Francisco Bay Area artists including Graciela Carrillo, Anthony Machado, Robert Mendoza, Irene Perez, Mike Rios. Well Illustrated.

1460 Santa Ana College, Santa Ana, CA and Goldman, Shifra M. Chicano art. Exhibition catalog, 1974. English.

AN: Thirteen California artists are presented in a short essay defining Chicano as a double mestizaje of Mexican mestizo and U.S. influences that exists in a state of "reconciled conflict." Its aim is communication. Artists included are Malaquias Montoya, Rupert Garcia, Manuel Hernandez, Esteban Villa, Robert Gomez, Harvey Tarango, Mary Helen Castro, Eduardo Carrillo, Graciela Carrillo, and "Los Four": Carlos Almaraz, Robert de la Rocha, Judithe Hernandez, Gilbert Lujan and Frank Romero.

1461 Stofflet-Santiago, Mary. The fifth sun: esthetic quality versus curatorial intent. ARTWEEK, Vol. 8, no. 37 (November 5, 1977), p. 6. English.

AN: Review of the exhibit THE FIFTH SUN at the University Art Museum in Berkeley, Calif., curated by Ralph Maradiaga of the Galeria de la Raza. It contains folk art, and posters by Chicano artists Maradiaga, Rupert Garcia, Juan Fuentes, mural studies by Graciela Carrillo and Mike Rios, ceramics by Anna de Leon, an altar by Amalia Mesa-Bains, and mural drawings by Mexican muralists. The writer criticizes the uneven quality of the show, but encourages better ones in the future. Illustrated.

1462 Time to greez: incantations from the Third World. San Francisco, CA: Glide Publications/Third World Communications, 1975. English.

AN: Rupert Garcia, drawing, p. 158; Xavier Viramontes, silkscreen, p. 181; Juan Fuentes, drawing, p. 188; Graciela Carrillo, drawing, p. 196.

1463 Valdez, Armando. El calendario chicano 1975. Hayward, CA: Southwest Network, 1975. English.

AN: Third in a series of historical calendars produced in 1972 and 1974 by La Causa Publications and Southwest Network. Artists included for each month are Carmen Lomas Garza, Sergio Hernandez, Malaquias Montoya, Mujeres Muralistas (Graciela Carrillo, Venezuelan Consuelo Mendez, Irene Perez, Patricia Rodriguez), Ramses Noriega, Ernie Palomino, Amado Maurilio Pena, Martin Perez. All but Texan Pena are California artists.

Carrillo, John

1464 Concilio de arte popular. CHISMEARTE, Vol. 1, no. 2 (Winter, Spring, 1977), p. 54. English.

AN: Report of a meeting February 12, 1977 by the Concilio de Arte Popular (CAP) which published CHISMEARTE. Introduces members of the Board and summarizes discussions of problems of the organization and their publication.

Carrillo, Juan

1465 R.C.A.F. artistas precursores del arte chicano. EL HISPANO, Vol. 8, no. 35 (February 17, 1976), p. 1. English.

AN: Information on the R.C.A.F. organization. Includes group photograph of R.C.A.F. members, Jose Montoya, Esteban Villa, John Carrillo, Ricardo Fabela, Rudy Cuellar, Juanishi Orozco and Frank Godena.

Carrillo, Patricia

1466 Lomas Garza, Carmen; Montoya, Jose E.; and Pinedo, Maria Vita. What we are...now. Exhibition catalog, n.d. English.

AN: Drawings by Sacramento women artists: Lorraine Garcia, Eva C. Garcia, Kathryn E. Garcia, Celia Rodriguez, Patricia Carrillo.

Carrillo, Sean

1467 Conversation on photography in the Los Angeles Latino community. OBSCURA, Vol. 2, no. 2 (December, February, 1981, 1982), p. 22-32. English.

AN: Interview on the nature and distinguishing characteristics of Chicano photography with Chicano photographers Isabel Castro (Council for Latino Photography), Lorenzo Hernandez (Director of Cityscape Gallery, publisher PHOTOSHOW magazine), Joseph G. Uribe (California State University, Los Angeles, Center for the Visual Arts, Director of West Colorado Gallery), Patssi Valdez, Becky Villasenor, and sculptor, curator, and Art Director for Academia Quinto Sol, Inc., Linda Vallejo, Portfolio of photography by Chicanos Don Anton, Louis Carlos Bernal, Sean Carrillo, Patssi Valdez, Ricardo Valverde, and by Morrie Camhi and Elizabeth Sisco on Chicano subjects.

Carter, Jimmy (President)

1468 Ramirez de Robe, Jose "Controll". Human rights defender [drawing]. CARACOL, Vol. 4, no. 4 (December 1977), p. FRNT COVER. Bilingual.

Carveo, Oscar

1469 Garcia, Rupert. Pulqueria art--defiant art of the barrios [Part II]. EL TECOLOTE, Vol. 8, no. 5 (February 1978), p. 8. Bilingual.

AN: In the Mission District of San Francisco, various artists like Irene Perez, Esther Fernandez, Chuy Campusano, Graciela Carrillo de Lopez, Consuelo Mendez Castillo, and Mike Rios have embellished business sites with wall decorations similar in spirit to the "Pulqueria" art of Mexico. Illustrated with three "Pulqueria"-type wall paintings: ATARDECER DE UN IMPERIO by Oscar Carveo at the Azteca Restaurant (Mission and

20th Sts.), El Buen Boricano Restaurant facade (24th and Harrison Sts.) and Fruitlandia facade (24th and Treat Sts.).

CASA AZTLAN'S NEW FACADE (MURAL)

1470 Sorell, Victor A. Barrio murals in Chicago: painting the Hispanic-American experience on "our community" walls. REVISTA CHICANO-RIQUENA, Vol. 4, no. 4 (Fall 1976), p. 51-72. English.

AN: Important survey of Chicago's Latino murals, with key works considered in detail. Among the Chicano art organizations and muralists mentioned are MARCH (Movimiento Artistico Chicano), and Yolanda Galvan, Juanita Jaramillo, Jose Nario, Raymond Patlan, Vicente Mendoza, Marcos Raya, Ricardo Alonzo, Jose G. Gonzalez and Mario Castillo, author of the earliest Latino mural in Chicago (1968). Puerto Rican and non-Latino muralists and mural groups are also discussed. Well illustrated.

Casa de la Raza, Santa Barbara, CA

1471 Chavez, Jaime. Rayaprofiles: Manuel Unzueta. RAYAS, Vol. 2, no. 3 (May, June, 1979), p. 5. Spanish.

AN: Brief biography of Mexican-born Chicano artist and muralist from Santa Barbara, California. Manuel Unzueta is active with La Casa de la Raza and its publication XALMAN. Unzueta is invited to paint a mural in Albuquerque. A Santa Barbara mural is illustrated.

1472 Reaves, John. Santa Barbara. NEWORLD, Vol. 6, no. 2 (March, April, 1980), p. 7+. English.

AN: Report on the activities of Casa de la Raza in Santa Barbara within social context. Erroneous attribution of murals, not all of which are by Vallejo.

1473 Rodriguez, Luis. A Center for Cultural Preservation and Human Resources. SOMOS, Vol. 1, no. 4 (September 1978), p. 26-29. English.

AN: Report on the founding, purposes, and continuing social and cultural activities of the Casa de La Raza. Illustrated.

1474 Unzueta, Manuel and La Casa de la Raza Gallery, Santa Barbara, CA. Murals art murals art: featuring the murals of la Casa de la Raza, Santa Barbara, California. Exhibition brochure, n.d. English.

AN: Illustrated booklet of Unzueta's murals and easel paintings.

Casa Hispana de Bellas Artes

1475 Albright, Thomas. Pre-Columbian art: New Galeria de la Raza. SAN FRANCISCO CHRONICLE, (July 15, 1970), p. 49. English.

AN: A new gallery is launched at 425 14th St. in San Francisco with an exhibit by Sacramento State College teacher Esteban Villa, with bold angular abstractions of roosters, comments on the Frito Bandito, and expressionist pen and pencil drawings. Other exhibits are also on display. The Galeria is sponsored by Casa Hispana de Bellas Artes.

Casa Hispana de Bellas Artes (cont.)

1476 Grimke, Angelina. Chicano art finds home in
     Mission galeria. PEOPLE'S WORLD, Vol. 33,
     no. 32 (August 8, 1970), p. 11. English.

     AN: Commentary on the exhibition
     CHICANOS, CUBA Y LOS 10 MILLONES held at the
     original Galeria de la Raza at 425 14th
     Street in San Francisco. The show presented
     photographs by Jay Ojeda and Roberto
     Perez-Diaz, drawings by Gloria Ozuna
     together with paintings and photographs by
     Cuban artist Mederos. Provides information
     about the goals of the Galeria as the visual
     arts department of Casa Hispana de Bellas
     Artes. Exhibition curator was Rolando
     Castellon.

1477 New Galeria de la Raza. EL HISPANO, (July
     28, 1970), p. 9. English.

     AN: Review of the first exhibit at the
     Galeria de la Raza at 425 14th St. in San
     Francisco. The inaugural exhibition featured
     Esteban Villa, Luis Gutierrez and Luis
     Cervantes. The new Galeria is sponsored by
     Casa Hispana de Bellas Artes assisted by San
     Francisco Art Commission through its
     Neighborhood Arts Program.

1478 Wilson, William. Art of barrios in East L.A.
     LOS ANGELES TIMES, (July 27, 1970), p.
     IV,1+. English.

     AN: Rather personalized view of ARTE DE
     LOS BARRIOS traveling exhibit organized by
     Casa Hispana de Bellas Artes with Artistas
     Latinos Americanos, San Francisco, and
     featuring "100 Chicano paintings,
     photographs, and other works of art".

Casa Zapata, Stanford University

1479 Hernandez, Manuel de Jesus. Zapata murals
     depict Chicano struggle. LA HONDA, Vol. 5,
     no. 3 (March, April, 1979). English.

     AN: Critical vignettes on the content of
     Chicano murals at Casa Zapata, a Chicano
     theme dorm at Stanford University. The
     muralists include Zarco Guerrero, Esteban
     Chavez, Hector Chacon, and Tina Alvarez.

Casanova, Stephen

1480 Galeria Tonantzin, Centro Cultural de LUCHA,
     Austin, TX. Young Chicano photographers from
     throughout Texas. Exhibition brochure, n.d.
     English.

     AN: This exhibition is the collection of
     the winners of the contest (by the same
     name) sponsored by the Extension Cultural
     SRE-UNAM in San Antonio. Photographers
     represented were: Grace Alvarez, David
     Cardenas, Hector Cardenas, Stephen Casanova,
     Ronald Cortez, Raul Espinosa, Felix Almanza,
     Carolina Flores, David Garza Perez, Xavier
     Garza, Conrad Guerra, Melinda Hasbrook, Juan
     Jose de Hoyes, Beverly Kennon, Art Moreno,
     David Perez, Isabelle Purden, Patricia
     Santell, Nancy de los Santos, Jose Soria,
     Richard Tichich, Kathy Vargas, Vivian Yaten,
     and Johnny Zamarria.

Casas, Mel

1481 The art of Mexican America. EMPIRE MAGAZINE,
     (November 1, 1970), p. 24-25. English.

     AN: Visual portfolio with minimal text.
     Includes paintings by Amado Pena, Mel Casas,
     Porfirio Salinas, and sculpture by Octavio

Medellin. On the same page, Dr. Jacinto
Quirarte gives views on the nature of
Mexican art, the Mexican American artist,
and the connection between Mexican and
Mexican American art.

1482 Ashford, Gerald. Artistic styles have no
     ethnic bonds. SUNDAY ONE, (October 18,
     1970), p. [18]. English.

     AN: Biographical information on
     Spanish-surnamed artists living and working
     in San Antonio. Includes commentary on
     Porfirio Salinas Jr. and Mel Casas.

1483 Con Safo. San Antonio, TX: Pintores Chicanos
     de San Antonio, [ca. 1975]. English.

     AN: Illustrated pamphlet issued by the
     San Antonio artists' group Con Safo.
     Includes a self-definition and a brief
     history of the group under the names El
     Grupo, Los Pintores de Aztlan, Los Pintores
     de la Nueva Raza, Con Safo (from 1967 on).
     Members include Jesse A. Almazan, Mel Casas,
     Jose Esquivel, Jose P. Garza, Cesar Augusto
     Martinez, Santos Martinez, Felipe Reyes,
     Roberto Rios, Jesus C. Trevino, and Vicente
     Velasquez.

1484 Con safo to hold Lutheran college exhibition
     at Texas. CHICANO TIMES, Vol. 7, no. 89
     (March 26, 1976), p. [15]. English.

     AN: Discusses the aims of "Con Safos"
     group: to interpret their environment and
     react to it; to act as spokespeople and give
     visual reality to the Chicano vision; to
     destroy stereotypes and demolish visual
     cliches. The participating artists include
     Rudy R. Trevino, Mel Casas, Lucas Hinojosa,
     Kathy Vargas, Joe Frank Acosta, Emilio
     Aguirre and Homero Ureste.

1485 Contemporary Arts Museum, Houston, TX. Dale
     gas: give it gas. The continued
     acceleration of Chicano art. Exhibition
     catalog, 1977. English.

     AN: A comprehensive catalog including 28
     works of art exhibited by 13 Texas artists:
     Melesio (Mel) Casas, Jose Esquivel,
     Francisco (Frank) Fajardo, Carmen Lomas
     Garza, Luis Jimenez, Cesar Augusto Martinez,
     Santos G. Martinez, Jr., Amado Pena, Roberto
     Rios, Jose Rivera, Joe B. Rodriguez, Jesus
     (Jesse) Trevino, and George Truan. Many
     illustrations, some in color. Introduction
     by James Harithas. Essay by Santos Martinez,
     Jr. Poetry, literature and essays by Chicano
     writers.

1486 Contemporary Arts Museum, Houston, TX. Fire!
     An exhibition of 100 Texas artists.
     Exhibition brochure, 1979. English.

     AN: Includes eleven Chicano artists.
     Unfortunately, not illustrated, though a
     checklist of works is included. Mel Casas,
     Carmen Lomas Garza, Xavier Gorena, Luis
     Jimenez, Cesar Martinez, Guillermo Z.
     Pulido, Philip Renteria, Jose L. Rivera, Joe
     Rodriguez, George Truan, Juan B. Vela.
     Introduction by James Surls. Statements by
     the artists.

Casas, Mel (cont.)

1487 Goldman, Shifra M. Chicano art alive and well in Texas: a 1981 update. REVISTA CHICANO-RIQUENA, Vol. 9, no. 1 (Winter 1981), p. 34-40. English.

AN: Reprint of article published as "Supervivencia y prosperidad del arte chicano en Texas: nueva revision" in COMUNIDAD (Los Angeles, CA) [Sunday Supplement to LA OPINION], September 21, 1980, p. 3, 15+.

1488 Goldman, Shifra M. Supervivencia y prosperidad del arte chicano en Texas: nueva revision. COMUNIDAD, Vol. 55, no. 5 (September 21, 1980), p. 3,15+. Spanish.

AN: Focuses on six Chicano artists from Austin, Houston, San Antonio, and Kingsville: Mel Casas, Cesar Martinez, Amado M. Pena, Leo Tanguma, Carmen Lomas Garza, and Santa Barraza. Well illustrated. This article was reprinted as "Chicano Art Alive and Well in Texas: A 1981 Update," in REVISTA CHICANO-RIQUENA (Houston), Vol. 9, no. 1, Winter 1981, p. 34-40.

1489 Mexican-American Institute of Cultural Exchange, San Antonio, TX and Alvarez Acosta, Miguel. Mel Casas paintings. Exhibition brochure, 1963. Bilingual.

AN: Exhibition brochure with biographical and exhibition chronology for El Paso born painter, Meliseo Casas. He is the first non-Mexican born artist invited to exhibit at the art gallery sponsored by the International Organization of Cultural Promotion for Foreign Relations in San Antonio.

1490 Moisan, Jim. Ancient roots, new visions. ARTWEEK, Vol. 9, no. 26 (July 29, 1978), p. 8. English.

AN: Review of the show held at the Municipal Arts Gallery of Los Angeles, the first national touring show of Latino artists in the United States. Includes commentary on work of Larry Fuente, Luis Jimenez, Frank Romero, Harry Gamboa, Gronk, Rudy Martinez, Benjamin Serrano, Ricardo Diaz, Patssi Valdez, Mel Casas, Luis Leroy, Pedro Lujan. A related show, NEW VISIONS, L.A., includes Robert Delgado, Ray Bravo, Joe Moran, Rosalyn Mesquita, Patricia Murillo and others.

1491 LA MOVIDA CON SAFO. no. 2 (February 1976). English.

AN: Mimeographed newsletter issued by Mel Casas about the San Antonio artists' group Con Safo. Reports on the exhibits, symposium, festival, TV appearance, film, and other activities of the group or its individual members. Illustrated.

1492 LA MOVIDA CON SAFO. no. 1 (Fall 1975). English.

AN: Mimeographed newletter issued by Mel Casas about the San Antonio artists' group Con Safo. Includes history of the group and its activities.

1493 Pena, Ruben R. Mel Casas - people in the arts. BUSINESS AND THE ARTS, (September, October, 1979), p. 15. English.

AN: Probing analysis of the work and life of San Antonio artist Mel Casas.

Article is divided into five sections in which the artist gives his views on culture, art, society, the Southwest and himself. Contains biographical information and artistic trajectory.

1494 Perez, Demetrio. Mel Casas - humanscapes. Houston, TX: Contemporary Arts Museum, 1976. English.

AN: Catalog for Mel Casas exhibition Oct. 22-Nov. 23, 1976. Artist calls his paintings "visual conundrums which play with our cultural concepts, with our cultural vision." Includes biographical information and exhibition chronology. Well illustrated with nine reproductions of artists work and two photos of the artist.

1495 S.A. site for National Symposium on Mexican American Art. CHICANO TIMES, Vol. 4, no. 30 (November 9, 1973), p. 5. English.

AN: Held at Trinity University, the Symposium discussed such issues as, creative evolution, art education, artistic relationships to Mexico and the evolution of Mexican American art in the California barrios. Participating artists included Rudy Trevino, Mel Casas, Octavio Medellin, Antonio Garcia, Carmen Garza, Esteban Villa, Jose Montoya, Ernesto Palomino, Michael Ponce de Leon, Luis Jimenez and Eugenio Quesada.

1496 Salazar, Veronica. Mel Casas sees things brown. SAN ANTONIO EXPRESS-NEWS, (December 23, 1973). English.

AN: Searching for "visual congruity," Mel Casas has slowly moved toward figurative art. Article traces aspects of his artistic trajectory and the philosophic basis of his aesthetic vision. Includes photograph of artist.

1497 Smith, Roberta. Twelve days of Texas. ART IN AMERICA, Vol. 64, no. 4 (July, August, 1976), p. 42-48. English.

AN: Overview of Texas art in Fort Worth/Dallas, Houston, San Antonio, Tyler, and Galveston. Includes reproductions of works by Luis Jimenez (color, on cover), Roberto Rios mural, Jesse Trevino, Mel Casas. Also mentioned in text are Phil Renteria and Cesar Martinez.

1498 Tannous, David. Problems of the artist as a hyphenated commodity. THE WASHINGTON STAR, (August 28, 1977), p. G-20. English.

AN: Review of ANCIENT ROOTS, NEW VISIONS show in Washington, D.C. describing Mel Casas' painting (San Antonio), Louis LeRoy's assemblage (Coolidge, Arizona), Amado Pena's silkscreen, Rogelio Ruiz Valdovin's costume (Tucson).

Casasola, Agustin V.

1499 Galeria de la Raza/Studio 24, San Francisco, CA; Sorell, Victor A.; and Vaughan, Kay. Images of the Mexican Revolution: photographs by Agustin V. Casasola. Exhibition catalog, 1980. English.

AN: Catalog of an exhibit of Mexican photographer Agustin V. Casasola from prints owned by the Martinezes of Lansing, MI. The exhibit traveled to Raza galleries in many parts of the United States. Illustrated.

Casasola, Agustin V.(cont.)

1500 Wasserman, Isabelle. Photos on exhibit
     capture Mexican revolution. SAN DIEGO UNION,
     (November 26, 1981), p. D10. English.

     AN: Report on the photographic
     exhibition of Mexican revolutionary
     photographer Agustin V. Casasola at the
     Centro Cultural de la Raza in San Diego.
     Illustrated.

Cassiano Homes murals, San Antonio, TX

1501 Minutaglio, Bill. Chicano take the art to
     the street of S.A. SAN ANTONIO EXPRESS-NEWS,
     (January 11, 1981), p. M, 1-2. English.

     AN: Survey of Chicano murals in San
     Antonio including 30 two-story murals at
     Westside Cassiano Homes by students from the
     commercial art program of Lanier High
     directed by Anastacio "Tache" Torres and
     Rudy Trevino; 8 murals at Lanier High
     School; one at the City Hall offices; and
     others throughout the city. Illustrated.

Castaneda, Carlos

1502 Martinez, Cesar Augusto; Garcia-Camarillo,
     Mia; and Garcia-Camarillo, Cecilio. Don Juan
     Volador, Platica con Cesar Augusto Martinez.
     CARACOL, Vol. 2, no. 4 (December 1975), p.
     3-5. Spanish.

     AN: Interview with Cesar Martinez about
     his acrylic painting DON JUAN VOLADOR. Based
     on themes suggested by the writings of
     Carlos Castaneda, the painting deals with
     the spiritual nature of Chicanismo. This
     issue of CARACOL is illustrated by the
     painting in question.

Castaneda, Sal

1503 Hartnell College Studio Gallery, Salinas,
     CA. Paintings, drawings, prints by San
     Francisco Bay Area Chicano artists. Exhibit
     brochure, 1971. English.

     AN: Brochure for exhibit featuring
     Francisco Camplis, Graciela Carrillo, Sal
     Castaneda, Priscilla Dominguez, J. Duarte,
     Rupert Garcia, Carlos Loarca, Irene Perez,
     Vincent Rascon, Michael Rios, Peter
     Rodriguez, Luis Valsoto, Esteban Villa, Rene
     Yanez, Zala. Illustrated by Rupert Carcia
     print.

Castaneda, Tomas

1504 Murphy, Patricia Lee. Artists renew Toltecas
     crafts heritage. LOS ANGELES TIMES, (May
     23, 1971), p. E, 10. English.

     AN: The Toltecas en Aztlan, creative arm
     of the Chicano Federation of San Diego
     County, Inc., will shortly move into their
     new Centro Cultural de la Raza in Balboa
     Park, San Diego. The group includes Mario
     Acevedo (Peruvian), Guillermo Aranda, Tomas
     Castaneda, Victor Ochoa and Salvador Torres
     (visual artists) and poet Alurista.

Castano, Wilfred

1505 San Francisco Museum of Modern Art, San
     Francisco, CA and Pearlstein, Howard.
     Aesthetics of graffiti. Exhibition catalog,
     1978. English.

     AN: Graffiti are defined as any
     coherently-intended presence written,
     scratched, painted, engraved, printed,

pasted or otherwise impressed in a public
place. Graffiti have been incorporated into
works by artists. In this catalog, works by
Chicano artists Carlos Almaraz, Wilfred
Castano, Judithe Hernandez, Gilbert Lujan,
Gustavo Rivera, Frank Romero, John M.
Valadez, Victor M. Valle, Xavier Viramontes
- as well as many Latino and non-Latino
artist, appear.

Castellanos, Leonard

1506 Blaine, John and Baker, Decia. Finding
     community through the arts: spotlight on
     cultural pluralism in Los Angeles. ARTS IN
     SOCIETY, Vol. 10, no. 1 (Spring, Summer,
     1973), p. 125-138. English.

     AN: Community arts expression by ethnic
     minorities is burgeoning everywhere,
     especially in Los Angeles. Various Black,
     Asian, and Chicano art administrators are
     interviewed, including Frank Lopez of Plaza
     de la Raza and Leonard Castellanos of
     Mechicano Art Center. Illustrated.

1507 California. State College. Los Angeles. Art
     Gallery. Twelve Chicano artists. Exhibition
     invitation, n.d. English.

     AN: Invitation to an exhibit: Jose
     Montoya, Gilbert Sanchez Lujan, Esteban
     Villa, Rene Yanez, Joe Moran, Armando Cid,
     Leonard Castellas, Juanishi Orozco, Rudy
     Cuellar, Beltran, Lopez and Cabrera.

1508 Concilio de arte popular. CHISMEARTE, Vol.
     1, no. 2 (Winter, Spring, 1977), p. 54.
     English.

     AN: Report of a meeting February 12,
     1977 by the Concilio de Arte Popular (CAP)
     which published CHISMEARTE. Introduces
     members of the Board and summarizes
     discussions of problems of the organization
     and their publication.

1509 Frankenstein, Alfred. Prison's artist in
     residence. SAN FRANCISCO CHRONICLE, (May 5,
     1978), p. 60. English.

     AN: Review of the exhibition MUNDOS
     PERDIDOS, curated at the Galeria de la Raza
     by Leonard Castellanos. Show consisted of
     work by Castellanos and inmates at Lompoc
     Federal Correctional Institution near Santa
     Barbara. Documents a prison mural, tattoos
     and silkscreen prints with socially critical
     themes.

1510 Galeria de la Raza/Studio 24, San Francisco,
     CA. Mundos perdidos/lost worlds. Exhibition
     invitation, 1978. English.

     AN: Invitatiion to a multi-media exhibit
     from a cultural workshop inside Lompoc
     Federal Correctional Institution by Leonard
     Castellanos, National Endowment for the Arts
     Artist in Residence. Included are murals and
     tattoo documentation, and silkscreen
     posters.

Castellanos, Leonard (cont.)

1511 Greenberg, David; Smith, Kathryn; and Teacher, Stuart. Megamurals & supergraphics: big art. Philadelphia, PN: Running Press, 1977. English.

AN: A full-color picture book of murals throughout the United States. Chicano murals include Michael Rios (San Francisco), Mujeres Muralistas (San Francisco), Leonard Castellanos and Tomas Gonzales with others (Los Angeles), Los Artes Guadalupanos de Aztlan (New Mexico), Willie Herron (Los Angeles), Toltecas en Aztlan (San Diego), David Botello (Los Angeles), David Lopez and Arizona Mara Gang (Los Angeles), Vatos de Maravilla (Los Angeles), Carlito Gaegos (Los Angeles), Gil Hernandez (Los Angeles), Wayne [Alaniz] Healy (Los Angeles).

1512 Images of Aztlan at Mechicano. CHISMEARTE, Vol. 1, no. 1 (Fall 1976), p. 3-4. English.

AN: History of Mechicano Art Center from its opening in West Los Angeles in 1969 through its 1976 location during which it decided to become a center serving its own community in East Los Angeles. Led by Leonard Castellanos, Victor Franco and Ray Atilano, the Center developed programs in supergraphics, silkscreen, and mural painting, as well as an "open-wall" art gallery for artists not allowed in establishment galleries.

1513 Mascorro, Julie. Mechicano Art Center exhibit to grace Price gallery walls. CAMPUS NEWS, (November 24, 1971). English.

AN: Brief history of Mechicano Art Center activities from its establishment in 1969 to 1971. Exhibiting are Charles Almaraz, Roberto Amaral, Raymond Atilano, William Bejarano, Armando Cabrera, Edward Carbajal, Leonard Castellanos, Henry de Vega, Antonio Esparza, Bob Gomez, Lucila V. Grijalva, Jesus Gutierrez, Santos Lira, Frank Martinez, Ernest Palomino, Louis Quijada, Richard Raya, Frank Romero. Illustrated.

1514 Mechicano Art Center attracts community artists. EL HISPANO, Vol. 5, no. 2 (June 10, 1972). English.

AN: Commentary by Leonard Castellanos, Director of Mechicano Art Center, who explains funding sources and programs of the Centro.

1515 Symposium on the politics of the arts: minorities and the arts. ARTS IN SOCIETY, Vol. 10, no. 3 (Fall , Winter, 1973), p. 66-73. English.

AN: One panel from the Colloquium "Politics of the Arts" presented by the UCLA Management in the Arts Program, Graduate School of Management, 1972, included, among others, Leonard Castellanos of Mechicano Art Center, and James Woods of Studio Watts Workshop, both in Los Angeles. A major topic was how minorities dealing with the corporate capitalist structure can keep control of their art programs.

Castellanos-Sanchez, Eloisa

1516 Raices y visiones [portfolio]. REVISTA CHICANO-RIQUENA, Vol. 7, no. 2 (Spring 1979), p. 29-44.

AN: Portfolio of works from the exhibit RAICES ANTIGUAS/VISIONES NUEVAS: ANCIENT ROOTS/NEW VISIONS. Artists included are Patssi Valdez (Los Angeles), Eloisa Castellanos-Sanchez (New York), Benjamin Serrano, Jr. (Tijuana, Mexico), Alex Garza (Chicago), Martin Y. Moreno (Michigan), Luis A. Jimenez (New Mexico), Rene Castro (Oakland, CA), Sita Gomez de Kanelba (New York), Susana Lasta (Tucson, AZ), Domingo Garcia (New York), Consuelo Mendez Castillo (Caracas, Venezuela), Naomi Castillo Simonetti (New Jersey), Louis Carlos Bernal, and Eddie Comptis.

Castillo, Mario E.

1517 Calendario de March: 1977. Chicago, IL: MARCH, Inc., 1976. English.

AN: Historical calendar with photos and biographies of artists. Illustrations of artwork by Ray Patlan, Jose Nario, Frank J. Sanchez, Salvador Dominguez, Salvador Vega, Marguerite Ortega, Aurelio Diaz, Carlos Cortez, Mario E. Castillo, Francisco Blasco, Rey Vasquez, and Efrain Martinez. History of MARCH (Movimiento Artistico Chicano).

1518 Canto al pueblo: an anthology of experiences. San Antonio, TX: Penca Books, 1978. English.

AN: Includes works by: Mario E. Castillo, Carlos Rosas, Jose G. Gonzalez, Santos Martinez, Gilbert Munoz, Fred Loa, Armando Ibanez and others.

1519 Cockcroft, Eva; Weber, John; and Cockcroft, James D. Towards a people's art: the contemporary mural movement. New York: E.P. Dutton, 1977. English.

AN: A survey of the street mural movement in the United States, from about 1967 on. Several chapters are written by the artists themselves: John Weber on the Chicago mural group; Susan Shapiro-Kiok on Cityarts Workshop of New York; Eva Cockcroft on People's painters of New Jersey; Geronimo Garduno on Artes Guadalupanos de Aztlan of New Mexico. Chicano murals illustrated include those of Mujeres Muralistas, Ray Patlan, William F. Herron, Hoyo-Mara Gang, Artes Guadalupanos de Aztlan, Vicente Mendoza and Jose Nario (with Patlan) Mario Castillo, Michael Rios, Toltecas en Aztlan, Roberto Chavez, Ernie Palomino, Chuy Campusano and Luis Cortazar (with Rios).

1520 Perales Leven, Humberto. Marcos Raya - Mexican painter. IMAGENES, Vol. 1, no. 1 (July 1976). Bilingual.

AN: Mexican born Chicago muralist Marcos Raya painted a mural titled HOMAGE TO RIVERA in the Pilsen barrio of Chicago at the corner of 18th Street and May. Raya articulates the role of the muralist and his function within the working class community. Also in this issue is an article on the formation of MARCH (Movimiento Artistico Chicano) in 1972 in East Chicago Indiana. Portfolio of drawings by Marcos Raya and photographs by Mario Castillo. Bilingual text.

Castillo, Oscar R.

1521 Wilson, William. 30 works from the grass roots. LOS ANGELES TIMES, (June 4, 1973), p. IV,2. English.

AN: Review of a show at the Junior Arts Center in Barnsdall Park by 15 members of the Mechicano Art Center. The critic feels contemporary groups that aim for change today (unlike past groups) are unable to articulate their spirit in a cohesive style. The top talent in this show is Charles Almaraz; also on exhibit are paintings by Jose Cervantes, Guillermo Martinez, Ray Atilano, sculpture by Manuel Cruz, and photography by (Oscar) R. Castillo.

Castillo Simonetti, Naomi

1522 Raices y visiones [portfolio]. REVISTA CHICANO-RIQUENA, Vol. 7, no. 2 (Spring 1979), p. 29-44.

AN: Portfolio of works from the exhibit RAICES ANTIGUAS/VISIONES NUEVAS: ANCIENT ROOTS/NEW VISIONS. Artists included are Patssi Valdez (Los Angeles), Eloisa Castellanos-Sanchez (New York), Benjamin Serrano, Jr. (Tijuana, Mexico), Alex Garza (Chicago), Martin Y. Moreno (Michigan), Luis A. Jimenez (New Mexico), Rene Castro (Oakland, CA), Sita Gomez de Kanelba (New York), Susana Lasta (Tucson, AZ), Domingo Garcia (New York), Consuelo Mendez Castillo (Caracas, Venezuela), Naomi Castillo Simonetti (New Jersey), Louis Carlos Bernal, and Eddie Comptis.

Castro, Fidel

1523 De la Torre, Susana. [Untitled drawing of Salvador Allende and Fidel Castro]. CARACOL, Vol. 3, no. 11 (July 1977), p. 23.

Castro, Isabel

1524 Consejo Mexicano de Fotografia, A.C., Mexico City and Tibol, Raquel. Hecho en Latinoamerica: primera muestra de la fotografia latinoamericana contemporanea. Exhibition catalog, 1978. Spanish.

AN: Catalog/book of the first colloquium and exhibit of Latin American photography. Among the Chicano artists in the exhibit were Francisco X. Camplis, Louis Carlos Bernal, Harry Gamboa, Jose P. Romero, Harvey J. Tarango, Isabel Castro. Statements by some of the artists. Great number of illustrations.

1525 Consejo Mexicano de Fotografia, A.C., Mexico City. Hecho en latinoamerica: segundo coloquio latinoamericano de fotografia. Exhibition catalog, 1982. Spanish.

AN: Catalog/book of the second colloquium and exhibit of Latin American photography. Among the Chicano artists whose work is reproduced are Louis Carlos Bernal, Robert C. Buitron, David Cardenas, Isabel Castro, Harry Gamboa, Jr., Luis Garza, Roberto Gil de Montes, John M. Valadez, Kathy Vargas. In the exhibit were also Porfirio Aguilar, Elsa Marie Flores, Ricardo Valverde. Great number of illustrations. In Spanish.

1526 Conversation on photography in the Los Angeles Latino community. OBSCURA, Vol. 2, no. 2 (December, February, 1981, 1982), p. 22-32. English.

AN: Interview on the nature and distinguishing characteristics of Chicano photography with Chicano photographers Isabel Castro (Council for Latino Photography), Lorenzo Hernandez (Director of Cityscape Gallery, publisher PHOTOSHOW magazine), Joseph G. Uribe (California State University, Los Angeles, Center for the Visual Arts, Director of West Colorado Gallery), Patssi Valdez, Becky Villasenor, and sculptor, curator, and Art Director for Academia Quinto Sol, Inc., Linda Vallejo, Portfolio of photography by Chicanos Don Anton, Louis Carlos Bernal, Sean Carrillo, Patssi Valdez, Ricardo Valverde, and by Morrie Camhi and Elizabeth Sisco on Chicano subjects.

1527 COUNCIL OF LATINO PHOTOGRAPHY/USA NEWSLETTER. no. 1 (January 1979). English.

AN: First number of photocopied newsletter produced by the Council of Latino Photography/USA announcing the formation of the organization and its affiliation with the Consejo Latinoamericano de Fotografia established in Mexico City in May 1978. Organizers of CLP/USA were photographers Isabel Castro, Harry Gamboa, Jr., Adam Avila, Luis Garza, and art historian Shifra Goldman.

1528 Documentary to include work by Cuate Santos. LAREDO NEWS, (July 17, 1980). English.

AN: Photography by Laredo News photographer Cuate Santos included in exhibit "Un encuentro sin palabras," a documentary show on Mexican American life in Texas sponsored by Mujeres Artistas del Suroeste (MAS). The state-wide show was juried by Los Angeles photographer Isabel Castro. Illustrated.

1529 Guggenheim Gallery, Chapman College, Orange, CA. Hexagono: paintings, sculpture, drawings, prints. Exhibit invitation, 1977. English.

AN: Invitation to an exhibit for artists Tito Aguirre, Isabel Castro, Rick Martinez, Esau Quiroz, Linda Vallejo, Emigdio Vasquez, Barrows, and Shanahan, sponsored by MEChA. Profiles and pictures of the artists.

1530 William Grant Still Community Arts Center, Los Angeles, CA. Latin American artists exhibition. Exhibition brochure, 1978. English.

AN: Exhibit curated by Linda Vallejo including Carlos Almaraz, Michael M. Amescua, Ray Bravo, Isabel Castro, Yreina Cervantez, Luis Serrano-Cordero, Cynthia Honesto, Judith Miranda, Teddy Sandoval, John Taboada, Emigdio Vasquez. Illustrated.

Castro Nagata, Grace

1531 Fourth annual San Antonio film festival. San Antonio, TX: Oblate College of the Southwest, 1979. Bilingual.

AN: Symposium and film festival catalog featuring motion pictures and videocassettes made by and about Mexicans, Chicanos and Latinos. The Symposium focused on Latina women in film and television, Margarita Galban, Carmen Tafolla, Leticia Ponce, Grace Castro Nagata, Marcela Fernandez Violante of Mexico, and Sylvia Morales.

Castro, Rene

1532 Raices y visiones [portfolio]. REVISTA
     CHICANO-RIQUENA, Vol. 7, no. 2 (Spring
     1979), p. 29-44.

     AN: Portfolio of works from the exhibit
     RAICES ANTIGUAS/VISIONES NUEVAS: ANCIENT
     ROOTS/NEW VISIONS. Artists included are
     Patssi Valdez (Los Angeles), Eloisa
     Castellanos-Sanchez (New York), Benjamin
     Serrano, Jr. (Tijuana, Mexico), Alex Garza
     (Chicago), Martin Y. Moreno (Michigan), Luis
     A. Jimenez (New Mexico), Rene Castro
     (Oakland, CA), Sita Gomez de Kanelba (New
     York), Susana Lasta (Tucson, AZ), Domingo
     Garcia (New York), Consuelo Mendez Castillo
     (Caracas, Venezuela), Naomi Castillo
     Simonetti (New Jersey), Louis Carlos Bernal,
     and Eddie Comptis.

Catalogues

1533 Ackerman Student Union, University of
     California, Los Angeles. Raza women in the
     arts: brotando del silencio. Exhibit
     invitation, 1979. English.

     AN: Invitation to a MEChA-sponsored
     exhibit of women's art. Illustrated.

1534 Amalgamated Meat Cutters and Butcher Workmen
     of North America. Cry for justice. 1972.
     English.

     AN: Well-illustrated catalog of Chicago
     street murals by Black, Chicano, White and
     Puerto Rican artists.

1535 Baxter Art Gallery, California Institute of
     Technology and Rosenstone, Robert A. In
     search of...four women/four cultures.
     Exhibition catalog, 1976. English.

     AN: Catalog of an exhibit including
     Donna Nakao, Cheri Pann, Betye Saar, and Los
     Angeles Chicana artist Judithe E. Hernandez.
     One work of each artist illustrated.

1536 Bellevue Art Museum, Bellevue, WA. Alfredo
     Arreguin. s.n.:s.l., n.d. English.

     AN: Profusely illustrated exhibition
     catalog for a one-man retrospective of
     paintings by Alfredo Arreguin. Exploring the
     possibilities of pattern painting, the
     intent of his art is to be visionary. His
     paintings have affinity with Pre-Columbian
     and Colonial Mexican designs and is related
     to decorative emotional images of various
     cultures. Includes photograph of artist and
     a selected bibliography.

1537 Bernal, Luis Carlos. La fotografia como
     reflejo de las estructuras sociales. In
     HECHO EN LATINOAMERICA: SEGUNDO COLOQUIO
     LATINOAMERICANO DE FOTOGRAFIA, MEXICO CITY,
     1982, p. 92-94. Spanish.

     AN: Presentation made by Tucson, AZ
     photographer Louis Carlos Bernal at the
     Second Latin American Colloquium of
     Photography and exhibit in 1981.

1538 Le Bistro Restaurant, San Antonio, TX.
     Contemporary paintings by Cesar Augusto
     Martinez. Exhibition catalog, 1980. English.

     AN: Catalog of an exhibit. Blurb about
     the artist.

1539 Brand Library Art Center, Glendale, CA. Los
     hermanos: Jesus, Jacob & Frank Gutierrez,
     sculpture, paintings, drawings, &

photographs. Exhibition catalog, 1974.
English.

     AN: Exhibit of the work of three
     brothers living in the Los Angeles area.

1540 California. State College. Los Angeles. Art
     Department. Fifth California small images
     exhibition. Exhibition catalog, [1972].
     English.

     AN: Catalog for an exhibit including the
     work of Charles D. Almaraz, Mary Lynn
     Dominguez, Gilbert Sanchez Lujan (who won
     Purchase Awards), Stephen Anaya, Martha
     Villegas. Illustrated.

1541 California. University. Los Angeles.
     Instructional Media Library. 1975-76 film
     catalog. Film catalog, 1976, p. 30-31.
     English.

     AN: List of films available from the
     Chicano Film Collection. 34 films on Chicano
     and Mexican subjects by Chicano and
     non-Chicano film makers.

1542 California. University. Santa Cruz. College
     Eight Gallery. Four artists: Edward
     Carrillo, Consuelo Mendez Castillo, Louis
     Gutierrez, Jose Montoya. Exhibition catalog,
     n.d. English.

     AN: Exhibit of three Chicano artists and
     Venezuelan-born artist Consuelo Mendez de
     Castillo.

1543 California. University. Santa Barbara.
     Coleccion Tloque Nahuaque. Mexican
     soldaderas and workers during the
     revolution. Exhibition catalog, 1979.
     English.

     AN: Well illustrated catalog of an
     exhibition of original lithographs by
     artists associated with the Taller de
     Grafica Popular of Mexico. Biographical
     information and illustrations by Raul
     Anguiano, Luis Arenal, Alberto Beltran,
     Angel Bracho, photographer, Agustin V.
     Casasola, Fernando Castro Pacheco, Jesus
     Escobedo, Arturo Garcia Bustos, Leopolda
     Mendez, Francisco Mora, Isidoro Ocampo,
     Pablo O'Higgins, Mariana Yampolsky and
     Alfredo Zolca.

1544 El Centro Cultural de La Raza, San Diego,
     CA. Reflexions: a Chicano-Latin art exhibit.
     San Diego, CA: El Centro Cultural de la
     Raza, 1978. English.

     AN: Statewide art exhibit of 126 works
     by 46 artists from all parts of CA.

1545 Centro Cultural Rafael Cintron Ortiz,
     University of Illinois, Chicago. Alejandro
     Romero. Exhibition catalog, 1978. English.

     AN: Full color catalog of drawings and
     paintings by Mexican-born artist living in
     Chicago.

1546 Comite Chicanarte and Los Angeles Municipal
     Art Gallery, Los Angeles, CA. Chicanarte.
     Exhibition catalog, 1975. English.

     AN: Catalog of an exhibit of 102
     California artists. 86 illustrations of
     works of art.

Catalogues (cont.)

1547 Consejo Mexicano de Fotografia, A.C., Mexico City and Tibol, Raquel. Hecho en Latinoamerica: primera muestra de la fotografia latinoamericana contemporanea. Exhibition catalog, 1978. Spanish.

AN: Catalog/book of the first colloquium and exhibit of Latin American photography. Among the Chicano artists in the exhibit were Francisco X. Camplis, Louis Carlos Bernal, Harry Gamboa, Jose P. Romero, Harvey J. Tarango, Isabel Castro. Statements by some of the artists. Great number of illustrations.

1548 Consejo Mexicano de Fotografia, A.C., Mexico City. Hecho en latinoamerica: segundo coloquio latinoamericano de fotografia. Exhibition catalog, 1982. Spanish.

AN: Catalog/book of the second colloquium and exhibit of Latin American photography. Among the Chicano artists whose work is reproduced are Louis Carlos Bernal, Robert C. Buitron, David Cardenas, Isabel Castro, Harry Gamboa, Jr., Luis Garza, Roberto Gil de Montes, John M. Valadez, Kathy Vargas. In the exhibit were also Porfirio Aguilar, Elsa Marie Flores, Ricardo Valverde. Great number of illustrations. In Spanish.

1549 Contemporary Arts Museum, Houston, TX. Dale gas: give it gas. The continued acceleration of Chicano art. Exhibition catalog, 1977. English.

AN: A comprehensive catalog including 28 works of art exhibited by 13 Texas artists: Melesio (Mel) Casas, Jose Esquivel, Francisco (Frank) Fajardo, Carmen Lomas Garza, Luis Jimenez, Cesar Augusto Martinez, Santos G. Martinez, Jr., Amado Pena, Roberto Rios, Jose Rivera, Joe B. Rodriguez, Jesus (Jesse) Trevino, and George Truan. Many illustrations, some in color. Introduction by James Harithas. Essay by Santos Martinez, Jr. Poetry, literature and essays by Chicano writers.

1550 Contemporary Arts Museum, Houston, TX and Harithas, James. Luis Jimenez: Progress I. Exhibition catalog, 1974-75. English.

AN: Catalog for a major exhibit of Jimenez sculptures, drawings and studies for sculptural works from 1967 to 1974. The latest project, PROGRESS, involves a series of monumental sculptures depicting the history of the West. Jimenez combines social comment with advanced plastic values. Well illustrated.

1551 Corcoran Gallery of Art, Washington, D.C. Images of an era: the American poster 1945-75. Washington, D.C.: Corcoran Gallery of Art, 1976. English.

AN: Uncredited poster [La Raza Silkscreen Center, San Francisco], (centerfold). Posters by Rupert Garcia, Linda Lucero, and Ralph Maradiaga, all of San Francisco, CA. Introduction by John Garriga. Essays by Margaret Cogswell, Milton Glaser, Dore Ashton, Alan Gowens.

1552 Craft and Folk Art Museum, Los Angeles, CA and Shapira, Nathan. From flat to form: Ben Gurule and Carlo Cattaneo. Exhibition catalog, 1978. English.

AN: Catalog for an exhibit by Los Angeles Chicano artist Ben Gurule and Italian artist Cattaneo, both involved with three-dimensional expression in paper. Gurule's works examine the interwoven families of waves, polygons, and circles, exploring relationships between geometry, wave mechanics and quantum mechanics. Well illustrated.

1553 Dittmar Memorial Gallery, Northwestern University, Evanston, IL and King, Elaine A. Alejandro Romero: new works. Exhibit catalog, 1981. English.

AN: Full color illustrated catalog of paintings by the Mexican-born artist who has been living in the United States since the early 1970s. His images appear to be grounded in the work of Bosch, Goya, Brueghel, and Diego Rivera. There is a synthesis of personal symbolism and expressionism.

1554 Dougherty Arts Center, Austin, TX. From the fringe: artists choose artists. Exhibition catalog, 1981. English.

AN: Catalog of an exhibit featuring eight women artists, including Santa Barraza of Austin. Barraza also designed the catalog.

1555 Encanto Pavilion, Encanto Park, Phoenix, AZ. Exposicion de arte para la raza: Arizona Chicano art show. Exhibition catalog, [ca. 1978]. English.

AN: Catalog for an exhibit organized by MARS (Movimiento Artistico del Rio Salado). Colombian-born Antonio L. Tocora, Jim Covarrubias, Ed Dias, Robert C. Buitron, Armando Leon Hernandez, Guillermo Galindo, Richard Luna Cisneros, Jose Andres Giron, Robert L. Matta included.

1556 Environmental Communications, Venice, CA. Street paintings of Los Angeles: a study of environmental reactionism. Slide catalog, n.d. English.

AN: Well illustrated annotated slide catalog of greater Los Angeles murals. Includes 7 Chicano murals. Articles reprinted from NEWSWEEK, LOS ANGELES TIMES, EARTH (Mar. 1972), ARTWORKERS NEWS (Oct. 1973), ARTFORUM (Feb. 1971), LOS ANGELES FREE PRESS (9/4/70), EVENING OUTLOOK (5/4/72), SUNSET (April 1973).

1557 Estudios Rio: gallery of contemporary arts and crafts. Exhibition catalog, 1976. English.

AN: Catalog including identification, portraits and works of participating artists: Joe Bova, Enrique Flores, Carmen Lomas Garza, Xavier Gorena, Erik Gronborg, Lucas Hinojosa, Ben Holland, Kris Hotvedt, William Kaars-Sijpesteijn, Cesar Martinez, Chris Mende, Roberto Mungia, Steve Reynolds, Vicente Rodriguez, William Wilhelmi.

1558 Fine Arts Gallery, California State University, Los Angeles and Goldberg, Aron. Edward Carrillo: selected works, 1960-1975. Exhibition catalog, 1975. English.

AN: Catalog of exhibit covering fifteen years of this California figurative painter's work. Eight illustrations, including one in color. (A printing error reproduced the same illustrations twice.).

Catalogues (cont.)

1559 Fine Arts Society of San Diego, CA. The cross and the sword. Exhibition catalog, 1976. Bilingual.

AN: Bi-lingual exhibition catalog of Southwestern art forms; santero art, vernacular architecture and traditional folk art. Important essays by experts in each field. Contains an iconographical summary of santos and a good bibliography. Profusely illustrated.

1560 Fondo del Sol, Washington, D.C. Raices antiguas/visiones nuevas; ancient roots/new visions. Exhibition catalog, 1977. English.

AN: Well illustrated catalog of traveling exhibition featuring Latin American and Latino artists living in the United States. Supplemental regional catalogs of local artists.

1561 Fourth annual San Antonio film festival. San Antonio, TX: Oblate College of the Southwest, 1979. Bilingual.

AN: Symposium and film festival catalog featuring motion pictures and videocassettes made by and about Mexicans, Chicanos and Latinos. The Symposium focused on Latina women in film and television, Margarita Galban, Carmen Tafolla, Leticia Ponce, Grace Castro Nagata, Marcela Fernandez Violante of Mexico, and Sylvia Morales.

1562 Friendly Center, Inc., Orange, CA / Galeria. The last Chicano art show. Exhibition brochure, 1981. English.

AN: Exhibit of 15 artists from Los Angeles and Orange Counties at the inauguration of the Galeria in Santa Ana, California. Statement and list of sponsors.

1563 Galeria Almazan, Inc., San Antonio, TX. Ray Chavez. Exhibition catalog, 1968. English.

AN: Exhibition catalog with biographical information on San Antonio painter Ray Chavez.

1564 Galeria de la Raza, San Antonio, TX. Celebration seventy-four. Exhibition catalog, [ca. 1974]. English.

AN: Catalog of extensive exhibition including European, Mexican, and the following Texan Chicano artists: Rolando Garces, Cesar Martinez, Ray Chavez, Vicente Rodriguez, Jorge Garza, Alfred Rodriguez, Luis Guerra, Carmen Lomas Garza, Bruno Andrade, Jr., Amado M. Pena Jr., Roberto Rios, Jose Trevino, Rudy Trevino, Luis Santoyo, Tati Rubio, Eduardo C. Garza, Arthur de la Fuente, and Jesus Campos Trevino.

1565 Galeria de la Raza/Studio 24, San Francisco, CA and Milkie, Anne. Carnaval '80. Exhibition catalog, 1980. English.

AN: Catalog of an exhibit of photographs and other media recording San Francisco's multi-ethnic CARNAVAL, organized in 1978 by Panamanian-born dancer. Included in the exhibit were the photographs of Chicana Maria V. Pinedo, who also designed the catalog.

1566 Galeria de la Raza/Studio 24, San Francisco, CA and Garcia, Rupert. Community art-murals: an exhibition of original drawings, sketches, and designs. Exhibition brochure, 1978. English.

AN: The current crisis of contemporary art is relatively resolved by community-based muralists who engage themselves against repressive forces as artists, organizers, propagandists. However, art and politics are not identical, though they may overlap. Color xerox illustrations of murals.

1567 Galeria de la Raza/Studio 24, San Francisco, CA. Homenaje a Frida Kahlo. Exhibition brochure, 1978.

AN: 51 artists, Chicano and non-Chicano.

1568 Galeria de la Raza/Studio 24, San Francisco, CA; Sorell, Victor A.; and Vaughan, Kay. Images of the Mexican Revolution: photographs by Agustin V. Casasola. Exhibition catalog, 1980. English.

AN: Catalog of an exhibit of Mexican photographer Agustin V. Casasola from prints owned by the Martinezes of Lansing, MI. The exhibit traveled to Raza galleries in many parts of the United States. Illustrated.

1569 Galeria de la Raza/Studio 24, San Francisco, CA. Images of the Southwest. Exhibition catalog, 1977. English.

AN: Invitation/catalog for an exhibit including Rudy M. Fernandez(Utah), Enrique Flores(Texas), Xavier Gorena(Texas), C.A.[Cesar] Martinez(Texas), Santos Martinez, Jr.(Texas), Pedro Rodriguez(Texas), Arnold Trujillo(New Mexico). Block prints, paper cut-outs, drawings, photographs, copper enamels, and sculpture were shown. Five illustrations.

1570 Galeria de la Raza/Studio 24, San Francisco, CA and Franco, Jean. Juan Fuentes y Rupert Garcia: posters, drawings, prints. Exhibition catalog, 1975. English.

AN: Catalog of an exhibit. Illustrated with drawings and posters.

1571 Galeria de la Raza/Studio 24, San Francisco, CA. Photographs by Angel Del Valle. Los sembradores: the marijuana growers. Exhibition catalog, 1976. English.

AN: Illustrated catalog. Del Valle documents the growing, customs, and merchandising of marijuana in the Sierras of Mexico.

1572 Galeria de la Raza/Studio 24, San Francisco, CA and Garcia, Rupert. La Raza Silkscreen Center: "Images of a community", an exhibit of silkscreen posters and graphic works from 1971 to 1979. Exhibition catalog, 1979. English.

AN: First large scale retrospective exhibit of the La Raza Silkscreen Center's eight years of postermaking. Includes list of 90 artists.

Catalogues (cont.)

1573 Galeria Museo, Mission Cultural Center, San
Francisco, CA and Rodriguez, Patricia.
Patricia Rodriguez: simbolos y fantasias
culturales. Exhibition catalog, 1981.
English.

AN: Catalog of an exhibition of
sculpture and painting. Autobiographical
information about the Texas-born artist who
lives in San Francisco and was a co-founder
of Mujeres Muralistas. She explains her
techniques in making portrait masks of
Chicano/a artists in plaster and mixed
media. Well illustrated.

1574 Galeria Museo, Mission Cultural Center, San
Francisco, CA. La sirena y el nopal:
Graciela Carrillo - Juan R. Fuentes. An
exhibition of paintings, drawings, and
graphics. Exhibition catalog, 1981. English.

AN: Invitation/catalog for an exhibit.
Includes reproductions and statements by the
two San Francisco artists. Well illustrated.

1575 Graham Gallery, New York, NY and Amaya,
Mario. Luis Jimenez. Exhibition catalog,
1969. English.

AN: Well-illustrated catalog of an
exhibit by El Paso-born sculptor. Some
biographical material.

1576 Graham Gallery, New York, NY and Perreault,
John. Luis Jimenez. Exhibition catalog,
1970. English.

AN: Well-illustrated catalog of an
exhibit by El Paso-born sculptor. Some
biographical material.

1577 Helen Euphrat Gallery, De Anza College,
Cupertino, CA. Staying visible: the
importance of archives. Art and "saved
stuff" of eleven 20th century California
artists. Cupertino, CA: Helen Euphrat
Gallery, De Anza College, 1981. English.

AN: Catalog issued in conjunction with
an exhibit held in the gallery Sept. 22 to
October 23, 1981 which included
documentation on Chicana artists Patricia
Rodriguez and Carmen Lomas Garza. Each
artist explains her method of saving,
storing and using cultural material in her
creations. Includes biographical sketch,
photograph of the artist and reproduction of
artwork.

1578 Incorporated Artes Monumentales/Inc.,
Denver, CO. IAM: art exhibit. Exhibition
brochure, n.d. English.

AN: Large format, well illustrated
brochure with information on muralists
Roberto Lucero, Al Sanchez, Andrew Manning,
Ricardo Barrera and Bob Reyes. Includes some
biographical information situating these
artists within the dynamic artistic
traditions of the Mexican and the Chicano
mural movements.

1579 Institute of American Indian Arts Museum,
Santa Fe, NM. Native American/Hispanic
festival, contemporary & historic visions.
Santa Fe, NM: Institute of American Indian
Arts Museum, 1981. English.

AN: Catalog for exhibit co-sponsored by
La Cofradia de Artes y Artesanos Hispanicos,
the Institute of American Indian Arts, and
the Santa Fe Council for the Arts. Exhibit

stresses the inter-relationship between the
Indian and Hispano peoples of New Mexico. 31
contemporary Hispano artists included.
Illustrated.

1580 Instituto Chicano de Artes y Artesanias
(Texas Instit. Educational Development).
Chicano art of the Southwest. San Antonio,
TX: Texas Institute for Educational
Development, [ca. 1975]. English.

AN: Illustrated brochure announcing a
color slide library on Chicano art
supplemented by slide annotation and artists
biographies available to institutions.
Statement of purpose by Executive Director
of program, Cesar Augusto Martinez.

1581 Instituto Cultural Mexicano (SER/UNAM), San
Antonio, TX. Jesse Trevino's one man
exhibit. San Antonio, TX: Instituto Cultural
Mexicano, 1981. Bilingual.

AN: Bilingual statement on the work of
Jesse Trevino; biography and list of
selected exhibitions; quotations from
several publications about his work.

1582 Intar, International Art Relations, Inc.,
New York, NY and Ferez Kuri, F. Jose.
Alejandro E. Romero. Exhibition catalog,
1977. English.

AN: Exhibit catalog of drawings and
paintings by Mexican-born painter and
muralist living in Chicago. Illustrated in
color.

1583 Laguna Gloria Art Museum, Austin, TX.
Tierra, familia sociedad, Amado Pena's
themes. Exhibition catalog, 1980. Bilingual.

AN: Illustrated exhibition catalog with
artist's biography and chronology of
exhibitions. The bi-lingual text by Santos
G. Martinez, Jr. situates the artist's work
within a dual phased trajectory. First a
period (1971-1975) in which the artist
creates images armed with a social-political
focus and (1975-present), a period starting
with the PEOPLESCAPE series in which the
artist enters a more lyrical introspective
phase.

1584 Lomas Garza, Carmen; Montoya, Jose E.; and
Pinedo, Maria Vita. What we are...now.
Exhibition catalog, n.d. English.

AN: Drawings by Sacramento women
artists: Lorraine Garcia, Eva C. Garcia,
Kathryn E. Garcia, Celia Rodriguez, Patricia
Carrillo.

1585 Los Angeles Municipal Art Gallery, Los
Angeles, CA and Comite Chicanarte.
Chicanarte: statewide exposition of Chicano
art. exhibit catalog, 1975. English.

AN: Exhibition by 101 artists,
accompanied by month-long performances of
films, theatre, music, poetry readings,
dance.

1586 Mandeville Art Gallery, University of
California, San Diego. Five photographers:
contemporary views of Mexican and
Mexican-American culture. Exhibition
catalog, 1981. English.

AN: Catalog of exhibit including Louis
Carlos Bernal, Robert C. Buitron, Alberto
Lau, Richard Tichich, and Meridel
Rubenstein. Illustrated.

Catalogues (cont.)

1587 Mandeville Center for the Arts, La Jolla, CA
and Lopez, Yolanda M. Yolanda M. Lopez
works: 1975-1978. Exhibition catalog, 1978.
English.

AN: Catalog of an exhibit dedicated to
Lopez's female family members, expecially
her grandmother and mother, to the artist
herself as a track runner, and to the
Guadalupe series, icons of the Virgin
transformed to reflect the life of
contemporary women. Well illustrated.

1588 Marion Koogler McNay Art Institute, San
Antonio, TX and Lee, Amy Freeman. Filigree
drawings by Consuelo Gonzalez Amezcua.
Exhibition catalog, 1968. English.

AN: Illustrated catalog for an
exhibition of 42 filigree drawings by Texas
artist "Chelo" Amezcua. Apart from
biographical and historical information, the
text evokes the ambiance of magic and
mysticism surrounding the artist.

1589 Menyah Productions. [Untitled catalog]. San
Juan Bautista, CA: El Centro Campesino
Cultural, 1977. English.

AN: Catalog of films and other cultural
materials available. Films listed are I AM
JOAQUIN (by Corky Gonzales), with Luis
Valdez, Daniel Valdez, El Teatro Campesino,
and photography by George Ballis; EL TEATRO
CAMPESINO, produced in 1970 by National
Educational Television; and LOS VENDIDOS, by
Luis Valdez, Luis Ruiz, George Paul, Daniel
Valdez and Loring d'Usseau.

1590 The Mexican Museum, San Francisco, CA and
Quirarte, Jacinto. 17 artists:
Hispano/Mexican-American/Chicano. Exhibition
catalog, 1977. English.

AN: Catalog of an exhibit for artists
Emilio Aguirre, Consuelo Gonzalez Amezcua,
Al Barela, Pedro Cervantez, Edward Chavez,
Antonio Garcia, Louis Gutierrez, Harry
Louie, Vincent Perez, Michael Ponce de Leon,
Eugenio Quesada, Gustavo Rivera, Peter
Rodriguez, Alex Sanchez, Darryl Sapien, Rudy
Trevino, Manuel Villamor. Illustrated.

1591 Mexican-American Institute of Cultural
Exchange, San Antonio, TX and Alvarez
Acosta, Miguel. Mel Casas paintings.
Exhibition brochure, 1963. Bilingual.

AN: Exhibition brochure with
biographical and exhibition chronology for
El Paso born painter, Meliseo Casas. He is
the first non-Mexican born artist invited to
exhibit at the art gallery sponsored by the
International Organization of Cultural
Promotion for Foreign Relations in San
Antonio.

1592 Mexico. Secretaria de Relaciones Exteriores.
Direccion General de Asuntos.. Exposicion:
estampas y remembranzas; Admonty y Geomonte.
Exhibition catalog, 1979. Bilingual.

AN: Catalog of an exhibit by Alice
Dickerson Montemayor (Admonty). Born in
Laredo, Texas in 1902, she began painting in
1976. Her nephew, George A. Montemayor, who
resides in Houston, is the Coordinator for
the La Porte Independent School District.

1593 Museum of Contemporary Art, Chicago, IL.
Raices antiguas/visiones nuevas; ancient
roots/new visions. Exhibition catalog, 1979.

English.

AN: Catalog produced for the mid-West
exhibit of RAICES ANTIGUAS. Includes 12
illustrations.

1594 New Mexico State University, University Art
Gallery, Las Cruces, NM. Luis Jimenez:
sculpture, drawings and prints. Exhibition
catalog, 1977. English.

AN: Well illustrated catalog, some
illustrations in color. Text is interview
tracing Jimenez's artistic development.
Artists identifies Mexican American
connections in his work.

1595 Newport Harbor Art Museum, Newport Beach,
CA. Our own artists: art in Orange County.
Exhibition catalog, 1979. English.

AN: Includes Patricia Murillo and
Emigdio Vasquez with illustrations of one
work each. Biographies of the artists.

1596 Oakes College, University of California,
Santa Cruz, CA and Carrillo, Eduardo.
Corazon de Aztlan: a Chicano arts show.
Exhibition catalog, 1981. English.

AN: Catalog of exhibit including works
by Eduardo Carrillo, Juana Franklin, Cruz
Zamarron, Jerry Astorga, Jaime Valadez,
Ernesto Palomino, Sal Garcia, Roger Sierra,
Jose Montoya, Esteban Villa, Juanishi
Orozco, from Santa Cruz, San Jose, Fresno
and Sacramento. Presentations of films and
by the Teatro de la Tierra Morena of Santa
Cruz County.

1597 Oakland Museum, Oakland, CA. Espejo:
reflections of the Mexican American: Louis
Carlos Bernal, Morrie Camhi, Abigail Heyman,
Roger Minick, Neal Slavin. Exhibit brochure,
1978. English.

AN: Twenty-five photographs from the
documentary series commissioned by the
Mexican American Legal Defense and Education
Fund. Only Bernal is Chicano.

1598 Ohlone College Art Department Gallery,
Fremont, CA. Impressions: a California print
invitational. Exhibition catalog, 1976.
English.

AN: Exhibition catalog includes
commentary on the artist and reproduction of
two silkscreen posters "El Grito Rebelde"
and "The Bicentennial Art Poster" by Rupert
Garcia.

1599 Orange Co. Library. El Modena Branch.
Empanada: a tasty Mexican group art exhibit
filled with a variety of digestable treats.
Exhibition catalog, [1979]. English.

AN: Catalog of an exhibit by 15 artists:
Dolores Grajeda, William Hernandez-M.,
Marylee Montano, Patricia Murillo, Eduardo
Navarro, Susana A. Zaccagnino, Esau Quiroz,
Juan Elias Ramos, Ricardo M. Serrato,
Benjamin Valenzuela, Emigdio C. Vasquez,
Arthur Valenzuela, Jack Vargas, Alonso
Whitney, and Mexican artist Artemio
Sepulveda living in Orange County. Brief
profiles of the artists.

Catalogues (cont.)

1600 Otis/Parsons Gallery, Los Angeles, CA;
Nieto, Margarita; and Price, Aimee Brown.
L.A. parks & wrecks: a reflection of urban
life/parques y choques: un reflejo de la
vida urbana. Exhibition catalog, [1979].
Bilingual.

AN: Catalog poster discussing the works
of the three artists on exhibit: Carlos
Almaraz, John Valadez and John Woods who
concentrate on urban images. Detailed
descriptions of each artist's work accompany
the many illustrations. Essays in English
and Spanish.

1601 Palacio de Mineria, Mexico, D.F. Raices
antiguas/visiones nuevas: arte chicano y
latinoamericano en los estados unidos.
Exhibition catalog, 1980. Spanish.

AN: Catalog of an exhibit circulated by
the Fondo del Sol in the United States, and
in Mexico. Included are Chicanos and Latin
Americans living in the United States. Well
illustrated.

1602 Perez, Demetrio. Mel Casas - humanscapes.
Houston, TX: Contemporary Arts Museum, 1976.
English.

AN: Catalog for Mel Casas exhibition
Oct. 22-Nov. 23, 1976. Artist calls his
paintings "visual conundrums which play with
our cultural concepts, with our cultural
vision." Includes biographical information
and exhibition chronology. Well illustrated
with nine reproductions of artists work and
two photos of the artist.

1603 Philip Renteria drawings, 1974-77. In YOUNG
TEXAS ARTISTS SERIES. Amarillo, TX: Amarillo
Art Center, 1977. English.

AN: Catalog of series of exhibits
co-sponsored by the Texas commission of the
Arts and Humanities and the Amarillo Art
Center. Illustrated with a biography of the
artist.

1604 Pomona College Gallery of Montgomery Art
Center, Claremont, CA; Allikas, Bob; and
Glickman, Hal. Chicano graffiti: the
signatures and symbols of Mexican-American
youth. Exhibition catalog, [1970]. English.

AN: Catalog of exhibit based on
photographs of Los Angeles graffiti.

1605 President's Gallery, Chicago State
University and Sorell, Victor A. Alejandro
Romero. Exhibition catalog, 1979. English.

AN: Catalog of an exhibit by
Mexican-born painter and muralist who has
been working in the United States since
about 1973. He has lived in Chicago since
1976. Illustrated.

1606 Ruiz Productions. Los Angeles, CA: Ruiz
Productions [ca. 1977]. English.

AN: Illustrated catalog of films
produced by or about Chicanos and Mexicans,
including LOS FOUR (artists group) by Jim
Tartan; MESSAGES IN CLAY (pre-Columbian) by
Ed Moreno and Barry Nye; LOS CARROS (cars)
part I: EL CARRO NUEVO and part II: LOW
RIDER by Frank Lisciandro and Alejandro
Nogales.

1607 San Antonio Museum Association, San Antonio,
TX. Visiones nuevas en Tejas/new visions in
Texas. Exhibition catalog, 1979. English.

AN: Supplementary regional catalog for
the exhibit RAICES ANTIGUAS/VISIONES NUEVAS;
ANCIENT ROOTS/NEW VISIONS. Illustrations for
works by George Cisneros, Francisco (Frank)
Fajardo, Robert Gonzalez, Cesar Augusto
Martinez, Roland Mazuca, Guillermo Pulido,
Felipe Reyes, Jesus (Jesse) Trevino.

1608 San Francisco Art Commission Gallery.
Rolando Castellon, Gustavo Rivera, Jerry
Concha. Exhibition brochure, 1971. English.

AN: Brochure for exhibit by
Sacramento-born Jerry Concha, Mexican-born
Gustavo Rivera, and Nicaraguan-born Rolando
Castellon titled CAPRICORN ASUNDER. Brief
biographies of the artists.

1609 San Francisco Art Institute. Other sources:
an American essay. Exhibition catalog, 1976.
English.

AN: Catalog for an exhibit of painting,
printmaking, film, photography, and
sculpture - as well as performing arts - by
300 artists of Chinese, Japanese, Oceanic,
Central and South American and African
descent. The work of over twenty Chicano
artists is included.

1610 San Francisco Museum of Modern Art, San
Francisco, CA; Chavez, Ray; and Gordon,
Allan M. Carmen Lomas Garza/prints and
gouaches: Margo Humphrey/monotypes.
Exhibition catalog, 1980. English.

AN: Carmen Lomas Garza, though working
in a "naive" style is technically adept and
academically trained, though she draws
motifs from folk production of her native
Texas. Her themes in this exhibit are
memories of her childhood. Well illustrated.

1611 San Francisco Museum of Modern Art, San
Francisco, CA and Castellon, Rolando.
People's murals: some events in American
history. Exhibition catalog, 1976. English.

AN: Eight portable murals by San
Francisco Bay Area artists including
Graciela Carrillo, Anthony Machado, Robert
Mendoza, Irene Perez, Mike Rios. Well
Illustrated.

1612 San Francisco Museum of Modern Art, San
Francisco, CA and Castellon, Rolando.
Posters and society. Exhibition catalog,
1975. English.

AN: 26 artists exhibiting public
announcement and social political commentary
posters. Includes 14 Bay Area and
Sacramento, Calif. Latino artists.

1613 San Francisco Museum of Modern Art, San
Francisco, CA and Castellon, Rolando. Rupert
Garcia/pastel drawings. Exhibition catalog,
1978. English.

AN: Exhibit by San Francisco artist
Rupert Garcia.

Catalogues (cont.)

1614 San Jose Museum of Art. Cinco de Mayo: el arte chicano de hoy, the works of Mexican American artists. Exhibition catalog, 1974. English.

AN: Bilingual, illustrated, small exhibition catalogue. Includes collective work by Centro de la Gente of San Jose and the Royal Chicano Air Force (R.C.A.F.) of Sacramento, California. Also lists more than twenty other exhibiting artists.

1615 Santa Ana College, Santa Ana, CA and Goldman, Shifra M. Chicano art. Exhibition catalog, 1974. English.

AN: Thirteen California artists are presented in a short essay defining Chicano as a double mestizaje of Mexican mestizo and U.S. influences that exists in a state of "reconciled conflict." Its aim is communication. Artists included are Malaquias Montoya, Rupert Garcia, Manuel Hernandez, Esteban Villa, Robert Gomez, Harvey Tarango, Mary Helen Castro, Eduardo Carrillo, Graciela Carrillo, and "Los Four": Carlos Almaraz, Robert de la Rocha, Judithe Hernandez, Gilbert Lujan and Frank Romero.

1616 Seattle Art Museum, Seattle, WA and Dickson, Joanne. Manuel Neri, sculpture and drawings. Exhibition catalog, 1981. English.

AN: Beautifully illustrated catalog. Text by Joanne Dickson from Oakland California, biography and very complete chronology of Neri exhibitions.

1617 Southwest Texas State University, San Marcos, TX and Carlisle, Charles Richard. Cuatro caminos: four perspectives on Chicano art. Exhibition catalog, 1980. English.

AN: Exhibition pamphlet with photographs of the artists. Alex Flores, Luis Jimenez, Cesar Augusto Martinez and Amado Pena, Jr. comment on their work and the Chicano art movement.

1618 Taylor Museum of the Colorado Springs Fine Arts Center, Colorado Springs, CO. Hispanic crafts of the Southwest. Catalog, 1977. English.

AN: An excellent and profusely illustrated catalog covering weaving, embroidery, furniture making, woodcarving, jewelry making, tinwork and straw inlay, both past and present. Historical background of crafts production, techniques, and biographies of the artists are provided.

1619 Texas Memorial Museum, University of Texas, Austin, TX. La vela prendida: Mexican-American women's home altars. Exhibition catalog, 1980. Bilingual.

AN: Bilingual illustrated brochure-catalog of exhibit. Includes home altars and graveyard headstones.

1620 Tucson Museum of Art. Raices antiguas/visiones nuevas; ancient roots/new visions. Exhibition catalog, 1977-78. English.

AN: An exhibit of Chicano and Latino artists living in the United States. The exhibit traveled continuously for several years and was supplemented by local artists. Statements by the artists. 59 illustrations, some in color.

1621 Union Gallery, University of Arizona Student Union, Tucson, AZ. Chicanarte: Cynthia Reyes Aponte, Zarco Guerrero, Virginia Federico Olivares, Antonio Pazos. Exhibition catalog, 1981. English.

AN: Illustrated catalog of exhibit featuring four artists.

1622 University Art Museum, Berkeley, CA. The Fifth Sun: Contemporary/Traditional Chicano & Latino Art. Exhibition catalog, 1977. English.

AN: Catalog of exhibit including 45 artists of northern California. Texts deal with Mexican muralists, Mujeres Muralistas & other muralists, posters, the Chicano art movement, altars, La Raza Silkscreen Center, Galeria de la Raza, the Mexican Museum, the Sacramento Centro de Artistas Chicanos/RCAF. Mural maps of S.F. Bay Area and Sacramento. Many illustrations.

1623 University Gallery, Chicago State University and Sorell, Victor A. Hispano American art in Chicago. Exhibition catalog, 1980. English.

AN: Includes 20 Latino artists living in the Chicago area: six from Mexico, five Chicanos, five from Cuba, three from Puerto Rico, one from Venezuela. 20 illustrations.

1624 University of Houston/Lawndale Annex and Xochil Art and Culture Center, Mission, TX. The instant image: an exhibition of polaroid photography. Exhibition catalog, 1980. English.

AN: Exhibit of 14 artists including Tejanos Frank Fajardo, Guillermo Pulido, Gregorio Salazar and Armando Rodriguez.

1625 University of Texas. San Antonio. Medical School and Lee, Amy Freeman. Consuelo Gonzales Amezcua. Exhibition catalog, n.d. English.

AN: Exhibition catalog with a text by Amy Freeman Lee. This major exhibit presented 110 of the artist's works. Price list included.

1626 Vasquez Tagle, Jose Jorge. Museo Mexicano, un rincon de nuestra cultura en San Francisco, California. EL OCCIDENTAL, (October 19, 1980). Spanish.

AN: Rotogravure with twelve colored illustrations of works from the Mexican Museum collections. Text is a mini catalog of the museum's holdings and includes information on funding sources.

1627 Winn Galleries, Seattle, WA. Alfredo Arreguin. Exhibition catalog, 1981. English.

AN: Catalog of an exhibit by Mexican-born Washington painter. Many reproductions, some in color.

Catholic Church

1628 Rafas. [Untitled drawing]. CON SAFOS, Vol. 2, no. 5 (1970), p. 36.

Caughlan, John

1629 The stolen art: the O'Higgins mural.
RECOBRANDO, Vol. 1, no. 2, p. 15, 16.
English.

AN: Historical documentation on 60-foot
long 8-foot high fresco mural painted for
the Seattle Shipscalers Union by Mexican
artist Pablo O'Higgins in 1949. In 1974,
John Caughlan, a people's lawyer documented
the existence of the mural to Chicano
community groups. M.E.C.H.A. students at the
University of Washington lobbied for the
murals restoration and permanent exhibition.

Ceja, David

1630 Art Gallery, California State University,
Long Beach and Lujan, Gilbert Sanchez
"Magu". El arte del pocho. Exhibit brochure,
October 1968. English.

AN: Information about Southern
California artists John Deheras, Marcus
Villagran, Roberto de la Rocha, Santos
Zuniga, Crispin Gonzales, Richard Martinez,
Jesus Gutierrez, Ed Oropeza, Pete Mendez,
David Ramirez, Gilbert Sanchez Lujan, Willie
Hernandez, Art Ponce, Carmen Tostado, Al
Almeida, David Ceja, Robert E. Chavez,
Thomas A. Ferriera. All art students,
graduates, or faculty.

Centro Cultural de la Raza, San Diego, CA

1631 Centro Cultural de La Raza [mural]. MAIZE,
Vol. 5, no. 1-2 (Fall , Winter, 1981,
1982), p. Bk cover. Spanish.

1632 Centro mural recipient of orchid award. LA
PRENSA SAN DIEGO, (November 20, 1981), p.
5. English.

AN: The American Institute of
Architects, the American Society of Interior
Designers, the American Planning Association
and the American Society of Landscape
Architects award the Centro Cultural de la
Raza of Balboa Park, San Diego, CA for
Victor Ochoa's mural on its walls.
Illustrated.

1633 Gardiner, Henry G. Painted exterior walls of
Southern California. CURRANT ART MAGAZINE,
Vol. 1, no. 2 (June, July, 1975), p. 16-23+.
English.

AN: Good survey of street muralism,
primarily in Los Angeles and San Diego,
which started in 1968. Divided into eight
"schools," including Chicano and non-Chicano
muralists. Most Chicano murals associated
with Goez Brothers Art Gallery and Mechicano
Art Center in Los Angeles, the Coronado Bay
Bridge group [Chicano Park] and Balboa Park
group [Centro Cultural de la Raza]. Mural
discussed in detail. Well illustrated.

1634 Lyle, Cindy. Chicano mural art: a mixture of
the barrio's rage and pride. NEW YORK TIMES,
(August 17, 1975), p. Sec.2, 21. English.

AN: Brief history of San Diego's Chicano
Park, why and how it was established, and
the establishment of the Centro Cultural de
la Raza in Balboa Park. Iconography of
several murals is examined, and the
longevity of outdoor murals discussed.
Illustrated.

1635 Murphy, Patricia Lee. Artists renew Toltecas
crafts heritage. LOS ANGELES TIMES, (May
23, 1971), p. E, 10. English.

AN: The Toltecas en Aztlan, creative arm
of the Chicano Federation of San Diego
County, Inc., will shortly move into their
new Centro Cultural de la Raza in Balboa
Park, San Diego. The group includes Mario
Acevedo (Peruvian), Guillermo Aranda, Tomas
Castaneda, Victor Ochoa and Salvador Torres
(visual artists) and poet Alurista.

1636 Rangel, Jesus. Heirs of Jose Posada:
revolution lives in Chicano art. SAN DIEGO
UNION, (February 24, 1980), p. D6. English.

AN: 19th century Mexican engraver Jose
Guadalupe Posada has been an inspiration to
Chicano artists. Along with two exhibits of
his work, the Centro Cultural de la Raza is
also showing calavera (skeleton) images by
Chicano artists: skull-masks from the Teatro
Campesino, a print by Amalia Mesa-Baines of
Frida Kahlo, and a collaged box by Jose
Antonio Burciaga. Illustration: Salvador
Roberto Torres work.

1637 Tang, Paul. Artist sustains proud Hispanic
mural tradition. ARIZONA DAILY
WILDCAT-ENCORE, (March 29, 1979), p. 1.
English.

AN: Born and educated in Hermosillo,
Sonora, Mexico, Antonio Pazos is painting
murals around Tucson. Pazos got his first
mural experience helping paint the Centro
Cultural de la Raza building in San Diego,
CA in the early 1970s. He also spent a
summer at Paolo Soleri's city north of
Phoenix, Arcosanti. Illustrated.

1638 Testimonios de Latinoamerica. LA PRENSA SAN
DIEGO, (October 26, 1979), p. 3. Spanish.

AN: Announcement of an exhibit at the
Centro Cultural de la Raza, San Diego,
"Testimonios de Latino America" and "America
en la mira," political graphics organized by
Mexican artist Felipe Ehrenberg and also
shown at the Los Angeles Contemporary
Exhibitions gallery (LACE).

1639 Thwaites, Lynette. Art on the border.
COMMUNITY ARTS NEWSLETTER, Vol. 3, no. 3
(July 1981). English.

AN: The Centro Cultural de la Raza has
been a pioneer of intercultural activity
between Mexico and the United States in the
San Diego area. The Arizona Commission on
the Arts has promoted numerous exchanges and
publishes a bilingual quarterly bulletin. In
Mission, Texas, Xavier Gorena of the Xochil
Art Center is forging ties with Mexico City.

1640 Wasserman, Isabelle. Photos on exhibit
capture Mexican revolution. SAN DIEGO UNION,
(November 26, 1981), p. D10. English.

AN: Report on the photographic
exhibition of Mexican revolutionary
photographer Agustin V. Casasola at the
Centro Cultural de la Raza in San Diego.
Illustrated.

Centro Cultural de League of Chicano Artists (LUCHA), Austin, TX

1641 Conferencia plastica chicana. Conference brochure, 1979. English.

AN: Schedule of proceedings at internationally attended conference on Chicano and Mexican art and photography sponsored by the Centro Cultural de LUCHA (League of United Chicano Artistas) and MAS (Mujeres Artistas del Suroeste). Brief biographies of presentors. Illustrated.

1642 League of United Chicano Artists, Austin, TX. La cultura es el derecho del pueblo. Brochure-poster, [ca. 1970]. Bilingual.

AN: Bilingual brochure-color poster describing activities of the Centro Cultural de LUCHA: an umbrella organization of the arts in Austin which also published the magazine TEJIDOS.

1643 Murales - 'expresan nuestra realidad'. AYUDA, Vol. 1, no. 6 (September 1977). English.

AN: Brief illustrated article on Raul Valdez's 1977 mural LOS ELEMENTOS on the outside wall of Antioch's Juarez-Lincoln College (Centro Cultural de LUCHA). Explains the iconography of the mural. Includes brief biography of the artist.

1644 Valdez, Raul. Hombre de bronce [mural]. VILLAGER, no. 48 (April 9, 1976), p. 9. English.

AN: Illustration and description of Raul Valdez's indoor mural HOMBRE DE BRONCE at Antioch Juarez-Lincoln College (Centro Cultural de LUCHA).

1645 Woman who began at 73 is shaping Chicano art. SAN ANTONIO EXPRESS-NEWS, (August 18, 1978), p. 6-W. English.

AN: 76-year-old Laredoan Alicia Dickerson Montemayor who began painting on guajes (gourds) from her garden three years ago, now paints on canvas stories from her life in the Valley, nature, and people. An exhibit of her work, referred to by Chicano art critics as "el arte de la inocencia" opens at Gallery of El Centro Cultural de LUCHA, in Austin, TX.

El Centro Cultural de la Gente, San Jose, CA

1646 NATIONAL MURALS NETWORK COMMUNITY NEWSLETTER. (Fall 1979). English.

AN: Reports on mural projects by Fermin Coronado working with students in Houston; Galeria de la Raza's billboard used as a mural surface for changing images; murals under the Flor en la Comunidad program of El Centro Cultural de la Gente in San Jose, California and led by artist Jaime Valadez; murals in Grand Rapids and other cities of western Michigan; murals by Jose Guerrero and others from the Chicago Mural Group; a survey of Chicano murals in the Pilsen area of Chicago guided by Jose Gonzalez.

El Centro Cultural de la Raza, San Diego, CA

1647 Avalos, David. A pure Mexican accent: the popular engravings of Jose Guadalupe Posada. PROCEEDINGS OF THE PACIFIC COAST COUNCIL ON LATIN AMER STUDIES, Vol. 7, (1980, 1981), p. 123-138. English.

AN: As a documentor of injustice and oppression, Posada, 19th century Mexican engraver, is a master who inspires Chicano artists. Appreciation for his art has been expressed by Sacramento artist Jose E. Montoya. Arsacio Vanegas Arroyo, grandson of Posada's publisher, has made his private collection available to Chicano cultural centers, including El Centro Cultural de la Raza, San Diego. Illustrated.

1648 Camacho, Eduardo. Por los cien anos de la fundacion de su editorial: inauguraran hoy en San Diego la exposicion 'Homenaje a Posada, Manilla y Vanegas Arroyo'. EXCELSIOR, (February 14, 1980). Spanish.

AN: Announcing the exhibit of 19th Century Mexican engravers Jose Guadalupe Posada and Manuel Manilla, with publisher Antonio Vanegas Arroyo, at the Centro Cultural de la Raza and Southwestern College, of San Diego, CA.

1649 El Centro Cultural de La Raza, San Diego, CA. Espejo del barrio-art exposition. Exhibition brochure, June 1975. English.

AN: Illustrated brochure announcement for a cultural exposition of Chicano music, art and drama. Includes some biographical information and one reproduction of painter Manuel Unzueta, woodworker Ambriz, muralist Victor Orozco Ochoa and designer/illustrator J. Armando Nunez.

1650 El Centro Cultural de La Raza, San Diego, CA. One hundred year anniversary: Jose Guadalupe Posada, Antonio Vanegas Arroyo. Exhibition invitation, 1980. English.

AN: Invitation to an exhibition of Mexican engravers Posada and Manuel Manilla and an homage to their publisher. Also, a "Chicano Tribute to Jose Guadalupe Posada," with contemporary works influenced by Posada. At the Centro, and at Southwestern College in Chula Vista.

1651 El Centro Cultural de La Raza, San Diego, CA and Enrique, Veronica. Tenth anniversary celebration, July 11, 1981. San Diego, CA: El Centro Cultural de la Raza, 1981. English.

AN: Anniversary brochure of the Centro, founded in 1970 by the Toltecas en Aztlan artistic collective and established at its Balboa Park location in 1971. Briefly reviews the history and activities of the Centro, including the establishment of Chicano Park in 1970 and the painting of murals at the Park and at the Centro. Well illustrated.

1652 Harper, Hilliard. Native Americans stand tall again as Balboa Park mural takes shape. LOS ANGELES TIMES [San Diego County edition], (March 2, 1981), p. II, 5. English.

AN: Victor Ochoa paints the figure of Geronimo on the wall of San Diego's Balboa Park Centro Cultural de la Raza to replace a skeletal calavera figure disturbing patients at a hospital across the street. The central figure is part of a planned 70 x 18 foot mural promoting Mexican, Chicano and Indian art. Activities at the Centro are described. Illustrated.

El Centro Cultural y Museo del Barrio, Taos, NM

1653 El centro cultural y museo del barrio, history and activities. Taos, NM: El Centro Cultural y Museo del Barrio, n.d.. English.

AN: Photo-copied history of the New Mexico organization which is a centro and museo "without walls" begun in 1973. Founded by Juan and Patricia Navarrete, it collaborates with established museums for community art events.

Centro de Arte, Long Beach, CA

1654 Quinonez, Naomi H. In her own backyard = En su propio traspatio. CAMINOS, Vol. 2, no. 2 (March 1981), p. 34-36,62. Bilingual.

AN: Describes the establishment of the Centro de Arte in Long Beach, CA by Chicana artist Lola de la Riva and her family. The Centro, which is in de la Riva's Long Beach home, is designed to give members of her barrio a chance to develop and display their artistic talents. Frequent workshops in mask making, clay sculpture, painting, and graphics are held at the Centro, and the works of local artists are usually on display in her backyard.

Centro de Artistas Chicanos, Sacramento, CA

1655 Case study: Centro de Artistas Chicanos, Sacramento, California. Washington, D.C.: Neighborhood Art Program National Organizing Committee, n.d. English.

AN: In various regions of the Southwest, local artists have started Centros Culturales "whose primary purpose is the proliferation and safeguarding of Chicano art and culture." This case study presents pertinent information on the Centro de Artistas Chicanos founded in 1972 in Sacramento, California. It spells out the philosophy, goals, programs, components and management structure of the R.C.A.F. (Royal Chicano Air Force) and Centro de Artistas. A useful and important document. Illustrated.

1656 Centro de artistas chicanos. EL HISPANO, Vol. 6, no. 39 (March 19, 1974). English.

AN: Description of goals and community oriented programs of the Centro. Illustrated with an R.C.A.F. poster announcing Teatro Campesino production of "LA CARPA DE LOS RASQUACHIS".

1657 Centro de Artistas Chicanos, Sacramento, CA. La arte cosmica [sic] de Esteban Villa: Chicano art exposition. Sacramento, CA: Centro de Artistas Chicanos, 1973. English.

AN: Invitation to an exhibition of works by Esteban Villa at the RCAF's center.

1658 Centro de artistas, Sacra: recuerdo ... descubrimiento ... voluntad. CHISMEARTE, Vol. 1, no. 1 (Fall 1976), p. 6-7. English.

AN: Summary of activities of the Centro de Artistas Chicanos, made up of artists from the Royal Chicano Air Force and other groups. The Centro makes posters, T-shirts, decals, murals and puts on a number of cultural and social events. Report on a "mass migration" July 1976 to the Academia de la Nueva Raza in Dixon, NM for two weeks of communion.

1659 A Chicano artist: Emigdio Vasquez. CANNERY

WORKER, Vol. 1, no. 4 (February 1977), p. 5. Bilingual.

AN: Story on an exhibit by Esteban Villa in the Galeria Barrios of Sacramento, California, which is dedicated to the Cannery Workers Committee on its eighth anniversary. Five works by Villa are illustrated, and a group photograph of the Centro de Artistas Chicanos is included.

1660 Cuellar, Rodolfo. Esteban Villa-maximo exponente del arte indigena mexicano. EL HISPANO, Vol. 8, no. 23 (January 27, 1976), p. 3. Spanish.

AN: Biographical data on the artist focusing on his activism in the formation of the Centro de Artistas Chicanos in Sacramento and the coalition of Centros Chicanos in California. Illustrated with photographs of the artist, one of his murals and a special emblem for the "Esteban Villa Fan Club" designed by the R.C.A.F.

1661 Goldman, Jane. Art against the wall. SACRAMENTO MAGAZINE, (August 1980). English.

AN: Muralists Esteban Villa, Stan Padilla and Juanishi Orozco from the Centro de Artistas Chicanos are planning a symbolic 65 foot, four-story mural on the parking structure opposite Macy's. The mural is described in detail. Illustrated.

1662 Gonzalez, Hector. El arte de Esteban Villa. EL HISPANO, Vol. 6, no. 20 (November 6, 1973). Spanish.

AN: Commenting on Esteban Villa's one man show at the Centro de Artistas Chicanos that presented sixty-five pieces of art ranging from acrylics, watercolors, woodcuts, to pen and ink drawings. Villa fuses Indian symbols, mythology, folklore and customs to create a new "cosmic" dimension for the Chicano experience.

1663 MacLatchie, Sharon. Art in the barrios: one man's commitment. LA LUZ, Vol. 3, no. 9 (December 1974), p. 17-18. English.

AN: Describes the Centro de Artistas Chicanos in Sacramento, California. Highlights the program for art in the Barrio and focuses on the work and personality of Jose Montoya.

1664 Rios, Sam. Chicano muralist: Toltecotl in Aztlan. Unpublished paper, 1980. English.

AN: History of pre-Columbian, Mexican, and Chicano wall paintings. Describes in detail murals by Jose Montoya, Juanishi Orozco, Esteban Villa, Stan Padilla, Juan Cervantes, Lorraine Garcia of the Centro de Artistas Chicanos, Royal Chicano Air Force, painted in 1977 at Southside Park, Sacramento, Calif. Symbolism is explained.

Centro de Artistas Chicanos, Sacramento, CA
(cont.)

1665 University Art Museum, Berkeley, CA. The
Fifth Sun: Contemporary/Traditional Chicano
& Latino Art. Exhibition catalog, 1977.
English.

AN: Catalog of exhibit including 45
artists of northern California. Texts deal
with Mexican muralists, Mujeres Muralistas &
other muralists, posters, the Chicano art
movement, altars, La Raza Silkscreen Center,
Galeria de la Raza, the Mexican Museum, the
Sacramento Centro de Artistas Chicanos/RCAF.
Mural maps of S.F. Bay Area and Sacramento.
Many illustrations.

1666 Valencia, Manuel. Store front academy for
Chicano artists. SACRAMENTO UNION, (January
17, 1973). English.

AN: Article includes comments by Armando
Cid, Ricardo Fabela and Jose Montoya in a
free-wheeling discussion of the goals and
underlying philosophy of the Centro de
Artistas Chicanos in Sacramento. More than
simply exposing the people to art, the
artists explain that they are looking for an
alternative art expression and method of
instruction never offered in traditional art
schools or university departments of art.

El Centro de Artistas Chicanos

1667 Venegas, Sybil. Dia de los muertos. SOMOS,
Vol. 1, no. 5 (October 1978), p. 42-47.
English.

AN: Brief history of Dia de los muertos
ceremonies. While the custom is dying in
Mexico (except for tourists), Chicano
organizations like Galeria de la Raza
(S.F.), El Centro de Artistas Chicanos
(Sacramento, Ca.) celebrate the event
annually, as does [Self-Help Graphics and
Art, Inc.] in East Los Angeles. Well
illustrated with photographs by Guillermo
Bejarano and Daniel Duran.

Centro de Cambio

1668 Dunsmore de Carrillo, Patricia. On Rene
Yanez of the Galeria de la Raza. CHISMEARTE,
Vol. 1, no. 1 (Fall 1976), p. 8-9.
English.

AN: Report on Yanez's negotiations with
the Foster Kleiser Company to take over a
billboard located outside the Galeria in San
Fancisco which has been painted by Michael
Rios, the Centro de Cambio and TIN TAN
magazine, Zaiver (Xavier) Viramontes, and
others.

Centro de la Gente, San Jose, CA

1669 San Jose Museum of Art. Cinco de Mayo: el
arte chicano de hoy, the works of Mexican
American artists. Exhibition catalog, 1974.
English.

AN: Bilingual, illustrated, small
exhibition catalogue. Includes collective
work by Centro de la Gente of San Jose and
the Royal Chicano Air Force (R.C.A.F.) of
Sacramento, California. Also lists more than
twenty other exhibiting artists.

El Centro de la Raza, Seattle, WA

1670 Contreras, Carlos. Nuestra cultura. LA VOZ:
Concilio for the Spanish Speaking of King
Co., Seattle, no. 7 (August 1979).

AN: Information of Washington state
murals painted by members of La Extension
Cultural; Armando Lara's autobiographical
mural titled "El Rio" is installed at the
Concilio offices, 107 Cherry St. Suite 210.
Arturo Artorez completed a wall painting
using the image of Quetzalcoatl at El Centro
de la Raza with funding from the Seattle
Arts Commission. Francisco Siqueiros used
the themes of ecology and Mexican mythology
for two murals at Seattle Community College.
Commentary on Alfredo Arreguin's painting
exhibition at the Kiku Gallery and his wall
painting at the Childrens Orthopedic
Hospital in Seattle.

1671 Cultural department. RECOBRANDO, Vol. 1, no.
15. Spanish.

AN: The development of "Raza" culture in
the Northwest and the role played by the
Centro de la Raza. Mentions the "talleres de
arte" set up by Carlos Contreras and Arturo
Artorez, artists from Mexico who moved to
Seattle in 1978. Details cultural events
sponsored by the Centro in the fields of
art, music, dance, and theater.

El Centro Inc. [art group], San Antonio, TX

1672 De la Torre, Alfredo. Editorial. CARACOL,
Vol. 4, no. 6 (February 1978), p. 3.
Bilingual.

AN: An editorial seeking support for a
proposal by El Centro Inc., a Chicano art
center in San Antonio, TX to commission
murals and decorations in the downtown San
Antonio area.

Ceramics

1673 Galeria de la Raza/Studio 24, San Francisco,
CA. Licita Fernandez (watercolor paintings),
Pete Davalos (ceramic pots). Exhibition
invitation, 1981. English.

AN: Invitation to an exhibit.

1674 Memorial Union Display Cases, Arizona State
University, Tempe, AZ. The material culture
of the Cabezas Redondas, reconstructed by
Liz Lerma Bowerman. Exhibition invitation,
1977. English.

AN: Invitation to an exhibit of pottery
helmets and other artifacts of an imaginary
Bronze Age people, conceived and created by
Liz Lerma Bowerman from Mesa, AZ.

1675 Stofflet-Santiago, Mary. The fifth sun:
esthetic quality versus curatorial intent.
ARTWEEK, Vol. 8, no. 37 (November 5, 1977),
p. 6. English.

AN: Review of the exhibit THE FIFTH SUN
at the University Art Museum in Berkeley,
Calif., curated by Ralph Maradiaga of the
Galeria de la Raza. It contains folk art,
and posters by Chicano artists Maradiaga,
Rupert Garcia, Juan Fuentes, mural studies
by Graciela Carrillo and Mike Rios, ceramics
by Anna de Leon, an altar by Amalia
Mesa-Bains, and mural drawings by Mexican
muralists. The writer criticizes the uneven
quality of the show, but encourages better
ones in the future. Illustrated.

Ceramics (cont.)

1676 Tsutakaua, Mayumi. Despite hostilities, Arreguin is transcending. SEATTLE TIMES, Exhibition brochure, n.d. English.

AN: Biographical sketch of Northwest Chicano painter and ceramicist Alfredo Arreguin. Artistic chronology and negative relationship with local mainstream art institutions.

Cernero, Franco

1677 San Antonio Museum of Modern Art. Zarzamora: inaugural exhibition of Ladrones de la Luz. Exhibition invitation, 1979. English.

AN: Illustrated invitation to photographic exhibition including Norman Avila, David Cardenas, Franco Cernero, Enrique Hernandez, Robert Maxham, James Newberry, Isaac Rodriguez, Daryl Studebaker, Richard Tichich, Beverly Ulmer, Kathy Vargas.

Cervantes, Joe

1678 Mechicano Art Center, Los Angeles, CA. Recent works of Armando Cabrera, Ed Carbajal, Joe Cervantes. Exhibition invitation, 1971. English.

AN: Invitation to an exhibit.

1679 Wilson, William. 30 works from the grass roots. LOS ANGELES TIMES, (June 4, 1973), p. IV,2. English.

AN: Review of a show at the Junior Arts Center in Barnsdall Park by 15 members of the Mechicano Art Center. The critic feels contemporary groups that aim for change today (unlike past groups) are unable to articulate their spirit in a cohesive style. The top talent in this show is Charles Almaraz; also on exhibit are paintings by Jose Cervantes, Guillermo Martinez, Ray Atilano, sculpture by Manuel Cruz, and photography by (Oscar) R. Castillo.

Cervantes, Juan

1680 Rios, Sam. Chicano muralist: Toltecotl in Aztlan. Unpublished paper, 1980. English.

AN: History of pre-Columbian, Mexican, and Chicano wall paintings. Describes in detail murals by Jose Montoya, Juanishi Orozco, Esteban Villa, Stan Padilla, Juan Cervantes, Lorraine Garcia of the Centro de Artistas Chicanos, Royal Chicano Air Force, painted in 1977 at Southside Park, Sacramento, Calif. Symbolism is explained.

Cervantez, Luis

1681 Albright, Thomas. Oakland Museum: a wide range in Latin art. SAN FRANCISCO CHRONICLE, (September 12, 1970), p. 33. English.

AN: A large show called ARTES DE LA RAZA at the Oakland Museum includes Mercedes Gutierrez-McDermid, Louis Gutierrez, Luis Cervantez, Calvin Tondre, Manuel Villamor, Rene Yanez, Jose Ramirez, Jorge Lerma, Rolando Castellon, Esteban Villa, Rupert Garcia, and Gustavo Rivera who is also having an exhibit at the Galeria de la Raza.

1682 Artes 6 Gallery, San Francisco, CA. Mixed media. Exhibition announcement, [ca. 1969-70]. English.

AN: Announcement of exhibit including Jim Cortez, Luis Cervantez, Vicente Rascon, Rene Yanes, Graciela Carrillo, Lorenza Camplis. The Artes 6 artists eventually formed the Galeria de la Raza of San Francisco.

1683 New Galeria de la Raza. EL HISPANO, (July 28, 1970), p. 9. English.

AN: Review of the first exhibit at the Galeria de la Raza at 425 14th St. in San Francisco. The inaugural exhibition featured Esteban Villa, Luis Gutierrez and Luis Cervantes. The new Galeria is sponsored by Casa Hispana de Bellas Artes assisted by San Francisco Art Commission through its Neighborhood Arts Program.

Cervantez, Pedro

1684 The Mexican Museum, San Francisco, CA and Quirarte, Jacinto. 17 artists: Hispano/Mexican-American/Chicano. Exhibition catalog, 1977. English.

AN: Catalog of an exhibit for artists Emilio Aguirre, Consuelo Gonzalez Amezcua, Al Barela, Pedro Cervantez, Edward Chavez, Antonio Garcia, Louis Gutierrez, Harry Louie, Vincent Perez, Michael Ponce de Leon, Eugenio Quesada, Gustavo Rivera, Peter Rodriguez, Alex Sanchez, Darryl Sapien, Rudy Trevino, Manuel Villamor. Illustrated.

Cervantez, Yreina

1685 Almaraz, Carlos. Introduccion: vida urbana y artistas chicanos. COMUNIDAD, Vol. 55, no. 22 (May 3, 1981), p. 2. Spanish.

AN: In the controversial period of the early 1980s, Chicano advances are being attacked. In this political climate, some Los Angeles artists are interested in beauty and artistic creation: Carlos Almaraz, best-known of the Los Four group; Yreina Cervantez; Elsa Flores; John Valadez, presently working on a mural; and musicians Louie Perez and Tito Rodriguez Larriva.

1686 Arte chicano y el pueblo. COMUNIDAD, no. 41 (May 3, 1981), p. 1-15. Spanish.

AN: The whole issue of the Sunday Supplement deals with Los Angeles Chicano art and music. Works by painter Carlos Almaraz, photographer Elsa Flores, painter Yreina Cervantez, muralist and draftsman John Valadez, and a performance piece by Elsa Flores and Louie Perez are featured. Biographical information, and statements by the artists.

1687 Mission to honor Frida Kahlo: famous Mexican artist. EL TECOLOTE, Vol. 9, no. 3 (November 1978), p. 1. Bilingual.

AN: Announcement of an homage to Mexican painter Frida Kahlo at the Galeria de la Raza's annual celebration of Dia de los Muertos. Works reproduced with the article include those of Emmanuel C. Montoya, Yreina Cervantez, Jose Antonio Burciaga, Nina Serrano and Lisa Kokin. Bilingual.

Cervantez, Yreina (cont.)

1688 William Grant Still Community Arts Center,
Los Angeles, CA. Latin American artists
exhibition. Exhibition brochure, 1978.
English.

AN: Exhibit curated by Linda Vallejo
including Carlos Almaraz, Michael M.
Amescua, Ray Bravo, Isabel Castro, Yreina
Cervantez, Luis Serrano-Cordero, Cynthia
Honesto, Judith Miranda, Teddy Sandoval,
John Taboada, Emigdio Vasquez. Illustrated.

Chacon, Gloria

1689 Una galeria de artistas = A gallery of
artists. CAMINOS, Vol. 1, no. 6 (October
1980), p. 20-26. Bilingual.

AN: Features California artists Domingo
O. Ulloa (Imperial Valley images), Gloria
Chacon, photographer Maria Pinedo (San
Francisco), Willie Herron (Los Angeles),
Joaquin Patino (Delano), Pedro Pelayo (Long
Beach), sculptor Rudi Sigala (San Diego),
Mario Torero (San Diego), sculptor Michael
M. Amescua (Los Angeles), and the East Los
Streetscapers. Illustrated.

Chacon, Hector

1690 Hernandez, Manuel de Jesus. Zapata murals
depict Chicano struggle. LA HONDA, Vol. 5,
no. 3 (March, April, 1979). English.

AN: Critical vignettes on the content of
Chicano murals at Casa Zapata, a Chicano
theme dorm at Stanford University. The
muralists include Zarco Guerrero, Esteban
Chavez, Hector Chacon, and Tina Alvarez.

Chacon, Juan

1691 Wilson, Michael and Biberman, Herbert. Salt
of the earth [film]. 16mm, 94 min., b&w.
English.

AN: The first feature film made in the
U.S. of, by and for labor, it deals with a
real strike of Mexican American miners in
New Mexico in which women played a key role
in the men's victory and their own demands.
Mexican actress Rosaura Revueltas starred
with labor leader Juan Chacon. One of the
best films on the subject.

Chapa Mendoza, Nora
USE: Mendoza, Nora Chapa

Charlot, Jean

1692 Patterson, Ann. Exhibit at Unitarian: Smith,
Quesada art black, white contrast. TEMPE
DAILY NEWS, (March 16, 1976). English.

AN: Eugenio Quesada presented drawings
of female torsos along with Smith. Both are
industrial design faculty members at Arizona
State University. Article mentions other
Quesada shows, and his participation on the
Jean Charlot mural at the University.

CHATO [cartoon strip]

1693 Lucas, Costa Ben. Chato [comic strip].
ABRAZO, Vol. 1, no. 2 (Summer 1979), p.
16-17. English.

AN: One installment of CHATO, the
cartoon strip created by Costa Ben Lucas.
Also provides a brief explanation of how the
character was created and his principal
characteristics.

Chavez, Cesar E.

1694 De la Rocha, Roberto. [Untitled woodcuts].
CON SAFOS, no. 7 (Winter 1971), p. 12-13.

1695 Hernandez, Sergio. Cesar [drawing]. CON
SAFOS, Vol. 2, no. 5 (1970), p. COVER.

Chavez, Edward

1696 Edward Chavez: sculptor-painter. LA LUZ,
Vol. 2, no. 2 (May 1973), p. 28-31. English.

AN: Lavishly illustrated biographical
account of Edward Chavez. Born in Ocate, New
Mexico in 1917, Chavez has a distinguished
career as a painter and sculptor. During the
1940's he executed a number of murals under
sponsorship of various government art
projects. These murals were placed in public
buildings in Nebraska, Colorado and Wyoming.
Although living and working in New York most
of his adult life, the work of Edward Chavez
has always been influenced by the Southwest.

1697 The Mexican Museum, San Francisco, CA and
Quirarte, Jacinto. 17 artists:
Hispano/Mexican-American/Chicano. Exhibition
catalog, 1977. English.

AN: Catalog of an exhibit for artists
Emilio Aguirre, Consuelo Gonzalez Amezcua,
Al Barela, Pedro Cervantez, Edward Chavez,
Antonio Garcia, Louis Gutierrez, Harry
Louie, Vincent Perez, Michael Ponce de Leon,
Eugenio Quesada, Gustavo Rivera, Peter
Rodriguez, Alex Sanchez, Darryl Sapien, Rudy
Trevino, Manuel Villamor. Illustrated.

Chavez, Esteban

1698 Hernandez, Manuel de Jesus. Zapata murals
depict Chicano struggle. LA HONDA, Vol. 5,
no. 3 (March, April, 1979). English.

AN: Critical vignettes on the content of
Chicano murals at Casa Zapata, a Chicano
theme dorm at Stanford University. The
muralists include Zarco Guerrero, Esteban
Chavez, Hector Chacon, and Tina Alvarez.

Chavez, Hernando

1699 Teatro de la Tierra Morena, Santa Cruz, CA.
Fuego en Aztlan: a Chicano arts show.
Exhibition brochure, 1980. English.

AN: Folder of information on the
exhibition curated by Cruz Zamarron and
Eduardo Carrillo. Exhibiting artists were:
Justina Avila, Terry Benitez, Eduardo
Carrillo, Hernando Chavez, Bob Cruz, Juanita
Estrada, Juana Franklin, Sal Garcia, Leticia
Hernandez, David "Sir Loco" Jimenez, Raoul
Mendez, Vicente Mendez, Maria V. Pinedo,
Gonzalo Placencia, Ramon Rodriguez, Roberto
Salas, George Silva and Cruz Zamarron. A
special feature was a live tattoo
demonstration entitled "Walking Art".

Chavez, Joseph A.

1700 Wilks, Flo. Joseph A. Chavez. ART VOICES
SOUTH, Vol. 3, no. 1 (January, February,
1980), p. 30. English.

AN: Brief resume on art and life of
Albuquerque sculptor. Illustrated.

Chavez, Ray

1701 Galeria Almazan, Inc., San Antonio, TX. Ray Chavez. Exhibition flyer, 1959. English.

AN: Single page flyer announcement for a one-man exhibition by Ray Chavez (born 1938 in San Antonio). Includes a photograph of the artist and a list of awards and exhibitions.

1702 Galeria Almazan, Inc., San Antonio, TX. Ray Chavez. Exhibition catalog, 1968. English.

AN: Exhibition catalog with biographical information on San Antonio painter Ray Chavez.

1703 Galeria de la Raza, San Antonio, TX. Celebration seventy-four. Exhibition catalog, [ca. 1974]. English.

AN: Catalog of extensive exhibition including European, Mexican, and the following Texan Chicano artists: Rolando Garces, Cesar Martinez, Ray Chavez, Vicente Rodriguez, Jorge Garza, Alfred Rodriguez, Luis Guerra, Carmen Lomas Garza, Bruno Andrade, Jr., Amado M. Pena Jr., Roberto Rios, Jose Trevino, Rudy Trevino, Luis Santoyo, Tati Rubio, Eduardo C. Garza, Arthur de la Fuente, and Jesus Campos Trevino.

Chavez, Robert E.

1704 Art Gallery, California State University, Long Beach and Lujan, Gilbert Sanchez "Magu". El arte del pocho. Exhibit brochure, October 1968. English.

AN: Information about Southern California artists John Deheras, Marcus Villagran, Roberto de la Rocha, Santos Zuniga, Crispin Gonzales, Richard Martinez, Jesus Gutierrez, Ed Oropeza, Pete Mendez, David Ramirez, Gilbert Sanchez Lujan, Willie Hernandez, Art Ponce, Carmen Tostado, Al Almeida, David Ceja, Robert E. Chavez, Thomas A. Ferriera. All art students, graduates, or faculty.

Chavez, Roberto

1705 Cockcroft, Eva; Weber, John; and Cockcroft, James D. Towards a people's art: the contemporary mural movement. New York: E.P. Dutton, 1977. English.

AN: A survey of the street mural movement in the United States, from about 1967 on. Several chapters are written by the artists themselves: John Weber on the Chicago mural group; Susan Shapiro-Kiok on Cityarts Workshop of New York; Eva Cockcroft on People's painters of New Jersey; Geronimo Garduno on Artes Guadalupanos de Aztlan of New Mexico. Chicano murals illustrated include those of Mujeres Muralistas, Ray Patlan, William F. Herron, Hoyo-Mara Gang, Artes Guadalupanos de Aztlan, Vicente Mendoza and Jose Nario (with Patlan) Mario Castillo, Michael Rios, Toltecas en Aztlan, Roberto Chavez, Ernie Palomino, Chuy Campusano and Luis Cortazar (with Rios).

1706 Exxon Company, Houston, TX and Quirarte, Jacinto. Chicano art of the barrio. Exhibition brochure, n.d. [c.1976]. English.

AN: Brochure for a traveling exhibit of photographically-reproduced Chicano murals: Leo Limon, Lucila Villasenor Grijalva, Antonio Esparza, Susan Saenz, Charles Felix,

Hoyo-Mara gang, David A. Lopez and team, Roberto Chavez and team (Los Angeles); Jerry Concha, Ruben Guzman, Chuy Campusano (San Francisco); Manuel Unzueta (Santa Barbara). Ernie Palomino and Leo Esequiel Ozona (Fresno). Leo Tanguma (Houston), Roberto Lucero, Manuel Martinez and Al Sanchez (Denver).

1707 Ross, Bob and Lyndon, George. The case of three California muralists: Roberto Chavez, Eduardo Carrillo, John Chamberlin. ARTS AND ENTERTAINMENT, (July 1981). English.

AN: Well documented reports on the destruction of the Carrillo, Chavez and Chamberlin murals. Focus is on the legal implications of mural effacement in relation to present California law.

1708 Sanchez, Jesus. Auditorium mural "wipe out" during recent renovation move. EAST LOS ANGELES COLLEGE NEWS, (September 26, 1979). English.

AN: "The Path to Knowledge and the False University," a mural by Roberto Chavez on the facade of ELAC's Ingalls Auditorium was painted over on Sept. 11, 1979. Contrasting views on the mural's fate are offered by the Chicano Faculty Association President and the Dean of Educational Services.

1709 Sanchez, Jesus. Resolution passed to support artist's paintings of new mural. EAST LOS ANGELES COLLEGE NEWS, (October 3, 1979). English.

AN: Statements and counter-statements between Arthur Avila, president of East Los Angeles College, Roberto Chavez, artist, and the Chicano Faculty Association about the controversial painting over of a Chavez mural on the exterior of the college auditorium.

1710 Street art explosion in Los Angeles. SUNSET, (April 1973), p. 110-113. English.

AN: Illustrated article on Los Angeles street murals including those by Roberto Chavez, Willie Herron, Frank Romero, Richard Jimenez, William Bejarano, Gilbert Lujan, Armando Cabrera, Frank Martinez, Charles Felix, and others.

1711 Street, Sharon. Califas - a celebration of Chicano culture and art. CITY ON A HILL, (April 16, 1981). English.

AN: Review of an exhibit at College V's Sesnon Gallery featuring 15 California artists: Ramses Noriega, Judy Baca, Salvador Roberto Torres, Malaquias Montoya, Rene Yanez, Ralph Maradiaga, Jose Montoya, Esteban Villa, Carmen Lomas Garza, Robert Chavez, among others. Illustrated.

1712 Tovar, Carlos. Chicano muralist interviewed. NUESTRA COSA, Vol. 8, no. 1 (November, December, 1979), p. 7. English.

AN: Interview with artist Roberto Chavez concerning the white-washing of a mural he painted on the outside front wall of the campus auditorium at East Los Angeles College.

Chavez, Santiago

1713 La Sociedad Historica de Nuestra Senora de
     Guadalupe, Santa Fe, NM. Meditacion.
     Exhibition invitation, 1980. English.

     AN: Invitation to an exhibit by four
     artists: Filomeno Martinez (graphic artist,
     Albuquerque), Ruben Montoya (santero, Santa
     Fe), Santiago Chavez (painter, Santa Rosa),
     Jose Alberto Baros (sculptor, Espanola).

Chicago, IL

1714 Alba-King Kong Studios, Chicago, IL. Latina
     Art Expo '77. Chicago, IL: ALBA-King Kong
     Studios, 1977. English.

     AN: An exhibit by 16 Chicana, Mexican,
     Puerto Rican and other Latina artists. Brief
     biographies of the artists.

1715 Allen, Jane and Guthrie, Derek. La mujer: a
     visual dialogue. NEW ART EXAMINER, Vol. 5,
     no. 10 (July 1978), p. 14. English.

     AN: Review of international show by
     MARCH of Chicago on women's themes.
     Criticizes male Chicano artistic stereotypes
     of women compared to women's art on women
     from California.

1716 Amalgamated Meat Cutters and Butcher Workmen
     of North America. Cry for justice. 1972.
     English.

     AN: Well-illustrated catalog of Chicago
     street murals by Black, Chicano, White and
     Puerto Rican artists.

1717 Chicago. Public Library Cultural Center,
     Chicago, IL. La mujer: a visual dialogue.
     Exhibition invitation, 1978. English.

     AN: Invitation to an exhibit
     spotlighting women artists from Mexico and
     the United States. Organized by the
     Movimiento Artistico Chicano (MARCH) of
     Chicago. 40 paintings by women artists
     included, and 50 works based on the theme of
     women. Poetry readings, music, dance, film,
     theatre, and panels of men and women artists
     included. Illustrated by work by Linda
     Vallejo.

1718 Chicago-Raza murals. NATIONAL MURALS NETWORK
     COMMUNITY NEWSLETTER, (Fall   1979), p. 22.
     English.

     AN: Murals by Ray Patlan, Aurelio Diaz,
     Marcos Raya, Salvador Vega, Jaime Longoria,
     Malu Ortega y Alberro, Oscar Moya in
     Chicago's Pilsen district.

1719 Dittmar Memorial Gallery, Northwestern
     University, Evanston, IL and King, Elaine A.
     Alejandro Romero: new works. Exhibit
     catalog, 1981. English.

     AN: Full color illustrated catalog of
     paintings by the Mexican-born artist who has
     been living in the United States since the
     early 1970s. His images appear to be
     grounded in the work of Bosch, Goya,
     Brueghel, and Diego Rivera. There is a
     synthesis of personal symbolism and
     expressionism.

1720 Elitzik, Paul. Mural magic. AMERICAS,
     (June, July, 1981). English.

     AN: Brief illustrated account of murals
     in the Pilsen barrio of Chicago. Mentions
     work by Aurelio Diaz, Marcos Raya, and

Salvador Vega. Focuses on the controversial
mural at Benito Juarez High School painted
by Jaime Longoria and Malu Ortega.

1721 Garza, Alex. Entrevista con Alex Garza.
     ABRAZO, Vol. 1, no. 2 (Summer 1979), p.
     27-29. English.

     AN: Brief article exploring Alex Garza's
     technique, philosophy, and setting for his
     sculptural work. The artist expresses his
     desire to see artists break with tradition
     and not allow the political rhetoric of the
     early Chicano Movement to promote
     stagnation. His connection to the art
     organization ALBA is also briefly mentioned.

1722 Mendoza, Vicente; Nario, Jose; and Patlan,
     Ray. The history of the Mexican-American
     worker (1974-75) [detail of mural]. REVISTA
     CHICANO-RIQUENA, Vol. 4, no. 4 (Fall
     1976), p. 50,54. English.

1723 Mexican-American Advisory Committee of the
     Museum of Science and Industry.. Second
     annual Mexican-American art fiesta.
     Exhibition brochure, 1975. English.

     AN: Exhibit of paintings, sculpture,
     crafts, and photography by 49 artists from
     Illinois, Indiana, and Mexico. Includes many
     of the most important Chicano artists of the
     Chicago area.

1724 Mitchell, Raye Bemis. March to an aesthetic
     of revolution. NEW ART EXAMINER, (February
     1977). English.

     AN: Interesting article that defines
     Chicano social-realism as a compelling
     aesthetic in opposition to avant-garde
     formalism. Exhibit by members of Chicago's
     MARCH group. Illustrated.

1725 Movimiento Artistico Chicano (MARCH),
     Chicago, IL. Letter to CARACOL. CARACOL,
     Vol. 4, no. 10 (June 1978), p. 3. Spanish.

     AN: Press release announcing LA MUJER:
     UN DIALOGO VISUAL, an art exhibit focusing
     on women sponsored by MARCH of the Chicago
     Public Library.

1726 NATIONAL MURALS NETWORK COMMUNITY
     NEWSLETTER. (Fall   1980). English.

     AN: Reports on murals in San Francisco,
     CA, by the Chicano Moratorium Coalition; in
     Chicago about the Anti-War Preparations
     mural; in Houston by a student at the
     Association for Advancement of Mexican
     Americans; on Michael Schorr's mural in
     Chicanok, San Diego, CA; on a segment being
     painted at the Tujunga Wash mural in Los
     Angeles under Judy Baca; on south San Diego
     murals being painted out; Alan Barnett's
     survey of Southwest murals. Illustrated.

Chicago, IL (cont.)

1727 NATIONAL MURALS NETWORK COMMUNITY
NEWSLETTER. (1978). English.

AN: This issue features reports from
muralists. Includes information about murals
at: La Pena Cultural Center in Berkeley, CA;
the Social and Public Art Resource Center's
Tujunga Wash Mural in Venice, CA; the
Citywide Mural Project in Los Angeles, CA;
activities at Chicano Park, and of the
Congress of American Cosmic Artists (CACA),
both in San Diego, CA; murals in San Mateo
County, CA; the Task Force on Hispanic
American Arts headed by Jacinto Quirarte of
San Antonio; the 1978 Canto Al Pueblo in
Corpus Christi, TX; murals in Chicago; and
other works by non-Chicano artists.

1728 Perales Leven, Humberto. Marcos Raya -
Mexican painter. IMAGENES, Vol. 1, no. 1
(July 1976). Bilingual.

AN: Mexican born Chicago muralist Marcos
Raya painted a mural titled HOMAGE TO RIVERA
in the Pilsen barrio of Chicago at the
corner of 18th Street and May. Raya
articulates the role of the muralist and his
function within the working class community.
Also in this issue is an article on the
formation of MARCH (Movimiento Artistico
Chicano) in 1972 in East Chicago Indiana.
Portfolio of drawings by Marcos Raya and
photographs by Mario Castillo. Bilingual
text.

1729 Plous, F.K. Street scenes. MIDWEST MAGAZINE,
(September 1, 1974), p. 10. English.

AN: Article focusing on the mural
production of Ray Patlan in the Pilsen
barrio of Chicago. Description of the
community and how Patlan functions as a
community worker and muralist. Includes a
directory of Chicago's murals. Well
illustrated with photographs, some in color.

1730 Sorell, Victor A. Barrio murals in Chicago:
painting the Hispanic-American experience on
"our community" walls. REVISTA
CHICANO-RIQUENA, Vol. 4, no. 4 (Fall
1976), p. 51-72. English.

AN: Important survey of Chicago's Latino
murals, with key works considered in detail.
Among the Chicano art organizations and
muralists mentioned are MARCH (Movimiento
Artistico Chicano), and Yolanda Galvan,
Juanita Jaramillo, Jose Nario, Raymond
Patlan, Vicente Mendoza, Marcos Raya,
Ricardo Alonzo, Jose G. Gonzalez and Mario
Castillo, author of the earliest Latino
mural in Chicago (1968). Puerto Rican and
non-Latino muralists and mural groups are
also discussed. Well illustrated.

1731 Sorell, Victor A. and Bernstein, Barbara.
Guide to Chicago murals: yesterday and
today. Chicago, IL: Chicago Council on the
Fine Arts, 1978. English.

AN: Valuable compendium of New Deal and
contemporary murals in Chicago giving
titles, artists' names, dates and locations.
Well illustrated.

1732 University Gallery, Chicago State University
and Sorell, Victor A. Hispano American art
in Chicago. Exhibition catalog, 1980.
English.

AN: Includes 20 Latino artists living in
the Chicago area: six from Mexico, five

Chicanos, five from Cuba, three from Puerto
Rico, one from Venezuela. 20 illustrations.

1733 "Viva la causa", a documentary film on the
Mexican mural movement in Chicago. Chicago,
IL: Kartemquin Films, [1974]. English.

AN: Advertising brochure for a film made
of Chicano muralist Ray Patlan working with
young people in Chicago. The film shows
murals in Mexico and Chicago, and follows
one mural from its sketch to its completion.

1734 Weber, John. A wall mural belongs to
everyone. YOUTH MAGAZINE, Vol. 23, no. 9
(September 1972), p. 58-66. English.

AN: Illustrated article by muralist
about Chicago street murals.

1735 Weiss, Margaret R. and Sommer, Robert.
Camera assignment: documenting street art.
SATURDAY REVIEW, (May 17, 1975), p. 41-43.
English.

AN: Interview with Robert Sommer.
Illustrations of six murals: in Santa Fe,
NM; Estrada Courts in Los Angeles; a John
Weber mural in Chicago; and Cityarts mural
in New York.

1736 Woodblock and linoleum prints by Carlos
Cortez, member of the Chicago mural group.
TIN TAN, Vol. 2, no. 6 (December 1, 1977).
English.

AN: Seven works reproduced from prints
by Cortez, also an active member of the
Movimiento Artistico Chicano of Chicago,
dating from 1971 to 1976.

Chicago Mural Group, Chicago, IL

1737 Cockcroft, Eva; Weber, John; and Cockcroft,
James D. Towards a people's art: the
contemporary mural movement. New York: E.P.
Dutton, 1977. English.

AN: A survey of the street mural
movement in the United States, from about
1967 on. Several chapters are written by the
artists themselves: John Weber on the
Chicago mural group; Susan Shapiro-Kiok on
Cityarts Workshop of New York; Eva Cockcroft
on People's painters of New Jersey; Geronimo
Garduno on Artes Guadalupanos de Aztlan of
New Mexico. Chicano murals illustrated
include those of Mujeres Muralistas, Ray
Patlan, William F. Herron, Hoyo-Mara Gang,
Artes Guadalupanos de Aztlan, Vicente
Mendoza and Jose Nario (with Patlan) Mario
Castillo, Michael Rios, Toltecas en Aztlan,
Roberto Chavez, Ernie Palomino, Chuy
Campusano and Luis Cortazar (with Rios).

Chicago Public Library

1738 Movimiento Artistico Chicano (MARCH),
Chicago, IL. Letter to CARACOL. CARACOL,
Vol. 4, no. 10 (June 1978), p. 3. Spanish.

AN: Press release announcing LA MUJER:
UN DIALOGO VISUAL, an art exhibit focusing
on women sponsored by MARCH of the Chicago
Public Library.

LA CHICANA DE AZTLAN [mural]

1739 Kim, Howard. Judithe Hernandez and a glimpse at the Chicana artist. SOMOS, (October, November, 1979), p. 6-11. English.

AN: Biographical information on Chicana artist Judithe Hernandez. Commentary on her contributions to Plaza de la Raza, Los Angeles Citywide Mural Project and her work as designer consultant to AZTLAN: INTERNATIONAL JOURNAL OF CHICANO RESEARCH. The article focuses on her mural activity, particularly two murals: EL MUNDO DE BARRIO SOTEL and LA CHICANA DE AZTLAN. Her personal art philosophy is presented in relation to Third World Art.

CHICANA [film]

1740 CHICANO CINEMA NEWSLETTER. Vol. 1, no. 4 (June 1979). English.

AN: Report and cautionary note on the upcoming Alternative Cinema Conference; announcement of ONLY ONCE IN A LIFETIME and CHICANA film releases; other new films and TV programs; a Chicano cinema bibliography; a list of Chicano production companies and distributors; a theoretical article on the nature (proposed) of Chicano cinema as an alternative cinema; statement of purpose of the Los Angeles Chicano Cinema Coalition.

Chicana Service Action Center, Los Angeles, CA

1741 Gonzalez, Ellen. U.S. art project: Chicanas painting 'future history'. LOS ANGELES TIMES, (March 16, 1978), p. II, 4. English.

AN: Women muralists from the murals workshop of the Chicana Service Action Center working on murals at City Terrace and Humphrey Avenue elementary schools in East Los Angeles. Illustrated.

1742 Marquez, Rosa Maria. Artistas chicanas together at C.S.A.C., an interview by Rosa Maria Marquez. CHISMEARTE, Vol. 1, no. 4 (Fall , Winter, 1977), p. 39. English.

AN: An interview with several women doing murals as part of the East Los Angeles Senior Citizens Housing and Mural Beautification Program under the sponsorship of the Chicana Service Action Center. Funding for the project through CETA (Comprehensive Employment Training Act).

CHICANARTE exhibit, Los Angeles Municipal Art Gallery

1743 Comite Chicanarte and Los Angeles Municipal Art Gallery, Los Angeles, CA. Chicanarte. Exhibition catalog, 1975. English.

AN: Catalog of an exhibit of 102 California artists. 86 illustrations of works of art.

1744 Gamboa, Harry, Jr. Seis imaginaciones: artistas chicanos en Los Angeles. COMUNIDAD, (July 13, 1980), p. 10. Spanish.

AN: A limited flow of media information about Los Angeles Chicanos has produced a "ghost" culture. Only sensational events are published. Alternative magazines like LA RAZA, CON SAFOS, and REGENERACION have disseminated Chicano ideas of the 1970s. The Chicano imagination has appeared in murals by Willie Herron, Gronk, Carlos Almaraz, John Valadez; in pieces like "walking" and "instant" murals by the group ASCO; by the

group Los Four; by group exhibits like "Chicanismo en el arte," and "Chicanarte." Patssi Valdez showed Photobooth Piece at the "Chicanismo" show. Gronk and Jerry Dreva exhibited their mail art at "Punk Meets Art." In Spanish.

1745 Los Angeles Municipal Art Gallery, Los Angeles, CA and Comite Chicanarte. Chicanarte: statewide exposition of Chicano art. exhibit catalog, 1975. English.

AN: Exhibition by 101 artists, accompanied by month-long performances of films, theatre, music, poetry readings, dance.

1746 Romero, Raul V. Chicanarte, a major exposition of California arts. NEWORLD, (Fall 1975). English.

AN: CHICANARTE at the Los Angeles Municipal Gallery, Barnsdall Park from Sept. 14 -Oct. 12, 1975 remains the most comprehensive statewide exposition of Chicano arts in California. This article details the production apparatus and history of the exposition. In particular, the contributions of Al Frente Communications, Inc., the Chicano Arts Council of U.C.L.A. and the Comite Chicanarte. Illustrated.

1747 Sotomayor, Frank. Chicanarte exposition opening in Barnsdall. CALENDAR, (September 14, 1975), p. 24. English.

AN: Review of the "Chicanarte" exhibit at Los Angeles Municipal Art Gallery. Illustrated.

Chicanas

1748 59th Street Gallery, St. Louis, MO. Midwest Mexican-American art exhibit: Mexico and its artists. Exhibition brochure, 1981. English.

AN: Sponsored by the Sociedad Mexicana "Benito Juarez" and the international Institute of St. Louis, this three-part exhibit includes 1) MEXICO AS SEEN BY HER CHILDREN, a bilingual exhibit from Mexico traveling under Smithsonian Institution auspices, 2) MEXICAN CHILDREN IN THE U.S.A., 3) MEXICAN AMERICAN ARTISTS. In the latter are included Stephen Capiz (Roseville, Minn.), Jose Gonzalez (Chicago), Cesar A. Martinez (San Antonio), Ada Medina (Des Moines), Nora Chapa Mendoza (West Bloomfield, Mich.), Rene David Michel-Trapaga (St. Louis), David Munoz (Kansas City, Mo.), Jose Luis Narezo (Grand Rapids, Mich.), Benny Ordonez, Roman Villarreal (Chicago), Alejandro Romero (Chicago), Aurelio Diaz "Tekpankalli" (Chicago), Simon Ybarra (St. Louis).

1749 Ackerman Student Union, University of California, Los Angeles. Raza women in the arts: brotando del silencio. Exhibit invitation, 1979. English.

AN: Invitation to a MEChA-sponsored exhibit of women's art. Illustrated.

Chicanas (cont.)

1750 Acosta, Dan. Paintings reflect life
experiences. THE ECCENTRIC, (June 26,
1980). English.

AN: Review of one-woman show by Nora
Chapa Mendoza at the Heritage Art Gallery,
Ypsilanti, MI. Mendoza works in abstract
impressionist style with wet streams of
colors that express energy. Her subjects are
landscapes, moods, nudes, and Hispanic
themes. She is active in the Detroit Latino
Artist Association, Nuestras Artes de
Michigan, and the New Detroit Art Council.

1751 Alba-King Kong Studios, Chicago, IL. Latina
Art Expo '77. Chicago, IL: ALBA-King Kong
Studios, 1977. English.

AN: An exhibit by 16 Chicana, Mexican,
Puerto Rican and other Latina artists. Brief
biographies of the artists.

1752 Allen, Jane and Guthrie, Derek. La mujer: a
visual dialogue. NEW ART EXAMINER, Vol. 5,
no. 10 (July 1978), p. 14. English.

AN: Review of international show by
MARCH of Chicago on women's themes.
Criticizes male Chicano artistic stereotypes
of women compared to women's art on women
from California.

1753 Almaraz, Carlos. Introduccion: vida urbana y
artistas chicanos. COMUNIDAD, Vol. 55, no.
22 (May 3, 1981), p. 2. Spanish.

AN: In the controversial period of the
early 1980s, Chicano advances are being
attacked. In this political climate, some
Los Angeles artists are interested in beauty
and artistic creation: Carlos Almaraz,
best-known of the Los Four group; Yreina
Cervantez; Elsa Flores; John Valadez,
presently working on a mural; and musicians
Louie Perez and Tito Rodriguez Larriva.

1754 Altars as folk art. ARRIBA, Vol. 1, no. 1
(July 1980), p. 4. English.

AN: Focusing on the home altar of
Josefina De Leon from Cuero, Texas, the
article describes this folk expression on
two levels: first as a subjective religious
intermediator and secondly as a masterpiece
of collected objects. Contains interesting
information on the form, function and
meaning of altars. Illustrated with
photographs.

1755 Amor sin fronteras. Los Angeles, CA:
Colectivo El Ojo, n.d.. English.

AN: Fotonovela with Josefina Arce,
Eduardo Dominguez and Mike Jauregui produced
by the Colectivo: Eduardo Dominguez, Roberto
Gil de Montes, Jerry Lucas, Kay Torres,
students at California State University, Los
Angeles.

1756 Art in public places. Program statement,
1977-78. English.

AN: Documents an eleven-month program
funded by CETA for 21 artists to produce
murals, prints and weavings as public art.
Includes murals by Gilberto Guzman and
Graciela Carrillo-Lopez in Santa Fe.
Statements by the artists. Illustrated.

1757 Artes 6 Gallery, San Francisco, CA. Mixed
media. Exhibition announcement, [ca.
1969-70]. English.

AN: Announcement of exhibit including
Jim Cortez, Luis Cervantez, Vicente Rascon,
Rene Yanes, Graciela Carrillo, Lorenza
Camplis. The Artes 6 artists eventually
formed the Galeria de la Raza of San
Francisco.

1758 Baciu, Joyce A. Hispanic artists: combining
energy and emotion. CAMINOS, Vol. 2, no. 5
(October 1981), p. 14-17. English.

AN: Brief profiles of Mario Uribe,
Ernest De Soto, Peter Rodriguez, Margarita
Jauregui Weiner, Virginia Jaramillo, Luis
Urrea, Ramses Noriega, Jose Lopez, Olivia
Sanchez.

1759 Barnett, Alan. Southern journey. NATIONAL
MURALS NETWORK COMMUNITY NEWSLETTER, (Fall
1980), p. 22-32. English.

AN: Rather gossipy account of murals
seen in a swing of the southern United
States. Includes the work of dozens of
artists and arts groups from California,
Arizona, New Mexico, Texas, and Colorado.

1760 Baxter Art Gallery, California Institute of
Technology and Rosenstone, Robert A. In
search of...four women/four cultures.
Exhibition catalog, 1976. English.

AN: Catalog of an exhibit including
Donna Nakao, Cheri Pann, Betye Saar, and Los
Angeles Chicana artist Judithe E. Hernandez.
One work of each artist illustrated.

1761 Bejarano, William. Utah Chicano forum.
CHISMEARTE, Vol. 1, no. 1 (Fall 1976), p.
9-10. English.

AN: Report on the CULTURE, ARTE Y MEDIOS
DE COMUNICACION workshop at the Third
National Chicano Forum at the University of
Utah, Salt Lake City. The panel, moderated
by artist Carmen Lomas Garza, set up a plan
of action for the visual, literary,
performing arts and the mass media which
included planning a national conference to
discuss cultural work, financial support,
recognition and moral support, among other
issues.

1762 Bendau, Clifford P. Preserving an ancient
craft. MS.MAGAZINE, Vol. 9, no. 11 (May
1981), p. 26. English.

AN: 40-year-old native Taos, NM resident
Anita Otilia Rodriguez travels the Southwest
as a professional enjarradora building homes
and fireplaces from earth and straw. Article
discusses the history of adobe construction,
Rodriguez's innovations with the ancient
technique. Illustrated.

1763 Beronius, George. The murals of East Los
Angeles. HOME MAGAZINE, (April 11, 1976),
p. 10-11+. English.

AN: Well-illustrated historical article
focusing on murals at Estrada Courts and
those produced through Goez Gallery and
Judith Baca in East Los Angeles.

Chicanas (cont.)

1764 Burkhardt, Dorothy. Chicano pride and anger
     mix at 'Califas'. THE TAB, (April 12,
     1981), p. 34. English.

     AN: CALIFAS: AN EXHIBITION OF CHICANO
     ARTISTS IN CALIFORNIA represents a
     cross-section of artists exhibiting work for
     at least ten years: Rupert Garcia, Ernie
     Palomino, Eduardo Carrillo, Judy Baca, Rene
     Yanez, Carmen Lomas Garza, Salvador Roberto
     Torres, Roberto Chavez, Willie Herron, Ralph
     Maradiaga, Sue Martinez, Jose Montoya,
     Malaquias Montoya, Ramses Noriega and
     Esteban Villa. Illustrated.

1765 Calendario de comida 1976. San Francisco,
     CA: Galeria de la Raza, 1976. English.

     AN: Handprinted silkscreen calendar
     consisting of twelve sheets and a cover. The
     work of the following artists is included:
     Ralph Maradiaga, Juanishi Orozco, Francisco
     Camplis, Ruben Guzman, Rodolfo Cuellar,
     Xavier Viramontes, Jose Montoya, Esteban
     Villa, Rene Yanez, Max Garcia and Louis "The
     Foot" Gonzalez, Patricia Rodriguez, and
     Ricardo Favela. All of the above are
     associated with the Galeria de la Raza, or
     the Royal Chicano Air Force of Sacramento,
     CA.

1766 Calendario de March: 1977. Chicago, IL:
     MARCH, Inc., 1976. English.

     AN: Historical calendar with photos and
     biographies of artists. Illustrations of
     artwork by Ray Patlan, Jose Nario, Frank J.
     Sanchez, Salvador Dominguez, Salvador Vega,
     Marguerite Ortega, Aurelio Diaz, Carlos
     Cortez, Mario E. Castillo, Francisco Blasco,
     Rey Vasquez, and Efrain Martinez. History of
     MARCH (Movimiento Artistico Chicano).

1767 El calendario hispano de Michigan, 1981.
     Stanton, MI: Montcalm Intermediate School
     District and Nuestras Artes de Michigan,
     1981. English.

     AN: Months of historical calendar
     illustrated with art works by George Vargas,
     Nora Chapa Mendoza, Jesse Gonzalez, Julio
     Perazza(Puerto Rican), Hector Valdez, Pamela
     M. Gonzalez, Isabell Escojico (7-year-old
     child), Jose Narezo, Martin Moreno, Laurie
     Mendoza Psarianos, Rosa Maria Arenas.

1768 California. State College. Los Angeles. Art
     Department. Fifth California small images
     exhibition. Exhibition catalog, [1972].
     English.

     AN: Catalog for an exhibit including the
     work of Charles D. Almaraz, Mary Lynn
     Dominguez, Gilbert Sanchez Lujan (who won
     Purchase Awards), Stephen Anaya, Martha
     Villegas. Illustrated.

1769 Capitol Art Gallery, Lansing, MI. Arte de
     Nora Mendoza, Hector Perez, George Vargas,
     Martin Moreno. Exhibition invitation [1979].
     English.

     AN: Invitation to an art exhibit
     organized by Nuestras Artes de Michigan.

1770 Cardona, Patricia. Gana adeptos de Museo
     Mexicano de San Francisco: Pedro Rodriguez.
     UNO MAS UNO, (February 6, 1978), p. 18.
     Spanish.

     AN: Report and brief history of the
     Mexican Museum which opened in 1975 with a

collection of colonial santos. The museum
offers a vista of Mexican culture to people
in the United States. Director Peter
Rodriguez says that Chicano artists Roberto
Gonzalez, Felipe Reyes, Alfredo Arreguin,
Gustavo Rivera, and Carmen Lomas Garza are
some of the best. Illustrated.

1771 Carrillo, Eduardo. Califas, is Chicano art
     safe in Santa Cruz? ARTS AT SANTA CRUZ, Vol.
     1, no. 1 (1981). English.

     AN: Illustrated essay surveying Chicano
     art in Santa Cruz with details about the
     planning and presentation of the CALIFAS
     exhibit at the Mary Porter Seanon Gallery.
     This exhibition presented the work of
     fifteen Chicano(a) artists united and
     defined by a shared vision: a conscious
     identification with Mexican/Chicano culture
     and an alliance with art circuits outside
     the mainstream.

1772 La Casa de la Raza Gallery, Santa Barbara,
     CA. Judithe Hernandez: virgen, madre, mujer;
     imagenes de la mujer chicana. Exhibition
     invitation [1979]. English.

     AN: Invitation to an exhibit with a list
     of projects, murals, and exhibitions.
     Illustrated.

1773 Celebracion Chican-india. CAMINOS, Vol. 1,
     no. 3 (May 1980), p. 38-39+. English.

     AN: Portfolio of works exhibited at the
     Galeria Capistrano in southern California:
     Zarco Guerrero, Domingo Ulloa, Mario Torero,
     Guillermo Acevedo. Judithe Hernandez, who
     also exhibited, is not included in the
     portfolio.

1774 Chavez, Lucy. A Chicano muralist. REVISTA
     MARYKNOLL, (July 1981). English.

     AN: Denver artist Carlotta Espinosa
     decided early in life that she was going to
     be an artist. Espinosa has painted murals in
     Arizona, Texas and the San Luis Valley in
     Colorado. Illustrated with photographs of
     artist and details from her murals.

1775 Chicago. Public Library Cultural Center,
     Chicago, IL. La mujer: a visual dialogue.
     Exhibition invitation, 1978. English.

     AN: Invitation to an exhibit
     spotlighting women artists from Mexico and
     the United States. Organized by the
     Movimiento Artistico Chicano (MARCH) of
     Chicago. 40 paintings by women artists
     included, and 50 works based on the theme of
     women. Poetry readings, music, dance, film,
     theatre, and panels of men and women artists
     included. Illustrated by work by Linda
     Vallejo.

1776 Clark, Yoko and Hama, Chizu. California
     murals. Berkeley, CA: Lancaster-Miller,
     1979. English.

     AN: Picture book of Bay Area and Los
     Angeles murals with brief descriptions.
     Chicano artists included: Daniel Galvez,
     Irene Perez, Patricia Rodriguez, Graciela
     Carrillo (Mujeres Muralistas), Ray Patlan.

Chicanas (cont.)

1777 Cockcroft, Eva. Women in the community mural movement. HERESIES, no. 1 (January 1977), p. 14-22. English.

AN: Women's role in the community mural movement is much greater than generally recognized. Among the many women muralists discussed are included the Mujeres Muralistas (Patricia Rodriguez, Irene Perez, Graciela Carrillo de Lopez, and Venezuelan Consuelo Mendez Castillo) of San Francisoc, and Judy Baca of Los Angeles. Illustrated.

1778 CODEX NEWSLETTER (Galeria de la Raza, San Francisco, CA). Vol. 1, no. 2 (September 1973). English.

AN: An in-house bulletin of upcoming events: EL SOL NUNCA MUERE, photography/poster exhibit, Rolando Garces, and Peruvian posters; Mujeres de Aztlan, women artists' collective exhibit; Filipino/Samoan art exhibit; Galeria Christmas art sale; Galeria pavilion at S.F. annual art festival; Rockefeller scholarship for Galeria curator Luis Santana; Galeria coloring book; Balmy Alley mural project; Diego Rivera exhibit; first installment of Rupert Garcia's RAZA MURALS AND MURALISTS: AN HISTORICAL VIEW.

1779 Colectivo El Ojo. CHOQUE DE AMOR: fotonovela by Lamp. CHISMEARTE, Vol. 1, no. 4 (Fall , Winter, 1977), p. 35-37. Bilingual.

AN: Several students with the help of the Latin American Media Project (LAMP) and the Latin American Studies Department of California State University, Los Angeles produced the fotonovela CHOQUE DE AMOR, a variation on the typical "fotonovela" romance. This one encourages readers to reevaluate traditional female roles. The group also includes Kay Torres. Six frames of the fotonovela are reproduced.

1780 Conferencia plastica chicana. Conference brochure, 1979. English.

AN: Schedule of proceedings at internationally attended conference on Chicano and Mexican art and photography sponsored by the Centro Cultural de LUCHA (League of United Chicano Artistas) and MAS (Mujeres Artistas del Suroeste). Brief biographies of presentors. Illustrated.

1781 Contemporary Arts Museum, Houston, TX. Fire! An exhibition of 100 Texas artists. Exhibition brochure, 1979. English.

AN: Includes eleven Chicano artists. Unfortunately, not illustrated, though a checklist of works is included. Mel Casas, Carmen Lomas Garza, Xavier Gorena, Luis Jimenez, Cesar Martinez, Guillermo Z. Pulido, Philip Renteria, Jose L. Rivera, Joe Rodriguez, George Truan, Juan B. Vela. Introduction by James Surls. Statements by the artists.

1782 Conversation on photography in the Los Angeles Latino community. OBSCURA, Vol. 2, no. 2 (December, February, 1981, 1982), p. 22-32. English.

AN: Interview on the nature and distinguishing characteristics of Chicano photography with Chicano photographers Isabel Castro (Council for Latino Photography), Lorenzo Hernandez (Director of Cityscape Gallery, publisher PHOTOSHOW magazine), Joseph G. Uribe (California State University, Los Angeles, Center for the Visual Arts, Director of West Colorado Gallery), Patssi Valdez, Becky Villasenor, and sculptor, curator, and Art Director for Academia Quinto Sol, Inc., Linda Vallejo, Portfolio of photography by Chicanos Don Anton, Louis Carlos Bernal, Sean Carrillo, Patssi Valdez, Ricardo Valverde, and by Morrie Camhi and Elizabeth Sisco on Chicano subjects.

1783 Corazon del norte: wood carving. GRITO DEL NORTE, Vol. 2, no. 5 (March 28, 1969), p. 11. English.

AN: Focus on the Aguilar family, folk artists from Los Ojos (Parkview), northern New Mexico. Sr. Cruz Aguilar is a sculptor and furniture maker, his 80-year-old mother Dona Cresanta Cruz is a quilter. Illustrated with photographs of the Aguilars and examples of their work.

1784 Corpus Christy State University for the Arts and Weil Gallery Center for the Arts, Corpus Christi State University. Southwest artists invitational: an exhibition of contemporary art by seven Texas artists of Hispanic American descent. Ehxibition brochure, 1980. English.

AN: Artists Jesse Almazan, Luis Jimenez, Cesar Martinez, Lydia Martinez, Manuel Mauricio, Guillermo Pulido, and Jesse Trevino show a variety of techniques and styles. Text by Roberto Tomas Esparza. Statements by and about the artists. Illustrated.

1785 Cox, Sue. Female psychology: the emerging self. New York: St. Martin's Press, 2nd ed., 1981, p. 138+. English.

AN: Reproductions of works by Carmen Lomas Garza, Graciela Carrillo, Consuelo Gonzalez Amezcua.

1786 Cultura chicana: Los Angeles. COMUNIDAD, no. 11 (July 13, 1980), p. 1-15. Spanish.

AN: The whole issue of the Cultural Supplement concerns Chicano art and music. Captioned photographs deal with visual artists Carlos Almaraz, Jerry Dreva [not Chicano], Glugio Gronk, Willie Herron, John Valadez, Patssi Valdez, with examples of their work. With the exception of Dreva, all the artists are members of Los Four or Asco. Asco member Harry Gamboa, Jr. sums up the 1960s and 1970s and activities of artists in his essay "Seis imaginaciones: Artistas chicanos en Los Angeles." Well illustrated.

1787 De Hoyos, Angela. Pa' delante vamos [drawing]. CARACOL, Vol. 4, no. 5 (January 1978), p. FRNT COVER. Spanish.

1788 Diaz, Aurelio. Yo soy chicana [drawing]. CARACOL, Vol. 4, no. 12 (August 1978), p. Bk cover.

1789 Diseno Studios, Austin, TX. Diseno Studios Gallery. Brochure, 1981. English.

Chicanas (cont.)

1790 Ditmar, Joanne. A new industry, done the old way. EMPIRE MAGAZINE, (September 26, 1976), p. 22-25. English.

AN: The Virginia Blue Resource Center for Colorado Women is embarked on a project to revive handicrafts and skills among Hispano women in the San Luis Valley. Igniting interest in traditional crafts like embroideries, tin work, straw mosaic and filigree jewelry, the Center hopes to revive or maintain these traditions. Detailed information on a project to create a group of embroidered wall hangings depicting San Luis Valley life past and present. Illustrated with examples of the completed wall hangings.

1791 Documentary to include work by Cuate Santos. LAREDO NEWS, (July 17, 1980). English.

AN: Photography by Laredo News photographer Cuate Santos included in exhibit "Un encuentro sin palabras," a documentary show on Mexican American life in Texas sponsored by Mujeres Artistas del Suroeste (MAS). The state-wide show was juried by Los Angeles photographer Isabel Castro. Illustrated.

1792 Dougherty Arts Center, Austin, TX. From the fringe: artists choose artists. Exhibition catalog, 1981. English.

AN: Catalog of an exhibit featuring eight women artists, including Santa Barraza of Austin. Barraza also designed the catalog.

1793 Drescher, Tim and Garcia, Rupert. Recent Raza murals in the U.S. RADICAL AMERICA, Vol. 12, no. 2 (March, April, 1978), p. 14-31. English.

AN: Like the cultural revolution of Mexico in the 1920s, La Raza of Aztlan emphasizes the Native American and mestizo heritage as well as the Mexican revolutionary heritage. Witnn a social context, the authors discuss Chicano and Latino murals nationally. Iconography and its relation to Chicano experience is explored, as well as images by and about women. Illustrations.

1794 Encuentro artistico femenil. Austin, TX: Juarez-Lincoln Institute, Centro Cultural de LUCHA, 1977. English.

AN: Program of music, literature and visual art. Lists works by 12 Latina artists and brief biographies. Part of "Women & Their Work" festival.

1795 ENCUENTRO FEMENIL (San Fernando, CA). Vol. 1, no. 1 (Spring 1973), p. 1+. English.

AN: Publication sponsored by Hijas de Cuauhtemoc, a Chicana femenist group. Black and white drawings on cover by Pat Portera Crary. Art work by Vicki Thrall, Adelaida del Castillo, and Maria Hortencia Garcia. Photography by Cindy Honesto and David Lazarin.

1796 Exhibit at UCSD: Chicana artist to show works. LOS ANGELES TIMES [San Diego County edition], (December 6, 1978), p. II, 8. English.

AN: Artist and activist from San Diego, Yolanda Lopez, will be showing sketches and paintings at the Mandeville Center, University of California, San Diego, from which she was the first Chicana to graduate with a Master's degree in visual arts. Her show is based on her family, and the icon of the Virgin of Guadalupe. Illustrated.

1797 Extension Cultural SRE/UNAM, San Antonio, TX. Second non professional (black & white) photography contest: Mexican women in Texas. Competition announcement, [ca. 1980]. English.

AN: Announcement of photographic competition sponsored by the Extension arm of the Secretaria de Relaciones Exteriores/Universidad Nacional Autonoma de Mexico in San Antonio. The theme specified an homage to the Mexican woman in Texas.

1798 Exxon Company, Houston, TX and Quirarte, Jacinto. Chicano art of the barrio. Exhibition brochure, n.d. [c.1976]. English.

AN: Brochure for a traveling exhibit of photographically-reproduced Chicano murals: Leo Limon, Lucila Villasenor Grijalva, Antonio Esparza, Susan Saenz, Charles Felix, Hoyo-Mara gang, David A. Lopez and team, Roberto Chavez and team (Los Angeles); Jerry Concha, Ruben Guzman, Chuy Campusano (San Francisco); Manuel Unzueta (Santa Barbara). Ernie Palomino and Leo Esequiel Ozona (Fresno). Leo Tanguma (Houston), Roberto Lucero, Manuel Martinez and Al Sanchez (Denver).

1799 Fenwick, Red. Why gifted artist's works won't sell. DENVER POST, (October 28, 1979), p. F, 75. English.

AN: Profile of Denver artist Carlota Espinoza--a painter, sculptor and creator of historic dioramas. Espinoza is mainly self-taught. A mural she created for the Byers branch library in Denver portraying "Hispanic" history in America was selected from more than 2,000 entries for national honors. She was chosen to do a stained glass window in the Colorado State House portraying the state's Spanish heritage, and has done art work for the Denver Museum of Natural History and other institutions. The article laments that such a talented artist has been unable to penetrate the mainstream art market.

1800 Focus: Yolanda Lopez. CITYBENDER, Vol. 2, no. 5 (1978). English.

AN: Brief biography and illustrations of drawings by San Diego/San Francisco artist Yolanda Lopez titled THREE GENERATIONS: TRES MUJERES.

1801 Los Four [art group]. Tales from the barrio by Los Four and friends. Los Angeles, CA: Los Four, Liberty Hill Foundation, United Steel Workers, [1977]. English.

AN: Comic book designed with drawings, comic strips, and calligraphy by Frank Romero, George Yepes, Carlos D. Almaraz, Leo Limon, Judithe Hernandez.

Chicanas (cont.)

1802 Los Four exhibit in Union Gallery.
UNIVERSITY TIMES, (November 6, 1975), p. 4.
English.

AN: "Los Four," a group of four Chicano
artists - Frank Romero, Roberto "Beto" de la
Rocha, Gilbert Lujan, and Carlos Almaraz,
with newcomer Judithe Hernandez - work with
political cartoons, Catholic symbols, works
of sardonic humor. They also paint street
murals: several have been done recently in
Los Angeles, La Puente, and Long Beach.
Illustrated.

1803 Fourth annual San Antonio film festival. San
Antonio, TX: Oblate College of the
Southwest, 1979. Bilingual.

AN: Symposium and film festival catalog
featuring motion pictures and videocassettes
made by and about Mexicans, Chicanos and
Latinos. The Symposium focused on Latina
women in film and television, Margarita
Galban, Carmen Tafolla, Leticia Ponce, Grace
Castro Nagata, Marcela Fernandez Violante of
Mexico, and Sylvia Morales.

1804 Frankenstein, Alfred. Report from New
Mexico. Needlework narrative of parish
life. ART IN AMERICA, Vol. 66, no. 5
(September, October, 1978), p. 52-55.
English.

AN: Illustrated report on the Villanueva
Tapestry: an embroidered history of a New
Mexico town by women residents, coached
through and documented by the Museum of
International Folk Art of Santa Fe.

1805 Galeria Capistrano, San Juan Capistrano, CA.
Celebracion Chican-india 1980: Acevedo,
Hernandez, Torero, Ulloa, Zarco. Exhibition
brochure, 1980. English.

AN: Exhibition of Chicano artists
Judithe Hernandez, Domingo Ulloa, El Zarco
Guerrero, and Peruvian-born artists
Guillermo Acevedo and Mario Acevedo Torero.
Color illustration by Torero.

1806 La Galeria de Colores, Las Vegas, NM. La
galeria de colores. Gallery brochure,
[1980]. English.

AN: Brochure for a gallery/studio run by
painter Pola Lopez de Jaramillo since 1980.

1807 Galeria de la Raza/Studio 24, San Francisco,
CA. Blanca Flor Gutierrez - oil pastels.
Exhibition announcement, 1981.

AN: Color xeroxed announcement for a
window display of oil pastels by Gutierrez.

1808 Galeria de la Raza/Studio 24, San Francisco,
CA and Milkie, Anne. Carnaval '80.
Exhibition catalog, 1980. English.

AN: Catalog of an exhibit of photographs
and other media recording San Francisco's
multi-ethnic CARNAVAL, organized in 1978 by
Panamanian-born dancer. Included in the
exhibit were the photographs of Chicana
Maria V. Pinedo, who also designed the
catalog.

1809 Galeria de la Raza/Studio 24, San Francisco,
CA. Third world women arts exhibit:
literary, performing & visual arts.
Exhibition invitation [1971]. English.

AN: Invitation to an exhibit.

1810 Galeria Museo, Mission Cultural Center, San
Francisco, CA and Rodriguez, Patricia.
Patricia Rodriguez: simbolos y fantasias
culturales. Exhibition catalog, 1981.
English.

AN: Catalog of an exhibition of
sculpture and painting. Autobiographical
information about the Texas-born artist who
lives in San Francisco and was a co-founder
of Mujeres Muralistas. She explains her
techniques in making portrait masks of
Chicano/a artists in plaster and mixed
media. Well illustrated.

1811 Galeria Otra Vez, Los Angeles, CA. Rosemary
Quesada-Weiner, Mary McNally: a photographic
exhibition. Exhibition invitation, [1981].
English.

AN: Invitation to an exhibition
including Chicana photographer
Quesada-Weiner. Illustrated.

1812 Galeria Tonantzin, Centro Cultural de LUCHA,
Austin, TX. Visiones Chicanas: images and
demonstrations by Chicana and Latina visual
artists. Exhibition invitation, 1979.
English.

AN: Invitational poster for an exhibit
and a series of workshops organized by
Mujeres Artistas del Suroeste (MAS),
affiliated with LUCHA, League of United
Chicano Artists of Austin, TX.

1813 Galeria Tonantzin, Centro Cultural de LUCHA,
Austin, TX. Young Chicano photographers from
throughout Texas. Exhibition brochure, n.d.
English.

AN: This exhibition is the collection of
the winners of the contest (by the same
name) sponsored by the Extension Cultural
SRE-UNAM in San Antonio. Photographers
represented were: Grace Alvarez, David
Cardenas, Hector Cardenas, Stephen Casanova,
Ronald Cortez, Raul Espinosa, Felix Almanza,
Carolina Flores, David Garza Perez, Xavier
Garza, Conrad Guerra, Melinda Hasbrook, Juan
Jose de Hoyes, Beverly Kennon, Art Moreno,
David Perez, Isabelle Purden, Patricia
Santell, Nancy de los Santos, Jose Soria,
Richard Tichich, Kathy Vargas, Vivian Yaten,
and Johnny Zamarria.

1814 Galerias Paco, New York, NY. Consuelo
Gonzalez Amezcua - filigree art. Exhibition
announcement, n.d. English.

AN: Two-page exhibition announcement
illustrated with two examples of the Texas
artist's "filigree art" and a sample of her
poetry.

1815 Gamboa, Harry, Jr. and Gronk. Gronk:
off-the-wall artist. NEWORLD, Vol. 6, no. 4
(1980), p. 33-43. English.

AN: Interview with Gronk about his No
Movies, by Harry Gamboa, Jr., both members
(with Willie Herron and Patssi Valdez) of
ASCO. The interview itself can be seen as an
"art piece" with photographs by Gamboa; it
contains valuable information about the
ideas and activities of the group.

Chicanas (cont.)

1816 Gamboa, Harry, Jr. Los murales de Aztlan.
COMUNIDAD, (June 28, 1981), p. 8-9+.
Spanish.

AN: Review of the exhibit at the Craft
and Folk Art Museum of Los Angeles of MURALS
OF AZTLAN: THE STREET PAINTERS OF EAST LOS
in which Carlos Almaraz, Gronk, Judithe
Hernandez, Willie Herron, Frank Romero, John
Valadez and the East Los Streetscapers
(David Botello, Wayne Healy, George Yepes)
painted portable murals in the gallery. The
murals are described and illustrated.

1817 Gamboa, Harry, Jr. Seis imaginaciones:
artistas chicanos en Los Angeles. COMUNIDAD,
(July 13, 1980), p. 10. Spanish.

AN: A limited flow of media information
about Los Angeles Chicanos has produced a
"ghost" culture. Only sensational events are
published. Alternative magazines like LA
RAZA, CON SAFOS, and REGENERACION have
disseminated Chicano ideas of the 1970s. The
Chicano imagination has appeared in murals
by Willie Herron, Gronk, Carlos Almaraz,
John Valadez; in pieces like "walking" and
"instant" murals by the group ASCO; by the
group Los Four; by group exhibits like
"Chicanismo en el arte," and "Chicanarte."
Patssi Valdez showed Photobooth Piece at the
"Chicanismo" show. Gronk and Jerry Dreva
exhibited their mail art at "Punk Meets
Art." In Spanish.

1818 Gamboa, Harry, Jr. [Woman (drawing)].
REGENERACION, Vol. 2, no. 3 (1973), p. 26.

1819 Garcia, Ruperto. Las companeras art exhibit.
ARRIBA, Vol. 1, no. 4 (October 1980), p. 9.
English.

AN: Illustrated story on an art show
featuring Texas Latinas organized by MAS
(Mujeres Artistas del Suroeste) in Austin.
More than 18 women were represented.

1820 Garza, Sabino. [Untitled graphic]. CARACOL,
Vol. 1, no. 3 (November 1974), p. 12.

1821 Goldman, Shifra M. Artistas en accion:
conferencia de las mujeres chicanas.
COMUNIDAD, (August 10, 1980), p. 15.
Spanish.

AN: In Chicano Studies programs, the
fine arts have had second class status to
social sciences and literature. Similarly a
Chicano Issues Conference overlooked artists
until a special effort was made. A round
table, which included visual artists
Gloriamalia Flores and Carmen Lomas Garza,
discussed the social functions of art, woman
as an image maker, problems of the Chicana
as creator and cultural worker, and
professionalism in the arts.

1822 Goldman, Shifra M. Canto de unidad: nuevo
mural de Berkeley. PLURAL, Vol. 8, no. 96
(September 1979), p. 33-44. Spanish.

AN: Report on significance,
inconography, and new technical
experimentation in street mural on facade of
La Pena Cultural Center, Berkeley, CA. Deals
with Latin American "nueva cancion." Ray
Patlan and Anna de Leon on team of four
muralists. Illustrated. This article was
reprinted as "Song of Unity: Berkeley's New
Raza Mural," in ARTWORKERS NEWS (New York),
Vol. 11, no. 30, September 20, 1980, p. 1.

1823 Goldman, Shifra M. Chicana artists at work.
ARRIBA, [n.d.], p. 3+. English.

AN: Excerpt of a longer article on the
Texas women's group Mujeres Artistas del
Suroeste (MAS). Integral to the group are
artists Santa Barraza, Nora Gonzalez-Dodson,
Alicia Arredondo, Maria Flores, Sylvia
Orozco, and Modesta Trevino.

1824 Goldman, Shifra M. Chicano art alive and
well in Texas: a 1981 update. REVISTA
CHICANO-RIQUENA, Vol. 9, no. 1 (Winter
1981), p. 34-40. English.

AN: Reprint of article published as
"Supervivencia y prosperidad del arte
chicano en Texas: nueva revision" in
COMUNIDAD (Los Angeles, CA) [Sunday
Supplement to LA OPINION], September 21,
1980, p. 3, 15+.

1825 Goldman, Shifra M. Song of unity: Berkeley's
new raza mural. ARTWORKERS NEWS, Vol. 11,
no. 30 (September 20, 1980), p. 1. English.

AN: Reprint of article published as
"Canto de unidad: nuevo mural de Berkeley"
in PLURAL (Mexico, D.F.), Vol. 8, no. 96,
September 1979, p. 33-44.

1826 Goldman, Shifra M. Supervivencia y
prosperidad del arte chicano en Texas: nueva
revision. COMUNIDAD, Vol. 55, no. 5
(September 21, 1980), p. 3,15+. Spanish.

AN: Focuses on six Chicano artists from
Austin, Houston, San Antonio, and
Kingsville: Mel Casas, Cesar Martinez, Amado
M. Pena, Leo Tanguma, Carmen Lomas Garza,
and Santa Barraza. Well illustrated. This
article was reprinted as "Chicano Art Alive
and Well in Texas: A 1981 Update," in
REVISTA CHICANO-RIQUENA (Houston), Vol. 9,
no. 1, Winter 1981, p. 34-40.

1827 Goldman, Shifra M. Thorns and roses.
ARTWEEK, Vol. 11, no. 30 (September 20,
1980), p. 1. English.

AN: Report on four Chicano artists
exhibiting at L.A.C.E. Gallery, Los Angeles:
Carlos Almaraz, Teddy Sandoval, John
Valadez, and Linda Vallejo. Illustrated.

1828 Goldman, Shifra M. Women artists of Texas:
MAS = More + Artists + Women = MAS.
CHISMEARTE, no. 7 (January 1981), p. 21-22.
English.

AN: History of Texas Chicana women
artists' organization, Mujeres Artistas del
Suroeste (MAS), co-founded in 1977 by Santa
Barraza and Nora Gonzalez-Dodson in the
framework of the burgeoning feminist art
movement, particularly Women and Their Work
of Texas. Brief history of Chicano politics
and the corresponding art movement of
southern and central Texas. In addition to
Barraza and Gonzalez-Dodson, Alicia
Arredondo, Modesta Trevino, and Maria Flores
are considered. Illustrated.

1829 Gonzalez, Ellen. U.S. art project: Chicanas
painting 'future history'. LOS ANGELES
TIMES, (March 16, 1978), p. II, 4. English.

AN: Women muralists from the murals
workshop of the Chicana Service Action
Center working on murals at City Terrace and
Humphrey Avenue elementary schools in East
Los Angeles. Illustrated.

Chicanas (cont.)

1830 The Green Line Gallery, San Pedro, CA.
     Lithographs and woodcuts by Muriel Olguin.
     Exhibit invitation, 1980. English.

     AN: Invitation to an exhibit.
     Illustrated.

1831 Gronk. The Tortuga paints a new mural.
     REGENERACION, Vol. 2, no. 3 (1973), p. 22.

1832 Gronk. [Women (drawing)]. REGENERACION, Vol.
     2, no. 3 (1973), p. 21.

1833 Gronk. [Women (drawing)]. REGENERACION, Vol.
     2, no. 3 (1973), p. 23.

1834 Guadalupe Historic Foundation, Santa Fe, NM.
     Artes en la primavera. (1981). English.

     AN: Catalog of exhibit by four New
     Mexico artists: Manuel Lopez, sculptor from
     Chili; Andres Martinez, painter from Santa
     Cruz; Victoria Lopez, colcha embroiderer
     from San Pedro; Sam Quintana, jeweler from
     La Mesilla.

1835 Guggenheim Gallery, Chapman College, Orange,
     CA. Hexagono: paintings, sculpture,
     drawings, prints. Exhibit invitation, 1977.
     English.

     AN: Invitation to an exhibit for artists
     Tito Aguirre, Isabel Castro, Rick Martinez,
     Esau Quiroz, Linda Vallejo, Emigdio Vasquez,
     Barrows, and Shanahan, sponsored by MEChA.
     Profiles and pictures of the artists.

1836 Hagen, Carol. Mission murals. ARTWEEK, Vol.
     5, no. 30 (September 14, 1974), p. 6.
     English.

     AN: Report on two recently completed
     murals in San Francisco's Mission District:
     Jesus Campusano's 90x10-ft mural in the Bank
     of America branch, and the Mujeres
     Muralistas' mural adjacent to the Mission
     Model Cities building. Illustrated.

1837 Harbor Area Community Art Center, San Pedro,
     CA. Mi arte, mi raza: an exhibition of
     current work by Judithe Hernandez.
     Exhibition invitation, 1979. English.

     AN: Invitation to an exhibit.

1838 Helen Euphrat Gallery, De Anza College,
     Cupertino, CA. Staying visible: the
     importance of archives. Art and "saved
     stuff" of eleven 20th century California
     artists. Cupertino, CA: Helen Euphrat
     Gallery, De Anza College, 1981. English.

     AN: Catalog issued in conjunction with
     an exhibit held in the gallery Sept. 22 to
     October 23, 1981 which included
     documentation on Chicana artists Patricia
     Rodriguez and Carmen Lomas Garza. Each
     artist explains her method of saving,
     storing and using cultural material in her
     creations. Includes biographical sketch,
     photograph of the artist and reproduction of
     artwork.

1839 HEMBRA: HERMANAS EN MOVIMIENTO BROTANDO
     RAICES DE AZTLAN (University of Texas,
     Austin). (Spring 1976).

     AN: Raul Valdez, drawing, p. 3; Carolina
     Flores, drawing, p. 5; Maria Flores,
     photograph, pp. 7, 11, 30; M.E.
     Secrest-Ramirez, drawing, p. 12; Amacio
     Zarate, drawing, p. 15; Santa Barraza,

drawings, pp. 16, 17, 18, 26, 32; Nora
Gonzales-Dodson, painting, p. 19; Gilberto
Cardenas, photograph, pp. 22, 28; Nanci de
los Santos, photograph, p. 23, 29; Amado
Maurilio Pena, Jr. p. 31.

1840 Hernandez, Judithe Elena. Mujer en Aztlan
     [drawing]. CHISMEARTE, Vol. 1, no. 4 (Fall,
     Winter, 1977, 1978), p. [32-33].

1841 Hernandez, Judithe Elena and Goldman, Shifra
     M. Readers' forum. ARTWEEK, Vol. 12, no. 25
     (August 1, 1981), p. 16. English.

     AN: Critical interchange between artist
     Judithe Elena Hernandez de Neikrug and
     critic Shifra M. Goldman concerning the
     latter's review of MURALS OF AZTLAN exhibit.

1842 Hernandez, Manuel de Jesus. Zapata murals
     depict Chicano struggle. LA HONDA, Vol. 5,
     no. 3 (March, April, 1979). English.

     AN: Critical vignettes on the content of
     Chicano murals at Casa Zapata, a Chicano
     theme dorm at Stanford University. The
     muralists include Zarco Guerrero, Esteban
     Chavez, Hector Chacon, and Tina Alvarez.

1843 Herrera, Juan Felipe. The four quarters of
     the heart: a photographic portfolio by Maria
     Pinedo. METAMORFOSIS, Vol. 3, no. 2 (1980,
     1981), p. 66-74. English.

     AN: Statement by San Francisco
     photographer Maria Pineda and review of her
     photography by Herrera. Fourteen
     illustrations.

1844 Hispanic artists' [sic] mural unveiled.
     SOUTHFIELD ECCENTRIC, Exhibition catalog,
     1980. English.

     AN: A mural titled SYNERGY by Michigan
     artist Nora Mendoza is unveiled at the R.J.
     Sullivan Funeral Home. Mendoza has exhibited
     at numerous one-person shows.

1845 La historia de California, 1977. San
     Francisco, CA: Galeria de la Raza, 1977.
     English.

     AN: Handprinted silkscreen calendar of
     history seen from a Mexican point of view.
     Twelve sheets and a cover. Artists are:
     Ralph Maradiaga, Irene Perez, Louie "The
     Foot" Gonzalez, Max Garcia, Patricia
     Rodriguez, Jose Romero, Esteban Villa,
     Juanishi Orozco, Rodolfo Cuellar, Jose
     Montoya, Xavier Viramontes, Rene Yanez,
     Ricardo Favela, associated with the Galeria
     de la Raza, or the Royal Chicano Air Force
     of Sacramento.

1846 Hollister, Kelly. Linda Vallejo. CAMINOS,
     Vol. 1, no. 6 (October 1980), p. 19.
     Bilingual.

     AN: Story on Long Beach, California
     artist Linda Vallejo who also works with
     Self-Help Graphics in Los Angeles and has
     curated a number of exhibits. Vallejo
     describes her work as containing
     "archetypal, mythological or dream-world
     imagery" combined with the "modern idea of
     self-knowledge." Illustrated on p. 17.

Chicanas (cont.)

1847 Hunt, Annette and McNally, Mary. Community
      art centers in Los Angeles. SPINNING OFF,
      Vol. 2, no. 19 (January 1980), p. 1.
      English.

      AN: Article includes an interview with
      Linda Vallejo on the community artistic work
      of Self-Help Graphics and Art, Inc.

1848 Imagenes de la Chicana. Menlo Park, CA:
      Nowels Publications (Stanford University
      Chicano Press), [ca 1975]. English.

      AN: Collections of writings by Chicanas;
      illustrated by unsigned drawings, and
      photographs by Lena Bugarin, Martina Puente,
      Francisco Camplis, Mario Anzaldua.

1849 Inner City Mural Program. Glendale, CA: Los
      Angeles County Dept. of Parks and
      Recreation, [ca. 1974]. English.

      AN: Brief history and philosophy of the
      Inner City Mural Program from June 1, 1973
      to May 31, 1974, when it was sponsored by
      the Cultural Arts Section of the Los Angeles
      County Department of Parks and Recreation,
      and coordinated by Lukman Glasgow. Artists
      Judithe Hernandez and Frank Romero included.
      20 illustrations, some in color.

1850 Instituto Chicano de Artes y Artesanias
      (Texas Instit. Educational Development) and
      Instituto Cultural Mexicano (SER/UNAM), San
      Antonio, TX. Artistas chicanos: Los
      Quemados. San Antonio, TX: Instituto
      Chicano, Texas Institute for Educational
      Development, 1975. English.

      AN: Invitation to an exhibit and
      manifesto of 1975 Austin-San Antonio
      artists' group, Los Quemados. Included Santa
      Barraza, Carolina Flores, Carmen Lomas
      Garza, Luis Guerra, Cesar Augusto Martinez,
      Santos Martinez, Amado Maurilio Pena, Jr.,
      Jose Rivera, Vicente Rodriguez, Jose
      Trevino.

1851 Jesus Gutierrez Gallery, San Pedro, CA. "Two
      of a kind" prints by Linda Vallejo, Muriel
      Olguin. Exhibition invitation [1978].
      English.

      AN: Invitation to an exhibit.

1852 Joslyn Art Center. Multi-media art exhibit:
      Muriel Olguin (printmaking), Myrna Shiras
      (mixed media), Linda Vallejo (painting).
      Exhibition invitation, 1979. English.

      AN: Invitation to an exhibit.

1853 Kim, Howard. Judithe Hernandez and a glimpse
      at the Chicana artist. SOMOS, (October,
      November, 1979), p. 6-11. English.

      AN: Biographical information on Chicana
      artist Judithe Hernandez. Commentary on her
      contributions to Plaza de la Raza, Los
      Angeles Citywide Mural Project and her work
      as designer consultant to AZTLAN:
      INTERNATIONAL JOURNAL OF CHICANO RESEARCH.
      The article focuses on her mural activity,
      particularly two murals: EL MUNDO DE BARRIO
      SOTEL and LA CHICANA DE AZTLAN. Her personal
      art philosophy is presented in relation to
      Third World Art.

1854 Kleinhaus, Chuck; Seiter, Ellen; and Steven,
      Peter. Conference report: struggling for
      unity. JUMP CUT, no. 21 (November 1979), p.
      35-37. English.

      AN: Report and critique of the U.S.
      Conference for an Alternative Cinema held in
      mid-June 1979 at Bard College in New York
      state to chart a course for independent
      filmmakers. Chicano, Black, Asian and Puerto
      Rican film people attended, including Jesus
      Salvador Trevino and Sylvia Morales from the
      Chicano Cinema Coalition of Los Angeles.

1855 L.A.C.E. (Los Angeles Contemporary
      Exhibitions), Los Angeles, CA. Espina
      (Thorn): Carlos Almaraz, Elsa Flores, Louie
      Perez, Teddy Sandoval, John Valadez, Linda
      Vallejo. Exhibition announcement, 1980.
      English.

      AN: Announcement of an exhibition and a
      performance piece by six Los Angeles
      artists.

1856 Lomas Garza, Carmen. Altares: arte
      espiritual del hogar. HOJAS, (1976).
      English.

      AN: Commentary and five photographs from
      the author's visual documentation of home
      altars in Kingsville, Texas. Brief analysis
      of the form, meaning and function of home
      altars in Chicano daily life.

1857 Lomas Garza, Carmen; Montoya, Jose E.; and
      Pinedo, Maria Vita. What we are...now.
      Exhibition catalog, n.d. English.

      AN: Drawings by Sacramento women
      artists: Lorraine Garcia, Eva C. Garcia,
      Kathryn E. Garcia, Celia Rodriguez, Patricia
      Carrillo.

1858 Lopez, Yolanda M. Portrait of my
      grandmother. CONNEXIONS, no. 2 (Fall
      1981). English.

      AN: Four mixed-media images representing
      different ages in the life of the artist's
      grandmother. A hand written text by the
      artist provides biographical and social
      commentary.

1859 Los Angeles City College. Latinos de tres
      mundos. Exhibition invitation, 1980.
      English.

      AN: Invitation to an exhibit featuring
      the work of ASCO members Harry Gamboa, Jr.,
      Gronk, Willie Herron; painters Xavier Mendez
      and Olivia Sanchez; and photographer Ricardo
      Valverde.

1860 Lucas, Jerry and Gil de Montes, Roberto, et
      al. CHOQUE DE AMOR: fotonovela by Lamp. Los
      Angeles, CA: Colectivo El Ojo, Latin
      American Studies Dept., CSULA, 1979.
      English.

      AN: "Fotonovela" featuring Elsa Flores,
      Rosa Marin, and Jerry Lucas produced by the
      collective work of Lucas, Roberto Gil de
      Montes, Mario Massinelli, Luis Soto, and Kay
      Torres.

1861 Lucero, Linda. Compositions from my
      kitchen/composiciones de mi cocina: an
      international cookbook. San Francisco, CA:
      La Raza Graphic Center, 1981. English.

      AN: International recipes illustrated
      with drawings and a poster by Linda Lucero,
      as well as other artists.

Chicanas (cont.)

1862 Lugavere, Joel P. Artists to add '40s to
Great Wall mural. LOS ANGELES TIMES
[Glendale/Burbank edition], (September 20,
1981), p. 1. English.

AN: Brief illustrated story on 1981
extension of the Tujunga Wash mural, THE
GREAT WALL OF LOS ANGELES, directed by Judy
Baca of SPARC, (Social and Public Arts
Resource Center in Venice California).

1863 Mandeville Center for the Arts, La Jolla, CA
and Lopez, Yolanda M. Yolanda M. Lopez
works: 1975-1978. Exhibition catalog, 1978.
English.

AN: Catalog of an exhibit dedicated to
Lopez's female family members, expecially
her grandmother and mother, to the artist
herself as a track runner, and to the
Guadalupe series, icons of the Virgin
transformed to reflect the life of
contemporary women. Well illustrated.

1864 Marion Koogler McNay Art Institute, San
Antonio, TX and Lee, Amy Freeman. Filigree
drawings by Consuelo Gonzalez Amezcua.
Exhibition catalog, 1968. English.

AN: Illustrated catalog for an
exhibition of 42 filigree drawings by Texas
artist "Chelo" Amezcua. Apart from
biographical and historical information, the
text evokes the ambiance of magic and
mysticism surrounding the artist.

1865 Marquez, Rosa Maria. Artistas chicanas
together at C.S.A.C., an interview by Rosa
Maria Marquez. CHISMEARTE, Vol. 1, no. 4
(Fall , Winter, 1977), p. 39. English.

AN: An interview with several women
doing murals as part of the East Los Angeles
Senior Citizens Housing and Mural
Beautification Program under the sponsorship
of the Chicana Service Action Center.
Funding for the project through CETA
(Comprehensive Employment Training Act).

1866 Martinez, Anita. Raza! Arte! Raza! Arte!
EL TECOLOTE, Vol. 1, no. 2 (September 7,
1970), p. 3. Bilingual.

AN: Galeria de la Raza opened on July,
1970 at 425 14th St. San Francisco. It was
an outgrowth of the Arte Seis organization
(an art effort established in the Mission
District in 1967 by Francisco Camplis,
Rupert Garcia, Ralph McNeil, Jay Ojeda and
Jack Ruiz). These and other artists brought
together by the Neighborhood Arts Program
have coalesced in the new Galeria de la
Raza. Article gives goals, organizational
scheme and plans for the Galeria. It's first
exhibit was a one man show by Esteban Villa
together with a photo and sketch exhibit on
Cuba by Jay Ojeda, Roberto Diaz Perez and
Gloria Ozuna. Illustrated with installation
view of new Galeria.

1867 Mascorro, Julie. Mechicano Art Center
exhibit to grace Price gallery walls. CAMPUS
NEWS, (November 24, 1971). English.

AN: Brief history of Mechicano Art
Center activities from its establishment in
1969 to 1971. Exhibiting are Charles
Almaraz, Roberto Amaral, Raymond Atilano,
William Bejarano, Armando Cabrera, Edward
Carbajal, Leonard Castellanos, Henry de
Vega, Antonio Esparza, Bob Gomez, Lucila V.
Grijalva, Jesus Gutierrez, Santos Lira,

Frank Martinez, Ernest Palomino, Louis
Quijada, Richard Raya, Frank Romero.
Illustrated.

1868 Mechicano Art Center, Los Angeles, CA.
Lucila [V. Grijalva] reception. Exhibition
announcement [1976]. English.

AN: Flyer announcing an exhibit for the
Los Angeles painter and muralist.

1869 Memorial Union Display Cases, Arizona State
University, Tempe, AZ. The material culture
of the Cabezas Redondas, reconstructed by
Liz Lerma Bowerman. Exhibition invitation,
1977. English.

AN: Invitation to an exhibit of pottery
helmets and other artifacts of an imaginary
Bronze Age people, conceived and created by
Liz Lerma Bowerman from Mesa, AZ.

1870 Mesa-Bains, Amalia. Homage to Frida Kahlo
opens Nov. 2, at Galeria de la Raza. EL
TECOLOTE, Vol. 9, no. 1 (September 1978), p.
7. English.

AN: Announcement and call for artwork to
Galeria de la Raza's exhibition honoring
Frida Kahlo on Nov. 2, 1978. The proposed
"Homage to Frida Kahlo" will encompass four
major areas; artists' work,
documentation/publication, related art
productions, and educational activities. The
Galeria educated participating artists to
the life and art of Frida Kahlo through
slide presentations and written material.
The exhibition became a milestone in the
Galeria de la Raza history.

1871 MEXICAN MUSEUM NEWSLETTER. Vol. 6, no. 1
(Winter 1980, 1981). English.

AN: Regular report on the activities,
finances, membership, and other information
about the Museum. Announces several upcoming
shows: Rupert Garcia, six Mexican geometric
artists, paintings and prints by Mexican
American and Mexican women artists, Mexican
Leonel Maciel and Chicano Carlos Almaraz,
Mexican folk art, Manuel Neri sculpture, and
Mexican Luis Jaso.

1872 The Mexican Museum, San Francisco, CA. Los
primeros cinco anos: fifth anniversary
exhibit. Exhibition brochure, 1980-81.
English.

AN: 65 Mexican, Chicano, and Latino
artists exhibited for the fifth anniversary
of the Mexican Museum, directed by artist
Peter Rodriguez. Cover is drawing by Carmen
Lomas Garza.

1873 The Mexican Museum, San Francisco, CA.
Virginia Jaramillo. Exhibition brochure,
1980. English.

AN: Exhibition brochure with
biographical information, exhibition
chronology and an artist's statement.

1874 Mexico. Secretaria de Relaciones Exteriores.
Direccion General de Asuntos.. Exposicion:
estampas y remembranzas; Admonty y Geomonte.
Exhibition catalog, 1979. Bilingual.

AN: Catalog of an exhibit by Alice
Dickerson Montemayor (Admonty). Born in
Laredo, Texas in 1902, she began painting in
1976. Her nephew, George A. Montemayor, who
resides in Houston, is the Coordinator for
the La Porte Independent School District.

Chicanas (cont.)

1875 Mills House Visual Arts Complex, Garden Grove, CA. Menudo: artistas latinos de Orange County. Exhibit invitation, 1980. English.

AN: Invitation to an exhibit organized for the first anniversary of Artistas Latinos de Orange County including Delores Grajeda, William Hernandez, Marylee Montano, Patricia Murillo, Irene Ramos, Juan Ramos, Ricardo Serrato, Miguel Shanahan, Arthur Valenzuela, Benjamin Valenzuela, Jack Vargas, Alonzo Whitney, Emigdio Vasquez, Susana Zaccagnino, and Mexican artist Artemio Sepulveda.

1876 Mills, James. Hispano history mural ready. DENVER POST, (October 17, 1975), p. 27+. English.

AN: PASADO, PRESENTE Y FUTURO, a 20-ft. mural by Denver artist Carlota Espinoza was commissioned by the Friends of the Denver Public Library for the Byers Branch (W. 7th Ave. and Santa Fe Drive). Blending myth and reality, the mural progresses from Aztec empires through the Spanish conquest, from alienation to the struggle for a collective identity and heritage by the Mexican American. Brief commentary by the artist on the mural's significance. Ms. Espinoza's mural was designated as an official Centennial-Bicentennial creation. Illustrated with photograph of artist.

1877 Mills, Kay. The great wall of Los Angeles. MS.MAGAZINE, (October 1981), p. 66-69+. English.

AN: THE GREAT WALL OF LOS ANGELES in the Tujunga flood control channel in the San Fernando Valley, was started as a Bicentennial project in 1976. Artistic director Judy Baca of the Social and Public Art Resource Center, works with crews of young people painting aspects of Los Angeles history that is not generally found in textbooks. Well illustrated.

1878 Montoya, Emmanuel; Rodriguez, Patricia; and Acevedo, Mario (Torero). Canto al pueblo '78. NATIONAL MURALS NETWORK COMMUNITY NEWSLETTER, (1978). English.

AN: The second annual Canto al Pueblo took place in Corpus Christi, Texas, where more than six murals were painted: "Wall of Cultural Education" by 13 artists headed by Roel Montealva; Carlota Espinoza, with children; Gilberto Romero, Jose Antonio Burciaga and Patricia Rodriguez, "Incomprehension al arte"; "Madre Tierra" by Manuel Martinez of Denver with Amador Hinojosa (Corpus Christi) and Enriquette Vasquez (New Mexico); Mario Torero; Salvador Vega of Chicago whose mural some Canto participants considered "insulting".

1879 Moody Hall, St. Edwards University, Austin, TX. Las companeras. Exhibition invitation, 1980. English.

AN: Invitation to an exhibition of Chicana/Latina artists sponsored by Mujeres Muralistas del Suroeste (MAS). Illustrated.

1880 Morales, Sylvia. Chicana. 20 min., 16 mm, color, 1979. English.

AN: Color film tracing the history of the Chicana back to pre-Columbian women's history. Utilizes images of pre-Columbian and modern Mexican murals, as well as filming of contemporary Chicanas and their activities. Based on a slide show by Anna Nieto-Gomez, adapted for the screen by Morales.

1881 Moreno, Dorinda. La mujer y el arte. TEJIDOS, Vol. 3, no. 1 (Spring 1976), p. 17. Spanish.

AN: Brief introduction to the collection of poems by Dorinda Moreno published in this issue of TEJIDOS. She also dedicates the collection by alluding to the significance and influence of two artists: Frida Kahlo and Rosaura Revueltas.

1882 Movimiento Artistico Chicano (MARCH), Chicago, IL. Letter to CARACOL. CARACOL, Vol. 4, no. 10 (June 1978), p. 3. Spanish.

AN: Press release announcing LA MUJER: UN DIALOGO VISUAL, an art exhibit focusing on women sponsored by MARCH of the Chicago Public Library.

1883 Muchnic, Suzanne. LAICA looks at social works. CALENDAR, (October 7, 1979), p. 93. English.

AN: Review of the exhibit SOCIAL WORKS at the Los Angeles Institute of Contemporary Art. Illustration and discussion of Judith F. Baca's mural UPRISING OF THE MUJERES, a four-part portable canvas mural in the style of Siqueiros.

1884 Mujeres de Aztlan. EL TECOLOTE, Vol. 4, no. 1 (October 10, 1973), p. 3. English.

AN: A collective of Third World women artists plan an art show at Galeria de la Raza in San Francisco. Stressing the need for art forms that bring awareness and present the true nature of women's living conditions, this call for submission of art work reflects some feminist concerns of the period.

1885 Las mujeres muralistas. Exhibition invitation, 1974. English.

AN: Invitation to the inauguration of the mural PARA EL MERCADO at Paco's Tacos in San Francisco's Mission District by the Mujeres Muralistas, Sept. 15, 1974. Illustrated by Venezuelan artist Consuelo Mendez.

1886 Mujeres muralistas de San Diego. CITYBENDER, Vol. 2, no. 7 (1978). English.

AN: Photographic essay on four women working on their mural at Chicano Park, San Diego.

1887 Mural Resource Center, Los Angeles, CA. Woman's manual: how to assemble scaffolding. Mimeographed booklet, n.d. English.

AN: Publication to service increasing number of women participating in muralism.

Chicanas (cont.)

1888 Las muralistas del barrio. CHISMEARTE, no. 2
     (Winter, Spring, 1977), p. 48-49. English.

     AN: Brief announcement about a Chicana
     artists' organization formed in Fresno,
     California which started work on a
     billboard-like mural, 60x8 feet on the theme
     of women. The mural received funding through
     Fresno's La Brocha del Valle. About fifteen
     women are involved, including Helen Gonzalez
     and Cecelia Risco.

1889 Las muralistas: Patricia Rodriguez, Consuelo
     Mendez, Graciela Carrillo, Irene Perez.
     Exhibition invitation, 1974. English.

     AN: Invitation to the inauguration of
     the mural LATINO AMERICA by the Mujeres
     Muralistas at the Mission Neighborhood Model
     Cities in San Francisco's Mission District,
     May 31, 1974.

1890 Musica hispana en nuestras vidas/Hispanic
     music in our lives: almanaque 1982/calendar.
     Milwaukee, WI: Miller Brewing Co., 1981.
     English.

     AN: Twelve Latino artists were
     commissioned to illustrate a calendar with
     paintings on Hispanic music. The Chicano
     artists include Frederico Vigil (New
     Mexico), Joe Bastida Rodriguez
     (Texas/Washington, D.C.), Manuel Martinez
     (Colorado), Jose Antonio Burciaga
     (California), Ignacio Gomez (California),
     Carolina Flores (Texas), Frank Martinez
     (California). Color.

1891 NATIONAL MURALS NETWORK COMMUNITY
     NEWSLETTER. (Fall   1980). English.

     AN: Reports on murals in San Francisco,
     CA, by the Chicano Moratorium Coalition; in
     Chicago about the Anti-War Preparations
     mural; in Houston by a student at the
     Association for Advancement of Mexican
     Americans; on Michael Schorr's mural in
     Chicanok, San Diego, CA; on a segment being
     painted at the Tujunga Wash mural in Los
     Angeles under Judy Baca; on south San Diego
     murals being painted out; Alan Barnett's
     survey of Southwest murals. Illustrated.

1892 Navar, M. Margarita. La vela prendida: home
     altars. ARRIBA, Vol. 1, no. 5 (February
     1980), p. 12. English.

     AN: Brief commentary on the exhibit LA
     VELA PRENDIDA: MEXICAN AMERICAN WOMEN'S HOME
     ALTARS at the Texas Memorial Museum during
     December 1980. Aside from altars, the
     exhibit focused on nichos, grutas and
     lapidas.

1893 Nelson, Kathryn J. Excerpts from los
     testamentos: Hispanic women folk artists of
     the San Luis Valley, Colorado. FRONTIERS,
     Vol. 5, no. 3 (Fall   1980), p. 34-43.
     English.

     AN: Eppie Archuleta, weaver from the San
     Luis Valley in Southern Colorado talks
     about her life philosophy, Hispanic cultural
     traditions and her role as a community
     artist. First person account amply
     illustrated with photographs.

1894 New mural on Mission Street. EL HISPANO,
     Vol. 7, no. 13 (September 19, 1974), p. 5.
     English.

     AN: Description of mural at the corner
     of 24th Street and South Van Ness in San
     Francisco. Painted by Mujeres
     Muralistas--Consuelo Mendez, Graciela
     Carrillo, Susan Cervantes and Miriam Olivo,
     the 30-foot mural depicts people in a
     tropical, Latin American setting.

1895 Newport Harbor Art Museum, Newport Beach,
     CA. Our own artists: art in Orange County.
     Exhibition catalog, 1979. English.

     AN: Includes Patricia Murillo and
     Emigdio Vasquez with illustrations of one
     work each. Biographies of the artists.

1896 Nora Mendoza: pintora de ascendencia
     mexicana triunfa en los EE. UU. BUENHOGAR,
     (May 1979), p. 7. Spanish.

     AN: Profile of Texas-born Nora Mendoza
     of Michigan, a painter of abstractions in
     acrylic. She is an active member of many
     Detroit and Michigan organizations,
     including Nuestras Artes de Michigan which
     she co-founded with Jorge Vargas, Martin
     Moreno and Jessie Gonzalez.

1897 Oakes College, University of California,
     Santa Cruz, CA and Carrillo, Eduardo.
     Corazon de Aztlan: a Chicano arts show.
     Exhibition catalog, 1981. English.

     AN: Catalog of exhibit including works
     by Eduardo Carrillo, Juana Franklin, Cruz
     Zamarron, Jerry Astorga, Jaime Valadez,
     Ernesto Palomino, Sal Garcia, Roger Sierra,
     Jose Montoya, Esteban Villa, Juanishi
     Orozco, from Santa Cruz, San Jose, Fresno
     and Sacramento. Presentations of films and
     by the Teatro de la Tierra Morena of Santa
     Cruz County.

1898 Oakland County Cultural Affairs, MI. Nora
     Mendoza: an exhibition of
     abstract/impressionism. Exhibition brochure,
     [1981]. English.

     AN: Exhibit brochure for Texas-born Nora
     Chapa Mendoza who studied
     abstract-impressionism with Michigan artist
     Ljubo Biro. She is a leader in the artistic
     and Hispanic communities and runs galleries
     in Clarkston and Detroit.

1899 Oakland Museum, Oakland, CA and Laney
     College, Oakland, CA. In search of Aztlan.
     Exhibition brochure, 1974. English.

     AN: Brochure for exhibit featuring Los
     Four: Carlos Almaraz, Gilbert Lujan, Roberto
     de la Rocha, Frank Romero, Judithe
     Hernandez.

1900 Oakland Museum, Oakland, CA. In search of
     Aztlan. Exhibition invitation, 1974.
     English.

     AN: Invitation to an exhibit by Los
     Four, a Chicano art group started about 1973
     in Los Angeles. On exhibit are the original
     members, Carlos Almaraz, Gilbert Lujan,
     Roberto de la Rocha, Frank Romero, and new
     member Judithe Hernandez.

Chicanas (cont.)

1901 Oakland Museum presents 5 L.A. Chicano artists. EL MUNDO (Hayward, CA), (August 1974). English.

AN: Report on the exhibit THE SEARCH FOR AZTLAN, featuring paintings, murals, tortilla art, folk and religious symbols and totems by Carlos Almaraz, Roberto de la Rocha, Gilbert Lujan, Frank Romero and Judithe Hernandez. Included in the more than 100 works are a wall mural, a folk art pyramid, and part of a primed '51 Chevy lowrider. Illustrated.

1902 La onda artistica de Carmen Lomas Garza. MAGAZIN, Vol. 1, no. 2 (November 1971), p. 29-37. Spanish.

AN: Short biographical sketch of artist and reproduction of seven early drawings. The art of Carmen Lomas Garza is situated within important events of the Chicano Movement in Texas: the student walkouts in Kingsville, and the formation of Colegio Jacinto Trevino.

1903 Orange Co. Library. El Modena Branch. Empanada: a tasty Mexican group art exhibit filled with a variety of digestable treats. Exhibition catalog, [1979]. English.

AN: Catalog of an exhibit by 15 artists: Dolores Grajeda, William Hernandez-M., Marylee Montano, Patricia Murillo, Eduardo Navarro, Susana A. Zaccagnino, Esau Quiroz, Juan Elias Ramos, Ricardo M. Serrato, Benjamin Valenzuela, Emigdio C. Vasquez, Arthur Valenzuela, Jack Vargas, Alonso Whitney, and Mexican artist Artemio Sepulveda living in Orange County. Brief profiles of the artists.

1904 Orozco, Irma. Women & their work. PARA LA GENTE, Vol. 1, no. 4 (October 1977), p. 12. English.

AN: Illustrated story about "Women & Their Work" festival in Austin, Texas, Oct-Dec 1977. Photographers Maria Flores and Teresina Guerra, Santa Barraza, Nora Gonzalez Dodson, Sylvia Orozco, and Modesta Trevino exhibited.

1905 Orozco, Sylvia. Las mujeres - Chicana artists come into their own. MOVING ON, Vol. 2, no. 3 (May 1978), p. 14-16. English.

AN: Illustrated feature prepared by artist Sylvia Orozco on the founding of Mujeres Artistas del Suroeste in Austin, September 1977. Artworks and statements by Nora Gonzalez Dodson, Maria Flores, Modesta Trevino, Santa Barraza, as well as musicians and singers.

1906 Orozco, Sylvia and Trevino, Jose. Trevino's arte interprets el mundo Chicano. PARA LA GENTE, Vol. 1, no. 10 (May 1978), p. 7-9. English.

AN: Interview with Jose Trevino of Austin and his artist wife, Modesta. Reproduction and discussion of four works. Centerspread reproduction of a Trevino poster, part of a set of 10 designed for bilingual classrooms.

1907 Painting changes woman's life at age when most ready to retire. LAREDO NEWS, (November 4, 1979), p. 1-C. English.

AN: Interview with 77 year old Alice D. Montemayor "Admonty" on the occasion of her San Antonio exhibit with her nephew George "Geomonte" Montemayor.

1908 Palma Castroman, Janis. ENCUENTRO ARTISTICO FEMENIL [exhibit], Austin, TX, November 28, 1977. TEJIDOS, Vol. 5, no. 1 (1978), p. 1-47. Bilingual.

AN: A multimedia, multicultural exposition by 26 Chicana artists held at Juarez-Lincoln University. The exhibit was sponsored by Chicanos Artistas Sirviendo a Aztlan (CASA) and Mujeres Artistas del Suroeste (MAS).

1909 Palma Castroman, Janis. Introduccion. TEJIDOS, Vol. 5, no. 1 (1978), p. i. Spanish.

AN: One-page introduction to theme issue featuring the work of Chicana artists exhibited at the ENCUENTRO ARTISTICO FEMENIL exposition held on November 28, 1977 in Austin, TX.

1910 Parachini, Allan. Tujunga wash mural stands up to storm. LOS ANGELES TIMES, (March 13, 1980), p. V, 1. English.

AN: Information about the mural project near Los Angeles Valley College in Van Nuys, Calif. sponsored by SPARC (Social and Public Art Resource Center) of Venice, Calif. and coordinated by Judy Baca. Illustrated.

1911 Petersen, Karen and Wilson, J.J. Women artists: Third World. New York, NY: Harper & Row, 1975. English.

AN: Catalog of slides with accompanying notes. Slides of Chicana artists available: Margaret Herrera (Chavez), Consuelo (Chelo) Gonzalez Amezcua, Santa Barraza, Mujeres Muralistas, El Grupo de Santa Ana, Carmen Lomas Garza, Carolina Flores.

1912 EL PLAYANO (Loyola University, Los Angeles). (Spring 1972).

AN: Illustrations by Willie Herron, Harry Gamboa, Jr., Gronk, Diane Gamboa, William A. Bejarano, Eddie Garcia.

1913 EL PLAYANO (Loyola University, Los Angeles). (Spring 1973).

AN: Illustrations by Simon Gonzales, Gronk, Harry Gamboa, Jr., Willie Herron, Charles Almaraz, Sister Teresa Munoz, Patsy Valdez, Diane Gamboa.

1914 The Point Gallery, Santa Monica, CA. ASCO (Gronk, Patssi, Gamboa, Herron), Los Four (Almaraz, de la Rocha, Judithe Hernandez, Gloriamalia Flores, Mauricio Ramirez, John Valadez. Exhibition invitation, [1975]. English.

AN: Illustrated invitation to an exhibit of Los Angeles artists.

1915 Popcorn. [Two women (drawing)]. REGENERACION, Vol. 2, no. 4 (1975), p. 16.

Chicanas (cont.)

1916 Portraying Latino women in the Mission. SAN
      FRANCISCO EXAMINER, (September 10, 1974),
      p. 26. English.

      AN: Three muralists of the Mission
      District, Irene Perez, Patricia Rodriguez,
      and Venezuelan Consuelo Mendez, are
      preparing a six-paneled
      painting-construction, the RHOMBOIDAL
      PARALLELOGRAM, for the 28th annual San
      Francisco Art Festival. It will illustrate
      the life of women in the Mission.
      Illustrated.

1917 Preuss, Karen. The new Mission murals. SAN
      FRANCISCO BAY GUARDIAN, (June 28, 1975), p.
      14-15. English.

      AN: Mural art in San Francisco's Mission
      District has covered nearly every wall and
      alley on lower 24th Street. Murals by Mike
      Rios, the Mujeres Muralistas (Patricia
      Rodriguez, Graciela Carrillo, Consuelo
      Mendez, Miriam Olivo, Irene Perez, Susan
      Cervantes) appear in the area. Others have
      been painted by artists associated with the
      Galeria de la Raza. Illustrations.

1918 Quesada-Weiner, Rosemary. Las mujeres: 1977
      National Women's Conference. Los Angeles,
      CA: Rosemary Quesada-Weiner, 1978. English.

      AN: Portfolio (with captions) of
      photographs taken by Quesada-Weiner.

1919 Quesada-Weiner, Rosemary. [Untitled
      collection of photographs]. COMUNIDAD,
      (August 24, 1980), p. 15.

      AN: Photographs of the CONFERENCIA DE
      LAS MUJERES CHICANAS taken by Rosemary
      Quesada-Weiner.

1920 Quintana, Helena. Sketches [drawing]. DE
      COLORES, Vol. 2, no. 3 (1975), p. 53-56.

1921 Quintero, Victoria. Mujeres muralistas. LA
      RAZON MESTIZA, Vol. 11, (Summer 1975).

      AN: Goals and artistic procedures of the
      Mujeres Muralistas Collective. Article
      emphasizes the solidarity of Latin American
      women and Chicanas and how their joint
      artistic production reflects a woman's
      viewpoint in aesthetic terms.

1922 Quintero, Victoria. A mural is a painting on
      a wall done by human hands. EL TECOLOTE,
      Vol. 5, no. 1 (September 13, 1974), p. 6+.
      English.

      AN: The women's collective, Mujeres
      Muralistas, exists within the strong San
      Francisco mural movement. Originally the
      group included Graciela Carrillo, Consuelo
      Mendez, Irene Perez, and Patricia Rodriguez.
      The group has expanded to include Susan
      Cervantes, Ester Hernandez, and Miriam
      Olivo. The two murals completed have been
      criticized for not being political; the
      women answer that they want the atmosphere
      to be surrounded with life, with colors.
      Illustrated.

1923 Quirarte, Jacinto. Chelo Gonzalez Amezcua.
      QUETZAL, Vol. 1, no. 2 (Winter 1970, 1971),
      p. 33-36.

      AN: Biographical information based on a
      taped interview with the Del Rio, Texas
      artist. As a self-taught artist, Chelo
      Gonzalez Amezcua developed a drawing style
      using colored ball point pens which she
      calls "Filigree Art", a new Texas culture.
      Poorly illustrated.

1924 Quirarte, Jacinto. Image and text (poetry)
      in the work of Consuelo (Chelo) Gonzalez
      Amezcua, a Texas artist (1903-1975).
      RESEARCH CENTER FOR THE ARTS REVIEW, Vol. 5,
      no. 1 (January 1982), p. 1-3. English.

      AN: The use of images and poetry in the
      work of self-taught Del Rio, Texas artist
      Chelo Gonzalez Amezcua is demonstrated by
      focusing on her drawing EL MOSAICO DE LAS
      AVES of 1972, in which her use of both sides
      of the paper is contrasted with similar uses
      in Aztec sculpture. Illustrated.

1925 Quirarte, Jacinto. Mexican-American artists.
      Austin, TX: University of Texas Press, 1973.
      English.

      AN: First comprehensive historical text
      on artists of Mexican descent in the United
      States. Sets up the antecedents from
      settlement to the visits of Mexican
      muralists Rivera, Siqueiros, Orozco and
      Tamayo in the U.S., though only Orozco and
      Tamayo are considered at length. Mexican
      American artists are divided by decades of
      birth, from 1901 to 1946. Twenty-seven
      artists (two women) are discussed. The
      epilogue is a discussion on the terms
      "Mexican American" and "Chicano," the latter
      articulated by Esteban Villa, who is not in
      the text.

1926 Rangel, Jesus. Heirs of Jose Posada:
      revolution lives in Chicano art. SAN DIEGO
      UNION, (February 24, 1980), p. D6. English.

      AN: 19th century Mexican engraver Jose
      Guadalupe Posada has been an inspiration to
      Chicano artists. Along with two exhibits of
      his work, the Centro Cultural de la Raza is
      also showing calavera (skeleton) images by
      Chicano artists: skull-masks from the Teatro
      Campesino, a print by Amalia Mesa-Baines of
      Frida Kahlo, and a collaged box by Jose
      Antonio Burciaga. Illustration: Salvador
      Roberto Torres work.

1927 Rickey, Carrie. The passion of Ana. VILLAGE
      VOICE, Vol. 25, no. 37 (September 10, 1980),
      p. 75. English.

      AN: Review of the exhibition DIALECTICS
      OF ISOLATION, AN EXHIBITION OF THIRD WORLD
      WOMEN ARTISTS OF THE UNITED STATES at the
      A.I.R Gallery in New York, September 1980.
      Includes a capsule analysis of Judith Baca's
      colossal mural in Tujunga Wash in Los
      Angeles. The mural "proposes to restore to
      public consciousness the ethnic and cultural
      history of the city's minorities." Details
      work procedures, content and political aims
      of the project. Eleven blue prints of mural
      cartoons detailing highlights of the mural's
      visual narrative were displayed in the
      exhibit.

1928 Rickey, Carrie. The writing on the wall. ART
      IN AMERICA, Vol. 69, no. 5 (May 1981), p.
      54-57. English.

      AN: Detailed article on the career of
      Judy Baca, director of SPARC (Social and
      Public Arts Resource Center) in Venice,
      Calif., and of the Great Wall of Los
      Angeles, a five year mural project at the
      Tujunga Wash. Well illustrated in black and
      white and color.

Chicanas (cont.)

1929 Rodriguez, Anita. Las enjarradoras: women of the earth. NEW MEXICO, (February 1980), p. 46-47+. English.

AN: History of adobe construction in New Mexico, its decline and its present revival in Arizona and New Mexico. Written by a professional adobe architect and feminist who defines the traditional terms and techniques of this woman's craft. Illustrated.

1930 Rodriguez, Anita. Tradiciones de adobe en Nuevo Mejico norteno = adobe traditions in Northern New Mexico. ADOBE NEWS, no. 15 (1977). Bilingual.

AN: History of adobe construction in New Mexico, from primarily Indian sources with Spanish input. For 400 years, women were builders and architects of the Southwest; today they are "enjarradoras" (plasterers). Written by a professional enjarradora from New Mexico. Illustrated.

1931 Rodriguez, Patricia. Portfolio: Patricia Rodriguez; the visual interview. METAMORFOSIS, Vol. 3, no. 1-2 (1980, 1981), p. 38-45. English.

AN: Statement by the artist reprinted from her exhibit "The Visual Interview" at the Mission Cultural Center, San Francisco. Discusses her fifteen mask-box-sculptures of Chicano artists from northern California. Illustrated with photographs of the artist at work and five of her sculptures. This issue of METAMORFOSIS combines volumes 3 and 4.

1932 Rodriguez, Patricia, ed. Selected readings on Chicano art. Berkeley, CA: Chicano Studies Department, University of California, 1977. English.

AN: Compendium of mechanically reproduced articles on Chicano and Latin American art prepared for Chicano Studies 130--Introduction to Chicano Art. Includes sections on Mexican Muralists in the U.S: Contemporary Chicano Art; Views on Chicano Art; Chicano Artists; Pinto Art: Raza Murals and Muralists; Plaqueasos (Graffiti); Chicana Artists: Art, Politics and the Community, Two Historical Examples: Cuba and Chile; Chicano Art Reproductions, 557 pp.

1933 Romotsky, Jerry and Romotsky, Sally R. Placas and murals. ARTS IN SOCIETY, Vol. 2, no. 1 (Summer, Fall , 1974), p. 286-299. English.

AN: Details how Chicano muralists have recognized the aesthetics of graffiti and incorporated them into their murals. Among the earliest to do so were Lucille Grijalva and Willie Herron. Illustrated.

1934 Ruben Salazar Library, Sonoma State University, Sonoma, CA. Patricia Rodriguez: Chicano sculpture and masks. Exhibition invitation, 1981. English.

AN: Invitation to an exhibit.

1935 Ruiz, Elvia. Whitewashed mural. SENTIMIENTOS, Vol. 1, no. 2 (May 1978), p. 7-10. English.

AN: Illustrated article about Las Mujeres Muralistas del Valle. Their mural titled, "History of the Chicanos From a Woman's Perspective" was vandalized. Members of the mural group recall its creation and comment on its destruction.

1936 Salazar, Veronica. Aspiration comes true. SAN ANTONIO EXPRESS-NEWS, (October 28, 1979), p. 8-H. English.

AN: History of Alice Dickerson Montemayor of Laredo, Texas (known as "Admonty") who started to paint at 74 on the occasion of her second exhibit at the Mexican government's Instituto Cultural.

1937 San Antonio Museum of Modern Art. Zarzamora: inaugural exhibition of Ladrones de la Luz. Exhibition invitation, 1979. English.

AN: Illustrated invitation to photographic exhibition including Norman Avila, David Cardenas, Franco Cernero, Enrique Hernandez, Robert Maxham, James Newberry, Isaac Rodriguez, Daryl Studebaker, Richard Tichich, Beverly Ulmer, Kathy Vargas.

1938 San Francisco Museum of Modern Art, San Francisco, CA; Chavez, Ray; and Gordon, Allan M. Carmen Lomas Garza/prints and gouaches: Margo Humphrey/monotypes. Exhibition catalog, 1980. English.

AN: Carmen Lomas Garza, though working in a "naive" style is technically adept and academically trained, though she draws motifs from folk production of her native Texas. Her themes in this exhibit are memories of her childhood. Well illustrated.

1939 San Francisco Museum of Modern Art, San Francisco, CA and Marra, Patricia. Day of the dead. Exhibition catalog, 1980. English.

AN: Broadside announcement in the manner of Jose Gudalupe Posada for an exhibit of prints by Posada and an altar by Amalia Mesa-Baines and Friends. Text presents customs and traditions for celebrating the Day of the Dead in Mexico and among the Chicano community.

1940 San Francisco Museum of Modern Art, San Francisco, CA and Castellon, Rolando. People's murals: some events in American history. Exhibition catalog, 1976. English.

AN: Eight portable murals by San Francisco Bay Area artists including Graciela Carrillo, Anthony Machado, Robert Mendoza, Irene Perez, Mike Rios. Well Illustrated.

1941 San Pedro Municipal Art Gallery, San Pedro, CA. Celebration: Muriel Olguin and Linda Vallejo. San Pedro, CA: San Pedro Municipal Art Gallery, [1978]. English.

AN: Invitation to an exhibit. Illustrated.

Chicanas (cont.)

1942 Santa Ana College, Santa Ana, CA and
     Goldman, Shifra M. Chicano art. Exhibition
     catalog, 1974. English.

     AN: Thirteen California artists are
     presented in a short essay defining Chicano
     as a double mestizaje of Mexican mestizo and
     U.S. influences that exists in a state of
     "reconciled conflict." Its aim is
     communication. Artists included are
     Malaquias Montoya, Rupert Garcia, Manuel
     Hernandez, Esteban Villa, Robert Gomez,
     Harvey Tarango, Mary Helen Castro, Eduardo
     Carrillo, Graciela Carrillo, and "Los Four":
     Carlos Almaraz, Robert de la Rocha, Judithe
     Hernandez, Gilbert Lujan and Frank Romero.

1943 Santa Ana Public Library, Newhope Branch,
     Santa Ana, CA. Artistas latinos de Orange
     County. Exhibition brochure, 1979. English.

     AN: Exhibit of six artists: Dolores
     Grajeda, Eduardo Navarro, Arthur Valenzuela,
     Benjamin Valenzuela, Emigdio Vasquez, Susana
     A. Zaccagnino.

1944 Shakti Gallery, Long Beach, CA. "Fire in the
     lodge," paper sculptures by Linda Vallejo.
     Exhibit invitation, 1981. English.

     AN: Invitation to an exhibit by Long
     Beach, CA artist Linda Vallejo. Illustrated.

1945 Simpson, Claudette. An adobe fireplace:
     Anita Rodriguez has built many - each one
     different. PRESCOTT COURIER-WEEKLY FEATURE,
     (December 1, 1978). English.

     AN: Anita Rodriguez is an enjarradora--a
     professional specializing in adobe
     architecture--in New Mexico. She builds
     fireplaces, lays mud floors, builds hornos
     (outdoor ovens) and does interior and
     exterior plastering. Well illustrated.

1946 Soberon, Mercedes. La revolucion se trata de
     amor: Mercedes Soberon. CHISMEARTE, Vol. 1,
     no. 1 (Fall   1976), p. 14-18. Spanish.

     AN: Short interview with Mercedes
     Soberon, San Francisco artist involved with
     the art group Mission Media Arts. Mercedes
     talks about the role of women as organizers
     and artists, the sacrifices associated with
     this role, and the politics of San Francisco
     museums.

1947 Social and public art resource center.
     Brochure, [1977]. English.

     AN: Brochure including the history,
     philosophy, and resources of SPARC, an
     outgrowth of the Los Angeles Citywide Mural
     Project/Mural Resource Center headed by Judy
     Baca. Illustrated.

1948 Sorell, Victor A. Barrio murals in Chicago:
     painting the Hispanic-American experience on
     "our community" walls. REVISTA
     CHICANO-RIQUENA, Vol. 4, no. 4 (Fall
     1976), p. 51-72. English.

     AN: Important survey of Chicago's Latino
     murals, with key works considered in detail.
     Among the Chicano art organizations and
     muralists mentioned are MARCH (Movimiento
     Artistico Chicano), and Yolanda Galvan,
     Juanita Jaramillo, Jose Nario, Raymond
     Patlan, Vicente Mendoza, Marcos Raya,
     Ricardo Alonzo, Jose G. Gonzalez and Mario
     Castillo, author of the earliest Latino
     mural in Chicago (1968). Puerto Rican and

non-Latino muralists and mural groups are
also discussed. Well illustrated.

1949 Street, Sharon. Califas - a celebration of
     Chicano culture and art. CITY ON A HILL,
     (April 16, 1981). English.

     AN: Review of an exhibit at College V's
     Sesnon Gallery featuring 15 California
     artists: Ramses Noriega, Judy Baca, Salvador
     Roberto Torres, Malaquias Montoya, Rene
     Yanez, Ralph Maradiaga, Jose Montoya,
     Esteban Villa, Carmen Lomas Garza, Robert
     Chavez, among others. Illustrated.

1950 Texas Memorial Museum, University of Texas,
     Austin, TX. La vela prendida:
     Mexican-American women's home altars.
     Exhibition catalog, 1980. Bilingual.

     AN: Bilingual illustrated
     brochure-catalog of exhibit. Includes home
     altars and graveyard headstones.

1951 Time to greez: incantations from the Third
     World. San Francisco, CA: Glide
     Publications/Third World Communications,
     1975. English.

     AN: Rupert Garcia, drawing, p. 158;
     Xavier Viramontes, silkscreen, p. 181; Juan
     Fuentes, drawing, p. 188; Graciela Carrillo,
     drawing, p. 196.

1952 Trujillo, Marcella. The dilemma of the
     modern Chicana artist and critic. HERESIES,
     Vol. 2, no. 4 (1979), p. 5-10. English.

     AN: Recommended for its application to
     the visual arts in its discussion of
     iconography common to literature and art,
     and symbols popular with Chicana artists: La
     Malinche, the Virgin of Guadalupe,
     Tonantzin, Mother Earth, etc.

1953 University Art Museum, Berkeley, CA. The
     Fifth Sun: Contemporary/Traditional Chicano
     & Latino Art. Exhibition catalog, 1977.
     English.

     AN: Catalog of exhibit including 45
     artists of northern California. Texts deal
     with Mexican muralists, Mujeres Muralistas &
     other muralists, posters, the Chicano art
     movement, altars, La Raza Silkscreen Center,
     Galeria de la Raza, the Mexican Museum, the
     Sacramento Centro de Artistas Chicanos/RCAF.
     Mural maps of S.F. Bay Area and Sacramento.
     Many illustrations.

1954 University of Texas. San Antonio. Medical
     School and Lee, Amy Freeman. Consuelo
     Gonzales Amezcua. Exhibition catalog, n.d.
     English.

     AN: Exhibition catalog with a text by
     Amy Freeman Lee. This major exhibit
     presented 110 of the artist's works. Price
     list included.

Chicanas (cont.)

1955 Valdez, Armando. El calendario chicano 1975. Hayward, CA: Southwest Network, 1975. English.

AN: Third in a series of historical calendars produced in 1972 and 1974 by La Causa Publications and Southwest Network. Artists included for each month are Carmen Lomas Garza, Sergio Hernandez, Malaquias Montoya, Mujeres Muralistas (Graciela Carrillo, Venezuelan Consuelo Mendez, Irene Perez, Patricia Rodriguez), Ramses Noriega, Ernie Palomino, Amado Maurilio Pena, Martin Perez. All but Texan Pena are California artists.

1956 Valdez, Armando. El calendario chicano 1977. Hayward, CA: Southwest Network, 1977. English.

AN: Fifth in a series of historical calendars produced in 1972, 1974, 1975, 1976 by La Causa Publications and Southwest Network. Artists whose work is reproduced are Malaquias Montoya, Amado Maurilio Pena, Ramori Zamora, Glugio J.L. Nicandro [Gronk], Etta Delgado, Ricardo Alaniz, Diane Gamboa, Elisa Marina Coleman, Margarita Calderon, Jose Antonio Burciaga, Cesar Augusto Martinez, Maria Ochoa y Valtierra, Juan Renteria Fuentes, from California, New Mexico, and Texas.

1957 Valdez, Patssi and Gamboa, Diane. [Chicanas (drawing)]. REGENERACION, Vol. 2, no. 3 (1973), p. Cover.

1958 Valle, Victor Manuel. Rosemary Quesada-Weiner. SOMOS, Vol. 1, no. 3 (August 1978), p. 36-39. English.

AN: Profile of photographer, feminist, community activist Rosemary Quesada-Weiner who was a school "drop-out" at 13, but received her journalism degree and discovered photography at La Verne College. She is a freelance photo-journalist who specializes in Chicana/Latina women's images, but is not limited to that theme. Well illustrated.

1959 Vallejo, Linda. I am...Linda Vallejo. CHISMEARTE, Vol. 1, no. 4 (Fall , Winter, 1977, 1978), p. 27-30.

AN: Brief autobiographical sketch illustrated with three drawings.

1960 Varda, Agnes. Mur murs/mural murals on the wall ... Film, Cine Tamaris, Paris, 1980. English.

AN: Full length documentary film produced for French television; also available with English subtitles. Deals impressionistically with the murals and muralists of Los Angeles. Included are Wayne Alaniz Healy, David Botello, Willie Herron, Manuel Cruz, Judy Baca, the murals in Venice, CA, graffiti - among others. Color.

1961 Vasquez, Esperanza and Esparza, Moctezuma. Agueda Martinez. 16 mm. color film. English.

AN: Sixteen-minute film directed by Esperanza Vasquez and produced by Moctezuma Esparza concerning the life and weaving of an elderly New Mexican woman. Martinez carries on the tradition of floor loom weaving, as well as farming.

1962 Vasquez y Sanchez, Ramon. La Adelita.

CARACOL, Vol. 1, no. 9 (May 1975), p. 1.

1963 Venegas, Sybil. The artists and their work--the role of the Chicana artist. CHISMEARTE, Vol. 1, no. 4 (Fall , Winter, 1977), p. 3, 5. English.

1964 Venegas, Sybil. Conditions for producing Chicana art. CHISMEARTE, Vol. 1, no. 4 (Fall, Winter, 1977, 1978), p. 2, 4. English.

AN: Chicana artists face more obstacles than white women or Chicano counterparts in the arts. Mexican life style has portrayed the ideal of a submissive woman, but the values have changed. Chicana artists are concerned with women and their struggles. Muralists include Patricia Rodriguez, Irene Perez, Consuelo Mendez de Castillo, Susan Cervantes, Ester Hernandez, Miriam Olivo, Ruth Rodriguez, of the Mujeres Muralistas (San Francisco). Other artists are Etta Delgado and Barbara Carrasco.

1965 Vincent, Kathy Ariana. Monty Montemayor: portrait of an artist. ARRIBA, Vol. 1, no. 7 (1980). English.

AN: Born in Laredo, TX, in 1902, "Monty" Montemayor paints in the naif tradition. As an older artist, she has been a role model for younger Chicana artists. Brief profile of the self-taught artist. Illustrated.

1966 Walking tour and guide to the Great Wall at Tujunga Wash. Venice, CA: Social and Public Art Resource Center, [1981]. English.

AN: History and symbolism of the GREAT WALL, directed by Judy Baca, and created by teams of young people working on the mural since 1976. Illustrated.

1967 Wilson, Michael and Biberman, Herbert. Salt of the earth [film]. 16mm, 94 min., b&w. English.

AN: The first feature film made in the U.S. of, by and for labor, it deals with a real strike of Mexican American miners in New Mexico in which women played a key role in the men's victory and their own demands. Mexican actress Rosaura Revueltas starred with labor leader Juan Chacon. One of the best films on the subject.

1968 Wilson, William. Chicana artists still seeking identification. LOS ANGELES TIMES, (June 23, 1975), p. VI, 5. English.

AN: Ten Chicana artists are exhibiting their work in the Boathouse Gallery of Plaza de la Raza in Lincoln Park: Judithe Hernandez, Patssi Valdez, Judy Baca, Josefina Quesada, Victoria del Castillo-Leon, Olga Muniz, Gloria Flores, Sylvia Morales, Isabel Castro and Celia Tejadak. The work is still tentative and may develop.

1969 Wine and cheese: foto fun. Berkeley, CA: Exhibition invitation, 1979. English.

AN: Invitation to an evening of photographic slides and prints and discussion by photographers Jose Romero and Maria Pinedo.

Chicanas (cont.)

1970 Woman who began at 73 is shaping Chicano
art. SAN ANTONIO EXPRESS-NEWS, (August 18,
1978), p. 6-W. English.

AN: 76-year-old Laredoan Alicia
Dickerson Montemayor who began painting on
guajes (gourds) from her garden three years
ago, now paints on canvas stories from her
life in the Valley, nature, and people. An
exhibit of her work, referred to by Chicano
art critics as "el arte de la inocencia"
opens at Gallery of El Centro Cultural de
LUCHA, in Austin, TX.

1971 Woman's Building, Los Angeles, CA.
Crosspollination: a blending of traditional
and contemporary art by Asian, Black and
Chicana women. Los Angeles, CA: Woman's
Building, 1979. English.

AN: Invitation to an exhibit in which
are included Patricia Murillo and Linda
Vallejo.

1972 Women artists: forming a Texas network.
Brochure, 1979. English.

AN: Biographic and bibliographic
information on women artists groups from
Austin, Dallas, Houston and San Antonio.
Includes brief history of MAS (Mujeres
Artistas del Suroeste), a list of members,
and biographies of Alicia Arredondo, Santa
Barraza, Mary Ann Ambray Gonzalez, and
Sylvia Orozco.

1973 Xochil Art and Culture Center, Mission, TX.
Besame mucho. Exhibition invitation, 1979.
English.

AN: Invitation to exhibit of Texas
artists from Mujeres Artistas del Suroeste
(MAS): Mary Ann Anguiano, Alicia Arredondo,
Santa Barraza, Nora Gonzales-Dodson, Maria
Flores, Carolina Flores, Mary Ann Ambray
Gonzales, Sylvia Orozco, Nancy de los
Santos, Modesta Barbina Trevino.
Illustrated.

Chicanismo

1974 Martinez, Cesar Augusto; Garcia-Camarillo,
Mia; and Garcia-Camarillo, Cecilio. Don Juan
Volador, Platica con Cesar Augusto Martinez.
CARACOL, Vol. 2, no. 4 (December 1975), p.
3-5. Spanish.

AN: Interview with Cesar Martinez about
his acrylic painting DON JUAN VOLADOR. Based
on themes suggested by the writings of
Carlos Castaneda, the painting deals with
the spiritual nature of Chicanismo. This
issue of CARACOL is illustrated by the
painting in question.

CHICANISMO EN EL ARTE [exhibit]

1975 Gamboa, Harry, Jr. Seis imaginaciones:
artistas chicanos en Los Angeles. COMUNIDAD,
(July 13, 1980), p. 10. Spanish.

AN: A limited flow of media information
about Los Angeles Chicanos has produced a
"ghost" culture. Only sensational events are
published. Alternative magazines like LA
RAZA, CON SAFOS, and REGENERACION have
disseminated Chicano ideas of the 1970s. The
Chicano imagination has appeared in murals
by Willie Herron, Gronk, Carlos Almaraz,
John Valadez; in pieces like "walking" and
"instant" murals by the group ASCO; by the
group Los Four; by group exhibits like

"Chicanismo en el arte," and "Chicanarte."
Patssi Valdez showed Photobooth Piece at the
"Chicanismo" show. Gronk and Jerry Dreva
exhibited their mail art at "Punk Meets
Art." In Spanish.

Chicano Arts Council, UCLA

1976 Romero, Raul V. Chicanarte, a major
exposition of California arts. NEWORLD,
(Fall   1975). English.

AN: CHICANARTE at the Los Angeles
Municipal Gallery, Barnsdall Park from Sept.
14 -Oct. 12, 1975 remains the most
comprehensive statewide exposition of
Chicano arts in California. This article
details the production apparatus and history
of the exposition. In particular, the
contributions of Al Frente Communications,
Inc., the Chicano Arts Council of U.C.L.A.
and the Comite Chicanarte. Illustrated.

Chicano Cinema Coalition

1977 Chicano cinema coalition. Mimeographed copy,
September 1, 1979. English.

AN: An informational bulletin about the
Coalition founded July 1978 in Los Angeles
of forty independent producers and
filmmakers who joined together for "the
development, production, distribution,
promotion and exhibition...of film and video
productions which meaningfully
address...needs and concerns of the Latino
people in the United States." Professionals
with their own companies (Amanecer Films,
Bilingual Educational Services, Luis Ruiz
Productions), television producers, and
post-graduate film students make up the
group. The Coalition published the CHICANO
CINEMA NEWSLETTER. Ties are promoted with
Latin American cinema people.

1978 CHICANO CINEMA NEWSLETTER. Vol. 1, no. 6
(August 1979). English.

AN: Announcements of the San Antonio
Chicano Film Festival, a seminar on the
business of art, the receipt of a report of
the Task Force on Minorities in Public
Broadcasting, a critical report on the
Alternative Cinema Conference in New York,
which was attended by eleven members of the
Chicano Cinema Coalition, and a report and
critique of the report by the Task Force.

1979 CHICANO CINEMA NEWSLETTER. Vol. 1, no. 4
(June 1979). English.

AN: Report and cautionary note on the
upcoming Alternative Cinema Conference;
announcement of ONLY ONCE IN A LIFETIME and
CHICANA film releases; other new films and
TV programs; a Chicano cinema bibliography;
a list of Chicano production companies and
distributors; a theoretical article on the
nature (proposed) of Chicano cinema as an
alternative cinema; statement of purpose of
the Los Angeles Chicano Cinema Coalition.

---   --

Chicano Cinema Coalition (cont.)

1980 Kleinhaus, Chuck; Seiter, Ellen; and Steven, Peter. Conference report: struggling for unity. JUMP CUT, no. 21 (November 1979), p. 35-37. English.

AN: Report and critique of the U.S. Conference for an Alternative Cinema held in mid-June 1979 at Bard College in New York state to chart a course for independent filmmakers. Chicano, Black, Asian and Puerto Rican film people attended, including Jesus Salvador Trevino and Sylvia Morales from the Chicano Cinema Coalition of Los Angeles.

CHICANO CINEMA NEWSLETTER, Los Angeles, CA

1981 Chicano cinema coalition. Mimeographed copy, September 1, 1979. English.

AN: An informational bulletin about the Coalition founded July 1978 in Los Angeles of forty independent producers and filmmakers who joined together for "the development, production, distribution, promotion and exhibition...of film and video productions which meaningfully address...needs and concerns of the Latino people in the United States." Professionals with their own companies (Amanecer Films, Bilingual Educational Services, Luis Ruiz Productions), television producers, and post-graduate film students make up the group. The Coalition published the CHICANO CINEMA NEWSLETTER. Ties are promoted with Latin American cinema people.

Chicano Film Festival (III), San Antonio, TX, August 24-25, 1978

1982 Gloria, Juan J. En San Antonio: se celebrara el tercer festival de cine, 'La vida chicana a traves del celuloide'. EL VISITANTE DOMINICAL, (August 20, 1978), p. 6-8, 12. Spanish.

AN: The Third Chicano Film Festival honors the only two feature-length films made by Chicanos: Moctezuma Esparza's ONLY ONCE IN A LIFETIME (made in Hollywood) and Jesus Salvador Trevino's RAICES DE SANGRE (Blood Roots), (made with CONACINE in Mexico). Illustrated.

CHICANO FROM THE SOUTHWEST [film]

1983 Films for the inner city. Los Angeles, CA: Los Angeles Public Library Federal Project, 1971. English.

AN: Annotated catalog of 16mm films and filmstrips, educational and documentary. Those concerning Mexican heritage include CHICANO FROM THE SOUTHWEST (1970), HENRY...BOY OF THE BARRIO (1969); HOW'S SCHOOL, ENRIQUE (1970), I AM JOAQUIN (1970), THE MEXICAN AMERICAN: HERITAGE AND DESTINY (1970), A MEXICAN AMERICAN FAMILY (1970), MEXICAN AMERICANS: QUEST FOR EQUALITY (1968), MEXICAN OR AMERICAN (1970), SIQUEIROS: "EL MAESTRO" (THE MARCH OF HUMANITY IN LATIN AMERICA) (1969). Filmstrips include THE AWAKENING (LA RAZA) - Part IV, CONFLICT OF CULTURES (LA RAZA) - Part III, MASTERWORKS OF MEXICAN ART, OUT OF THE MAINSTREAM, PILGRIMAGE (GRAPE STRIKERS). Also listed are films and filmstrips for children.

CHICANO MORATORIUM AFTERMATH [film]

1984 Gamboa, Harry, Jr. Film, television, and Trevino. LA LUZ, Vol. 6, no. 10 (October

1977), p. 7-8. English.

AN: Jesus Salvador Trevino has been an active proponent and participant in transforming cultural inaccuracy about Chicanos in the media to accurate mass media models. A biography of Trevino follows, including discussion of some of his films: THE SALAZAR INQUEST, CHICANO MORATORIUM AFTERMATH, SOLEDAD, AMERICA TROPICAL, YO SOY CHICANO, RAICES DE SANGRE, as well as television series like ACCION CHICANO, AHORA, and INFINITY FACTORY.

Chicano Moratorium Coalition

1985 NATIONAL MURALS NETWORK COMMUNITY NEWSLETTER. (Fall 1980). English.

AN: Reports on murals in San Francisco, CA, by the Chicano Moratorium Coalition; in Chicago about the Anti-War Preparations mural; in Houston by a student at the Association for Advancement of Mexican Americans; on Michael Schorr's mural in Chicanok, San Diego, CA; on a segment being painted at the Tujunga Wash mural in Los Angeles under Judy Baca; on south San Diego murals being painted out; Alan Barnett's survey of Southwest murals. Illustrated.

Chicano Movement

1986 Barrios, Lex. The barrio as a work of art: Chicano muralism in Laredo, Texas? REVISTA RIO BRAVO, Vol. 1, no. 3 (Fall 1981), p. 5, 15-16. English.

AN: Report by Laredo sociologist on local conservative attitudes toward the Chicano movement and muralism, and a meeting held to plan a mural project in Laredo so it could finally enter the mural movement. Illustrated.

1987 Chavez, Jaime and Vallecillo, Ana Maria. A political, historical, philosophical perspective of muralist art in the Southwest. RAYAS, Vol. 1, no. 3 (May, June, 1978), p. 6. English.

AN: Relates Chicano mural art to main issues of the Chicano movement. The Mechicano Art Center in Los Angeles and Artes Guadalupanos de Aztlan in Santa Fe are seen as examples of groups creating a new people's art; art forms where esthetics are allied to politics.

1988 Crusade for Justice, Denver, CO. Los artistas de Aztlan. Mimeographed copy, 1969. English.

AN: Resolutions from the Chicano Youth Conference (March-April, 1969) on the role of art and artists within the Chicano movement. An important document.

1989 Freedom of expression and the Chicano Movement: an open letter to Dr. Philip Ortego. LA LUZ, Vol. 2, no. 5 (September 1973), p. 28-29. English.

AN: An unattributed letter questioning the imposition of norms on Chicano art. The author criticizes the practice of unquestioningly assigning rubrics like "Mexican" or "Chicano" to certain styles while excluding others produced by Mexican American artists.

Chicano Movement (cont.)

1990 Garcia, Rupert. La Raza murals of
California, 1963 to 1970: a period of social
change and protest. Master's thesis, UC
Berkeley, 1981. English.

AN: Important introduction to a selected
group of murals from Northern and Southern
California. Garcia deals with murals of
"accommodation" from 1960 to 1965; the
Chicano protest movement, 1965 and 1970; and
Chicano protest murals from 1968 to 1970.
Murals are discussed within historical,
political and cultural contexts.
Illustrated.

1991 Jose Montoya: poeta, pintor, profesor,
humanista, padre, abuelo. EL HISPANO, Vol.
8, no. 27 (December 23, 1975), p. 5.
Spanish.

AN: Biographical data on the Sacramento
artist, his contributions to the Chicano
Movement and his life as an artist-activist.
Photographs of his family and reproduction
of one drawing.

1992 Martinez, Manuel. The art of the Chicano
movement, and the movement of Chicano art.
In: Valdez, Luis and Steiner, Stan eds.
AZTLAN: AN ANTHOLOGY OF MEXICAN AMERICAN
LITERATURE. New York: Vintage, 1972,
p.349-353. English.

AN: "Like the modern art of Mexico, the
new Chicano art is essentially an art of
social protest," writes Denver, Colorado
muralist and easel painter Martinez. He
traces the roots of Chicano art back into
Indian, colonial and modern Mexican art, and
defines two kinds of Chicano art.

1993 Monteverde, Mildred. Contemporary Chicano
art. AZTLAN, Vol. 2, no. 2 (Fall   1971), p.
51-61. Bibliography. English.

AN: An historical survey of trends and
influences on contemporary Chicano art.
Discusses San Diego's Toltecas en Aztlan and
the projected Centro Cultural de la Raza;
Los Angeles' Mechicano Art Center, Goez
Gallery and Plaza de la Raza; pinto (prison)
art; New Mexican art. Many artists are
mentioned.

1994 La onda artistica de Carmen Lomas Garza.
MAGAZIN, Vol. 1, no. 2 (November 1971), p.
29-37. Spanish.

AN: Short biographical sketch of artist
and reproduction of seven early drawings.
The art of Carmen Lomas Garza is situated
within important events of the Chicano
Movement in Texas: the student walkouts in
Kingsville, and the formation of Colegio
Jacinto Trevino.

**Chicano National Congress for Land and Cultural
Reform, Albuquerque, NM**

1995 Pepe and Pepito. SANTA FE NEW MEXICAN,
(October 11, 1972), p. A7. English.

AN: The unveiling of a mural entitled
"Rebirth of the Chicano" will take places on
the eve (Oct., 19) of the First Chicano
National Congress for Land and Cultural
Reform held in Albuquerque Oct., 20-22. (See
"Chicano Congress Set for Albuquerque" SFNM
6/21/72).

Chicano Park, San Diego, CA

1996 Cabaniss, Joe H. Mural painters believes
vandalism political act. CHULA VISTA STAR
NEWS, (March 16, 1980), p. 40-41. English.

AN: Recent vandalism on Chicano Park's
twenty outdoor murals left seven splattered
with paint. It was the second such incident
in five months. Michael Schnorr,
Southwestern College art instructor and
painter of two murals, believes the attack
was politically motivated. Illustrated.
Reprinted in COMMUNITY MURALISTS NEWSLETTER,
Spring 1981.

1997 El Centro Cultural de La Raza, San Diego, CA
and Enrique, Veronica. Tenth anniversary
celebration, July 11, 1981. San Diego, CA:
El Centro Cultural de la Raza, 1981.
English.

AN: Anniversary brochure of the Centro,
founded in 1970 by the Toltecas en Aztlan
artistic collective and established at its
Balboa Park location in 1971. Briefly
reviews the history and activities of the
Centro, including the establishment of
Chicano Park in 1970 and the painting of
murals at the Park and at the Centro. Well
illustrated.

1998 Gardiner, Henry G. Painted exterior walls of
Southern California. CURRANT ART MAGAZINE,
Vol. 1, no. 2 (June, July, 1975), p. 16-23+.
English.

AN: Good survey of street muralism,
primarily in Los Angeles and San Diego,
which started in 1968. Divided into eight
"schools," including Chicano and non-Chicano
muralists. Most Chicano murals associated
with Goez Brothers Art Gallery and Mechicano
Art Center in Los Angeles, the Coronado Bay
Bridge group [Chicano Park] and Balboa Park
group [Centro Cultural de la Raza]. Mural
discussed in detail. Well illustrated.

1999 Herrera, Barbara. Bisected barrio seeks new
unity: Chicano part bridges past and future.
EVENING TRIBUNE, (August 7, 1974), p. E-1.
English.

AN: Bisected by the Coronado bridge,
remains of the Logan barrio are unified by
Chicano Park and its murals recording
Chicano culture. Inspired by Salvador
Torres, who returned to Logan in 1967,
barrio activists are working to restore
community spirit and dignity. Illustrated.

2000 Herrera, Barbara. Chicano park expansion
sought: barrio idealists face strong
barriers. EVENING TRIBUNE, (August 10,
1974), p. A-10. English.

AN: Last of a three part series on
Chicano Park. Barrio activists of the
Chicano Park Steering Committee plan to
extend the Chicano Park under the Coronado
bridge from 5.8 acres to the bay, painting
all the pillars with murals, and ending with
a small marina. They are facing opposition
from government officials, but are hopeful
of success.

Chicano Park, San Diego, CA (cont.)

2001 Herrera, Barbara. The pillars are our trees: Chicano park needs planning, power. EVENING TRIBUNE, (August 8, 1974), p. D-1. English.

AN: In the face of government and business opposition, activists obtained the land under the Coronado bridge to establish Chicano Park. They want to extend the park to the waterfront. Illustrated.

2002 Knilli, Monika and Knilli, Friedrich. Linke allegorien & lebende bilder der ghettos: das Americanische mural-movement. TENDENZEN, (November, December, 1977), p. 27-32. Other.

AN: Illustrated story on U.S. murals including those of East Los Angeles and Chicano Park, San Diego. The November-December issue of 1977 is numbered 116.

2003 Lyle, Cindy. Chicano mural art: a mixture of the barrio's rage and pride. NEW YORK TIMES, (August 17, 1975), p. Sec.2, 21. English.

AN: Brief history of San Diego's Chicano Park, why and how it was established, and the establishment of the Centro Cultural de la Raza in Balboa Park. Iconography of several murals is examined, and the longevity of outdoor murals discussed. Illustrated.

2004 Mujeres muralistas de San Diego. CITYBENDER, Vol. 2, no. 7 (1978). English.

AN: Photographic essay on four women working on their mural at Chicano Park, San Diego.

2005 NATIONAL MURALS NETWORK COMMUNITY NEWSLETTER. (Spring 1981). English.

AN: Reports, or illustrations, of murals by Guillermo Aranda (Calif.), Francisco Lefebre (New Mexico); Marcos Raya's section of Chicago's anti-war mural; Gilberto Guzman's mural (New Mexico); vandalism on a Michael Schnorr mural at Chicano Park, San Diego, Calif.

2006 NATIONAL MURALS NETWORK COMMUNITY NEWSLETTER. (Fall 1980). English.

AN: Reports on murals in San Francisco, CA, by the Chicano Moratorium Coalition; in Chicago about the Anti-War Preparations mural; in Houston by a student at the Association for Advancement of Mexican Americans; on Michael Schorr's mural in Chicanok, San Diego, CA; on a segment being painted at the Tujunga Wash mural in Los Angeles under Judy Baca; on south San Diego murals being painted out; Alan Barnett's survey of Southwest murals. Illustrated.

2007 NATIONAL MURALS NETWORK COMMUNITY NEWSLETTER. (1978). English.

AN: This issue features reports from muralists. Includes information about murals at: La Pena Cultural Center in Berkeley, CA; the Social and Public Art Resource Center's Tujunga Wash Mural in Venice, CA; the Citywide Mural Project in Los Angeles, CA; activities at Chicano Park, and of the Congress of American Cosmic Artists (CACA), both in San Diego, CA; murals in San Mateo County, CA; the Task Force on Hispanic American Arts headed by Jacinto Quirarte of San Antonio; the 1978 Canto Al Pueblo in Corpus Christi, TX; murals in Chicago; and

other works by non-Chicano artists.

2008 Ordorica, Leticia. Community expression in muralism. VOZ FRONTERIZA, Vol. 3, no. 5 (March 1978). English.

AN: Brief history of Chicano Park in San Diego. Announcement of the "Mural Marathon" from April 1 to April 20, two days before the Eighth Annual Chicano Park Celebration. Five pillars and the kiosk will be painted. Illustration.

2009 Orth, Maureen. The soaring spirit of Chicano arts. NEW WEST MAGAZINE, Vol. 3, no. 19 (September 11, 1978), p. 41-46. English.

AN: Overview of California Chicano culture. Color illustrations of works by Mexican muralist David Alfaro Siqueiros, Rupert Garcia, Mujeres Muralistas, Willie Herron, Rene Yanez, Rudy Martinez, San Diego's Chicano Park, ASCO, Jose Montoya.

Chicano Park Steering Committee

2010 Herrera, Barbara. Chicano park expansion sought: barrio idealists face strong barriers. EVENING TRIBUNE, (August 10, 1974), p. A-10. English.

AN: Last of a three part series on Chicano Park. Barrio activists of the Chicano Park Steering Committee plan to extend the Chicano Park under the Coronado bridge from 5.8 acres to the bay, painting all the pillars with murals, and ending with a small marina. They are facing opposition from government officials, but are hopeful of success.

EL CHICANO (San Bernardino, CA)

2011 Garcia, Rupert. A source for mural art education: an annotated bibliography of three Chicano newspapers. Unpublished paper, 1974 (Chicano Studies Library, Univ. of California, Berkeley). English.

AN: A research project showing how Chicano newspapers reported and educated their readers to mural activity by Raza artists during the period 1968-1978. The newspapers analized are EL GALLO (Denver, CO), EL CHICANO (San Bernardino, CA), and EL TECOLOTE (San Francisco, CA). Author draws eight conclusions about the form, meaning and significance of mural activity in Chicano barrios and the importance of community newspapers as a fruitful and meaningful source for art education.

Chicano Studies

2012 Goldman, Shifra M. Artistas en accion: conferencia de las mujeres chicanas. COMUNIDAD, (August 10, 1980), p. 15. Spanish.

AN: In Chicano Studies programs, the fine arts have had second class status to social sciences and literature. Similarly a Chicano Issues Conference overlooked artists until a special effort was made. A round table, which included visual artists Gloriamalia Flores and Carmen Lomas Garza, discussed the social functions of art, woman as an image maker, problems of the Chicana as creator and cultural worker, and professionalism in the arts.

Chicano Studies Department, University of California, Berkeley

2013 Garcia, Rupert. 'Fifth Sun' Raza art show at UC Berkeley Museum. EL TECOLOTE, Vol. 8, no. 3 (November 1977), p. 8+. English.

AN: Review of THE FIFTH SUN: CONTEMPORARY TRADITIONAL CHICANO AND LATINO ART, co-sponsored by University of California, Berkeley Chicano Studies and Arte Popular, and curated by artist Ralph Maradiaga, co-director of Galeria de la Raza, showing at the UC Berkeley Museum. It will travel to the University of California, Santa Barbara's Art Museum. Illustrated.

Chicano Studies Research Center, UCLA

2014 Film collection of the Chicano Library. Chicano Studies Research Center, UCLA, 1972. English.

AN: Description, producers, rentals of 15 films made by or about Chicanos and Mexicans, and available through the Center.

Chicano Studies Research Library, UCLA

2015 Carrillo, Eduardo; Hernandez, Sergio; and Noriega, Ramses. Mural, Chicano Research Library, UCLA [photograph]. AZTLAN, Vol. 3, no. 1 (Spring 1972), p. [VIII-IX].

2016 Depicts Chicano attitudes: library receives new mural. DAILY BRUIN, (September 29, 1970), p. 6. English.

AN: Illustrated story of mural painted in UCLA's Mexican American Library by Eduardo Carrillo, Ramses Noriega, Sergio Hernandez, Saul Solache.

2017 Kahn, David. Chicano street murals: people's art in the East Los Angeles barrio. AZTLAN, Vol. 6, no. 1 (Spring 1975), p. 117-121. Bibliography. English.

AN: A study of Chicano mural painting starting with the 1970 mural at UCLA by Eduardo Carrillo, Ramses Noriega, Sergio Hernandez, and Saul Solache. Deals with mural symbols, graffiti, and works by John Alverer [sic] and Willie Herron's murals in the Ramona Gardens Housing Project.

2018 Mural at U.C.L.A.'s Chicano Library: detail. LA GENTE DE AZTLAN, Vol. 1, no. 6 (May 31, 1971), p. 1. English.

AN: Reproduction of detail, Chicano Library mural painted in 1971.

2019 Mural at U.C.L.A.'s Chicano Library: detail. LA GENTE DE AZTLAN, Vol. 1, no. 6 (May 31, 1971), p. Ft cover,4.

AN: UCLA's Chicano Library mural: details of the mural on the front page and p. 4.

CHICANO TIME TRIP [mural]

2020 Los Dos Streetscapers. Los Dos Streetscapers, mural detail. NATIONAL GEOGRAPHIC, Vol. 155, no. 1 (January 1979), p. 38-39. English.

AN: One panel of Los Angeles mural by Wayne Alaniz Healey and David Botello, CHICANO TIME TRIP.

Chicano Youth Conference, March-April, 1969

2021 Crusade for Justice, Denver, CO. Los artistas de Aztlan. Mimeographed copy, 1969. English.

AN: Resolutions from the Chicano Youth Conference (March-April, 1969) on the role of art and artists within the Chicano movement. An important document.

Chicanos Artistas Sirviendo a Aztlan (CASA), Austin, TX

2022 Palma Castroman, Janis. ENCUENTRO ARTISTICO FEMENIL [exhibit], Austin, TX, November 28, 1977. TEJIDOS, Vol. 5, no. 1 (1978), p. 1-47. Bilingual.

AN: A multimedia, multicultural exposition by 26 Chicana artists held at Juarez-Lincoln University. The exhibit was sponsored by Chicanos Artistas Sirviendo a Aztlan (CASA) and Mujeres Artistas del Suroeste (MAS).

2023 Palma Castroman, Janis. Introduccion. TEJIDOS, Vol. 5, no. 1 (1978), p. 1. Spanish.

AN: One-page introduction to theme issue featuring the work of Chicana artists exhibited at the ENCUENTRO ARTISTICO FEMENIL exposition held on November 28, 1977 in Austin, TX.

CHICANOS, CUBA Y LOS 10 MILLONES [exhibit]

2024 Grimke, Angelina. Chicano art finds home in Mission galeria. PEOPLE'S WORLD, Vol. 33, no. 32 (August 8, 1970), p. 11. English.

AN: Commentary on the exhibition CHICANOS, CUBA Y LOS 10 MILLONES held at the original Galeria de la Raza at 425 14th Street in San Francisco. The show presented photographs by Jay Ojeda and Roberto Perez-Diaz, drawings by Gloria Ozuna together with paintings and photographs by Cuban artist Mederos. Provides information about the goals of the Galeria as the visual arts department of Casa Hispana de Bellas Artes. Exhibition curator was Rolando Castellon.

Children

2025 Gonzalez, Hector. Aztlandia. EL HISPANO, Vol. 5, no. 2 (June 20, 1972).

AN: Story and photographs of a childrens sculptural park created by Pedro Ximenez.

2026 Ozuna, Gloria. El tamal [drawing]. CARACOL, Vol. 3, no. 7 (March 1977), p. Cover 4-21.

2027 Torres, Louis R. An innovation in children's t.v.: THE INFINITY FACTORY. LA LUZ, Vol. 6, no. 2 (February 1977), p. 10-11. English.

AN: Illustrated report on a new television series for children aimed at teaching mathematics fundamentals in a crisply-paced series of half-hour programs. The executive producer, Jesus Salvador Trevino, filmed the segments in a New York Black community and in the East Los Angeles Chicano barrio. In one segment, muralist Willie Herron works with youngsters to design and paint an outdoor mural.

CHILDREN OF THE STATE [film]

2028 Rivera, Humberto R. Film notes. CHISMEARTE,
Vol. 1, no. 2 (Winter, Spring, 1977), p.
20-24. English.

AN: Summary of films produced by and/or
about Chicanos for cinema and television.
Includes REALIDADES (TV) by David Sandoval,
Rudy Vargas, Luis Torres, Jose Luis Ruiz,
Antonio Reyes; A POLITICAL RENAISSANCE from
the LA RAZA series (TV) by Moctezuma
Esparza; CHILDREN OF THE STATE by Andres
Markovits, Richard Trubo, Frank Christopher
(film); LA RAZA UNIDA (released as RAICES DE
SANGRE) by Jesus Salvador Trevino (Mexican
film by a Chicano); CHULAS FRONTERAS (film)
by Les Blank; THE MURALS OF EAST LOS
ANGELES, A MUSEUM WITHOUT WALLS by Humberto
R. Rivera and Heather R. Howell.
Announcement for the National Latino Media
Coalition.

Children's Literature

2029 Carrillo, Graciela. El frijol magico.
Berkeley, CA: Center for Open Learning and
Teaching, 1974. Spanish.

AN: Children's book conceived and
illustrated in color by Carrillo.

2030 Johnston, Jerry. A man with a message: let's
build strength, pride. DESERET NEWS, (June
28, 1980), p. S3. English.

AN: Story on Nephtali De Leon,
playwright, poet, and illustrator of
children's literature. In addition to I WILL
CATCH THE SUN and I COLOR MY GARDEN
children's books, he works with oil
painting, stained glass and woodcuts.

Chile

2031 Galeria de la Raza/Studio 24, San Francisco,
CA. Por Chile: silkscreens from President
Allende cultural campaign. Exhibition
invitation, [1973]. English.

AN: Invitation to an exhibit: the first
U.S. showing of Chilean posters.

CHISMEARTE Magazine

2032 Concilio de arte popular. CHISMEARTE, Vol.
1, no. 2 (Winter, Spring, 1977), p. 54.
English.

AN: Report of a meeting February 12,
1977 by the Concilio de Arte Popular (CAP)
which published CHISMEARTE. Introduces
members of the Board and summarizes
discussions of problems of the organization
and their publication.

2033 Yarbro-Bejarano, Yvonne. Resena critica de
revistas literarias chicanas: problemas y
tendencias. LA PALABRA, Vol. 3, no. 1-2
(Spring, Fall , 1981), p. 123-137. Spanish.

AN: Continuation of review of Chicano
magazines from Texas, California, and
Washington. The article discusses content,
literary and artistic format, and other
aspects, taking a critical stance (See LA
PALABRA, Spring 1980).

Cholos
USE: Batos Locos

Cholos, Images by
USE: Pachuco Images

CHOQUE DE AMOR [fotonovela]

2034 Colectivo El Ojo. CHOQUE DE AMOR: fotonovela
by Lamp. CHISMEARTE, Vol. 1, no. 4 (Fall ,
Winter, 1977), p. 35-37. Bilingual.

AN: Several students with the help of
the Latin American Media Project (LAMP) and
the Latin American Studies Department of
California State University, Los Angeles
produced the fotonovela CHOQUE DE AMOR, a
variation on the typical "fotonovela"
romance. This one encourages readers to
reevaluate traditional female roles. The
group also includes Kay Torres. Six frames
of the fotonovela are reproduced.

Christmas

2035 Burciaga, Jose Antonio. Adoracion [drawing].
REVISTA CHICANO-RIQUENA, Vol. 3, no. 4 (Fall
1975), p. 31. Spanish.

2036 Burciaga, Jose Antonio. Nacimiento
[drawing]. REVISTA CHICANO-RIQUENA, Vol. 3,
no. 4 (Fall 1975), p. 21. Spanish.

2037 Burciaga, Jose Antonio. La posada [drawing].
REVISTA CHICANO-RIQUENA, Vol. 3, no. 4 (Fall
1975), p. COVER. Spanish.

2038 Burciaga, Jose Antonio. Los tres magos
[drawing]. REVISTA CHICANO-RIQUENA, Vol. 3,
no. 4 (Fall 1975), p. 2. Spanish.

Chronology
USE: Calendars

CHULAS FRONTERAS [film]

2039 Rivera, Humberto R. Film notes. CHISMEARTE,
Vol. 1, no. 2 (Winter, Spring, 1977), p.
20-24. English.

AN: Summary of films produced by and/or
about Chicanos for cinema and television.
Includes REALIDADES (TV) by David Sandoval,
Rudy Vargas, Luis Torres, Jose Luis Ruiz,
Antonio Reyes; A POLITICAL RENAISSANCE from
the LA RAZA series (TV) by Moctezuma
Esparza; CHILDREN OF THE STATE by Andres
Markovits, Richard Trubo, Frank Christopher
(film); LA RAZA UNIDA (released as RAICES DE
SANGRE) by Jesus Salvador Trevino (Mexican
film by a Chicano); CHULAS FRONTERAS (film)
by Les Blank; THE MURALS OF EAST LOS
ANGELES, A MUSEUM WITHOUT WALLS by Humberto
R. Rivera and Heather R. Howell.
Announcement for the National Latino Media
Coalition.

Cid, Armando

2040 And/Or Gallery, Seattle, WA. Artistas de
Aztlan. Exhibition announcement, 1975.
English.

AN: Exhibition announcement for an
important exhibit of Northwest Chicano art.
Co-sponsored by MEChA and the Chicano
Studies Program at the University of
Washington, the exhibit presented works by
Emilio Aguayo, Danny Desiga, Ricardo
Aguirre, Ramiro Benavidez, Elma Herada,
Pedro Rodriguez and others. A selection of
posters by Armando Cid of the R.C.A.F. group
from Sacramento, California was also
presented. Concurrently, at the Heny Gallery
of the University of Washington, Esteban
Villa presented a one-man show.

Cid, Armando (cont.)

2041 Armando Cid art works on display at Barrio Gallery. EL HISPANO, Vol. 5, no. 44 (April 24, 1973). English.

AN: Description of Armando Cid's M.A. thesis exhibition. The dominant impulse in the paintings is an attempt to define and reflect a Chicano style.

2042 California. State College. Los Angeles. Art Gallery. Twelve Chicano artists. Exhibition invitation, n.d. English.

AN: Invitation to an exhibit: Jose Montoya, Gilbert Sanchez Lujan, Esteban Villa, Rene Yanez, Joe Moran, Armando Cid, Leonard Castellas, Juanishi Orozco, Rudy Cuellar, Beltran, Lopez and Cabrera.

2043 Gonzalez, Hector and Cid, Armando. An interview with Armando Cid. EL HISPANO, Vol. 5, no. 32 (January 23, 1973). English.

AN: Biographical information and commentary on Cid's career and his art style which is described as containing pre-Columbian motifs and mannerisms of the people in the barrio.

2044 Montoya, Jose E. and Murguia, Alejandro. El sol y los de abajo and other R.C.A.F. poems / oracion a la mano poderosa. San Francisco, CA: Ediciones Pocho-Che, 1972. English.

AN: 10 illustrations by Sacramento, CA artist Armando Cid.

2045 Valencia, Manuel. Store front academy for Chicano artists. SACRAMENTO UNION, (January 17, 1973). English.

AN: Article includes comments by Armando Cid, Ricardo Fabela and Jose Montoya in a free-wheeling discussion of the goals and underlying philosophy of the Centro de Artistas Chicanos in Sacramento. More than simply exposing the people to art, the artists explain that they are looking for an alternative art expression and method of instruction never offered in traditional art schools or university departments of art.

Cinco de Mayo

2046 Chairez, Bob. Bob's Chicano chronicles: the spirit of Cinco de Mayo=el espiritu de Cinco de Mayo [drawing]. CAMINOS, Vol. 1, no. 3 (May 1980), p. 46.

2047 The Mexican Museum, San Francisco, CA. Cinco de Mayo exhibit at the Cannery. Exhibition brochure, 1980. English.

AN: Well-illustrated brochure with text by Nora Wagner and Bea Carrillo Hocker. Succinct statements on the history, purpose and programs of the Mexican Museum.

Cine Chicanesco

2048 Vasquez, Richard. Mojado power: a boost for illegal aliens. CALENDAR, (February 22, 1981), p. 41. English.

AN: An uncritical review of the commercial film made by Mexican film star and comedian Alfonso Arau in the United States primarily for the "American-Hispanic" market on a low-cost budget. Arau planned to distribute in Mexico, Latin America and Spain. The film is a light-weight comedy about a "wetback" who launches a campaign for "mojado power" but falls victim to dope smugglers and is sent to jail.

2049 "Viva la causa", a documentary film on the Mexican mural movement in Chicago. Chicago, IL: Kartemquin Films, [1974]. English.

AN: Advertising brochure for a film made of Chicano muralist Ray Patlan working with young people in Chicago. The film shows murals in Mexico and Chicago, and follows one mural from its sketch to its completion.

Cisneros, George

2050 San Antonio Museum Association, San Antonio, TX. Visiones nuevas en Tejas/new visions in Texas. Exhibtion catalog, 1979. English.

AN: Supplementary regional catalog for the exhibit RAICES ANTIGUAS/VISIONES NUEVAS; ANCIENT ROOTS/NEW VISIONS. Illustrations for works by George Cisneros, Francisco (Frank) Fajardo, Robert Gonzalez, Cesar Augusto Martinez, Roland Mazuca, Guillermo Pulido, Felipe Reyes, Jesus (Jesse) Trevino.

Cisneros, Jose

2051 Cisneros, Jose. Riders of the border. El Paso, TX: Texas Western Press, 1971. English.

AN: Jose Cisneros, El Paso artist has illustrated (in total or in part) over forty books, most of which deal with the Southwest. This collection ia a picture book rendering the picturesqueness and pagentry of the various riders along the border. Illustrated with 30 black and white drawings and text by the artist.

2052 Hertzog, Carl. Tribute to Jose Cisneros. THE PASSWORD, Vol. 19, no. 4 (Winter 1974). English.

AN: Tribute to artist-illustrator Jose Cisneros, who has "enhanced the appearance of programs, exhibition catalogs, newspaper articles, magazines and special stationery. He has designed emblems such as the seal of the University of Texas at El Paso, the seal of the city of Juarez, Mexico, and the emblem of the Western History Association".

2053 Samuels, Peggy and Samuels, Harold. Cisneros, Jose. In: THE ILLUSTRATED BIOGRAPHICAL ENCYCLOPEDIA OF ARTISTS OF THE AMERICAN WEST. Garden City, NY: Doubleday, 1976, p. 95. English.

AN: Brief biography on book illustrator, Jose Cisneros, who is a leading authority on the costume, weapons, and trappings of Mexican border horsemen.

Cisneros, Ramon

2054 Temko, Allan. Teen Angel's low riders -
Chicano art on the rise. THIS WORLD,
(August 26, 1979), p. 42-43. English.

AN: Important and insightful analysis of
the lowrider phenomenon among Chicano youth
in California. Analysis of publications like
LOW RIDER Magazine of San Jose, information
on graphic artists like "Teen Angel" and
Ramon Cisneros and thematic relationship of
recognized Chicano artists like Gilbert
Lujan, John Valadez, and Luis Jimenez to the
lowrider movement. The lowrider is
provocatively related to world wide cultural
manifestations from diverse epochs.

Cisneros, Rene

2055 Gaytan, Ray; Leone, Betty; and Cisneros,
Rene. An interview. TEJIDOS, Vol. 2, no. 6
(Summer 1975), p. 29-38. English.

AN: Interview with Texas artists Ray
Gaytan, Trini Perez, and Sam Coronado on the
topic "What Is Chicano Art?".

Cities
USE: Urban Communities

CITYARTS [mural]

2056 Weiss, Margaret R. and Sommer, Robert.
Camera assignment: documenting street art.
SATURDAY REVIEW, (May 17, 1975), p. 41-43.
English.

AN: Interview with Robert Sommer.
Illustrations of six murals: in Santa Fe,
NM; Estrada Courts in Los Angeles; a John
Weber mural in Chicago; and Cityarts mural
in New York.

Cityarts Workshop, NY

2057 Cockcroft, Eva; Weber, John; and Cockcroft,
James D. Towards a people's art: the
contemporary mural movement. New York: E.P.
Dutton, 1977. English.

AN: A survey of the street mural
movement in the United States, from about
1967 on. Several chapters are written by the
artists themselves: John Weber on the
Chicago mural group; Susan Shapiro-Kiok on
Cityarts Workshop of New York; Eva Cockcroft
on People's painters of New Jersey; Geronimo
Garduno on Artes Guadalupanos de Aztlan of
New Mexico. Chicano murals illustrated
include those of Mujeres Muralistas, Ray
Patlan, William F. Herron, Hoyo-Mara Gang,
Artes Guadalupanos de Aztlan, Vicente
Mendoza and Jose Nario (with Patlan) Mario
Castillo, Michael Rios, Toltecas en Aztlan,
Roberto Chavez, Ernie Palomino, Chuy
Campusano and Luis Cortazar (with Rios).

CITYBENDER [magazine]

2058 Yarbro-Bejarano, Yvonne. Resena critica de
revistas literarias chicanas: problemas y
tendencias. LA PALABRA, Vol. 3, no. 1-2
(Spring, Fall , 1981), p. 123-137. Spanish.

AN: Continuation of review of Chicano
magazines from Texas, California, and
Washington. The article discusses content,
literary and artistic format, and other
aspects, taking a critical stance (See LA
PALABRA, Spring 1980).

Cityscape Photo Gallery, Pasadena, CA

2059 Four and four: Mexican and Latino
photography, April 25 through June 14 on the
balcony. CALENDAR: SANTA BARBARA MUSEUM OF
ART, (April 1981). English.

AN: Announcement of exhibit organized by
Lorenzo Hernandez of the Cityscape Foto
Gallery, Pasadena, Calif. Sought to present
"the observable differences between the
'classic' vision of the Mexican National and
the 'realistic' vision of the re-rooted
Mexican/American." The latter included Louis
Bernal (Tucson) and Ricardo Valverde (Los
Angeles) as well as two Spanish Sephardics
of Los Angeles, Camhi and Sisco.

2060 Geyer, Anne; Hernandez, Lorenzo; and
Valverde, Ricardo. Latino photographers of
U.S. still seeking identity. THE NEWS,
(September 5, 1981), p. 17. English.

AN: Interview with Lorenzo Hernandez,
photo dealer and owner of Cityscape Foto
Gallery, Pasadena, Calif. in which he
compares Mexican with U.S. Latino
photography. Interview with Ricardo
Valverde, Chicano photographer and co-chair
of the Council of Latino Photography/USA,
discussing his work. Illustrated.

2061 Gonzalez, Jose Carlos. Consejo mexicano de
fotografia: foto latino en el suroeste de
los Estado Unidos. ARTES VISUALES, Vol. 29,
no. 29 (June 1981), p. 55-56. Spanish.

AN: Review of a photography show in
Mexico City organized by Lorenzo Hernandez,
Cityscape Photo Gallery of Pasadena, and the
Council of Latino Photography/USA. The show
featured Latinos of the Southwest and Latino
themes by non-Latino photographers.

Coalition of Centros Chicanos in California

2062 Cuellar, Rodolfo. Esteban Villa-maximo
exponente del arte indigena mexicano. EL
HISPANO, Vol. 8, no. 23 (January 27, 1976),
p. 3. Spanish.

AN: Biographical data on the artist
focusing on his activism in the formation of
the Centro de Artistas Chicanos in
Sacramento and the coalition of Centros
Chicanos in California. Illustrated with
photographs of the artist, one of his murals
and a special emblem for the "Esteban Villa
Fan Club" designed by the R.C.A.F.

CODEX BORGIA

2063 [Untitled drawing]. ATISBOS, no. 2 (Winter
1976, 1977), p. 15.

2064 [Untitled drawing]. ATISBOS, no. 2 (Winter
1976, 1977), p. 27.

2065 [Untitled drawing]. ATISBOS, no. 2 (Winter
1976, 1977), p. 35.

2066 [Untitled drawing]. ATISBOS, no. 2 (Winter
1976, 1977), p. 61.

2067 [Untitled drawing]. ATISBOS, no. 2 (Winter
1976, 1977), p. 71.

2068 [Untitled drawing]. ATISBOS, Vol. 2,
(Winter 1976, 1977), p. 97.

2069 [Untitled drawing]. ATISBOS, no. 2 (Winter
1976, 1977), p. 107.

CODEX NUTTAL

2070 Rodriguez, Vicente. Mayan gods [drawing].
TEJIDOS, Vol. 4, no. 2 (Summer 1977), p. 20.
Spanish.

2071 Rodriguez, Vicente. Mayan gods [drawing].
TEJIDOS, Vol. 4, no. 2 (Summer 1977), p. 21.
English.

La Cofradia de Artes y Artesanos Hispanicos, Santa Fe, NM

2072 La Cofradia de Artes y Artesanos Hispanicos
and Santa Fe Council for the Arts. El
festival hispanico. Festival program, [ca.
1979]. English.

AN: Program for the festival which
included over 70 visual artists from
northern New Mexico selected and hung by the
Cofradia at the Armory for the Arts gallery
in Santa Fe. The poster for the festival,
reproduced on the program cover, is taken
from a painting by Gilberto Guzman. The
festival also featured music, cuentos,
dance, slide show, poetry, films.

2073 Daigh, Janice. Old church alive with art.
TAOS NEWS BULLETIN, (January 25, 1979), p.
B, 1. English.

AN: Commentary on the formation of the
Cofradia de Artes y Artesanos Hispanicos.
The organization projects an ambitious
program including the expansion of artistic
endeavors by contemporary crafts people and
artists, the restoration of historic
buildings and the education of Hispanic
children in their artistic heritage as well
as providing information to the general
public.

2074 Eichstaedt, Peter. Hispanic festival
cultural showcase. NEW MEXICAN WEEKEND,
(May 25, 1979), p. 3. English.

AN: Announcement of the week-long
HISPANIC HERITAGE FESTIVAL/EL FESTIVAL
HISPANICO co-sponsored by La Cofradia de
Artes y Artesanos Hispanicos and the Santa
Fe Council fo the Arts at the Armory for the
Arts in Santa Fe. Outlines the cultural
activities, including a visual arts exhibit.
La Cofradia is a recently formed
organization which has assembled regional
shows at the Santuario de Guadalupe which
gave opportunities to local artists to show
their work. Festival artists are primarily
from the upper Rio Grande but also include
artists from the State Penitentiary, as well
as Albuquerque and Las Cruces. Illustration
of painting by Sam Leyba.

2075 Fabricant, Don. Show reveals Hispanic art.
NEW MEXICAN WEEKEND, (June 1, 1979).
English.

AN: Review of two exhibits in Santa Fe:
EL FESTIVAL HISPANICO, mounted by La
Cofradia de Artes y Artesanos Hispanicos and
Gilberto Guzman at the Black Kachina
Gallery. The reviewer feels the
traditional-style woodcarving done by
contemporaries is the strongest part of the
show; works that break with these forms seem
weaker, less skillful and cliche-ridden.
Crafts are excellent. Muralist Guzman has
blossomed in murals and easel paintings
since he was employed by the 1978 Art in
Public Places project. His work is intense
and expressive, sometimes erotic.
Illustration of work by sculptor Ruben
Montoya.

2076 Guadalupe Historic Foundation, Santa Fe, NM.
Cofradia de artes y artesanos hispanicos.
Mimeograph, 1979. Spanish.

AN: Mimeographed call to join and
support the Cofradia, an organization begun
by and sustained by artists and craftsmen to
help support each other. Stated aims: "to
encourage the revival, continuation, and
growth of traditional and contemporary
Hispanic arts and crafts, to serve as a
source of public information for these
crafts and their producers, and to promote
the general social, cultural, and economic
welfare of the Hispanic arts and crafts".

2077 Institute of American Indian Arts Museum,
Santa Fe, NM. Native American/Hispanic
festival, contemporary & historic visions.
Santa Fe, NM: Institute of American Indian
Arts Museum, 1981. English.

AN: Catalog for exhibit co-sponsored by
La Cofradia de Artes y Artesanos Hispanicos,
the Institute of American Indian Arts, and
the Santa Fe Council for the Arts. Exhibit
stresses the inter-relationship between the
Indian and Hispano peoples of New Mexico. 31
contemporary Hispano artists included.
Illustrated.

2078 Loniak, Walter. The true New Mexico
contemporary style. SANTA FE REPORTER, (May
31, 1979). English.

AN: Review of three exhibits in Santa
Fe, EL FESTIVAL HISPANICO co-sponsored by
the Cofradia de Artes y Artesanos Hispanicos
and the Santa Fe Council for the Arts; a
wood carving exhibit at Elaine Horwitch
Gallery, and easel paintings by muralist
Gilberto Guzman at the Black Kachina
Gallery. Concerning the Festival exhibit,
the critic states that the sculptural pieces
are the strongest; two dimensional work is
inconsistent or unimpressive, weaving is not
well represented (though usually the
strongest medium), and there are few
photographs or prints. Illustration.

2079 Museum of Fine Arts, Santa Fe, NM. Luis
Jimenez, sculpture, drawings and prints: La
Cofradia de Artes y Artesanos Hispanicos,
selected works. Exhibition invitation, 1979.
English.

AN: Invitation to an exhibit of Texas
sculptor and printmaker Luis Jimenez, and
New Mexican artists and artisans.

Colectivo El Ojo, Los Angeles, CA

2080 Amor sin fronteras. Los Angeles, CA:
Colectivo El Ojo, n.d.. English.

AN: Fotonovela with Josefina Arce,
Eduardo Dominguez and Mike Jauregui produced
by the Colectivo: Eduardo Dominguez, Roberto
Gil de Montes, Jerry Lucas, Kay Torres,
students at California State University, Los
Angeles.

Coleman, Elisa Marina

2081 Valdez, Armando. El calendario chicano 1977.
Hayward, CA: Southwest Network, 1977.
English.

AN: Fifth in a series of historical
calendars produced in 1972, 1974, 1975, 1976
by La Causa Publications and Southwest
Network. Artists whose work is reproduced
are Malaquias Montoya, Amado Maurilio Pena,
Ramori Zamora, Glugio J.L. Nicandro [Gronk],
Etta Delgado, Ricardo Alaniz, Diane Gamboa,
Elisa Marina Coleman, Margarita Calderon,
Jose Antonio Burciaga, Cesar Augusto
Martinez, Maria Ochoa y Valtierra, Juan
Renteria Fuentes, from California, New
Mexico, and Texas.

Collage

2082 De Leon, Hector. Promises, promises
[collage]. CARACOL, Vol. 2, no. 5 (January
1976), p. 10. English.

2083 Fuentes, Juan. [Untitled collage]. TIN TAN,
Vol. 1, no. 2 (September 1975), p. In
BkCover.

2084 Gonzalez, Hector. [Untitled photo collage].
TIN TAN, Vol. 1, no. 2 (September 1975), p.
[24-25].

2085 Munoz, Victor. One way [collage]. TEJIDOS,
Vol. 2, no. 6 (Summer 1975), p. 39. English.

2086 Royal Chicano Air Force (RCAF), Sacramento,
CA. [Untitled collage]. CHISMEARTE, no. 1
(Fall 1976), p. 52-53.

Colonia
USE: Barrios

Colonia Juarez, Fountain Valley, CA

2087 Chapple, Paul. FV [Fountain Valley] wall
mural stirs contention. THE REGISTER,
(December 29, 1974), p. A3. English.

AN: Artist Sergio O'Cadiz has included a
panel showing gas-masked police dragging off
a Chicano youth. The panel has caused
controversy in Fountain Valley, CA; police
object to the image.

2088 Chapple, Paul. Mural, graffiti painters wage
endurance contest in F.V. [Fountain Valley].
THE REGISTER, (December 4, 1975), p. B5.
English.

AN: Mexican-born architect and designer
Sergio O'Cadiz, with a team, paints a 600
foot mural in Colonia Juarez, an older
section of Fountain Valley in Orange County,
CA. Local police objected to a scene showing
police brutality. White paint was hurled at
this panel one night, and the mural was
constantly attacked by vandals. Illustrated.

2089 Fortune, Thomas. Mural will mirror barrio
pride. LOS ANGELES TIMES, (December 27,
1974), p. II, 1, 8. English.

AN: Artist Sergio O'Cadiz has been
painting a 625-foot concrete wall
constructed to separate old Colonia Juarez
and a new Anglo housing complex in Fountain
Valley (Orange County), Calif., to eliminate
graffiti. The mural depicts the barrio's
history: Mexican Americans try on white
masks for Anglo acceptance. Other scenes
will show the arrival of the surrounding
city, and resident's awareness of their
Chicano identity. O'Cadiz is assisted by 40

students from surrounding colleges and
universities. Illustrated.

Colorado

2090 Adams, Robert. The architecture and art of
early Hispanic Colorado. Boulder, CO:
Colorado Associated University Press in
cooperation with the State Historical
Society of Colorado, 1974. English.

AN: Robert Adams is a photographer and
writer from Longmont, CO who has evocatively
captured scenes in the San Luis and
Purgatory Valleys of Southern Colorado. The
text and photographs focus on "Hispano"
village life, customs and traditions.

2091 Barnett, Alan. Southern journey. NATIONAL
MURALS NETWORK COMMUNITY NEWSLETTER, (Fall
1980), p. 22-32. English.

AN: Rather gossipy account of murals
seen in a swing of the southern United
States. Includes the work of dozens of
artists and arts groups from California,
Arizona, New Mexico, Texas, and Colorado.

2092 Barrett, Marjorie. Ray Espinoza: versatile
artist. ROCKY MOUNTAIN NEWS, (February 12,
1973), p. 44. English.

AN: Ray Espinoza whose family spans six
generations in the San Luis Valley of
Colorado is steeped in Southwestern art
traditions. Drawing from his ancestral
heritage, he has become a prominent sculptor
working in wax. Illustrated with photograph
of artist and two of his sculptures.

2093 Edward Chavez: sculptor-painter. LA LUZ,
Vol. 2, no. 2 (May 1973), p. 28-31. English.

AN: Lavishly illustrated biographical
account of Edward Chavez. Born in Ocate, New
Mexico in 1917, Chavez has a distinguished
career as a painter and sculptor. During the
1940's he executed a number of murals under
sponsorship of various government art
projects. These murals were placed in public
buildings in Nebraska, Colorado and Wyoming.
Although living and working in New York most
of his adult life, the work of Edward Chavez
has always been influenced by the Southwest.

2094 Espinoza. EMPIRE MAGAZINE, (October 22,
1972), p. 28. English.

AN: Biographical information and
artistic trajectory of Ray Espinoza from
Colorado's San Luis Valley. Focus on
Espinoza as a community artist who expresses
aspects of Southwestern culture. Illustrated
with photographs of three wax sculptures by
Ray Espinoza.

2095 Sharing a bit of magic with John Mendoza.
ARTISTS OF THE ROCKIES, Vol. 1, no. 2
(Spring 1974), p. 14-17. English.

AN: Growing up in the St. Charles Mesa
east of Pueblo Colorado, John Mendoza has
sought to capture the essence of nature in
that part of the country in his paintings.
Blending realism and abstraction, Mendoza
has evolved a distinctive personal idiom.
Illustrated with reproductions of two
watercolors and six drawings. Includes two
photos of the artist and his pupils.

Colorado Springs Fine Arts Center, Taylor Museum

2096 Miller, Marlan. Heard speaks Spanish through art. PHOENIX GAZETTE, (September 23, 1978). English.

AN: Four new exhibits at the Heard Museum of Phoenix include "Hispanic crafts of the Southwest", and "Southwest Chicano Art Invitational". The former focuses on New Mexico and Colorado crafts, organized by the Taylor Museum if the Colorado Springs Fine Arts Center; the latter includes Rupert Garcia and Xavier Miramontes of San Francisco, Rudy Fernandez of Salt Lake City (now in Scottsdale, AZ), and Antonio Pazos of Tucson.

Colton, CA

2097 Valadez, Kathy L. Colton history told in mural. EL CHICANO, Vol. 8, no. 7 (July 19, 1973), p. 3, 9. English.

AN: Esau Quiroz was commissioned by the Mexican American Political Association to paint mural for their 1973 Convention. Mural portrays arrival of Mexican workers after the Revolution of 1910, the railroad industry in Colton, and the labor struggles organized by "La Cruz Azul".

Columbus, Christopher

2098 Limon, Leo. Christopher's movement. CHISMEARTE, Vol. 1, no. 2 (Winter, Spring, 1977), p. 28-29. English.

AN: Caricatures illustrating a poem written by Olivia Sanchez. The poem makes allusion to Christopher Columbus as the originator of the "Wetback Problem" by bringing his European compatriots across the sea to the American continent.

Comite Chicanarte

2099 Romero, Raul V. Chicanarte, a major exposition of California arts. NEWORLD, (Fall 1975). English.

AN: CHICANARTE at the Los Angeles Municipal Gallery, Barnsdall Park from Sept. 14 -Oct. 12, 1975 remains the most comprehensive statewide exposition of Chicano arts in California. This article details the production apparatus and history of the exposition. In particular, the contributions of Al Frente Communications, Inc., the Chicano Arts Council of U.C.L.A. and the Comite Chicanarte. Illustrated.

Commercial Design

2100 Neumeier, Marty. Ignacio Gomez. COMMUNICATION ARTS MAGAZINE, Vol. 21, no. 6 (January, February, 1980), p. 78-87. English.

AN: Story on commercial designer and illustrator Ignacio Gomez of Los Angeles which describes his background, education and life style. 17 full-color illustrations of his art work, including the ZOOT SUIT poster for the Mark Taper Forum play.

Commonarts

2101 Mural celebration. GRASSROOTS, (September 6, 1978), p. 8. English.

AN: Illustrated story on the new mural of plywood, papier mache and ceramic painted and modeled by artists from Commonarts for la Pena Cultural Center. The mural depicts peoples of the Americas coming together, singing and playing musical instruments, with Chilean musician Victor Jara as the major symbol.

2102 New radical wall art. PEOPLE'S WORLD, Vol. 41, no. 37 (September 16, 1978), p. 10. English.

AN: Illustrated story and explanation of the imagery on the new mural resulting from a collaboration of Commonarts and La Pena Cultural Center. The artists are Ray Patlan, O'Brien Thiele, Osha Neumann, and Anna de Leon.

Community Art

2103 Blaine, John and Baker, Decia. Finding community through the arts: spotlight on cultural pluralism in Los Angeles. ARTS IN SOCIETY, Vol. 10, no. 1 (Spring, Summer, 1973), p. 125-138. English.

AN: Community arts expression by ethnic minorities is burgeoning everywhere, especially in Los Angeles. Various Black, Asian, and Chicano art administrators are interviewed, including Frank Lopez of Plaza de la Raza and Leonard Castellanos of Mechicano Art Center. Illustrated.

2104 Karam, Bruce G. The murals of Tucson. NUESTRO, Vol. 5, no. 8 (November 1981), p. 58-60. English.

AN: Themes of ethnic pride, cultural unity and cooperation define the murals of Tucson. Brief commentary on the relationship of artists and the community. Illustrated with color photographs.

2105 Lopez, Gerard. Estrada murals. LA GENTE DE AZTLAN, Vol. 4, no. 6 (May, June, 1974), p. 4. English.

AN: Article explains how the community at Estrada Courts was mobilized to support a mural project uniting artists with residents. Includes interview with artist C.W. Felix who comments on the goals of the mural program and cites the themes and symbolism of the murals.

Community Development

2106 A new cultural center for Houston. AGENDA, Vol. 7, no. 2 (March, April, 1977), p. 17-18. English.

AN: Goals and programs of a proposed Mexican American cultural center for Houston, Texas. Since August of 1976, the center has been operating from a temporary location and has sponsored various art exhibits. Expected to be in full operation by 1980, the Houston Bellas Artes will sponsor workshops, symposia, performances and exhibits related to Mexican American culture. Illustrated with two photographs of the cultural activities of the Houston Bellas Artes Center.

Community Organizations
USE: Cultural Organizations

Comprehensive Employment and Training Act (CETA)

2107 Art in public places. Program statement, 1977-78. English.

AN: Documents an eleven-month program funded by CETA for 21 artists to produce murals, prints and weavings as public art. Includes murals by Gilberto Guzman and Graciela Carrillo-Lopez in Santa Fe. Statements by the artists. Illustrated.

2108 Barnes, Peter. Fringe benefits of a depression: bringing back the WPA. NEW REPUBLIC, Vol. 172, no. 11 (March 15, 1975), p. 19-21. English.

AN: A well-researched and comprehensive analysis of the CETA (Comprehensive Employment and Training Act) impact on public art in San Francisco. Material on Chicano-Latino murals in the Mission district. Includes viewpoints by artist-activists Patricia Rodriguez, Mike Rios, and writer Roberto Vargas. Important compendium on funding sources of various neighborhood art programs stressing their value as community assets.

2109 Marquez, Rosa Maria. Artistas chicanas together at C.S.A.C., an interview by Rosa Maria Marquez. CHISMEARTE, Vol. 1, no. 4 (Fall , Winter, 1977), p. 39. English.

AN: An interview with several women doing murals as part of the East Los Angeles Senior Citizens Housing and Mural Beautification Program under the sponsorship of the Chicana Service Action Center. Funding for the project through CETA (Comprehensive Employment Training Act).

Compton, CA

2110 [Untitled photograph]. LOS ANGELES TIMES, (May 5, 1972), p. II, 1. English.

AN: Captioned illustration of Chicano high school students' 25x5 foot mural at Compton's Thomas Jefferson Elementary School. The mural, which took a year to paint, is based on Mexican history.

Con Safo [art group], San Antonio, TX

2111 Con Safo. San Antonio, TX: Pintores Chicanos de San Antonio, [ca. 1975]. English.

AN: Illustrated pamphlet issued by the San Antonio artists' group Con Safo. Includes a self-definition and a brief history of the group under the names El Grupo, Los Pintores de Aztlan, Los Pintores de la Nueva Raza, Con Safo (from 1967 on). Members include Jesse A. Almazan, Mel Casas, Jose Esquivel, Jose P. Garza, Cesar Augusto Martinez, Santos Martinez, Felipe Reyes, Roberto Rios, Jesus C. Trevino, and Vicente Velasquez.

2112 Con safo to hold Lutheran college exhibition at Texas. CHICANO TIMES, Vol. 7, no. 89 (March 26, 1976), p. [15]. English.

AN: Discusses the aims of "Con Safos" group: to interpret their environment and react to it; to act as spokespeople and give visual reality to the Chicano vision; to destroy stereotypes and demolish visual cliches. The participating artists include Rudy R. Trevino, Mel Casas, Lucas Hinojosa, Kathy Vargas, Joe Frank Acosta, Emilio Aguirre and Homero Ureste.

2113 LA MOVIDA CON SAFO. no. 2 (February 1976). English.

AN: Mimeographed newsletter issued by Mel Casas about the San Antonio artists' group Con Safo. Reports on the exhibits, symposium, festival, TV appearance, film, and other activities of the group or its individual members. Illustrated.

2114 LA MOVIDA CON SAFO. no. 1 (Fall 1975). English.

AN: Mimeographed newletter issued by Mel Casas about the San Antonio artists' group Con Safo. Includes history of the group and its activities.

CON SAFOS [magazine]

2115 Gamboa, Harry, Jr. Seis imaginaciones: artistas chicanos en Los Angeles. COMUNIDAD, (July 13, 1980), p. 10. Spanish.

AN: A limited flow of media information about Los Angeles Chicanos has produced a "ghost" culture. Only sensational events are published. Alternative magazines like LA RAZA, CON SAFOS, and REGENERACION have disseminated Chicano ideas of the 1970s. The Chicano imagination has appeared in murals by Willie Herron, Gronk, Carlos Almaraz, John Valadez; in pieces like "walking" and "instant" murals by the group ASCO; by the group Los Four; by group exhibits like "Chicanismo en el arte," and "Chicanarte." Patssi Valdez showed Photobooth Piece at the "Chicanismo" show. Gronk and Jerry Dreva exhibited their mail art at "Punk Meets Art." In Spanish.

2116 La razon [montage]. CON SAFOS, no. 8 (1972), p. 52.

Conacine [film studio]

2117 Torres, Louis R. RAICES DE SANGRE: first full length film directed by a Chicano. SOMOS, Vol. 1, no. 2 (July 1978), p. 16-19. English.

AN: Report on Jesus Salvador Trevino's RAICES DE SANGRE, the only film made by a Chicano at the Mexican film studio, CONACINE. Deals with the efforts of Chicanos and Mexicans living in border cities to organize an international labor union. Trevino's previous work is briefly mentioned. Illustrated.

Conceptual Art

2118 Exploratorium, Student Union, California State University, Los Angeles. Herron/Gronk in ILLEGAL LANDSCAPE. Exhibition catalog, 1980. English.

AN: Invitation to a "performance" piece NO MOVIE by Willie Herron and Gronk, two members of ASCO. Illustrated.

2119 Gamboa, Harry, Jr. ASCO: no phantoms. HIGH PERFORMANCE, Vol. 4, no. 2 (Summer 1981), p. 15. English.

AN: "The media's hit and run attitude has generally relegated the influence by Chicanos on Los Angeles to that of a phantom culture," says Gamboa's introduction to an ASCO No Movie event, NO PHANTOMS: "various overt acts of communal alienation." Illustrated.

Conceptual Art (cont.)

2120 Gamboa, Harry, Jr.

Fadein. CHISMEARTE, Vol. 1, no. 2 (Winter, Spring, 1977), p. 38. English.

AN: A conceptual art piece by Harry Gamboa, Jr. of ASCO. The piece consists of drawings and text.

2121 Gamboa, Harry, Jr.; Gronk; and Herron, Willie. Gronk and Herron. NEWORLD, Vol. 2, no. 3 (Spring 1976), p. 28-30. English.

AN: An interview with ASCO members Gronk and Willie Herron by a third member, Gamboa. Brief historical introduction (1970 on). The witty tongue-in-cheek interview can be considered an artwork by this performance art group. Illustrated.

2122 Gamboa, Harry, Jr. and Gronk. Gronk: off-the-wall artist. NEWORLD, Vol. 6, no. 4 (1980), p. 33-43. English.

AN: Interview with Gronk about his No Movies, by Harry Gamboa, Jr., both members (with Willie Herron and Patssi Valdez) of ASCO. The interview itself can be seen as an "art piece" with photographs by Gamboa; it contains valuable information about the ideas and activities of the group.

2123 Gamboa, Harry, Jr. Phobia friend. TIN TAN, Vol. 2, no. 6 (December 1, 1977), p. 13-14. English.

AN: Short story written and illustrated as a conceptual art piece by ASCO member, Gamboa, as a "Cinema Chicano" work.

2124 Gamboa, Harry, Jr. Seis imaginaciones: artistas chicanos en Los Angeles. COMUNIDAD, (July 13, 1980), p. 10. Spanish.

AN: A limited flow of media information about Los Angeles Chicanos has produced a "ghost" culture. Only sensational events are published. Alternative magazines like LA RAZA, CON SAFOS, and REGENERACION have disseminated Chicano ideas of the 1970s. The Chicano imagination has appeared in murals by Willie Herron, Gronk, Carlos Almaraz, John Valadez; in pieces like "walking" and "instant" murals by the group ASCO; by the group Los Four; by group exhibits like "Chicanismo en el arte," and "Chicanarte." Patssi Valdez showed Photobooth Piece at the "Chicanismo" show. Gronk and Jerry Dreva exhibited their mail art at "Punk Meets Art." In Spanish.

2125 Geyer, Anne and Gamboa, Harry, Jr. Artists' exhibits are street performances. THE NEWS, (September 11, 1981), p. 18. English.

AN: Illustrated interview with photographer/writer Harry Gamboa, Jr., member and documenter of the performance art group ASCO. Description of the NO MOVIE, NO PHANTOM, walking and instant murals of the group, and other performance street art which Gamboa considers as Chicano self-documentation and expression.

2126 L.A.C.E. (Los Angeles Contemporary Exhibitions), Los Angeles, CA. No Movie: Gil de Montes, Teddy, Glugio [Gronk], Patssi, Gamboa. Exhibition invitation, 1978. English.

AN: Invitation to "performance" piece by Roberto Gil de Montes, Teddy Sandoval,

Gronk, Patssi Valdez and Harry Gamboa, Jr., the latter three of the ASCO group. Illustrated.

2127 Literally live movie at NO MOVIE exhibit. CIVIC CENTER NEWS, Vol. 7, no. 17 (April 25, 1978), p. 1. English.

AN: Story on the ASCO "performance" NO MOVIE, described by "Glugio" Gronk as "movies without celluloid" to be held at LACE Gallery. Illustrated.

2128 Mechicano Art Center, Los Angeles, CA. Schizophrenibeneficial. Exhibition invitation, 1977. English.

AN: Invitation to an ASCO "performance" work: "Projecting of Visual and/or Verbal Personality Disorders Onto Person or Persons Unknown." Glugio (Gronk), Teddy (Sandoval), (Roberto) Gil de Montes, Patssi (Valdez), (Harry) Gamboa.

2129 Out in the open/Allen Parkway: Frank Fajardo, Jesse Lott, Guillermo Pulido, Jana Vander Lee. Exhibit invitation, 1979. English.

AN: Invitation to the installation of conceptual pieces in public areas of Houston. Includes Chicano artist Frank Fajardo and Bolivian-born Pulido.

2130 Tennant, Donna. Conceptual art dots city landscape. HOUSTON CHRONICLE, (October 27, 1979), p. II, 7. English.

AN: Frank Fajardo and Bolivian-born Guillermo Pulido are two of several artists creating conceptual art pieces in various parts of Houston. Fajardo marked out space with 25 stakes tipped with day-glo orange paint. Pulido constructed two large triangles on opposite hillsides, like giant markers.

Concha, Jerry

2131 Exxon Company, Houston, TX and Quirarte, Jacinto. Chicano art of the barrio. Exhibition brochure, n.d. [c.1976]. English.

AN: Brochure for a traveling exhibit of photographically-reproduced Chicano murals: Leo Limon, Lucila Villasenor Grijalva, Antonio Esparza, Susan Saenz, Charles Felix, Hoyo-Mara gang, David A. Lopez and team, Roberto Chavez and team (Los Angeles); Jerry Concha, Ruben Guzman, Chuy Campusano (San Francisco); Manuel Unzueta (Santa Barbara). Ernie Palomino and Leo Esequiel Ozona (Fresno). Leo Tanguma (Houston), Roberto Lucero, Manuel Martinez and Al Sanchez (Denver).

2132 Los Medanos College Gallery, [CA]. Cinco/five: an exhibit of five Bay Area artists. Exhibition brochure, n.d. English.

AN: Artists Gerry Concha, Gustavo Rivera, Raoul Mora, Manuel Villamor and Peter Rodriguez included in the show. Illustrated by Peter Rodriguez's portraits of the five.

Concha, Jerry (cont.)

2133 Morch, Albert. He put down his brushes for a
     dream. SAN FRANCISCO SUNDAY EXAMINER AND
     CHRONICLE, (October 2, 1977), p. Scene, 3.
     English.

     AN: Brief profile of painter Peter
     Rodriguez, founder and director of the
     Mexican Museum in San Francisco which opened
     in 1975. On exhibit are the works of San
     Francisco artist Jerry Concha. Illustrated.

2134 Opton, Suzanne. Short strokes. SAN FRANCISCO
     FAULT, (December 29, 1971), p. 9-10.
     English.

     AN: The currently homeless Galeria de la
     Raza has begun a series of wall painting
     projects. Artist "Spain" did a Horizons
     mural; Puerto Rican photographer Adal
     Maldonado did photographic murals; Jerry
     Concha, Tom Rios, did rooms in the Center
     for Change drug program building, Chuy
     Campusano, working with cartoonist R. Crumb,
     and the Mission Rebel Kids did a cartoon
     mural. Model Cities day care centers are
     next to be painted.

2135 San Francisco Art Commission Gallery.
     Rolando Castellon, Gustavo Rivera, Jerry
     Concha. Exhibition brochure, 1971. English.

     AN: Brochure for exhibit by
     Sacramento-born Jerry Concha, Mexican-born
     Gustavo Rivera, and Nicaraguan-born Rolando
     Castellon titled CAPRICORN ASUNDER. Brief
     biographies of the artists.

Concilio de Arte Popular, Los Angeles, CA

2136 Concilio de Arte Popular (State Coalition of
     La Raza Artists). CHISMEARTE, Vol. 1, no. 1
     (Fall   1976), p. 56. English.

     AN: Announcement of the formation of the
     Concilio de Arte Popular on March 13, 1976,
     and a brief statement about the goals of the
     organization.

2137 Concilio de arte popular. CHISMEARTE, Vol.
     1, no. 2 (Winter, Spring, 1977), p. 54.
     English.

     AN: Report of a meeting February 12,
     1977 by the Concilio de Arte Popular (CAP)
     which published CHISMEARTE. Introduces
     members of the Board and summarizes
     discussions of problems of the organization
     and their publication.

2138 Garcia, Sol. Vato Loco y Chata La Gata
     [comic strip]. CHISMEARTE, no. 2 (Winter,
     Spring, 1977), p. Bk cover. Calo.

     AN: Comic strip format utilized to
     invite all interested persons to meeting of
     the Concilio de Arte Popular. The artist is
     a member of the Brocha del Valle group from
     Fresno, CA.

2139 Soberon, Mercedes. La revolucion se trata de
     amor: Mercedes Soberon. CHISMEARTE, Vol. 1,
     no. 1 (Fall   1976), p. 14-18. Spanish.

     AN: Short interview with Mercedes
     Soberon, San Francisco artist involved with
     the art group Mission Media Arts. Mercedes
     talks about the role of women as organizers
     and artists, the sacrifices associated with
     this role, and the politics of San Francisco
     museums.

Conferences and Meetings

2140 Association for Resources and Technical
     Services, Inc. (ARTS); Tejano Artists, Inc.;
     and Performing Artists Nucleus, Inc. (PAN).
     Tejano arts workshop. Brochure, 1981.
     English.

     AN: Call to a two-day arts workshop in
     San Antonio designed to inform participants
     on organizational development, networking,
     fundraising, touring, marketing, public
     relations, and audience development.
     Southwest in scope, with input and
     organization from Washington, D.C. and New
     York.

2141 Bejarano, William. Utah Chicano forum.
     CHISMEARTE, Vol. 1, no. 1 (Fall   1976), p.
     9-10. English.

     AN: Report on the CULTURE, ARTE Y MEDIOS
     DE COMUNICACION workshop at the Third
     National Chicano Forum at the University of
     Utah, Salt Lake City. The panel, moderated
     by artist Carmen Lomas Garza, set up a plan
     of action for the visual, literary,
     performing arts and the mass media which
     included planning a national conference to
     discuss cultural work, financial support,
     recognition and moral support, among other
     issues.

2142 CHICANO CINEMA NEWSLETTER. Vol. 1, no. 4
     (June 1979). English.

     AN: Report and cautionary note on the
     upcoming Alternative Cinema Conference;
     announcement of ONLY ONCE IN A LIFETIME and
     CHICANA film releases; other new films and
     TV programs; a Chicano cinema bibliography;
     a list of Chicano production companies and
     distributors; a theoretical article on the
     nature (proposed) of Chicano cinema as an
     alternative cinema; statement of purpose of
     the Los Angeles Chicano Cinema Coalition.

2143 Crusade for Justice, Denver, CO. Los
     artistas de Aztlan. Mimeographed copy, 1969.
     English.

     AN: Resolutions from the Chicano Youth
     Conference (March-April, 1969) on the role
     of art and artists within the Chicano
     movement. An important document.

2144 Goldman, Shifra M. Artistas en accion:
     conferencia de las mujeres chicanas.
     COMUNIDAD, (August 10, 1980), p. 15.
     Spanish.

     AN: In Chicano Studies programs, the
     fine arts have had second class status to
     social sciences and literature. Similarly a
     Chicano Issues Conference overlooked artists
     until a special effort was made. A round
     table, which included visual artists
     Gloriamalia Flores and Carmen Lomas Garza,
     discussed the social functions of art, woman
     as an image maker, problems of the Chicana
     as creator and cultural worker, and
     professionalism in the arts.

Conferences and Meetings (cont.)

2145 Kleinhaus, Chuck; Seiter, Ellen; and Steven, Peter. Conference report: struggling for unity. JUMP CUT, no. 21 (November 1979), p. 35-37. English.

AN: Report and critique of the U.S. Conference for an Alternative Cinema held in mid-June 1979 at Bard College in New York state to chart a course for independent filmmakers. Chicano, Black, Asian and Puerto Rican film people attended, including Jesus Salvador Trevino and Sylvia Morales from the Chicano Cinema Coalition of Los Angeles.

2146 Notes on 2nd National Community Muralists' Network Conference, Chicago, Ill. April 20-23, 1978. San Francisco, CA, 1978. English.

AN: Rupert Garcia, Raul Martinez, Patricia Rodriguez, Ray Patlan (San Francisco Bay Area) and Jaime Valadez (San Jose), among others, attended the conference in Chicago. Reports were heard from many parts of the United States on mural activities, including that of Aurelio Diaz of Chicago, representing MARCH (Movimiento Artistico Chicano). A workshop presentation was made by Luis Arenal and others from the Taller Siqueiros of Cuernavaca, Mexico. An experimental mural to try Siqueiros' techniques was created. Illustrated.

2147 Quesada-Weiner, Rosemary. [Untitled collection of photographs]. COMUNIDAD, (August 24, 1980), p. 15.

AN: Photographs of the CONFERENCIA DE LAS MUJERES CHICANAS taken by Rosemary Quesada-Weiner.

2148 Romero, Ernestina. Chicano art movement: conference celebrates transformation. DAILY TEXAN, (September 17, 1979). English.

AN: Report on the internationally attended CONFERENCIA PLASTICA CHICANA. Some confusing definitions.

2149 Romero, Ernestina. Chicano culture to be explored at conference. DAILY TEXAN, (September 10, 1979). English.

AN: Announcement of the internationally attended CONFERENCIA PLASTICA CHICANA. Statements by organizers Santa Barraza and Pedro Rodriguez.

2150 Semana de la Raza: international panel of the arts, Mexico and the United States. Santa Ana, CA: MEChA, Santa Ana College, 1972. English.

AN: An International Panel of the Arts, organized by art historian Shifra Goldman, featured Mexicans Hector Garcia, prize-winning photographer; Jaime Mejia, painter, restorer, filmmaker; Alejandro Vichir, director of Teatro Trashumante; and Chicanos Gilbert Sanchez Lujan, sculptor and painter; Gloria Osuna, painter and artist for Teatro Campesino; and Jesus Salvador Trevino, filmmaker.

2151 Symposium on the politics of the arts: minorities and the arts. ARTS IN SOCIETY, Vol. 10, no. 3 (Fall , Winter, 1973), p. 66-73. English.

AN: One panel from the Colloquium "Politics of the Arts" presented by the UCLA Management in the Arts Program, Graduate School of Management, 1972, included, among others, Leonard Castellanos of Mechicano Art Center, and James Woods of Studio Watts Workshop, both in Los Angeles. A major topic was how minorities dealing with the corporate capitalist structure can keep control of their art programs.

2152 Tibol, Raquel. Primera conferencia de plastica chicana. PROCESO, (September 24, 1979). p. 57-58. Spanish.

AN: Report on the internationally attended CONFERENCIA PLASTICA CHICANA held in Austin, Texas September 13th to 16th, 1979.

CONFERENCIA DE LAS MUJERES CHICANAS

2153 Quesada-Weiner, Rosemary. [Untitled collection of photographs]. COMUNIDAD, (August 24, 1980), p. 15.

AN: Photographs of the CONFERENCIA DE LAS MUJERES CHICANAS taken by Rosemary Quesada-Weiner.

CONFERENCIA PLASTICA CHICANA, Austin, TX, Sept. 13-16, 1979

2154 Chicano art conference kicks off. AUSTIN AMERICAN STATESMAN, (September 14, 1979). English.

AN: Announcement of upcoming CONFERENCIA PLASTICA CHICANA to be held in Austin, TX.

2155 Conferencia plastica chicana. Conference brochure, 1979. English.

AN: Schedule of proceedings at internationally attended conference on Chicano and Mexican art and photography sponsored by the Centro Cultural de LUCHA (League of United Chicano Artistas) and MAS (Mujeres Artistas del Suroeste). Brief biographies of presentors. Illustrated.

2156 Romero, Ernestina. Chicano art movement: conference celebrates transformation. DAILY TEXAN, (September 17, 1979). English.

AN: Report on the internationally attended CONFERENCIA PLASTICA CHICANA. Some confusing definitions.

2157 Romero, Ernestina. Chicano culture to be explored at conference. DAILY TEXAN, (September 10, 1979). English.

AN: Announcement of the internationally attended CONFERENCIA PLASTICA CHICANA. Statements by organizers Santa Barraza and Pedro Rodriguez.

2158 Tibol, Raquel. Primera conferencia de plastica chicana. PROCESO, (September 24, 1979), p. 57-58. Spanish.

AN: Report on the internationally attended CONFERENCIA PLASTICA CHICANA held in Austin, Texas September 13th to 16th, 1979.

CONFLICT OF CULTURES (LA RAZA - PART III) [film]

2159 Films for the inner city. Los Angeles, CA: Los Angeles Public Library Federal Project, 1971. English.

AN: Annotated catalog of 16mm films and filmstrips, educational and documentary. Those concerning Mexican heritage include CHICANO FROM THE SOUTHWEST (1970), HENRY...BOY OF THE BARRIO (1969); HOW'S SCHOOL, ENRIQUE (1970), I AM JOAQUIN (1970), THE MEXICAN AMERICAN: HERITAGE AND DESTINY (1970), A MEXICAN AMERICAN FAMILY (1970), MEXICAN AMERICANS: QUEST FOR EQUALITY (1968), MEXICAN OR AMERICAN (1970), SIQUEIROS: "EL MAESTRO" (THE MARCH OF HUMANITY IN LATIN AMERICA) (1969). Filmstrips include THE AWAKENING (LA RAZA) - Part IV, CONFLICT OF CULTURES (LA RAZA) - Part III, MASTERWORKS OF MEXICAN ART, OUT OF THE MAINSTREAM, PILGRIMAGE (GRAPE STRIKERS). Also listed are films and filmstrips for children.

Congreso de Artistas Chicanos

2160 Congreso de Artistas Chicanos en Aztlan, San Diego, CA. Diego Rivera, David Alfaro Siqueiros, Jose Clemente Orozco: exhibit of local artists, La Logan [San Diego]. Exhibition brochure, n.d. [c.1974]. English.

AN: Announcement of a traveling exhibit organized by Galeria de la Raza, San Francisco, from the collection of the San Francisco Museum of Art. Illustrated with a San Diego mural.

2161 Salvador R. Torres Chicano Underground Studio-Gallery, San Diego, CA. Diego Rivera, David Alfaro Siqueiros, Jose Clemente Orozco, from the collection of the S.F. Museum of Art. Exhibition invitation, [1974]. English.

AN: Illustrated invitation of an exhibit organized by the Galeria de la Raza of San Francisco loaned to the Congreso de Artistas Chicanos en Aztlan, and held in artist Torres' studio.

Congress of American Cosmic Artists (CACA), San Diego, CA

2162 NATIONAL MURALS NETWORK COMMUNITY NEWSLETTER. (1978). English.

AN: This issue features reports from muralists. Includes information about murals at: La Pena Cultural Center in Berkeley, CA; the Social and Public Art Resource Center's Tujunga Wash Mural in Venice, CA; the Citywide Mural Project in Los Angeles, CA; activities at Chicano Park, and of the Congress of American Cosmic Artists (CACA), both in San Diego, CA; murals in San Mateo County, CA; the Task Force on Hispanic American Arts headed by Jacinto Quirarte of San Antonio; the 1978 Canto Al Pueblo in Corpus Christi, TX; murals in Chicago; and other works by non-Chicano artists.

Consejo Latinoamericano de Fotografia (CLAF)

2163 Goldman, Shifra M. Hecho en Latino America: first photography colloquium and exhibition. CHISMEARTE, no. 6 (February 1980), p. 16-25. English.

AN: Report on the first colloquium of Latin American photography, Mexico City, May 1978. Analysis and critique of U.S. Latino photographers' work presented in exhibition.

Well illustrated.

Consejo Mexicano de Fotografia

2164 COUNCIL OF LATINO PHOTOGRAPHY/USA NEWSLETTER. no. 2 (January 1980). English.

AN: Photocopied newsletter reporting on the "First Communication" meeting of the organization, the opening of a Council gallery and darkroom in Pasadena, news from San Francisco/Berkeley group, news of the activities of the Consejo Mexicano de Fotografia, Mexico, and an announcement of the II COLLOQUIUM OF LATIN AMERICAN PHOTOGRAPHY for 1981.

Contra Costa, CA

2165 Chicano art show at Contra Costa College. EL HISPANO, Vol. 8, no. 25 (December 11, 1973). English.

AN: Information on exhibition organized by Ramses Noriega that included the work of Jose Montoya, Esteban Villa, Mario Sinape, Ricardo Rios, Malaquias Montoya, Fuchi Queso, and Joe Palomino.

Contreras, Carlos

2166 Cultural department. RECOBRANDO, Vol. 1, no. 15. Spanish.

AN: The development of "Raza" culture in the Northwest and the role played by the Centro de la Raza. Mentions the "talleres de arte" set up by Carlos Contreras and Arturo Artorez, artists from Mexico who moved to Seattle in 1978. Details cultural events sponsored by the Centro in the fields of art, music, dance, and theater.

Cordoba, NM

2167 Briggs, Charles L. The wood carvers of Cordova, New Mexico: social dimensions of an artistic "revival". Knoxville, TN: University of Tennessee Press, 1980. English.

AN: One of the few books that deals with the traditional and contemporary-traditional religious art of New Mexico within social context. The author explores the influence of Anglo patronage and tourism on the meaning, aesthetics and distribution of the santos, and non-religious carving of the town of Cordoba.

Cordova, Carlos Chavez

2168 The Mexican Museum, San Francisco, CA. Recent works of Luis Jaso from Mexico City and Carlos Chavez Cordova from Los Angeles. Exhibition invitation, 1981. English.

AN: Invitation to an exhibit.

Coronado, Sam

2169 Gaytan, Ray; Leone, Betty; and Cisneros, Rene. An interview. TEJIDOS, Vol. 2, no. 6 (Summer 1975), p. 29-38. English.

AN: Interview with Texas artists Ray Gaytan, Trini Perez, and Sam Coronado on the topic "What Is Chicano Art?".

Corporate Funding Sources

2170 Monroe, Julie T. A splash of art from
     Idaho's Mexican-Americans. IDAHO STATESMAN,
     (March 11, 1977), p. 4D. English.

   AN: As a Bicentennial tribute to all
   people of Latin American heritage, Illinois
   Bell Telephone Company organized a national
   exhiibit of 17 Mexican-American/Chicano
   artists. In Idaho, the touring exhibition
   was augmented by a local presentation,
   MEXICAN-AMERICAN: IDAHO, shown at the Boise
   Gallery of Art under sponsorship of Boise
   Cascade. Jose Rodriguez, local artist
   presents his views on the meanings of the
   word "Chicano" and "Chicano Art."
   Illustrated with a photograph of Jose
   Rodriguez and a reproduction of one of his
   oil paintings entitled THE HOE.

Corporations and Art

2171 Boise Gallery of Art, Idaho Migrant Council
     and Boise Cascade Corp. 17 artists:
     Hispano/Mexican-American/Chicano. Boise, ID:
     1977. English.

   AN: Announcement of a national
   exhibition organized and toured by Illinois
   Bell Telephone. In Idaho, the exhibit (March
   12 to April 10, 1977) also included local
   Chicano artists.

2172 Kutner, Janet. Total freedom in Chicano art.
     DALLAS MORNING STAR, (December 18, 1977),
     p. 10C. English.

   AN: Review of traveling photo-exhibition
   of Chicano murals organized by Jacinto
   Quirarte for Exxon USA.

2173 The Mexican Museum, San Francisco, CA and
     Quirarte, Jacinto. 17 artists:
     Hispano/Mexican-American/Chicano. Exhibition
     catalog, 1977. English.

   AN: Catalog of an exhibit for artists
   Emilio Aguirre, Consuelo Gonzalez Amezcua,
   Al Barela, Pedro Cervantez, Edward Chavez,
   Antonio Garcia, Louis Gutierrez, Harry
   Louie, Vincent Perez, Michael Ponce de Leon,
   Eugenio Quesada, Gustavo Rivera, Peter
   Rodriguez, Alex Sanchez, Darryl Sapien, Rudy
   Trevino, Manuel Villamor. Illustrated.

2174 Quirarte, Jacinto. The art of Mexican
     America. HUMBLE WAY, Vol. 9, no. 2 (1970),
     p. 2-9. English.

   AN: One of the earliest surveys of
   Mexican American/Chicano artists. Provided
   the framework for Quirarte's book, Mexican
   American Artists.

2175 Quirarte, Jacinto. The murals of el barrio.
     EXXON USA, (February 1974), p. 2-9.
     English.

   AN: Well illustrated article on
   California murals from Santa Barbara, San
   Diego, Los Angeles, Fresno, and San
   Francisco.

2176 Rivas, Maggie. Art of the barrio: Exxon's
     traveling art show comes to headquarters. HQ
     HOUSTON, (August 1976), p. 6-7. English.

   AN: Report on traveling photo-exhibition
   of 29 Chicano murals organized by Jacinto
   Quirarte for Exxon USA.

2177 Symposium on the politics of the arts:
     minorities and the arts. ARTS IN SOCIETY,

Vol. 10, no. 3 (Fall   , Winter, 1973), p.
66-73. English.

   AN: One panel from the Colloquium
   "Politics of the Arts" presented by the UCLA
   Management in the Arts Program, Graduate
   School of Management, 1972, included, among
   others, Leonard Castellanos of Mechicano Art
   Center, and James Woods of Studio Watts
   Workshop, both in Los Angeles. A major topic
   was how minorities dealing with the
   corporate capitalist structure can keep
   control of their art programs.

Corpus Christi, TX

2178 Canto al Pueblo Steering Committee. Canto al
     Pueblo [poster]. CARACOL, Vol. 4, no. 9 (May
     1978), p. 23.

2179 Rodriguez, Alfred. A historical survey of
     Chicano murals in the Southwest: an
     interdisciplinary teaching unit. Unpublished
     paper, 1980. English.

   AN: Lists murals by title, artist and
   date (when known), location and subject. Los
   Angeles, San Francisco, San Diego, Fresno,
   San Antonio, Austin, Corpus Christi, Santa
   Fe, New Mexico murals are included.
   Circulated by the Institute of Latin
   American Studies, University of Austin,
   Texas.

Cortazar, Luis J.

2180 Albright, Thomas. Three remarkable Latin
     murals. SAN FRANCISCO CHRONICLE, (June 7,
     1974), p. 48. English.

   AN: The myth of the melting pot is
   vanishing: we recognize a variety of
   "publics" today. This is shown in three
   remarkable murals in the San Francisco
   Mission District. The Mission branch of the
   Bank of America has a 90 foot mural designed
   by Jesus Campusano, assisted by Luis
   Cortazar and Michael Rios, with technical
   advice from Emmy Lou Packard. Another mural
   is by the Mujeres Muralistas (Graciela
   Carrillo, Consuelo Mendez, Irene Perez,
   Patricia Rodriguez); the third by Michael
   Rios on the 24th St. mini-park.

2181 Bank of America, Mission-23rd St. Branch,
     San Francisco, CA. A community mural
     dedicated by the artists to Mexican muralist
     David Alfaro Siqueiros. 1974. English.

   AN: Brochure about the Bank of America
   mural in the Mission District of San
   Francisco designed by Jesus Campusano and
   Luis J. Cortazar, assisted by Michael Rios,
   Jaime Carrillo, Candice Ho, Julio Lopez,
   Anthony Machado, Jack Nevarez. Technical
   advisor, Emmy Lou Packard. Well illustrated.

Cortazar, Luis J.(cont.)

2182 Barrio heritage reflected in bank mural. EL
     CHICANO, Vol. 8, no. 50 (May 30, 1974), p.
     8-9. English.

     AN: Jesus Campusano and Luis J. Cortazar
     were artist-designers of a monumental mural
     painted inside the Mission Branch of the
     Bank of America. Michael Rios was color
     coordinator and five young artists worked
     collectively on the project for four months.
     Realistic scenes of everyday life in the
     Mission barrio are contrasted to heroic
     personalities from Latin America. Folk art
     imagery, Indian and Spanish cultural symbols
     and historical personages form a pageant of
     Latin American history. Mural was
     inaugurated on June 4, 1974.

Cortez, Carlos

2183 Calendario de March: 1977. Chicago, IL:
     MARCH, Inc., 1976. English.

     AN: Historical calendar with photos and
     biographies of artists. Illustrations of
     artwork by Ray Patlan, Jose Nario, Frank J.
     Sanchez, Salvador Dominguez, Salvador Vega,
     Marguerite Ortega, Aurelio Diaz, Carlos
     Cortez, Mario E. Castillo, Francisco Blasco,
     Rey Vasquez, and Efrain Martinez. History of
     MARCH (Movimiento Artistico Chicano).

2184 Nelson, Eugene. Pablo Cruz and the American
     dream. Salt Lake City, UT: Peregrine Smith,
     1975. English.

     AN: A first-person account of a typical
     "alambrista" (a wire jumper or undocumented
     Mexican worker in the U.S.) compiled from
     several accounts by the author. Illustrated
     with 14 prints by Carlos Cortez, Chicago
     artist, then the editor of THE INDUSTRIAL
     WORKER.

2185 Rayaprofile: Carlos Cortez. RAYAS, Vol. 1,
     no. 6 (November, December, 1978), p. 3.
     English.

     AN: Biographical profile of Chicago
     artist Carlos Cortez.

2186 Woodblock and linoleum prints by Carlos
     Cortez, member of the Chicago mural group.
     TIN TAN, Vol. 2, no. 6 (December 1, 1977).
     English.

     AN: Seven works reproduced from prints
     by Cortez, also an active member of the
     Movimiento Artistico Chicano of Chicago,
     dating from 1971 to 1976.

Cortez, Jim

2187 Artes 6 Gallery, San Francisco, CA. Mixed
     media. Exhibition announcement, [ca.
     1969-70]. English.

     AN: Announcement of exhibit including
     Jim Cortez, Luis Cervantez, Vicente Rascon,
     Rene Yanes, Graciela Carrillo, Lorenza
     Camplis. The Artes 6 artists eventually
     formed the Galeria de la Raza of San
     Francisco.

Cortez, Ronald

2188 Galeria Tonantzin, Centro Cultural de LUCHA,
     Austin, TX. Young Chicano photographers from
     throughout Texas. Exhibition brochure, n.d.
     English.

     AN: This exhibition is the collection of

the winners of the contest (by the same
name) sponsored by the Extension Cultural
SRE-UNAM in San Antonio. Photographers
represented were: Grace Alvarez, David
Cardenas, Hector Cardenas, Stephen Casanova,
Ronald Cortez, Raul Espinosa, Felix Almanza,
Carolina Flores, David Garza Perez, Xavier
Garza, Conrad Guerra, Melinda Hasbrook, Juan
Jose de Hoyes, Beverly Kennon, Art Moreno,
David Perez, Isabelle Purden, Patricia
Santell, Nancy de los Santos, Jose Soria,
Richard Tichich, Kathy Vargas, Vivian Yaten,
and Johnny Zamarria.

Council of Latino Photography/USA, Los Angeles, CA

2189 COUNCIL OF LATINO PHOTOGRAPHY/USA
     NEWSLETTER. no. 1 (January 1979). English.

     AN: First number of photocopied
     newsletter produced by the Council of Latino
     Photography/USA announcing the formation of
     the organization and its affiliation with
     the Consejo Latinoamericano de Fotografia
     established in Mexico City in May 1978.
     Organizers of CLP/USA were photographers
     Isabel Castro, Harry Gamboa, Jr., Adam
     Avila, Luis Garza, and art historian Shifra
     Goldman.

2190 COUNCIL OF LATINO PHOTOGRAPHY/USA
     NEWSLETTER. no. 2 (January 1980). English.

     AN: Photocopied newsletter reporting on
     the "First Communication" meeting of the
     organization, the opening of a Council
     gallery and darkroom in Pasadena, news from
     San Francisco/Berkeley group, news of the
     activities of the Consejo Mexicano de
     Fotografia, Mexico, and an announcement of
     the II COLLOQUIUM OF LATIN AMERICAN
     PHOTOGRAPHY for 1981.

2191 Geyer, Anne; Hernandez, Lorenzo; and
     Valverde, Ricardo. Latino photographers of
     U.S. still seeking identity. THE NEWS,
     (September 5, 1981), p. 17. English.

     AN: Interview with Lorenzo Hernandez,
     photo dealer and owner of Cityscape Foto
     Gallery, Pasadena, Calif. in which he
     compares Mexican with U.S. Latino
     photography. Interview with Ricardo
     Valverde, Chicano photographer and co-chair
     of the Council of Latino Photography/USA,
     discussing his work. Illustrated.

2192 Goldman, Shifra M. Hecho en Latino America:
     first photography colloquium and exhibition.
     CHISMEARTE, no. 6 (February 1980), p. 16-25.
     English.

     AN: Report on the first colloquium of
     Latin American photography, Mexico City, May
     1978. Analysis and critique of U.S. Latino
     photographers' work presented in exhibition.
     Well illustrated.

2193 Gonzalez, Jose Carlos. Consejo mexicano de
     fotografia: foto latino en el suroeste de
     los Estado Unidos. ARTES VISUALES, Vol. 29,
     no. 29 (June 1981), p. 55-56. Spanish.

     AN: Review of a photography show in
     Mexico City organized by Lorenzo Hernandez,
     Cityscape Photo Gallery of Pasadena, and the
     Council of Latino Photography/USA. The show
     featured Latinos of the Southwest and Latino
     themes by non-Latino photographers.

Council of Latino Photography/USA, Los Angeles, CA
(cont.)

2194 L.A.C.E. (Los Angeles Contemporary
Exhibitions), Los Angeles, CA. First
communication. Exhibition invitation, 1979.
English.

AN: Invitation to a showing of
photographic slides and prints organized by
the Council of Latino Photography/USA.

Covarrubias, Jim

2195 Donaghy, Kathleen. Two Arizona firsts:
Chicano gallery and Spanish theatre. ARIZONA
ARTS AND LIFESTYLE, (1981). English.

AN: The MARS (Movimiento Artistico del
Rio Salado) Gallery has opened in downtown
Phoenix, run by MARS founder Jim
Covarrubias. Louis Leroy, expansion arts
coordinator for the Arizona Commission on
the Arts, says it is the only arts-oriented
space that caters to Chicanos in Arizona.

2196 Encanto Pavilion, Encanto Park, Phoenix, AZ.
Exposicion de arte para la raza: Arizona
Chicano art show. Exhibition catalog, [ca.
1978]. English.

AN: Catalog for an exhibit organized by
MARS (Movimiento Artistico del Rio Salado).
Colombian-born Antonio L. Tocora, Jim
Covarrubias, Ed Dias, Robert C. Buitron,
Armando Leon Hernandez, Guillermo Galindo,
Richard Luna Cisneros, Jose Andres Giron,
Robert L. Matta included.

2197 MARS: Movimiento Artistico del Rio Salado.
Phoenix, AZ: Mars Studio/Gallery, 1978.
English.

AN: History and manifesto of MARS, 13
member group of Arizona painters, sculptors,
designers, and photographers: Jose Andres
Giron, Jose Jimenez Rodriguez, Antonio
Tocora (Colombian-born), Ramon Delgadillo,
Francisco Zuniga, Jim Covarrubias, Ed Diaz,
David Martinez, Roberto Buitron, Juan
Rodriguez, Eddie Lopez, Zarco Guerrero, Joe
Sanchez.

Craft and Folk Art Museum, Los Angeles, CA

2198 Gamboa, Harry, Jr. Los murales de Aztlan.
COMUNIDAD, (June 28, 1981), p. 8-9+.
Spanish.

AN: Review of the exhibit at the Craft
and Folk Art Museum of Los Angeles of MURALS
OF AZTLAN: THE STREET PAINTERS OF EAST LOS
in which Carlos Almaraz, Gronk, Judithe
Hernandez, Willie Herron, Frank Romero, John
Valadez and the East Los Streetscapers
(David Botello, Wayne Healy, George Yepes)
painted portable murals in the gallery. The
murals are described and illustrated.

2199 Knight, Christopher. Urban eye sites up
against the wall. HERALD EXAMINER, (May 31,
1981). English.

AN: Review of the exhibit MURALS OF
AZTLAN: THE STREET PAINTERS OF EAST LOS at
the Craft and Folk Art Museum of Los
Angeles. Illustration.

2200 Muchnic, Suzanne. Passion, paint splatter
folk art museum show. LOS ANGELES TIMES,
(June 25, 1981), p. VI, 1. English.

AN: Review of the MURALS OF AZTLAN:
STREET PAINTERS OF EAST LOS exhibit at the

Craft and Folk Art Museum in Los Angeles.
The critic considered the show "revved-up,
highly emotional art descended from Mexico's
political muralists" that made up what it
lacked in subtlety with passion, and one of
the most visually exciting shows of the
Museum. Illustrations.

Crary, Pat Portera

2201 ENCUENTRO FEMENIL (San Fernando, CA). Vol.
1, no. 1 (Spring 1973), p. 1+. English.

AN: Publication sponsored by Hijas de
Cuauhtemoc, a Chicana femenist group. Black
and white drawings on cover by Pat Portera
Crary. Art work by Vicki Thrall, Adelaida
del Castillo, and Maria Hortencia Garcia.
Photography by Cindy Honesto and David
Lazarin.

THE CREATION OF CULTURES [mural]

2202 Huge mural displayed at El Con Shopping
Center. ARIZONA DAILY STAR, (January 31,
1979). English.

AN: A 15 x 50 foot mural called The
Creation of Cultures, a latex-enamel on
panels, was painted by Tucson muralist
Roberto Borboa. Its final site has not been
determined. Illustrated.

LA CRUCIFIXION DE DON PEDRO ALBIZU CAMPOS [mural]

2203 Sorell, Victor A. Barrio murals in Chicago:
painting the Hispanic-American experience on
"our community" walls. REVISTA
CHICANO-RIQUENA, Vol. 4, no. 4 (Fall
1976), p. 51-72. English.

AN: Important survey of Chicago's Latino
murals, with key works considered in detail.
Among the Chicano art organizations and
muralists mentioned are MARCH (Movimiento
Artistico Chicano), and Yolanda Galvan,
Juanita Jaramillo, Jose Nario, Raymond
Patlan, Vicente Mendoza, Marcos Raya,
Ricardo Alonzo, Jose G. Gonzalez and Mario
Castillo, author of the earliest Latino
mural in Chicago (1968). Puerto Rican and
non-Latino muralists and mural groups are
also discussed. Well illustrated.

Cruz, Bob

2204 Pimentel, Ricardo. Graffiti: expression or
scourge? FRESNO BEE, (February 23, 1981),
p. Metro, B1+. English.

AN: A rapid review of graffiti symbols,
their meaning and social context. Commentary
by various young people explaining the
value, style and meanings of plaqueasos
(spray painted graffiti). Some Chicano
artists like Bob Cruz, director of La Brocha
del Valle, see mural painting as a positive
alternative to graffiti art forms. Article
also provides views of local businessmen to
the graffiti phenomenon.

Cruz, Bob (cont.)

2205 Teatro de la Tierra Morena, Santa Cruz, CA.
Fuego en Aztlan: a Chicano arts show.
Exhibition brochure, 1980. English.

AN: Folder of information on the
exhibition curated by Cruz Zamarron and
Eduardo Carrillo. Exhibiting artists were:
Justina Avila, Terry Benitez, Eduardo
Carrillo, Hernando Chavez, Bob Cruz, Juanita
Estrada, Juana Franklin, Sal Garcia, Leticia
Hernandez, David "Sir Loco" Jimenez, Raoul
Mendez, Vicente Mendez, Maria V. Pinedo,
Gonzalo Placencia, Ramon Rodriguez, Roberto
Salas, George Silva and Cruz Zamarron. A
special feature was a live tattoo
demonstration entitled "Walking Art".

Cruz, Cresanta

2206 Corazon del norte: wood carving. GRITO DEL
NORTE, Vol. 2, no. 5 (March 28, 1969), p.
11. English.

AN: Focus on the Aguilar family, folk
artists from Los Ojos (Parkview), northern
New Mexico. Sr. Cruz Aguilar is a sculptor
and furniture maker, his 80-year-old mother
Dona Cresanta Cruz is a quilter. Illustrated
with photographs of the Aguilars and
examples of their work.

Cruz, Manuel

2207 Collection by Mexican American artist:
Manuel Cruz. EL CHICANO, Vol. 3, no. 15
(December 5, 1969), p. [3]. English.

AN: Manuel Cruz creates ceramic
figurines of Chicano types. The small,
painted and glazed figures depict aspects of
the daily life of the Mexican people from
pre-Colombian times to the present.
Illustrated with photographs of more than
two dozen of the figurines.

2208 Creations by Cruz. Color brochure, n.d.
English.

AN: Color brochure of genre-like figures
produced for sale by Los Angeles sculptor
Manuel Cruz in hydro-stone. The figures,
which run from 3" to 12" high depict images
from Aztec legends to Pachucos, Brown
Berets, and hippies.

2209 Varda, Agnes. Mur murs/mural murals on the
wall ... Film, Cine Tamaris, Paris, 1980.
English.

AN: Full length documentary film
produced for French television; also
available with English subtitles. Deals
impressionistically with the murals and
muralists of Los Angeles. Included are Wayne
Alaniz Healy, David Botello, Willie Herron,
Manuel Cruz, Judy Baca, the murals in
Venice, CA, graffiti - among others. Color.

2210 Wilson, William. 30 works from the grass
roots. LOS ANGELES TIMES, (June 4, 1973),
p. IV,2. English.

AN: Review of a show at the Junior Arts
Center in Barnsdall Park by 15 members of
the Mechicano Art Center. The critic feels
contemporary groups that aim for change
today (unlike past groups) are unable to
articulate their spirit in a cohesive style.
The top talent in this show is Charles
Almaraz; also on exhibit are paintings by
Jose Cervantes, Guillermo Martinez, Ray
Atilano, sculpture by Manuel Cruz, and

photography by (Oscar) R. Castillo.

Cuba

2211 Galeria de la Raza/Studio 24, San Francisco,
CA. Canto a Cuba. Exhibition invitation,
[1974]. English.

AN: Invitation to an exhibit of prints,
posters, paintings and drawings by two Cuban
artists.

Cuellar, Rodolfo

2212 Anaya, Rudolfo A. and Ortiz, Simon J.
1680-1980: a ceremony of brotherhood.
Albuquerque, NM: Academic, 1981. English.

AN: A cooperative publication by members
of the former La Academia de la Nueva Raza
(1969-1976) formed of writers and artists,
and the Tri-Centennial Commission of the
All-Indian Pueblo Council. Includes writings
and artworks by Chicanos and Indians from
New Mexico, California, Texas, and Arizona.
Chicano artists works included are by Ellen
Arellano, Juan Estevan Arellano, Alberto
Baros, Jose Antonio Burciaga, Juan Reyes
Cervantes, Rudy Cuellar, Ricardo Favela, El
Zarco Guerrero, Luis Jimenez, Jr., Carlos
Quinto Kemm, Alejandro Lopez, Floyd Lujan,
Jose Montoya, Juanishi Orozco, Leo Romero,
Secundino Sandoval, Jaime Valdez, Maria
Varela, Esteban Villa.

2213 Calendario de comida 1976. San Francisco,
CA: Galeria de la Raza, 1976. English.

AN: Handprinted silkscreen calendar
consisting of twelve sheets and a cover. The
work of the following artists is included:
Ralph Maradiaga, Juanishi Orozco, Francisco
Camplis, Ruben Guzman, Rodolfo Cuellar,
Xavier Viramontes, Jose Montoya, Esteban
Villa, Rene Yanez, Max Garcia and Louis "The
Foot" Gonzalez, Patricia Rodriguez, and
Ricardo Favela. All of the above are
associated with the Galeria de la Raza, or
the Royal Chicano Air Force of Sacramento,
CA.

2214 California. State College. Los Angeles. Art
Gallery. Twelve Chicano artists. Exhibition
invitation, n.d. English.

AN: Invitation to an exhibit: Jose
Montoya, Gilbert Sanchez Lujan, Esteban
Villa, Rene Yanez, Joe Moran, Armando Cid,
Leonard Castellas, Juanishi Orozco, Rudy
Cuellar, Beltran, Lopez and Cabrera.

2215 La historia de California, 1977. San
Francisco, CA: Galeria de la Raza, 1977.
English.

AN: Handprinted silkscreen calendar of
history seen from a Mexican point of view.
Twelve sheets and a cover. Artists are:
Ralph Maradiaga, Irene Perez, Louie "The
Foot" Gonzalez, Max Garcia, Patricia
Rodriguez, Jose Romero, Esteban Villa,
Juanishi Orozco, Rodolfo Cuellar, Jose
Montoya, Xavier Viramontes, Rene Yanez,
Ricardo Favela, associated with the Galeria
de la Raza, or the Royal Chicano Air Force
of Sacramento.

Cuellar, Rodolfo (cont.)

2216 R.C.A.F. artistas precursores del arte
chicano. EL HISPANO, Vol. 8, no. 35
(February 17, 1976), p. 1. English.

AN: Information on the R.C.A.F.
organization. Includes group photograph of
R.C.A.F. members, Jose Montoya, Esteban
Villa, John Carrillo, Ricardo Fabela, Rudy
Cuellar, Juanishi Orozco and Frank Godena.

Cuentos

2217 Gamboa, Harry, Jr. Phobia friend. TIN TAN,
Vol. 2, no. 6 (December 1, 1977), p. 13-14.
English.

AN: Short story written and illustrated
as a conceptual art piece by ASCO member,
Gamboa, as a "Cinema Chicano" work.

2218 Salinas, Porfirio. Bluebonnets and cactus:
an album of southwestern paintings. Austin,
TX: Pemberton Press, 1967. English.

AN: Portfolio of Salinas landscape
paintings and five short stories. Lavishly
illustrated as a special edition.

Cuevas, Jose Luis

2219 Quiroz, Esau and Cuevas, Jose Luis. Chicano
art: an identity crisis. NEWORLD, Vol. 1,
no. 4 (Summer 1975). English.

AN: Interview between Chicano muralist
Esau Quiroz and Mexican artist Jose Luis
Cuevas. Chicano art is described as a search
for pictorial roots in Mexico expressed
through contemporary forms adopted from
United States art movements. Cuevas suggests
that Chicanos travel, exhibit and "project
to the United States from Latin America."
Illustrated with one drawing by Cuevas and
photographs of Quiroz.

Cultural Organizations

2220 Centro de artistas, Sacra: recuerdo ...
descubrimiento ... voluntad. CHISMEARTE,
Vol. 1, no. 1 (Fall   1976), p. 6-7.
English.

AN: Summary of activities of the Centro
de Artistas Chicanos, made up of artists
from the Royal Chicano Air Force and other
groups. The Centro makes posters, T-shirts,
decals, murals and puts on a number of
cultural and social events. Report on a
"mass migration" July 1976 to the Academia
de la Nueva Raza in Dixon, NM for two weeks
of communion.

2221 Concilio de Arte Popular (State Coalition of
La Raza Artists). CHISMEARTE, Vol. 1, no. 1
(Fall   1976), p. 56. English.

AN: Announcement of the formation of the
Concilio de Arte Popular on March 13, 1976,
and a brief statement about the goals of the
organization.

2222 Eichstaedt, Peter. Hispanic festival
cultural showcase. NEW MEXICAN WEEKEND,
(May 25, 1979), p. 3. English.

AN: Announcement of the week-long
HISPANIC HERITAGE FESTIVAL/EL FESTIVAL
HISPANICO co-sponsored by La Cofradia de
Artes y Artesanos Hispanicos and the Santa
Fe Council fo the Arts at the Armory for the
Arts in Santa Fe. Outlines the cultural
activities, including a visual arts exhibit.

La Cofradia is a recently formed
organization which has assembled regional
shows at the Santuario de Guadalupe which
gave opportunities to local artists to show
their work. Festival artists are primarily
from the upper Rio Grande but also include
artists from the State Penitentiary, as well
as Albuquerque and Las Cruces. Illustration
of painting by Sam Leyba.

2223 Images of Aztlan at Mechicano. CHISMEARTE,
Vol. 1, no. 1 (Fall   1976), p. 3-4.
English.

AN: History of Mechicano Art Center from
its opening in West Los Angeles in 1969
through its 1976 location during which it
decided to become a center serving its own
community in East Los Angeles. Led by
Leonard Castellanos, Victor Franco and Ray
Atilano, the Center developed programs in
supergraphics, silkscreen, and mural
painting, as well as an "open-wall" art
gallery for artists not allowed in
establishment galleries.

2224 A new cultural center for Houston. AGENDA,
Vol. 7, no. 2 (March, April, 1977), p.
17-18. English.

AN: Goals and programs of a proposed
Mexican American cultural center for
Houston, Texas. Since August of 1976, the
center has been operating from a temporary
location and has sponsored various art
exhibits. Expected to be in full operation
by 1980, the Houston Bellas Artes will
sponsor workshops, symposia, performances
and exhibits related to Mexican American
culture. Illustrated with two photographs of
the cultural activities of the Houston
Bellas Artes Center.

2225 Rodriguez, Luis. A Center for Cultural
Preservation and Human Resources. SOMOS,
Vol. 1, no. 4 (September 1978), p. 26-29.
English.

AN: Report on the founding, purposes,
and continuing social and cultural
activities of the Casa de La Raza.
Illustrated.

2226 Soberon, Mercedes. La revolucion se trata de
amor: Mercedes Soberon. CHISMEARTE, Vol. 1,
no. 1 (Fall   1976), p. 14-18. Spanish.

AN: Short interview with Mercedes
Soberon, San Francisco artist involved with
the art group Mission Media Arts. Mercedes
talks about the role of women as organizers
and artists, the sacrifices associated with
this role, and the politics of San Francisco
museums.

Culture

2227 Acosta, a man and his art. NOSOTROS, Vol. 2,
no. 6. English.

AN: Biographical information and
thematic analysis of the work of El Paso
artist Manuel Acosta. He is especially
noted for genre paintings of humble people
reflecting social life and cultural
traditions.

Culture (cont.)

2228 Adams, Robert. The architecture and art of
early Hispanic Colorado. Boulder, CO:
Colorado Associated University Press in
cooperation with the State Historical
Society of Colorado, 1974. English.

AN: Robert Adams is a photographer and
writer from Longmont, CO who has evocatively
captured scenes in the San Luis and
Purgatory Valleys of Southern Colorado. The
text and photographs focus on "Hispano"
village life, customs and traditions.

2229 Bolger, Kathryn McKenna. Amado Pena's art.
AUSTIN AMERICAN STATESMAN, (March 29,
1980), p. 10-11. English.

AN: A review of Pena's show of
silkscreens, watercolors, and drawings at
the Laguna Gloria Art Museum in Austin,
Texas, March-May, 1980. Suggests that the
artist has turned from a confrontational to
an assimilationist stance. At present he
visually documents the peaceful amalgamation
of the cultural heritage on both sides of
the Rio Grande.

2230 Carlos Sandoval to complete mural in
Zihuatanejo, Mexico. TIERRA Y LIBERTAD, Vol.
2, no. 4 (July 1980), p. 3, 10. English.

AN: Biographical information on Colorado
artist Carlos Sandoval. The Municipal
Library in the city of Zihuatanejo in the
state of Guerrero is the site of Sandoval's
mural which visually and symbolically
projects the cultural and historical unity
between Mejicanos and Chicanos.

2231 Johansen, Jason. Preliminaries toward an
Hispanic media: a cultural imperative.
Unpublished manuscript, 1980. English.

AN: Presentation made at the Hispanic
Southwest Conference on Media and the
Humanities. Johansen outlines the
culturally-leveling and stereotypical roles
for men and women of mass media in our
century which is dominated by communication
means owned by industries interested in
profits from products. Within this context,
Hispanic media producers must find new ways
of relaying values, judgements and ideas
that combat the dominant culture and
strengthen humanity and social change.

2232 Montoya, Jose E. Thoughts on la cultura, the
media, con safos and survival. Sacramento,
CA: Royal Chicano Air Force, 1979. English.

AN: Important theoretical article on the
state of Chicano culture. Reprinted in
METAMORFOSIS (Seattle, WA), vol. 3, no.
1(Spring/Summer 1980), p. 28-31.

2233 Mural depicts history of Mexican Americans.
EASTSIDE JRNL, (December 16, 1971), p. 1.
English.

AN: Richard Jimenez of the Goez Gallery
depicts the past and present of Mexican
American culture on an interior mural at the
First Street Store (3640 E. First St.) The 6
ft. by 15 ft. mural has central image of a
clock with a faceless figure (The Mexican
American of the future). Artist comments on
another of his murals titled EDUCATION OF
LIFE.

2234 Salazar, Juan Albert. Entelequia. 16 MM
Film, 1978. Bilingual.

AN: This production is Salazar's MFA
thesis from the Department of Art,
University of Utah. Its purpose is to
explore the Chicano mentality. Based on the
shooting of Santos Rodriguez in Texas, the
historical fact is abstracted and the
emotional impact transformed to an
analytical examination of the whys and hows
raised by such a situation.

2235 Venegas, Sybil. Towards a Chicano cultural
renaissance. LA GENTE DE AZTLAN, Vol. 8, no.
1 (November 2, 1977), p. 12. English.

AN: The revival of celebrations like El
Dia de Los Muertos are seen as catalysts for
barrio unification. Detailed information on
how Self Help Graphics in East Los Angeles
mobilizes artists and community for a
communal celebration.

**CULTURE, ARTE Y MEDIOS DE COMUNICACION [art
workshop]**

2236 Bejarano, William. Utah Chicano forum.
CHISMEARTE, Vol. 1, no. 1 (Fall   1976), p.
9-10. English.

AN: Report on the CULTURE, ARTE Y MEDIOS
DE COMUNICACION workshop at the Third
National Chicano Forum at the University of
Utah, Salt Lake City. The panel, moderated
by artist Carmen Lomas Garza, set up a plan
of action for the visual, literary,
performing arts and the mass media which
included planning a national conference to
discuss cultural work, financial support,
recognition and moral support, among other
issues.

Curanderismo

2237 Lomas Garza, Carmen. Don Pedrito Jaramillo,
Falfurrias, Texas, 1829-1907 [etching].
TEJIDOS, Vol. 3, no. 4 (Winter 1976), p. 22.

Curriculum Materials

2238 450 anos del pueblo chicano/450 years of
Chicano history in pictures. Albuquerque,
NM: Chicano Communications Center, 1976.
English.

AN: A pictorial history of Mexico,
Mexican Americans and Chicanos through
photographs and art works. P. 138 is
dedicated to murals, graphics, cartoons and
photographs from Chicago and the Southwest,
but other murals, graphics, cartoons and
photographs by Chicanos and non-Chicanos are
scattered throughout. In addition, 450 ANOS
has been a rich source book of imagery for
Chicano artists, especially historical works
of art.

2239 An.i.ma.tion: the arts, techniques, and
processes involved in giving apparent life
and movement to inanimate objects by means
of cinematography. San Francisco, CA:
Galeria de la Raza, n.d. English.

AN: Illustrated booklet on animation.
Reproductions and sequences illustrated by
Leslie Cabarga, Xavier Viramontes and Ralph
Maradiaga.

Curriculum Materials (cont.)

2240 California. University. Los Angeles. Instructional Media Library. 1975-76 film catalog. Film catalog, 1976, p. 30-31. English.

AN: List of films available from the Chicano Film Collection. 34 films on Chicano and Mexican subjects by Chicano and non-Chicano film makers.

2241 Chicano art of the Southwest. San Antonio, TX: Instituto Chicano de Artes y Artesanias of the Texas Institute for Educational Development, 1975. English.

AN: Collection of 220 slides supplemented by slide annotation and artists' biographies researched and photographed by Texas artist Cesar A. Martinez over two years. Biographies cover 20 Texas, 6 New Mexico, and 15 northern California artists. Slides include, in addition, murals from Los Angeles and San Diego.

2242 Corneil, Paul. Militant barrio murals of Santa Fe. Venice, CA: Environmental Communications, n.d. English.

AN: Annotated slide catalog with introductory text about the mural group Los Artes Guadalupanos de Aztlan of Santa Fe. Gilberto Guzman is mentioned as one of the group.

2243 Environmental Communications, Venice, CA. Street paintings of Los Angeles: a study of environmental reactionism. Slide catalog, n.d. English.

AN: Well illustrated annotated slide catalog of greater Los Angeles murals. Includes 7 Chicano murals. Articles reprinted from NEWSWEEK, LOS ANGELES TIMES, EARTH (Mar. 1972), ARTWORKERS NEWS (Oct. 1973), ARTFORUM (Feb. 1971), LOS ANGELES FREE PRESS (9/4/70), EVENING OUTLOOK (5/4/72), SUNSET (April 1973).

2244 Film collection of the Chicano Library. Chicano Studies Research Center, UCLA, 1972. English.

AN: Description, producers, rentals of 15 films made by or about Chicanos and Mexicans, and available through the Center.

2245 Films for the inner city. Los Angeles, CA: Los Angeles Public Library Federal Project, 1971. English.

AN: Annotated catalog of 16mm films and filmstrips, educational and documentary. Those concerning Mexican heritage include CHICANO FROM THE SOUTHWEST (1970), HENRY...BOY OF THE BARRIO (1969); HOW'S SCHOOL, ENRIQUE (1970), I AM JOAQUIN (1970), THE MEXICAN AMERICAN: HERITAGE AND DESTINY (1970), A MEXICAN AMERICAN FAMILY (1970), MEXICAN AMERICANS: QUEST FOR EQUALITY (1968), MEXICAN OR AMERICAN (1970), SIQUEIROS: "EL MAESTRO" (THE MARCH OF HUMANITY IN LATIN AMERICA) (1969). Filmstrips include THE AWAKENING (LA RAZA) - Part IV, CONFLICT OF CULTURES (LA RAZA) - Part III, MASTERWORKS OF MEXICAN ART, OUT OF THE MAINSTREAM, PILGRIMAGE (GRAPE STRIKERS). Also listed are films and filmstrips for children.

2246 Instituto Chicano de Artes y Artesanias (Texas Instit. Educational Development).

Chicano art of the Southwest. San Antonio, TX: Texas Institute for Educational Development, [ca. 1975]. English.

AN: Illustrated brochure announcing a color slide library on Chicano art supplemented by slide annotation and artists biographies available to institutions. Statement of purpose by Executive Director of program, Cesar Augusto Martinez.

2247 Morales, Sylvia. Chicana. 20 min., 16 mm, color, 1979. English.

AN: Color film tracing the history of the Chicana back to pre-Columbian women's history. Utilizes images of pre-Columbian and modern Mexican murals, as well as filming of contemporary Chicanas and their activities. Based on a slide show by Anna Nieto-Gomez, adapted for the screen by Morales.

2248 Petersen, Karen and Wilson, J.J. Women artists: Third World. New York, NY: Harper & Row, 1975. English.

AN: Catalog of slides with accompanying notes. Slides of Chicana artists available: Margaret Herrera (Chavez), Consuelo (Chelo) Gonzalez Amezcua, Santa Barraza, Mujeres Muralistas, El Grupo de Santa Ana, Carmen Lomas Garza, Carolina Flores.

2249 Peyton, Patricia, ed. Reel change: a guide to social issue films. San Francisco, CA: Film Fund, 1979. English.

AN: Includes a section on Hispanic film with descriptions, sources, and rentals. Listed are Esperanza Vasquez's AGUEDA MARTINEZ, Sylvia Morales' CHICANA, Adolfo Vargas' CONSUELO: QUIENES SOMOS?/WHO ARE WE?, El Teatro Campesino's I AM JOAQUIN, Jose Luis Ruiz's THE UNWANTED, Jesus Salvador Trevino's YO SOY CHICANO, and others. Listings are international in scope.

2250 Rodriguez, Alfred. A historical survey of Chicano murals in the Southwest: an interdisciplinary teaching unit. Unpublished paper, 1980. English.

AN: Lists murals by title, artist and date (when known), location and subject. Los Angeles, San Francisco, San Diego, Fresno, San Antonio, Austin, Corpus Christi, Santa Fe, New Mexico murals are included. Circulated by the Institute of Latin American Studies, University of Austin, Texas.

2251 Rodriguez, Patricia. Chicano Studies 130. Course reader, 1978. English.

AN: Unpublished compendium of articles on Chicano art. Includes section on Contemporary Chicano Art; Historical Cultural Perspectives of the Chicano; Mexican Muralists in the United States; and Views on Chicano Art, 352 pp.

Curriculum Materials (cont.)

2252 Rodriguez, Patricia, ed. Selected readings
on Chicano art. Berkeley, CA: Chicano
Studies Department, University of
California, 1977. English.

AN: Compendium of mechanically
reproduced articles on Chicano and Latin
American art prepared for Chicano Studies
130--Introduction to Chicano Art. Includes
sections on Mexican Muralists in the U.S:
Contemporary Chicano Art; Views on Chicano
Art; Chicano Artists; Pinto Art: Raza Murals
and Muralists; Plaqueasos (Graffiti);
Chicana Artists: Art, Politics and the
Community, Two Historical Examples: Cuba and
Chile; Chicano Art Reproductions, 557 pp.

2253 Rogovin, Mark and Burton, Marie. Mural
manual: how to paint murals for the
classroom, community center and street
corner. Boston, MA: Beacon Press, 1975.
English.

AN: The aesthetics, methodology,
techniques, materials and equipment for
producing popular murals, indoors and out.
Also deals with documentation, finances,
copyright laws and the history of modern
murals. Source book for muralists throughout
U.S. Well illustrated with murals and work
diagrams.

2254 Romotsky, Jerry and Romotsky, Sally R.
Chicano graffiti. Venice, CA: Environmental
Communications, 1974. English.

AN: Annotated slide catalog with text
and glossary of terms. Well illustrated.

2255 Rosenthal art slides. Chicago, IL: Rosenthal
Art Slides, 1978. English.

AN: Includes a selection on murals from
Canada, Chile, Cuba, Mexico, and murals from
the United States including the cities of
Los Angeles, Chicago, and New York, and the
states of Massachusetts, New Jersey, New
York, and New Mexico. Many slides of Chicano
murals from Los Angeles, Chicago and New
Mexico are available, fully documented.

2256 Varda, Agnes. Mur murs/mural murals on the
wall ... Film, Cine Tamaris, Paris, 1980.
English.

AN: Full length documentary film
produced for French television; also
available with English subtitles. Deals
impressionistically with the murals and
muralists of Los Angeles. Included are Wayne
Alaniz Healy, David Botello, Willie Herron,
Manuel Cruz, Judy Baca, the murals in
Venice, CA, graffiti - among others. Color.

DALE GAS [exhibit]

2257 Contemporary Arts Museum, Houston, TX. Dale
gas: give it gas. The continued
acceleration of Chicano art. Exhibition
catalog, 1977. English.

AN: A comprehensive catalog including 28
works of art exhibited by 13 Texas artists:
Melesio (Mel) Casas, Jose Esquivel,
Francisco (Frank) Fajardo, Carmen Lomas
Garza, Luis Jimenez, Cesar Augusto Martinez,
Santos G. Martinez, Jr., Amado Pena, Roberto
Rios, Jose Rivera, Joe B. Rodriguez, Jesus
(Jesse) Trevino, and George Truan. Many
illustrations, some in color. Introduction
by James Harithas. Essay by Santos Martinez,
Jr. Poetry, literature and essays by Chicano

writers.

Dance

2258 Cultural department. RECOBRANDO, Vol. 1, no.
15. Spanish.

AN: The development of "Raza" culture in
the Northwest and the role played by the
Centro de la Raza. Mentions the "talleres de
arte" set up by Carlos Contreras and Arturo
Artorez, artists from Mexico who moved to
Seattle in 1978. Details cultural events
sponsored by the Centro in the fields of
art, music, dance, and theater.

2259 Public invited to weekend fiesta at Lincoln
High. LOS ANGELES TIMES, (April 29, 1969),
p. II. English.

AN: Fiesta of art, music, dance and
literature organized by the committee formed
after the East Los Angeles high school
"blowouts" to press for better and more
relevant education. Hundreds of works of art
were collected for display at the "Fiesta de
los Barrios".

DANZANTES [mural]

2260 Danzantes. LA GENTE DE AZTLAN, Vol. 8, no. 5
(May 31, 1978), p. 12. English.

AN: Ernie de la Torre, muralist from El
Sereno, Los Angeles, CA, describes style and
meaning of his mural DANZANTES. Painted on
the wall of the Alameda Theatre (Woods and
Whittier Blvd.), the mural portrays cultural
and historic aspects of Chicano culture.
Illustrated with photographs.

DANZAS MEXICANAS [mural], Recwood City, CA

2261 Bauer, Bernard. Angry artists deface own
mural. BERKELEY BARB, (March 1978), p. 7.
English.

AN: Chicano artists Jose Antonio
Burciaga and Gilberto Romero Rodriguez
recall a few struggles to sensitize local
arts organizations to Raza art. Financial
and political aspects of their painting a
patriotic mural, "Danzas mexicanas" in
Redwood City. Artists explain why they
defaced their own mural as an act of
protest.

2262 Burciaga, Jose Antonio. Mural protest.
CHISMEARTE, Vol. 2, no. 1 (Summer 1978), p.
27-28. English.

AN: Mexican muralist Gilberto Romero
Rodriguez and Chicano poet and artist
Burciaga splatter their own mural at
dedication ceremonies to protest their
exploitation as artists and the opportunism
and insensitivity of the commissioning
organization, The Multicultural Arts Council
of San Mateo County, CA. The mural was
painted in Redwood City, CA. Illustrated.

2263 Danzas mexicanas. Flyer, 1978. English.

AN: Illustrated flyer about a mural
designed and painted by Chicano artist and
poet Jose Antonio Burciaga and Mexican
muralist Gilberto Romero Rodriguez. Detail
of the 147 x 22 feet mural in Redwood City,
California is reproduced.

DANZAS MEXICANAS [mural], Redwood City, CA (cont.)

2264 Frankenstein, Alfred. One artist's self-defense. SAN FRANCISCO CHRONICLE, (March 9, 1978), p. 44. English.

AN: Art critic Frankenstein opens his columns to Jose Antonio Burciaga to explain why he, and fellow muralist Gilberto Romero Rodriguez, splattered red, white and blue paint on their completed mural at the dedication ceremony. They were protesting the exploitation, use and abuse of artists, particularly by arts councils.

2265 Largest mural in San Mateo County becomes official Saturday. REDWOOD CITY TRIBUNE, (February 23, 1978), p. 12. English.

AN: Mural DANZAS MEXICANAS by Chicano artist and poet Jose Antonio Burciaga and Mexican muralist Gilberto Romero Rodriguez was commissioned by the Multi-cultural Arts Council of San Mateo County. Color illustration.

2266 Martinez, Sue. New mural unveiled in Redwood City. EL TECOLOTE, Vol. 8, no. 7 (April 1978), p. 7. English.

AN: Commentary on the 147x22-ft. mural, DANZAS MEXICANAS, painted by Chicano artist Jose Antonio Burciaga and Mexican artist Gilberto Romero at the Redwood City Civic Center. The mural depicts dance rituals from various Mexican regions and the flora and fauna of Mexico. The mural became a subject of controversy when its creators splattered paint on it during its unveiling as a form of protest against the San Mateo Arts Council for its exploitation of Third World artists. Detail of mural showing "La Danza De Los Viejitos".

DAR LUZ [mural] (Austin, TX)

2267 COMMUNITY MURALS (San Francisco, CA). (Fall 1981). English.

AN: Citywide Murals Group of Denver, Colorado assisted the Chilean-oriented Brigada Orlando Letelier with a mural in their city; Carlos Sandoval of Denver doing mural in Guerrero, Mexico; Ray Patlan of Berkeley, California assisting with mural in Mexico painted by Arnold Belkin's class at the Academy of San Carlos; report on the exhibit MURALS OF AZTLAN: THE STREET PAINTERS OF EAST LOS with a reprint of debate on the event by Shifra M. Goldman, Judithe Elena Hernandez de Neikrug, and comments by John Pitman Weber and Tim Drescher; report on DAR LUZ mural directed by Santa Barraza in Austin, Texas, and a new mural in Hayward, California directed by Enrique Romero; a mural sponsored by the Chicano Youth Center of Fresno, California showing the influence of Mexican calendars; a new mural, OAKLAND'S PORTRAIT by Daniel Galvez in Oakland, California; pro-and-con discussion of social function of graffiti in response to letter from Belgian source; reprint of story on spray paint crime bill (anti-graffiti) sponsored by California Assemblyman Richard Alatorre. Entire issue illustrated.

Davalos, Pete

2268 Galeria de la Raza/Studio 24, San Francisco, CA. Licita Fernandez (watercolor paintings), Pete Davalos (ceramic pots). Exhibition invitation, 1981. English.

AN: Invitation to an exhibit.

Davila, Atanacio

2269 Houston Chicanismo. LA PRENSA, Vol. 1, no. 2 (March 31, 1978). English.

AN: In Houston, Texas, the AMA Gallery (Association for the Advancement of Mexican Americans) was opened in February 1976 to showcase Chicano art. Noel Rodriguez, gallery director, informs about the goals and objectives of the gallery. A current exhibit presents paintings by Josie Mendoza and Atanacio Davila, ceramics by Jesse Sifuentes and mixed-media works by Joe Ramirez. Illustrated with two pieces from exhibit, THANKSGIVING, an acrylic painting by Josie Mendoza and BIRDS, a ceramic piece.

2270 Karkabi, Barbara. For artist Atanacio P. Davila, mural is way to express love for children. HOUSTON CHRONICLE, (May 14, 1980), p. IV-I. English.

AN: Color-illustrated story on mural-in-progress at the Ripley House medical clinic by 70 year old Davila titled THE HEALTHY FAMILY. Son of an artist, Mexican-born Davila was raised in Texas and did commercial art and painting until 1938. After retirement, he has resumed his art.

2271 Mencion Don Quijote: Atanasio P. Davila. LA VOZ DE HOUSTON, (June 5, 1980). English.

AN: Illustrated biography of 70-year-old Mexican-born Texas painter who returned to art after his retirement and had just completed a mural for Houston's Ripley House medical clinic.

Davis, Mike

2272 M.E.C.H.A. cultura y evolucion mexicana. EL CLARIN, (May 2, 1974), p. 3. Spanish.

AN: Report on the mural designed and painted under the direction of Mexican-born designer Sergio O'Cadiz at Santa Ana College, Santa Ana, Calif. Collaborators were instructor Shifra Goldman and gallery director Mike Davis, with members of the MEChA Club and other students. The mural concerns the history of Mexico and of the Chicano and includes a tribute to David Alfaro Siqueiros' Los Angeles mural AMERICA TROPICAL, painted and white-washed in the 1930s. Illustrated.

Day of the Dead
USE: Dia de los Muertos

De Albuquerque, Veronica Dalia

2273 Lansing Community College, Lansing, MI. Festival! Festival program, [1978]. English.

AN: Program of a festival which includes an Hispanic Arts Exhibit, including Juan Ortega, Nora Mendoza, Jose Luis Narezo, and Brazilian-born Veronica Dalia de Albuquerque.

--   --

De Avila, Alfred

2274 Smith, Arva. CEU unveils Chicano mural.
DESERET NEWS, (May 13, 1978), p. 12A.
English.

AN: On Cinco de Mayo 1978, a 14x5-ft.
mural was unveiled in the library of the
College of Eastern Utah. Painted by Salt
Lake City artist Alfred de Avila, the mural
focuses on incidents from Mexican and
Chicano history including a panel on Carbon
County's coal mining industry. Mural was a
bicentennial community art project.
Illustrated with photograph of artist and
section of mural.

De Colores Gallery, Denver, CO

2275 Andrews, Rena. The fine arts. ROUNDUP,
(November 25, 1973), p. 22. English.

AN: Article places work of Ramon Kelley
within the impressionist mode. At the De
Colores Gallery in his hometown of Denver,
Kelley's exhibit titled, "Faces of the
Southwest" included drawings, water color
and pastel painting, oils and acrylics.

2276 Barrett, Marjorie and Flores, John. Flores:
artist's gamble paid off. ROCKY MOUNTAIN
NEWS, (May 18, 1980), p. 27. English.

AN: In less than a decade, John Flores
has gone from being a part-time painter
working in a meat packing plant to a
prolific fulltime artist. This interview on
the occasion of Flores' one person show at
the De Colores Gallery reviews his artistic
trajectory. The 30 odd paintings in the
exhibit include still lifes, pastel
portraits, street scenes and landscapes in
oil. Experimenting with vivid color, Flores
is turning to his own cultural roots.

2277 Kelley sparks Chicano growth. EMPIRE
MAGAZINE, (December 19, 1971), p. 32.
English.

AN: Ramon Kelley, successful and well
known Denver artist is credited with
fomenting and developing a small but strong
Chicano art colony in Denver. As owner of
the De Colores Gallery, Kelley has sponsored
exhibits and personally encouraged many
Chicano artists. John Flores, one of
Kelley's proteges talks about his artistic
development within the Chicano art and
political milieu in Denver. Artist provides
information on his daily life and work
habits on the occasion of an exhibit of his
work at the De Colores Gallery. Flores is a
member of the Denver Arts and Humanities
Commission. Illustrated with a reproduction
of a pastel drawing by John Flores.

De Colores Mural Team

2278 De colores mural team. Brochure, [ca. 1975].
English.

AN: Brochure giving brief history of the
De Colores Mural Team established in 1972 as
part of the Horizons Unlimited program with
Chuy Campusano as coordinator. The team
participated in murals at the Jamestown
Center, Balmy Alley, Redding Elementary
School, Mission Childcare Center, Mission
Branch Bank of America and Horizons
Unlimited from 1972 to 1975.

De la Fuente, Roberto

2279 Trevino, Rudy. San Antonio murals a self

portrait. PICANTE, Vol. 1, no. 3, p. 60-61.
English.

AN: Commentary on the San Antonio Mural
Project assisted by the CETA program and the
Barrio Betterment and Development
Corporation (BBDC). Goals and information on
the light murals in progress in the Casiano
Housing Project. Participating artists: Juan
Hernandez, Esteban Adame, Andrew Gutierrez,
Bob Tate, and Roberto de La Fuente.

De la Huerta, Sylvia

2280 Silent protest. ARIZONA DAILY STAR, (May
18, 1978), p. 6-H. English.

AN: Outdoor murals in Tucson by Ausberto
Sandoval, Antonio Pazos and Sylvia de la
Huerta on a house in community being
displaced by urban renewal. Illustrated.

De la Riva, Lola

2281 Quinonez, Naomi H. In her own backyard = En
su propio traspatio. CAMINOS, Vol. 2, no. 2
(March 1981), p. 34-36,62. Bilingual.

AN: Describes the establishment of the
Centro de Arte in Long Beach, CA by Chicana
artist Lola de la Riva and her family. The
Centro, which is in de la Riva's Long Beach
home, is designed to give members of her
barrio a chance to develop and display their
artistic talents. Frequent workshops in mask
making, clay sculpture, painting, and
graphics are held at the Centro, and the
works of local artists are usually on
display in her backyard.

De la Rocha, Roberto

2282 Art Gallery, California State University,
Long Beach and Lujan, Gilbert Sanchez
"Magu". El arte del pocho. Exhibit brochure,
October 1968. English.

AN: Information about Southern
California artists John Deheras, Marcus
Villagran, Roberto de la Rocha, Santos
Zuniga, Crispin Gonzales, Richard Martinez,
Jesus Gutierrez, Ed Oropeza, Pete Mendez,
David Ramirez, Gilbert Sanchez Lujan, Willie
Hernandez, Art Ponce, Carmen Tostado, Al
Almeida, David Ceja, Robert E. Chavez,
Thomas A. Ferriera. All art students,
graduates, or faculty.

2283 Art Gallery, University of California,
Irvine and Los Angeles County Museum of Art,
Los Angeles, CA. Los Four: Almaraz, de la
Rocha, Lujan, Romero. Exhibition brochure,
1973-74. English.

AN: Photographs and biographies of
Carlos Almaraz, Roberto de la Rocha, Gilbert
S. Lujan, Frank Romero.

2284 Los Four exhibit in Union Gallery.
UNIVERSITY TIMES, (November 6, 1975), p. 4.
English.

AN: "Los Four," a group of four Chicano
artists - Frank Romero, Roberto "Beto" de la
Rocha, Gilbert Lujan, and Carlos Almaraz,
with newcomer Judithe Hernandez - work with
political cartoons, Catholic symbols, works
of sardonic humor. They also paint street
murals: several have been done recently in
Los Angeles, La Puente, and Long Beach.
Illustrated.

De la Rocha, Roberto (cont.)

2285 Lujan, Gilbert Sanchez "Magu". El arte del Chicano - "The Spirit of the Experience". CON SAFOS, no. 7 (Winter 1971), p. 11-13. English.

AN: Definition of Chicano Art by artist Lujan as the expression of an unique experience that is neither Mexican nor U.S. Anglo, that has its own vitality and dynamics. Chicanos can draw upon common cultural elements and transform them into images and art forms such as sculptured menudo bones, tortilla drawings, vato loco portraits, etc. Four woodcuts by Roberto de la Rocha are shown as examples.

2286 Moreno, Eduardo. Los Four. Half-hour 16mm film. English.

AN: Film about the Los Angeles group of artists known as Los Four (originally Carlos Almaraz, Gilbert Sanchez Lujan, Roberto de la Rocha, Frank Romero), at the time of their exhibit at the Los Angeles County Museum of Art - the first time Chicano art was shown at the Museum.

2287 Oakland Museum, Oakland, CA and Laney College, Oakland, CA. In search of Aztlan. Exhibition brochure, 1974. English.

AN: Brochure for exhibit featuring Los Four: Carlos Almaraz, Gilbert Lujan, Roberto de la Rocha, Frank Romero, Judithe Hernandez.

2288 Oakland Museum, Oakland, CA. In search of Aztlan. Exhibition invitation, 1974. English.

AN: Invitation to an exhibit by Los Four, a Chicano art group started about 1973 in Los Angeles. On exhibit are the original members, Carlos Almaraz, Gilbert Lujan, Roberto de la Rocha, Frank Romero, and new member Judithe Hernandez.

2289 Oakland Museum presents 5 L.A. Chicano artists. EL MUNDO (Hayward, CA), (August 1974). English.

AN: Report on the exhibit THE SEARCH FOR AZTLAN, featuring paintings, murals, tortilla art, folk and religious symbols and totems by Carlos Almaraz, Roberto de la Rocha, Gilbert Lujan, Frank Romero and Judithe Hernandez. Included in the more than 100 works are a wall mural, a folk art pyramid, and part of a primed '51 Chevy lowrider. Illustrated.

2290 Plagens, Peter. Los Four (Roberto de la Rocha, Carlos Almaraz, Gilbert Lujan and Frank Romero) at LACMA. ARTFORUM, (September 1974), p. 87-88. English.

AN: Review of Los Four exhibit at Los Angeles County Museum of Art which calls it a "sociological bazaar" in which Chicanos have been "corrupted" by art schools and "museumized".

2291 The Point Gallery, Santa Monica, CA. ASCO (Gronk, Patssi, Gamboa, Herron), Los Four (Almaraz, de la Rocha, Judithe Hernandez, Gloriamalia Flores, Mauricio Ramirez, John Valadez. Exhibition invitation, [1975]. English.

AN: Illustrated invitation to an exhibit of Los Angeles artists.

2292 Polack, Clark. A question of style - Los Four and the Los Angeles County Museum of Art. SOUTHWEST ART, (July, August, 1974). English.

AN: A double-edged assessment of the "Los Four" exhibit. The exhibition is at once lauded for being provocative and stimulating while at the same time failing artistically. Author feels that special treatment given Carlos Almaraz, Gilbert Lujan, Roberto de la Rocha and Frank Romero by the L.A. County Art Museum has not been extended to other young Los Angeles artists.

2293 Santa Ana College, Santa Ana, CA and Goldman, Shifra M. Chicano art. Exhibition catalog, 1974. English.

AN: Thirteen California artists are presented in a short essay defining Chicano as a double mestizaje of Mexican mestizo and U.S. influences that exists in a state of "reconciled conflict." Its aim is communication. Artists included are Malaquias Montoya, Rupert Garcia, Manuel Hernandez, Esteban Villa, Robert Gomez, Harvey Tarango, Mary Helen Castro, Eduardo Carrillo, Graciela Carrillo, and "Los Four": Carlos Almaraz, Robert de la Rocha, Judithe Hernandez, Gilbert Lujan and Frank Romero.

De la Torre, Ernie

2294 Danzantes. LA GENTE DE AZTLAN, Vol. 8, no. 5 (May 31, 1978), p. 12. English.

AN: Ernie de la Torre, muralist from El Sereno, Los Angeles, CA, describes style and meaning of his mural DANZANTES. Painted on the wall of the Alameda Theatre (Woods and Whittier Blvd.), the mural portrays cultural and historic aspects of Chicano culture. Illustrated with photographs.

De Leon, Anna

2295 Erickson, Barbara. La Pena's new face. NORTH EAST BAY INDEPENDENT, no. 4 (September 5, 1978), p. 11. English.

AN: Illustrated story on the relief mural SONG OF UNITY by Ray Patlan, O'Brien Thiele, Osha Neumann, and Anna de Leon on the facade of La Pena cultural center in Berkeley, California. Chilean songwriter Victor Jara and the music of North and South America are the motifs.

2296 Goldman, Shifra M. Canto de unidad: nuevo mural de Berkeley. PLURAL, Vol. 8, no. 96 (September 1979), p. 33-44. Spanish.

AN: Report on significance, inconography, and new technical experimentation in street mural on facade of La Pena Cultural Center, Berkeley, CA. Deals with Latin American "nueva cancion." Ray Patlan and Anna de Leon on team of four muralists. Illustrated. This article was reprinted as "Song of Unity: Berkeley's New Raza Mural," in ARTWORKERS NEWS (New York), Vol. 11, no. 30, September 20, 1980, p. 1.

2297 Goldman, Shifra M. Song of unity: Berkeley's new raza mural. ARTWORKERS NEWS, Vol. 11, no. 30 (September 20, 1980), p. 1. English.

AN: Reprint of article published as "Canto de unidad: nuevo mural de Berkeley" in PLURAL (Mexico, D.F.), Vol. 8, no. 96, September 1979, p. 33-44.

De Leon, Anna (cont.)

2298 New radical wall art. PEOPLE'S WORLD, Vol. 41, no. 37 (September 16, 1978), p. 10. English.

AN: Illustrated story and explanation of the imagery on the new mural resulting from a collaboration of Commonarts and La Pena Cultural Center. The artists are Ray Patlan, O'Brien Thiele, Osha Neumann, and Anna de Leon.

De Leon, Josefina

2299 Altars as folk art. ARRIBA, Vol. 1, no. 1 (July 1980, 194), p. 4. English.

AN: Focusing on the home altar of Josefina De Leon from Cuero, Texas, the article describes this folk expression on two levels: first as a subjective religious intermediator and secondly as a masterpiece of collected objects. Contains interesting information on the form, function and meaning of altars. Illustrated with photographs.

De Leon, Nephtali

2300 De La Zerda, Nancy and De Leon, Nephtali. Entrevista con Nephtali de Leon. CARACOL, Vol. 5, no. 9 (May 1979), p. 12-13, 19. Spanish.

AN: Discusses the iconography of his painting EL DESTINO DE LAS AMERICAS.

2301 Johnston, Jerry. A man with a message: let's build strength, pride. DESERET NEWS, (June 28, 1980), p. S3. English.

AN: Story on Nephtali De Leon, playwright, poet, and illustrator of children's literature. In addition to I WILL CATCH THE SUN and I COLOR MY GARDEN children's books, he works with oil painting, stained glass and woodcuts.

De los Santos, Nanci

2302 HEMBRA: HERMANAS EN MOVIMIENTO BROTANDO RAICES DE AZTLAN (University of Texas, Austin). (Spring 1976).

AN: Raul Valdez, drawing, p. 3; Carolina Flores, drawing, p. 5; Maria Flores, photograph, pp. 7, 11, 30; M.E. Secrest-Ramirez, drawing, p. 12; Amacio Zarate, drawing, p. 15; Santa Barraza, drawings, pp. 16, 17, 18, 26, 32; Nora Gonzales-Dodson, painting, p. 19; Gilberto Cardenas, photograph, pp. 22, 28; Nanci de los Santos, photograph, p. 23, 29; Amado Maurilio Pena, Jr. p. 31.

2303 Xochil Art and Culture Center, Mission, TX. Besame mucho. Exhibition invitation, 1979. English.

AN: Invitation to exhibit of Texas artists from Mujeres Artistas del Suroeste (MAS): Mary Ann Anguiano, Alicia Arredondo, Santa Barraza, Nora Gonzales-Dodson, Maria Flores, Carolina Flores, Mary Ann Ambray Gonzales, Sylvia Orozco, Nancy de los Santos, Modesta Barbina Trevino. Illustrated.

De Soto, Ernest

2304 Baciu, Joyce A. Hispanic artists: combining energy and emotion. CAMINOS, Vol. 2, no. 5 (October 1981), p. 14-17. English.

AN: Brief profiles of Mario Uribe, Ernest De Soto, Peter Rodriguez, Margarita Jauregui Weiner, Virginia Jaramillo, Luis Urrea, Ramses Noriega, Jose Lopez, Olivia Sanchez.

Decorative Arts
USE: Arts and Crafts

Del Castillo, Adelaida R.

2305 ENCUENTRO FEMENIL (San Fernando, CA). Vol. 1, no. 1 (Spring 1973), p. 1+. English.

AN: Publication sponsored by Hijas de Cuauhtemoc, a Chicana femenist group. Black and white drawings on cover by Pat Portera Crary. Art work by Vicki Thrall, Adelaida del Castillo, and Maria Hortencia Garcia. Photography by Cindy Honesto and David Lazarin.

Del Castillo-Leon, Victoria

2306 Wilson, William. Chicana artists still seeking identification. LOS ANGELES TIMES, (June 23, 1975), p. VI, 5. English.

AN: Ten Chicana artists are exhibiting their work in the Boathouse Gallery of Plaza de la Raza in Lincoln Park: Judithe Hernandez, Patssi Valdez, Judy Baca, Josefina Quesada, Victoria del Castillo-Leon, Olga Muniz, Gloria Flores, Sylvia Morales, Isabel Castro and Celia Tejadak. The work is still tentative and may develop.

Del Valle, Angel

2307 Frankenstein, Alfred. Just for the record. SAN FRANCISCO CHRONICLE, (May 27, 1976), p. 48. English.

AN: Positive review of exhibit at the Mexican Museum featuring the work of Jesus Reyes Ferreira from Mexico and Gustavo Rivera from San Francisco. Ninety-five-year-old Ferreira uses tempera on tissue paper to render brilliant paintings focusing on Mexican folk motifs. Rivera paints in the abstract expressionist mode with power and passion. Article also lauds the photographic work of Angel del Valle in his exhibition: SEMBRADORES at the Galeria de la Raza.

2308 Frankenstein, Alfred. A senior senor's approach. SAN FRANCISCO CHRONICLE, (May 27, 1976), p. 48. English.

AN: Review of an exhibit of Mexican painter Jesus Reyes Ferreira at the Mexican Museum of San Francisco, as well as that of San Francisco artist Gustavo Rivera, an abstract expressionist painter. Also mentions the Museum's mural map, and Angel del Valle's photography show at the Galeria de la Raza.

2309 Galeria de la Raza/Studio 24, San Francisco, CA. Photographs by Angel Del Valle. Los sembradores: the marijuana growers. Exhibition catalog, 1976. English.

AN: Illustrated catalog. Del Valle documents the growing, customs, and merchandising of marijuana in the Sierras of Mexico.

Delano, CA

2310 Zermeno, Andy. Don Sotaco: caricaturas de la huelga de Delano. Delano, CA: Farmworkers Press, 1966. English.

AN: Short vignettes depicting the farmworkers' struggle and how Don Sotaco comes to understand his role in that social movement. Illustrated with caricatures of the various personages in the struggle; patrones, coyotes, esquiroles, campesinos and huelguistas. Centerfold and back cover photographs by Jon Lewis.

Delgadillo, Ramon

2311 MARS: Movimiento Artistico del Rio Salado. Phoenix, AZ: Mars Studio/Gallery, 1978. English.

AN: History and manifesto of MARS, 13 member group of Arizona painters, sculptors, designers, and photographers: Jose Andres Giron, Jose Jimenez Rodriguez, Antonio Tocora (Colombian-born), Ramon Delgadillo, Francisco Zuniga, Jim Covarrubias, Ed Diaz, David Martinez, Roberto Buitron, Juan Rodriguez, Eddie Lopez, Zarco Guerrero, Joe Sanchez.

Delgado, Etta

2312 Valdez, Armando. El calendario chicano 1977. Hayward, CA: Southwest Network, 1977. English.

AN: Fifth in a series of historical calendars produced in 1972, 1974, 1975, 1976 by La Causa Publications and Southwest Network. Artists whose work is reproduced are Malaquias Montoya, Amado Maurilio Pena, Ramori Zamora, Glugio J.L. Nicandro [Gronk], Etta Delgado, Ricardo Alaniz, Diane Gamboa, Elisa Marina Coleman, Margarita Calderon, Jose Antonio Burciaga, Cesar Augusto Martinez, Maria Ochoa y Valtierra, Juan Renteria Fuentes, from California, New Mexico, and Texas.

2313 Venegas, Sybil. The artists and their work--the role of the Chicana artist. CHISMEARTE, Vol. 1, no. 4 (Fall , Winter, 1977), p. 3, 5. English.

2314 Venegas, Sybil. Conditions for producing Chicana art. CHISMEARTE, Vol. 1, no. 4 (Fall, Winter, 1977, 1978), p. 2, 4. English.

AN: Chicana artists face more obstacles than white women or Chicano counterparts in the arts. Mexican life style has portrayed the ideal of a submissive woman, but the values have changed. Chicana artists are concerned with women and their struggles. Muralists include Patricia Rodriguez, Irene Perez, Consuelo Mendez de Castillo, Susan Cervantes, Ester Hernandez, Miriam Olivo, Ruth Rodriguez, of the Mujeres Muralistas (San Francisco). Other artists are Etta Delgado and Barbara Carrasco.

Delgado, Roberto

2315 Kim, Howard. Chicano art: is it an art form? Or simply art by Chicanos. NEWORLD, Vol. 6, no. 4 (1980), p. 26-30. English.

AN: An attempt to define Chicano art through interviews with Carlos Almaraz, John Valadez, (Los Four), Robert Delgado, Sister Karen Boccalero (Self-Help Graphics), Harry Gamboa, Jr. (ASCO), Ricardo Duardo, Ignacio Gomez, and others. Well illustrated.

Denver City Walls Project, Denver, CO

2316 Metro Denver Urban Coalition, Denver, CO. City walls. Brochure, 1979. English.

AN: Brochure/poster giving history of City Walls Project and biographies of seven artists: Jon Howe, Jerry Jaramillo, Steve Lucero, Jowinnie Moore, Al Sanchez, Fred Sanchez, Carlos M. Sandoval. Illustrated.

2317 Sinisi, J. Sebastian J. Following footsteps of Diego Rivera. CONTEMPORARY, (January 13, 1980), p. 28-30. English.

AN: Story on West Denver murals, particularly by Manuel Martinez and Carlos Sandoval at the La Alma Recreation Center, Summer 1979. Murals done through the Denver City Walls Project by artists belonging to Incorporated Artes Monumentales. Illustrated.

Denver, CO

2318 Andrews, Rena. The fine arts. ROUNDUP, (March 15, 1970), p. 16+. English.

AN: Biographical information on Chicano artist Ramon Kelley. Described as an impressionist, his work has affinity with Monet and Manet.

2319 Andrews, Rena. The fine arts. EMPIRE MAGAZINE, (December 19, 1971), p. 32. English.

AN: Review of first one person show by John Flores at the Nathan Galleries in Denver. Born in El Paso, Texas but reared in Denver, Flores depicts his Indo-Hispanic heritage in his creations. Concentrating on portraits, still-lifes, and landscapes, Flores paints within the Impressionistic mode. Critic feels Flores is not fully realized, yet has some impressive work and is a promising younger artist.

2320 Barrett, Marjorie. Experimental art of a realist. ROCKY MOUNTAIN NEWS, (August 2, 1970), p. 74. English.

AN: Recognized as one of the area's top realist painters, Ramon Kelley is a diligent, hard-working artist. Current work includes experiments with abstraction, strong facial studies and landscapes. Includes photograph of artist and three examples of his work.

2321 Chavez, Lucy. A Chicano muralist. REVISTA MARYKNOLL, (July 1981). English.

AN: Denver artist Carlotta Espinosa decided early in life that she was going to be an artist. Espinosa has painted murals in Arizona, Texas and the San Luis Valley in Colorado. Illustrated with photographs of artist and details from her murals.

Denver, CO (cont.)

2322 Culver, Virginia. Church's secession depicted on canvas. DENVER POST: RELIGION NEWS WEEKLY, (June 24, 1977). English.

AN: Article commenting on mural created by Manuel Martinez as part of a secession movement by St. Mary's Episcopal Church in Denver whose members voted to leave the Episcopal Diocese of Colorado and the national Episcopal Church. Details of the controversy and examination of the iconography in Martinez's mural. Illustrated with photograph of controversial mural.

2323 Dean, Nancy. Denver artist dues are paid in full. ROCKY MOUNTAIN NEWS, (April 5, 1981), p. 6. English.

AN: Profile of artist Ramon Kelley focusing on his successful career and detailing his rise on the art market. Includes photograph of the artist.

2324 Denver. NATIONAL MURALS NETWORK COMMUNITY NEWSLETTER, (Spring 1980), p. 10. English.

AN: Denver, Colorado murals by Manuel Martinez, the Chilean Orlando Letelier Brigade, Roberto Lucero, Al Sanchez, Jerry Jaramillo. Illustrated.

2325 Denver muralist here for workshop. TEMPE DAILY NEWS, (March 28, 1975). English.

AN: Denver muralist Roberto Lucero is invited to give a weekend mural workshop for the Quetzalcoatl Youth Organization of Escalante Community Center in Tempe, Arizona.

2326 Fenwick, Red. Why gifted artist's works won't sell. DENVER POST, (October 28, 1979), p. F, 75. English.

AN: Profile of Denver artist Carlota Espinoza--a painter, sculptor and creator of historic dioramas. Espinoza is mainly self-taught. A mural she created for the Byers branch library in Denver portraying "Hispanic" history in America was selected from more than 2,000 entries for national honors. She was chosen to do a stained glass window in the Colorado State House portraying the state's Spanish heritage, and has done art work for the Denver Museum of Natural History and other institutions. The article laments that such a talented artist has been unable to penetrate the mainstream art market.

2327 Incorporated Artes Monumentales/Inc., Denver, CO. IAM: art exhibit. Exhibition brochure, n.d. English.

AN: Large format, well illustrated brochure with information on muralists Roberto Lucero, Al Sanchez, Andrew Manning, Ricardo Barrera and Bob Reyes. Includes some biographical information situating these artists within the dynamic artistic traditions of the Mexican and the Chicano mural movements.

2328 Kelley sparks Chicano growth. ROCKY MOUNTAIN NEWS, (February 18, 1973), p. Festival,7. English.

AN: Denver artist John Flores speaks about his work and provides details about the small but strong Chicano art colony in Denver. Flores credits Ramon Kelley, an established Chicano artist, with providing much leadership and encouragement in the development of Chicano art in Colorado.

2329 Martinez, Manuel. The art of the Chicano movement, and the movement of Chicano art. In: Valdez, Luis and Steiner, Stan eds. AZTLAN: AN ANTHOLOGY OF MEXICAN AMERICAN LITERATURE. New York: Vintage, 1972, p.349-353. English.

AN: "Like the modern art of Mexico, the new Chicano art is essentially an art of social protest," writes Denver, Colorado muralist and easel painter Martinez. He traces the roots of Chicano art back into Indian, colonial and modern Mexican art, and defines two kinds of Chicano art.

2330 Meta studio I. Denver, CO: s.n., [1980]. English.

AN: Portfolio of colored prints by Colorado artists Ernie Gallegos, Jerry Jaramillo, Steve Lucero and Carlos M. Sandoval. Biographical information and photograph of each artist. Presentation of the group under the rubric of "metarealism" by Stephen Pascual Lucero.

2331 Mills, James. Hispano history mural ready. DENVER POST, (October 17, 1975), p. 27+. English.

AN: PASADO, PRESENTE Y FUTURO, a 20-ft. mural by Denver artist Carlota Espinoza was commissioned by the Friends of the Denver Public Library for the Byers Branch (W. 7th Ave. and Santa Fe Drive). Blending myth and reality, the mural progresses from Aztec empires through the Spanish conquest, from alienation to the struggle for a collective identity and heritage by the Mexican American. Brief commentary by the artist on the mural's significance. Ms. Espinoza's mural was designated as an official Centennial-Bicentennial creation. Illustrated with photograph of artist.

2332 Minority artists exhibit works at Auraria. ROUNDUP, (January 13, 1980), p. 27. English.

AN: Gala art exhibit organized by the Resource Coalition for Minority Artists of Denver. Included Black, Chicano and Native American visual artists as well as film makers and musicians.

2333 Park murals to be censored. EL DIARIO DE LA GENTE, Vol. 1, no. 1 (October 20, 1972), p. 3. English.

AN: Controversy over Chicano murals at La Raza Park in North Denver caused the Denver City Council to pass an ordinance which requires all artists wishing to paint a mural on a public building to secure a permit and obtain approval from the department in question. The disputed mural is one of Aztec symbols that express the elements of an eternal struggle. Illustrated with photograph of controversial mural.

Denver, CO (cont.)

2334 Pollock, Duncan. He sallied forth to paint.
ROCKY MOUNTAIN NEWS, (February 7, 1971), p.
1. English.

AN: Biographical information about
Martin Saldana, an eccentric personality
labeled as Denver's answer to Grandma Moses.
Saldana died in 1965 leaving behind a cache
of "primitive" paintings that soon became
much sought after by collectors. His work
portrayed the rural pageant of Mexican life.
Illustrated with self-portrait.

2335 Pollock, Duncan. Recognition arrives for
Martin Saldana. ROCKY MOUNTAIN NEWS,
(January 13, 1972), p. 55. English.

AN: After a long career as a vegetable
cook at the venerable Brown Palace Hotel in
Denver, Martin Saldana started art classes
at the Denver Art Museum. His work was
fresh, imaginative and totally naive. After
the artist's death in 1965 at age 90, his
paintings started to receive critical
acclaim. Article details Saldana's rise to
prominence and compares his artwork to that
of Henry Rousseau. Illustrated with
photograph of Martin Saldana.

2336 Sanchez, Al. Murals destroyed. EL DIARIO DE
LA GENTE, Vol. 4, no. 14 (August 13, 1976),
p. 7. English.

AN: Open letter from Al Sanchez,
originator of the cartoon "The Tortilla Kid"
and graphics contributor to EL DIARIO.
Letter details events which led to painting
over of six "cultural" paintings at the
Denver Community Development Corporation
Building (4142 Tejon, Denver, CO). Artist
wants due compensation, specifically monies
for "the replacement of artwork to be done
by a community artist on portable murals".

2337 Sinisi, J. Sebastian J. Following footsteps
of Diego Rivera. CONTEMPORARY, (January 13,
1980), p. 28-30. English.

AN: Story on West Denver murals,
particularly by Manuel Martinez and Carlos
Sandoval at the La Alma Recreation Center,
Summer 1979. Murals done through the Denver
City Walls Project by artists belonging to
Incorporated Artes Monumentales.
Illustrated.

2338 Troelstrup, Glenn. Former delinquent paints
his way out of corner. DENVER POST, (April
23, 1977), p. 2. English.

AN: Manuel Martinez started sketching at
13; at 29, after studying with Siqueiros
(1967-68), he painted a number of murals in
Denver and Albuquerque. In 1977 he organized
Incorporated Artists Monumentales. Color
illustration.

Denver Community Development Corporation Building

2339 Sanchez, Al. Murals destroyed. EL DIARIO DE
LA GENTE, Vol. 4, no. 14 (August 13, 1976),
p. 7. English.

AN: Open letter from Al Sanchez,
originator of the cartoon "The Tortilla Kid"
and graphics contributor to EL DIARIO.
Letter details events which led to painting
over of six "cultural" paintings at the
Denver Community Development Corporation
Building (4142 Tejon, Denver, CO). Artist
wants due compensation, specifically monies
for "the replacement of artwork to be done

by a community artist on portable murals".

THE DENVER HARBOR ARTISTS [exhibit]

2340 De Marroquin, Moron. Denver Harbor artists.
LA PRENSA, (June 2, 1978). Spanish.

AN: Commentary on two exhibitions. THE
DENVER HARBOR ARTISTS includes information
on paintings by Lupe Aguirre, Josie Mendoza
and Abel Gonzalez--all from Houston. The
solo show MAGIC BLANCA featured the work of
Brownsville, Texas artist Jorge Truan.
Truan's work is mystical and visionary.

Desiga, Daniel

2341 And/Or Gallery, Seattle, WA. Artistas de
Aztlan. Exhibition announcement, 1975.
English.

AN: Exhibition announcement for an
important exhibit of Northwest Chicano art.
Co-sponsored by MEChA and the Chicano
Studies Program at the University of
Washington, the exhibit presented works by
Emilio Aguayo, Danny Desiga, Ricardo
Aguirre, Ramiro Benavidez, Elma Herada,
Pedro Rodriguez and others. A selection of
posters by Armando Cid of the R.C.A.F. group
from Sacramento, California was also
presented. Concurrently, at the Heny Gallery
of the University of Washington, Esteban
Villa presented a one-man show.

Design

2342 Cantu, Jesus "Chista". Entrevista con
"Chista" Cantu. SIN FRONTERAS, Vol. 1, no.
12 (November 15, 1974), p. 16. Spanish.

AN: Conversation in which Cantu speaks
about his art which is based on the
essential duality of all things. Includes
photograph of design for an album cover
CANTOS SIN FRONTERAS and a photograph of one
of his murals representing the "cosmic unity
of things as seen by people of the corn
culture".

2343 Flores, Gloriamalia and Herrera, Juan
Felipe. Rebozos of love/we have woven/sudor
de pueblos/on our back. San Diego, CA:
Toltecas en Aztlan, 1974. English.

AN: Designs by Gloria Amalia Flores.

EL DESTINO DE LAS AMERICAS [painting]

2344 De La Zerda, Nancy and De Leon, Nephtali.
Entrevista con Nephtali de Leon. CARACOL,
Vol. 5, no. 9 (May 1979), p. 12-13, 19.
Spanish.

AN: Discusses the iconography of his
painting EL DESTINO DE LAS AMERICAS.

Detroit Latino Artist Association

2345 Acosta, Dan. Paintings reflect life
experiences. THE ECCENTRIC, (June 26,
1980). English.

AN: Review of one-woman show by Nora
Chapa Mendoza at the Heritage Art Gallery,
Ypsilanti, MI. Mendoza works in abstract
impressionist style with wet streams of
colors that express energy. Her subjects are
landscapes, moods, nudes, and Hispanic
themes. She is active in the Detroit Latino
Artist Association, Nuestras Artes de
Michigan, and the New Detroit Art Council.

Dia de los Muertos

2346 Amescua, Michael M. Dia de los muertos.
SOMOS, Vol. 1, no. 6 (November 1978), p.
39-40. English.

AN: Report on Self-Help Graphics'
project involving fifteen humanists who
explored history, literature, philosophy and
religion as they relate to the Dia de los
Muertos, an annual program of Self-Help.
Illustrated.

2347 Galeria de la Raza/Studio 24, San Francisco,
CA. Calacas huesudas. Exhibition brochure,
1980.

AN: Exhibition of Chicano artists for El
Dia de los Muertos with brochure using text
adapted from POSADA'S MEXICO, edited by Ron
Tyler, Library of Congress, Washington,
D.C., 1979. The Galeria exhibit was curated
by Kate Connell, Maria Pinedo and Galeria
staff.

2348 Galeria de la Raza/Studio 24, San Francisco,
CA. Dia de los muertos/day of the dead.
Exhibition invitation, 1981. English.

AN: Invitation to the Galeria's annual
Dia de los Muertos exhibition.

2349 Hansen, Barbara. Food for the soul: an
earthly delight. HOME MAGAZINE, (October
22, 1978), p. 53-54. English.

AN: Story on El Dia de los Muertos.
Color illustrations of annual celebration by
Self-Help Graphics and Art, Inc. with
costumes, masks, floats.

2350 Mission to honor Frida Kahlo: famous Mexican
artist. EL TECOLOTE, Vol. 9, no. 3 (November
1978), p. 1. Bilingual.

AN: Announcement of an homage to Mexican
painter Frida Kahlo at the Galeria de la
Raza's annual celebration of Dia de los
Muertos. Works reproduced with the article
include those of Emmanuel C. Montoya, Yreina
Cervantez, Jose Antonio Burciaga, Nina
Serrano and Lisa Kokin. Bilingual.

2351 San Francisco Museum of Modern Art, San
Francisco, CA and Marra, Patricia. Day of
the dead. Exhibition catalog, 1980. English.

AN: Broadside announcement in the manner
of Jose Gudalupe Posada for an exhibit of
prints by Posada and an altar by Amalia Mesa
-Baines and Friends. Text presents customs
and traditions for celebrating the Day of
the Dead in Mexico and among the Chicano
community.

2352 Venegas, Sybil. Dia de los muertos. SOMOS,
Vol. 1, no. 5 (October 1978), p. 42-47.
English.

AN: Brief history of Dia de los muertos
ceremonies. While the custom is dying in
Mexico (except for tourists), Chicano
organizations like Galeria de la Raza
(S.F.), El Centro de Artistas Chicanos
(Sacramento, Ca.) celebrate the event
annually, as does [Self-Help Graphics and
Art, Inc.] in East Los Angeles. Well
illustrated with photographs by Guillermo
Bejarano and Daniel Duran.

2353 Venegas, Sybil. Towards a Chicano cultural
renaissance. LA GENTE DE AZTLAN, Vol. 8, no.
1 (November 2, 1977), p. 12. English.

AN: The revival of celebrations like El
Dia de Los Muertos are seen as catalysts for
barrio unification. Detailed information on
how Self Help Graphics in East Los Angeles
mobilizes artists and community for a
communal celebration.

DIALECTICS OF ISOLATION [exhibit]

2354 Rickey, Carrie. The passion of Ana. VILLAGE
VOICE, Vol. 25, no. 37 (September 10, 1980),
p. 75. English.

AN: Review of the exhibition DIALECTICS
OF ISOLATION, AN EXHIBITION OF THIRD WORLD
WOMEN ARTISTS OF THE UNITED STATES at the
A.I.R Gallery in New York, September 1980.
Includes a capsule analysis of Judith Baca's
colossal mural in Tujunga Wash in Los
Angeles. The mural "proposes to restore to
public consciousness the ethnic and cultural
history of the city's minorities." Details
work procedures, content and political aims
of the project. Eleven blue prints of mural
cartoons detailing highlights of the mural's
visual narrative were displayed in the
exhibit.

Diaz, Aurelio

2355 59th Street Gallery, St. Louis, MO. Midwest
Mexican-American art exhibit: Mexico and its
artists. Exhibition brochure, 1981. English.

AN: Sponsored by the Sociedad Mexicana
"Benito Juarez" and the international
Institute of St. Louis, this three-part
exhibit includes 1) MEXICO AS SEEN BY HER
CHILDREN, a bilingual exhibit from Mexico
traveling under Smithsonian Institution
auspices, 2) MEXICAN CHILDREN IN THE U.S.A.,
3) MEXICAN AMERICAN ARTISTS. In the latter
are included Stephen Capiz (Roseville,
Minn.), Jose Gonzalez (Chicago), Cesar A.
Martinez (San Antonio), Ada Medina (Des
Moines), Nora Chapa Mendoza (West
Bloomfield, Mich.), Rene David
Michel-Trapaga (St. Louis), David Munoz
(Kansas City, Mo.), Jose Luis Narezo (Grand
Rapids, Mich.), Benny Ordonez, Roman
Villarreal (Chicago), Alejandro Romero
(Chicago), Aurelio Diaz "Tekpankalli"
(Chicago), Simon Ybarra (St. Louis).

2356 Calendario de March: 1977. Chicago, IL:
MARCH, Inc., 1976. English.

AN: Historical calendar with photos and
biographies of artists. Illustrations of
artwork by Ray Patlan, Jose Nario, Frank J.
Sanchez, Salvador Dominguez, Salvador Vega,
Marguerite Ortega, Aurelio Diaz, Carlos
Cortez, Mario E. Castillo, Francisco Blasco,
Rey Vasquez, and Efrain Martinez. History of
MARCH (Movimiento Artistico Chicano).

2357 Chicago-Raza murals. NATIONAL MURALS NETWORK
COMMUNITY NEWSLETTER, (Fall 1979), p. 22.
English.

AN: Murals by Ray Patlan, Aurelio Diaz,
Marcos Raya, Salvador Vega, Jaime Longoria,
Malu Ortega y Alberro, Oscar Moya in
Chicago's Pilsen district.

Diaz, Aurelio (cont.)

2358 Elitzik, Paul. Mural magic. AMERICAS,
     (June, July, 1981). English.

     AN: Brief illustrated account of murals
     in the Pilsen barrio of Chicago. Mentions
     work by Aurelio Diaz, Marcos Raya, and
     Salvador Vega. Focuses on the controversial
     mural at Benito Juarez High School painted
     by Jaime Longoria and Malu Ortega.

2359 Notes on 2nd National Community Muralists'
     Network Conference, Chicago, Ill. April
     20-23, 1978. San Francisco, CA, 1978.
     English.

     AN: Rupert Garcia, Raul Martinez,
     Patricia Rodriguez, Ray Patlan (San
     Francisco Bay Area) and Jaime Valadez (San
     Jose), among others, attended the conference
     in Chicago. Reports were heard from many
     parts of the United States on mural
     activities, including that of Aurelio Diaz
     of Chicago, representing MARCH (Movimiento
     Artistico Chicano). A workshop presentation
     was made by Luis Arenal and others from the
     Taller Siqueiros of Cuernavaca, Mexico. An
     experimental mural to try Siqueiros'
     techniques was created. Illustrated.

Diaz, Ed

2360 Encanto Pavilion, Encanto Park, Phoenix, AZ.
     Exposicion de arte para la raza: Arizona
     Chicano art show. Exhibition catalog, [ca.
     1978]. English.

     AN: Catalog for an exhibit organized by
     MARS (Movimiento Artistico del Rio Salado).
     Colombian-born Antonio L. Tocora, Jim
     Covarrubias, Ed Dias, Robert C. Buitron,
     Armando Leon Hernandez, Guillermo Galindo,
     Richard Luna Cisneros, Jose Andres Giron,
     Robert L. Matta included.

2361 MARS: Movimiento Artistico del Rio Salado.
     Phoenix, AZ: Mars Studio/Gallery, 1978.
     English.

     AN: History and manifesto of MARS, 13
     member group of Arizona painters, sculptors,
     designers, and photographers: Jose Andres
     Giron, Jose Jimenez Rodriguez, Antonio
     Tocora (Colombian-born), Ramon Delgadillo,
     Francisco Zuniga, Jim Covarrubias, Ed Diaz,
     David Martinez, Roberto Buitron, Juan
     Rodriguez, Eddie Lopez, Zarco Guerrero, Joe
     Sanchez.

Diaz, Jean

2362 Diaz, Jean; Dominguez, Edward; and Torres,
     Kay. Bi-Lingual blues [fotonovela]. SOMOS,
     Vol. 1, no. 1 (April, May, 1978), p. 33-36.
     English.

     AN: Reproduction of a "fotonovela",
     BI-LINGUAL BLUES by Ojo Productions, a group
     of students connected with the Latin
     American Studies Department of California
     State University, Los Angeles.

Diaz Perez, Roberto

2363 Martinez, Anita. Raza! Arte! Raza! Arte!
     EL TECOLOTE, Vol. 1, no. 2 (September 7,
     1970), p. 3. Bilingual.

     AN: Galeria de la Raza opened on July,
     1970 at 425 14th St. San Francisco. It was
     an outgrowth of the Arte Seis organization
     (an art effort established in the Mission
     District in 1967 by Francisco Camplis,

Rupert Garcia, Ralph McNeil, Jay Ojeda and
Jack Ruiz). These and other artists brought
together by the Neighborhood Arts Program
have coalesced in the new Galeria de la
Raza. Article gives goals, organizational
scheme and plans for the Galeria. It's first
exhibit was a one man show by Esteban Villa
together with a photo and sketch exhibit on
Cuba by Jay Ojeda, Roberto Diaz Perez and
Gloria Ozuna. Illustrated with installation
view of new Galeria.

Diaz, Ricardo

2364 Garcia, Rupert. Laminas de la Raza. San
     Francisco: Garcia Litho and Printing
     Service, 1975. English.

     AN: Portfolio of drawings and prints by
     Patricia Rodriguez, Ricardo Apodaca,
     Xochitl, Domingo Rivera, Francisco Camplis,
     Rafael Maradiaga, Tom Rios, Juan Fuentes,
     Ricardo Diaz, Jose Romero, Consuelo Mendez,
     Jose Antonio Burciaga, Irene Perez, Ricardo
     Rios, Mike Rios, Graciela Carrillo, Rene
     Yanez, Luis Talamantez, Guillermo Bermudez,
     all from Northern California.

2365 Moisan, Jim. Ancient roots, new visions.
     ARTWEEK, Vol. 9, no. 26 (July 29, 1978), p.
     8. English.

     AN: Review of the show held at the
     Municipal Arts Gallery of Los Angeles, the
     first national touring show of Latino
     artists in the United States. Includes
     commentary on work of Larry Fuente, Luis
     Jimenez, Frank Romero, Harry Gamboa, Gronk,
     Rudy Martinez, Benjamin Serrano, Ricardo
     Diaz, Patssi Valdez, Mel Casas, Luis Leroy,
     Pedro Lujan. A related show, NEW VISIONS,
     L.A., includes Robert Delgado, Ray Bravo,
     Joe Moran, Rosalyn Mesquita, Patricia
     Murillo and others.

Dichos

2366 Garcia-Camarillo, Mia. [Untitled drawings].
     CARACOL, Vol. 3, no. 4 (December 1976), p.
     8-9, 12.

DIRECTAMENTE DEL BARRIO [exhibit]

2367 Garcia, Ignacio. Senior exhibit attempts to
     define Chicano art. SOUTH TEXAN, (August 1,
     1975). English.

     AN: DIRECTAMENTE DEL BARRIO, a senior
     art exhibit at Texas A & I University by art
     majors Raul Valdez and Jesus Reyes. Sets
     forth their ideas about Chicano arts and
     their future plans.

Discrimination
     USE: Racism

Diseno Studios Gallery, Austin, TX

2368 Diseno Studios, Austin, TX. Diseno Studios
     Gallery. Brochure, 1981. English.

Doctor's Hospital, East Los Angeles

2369 [Untitled photograph]. LOS ANGELES TIMES,
     (June 4, 1971), p. II, 2. English.

     AN: Captioned illustration of Frank
     Martinez's mural painting of slain LOS
     ANGELES TIMES reporter Ruben Salazar.
     Unveiling of the mural at the Doctor's
     Hospital, East Los Angeles, during
     groundbreaking ceremonies for a new wing.

Dohrenwend, Bruce P.

2370 Sanchez, Jesus. Auditorium mural "wipe out" during recent renovation move. EAST LOS ANGELES COLLEGE NEWS, (September 26, 1979). English.

AN: "The Path to Knowledge and the False University," a mural by Roberto Chavez on the facade of ELAC's Ingalls Auditorium was painted over on Sept. 11, 1979. Contrasting views on the mural's fate are offered by the Chicano Faculty Association President and the Dean of Educational Services.

Dominguez, Eduardo

2371 Amor sin fronteras. Los Angeles, CA: Colectivo El Ojo, n.d.. English.

AN: Fotonovela with Josefina Arce, Eduardo Dominguez and Mike Jauregui produced by the Colectivo: Eduardo Dominguez, Roberto Gil de Montes, Jerry Lucas, Kay Torres, students at California State University, Los Angeles.

Dominguez, Mary Lynn

2372 California. State College. Los Angeles. Art Department. Fifth California small images exhibition. Exhibition catalog, [1972]. English.

AN: Catalog for an exhibit including the work of Charles D. Almaraz, Mary Lynn Dominguez, Gilbert Sanchez Lujan (who won Purchase Awards), Stephen Anaya, Martha Villegas. Illustrated.

Dominguez, Priscilla

2373 Hartnell College Studio Gallery, Salinas, CA. Paintings, drawings, prints by San Francisco Bay Area Chicano artists. Exhibit brochure, 1971. English.

AN: Brochure for exhibit featuring Francisco Camplis, Graciela Carrillo, Sal Castaneda, Priscilla Dominguez, J. Duarte, Rupert Garcia, Carlos Loarca, Irene Perez, Vincent Rascon, Michael Rios, Peter Rodriguez, Luis Valsoto, Esteban Villa, Rene Yanez, Zala. Illustrated by Rupert Carcia print.

Dominguez, Salvador

2374 Calendario de March: 1977. Chicago, IL: MARCH, Inc., 1976. English.

AN: Historical calendar with photos and biographies of artists. Illustrations of artwork by Ray Patlan, Jose Nario, Frank J. Sanchez, Salvador Dominguez, Salvador Vega, Marguerite Ortega, Aurelio Diaz, Carlos Cortez, Mario E. Castillo, Francisco Blasco, Rey Vasquez, and Efrain Martinez. History of MARCH (Movimiento Artistico Chicano).

DON JUAN VOLADOR [painting]

2375 Martinez, Cesar Augusto; Garcia-Camarillo, Mia; and Garcia-Camarillo, Cecilio. Don Juan Volador, Platica con Cesar Augusto Martinez. CARACOL, Vol. 2, no. 4 (December 1975), p. 3-5. Spanish.

AN: Interview with Cesar Martinez about his acrylic painting DON JUAN VOLADOR. Based on themes suggested by the writings of Carlos Castaneda, the painting deals with the spiritual nature of Chicanismo. This issue of CARACOL is illustrated by the painting in question.

Los Dos Streetscapers [art group]

2376 Botello, David Rivas and Healy, Wayne Alaniz. Los Dos Streetscapers. SOMOS, Vol. 1, no. 3 (August 1978), p. 12-17. English.

AN: Autobiographical material by Los Angeles street muralists Botello and Healy. Illustrated.

2377 Los Dos Streetscapers. Los Dos Streetscapers, mural detail. NATIONAL GEOGRAPHIC, Vol. 155, no. 1 (January 1979), p. 38-39. English.

AN: One panel of Los Angeles mural by Wayne Alaniz Healey and David Botello, CHICANO TIME TRIP.

Drawings

2378 La abuela [drawing]. REVISTA RIO BRAVO, Vol. 1, no. 1 (Winter 1981), p. Bk cover.

2379 Acevedo, Esperanza "Inky". [Untitled drawing]. REVISTA CHICANO-RIQUENA, Vol. 5, no. 1 (Winter 1977), p. 44. English.

2380 Acevedo, Esperanza "Inky". [Untitled drawing]. REVISTA CHICANO-RIQUENA, Vol. 5, no. 1 (Winter 1977), p. 93. English.

2381 Acevedo, Esperanza "Inky". Untitled [drawing]. REVISTA CHICANO-RIQUENA, Vol. 5, no. 1 (Winter 1977), p. 113. English.

2382 Acosta, Tom. [Untitled drawing]. CON SAFOS, no. 8 (1972), p. 63.

2383 Acosta, Tom. [Untitled drawing]. CON SAFOS, no. 8 (1972), p. 59,63. Bilingual.

2384 Aguayo, Emilio. Chicano art: a new art-style of the future. (Unpublished Study Project for Prof. Brauman, Art Dept., Univ. of Washington, Seattle), June 6, 1972. English.

AN: Autobiographical account and self-analysis of artist's work. Beginning in 1965 the artist has created 40,000 small ink drawings in a contour line technique. Situating himself within the Chicano Arts Movement, Aguayo describes his dominant themes, symbols, and stylistic preoccupations.

2385 Alegria, Isabel. [Untitled drawing]. MAIZE, Vol. 4, no. 3-4 (Spring, Summer, 1981), p. 46. Bilingual.

2386 Almaraz, Carlos. [Untitled drawing]. CON SAFOS, no. 8 (1972), p. 29.

2387 Alonzo, R. Honey boom USA [drawing]. REVISTA CHICANO-RIQUENA, Vol. 2, no. 1 (Winter 1974), p. 38. English.

2388 Alonzo, R. Late sleeper [drawing]. REVISTA CHICANO-RIQUENA, Vol. 2, no. 1 (Winter 1974), p. COVER. English.

2389 Alonzo, R. [Untitled drawing]. REVISTA CHICANO-RIQUENA, Vol. 2, no. 1 (Winter 1974), p. 23. English.

2390 Alurista. Nationchild plumaroja: 1969-1972. San Diego, CA: Toltecas en Aztlan, Centro Cultural de La Raza, 1972. English.

AN: Drawings by Esteban Villa and Armando Nunez.

Drawings (cont.)

2391 Andrews, Rena. The fine arts. ROUNDUP,
(November 25, 1973), p. 22. English.

AN: Article places work of Ramon Kelley
within the impressionist mode. At the De
Colores Gallery in his hometown of Denver,
Kelley's exhibit titled, "Faces of the
Southwest" included drawings, water color
and pastel painting, oils and acrylics.

2392 Angulo, Hector "H". U-NIDA [drawing].
CARACOL, Vol. 2, no. 12 (August 1976), p.
FRNT COVER. Bilingual.

2393 Angulo, Hector "H". [Untitled drawing].
CARACOL, Vol. 2, no. 12 (August 1976), p. Bk
cover. English.

2394 Angulo, Hector "H". [Untitled drawing].
CARACOL, Vol. 4, no. 3 (November 1977), p.
7.

2395 Arreola, Tomas. Genesis [drawing]. XALMAN,
Vol. 1, no. 5 (Fall   1977), p. iv.

2396 Arreola, Tomas. [Untitled drawing]. XALMAN,
Vol. 1, no. 5 (Fall   1977), p. 12.

2397 Arreola, Tomas. La viuda [drawing]. XALMAN,
Vol. 1, no. 5 (Fall   1977), p. 22.

2398 Art directors, take note. INTERRACIAL BOOKS
FOR CHILDREN, Vol. 5, no. 7-8 (1975), p. 19.
English.

AN: Focus on the work of three Chicano
illustrators: Salvador Barajas V., Arturo
Roman, and Guillermo Aranda. Includes
representative examples of their work.

2399 The art of Rodolfo Leal. TIN TAN, Vol. 2,
no. 6 (December 1, 1977), p. 15-18. English.

AN: Two calligraphic ink drawings and a
serigraph by Texas-born Leal who lives in
San Francisco.

2400 Artista de Aztlan. EL DIARIO DE LA GENTE,
Vol. 4, no. 8 (April 1976), p. 7. Spanish.

AN: Interview with Mike Garcia, staff
artist for the DIARIO. Born in Alamosa,
Colorado, the artist defines his work as
"mestizo art because it expresses our Indian
heritage, using motifs of the revolutionary
struggles to reflect the possibilities of
the future." Well illustrated.

2401 Avalos, David. [Untitled drawing]. EL
TECOLOTE LITERARY MAGAZINE, Vol. 1, no. 1
(April 1980), p. 4.

2402 Baca, Judith F. Study for figure one: the
uprising of the mujeres [drawing]. EL
TECOLOTE LITERARY MAGAZINE, Vol. 2, no. 2
(July 1981), p. 4.

2403 Barraza, Santa. Arte de Santa Barraza.
TEJIDOS, Vol. 5, no. 2-4 (1978), p. 14-21.
Bilingual.

2404 Barraza, Santa. Israelita [drawing].
TEJIDOS, Vol. 1, no. 4 (Fall   1974), p. 11.
Spanish.

2405 Barraza, Santa. Life drawing study
[drawing]. TEJIDOS, Vol. 1, no. 4 (Fall
1974), p. 7. English.

2406 Barraza, Santa. Madonna & child [drawing].
TEJIDOS, Vol. 1, no. 4 (Fall   1974), p. 19.
English.

2407 Barraza, Santa. Maria Elena [drawing].
TEJIDOS, Vol. 5, no. 1 (1978), p. 48.
Bilingual.

2408 Barraza, Santa. Self portrait [drawing].
TEJIDOS, Vol. 1, no. 4 (Fall   1974), p. 26.

2409 Barraza, Santa. [Untitled drawing]. TEJIDOS,
Vol. 1, no. 4 (Fall   1974), p. COVER.
English.

2410 Barraza, Santa. [Untitled drawing]. CARACOL,
Vol. 2, no. 11 (July 1976), p. 4. English.

2411 Barraza, Santa. Villa y Cortina [drawing].
TEJIDOS, Vol. 1, no. 4 (Fall   1974), p. 34.
Spanish.

2412 Bejarano, William. [Untitled drawing]. CON
SAFOS, Vol. 2, no. 5 (1970), p. 10.

2413 Bejarano, William. [Women (drawing)].
REGENERACION, Vol. 2, no. 3 (1973), p. 34.

2414 Berry, Miguel. Now showing: outer space
[drawing]. CARACOL, Vol. 2, no. 5 (January
1976), p. 10. English.

2415 Borajas, Carlos. Images of my mind
[drawing]. XALMAN, Vol. 1, no. 4 (Spring
1977), p. 19.

2416 [Boycott non-union lettuce (graphic)].
REGENERACION, Vol. 1, (1970), p. BACK
COVER. English.

2417 Brand Library Art Center, Glendale, CA. Los
hermanos: Jesus, Jacob & Frank Gutierrez,
sculpture, paintings, drawings, &
photographs. Exhibition catalog, 1974.
English.

AN: Exhibit of the work of three
brothers living in the Los Angeles area.

2418 Burciaga, Jose Antonio. Adoracion [drawing].
REVISTA CHICANO-RIQUENA, Vol. 3, no. 4 (Fall
1975), p. 31. Spanish.

2419 Burciaga, Jose Antonio. Al frente [drawing].
EL GRITO, Vol. 7, no. 3 (March, May, 1974),
p. 52. Bilingual.

2420 Burciaga, Jose Antonio. Aliens [drawing].
CARACOL, Vol. 4, no. 2 (October 1977), p.
FRNT COVER.

2421 Burciaga, Jose Antonio. [Inside the public
school (drawing)]. ATISBOS, no. 3 (Summer,
Fall , 1978), p. 85.

2422 Burciaga, Jose Antonio. Mestizo [drawing].
CARACOL, Vol. 3, no. 2 (October 1976), p.
FRNT COVER. Spanish.

2423 Burciaga, Jose Antonio. Nacimiento
[drawing]. REVISTA CHICANO-RIQUENA, Vol. 3,
no. 4 (Fall   1975), p. 21. Spanish.

2424 Burciaga, Jose Antonio. La posada [drawing].
REVISTA CHICANO-RIQUENA, Vol. 3, no. 4 (Fall
1975), p. COVER. Spanish.

2425 Burciaga, Jose Antonio and Zamora, Bernice.
Restless serpents. Menlo Park, CA: Disenos
Literarios, 1976. English.

AN: Includes numerous drawings by
northern California artist and poet Jose
Antonio Burciaga.

Drawings (cont.)

2426 Burciaga, Jose Antonio. Spirit of '76 [drawing]. CARACOL, Vol. 2, no. 10 (June 1976), p. 12. English.

2427 Burciaga, Jose Antonio. Los tres magos [drawing]. REVISTA CHICANO-RIQUENA, Vol. 3, no. 4 (Fall 1975), p. 2. Spanish.

2428 Burciaga, Jose Antonio. [Untitled drawing]. ATISBOS, no. 3 (Summer, Fall , 1978), p. 1.

2429 Burciaga, Jose Antonio. [Untitled drawing]. ATISBOS, no. 3 (Summer, Fall , 1978), p. 19.

2430 Burciaga, Jose Antonio. [Untitled drawing]. ATISBOS, no. 3 (Summer, Fall , 1978), p. 35.

2431 Burciaga, Jose Antonio. [Untitled drawing]. ATISBOS, no. 3 (Summer, Fall , 1978), p. 61.

2432 Burciaga, Jose Antonio. [Untitled drawing]. ATISBOS, no. 3 (Summer, Fall , 1978), p. 101.

2433 Burciaga, Jose Antonio. [Untitled drawing]. ATISBOS, no. 3 (Summer, Fall , 1978), p. 125.

2434 Burciaga, Jose Antonio. [Untitled drawing]. ATISBOS, no. 3 (Summer, Fall , 1978), p. 141.

2435 Burciaga, Jose Antonio. [Untitled drawing]. ATISBOS, no. 3 (Summer, Fall , 1978), p. 155.

2436 Burciaga, Jose Antonio. [Untitled drawing]. ATISBOS, no. 3 (Summer, Fall , 1978), p. 179.

2437 Burciaga, Jose Antonio. [Untitled drawing]. ATISBOS, no. 3 (Summer, Fall , 1978), p. 192.

2438 Burciaga, Jose Antonio. [Untitled drawing]. ATISBOS, no. 3 (Summer, Fall , 1978), p. 193.

2439 Burciaga, Jose Antonio. [Untitled drawing]. ATISBOS, no. 3 (Summer, Fall , 1978), p. 201.

2440 Burciaga, Jose Antonio. [Untitled drawing]. ATISBOS, no. 3 (Summer, Fall , 1978), p. 215.

2441 Burciaga, Jose Antonio. [Untitled drawing]. ATISBOS, no. 3 (Summer, Fall , 1978), p. 221.

2442 Burciaga, Jose Antonio. [Untitled drawing]. MANGO, Vol. 1, no. 1 (Fall 1976), p. Ft Cover.

2443 Burciaga, Jose Antonio. [Untitled drawing]. EL GRITO, Vol. 7, no. 3 (March, May, 1974), p. 74. Bilingual.

2444 Burciaga, Jose Antonio. [Untitled drawing]. EL GRITO, Vol. 7, no. 3 (March, May, 1974), p. 64. Bilingual.

2445 Burciaga, Jose Antonio. [Untitled drawing]. EL GRITO, Vol. 7, no. 3 (March, May, 1974), p. 59. Bilingual.

2446 Burciaga, Jose Antonio. [Untitled drawing]. EL GRITO, Vol. 7, no. 3 (March, May, 1974), p. 26. Bilingual.

2447 Burciaga, Jose Antonio. [Untitled drawing]. EL TECOLOTE LITERARY MAGAZINE, Vol. 1, no. 1 (April 1980), p. 8.

2448 Burciaga, Jose Antonio. [Untitled drawing]. EL TECOLOTE LITERARY MAGAZINE, Vol. 1, no. 1 (April 1980), p. 10.

2449 Burciaga, Jose Antonio. [Untitled drawing]. MANGO, Vol. 1, no. 1 (Fall 1976), p. Bk cover.

2450 Burciaga, Jose Antonio. [Untitled drawings]. EL GRITO, Vol. 7, no. 3 (March, May, 1974), p. 4-74.

2451 Burciaga, Jose Antonio. [Untitled drawings]. CARACOL, Vol. 2, no. 11 (July 1976), p. 24.

2452 Burciaga, Jose Antonio. [Untitled drawings]. MANGO, Vol. 1, no. 1 (Fall 1976), p. 9,16,18,30.

2453 Burciaga, Jose Antonio. Which way did they go, slim? [drawing]. CARACOL, Vol. 5, no. 2 (October 1978), p. 9. English.

2454 Camacho, Jose. [Untitled drawing]. EL POCHO CHE, Vol. 1, no. 2 (1970), p. 69.

2455 Camargo, Arturo. [Untitled drawing]. CON SAFOS, Vol. 1, no. 3 (March 1969), p. 46.

2456 [Camarillo (drawing)]. REVISTA RIO BRAVO, Vol. 1, no. 1 (Winter 1981), p. 7.

2457 Campbell, Roberto Bruce. [Untitled drawings]. CARACOL, Vol. 5, no. 10 (June 1979), p. 5. English.

2458 Canto al pueblo: an anthology of experiences. San Antonio, TX: Penca Books, 1978. English.

   AN: Includes works by: Mario E. Castillo, Carlos Rosas, Jose G. Gonzalez, Santos Martinez, Gilbert Munoz, Fred Loa, Armando Ibanez and others.

2459 Cantu, Jesus "Chista". [Una interpretacion de la Raza Cosmica en armonia con la tierra y el cosmos (drawing)]. CARACOL, Vol. 4, no. 9 (May 1978), p. FRNT COVER. Spanish.

2460 Cardenas de Dwyer, Carlota, ed. Chicano voices. Boston, MS: Houghton Mifflin, 1975. English.

   AN: Includes artwork by: Peter Rodriguez, Arturo Anselmo Roman, Carmen Lomas Garza, Santa Barraza, and Cesar Augusto Martinez.

2461 Cardenas, Valentin. Arte de Valentin Cardenas [drawing]. CARACOL, Vol. 2, no. 1 (September 1975), p. 4. English.

2462 Cardenas, Valentin. [Untitled drawing]. CARACOL, Vol. 2, no. 1 (September 1975), p. 1.

2463 Cardenas, Valentin. [Untitled drawing]. CARACOL, Vol. 3, no. 11 (July 1977), p. 20.

2464 Cardenas, Valentin. [Untitled drawings]. CARACOL, Vol. 1, no. 8 (April 1975), p. 12-13.

2465 Carrasco, Barbara. Untitled [drawing]. REVISTA CHICANO-RIQUENA, Vol. 6, no. 2 (Spring 1978), p. 2. English.

Drawings (cont.)

2466 Carrasco, Barbara. [Untitled drawing]. In
ESSAYS ON LA MUJER. Los Angeles, CA: Chicano
Studies Center Publications, UCLA, 1977,
cover.

2467 Carrasco, Barbara. [Untitled drawing]. LA
GENTE DE AZTLAN, Vol. 8, no. 4 (March,
April, 1978), p. Ft cover.

2468 Carrasco, Barbara. [Untitled drawings].
CHISMEARTE, Vol. 1, no. 4 (Fall , Winter,
1977, 1978), p. 2-4.

   AN: 134.

2469 Castellon, Rolando. Untitled [drawing]. TIN
TAN, Vol. 1, no. 2 (September 1975), p.
[19].

2470 Castillo, Mario. [Untitled drawing]. REVISTA
CHICANO-RIQUENA, Vol. 3, no. 3 (Summer
1976), p. COVER. Spanish.

2471 Castillo, Mario. Untitled [drawing]. REVISTA
CHICANO-RIQUENA, Vol. 3, no. 3 (Spring
1975), p. 2.

2472 Castillo, Mario. Untitled [drawing]. REVISTA
CHICANO-RIQUENA, Vol. 3, no. 3 (Summer
1975), p. 11.

2473 Castillo, Mario. Untitled [drawing]. REVISTA
CHICANO-RIQUENA, Vol. 3, no. 3 (Summer
1975), p. 21.

2474 Castro, Monica. Una nina jugando con el
"jump rope" [drawing]. TEJIDOS, Vol. 4, no.
3 (Fall 1977), p. 17. Bilingual.

2475 Centro Cultural Rafael Cintron Ortiz,
University of Illinois, Chicago. Alejandro
Romero. Exhibition catalog, 1978. English.

   AN: Full color catalog of drawings and
   paintings by Mexican-born artist living in
   Chicago.

2476 Chairez, Bob. Bob's Chicano chronicles:
putting the pieces back together=pegando las
piezas otra vez [drawing]. CAMINOS, Vol. 1,
no. 2 (April 1980), p. 46. Bilingual.

2477 Chairez, Bob. Bob's Chicano chronicles: the
spirit of Cinco de Mayo=el espiritu de Cinco
de Mayo [drawing]. CAMINOS, Vol. 1, no. 3
(May 1980), p. 46.

2478 Chairez, Bob. Bob's Chicano chronicles: The
Latino athlete, then and now. CAMINOS, Vol.
1, no. 4 (July, August, 1980), p. 46.
Bilingual.

2479 Chairez, Bob. Bob's Chicano chronicles: the
Chicano in art [drawing]. CAMINOS, Vol. 1,
no. 6 (October 1980), p. 40. Bilingual.

2480 Chairez, Bob. [Untitled drawing]. CAMINOS,
Vol. 1, no. 1 (March 1980), p. 14.
Bilingual.

2481 Chairez, Bob. [Untitled drawing]. CAMINOS,
Vol. 1, no. 1 (March 1980), p. 32.

2482 Chano. A social comment in Chicano realism
[drawing]. CON SAFOS, Vol. 1, no. 4 (1969),
p. 15.

2483 Chapa, Xavier "Mimo". Enamorados en
primavera [drawing]. TEJIDOS, Vol. 4, no. 3
(Fall 1977), p. 19. Spanish.

2484 Chavez, Esteban. Caballos & the pollution of

time [drawings]. VORTICE, Vol. 2, no. 1
(Spring 1978), p. 15-22.

   AN: Esteban Chavez: portfolio of six
   intaglios entitled CABALLOS & THE POLLUTION
   OF TIME. The works have lost clarity because
   they are printed on textured paper with
   sepia ink. Chavez is a Denver-born sculptor
   and graphic artist living in California.

2485 Chavez, Sharon. [Untitled drawing]. RAYAS,
Vol. 1, no. 3 (May, June, 1978), p. Ft
cover. English.

2486 Chicano artists exhibit at USC. CALENDAR,
(September 23, 1973), p. 61. English.

   AN: Announcement of an exhibit of
   paintings, drawings, sculpture and graphics
   by artists from the Mechicano Art Center of
   Los Angeles at the University of Southern
   California Art Galleries. Slide
   presentations of murals and supergraphics.

2487 Chicano Studies Library, University of
California, Berkeley and Garcia, Rupert.
Realismo: Chicano drawings by Juan Fuentes.
Berkeley, CA: Chicano Studies Library
Publications, UC Berkeley, 1976. English.

   AN: Exhibition pamphlet with one drawing
   by Juan Fuentes. Text situates the drawings
   within artistic experiments using the
   photograph as part of the artists visual
   vocabulary. Different from "avant-garde new
   realists," Fuentes' "Realismo Chicano" is
   subjective in using selected photographs
   that present a reality of struggle.

2488 Cisneros, Ben. Bleached inked woods
[drawing]. TEJIDOS, Vol. 4, no. 3 (Fall
1977), p. 29. English.

2489 Cisneros, Luis. La bicicleta chicana
[drawing]. TEJIDOS, Vol. 1, no. 1 (Fall
1973), p. 38. Spanish.

2490 Cisneros, Rene. [Untitled drawing]. TEJIDOS,
Vol. 1, no. 1 (Fall 1973), p. COVER.
English.

2491 Contemporary Arts Museum, Houston, TX and
Harithas, James. Luis Jimenez: Progress I.
Exhibition catalog, 1974-75. English.

   AN: Catalog for a major exhibit of
   Jimenez sculptures, drawings and studies for
   sculptural works from 1967 to 1974. The
   latest project, PROGRESS, involves a series
   of monumental sculptures depicting the
   history of the West. Jimenez combines social
   comment with advanced plastic values. Well
   illustrated.

2492 Contreras, Hilario H. The Chicano's search
for identity [drawing]. CON SAFOS, Vol. 2,
no. 5 (1970), p. 26.

2493 Coronado, Sam. The American way [drawing].
TEJIDOS, Vol. 4, no. 1 (Spring 1977), p. 27.
English.

2494 Coronado, Sam. Leticia [drawing]. TEJIDOS,
Vol. 4, no. 1 (Spring 1977), p. 18. English.

2495 Coronado, Sam. Leticia [drawing]. TEJIDOS,
Vol. 4, no. 1 (Spring 1977), p. 19. English.

2496 Coronado, Sam. [Untitled drawing]. TEJIDOS,
Vol. 4, no. 1 (Spring 1977), p. 20. English.

2497 Coronado, Sam. [Untitled drawing]. TEJIDOS,
Vol. 4, no. 1 (Spring 1977), p. 21. English.

Drawings (cont.)

2498 Cortez, Carlos. [Untitled drawing]. REVISTA CHICANO-RIQUENA, Vol. 8, no. 1 (Winter 1980), p. x. English.

2499 Cotera, Martha P. The Chicana feminist. Austin, TX: Information Systems Development, 1977. English.

   AN: Cover art on this pamphlet is by Nora Gonzalez-Dodson.

2500 Cox, Vic. Beauty in the barrio. WESTWAYS, Vol. 67, no. 2 (February 1975), p. 50-53. English.

   AN: "Tooner Flats" is another name for the barrio of East Los Angeles. These streets are the home and inspiration to Frank Hernandez who illustrates the article with pen and ink sketches of buildings.

2501 Cozmos. [Skull with bandanna (drawing)]. MAIZE, Vol. 1, no. 2 (Winter 1978), p. In FtCover. English.

2502 Cruz, Ruben. [Untitled drawing]. REVISTA CHICANO-RIQUENA, Vol. 1, no. 1 (Spring 1973), p. Cover. Spanish.

2503 Cruz, Ruben. Untitled drawing from the Series "Chicago". REVISTA CHICANO-RIQUENA, Vol. 1, no. 1 (Spring 1973), p. 12. Spanish.

2504 Cruz, Ruben. Untitled drawing from the Series "Chicago". REVISTA CHICANO-RIQUENA, Vol. 1, no. 1 (Fall 1973), p. 31. Spanish.

2505 Cuadra, Ricardo. Portfolio. EL GRITO, Vol. 3, no. 2 (Winter 1970), p. 56-64. English.

2506 Cuadra, Ricardo. [Untitled drawing]. EL GRITO, Vol. 3, no. 2 (Winter 1970), p. [57]. Bilingual.

2507 Cuevas, Jose Luis. [Untitled drawing]. TIN TAN, Vol. 2, no. 5 (June 1, 1977), p. 24-25.

2508 DE COLORES. Vol. 2, no. 4 (1976), p. 1-68. English.

   AN: Photographs by Moises Medina, Jose Luis Sedano; drawings by Jerry Lujan, Gilbert "Sparky" Espinoza, Rebecca Polanco; paintings by John Herrera, Sonny Duran, Larry Martinez. Cover by Fernando Penalosa.

2509 De Cordova, Lorenzo. Echoes of the flute. Santa Fe, NM: Ancient City Press, 1972. English.

   AN: First person reminiscences on Penitente traditions in northern New Mexico at the turn of the century. Reprints two Works progress Administration (WPA) manuscripts: "Lent in Cordoba" (n.d.) and "The Wake" (1937). Illustrated with drawings by Eliseo Rodriguez. Notes by Marta Weigle.

2510 De Hoyos, Angela. Pa' delante vamos [drawing]. CARACOL, Vol. 4, no. 5 (January 1978), p. FRNT COVER. Spanish.

2511 De la Rocha, Roberto. [Untitled drawings]. CON SAFOS, no. 8 (1972), p. 21-24.

2512 De la Torre, Susana. La Conquista [drawing]. CARACOL, Vol. 4, no. 5 (January 1978), p. BACK COVER. Bilingual.

2513 De la Torre, Susana. [Untitled drawing]. CARACOL, Vol. 3, no. 8 (April 1977), p. 14.

2514 De la Torre, Susana. [Untitled drawing]. CARACOL, Vol. 4, no. 3 (November 1977), p. 19. Bilingual.

2515 De la Torre, Susana. [Untitled drawing of Salvador Allende and Fidel Castro]. CARACOL, Vol. 3, no. 11 (July 1977), p. 23.

2516 De la Torre, Susana. [Untitled drawings]. CARACOL, Vol. 2, no. 11 (July 1976), p. 20.

2517 De la Torre, Susana. [Untitled portrait]. CARACOL, Vol. 5, no. 1 (September 1978), p. 18. Bilingual.

2518 De Leon, Nephtali. No, Mr. Boa [drawing]. CARACOL, Vol. 3, no. 7 (March 1977), p. 22.

2519 De Leon, Nephtali. Raquel and the umbrellas [drawing]. CARACOL, Vol. 3, no. 7 (March 1977), p. 23.

2520 Delgado, Abelardo "Lalo". Chicano: 25 pieces of a Chicano mind. El Paso, TX: Barrio Publications, 1972. English.

   AN: Three drawings by Ernesto Palomino.

2521 Diaz, Aurelio. Arte de Aurelio Diaz [drawings]. CARACOL, Vol. 5, no. 5 (January 1979), p. 1,6,18,24. English.

2522 Diaz, Aurelio. Yo soy chicana [drawing]. CARACOL, Vol. 4, no. 12 (August 1978), p. Bk cover.

2523 Eloy. Cheshire cat [drawing]. TEJIDOS, Vol. 1, no. 2 (Spring 1974), p. 17. English.

2524 Eloy. The hunchback giraffe [drawing]. TEJIDOS, Vol. 1, no. 2 (Spring 1974), p. 18. English.

2525 Eloy. [Untitled drawing]. TEJIDOS, Vol. 1, no. 2 (Spring 1974), p. COVER. English.

2526 Eloy. [Untitled drawing]. TEJIDOS, Vol. 1, no. 2 (Spring 1974), p. 19-20. English.

2527 ENCUENTRO FEMENIL (San Fernando, CA). Vol. 1, no. 1 (Spring 1973), p. 1+. English.

   AN: Publication sponsored by Hijas de Cuauhtemoc, a Chicana femenist group. Black and white drawings on cover by Pat Portera Crary. Art work by Vicki Thrall, Adelaida del Castillo, and Maria Hortencia Garcia. Photography by Cindy Honesto and David Lazarin.

2528 Espinoza, Gilbert "Sparky". [Untitled drawing]. DE COLORES, Vol. 2, no. 4 (1976), p. 13.

2529 Espinoza, Gilbert "Sparky". [Untitled drawing]. DE COLORES, Vol. 2, no. 4 (1976), p. 14.

2530 Espinoza, Gilbert "Sparky". [Untitled drawing]. DE COLORES, Vol. 2, no. 4 (1976), p. 15.

2531 Espinoza, Gilbert "Sparky". [Untitled drawing]. DE COLORES, Vol. 2, no. 4 (1976), p. 16.

2532 Espinoza, Gilbert "Sparky". [Untitled drawing]. DE COLORES, Vol. 2, no. 4 (1976), p. 17.

2533 Espinoza, Gilbert "Sparky". [Untitled drawing]. DE COLORES, Vol. 2, no. 4 (1976), p. 18.

Drawings (cont.)

2534 Espinoza, Gilbert "Sparky". [Untitled drawing]. DE COLORES, Vol. 2, no. 4 (1976), p. 19.

2535 Espinoza, Gilbert "Sparky". [Untitled drawing]. DE COLORES, Vol. 2, no. 4 (1976), p. 20.

2536 Espinoza, Gilbert "Sparky". [Untitled drawing]. DE COLORES, Vol. 2, no. 4 (1976), p. 21.

2537 Espinoza, Gilbert "Sparky". [Untitled drawing]. DE COLORES, Vol. 2, no. 4 (1976), p. 22.

2538 Espinoza, Gilbert "Sparky". [Untitled drawing]. DE COLORES, Vol. 2, no. 4 (1976), p. 23.

2539 Espinoza, Gilbert "Sparky". [Untitled drawing]. DE COLORES, Vol. 2, no. 4 (1976), p. 25.

2540 Espinoza, Gilbert "Sparky". Untitled pen and ink drawings from la pinta [portfolio]. DE COLORES, Vol. 2, no. 4 (1976), p. [12]-25. English.

2541 Espinoza, Gilbert "Sparky". [Untitled pen and ink drawing from la pinta]. DE COLORES, Vol. 2, no. 4 (1976), p. 24.

2542 Espinoza, Raul. Portfolio: mortification of ambivalence [drawings]. EL GRITO, Vol. 2, no. 4 (Summer 1969), p. 57-63. English.

2543 Espinoza, Raul. [Untitled drawing]. EL GRITO, Vol. 2, no. 4 (Summer 1969), p. [64]. Bilingual.

2544 Espinoza, Raul. [Untitled drawing]. EL GRITO, Vol. 2, no. 4 (Summer 1969), p. [63]. Bilingual.

2545 Espinoza, Raul. [Untitled drawing]. EL GRITO, Vol. 2, no. 4 (Summer 1969), p. [62]. Bilingual.

2546 Espinoza, Raul. [Untitled drawing]. EL GRITO, Vol. 2, no. 4 (Summer 1969), p. [61]. Bilingual.

2547 Espinoza, Raul. [Untitled drawing]. EL GRITO, Vol. 2, no. 4 (Summer 1969), p. [60]. Bilingual.

2548 Espinoza, Raul. [Untitled drawing]. EL GRITO, Vol. 2, no. 4 (Summer 1969), p. [59]. Bilingual.

2549 Espinoza, Raul. [Untitled drawing]. EL GRITO, Vol. 2, no. 4 (Summer 1969), p. [58]. Bilingual.

2550 Esqueda, Hilda. Give us this day our daily bread... [drawing]. XALMAN, Vol. 1, no. 4 (Spring 1977), p. 53.

2551 Esquivel, Renato. [Untitled drawing]. REVISTA CHICANO-RIQUENA, Vol. 8, no. 1 (Winter 1980), p. 44. English.

2552 Esteban Jordan [drawing]. CARACOL, Vol. 1, no. 6 (February 1975), p. 18.

2553 Figoten, Sheldon. Building and painting the figure. ARTWEEK, Vol. 12, no. 22 (June 20, 1981), p. 5-6. English.

AN: Review of eight sculptures and 25 drawings by Manuel Neri at the Redding Art

Museum. Neri was influenced as a student in the San Francisco Bay Area in the 1950s by abstract expressionist philosophy and methodology, which he transferred to sculpture. Plaster, bronze, and marble figures are freely and loosely painted in areas. Illustration.

2554 Fiske, Wanda. Cat [drawing]. TEJIDOS, Vol. 4, no. 3 (Fall 1977), p. 35. English.

2555 Flores, Carolina. House [drawing]. TEJIDOS, Vol. 1, no. 3 (Summer 1974), p. 12. English.

2556 Flores, Carolina. Self portrait [drawing]. TEJIDOS, Vol. 1, no. 3 (Summer 1974), p. Cover.

2557 Flores, Carolina. Self portrait [drawing]. TEJIDOS, Vol. 1, no. 3 (Summer 1974), p. 6.

2558 Flores, Carolina. Street scene [drawing]. TEJIDOS, Vol. 1, no. 3 (Summer 1974), p. 20. English.

2559 Flores, Jose. Peregrino [drawing]. In MESQUI + TIERRA. Albuquerque, NM: Pajarito Publications, 1977. English.

AN: Drawings by Jose F. Trevino of Austin, Texas.

2560 Flores-Morales, Gina. [Untitled drawing]. TEJIDOS, Vol. 5, no. 1 (1978), p. 35. English.

2561 Focus: Yolanda Lopez. CITYBENDER, Vol. 2, no. 5 (1978). English.

AN: Brief biography and illustrations of drawings by San Diego/San Francisco artist Yolanda Lopez titled THREE GENERATIONS: TRES MUJERES.

2562 Fong, Katheryn M. Pachuco art records era of zootsuits and anti-Mexican riots. SAN FRANCISCO JRNL, Vol. 2, no. 32 (March 1, 1978), p. 6. English.

AN: Review of Galeria de la Raza exhibit of Jose Montoya's Pachuco Art. Installation included historical photographs and documents. Montoya work (drawings and paintings) were contextualized by written commentary aiming to re-interpret an important aspect of Chicano cultural history.

2563 Frankenstein, Alfred. Montoya's artistic update on Chicano zoot suiters. SAN FRANCISCO CHRONICLE, (February 18, 1978), p. 36. English.

AN: Review of Pachuco show at San Francisco's Galeria de la Raza, especially Jose Montoya's sketches and paintings.

2564 Fuentes, Juan. [Untitled drawing]. EL TECOLOTE LITERARY MAGAZINE, Vol. 1, no. 1 (April 1980), p. 6-7.

2565 Fuentes, Juan. [Untitled drawing]. EL TECOLOTE LITERARY MAGAZINE, Vol. 2, no. 2 (July 1981), p. 6-7.

2566 Fuentes, Juan. [Untitled drawing]. TIN TAN, Vol. 1, no. 2 (September 1975), p. In FtCover.

Drawings (cont.)

2567 Galeria de arte de Aztlan. AZTLAN (U.S. Penitentiary, Leavenworth, KA), Vol. 1, no. 2. English.

AN: Pictorial supplement with reproductions of pinto art by Manuel Aguilera, Jessie Hernandez, Ruben Estrella, Tomas Torres and Jose D. Marin. Many of these works were reproduced in other Chicano newspapers demonstrating the solidarity that existed in the Chicano movement inside and outside the prison walls.

2568 Galeria de la Raza/Studio 24, San Francisco, CA. Images of the Southwest. Exhibition catalog, 1977. English.

AN: Invitation/catalog for an exhibit including Rudy M. Fernandez(Utah), Enrique Flores(Texas), Xavier Gorena(Texas), C.A.[Cesar] Martinez(Texas), Santos Martinez, Jr.(Texas), Pedro Rodriguez(Texas), Arnold Trujillo(New Mexico). Block prints, paper cut-outs, drawings, photographs, copper enamels, and sculpture were shown. Five illustrations.

2569 Galeria de la Raza/Studio 24, San Francisco, CA and Franco, Jean. Juan Fuentes y Rupert Garcia: posters, drawings, prints. Exhibition catalog, 1975. English.

AN: Catalog of an exhibit. Illustrated with drawings and posters.

2570 Galeria de la Raza/Studio 24, San Francisco, CA. "Low 'n slow": checking out low rider art. Exhibition invitation, 1979. English.

AN: Invitation to an exhibit of drawings, photographs, and graphics. Participation by LOWRIDER MAGAZINE and local car and bike clubs.

2571 Galerias Paco, New York, NY. Consuelo Gonzalez Amezcua - filigree art. Exhibition announcement, n.d. English.

AN: Two-page exhibition announcement illustrated with two examples of the Texas artist's "filigree art" and a sample of her poetry.

2572 Galvan, Diane. [Untitled drawing]. REGENERACION, Vol. 2, no. 4 (1975), p. 2.

2573 Galvan, Diane. [Untitled drawing]. REGENERACION, Vol. 2, no. 4 (1973), p. 8.

2574 Galvan, Diane. [Untitled drawing]. REGENERACION, Vol. 2, no. 4 (1975), p. 32.

2575 Galvan, Diane. [Untitled drawing]. REGENERACION, Vol. 2, no. 4 (1975), p. 49.

2576 Galvan, Diane. [Woman sitting with rabbit (drawing)]. REGENERACION, Vol. 2, no. 4 (1975), p. 55.

2577 Galvan, Diane. [Women (drawing)]. REGENERACION, Vol. 2, no. 4 (1975), p. BACK COVER.

2578 Galvan, Yolanda. Breathe [drawing]. REVISTA CHICANO-RIQUENA, Vol. 5, no. 1 (Winter 1977), p. 70. English.

2579 Gamboa, Diane. [Man (drawing)]. REGENERACION, Vol. 2, no. 3 (1973), p. 13.

2580 Gamboa, Diane. [Mother and child (drawing)]. REGENERACION, Vol. 2, no. 3 (1973), p. 26.

2581 Gamboa, Diane. [Untitled drawing]. REGENERACION, Vol. 2, no. 3 (1973), p. 24.

2582 Gamboa, Harry, Jr. [Chicana (drawing)]. REGENERACION, Vol. 2, no. 3 (1973), p. 5.

2583 Gamboa, Harry, Jr. [Chicana in pen and ink (drawing)]. REGENERACION, Vol. 2, no. 2 (1972), p. 5.

2584 Gamboa, Harry, Jr. [Chicana portrait (drawing)]. REGENERACION, Vol. 2, no. 2 (1972), p. 19.

2585 Gamboa, Harry, Jr. [Chicano in shadow (drawing)]. REGENERACION, Vol. 2, no. 2 (1972), p. 7.

2586 Gamboa, Harry, Jr. Chicano power [drawing]. REGENERACION, Vol. 1, no. 9 (1970), p. 16.

2587 Gamboa, Harry, Jr. [Crying (drawing)]. REGENERACION, Vol. 2, no. 3 (1973), p. 10.

2588 Gamboa, Harry, Jr. He threw a rock at me [drawing]. REGENERACION, Vol. 1, no. 9 (1970), p. 12-13.

2589 Gamboa, Harry, Jr. [Old man (drawing)]. REGENERACION, Vol. 2, no. 2 (1972), p. 11.

2590 Gamboa, Harry, Jr. [Split head (drawing)]. REGENERACION, Vol. 2, no. 2 (1972), p. 18.

2591 Gamboa, Harry, Jr. [Untitled drawing]. REGENERACION, Vol. 2, no. 2 (1972), p. i.

2592 Gamboa, Harry, Jr. [Untitled drawing]. REGENERACION, Vol. 2, no. 2 (1972), p. 20.

2593 Gamboa, Harry, Jr. [Untitled drawing]. REGENERACION, Vol. 2, no. 3 (1973), p. 35.

2594 Gamboa, Harry, Jr. [Untitled drawing]. REGENERACION, Vol. 2, no. 4 (1975), p. 18.

2595 Gamboa, Harry, Jr. [Untitled drawing]. REGENERACION, Vol. 2, no. 4 (1975), p. 18.

2596 Gamboa, Harry, Jr. [Untitled drawing]. REGENERACION, Vol. 2, no. 4 (1975), p. 25.

2597 Gamboa, Harry, Jr. [Untitled drawing]. REGENERACION, Vol. 2, no. 4 (1975), p. 32.

2598 Gamboa, Harry, Jr. [Untitled drawing]. REGENERACION, Vol. 2, no. 4 (1975), p. 43.

2599 Gamboa, Harry, Jr. [Woman (drawing)]. REGENERACION, Vol. 2, no. 3 (1973), p. 26.

2600 Gamboa, Harry, Jr. [Women (drawing)]. REGENERACION, Vol. 2, no. 3 (1973), p. 32.

2601 Gamez, Eddie. [Untitled drawing]. CARACOL, Vol. 4, no. 6 (February 1978), p. 12. Spanish.

2602 Garcia, Daniel C. Pan dulce [drawing]. CON SAFOS, no. 6 (Summer 1970), p. 11.

2603 Garcia, Edward E. Chicano art. LA RAZA, Vol. 1, no. 6 (1971), p. 76-80. English.

2604 Garcia, Edward E. [Untitled drawing]. LA RAZA, Vol. 2, no. 1 (February 1974), p. Ft cover.

2605 Garcia Perez, Linda Mary. Mejico [drawing]. MAIZE, Vol. 2, no. 3 (Spring 1979), p. 32-33. English.

Drawings (cont.)

2606 Garcia, Raul Roy. La justicia. CARACOL, Vol. 5, no. 2 (October 1978), p. FRNT COVER. English.

2607 Garcia, Rupert. Laminas de la Raza. San Francisco: Garcia Litho and Printing Service, 1975. English.

   AN: Portfolio of drawings and prints by Patricia Rodriguez, Ricardo Apodaca, Xochitl, Domingo Rivera, Francisco Camplis, Rafael Maradiaga, Tom Rios, Juan Fuentes, Ricardo Diaz, Jose Romero, Consuelo Mendez, Jose Antonio Burciaga, Irene Perez, Ricardo Rios, Mike Rios, Graciela Carrillo, Rene Yanez, Luis Talamantez, Guillermo Bermudez, all from Northern California.

2608 Garcia, Rupert. Para Olga Talamante [drawing]. TIN TAN, Vol. 1, no. 2 (September 1975), p. [17].

2609 Garcia, Rupert. Portfolio [drawings]. EL GRITO, Vol. 3, no. 1 (Fall 1969), p. 64-68. English.

2610 Garcia, Rupert. [Untitled drawing]. EL GRITO, Vol. 3, no. 1 (Fall 1969), p. [65]. Bilingual.

2611 Garcia, Rupert. [Untitled drawing]. EL GRITO, Vol. 3, no. 1 (Fall 1969), p. [66]. Bilingual.

2612 Garcia, Rupert. [Untitled drawing]. EL GRITO, Vol. 3, no. 1 (Fall 1969), p. [67]. Bilingual.

2613 Garcia, Rupert. [Untitled drawing]. EL GRITO, Vol. 3, no. 1 (Fall 1969), p. [68]. Bilingual.

2614 Garcia, Rupert. [Untitled drawing]. CHISMEARTE, Vol. 2, no. 1 (Summer 1978), p. 3. English.

2615 Garcia-Camarillo, Cecilio and Martinez, Dennis. Platicando con Dennis Martinez. RAYAS, Vol. 1, no. 5 (September, October, 1978), p. 12, 11. Bilingual.

   AN: Interview with Dennis Martinez, illustrator of BLESS ME ULTIMA, NAMBE: YEAR ONE, and MI ABUELA FUMABA PUROS. The books share New Mexican setting and their illustrator seeks to capture the essence of the landscape in that region. In his drawings Dennis Martinez hopes to evoke history in relation to landscape and culture. Illustrated.

2616 Garcia-Camarillo, Mia. Don Pedrito Jaramillo [drawing]. CARACOL, Vol. 2, no. 9 (May 1976), p. 24.

2617 Garcia-Camarillo, Mia. [Five men (drawing)]. CARACOL, Vol. 1, no. 2 (October 1974), p. 20.

2618 Garcia-Camarillo, Mia. [Jose Angel Gutierrez (drawing)]. CARACOL, Vol. 1, no. 3 (November 1974), p. 4.

2619 Garcia-Camarillo, Mia. [Jose Angel Gutierrez (drawing)]. CARACOL, Vol. 1, no. 3 (November 1974), p. 5.

2620 Garcia-Camarillo, Mia. [Jose Angel Gutierrez (drawing)]. CARACOL, Vol. 1, no. 3 (November 1974), p. 6.

2621 Garcia-Camarillo, Mia. Oscarin y Lorina

[drawing]. CARACOL, Vol. 2, no. 7 (March 1976), p. 24.

2622 Garcia-Camarillo, Mia. Pen and Ink Drawings. CARACOL, Vol. 2, no. 9 (May 1976), p. 11.

2623 Garcia-Camarillo, Mia. [Untitled drawing]. CARACOL, Vol. 2, no. 7 (March 1976), p. 1.

2624 Garcia-Camarillo, Mia. [Untitled drawing]. CARACOL, Vol. 2, no. 12 (August 1976), p. 3. Spanish.

2625 Garcia-Camarillo, Mia. [Untitled drawing]. CARACOL, Vol. 3, no. 5 (January 1977), p. FRNT COVER.

2626 Garcia-Camarillo, Mia. [Untitled drawing]. CARACOL, Vol. 3, no. 5 (January 1977), p. BACK COVER.

2627 Garcia-Camarillo, Mia. [Untitled drawing]. CARACOL, Vol. 3, no. 8 (April 1977), p. 18.

2628 Garcia-Camarillo, Mia. [Untitled drawing]. CARACOL, Vol. 3, no. 11 (July 1977), p. 7.

2629 Garcia-Camarillo, Mia. [Untitled drawing]. MAIZE, Vol. 1, no. 1 (Fall 1977), p. Bk cover. Spanish.

2630 Garcia-Camarillo, Mia. [Untitled drawings]. CARACOL, Vol. 2, no. 8 (April 1976), p. 12-13.

2631 Garcia-Camarillo, Mia. [Untitled drawings]. CARACOL, Vol. 2, no. 10 (June 1976), p. 10-11.

2632 Garcia-Camarillo, Mia. [Untitled drawings]. CARACOL, Vol. 2, no. 11 (July 1976), p. 8-9.

2633 Garcia-Camarillo, Mia. [Untitled drawings]. CARACOL, Vol. 3, no. 4 (December 1976), p. 8-9, 12.

2634 Garza, Eduardo C. The awakening of la teqnica chit [drawing]. CARACOL, Vol. 3, no. 6 (February 1977), p. 12.

2635 Garza, Eduardo C. Chispas reales [drawing]. CARACOL, Vol. 3, no. 6 (February 1977), p. 13.

2636 Garza, Eduardo C. [Untitled drawing]. CARACOL, Vol. 2, no. 10 (June 1976), p. 13.

2637 Garza, Efrain and Tijerina, Ramon. Caracol azteca - el tiempo limitado del hombre de la ciencia [drawing]. CARACOL, Vol. 4, no. 12 (August 1978), p. 8. Spanish.

2638 Garza, Rose. [Untitled drawing]. TEJIDOS, Vol. 2, no. 6 (Summer 1975), p. 20. English.

2639 Gaytan, Ray. B.I.T.C.H. [drawing]. TEJIDOS, Vol. 3, no. 1 (Spring 1976), p. COVER. English.

2640 Gaytan, Ray. Fallen leaves [drawing]. TEJIDOS, Vol. 3, no. 1 (Spring 1976), p. 39. English.

2641 Gaytan, Ray. La vida [drawing]. TEJIDOS, Vol. 2, no. 6 (Summer 1975), p. 37. Spanish.

2642 Gomez, Gricelle. Chicano soy [drawing]. CARACOL, Vol. 3, no. 11 (July 1977), p. 21.

Drawings (cont.)

2643 Gomez, Linda. Malaquias Montoya exhibit opens at La Pena. EL MUNDO (San Francisco, CA), (October 29, 1975), p. 3. English.

AN: Over 50 paintings, silkscreens, and drawings by Montoya at La Pena Cultural Center, Berkeley, CA. Statement by the artist who refuses to exhibit in museums and is opposed to murals that are "pretty decorations.".

2644 Gonzalez, David M. Al sol y la luna [drawing]. CARACOL, Vol. 5, no. 10 (June 1979), p. 1. Spanish.

2645 Gonzalez Dodson, Nora. Terrestrial flight II [drawing]. TEJIDOS, Vol. 2, no. 8 (Winter 1975), p. 14. English.

2646 Gonzalez Dodson, Nora. [Untitled drawing]. TEJIDOS, Vol. 5, no. 1 (1978), p. 28. English.

2647 Gonzalez Dodson, Nora. [Untitled drawing]. TEJIDOS, Vol. 2, no. 8 (Winter 1975), p. 19. English.

2648 Gonzalez Dodson, Nora. [Untitled drawing]. TEJIDOS, Vol. 2, no. 8 (Winter 1975), p. 33. English.

2649 Gonzalez Dodson, Nora. El vendedor [drawing]. TEJIDOS, Vol. 2, no. 8 (Winter 1975), p. 39. Spanish.

2650 Gonzalez, Gracie. The Chicano singers [drawing]. TEJIDOS, Vol. 4, no. 3 (Fall 1977), p. 24. English.

2651 Gonzalez, Jose Gamaliel. Boycott [drawing]. REVISTA CHICANO-RIQUENA, Vol. 5, no. 1 (Winter 1977), p. 9. English.

2652 Gonzalez, Jose Gamaliel. Lenina of BRAVE NEW WORLD [drawing]. REVISTA CHICANO-RIQUENA, Vol. 1, no. 2 (Fall 1973), p. 21. English.

2653 Gonzalez, Jose Gamaliel. La LLorona [drawing]. REVISTA CHICANO-RIQUENA, Vol. 1, no. 2 (Fall 1973), p. 35. Spanish.

2654 Gonzalez, Jose Gamaliel. Metamorphosis [drawing]. REVISTA CHICANO-RIQUENA, Vol. 1, no. 2 (Fall 1973), p. COVER. English.

2655 Gonzalez, Jose Gamaliel. Three ages of man [drawing]. REVISTA CHICANO-RIQUENA, Vol. 1, no. 2 (Fall 1973), p. 10. English.

2656 Gonzalez, Jose Gamaliel. Yo soy chicana [drawing]. REVISTA CHICANO-RIQUENA, Vol. 5, no. 1 (Winter 1977), p. 111.

2657 Gonzalez, Reveca; Gonzalez, Johnny; and Valdez, Sylvia. Arte de ninos coloring book. CARACOL, Vol. 4, no. 1 (September 1977), p. 12-13. English.

2658 Gonzalez, Tobias and Gonzalez, Sandra. Perspectives on Chicano education. Stanford, CA: Stanford University, 1975. English.

AN: Reproductions of artworks by Ralph Maradiaga, Patricia Rodriguez, Roberto Bonilla, Francisco Camplis, Graciela Carrillo-Lopez, Juan Fuentes, Irene Perez, Roger Reyes, Carlos Loarca, Xavier Viramontes, Ralph McNeill, Rupert Garcia, Jose Romero.

2659 Grimke, Angelina. Chicano art finds home in Mission galeria. PEOPLE'S WORLD, Vol. 33, no. 32 (August 8, 1970), p. 11. English.

AN: Commentary on the exhibition CHICANOS, CUBA Y LOS 10 MILLONES held at the original Galeria de la Raza at 425 14th Street in San Francisco. The show presented photographs by Jay Ojeda and Roberto Perez-Diaz, drawings by Gloria Ozuna together with paintings and photographs by Cuban artist Mederos. Provides information about the goals of the Galeria as the visual arts department of Casa Hispana de Bellas Artes. Exhibition curator was Rolando Castellon.

2660 Gronk. [Agony (drawing)]. REGENERACION, Vol. 2, no. 3 (1973), p. 20.

2661 Gronk. [Chicana (drawing)]. REGENERACION, Vol. 2, no. 3 (1973), p. 1.

2662 Gronk and Valdez, Patssi. [Faces (drawing)]. REGENERACION, Vol. 2, no. 3 (1973), p. 30.

2663 Gronk. [Nude (drawing)]. REGENERACION, Vol. 2, no. 3 (1973), p. 16.

2664 Gronk. The Tortuga paints a new mural. REGENERACION, Vol. 2, no. 3 (1973), p. 22.

2665 Gronk. [Untitled drawing]. REGENERACION, Vol. 2, no. 2 (1972), p. 16.

2666 Gronk. [Untitled drawing]. REGENERACION, Vol. 2, no. 2 (1972), p. 21.

2667 Gronk. [Untitled drawing]. REGENERACION, Vol. 2, no. 3 (1973), p. 9.

2668 Gronk. [Untitled drawing]. REGENERACION, Vol. 2, no. 3 (1973), p. 12.

2669 Gronk. [Untitled drawing]. REGENERACION, Vol. 2, no. 3 (1973), p. 23.

2670 Gronk. [Untitled drawing]. REGENERACION, Vol. 2, no. 3 (1973), p. 24-25.

2671 Gronk. [Untitled drawing]. REGENERACION, Vol. 2, no. 3 (1973), p. 28.

2672 Gronk. [Untitled drawing]. REGENERACION, Vol. 2, no. 3 (1973), p. 29.

2673 Gronk. [Untitled drawing]. REGENERACION, Vol. 2, no. 3 (1973), p. 29.

2674 Gronk. [Untitled drawing]. REGENERACION, Vol. 2, no. 3 (1973), p. 31.

2675 Gronk. [Untitled drawing]. AZTLAN, Vol. 2, no. 3 (1973), p. 36.

2676 Gronk. [Untitled drawing]. REGENERACION, Vol. 2, no. 3 (1973), p. 36.

2677 Gronk. [Woman (drawing)]. REGENERACION, Vol. 2, no. 3 (1973), p. 17.

2678 Gronk. [Women (drawing)]. REGENERACION, Vol. 2, no. 3 (1973), p. 21.

2679 Gronk. [Women (drawing)]. REGENERACION, Vol. 2, no. 3 (1973), p. 23.

2680 Gronk and Gamboa, Harry, Jr. [Women (drawing)]. REGENERACION, Vol. 2, no. 3 (1973), p. 30. English.

2681 Guerra, Luis. Hasta la gloria [drawing]. TEJIDOS, Vol. 4, no. 2 (Summer 1977), p. COVER. Spanish.

Drawings (cont.)

2682 Guerra, Victor. Primavera: happy in Khaki. TEJIDOS, Vol. 5, no. 2-4 (1978), p. 68. English.

2683 Guerra, Victor, ed. El camino de la cruz. Austin, TX: Tejidos Publications, 1981. Spanish.

   AN: Carlos Andres Guerra, portfolio; painting (in color), sculpture, drawing, jewelry. Luis Guerra drawing on cover.

2684 Guerrero, Jose. [Untitled drawing]. REVISTA CHICANO-RIQUENA, Vol. 8, no. 1 (Winter 1980), p. 70. English.

2685 Guerrero, Xochitl Nevel. Avatar de la paloma de la paz: las naciones la van a convertir en monstruo [drawing]. CARACOL, Vol. 4, no. 12 (August 1978), p. 18. Spanish.

2686 Guggenheim Gallery, Chapman College, Orange, CA. Hexagono: paintings, sculpture, drawings, prints. Exhibit invitation, 1977. English.

   AN: Invitation to an exhibit for artists Tito Aguirre, Isabel Castro, Rick Martinez, Esau Quiroz, Linda Vallejo, Emigdio Vasquez, Barrows, and Shanahan, sponsored by MEChA. Profiles and pictures of the artists.

2687 Gutierrez, Juan Pablo. Bird [yarn drawing]. TEJIDOS, Vol. 2, no. 6 (Summer 1975), p. 28. English.

2688 Haines, Bruce J. Gonzales' works are controlled and full of detail. ANCHORAGE DAILY NEWS, (May 23, 1980). English.

   AN: Positive review of an exhibit titled THE HEAD TASTES BEST by Mariano Gonzales. Born in El Paso, Texas but reared in Alaska, Gonzales' works in various media from drawings and paintings to metals, ivory, enamel and plastics. The critic praises the artist for his "volatile intricacy" and his fusion of materials "always with craft and finesse". Includes reproductions of two paintings.

2689 Help the Delano farm workers. Flyer, 1966. English.

   AN: Adolph Villalvazo drawing reproduced.

2690 HEMBRA: HERMANAS EN MOVIMIENTO BROTANDO RAICES DE AZTLAN (University of Texas, Austin). (Spring 1976).

   AN: Raul Valdez, drawing, p. 3; Carolina Flores, drawing, p. 5; Maria Flores, photograph, pp. 7, 11, 30; M.E. Secrest-Ramirez, drawing, p. 12; Amacio Zarate, drawing, p. 15; Santa Barraza, drawings, pp. 16, 17, 18, 26, 32; Nora Gonzales-Dodson, painting, p. 19; Gilberto Cardenas, photograph, pp. 22, 28; Nanci de los Santos, photograph, p. 23, 29; Amado Maurilio Pena, Jr. p. 31.

2691 Hernandez, Judithe Elena. Calavera de azucar [drawing]. AZTLAN, Vol. 4, no. 1 (Spring 1973), p. COVER. Spanish.

2692 Hernandez, Judithe Elena. La familia [drawing]. AZTLAN, Vol. 6, no. 1 (Spring 1975), p. COVER. Spanish.

2693 Hernandez, Judithe Elena. In her house [illustration]. CHISMEARTE, Vol. 1, no. 4 (Fall , Winter, 1977, 1978), p. 31,34.

   AN: Illustration of poem by Olivia Sanchez.

2694 Hernandez, Judithe Elena. Mujer en Aztlan [drawing]. CHISMEARTE, Vol. 1, no. 4 (Fall, Winter, 1977, 1978), p. [32-33].

2695 Hernandez, Judithe Elena. Pajaro de lluvia [print]. AZTLAN, Vol. 2, no. 2 (Fall 1971), p. COVER. Spanish.

2696 Hernandez, Judithe Elena. Thunderbird [print]. AZTLAN, Vol. 3, no. 1 (Spring 1972), p. COVER. English.

2697 Hernandez, Sergio. American Consul General, visa section [drawing]. CON SAFOS, Vol. 2, no. 5 (1970), p. 16-17.

2698 Hernandez, Sergio. El barrio - love it or leave it (si puedes) [drawing]. CON SAFOS, Vol. 1, no. 4 (1969), p. 24-25.

2699 Hernandez, Sergio. [Brown Buffalo (painting)]. CON SAFOS, no. 7 (Winter 1971), p. COVER.

2700 Hernandez, Sergio. Cesar [drawing]. CON SAFOS, Vol. 2, no. 5 (1970), p. COVER.

2701 Hernandez, Sergio. Hero worship poster pop [drawing]. CON SAFOS, Vol. 2, no. 5 (1970), p. 24-25.

2702 Hernandez, Sergio. Justicia. REGENERACION, Vol. 1, no. 8 (1970), p. FRNT COVER.

2703 Hernandez, Sergio. Mexico, U.S. [drawing]. CON SAFOS, Vol. 2, no. 5 (1970), p. 19.

2704 Hernandez, Sergio. Peace on you too [drawing]. CON SAFOS, Vol. 2, no. 5 (1970), p. 21.

2705 Hernandez, Sergio. [Por mi raza habla el espiritu (drawing)]. CON SAFOS, Vol. 2, no. 5 (1970), p. 30.

2706 Hernandez, Sergio. Retrato de un bato loco [drawing]. CON SAFOS, Vol. 2, no. 5 (1970), p. 22.

2707 Hernandez, Sergio. Speak English [drawing]. CON SAFOS, Vol. 1, no. 2 (Fall 1968), p. 7.

2708 Hernandez, Sergio. [Untitled drawing]. CON SAFOS, Vol. 1, no. 2 (Fall 1968), p. 12.

2709 Hernandez, Sergio. [Untitled drawing]. CON SAFOS, Vol. 1, no. 2 (Fall 1968), p. 23.

2710 Hernandez, Sergio. [Untitled drawing]. CON SAFOS, Vol. 1, no. 2 (Fall 1968), p. 25.

2711 Hernandez, Sergio. [Untitled drawing]. CON SAFOS, Vol. 1, no. 2 (Fall 1968), p. 29.

2712 Hernandez, Sergio. [Untitled drawing]. CON SAFOS, Vol. 1, no. 3 (March 1969), p. COVER.

2713 Hernandez, Sergio. [Untitled drawing]. CON SAFOS, Vol. 1, no. 3 (March 1969), p. 9.

2714 Hernandez, Sergio. [Untitled drawing]. CON SAFOS, Vol. 1, no. 3 (March 1969), p. 28.

2715 Hernandez, Sergio. [Untitled drawing]. CON SAFOS, Vol. 1, no. 4 (1969), p. 28-29.

Drawings (cont.)

2716 Hernandez, Sergio. [Untitled drawing]. CON
     SAFOS, Vol. 1, no. 4 (1969), p. 44.

2717 Hernandez, Sergio. [Untitled drawing]. CON
     SAFOS, no. 8 (1972), p. COVER.

2718 Hernandez, Sergio. [Untitled drawing].
     REGENERACION, Vol. 1, no. 3 (1970), p.
     COVER. English.

2719 Hernandez, Sergio. [Untitled drawing].
     REGENERACION, Vol. 1, no. 2 (1970), p.
     COVER.

2720 Hernandez, Sergio. [Untitled drawing].
     REGENERACION, Vol. 1, no. 1 (1970), p. FRNT
     COVER.

2721 Hernandez, Sergio. [Untitled drawing]. CON
     SAFOS, Vol. 2, no. 6 (Summer 1970), p. 19.

2722 Hernandez, Sergio. [Untitled drawing]. CON
     SAFOS, Vol. 2, no. 6 (Summer 1970), p. 18.

2723 Hernandez, Sergio. [Untitled drawing]. CON
     SAFOS, Vol. 2, no. 6 (Summer 1970), p. 17.

2724 Hernandez, Sergio. [Untitled drawing]. CON
     SAFOS, Vol. 2, no. 6 (Summer 1970), p. 15.

2725 Hernandez-Trujillo, Manuel. Dibujo de mujer
     y nino [drawing]. EL GRITO, Vol. 2, no. 3
     (Spring 1969), p. 28. Spanish.

2726 Hernandez-Trujillo, Manuel. Donde esta la
     perra? [drawing]. EL GRITO, Vol. 2, no. 3
     (Spring 1969), p. [36]. Spanish.

2727 Hernandez-Trujillo, Manuel. Portfolio:
     Sangrandose; Xochitl; Ejecutado; Dibujo de
     Mujer y Nino; Conejo; Vida y Muerte;
     Chicano; Nina y Gati; Retrato Femenil; La
     Cruz; Slayer of Light; One and One Equals
     Me; Donde esta la Perra? EL GRITO, Vol. 2,
     no. 3 (Spring 1969), p. 25-38. Spanish.

2728 Hernandez-Trujillo, Manuel. [Untitled
     drawing]. EL POCHO CHE, Vol. 1, no. 2
     (1970), p. 32.

2729 Herron, Willie. [Anglo meets three Chicano
     youths (drawing)]. REGENERACION, Vol. 2, no.
     1 (1971), p. 21. English.

2730 Herron, Willie. [Ese vato va marchar
     (drawing)]. REGENERACION, Vol. 2, no. 2
     (1972), p. 25.

2731 Herron, Willie. [The foundation of
     capitalism (drawing)]. REGENERACION, Vol. 2,
     no. 1 (1971), p. 8.

2732 Herron, Willie. [Untitled drawing].
     REGENERACION, Vol. 2, no. 2 (1972), p. 22.

2733 Herron, Willie and Gronk. [Untitled
     drawing]. REGENERACION, Vol. 2, no. 3
     (1973), p. 18-19.

2734 Herron, Willie. [Untitled drawing].
     REGENERACION, Vol. 2, no. 3 (1973), p. 27.

2735 Herron, Willie. [Untitled drawing].
     REGENERACION, Vol. 2, no. 4 (1975), p. 10.

2736 Herron, Willie. [Untitled drawing].
     REGENERACION, Vol. 2, no. 4 (1975), p. 47.

2737 Herron, Willie. [Untitled painting].
     REGENERACION, Vol. 2, no. 1 (1971), p. 9.

2738 Herron, Willie. [Women in chains

(painting)]. REGENERACION, Vol. 2, no. 1
(1971), p. 4.

2739 Huerta, Rebecca. The present is a time for
     struggle: the future is ours [drawing].
     CARACOL, Vol. 5, no. 1 (September 1978), p.
     FRNT COVER. Spanish.

2740 Huerta, Rebecca. La tierra [drawing].
     CARACOL, Vol. 4, no. 3 (November 1977), p.
     BACK COVER. Bilingual.

2741 Hurtado, Debbie. A historical update:
     Montoya's vindication of fabricated biases.
     THE STATE HORNET, (December 13, 1977), p.
     6. English.

     AN: Review of Jose Montoya's show
     "Pachuco Art - A Historical Update; "a
     rekindling of pachuquismo from the 1940s
     prevalent in Montoya's paintings and
     pen-and-ink drawings. The show featured
     historical photographs, and an animated
     hologram. Visitors wore zoot suit outfits to
     the opening. Illustrated.

2742 Imagenes de la Chicana. Menlo Park, CA:
     Nowels Publications (Stanford University
     Chicano Press), [ca 1975]. English.

     AN: Collections of writings by Chicanas;
     illustrated by unsigned drawings, and
     photographs by Lena Bugarin, Martina Puente,
     Francisco Camplis, Mario Anzaldua.

2743 Intar, International Art Relations, Inc.,
     New York, NY and Ferez Kuri, F. Jose.
     Alejandro E. Romero. Exhibition catalog,
     1977. English.

     AN: Exhibit catalog of drawings and
     paintings by Mexican-born painter and
     muralist living in Chicago. Illustrated in
     color.

2744 Israel, Harry S. Portfolio [drawings]. EL
     GRITO, Vol. 1, no. 1 (Fall 1967), p.
     32-39. English.

2745 Jaramillo, Juanita. Descanso [drawing].
     REVISTA CHICANO-RIQUENA, Vol. 4, no. 3
     (Summer 1976), p. 2. Spanish.

2746 Jaramillo, Juanita. Moods [drawing]. REVISTA
     CHICANO-RIQUENA, Vol. 5, no. 1 (Winter
     1977), p. 88. English.

2747 Jaramillo, Juanita. Mujer Lucandona
     [drawing]. REVISTA CHICANO-RIQUENA, Vol. 4,
     no. 3 (Summer 1976), p. Cover. Spanish.

2748 Jaramillo, Juanita. Sunflower [drawing].
     REVISTA CHICANO-RIQUENA, Vol. 4, no. 3
     (Summer 1976), p. 13. English.

2749 Jaramillo, Juanita. Tierra madre [drawing].
     REVISTA CHICANO-RIQUENA, Vol. 5, no. 1
     (Winter 1977), p. 60. Spanish.

2750 Jaramillo, Juanita. La voladora [drawing].
     REVISTA CHICANO-RIQUENA, Vol. 5, no. 1
     (Winter 1977), p. 112. Bilingual.

Drawings (cont.)

2751 Johnson, Charles. J street galleries: politics flavor alternative art shows. SACRAMENTO BEE, (December 20, 1977), p. A13. English.

AN: Review of a Pachuco show by Jose Montoya that is half drawings and paintings, and half politics - photographs of Pachucos of the 1940s. Montoya's essay that accompanies the exhibit attempts to dispel the image of Pachucos as gangsters, and declares that Pachucos were the first "freedom Fighters." The reviewer feels this is one-sided. Illustrated.

2752 Jose Montoya: poeta, pintor, profesor, humanista, padre, abuelo. EL HISPANO, Vol. 8, no. 27 (December 23, 1975), p. 5. Spanish.

AN: Biographical data on the Sacramento artist, his contributions to the Chicano Movement and his life as an artist-activist. Photographs of his family and reproduction of one drawing.

2753 Kelley, Ramon. Pobrecita [drawing]. DE COLORES, Vol. 1, no. 3 (Summer 1974), p. COVER. Spanish.

2754 Lomas Garza, Carmen. Curandera II [etching]. EL TECOLOTE LITERARY MAGAZINE, Vol. 1, no. 1 (April 1980), p. 5.

2755 Lomas Garza, Carmen. Killed in Pharr, Texas [drawing]. EL GRITO, Vol. 4, no. 4 (Spring 1971), p. 71. English.

2756 Lomas Garza, Carmen. Lo que nos espera [drawing]. EL GRITO, Vol. 4, no. 4 (Spring 1971), p. 70. English.

2757 Lomas Garza, Carmen. Portrait of a pregnant woman. EL GRITO, Vol. 4, no. 4 (Spring 1971), p. 72. English.

2758 Lomas Garza, Carmen. Semillas (de liberacion) [drawing]. HOJAS, (1976), p. 47.

2759 Lomas Garza, Carmen. Semillas [drawing]. EL GRITO, Vol. 4, no. 4 (Spring 1971), p. 73. English.

2760 Lomas Garza, Carmen. Tabla llena [etching]. EL TECOLOTE LITERARY MAGAZINE, Vol. 2, no. 2 (July 1981), p. 5.

2761 Lomas Garza, Carmen. [Untitled drawing]. EL GRITO, Vol. 6, no. 1 (Fall 1972), p. 92.

2762 Lomas Garza, Carmen. [Untitled etching]. TIN TAN, Vol. 2, no. 5 (June 1, 1977), p. In Ftcover.

2763 Lomas Garza, Carmen. [Untitled etching]. TIN TAN, Vol. 2, no. 5 (June 1, 1977), p. In Bkcover.

2764 Lomas Garza, Carmen; Montoya, Jose E.; and Pinedo, Maria Vita. What we are...now. Exhibition catalog, n.d. English.

AN: Drawings by Sacramento women artists: Lorraine Garcia, Eva C. Garcia, Kathryn E. Garcia, Celia Rodriguez, Patricia Carrillo.

2765 Lomeli, Filiberto. [Untitled drawing]. XALMAN, Vol. 1, no. 4 (Spring 1977), p. C.

2766 Lopez Castro, Rafael. [Untitled drawing].

2767 Lopez Castro, Rafael. [Untitled drawing]. ATISBOS, no. 1 (Summer 1975), p. COVER.

2767 Lopez Castro, Rafael. [Untitled drawing]. ATISBOS, no. 1 (Summer 1975), p. 1.

2768 Lopez Castro, Rafael. [Untitled drawing]. ATISBOS, no. 1 (Summer 1975), p. 9.

2769 Lopez Castro, Rafael. [Untitled drawing]. ATISBOS, no. 1 (Summer 1975), p. 31.

2770 Lopez Castro, Rafael. [Untitled drawing]. ATISBOS, no. 1 (Summer 1975), p. 53.

2771 Lopez Castro, Rafael. [Untitled drawing]. ATISBOS, no. 1 (Summer 1975), p. 66.

2772 Lopez Castro, Rafael. [Untitled drawing]. ATISBOS, no. 1 (Summer 1975), p. 67.

2773 Lopez Castro, Rafael. [Untitled drawing]. ATISBOS, no. 1 (Summer 1975), p. 79.

2774 Lopez Castro, Rafael. [Untitled drawing]. ATISBOS, no. 1 (Summer 1975), p. 93.

2775 Lopez, Oscar. [Untitled drawing]. MAIZE, Vol. 5, no. 1-2 (Fall , Winter, 1981, 1982), p. 32. English.

2776 Lopez, Oscar. [Untitled drawing]. MAIZE, Vol. 5, no. 1-2 (Fall , Winter, 1981, 1982), p. 47. English.

2777 Lopez, Yolanda M. Three generations [drawings]. HERESIES, Vol. 2, no. 4 (1979), p. 83.

2778 Lucas, Costa Ben. Chato [comic strip]. ABRAZO, Vol. 1, no. 2 (Summer 1979), p. 16-17. English.

AN: One installment of CHATO, the cartoon strip created by Costa Ben Lucas. Also provides a brief explanation of how the character was created and his principal characteristics.

2779 Lucero, Linda. Compositions from my kitchen/composiciones de mi cocina: an international cookbook. San Francisco, CA: La Raza Graphic Center, 1981. English.

AN: International recipes illustrated with drawings and a poster by Linda Lucero, as well as other artists.

2780 Lujan, Gilbert Sanchez "Magu". [C/S nudes (drawing)]. CON SAFOS, no. 8 (1972), p. 27.

2781 Lujan, Gilbert Sanchez "Magu". [Untitled drawing]. CON SAFOS, no. 7 (Winter 1971), p. 36.

2782 Lujan, Gilbert Sanchez "Magu". [Untitled drawing]. RAYAS, Vol. 1, no. 2 (March, April, 1978), p. Ft cover. English.

2783 Lujan, Gilbert Sanchez "Magu". [Untitled drawing]. CHISMEARTE, Vol. 1, no. 1 (Fall 1976), p. 28-29. English.

2784 Lujan, Gilbert Sanchez "Magu". [Untitled drawings]. CON SAFOS, no. 7 (Winter 1971), p. 43.

2785 Lujan, Gilbert Sanchez "Magu". [Untitled drawings]. CON SAFOS, no. 7 (Winter 1971), p. 41.

2786 Lujan, Gilbert Sanchez "Magu". [Untitled drawings]. CON SAFOS, no. 7 (Winter 1971), p. 39.

Drawings (cont.)

2787 Lujan, Gilbert Sanchez "Magu". [Untitled drawings]. RAYAS, (Spring 1977), p. 4,5,12-15.

2788 Lujan, Jerry. Vida y muerte [drawing]. DE COLORES, Vol. 2, no. 4 (1976), p. 54.

2789 Luna, Benjamin R. [Chicanos and police clash - a drawing]. REGENERACION, Vol. 1, no. 6 (1970), p. 10-11. English.

2790 Luna, Benjamin R. Homshuk [drawing]. REGENERACION, Vol. 1, no. 7 (1970), p. 10-11.

2791 Luna, Benjamin R. [Untitled drawing]. CON SAFOS, Vol. 1, no. 2 (Fall 1968), p. BACK COVER.

2792 Luna, Benjamin R. [Untitled drawing]. REGENERACION, Vol. 1, no. 6 (1970), p. 21.

2793 Madrid, Lydia Rede. [Untitled drawing]. EL GRITO, Vol. 7, no. 1 (September 1973), p. Ft cover. Bilingual.

2794 Madrid, Lydia Rede. [Untitled drawing]. EL GRITO, Vol. 7, no. 1 (September 1973), p. [79]. Bilingual.

2795 Madrid, Lydia Rede. [Untitled drawing]. EL GRITO, Vol. 7, no. 1 (September 1973), p. [75]. Bilingual.

2796 Madrid, Lydia Rede. [Untitled drawing]. EL GRITO, Vol. 7, no. 1 (September 1973), p. [68]. Bilingual.

2797 Madrid, Lydia Rede. [Untitled drawing]. EL GRITO, Vol. 7, no. 1 (September 1973), p. [65]. Bilingual.

2798 Madrid, Lydia Rede. [Untitled drawing]. EL GRITO, Vol. 7, no. 1 (September 1973), p. [59]. Bilingual.

2799 Madrid, Lydia Rede. [Untitled drawing]. EL GRITO, Vol. 7, no. 1 (September 1973), p. 38. Bilingual.

2800 Madrid, Lydia Rede. [Untitled drawing]. EL GRITO, Vol. 7, no. 1 (September 1973), p. 35. Bilingual.

2801 Madrid, Lydia Rede. [Untitled drawing]. EL GRITO, Vol. 7, no. 1 (September 1973), p. [4]. Bilingual.

2802 Madrid, Lydia Rede. [Untitled drawing]. EL GRITO, Vol. 7, no. 1 (September 1973), p. [3]. Bilingual.

2803 Malaquias Montoya. ARTE, (Fall 1977). English.

   AN: Interview with northern California printmaker, painter and muralist, Malaquias Montoya. He discusses his life, his dedication to Chicano art, his resistance to the institutionalization of the Chicano struggle and its art, their cooptation by the establishment. He says he transcended nationalism at one period and became a Third World internationalist. Four drawings and two posters reproduced.

2804 Martinez, Cesar Augusto. Caravana Internacional Chicano del Tratado de Guadalupe Hidalgo [drawing]. CARACOL, Vol. 2, no. 10 (June 1976), p. 1.

2805 Martinez, Cesar Augusto. Coco de choco,

Socorro [drawing]. CARACOL, Vol. 4, no. 10 (June 1978), p. FRNT COVER. Spanish.

2806 Martinez, Cesar Augusto. Manito [drawing]. CARACOL, Vol. 4, no. 10 (June 1978), p. 19. Bilingual.

2807 Martinez, Cesar Augusto. La papa [drawing]. CARACOL, Vol. 4, no. 10 (June 1978), p. BACK COVER. Spanish.

2808 Martinez, Cesar Augusto. El Sonny [drawing]. CARACOL, Vol. 4, no. 10 (June 1978), p. 7. Bilingual.

2809 Martinez, Dennis. [Drawing for BOOK OF THAILAND]. EL GRITO DEL SOL, Vol. 2, no. 2 (April, June, 1977), p. [71].

2810 Martinez, Dennis. [Drawing for BOOK OF THAILAND]. EL GRITO DEL SOL, Vol. 2, no. 2 (April, June, 1977), p. [75].

2811 Martinez, Dennis. [Drawing for BOOK OF THAILAND]. EL GRITO DEL SOL, Vol. 2, no. 2 (April, June, 1977), p. [79].

2812 Martinez, Dennis. [Drawing for PELON DROPS OUT]. EL GRITO DEL SOL, Vol. 2, no. 2 (April, June, 1977), p. [51].

2813 Martinez, Dennis. [Drawing for PELON DROPS OUT]. EL GRITO DEL SOL, Vol. 2, no. 2 (April, June, 1977), p. [55].

2814 Martinez, Dennis. [Drawing for PELON DROPS OUT]. EL GRITO DEL SOL, Vol. 2, no. 2 (April, June, 1977), p. [59].

2815 Martinez, Dennis. [Drawing for PELON DROPS OUT]. EL GRITO DEL SOL, Vol. 2, no. 2 (April, June, 1977), p. [65].

2816 Martinez, Dennis. A New Mexico scene [drawing]. EL GRITO DEL SOL, Vol. 2, no. 2 (April, June, 1977), p. [13].

2817 Martinez, Dennis. A New Mexico scene [drawing]. EL GRITO DEL SOL, Vol. 2, no. 2 (April, June, 1977), p. [17].

2818 Martinez, Dennis. A New Mexico scene [drawing]. EL GRITO DEL SOL, Vol. 2, no. 2 (April, June, 1977), p. 25.

2819 Martinez, Dennis. A New Mexico scene [drawing]. EL GRITO DEL SOL, Vol. 2, no. 2 (April, June, 1977), p. [29].

2820 Martinez, Dennis. [Untitled drawing]. EL GRITO, Vol. 6, no. 1 (Fall 1972), p. 91.

2821 Martinez, Oscar. Dona Paula Ortiz Baez [drawing]. REVISTA CHICANO-RIQUENA, Vol. 5, no. 1 (Winter 1977), p. 115. Spanish.

2822 Martinez, Oscar. In the mist of isolation. REVISTA CHICANO-RIQUENA, Vol. 5, no. 1 (Winter 1977), p. 75. English.

2823 Martinez, Oscar. [Untitled drawing]. REVISTA CHICANO-RIQUENA, Vol. 8, no. 1 (Winter 1980), p. 30. English.

2824 Martinez, Oscar. Victoria Maria Nodai: a life's endless torture; an obsession of one's heart. REVISTA CHICANO-RIQUENA, Vol. 5, no. 1 (Winter 1977), p. 116. English.

2825 Martinez, Pedro. [Self-portrait (drawing)]. REVISTA RIO BRAVO, Vol. 1, no. 1 (Winter 1981), p. 2.

Drawings (cont.)

2826 Martinez, Santos G., Jr. La cucaracha
[drawing]. TEJIDOS, Vol. 3, no. 3 (Fall
1976), p. 5. Spanish.

2827 Martinez, Santos G., Jr. El mundo es una
cantina tan grande como el dolor [drawing].
TEJIDOS, Vol. 3, no. 3 (Fall   1976), p. 22.
Spanish.

2828 Martinez, Santos G., Jr. Por la calle
Guadalupe o el Chavalito Lounge 2 [drawing].
TEJIDOS, Vol. 3, no. 3 (Fall   1976), p. 18.
Spanish.

2829 Martinez, Santos G., Jr. Por la calle
Guadalupe o el Chavalito Lounge 1 [drawing].
TEJIDOS, Vol. 3, no. 3 (Fall   1976), p. 45.
Spanish.

2830 Martinez, Santos G., Jr. Por la Calle Perez,
#1 [drawing]. REVISTA CHICANO-RIQUENA, Vol.
4, no. 1 (Winter 1976), p. Cover. Spanish.

2831 Martinez, Santos G., Jr. Por la calle Perez
1 [drawing]. TEJIDOS, Vol. 3, no. 3 (Fall
1976), p. 28. Spanish.

2832 Martinez, Santos G., Jr. Por la Calle Perez
[drawing]. REVISTA CHICANO-RIQUENA, Vol. 4,
no. 1 (Winter 1976), p. 26. Spanish.

2833 Martinez, Santos G., Jr. Por las calles
Green y Nogalitos [drawing]. REVISTA
CHICANO-RIQUENA, Vol. 4, no. 1 (Winter
1976), p. 15. Spanish.

2834 Martinez, Santos G., Jr. Por las calles
Nogalitos y Green [drawing]. TEJIDOS, Vol.
3, no. 3 (Fall   1976), p. 14. Spanish.

2835 Martinez, Santos G., Jr. Por las calles
Nogalitos y Lubbock [drawing]. TEJIDOS, Vol.
3, no. 3 (Fall   1976), p. 36. Spanish.

2836 Martinez, Santos G., Jr. Por las calles S.
Zarzamora y Chihuahua #2 [drawing]. CARACOL,
Vol. 2, no. 4 (December 1975), p. 24.
Spanish.

2837 Martinez, Santos G., Jr. Por las calles San
Fernando y S. Frio [drawing]. REVISTA
CHICANO-RIQUENA, Vol. 4, no. 1 (Winter
1976), p. 2. Spanish.

2838 Martinez, Santos G., Jr. La Raza 1
[drawing]. TEJIDOS, Vol. 3, no. 3 (Fall
1976), p. 9. Spanish.

2839 Martinez, Santos G., Jr. La Raza 2
[drawing]. TEJIDOS, Vol. 3, no. 3 (Fall
1976), p. 40. Spanish.

2840 Martinez, Santos G., Jr. [Untitled drawing].
R.A.M. COLLECTIVE, Vol. 1, no. 2 (March 1,
1976), p. 5.

2841 Martinez, Santos G., Jr. Vuela la paloma
[drawing]. TEJIDOS, Vol. 3, no. 3 (Fall
1976), p. 33. Spanish.

2842 Martinez, Sue. [Untitled drawing]. EL
TECOLOTE LITERARY MAGAZINE, Vol. 1, no. 1
(April 1980), p. Cover.

2843 Mendez, Xavier. [Untitled drawing]. LO
SENCILLO, Vol. 1, no. 1 (1976), p. [2].

2844 Mendez, Xavier. [Untitled drawing]. LO
SENCILLO, Vol. 1, no. 1 (1976), p. [8].

2845 Mendez, Xavier. [Untitled drawing]. LO
SENCILLO, Vol. 1, no. 1 (1976), p. [28].

2846 Mendez, Xavier. [Untitled drawing]. LO
SENCILLO, Vol. 1, no. 1 (1976), p. [39].

2847 Mendoza, Enrique. [Untitled drawing].
XALMAN, Vol. 1, no. 4 (Spring 1977), p. 16.

2848 Mestiza [drawing]. LA LUZ, Vol. 8, no. 8
(October, November, 1980), p. 10. English.

2849 The Mexican Museum, San Francisco, CA.
Manuel Neri: sculpture and drawings.
Exhibition invitation, 1981. English.

AN: Illustrated invitation to an
exhibit.

2850 Montoya, Emmanuel. [Untitled drawing]. EL
TECOLOTE LITERARY MAGAZINE, Vol. 2, no. 2
(July 1981), p. 11.

2851 Montoya, Jose E. Chuco series [drawings].
MAIZE, Vol. 2, no. 1 (Fall   1978), p. Bk
cover. English.

2852 Montoya, Jose E. Pachuco art: a historical
update. Sacramento, CA: Royal Chicano Air
Force, 1977. English.

AN: Booklet outlining the history of the
Zoot Suit Riots of 1943 and the making of
the Pachuco myth, written by Montoya and
illustrated with his pen-and-ink drawings of
Pachucos and Pachucas.

2853 Montoya, Jose E. Portfolio 5: Campesinos;
The Journey; Untitled; The Year of the Pigs;
The General; The Priest; Visiting Day; Girl
Learning. EL GRITO, Vol. 2, no. 3 (Spring 1969),
p. 48-57. English.

2854 Montoya, Jose E. and Murguia, Alejandro. El
sol y los de abajo and other R.C.A.F. poems
/ oracion a la mano poderosa. San Francisco,
CA: Ediciones Pocho-Che, 1972. English.

AN: 10 illustrations by Sacramento, CA
artist Armando Cid.

2855 Montoya, Jose E. [Untitled drawing]. MAIZE,
Vol. 3, no. 3-4 (Spring, Summer, 1980), p.
Ft cover. Bilingual.

2856 Montoya, Jose E. [Untitled drawing]. MAIZE,
Vol. 3, no. 3-4 (Spring, Summer, 1980), p.
63. Bilingual.

2857 Montoya, Jose E. [Untitled drawing]. MAIZE,
Vol. 3, no. 3-4 (Spring, Summer, 1980), p.
77. Bilingual.

2858 Montoya, Jose E. [Untitled drawing]. MAIZE,
Vol. 4, no. 1-2 (Fall , Winter, 1980,
1981), p. Ft cover. Bilingual.

2859 Montoya, Jose E. [Untitled drawing]. MAIZE,
Vol. 4, no. 1-2 (Fall , Winter, 1980,
1981), p. 13. Bilingual.

2860 Montoya, Jose E. [Untitled drawing]. EL
GRITO, Vol. 2, no. 3 (Spring 1969), p. [51].
Bilingual.

2861 Montoya, Jose E. [Untitled drawings from the
CHUCO SERIES]. MAIZE, Vol. 2, no. 1 (Fall
1978), p. 32-35. English.

2862 Montoya, Jose E. [Untitled drawings from the
CHUCO SERIES]. MAIZE, Vol. 2, no. 1 (Fall
1978), p. Ft cover. English.

Drawings (cont.)

2863 Montoya, Jose E. The year of the pigs
[drawing]. EL GRITO, Vol. 2, no. 3 (Spring
1969), p. [52]. English.

2864 Montoya, Malaquias. [El Pocho Che (logo)].
EL POCHO CHE, Vol. 1, no. 2 (1970), p.
Cover.

2865 Montoya, Malaquias. El sabado en la tarde
[drawing]. EL GRITO, Vol. 2, no. 3 (Spring
1969), p. [4]. English.

2866 Montoya, Malaquias. [Untitled drawing]. EL
GRITO, Vol. 6, no. 1 (Fall 1972), p. 88.

2867 Montoya, Malaquias. [Untitled drawing]. EL
POCHO CHE, Vol. 1, no. 2 (1970), p. 56.

2868 Montoya, Malaquias. [Untitled drawing]. TIN
TAN, no. 4 (Fall 1976), p. In FtCover.

2869 Montoya, Malaquias. [Untitled drawing]. TIN
TAN, no. 4 (Fall 1976), p. In BkCover.

2870 Moreno, Juan M. [Untitled drawings]. MAIZE,
Vol. 2, no. 1 (Fall 1978), p. 18-19.
English.

2871 Muchnic, Suzanne. Damaged goods in the big
city. LOS ANGELES TIMES, (July 23, 1979),
p. IV-11. English.

AN: Review of the exhibit at Otis Art
Institute of Parsons School of Design of
L.A. PARKS AND WRECKS, featuring Carlos
Almaraz, John Valadez, and Black artist John
Woods. Almaraz paints auto wrecks, and
landscapes of Echo Park. Valadez does pencil
portraits of young Chicanos. Illustrated.

2872 Museum of Fine Arts, Santa Fe, NM. Luis
Jimenez, sculpture, drawings and prints: La
Cofradia de Artes y Artesanos Hispanicos,
selected works. Exhibition invitation, 1979.
English.

AN: Invitation to an exhibit of Texas
sculptor and printmaker Luis Jimenez, and
New Mexican artists and artisans.

2873 Narezo, Jose. [Drawing for CRONICA DE
AZTLAN]. EL GRITO DEL SOL, Vol. 2, no. 2
(April, June, 1977), p. [35].

2874 Narezo, Jose. [Drawing for CRONICA DE
AZTLAN]. EL GRITO DEL SOL, Vol. 2, no. 2
(April, June, 1977), p. [39].

2875 Narezo, Jose. [Drawing for CRONICA DE
AZTLAN]. EL GRITO DEL SOL, Vol. 2, no. 2
(April, June, 1977), p. [43].

2876 Narezo, Jose. [Drawing for CRONICA DE
AZTLAN]. EL GRITO DEL SOL, Vol. 2, no. 2
(April, June, 1977), p. [47].

2877 New Mexico State University, University Art
Gallery, Las Cruces, NM. Luis Jimenez:
sculpture, drawings and prints. Exhibition
catalog, 1977. English.

AN: Well illustrated catalog, some
illustrations in color. Text is interview
tracing Jimenez's artistic development.
Artists identifies Mexican American
connections in his work.

2878 Noriega, Ramses. [Untitled drawing]. EL
GRITO, Vol. 6, no. 1 (Fall 1972), p. 90.

2879 Noriega, Ramses. [Untitled drawing]. EL
GRITO, Vol. 5, no. 3 (Spring 1972), p. [83].

Bilingual.

2880 Noriega, Ramses. [Untitled drawing]. EL
GRITO, Vol. 5, no. 3 (Spring 1972), p. [82].
Bilingual.

2881 Noriega, Ramses. [Untitled drawing]. EL
GRITO, Vol. 5, no. 3 (Spring 1972), p. [81].
Bilingual.

2882 Noriega, Ramses. [Untitled drawing]. EL
GRITO, Vol. 5, no. 3 (Spring 1972), p. [80].
Bilingual.

2883 Noriega, Ramses. [Untitled drawings]. EL
GRITO, Vol. 5, no. 3 (Spring 1972), p.
80-83. English.

2884 Oakland Museum, Oakland, CA and Laney
College, Oakland, CA. In search of Aztlan.
Exhibition brochure, 1974. English.

AN: Brochure for exhibit featuring Los
Four: Carlos Almaraz, Gilbert Lujan, Roberto
de la Rocha, Frank Romero, Judithe
Hernandez.

2885 Ochoa, Victor Orozco. Centerfold-arte
[drawing]. MAIZE, Vol. 1, no. 1 (Fall
1977), p. 32-33. English.

2886 Ochoa, Victor Orozco. [Resistencia!
(drawing)]. MAIZE, Vol. 2, no. 2 (Winter
1979), p. 61. Spanish.

2887 Ochoa, Victor Orozco. [La tierra mia, all
the way to the Bay (drawing)]. MAIZE, Vol.
2, no. 2 (Winter 1979), p. 6. English.

2888 Ochoa, Victor Orozco. [Untitled drawing].
MAIZE, Vol. 2, no. 1 (Fall 1978), p. 8.
English.

2889 Ojeda, Jay. Galeria de la Raza--art for the
community. SAN FRANCISCO PROGRESS, (March
24, 1972). English.

AN: Analysis of group exhibition by
thirty-four Raza artists. Commentary on the
work of Latin American artists Consuelo
Mendez, Rolando Castellon, and Chicano
artists Rupert Garcia, Chuy Campusano and
Peter Rodriguez.

2890 La onda artistica de Carmen Lomas Garza.
MAGAZIN, Vol. 1, no. 2 (November 1971), p.
29-37. Spanish.

AN: Short biographical sketch of artist
and reproduction of seven early drawings.
The art of Carmen Lomas Garza is situated
within important events of the Chicano
Movement in Texas: the student walkouts in
Kingsville, and the formation of Colegio
Jacinto Trevino.

2891 Orozco, Juan Ishi. [Untitled drawing].
MAIZE, Vol. 4, no. 1-2 (Fall , Winter,
1980, 1981), p. 31. Bilingual.

2892 Orozco, Sylvia. [Untitled painting].
TEJIDOS, Vol. 5, no. 1 (1978), p. 9.
English.

2893 Ortegon, Veronica. [Illustration of Orozco's
mural HERNAN CORTEZ]. REVISTA RIO BRAVO,
Vol. 1, no. 3 (Fall 1981), p. 11.

2894 Ortegon, Veronica. [Low riders c/s
(drawing)]. REVISTA RIO BRAVO, Vol. 1, no. 3
(Fall 1981), p. Bk cover.

Drawings (cont.)

2895 Ortegon, Veronica. [Photographs and
     drawings]. REVISTA RIO BRAVO, Vol. 1, no. 3
     (Fall 1981), p. Passim.

2896 Ortegon, Veronica. [Untitled drawing].
     REVISTA RIO BRAVO, Vol. 1, no. 3 (Fall
     1981), p. 8.

2897 Ortegon, Veronica. [Untitled drawing].
     REVISTA RIO BRAVO, Vol. 1, no. 3 (Fall
     1981), p. 7.

2898 Ortiz, Leo. [Untitled drawing].
     REGENERACION, Vol. 1, no. 4 (1970), p.
     COVER. English.

2899 Ozuna, Gloria. Un companero de lejos
     [drawing]. CARACOL, Vol. 3, no. 3 (November
     1976), p. BACK COVER. Spanish.

2900 Ozuna, Gloria. [Familia (drawing)]. CARACOL,
     Vol. 3, no. 7 (March 1977), p. 24.

2901 Ozuna, Gloria. La Senora Soliz de la Calle
     "D" [drawing]. CARACOL, Vol. 3, no. 3
     (November 1976), p. FRNT COVER. Spanish.

2902 Ozuna, Gloria. El tamal [drawing]. CARACOL,
     Vol. 3, no. 7 (March 1977), p. Cover 4-21.

2903 Palma Castroman, Janis. [Untitled drawing].
     TEJIDOS, Vol. 5, no. 2 (1978), p. 100.

2904 Palma Castroman, Janis. [Untitled drawing].
     TEJIDOS, Vol. 5, no. 2 (1978), p. 101.

2905 Palma Castroman, Janis. [Untitled drawing].
     TEJIDOS, Vol. 5, no. 2 (1978), p. 102.

2906 Palma Castroman, Janis. [Untitled drawing].
     TEJIDOS, Vol. 5, no. 2 (1978), p. 103.

2907 Palomino, Ernesto ("Ernie"). In black and
     white: evolution of an artist. Fresno, CA:
     Academy Library Guild, 1956. English.

     AN: Illustrations of Palomino's work
     between 1945 and 1955 when he was a student
     in Fresno's Edison High and Adult Schools
     with art teacher Elizabeth Daniels Baldwin,
     who promoted the publication of the book.
     Drawings show extraordinary power and the
     social commentary of a young, essentially
     self-taught artist.

2908 Patterson, Ann. Exhibit at Unitarian: Smith,
     Quesada art black, white contrast. TEMPE
     DAILY NEWS, (March 16, 1976). English.

     AN: Eugenio Quesada presented drawings
     of female torsos along with Smith. Both are
     industrial design faculty members at Arizona
     State University. Article mentions other
     Quesada shows, and his participation on the
     Jean Charlot mural at the University.

2909 Pazos, Antonio. [Con el poncho embravecido
     (drawing)]. LLUEVE TLALOC, no. 5 (1978), p.
     15.

2910 Pazos, Antonio. [Loui Romero (drawing)].
     LLUEVE TLALOC, no. 6 (1979), p. 43.

2911 Pazos, Antonio. El poeta suena... [drawing].
     LLUEVE TLALOC, no. 5 (1978), p. 6. Spanish.

2912 Pazos, Antonio. [Untitled drawing]. MAIZE,
     Vol. 2, no. 1 (Fall 1978), p. In BkCover.
     English.

2913 Pazos, Antonio. [Untitled drawing]. LLUEVE
     TLALOC, no. 4 (1977), p. Cover.

2914 Pazos, Antonio. [Untitled drawing]. LLUEVE
     TLALOC, no. 4 (1977), p. 22.

2915 Pazos, Antonio. [Untitled drawing]. LLUEVE
     TLALOC, no. 4 (1977), p. [25].

2916 Pazos, Antonio. [Untitled drawing]. LLUEVE
     TLALOC, no. 4 (1977), p. 34.

2917 Pazos, Antonio. [Untitled drawing]. LLUEVE
     TLALOC, no. 4 (1977), p. 45.

2918 Pazos, Antonio. [Untitled drawing]. LLUEVE
     TLALOC, no. 4 (1977), p. 53.

2919 Pazos, Antonio. [Untitled drawing]. LLUEVE
     TLALOC, no. 4 (1977), p. [55].

2920 Pazos, Antonio. [Untitled drawing]. LLUEVE
     TLALOC, no. 4 (1977), p. [61].

2921 Pazos, Antonio. [Untitled drawing]. LLUEVE
     TLALOC, no. 4 (1977), p. [66].

2922 Pazos, Antonio. [Untitled drawing]. LLUEVE
     TLALOC, no. 4 (1977), p. [71].

2923 Pazos, Antonio. [Untitled drawing]. LLUEVE
     TLALOC, no. 4 (1977), p. 90.

2924 Pazos, Antonio. [Untitled drawing]. LLUEVE
     TLALOC, no. 4 (1977), p. 91.

2925 Pazos, Antonio. [Untitled drawing]. LLUEVE
     TLALOC, no. 4 (1977), p. 92.

2926 Pazos, Antonio. [Untitled drawing]. LLUEVE
     TLALOC, no. 4 (1977), p. 95.

2927 Pazos, Antonio. [Untitled drawing]. LLUEVE
     TLALOC, no. 4 (1977), p. 106.

2928 Pazos, Antonio. [Untitled drawing]. LLUEVE
     TLALOC, no. 5 (1978), p. Cover.

2929 Pazos, Antonio. [Untitled drawing]. LLUEVE
     TLALOC, no. 5 (1978), p. 9.

2930 Pazos, Antonio. [Untitled drawing]. LLUEVE
     TLALOC, no. 5 (1978), p. 21.

2931 Pazos, Antonio. [Untitled drawing]. LLUEVE
     TLALOC, no. 5 (1978), p. 25.

2932 Pazos, Antonio. [Untitled drawing]. LLUEVE
     TLALOC, no. 6 (1979), p. [25].

2933 Pazos, Antonio. [Untitled drawing]. LLUEVE
     TLALOC, no. 6 (1979), p. 27.

2934 Pazos, Antonio. [Untitled drawing]. LLUEVE
     TLALOC, no. 6 (1979), p. 31.

2935 Pazos, Antonio. [Untitled drawing]. LLUEVE
     TLALOC, no. 6 (1979), p. 33.

2936 Pazos, Antonio. [Untitled drawing]. LLUEVE
     TLALOC, no. 6 (1979), p. 37.

2937 Pazos, Antonio. [Untitled drawing]. LLUEVE
     TLALOC, no. 6 (1979), p. 44.

2938 Pazos, Antonio. [Untitled drawing]. LLUEVE
     TLALOC, no. 7 (1980), p. 9.

2939 Pazos, Antonio. [Untitled drawing]. LLUEVE
     TLALOC, no. 7 (1980), p. 11.

2940 Pazos, Antonio. [Untitled drawing]. LLUEVE
     TLALOC, no. 7 (1980), p. 13.

Drawings (cont.)

2941 Pazos, Antonio. [Untitled drawing]. LLUEVE TLALOC, no. 7 (1980), p. 16.

2942 Pazos, Antonio. [Untitled drawing]. LLUEVE TLALOC, no. 7 (1980), p. 18.

2943 Pazos, Antonio. [Untitled drawing]. LLUEVE TLALOC, no. 7 (1980), p. 20.

2944 Pazos, Antonio. [Untitled drawing]. LLUEVE TLALOC, no. 7 (1980), p. 22.

2945 Pazos, Antonio. [Untitled drawing]. LLUEVE TLALOC, no. 7 (1980), p. 23.

2946 Pazos, Antonio. [Untitled drawing]. LLUEVE TLALOC, no. 7 (1980), p. 26.

2947 Pazos, Antonio. [Untitled drawing]. LLUEVE TLALOC, no. 7 (1980), p. 27.

2948 Pazos, Antonio. [Untitled drawing]. LLUEVE TLALOC, no. 7 (1980), p. 30.

2949 Pazos, Antonio. [Untitled drawing]. LLUEVE TLALOC, no. 7 (1980), p. 32.

2950 Pazos, Antonio. [Untitled drawing]. LLUEVE TLALOC, no. 7 (1980), p. 33.

2951 Pazos, Antonio. [Untitled drawing]. LLUEVE TLALOC, no. 7 (1980), p. 35.

2952 Pazos, Antonio. [Untitled drawing]. LLUEVE TLALOC, no. 7 (1980), p. 36.

2953 Pazos, Antonio. [Untitled drawing]. LLUEVE TLALOC, no. 7 (1980), p. 40.

2954 Pazos, Antonio. [Untitled drawing]. LLUEVE TLALOC, no. 8 (1981), p. 5.

2955 Pazos, Antonio. [Untitled drawing]. LLUEVE TLALOC, no. 8 (1981), p. 11.

2956 Pazos, Antonio. [Untitled drawing]. LLUEVE TLALOC, no. 8 (1981), p. 17.

2957 Pazos, Antonio. [Untitled drawing]. LLUEVE TLALOC, no. 8 (1981), p. [19].

2958 Pazos, Antonio. [Untitled drawing]. LLUEVE TLALOC, no. 8 (1981), p. 23.

2959 Pazos, Antonio. [Untitled drawing]. LLUEVE TLALOC, no. 8 (1981), p. 25.

2960 Pazos, Antonio. [Untitled drawing]. LLUEVE TLALOC, no. 8 (1981), p. 27.

2961 Pazos, Antonio. [Untitled drawing]. LLUEVE TLALOC, no. 8 (1981), p. 29.

2962 Pazos, Antonio. [Untitled drawing]. LLUEVE TLALOC, no. 8 (1981), p. [33].

2963 Penalosa, Fernando. [Graphic for SOL Y SANGRE (drawing)]. CARACOL, Vol. 3, no. 6 (February 1977), p. 24.

2964 Perales, Tony. [Mexico age four (drawing)]. In: Salinas, Luis Omar. CRAZY GYPSY. Fresno, CA: Origenes Publications, c1970, p. [54]..

2965 Perales, Tony. [Pedro Infante (drawing)]. In: Salinas, Luis Omar. CRAZY GYPSY. Fresno, CA: Origenes Publications, c1970, p. [40]..

2966 Perales, Tony. [Robstown (drawing)]. In: Salinas, Luis Omar. CRAZY GYPSY. Fresno,

CA: Origenes Publications, c1970, p. [60].

2967 Perez, Raymond. Mexican singing [drawing]. TEJIDOS, Vol. 4, no. 3 (Fall 1977), p. 25. English.

2968 Philip Renteria drawings, 1974-77. In YOUNG TEXAS ARTISTS SERIES. Amarillo, TX: Amarillo Art Center, 1977. English.

AN: Catalog of series of exhibits co-sponsored by the Texas commission of the Arts and Humanities and the Amarillo Art Center. Illustrated with a biography of the artist.

2969 Photo-graphics/foto-grafica. MAIZE, Vol. 4, no. 1-2 (Fall , Winter, 1980, 1981). Bilingual.

AN: 9 drawings and prints by Royal Chicano Air Force (Sacramento, Calif.) artists Jose Montoya, Juanishi Orozco, Esteban Villa.

2970 The plan of Delano. Brochure, n.d. English.

AN: Los Angeles artist Adolph Villavazo, Charcoal drawing, 1966.

2971 EL PLAYANO (Loyola University, Los Angeles). (Spring 1972).

AN: Illustrations by Willie Herron, Harry Gamboa, Jr., Gronk, Diane Gamboa, William A. Bejarano, Eddie Garcia.

2972 EL PLAYANO (Loyola University, Los Angeles). (Spring 1973).

AN: Illustrations by Simon Gonzales, Gronk, Harry Gamboa, Jr., Willie Herron, Charles Almaraz, Sister Teresa Munoz, Patsy Valdez, Diane Gamboa.

2973 Popcorn. [Two women (drawing)]. REGENERACION, Vol. 2, no. 4 (1975), p. 16.

2974 Popcorn. [Untitled drawing]. REGENERACION, Vol. 2, no. 4 (1975), p. 5.

2975 Popcorn. [Untitled drawing]. REGENERACION, Vol. 2, no. 4 (1975), p. 6.

2976 Popcorn. [Untitled drawing]. REGENERACION, Vol. 2, no. 4 (1975), p. 15.

2977 Popcorn. [Untitled drawing]. REGENERACION, Vol. 2, no. 4 (1975), p. 51.

2978 Quintana, Helena. Sketches [drawing]. DE COLORES, Vol. 2, no. 3 (1975), p. 53-56.

2979 Quirarte, Jacinto. Chelo Gonzalez Amezcua. QUETZAL, Vol. 1, no. 2 (Winter 1970, 1971), p. 33-36.

AN: Biographical information based on a taped interview with the Del Rio, Texas artist. As a self-taught artist, Chelo Gonzalez Amezcua developed a drawing style using colored ball point pens which she calls "Filigree Art", a new Texas culture. Poorly illustrated.

Drawings (cont.)

2980 Quirarte, Jacinto. Image and text (poetry)
     in the work of Consuelo (Chelo) Gonzalez
     Amezcua, a Texas artist (1903-1975).
     RESEARCH CENTER FOR THE ARTS REVIEW, Vol. 5,
     no. 1 (January 1982), p. 1-3. English.

     AN: The use of images and poetry in the
     work of self-taught Del Rio, Texas artist
     Chelo Gonzalez Amezcua is demonstrated by
     focusing on her drawing EL MOSAICO DE LAS
     AVES of 1972, in which her use of both sides
     of the paper is contrasted with similar uses
     in Aztec sculpture. Illustrated.

2981 Quiroz, Martin, III. Cuauhtemoc [drawing].
     REGENERACION, Vol. 1, no. 5 (1970), p.
     COVER. English.

2982 Rafas. Social comment in barrio pop
     [drawing]. CON SAFOS, no. 7 (Winter 1971),
     p. 22.

2983 Rafas. Social comment in barrio pop
     [drawing]. CON SAFOS, no. 8 (1972), p. 34.

2984 Rafas. A social comment in Chicano pop
     [drawing]. CON SAFOS, Vol. 1, no. 4 (1969),
     p. 10.

2985 Rafas. Social commentary in Chicano pop art
     [drawing]. CON SAFOS, Vol. 2, no. 5 (1970),
     p. 31.

2986 Rafas. Social commentary in Chicano pop art
     [drawing]. CON SAFOS, no. 6 (Summer 1970),
     p. 43.

2987 Rafas. [Untitled drawing]. CON SAFOS, Vol.
     2, no. 5 (1970), p. 36.

2988 Raffel, Stefan. [Portfolio (drawings)].
     CARACOL, Vol. 1, no. 5 (January 1975), p.
     4-5. English.

2989 Ramirez de Robe, Jose "Controll". Carton de
     Jose "Controll" Ramirez. CARACOL, Vol. 3,
     no. 11 (July 1977), p. 14. Spanish.

2990 Ramirez de Robe, Jose "Controll". Human
     rights defender [drawing]. CARACOL, Vol. 4,
     no. 4 (December 1977), p. FRNT COVER.
     Bilingual.

2991 Ramirez de Robe, Jose "Controll". Police
     scoreboard [drawing]. CARACOL, Vol. 4, no. 2
     (October 1977), p. 20.

2992 Ramirez de Robe, Jose "Controll". [Which way
     to the revolution, ese? (caricature)].
     CARACOL, Vol. 1, no. 7 (March 1975), p. 2.
     Bilingual.

2993 Ramirez, Fern. [Untitled drawings]. CARACOL,
     Vol. 3, no. 11 (July 1977), p. 18.

2994 Ramirez, Mickey. A letter in depth
     [drawing]. TEJIDOS, Vol. 5, no. 1 (1978), p.
     17. English.

2995 Raya, Marcos. Ladies and gentlemen, we got a
     new pope [drawing]. REVISTA CHICANO-RIQUENA,
     Vol. 6, no. 4 (Fall 1978), p. 50. English.

2996 Raya, Marcos. [Untitled drawing]. REVISTA
     CHICANO-RIQUENA, Vol. 8, no. 1 (Winter
     1980), p. 80. English.

2997 Resendez, Izabel. Christ [drawing]. TEJIDOS,
     Vol. 4, no. 3 (Fall 1977), p. 31. English.

2998 Reyes Aponte, Cynthia. Untitled [drawing].
     LA PALABRA, Vol. 2, no. 2 (Fall 1980), p.
     10.

2999 Reyes Aponte, Cynthia. Untitled [drawing].
     LA PALABRA, Vol. 2, no. 2 (Fall 1980), p.
     10.

3000 Reyes, Felipe. Malinche complex [drawing].
     REVISTA CHICANO-RIQUENA, Vol. 2, no. 3
     (Summer 1974), p. 26. English.

3001 Reyes, Felipe. La Malinche [drawing].
     REVISTA CHICANO-RIQUENA, Vol. 2, no. 3
     (Summer 1974), p. 12. Spanish.

3002 Reyes, Felipe. [Untitled drawing]. REVISTA
     CHICANO-RIQUENA, Vol. 2, no. 3 (Summer
     1974), p. COVER. Spanish.

3003 Reyes, Felipe. Untitled [drawing]. REVISTA
     CHICANO-RIQUENA, Vol. 2, no. 3 (Summer
     1974), p. 40. English.

3004 Rezendez, Mark. Christian cross [drawing].
     TEJIDOS, Vol. 4, no. 3 (Fall 1977), p. 32.
     English.

3005 Rivera, Domingo. [Untitled drawing]. EL
     POCHO CHE, Vol. 1, no. 2 (1970), p. 40.

3006 Rivera, Domingo. [Untitled drawing]. EL
     POCHO CHE, Vol. 1, no. 2 (1970), p. 42.

3007 Rivera, Domingo. [Untitled drawing]. EL
     POCHO CHE, Vol. 1, no. 2 (1970), p. 49.

3008 Rocha, Adrian. [Untitled drawings]. MANGO,
     Vol. 1, no. 1 (Fall 1976), p. 14,23.

3009 Rodriguez, Jose. El hombre pequeno
     [drawing]. LA PALABRA, Vol. 3, no. 1-2
     (Spring, Fall , 1981), p. 91. Spanish.

3010 Rodriguez, Jose. Remigia, la mama de Manuel
     [drawing]. LA PALABRA, Vol. 3, no. 1-2
     (Spring, Fall , 1981), p. 117. Spanish.

3011 Rodriguez, Jose. Timoteo y su burro
     [drawing]. LA PALABRA, Vol. 3, no. 1-2
     (Spring, Fall , 1981), p. 101. Spanish.

3012 Rodriguez, Julia. El control humano
     [drawing]. RAYAS, Vol. 1, no. 5 (September,
     October, 1978), p. Ft cover. Spanish.

3013 Rodriguez, Patricia. Untitled [drawing]. LA
     PALABRA, Vol. 2, no. 2 (Fall 1980), p. 42.
     Bilingual.

3014 Rodriguez, Patricia. Untitled [drawing]. TIN
     TAN, Vol. 1, no. 2 (September 1975), p.
     [22].

3015 Rodriguez, Vicente. Dia de la coneja
     [drawing]. TEJIDOS, Vol. 4, no. 2 (Summer
     1977), p. 24. Bilingual.

3016 Rodriguez, Vicente. Drawing commemorating
     the 16th of September, Mexico's Independence
     Day. TEJIDOS, Vol. 4, no. 2 (Summer 1977),
     p. 22. English.

3017 Rodriguez, Vicente. La hormiga [drawing].
     CARACOL, Vol. 2, no. 11 (July 1976), p. 12.

3018 Rodriguez, Vicente. Mayan gods [drawing].
     TEJIDOS, Vol. 4, no. 2 (Summer 1977), p. 20.
     Spanish.

3019 Rodriguez, Vicente. Mayan gods [drawing].
     TEJIDOS, Vol. 4, no. 2 (Summer 1977), p. 21.
     English.

Drawings (cont.)

3020 Rodriguez, Vicente. Mayan religious ceremonies [drawing]. TEJIDOS, Vol. 4, no. 2 (Summer 1977), p. 18. English.

3021 Rodriguez, Vicente. Mayas cazando ganado para comer=Mayas hunting game for food [drawing]. TEJIDOS, Vol. 4, no. 2 (Summer 1977), p. 19. Bilingual.

3022 Rodriguez, Vicente. Mayas plantando maiz=Mayas planting corn [drawing]. TEJIDOS, Vol. 4, no. 2 (Summer 1977), p. 17. Bilingual.

3023 Rodriguez, Vicente. Nuestra Senora de Guadalupe=Our Lady of Guadalupe [drawing]. TEJIDOS, Vol. 4, no. 2 (Summer 1977), p. 23. Bilingual.

3024 Rodriguez, Vicente. El pajaro grande [drawing]. CARACOL, Vol. 2, no. 10 (June 1976), p. 17.

3025 Rodriguez, Vicente. Por ahi en la luna [drawing]. CARACOL, Vol. 2, no. 11 (July 1976), p. 13.

3026 Romero, Alejandro E. [Untitled drawing]. REVISTA CHICANO-RIQUENA, Vol. 8, no. 1 (Winter 1980), p. COVER. Bilingual.

3027 Romero, Alejandro E. [Untitled drawing]. REVISTA CHICANO-RIQUENA, Vol. 8, no. 1 (Winter 1980), p. 50. English.

3028 Romero, Alejandro E. [Untitled drawing]. REVISTA CHICANO-RIQUENA, Vol. 8, no. 1 (Winter 1980), p. 60. English.

3029 Romero, Leo. Celso: poetry by Leo Romero, New Mexico. Berkeley, CA: Tonatiuh International, 1980. English.

AN: Book illustrated by poet-artist Leo Romero from New Mexico. Drawings.

3030 Romero, Orlando and Cumpian, Carlos. A Canto al Pueblo artist at the second "Canto" en 1978, Corpus Christi, Tex Aztlan, enjoying the fruits of the struggle on to the third ... Canto al Pueblo!!! CARACOL, Vol. 5, no. 1 (September 1978), p. 19.

3031 Romero, Orlando. Nambe - year one. Berkeley, Ca: Tonatiuh International, 1976. English.

AN: Illustrations by Dennis Martinez.

3032 Rosas, Carlos. 3er paisaje [drawing]. CARACOL, Vol. 3, no. 1 (September 1976), p. Ft cover. Spanish.

3033 Rosas, Carlos. Miseria [drawing]. CARACOL, Vol. 5, no. 1 (September 1978), p. BACK COVER. English.

3034 Salinas, Paula. Easter egg breaktime [drawing]. TEJIDOS, Vol. 4, no. 3 (Fall 1977), p. 21. English.

3035 Sanchez, James. Fighters [drawing]. TEJIDOS, Vol. 4, no. 3 (Fall 1977), p. 36. English.

3036 Sanchez, Ricardo. Hechizo/spells. Los Angeles, CA: Chicano Studies Publications, UCLA, 1976. English.

AN: Willie Herron, drawings and paintings on pp. 68, 70, 75, 89, 93, 97, 99, 123, 129, 135, 137, 151, 165, 167, 170, 181, 195, 229, 231, 235, 236, 238, 256, 258, 261, 268, 279, 284, 288, 312 and inside front and back covers.

3037 Sanchez, Rita. [Untitled drawing]. MAIZE, Vol. 1, no. 4 (Summer 1978), p. 32-33. English.

3038 Santos, Mauricio. [Untitled drawing]. TIN TAN, Vol. 2, no. 5 (June 1, 1977), p. 32.

3039 Saunders, Jaime. Hauling a load [drawing]. TEJIDOS, Vol. 4, no. 3 (Fall 1977), p. 22. English.

3040 Seattle Art Museum, Seattle, WA and Dickson, Joanne. Manuel Neri, sculpture and drawings. Exhibition catalog, 1981. English.

AN: Beautifully illustrated catalog. Text by Joanne Dickson from Oakland California, biography and very complete chronology of Neri exhibitions.

3041 Sierra, John. Aztec Angel [drawing]. In: Salinas, Luis Omar. CRAZY GYPSY. Fresno, CA: Origenes Publications, c1970, p. [16]..

3042 Sierra, John. Quixotic expectation [drawing]. In: Salinas, Luis Omar. CRAZY GYPSY. Fresno, CA: Origenes Publications, c1970, p. [29]..

3043 Sierra, John. Stardust vigil [drawing]. In: Salinas, Luis Omar. CRAZY GYPSY. Fresno, CA: Origenes Publications, c1970, p. [73]..

3044 Sierra, John. [Untitled drawing]. In: Salinas, Luis Omar. CRAZY GYPSY. Fresno, CA: Origenes Publications, c1970, p. [14]..

3045 [Soldadera (drawing)]. REGENERACION, Vol. 2, no. 3 (1973), p. 3.

3046 Stamper, Frances. Fluid washes of ink and acrylic. TEXAS HOMES MAGAZINE, Vol. 4, no. 1 (January, February, 1980), p. 104-112. English.

AN: Well illustrated article with color reproductions of the work of Philip Renteria. Provides biographical information and focuses on the consumate craftsmanship of his drawings and paintings.

3047 Taller de Arte, San Antonio, TX. Felipe Varelas Reyes. Exhibition announcement, n.d. English.

AN: Artist statement and reproduction of one drawing in an announcement for a one man show at the Taller.

3048 Terronez, Irene R. [Untitled drawing]. MAIZE, Vol. 2, no. 4 (Summer 1979), p. 34. English.

3049 Tijerina, Jose A. [Untitled drawings]. CARACOL, Vol. 2, no. 12 (August 1976), p. 12.

3050 Time to greez: incantations from the Third World. San Francisco, CA: Glide Publications/Third World Communications, 1975. English.

AN: Rupert Garcia, drawing, p. 158; Xavier Viramontes, silkscreen, p. 181; Juan Fuentes, drawing, p. 188; Graciela Carrillo, drawing, p. 196.

3051 Tizoc. Arte. MAIZE, Vol. 1, no. 1 (Fall 1977), p. 45.

Drawings (cont.)

3052 Tizoc. Breaking the needle [drawing]. MAIZE, Vol. 1, no. 2 (Winter 1978), p. 37. English.

3053 Tizoc. [Levantate campesino! (drawing)]. MAIZE, Vol. 1, no. 1 (Fall 1977), p. 48. English.

3054 Torres, Salvador Roberto. Chicharra. EL GRITO, Vol. 1, no. 2 (Winter 1968), p. 21. Spanish.

3055 Torres, Salvador Roberto. Arte de la Raza [portfolio]. DE COLORES, Vol. 1, no. 1 (Winter 1973), p. 34-43. Bilingual.

AN: A portfolio consisting of four drawings representing the "progression" of the symbol of the banner adopted by the United Farm Workers (UFW). Included are four out of six drawings, each with its own explication in English and Spanish, and brief biographical data about the artist.

3056 Torres, Salvador Roberto. El bato de San Anto [drawing]. EL GRITO, Vol. 1, no. 2 (Winter 1968), p. 18. Spanish.

3057 Torres, Salvador Roberto. Cachetes de TJ [drawing]. EL GRITO, Vol. 1, no. 2 (Winter 1968), p. 17. Spanish.

3058 Torres, Salvador Roberto. Chapo con TB [drawing]. EL GRITO, Vol. 1, no. 2 (Winter 1968), p. 28. Bilingual.

3059 Torres, Salvador Roberto. Chon [drawing]. EL GRITO, Vol. 1, no. 2 (Winter 1968), p. 16. Spanish.

3060 Torres, Salvador Roberto. Coraje [drawing]. DE COLORES, Vol. 1, no. 1 (Winter 1973), p. 42.

3061 Torres, Salvador Roberto. Creative aspects of la Raza inspired by Chicano experiences. Unpublished thesis, 1973. Bilingual.

AN: Project presents six paintings and six drawings by San Diego artist Torres based on the feeling and impact of United Farm Workers Huelga banner, used on a personal level. Torres wants to make an "imaginary theatre" of the ideas drawn from the Chicano movement. Bilingual. Illustrated.

3062 Torres, Salvador Roberto. La del Piquito [drawing]. EL GRITO, Vol. 1, no. 2 (Winter 1968), p. 20. Spanish.

3063 Torres, Salvador Roberto. Oso State [drawing]. DE COLORES, Vol. 1, no. 1 (Winter 1973), p. 40.

3064 Torres, Salvador Roberto. El pedorro [drawing]. EL GRITO, Vol. 1, no. 2 (Winter 1968), p. 19. Spanish.

3065 Torres, Salvador Roberto. Portfolio I [drawings]. EL GRITO, Vol. 1, no. 2 (Winter 1968), p. 15-21. Bilingual.

3066 Torres, Salvador Roberto. Portfolio II: day dreams from a hospital bed [drawings]. EL GRITO, Vol. 1, no. 2 (Winter 1968), p. 33-48. English.

3067 Torres, Salvador Roberto. Teatro Mono meets Teatro Mascarones [drawing]. DE COLORES, Vol. 1, no. 1 (Winter 1973), p. 36.

3068 Torres, Salvador Roberto. Teatro Mono meets Teatro Mestizo. DE COLORES, Vol. 1, no. 1 (Winter 1973), p. 38.

3069 Torres, Salvador Roberto. [Untitled drawing]. EL GRITO, Vol. 1, no. 2 (Winter 1968), p. 35. Bilingual.

3070 Torres, Salvador Roberto. [Untitled drawing]. EL GRITO, Vol. 1, no. 2 (Winter 1968), p. 37. Bilingual.

3071 Torres, Salvador Roberto. [Untitled drawing]. EL GRITO, Vol. 1, no. 2 (Winter 1968), p. 39. Bilingual.

3072 Torres, Salvador Roberto. [Untitled drawing]. EL GRITO, Vol. 1, no. 2 (Winter 1968), p. 41. Bilingual.

3073 Torres, Salvador Roberto. [Untitled drawing]. EL GRITO, Vol. 1, no. 2 (Winter 1968), p. 43. Bilingual.

3074 Torres, Salvador Roberto. [Untitled drawing]. EL GRITO, Vol. 1, no. 2 (Winter 1968), p. 45. Bilingual.

3075 Torres, Salvador Roberto. [Untitled drawing]. EL GRITO, Vol. 1, no. 2 (Winter 1968), p. 47. Bilingual.

3076 Trevino, Jose. La canicula=Equinox [drawing]. TEJIDOS, Vol. 4, no. 2 (Summer 1977), p. 28. Bilingual.

3077 Trevino, Jose. Celebracion de los muertos [drawing]. TEJIDOS, Vol. 4, no. 2 (Summer 1977), p. 26. Bilingual.

3078 Trevino, Jose. La cruda=The hangover [drawing]. CARACOL, Vol. 5, no. 6 (February 1979), p. 5. Bilingual.

3079 Trevino, Jose. Devocion al sol [drawing]. TEJIDOS, Vol. 4, no. 2 (Summer 1977), p. 25. Bilingual.

3080 Trevino, Jose. [Drawings]. REVISTA RIO BRAVO, (Fall 1980), p. 6-7.

AN: Drawings by Austin artist Jose Trevino. Includes samples from his SKETCH FROM MESQUITIERRA series.

3081 Trevino, Jose. Los enamorados - dia de St. Valentino [drawing]. TEJIDOS, Vol. 4, no. 2 (Summer 1977), p. 27. Bilingual.

3082 Trevino, Jose. [Indio caminando (drawing)]. CARACOL, Vol. 4, no. 8 (April 1978), p. FRNT COVER. Spanish.

3083 Trevino, Jose. Sketch from MESQUITIERRA. REVISTA RIO BRAVO, no. 1 (Fall 1980), p. 7.

3084 Trevino, Jose. Sketch from MESQUITIERRA. REVISTA RIO BRAVO, no. 1 (Fall 1980), p. 6.

3085 Trevino, Jose. [Untitled drawing]. TEJIDOS, Vol. 5, no. 2-4 (1978), p. 105. Bilingual.

3086 Ulloa, Domingo. [Untitled drawing]. MAIZE, Vol. 1, no. 1 (Fall 1977), p. 40. English.

Drawings (cont.)

3087 University of Texas. El Paso. Chicano
     Studies Program. "Chicanotations": paintings
     and drawings by Manuel Unzueta. Exhibition
     brochure, 1979. English.

     AN: Exhibition handout includes
     biographical data and a listing of the 20
     works exhibited by Unzueta.

3088 [Untitled drawing]. REVISTA CHICANO-RIQUENA,
     Vol. 4, no. 3 (Summer 1976), p. 36.

3089 [Untitled drawing]. CARACOL, Vol. 5, no. 1
     (September 1978), p. 22. Bilingual.

3090 [Untitled drawing]. ATISBOS, no. 2 (Winter
     1976, 1977), p. 15.

3091 [Untitled drawing]. ATISBOS, no. 2 (Winter
     1976, 1977), p. 27.

3092 [Untitled drawing]. ATISBOS, no. 2 (Winter
     1976, 1977), p. 35.

3093 [Untitled drawing]. ATISBOS, no. 2 (Winter
     1976, 1977), p. 61.

3094 [Untitled drawing]. ATISBOS, no. 2 (Winter
     1976, 1977), p. 71.

3095 [Untitled drawing]. ATISBOS, Vol. 2,
     (Winter 1976, 1977), p. 97.

3096 [Untitled drawing]. ATISBOS, no. 2 (Winter
     1976, 1977), p. 107.

3097 [Untitled drawing]. CARACOL, Vol. 3, no. 8
     (April 1977), p. 6.

3098 Unzueta, Manuel. [Angel baby (drawing)].
     XALMAN, Vol. 1, no. 3 (July 1975), p. [3].

3099 Unzueta, Manuel. [Chicana! (drawing)].
     CHISMEARTE, Vol. 1, no. 1 (Fall   1976), p.
     45. English.

3100 Unzueta, Manuel. La chiclera [drawing].
     MAIZE, Vol. 1, no. 3 (Spring 1978), p. 37.
     English.

3101 Unzueta, Manuel. City rat [drawing]. XALMAN,
     Vol. 1, no. 4 (Spring 1977), p. 45.

3102 Unzueta, Manuel. Con la gente [drawing].
     XALMAN, Vol. 1, no. 4 (Spring 1977), p. 20.

3103 Unzueta, Manuel. Field's butterfly
     [drawing]. XALMAN, Vol. 1, no. 4 (Spring
     1977), p. 51.

3104 Unzueta, Manuel. Mayan ode [drawing].
     XALMAN, Vol. 2, no. 1 (Spring 1978), p. 10.

3105 Unzueta, Manuel. Music, my only company
     [drawing]. XALMAN, Vol. 2, no. 1 (Spring
     1978), p. 56.

3106 Unzueta, Manuel. Nicaragua's eyes [drawing].
     XALMAN, Vol. 2, no. 1 (Spring 1978), p. 16.

3107 Unzueta, Manuel. Perfect song [drawing].
     XALMAN, Vol. 2, no. 2 (Spring 1979), p. 18.

3108 Unzueta, Manuel. [Raza in pain...(drawing)].
     XALMAN, Vol. 1, no. 4 (Spring 1977), p. 1.

3109 Unzueta, Manuel. Siempre [drawing]. XALMAN,
     Vol. 2, no. 1 (Spring 1978), p. 50.

3110 Unzueta, Manuel. [Untitled drawing]. XALMAN,
     Vol. 1, no. 3 (July 1975), p. 13.

3111 Unzueta, Manuel. [Untitled drawing]. XALMAN,
     Vol. 1, no. 3 (July 1975), p. 21.

3112 Unzueta, Manuel. [Untitled drawing]. XALMAN,
     Vol. 1, no. 3 (July 1975), p. 26.

3113 Unzueta, Manuel. [Untitled drawing]. XALMAN,
     Vol. 1, no. 3 (July 1975), p. 32.

3114 Unzueta, Manuel. [Untitled drawing]. XALMAN,
     Vol. 1, no. 3 (July 1975), p. 37.

3115 Unzueta, Manuel. [Untitled drawing]. XALMAN,
     Vol. 1, no. 4 (Spring 1977), p. A.

3116 Unzueta, Manuel. [Untitled drawing]. XALMAN,
     Vol. 1, no. 1 (July 1975), p. Cover.

3117 Unzueta, Manuel. [Untitled drawing]. XALMAN,
     Vol. 1, no. 5 (Fall   1977), p. 57.

3118 Unzueta, Manuel. Worlds of make believe...
     [drawings]. XALMAN, Vol. 2, no. 2 (Spring
     1979), p. 20.

3119 Uriegas, Johnny. [Untitled drawing].
     CARACOL, Vol. 4, no. 3 (November 1977), p.
     17. Bilingual.

3120 Urrea, Luis. Maiz [drawing]. MAIZE, Vol. 4,
     no. 3-4 (Spring, Summer, 1981), p. 69.
     Bilingual.

3121 Urrea, Luis. [Untitled drawing]. MAIZE, Vol.
     4, no. 3-4 (Spring, Summer, 1981), p. Bk
     cover. Bilingual.

3122 Urrea, Luis. [Untitled drawing]. MAIZE, Vol.
     4, no. 3-4 (Spring, Summer, 1981), p. 84.
     English.

3123 Valadez, John. La hermosura de nuestra raza
     [drawing]. SOMOS, Vol. 1, no. 1 (April, May,
     1978), p. 24-25. English.

3124 Valadez, John. Unidad [drawing]. CHISMEARTE,
     Vol. 1, no. 4 (Fall , Winter, 1977, 1978),
     p. Ft cover.

3125 Valadez, John. [Untitled drawing].
     CHISMEARTE, Vol. 2, no. 1 (Summer 1978), p.
     5. English.

3126 Valdes, Rosalia Hayakawa. [Untitled
     drawing]. MAIZE, Vol. 2, no. 2 (Winter
     1979), p. 49. English.

3127 Valdes, Rosalia Hayakawa. [Untitled
     drawing]. MAIZE, Vol. 2, no. 2 (Winter
     1979), p. 50. English.

3128 Valdez, Patssi and Gamboa, Diane. [Chicanas
     (drawing)]. REGENERACION, Vol. 2, no. 3
     (1973), p. Cover.

3129 Valdez, Patssi. [Faces (drawing)].
     REGENERACION, Vol. 2, no. 3 (1973), p. 8.

3130 Valdez, Patssi. [Pen and ink drawing of two
     faces]. REGENERACION, Vol. 2, no. 2 (1972),
     p. 8.

3131 Valdez, Patssi. [Untitled drawing].
     REGENERACION, Vol. 2, no. 1 (1971), p. 2.

3132 Valdez, Patssi. [Untitled drawing].
     REGENERACION, Vol. 2, no. 2 (1972), p. 1.

3133 Valdez, Patssi. [Untitled drawing].
     REGENERACION, Vol. 2, no. 3 (1973), p. 29.

3134 Valdez, Patssi. [Untitled drawing].
     REGENERACION, Vol. 2, no. 4 (1975), p. 31.

Drawings (cont.)

3135 Valdez, Sylvia. The make believe animal book [drawing]. CARACOL, Vol. 3, no. 8 (April 1977), p. 17. English.

3136 Vallecillo, Ricardo. [Untitled drawing]. RAYAS, Vol. 1, no. 6 (November, December, 1978), p. Ft cover. English.

3137 Vallejo, Armando. Luna llena: ocho anos de poesia chicana, 1971-1979. Santa Barbara, CA: Ediciones Aztlan, 1979. English.

   AN: Cover and illustrations Manuel Unzueta of Santa Barbara, Calif.

3138 Vallejo, Armando. Y aqui estamos de nuevo... [drawing]. XALMAN, Vol. 1, no. 4 (Spring 1977), p. 39.

3139 Vallejo, Linda. Beneath the skin [drawing]. CHISMEARTE, Vol. 1, no. 4 (Fall , Winter, 1977, 1978), p. 27.

3140 Vallejo, Linda. Self-portrait [drawing]. CHISMEARTE, Vol. 1, no. 4 (Fall , Winter, 1977, 1978), p. 30.

3141 Vallejo, Linda. [Untitled drawing]. CHISMEARTE, Vol. 1, no. 4 (Fall , Winter, 1977, 1978), p. [28-29].

3142 Vasquez y Sanchez, Ramon. La Adelita. CARACOL, Vol. 1, no. 9 (May 1975), p. 1.

3143 Vasquez y Sanchez, Ramon. Campesina [drawing]. CARACOL, Vol. 2, no. 6 (February 1976), p. 1.

3144 Vasquez y Sanchez, Ramon. Documentacion del ejercito mexicano en la campana del Alamo [drawings]. CARACOL, Vol. 1, no. 9 (May 1975), p. 12-13.

3145 Vasquez y Sanchez, Ramon. El nino y los cosmos [drawing]. CARACOL, Vol. 4, no. 12 (August 1978), p. FRNT COVER. Spanish.

3146 Vasquez y Sanchez, Ramon. El poeta [drawing]. CARACOL, Vol. 1, no. 8 (April 1975), p. 18.

3147 Vega, Salvador. Crooked flag [drawing]. REVISTA CHICANO-RIQUENA, Vol. 5, no. 3 (Summer 1977), p. 2. English.

3148 Vega, Salvador. Man and machine [drawing]. REVISTA CHICANO-RIQUENA, Vol. 5, no. 3 (Summer 1977), p. 25. English.

3149 Vega, Salvador. [Untitled drawing]. REVISTA CHICANO-RIQUENA, Vol. 5, no. 3 (Summer 1977), p. COVER. Spanish.

3150 Vega, Salvador. [Untitled drawing]. REVISTA CHICANO-RIQUENA, Vol. 8, no. 1 (Winter 1980), p. 34. English.

3151 Vergara, Dora Maria. New artist del barrio Canta Ranas. REVISTA RIO BRAVO, Vol. 1, no. 1 (Winter 1981), p. 2. English.

   AN: Biography of self-taught artist Pedro Martinez who lives in and records the life and people of the westide barrio "Cantaranas" in Laredo, Texas. Five drawings reproduced in this issue.

3152 Villa, Esteban. Chicanito science [drawing]. EL GRITO DEL SOL, Vol. 3, no. 1 (Winter 1978), p. 66. English.

3153 Villa, Esteban. Elitism/creativa c/s

[drawing]. EL GRITO DEL SOL, Vol. 3, no. 1 (Winter 1978), p. 7. English.

3154 Villa, Esteban. The hallway [drawing]. EL GRITO, Vol. 2, no. 3 (Spring 1969), p. [16]. English.

3155 Villa, Esteban. Un hombre [drawing]. EL GRITO, Vol. 2, no. 3 (Spring 1969), p. [22]. English.

3156 Villa, Esteban. Indigena [drawing]. EL GRITO, Vol. 2, no. 3 (Spring 1969), p. [18]. English.

3157 Villa, Esteban. Mas caras mascaras [drawing]. EL GRITO DEL SOL, Vol. 3, no. 1 (Winter 1978), p. 105. Spanish.

3158 Villa, Esteban. Nino [drawing]. EL GRITO, Vol. 2, no. 3 (Spring 1969), p. [20]. English.

3159 Villa, Esteban. Patroncito [drawing]. EL GRITO, Vol. 2, no. 3 (Spring 1969), p. [19]. English.

3160 Villa, Esteban. Portfolio 2: Profile; The Hallway; Durmiente; Portrait of Manuel; Indigena; Patroncito; Nino; The Bride; Un hombre. EL GRITO, Vol. 2, no. 3 (Spring 1969), p. 15-24. Bilingual.

3161 Villa, Esteban. Portrait of Manuel [drawing]. EL GRITO, Vol. 2, no. 3 (Spring 1969), p. [17]. English.

3162 Villa, Esteban. Profile [drawing]. EL GRITO, Vol. 2, no. 3 (Spring 1969), p. [15]. English.

3163 Villa, Esteban. La solution [drawing]. EL GRITO DEL SOL, Vol. 3, no. 1 (Winter 1978), p. 18. Spanish.

3164 Villa, Esteban. [Untitled drawing]. EL GRITO, Vol. 1, no. 3 (Spring 1968), p. 23. Bilingual.

3165 Villa, Esteban. [Untitled drawing]. EL GRITO, Vol. 1, no. 3 (Spring 1968), p. 24. Bilingual.

3166 Villa, Esteban. [Untitled drawing]. EL GRITO, Vol. 1, no. 3 (Spring 1968), p. 25. Bilingual.

3167 Villa, Esteban. [Untitled drawing]. EL GRITO, Vol. 1, no. 3 (Spring 1968), p. 26. Bilingual.

3168 Villa, Esteban. [Untitled drawing]. EL GRITO, Vol. 1, no. 3 (Spring 1968), p. 27. Bilingual.

3169 Villa, Esteban. [Untitled drawing]. EL GRITO, Vol. 1, no. 3 (Spring 1968), p. 28-29. Bilingual.

3170 Villa, Esteban. [Untitled drawing]. EL GRITO, Vol. 1, no. 3 (Spring 1968), p. 30. Bilingual.

3171 Villa, Esteban. [Untitled drawing]. EL POCHO CHE, Vol. 1, no. 2 (1970), p. 59.

3172 Villa, Esteban. [Untitled drawing]. EL POCHO CHE, Vol. 1, no. 2 (1970), p. 68.

3173 Villa, Esteban. [Untitled drawing]. EL POCHO CHE, Vol. 1, no. 2 (1970), p. Bk Cover.

Drawings (cont.)

3174 Villa, Esteban. Viet Nam! [drawings]. EL GRITO, Vol. 1, no. 3 (Spring 1968), p. 22-30. English.

3175 Washington State University, Pullman. Fine Arts Center Gallery II. Ruben M. Trejo-mi ultimo fracaso. Exhibition announcement, 1976. English.

AN: Exhibit announcement for Trejo's show of sculpture and drawings. Illustrated with a Trejo "jalapeno" sculpture.

3176 Yanez, Rene. [Free Los 7 (drawing)]. EL POCHO CHE, Vol. 1, no. 2 (1970), p. 14.

3177 Yanez, Rene. Portfolio 4: 1; 2; 3; 4; 5; 6; 7; 8; 9; 10. EL GRITO, Vol. 2, no. 3 (Spring 1969), p. 39-47. English.

3178 Yanez, Rene. Portfolio [mixed media]. EL GRITO, Vol. 1, no. 4 (Summer 1968), p. 21-28. English.

3179 Yanez, Rene. [Untitled drawing]. EL POCHO CHE, Vol. 1, no. 2 (1970), p. 19.

3180 Yanez, Rene. [Untitled drawing]. EL POCHO CHE, Vol. 1, no. 2 (1970), p. 50.

3181 Yanez, Rene. [Untitled drawing]. EL POCHO CHE, Vol. 1, no. 2 (1970), p. 55.

3182 Yanez, Rene. [Untitled painting]. EL GRITO, Vol. 1, no. 4 (Summer 1968), p. 28. Bilingual.

3183 Zapata, Eloy. [Untitled drawing]. CARACOL, Vol. 1, no. 9 (May 1975), p. 18.

3184 Zufelt, Wilma. Untitled [drawing]. LA PALABRA, Vol. 2, no. 2 (Fall 1980), p. 77.

3185 Zufelt, Wilma. Untitled [drawing]. LA PALABRA, Vol. 2, no. 2 (Fall 1980), p. 78.

3186 Zufelt, Wilma. Untitled [drawing]. LA PALABRA, Vol. 2, no. 2 (Fall 1980), p. 78.

3187 Zuniga, Ramiro. Losing hold [drawing]. XALMAN, Vol. 1, no. 5 (Fall 1977), p. 69.

3188 Zuniga, Ramiro. [Untitled drawing]. XALMAN, Vol. 1, no. 5 (Fall 1977), p. 19.

3189 Zuniga, Ramiro. [Untitled drawing]. XALMAN, Vol. 1, no. 5 (Fall 1977), p. 62.

Drug Abuse

3190 Baca, Walter R. Vicios [mural]. DE COLORES, Vol. 1, no. 2 (Spring 1974), p. 62. Spanish.

Duardo, Richard

3191 Exploratorium, Student Union, California State University, Los Angeles. An exhibit of published prints of Aztlan Multiples. Exhibition catalog, 1981. English.

AN: The published silkscreen prints of Aztlan Multiples, a small business run by Richard Duardo of Los Angeles, features works by Duardo, John Valadez, and Carlos Almaraz, among others. Illustrations.

3192 Galeria de la Raza/Studio 24, San Francisco, CA. Published prints of Hecho en Aztlan Multiples. Exhibition announcement, 1980. English.

AN: Announcement of exhibit of the published silkscreen prints of Hecho en Aztlan Multiples; a small business run by Richard Duardo of Los Angeles.

3193 Kim, Howard. Chicano art: is it an art form? Or simply art by Chicanos. NEWORLD, Vol. 6, no. 4 (1980), p. 26-30. English.

AN: An attempt to define Chicano art through interviews with Carlos Almaraz, John Valadez, (Los Four), Robert Delgado, Sister Karen Boccalero (Self-Help Graphics), Harry Gamboa, Jr. (ASCO), Ricardo Duardo, Ignacio Gomez, and others. Well illustrated.

3194 Sol Art Gallery, San Diego, CA. Group showing of Southern California artists. Exhibition brochure, 1980. English.

AN: First exhibit of new Chicano art gallery showing Los Angeles artists Carlos Almaraz, Judithe Hernandez, John Valadez, Linda Vallejo, Ricardo Duardo, Barbara Carrasco.

3195 SPARC (Social and Public Arts Resource Center), Venice, CA and Los Angeles. Ceta VI, Venice, CA. Hecho en Aztlan multiples: screen printed works. Exhibition invitation, 1980. English.

AN: Invitation to an exhibit of silkscreen prints by Hecho en Aztlan Multiples, a small business run by Richard Duardo. At the Social and Public Art Resource Center, Venice, Calif.

Duarte, J.

3196 Hartnell College Studio Gallery, Salinas, CA. Paintings, drawings, prints by San Francisco Bay Area Chicano artists. Exhibit brochure, 1971. English.

AN: Brochure for exhibit featuring Francisco Camplis, Graciela Carrillo, Sal Castaneda, Priscilla Dominguez, J. Duarte, Rupert Garcia, Carlos Loarca, Irene Perez, Vincent Rascon, Michael Rios, Peter Rodriguez, Luis Valsoto, Esteban Villa, Rene Yanez, Zala. Illustrated by Rupert Carcia print.

Duarte, Roy

3197 Valadez, Kathy L. Chicano murals tell of Mexican heritage. EL CHICANO, Vol. 7, no. 34 (January 25, 1973), p. 10-11. English.

AN: Focus on Roy Duarte's murals in the Casa Blanca area of Riverside, California.

Duppa Villa Housing Project, Phoenix, AZ

3198 McClellan, Bill. Army of volunteers paints a little history in Phoenix. PHOENIX GAZETTE, (April 20, 1977). English.

AN: Adolfo "El Zarco" Guerrero with 100 residents from the Duppa Villa Housing Project completes a mural funded by the Arizona Commission on Arts and Humanities. Guerrero completed six murals, but prefers sculpture.

Duran, Bernardo

3199 Chicano muralists maintain traditions. LA
     CUCARACHA, (November 20, 1979), p. 7.
     English.

     AN: Introduction to Chicano muralism in
     Pueblo and comparison to the Mexican mural
     movement from which it draws inspiration. 20
     murals painted from 1977 to 1979. The
     muralists include Bernardo Duran, Juan
     Espinoza, Miguel "Freeloader" Garcia, Lola
     Gutierrez, Leo Lucero, Juan Pacheco, Dolores
     Pena, Pedro Romero, Stan Salazar, David
     Sandoval. Diego Rivera murals illustrated.

Duran, Daniel

3200 Venegas, Sybil. Dia de los muertos. SOMOS,
     Vol. 1, no. 5 (October 1978), p. 42-47.
     English.

     AN: Brief history of Dia de los muertos
     ceremonies. While the custom is dying in
     Mexico (except for tourists), Chicano
     organizations like Galeria de la Raza
     (S.F.), El Centro de Artistas Chicanos
     (Sacramento, Ca.) celebrate the event
     annually, as does [Self-Help Graphics and
     Art, Inc.] in East Los Angeles. Well
     illustrated with photographs by Guillermo
     Bejarano and Daniel Duran.

Duran, Gonzalo

3201 Davis, Alonzo, ed. Los Angeles street
     graphics. Los Angeles, CA: Brockman Gallery
     Productions, [ca. 1975]. English.

     AN: Portfolio of art in public places.
     Includes Charles Felix (murals), Leo Limon
     (mural), Charles Almaraz (billboard mural),
     Johnny Alvarez (mural), Mexican artist
     Gonzalo Duran, and graffiti.

East Los Angeles, CA

3202 Bright, John; Bright, Mura; and Castellanos,
     Leonard. L.A. Chicano street art. Venice,
     CA: Environmental Communications, 1974.
     English.

     AN: Annotated slide catalog of Chicano
     murals in East Los Angeles compiled by staff
     of Mechicano Art Center. Also includes
     article reprints on painted bus benches by
     Mechicano artists (SUNSET Magazine, n.d.),
     murals of East Los Angeles (LOS ANGELES
     TIMES, 12/3/73, and SUNSET Magazine, April
     1973). Well illustrated.

3203 Chicano art: East Los Angeles graffiti. LA
     GENTE DE AZTLAN, Vol. 6, no. 5 (May 1976),
     p. 5. English.

     AN: The particular forms and styles of
     Chicano graffiti are affirmed as stemming
     from the social conditions of the barrio
     circa 1930. Gangs and their social world are
     examined as contributors to the creation of
     graffiti, tattoos and "calo," a dialect of
     Chicano Spanish.

3204 Cox, Vic. Beauty in the barrio. WESTWAYS,
     Vol. 67, no. 2 (February 1975), p. 50-53.
     English.

     AN: "Tooner Flats" is another name for
     the barrio of East Los Angeles. These
     streets are the home and inspiration to
     Frank Hernandez who illustrates the article
     with pen and ink sketches of buildings.

3205 Del Olmo, Frank. Chicano gang turns to art.

LOS ANGELES TIMES, (September 11, 1973), p.
II, 3. English.

     AN: Residents of the East Los Angeles
     barrio "Lil' Valley" dedicate a mural
     memorializing Chicano gang members who have
     died violently. The mural was painted by 40
     gang members guided by professional artist
     Bill Butler.

3206 Del Olmo, Frank. Murals changing face of
     East L.A. LOS ANGELES TIMES, (December 3,
     1973), p. II, 1+. English.

     AN: First Los Angeles Times report on
     burgeoning Los Angeles mural movement with a
     map of 15 mural sites. Mentioned are C.W.
     Felix (originator of Estrada Courts
     project), Willie Herron, David Botello,
     Armando Campero, Edward Carbajal. (Chicano
     Art Committee).

3207 Edy. A true barrio art. EL CHICANO,
     (December 7, 1972), p. 9. English.

     AN: Interview with East Los Angeles
     artists Harry Gamboa, Robert Gronk and
     Willie Herron (also included in the
     conversation are Patsy Valdez and Eddie
     Ytuarte). Suffering, fatalism, existential
     reality and the awareness of cultural
     colonialism are cited as sources of
     inspiration for urban barrio art.
     Illustrated with a photograph of Willie
     Herron's Quetzalcoatl mural in City Terrace
     barrio and two drawings by Robert Gronk and
     Harry Gamboa.

3208 Fiesta de los barrios observes Cinco de
     Mayo. EASTSIDE SUN, (May 1, 1969). English.

     AN: The Fiesta de los Barrios is a
     cultural festival organized by the committee
     pressuring the Los Angeles Board of
     Education for better and more relevant
     education after the East Los Angeles high
     school "blowouts." The Fiesta features art,
     music, dance and literature.

3209 Finalists in $540 E.L.A. art contest provide
     dazzling show at local hospital. EASTSIDE
     SUN, (November 21, 1968). English.

     AN: First East Los Angeles art festival.
     Juried by artists Donald Manion, John Bene,
     Rubin Holguin. Show hung at Doctors'
     Hospital by Garfield High School art teacher
     David Ramirez.

3210 The Goez map guide to the murals of East Los
     Angeles. Los Angeles, CA: Goez, 1975.
     English.

     AN: Street map indicating location of
     murals in the vicinity of East Los Angeles,
     CA.

3211 Gonzalez, Ellen. U.S. art project: Chicanas
     painting 'future history'. LOS ANGELES
     TIMES, (March 16, 1978), p. II, 4. English.

     AN: Women muralists from the murals
     workshop of the Chicana Service Action
     Center working on murals at City Terrace and
     Humphrey Avenue elementary schools in East
     Los Angeles. Illustrated.

East Los Angeles, CA (cont.)

3212 Graffiti gone: murals in full bloom. PHOENIX GAZETTE, (April 13, 1974). English.

AN: Mural explosion at Estrada Courts Housing Project in Los Angeles led by C.W. Felix. Estimates 60 murals in East Los Angeles. Illustrated.

3213 Hebert, Ray. $10 million Latin cultural center: Lincoln Park to get new life. LOS ANGELES TIMES, (March 19, 1972), p. B-7. English.

AN: Report on the start of East Los Angeles cultural center Plaza de la Raza, intended as a showcase for Model Cities agency funding.

3214 Kahn, David. Chicano street murals: people's art in the East Los Angeles barrio. AZTLAN, Vol. 6, no. 1 (Spring 1975), p. 117-121. Bibliography. English.

AN: A study of Chicano mural painting starting with the 1970 mural at UCLA by Eduardo Carrillo, Ramses Noriega, Sergio Hernandez, and Saul Solache. Deals with mural symbols, graffiti, and works by John Alverer [sic] and Willie Herron's murals in the Ramona Gardens Housing Project.

3215 Knight, Christopher. Urban eye sites up against the wall. HERALD EXAMINER, (May 31, 1981). English.

AN: Review of the exhibit MURALS OF AZTLAN: THE STREET PAINTERS OF EAST LOS at the Craft and Folk Art Museum of Los Angeles. Illustration.

3216 Knilli, Monika and Knilli, Friedrich. Linke allegorien & lebende bilder der ghettos: das Americanische mural-movement. TENDENZEN, (November, December, 1977), p. 27-32. Other.

AN: Illustrated story on U.S. murals including those of East Los Angeles and Chicano Park, San Diego. The November-December issue of 1977 is numbered 116.

3217 Kushner, Sam. It was a meat market in East L.A. LOS ANGELES FREE PRESS, Vol. 11, no. 34 (August 23, 1974), p. 17. English.

AN: Data on the formation of Goez Gallery by John Gonzalez and David Botello in 1970. Created in what once was a meat market in the East Los Angeles barrio, Goez became an important showcase for Chicano art.

3218 Marquez, Rosa Maria. Artistas chicanas together at C.S.A.C., an interview by Rosa Maria Marquez. CHISMEARTE, Vol. 1, no. 4 (Fall , Winter, 1977), p. 39. English.

AN: An interview with several women doing murals as part of the East Los Angeles Senior Citizens Housing and Mural Beautification Program under the sponsorship of the Chicana Service Action Center. Funding for the project through CETA (Comprehensive Employment Training Act).

3219 Muchnic, Suzanne. Passion, paint splatter folk art museum show. LOS ANGELES TIMES, (June 25, 1981), p. VI, 1. English.

AN: Review of the MURALS OF AZTLAN: STREET PAINTERS OF EAST LOS exhibit at the Craft and Folk Art Museum in Los Angeles.

The critic considered the show "revved-up, highly emotional art descended from Mexico's political muralists" that made up what it lacked in subtlety with passion, and one of the most visually exciting shows of the Museum. Illustrations.

3220 The mural message. TIME, Vol. 105, no. 14 (April 7, 1975), p. 79. English.

AN: Brief illustrated story of murals painted in East Los Angeles during the 1970s. Spotlights activities of Goez Gallery.

3221 A new gallery of art on city streets. U.S. NEWS & WORLD REPORT, Vol. 50, no. 18 (May 8, 1978), p. 86-87. English.

AN: Brief illustrated story on street murals across the U.S. including Chicano murals in East Los Angeles and Santa Ana College, Calif.

3222 Plaza de la Raza: place of the people. Brochure, n.d. English.

AN: Glossy promotional brochure for Plaza de la Raza, a cultural center in East Los Angeles. Brief history of the Plaza and photographs of its activities with children.

3223 Public invited to weekend fiesta at Lincoln High. LOS ANGELES TIMES, (April 29, 1969), p. II. English.

AN: Fiesta of art, music, dance and literature organized by the committee formed after the East Los Angeles high school "blowouts" to press for better and more relevant education. Hundreds of works of art were collected for display at the "Fiesta de los Barrios".

3224 Rivera, Humberto R. and Howell, Heather R. The murals of East Los Angeles. Film. English.

AN: Puerto Rican filmmaker Rivera deals with Chicano murals and their makers. Views of the murals and interviews with the artists make up the bulk of the film. Unfortunately Rivera focuses the camera on the artists and the streets and seldom gives the viewer a detailed look at the mural under discussion.

3225 Saenz, John. Felix completes art project: artist's murals mask East LA graffitti [sic]. EAST LOS ANGELES TRIBUNE, (November 30, 1972), p. A-4. English.

AN: Charles Felix is doing murals as part of a community beautification "Wall Project" to cover graffiti. His present project is a series of murals intended to make Whittier Blvd. into a street gallery. Illustrated.

3226 Wilson, William. Art of barrios in East L.A. LOS ANGELES TIMES, (July 27, 1970), p. IV,1+. English.

AN: Rather personalized view of ARTE DE LOS BARRIOS traveling exhibit organized by Casa Hispana de Bellas Artes with Artistas Latinos Americanos, San Francisco, and featuring "100 Chicano paintings, photographs, and other works of art".

East Los Angeles, CA (cont.)

3227 Zucker, Martin. Walls of barrio are brought to life by street gang art. SMITHSONIAN, Vol. 9, no. 7 (October 1978), p. 105-111. English.

AN: Illustrated survey of East Los Angeles murals.

East Los Angeles College Library

3228 Xap, Pablo. The wall of art. Q-VO, (August 1981). English.

AN: 1980 competition for East Los Angeles College Library mural awarded to East Los Streetscapers who did the three walls totaling 51x24 feet, THE EDUCATION SUITE - ARTE, CIENCIA Y FILOSOFIA on canvas bonded to wall. Illustrated.

East Los Angeles College

3229 Los Angeles City College. Latinos de tres mundos. Exhibition invitation, 1980. English.

AN: Invitation to an exhibit featuring the work of ASCO members Harry Gamboa, Jr., Gronk, Willie Herron; painters Xavier Mendez and Olivia Sanchez; and photographer Ricardo Valverde.

3230 Los Angeles County Museum of Art, Los Angeles, CA and D'Andrea, Jeanne. Chicanismo en el arte. Exhibit brochure, 1975. English.

AN: An exhibit of Southern California Chicano student artists organized in cooperation with East Los Angeles College. Thirty-one artists displayed 73 works. The show was exhibited at the Vincent Price Gallery of East Los Angeles College prior to moving to the Los Angeles County Museum of Art. 70 illustrations.

3231 Sanchez, Jesus. Auditorium mural "wipe out" during recent renovation move. EAST LOS ANGELES COLLEGE NEWS, (September 26, 1979). English.

AN: "The Path to Knowledge and the False University," a mural by Roberto Chavez on the facade of ELAC's Ingalls Auditorium was painted over on Sept. 11, 1979. Contrasting views on the mural's fate are offered by the Chicano Faculty Association President and the Dean of Educational Services.

3232 Sanchez, Jesus. Resolution passed to support artist's paintings of new mural. EAST LOS ANGELES COLLEGE NEWS, (October 3, 1979). English.

AN: Statements and counter-statements between Arthur Avila, president of East Los Angeles College, Roberto Chavez, artist, and the Chicano Faculty Association about the controversial painting over of a Chavez mural on the exterior of the college auditorium.

3233 Tovar, Carlos. Chicano muralist interviewed. NUESTRA COSA, Vol. 8, no. 1 (November, December, 1979), p. 7. English.

AN: Interview with artist Roberto Chavez concerning the white-washing of a mural he painted on the outside front wall of the campus auditorium at East Los Angeles College.

East Los Angeles Senior Citizens Housing and Mural Beautification Program

3234 Marquez, Rosa Maria. Artistas chicanas together at C.S.A.C., an interview by Rosa Maria Marquez. CHISMEARTE, Vol. 1, no. 4 (Fall , Winter, 1977), p. 39. English.

AN: An interview with several women doing murals as part of the East Los Angeles Senior Citizens Housing and Mural Beautification Program under the sponsorship of the Chicana Service Action Center. Funding for the project through CETA (Comprehensive Employment Training Act).

East Los Streetscapers

3235 Una galeria de artistas = A gallery of artists. CAMINOS, Vol. 1, no. 6 (October 1980), p. 20-26. Bilingual.

AN: Features California artists Domingo O. Ulloa (Imperial Valley images), Gloria Chacon, photographer Maria Pinedo (San Francisco), Willie Herron (Los Angeles), Joaquin Patino (Delano), Pedro Pelayo (Long Beach), sculptor Rudi Sigala (San Diego), Mario Torero (San Diego), sculptor Michael M. Amescua (Los Angeles), and the East Los Streetscapers. Illustrated.

3236 Gamboa, Harry, Jr. Los murales de Aztlan. COMUNIDAD, (June 28, 1981), p. 8-9+. Spanish.

AN: Review of the exhibit at the Craft and Folk Art Museum of Los Angeles of MURALS OF AZTLAN: THE STREET PAINTERS OF EAST LOS in which Carlos Almaraz, Gronk, Judithe Hernandez, Willie Herron, Frank Romero, John Valadez and the East Los Streetscapers (David Botello, Wayne Healy, George Yepes) painted portable murals in the gallery. The murals are described and illustrated.

3237 Xap, Pablo. The wall of art. Q-VO, (August 1981). English.

AN: 1980 competition for East Los Angeles College Library mural awarded to East Los Streetscapers who did the three walls totaling 51x24 feet, THE EDUCATION SUITE - ARTE, CIENCIA Y FILOSOFIA on canvas bonded to wall. Illustrated.

Edificio Quinto Sol, Lansing, MI

3238 Mural en Quinto Sol. SOL DE AZTLAN, Vol. 2, no. 3 (July 1971). English.

AN: Full-page illustrated article describing mural by Jose Mojica at the Edificio Quinto Sol in Lansing. Mural traces the history of La Raza and was painted by the self-taught artist with the assistance of his brother Adolfo.

EDUCATION SUITE--ARTE, CIENCIA Y FILOSOFIA [mural]

3239 Xap, Pablo. The wall of art. Q-VO, (August 1981). English.

AN: 1980 competition for East Los Angeles College Library mural awarded to East Los Streetscapers who did the three walls totaling 51x24 feet, THE EDUCATION SUITE - ARTE, CIENCIA Y FILOSOFIA on canvas bonded to wall. Illustrated.

Educational Materials
    USE: Curriculum Materials

Ehrenberg, Felipe

3240 Lucas, Jerry. Testimonios de Latinoamerica.
CHISMEARTE, no. 6 (February 1980), p. 6-9.
English.

AN: Review of the exhibits TESTIMONIOS
DE LATINOAMERICA and AMERICA EN LA MIRA,
brought to Los Angeles Contemporary
Exhibitions Gallery by Chicano curator
Roberto Gil de Montes, as part of a cultural
exchange between the Mexican Cultural
Workers Front and Felipe Ehrenberg of the
Grupo Proceso Pentagono of Mexico, and
Chicano artists and photographers from the
Council of Latino Photography/USA in Los
Angeles. Well illustrated.

3241 Testimonios de Latinoamerica. LA PRENSA SAN
DIEGO, (October 26, 1979), p. 3. Spanish.

AN: Announcement of an exhibit at the
Centro Cultural de la Raza, San Diego,
"Testimonios de Latino America" and "America
en la mira," political graphics organized by
Mexican artist Felipe Ehrenberg and also
shown at the Los Angeles Contemporary
Exhibitions gallery (LACE).

El Paso, TX

3242 Carlos Pineda shows art in Centennial
Museum. EL PASO TIMES, (November 5, 1972).
English.

AN: Themes from Mexican folk culture
predominate in paintings by Carlos R. Pineda
shown at the El Paso Centennial Museum. He
has exhibited in Panama, Guadalajara,
Phoenix, Tucson, and Dallas and is
represented by the Jinx Gallery in El Paso.

3243 Garcia-Camarillo, Cecilio and Rosas, Carlos.
Platicando con Carlos Rosas. RAYAS, Vol. 1,
no. 6 (November, December, 1978), p. 12, 11.
Spanish.

AN: Muralist Carlos Rosas painted murals
in Boulder and Denver, Colorado; Milwaukee,
Wisconsin, and El Paso, Texas. Commentary on
cross ethnic murals, views on art in
socialist countries, influence of Mexican
murals and information on his personal
preocupation as a politically engaged
artist.

3244 Hamm, Madeline McDermott. Artist envisions a
'Sistine' ceiling. HOUSTON CHRONICLE,
(September 19, 1978), p. III, 1-3. English.

AN: Illustrated article on mural that
Ernesto Pedregon Martinez (who was active in
El Paso in the 1950s) was doing for St.
Joseph Catholic Church in Houston. The mural
depicts the crucifixion.

3245 Hertzog, Carl. Tribute to Jose Cisneros. THE
PASSWORD, Vol. 19, no. 4 (Winter 1974).
English.

AN: Tribute to artist-illustrator Jose
Cisneros, who has "enhanced the appearance
of programs, exhibition catalogs, newspaper
articles, magazines and special stationery.
He has designed emblems such as the seal of
the University of Texas at El Paso, the seal
of the city of Juarez, Mexico, and the
emblem of the Western History Association".

3246 Manuel Acosta. LA LUZ, Vol. 3, no. 10-11
(January, February, 1975), p. 30. English.

AN: Biographical and exhibition data
focusing on Acosta's ability to paint
Mexican American types from the border area.

3247 Phelon, Craig. Sculptor survives on the edge
of a concrete canyon. EL PASO TIMES, (July
11, 1980). English.

AN: 84 year old Jesus Barrera sculpted
and painted hundreds of religious plaster
statues until forced to abandon sculpture in
1962 because lead-based paint ruined his
health.

3248 Renteria, Ramon. Struggle of barrio life
reflected in mural. EL PASO TIMES,
(November 21, 1976). English.

AN: Carlos Rosas paints a 100x35-foot
mural on the El Paso Boys Club building, as
an homage to a child. It also reflects the
artist's roots in El Paso. Iconography of
the mural is discussed. Illustrated.

Elaine Horwitch Gallery, Santa Fe, NM

3249 Loniak, Walter. The true New Mexico
contemporary style. SANTA FE REPORTER, (May
31, 1979). English.

AN: Review of three exhibits in Santa
Fe, EL FESTIVAL HISPANICO co-sponsored by
the Cofradia de Artes y Artesanos Hispanicos
and the Santa Fe Council for the Arts; a
wood carving exhibit at Elaine Horwitch
Gallery, and easel paintings by muralist
Gilberto Guzman at the Black Kachina
Gallery. Concerning the Festival exhibit,
the critic states that the sculptural pieces
are the strongest; two dimensional work is
inconsistent or unimpressive, weaving is not
well represented (though usually the
strongest medium), and there are few
photographs or prints. Illustration.

Electro-Arts Gallery, San Francisco, CA

3250 Reser, Phil. Rene Yanez: state-of-the-xerox
art. CITY ARTS, Vol. 3, no. 8 (August 1981).
English.

AN: Five years ago when Xerox came out
with a color copier, Yanez started
experimenting with the machine's color
buttons, which he uses like a musical
instrument or a paint brush. Yanez's work is
showing at the Electro-Arts Gallery in San
Francisco. Brief profile of the artist,
whose father and grandfather were both
artists.

LOS ELEMENTOS [mural]

3251 Murales - 'expresan nuestra realidad'.
AYUDA, Vol. 1, no. 6 (September 1977).
English.

AN: Brief illustrated article on Raul
Valdez's 1977 mural LOS ELEMENTOS on the
outside wall of Antioch's Juarez-Lincoln
College (Centro Cultural de LUCHA). Explains
the iconography of the mural. Includes brief
biography of the artist.

EMERGING [sculpture]

3252 Garza, Alex. Entrevista con Alex Garza.
ABRAZO, Vol. 1, no. 2 (Summer 1979), p.
27-29. English.

AN: Brief article exploring Alex Garza's
technique, philosophy, and setting for his
sculptural work. The artist expresses his
desire to see artists break with tradition
and not allow the political rhetoric of the
early Chicano Movement to promote
stagnation. His connection to the art
organization ALBA is also briefly mentioned.

EMPANADA [exhibit]

3253 Orange Co. Library. El Modena Branch. The
Hispanic Artist Association of Orange County
presents "Empanada," a tasty Mexican group
art exhibit filled with a variety of
digestible treats. Exhibition invitation,
1979. English.

AN: Poster/invitation to an exhibit of
artists (See "Empanada").

3254 Roberts, Tim. For art's sake, for the
community, for the working class. ORANGE
CITY NEWS, Vol. 10, (March 14, 1979), p.
1,8-9. English.

AN: Illustrated article on Orange
County, Calif. realist painter Emigdio
Vasquez. Focuses on his community murals,
and his attitudes toward his art. Also
announces the first exhibit, "Empanada" of
the newly formed Hispanic Artists
Association of Orange County. 13
participants including Vasquez.

**ENCUENTRO ARTISTICO FEMENIL [exhibit], Austin, TX,
November 28, 1977**

3255 Palma Castroman, Janis. ENCUENTRO ARTISTICO
FEMENIL [exhibit], Austin, TX, November 28,
1977. TEJIDOS, Vol. 5, no. 1 (1978), p.
1-47. Bilingual.

AN: A multimedia, multicultural
exposition by 26 Chicana artists held at
Juarez-Lincoln University. The exhibit was
sponsored by Chicanos Artistas Sirviendo a
Aztlan (CASA) and Mujeres Artistas del
Suroeste (MAS).

3256 Palma Castroman, Janis. Introduccion.
TEJIDOS, Vol. 5, no. 1 (1978), p. i.
Spanish.

AN: One-page introduction to theme issue
featuring the work of Chicana artists
exhibited at the ENCUENTRO ARTISTICO FEMENIL
exposition held on November 28, 1977 in
Austin, TX.

UN ENCUENTRO SIN PALABRAS [exhibit]

3257 Bolger, Kathryn McKenna. Photo exhibit
direct, human. AUSTIN AMERICAN STATESMAN,
(July 25, 1980), p. E-4. English.

AN: Review of photo-documentary group
exhibit "Un Encuentro Sin Palabras." The
reviewer felt that there was nothing
"unique" about the Chicano experience, as
claimed by the show's organizers.

3258 Documentary to include work by Cuate Santos.
LAREDO NEWS, (July 17, 1980). English.

AN: Photography by Laredo News
photographer Cuate Santos included in
exhibit "Un encuentro sin palabras," a

documentary show on Mexican American life in
Texas sponsored by Mujeres Artistas del
Suroeste (MAS). The state-wide show was
juried by Los Angeles photographer Isabel
Castro. Illustrated.

Environmental Pollution
USE: Pollution

Escalante Community Center, Tempe, AZ

3259 Denver muralist here for workshop. TEMPE
DAILY NEWS, (March 28, 1975). English.

AN: Denver muralist Roberto Lucero is
invited to give a weekend mural workshop for
the Quetzalcoatl Youth Organization of
Escalante Community Center in Tempe,
Arizona.

Escalante, Mariana

3260 Renacimiento del arte chicano en Texas. EL
HISPANO, Vol. 6, no. 3 (July 10, 1973).
English.

AN: Remigio Garcia and Mariana
Escalante, young muralists, describe their
work and the collective goals of a mural
workshop begun by Leo Tanguma in Houston,
TX.

Escojico, Isabell

3261 El calendario hispano de Michigan, 1981.
Stanton, MI: Montcalm Intermediate School
District and Nuestras Artes de Michigan,
1981. English.

AN: Months of historical calendar
illustrated with art works by George Vargas,
Nora Chapa Mendoza, Jesse Gonzalez, Julio
Perazza(Puerto Rican), Hector Valdez, Pamela
M. Gonzalez, Isabell Escojico (7-year-old
child), Jose Narezo, Martin Moreno, Laurie
Mendoza Psarianos, Rosa Maria Arenas.

Esparza, Antonio

3262 Exxon Company, Houston, TX and Quirarte,
Jacinto. Chicano art of the barrio.
Exhibition brochure, n.d. [c.1976]. English.

AN: Brochure for a traveling exhibit of
photographically-reproduced Chicano murals:
Leo Limon, Lucila Villasenor Grijalva,
Antonio Esparza, Susan Saenz, Charles Felix,
Hoyo-Mara gang, David A. Lopez and team,
Roberto Chavez and team (Los Angeles); Jerry
Concha, Ruben Guzman, Chuy Campusano (San
Francisco); Manuel Unzueta (Santa Barbara).
Ernie Palomino and Leo Esequiel Ozona
(Fresno). Leo Tanguma (Houston), Roberto
Lucero, Manuel Martinez and Al Sanchez
(Denver).

3263 Mascorro, Julie. Mechicano Art Center
exhibit to grace Price gallery walls. CAMPUS
NEWS, (November 24, 1971). English.

AN: Brief history of Mechicano Art
Center activities from its establishment in
1969 to 1971. Exhibiting are Charles
Almaraz, Roberto Amaral, Raymond Atilano,
William Bejarano, Armando Cabrera, Edward
Carbajal, Leonard Castellanos, Henry de
Vega, Antonio Esparza, Bob Gomez, Lucila V.
Grijalva, Jesus Gutierrez, Santos Lira,
Frank Martinez, Ernest Palomino, Louis
Quijada, Richard Raya, Frank Romero.
Illustrated.

Esparza, Moctezuma

3264 California. University. Los Angeles. Cine sin fronteras. Festival brochure, 1981. English.

   AN: Brochure program for a cinema festival and series of seminars and discussions featuring films and discussants from Mexico and Chicanos of the United States. Participating were Chicano directors Moctezuma Esparza, Richard Soto, David Sandoval, and Robert Young, and film historian David Maciel.

3265 Gloria, Juan J. En San Antonio: se celebrara el tercer festival de cine, 'La vida chicana a traves del celuloide'. EL VISITANTE DOMINICAL, (August 20, 1978), p. 6-8, 12. Spanish.

   AN: The Third Chicano Film Festival honors the only two feature-length films made by Chicanos: Moctezuma Esparza's ONLY ONCE IN A LIFETIME (made in Hollywood) and Jesus Salvador Trevino's RAICES DE SANGRE (Blood Roots), (made with CONACINE in Mexico). Illustrated.

3266 Vasquez, Esperanza and Esparza, Moctezuma. Agueda Martinez. 16 mm. color film. English.

   AN: Sixteen-minute film directed by Esperanza Vasquez and produced by Moctezuma Esparza concerning the life and weaving of an elderly New Mexican woman. Martinez carries on the tradition of floor loom weaving, as well as farming.

Esparza, Raul S.

3267 [Untitled photograph]. HISPANIC BUSINESS, (September 16, 1975). English.

   AN: Captioned illustration of Raul Esparza's 24x60 foot ceramic mural on the wall of the Exposition Park Museum of Science and Industry. Esparza worked a year and a half on the mural, MEXICO Y EL GENERO HUMANO.

ESPEJO DEL BARRIO [exhibit]

3268 El Centro Cultural de La Raza, San Diego, CA. Espejo del barrio-art exposition. Exhibition brochure, June 1975. English.

   AN: Illustrated brochure announcement for a cultural exposition of Chicano music, art and drama. Includes some biographical information and one reproduction of painter Manuel Unzueta, woodworker Ambriz, muralist Victor Orozco Ochoa and designer/illustrator J. Armando Nunez.

ESPEJO: REFLECTIONS OF THE MEXICAN AMERICAN

3269 Blum, Walter. The vision behind the mirror. CALIFORNIA LIVING, (November 26, 1978), p. 40-44. English.

   AN: Illustrated article with background information on the non-Chicano photographers (Roger Minick, Morrie Camhi, and Abigail Heyman) who spent a year documenting the Chicano community. Their work was issued as a portfolio, "Espejo: Reflections of the Mexican American," by the Mexican-American Legal Defense and Educational Fund (MALDEF). It is one of the most extensive photographic records made of the Chicano experience.

3270 Fischer, Hal. Espejo: reflections of the Mexican American: Louis Carlos Bernal,

Morrie Camhi, Abigail Heyman, Roger Minick, Neal Slavin. PICTURE MAGAZINE, no. 9 (1978). English.

   AN: Oversize portfolio of photographs recording contemporary Mexican American life commissioned by the Mexican American Legal Defense and Education Fund. Three photographers, Louis Carlos Bernal (from Arizona), Morrie Camhi and Abagail Heyman focus on the family and the home; the fourth, Roger Minick, juxtaposes the Mexican American against "barrio" murals. Only Bernal is Chicano. 24 photographs, six of which (Bernal's) are in color.

3271 Oakland Museum, Oakland, CA. Espejo: reflections of the Mexican American: Louis Carlos Bernal, Morrie Camhi, Abigail Heyman, Roger Minick, Neal Slavin. Exhibit brochure, 1978. English.

   AN: Twenty-five photographs from the documentary series commissioned by the Mexican American Legal Defense and Education Fund. Only Bernal is Chicano.

Espinoza, Al

3272 Mexican American Community Service Organization, San Jose, CA. Exhibition of contemporary art. Exhibition brochure, 1968. English.

   AN: Biographical and exhibition data for Al Barela, Bert Hermosillo, Octavio Romano, Luis Valdez, Vincent P. Rascon, John Soares and Al Espinoza.

Espinoza, Carlota

3273 Chavez, Lucy. A Chicano muralist. REVISTA MARYKNOLL, (July 1981). English.

   AN: Denver artist Carlotta Espinosa decided early in life that she was going to be an artist. Espinosa has painted murals in Arizona, Texas and the San Luis Valley in Colorado. Illustrated with photographs of artist and details from her murals.

3274 Fenwick, Red. Why gifted artist's works won't sell. DENVER POST, (October 28, 1979), p. F, 75. English.

   AN: Profile of Denver artist Carlota Espinoza--a painter, sculptor and creator of historic dioramas. Espinoza is mainly self-taught. A mural she created for the Byers branch library in Denver portraying "Hispanic" history in America was selected from more than 2,000 entries for national honors. She was chosen to do a stained glass window in the Colorado State House portraying the state's Spanish heritage, and has done art work for the Denver Museum of Natural History and other institutions. The article laments that such a talented artist has been unable to penetrate the mainstream art market.

Espinoza, Carlota (cont.)

3275 Mills, James. Hispano history mural ready.
DENVER POST, (October 17, 1975), p. 27+.
English.

AN: PASADO, PRESENTE Y FUTURO, a 20-ft.
mural by Denver artist Carlota Espinoza was
commissioned by the Friends of the Denver
Public Library for the Byers Branch (W. 7th
Ave. and Santa Fe Drive). Blending myth and
reality, the mural progresses from Aztec
empires through the Spanish conquest, from
alienation to the struggle for a collective
identity and heritage by the Mexican
American. Brief commentary by the artist on
the mural's significance. Ms. Espinoza's
mural was designated as an official
Centennial-Bicentennial creation.
Illustrated with photograph of artist.

3276 Montoya, Emmanuel; Rodriguez, Patricia; and
Acevedo, Mario (Torero). Canto al pueblo
'78. NATIONAL MURALS NETWORK COMMUNITY
NEWSLETTER, (1978). English.

AN: The second annual Canto al Pueblo
took place in Corpus Christi, Texas, where
more than six murals were painted: "Wall of
Cultural Education" by 13 artists headed by
Roel Montealva; Carlota Espinoza, with
children; Gilberto Romero, Jose Antonio
Burciaga and Patricia Rodriguez,
"Incomprehension al arte"; "Madre Tierra" by
Manuel Martinez of Denver with Amador
Hinojosa (Corpus Christi) and Enriquette
Vasquez (New Mexico); Mario Torero; Salvador
Vega of Chicago whose mural some Canto
participants considered "insulting".

Espinoza, Gilbert "Sparky"

3277 DE COLORES. Vol. 2, no. 4 (1976), p. 1-68.
English.

AN: Photographs by Moises Medina, Jose
Luis Sedano; drawings by Jerry Lujan,
Gilbert "Sparky" Espinoza, Rebecca Polanco;
paintings by John Herrera, Sonny Duran,
Larry Martinez. Cover by Fernando Penalosa.

Espinoza, Juan

3278 Chicano muralists maintain traditions. LA
CUCARACHA, (November 20, 1979), p. 7.
English.

AN: Introduction to Chicano muralism in
Pueblo and comparison to the Mexican mural
movement from which it draws inspiration. 20
murals painted from 1977 to 1979. The
muralists include Bernardo Duran, Juan
Espinoza, Miguel "Freeloader" Garcia, Lola
Gutierrez, Leo Lucero, Juan Pacheco, Dolores
Pena, Pedro Romero, Stan Salazar, David
Sandoval. Diego Rivera murals illustrated.

Espinoza, Raul

3279 Galeria Tonantzin, Centro Cultural de LUCHA,
Austin, TX. Young Chicano photographers from
throughout Texas. Exhibition brochure, n.d.
English.

AN: This exhibition is the collection of
the winners of the contest (by the same
name) sponsored by the Extension Cultural
SRE-UNAM in San Antonio. Photographers
represented were: Grace Alvarez, David
Cardenas, Hector Cardenas, Stephen Casanova,
Ronald Cortez, Raul Espinosa, Felix Almanza,
Carolina Flores, David Garza Perez, Xavier
Garza, Conrad Guerra, Melinda Hasbrook, Juan
Jose de Hoyes, Beverly Kennon, Art Moreno,

David Perez, Isabelle Purden, Patricia
Santell, Nancy de los Santos, Jose Soria,
Richard Tichich, Kathy Vargas, Vivian Yaten,
and Johnny Zamarria.

Espinoza, Ray

3280 Barrett, Marjorie. Ray Espinoza: versatile
artist. ROCKY MOUNTAIN NEWS, (February 12,
1973), p. 44. English.

AN: Ray Espinoza whose family spans six
generations in the San Luis Valley of
Colorado is steeped in Southwestern art
traditions. Drawing from his ancestral
heritage, he has become a prominent sculptor
working in wax. Illustrated with photograph
of artist and two of his sculptures.

3281 Espinoza. EMPIRE MAGAZINE, (October 22,
1972), p. 28. English.

AN: Biographical information and
artistic trajectory of Ray Espinoza from
Colorado's San Luis Valley. Focus on
Espinoza as a community artist who expresses
aspects of Southwestern culture. Illustrated
with photographs of three wax sculptures by
Ray Espinoza.

3282 Haddad, Barbara. The fine arts. ROUNDUP,
(January 25, 1970), p. 12. English.

AN: Mixed review of Ray Espinoza's
one-person show at the International House
Gallery in Denver. The exhibition included
drawings, paintings, prints, assemblages and
sculptures. Selecting work from each medium,
the critic comments on pieces that are
successful and those not fully realized.
Illustrated with a wood and metal relief of
a guitar and a graphic of "Che" Guevara.

Espinoza, Roberto

3283 Heard Museum, Phoenix, AZ. Second Southwest
Chicano Art Invitational. Exhibit catalog,
1978. English.

AN: Exhibit by eight artists: Antonio
Pazos (Tucson), Rudy Fernandez (Salt Lake
City), Harry Gamboa (Los Angeles), Rupert
Garcia and Xavier Viramontes (San
Francisco), Roberto Rios (San Antonio),
Roberto Espinoza (Yuma), and Roberto Borboa
(Tucson). Brief biographies of all but Rios.
29 illustrations.

Esquivel, Jose

3284 Con Safo. San Antonio, TX: Pintores Chicanos
de San Antonio, [ca. 1975]. English.

AN: Illustrated pamphlet issued by the
San Antonio artists' group Con Safo.
Includes a self-definition and a brief
history of the group under the names El
Grupo, Los Pintores de Aztlan, Los Pintores
de la Nueva Raza, Con Safo (from 1967 on).
Members include Jesse A. Almazan, Mel Casas,
Jose Esquivel, Jose P. Garza, Cesar Augusto
Martinez, Santos Martinez, Felipe Reyes,
Roberto Rios, Jesus C. Trevino, and Vicente
Velasquez.

Esquivel, Jose (cont.)

3285 Contemporary Arts Museum, Houston, TX. Dale
gas: give it gas. The continued
acceleration of Chicano art. Exhibition
catalog, 1977. English.

AN: A comprehensive catalog including 28
works of art exhibited by 13 Texas artists:
Melesio (Mel) Casas, Jose Esquivel,
Francisco (Frank) Fajardo, Carmen Lomas
Garza, Luis Jimenez, Cesar Augusto Martinez,
Santos G. Martinez, Jr., Amado Pena, Roberto
Rios, Jose Rivera, Joe B. Rodriguez, Jesus
(Jesse) Trevino, and George Truan. Many
illustrations, some in color. Introduction
by James Harithas. Essay by Santos Martinez,
Jr. Poetry, literature and essays by Chicano
writers.

Estrada Courts, Los Angeles, CA

3286 Beronius, George. The murals of East Los
Angeles. HOME MAGAZINE, (April 11, 1976),
p. 10-11+. English.

AN: Well-illustrated historical article
focusing on murals at Estrada Courts and
those produced through Goez Gallery and
Judith Baca in East Los Angeles.

3287 Blanco, Gil. Art on the walls: a vehicle for
positive change. LATIN QUARTER, Vol. 1, no.
2 (October 1974), p. 26-30. English.

AN: East Los Angeles artists Ismael
"Smiley" Pereira and C.W. (Charles) Felix
started painting murals with young people at
the Estrada Courts Housing Project in May
1973. There are now 30 murals, and the
residents are more receptive, noting the
changes that are taking place. Illustrated
with murals by Herron and Gronk, and Daniel
Martinez.

3288 Graffiti gone: murals in full bloom. PHOENIX
GAZETTE, (April 13, 1974). English.

AN: Mural explosion at Estrada Courts
Housing Project in Los Angeles led by C.W.
Felix. Estimates 60 murals in East Los
Angeles. Illustrated.

3289 Gutierrez, Helga. The walls of Estrada
Courts. LA GENTE DE AZTLAN, Vol. 7, no. 3
(February 1977), p. 19. English.

AN: Photographic essay of Estrada murals
by Helga Gutierrez.

3290 Lopez, Gerard. Estrada murals. LA LUZ, Vol.
4, no. 3 (June 1975), p. 21. English.

AN: Describes goals and procedures of a
barrio mural project under the guidance of
"Los Ninos del Mundo", a group of Chicano
artists, musicians and social workers.

3291 Lopez, Gerard. Estrada murals. LA GENTE DE
AZTLAN, Vol. 4, no. 6 (May, June, 1974), p.
4. English.

AN: Article explains how the community
at Estrada Courts was mobilized to support a
mural project uniting artists with
residents. Includes interview with artist
C.W. Felix who comments on the goals of the
mural program and cites the themes and
symbolism of the murals.

3292 Weiss, Margaret R. and Sommer, Robert.
Camera assignment: documenting street art.
SATURDAY REVIEW, (May 17, 1975), p. 41-43.
English.

AN: Interview with Robert Sommer.
Illustrations of six murals: in Santa Fe,
NM; Estrada Courts in Los Angeles; a John
Weber mural in Chicago; and Cityarts mural
in New York.

Estrada, Juanita

3293 Teatro de la Tierra Morena, Santa Cruz, CA.
Fuego en Aztlan: a Chicano arts show.
Exhibition brochure, 1980. English.

AN: Folder of information on the
exhibition curated by Cruz Zamarron and
Eduardo Carrillo. Exhibiting artists were:
Justina Avila, Terry Benitez, Eduardo
Carrillo, Hernando Chavez, Bob Cruz, Juanita
Estrada, Juana Franklin, Sal Garcia, Leticia
Hernandez, David "Sir Loco" Jimenez, Raoul
Mendez, Vicente Mendez, Maria V. Pinedo,
Gonzalo Placencia, Ramon Rodriguez, Roberto
Salas, George Silva and Cruz Zamarron. A
special feature was a live tattoo
demonstration entitled "Walking Art".

Estrella, Armando

3294 Community Programs in the Arts and Sciences
(COMPAS). Artists in the city: a report on
C.E.T.A. artists in St. Paul. St. Paul, MN:
COMPAS, 1978. English.

AN: Includes data on Chicano muralists
John Acosta, Thomas Acosta, Paul Basquez,
Armando Estrella, and photographer Raphael
Romo.

3295 Community Programs in the Arts and Sciences
(COMPAS). Flor y Canto in Minnesota. St.
Paul, MN: Northwestern Press, 1978. English.

AN: Survey of community arts projects.
Includes commentary on Chicano mural
activity in Minnesota. Cover design by
Chicano artist Armando Estrella.

3296 Flanagan, Barbara. Murals warm up west St.
Paul. MINNEAPOLIS STAR, (December 20,
1977). English.

AN: Discussion of mural activity in West
St. Paul, Minnesota by Armando Estrella,
Paul Basquez and John Acosta. The subject of
most murals in Minnesota is either
political, religious or historic. Of the
three artists involved, Paul Basquez grew up
in the barrio of West St. Paul. He tells how
mural activity in the region is related to
the Chicano art movement. About a half-dozen
murals have been painted in St. Paul.

3297 Knapp, Martha. West side is part of mural
art renaissance. WEST SAINT PAUL VOICE, Vol.
5, no. 19 (November 21, 1977). English.

AN: Pre-Columbian symbology in the mural
program painted by Paul Basquez and Armando
Estrella in the Chicano barrio; information
and data on the mural renaissance in
Minnesota.

Estrella, Ruben

3298 Galeria de arte de Aztlan. AZTLAN (U.S.
Penitentiary, Leavenworth, KA), Vol. 1, no.
2. English.

AN: Pictorial supplement with
reproductions of pinto art by Manuel
Aguilera, Jessie Hernandez, Ruben Estrella,
Tomas Torres and Jose D. Marin. Many of
these works were reproduced in other Chicano
newspapers demonstrating the solidarity that
existed in the Chicano movement inside and
outside the prison walls.

3299 NEW ERA (U.S. Penitentiary, Leavenworth,
KA). (Fall , Winter, 1970). English.

AN: Under the art direction of Ruben
Estrella from San Antonio, Texas, NEW ERA, a
prison cultural magazine also featured the
caricatures and cartoons of Tone Briones
from Laredo, Texas. Raul Salinas, poet from
Austin, Texas was Associate Editor for both
issues.

3300 Salinas, Raul. Nueva estrella en el
horizonte. LA RAZA, Vol. 1, no. 2 (1970), p.
79. Spanish.

AN: Brief introduction to the work of
painter Ruben Estrella, a native of San
Antonio, who at the time was serving out his
penalty at Leavenworth State Prison.

3301 Salinas, Raul. Nueva estrella en el
horizonte. AZTLAN (U.S. Penitentiary,
Leavenworth, KA), Vol. 1, no. 1 (May 5,
1970). English.

AN: Brief article on San Antonio artist
Ruben Estrella who perfected his art within
the walls of Leavenworth. Especially noted
for his portraits, Estrella was illustrator
of NEW ERA, the prison's literary journal.
Illustrated with photograph of artist and
four of his oil paintings.

3302 Salinas, Raul. Portrait of an artist.
ENTRELINEAS, Vol. 1, no. 5-6 (October,
December, 1971), p. 3-5. English.

AN: Biographical and artistic
information on Ruben Estrella who developed
as a "pinto" artist within Leavenworth
Penitentiary.

Estudios Rio: Gallery of Contemporary Arts and Crafts, Mission, TX

3303 Estudios Rio: gallery of contemporary arts
and crafts. Exhibition catalog, 1976.
English.

AN: Catalog including identification,
portraits and works of participating
artists: Joe Bova, Enrique Flores, Carmen
Lomas Garza, Xavier Gorena, Erik Gronborg,
Lucas Hinojosa, Ben Holland, Kris Hotvedt,
William Kaars-Sijpesteijn, Cesar Martinez,
Chris Mende, Roberto Mungia, Steve Reynolds,
Vicente Rodriguez, William Wilhelmi.

Ethnic Identity
USE: Identity

Ethnicity
USE: Identity

Exhibits

3304 11 reproduccion - significacion politica:
arte fotocopia. Exhibition invitation, 1979.
English.

AN: Invitation to an international
exhibit of photocopy artists from Europe,
Latin America and the United States.
Includes Rene Yanez of San Francisco.

3305 59th Street Gallery, St. Louis, MO. Midwest
Mexican-American art exhibit: Mexico and its
artists. Exhibition brochure, 1981. English.

AN: Sponsored by the Sociedad Mexicana
"Benito Juarez" and the international
Institute of St. Louis, this three-part
exhibit includes 1) MEXICO AS SEEN BY HER
CHILDREN, a bilingual exhibit from Mexico
traveling under Smithsonian Institution
auspices, 2) MEXICAN CHILDREN IN THE U.S.A.,
3) MEXICAN AMERICAN ARTISTS. In the latter
are included Stephen Capiz (Roseville,
Minn.), Jose Gonzalez (Chicago), Cesar A.
Martinez (San Antonio), Ada Medina (Des
Moines), Nora Chapa Mendoza (West
Bloomfield, Mich.), Rene David
Michel-Trapaga (St. Louis), David Munoz
(Kansas City, Mo.), Jose Luis Narezo (Grand
Rapids, Mich.), Benny Ordonez, Roman
Villarreal (Chicago), Alejandro Romero
(Chicago), Aurelio Diaz "Tekpankalli"
(Chicago), Simon Ybarra (St. Louis).

3306 Ackerman Student Union, University of
California, Los Angeles. Raza women in the
arts: brotando del silencio. Exhibit
invitation, 1979. English.

AN: Invitation to a MEChA-sponsored
exhibit of women's art. Illustrated.

3307 Acosta, Dan. Paintings reflect life
experiences. THE ECCENTRIC, (June 26,
1980). English.

AN: Review of one-woman show by Nora
Chapa Mendoza at the Heritage Art Gallery,
Ypsilanti, MI. Mendoza works in abstract
impressionist style with wet streams of
colors that express energy. Her subjects are
landscapes, moods, nudes, and Hispanic
themes. She is active in the Detroit Latino
Artist Association, Nuestras Artes de
Michigan, and the New Detroit Art Council.

3308 Adams Hotel, Phoenix, AZ. Chicano and Indian
art exhibit. Exhibit invitation, 1979.
English.

AN: Invitation to an exhibit of 16
artists. Brief history of the organization
MARS (Moviemiento Artistico del Rio Salado)
of Phoenix, AZ, formed in Summer 1978 after
a Floricanto Culture Week. 98% of MARS
members are Chicano or Indian. Their purpose
is to build the Salt River Valley as a
cultural center of the Southwest.

3309 Adrienne Simard Gallery, Los Angeles, CA.
Presenting Carlos Almaraz: pastel drawings,
1969-1981. Exhibition invitation, 1981.
English.

AN: Invitation to exhibit of Los Angeles
painter Carlos Almaraz. includes color
illustration.

-- --

Exhibits (cont.)

1979), p. 118. English.

3310 Alarcon, Francisco X. El Museo Mexicano,
     quinto aniversario. EL TECOLOTE LITERARY
     MAGAZINE, (December 10, 1981). Spanish.

   AN: Goals of the Mexican Museum in San
   Francisco are contextualized within the
   social nexus of the Chicano Art Movement of
   the 1960s. Explains functional difference
   between Mexican Museum and community art
   galleries.

3311 Alarcon, Francisco X. and Herrera, Juan
     Felipe. Portraits plus struggles plus
     consciousness: nine pastels by Rupert
     Garcia. METAMORFOSIS, Vol. 3, no. 2 (1980),
     p. 104-106. English.

   AN: Reprint of article published as
   "Rupert Garcia: portraits/retratos" in EL
   TECOLOTE LITERARY MAGAZINE (San Francisco,
   CA), Vol. 2, no. 1, March 1981, p. 6.

3312 Alarcon, Francisco X. Rupert Garcia:
     portraits/retratos. EL TECOLOTE LITERARY
     MAGAZINE, Vol. 2, no. 1 (March 1981), p. 6+.
     Bilingual.

   AN: Review of Garcia exhibit at the
   Mexican Museum (S.F.) in 1981. Includes
   portraits of Frida Kahlo and the Flores
   Magon brothers, Goya, Van Gogh, Ethel and
   Julius Rosenberg, etc. Illustrated. This
   article has been reprinted in METAMORFOSIS
   under a different title: "Portraits Plus
   Struggles Plus Consciousness: Nine Pastels
   by Rupert Garcia," Vol. 3-4, no. 1-2,
   (1980-81), p. 104-106.

3313 Alba-King Kong Studios, Chicago, IL. Latina
     Art Expo '77. Chicago, IL: ALBA-King Kong
     Studios, 1977. English.

   AN: An exhibit by 16 Chicana, Mexican,
   Puerto Rican and other Latina artists. Brief
   biographies of the artists.

3314 Albright, Thomas. Forceful masterpieces from
     Manuel Neri. SAN FRANCISCO CHRONICLE, (May
     17, 1979), p. 47. English.

   AN: A rave review of Neri's one-person
   sculpture show at the Paula Anglum Gallery.

3315 Albright, Thomas. Oakland Museum: a wide
     range in Latin art. SAN FRANCISCO CHRONICLE,
     (September 12, 1970), p. 33. English.

   AN: A large show called ARTES DE LA RAZA
   at the Oakland Museum includes Mercedes
   Gutierrez-McDermid, Louis Gutierrez, Luis
   Cervantez, Calvin Tondre, Manuel Villamor,
   Rene Yanez, Jose Ramirez, Jorge Lerma,
   Rolando Castellon, Esteban Villa, Rupert
   Garcia, and Gustavo Rivera who is also
   having an exhibit at the Galeria de la Raza.

3316 Albright, Thomas. Pre-Columbian art: New
     Galeria de la Raza. SAN FRANCISCO CHRONICLE,
     (July 15, 1970), p. 49. English.

   AN: A new gallery is launched at 425
   14th St. in San Francisco with an exhibit by
   Sacramento State College teacher Esteban
   Villa, with bold angular abstractions of
   roosters, comments on the Frito Bandito, and
   expressionist pen and pencil drawings. Other
   exhibits are also on display. The Galeria is
   sponsored by Casa Hispana de Bellas Artes.

3317 Albright, Thomas. San Francisco: sleepers
     and spectacles [Manuel Neri exhibit review].
     ART NEWS MAGAZINE, Vol. 78, no. 7 (September

   AN: Review of an exhibit at the Paula
   Anglum Gallery of San Francisco by Manuel
   Neri who has been developing over the last
   twenty years into one of the country's most
   profound and compelling sculptors. These
   pieces are life-sized plaster figures of
   nude female models.

3318 Albright, Thomas. San Francisco: the force
     of universals. ART NEWS MAGAZINE, Vol. 77,
     no. 6 (Summer 1978), p. 174. English.

   AN: Review of Rupert Garcia pastel show
   at the San Francisco Museum of Modern Art.
   Reviewer suggests he is one of the very few
   real artists to emerge from the "unfortunate
   genre" of poster art. His images are highly
   charged: political prisoners, corpses,
   revolutionary martyrs.

3319 Albright, Thomas. The sensual moods of
     nature. SAN FRANCISCO CHRONICLE, (January
     23, 1971), p. 34. English.

   AN: Review of an exhibition of paintings
   by Pedro Rodriguez of San Francisco at the
   Galeria de La Raza. Work classified as
   lyrical abstractions "in the vein of
   introspective lyric poetry".

3320 Albright, Thomas. 'Unspoiled' Bay Area art.
     SAN FRANCISCO CHRONICLE, (August 29, 1974),
     p. 40. English.

   AN: Review of an exhibit titled ART NAIF
   curated by Rolando Castellon. The show
   featured 15 Bay Area painters who are
   basically self-taught and share a personal
   expression unhampered by prevailing art
   conventions and trends. Includes material on
   Alexander Maldonado, 72-year-old "primitive"
   painter from San Francisco. Some of
   Maldonado's work includes references to his
   childhood and youth in Mexico.

3321 Amado Maurilio Pena, Jr. PAPEL CHICANO, Vol.
     1, no. 13 (July 21, 1978). Spanish.

   AN: Includes the artist's resume, an
   exhibition list, and a gallery statement
   situating the work of Pena within both
   Native American and Chicano art traditions.
   Includes reproduction of four works.

3322 And/Or Gallery, Seattle, WA. Artistas de
     Aztlan. Exhibition announcement, 1975.
     English.

   AN: Exhibition announcement for an
   important exhibit of Northwest Chicano art.
   Co-sponsored by MEChA and the Chicano
   Studies Program at the University of
   Washington, the exhibit presented works by
   Emilio Aguayo, Danny Desiga, Ricardo
   Aguirre, Ramiro Benavidez, Elma Herada,
   Pedro Rodriguez and others. A selection of
   posters by Armando Cid of the R.C.A.F. group
   from Sacramento, California was also
   presented. Concurrently, at the Heny Gallery
   of the University of Washington, Esteban
   Villa presented a one-man show.

Exhibits (cont.)

3323 Andrews, Rena. The fine arts. ROUNDUP,
     (September 27, 1970), p. 18. English.

     AN: Commentary on one-man exhibition by
     John L. Mendoza at the International House
     Gallery in Denver. Noted for his water-color
     landscapes, the artists is a full time art
     teacher at East High School in Pueblo
     Colorado. Illustrated with photograph of the
     artist and one of his paintings.

3324 Andrews, Rena. The fine arts. ROUNDUP,
     (November 25, 1973), p. 22. English.

     AN: Article places work of Ramon Kelley
     within the impressionist mode. At the De
     Colores Gallery in his hometown of Denver,
     Kelley's exhibit titled, "Faces of the
     Southwest" included drawings, water color
     and pastel painting, oils and acrylics.

3325 Andrews, Rena. The fine arts. EMPIRE
     MAGAZINE, (December 19, 1971), p. 32.
     English.

     AN: Review of first one person show by
     John Flores at the Nathan Galleries in
     Denver. Born in El Paso, Texas but reared in
     Denver, Flores depicts his Indo-Hispanic
     heritage in his creations. Concentrating on
     portraits, still-lifes, and landscapes,
     Flores paints within the Impressionistic
     mode. Critic feels Flores is not fully
     realized, yet has some impressive work and
     is a promising younger artist.

3326 Arizona. ARIZONA REPUBLIC, (September 11,
     1977), p. 50. English.

     AN: Exhibit of photographs by Louis
     Carlos Bernal from Tucson in the Heard
     Museum in Phoenix, Arizona. Includes 6
     illustrations.

3327 Armando Cid art works on display at Barrio
     Gallery. EL HISPANO, Vol. 5, no. 44 (April
     24, 1973). English.

     AN: Description of Armando Cid's M.A.
     thesis exhibition. The dominant impulse in
     the paintings is an attempt to define and
     reflect a Chicano style.

3328 Arnold, Frank. Posters and society. PEOPLE'S
     WORLD, Vol. 23, no. 2. English.

     AN: An exhibit at the San Francisco
     Museum of Art curated by Rolando Castellon.
     The article focuses on the posters of Xavier
     Viramontes and Rupert Garcia of San
     Francisco.

3329 Around the Bay. METAMORFOSIS, Vol. 3, no. 2
     (1980), p. 101-108. English.

     AN: Cultural review of activities in the
     Bay Area, northern California, and
     Sacramento. Includes history of the Galeria
     de la Raza/Studio 24 (San Francisco), the
     Centro de Artistas Chicanos/RCAF, Royal
     Chicano Air Force (Sacramento), and a review
     of Rupert Garcia's pastel portraits exhibit
     at the Mexican Museum (S.F.) in 1981.
     Illustrated. Continued in Vol. 4, no. 1,
     1981.

3330 Art Gallery, California State University,
     Long Beach and Lujan, Gilbert Sanchez
     "Magu". El arte del pocho. Exhibit brochure,
     October 1968. English.

     AN: Information about Southern

California artists John Deheras, Marcus
Villagran, Roberto de la Rocha, Santos
Zuniga, Crispin Gonzales, Richard Martinez,
Jesus Gutierrez, Ed Oropeza, Pete Mendez,
David Ramirez, Gilbert Sanchez Lujan, Willie
Hernandez, Art Ponce, Carmen Tostado, Al
Almeida, David Ceja, Robert E. Chavez,
Thomas A. Ferriera. All art students,
graduates, or faculty.

3331 Art Gallery, University of California,
     Irvine and Los Angeles County Museum of Art,
     Los Angeles, CA. Los Four: Almaraz, de la
     Rocha, Lujan, Romero. Exhibition brochure,
     1973-74. English.

     AN: Photographs and biographies of
     Carlos Almaraz, Roberto de la Rocha, Gilbert
     S. Lujan, Frank Romero.

3332 The art of Mexican America. EMPIRE MAGAZINE,
     (November 1, 1970), p. 24-25. English.

     AN: Visual portfolio with minimal text.
     Includes paintings by Amado Pena, Mel Casas,
     Porfirio Salinas, and sculpture by Octavio
     Medellin. On the same page, Dr. Jacinto
     Quirarte gives views on the nature of
     Mexican art, the Mexican American artist,
     and the connection between Mexican and
     Mexican American art.

3333 Art Space - Open Ring Gallery, Sacramento,
     CA. El Pachuco art de Jose Montoya: a
     historical update. Exhibition invitation,
     1977. English.

     AN: Invitation to an exhibit.
     Illustrated with a reproduction of a 1977
     silkscreen calendar page in color by
     Montoya.

3334 Artes 6 Gallery, San Francisco, CA. Mixed
     media. Exhibition announcement, [ca.
     1969-70]. English.

     AN: Announcement of exhibit including
     Jim Cortez, Luis Cervantez, Vicente Rascon,
     Rene Yanes, Graciela Carrillo, Lorenza
     Camplis. The Artes 6 artists eventually
     formed the Galeria de la Raza of San
     Francisco.

3335 Arts review. ARTS REVIEW, Vol. 31, no. 20
     (October 12, 1979), p. 558. English.

     AN: Review of show in October Gallery
     London by Gilberto Guzman of Santa Fe, New
     Mexico. Guzman is characterized as a
     "figurative expressionist."

3336 Barrett, Marjorie and Flores, John. Flores:
     artist's gamble paid off. ROCKY MOUNTAIN
     NEWS, (May 18, 1980), p. 27. English.

     AN: In less than a decade, John Flores
     has gone from being a part-time painter
     working in a meat packing plant to a
     prolific fulltime artist. This interview on
     the occasion of Flores' one person show at
     the De Colores Gallery reviews his artistic
     trajectory. The 30 odd paintings in the
     exhibit include still lifes, pastel
     portraits, street scenes and landscapes in
     oil. Experimenting with vivid color, Flores
     is turning to his own cultural roots.

Exhibits (cont.)

3337 Baxter Art Gallery, California Institute of
     Technology and Rosenstone, Robert A. In
     search of...four women/four cultures.
     Exhibition catalog, 1976. English.

     AN: Catalog of an exhibit including
     Donna Nakao, Cheri Pann, Betye Saar, and Los
     Angeles Chicana artist Judithe E. Hernandez.
     One work of each artist illustrated.

3338 Bellevue Art Museum, Bellevue, WA. Alfredo
     Arreguin. s.n.:s.l., n.d. English.

     AN: Profusely illustrated exhibition
     catalog for a one-man retrospective of
     paintings by Alfredo Arreguin. Exploring the
     possibilities of pattern painting, the
     intent of his art is to be visionary. His
     paintings have affinity with Pre-Columbian
     and Colonial Mexican designs and is related
     to decorative emotional images of various
     cultures. Includes photograph of artist and
     a selected bibliography.

3339 Bernal, Luis Carlos. La fotografia como
     reflejo de las estructuras sociales. In
     HECHO EN LATINOAMERICA: SEGUNDO COLOQUIO
     LATINOAMERICANO DE FOTOGRAFIA, MEXICO CITY,
     1982, p. 92-94. Spanish.

     AN: Presentation made by Tucson, AZ
     photographer Louis Carlos Bernal at the
     Second Latin American Colloquium of
     Photography and exhibit in 1981.

3340 Le Bistro Restaurant, San Antonio, TX.
     Contemporary paintings by Cesar Augusto
     Martinez. Exhibition catalog, 1980. English.

     AN: Catalog of an exhibit. Blurb about
     the artist.

3341 Bloomfield, Arthur. Zesty show at Mexican
     museum. SAN FRANCISCO EXAMINER, (February
     1, 1977), p. 24. English.

     AN: Review of an exhibit of Mexican and
     Mexican American artists from the Southwest
     and the San Francisco area. Commentary and
     analysis on artists Vincent Perez and
     Gustavo Rivera, Rudy Trevino and Al Barela.
     The work selected focused on aesthetic
     quality rather than the ethnic
     identification of the artist.

3342 Blum, Walter. The vision behind the mirror.
     CALIFORNIA LIVING, (November 26, 1978), p.
     40-44. English.

     AN: Illustrated article with background
     information on the non-Chicano photographers
     (Roger Minick, Morrie Camhi, and Abigail
     Heyman) who spent a year documenting the
     Chicano community. Their work was issued as
     a portfolio, "Espejo: Reflections of the
     Mexican American," by the Mexican-American
     Legal Defense and Educational Fund (MALDEF).
     It is one of the most extensive photographic
     records made of the Chicano experience.

3343 Boise Gallery of Art, Idaho Migrant Council
     and Boise Cascade Corp. 17 artists:
     Hispano/Mexican-American/Chicano. Boise, ID:
     1977. English.

     AN: Announcement of a national
     exhibition organized and toured by Illinois
     Bell Telephone. In Idaho, the exhibit (March
     12 to April 10, 1977) also included local
     Chicano artists.

3344 Bolger, Kathryn McKenna. Photo exhibit

direct, human. AUSTIN AMERICAN STATESMAN,
(July 25, 1980), p. E-4. English.

     AN: Review of photo-documentary group
     exhibit "Un Encuentro Sin Palabras." The
     reviewer felt that there was nothing
     "unique" about the Chicano experience, as
     claimed by the show's organizers.

3345 Brand Library Art Center, Glendale, CA. Los
     hermanos: Jesus, Jacob & Frank Gutierrez,
     sculpture, paintings, drawings, &
     photographs. Exhibition catalog, 1974.
     English.

     AN: Exhibit of the work of three
     brothers living in the Los Angeles area.

3346 Bravo, Antonio. Manuel Alvarez Bravo at the
     San Francisco Art Institute. CHISMEARTE,
     Vol. 2, no. 1 (Summer 1978), p. 37. English.

     AN: Presentation of the Mexican
     photographer's work in relation to a
     visiting exhibit in the United States.
     Illustrated.

3347 Burkhardt, Dorothy. Chicano pride and anger
     mix at 'Califas'. THE TAB, (April 12,
     1981), p. 34. English.

     AN: CALIFAS: AN EXHIBITION OF CHICANO
     ARTISTS IN CALIFORNIA represents a
     cross-section of artists exhibiting work for
     at least ten years: Rupert Garcia, Ernie
     Palomino, Eduardo Carrillo, Judy Baca, Rene
     Yanez, Carmen Lomas Garza, Salvador Roberto
     Torres, Roberto Chavez, Willie Herron, Ralph
     Maradiaga, Sue Martinez, Jose Montoya,
     Malaquias Montoya, Ramses Noriega and
     Esteban Villa. Illustrated.

3348 California. State College. Los Angeles. Art
     Department. Fifth California small images
     exhibition. Exhibition catalog, [1972].
     English.

     AN: Catalog for an exhibit including the
     work of Charles D. Almaraz, Mary Lynn
     Dominguez, Gilbert Sanchez Lujan (who won
     Purchase Awards), Stephen Anaya, Martha
     Villegas. Illustrated.

3349 California. State College. Los Angeles. Art
     Gallery. Twelve Chicano artists. Exhibition
     invitation, n.d. English.

     AN: Invitation to an exhibit: Jose
     Montoya, Gilbert Sanchez Lujan, Esteban
     Villa, Rene Yanez, Joe Moran, Armando Cid,
     Leonard Castellanos, Juanishi Orozco, Rudy
     Cuellar, Beltran, Lopez and Cabrera.

3350 California. University. Santa Cruz. College
     Eight Gallery. Four artists: Edward
     Carrillo, Consuelo Mendez Castillo, Louis
     Gutierrez, Jose Montoya. Exhibition catalog,
     n.d. English.

     AN: Exhibit of three Chicano artists and
     Venezuelan-born artist Consuelo Mendez de
     Castillo.

Exhibits (cont.)

3351 California. University. Santa Barbara. Coleccion Tloque Nahuaque. Mexican soldaderas and workers during the revolution. Exhibition catalog, 1979. English.

AN: Well illustrated catalog of an exhibition of original lithographs by artists associated with the Taller de Grafica Popular of Mexico. Biographical information and illustrations by Raul Anguiano, Luis Arenal, Alberto Beltran, Angel Bracho, photographer, Agustin V. Casasola, Fernando Castro Pacheco, Jesus Escobedo, Arturo Garcia Bustos, Leopolda Mendez, Francisco Mora, Isidoro Ocampo, Pablo O'Higgins, Mariana Yampolsky and Alfredo Zolca.

3352 Camacho, Eduardo. Por los cien anos de la fundacion de su editorial: inauguraran hoy en San Diego la exposicion 'Homenaje a Posada, Manilla y Vanegas Arroyo'. EXCELSIOR, (February 14, 1980). Spanish.

AN: Announcing the exhibit of 19th Century Mexican engravers Jose Guadalupe Posada and Manuel Manilla, with publisher Antonio Vanegas Arroyo, at the Centro Cultural de la Raza and Southwestern College, of San Diego, CA.

3353 Campesino Business and Joint Enterprise Building, Fresno, CA. Sabor a Fresno. Arte chicano: los Four and la Brocha. Exhibition invitation [1976]. English.

AN: Invitation to an exhibit of works by Los Four of Los Angeles and members of La Brocha del Valle of Fresno: Arturo Roman, Sal Garcia, John Sierra, Juan Truner, Sapo de Aztlan, Fernando Hernandez, Alberto Reyes, Ernesto Palomino, Lee Orona, Francisco Barrios, Juan Ybarra, Bobby Reyes, Alberto Hernandez. Brocha was started by Palomino (California State University, Fresno professor) to pool talents of Central Valley artists.

3354 Canavier, Elena Karina. Los Four. ARTWEEK, Vol. 5, no. 10 (March 9, 1974), p. 1, 16. English.

AN: Illustrated review, with detailed description of work of the Los Four exhibit at the Los Angeles County Museum of Art.

3355 Capitol Art Gallery, Lansing, MI. Arte de Nora Mendoza, Hector Perez, George Vargas, Martin Moreno. Exhibition invitation [1979]. English.

AN: Invitation to an art exhibit organized by Nuestras Artes de Michigan.

3356 Cardona, Patricia. El museo mexicano de San Francisco. EL DIA, (July 6, 1977), p. 10. Spanish.

AN: Report on the Mexican Museum giving a brief overview of its programs. The Mexican Museum opened Nov. 20, 1975 and has been a vital force in the cultural life of San Francisco, showing the work of one Mexican and one Chicano artist every two months.

3357 Carlos Pineda shows art in Centennial Museum. EL PASO TIMES, (November 5, 1972). English.

AN: Themes from Mexican folk culture

predominate in paintings by Carlos R. Pineda shown at the El Paso Centennial Museum. He has exhibited in Panama, Guadalajara, Phoenix, Tucson, and Dallas and is represented by the Jinx Gallery in El Paso.

3358 Carrillo, Eduardo. Califas, is Chicano art safe in Santa Cruz? ARTS AT SANTA CRUZ, Vol. 1, no. 1 (1981). English.

AN: Illustrated essay surveying Chicano art in Santa Cruz with details about the planning and presentation of the CALIFAS exhibit at the Mary Porter Seanon Gallery. This exhibition presented the work of fifteen Chicano(a) artists united and defined by a shared vision: a conscious identification with Mexican/Chicano culture and an alliance with art circuits outside the mainstream.

3359 La Casa de la Raza Gallery, Santa Barbara, CA. Judithe Hernandez: virgen, madre, mujer; imagenes de la mujer chicana. Exhibition invitation [1979]. English.

AN: Invitation to an exhibit with a list of projects, murals, and exhibitions. Illustrated.

3360 Castro, Mike. Climb from barrio is tough: artist finds life a waiting game. LOS ANGELES TIMES [Central Section], (November 2, 1973), p. IV, 1+. English.

AN: Edward Carbajal, graduate of Chouinard Institute of the Arts in Valencia, has a hard time making a living. He approached the Los Angeles County Museum of Art about exhibits for Chicano artists, with no result, though the Museum says it is still interested. Illustrated.

3361 La Causa Publications, Oakland, CA. New symbols for la Nueva Raza. Exhibition announcement, [ca. 1969]. English.

AN: Announcement for exhibition of the four founding artists of the Mexican American Liberation Art Front (MALAF): Esteban Villa, Rene Yanez, Manuel Hernandez, Malaquias Montoya. Collage of portraits by the artists.

3362 La Causa Publications, Oakland, CA. Rene Yanez: paintings. Exhibition invitation, [ca. 1968]. English.

AN: Invitation to an exhibit of paintings by San Francisco artist Rene Yanez. Illustrated.

3363 Celebracion Chican-india. CAMINOS, Vol. 1, no. 3 (May 1980), p. 38-39+. English.

AN: Portfolio of works exhibited at the Galeria Capistrano in southern California: Zarco Guerrero, Domingo Ulloa, Mario Torero, Guillermo Acevedo. Judithe Hernandez, who also exhibited, is not included in the portfolio.

3364 El Centro Cultural de La Raza, San Diego, CA. Espejo del barrio-art exposition. Exhibition brochure, June 1975. English.

AN: Illustrated brochure announcement for a cultural exposition of Chicano music, art and drama. Includes some biographical information and one reproduction of painter Manuel Unzueta, woodworker Ambriz, muralist Victor Orozco Ochoa and designer/illustrator J. Armando Nunez.

Exhibits (cont.)

3365 El Centro Cultural de La Raza, San Diego,
CA. One hundred year anniversary: Jose
Guadalupe Posada, Antonio Vanegas Arroyo.
Exhibition invitation, 1980. English.

AN: Invitation to an exhibition of
Mexican engravers Posada and Manuel Manilla
and an homage to their publisher. Also, a
"Chicano Tribute to Jose Guadalupe Posada,"
with contemporary works influenced by
Posada. At the Centro, and at Southwestern
College in Chula Vista.

3366 El Centro Cultural de La Raza, San Diego,
CA. Reflexions: a Chicano-Latin art exhibit.
San Diego, CA: El Centro Cultural de la
Raza, 1978. English.

AN: Statewide art exhibit of 126 works
by 46 artists from all parts of CA.

3367 Centro Cultural Rafael Cintron Ortiz,
University of Illinois, Chicago. Alejandro
Romero. Exhibition catalog, 1978. English.

AN: Full color catalog of drawings and
paintings by Mexican-born artist living in
Chicago.

3368 Centro de Artistas Chicanos, Sacramento, CA.
La arte cosmica [sic] de Esteban Villa:
Chicano art exposition. Sacramento, CA:
Centro de Artistas Chicanos, 1973. English.

AN: Invitation to an exhibition of works
by Esteban Villa at the RCAF's center.

3369 Charles Cowles Gallery. Manuel Neri. New
York: Charles Cowles Gallery, 1981. English.

AN: Brochure for one-person show with
two color photographs of Neri's sculpture.
Exhibition chronology and bibliography.

3370 Chicago. Public Library Cultural Center,
Chicago, IL. La mujer: a visual dialogue.
Exhibition invitation, 1978. English.

AN: Invitation to an exhibit
spotlighting women artists from Mexico and
the United States. Organized by the
Movimiento Artistico Chicano (MARCH) of
Chicago. 40 paintings by women artists
included, and 50 works based on the theme of
women. Poetry readings, music, dance, film,
theatre, and panels of men and women artists
included. Illustrated by work by Linda
Vallejo.

3371 Chicano art show. EL DIARIO DE LA GENTE,
Vol. 1, no. 7 (February 6, 1973), p. 4.
English.

AN: Fine arts students at the University
of Colorado led by Rudy Fernandez hope to
educate high school students about Chicano
art. This article documents an exhibit held
at Lafayette, CO. Members of the group are
Bob Maez, Jerry Jaramillo, Anthony Mendoza,
and Rudy Fernandez. Illustrated by four
exhibition photographs by John L. Espinosa.

3372 Chicano art show at Contra Costa College. EL
HISPANO, Vol. 8, no. 25 (December 11, 1973).
English.

AN: Information on exhibition organized
by Ramses Noriega that included the work of
Jose Montoya, Esteban Villa, Mario Sinape,
Ricardo Rios, Malaquias Montoya, Fuchi
Queso, and Joe Palomino.

3373 A Chicano artist: Emigdio Vasquez. CANNERY
WORKER, Vol. 1, no. 4 (February 1977), p. 5.
Bilingual.

AN: Story on an exhibit by Esteban Villa
in the Galeria Barrios of Sacramento,
California, which is dedicated to the
Cannery Workers Committee on its eighth
anniversary. Five works by Villa are
illustrated, and a group photograph of the
Centro de Artistas Chicanos is included.

3374 Chicano artists exhibit at USC. CALENDAR,
(September 23, 1973), p. 61. English.

AN: Announcement of an exhibit of
paintings, drawings, sculpture and graphics
by artists from the Mechicano Art Center of
Los Angeles at the University of Southern
California Art Galleries. Slide
presentations of murals and supergraphics.

3375 Chicano exhibit set. SANTA FE NEW MEXICAN,
(September 22, 1972), p. A4. English.

AN: A Chicano art show organized by El
Instituto Chicano de Artes y Artesanias of
San Antonio, TX is scheduled for Highlands
University Gallery, Las Vegas, NM.

3376 Chicano Studies Library, University of
California, Berkeley and Garcia, Rupert.
Realismo: Chicano drawings by Juan Fuentes.
Berkeley, CA: Chicano Studies Library
Publications, UC Berkeley, 1976. English.

AN: Exhibition pamphlet with one drawing
by Juan Fuentes. Text situates the drawings
within artistic experiments using the
photograph as part of the artists visual
vocabulary. Different from "avant-garde new
realists," Fuentes' "Realismo Chicano" is
subjective in using selected photographs
that present a reality of struggle.

3377 CODEX NEWSLETTER (Galeria de la Raza, San
Francisco, CA). Vol. 1, no. 2 (September
1973). English.

AN: An in-house bulletin of upcoming
events: EL SOL NUNCA MUERE,
photography/poster exhibit, Rolando Garces,
and Peruvian posters; Mujeres de Aztlan,
women artists' collective exhibit;
Filipino/Samoan art exhibit; Galeria
Christmas art sale; Galeria pavilion at S.F.
annual art festival; Rockefeller scholarship
for Galeria curator Luis Santana; Galeria
coloring book; Balmy Alley mural project;
Diego Rivera exhibit; first installment of
Rupert Garcia's RAZA MURALS AND MURALISTS:
AN HISTORICAL VIEW.

3378 Coffman Gallery I, The University of
Minnesota, Minneapolis, MN. Ruben Trejo:
visiting Chicano artist. Exhibition
brochure, 1981. English.

AN: Exhibition brochure of a sculpture
show by Ruben Trejo presented from April 25
to May 6. Trejo's sculptures are created
from laminated wood, metal and plastic.
Dominant motifs in this exhibit were the
skull, the pepper and the heart. Brochure
includes biographical information, checklist
of the 28 works exhibited and one black and
white photograph.

Exhibits (cont.)

3379 La Cofradia de Artes y Artesanos Hispanicos
and Santa Fe Council for the Arts. El
festival hispanico. Festival program, [ca.
1979]. English.

AN: Program for the festival which
included over 70 visual artists from
northern New Mexico selected and hung by the
Cofradia at the Armory for the Arts gallery
in Santa Fe. The poster for the festival,
reproduced on the program cover, is taken
from a painting by Gilberto Guzman. The
festival also featured music, cuentos,
dance, slide show, poetry, films.

3380 Comite Chicanarte and Los Angeles Municipal
Art Gallery, Los Angeles, CA. Chicanarte.
Exhibition catalog, 1975. English.

AN: Catalog of an exhibit of 102
California artists. 86 illustrations of
works of art.

3381 Congreso de Artistas Chicanos en Aztlan, San
Diego, CA. Diego Rivera, David Alfaro
Siqueiros, Jose Clemente Orozco: exhibit of
local artists, La Logan [San Diego].
Exhibition brochure, n.d. [c.1974]. English.

AN: Announcement of a traveling exhibit
organized by Galeria de la Raza, San
Francisco, from the collection of the San
Francisco Museum of Art. Illustrated with a
San Diego mural.

3382 Consejo Mexicano de Fotografia, A.C., Mexico
City and Tibol, Raquel. Hecho en
Latinoamerica: primera muestra de la
fotografia latinoamericana contemporanea.
Exhibition catalog, 1978. Spanish.

AN: Catalog/book of the first colloquium
and exhibit of Latin American photography.
Among the Chicano artists in the exhibit
were Francisco X. Camplis, Louis Carlos
Bernal, Harry Gamboa, Jose P. Romero, Harvey
J. Tarango, Isabel Castro. Statements by
some of the artists. Great number of
illustrations.

3383 Consejo Mexicano de Fotografia, A.C., Mexico
City. Hecho en latinoamerica: segundo
coloquio latinoamericano de fotografia.
Exhibition catalog, 1982. Spanish.

AN: Catalog/book of the second
colloquium and exhibit of Latin American
photography. Among the Chicano artists whose
work is reproduced are Louis Carlos Bernal,
Robert C. Buitron, David Cardenas, Isabel
Castro, Harry Gamboa, Jr., Luis Garza,
Roberto Gil de Montes, John M. Valadez,
Kathy Vargas. In the exhibit were also
Porfirio Aguilar, Elsa Marie Flores, Ricardo
Valverde. Great number of illustrations. In
Spanish.

3384 Contemporary Arts Museum, Houston, TX. Dale
gas: give it gas. The continued
acceleration of Chicano art. Exhibition
catalog, 1977. English.

AN: A comprehensive catalog including 28
works of art exhibited by 13 Texas artists:
Melesio (Mel) Casas, Jose Esquivel,
Francisco (Frank) Fajardo, Carmen Lomas
Garza, Luis Jimenez, Cesar Augusto Martinez,
Santos G. Martinez, Jr., Amado Pena, Roberto
Rios, Jose Rivera, Joe B. Rodriguez, Jesus
(Jesse) Trevino, and George Truan. Many
illustrations, some in color. Introduction
by James Harithas. Essay by Santos Martinez,

Jr. Poetry, literature and essays by Chicano
writers.

3385 Contemporary Arts Museum, Houston, TX. Fire!
An exhibition of 100 Texas artists.
Exhibition brochure, 1979. English.

AN: Includes eleven Chicano artists.
Unfortunately, not illustrated, though a
checklist of works is included. Mel Casas,
Carmen Lomas Garza, Xavier Gorena, Luis
Jimenez, Cesar Martinez, Guillermo Z.
Pulido, Philip Renteria, Jose L. Rivera, Joe
Rodriguez, George Truan, Juan B. Vela.
Introduction by James Surls. Statements by
the artists.

3386 Contemporary Arts Museum, Houston, TX and
Harithas, James. Luis Jimenez: Progress I.
Exhibition catalog, 1974-75. English.

AN: Catalog for a major exhibit of
Jimenez sculptures, drawings and studies for
sculptural works from 1967 to 1974. The
latest project, PROGRESS, involves a series
of monumental sculptures depicting the
history of the West. Jimenez combines social
comment with advanced plastic values. Well
illustrated.

3387 Contemporary Arts Museum, Houston, TX and
Martinez, Santos G., Jr. Mexican movie
posters. Exhibition invitation, 1979.
English.

AN: Invitation to an exhibit of posters
primarily from the collecttion of Enrique
Flores and Xavier Gorena of Xochil Art
Center, Mission, Texas. Martinez considers
the posters monumental, with expressive
qualities that have influenced Chicano
poster makers like the Royal Chicano Air
Force, and Rupert Garcia, and Texas artists
like Luis Jimenez, Jesse Trevino and Cesar
Martinez. One illustration. Introduction by
guest curator Santos G. Martinez, Jr. (See
Rupert Garcia's essay in the exhibition
catalog: POSTERS FROM THE GOLDEN AGE OF
MEXICAN CINEMA, for another point of view).

3388 Corcoran Gallery of Art, Washington, D.C.
Images of an era: the American poster
1945-75. Washington, D.C.: Corcoran Gallery
of Art, 1976. English.

AN: Uncredited poster [La Raza
Silkscreen Center, San Francisco],
(centerfold). Posters by Rupert Garcia,
Linda Lucero, and Ralph Maradiaga, all of
San Francisco, CA. Introduction by John
Garriga. Essays by Margaret Cogswell, Milton
Glaser, Dore Ashton, Alan Gowens.

3389 Corpus Christy State University for the Arts
and Weil Gallery Center for the Arts, Corpus
Christi State University. Southwest artists
invitational: an exhibition of contemporary
art by seven Texas artists of Hispanic
American descent. Ehxibition brochure, 1980.
English.

AN: Artists Jesse Almazan, Luis Jimenez,
Cesar Martinez, Lydia Martinez, Manuel
Mauricio, Guillermo Pulido, and Jesse
Trevino show a variety of techniques and
styles. Text by Roberto Tomas Esparza.
Statements by and about the artists.
Illustrated.

Exhibits (cont.)

3390 Craft and Folk Art Museum, Los Angeles, CA
and Shapira, Nathan. From flat to form: Ben
Gurule and Carlo Cattaneo. Exhibition
catalog, 1978. English.

AN: Catalog for an exhibit by Los
Angeles Chicano artist Ben Gurule and
Italian artist Cattaneo, both involved with
three-dimensional expression in paper.
Gurule's works examine the interwoven
families of waves, polygons, and circles,
exploring relationships between geometry,
wave mechanics and quantum mechanics. Well
illustrated.

3391 Crossley, Mimi. Tejano artists. HOUSTON
POST, (August 19, 1976). English.

AN: Exhibition of 19 Texas artists
organized by Joe Rodriguez of the AAMA
(Association for the Advancement of Mexican
Americans) Art Center in Houston, Texas.
Working within a wide range of styles and a
great scope of subject matter. Includes
brief commentary on the work of Amado Pena,
Carmen Lomas Garza, Cesar Martinez, Enrique
Campos, Carolina Flores, Jesus Trevino and a
host of others.

3392 Curtis, Cathy. Six aspiring watercolorists.
SUNDAY MAGAZINE [Supplement to CONTRA COSTA
COUNTY TIMES, CA], (October 14, 1979), p.
19. English.

AN: In a recent show at the Richmond Art
Center (Calif.), David Gallegos was one of
the watercolorists. Working in a traditional
modernist style, Gallegos deals with light
and air in his views of the waterfront.

3393 Day, Orman. Hispanic life mirrored by ethnic
artists. THE REGISTER, (July 5, 1981), p.
B1+. English.

AN: Story on artists Manuel Hernandez
Trujillo and Emigdio Vasquez whose work
opened the new Galeria in Santa Ana, and
poet Manuel Gomez. Color illustrations.

3394 De Lappe, Pele. Gordo plus folk art.
PEOPLE'S WORLD, Vol. 42, no. 41 (October 13,
1979), p. 10. English.

AN: Announcement of an exhibit at the
Mexican Museum of Gus Arriola's syndicated
comic strip "Gordo." Arizona-born Arriola
was an animator for Columbia and MGM
cartoons until he created "Gordo" in 1941.
Illustrated.

3395 De Marroquin, Moron. Arte negativo en
exposicion. LA PRENSA, Vol. 1, no. 18
(September 18, 1978). Spanish.

AN: Florida-born Jesus G. Moron produces
art within the canons of surrealism and
mystical art. Strongly influenced by ancient
cultures like those of the Mayas, Olmecs and
"Lemurians". Illustrated with an ink on
paper drawing titled CAIDA DEL CONSCIENTE.

3396 De Marroquin, Moron. Denver Harbor artists.
LA PRENSA, (June 2, 1978). Spanish.

AN: Commentary on two exhibitions. THE
DENVER HARBOR ARTISTS includes information
on paintings by Lupe Aguirre, Josie Mendoza
and Abel Gonzalez--all from Houston. The
solo show MAGIC BLANCA featured the work of
Brownsville, Texas artist Jorge Truan.
Truan's work is mystical and visionary.

3397 Diseno Studios, Austin, TX. Diseno Studios
Gallery. Brochure, 1981. English.

3398 Dittmar Memorial Gallery, Northwestern
University, Evanston, IL and King, Elaine A.
Alejandro Romero: new works. Exhibit
catalog, 1981. English.

AN: Full color illustrated catalog of
paintings by the Mexican-born artist who has
been living in the United States since the
early 1970s. His images appear to be
grounded in the work of Bosch, Goya,
Brueghel, and Diego Rivera. There is a
synthesis of personal symbolism and
expressionism.

3399 Documentary to include work by Cuate Santos.
LAREDO NEWS, (July 17, 1980). English.

AN: Photography by Laredo News
photographer Cuate Santos included in
exhibit "Un encuentro sin palabras," a
documentary show on Mexican American life in
Texas sponsored by Mujeres Artistas del
Suroeste (MAS). The state-wide show was
juried by Los Angeles photographer Isabel
Castro. Illustrated.

3400 Donnell-Kotrozo, Carol. Containment and
discovery. ARTWEEK, Vol. 11, no. 41
(December 6, 1980), p. 12. English.

AN: Review of an exhibit at Scottsdale,
Arizona gallery, C.G. Rein by Rudy
Fernandez. Discussed in detail is one of his
altar-like boxes of mixed media which
contain personal symbolisms. Illustrated.

3401 Doty, Robert. Human concern/personal
torment: the grotesque in American art. New
York: Praeger, 1969. English.

AN: Acknowledging the revival of realism
after fifty years of abstraction, the
Whitney Museum of American Art in New York
mounted a controversial show of modern and
contemporary painters and sculptors. Two
sculptures and a drawing by Luis Jimenez
were included, one of which, THE AMERICAN
DREAM, (1968) is illustrated.

3402 Dougherty Arts Center, Austin, TX. From the
fringe: artists choose artists. Exhibition
catalog, 1981. English.

AN: Catalog of an exhibit featuring
eight women artists, including Santa Barraza
of Austin. Barraza also designed the
catalog.

3403 Dreva & Gronk exhibit at L.A.C.E.: Gronkart
live; Bonbon returns. Exhibition invitation,
1978. English.

AN: Illustrated invitation/poster to
exhibit of Asco's Gronk, and Jerry Dreva, a
collaborative show featuring ten years of
work:photos, correspondence, documents,
ephemera and other art.

Exhibits (cont.)

3404 Dunham, Judith L. Manuel Neri: life with the figure. ARTWEEK, Vol. 7, no. 39 (November 13, 1976), p. 1+. English.

AN: Favorable review of Neri's exhibition of more than 80 figures or fragments of figures at the Oakland Museum. Explores relationship of Neri's sculpture with developments in Bay Area figurative painting and expressionism. Inventories Neri's thematic and material concerns. Analysis of his work in plaster, bronze and fiberglass. An important assessment of Neri's contribution to Bay Area art.

3405 Elaine Horwitch Galleries, Santa Fe, NM. New Mexico woodcarving. Exhibition catalog, 1980. English.

AN: Invitation to an exhibit at the Horwitch galleries of Scottsdale, Arizona, and Santa Fe, NM of sculptors Felipe Archuleta, Leroy Archuleta, Frank Brito, Alonso Jimenez, Horatio Valdez, and others. Illustration.

3406 Electro Arts Gallery, San Francisco, CA. Electric realizations: an exhibition by Rene Yanez & Carl Heyward. Exhibition invitation, 1981. English.

AN: Invitation to an exhibit of color Xerox prints by Rene Yanez, Co-director of the Galeria de la Raza of San Francisco. Yanez feels that Xerox has opened new frontiers in presenting graphic work at a different scale and size.

3407 Encanto Pavilion, Encanto Park, Phoenix, AZ. Exposicion de arte para la raza: Arizona Chicano art show. Exhibition catalog, [ca. 1978]. English.

AN: Catalog for an exhibit organized by MARS (Movimiento Artistico del Rio Salado). Colombian-born Antonio L. Tocora, Jim Covarrubias, Ed Dias, Robert C. Buitron, Armando Leon Hernandez, Guillermo Galindo, Richard Luna Cisneros, Jose Andres Giron, Robert L. Matta included.

3408 Espejo: reflections of the Mexican American: Louis Carlos Bernal, Morrie Camhi, Abigail Heyman, Roger Minick, Neal Slavin. SOMOS, Vol. 2, no. 1 (February 1978), p. 26-35. English.

AN: Announcement of the ESPEJO photographic exhibit to be held at Goez Gallery in East Los Angeles. Statements by the four artists and a portfolio of their works: Abigail Heyman, Roger Minick, Morrie Camhi, and Arizona Chicano photographer Louis Carlos Bernal. Includes color photographs by Bernal on cover. This 1979 issue is erroneously dated 1978.

3409 Exhibit at UCSD: Chicana artist to show works. LOS ANGELES TIMES [San Diego County edition], (December 6, 1978), p. II, 8. English.

AN: Artist and activist from San Diego, Yolanda Lopez, will be showing sketches and paintings at the Mandeville Center, University of California, San Diego, from which she was the first Chicana to graduate with a Master's degree in visual arts. Her show is based on her family, and the icon of the Virgin of Guadalupe. Illustrated.

3410 Exploratorium, Student Union, California

State University, Los Angeles. An exhibit of published prints of Aztlan Multiples. Exhibition catalog, 1981. English.

AN: The published silkscreen prints of Aztlan Multiples, a small business run by Richard Duardo of Los Angeles, features works by Duardo, John Valadez, and Carlos Almaraz, among others. Illustrations.

3411 Exploratorium, Student Union, California State University, Los Angeles. Herron/Gronk in ILLEGAL LANDSCAPE. Exhibition catalog, 1980. English.

AN: Invitation to a "performance" piece NO MOVIE by Willie Herron and Gronk, two members of ASCO. Illustrated.

3412 Exxon Company, Houston, TX and Quirarte, Jacinto. Chicano art of the barrio. Exhibition brochure, n.d. [c.1976]. English.

AN: Brochure for a traveling exhibit of photographically-reproduced Chicano murals: Leo Limon, Lucila Villasenor Grijalva, Antonio Esparza, Susan Saenz, Charles Felix, Hoyo-Mara gang, David A. Lopez and team, Roberto Chavez and team (Los Angeles); Jerry Concha, Ruben Guzman, Chuy Campusano (San Francisco); Manuel Unzueta (Santa Barbara). Ernie Palomino and Leo Esequiel Ozona (Fresno). Leo Tanguma (Houston), Roberto Lucero, Manuel Martinez and Al Sanchez (Denver).

3413 Fabricant, Don. Show reveals Hispanic art. NEW MEXICAN WEEKEND, (June 1, 1979). English.

AN: Review of two exhibits in Santa Fe: EL FESTIVAL HISPANICO, mounted by La Cofradia de Artes y Artesanos Hispanicos and Gilberto Guzman at the Black Kachina Gallery. The reviewer feels the traditional-style woodcarving done by contemporaries is the strongest part of the show; works that break with these forms seem weaker, less skillful and cliche-ridden. Crafts are excellent. Muralist Guzman has blossomed in murals and easel paintings since he was employed by the 1978 Art in Public Places project. His work is intense and expressive, sometimes erotic. Illustration of work by sculptor Ruben Montoya.

3414 La Familia Recreation Center, Denver, CO. Mural unveiling and swim party. Exhibition invitation, 1980. English.

AN: Invitation to the unveiling of La Familia Cosmica, a mural by Jerry Jaramillo assisted by Carlos Sandoval, Al Sanchez, Stephen Lucero. An art exhibit featured the muralists, Jon Howe, and Fred Sanchez, all of the Metro Denver Urban Coalition's City Walls artists. Illustrated.

3415 'Fashion Moda' at Galeria de la Raza. PEOPLE'S WORLD, Vol. 44, no. 48 (November 29, 1981), p. 10. English.

AN: A joint exhibit, FASHION MODA AT GALERIA DE LA RAZA, focuses on people interested in cross-cultural interaction. 50 artists from the San Francisco Bay Area, the South Bronx, Los Angeles, and New York City were shown. Fashion Moda is located in the South Bronx, an area of severe urban devastation. Illustrated.

Exhibits (cont.)

3416 Figoten, Sheldon. Building and painting the
     figure. ARTWEEK, Vol. 12, no. 22 (June 20,
     1981), p. 5-6. English.

     AN: Review of eight sculptures and 25
     drawings by Manuel Neri at the Redding Art
     Museum. Neri was influenced as a student in
     the San Francisco Bay Area in the 1950s by
     abstract expressionist philosophy and
     methodology, which he transferred to
     sculpture. Plaster, bronze, and marble
     figures are freely and loosely painted in
     areas. Illustration.

3417 Fine Arts Gallery, California State
     University, Los Angeles and Goldberg, Aron.
     Edward Carrillo: selected works, 1960-1975.
     Exhibition catalog, 1975. English.

     AN: Catalog of exhibit covering fifteen
     years of this California figurative
     painter's work. Eight illustrations,
     including one in color. (A printing error
     reproduced the same illustrations twice.).

3418 Fine Arts Society of San Diego, CA. The
     cross and the sword. Exhibition catalog,
     1976. Bilingual.

     AN: Bi-lingual exhibition catalog of
     Southwestern art forms; santero art,
     vernacular architecture and traditional folk
     art. Important essays by experts in each
     field. Contains an iconographical summary of
     santos and a good bibliography. Profusely
     illustrated.

3419 First Federal Plaza Display Gallery, Austin,
     TX. Tejano artists: an exhibit of
     Mexican-American art. Exhibit brochure,
     1976. English.

     AN: Announcement of exhibit illustrated
     by Cesar A. Martinez's woodcut.

3420 The First Unitarian Universalist Church,
     Paradise Valley, AZ. Five Chicano artists.
     Exhibition brochure, 1971. English.

     AN: Exhibit organized by L. Eugene
     Grigsby, Jr., Art Department of Arizona
     State University, Tempe, AZ. 21 works by
     Eugene Quesada, David Nunez, Fernando
     Navarro, Luis Baiz (of Arizona) and Saul
     Solache (of Los Angeles). Brief biographies
     of the artists.

3421 Five views on Mexican culture. LA JOLLA
     LIGHT, (September 10, 1981), p. B-6.
     English.

     AN: Review of a show at the University
     of California, San Diego's Mandeville Art
     Gallery called FIVE PHOTOGRAPHERS:
     CONTEMPORARY VIEWS OF MEXICAN AND
     MEXICAN-AMERICAN CULTURE and featuring
     Arizona photographers Louis Carlos Bernal,
     Robert C. Buitron, and three others.

3422 Flaco, Eduardo. Chicanismo en el arte.
     ARTWEEK, Vol. 6, no. 20 (May 17, 1975), p.
     3. English.

     AN: Review of competitive exhibition
     composed of Chicano artists between
     seventeen and twenty-six from Los Angeles
     colleges, universities and art schools.
     Focuses on work of ASCO, the only noteworthy
     art in the show, according to the critic.

3423 Fondo del Sol, Washington, D.C. Raices
     antiguas/visiones nuevas; ancient roots/new
     visions. Exhibition catalog, 1977. English.

     AN: Well illustrated catalog of
     traveling exhibition featuring Latin
     American and Latino artists living in the
     United States. Supplemental regional
     catalogs of local artists.

3424 Fong, Katheryn M. Pachuco art records era of
     zootsuits and anti-Mexican riots. SAN
     FRANCISCO JRNL, Vol. 2, no. 32 (March 1,
     1978), p. 6. English.

     AN: Review of Galeria de la Raza exhibit
     of Jose Montoya's Pachuco Art. Installation
     included historical photographs and
     documents. Montoya work (drawings and
     paintings) were contextualized by written
     commentary aiming to re-interpret an
     important aspect of Chicano cultural
     history.

3425 Forest Home Library, Milwaukee, WI. Arte
     chicano de Carlos Rosas, Chicano muralist.
     Exhibition invitation, 1978. English.

     AN: Invitation to an exhibit by Carlos
     Rosas [originally from El Paso, TX] who has
     created murals with Chicano themes in many
     parts of the United States. Sponsored by El
     Taller Obrero Cultural de Milwaukee.

3426 Four and four: Mexican and Latino
     photography, April 25 through June 14 on the
     balcony. CALENDAR: SANTA BARBARA MUSEUM OF
     ART, (April 1981). English.

     AN: Announcement of exhibit organized by
     Lorenzo Hernandez of the Cityscape Foto
     Gallery, Pasadena, Calif. Sought to present
     "the observable differences between the
     'classic' vision of the Mexican National and
     the 'realistic' vision of the re-rooted
     Mexican/American." The latter included Louis
     Bernal (Tucson) and Ricardo Valverde (Los
     Angeles) as well as two Spanish Sephardics
     of Los Angeles, Camhi and Sisco.

3427 Los Four exhibit in Union Gallery.
     UNIVERSITY TIMES, (November 6, 1975), p. 4.
     English.

     AN: "Los Four," a group of four Chicano
     artists - Frank Romero, Roberto "Beto" de la
     Rocha, Gilbert Lujan, and Carlos Almaraz,
     with newcomer Judithe Hernandez - work with
     political cartoons, Catholic symbols, works
     of sardonic humor. They also paint street
     murals: several have been done recently in
     Los Angeles, La Puente, and Long Beach.
     Illustrated.

3428 Frankenstein, Alfred. An artistic taste of
     Mexico in the city. SAN FRANCISCO CHRONICLE,
     (November 29, 1975), p. 29. English.

     AN: A very favorable review of the
     inaugural exhibit at the Mexican Museum. The
     opening show was a panoramic view of Mexican
     art including pre-Hispanic, colonial, folk
     art and fine art. Among the Mexican American
     artists presented were Roberto Gonzalez,
     Raul Mora and Gustavo Rivera.

Exhibits (cont.)

3429 Frankenstein, Alfred. At the museum: when politics and art do mix. SAN FRANCISCO CHRONICLE, (March 15, 1978), p. 54. English.

AN: Glowing review of exhibit at the San Francisco Museum of Modern Art by Rupert Garcia who, the critic says, has a genius for saying the essential thing without a line, a gesture or a touch of color more than necessary. Illustrated.

3430 Frankenstein, Alfred. Just for the record. SAN FRANCISCO CHRONICLE, (May 27, 1976), p. 48. English.

AN: Positive review of exhibit at the Mexican Museum featuring the work of Jesus Reyes Ferreira from Mexico and Gustavo Rivera from San Francisco. Ninety-five-year-old Ferreira uses tempera on tissue paper to render brilliant paintings focusing on Mexican folk motifs. Rivera paints in the abstract expressionist mode with power and passion. Article also lauds the photographic work of Angel del Valle in his exhibition: SEMBRADORES at the Galeria de la Raza.

3431 Frankenstein, Alfred. A long-range view of Latino art: at the UC Art Museum. SAN FRANCISCO CHRONICLE, (October 15, 1977), p. 34. English.

AN: Controversial critical review of the exhibit THE FIFTH SUN: CONTEMPORARY TRADITIONAL CHICANO & LATINO ART.

3432 Frankenstein, Alfred. Montoya's artistic update on Chicano zoot suiters. SAN FRANCISCO CHRONICLE, (February 18, 1978), p. 36. English.

AN: Review of Pachuco show at San Francisco's Galeria de la Raza, especially Jose Montoya's sketches and paintings.

3433 Frankenstein, Alfred. Prison's artist in residence. SAN FRANCISCO CHRONICLE, (May 5, 1978), p. 60. English.

AN: Review of the exhibition MUNDOS PERDIDOS, curated at the Galeria de la Raza by Leonard Castellanos. Show consisted of work by Castellanos and inmates at Lompoc Federal Correctional Institution near Santa Barbara. Documents a prison mural, tattoos and silkscreen prints with socially critical themes.

3434 Frankenstein, Alfred. A senior senor's approach. SAN FRANCISCO CHRONICLE, (May 27, 1976), p. 48. English.

AN: Review of an exhibit of Mexican painter Jesus Reyes Ferreira at the Mexican Museum of San Francisco, as well as that of San Francisco artist Gustavo Rivera, an abstract expressionist painter. Also mentions the Museum's mural map, and Angel del Valle's photography show at the Galeria de la Raza.

3435 Friendly Center, Inc., Orange, CA / Galeria. The last Chicano art show. Exhibition brochure, 1981. English.

AN: Exhibit of 15 artists from Los Angeles and Orange Counties at the inauguration of the Galeria in Santa Ana, California. Statement and list of sponsors.

3436 From the barrios. OBSERVER, (September 23, 1979), p. 16+. English.

AN: Short story on Gilberto Guzman from Santa Fe, New Mexico, announcing an exhibit of his work in the October Gallery, London. Two color reproductions of his paintings.

3437 Fuegos en Aztlan (fires in Aztlan): a Chicano arts show. Unpublished program, 1980. English.

AN: Program for a Chicano arts event, including an art show of 23 artists working in all media. Unpublished program.

3438 Gala evening at OAS. NUESTRO, Vol. 5, no. 7 (October 1981), p. 21. English.

AN: Brief description of "Salute to Hispanic Arts" held as part of Hispanic Heritage Week festivities in Washington, D.C. Special guest at the affair was Amado Pena who was there to be recognized and to unveil his work LA FAMILIA which was used on the posters announcing Hispanic Heritage Week nationwide.

3439 Galeria Almazan, Inc., San Antonio, TX. Ray Chavez. Exhibition flyer, 1959. English.

AN: Single page flyer announcement for a one-man exhibition by Ray Chavez (born 1938 in San Antonio). Includes a photograph of the artist and a list of awards and exhibitions.

3440 Galeria Almazan, Inc., San Antonio, TX. Ray Chavez. Exhibition catalog, 1968. English.

AN: Exhibition catalog with biographical information on San Antonio painter Ray Chavez.

3441 Galeria Capistrano, San Juan Capistrano, CA. Celebracion Chican-india 1980: Acevedo, Hernandez, Torero, Ulloa, Zarco. Exhibition brochure, 1980. English.

AN: Exhibition of Chicano artists Judithe Hernandez, Domingo Ulloa, El Zarco Guerrero, and Peruvian-born artists Guillermo Acevedo and Mario Acevedo Torero. Color illustration by Torero.

3442 Galeria de la Raza, San Antonio, TX. Celebration seventy-four. Exhibition catalog, [ca. 1974]. English.

AN: Catalog of extensive exhibition including European, Mexican, and the following Texan Chicano artists: Rolando Garces, Cesar Martinez, Ray Chavez, Vicente Rodriguez, Jorge Garza, Alfred Rodriguez, Luis Guerra, Carmen Lomas Garza, Bruno Andrade, Jr., Amado M. Pena Jr., Roberto Rios, Jose Trevino, Rudy Trevino, Luis Santoyo, Tati Rubio, Eduardo C. Garza, Arthur de la Fuente, and Jesus Campos Trevino.

3443 Galeria de la Raza/Studio 24, San Francisco, CA. 2001: a group exhibit of mixed media. Exhibit invitation, n.d. English.

AN: Invitation to an exhibit featuring the work of 40 artists.

Exhibits (cont.)

3444 Galeria de la Raza/Studio 24, San Francisco, CA. Ajo, granadas y tres flores. Exhibition announcement, 1981.

AN: Announcement for an exhibition featuring Ruben Trejo, sculpture (Spokane, Washington), Cesar A. Martinez, paintings (San Antonio, Texas), Xavier Gorena, paper cut-outs (Mission, Texas).

3445 Galeria de la Raza/Studio 24, San Francisco, CA. Blanca Flor Gutierrez - oil pastels. Exhibition announcement, 1981.

AN: Color xeroxed announcement for a window display of oil pastels by Gutierrez.

3446 Galeria de la Raza/Studio 24, San Francisco, CA. Calacas huesudas. Exhibition brochure, 1980.

AN: Exhibition of Chicano artists for El Dia de los Muertos with brochure using text adapted from POSADA'S MEXICO, edited by Ron Tyler, Library of Congress, Washington, D.C., 1979. The Galeria exhibit was curated by Kate Connell, Maria Pinedo and Galeria staff.

3447 Galeria de la Raza/Studio 24, San Francisco, CA. Canto a Cuba. Exhibition invitation, [1974]. English.

AN: Invitation to an exhibit of prints, posters, paintings and drawings by two Cuban artists.

3448 Galeria de la Raza/Studio 24, San Francisco, CA and Milkie, Anne. Carnaval '80. Exhibition catalog, 1980. English.

AN: Catalog of an exhibit of photographs and other media recording San Francisco's multi-ethnic CARNAVAL, organized in 1978 by Panamanian-born dancer. Included in the exhibit were the photographs of Chicana Maria V. Pinedo, who also designed the catalog.

3449 Galeria de la Raza/Studio 24, San Francisco, CA and Garcia, Rupert. Community art-murals: an exhibition of original drawings, sketches, and designs. Exhibition brochure, 1978. English.

AN: The current crisis of contemporary art is relatively resolved by community-based muralists who engage themselves against repressive forces as artists, organizers, propagandists. However, art and politics are not identical, though they may overlap. Color xerox illustrations of murals.

3450 Galeria de la Raza/Studio 24, San Francisco, CA. Dia de los muertos/day of the dead. Exhibition invitation, 1981. English.

AN: Invitation to the Galeria's annual Dia de los Muertos exhibition.

3451 Galeria de la Raza/Studio 24, San Francisco, CA. Homenaje a Frida Kahlo. Exhibition brochure, 1978.

AN: 51 artists, Chicano and non-Chicano.

3452 Galeria de la Raza/Studio 24, San Francisco, CA; Sorell, Victor A.; and Vaughan, Kay. Images of the Mexican Revolution: photographs by Agustin V. Casasola. Exhibition catalog, 1980. English.

AN: Catalog of an exhibit of Mexican photographer Agustin V. Casasola from prints owned by the Martinezes of Lansing, MI. The exhibit traveled to Raza galleries in many parts of the United States. Illustrated.

3453 Galeria de la Raza/Studio 24, San Francisco, CA. Images of the Southwest. Exhibition catalog, 1977. English.

AN: Invitation/catalog for an exhibit including Rudy M. Fernandez(Utah), Enrique Flores(Texas), Xavier Gorena(Texas), C.A.[Cesar] Martinez(Texas), Santos Martinez, Jr.(Texas), Pedro Rodriguez(Texas), Arnold Trujillo(New Mexico). Block prints, paper cut-outs, drawings, photographs, copper enamels, and sculpture were shown. Five illustrations.

3454 Galeria de la Raza/Studio 24, San Francisco, CA and Franco, Jean. Juan Fuentes y Rupert Garcia: posters, drawings, prints. Exhibition catalog, 1975. English.

AN: Catalog of an exhibit. Illustrated with drawings and posters.

3455 Galeria de la Raza/Studio 24, San Francisco, CA. Licita Fernandez (watercolor paintings), Pete Davalos (ceramic pots). Exhibition invitation, 1981. English.

AN: Invitation to an exhibit.

3456 Galeria de la Raza/Studio 24, San Francisco, CA. "Low 'n slow": checking out low rider art. Exhibition invitation, 1979. English.

AN: Invitation to an exhibit of drawings, photographs, and graphics. Participation by LOWRIDER MAGAZINE and local car and bike clubs.

3457 Galeria de la Raza/Studio 24, San Francisco, CA. Mexican film poster (1943-71): an exhibition/exhibicion de fotos/cartelones del cine mexicano. Exhibition invitation, 1971. English.

AN: Invitation to an exhibit.

3458 Galeria de la Raza/Studio 24, San Francisco, CA. Mundos perdidos/lost worlds. Exhibition invitation, 1978. English.

AN: Invitatiion to a multi-media exhibit from a cultural workshop inside Lompoc Federal Correctional Institution by Leonard Castellanos, National Endowment for the Arts Artist in Residence. Included are murals and tattoo documentation, and silkscreen posters.

3459 Galeria de la Raza/Studio 24, San Francisco, CA. Otra onda (the other wave): an exhibition of the Mission scene. Exhibition invitation, [1981]. English.

AN: Invitation to an exhibit.

3460 Galeria de la Raza/Studio 24, San Francisco, CA. Photographs by Angel Del Valle. Los sembradores: the marijuana growers. Exhibition catalog, 1976. English.

AN: Illustrated catalog. Del Valle documents the growing, customs, and merchandising of marijuana in the Sierras of Mexico.

Exhibits (cont.)

3461 Galeria de la Raza/Studio 24, San Francisco, CA. Por Chile: silkscreens from President Allende cultural campaign. Exhibition invitation, [1973]. English.

AN: Invitation to an exhibit: the first U.S. showing of Chilean posters.

3462 Galeria de la Raza/Studio 24, San Francisco, CA and Garcia, Rupert. Posters from the golden age of Mexican cinema. Exhibition catalog, 1979. English.

AN: The Galeria's second exhibit of Mexican movie posters features those of the 1940s and early 1950s (in 1971, the exhibit covered 1943-1971) from the collection of Enrique Flores, owner of the Rio Theatre, Mission, Texas, and the Xochil Art Center. Garcia's essay includes a history of Mexican cinema, and the mythologizing period of the "Golden Age" reflected in the posters which promoted movie-consumership. One illustration. (See Santos G. Martinez, Jr.'s essay in the exhibition catalog: MEXICAN MOVIE POSTERS, for another point of view).

3463 Galeria de la Raza/Studio 24, San Francisco, CA. Published prints of Hecho en Aztlan Multiples. Exhibition announcement, 1980. English.

AN: Announcement of exhibit of the published silkscreen prints of Hecho en Aztlan Multiples; a small business run by Richard Duardo of Los Angeles.

3464 Galeria de la Raza/Studio 24, San Francisco, CA and Garcia, Rupert. La Raza Silkscreen Center: "Images of a community", an exhibit of silkscreen posters and graphic works from 1971 to 1979. Exhibition catalog, 1979. English.

AN: First large scale retrospective exhibit of the La Raza Silkscreen Center's eight years of postermaking. Includes list of 90 artists.

3465 Galeria de la Raza/Studio 24, San Francisco, CA. Royal Chicano Air Force presents "Chicanos del Valle Tortilla Opening". Exhibition invitation, 1971. English.

3466 Galeria de la Raza/Studio 24, San Francisco, CA and Lomas Garza, Carmen. Self-portraits by Chicano and Latino artists. Exhibition catalog, 1980. English.

AN: Catalog of a national exhibition by 66 artists. Gives names, residence, date of birth, and information on the work shown for each of the artists. 45 are from California, and 3 each from Puerto Rico, Arizona, New York, 9 from Texas, 2 from Washington, 1 from Virginia. 9 are women.

3467 Galeria de la Raza/Studio 24, San Francisco, CA. Third world women arts exhibit: literary, performing & visual arts. Exhibition invitation [1971]. English.

AN: Invitation to an exhibit.

3468 Galeria Museo - new art gallery opens in the Mission. EL TECOLOTE, Vol. 8, no. 1 (September 1977), p. 8. Bilingual.

AN: Brief article on the inauguration of the Art Gallery at the Mission Cultural Center. The opening Exhibit (August 13, 1977) was entitled SIXTY-THREE SHOW and included work in various media by Sixty three Bay Area Latino artists. Gilberto Osorio was designated as the first artist-in-residence. Information on future plans for the Galeria-Museo.

3469 Galeria Museo, Mission Cultural Center, San Francisco, CA and Rodriguez, Patricia. Patricia Rodriguez: simbolos y fantasias culturales. Exhibition catalog, 1981. English.

AN: Catalog of an exhibition of sculpture and painting. Autobiographical information about the Texas-born artist who lives in San Francisco and was a co-founder of Mujeres Muralistas. She explains her techniques in making portrait masks of Chicano/a artists in plaster and mixed media. Well illustrated.

3470 Galeria Museo, Mission Cultural Center, San Francisco, CA. La sirena y el nopal: Graciela Carrillo - Juan R. Fuentes. An exhibition of paintings, drawings, and graphics. Exhibition catalog, 1981. English.

AN: Invitation/catalog for an exhibit. Includes reproductions and statements by the two San Francisco artists. Well illustrated.

3471 Galeria Otra Vez, Los Angeles, CA. Inner/urban landscapes: Ricardo Valverde, Suda House, David Feldman. Exhibition invitation, 1979. English.

AN: Invitation to a photography exhibition held at Self-Help Graphic's gallery.

3472 Galeria Otra Vez, Los Angeles, CA. Rosemary Quesada-Weiner, Mary McNally: a photographic exhibition. Exhibition invitation, [1981]. English.

AN: Invitation to an exhibition including Chicana photographer Quesada-Weiner. Illustrated.

3473 Galeria, Santa Ana, CA. Diez anos con Emigdio (ten years with Emigdio), works by Emigdio Vasquez: 1971-1981. Exhibition invitation, 1982.

AN: Invitation to exhibit by Emigdio Vasquez. Illustrated.

3474 Galeria, Santa Ana, CA. Egg-sploration: a comprehensive exhibit by Art & Ben Valenzuela. Exhibition invitation, 1981. English.

AN: Invitation to an exhibit of two Orange County, CA artists in a new Chicano-run gallery. Illustrated with work of art by Art Valenzuela.

3475 Galeria, Santa Ana, CA. The last Chicano art show. Exhibition brochure, 1981. English.

AN: Invitation-brochure for an exhibit of Los Angeles and Orange County artists in a gallery underwritten by the Friendly Center, Inc. with grants from local government and from businesses. Exhibiting are (Roberto) Gil de Montes, Gilbert Lujan, Judy Miranda, Patricia Murillo, Alonso Pardo, Teddy Sandoval, Mexican artist Artemio Sepulveda, Joey Terrill, Art Valenzuela, Ben Valenzuela, Linda Vallejo, Jack A. Vargas, Emigdio Vasquez, Richard Serrato, and J. William Hernandez, who is the gallery director.

Exhibits (cont.)

their future plans.

3476 Galeria Tonantzin, Centro Cultural de LUCHA, Austin, TX. Mexican faces in San Antonio. Exhibition brochure, [1980]. English.

AN: Photography show by 24 young Chicanos from Texas sponsored by the Secretaria de Relaciones Exteriores and the Universidad Autonoma de Mexico, Cultural Extension program (SRE-UNAM) in San Antonio.

3477 Galeria Tonantzin, Centro Cultural de LUCHA, Austin, TX. Visiones Chicanas: images and demonstrations by Chicana and Latina visual artists. Exhibition invitation, 1979. English.

AN: Invitational poster for an exhibit and a series of workshops organized by Mujeres Artistas del Suroeste (MAS), affiliated with LUCHA, League of United Chicano Artists of Austin, TX.

3478 Galeria Tonantzin, Centro Cultural de LUCHA, Austin, TX. Young Chicano photographers from throughout Texas. Exhibition brochure, n.d. English.

AN: This exhibition is the collection of the winners of the contest (by the same name) sponsored by the Extension Cultural SRE-UNAM in San Antonio. Photographers represented were: Grace Alvarez, David Cardenas, Hector Cardenas, Stephen Casanova, Ronald Cortez, Raul Espinosa, Felix Almanza, Carolina Flores, David Garza Perez, Xavier Garza, Conrad Guerra, Melinda Hasbrook, Juan Jose de Hoyes, Beverly Kennon, Art Moreno, David Perez, Isabelle Purden, Patricia Santell, Nancy de los Santos, Jose Soria, Richard Tichich, Kathy Vargas, Vivian Yaten, and Johnny Zamarria.

3479 Galerias Paco, New York, NY. Consuelo Gonzalez Amezcua - filigree art. Exhibition announcement, n.d. English.

AN: Two-page exhibition announcement illustrated with two examples of the Texas artist's "filigree art" and a sample of her poetry.

3480 Gallery Sanchez, San Francisco, CA. Xerox art: an exhibit of local color xerox artists. Exhibition invitation, 1981. English.

AN: Invitation to an exhibit featuring Rene Yanez and eight other artists working in color Xerox.

3481 Gamboa, Harry, Jr. Los murales de Aztlan. COMUNIDAD, (June 28, 1981), p. 8-9+. Spanish.

AN: Review of the exhibit at the Craft and Folk Art Museum of Los Angeles of MURALS OF AZTLAN: THE STREET PAINTERS OF EAST LOS in which Carlos Almaraz, Gronk, Judithe Hernandez, Willie Herron, Frank Romero, John Valadez and the East Los Streetscapers (David Botello, Wayne Healy, George Yepes) painted portable murals in the gallery. The murals are described and illustrated.

3482 Garcia, Ignacio. Senior exhibit attempts to define Chicano art. SOUTH TEXAN, (August 1, 1975). English.

AN: DIRECTAMENTE DEL BARRIO, a senior art exhibit at Texas A & I University by art majors Raul Valdez and Jesus Reyes. Sets forth their ideas about Chicano arts and

3483 Garcia, Rupert. 'Fifth Sun' Raza art show at UC Berkeley Museum. EL TECOLOTE, Vol. 8, no. 3 (November 1977), p. 8+. English.

AN: Review of THE FIFTH SUN: CONTEMPORARY TRADITIONAL CHICANO AND LATINO ART, co-sponsored by University of California, Berkeley Chicano Studies and Arte Popular, and curated by artist Ralph Maradiaga, co-director of Galeria de la Raza, showing at the UC Berkeley Museum. It will travel to the University of California, Santa Barbara's Art Museum. Illustrated.

3484 Garcia, Ruperto. Las companeras art exhibit. ARRIBA, Vol. 1, no. 4 (October 1980), p. 9. English.

AN: Illustrated story on an art show featuring Texas Latinas organized by MAS (Mujeres Artistas del Suroeste) in Austin. More than 18 women were represented.

3485 Goez proudly presents. Exhibit brochure, n.d. [1970]. English.

AN: Brochure produced by the Goez Gallery of Los Angeles for an inaugural exhibit showing the work of 76 artists.

3486 Goldman, Shifra M. Chicano art - looking backward. ARTWEEK, Vol. 12, no. 22 (June 20, 1981), p. 3-4. English.

AN: Review of Chicano art shows in Santa Cruz (CALIFAS) and Los Angeles (MURALS OF AZTLAN: THE STREET PAINTERS OF EAST LOS) featuring a total of 24 artists and how the shows reflect the critical crossroad at which Chicano artists presently find themselves.

3487 Goldman, Shifra M. Hecho en Latino America: first photography colloquium and exhibition. CHISMEARTE, no. 6 (February 1980), p. 16-25. English.

AN: Report on the first colloquium of Latin American photography, Mexico City, May 1978. Analysis and critique of U.S. Latino photographers' work presented in exhibition. Well illustrated.

3488 Goldman, Shifra M. Thorns and roses. ARTWEEK, Vol. 11, no. 30 (September 20, 1980), p. 1. English.

AN: Report on four Chicano artists exhibiting at L.A.C.E. Gallery, Los Angeles: Carlos Almaraz, Teddy Sandoval, John Valadez, and Linda Vallejo. Illustrated.

3489 Goldman, Shifra M. Women artists of Texas: MAS = More + Artists + Women = MAS. CHISMEARTE, no. 7 (January 1981), p. 21-22. English.

AN: History of Texas Chicana women artists' organization, Mujeres Artistas del Suroeste (MAS), co-founded in 1977 by Santa Barraza and Nora Gonzalez-Dodson in the framework of the burgeoning feminist art movement, particularly Women and Their Work of Texas. Brief history of Chicano politics and the corresponding art movement of southern and central Texas. In addition to Barraza and Gonzalez-Dodson, Alicia Arredondo, Modesta Trevino, and Maria Flores are considered. Illustrated.

Exhibits (cont.)

3490 Gomez, Linda. Malaquias Montoya exhibit
opens at La Pena. EL MUNDO (San Francisco,
CA), (October 29, 1975), p. 3. English.

AN: Over 50 paintings, silkscreens, and
drawings by Montoya at La Pena Cultural
Center, Berkeley, CA. Statement by the
artist who refuses to exhibit in museums and
is opposed to murals that are "pretty
decorations.".

3491 Gonzales, Juan. Galeria de la Raza: "our
people deserve the best". EL TECOLOTE, Vol.
7, no. 11 (July 1977), p. 14. English.

AN: "We are not here to sell our art,
but to sell the idea of art." This could
well be the motto of Galeria de la Raza who
under co-directors Rene Yanez and Ralph
Maradiaga has become a key cultural
institution in the Mission District of San
Francisco. The two directors have a broad
definition of art that encompasses
everything from cartoons to craftwork. The
article details past exhibits and future
goals. A half-page photograph of the
exterior of Galeria de la Raza by Pilar
Mejia illustrates the article. Reprint of
article entitled "Our people deserve the
best" which appeared in NUESTRO, Vol. 1, no.
2 (May, 1977), p. 56-57.

3492 Gonzalez, Hector. El arte de Esteban Villa.
EL HISPANO, Vol. 6, no. 20 (November 6,
1973). Spanish.

AN: Commenting on Esteban Villa's one
man show at the Centro de Artistas Chicanos
that presented sixty-five pieces of art
ranging from acrylics, watercolors,
woodcuts, to pen and ink drawings. Villa
fuses Indian symbols, mythology, folklore
and customs to create a new "cosmic"
dimension for the Chicano experience.

3493 Gonzalez, Jose Carlos. Consejo mexicano de
fotografia: foto latino en el suroeste de
los Estado Unidos. ARTES VISUALES, Vol. 29,
no. 29 (June 1981), p. 55-56. Spanish.

AN: Review of a photography show in
Mexico City organized by Lorenzo Hernandez,
Cityscape Photo Gallery of Pasadena, and the
Council of Latino Photography/USA. The show
featured Latinos of the Southwest and Latino
themes by non-Latino photographers.

3494 Gonzalez, Lila. Ideas on a Third World art
exhibit. SAN FRANCISCO ODALISQUE, (October,
November, 1976), p. 5-6. English.

AN: Review essay on the exhibition
"Other Sources: An American Essay" sponsored
by the San Francisco Art Institute.

3495 Graham Gallery, New York, NY and Amaya,
Mario. Luis Jimenez. Exhibition catalog,
1969. English.

AN: Well-illustrated catalog of an
exhibit by El Paso-born sculptor. Some
biographical material.

3496 Graham Gallery, New York, NY and Perreault,
John. Luis Jimenez. Exhibition catalog,
1970. English.

AN: Well-illustrated catalog of an
exhibit by El Paso-born sculptor. Some
biographical material.

3497 Grand Rapids Art Museum, Grand Rapids, MI.
Jose Narezo: paintings on paper. Exhibition
announcement, 1979. English.

AN: Announcement of an exhibit of
paintings by Michigan abstractionist Jose
Narezo. Illustrated.

3498 The Green Line Gallery, San Pedro, CA.
Lithographs and woodcuts by Muriel Olguin.
Exhibit invitation, 1980. English.

AN: Invitation to an exhibit.
Illustrated.

3499 Grimke, Angelina. Chicano art finds home in
Mission galeria. PEOPLE'S WORLD, Vol. 33,
no. 32 (August 8, 1970), p. 11. English.

AN: Commentary on the exhibition
CHICANOS, CUBA Y LOS 10 MILLONES held at the
original Galeria de la Raza at 425 14th
Street in San Francisco. The show presented
photographs by Jay Ojeda and Roberto
Perez-Diaz, drawings by Gloria Ozuna
together with paintings and photographs by
Cuban artist Mederos. Provides information
about the goals of the Galeria as the visual
arts department of Casa Hispana de Bellas
Artes. Exhibition curator was Rolando
Castellon.

3500 Guadalupe Historic Foundation, Santa Fe, NM.
Artes en la primavera. (1981). English.

AN: Catalog of exhibit by four New
Mexico artists: Manuel Lopez, sculptor from
Chili; Andres Martinez, painter from Santa
Cruz; Victoria Lopez, colcha embroiderer
from San Pedro; Sam Quintana, jeweler from
La Mesilla.

3501 Guggenheim Gallery, Chapman College, Orange,
CA. Hexagono: paintings, sculpture,
drawings, prints. Exhibit invitation, 1977.
English.

AN: Invitation to an exhibit for artists
Tito Aguirre, Isabel Castro, Rick Martinez,
Esau Quiroz, Linda Vallejo, Emigdio Vasquez,
Barrows, and Shanahan, sponsored by MEChA.
Profiles and pictures of the artists.

3502 Haddad, Barbara. The fine arts. ROUNDUP,
(January 25, 1970), p. 12. English.

AN: Mixed review of Ray Espinoza's
one-person show at the International House
Gallery in Denver. The exhibition included
drawings, paintings, prints, assemblages and
sculptures. Selecting work from each medium,
the critic comments on pieces that are
successful and those not fully realized.
Illustrated with a wood and metal relief of
a guitar and a graphic of "Che" Guevara.

3503 Haines, Bruce J. Gonzales' works are
controlled and full of detail. ANCHORAGE
DAILY NEWS, (May 23, 1980). English.

AN: Positive review of an exhibit titled
THE HEAD TASTES BEST by Mariano Gonzales.
Born in El Paso, Texas but reared in Alaska,
Gonzales' works in various media from
drawings and paintings to metals, ivory,
enamel and plastics. The critic praises the
artist for his "volatile intricacy" and his
fusion of materials "always with craft and
finesse". Includes reproductions of two
paintings.

Exhibits (cont.)

3504 Hale, David. La Brocha del Valle artists deal with Chicano reality. FRESNO BEE, (October 1, 1978), p. G, 5. English.

AN: Positive critique of a collective exhibition by members of La Brocha del Valle Group held at Fresno State University's Phebe Conley Art Building Gallery. With divergent attitudes, styles and ideas, the group is united by their focus on subject matter that deals with the diverse realities of being Chicano. Illustrated with photograph of Juan Ybarra's bronze sculpture, ONLY ONE TIME.

3505 Hale, David. Exhibit backers hope for Chicano cultural center plan. FRESNO BEE, (July 14, 1974), p. K5. English.

AN: Review of a Chicano art exhibition in the Sarah McCardle Room of the downtown Fresno County Public Library. According to artist-organizer Ernie Palomino, the exhibit is a trial balloon to see if enough Chicano artists can surface and cooperate in the establishment of a Chicano Cultural Center in Southeast Fresno. Illustrated with reproduction of a portrait by Romero Arroyo of Mendota, California and a painting by Victor Hernandez from Visalia, California.

3506 Harbor Area Community Art Center, San Pedro, CA. Mi arte, mi raza: an exhibition of current work by Judithe Hernandez. Exhibition invitation, 1979. English.

AN: Invitation to an exhibit.

3507 Hartnell College Studio Gallery, Salinas, CA. Paintings, drawings, prints by San Francisco Bay Area Chicano artists. Exhibit brochure, 1971. English.

AN: Brochure for exhibit featuring Francisco Camplis, Graciela Carrillo, Sal Castaneda, Priscilla Dominguez, J. Duarte, Rupert Garcia, Carlos Loarca, Irene Perez, Vincent Rascon, Michael Rios, Peter Rodriguez, Luis Valsoto, Esteban Villa, Rene Yanez, Zala. Illustrated by Rupert Carcia print.

3508 Heard Museum, Phoenix, AZ. First Annual Southwest Chicano Art Invitational Exposition. Invitation for reception, 1976. English.

AN: Invitation to a reception for artists Luis Jimenez (Roswell, New Mexico), Eugenio Quesada (Phoenix), Felipe Reyes (San Antonio), Pedro Rodriguez (San Francisco), Pedro Romero (Cannon City, Colo.) One illustration.

3509 Heard Museum, Phoenix, AZ. Second Southwest Chicano Art Invitational. Exhibit catalog, 1978. English.

AN: Exhibit by eight artists: Antonio Pazos (Tucson), Rudy Fernandez (Salt Lake City), Harry Gamboa (Los Angeles), Rupert Garcia and Xavier Viramontes (San Francisco), Roberto Rios (San Antonio), Roberto Espinoza (Yuma), and Roberto Borboa (Tucson). Brief biographies of all but Rios. 29 illustrations.

3510 Helen Euphrat Gallery, De Anza College, Cupertino, CA. Staying visible: the importance of archives. Art and "saved stuff" of eleven 20th century California artists. Cupertino, CA: Helen Euphrat Gallery, De Anza College, 1981. English.

AN: Catalog issued in conjunction with an exhibit held in the gallery Sept. 22 to October 23, 1981 which included documentation on Chicana artists Patricia Rodriguez and Carmen Lomas Garza. Each artist explains her method of saving, storing and using cultural material in her creations. Includes biographical sketch, photograph of the artist and reproduction of artwork.

3511 Henry Gallery, University of Washington, Seattle, WA and Ybarra-Frausto, Tomas. Arte prehispanico, arte popular. Exhibit Catalog, 19. English.

AN: Exhibition catalog for an exhibit prepared almost entirely by students from the School of Art with assistance from MEChA and members of the faculty of the School of Art. The pre-Columbian sections presented objects from sites in Mexico and Peru from pre-classic, classic and post-classic periods. The arte popular sections exhibited wares from craft centers in Mexico, Peru, Ecuador and Guatemala. Includes statement by Tomas Ybarra-Frausto on the relevance of this exhibition to the cultural identity of Chicanos in the Pacific Northwest.

3512 Herrera, Philip. The Latino eye. NUESTRO, Vol. 2, no. 4 (April 1978), p. 46-48. English.

AN: Commentary on the traveling exhibition ANTIGUAS RAICES/NUEVAS VISIONES. Illustrated with selections from the exhibition that included several Chicano artists.

3513 Highfill, Holly. MARCH (Movimiento Artistico Chicano). NEW ART EXAMINER, (June 1975), p. 4. English.

AN: Brief history of MARCH (started 1972; chartered 1975). Resume of its activities, including report on most ambitious show of 25 Mexican artists, MEXPOSICION.

3514 Incorporated Artes Monumentales/Inc., Denver, CO. IAM: art exhibit. Exhibition brochure, n.d. English.

AN: Large format, well illustrated brochure with information on muralists Roberto Lucero, Al Sanchez, Andrew Manning, Ricardo Barrera and Bob Reyes. Includes some biographical information situating these artists within the dynamic artistic traditions of the Mexican and the Chicano mural movements.

3515 Institute of American Indian Arts Museum, Santa Fe, NM. Native American/Hispanic festival, contemporary & historic visions. Santa Fe, NM: Institute of American Indian Arts Museum, 1981. English.

AN: Catalog for exhibit co-sponsored by La Cofradia de Artes y Artesanos Hispanicos, the Institute of American Indian Arts, and the Santa Fe Council for the Arts. Exhibit stresses the inter-relationship between the Indian and Hispano peoples of New Mexico. 31 contemporary Hispano artists included. Illustrated.

Exhibits (cont.)

3516 Instituto Chicano de Artes y Artesanias
     (Texas Instit. Educational Development) and
     Instituto Cultural Mexicano (SER/UNAM), San
     Antonio, TX. Artistas chicanos: Los
     Quemados. San Antonio, TX: Instituto
     Chicano, Texas Institute for Educational
     Development, 1975. English.

     AN: Invitation to an exhibit and
     manifesto of 1975 Austin-San Antonio
     artists' group, Los Quemados. Included Santa
     Barraza, Carolina Flores, Carmen Lomas
     Garza, Luis Guerra, Cesar Augusto Martinez,
     Santos Martinez, Amado Maurilio Pena, Jr.,
     Jose Rivera, Vicente Rodriguez, Jose
     Trevino.

3517 Instituto Cultural Mexicano (SER/UNAM), San
     Antonio, TX. Jesse Trevino's one man
     exhibit. San Antonio, TX: Instituto Cultural
     Mexicano, 1981. Bilingual.

     AN: Bilingual statement on the work of
     Jesse Trevino; biography and list of
     selected exhibitions; quotations from
     several publications about his work.

3518 Intar, International Art Relations, Inc.,
     New York, NY and Ferez Kuri, F. Jose.
     Alejandro E. Romero. Exhibition catalog,
     1977. English.

     AN: Exhibit catalog of drawings and
     paintings by Mexican-born painter and
     muralist living in Chicago. Illustrated in
     color.

3519 Invitational art exhibition/exposicion
     artistas invitados. Exhibition invitation,
     [ca. 1976]. English.

     AN: A benefit night for the Chicano
     Health Clinic included an exhibit of San
     Diego, as well as Ensenada, Mexicali and
     Tijuana (Mexico) artists. San Diego Latino
     artists include Peruvians Guillermo Acevedo
     and Mario Acevedo Torero, Chicano Salvador
     Roberto Torres, and Mexican-born Raul Trejo.

3520 Jesus Gutierrez Gallery, San Pedro, CA. "Two
     of a kind" prints by Linda Vallejo, Muriel
     Olguin. Exhibition invitation [1978].
     English.

     AN: Invitation to an exhibit.

3521 Joe B. Rodriguez. LA PRENSA, Vol. 1, no. 13
     (July 21, 1978). Spanish.

     AN: Commentary on an exhibition by Joe
     B. Rodriguez at the George I. Sanchez Center
     in Houston, Texas. Rodriguez's work is seen
     as having affinity with the art of Diego
     Rivera and Raul Anguiano. Illustrated with a
     reproduction of a watercolor, THE LANDING OF
     THE SALSA PEOPLE.

3522 Johnson, Charles. J street galleries:
     politics flavor alternative art shows.
     SACRAMENTO BEE, (December 20, 1977), p.
     A13. English.

     AN: Review of a Pachuco show by Jose
     Montoya that is half drawings and paintings,
     and half politics - photographs of Pachucos
     of the 1940s. Montoya's essay that
     accompanies the exhibit attempts to dispel
     the image of Pachucos as gangsters, and
     declares that Pachucos were the first
     "freedom fighters." The reviewer feels this
     is one-sided. Illustrated.

3523 Joseph Chowning Gallery; Laguna Beach Museum
     of Art; and Fitzgibbon, John. California
     connections: Sacramento State College, the
     early 1970s. Exhibit brochure, 1982.
     English.

     AN: Works by 35 artists, teachers and
     students at Sacramento State College. Color
     plate by Eduardo Carrillo and anecdotal
     material about Carrillo in text. Time frame
     is important for Jose Montoya and Esteban
     Villa, co-founders of the Royal Chicano Air
     Force in Sacramento.

3524 Joslyn Art Center. Multi-media art exhibit:
     Muriel Olguin (printmaking), Myrna Shiras
     (mixed media), Linda Vallejo (painting).
     Exhibition invitation, 1979. English.

     AN: Invitation to an exhibit.

3525 Kamin, Ira. Come on in, bring your paint.
     PACIFIC SUN, (May 30, 1974), p. 11-12.
     English.

     AN: Chatty report on murals and art
     exhibit in San Francisco's Mission District:
     murals by Chuy Campusano, Michael Rios,
     Richard Montez, Trish (Patricia) Rodriguez,
     Graciela Carrillo, Consuelo Mendez and Irene
     Perez. Illustrated.

3526 Kamin, Ira. Memories of Frida Kahlo.
     CALIFORNIA LIVING, (May 6, 1979), p. 44-50.
     English.

     AN: Chatty review of the sixth annual
     Dia de los Muertos, celebrated by the
     Galeria de la Raza this year with an homage
     to Mexican painter Frida Kahlo. Local
     artists filled the gallery with their
     homages; the Galeria's outdoor billboard was
     painted with her image; guests brought gifts
     and dressed in Kahlo style, including older
     women who wore jewelry given them by Kahlo.
     Biographical material on Kahlo and Diego
     Rivera should be read with caution. Well
     illustrated.

3527 Kelley sparks Chicano growth. EMPIRE
     MAGAZINE, (December 19, 1971), p. 32.
     English.

     AN: Ramon Kelley, successful and well
     known Denver artist is credited with
     fomenting and developing a small but strong
     Chicano art colony in Denver. As owner of
     the De Colores Gallery, Kelley has sponsored
     exhibits and personally encouraged many
     Chicano artists. John Flores, one of
     Kelley's proteges talks about his artistic
     development within the Chicano art and
     political milieu in Denver. Artist provides
     information on his daily life and work
     habits on the occasion of an exhibit of his
     work at the De Colores Gallery. Flores is a
     member of the Denver Arts and Humanities
     Commission. Illustrated with a reproduction
     of a pastel drawing by John Flores.

3528 Knight, Christopher. Urban eye sites up
     against the wall. HERALD EXAMINER, (May 31,
     1981). English.

     AN: Review of the exhibit MURALS OF
     AZTLAN: THE STREET PAINTERS OF EAST LOS at
     the Craft and Folk Art Museum of Los
     Angeles. Illustration.

Exhibits (cont.)

3529 Kutner, Janet. Total freedom in Chicano art. DALLAS MORNING STAR, (December 18, 1977), p. 10C. English.

AN: Review of traveling photo-exhibition of Chicano murals organized by Jacinto Quirarte for Exxon USA.

3530 L.A.C.E. (Los Angeles Contemporary Exhibitions), Los Angeles, CA. Espina (Thorn): Carlos Almaraz, Elsa Flores, Louie Perez, Teddy Sandoval, John Valadez, Linda Vallejo. Exhibition announcement, 1980. English.

AN: Announcement of an exhibition and a performance piece by six Los Angeles artists.

3531 L.A.C.E. (Los Angeles Contemporary Exhibitions), Los Angeles, CA. First communication. Exhibition invitation, 1979. English.

AN: Invitation to a showing of photographic slides and prints organized by the Council of Latino Photography/USA.

3532 L.A.C.E. (Los Angeles Contemporary Exhibitions), Los Angeles, CA. Gronk/Dreva, 1968-1978: ten years of art/life. Exhibition brochure, 1978. English.

AN: Exhibit and other acitivities by Gronk of the group ASCO and Jerry Dreva.

3533 Laguna Gloria Art Museum, Austin, TX. Tierra, familia sociedad, Amado Pena's themes. Exhibition catalog, 1980. Bilingual.

AN: Illustrated exhibition catalog with artist's biography and chronology of exhibitions. The bi-lingual text by Santos G. Martinez, Jr. situates the artist's work within a dual phased trajectory. First a period (1971-1975) in which the artist creates images armed with a social-political focus and (1975-present), a period starting with the PEOPLESCAPE series in which the artist enters a more lyrical introspective phase.

3534 Literally live movie at NO MOVIE exhibit. CIVIC CENTER NEWS, Vol. 7, no. 17 (April 25, 1978), p. 1. English.

AN: Story on the ASCO "performance" NO MOVIE, described by "Glugio" Gronk as "movies without celluloid" to be held at LACE Gallery. Illustrated.

3535 Lomas Garza, Carmen; Montoya, Jose E.; and Pinedo, Maria Vita. What we are...now. Exhibition catalog, n.d. English.

AN: Drawings by Sacramento women artists: Lorraine Garcia, Eva C. Garcia, Kathryn E. Garcia, Celia Rodriguez, Patricia Carrillo.

3536 Loniak, Walter. The true New Mexico contemporary style. SANTA FE REPORTER, (May 31, 1979). English.

AN: Review of three exhibits in Santa Fe, EL FESTIVAL HISPANICO co-sponsored by the Cofradia de Artes y Artesanos Hispanicos and the Santa Fe Council for the Arts; a wood carving exhibit at Elaine Horwitch Gallery, and easel paintings by muralist Gilberto Guzman at the Black Kachina Gallery. Concerning the Festival exhibit,

the critic states that the sculptural pieces are the strongest; two dimensional work is inconsistent or unimpressive, weaving is not well represented (though usually the strongest medium), and there are few photographs or prints. Illustration.

3537 Los Angeles City College. Contemporary times 2. Exhibition announcement, 1980. English.

AN: Illustrated announcement for photography show of Monticello Miller and William Ortiz.

3538 Los Angeles City College. Latinos de tres mundos. Exhibition invitation, 1980. English.

AN: Invitation to an exhibit featuring the work of ASCO members Harry Gamboa, Jr., Gronk, Willie Herron; painters Xavier Mendez and Olivia Sanchez; and photographer Ricardo Valverde.

3539 Los Angeles County Museum of Art, Los Angeles, CA and D'Andrea, Jeanne. Chicanismo en el arte. Exhibit brochure, 1975. English.

AN: An exhibit of Southern California Chicano student artists organized in cooperation with East Los Angeles College. Thirty-one artists displayed 73 works. The show was exhibited at the Vincent Price Gallery of East Los Angeles College prior to moving to the Los Angeles County Museum of Art. 70 illustrations.

3540 Los Angeles Municipal Art Gallery, Los Angeles, CA and Comite Chicanarte. Chicanarte: statewide exposition of Chicano art. exhibit catalog, 1975. English.

AN: Exhibition by 101 artists, accompanied by month-long performances of films, theatre, music, poetry readings, dance.

3541 Los Angeles Municipal Art Gallery, Los Angeles, CA. Multicultural focus: a photography exhibition for the Los Angeles Bicentennial. Exhibition catalog, 1981. English.

AN: Catalog of an exhibit demonstrating the multi-ethnic character of Los Angeles. Chicano photographers include Don Anton, Ron Bernal, Daniel Martinez, Rick Tejada-Flores. Illustrated.

3542 Low n slow - lowrider art. PEOPLE'S WORLD, Vol. 42, no. 34 (August 25, 1979), p. 10. English.

AN: Announcement of the Galeria de la Raza's exhibit of lowrider art. The article mentions the history of the lowrider car from the 1940s Pachuco zootsuiters, to the 1950s car clubs. The lowrider exhibit was prepared by the Galeria in response to white neighbors' recent protests against Saturday night cruising in the Mission District.

Exhibits (cont.)

3543 Lucas, Jerry. Testimonios de Latinoamerica. CHISMEARTE, no. 6 (February 1980), p. 6-9. English.

AN: Review of the exhibits TESTIMONIOS DE LATINOAMERICA and AMERICA EN LA MIRA, brought to Los Angeles Contemporary Exhibitions Gallery by Chicano curator Roberto Gil de Montes, as part of a cultural exchange between the Mexican Cultural Workers Front and Felipe Ehrenberg of the Grupo Proceso Pentagono of Mexico, and Chicano artists and photographers from the Council of Latino Photography/USA in Los Angeles. Well illustrated.

3544 Mandeville Art Gallery, University of California, San Diego. Five photographers: contemporary views of Mexican and Mexican-American culture. Exhibition catalog, 1981. English.

AN: Catalog of exhibit including Louis Carlos Bernal, Robert C. Buitron, Alberto Lau, Richard Tichich, and Meridel Rubenstein. Illustrated.

3545 Mandeville Center for the Arts, La Jolla, CA and Lopez, Yolanda M. Yolanda M. Lopez works: 1975-1978. Exhibition catalog, 1978. English.

AN: Catalog of an exhibit dedicated to Lopez's female family members, expecially her grandmother and mother, to the artist herself as a track runner, and to the Guadalupe series, icons of the Virgin transformed to reflect the life of contemporary women. Well illustrated.

3546 Marion Koogler McNay Art Institute, San Antonio, TX and Lee, Amy Freeman. Filigree drawings by Consuelo Gonzalez Amezcua. Exhibition catalog, 1968. English.

AN: Illustrated catalog for an exhibition of 42 filigree drawings by Texas artist "Chelo" Amezcua. Apart from biographical and historical information, the text evokes the ambiance of magic and mysticism surrounding the artist.

3547 Martinez, Anita. Raza art. EL TECOLOTE, Vol. 1, no. 8 (November 30, 1970), p. 1. English.

AN: Jay Ojeda, newly selected director of Galeria de la Raza, describes the memorial exhibition dedicated to Ruben Salazar installed at the Galeria on Dec. 12, 1970. Salazar symbolized and synthesized many of the goals subscribed to by artist members of La Galeria. The exhibit included work by Chicano and Latino artists Francisco Camplis, Jay Ojeda, Jose Romero, Rolando Castellon, Rene Yanez, Luis Valsoto, Mike Ruiz, Carlos Perez, Gustavo Rivera, Peter Rodriguez, Carlos Loarca and Ralph Maradiaga.

3548 Mascorro, Julie. Mechicano Art Center exhibit to grace Price gallery walls. CAMPUS NEWS, (November 24, 1971). English.

AN: Brief history of Mechicano Art Center activities from its establishment in 1969 to 1971. Exhibiting are Charles Almaraz, Roberto Amaral, Raymond Atilano, William Bejarano, Armando Cabrera, Edward Carbajal, Leonard Castellanos, Henry de Vega, Antonio Esparza, Bob Gomez, Lucila V. Grijalva, Jesus Gutierrez, Santos Lira, Frank Martinez, Ernest Palomino, Louis

Quijada, Richard Raya, Frank Romero. Illustrated.

3549 McAlister, John. Carrillo paintings on view in art gallery. UNIVERSITY TIMES, (April 2, 1975), p. 7. English.

AN: Review of 25 works by California painter Eduardo Carrillo. Illustrated.

3550 Mechicano Art Center. Los Angeles, CA: Mechicano Art Center, 1971. English.

AN: Announcement of an exhibit by painters Ramon Atilano, Xavier Lopez Ortega, and Frank A. Martinez. Martinez and Lopez Ortega are also muralists. Brief profiles of the artists. Illustrated.

3551 Mechicano Art Center, Los Angeles, CA. Lucila [V. Grijalva] reception. Exhibition announcement [1976]. English.

AN: Flyer announcing an exhibit for the Los Angeles painter and muralist.

3552 Mechicano Art Center, Los Angeles, CA. Paper pieces by C.D.A. [Carlos D. Almaraz]. Exhibition invitation, [1973]. English.

AN: Invitation to a gallery exhibit by the artist, with his manifesto, "Notes on an Aesthetic Alternative".

3553 Mechicano Art Center, Los Angeles, CA. Recent works of Armando Cabrera, Ed Carbajal, Joe Cervantes. Exhibition invitation, 1971. English.

AN: Invitation to an exhibit.

3554 Mechicano Art Center, Los Angeles, CA. Schizophrenibeneficial. Exhibition invitation, 1977. English.

AN: Invitation to an ASCO "performance" work: "Projecting of Visual and/or Verbal Personality Disorders Onto Person or Persons Unknown." Glugio (Gronk), Teddy (Sandoval), (Roberto) Gil de Montes, Patssi (Valdez), (Harry) Gamboa.

3555 Los Medanos College Gallery, [CA]. Cinco/five: an exhibit of five Bay Area artists. Exhibition brochure, n.d. English.

AN: Artists Gerry Concha, Gustavo Rivera, Raoul Mora, Manuel Villamor and Peter Rodriguez included in the show. Illustrated by Peter Rodriguez's portraits of the five.

3556 Memorial Union Display Cases, Arizona State University, Tempe, AZ. The material culture of the Cabezas Redondas, reconstructed by Liz Lerma Bowerman. Exhibition invitation, 1977. English.

AN: Invitation to an exhibit of pottery helmets and other artifacts of an imaginary Bronze Age people, conceived and created by Liz Lerma Bowerman from Mesa, AZ.

Exhibits (cont.)

3557 Mendiville, Miguel and Saavedra-Vela, Pilar.
A time for less talk and more action.
AGENDA, Vol. 7, no. 5 (September, October,
1977), p. 33-34. English.

AN: The exhibit RAICES Y VISIONES,
funded by the National Endowment for the
Arts, was composed of more than 100 artworks
by Chicano and Latino artists and toured the
United States in 1977. The exposition was
organized in four sections; artists whose
work is influenced or related to
Pre-Columbian art, art that explores social
and political realities, and works that are
more personal and introspective. Gives
itinerary and listing of participating
artists. Illustrated by photographs of the
work of Rudy Trevino, Cesar Martinez, Luis
Jimenez from Texas and Larry Fuente from
California.

3558 Mesa-Bains, Amalia. Homage to Frida Kahlo
opens Nov. 2, at Galeria de la Raza. EL
TECOLOTE, Vol. 9, no. 1 (September 1978), p.
7. English.

AN: Announcement and call for artwork to
Galeria de la Raza's exhibition honoring
Frida Kahlo on Nov. 2, 1978. The proposed
"Homage to Frida Kahlo" will encompass four
major areas; artists' work,
documentation/publication, related art
productions, and educational activities. The
Galeria educated participating artists to
the life and art of Frida Kahlo through
slide presentations and written material.
The exhibition became a milestone in the
Galeria de la Raza history.

3559 Mexican American Community Service
Organization, San Jose, CA. Exhibition of
contemporary art. Exhibition brochure, 1968.
English.

AN: Biographical and exhibition data for
Al Barela, Bert Hermosillo, Octavio Romano,
Luis Valdez, Vincent P. Rascon, John Soares
and Al Espinoza.

3560 Mexican American liberation art front: la
Raza Nueva, Rene Yanez, Esteban Villa,
Malaquias Montoya, Manuel Hernandez. BRONCE,
Vol. 1, no. 3 (March 1969), p. 6-7. English.

AN: Manifesto of MALAF, a germinal
Chicano art group in northern California.
Compares revolutionary Chicanos of 1968 with
the Mexicans of 1910; equally Chicano
artists reject European-influenced art.
Announces the exhibit NEW SYMBOLS FOR LA
RAZA NUEVA, at La Causa in Oakland, March 22
to April 5, 1969. Puts forth the group's
philosophy and goals, particularly exhibits
and art services to the "barrio".
Illustrated.

3561 MEXICAN MUSEUM NEWSLETTER. Vol. 6, no. 1
(Winter 1980, 1981). English.

AN: Regular report on the activities,
finances, membership, and other information
about the Museum. Announces several upcoming
shows: Rupert Garcia, six Mexican geometric
artists, paintings and prints by Mexican
American and Mexican women artists, Mexican
Leonel Maciel and Chicano Carlos Almaraz,
Mexican folk art, Manuel Neri sculpture, and
Mexican Luis Jaso.

3562 The Mexican Museum, San Francisco, CA and
Quirarte, Jacinto. 17 artists:
Hispano/Mexican-American/Chicano. Exhibition

catalog, 1977. English.

AN: Catalog of an exhibit for artists
Emilio Aguirre, Consuelo Gonzalez Amezcua,
Al Barela, Pedro Cervantez, Edward Chavez,
Antonio Garcia, Louis Gutierrez, Harry
Louie, Vincent Perez, Michael Ponce de Leon,
Eugenio Quesada, Gustavo Rivera, Peter
Rodriguez, Alex Sanchez, Darryl Sapien, Rudy
Trevino, Manuel Villamor. Illustrated.

3563 The Mexican Museum, San Francisco, CA.
Alexander Maldonado. Exhibition brochure,
1979. English.

AN: One page autobiographical statement
by Alexander Maldonado. Includes sources of
his imagery.

3564 The Mexican Museum, San Francisco, CA. Bruno
Andrade (from Missouri) and Antonio Lopez
Saenz (from Mexico). Exhibition
announcement, 1978. English.

AN: Flyer announcing an exhibit at the
Mexican Museum of Texas-born Andrade who is
exhibiting large abstract landscapes.
Andrade teaches in Columbia, Missouri; this
is his first California exhibit.

3565 The Mexican Museum, San Francisco, CA. Cinco
de Mayo exhibit at the Cannery. Exhibition
brochure, 1980. English.

AN: Well-illustrated brochure with text
by Nora Wagner and Bea Carrillo Hocker.
Succinct statements on the history, purpose
and programs of the Mexican Museum.

3566 The Mexican Museum, San Francisco, CA.
Manuel Neri: sculpture and drawings.
Exhibition invitation, 1981. English.

AN: Illustrated invitation to an
exhibit.

3567 The Mexican Museum, San Francisco, CA. Los
primeros cinco anos: fifth anniversary
exhibit. Exhibition brochure, 1980-81.
English.

AN: 65 Mexican, Chicano, and Latino
artists exhibited for the fifth anniversary
of the Mexican Museum, directed by artist
Peter Rodriguez. Cover is drawing by Carmen
Lomas Garza.

3568 The Mexican Museum, San Francisco, CA.
Recent works of Leonel Maciel and Carlos
Almaraz. Exhibition invitation, 1981.
English.

AN: Invitation to an exhibit of works by
Mexican artist Maciel and Chicano painter
Almaraz.

3569 The Mexican Museum, San Francisco, CA.
Recent works of Luis Jaso from Mexico City
and Carlos Chavez Cordova from Los Angeles.
Exhibition invitation, 1981. English.

AN: Invitation to an exhibit.

3570 The Mexican Museum, San Francisco, CA.
Rupert Garcia: portraits/retratos.
Exhibition brochure, 1981. English.

AN: Exhibition brochure with
biographical information and exhibition
chronology for Rupert Garcia.

Exhibits (cont.)

3571 The Mexican Museum, San Francisco, CA.
Virginia Jaramillo. Exhibition brochure,
1980. English.

AN: Exhibition brochure with
biographical information, exhibition
chronology and an artist's statement.

3572 Mexican-American Advisory Committee of the
Museum of Science and Industry.. Second
annual Mexican-American art fiesta.
Exhibition brochure, 1975. English.

AN: Exhibit of paintings, sculpture,
crafts, and photography by 49 artists from
Illinois, Indiana, and Mexico. Includes many
of the most important Chicano artists of the
Chicago area.

3573 Mexican-American Institute of Cultural
Exchange, San Antonio, TX and Alvarez
Acosta, Miguel. Mel Casas paintings.
Exhibition brochure, 1963. Bilingual.

AN: Exhibition brochure with
biographical and exhibition chronology for
El Paso born painter, Meliseo Casas. He is
the first non-Mexican born artist invited to
exhibit at the art gallery sponsored by the
International Organization of Cultural
Promotion for Foreign Relations in San
Antonio.

3574 Mexico. Secretaria de Relaciones Exteriores.
Direccion General de Asuntos.. Exposicion:
estampas y remembranzas; Admonty y Geomonte.
Exhibition catalog, 1979. Bilingual.

AN: Catalog of an exhibit by Alice
Dickerson Montemayor (Admonty). Born in
Laredo, Texas in 1902, she began painting in
1976. Her nephew, George A. Montemayor, who
resides in Houston, is the Coordinator for
the La Porte Independent School District.

3575 Miller, Marlan. Heard speaks Spanish through
art. PHOENIX GAZETTE, (September 23, 1978).
English.

AN: Four new exhibits at the Heard
Museum of Phoenix include "Hispanic crafts
of the Southwest", and "Southwest Chicano
Art Invitational". The former focuses on New
Mexico and Colorado crafts, organized by the
Taylor Museum if the Colorado Springs Fine
Arts Center; the latter includes Rupert
Garcia and Xavier Miramontes of San
Francisco, Rudy Fernandez of Salt Lake City
(now in Scottsdale, AZ), and Antonio Pazos
of Tucson.

3576 Miller, Marlan. Vigil paintings examine
Indian life. PHOENIX GAZETTE, (November 29,
1975), p. 20. English.

AN: Review of an exhibit by Denver-born
Veloy Vigil at the Sue Brown Galley in
Scottsdale, Arizona. The artist works in
watercolor, gouache and acrylic. Several
works are discussed in detail.

3577 Mills House Visual Arts Complex, Garden
Grove, CA. Menudo: artistas latinos de
Orange County. Exhibit invitation, 1980.
English.

AN: Invitation to an exhibit organized
for the first anniversary of Artistas
Latinos de Orange County including Delores
Grajeda, William Hernandez, Marylee Montano,
Patricia Murillo, Irene Ramos, Juan Ramos,
Ricardo Serrato, Miguel Shanahan, Arthur

Valenzuela, Benjamin Valenzuela, Jack
Vargas, Alonzo Whitney, Emigdio Vasquez,
Susana Zaccagnino, and Mexican artist
Artemio Sepulveda.

3578 Minority artists exhibit works at Auraria.
ROUNDUP, (January 13, 1980), p. 27.
English.

AN: Gala art exhibit organized by the
Resource Coalition for Minority Artists of
Denver. Included Black, Chicano and Native
American visual artists as well as film
makers and musicians.

3579 Mission to honor Frida Kahlo: famous Mexican
artist. EL TECOLOTE, Vol. 9, no. 3 (November
1978), p. 1. Bilingual.

AN: Announcement of an homage to Mexican
painter Frida Kahlo at the Galeria de la
Raza's annual celebration of Dia de los
Muertos. Works reproduced with the article
include those of Emmanuel C. Montoya, Yreina
Cervantez, Jose Antonio Burciaga, Nina
Serrano and Lisa Kokin. Bilingual.

3580 Moisan, Jim. Ancient roots, new visions.
ARTWEEK, Vol. 9, no. 26 (July 29, 1978), p.
8. English.

AN: Review of the show held at the
Municipal Arts Gallery of Los Angeles, the
first national touring show of Latino
artists in the United States. Includes
commentary on work of Larry Fuente, Luis
Jimenez, Frank Romero, Harry Gamboa, Gronk,
Rudy Martinez, Benjamin Serrano, Ricardo
Diaz, Patssi Valdez, Mel Casas, Luis Leroy,
Pedro Lujan. A related show, NEW VISIONS,
L.A., includes Robert Delgado, Ray Bravo,
Joe Moran, Rosalyn Mesquita, Patricia
Murillo and others.

3581 Monroe, Julie T. A splash of art from
Idaho's Mexican-Americans. IDAHO STATESMAN,
(March 11, 1977), p. 4D. English.

AN: As a Bicentennial tribute to all
people of Latin American heritage, Illinois
Bell Telephone Company organized a national
exhiibit of 17 Mexican-American/Chicano
artists. In Idaho, the touring exhibition
was augmented by a local presentation,
MEXICAN-AMERICAN: IDAHO, shown at the Boise
Gallery of Art under sponsorship of Boise
Cascade. Jose Rodriguez, local artist
presents his views on the meanings of the
word "Chicano" and "Chicano Art."
Illustrated with a photograph of Jose
Rodriguez and a reproduction of one of his
oil paintings entitled THE HOE.

3582 Montoya, Jose E. Rupert Garcia and the SF
Museum of Modern Art. RAYAS, Vol. 2, no. 2
(March, April, 1979), p. 5,11. English.

AN: Commentary apropos an exhibit of
pastel drawings by Rupert Garcia at the San
Francisco Museum of Modern Art. Author
gives a capsule history of the relationship
between Raza artists and mainstream cultural
institutions. Rupert Garcia is seen as
belonging to a stalwart group of Chicano
artists.

3583 Moody Hall, St. Edwards University, Austin,
TX. Las companeras. Exhibition invitation,
1980. English.

AN: Invitation to an exhibition of
Chicana/Latina artists sponsored by Mujeres
Muralistas del Suroeste (MAS). Illustrated.

Exhibits (cont.)

3584 Morch, Albert. Mexican art through a
cartoonist's eyes. SAN FRANCISCO EXAMINER,
(September 24, 1979), p. 28. English.

AN: Review of "GORDO'S WORLD" and the
paintings of Alexander Maldonado, an
exhibition at the Mexican Museum.
Biographical information on Gustavo Montano
Arriola, creator of the Gordo cartoon in
1941. The exhibit conceived and designed by
the San Diego Museum of Art, had
representative blow-ups of the strip along
with artifacts. Maldonado, a self-taught
artist started painting at age 60. His
canvases embrace a fascination with towers,
unique buildings, underground cities and
skylines from an imagined urban environment.

3585 Moreno, Eduardo. Los Four. Half-hour 16mm
film. English.

AN: Film about the Los Angeles group of
artists known as Los Four (originally Carlos
Almaraz, Gilbert Sanchez Lujan, Roberto de
la Rocha, Frank Romero), at the time of
their exhibit at the Los Angeles County
Museum of Art - the first time Chicano art
was shown at the Museum.

3586 Movimiento Artistico Chicano (MARCH),
Chicago, IL. Letter to CARACOL. CARACOL,
Vol. 4, no. 10 (June 1978), p. 3. Spanish.

AN: Press release announcing LA MUJER:
UN DIALOGO VISUAL, an art exhibit focusing
on women sponsored by MARCH of the Chicago
Public Library.

3587 Muchnic, Suzanne. Damaged goods in the big
city. LOS ANGELES TIMES, (July 23, 1979),
p. IV-11. English.

AN: Review of the exhibit at Otis Art
Institute of Parsons School of Design of
L.A. PARKS AND WRECKS, featuring Carlos
Almaraz, John Valadez, and Black artist John
Woods. Almaraz paints auto wrecks, and
landscapes of Echo Park. Valadez does pencil
portraits of young Chicanos. Illustrated.

3588 Muchnic, Suzanne. LAICA looks at social
works. CALENDAR, (October 7, 1979), p. 93.
English.

AN: Review of the exhibit SOCIAL WORKS
at the Los Angeles Institute of Contemporary
Art. Illustration and discussion of Judith
F. Baca's mural UPRISING OF THE MUJERES, a
four-part portable canvas mural in the style
of Siqueiros.

3589 Muchnic, Suzanne. Passion, paint splatter
folk art museum show. LOS ANGELES TIMES,
(June 25, 1981), p. VI, 1. English.

AN: Review of the MURALS OF AZTLAN:
STREET PAINTERS OF EAST LOS exhibit at the
Craft and Folk Art Museum in Los Angeles.
The critic considered the show "revved-up,
highly emotional art descended from Mexico's
political muralists" that made up what it
lacked in subtlety with passion, and one of
the most visually exciting shows of the
Museum. Illustrations.

3590 Mujeres de Aztlan. EL TECOLOTE, Vol. 4, no.
1 (October 10, 1973), p. 3. English.

AN: A collective of Third World women
artists plan an art show at Galeria de la
Raza in San Francisco. Stressing the need
for art forms that bring awareness and

present the true nature of women's living
conditions, this call for submission of art
work reflects some feminist concerns of the
period.

3591 Museum of Contemporary Art, Chicago, IL.
Raices antiguas/visiones nuevas; ancient
roots/new visions. Exhibition catalog, 1979.
English.

AN: Catalog produced for the mid-West
exhibit of RAICES ANTIGUAS. Includes 12
illustrations.

3592 Museum of Fine Arts, Santa Fe, NM. John
Hernandez, Douglas Johnson. Exhibition
invitation, 1979. English.

AN: Invitation to an exhibit including
the jeweled sculpture of John Hernandez from
New Mexico.

3593 Museum of Fine Arts, Santa Fe, NM. Luis
Jimenez, sculpture, drawings and prints: La
Cofradia de Artes y Artesanos Hispanicos,
selected works. Exhibition invitation, 1979.
English.

AN: Invitation to an exhibit of Texas
sculptor and printmaker Luis Jimenez, and
New Mexican artists and artisans.

3594 Navar, M. Margarita. La vela prendida: home
altars. ARRIBA, Vol. 1, no. 5 (February
1980), p. 12. English.

AN: Brief commentary on the exhibit LA
VELA PRENDIDA: MEXICAN AMERICAN WOMEN'S HOME
ALTARS at the Texas Memorial Museum during
December 1980. Aside from altars, the
exhibit focused on nichos, grutas and
lapidas.

3595 New Mexico State University, University Art
Gallery, Las Cruces, NM. Luis Jimenez:
sculpture, drawings and prints. Exhibition
catalog, 1977. English.

AN: Well illustrated catalog, some
illustrations in color. Text is interview
tracing Jimenez's artistic development.
Artists identifies Mexican American
connections in his work.

3596 Newport Harbor Art Museum, Newport Beach,
CA. Our own artists: art in Orange County.
Exhibition catalog, 1979. English.

AN: Includes Patricia Murillo and
Emigdio Vasquez with illustrations of one
work each. Biographies of the artists.

3597 Oakes College, University of California,
Santa Cruz, CA and Carrillo, Eduardo.
Corazon de Aztlan: a Chicano arts show.
Exhibition catalog, 1981. English.

AN: Catalog of exhibit including works
by Eduardo Carrillo, Juana Franklin, Cruz
Zamarron, Jerry Astorga, Jaime Valadez,
Ernesto Palomino, Sal Garcia, Roger Sierra,
Jose Montoya, Esteban Villa, Juanishi
Orozco, from Santa Cruz, San Jose, Fresno
and Sacramento. Presentations of films and
by the Teatro de la Tierra Morena of Santa
Cruz County.

Exhibits (cont.)

3598 Oakland County Cultural Affairs, MI. Nora
     Mendoza: an exhibition of
     abstract/impressionism. Exhibition brochure,
     [1981]. English.

     AN: Exhibit brochure for Texas-born Nora
     Chapa Mendoza who studied
     abstract-impressionism with Michigan artist
     Ljubo Biro. She is a leader in the artistic
     and Hispanic communities and runs galleries
     in Clarkston and Detroit.

3599 Oakland Museum, Oakland, CA. Espejo:
     reflections of the Mexican American: Louis
     Carlos Bernal, Morrie Camhi, Abigail Heyman,
     Roger Minick, Neal Slavin. Exhibit brochure,
     1978. English.

     AN: Twenty-five photographs from the
     documentary series commissioned by the
     Mexican American Legal Defense and Education
     Fund. Only Bernal is Chicano.

3600 Oakland Museum, Oakland, CA and Laney
     College, Oakland, CA. In search of Aztlan.
     Exhibition brochure, 1974. English.

     AN: Brochure for exhibit featuring Los
     Four: Carlos Almaraz, Gilbert Lujan, Roberto
     de la Rocha, Frank Romero, Judithe
     Hernandez.

3601 Oakland Museum, Oakland, CA. In search of
     Aztlan. Exhibition invitation, 1974.
     English.

     AN: Invitation to an exhibit by Los
     Four, a Chicano art group started about 1973
     in Los Angeles. On exhibit are the original
     members, Carlos Almaraz, Gilbert Lujan,
     Roberto de la Rocha, Frank Romero, and new
     member Judithe Hernandez.

3602 Oakland Museum presents 5 L.A. Chicano
     artists. EL MUNDO (Hayward, CA), (August
     1974). English.

     AN: Report on the exhibit THE SEARCH FOR
     AZTLAN, featuring paintings, murals,
     tortilla art, folk and religious symbols and
     totems by Carlos Almaraz, Roberto de la
     Rocha, Gilbert Lujan, Frank Romero and
     Judithe Hernandez. Included in the more than
     100 works are a wall mural, a folk art
     pyramid, and part of a primed '51 Chevy
     lowrider. Illustrated.

3603 Ohlone College Art Department Gallery,
     Fremont, CA. Impressions: a California print
     invitational. Exhibition catalog, 1976.
     English.

     AN: Exhibition catalog includes
     commentary on the artist and reproduction of
     two silkscreen posters "El Grito Rebelde"
     and "The Bicentennial Art Poster" by Rupert
     Garcia.

3604 Orange Co. Library. El Modena Branch.
     Empanada: a tasty Mexican group art exhibit
     filled with a variety of digestable treats.
     Exhibition catalog, [1979]. English.

     AN: Catalog of an exhibit by 15 artists:
     Dolores Grajeda, William Hernandez-M.,
     Marylee Montano, Patricia Murillo, Eduardo
     Navarro, Susana A. Zaccagnino, Esau Quiroz,
     Juan Elias Ramos, Ricardo M. Serrato,
     Benjamin Valenzuela, Emigdio C. Vasquez,
     Arthur Valenzuela, Jack Vargas, Alonso
     Whitney, and Mexican artist Artemio
     Sepulveda living in Orange County. Brief

profiles of the artists.

3605 Orange Co. Library. El Modena Branch. The
     Hispanic Artist Association of Orange County
     presents "Empanada," a tasty Mexican group
     art exhibit filled with a variety of
     digestible treats. Exhibition invitation,
     1979. English.

     AN: Poster/invitation to an exhibit of
     artists (See "Empanada").

3606 Orozco, Irma. Women & their work. PARA LA
     GENTE, Vol. 1, no. 4 (October 1977), p. 12.
     English.

     AN: Illustrated story about "Women &
     Their Work" festival in Austin, Texas,
     Oct-Dec 1977. Photographers Maria Flores and
     Teresina Guerra, Santa Barraza, Nora
     Gonzalez Dodson, Sylvia Orozco, and Modesta
     Trevino exhibited.

3607 Otis/Parsons Gallery, Los Angeles, CA;
     Nieto, Margarita; and Price, Aimee Brown.
     L.A. parks & wrecks: a reflection of urban
     life/parques y choques: un reflejo de la
     vida urbana. Exhibition catalog, [1979].
     Bilingual.

     AN: Catalog poster discussing the works
     of the three artists on exhibit: Carlos
     Almaraz, John Valadez and John Woods who
     concentrate on urban images. Detailed
     descriptions of each artist's work accompany
     the many illustrations. Essays in English
     and Spanish.

3608 Out in the open/Allen Parkway: Frank
     Fajardo, Jesse Lott, Guillermo Pulido, Jana
     Vander Lee. Exhibit invitation, 1979.
     English.

     AN: Invitation to the installation of
     conceptual pieces in public areas of
     Houston. Includes Chicano artist Frank
     Fajardo and Bolivian-born Pulido.

3609 Painting changes woman's life at age when
     most ready to retire. LAREDO NEWS,
     (November 4, 1979), p. 1-C. English.

     AN: Interview with 77 year old Alice D.
     Montemayor "Admonty" on the occasion of her
     San Antonio exhibit with her nephew George
     "Geomonte" Montemayor.

3610 Palacio de Mineria, Mexico, D.F. Raices
     antiguas/visiones nuevas: arte chicano y
     latinoamericano en los estados unidos.
     Exhibition catalog, 1980. Spanish.

     AN: Catalog of an exhibit circulated by
     the Fondo del Sol in the United States, and
     in Mexico. Included are Chicanos and Latin
     Americans living in the United States. Well
     illustrated.

3611 Palma Castroman, Janis. ENCUENTRO ARTISTICO
     FEMENIL [exhibit], Austin, TX, November 28,
     1977. TEJIDOS, Vol. 5, no. 1 (1978), p.
     1-47. Bilingual.

     AN: A multimedia, multicultural
     exposition by 26 Chicana artists held at
     Juarez-Lincoln University. The exhibit was
     sponsored by Chicanos Artistas Sirviendo a
     Aztlan (CASA) and Mujeres Artistas del
     Suroeste (MAS).

Exhibits (cont.)

3612 Palma Castroman, Janis. Introduccion.
     TEJIDOS, Vol. 5, no. 1 (1978), p. i.
     Spanish.

     AN: One-page introduction to theme issue
     featuring the work of Chicana artists
     exhibited at the ENCUENTRO ARTISTICO FEMENIL
     exposition held on November 28, 1977 in
     Austin, TX.

3613 Patterson, Ann. Exhibit at Unitarian: Smith,
     Quesada art black, white contrast. TEMPE
     DAILY NEWS, (March 16, 1976). English.

     AN: Eugenio Quesada presented drawings
     of female torsos along with Smith. Both are
     industrial design faculty members at Arizona
     State University. Article mentions other
     Quesada shows, and his participation on the
     Jean Charlot mural at the University.

3614 Perez, Demetrio. Mel Casas - humanscapes.
     Houston, TX: Contemporary Arts Museum, 1976.
     English.

     AN: Catalog for Mel Casas exhibition
     Oct. 22-Nov. 23, 1976. Artist calls his
     paintings "visual conundrums which play with
     our cultural concepts, with our cultural
     vision." Includes biographical information
     and exhibition chronology. Well illustrated
     with nine reproductions of artists work and
     two photos of the artist.

3615 Philip Renteria drawings, 1974-77. In YOUNG
     TEXAS ARTISTS SERIES. Amarillo, TX: Amarillo
     Art Center, 1977. English.

     AN: Catalog of series of exhibits
     co-sponsored by the Texas commission of the
     Arts and Humanities and the Amarillo Art
     Center. Illustrated with a biography of the
     artist.

3616 Plagens, Peter. Los Four (Roberto de la
     Rocha, Carlos Almaraz, Gilbert Lujan and
     Frank Romero) at LACMA. ARTFORUM,
     (September 1974), p. 87-88. English.

     AN: Review of Los Four exhibit at Los
     Angeles County Museum of Art which calls it
     a "sociological bazaar" in which Chicanos
     have been "corrupted" by art schools and
     "museumized".

3617 The Point Gallery, Santa Monica, CA. ASCO
     (Gronk, Patssi, Gamboa, Herron), Los Four
     (Almaraz, de la Rocha, Judithe Hernandez,
     Gloriamalia Flores, Mauricio Ramirez, John
     Valadez. Exhibition invitation, [1975].
     English.

     AN: Illustrated invitation to an exhibit
     of Los Angeles artists.

3618 Polack, Clark. A question of style - Los
     Four and the Los Angeles County Museum of
     Art. SOUTHWEST ART, (July, August, 1974).
     English.

     AN: A double-edged assessment of the
     "Los Four" exhibit. The exhibition is at
     once lauded for being provocative and
     stimulating while at the same time failing
     artistically. Author feels that special
     treatment given Carlos Almaraz, Gilbert
     Lujan, Roberto de la Rocha and Frank Romero
     by the L.A. County Art Museum has not been
     extended to other young Los Angeles artists.

3619 Pomona College Gallery of Montgomery Art
     Center, Claremont, CA; Allikas, Bob; and

Glickman, Hal. Chicano graffiti: the
signatures and symbols of Mexican-American
youth. Exhibition catalog, [1970]. English.

     AN: Catalog of exhibit based on
     photographs of Los Angeles graffiti.

3620 President's Gallery, Chicago State
     University and Sorell, Victor A. Alejandro
     Romero. Exhibition catalog, 1979. English.

     AN: Catalog of an exhibit by
     Mexican-born painter and muralist who has
     been working in the United States since
     about 1973. He has lived in Chicago since
     1976. Illustrated.

3621 Pro Arts Gallery, Oakland, CA. Si se puede!
     We can do it!: an exhibition of silkscreen
     prints and posters by Malaquias Montoya.
     Exhibition announcement, [1981]. English.

     AN: Announcement of a traveling exhibit
     of prints and posters in Oakland,
     California. Illustrated.

3622 Rabyor, Jozanne. Luis Jimenez at
     Contemporary Arts Museum. ART IN AMERICA,
     Vol. 63, no. 1 (January, February, 1975), p.
     88. English.

     AN: Texas-born Luis Jimenez's first
     major museum show of 77 pieces spanning
     eight years of production is dazzling.
     Superbly crafted fiberglass sculptures
     comment on indigenous mythologies often with
     macabre humor. His work, according to the
     critic, is too moralistic to be Pop, and
     too passionate to be dumped into the
     California-plastic bag.

3623 Raices y visiones [portfolio]. REVISTA
     CHICANO-RIQUENA, Vol. 7, no. 2 (Spring
     1979), p. 29-44.

     AN: Portfolio of works from the exhibit
     RAICES ANTIGUAS/VISIONES NUEVAS: ANCIENT
     ROOTS/NEW VISIONS. Artists included are
     Patssi Valdez (Los Angeles), Eloisa
     Castellanos-Sanchez (New York), Benjamin
     Serrano, Jr. (Tijuana, Mexico), Alex Garza
     (Chicago), Martin Y. Moreno (Michigan), Luis
     A. Jimenez (New Mexico), Rene Castro
     (Oakland, CA), Sita Gomez de Kanelba (New
     York), Susana Lasta (Tucson, AZ), Domingo
     Garcia (New York), Consuelo Mendez Castillo
     (Caracas, Venezuela), Naomi Castillo
     Simonetti (New Jersey), Louis Carlos Bernal,
     and Eddie Comptis.

3624 Ramon Kelley. ARTISTS OF THE ROCKIES, Vol.
     1, no. 1 (Spring 1974), p. 6-11. English.

     AN: Biographical information on Ramon
     Kelley and a listing of his invitational
     shows. Illustrated with a photograph of the
     artist and a portfolio of ten works (three
     in color).

3625 Rand, Steve. Carlos David Almaraz. LOS
     ANGELES FREE PRESS, Vol. 11, no. 10 (March
     8, 1974), p. 14. English.

     AN: Brief biographical sketch on
     Mexican-born, Los Angeles artist Carlos
     Almaraz on the occasion of the Los Four
     exhibit at the Los Angeles County Museum of
     Art, artists who are, the author says
     inaccurately, largely self-taught. Almaraz
     studied at Garfield High School with David
     Ramirez, and at Otis Art Institute. One
     illustration.

Exhibits (cont.)

3626 Rangel, Jesus. Heirs of Jose Posada: revolution lives in Chicano art. SAN DIEGO UNION, (February 24, 1980), p. D6. English.

AN: 19th century Mexican engraver Jose Guadalupe Posada has been an inspiration to Chicano artists. Along with two exhibits of his work, the Centro Cultural de la Raza is also showing calavera (skeleton) images by Chicano artists: skull-masks from the Teatro Campesino, a print by Amalia Mesa-Baines of Frida Kahlo, and a collaged box by Jose Antonio Burciaga. Illustration: Salvador Roberto Torres work.

3627 La Raza art festival. PAPEL CHICANO, Vol. 1, no. 6 (May 21, 1971), p. 8-9. English.

AN: Two-page centerfold of photographs by Johnny Almendarez of the LA RAZA ART FESTIVAL held at Ripley House in Segundo Barrio of Houston, Texas, May 5-9, 1971. Includes installation view of the exhibit, two photos of artists in action and a cover photograph of artist Pedro Rodriguez conducting a silkscreen workshop.

3628 Riches of the barrios. ARIZONA [supplement to ARIZONA REPUBLIC], (September 11, 1977), p. 50. English.

AN: Louis Carlos Bernal of Tucson shows his collection of photographic portratis of the barrios at the Heard Museum in Phoenix. Well illustrated.

3629 Rivas, Maggie. Art of the barrio: Exxon's traveling art show comes to headquarters. HQ HOUSTON, (August 1976), p. 6-7. English.

AN: Report on traveling photo-exhibition of 29 Chicano murals organized by Jacinto Quirarte for Exxon USA.

3630 Roberts, Tim. For art's sake, for the community, for the working class. ORANGE CITY NEWS, Vol. 10, (March 14, 1979), p. 1,8-9. English.

AN: Illustrated article on Orange County, Calif. realist painter Emigdio Vasquez. Focuses on his community murals, and his attitudes toward his art. Also announces the first exhibit, "Empanada" of the newly formed Hispanic Artists Association of Orange County. 13 participants including Vasquez.

3631 Rodriguez, Patricia. Portfolio: Patricia Rodriguez; the visual interview. METAMORFOSIS, Vol. 3, no. 1-2 (1980, 1981), p. 38-45. English.

AN: Statement by the artist reprinted from her exhibit "The Visual Interview" at the Mission Cultural Center, San Francisco. Discusses her fifteen mask-box-sculptures of Chicano artists from northern California. Illustrated with photographs of the artist at work and five of her sculptures. This issue of METAMORFOSIS combines volumes 3 and 4.

3632 Rodriguez, Pedro and Walla Walla Community College, Walla Walla, WA. Chicano art exhibition. Exhibition invitation, 1981. English.

AN: Poster invitation to exhibition by Pedro Rodriguez, Associate professor of Chicano Studies at Washington State University, Pullman, Washington. Rodriguez

presented a lecture in English, "Chicano Art and Its Mexican Antecedents," and one in Spanish, "El Muralismo en Mexico y Mexico-America." Illustrated with painting of woman shrouded in a rebozo.

3633 Romero, Raul V. Chicanarte, a major exposition of California arts. NEWORLD, (Fall 1975). English.

AN: CHICANARTE at the Los Angeles Municipal Gallery, Barnsdall Park from Sept. 14 -Oct. 12, 1975 remains the most comprehensive statewide exposition of Chicano arts in California. This article details the production apparatus and history of the exposition. In particular, the contributions of Al Frente Communications, Inc., the Chicano Arts Council of U.C.L.A. and the Comite Chicanarte. Illustrated.

3634 Ruben Salazar Library, Sonoma State University, Sonoma, CA. Patricia Rodriguez: Chicano sculpture and masks. Exhibition invitation, 1981. English.

AN: Invitation to an exhibit.

3635 Saavedra-Vela, Pilar. Exposicion nacional de raices hispanicas. AGENDA, Vol. 7, no. 5 (September, October, 1977), p. 33-34. Spanish.

AN: Announcement of the national tour of the exhibition entitled: RAICES Y VISIONES organized by the group Fondo del Sol, from Washington, D.C.

3636 Saks Galleries, Denver, CO. Ramon K. Exhibition brochure, 1971. English.

AN: Promotional brochure for major one-man exhibition. Ramon Kelley is a Chicano artist of international stature whose artistic roots are firmly planted in the American west. The Gallery director states, "His impressionistic paintings reveal a strong affinity to the land and people of the southwest and they are the major subject of his work. Lavishly illustrated with full color reproductions of several pastel and oil paintings.

3637 Salazar, Veronica. Aspiration comes true. SAN ANTONIO EXPRESS-NEWS, (October 28, 1979), p. 8-H. English.

AN: History of Alice Dickerson Montemayor of Laredo, Texas (known as "Admonty") who started to paint at 74 on the occasion of her second exhibit at the Mexican government's Instituto Cultural.

3638 Salvador R. Torres Chicano Underground Studio-Gallery, San Diego, CA. Diego Rivera, David Alfaro Siqueiros, Jose Clemente Orozco, from the collection of the S.F. Museum of Art. Exhibition invitation, [1974]. English.

AN: Illustrated invitation of an exhibit organized by the Galeria de la Raza of San Francisco loaned to the Congreso de Artistas Chicanos en Aztlan, and held in artist Torres' studio.

Exhibits (cont.)

3639 San Antonio Museum Association, San Antonio,
      TX. Visiones nuevas en Tejas/new visions in
      Texas. Exhibtion catalog, 1979. English.

      AN: Supplementary regional catalog for
      the exhibit RAICES ANTIGUAS/VISIONES NUEVAS;
      ANCIENT ROOTS/NEW VISIONS. Illustrations for
      works by George Cisneros, Francisco (Frank)
      Fajardo, Robert Gonzalez, Cesar Augusto
      Martinez, Roland Mazuca, Guillermo Pulido,
      Felipe Reyes, Jesus (Jesse) Trevino.

3640 San Antonio Museum of Modern Art. Paperwork:
      an exhibition of Texas artists. San Antonio,
      TX: San Antonio Museum of Modern Art, 1979.
      English.

      AN: Includes Roberto Munguia, Mexican
      American artist from Kingsville, Texas.
      Working with shaped paper, the artist
      describes his material and methods of
      creation. Includes biography of artist
      together with an exhibition list.
      Illustrated with photographs of five paper
      constructions by Roberto Munguia.

3641 San Antonio Museum of Modern Art. Zarzamora:
      inaugural exhibition of Ladrones de la Luz.
      Exhibition invitation, 1979. English.

      AN: Illustrated invitation to
      photographic exhibition including Norman
      Avila, David Cardenas, Franco Cernero,
      Enrique Hernandez, Robert Maxham, James
      Newberry, Isaac Rodriguez, Daryl Studebaker,
      Richard Tichich, Beverly Ulmer, Kathy
      Vargas.

3642 San Francisco. ART NEWS MAGAZINE, Vol. 69,
      no. 6 (October 1970), p. 83. English.

      AN: Review of Esteban Villa's show, the
      first held by the newly constituted Galeria
      de la Raza in San Francisco. Illustrated.

3643 San Francisco Art Commission Gallery.
      Rolando Castellon, Gustavo Rivera, Jerry
      Concha. Exhibition brochure, 1971. English.

      AN: Brochure for exhibit by
      Sacramento-born Jerry Concha, Mexican-born
      Gustavo Rivera, and Nicaraguan-born Rolando
      Castellon titled CAPRICORN ASUNDER. Brief
      biographies of the artists.

3644 San Francisco Art Institute. Other sources:
      an American essay. Exhibition catalog, 1976.
      English.

      AN: Catalog for an exhibit of painting,
      printmaking, film, photography, and
      sculpture - as well as performing arts - by
      300 artists of Chinese, Japanese, Oceanic,
      Central and South American and African
      descent. The work of over twenty Chicano
      artists is included.

3645 San Francisco Museum of Modern Art, San
      Francisco, CA; Chavez, Ray; and Gordon,
      Allan M. Carmen Lomas Garza/prints and
      gouaches: Margo Humphrey/monotypes.
      Exhibition catalog, 1980. English.

      AN: Carmen Lomas Garza, though working
      in a "naive" style is technically adept and
      academically trained, though she draws
      motifs from folk production of her native
      Texas. Her themes in this exhibit are
      memories of her childhood. Well illustrated.

3646 San Francisco Museum of Modern Art, San
      Francisco, CA and Marra, Patricia. Day of

the dead. Exhibition catalog, 1980. English.

      AN: Broadside announcement in the manner
      of Jose Gudalupe Posada for an exhibit of
      prints by Posada and an altar by Amalia Mesa
      -Baines and Friends. Text presents customs
      and traditions for celebrating the Day of
      the Dead in Mexico and among the Chicano
      community.

3647 San Francisco Museum of Art, San Francisco,
      CA. M.I.X. graphics I: prints. Exhibition
      invitation, 1974. English.

      AN: Invitation to an exhibit of 15
      multi-ethnic artists, including San
      Francisco artists Ralph Maradiaga and Rupert
      Garcia.

3648 San Francisco Museum of Modern Art, San
      Francisco, CA and Castellon, Rolando.
      People's murals: some events in American
      history. Exhibition catalog, 1976. English.

      AN: Eight portable murals by San
      Francisco Bay Area artists including
      Graciela Carrillo, Anthony Machado, Robert
      Mendoza, Irene Perez, Mike Rios. Well
      Illustrated.

3649 San Francisco Museum of Modern Art, San
      Francisco, CA and Castellon, Rolando.
      Posters and society. Exhibition catalog,
      1975. English.

      AN: 26 artists exhibiting public
      announcement and social political commentary
      posters. Includes 14 Bay Area and
      Sacramento, Calif. Latino artists.

3650 San Francisco Museum of Modern Art, San
      Francisco, CA and Castellon, Rolando. Rupert
      Garcia/pastel drawings. Exhibition catalog,
      1978. English.

      AN: Exhibit by San Francisco artist
      Rupert Garcia.

3651 San Jose Museum of Art. Cinco de Mayo: el
      arte chicano de hoy, the works of Mexican
      American artists. Exhibition catalog, 1974.
      English.

      AN: Bilingual, illustrated, small
      exhibition catalogue. Includes collective
      work by Centro de la Gente of San Jose and
      the Royal Chicano Air Force (R.C.A.F.) of
      Sacramento, California. Also lists more than
      twenty other exhibiting artists.

3652 San Pedro Municipal Art Gallery, San Pedro,
      CA. Celebration: Muriel Olguin and Linda
      Vallejo. San Pedro, CA: San Pedro Municipal
      Art Gallery, [1978]. English.

      AN: Invitation to an exhibit.
      Illustrated.

Exhibits (cont.)

3653 Santa Ana College, Santa Ana, CA and
     Goldman, Shifra M. Chicano art. Exhibition
     catalog, 1974. English.

     AN: Thirteen California artists are
     presented in a short essay defining Chicano
     as a double mestizaje of Mexican mestizo and
     U.S. influences that exists in a state of
     "reconciled conflict." Its aim is
     communication. Artists included are
     Malaquias Montoya, Rupert Garcia, Manuel
     Hernandez, Esteban Villa, Robert Gomez,
     Harvey Tarango, Mary Helen Castro, Eduardo
     Carrillo, Graciela Carrillo, and "Los Four":
     Carlos Almaraz, Robert de la Rocha, Judithe
     Hernandez, Gilbert Lujan and Frank Romero.

3654 Santa Ana College, Santa Ana, CA. MECHA
     presents la semana de la Raza. Exhibition
     brochure, 1970. English.

     AN: Program for the week's activities,
     including EL ARTE DE LA RAZA exhibition,
     Gilbert Sanchez Lujan speaking on "Chicano
     Art in the Barrio," art demonstrations by
     Gilbert Vasquez, Emigdio Vasquez, Esau
     Quiroz, and Richard Garcia.

3655 Santa Ana Public Library, Newhope Branch,
     Santa Ana, CA. Artistas latinos de Orange
     County. Exhibition brochure, 1979. English.

     AN: Exhibit of six artists: Dolores
     Grajeda, Eduardo Navarro, Arthur Valenzuela,
     Benjamin Valenzuela, Emigdio Vasquez, Susana
     A. Zaccagnino.

3656 Santuario de N.S. [Nuestra Senora] de
     Guadalupe, Santa Fe, NM. Artes Guadalupanos
     de Aztlan: Samuel Leyba, Gilberto Guzman,
     Geronimo Garduno, Carlos Leyba, Pancho
     Hunter. Exhibition invitation, 1979.
     English.

3657 Schlesinger, Ellen. At the Galeria Posada
     there is sophistication, machismo and humor:
     Villa has varied impact. SACRAMENTO BEE,
     (August 23, 1981), p. Scene, 3. English.

     AN: Favorable review of exhibit by
     Esteban Villa showing etchings, xerox
     prints, lithographs and other graphics.
     Villa's world view is broad, critical,
     political and romantic and encompasses
     comments of computerized society to stylized
     landscapes. Illustrated.

3658 Seattle Art Museum, Seattle, WA and Dickson,
     Joanne. Manuel Neri, sculpture and drawings.
     Exhibition catalog, 1981. English.

     AN: Beautifully illustrated catalog.
     Text by Joanne Dickson from Oakland
     California, biography and very complete
     chronology of Neri exhibitions.

3659 Shakti Gallery, Long Beach, CA. "Fire in the
     lodge," paper sculptures by Linda Vallejo.
     Exhibit invitation, 1981. English.

     AN: Invitation to an exhibit by Long
     Beach, CA artist Linda Vallejo. Illustrated.

3660 La Sociedad Historica de Nuestra Senora de
     Guadalupe, Santa Fe, NM. Meditacion.
     Exhibition invitation, 1980. English.

     AN: Invitation to an exhibit by four
     artists: Filomeno Martinez (graphic artist,
     Albuquerque), Ruben Montoya (santero, Santa
     Fe), Santiago Chavez (painter, Santa Rosa),
     Jose Alberto Baros (sculptor, Espanola).

3661 Sol Art Gallery, San Diego, CA. Group
     showing of Southern California artists.
     Exhibition brochure, 1980. English.

     AN: First exhibit of new Chicano art
     gallery showing Los Angeles artists Carlos
     Almaraz, Judithe Hernandez, John Valadez,
     Linda Vallejo, Ricardo Duardo, Barbara
     Carrasco.

3662 Sotomayor, Frank. Chicanarte exposition
     opening in Barnsdall. CALENDAR, (September
     14, 1975), p. 24. English.

     AN: Review of the "Chicanarte" exhibit
     at Los Angeles Municipal Art Gallery.
     Illustrated.

3663 Southern Colorado State College, Pueblo, CO
     and Monteverde, Mildred. Chicanos graficos
     [sic]...California. Exhibition brochure,
     [1974]. Spanish.

     AN: Brief background of California art
     movement and 13 artists from San Francisco,
     Los Angeles, Sacramento, Fresno. Important
     factual information despite numerous errors
     with names and Spanish terms. 16
     illustrations of silkscreens, lithograph,
     etching.

3664 Southwest Chicano Arts Center, Houston, TX.
     Chicano youth in art. Exhibition invitation,
     1978. English.

     AN: Invitation to exhibit featuring
     works from Chicano youth in the Houston
     area.

3665 Southwest Chicano Arts Center, Houston, TX.
     The oil and acrylic paintings of Jose Perez.
     Exhibition invitation, 1977. English.

     AN: Illustrated invitation to exhibit.

3666 Southwest Chicano Arts Center, Houston, TX.
     Pilar C. Rubin. Exhibition invitation, 1977.
     English.

     AN: Illustrated invitation to exhibit of
     sculpture.

3667 Southwest Texas State University, San
     Marcos, TX and Carlisle, Charles Richard.
     Cuatro caminos: four perspectives on Chicano
     art. Exhibition catalog, 1980. English.

     AN: Exhibition pamphlet with photographs
     of the artists. Alex Flores, Luis Jimenez,
     Cesar Augusto Martinez and Amado Pena, Jr.
     comment on their work and the Chicano art
     movement.

3668 Southwest Texas State University, San
     Marcos, TX and Carlisle, Charles Richard. El
     mundo de Luis Santiago. Exhibition brochure,
     n.d. English.

     AN: Illustrated exhibition brochure with
     biographical data and exhibition chronology
     on Luis Santiago. Both as a sculptor and
     painter, Santiago works in various
     techniques and styles to project the dynamic
     and multi-faceted aspects of Chicano life.

Exhibits (cont.)

3669 SPARC (Social and Public Arts Resource
     Center), Venice, CA and Los Angeles. Ceta
     VI, Venice, CA. Hecho en Aztlan multiples:
     screen printed works. Exhibition invitation,
     1980. English.

     AN: Invitation to an exhibit of
     silkscreen prints by Hecho en Aztlan
     Multiples, a small business run by Richard
     Duardo. At the Social and Public Art
     Resource Center, Venice, Calif.

3670 Stofflet-Santiago, Mary. The fifth sun:
     esthetic quality versus curatorial intent.
     ARTWEEK, Vol. 8, no. 37 (November 5, 1977),
     p. 6. English.

     AN: Review of the exhibit THE FIFTH SUN
     at the University Art Museum in Berkeley,
     Calif., curated by Ralph Maradiaga of the
     Galeria de la Raza. It contains folk art,
     and posters by Chicano artists Maradiaga,
     Rupert Garcia, Juan Fuentes, mural studies
     by Graciela Carrillo and Mike Rios, ceramics
     by Anna de Leon, an altar by Amalia
     Mesa-Bains, and mural drawings by Mexican
     muralists. The writer criticizes the uneven
     quality of the show, but encourages better
     ones in the future. Illustrated.

3671 Street, Sharon. Califas - a celebration of
     Chicano culture and art. CITY ON A HILL,
     (April 16, 1981). English.

     AN: Review of an exhibit at College V's
     Sesnon Gallery featuring 15 California
     artists: Ramses Noriega, Judy Baca, Salvador
     Roberto Torres, Malaquias Montoya, Rene
     Yanez, Ralph Maradiaga, Jose Montoya,
     Esteban Villa, Carmen Lomas Garza, Robert
     Chavez, among others. Illustrated.

3672 Taller de Arte, San Antonio, TX. Felipe
     Varelas Reyes. Exhibition announcement, n.d.
     English.

     AN: Artist statement and reproduction of
     one drawing in an announcement for a one man
     show at the Taller.

3673 El Taller, Inc., Chicago, IL and Movimiento
     Artistico Chicano (MARCH), Chicago, IL.
     Skyjacked: screenprinted posters from
     California by the Royal Chicano Air Force
     (R.C.A.F.), 1980. Exhibition invitation,
     1980. English.

     AN: Invitation to an exhibit at the El
     Taller Gallery, co-sponsored by MARCH.
     Illustrated with a print by San Francisco
     artist Xavier Viramontes.

3674 Tannous, David. Problems of the artist as a
     hyphenated commodity. THE WASHINGTON STAR,
     (August 28, 1977), p. G-20. English.

     AN: Review of ANCIENT ROOTS, NEW VISIONS
     show in Washington, D.C. describing Mel
     Casas' painting (San Antonio), Louis LeRoy's
     assemblage (Coolidge, Arizona), Amado Pena's
     silkscreen, Rogelio Ruiz Valdovin's costume
     (Tucson).

3675 [Tapia exhibit invitation]. Exhibition
     invitation. Santa Fe, NM: Santuario de
     Nuestra Senora de Guadalupe, 1979. English.

     AN: Invitation to an exhibit of works by
     Luis and Star Tapia.

3676 Teatro de la Tierra Morena, Santa Cruz, CA.
     Fuego en Aztlan: a Chicano arts show.

Exhibition brochure, 1980. English.

     AN: Folder of information on the
     exhibition curated by Cruz Zamarron and
     Eduardo Carrillo. Exhibiting artists were:
     Justina Avila, Terry Benitez, Eduardo
     Carrillo, Hernando Chavez, Bob Cruz, Juanita
     Estrada, Juana Franklin, Sal Garcia, Leticia
     Hernandez, David "Sir Loco" Jimenez, Raoul
     Mendez, Vicente Mendez, Maria V. Pinedo,
     Gonzalo Placencia, Ramon Rodriguez, Roberto
     Salas, George Silva and Cruz Zamarron. A
     special feature was a live tattoo
     demonstration entitled "Walking Art".

3677 Temko, Allan. Ole! It's already a triumph.
     REVIEW [supplement to SAN FRANCISCO SUNDAY
     EXAMINER], (December 28, 1980), p. 13-14.
     English.

     AN: A glowing report on the Mexican
     Museum as it celebrates its fifth
     anniversary. Provides details about
     programs, financing and goals. Brief
     analysis of the work of sculptor Manuel Neri
     and painters Manuel Villamor, Gustavo
     Rivera, Alfredo Arreguin and Miguel
     Almaguer. Informative profile on Peter
     Rodriguez, founder and Executive Director of
     the Museum.

3678 Testimonios de Latinoamerica. LA PRENSA SAN
     DIEGO, (October 26, 1979), p. 3. Spanish.

     AN: Announcement of an exhibit at the
     Centro Cultural de la Raza, San Diego,
     "Testimonios de Latino America" and "America
     en la mira," political graphics organized by
     Mexican artist Felipe Ehrenberg and also
     shown at the Los Angeles Contemporary
     Exhibitions gallery (LACE).

3679 Texas Memorial Museum, University of Texas,
     Austin, TX. La vela prendida:
     Mexican-American women's home altars.
     Exhibition catalog, 1980. Bilingual.

     AN: Bilingual illustrated
     brochure-catalog of exhibit. Includes home
     altars and graveyard headstones.

3680 Through the eyes of Joe Giron. NUESTRO, Vol.
     5, no. 9 (December 1981), p. 34-40. English.

     AN: A 9-photo collection of the work of
     Las Cruces, NM photographer, Joe Giron.
     Typical scenes in Texas, NM, and Ohio.

3681 Tolin Fine Art Gallery, Lancaster, CA.
     Presentation of photographic works by David
     Feldman, Richard Valverde. Exhibition
     invitation, 1979. English.

     AN: Invitation to an exhibit.

3682 Trejo, Frank. S.A. mission doors inspired
     wood carver. SAN ANTONIO LIGHT, (January
     10, 1971), p. 18. English.

     AN: Biographical and exhibition
     information on San Antonio woodcarver Jesse
     V. Garcia. Illustrated by photograph of
     artist.

3683 Tucker, Glen. Art scene. TODAY MAGAZINE,
     (April 16, 1978), p. 3. English.

     AN: Commentary on photographic exhibit
     by Robert Tapias and the gift to the Witte
     Museum from the American Academy and
     Institute of Arts and Letters of a colored
     pencil drawing titled "El Filos Lowrider" by
     Luis Jimenez.

Exhibits (cont.)

3684 Tucson Museum of Art and Pima Community
College, Tucson, AZ. Raices
antiguas/visiones nuevas; ancient roots/new
visions. Exhibition invitation, 1977.
English.

AN: Invitation to "Raices" exhibit of
Chicano and Latino artists living in the
United States originated by the Washington
D.C.-based Fondo del Sol and the concurrent
exhibit at Pima, "Art of the Barrio and
Political Art." Illustrated.

3685 Tucson Museum of Art. Raices
antiguas/visiones nuevas; ancient roots/new
visions. Exhibition catalog, 1977-78.
English.

AN: An exhibit of Chicano and Latino
artists living in the United States. The
exhibit traveled continuously for several
years and was supplemented by local artists.
Statements by the artists. 59 illustrations,
some in color.

3686 Union Gallery, University of Arizona Student
Union, Tucson, AZ. Chicanarte: Cynthia Reyes
Aponte, Zarco Guerrero, Virginia Federico
Olivares, Antonio Pazos. Exhibition catalog,
1981. English.

AN: Illustrated catalog of exhibit
featuring four artists.

3687 University Art Museum, Berkeley, CA. The
Fifth Sun: Contemporary/Traditional Chicano
& Latino Art. Exhibition catalog, 1977.
English.

AN: Catalog of exhibit including 45
artists of northern California. Texts deal
with Mexican muralists, Mujeres Muralistas &
other muralists, posters, the Chicano art
movement, altars, La Raza Silkscreen Center,
Galeria de la Raza, the Mexican Museum, the
Sacramento Centro de Artistas Chicanos/RCAF.
Mural maps of S.F. Bay Area and Sacramento.
Many illustrations.

3688 University Gallery, Chicago State University
and Sorell, Victor A. Hispano American art
in Chicago. Exhibition catalog, 1980.
English.

AN: Includes 20 Latino artists living in
the Chicago area: six from Mexico, five
Chicanos, five from Cuba, three from Puerto
Rico, one from Venezuela. 20 illustrations.

3689 University of Houston/Lawndale Annex and
Xochil Art and Culture Center, Mission, TX.
The instant image: an exhibition of polaroid
photography. Exhibition catalog, 1980.
English.

AN: Exhibit of 14 artists including
Tejanos Frank Fajardo, Guillermo Pulido,
Gregorio Salazar and Armando Rodriguez.

3690 University of Texas. El Paso. Chicano
Studies Program. "Chicanotations": paintings
and drawings by Manuel Unzueta. Exhibition
brochure, 1979. English.

AN: Exhibition handout includes
biographical data and a listing of the 20
works exhibited by Unzueta.

3691 University of Texas. San Antonio. Medical
School and Lee, Amy Freeman. Consuelo
Gonzales Amezcua. Exhibition catalog, n.d.
English.

AN: Exhibition catalog with a text by
Amy Freeman Lee. This major exhibit
presented 110 of the artist's works. Price
list included.

3692 [Untitled]. Exhibition invitation. Santa Fe,
NM: Santuario de Nuestra Senora de
Guadalupe, 1980. English.

AN: Invitation to an exhibit by three
northern New Mexico artists: Claudio Salazar
(sculptor from Espanola), Eliud Salazar
(painter from Canones)--both members of the
Escuela Artesana--and Donald Romero (painter
from Santa Fe).

3693 [Untitled photograph]. CHISMEARTE, no. 2
(Winter, Spring, 1977), p. 34.

AN: Reproduction of the invitation to a
Los Four exhibit at Mount San Antonio
College Art Gallery, BANNERS AND PAPER,
April 12 - May 6, 1977.

3694 U.S. Department of Health, Education, and
Welfare. Salud, dinero y amor y tiempo para
gozarlos. Exhibit brochure, n.d. English.

AN: Brochure announcement with statement
by Joseph A. Califano H.E. W. Secretary and
list of participating artists.

3695 Washington State University, Pullman. Fine
Arts Center Gallery II. Ruben M. Trejo-mi
ultimo fracaso. Exhibition announcement,
1976. English.

AN: Exhibit announcement for Trejo's
show of sculpture and drawings. Illustrated
with a Trejo "jalapeno" sculpture.

3696 Wasserman, Isabelle. Photos on exhibit
capture Mexican revolution. SAN DIEGO UNION,
(November 26, 1981), p. D10. English.

AN: Report on the photographic
exhibition of Mexican revolutionary
photographer Agustin V. Casasola at the
Centro Cultural de la Raza in San Diego.
Illustrated.

3697 Weegar, Sally. Native Mexican images. DAILY
TEXAN, (October 23, 1978), p. 16. English.

AN: Review of an exhibit of watercolors,
tiles, and silkscreen prints by Amado Pena
at the Wagner Gallery in Austin. Earlier
work of Laredo-born Pena were politically
oriented toward La Raza. Recent work
concentrates on New Mexican landscape and
Indian peoples. Illustrated.

3698 Weil Gallery Center for the Arts, Corpus
Christi State University. Caras y mascaras:
the art of El Zarco Guerrero. Exhibition
invitation, 1981. English.

AN: Invitation to exhibit of Arizona
artist. Color illustration.

3699 West Colorado Gallery, Pasadena, CA.
Gronk/Patssi. Exhibition brochure, 1979.
English.

AN: Works on exhibit by ASCO members
Gronk and Patssi Valdez. Photo of artists.

Exhibits (cont.)

3700 William Grant Still Community Arts Center,
      Los Angeles, CA. Latin American artists
      exhibition. Exhibition brochure, 1978.
      English.

      AN: Exhibit curated by Linda Vallejo
      including Carlos Almaraz, Michael M.
      Amescua, Ray Bravo, Isabel Castro, Yreina
      Cervantez, Luis Serrano-Cordero, Cynthia
      Honesto, Judith Miranda, Teddy Sandoval,
      John Taboada, Emigdio Vasquez. Illustrated.

3701 Wilson, William. 30 works from the grass
      roots. LOS ANGELES TIMES, (June 4, 1973),
      p. IV,2. English.

      AN: Review of a show at the Junior Arts
      Center in Barnsdall Park by 15 members of
      the Mechicano Art Center. The critic feels
      contemporary groups that aim for change
      today (unlike past groups) are unable to
      articulate their spirit in a cohesive style.
      The top talent in this show is Charles
      Almaraz; also on exhibit are paintings by
      Jose Cervantes, Guillermo Martinez, Ray
      Atilano, sculpture by Manuel Cruz, and
      photography by (Oscar) R. Castillo.

3702 Wilson, William. Art of barrios in East L.A.
      LOS ANGELES TIMES, (July 27, 1970), p.
      IV,1+. English.

      AN: Rather personalized view of ARTE DE
      LOS BARRIOS traveling exhibit organized by
      Casa Hispana de Bellas Artes with Artistas
      Latinos Americanos, San Francisco, and
      featuring "100 Chicano paintings,
      photographs, and other works of art".

3703 Wilson, William. Artistic get-together in
      Orange County exhibit. CALENDAR, (November
      4, 1979), p. 99. English.

      AN: Review of exhibit OUR OWN ARTISTS:
      ART IN ORANGE COUNTY at the Newport Harbor
      Art Museum. Mention of Patricia Murillo and
      Emigdio Vasquez.

3704 Wilson, William. A bit of the barrio at
      County Museum. LOS ANGELES TIMES, (February
      27, 1974), p. IV, 1+. English.

      AN: Review of the Los Four exhibit at
      the Los Angeles County Museum of Art. Quotes
      from artists, history of group's formation
      in 1973.

3705 Wilson, William. A blending of Hispanic
      roots, visions. CALENDAR, (July 30, 1978),
      p. 90. English.

      AN: Review of ANCIENT ROOTS/NEW VISIONS
      exhibit held at the Municipal Art Gallery in
      Los Angeles.

3706 Wilson, William. Chicana artists still
      seeking identification. LOS ANGELES TIMES,
      (June 23, 1975), p. VI, 5. English.

      AN: Ten Chicana artists are exhibiting
      their work in the Boathouse Gallery of Plaza
      de la Raza in Lincoln Park: Judithe
      Hernandez, Patssi Valdez, Judy Baca,
      Josefina Quesada, Victoria del
      Castillo-Leon, Olga Muniz, Gloria Flores,
      Sylvia Morales, Isabel Castro and Celia
      Tejadak. The work is still tentative and may
      develop.

3707 Wilson, William. 'Los Four' a statement of
      Chicano spirit. CALENDAR, (March 10, 1974),
      p. 64+. English.

      AN: Lengthy critical review of Los Four
      exhibit at Los Angeles County Museum of Art.
      Illustrated.

3708 Wilson, William. A multicultural celebration
      of photos. CALENDAR, (February 8, 1981), p.
      89-90. English.

      AN: Review of multi-ethnic photography
      show at the Los Angeles Municipal Art
      Gallery. Wilson finds the photographs about
      equally divided between sociological reality
      and expression/art for its own sake.

3709 Winn Galleries, Seattle, WA. Alfredo
      Arreguin. Exhibition catalog, 1981. English.

      AN: Catalog of an exhibit by
      Mexican-born Washington painter. Many
      reproductions, some in color.

3710 Woman who began at 73 is shaping Chicano
      art. SAN ANTONIO EXPRESS-NEWS, (August 18,
      1978), p. 6-W. English.

      AN: 76-year-old Laredoan Alicia
      Dickerson Montemayor who began painting on
      guajes (gourds) from her garden three years
      ago, now paints on canvas stories from her
      life in the Valley, nature, and people. An
      exhibit of her work, referred to by Chicano
      art critics as "el arte de la inocencia"
      opens at Gallery of El Centro Cultural de
      LUCHA, in Austin, TX.

3711 Woman's Building, Los Angeles, CA.
      Crosspollination: a blending of traditional
      and contemporary art by Asian, Black and
      Chicana women. Los Angeles, CA: Woman's
      Building, 1979. English.

      AN: Invitation to an exhibit in which
      are included Patricia Murillo and Linda
      Vallejo.

3712 Wood carving art. EASTSIDE JRNL, (January
      7, 1971), p. 2. English.

      AN: Two photographs and commentary on
      woodcarver Roberto H. Rodriguez on the
      occasion of his one man show at the East Los
      Angeles Library. Illustrated work shows
      pre-Columbian motifs.

3713 Xerox Reproductions Center, San Francisco,
      CA. Fine arts exhibitions of color xerox.
      Exhibition invitation, 1978-79. English.

      AN: Invitation to an exhibit featuring
      Rene Yanez and 11 other artists working in
      color Xerox.

3714 XIe festival international de la peinture.
      Exhibition catalog, 1980. English.

      AN: Catalog of an international
      exposition in Cagnes-Sur-Mer, France. The
      United States exhibit included the work of
      Seattle artist Alfredo Mendoza Arreguin.
      Biographical information and reproduction of
      Arreguin's oil painting URUAPAN.

Exhibits (cont.)

3715 Xochil Art and Culture Center, Mission, TX.
Besame mucho. Exhibition invitation, 1979.
English.

AN: Invitation to exhibit of Texas
artists from Mujeres Artistas del Suroeste
(MAS): Mary Ann Anguiano, Alicia Arredondo,
Santa Barraza, Nora Gonzales-Dodson, Maria
Flores, Carolina Flores, Mary Ann Ambray
Gonzales, Sylvia Orozco, Nancy de los
Santos, Modesta Barbina Trevino.
Illustrated.

3716 Xochil Art and Culture Center, Mission, TX.
¡Que te vaya pretty nice! Exhibition
brochure, 1979. English.

AN: Exhibition of Chicano art including
Carmen Lomas Garza, Luis Jimenez, Cesar
Martinez, Guillermo Pulido, Roberto Rios,
Jose Rivera and Jesse Trevino. [See also
Estudios Rio].

**Exposition Park Museum of Science and Industry,
Los Angeles, CA**

3717 [Untitled photograph]. HISPANIC BUSINESS,
(September 16, 1975). English.

AN: Captioned illustration of Raul
Esparza's 24x60 foot ceramic mural on the
wall of the Exposition Park Museum of
Science and Industry. Esparza worked a year
and a half on the mural, MEXICO Y EL GENERO
HUMANO.

La Extension Cultural, Seattle, WA

3718 Contreras, Carlos. Nuestra cultura. LA VOZ:
Concilio for the Spanish Speaking of King
Co., Seattle, no. 7 (August 1979).

AN: Information of Washington state
murals painted by members of La Extension
Cultural; Armando Lara's autobiographical
mural titled "El Rio" is installed at the
Concilio offices, 107 Cherry St. Suite 210.
Arturo Artorez completed a wall painting
using the image of Quetzalcoatl at El Centro
de la Raza with funding from the Seattle
Arts Commission. Francisco Siqueiros used
the themes of ecology and Mexican mythology
for two murals at Seattle Community College.
Commentary on Alfredo Arreguin's painting
exhibition at the Kiku Gallery and his wall
painting at the Childrens Orthopedic
Hospital in Seattle.

3719 The new logo. LA VOZ: Concilio for the
Spanish Speaking of King Co., Seattle, no. 5
(June 1979). English.

AN: Biographical information on artist
Alfredo Arreguin. Born in Uruapan, Michoacan
Mexico and residing in Seattle for eighteen
years, Arrequin is active in La Extension
Cultural, an agency formed to meet the
cultural needs of "Hispanics" in the Pacific
Northwest. In his logo for the "Concilio,"
Arreguin employs symbols representing
history, beauty, unity, ethnicity and
communication.

**LAS EXTRAORDINARIAS HISTORIAS DE LOS CODICES
MEXICANOS**

3720 Lopez Castro, Rafael. [Untitled drawing].
ATISBOS, no. 1 (Summer 1975), p. COVER.

3721 Lopez Castro, Rafael. [Untitled drawing].
ATISBOS, no. 1 (Summer 1975), p. 1.

3722 Lopez Castro, Rafael. [Untitled drawing].
ATISBOS, no. 1 (Summer 1975), p. 9.

3723 Lopez Castro, Rafael. [Untitled drawing].
ATISBOS, no. 1 (Summer 1975), p. 31.

3724 Lopez Castro, Rafael. [Untitled drawing].
ATISBOS, no. 1 (Summer 1975), p. 53.

3725 Lopez Castro, Rafael. [Untitled drawing].
ATISBOS, no. 1 (Summer 1975), p. 66.

3726 Lopez Castro, Rafael. [Untitled drawing].
ATISBOS, no. 1 (Summer 1975), p. 67.

3727 Lopez Castro, Rafael. [Untitled drawing].
ATISBOS, no. 1 (Summer 1975), p. 79.

3728 Lopez Castro, Rafael. [Untitled drawing].
ATISBOS, no. 1 (Summer 1975), p. 93.

EXXON U.S.A

3729 Rivas, Maggie. Art of the barrio: Exxon's
traveling art show comes to headquarters. HQ
HOUSTON, (August 1976), p. 6-7. English.

AN: Report on traveling photo-exhibition
of 29 Chicano murals organized by Jacinto
Quirarte for Exxon USA.

Fables
USE: Cuentos

Fairytales
USE: Cuentos

Fajardo, Francisco (Frank)

3730 Contemporary Arts Museum, Houston, TX. Dale
gas: give it gas. The continued
acceleration of Chicano art. Exhibition
catalog, 1977. English.

AN: A comprehensive catalog including 28
works of art exhibited by 13 Texas artists:
Melesio (Mel) Casas, Jose Esquivel,
Francisco (Frank) Fajardo, Carmen Lomas
Garza, Luis Jimenez, Cesar Augusto Martinez,
Santos G. Martinez, Jr., Amado Pena, Roberto
Rios, Jose B. Rodriguez, Jesus
(Jesse) Trevino, and George Truan. Many
illustrations, some in color. Introduction
by James Harithas. Essay by Santos Martinez,
Jr. Poetry, literature and essays by Chicano
writers.

3731 Out in the open/Allen Parkway: Frank
Fajardo, Jesse Lott, Guillermo Pulido, Jana
Vander Lee. Exhibit invitation, 1979.
English.

AN: Invitation to the installation of
conceptual pieces in public areas of
Houston. Includes Chicano artist Frank
Fajardo and Bolivian-born Pulido.

3732 San Antonio Museum Association, San Antonio,
TX. Visiones nuevas en Tejas/new visions in
Texas. Exhibtion catalog, 1979. English.

AN: Supplementary regional catalog for
the exhibit RAICES ANTIGUAS/VISIONES NUEVAS;
ANCIENT ROOTS/NEW VISIONS. Illustrations for
works by George Cisneros, Francisco (Frank)
Fajardo, Robert Gonzalez, Cesar Augusto
Martinez, Roland Mazuca, Guillermo Pulido,
Felipe Reyes, Jesus (Jesse) Trevino.

Fajardo, Francisco (Frank) (cont.)

3733 Tennant, Donna. Conceptual art dots city landscape. HOUSTON CHRONICLE, (October 27, 1979), p. II, 7. English.

AN: Frank Fajardo and Bolivian-born Guillermo Pulido are two of several artists creating conceptual art pieces in various parts of Houston. Fajardo marked out space with 25 stakes tipped with day-glo orange paint. Pulido constructed two large triangles on opposite hillsides, like giant markers.

3734 University of Houston/Lawndale Annex and Xochil Art and Culture Center, Mission, TX. The instant image: an exhibition of polaroid photography. Exhibition catalog, 1980. English.

AN: Exhibit of 14 artists including Tejanos Frank Fajardo, Guillermo Pulido, Gregorio Salazar and Armando Rodriguez.

Falcon, Mario

3735 Mario Falcon. CHISMEARTE, Vol. 2, no. 1 (Summer 1978), p. 29. Spanish.

AN: Mexican muralist Mario Falcon, who has painted murals in Long Beach and Wilmington (Los Angeles, County), is a political exile in the U. S. Support is asked to prevent his return to Mexico. Illustrated.

LA FAMILIA COSMICA [mural]

3736 La Familia Recreation Center, Denver, CO. Mural unveiling and swim party. Exhibition invitation, 1980. English.

AN: Invitation to the unveiling of La Familia Cosmica, a mural by Jerry Jaramillo assisted by Carlos Sandoval, Al Sanchez, Stephen Lucero. An art exhibit featured the muralists, Jon Howe, and Fred Sanchez, all of the Metro Denver Urban Coalition's City Walls artists. Illustrated.

LA FAMILIA [poster]

3737 Gala evening at OAS. NUESTRO, Vol. 5, no. 7 (October 1981), p. 21. English.

AN: Brief description of "Salute to Hispanic Arts" held as part of Hispanic Heritage Week festivities in Washington, D.C. Special guest at the affair was Amado Pena who was there to be recognized and to unveil his work LA FAMILIA which was used on the posters announcing Hispanic Heritage Week nationwide.

Farm Workers
USE: Agricultural Laborers

Farmworkers, Images of

3738 Help the Delano farm workers. Flyer, 1966. English.

AN: Adolph Villalvazo, drawing reproduced.

3739 Pazos, Antonio. [Untitled drawing]. LLUEVE TLALOC, no. 4 (1977), p. [66].

3740 Pazos, Antonio. [Untitled drawing]. LLUEVE TLALOC, no. 4 (1977), p. [71].

3741 Pazos, Antonio. [Untitled drawing]. LLUEVE TLALOC, no. 6 (1979), p. 33.

3742 Ulloa, Domingo. [Untitled drawing]. MAIZE, Vol. 1, no. 1 (Fall 1977), p. 40. English.

3743 [Untitled drawing]. CARACOL, Vol. 5, no. 1 (September 1978), p. 22. Bilingual.

3744 Vasquez y Sanchez, Ramon. Campesina [drawing]. CARACOL, Vol. 2, no. 6 (February 1976), p. 1.

Fashion

3745 Johnston, Tracy. La vida loca. NEW WEST MAGAZINE, (January 29, 1979), p. 38-46. English.

AN: A journalistic account of barrio lifestyles composed from conversations with young Cholos in Los Angeles. Amid poverty, unemployment, drug abuse and familial disintegration, codes of group solidarity and rituals of connection occur. Information on urban Chicano forms of self expression such as mascaras (chola make up), tattoos and graffiti. Well illustrated with photographs.

Fashion Moda, South Bronx, NY

3746 'Fashion Moda' at Galeria de la Raza. PEOPLE'S WORLD, Vol. 44, no. 48 (November 29, 1981), p. 10. English.

AN: A joint exhibit, FASHION MODA AT GALERIA DE LA RAZA, focuses on people interested in cross-cultural interaction. 50 artists from the San Francisco Bay Area, the South Bronx, Los Angeles, and New York City were shown. Fashion Moda is located in the South Bronx, an area of severe urban devastation. Illustrated.

Favela, Ricardo V.

3747 Calendario de comida 1976. San Francisco, CA: Galeria de la Raza, 1976. English.

AN: Handprinted silkscreen calendar consisting of twelve sheets and a cover. The work of the following artists is included: Ralph Maradiaga, Juanishi Orozco, Francisco Camplis, Ruben Guzman, Rodolfo Cuellar, Xavier Viramontes, Jose Montoya, Esteban Villa, Rene Yanez, Max Garcia and Louis "The Foot" Gonzalez, Patricia Rodriguez, and Ricardo Favela. All of the above are associated with the Galeria de la Raza, or the Royal Chicano Air Force of Sacramento, CA.

3748 R.C.A.F. artistas precursores del arte chicano. EL HISPANO, Vol. 8, no. 35 (February 17, 1976), p. 1. English.

AN: Information on the R.C.A.F. organization. Includes group photograph of R.C.A.F. members, Jose Montoya, Esteban Villa, John Carrillo, Ricardo Fabela, Rudy Cuellar, Juanishi Orozco and Frank Godena.

Favela, Ricardo V.(cont.)

3749 Valencia, Manuel. Store front academy for
     Chicano artists. SACRAMENTO UNION, (January
     17, 1973). English.

     AN: Article includes comments by Armando
     Cid, Ricardo Fabela and Jose Montoya in a
     free-wheeling discussion of the goals and
     underlying philosophy of the Centro de
     Artistas Chicanos in Sacramento. More than
     simply exposing the people to art, the
     artists explain that they are looking for an
     alternative art expression and method of
     instruction never offered in traditional art
     schools or university departments of art.

Felix, Charles "Clavos"

3750 Blanco, Gil. Art on the walls: a vehicle for
     positive change. LATIN QUARTER, Vol. 1, no.
     2 (October 1974), p. 26-30. English.

     AN: East Los Angeles artists Ismael
     "Smiley" Pereira and C.W. (Charles) Felix
     started painting murals with young people at
     the Estrada Courts Housing Project in May
     1973. There are now 30 murals, and the
     residents are more receptive, noting the
     changes that are taking place. Illustrated
     with murals by Herron and Gronk, and Daniel
     Martinez.

3751 Davis, Alonzo, ed. Los Angeles street
     graphics. Los Angeles, CA: Brockman Gallery
     Productions, [ca. 1975]. English.

     AN: Portfolio of art in public places.
     Includes Charles Felix (murals), Leo Limon
     (mural), Charles Almaraz (billboard mural),
     Johnny Alvarez (mural), Mexican artist
     Gonzalo Duran, and graffiti.

3752 Exxon Company, Houston, TX and Quirarte,
     Jacinto. Chicano art of the barrio.
     Exhibition brochure, n.d. [c.1976]. English.

     AN: Brochure for a traveling exhibit of
     photographically-reproduced Chicano murals:
     Leo Limon, Lucila Villasenor Grijalva,
     Antonio Esparza, Susan Saenz, Charles Felix,
     Hoyo-Mara gang, David A. Lopez and team,
     Roberto Chavez and team (Los Angeles); Jerry
     Concha, Ruben Guzman, Chuy Campusano (San
     Francisco); Manuel Unzueta (Santa Barbara).
     Ernie Palomino and Leo Esequiel Ozona
     (Fresno). Leo Tanguma (Houston), Roberto
     Lucero, Manuel Martinez and Al Sanchez
     (Denver).

3753 Saenz, John. Felix completes art project:
     artist's murals mask East LA graffitti
     [sic]. EAST LOS ANGELES TRIBUNE, (November
     30, 1972), p. A-4. English.

     AN: Charles Felix is doing murals as
     part of a community beautification "Wall
     Project" to cover graffiti. His present
     project is a series of murals intended to
     make Whittier Blvd. into a street gallery.
     Illustrated.

3754 Sommer, Robert. Street art. New York: Quick
     Fox, 1975. English.

     AN: Introductory essay covering the
     history of the new mural movement, forms of
     street art, politics, street sculpture, how
     to locate and photograph street art. Chicano
     murals include Charles Felix and others at
     Estrada Courts (L.A.), RCAF murals in
     Sacramento, Jose Montoya and others
     (Broderick, Ca.) Marcos Raya (Chicago), Mike
     Rios (Neighborhood Legal Aid, S.F.)

Mechicano Art Center (L.A.) Johnny Alvarez
(L.A.), New Mexico State Employment Bldg.,
Albuquerque mural, Lorena Street School
(L.A.), two murals, Casa de la Raza
Alternative School (Berkeley), Santa Fe, New
Mexico mural, Francisco Hernandez (L.A.),
Artes Guadalupanos de Aztlan (N. Mexico),
Willie Herron (L.A.). Better documentation
would have been welcome.

3755 Street art explosion in Los Angeles. SUNSET,
     (April 1973), p. 110-113. English.

     AN: Illustrated article on Los Angeles
     street murals including those by Roberto
     Chavez, Willie Herron, Frank Romero, Richard
     Jimenez, William Bejarano, Gilbert Lujan,
     Armando Cabrera, Frank Martinez, Charles
     Felix, and others.

3756 Torres, Louis R. A Profile of an Hispano
     Artist: Charlie "Clavos" Felix. LA LUZ, Vol.
     4, no. 6-7 (September, October, 1975), p.
     3-4. English.

     AN: Biographical data on artist and his
     unique nail relief sculpture.

Felix, Charles W.

3757 Del Olmo, Frank. Murals changing face of
     East L.A. LOS ANGELES TIMES, (December 3,
     1973), p. II, 1+. English.

     AN: First Los Angeles Times report on
     burgeoning Los Angeles mural movement with a
     map of 15 mural sites. Mentioned are C.W.
     Felix (originator of Estrada Courts
     project), Willie Herron, David Botello,
     Armando Campero, Edward Carbajal. (Chicano
     Art Committee).

3758 Graffiti gone: murals in full bloom. PHOENIX
     GAZETTE, (April 13, 1974). English.

     AN: Mural explosion at Estrada Courts
     Housing Project in Los Angeles led by C.W.
     Felix. Estimates 60 murals in East Los
     Angeles. Illustrated.

3759 Lopez, Gerard. Estrada murals. LA GENTE DE
     AZTLAN, Vol. 4, no. 6 (May, June, 1974), p.
     4. English.

     AN: Article explains how the community
     at Estrada Courts was mobilized to support a
     mural project uniting artists with
     residents. Includes interview with artist
     C.W. Felix who comments on the goals of the
     mural program and cites the themes and
     symbolism of the murals.

Fellowship
     USE: Financial Aid

Females
     USE: Chicanas

Feminism
     USE: Women's Rights

Fenner-Lopez, Claudio

3760 Knapp, Dan. KCET's show for Chicano viewers. LOS ANGELES TIMES, (April 3, 1970), p. IV, 18. English.

AN: Story on the television series AHORA! started September 1969 on KCET, Los Angeles' National Educational Television. Edward Moreno is program director and host; Victor Millan is producer-director; Claudio Fenner-Lopez, senior producer, has staff including set-designer David Villasenor, production manager James Val, and alternate host-narrator Jesus Trevino. The program has shown exhibits of artists Gilberto Lujan and Daniel Ramirez.

Fernandez, Esther

3761 Garcia, Rupert. Pulqueria art--defiant art of the barrios [Part II]. EL TECOLOTE, Vol. 8, no. 5 (February 1978), p. 8. Bilingual.

AN: In the Mission District of San Francisco, various artists like Irene Perez, Esther Fernandez, Chuy Campusano, Graciela Carrillo de Lopez, Consuelo Mendez Castillo, and Mike Rios have embellished business sites with wall decorations similar in spirit to the "Pulqueria" art of Mexico. Illustrated with three "Pulqueria"-type wall paintings: ATARDECER DE UN IMPERIO by Oscar Carveo at the Azteca Restaurant (Mission and 20th Sts.), El Buen Boricano Restaurant facade (24th and Harrison Sts.) and Fruitlandia facade (24th and Treat Sts.).

Fernandez, Licita

3762 Galeria de la Raza/Studio 24, San Francisco, CA. Licita Fernandez (watercolor paintings), Pete Davalos (ceramic pots). Exhibition invitation, 1981. English.

AN: Invitation to an exhibit.

Fernandez, Rudy

3763 Chicano art show. EL DIARIO DE LA GENTE, Vol. 1, no. 7 (February 6, 1973), p. 4. English.

AN: Fine arts students at the University of Colorado led by Rudy Fernandez hope to educate high school students about Chicano art. This article documents an exhibit held at Lafayette, CO. Members of the group are Bob Maez, Jerry Jaramillo, Anthony Mendoza, and Rudy Fernandez. Illustrated by four exhibition photographs by John L. Espinosa.

3764 Coe, Kathryn. Heritage plus science yields art. SCOTTSDALE DAILY PROGRESS, (August 28, 1981), p. 27. English.

AN: Biography of Colorado-born Rudy Fernandez who bases many of his paintings and mixed media boxes on the religious imagery of Colorado. He studied geology; travelled to Spain and Mexico to know his heritage. All these factors influence his art, in which he uses symbols personally.

3765 Donnell-Kotrozo, Carol. Containment and discovery. ARTWEEK, Vol. 11, no. 41 (December 6, 1980), p. 12. English.

AN: Review of an exhibit at Scottsdale, Arizona gallery, C.G. Rein by Rudy Fernandez. Discussed in detail is one of his altar-like boxes of mixed media which contain personal symbolisms. Illustrated.

3766 Donnell-Kotrozo, Carol and Perlman, Barbara. Male passages: a secular santero of the '80s interprets machismo. ARIZONA ARTS AND LIFESTYLE, Vol. 4, no. 1 (1982), p. 32-39. English.

AN: Rudy Fernandez moves freely between two- and three-dimensional forms using personal symbols such as cacti, roosters, flying hearts, trout, in paintings or lead-covered shelves of boxes reminiscent of retablos. Colorado-born Fernandez has lived in Arizona, Utah, New Mexico, and Washington. His art is not religious, but is influenced by a strong Catholic background. Many color illustrations, including the cover.

3767 Donnell-Kotrozo, Carol. Rudy Fernandez. SOUTHWESTERN CONTEMPORARY ARTS QUARTERLY, (Fall 1981). English.

AN: Well-illustrated article on the mixed media creations of Rudy Fernandez who lives in Scottsdale, AZ.

3768 Donnell-Kotrozo, Carol. Rudy Fernandez. ARTSPACE, Vol. 5, no. 4 (Fall 1981), p. 18-23. English.

AN: Scottsdale, Arizona resident Rudy Fernandez converts cultural symbols into a private system language that revolves around love, family, manhood and self-identity. His mixed media altar-like forms are based on interest in Southwest santos, their format and presentation. Fernandez does paintings, and assembled wood pieces. Handsomely illustrated, with color.

3769 Galeria de la Raza/Studio 24, San Francisco, CA. Images of the Southwest. Exhibition catalog, 1977. English.

AN: Invitation/catalog for an exhibit including Rudy M. Fernandez(Utah), Enrique Flores(Texas), Xavier Gorena(Texas), C.A.[Cesar] Martinez(Texas), Santos Martinez, Jr.(Texas), Pedro Rodriguez(Texas), Arnold Trujillo(New Mexico). Block prints, paper cut-outs, drawings, photographs, copper enamels, and sculpture were shown. Five illustrations.

3770 Heard Museum, Phoenix, AZ. Second Southwest Chicano Art Invitational. Exhibit catalog, 1978. English.

AN: Exhibit by eight artists: Antonio Pazos (Tucson), Rudy Fernandez (Salt Lake City), Harry Gamboa (Los Angeles), Rupert Garcia and Xavier Viramontes (San Francisco), Roberto Rios (San Antonio), Roberto Espinoza (Yuma), and Roberto Borboa (Tucson). Brief biographies of all but Rios. 29 illustrations.

3771 Miller, Marlan. Heard speaks Spanish through art. PHOENIX GAZETTE, (September 23, 1978). English.

AN: Four new exhibits at the Heard Museum of Phoenix include "Hispanic crafts of the Southwest", and "Southwest Chicano Art Invitational". The former focuses on New Mexico and Colorado crafts, organized by the Taylor Museum if the Colorado Springs Fine Arts Center; the latter includes Rupert Garcia and Xavier Miramontes of San Francisco, Rudy Fernandez of Salt Lake City (now in Scottsdale, AZ), and Antonio Pazos of Tucson.

Fernandez, Rudy (cont.)

3772 Scottsdale resident wins art fellowship.
SCOTTSDALE DAILY PROGRESS, (April 10,
1981), p. 29. English.

AN: Rudy M. Fernandez, Jr. awarded the
1981 Visual Arts Fellowship in painting by
the Arizona Commission on the arts.
Fernandez holds an M.F.A. from Washington
State University, and is affiliated with the
Elaine Horwitch Gallery in Scottsdale and
the Galeria de la Raza in San Francisco.

3773 Valley artist is basking in rosy glory.
ARIZONA REPUBLIC, (October 14, 1981), p.
Extra,11. English.

AN: Rudy M. Fernandez has been invited
to the White House, selected to create a
Festival poster, included in a group show of
emerging artists. He is presently working on
a series called TROPHIES featuring roses,
and sometimes trout--both trophies of sorts.
Illustrated.

FESTIVAL ESTUDIANTIL CHICANO DE ARTE Y LITERATURA, Austin, TX, 1977

3774 Cavazos, David S. FESTIVAL ESTUDIANTIL
CHICANO DE ARTE Y LITERATURA, Austin, TX,
1976. TEJIDOS, Vol. 4, no. 3 (Fall 1977),
p. i-ii. English.

AN: Brief description of the goals and
objectives of this artistic festival geared
towards school-aged children.

EL FESTIVAL HISPANICO

3775 Eichstaedt, Peter. Hispanic festival
cultural showcase. NEW MEXICAN WEEKEND,
(May 25, 1979), p. 3. English.

AN: Announcement of the week-long
HISPANIC HERITAGE FESTIVAL/EL FESTIVAL
HISPANICO co-sponsored by La Cofradia de
Artes y Artesanos Hispanicos and the Santa
Fe Council fo the Arts at the Armory for the
Arts in Santa Fe. Outlines the cultural
activities, including a visual arts exhibit.
La Cofradia is a recently formed
organization which has assembled regional
shows at the Santuario de Guadalupe which
gave opportunities to local artists to show
their work. Festival artists are primarily
from the upper Rio Grande but also include
artists from the State Penitentiary, as well
as Albuquerque and Las Cruces. Illustration
of painting by Sam Leyba.

3776 Fabricant, Don. Show reveals Hispanic art.
NEW MEXICAN WEEKEND, (June 1, 1979).
English.

AN: Review of two exhibits in Santa Fe:
EL FESTIVAL HISPANICO, mounted by La
Cofradia de Artes y Artesanos Hispanicos and
Gilberto Guzman at the Black Kachina
Gallery. The reviewer feels the
traditional-style woodcarving done by
contemporaries is the strongest part of the
show; works that break with these forms seem
weaker, less skillful and cliche-ridden.
Crafts are excellent. Muralist Guzman has
blossomed in murals and easel paintings
since he was employed by the 1978 Art in
Public Places project. His work is intense
and expressive, sometimes erotic.
Illustration of work by sculptor Ruben
Montoya.

3777 Loniak, Walter. The true New Mexico
contemporary style. SANTA FE REPORTER, (May

31, 1979). English.

AN: Review of three exhibits in Santa
Fe, EL FESTIVAL HISPANICO co-sponsored by
the Cofradia de Artes y Artesanos Hispanicos
and the Santa Fe Council for the Arts; a
wood carving exhibit at Elaine Horwitch
Gallery, and easel paintings by muralist
Gilberto Guzman at the Black Kachina
Gallery. Concerning the Festival exhibit,
the critic states that the sculptural pieces
are the strongest; two dimensional work is
inconsistent or unimpressive, weaving is not
well represented (though usually the
strongest medium), and there are few
photographs or prints. Illustration.

Festivals
USE: Fiestas

Fiction and Juvenile Literature
USE: Children's Literature

Fiesta de los Barrios, Los Angeles

3778 Fiesta de los barrios observes Cinco de
Mayo. EASTSIDE SUN, (May 1, 1969). English.

AN: The Fiesta de los Barrios is a
cultural festival organized by the committee
pressuring the Los Angeles Board of
Education for better and more relevant
education after the East Los Angeles high
school "blowouts." The Fiesta features art,
music, dance and literature.

3779 Public invited to weekend fiesta at Lincoln
High. LOS ANGELES TIMES, (April 29, 1969),
p. II. English.

AN: Fiesta of art, music, dance and
literature organized by the committee formed
after the East Los Angeles high school
"blowouts" to press for better and more
relevant education. Hundreds of works of art
were collected for display at the "Fiesta de
los Barrios".

Fiestas

3780 Arts Council Center for the Arts of Greater
Lansing, Lansing, MI. Raza fine arts
festival. Festival program, 1978. English.

AN: This festival program mentions Jose
Narezo's mural at the Holland National Guard
Armory, Grand Rapids; includes a statement
of the Raza Art/Media Collective, Inc.; the
philosophy of artists Zaragosa Vargas and S.
Kaneta Kosiba-Vargas; and profiles of
exhibiting artists George Vargas, Martin
Moreno, Hector Perez, Michael L. Selley,
Jesse Gonzales, Nora Chapa Mendoza, Jesse
Soriano, Jose Luis Narezo.

3781 'Barrios fiesta' due May 2-5. EL SERENO
STAR, (May 1, 1969). English.

AN: Details of the FIESTA DE LOS BARRIOS
held at Lincoln High School a year after the
school "blowouts" in East Los Angeles.
Featured 250 community visual artists from
primary school through professional
categories.

Fiestas (cont.)

3782 California. University. Los Angeles. Cine sin fronteras. Festival brochure, 1981. English.

AN: Brochure program for a cinema festival and series of seminars and discussions featuring films and discussants from Mexico and Chicanos of the United States. Participating were Chicano directors Moctezuma Esparza, Richard Soto, David Sandoval, and Robert Young, and film historian David Maciel.

3783 Cinefestival. ARRIBA, , p. 5. English.

AN: Announcement of the 6th Annual International Hispanic Film Festival in San Antonio, TX. Willie Varela will conduct a workshop, and Jesus Trevino will premiere his hour-long production, SEGUIN.

3784 La Cofradia de Artes y Artesanos Hispanicos and Santa Fe Council for the Arts. El festival hispanico. Festival program, [ca. 1979]. English.

AN: Program for the festival which included over 70 visual artists from northern New Mexico selected and hung by the Cofradia at the Armory for the Arts gallery in Santa Fe. The poster for the festival, reproduced on the program cover, is taken from a painting by Gilberto Guzman. The festival also featured music, cuentos, dance, slide show, poetry, films.

3785 Eichstaedt, Peter. Hispanic festival cultural showcase. NEW MEXICAN WEEKEND, (May 25, 1979), p. 3. English.

AN: Announcement of the week-long HISPANIC HERITAGE FESTIVAL/EL FESTIVAL HISPANICO co-sponsored by La Cofradia de Artes y Artesanos Hispanicos and the Santa Fe Council fo the Arts at the Armory for the Arts in Santa Fe. Outlines the cultural activities, including a visual arts exhibit. La Cofradia is a recently formed organization which has assembled regional shows at the Santuario de Guadalupe which gave opportunities to local artists to show their work. Festival artists are primarily from the upper Rio Grande but also include artists from the State Penitentiary, as well as Albuquerque and Las Cruces. Illustration of painting by Sam Leyba.

3786 'Festival of arts' planned by Arthritis Foundation. SANTA FE NEW MEXICAN, (October 11, 1972), p. B6. English.

AN: The Albuquerque Arthritis Foundation has invited professional artists and craftsmen from New Mexico to display their paintings, watercolors, sculpture, prints, lithographs, jewelry. Joel Ramirez's painting THE WEAVERS is selected for full color art prints. Illustrated.

3787 Fiesta de los barrios observes Cinco de Mayo. EASTSIDE SUN, (May 1, 1969). English.

AN: The Fiesta de los Barrios is a cultural festival organized by the committee pressuring the Los Angeles Board of Education for better and more relevant education after the East Los Angeles high school "blowouts." The Fiesta features art, music, dance and literature.

3788 Finalists in $540 E.L.A. art contest provide dazzling show at local hospital. EASTSIDE

SUN, (November 21, 1968). English.

AN: First East Los Angeles art festival. Juried by artists Donald Manion, John Bene, Rubin Holguin. Show hung at Doctors' Hospital by Garfield High School art teacher David Ramirez.

3789 Fourth annual San Antonio film festival. San Antonio, TX: Oblate College of the Southwest, 1979. Bilingual.

AN: Symposium and film festival catalog featuring motion pictures and videocassettes made by and about Mexicans, Chicanos and Latinos. The Symposium focused on Latina women in film and television, Margarita Galban, Carmen Tafolla, Leticia Ponce, Grace Castro Nagata, Marcela Fernandez Violante of Mexico, and Sylvia Morales.

3790 Galeria de la Raza/Studio 24, San Francisco, CA and Milkie, Anne. Carnaval '80. Exhibition catalog, 1980. English.

AN: Catalog of an exhibit of photographs and other media recording San Francisco's multi-ethnic CARNAVAL, organized in 1978 by Panamanian-born dancer. Included in the exhibit were the photographs of Chicana Maria V. Pinedo, who also designed the catalog.

3791 Gloria, Juan J. En San Antonio: se celebrara el tercer festival de cine, 'La vida chicana a traves del celuloide'. EL VISITANTE DOMINICAL, (August 20, 1978), p. 6-8, 12. Spanish.

AN: The Third Chicano Film Festival honors the only two feature-length films made by Chicanos: Moctezuma Esparza's ONLY ONCE IN A LIFETIME (made in Hollywood) and Jesus Salvador Trevino's RAICES DE SANGRE (Blood Roots), (made with CONACINE in Mexico). Illustrated.

3792 Gonzales, Juan. Chicano film festival earns pluses and minuses. EL TECOLOTE, Vol. 9, no. 3 (November 1978), p. 7. English.

AN: Critical review of the Third Annual Chicano Film Festival in San Antonio, TX. The writer criticizes lack of critical exchange and dialogue between filmmakers and audience; expresses disappointment at the exploitive nature of Cheech and Chong film; reports audience tribute to Jesus S. Trevino's RAICES DE SANGRE; feels ONLY ONCE IN A LIFETIME was technically excellent, but passive and without a significant message. Question is posed about the role and expected audience of Chicano filmmakers.

Fiestas (cont.)

3793 Guernica, Antonio Jose and Saavedra-Vela,
     Pilar. El Midwest Canto al pueblo: "Otra
     Vez, C/S". AGENDA, Vol. 7, no. 3 (May, June,
     1977), p. 4-13. Bilingual.

     AN: A thorough report on the various
     phases and events of the Midwest Canto al
     Pueblo in Milwaukee, Wisconsin on April 28
     to May 8, 1977. The festival brought
     together artists, poets, musicians, and
     cultural workers to reaffirm, share, and
     celebrate the identity of La Raza with El
     Pueblo. Includes a thematic and iconographic
     overview of Chicano murals in California by
     Jose Montoya, and an analysis of his
     sculpture by Zarco Guerrero from Meza,
     Arizona. Well illustrated. Includes a
     photograph of the collective mural painted
     at 5th St. and National Avenue in Milwaukee,
     Wisconsin during the course of the
     conference.

3794 Hansen, Barbara. Food for the soul: an
     earthly delight. HOME MAGAZINE, (October
     22, 1978), p. 53-54. English.

     AN: Story on El Dia de los Muertos.
     Color illustrations of annual celebration by
     Self-Help Graphics and Art, Inc. with
     costumes, masks, floats.

3795 Lansing Community College, Lansing, MI.
     Festival! Festival program, [1978]. English.

     AN: Program of a festival which includes
     an Hispanic Arts Exhibit, including Juan
     Ortega, Nora Mendoza, Jose Luis Narezo, and
     Brazilian-born Veronica Dalia de
     Albuquerque.

3796 Montoya, Emmanuel; Rodriguez, Patricia; and
     Acevedo, Mario (Torero). Canto al pueblo
     '78. NATIONAL MURALS NETWORK COMMUNITY
     NEWSLETTER, (1978). English.

     AN: The second annual Canto al Pueblo
     took place in Corpus Christi, Texas, where
     more than six murals were painted: "Wall of
     Cultural Education" by 13 artists headed by
     Roel Montealva; Carlota Espinoza, with
     children; Gilberto Romero, Jose Antonio
     Burciaga and Patricia Rodriguez,
     "Incomprehension al arte"; "Madre Tierra" by
     Manuel Martinez of Denver with Amador
     Hinojosa (Corpus Christi) and Enriquette
     Vasquez (New Mexico); Mario Torero; Salvador
     Vega of Chicago whose mural some Canto
     participants considered "insulting".

3797 Ordorica, Leticia. Community expression in
     muralism. VOZ FRONTERIZA, Vol. 3, no. 5
     (March 1978). English.

     AN: Brief history of Chicano Park in San
     Diego. Announcement of the "Mural Marathon"
     from April 1 to April 20, two days before
     the Eighth Annual Chicano Park Celebration.
     Five pillars and the kiosk will be painted.
     Illustration.

3798 Poster, Corky. Cuba welcomes Latin film
     festival. GUARDIAN, (January 16, 1980), p.
     21. English.

     AN: Report on the First International
     Festival of New Latin American Cinema held
     in Havana December 3-10, 1979. The Festival
     focused on emerging cinema of Latin America,
     especially of Nicaraguans and Chicanos.
     Festival organizers hoped to
     "internationalize" the Chicano struggle by
     encouraging it toward a Latin American

political perspective and moving it from a
limited "la raza" view to one of class
analysis and solidarity. Jesus Trevino's
film RAICES DE SANGRE was shown.

3799 Public invited to weekend fiesta at Lincoln
     High. LOS ANGELES TIMES, (April 29, 1969),
     p. II. English.

     AN: Fiesta of art, music, dance and
     literature organized by the committee formed
     after the East Los Angeles high school
     "blowouts" to press for better and more
     relevant education. Hundreds of works of art
     were collected for display at the "Fiesta de
     los Barrios".

3800 Santa Ana College, Santa Ana, CA. MECHA
     presents la semana de la Raza. Exhibition
     brochure, 1970. English.

     AN: Program for the week's activities,
     including EL ARTE DE LA RAZA exhibition,
     Gilbert Sanchez Lujan speaking on "Chicano
     Art in the Barrio," art demonstrations by
     Gilbert Vasquez, Emigdio Vasquez, Esau
     Quiroz, and Richard Garcia.

3801 Tanguma, Leo. Raza art festival. PAPEL
     CHICANO, Vol. 1, no. 6 (May 21, 1971), p.
     10. English.

     AN: Purpose of festival was to bring
     Chicano artists together to exhibit their
     work. Contingents of artists from throughout
     Texas participated. Barrio people were
     invited to present their arts and crafts and
     show their creativity. Artist Leo Tanguma
     affirms festival goal as "the idea of
     Chicano artists getting together to use art
     as a tool for mass education of our heritage
     and culture or in whatever way La Raza's
     needs direct us".

3802 Venegas, Sybil. Dia de los muertos. SOMOS,
     Vol. 1, no. 5 (October 1978), p. 42-47.
     English.

     AN: Brief history of Dia de los muertos
     ceremonies. While the custom is dying in
     Mexico (except for tourists), Chicano
     organizations like Galeria de la Raza
     (S.F.), El Centro de Artistas Chicanos
     (Sacramento, Ca.) celebrate the event
     annually, as does [Self-Help Graphics and
     Art, Inc.] in East Los Angeles. Well
     illustrated with photographs by Guillermo
     Bejarano and Daniel Duran.

3803 Venegas, Sybil. Towards a Chicano cultural
     renaissance. LA GENTE DE AZTLAN, Vol. 8, no.
     1 (November 2, 1977), p. 12. English.

     AN: The revival of celebrations like El
     Dia de Los Muertos are seen as catalysts for
     barrio unification. Detailed information on
     how Self Help Graphics in East Los Angeles
     mobilizes artists and community for a
     communal celebration.

3804 Amescua, Michael M. Dia de los muertos.
     SOMOS, Vol. 1, no. 6 (November 1978), p.
     39-40. English.

     AN: Report on Self-Help Graphics'
     project involving fifteen humanists who
     explored history, literature, philosophy and
     religion as they relate to the Dia de los
     Muertos, an annual program of Self-Help.
     Illustrated.

FIFTH SUN: CONTEMPORARY/TRADITIONAL CHICANO & LATINO ART [exhibit], Berkeley, CA

3805 Frankenstein, Alfred. A long-range view of Latino art: at the UC Art Museum. SAN FRANCISCO CHRONICLE, (October 15, 1977), p. 34. English.

AN: Controversial critical review of the exhibit THE FIFTH SUN: CONTEMPORARY TRADITIONAL CHICANO & LATINO ART.

3806 Stofflet-Santiago, Mary. The fifth sun: esthetic quality versus curatorial intent. ARTWEEK, Vol. 8, no. 37 (November 5, 1977), p. 6. English.

AN: Review of the exhibit THE FIFTH SUN at the University Art Museum in Berkeley, Calif., curated by Ralph Maradiaga of the Galeria de la Raza. It contains folk art, and posters by Chicano artists Maradiaga, Rupert Garcia, Juan Fuentes, mural studies by Graciela Carrillo and Mike Rios, ceramics by Anna de Leon, an altar by Amalia Mesa-Bains, and mural drawings by Mexican muralists. The writer criticizes the uneven quality of the show, but encourages better ones in the future. Illustrated.

Film Reviews

3807 Camplis, Francisco X. Towards the development of a Raza cinema. TIN TAN, Vol. 2, no. 5 (June 1, 1977), p. 5-7. English.

AN: Chicanos and other minorities remain invisible to white America, an expression of neo-colonialism. Camplis defines "Chicano" and "Raza" as terms, and states there are few, if any, full-length feature films available. Without role models, Chicano/Raza filmmakers can learn from contemporary revolutionary Latin American filmmakers, be familiar with European and Hollywood films, though the latter are alien models. Camplis suggests directions for Chicano films, and reviews films by Jesus Trevino, Jose Camacho, and Luis Valdez.

Filmography

3808 Cine chicano: primer acercamiento. COMUNIDAD, no. 20 (November 16, 1980), p. 1-15. Spanish.

AN: The entire cultural supplement of LA OPINION is dedicated to Chicano film. Includes articles by Jason Johansen, Jeff Penichet, Harry Gamboa, Jr., Jesus Salvador Trevino, Carlos Penichet, Sylvia Morales, Julio Moran, and Jose Luis Borau. Also includes a declaration of purpose by the Asociacion Chicana de Cineastas, and a filmography of Chicano cinema compiled by Trevino.

Films

3809 An.i.ma.tion: the arts, techniques, and processes involved in giving apparent life and movement to inanimate objects by means of cinematography. San Francisco, CA: Galeria de la Raza, n.d. English.

AN: Illustrated booklet on animation. Reproductions and sequences illustrated by Leslie Cabarga, Xavier Viramontes and Ralph Maradiaga.

3810 Blue Sky Productions. Los santeros. Color film, 29 min., 1979. English.

AN: A 29 minute color film produced with funding assistance from New Mexico Highlands University and the National Endowment for the Arts. Features santeros Luis Tapia, Orlando Romero, Horacio Valdez.

3811 California. University. Los Angeles. Instructional Media Library. 1975-76 film catalog. Film catalog, 1976, p. 30-31. English.

AN: List of films available from the Chicano Film Collection. 34 films on Chicano and Mexican subjects by Chicano and non-Chicano film makers.

3812 California. University. Los Angeles. Cine sin fronteras. Festival brochure, 1981. English.

AN: Brochure program for a cinema festival and series of seminars and discussions featuring films and discussants from Mexico and Chicanos of the United States. Participating were Chicano directors Moctezuma Esparza, Richard Soto, David Sandoval, and Robert Young, and film historian David Maciel.

3813 Camplis, Francisco X. Towards the development of a Raza cinema. TIN TAN, Vol. 2, no. 5 (June 1, 1977), p. 5-7. English.

AN: Chicanos and other minorities remain invisible to white America, an expression of neo-colonialism. Camplis defines "Chicano" and "Raza" as terms, and states there are few, if any, full-length feature films available. Without role models, Chicano/Raza filmmakers can learn from contemporary revolutionary Latin American filmmakers, be familiar with European and Hollywood films, though the latter are alien models. Camplis suggests directions for Chicano films, and reviews films by Jesus Trevino, Jose Camacho, and Luis Valdez.

3814 Champlin, Chuck, Jr. Working for more than peanuts. LOS ANGELES TIMES, (June 21, 1980), p. II, 8, 10. English.

AN: Bill Melendez has been an animator 21 years for Charles Schulz's Charlie Brown and Peanuts comic strips, TV specials, and feature films. Melendez began his career with Walt Disney Productions in 1938.

3815 Chicano cinema coalition. Mimeographed copy, September 1, 1979. English.

AN: An informational bulletin about the Coalition founded July 1978 in Los Angeles of forty independent producers and filmmakers who joined together for "the development, production, distribution, promotion and exhibition...of film and video productions which meaningfully address...needs and concerns of the Latino people in the United States." Professionals with their own companies (Amanecer Films, Bilingual Educational Services, Luis Ruiz Productions), television producers, and post-graduate film students make up the group. The Coalition published the CHICANO CINEMA NEWSLETTER. Ties are promoted with Latin American cinema people.

Films (cont.)

3816 CHICANO CINEMA NEWSLETTER. Vol. 2, no. 1
     (January 1, 1980). English.

     AN: 17 Chicano filmmakers from Los
     Angeles, Albuquerque, Sacramento, San
     Francisco and Boston attended the First
     Annual International Festival of New Latin
     American Cinema in Cuba. Chicano cinema
     received the "Black Coral" award for a
     retrospective screened as part of the
     festival. Includes reports on coming events.

3817 CHICANO CINEMA NEWSLETTER. Vol. 1, no. 6
     (August 1979). English.

     AN: Announcements of the San Antonio
     Chicano Film Festival, a seminar on the
     business of art, the receipt of a report of
     the Task Force on Minorities in Public
     Broadcasting, a critical report on the
     Alternative Cinema Conference in New York,
     which was attended by eleven members of the
     Chicano Cinema Coalition, and a report and
     critique of the report by the Task Force.

3818 CHICANO CINEMA NEWSLETTER. Vol. 1, no. 4
     (June 1979). English.

     AN: Report and cautionary note on the
     upcoming Alternative Cinema Conference;
     announcement of ONLY ONCE IN A LIFETIME and
     CHICANA film releases; other new films and
     TV programs; a Chicano cinema bibliography;
     a list of Chicano production companies and
     distributors; a theoretical article on the
     nature (proposed) of Chicano cinema as an
     alternative cinema; statement of purpose of
     the Los Angeles Chicano Cinema Coalition.

3819 CHICANO CINEMA NEWSLETTER. Vol. 1, no. 3
     (May 1979). English.

     AN: Announcements for the U.S.
     Conference for an Alternative Cinema (N.Y.),
     a "Nosotros" banquet, application dates for
     the Film Fund, deadlines for the National
     Endowment for the Humanities, and criticism
     of the Hollywood feature film BOULEVARD
     NIGHTS.

3820 CHICANO CINEMA NEWSLETTER. Vol. 1, no. 1
     (December 1978). English.

     AN: Reports on activities of Chicano
     filmmakers in producing films, meeting with
     organizations like the American Film
     Institute, the Hispanic Task Force of the
     National Endowment for the Arts, the WNET
     Independent Documentary Film Fund.
     International film news also included.

3821 Cine chicano: primer acercamiento.
     COMUNIDAD, no. 20 (November 16, 1980), p.
     1-15. Spanish.

     AN: The entire cultural supplement of LA
     OPINION is dedicated to Chicano film.
     Includes articles by Jason Johansen, Jeff
     Penichet, Harry Gamboa, Jr., Jesus Salvador
     Trevino, Carlos Penichet, Sylvia Morales,
     Julio Moran, and Jose Luis Borau. Also
     includes a declaration of purpose by the
     Asociacion Chicana de Cineastas, and a
     filmography of Chicano cinema compiled by
     Trevino.

3822 Cinefestival. ARRIBA, [n.d.], p. 5. English.

     AN: Announcement of the 6th Annual
     International Hispanic Film Festival in San
     Antonio, TX. Willie Varela will conduct a
     workshop, and Jesus Trevino will premiere

his hour-long production, SEGUIN.

3823 Contemporary Arts Museum, Houston, TX and
     Martinez, Santos G., Jr. Mexican movie
     posters. Exhibition invitation, 1979.
     English.

     AN: Invitation to an exhibit of posters
     primarily from the collecttion of Enrique
     Flores and Xavier Gorena of Xochil Art
     Center, Mission, Texas. Martinez considers
     the posters monumental, with expressive
     qualities that have influenced Chicano
     poster makers like the Royal Chicano Air
     Force, and Rupert Garcia, and Texas artists
     like Luis Jimenez, Jesse Trevino and Cesar
     Martinez. One illustration. Introduction by
     guest curator Santos G. Martinez, Jr. (See
     Rupert Garcia's essay in the exhibition
     catalog: POSTERS FROM THE GOLDEN AGE OF
     MEXICAN CINEMA, for another point of view).

3824 De Lappe, Pele. Gordo plus folk art.
     PEOPLE'S WORLD, Vol. 42, no. 41 (October 13,
     1979), p. 10. English.

     AN: Announcement of an exhibit at the
     Mexican Museum of Gus Arriola's syndicated
     comic strip "Gordo." Arizona-born Arriola
     was an animator for Columbia and MGM
     cartoons until he created "Gordo" in 1941.
     Illustrated.

3825 Deitch, Donna. The great wall of Los
     Angeles. Film, 1976. Bilingual.

     AN: Eight minute 16 mm film produced by
     SPARC (Social and Public Art Resource
     Center) on the GREAT WALL OF LOS ANGELES
     mural. In English with Spanish subtitles.

3826 Film collection of the Chicano Library.
     Chicano Studies Research Center, UCLA, 1972.
     English.

     AN: Description, producers, rentals of
     15 films made by or about Chicanos and
     Mexicans, and available through the Center.

3827 Films for the inner city. Los Angeles, CA:
     Los Angeles Public Library Federal Project,
     1971. English.

     AN: Annotated catalog of 16mm films and
     filmstrips, educational and documentary.
     Those concerning Mexican heritage include
     CHICANO FROM THE SOUTHWEST (1970),
     HENRY...BOY OF THE BARRIO (1969); HOW'S
     SCHOOL, ENRIQUE (1970), I AM JOAQUIN (1970),
     THE MEXICAN AMERICAN: HERITAGE AND DESTINY
     (1970), A MEXICAN AMERICAN FAMILY (1970),
     MEXICAN AMERICANS: QUEST FOR EQUALITY
     (1968), MEXICAN OR AMERICAN (1970),
     SIQUEIROS: "EL MAESTRO" (THE MARCH OF
     HUMANITY IN LATIN AMERICA) (1969).
     Filmstrips include THE AWAKENING (LA RAZA) -
     Part IV, CONFLICT OF CULTURES (LA RAZA) -
     Part III, MASTERWORKS OF MEXICAN ART, OUT OF
     THE MAINSTREAM, PILGRIMAGE (GRAPE STRIKERS).
     Also listed are films and filmstrips for
     children.

Films (cont.)

3828 Fourth annual San Antonio film festival. San
     Antonio, TX: Oblate College of the
     Southwest, 1979. Bilingual.

     AN: Symposium and film festival catalog
     featuring motion pictures and videocassettes
     made by and about Mexicans, Chicanos and
     Latinos. The Symposium focused on Latina
     women in film and television, Margarita
     Galban, Carmen Tafolla, Leticia Ponce, Grace
     Castro Nagata, Marcela Fernandez Violante of
     Mexico, and Sylvia Morales.

3829 Galeria de la Raza/Studio 24, San Francisco,
     CA. Mexican film poster (1943-71): an
     exhibition/exhibicion de fotos/cartelones
     del cine mexicano. Exhibition invitation,
     1971. English.

     AN: Invitation to an exhibit.

3830 Galeria de la Raza/Studio 24, San Francisco,
     CA and Garcia, Rupert. Posters from the
     golden age of Mexican cinema. Exhibition
     catalog, 1979. English.

     AN: The Galeria's second exhibit of
     Mexican movie posters features those of the
     1940s and early 1950s (in 1971, the exhibit
     covered 1943-1971) from the collection of
     Enrique Flores, owner of the Rio Theatre,
     Mission, Texas, and the Xochil Art Center.
     Garcia's essay includes a history of Mexican
     cinema, and the mythologizing period of the
     "Golden Age" reflected in the posters which
     promoted movie-consumership. One
     illustration. (See Santos G. Martinez, Jr.'s
     essay in the exhibition catalog: MEXICAN
     MOVIE POSTERS, for another point of view).

3831 Gamboa, Harry, Jr. Film, television, and
     Trevino. LA LUZ, Vol. 6, no. 10 (October
     1977), p. 7-8. English.

     AN: Jesus Salvador Trevino has been an
     active proponent and participant in
     transforming cultural inaccuracy about
     Chicanos in the media to accurate mass media
     models. A biography of Trevino follows,
     including discussion of some of his films:
     THE SALAZAR INQUEST, CHICANO MORATORIUM
     AFTERMATH, SOLEDAD, AMERICA TROPICAL, YO SOY
     CHICANO, RAICES DE SANGRE, as well as
     television series like ACCION CHICANO,
     AHORA, and INFINITY FACTORY.

3832 Gloria, Juan J. En San Antonio: se celebrara
     el tercer festival de cine, 'La vida chicana
     a traves del celuloide'. EL VISITANTE
     DOMINICAL, (August 20, 1978), p. 6-8, 12.
     Spanish.

     AN: The Third Chicano Film Festival
     honors the only two feature-length films
     made by Chicanos: Moctezuma Esparza's ONLY
     ONCE IN A LIFETIME (made in Hollywood) and
     Jesus Salvador Trevino's RAICES DE SANGRE
     (Blood Roots), (made with CONACINE in
     Mexico). Illustrated.

3833 Gonzales, Juan. Chicano film festival earns
     pluses and minuses. EL TECOLOTE, Vol. 9, no.
     3 (November 1978), p. 7. English.

     AN: Critical review of the Third Annual
     Chicano Film Festival in San Antonio, TX.
     The writer criticizes lack of critical
     exchange and dialogue between filmmakers and
     audience; expresses disappointment at the
     exploitive nature of Cheech and Chong film;
     reports audience tribute to Jesus S.
     Trevino's RAICES DE SANGRE; feels ONLY ONCE

IN A LIFETIME was technically excellent, but
passive and without a significant message.
Question is posed about the role and
expected audience of Chicano filmmakers.

3834 Gronk and Gamboa, Harry, Jr. Interview:
     Gronk and Gamboa. CHISMEARTE, Vol. 1, no. 1
     (Fall 1976), p. 31-33. English.

     AN: Interview with two members of the
     group Asco concerning their NO MOVIE series.
     Questions and answers were probably written
     by the artists themselves as a performance
     art piece. Includes a description of the
     group and their 1972 ACTION PROJECT PIE IN
     DEFACE: L.A. COUNTY MUSEUM OF ART.
     Illustrations.

3835 Herrera, Juan Felipe and Paramo, Bobby.
     Cerco Blanco, the balloon man and fighting
     City Hall: on being a Chicano filmmaker.
     METAMORFOSIS, Vol. 3, no. 2 (1980, 1981), p.
     77-82. English.

     AN: Autobiographical article about his
     life and his introduction and immersion in
     filmmaking by Bobby Paramo. His experiences
     with documentary films, television, the Los
     Angeles Chicano film movement, are recorded.

3836 Johansen, Jason. Preliminaries toward an
     Hispanic media: a cultural imperative.
     Unpublished manuscript, 1980. English.

     AN: Presentation made at the Hispanic
     Southwest Conference on Media and the
     Humanities. Johansen outlines the
     culturally-leveling and stereotypical roles
     for men and women of mass media in our
     century which is dominated by communication
     means owned by industries interested in
     profits from products. Within this context,
     Hispanic media producers must find new ways
     of relaying values, judgements and ideas
     that combat the dominant culture and
     strengthen humanity and social change.

3837 Kleinhaus, Chuck; Seiter, Ellen; and Steven,
     Peter. Conference report: struggling for
     unity. JUMP CUT, no. 21 (November 1979), p.
     35-37. English.

     AN: Report and critique of the U.S.
     Conference for an Alternative Cinema held in
     mid-June 1979 at Bard College in New York
     state to chart a course for independent
     filmmakers. Chicano, Black, Asian and Puerto
     Rican film people attended, including Jesus
     Salvador Trevino and Sylvia Morales from the
     Chicano Cinema Coalition of Los Angeles.

3838 Lopez Oliva, Manuel. Proyeccion chicana en
     RAICES DE SANGRE. CINE CUBANO, (1981), p.
     75-80. Spanish.

     AN: A Latin American view of Jesus
     Salvador Trevino's 1976 film RAICES DE
     SANGRE, particularly its concern with the
     exploitation by U.S. multinationals of
     Mexicans and Chicanos on both sides of the
     border. The author notes Trevino's tendency
     to relate Chicano culture and problems to
     continental and world problems of workers.
     Illustrated.

Films (cont.)

3839 Menyah Productions. [Untitled catalog]. San
      Juan Bautista, CA: El Centro Campesino
      Cultural, 1977. English.

      AN: Catalog of films and other cultural
      materials available. Films listed are I AM
      JOAQUIN (by Corky Gonzales), with Luis
      Valdez, Daniel Valdez, El Teatro Campesino,
      and photography by George Ballis; EL TEATRO
      CAMPESINO, produced in 1970 by National
      Educational Television; and LOS VENDIDOS, by
      Luis Valdez, Luis Ruiz, George Paul, Daniel
      Valdez and Loring d'Usseau.

3840 Minority artists exhibit works at Auraria.
      ROUNDUP, (January 13, 1980), p. 27.
      English.

      AN: Gala art exhibit organized by the
      Resource Coalition for Minority Artists of
      Denver. Included Black, Chicano and Native
      American visual artists as well as film
      makers and musicians.

3841 Morales, Sylvia. Chicana. 20 min., 16 mm,
      color, 1979. English.

      AN: Color film tracing the history of
      the Chicana back to pre-Columbian women's
      history. Utilizes images of pre-Columbian
      and modern Mexican murals, as well as
      filming of contemporary Chicanas and their
      activities. Based on a slide show by Anna
      Nieto-Gomez, adapted for the screen by
      Morales.

3842 Moreno, Eduardo. Los Four. Half-hour 16mm
      film. English.

      AN: Film about the Los Angeles group of
      artists known as Los Four (originally Carlos
      Almaraz, Gilbert Sanchez Lujan, Roberto de
      la Rocha, Frank Romero), at the time of
      their exhibit at the Los Angeles County
      Museum of Art - the first time Chicano art
      was shown at the Museum.

3843 Palomino, Ernesto ("Ernie"). My trip in a
      '52 Ford. San Francisco State College:
      Unpublished typescript for film, 1966.
      English.

      AN: Script for film of the same name by
      Fresno artist Ernesto Palomino. Master's
      project.

3844 Palomino, Ernesto ("Ernie"). My trip in a
      '52 Ford. 16 mm. film, 1966. English.

      AN: Animated film based on works of junk
      sculpture produced by Fresno-based artist.
      Features "Mary '52 Ford, an immortal mother
      having children after death," George Go,
      Dorothy Dresser, Carol Chair, Steve Stove,
      and other characters.

3845 Petraitis, Louise. Student union murals:
      walls with tongues. PHOENIX MAGAZINE,
      (April 21, 1977), p. 12. English.

      AN: San Francisco State University
      instructor Ray Patlan and his La Raza Mural
      Workshop are painting murals in the Student
      Union basement. The relationship of a mural
      to architecture, the process of transferring
      a sketch to the wall, the underpainting, and
      the finishing painting processes are
      explained. A videotape of the mural is being
      made. Illustrated.

3846 Pettit, Arthur G. Images of the Mexican
      American in fiction and film. College

Station, TX: Texas A & M Univ. Press, 1980.
English.

      AN: A study on Anglo-American attitudes
toward Mexican people in the Southwest as
reflected in the sterotypes of popular
literature and film. Most of the book is
historical. The afterword (by Dennis
Showalter) argues that these patterns have
not improved, citing television series such
as CHICO AND THE MAN and CHIPS.

3847 Peyton, Patricia, ed. Reel change: a guide
      to social issue films. San Francisco, CA:
      Film Fund, 1979. English.

      AN: Includes a section on Hispanic film
with descriptions, sources, and rentals.
Listed are Esperanza Vasquez's AGUEDA
MARTINEZ, Sylvia Morales' CHICANA, Adolfo
Vargas' CONSUELO: QUIENES SOMOS?/WHO ARE
WE?, El Teatro Campesino's I AM JOAQUIN,
Jose Luis Ruiz's THE UNWANTED, Jesus
Salvador Trevino's YO SOY CHICANO, and
others. Listings are international in scope.

3848 Poster, Corky. Cuba welcomes Latin film
      festival. GUARDIAN, (January 16, 1980), p.
      21. English.

      AN: Report on the First International
Festival of New Latin American Cinema held
in Havana December 3-10, 1979. The Festival
focused on emerging cinema of Latin America,
especially of Nicaraguans and Chicanos.
Festival organizers hoped to
"internationalize" the Chicano struggle by
encouraging it toward a Latin American
political perspective and moving it from a
limited "la raza" view to one of class
analysis and solidarity. Jesus Trevino's
film RAICES DE SANGRE was shown.

3849 Reyes, Luis. Seguin: traidor o heroe.
      COMUNIDAD, (April 12, 1981), p. 8-9.
      Spanish.

      AN: Report on the pilot film for an
eight-part series called LA HISTORIA made by
Jesus Trevino for the Public Broadcasting
Service. The pilot treats the life of an
"anti-hero," Juan Seguin, during the Texas
war for independence from Mexico, and
relates the little-known history of the
Mexican defenders of the Alamo. Trevino
chose this controversial subject because it
exemplified an early case of the dual nature
of bilingualism and biculturalism.
Description of the research and filming of
the pilot. Illustrated.

3850 Rivera, Humberto R. Film notes. CHISMEARTE,
      Vol. 1, no. 2 (Winter, Spring, 1977), p.
      20-24. English.

      AN: Summary of films produced by and/or
about Chicanos for cinema and television.
Includes REALIDADES (TV) by David Sandoval,
Rudy Vargas, Luis Torres, Jose Luis Ruiz,
Antonio Reyes; A POLITICAL RENAISSANCE from
the LA RAZA series (TV) by Moctezuma
Esparza; CHILDREN OF THE STATE by Andres
Markovits, Richard Trubo, Frank Christopher
(film); LA RAZA UNIDA (released as RAICES DE
SANGRE) by Jesus Salvador Trevino (Mexican
film by a Chicano); CHULAS FRONTERAS (film)
by Les Blank; THE MURALS OF EAST LOS
ANGELES, A MUSEUM WITHOUT WALLS by Humberto
R. Rivera and Heather R. Howell.
Announcement for the National Latino Media
Coalition.

Films (cont.)

3851 Rivera, Humberto R. and Howell, Heather R.
The murals of East Los Angeles. Film.
English.

AN: Puerto Rican filmmaker Rivera deals
with Chicano murals and their makers. Views
of the murals and interviews with the
artists make up the bulk of the film.
Unfortunately Rivera focuses the camera on
the artists and the streets and seldom gives
the viewer a detailed look at the mural
under discussion.

3852 Ruiz Productions. Los Angeles, CA: Ruiz
Productions [ca. 1977]. English.

AN: Illustrated catalog of films
produced by or about Chicanos and Mexicans,
including LOS FOUR (artists group) by Jim
Tartan; MESSAGES IN CLAY (pre-Columbian) by
Ed Moreno and Barry Nye; LOS CARROS (cars)
part I: EL CARRO NUEVO and part II: LOW
RIDER by Frank Lisciandro and Alejandro
Nogales.

3853 Salazar, Juan Albert. Entelequia. 16 MM
Film, 1978. Bilingual.

AN: This production is Salazar's MFA
thesis from the Department of Art,
University of Utah. Its purpose is to
explore the Chicano mentality. Based on the
shooting of Santos Rodriguez in Texas, the
historical fact is abstracted and the
emotional impact transformed to an
analytical examination of the whys and hows
raised by such a situation.

3854 Smith, Cecil. YO SOY captures the Chicano
soul. LOS ANGELES TIMES, (August 17, 1972),
p. IV, 20. English.

AN: Trevino's films YO SOY CHICANO and
AMERICA TROPICAL shown on KCET.

3855 SPARC (Social and Public Arts Resource
Center), Venice, CA. The great wall of Los
Angeles. Brochure, n.d. English.

AN: Publicity brochure for the rental or
purchase of the film The Great Wall of Los
Angeles. Reproduces photographs of the
mural, statements of youth participants, and
names of the mural director and supervisors.

3856 Torres, Louis R. RAICES DE SANGRE: first
full length film directed by a Chicano.
SOMOS, Vol. 1, no. 2 (July 1978), p. 16-19.
English.

AN: Report on Jesus Salvador Trevino's
RAICES DE SANGRE, the only film made by a
Chicano at the Mexican film studio,
CONACINE. Deals with the efforts of Chicanos
and Mexicans living in border cities to
organize an international labor union.
Trevino's previous work is briefly
mentioned. Illustrated.

3857 Trevino, Jesus Salvador. America tropical.
(1971). English.

AN: Half-hour 16mm color film produced
and written by Jesus Salvador Trevino and
directed by Barry Nye about the painting and
whitewashing in 1932-34 of Mexican muralist
David Alfaro Siqueiros' mural AMERICA
TROPICAL in Olvera Street, Los Angeles.
Traces the attempts at restoration of the
mural starting in the late 1960s and
continuing in the 1970s. History of the
mural set within social/political context of

Mexican Americans in the 1930s, and
counterpart struggles of Chicanos in the
1970s.

3858 Varda, Agnes. Mur murs/mural murals on the
wall ... Film, Cine Tamaris, Paris, 1980.
English.

AN: Full length documentary film
produced for French television; also
available with English subtitles. Deals
impressionistically with the murals and
muralists of Los Angeles. Included are Wayne
Alaniz Healy, David Botello, Willie Herron,
Manuel Cruz, Judy Baca, the murals in
Venice, CA, graffiti - among others. Color.

3859 Vasquez, Esperanza and Esparza, Moctezuma.
Agueda Martinez. 16 mm. color film. English.

AN: Sixteen-minute film directed by
Esperanza Vasquez and produced by Moctezuma
Esparza concerning the life and weaving of
an elderly New Mexican woman. Martinez
carries on the tradition of floor loom
weaving, as well as farming.

3860 Vasquez, Richard. Mojado power: a boost for
illegal aliens. CALENDAR, (February 22,
1981), p. 41. English.

AN: An uncritical review of the
commercial film made by Mexican film star
and comedian Alfonso Arau in the United
States primarily for the "American-Hispanic"
market on a low-cost budget. Arau planned to
distribute in Mexico, Latin America and
Spain. The film is a light-weight comedy
about a "wetback" who launches a campaign
for "mojado power" but falls victim to dope
smugglers and is sent to jail.

3861 "Viva la causa", a documentary film on the
Mexican mural movement in Chicago. Chicago,
IL: Kartemquin Films, [1974]. English.

AN: Advertising brochure for a film made
of Chicano muralist Ray Patlan working with
young people in Chicago. The film shows
murals in Mexico and Chicago, and follows
one mural from its sketch to its completion.

3862 Wilson, Michael and Biberman, Herbert. Salt
of the earth [film]. 16mm, 94 min., b&w.
English.

AN: The first feature film made in the
U.S. of, by and for labor, it deals with a
real strike of Mexican American miners in
New Mexico in which women played a key role
in the men's victory and their own demands.
Mexican actress Rosaura Revueltas starred
with labor leader Juan Chacon. One of the
best films on the subject.

Films (cont.)

3863 Wu, Ying Ying. Mural, mural on the Great
Wall. LOS ANGELES TIMES, (September 16,
1980), p. VI,4. English.

AN: Information on a video project
directed by John Rier to document work on
the 1700-ft. mural THE GREAT WALL OF LOS
ANGELES which depicts California history
with an emphasis on the role that minorities
had in forging that history. Three
teen-agers were trained in video production
while assisting with taping the mural
project. Simultaneously, 40 other youngsters
hired from the Summer Program for the
Employment of Disadvantaged Youth painted a
400-ft. section of the mural in 1980.
Article describes the various skills
mathematical, social and artistic developed
by youth involved in the project. The mural
was started as a Bicentennial Project in
1976 by Judy Baca for the Social and Public
Art Resources Center in Venice, California.
Illustrated with 3 photographs of various
aspects of the Project.

3864 Zheutlin, Barbara and Talbot, David. Jesus
Salvador Trevino. In: CREATIVE DIFFERENCES:
PROFILES OF HOLLYWOOD DISSIDENTS. Boston,
MS: South End Press, 1978, p. 345-352.
English.

AN: Within the context of New Left
alternative filmmakers who chose to work
within Hollywood, Trevino sets forth his
standards and goals. His films and TV
productions include SOLEDAD (1971), AMERICA
TROPICAL (1971), YO SOY CHICANO (1972),
RAICES DE SANGRE (1977) and INFINITY FACTORY
(1975-1976).

Financial Aid

3865 Scottsdale resident wins art fellowship.
SCOTTSDALE DAILY PROGRESS, (April 10,
1981), p. 29. English.

AN: Rudy M. Fernandez, Jr. awarded the
1981 Visual Arts Fellowship in painting by
the Arizona Commission on the arts.
Fernandez holds an M.F.A. from Washington
State University, and is affiliated with the
Elaine Horwitch Gallery in Scottsdale and
the Galeria de la Raza in San Francisco.

Fine Arts Gallery, San Diego, CA

3866 Fine Arts Society of San Diego, CA. The
cross and the sword. Exhibition catalog,
1976. Bilingual.

AN: Bi-lingual exhibition catalog of
Southwestern art forms; santero art,
vernacular architecture and traditional folk
art. Important essays by experts in each
field. Contains an iconographical summary of
santos and a good bibliography. Profusely
illustrated.

FIRE! AN EXHIBITION OF 100 TEXAS ARTISTS [exhibit]

3867 Contemporary Arts Museum, Houston, TX. Fire!
An exhibition of 100 Texas artists.
Exhibition brochure, 1979. English.

AN: Includes eleven Chicano artists.
Unfortunately, not illustrated, though a
checklist of works is included. Mel Casas,
Carmen Lomas Garza, Xavier Gorena, Luis
Jimenez, Cesar Martinez, Guillermo Z.
Pulido, Philip Renteria, Jose L. Rivera, Joe
Rodriguez, George Truan, Juan B. Vela.
Introduction by James Surls. Statements by

the artists.

FIRME MAGAZINE

3868 Gamboa, Harry, Jr. Fantasias moviles.
COMUNIDAD, (August 30, 1981), p. 8-9.
Spanish.

AN: An illustrated article by ASCO
artist Harry Gamboa, Jr. on lowriders, and
the magazines LOWRIDER, Q-VO and FIRME.

FIRST DECADE OF THE CHICANO RENAISSANCE [lecture]

3869 Lopez, Armando. 'Chicano' art gains
cross-culture recognition: 'the street mural
has flourished in the barrio'. LAREDO NEWS,
(July 20, 1980), p. 6-A. English.

AN: Report on a lecture "The First
Decade of the Chicano Renaissance: Mexican
American Art in the United States" given by
Dr. Shifra M. Goldman under the sponsorship
of the Laredo Philosophical Society.
Mentions the "delicate Issue" of using the
word "Chicano" in conservative Laredo.
Illustrated with works of Laredo-born Amado
M. Pena.

**First International Festival of New Latin American
Cinema, Havana, Cuba, Dec. 3-10, 1979**

3870 CHICANO CINEMA NEWSLETTER. Vol. 2, no. 1
(January 1, 1980). English.

AN: 17 Chicano filmmakers from Los
Angeles, Albuquerque, Sacramento, San
Francisco and Boston attended the First
Annual International Festival of New Latin
American Cinema in Cuba. Chicano cinema
received the "Black Coral" award for a
retrospective screened as part of the
festival. Includes reports on coming events.

3871 Poster, Corky. Cuba welcomes Latin film
festival. GUARDIAN, (January 16, 1980), p.
21. English.

AN: Report on the First International
Festival of New Latin American Cinema held
in Havana December 3-10, 1979. The Festival
focused on emerging cinema of Latin America,
especially of Nicaraguans and Chicanos.
Festival organizers hoped to
"internationalize" the Chicano struggle by
encouraging it toward a Latin American
political perspective and moving it from a
limited "la raza" view to one of class
analysis and solidarity. Jesus Trevino's
film RAICES DE SANGRE was shown.

**First Latin American Colloquium and Exhibition of
Contemporary Photography, Mexico City, May,
1978**

3872 Goldman, Shifra M. Hecho en Latino America:
first photography colloquium and exhibition.
CHISMEARTE, no. 6 (February 1980), p. 16-25.
English.

AN: Report on the first colloquium of
Latin American photography, Mexico City, May
1978. Analysis and critique of U.S. Latino
photographers' work presented in exhibition.
Well illustrated.

FIVE PHOTOGRAPHERS [exhibit]

3873 Chu, Amy. Focus on cultural heritage.
     READER: SAN DIEGO WEEKLY, (September 17,
     1981). English.

     AN: Review of exhibit FIVE
     PHOTOGRAPHERS: CONTEMPORARY VIEWS OF MEXICAN
     AND MEXICAN-AMERICAN CULTURE which includes
     two Chicano photographers from Arizona:
     Louis Carlos Bernal (Tucson), and Robert C.
     Buitron (Tempe). Details some of Bernal's
     work between 1973 and 1980; Buitron's more
     personal work (1978-1981) is from his FAMILY
     AND PHOTOGRAPHY book-in-progress.

Flagellants and Flagellation
     USE: Hermanos Penitentes

Flor en la Comunidad [mural] Program, San Jose, CA

3874 NATIONAL MURALS NETWORK COMMUNITY
     NEWSLETTER. (Fall 1979). English.

     AN: Reports on mural projects by Fermin
     Coronado working with students in Houston;
     Galeria de la Raza's billboard used as a
     mural surface for changing images; murals
     under the Flor en la Comunidad program of El
     Centro Cultural de la Gente in San Jose,
     California and led by artist Jaime Valadez;
     murals in Grand Rapids and other cities of
     western Michigan; murals by Jose Guerrero
     and others from the Chicago Mural Group; a
     survey of Chicano murals in the Pilsen area
     of Chicago guided by Jose Gonzalez.

Flores, Alex

3875 Southwest Texas State University, San
     Marcos, TX and Carlisle, Charles Richard.
     Cuatro caminos: four perspectives on Chicano
     art. Exhibition catalog, 1980. English.

     AN: Exhibition pamphlet with photographs
     of the artists. Alex Flores, Luis Jimenez,
     Cesar Augusto Martinez and Amado Pena, Jr.
     comment on their work and the Chicano art
     movement.

Flores, Carolina G.

3876 Crossley, Mimi. Tejano artists. HOUSTON
     POST, (August 19, 1976). English.

     AN: Exhibition of 19 Texas artists
     organized by Joe Rodriguez of the AAMA
     (Association for the Advancement of Mexican
     Americans) Art Center in Houston, Texas.
     Working within a wide range of styles and a
     great scope of subject matter. Includes
     brief commentary on the work of Amado Pena,
     Carmen Lomas Garza, Cesar Martinez, Enrique
     Campos, Carolina Flores, Jesus Trevino and a
     host of others.

3877 Flores, Carolina. Self portrait [drawing].
     TEJIDOS, Vol. 1, no. 3 (Summer 1974), p.
     Cover.

3878 Galeria Tonantzin, Centro Cultural de LUCHA,
     Austin, TX. Young Chicano photographers from
     throughout Texas. Exhibition brochure, n.d.
     English.

     AN: This exhibition is the collection of
     the winners of the contest (by the same
     name) sponsored by the Extension Cultural
     SRE-UNAM in San Antonio. Photographers
     represented were: Grace Alvarez, David
     Cardenas, Hector Cardenas, Stephen Casanova,
     Ronald Cortez, Raul Espinosa, Felix Almanza,
     Carolina Flores, David Garza Perez, Xavier
     Garza, Conrad Guerra, Melinda Hasbrook, Juan

Jose de Hoyes, Beverly Kennon, Art Moreno,
David Perez, Isabelle Purden, Patricia
Santell, Nancy de los Santos, Jose Soria,
Richard Tichich, Kathy Vargas, Vivian Yaten,
and Johnny Zamarria.

3879 HEMBRA: HERMANAS EN MOVIMIENTO BROTANDO
     RAICES DE AZTLAN (University of Texas,
     Austin). (Spring 1976).

     AN: Raul Valdez, drawing, p. 3; Carolina
     Flores, drawing, p. 5; Maria Flores,
     photograph, pp. 7, 11, 30; M.E.
     Secrest-Ramirez, drawing, p. 12; Amacio
     Zarate, drawing, p. 15; Santa Barraza,
     drawings, pp. 16, 17, 18, 26, 32; Nora
     Gonzales-Dodson, painting, p. 19; Gilberto
     Cardenas, photograph, pp. 22, 28; Nanci de
     los Santos, photograph, p. 23, 29; Amado
     Maurilio Pena, Jr. p. 31.

3880 Instituto Chicano de Artes y Artesanias
     (Texas Instit. Educational Development) and
     Instituto Cultural Mexicano (SER/UNAM), San
     Antonio, TX. Artistas chicanos: Los
     Quemados. San Antonio, TX: Instituto
     Chicano, Texas Institute for Educational
     Development, 1975. English.

     AN: Invitation to an exhibit and
     manifesto of 1975 Austin-San Antonio
     artists' group, Los Quemados. Included Santa
     Barraza, Carolina Flores, Carmen Lomas
     Garza, Luis Guerra, Cesar Augusto Martinez,
     Santos Martinez, Amado Maurilio Pena, Jr.,
     Jose Rivera, Vicente Rodriguez, Jose
     Trevino.

3881 Musica hispana en nuestras vidas/Hispanic
     music in our lives: almanaque 1982/calendar.
     Milwaukee, WI: Miller Brewing Co., 1981.
     English.

     AN: Twelve Latino artists were
     commissioned to illustrate a calendar with
     paintings on Hispanic music. The Chicano
     artists include Frederico Vigil (New
     Mexico), Joe Bastida Rodriguez
     (Texas/Washington, D.C.), Manuel Martinez
     (Colorado), Jose Antonio Burciaga
     (California), Ignacio Gomez (California),
     Carolina Flores (Texas), Frank Martinez
     (California). Color.

3882 Petersen, Karen and Wilson, J.J. Women
     artists: Third World. New York, NY: Harper &
     Row, 1975. English.

     AN: Catalog of slides with accompanying
     notes. Slides of Chicana artists available:
     Margaret Herrera (Chavez), Consuelo (Chelo)
     Gonzalez Amezcua, Santa Barraza, Mujeres
     Muralistas, El Grupo de Santa Ana, Carmen
     Lomas Garza, Carolina Flores.

3883 Xochil Art and Culture Center, Mission, TX.
     Besame mucho. Exhibition invitation, 1979.
     English.

     AN: Invitation to exhibit of Texas
     artists from Mujeres Artistas del Suroeste
     (MAS): Mary Ann Anguiano, Alicia Arredondo,
     Santa Barraza, Nora Gonzales-Dodson, Maria
     Flores, Carolina Flores, Mary Ann Ambray
     Gonzales, Sylvia Orozco, Nancy de los
     Santos, Modesta Barbina Trevino.
     Illustrated.

Flores, Elsa Marie

3884 Almaraz, Carlos. Introduccion: vida urbana y artistas chicanos. COMUNIDAD, Vol. 55, no. 22 (May 3, 1981), p. 2. Spanish.

AN: In the controversial period of the early 1980s, Chicano advances are being attacked. In this political climate, some Los Angeles artists are interested in beauty and artistic creation: Carlos Almaraz, best-known of the Los Four group; Yreina Cervantez; Elsa Flores; John Valadez, presently working on a mural; and musicians Louie Perez and Tito Rodriguez Larriva.

3885 Arte chicano y el pueblo. COMUNIDAD, no. 41 (May 3, 1981), p. 1-15. Spanish.

AN: The whole issue of the Sunday Supplement deals with Los Angeles Chicano art and music. Works by painter Carlos Almaraz, photographer Elsa Flores, painter Yreina Cervantez, muralist and draftsman John Valadez, and a performance piece by Elsa Flores and Louie Perez are featured. Biographical information, and statements by the artists.

3886 Chicano art. ARTES VISUALES, no. 29 (1981). English.

AN: Issue on Chicano art, introduced by Los Angeles artist Roberto Gil de Montes. Includes works and statements by: Pedro Lujan (Texas); Raul M. Guerrero (Calif.); Sylvia Salazar Simpson (New Mexico/Calif.); Carlos Almaraz (Calif.); Rene Yanez (Calif.); Jack Vargas (Calif.); Ray Bravo (Calif.); John Valadez (Calif.); Gloria Maya (Calif.); Elsa Flores (Calif.); Willie Herron (Calif.); Gilbert "Magu" Lujan (Calif.); Kay Torres, Jerry Lucas, and Louis Perez (Calif.).

3887 Colectivo El Ojo. CHOQUE DE AMOR: fotonovela by Lamp. CHISMEARTE, Vol. 1, no. 4 (Fall , Winter, 1977), p. 35-37. Bilingual.

AN: Several students with the help of the Latin American Media Project (LAMP) and the Latin American Studies Department of California State University, Los Angeles produced the fotonovela CHOQUE DE AMOR, a variation on the typical "fotonovela" romance. This one encourages readers to reevaluate traditional female roles. The group also includes Kay Torres. Six frames of the fotonovela are reproduced.

3888 Consejo Mexicano de Fotografia, A.C., Mexico City. Hecho en latinoamerica: segundo coloquio latinoamericano de fotografia. Exhibition catalog, 1982. Spanish.

AN: Catalog/book of the second colloquium and exhibit of Latin American photography. Among the Chicano artists whose work is reproduced are Louis Carlos Bernal, Robert C. Buitron, David Cardenas, Isabel Castro, Harry Gamboa, Jr., Luis Garza, Roberto Gil de Montes, John M. Valadez, Kathy Vargas. In the exhibit were also Porfirio Aguilar, Elsa Marie Flores, Ricardo Valverde. Great number of illustrations. In Spanish.

3889 L.A.C.E. (Los Angeles Contemporary Exhibitions), Los Angeles, CA. Espina (Thorn): Carlos Almaraz, Elsa Flores, Louie Perez, Teddy Sandoval, John Valadez, Linda Vallejo. Exhibition announcement, 1980. English.

AN: Announcement of an exhibition and a performance piece by six Los Angeles artists.

3890 Lucas, Jerry and Gil de Montes, Roberto, et al. CHOQUE DE AMOR: fotonovela by Lamp. Los Angeles, CA: Colectivo El Ojo, Latin American Studies Dept., CSULA, 1979. English.

AN: "Fotonovela" featuring Elsa Flores, Rosa Marin, and Jerry Lucas produced by the collective work of Lucas, Roberto Gil de Montes, Mario Massinelli, Luis Soto, and Kay Torres.

Flores, Enrique

3891 Contemporary Arts Museum, Houston, TX and Martinez, Santos G., Jr. Mexican movie posters. Exhibition invitation, 1979. English.

AN: Invitation to an exhibit of posters primarily from the collecttion of Enrique Flores and Xavier Gorena of Xochil Art Center, Mission, Texas. Martinez considers the posters monumental, with expressive qualities that have influenced Chicano poster makers like the Royal Chicano Air Force, and Rupert Garcia, and Texas artists like Luis Jimenez, Jesse Trevino and Cesar Martinez. One illustration. Introduction by guest curator Santos G. Martinez, Jr. (See Rupert Garcia's essay in the exhibition catalog: POSTERS FROM THE GOLDEN AGE OF MEXICAN CINEMA, for another point of view).

3892 Estudios Rio: gallery of contemporary arts and crafts. Exhibition catalog, 1976. English.

AN: Catalog including identification, portraits and works of participating artists: Joe Bova, Enrique Flores, Carmen Lomas Garza, Xavier Gorena, Erik Gronborg, Lucas Hinojosa, Ben Holland, Kris Hotvedt, William Kaars-Sijpesteijn, Cesar Martinez, Chris Mende, Roberto Mungia, Steve Reynolds, Vicente Rodriguez, William Wilhelmi.

3893 Galeria de la Raza/Studio 24, San Francisco, CA. Images of the Southwest. Exhibition catalog, 1977. English.

AN: Invitation/catalog for an exhibit including Rudy M. Fernandez(Utah), Enrique Flores(Texas), Xavier Gorena(Texas), C.A.[Cesar] Martinez(Texas), Santos Martinez, Jr.(Texas), Pedro Rodriguez(Texas), Arnold Trujillo(New Mexico). Block prints, paper cut-outs, drawings, photographs, copper enamels, and sculpture were shown. Five illustrations.

3894 Galeria de la Raza/Studio 24, San Francisco, CA and Garcia, Rupert. Posters from the golden age of Mexican cinema. Exhibition catalog, 1979. English.

AN: The Galeria's second exhibit of Mexican movie posters features those of the 1940s and early 1950s (in 1971, the exhibit covered 1943-1971) from the collection of Enrique Flores, owner of the Rio Theatre, Mission, Texas, and the Xochil Art Center. Garcia's essay includes a history of Mexican cinema, and the mythologizing period of the "Golden Age" reflected in the posters which promoted movie-consumership. One illustration. (See Santos G. Martinez, Jr.'s essay in the exhibition catalog: MEXICAN MOVIE POSTERS, for another point of view).

Flores, Enrique (cont.)

3895 Giepen, Hubert. Xochil Art Center taking big steps. PROGRESS, Vol. 10, no. 1 (August 12, 1981). English.

AN: Brief history of the founding and expansion plans of the Xochil Art Institute in Mission which includes an old theatre, workshop. studio, and gallery. Artists Xavier Gorena and Enrique Flores are responsible for the development.

Flores, Gloria

3896 Concilio de arte popular. CHISMEARTE, Vol. 1, no. 2 (Winter, Spring, 1977), p. 54. English.

AN: Report of a meeting February 12, 1977 by the Concilio de Arte Popular (CAP) which published CHISMEARTE. Introduces members of the Board and summarizes discussions of problems of the organization and their publication.

3897 Wilson, William. Chicana artists still seeking identification. LOS ANGELES TIMES, (June 23, 1975), p. VI, 5. English.

AN: Ten Chicana artists are exhibiting their work in the Boathouse Gallery of Plaza de la Raza in Lincoln Park: Judithe Hernandez, Patssi Valdez, Judy Baca, Josefina Quesada, Victoria del Castillo-Leon, Olga Muniz, Gloria Flores, Sylvia Morales, Isabel Castro and Celia Tejadak. The work is still tentative and may develop.

Flores, Gloriamalia

3898 Flores, Gloriamalia and Herrera, Juan Felipe. Rebozos of love/we have woven/sudor de pueblos/on our back. San Diego, CA: Toltecas en Aztlan, 1974. English.

AN: Designs by Gloria Amalia Flores.

3899 Goldman, Shifra M. Artistas en accion: conferencia de las mujeres chicanas. COMUNIDAD, (August 10, 1980), p. 15. Spanish.

AN: In Chicano Studies programs, the fine arts have had second class status to social sciences and literature. Similarly a Chicano Issues Conference overlooked artists until a special effort was made. A round table, which included visual artists Gloriamalia Flores and Carmen Lomas Garza, discussed the social functions of art, woman as an image maker, problems of the Chicana as creator and cultural worker, and professionalism in the arts.

3900 The Point Gallery, Santa Monica, CA. ASCO (Gronk, Patssi, Gamboa, Herron), Los Four (Almaraz, de la Rocha, Judithe Hernandez, Gloriamalia Flores, Mauricio Ramirez, John Valadez. Exhibition invitation, [1975]. English.

AN: Illustrated invitation to an exhibit of Los Angeles artists.

Flores, John

3901 Andrews, Rena. The fine arts. EMPIRE MAGAZINE, (December 19, 1971), p. 32. English.

AN: Review of first one person show by John Flores at the Nathan Galleries in Denver. Born in El Paso, Texas but reared in Denver, Flores depicts his Indo-Hispanic heritage in his creations. Concentrating on portraits, still-lifes, and landscapes, Flores paints within the Impressionistic mode. Critic feels Flores is not fully realized, yet has some impressive work and is a promising younger artist.

3902 Barrett, Marjorie and Flores, John. Flores: artist's gamble paid off. ROCKY MOUNTAIN NEWS, (May 18, 1980), p. 27. English.

AN: In less than a decade, John Flores has gone from being a part-time painter working in a meat packing plant to a prolific fulltime artist. This interview on the occasion of Flores' one person show at the De Colores Gallery reviews his artistic trajectory. The 30 odd paintings in the exhibit include still lifes, pastel portraits, street scenes and landscapes in oil. Experimenting with vivid color, Flores is turning to his own cultural roots.

3903 Kelley sparks Chicano growth. ROCKY MOUNTAIN NEWS, (February 18, 1973), p. Festival,7. English.

AN: Denver artist John Flores speaks about his work and provides details about the small but strong Chicano art colony in Denver. Flores credits Ramon Kelley, an established Chicano artist, with providing much leadership and encouragement in the development of Chicano art in Colorado.

3904 Kelley sparks Chicano growth. EMPIRE MAGAZINE, (December 19, 1971), p. 32. English.

AN: Ramon Kelley, successful and well known Denver artist is credited with fomenting and developing a small but strong Chicano art colony in Denver. As owner of the De Colores Gallery, Kelley has sponsored exhibits and personally encouraged many Chicano artists. John Flores, one of Kelley's proteges talks about his artistic development within the Chicano art and political milieu in Denver. Artist provides information on his daily life and work habits on the occasion of an exhibit of his work at the De Colores Gallery. Flores is a member of the Denver Arts and Humanities Commission. Illustrated with a reproduction of a pastel drawing by John Flores.

Flores Magon, Enrique

3905 Alarcon, Francisco X. and Herrera, Juan Felipe. Portraits plus struggles plus consciousness: nine pastels by Rupert Garcia. METAMORFOSIS, Vol. 3, no. 2 (1980), p. 104-106. English.

AN: Reprint of article published as "Rupert Garcia: portraits/retratos" in EL TECOLOTE LITERARY MAGAZINE (San Francisco, CA), Vol. 2, no. 1, March 1981, p. 6.

Flores Magon, Enrique (cont.)

3906 Alarcon, Francisco X. Rupert Garcia:
portraits/retratos. EL TECOLOTE LITERARY
MAGAZINE, Vol. 2, no. 1 (March 1981), p. 6+.
Bilingual.

AN: Review of Garcia exhibit at the
Mexican Museum (S.F.) in 1981. Includes
portraits of Frida Kahlo and the Flores
Magon brothers, Goya, Van Gogh, Ethel and
Julius Rosenberg, etc. Illustrated. This
article has been reprinted in METAMORFOSIS
under a different title: "Portraits Plus
Struggles Plus Consciousness: Nine Pastels
by Rupert Garcia," Vol. 3-4, no. 1-2,
(1980-81), p. 104-106.

Flores Magon, Ricardo

3907 Alarcon, Francisco X. and Herrera, Juan
Felipe. Portraits plus struggles plus
consciousness: nine pastels by Rupert
Garcia. METAMORFOSIS, Vol. 3, no. 2 (1980),
p. 104-106. English.

AN: Reprint of article published as
"Rupert Garcia: portraits/retratos" in EL
TECOLOTE LITERARY MAGAZINE (San Francisco,
CA), Vol. 2, no. 1, March 1981, p. 6.

3908 Alarcon, Francisco X. Rupert Garcia:
portraits/retratos. EL TECOLOTE LITERARY
MAGAZINE, Vol. 2, no. 1 (March 1981), p. 6+.
Bilingual.

AN: Review of Garcia exhibit at the
Mexican Museum (S.F.) in 1981. Includes
portraits of Frida Kahlo and the Flores
Magon brothers, Goya, Van Gogh, Ethel and
Julius Rosenberg, etc. Illustrated. This
article has been reprinted in METAMORFOSIS
under a different title: "Portraits Plus
Struggles Plus Consciousness: Nine Pastels
by Rupert Garcia," Vol. 3-4, no. 1-2,
(1980-81), p. 104-106.

3909 Cortez, Carlos. Ricardo Flores-Magon
[graphic]. CARACOL, Vol. 5, no. 2 (October
1978), p. BACK COVER. Spanish.

Flores, Maria

3910 Goldman, Shifra M. Women artists of Texas:
MAS = More + Artists + Women = MAS.
CHISMEARTE, no. 7 (January 1981), p. 21-22.
English.

AN: History of Texas Chicana women
artists' organization, Mujeres Artistas del
Suroeste (MAS), co-founded in 1977 by Santa
Barraza and Nora Gonzalez-Dodson in the
framework of the burgeoning feminist art
movement, particularly Women and Their Work
of Texas. Brief history of Chicano politics
and the corresponding art movement of
southern and central Texas. In addition to
Barraza and Gonzalez-Dodson, Alicia
Arredondo, Modesta Trevino, and Maria Flores
are considered. Illustrated.

3911 HEMBRA: HERMANAS EN MOVIMIENTO BROTANDO
RAICES DE AZTLAN (University of Texas,
Austin). (Spring 1976).

AN: Raul Valdez, drawing, p. 3; Carolina
Flores, drawing, p. 5; Maria Flores,
photograph, pp. 7, 11, 30; M.E.
Secrest-Ramirez, drawing, p. 12; Amacio
Zarate, drawing, p. 15; Santa Barraza,
drawings, pp. 16, 17, 18, 26, 32; Nora
Gonzales-Dodson, painting, p. 19; Gilberto
Cardenas, photograph, pp. 22, 28; Nanci de
los Santos, photograph, p. 23, 29; Amado

Maurilio Pena, Jr. p. 31.

3912 Orozco, Irma. Women & their work. PARA LA
GENTE, Vol. 1, no. 4 (October 1977), p. 12.
English.

AN: Illustrated story about "Women &
Their Work" festival in Austin, Texas,
Oct-Dec 1977. Photographers Maria Flores and
Teresina Guerra, Santa Barraza, Nora
Gonzalez Dodson, Sylvia Orozco, and Modesta
Trevino exhibited.

3913 Orozco, Sylvia. Las mujeres - Chicana
artists come into their own. MOVING ON, Vol.
2, no. 3 (May 1978), p. 14-16. English.

AN: Illustrated feature prepared by
artist Sylvia Orozco on the founding of
Mujeres Artistas del Suroeste in Austin,
September 1977. Artworks and statements by
Nora Gonzalez Dodson, Maria Flores, Modesta
Trevino, Santa Barraza, as well as musicians
and singers.

3914 Xochil Art and Culture Center, Mission, TX.
Besame mucho. Exhibition invitation, 1979.
English.

AN: Invitation to exhibit of Texas
artists from Mujeres Artistas del Suroeste
(MAS): Mary Ann Anguiano, Alicia Arredondo,
Santa Barraza, Nora Gonzales-Dodson, Maria
Flores, Carolina Flores, Mary Ann Ambray
Gonzales, Sylvia Orozco, Nancy de los
Santos, Modesta Barbina Trevino.
Illustrated.

Folk Art

3915 Adams, Robert. The architecture and art of
early Hispanic Colorado. Boulder, CO:
Colorado Associated University Press in
cooperation with the State Historical
Society of Colorado, 1974. English.

AN: Robert Adams is a photographer and
writer from Longmont, CO who has evocatively
captured scenes in the San Luis and
Purgatory Valleys of Southern Colorado. The
text and photographs focus on "Hispano"
village life, customs and traditions.

3916 Ahlborn, Richard E. The Penitente Moradas of
Abiquiu. Washington, D.C.: Smithsonian
Institution Press, 1968 (Contributions from
the Museum of History and Technology, Paper
63). English.

AN: The history and organization of the
Penitente Brotherhood. Detailed analysis of
the architecture of Penitente moradas and
the artifacts within them. Illustrated with
many ethnographic photographs.

3917 Alex Maldonado, primitive painter. SAN
FRANCISCO FOCUS MAGAZINE, (1973). English.

AN: Biographical information on 72 year
old Alexander Maldonado who started painting
upon his retirement. His "naif" work has
gained wide critical acclaim and he has had
more than 200 exhibitions throughout the
United States. Illustrated with reproduction
of one of Maldonado's paintings.

Folk Art (cont.)

3918 Altars as folk art. ARRIBA, Vol. 1, no. 1 (July 1980, 194), p. 4. English.

   AN: Focusing on the home altar of Josefina De Leon from Cuero, Texas, the article describes this folk expression on two levels: first as a subjective religious intermediator and secondly as a masterpiece of collected objects. Contains interesting information on the form, function and meaning of altars. Illustrated with photographs.

3919 Barrett, Marjorie. Carving out a living - a primitive process. ROCKY MOUNTAIN NEWS, (December 15, 1979), p. 90. English.

   AN: In the village of Teseque outside Santa Fe, NM, Felipe Archuleta, a 69-year-old folk carver has emerged as an international art celebrity, famous for his naive animal carvings. His work expecially life-sized renditions of animals, is represented in many distinguished collections and is prized for its wit and lack of predictability. Illustrated with photograph of carver and one of his creations.

3920 Blue Sky Productions. Los santeros. Color film, 29 min., 1979. English.

   AN: A 29 minute color film produced with funding assistance from New Mexico Highlands University and the National Endowment for the Arts. Features santeros Luis Tapia, Orlando Romero, Horacio Valdez.

3921 Corazon del norte: Jose Alfredo Maestas. GRITO DEL NORTE, Vol. 2, no. 7 (May 19, 1969), p. 13. English.

   AN: Jose Alfredo Maestas, born in San Juan Pueblo is a folk carver imbued with the mythical and spiritual Indo-Hispano tradition. His carved figurines made from cotton wood roots, balsam and driftwood are in many museums and private collections. Illustrated with photographs of artist at work and two photographs of his sculpture.

3922 Corazon del norte: wood carving. GRITO DEL NORTE, Vol. 2, no. 5 (March 28, 1969), p. 11. English.

   AN: Focus on the Aguilar family, folk artists from Los Ojos (Parkview), northern New Mexico. Sr. Cruz Aguilar is a sculptor and furniture maker, his 80-year-old mother Dona Cresanta Cruz is a quilter. Illustrated with photographs of the Aguilars and examples of their work.

3923 Crews, Mildred T. Saint-maker from Taos. AMERICAS, Vol. 21, no. 3 (March 1969). English.

   AN: An in-depth study of woodcarver Patrocino Barela (died 1964). Barela's work is an evolvement of the "santero" tradition filtered through an intensely personal style. His work was widely collected by institutions like The Museum of Modern Art, New York, The San Francisco Museum of Art and The New Mexico Fine Arts Museum. Well-illustrated with photographs of the artist and example of his work.

3924 Daigh, Janice. Old church alive with art. TAOS NEWS BULLETIN, (January 25, 1979), p. B, 1. English.

   AN: Commentary on the formation of the Cofradia de Artes y Artesanos Hispanicos. The organization projects an ambitious program including the expansion of artistic endeavors by contemporary crafts people and artists, the restoration of historic buildings and the education of Hispanic children in their artistic heritage as well as providing information to the general public.

3925 Ditmar, Joanne. A new industry, done the old way. EMPIRE MAGAZINE, (September 26, 1976), p. 22-25. English.

   AN: The Virginia Blue Resource Center for Colorado Women is embarked on a project to revive handicrafts and skills among Hispano women in the San Luis Valley. Igniting interest in traditional crafts like embroideries, tin work, straw mosaic and filigree jewelry, the Center hopes to revive or maintain these traditions. Detailed information on a project to create a group of embroidered wall hangings depicting San Luis Valley life past and present. Illustrated with examples of the completed wall hangings.

3926 Evans, Marylin. Tucson barrio janitor designs authentic Aztec costumes. LA PRENSA, Vol. 1, no. 6 (October 11, 1978). English.

   AN: Rogelio Valdovin, self-taught artist from Tucson, Arizona feels he has received a spiritual call to create authentic Pre-Columbian costumes and regalia. Specializing in Aztec costumes, the artist works with metal, beads, feathers, leather and many fabrics and fibers in designing and making his creations. He exhibits them as a form of body art.

3927 Fine Arts Society of San Diego, CA. The cross and the sword. Exhibition catalog, 1976. Bilingual.

   AN: Bi-lingual exhibition catalog of Southwestern art forms; santero art, vernacular architecture and traditional folk art. Important essays by experts in each field. Contains an iconographical summary of santos and a good bibliography. Profusely illustrated.

3928 Garcia, Rupert. The politics of popular art. CHISMEARTE, Vol. 2, no. 1 (Summer 1978), p. 2-4. English.

   AN: Defines and discusses the terms "Popular Art", "Mass Art", and "Folk Art" and gives examples of their correct and incorrect usages.

3929 Garcia, Rupert. Pulqueria art--defiant art of the barrios [Part I]. EL TECOLOTE, Vol. 8, no. 4 (December 1977), p. 7. Bilingual.

   AN: In contrast to billboards that function as calculated visual corporate advertisements, Chicano-Latino communities have evolved a form of colorful wall paintings that draw attention to goods available in the neighborhood. Related to the "Pulqueria" paintings of Mexico, these wall paintings are validated as a true people's art. In the best examples, pulqueria art functions to provide images of a positive and innovative nature.

Folk Art (cont.)

3930 Garcia, Rupert. Pulqueria art--defiant art of the barrios [Part II]. EL TECOLOTE, Vol. 8, no. 5 (February 1978), p. 8. Bilingual.

AN: In the Mission District of San Francisco, various artists like Irene Perez, Esther Fernandez, Chuy Campusano, Graciela Carrillo de Lopez, Consuelo Mendez Castillo, and Mike Rios have embellished business sites with wall decorations similar in spirit to the "Pulqueria" art of Mexico. Illustrated with three "Pulqueria"-type wall paintings: ATARDECER DE UN IMPERIO by Oscar Carveo at the Azteca Restaurant (Mission and 20th Sts.), El Buen Boricano Restaurant facade (24th and Harrison Sts.) and Fruitlandia facade (24th and Treat Sts.)

3931 Goldman, Shifra M. Women artists of Texas: MAS = More + Artists + Women = MAS. CHISMEARTE, no. 7 (January 1981), p. 21-22. English.

AN: History of Texas Chicana women artists' organization, Mujeres Artistas del Suroeste (MAS), co-founded in 1977 by Santa Barraza and Nora Gonzalez-Dodson in the framework of the burgeoning feminist art movement, particularly Women and Their Work of Texas. Brief history of Chicano politics and the corresponding art movement of southern and central Texas. In addition to Barraza and Gonzalez-Dodson, Alicia Arredondo, Modesta Trevino, and Maria Flores are considered. Illustrated.

3932 Henry Gallery, University of Washington, Seattle, WA and Ybarra-Frausto, Tomas. Arte prehispanico, arte popular. Exhibit Catalog, 19. English.

AN: Exhibition catalog for an exhibit prepared almost entirely by students from the School of Art with assistance from MEChA and members of the faculty of the School of Art. The pre-Columbian sections presented objects from sites in Mexico and Peru from pre-classic, classic and post-classic periods. The arte popular sections exhibited wares from craft centers in Mexico, Peru, Ecuador and Guatemala. Includes statement by Tomas Ybarra-Frausto on the relevance of this exhibition to the cultural identity of Chicanos in the Pacific Northwest.

3933 Lomas Garza, Carmen. Altares: arte espiritual del hogar. HOJAS, (1976). English.

AN: Commentary and five photographs from the author's visual documentation of home altars in Kingsville, Texas. Brief analysis of the form, meaning and function of home altars in Chicano daily life.

3934 Martinez, Eluid Levi. What is a New Mexico santo? Santa Fe, NM: Sunstone Press, 1978. Bilingual.

AN: Martinez is a carver of saints from the well-known Lopez family of·santeros of Cordova, New Mexico, who have carved for seven generations. An oversimplified history of the settlement of New Mexico and the rise of religious imagery production. Of interest are the illustrated steps of the carving process. Many reproductions.

3935 Miller, Marlan. Heard speaks Spanish through art. PHOENIX GAZETTE, (September 23, 1978). English.

AN: Four new exhibits at the Heard Museum of Phoenix include "Hispanic crafts of the Southwest", and "Southwest Chicano Art Invitational". The former focuses on New Mexico and Colorado crafts, organized by the Taylor Museum if the Colorado Springs Fine Arts Center; the latter includes Rupert Garcia and Xavier Miramontes of San Francisco, Rudy Fernandez of Salt Lake City (now in Scottsdale, AZ), and Antonio Pazos of Tucson.

3936 Navar, M. Margarita. La vela prendida: home altars. ARRIBA, Vol. 1, no. 5 (February 1980), p. 12. English.

AN: Brief commentary on the exhibit LA VELA PRENDIDA: MEXICAN AMERICAN WOMEN'S HOME ALTARS at the Texas Memorial Museum during December 1980. Aside from altars, the exhibit focused on nichos, grutas and lapidas.

3937 Nelson, Kathryn J. Excerpts from los testamentos: Hispanic women folk artists of the San Luis Valley, Colorado. FRONTIERS, Vol. 5, no. 3 (Fall 1980), p. 34-43. English.

AN: Eppie Archuleta, weaver from the San Luis Valley in Southern Colorado talks about her life philosophy, Hispanic cultural traditions and her role as a community artist. First person account amply illustrated with photographs.

3938 Pollock, Duncan. He sallied forth to paint. ROCKY MOUNTAIN NEWS, (February 7, 1971), p. 1. English.

AN: Biographical information about Martin Saldana, an eccentric personality labeled as Denver's answer to Grandma Moses. Saldana died in 1965 leaving behind a cache of "primitive" paintings that soon became much sought after by collectors. His work portrayed the rural pageant of Mexican life. Illustrated with self-portrait.

3939 Sanchez, Arley. Santeros. ALBUQUERQUE JRNL, (August 21, 1977), p. C, 1. English.

AN: Review of THE SANTERO EXPERIENCE, an exhibition of contemporary folk art by eleven New Mexican santeros, most in their 30s, at the Albuquerque Museum. The carvers include Juan Lucero, Ben Lopez, Luisito Lujan, Horacio Valdez, C. Garcia, George Lopez. A revival of the art has been taking place within last several years due to cultural awareness being experienced by Hispanos. Contemporary santeros still donate some pieces to the church, but most are marketed to private collectors, displayed in museums, or kept.

3940 Santos of New Mexico, art of our people. GRITO DEL NORTE, Vol. 3, no. 1 (January 17, 1970), p. 8-9. English.

AN: Historical trajectory of santero tradition in New Mexico. Distinguished santeros like Rafael Aragon of Cordova, Miguel Herrera of Arroyo Hondo, Juan Ramon Velasquez of Conjilon, Jose Benito Ortega of La Cueva all created art wedded to the environment of the Southwest. Illustrated with a portfolio of santos and retablos from the Folk Art Museum of Santa Fe, NM.

Folk Art (cont.)

3941 Stofflet-Santiago, Mary. The fifth sun:
      esthetic quality versus curatorial intent.
      ARTWEEK, Vol. 8, no. 37 (November 5, 1977),
      p. 6. English.

      AN: Review of the exhibit THE FIFTH SUN
      at the University Art Museum in Berkeley,
      Calif., curated by Ralph Maradiaga of the
      Galeria de la Raza. It contains folk art,
      and posters by Chicano artists Maradiaga,
      Rupert Garcia, Juan Fuentes, mural studies
      by Graciela Carrillo and Mike Rios, ceramics
      by Anna de Leon, an altar by Amalia
      Mesa-Bains, and mural drawings by Mexican
      muralists. The writer criticizes the uneven
      quality of the show, but encourages better
      ones in the future. Illustrated.

3942 Sutherland-Martinez, Elizabeth. Corazon del
      norte: Baltasar Martinez. GRITO DEL NORTE,
      Vol. 2, no. 2 (January 29, 1968), p. 5.
      English.

      AN: Baltazar Martinez from Conjilon (one
      of the defendants in the Tierra Amarilla
      Courthouse "Raid" Case) is a noted naif
      painter. This article focuses on his
      methods, techniques and subject matter. His
      work is related to that current of cultural
      production outside mainstream channels.
      Illustrated with photograph of artist and
      several of his paintings.

3943 Taylor Museum of the Colorado Springs Fine
      Arts Center, Colorado Springs, CO. Hispanic
      crafts of the Southwest. Catalog, 1977.
      English.

      AN: An excellent and profusely
      illustrated catalog covering weaving,
      embroidery, furniture making, woodcarving,
      jewelry making, tinwork and straw inlay,
      both past and present. Historical background
      of crafts production, techniques, and
      biographies of the artists are provided.

3944 Texas Memorial Museum, University of Texas,
      Austin, TX. La vela prendida:
      Mexican-American women's home altars.
      Exhibition catalog, 1980. Bilingual.

      AN: Bilingual illustrated
      brochure-catalog of exhibit. Includes home
      altars and graveyard headstones.

3945 Trejo, Frank. S.A. mission doors inspired
      wood carver. SAN ANTONIO LIGHT, (January
      10, 1971), p. 18. English.

      AN: Biographical and exhibition
      information on San Antonio woodcarver Jesse
      V. Garcia. Illustrated by photograph of
      artist.

3946 Vincent, Kathy Ariana. Monty Montemayor:
      portrait of an artist. ARRIBA, Vol. 1, no. 7
      (1980). English.

      AN: Born in Laredo, TX, in 1902, "Monty"
      Montemayor paints in the naif tradition. As
      an older artist, she has been a role model
      for younger Chicana artists. Brief profile
      of the self-taught artist. Illustrated.

Folk Dancing
      USE: Dance

Folk Healing
      USE: Curanderismo

Folktales
      USE: Cuentos

FONDO DEL SOL [journal] (Washington, D.C.)

3947 Fondo del Sol, Washington, D.C. Raices
      antiguas/visiones nuevas; ancient roots/new
      visions. Exhibition catalog, 1977. English.

      AN: Well illustrated catalog of
      traveling exhibition featuring Latin
      American and Latino artists living in the
      United States. Supplemental regional
      catalogs of local artists.

3948 Palacio de Mineria, Mexico, D.F. Raices
      antiguas/visiones nuevas: arte chicano y
      latinoamericano en los estados unidos.
      Exhibition catalog, 1980. Spanish.

      AN: Catalog of an exhibit circulated by
      the Fondo del Sol in the United States, and
      in Mexico. Included are Chicanos and Latin
      Americans living in the United States. Well
      illustrated.

3949 Saavedra-Vela, Pilar. Exposicion nacional de
      raices hispanicas. AGENDA, Vol. 7, no. 5
      (September, October, 1977), p. 33-34.
      Spanish.

      AN: Announcement of the national tour of
      the exhibition entitled: RAICES Y VISIONES
      organized by the group Fondo del Sol, from
      Washington, D.C.

Foster Kleiser Co.

3950 Dunsmore de Carrillo, Patricia. On Rene
      Yanez of the Galeria de la Raza. CHISMEARTE,
      Vol. 1, no. 1 (Fall 1976), p. 8-9.
      English.

      AN: Report on Yanez's negotiations with
      the Foster Kleiser Company to take over a
      billboard located outside the Galeria in San
      Fancisco which has been painted by Michael
      Rios, the Centro de Cambio and TIN TAN
      magazine, Zaiver (Xavier) Viramontes, and
      others.

Fotonovelas

3951 Colectivo El Ojo. CHOQUE DE AMOR: fotonovela
      by Lamp. CHISMEARTE, Vol. 1, no. 4 (Fall ,
      Winter, 1977), p. 35-37. Bilingual.

      AN: Several students with the help of
      the Latin American Media Project (LAMP) and
      the Latin American Studies Department of
      California State University, Los Angeles
      produced the fotonovela CHOQUE DE AMOR, a
      variation on the typical "fotonovela"
      romance. This one encourages readers to
      reevaluate traditional female roles. The
      group also includes Kay Torres. Six frames
      of the fotonovela are reproduced.

3952 Lucas, Jerry and Gil de Montes, Roberto, et
      al. CHOQUE DE AMOR: fotonovela by Lamp. Los
      Angeles, CA: Colectivo El Ojo, Latin
      American Studies Dept., CSULA, 1979.
      English.

      AN: "Fotonovela" featuring Elsa Flores,
      Rosa Marin, and Jerry Lucas produced by the
      collective work of Lucas, Roberto Gil de
      Montes, Mario Massinelli, Luis Soto, and Kay
      Torres.

Los Four [art group], Los Angeles, CA

3953 Almaraz, Carlos. Introduccion: vida urbana y artistas chicanos. COMUNIDAD, Vol. 55, no. 22 (May 3, 1981), p. 2. Spanish.

AN: In the controversial period of the early 1980s, Chicano advances are being attacked. In this political climate, some Los Angeles artists are interested in beauty and artistic creation: Carlos Almaraz, best-known of the Los Four group; Yreina Cervantez; Elsa Flores; John Valadez, presently working on a mural; and musicians Louie Perez and Tito Rodriguez Larriva.

3954 Campesino Business and Joint Enterprise Building, Fresno, CA. Sabor a Fresno. Arte chicano: los Four and la Brocha. Exhibition invitation [1976]. English.

AN: Invitation to an exhibit of works by Los Four of Los Angeles and members of La Brocha del Valle of Fresno: Arturo Roman, Sal Garcia, John Sierra, Juan Truner, Sapo de Aztlan, Fernando Hernandez, Alberto Reyes, Ernesto Palomino, Lee Orona, Francisco Barrios, Juan Ybarra, Bobby Reyes, Alberto Hernandez. Brocha was started by Palomino (California State University, Fresno professor) to pool talents of Central Valley artists.

3955 Canavier, Elena Karina. Los Four. ARTWEEK, Vol. 5, no. 10 (March 9, 1974), p. 1, 16. English.

AN: Illustrated review, with detailed description of work of the Los Four exhibit at the Los Angeles County Museum of Art.

3956 Cultura chicana: Los Angeles. COMUNIDAD, no. 11 (July 13, 1980), p. 1-15. Spanish.

AN: The whole issue of the Cultural Supplement concerns Chicano art and music. Captioned photographs deal with visual artists Carlos Almaraz, Jerry Dreva [not Chicano], Glugio Gronk, Willie Herron, John Valadez, Patssi Valdez, with examples of their work. With the exception of Dreva, all the artists are members of Los Four or Asco. Asco member Harry Gamboa, Jr. sums up the 1960s and 1970s and activities of artists in his essay "Seis imaginaciones: Artistas chicanos en Los Angeles." Well illustrated.

3957 Los Four exhibit in Union Gallery. UNIVERSITY TIMES, (November 6, 1975), p. 4. English.

AN: "Los Four," a group of four Chicano artists - Frank Romero, Roberto "Beto" de la Rocha, Gilbert Lujan, and Carlos Almaraz, with newcomer Judithe Hernandez - work with political cartoons, Catholic symbols, works of sardonic humor. They also paint street murals: several have been done recently in Los Angeles, La Puente, and Long Beach. Illustrated.

3958 Gamboa, Harry, Jr. Seis imaginaciones: artistas chicanos en Los Angeles. COMUNIDAD, (July 13, 1980), p. 10. Spanish.

AN: A limited flow of media information about Los Angeles Chicanos has produced a "ghost" culture. Only sensational events are published. Alternative magazines like LA RAZA, CON SAFOS, and REGENERACION have disseminated Chicano ideas of the 1970s. The Chicano imagination has appeared in murals by Willie Herron, Gronk, Carlos Almaraz, John Valadez; in pieces like "walking" and "instant" murals by the group ASCO; by the group Los Four; by group exhibits like "Chicanismo en el arte," and "Chicanarte." Patssi Valdez showed Photobooth Piece at the "Chicanismo" show. Gronk and Jerry Dreva exhibited their mail art at "Punk Meets Art." In Spanish.

3959 Moreno, Eduardo. Los Four. Half-hour 16mm film. English.

AN: Film about the Los Angeles group of artists known as Los Four (originally Carlos Almaraz, Gilbert Sanchez Lujan, Roberto de la Rocha, Frank Romero), at the time of their exhibit at the Los Angeles County Museum of Art - the first time Chicano art was shown at the Museum.

3960 Oakland Museum, Oakland, CA and Laney College, Oakland, CA. In search of Aztlan. Exhibition brochure, 1974. English.

AN: Brochure for exhibit featuring Los Four: Carlos Almaraz, Gilbert Lujan, Roberto de la Rocha, Frank Romero, Judithe Hernandez.

3961 Oakland Museum, Oakland, CA. In search of Aztlan. Exhibition invitation, 1974. English.

AN: Invitation to an exhibit by Los Four, a Chicano art group started about 1973 in Los Angeles. On exhibit are the original members, Carlos Almaraz, Gilbert Lujan, Roberto de la Rocha, Frank Romero, and new member Judithe Hernandez.

3962 Oakland Museum presents 5 L.A. Chicano artists. EL MUNDO (Hayward, CA), (August 1974). English.

AN: Report on the exhibit THE SEARCH FOR AZTLAN, featuring paintings, murals, tortilla art, folk and religious symbols and totems by Carlos Almaraz, Roberto de la Rocha, Gilbert Lujan, Frank Romero and Judithe Hernandez. Included in the more than 100 works are a wall mural, a folk art pyramid, and part of a primed '51 Chevy lowrider. Illustrated.

3963 Plagens, Peter. Los Four (Roberto de la Rocha, Carlos Almaraz, Gilbert Lujan and Frank Romero) at LACMA. ARTFORUM, (September 1974), p. 87-88. English.

AN: Review of Los Four exhibit at Los Angeles County Museum of Art which calls it a "sociological bazaar" in which Chicanos have been "corrupted" by art schools and "museumized".

3964 The Point Gallery, Santa Monica, CA. ASCO (Gronk, Patssi, Gamboa, Herron), Los Four (Almaraz, de la Rocha, Judithe Hernandez, Gloriamalia Flores, Mauricio Ramirez, John Valadez. Exhibition invitation, [1975]. English.

AN: Illustrated invitation to an exhibit of Los Angeles artists.

Los Four [art group], Los Angeles, CA (cont.)

3965 Polack, Clark. A question of style - Los
Four and the Los Angeles County Museum of
Art. SOUTHWEST ART, (July, August, 1974).
English.

> **AN:** A double-edged assessment of the
> "Los Four" exhibit. The exhibition is at
> once lauded for being provocative and
> stimulating while at the same time failing
> artistically. Author feels that special
> treatment given Carlos Almaraz, Gilbert
> Lujan, Roberto de la Rocha and Frank Romero
> by the L.A. County Art Museum has not been
> extended to other young Los Angeles artists.

3966 Rand, Steve. Carlos David Almaraz. LOS
ANGELES FREE PRESS, Vol. 11, no. 10 (March
8, 1974), p. 14. English.

> **AN:** Brief biographical sketch on
> Mexican-born, Los Angeles artist Carlos
> Almaraz on the occasion of the Los Four
> exhibit at the Los Angeles County Museum of
> Art, artists who are, the author says
> inaccurately, largely self-taught. Almaraz
> studied at Garfield High School with David
> Ramirez, and at Otis Art Institute. One
> illustration.

3967 [Untitled photograph]. CHISMEARTE, no. 2
(Winter, Spring, 1977), p. 34.

> **AN:** Reproduction of the invitation to a
> Los Four exhibit at Mount San Antonio
> College Art Gallery, BANNERS AND PAPER,
> April 12 - May 6, 1977.

3968 Wilson, William. A bit of the barrio at
County Museum. LOS ANGELES TIMES, (February
27, 1974), p. IV, 1+. English.

> **AN:** Review of the Los Four exhibit at
> the Los Angeles County Museum of Art. Quotes
> from artists, history of group's formation
> in 1973.

3969 Wilson, William. 'Los Four' a statement of
Chicano spirit. CALENDAR, (March 10, 1974),
p. 64+. English.

> **AN:** Lengthy critical review of Los Four
> exhibit at Los Angeles County Museum of Art.
> Illustrated.

Franco, Victor

3970 Images of Aztlan at Mechicano. CHISMEARTE,
Vol. 1, no. 1 (Fall   1976), p. 3-4.
English.

> **AN:** History of Mechicano Art Center from
> its opening in West Los Angeles in 1969
> through its 1976 location during which it
> decided to become a center serving its own
> community in East Los Angeles. Led by
> Leonard Castellanos, Victor Franco and Ray
> Atilano, the Center developed programs in
> supergraphics, silkscreen, and mural
> painting, as well as an "open-wall" art
> gallery for artists not allowed in
> establishment galleries.

Franklin, Juana

3971 Oakes College, University of California,
Santa Cruz, CA and Carrillo, Eduardo.
Corazon de Aztlan: a Chicano arts show.
Exhibition catalog, 1981. English.

> **AN:** Catalog of exhibit including works
> by Eduardo Carrillo, Juana Franklin, Cruz
> Zamarron, Jerry Astorga, Jaime Valadez,

Ernesto Palomino, Sal Garcia, Roger Sierra,
Jose Montoya, Esteban Villa, Juanishi
Orozco, from Santa Cruz, San Jose, Fresno
and Sacramento. Presentations of films and
by the Teatro de la Tierra Morena of Santa
Cruz County.

3972 Teatro de la Tierra Morena, Santa Cruz, CA.
Fuego en Aztlan: a Chicano arts show.
Exhibition brochure, 1980. English.

> **AN:** Folder of information on the
> exhibition curated by Cruz Zamarron and
> Eduardo Carrillo. Exhibiting artists were:
> Justina Avila, Terry Benitez, Eduardo
> Carrillo, Hernando Chavez, Bob Cruz, Juanita
> Estrada, Juana Franklin, Sal Garcia, Leticia
> Hernandez, David "Sir Loco" Jimenez, Raoul
> Mendez, Vicente Mendez, Maria V. Pinedo,
> Gonzalo Placencia, Ramon Rodriguez, Roberto
> Salas, George Silva and Cruz Zamarron. A
> special feature was a live tattoo
> demonstration entitled "Walking Art".

Fresno, CA

3973 Artist's vow: delay-plagued state building
mural will be finished. FRESNO BEE,
(November 10, 1980), p. B4. English.

> **AN:** Five-story-high mural "PLANTING OF
> CULTURES" by John Sierra. Illustrated.

3974 Hale, David. Exhibit backers hope for
Chicano cultural center plan. FRESNO BEE,
(July 14, 1974), p. K5. English.

> **AN:** Review of a Chicano art exhibition
> in the Sarah McCardle Room of the downtown
> Fresno County Public Library. According to
> artist-organizer Ernie Palomino, the exhibit
> is a trial balloon to see if enough Chicano
> artists can surface and cooperate in the
> establishment of a Chicano Cultural Center
> in Southeast Fresno. Illustrated with
> reproduction of a portrait by Romero Arroyo
> of Mendota, California and a painting by
> Victor Hernandez from Visalia, California.

3975 Hale, David. Fresnan gets grant to create
five story high mural. FRESNO BEE, (April
16, 1978), p. Forum, C4. English.

> **AN:** Details on the awarding of a grant
> to John Sierra, Fresno artist, for the
> creation of what will be the largest piece
> of public art in that city. The artwork is a
> 6000 square foot mural titled THE PLANTING
> OF THE CULTURES. Article contains
> biographical information on the artist and
> presents goals of his mural project.

3976 Las muralistas del barrio. CHISMEARTE, no. 2
(Winter, Spring, 1977), p. 48-49. English.

> **AN:** Brief announcement about a Chicana
> artists' organization formed in Fresno,
> California which started work on a
> billboard-like mural, 60x8 feet on the theme
> of women. The mural received funding through
> Fresno's La Brocha del Valle. About fifteen
> women are involved, including Helen Gonzalez
> and Cecelia Risco.

Fresno, CA (cont.)

3977 Rodriguez, Alfred. A historical survey of
Chicano murals in the Southwest: an
interdisciplinary teaching unit. Unpublished
paper, 1980. English.

AN: Lists murals by title, artist and
date (when known), location and subject. Los
Angeles, San Francisco, San Diego, Fresno,
San Antonio, Austin, Corpus Christi, Santa
Fe, New Mexico murals are included.
Circulated by the Institute of Latin
American Studies, University of Austin,
Texas.

FUEGO DE AZTLAN [journal] (UC Berkeley, CA)

3978 Yarbro-Bejarano, Yvonne. Resena de revistas
chicanas: problemas y tendencias, Part I. LA
PALABRA, Vol. 2, no. 1 (Spring 1980), p.
76-85. Spanish.

AN: Review of five Chicano magazines of
California discussing their contents, both
literary and artistic, taking a critical
attitude toward both. The five are FUEGO DE
AZTLAN, VORTICE, PRISMA, MAIZE, and MANGO.

FUEGOS EN AZTLAN [exhibit]

3979 Teatro de la Tierra Morena, Santa Cruz, CA.
Fuego en Aztlan: a Chicano arts show.
Exhibition brochure, 1980. English.

AN: Folder of information on the
exhibition curated by Cruz Zamarron and
Eduardo Carrillo. Exhibiting artists were:
Justina Avila, Terry Benitez, Eduardo
Carrillo, Hernando Chavez, Bob Cruz, Juanita
Estrada, Juana Franklin, Sal Garcia, Leticia
Hernandez, David "Sir Loco" Jimenez, Raoul
Mendez, Vicente Mendez, Maria V. Pinedo,
Gonzalo Placencia, Ramon Rodriguez, Roberto
Salas, George Silva and Cruz Zamarron. A
special feature was a live tattoo
demonstration entitled "Walking Art".

Fuentes, Juan

3980 Chicano Studies Library, University of
California, Berkeley and Garcia, Rupert.
Realismo: Chicano drawings by Juan Fuentes.
Berkeley, CA: Chicano Studies Library
Publications, UC Berkeley, 1976. English.

AN: Exhibition pamphlet with one drawing
by Juan Fuentes. Text situates the drawings
within artistic experiments using the
photograph as part of the artists visual
vocabulary. Different from "avant-garde new
realists," Fuentes' "Realismo Chicano" is
subjective in using selected photographs
that present a reality of struggle.

3981 Galeria de la Raza/Studio 24, San Francisco,
CA and Franco, Jean. Juan Fuentes y Rupert
Garcia: posters, drawings, prints.
Exhibition catalog, 1975. English.

AN: Catalog of an exhibit. Illustrated
with drawings and posters.

3982 Galeria Museo, Mission Cultural Center, San
Francisco, CA. La sirena y el nopal:
Graciela Carrillo - Juan R. Fuentes. An
exhibition of paintings, drawings, and
graphics. Exhibition catalog, 1981. English.

AN: Invitation/catalog for an exhibit.
Includes reproductions and statements by the
two San Francisco artists. Well illustrated.

3983 Garcia, Rupert. Laminas de la Raza. San

Francisco: Garcia Litho and Printing
Service, 1975. English.

AN: Portfolio of drawings and prints by
Patricia Rodriguez, Ricardo Apodaca,
Xochitl, Domingo Rivera, Francisco Camplis,
Rafael Maradiaga, Tom Rios, Juan Fuentes,
Ricardo Diaz, Jose Romero, Consuelo Mendez,
Jose Antonio Burciaga, Irene Perez, Ricardo
Rios, Mike Rios, Graciela Carrillo, Rene
Yanez, Luis Talamantez, Guillermo Bermudez,
all from Northern California.

3984 Gonzalez, Tobias and Gonzalez, Sandra.
Perspectives on Chicano education. Stanford,
CA: Stanford University, 1975. English.

AN: Reproductions of artworks by Ralph
Maradiaga, Patricia Rodriguez, Roberto
Bonilla, Francisco Camplis, Graciela
Carrillo-Lopez, Juan Fuentes, Irene Perez,
Roger Reyes, Carlos Loarca, Xavier
Viramontes, Ralph McNeill, Rupert Garcia,
Jose Romero.

3985 Stofflet-Santiago, Mary. The fifth sun:
esthetic quality versus curatorial intent.
ARTWEEK, Vol. 8, no. 37 (November 5, 1977),
p. 6. English.

AN: Review of the exhibit THE FIFTH SUN
at the University Art Museum in Berkeley,
Calif., curated by Ralph Maradiaga of the
Galeria de la Raza. It contains folk art,
and posters by Chicano artists Maradiaga,
Rupert Garcia, Juan Fuentes, mural studies
by Graciela Carrillo and Mike Rios, ceramics
by Anna de Leon, an altar by Amalia
Mesa-Bains, and mural drawings by Mexican
muralists. The writer criticizes the uneven
quality of the show, but encourages better
ones in the future. Illustrated.

3986 Time to greez: incantations from the Third
World. San Francisco, CA: Glide
Publications/Third World Communications,
1975. English.

AN: Rupert Garcia, drawing, p. 158;
Xavier Viramontes, silkscreen, p. 181; Juan
Fuentes, drawing, p. 188; Graciela Carrillo,
drawing, p. 196.

Fuentes, Larry

3987 Mendiville, Miguel and Saavedra-Vela, Pilar.
A time for less talk and more action.
AGENDA, Vol. 7, no. 5 (September, October,
1977), p. 33-34. English.

AN: The exhibit RAICES Y VISIONES,
funded by the National Endowment for the
Arts, was composed of more than 100 artworks
by Chicano and Latino artists and toured the
United States in 1977. The exposition was
organized in four sections; artists whose
work is influenced or related to
Pre-Columbian art, art that explores social
and political realities, and works that are
more personal and introspective. Gives
itinerary and listing of participating
artists. Illustrated by photographs of the
work of Rudy Trevino, Cesar Martinez, Luis
Jimenez from Texas and Larry Fuente from
California.

Fuentes, Larry (cont.)

3988 Moisan, Jim. Ancient roots, new visions. ARTWEEK, Vol. 9, no. 26 (July 29, 1978), p. 8. English.

AN: Review of the show held at the Municipal Arts Gallery of Los Angeles, the first national touring show of Latino artists in the United States. Includes commentary on work of Larry Fuente, Luis Jimenez, Frank Romero, Harry Gamboa, Gronk, Rudy Martinez, Benjamin Serrano, Ricardo Diaz, Patssi Valdez, Mel Casas, Luis Leroy, Pedro Lujan. A related show, NEW VISIONS, L.A., includes Robert Delgado, Ray Bravo, Joe Moran, Rosalyn Mesquita, Patricia Murillo and others.

3989 Ripley, Deborah. A sticky business. NEW WEST MAGAZINE, (July 28, 1980). English.

AN: Essay on California artists who take discarded objects and upgrade them into art works. Includes photographs of Larry Fuentes and three of his creations.

Funding Sources

3990 CHICANO CINEMA NEWSLETTER. Vol. 1, no. 1 (December 1978). English.

AN: Reports on activities of Chicano filmmakers in producing films, meeting with organizations like the American Film Institute, the Hispanic Task Force of the National Endowment for the Arts, the WNET Independent Documentary Film Fund. International film news also included.

3991 Goldman, Shifra M. Resistance and identity: street murals of occupied Aztlan. LATIN AMERICAN LITERARY REVIEW, Vol. 5, no. 10 (Spring, Summer, 1977), p. 124-128. English.

AN: Two periods of Mexican muralism's influence in the U.S.: 1930s and 1960s. Differences between Mexican and Chicano murals nationally. Comparison of the respective iconographies and funding sources. This article was reprinted as "Resistencia e Identidad: Los Murales Callejeros de Aztlan, La Ciudad (sic) Ocupada," in ARTES VISUALES (Mexico, D.F.), no. 16, Fall-Winter, 1977, p. 22-25.

3992 Goldman, Shifra M. Resistencia e identidad: los murales callejeros de Aztlan, la ciudad (sic) ocupada. ARTES VISUALES, no. 16 (Fall, Winter, 1977), p. 22-25. Spanish.

AN: Reprint of article published as "Resistance and identity: street murals of occupied Aztlan" in LATIN AMERICAN LITERARY REVIEW, Vol. 5, no. 10, Spring-Summer 1977, p. 124-128.

3993 Hanson, Matt. Barren walls toned into bold works of art. ARIZONA DAILY STAR, (May 24, 1979). English.

AN: Tucson high school students under direction of Antonio Pazos paint murals with a $10,000 grant from the Law Enforcement Assistance Administration. Color illustrations.

Gaegos, Carlito

3994 Greenberg, David; Smith, Kathryn; and Teacher, Stuart. Megamurals & supergraphics: big art. Philadelphia, PN: Running Press, 1977. English.

AN: A full-color picture book of murals throughout the United States. Chicano murals include Michael Rios (San Francisco), Mujeres Muralistas (San Francisco), Leonard Castellanos and Tomas Gonzales with others (Los Angeles), Los Artes Guadalupanos de Aztlan (New Mexico), Willie Herron (Los Angeles), Toltecas en Aztlan (San Diego), David Botello (Los Angeles), David Lopez and Arizona Mara Gang (Los Angeles), Vatos de Maravilla (Los Angeles), Carlito Gaegos (Los Angeles), Gil Hernandez (Los Angeles), Wayne [Alaniz] Healy (Los Angeles).

Galban, Margarita

3995 Fourth annual San Antonio film festival. San Antonio, TX: Oblate College of the Southwest, 1979. Bilingual.

AN: Symposium and film festival catalog featuring motion pictures and videocassettes made by and about Mexicans, Chicanos and Latinos. The Symposium focused on Latina women in film and television, Margarita Galban, Carmen Tafolla, Leticia Ponce, Grace Castro Nagata, Marcela Fernandez Violante of Mexico, and Sylvia Morales.

Galeria Almazan, Inc., San Antonio, TX

3996 Galeria Almazan, Inc., San Antonio, TX. Ray Chavez. Exhibition flyer, 1959. English.

AN: Single page flyer announcement for a one-man exhibition by Ray Chavez (born 1938 in San Antonio). Includes a photograph of the artist and a list of awards and exhibitions.

3997 Galeria Almazan, Inc., San Antonio, TX. Ray Chavez. Exhibition catalog, 1968. English.

AN: Exhibition catalog with biographical information on San Antonio painter Ray Chavez.

Galeria Barrios, Sacramento, CA

3998 A Chicano artist: Emigdio Vasquez. CANNERY WORKER, Vol. 1, no. 4 (February 1977), p. 5. Bilingual.

AN: Story on an exhibit by Esteban Villa in the Galeria Barrios of Sacramento, California, which is dedicated to the Cannery Workers Committee on its eighth anniversary. Five works by Villa are illustrated, and a group photograph of the Centro de Artistas Chicanos is included.

Galeria Capistrano

3999 Celebracion Chican-india. CAMINOS, Vol. 1, no. 3 (May 1980), p. 38-39+. English.

AN: Portfolio of works exhibited at the Galeria Capistrano in southern California: Zarco Guerrero, Domingo Ulloa, Mario Torero, Guillermo Acevedo. Judithe Hernandez, who also exhibited, is not included in the portfolio.

La Galeria de Colores, Las Vegas, NM

4000 La Galeria de Colores, Las Vegas, NM. La galeria de colores. Gallery brochure, [1980]. English.

AN: Brochure for a gallery/studio run by painter Pola Lopez de Jaramillo since 1980.

Galeria de la Comunidad, San Francisco, CA

4001 San Francisco's neighborhood arts program. San Francisco, CA: San Francisco Art Commission, [1971]. English.

AN: Booklet in pictures describing the activities underwritten by the city and county of San Francisco, the National Endowment for the Arts, the San Francisco Foundation, and the Zellerbach Family Fund. The interracial, interethnic staff includes Rene Yanez. Organizations listed are Galeria de la Raza, Galeria de la Comunidad, Galeria de las Bellas Artes, Galeria de las Pinturas, Galeria de la Musica, Galeria de la Poesia, Galeria de la Instruccion.

Galeria de la Instruccion

4002 San Francisco's neighborhood arts program. San Francisco, CA: San Francisco Art Commission, [1971]. English.

AN: Booklet in pictures describing the activities underwritten by the city and county of San Francisco, the National Endowment for the Arts, the San Francisco Foundation, and the Zellerbach Family Fund. The interracial, interethnic staff includes Rene Yanez. Organizations listed are Galeria de la Raza, Galeria de la Comunidad, Galeria de las Bellas Artes, Galeria de las Pinturas, Galeria de la Musica, Galeria de la Poesia, Galeria de la Instruccion.

Galeria de la Musica, San Francisco, CA

4003 San Francisco's neighborhood arts program. San Francisco, CA: San Francisco Art Commission, [1971]. English.

AN: Booklet in pictures describing the activities underwritten by the city and county of San Francisco, the National Endowment for the Arts, the San Francisco Foundation, and the Zellerbach Family Fund. The interracial, interethnic staff includes Rene Yanez. Organizations listed are Galeria de la Raza, Galeria de la Comunidad, Galeria de las Bellas Artes, Galeria de las Pinturas, Galeria de la Musica, Galeria de la Poesia, Galeria de la Instruccion.

Galeria de la Poesia

4004 San Francisco's neighborhood arts program. San Francisco, CA: San Francisco Art Commission, [1971]. English.

AN: Booklet in pictures describing the activities underwritten by the city and county of San Francisco, the National Endowment for the Arts, the San Francisco Foundation, and the Zellerbach Family Fund. The interracial, interethnic staff includes Rene Yanez. Organizations listed are Galeria de la Raza, Galeria de la Comunidad, Galeria de las Bellas Artes, Galeria de las Pinturas, Galeria de la Musica, Galeria de la Poesia, Galeria de la Instruccion.

Galeria de la Raza, San Antonio, TX

4005 Galeria de la Raza, San Antonio, TX. Celebration seventy-four. Exhibition catalog, [ca. 1974]. English.

AN: Catalog of extensive exhibition including European, Mexican, and the following Texan Chicano artists: Rolando Garces, Cesar Martinez, Ray Chavez, Vicente Rodriguez, Jorge Garza, Alfred Rodriguez, Luis Guerra, Carmen Lomas Garza, Bruno Andrade, Jr., Amado M. Pena Jr., Roberto Rios, Jose Trevino, Rudy Trevino, Luis Santoyo, Tati Rubio, Eduardo C. Garza, Arthur de la Fuente, and Jesus Campos Trevino.

Galeria de la Raza, San Francisco, CA

4006 Albright, Thomas. Pre-Columbian art: New Galeria de la Raza. SAN FRANCISCO CHRONICLE, (July 15, 1970), p. 49. English.

AN: A new gallery is launched at 425 14th St. in San Francisco with an exhibit by Sacramento State College teacher Esteban Villa, with bold angular abstractions of roosters, comments on the Frito Bandito, and expressionist pen and pencil drawings. Other exhibits are also on display. The Galeria is sponsored by Casa Hispana de Bellas Artes.

4007 Albright, Thomas. The sensual moods of nature. SAN FRANCISCO CHRONICLE, (January 23, 1971), p. 34. English.

AN: Review of an exhibition of paintings by Pedro Rodriguez of San Francisco at the Galeria de La Raza. Work classified as lyrical abstractions "in the vein of introspective lyric poetry".

4008 Around the Bay. METAMORFOSIS, Vol. 3, no. 2 (1980), p. 101-108. English.

AN: Cultural review of activities in the Bay Area, northern California, and Sacramento. Includes history of the Galeria de la Raza/Studio 24 (San Francisco), the Centro de Artistas Chicanos/RCAF, Royal Chicano Air Force (Sacramento), and a review of Rupert Garcia's pastel portraits exhibit at the Mexican Museum (S.F.) in 1981. Illustrated. Continued in Vol. 4, no. 1, 1981.

4009 Artes 6 Gallery, San Francisco, CA. Mixed media. Exhibition announcement, [ca. 1969-70]. English.

AN: Announcement of exhibit including Jim Cortez, Luis Cervantez, Vicente Rascon, Rene Yanes, Graciela Carrillo, Lorenza Camplis. The Artes 6 artists eventually formed the Galeria de la Raza of San Francisco.

4010 Calendar 1977. CHISMEARTE, no. 2 (Winter, Spring, 1977), p. 26-27. English.

AN: Reproduction of one month of the 1977 silkscreen calendar produced in limited edition by the Galeria de la Raza of San Francisco and the Royal Chicano Air Force of Sacramento, California. Displayed is Rene Yanez's screen HISTORICAL PHOTO-SILKSCREENMOVIE.

4011 Calendario 1973. San Francisco, CA: Galeria de la Raza, 1973. English.

AN: Handprinted silkscreen calendar by artists of the Galeria de la Raza.

Galeria de la Raza, San Francisco, CA (cont.)

4012 Calendario de comida 1976. San Francisco, CA: Galeria de la Raza, 1976. English.

AN: Handprinted silkscreen calendar consisting of twelve sheets and a cover. The work of the following artists is included: Ralph Maradiaga, Juanishi Orozco, Francisco Camplis, Ruben Guzman, Rodolfo Cuellar, Xavier Viramontes, Jose Montoya, Esteban Villa, Rene Yanez, Max Garcia and Louis "The Foot" Gonzalez, Patricia Rodriguez, and Ricardo Favela. All of the above are associated with the Galeria de la Raza, or the Royal Chicano Air Force of Sacramento, CA.

4013 CODEX NEWSLETTER (Galeria de la Raza, San Francisco, CA). Vol. 1, no. 2 (September 1973). English.

AN: An in-house bulletin of upcoming events: EL SOL NUNCA MUERE, photography/poster exhibit, Rolando Garces, and Peruvian posters; Mujeres de Aztlan, women artists' collective exhibit; Filipino/Samoan art exhibit; Galeria Christmas art sale; Galeria pavilion at S.F. annual art festival; Rockefeller scholarship for Galeria curator Luis Santana; Galeria coloring book; Balmy Alley mural project; Diego Rivera exhibit; first installment of Rupert Garcia's RAZA MURALS AND MURALISTS: AN HISTORICAL VIEW.

4014 Congreso de Artistas Chicanos en Aztlan, San Diego, CA. Diego Rivera, David Alfaro Siqueiros, Jose Clemente Orozco: exhibit of local artists, La Logan [San Diego]. Exhibition brochure, n.d. [c.1974]. English.

AN: Announcement of a traveling exhibit organized by Galeria de la Raza, San Francisco, from the collection of the San Francisco Museum of Art. Illustrated with a San Diego mural.

4015 Dunsmore de Carrillo, Patricia. On Rene Yanez of the Galeria de la Raza. CHISMEARTE, Vol. 1, no. 1 (Fall 1976), p. 8-9. English.

AN: Report on Yanez's negotiations with the Foster Kleiser Company to take over a billboard located outside the Galeria in San Fancisco which has been painted by Michael Rios, the Centro de Cambio and TIN TAN magazine, Zaiver (Xavier) Viramontes, and others.

4016 Electro Arts Gallery, San Francisco, CA. Electric realizations: an exhibition by Rene Yanez & Carl Heyward. Exhibition invitation, 1981. English.

AN: Invitation to an exhibit of color Xerox prints by Rene Yanez, Co-director of the Galeria de la Raza of San Francisco. Yanez feels that Xerox has opened new frontiers in presenting graphic work at a different scale and size.

4017 'Fashion Moda' at Galeria de la Raza. PEOPLE'S WORLD, Vol. 44, no. 48 (November 29, 1981), p. 10. English.

AN: A joint exhibit, FASHION MODA AT GALERIA DE LA RAZA, focuses on people interested in cross-cultural interaction. 50 artists from the San Francisco Bay Area, the South Bronx, Los Angeles, and New York City were shown. Fashion Moda is located in the South Bronx, an area of severe urban devastation. Illustrated.

4018 Fong, Katheryn M. Pachuco art records era of zootsuits and anti-Mexican riots. SAN FRANCISCO JRNL, Vol. 2, no. 32 (March 1, 1978), p. 6. English.

AN: Review of Galeria de la Raza exhibit of Jose Montoya's Pachuco Art. Installation included historical photographs and documents. Montoya work (drawings and paintings) were contextualized by written commentary aiming to re-interpret an important aspect of Chicano cultural history.

4019 Frankenstein, Alfred. Montoya's artistic update on Chicano zoot suiters. SAN FRANCISCO CHRONICLE, (February 18, 1978), p. 36. English.

AN: Review of Pachuco show at San Francisco's Galeria de la Raza, especially Jose Montoya's sketches and paintings.

4020 Frankenstein, Alfred. Prison's artist in residence. SAN FRANCISCO CHRONICLE, (May 5, 1978), p. 60. English.

AN: Review of the exhibition MUNDOS PERDIDOS, curated at the Galeria de la Raza by Leonard Castellanos. Show consisted of work by Castellanos and inmates at Lompoc Federal Correctional Institution near Santa Barbara. Documents a prison mural, tattoos and silkscreen prints with socially critical themes.

4021 Frankenstein, Alfred. A senior senor's approach. SAN FRANCISCO CHRONICLE, (May 27, 1976), p. 48. English.

AN: Review of an exhibit of Mexican painter Jesus Reyes Ferreira at the Mexican Museum of San Francisco, as well as that of San Francisco artist Gustavo Rivera, an abstract expressionist painter. Also mentions the Museum's mural map, and Angel del Valle's photography show at the Galeria de la Raza.

4022 Galeria de la Raza/Studio 24. Mimeograph, [1980]. English.

AN: Mimeographed history of the Galeria de la Raza/Studio 24 which opened in 1970 as a showcase for Chicano/Latino artists. Its programs include exhibitions, murals and billboads, beautification of the community, education. Along with public grants, the Galeria strives to be self-sustaining through Studio 24 with retail sales and printing services.

4023 Galeria de la Raza/Studio 24, San Francisco, CA. Ajo, granadas y tres flores. Exhibition announcement, 1981.

AN: Announcement for an exhibition featuring Ruben Trejo, sculpture (Spokane, Washington), Cesar A. Martinez, paintings (San Antonio, Texas), Xavier Gorena, paper cut-outs (Mission, Texas).

4024 Galeria de la Raza/Studio 24, San Francisco, CA. Blanca Flor Gutierrez - oil pastels. Exhibition announcement, 1981.

AN: Color xeroxed announcement for a window display of oil pastels by Gutierrez.

Galeria de la Raza, San Francisco, CA (cont.)

4025 Galeria de la Raza/Studio 24, San Francisco,
     CA. Calacas huesudas. Exhibition brochure,
     1980.

     AN: Exhibition of Chicano artists for El
     Dia de los Muertos with brochure using text
     adapted from POSADA'S MEXICO, edited by Ron
     Tyler, Library of Congress, Washington,
     D.C., 1979. The Galeria exhibit was curated
     by Kate Connell, Maria Pinedo and Galeria
     staff.

4026 Galeria de la Raza/Studio 24, San Francisco,
     CA and Garcia, Rupert. Community art-murals:
     an exhibition of original drawings,
     sketches, and designs. Exhibition brochure,
     1978. English.

     AN: The current crisis of contemporary
     art is relatively resolved by
     community-based muralists who engage
     themselves against repressive forces as
     artists, organizers, propagandists. However,
     art and politics are not identical, though
     they may overlap. Color xerox illustrations
     of murals.

4027 Galeria de la Raza/Studio 24, San Francisco,
     CA. Dia de los muertos/day of the dead.
     Exhibition invitation, 1981. English.

     AN: Invitation to the Galeria's annual
     Dia de los Muertos exhibition.

4028 Galeria de la Raza/Studio 24, San Francisco,
     CA. Homenaje a Frida Kahlo. Exhibition
     brochure, 1978.

     AN: 51 artists, Chicano and non-Chicano.

4029 Galeria de la Raza/Studio 24, San Francisco,
     CA. Mexican film poster (1943-71): an
     exhibition/exhibicion de fotos/cartelones
     del cine mexicano. Exhibition invitation,
     1971. English.

     AN: Invitation to an exhibit.

4030 Galeria de la Raza/Studio 24, San Francisco,
     CA. Photographs by Angel Del Valle. Los
     sembradores: the marijuana growers.
     Exhibition catalog, 1976. English.

     AN: Illustrated catalog. Del Valle
     documents the growing, customs, and
     merchandising of marijuana in the Sierras of
     Mexico.

4031 Galeria de la Raza/Studio 24, San Francisco,
     CA and Garcia, Rupert. Posters from the
     golden age of Mexican cinema. Exhibition
     catalog, 1979. English.

     AN: The Galeria's second exhibit of
     Mexican movie posters features those of the
     1940s and early 1950s (in 1971, the exhibit
     covered 1943-1971) from the collection of
     Enrique Flores, owner of the Rio Theatre,
     Mission, Texas, and the Xochil Art Center.
     Garcia's essay includes a history of Mexican
     cinema, and the mythologizing period of the
     "Golden Age" reflected in the posters which
     promoted movie-consummership. One
     illustration. (See Santos G. Martinez, Jr.'s
     essay in the exhibition catalog: MEXICAN
     MOVIE POSTERS, for another point of view).

4032 Galeria de la Raza/Studio 24, San Francisco,
     CA. Published prints of Hecho en Aztlan
     Multiples. Exhibition announcement, 1980.
     English.

     AN: Announcement of exhibit of the
     published silkscreen prints of Hecho en
     Aztlan Multiples; a small business run by
     Richard Duardo of Los Angeles.

4033 Galeria de la Raza/Studio 24, San Francisco,
     CA and Garcia, Rupert. La Raza Silkscreen
     Center: "Images of a community", an exhibit
     of silkscreen posters and graphic works from
     1971 to 1979. Exhibition catalog, 1979.
     English.

     AN: First large scale retrospective
     exhibit of the La Raza Silkscreen Center's
     eight years of postermaking. Includes list
     of 90 artists.

4034 Galeria de la Raza/Studio 24, San Francisco,
     CA. Royal Chicano Air Force presents
     "Chicanos del Valle Tortilla Opening".
     Exhibition invitation, 1971. English.

4035 Galeria de la Raza/Studio 24, San Francisco,
     CA and Lomas Garza, Carmen. Self-portraits
     by Chicano and Latino artists. Exhibition
     catalog, 1980. English.

     AN: Catalog of a national exhibition by
     66 artists. Gives names, residence, date of
     birth, and information on the work shown for
     each of the artists. 45 are from California,
     and 3 each from Puerto Rico, Arizona, New
     York, 9 from Texas, 2 from Washington, 1
     from Virginia. 9 are women.

4036 Gonzales, Juan. Galeria de la Raza: "our
     people deserve the best". EL TECOLOTE, Vol.
     7, no. 11 (July 1977), p. 14. English.

     AN: "We are not here to sell our art,
     but to sell the idea of art." This could
     well be the motto of Galeria de la Raza who
     under co-directors Rene Yanez and Ralph
     Maradiaga has become a key cultural
     institution in the Mission District of San
     Francisco. The two directors have a broad
     definition of art that encompasses
     everything from cartoons to craftwork. The
     article details past exhibits and future
     goals. A half-page photograph of the
     exterior of Galeria de la Raza by Pilar
     Mejia illustrates the article. Reprint of
     article entitled "Our people deserve the
     best" which appeared in NUESTRO, Vol. 1, no.
     2 (May, 1977), p. 56-57.

4037 Gonzales, Juan. Regional report, The arts:
     "Our people deserve the best". NUESTRO, Vol.
     1, no. 2 (May 1977), p. 56-57. English.

     AN: Activities of San Francisco's
     Galeria de la Raza; interviews with its
     directors, Rene Yanez and Ralph Maradiaga.
     Reprinted as "Galeria de la Raza: our people
     deserve the best" in EL TECOLOTE (San
     Francisco, CA), Vol. 7, no. 11 (July, 1977),
     p. 14.

Galeria de la Raza, San Francisco, CA (cont.)

4038 Grimke, Angelina. Chicano art finds home in Mission galeria. PEOPLE'S WORLD, Vol. 33, no. 32 (August 8, 1970), p. 11. English.

AN: Commentary on the exhibition CHICANOS, CUBA Y LOS 10 MILLONES held at the original Galeria de la Raza at 425 14th Street in San Francisco. The show presented photographs by Jay Ojeda and Roberto Perez-Diaz, drawings by Gloria Ozuna together with paintings and photographs by Cuban artist Mederos. Provides information about the goals of the Galeria as the visual arts department of Casa Hispana de Bellas Artes. Exhibition curator was Rolando Castellon.

4039 La historia de California, 1977. San Francisco, CA: Galeria de la Raza, 1977. English.

AN: Handprinted silkscreen calendar of history seen from a Mexican point of view. Twelve sheets and a cover. Artists are: Ralph Maradiaga, Irene Perez, Louie "The Foot" Gonzalez, Max Garcia, Patricia Rodriguez, Jose Romero, Esteban Villa, Juanishi Orozco, Rodolfo Cuellar, Jose Montoya, Xavier Viramontes, Rene Yanez, Ricardo Favela, associated with the Galeria de la Raza, or the Royal Chicano Air Force of Sacramento.

4040 Kamin, Ira. Memories of Frida Kahlo. CALIFORNIA LIVING, (May 6, 1979), p. 44-50. English.

AN: Chatty review of the sixth annual Dia de los Muertos, celebrated by the Galeria de la Raza this year with an homage to Mexican painter Frida Kahlo. Local artists filled the gallery with their homages; the Galeria's outdoor billboard was painted with her image; guests brought gifts and dressed in Kahlo style, including older women who wore jewelry given them by Kahlo. Biographical material on Kahlo and Diego Rivera should be read with caution. Well illustrated.

4041 Lomas Garza, Carmen; Montoya, Jose E.; and Pinedo, Maria Vita. What we are...now. Exhibition catalog, n.d. English.

AN: Drawings by Sacramento women artists: Lorraine Garcia, Eva C. Garcia, Kathryn E. Garcia, Celia Rodriguez, Patricia Carrillo.

4042 Low n slow - lowrider art. PEOPLE'S WORLD, Vol. 42, no. 34 (August 25, 1979), p. 10. English.

AN: Announcement of the Galeria de la Raza's exhibit of lowrider art. The article mentions the history of the lowrider car from the 1940s Pachuco zootsuiters, to the 1950s car clubs. The lowrider exhibit was prepared by the Galeria in response to white neighbors' recent protests against Saturday night cruising in the Mission District.

4043 Martinez, Anita. Raza! Arte! Raza! Arte! EL TECOLOTE, Vol. 1, no. 2 (September 7, 1970), p. 3. Bilingual.

AN: Galeria de la Raza opened on July, 1970 at 425 14th St. San Francisco. It was an outgrowth of the Arte Seis organization (an art effort established in the Mission District in 1967 by Francisco Camplis, Rupert Garcia, Ralph McNeil, Jay Ojeda and

Jack Ruiz). These and other artists brought together by the Neighborhood Arts Program have coalesced in the new Galeria de la Raza. Article gives goals, organizational scheme and plans for the Galeria. It's first exhibit was a one man show by Esteban Villa together with a photo and sketch exhibit on Cuba by Jay Ojeda, Roberto Diaz Perez and Gloria Ozuna. Illustrated with installation view of new Galeria.

4044 Martinez, Anita. Raza art. EL TECOLOTE, Vol. 1, no. 8 (November 30, 1970), p. 1. English.

AN: Jay Ojeda, newly selected director of Galeria de la Raza, describes the memorial exhibition dedicated to Ruben Salazar installed at the Galeria on Dec. 12, 1970. Salazar symbolized and synthesized many of the goals subscribed to by artist members of La Galeria. The exhibit included work by Chicano and Latino artists Francisco Camplis, Jay Ojeda, Jose Romero, Rolando Castellon, Rene Yanez, Luis Valsoto, Mike Ruiz, Carlos Perez, Gustavo Rivera, Peter Rodriguez, Carlos Loarca and Ralph Maradiaga.

4045 Mesa-Bains, Amalia. Homage to Frida Kahlo opens Nov. 2, at Galeria de la Raza. EL TECOLOTE, Vol. 9, no. 1 (September 1978), p. 7. English.

AN: Announcement and call for artwork to Galeria de la Raza's exhibition honoring Frida Kahlo on Nov. 2, 1978. The proposed "Homage to Frida Kahlo" will encompass four major areas; artists' work, documentation/publication, related art productions, and educational activities. The Galeria educated participating artists to the life and art of Frida Kahlo through slide presentations and written material. The exhibition became a milestone in the Galeria de la Raza history.

4046 Mission to honor Frida Kahlo: famous Mexican artist. EL TECOLOTE, Vol. 9, no. 3 (November 1978), p. 1. Bilingual.

AN: Announcement of an homage to Mexican painter Frida Kahlo at the Galeria de la Raza's annual celebration of Dia de los Muertos. Works reproduced with the article include those of Emmanuel C. Montoya, Yreina Cervantez, Jose Antonio Burciaga, Nina Serrano and Lisa Kokin. Bilingual.

4047 Mujeres de Aztlan. EL TECOLOTE, Vol. 4, no. 1 (October 10, 1973), p. 3. English.

AN: A collective of Third World women artists plan an art show at Galeria de la Raza in San Francisco. Stressing the need for art forms that bring awareness and present the true nature of women's living conditions, this call for submission of art work reflects some feminist concerns of the period.

Galeria de la Raza, San Francisco, CA (cont.)

4048 NATIONAL MURALS NETWORK COMMUNITY
NEWSLETTER. (Fall 1979). English.

AN: Reports on mural projects by Fermin
Coronado working with students in Houston;
Galeria de la Raza's billboard used as a
mural surface for changing images; murals
under the Flor en la Comunidad program of El
Centro Cultural de la Gente in San Jose,
California and led by artist Jaime Valadez;
murals in Grand Rapids and other cities of
western Michigan; murals by Jose Guerrero
and others from the Chicago Mural Group; a
survey of Chicano murals in the Pilsen area
of Chicago guided by Jose Gonzalez.

4049 New Galeria de la Raza. EL HISPANO, (July
28, 1970), p. 9. English.

AN: Review of the first exhibit at the
Galeria de la Raza at 425 14th St. in San
Francisco. The inaugural exhibition featured
Esteban Villa, Luis Gutierrez and Luis
Cervantes. The new Galeria is sponsored by
Casa Hispana de Bellas Artes assisted by San
Francisco Art Commission through its
Neighborhood Arts Program.

4050 Ojeda, Jay. Galeria de la Raza--art for the
community. SAN FRANCISCO PROGRESS, (March
24, 1972). English.

AN: Analysis of group exhibition by
thirty-four Raza artists. Commentary on the
work of Latin American artists Consuelo
Mendez, Rolando Castellon, and Chicano
artists Rupert Garcia, Chuy Campusano and
Peter Rodriguez.

4051 Opton, Suzanne. Short strokes. SAN FRANCISCO
FAULT, (December 29, 1971), p. 9-10.
English.

AN: The currently homeless Galeria de la
Raza has begun a series of wall painting
projects. Artist "Spain" did a Horizons
mural; Puerto Rican photographer Adal
Maldonado did photographic murals; Jerry
Concha, Tom Rios, did rooms in the Center
for Change drug program building, Chuy
Campusano, working with cartoonist R. Crumb,
and the Mission Rebel Kids did a cartoon
mural. Model Cities day care centers are
next to be painted.

4052 Pinedo, Maria Vita. Galeria de la Raza. KPFA
FOLIO, Vol. 28, no. 2 (February 1977).
English.

AN: Brief history of San Francisco's
Galeria de la Raza.

4053 Preuss, Karen. The new Mission murals. SAN
FRANCISCO BAY GUARDIAN, (June 28, 1975), p.
14-15. English.

AN: Mural art in San Francisco's Mission
District has covered nearly every wall and
alley on lower 24th Street. Murals by Mike
Rios, the Mujeres Muralistas (Patricia
Rodriguez, Graciela Carrillo, Consuelo
Mendez, Miriam Olivo, Irene Perez, Susan
Cervantes) appear in the area. Others have
been painted by artists associated with the
Galeria de la Raza. Illustrations.

4054 Salvador R. Torres Chicano Underground
Studio-Gallery, San Diego, CA. Diego Rivera,
David Alfaro Siqueiros, Jose Clemente
Orozco, from the collection of the S.F.
Museum of Art. Exhibition invitation,
[1974]. English.

AN: Illustrated invitation of an exhibit
organized by the Galeria de la Raza of San
Francisco loaned to the Congreso de Artistas
Chicanos en Aztlan, and held in artist
Torres' studio.

4055 San Francisco. ART NEWS MAGAZINE, Vol. 69,
no. 6 (October 1970), p. 83. English.

AN: Review of Esteban Villa's show, the
first held by the newly constituted Galeria
de la Raza in San Francisco. Illustrated.

4056 San Francisco's neighborhood arts program.
San Francisco, CA: San Francisco Art
Commission, [1971]. English.

AN: Booklet in pictures describing the
activities underwritten by the city and
county of San Francisco, the National
Endowment for the Arts, the San Francisco
Foundation, and the Zellerbach Family Fund.
The interracial, interethnic staff includes
Rene Yanez. Organizations listed are Galeria
de la Raza, Galeria de la Comunidad, Galeria
de las Bellas Artes, Galeria de las
Pinturas, Galeria de la Musica, Galeria de
la Poesia, Galeria de la Instruccion.

4057 University Art Museum, Berkeley, CA. The
Fifth Sun: Contemporary/Traditional Chicano
& Latino Art. Exhibition catalog, 1977.
English.

AN: Catalog of exhibit including 45
artists of northern California. Texts deal
with Mexican muralists, Mujeres Muralistas &
other muralists, posters, the Chicano art
movement, altars, La Raza Silkscreen Center,
Galeria de la Raza, the Mexican Museum, the
Sacramento Centro de Artistas Chicanos/RCAF.
Mural maps of S.F. Bay Area and Sacramento.
Many illustrations.

4058 Venegas, Sybil. Dia de los muertos. SOMOS,
Vol. 1, no. 5 (October 1978), p. 42-47.
English.

AN: Brief history of Dia de los muertos
ceremonies. While the custom is dying in
Mexico (except for tourists), Chicano
organizations like Galeria de la Raza
(S.F.), El Centro de Artistas Chicanos
(Sacramento, Ca.) celebrate the event
annually, as does [Self-Help Graphics and
Art, Inc.] in East Los Angeles. Well
illustrated with photographs by Guillermo
Bejarano and Daniel Duran.

Galeria de las Bellas Artes, San Francisco, CA

4059 San Francisco's neighborhood arts program.
San Francisco, CA: San Francisco Art
Commission, [1971]. English.

AN: Booklet in pictures describing the
activities underwritten by the city and
county of San Francisco, the National
Endowment for the Arts, the San Francisco
Foundation, and the Zellerbach Family Fund.
The interracial, interethnic staff includes
Rene Yanez. Organizations listed are Galeria
de la Raza, Galeria de la Comunidad, Galeria
de las Bellas Artes, Galeria de las
Pinturas, Galeria de la Musica, Galeria de
la Poesia, Galeria de la Instruccion.

Galeria de las Pinturas, San Francisco, CA

4060 San Francisco's neighborhood arts program.
San Francisco, CA: San Francisco Art
Commission, [1971]. English.

AN: Booklet in pictures describing the
activities underwritten by the city and
county of San Francisco, the National
Endowment for the Arts, the San Francisco
Foundation, and the Zellerbach Family Fund.
The interracial, interethnic staff includes
Rene Yanez. Organizations listed are Galeria
de la Raza, Galeria de la Comunidad, Galeria
de las Bellas Artes, Galeria de las
Pinturas, Galeria de la Musica, Galeria de
la Poesia, Galeria de la Instruccion.

Galeria Museo, Mission Cultural Center, San Francisco, CA

4061 Galeria Museo - new art gallery opens in the
Mission. EL TECOLOTE, Vol. 8, no. 1
(September 1977), p. 8. Bilingual.

AN: Brief article on the inauguration of
the Art Gallery at the Mission Cultural
Center. The opening Exhibit (August 13,
1977) was entitled SIXTY-THREE SHOW and
included work in various media by Sixty
three Bay Area Latino artists. Gilberto
Osorio was designated as the first
artist-in-residence. Information on future
plans for the Galeria-Museo.

4062 Galeria Museo, Mission Cultural Center, San
Francisco, CA. La sirena y el nopal:
Graciela Carrillo - Juan R. Fuentes. An
exhibition of paintings, drawings, and
graphics. Exhibition catalog, 1981. English.

AN: Invitation/catalog for an exhibit.
Includes reproductions and statements by the
two San Francisco artists. Well illustrated.

Galeria Otra Vez, Los Angeles, CA

4063 Galeria Otra Vez, Los Angeles, CA.
Inner/urban landscapes: Ricardo Valverde,
Suda House, David Feldman. Exhibition
invitation, 1979. English.

AN: Invitation to a photography
exhibition held at Self-Help Graphic's
gallery.

Galeria, Santa Ana, CA

4064 Day, Orman. Hispanic life mirrored by ethnic
artists. THE REGISTER, (July 5, 1981), p.
B1+. English.

AN: Story on artists Manuel Hernandez
Trujillo and Emigdio Vasquez whose work
opened the new Galeria in Santa Ana, and
poet Manuel Gomez. Color illustrations.

4065 Dietmeier, R. C. City artist finds his
inspiration where he lives. ORANGE CITY
NEWS, (December 23, 1981), p. 2. English.

AN: Illustrated story on Emigdio
Vasquez's ten year retrospective of
realistic paintings taken from photographs,
held at the Galeria in Santa Ana, Calif.
Vasquez records his environment and events
from the 1940s and 1950s as an artistic and
documentary statement.

4066 Friendly Center, Inc., Orange, CA / Galeria.
The last Chicano art show. Exhibition
brochure, 1981. English.

AN: Exhibit of 15 artists from Los
Angeles and Orange Counties at the
inauguration of the Galeria in Santa Ana,
California. Statement and list of sponsors.

4067 Galeria: a place you should visit. CAMINOS,
Vol. 2, no. 5 (October 1981), p. 24-25.
English.

AN: Announcement of the opening of
Galeria, specializing in Hispanic art, in
Orange County, California. Illustrations of
sculpture by Richard G. Villa and Eduardo
Oropeza.

4068 Galeria, Santa Ana, CA. Diez anos con
Emigdio (ten years with Emigdio), works by
Emigdio Vasquez: 1971-1981. Exhibition
invitation, 1982.

AN: Invitation to exhibit by Emigdio
Vasquez. Illustrated.

4069 Galeria, Santa Ana, CA. Egg-sploration: a
comprehensive exhibit by Art & Ben
Valenzuela. Exhibition invitation, 1981.
English.

AN: Invitation to an exhibit of two
Orange County, CA artists in a new
Chicano-run gallery. Illustrated with work
of art by Art Valenzuela.

4070 Galeria, Santa Ana, CA. The last Chicano art
show. Exhibition brochure, 1981. English.

AN: Invitation-brochure for an exhibit
of Los Angeles and Orange County artists in
a gallery underwritten by the Friendly
Center, Inc. with grants from local
government and from businesses. Exhibiting
are (Roberto) Gil de Montes, Gilbert Lujan,
Judy Miranda, Patricia Murillo, Alonso
Pardo, Teddy Sandoval, Mexican artist
Artemio Sepulveda, Joey Terrill, Art
Valenzuela, Ben Valenzuela, Linda Vallejo,
Jack A. Vargas, Emigdio Vasquez, Richard
Serrato, and J. William Hernandez, who is
the gallery director.

Galeria Tonantzin, Centro Cultural de LUCHA, Austin, TX

4071 Galeria Tonantzin, Centro Cultural de LUCHA,
Austin, TX. Mexican faces in San Antonio.
Exhibition brochure, [1980]. English.

AN: Photography show by 24 young
Chicanos from Texas sponsored by the
Secretaria de Relaciones Exteriores and the
Universidad Autonoma de Mexico, Cultural
Extension program (SRE-UNAM) in San Antonio.

4072 Galeria Tonantzin, Centro Cultural de LUCHA,
Austin, TX. Visiones Chicanas: images and
demonstrations by Chicana and Latina visual
artists. Exhibition invitation, 1979.
English.

AN: Invitational poster for an exhibit
and a series of workshops organized by
Mujeres Artistas del Suroeste (MAS),
affiliated with LUCHA, League of United
Chicano Artists of Austin, TX.

Galeria Tonantzin, Centro Cultural de LUCHA, Austin, TX (cont.)

4073 Galeria Tonantzin, Centro Cultural de LUCHA, Austin, TX. Young Chicano photographers from throughout Texas. Exhibition brochure, n.d. English.

AN: This exhibition is the collection of the winners of the contest (by the same name) sponsored by the Extension Cultural SRE-UNAM in San Antonio. Photographers represented were: Grace Alvarez, David Cardenas, Hector Cardenas, Stephen Casanova, Ronald Cortez, Raul Espinosa, Felix Almanza, Carolina Flores, David Garza Perez, Xavier Garza, Conrad Guerra, Melinda Hasbrook, Juan Jose de Hoyes, Beverly Kennon, Art Moreno, David Perez, Isabelle Purden, Patricia Santell, Nancy de los Santos, Jose Soria, Richard Tichich, Kathy Vargas, Vivian Yaten, and Johnny Zamarria.

Galerias Paco, New York, NY

4074 Galerias Paco, New York, NY. Consuelo Gonzalez Amezcua - filigree art. Exhibition announcement, n.d. English.

AN: Two-page exhibition announcement illustrated with two examples of the Texas artist's "filigree art" and a sample of her poetry.

Galindo, Guillermo

4075 Encanto Pavilion, Encanto Park, Phoenix, AZ. Exposicion de arte para la raza: Arizona Chicano art show. Exhibition catalog, [ca. 1978]. English.

AN: Catalog for an exhibit organized by MARS (Movimiento Artistico del Rio Salado). Colombian-born Antonio L. Tocora, Jim Covarrubias, Ed Dias, Robert C. Buitron, Armando Leon Hernandez, Guillermo Galindo, Richard Luna Cisneros, Jose Andres Giron, Robert L. Matta included.

Gallegos, David

4076 Curtis, Cathy. Six aspiring watercolorists. SUNDAY MAGAZINE [Supplement to CONTRA COSTA COUNTY TIMES, CA], (October 14, 1979), p. 19. English.

AN: In a recent show at the Richmond Art Center (Calif.), David Gallegos was one of the watercolorists. Working in a traditional modernist style, Gallegos deals with light and air in his views of the waterfront.

4077 Fowler, Carol. A study on contrasts at valley art. SUNDAY MAGAZINE [Supplement to CONTRA COSTA COUNTY TIMES, CA], (October 9, 1980). English.

AN: David Gallegos' unpeopled landscapes are composed of large color patches which portray the industrial fringes of San Francisco Bay. He works within a luminist tradition, stressing light. Illustrated.

Gallegos, Ernie

4078 Meta studio I. Denver, CO: s.n., [1980]. English.

AN: Portfolio of colored prints by Colorado artists Ernie Gallegos, Jerry Jaramillo, Steve Lucero and Carlos M. Sandoval. Biographical information and photograph of each artist. Presentation of the group under the rubric of "metarealism"

by Stephen Pascual Lucero.

Galleries, Chicano

4079 Albright, Thomas. Pre-Columbian art: New Galeria de la Raza. SAN FRANCISCO CHRONICLE, (July 15, 1970), p. 49. English.

AN: A new gallery is launched at 425 14th St. in San Francisco with an exhibit by Sacramento State College teacher Esteban Villa, with bold angular abstractions of roosters, comments on the Frito Bandito, and expressionist pen and pencil drawings. Other exhibits are also on display. The Galeria is sponsored by Casa Hispana de Bellas Artes.

4080 Albright, Thomas. The sensual moods of nature. SAN FRANCISCO CHRONICLE, (January 23, 1971), p. 34. English.

AN: Review of an exhibition of paintings by Pedro Rodriguez of San Francisco at the Galeria de La Raza. Work classified as lyrical abstractions "in the vein of introspective lyric poetry".

4081 Around the Bay. METAMORFOSIS, Vol. 3, no. 2 (1980), p. 101-108. English.

AN: Cultural review of activities in the Bay Area, northern California, and Sacramento. Includes history of the Galeria de la Raza/Studio 24 (San Francisco), the Centro de Artistas Chicanos/RCAF, Royal Chicano Air Force (Sacramento), and a review of Rupert Garcia's pastel portraits exhibit at the Mexican Museum (S.F.) in 1981. Illustrated. Continued in Vol. 4, no. 1, 1981.

4082 Artes 6 Gallery, San Francisco, CA. Mixed media. Exhibition announcement, [ca. 1969-70]. English.

AN: Announcement of exhibit including Jim Cortez, Luis Cervantez, Vicente Rascon, Rene Yanes, Graciela Carrillo, Lorenza Camplis. The Artes 6 artists eventually formed the Galeria de la Raza of San Francisco.

4083 Beronius, George. The murals of East Los Angeles. HOME MAGAZINE, (April 11, 1976), p. 10-11+. English.

AN: Well-illustrated historical article focusing on murals at Estrada Courts and those produced through Goez Gallery and Judith Baca in East Los Angeles.

4084 A Chicano artist: Emigdio Vasquez. CANNERY WORKER, Vol. 1, no. 4 (February 1977), p. 5. Bilingual.

AN: Story on an exhibit by Esteban Villa in the Galeria Barrios of Sacramento, California, which is dedicated to the Cannery Workers Committee on its eighth anniversary. Five works by Villa are illustrated, and a group photograph of the Centro de Artistas Chicanos is included.

Galleries, Chicano (cont.)

4085 Congreso de Artistas Chicanos en Aztlan, San
     Diego, CA. Diego Rivera, David Alfaro
     Siqueiros, Jose Clemente Orozco: exhibit of
     local artists, La Logan [San Diego].
     Exhibition brochure, n.d. [c.1974]. English.

     AN: Announcement of a traveling exhibit
     organized by Galeria de la Raza, San
     Francisco, from the collection of the San
     Francisco Museum of Art. Illustrated with a
     San Diego mural.

4086 Contemporary Arts Museum, Houston, TX and
     Martinez, Santos G., Jr. Mexican movie
     posters. Exhibition invitation, 1979.
     English.

     AN: Invitation to an exhibit of posters
     primarily from the collecttion of Enrique
     Flores and Xavier Gorena of Xochil Art
     Center, Mission, Texas. Martinez considers
     the posters monumental, with expressive
     qualities that have influenced Chicano
     poster makers like the Royal Chicano Air
     Force, and Rupert Garcia, and Texas artists
     like Luis Jimenez, Jesse Trevino and Cesar
     Martinez. One illustration. Introduction by
     guest curator Santos G. Martinez, Jr. (See
     Rupert Garcia's essay in the exhibition
     catalog: POSTERS FROM THE GOLDEN AGE OF
     MEXICAN CINEMA, for another point of view).

4087 Conversation on photography in the Los
     Angeles Latino community. OBSCURA, Vol. 2,
     no. 2 (December, February, 1981, 1982), p.
     22-32. English.

     AN: Interview on the nature and
     distinguishing characteristics of Chicano
     photography with Chicano photographers
     Isabel Castro (Council for Latino
     Photography), Lorenzo Hernandez (Director of
     Cityscape Gallery, publisher PHOTOSHOW
     magazine), Joseph G. Uribe (California State
     University, Los Angeles, Center for the
     Visual Arts, Director of West Colorado
     Gallery), Patssi Valdez, Becky Villasenor,
     and sculptor, curator, and Art Director for
     Academia Quinto Sol, Inc., Linda Vallejo,
     Portfolio of photography by Chicanos Don
     Anton, Louis Carlos Bernal, Sean Carrillo,
     Patssi Valdez, Ricardo Valverde, and by
     Morrie Camhi and Elizabeth Sisco on Chicano
     subjects.

4088 Day, Orman. Hispanic life mirrored by ethnic
     artists. THE REGISTER, (July 5, 1981), p.
     B1+. English.

     AN: Story on artists Manuel Hernandez
     Trujillo and Emigdio Vasquez whose work
     opened the new Galeria in Santa Ana, and
     poet Manuel Gomez. Color illustrations.

4089 Diaz, Katherine A. Art is business: an
     interview with Joe L. Gonzalez. CAMINOS,
     Vol. 2, no. 5 (October 1981), p. 21-22.
     English.

     AN: Business advice to the artist and to
     the collector from the owner of the two Goez
     art galleries in Los Angeles. How to
     merchandise or buy art as a good investment.

4090 Dietmeier, R. C. City artist finds his
     inspiration where he lives. ORANGE CITY
     NEWS, (December 23, 1981), p. 2. English.

     AN: Illustrated story on Emigdio
     Vasquez's ten year retrospective of
     realistic paintings taken from photographs,
     held at the Galeria in Santa Ana, Calif.

Vasquez records his environment and events
from the 1940s and 1950s as an artistic and
documentary statement.

4091 Diseno Studios, Austin, TX. Diseno Studios
     Gallery. Brochure, 1981. English.

4092 Donaghy, Kathleen. Two Arizona firsts:
     Chicano gallery and Spanish theatre. ARIZONA
     ARTS AND LIFESTYLE, (1981). English.

     AN: The MARS (Movimiento Artistico del
     Rio Salado) Gallery has opened in downtown
     Phoenix, run by MARS founder Jim
     Covarrubias. Louis Leroy, expansion arts
     coordinator for the Arizona Commission on
     the Arts, says it is the only arts-oriented
     space that caters to Chicanos in Arizona.

4093 Estudios Rio: gallery of contemporary arts
     and crafts. Exhibition catalog, 1976.
     English.

     AN: Catalog including identification,
     portraits and works of participating
     artists: Joe Bova, Enrique Flores, Carmen
     Lomas Garza, Xavier Gorena, Erik Gronborg,
     Lucas Hinojosa, Ben Holland, Kris Hotvedt,
     William Kaars-Sijpesteijn, Cesar Martinez,
     Chris Mende, Roberto Mungia, Steve Reynolds,
     Vicente Rodriguez, William Wilhelmi.

4094 Fong, Katheryn M. Pachuco art records era of
     zootsuits and anti-Mexican riots. SAN
     FRANCISCO JRNL, Vol. 2, no. 32 (March 1,
     1978), p. 6. English.

     AN: Review of Galeria de la Raza exhibit
     of Jose Montoya's Pachuco Art. Installation
     included historical photographs and
     documents. Montoya work (drawings and
     paintings) were contextualized by written
     commentary aiming to re-interpret an
     important aspect of Chicano cultural
     history.

4095 Four and four: Mexican and Latino
     photography, April 25 through June 14 on the
     balcony. CALENDAR: SANTA BARBARA MUSEUM OF
     ART, (April 1981). English.

     AN: Announcement of exhibit organized by
     Lorenzo Hernandez of the Cityscape Foto
     Gallery, Pasadena, Calif. Sought to present
     "the observable differences between the
     'classic' vision of the Mexican National and
     the 'realistic' vision of the re-rooted
     Mexican/American." The latter included Louis
     Bernal (Tucson) and Ricardo Valverde (Los
     Angeles) as well as two Spanish Sephardics
     of Los Angeles, Camhi and Sisco.

4096 Frankenstein, Alfred. Montoya's artistic
     update on Chicano zoot suiters. SAN
     FRANCISCO CHRONICLE, (February 18, 1978),
     p. 36. English.

     AN: Review of Pachuco show at San
     Francisco's Galeria de la Raza, especially
     Jose Montoya's sketches and paintings.

4097 Frankenstein, Alfred. Prison's artist in
     residence. SAN FRANCISCO CHRONICLE, (May 5,
     1978), p. 60. English.

     AN: Review of the exhibition MUNDOS
     PERDIDOS, curated at the Galeria de la Raza
     by Leonard Castellanos. Show consisted of
     work by Castellanos and inmates at Lompoc
     Federal Correctional Institution near Santa
     Barbara. Documents a prison mural, tattoos
     and silkscreen prints with socially critical
     themes.

Galleries, Chicano (cont.)

4098 Frankenstein, Alfred. A senior senor's approach. SAN FRANCISCO CHRONICLE, (May 27, 1976), p. 48. English.

AN: Review of an exhibit of Mexican painter Jesus Reyes Ferreira at the Mexican Museum of San Francisco, as well as that of San Francisco artist Gustavo Rivera, an abstract expressionist painter. Also mentions the Museum's mural map, and Angel del Valle's photography show at the Galeria de la Raza.

4099 Galeria: a place you should visit. CAMINOS, Vol. 2, no. 5 (October 1981), p. 24-25. English.

AN: Announcement of the opening of Galeria, specializing in Hispanic art, in Orange County, California. Illustrations of sculpture by Richard G. Villa and Eduardo Oropeza.

4100 La Galeria de Colores, Las Vegas, NM. La galeria de colores. Gallery brochure, [1980]. English.

AN: Brochure for a gallery/studio run by painter Pola Lopez de Jaramillo since 1980.

4101 Galeria de la Raza/Studio 24. Mimeograph, [1980]. English.

AN: Mimeographed history of the Galeria de la Raza/Studio 24 which opened in 1970 as a showcase for Chicano/Latino artists. Its programs include exhibitions, murals and billboads, beautification of the community, education. Along with public grants, the Galeria strives to be self-sustaining through Studio 24 with retail sales and printing services.

4102 Galeria de la Raza/Studio 24, San Francisco, CA. Ajo, granadas y tres flores. Exhibition announcement, 1981.

AN: Announcement for an exhibition featuring Ruben Trejo, sculpture (Spokane, Washington), Cesar A. Martinez, paintings (San Antonio, Texas), Xavier Gorena, paper cut-outs (Mission, Texas).

4103 Galeria de la Raza/Studio 24, San Francisco, CA. Blanca Flor Gutierrez - oil pastels. Exhibition announcement, 1981.

AN: Color xeroxed announcement for a window display of oil pastels by Gutierrez.

4104 Galeria de la Raza/Studio 24, San Francisco, CA. Calacas huesudas. Exhibition brochure, 1980.

AN: Exhibition of Chicano artists for El Dia de los Muertos with brochure using text adapted from POSADA'S MEXICO, edited by Ron Tyler, Library of Congress, Washington, D.C., 1979. The Galeria exhibit was curated by Kate Connell, Maria Pinedo and Galeria staff.

4105 Galeria de la Raza/Studio 24, San Francisco, CA and Garcia, Rupert. Community art-murals: an exhibition of original drawings, sketches, and designs. Exhibition brochure, 1978. English.

AN: The current crisis of contemporary art is relatively resolved by community-based muralists who engage themselves against repressive forces as artists, organizers, propagandists. However, art and politics are not identical, though they may overlap. Color xerox illustrations of murals.

4106 Galeria de la Raza/Studio 24, San Francisco, CA. Homenaje a Frida Kahlo. Exhibition brochure, 1978.

AN: 51 artists, Chicano and non-Chicano.

4107 Galeria de la Raza/Studio 24, San Francisco, CA; Sorell, Victor A.; and Vaughan, Kay. Images of the Mexican Revolution: photographs by Agustin V. Casasola. Exhibition catalog, 1980. English.

AN: Catalog of an exhibit of Mexican photographer Agustin V. Casasola from prints owned by the Martinezes of Lansing, MI. The exhibit traveled to Raza galleries in many parts of the United States. Illustrated.

4108 Galeria de la Raza/Studio 24, San Francisco, CA. Mexican film poster (1943-71): an exhibition/exhibicion de fotos/cartelones del cine mexicano. Exhibition invitation, 1971. English.

AN: Invitation to an exhibit.

4109 Galeria de la Raza/Studio 24, San Francisco, CA. Photographs by Angel Del Valle. Los sembradores: the marijuana growers. Exhibition catalog, 1976. English.

AN: Illustrated catalog. Del Valle documents the growing, customs, and merchandising of marijuana in the Sierras of Mexico.

4110 Galeria de la Raza/Studio 24, San Francisco, CA and Garcia, Rupert. Posters from the golden age of Mexican cinema. Exhibition catalog, 1979. English.

AN: The Galeria's second exhibit of Mexican movie posters features those of the 1940s and early 1950s (in 1971, the exhibit covered 1943-1971) from the collection of Enrique Flores, owner of the Rio Theatre, Mission, Texas, and the Xochil Art Center. Garcia's essay includes a history of Mexican cinema, and the mythologizing period of the "Golden Age" reflected in the posters which promoted movie-consumership. One illustration. (See Santos G. Martinez, Jr.'s essay in the exhibition catalog: MEXICAN MOVIE POSTERS, for another point of view).

4111 Galeria de la Raza/Studio 24, San Francisco, CA. Published prints of Hecho en Aztlan Multiples. Exhibition announcement, 1980. English.

AN: Announcement of exhibit of the published silkscreen prints of Hecho en Aztlan Multiples; a small business run by Richard Duardo of Los Angeles.

4112 Galeria de la Raza/Studio 24, San Francisco, CA and Garcia, Rupert. La Raza Silkscreen Center: "Images of a community", an exhibit of silkscreen posters and graphic works from 1971 to 1979. Exhibition catalog, 1979. English.

AN: First large scale retrospective exhibit of the La Raza Silkscreen Center's eight years of postermaking. Includes list of 90 artists.

Galleries, Chicano (cont.)

4113 Galeria de la Raza/Studio 24, San Francisco, CA. Royal Chicano Air Force presents "Chicanos del Valle Tortilla Opening". Exhibition invitation, 1971. English.

4114 Galeria de la Raza/Studio 24, San Francisco, CA and Lomas Garza, Carmen. Self-portraits by Chicano and Latino artists. Exhibition catalog, 1980. English.

AN: Catalog of a national exhibition by 66 artists. Gives names, residence, date of birth, and information on the work shown for each of the artists. 45 are from California, and 3 each from Puerto Rico, Arizona, New York, 9 from Texas, 2 from Washington, 1 from Virginia. 9 are women.

4115 Galeria Museo - new art gallery opens in the Mission. EL TECOLOTE, Vol. 8, no. 1 (September 1977), p. 8. Bilingual.

AN: Brief article on the inauguration of the Art Gallery at the Mission Cultural Center. The opening Exhibit (August 13, 1977) was entitled SIXTY-THREE SHOW and included work in various media by Sixty three Bay Area Latino artists. Gilberto Osorio was designated as the first artist-in-residence. Information on future plans for the Galeria-Museo.

4116 Galeria, Santa Ana, CA. Diez anos con Emigdio (ten years with Emigdio), works by Emigdio Vasquez: 1971-1981. Exhibition invitation, 1982.

AN: Invitation to exhibit by Emigdio Vasquez. Illustrated.

4117 Galeria, Santa Ana, CA. Egg-sploration: a comprehensive exhibit by Art & Ben Valenzuela. Exhibition invitation, 1981. English.

AN: Invitation to an exhibit of two Orange County, CA artists in a new Chicano-run gallery. Illustrated with work of art by Art Valenzuela.

4118 Galeria, Santa Ana, CA. The last Chicano art show. Exhibition brochure, 1981. English.

AN: Invitation-brochure for an exhibit of Los Angeles and Orange County artists in a gallery underwritten by the Friendly Center, Inc. with grants from local government and from businesses. Exhibiting are (Roberto) Gil de Montes, Gilbert Lujan, Judy Miranda, Patricia Murillo, Alonso Pardo, Teddy Sandoval, Mexican artist Artemio Sepulveda, Joey Terrill, Art Valenzuela, Ben Valenzuela, Linda Vallejo, Jack A. Vargas, Emigdio Vasquez, Richard Serrato, and J. William Hernandez, who is the gallery director.

4119 Galeria Tonantzin, Centro Cultural de LUCHA, Austin, TX. Mexican faces in San Antonio. Exhibition brochure, [1980]. English.

AN: Photography show by 24 young Chicanos from Texas sponsored by the Secretaria de Relaciones Exteriores and the Universidad Autonoma de Mexico, Cultural Extension program (SRE-UNAM) in San Antonio.

4120 Galeria Tonantzin, Centro Cultural de LUCHA, Austin, TX. Visiones Chicanas: images and demonstrations by Chicana and Latina visual artists. Exhibition invitation, 1979. English.

AN: Invitational poster for an exhibit and a series of workshops organized by Mujeres Artistas del Suroeste (MAS), affiliated with LUCHA, League of United Chicano Artists of Austin, TX.

4121 Galeria Tonantzin, Centro Cultural de LUCHA, Austin, TX. Young Chicano photographers from throughout Texas. Exhibition brochure, n.d. English.

AN: This exhibition is the collection of the winners of the contest (by the same name) sponsored by the Extension Cultural SRE-UNAM in San Antonio. Photographers represented were: Grace Alvarez, David Cardenas, Hector Cardenas, Stephen Casanova, Ronald Cortez, Raul Espinosa, Felix Almanza, Carolina Flores, David Garza Perez, Xavier Garza, Conrad Guerra, Melinda Hasbrook, Juan Jose de Hoyes, Beverly Kennon, Art Moreno, David Perez, Isabelle Purden, Patricia Santell, Nancy de los Santos, Jose Soria, Richard Tichich, Kathy Vargas, Vivian Yaten, and Johnny Zamarria.

4122 Garcia's art. Gallery brochure, n.d.. English.

AN: Brochure of a non-profit center featuring an art gallery and other cultural activities to promote knowledge and education about Chicano and Mexican arts. [Headed by Ralph Garcia who in 1981 is director of PAN, Performance Artists Nucleus.].

4123 Gardiner, Henry G. Painted exterior walls of Southern California. CURRANT ART MAGAZINE, Vol. 1, no. 2 (June, July, 1975), p. 16-23+. English.

AN: Good survey of street muralism, primarily in Los Angeles and San Diego, which started in 1968. Divided into eight "schools," including Chicano and non-Chicano muralists. Most Chicano murals associated with Goez Brothers Art Gallery and Mechicano Art Center in Los Angeles, the Coronado Bay Bridge group [Chicano Park] and Balboa Park group [Centro Cultural de la Raza]. Mural discussed in detail. Well illustrated.

4124 Geyer, Anne; Hernandez, Lorenzo; and Valverde, Ricardo. Latino photographers of U.S. still seeking identity. THE NEWS, (September 5, 1981), p. 17. English.

AN: Interview with Lorenzo Hernandez, photo dealer and owner of Cityscape Foto Gallery, Pasadena, Calif. in which he compares Mexican with U.S. Latino photography. Interview with Ricardo Valverde, Chicano photographer and co-chair of the Council of Latino Photography/USA, discussing his work. Illustrated.

4125 Giepen, Hubert. Xochil Art Center taking big steps. PROGRESS, Vol. 10, no. 1 (August 12, 1981). English.

AN: Brief history of the founding and expansion plans of the Xochil Art Institute in Mission which includes an old theatre, workshop. studio, and gallery. Artists Xavier Gorena and Enrique Flores are responsible for the development.

Galleries, Chicano (cont.)

4126 Goez Imports & Fine Arts, Los Angeles, CA.
We invite you to see the birth of our art.
Gallery brochure, 1971. English.

> **AN:** Brochure with history of gallery,
> mural map, iconography of Goez mural.

4127 Goez proudly presents. Exhibit brochure,
n.d. [1970]. English.

> **AN:** Brochure produced by the Goez
> Gallery of Los Angeles for an inaugural
> exhibit showing the work of 76 artists.

4128 Gonzales, Juan. Galeria de la Raza: "our
people deserve the best". EL TECOLOTE, Vol.
7, no. 11 (July 1977), p. 14. English.

> **AN:** "We are not here to sell our art,
> but to sell the idea of art." This could
> well be the motto of Galeria de la Raza who
> under co-directors Rene Yanez and Ralph
> Maradiaga has become a key cultural
> institution in the Mission District of San
> Francisco. The two directors have a broad
> definition of art that encompasses
> everything from cartoons to craftwork. The
> article details past exhibits and future
> goals. A half-page photograph of the
> exterior of Galeria de la Raza by Pilar
> Mejia illustrates the article. Reprint of
> article entitled "Our people deserve the
> best" which appeared in NUESTRO, Vol. 1, no.
> 2 (May, 1977), p. 56-57.

4129 Gonzales, Juan. Regional report, The arts:
"Our people deserve the best". NUESTRO, Vol.
1, no. 2 (May 1977), p. 56-57. English.

> **AN:** Activities of San Francisco's
> Galeria de la Raza; interviews with its
> directors, Rene Yanez and Ralph Maradiaga.
> Reprinted as "Galeria de la Raza: our people
> deserve the best" in EL TECOLOTE (San
> Francisco, CA), Vol. 7, no. 11 (July, 1977),
> p. 14.

4130 Grimke, Angelina. Chicano art finds home in
Mission galeria. PEOPLE'S WORLD, Vol. 33,
no. 32 (August 8, 1970), p. 11. English.

> **AN:** Commentary on the exhibition
> CHICANOS, CUBA Y LOS 10 MILLONES held at the
> original Galeria de la Raza at 425 14th
> Street in San Francisco. The show presented
> photographs by Jay Ojeda and Roberto
> Perez-Diaz, drawings by Gloria Ozuna
> together with paintings and photographs by
> Cuban artist Mederos. Provides information
> about the goals of the Galeria as the visual
> arts department of Casa Hispana de Bellas
> Artes. Exhibition curator was Rolando
> Castellon.

4131 Houston Chicanismo. LA PRENSA, Vol. 1, no. 2
(March 31, 1978). English.

> **AN:** In Houston, Texas, the AMA Gallery
> (Association for the Advancement of Mexican
> Americans) was opened in February 1976 to
> showcase Chicano art. Noel Rodriguez,
> gallery director, informs about the goals
> and objectives of the gallery. A current
> exhibit presents paintings by Josie Mendoza
> and Atanacio Davila, ceramics by Jesse
> Sifuentes and mixed-media works by Joe
> Ramirez. Illustrated with two pieces from
> exhibit, THANKSGIVING, an acrylic painting
> by Josie Mendoza and BIRDS, a ceramic piece.

4132 Jesus Gutierrez Gallery, San Pedro, CA. "Two
of a kind" prints by Linda Vallejo, Muriel

Olguin. Exhibition invitation [1978].
English.

> **AN:** Invitation to an exhibit.

4133 Kamin, Ira. Memories of Frida Kahlo.
CALIFORNIA LIVING, (May 6, 1979), p. 44-50.
English.

> **AN:** Chatty review of the sixth annual
> Dia de los Muertos, celebrated by the
> Galeria de la Raza this year with an homage
> to Mexican painter Frida Kahlo. Local
> artists filled the gallery with their
> homages; the Galeria's outdoor billboard was
> painted with her image; guests brought gifts
> and dressed in Kahlo style, including older
> women who wore jewelry given them by Kahlo.
> Biographical material on Kahlo and Diego
> Rivera should be read with caution. Well
> illustrated.

4134 Kushner, Sam. It was a meat market in East
L.A. LOS ANGELES FREE PRESS, Vol. 11, no. 34
(August 23, 1974), p. 17. English.

> **AN:** Data on the formation of Goez
> Gallery by John Gonzalez and David Botello
> in 1970. Created in what once was a meat
> market in the East Los Angeles barrio, Goez
> became an important showcase for Chicano
> art.

4135 Lomas Garza, Carmen; Montoya, Jose E.; and
Pinedo, Maria Vita. What we are...now.
Exhibition catalog, n.d. English.

> **AN:** Drawings by Sacramento women
> artists: Lorraine Garcia, Eva C. Garcia,
> Kathryn E. Garcia, Celia Rodriguez, Patricia
> Carrillo.

4136 MARS: Movimiento Artistico del Rio Salado.
Phoenix, AZ: [MARS], n.d. English.

> **AN:** Illustrated brochure for the MARS
> organization and its studio-gallery.
> Includes a brief history, list of
> exhibitions from 1978 to 1981, news about
> its studio-workshop for the community, and
> its goals.

4137 Martinez, Anita. Raza! Arte! Raza! Arte!
EL TECOLOTE, Vol. 1, no. 2 (September 7,
1970), p. 3. Bilingual.

> **AN:** Galeria de la Raza opened on July,
> 1970 at 425 14th St. San Francisco. It was
> an outgrowth of the Arte Seis organization
> (an art effort established in the Mission
> District in 1967 by Francisco Camplis,
> Rupert Garcia, Ralph McNeil, Jay Ojeda and
> Jack Ruiz). These and other artists brought
> together by the Neighborhood Arts Program
> have coalesced in the new Galeria de la
> Raza. Article gives goals, organizational
> scheme and plans for the Galeria. It's first
> exhibit was a one man show by Esteban Villa
> together with a photo and sketch exhibit on
> Cuba by Jay Ojeda, Roberto Diaz Perez and
> Gloria Ozuna. Illustrated with installation
> view of new Galeria.

4138 Mechicano Art Center. Los Angeles, CA:
Mechicano Art Center, 1971. English.

> **AN:** Announcement of an exhibit by
> painters Ramon Atilano, Xavier Lopez Ortega,
> and Frank A. Martinez. Martinez and Lopez
> Ortega are also muralists. Brief profiles of
> the artists. Illustrated.

Galleries, Chicano (cont.)

4139 Mesa-Bains, Amalia. Homage to Frida Kahlo opens Nov. 2, at Galeria de la Raza. EL TECOLOTE, Vol. 9, no. 1 (September 1978), p. 7. English.

> **AN:** Announcement and call for artwork to Galeria de la Raza's exhibition honoring Frida Kahlo on Nov. 2, 1978. The proposed "Homage to Frida Kahlo" will encompass four major areas; artists' work, documentation/publication, related art productions, and educational activities. The Galeria educated participating artists to the life and art of Frida Kahlo through slide presentations and written material. The exhibition became a milestone in the Galeria de la Raza history.

4140 The Mexican Museum, San Francisco, CA and Quirarte, Jacinto. 17 artists: Hispano/Mexican-American/Chicano. Exhibition catalog, 1977. English.

> **AN:** Catalog of an exhibit for artists Emilio Aguirre, Consuelo Gonzalez Amezcua, Al Barela, Pedro Cervantez, Edward Chavez, Antonio Garcia, Louis Gutierrez, Harry Louie, Vincent Perez, Michael Ponce de Leon, Eugenio Quesada, Gustavo Rivera, Peter Rodriguez, Alex Sanchez, Darryl Sapien, Rudy Trevino, Manuel Villamor. Illustrated.

4141 The Mexican Museum, San Francisco, CA. Alexander Maldonado. Exhibition brochure, 1979. English.

> **AN:** One page autobiographical statement by Alexander Maldonado. Includes sources of his imagery.

4142 The Mexican Museum, San Francisco, CA. Cinco de Mayo exhibit at the Cannery. Exhibition brochure, 1980. English.

> **AN:** Well-illustrated brochure with text by Nora Wagner and Bea Carrillo Hocker. Succinct statements on the history, purpose and programs of the Mexican Museum.

4143 The Mexican Museum, San Francisco, CA. Manuel Neri: sculpture and drawings. Exhibition invitation, 1981. English.

> **AN:** Illustrated invitation to an exhibit.

4144 The Mexican Museum, San Francisco, CA. Los primeros cinco anos: fifth anniversary exhibit. Exhibition brochure, 1980-81. English.

> **AN:** 65 Mexican, Chicano, and Latino artists exhibited for the fifth anniversary of the Mexican Museum, directed by artist Peter Rodriguez. Cover is drawing by Carmen Lomas Garza.

4145 The Mexican Museum, San Francisco, CA. Recent works of Leonel Maciel and Carlos Almaraz. Exhibition invitation, 1981. English.

> **AN:** Invitation to an exhibit of works by Mexican artist Maciel and Chicano painter Almaraz.

4146 The Mexican Museum, San Francisco, CA. Recent works of Luis Jaso from Mexico City and Carlos Chavez Cordova from Los Angeles. Exhibition invitation, 1981. English.

> **AN:** Invitation to an exhibit.

4147 The Mexican Museum, San Francisco, CA. Rupert Garcia: portraits/retratos. Exhibition brochure, 1981. English.

> **AN:** Exhibition brochure with biographical information and exhibition chronology for Rupert Garcia.

4148 The Mexican Museum, San Francisco, CA. Virginia Jaramillo. Exhibition brochure, 1980. English.

> **AN:** Exhibition brochure with biographical information, exhibition chronology and an artist's statement.

4149 Minutaglio, Bill. S.A. aims at becoming Hispanic art center. SAN ANTONIO EXPRESS-NEWS, (January 18, 1981), p. 3-M+. English.

> **AN:** Rick Reyna is director of the fledging San Antonio Consortium for Hispanic Arts (SACHA), a city-funded umbrella organization covering seven art groups, three of which - Centro Cultural del Pueblo (instruction for young people), Community Cultural Arts Program (murals), and Performance Artists Nucleus (displays and exhibits) - concern the visual arts. Rudy Garcia, Anastacio "Tache" Torres, and Ralph Garcia (formerly of Garcia's Art Gallery) head the three groups respectively.

4150 Morch, Albert. Mexican art through a cartoonist's eyes. SAN FRANCISCO EXAMINER, (September 24, 1979), p. 28. English.

> **AN:** Review of "GORDO'S WORLD" and the paintings of Alexander Maldonado, an exhibition at the Mexican Museum. Biographical information on Gustavo Montano Arriola, creator of the Gordo cartoon in 1941. The exhibit conceived and designed by the San Diego Museum of Art, had representative blow-ups of the strip along with artifacts. Maldonado, a self-taught artist started painting at age 60. His canvases embrace a fascination with towers, unique buildings, underground cities and skylines from an imagined urban environment.

4151 Mural depicts history of Mexican Americans. EASTSIDE JRNL, (December 16, 1971), p. 1. English.

> **AN:** Richard Jimenez of the Goez Gallery depicts the past and present of Mexican American culture on an interior mural at the First Street Store (3640 E. First St.) The 6 ft. by 15 ft. mural has central image of a clock with a faceless figure (The Mexican American of the future). Artist comments on another of his murals titled EDUCATION OF LIFE.

4152 The mural message. TIME, Vol. 105, no. 14 (April 7, 1975), p. 79. English.

> **AN:** Brief illustrated story of murals painted in East Los Angeles during the 1970s. Spotlights activities of Goez Gallery.

Galleries, Chicano (cont.)

4153 Nevarez, Joe R. Chicano art blooms in barrio warehouse. LOS ANGELES TIMES, (December 26, 1974), p. I, 32. English.

AN: Former meat packing warehouse transformed into Goez Art Studios by Joe and John Gonzalez. Exhibiting David Negron, Eddie Martinez, David Lopez (Hollywood scenic artists) and Roberto Arenivar. Lists activities of the gallery: exhibits, murals, restoration.

4154 New Galeria de la Raza. EL HISPANO, (July 28, 1970), p. 9. English.

AN: Review of the first exhibit at the Galeria de la Raza at 425 14th St. in San Francisco. The inaugural exhibition featured Esteban Villa, Luis Gutierrez and Luis Cervantes. The new Galeria is sponsored by Casa Hispana de Bellas Artes assisted by San Francisco Art Commission through its Neighborhood Arts Program.

4155 Oakland County Cultural Affairs, MI. Nora Mendoza: an exhibition of abstract/impressionism. Exhibition brochure, [1981]. English.

AN: Exhibit brochure for Texas-born Nora Chapa Mendoza who studied abstract-impressionism with Michigan artist Ljubo Biro. She is a leader in the artistic and Hispanic communities and runs galleries in Clarkston and Detroit.

4156 Opton, Suzanne. Short strokes. SAN FRANCISCO FAULT, (December 29, 1971), p. 9-10. English.

AN: The currently homeless Galeria de la Raza has begun a series of wall painting projects. Artist "Spain" did a Horizons mural; Puerto Rican photographer Adal Maldonado did photographic murals; Jerry Concha, Tom Rios, did rooms in the Center for Change drug program building, Chuy Campusano, working with cartoonist R. Crumb, and the Mission Rebel Kids did a cartoon mural. Model Cities day care centers are next to be painted.

4157 Parr, June. Amado Maurilio Pena, Jr.: a talented and dedicated artist. ARRIBA, (October 1980), p. 1. English.

AN: Pena is represented in forty-two galleries internationally. Recently, Pena opened his studio and gallery, El Taller, in Austin. His latest works focus on the Indian heritage and are based on trips to New Mexico. Illustrated.

4158 Pinedo, Maria Vita. Galeria de la Raza. KPFA FOLIO, Vol. 28, no. 2 (February 1977). English.

AN: Brief history of San Francisco's Galeria de la Raza.

4159 Quinonez, Naomi H. In her own backyard = En su propio traspatio. CAMINOS, Vol. 2, no. 2 (March 1981), p. 34-36,62. Bilingual.

AN: Describes the establishment of the Centro de Arte in Long Beach, CA by Chicana artist Lola de la Riva and her family. The Centro, which is in de la Riva's Long Beach home, is designed to give members of her barrio a chance to develop and display their artistic talents. Frequent workshops in mask making, clay sculpture, painting, and graphics are held at the Centro, and the works of local artists are usually on display in her backyard.

4160 Sol Art Gallery, San Diego, CA. Group showing of Southern California artists. Exhibition brochure, 1980. English.

AN: First exhibit of new Chicano art gallery showing Los Angeles artists Carlos Almaraz, Judithe Hernandez, John Valadez, Linda Vallejo, Ricardo Duardo, Barbara Carrasco.

4161 Valadez, Kathy L. Ten hints in buying Chicano and Mexican art/10 ideas para la compra de obras de arte. CAMINOS, Vol. 1, no. 6 (October 1980), p. 15-17. Bilingual.

AN: An interior design/investment approach to Mexican and Chicano art. Some of the characterizations of both types of art are unfortunate and uninformed. Seems to be an article to boost sales for Joe Gonzales' Goez Gallery, but lists a number of other locations in California to purchase art. Illustrated.

Gallery Sanchez, San Francisco, CA

4162 Gallery Sanchez, San Francisco, CA. Xerox art: an exhibit of local color xerox artists. Exhibition invitation, 1981. English.

AN: Invitation to an exhibit featuring Rene Yanez and eight other artists working in color Xerox.

EL GALLO (Denver, CO)

4163 Garcia, Rupert. A source for mural art education: an annotated bibliography of three Chicano newspapers. Unpublished paper, 1974 (Chicano Studies Library, Univ. of California, Berkeley). English.

AN: A research project showing how Chicano newspapers reported and educated their readers to mural activity by Raza artists during the period 1968-1978. The newspapers analized are EL GALLO (Denver, CO), EL CHICANO (San Bernardino, CA), and EL TECOLOTE (San Francisco, CA). Author draws eight conclusions about the form, meaning and significance of mural activity in Chicano barrios and the importance of community newspapers as a fruitful and meaningful source for art education.

Gallo Wines

4164 Gonzalez, Jose Gamaliel. Boycott [drawing]. REVISTA CHICANO-RIQUENA, Vol. 5, no. 1 (Winter 1977), p. 9. English.

Galvan, Yolanda

4165 Sorell, Victor A. Barrio murals in Chicago:
painting the Hispanic-American experience on
"our community" walls. REVISTA
CHICANO-RIQUENA, Vol. 4, no. 4 (Fall
1976), p. 51-72. English.

> **AN:** Important survey of Chicago's Latino
> murals, with key works considered in detail.
> Among the Chicano art organizations and
> muralists mentioned are MARCH (Movimiento
> Artistico Chicano), and Yolanda Galvan,
> Juanita Jaramillo, Jose Nario, Raymond
> Patlan, Vicente Mendoza, Marcos Raya,
> Ricardo Alonzo, Jose G. Gonzalez and Mario
> Castillo, author of the earliest Latino
> mural in Chicago (1968). Puerto Rican and
> non-Latino muralists and mural groups are
> also discussed. Well illustrated.

Galvez, Daniel

4166 Clark, Yoko and Hama, Chizu. California
murals. Berkeley, CA: Lancaster-Miller,
1979. English.

> **AN:** Picture book of Bay Area and Los
> Angeles murals with brief descriptions.
> Chicano artists included: Daniel Galvez,
> Irene Perez, Patricia Rodriguez, Graciela
> Carrillo (Mujeres Muralistas), Ray Patlan.

4167 Cockcroft, Eva; Weber, John; and Cockcroft,
James D. Towards a people's art: the
contemporary mural movement. New York: E.P.
Dutton, 1977. English.

> **AN:** A survey of the street mural
> movement in the United States, from about
> 1967 on. Several chapters are written by the
> artists themselves: John Weber on the
> Chicago mural group; Susan Shapiro-Kiok on
> Cityarts Workshop of New York; Eva Cockcroft
> on People's painters of New Jersey; Geronimo
> Garduno on Artes Guadalupanos de Aztlan of
> New Mexico. Chicano murals illustrated
> include those of Mujeres Muralistas, Ray
> Patlan, William F. Herron, Hoyo-Mara Gang,
> Artes Guadalupanos de Aztlan, Vicente
> Mendoza and Jose Nario (with Patlan) Mario
> Castillo, Michael Rios, Toltecas en Aztlan,
> Roberto Chavez, Ernie Palomino, Chuy
> Campusano and Luis Cortazar (with Rios).

4168 COMMUNITY MURALS (San Francisco, CA). (Fall
1981). English.

> **AN:** Citywide Murals Group of Denver,
> Colorado assisted the Chilean-oriented
> Brigada Orlando Letelier with a mural in
> their city; Carlos Sandoval of Denver doing
> mural in Guerrero, Mexico; Ray Patlan of
> Berkeley, California assisting with mural in
> Mexico painted by Arnold Belkin's class at
> the Academy of San Carlos; report on the
> exhibit MURALS OF AZTLAN: THE STREET
> PAINTERS OF EAST LOS with a reprint of
> debate on the event by Shifra M. Goldman,
> Judithe Elena Hernandez de Neikrug, and
> comments by John Pitman Weber and Tim
> Drescher; report on DAR LUZ mural directed
> by Santa Barraza in Austin, Texas, and a new
> mural in Hayward, California directed by
> Enrique Romero; a mural sponsored by the
> Chicano Youth Center of Fresno, California
> showing the influence of Mexican calendars;
> a new mural, OAKLAND'S PORTRAIT by Daniel
> Galvez in Oakland, California; pro-and-con
> discussion of social function of graffiti in
> response to letter from Belgian source;
> reprint of story on spray paint crime bill
> (anti-graffiti) sponsored by California
> Assemblyman Richard Alatorre. Entire issue

illustrated.

4169 Mural. ARTE, no. 1 (1977). English.

> **AN:** Describes a section of the mural A
> PEOPLE'S HISTORY OF TELEGRAPH AVENUE painted
> by Daniel Galvez and Brian Thiele. The mural
> represents the work of dozens of additional
> artists.

Gamboa, Diane

4170 EL PLAYANO (Loyola University, Los Angeles).
(Spring 1972).

> **AN:** Illustrations by Willie Herron,
> Harry Gamboa, Jr., Gronk, Diane Gamboa,
> William A. Bejarano, Eddie Garcia.

4171 EL PLAYANO (Loyola University, Los Angeles).
(Spring 1973).

> **AN:** Illustrations by Simon Gonzales,
> Gronk, Harry Gamboa, Jr., Willie Herron,
> Charles Almaraz, Sister Teresa Munoz, Patsy
> Valdez, Diane Gamboa.

4172 Valdez, Armando. El calendario chicano 1977.
Hayward, CA: Southwest Network, 1977.
English.

> **AN:** Fifth in a series of historical
> calendars produced in 1972, 1974, 1975, 1976
> by La Causa Publications and Southwest
> Network. Artists whose work is reproduced
> are Malaquias Montoya, Amado Maurilio Pena,
> Ramori Zamora, Glugio J.L. Nicandro [Gronk],
> Etta Delgado, Ricardo Alaniz, Diane Gamboa,
> Elisa Marina Coleman, Margarita Calderon,
> Jose Antonio Burciaga, Cesar Augusto
> Martinez, Maria Ochoa y Valtierra, Juan
> Renteria Fuentes, from California, New
> Mexico, and Texas.

Gamboa, Harry, Jr.

4173 Cine chicano: primer acercamiento.
COMUNIDAD, no. 20 (November 16, 1980), p.
1-15. Spanish.

> **AN:** The entire cultural supplement of LA
> OPINION is dedicated to Chicano film.
> Includes articles by Jason Johansen, Jeff
> Penichet, Harry Gamboa, Jr., Jesus Salvador
> Trevino, Carlos Penichet, Sylvia Morales,
> Julio Moran, and Jose Luis Borau. Also
> includes a declaration of purpose by the
> Asociacion Chicana de Cineastas, and a
> filmography of Chicano cinema compiled by
> Trevino.

4174 Consejo Mexicano de Fotografia, A.C., Mexico
City and Tibol, Raquel. Hecho en
Latinoamerica: primera muestra de la
fotografia latinoamericana contemporanea.
Exhibition catalog, 1978. Spanish.

> **AN:** Catalog/book of the first colloquium
> and exhibit of Latin American photography.
> Among the Chicano artists in the exhibit
> were Francisco X. Camplis, Louis Carlos
> Bernal, Harry Gamboa, Jose P. Romero, Harvey
> J. Tarango, Isabel Castro. Statements by
> some of the artists. Great number of
> illustrations.

Gamboa, Harry, Jr.(cont.)

4175 Consejo Mexicano de Fotografia, A.C., Mexico City. Hecho en latinoamerica: segundo coloquio latinoamericano de fotografia. Exhibition catalog, 1982. Spanish.

AN: Catalog/book of the second colloquium and exhibit of Latin American photography. Among the Chicano artists whose work is reproduced are Louis Carlos Bernal, Robert C. Buitron, David Cardenas, Isabel Castro, Harry Gamboa, Jr., Luis Garza, Roberto Gil de Montes, John M. Valadez, Kathy Vargas. In the exhibit were also Porfirio Aguilar, Elsa Marie Flores, Ricardo Valverde. Great number of illustrations. In Spanish.

4176 COUNCIL OF LATINO PHOTOGRAPHY/USA NEWSLETTER. no. 1 (January 1979). English.

AN: First number of photocopied newsletter produced by the Council of Latino Photography/USA announcing the formation of the organization and its affiliation with the Consejo Latinoamericano de Fotografia established in Mexico City in May 1978. Organizers of CLP/USA were photographers Isabel Castro, Harry Gamboa, Jr., Adam Avila, Luis Garza, and art historian Shifra Goldman.

4177 Cultura chicana: Los Angeles. COMUNIDAD, no. 11 (July 13, 1980), p. 1-15. Spanish.

AN: The whole issue of the Cultural Supplement concerns Chicano art and music. Captioned photographs deal with visual artists Carlos Almaraz, Jerry Dreva [not Chicano], Glugio Gronk, Willie Herron, John Valadez, Patssi Valdez, with examples of their work. With the exception of Dreva, all the artists are members of Los Four or Asco. Asco member Harry Gamboa, Jr. sums up the 1960s and 1970s and activities of artists in his essay "Seis imaginaciones: Artistas chicanos en Los Angeles." Well illustrated.

4178 Edy. A true barrio art. EL CHICANO, (December 7, 1972), p. 9. English.

AN: Interview with East Los Angeles artists Harry Gamboa, Robert Gronk and Willie Herron (also included in the conversation are Patsy Valdez and Eddie Ytuarte). Suffering, fatalism, existential reality and the awareness of cultural colonialism are cited as sources of inspiration for urban barrio art. Illustrated with a photograph of Willie Herron's Quetzalcoatl mural in City Terrace barrio and two drawings by Robert Gronk and Harry Gamboa.

4179 Gamboa, Harry, Jr.; Gronk; and Herron, Willie. Gronk and Herron. NEWORLD, Vol. 2, no. 3 (Spring 1976), p. 28-30. English.

AN: An interview with ASCO members Gronk and Willie Herron by a third member, Gamboa. Brief historical introduction (1970 on). The witty tongue-in-cheek interview can be considered an artwork by this performance art group. Illustrated.

4180 Gamboa, Harry, Jr. Phobia friend. TIN TAN, Vol. 2, no. 6 (December 1, 1977), p. 13-14. English.

AN: Short story written and illustrated as a conceptual art piece by ASCO member, Gamboa, as a "Cinema Chicano" work.

4181 Gamboa, Harry, Jr. Pistol whippersnapper. R.A.M. COLLECTIVE, Vol. 2, no. 1 (June 1, 1977), p. 10-11. English.

AN: Photography and poetry by Harry Gamboa, Jr., member of ASCO, Los Angeles.

4182 Geyer, Anne and Gamboa, Harry, Jr. Artists' exhibits are street performances. THE NEWS, (September 11, 1981), p. 18. English.

AN: Illustrated interview with photographer/writer Harry Gamboa, Jr., member and documenter of the performance art group ASCO. Description of the NO MOVIE, NO PHANTOM, walking and instant murals of the group, and other performance street art which Gamboa considers as Chicano self-documentation and expression.

4183 Gronk and Gamboa, Harry, Jr. Interview: Gronk and Gamboa. CHISMEARTE, Vol. 1, no. 1 (Fall 1976), p. 31-33. English.

AN: Interview with two members of the group Asco concerning their NO MOVIE series. Questions and answers were probably written by the artists themselves as a performance art piece. Includes a description of the group and their 1972 ACTION PROJECT PIE IN DEFACE: L.A. COUNTY MUSEUM OF ART. Illustrations.

4184 Heard Museum, Phoenix, AZ. Second Southwest Chicano Art Invitational. Exhibit catalog, 1978. English.

AN: Exhibit by eight artists: Antonio Pazos (Tucson), Rudy Fernandez (Salt Lake City), Harry Gamboa (Los Angeles), Rupert Garcia and Xavier Viramontes (San Francisco), Roberto Rios (San Antonio), Roberto Espinoza (Yuma), and Roberto Borboa (Tucson). Brief biographies of all but Rios. 29 illustrations.

4185 Kim, Howard. Chicano art: is it an art form? Or simply art by Chicanos. NEWORLD, Vol. 6, no. 4 (1980), p. 26-30. English.

AN: An attempt to define Chicano art through interviews with Carlos Almaraz, John Valadez, (Los Four), Robert Delgado, Sister Karen Boccalero (Self-Help Graphics), Harry Gamboa, Jr. (ASCO), Ricardo Duardo, Ignacio Gomez, and others. Well illustrated.

4186 L.A.C.E. (Los Angeles Contemporary Exhibitions), Los Angeles, CA. No Movie: Gil de Montes, Teddy, Glugio [Gronk], Patssi, Gamboa. Exhibition invitation, 1978. English.

AN: Invitation to "performance" piece by Roberto Gil de Montes, Teddy Sandoval, Gronk, Patssi Valdez and Harry Gamboa, Jr., the latter three of the ASCO group. Illustrated.

4187 Los Angeles City College. Latinos de tres mundos. Exhibition invitation, 1980. English.

AN: Invitation to an exhibit featuring the work of ASCO members Harry Gamboa, Jr., Gronk, Willie Herron; painters Xavier Mendez and Olivia Sanchez; and photographer Ricardo Valverde.

Gamboa, Harry, Jr.(cont.)

4188 Mechicano Art Center, Los Angeles, CA.
Schizophrenibeneficial. Exhibition
invitation, 1977. English.

AN: Invitation to an ASCO "performance"
work: "Projecting of Visual and/or Verbal
Personality Disorders Onto Person or Persons
Unknown." Glugio (Gronk), Teddy (Sandoval),
(Roberto) Gil de Montes, Patssi (Valdez),
(Harry) Gamboa.

4189 Moisan, Jim. Ancient roots, new visions.
ARTWEEK, Vol. 9, no. 26 (July 29, 1978), p.
8. English.

AN: Review of the show held at the
Municipal Arts Gallery of Los Angeles, the
first national touring show of Latino
artists in the United States. Includes
commentary on work of Larry Fuente, Luis
Jimenez, Frank Romero, Harry Gamboa, Gronk,
Rudy Martinez, Benjamin Serrano, Ricardo
Diaz, Patssi Valdez, Mel Casas, Luis Leroy,
Pedro Lujan. A related show, NEW VISIONS,
L.A., includes Robert Delgado, Ray Bravo,
Joe Moran, Rosalyn Mesquita, Patricia
Murillo and others.

4190 EL PLAYANO (Loyola University, Los Angeles).
(Spring 1972).

AN: Illustrations by Willie Herron,
Harry Gamboa, Jr., Gronk, Diane Gamboa,
William A. Bejarano, Eddie Garcia.

4191 EL PLAYANO (Loyola University, Los Angeles).
(Spring 1973).

AN: Illustrations by Simon Gonzales,
Gronk, Harry Gamboa, Jr., Willie Herron,
Charles Almaraz, Sister Teresa Munoz, Patsy
Valdez, Diane Gamboa.

4192 The Point Gallery, Santa Monica, CA. ASCO
(Gronk, Patssi, Gamboa, Herron), Los Four
(Almaraz, de la Rocha, Judithe Hernandez,
Gloriamalia Flores, Mauricio Ramirez, John
Valadez. Exhibition invitation, [1975].
English.

AN: Illustrated invitation to an exhibit
of Los Angeles artists.

Gangs

4193 Chicano art: East Los Angeles graffiti. LA
GENTE DE AZTLAN, Vol. 6, no. 5 (May 1976),
p. 5. English.

AN: The particular forms and styles of
Chicano graffiti are affirmed as stemming
from the social conditions of the barrio
circa 1930. Gangs and their social world are
examined as contributors to the creation of
graffiti, tattoos and "calo," a dialect of
Chicano Spanish.

4194 Del Olmo, Frank. Chicano gang turns to art.
LOS ANGELES TIMES, (September 11, 1973), p.
II, 3. English.

AN: Residents of the East Los Angeles
barrio "Lil' Valley" dedicate a mural
memorializing Chicano gang members who have
died violently. The mural was painted by 40
gang members guided by professional artist
Bill Butler.

4195 Del Olmo, Frank. Gang-inspired mural now a
shrine. LOS ANGELES TIMES, (March 27,
1975), p. II, 1, 6. English.

AN: Two 1973 murals by David Lopez in
the old Maravilla Housing Project which
received a papal blessing and continue to be
shrines at new housing location.

4196 Zahn, Debbie. Citywide murals: outlook bleak
for funding of art work by Chicanos.
FORTY-NINER, (May 4, 1976). English.

AN: The Los Angeles City Council decides
to terminate the 1974 program, Citywide
Murals, which provided funds for Chicano
artists. Description of Joe Bravo's 2000 sq
ft mural at the Wilmington Recreation
Center, painted with a team, which makes a
positive statement against gang warfare.
Illustrated.

4197 Zucker, Martin. Walls of barrio are brought
to life by street gang art. SMITHSONIAN,
Vol. 9, no. 7 (October 1978), p. 105-111.
English.

AN: Illustrated survey of East Los
Angeles murals.

Garces, Rolando

4198 CODEX NEWSLETTER (Galeria de la Raza, San
Francisco, CA). Vol. 1, no. 2 (September
1973). English.

AN: An in-house bulletin of upcoming
events: EL SOL NUNCA MUERE,
photography/poster exhibit, Rolando Garces,
and Peruvian posters; Mujeres de Aztlan,
women artists' collective exhibit;
Filipino/Samoan art exhibit; Galeria
Christmas art sale; Galeria pavilion at S.F.
annual art festival; Rockefeller scholarship
for Galeria curator Luis Santana; Galeria
coloring book; Balmy Alley mural project;
Diego Rivera exhibit; first installment of
Rupert Garcia's RAZA MURALS AND MURALISTS:
AN HISTORICAL VIEW.

4199 Galeria de la Raza, San Antonio, TX.
Celebration seventy-four. Exhibition
catalog, [ca. 1974]. English.

AN: Catalog of extensive exhibition
including European, Mexican, and the
following Texan Chicano artists: Rolando
Garces, Cesar Martinez, Ray Chavez, Vicente
Rodriguez, Jorge Garza, Alfred Rodriguez,
Luis Guerra, Carmen Lomas Garza, Bruno
Andrade, Jr., Amado M. Pena Jr., Roberto
Rios, Jose Trevino, Rudy Trevino, Luis
Santoyo, Tati Rubio, Eduardo C. Garza,
Arthur de la Fuente, and Jesus Campos
Trevino.

Garcia, Antonio

4200 The Mexican Museum, San Francisco, CA and
Quirarte, Jacinto. 17 artists:
Hispano/Mexican-American/Chicano. Exhibition
catalog, 1977. English.

AN: Catalog of an exhibit for artists
Emilio Aguirre, Consuelo Gonzalez Amezcua,
Al Barela, Pedro Cervantez, Edward Chavez,
Antonio Garcia, Louis Gutierrez, Harry
Louie, Vincent Perez, Michael Ponce de Leon,
Eugenio Quesada, Gustavo Rivera, Peter
Rodriguez, Alex Sanchez, Darryl Sapien, Rudy
Trevino, Manuel Villamor. Illustrated.

Garcia, Antonio (cont.)

4201 S.A. site for National Symposium on Mexican American Art. CHICANO TIMES, Vol. 4, no. 30 (November 9, 1973), p. 5. English.

AN: Held at Trinity University, the Symposium discussed such issues as, creative evolution, art education, artistic relationships to Mexico and the evolution of Mexican American art in the California barrios. Participating artists included Rudy Trevino, Mel Casas, Octavio Medellin, Antonio Garcia, Carmen Garza, Esteban Villa, Jose Montoya, Ernesto Palomino, Michael Ponce de Leon, Luis Jimenez and Eugenio Quesada.

Garcia, C.

4202 Sanchez, Arley. Santeros. ALBUQUERQUE JRNL, (August 21, 1977), p. C, 1. English.

AN: Review of THE SANTERO EXPERIENCE, an exhibition of contemporary folk art by eleven New Mexican santeros, most in their 30s, at the Albuquerque Museum. The carvers include Juan Lucero, Ben Lopez, Luisito Lujan, Horacio Valdez, C. Garcia, George Lopez. A revival of the art has been taking place within last several years due to cultural awareness being experienced by Hispanos. Contemporary santeros still donate some pieces to the church, but most are marketed to private collectors, displayed in museums, or kept.

Garcia, Domingo

4203 Raices y visiones [portfolio]. REVISTA CHICANO-RIQUENA, Vol. 7, no. 2 (Spring 1979), p. 29-44.

AN: Portfolio of works from the exhibit RAICES ANTIGUAS/VISIONES NUEVAS: ANCIENT ROOTS/NEW VISIONS. Artists included are Patssi Valdez (Los Angeles), Eloisa Castellanos-Sanchez (New York), Benjamin Serrano, Jr. (Tijuana, Mexico), Alex Garza (Chicago), Martin Y. Moreno (Michigan), Luis A. Jimenez (New Mexico), Rene Castro (Oakland, CA), Sita Gomez de Kanelba (New York), Susana Lasta (Tucson, AZ), Domingo Garcia (New York), Consuelo Mendez Castillo (Caracas, Venezuela), Naomi Castillo Simonetti (New Jersey), Louis Carlos Bernal, and Eddie Comptis.

Garcia, Eva C.

4204 Lomas Garza, Carmen; Montoya, Jose E.; and Pinedo, Maria Vita. What we are...now. Exhibition catalog, n.d. English.

AN: Drawings by Sacramento women artists: Lorraine Garcia, Eva C. Garcia, Kathryn E. Garcia, Celia Rodriguez, Patricia Carrillo.

Garcia, Francisco

4205 Echos de la Mision: the newest in Mission murals. EL TECOLOTE, Vol. 6, no. 4 (January 1976), p. 11. English.

AN: Panoramic view of new murals in the Mission District of San Francisco. Contains brief descriptions and photographs of mural art at Valencia Gardens, Garfield Park, Folsom Project and The Bart mural at 24th and Mission streets. Includes five photos by Francisco Garcia.

Garcia, Hector

4206 Semana de la Raza: international panel of the arts, Mexico and the United States. Santa Ana, CA: MEChA, Santa Ana College, 1972. English.

AN: An International Panel of the Arts, organized by art historian Shifra Goldman, featured Mexicans Hector Garcia, prize-winning photographer; Jaime Mejia, painter, restorer, filmmaker; Alejandro Vichir, director of Teatro Trashumante; and Chicanos Gilbert Sanchez Lujan, sculptor and painter; Gloria Osuna, painter and artist for Teatro Campesino; and Jesus Salvador Trevino, filmmaker.

Garcia, Jesse V.

4207 Trejo, Frank. S.A. mission doors inspired wood carver. SAN ANTONIO LIGHT, (January 10, 1971), p. 18. English.

AN: Biographical and exhibition information on San Antonio woodcarver Jesse V. Garcia. Illustrated by photograph of artist.

Garcia, Kathryn E.

4208 Lomas Garza, Carmen; Montoya, Jose E.; and Pinedo, Maria Vita. What we are...now. Exhibition catalog, n.d. English.

AN: Drawings by Sacramento women artists: Lorraine Garcia, Eva C. Garcia, Kathryn E. Garcia, Celia Rodriguez, Patricia Carrillo.

Garcia, Lorraine

4209 Lomas Garza, Carmen; Montoya, Jose E.; and Pinedo, Maria Vita. What we are...now. Exhibition catalog, n.d. English.

AN: Drawings by Sacramento women artists: Lorraine Garcia, Eva C. Garcia, Kathryn E. Garcia, Celia Rodriguez, Patricia Carrillo.

4210 Rios, Sam. Chicano muralist: Toltecotl in Aztlan. Unpublished paper, 1980. English.

AN: History of pre-Columbian, Mexican, and Chicano wall paintings. Describes in detail murals by Jose Montoya, Juanishi Orozco, Esteban Villa, Stan Padilla, Juan Cervantes, Lorraine Garcia of the Centro de Artistas Chicanos, Royal Chicano Air Force, painted in 1977 at Southside Park, Sacramento, Calif. Symbolism is explained.

Garcia, Maria Hortencia

4211 ENCUENTRO FEMENIL (San Fernando, CA). Vol. 1, no. 1 (Spring 1973), p. 1+. English.

AN: Publication sponsored by Hijas de Cuauhtemoc, a Chicana femenist group. Black and white drawings on cover by Pat Portera Crary. Art work by Vicki Thrall, Adelaida del Castillo, and Maria Hortencia Garcia. Photography by Cindy Honesto and David Lazarin.

Garcia, Max

4212 Calendario de comida 1976. San Francisco,
     CA: Galeria de la Raza, 1976. English.

     AN: Handprinted silkscreen calendar
     consisting of twelve sheets and a cover. The
     work of the following artists is included:
     Ralph Maradiaga, Juanishi Orozco, Francisco
     Camplis, Ruben Guzman, Rodolfo Cuellar,
     Xavier Viramontes, Jose Montoya, Esteban
     Villa, Rene Yanez, Max Garcia and Louis "The
     Foot" Gonzalez, Patricia Rodriguez, and
     Ricardo Favela. All of the above are
     associated with the Galeria de la Raza, or
     the Royal Chicano Air Force of Sacramento,
     CA.

4213 La historia de California, 1977. San
     Francisco, CA: Galeria de la Raza, 1977.
     English.

     AN: Handprinted silkscreen calendar of
     history seen from a Mexican point of view.
     Twelve sheets and a cover. Artists are:
     Ralph Maradiaga, Irene Perez, Louie "The
     Foot" Gonzalez, Max Garcia, Patricia
     Rodriguez, Jose Romero, Esteban Villa,
     Juanishi Orozco, Rodolfo Cuellar, Jose
     Montoya, Xavier Viramontes, Rene Yanez,
     Ricardo Favela, associated with the Galeria
     de la Raza, or the Royal Chicano Air Force
     of Sacramento.

Garcia, Miguel "Freeloader"

4214 Chicano muralists maintain traditions. LA
     CUCARACHA, (November 20, 1979), p. 7.
     English.

     AN: Introduction to Chicano muralism in
     Pueblo and comparison to the Mexican mural
     movement from which it draws inspiration. 20
     murals painted from 1977 to 1979. The
     muralists include Bernardo Duran, Juan
     Espinoza, Miguel "Freeloader" Garcia, Lola
     Gutierrez, Leo Lucero, Juan Pacheco, Dolores
     Pena, Pedro Romero, Stan Salazar, David
     Sandoval. Diego Rivera murals illustrated.

Garcia, Mike

4215 Artista de Aztlan. EL DIARIO DE LA GENTE,
     Vol. 4, no. 8 (April 1976), p. 7. Spanish.

     AN: Interview with Mike Garcia, staff
     artist for the DIARIO. Born in Alamosa,
     Colorado, the artist defines his work as
     "mestizo art because it expresses our Indian
     heritage, using motifs of the revolutionary
     struggles to reflect the possibilities of
     the future." Well illustrated.

Garcia, Ralph

4216 Garcia's art. Gallery brochure, n.d..
     English.

     AN: Brochure of a non-profit center
     featuring an art gallery and other cultural
     activities to promote knowledge and
     education about Chicano and Mexican arts.
     [Headed by Ralph Garcia who in 1981 is
     director of PAN, Performance Artists
     Nucleus.].

4217 Minutaglio, Bill. S.A. aims at becoming
     Hispanic art center. SAN ANTONIO
     EXPRESS-NEWS, (January 18, 1981), p. 3-M+.
     English.

     AN: Rick Reyna is director of the
     fledging San Antonio Consortium for Hispanic
     Arts (SACHA), a city-funded umbrella

organization covering seven art groups,
three of which - Centro Cultural del Pueblo
(instruction for young people), Community
Cultural Arts Program (murals), and
Performance Artists Nucleus (displays and
exhibits) - concern the visual arts. Rudy
Garcia, Anastacio "Tache" Torres, and Ralph
Garcia (formerly of Garcia's Art Gallery)
head the three groups respectively.

Garcia, Remigio

4218 Renacimiento del arte chicano en Texas. EL
     HISPANO, Vol. 6, no. 3 (July 10, 1973).
     English.

     AN: Remigio Garcia and Mariana
     Escalante, young muralists, describe their
     work and the collective goals of a mural
     workshop begun by Leo Tanguma in Houston,
     TX.

Garcia, Richard

4219 Santa Ana College, Santa Ana, CA. MECHA
     presents la semana de la Raza. Exhibition
     brochure, 1970. English.

     AN: Program for the week's activities,
     including EL ARTE DE LA RAZA exhibition,
     Gilbert Sanchez Lujan speaking on "Chicano
     Art in the Barrio," art demonstrations by
     Gilbert Vasquez, Emigdio Vasquez, Esau
     Quiroz, and Richard Garcia.

Garcia, Rudy

4220 Minutaglio, Bill. S.A. aims at becoming
     Hispanic art center. SAN ANTONIO
     EXPRESS-NEWS, (January 18, 1981), p. 3-M+.
     English.

     AN: Rick Reyna is director of the
     fledging San Antonio Consortium for Hispanic
     Arts (SACHA), a city-funded umbrella
     organization covering seven art groups,
     three of which - Centro Cultural del Pueblo
     (instruction for young people), Community
     Cultural Arts Program (murals), and
     Performance Artists Nucleus (displays and
     exhibits) - concern the visual arts. Rudy
     Garcia, Anastacio "Tache" Torres, and Ralph
     Garcia (formerly of Garcia's Art Gallery)
     head the three groups respectively.

Garcia, Rupert

4221 Alarcon, Francisco X. and Herrera, Juan
     Felipe. Portraits plus struggles plus
     consciousness: nine pastels by Rupert
     Garcia. METAMORFOSIS, Vol. 3, no. 2 (1980),
     p. 104-106. English.

     AN: Reprint of article published as
     "Rupert Garcia: portraits/retratos" in EL
     TECOLOTE LITERARY MAGAZINE (San Francisco,
     CA), Vol. 2, no. 1, March 1981, p. 6.

4222 Alarcon, Francisco X. Rupert Garcia:
     portraits/retratos. EL TECOLOTE LITERARY
     MAGAZINE, Vol. 2, no. 1 (March 1981), p. 6+.
     Bilingual.

     AN: Review of Garcia exhibit at the
     Mexican Museum (S.F.) in 1981. Includes
     portraits of Frida Kahlo and the Flores
     Magon brothers, Goya, Van Gogh, Ethel and
     Julius Rosenberg, etc. Illustrated. This
     article has been reprinted in METAMORFOSIS
     under a different title: "Portraits Plus
     Struggles Plus Consciousness: Nine Pastels
     by Rupert Garcia," Vol. 3-4, no. 1-2,
     (1980-81), p. 104-106.

Garcia, Rupert (cont.)

4223 Albright, Thomas. Oakland Museum: a wide
     range in Latin art. SAN FRANCISCO CHRONICLE,
     (September 12, 1970), p. 33. English.

     AN: A large show called ARTES DE LA RAZA
     at the Oakland Museum includes Mercedes
     Gutierrez-McDermid, Louis Gutierrez, Luis
     Cervantez, Calvin Tondre, Manuel Villamor,
     Rene Yanez, Jose Ramirez, Jorge Lerma,
     Rolando Castellon, Esteban Villa, Rupert
     Garcia, and Gustavo Rivera who is also
     having an exhibit at the Galeria de la Raza.

4224 Albright, Thomas. San Francisco: the force
     of universals. ART NEWS MAGAZINE, Vol. 77,
     no. 6 (Summer 1978), p. 174. English.

     AN: Review of Rupert Garcia pastel show
     at the San Francisco Museum of Modern Art.
     Reviewer suggests he is one of the very few
     real artists to emerge from the "unfortunate
     genre" of poster art. His images are highly
     charged: political prisoners, corpses,
     revolutionary martyrs.

4225 Arnold, Frank. Posters and society. PEOPLE'S
     WORLD, Vol. 23, no. 2. English.

     AN: An exhibit at the San Francisco
     Museum of Art curated by Rolando Castellon.
     The article focuses on the posters of Xavier
     Viramontes and Rupert Garcia of San
     Francisco.

4226 Around the Bay. METAMORFOSIS, Vol. 3, no. 2
     (1980), p. 101-108. English.

     AN: Cultural review of activities in the
     Bay Area, northern California, and
     Sacramento. Includes history of the Galeria
     de la Raza/Studio 24 (San Francisco), the
     Centro de Artistas Chicanos/RCAF, Royal
     Chicano Air Force (Sacramento), and a review
     of Rupert Garcia's pastel portraits exhibit
     at the Mexican Museum (S.F.) in 1981.
     Illustrated. Continued in Vol. 4, no. 1,
     1981.

4227 Burkhardt, Dorothy. Chicano pride and anger
     mix at 'Califas'. THE TAB, (April 12,
     1981), p. 34. English.

     AN: CALIFAS: AN EXHIBITION OF CHICANO
     ARTISTS IN CALIFORNIA represents a
     cross-section of artists exhibiting work for
     at least ten years: Rupert Garcia, Ernie
     Palomino, Eduardo Carrillo, Judy Baca, Rene
     Yanez, Carmen Lomas Garza, Salvador Roberto
     Torres, Roberto Chavez, Willie Herron, Ralph
     Maradiaga, Sue Martinez, Jose Montoya,
     Malaquias Montoya, Ramses Noriega and
     Esteban Villa. Illustrated.

4228 CODEX NEWSLETTER (Galeria de la Raza, San
     Francisco, CA). Vol. 1, no. 2 (September
     1973). English.

     AN: An in-house bulletin of upcoming
     events: EL SOL NUNCA MUERE,
     photography/poster exhibit, Rolando Garces,
     and Peruvian posters; Mujeres de Aztlan,
     women artists' collective exhibit;
     Filipino/Samoan art exhibit; Galeria
     Christmas art sale; Galeria pavilion at S.F.
     annual art festival; Rockefeller scholarship
     for Galeria curator Luis Santana; Galeria
     coloring book; Balmy Alley mural project;
     Diego Rivera exhibit; first installment of
     Rupert Garcia's RAZA MURALS AND MURALISTS:
     AN HISTORICAL VIEW.

4229 Contemporary Arts Museum, Houston, TX and

Martinez, Santos G., Jr. Mexican movie
posters. Exhibition invitation, 1979.
English.

     AN: Invitation to an exhibit of posters
     primarily from the collecttion of Enrique
     Flores and Xavier Gorena of Xochil Art
     Center, Mission, Texas. Martinez considers
     the posters monumental, with expressive
     qualities that have influenced Chicano
     poster makers like the Royal Chicano Air
     Force, and Rupert Garcia, and Texas artists
     like Luis Jimenez, Jesse Trevino and Cesar
     Martinez. One illustration. Introduction by
     guest curator Santos G. Martinez, Jr. (See
     Rupert Garcia's essay in the exhibition
     catalog: POSTERS FROM THE GOLDEN AGE OF
     MEXICAN CINEMA, for another point of view).

4230 Corcoran Gallery of Art, Washington, D.C.
     Images of an era: the American poster
     1945-75. Washington, D.C.: Corcoran Gallery
     of Art, 1976. English.

     AN: Uncredited poster [La Raza
     Silkscreen Center, San Francisco],
     (centerfold). Posters by Rupert Garcia,
     Linda Lucero, and Ralph Maradiaga, all of
     San Francisco, CA. Introduction by John
     Garriga. Essays by Margaret Cogswell, Milton
     Glaser, Dore Ashton, Alan Gowens.

4231 Cross, Miriam Dungan. A satirical brutal
     view of pollution. THE TRIBUNE (Oakland,
     CA), (January 25, 1970), p. 26-EN. English.

     AN: (Includes reproduction of Rupert
     Garcia's silkscreen print "D.D.T." dated
     1969).

4232 De Lappe, Pele. Saga of Rupert Garcia's
     poster: from pen to UN. PEOPLE'S WORLD, Vol.
     44, no. 28 (July 11, 1981), p. 10. English.

     AN: Desiring to produce a poster on
     Nelson Mandela and South African political
     prisoners, San Francisco artist Rupert
     Garcia, appealed for support to the African
     National Congress, and the Liberation
     Support Movement. The United Nations Center
     Against Apartheid provided a grant for
     production, indicating it should be
     distributed free. Illustrated.

4233 Frankenstein, Alfred. At the museum: when
     politics and art do mix. SAN FRANCISCO
     CHRONICLE, (March 15, 1978), p. 54.
     English.

     AN: Glowing review of exhibit at the San
     Francisco Museum of Modern Art by Rupert
     Garcia who, the critic says, has a genius
     for saying the essential thing without a
     line, a gesture or a touch of color more
     than necessary. Illustrated.

4234 Galeria de la Raza/Studio 24, San Francisco,
     CA and Franco, Jean. Juan Fuentes y Rupert
     Garcia: posters, drawings, prints.
     Exhibition catalog, 1975. English.

     AN: Catalog of an exhibit. Illustrated
     with drawings and posters.

4235 Garcia, Rupert. Assassination of a striking
     Mexican worker [painting]. PEOPLE'S WORLD,
     (January 31, 1981), p. 10.

     AN: Reproduction of a Rupert Garcia
     pastel being exhibited at the Mexican Museum
     in San Francisco, CA.

Garcia, Rupert (cont.)

4236 Garcia, Rupert. Echos de la Mision - Alfaro
Siqueiros (1896-1974). EL TECOLOTE, Vol. 4,
no. 3 (February 22, 1974), p. 11. English.

AN: Biographical and artistic trajectory
of Mexican artist David Alfaro Siqueiros.
Artist painted three murals in Southern
California in 1932 (MEETING IN THE STREET
and TROPICAL AMERICA were done in Los
Angeles on the walls of the Chouinard School
of Art and the Plaza Art Center, Olvera
Street area respectively. The third mural
PORTRAIT OF MEXICO was privately
commissioned in Santa Monica). The three
California murals deal with themes of
censorship, racism, colonialism, capitalism,
and imperialism. Article suggests that Raza
artists are much influenced by the ideas and
work of Siqueiros. Illustrated with Rupert
Garcia's silkscreen poster SIQUEIROS.

4237 Garcia, Rupert. Portfolio [drawings]. EL
GRITO, Vol. 3, no. 1 (Fall 1969), p.
64-68. English.

4238 Garcia, Rupert. Rupert Garcia. TRA, Vol. 2,
no. 6 (1975), p. 20-27. English.

AN: Statement by the artist and
portfolio of nine silkscreen posters, five
in color.

4239 Gonzalez, Tobias and Gonzalez, Sandra.
Perspectives on Chicano education. Stanford,
CA: Stanford University, 1975. English.

AN: Reproductions of artworks by Ralph
Maradiaga, Patricia Rodriguez, Roberto
Bonilla, Francisco Camplis, Graciela
Carrillo-Lopez, Juan Fuentes, Irene Perez,
Roger Reyes, Carlos Loarca, Xavier
Viramontes, Ralph McNeill, Rupert Garcia,
Jose Romero.

4240 Hartnell College Studio Gallery, Salinas,
CA. Paintings, drawings, prints by San
Francisco Bay Area Chicano artists. Exhibit
brochure, 1971. English.

AN: Brochure for exhibit featuring
Francisco Camplis, Graciela Carrillo, Sal
Castaneda, Priscilla Dominguez, J. Duarte,
Rupert Garcia, Carlos Loarca, Irene Perez,
Vincent Rascon, Michael Rios, Peter
Rodriguez, Luis Valsoto, Esteban Villa, Rene
Yanez, Zala. Illustrated by Rupert Carcia
print.

4241 Heard Museum, Phoenix, AZ. Second Southwest
Chicano Art Invitational. Exhibit catalog,
1978. English.

AN: Exhibit by eight artists: Antonio
Pazos (Tucson), Rudy Fernandez (Salt Lake
City), Harry Gamboa (Los Angeles), Rupert
Garcia and Xavier Viramontes (San
Francisco), Roberto Rios (San Antonio),
Roberto Espinoza (Yuma), and Roberto Borboa
(Tucson). Brief biographies of all but Rios.
29 illustrations.

4242 Martinez, Anita. Raza! Arte! Raza! Arte!
EL TECOLOTE, Vol. 1, no. 2 (September 7,
1970), p. 3. Bilingual.

AN: Galeria de la Raza opened on July,
1970 at 425 14th St. San Francisco. It was
an outgrowth of the Arte Seis organization
(an art effort established in the Mission
District in 1967 by Francisco Camplis,
Rupert Garcia, Ralph McNeil, Jay Ojeda and
Jack Ruiz). These and other artists brought

together by the Neighborhood Arts Program
have coalesced in the new Galeria de la
Raza. Article gives goals, organizational
scheme and plans for the Galeria. It's first
exhibit was a one man show by Esteban Villa
together with a photo and sketch exhibit on
Cuba by Jay Ojeda, Roberto Diaz Perez and
Gloria Ozuna. Illustrated with installation
view of new Galeria.

4243 MEXICAN MUSEUM NEWSLETTER. Vol. 6, no. 1
(Winter 1980, 1981). English.

AN: Regular report on the activities,
finances, membership, and other information
about the Museum. Announces several upcoming
shows: Rupert Garcia, six Mexican geometric
artists, paintings and prints by Mexican
American and Mexican women artists, Mexican
Leonel Maciel and Chicano Carlos Almaraz,
Mexican folk art, Manuel Neri sculpture, and
Mexican Luis Jaso.

4244 The Mexican Museum, San Francisco, CA.
Rupert Garcia: portraits/retratos.
Exhibition brochure, 1981. English.

AN: Exhibition brochure with
biographical information and exhibition
chronology for Rupert Garcia.

4245 Miller, Marlan. Heard speaks Spanish through
art. PHOENIX GAZETTE, (September 23, 1978).
English.

AN: Four new exhibits at the Heard
Museum of Phoenix include "Hispanic crafts
of the Southwest", and "Southwest Chicano
Art Invitational". The former focuses on New
Mexico and Colorado crafts, organized by the
Taylor Museum if the Colorado Springs Fine
Arts Center; the latter includes Rupert
Garcia and Xavier Miramontes of San
Francisco, Rudy Fernandez of Salt Lake City
(now in Scottsdale, AZ), and Antonio Pazos
of Tucson.

4246 Montoya, Jose E. Rupert Garcia and the SF
Museum of Modern Art. RAYAS, Vol. 2, no. 2
(March, April, 1979), p. 5,11. English.

AN: Commentary apropos an exhibit of
pastel drawings by Rupert Garcia at the San
Francisco Museum of Modern Art. Author
gives a capsule history of the relationship
between Raza artists and mainstream cultural
institutions. Rupert Garcia is seen as
belonging to a stalwart group of Chicano
artists.

4247 Notes on 2nd National Community Muralists'
Network Conference, Chicago, Ill. April
20-23, 1978. San Francisco, CA, 1978.
English.

AN: Rupert Garcia, Raul Martinez,
Patricia Rodriguez, Ray Patlan (San
Francisco Bay Area) and Jaime Valadez (San
Jose), among others, attended the conference
in Chicago. Reports were heard from many
parts of the United States on mural
activities, including that of Aurelio Diaz
of Chicago, representing MARCH (Movimiento
Artistico Chicano). A workshop presentation
was made by Luis Arenal and others from the
Taller Siqueiros of Cuernavaca, Mexico. An
experimental mural to try Siqueiros'
techniques was created. Illustrated.

Garcia, Rupert (cont.)

4248 Ohlone College Art Department Gallery,
Fremont, CA. Impressions: a California print
invitational. Exhibition catalog, 1976.
English.

AN: Exhibition catalog includes
commentary on the artist and reproduction of
two silkscreen posters "El Grito Rebelde"
and "The Bicentennial Art Poster" by Rupert
Garcia.

4249 Ojeda, Jay. Galeria de la Raza--art for the
community. SAN FRANCISCO PROGRESS, (March
24, 1972). English.

AN: Analysis of group exhibition by
thirty-four Raza artists. Commentary on the
work of Latin American artists Consuelo
Mendez, Rolando Castellon, and Chicano
artists Rupert Garcia, Chuy Campusano and
Peter Rodriguez.

4250 Orth, Maureen. The soaring spirit of Chicano
arts. NEW WEST MAGAZINE, Vol. 3, no. 19
(September 11, 1978), p. 41-46. English.

AN: Overview of California Chicano
culture. Color illustrations of works by
Mexican muralist David Alfaro Siqueiros,
Rupert Garcia, Mujeres Muralistas, Willie
Herron, Rene Yanez, Rudy Martinez, San
Diego's Chicano Park, ASCO, Jose Montoya.

4251 Rupert Garcia. SAN FRANCISCO BAY GUARDIAN,
(October 3, 1975), p. 22-23. English.

AN: Informative piece focusing on the
artist's work procedures; his techniques of
image selection, transformation and
manipulation. Presents Garcia's political
and aesthetic credo and situates him as a
community activist and artist. Illustrated
with reproduction of Garcia's BICENTENNIAL
POSTER.

4252 San Francisco Museum of Art, San Francisco,
CA. M.I.X. graphics I: prints. Exhibition
invitation, 1974. English.

AN: Invitation to an exhibit of 15
multi-ethnic artists, including San
Francisco artists Ralph Maradiaga and Rupert
Garcia.

4253 San Francisco Museum of Modern Art, San
Francisco, CA and Castellon, Rolando. Rupert
Garcia/pastel drawings. Exhibition catalog,
1978. English.

AN: Exhibit by San Francisco artist
Rupert Garcia.

4254 Santa Ana College, Santa Ana, CA and
Goldman, Shifra M. Chicano art. Exhibition
catalog, 1974. English.

AN: Thirteen California artists are
presented in a short essay defining Chicano
as a double mestizaje of Mexican mestizo and
U.S. influences that exists in a state of
"reconciled conflict." Its aim is
communication. Artists included are
Malaquias Montoya, Rupert Garcia, Manuel
Hernandez, Esteban Villa, Robert Gomez,
Harvey Tarango, Mary Helen Castro, Eduardo
Carrillo, Graciela Carrillo, and "Los Four":
Carlos Almaraz, Robert de la Rocha, Judithe
Hernandez, Gilbert Lujan and Frank Romero.

4255 Stofflet-Santiago, Mary. The fifth sun:
esthetic quality versus curatorial intent.
ARTWEEK, Vol. 8, no. 37 (November 5, 1977),
p. 6. English.

AN: Review of the exhibit THE FIFTH SUN
at the University Art Museum in Berkeley,
Calif., curated by Ralph Maradiaga of the
Galeria de la Raza. It contains folk art,
and posters by Chicano artists Maradiaga,
Rupert Garcia, Juan Fuentes, mural studies
by Graciela Carrillo and Mike Rios, ceramics
by Anna de Leon, an altar by Amalia
Mesa-Bains, and mural drawings by Mexican
muralists. The writer criticizes the uneven
quality of the show, but encourages better
ones in the future. Illustrated.

4256 Time to greez: incantations from the Third
World. San Francisco, CA: Glide
Publications/Third World Communications,
1975. English.

AN: Rupert Garcia, drawing, p. 158;
Xavier Viramontes, silkscreen, p. 181; Juan
Fuentes, drawing, p. 188; Graciela Carrillo,
drawing, p. 196.

Garcia, Ruperto

4257 Garcia, Ruperto. Photography. ARRIBA, Vol.
1, no. 6 (1980). English.

AN: Statement of photographic credo and
portfolio of photographs by Ruperto Garcia,
photographer from the Rio Grande Valley.

Garcia, Sal

4258 Campesino Business and Joint Enterprise
Building, Fresno, CA. Sabor a Fresno. Arte
chicano: los Four and la Brocha. Exhibition
invitation [1976]. English.

AN: Invitation to an exhibit of works by
Los Four of Los Angeles and members of La
Brocha del Valle of Fresno: Arturo Roman,
Sal Garcia, John Sierra, Juan Truner, Sapo
de Aztlan, Fernando Hernandez, Alberto
Reyes, Ernesto Palomino, Lee Orona,
Francisco Barrios, Juan Ybarra, Bobby Reyes,
Alberto Hernandez. Brocha was started by
Palomino (California State University,
Fresno professor) to pool talents of Central
Valley artists.

4259 Oakes College, University of California,
Santa Cruz, CA and Carrillo, Eduardo.
Corazon de Aztlan: a Chicano arts show.
Exhibition catalog, 1981. English.

AN: Catalog of exhibit including works
by Eduardo Carrillo, Juana Franklin, Cruz
Zamarron, Jerry Astorga, Jaime Valadez,
Ernesto Palomino, Sal Garcia, Roger Sierra,
Jose Montoya, Esteban Villa, Juanishi
Orozco, from Santa Cruz, San Jose, Fresno
and Sacramento. Presentations of films and
by the Teatro de la Tierra Morena of Santa
Cruz County.

Garcia, Sal (cont.)

4260 Teatro de la Tierra Morena, Santa Cruz, CA.
Fuego en Aztlan: a Chicano arts show.
Exhibition brochure, 1980. English.

AN: Folder of information on the
exhibition curated by Cruz Zamarron and
Eduardo Carrillo. Exhibiting artists were:
Justina Avila, Terry Benitez, Eduardo
Carrillo, Hernando Chavez, Bob Cruz, Juanita
Estrada, Juana Franklin, Sal Garcia, Leticia
Hernandez, David "Sir Loco" Jimenez, Raoul
Mendez, Vicente Mendez, Maria V. Pinedo,
Gonzalo Placencia, Ramon Rodriguez, Roberto
Salas, George Silva and Cruz Zamarron. A
special feature was a live tattoo
demonstration entitled "Walking Art".

Garcia-Camarillo, Cecilio

4261 [Camarillo (drawing)]. REVISTA RIO BRAVO,
Vol. 1, no. 1 (Winter 1981), p. 7.

Garcia's Art Gallery, San Antonio, TX

4262 Minutaglio, Bill. S.A. aims at becoming
Hispanic art center. SAN ANTONIO
EXPRESS-NEWS, (January 18, 1981), p. 3-M+.
English.

AN: Rick Reyna is director of the
fledging San Antonio Consortium for Hispanic
Arts (SACHA), a city-funded umbrella
organization covering seven art groups,
three of which - Centro Cultural del Pueblo
(instruction for young people), Community
Cultural Arts Program (murals), and
Performance Artists Nucleus (displays and
exhibits) - concern the visual arts. Rudy
Garcia, Anastacio "Tache" Torres, and Ralph
Garcia (formerly of Garcia's Art Gallery)
head the three groups respectively.

Garduno, Geronimo

4263 Cockcroft, Eva; Weber, John; and Cockcroft,
James D. Towards a people's art: the
contemporary mural movement. New York: E.P.
Dutton, 1977. English.

AN: A survey of the street mural
movement in the United States, from about
1967 on. Several chapters are written by the
artists themselves: John Weber on the
Chicago mural group; Susan Shapiro-Kiok on
Cityarts Workshop of New York; Eva Cockcroft
on People's painters of New Jersey; Geronimo
Garduno on Artes Guadalupanos de Aztlan of
New Mexico. Chicano murals illustrated
include those of Mujeres Muralistas, Ray
Patlan, William F. Herron, Hoyo-Mara Gang,
Artes Guadalupanos de Aztlan, Vicente
Mendoza and Jose Nario (with Patlan) Mario
Castillo, Michael Rios, Toltecas en Aztlan,
Roberto Chavez, Ernie Palomino, Chuy
Campusano and Luis Cortazar (with Rios).

4264 Painted walls - a New Mexico folk art. NEW
MEXICO, (January 1977), p. 34-35. English.

AN: Five color illustrations of murals
from New Mexico including those done by
Gilberto Guzman, Geronimo Garduno, and Sam
Leyba. The murals are located in Santa Fe,
Chimayo, Embudo and Albuquerque.

4265 SF muralists display paintings. VIVA,
(October 8, 1972), p. 19. English.

AN: Paintings, and photos of murals
taken by Gilberto Romero, on display at the
New Mexico Arts Commission. Artists Sammy,
Carlos and Albert Leyba (the original

members), Gilberto Guzman and Geronimo
Garduno, part of the Artes Guadalupanos de
Aztlan, finished a mural at Tot Lot in 1971
and are team-painting La Clinica de la
Gente. They have also painted a mural for
West Las Vegas High School.

Garry, Susan

4266 Garcia-Camarillo, Mia. [Untitled drawing].
CARACOL, Vol. 3, no. 8 (April 1977), p. 18.

Garza, Alex

4267 Garza, Alex. Entrevista con Alex Garza.
ABRAZO, Vol. 1, no. 2 (Summer 1979), p.
27-29. English.

AN: Brief article exploring Alex Garza's
technique, philosophy, and setting for his
sculptural work. The artist expresses his
desire to see artists break with tradition
and not allow the political rhetoric of the
early Chicano Movement to promote
stagnation. His connection to the art
organization ALBA is also briefly mentioned.

4268 Raices y visiones [portfolio]. REVISTA
CHICANO-RIQUENA, Vol. 7, no. 2 (Spring
1979), p. 29-44.

AN: Portfolio of works from the exhibit
RAICES ANTIGUAS/VISIONES NUEVAS: ANCIENT
ROOTS/NEW VISIONS. Artists included are
Patssi Valdez (Los Angeles), Eloisa
Castellanos-Sanchez (New York), Benjamin
Serrano, Jr. (Tijuana, Mexico), Alex Garza
(Chicago), Martin Y. Moreno (Michigan), Luis
A. Jimenez (New Mexico), Rene Castro
(Oakland, CA), Sita Gomez de Kanelba (New
York), Susana Lasta (Tucson, AZ), Domingo
Garcia (New York), Consuelo Mendez Castillo
(Caracas, Venezuela), Naomi Castillo
Simonetti (New Jersey), Louis Carlos Bernal,
and Eddie Comptis.

Garza, Danny

4269 Tucson Public Library; Sonoran Heritage; and
De la Cruz, Frank. Mexican American mural
art: the power of cultural identity.
Brochure, 1980. English.

AN: Brochure on Tucson murals painted by
Antonio Pazos, David Tineo, Danny Garza,
Cynthia Reyes, Darlene Marcos, Roberto
Borboa, and others.

Garza, Jorge

4270 Galeria de la Raza, San Antonio, TX.
Celebration seventy-four. Exhibition
catalog, [ca. 1974]. English.

AN: Catalog of extensive exhibition
including European, Mexican, and the
following Texan Chicano artists: Rolando
Garces, Cesar Martinez, Ray Chavez, Vicente
Rodriguez, Jorge Garza, Alfred Rodriguez,
Luis Guerra, Carmen Lomas Garza, Bruno
Andrade, Jr., Amado M. Pena Jr., Roberto
Rios, Jose Trevino, Rudy Trevino, Luis
Santoyo, Tati Rubio, Eduardo C. Garza,
Arthur de la Fuente, and Jesus Campos
Trevino.

Garza, Luis

4271 Consejo Mexicano de Fotografia, A.C., Mexico
     City. Hecho en latinoamerica: segundo
     coloquio latinoamericano de fotografia.
     Exhibition catalog, 1982. Spanish.

     AN: Catalog/book of the second
     colloquium and exhibit of Latin American
     photography. Among the Chicano artists whose
     work is reproduced are Louis Carlos Bernal,
     Robert C. Buitron, David Cardenas, Isabel
     Castro, Harry Gamboa, Jr., Luis Garza,
     Roberto Gil de Montes, John M. Valadez,
     Kathy Vargas. In the exhibit were also
     Porfirio Aguilar, Elsa Marie Flores, Ricardo
     Valverde. Great number of illustrations. In
     Spanish.

4272 COUNCIL OF LATINO PHOTOGRAPHY/USA
     NEWSLETTER. no. 1 (January 1979). English.

     AN: First number of photocopied
     newsletter produced by the Council of Latino
     Photography/USA announcing the formation of
     the organization and its affiliation with
     the Consejo Latinoamericano de Fotografia
     established in Mexico City in May 1978.
     Organizers of CLP/USA were photographers
     Isabel Castro, Harry Gamboa, Jr., Adam
     Avila, Luis Garza, and art historian Shifra
     Goldman.

Garza, Manuel

4273 Wagner Gallery presents paintings by Manuel
     Garza. SOUTHWEST ART COLLECTOR, Vol. 1, no.
     3 (March, April, 1980), p. 3. English.

     AN: Story on Texas landscape and
     blue-bonnet painter influenced by Porfirio
     Salinas.

Garza Perez, David

4274 Galeria Tonantzin, Centro Cultural de LUCHA,
     Austin, TX. Young Chicano photographers from
     throughout Texas. Exhibition brochure, n.d.
     English.

     AN: This exhibition is the collection of
     the winners of the contest (by the same
     name) sponsored by the Extension Cultural
     SRE-UNAM in San Antonio. Photographers
     represented were: Grace Alvarez, David
     Cardenas, Hector Cardenas, Stephen Casanova,
     Ronald Cortez, Raul Espinosa, Felix Almanza,
     Carolina Flores, David Garza Perez, Xavier
     Garza, Conrad Guerra, Melinda Hasbrook, Juan
     Jose de Hoyes, Beverly Kennon, Art Moreno,
     David Perez, Isabelle Purden, Patricia
     Santell, Nancy de los Santos, Jose Soria,
     Richard Tichich, Kathy Vargas, Vivian Yaten,
     and Johnny Zamarria.

Gaytan, Ray

4275 Gaytan, Ray; Leone, Betty; and Cisneros,
     Rene. An interview. TEJIDOS, Vol. 2, no. 6
     (Summer 1975), p. 29-38. English.

     AN: Interview with Texas artists Ray
     Gaytan, Trini Perez, and Sam Coronado on the
     topic "What Is Chicano Art?".

Geomonte
     USE: Montemayor, George A. "Geomonte"

Geronimo (Native American Chief)

4276 Harper, Hilliard. Native Americans stand
     tall again as Balboa Park mural takes shape.
     LOS ANGELES TIMES [San Diego County
     edition], (March 2, 1981), p. II, 5.

English.

     AN: Victor Ochoa paints the figure of
     Geronimo on the wall of San Diego's Balboa
     Park Centro Cultural de la Raza to replace a
     skeletal calavera figure disturbing patients
     at a hospital across the street. The central
     figure is part of a planned 70 x 18 foot
     mural promoting Mexican, Chicano and Indian
     art. Activities at the Centro are described.
     Illustrated.

Ghetto
     USE: Barrios

Gil de Montes, Roberto

4277 Colectivo El Ojo. CHOQUE DE AMOR: fotonovela
     by Lamp. CHISMEARTE, Vol. 1, no. 4 (Fall ,
     Winter, 1977), p. 35-37. Bilingual.

     AN: Several students with the help of
     the Latin American Media Project (LAMP) and
     the Latin American Studies Department of
     California State University, Los Angeles
     produced the fotonovela CHOQUE DE AMOR, a
     variation on the typical "fotonovela"
     romance. This one encourages readers to
     reevaluate traditional female roles. The
     group also includes Kay Torres. Six frames
     of the fotonovela are reproduced.

4278 Consejo Mexicano de Fotografia, A.C., Mexico
     City. Hecho en latinoamerica: segundo
     coloquio latinoamericano de fotografia.
     Exhibition catalog, 1982. Spanish.

     AN: Catalog/book of the second
     colloquium and exhibit of Latin American
     photography. Among the Chicano artists whose
     work is reproduced are Louis Carlos Bernal,
     Robert C. Buitron, David Cardenas, Isabel
     Castro, Harry Gamboa, Jr., Luis Garza,
     Roberto Gil de Montes, John M. Valadez,
     Kathy Vargas. In the exhibit were also
     Porfirio Aguilar, Elsa Marie Flores, Ricardo
     Valverde. Great number of illustrations. In
     Spanish.

4279 Diaz, Jean; Dominguez, Edward; and Torres,
     Kay. Bi-Lingual blues [fotonovela]. SOMOS,
     Vol. 1, no. 1 (April, May, 1978), p. 33-36.
     English.

     AN: Reproduction of a "fotonovela",
     BI-LINGUAL BLUES by Ojo Productions, a group
     of students connected with the Latin
     American Studies Department of California
     State University, Los Angeles.

4280 Galeria, Santa Ana, CA. The last Chicano art
     show. Exhibition brochure, 1981. English.

     AN: Invitation-brochure for an exhibit
     of Los Angeles and Orange County artists in
     a gallery underwritten by the Friendly
     Center, Inc. with grants from local
     government and from businesses. Exhibiting
     are (Roberto) Gil de Montes, Gilbert Lujan,
     Judy Miranda, Patricia Murillo, Alonso
     Pardo, Teddy Sandoval, Mexican artist
     Artemio Sepulveda, Joey Terrill, Art
     Valenzuela, Ben Valenzuela, Linda Vallejo,
     Jack A. Vargas, Emigdio Vasquez, Richard
     Serrato, and J. William Hernandez, who is
     the gallery director.

Gil de Montes, Roberto (cont.)

4281 L.A.C.E. (Los Angeles Contemporary
Exhibitions), Los Angeles, CA. No Movie: Gil
de Montes, Teddy, Glugio [Gronk], Patssi,
Gamboa. Exhibition invitation, 1978.
English.

AN: Invitation to "performance" piece by
Roberto Gil de Montes, Teddy Sandoval,
Gronk, Patssi Valdez and Harry Gamboa, Jr.,
the latter three of the ASCO group.
Illustrated.

4282 Lucas, Jerry and Gil de Montes, Roberto, et
al. CHOQUE DE AMOR: fotonovela by Lamp. Los
Angeles, CA: Colectivo El Ojo, Latin
American Studies Dept., CSULA, 1979.
English.

AN: "Fotonovela" featuring Elsa Flores,
Rosa Marin, and Jerry Lucas produced by the
collective work of Lucas, Roberto Gil de
Montes, Mario Massinelli, Luis Soto, and Kay
Torres.

4283 Lucas, Jerry. Testimonios de Latinoamerica.
CHISMEARTE, no. 6 (February 1980), p. 6-9.
English.

AN: Review of the exhibits TESTIMONIOS
DE LATINOAMERICA and AMERICA EN LA MIRA,
brought to Los Angeles Contemporary
Exhibitions Gallery by Chicano curator
Roberto Gil de Montes, as part of a cultural
exchange between the Mexican Cultural
Workers Front and Felipe Ehrenberg of the
Grupo Proceso Pentagono of Mexico, and
Chicano artists and photographers from the
Council of Latino Photography/USA in Los
Angeles. Well illustrated.

4284 Mechicano Art Center, Los Angeles, CA.
Schizophrenibeneficial. Exhibition
invitation, 1977. English.

AN: Invitation to an ASCO "performance"
work: "Projecting of Visual and/or Verbal
Personality Disorders Onto Person or Persons
Unknown." Glugio (Gronk), Teddy (Sandoval),
(Roberto) Gil de Montes, Patssi (Valdez),
(Harry) Gamboa.

Gilroy, CA

4285 Gilroy's public art form. THE VALLEY WORLD,
(July 19, 1978). English.

AN: Article cites activities of "The
Tortuga Patrol" a Chicano muralist group
from the Watsonville California area.

4286 The Tortuga paints a new mural. CHISMEARTE,
Vol. 2, no. 1 (Summer 1978), p. 12-13.
English.

AN: Black and white details of new
indoor mural painted at the Gilroy's
Recreation Center.

Giron, Jose

4287 Encanto Pavilion, Encanto Park, Phoenix, AZ.
Exposicion de arte para la raza: Arizona
Chicano art show. Exhibition catalog, [ca.
1978]. English.

AN: Catalog for an exhibit organized by
MARS (Movimiento Artistico del Rio Salado).
Colombian-born Antonio L. Tocora, Jim
Covarrubias, Ed Dias, Robert C. Buitron,
Armando Leon Hernandez, Guillermo Galindo,
Richard Luna Cisneros, Jose Andres Giron,
Robert L. Matta included.

4288 MARS: Movimiento Artistico del Rio Salado.
Phoenix, AZ: Mars Studio/Gallery, 1978.
English.

AN: History and manifesto of MARS, 13
member group of Arizona painters, sculptors,
designers, and photographers: Jose Andres
Giron, Jose Jimenez Rodriguez, Antonio
Tocora (Colombian-born), Ramon Delgadillo,
Francisco Zuniga, Jim Covarrubias, Ed Diaz,
David Martinez, Roberto Buitron, Juan
Rodriguez, Eddie Lopez, Zarco Guerrero, Joe
Sanchez.

4289 Through the eyes of Joe Giron. NUESTRO, Vol.
5, no. 9 (December 1981), p. 34-40. English.

AN: A 9-photo collection of the work of
Las Cruces, NM photographer, Joe Giron.
Typical scenes in Texas, NM, and Ohio.

Godean, Frank

4290 R.C.A.F. artistas precursores del arte
chicano. EL HISPANO, Vol. 8, no. 35
(February 17, 1976), p. 1. English.

AN: Information on the R.C.A.F.
organization. Includes group photograph of
R.C.A.F. members, Jose Montoya, Esteban
Villa, John Carrillo, Ricardo Fabela, Rudy
Cuellar, Juanishi Orozco and Frank Godena.

Goez Art Gallery, Los Angeles, CA

4291 Beronius, George. The murals of East Los
Angeles. HOME MAGAZINE, (April 11, 1976),
p. 10-11+. English.

AN: Well-illustrated historical article
focusing on murals at Estrada Courts and
those produced through Goez Gallery and
Judith Baca in East Los Angeles.

4292 Gardiner, Henry G. Painted exterior walls of
Southern California. CURRANT ART MAGAZINE,
Vol. 1, no. 2 (June, July, 1975), p. 16-23+.
English.

AN: Good survey of street muralism,
primarily in Los Angeles and San Diego,
which started in 1968. Divided into eight
"schools," including Chicano and non-Chicano
muralists. Most Chicano murals associated
with Goez Brothers Art Gallery and Mechicano
Art Center in Los Angeles, the Coronado Bay
Bridge group [Chicano Park] and Balboa Park
group [Centro Cultural de la Raza]. Mural
discussed in detail. Well illustrated.

4293 Goez proudly presents. Exhibit brochure,
n.d. [1970]. English.

AN: Brochure produced by the Goez
Gallery of Los Angeles for an inaugural
exhibit showing the work of 76 artists.

4294 Kushner, Sam. It was a meat market in East
L.A. LOS ANGELES FREE PRESS, Vol. 11, no. 34
(August 23, 1974), p. 17. English.

AN: Data on the formation of Goez
Gallery by John Gonzalez and David Botello
in 1970. Created in what once was a meat
market in the East Los Angeles barrio, Goez
became an important showcase for Chicano
art.

Goez Art Gallery, Los Angeles, CA (cont.)

4295 Mural depicts history of Mexican Americans. EASTSIDE JRNL, (December 16, 1971), p. 1. English.

AN: Richard Jimenez of the Goez Gallery depicts the past and present of Mexican American culture on an interior mural at the First Street Store (3640 E. First St.) The 6 ft. by 15 ft. mural has central image of a clock with a faceless figure (The Mexican American of the future). Artist comments on another of his murals titled EDUCATION OF LIFE.

4296 The mural message. TIME, Vol. 105, no. 14 (April 7, 1975), p. 79. English.

AN: Brief illustrated story of murals painted in East Los Angeles during the 1970s. Spotlights activities of Goez Gallery.

Goez Art Studios, Los Angeles

4297 Diaz, Katherine A. Art is business: an interview with Joe L. Gonzalez. CAMINOS, Vol. 2, no. 5 (October 1981), p. 21-22. English.

AN: Business advice to the artist and to the collector from the owner of the two Goez art galleries in Los Angeles. How to merchandise or buy art as a good investment.

4298 Espejo: reflections of the Mexican American: Louis Carlos Bernal, Morrie Camhi, Abigail Heyman, Roger Minick, Neal Slavin. SOMOS, Vol. 2, no. 1 (February 1978), p. 26-35. English.

AN: Announcement of the ESPEJO photographic exhibit to be held at Goez Gallery in East Los Angeles. Statements by the four artists and a portfolio of their works: Abigail Heyman, Roger Minick, Morrie Camhi, and Arizona Chicano photographer Louis Carlos Bernal. Includes color photographs by Bernal on cover. This 1979 issue is erroneously dated 1978.

4299 Nevarez, Joe R. Chicano art blooms in barrio warehouse. LOS ANGELES TIMES, (December 26, 1974), p. I, 32. English.

AN: Former meat packing warehouse transformed into Goez Art Studios by Joe and John Gonzalez. Exhibiting David Negron, Eddie Martinez, David Lopez (Hollywood scenic artists) and Roberto Arenivar. Lists activities of the gallery: exhibits, murals, restoration.

4300 Torres, Louis R. A Profile of an Hispano Artist: Charlie "Clavos" Felix. LA LUZ, Vol. 4, no. 6-7 (September, October, 1975), p. 3-4. English.

AN: Biographical data on artist and his unique nail relief sculpture.

4301 Valadez, Kathy L. Ten hints in buying Chicano and Mexican art/10 ideas para la compra de obras de arte. CAMINOS, Vol. 1, no. 6 (October 1980), p. 15-17. Bilingual.

AN: An interior design/investment approach to Mexican and Chicano art. Some of the characterizations of both types of art are unfortunate and uninformed. Seems to be an article to boost sales for Joe Gonzales' Goez Gallery, but lists a number of other locations in California to purchase art.

Illustrated.

Goez Imports & Fine Arts, Los Angeles, CA

4302 Goez Imports & Fine Arts, Los Angeles, CA. We invite you to see the birth of our art. Gallery brochure, 1971. English.

AN: Brochure with history of gallery, mural map, iconography of Goez mural.

Goldman, Shifra M.

4303 COUNCIL OF LATINO PHOTOGRAPHY/USA NEWSLETTER. no. 1 (January 1979). English.

AN: First number of photocopied newsletter produced by the Council of Latino Photography/USA announcing the formation of the organization and its affiliation with the Consejo Latinoamericano de Fotografia established in Mexico City in May 1978. Organizers of CLP/USA were photographers Isabel Castro, Harry Gamboa, Jr., Adam Avila, Luis Garza, and art historian Shifra Goldman.

4304 Lopez, Armando. 'Chicano' art gains cross-culture recognition: 'the street mural has flourished in the barrio'. LAREDO NEWS, (July 20, 1980), p. 6-A. English.

AN: Report on a lecture "The First Decade of the Chicano Renaissance: Mexican American Art in the United States" given by Dr. Shifra M. Goldman under the sponsorship of the Laredo Philosophical Society. Mentions the "delicate Issue" of using the word "Chicano" in conservative Laredo. Illustrated with works of Laredo-born Amado M. Pena.

4305 M.E.C.H.A. cultura y evolucion mexicana. EL CLARIN, (May 2, 1974), p. 3. Spanish.

AN: Report on the mural designed and painted under the direction of Mexican-born designer Sergio O'Cadiz at Santa Ana College, Santa Ana, Calif. Collaborators were instructor Shifra Goldman and gallery director Mike Davis, with members of the MEChA Club and other students. The mural concerns the history of Mexico and of the Chicano and includes a tribute to David Alfaro Siqueiros' Los Angeles mural AMERICA TROPICAL, painted and white-washed in the 1930s. Illustrated.

4306 Rowe, Richard. On Olvera Street: one vision realized, another white washed. REVIEW (Society of Architectural Historians, Pasadena, CA), Vol. 1, no. 1 (Fall 1981), p. 7. English.

AN: Documentation about AMERICA TROPICAL, 1932 mural by David Alfaro Siqueiros. The mural, commissioned by F.K. Ferenz of the Plaza Art Center on Olvera Street in Los Angeles, was a 16' by 80' painting on the second-story wall of the old Italian Hall. From 1968 on, art historian Shifra M. Goldman, working with a small committee, has been actively involved in the attempt to restore the mural. Article details the travails of restoration and underscores the mural's importance. Illustrated.

Gomez, Bob

4307 Mascorro, Julie. Mechicano Art Center
exhibit to grace Price gallery walls. CAMPUS
NEWS, (November 24, 1971). English.

AN: Brief history of Mechicano Art
Center activities from its establishment in
1969 to 1971. Exhibiting are Charles
Almaraz, Roberto Amaral, Raymond Atilano,
William Bejarano, Armando Cabrera, Edward
Carbajal, Leonard Castellanos, Henry de
Vega, Antonio Esparza, Bob Gomez, Lucila V.
Grijalva, Jesus Gutierrez, Santos Lira,
Frank Martinez, Ernest Palomino, Louis
Quijada, Richard Raya, Frank Romero.
Illustrated.

Gomez, Ignacio

4308 Musica hispana en nuestras vidas/Hispanic
music in our lives: almanaque 1982/calendar.
Milwaukee, WI: Miller Brewing Co., 1981.
English.

AN: Twelve Latino artists were
commissioned to illustrate a calendar with
paintings on Hispanic music. The Chicano
artists include Frederico Vigil (New
Mexico), Joe Bastida Rodriguez
(Texas/Washington, D.C.), Manuel Martinez
(Colorado), Jose Antonio Burciaga
(California), Ignacio Gomez (California),
Carolina Flores (Texas), Frank Martinez
(California). Color.

4309 Neumeier, Marty. Ignacio Gomez.
COMMUNICATION ARTS MAGAZINE, Vol. 21, no. 6
(January, February, 1980), p. 78-87.
English.

AN: Story on commercial designer and
illustrator Ignacio Gomez of Los Angeles
which describes his background, education
and life style. 17 full-color illustrations
of his art work, including the ZOOT SUIT
poster for the Mark Taper Forum play.

4310 Posters by Ignacio Gomez: in full color
suitable for framing. CAMINOS, (May 1981),
p. 49. English.

AN: Six full-color posters on Latino
subjects by illustrator Gomez advertised for
sale. The best-known is Gomez's poster for
ZOOT SUIT, a play by Luis Valdez.

4311 Valadez, Kathy L. and Valadez, Kathy L.
Living in the understanding of success/el
endendimiento [sic] del exito. CAMINOS, Vol.
1, no. 6 (October 1980), p. 12-14, 40.
Bilingual.

AN: Story about financially successful
Los Angeles illustrator Ignacio Gomez who
produced the illustration for the play ZOOT
SUIT and designs posters, catalogs, magazine
covers and layouts. Also see front cover and
inside of front cover for illustrations.

Gomez, Robert

4312 Monteverde, Mildred. Contemporary Chicano
art. AZTLAN, Vol. 2, no. 2 (Fall 1971), p.
51-61. Bibliography. English.

AN: An historical survey of trends and
influences on contemporary Chicano art.
Discusses San Diego's Toltecas en Aztlan and
the projected Centro Cultural de la Raza;
Los Angeles' Mechicano Art Center, Goez
Gallery and Plaza de la Raza; pinto (prison)
art; New Mexican art. Many artists are
mentioned.

4313 Santa Ana College, Santa Ana, CA and
Goldman, Shifra M. Chicano art. Exhibition
catalog, 1974. English.

AN: Thirteen California artists are
presented in a short essay defining Chicano
as a double mestizaje of Mexican mestizo and
U.S. influences that exists in a state of
"reconciled conflict." Its aim is
communication. Artists included are
Malaquias Montoya, Rupert Garcia, Manuel
Hernandez, Esteban Villa, Robert Gomez,
Harvey Tarango, Mary Helen Castro, Eduardo
Carrillo, Graciela Carrillo, and "Los Four":
Carlos Almaraz, Robert de la Rocha, Judithe
Hernandez, Gilbert Lujan and Frank Romero.

Gonzales, Jesse

4314 Arts Council Center for the Arts of Greater
Lansing, Lansing, MI. Raza fine arts
festival. Festival program, 1978. English.

AN: This festival program mentions Jose
Narezo's mural at the Holland National Guard
Armory, Grand Rapids; includes a statement
of the Raza Art/Media Collective, Inc.; the
philosophy of artists Zaragosa Vargas and S.
Kaneta Kosiba-Vargas; and profiles of
exhibiting artists George Vargas, Martin
Moreno, Hector Perez, Michael L. Selley,
Jesse Gonzales, Nora Chapa Mendoza, Jesse
Soriano, Jose Luis Narezo.

Gonzales, Mariano

4315 Haines, Bruce J. Gonzales' works are
controlled and full of detail. ANCHORAGE
DAILY NEWS, (May 23, 1980). English.

AN: Positive review of an exhibit titled
THE HEAD TASTES BEST by Mariano Gonzales.
Born in El Paso, Texas but reared in Alaska,
Gonzales' works in various media from
drawings and paintings to metals, ivory,
enamel and plastics. The critic praises the
artist for his "volatile intricacy" and his
fusion of materials "always with craft and
finesse". Includes reproductions of two
paintings.

4316 McCullom, Pat. Gonzales: his paintings are
like hieroglyphs. ANCHORAGE TIMES, (June
25, 1978), p. I, 3. English.

AN: Mariano Gonzales born in El Paso
Texas, reared in Anchorage and trained at
the Rhode Island School of Design has a
developing reputation as an artist from the
far north. This positive review is for an
exhibit of paintings, jewelry and metal work
pieces. Gonzales' paintings are heavily
saturated with subconscious symbolism and
his sculptures generally feature mechanical,
movable parts.

Gonzales, Rodolfo (Corky)

4317 De la Rocha, Roberto. [Untitled woodcuts].
CON SAFOS, no. 7 (Winter 1971), p. 12-13.

Gonzales, Tomas

4318 Greenberg, David; Smith, Kathryn; and
Teacher, Stuart. Megamurals & supergraphics:
big art. Philadelphia, PN: Running Press,
1977. English.

AN: A full-color picture book of murals
throughout the United States. Chicano murals
include Michael Rios (San Francisco),
Mujeres Muralistas (San Francisco), Leonard
Castellanos and Tomas Gonzales with others
(Los Angeles), Los Artes Guadalupanos de
Aztlan (New Mexico), Willie Herron (Los
Angeles), Toltecas en Aztlan (San Diego),
David Botello (Los Angeles), David Lopez and
Arizona Mara Gang (Los Angeles), Vatos de
Maravilla (Los Angeles), Carlito Gaegos (Los
Angeles), Gil Hernandez (Los Angeles), Wayne
[Alaniz] Healy (Los Angeles).

Gonzalez, Abel

4319 De Marroquin, Moron. Denver Harbor artists.
LA PRENSA, (June 2, 1978). Spanish.

AN: Commentary on two exhibitions. THE
DENVER HARBOR ARTISTS includes information
on paintings by Lupe Aguirre, Josie Mendoza
and Abel Gonzalez--all from Houston. The
solo show MAGIC BLANCA featured the work of
Brownsville, Texas artist Jorge Truan.
Truan's work is mystical and visionary.

Gonzalez, Crispin

4320 Art Gallery, California State University,
Long Beach and Lujan, Gilbert Sanchez
"Magu". El arte del pocho. Exhibit brochure,
October 1968. English.

AN: Information about Southern
California artists John Deheras, Marcus
Villagran, Roberto de la Rocha, Santos
Zuniga, Crispin Gonzales, Richard Martinez,
Jesus Gutierrez, Ed Oropeza, Pete Mendez,
David Ramirez, Gilbert Sanchez Lujan, Willie
Hernandez, Art Ponce, Carmen Tostado, Al
Almeida, David Ceja, Robert E. Chavez,
Thomas A. Ferriera. All art students,
graduates, or faculty.

Gonzalez Dodson, Nora

4321 Goldman, Shifra M. Chicana artists at work.
ARRIBA, [n.d.], p. 3+. English.

AN: Excerpt of a longer article on the
Texas women's group Mujeres Artistas del
Suroeste (MAS). Integral to the group are
artists Santa Barraza, Nora Gonzalez-Dodson,
Alicia Arredondo, Maria Flores, Sylvia
Orozco, and Modesta Trevino.

4322 Goldman, Shifra M. Women artists of Texas:
MAS = More + Artists + Women = MAS.
CHISMEARTE, no. 7 (January 1981), p. 21-22.
English.

AN: History of Texas Chicana women
artists' organization, Mujeres Artistas del
Suroeste (MAS), co-founded in 1977 by Santa
Barraza and Nora Gonzalez-Dodson in the
framework of the burgeoning feminist art
movement, particularly Women and Their Work
of Texas. Brief history of Chicano politics
and the corresponding art movement of
southern and central Texas. In addition to
Barraza and Gonzalez-Dodson, Alicia
Arredondo, Modesta Trevino, and Maria Flores
are considered. Illustrated.

4323 HEMBRA: HERMANAS EN MOVIMIENTO BROTANDO
RAICES DE AZTLAN (University of Texas,
Austin). (Spring 1976).

AN: Raul Valdez, drawing, p. 3; Carolina
Flores, drawing, p. 5; Maria Flores,
photograph, pp. 7, 11, 30; M.E.
Secrest-Ramirez, drawing, p. 12; Amacio
Zarate, drawing, p. 15; Santa Barraza,
drawings, pp. 16, 17, 18, 26, 32; Nora
Gonzales-Dodson, painting, p. 19; Gilberto
Cardenas, photograph, pp. 22, 28; Nanci de
los Santos, photograph, p. 23, 29; Amado
Maurilio Pena, Jr. p. 31.

4324 Orozco, Irma. Women & their work. PARA LA
GENTE, Vol. 1, no. 4 (October 1977), p. 12.
English.

AN: Illustrated story about "Women &
Their Work" festival in Austin, Texas,
Oct-Dec 1977. Photographers Maria Flores and
Teresina Guerra, Santa Barraza, Nora
Gonzalez Dodson, Sylvia Orozco, and Modesta
Trevino exhibited.

4325 Orozco, Sylvia. Las mujeres - Chicana
artists come into their own. MOVING ON, Vol.
2, no. 3 (May 1978), p. 14-16. English.

AN: Illustrated feature prepared by
artist Sylvia Orozco on the founding of
Mujeres Artistas del Suroeste in Austin,
September 1977. Artworks and statements by
Nora Gonzalez Dodson, Maria Flores, Modesta
Trevino, Santa Barraza, as well as musicians
and singers.

4326 Xochil Art and Culture Center, Mission, TX.
Besame mucho. Exhibition invitation, 1979.
English.

AN: Invitation to exhibit of Texas
artists from Mujeres Artistas del Suroeste
(MAS): Mary Ann Anguiano, Alicia Arredondo,
Santa Barraza, Nora Gonzales-Dodson, Maria
Flores, Carolina Flores, Mary Ann Ambray
Gonzales, Sylvia Orozco, Nancy de los
Santos, Modesta Barbina Trevino.
Illustrated.

Gonzalez, Helen

4327 Las muralistas del barrio. CHISMEARTE, no. 2
(Winter, Spring, 1977), p. 48-49. English.

AN: Brief announcement about a Chicana
artists' organization formed in Fresno,
California which started work on a
billboard-like mural, 60x8 feet on the theme
of women. The mural received funding through
Fresno's La Brocha del Valle. About fifteen
women are involved, including Helen Gonzalez
and Cecelia Risco.

Gonzalez, Jesse

4328 El calendario hispano de Michigan, 1981.
Stanton, MI: Montcalm Intermediate School
District and Nuestras Artes de Michigan,
1981. English.

AN: Months of historical calendar
illustrated with art works by George Vargas,
Nora Chapa Mendoza, Jesse Gonzalez, Julio
Perazza(Puerto Rican), Hector Valdez, Pamela
M. Gonzalez, Isabell Escojico (7-year-old
child), Jose Narezo, Martin Moreno, Laurie
Mendoza Psarianos, Rosa Maria Arenas.

Gonzalez, Jesse (cont.)

4329 Nora Mendoza: pintora de ascendencia
     mexicana triunfa en los EE. UU. BUENHOGAR,
     (May 1979), p. 7. Spanish.

     AN: Profile of Texas-born Nora Mendoza
     of Michigan, a painter of abstractions in
     acrylic. She is an active member of many
     Detroit and Michigan organizations,
     including Nuestras Artes de Michigan which
     she co-founded with Jorge Vargas, Martin
     Moreno and Jessie Gonzalez.

Gonzalez, Joe L.

4330 Diaz, Katherine A. Art is business: an
     interview with Joe L. Gonzalez. CAMINOS,
     Vol. 2, no. 5 (October 1981), p. 21-22.
     English.

     AN: Business advice to the artist and to
     the collector from the owner of the two Goez
     art galleries in Los Angeles. How to
     merchandise or buy art as a good investment.

4331 Nevarez, Joe R. Chicano art blooms in barrio
     warehouse. LOS ANGELES TIMES, (December 26,
     1974), p. I, 32. English.

     AN: Former meat packing warehouse
     transformed into Goez Art Studios by Joe and
     John Gonzalez. Exhibiting David Negron,
     Eddie Martinez, David Lopez (Hollywood
     scenic artists) and Roberto Arenivar. Lists
     activities of the gallery: exhibits, murals,
     restoration.

Gonzalez, John

4332 Kushner, Sam. It was a meat market in East
     L.A. LOS ANGELES FREE PRESS, Vol. 11, no. 34
     (August 23, 1974), p. 17. English.

     AN: Data on the formation of Goez
     Gallery by John Gonzalez and David Botello
     in 1970. Created in what once was a meat
     market in the East Los Angeles barrio, Goez
     became an important showcase for Chicano
     art.

4333 Nevarez, Joe R. Chicano art blooms in barrio
     warehouse. LOS ANGELES TIMES, (December 26,
     1974), p. I, 32. English.

     AN: Former meat packing warehouse
     transformed into Goez Art Studios by Joe and
     John Gonzalez. Exhibiting David Negron,
     Eddie Martinez, David Lopez (Hollywood
     scenic artists) and Roberto Arenivar. Lists
     activities of the gallery: exhibits, murals,
     restoration.

Gonzalez, Jose G.

4334 59th Street Gallery, St. Louis, MO. Midwest
     Mexican-American art exhibit: Mexico and its
     artists. Exhibition brochure, 1981. English.

     AN: Sponsored by the Sociedad Mexicana
     "Benito Juarez" and the international
     Institute of St. Louis, this three-part
     exhibit includes 1) MEXICO AS SEEN BY HER
     CHILDREN, a bilingual exhibit from Mexico
     traveling under Smithsonian Institution
     auspices, 2) MEXICAN CHILDREN IN THE U.S.A.,
     3) MEXICAN AMERICAN ARTISTS. In the latter
     are included Stephen Capiz (Roseville,
     Minn.), Jose Gonzalez (Chicago), Cesar A.
     Martinez (San Antonio), Ada Medina (Des
     Moines), Nora Chapa Mendoza (West
     Bloomfield, Mich.), Rene David
     Michel-Trapaga (St. Louis), David Munoz
     (Kansas City, Mo.), Jose Luis Narezo (Grand

Rapids, Mich.), Benny Ordonez, Roman
Villarreal (Chicago), Alejandro Romero
(Chicago), Aurelio Diaz "Tekpankalli"
(Chicago), Simon Ybarra (St. Louis).

4335 Canto al pueblo: an anthology of
     experiences. San Antonio, TX: Penca Books,
     1978. English.

     AN: Includes works by: Mario E.
     Castillo, Carlos Rosas, Jose G. Gonzalez,
     Santos Martinez, Gilbert Munoz, Fred Loa,
     Armando Ibanez and others.

4336 MARCH: Movimiento artistico Chicano
     (Mexican-American Art Movement). QUARTERLY,
     (Spring 1976), p. 10. English.

     AN: Brief history of MARCH.
     Illustrations of murals by Ricarco Alonzo,
     Jose Gonzalez, Vicente Mendoza. Ray Patlan.

4337 NATIONAL MURALS NETWORK COMMUNITY
     NEWSLETTER. (Fall 1979). English.

     AN: Reports on mural projects by Fermin
     Coronado working with students in Houston;
     Galeria de la Raza's billboard used as a
     mural surface for changing images; murals
     under the Flor en la Comunidad program of El
     Centro Cultural de la Gente in San Jose,
     California and led by artist Jaime Valadez;
     murals in Grand Rapids and other cities of
     western Michigan; murals by Jose Guerrero
     and others from the Chicago Mural Group; a
     survey of Chicano murals in the Pilsen area
     of Chicago guided by Jose Gonzalez.

Gonzalez, Louis "The Foot"

4338 Calendario de comida 1976. San Francisco,
     CA: Galeria de la Raza, 1976. English.

     AN: Handprinted silkscreen calendar
     consisting of twelve sheets and a cover. The
     work of the following artists is included:
     Ralph Maradiaga, Juanishi Orozco, Francisco
     Camplis, Ruben Guzman, Rodolfo Cuellar,
     Xavier Viramontes, Jose Montoya, Esteban
     Villa, Rene Yanez, Max Garcia and Louis "The
     Foot" Gonzalez, Patricia Rodriguez, and
     Ricardo Favela. All of the above are
     associated with the Galeria de la Raza, or
     the Royal Chicano Air Force of Sacramento,
     CA.

4339 La historia de California, 1977. San
     Francisco, CA: Galeria de la Raza, 1977.
     English.

     AN: Handprinted silkscreen calendar of
     history seen from a Mexican point of view.
     Twelve sheets and a cover. Artists are:
     Ralph Maradiaga, Irene Perez, Louie "The
     Foot" Gonzalez, Max Garcia, Patricia
     Rodriguez, Jose Romero, Esteban Villa,
     Juanishi Orozco, Rodolfo Cuellar, Jose
     Montoya, Xavier Viramontes, Rene Yanez,
     Ricardo Favela, associated with the Galeria
     de la Raza, or the Royal Chicano Air Force
     of Sacramento.

Gonzalez, Mary Ann Ambray

4340 Women artists: forming a Texas network.
Brochure, 1979. English.

AN: Biographic and bibliographic
information on women artists groups from
Austin, Dallas, Houston and San Antonio.
Includes brief history of MAS (Mujeres
Artistas del Suroeste), a list of members,
and biographies of Alicia Arredondo, Santa
Barraza, Mary Ann Ambray Gonzalez, and
Sylvia Orozco.

4341 Xochil Art and Culture Center, Mission, TX.
Besame mucho. Exhibition invitation, 1979.
English.

AN: Invitation to exhibit of Texas
artists from Mujeres Artistas del Suroeste
(MAS): Mary Ann Anguiano, Alicia Arredondo,
Santa Barraza, Nora Gonzales-Dodson, Maria
Flores, Carolina Flores, Mary Ann Ambray
Gonzales, Sylvia Orozco, Nancy de los
Santos, Modesta Barbina Trevino.
Illustrated.

Gonzalez, Pamela M.

4342 El calendario hispano de Michigan, 1981.
Stanton, MI: Montcalm Intermediate School
District and Nuestras Artes de Michigan,
1981. English.

AN: Months of historical calendar
illustrated with art works by George Vargas,
Nora Chapa Mendoza, Jesse Gonzalez, Julio
Perazza(Puerto Rican), Hector Valdez, Pamela
M. Gonzalez, Isabell Escojico (7-year-old
child), Jose Narezo, Martin Moreno, Laurie
Mendoza Psarianos, Rosa Maria Arenas.

Gonzalez, Robert H.

4343 Heymann, Ann W. Robert Gonzalez. ART VOICES
SOUTH, Vol. 3, no. 1 (January, February,
1980), p. 68. English.

AN: Brief resume on art and life of San
Francisco painter. Illustrated.

Gonzalez, Roberto

4344 Cardona, Patricia. Gana adeptos de Museo
Mexicano de San Francisco: Pedro Rodriguez.
UNO MAS UNO, (February 6, 1978), p. 18.
Spanish.

AN: Report and brief history of the
Mexican Museum which opened in 1975 with a
collection of colonial santos. The museum
offers a vista of Mexican culture to people
in the United States. Director Peter
Rodriguez says that Chicano artists Roberto
Gonzalez, Felipe Reyes, Alfredo Arreguin,
Gustavo Rivera, and Carmen Lomas Garza are
some of the best. Illustrated.

4345 Frankenstein, Alfred. An artistic taste of
Mexico in the city. SAN FRANCISCO CHRONICLE,
(November 29, 1975), p. 29. English.

AN: A very favorable review of the
inaugural exhibit at the Mexican Museum. The
opening show was a panoramic view of Mexican
art including pre-Hispanic, colonial, folk
art and fine art. Among the Mexican American
artists presented were Roberto Gonzalez,
Raul Mora and Gustavo Rivera.

4346 San Antonio Museum Association, San Antonio,
TX. Visiones nuevas en Tejas/new visions in
Texas. Exhibtion catalog, 1979. English.

AN: Supplementary regional catalog for
the exhibit RAICES ANTIGUAS/VISIONES NUEVAS;
ANCIENT ROOTS/NEW VISIONS. Illustrations for
works by George Cisneros, Francisco (Frank)
Fajardo, Robert Gonzalez, Cesar Augusto
Martinez, Roland Mazuca, Guillermo Pulido,
Felipe Reyes, Jesus (Jesse) Trevino.

GORDO [comic strip]

4347 De Lappe, Pele. Gordo plus folk art.
PEOPLE'S WORLD, Vol. 42, no. 41 (October 13,
1979), p. 10. English.

AN: Announcement of an exhibit at the
Mexican Museum of Gus Arriola's syndicated
comic strip "Gordo." Arizona-born Arriola
was an animator for Columbia and MGM
cartoons until he created "Gordo" in 1941.
Illustrated.

4348 Morch, Albert. Mexican art through a
cartoonist's eyes. SAN FRANCISCO EXAMINER,
(September 24, 1979), p. 28. English.

AN: Review of "GORDO'S WORLD" and the
paintings of Alexander Maldonado, an
exhibition at the Mexican Museum.
Biographical information on Gustavo Montano
Arriola, creator of the Gordo cartoon in
1941. The exhibit conceived and designed by
the San Diego Museum of Art, had
representative blow-ups of the strip along
with artifacts. Maldonado, a self-taught
artist started painting at age 60. His
canvases embrace a fascination with towers,
unique buildings, underground cities and
skylines from an imagined urban environment.

Gorena, Xavier

4349 Contemporary Arts Museum, Houston, TX. Fire!
An exhibition of 100 Texas artists.
Exhibition brochure, 1979. English.

AN: Includes eleven Chicano artists.
Unfortunately, not illustrated, though a
checklist of works is included. Mel Casas,
Carmen Lomas Garza, Xavier Gorena, Luis
Jimenez, Cesar Martinez, Guillermo Z.
Pulido, Philip Renteria, Jose L. Rivera, Joe
Rodriguez, George Truan, Juan B. Vela.
Introduction by James Surls. Statements by
the artists.

4350 Contemporary Arts Museum, Houston, TX and
Martinez, Santos G., Jr. Mexican movie
posters. Exhibition invitation, 1979.
English.

AN: Invitation to an exhibit of posters
primarily from the collecttion of Enrique
Flores and Xavier Gorena of Xochil Art
Center, Mission, Texas. Martinez considers
the posters monumental, with expressive
qualities that have influenced Chicano
poster makers like the Royal Chicano Air
Force, and Rupert Garcia, and Texas artists
like Luis Jimenez, Jesse Trevino and Cesar
Martinez. One illustration. Introduction by
guest curator Santos G. Martinez, Jr. (See
Rupert Garcia's essay in the exhibition
catalog: POSTERS FROM THE GOLDEN AGE OF
MEXICAN CINEMA, for another point of view).

Gorena, Xavier (cont.)

4351 Estudios Rio: gallery of contemporary arts and crafts. Exhibition catalog, 1976. English.

AN: Catalog including identification, portraits and works of participating artists: Joe Bova, Enrique Flores, Carmen Lomas Garza, Xavier Gorena, Erik Gronborg, Lucas Hinojosa, Ben Holland, Kris Hotvedt, William Kaars-Sijpesteijn, Cesar Martinez, Chris Mende, Roberto Mungia, Steve Reynolds, Vicente Rodriguez, William Wilhelmi.

4352 Galeria de la Raza/Studio 24, San Francisco, CA. Ajo, granadas y tres flores. Exhibition announcement, 1981.

AN: Announcement for an exhibition featuring Ruben Trejo, sculpture (Spokane, Washington), Cesar A. Martinez, paintings (San Antonio, Texas), Xavier Gorena, paper cut-outs (Mission, Texas).

4353 Galeria de la Raza/Studio 24, San Francisco, CA. Images of the Southwest. Exhibition catalog, 1977. English.

AN: Invitation/catalog for an exhibit including Rudy M. Fernandez(Utah), Enrique Flores(Texas), Xavier Gorena(Texas), C.A.[Cesar] Martinez(Texas), Santos Martinez, Jr.(Texas), Pedro Rodriguez(Texas), Arnold Trujillo(New Mexico). Block prints, paper cut-outs, drawings, photographs, copper enamels, and sculpture were shown. Five illustrations.

4354 Giepen, Hubert. Xochil Art Center taking big steps. PROGRESS, Vol. 10, no. 1 (August 12, 1981). English.

AN: Brief history of the founding and expansion plans of the Xochil Art Institute in Mission which includes an old theatre, workshop. studio, and gallery. Artists Xavier Gorena and Enrique Flores are responsible for the development.

4355 Thwaites, Lynette. Art on the border. COMMUNITY ARTS NEWSLETTER, Vol. 3, no. 3 (July 1981). English.

AN: The Centro Cultural de la Raza has been a pioneer of intercultural activity between Mexico and the United States in the San Diego area. The Arizona Commission on the Arts has promoted numerous exchanges and publishes a bilingual quarterly bulletin. In Mission, Texas, Xavier Gorena of the Xochil Art Center is forging ties with Mexico City.

Government and Art

4356 Barnes, Peter. Fringe benefits of a depression: bringing back the WPA. NEW REPUBLIC, Vol. 172, no. 11 (March 15, 1975), p. 19-21. English.

AN: A well-researched and comprehensive analysis of the CETA (Comprehensive Employment and Training Act) impact on public art in San Francisco. Material on Chicano-Latino murals in the Mission district. Includes viewpoints by artist-activists Patricia Rodriguez, Mike Rios, and writer Roberto Vargas. Important compendium on funding sources of various neighborhood art programs stressing their value as community assets.

4357 CHICANO CINEMA NEWSLETTER. Vol. 1, no. 3

(May 1979). English.

AN: Announcements for the U.S. Conference for an Alternative Cinema (N.Y.), a "Nosotros" banquet, application dates for the Film Fund, deadlines for the National Endowment for the Humanities, and criticism of the Hollywood feature film BOULEVARD NIGHTS.

4358 CHICANO CINEMA NEWSLETTER. Vol. 1, no. 1 (December 1978). English.

AN: Reports on activities of Chicano filmmakers in producing films, meeting with organizations like the American Film Institute, the Hispanic Task Force of the National Endowment for the Arts, the WNET Independent Documentary Film Fund. International film news also included.

4359 Holliday-Abbott, Anne. Suitcase is 2nd home for arts liaison. ARIZONA DAILY STAR, (June 18, 1981), p. H-3. English.

AN: Arizona artist Louis LeRoy who paints, makes prints, and does assemblage is also a regional representative for the National Endowment for the Arts in Arizona, New Mexico, Colorado, Utah, and Wyoming. LeRoy has always been an "advocate of people being proud of their ethnic backgrounds." He feels artists can be self-supporting without commercializing.

4360 Inner City Mural Program. Glendale, CA: Los Angeles County Dept. of Parks and Recreation, [ca. 1974]. English.

AN: Brief history and philosophy of the Inner City Mural Program from June 1, 1973 to May 31, 1974, when it was sponsored by the Cultural Arts Section of the Los Angeles County Department of Parks and Recreation, and coordinated by Lukman Glasgow. Artists Judithe Hernandez and Frank Romero included. 20 illustrations, some in color.

4361 McClellan, Bill. Army of volunteers paints a little history in Phoenix. PHOENIX GAZETTE, (April 20, 1977). English.

AN: Adolfo "El Zarco" Guerrero with 100 residents from the Duppa Villa Housing Project completes a mural funded by the Arizona Commission on Arts and Humanities. Guerrero completed six murals, but prefers sculpture.

4362 Mendiville, Miguel and Saavedra-Vela, Pilar. A time for less talk and more action. AGENDA, Vol. 7, no. 5 (September, October, 1977), p. 33-34. English.

AN: The exhibit RAICES Y VISIONES, funded by the National Endowment for the Arts, was composed of more than 100 artworks by Chicano and Latino artists and toured the United States in 1977. The exposition was organized in four sections; artists whose work is influenced or related to Pre-Columbian art, art that explores social and political realities, and works that are more personal and introspective. Gives itinerary and listing of participating artists. Illustrated by photographs of the work of Rudy Trevino, Cesar Martinez, Luis Jimenez from Texas and Larry Fuente from California.

Government and Art (cont.)

4363 New Galeria de la Raza. EL HISPANO, (July 28, 1970), p. 9. English.

   AN: Review of the first exhibit at the Galeria de la Raza at 425 14th St. in San Francisco. The inaugural exhibition featured Esteban Villa, Luis Gutierrez and Luis Cervantes. The new Galeria is sponsored by Casa Hispana de Bellas Artes assisted by San Francisco Art Commission through its Neighborhood Arts Program.

4364 New Mexico Arts Division, Santa Fe, NM. Art in public places. Catalog, 1977-78, p. 9, 11. English.

   AN: Catalog of CETA-funded project. Illustrated murals by Graciela Carrillo of San Francisco, and Gilbert Guzman of Santa Fe.

4365 Pepe and Pepito. SANTA FE NEW MEXICAN, (August 16, 1972), p. A2. English.

   AN: Among the barrio groups receiving funding from the COPAS Cultural Awareness Program of the Model Cities program are Los Artesanos and Los Artes Guadalupanos.

4366 Thwaites, Lynette. Art on the border. COMMUNITY ARTS NEWSLETTER, Vol. 3, no. 3 (July 1981). English.

   AN: The Centro Cultural de la Raza has been a pioneer of intercultural activity between Mexico and the United States in the San Diego area. The Arizona Commission on the Arts has promoted numerous exchanges and publishes a bilingual quarterly bulletin. In Mission, Texas, Xavier Gorena of the Xochil Art Center is forging ties with Mexico City.

Government Funding Sources

4367 Art in public places. Program statement, 1977-78. English.

   AN: Documents an eleven-month program funded by CETA for 21 artists to produce murals, prints and weavings as public art. Includes murals by Gilberto Guzman and Graciela Carrillo-Lopez in Santa Fe. Statements by the artists. Illustrated.

4368 Artist registry financed. RIO GRANDE SUN, (January 17, 1980). English.

   AN: A $15,000 grant received from the National Endowment for the Arts to begin a New Mexico Hispanic Arts Community Outreach project, which will include a central registry of New Mexico Hispanic artists with current resume, documentation of work, and other information. In charge will be artists Estevan Arellano, Albert Baros, and Susan Jamison of the Santa Fe Council for the Arts.

4369 Barnes, Peter. Fringe benefits of a depression: bringing back the WPA. NEW REPUBLIC, Vol. 172, no. 11 (March 15, 1975), p. 19-21. English.

   AN: A well-researched and comprehensive analysis of the CETA (Comprehensive Employment and Training Act) impact on public art in San Francisco. Material on Chicano-Latino murals in the Mission district. Includes viewpoints by artist-activists Patricia Rodriguez, Mike Rios, and writer Roberto Vargas. Important

compendium on funding sources of various neighborhood art programs stressing their value as community assets.

4370 Case study: Centro de Artistas Chicanos, Sacramento, California. Washington, D.C.: Neighborhood Art Program National Organizing Committee, n.d. English.

   AN: In various regions of the Southwest, local artists have started Centros Culturales "whose primary purpose is the proliferation and safeguarding of Chicano art and culture." This case study presents pertinent information on the Centro de Artistas Chicanos founded in 1972 in Sacramento, California. It spells out the philosophy, goals, programs, components and management structure of the R.C.A.F. (Royal Chicano Air Force) and Centro de Artistas. A useful and important document. Illustrated.

4371 Espinosa, Juan. Carlos Sandoval completing mural in Mexico. LA CUCARACHA, (June 1980). English.

   AN: Details how Carlos Sandoval, Denver Chicano artist was invited by the Mexican government to paint mural in Zihuantanejo, Mexico. The mayor of the Mexican town states, "this work represents an expression of two pueblos who want to expand their relations, as a product of one common people." Illustrated with photograph of Carlos Sandoval and one preliminary drawing of the mural.

4372 Galeria de la Raza/Studio 24, San Francisco, CA. Mundos perdidos/lost worlds. Exhibition invitation, 1978. English.

   AN: Invitatiion to a multi-media exhibit from a cultural workshop inside Lompoc Federal Correctional Institution by Leonard Castellanos, National Endowment for the Arts Artist in Residence. Included are murals and tattoo documentation, and silkscreen posters.

4373 Goll, Dave. More than handball on this court. MENLO-ATHERTON RECORDER, (May 23, 1978), p. 15. English.

   AN: Emmanuel Montoya is painting a mural on African and Chicano unity at the handball court of Fair Oaks Community Center in Redwood City, CA. Montoya is working because of CETA (Comprehensive Employment Training Act) funds. Illustrated.

4374 Gustaitis, Rasa. Arts imperiled. PEOPLE'S WORLD, Vol. 44, no. 26 (June 27, 1981), p. 10. English.

   AN: A decade ago the San Francisco Neighborhood Arts Program received new commitments from the National Endowment for the Arts to fund local, unknown and chronically poor neighborhood artists. With these funds, murals were painted on the walls and other art events were created with young people, minorities, old people. This program piloted the Expansion Arts Program of NEA. These funds are now being cut, especially with the Reagan administration's proposed cuts for 1981 and 1982.

Government Funding Sources (cont.)

4375 Johnson, Richard. The mural at Zihuatanejo.
EMPIRE MAGAZINE, (October 12, 1980).
English.

AN: Denver artist Carlos M. Sandoval is
said to be the first Chicano commissioned by
the Mexican government to paint a mural in
Mexico. Sandoval's mural is on the facade of
the public library in Zihuatanejo. Its theme
is unity and synthesis and its title is
MESTIZO. Article contains much information
on mural act ivity in Denver, Colorado. Well
illustrated with color and black and white
photographs.

4376 San Francisco's neighborhood arts program.
San Francisco, CA: San Francisco Art
Commission, [1971]. English.

AN: Booklet in pictures describing the
activities underwritten by the city and
county of San Francisco, the National
Endowment for the Arts, the San Francisco
Foundation, and the Zellerbach Family Fund.
The interracial, interethnic staff includes
Rene Yanez. Organizations listed are Galeria
de la Raza, Galeria de la Comunidad, Galeria
de las Bellas Artes, Galeria de las
Pinturas, Galeria de la Musica, Galeria de
la Poesia, Galeria de la Instruccion.

4377 Smith, Arva. CEU unveils Chicano mural.
DESERET NEWS, (May 13, 1978), p. 12A.
English.

AN: On Cinco de Mayo 1978, a 14x5-ft.
mural was unveiled in the library of the
College of Eastern Utah. Painted by Salt
Lake City artist Alfred de Avila, the mural
focuses on incidents from Mexican and
Chicano history including a panel on Carbon
County's coal mining industry. Mural was a
bicentennial community art project.
Illustrated with photograph of artist and
section of mural.

4378 U.S. Department of Health, Education, and
Welfare. Salud, dinero y amor y tiempo para
gozarlos. Exhibit brochure, n.d. English.

AN: Brochure announcement with statement
by Joseph A. Califano H.E. W. Secretary and
list of participating artists.

4379 Werley, Lenora. Murals give young artists
community pride, sculptor says. YUMA DAILY
SUN, (February 4, 1981). English.

AN: Mesa, Arizona sculptor Adolfo
"Zarco" Guerrero feels murals give young
people pride in their community. Guerrero is
part of the Xicanindio Artist Coalition that
is CETA-contracted to run summer art
programs for high school students.

4380 Zahn, Debbie. Citywide murals: outlook bleak
for funding of art work by Chicanos.
FORTY-NINER, (May 4, 1976). English.

AN: The Los Angeles City Council decides
to terminate the 1974 program, Citywide
Murals, which provided funds for Chicano
artists. Description of Joe Bravo's 2000 sq
ft mural at the Wilmington Recreation
Center, painted with a team, which makes a
positive statement against gang warfare.
Illustrated.

Graffiti

4381 Arte del varrio. San Jose: A.T.M

Communications, Inc., Nos. 1-3, 1979-81..
English.

AN: Large format color illustrated
albums of "Varrio art." Includes examples of
tattoo art, placasos (graffiti) and barrio
murals.

4382 Barrio graffiti. In Castaneda-Shular,
Ybarra-Frausto, and Sommers, eds. LITERATURA
CHICANA. Englewood Cliffs, NJ:
Prentice-Hall, 1972. Spanish.

AN: Drawings and explanations of Chicano
graffiti that originated in the Pachuco era.

4383 Boettner, Jack. Youths help in fight against
graffiti: muralist fights spray cans with
brushes. LOS ANGELES TIMES [Orange County
edition], (May 26, 1979), p. II, 12-13.
English.

AN: Illustrated and descriptive story
about Orange County painter Emigdio Vasquez
working on a series of murals with youth.
Locations of murals by the group,
biographical information about Vasquez, and
his statement about art are given.
Illustrated.

4384 Bright, John; Bright, Mura; and Castellanos,
Leonard. "Placas": graffiti and the
environment. Venice, CA: Environmental
Communications, 1974. English.

AN: Annotated slide catalog of Chicano
graffiti on walls, murals, and tattoos,
compiled by staff of Mechicano Art Center.

4385 Cesaretti, Gusmano. Street writers: a guided
tour of Chicano graffiti. Los Angeles, CA:
Acrobat Books, 1975. English.

AN: A photographic essay of graffiti and
Mexican/Chicano peoples in Los Angeles.
Introductions by author to each geographical
part of the city.

4386 Chicano art: East Los Angeles graffiti. LA
GENTE DE AZTLAN, Vol. 6, no. 5 (May 1976),
p. 5. English.

AN: The particular forms and styles of
Chicano graffiti are affirmed as stemming
from the social conditions of the barrio
circa 1930. Gangs and their social world are
examined as contributors to the creation of
graffiti, tattoos and "calo," a dialect of
Chicano Spanish.

4387 Chicano graffiti. LA GENTE DE AZTLAN, Vol.
3, no. 3 (January 24, 1973), p. 4. English.

AN: Short article on the forms,
techniques and meaning of Chicano graffiti.

4388 Davis, Alonzo, ed. Los Angeles street
graphics. Los Angeles, CA: Brockman Gallery
Productions, [ca. 1975]. English.

AN: Portfolio of art in public places.
Includes Charles Felix (murals), Leo Limon
(mural), Charles Almaraz (billboard mural),
Johnny Alvarez (mural), Mexican artist
Gonzalo Duran, and graffiti.

Graffiti (cont.)

4389 De Leon, Hector. Barrio art--the community's reflection of itself. AGENDA, Vol. 9, no. 4 (July, August, 1979), p. 7, 38. English.

AN: Barrio art is communal, its forms such as posters, pamphlets, graffiti, and murals have an educative function. Its style is eclectic and its content is stark and direct. Through various forms of graphic representation, people in the barrio have reappropriated art forms to give meaning to their daily experiences. Includes nine illustrations of barrio art.

4390 Fortune, Thomas. Mural will mirror barrio pride. LOS ANGELES TIMES, (December 27, 1974), p. II, 1, 8. English.

AN: Artist Sergio O'Cadiz has been painting a 625-foot concrete wall constructed to separate old Colonia Juarez and a new Anglo housing complex in Fountain Valley (Orange County), Calif., to eliminate graffiti. The mural depicts the barrio's history: Mexican Americans try on white masks for Anglo acceptance. Other scenes will show the arrival of the surrounding city, and resident's awareness of their Chicano identity. O'Cadiz is assisted by 40 students from surrounding colleges and universities. Illustrated.

4391 Graffiti gone: murals in full bloom. PHOENIX GAZETTE, (April 13, 1974). English.

AN: Mural explosion at Estrada Courts Housing Project in Los Angeles led by C.W. Felix. Estimates 60 murals in East Los Angeles. Illustrated.

4392 Johnston, Tracy. La vida loca. NEW WEST MAGAZINE, (January 29, 1979), p. 38-46. English.

AN: A journalistic account of barrio lifestyles composed from conversations with young Cholos in Los Angeles. Amid poverty, unemployment, drug abuse and familial disintegration, codes of group solidarity and rituals of connection occur. Information on urban Chicano forms of self expression such as mascaras (chola make up), tattoos and graffiti. Well illustrated with photographs.

4393 Kahn, David. Chicano street murals: people's art in the East Los Angeles barrio. AZTLAN, Vol. 6, no. 1 (Spring 1975), p. 117-121. Bibliography. English.

AN: A study of Chicano mural painting starting with the 1970 mural at UCLA by Eduardo Carrillo, Ramses Noriega, Sergio Hernandez, and Saul Solache. Deals with mural symbols, graffiti, and works by John Alverer [sic] and Willie Herron's murals in the Ramona Gardens Housing Project.

4394 Lowrider: arte del varrio. A.T.M. Communications, Inc., 1979. English.

AN: Issue of LOWRIDER Magazine dedicated to drawings and paintings by "cholos" sent in to the editor for publication. Good example of a popular art form by largely self-taught neighborhood youth, with a distinctive style and symbolism. Related to graffiti and tattoos. Most images are of lowrider cars, young women and men.

4395 Lowrider: arte del varrio. San Jose, CA: A.T.M. Communications, 1980. English.

AN: Second issue of LOWRIDER Magazine dedicated to drawings and pantings by "cholos" sent in to the editor for publication.

4396 Mirando tras las rejas [graffiti]. DE COLORES, Vol. 3, no. 1 (1976), p. 28. Bilingual.

4397 Orozco, Sylvia. Chicano tattoos, dibujos de mano - an expression of Chicano life. ARRIBA, Vol. 1, no. 2 (August 1980), p. 9. English.

AN: Detailing the barrio tradition of handmade tatoos, the article describes techniques of application, subject matter and tatoo art traditions. Illustrated with one photograph by author.

4398 Ortega, Gil. The 50's and other assorted Chicano graffiti. La Habra, CA: s.n., 1981. English.

AN: Album of caricatures of barrio types; black and white drawings in six categories: The Parties and Dances, Schooldays, Oldtime Lowriders, Refine, Los Veteranos, Los Vatos. Some drawings accompanied by commentary.

4399 Pimentel, Ricardo. Graffiti: expression or scourge? FRESNO BEE, (February 23, 1981), p. Metro, B1+. English.

AN: A rapid review of graffiti symbols, their meaning and social context. Commentary by various young people explaining the value, style and meanings of plaqueasos (spray painted graffiti). Some Chicano artists like Bob Cruz, director of La Brocha del Valle, see mural painting as a positive alternative to graffiti art forms. Article also provides views of local businessmen to the graffiti phenomenon.

4400 Pomona College Gallery of Montgomery Art Center, Claremont, CA; Allikas, Bob; and Glickman, Hal. Chicano graffiti: the signatures and symbols of Mexican-American youth. Exhibition catalog, [1970]. English.

AN: Catalog of exhibit based on photographs of Los Angeles graffiti.

4401 Rafas. Social comment in barrio pop [drawing]. CON SAFOS, no. 7 (Winter 1971), p. 22.

4402 Rafas. Social comment in barrio pop [drawing]. CON SAFOS, no. 8 (1972), p. 34.

4403 Rafas. A social comment in Chicano pop [drawing]. CON SAFOS, Vol. 1, no. 4 (1969), p. 10.

4404 Rafas. Social commentary in Chicano pop art [drawing]. CON SAFOS, Vol. 2, no. 5 (1970), p. 31.

4405 Rafas. Social commentary in Chicano pop art [drawing]. CON SAFOS, no. 6 (Summer 1970), p. 43.

Graffiti (cont.)

4406 Rodriguez, Patricia, ed. Selected readings on Chicano art. Berkeley, CA: Chicano Studies Department, University of California, 1977. English.

AN: Compendium of mechanically reproduced articles on Chicano and Latin American art prepared for Chicano Studies 130--Introduction to Chicano Art. Includes sections on Mexican Muralists in the U.S: Contemporary Chicano Art; Views on Chicano Art; Chicano Artists; Pinto Art: Raza Murals and Muralists; Plaqueasos (Graffiti); Chicana Artists: Art, Politics and the Community, Two Historical Examples: Cuba and Chile; Chicano Art Reproductions, 557 pp.

4407 Romotsky, Jerry and Romotsky, Sally R. Chicano graffiti. Venice, CA: Environmental Communications, 1974. English.

AN: Annotated slide catalog with text and glossary of terms. Well illustrated.

4408 Romotsky, Jerry and Romotsky, Sally R. Los Angeles barrio calligraphy. Los Angeles, CA: Dawson's Book Shop, 1976. English.

AN: Deals with visual quality, styles, and meanings of Los Angeles "placas," or graffiti. Well illustrated.

4409 Romotsky, Jerry and Romotsky, Sally R. Placas and murals. ARTS IN SOCIETY, Vol. 2, no. 1 (Summer, Fall , 1974), p. 286-299. English.

AN: Details how Chicano muralists have recognized the aesthetics of graffiti and incorporated them into their murals. Among the earliest to do so were Lucille Grijalva and Willie Herron. Illustrated.

4410 Romotsky, Sally R. and Romotsky, Jerry. Plaqueaso on the wall. HUMAN BEHAVIOR, Vol. 4, no. 5 (May 1975), p. 64-69. English.

AN: Detailed discussion of meaning of Los Angeles Chicano graffiti. Many illustrations, one in color.

4411 Saenz, John. Felix completes art project: artist's murals mask East LA graffitti [sic]. EAST LOS ANGELES TRIBUNE, (November 30, 1972), p. A-4. English.

AN: Charles Felix is doing murals as part of a community beautification "Wall Project" to cover graffiti. His present project is a series of murals intended to make Whittier Blvd. into a street gallery. Illustrated.

4412 San Francisco Museum of Modern Art, San Francisco, CA and Pearlstein, Howard. Aesthetics of graffiti. Exhibition catalog, 1978. English.

AN: Graffiti are defined as any coherently-intended presence written, scratched, painted, engraved, printed, pasted or otherwise impressed in a public place. Graffiti have been incorporated into works by artists. In this catalog, works by Chicano artists Carlos Almaraz, Wilfred Castano, Judithe Hernandez, Gilbert Lujan, Gustavo Rivera, Frank Romero, John M. Valadez, Victor M. Valle, Xavier Viramontes - as well as many Latino and non-Latino artist, appear.

4413 Teatro de la Tierra Morena, Santa Cruz, CA.

Fuego en Aztlan: a Chicano arts show. Exhibition brochure, 1980. English.

AN: Folder of information on the exhibition curated by Cruz Zamarron and Eduardo Carrillo. Exhibiting artists were: Justina Avila, Terry Benitez, Eduardo Carrillo, Hernando Chavez, Bob Cruz, Juanita Estrada, Juana Franklin, Sal Garcia, Leticia Hernandez, David "Sir Loco" Jimenez, Raoul Mendez, Vicente Mendez, Maria V. Pinedo, Gonzalo Placencia, Ramon Rodriguez, Roberto Salas, George Silva and Cruz Zamarron. A special feature was a live tattoo demonstration entitled "Walking Art".

4414 Varda, Agnes. Mur murs/mural murals on the wall ... Film, Cine Tamaris, Paris, 1980. English.

AN: Full length documentary film produced for French television; also available with English subtitles. Deals impressionistically with the murals and muralists of Los Angeles. Included are Wayne Alaniz Healy, David Botello, Willie Herron, Manuel Cruz, Judy Baca, the murals in Venice, CA, graffiti - among others. Color.

Grajeda, Dolores

4415 Mills House Visual Arts Complex, Garden Grove, CA. Menudo: artistas latinos de Orange County. Exhibit invitation, 1980. English.

AN: Invitation to an exhibit organized for the first anniversary of Artistas Latinos de Orange County including Delores Grajeda, William Hernandez, Marylee Montano, Patricia Murillo, Irene Ramos, Juan Ramos, Ricardo Serrato, Miguel Shanahan, Arthur Valenzuela, Benjamin Valenzuela, Jack Vargas, Alonzo Whitney, Emigdio Vasquez, Susana Zaccagnino, and Mexican artist Artemio Sepulveda.

4416 Orange Co. Library. El Modena Branch. Empanada: a tasty Mexican group art exhibit filled with a variety of digestable treats. Exhibition catalog, [1979]. English.

AN: Catalog of an exhibit by 15 artists: Dolores Grajeda, William Hernandez-M., Marylee Montano, Patricia Murillo, Eduardo Navarro, Susana A. Zaccagnino, Esau Quiroz, Juan Elias Ramos, Ricardo M. Serrato, Benjamin Valenzuela, Emigdio C. Vasquez, Arthur Valenzuela, Jack Vargas, Alonso Whitney, and Mexican artist Artemio Sepulveda living in Orange County. Brief profiles of the artists.

4417 Santa Ana Public Library, Newhope Branch, Santa Ana, CA. Artistas latinos de Orange County. Exhibition brochure, 1979. English.

AN: Exhibit of six artists: Dolores Grajeda, Eduardo Navarro, Arthur Valenzuela, Benjamin Valenzuela, Emigdio Vasquez, Susana A. Zaccagnino.

Grand Rapids, MI

4418 Grand Rapids Jr. College, MI. Dedication "El Centro de Vida". Brochure, 1977. English.

AN: Brochure announcing unveiling of a mural by painter Jose Narezo working with a team of young people.

Grand Rapids, MI (cont.)

4419 NATIONAL MURALS NETWORK COMMUNITY
NEWSLETTER. (Fall 1979). English.

AN: Reports on mural projects by Fermin
Coronado working with students in Houston;
Galeria de la Raza's billboard used as a
mural surface for changing images; murals
under the Flor en la Comunidad program of El
Centro Cultural de la Gente in San Jose,
California and led by artist Jaime Valadez;
murals in Grand Rapids and other cities of
western Michigan; murals by Jose Guerrero
and others from the Chicago Mural Group; a
survey of Chicano murals in the Pilsen area
of Chicago guided by Jose Gonzalez.

Grandee, Joe Ruiz

4420 Samuels, Peggy and Samuels, Harold. Grandee,
Joe Ruiz. In: THE ILLUSTRATED BIOGRAPHICAL
ENCYCLOPEDIA OF ARTISTS OF THE AMERICAN
WEST. NY: Doubleday, 1976, p. 193. English.

AN: Brief biography of third generation
Texan, Western painter of history, military,
portrait subjects and illustrator living in
Arlington, TX where his collection of
Western artifacts is at the "Joe Grandee
Gallery and Museum of the Old West." 1974
one person retrospective in Washington, DC.

Grape Boycott
USE: Boycotts

Graphics

4421 11 reproduccion - significacion politica:
arte fotocopia. Exhibition invitation, 1979.
English.

AN: Invitation to an international
exhibit of photocopy artists from Europe,
Latin America and the United States.
Includes Rene Yanez of San Francisco.

4422 450 anos del pueblo chicano/450 years of
Chicano history in pictures. Albuquerque,
NM: Chicano Communications Center, 1976.
English.

AN: A pictorial history of Mexico,
Mexican Americans and Chicanos through
photographs and art works. P. 138 is
dedicated to murals, graphics, cartoons and
photographs from Chicago and the Southwest,
but other murals, graphics, cartoons and
photographs by Chicanos and non-Chicanos are
scattered throughout. In addition, 450 ANOS
has been a rich source book of imagery for
Chicano artists, especially historical works
of art.

4423 Aguila, Pancho. 11 poems. MANGO, (1977).
English.

AN: Art works by Northern California
artists Emmanuel Montoya and Jose Antonio
Burciaga.

4424 Aguirre, Ignacio. [Untitled woodcut].
REGENERACION, Vol. 1, no. 7 (1970), p. 7.

4425 Almaraz, Carlos. The artist as a
revolutionary. CHISMEARTE, no. 1 (Fall
1976), p. 47-55. English.

AN: Los Angeles painter Carlos D.
Almaraz gives a detailed history of a
cartoon-banner he made for the first
constitutional convention of the United Farm
Workers of America while he was an
illustrator for EL MALCRIADO, and a mural he

did for the UFWA administration building in
La Paz. He also elucidates his philosophy
about politics, the role of the
revolutionary artist in our time, and the
artist's relation to the bourgeois art
market.

4426 Alurista. Timespace huracan: poems,
1972-1975. Albuquerque, NM: Pajarito
Publications, 1976. English.

AN: Seven woodcuts by Cesar Augusto
Martinez.

4427 Amado Maurilio Pena, Jr. PAPEL CHICANO, Vol.
1, no. 13 (July 21, 1978). Spanish.

AN: Includes the artist's resume, an
exhibition list, and a gallery statement
situating the work of Pena within both
Native American and Chicano art traditions.
Includes reproduction of four works.

4428 Anderson, Howard J.; Young, Robert S.; and
Kilgore, Andrew. Amado Maurilio Pena, Jr.
Albuquerque, NM: Robert Stephan Young
Publishing Co., 1981. English.

AN: Coffee-table type of art book about
the Laredo-born painter and printmaker. The
text includes impressionistic writing about
Pena's life, interlaced with statements by
the artist about his life and work. Though
including a few plates from his early
(1974-1978) political and family
silkscreens, over 50 color plates reproduce
his "Santa Fe Indian" works from 1978 to the
present.

4429 The art of Rodolfo Leal. TIN TAN, Vol. 2,
no. 6 (December 1, 1977), p. 15-18. English.

AN: Two calligraphic ink drawings and a
serigraph by Texas-born Leal who lives in
San Francisco.

4430 Art Space - Open Ring Gallery, Sacramento,
CA. El Pachuco art de Jose Montoya: a
historical update. Exhibition invitation,
1977. English.

AN: Invitation to an exhibit.
Illustrated with a reproduction of a 1977
silkscreen calendar page in color by
Montoya.

4431 Art wall for Plaza de la Raza March 28.
EASTSIDE JRNL, (March 11, 1971), p. 1.
English.

AN: On March 28, 1971, the art dealers
of Los Angeles sponsored an "art walk" on
"Gallery Row" on Melrose Place and La
Cienega Blvds as a benefit for Plaza de la
Raza, Mexican American cultural Center at
Lincoln Park. Art dealers financed a limited
edition lithograph by Mexican muralist David
Alfaro Siqueiros. The print shows Ruben
Salazar, slain Mexican American journalist
and community leader with the famous figure
from Siqueiros' mural "New Democracy" below
it. Illustrated.

4432 Astorga, Jerry. [Untitled graphic]. EL
TECOLOTE LITERARY MAGAZINE, Vol. 1, no. 1
(April 1980), p. 4.

Graphics (cont.)

4433 Avalos, David. A pure Mexican accent: the popular engravings of Jose Guadalupe Posada. PROCEEDINGS OF THE PACIFIC COAST COUNCIL ON LATIN AMER STUDIES, Vol. 7, (1980, 1981), p. 123-138. English.

AN: As a documentor of injustice and oppression, Posada, 19th century Mexican engraver, is a master who inspires Chicano artists. Appreciation for his art has been expressed by Sacramento artist Jose E. Montoya. Arsacio Vanegas Arroyo, grandson of Posada's publisher, has made his private collection available to Chicano cultural centers, including El Centro Cultural de la Raza, San Diego. Illustrated.

4434 Beltran. [Dancers (graphic)]. REGENERACION, Vol. 1, no. 3 (1970), p. 5. English.

4435 Beltran, Alberto. [Untitled woodcut]. CARACOL, Vol. 1, no. 12 (August 1975), p. 13.

4436 Bolger, Kathryn McKenna. Amado Pena's art. AUSTIN AMERICAN STATESMAN, (March 29, 1980), p. 10-11. English.

AN: A review of Pena's show of silkscreens, watercolors, and drawings at the Laguna Gloria Art Museum in Austin, Texas, March-May, 1980. Suggests that the artist has turned from a confrontational to an assimilationist stance. At present he visually documents the peaceful amalgamation of the cultural heritage on both sides of the Rio Grande.

4437 Bonilla, Guillermo. [Untitled woodcut]. CARACOL, Vol. 1, no. 12 (August 1975), p. 10.

4438 [Bride and groom (graphic)]. REGENERACION, Vol. 2, no. 4 (1975), p. 35.

4439 Burciaga, Jose Antonio. Batos locos [graphic]. CARACOL, Vol. 2, no. 8 (April 1976), p. Cover.

4440 Burciaga, Jose Antonio. Mujeres [woodcut]. CARACOL, Vol. 2, no. 5 (January 1976), p. 1.

4441 Calendar 1977. CHISMEARTE, no. 2 (Winter, Spring, 1977), p. 26-27. English.

AN: Reproduction of one month of the 1977 silkscreen calendar produced in limited edition by the Galeria de la Raza of San Francisco and the Royal Chicano Air Force of Sacramento, California. Displayed is Rene Yanez's screen HISTORICAL PHOTO-SILKSCREENMOVIE.

4442 Calendario 1973. San Francisco, CA: Galeria de la Raza, 1973. English.

AN: Handprinted silkscreen calendar by artists of the Galeria de la Raza.

4443 Calendario de comida 1976. San Francisco, CA: Galeria de la Raza, 1976. English.

AN: Handprinted silkscreen calendar consisting of twelve sheets and a cover. The work of the following artists is included: Ralph Maradiaga, Juanishi Orozco, Francisco Camplis, Ruben Guzman, Rodolfo Cuellar, Xavier Viramontes, Jose Montoya, Esteban Villa, Rene Yanez, Max Garcia and Louis "The Foot" Gonzalez, Patricia Rodriguez, and Ricardo Favela. All of the above are associated with the Galeria de la Raza, or

the Royal Chicano Air Force of Sacramento, CA.

4444 Canto al pueblo: an anthology of experiences. San Antonio, TX: Penca Books, 1978. English.

AN: Includes works by: Mario E. Castillo, Carlos Rosas, Jose G. Gonzalez, Santos Martinez, Gilbert Munoz, Fred Loa, Armando Ibanez and others.

4445 Cardenas de Dwyer, Carlota, ed. Chicano voices. Boston, MS: Houghton Mifflin, 1975. English.

AN: Includes artwork by: Peter Rodriguez, Arturo Anselmo Roman, Carmen Lomas Garza, Santa Barraza, and Cesar Augusto Martinez.

4446 Carraro, Francine. Refined rhythmic references: Amado Pena, Jr. SOUTHWEST ART, Vol. 9, no. 6 (November 1979), p. 70-75. English.

AN: Well-illustrated (including 4 color) story on Austin silkscreen artist Amado M. Pena. Features his recent stylized work based on New Mexican indian motifs.

4447 Carrillo, Graciela. El frijol magico. Berkeley, CA: Center for Open Learning and Teaching, 1974. Spanish.

AN: Children's book conceived and illustrated in color by Carrillo.

4448 Castellanos, Leonard. Chicano centros, murals, and art. CHISMEARTE, Vol. 1, no. 1 (Fall 1976), p. 26-27. English.

AN: Excerpt of an article originally published under the same title in ARTS IN SOCIETY (Spring-Summer 1975).

4449 Cattleth, Elizabeth. [Untitled woodcut]. CARACOL, Vol. 1, no. 12 (August 1975), p. 1.

4450 El Centro Cultural de La Raza, San Diego, CA. Espejo del barrio-art exposition. Exhibition brochure, June 1975. English.

AN: Illustrated brochure announcement for a cultural exposition of Chicano music, art and drama. Includes some biographical information and one reproduction of painter Manuel Unzueta, woodworker Ambriz, muralist Victor Orozco Ochoa and designer/illustrator J. Armando Nunez.

4451 El Centro Cultural de La Raza, San Diego, CA. One hundred year anniversary: Jose Guadalupe Posada, Antonio Vanegas Arroyo. Exhibition invitation, 1980. English.

AN: Invitation to an exhibition of Mexican engravers Posada and Manuel Manilla and an homage to their publisher. Also, a "Chicano Tribute to Jose Guadalupe Posada," with contemporary works influenced by Posada. At the Centro, and at Southwestern College in Chula Vista.

4452 Centro de artistas chicanos. EL HISPANO, Vol. 6, no. 39 (March 19, 1974). English.

AN: Description of goals and community oriented programs of the Centro. Illustrated with an R.C.A.F. poster announcing Teatro Campesino production of "LA CARPA DE LOS RASQUACHIS".

Graphics (cont.)

4453 Centro de artistas, Sacra: recuerdo ...
     descubrimiento ... voluntad. CHISMEARTE,
     Vol. 1, no. 1 (Fall 1976), p. 6-7.
     English.

   AN: Summary of activities of the Centro
   de Artistas Chicanos, made up of artists
   from the Royal Chicano Air Force and other
   groups. The Centro makes posters, T-shirts,
   decals, murals and puts on a number of
   cultural and social events. Report on a
   "mass migration" July 1976 to the Academia
   de la Nueva Raza in Dixon, NM for two weeks
   of communion.

4454 Cervantez, Yreina. Huelga in the morning
     [lithograph]. AZTLAN, Vol. 9, no. 1 (1978),
     p. COVER. Bilingual.

4455 Chicano artists exhibit at USC. CALENDAR,
     (September 23, 1973), p. 61. English.

   AN: Announcement of an exhibit of
   paintings, drawings, sculpture and graphics
   by artists from the Mechicano Art Center of
   Los Angeles at the University of Southern
   California Art Galleries. Slide
   presentations of murals and supergraphics.

4456 CJL. Artist profile-Amado Pena. FOUR WINDS,
     Vol. 1, no. 4 (1980), p. 10. English.

   AN: Amado Pena works within the
   expectations of an American Indian artist,
   but also within the context of the Mexican
   American culture. The article treats Pena's
   artistic trajectory and provides
   biographical information. Illustrated with
   photograph of the artist and reproductions
   of one lithograph and one mixed-media
   drawing.

4457 Contemporary Arts Museum, Houston, TX and
     Martinez, Santos G., Jr. Mexican movie
     posters. Exhibition invitation, 1979.
     English.

   AN: Invitation to an exhibit of posters
   primarily from the collecttion of Enrique
   Flores and Xavier Gorena of Xochil Art
   Center, Mission, Texas. Martinez considers
   the posters monumental, with expressive
   qualities that have influenced Chicano
   poster makers like the Royal Chicano Air
   Force, and Rupert Garcia, and Texas artists
   like Luis Jimenez, Jesse Trevino and Cesar
   Martinez. One illustration. Introduction by
   guest curator Santos G. Martinez, Jr. (See
   Rupert Garcia's essay in the exhibition
   catalog: POSTERS FROM THE GOLDEN AGE OF
   MEXICAN CINEMA, for another point of view).

4458 Cortez, Carlos. [Cover design]. INDUSTRIAL
     WORKER, Vol. 67, no. 5 (May 1970), p. Cover.

4459 Cortez, Carlos. Las dos esperanzas [print].
     REVISTA CHICANO-RIQUENA, Vol. 5, no. 2
     (Spring 1977), p. 21. Spanish.

4460 Cortez, Carlos. Gente de la tierra [print].
     REVISTA CHICANO-RIQUENA, Vol. 5, no. 2
     (Winter 1977), p. 5. Spanish.

4461 Cortez, Carlos. Ricardo Flores-Magon
     [graphic]. CARACOL, Vol. 5, no. 2 (October
     1978), p. BACK COVER. Spanish.

4462 Cortez, Carlos. Untitled [print]. REVISTA
     CHICANO-RIQUENA, Vol. 5, no. 2 (Spring
     1977), p. COVER. Bilingual.

4463 Cross, Miriam Dungan. A satirical brutal

view of pollution. THE TRIBUNE (Oakland,
CA), (January 25, 1970), p. 26-EN. English.

   AN: (Includes reproduction of Rupert
   Garcia's silkscreen print "D.D.T." dated
   1969).

4464 Cuadra, Ricardo. [Untitled print]. EL GRITO,
     Vol. 3, no. 2 (Winter 1970), p. [58].
     Bilingual.

4465 Cuadra, Ricardo. [Untitled print]. EL GRITO,
     Vol. 3, no. 2 (Winter 1970), p. [59].
     Bilingual.

4466 Cuadra, Ricardo. [Untitled print]. EL GRITO,
     Vol. 3, no. 2 (Winter 1970), p. [60].
     Bilingual.

4467 Cuadra, Ricardo. [Untitled print]. EL GRITO,
     Vol. 3, no. 2 (Winter 1970), p. [61].
     Bilingual.

4468 Cuadra, Ricardo. [Untitled print]. EL GRITO,
     Vol. 3, no. 2 (Winter 1970), p. [62].
     Bilingual.

4469 Cuadra, Ricardo. [Untitled print]. EL GRITO,
     Vol. 3, no. 2 (Winter 1970), p. [63].
     Bilingual.

4470 Cuadra, Ricardo. [Untitled print]. EL GRITO,
     Vol. 3, no. 2 (Winter 1970), p. [64].
     Bilingual.

4471 De la Rocha, Roberto. [Untitled woodcuts].
     CON SAFOS, no. 7 (Winter 1971), p. 12-13.

4472 De Leon, Hector. Barrio art--the community's
     reflection of itself. AGENDA, Vol. 9, no. 4
     (July, August, 1979), p. 7, 38. English.

   AN: Barrio art is communal, its forms
   such as posters, pamphlets, graffiti, and
   murals have an educative function. Its style
   is eclectic and its content is stark and
   direct. Through various forms of graphic
   representation, people in the barrio have
   reappropriated art forms to give meaning to
   their daily experiences. Includes nine
   illustrations of barrio art.

4473 De Leon, Hector. [Untitled graphic].
     CARACOL, Vol. 2, no. 3 (November 1975), p.
     Bk cover.

4474 De Leon, Nephtali. Coca cola dreams.
     Lubbock, TX: Trucha Publications, 1976.
     English.

   AN: Poems and illustrations by Nephtali
   de Leon.

4475 Electro Arts Gallery, San Francisco, CA.
     Electric realizations: an exhibition by Rene
     Yanez & Carl Heyward. Exhibition invitation,
     1981. English.

   AN: Invitation to an exhibit of color
   Xerox prints by Rene Yanez, Co-director of
   the Galeria de la Raza of San Francisco.
   Yanez feels that Xerox has opened new
   frontiers in presenting graphic work at a
   different scale and size.

Graphics (cont.)

4476 Exploratorium, Student Union, California
State University, Los Angeles. An exhibit of
published prints of Aztlan Multiples.
Exhibition catalog, 1981. English.

AN: The published silkscreen prints of
Aztlan Multiples, a small business run by
Richard Duardo of Los Angeles, features
works by Duardo, John Valadez, and Carlos
Almaraz, among others. Illustrations.

4477 'Festival of arts' planned by Arthritis
Foundation. SANTA FE NEW MEXICAN, (October
11, 1972), p. B6. English.

AN: The Albuquerque Arthritis Foundation
has invited professional artists and
craftsmen from New Mexico to display their
paintings, watercolors, sculpture, prints,
lithographs, jewelry. Joel Ramirez's
painting THE WEAVERS is selected for full
color art prints. Illustrated.

4478 First Federal Plaza Display Gallery, Austin,
TX. Tejano artists: an exhibit of
Mexican-American art. Exhibit brochure,
1976. English.

AN: Announcement of exhibit illustrated
by Cesar A. Martinez's woodcut.

4479 Frankenstein, Alfred. Prison's artist in
residence. SAN FRANCISCO CHRONICLE, (May 5,
1978), p. 60. English.

AN: Review of the exhibition MUNDOS
PERDIDOS, curated at the Galeria de la Raza
by Leonard Castellanos. Show consisted of
work by Castellanos and inmates at Lompoc
Federal Correctional Institution near Santa
Barbara. Documents a prison mural, tattoos
and silkscreen prints with socially critical
themes.

4480 Galeria de la Raza/Studio 24, San Francisco,
CA. Images of the Southwest. Exhibition
catalog, 1977. English.

AN: Invitation/catalog for an exhibit
including Rudy M. Fernandez(Utah), Enrique
Flores(Texas), Xavier Gorena(Texas),
C.A.[Cesar] Martinez(Texas), Santos
Martinez, Jr.(Texas), Pedro
Rodriguez(Texas), Arnold Trujillo(New
Mexico). Block prints, paper cut-outs,
drawings, photographs, copper enamels, and
sculpture were shown. Five illustrations.

4481 Galeria de la Raza/Studio 24, San Francisco,
CA and Franco, Jean. Juan Fuentes y Rupert
Garcia: posters, drawings, prints.
Exhibition catalog, 1975. English.

AN: Catalog of an exhibit. Illustrated
with drawings and posters.

4482 Galeria de la Raza/Studio 24, San Francisco,
CA. "Low 'n slow": checking out low rider
art. Exhibition invitation, 1979. English.

AN: Invitation to an exhibit of
drawings, photographs, and graphics.
Participation by LOWRIDER MAGAZINE and local
car and bike clubs.

4483 Galeria de la Raza/Studio 24, San Francisco,
CA. Published prints of Hecho en Aztlan
Multiples. Exhibition announcement, 1980.
English.

AN: Announcement of exhibit of the
published silkscreen prints of Hecho en
Aztlan Multiples; a small business run by
Richard Duardo of Los Angeles.

4484 Galeria de la Raza/Studio 24, San Francisco,
CA and Garcia, Rupert. La Raza Silkscreen
Center: "Images of a community", an exhibit
of silkscreen posters and graphic works from
1971 to 1979. Exhibition catalog, 1979.
English.

AN: First large scale retrospective
exhibit of the La Raza Silkscreen Center's
eight years of postermaking. Includes list
of 90 artists.

4485 Gallery Sanchez, San Francisco, CA. Xerox
art: an exhibit of local color xerox
artists. Exhibition invitation, 1981.
English.

AN: Invitation to an exhibit featuring
Rene Yanez and eight other artists working
in color Xerox.

4486 Galvan, Yolanda. Coming out [print]. REVISTA
CHICANO-RIQUENA, Vol. 5, no. 1 (Winter
1977), p. 52. English.

4487 Galvan, Yolanda. Penetration [print].
REVISTA CHICANO-RIQUENA, Vol. 5, no. 1
(Winter 1977), p. 6. English.

4488 Gamboa, Harry, Jr. Chile [graphic].
REGENERACION, Vol. 2, no. 4 (1975), p. 7.

4489 Gamboa, Harry, Jr. [Untitled graphic].
REGENERACION, Vol. 1, no. 9 (1970), p. FRNT
COVER.

4490 Gamboa, Harry, Jr. [Untitled graphic].
REGENERACION, Vol. 2, no. 1 (1971), p. i.

4491 Gamboa, Harry, Jr. [Untitled graphic].
REGENERACION, Vol. 2, no. 4 (1975), p. 48.

4492 Garcia Perez, Linda Mary. Cactus prisoner.
MAIZE, Vol. 2, no. 3 (Spring 1979), p. 35.
English.

4493 Garcia, Rupert. Laminas de la Raza. San
Francisco: Garcia Litho and Printing
Service, 1975. English.

AN: Portfolio of drawings and prints by
Patricia Rodriguez, Ricardo Apodaca,
Xochitl, Domingo Rivera, Francisco Camplis,
Rafael Maradiaga, Tom Rios, Juan Fuentes,
Ricardo Diaz, Jose Romero, Consuelo Mendez,
Jose Antonio Burciaga, Irene Perez, Ricardo
Rios, Mike Rios, Graciela Carrillo, Rene
Yanez, Luis Talamantez, Guillermo Bermudez,
all from Northern California.

4494 Garcia-Camarillo, Cecilio. Aire triste
[poetry in graphic design]. EL GRITO, Vol.
7, no. 3 (Spring 1974), p. 44. Spanish.

4495 Garcia-Camarillo, Cecilio. Frio [poetry in
graphic design]. EL GRITO, Vol. 7, no. 3
(Spring 1974), p. 41. English.

4496 Garcia-Camarillo, Cecilio. Hormiguero
[poetry in graphic design]. EL GRITO, Vol.
7, no. 3 (Spring 1974), p. 43. English.

4497 Garcia-Camarillo, Cecilio. Lluvia Marxista
[poetry in graphic design]. EL GRITO, Vol.
7, no. 3 (Spring 1974), p. 40. English.

4498 Garcia-Camarillo, Cecilio. Medianoche
[graphic]. MAIZE, Vol. 1, no. 4 (Summer
1978), p. 42. Spanish.

Graphics (cont.)

4499 Garcia-Camarillo, Cecilio. Naturaleza es
cadaver [poetry in graphic design]. EL
GRITO, Vol. 7, no. 3 (Spring 1974), p. 45.
Spanish.

4500 Garcia-Camarillo, Cecilio. Nopal y piedras
[graphic]. MAIZE, Vol. 1, no. 4 (Summer,
1978), p. 40. Spanish.

4501 Garcia-Camarillo, Cecilio. Sol y nube.
MAIZE, Vol. 1, no. 4 (Summer 1978), p. 41.
Spanish.

4502 Garcia-Camarillo, Cecilio. [Untitled poetry
in graphic design]. EL GRITO, Vol. 7, no. 3
(Spring 1974), p. 42. English.

4503 Garcia-Camarillo, Cecilio. Viendo un lago
[graphic]. MAIZE, Vol. 1, no. 4 (Summer
1978), p. 39. Spanish.

4504 Garza, Sabino. [Family (graphic)]. CARACOL,
Vol. 1, no. 3 (November 1974), p. 12.

4505 Garza, Sabino. [Untitled graphic]. CARACOL,
Vol. 1, no. 3 (November 1974), p. 12.

4506 Gonzalez Dodson, Nora. Maternity [graphic].
TEJIDOS, Vol. 2, no. 8 (Winter 1975), p. 1.
English.

4507 Gonzalez Dodson, Nora. [Untitled graphic].
TEJIDOS, Vol. 2, no. 8 (Winter 1975), p.
COVER. English.

4508 Gonzalez, Jose Gamaliel. Zapata [print].
REVISTA CHICANO-RIQUENA, Vol. 5, no. 1
(Winter 1977), p. 36. English.

4509 The Green Line Gallery, San Pedro, CA.
Lithographs and woodcuts by Muriel Olguin.
Exhibit invitation, 1980. English.

   AN: Invitation to an exhibit.
   Illustrated.

4510 Gronk. [Faces (graphic)]. REGENERACION, Vol.
2, no. 3 (1973), p. 15.

4511 Gronk. The same cave down the street
[graphic]. REGENERACION, Vol. 2, no. 2
(1972), p. 9.

4512 Haddad, Barbara. The fine arts. ROUNDUP,
(January 25, 1970), p. 12. English.

   AN: Mixed review of Ray Espinoza's
   one-person show at the International House
   Gallery in Denver. The exhibition included
   drawings, paintings, prints, assemblages and
   sculptures. Selecting work from each medium,
   the critic comments on pieces that are
   successful and those not fully realized.
   Illustrated with a wood and metal relief of
   a guitar and a graphic of "Che" Guevara.

4513 Hennessey, Kathy. Amado Pena, Chicano
artist. REVISTA RIO BRAVO, no. 1 (Fall
1980), p. 2+. English.

   AN: Review of the life and art of
   Laredo-born artist Pena whose early work in
   the 1960s was abstracted figures in bright
   colors; in the 1970s his work became
   political commentary for the Chicano
   movement; most recently he is doing
   paintings and silkscreens about New Mexican
   Indian life. As a teacher he influenced many
   students, especially in Anderson High School
   (Austin). Illustrations throughout the
   issue.

4514 Hernandez, Ester. Homenaje a mi tio.
CHISMEARTE, Vol. 1, no. 4 (Fall , Winter,
1977, 1978), p. 6.

4515 Hernandez, Ester. Mujer con fuego [etching].
CHISMEARTE, Vol. 1, no. 4 (Fall , Winter,
1977, 1978), p. 7.

4516 Hernandez, Judithe Elena. Concepto de Aztlan
[print]. AZTLAN, Vol. 1, no. 1 (Spring
1970), p. COVER. Spanish.

4517 Hernandez, Judithe Elena. La lechuza de
antano en el presente [print]. AZTLAN, Vol.
1, no. 2 (Fall 1970), p. COVER. Spanish.

4518 Hernandez, Judithe Elena. Rain Bird, Zuni
[print]. AZTLAN, Vol. 3, no. 2 (Fall
1972), p. COVER. English.

4519 Hernandez, Judithe Elena. Tribu Acoma
[print]. AZTLAN, Vol. 2, no. 1 (Spring
1971), p. COVER. Spanish.

4520 Hernandez-Trujillo, Manuel. Chicano [print].
EL GRITO, Vol. 2, no. 3 (Spring 1969), p.
[29-30]. Bilingual.

4521 Hernandez-Trujillo, Manuel. Conejo [print].
EL GRITO, Vol. 2, no. 3 (Spring 1969), p.
[28]. Spanish.

4522 Hernandez-Trujillo, Manuel. Nina y gato
[print]. EL GRITO, Vol. 2, no. 3 (Spring
1969), p. [31]. Spanish.

4523 Hernandez-Trujillo, Manuel. One and one
equals me [print]. EL GRITO, Vol. 2, no. 3
(Spring 1969), p. [35]. English.

4524 Hernandez-Trujillo, Manuel. Sangrandose
[print]. EL GRITO, Vol. 2, no. 3 (Spring
1969), p. [25]. Spanish.

4525 Hernandez-Trujillo, Manuel. Retrato femenil
[print]. EL GRITO, Vol. 2, no. 3 (Spring
1969), p. [32]. Spanish.

4526 Hernandez-Trujillo, Manuel. Slayer of night
[print]. EL GRITO, Vol. 2, no. 3 (Spring
1969), p. 34. English.

4527 Hernandez-Trujillo, Manuel. Vida y muerte
[print]. EL GRITO, Vol. 2, no. 3 (Spring
1969), p. [28]. Spanish.

4528 Hernandez-Trujillo, Manuel. Xochitl [print].
EL GRITO, Vol. 2, no. 3 (Spring 1969), p.
[26]. English.

4529 Herrera, Estela. La mujer en el mundo: una
chicana en las artes. LA OPINION, (March
25, 1982), p. III,6. Spanish.

   AN: Illustrated interview with Judith
   Elena Hernandez de Niekrug including
   biographical information and discussion of
   her attitudes toward her murals, paintings,
   and graphics.

4530 Herron, Willie and Gamboa, Harry, Jr.
[Eagle, serpent and man (graphic)].
REGENERACION, Vol. 2, no. 2 (1972), p.
COVER.

4531 Herron, Willie. [The face in the skull's
mouth (graphic)]. REGENERACION, Vol. 2, no.
2 (1972), p. 3.

4532 Herron, Willie and Gamboa, Harry, Jr. [Man,
woman and child (graphic)]. REGENERACION,
Vol. 2, no. 2 (1972), p. BACK COVER.

Graphics (cont.)

4533 Herron, Willie. [Old man (graphic)].
     REGENERACION, Vol. 2, no. 2 (1972), p. 15.

4534 Herron, Willie. [People in poverty
     (graphic)]. REGENERACION, Vol. 2, no. 2
     (1972), p. 16.

4535 Hertzog, Carl. Tribute to Jose Cisneros. THE
     PASSWORD, Vol. 19, no. 4 (Winter 1974).
     English.

     AN: Tribute to artist-illustrator Jose
     Cisneros, who has "enhanced the appearance
     of programs, exhibition catalogs, newspaper
     articles, magazines and special stationery.
     He has designed emblems such as the seal of
     the University of Texas at El Paso, the seal
     of the city of Juarez, Mexico, and the
     emblem of the Western History Association".

4536 La historia de California, 1977. San
     Francisco, CA: Galeria de la Raza, 1977.
     English.

     AN: Handprinted silkscreen calendar of
     history seen from a Mexican point of view.
     Twelve sheets and a cover. Artists are:
     Ralph Maradiaga, Irene Perez, Louie "The
     Foot" Gonzalez, Max Garcia, Patricia
     Rodriguez, Jose Romero, Esteban Villa,
     Juanishi Orozco, Rodolfo Cuellar, Jose
     Montoya, Xavier Viramontes, Rene Yanez,
     Ricardo Favela, associated with the Galeria
     de la Raza, or the Royal Chicano Air Force
     of Sacramento.

4537 Holliday-Abbott, Anne. Suitcase is 2nd home
     for arts liaison. ARIZONA DAILY STAR, (June
     18, 1981), p. H-3. English.

     AN: Arizona artist Louis LeRoy who
     paints, makes prints, and does assemblage is
     also a regional representative for the
     National Endowment for the Arts in Arizona,
     New Mexico, Colorado, Utah, and Wyoming.
     LeRoy has always been an "advocate of people
     being proud of their ethnic backgrounds." He
     feels artists can be self-supporting without
     commercializing.

4538 How we came to the Fifth World = Como
     vinimos al quinto mundo. San Francisco, CA:
     Children's Book Press/Imprenta de Libros
     Infantiles, 1976. Bilingual.

     AN: Children's book illustrated by
     Graciela Carrillo de Lopez. Color.

4539 Huerta, Elena. [Untitled woodcut]. CARACOL,
     Vol. 1, no. 12 (August 1975), p. 11.

4540 Images of Aztlan at Mechicano. CHISMEARTE,
     Vol. 1, no. 1 (Fall 1976), p. 3-4.
     English.

     AN: History of Mechicano Art Center from
     its opening in West Los Angeles in 1969
     through its 1976 location during which it
     decided to become a center serving its own
     community in East Los Angeles. Led by
     Leonard Castellanos, Victor Franco and Ray
     Atilano, the Center developed programs in
     supergraphics, silkscreen, and mural
     painting, as well as an "open-wall" art
     gallery for artists not allowed in
     establishment galleries.

4541 Iniguez, Javier. [Untitled woodcut].
     CARACOL, Vol. 1, no. 12 (August 1975), p.
     14.

4542 Iniguez, Javier. [Untitled woodcut].

CARACOL, Vol. 1, no. 12 (August 1975), p.
13.

4543 Jimenez, Sarah. [Untitled woodcut]. CARACOL,
     Vol. 1, no. 12 (August 1975), p. 12.

4544 Johnston, Jerry. A man with a message: let's
     build strength, pride. DESERET NEWS, (June
     28, 1980), p. S3. English.

     AN: Story on Nephtali De Leon,
     playwright, poet, and illustrator of
     children's literature. In addition to I WILL
     CATCH THE SUN and I COLOR MY GARDEN
     children's books, he works with oil
     painting, stained glass and woodcuts.

4545 Joslyn Art Center. Multi-media art exhibit:
     Muriel Olguin (printmaking), Myrna Shiras
     (mixed media), Linda Vallejo (painting).
     Exhibition invitation, 1979. English.

     AN: Invitation to an exhibit.

4546 Kagawa, Paul and Rilkin, Scott. La Raza
     Silkscreen Center, in step with the Mission.
     ARTS BIWEEKLY, no. 44 (March 15, 1977).
     English.

     AN: Concise history and goals of the
     Silkscreen Center: the Center's values are
     reflected in the collective process that
     produces the posters, as well as in the
     collective style of the art; in the emphasis
     upon education. The Center trains
     apprentices, educates the student community
     about the silkscreen process and Raza
     history and produces posters that have an
     information impact. The Silkscreen Center is
     part of a coalition of La Raza Information
     Center, Tutorial Center, and Centro Legal
     which evolved from La Raza En Accion Social
     founded in 1970.

4547 Lomas Garza, Carmen. Abuelita [etching].
     TEJIDOS, Vol. 3, no. 4 (Winter 1976), p. 28.
     Spanish.

4548 Lomas Garza, Carmen. La curandera [etching].
     TEJIDOS, Vol. 3, no. 4 (Winter 1976), p. 45.
     Spanish.

4549 Lomas Garza, Carmen. La curandera [etching].
     HOJAS, (1976), p. 51.

4550 Lomas Garza, Carmen. Don Pedrito Jaramillo,
     Falfurrias, Texas, 1829-1907 [etching].
     TEJIDOS, Vol. 3, no. 4 (Winter 1976), p. 22.

4551 Lomas Garza, Carmen. Flor de un color
     [etching]. TEJIDOS, Vol. 3, no. 4 (Winter
     1976), p. 4. Spanish.

4552 Lomas Garza, Carmen. El jardin [etching].
     TEJIDOS, Vol. 3, no. 4 (Winter 1976), p. 36.
     Spanish.

4553 Lomas Garza, Carmen. Lo que nos espera =
     What awaits us [lithograph]. HOJAS, (1976),
     p. 49.

4554 Lomas Garza, Carmen. Loteria tabla llena
     [etching]. TEJIDOS, Vol. 3, no. 4 (Winter
     1976), p. 26. Spanish.

4555 Lomas Garza, Carmen. Luna nene [etching].
     TEJIDOS, Vol. 3, no. 4 (Winter 1976), p. 9.
     Spanish.

4556 Lomas Garza, Carmen. Luna nene [etching].
     TEJIDOS, Vol. 3, no. 4 (Winter 1976), p. 13.
     Spanish.

Graphics (cont.)

4557 Lomas Garza, Carmen. Luna nene [etching].
TEJIDOS, Vol. 3, no. 4 (Winter 1976), p. 18.
Spanish.

4558 Lomas Garza, Carmen. Pobreza - la perra
entre la raza = Poverty the bitch
[lithograph]. HOJAS, (1976), p. 48.

4559 Lomas Garza, Carmen. Raspas con nieve
[etching]. TEJIDOS, Vol. 3, no. 4 (Winter
1976), p. 40. Spanish.

4560 Lomas Garza, Carmen. Riqueza [etching].
TEJIDOS, Vol. 3, no. 4 (Winter 1976), p. 32.
Spanish.

4561 Lomas Garza, Carmen. [Untitled etching].
TEJIDOS, Vol. 3, no. 4 (Winter 1976), p. 1.
English.

4562 Lomas Garza, Carmen. La Virgen de San Juan
de los Lagos [etching]. HOJAS, (1976), p.
50.

4563 La Lomita. [Emiliano Zapata (graphic)].
CARACOL, Vol. 1, no. 4 (December 1974), p.
9.

4564 Lujan, Gilbert Sanchez "Magu". El arte del
Chicano - "The Spirit of the Experience".
CON SAFOS, no. 7 (Winter 1971), p. 11-13.
English.

   AN: Definition of Chicano Art by artist
   Lujan as the expression of an unique
   experience that is neither Mexican nor U.S.
   Anglo, that has its own vitality and
   dynamics. Chicanos can draw upon common
   cultural elements and transform them into
   images and art forms such as sculptured
   menudo bones, tortilla drawings, vato loco
   portraits, etc. Four woodcuts by Roberto de
   la Rocha are shown as examples.

4565 Marta. [Untitled graphic]. MAIZE, Vol. 1,
no. 2 (Winter 1978), p. 32-33. English.

4566 Martin, Maria Luisa. [Untitled woodcut].
CARACOL, Vol. 1, no. 12 (August 1975), p.
12.

4567 Martinez, Cesar Augusto. Arte chicano.
CARACOL, Vol. 1, no. 6 (February 1975), p.
3. English.

   AN: Thoughts on the form, function and
   meaning of Chicano Art. Stylistically, it is
   seen as a fusion. It is dynamic, expressing
   multiple political sentiments and has an
   irreverent attitude towards dominant
   culture. Front cover of issue is a black and
   white reproduction of a silkscreen print by
   Amado Maurilio Pena, Jr.

4568 Martinez, Cesar Augusto. Brujerias
[woodcut]. CARACOL, Vol. 2, no. 2 (October
1975), p. 1.

4569 Martinez, Cesar Augusto. Don Pedrito
Jaramillo [woodcut]. CARACOL, Vol. 2, no. 9
(May 1976), p. Ft Cover. English.

4570 Martinez, Cesar Augusto. Don Pedrito
Jaramillo [woodcut]. CARACOL, Vol. 3, no. 4
(December 1976), p. Bk Cover.

4571 Martinez, Cesar Augusto. Liberacion de lo
que esta debajo los huesos [woodcut].
CARACOL, Vol. 1, no. 4 (December 1974), p.
24. Spanish.

4572 Maya, Gloria. Telephone booth no 347

[graphic]. TIN TAN, Vol. 2, no. 5 (June 1,
1977), p. Cover.

4573 Mechicano art posters. CON SAFOS, no. 8
(1972), p. 38. Bilingual.

4574 Mendez, Leopoldo. [Untitled woodcut].
CARACOL, Vol. 1, no. 7 (March 1975), p. 12.

4575 Mendez, Leopoldo. [Untitled woodcut].
CARACOL, Vol. 1, no. 7 (March 1975), p. 3.

4576 Los mesquites [etching]. TEJIDOS, Vol. 3,
no. 4 (Winter 1976), p. COVER. Spanish.

4577 Meta studio I. Denver, CO: s.n., [1980].
English.

   AN: Portfolio of colored prints by
   Colorado artists Ernie Gallegos, Jerry
   Jaramillo, Steve Lucero and Carlos M.
   Sandoval. Biographical information and
   photograph of each artist. Presentation of
   the group under the rubric of "metarealism"
   by Stephen Pascual Lucero.

4578 Mexiac, Adolfo. [Untitled woodcut]. CARACOL,
Vol. 1, no. 12 (August 1975), p. 14.

4579 Michigan State University, East Lansing, MI.
Voces del norte. Brochure, 1978. English.

   AN: Photos and graphics by 11 Chicanos
   residing in Michigan.

4580 Miller, Marlan. Heard speaks Spanish through
art. PHOENIX GAZETTE, (September 23, 1978).
English.

   AN: Four new exhibits at the Heard
   Museum of Phoenix include "Hispanic crafts
   of the Southwest", and "Southwest Chicano
   Art Invitational". The former focuses on New
   Mexico and Colorado crafts, organized by the
   Taylor Museum if the Colorado Springs Fine
   Arts Center; the latter includes Rupert
   Garcia and Xavier Miramontes of San
   Francisco, Rudy Fernandez of Salt Lake City
   (now in Scottsdale, AZ), and Antonio Pazos
   of Tucson.

4581 Mora, Francisco. [Woodcut of Emiliano
Zapata]. REGENERACION, Vol. 1, no. 7 (1970),
p. 5.

4582 Muralist Campero shows works. EASTSIDE JRNL,
(June 3, 1971), p. 6. English.

   AN: Photograph of artist Armando Campero
   with samples of his graphic work. The artist
   was completing a 3,000 square foot mural,
   JOHN KENNEDY SAGA NUMBER 2 for installation
   at the City Terrace Social Hall.

4583 Museum of Fine Arts, Santa Fe, NM. Luis
Jimenez, sculpture, drawings and prints: La
Cofradia de Artes y Artesanos Hispanicos,
selected works. Exhibition invitation, 1979.
English.

   AN: Invitation to an exhibit of Texas
   sculptor and printmaker Luis Jimenez, and
   New Mexican artists and artisans.

Graphics (cont.)

4584 Nelson, Eugene. Pablo Cruz and the American dream. Salt Lake City, UT: Peregrine Smith, 1975. English.

AN: A first-person account of a typical "alambrista" (a wire jumper or undocumented Mexican worker in the U.S.) compiled from several accounts by the author. Illustrated with 14 prints by Carlos Cortez, Chicago artist, then the editor of THE INDUSTRIAL WORKER.

4585 New co-op in San Cristobal. GRITO DEL NORTE, Vol. 3, no. 8 (July 5, 1970), p. 13. English.

AN: Details formation of the San Cristobal Valley Arts Inc., a community corporation formed to train people in a silkscreen business venture. Aiming to use expressive forms as a source of economic development, the corporation published and distributed a line of Chicano silkscreen posters. Illustrated by three posters, WE SHALL ENDURE, SOMOS AZTLAN, and TAOS PUEBLO.

4586 The new logo. LA VOZ: Concilio for the Spanish Speaking of King Co., Seattle, no. 5 (June 1979). English.

AN: Biographical information on artist Alfredo Arreguin. Born in Uruapan, Michoacan Mexico and residing in Seattle for eighteen years, Arrequin is active in La Extension Cultural, an agency formed to meet the cultural needs of "Hispanics" in the Pacific Northwest. In his logo for the "Concilio," Arreguin employs symbols representing history, beauty, unity, ethnicity and communication.

4587 New Mexico State University, University Art Gallery, Las Cruces, NM. Luis Jimenez: sculpture, drawings and prints. Exhibition catalog, 1977. English.

AN: Well illustrated catalog, some illustrations in color. Text is interview tracing Jimenez's artistic development. Artists identifies Mexican American connections in his work.

4588 Oakland Museum, Oakland, CA and Laney College, Oakland, CA. In search of Aztlan. Exhibition brochure, 1974. English.

AN: Brochure for exhibit featuring Los Four: Carlos Almaraz, Gilbert Lujan, Roberto de la Rocha, Frank Romero, Judithe Hernandez.

4589 Ochoa, Victor Orozco. Posadas [graphic]. MAIZE, Vol. 1, no. 2 (Winter 1978), p. Ft cover. English.

4590 Ohlone College Art Department Gallery, Fremont, CA. Impressions: a California print invitational. Exhibition catalog, 1976. English.

AN: Exhibition catalog includes commentary on the artist and reproduction of two silkscreen posters "El Grito Rebelde" and "The Bicentennial Art Poster" by Rupert Garcia.

4591 Ojeda, Jay. Galeria de la Raza--art for the community. SAN FRANCISCO PROGRESS, (March 24, 1972). English.

AN: Analysis of group exhibition by thirty-four Raza artists. Commentary on the work of Latin American artists Consuelo Mendez, Rolando Castellon, and Chicano artists Rupert Garcia, Chuy Campusano and Peter Rodriguez.

4592 Palacios, Procopio. Partido Liberal Mexicano [print]. AZTLAN, Vol. 4, no. 2 (Fall 1973), p. Cover. Spanish.

4593 Pazos, Antonio. [Untitled graphic]. LLUEVE TLALOC, no. 4 (1977), p. [79].

4594 Pazos, Antonio. [Untitled graphic]. LLUEVE TLALOC, no. 4 (1977), p. [82].

4595 Pazos, Antonio. [Untitled graphic]. LLUEVE TLALOC, no. 4 (1977), p. [108].

4596 Pazos, Antonio. [Untitled graphic]. LLUEVE TLALOC, no. 5 (1978), p. 5.

4597 Pazos, Antonio. [Untitled graphic]. LLUEVE TLALOC, no. 5 (1978), p. 13.

4598 Pazos, Antonio. [Untitled graphic]. LLUEVE TLALOC, no. 5 (1978), p. 17.

4599 Pazos, Antonio. [Untitled graphic]. LLUEVE TLALOC, no. 5 (1978), p. 19.

4600 Pazos, Antonio. [Untitled graphic]. LLUEVE TLALOC, no. 5 (1978), p. 23.

4601 Pazos, Antonio. [Untitled graphic]. LLUEVE TLALOC, no. 5 (1978), p. 27.

4602 Pazos, Antonio. [Untitled graphic]. LLUEVE TLALOC, no. 5 (1978), p. 31.

4603 Pazos, Antonio. [Untitled graphic]. LLUEVE TLALOC, no. 5 (1978), p. 34.

4604 Pazos, Antonio. [Untitled graphic]. LLUEVE TLALOC, no. 5 (1978), p. 38.

4605 Pazos, Antonio. [Untitled graphic]. LLUEVE TLALOC, no. 5 (1978), p. 40.

4606 Pazos, Antonio. [Untitled graphic]. LLUEVE TLALOC, no. 6 (1979), p. Cover.

4607 Pazos, Antonio. [Untitled graphic]. LLUEVE TLALOC, no. 6 (1979), p. 10.

4608 Pazos, Antonio. [Untitled graphic]. LLUEVE TLALOC, no. 6 (1979), p. 12.

4609 Pazos, Antonio. [Untitled graphic]. LLUEVE TLALOC, no. 6 (1979), p. 15.

4610 Pazos, Antonio. [Untitled graphic]. LLUEVE TLALOC, no. 6 (1979), p. 17.

4611 Pazos, Antonio. [Untitled graphic]. LLUEVE TLALOC, no. 6 (1979), p. 19.

4612 Pazos, Antonio. [Untitled graphic]. LLUEVE TLALOC, no. 6 (1979), p. 21.

4613 Pazos, Antonio. [Untitled graphic]. LLUEVE TLALOC, no. 6 (1979), p. 23.

4614 Pazos, Antonio. [Untitled graphic]. LLUEVE TLALOC, no. 6 (1979), p. 29.

4615 Pazos, Antonio. [Untitled graphic]. LLUEVE TLALOC, no. 6 (1979), p. 35.

4616 Pazos, Antonio. [Untitled graphic]. LLUEVE TLALOC, no. 7 (1980), p. Cover.

4617 Pazos, Antonio. [Untitled graphic]. LLUEVE TLALOC, no. 8 (1981), p. Cover.

Graphics (cont.)

4618 Pazos, Antonio. [Untitled graphics]. MAIZE, Vol. 2, no. 1 (Fall   1978), p. 59-60,[65]. English.

4619 Pena, Amado Maurilio, Jr. Amado Maurilio Pena, Jr. Brochure [1980]. English.

AN: Promotional brochure including a biographical profile of the artist, a list of representing galleries throughout the United States, and eight good quality reproductions of serigraphs and mixed media drawings, six in color, on the theme of New Mexican Pueblo Indians.

4620 Pena, Amado Maurilio, Jr. Huelga [print]. CARACOL, Vol. 3, no. 8 (April 1977), p. 24.

4621 Pena, Amado Maurilio, Jr. Support Texas farm workers [print]. CARACOL, Vol. 3, no. 8 (April 1977), p. 1.

4622 Pena, Amado Maurilio, Jr. [Untitled graphic]. REVISTA RIO BRAVO, no. 1 (Fall 1980), p. Bk cover.

4623 Pena, Amado Maurilio, Jr. [Untitled graphic]. REVISTA RIO BRAVO, no. 1 (Fall 1980), p. 19.

4624 Pena, Amado Maurilio, Jr. [Untitled graphic]. REVISTA RIO BRAVO, no. 1 (Fall 1980), p. 16, 17.

4625 Pena, Amado Maurilio, Jr. [Untitled graphic]. REVISTA RIO BRAVO, no. 1 (Fall 1980), p. Ft cover.

4626 Pena, Amado Maurilio, Jr. [Untitled silkscreen]. CARACOL, Vol. 1, no. 6 (February 1975), p. COVER.

4627 Penalosa, Fernando. [Untitled graphic]. DE COLORES, Vol. 2, no. 4 (1976), p. Cover.

4628 Perez, Irene. La huichola [graphic]. CHISMEARTE, Vol. 1, no. 4 (Fall , Winter, 1977, 1978), p. [20-21].

4629 Photo-graphics/foto-grafica. MAIZE, Vol. 4, no. 1-2 (Fall , Winter, 1980, 1981). Bilingual.

AN: 9 drawings and prints by Royal Chicano Air Force (Sacramento, Calif.) artists Jose Montoya, Juanishi Orozco, Esteban Villa.

4630 Posada, Jose Guadalupe. Calavera huertista [graphic]. REGENERACION, Vol. 1, no. 7 (1970), p. COVER.

4631 Posada, Jose Guadalupe. [El jarabe en ultratumba (graphic)]. CARACOL, Vol. 1, no. 3 (November 1974), p. Cover.

4632 Pro Arts Gallery, Oakland, CA. Si se puede! We can do it!: an exhibition of silkscreen prints and posters by Malaquias Montoya. Exhibition announcement, [1981]. English.

AN: Announcement of a traveling exhibit of prints and posters in Oakland, California. Illustrated.

4633 Rabel, Fanny. [Untitled woodcut]. CARACOL, Vol. 1, no. 12 (August 1975), p. 11.

4634 Rangel, Jesus. Heirs of Jose Posada: revolution lives in Chicano art. SAN DIEGO UNION, (February 24, 1980), p. D6. English.

AN: 19th century Mexican engraver Jose Guadalupe Posada has been an inspiration to Chicano artists. Along with two exhibits of his work, the Centro Cultural de la Raza is also showing calavera (skeleton) images by Chicano artists: skull-masks from the Teatro Campesino, a print by Amalia Mesa-Baines of Frida Kahlo, and a collaged box by Jose Antonio Burciaga. Illustration: Salvador Roberto Torres work.

4635 Raoul Mora. ESENCIA, Vol. 1, no. 3 (March, April, 1982).

AN: Brief article on Stockton-born landscape painter and lithographer who records the beauties of Northern California in flat patterns and strong color. Illustrated.

4636 Raza Unida Party [graphic]. CARACOL, Vol. 4, no. 5 (January 1978), p. 5. Bilingual.

4637 Reser, Phil. Rene Yanez: state-of-the-xerox art. CITY ARTS, Vol. 3, no. 8 (August 1981). English.

AN: Five years ago when Xerox came out with a color copier, Yanez started experimenting with the machine's color buttons, which he uses like a musical instrument or a paint brush. Yanez's work is showing at the Electro-Arts Gallery in San Francisco. Brief profile of the artist, whose father and grandfather were both artists.

4638 Rios, Roberto. La familia [silkscreen]. CARACOL, Vol. 3, no. 1 (September 1976), p. 3. Spanish.

4639 Rodriguez, Patricia. Untitled [graphic]. LA PALABRA, Vol. 2, no. 2 (Fall 1980), p. 41.

4640 Rupert Garcia. SAN FRANCISCO BAY GUARDIAN, (October 3, 1975), p. 22-23. English.

AN: Informative piece focusing on the artist's work procedures; his techniques of image selection, transformation and manipulation. Presents Garcia's political and aesthetic credo and situates him as a community activist and artist. Illustrated with reproduction of Garcia's BICENTENNIAL POSTER.

4641 Sagel, Jaime. Art of brothers taps New Mexico heritage. JOURNAL NORTH, (December 16, 1981). English.

AN: Three brothers, graphics artist, painter, photographer, potter and poet Alejandro Lopez and his older self-taught brothers Felix and Manuel, are working with traditional New Mexican art forms (bultos, straw inlay crosses) and with newer innovative forms - reflecting the fusion of traditional-experimental art developing in New Mexico among young artists.

4642 San Francisco Museum of Art, San Francisco, CA. M.I.X. graphics I: prints. Exhibition invitation, 1974. English.

AN: Invitation to an exhibit of 15 multi-ethnic artists, including San Francisco artists Ralph Maradiaga and Rupert Garcia.

Graphics (cont.)

Exhibitions gallery (LACE).

4643 Schlesinger, Ellen. At the Galeria Posada there is sophistication, machismo and humor: Villa has varied impact. SACRAMENTO BEE, (August 23, 1981), p. Scene, 3. English.

AN: Favorable review of exhibit by Esteban Villa showing etchings, xerox prints, lithographs and other graphics. Villa's world view is broad, critical, political and romantic and encompasses comments of computerized society to stylized landscapes. Illustrated.

4644 La Sociedad Historica de Nuestra Senora de Guadalupe, Santa Fe, NM. Meditacion. Exhibition invitation, 1980. English.

AN: Invitation to an exhibit by four artists: Filomeno Martinez (graphic artist, Albuquerque), Ruben Montoya (santero, Santa Fe), Santiago Chavez (painter, Santa Rosa), Jose Alberto Baros (sculptor, Espanola).

4645 Southern Colorado State College, Pueblo, CO and Monteverde, Mildred. Chicanos graficos [sic]...California. Exhibition brochure, [1974]. Spanish.

AN: Brief background of California art movement and 13 artists from San Francisco, Los Angeles, Sacramento, Fresno. Important factual information despite numerous errors with names and Spanish terms. 16 illustrations of silkscreens, lithograph, etching.

4646 SPARC (Social and Public Arts Resource Center), Venice, CA and Los Angeles. Ceta VI, Venice, CA. Hecho en Aztlan multiples: screen printed works. Exhibition invitation, 1980. English.

AN: Invitation to an exhibit of silkscreen prints by Hecho en Aztlan Multiples, a small business run by Richard Duardo. At the Social and Public Art Resource Center, Venice, Calif.

4647 Spurgin, Judy. Amado Maurilio Pena, Jr. ULTRA MAGAZINE, Vol. 1, no. 1 (September 1981). English.

AN: Succinct treatment of Pena's artistic trajectory and a superficial analysis of his work. Information on his patrons and supporters.

4648 Temko, Allan. Teen Angel's low riders - Chicano art on the rise. THIS WORLD, (August 26, 1979), p. 42-43. English.

AN: Important and insightful analysis of the lowrider phenomenon among Chicano youth in California. Analysis of publications like LOW RIDER Magazine of San Jose, information on graphic artists like "Teen Angel" and Ramon Cisneros and thematic relationship of recognized Chicano artists like Gilbert Lujan, John Valadez, and Luis Jimenez to the lowrider movement. The lowrider is provocatively related to world wide cultural manifestations from diverse epochs.

4649 Testimonios de Latinoamerica. LA PRENSA SAN DIEGO, (October 26, 1979), p. 3. Spanish.

AN: Announcement of an exhibit at the Centro Cultural de la Raza, San Diego, "Testimonios de Latino America" and "America en la mira," political graphics organized by Mexican artist Felipe Ehrenberg and also shown at the Los Angeles Contemporary

4650 Time to greez: incantations from the Third World. San Francisco, CA: Glide Publications/Third World Communications, 1975. English.

AN: Rupert Garcia, drawing, p. 158; Xavier Viramontes, silkscreen, p. 181; Juan Fuentes, drawing, p. 188; Graciela Carrillo, drawing, p. 196.

4651 Torres, Pablo, Jr. La Cena [silkscreen]. CARACOL, Vol. 3, no. 4 (December 1976), p. 13.

4652 Valadez, Kathy L. and Valadez, Kathy L. Living in the understanding of success/el endendimiento [sic] del exito. CAMINOS, Vol. 1, no. 6 (October 1980), p. 12-14, 40. Bilingual.

AN: Story about financially successful Los Angeles illustrator Ignacio Gomez who produced the illustration for the play ZOOT SUIT and designs posters, catalogs, magazine covers and layouts. Also see front cover and inside of front cover for illustrations.

4653 Valdez, Patssi. [Skulls (graphic)]. REGENERACION, Vol. 2, no. 2 (1972), p. 2.

4654 Valdez, Patssi. [Skulls (graphic)]. REGENERACION, Vol. 2, no. 2 (1972), p. 17.

4655 Villa, Esteban. Mujer with taco on her head [graphic]. MAIZE, Vol. 4, no. 1-2 (Fall , Winter, 1980, 1981), p. 85. Bilingual.

4656 Villa, Esteban. [Untitled graphic]. MAIZE, Vol. 4, no. 1-2 (Fall , Winter, 1980, 1981), p. 65. Bilingual.

4657 Villa, Esteban. [Untitled graphic]. MAIZE, Vol. 4, no. 1-2 (Fall , Winter, 1980, 1981), p. 71. English.

4658 Villa, Esteban. [Untitled graphic]. MAIZE, Vol. 4, no. 1-2 (Fall , Winter, 1980, 1981), p. 81. English.

4659 Woodblock and linoleum prints by Carlos Cortez, member of the Chicago mural group. TIN TAN, Vol. 2, no. 6 (December 1, 1977). English.

AN: Seven works reproduced from prints by Cortez, also an active member of the Movimiento Artistico Chicano of Chicago, dating from 1971 to 1976.

4660 Woodcuts by Cesar Augusto Martinez. Albuquerque, NM: Pajarito Publications, 1976, p. 13, 29, 43, 54, 74, 90, 96. English.

AN: Seven woodcuts from 1975-1976 by the San Antonio artist.

4661 Xerox Reproductions Center, San Francisco, CA. Fine arts exhibitions of color xerox. Exhibition invitation, 1978-79. English.

AN: Invitation to an exhibit featuring Rene Yanez and 11 other artists working in color Xerox.

4662 Xochipilli Macuilxochitl [graphic]. REGENERACION, Vol. 1, no. 9 (1970), p. 22.

4663 Yanez, Rene. 10 [print]. EL GRITO, Vol. 2, no. 3 (Spring 1969), p. [46]. Bilingual.

Graphics (cont.)

4664 Yanez, Rene. 8 [print]. EL GRITO, Vol. 2,
     no. 3 (Spring 1969), p. [45]. Bilingual.

4665 Yanez, Rene. 9 [print]. EL GRITO, Vol. 2,
     no. 3 (Spring 1969), p. [46]. Bilingual.

4666 Zuniga, Ramiro. Calle [graphic]. XALMAN,
     Vol. 2, no. 1 (Spring 1978), p. III.

4667 Zuniga, Ramiro. Red and blue [graphic].
     XALMAN, Vol. 2, no. 1 (Spring 1978), p. 69.

4668 Zuniga, Ramiro. [Untitled graphic]. XALMAN,
     Vol. 2, no. 1 (Spring 1978), p. 32-33.

GREAT WALL OF LOS ANGELES [film]

4669 Deitch, Donna. The great wall of Los
     Angeles. Film, 1976. Bilingual.

     AN: Eight minute 16 mm film produced by
     SPARC (Social and Public Art Resource
     Center) on the GREAT WALL OF LOS ANGELES
     mural. In English with Spanish subtitles.

4670 SPARC (Social and Public Arts Resource
     Center), Venice, CA. The great wall of Los
     Angeles. Brochure, n.d. English.

     AN: Publicity brochure for the rental or
     purchase of the film The Great Wall of Los
     Angeles. Reproduces photographs of the
     mural, statements of youth participants, and
     names of the mural director and supervisors.

GREAT WALL OF LOS ANGELES [mural]

4671 Lugavere, Joel P. Artists to add '40s to
     Great Wall mural. LOS ANGELES TIMES
     [Glendale/Burbank edition], (September 20,
     1981), p. 1. English.

     AN: Brief illustrated story on 1981
     extension of the Tujunga Wash mural, THE
     GREAT WALL OF LOS ANGELES, directed by Judy
     Baca of SPARC, (Social and Public Arts
     Resource Center in Venice California).

4672 Mills, Kay. The great wall of Los Angeles.
     MS.MAGAZINE, (October 1981), p. 66-69+.
     English.

     AN: THE GREAT WALL OF LOS ANGELES in the
     Tujunga flood control channel in the San
     Fernando Valley, was started as a
     Bicentennial project in 1976. Artistic
     director Judy Baca of the Social and Public
     Art Resource Center, works with crews of
     young people painting aspects of Los Angeles
     history that is not generally found in
     textbooks. Well illustrated.

4673 Mitchell, John L. History restarted with
     mural grant. LOS ANGELES TIMES [Valley
     edition], (February 3, 1980), p. XI,1,4.
     English.

     AN: Interview with Judith Baca on the
     goals and purposes of the "Great Wall of Los
     Angeles" mural project. The central aim is
     to provide work, educational experience and
     skills for 40 ethnically-mixed unemployed
     youngsters between the ages of 14-21.
     Article details evolution of the project and
     funding sources. Illustrated.

4674 NATIONAL MURALS NETWORK COMMUNITY
     NEWSLETTER. (Fall 1980). English.

     AN: Reports on murals in San Francisco,
     CA, by the Chicano Moratorium Coalition; in

Chicago about the Anti-War Preparations
mural; in Houston by a student at the
Association for Advancement of Mexican
Americans; on Michael Schorr's mural in
Chicanok, San Diego, CA; on a segment being
painted at the Tujunga Wash mural in Los
Angeles under Judy Baca; on south San Diego
murals being painted out; Alan Barnett's
survey of Southwest murals. Illustrated.

4675 NATIONAL MURALS NETWORK COMMUNITY
     NEWSLETTER. (1978). English.

     AN: This issue features reports from
     muralists. Includes information about murals
     at: La Pena Cultural Center in Berkeley, CA;
     the Social and Public Art Resource Center's
     Tujunga Wash Mural in Venice, CA; the
     Citywide Mural Project in Los Angeles, CA;
     activities at Chicano Park, and of the
     Congress of American Cosmic Artists (CACA),
     both in San Diego, CA; murals in San Mateo
     County, CA; the Task Force on Hispanic
     American Arts headed by Jacinto Quirarte of
     San Antonio; the 1978 Canto Al Pueblo in
     Corpus Christi, TX; murals in Chicago; and
     other works by non-Chicano artists.

4676 Parachini, Allan. Tujunga wash mural stands
     up to storm. LOS ANGELES TIMES, (March 13,
     1980), p. V, 1. English.

     AN: Information about the mural project
     near Los Angeles Valley College in Van Nuys,
     Calif. sponsored by SPARC (Social and Public
     Art Resource Center) of Venice, Calif. and
     coordinated by Judy Baca. Illustrated.

4677 Rickey, Carrie. The passion of Ana. VILLAGE
     VOICE, Vol. 25, no. 37 (September 10, 1980),
     p. 75. English.

     AN: Review of the exhibition DIALECTICS
     OF ISOLATION, AN EXHIBITION OF THIRD WORLD
     WOMEN ARTISTS OF THE UNITED STATES at the
     A.I.R Gallery in New York, September 1980.
     Includes a capsule analysis of Judith Baca's
     colossal mural in Tujunga Wash in Los
     Angeles. The mural "proposes to restore to
     public consciousness the ethnic and cultural
     history of the city's minorities." Details
     work procedures, content and political aims
     of the project. Eleven blue prints of mural
     cartoons detailing highlights of the mural's
     visual narrative were displayed in the
     exhibit.

4678 Rickey, Carrie. The writing on the wall. ART
     IN AMERICA, Vol. 69, no. 5 (May 1981), p.
     54-57. English.

     AN: Detailed article on the career of
     Judy Baca, director of SPARC (Social and
     Public Arts Resource Center) in Venice,
     Calif., and of the Great Wall of Los
     Angeles, a five year mural project at the
     Tujunga Wash. Well illustrated in black and
     white and color.

4679 SPARC (Social and Public Arts Resource
     Center), Venice, CA. The great wall of Los
     Angeles. Brochure, n.d. English.

     AN: Publicity brochure for the rental or
     purchase of the film The Great Wall of Los
     Angeles. Reproduces photographs of the
     mural, statements of youth participants, and
     names of the mural director and supervisors.

GREAT WALL OF LOS ANGELES [mural] (cont.)

4680 Walking tour and guide to the Great Wall at Tujunga Wash. Venice, CA: Social and Public Art Resource Center, [1981]. English.

AN: History and symbolism of the GREAT WALL, directed by Judy Baca, and created by teams of young people working on the mural since 1976. Illustrated.

4681 Wu, Ying Ying. Mural, mural on the Great Wall. LOS ANGELES TIMES, (September 16, 1980), p. VI,4. English.

AN: Information on a video project directed by John Rier to document work on the 1700-ft. mural THE GREAT WALL OF LOS ANGELES which depicts California history with an emphasis on the role that minorities had in forging that history. Three teen-agers were trained in video production while assisting with taping the mural project. Simultaneously, 40 other youngsters hired from the Summer Program for the Employment of Disadvantaged Youth painted a 400-ft. section of the mural in 1980. Article describes the various skills mathematical, social and artistic developed by youth involved in the project. The mural was started as a Bicentennial Project in 1976 by Judy Baca for the Social and Public Art Resources Center in Venice, California. Illustrated with 3 photographs of various aspects of the Project.

Grigsby, J. Eugene, Jr.

4682 The First Unitarian Universalist Church, Paradise Valley, AZ. Five Chicano artists. Exhibition brochure, 1971. English.

AN: Exhibit organized by L. Eugene Grigsby, Jr., Art Department of Arizona State University, Tempe, AZ. 21 works by Eugene Quesada, David Nunez, Fernando Navarro, Luis Baiz (of Arizona) and Saul Solache (of Los Angeles). Brief biographies of the artists.

Grijalva, Lucila V.

4683 Exxon Company, Houston, TX and Quirarte, Jacinto. Chicano art of the barrio. Exhibition brochure, n.d. [c.1976]. English.

AN: Brochure for a traveling exhibit of photographically-reproduced Chicano murals: Leo Limon, Lucila Villasenor Grijalva, Antonio Esparza, Susan Saenz, Charles Felix, Hoyo-Mara gang, David A. Lopez and team, Roberto Chavez and team (Los Angeles); Jerry Concha, Ruben Guzman, Chuy Campusano (San Francisco); Manuel Unzueta (Santa Barbara). Ernie Palomino and Leo Esequiel Ozona (Fresno). Leo Tanguma (Houston), Roberto Lucero, Manuel Martinez and Al Sanchez (Denver).

4684 Mascorro, Julie. Mechicano Art Center exhibit to grace Price gallery walls. CAMPUS NEWS, (November 24, 1971). English.

AN: Brief history of Mechicano Art Center activities from its establishment in 1969 to 1971. Exhibiting are Charles Almaraz, Roberto Amaral, Raymond Atilano, William Bejarano, Armando Cabrera, Edward Carbajal, Leonard Castellanos, Henry de Vega, Antonio Esparza, Bob Gomez, Lucila V. Grijalva, Jesus Gutierrez, Santos Lira, Frank Martinez, Ernest Palomino, Louis Quijada, Richard Raya, Frank Romero. Illustrated.

4685 Mechicano Art Center, Los Angeles, CA. Lucila [V. Grijalva] reception. Exhibition announcement [1976]. English.

AN: Flyer announcing an exhibit for the Los Angeles painter and muralist.

4686 Romotsky, Jerry and Romotsky, Sally R. Placas and murals. ARTS IN SOCIETY, Vol. 2, no. 1 (Summer, Fall , 1974), p. 286-299. English.

AN: Details how Chicano muralists have recognized the aesthetics of graffiti and incorporated them into their murals. Among the earliest to do so were Lucille Grijalva and Willie Herron. Illustrated.

Gronk (Pseud.)

4687 Blanco, Gil. Art on the walls: a vehicle for positive change. LATIN QUARTER, Vol. 1, no. 2 (October 1974), p. 26-30. English.

AN: East Los Angeles artists Ismael "Smiley" Pereira and C.W. (Charles) Felix started painting murals with young people at the Estrada Courts Housing Project in May 1973. There are now 30 murals, and the residents are more receptive, noting the changes that are taking place. Illustrated with murals by Herron and Gronk, and Daniel Martinez.

4688 Cultura chicana: Los Angeles. COMUNIDAD, no. 11 (July 13, 1980), p. 1-15. Spanish.

AN: The whole issue of the Cultural Supplement concerns Chicano art and music. Captioned photographs deal with visual artists Carlos Almaraz, Jerry Dreva [not Chicano], Glugio Gronk, Willie Herron, John Valadez, Patssi Valdez, with examples of their work. With the exception of Dreva, all the artists are members of Los Four or Asco. Asco member Harry Gamboa, Jr. sums up the 1960s and 1970s and activities of artists in his essay "Seis imaginaciones: Artistas chicanos en Los Angeles." Well illustrated.

4689 Dreva & Gronk exhibit at L.A.C.E.: Gronkart live; Bonbon returns. Exhibition invitation, 1978. English.

AN: Illustrated invitation/poster to exhibit of Asco's Gronk, and Jerry Dreva, a collaborative show featuring ten years of work:photos, correspondence, documents, ephemera and other art.

4690 Edy. A true barrio art. EL CHICANO, (December 7, 1972), p. 9. English.

AN: Interview with East Los Angeles artists Harry Gamboa, Robert Gronk and Willie Herron (also included in the conversation are Patsy Valdez and Eddie Ytuarte). Suffering, fatalism, existential reality and the awareness of cultural colonialism are cited as sources of inspiration for urban barrio art. Illustrated with a photograph of Willie Herron's Quetzalcoatl mural in City Terrace barrio and two drawings by Robert Gronk and Harry Gamboa.

Gronk (Pseud.) (cont.)

4691 Exploratorium, Student Union, California
State University, Los Angeles. Herron/Gronk
in ILLEGAL LANDSCAPE. Exhibition catalog,
1980. English.

AN: Invitation to a "performance" piece
NO MOVIE by Willie Herron and Gronk, two
members of ASCO. Illustrated.

4692 Gamboa, Harry, Jr.; Gronk; and Herron,
Willie. Gronk and Herron. NEWORLD, Vol. 2,
no. 3 (Spring 1976), p. 28-30. English.

AN: An interview with ASCO members Gronk
and Willie Herron by a third member, Gamboa.
Brief historical introduction (1970 on). The
witty tongue-in-cheek interview can be
considered an artwork by this performance
art group. Illustrated.

4693 Gamboa, Harry, Jr. and Gronk. Gronk:
off-the-wall artist. NEWORLD, Vol. 6, no. 4
(1980), p. 33-43. English.

AN: Interview with Gronk about his No
Movies, by Harry Gamboa, Jr., both members
(with Willie Herron and Patssi Valdez) of
ASCO. The interview itself can be seen as an
"art piece" with photographs by Gamboa; it
contains valuable information about the
ideas and activities of the group.

4694 Gamboa, Harry, Jr. Los murales de Aztlan.
COMUNIDAD, (June 28, 1981), p. 8-9+.
Spanish.

AN: Review of the exhibit at the Craft
and Folk Art Museum of Los Angeles of MURALS
OF AZTLAN: THE STREET PAINTERS OF EAST LOS
in which Carlos Almaraz, Gronk, Judithe
Hernandez, Willie Herron, Frank Romero, John
Valadez and the East Los Streetscapers
(David Botello, Wayne Healy, George Yepes)
painted portable murals in the gallery. The
murals are described and illustrated.

4695 Gamboa, Harry, Jr. Seis imaginaciones:
artistas chicanos en Los Angeles. COMUNIDAD,
(July 13, 1980), p. 10. Spanish.

AN: A limited flow of media information
about Los Angeles Chicanos has produced a
"ghost" culture. Only sensational events are
published. Alternative magazines like LA
RAZA, CON SAFOS, and REGENERACION have
disseminated Chicano ideas of the 1970s. The
Chicano imagination has appeared in murals
by Willie Herron, Gronk, Carlos Almaraz,
John Valadez; in pieces like "walking" and
"instant" murals by the group ASCO; by the
group Los Four; by group exhibits like
"Chicanismo en el arte," and "Chicanarte."
Patssi Valdez showed Photobooth Piece at the
"Chicanismo" show. Gronk and Jerry Dreva
exhibited their mail art at "Punk Meets
Art." In Spanish.

4696 Gronk and Gamboa, Harry, Jr. Interview:
Gronk and Gamboa. CHISMEARTE, Vol. 1, no. 1
(Fall 1976), p. 31-33. English.

AN: Interview with two members of the
group Asco concerning their NO MOVIE series.
Questions and answers were probably written
by the artists themselves as a performance
art piece. Includes a description of the
group and their 1972 ACTION PROJECT PIE IN
DEFACE: L.A. COUNTY MUSEUM OF ART.
Illustrations.

4697 L.A.C.E. (Los Angeles Contemporary
Exhibitions), Los Angeles, CA. Gronk/Dreva,

1968-1978: ten years of art/life. Exhibition
brochure, 1978. English.

AN: Exhibit and other acitivities by
Gronk of the group ASCO and Jerry Dreva.

4698 L.A.C.E. (Los Angeles Contemporary
Exhibitions), Los Angeles, CA. No Movie: Gil
de Montes, Teddy, Glugio [Gronk], Patssi,
Gamboa. Exhibition invitation, 1978.
English.

AN: Invitation to "performance" piece by
Roberto Gil de Montes, Teddy Sandoval,
Gronk, Patssi Valdez and Harry Gamboa, Jr.,
the latter three of the ASCO group.
Illustrated.

4699 Literally live movie at NO MOVIE exhibit.
CIVIC CENTER NEWS, Vol. 7, no. 17 (April 25,
1978), p. 1. English.

AN: Story on the ASCO "performance" NO
MOVIE, described by "Glugio" Gronk as
"movies without celluloid" to be held at
LACE Gallery. Illustrated.

4700 Los Angeles City College. Latinos de tres
mundos. Exhibition invitation, 1980.
English.

AN: Invitation to an exhibit featuring
the work of ASCO members Harry Gamboa, Jr.,
Gronk, Willie Herron; painters Xavier Mendez
and Olivia Sanchez; and photographer Ricardo
Valverde.

4701 Mechicano Art Center, Los Angeles, CA.
Schizophrenibeneficial. Exhibition
invitation, 1977. English.

AN: Invitation to an ASCO "performance"
work: "Projecting of Visual and/or Verbal
Personality Disorders Onto Person or Persons
Unknown." Glugio (Gronk), Teddy (Sandoval),
(Roberto) Gil de Montes, Patssi (Valdez),
(Harry) Gamboa.

4702 Moisan, Jim. Ancient roots, new visions.
ARTWEEK, Vol. 9, no. 26 (July 29, 1978), p.
8. English.

AN: Review of the show held at the
Municipal Arts Gallery of Los Angeles, the
first national touring show of Latino
artists in the United States. Includes
commentary on work of Larry Fuente, Luis
Jimenez, Frank Romero, Harry Gamboa, Gronk,
Rudy Martinez, Benjamin Serrano, Ricardo
Diaz, Patssi Valdez, Mel Casas, Luis Leroy,
Pedro Lujan. A related show, NEW VISIONS,
L.A., includes Robert Delgado, Ray Bravo,
Joe Moran, Rosalyn Mesquita, Patricia
Murillo and others.

4703 EL PLAYANO (Loyola University, Los Angeles).
(Spring 1972).

AN: Illustrations by Willie Herron,
Harry Gamboa, Jr., Gronk, Diane Gamboa,
William A. Bejarano, Eddie Garcia.

4704 EL PLAYANO (Loyola University, Los Angeles).
(Spring 1973).

AN: Illustrations by Simon Gonzales,
Gronk, Harry Gamboa, Jr., Willie Herron,
Charles Almaraz, Sister Teresa Munoz, Patsy
Valdez, Diane Gamboa.

Gronk (Pseud.) (cont.)

4705 The Point Gallery, Santa Monica, CA. ASCO
(Gronk, Patssi, Gamboa, Herron), Los Four
(Almaraz, de la Rocha, Judithe Hernandez,
Gloriamalia Flores, Mauricio Ramirez, John
Valadez. Exhibition invitation, [1975].
English.

AN: Illustrated invitation to an exhibit
of Los Angeles artists.

4706 Valdez, Armando. El calendario chicano 1977.
Hayward, CA: Southwest Network, 1977.
English.

AN: Fifth in a series of historical
calendars produced in 1972, 1974, 1975, 1976
by La Causa Publications and Southwest
Network. Artists whose work is reproduced
are Malaquias Montoya, Amado Maurilio Pena,
Ramori Zamora, Glugio J.L. Nicandro [Gronk],
Etta Delgado, Ricardo Alaniz, Diane Gamboa,
Elisa Marina Coleman, Margarita Calderon,
Jose Antonio Burciaga, Cesar Augusto
Martinez, Maria Ochoa y Valtierra, Juan
Renteria Fuentes, from California, New
Mexico, and Texas.

4707 West Colorado Gallery, Pasadena, CA.
Gronk/Patssi. Exhibition brochure, 1979.
English.

AN: Works on exhibit by ASCO members
Gronk and Patssi Valdez. Photo of artists.

El Grupo [art group], San Antonio, TX

4708 Con Safo. San Antonio, TX: Pintores Chicanos
de San Antonio, [ca. 1975]. English.

AN: Illustrated pamphlet issued by the
San Antonio artists' group Con Safo.
Includes a self-definition and a brief
history of the group under the names El
Grupo, Los Pintores de Aztlan, Los Pintores
de la Nueva Raza, Con Safo (from 1967 on).
Members include Jesse A. Almazan, Mel Casas,
Jose Esquivel, Jose P. Garza, Cesar Augusto
Martinez, Santos Martinez, Felipe Reyes,
Roberto Rios, Jesus C. Trevino, and Vicente
Velasquez.

El Grupo de Santa Ana, CA

4709 Petersen, Karen and Wilson, J.J. Women
artists: Third World. New York, NY: Harper &
Row, 1975. English.

AN: Catalog of slides with accompanying
notes. Slides of Chicana artists available:
Margaret Herrera (Chavez), Consuelo (Chelo)
Gonzalez Amezcua, Santa Barraza, Mujeres
Muralistas, El Grupo de Santa Ana, Carmen
Lomas Garza, Carolina Flores.

Guerra, Carlos Andres

4710 Guerra, Victor, ed. El camino de la cruz.
Austin, TX: Tejidos Publications, 1981.
Spanish.

AN: Carlos Andres Guerra, portfolio;
painting (in color), sculpture, drawing,
jewelry. Luis Guerra drawing on cover.

Guerra, Luis

4711 Galeria de la Raza, San Antonio, TX.
Celebration seventy-four. Exhibition
catalog, [ca. 1974]. English.

AN: Catalog of extensive exhibition
including European, Mexican, and the

following Texan Chicano artists: Rolando
Garces, Cesar Martinez, Ray Chavez, Vicente
Rodriguez, Jorge Garza, Alfred Rodriguez,
Luis Guerra, Carmen Lomas Garza, Bruno
Andrade, Jr., Amado M. Pena Jr., Roberto
Rios, Jose Trevino, Rudy Trevino, Luis
Santoyo, Tati Rubio, Eduardo C. Garza,
Arthur de la Fuente, and Jesus Campos
Trevino.

4712 Guerra, Victor, ed. El camino de la cruz.
Austin, TX: Tejidos Publications, 1981.
Spanish.

AN: Carlos Andres Guerra, portfolio;
painting (in color), sculpture, drawing,
jewelry. Luis Guerra drawing on cover.

4713 Instituto Chicano de Artes y Artesanias
(Texas Instit. Educational Development) and
Instituto Cultural Mexicano (SER/UNAM), San
Antonio, TX. Artistas chicanos: Los
Quemados. San Antonio, TX: Instituto
Chicano, Texas Institute for Educational
Development, 1975. English.

AN: Invitation to an exhibit and
manifesto of 1975 Austin-San Antonio
artists' group, Los Quemados. Included Santa
Barraza, Carolina Flores, Carmen Lomas
Garza, Luis Guerra, Cesar Augusto Martinez,
Santos Martinez, Amado Maurilio Pena, Jr.,
Jose Rivera, Vicente Rodriguez, Jose
Trevino.

Guerra, Teresina

4714 Orozco, Irma. Women & their work. PARA LA
GENTE, Vol. 1, no. 4 (October 1977), p. 12.
English.

AN: Illustrated story about "Women &
Their Work" festival in Austin, Texas,
Oct-Dec 1977. Photographers Maria Flores and
Teresina Guerra, Santa Barraza, Nora
Gonzalez Dodson, Sylvia Orozco, and Modesta
Trevino exhibited.

Guerrero, Adolfo "El Zarco"

4715 Anaya, Rudolfo A. and Ortiz, Simon J.
1680-1980: a ceremony of brotherhood.
Albuquerque, NM: Academic, 1981. English.

AN: A cooperative publication by members
of the former La Academia de la Nueva Raza
(1969-1976) formed of writers and artists,
and the Tri-Centennial Commission of the
All-Indian Pueblo Council. Includes writings
and artworks by Chicanos and Indians from
New Mexico, California, Texas, and Arizona.
Chicano artists works included are by Ellen
Arellano, Juan Estevan Arellano, Alberto
Baros, Jose Antonio Burciaga, Juan Reyes
Cervantes, Rudy Cuellar, Ricardo Favela, El
Zarco Guerrero, Luis Jimenez, Jr., Carlos
Quinto Kemm, Alejandro Lopez, Floyd Lujan,
Jose Montoya, Juanishi Orozco, Leo Romero,
Secundino Sandoval, Jaime Valdez, Maria
Varela, Esteban Villa.

4716 Arizona Commission on the Arts and
Humanities. Humanizarte: the art of Zarco
Guerrero. Exhibition brochure, 1978.
English.

AN: Illustrated brochure of ceramic
masks and bronze sculptures by Zarco
Guerrero. The exhibit traveled throughout
Arizona.

Guerrero, Adolfo "El Zarco" (cont.)

4717 Arizona Commission on the Arts and
     Humanities. Humanizarte: the art of Zarco
     Guerrero. Announcement, n.d. English.

     AN: Poster announcement for an
     exhibition of bronze sculptures and ceramic
     masks by Zarco Guerrero.

4718 Celebracion Chican-india. CAMINOS, Vol. 1,
     no. 3 (May 1980), p. 38-39+. English.

     AN: Portfolio of works exhibited at the
     Galeria Capistrano in southern California:
     Zarco Guerrero, Domingo Ulloa, Mario Torero,
     Guillermo Acevedo. Judithe Hernandez, who
     also exhibited, is not included in the
     portfolio.

4719 Galeria Capistrano, San Juan Capistrano, CA.
     Celebracion Chican-india 1980: Acevedo,
     Hernandez, Torero, Ulloa, Zarco. Exhibition
     brochure, 1980. English.

     AN: Exhibition of Chicano artists
     Judithe Hernandez, Domingo Ulloa, El Zarco
     Guerrero, and Peruvian-born artists
     Guillermo Acevedo and Mario Acevedo Torero.
     Color illustration by Torero.

4720 Guernica, Antonio Jose and Saavedra-Vela,
     Pilar. El Midwest Canto al pueblo: "Otra
     Vez, C/S". AGENDA, Vol. 7, no. 3 (May, June,
     1977), p. 4-13. Bilingual.

     AN: A thorough report on the various
     phases and events of the Midwest Canto al
     Pueblo in Milwaukee, Wisconsin on April 28
     to May 8, 1977. The festival brought
     together artists, poets, musicians, and
     cultural workers to reaffirm, share, and
     celebrate the identity of La Raza with El
     Pueblo. Includes a thematic and iconographic
     overview of Chicano murals in California by
     Jose Montoya, and an analysis of his
     sculpture by Zarco Guerrero from Meza,
     Arizona. Well illustrated. Includes a
     photograph of the collective mural painted
     at 5th St. and National Avenue in Milwaukee,
     Wisconsin during the course of the
     conference.

4721 Guerrero, Adolfo "El Zarco". The new vision
     of Xicanindio art. RAYAS, Vol. 2, no. 1
     (January, February, 1979), p. 3. Bilingual.

     AN: Zarco Guerrero explains his personal
     artistic philosophy that unites Amerindian
     concepts of art to contemporary art forms,
     especially in sculpture. For Guerrero, "the
     Chicano artist is making a monumental effort
     to arrive at a new universal language and to
     create a new meaning of community through
     art.

4722 Hernandez, Manuel de Jesus. Zapata murals
     depict Chicano struggle. LA HONDA, Vol. 5,
     no. 3 (March, April, 1979). English.

     AN: Critical vignettes on the content of
     Chicano murals at Casa Zapata, a Chicano
     theme dorm at Stanford University. The
     muralists include Zarco Guerrero, Esteban
     Chavez, Hector Chacon, and Tina Alvarez.

4723 McClellan, Bill. Army of volunteers paints a
     little history in Phoenix. PHOENIX GAZETTE,
     (April 20, 1977). English.

     AN: Adolfo "El Zarco" Guerrero with 100
     residents from the Duppa Villa Housing
     Project completes a mural funded by the
     Arizona Commission on Arts and Humanities.

Guerrero completed six murals, but prefers
sculpture.

4724 Montini, Ed. Masks reflect the spirit of an
     artist. ARIZONA REPUBLIC, (May 31, 1981),
     p. G-1,G-3. English.

     AN: The paper and ceramic masks of Zarco
     Guerrero reflect many different emotions.
     Masking has long been a tradition in Mexico,
     where Guerrero got his inspiration. Guerrero
     uses his masks for theatre and as an
     educational tool. Illustrated.

4725 Muralist helps youth paint better world.
     YUMA DAILY SUN, (November 14, 1980).
     English.

     AN: Adolfo "Zarco" Guerrero meeting with
     students, educators, officials, and the
     community in Yuma.

4726 Union Gallery, University of Arizona Student
     Union, Tucson, AZ. Chicanarte: Cynthia Reyes
     Aponte, Zarco Guerrero, Virginia Federico
     Olivares, Antonio Pazos. Exhibition catalog,
     1981. English.

     AN: Illustrated catalog of exhibit
     featuring four artists.

4727 Weil Gallery Center for the Arts, Corpus
     Christi State University. Caras y mascaras:
     the art of El Zarco Guerrero. Exhibition
     invitation, 1981. English.

     AN: Invitation to exhibit of Arizona
     artist. Color illustration.

4728 Werley, Lenora. Murals give young artists
     community pride, sculptor says. YUMA DAILY
     SUN, (February 4, 1981). English.

     AN: Mesa, Arizona sculptor Adolfo
     "Zarco" Guerrero feels murals give young
     people pride in their community. Guerrero is
     part of the Xicanindio Artist Coalition that
     is CETA-contracted to run summer art
     programs for high school students.
     Illustrated.

Guerrero, Jose

4729 NATIONAL MURALS NETWORK COMMUNITY
     NEWSLETTER. (Fall 1979). English.

     AN: Reports on mural projects by Fermin
     Coronado working with students in Houston;
     Galeria de la Raza's billboard used as a
     mural surface for changing images; murals
     under the Flor en la Comunidad program of El
     Centro Cultural de la Gente in San Jose,
     California and led by artist Jaime Valadez;
     murals in Grand Rapids and other cities of
     western Michigan; murals by Jose Guerrero
     and others from the Chicago Mural Group; a
     survey of Chicano murals in the Pilsen area
     of Chicago guided by Jose Gonzalez.

Guerrero, Raul M

4730 Chicano art. ARTES VISUALES, no. 29 (1981).
English.

AN: Issue on Chicano art, introduced by
Los Angeles artist Roberto Gil de Montes.
Includes works and statements by: Pedro
Lujan (Texas); Raul M. Guerrero (Calif.);
Sylvia Salazar Simpson (New Mexico/Calif.);
Carlos Almaraz (Calif.); Rene Yanez
(Calif.); Jack Vargas (Calif.); Ray Bravo
(Calif.); John Valadez (Calif.); Gloria Maya
(Calif.); Elsa Flores (Calif.); Willie
Herron (Calif.); Gilbert "Magu" Lujan
(Calif.); Kay Torres, Jerry Lucas, and Louis
Perez (Calif.).

Guerrero, Xochitl Nevel

4731 Garcia, Rupert. Laminas de la Raza. San
Francisco: Garcia Litho and Printing
Service, 1975. English.

AN: Portfolio of drawings and prints by
Patricia Rodriguez, Ricardo Apodaca,
Xochitl, Domingo Rivera, Francisco Camplis,
Rafael Maradiaga, Tom Rios, Juan Fuentes,
Ricardo Diaz, Jose Romero, Consuelo Mendez,
Jose Antonio Burciaga, Irene Perez, Ricardo
Rios, Mike Rios, Graciela Carrillo, Rene
Yanez, Luis Talamantez, Guillermo Bermudez,
all from Northern California.

Guevara, Che

4732 Huerta, Rebecca. The present is a time for
struggle: the future is ours [drawing].
CARACOL, Vol. 5, no. 1 (September 1978), p.
FRNT COVER. Spanish.

A GUIDE TO MURAL ART IN EAST AUSTIN

4733 Barrios, Greg. Big art comes of age. RIVER
CITY SUN, (July 21, 1978), p. 9. English.

AN: Report on the meeting of Mexican and
Chicano muralists at a mural conference in
Austin. Includes a "Guide to Mural Art in
East Austin," most of whose murals were done
by Raul Valdez. Illustrated.

Gurule, Ben

4734 Craft and Folk Art Museum, Los Angeles, CA
and Shapira, Nathan. From flat to form: Ben
Gurule and Carlo Cattaneo. Exhibition
catalog, 1978. English.

AN: Catalog for an exhibit by Los
Angeles Chicano artist Ben Gurule and
Italian artist Cattaneo, both involved with
three-dimensional expression in paper.
Gurule's works examine the interwoven
families of waves, polygons, and circles,
exploring relationships between geometry,
wave mechanics and quantum mechanics. Well
illustrated.

Gutierrez, Andrew

4735 Trevino, Rudy. San Antonio murals a self
portrait. PICANTE, Vol. 1, no. 3, p. 60-61.
English.

AN: Commentary on the San Antonio Mural
Project assisted by the CETA program and the
Barrio Betterment and Development
Corporation (BBDC). Goals and information on
the light murals in progress in the Casiano
Housing Project. Participating artists: Juan
Hernandez, Esteban Adame, Andrew Gutierrez,
Bob Tate, and Roberto de La Fuente.

Gutierrez, Blanca Flor

4736 Galeria de la Raza/Studio 24, San Francisco,
CA. Blanca Flor Gutierrez - oil pastels.
Exhibition announcement, 1981.

AN: Color xeroxed announcement for a
window display of oil pastels by Gutierrez.

Gutierrez, Frank

4737 Brand Library Art Center, Glendale, CA. Los
hermanos: Jesus, Jacob & Frank Gutierrez,
sculpture, paintings, drawings, &
photographs. Exhibition catalog, 1974.
English.

AN: Exhibit of the work of three
brothers living in the Los Angeles area.

Gutierrez, Jacob

4738 Brand Library Art Center, Glendale, CA. Los
hermanos: Jesus, Jacob & Frank Gutierrez,
sculpture, paintings, drawings, &
photographs. Exhibition catalog, 1974.
English.

AN: Exhibit of the work of three
brothers living in the Los Angeles area.

Gutierrez, Jesus

4739 Art Gallery, California State University,
Long Beach and Lujan, Gilbert Sanchez
"Magu". El arte del pocho. Exhibit brochure,
October 1968. English.

AN: Information about Southern
California artists John Deheras, Marcus
Villagran, Roberto de la Rocha, Santos
Zuniga, Crispin Gonzales, Richard Martinez,
Jesus Gutierrez, Ed Oropeza, Pete Mendez,
David Ramirez, Gilbert Sanchez Lujan, Willie
Hernandez, Art Ponce, Carmen Tostado, Al
Almeida, David Ceja, Robert E. Chavez,
Thomas A. Ferriera. All art students,
graduates, or faculty.

4740 Brand Library Art Center, Glendale, CA. Los
hermanos: Jesus, Jacob & Frank Gutierrez,
sculpture, paintings, drawings, &
photographs. Exhibition catalog, 1974.
English.

AN: Exhibit of the work of three
brothers living in the Los Angeles area.

4741 Mascorro, Julie. Mechicano Art Center
exhibit to grace Price gallery walls. CAMPUS
NEWS, (November 24, 1971). English.

AN: Brief history of Mechicano Art
Center activities from its establishment in
1969 to 1971. Exhibiting are Charles
Almaraz, Roberto Amaral, Raymond Atilano,
William Bejarano, Armando Cabrera, Edward
Carbajal, Leonard Castellanos, Henry de
Vega, Antonio Esparza, Bob Gomez, Lucila V.
Grijalva, Jesus Gutierrez, Santos Lira,
Frank Martinez, Ernest Palomino, Louis
Quijada, Richard Raya, Frank Romero.
Illustrated.

Gutierrez, Jose Angel

4742 Garcia-Camarillo, Mia. [Jose Angel Gutierrez
(drawing)]. CARACOL, Vol. 1, no. 3 (November
1974), p. 4.

Gutierrez, Jose Angel (cont.)

4743 Garcia-Camarillo, Mia. [Jose Angel Gutierrez (drawing)]. CARACOL, Vol. 1, no. 3 (November 1974), p. 5.

4744 Garcia-Camarillo, Mia. [Jose Angel Gutierrez (drawing)]. CARACOL, Vol. 1, no. 3 (November 1974), p. 6.

Gutierrez, Lola

4745 Chicano muralists maintain traditions. LA CUCARACHA, (November 20, 1979), p. 7. English.

AN: Introduction to Chicano muralism in Pueblo and comparison to the Mexican mural movement from which it draws inspiration. 20 murals painted from 1977 to 1979. The muralists include Bernardo Duran, Juan Espinoza, Miguel "Freeloader" Garcia, Lola Gutierrez, Leo Lucero, Juan Pacheco, Dolores Pena, Pedro Romero, Stan Salazar, David Sandoval. Diego Rivera murals illustrated.

Gutierrez, Louis

4746 Albright, Thomas. Oakland Museum: a wide range in Latin art. SAN FRANCISCO CHRONICLE, (September 12, 1970), p. 33. English.

AN: A large show called ARTES DE LA RAZA at the Oakland Museum includes Mercedes Gutierrez-McDermid, Louis Gutierrez, Luis Cervantez, Calvin Tondre, Manuel Villamor, Rene Yanez, Jose Ramirez, Jorge Lerma, Rolando Castellon, Esteban Villa, Rupert Garcia, and Gustavo Rivera who is also having an exhibit at the Galeria de la Raza.

4747 California. University. Santa Cruz. College Eight Gallery. Four artists: Edward Carrillo, Consuelo Mendez Castillo, Louis Gutierrez, Jose Montoya. Exhibition catalog, n.d. English.

AN: Exhibit of three Chicano artists and Venezuelan-born artist Consuelo Mendez de Castillo.

4748 The Mexican Museum, San Francisco, CA and Quirarte, Jacinto. 17 artists: Hispano/Mexican-American/Chicano. Exhibition catalog, 1977. English.

AN: Catalog of an exhibit for artists Emilio Aguirre, Consuelo Gonzalez Amezcua, Al Barela, Pedro Cervantez, Edward Chavez, Antonio Garcia, Louis Gutierrez, Harry Louie, Vincent Perez, Michael Ponce de Leon, Eugenio Quesada, Gustavo Rivera, Peter Rodriguez, Alex Sanchez, Darryl Sapien, Rudy Trevino, Manuel Villamor. Illustrated.

4749 New Galeria de la Raza. EL HISPANO, (July 28, 1970), p. 9. English.

AN: Review of the first exhibit at the Galeria de la Raza at 425 14th St. in San Francisco. The inaugural exhibition featured Esteban Villa, Luis Gutierrez and Luis Cervantes. The new Galeria is sponsored by Casa Hispana de Bellas Artes assisted by San Francisco Art Commission through its Neighborhood Arts Program.

Gutierrez, Raul

4750 Salazar, Veronica. Artist doesn't starve now. SAN ANTONIO EXPRESS-NEWS, (June 13, 1976), p. 18-A. English.

AN: Raul Gutierrez, water colorist from

Laredo, Texas, has emerged as a nationally recognized master painter of western and wildlife themes. His work is avidly collected and exhibited. Article details his artistic trajectory and provides biographical information.

Gutierrez-McDermid, Mercedes

4751 Albright, Thomas. Oakland Museum: a wide range in Latin art. SAN FRANCISCO CHRONICLE, (September 12, 1970), p. 33. English.

AN: A large show called ARTES DE LA RAZA at the Oakland Museum includes Mercedes Gutierrez-McDermid, Louis Gutierrez, Luis Cervantez, Calvin Tondre, Manuel Villamor, Rene Yanez, Jose Ramirez, Jorge Lerma, Rolando Castellon, Esteban Villa, Rupert Garcia, and Gustavo Rivera who is also having an exhibit at the Galeria de la Raza.

Guzman, Gilberto

4752 Art in public places. Program statement, 1977-78. English.

AN: Documents an eleven-month program funded by CETA for 21 artists to produce murals, prints and weavings as public art. Includes murals by Gilberto Guzman and Graciela Carrillo-Lopez in Santa Fe. Statements by the artists. Illustrated.

4753 Arts review. ARTS REVIEW, Vol. 31, no. 20 (October 12, 1979), p. 558. English.

AN: Review of show in October Gallery London by Gilberto Guzman of Santa Fe, New Mexico. Guzman is characterized as a "figurative expressionist.".

4754 Barrio, Raymond. Art for our sake. NUESTRO, Vol. 1, no. 6 (September 1977), p. 30-34. English.

AN: Brief text with three color reproductions of murals by Mike Rios (Bart Mural, San Francisco), Gilberto Guzman (West Las Vegas High School, NM), Willie Herron (Farmacia Hidalgo, East Los Angeles, CA).

4755 Callum, Diane. Regional report, The arts: walls of passion. NUESTRO, Vol. 3, no. 11 (December 1979), p. 16, 51. English.

AN: Focusing on muralist Gilberto Guzman, one of the founders of Artes Guadalupanos in Santa Fe, the article details his efforts in the promotion and preservation of Chicano murals in New Mexico.

4756 La Cofradia de Artes y Artesanos Hispanicos and Santa Fe Council for the Arts. El festival hispanico. Festival program, [ca. 1979]. English.

AN: Program for the festival which included over 70 visual artists from northern New Mexico selected and hung by the Cofradia at the Armory for the Arts gallery in Santa Fe. The poster for the festival, reproduced on the program cover, is taken from a painting by Gilberto Guzman. The festival also featured music, cuentos, dance, slide show, poetry, films.

Guzman, Gilberto (cont.)

4757 Corneil, Paul. Militant barrio murals of
     Santa Fe. Venice, CA: Environmental
     Communications, n.d. English.

    AN: Annotated slide catalog with
    introductory text about the mural group Los
    Artes Guadalupanos de Aztlan of Santa Fe.
    Gilberto Guzman is mentioned as one of the
    group.

4758 Fabricant, Don. Show reveals Hispanic art.
     NEW MEXICAN WEEKEND, (June 1, 1979).
     English.

    AN: Review of two exhibits in Santa Fe:
    EL FESTIVAL HISPANICO, mounted by La
    Cofradia de Artes y Artesanos Hispanicos and
    Gilberto Guzman at the Black Kachina
    Gallery. The reviewer feels the
    traditional-style woodcarving done by
    contemporaries is the strongest part of the
    show; works that break with these forms seem
    weaker, less skillful and cliche-ridden.
    Crafts are excellent. Muralist Guzman has
    blossomed in murals and easel paintings
    since he was employed by the 1978 Art in
    Public Places project. His work is intense
    and expressive, sometimes erotic.
    Illustration of work by sculptor Ruben
    Montoya.

4759 From the barrios. OBSERVER, (September 23,
     1979), p. 16+. English.

    AN: Short story on Gilberto Guzman from
    Santa Fe, New Mexico, announcing an exhibit
    of his work in the October Gallery, London.
    Two color reproductions of his paintings.

4760 Loniak, Walter. The true New Mexico
     contemporary style. SANTA FE REPORTER, (May
     31, 1979). English.

    AN: Review of three exhibits in Santa
    Fe, EL FESTIVAL HISPANICO co-sponsored by
    the Cofradia de Artes y Artesanos Hispanicos
    and the Santa Fe Council for the Arts; a
    wood carving exhibit at Elaine Horwitch
    Gallery, and easel paintings by muralist
    Gilberto Guzman at the Black Kachina
    Gallery. Concerning the Festival exhibit,
    the critic states that the sculptural pieces
    are the strongest; two dimensional work is
    inconsistent or unimpressive, weaving is not
    well represented (though usually the
    strongest medium), and there are few
    photographs or prints. Illustration.

4761 NATIONAL MURALS NETWORK COMMUNITY
     NEWSLETTER. (Spring 1981). English.

    AN: Reports, or illustrations, of murals
    by Guillermo Aranda (Calif.), Francisco
    Lefebre (New Mexico); Marcos Raya's section
    of Chicago's anti-war mural; Gilberto
    Guzman's mural (New Mexico); vandalism on a
    Michael Schnorr mural at Chicano Park, San
    Diego, Calif.

4762 New Mexico Arts Division, Santa Fe, NM. Art
     in public places. Catalog, 1977-78, p. 9,
     11. English.

    AN: Catalog of CETA-funded project.
    Illustrated murals by Graciela Carrillo of
    San Francisco, and Gilbert Guzman of Santa
    Fe.

4763 Painted walls - a New Mexico folk art. NEW
     MEXICO, (January 1977), p. 34-35. English.

    AN: Five color illustrations of murals

from New Mexico including those done by
Gilberto Guzman, Geronimo Garduno, and Sam
Leyba. The murals are located in Santa Fe,
Chimayo, Embudo and Albuquerque.

4764 SF muralists display paintings. VIVA,
     (October 8, 1972), p. 19. English.

    AN: Paintings, and photos of murals
    taken by Gilberto Romero, on display at the
    New Mexico Arts Commission. Artists Sammy,
    Carlos and Albert Leyba (the original
    members), Gilberto Guzman and Geronimo
    Garduno, part of the Artes Guadalupanos de
    Aztlan, finished a mural at Tot Lot in 1971
    and are team-painting La Clinica de la
    Gente. They have also painted a mural for
    West Las Vegas High School.

4765 [Untitled photograph]. NUESTRO, Vol. 1, no.
     4 (July 1977), p. 31. English.

    AN: Color reproduction of mural (now
    destroyed) in Santa Fe, New Mexico by
    Gilberto Guzman.

Guzman, Leo

4766 Directo, Cyril. Leo Guzman:
     woodcarver/tallador in madera. ENTRELINEAS,
     Vol. 1, no. 2 (February, March, 1968), p. 8.
     English.

    AN: Biographical facts and commentary on
    artist's work. Illustrated with photographs
    of artist and examples of his work.

Guzman, Ruben

4767 Calendario de comida 1976. San Francisco,
     CA: Galeria de la Raza, 1976. English.

    AN: Handprinted silkscreen calendar
    consisting of twelve sheets and a cover. The
    work of the following artists is included:
    Ralph Maradiaga, Juanishi Orozco, Francisco
    Camplis, Ruben Guzman, Rodolfo Cuellar,
    Xavier Viramontes, Jose Montoya, Esteban
    Villa, Rene Yanez, Max Garcia and Louis "The
    Foot" Gonzalez, Patricia Rodriguez, and
    Ricardo Favela. All of the above are
    associated with the Galeria de la Raza, or
    the Royal Chicano Air Force of Sacramento,
    CA.

4768 Exxon Company, Houston, TX and Quirarte,
     Jacinto. Chicano art of the barrio.
     Exhibition brochure, n.d. [c.1976]. English.

    AN: Brochure for a traveling exhibit of
    photographically-reproduced Chicano murals:
    Leo Limon, Lucila Villasenor Grijalva,
    Antonio Esparza, Susan Saenz, Charles Felix,
    Hoyo-Mara gang, David A. Lopez and team,
    Roberto Chavez and team (Los Angeles); Jerry
    Concha, Ruben Guzman, Chuy Campusano (San
    Francisco); Manuel Unzueta (Santa Barbara).
    Ernie Palomino and Leo Esequiel Ozona
    (Fresno). Leo Tanguma (Houston), Roberto
    Lucero, Manuel Martinez and Al Sanchez
    (Denver).

Handicrafts
     USE: Arts and Crafts

HAY CULTURA EN NUESTRA COMUNIDAD [mural]

4769 Sorell, Victor A. Barrio murals in Chicago:
painting the Hispanic-American experience on
"our community" walls. REVISTA
CHICANO-RIQUENA, Vol. 4, no. 4 (Fall
1976), p. 51-72. English.

AN: Important survey of Chicago's Latino
murals, with key works considered in detail.
Among the Chicano art organizations and
muralists mentioned are MARCH (Movimiento
Artistico Chicano), and Yolanda Galvan,
Juanita Jaramillo, Jose Nario, Raymond
Patlan, Vicente Mendoza, Marcos Raya,
Ricardo Alonzo, Jose G. Gonzalez and Mario
Castillo, author of the earliest Latino
mural in Chicago (1968). Puerto Rican and
non-Latino muralists and mural groups are
also discussed. Well illustrated.

Hayward, CA

4770 Rogelio Cardenas--making murals. EL MUNDO
(San Francisco, CA), (September 14, 1978).
English.

AN: Rogelio Cardenas' fourth mural, LA
MUJER, on the La Mexicana Tortilleria in
Hayward, California. Interview with the
artist who explains the mural's symbolism
and his future plans. Illustrated.

HEALTHY FAMILY [mural]

4771 Karkabi, Barbara. For artist Atanacio P.
Davila, mural is way to express love for
children. HOUSTON CHRONICLE, (May 14,
1980), p. IV-I. English.

AN: Color-illustrated story on
mural-in-progress at the Ripley House
medical clinic by 70 year old Davila titled
THE HEALTHY FAMILY. Son of an artist,
Mexican-born Davila was raised in Texas and
did commercial art and painting until 1938.
After retirement, he has resumed his art.

Healy, Wayne Alaniz

4772 Botello, David Rivas and Healy, Wayne
Alaniz. Los Dos Streetscapers. SOMOS, Vol.
1, no. 3 (August 1978), p. 12-17. English.

AN: Autobiographical material by Los
Angeles street muralists Botello and Healy.
Illustrated.

4773 Los Dos Streetscapers. Los Dos
Streetscapers, mural detail. NATIONAL
GEOGRAPHIC, Vol. 155, no. 1 (January 1979),
p. 38-39. English.

AN: One panel of Los Angeles mural by
Wayne Alaniz Healey and David Botello,
CHICANO TIME TRIP.

4774 Una galeria de artistas = A gallery of
artists. CAMINOS, Vol. 1, no. 6 (October
1980), p. 20-26. Bilingual.

AN: Features California artists Domingo
O. Ulloa (Imperial Valley images), Gloria
Chacon, photographer Maria Pinedo (San
Francisco), Willie Herron (Los Angeles),
Joaquin Patino (Delano), Pedro Pelayo (Long
Beach), sculptor Rudi Sigala (San Diego),
Mario Torero (San Diego), sculptor Michael
M. Amescua (Los Angeles), and the East Los
Streetscapers. Illustrated.

4775 Gamboa, Harry, Jr. Los murales de Aztlan.
COMUNIDAD, (June 28, 1981), p. 8-9+.
Spanish.

AN: Review of the exhibit at the Craft
and Folk Art Museum of Los Angeles of MURALS
OF AZTLAN: THE STREET PAINTERS OF EAST LOS
in which Carlos Almaraz, Gronk, Judithe
Hernandez, Willie Herron, Frank Romero, John
Valadez and the East Los Streetscapers
(David Botello, Wayne Healy, George Yepes)
painted portable murals in the gallery. The
murals are described and illustrated.

4776 Greenberg, David; Smith, Kathryn; and
Teacher, Stuart. Megamurals & supergraphics:
big art. Philadelphia, PN: Running Press,
1977. English.

AN: A full-color picture book of murals
throughout the United States. Chicano murals
include Michael Rios (San Francisco),
Mujeres Muralistas (San Francisco), Leonard
Castellanos and Tomas Gonzales with others
(Los Angeles), Los Artes Guadalupanos de
Aztlan (New Mexico), Willie Herron (Los
Angeles), Toltecas en Aztlan (San Diego),
David Botello (Los Angeles), David Lopez and
Arizona Mara Gang (Los Angeles), Vatos de
Maravilla (Los Angeles), Carlito Gaegos (Los
Angeles), Gil Hernandez (Los Angeles), Wayne
[Alaniz] Healy (Los Angeles).

4777 Varda, Agnes. Mur murs/mural murals on the
wall ... Film, Cine Tamaris, Paris, 1980.
English.

AN: Full length documentary film
produced for French television; also
available with English subtitles. Deals
impressionistically with the murals and
muralists of Los Angeles. Included are Wayne
Aniz Healy, David Botello, Willie Herron,
Manuel Cruz, Judy Baca, the murals in
Venice, CA, graffiti - among others. Color.

Heard Museum, Phoenix, AZ

4778 Arizona. ARIZONA REPUBLIC, (September 11,
1977), p. 50. English.

AN: Exhibit of photographs by Louis
Carlos Bernal from Tucson in the Heard
Museum in Phoenix, Arizona. Includes 6
illustrations.

4779 Heard Museum, Phoenix, AZ. First Annual
Southwest Chicano Art Invitational
Exposition. Invitation for reception, 1976.
English.

AN: Invitation to a reception for
artists Luis Jimenez (Roswell, New Mexico),
Eugenio Quesada (Phoenix), Felipe Reyes (San
Antonio), Pedro Rodriguez (San Francisco),
Pedro Romero (Cannon City, Colo.) One
illustration.

4780 Heard Museum, Phoenix, AZ. Second Southwest
Chicano Art Invitational. Exhibit catalog,
1978. English.

AN: Exhibit by eight artists: Antonio
Pazos (Tucson), Rudy Fernandez (Salt Lake
City), Harry Gamboa (Los Angeles), Rupert
Garcia and Xavier Viramontes (San
Francisco), Roberto Rios (San Antonio),
Roberto Espinoza (Yuma), and Roberto Borboa
(Tucson). Brief biographies of all but Rios.
29 illustrations.

Heard Museum, Phoenix, AZ (cont.)

4781 Miller, Marlan. Heard speaks Spanish through art. PHOENIX GAZETTE, (September 23, 1978). English.

AN: Four new exhibits at the Heard Museum of Phoenix include "Hispanic crafts of the Southwest", and "Southwest Chicano Art Invitational". The former focuses on New Mexico and Colorado crafts, organized by the Taylor Museum if the Colorado Springs Fine Arts Center; the latter includes Rupert Garcia and Xavier Miramontes of San Francisco, Rudy Fernandez of Salt Lake City (now in Scottsdale, AZ), and Antonio Pazos of Tucson.

4782 Riches of the barrios. ARIZONA [supplement to ARIZONA REPUBLIC], (September 11, 1977), p. 50. English.

AN: Louis Carlos Bernal of Tucson shows his collection of photographic portratis of the barrios at the Heard Museum in Phoenix. Well illustrated.

Hecho en Aztlan Multiples

4783 Galeria de la Raza/Studio 24, San Francisco, CA. Published prints of Hecho en Aztlan Multiples. Exhibition announcement, 1980. English.

AN: Announcement of exhibit of the published silkscreen prints of Hecho en Aztlan Multiples; a small business run by Richard Duardo of Los Angeles.

4784 SPARC (Social and Public Arts Resource Center), Venice, CA and Los Angeles. Ceta VI, Venice, CA. Hecho en Aztlan multiples: screen printed works. Exhibition invitation, 1980. English.

AN: Invitation to an exhibit of silkscreen prints by Hecho en Aztlan Multiples, a small business run by Richard Duardo. At the Social and Public Art Resource Center, Venice, Calif.

HECHO EN LATINO AMERICA [exhibit]

4785 Goldman, Shifra M. Hecho en Latino America: first photography colloquium and exhibition. CHISMEARTE, no. 6 (February 1980), p. 16-25. English.

AN: Report on the first colloquium of Latin American photography, Mexico City, May 1978. Analysis and critique of U.S. Latino photographers' work presented in exhibition. Well illustrated.

HENRY...BOY OF THE BARRIO [film]

4786 Films for the inner city. Los Angeles, CA: Los Angeles Public Library Federal Project, 1971. English.

AN: Annotated catalog of 16mm films and filmstrips, educational and documentary. Those concerning Mexican heritage include CHICANO FROM THE SOUTHWEST (1970), HENRY...BOY OF THE BARRIO (1969); HOW'S SCHOOL, ENRIQUE (1970), I AM JOAQUIN (1970), THE MEXICAN AMERICAN: HERITAGE AND DESTINY (1970), A MEXICAN AMERICAN FAMILY (1970), MEXICAN AMERICANS: QUEST FOR EQUALITY (1968), MEXICAN OR AMERICAN (1970), SIQUEIROS: "EL MAESTRO" (THE MARCH OF HUMANITY IN LATIN AMERICA) (1969). Filmstrips include THE AWAKENING (LA RAZA) - Part IV, CONFLICT OF CULTURES (LA RAZA) -

Part III, MASTERWORKS OF MEXICAN ART, OUT OF THE MAINSTREAM, PILGRIMAGE (GRAPE STRIKERS). Also listed are films and filmstrips for children.

Herada, Elma

4787 And/Or Gallery, Seattle, WA. Artistas de Aztlan. Exhibition announcement, 1975. English.

AN: Exhibition announcement for an important exhibit of Northwest Chicano art. Co-sponsored by MEChA and the Chicano Studies Program at the University of Washington, the exhibit presented works by Emilio Aguayo, Danny Desiga, Ricardo Aguirre, Ramiro Benavidez, Elma Herada, Pedro Rodriguez and others. A selection of posters by Armando Cid of the R.C.A.F. group from Sacramento, California was also presented. Concurrently, at the Heny Gallery of the University of Washington, Esteban Villa presented a one-man show.

Heritage Art Gallery, Ypsilanti, MI

4788 Acosta, Dan. Paintings reflect life experiences. THE ECCENTRIC, (June 26, 1980). English.

AN: Review of one-woman show by Nora Chapa Mendoza at the Heritage Art Gallery, Ypsilanti, MI. Mendoza works in abstract impressionist style with wet streams of colors that express energy. Her subjects are landscapes, moods, nudes, and Hispanic themes. She is active in the Detroit Latino Artist Association, Nuestras Artes de Michigan, and the New Detroit Art Council.

Hermanos de Luz
    USE: Hermanos Penitentes

Hermanos de Sangre de Cristo
    USE: Hermanos Penitentes

Hermanos Penitentes

4789 Ahlborn, Richard E. The Penitente Moradas of Abiquiu. Washington, D.C.: Smithsonian Institution Press, 1968 (Contributions from the Museum of History and Technology, Paper 63). English.

AN: The history and organization of the Penitente Brotherhood. Detailed analysis of the architecture of Penitente moradas and the artifacts within them. Illustrated with many ethnographic photographs.

4790 De Cordova, Lorenzo. Echoes of the flute. Santa Fe, NM: Ancient City Press, 1972. English.

AN: First person reminiscences on Penitente traditions in northern New Mexico at the turn of the century. Reprints two Works progress Administration (WPA) manuscripts: "Lent in Cordoba" (n.d.) and "The Wake" (1937). Illustrated with drawings by Eliseo Rodriguez. Notes by Marta Weigle.

Hermosillo, Bert

4791 Mexican American Community Service
Organization, San Jose, CA. Exhibition of
contemporary art. Exhibition brochure, 1968.
English.

AN: Biographical and exhibition data for
Al Barela, Bert Hermosillo, Octavio Romano,
Luis Valdez, Vincent P. Rascon, John Soares
and Al Espinoza.

Hernandez, Armando Leon

4792 Encanto Pavilion, Encanto Park, Phoenix, AZ.
Exposicion de arte para la raza: Arizona
Chicano art show. Exhibition catalog, [ca.
1978]. English.

AN: Catalog for an exhibit organized by
MARS (Movimiento Artistico del Rio Salado).
Colombian-born Antonio L. Tocora, Jim
Covarrubias, Ed Dias, Robert C. Buitron,
Armando Leon Hernandez, Guillermo Galindo,
Richard Luna Cisneros, Jose Andres Giron,
Robert L. Matta included.

Hernandez, Enrique

4793 San Antonio Museum of Modern Art. Zarzamora:
inaugural exhibition of Ladrones de la Luz.
Exhibition invitation, 1979. English.

AN: Illustrated invitation to
photographic exhibition including Norman
Avila, David Cardenas, Franco Cernero,
Enrique Hernandez, Robert Maxham, James
Newberry, Isaac Rodriguez, Daryl Studebaker,
Richard Tichich, Beverly Ulmer, Kathy
Vargas.

Hernandez, Ester

4794 Quintero, Victoria. A mural is a painting on
a wall done by human hands. EL TECOLOTE,
Vol. 5, no. 1 (September 13, 1974), p. 6+.
English.

AN: The women's collective, Mujeres
Muralistas, exists within the strong San
Francisco mural movement. Originally the
group included Graciela Carrillo, Consuelo
Mendez, Irene Perez, and Patricia Rodriguez.
The group has expanded to include Susan
Cervantes, Ester Hernandez, and Miriam
Olivo. The two murals completed have been
criticized for not being political; the
women answer that they want the atmosphere
to be surrounded with life, with colors.
Illustrated.

4795 Venegas, Sybil. The artists and their
work--the role of the Chicana artist.
CHISMEARTE, Vol. 1, no. 4 (Fall , Winter,
1977), p. 3, 5. English.

4796 Venegas, Sybil. Conditions for producing
Chicana art. CHISMEARTE, Vol. 1, no. 4 (Fall
, Winter, 1977, 1978), p. 2, 4. English.

AN: Chicana artists face more obstacles
than white women or Chicano counterparts in
the arts. Mexican life style has portrayed
the ideal of a submissive woman, but the
values have changed. Chicana artists are
concerned with women and their struggles.
Muralists include Patricia Rodriguez, Irene
Perez, Consuelo Mendez de Castillo, Susan
Cervantes, Ester Hernandez, Miriam Olivo,
Ruth Rodriguez, of the Mujeres Muralistas
(San Francisco). Other artists are Etta
Delgado and Barbara Carrasco.

Hernandez, Fernando

4797 Campesino Business and Joint Enterprise
Building, Fresno, CA. Sabor a Fresno. Arte
chicano: los Four and la Brocha. Exhibition
invitation [1976]. English.

AN: Invitation to an exhibit of works by
Los Four of Los Angeles and members of La
Brocha del Valle of Fresno: Arturo Roman,
Sal Garcia, John Sierra, Juan Truner, Sapo
de Aztlan, Fernando Hernandez, Alberto
Reyes, Ernesto Palomino, Lee Orona,
Francisco Barrios, Juan Ybarra, Bobby Reyes,
Alberto Hernandez. Brocha was started by
Palomino (California State University,
Fresno professor) to pool talents of Central
Valley artists.

Hernandez, Francisco (Los Angeles)

4798 Sommer, Robert. Street art. New York: Quick
Fox, 1975. English.

AN: Introductory essay covering the
history of the new mural movement, forms of
street art, politics, street sculpture, how
to locate and photograph street art. Chicano
murals include Charles Felix and others at
Estrada Courts (L.A.), RCAF murals in
Sacramento, Jose Montoya and others
(Broderick, Ca.) Marcos Raya (Chicago), Mike
Rios (Neighborhood Legal Aid, S.F.)
Mechicano Art Center (L.A.) Johnny Alvarez
(L.A.), New Mexico State Employment Bldg.,
Albuquerque mural, Lorena Street School
(L.A.), two murals, Casa de la Raza
Alternative School (Berkeley), Santa Fe, New
Mexico mural, Francisco Hernandez (L.A.),
Artes Guadalupanos de Aztlan (N. Mexico),
Willie Herron (L.A.). Better documentation
would have been welcome.

Hernandez, Frank

4799 Cox, Vic. Beauty in the barrio. WESTWAYS,
Vol. 67, no. 2 (February 1975), p. 50-53.
English.

AN: "Tooner Flats" is another name for
the barrio of East Los Angeles. These
streets are the home and inspiration to
Frank Hernandez who illustrates the article
with pen and ink sketches of buildings.

Hernandez, Gil

4800 Greenberg, David; Smith, Kathryn; and
Teacher, Stuart. Megamurals & supergraphics:
big art. Philadelphia, PN: Running Press,
1977. English.

AN: A full-color picture book of murals
throughout the United States. Chicano murals
include Michael Rios (San Francisco),
Mujeres Muralistas (San Francisco), Leonard
Castellanos and Tomas Gonzales with others
(Los Angeles), Los Artes Guadalupanos de
Aztlan (New Mexico), Willie Herron (Los
Angeles), Toltecas en Aztlan (San Diego),
David Botello (Los Angeles), David Lopez and
Arizona Mara Gang (Los Angeles), Vatos de
Maravilla (Los Angeles), Carlito Gaegos (Los
Angeles), Gil Hernandez (Los Angeles), Wayne
[Alaniz] Healy (Los Angeles).

Hernandez, Jessie

4801 Galeria de arte de Aztlan. AZTLAN (U.S.
     Penitentiary, Leavenworth, KA), Vol. 1, no.
     2. English.

     AN: Pictorial supplement with
     reproductions of pinto art by Manuel
     Aguilera, Jessie Hernandez, Ruben Estrella,
     Tomas Torres and Jose D. Marin. Many of
     these works were reproduced in other Chicano
     newspapers demonstrating the solidarity that
     existed in the Chicano movement inside and
     outside the prison walls.

Hernandez, John

4802 Museum of Fine Arts, Santa Fe, NM. John
     Hernandez, Douglas Johnson. Exhibition
     invitation, 1979. English.

     AN: Invitation to an exhibit including
     the jeweled sculpture of John Hernandez from
     New Mexico.

Hernandez, Juan

4803 Trevino, Rudy. San Antonio murals a self
     portrait. PICANTE, Vol. 1, no. 3, p. 60-61.
     English.

     AN: Commentary on the San Antonio Mural
     Project assisted by the CETA program and the
     Barrio Betterment and Development
     Corporation (BBDC). Goals and information on
     the light murals in progress in the Casiano
     Housing Project. Participating artists: Juan
     Hernandez, Esteban Adame, Andrew Gutierrez,
     Bob Tate, and Roberto de La Fuente.

Hernandez, Judithe E.

4804 Baxter Art Gallery, California Institute of
     Technology and Rosenstone, Robert A. In
     search of...four women/four cultures.
     Exhibition catalog, 1976. English.

     AN: Catalog of an exhibit including
     Donna Nakao, Cheri Pann, Betye Saar, and Los
     Angeles Chicana artist Judithe E. Hernandez.
     One work of each artist illustrated.

4805 La Casa de la Raza Gallery, Santa Barbara,
     CA. Judithe Hernandez: virgen, madre, mujer;
     imagenes de la mujer chicana. Exhibition
     invitation [1979]. English.

     AN: Invitation to an exhibit with a list
     of projects, murals, and exhibitions.
     Illustrated.

4806 Los Four [art group]. Tales from the barrio
     by Los Four and friends. Los Angeles, CA:
     Los Four, Liberty Hill Foundation, United
     Steel Workers, [1977]. English.

     AN: Comic book designed with drawings,
     comic strips, and calligraphy by Frank
     Romero, George Yepes, Carlos D. Almaraz, Leo
     Limon, Judithe Hernandez.

4807 Los Four exhibit in Union Gallery.
     UNIVERSITY TIMES, (November 6, 1975), p. 4.
     English.

     AN: "Los Four," a group of four Chicano
     artists - Frank Romero, Roberto "Beto" de la
     Rocha, Gilbert Lujan, and Carlos Almaraz,
     with newcomer Judithe Hernandez - work with
     political cartoons, Catholic symbols, works
     of sardonic humor. They also paint street
     murals: several have been done recently in
     Los Angeles, La Puente, and Long Beach.
     Illustrated.

4808 Galeria Capistrano, San Juan Capistrano, CA.
     Celebracion Chican-india 1980: Acevedo,
     Hernandez, Torero, Ulloa, Zarco. Exhibition
     brochure, 1980. English.

     AN: Exhibition of Chicano artists
     Judithe Hernandez, Domingo Ulloa, El Zarco
     Guerrero, and Peruvian-born artists
     Guillermo Acevedo and Mario Acevedo Torero.
     Color illustration by Torero.

4809 Gamboa, Harry, Jr. Los murales de Aztlan.
     COMUNIDAD, (June 28, 1981), p. 8-9+.
     Spanish.

     AN: Review of the exhibit at the Craft
     and Folk Art Museum of Los Angeles of MURALS
     OF AZTLAN: THE STREET PAINTERS OF EAST LOS
     in which Carlos Almaraz, Gronk, Judithe
     Hernandez, Willie Herron, Frank Romero, John
     Valadez and the East Los Streetscapers
     (David Botello, Wayne Healy, George Yepes)
     painted portable murals in the gallery. The
     murals are described and illustrated.

4810 Harbor Area Community Art Center, San Pedro,
     CA. Mi arte, mi raza: an exhibition of
     current work by Judithe Hernandez.
     Exhibition invitation, 1979. English.

     AN: Invitation to an exhibit.

4811 Hernandez, Judithe Elena and Goldman, Shifra
     M. Readers' forum. ARTWEEK, Vol. 12, no. 25
     (August 1, 1981), p. 16. English.

     AN: Critical interchange between artist
     Judithe Elena Hernandez de Neikrug and
     critic Shifra M. Goldman concerning the
     latter's review of MURALS OF AZTLAN exhibit.

4812 Herrera, Estela. La mujer en el mundo: una
     chicana en las artes. LA OPINION, (March
     25, 1982), p. III,6. Spanish.

     AN: Illustrated interview with Judith
     Elena Hernandez de Niekrug including
     biographical information and discussion of
     her attitudes toward her murals, paintings,
     and graphics.

4813 Inner City Mural Program. Glendale, CA: Los
     Angeles County Dept. of Parks and
     Recreation, [ca. 1974]. English.

     AN: Brief history and philosophy of the
     Inner City Mural Program from June 1, 1973
     to May 31, 1974, when it was sponsored by
     the Cultural Arts Section of the Los Angeles
     County Department of Parks and Recreation,
     and coordinated by Lukman Glasgow. Artists
     Judithe Hernandez and Frank Romero included.
     20 illustrations, some in color.

4814 Kim, Howard. Judithe Hernandez and a glimpse
     at the Chicana artist. SOMOS, (October,
     November, 1979), p. 6-11. English.

     AN: Biographical information on Chicana
     artist Judithe Hernandez. Commentary on her
     contributions to Plaza de la Raza, Los
     Angeles Citywide Mural Project and her work
     as designer consultant to AZTLAN:
     INTERNATIONAL JOURNAL OF CHICANO RESEARCH.
     The article focuses on her mural activity,
     particularly two murals: EL MUNDO DE BARRIO
     SOTEL and LA CHICANA DE AZTLAN. Her personal
     art philosophy is presented in relation to
     Third World Art.

Hernandez, Judithe E.(cont.)

4815 Oakland Museum, Oakland, CA and Laney College, Oakland, CA. In search of Aztlan. Exhibition brochure, 1974. English.

> **AN:** Brochure for exhibit featuring Los Four: Carlos Almaraz, Gilbert Lujan, Roberto de la Rocha, Frank Romero, Judithe Hernandez.

4816 Oakland Museum, Oakland, CA. In search of Aztlan. Exhibition invitation, 1974. English.

> **AN:** Invitation to an exhibit by Los Four, a Chicano art group started about 1973 in Los Angeles. On exhibit are the original members, Carlos Almaraz, Gilbert Lujan, Roberto de la Rocha, Frank Romero, and new member Judithe Hernandez.

4817 Oakland Museum presents 5 L.A. Chicano artists. EL MUNDO (Hayward, CA), (August 1974). English.

> **AN:** Report on the exhibit THE SEARCH FOR AZTLAN, featuring paintings, murals, tortilla art, folk and religious symbols and totems by Carlos Almaraz, Roberto de la Rocha, Gilbert Lujan, Frank Romero and Judithe Hernandez. Included in the more than 100 works are a wall mural, a folk art pyramid, and part of a primed '51 Chevy lowrider. Illustrated.

4818 The Point Gallery, Santa Monica, CA. ASCO (Gronk, Patssi, Gamboa, Herron), Los Four (Almaraz, de la Rocha, Judithe Hernandez, Gloriamalia Flores, Mauricio Ramirez, John Valadez. Exhibition invitation, [1975]. English.

> **AN:** Illustrated invitation to an exhibit of Los Angeles artists.

4819 San Francisco Museum of Modern Art, San Francisco, CA and Pearlstein, Howard. Aesthetics of graffiti. Exhibition catalog, 1978. English.

> **AN:** Graffiti are defined as any coherently-intended presence written, scratched, painted, engraved, printed, pasted or otherwise impressed in a public place. Graffiti have been incorporated into works by artists. In this catalog, works by Chicano artists Carlos Almaraz, Wilfred Castano, Judithe Hernandez, Gilbert Lujan, Gustavo Rivera, Frank Romero, John M. Valadez, Victor M. Valle, Xavier Viramontes - as well as many Latino and non-Latino artist, appear.

4820 Santa Ana College, Santa Ana, CA and Goldman, Shifra M. Chicano art. Exhibition catalog, 1974. English.

> **AN:** Thirteen California artists are presented in a short essay defining Chicano as a double mestizaje of Mexican mestizo and U.S. influences that exists in a state of "reconciled conflict." Its aim is communication. Artists included are Malaquias Montoya, Rupert Garcia, Manuel Hernandez, Esteban Villa, Robert Gomez, Harvey Tarango, Mary Helen Castro, Eduardo Carrillo, Graciela Carrillo, and "Los Four": Carlos Almaraz, Robert de la Rocha, Judithe Hernandez, Gilbert Lujan and Frank Romero.

4821 Sol Art Gallery, San Diego, CA. Group showing of Southern California artists. Exhibition brochure, 1980. English.

> **AN:** First exhibit of new Chicano art gallery showing Los Angeles artists Carlos Almaraz, Judithe Hernandez, John Valadez, Linda Vallejo, Ricardo Duardo, Barbara Carrasco.

4822 Wilson, William. Chicana artists still seeking identification. LOS ANGELES TIMES, (June 23, 1975), p. VI, 5. English.

> **AN:** Ten Chicana artists are exhibiting their work in the Boathouse Gallery of Plaza de la Raza in Lincoln Park: Judithe Hernandez, Patssi Valdez, Judy Baca, Josefina Quesada, Victoria del Castillo-Leon, Olga Muniz, Gloria Flores, Sylvia Morales, Isabel Castro and Celia Tejadak. The work is still tentative and may develop.

Hernandez, Leticia

4823 Teatro de la Tierra Morena, Santa Cruz, CA. Fuego en Aztlan: a Chicano arts show. Exhibition brochure, 1980. English.

> **AN:** Folder of information on the exhibition curated by Cruz Zamarron and Eduardo Carrillo. Exhibiting artists were: Justina Avila, Terry Benitez, Eduardo Carrillo, Hernando Chavez, Bob Cruz, Juanita Estrada, Juana Franklin, Sal Garcia, Leticia Hernandez, David "Sir Loco" Jimenez, Raoul Mendez, Vicente Mendez, Maria V. Pinedo, Gonzalo Placencia, Ramon Rodriguez, Roberto Salas, George Silva and Cruz Zamarron. A special feature was a live tattoo demonstration entitled "Walking Art".

Hernandez, Lorenzo

4824 Conversation on photography in the Los Angeles Latino community. OBSCURA, Vol. 2, no. 2 (December, February, 1981, 1982), p. 22-32. English.

> **AN:** Interview on the nature and distinguishing characteristics of Chicano photography with Chicano photographers Isabel Castro (Council for Latino Photography), Lorenzo Hernandez (Director of Cityscape Gallery, publisher PHOTOSHOW magazine), Joseph G. Uribe (California State University, Los Angeles, Center for the Visual Arts, Director of West Colorado Gallery), Patssi Valdez, Becky Villasenor, and sculptor, curator, and Art Director for Academia Quinto Sol, Inc., Linda Vallejo, Portfolio of photography by Chicanos Don Anton, Louis Carlos Bernal, Sean Carrillo, Patssi Valdez, Ricardo Valverde, and by Morrie Camhi and Elizabeth Sisco on Chicano subjects.

4825 Four and four: Mexican and Latino photography, April 25 through June 14 on the balcony. CALENDAR: SANTA BARBARA MUSEUM OF ART, (April 1981). English.

> **AN:** Announcement of exhibit organized by Lorenzo Hernandez of the Cityscape Foto Gallery, Pasadena, Calif. Sought to present "the observable differences between the 'classic' vision of the Mexican National and the 'realistic' vision of the re-rooted Mexican/American." The latter included Louis Bernal (Tucson) and Ricardo Valverde (Los Angeles) as well as two Spanish Sephardics of Los Angeles, Camhi and Sisco.

Hernandez, Lorenzo (cont.)

4826 Geyer, Anne; Hernandez, Lorenzo; and
Valverde, Ricardo. Latino photographers of
U.S. still seeking identity. THE NEWS,
(September 5, 1981), p. 17. English.

AN: Interview with Lorenzo Hernandez,
photo dealer and owner of Cityscape Foto
Gallery, Pasadena, Calif. in which he
compares Mexican with U.S. Latino
photography. Interview with Ricardo
Valverde, Chicano photographer and co-chair
of the Council of Latino Photography/USA,
discussing his work. Illustrated.

4827 Gonzalez, Jose Carlos. Consejo mexicano de
fotografia: foto latino en el suroeste de
los Estado Unidos. ARTES VISUALES, Vol. 29,
no. 29 (June 1981), p. 55-56. Spanish.

AN: Review of a photography show in
Mexico City organized by Lorenzo Hernandez,
Cityscape Photo Gallery of Pasadena, and the
Council of Latino Photography/USA. The show
featured Latinos of the Southwest and Latino
themes by non-Latino photographers.

Hernandez, Manuel

4828 La Causa Publications, Oakland, CA. New
symbols for la Nueva Raza. Exhibition
announcement, [ca. 1969]. English.

AN: Announcement for exhibition of the
four founding artists of the Mexican
American Liberation Art Front (MALAF):
Esteban Villa, Rene Yanez, Manuel Hernandez,
Malaquias Montoya. Collage of portraits by
the artists.

4829 Mexican American liberation art front: la
Raza Nueva, Rene Yanez, Esteban Villa,
Malaquias Montoya, Manuel Hernandez. BRONCE,
Vol. 1, no. 3 (March 1969), p. 6-7. English.

AN: Manifesto of MALAF, a germinal
Chicano art group in northern California.
Compares revolutionary Chicanos of 1968 with
the Mexicans of 1910; equally Chicano
artists reject European-influenced art.
Announces the exhibit NEW SYMBOLS FOR LA
RAZA NUEVA, at La Causa in Oakland, March 22
to April 5, 1969. Puts forth the group's
philosophy and goals, particularly exhibits
and art services to the "barrio".
Illustrated.

4830 Santa Ana College, Santa Ana, CA and
Goldman, Shifra M. Chicano art. Exhibition
catalog, 1974. English.

AN: Thirteen California artists are
presented in a short essay defining Chicano
as a double mestizaje of Mexican mestizo and
U.S. influences that exists in a state of
"reconciled conflict." Its aim is
communication. Artists included are
Malaquias Montoya, Rupert Garcia, Manuel
Hernandez, Esteban Villa, Robert Gomez,
Harvey Tarango, Mary Helen Castro, Eduardo
Carrillo, Graciela Carrillo, and "Los Four":
Carlos Almaraz, Robert de la Rocha, Judithe
Hernandez, Gilbert Lujan and Frank Romero.

Hernandez, Sergio

4831 Depicts Chicano attitudes: library receives
new mural. DAILY BRUIN, (September 29,
1970), p. 6. English.

AN: Illustrated story of mural painted
in UCLA's Mexican American Library by
Eduardo Carrillo, Ramses Noriega, Sergio

Hernandez, Saul Solache.

4832 Valdez, Armando. El calendario chicano 1975.
Hayward, CA: Southwest Network, 1975.
English.

AN: Third in a series of historical
calendars produced in 1972 and 1974 by La
Causa Publications and Southwest Network.
Artists included for each month are Carmen
Lomas Garza, Sergio Hernandez, Malaquias
Montoya, Mujeres Muralistas (Graciela
Carrillo, Venezuelan Consuelo Mendez, Irene
Perez, Patricia Rodriguez), Ramses Noriega,
Ernie Palomino, Amado Maurilio Pena, Martin
Perez. All but Texan Pena are California
artists.

Hernandez, Victor

4833 Hale, David. Exhibit backers hope for
Chicano cultural center plan. FRESNO BEE,
(July 14, 1974), p. K5. English.

AN: Review of a Chicano art exhibition
in the Sarah McCardle Room of the downtown
Fresno County Public Library. According to
artist-organizer Ernie Palomino, the exhibit
is a trial balloon to see if enough Chicano
artists can surface and cooperate in the
establishment of a Chicano Cultural Center
in Southeast Fresno. Illustrated with
reproduction of a portrait by Romero Arroyo
of Mendota, California and a painting by
Victor Hernandez from Visalia, California.

Hernandez-M, William

4834 Orange Co. Library. El Modena Branch.
Empanada: a tasty Mexican group art exhibit
filled with a variety of digestable treats.
Exhibition catalog, [1979]. English.

AN: Catalog of an exhibit by 15 artists:
Dolores Grajeda, William Hernandez-M.,
Marylee Montano, Patricia Murillo, Eduardo
Navarro, Susana A. Zaccagnino, Esau Quiroz,
Juan Elias Ramos, Ricardo M. Serrato,
Benjamin Valenzuela, Emigdio C. Vasquez,
Arthur Valenzuela, Jack Vargas, Alonso
Whitney, and Mexican artist Artemio
Sepulveda living in Orange County. Brief
profiles of the artists.

Hernandez-Trujillo, Manuel

4835 Day, Orman. Hispanic life mirrored by ethnic
artists. THE REGISTER, (July 5, 1981), p.
B1+. English.

AN: Story on artists Manuel Hernandez
Trujillo and Emigdio Vasquez whose work
opened the new Galeria in Santa Ana, and
poet Manuel Gomez. Color illustrations.

Herrera (Chavez), Margaret

4836 Petersen, Karen and Wilson, J.J. Women
artists: Third World. New York, NY: Harper &
Row, 1975. English.

AN: Catalog of slides with accompanying
notes. Slides of Chicana artists available:
Margaret Herrera (Chavez), Consuelo (Chelo)
Gonzalez Amezcua, Santa Barraza, Mujeres
Muralistas, El Grupo de Santa Ana, Carmen
Lomas Garza, Carolina Flores.

Herrera, Miguel

4837 Santos of New Mexico, art of our people.
GRITO DEL NORTE, Vol. 3, no. 1 (January 17,
1970), p. 8-9. English.

AN: Historical trajectory of santero
tradition in New Mexico. Distinguished
santeros like Rafael Aragon of Cordova,
Miguel Herrera of Arroyo Hondo, Juan Ramon
Velasquez of Conjilon, Jose Benito Ortega of
La Cueva all created art wedded to the
environment of the Southwest. Illustrated
with a portfolio of santos and retablos from
the Folk Art Museum of Santa Fe, NM.

Herron, Willie, Jr.

4838 Barrio, Raymond. Art for our sake. NUESTRO,
Vol. 1, no. 6 (September 1977), p. 30-34.
English.

AN: Brief text with three color
reproductions of murals by Mike Rios (Bart
Mural, San Francisco), Gilberto Guzman (West
Las Vegas High School, NM), Willie Herron
(Farmacia Hidalgo, East Los Angeles, CA).

4839 Blanco, Gil. Art on the walls: a vehicle for
positive change. LATIN QUARTER, Vol. 1, no.
2 (October 1974), p. 26-30. English.

AN: East Los Angeles artists Ismael
"Smiley" Pereira and C.W. (Charles) Felix
started painting murals with young people at
the Estrada Courts Housing Project in May
1973. There are now 30 murals, and the
residents are more receptive, noting the
changes that are taking place. Illustrated
with murals by Herron and Gronk, and Daniel
Martinez.

4840 Burkhardt, Dorothy. Chicano pride and anger
mix at 'Califas'. THE TAB, (April 12,
1981), p. 34. English.

AN: CALIFAS: AN EXHIBITION OF CHICANO
ARTISTS IN CALIFORNIA represents a
cross-section of artists exhibiting work for
at least ten years: Rupert Garcia, Ernie
Palomino, Eduardo Carrillo, Judy Baca, Rene
Yanez, Carmen Lomas Garza, Salvador Roberto
Torres, Roberto Chavez, Willie Herron, Ralph
Maradiaga, Sue Martinez, Jose Montoya,
Malaquias Montoya, Ramses Noriega and
Esteban Villa. Illustrated.

4841 Chicano art. ARTES VISUALES, no. 29 (1981).
English.

AN: Issue on Chicano art, introduced by
Los Angeles artist Roberto Gil de Montes.
Includes works and statements by: Pedro
Lujan (Texas); Raul M. Guerrero (Calif.);
Sylvia Salazar Simpson (New Mexico/Calif.);
Carlos Almaraz (Calif.); Rene Yanez
(Calif.); Jack Vargas (Calif.); Ray Bravo
(Calif.); John Valadez (Calif.); Gloria Maya
(Calif.); Elsa Flores (Calif.); Willie
Herron (Calif.); Gilbert "Magu" Lujan
(Calif.); Kay Torres, Jerry Lucas, and Louis
Perez (Calif.).

4842 Cockcroft, Eva; Weber, John; and Cockcroft,
James D. Towards a people's art: the
contemporary mural movement. New York: E.P.
Dutton, 1977. English.

AN: A survey of the street mural
movement in the United States, from about
1967 on. Several chapters are written by the
artists themselves: John Weber on the
Chicago mural group; Susan Shapiro-Kiok on
Cityarts Workshop of New York; Eva Cockcroft

on People's painters of New Jersey; Geronimo
Garduno on Artes Guadalupanos de Aztlan of
New Mexico. Chicano murals illustrated
include those of Mujeres Muralistas, Ray
Patlan, William F. Herron, Hoyo-Mara Gang,
Artes Guadalupanos de Aztlan, Vicente
Mendoza and Jose Nario (with Patlan) Mario
Castillo, Michael Rios, Toltecas en Aztlan,
Roberto Chavez, Ernie Palomino, Chuy
Campusano and Luis Cortazar (with Rios).

4843 Cultura chicana: Los Angeles. COMUNIDAD, no.
11 (July 13, 1980), p. 1-15. Spanish.

AN: The whole issue of the Cultural
Supplement concerns Chicano art and music.
Captioned photographs deal with visual
artists Carlos Almaraz, Jerry Dreva [not
Chicano], Glugio Gronk, Willie Herron, John
Valadez, Patssi Valdez, with examples of
their work. With the exception of Dreva, all
the artists are members of Los Four or Asco.
Asco member Harry Gamboa, Jr. sums up the
1960s and 1970s and activities of artists in
his essay "Seis imaginaciones: Artistas
chicanos en Los Angeles." Well illustrated.

4844 Del Olmo, Frank. Murals changing face of
East L.A. LOS ANGELES TIMES, (December 3,
1973), p. II, 1+. English.

AN: First Los Angeles Times report on
burgeoning Los Angeles mural movement with a
map of 15 mural sites. Mentioned are C.W.
Felix (originator of Estrada Courts
project), Willie Herron, David Botello,
Armando Campero, Edward Carbajal. (Chicano
Art Committee).

4845 Delgado, Sylvia. My people never smile: a
profile of a young Chicano artist.
REGENERACION, Vol. 2, no. 1 (1971), p. 23.
English.

AN: Very brief biographical sketch of
Willie Herron.

4846 Edy. A true barrio art. EL CHICANO,
(December 7, 1972), p. 9. English.

AN: Interview with East Los Angeles
artists Harry Gamboa, Robert Gronk and
Willie Herron (also included in the
conversation are Patsy Valdez and Eddie
Ytuarte). Suffering, fatalism, existential
reality and the awareness of cultural
colonialism are cited as sources of
inspiration for urban barrio art.
Illustrated with a photograph of Willie
Herron's Quetzalcoatl mural in City Terrace
barrio and two drawings by Robert Gronk and
Harry Gamboa.

4847 Exploratorium, Student Union, California
State University, Los Angeles. Herron/Gronk
in ILLEGAL LANDSCAPE. Exhibition catalog,
1980. English.

AN: Invitation to a "performance" piece
NO MOVIE by Willie Herron and Gronk, two
members of ASCO. Illustrated.

Herron, Willie, Jr.(cont.)

4848 Una galeria de artistas = A gallery of
artists. CAMINOS, Vol. 1, no. 6 (October
1980), p. 20-26. Bilingual.

AN: Features California artists Domingo
O. Ulloa (Imperial Valley images), Gloria
Chacon, photographer Maria Pinedo (San
Francisco), Willie Herron (Los Angeles),
Joaquin Patino (Delano), Pedro Pelayo (Long
Beach), sculptor Rudi Sigala (San Diego),
Mario Torero (San Diego), sculptor Michael
M. Amescua (Los Angeles), and the East Los
Streetscapers. Illustrated.

4849 Gamboa, Harry, Jr.; Gronk; and Herron,
Willie. Gronk and Herron. NEWORLD, Vol. 2,
no. 3 (Spring 1976), p. 28-30. English.

AN: An interview with ASCO members Gronk
and Willie Herron by a third member, Gamboa.
Brief historical introduction (1970 on). The
witty tongue-in-cheek interview can be
considered an artwork by this performance
art group. Illustrated.

4850 Gamboa, Harry, Jr. and Gronk. Gronk:
off-the-wall artist. NEWORLD, Vol. 6, no. 4
(1980), p. 33-43. English.

AN: Interview with Gronk about his No
Movies, by Harry Gamboa, Jr., both members
(with Willie Herron and Patssi Valdez) of
ASCO. The interview itself can be seen as an
"art piece" with photographs by Gamboa; it
contains valuable information about the
ideas and activities of the group.

4851 Gamboa, Harry, Jr. Los murales de Aztlan.
COMUNIDAD, (June 28, 1981), p. 8-9+.
Spanish.

AN: Review of the exhibit at the Craft
and Folk Art Museum of Los Angeles of MURALS
OF AZTLAN: THE STREET PAINTERS OF EAST LOS
in which Carlos Almaraz, Gronk, Judithe
Hernandez, Willie Herron, Frank Romero, John
Valadez and the East Los Streetscapers
(David Botello, Wayne Healy, George Yepes)
painted portable murals in the gallery. The
murals are described and illustrated.

4852 Gamboa, Harry, Jr. Seis imaginaciones:
artistas chicanos en Los Angeles. COMUNIDAD,
(July 13, 1980), p. 10. Spanish.

AN: A limited flow of media information
about Los Angeles Chicanos has produced a
"ghost" culture. Only sensational events are
published. Alternative magazines like LA
RAZA, CON SAFOS, and REGENERACION have
disseminated Chicano ideas of the 1970s. The
Chicano imagination has appeared in murals
by Willie Herron, Gronk, Carlos Almaraz,
John Valadez; in pieces like "walking" and
"instant" murals by the group ASCO; by the
group Los Four; by group exhibits like
"Chicanismo en el arte," and "Chicanarte."
Patssi Valdez showed Photobooth Piece at the
"Chicanismo" show. Gronk and Jerry Dreva
exhibited their mail art at "Punk Meets
Art." In Spanish.

4853 Greenberg, David; Smith, Kathryn; and
Teacher, Stuart. Megamurals & supergraphics:
big art. Philadelphia, PN: Running Press,
1977. English.

AN: A full-color picture book of murals
throughout the United States. Chicano murals
include Michael Rios (San Francisco),
Mujeres Muralistas (San Francisco), Leonard
Castellanos and Tomas Gonzales with others

(Los Angeles), Los Artes Guadalupanos de
Aztlan (New Mexico), Willie Herron (Los
Angeles), Toltecas en Aztlan (San Diego),
David Botello (Los Angeles), David Lopez and
Arizona Mara Gang (Los Angeles), Vatos de
Maravilla (Los Angeles), Carlito Gaegos (Los
Angeles), Gil Hernandez (Los Angeles), Wayne
[Alaniz] Healy (Los Angeles).

4854 Los Angeles City College. Latinos de tres
mundos. Exhibition invitation, 1980.
English.

AN: Invitation to an exhibit featuring
the work of ASCO members Harry Gamboa, Jr.,
Gronk, Willie Herron; painters Xavier Mendez
and Olivia Sanchez; and photographer Ricardo
Valverde.

4855 Manning, Andrew. Damaged mural inspires
community restoration project. CHISMEARTE,
Vol. 2, no. 1 (Summer 1978), p. 28. English.

AN: Describes the damage caused to a
Willie Herron mural by inclement weather
conditions and the community drive to fund a
restoration project. The project is being
directed by Ricardo Barrera.

4856 Orth, Maureen. The soaring spirit of Chicano
arts. NEW WEST MAGAZINE, Vol. 3, no. 19
(September 11, 1978), p. 41-46. English.

AN: Overview of California Chicano
culture. Color illustrations of works by
Mexican muralist David Alfaro Siqueiros,
Rupert Garcia, Mujeres Muralistas, Willie
Herron, Rene Yanez, Rudy Martinez, San
Diego's Chicano Park, ASCO, Jose Montoya.

4857 EL PLAYANO (Loyola University, Los Angeles).
(Spring 1972).

AN: Illustrations by Willie Herron,
Harry Gamboa, Jr., Gronk, Diane Gamboa,
William A. Bejarano, Eddie Garcia.

4858 EL PLAYANO (Loyola University, Los Angeles).
(Spring 1973).

AN: Illustrations by Simon Gonzales,
Gronk, Harry Gamboa, Jr., Willie Herron,
Charles Almaraz, Sister Teresa Munoz, Patsy
Valdez, Diane Gamboa.

4859 Romotsky, Jerry and Romotsky, Sally R.
Placas and murals. ARTS IN SOCIETY, Vol. 2,
no. 1 (Summer, Fall , 1974), p. 286-299.
English.

AN: Details how Chicano muralists have
recognized the aesthetics of graffiti and
incorporated them into their murals. Among
the earliest to do so were Lucille Grijalva
and Willie Herron. Illustrated.

4860 Sanchez, Ricardo. Hechizo/spells. Los
Angeles, CA: Chicano Studies Publications,
UCLA, 1976. English.

AN: Willie Herron, drawings and
paintings on pp. 68, 70, 75, 89, 93, 97,
99, 123, 129, 135, 137, 151, 165, 167, 170,
181, 195, 229, 231, 235, 236, 238, 256, 258,
261, 268, 279, 284, 288, 312 and inside
front and back covers.

Herron, Willie, Jr (cont.)

4861 Sommer, Robert. Street art. New York: Quick Fox, 1975. English.

AN: Introductory essay covering the history of the new mural movement, forms of street art, politics, street sculpture, how to locate and photograph street art. Chicano murals include Charles Felix and others at Estrada Courts (L.A.), RCAF murals in Sacramento, Jose Montoya and others (Broderick, Ca.) Marcos Raya (Chicago), Mike Rios (Neighborhood Legal Aid, S.F.) Mechicano Art Center (L.A.) Johnny Alvarez (L.A.), New Mexico State Employment Bldg., Albuquerque mural, Lorena Street School (L.A.), two murals, Casa de la Raza Alternative School (Berkeley), Santa Fe, New Mexico mural, Francisco Hernandez (L.A.), Artes Guadalupanos de Aztlan (N. Mexico), Willie Herron (L.A.). Better documentation would have been welcome.

4862 Street art explosion in Los Angeles. SUNSET, (April 1973), p. 110-113. English.

AN: Illustrated article on Los Angeles street murals including those by Roberto Chavez, Willie Herron, Frank Romero, Richard Jimenez, William Bejarano, Gilbert Lujan, Armando Cabrera, Frank Martinez, Charles Felix, and others.

4863 Torres, Louis R. An innovation in children's t.v.: THE INFINITY FACTORY. LA LUZ, Vol. 6, no. 2 (February 1977), p. 10-11. English.

AN: Illustrated report on a new television series for children aimed at teaching mathematics fundamentals in a crisply-paced series of half-hour programs. The executive producer, Jesus Salvador Trevino, filmed the segments in a New York Black community, and in the East Los Angeles Chicano barrio. In one segment, muralist Willie Herron works with youngsters to design and paint an outdoor mural.

4864 Varda, Agnes. Mur murs/mural murals on the wall ... Film, Cine Tamaris, Paris, 1980. English.

AN: Full length documentary film produced for French television; also available with English subtitles. Deals impressionistically with the murals and muralists of Los Angeles. Included are Wayne Alaniz Healy, David Botello, Willie Herron, Manuel Cruz, Judy Baca, the murals in Venice, CA, graffiti - among others. Color.

Hidalgo Mural, Farmacia Hidalgo, East Los Angeles, CA

4865 Manning, Andrew. Damaged mural inspires community restoration project. CHISMEARTE, Vol. 2, no. 1 (Summer 1978), p. 28. English.

AN: Describes the damage caused to a Willie Herron mural by inclement weather conditions and the community drive to fund a restoration project. The project is being directed by Ricardo Barrera.

Hidalgo y Costilla, Miguel

4866 Orozco, Jose Clemente. [Untitled painting]. CON SAFOS, no. 8 (1972), p. 35-36.

High School Education
    USE: Secondary School Education

High School Students

4867 [Untitled photograph]. LOS ANGELES TIMES, (May 5, 1972), p. II, 1. English.

AN: Captioned illustration of Chicano high school students' 25x5 foot mural at Compton's Thomas Jefferson Elementary School. The mural, which took a year to paint, is based on Mexican history.

Highlands University Gallery, Las Vegas, NM

4868 Chicano exhibit set. SANTA FE NEW MEXICAN, (September 22, 1972), p. A4. English.

AN: A Chicano art show organized by El Instituto Chicano de Artes y Artesanias of San Antonio, TX is scheduled for Highlands University Gallery, Las Vegas, NM.

Hijas de Cuauhtemoc

4869 ENCUENTRO FEMENIL (San Fernando, CA). Vol. 1, no. 1 (Spring 1973), p. 1+. English.

AN: Publication sponsored by Hijas de Cuauhtemoc, a Chicana femenist group. Black and white drawings on cover by Pat Portera Crary. Art work by Vicki Thrall, Adelaida del Castillo, and Maria Hortencia Garcia. Photography by Cindy Honesto and David Lazarin.

Hinojosa, Amador

4870 Montoya, Emmanuel; Rodriguez, Patricia; and Acevedo, Mario (Torero). Canto al pueblo '78. NATIONAL MURALS NETWORK COMMUNITY NEWSLETTER, (1978). English.

AN: The second annual Canto al Pueblo took place in Corpus Christi, Texas, where more than six murals were painted: "Wall of Cultural Education" by 13 artists headed by Roel Montealva; Carlota Espinoza, with children; Gilberto Romero, Jose Antonio Burciaga and Patricia Rodriguez, "Incomprehension al arte"; "Madre Tierra" by Manuel Martinez of Denver with Amador Hinojosa (Corpus Christi) and Enriquette Vasquez (New Mexico); Mario Torero; Salvador Vega of Chicago whose mural some Canto participants considered "insulting".

Hinojosa, Lucas

4871 Con safo to hold Lutheran college exhibition at Texas. CHICANO TIMES, Vol. 7, no. 89 (March 26, 1976), p. [15]. English.

AN: Discusses the aims of "Con Safos" group: to interpret their environment and react to it; to act as spokespeople and give visual reality to the Chicano vision; to destroy stereotypes and demolish visual cliches. The participating artists include Rudy R. Trevino, Mel Casas, Lucas Hinojosa, Kathy Vargas, Joe Frank Acosta, Emilio Aguirre and Homero Ureste.

Hinojosa, Lucas (cont.)

4872 Estudios Rio: gallery of contemporary arts
and crafts. Exhibition catalog, 1976.
English.

AN: Catalog including identification,
portraits and works of participating
artists: Joe Bova, Enrique Flores, Carmen
Lomas Garza, Xavier Gorena, Erik Gronborg,
Lucas Hinojosa, Ben Holland, Kris Hotvedt,
William Kaars-Sijpesteijn, Cesar Martinez,
Chris Mende, Roberto Mungia, Steve Reynolds,
Vicente Rodriguez, William Wilhelmi.

Hispanic Artist Association, Orange County, CA

4873 Orange Co. Library. El Modena Branch. The
Hispanic Artist Association of Orange County
presents "Empanada," a tasty Mexican group
art exhibit filled with a variety of
digestible treats. Exhibition invitation,
1979. English.

AN: Poster/invitation to an exhibit of
artists (See "Empanada").

4874 Roberts, Tim. For art's sake, for the
community, for the working class. ORANGE
CITY NEWS, Vol. 10, (March 14, 1979), p.
1,8-9. English.

AN: Illustrated article on Orange
County, Calif. realist painter Emigdio
Vasquez. Focuses on his community murals,
and his attitudes toward his art. Also
announces the first exhibit, "Empanada" of
the newly formed Hispanic Artists
Association of Orange County. 13
participants including Vasquez.

**Hispanic Southwest Conference on Media and the
Humanities**

4875 Johansen, Jason. Preliminaries toward an
Hispanic media: a cultural imperative.
Unpublished manuscript, 1980. English.

AN: Presentation made at the Hispanic
Southwest Conference on Media and the
Humanities. Johansen outlines the
culturally-leveling and stereotypical roles
for men and women of mass media in our
century which is dominated by communication
means owned by industries interested in
profits from products. Within this context,
Hispanic media producers must find new ways
of relaying values, judgements and ideas
that combat the dominant culture and
strengthen humanity and social change.

HISTORIA DE LA RAZA [mural]

4876 Los murales del pueblo. PAPEL CHICANO, Vol.
2, no. 12 (February 1973), p. 1+. Spanish.

AN: Analysis of Leo Tanguma's work as
"an expression not only of artistic creative
opinion but also of the suppressed and
accumulated feeling of La Raza in the United
States." Includes thematic and stylistic
information on four murals in the Houston
barrio: "The Rebirth of Our Nationality,"
"Towards a Humanitarian Technology for La
Raza," "Historia de la Raza," and "El
Mestizo Chicano".

LA HISTORIA [film series]

4877 Reyes, Luis. Seguin: traidor o heroe.
COMUNIDAD, (April 12, 1981), p. 8-9.
Spanish.

AN: Report on the pilot film for an

eight-part series called LA HISTORIA made by
Jesus Trevino for the Public Broadcasting
Service. The pilot treats the life of an
"anti-hero," Juan Seguin, during the Texas
war for independence from Mexico, and
relates the little-known history of the
Mexican defenders of the Alamo. Trevino
chose this controversial subject because it
exemplified an early case of the dual nature
of bilingualism and biculturalism.
Description of the research and filming of
the pilot. Illustrated.

History

4878 Cardona, Patricia. El museo mexicano de San
Francisco. EL DIA, (July 6, 1977), p. 10.
Spanish.

AN: Report on the Mexican Museum giving
a brief overview of its programs. The
Mexican Museum opened Nov. 20, 1975 and has
been a vital force in the cultural life of
San Francisco, showing the work of one
Mexican and one Chicano artist every two
months.

4879 El Centro Cultural de La Raza, San Diego, CA
and Enrique, Veronica. Tenth anniversary
celebration, July 11, 1981. San Diego, CA:
El Centro Cultural de la Raza, 1981.
English.

AN: Anniversary brochure of the Centro,
founded in 1970 by the Toltecas en Aztlan
artistic collective and established at its
Balboa Park location in 1971. Briefly
reviews the history and activities of the
Centro, including the establishment of
Chicano Park in 1970 and the painting of
murals at the Park and at the Centro. Well
illustrated.

4880 El centro cultural y museo del barrio,
history and activities. Taos, NM: El Centro
Cultural y Museo del Barrio, n.d.. English.

AN: Photo-copied history of the New
Mexico organization which is a centro and
museo "without walls" begun in 1973. Founded
by Juan and Patricia Navarrete, it
collaborates with established museums for
community art events.

4881 Chicano pride reflected in '75 calendar. LOS
ANGELES TIMES, (December 2, 1974), p. I,
34. English.

AN: The 1975 edition of EL CALENDARIO
CHICANO, developed for the Southwest Network
of Hayward, focuses on Chicano history and
dates that are significant to Mexican
Americans.

4882 Goldman, Shifra M. Affirmations of
existence, barrio murals of Los Angeles.
REVISTA CHICANO-RIQUENA, Vol. 4, no. 4 (Fall
1976), p. 73-76. Bibliography. English.

AN: Brief history, communicative thrust,
community orientation, and special
iconography of Chicano murals in Los
Angeles.

4883 Goldman, Shifra M. Les muraux chicanos aux
Etats-Unis: un double language. In L'ART
PUBLIC. Paris: Jacques Damase Editeur, 1981,
p. 20-32. Other.

AN: Updating of new artistic and social
developments surrounding Chicano mural
production. Illustrated.

History (cont.)

4884 La historia de California, 1977. San
Francisco, CA: Galeria de la Raza, 1977.
English.

AN: Handprinted silkscreen calendar of
history seen from a Mexican point of view.
Twelve sheets and a cover. Artists are:
Ralph Maradiaga, Irene Perez, Louie "The
Foot" Gonzalez, Max Garcia, Patricia
Rodriguez, Jose Romero, Esteban Villa,
Juanishi Orozco, Rodolfo Cuellar, Jose
Montoya, Xavier Viramontes, Rene Yanez,
Ricardo Favela, associated with the Galeria
de la Raza, or the Royal Chicano Air Force
of Sacramento.

4885 La historia de Mechicano. LA GENTE DE
AZTLAN, Vol. 8, no. 1 (November 2, 1977), p.
14. English.

AN: Excellent and complete account of
the formation and development of Mechicano
Art Center from 1968 to 1977. Explains
goals, activities and participating artists.

4886 Kagawa, Paul and Rilkin, Scott. La Raza
Silkscreen Center, in step with the Mission.
ARTS BIWEEKLY, no. 44 (March 15, 1977).
English.

AN: Concise history and goals of the
Silkscreen Center: the Center's values are
reflected in the collective process that
produces the posters, as well as in the
collective style of the art; in the emphasis
upon education. The Center trains
apprentices, educates the student community
about the silkscreen process and Raza
history and produces posters that have an
information impact. The Silkscreen Center is
part of a coalition of La Raza Information
Center, Tutorial Center, and Centro Legal
which evolved from La Raza En Accion Social
founded in 1970.

4887 MARCH: Movimiento artistico Chicano
(Mexican-American Art Movement). QUARTERLY,
(Spring 1976), p. 10. English.

AN: Brief history of MARCH.
Illustrations of murals by Ricarco Alonzo,
Jose Gonzalez, Vicente Mendoza, Ray Patlan.

4888 MARS: Movimiento Artistico del Rio Salado.
Exhibition brochure, [1981]. English.

AN: Illustrated brochure for the MARS
organization and its studio-gallery.
Includes a brief history, list of
exhibitions from 1978 to 1981, news about
its studio-workshop for the community, and
its goals.

4889 Martinez, Eluid Levi. What is a New Mexico
santo? Santa Fe, NM: Sunstone Press, 1978.
Bilingual.

AN: Martinez is a carver of saints from
the well-known Lopez family of santeros of
Cordova, New Mexico, who have carved for
seven generations. An oversimplified history
of the settlement of New Mexico and the rise
of religious imagery production. Of interest
are the illustrated steps of the carving
process. Many reproductions.

4890 Mascorro, Julie. Mechicano Art Center
exhibit to grace Price gallery walls. CAMPUS
NEWS, (November 24, 1971). English.

AN: Brief history of Mechicano Art
Center activities from its establishment in

1969 to 1971. Exhibiting are Charles
Almaraz, Roberto Amaral, Raymond Atilano,
William Bejarano, Armando Cabrera, Edward
Carbajal, Leonard Castellanos, Henry de
Vega, Antonio Esparza, Bob Gomez, Lucila V.
Grijalva, Jesus Gutierrez, Santos Lira,
Frank Martinez, Ernest Palomino, Louis
Quijada, Richard Raya, Frank Romero.
Illustrated.

4891 Metro Denver Urban Coalition, Denver, CO.
City walls. Brochure, 1979. English.

AN: Brochure/poster giving history of
City Walls Project and biographies of seven
artists: Jon Howe, Jerry Jaramillo, Steve
Lucero, Jowinnie Moore, Al Sanchez, Fred
Sanchez, Carlos M. Sandoval. Illustrated.

4892 The Mexican Museum, San Francisco, CA. Cinco
de Mayo exhibit at the Cannery. Exhibition
brochure, 1980. English.

AN: Well-illustrated brochure with text
by Nora Wagner and Bea Carrillo Hocker.
Succinct statements on the history, purpose
and programs of the Mexican Museum.

4893 Mills, Kay. The great wall of Los Angeles.
MS.MAGAZINE, (October 1981), p. 66-69+.
English.

AN: THE GREAT WALL OF LOS ANGELES in the
Tujunga flood control channel in the San
Fernando Valley, was started as a
Bicentennial project in 1976. Artistic
director Judy Baca of the Social and Public
Art Resource Center, works with crews of
young people painting aspects of Los Angeles
history that is not generally found in
textbooks. Well illustrated.

4894 Miranda, Keta. Refunding battle for mural
project. PEOPLE'S WORLD, Vol. 39, no. 20
(May 15, 1976), p. 5+. English.

AN: History of the Mural Arts and
Resource Center (Los Angeles Citywide Mural
Project) from 1974 to its imminent demise in
1976. Joe Bravo mural illustrated.

4895 Montoya, Jose E. Pachuco art: a historical
update. Sacramento, CA: Royal Chicano Air
Force, 1977. English.

AN: Booklet outlining the history of the
Zoot Suit Riots of 1943 and the making of
the Pachuco myth, written by Montoya and
illustrated with his pen-and-ink drawings of
Pachucos and Pachucas.

4896 Morales, Sylvia. Chicana. 20 min., 16 mm,
color, 1979. English.

AN: Color film tracing the history of
the Chicana back to pre-Columbian women's
history. Utilizes images of pre-Columbian
and modern Mexican murals, as well as
filming of contemporary Chicanas and their
activities. Based on a slide show by Anna
Nieto-Gomez, adapted for the screen by
Morales.

4897 Mural en Quinto Sol. SOL DE AZTLAN, Vol. 2,
no. 3 (July 1971). English.

AN: Full-page illustrated article
describing mural by Jose Mojica at the
Edificio Quinto Sol in Lansing. Mural traces
the history of La Raza and was painted by
the self-taught artist with the assistance
of his brother Adolfo.

History (cont.)

4898 Reyes, Luis. Seguin: traidor o heroe.
COMUNIDAD, (April 12, 1981), p. 8-9.
Spanish.

AN: Report on the pilot film for an
eight-part series called LA HISTORIA made by
Jesus Trevino for the Public Broadcasting
Service. The pilot treats the life of an
"anti-hero," Juan Seguin, during the Texas
war for independence from Mexico, and
relates the little-known history of the
Mexican defenders of the Alamo. Trevino
chose this controversial subject because it
exemplified an early case of the dual nature
of bilingualism and biculturalism.
Description of the research and filming of
the pilot. Illustrated.

4899 Rios, Sam. Chicano muralist: Toltecotl in
Aztlan. Unpublished paper, 1980. English.

AN: History of pre-Columbian, Mexican,
and Chicano wall paintings. Describes in
detail murals by Jose Montoya, Juanishi
Orozco, Esteban Villa, Stan Padilla, Juan
Cervantes, Lorraine Garcia of the Centro de
Artistas Chicanos, Royal Chicano Air Force,
painted in 1977 at Southside Park,
Sacramento, Calif. Symbolism is explained.

4900 Sommer, Robert. Street art. New York: Quick
Fox, 1975. English.

AN: Introductory essay covering the
history of the new mural movement, forms of
street art, politics, street sculpture, how
to locate and photograph street art. Chicano
murals include Charles Felix and others at
Estrada Courts (L.A.), RCAF murals in
Sacramento, Jose Montoya and others
(Broderick, Ca.) Marcos Raya (Chicago), Mike
Rios (Neighborhood Legal Aid, S.F.)
Mechicano Art Center (L.A.) Johnny Alvarez
(L.A.), New Mexico State Employment Bldg.,
Albuquerque mural, Lorena Street School
(L.A.), two murals, Casa de la Raza
Alternative School (Berkeley), Santa Fe, New
Mexico mural, Francisco Hernandez (L.A.),
Artes Guadalupanos de Aztlan (N. Mexico),
Willie Herron (L.A.). Better documentation
would have been welcome.

4901 Stellweg, Carla. De como el arte chicano es
tan indocumentado como los
indocumentados/the way in which Chicano art
is as undocumented as the 'undocumented'.
ARTES VISUALES, no. 29 (June 1981), p.
23-32. Bilingual.

AN: An overview of Chicano art from its
beginnings to the present. Suggestion that
present art is improved by abandoning the
nationalist, derivative and folkloric phase.
Statements and biographies of artists. Some
non-Chicanos included as Chicanos. Many
illustrations. Bilingual.

4902 The stolen art: the O'Higgins mural.
RECOBRANDO, Vol. 1, no. 2, p. 15, 16.
English.

AN: Historical documentation on 60-foot
long 8-foot high fresco mural painted for
the Seattle Shipscalers Union by Mexican
artist Pablo O'Higgins in 1949. In 1974,
John Caughlan, a people's lawyer documented
the existence of the mural to Chicano
community groups. M.E.C.H.A. students at the
University of Washington lobbied for the
murals restoration and permanent exhibition.

4903 Taylor Museum of the Colorado Springs Fine

Arts Center, Colorado Springs, CO. Hispanic
crafts of the Southwest. Catalog, 1977.
English.

AN: An excellent and profusely
illustrated catalog covering weaving,
embroidery, furniture making, woodcarving,
jewelry making, tinwork and straw inlay,
both past and present. Historical background
of crafts production, techniques, and
biographies of the artists are provided.

4904 Torres, Miguel. Mexican Museum - artifacts
and culture to open in S.F. EL TECOLOTE,
Vol. 6, no. 1 (October 1975), p. 4. English.

AN: On April 1972, the first
organizational meeting of a new Mexican
Museum was held. Later, a Board of Directors
was organized and fifteen months later, the
Museum was incorporated by the state of
California as a non-profit organization.
Pedro Rodriguez, founder-director of the
Museum tells his aspirations and goals for
this unique repository of Mexican culture in
the United States. Illustrated with
photograph of the Director and examples of
work from the Museum's collection.

4905 Venegas, Sybil. Dia de los muertos. SOMOS,
Vol. 1, no. 5 (October 1978), p. 42-47.
English.

AN: Brief history of Dia de los muertos
ceremonies. While the custom is dying in
Mexico (except for tourists), Chicano
organizations like Galeria de la Raza
(S.F.), El Centro de Artistas Chicanos
(Sacramento, Ca.) celebrate the event
annually, as does [Self-Help Graphics and
Art, Inc.] in East Los Angeles. Well
illustrated with photographs by Guillermo
Bejarano and Daniel Duran.

4906 Walking tour and guide to the Great Wall at
Tujunga Wash. Venice, CA: Social and Public
Art Resource Center, [1981]. English.

AN: History and symbolism of the GREAT
WALL, directed by Judy Baca, and created by
teams of young people working on the mural
since 1976. Illustrated.

**History and Traditions Museum, Lackland Air Force
Base, San Antonio, TX**

4907 History and Traditions Museum. San Antonio,
TX: Lackland Air Force Base, n.d. English.

AN: Brochure of the Museum with
reproduction of two murals (unattributed) by
Roberto Rios of San Antonio.

History, Cultural

4908 450 anos del pueblo chicano/450 years of
Chicano history in pictures. Albuquerque,
NM: Chicano Communications Center, 1976.
English.

AN: A pictorial history of Mexico,
Mexican Americans and Chicanos through
photographs and art works. P. 138 is
dedicated to murals, graphics, cartoons and
photographs from Chicago and the Southwest,
but other murals, graphics, cartoons and
photographs by Chicanos and non-Chicanos are
scattered throughout. In addition, 450 ANOS
has been a rich source book of imagery for
Chicano artists, especially historical works
of art.

History, Cultural (cont.)

4909 Adams, Robert. The architecture and art of
     early Hispanic Colorado. Boulder, CO:
     Colorado Associated University Press in
     cooperation with the State Historical
     Society of Colorado, 1974. English.

     AN: Robert Adams is a photographer and
     writer from Longmont, CO who has evocatively
     captured scenes in the San Luis and
     Purgatory Valleys of Southern Colorado. The
     text and photographs focus on "Hispano"
     village life, customs and traditions.

4910 Ahlborn, Richard E. The Penitente Moradas of
     Abiquiu. Washington, D.C.: Smithsonian
     Institution Press, 1968 (Contributions from
     the Museum of History and Technology, Paper
     63). English.

     AN: The history and organization of the
     Penitente Brotherhood. Detailed analysis of
     the architecture of Penitente moradas and
     the artifacts within them. Illustrated with
     many ethnographic photographs.

4911 Around the Bay. METAMORFOSIS, Vol. 3, no. 2
     (1980), p. 101-108. English.

     AN: Cultural review of activities in the
     Bay Area, northern California, and
     Sacramento. Includes history of the Galeria
     de la Raza/Studio 24 (San Francisco), the
     Centro de Artistas Chicanos/RCAF, Royal
     Chicano Air Force (Sacramento), and a review
     of Rupert Garcia's pastel portraits exhibit
     at the Mexican Museum (S.F.) in 1981.
     Illustrated. Continued in Vol. 4, no. 1,
     1981.

4912 Brunazzi, Ceci. Writing on the walls: murals
     in the mission. COMMON SENSE, (May 1975),
     p. 1, 8. English.

     AN: History of the early murals in the
     Mission District of San Francisco, CA.
     Illustrated.

4913 Celebrate!: the story of the Museum of
     International Folk Art. Santa Fe, NM: Museum
     of New Mexico Press, 1979. English.

     AN: History of the Museum; its founding
     in 1953 by Chicago philanthropist Florence
     Dibell Bartlett; its patronage of New Mexico
     Hispanic crafts as well as international
     crafts.

4914 Cisneros, Jose. Riders of the border. El
     Paso, TX: Texas Western Press, 1971.
     English.

     AN: Jose Cisneros, El Paso artist has
     illustrated (in total or in part) over forty
     books, most of which deal with the
     Southwest. This collection ia a picture book
     rendering the picturesqueness and pagentry
     of the various riders along the border.
     Illustrated with 30 black and white drawings
     and text by the artist.

4915 Cultural department. RECOBRANDO, Vol. 1, no.
     15. Spanish.

     AN: The development of "Raza" culture in
     the Northwest and the role played by the
     Centro de la Raza. Mentions the "talleres de
     arte" set up by Carlos Contreras and Arturo
     Artorez, artists from Mexico who moved to
     Seattle in 1978. Details cultural events
     sponsored by the Centro in the fields of
     art, music, dance, and theater.

4916 Danzantes. LA GENTE DE AZTLAN, Vol. 8, no. 5
     (May 31, 1978), p. 12. English.

     AN: Ernie de la Torre, muralist from El
     Sereno, Los Angeles, CA, describes style and
     meaning of his mural DANZANTES. Painted on
     the wall of the Alameda Theatre (Woods and
     Whittier Blvd.), the mural portrays cultural
     and historic aspects of Chicano culture.
     Illustrated with photographs.

4917 De Cordova, Lorenzo. Echoes of the flute.
     Santa Fe, NM: Ancient City Press, 1972.
     English.

     AN: First person reminiscences on
     Penitente traditions in northern New Mexico
     at the turn of the century. Reprints two
     Works progress Administration (WPA)
     manuscripts: "Lent in Cordoba" (n.d.) and
     "The Wake" (1937). Illustrated with drawings
     by Eliseo Rodriguez. Notes by Marta Weigle.

4918 Drescher, Tim and Garcia, Rupert. Recent
     Raza murals in the U.S. RADICAL AMERICA,
     Vol. 12, no. 2 (March, April, 1978), p.
     14-31. English.

     AN: Like the cultural revolution of
     Mexico in the 1920s, La Raza of Aztlan
     emphasizes the Native American and mestizo
     heritage as well as the Mexican
     revolutionary heritage. Within a social
     context, the authors discuss Chicano and
     Latino murals nationally. Iconography and
     its relation to Chicano experience is
     explored, as well as images by and about
     women. Illustrations.

4919 Fortune, Thomas. Mural will mirror barrio
     pride. LOS ANGELES TIMES, (December 27,
     1974), p. II, 1, 8. English.

     AN: Artist Sergio O'Cadiz has been
     painting a 625-foot concrete wall
     constructed to separate old Colonia Juarez
     and a new Anglo housing complex in Fountain
     Valley (Orange County), Calif., to eliminate
     graffiti. The mural depicts the barrio's
     history: Mexican Americans try on white
     masks for Anglo acceptance. Other scenes
     will show the arrival of the surrounding
     city, and resident's awareness of their
     Chicano identity. O'Cadiz is assisted by 40
     students from surrounding colleges and
     universities. Illustrated.

4920 Garcia, Rupert. Raza murals & muralists: an
     historical perspective. San Francisco, CA:
     Rupert Garcia, n.d.. English.

     AN: Basic assumptions are that
     socio-economic, political and cultural
     relationships exist between the Raza of
     Mexico and those of Aztlan (the Southwest
     United States) Half the text deals with
     Mexican murals, the other half sets Raza
     murals in social context, and focuses on
     murals in San Francisco's Mission District,
     in four locations. 19 illustrations; 9 of
     Raza murals. Mural map of the Mission
     district.

History, Cultural (cont.)

4921 Garcia, Rupert. La Raza murals of
California, 1963 to 1970: a period of social
change and protest. Master's thesis, UC
Berkeley, 1981. English.

AN: Important introduction to a selected
group of murals from Northern and Southern
California. Garcia deals with murals of
"accommodation" from 1960 to 1965; the
Chicano protest movement, 1965 and 1970; and
Chicano protest murals from 1968 to 1970.
Murals are discussed within historical,
political and cultural contexts.
Illustrated.

4922 Goldman, Shifra M. Canto de unidad: nuevo
mural de Berkeley. PLURAL, Vol. 8, no. 96
(September 1979), p. 33-44. Spanish.

AN: Report on significance,
inconography, and new technical
experimentation in street mural on facade of
La Pena Cultural Center, Berkeley, CA. Deals
with Latin American "nueva cancion." Ray
Patlan and Anna de Leon on team of four
muralists. Illustrated. This article was
reprinted as "Song of Unity: Berkeley's New
Raza Mural," in ARTWORKERS NEWS (New York),
Vol. 11, no. 30, September 20, 1980, p. 1.

4923 Goldman, Shifra M. Song of unity: Berkeley's
new raza mural. ARTWORKERS NEWS, Vol. 11,
no. 30 (September 20, 1980), p. 1. English.

AN: Reprint of article published as
"Canto de unidad: nuevo mural de Berkeley"
in PLURAL (Mexico, D.F.), Vol. 8, no. 96,
September 1979, p. 33-44.

4924 Gomez-Quinones, Juan. On culture. Los
Angeles, CA: UCLA-Chicano studies Center
Publications, 1977. English.

AN: Important essay which explores the
history and nature of culture produced by a
dominated people which has rejected the
dominating culture. The essay was reprinted
as "Toward a Concept of Culture," in Joseph
Sommers and Tomas Ybarra-Frausto (eds.)
MODERN CHICANO WRITERS: A COLLECTION OF
CRITICAL ESSAYS. Englewood Cliffs, N.J.:
Prentice-Hall, Inc., 1979, p. 54-66.

4925 Gomez-Quinones, Juan. Toward a concept of
culture. In Sommers and Ybarra-Frausto,
eds., MODERN CHICANO WRITERS. Englewood
Cliffs, NJ: Prentice-Hall, 1979, p. 54-66.
English.

AN: Reprint of essay published as ON
CULTURE. Los Angeles: UCLA-Chicano Studies
Center Publications, 1977. Popular Series
No. 1.

4926 Hurtado, Debbie. A historical update:
Montoya's vindication of fabricated biases.
THE STATE HORNET, (December 13, 1977), p.
6. English.

AN: Review of Jose Montoya's show
"Pachuco Art - A Historical Update; "a
rekindling of pachuquismo from the 1940s
prevalent in Montoya's paintings and
pen-and-ink drawings. The show featured
historical photographs, and an animated
hologram. Visitors wore zoot suit outfits to
the opening. Illustrated.

4927 Johnson, Charles. J street galleries:
politics flavor alternative art shows.
SACRAMENTO BEE, (December 20, 1977), p.
A13. English.

AN: Review of a Pachuco show by Jose
Montoya that is half drawings and paintings,
and half politics - photographs of Pachucos
of the 1940s. Montoya's essay that
accompanies the exhibit attempts to dispel
the image of Pachucos as gangsters, and
declares that Pachucos were the first
"freedom Fighters." The reviewer feels this
is one-sided. Illustrated.

4928 Low n slow - lowrider art. PEOPLE'S WORLD,
Vol. 42, no. 34 (August 25, 1979), p. 10.
English.

AN: Announcement of the Galeria de la
Raza's exhibit of lowrider art. The article
mentions the history of the lowrider car
from the 1940s Pachuco zootsuiters, to the
1950s car clubs. The lowrider exhibit was
prepared by the Galeria in response to white
neighbors' recent protests against Saturday
night cruising in the Mission District.

4929 Low riders of the urban range. LIFE, Vol. 3,
no. 5 (May 1980), p. 88-94. English.

AN: Visual documentation of lowrider
culture in Los Angeles. Car murals, custom
paint jobs, upholstery and clothing styles
are featured. Well illustrated with color
photography.

4930 Mills, James. Hispano history mural ready.
DENVER POST, (October 17, 1975), p. 27+.
English.

AN: PASADO, PRESENTE Y FUTURO, a 20-ft.
mural by Denver artist Carlota Espinoza was
commissioned by the Friends of the Denver
Public Library for the Byers Branch (W. 7th
Ave. and Santa Fe Drive). Blending myth and
reality, the mural progresses from Aztec
empires through the Spanish conquest, from
alienation to the struggle for a collective
identity and heritage by the Mexican
American. Brief commentary by the artist on
the mural's significance. Ms. Espinoza's
mural was designated as an official
Centennial-Bicentennial creation.
Illustrated with photograph of artist.

4931 Mural depicts history of Mexican Americans.
EASTSIDE JRNL, (December 16, 1971), p. 1.
English.

AN: Richard Jimenez of the Goez Gallery
depicts the past and present of Mexican
American culture on an interior mural at the
First Street Store (3640 E. First St.) The 6
ft. by 15 ft. mural has central image of a
clock with a faceless figure (The Mexican
American of the future). Artist comments on
another of his murals titled EDUCATION OF
LIFE.

4932 Orth, Maureen. The soaring spirit of Chicano
arts. NEW WEST MAGAZINE, Vol. 3, no. 19
(September 11, 1978), p. 41-46. English.

AN: Overview of California Chicano
culture. Color illustrations of works by
Mexican muralist David Alfaro Siqueiros,
Rupert Garcia, Mujeres Muralistas, Willie
Herron, Rene Yanez, Rudy Martinez, San
Diego's Chicano Park, ASCO, Jose Montoya.

History, Cultural (cont.)

4933 Plagens, Peter. Sunshine muse: contemporary art on the West Coast. New York: Praeger, 1974. English.

AN: Despite his rather "chic" art critical prose and mainstream orientation, Plagen's book is an important compendium of arts and cultural activities on the West Coast, primarily California. Gives the history of important artists, movements, and art schools. These set the institutional framework for the education of Chicano artists from the 1950s on. Manuel Neri discussed (p. 89, 94, 99) and illustrated (p. 92).

4934 Southwick, Marcia. Build with adobe. Chicago, IL: Swallow, 1965. English.

AN: Modern building techniques for construction of adobe homes with information on traditional building practices.

4935 Trillin, Calvin and Koren, Edward. Low and slow, mean and clean. NEW YORKER, Vol. 54, no. 21 (July 10, 1978), p. 70-74. English.

AN: An important in-depth account of Chicano lowriding culture in California. Detailed analysis of how cars are lowered and customized. Information on "cruising" and "low rider happenings -- car shows at which trophies are awarded for the best interior and the finest paint job and the highest hop off the ground." Distinctions and variations between "cholos" and car clubbers. Historical information on barrio youth subcultures in Los Angeles. Illustrated with cartoons.

4936 Valencia, Manuel. Store front academy for Chicano artists. SACRAMENTO UNION, (January 17, 1973). English.

AN: Article includes comments by Armando Cid, Ricardo Fabela and Jose Montoya in a free-wheeling discussion of the goals and underlying philosophy of the Centro de Artistas Chicanos in Sacramento. More than simply exposing the people to art, the artists explain that they are looking for an alternative art expression and method of instruction never offered in traditional art schools or university departments of art.

HISTORY OF THE CHICANOS FROM A WOMAN'S PERSPECTIVE [mural]

4937 Ruiz, Elvia. Whitewashed mural. SENTIMIENTOS, Vol. 1, no. 2 (May 1978), p. 7-10. English.

AN: Illustrated article about Las Mujeres Muralistas del Valle. Their mural titled, "History of the Chicanos From a Woman's Perspective" was vandalized. Members of the mural group recall its creation and comment on its destruction.

HISTORY OF THE CHICANO [mural]

4938 History traced in mural. THE REGISTER, (May 1, 1974), p. C-1. English.

AN: Illustrated story of History of the Chicano mural painted by Sergio O'Cadiz and fifty students from MEChA at Santa Ana College.

THE HISTORY OF THE MEXICAN-AMERICAN WORKER (1974-75) [mural]

4939 Mendoza, Vicente; Nario, Jose; and Patlan, Ray. The history of the Mexican-American worker (1974-75) [detail of mural]. REVISTA CHICANO-RIQUENA, Vol. 4, no. 4 (Fall 1976), p. 50,54. English.

4940 Sorell, Victor A. Barrio murals in Chicago: painting the Hispanic-American experience on "our community" walls. REVISTA CHICANO-RIQUENA, Vol. 4, no. 4 (Fall 1976), p. 51-72. English.

AN: Important survey of Chicago's Latino murals, with key works considered in detail. Among the Chicano art organizations and muralists mentioned are MARCH (Movimiento Artistico Chicano), and Yolanda Galvan, Juanita Jaramillo, Jose Nario, Raymond Patlan, Vicente Mendoza, Marcos Raya, Ricardo Alonzo, Jose G. Gonzalez and Mario Castillo, author of the earliest Latino mural in Chicago (1968). Puerto Rican and non-Latino muralists and mural groups are also discussed. Well illustrated.

Holguin, Ruben

4941 Finalists in $540 E.L.A. art contest provide dazzling show at local hospital. EASTSIDE SUN, (November 21, 1968). English.

AN: First East Los Angeles art festival. Juried by artists Donald Manion, John Bene, Rubin Holguin. Show hung at Doctors' Hospital by Garfield High School art teacher David Ramirez.

HOMAGE TO RIVERA [mural]

4942 Perales Leven, Humberto. Marcos Raya - Mexican painter. IMAGENES, Vol. 1, no. 1 (July 1976). Bilingual.

AN: Mexican born Chicago muralist Marcos Raya painted a mural titled HOMAGE TO RIVERA in the Pilsen barrio of Chicago at the corner of 18th Street and May. Raya articulates the role of the muralist and his function within the working class community. Also in this issue is an article on the formation of MARCH (Movimiento Artistico Chicano) in 1972 in East Chicago Indiana. Portfolio of drawings by Marcos Raya and photographs by Mario Castillo. Bilingual text.

4943 Sorell, Victor A. Barrio murals in Chicago: painting the Hispanic-American experience on "our community" walls. REVISTA CHICANO-RIQUENA, Vol. 4, no. 4 (Fall 1976), p. 51-72. English.

AN: Important survey of Chicago's Latino murals, with key works considered in detail. Among the Chicano art organizations and muralists mentioned are MARCH (Movimiento Artistico Chicano), and Yolanda Galvan, Juanita Jaramillo, Jose Nario, Raymond Patlan, Vicente Mendoza, Marcos Raya, Ricardo Alonzo, Jose G. Gonzalez and Mario Castillo, author of the earliest Latino mural in Chicago (1968). Puerto Rican and non-Latino muralists and mural groups are also discussed. Well illustrated.

Honesto, Cynthia

4944 ENCUENTRO FEMENIL (San Fernando, CA). Vol. 1, no. 1 (Spring 1973), p. 1+. English.

AN: Publication sponsored by Hijas de Cuauhtemoc, a Chicana femenist group. Black and white drawings on cover by Pat Portera Crary. Art work by Vicki Thrall, Adelaida del Castillo, and Maria Hortencia Garcia. Photography by Cindy Honesto and David Lazarin.

4945 William Grant Still Community Arts Center, Los Angeles, CA. Latin American artists exhibition. Exhibition brochure, 1978. English.

AN: Exhibit curated by Linda Vallejo including Carlos Almaraz, Michael M. Amescua, Ray Bravo, Isabel Castro, Yreina Cervantez, Luis Serrano-Cordero, Cynthia Honesto, Judith Miranda, Teddy Sandoval, John Taboada, Emigdio Vasquez. Illustrated.

Horwitch Galleries, Scottdale, AZ (and Santa Fe, NM)

4946 Elaine Horwitch Galleries, Santa Fe, NM. New Mexico woodcarving. Exhibition catalog, 1980. English.

AN: Invitation to an exhibit at the Horwitch galleries of Scottsdale, Arizona, and Santa Fe, NM of sculptors Felipe Archuleta, Leroy Archuleta, Frank Brito, Alonso Jimenez, Horatio Valdez, and others. Illustration.

Housing

4947 OMICA Housing Corp., Inc., Homestead (Miami), FL. Dedication of heritage village. Brochure, 1977. English.

AN: Brochure of non-profit housing corporation which built, with Housing and Urban Development (HUD) funds, public homeownership housing for farmworkers and low-income rural residents of South Dade County. Illustrated with a mural by Roberto Rios of San Antonio, one of three done in Florida.

Houston Bellas Artes Center

4948 A new cultural center for Houston. AGENDA, Vol. 7, no. 2 (March, April, 1977), p. 17-18. English.

AN: Goals and programs of a proposed Mexican American cultural center for Houston, Texas. Since August of 1976, the center has been operating from a temporary location and has sponsored various art exhibits. Expected to be in full operation by 1980, the Houston Bellas Artes will sponsor workshops, symposia, performances and exhibits related to Mexican American culture. Illustrated with two photographs of the cultural activities of the Houston Bellas Artes Center.

Houston Metropolitan Archives and Research Center

4949 Kreneck, Tom. With the eye of an artist: Jesus Murillo's Houston, 1927-1933. REVISTA CHICANO-RIQUENA, Vol. 8, no. 3 (Summer 1980), p. 104-105. English.

AN: Biographical sketch of Mexican-born commercial and portrait photographer who worked professionally in Texas from 1916 until his death in 1971. The illustrations concern his Houston stay.

Houston, TX

4950 Artist views murals as dialogue with oppressed. HOUSTON POST, (June 13, 1979), p. 3A. English.

AN: There are doubts that Houston muralist Leo Tanguma's latest structural mural about police brutality will ever see the light of day. Painted on three pointed plywood panels, it was originally destined for Moody Park. Other Tanguma murals have been painted over. Illustrated.

4951 Barnstone, Gertrude and Tanguma, Leo. The big picture: 'I want to indict the system that has condemned us!'. HOUSTON BREAKTHROUGH, (March 1980), p. 16-19. English.

AN: Houston muralist Leo Tanguma studied with John Biggers at Texas Southern University who encouraged him and other Chicanos to study Mexican murals. The article is an interview with Tanguma which details his strong political orientation and ideals, and the problems he has encountered as a result. Three illustrations.

4952 Beardsley, John. Personal sensibilities in public places. ARTFORUM, Vol. 19, no. 10 (June 1981), p. 43-45. English.

AN: Distinction is made between art in public places and public art. The latter is assumed to have content and symbolism accessible to the majority of the population. Luis Jimenez, sculptor of VAQUERO intended for Houston's Moody Park, feels people should be able to identify with art. Color illustration.

4953 Hamm, Madeline McDermott. Artist envisions a 'Sistine' ceiling. HOUSTON CHRONICLE, (September 19, 1978), p. III, 1-3. English.

AN: Illustrated article on mural that Ernesto Pedregon Martinez (who was active in El Paso in the 1950s) was doing for St. Joseph Catholic Church in Houston. The mural depicts the crucifixion.

4954 Kalil, Susie. Provocative painting: muralist Leo Tanguma advances the tradition of Mexico's masters. HOUSTON CITY MAGAZINE, (March 1980), p. 88+. English.

AN: 38 year old Leo Tanguma from Beeville, Texas joined the Mexican-American Youth Organization in Houston in 1968, which provided a stimulus to say what he felt in large paintings. His firsHouston mural was in 1970, followed by meeting Mexican muralisDavid Alfaro Siqueiros in 1972. A monumental mural for Continental Can Co. followed in 1973. Many of Tanguma's murals have been controversial and destroyed, or the commissions withdrawn. Color illustration of maquette for an ecology mural.

Houston, TX (cont.)

4955 Karkabi, Barbara. For artist Atanacio P.
Davila, mural is way to express love for
children. HOUSTON CHRONICLE, (May 14,
1980), p. IV-I. English.

AN: Color-illustrated story on
mural-in-progress at the Ripley House
medical clinic by 70 year old Davila titled
THE HEALTHY FAMILY. Son of an artist,
Mexican-born Davila was raised in Texas and
did commercial art and painting until 1938.
After retirement, he has resumed his art.

4956 Kreneck, Tom. With the eye of an artist:
Jesus Murillo's Houston, 1927-1933. REVISTA
CHICANO-RIQUENA, Vol. 8, no. 3 (Summer
1980), p. 104-105. English.

AN: Biographical sketch of Mexican-born
commercial and portrait photographer who
worked professionally in Texas from 1916
until his death in 1971. The illustrations
concern his Houston stay.

4957 Leo Tanguma and Houston murals. NATIONAL
MURALS NETWORK COMMUNITY NEWSLETTER,
(Spring 1980), p. 11. English.

AN: Report on environmental and police
brutality murals in Houston, Texas.
Illustrated.

4958 Mencion Don Quijote: Atanasio P. Davila. LA
VOZ DE HOUSTON, (June 5, 1980). English.

AN: Illustrated biography of 70-year-old
Mexican-born Texas painter who returned to
art after his retirement and had just
completed a mural for Houston's Ripley House
medical clinic.

4959 NATIONAL MURALS NETWORK COMMUNITY
NEWSLETTER. (Fall 1980). English.

AN: Reports on murals in San Francisco,
CA, by the Chicano Moratorium Coalition; in
Chicago about the Anti-War Preparations
mural; in Houston by a student at the
Association for Advancement of Mexican
Americans; on Michael Schorr's mural in
Chicanok, San Diego, CA; on a segment being
painted at the Tujunga Wash mural in Los
Angeles under Judy Baca; on south San Diego
murals being painted out; Alan Barnett's
survey of Southwest murals. Illustrated.

4960 A new cultural center for Houston. AGENDA,
Vol. 7, no. 2 (March, April, 1977), p.
17-18. English.

AN: Goals and programs of a proposed
Mexican American cultural center for
Houston, Texas. Since August of 1976, the
center has been operating from a temporary
location and has sponsored various art
exhibits. Expected to be in full operation
by 1980, the Houston Bellas Artes will
sponsor workshops, symposia, performances
and exhibits related to Mexican American
culture. Illustrated with two photographs of
the cultural activities of the Houston
Bellas Artes Center.

4961 Out in the open/Allen Parkway: Frank
Fajardo, Jesse Lott, Guillermo Pulido, Jana
Vander Lee. Exhibit invitation, 1979.
English.

AN: Invitation to the installation of
conceptual pieces in public areas of
Houston. Includes Chicano artist Frank
Fajardo and Bolivian-born Pulido.

4962 Painting pride for everyone to see - a
Chicano artist and his giant murals. TEXAS
MAGAZINE, (April 22, 1973), p. 4-6+.
English.

AN: Brief story and photographs of
31-year-old Leo Tanguma's murals at
Continental Can Co., Lamons Metal Gasket
Co., McAshan Community Center, and Casa de
Amigos Clinic, in Houston. His large murals
deal with Chicano history and oppression.
Tanguma is unpaid for his labor.

4963 Renacimiento del arte chicano en Texas. EL
HISPANO, Vol. 6, no. 3 (July 10, 1973).
English.

AN: Remigio Garcia and Mariana
Escalante, young muralists, describe their
work and the collective goals of a mural
workshop begun by Leo Tanguma in Houston,
TX.

4964 Southwest Chicano Arts Center, Houston, TX.
Chicano youth in art. Exhibition invitation,
1978. English.

AN: Invitation to exhibit featuring
works from Chicano youth in the Houston
area.

4965 Tennant, Donna. Conceptual art dots city
landscape. HOUSTON CHRONICLE, (October 27,
1979), p. II, 7. English.

AN: Frank Fajardo and Bolivian-born
Guillermo Pulido are two of several artists
creating conceptual art pieces in various
parts of Houston. Fajardo marked out space
with 25 stakes tipped with day-glo orange
paint. Pulido constructed two large
triangles on opposite hillsides, like giant
markers.

4966 Valenzuela-Crocker, Elvira. Tanguma: a man
and his murals. AGENDA, no. 5 (Summer 1974),
p. 14-17. English.

AN: Illustrated report on Houston
muralist Leo Tanguma's 1973 work REBIRTH OF
OUR NATIONALITY as well as other murals in
progress. Tanguma's social views and his
debt to Mexican muralist David Alfaro
Siqueiros are detailed.

HOW'S SCHOOL ENRIQUE? [film]

4967 Films for the inner city. Los Angeles, CA:
Los Angeles Public Library Federal Project,
1971. English.

AN: Annotated catalog of 16mm films and
filmstrips, educational and documentary.
Those concerning Mexican heritage include
CHICANO FROM THE SOUTHWEST (1970),
HENRY...BOY OF THE BARRIO (1969); HOW'S
SCHOOL, ENRIQUE (1970), I AM JOAQUIN (1970),
THE MEXICAN AMERICAN: HERITAGE AND DESTINY
(1970), A MEXICAN AMERICAN FAMILY (1970),
MEXICAN AMERICANS: QUEST FOR EQUALITY
(1968), MEXICAN OR AMERICAN (1970),
SIQUEIROS: "EL MAESTRO" (THE MARCH OF
HUMANITY IN LATIN AMERICA) (1969).
Filmstrips include THE AWAKENING (LA RAZA) -
Part IV, CONFLICT OF CULTURES (LA RAZA) -
Part III, MASTERWORKS OF MEXICAN ART, OUT OF
THE MAINSTREAM, PILGRIMAGE (GRAPE STRIKERS).
Also listed are films and filmstrips for
children.

Hoyo-Mara Gang, East Los Angeles, CA

4968 Cockcroft, Eva; Weber, John; and Cockcroft, James D. Towards a people's art: the contemporary mural movement. New York: E.P. Dutton, 1977. English.

AN: A survey of the street mural movement in the United States, from about 1967 on. Several chapters are written by the artists themselves: John Weber on the Chicago mural group; Susan Shapiro-Kiok on Cityarts Workshop of New York; Eva Cockcroft on People's painters of New Jersey; Geronimo Garduno on Artes Guadalupanos de Aztlan of New Mexico. Chicano murals illustrated include those of Mujeres Muralistas, Ray Patlan, William F. Herron, Hoyo-Mara Gang, Artes Guadalupanos de Aztlan, Vicente Mendoza and Jose Nario (with Patlan) Mario Castillo, Michael Rios, Toltecas en Aztlan, Roberto Chavez, Ernie Palomino, Chuy Campusano and Luis Cortazar (with Rios).

4969 Exxon Company, Houston, TX and Quirarte, Jacinto. Chicano art of the barrio. Exhibition brochure, n.d. [c.1976]. English.

AN: Brochure for a traveling exhibit of photographically-reproduced Chicano murals: Leo Limon, Lucila Villasenor Grijalva, Antonio Esparza, Susan Saenz, Charles Felix, Hoyo-Mara gang, David A. Lopez and team, Roberto Chavez and team (Los Angeles); Jerry Concha, Ruben Guzman, Chuy Campusano (San Francisco); Manuel Unzueta (Santa Barbara). Ernie Palomino and Leo Esequiel Ozona (Fresno). Leo Tanguma (Houston), Roberto Lucero, Manuel Martinez and Al Sanchez (Denver).

Huerta, Victoriano

4970 Posada, Jose Guadalupe. Calavera huertista [graphic]. REGENERACION, Vol. 1, no. 7 (1970), p. COVER.

I AM JOAQUIN [film]

4971 Films for the inner city. Los Angeles, CA: Los Angeles Public Library Federal Project, 1971. English.

AN: Annotated catalog of 16mm films and filmstrips, educational and documentary. Those concerning Mexican heritage include CHICANO FROM THE SOUTHWEST (1970), HENRY...BOY OF THE BARRIO (1969); HOW'S SCHOOL, ENRIQUE (1970), I AM JOAQUIN (1970), THE MEXICAN AMERICAN: HERITAGE AND DESTINY (1970), A MEXICAN AMERICAN FAMILY (1970), MEXICAN AMERICANS: QUEST FOR EQUALITY (1968), MEXICAN OR AMERICAN (1970), SIQUEIROS: "EL MAESTRO" (THE MARCH OF HUMANITY IN LATIN AMERICA) (1969). Filmstrips include THE AWAKENING (LA RAZA) - Part IV, CONFLICT OF CULTURES (LA RAZA) - Part III, MASTERWORKS OF MEXICAN ART, OUT OF THE MAINSTREAM, PILGRIMAGE (GRAPE STRIKERS). Also listed are films and filmstrips for children.

Ibanez, Armando

4972 Canto al pueblo: an anthology of experiences. San Antonio, TX: Penca Books, 1978. English.

AN: Includes works by: Mario E. Castillo, Carlos Rosas, Jose G. Gonzalez, Santos Martinez, Gilbert Munoz, Fred Loa, Armando Ibanez and others.

Iconography

4973 Donnell-Kotrozo, Carol and Perlman, Barbara. Male passages: a secular santero of the '80s interprets machismo. ARIZONA ARTS AND LIFESTYLE, Vol. 4, no. 1 (1982), p. 32-39. English.

AN: Rudy Fernandez moves freely between two- and three-dimensional forms using personal symbols such as cacti, roosters, flying hearts, trout, in paintings or lead-covered shelves of boxes reminiscent of retablos. Colorado-born Fernandez has lived in Arizona, Utah, New Mexico, and Washington. His art is not religious, but is influenced by a strong Catholic background. Many color illustrations, including the cover.

4974 Drescher, Tim and Garcia, Rupert. Recent Raza murals in the U.S. RADICAL AMERICA, Vol. 12, no. 2 (March, April, 1978), p. 14-31. English.

AN: Like the cultural revolution of Mexico in the 1920s, La Raza of Aztlan emphasizes the Native American and mestizo heritage as well as the Mexican revolutionary heritage. Witnn a social context, the authors discuss Chicano and Latino murals nationally. Iconography and its relation to Chicano experience is explored, as well as images by and about women. Illustrations.

4975 Fine Arts Society of San Diego, CA. The cross and the sword. Exhibition catalog, 1976. Bilingual.

AN: Bi-lingual exhibition catalog of Southwestern art forms; santero art, vernacular architecture and traditional folk art. Important essays by experts in each field. Contains an iconographical summary of santos and a good bibliography. Profusely illustrated.

4976 Los Four exhibit in Union Gallery. UNIVERSITY TIMES, (November 6, 1975), p. 4. English.

AN: "Los Four," a group of four Chicano artists - Frank Romero, Roberto "Beto" de la Rocha, Gilbert Lujan, and Carlos Almaraz, with newcomer Judithe Hernandez - work with political cartoons, Catholic symbols, works of sardonic humor. They also paint street murals: several have been done recently in Los Angeles, La Puente, and Long Beach. Illustrated.

4977 Goez Imports & Fine Arts, Los Angeles, CA. We invite you to see the birth of our art. Gallery brochure, 1971. English.

AN: Brochure with history of gallery, mural map, iconography of Goez mural.

Iconography (cont.)

4978 Goldman, Shifra M. Canto de unidad: nuevo mural de Berkeley. PLURAL, Vol. 8, no. 96 (September 1979), p. 33-44. Spanish.

AN: Report on significance, inconography, and new technical experimentation in street mural on facade of La Pena Cultural Center, Berkeley, CA. Deals with Latin American "nueva cancion." Ray Patlan and Anna de Leon on team of four muralists. Illustrated. This article was reprinted as "Song of Unity: Berkeley's New Raza Mural," in ARTWORKERS NEWS (New York), Vol. 11, no. 30, September 20, 1980, p. 1.

4979 Goldman, Shifra M. Resistance and identity: street murals of occupied Aztlan. LATIN AMERICAN LITERARY REVIEW, Vol. 5, no. 10 (Spring, Summer, 1977), p. 124-128. English.

AN: Two periods of Mexican muralism's influence in the U.S.: 1930s and 1960s. Differences between Mexican and Chicano murals nationally. Comparison of the respective iconographies and funding sources. This article was reprinted as "Resistencia e Identidad: Los Murales Callejeros de Aztlan, La Ciudad (sic) Ocupada," in ARTES VISUALES (Mexico, D.F.), no. 16, Fall-Winter, 1977, p. 22-25.

4980 Gonzalez, Hector. El arte de Esteban Villa. EL HISPANO, Vol. 6, no. 20 (November 6, 1973). Spanish.

AN: Commenting on Esteban Villa's one man show at the Centro de Artistas Chicanos that presented sixty-five pieces of art ranging from acrylics, watercolors, woodcuts, to pen and ink drawings. Villa fuses Indian symbols, mythology, folklore and customs to create a new "cosmic" dimension for the Chicano experience.

4981 Guernica, Antonio Jose and Saavedra-Vela, Pilar. El Midwest Canto al pueblo: "Otra Vez, C/S". AGENDA, Vol. 7, no. 3 (May, June, 1977), p. 4-13. Bilingual.

AN: A thorough report on the various phases and events of the Midwest Canto al Pueblo in Milwaukee, Wisconsin on April 28 to May 8, 1977. The festival brought together artists, poets, musicians, and cultural workers to reaffirm, share, and celebrate the identity of La Raza with El Pueblo. Includes a thematic and iconographic overview of Chicano murals in California by Jose Montoya, and an analysis of his sculpture by Zarco Guerrero from Meza, Arizona. Well illustrated. Includes a photograph of the collective mural painted at 5th St. and National Avenue in Milwaukee, Wisconsin during the course of the conference.

4982 Knapp, Martha. West side is part of mural art renaissance. WEST SAINT PAUL VOICE, Vol. 5, no. 19 (November 21, 1977). English.

AN: Pre-Columbian symbology in the mural program painted by Paul Basquez and Armando Estrella in the Chicano barrio; information and data on the mural renaissance in Minnesota.

4983 Lopez, Gerard. Estrada murals. LA GENTE DE AZTLAN, Vol. 4, no. 6 (May, June, 1974), p. 4. English.

AN: Article explains how the community at Estrada Courts was mobilized to support a mural project uniting artists with residents. Includes interview with artist C.W. Felix who comments on the goals of the mural program and cites the themes and symbolism of the murals.

4984 Lyle, Cindy. Chicano mural art: a mixture of the barrio's rage and pride. NEW YORK TIMES, (August 17, 1975), p. Sec.2, 21. English.

AN: Brief history of San Diego's Chicano Park, why and how it was established, and the establishment of the Centro Cultural de la Raza in Balboa Park. Iconography of several murals is examined, and the longevity of outdoor murals discussed. Illustrated.

4985 Mandeville Center for the Arts, La Jolla, CA and Lopez, Yolanda M. Yolanda M. Lopez works: 1975-1978. Exhibition catalog, 1978. English.

AN: Catalog of an exhibit dedicated to Lopez's female family members, expecially her grandmother and mother, to the artist herself as a track runner, and to the Guadalupe series, icons of the Virgin transformed to reflect the life of contemporary women. Well illustrated.

4986 Montoya, Jose E. and Carrillo, John M. Posada: the man and his art. A comparative analysis of Jose Guadalupe Posada and the current Chicano art movement as they apply toward social and cultural change: a visual resource unit for Chicano education. Unpublished thesis, 1975. English.

AN: Includes a historical background of 19th century Mexican engraver Posada, the significance of his work, a background of Chicano art, and the influence of Posada and the "calavera" on Chicano art. The unit includes 227 slides of Posada and other Mexican artists; and slides of Chicano artists using the calavera theme.

4987 Murales - 'expresan nuestra realidad'. AYUDA, Vol. 1, no. 6 (September 1977). English.

AN: Brief illustrated article on Raul Valdez's 1977 mural LOS ELEMENTOS on the outside wall of Antioch's Juarez-Lincoln College (Centro Cultural de LUCHA). Explains the iconography of the mural. Includes brief biography of the artist.

4988 The new logo. LA VOZ: Concilio for the Spanish Speaking of King Co., Seattle, no. 5 (June 1979). English.

AN: Biographical information on artist Alfredo Arreguin. Born in Uruapan, Michoacan Mexico and residing in Seattle for eighteen years, Arrequin is active in La Extension Cultural, an agency formed to meet the cultural needs of "Hispanics" in the Pacific Northwest. In his logo for the "Concilio," Arreguin employs symbols representing history, beauty, unity, ethnicity and communication.

4989 Pomona College Gallery of Montgomery Art Center, Claremont, CA; Allikas, Bob; and Glickman, Hal. Chicano graffiti: the signatures and symbols of Mexican-American youth. Exhibition catalog, [1970]. English.

AN: Catalog of exhibit based on photographs of Los Angeles graffiti.

Iconography (cont.)

oil paintings entitled THE HOE.

4990 Rios, Sam. Chicano muralist: Toltecotl in
Aztlan. Unpublished paper, 1980. English.

AN: History of pre-Columbian, Mexican,
and Chicano wall paintings. Describes in
detail murals by Jose Montoya, Juanishi
Orozco, Esteban Villa, Stan Padilla, Juan
Cervantes, Lorraine Garcia of the Centro de
Artistas Chicanos, Royal Chicano Air Force,
painted in 1977 at Southside Park,
Sacramento, Calif. Symbolism is explained.

4991 Rogelio Cardenas--making murals. EL MUNDO
(San Francisco, CA), (September 14, 1978).
English.

AN: Rogelio Cardenas' fourth mural, LA
MUJER, on the La Mexicana Tortilleria in
Hayward, California. Interview with the
artist who explains the mural's symbolism
and his future plans. Illustrated.

4992 Torres, Salvador Roberto. Arte de la Raza
[portfolio]. DE COLORES, Vol. 1, no. 1
(Winter 1973), p. 34-43. Bilingual.

AN: A portfolio consisting of four
drawings representing the "progression" of
the symbol of the banner adopted by the
United Farm Workers (UFW). Included are four
out of six drawings, each with its own
explication in English and Spanish, and
brief biographical data about the artist.

4993 Trujillo, Marcella. The dilemma of the
modern Chicana artist and critic. HERESIES,
Vol. 2, no. 4 (1979), p. 5-10. English.

AN: Recommended for its application to
the visual arts in its discussion of
iconography common to literature and art,
and symbols popular with Chicana artists: La
Malinche, the Virgin of Guadalupe,
Tonantzin, Mother Earth, etc.

4994 Unzueta, Manuel. Iconography: strictly
Chicano. XALMAN, Vol. 1, no. 4 (Spring
1977), p. 17-18. English.

AN: Only a Chicano artist can portray
the unique experience of being Chicano
through visual images of despair and self
pride: opinion of painter Unzueta.

4995 Walking tour and guide to the Great Wall at
Tujunga Wash. Venice, CA: Social and Public
Art Resource Center, [1981]. English.

AN: History and symbolism of the GREAT
WALL, directed by Judy Baca, and created by
teams of young people working on the mural
since 1976. Illustrated.

Idaho

4996 Monroe, Julie T. A splash of art from
Idaho's Mexican-Americans. IDAHO STATESMAN,
(March 11, 1977), p. 4D. English.

AN: As a Bicentennial tribute to all
people of Latin American heritage, Illinois
Bell Telephone Company organized a national
exhiibit of 17 Mexican-American/Chicano
artists. In Idaho, the touring exhibition
was augmented by a local presentation,
MEXICAN-AMERICAN: IDAHO, shown at the Boise
Gallery of Art under sponsorship of Boise
Cascade. Jose Rodriguez, local artist
presents his views on the meanings of the
word "Chicano" and "Chicano Art."
Illustrated with a photograph of Jose
Rodriguez and a reproduction of one of his

Identity

4997 Baeza, Armando M. In disagreement. CON
SAFOS, no. 7 (Winter 1971), p. 60-61.
Bilingual.

AN: Reply to a CON SAFOS editorial
(Vol.2, no.5) in which it is stated that
Chicanos have no "...body of visual
arts...no theatre...no music...", etc.

4998 Editorial. CON SAFOS, Vol. 2, no. 5 (1970),
p. 45-46. English.

AN: Editorial calling attention to the
greatest "weakness" of La Raza as the lack
of clear and tangible art forms.

4999 Gonzales, Juan. Regional report, The arts:
"Our people deserve the best". NUESTRO, Vol.
1, no. 2 (May 1977), p. 56-57. English.

AN: Activities of San Francisco's
Galeria de la Raza; interviews with its
directors, Rene Yanez and Ralph Maradiaga.
Reprinted as "Galeria de la Raza: our people
deserve the best" in EL TECOLOTE (San
Francisco, CA), Vol. 7, no. 11 (July, 1977),
p. 14.

5000 Lopez, Armando. 'Chicano' art gains
cross-culture recognition: 'the street mural
has flourished in the barrio'. LAREDO NEWS,
(July 20, 1980), p. 6-A. English.

AN: Report on a lecture "The First
Decade of the Chicano Renaissance: Mexican
American Art in the United States" given by
Dr. Shifra M. Goldman under the sponsorship
of the Laredo Philosophical Society.
Mentions the "delicate Issue" of using the
word "Chicano" in conservative Laredo.
Illustrated with works of Laredo-born Amado
M. Pena.

5001 Lujan, Gilbert Sanchez "Magu". El arte del
Chicano - "The Spirit of the Experience".
CON SAFOS, no. 7 (Winter 1971), p. 11-13.
English.

AN: Definition of Chicano Art by artist
Lujan as the expression of an unique
experience that is neither Mexican nor U.S.
Anglo, that has its own vitality and
dynamics. Chicanos can draw upon common
cultural elements and transform them into
images and art forms such as sculptured
menudo bones, tortilla drawings, vato loco
portraits, etc. Four woodcuts by Roberto de
la Rocha are shown as examples.

5002 Monroe, Julie T. A splash of art from
Idaho's Mexican-Americans. IDAHO STATESMAN,
(March 11, 1977), p. 4D. English.

AN: As a Bicentennial tribute to all
people of Latin American heritage, Illinois
Bell Telephone Company organized a national
exhiibit of 17 Mexican-American/Chicano
artists. In Idaho, the touring exhibition
was augmented by a local presentation,
MEXICAN-AMERICAN: IDAHO, shown at the Boise
Gallery of Art under sponsorship of Boise
Cascade. Jose Rodriguez, local artist
presents his views on the meanings of the
word "Chicano" and "Chicano Art."
Illustrated with a photograph of Jose
Rodriguez and a reproduction of one of his
oil paintings entitled THE HOE.

Identity (cont.)

5003 Quirarte, Jacinto. Mexican-American artists. Austin, TX: University of Texas Press, 1973. English.

AN: First comprehensive historical text on artists of Mexican descent in the United States. Sets up the antecedents from settlement to the visits of Mexican muralists Rivera, Siqueiros, Orozco and Tamayo in the U.S., though only Orozco and Tamayo are considered at length. Mexican American artists are divided by decades of birth, from 1901 to 1946. Twenty-seven artists (two women) are discussed. The epilogue is a discussion on the terms "Mexican American" and "Chicano," the latter articulated by Esteban Villa, who is not in the text.

5004 Rodriguez, Pedro. Chicano artist's paintings on display at WWC. UNION BULLETIN, (February 19, 1981). English.

AN: Commentary by artist Pedro Rodriguez stressing the social context of Chicano art and the role and function of the Chicano artist. Illustrated with a photograph of the artist and reproductions of two oil paintings: EL OBRERO and CIUDAD LIBERTAD.

5005 Santa Ana College, Santa Ana, CA and Goldman, Shifra M. Chicano art. Exhibition catalog, 1974. English.

AN: Thirteen California artists are presented in a short essay defining Chicano as a double mestizaje of Mexican mestizo and U.S. influences that exists in a state of "reconciled conflict." Its aim is communication. Artists included are Malaquias Montoya, Rupert Garcia, Manuel Hernandez, Esteban Villa, Robert Gomez, Harvey Tarango, Mary Helen Castro, Eduardo Carrillo, Graciela Carrillo, and "Los Four": Carlos Almaraz, Robert de la Rocha, Judithe Hernandez, Gilbert Lujan and Frank Romero.

5006 Tijerina lauds Chicano Congress results. SANTA FE NEW MEXICAN, (October 24, 1972), p. A3. English.

AN: At the First National Chicano Congress for Land and Cultural Reform in Albuquerque, it was pointed out that younger delegates are just coming to the realization of being Chicano but are behind in knowledge about the relationships between Spaniards, Mexicans and Indians. This was the reason for unveiling the mural BIRTH OF THE INDO-HISPANO [called elsewhere REBIRTH OF THE CHICANO] at the Alianza headquarters October 19, 1972.

5007 Unzueta, Manuel. Iconography: strictly Chicano. XALMAN, Vol. 1, no. 4 (Spring 1977), p. 17-18. English.

AN: Only a Chicano artist can portray the unique experience of being Chicano through visual images of despair and self pride: opinion of painter Unzueta.

5008 Valadez, Kathy L. What is Chicano art? A Chicano artist's concept. EL CHICANO, Vol. 7, no. 47 (April 26, 1973), p. 12-13. English.

AN: Esau Quiroz is a Chicano artist who states that Chicano art is that art by which a Chicano can be identified. He further defines Chicano art as that which contains a Chicano consciousness and portrays

Chicanismo in terms of the exploitation of Chicanos.

5009 Valdez, James. Analysis of Chicano aesthetics in visual art. Symposium paper, 1973 [unpublished]. English.

AN: The basic premise of this paper, presented at the Third Annual El Alma Symposium at California State University, San Jose, is that Chicano artists (as a group) are imitators and only by a process that develops self-knowledge can they transcend their situation. Of the six potential positions for the Chicano analyzed in this paper, only one articulates how Chicanos could create art reflective of their experience as truth. Only when Chicanos have an awareness of their identity can they function creatively in their environment.

5010 Yarbro-Bejarano, Yvonne. La forma del sueno: arte y pensamiento de Alfredo Arreguin. METAMORFOSIS, Vol. 3, no. 2 (1980, 1981), p. 10-24. Spanish.

AN: Interview and portfolio of Mexican-born painter who has been living in Seattle for more than 20 years. Contains biographical data and the artist's view on the role of the Chicano artist. Ten illustrations.

Ideology
    USE: Political Ideology

II Colloquium of Latin American Photography

5011 COUNCIL OF LATINO PHOTOGRAPHY/USA NEWSLETTER. no. 2 (January 1980). English.

AN: Photocopied newsletter reporting on the "First Communication" meeting of the organization, the opening of a Council gallery and darkroom in Pasadena, news from San Francisco/Berkeley group, news of the activities of the Consejo Mexicano de Fotografia, Mexico, and an announcement of the II COLLOQUIUM OF LATIN AMERICAN PHOTOGRAPHY for 1981.

Illegal Aliens
    USE: Undocumented Workers

Illinois Bell Telephone Co.

5012 Monroe, Julie T. A splash of art from Idaho's Mexican-Americans. IDAHO STATESMAN, (March 11, 1977), p. 4D. English.

AN: As a Bicentennial tribute to all people of Latin American heritage, Illinois Bell Telephone Company organized a national exhiibit of 17 Mexican-American/Chicano artists. In Idaho, the touring exhibition was augmented by a local presentation, MEXICAN-AMERICAN: IDAHO, shown at the Boise Gallery of Art under sponsorship of Boise Cascade. Jose Rodriguez, local artist presents his views on the meanings of the word "Chicano" and "Chicano Art." Illustrated with a photograph of Jose Rodriguez and a reproduction of one of his oil paintings entitled THE HOE.

Immigration

5013 Burciaga, Jose Antonio. Which way did they go, slim? [drawing]. CARACOL, Vol. 5, no. 2 (October 1978), p. 9. English.

Immigration (cont.)

5014 Marta. National Chicano/Latino Conference on Immigration and Public Policy [poster]. CARACOL, Vol. 4, no. 2 (October 1977), p. BACK COVER. Bilingual.

5015 Ochoa, Victor Orozco. [Resistencia! (drawing)]. MAIZE, Vol. 2, no. 2 (Winter 1979), p. 61. Spanish.

INCOMPREHENSION AL ARTE [mural]

5016 Montoya, Emmanuel; Rodriguez, Patricia; and Acevedo, Mario (Torero). Canto al pueblo '78. NATIONAL MURALS NETWORK COMMUNITY NEWSLETTER, (1978). English.

AN: The second annual Canto al Pueblo took place in Corpus Christi, Texas, where more than six murals were painted: "Wall of Cultural Education" by 13 artists headed by Roel Montealva; Carlota Espinoza, with children; Gilberto Romero, Jose Antonio Burciaga and Patricia Rodriguez, "Incomprehension al arte"; "Madre Tierra" by Manuel Martinez of Denver with Amador Hinojosa (Corpus Christi) and Enriquette Vasquez (New Mexico); Mario Torero; Salvador Vega of Chicago whose mural some Canto participants considered "insulting".

Incorporated Artes Monumentales, Denver, CO

5017 Incorporated Artes Monumentales/Inc., Denver, CO. IAM: art exhibit. Exhibition brochure, n.d. English.

AN: Large format, well illustrated brochure with information on muralists Roberto Lucero, Al Sanchez, Andrew Manning, Ricardo Barrera and Bob Reyes. Includes some biographical information situating these artists within the dynamic artistic traditions of the Mexican and the Chicano mural movements.

5018 Sinisi, J. Sebastian J. Following footsteps of Diego Rivera. CONTEMPORARY, (January 13, 1980), p. 28-30. English.

AN: Story on West Denver murals, particularly by Manuel Martinez and Carlos Sandoval at the La Alma Recreation Center, Summer 1979. Murals done through the Denver City Walls Project by artists belonging to Incorporated Artes Monumentales. Illustrated.

5019 Troelstrup, Glenn. Former delinquent paints his way out of corner. DENVER POST, (April 23, 1977), p. 2. English.

AN: Manuel Martinez started sketching at 13; at 29, after studying with Siqueiros (1967-68), he painted a number of murals in Denver and Albuquerque. In 1977 he organized Incorporated Artists Monumentales. Color illustration.

5020 Tully, Robert. City walls. LA VOZ (Denver, CO), (August 3, 1979), p. 7. English.

AN: In a project managed by Metro Denver Urban Coalition, several Chicano artists were hired to work consistently in creating murals for the inner city. Article focuses on the goals, procedures, and activities of the muralists. Grouped as Incorporated Artes Monumentales, the group included Jerry Jaramillo, Steve Lucero, Al Sanchez, Fred Sanchez, and Carlos Sandoval. Illustrated by a group photograph of artists and a photograph of a wall painting by the

Chilean-led Brigada Orlando Letelier in Denver.

Indiana

5021 Mexican-American Advisory Committee of the Museum of Science and Industry.. Second annual Mexican-American art fiesta. Exhibition brochure, 1975. English.

AN: Exhibit of paintings, sculpture, crafts, and photography by 49 artists from Illinois, Indiana, and Mexico. Includes many of the most important Chicano artists of the Chicago area.

Infante, Pedro

5022 Perales, Tony. [Pedro Infante (drawing)]. In: Salinas, Luis Omar. CRAZY GYPSY. Fresno, CA: Origenes Publications, c1970, p. [40].

INFINITY FACTORY

5023 Gamboa, Harry, Jr. Film, television, and Trevino. LA LUZ, Vol. 6, no. 10 (October 1977), p. 7-8. English.

AN: Jesus Salvador Trevino has been an active proponent and participant in transforming cultural inaccuracy about Chicanos in the media to accurate mass media models. A biography of Trevino follows, including discussion of some of his films: THE SALAZAR INQUEST, CHICANO MORATORIUM AFTERMATH, SOLEDAD, AMERICA TROPICAL, YO SOY CHICANO, RAICES DE SANGRE, as well as television series like ACCION CHICANO, AHORA, and INFINITY FACTORY.

5024 Torres, Louis R. An innovation in children's t.v.: THE INFINITY FACTORY. LA LUZ, Vol. 6, no. 2 (February 1977), p. 10-11. English.

AN: Illustrated report on a new television series for children aimed at teaching mathematics fundamentals in a crisply-paced series of half-hour programs. The executive producer, Jesus Salvador Trevino, filmed the segments in a New York Black community, and in the East Los Angeles Chicano barrio. In one segment, muralist Willie Herron works with youngsters to design and paint an outdoor mural.

5025 Zheutlin, Barbara and Talbot, David. Jesus Salvador Trevino. In: CREATIVE DIFFERENCES: PROFILES OF HOLLYWOOD DISSIDENTS. Boston, MS: South End Press, 1978, p. 345-352. English.

AN: Within the context of New Left alternative filmmakers who chose to work within Hollywood, Trevino sets forth his standards and goals. His films and TV productions include SOLEDAD (1971), AMERICA TROPICAL (1971), YO SOY CHICANO (1972), RAICES DE SANGRE (1977) and INFINITY FACTORY (1975-1976).

Inner City
USE: Urban Communities

Inner City Mural Program, Los Angeles, CA

5026 Citywide mural project. Los Angeles, CA:
     Citywide Mural Project, n.d. [c. 1975].
     English.

     AN: Brochure giving history, resources
     and procedures for doing a mural by the Los
     Angeles Citywide Mural Project/Mural
     Resource Mural Program of 1973-1974.
     Illustrated. Available in Social and Public
     Art Resource Center (Venice, CA) archives.

5027 Inner City Mural Program. Glendale, CA: Los
     Angeles County Dept. of Parks and
     Recreation, [ca. 1974]. English.

     AN: Brief history and philosophy of the
     Inner City Mural Program from June 1, 1973
     to May 31, 1974, when it was sponsored by
     the Cultural Arts Section of the Los Angeles
     County Department of Parks and Recreation,
     and coordinated by Lukman Glasgow. Artists
     Judithe Hernandez and Frank Romero included.
     20 illustrations, some in color.

Institute of American Indian Arts

5028 Institute of American Indian Arts Museum,
     Santa Fe, NM. Native American/Hispanic
     festival, contemporary & historic visions.
     Santa Fe, NM: Institute of American Indian
     Arts Museum, 1981. English.

     AN: Catalog for exhibit co-sponsored by
     La Cofradia de Artes y Artesanos Hispanicos,
     the Institute of American Indian Arts, and
     the Santa Fe Council for the Arts. Exhibit
     stresses the inter-relationship between the
     Indian and Hispano peoples of New Mexico. 31
     contemporary Hispano artists included.
     Illustrated.

El Instituto Chicano de Artes y Artesanias, San Antonio, TX

5029 Chicano art of the Southwest. San Antonio,
     TX: Instituto Chicano de Artes y Artesanias
     of the Texas Institute for Educational
     Development, 1975. English.

     AN: Collection of 220 slides
     supplemented by slide annotation and
     artists' biographies researched and
     photographed by Texas artist Cesar A.
     Martinez over two years. Biographies cover
     20 Texas, 6 New Mexico, and 15 northern
     California artists. Slides include, in
     addition, murals from Los Angeles and San
     Diego.

5030 Chicano exhibit set. SANTA FE NEW MEXICAN,
     (September 22, 1972), p. A4. English.

     AN: A Chicano art show organized by El
     Instituto Chicano de Artes y Artesanias of
     San Antonio, TX is scheduled for Highlands
     University Gallery, Las Vegas, NM.

Instituto Cultural Mexicano, San Antonio, TX

5031 Salazar, Veronica. Aspiration comes true.
     SAN ANTONIO EXPRESS-NEWS, (October 28,
     1979), p. 8-H. English.

     AN: History of Alice Dickerson
     Montemayor of Laredo, Texas (known as
     "Admonty") who started to paint at 74 on the
     occasion of her second exhibit at the
     Mexican government's Instituto Cultural.

International House Gallery, Denver, CO

5032 Andrews, Rena. The fine arts. ROUNDUP,

(September 27, 1970), p. 18. English.

     AN: Commentary on one-man exhibition by
     John L. Mendoza at the International House
     Gallery in Denver. Noted for his water-color
     landscapes, the artists is a full time art
     teacher at East High School in Pueblo
     Colorado. Illustrated with photograph of the
     artist and one of his paintings.

5033 Haddad, Barbara. The fine arts. ROUNDUP,
     (January 25, 1970), p. 12. English.

     AN: Mixed review of Ray Espinoza's
     one-person show at the International House
     Gallery in Denver. The exhibition included
     drawings, paintings, prints, assemblages and
     sculptures. Selecting work from each medium,
     the critic comments on pieces that are
     successful and those not fully realized.
     Illustrated with a wood and metal relief of
     a guitar and a graphic of "Che" Guevara.

International Institute of St. Louis, MO

5034 59th Street Gallery, St. Louis, MO. Midwest
     Mexican-American art exhibit: Mexico and its
     artists. Exhibition brochure, 1981. English.

     AN: Sponsored by the Sociedad Mexicana
     "Benito Juarez" and the international
     Institute of St. Louis, this three-part
     exhibit includes 1) MEXICO AS SEEN BY HER
     CHILDREN, a bilingual exhibit from Mexico
     traveling under Smithsonian Institution
     auspices, 2) MEXICAN CHILDREN IN THE U.S.A.,
     3) MEXICAN AMERICAN ARTISTS. In the latter
     are included Stephen Capiz (Roseville,
     Minn.), Jose Gonzalez (Chicago), Cesar A.
     Martinez (San Antonio), Ada Medina (Des
     Moines), Nora Chapa Mendoza (West
     Bloomfield, Mich.), Rene David
     Michel-Trapaga (St. Louis), David Munoz
     (Kansas City, Mo.), Jose Luis Narezo (Grand
     Rapids, Mich.), Benny Ordonez, Roman
     Villarreal (Chicago), Alejandro Romero
     (Chicago), Aurelio Diaz "Tekpankalli"
     (Chicago), Simon Ybarra (St. Louis).

Jails
USE: Prisons

James Monroe School, Santa Ana, CA

5035 Monroe mural brightens school. THE REGISTER,
     (December 13, 1973), p. G3. English.

     AN: James Monroe School in Santa Ana, CA
     has a huge mural painted by Costa Mesa
     artist Sergio O'Cadiz. The mural cost $4250,
     but the artist donated much time and talent.
     Illustrated.

Jara, Victor

5036 Erickson, Barbara. La Pena's new face. NORTH
     EAST BAY INDEPENDENT, no. 4 (September 5,
     1978), p. 11. English.

     AN: Illustrated story on the relief
     mural SONG OF UNITY by Ray Patlan, O'Brien
     Thiele, Osha Neumann, and Anna de Leon on
     the facade of La Pena cultural center in
     Berkeley, California. Chilean songwriter
     Victor Jara and the music of North and South
     America are the motifs.

Jara, Victor (cont.)

5037 Kerschen, Karen. Where politics and music mix: La Pena. BERKELEY BARB, (August 18, 1978), p. 12. English.

AN: A new three-dimensional mural has been completed on the outside of Berkeley's La Pena Community Center. It incorporates ceramic and papier mache relief in a painted mural. One side of the painting is dominated by a relief sculpture of Victor Jara, the Chilean musician and poet killed by the junta. Illustrated.

Jaramillo, Jerry

5038 Chicano art show. EL DIARIO DE LA GENTE, Vol. 1, no. 7 (February 6, 1973), p. 4. English.

AN: Fine arts students at the University of Colorado led by Rudy Fernandez hope to educate high school students about Chicano art. This article documents an exhibit held at Lafayette, CO. Members of the group are Bob Maez, Jerry Jaramillo, Anthony Mendoza, and Rudy Fernandez. Illustrated by four exhibition photographs by John L. Espinosa.

5039 Denver. NATIONAL MURALS NETWORK COMMUNITY NEWSLETTER, (Spring 1980), p. 10. English.

AN: Denver, Colorado murals by Manuel Martinez, the Chilean Orlando Letelier Brigade, Roberto Lucero, Al Sanchez, Jerry Jaramillo. Illustrated.

5040 La Familia Recreation Center, Denver, CO. Mural unveiling and swim party. Exhibition invitation, 1980. English.

AN: Invitation to the unveiling of La Familia Cosmica, a mural by Jerry Jaramillo assisted by Carlos Sandoval, Al Sanchez, Stephen Lucero. An art exhibit featured the muralists, Jon Howe, and Fred Sanchez, all of the Metro Denver Urban Coalition's City Walls artists. Illustrated.

5041 Meta studio I. Denver, CO: s.n., [1980]. English.

AN: Portfolio of colored prints by Colorado artists Ernie Gallegos, Jerry Jaramillo, Steve Lucero and Carlos M. Sandoval. Biographical information and photograph of each artist. Presentation of the group under the rubric of "metarealism" by Stephen Pascual Lucero.

5042 Metro Denver Urban Coalition, Denver, CO. City walls. Brochure, 1979. English.

AN: Brochure/poster giving history of City Walls Project and biographies of seven artists: Jon Howe, Jerry Jaramillo, Steve Lucero, Jowinnie Moore, Al Sanchez, Fred Sanchez, Carlos M. Sandoval. Illustrated.

5043 NATIONAL MURALS NETWORK COMMUNITY NEWSLETTER. (Spring 1980). English.

AN: Reports on the Sept. 1979 conference of Chicano visual arts held at UT Austin, organized by the Mujeres Artistas del Suroeste, and the Liga Unida de Chicanos Artistas, which brought together participants from the U.S. and Mexico City; on Manuel Martinez's five murals (1976-78); murals by Roberto Lucero, Al Sanchez, and Jerry Jaramillo; as well as by the Chilean group Orlando Letelier Brigade, all in Denver, Colorado; murals by Leo Tanguma in Houston; the story about the "forbidden" Chicano mural in Blue Island, Illinois. Illustrated.

5044 Tully, Robert. City walls. LA VOZ (Denver, CO), (August 3, 1979), p. 7. English.

AN: In a project managed by Metro Denver Urban Coalition, several Chicano artists were hired to work consistently in creating murals for the inner city. Article focuses on the goals, procedures, and activities of the muralists. Grouped as Incorporated Artes Monumentales, the group included Jerry Jaramillo, Steve Lucero, Al Sanchez, Fred Sanchez, and Carlos Sandoval. Illustrated by a group photograph of artists and a photograph of a wall painting by the Chilean-led Brigada Orlando Letelier in Denver.

Jaramillo, Pedrito

5045 Garcia-Camarillo, Mia. Don Pedrito Jaramillo [drawing]. CARACOL, Vol. 2, no. 9 (May 1976), p. 24.

5046 Lomas Garza, Carmen. Don Pedrito Jaramillo, Falfurrias, Texas, 1829-1907 [etching]. TEJIDOS, Vol. 3, no. 4 (Winter 1976), p. 22.

5047 Martinez, Cesar Augusto. Don Pedrito Jaramillo [woodcut]. CARACOL, Vol. 2, no. 9 (May 1976), p. Ft Cover. English.

5048 Martinez, Cesar Augusto. Don Pedrito Jaramillo [woodcut]. CARACOL, Vol. 3, no. 4 (December 1976), p. Bk Cover.

Jaramillo, Virginia

5049 Baciu, Joyce A. Hispanic artists: combining energy and emotion. CAMINOS, Vol. 2, no. 5 (October 1981), p. 14-17. English.

AN: Brief profiles of Mario Uribe, Ernest De Soto, Peter Rodriguez, Margarita Jauregui Weiner, Virginia Jaramillo, Luis Urrea, Ramses Noriega, Jose Lopez, Olivia Sanchez.

5050 The Mexican Museum, San Francisco, CA. Virginia Jaramillo. Exhibition brochure, 1980. English.

AN: Exhibition brochure with biographical information, exhibition chronology and an artist's statement.

Jaso, Luis

5051 MEXICAN MUSEUM NEWSLETTER. Vol. 6, no. 1 (Winter 1980, 1981). English.

AN: Regular report on the activities, finances, membership, and other information about the Museum. Announces several upcoming shows: Rupert Garcia, six Mexican geometric artists, paintings and prints by Mexican American and Mexican women artists, Mexican Leonel Maciel and Chicano Carlos Almaraz, Mexican folk art, Manuel Neri sculpture, and Mexican Luis Jaso.

5052 The Mexican Museum, San Francisco, CA. Recent works of Luis Jaso from Mexico City and Carlos Chavez Cordova from Los Angeles. Exhibition invitation, 1981. English.

AN: Invitation to an exhibit.

Jauregui Weiner, Margarita

5053 Baciu, Joyce A. Hispanic artists: combining energy and emotion. CAMINOS, Vol. 2, no. 5 (October 1981), p. 14-17. English.

AN: Brief profiles of Mario Uribe, Ernest De Soto, Peter Rodriguez, Margarita Jauregui Weiner, Virginia Jaramillo, Luis Urrea, Ramses Noriega, Jose Lopez, Olivia Sanchez.

Jauregui, Mike

5054 Amor sin fronteras. Los Angeles, CA: Colectivo El Ojo, n.d.. English.

AN: Fotonovela with Josefina Arce, Eduardo Dominguez and Mike Jauregui produced by the Colectivo: Eduardo Dominguez, Roberto Gil de Montes, Jerry Lucas, Kay Torres, students at California State University, Los Angeles.

Jesus Gutierrez Gallery, San Pedro, CA

5055 Jesus Gutierrez Gallery, San Pedro, CA. "Two of a kind" prints by Linda Vallejo, Muriel Olguin. Exhibition invitation [1978]. English.

AN: Invitation to an exhibit.

Jimenez, Alonso

5056 Elaine Horwitch Galleries, Santa Fe, NM. New Mexico woodcarving. Exhibition catalog, 1980. English.

AN: Invitation to an exhibit at the Horwitch galleries of Scottsdale, Arizona, and Santa Fe, NM of sculptors Felipe Archuleta, Leroy Archuleta, Frank Brito, Alonso Jimenez, Horatio Valdez, and others. Illustration.

Jimenez, David "Sir Loco"

5057 Teatro de la Tierra Morena, Santa Cruz, CA. Fuego en Aztlan: a Chicano arts show. Exhibition brochure, 1980. English.

AN: Folder of information on the exhibition curated by Cruz Zamarron and Eduardo Carrillo. Exhibiting artists were: Justina Avila, Terry Benitez, Eduardo Carrillo, Hernando Chavez, Bob Cruz, Juanita Estrada, Juana Franklin, Sal Garcia, Leticia Hernandez, David "Sir Loco" Jimenez, Raoul Mendez, Vicente Mendez, Maria V. Pinedo, Gonzalo Placencia, Ramon Rodriguez, Roberto Salas, George Silva and Cruz Zamarron. A special feature was a live tattoo demonstration entitled "Walking Art".

Jimenez, Luis

5058 Anaya, Rudolfo A. and Ortiz, Simon J. 1680-1980: a ceremony of brotherhood. Albuquerque, NM: Academic, 1981. English.

AN: A cooperative publication by members of the former La Academia de la Nueva Raza (1969-1976) formed of writers and artists, and the Tri-Centennial Commission of the All-Indian Pueblo Council. Includes writings and artworks by Chicanos and Indians from New Mexico, California, Texas, and Arizona. Chicano artists works included are by Ellen Arellano, Juan Estevan Arellano, Alberto Baros, Jose Antonio Burciaga, Juan Reyes Cervantes, Rudy Cuellar, Ricardo Favela, El Zarco Guerrero, Luis Jimenez, Jr., Carlos Quinto Kemm, Alejandro Lopez, Floyd Lujan,

Jose Montoya, Juanishi Orozco, Leo Romero, Secundino Sandoval, Jaime Valdez, Maria Varela, Esteban Villa.

5059 Beardsley, John. Personal sensibilities in public places. ARTFORUM, Vol. 19, no. 10 (June 1981), p. 43-45. English.

AN: Distinction is made between art in public places and public art. The latter is assumed to have content and symbolism accessible to the majority of the population. Luis Jimenez, sculptor of VAQUERO intended for Houston's Moody Park, feels people should be able to identify with art. Color illustration.

5060 Contemporary Arts Museum, Houston, TX. Dale gas: give it gas. The continued acceleration of Chicano art. Exhibition catalog, 1977. English.

AN: A comprehensive catalog including 28 works of art exhibited by 13 Texas artists: Melesio (Mel) Casas, Jose Esquivel, Francisco (Frank) Fajardo, Carmen Lomas Garza, Luis Jimenez, Cesar Augusto Martinez, Santos G. Martinez, Jr., Amado Pena, Roberto Rios, Jose Rivera, Joe B. Rodriguez, Jesus (Jesse) Trevino, and George Truan. Many illustrations, some in color. Introduction by James Harithas. Essay by Santos Martinez, Jr. Poetry, literature and essays by Chicano writers.

5061 Contemporary Arts Museum, Houston, TX. Fire! An exhibition of 100 Texas artists. Exhibition brochure, 1979. English.

AN: Includes eleven Chicano artists. Unfortunately, not illustrated, though a checklist of works is included. Mel Casas, Carmen Lomas Garza, Xavier Gorena, Luis Jimenez, Cesar Martinez, Guillermo Z. Pulido, Philip Renteria, Jose L. Rivera, Joe Rodriguez, George Truan, Juan B. Vela. Introduction by James Surls. Statements by the artists.

5062 Contemporary Arts Museum, Houston, TX and Harithas, James. Luis Jimenez: Progress I. Exhibition catalog, 1974-75. English.

AN: Catalog for a major exhibit of Jimenez sculptures, drawings and studies for sculptural works from 1967 to 1974. The latest project, PROGRESS, involves a series of monumental sculptures depicting the history of the West. Jimenez combines social comment with advanced plastic values. Well illustrated.

5063 Corpus Christy State University for the Arts and Weil Gallery Center for the Arts, Corpus Christi State University. Southwest artists invitational: an exhibition of contemporary art by seven Texas artists of Hispanic American descent. Ehxibition brochure, 1980. English.

AN: Artists Jesse Almazan, Luis Jimenez, Cesar Martinez, Lydia Martinez, Manuel Mauricio, Guillermo Pulido, and Jesse Trevino show a variety of techniques and styles. Text by Roberto Tomas Esparza. Statements by and about the artists. Illustrated.

Jimenez, Luis (cont.)

5064 Doty, Robert. Human concern/personal
     torment: the grotesque in American art. New
     York: Praeger, 1969. English.

     AN: Acknowledging the revival of realism
     after fifty years of abstraction, the
     Whitney Museum of American Art in New York
     mounted a controversial show of modern and
     contemporary painters and sculptors. Two
     sculptures and a drawing by Luis Jimenez
     were included, one of which, THE AMERICAN
     DREAM, (1968) is illustrated.

5065 Graham Gallery, New York, NY and Amaya,
     Mario. Luis Jimenez. Exhibition catalog,
     1969. English.

     AN: Well-illustrated catalog of an
     exhibit by El Paso-born sculptor. Some
     biographical material.

5066 Graham Gallery, New York, NY and Perreault,
     John. Luis Jimenez. Exhibition catalog,
     1970. English.

     AN: Well-illustrated catalog of an
     exhibit by El Paso-born sculptor. Some
     biographical material.

5067 Heard Museum, Phoenix, AZ. First Annual
     Southwest Chicano Art Invitational
     Exposition. Invitation for reception, 1976.
     English.

     AN: Invitation to a reception for
     artists Luis Jimenez (Roswell, New Mexico),
     Eugenio Quesada (Phoenix), Felipe Reyes (San
     Antonio), Pedro Rodriguez (San Francisco),
     Pedro Romero (Cannon City, Colo.) One
     illustration.

5068 Mendiville, Miguel and Saavedra-Vela, Pilar.
     A time for less talk and more action.
     AGENDA, Vol. 7, no. 5 (September, October,
     1977), p. 33-34. English.

     AN: The exhibit RAICES Y VISIONES,
     funded by the National Endowment for the
     Arts, was composed of more than 100 artworks
     by Chicano and Latino artists and toured the
     United States in 1977. The exposition was
     organized in four sections; artists whose
     work is influenced or related to
     Pre-Columbian art, art that explores social
     and political realities, and works that are
     more personal and introspective. Gives
     itinerary and listing of participating
     artists. Illustrated by photographs of the
     work of Rudy Trevino, Cesar Martinez, Luis
     Jimenez from Texas and Larry Fuente from
     California.

5069 Moisan, Jim. Ancient roots, new visions.
     ARTWEEK, Vol. 9, no. 26 (July 29, 1978), p.
     8. English.

     AN: Review of the show held at the
     Municipal Arts Gallery of Los Angeles, the
     first national touring show of Latino
     artists in the United States. Includes
     commentary on work of Larry Fuente, Luis
     Jimenez, Frank Romero, Harry Gamboa, Gronk,
     Rudy Martinez, Benjamin Serrano, Ricardo
     Diaz, Patssi Valdez, Mel Casas, Luis Leroy,
     Pedro Lujan. A related show, NEW VISIONS,
     L.A., includes Robert Delgado, Ray Bravo,
     Joe Moran, Rosalyn Mesquita, Patricia
     Murillo and others.

5070 Museum of Fine Arts, Santa Fe, NM. Luis
     Jimenez, sculpture, drawings and prints: La
     Cofradia de Artes y Artesanos Hispanicos,

selected works. Exhibition invitation, 1979.
English.

     AN: Invitation to an exhibit of Texas
     sculptor and printmaker Luis Jimenez, and
     New Mexican artists and artisans.

5071 New Mexico State University, University Art
     Gallery, Las Cruces, NM. Luis Jimenez:
     sculpture, drawings and prints. Exhibition
     catalog, 1977. English.

     AN: Well illustrated catalog, some
     illustrations in color. Text is interview
     tracing Jimenez's artistic development.
     Artists identifies Mexican American
     connections in his work.

5072 Rabyor, Jozanne. Luis Jimenez at
     Contemporary Arts Museum. ART IN AMERICA,
     Vol. 63, no. 1 (January, February, 1975), p.
     88. English.

     AN: Texas-born Luis Jimenez's first
     major museum show of 77 pieces spanning
     eight years of production is dazzling.
     Superbly crafted fiberglass sculptures
     comment on indigenous mythologies often with
     macabre humor. His work, according to the
     critic, is too moralistic to be Pop, and
     too passionate to be dumped into the
     California-plastic bag.

5073 Raices y visiones [portfolio]. REVISTA
     CHICANO-RIQUENA, Vol. 7, no. 2 (Spring
     1979), p. 29-44.

     AN: Portfolio of works from the exhibit
     RAICES ANTIGUAS/VISIONES NUEVAS: ANCIENT
     ROOTS/NEW VISIONS. Artists included are
     Patssi Valdez (Los Angeles), Eloisa
     Castellanos-Sanchez (New York), Benjamin
     Serrano, Jr. (Tijuana, Mexico), Alex Garza
     (Chicago), Martin Y. Moreno (Michigan), Luis
     A. Jimenez (New Mexico), Rene Castro
     (Oakland, CA), Sita Gomez de Kanelba (New
     York), Susana Lasta (Tucson, AZ), Domingo
     Garcia (New York), Consuelo Mendez Castillo
     (Caracas, Venezuela), Naomi Castillo
     Simonetti (New Jersey), Louis Carlos Bernal,
     and Eddie Comptis.

5074 S.A. site for National Symposium on Mexican
     American Art. CHICANO TIMES, Vol. 4, no. 30
     (November 9, 1973), p. 5. English.

     AN: Held at Trinity University, the
     Symposium discussed such issues as, creative
     evolution, art education, artistic
     relationships to Mexico and the evolution of
     Mexican American art in the California
     barrios. Participating artists included Rudy
     Trevino, Mel Casas, Octavio Medellin,
     Antonio Garcia, Carmen Garza, Esteban Villa,
     Jose Montoya, Ernesto Palomino, Michael
     Ponce de Leon, Luis Jimenez and Eugenio
     Quesada.

5075 Schwartz, Barry. The new humanism: art in a
     time of change. New York, Praeger, 1974.
     English.

     AN: Schwartz compiled an international
     roster of over 100 artists whom he believed
     formed a "movement" away from abstraction
     and toward an art expressing a belief in
     human values and human dignity. He divides
     humanism into categories like metaphysical,
     existential, absurd, etc. Included are Luis
     Jimenez's BARFLY and OLD WOMAN WITH CAT
     (illustrated p. 121), and a brief biography
     (p. 171).

Jimenez, Luis (cont.)

5076 Simon, Joan. Report from New Mexico. ART IN
     AMERICA, Vol. 68, no. 6 (Summer 1980), p.
     33-41. English.

     AN: Luis Jimenez worked four years as
     artist-in-residence at the Roswell Museum
     and Art Center, Roswell, NM, which enabled
     him to produce his PROGRESS series and other
     monumental sculpture.

5077 Smith, Roberta. Twelve days of Texas. ART IN
     AMERICA, Vol. 64, no. 4 (July, August,
     1976), p. 42-48. English.

     AN: Overview of Texas art in Fort
     Worth/Dallas, Houston, San Antonio, Tyler,
     and Galveston. Includes reproductions of
     works by Luis Jimenez (color, on cover),
     Roberto Rios mural, Jesse Trevino, Mel
     Casas. Also mentioned in text are Phil
     Renteria and Cesar Martinez.

5078 Southwest Texas State University, San
     Marcos, TX and Carlisle, Charles Richard.
     Cuatro caminos: four perspectives on Chicano
     art. Exhibition catalog, 1980. English.

     AN: Exhibition pamphlet with photographs
     of the artists. Alex Flores, Luis Jimenez,
     Cesar Augusto Martinez and Amado Pena, Jr.
     comment on their work and the Chicano art
     movement.

5079 Tannous, David. Report from Washington
     'directions' and the 'First Western
     Biennial'. ART IN AMERICA, Vol. 67, no. 8
     (December 1979), p. 29, 31. English.

     AN: Among the best and most eye-catching
     works at the First Western Biennial are
     three large fiberglass-and-epoxy sculptures
     by Luis A. Jimenez, Jr. from the series
     PROGRESS, PART II.

5080 Temko, Allan. Teen Angel's low riders -
     Chicano art on the rise. THIS WORLD,
     (August 26, 1979), p. 42-43. English.

     AN: Important and insightful analysis of
     the lowrider phenomenon among Chicano youth
     in California. Analysis of publications like
     LOW RIDER Magazine of San Jose, information
     on graphic artists like "Teen Angel" and
     Ramon Cisneros and thematic relationship of
     recognized Chicano artists like Gilbert
     Lujan, John Valadez, and Luis Jimenez to the
     lowrider movement. The lowrider is
     provocatively related to world wide cultural
     manifestations from diverse epochs.

5081 Tucker, Glen. Art scene. TODAY MAGAZINE,
     (April 16, 1978), p. 3. English.

     AN: Commentary on photographic exhibit
     by Robert Tapias and the gift to the Witte
     Museum from the American Academy and
     Institute of Arts and Letters of a colored
     pencil drawing titled "El Filos Lowrider" by
     Luis Jimenez.

5082 Xochil Art and Culture Center, Mission, TX.
     !Que te vaya pretty nice! Exhibition
     brochure, 1979. English.

     AN: Exhibition of Chicano art including
     Carmen Lomas Garza, Luis Jimenez, Cesar
     Martinez, Guillermo Pulido, Roberto Rios,
     Jose Rivera and Jesse Trevino. [See also
     Estudios Rio].

Jimenez, Richard

5083 Mural depicts history of Mexican Americans.
     EASTSIDE JRNL, (December 16, 1971), p. 1.
     English.

     AN: Richard Jimenez of the Goez Gallery
     depicts the past and present of Mexican
     American culture on an interior mural at the
     First Street Store (3640 E. First St.) The 6
     ft. by 15 ft. mural has central image of a
     clock with a faceless figure (The Mexican
     American of the future). Artist comments on
     another of his murals titled EDUCATION OF
     LIFE.

5084 Street art explosion in Los Angeles. SUNSET,
     (April 1973), p. 110-113. English.

     AN: Illustrated article on Los Angeles
     street murals including those by Roberto
     Chavez, Willie Herron, Frank Romero, Richard
     Jimenez, William Bejarano, Gilbert Lujan,
     Armando Cabrera, Frank Martinez, Charles
     Felix, and others.

**Joe Grandee Gallery and Museum of the Old West,
Arlington, TX**

5085 Samuels, Peggy and Samuels, Harold. Grandee,
     Joe Ruiz. In: THE ILLUSTRATED BIOGRAPHICAL
     ENCYCLOPEDIA OF ARTISTS OF THE AMERICAN
     WEST. NY: Doubleday, 1976, p. 193. English.

     AN: Brief biography of third generation
     Texan, Western painter of history, military,
     portrait subjects and illustrator living in
     Arlington, TX where his collection of
     Western artifacts is at the "Joe Grandee
     Gallery and Museum of the Old West." 1974
     one person retrospective in Washington, DC.

JOHN KENNEDY SAGA NUMBER 2 [mural]

5086 Muralist Campero shows works. EASTSIDE JRNL,
     (June 3, 1971), p. 6. English.

     AN: Photograph of artist Armando Campero
     with samples of his graphic work. The artist
     was completing a 3,000 square foot mural,
     JOHN KENNEDY SAGA NUMBER 2 for installation
     at the City Terrace Social Hall.

Jordan, Esteban

5087 Esteban Jordan [drawing]. CARACOL, Vol. 1,
     no. 6 (February 1975), p. 18.

Juarez, Benito

5088 Flores, Carolina. Benito Juarez [painting].
     TEJIDOS, Vol. 1, no. 3 (Summer 1974), p. 35.
     Spanish.

5089 Hernandez, Sergio. [Untitled drawing].
     REGENERACION, Vol. 1, no. 2 (1970), p.
     COVER.

Juarez-Lincoln University

5090 Palma Castroman, Janis. ENCUENTRO ARTISTICO
     FEMENIL [exhibit], Austin, TX, November 28,
     1977. TEJIDOS, Vol. 5, no. 1 (1978), p.
     1-47. Bilingual.

     AN: A multimedia, multicultural
     exposition by 26 Chicana artists held at
     Juarez-Lincoln University. The exhibit was
     sponsored by Chicanos Artistas Sirviendo a
     Aztlan (CASA) and Mujeres Artistas del
     Suroeste (MAS).

Juarez-Lincoln University (cont.)

5091 Palma Castroman, Janis. Introduccion.
TEJIDOS, Vol. 5, no. 1 (1978), p. i.
Spanish.

AN: One-page introduction to theme issue
featuring the work of Chicana artists
exhibited at the ENCUENTRO ARTISTICO FEMENIL
exposition held on November 28, 1977 in
Austin, TX.

Kahlo, Frida

5092 Alarcon, Francisco X. and Herrera, Juan
Felipe. Portraits plus struggles plus
consciousness: nine pastels by Rupert
Garcia. METAMORFOSIS, Vol. 3, no. 2 (1980),
p. 104-106. English.

AN: Reprint of article published as
"Rupert Garcia: portraits/retratos" in EL
TECOLOTE LITERARY MAGAZINE (San Francisco,
CA), Vol. 2, no. 1, March 1981, p. 6.

5093 Alarcon, Francisco X. Rupert Garcia:
portraits/retratos. EL TECOLOTE LITERARY
MAGAZINE, Vol. 2, no. 1 (March 1981), p. 6+.
Bilingual.

AN: Review of Garcia exhibit at the
Mexican Museum (S.F.) in 1981. Includes
portraits of Frida Kahlo and the Flores
Magon brothers, Goya, Van Gogh, Ethel and
Julius Rosenberg, etc. Illustrated. This
article has been reprinted in METAMORFOSIS
under a different title: "Portraits Plus
Struggles Plus Consciousness: Nine Pastels
by Rupert Garcia," Vol. 3-4, no. 1-2,
(1980-81), p. 104-106.

5094 Galeria de la Raza/Studio 24, San Francisco,
CA. Homenaje a Frida Kahlo. Exhibition
brochure, 1978.

AN: 51 artists, Chicano and non-Chicano.

5095 Goldman, Shifra M. The intense realism of
Frida Kahlo. CHISMEARTE, Vol. 1, no. 4 (Fall,
Winter, 1977), p. 8-11. English.

AN: A brief, one-page biographical
sketch of Frida Kahlo's life and work. This
is accompanied by black and white
reproductions of her paintings: AUTORRETRATO
COMO TEHUANA (1943), AUTORRETRATO (1946),
RAICES (1943), LA VENADITA (1946), and LA
NOVIA QUE SE ESPANTA DE VER LA VIDA ABIERTA
(n.d.).

5096 Kahlo, Frida and Del Solar, Daniel. Frida
Kahlo's THE BIRTH OF MOSES. TIN TAN, Vol. 1,
no. 2 (September 1975), p. 2-6. Bilingual.

AN: Mexican painter Frida Kahlo's
explanation of her painting THE BIRTH OF
MOSES in Spanish, with an error-ridden
translation to English. Source of the
original text not given. Illustrated.

5097 Kahlo, Frida. Henry Ford Hospital
[painting]. DE COLORES, Vol. 3, no. 3
(1977), p. 57. English.

5098 Kahlo, Frida. Mi nana y yo [painting]. DE
COLORES, Vol. 3, no. 3 (1977), p. 60.
Spanish.

5099 Kahlo, Frida. Pensando en la muerte
[painting]. DE COLORES, Vol. 3, no. 3
(1977), p. 63. Spanish.

5100 Kahlo, Frida. Retrato de la familia de Frida
[painting]. DE COLORES, Vol. 3, no. 3

(1977), p. 65. Spanish.

5101 Kamin, Ira. Memories of Frida Kahlo.
CALIFORNIA LIVING, (May 6, 1979), p. 44-50.
English.

AN: Chatty review of the sixth annual
Dia de los Muertos, celebrated by the
Galeria de la Raza this year with an homage
to Mexican painter Frida Kahlo. Local
artists filled the gallery with their
homages; the Galeria's outdoor billboard was
painted with her image; guests brought gifts
and dressed in Kahlo style, including older
women who wore jewelry given them by Kahlo.
Biographical material on Kahlo and Diego
Rivera should be read with caution. Well
illustrated.

5102 Mesa-Bains, Amalia. Homage to Frida Kahlo
opens Nov. 2, at Galeria de la Raza. EL
TECOLOTE, Vol. 9, no. 1 (September 1978), p.
7. English.

AN: Announcement and call for artwork to
Galeria de la Raza's exhibition honoring
Frida Kahlo on Nov. 2, 1978. The proposed
"Homage to Frida Kahlo" will encompass four
major areas; artists' work,
documentation/publication, related art
productions, and educational activities. The
Galeria educated participating artists to
the life and art of Frida Kahlo through
slide presentations and written material.
The exhibition became a milestone in the
Galeria de la Raza history.

5103 Mission to honor Frida Kahlo: famous Mexican
artist. EL TECOLOTE, Vol. 9, no. 3 (November
1978), p. 1. Bilingual.

AN: Announcement of an homage to Mexican
painter Frida Kahlo at the Galeria de la
Raza's annual celebration of Dia de los
Muertos. Works reproduced with the article
include those of Emmanuel C. Montoya, Yreina
Cervantez, Jose Antonio Burciaga, Nina
Serrano and Lisa Kokin. Bilingual.

5104 Moreno, Dorinda. La mujer y el arte.
TEJIDOS, Vol. 3, no. 1 (Spring 1976), p. 17.
Spanish.

AN: Brief introduction to the collection
of poems by Dorinda Moreno published in this
issue of TEJIDOS. She also dedicates the
collection by alluding to the significance
and influence of two artists: Frida Kahlo
and Rosaura Revueltas.

Kaneta Kosiba-Vargas, S.

5105 Arts Council Center for the Arts of Greater
Lansing, Lansing, MI. Raza fine arts
festival. Festival program, 1978. English.

AN: This festival program mentions Jose
Narezo's mural at the Holland National Guard
Armory, Grand Rapids; includes a statement
of the Raza Art/Media Collective, Inc.; the
philosophy of artists Zaragosa Vargas and S.
Kaneta Kosiba-Vargas; and profiles of
exhibiting artists George Vargas, Martin
Moreno, Hector Perez, Michael L. Selley,
Jesse Gonzales, Nora Chapa Mendoza, Jesse
Soriano, Jose Luis Narezo.

KCET-TV, Channel 28, Los Angeles, CA

5106 Knapp, Dan. KCET's show for Chicano viewers. LOS ANGELES TIMES, (April 3, 1970), p. IV, 18. English.

AN: Story on the television series AHORA! started September 1969 on KCET, Los Angeles' National Educational Television. Edward Moreno is program director and host; Victor Millan is producer-director; Claudio Fenner-Lopez, senior producer, has staff including set-designer David Villasenor, production manager James Val, and alternate host-narrator Jesus Trevino. The program has shown exhibits of artists Gilberto Lujan and Daniel Ramirez.

Kelley, Ramon

5107 Andrews, Rena. The fine arts. ROUNDUP, (March 15, 1970), p. 16+. English.

AN: Biographical information on Chicano artist Ramon Kelley. Described as an impressionist, his work has affinity with Monet and Manet.

5108 Andrews, Rena. The fine arts. ROUNDUP, (November 25, 1973), p. 22. English.

AN: Article places work of Ramon Kelley within the impressionist mode. At the De Colores Gallery in his hometown of Denver, Kelley's exhibit titled, "Faces of the Southwest" included drawings, water color and pastel painting, oils and acrylics.

5109 Barrett, Marjorie. Experimental art of a realist. ROCKY MOUNTAIN NEWS, (August 2, 1970), p. 74. English.

AN: Recognized as one of the area's top realist painters, Ramon Kelley is a diligent, hard-working artist. Current work includes experiments with abstraction, strong facial studies and landscapes. Includes photograph of artist and three examples of his work.

5110 Dean, Nancy. Denver artist dues are paid in full. ROCKY MOUNTAIN NEWS, (April 5, 1981), p. 6. English.

AN: Profile of artist Ramon Kelley focusing on his successful career and detailing his rise on the art market. Includes photograph of the artist.

5111 Kelley sparks Chicano growth. ROCKY MOUNTAIN NEWS, (February 18, 1973), p. Festival,7. English.

AN: Denver artist John Flores speaks about his work and provides details about the small but strong Chicano art colony in Denver. Flores credits Ramon Kelley, an established Chicano artist, with providing much leadership and encouragement in the development of Chicano art in Colorado.

5112 Kelley sparks Chicano growth. EMPIRE MAGAZINE, (December 19, 1971), p. 32. English.

AN: Ramon Kelley, successful and well known Denver artist is credited with fomenting and developing a small but strong Chicano art colony in Denver. As owner of the De Colores Gallery, Kelley has sponsored exhibits and personally encouraged many Chicano artists. John Flores, one of Kelley's proteges talks about his artistic development within the Chicano art and political milieu in Denver. Artist provides information on his daily life and work habits on the occasion of an exhibit of his work at the De Colores Gallery. Flores is a member of the Denver Arts and Humanities Commission. Illustrated with a reproduction of a pastel drawing by John Flores.

5113 Pino, Thomas E. Ramon Kelley: the business of art. LA LUZ, Vol. 7, no. 5 (May 1978), p. 24-26. English.

AN: Biographical information on Colorado artist Ramon Kelley. Business aspects of art: marketing, selling, art as investment.

5114 Ramon Kelley. ARTISTS OF THE ROCKIES, Vol. 1, no. 1 (Spring 1974), p. 6-11. English.

AN: Biographical information on Ramon Kelley and a listing of his invitational shows. Illustrated with a photograph of the artist and a portfolio of ten works (three in color).

5115 Saks Galleries, Denver, CO. Ramon K. Exhibition brochure, 1971. English.

AN: Promotional brochure for major one-man exhibition. Ramon Kelley is a Chicano artist of international stature whose artistic roots are firmly planted in the American west. The Gallery director states, "His impressionistic paintings reveal a strong affinity to the land and people of the southwest and they are the major subject of his work. Lavishly illustrated with full color reproductions of several pastel and oil paintings.

La Huelga
USE: Boycotts

La Migra
USE: Border Patrol

L.A. PARKS AND WRECKS [exhibit]

5116 Muchnic, Suzanne. Damaged goods in the big city. LOS ANGELES TIMES, (July 23, 1979), p. IV-11. English.

AN: Review of the exhibit at Otis Art Institute of Parsons School of Design of L.A. PARKS AND WRECKS, featuring Carlos Almaraz, John Valadez, and Black artist John Woods. Almaraz paints auto wrecks, and landscapes of Echo Park. Valadez does pencil portraits of young Chicanos. Illustrated.

5117 Otis/Parsons Gallery, Los Angeles, CA; Nieto, Margarita; and Price, Aimee Brown. L.A. parks & wrecks: a reflection of urban life/parques y choques: un reflejo de la vida urbana. Exhibition catalog, [1979]. Bilingual.

AN: Catalog poster discussing the works of the three artists on exhibit: Carlos Almaraz, John Valadez and John Woods who concentrate on urban images. Detailed descriptions of each artist's work accompany the many illustrations. Essays in English and Spanish.

Labor

5118 Wilson, Michael and Biberman, Herbert. Salt
of the earth [film]. 16mm, 94 min., b&w.
English.

AN: The first feature film made in the
U.S. of, by and for labor, it deals with a
real strike of Mexican American miners in
New Mexico in which women played a key role
in the men's victory and their own demands.
Mexican actress Rosaura Revueltas starred
with labor leader Juan Chacon. One of the
best films on the subject.

Labor Disputes

5119 Beltran, Alberto. [Untitled woodcut].
CARACOL, Vol. 1, no. 12 (August 1975), p.
13.

5120 Bonilla, Guillermo. [Untitled woodcut].
CARACOL, Vol. 1, no. 12 (August 1975), p.
10.

5121 Huerta, Elena. [Untitled woodcut]. CARACOL,
Vol. 1, no. 12 (August 1975), p. 11.

5122 Iniguez, Javier. [Untitled woodcut].
CARACOL, Vol. 1, no. 12 (August 1975), p.
14.

5123 Iniguez, Javier. [Untitled woodcut].
CARACOL, Vol. 1, no. 12 (August 1975), p.
13.

5124 Jimenez, Sarah. [Untitled woodcut]. CARACOL,
Vol. 1, no. 12 (August 1975), p. 12.

5125 Martin, Maria Luisa. [Untitled woodcut].
CARACOL, Vol. 1, no. 12 (August 1975), p.
12.

5126 Mexiac, Adolfo. [Untitled woodcut]. CARACOL,
Vol. 1, no. 12 (August 1975), p. 14.

5127 Rabel, Fanny. [Untitled woodcut]. CARACOL,
Vol. 1, no. 12 (August 1975), p. 11.

L.A.C.E. Gallery, Los Angeles, CA

5128 Goldman, Shifra M. Thorns and roses.
ARTWEEK, Vol. 11, no. 30 (September 20,
1980), p. 1. English.

AN: Report on four Chicano artists
exhibiting at L.A.C.E. Gallery, Los Angeles:
Carlos Almaraz, Teddy Sandoval, John
Valadez, and Linda Vallejo. Illustrated.

5129 Literally live movie at NO MOVIE exhibit.
CIVIC CENTER NEWS, Vol. 7, no. 17 (April 25,
1978), p. 1. English.

AN: Story on the ASCO "performance" NO
MOVIE, described by "Glugio" Gronk as
"movies without celluloid" to be held at
LACE Gallery. Illustrated.

Ladrones de la Luz [art group], San Antonio, TX

5130 The class of '79. SA: THE MAGAZINE OF SAN
ANTONIO, Vol. 3, no. 4 (June 1979). English.

AN: Well-illustrated article on students
of James Newberry, photography teacher at
the University of Texas, San Antonio.
Includes photos of top prizewinners and
members of Ladrones de la Luz, David
Cardenas and Kathy Vargas.

5131 San Antonio Museum of Modern Art. Zarzamora:
inaugural exhibition of Ladrones de la Luz.
Exhibition invitation, 1979. English.

AN: Illustrated invitation to
photographic exhibition including Norman
Avila, David Cardenas, Franco Cernero,
Enrique Hernandez, Robert Maxham, James
Newberry, Isaac Rodriguez, Daryl Studebaker,
Richard Tichich, Beverly Ulmer, Kathy
Vargas.

Laguna Gloria Art Museum, Austin, TX

5132 Bolger, Kathryn McKenna. Amado Pena's art.
AUSTIN AMERICAN STATESMAN, (March 29,
1980), p. 10-11. English.

AN: A review of Pena's show of
silkscreens, watercolors, and drawings at
the Laguna Gloria Art Museum in Austin,
Texas, March-May, 1980. Suggests that the
artist has turned from a confrontational to
an assimilationist stance. At present he
visually documents the peaceful amalgamation
of the cultural heritage on both sides of
the Rio Grande.

THE LANDING OF THE SALSA PEOPLE [painting]

5133 Joe B. Rodriguez. LA PRENSA, Vol. 1, no. 13
(July 21, 1978). Spanish.

AN: Commentary on an exhibition by Joe
B. Rodriguez at the George I. Sanchez Center
in Houston, Texas. Rodriguez's work is seen
as having affinity with the art of Diego
Rivera and Raul Anguiano. Illustrated with a
reproduction of a watercolor, THE LANDING OF
THE SALSA PEOPLE.

Lansing, MI

5134 Mural en Quinto Sol. SOL DE AZTLAN, Vol. 2,
no. 3 (July 1971). English.

AN: Full-page illustrated article
describing mural by Jose Mojica at the
Edificio Quinto Sol in Lansing. Mural traces
the history of La Raza and was painted by
the self-taught artist with the assistance
of his brother Adolfo.

Lara, Armando

5135 Contreras, Carlos. Nuestra cultura. LA VOZ:
Concilio for the Spanish Speaking of King
Co., Seattle, no. 7 (August 1979).

AN: Information of Washington state
murals painted by members of La Extension
Cultural; Armando Lara's autobiographical
mural titled "El Rio" is installed at the
Concilio offices, 107 Cherry St. Suite 210.
Arturo Artorez completed a wall painting
using the image of Quetzalcoatl at El Centro
de la Raza with funding from the Seattle
Arts Commission. Francisco Siqueiros used
the themes of ecology and Mexican mythology
for two murals at Seattle Community College.
Commentary on Alfredo Arreguin's painting
exhibition at the Kiku Gallery and his wall
painting at the Childrens Orthopedic
Hospital in Seattle.

5136 Tsutakaua, Mayumi. Artist paints from
heritage. SEATTLE TIMES, (September 15,
1980). English.

AN: Biographical information on Armond
Lara, Northwest Chicano-Navajo artist. He is
coordinating the restoration of a mural done
in Seattle by Mexican artist Pablo
O'Higgins. In his own work Lara is
experimenting with paper making and the use
of natural pigments.

Lara, Joseph

5137 Martinez, O.W. "Bill". Here comes la gente fragmented and fused [paintings]. LA LUZ, Vol. 1, no. 1 (April 1972), p. 56-57. English.

Laredo, TX

5138 Anderson, Howard J.; Young, Robert S.; and Kilgore, Andrew. Amado Maurilio Pena, Jr. Albuquerque, NM: Robert Stephan Young Publishing Co., 1981. English.

AN: Coffee-table type of art book about the Laredo-born painter and printmaker. The text includes impressionistic writing about Pena's life, interlaced with statements by the artist about his life and work. Though including a few plates from his early (1974-1978) political and family silkscreens, over 50 color plates reproduce his "Santa Fe Indian" works from 1978 to the present.

5139 Barrios, Lex. The barrio as a work of art: Chicano muralism in Laredo, Texas? REVISTA RIO BRAVO, Vol. 1, no. 3 (Fall 1981), p. 5, 15-16. English.

AN: Report by Laredo sociologist on local conservative attitudes toward the Chicano movement and muralism, and a meeting held to plan a mural project in Laredo so it could finally enter the mural movement. Illustrated.

5140 Hennessey, Kathy. Amado Pena, Chicano artist. REVISTA RIO BRAVO, no. 1 (Fall 1980), p. 2+. English.

AN: Review of the life and art of Laredo-born artist Pena whose early work in the 1960s was abstracted figures in bright colors; in the 1970s his work became political commentary for the Chicano movement; most recently he is doing paintings and silkscreens about New Mexican Indian life. As a teacher he influenced many students, especially in Anderson High School (Austin). Illustrations throughout the issue.

5141 Lopez, Armando. 'Chicano' art gains cross-culture recognition: 'the street mural has flourished in the barrio'. LAREDO NEWS, (July 20, 1980), p. 6-A. English.

AN: Report on a lecture "The First Decade of the Chicano Renaissance: Mexican American Art in the United States" given by Dr. Shifra M. Goldman under the sponsorship of the Laredo Philosophical Society. Mentions the "delicate Issue" of using the word "Chicano" in conservative Laredo. Illustrated with works of Laredo-born Amado M. Pena.

5142 Salazar, Veronica. Artist doesn't starve now. SAN ANTONIO EXPRESS-NEWS, (June 13, 1976), p. 18-A. English.

AN: Raul Gutierrez, water colorist from Laredo, Texas, has emerged as a nationally recognized master painter of western and wildlife themes. His work is avidly collected and exhibited. Article details his artistic trajectory and provides biographical information.

5143 Vergara, Dora Maria. New artist del barrio Canta Ranas. REVISTA RIO BRAVO, Vol. 1, no. 1 (Winter 1981), p. 2. English.

AN: Biography of self-taught artist Pedro Martinez who lives in and records the life and people of the westide barrio "Cantaranas" in Laredo, Texas. Five drawings reproduced in this issue.

Las Vegas, NM

5144 Barrio, Raymond. Art for our sake. NUESTRO, Vol. 1, no. 6 (September 1977), p. 30-34. English.

AN: Brief text with three color reproductions of murals by Mike Rios (Bart Mural, San Francisco), Gilberto Guzman (West Las Vegas High School, NM), Willie Herron (Farmacia Hidalgo, East Los Angeles, CA).

Lasta, Susana

5145 Raices y visiones [portfolio]. REVISTA CHICANO-RIQUENA, Vol. 7, no. 2 (Spring 1979), p. 29-44.

AN: Portfolio of works from the exhibit RAICES ANTIGUAS/VISIONES NUEVAS: ANCIENT ROOTS/NEW VISIONS. Artists included are Patssi Valdez (Los Angeles), Eloisa Castellanos-Sanchez (New York), Benjamin Serrano, Jr. (Tijuana, Mexico), Alex Garza (Chicago), Martin Y. Moreno (Michigan), Luis A. Jimenez (New Mexico), Rene Castro (Oakland, CA), Sita Gomez de Kanelba (New York), Susana Lasta (Tucson, AZ), Domingo Garcia (New York), Consuelo Mendez Castillo (Caracas, Venezuela), Naomi Castillo Simonetti (New Jersey), Louis Carlos Bernal, and Eddie Comptis.

Latin America

5146 Carlos Pineda shows art in Centennial Museum. EL PASO TIMES, (November 5, 1972). English.

AN: Themes from Mexican folk culture predominate in paintings by Carlos R. Pineda shown at the El Paso Centennial Museum. He has exhibited in Panama, Guadalajara, Phoenix, Tucson, and Dallas and is represented by the Jinx Gallery in El Paso.

5147 Consejo Mexicano de Fotografia, A.C., Mexico City and Tibol, Raquel. Hecho en Latinoamerica: primera muestra de la fotografia latinoamericana contemporanea. Exhibition catalog, 1978. Spanish.

AN: Catalog/book of the first colloquium and exhibit of Latin American photography. Among the Chicano artists in the exhibit were Francisco X. Camplis, Louis Carlos Bernal, Harry Gamboa, Jose P. Romero, Harvey J. Tarango, Isabel Castro. Statements by some of the artists. Great number of illustrations.

5148 Consejo Mexicano de Fotografia, A.C., Mexico City. Hecho en latinoamerica: segundo coloquio latinoamericano de fotografia. Exhibition catalog, 1982. Spanish.

AN: Catalog/book of the second colloquium and exhibit of Latin American photography. Among the Chicano artists whose work is reproduced are Louis Carlos Bernal, Robert C. Buitron, David Cardenas, Isabel Castro, Harry Gamboa, Jr., Luis Garza, Roberto Gil de Montes, John M. Valadez, Kathy Vargas. In the exhibit were also Porfirio Aguilar, Elsa Marie Flores, Ricardo Valverde. Great number of illustrations. In Spanish.

Latin America (cont.)

5149 COUNCIL OF LATINO PHOTOGRAPHY/USA
     NEWSLETTER. no. 1 (January 1979). English.

     AN: First number of photocopied
     newsletter produced by the Council of Latino
     Photography/USA announcing the formation of
     the organization and its affiliation with
     the Consejo Latinoamericano de Fotografia
     established in Mexico City in May 1978.
     Organizers of CLP/USA were photographers
     Isabel Castro, Harry Gamboa, Jr., Adam
     Avila, Luis Garza, and art historian Shifra
     Goldman.

5150 COUNCIL OF LATINO PHOTOGRAPHY/USA
     NEWSLETTER. no. 2 (January 1980). English.

     AN: Photocopied newsletter reporting on
     the "First Communication" meeting of the
     organization, the opening of a Council
     gallery and darkroom in Pasadena, news from
     San Francisco/Berkeley group, news of the
     activities of the Consejo Mexicano de
     Fotografia, Mexico, and an announcement of
     the II COLLOQUIUM OF LATIN AMERICAN
     PHOTOGRAPHY for 1981.

5151 Fondo del Sol, Washington, D.C. Raices
     antiguas/visiones nuevas; ancient roots/new
     visions. Exhibition catalog, 1977. English.

     AN: Well illustrated catalog of
     traveling exhibition featuring Latin
     American and Latino artists living in the
     United States. Supplemental regional
     catalogs of local artists.

5152 Goldman, Shifra M. Hecho en Latino America:
     first photography colloquium and exhibition.
     CHISMEARTE, no. 6 (February 1980), p. 16-25.
     English.

     AN: Report on the first colloquium of
     Latin American photography, Mexico City, May
     1978. Analysis and critique of U.S. Latino
     photographers' work presented in exhibition.
     Well illustrated.

5153 Kerschen, Karen. Where politics and music
     mix: La Pena. BERKELEY BARB, (August 18,
     1978), p. 12. English.

     AN: A new three-dimensional mural has
     been completed on the outside of Berkeley's
     La Pena Community Center. It incorporates
     ceramic and papier mache relief in a painted
     mural. One side of the painting is dominated
     by a relief sculpture of Victor Jara, the
     Chilean musician and poet killed by the
     junta. Illustrated.

5154 Latin American council bicentennial mural.
     Exhibition brochure, [1976]. English.

     AN: Brochure giving history and
     iconography of a 8 x 16 foot portable mural
     by Grand Rapids, Mich. artist Jose Narezo
     with a team of students. The mural honors
     North and South American revolutionaries
     with portraits of George Washington, Jose
     Marti, Eugenio Maria de Hostos, and Benito
     Juarez.

5155 Mural celebration. GRASSROOTS, (September
     6, 1978), p. 8. English.

     AN: Illustrated story on the new mural
     of plywood, papier mache and ceramic painted
     and modeled by artists from Commonarts for
     la Pena Cultural Center. The mural depicts
     peoples of the Americas coming together,
     singing and playing musical instruments,

with Chilean musician Victor Jara as the
major symbol.

5156 NATIONAL MURALS NETWORK COMMUNITY
     NEWSLETTER. (Spring 1980). English.

     AN: Reports on the Sept. 1979 conference
     of Chicano visual arts held at UT Austin,
     organized by the Mujeres Artistas del
     Suroeste, and the Liga Unida de Chicanos
     Artistas, which brought together
     participants from the U.S. and Mexico City;
     on Manuel Martinez's five murals (1976-78);
     murals by Roberto Lucero, Al Sanchez, and
     Jerry Jaramillo; as well as by the Chilean
     group Orlando Letelier Brigade, all in
     Denver, Colorado; murals by Leo Tanguma in
     Houston; the story about the "forbidden"
     Chicano mural in Blue Island, Illinois.
     Illustrated.

5157 Poster, Corky. Cuba welcomes Latin film
     festival. GUARDIAN, (January 16, 1980), p.
     21. English.

     AN: Report on the First International
     Festival of New Latin American Cinema held
     in Havana December 3-10, 1979. The Festival
     focused on emerging cinema of Latin America,
     especially of Nicaraguans and Chicanos.
     Festival organizers hoped to
     "internationalize" the Chicano struggle by
     encouraging it toward a Latin American
     political perspective and moving it from a
     limited "la raza" view to one of class
     analysis and solidarity. Jesus Trevino's
     film RAICES DE SANGRE was shown.

Latin America, Fraternal Ties

5158 Chicano cinema coalition. Mimeographed copy,
     September 1, 1979. English.

     AN: An informational bulletin about the
     Coalition founded July 1978 in Los Angeles
     of forty independent producers and
     filmmakers who joined together for "the
     development, production, distribution,
     promotion and exhibition...of film and video
     productions which meaningfully
     address...needs and concerns of the Latino
     people in the United States." Professionals
     with their own companies (Amanecer Films,
     Bilingual Educational Services, Luis Ruiz
     Productions), television producers, and
     post-graduate film students make up the
     group. The Coalition published the CHICANO
     CINEMA NEWSLETTER. Ties are promoted with
     Latin American cinema people.

5159 Goldman, Shifra M. Canto de unidad: nuevo
     mural de Berkeley. PLURAL, Vol. 8, no. 96
     (September 1979), p. 33-44. Spanish.

     AN: Report on significance,
     inconography, and new technical
     experimentation in street mural on facade of
     La Pena Cultural Center, Berkeley, CA. Deals
     with Latin American "nueva cancion." Ray
     Patlan and Anna de Leon on team of four
     muralists. Illustrated. This article was
     reprinted as "Song of Unity: Berkeley's New
     Raza Mural," in ARTWORKERS NEWS (New York),
     Vol. 11, no. 30, September 20, 1980, p. 1.

5160 Goldman, Shifra M. Song of unity: Berkeley's
     new raza mural. ARTWORKERS NEWS, Vol. 11,
     no. 30 (September 20, 1980), p. 1. English.

     AN: Reprint of article published as
     "Canto de unidad: nuevo mural de Berkeley"
     in PLURAL (Mexico, D.F.), Vol. 8, no. 96,
     September 1979, p. 33-44.

Latin America, Influence of

5161 Camplis, Francisco X. Towards the
development of a Raza cinema. TIN TAN, Vol.
2, no. 5 (June 1, 1977), p. 5-7. English.

AN: Chicanos and other minorities remain
invisible to white America, an expression of
neo-colonialism. Camplis defines "Chicano"
and "Raza" as terms, and states there are
few, if any, full-length feature films
available. Without role models, Chicano/Raza
filmmakers can learn from contemporary
revolutionary Latin American filmmakers, be
familiar with European and Hollywood films,
though the latter are alien models. Camplis
suggests directions for Chicano films, and
reviews films by Jesus Trevino, Jose
Camacho, and Luis Valdez.

5162 Rodriguez, Patricia, ed. Selected readings
on Chicano art. Berkeley, CA: Chicano
Studies Department, University of
California, 1977. English.

AN: Compendium of mechanically
reproduced articles on Chicano and Latin
American art prepared for Chicano Studies
130--Introduction to Chicano Art. Includes
sections on Mexican Muralists in the U.S:
Contemporary Chicano Art; Views on Chicano
Art; Chicano Artists; Pinto Art: Raza Murals
and Muralists; Plaqueasos (Graffiti);
Chicana Artists: Art, Politics and the
Community, Two Historical Examples: Cuba and
Chile; Chicano Art Reproductions, 557 pp.

LATINO AMERICA [mural]

5163 Las muralistas: Patricia Rodriguez, Consuelo
Mendez, Graciela Carrillo, Irene Perez.
Exhibition invitation, 1974. English.

AN: Invitation to the inauguration of
the mural LATINO AMERICA by the Mujeres
Muralistas at the Mission Neighborhood Model
Cities in San Francisco's Mission District,
May 31, 1974.

LATINO AND ASIAN-AMERICAN HISTORY [mural]

5164 Sorell, Victor A. Barrio murals in Chicago:
painting the Hispanic-American experience on
"our community" walls. REVISTA
CHICANO-RIQUENA, Vol. 4, no. 4 (Fall
1976), p. 51-72. English.

AN: Important survey of Chicago's Latino
murals, with key works considered in detail.
Among the Chicano art organizations and
muralists mentioned are MARCH (Movimiento
Artistico Chicano), and Yolanda Galvan,
Juanita Jaramillo, Jose Nario, Raymond
Patlan, Vicente Mendoza, Marcos Raya,
Ricardo Alonzo, Jose G. Gonzalez and Mario
Castillo, author of the earliest Latino
mural in Chicago (1968). Puerto Rican and
non-Latino muralists and mural groups are
also discussed. Well illustrated.

Lau, Alberto

5165 Mandeville Art Gallery, University of
California, San Diego. Five photographers:
contemporary views of Mexican and
Mexican-American culture. Exhibition
catalog, 1981. English.

AN: Catalog of exhibit including Louis
Carlos Bernal, Robert C. Buitron, Alberto
Lau, Richard Tichich, and Meridel
Rubenstein. Illustrated.

Law Enforcement Assistance Administration

5166 Hanson, Matt. Barren walls toned into bold
works of art. ARIZONA DAILY STAR, (May 24,
1979). English.

AN: Tucson high school students under
direction of Antonio Pazos paint murals with
a $10,000 grant from the Law Enforcement
Assistance Administration. Color
illustrations.

Lazarin, David

5167 ENCUENTRO FEMENIL (San Fernando, CA). Vol.
1, no. 1 (Spring 1973), p. 1+. English.

AN: Publication sponsored by Hijas de
Cuauhtemoc, a Chicana femenist group. Black
and white drawings on cover by Pat Portera
Crary. Art work by Vicki Thrall, Adelaida
del Castillo, and Maria Hortencia Garcia.
Photography by Cindy Honesto and David
Lazarin.

League of United Chicano Artists (LUCHA), Austin, TX

5168 Briseno, Rodolfo. Interview with a muralist.
ARRIBA, Vol. 1, no. 1 (July 1980), p. 5+.
English.

AN: Raul Valdez, muralist from Del Rio,
Texas has been painting murals in Austin and
was a founding member of LUCHA (League of
United Chicano Artists) in 1976. Having
studied with Siqueiros in Mexico, Valdez
sees strong affinities in content and form
between Chicano and Mexican muralism.
Illustrated with two photographs of Valdez's
Juarez-Lincoln mural.

5169 Conferencia plastica chicana. Conference
brochure, 1979. English.

AN: Schedule of proceedings at
internationally attended conference on
Chicano and Mexican art and photography
sponsored by the Centro Cultural de LUCHA
(League of United Chicano Artistas) and MAS
(Mujeres Artistas del Suroeste). Brief
biographies of presentors. Illustrated.

5170 Galeria Tonantzin, Centro Cultural de LUCHA,
Austin, TX. Visiones Chicanas: images and
demonstrations by Chicana and Latina visual
artists. Exhibition invitation, 1979.
English.

AN: Invitational poster for an exhibit
and a series of workshops organized by
Mujeres Artistas del Suroeste (MAS),
affiliated with LUCHA, League of United
Chicano Artists of Austin, TX.

5171 Manley, Paula. If walls could speak, a
festival of murals. DAILY TEXAN, (August 4,
1980). English.

AN: Commentary on community murals in
Austin, including murals painted by LUCHA
(The League of United Chicano Artists).

League of United Chicano Artists (LUCHA), Austin, TX (cont.)

5172 NATIONAL MURALS NETWORK COMMUNITY NEWSLETTER. (Spring 1980). English.

AN: Reports on the Sept. 1979 conference of Chicano visual arts held at UT Austin, organized by the Mujeres Artistas del Suroeste, and the Liga Unida de Chicanos Artistas, which brought together participants from the U.S. and Mexico City; on Manuel Martinez's five murals (1976-78); murals by Roberto Lucero, Al Sanchez, and Jerry Jaramillo; as well as by the Chilean group Orlando Letelier Brigade, all in Denver, Colorado; murals by Leo Tanguma in Houston; the story about the "forbidden" Chicano mural in Blue Island, Illinois. Illustrated.

Leal, Rodolfo

5173 The art of Rodolfo Leal. TIN TAN, Vol. 2, no. 6 (December 1, 1977), p. 15-18. English.

AN: Two calligraphic ink drawings and a serigraph by Texas-born Leal who lives in San Francisco.

Lefebre, Francisco

5174 Diaz, Katherine A. Murals of New Mexico. CAMINOS, Vol. 2, no. 5 (October 1981), p. 9-10. English.

AN: Illustrations of murals in Santa Fe and Albuquerque by Gilberto Guzman, Francisco Le Fevere[sic; Lefebre], Manuel Unzueta, and Fernando Penalosa.

5175 Lefebre, Francisco. El mural chicano en Nuevo Mexico. RAYAS, Vol. 1, no. 2 (March, April, 1978), p. 7. Spanish.

AN: Albuquerque muralist writes about Chicano murals which derive from pre-Columbian and modern Mexican murals. New Mexican muralism started in 1970 with the Muralistas Guadalupanos de Aztlan in Santa Fe. In 1971 and 1972 students at the Highlands University of Las Vegas, New Mexico also painted murals. In addition, murals have appeared in Albuquerque. Brief biography of Lefebre. Illustrated.

5176 NATIONAL MURALS NETWORK COMMUNITY NEWSLETTER. (Spring 1981). English.

AN: Reports, or illustrations, of murals by Guillermo Aranda (Calif.), Francisco Lefebre (New Mexico); Marcos Raya's section of Chicago's anti-war mural; Gilberto Guzman's mural (New Mexico); vandalism on a Michael Schnorr mural at Chicano Park, San Diego, Calif.

Lerma Bowerman, Liz

5177 Memorial Union Display Cases, Arizona State University, Tempe, AZ. The material culture of the Cabezas Redondas, reconstructed by Liz Lerma Bowerman. Exhibition invitation, 1977. English.

AN: Invitation to an exhibit of pottery helmets and other artifacts of an imaginary Bronze Age people, conceived and created by Liz Lerma Bowerman from Mesa, AZ.

LeRoy, Louis

5178 Donaghy, Kathleen. Two Arizona firsts: Chicano gallery and Spanish theatre. ARIZONA ARTS AND LIFESTYLE, (1981). English.

AN: The MARS (Movimiento Artistico del Rio Salado) Gallery has opened in downtown Phoenix, run by MARS founder Jim Covarrubias. Louis Leroy, expansion arts coordinator for the Arizona Commission on the Arts, says it is the only arts-oriented space that caters to Chicanos in Arizona.

5179 Holliday-Abbott, Anne. Suitcase is 2nd home for arts liaison. ARIZONA DAILY STAR, (June 18, 1981), p. H-3. English.

AN: Arizona artist Louis LeRoy who paints, makes prints, and does assemblage is also a regional representative for the National Endowment for the Arts in Arizona, New Mexico, Colorado, Utah, and Wyoming. LeRoy has always been an "advocate of people being proud of their ethnic backgrounds." He feels artists can be self-supporting without commercializing.

5180 Moisan, Jim. Ancient roots, new visions. ARTWEEK, Vol. 9, no. 26 (July 29, 1978), p. 8. English.

AN: Review of the show held at the Municipal Arts Gallery of Los Angeles, the first national touring show of Latino artists in the United States. Includes commentary on work of Larry Fuente, Luis Jimenez, Frank Romero, Harry Gamboa, Gronk, Rudy Martinez, Benjamin Serrano, Ricardo Diaz, Patssi Valdez, Mel Casas, Luis Leroy, Pedro Lujan. A related show, NEW VISIONS, L.A., includes Robert Delgado, Ray Bravo, Joe Moran, Rosalyn Mesquita, Patricia Murillo and others.

5181 Tannous, David. Problems of the artist as a hyphenated commodity. THE WASHINGTON STAR, (August 28, 1977), p. G-20. English.

AN: Review of ANCIENT ROOTS, NEW VISIONS show in Washington, D.C. describing Mel Casas' painting (San Antonio), Louis LeRoy's assemblage (Coolidge, Arizona), Amado Pena's silkscreen, Rogelio Ruiz Valdovin's costume (Tucson).

Lettuce Boycotts
USE: Boycotts

Leyba, Albert

5182 SF muralists display paintings. VIVA, (October 8, 1972), p. 19. English.

AN: Paintings, and photos of murals taken by Gilberto Romero, on display at the New Mexico Arts Commission. Artists Sammy, Carlos and Albert Leyba (the original members), Gilberto Guzman and Geronimo Garduno, part of the Artes Guadalupanos de Aztlan, finished a mural at Tot Lot in 1971 and are team-painting La Clinica de la Gente. They have also painted a mural for West Las Vegas High School.

Leyba, Carlos

5183 SF muralists display paintings. VIVA,
(October 8, 1972), p. 19. English.

AN: Paintings, and photos of murals
taken by Gilberto Romero, on display at the
New Mexico Arts Commission. Artists Sammy,
Carlos and Albert Leyba (the original
members), Gilberto Guzman and Geronimo
Garduno, part of the Artes Guadalupanos de
Aztlan, finished a mural at Tot Lot in 1971
and are team-painting La Clinica de la
Gente. They have also painted a mural for
West Las Vegas High School.

Leyba, Sam

5184 Eichstaedt, Peter. Hispanic festival
cultural showcase. NEW MEXICAN WEEKEND,
(May 25, 1979), p. 3. English.

AN: Announcement of the week-long
HISPANIC HERITAGE FESTIVAL/EL FESTIVAL
HISPANICO co-sponsored by La Cofradia de
Artes y Artesanos Hispanicos and the Santa
Fe Council fo the Arts at the Armory for the
Arts in Santa Fe. Outlines the cultural
activities, including a visual arts exhibit.
La Cofradia is a recently formed
organization which has assembled regional
shows at the Santuario de Guadalupe which
gave opportunities to local artists to show
their work. Festival artists are primarily
from the upper Rio Grande but also include
artists from the State Penitentiary, as well
as Albuquerque and Las Cruces. Illustration
of painting by Sam Leyba.

5185 Painted walls - a New Mexico folk art. NEW
MEXICO, (January 1977), p. 34-35. English.

AN: Five color illustrations of murals
from New Mexico including those done by
Gilberto Guzman, Geronimo Garduno, and Sam
Leyba. The murals are located in Santa Fe,
Chimayo, Embudo and Albuquerque.

5186 SF muralists display paintings. VIVA,
(October 8, 1972), p. 19. English.

AN: Paintings, and photos of murals
taken by Gilberto Romero, on display at the
New Mexico Arts Commission. Artists Sammy,
Carlos and Albert Leyba (the original
members), Gilberto Guzman and Geronimo
Garduno, part of the Artes Guadalupanos de
Aztlan, finished a mural at Tot Lot in 1971
and are team-painting La Clinica de la
Gente. They have also painted a mural for
West Las Vegas High School.

Liberation Support Movement

5187 De Lappe, Pele. Saga of Rupert Garcia's
poster: from pen to UN. PEOPLE'S WORLD, Vol.
44, no. 28 (July 11, 1981), p. 10. English.

AN: Desiring to produce a poster on
Nelson Mandela and South African political
prisoners, San Francisco artist Rupert
Garcia, appealed for support to the African
National Congress, and the Liberation
Support Movement. The United Nations Center
Against Apartheid provided a grant for
production, indicating it should be
distributed free. Illustrated.

Liga Unida de Chicano Artistas (LUCHA), Austin, TX

USE: League of United Chicano Artists
(LUCHA), Austin, TX

Lil' Valley Barrio, East Los Angeles, CA

5188 Del Olmo, Frank. Chicano gang turns to art.
LOS ANGELES TIMES, (September 11, 1973), p.
II, 3. English.

AN: Residents of the East Los Angeles
barrio "Lil' Valley" dedicate a mural
memorializing Chicano gang members who have
died violently. The mural was painted by 40
gang members guided by professional artist
Bill Butler.

Limon, Leo

5189 Davis, Alonzo, ed. Los Angeles street
graphics. Los Angeles, CA: Brockman Gallery
Productions, [ca. 1975]. English.

AN: Portfolio of art in public places.
Includes Charles Felix (murals), Leo Limon
(mural), Charles Almaraz (billboard mural),
Johnny Alvarez (mural), Mexican artist
Gonzalo Duran, and graffiti.

5190 Exxon Company, Houston, TX and Quirarte,
Jacinto. Chicano art of the barrio.
Exhibition brochure, n.d. [c.1976]. English.

AN: Brochure for a traveling exhibit of
photographically-reproduced Chicano murals:
Leo Limon, Lucila Villasenor Grijalva,
Antonio Esparza, Susan Saenz, Charles Felix,
Hoyo-Mara gang, David A. Lopez and team,
Roberto Chavez and team (Los Angeles); Jerry
Concha, Ruben Guzman, Chuy Campusano (San
Francisco); Manuel Unzueta (Santa Barbara).
Ernie Palomino and Leo Esequiel Ozona
(Fresno). Leo Tanguma (Houston), Roberto
Lucero, Manuel Martinez and Al Sanchez
(Denver).

5191 Los Four [art group]. Tales from the barrio
by Los Four and friends. Los Angeles, CA:
Los Four, Liberty Hill Foundation, United
Steel Workers, [1977]. English.

AN: Comic book designed with drawings,
comic strips, and calligraphy by Frank
Romero, George Yepes, Carlos D. Almaraz, Leo
Limon, Judithe Hernandez.

Lincoln High School

5192 'Barrios fiesta' due May 2-5. EL SERENO
STAR, (May 1, 1969). English.

AN: Details of the FIESTA DE LOS BARRIOS
held at Lincoln High School a year after the
school "blowouts" in East Los Angeles.
Featured 250 community visual artists from
primary school through professional
categories.

Lira, Santos

5193 Mascorro, Julie. Mechicano Art Center
exhibit to grace Price gallery walls. CAMPUS
NEWS, (November 24, 1971). English.

AN: Brief history of Mechicano Art
Center activities from its establishment in
1969 to 1971. Exhibiting are Charles
Almaraz, Roberto Amaral, Raymond Atilano,
William Bejarano, Armando Cabrera, Edward
Carbajal, Leonard Castellanos, Henry de
Vega, Antonio Esparza, Bob Gomez, Lucila V.
Grijalva, Jesus Gutierrez, Santos Lira,
Frank Martinez, Ernest Palomino, Louis
Quijada, Richard Raya, Frank Romero.
Illustrated.

Literature

5194 Anaya, Rudolfo A. and Ortiz, Simon J.
1680-1980: a ceremony of brotherhood.
Albuquerque, NM: Academic, 1981. English.

AN: A cooperative publication by members
of the former La Academia de la Nueva Raza
(1969-1976) formed of writers and artists,
and the Tri-Centennial Commission of the
All-Indian Pueblo Council. Includes writings
and artworks by Chicanos and Indians from
New Mexico, California, Texas, and Arizona.
Chicano artists works included are by Ellen
Arellano, Juan Estevan Arellano, Alberto
Baros, Jose Antonio Burciaga, Juan Reyes
Cervantes, Rudy Cuellar, Ricardo Favela, El
Zarco Guerrero, Luis Jimenez, Jr., Carlos
Quinto Kemm, Alejandro Lopez, Floyd Lujan,
Jose Montoya, Juanishi Orozco, Leo Romero,
Secundino Sandoval, Jaime Valdez, Maria
Varela, Esteban Villa.

5195 Cavazos, David S. FESTIVAL ESTUDIANTIL
CHICANO DE ARTE Y LITERATURA, Austin, TX,
1976. TEJIDOS, Vol. 4, no. 3 (Fall 1977),
p. i-ii. English.

AN: Brief description of the goals and
objectives of this artistic festival geared
towards school-aged children.

5196 Palma Castroman, Janis. ENCUENTRO ARTISTICO
FEMENIL [exhibit], Austin, TX, November 28,
1977. TEJIDOS, Vol. 5, no. 1 (1978), p.
1-47. Bilingual.

AN: A multimedia, multicultural
exposition by 26 Chicana artists held at
Juarez-Lincoln University. The exhibit was
sponsored by Chicanos Artistas Sirviendo a
Aztlan (CASA) and Mujeres Artistas del
Suroeste (MAS).

5197 Palma Castroman, Janis. Introduccion.
TEJIDOS, Vol. 5, no. 1 (1978), p. i.
Spanish.

AN: One-page introduction to theme issue
featuring the work of Chicana artists
exhibited at the ENCUENTRO ARTISTICO FEMENIL
exposition held on November 28, 1977 in
Austin, TX.

5198 Pettit, Arthur G. Images of the Mexican
American in fiction and film. College
Station, TX: Texas A & M Univ. Press, 1980.
English.

AN: A study on Anglo-American attitudes
toward Mexican people in the Southwest as
reflected in the sterotypes of popular
literature and film. Most of the book is
historical. The afterword (by Dennis
Showalter) argues that these patterns have
not improved, citing television series such
as CHICO AND THE MAN and CHIPS.

5199 Public invited to weekend fiesta at Lincoln
High. LOS ANGELES TIMES, (April 29, 1969),
p. II. English.

AN: Fiesta of art, music, dance and
literature organized by the committee formed
after the East Los Angeles high school
"blowouts" to press for better and more
relevant education. Hundreds of works of art
were collected for display at the "Fiesta de
los Barrios".

5200 SEGUNDO FESTIVAL ESTUDIANTIL CHICANO DE ARTE
Y LITERATURA, Austin, TX, 1977. TEJIDOS,
Vol. 4, no. 3 (Fall 1977), p. 1-2.
Bilingual.

AN: Introduction to this theme issue
which presents selected works of art and
literature submitted at the 2nd Annual
Festival Estudiantil.

5201 Yarbro-Bejarano, Yvonne. Resena critica de
revistas literarias chicanas: problemas y
tendencias. LA PALABRA, Vol. 3, no. 1-2
(Spring, Fall , 1981), p. 123-137. Spanish.

AN: Continuation of review of Chicano
magazines from Texas, California, and
Washington. The article discusses content,
literary and artistic format, and other
aspects, taking a critical stance (See LA
PALABRA, Spring 1980).

5202 Yarbro-Bejarano, Yvonne. Resena de revistas
chicanas: problemas y tendencias, Part I. LA
PALABRA, Vol. 2, no. 1 (Spring 1980), p.
76-85. Spanish.

AN: Review of five Chicano magazines of
California discussing their contents, both
literary and artistic, taking a critical
attitude toward both. The five are FUEGO DE
AZTLAN, VORTICE, PRISMA, MAIZE, and MANGO.

Lithographs

5203 Cuevas, Jose Luis. Lithographs. CON SAFOS,
no. 6 (Summer 1970), p. 32. Bilingual.

La Llorona

5204 Gonzalez, Jose Gamaliel. La LLorona
[drawing]. REVISTA CHICANO-RIQUENA, Vol. 1,
no. 2 (Fall 1973), p. 35. Spanish.

Loa, Fred

5205 Canto al pueblo: an anthology of
experiences. San Antonio, TX: Penca Books,
1978. English.

AN: Includes works by: Mario E.
Castillo, Carlos Rosas, Jose G. Gonzalez,
Santos Martinez, Gilbert Munoz, Fred Loa,
Armando Ibanez and others.

Loans (Student)
USE: Financial Aid

Logan Heights (San Diego, CA)

5206 Herrera, Barbara. Bisected barrio seeks new
unity: Chicano part bridges past and future.
EVENING TRIBUNE, (August 7, 1974), p. E-1.
English.

AN: Bisected by the Coronado bridge,
remains of the Logan barrio are unified by
Chicano Park and its murals recording
Chicano culture. Inspired by Salvador
Torres, who returned to Logan in 1967,
barrio activists are working to restore
community spirit and dignity. Illustrated.

Logos or Symbols
USE: Symbolism

Lomas Garza, Carmen

5207 Bejarano, William. Utah Chicano forum.
CHISMEARTE, Vol. 1, no. 1 (Fall 1976), p.
9-10. English.

AN: Report on the CULTURE, ARTE Y MEDIOS
DE COMUNICACION workshop at the Third
National Chicano Forum at the University of
Utah, Salt Lake City. The panel, moderated
by artist Carmen Lomas Garza, set up a plan
of action for the visual, literary,
performing arts and the mass media which
included planning a national conference to
discuss cultural work, financial support,
recognition and moral support, among other
issues.

5208 Burkhardt, Dorothy. Chicano pride and anger
mix at 'Califas'. THE TAB, (April 12,
1981), p. 34. English.

AN: CALIFAS: AN EXHIBITION OF CHICANO
ARTISTS IN CALIFORNIA represents a
cross-section of artists exhibiting work for
at least ten years: Rupert Garcia, Ernie
Palomino, Eduardo Carrillo, Judy Baca, Rene
Yanez, Carmen Lomas Garza, Salvador Roberto
Torres, Roberto Chavez, Willie Herron, Ralph
Maradiaga, Sue Martinez, Jose Montoya,
Malaquias Montoya, Ramses Noriega and
Esteban Villa. Illustrated.

5209 Cardenas de Dwyer, Carlota, ed. Chicano
voices. Boston, MS: Houghton Mifflin, 1975.
English.

AN: Includes artwork by: Peter
Rodriguez, Arturo Anselmo Roman, Carmen
Lomas Garza, Santa Barraza, and Cesar
Augusto Martinez.

5210 Cardona, Patricia. Gana adeptos de Museo
Mexicano de San Francisco: Pedro Rodriguez.
UNO MAS UNO, (February 6, 1978), p. 18.
Spanish.

AN: Report and brief history of the
Mexican Museum which opened in 1975 with a
collection of colonial santos. The museum
offers a vista of Mexican culture to people
in the United States. Director Peter
Rodriguez says that Chicano artists Roberto
Gonzalez, Felipe Reyes, Alfredo Arreguin,
Gustavo Rivera, and Carmen Lomas Garza are
some of the best. Illustrated.

5211 Contemporary Arts Museum, Houston, TX. Dale
gas: give it gas. The continued
acceleration of Chicano art. Exhibition
catalog, 1977. English.

AN: A comprehensive catalog including 28
works of art exhibited by 13 Texas artists:
Melesio (Mel) Casas, Jose Esquivel,
Francisco (Frank) Fajardo, Carmen Lomas
Garza, Luis Jimenez, Cesar Augusto Martinez,
Santos G. Martinez, Jr., Amado Pena, Roberto
Rios, Jose Rivera, Joe B. Rodriguez, Jesus
(Jesse) Trevino, and George Truan. Many
illustrations, some in color. Introduction
by James Harithas. Essay by Santos Martinez,
Jr. Poetry, literature and essays by Chicano
writers.

5212 Contemporary Arts Museum, Houston, TX. Fire!
An exhibition of 100 Texas artists.
Exhibition brochure, 1979. English.

AN: Includes eleven Chicano artists.
Unfortunately, not illustrated, though a
checklist of works is included. Mel Casas,
Carmen Lomas Garza, Xavier Gorena, Luis
Jimenez, Cesar Martinez, Guillermo Z.

Pulido, Philip Renteria, Jose L. Rivera, Joe
Rodriguez, George Truan, Juan B. Vela.
Introduction by James Surls. Statements by
the artists.

5213 Cox, Sue. Female psychology: the emerging
self. New York: St. Martin's Press, 2nd ed.,
1981, p. 138+. English.

AN: Reproductions of works by Carmen
Lomas Garza, Graciela Carrillo, Consuelo
Gonzalez Amezcua.

5214 Crossley, Mimi. Tejano artists. HOUSTON
POST, (August 19, 1976). English.

AN: Exhibition of 19 Texas artists
organized by Joe Rodriguez of the AAMA
(Association for the Advancement of Mexican
Americans) Art Center in Houston, Texas.
Working within a wide range of styles and a
great scope of subject matter. Includes
brief commentary on the work of Amado Pena,
Carmen Lomas Garza, Cesar Martinez, Enrique
Campos, Carolina Flores, Jesus Trevino and a
host of others.

5215 Estudios Rio: gallery of contemporary arts
and crafts. Exhibition catalog, 1976.
English.

AN: Catalog including identification,
portraits and works of participating
artists: Joe Bova, Enrique Flores, Carmen
Lomas Garza, Xavier Gorena, Erik Gronborg,
Lucas Hinojosa, Ben Holland, Kris Hotvedt,
William Kaars-Sijpesteijn, Cesar Martinez,
Chris Mende, Roberto Mungia, Steve Reynolds,
Vicente Rodriguez, William Wilhelmi.

5216 Galeria de la Raza, San Antonio, TX.
Celebration seventy-four. Exhibition
catalog, [ca. 1974]. English.

AN: Catalog of extensive exhibition
including European, Mexican, and the
following Texan Chicano artists: Rolando
Garces, Cesar Martinez, Ray Chavez, Vicente
Rodriguez, Jorge Garza, Alfred Rodriguez,
Luis Guerra, Carmen Lomas Garza, Bruno
Andrade, Jr., Amado M. Pena Jr., Roberto
Rios, Jose Trevino, Rudy Trevino, Luis
Santoyo, Tati Rubio, Eduardo C. Garza,
Arthur de la Fuente, and Jesus Campos
Trevino.

5217 Goldman, Shifra M. Artistas en accion:
conferencia de las mujeres chicanas.
COMUNIDAD, (August 10, 1980), p. 15.
Spanish.

AN: In Chicano Studies programs, the
fine arts have had second class status to
social sciences and literature. Similarly a
Chicano Issues Conference overlooked artists
until a special effort was made. A round
table, which included visual artists
Gloriamalia Flores and Carmen Lomas Garza,
discussed the social functions of art, woman
as an image maker, problems of the Chicana
as creator and cultural worker, and
professionalism in the arts.

Lomas Garza, Carmen (cont.)

5218 Goldman, Shifra M. Chicano art alive and
well in Texas: a 1981 update. REVISTA
CHICANO-RIQUENA, Vol. 9, no. 1 (Winter
1981), p. 34-40. English.

AN: Reprint of article published as
"Supervivencia y prosperidad del arte
chicano en Texas: nueva revision" in
COMUNIDAD (Los Angeles, CA) [Sunday
Supplement to LA OPINION], September 21,
1980, p. 3, 15+.

5219 Goldman, Shifra M. Supervivencia y
prosperidad del arte chicano en Texas: nueva
revision. COMUNIDAD, Vol. 55, no. 5
(September 21, 1980), p. 3,15+. Spanish.

AN: Focuses on six Chicano artists from
Austin, Houston, San Antonio, and
Kingsville: Mel Casas, Cesar Martinez, Amado
M. Pena, Leo Tanguma, Carmen Lomas Garza,
and Santa Barraza. Well illustrated. This
article was reprinted as "Chicano Art Alive
and Well in Texas: A 1981 Update," in
REVISTA CHICANO-RIQUENA (Houston), Vol. 9,
no. 1, Winter 1981, p. 34-40.

5220 Helen Euphrat Gallery, De Anza College,
Cupertino, CA. Staying visible: the
importance of archives. Art and "saved
stuff" of eleven 20th century California
artists. Cupertino, CA: Helen Euphrat
Gallery, De Anza College, 1981. English.

AN: Catalog issued in conjunction with
an exhibit held in the gallery Sept. 22 to
October 23, 1981 which included
documentation on Chicana artists Patricia
Rodriguez and Carmen Lomas Garza. Each
artist explains her method of saving,
storing and using cultural material in her
creations. Includes biographical sketch,
photograph of the artist and reproduction of
artwork.

5221 Instituto Chicano de Artes y Artesanias
(Texas Instit. Educational Development) and
Instituto Cultural Mexicano (SER/UNAM), San
Antonio, TX. Artistas chicanos: Los
Quemados. San Antonio, TX: Instituto
Chicano, Texas Institute for Educational
Development, 1975. English.

AN: Invitation to an exhibit and
manifesto of 1975 Austin-San Antonio
artists' group, Los Quemados. Included Santa
Barraza, Carolina Flores, Carmen Lomas
Garza, Luis Guerra, Cesar Augusto Martinez,
Santos Martinez, Amado Maurilio Pena, Jr.,
Jose Rivera, Vicente Rodriguez, Jose
Trevino.

5222 Lomas Garza, Carmen. Altares: arte
espiritual del hogar. HOJAS, (1976).
English.

AN: Commentary and five photographs from
the author's visual documentation of home
altars in Kingsville, Texas. Brief analysis
of the form, meaning and function of home
altars in Chicano daily life.

5223 The Mexican Museum, San Francisco, CA. Los
primeros cinco anos: fifth anniversary
exhibit. Exhibition brochure, 1980-81.
English.

AN: 65 Mexican, Chicano, and Latino
artists exhibited for the fifth anniversary
of the Mexican Museum, directed by artist
Peter Rodriguez. Cover is drawing by Carmen
Lomas Garza.

5224 La onda artistica de Carmen Lomas Garza.
MAGAZIN, Vol. 1, no. 2 (November 1971), p.
29-37. Spanish.

AN: Short biographical sketch of artist
and reproduction of seven early drawings.
The art of Carmen Lomas Garza is situated
within important events of the Chicano
Movement in Texas: the student walkouts in
Kingsville, and the formation of Colegio
Jacinto Trevino.

5225 Petersen, Karen and Wilson, J.J. Women
artists: Third World. New York, NY: Harper &
Row, 1975. English.

AN: Catalog of slides with accompanying
notes. Slides of Chicana artists available:
Margaret Herrera (Chavez), Consuelo (Chelo)
Gonzalez Amezcua, Santa Barraza, Mujeres
Muralistas, El Grupo de Santa Ana, Carmen
Lomas Garza, Carolina Flores.

5226 S.A. site for National Symposium on Mexican
American Art. CHICANO TIMES, Vol. 4, no. 30
(November 9, 1973), p. 5. English.

AN: Held at Trinity University, the
Symposium discussed such issues as, creative
evolution, art education, artistic
relationships to Mexico and the evolution of
Mexican American art in the California
barrios. Participating artists included Rudy
Trevino, Mel Casas, Octavio Medellin,
Antonio Garcia, Carmen Garza, Esteban Villa,
Jose Montoya, Ernesto Palomino, Michael
Ponce de Leon, Luis Jimenez and Eugenio
Quesada.

5227 San Francisco Museum of Modern Art, San
Francisco, CA; Chavez, Ray; and Gordon,
Allan M. Carmen Lomas Garza/prints and
gouaches: Margo Humphrey/monotypes.
Exhibition catalog, 1980. English.

AN: Carmen Lomas Garza, though working
in a "naive" style is technically adept and
academically trained, though she draws
motifs from folk production of her native
Texas. Her themes in this exhibit are
memories of her childhood. Well illustrated.

5228 Street, Sharon. Califas - a celebration of
Chicano culture and art. CITY ON A HILL,
(April 16, 1981). English.

AN: Review of an exhibit at College V's
Sesnon Gallery featuring 15 California
artists: Ramses Noriega, Judy Baca, Salvador
Roberto Torres, Malaquias Montoya, Rene
Yanez, Ralph Maradiaga, Jose Montoya,
Esteban Villa, Carmen Lomas Garza, Robert
Chavez, among others. Illustrated.

5229 Valdez, Armando. El calendario chicano 1975.
Hayward, CA: Southwest Network, 1975.
English.

AN: Third in a series of historical
calendars produced in 1972 and 1974 by La
Causa Publications and Southwest Network.
Artists included for each month are Carmen
Lomas Garza, Sergio Hernandez, Malaquias
Montoya, Mujeres Muralistas (Graciela
Carrillo, Venezuelan Consuelo Mendez, Irene
Perez, Patricia Rodriguez), Ramses Noriega,
Ernie Palomino, Amado Maurilio Pena, Martin
Perez. All but Texan Pena are California
artists.

Lomas Garza, Carmen (cont.)

5230 Xochil Art and Culture Center, Mission, TX.
!Que te vaya pretty nice! Exhibition
brochure, 1979. English.

AN: Exhibition of Chicano art including
Carmen Lomas Garza, Luis Jimenez, Cesar
Martinez, Guillermo Pulido, Roberto Rios,
Jose Rivera and Jesse Trevino. [See also
Estudios Rio].

**Lompoc Federal Correctional Institution, Lompoc,
CA**

5231 Frankenstein, Alfred. Prison's artist in
residence. SAN FRANCISCO CHRONICLE, (May 5,
1978), p. 60. English.

AN: Review of the exhibition MUNDOS
PERDIDOS, curated at the Galeria de la Raza
by Leonard Castellanos. Show consisted of
work by Castellanos and inmates at Lompoc
Federal Correctional Institution near Santa
Barbara. Documents a prison mural, tattoos
and silkscreen prints with socially critical
themes.

5232 Galeria de la Raza/Studio 24, San Francisco,
CA. Mundos perdidos/lost worlds. Exhibition
invitation, 1978. English.

AN: Invitatiion to a multi-media exhibit
from a cultural workshop inside Lompoc
Federal Correctional Institution by Leonard
Castellanos, National Endowment for the Arts
Artist in Residence. Included are murals and
tattoo documentation, and silkscreen
posters.

Long Beach, CA

5233 Quinonez, Naomi H. In her own backyard = En
su propio traspatio. CAMINOS, Vol. 2, no. 2
(March 1981), p. 34-36,62. Bilingual.

AN: Describes the establishment of the
Centro de Arte in Long Beach, CA by Chicana
artist Lola de la Riva and her family. The
Centro, which is in de la Riva's Long Beach
home, is designed to give members of her
barrio a chance to develop and display their
artistic talents. Frequent workshops in mask
making, clay sculpture, painting, and
graphics are held at the Centro, and the
works of local artists are usually on
display in her backyard.

Longoria, Jaime

5234 Chicago-Raza murals. NATIONAL MURALS NETWORK
COMMUNITY NEWSLETTER, (Fall 1979), p. 22.
English.

AN: Murals by Ray Patlan, Aurelio Diaz,
Marcos Raya, Salvador Vega, Jaime Longoria,
Malu Ortega y Alberro, Oscar Moya in
Chicago's Pilsen district.

5235 Elitzik, Paul. Mural magic. AMERICAS,
(June, July, 1981). English.

AN: Brief illustrated account of murals
in the Pilsen barrio of Chicago. Mentions
work by Aurelio Diaz, Marcos Raya, and
Salvador Vega. Focuses on the controversial
mural at Benito Juarez High School painted
by Jaime Longoria and Malu Ortega.

Lopez, Alejandro

5236 Anaya, Rudolfo A. and Ortiz, Simon J.
1680-1980: a ceremony of brotherhood.
Albuquerque, NM: Academic, 1981. English.

AN: A cooperative publication by members
of the former La Academia de la Nueva Raza
(1969-1976) formed of writers and artists,
and the Tri-Centennial Commission of the
All-Indian Pueblo Council. Includes writings
and artworks by Chicanos and Indians from
New Mexico, California, Texas, and Arizona.
Chicano artists works included are by Ellen
Arellano, Juan Estevan Arellano, Alberto
Baros, Jose Antonio Burciaga, Juan Reyes
Cervantes, Rudy Cuellar, Ricardo Favela, El
Zarco Guerrero, Luis Jimenez, Jr., Carlos
Quinto Kemm, Alejandro Lopez, Floyd Lujan,
Jose Montoya, Juanishi Orozco, Leo Romero,
Secundino Sandoval, Jaime Valdez, Maria
Varela, Esteban Villa.

5237 Sagel, Jaime. Art of brothers taps New
Mexico heritage. JOURNAL NORTH, (December
16, 1981). English.

AN: Three brothers, graphics artist,
painter, photographer, potter and poet
Alejandro Lopez and his older self-taught
brothers Felix and Manuel, are working with
traditional New Mexican art forms (bultos,
straw inlay crosses) and with newer
innovative forms - reflecting the fusion of
traditional-experimental art developing in
New Mexico among young artists.

Lopez, Ben

5238 Sanchez, Arley. Santeros. ALBUQUERQUE JRNL,
(August 21, 1977), p. C, 1. English.

AN: Review of THE SANTERO EXPERIENCE, an
exhibition of contemporary folk art by
eleven New Mexican santeros, most in their
30s, at the Albuquerque Museum. The carvers
include Juan Lucero, Ben Lopez, Luisito
Lujan, Horacio Valdez, C. Garcia, George
Lopez. A revival of the art has been taking
place within last several years due to
cultural awareness being experienced by
Hispanos. Contemporary santeros still donate
some pieces to the church, but most are
marketed to private collectors, displayed in
museums, or kept.

Lopez, David

5239 Del Olmo, Frank. Gang-inspired mural now a
shrine. LOS ANGELES TIMES, (March 27,
1975), p. II, 1, 6. English.

AN: Two 1973 murals by David Lopez in
the old Maravilla Housing Project which
received a papal blessing and continue to be
shrines at new housing location.

5240 Exxon Company, Houston, TX and Quirarte,
Jacinto. Chicano art of the barrio.
Exhibition brochure, n.d. [c.1976]. English.

AN: Brochure for a traveling exhibit of
photographically-reproduced Chicano murals:
Leo Limon, Lucila Villasenor Grijalva,
Antonio Esparza, Susan Saenz, Charles Felix,
Hoyo-Mara gang, David A. Lopez and team,
Roberto Chavez and team (Los Angeles); Jerry
Concha, Ruben Guzman, Chuy Campusano (San
Francisco); Manuel Unzueta (Santa Barbara).
Ernie Palomino and Leo Esequiel Ozona
(Fresno). Leo Tanguma (Houston), Roberto
Lucero, Manuel Martinez and Al Sanchez
(Denver).

Lopez, David (cont.)

5241 Greenberg, David; Smith, Kathryn; and Teacher, Stuart. Megamurals & supergraphics: big art. Philadelphia, PN: Running Press, 1977. English.

AN: A full-color picture book of murals throughout the United States. Chicano murals include Michael Rios (San Francisco), Mujeres Muralistas (San Francisco), Leonard Castellanos and Tomas Gonzales with others (Los Angeles), Los Artes Guadalupanos de Aztlan (New Mexico), Willie Herron (Los Angeles), Toltecas en Aztlan (San Diego), David Botello (Los Angeles), David Lopez and Arizona Mara Gang (Los Angeles), Vatos de Maravilla (Los Angeles), Carlito Gaegos (Los Angeles), Gil Hernandez (Los Angeles), Wayne [Alaniz] Healy (Los Angeles).

5242 Nevarez, Joe R. Chicano art blooms in barrio warehouse. LOS ANGELES TIMES, (December 26, 1974), p. I, 32. English.

AN: Former meat packing warehouse transformed into Goez Art Studios by Joe and John Gonzalez. Exhibiting David Negron, Eddie Martinez, David Lopez (Hollywood scenic artists) and Roberto Arenivar. Lists activities of the gallery: exhibits, murals, restoration.

Lopez de Jaramillo, Pola

5243 La Galeria de Colores, Las Vegas, NM. La galeria de colores. Gallery brochure, [1980]. English.

AN: Brochure for a gallery/studio run by painter Pola Lopez de Jaramillo since 1980.

Lopez, Felix

5244 Sagel, Jaime. Art of brothers taps New Mexico heritage. JOURNAL NORTH, (December 16, 1981). English.

AN: Three brothers, graphics artist, painter, photographer, potter and poet Alejandro Lopez and his older self-taught brothers Felix and Manuel, are working with traditional New Mexican art forms (bultos, straw inlay crosses) and with newer innovative forms - reflecting the fusion of traditional-experimental art developing in New Mexico among young artists.

Lopez, Frank

5245 Blaine, John and Baker, Decia. Finding community through the arts: spotlight on cultural pluralism in Los Angeles. ARTS IN SOCIETY, Vol. 10, no. 1 (Spring, Summer, 1973), p. 125-138. English.

AN: Community arts expression by ethnic minorities is burgeoning everywhere, especially in Los Angeles. Various Black, Asian, and Chicano art administrators are interviewed, including Frank Lopez of Plaza de la Raza and Leonard Castellanos of Mechicano Art Center. Illustrated.

Lopez, George

5246 Sanchez, Arley. Santeros. ALBUQUERQUE JRNL, (August 21, 1977), p. C, 1. English.

AN: Review of THE SANTERO EXPERIENCE, an exhibition of contemporary folk art by eleven New Mexican santeros, most in their 30s, at the Albuquerque Museum. The carvers include Juan Lucero, Ben Lopez, Luisito

Lujan, Horacio Valdez, C. Garcia, George Lopez. A revival of the art has been taking place within last several years due to cultural awareness being experienced by Hispanos. Contemporary santeros still donate some pieces to the church, but most are marketed to private collectors, displayed in museums, or kept.

Lopez, Jose

5247 Baciu, Joyce A. Hispanic artists: combining energy and emotion. CAMINOS, Vol. 2, no. 5 (October 1981), p. 14-17. English.

AN: Brief profiles of Mario Uribe, Ernest De Soto, Peter Rodriguez, Margarita Jauregui Weiner, Virginia Jaramillo, Luis Urrea, Ramses Noriega, Jose Lopez, Olivia Sanchez.

Lopez, Manuel

5248 Guadalupe Historic Foundation, Santa Fe, NM. Artes en la primavera. (1981). English.

AN: Catalog of exhibit by four New Mexico artists: Manuel Lopez, sculptor from Chili; Andres Martinez, painter from Santa Cruz; Victoria Lopez, colcha embroiderer from San Pedro; Sam Quintana, jeweler from La Mesilla.

5249 Sagel, Jaime. Art of brothers taps New Mexico heritage. JOURNAL NORTH, (December 16, 1981). English.

AN: Three brothers, graphics artist, painter, photographer, potter and poet Alejandro Lopez and his older self-taught brothers Felix and Manuel, are working with traditional New Mexican art forms (bultos, straw inlay crosses) and with newer innovative forms - reflecting the fusion of traditional-experimental art developing in New Mexico among young artists.

Lopez Ortega, Ramon

5250 Mechicano Art Center. Los Angeles, CA: Mechicano Art Center, 1971. English.

AN: Announcement of an exhibit by painters Ramon Atilano, Xavier Lopez Ortega, and Frank A. Martinez. Martinez and Lopez Ortega are also muralists. Brief profiles of the artists. Illustrated.

Lopez, Ruben

5251 Herbeck, Ray, Jr. Regional report, The arts: the many credits of Ruben Lopez. NUESTRO, Vol. 1, no. 4 (July 1977), p. 13-14. English.

AN: Brief biographical article about Ruben Orozco Lopez, a Chicano artist who is widely recognized for his court-room sketching and commercial art work for the Hollywood film industry. For the past few years, Lopez has been working with the Chicano News Media Association to recruit barrio youths into the news artist profession.

Lopez Saenz, Antonio

5252 The Mexican Museum, San Francisco, CA. Bruno
     Andrade (from Missouri) and Antonio Lopez
     Saenz (from Mexico). Exhibition
     announcement, 1978. English.

     AN: Flyer announcing an exhibit at the
     Mexican Museum of Texas-born Andrade who is
     exhibiting large abstract landscapes.
     Andrade teaches in Columbia, Missouri; this
     is his first California exhibit.

Lopez Tijerina, Reies
     USE: Tijerina, Reies Lopez

Lopez, Yolanda M.

5253 Exhibit at UCSD: Chicana artist to show
     works. LOS ANGELES TIMES [San Diego County
     edition], (December 6, 1978), p. II, 8.
     English.

     AN: Artist and activist from San Diego,
     Yolanda Lopez, will be showing sketches and
     paintings at the Mandeville Center,
     University of California, San Diego, from
     which she was the first Chicana to graduate
     with a Master's degree in visual arts. Her
     show is based on her family, and the icon of
     the Virgin of Guadalupe. Illustrated.

5254 Focus: Yolanda Lopez. CITYBENDER, Vol. 2,
     no. 5 (1978). English.

     AN: Brief biography and illustrations of
     drawings by San Diego/San Francisco artist
     Yolanda Lopez titled THREE GENERATIONS: TRES
     MUJERES.

5255 Lopez, Yolanda M. Portrait of my
     grandmother. CONNEXIONS, no. 2 (Fall
     1981). English.

     AN: Four mixed-media images representing
     different ages in the life of the artist's
     grandmother. A hand written text by the
     artist provides biographical and social
     commentary.

5256 Mandeville Center for the Arts, La Jolla, CA
     and Lopez, Yolanda M. Yolanda M. Lopez
     works: 1975-1978. Exhibition catalog, 1978.
     English.

     AN: Catalog of an exhibit dedicated to
     Lopez's female family members, expecially
     her grandmother and mother, to the artist
     herself as a track runner, and to the
     Guadalupe series, icons of the Virgin
     transformed to reflect the life of
     contemporary women. Well illustrated.

Los Angeles, CA

5257 Adrienne Simard Gallery, Los Angeles, CA.
     Presenting Carlos Almaraz: pastel drawings,
     1969-1981. Exhibition invitation, 1981.
     English.

     AN: Invitation to exhibit of Los Angeles
     painter Carlos Almaraz. includes color
     illustration.

5258 Almaraz, Carlos. Introduccion: vida urbana y
     artistas chicanos. COMUNIDAD, Vol. 55, no.
     22 (May 3, 1981), p. 2. Spanish.

     AN: In the controversial period of the
     early 1980s, Chicano advances are being
     attacked. In this political climate, some
     Los Angeles artists are interested in beauty
     and artistic creation: Carlos Almaraz,
     best-known of the Los Four group; Yreina

Cervantez; Elsa Flores; John Valadez,
presently working on a mural; and musicians
Louie Perez and Tito Rodriguez Larriva.

5259 Andrews, Colman. Art of the state:
     California. NEW WEST MAGAZINE, (January
     1981), p. 54-59. English.

     AN: Short text on California artists who
     are presumably influenced by the state's
     light, color, space, etc. Works of 16
     artists reproduced in full color, including
     one by Carlos Almaraz of Los Angeles.
     Statements by each artist.

5260 Art Gallery, University of California,
     Irvine and Los Angeles County Museum of Art,
     Los Angeles, CA. Los Four: Almaraz, de la
     Rocha, Lujan, Romero. Exhibition brochure,
     1973-74. English.

     AN: Photographs and biographies of
     Carlos Almaraz, Roberto de la Rocha, Gilbert
     S. Lujan, Frank Romero.

5261 Art wall for Plaza de la Raza March 28.
     EASTSIDE JRNL, (March 11, 1971), p. 1.
     English.

     AN: On March 28, 1971, the art dealers
     of Los Angeles sponsored an"art walk" on
     "Gallery Row" on Melrose Place and La
     Cienega Blvds as a benefit for Plaza de la
     Raza, Mexican American cultural Center at
     Lincoln Park. Art dealers financed a limited
     edition lithograph by Mexican muralist David
     Alfaro Siqueiros. The print shows Ruben
     Salazar, slain Mexican American journalist
     and community leader with the famous figure
     from Siqueiros' mural "New Democracy" below
     it. Illustrated.

5262 Arte chicano y el pueblo. COMUNIDAD, no. 41
     (May 3, 1981), p. 1-15. Spanish.

     AN: The whole issue of the Sunday
     Supplement deals with Los Angeles Chicano
     art and music. Works by painter Carlos
     Almaraz, photographer Elsa Flores, painter
     Yreina Cervantez, muralist and draftsman
     John Valadez, and a performance piece by
     Elsa Flores and Louie Perez are featured.
     Biographical information, and statements by
     the artists.

5263 Baca, Judith F. Judith F. Baca. In: SOCIAL
     WORKS: AN EXHIBITION OF ART CONCERNED WITH
     SOCIAL CHANGE. Los Angeles, CA: Institute of
     Contemporary Art, 1979, p. 44. English.

     AN: Statement of purpose and history of
     the Tujunga Wash Mural (San Fernando Valley,
     CA) in process from 1976 on, by muralist and
     founder of Social and Public Art Resource
     Center (SPARC), Judith Baca. Illustrated.

Los Angeles, CA (cont.)

section of the complete mural.

5264 Baciu, Joyce A. and Diaz, Katherine A. Margo Albert: a woman who gets things done = una mujer que realiza lo que desea. CAMINOS, Vol. 2, no. 5 (September 1981), p. 44-46. Bilingual.

AN: Mexican-born Margo Albert is a well-known Los Angeles, CA artist, dancer, and actress who has been most active on behalf of the Plaza de la Raza in East Los Angeles. This article describes her activities as Co-chairperson of the Los Angeles Bicentennial Committee. For Margo, the highlights of the celebration marking the 200th anniversary of the founding of Los Angeles, included a day-long Fiesta del Bicentenario; groundbreaking ceremonies for the Ruben Salazar Bicentennial Building; and the reception for an official delegation of charros, sponsored as a gift to the people of Los Angeles by the Mexican government.

5265 Barrio, Raymond. Art for our sake. NUESTRO, Vol. 1, no. 6 (September 1977), p. 30-34. English.

AN: Brief text with three color reproductions of murals by Mike Rios (Bart Mural, San Francisco), Gilberto Guzman (West Las Vegas High School, NM), Willie Herron (Farmacia Hidalgo, East Los Angeles, CA).

5266 'Barrios fiesta' due May 2-5. EL SERENO STAR, (May 1, 1969). English.

AN: Details of the FIESTA DE LOS BARRIOS held at Lincoln High School a year after the school "blowouts" in East Los Angeles. Featured 250 community visual artists from primary school through professional categories.

5267 Blaine, John and Baker, Decia. Finding community through the arts: spotlight on cultural pluralism in Los Angeles. ARTS IN SOCIETY, Vol. 10, no. 1 (Spring, Summer, 1973), p. 125-138. English.

AN: Community arts expression by ethnic minorities is burgeoning everywhere, especially in Los Angeles. Various Black, Asian, and Chicano art administrators are interviewed, including Frank Lopez of Plaza de la Raza and Leonard Castellanos of Mechicano Art Center. Illustrated.

5268 Botello, David Rivas and Healy, Wayne Alaniz. Los Dos Streetscapers. SOMOS, Vol. 1, no. 3 (August 1978), p. 12-17. English.

AN: Autobiographical material by Los Angeles street muralists Botello and Healy. Illustrated.

5269 Bright, John; Bright, Mura; and Castellanos, Leonard. "Placas": graffiti and the environment. Venice, CA: Environmental Communications, 1974. English.

AN: Annotated slide catalog of Chicano graffiti on walls, murals, and tattoos, compiled by staff of Mechicano Art Center.

5270 The Broadway mural, 1981, by John Manuel Valadez. Los Angeles, CA: Victor Clothing Co., n.d. English.

AN: Postcard/brochure about Valadez's 8x48-ft mural, oil on canvas, displayed at the Victor Clothing Co. in downtown Los Angeles. Brief profile of the photographer and muralist. Full color reproduction of a

5271 Cesaretti, Gusmano. Street writers: a guided tour of Chicano graffiti. Los Angeles, CA: Acrobat Books, 1975. English.

AN: A photographic essay of graffiti and Mexican/Chicano peoples in Los Angeles. Introductions by author to each geographical part of the city.

5272 Cesaretti, Gusmano and Hirtz, Jacqueline. Uplifting the city: the mural-painter's goal. HOME MAGAZINE, (May 8, 1977), p. 50-51. English.

AN: Illustrated report on murals in Los Angeles and Pasadena by Anthony Padilla.

5273 Chicano art of the Southwest. San Antonio, TX: Instituto Chicano de Artes y Artesanias of the Texas Institute for Educational Development, 1975. English.

AN: Collection of 220 slides supplemented by slide annotation and artists' biographies researched and photographed by Texas artist Cesar A. Martinez over two years. Biographies cover 20 Texas, 6 New Mexico, and 15 northern California artists. Slides include, in addition, murals from Los Angeles and San Diego.

5274 Chicano cinema coalition. Mimeographed copy, September 1, 1979. English.

AN: An informational bulletin about the Coalition founded July 1978 in Los Angeles of forty independent producers and filmmakers who joined together for "the development, production, distribution, promotion and exhibition...of film and video productions which meaningfully address...needs and concerns of the Latino people in the United States." Professionals with their own companies (Amanecer Films, Bilingual Educational Services, Luis Ruiz Productions), television producers, and post-graduate film students make up the group. The Coalition published the CHICANO CINEMA NEWSLETTER. Ties are promoted with Latin American cinema people.

5275 Citywide mural project. Los Angeles, CA: Citywide Mural Project, n.d. [c. 1975]. English.

AN: Brochure giving history, resources and procedures for doing a mural by the Los Angeles Citywide Mural Project/Mural Resource Mural Program of 1973-1974. Illustrated. Available in Social and Public Art Resource Center (Venice, CA) archives.

5276 Clark, Yoko and Hama, Chizu. California murals. Berkeley, CA: Lancaster-Miller, 1979. English.

AN: Picture book of Bay Area and Los Angeles murals with brief descriptions. Chicano artists included: Daniel Galvez, Irene Perez, Patricia Rodriguez, Graciela Carrillo (Mujeres Muralistas), Ray Patlan.

Los Angeles, CA (cont.)

5277 Cultura chicana: Los Angeles. COMUNIDAD, no. 11 (July 13, 1980), p. 1-15. Spanish.

AN: The whole issue of the Cultural Supplement concerns Chicano art and music. Captioned photographs deal with visual artists Carlos Almaraz, Jerry Dreva [not Chicano], Glugio Gronk, Willie Herron, John Valadez, Patssi Valdez, with examples of their work. With the exception of Dreva, all the artists are members of Los Four or Asco. Asco member Harry Gamboa, Jr. sums up the 1960s and 1970s and activities of artists in his essay "Seis imaginaciones: Artistas chicanos en Los Angeles." Well illustrated.

5278 Danzantes. LA GENTE DE AZTLAN, Vol. 8, no. 5 (May 31, 1978), p. 12. English.

AN: Ernie de la Torre, muralist from El Sereno, Los Angeles, CA, describes style and meaning of his mural DANZANTES. Painted on the wall of the Alameda Theatre (Woods and Whittier Blvd.), the mural portrays cultural and historic aspects of Chicano culture. Illustrated with photographs.

5279 Davis, Alonzo, ed. Los Angeles street graphics. Los Angeles, CA: Brockman Gallery Productions, [ca. 1975]. English.

AN: Portfolio of art in public places. Includes Charles Felix (murals), Leo Limon (mural), Charles Almaraz (billboard mural), Johnny Alvarez (mural), Mexican artist Gonzalo Duran, and graffiti.

5280 Del Olmo, Frank. Gang-inspired mural now a shrine. LOS ANGELES TIMES, (March 27, 1975), p. II, 1, 6. English.

AN: Two 1973 murals by David Lopez in the old Maravilla Housing Project which received a papal blessing and continue to be shrines at new housing location.

5281 Depicts Chicano attitudes: library receives new mural. DAILY BRUIN, (September 29, 1970), p. 6. English.

AN: Illustrated story of mural painted in UCLA's Mexican American Library by Eduardo Carrillo, Ramses Noriega, Sergio Hernandez, Saul Solache.

5282 Documentary to include work by Cuate Santos. LAREDO NEWS, (July 17, 1980). English.

AN: Photography by Laredo News photographer Cuate Santos included in exhibit "Un encuentro sin palabras," a documentary show on Mexican American life in Texas sponsored by Mujeres Artistas del Suroeste (MAS). The state-wide show was juried by Los Angeles photographer Isabel Castro. Illustrated.

5283 Los Dos Streetscapers. Los Dos Streetscapers, mural detail. NATIONAL GEOGRAPHIC, Vol. 155, no. 1 (January 1979), p. 38-39. English.

AN: One panel of Los Angeles mural by Wayne Alaniz Healey and David Botello, CHICANO TIME TRIP.

5284 Environmental Communications, Venice, CA. Street paintings of Los Angeles: a study of environmental reactionism. Slide catalog, n.d. English.

AN: Well illustrated annotated slide catalog of greater Los Angeles murals. Includes 7 Chicano murals. Articles reprinted from NEWSWEEK, LOS ANGELES TIMES, EARTH (Mar. 1972), ARTWORKERS NEWS (Oct. 1973), ARTFORUM (Feb. 1971), LOS ANGELES FREE PRESS (9/4/70), EVENING OUTLOOK (5/4/72), SUNSET (April 1973).

5285 The First Unitarian Universalist Church, Paradise Valley, AZ. Five Chicano artists. Exhibition brochure, 1971. English.

AN: Exhibit organized by L. Eugene Grigsby, Jr., Art Department of Arizona State University, Tempe, AZ. 21 works by Eugene Quesada, David Nunez, Fernando Navarro, Luis Baiz (of Arizona) and Saul Solache (of Los Angeles). Brief biographies of the artists.

5286 Galeria Otra Vez, Los Angeles, CA. Inner/urban landscapes: Ricardo Valverde, Suda House, David Feldman. Exhibition invitation, 1979. English.

AN: Invitation to a photography exhibition held at Self-Help Graphic's gallery.

5287 Gamboa, Harry, Jr. ASCO: no phantoms. HIGH PERFORMANCE, Vol. 4, no. 2 (Summer 1981), p. 15. English.

AN: "The media's hit and run attitude has generally relegated the influence by Chicanos on Los Angeles to that of a phantom culture," says Gamboa's introduction to an ASCO No Movie event, NO PHANTOMS: "various overt acts of communal alienation." Illustrated.

5288 Gamboa, Harry, Jr.; Gronk; and Herron, Willie. Gronk and Herron. NEWORLD, Vol. 2, no. 3 (Spring 1976), p. 28-30. English.

AN: An interview with ASCO members Gronk and Willie Herron by a third member, Gamboa. Brief historical introduction (1970 on). The witty tongue-in-cheek interview can be considered an artwork by this performance art group. Illustrated.

5289 Gamboa, Harry, Jr. and Gronk. Gronk: off-the-wall artist. NEWORLD, Vol. 6, no. 4 (1980), p. 33-43. English.

AN: Interview with Gronk about his No Movies, by Harry Gamboa, Jr., both members (with Willie Herron and Patssi Valdez) of ASCO. The interview itself can be seen as an "art piece" with photographs by Gamboa; it contains valuable information about the ideas and activities of the group.

5290 Gamboa, Harry, Jr. Los murales de Aztlan. COMUNIDAD, (June 28, 1981), p. 8-9+. Spanish.

AN: Review of the exhibit at the Craft and Folk Art Museum of Los Angeles of MURALS OF AZTLAN: THE STREET PAINTERS OF EAST LOS in which Carlos Almaraz, Gronk, Judithe Hernandez, Willie Herron, Frank Romero, John Valadez and the East Los Streetscapers (David Botello, Wayne Healy, George Yepes) painted portable murals in the gallery. The murals are described and illustrated.

Los Angeles, CA (cont.)

5291 Gamboa, Harry, Jr. Seis imaginaciones:
artistas chicanos en Los Angeles. COMUNIDAD,
(July 13, 1980), p. 10. Spanish.

AN: A limited flow of media information
about Los Angeles Chicanos has produced a
"ghost" culture. Only sensational events are
published. Alternative magazines like LA
RAZA, CON SAFOS, and REGENERACION have
disseminated Chicano ideas of the 1970s. The
Chicano imagination has appeared in murals
by Willie Herron, Gronk, Carlos Almaraz,
John Valadez; in pieces like "walking" and
"instant" murals by the group ASCO; by the
group Los Four; by group exhibits like
"Chicanismo en el arte," and "Chicanarte."
Patssi Valdez showed Photobooth Piece at the
"Chicanismo" show. Gronk and Jerry Dreva
exhibited their mail art at "Punk Meets
Art." In Spanish.

5292 Gardiner, Henry G. Painted exterior walls of
Southern California. CURRANT ART MAGAZINE,
Vol. 1, no. 2 (June, July, 1975), p. 16-23+.
English.

AN: Good survey of street muralism,
primarily in Los Angeles and San Diego,
which started in 1968. Divided into eight
"schools," including Chicano and non-Chicano
muralists. Most Chicano murals associated
with Goez Brothers Art Gallery and Mechicano
Art Center in Los Angeles, the Coronado Bay
Bridge group [Chicano Park] and Balboa Park
group [Centro Cultural de la Raza]. Mural
discussed in detail. Well illustrated.

5293 Geyer, Anne. Muralist works to dispel
negative Latino images. THE NEWS,
(September 2, 1981), p. 22. English.

AN: John Valadez is painting a mural on
canvas depicting the Latino people of
downtown Los Angeles. It will be housed in
Victor Clothing Co. Valadez is one of an
increasing number of artists and dealers who
have moved to the downtown area. Valadez
discusses the images he makes and his
attempt to correct media stereotypes about
Latinos. Illustrated.

5294 Goldman, Shifra M. Affirmations of
existence, barrio murals of Los Angeles.
REVISTA CHICANO-RIQUENA, Vol. 4, no. 4 (Fall
1976), p. 73-76. English.

AN: Brief history, communicative thrust,
community orientation, and special
iconography of Chicano murals in Los
Angeles.

5295 Goldman, Shifra M. Chicano art - looking
backward. ARTWEEK, Vol. 12, no. 22 (June 20,
1981), p. 3-4. English.

AN: Review of Chicano art shows in Santa
Cruz (CALIFAS) and Los Angeles (MURALS OF
AZTLAN: THE STREET PAINTERS OF EAST LOS)
featuring a total of 24 artists and how the
shows reflect the critical crossroad at
which Chicano artists presently find
themselves.

5296 Goldman, Shifra M. Resistance and identity:
street murals of occupied Aztlan. LATIN
AMERICAN LITERARY REVIEW, Vol. 5, no. 10
(Spring, Summer, 1977), p. 124-128. English.

AN: Two periods of Mexican muralism's
influence in the U.S.: 1930s and 1960s.
Differences between Mexican and Chicano
murals nationally. Comparison of the

respective iconographies and funding
sources. This article was reprinted as
"Resistencia e Identidad: Los Murales
Callejeros de Aztlan, La Ciudad (sic)
Ocupada," in ARTES VISUALES (Mexico, D.F.),
no. 16, Fall-Winter, 1977, p. 22-25.

5297 Goldman, Shifra M. Thorns and roses.
ARTWEEK, Vol. 11, no. 30 (September 20,
1980), p. 1. English.

AN: Report on four Chicano artists
exhibiting at L.A.C.E. Gallery, Los Angeles:
Carlos Almaraz, Teddy Sandoval, John
Valadez, and Linda Vallejo. Illustrated.

5298 Gutierrez, Helga. The walls of Estrada
Courts. LA GENTE DE AZTLAN, Vol. 7, no. 3
(February 1977), p. 19. English.

AN: Photographic essay of Estrada murals
by Helga Gutierrez.

5299 Hansen, Barbara. Food for the soul: an
earthly delight. HOME MAGAZINE, (October
22, 1978), p. 53-54. English.

AN: Story on El Dia de los Muertos.
Color illustrations of annual celebration by
Self-Help Graphics and Art, Inc. with
costumes, masks, floats.

5300 Images of Aztlan at Mechicano. CHISMEARTE,
Vol. 1, no. 1 (Fall 1976), p. 3-4.
English.

AN: History of Mechicano Art Center from
its opening in West Los Angeles in 1969
through its 1976 location during which it
decided to become a center serving its own
community in East Los Angeles. Led by
Leonard Castellanos, Victor Franco and Ray
Atilano, the Center developed programs in
supergraphics, silkscreen, and mural
painting, as well as an "open-wall" art
gallery for artists not allowed in
establishment galleries.

5301 Johnston, Beatriz. Valadez: exponente de la
vida urbana en mural contemporaneo. LA
OPINION, Vol. 56, no. 68 (November 22,
1981), p. II, 1. Spanish.

AN: Report on the mural in preparation
by John Valadez for Victor Clothing Co. in
downtown Los Angeles. It deals with people
walking in the streets of the downtown area.
Illustrated with the sketch for the mural
which Valadez has been painting in the
basement of the building for nine months.

5302 Johnston, Tracy. La vida loca. NEW WEST
MAGAZINE, (January 29, 1979), p. 38-46.
English.

AN: A journalistic account of barrio
lifestyles composed from conversations with
young Cholos in Los Angeles. Amid poverty,
unemployment, drug abuse and familial
disintegration, codes of group solidarity
and rituals of connection occur. Information
on urban Chicano forms of self expression
such as mascaras (chola make up), tattoos
and graffiti. Well illustrated with
photographs.

Los Angeles, CA (cont.)

5303 Kahn, David. Chicano street murals: people's
     art in the East Los Angeles barrio. AZTLAN,
     Vol. 6, no. 1 (Spring 1975), p. 117-121.
     Bibliography. English.

     AN: A study of Chicano mural painting
     starting with the 1970 mural at UCLA by
     Eduardo Carrillo, Ramses Noriega, Sergio
     Hernandez, and Saul Solache. Deals with
     mural symbols, graffiti, and works by John
     Alverer [sic] and Willie Herron's murals in
     the Ramona Gardens Housing Project.

5304 L.A.C.E. (Los Angeles Contemporary
     Exhibitions), Los Angeles, CA. No Movie: Gil
     de Montes, Teddy, Glugio [Gronk], Patssi,
     Gamboa. Exhibition invitation, 1978.
     English.

     AN: Invitation to "performance" piece by
     Roberto Gil de Montes, Teddy Sandoval,
     Gronk, Patssi Valdez and Harry Gamboa, Jr.,
     the latter three of the ASCO group.
     Illustrated.

5305 The legend of the five murals. [Los Angeles,
     CA]: Pan American Bank of East Los Angeles,
     [1966]. Spanish.

     AN: Iconography of the five murals in
     Venetian mosaic created for the Bank by
     Mexican artist Jose Reyes Meza, information
     about mosaics, and a brief biography of the
     artist are included in a biligual brochure.
     The murals are 10x14-ft each and adorn
     thefacade of the building.

5306 Lopez, Gerard. Estrada murals. LA GENTE DE
     AZTLAN, Vol. 4, no. 6 (May, June, 1974), p.
     4. English.

     AN: Article explains how the community
     at Estrada Courts was mobilized to support a
     mural project uniting artists with
     residents. Includes interview with artist
     C.W. Felix who comments on the goals of the
     mural program and cites the themes and
     symbolism of the murals.

5307 Los Angeles Municipal Art Gallery, Los
     Angeles, CA. Multicultural focus: a
     photography exhibition for the Los Angeles
     Bicentennial. Exhibition catalog, 1981.
     English.

     AN: Catalog of an exhibit demonstrating
     the multi-ethnic character of Los Angeles.
     Chicano photographers include Don Anton, Ron
     Bernal, Daniel Martinez, Rick Tejada-Flores.
     Illustrated.

5308 Mechicano Art Center attracts community
     artists. EL HISPANO, Vol. 5, no. 2 (June 10,
     1972). English.

     AN: Commentary by Leonard Castellanos,
     Director of Mechicano Art Center, who
     explains funding sources and programs of the
     Centro.

5309 Meza to paint Pan American National Bank
     murals. MEXICAN AMERICAN SUN, (October 14,
     1965). English.

     AN: Mexican painter Jose Reyes Meza is
     commissioned to create a mosaic mural titled
     OUR PAST, OUR PRESENT, AND OUR FUTURE for
     the facade of the Pan American National Bank
     of East Los Angeles being erected on First
     Street.

5310 Mills, Kay. The great wall of Los Angeles.

MS.MAGAZINE, (October 1981), p. 66-69+.
English.

     AN: THE GREAT WALL OF LOS ANGELES in the
     Tujunga flood control channel in the San
     Fernando Valley, was started as a
     Bicentennial project in 1976. Artistic
     director Judy Baca of the Social and Public
     Art Resource Center, works with crews of
     young people painting aspects of Los Angeles
     history that is not generally found in
     textbooks. Well illustrated.

5311 Muchnic, Suzanne. Mural: a lullaby of
     another Broadway. LOS ANGELES TIMES,
     (December 18, 1981), p. VI, 1+. English.

     AN: Commentary on the panoramic mural
     painted by John Valadez inside the Victor
     Clothing Company at 242 S. Broadway. Mural
     depicts Broadway street life. Photograph of
     the artist and the mural.

5312 Mural depicts history of Mexican Americans.
     EASTSIDE JRNL, (December 16, 1971), p. 1.
     English.

     AN: Richard Jimenez of the Goez Gallery
     depicts the past and present of Mexican
     American culture on an interior mural at the
     First Street Store (3640 E. First St.) The 6
     ft. by 15 ft. mural has central image of a
     clock with a faceless figure (The Mexican
     American of the future). Artist comments on
     another of his murals titled EDUCATION OF
     LIFE.

5313 Muralist Campero shows works. EASTSIDE JRNL,
     (June 3, 1971), p. 6. English.

     AN: Photograph of artist Armando Campero
     with samples of his graphic work. The artist
     was completing a 3,000 square foot mural,
     JOHN KENNEDY SAGA NUMBER 2 for installation
     at the City Terrace Social Hall.

5314 Nevarez, Joe R. Chicano art blooms in barrio
     warehouse. LOS ANGELES TIMES, (December 26,
     1974), p. I, 32. English.

     AN: Former meat packing warehouse
     transformed into Goez Art Studios by Joe and
     John Gonzalez. Exhibiting David Negron,
     Eddie Martinez, David Lopez (Hollywood
     scenic artists) and Roberto Arenivar. Lists
     activities of the gallery: exhibits, murals,
     restoration.

5315 Otis/Parsons Gallery, Los Angeles, CA;
     Nieto, Margarita; and Price, Aimee Brown.
     L.A. parks & wrecks: a reflection of urban
     life/parques y choques: un reflejo de la
     vida urbana. Exhibition catalog, [1979].
     Bilingual.

     AN: Catalog poster discussing the works
     of the three artists on exhibit: Carlos
     Almaraz, John Valadez and John Woods who
     concentrate on urban images. Detailed
     descriptions of each artist's work accompany
     the many illustrations. Essays in English
     and Spanish.

5316 Plagens, Peter. Los Four (Roberto de la
     Rocha, Carlos Almaraz, Gilbert Lujan and
     Frank Romero) at LACMA. ARTFORUM,
     (September 1974), p. 87-88. English.

     AN: Review of Los Four exhibit at Los
     Angeles County Museum of Art which calls it
     a "sociological bazaar" in which Chicanos
     have been "corrupted" by art schools and
     "museumized".

Los Angeles, CA (cont.)

5317 Pomona College Gallery of Montgomery Art
Center, Claremont, CA; Allikas, Bob; and
Glickman, Hal. Chicano graffiti: the
signatures and symbols of Mexican-American
youth. Exhibition catalog, [1970]. English.

AN: Catalog of exhibit based on
photographs of Los Angeles graffiti.

5318 Rickey, Carrie. The writing on the wall. ART
IN AMERICA, Vol. 69, no. 5 (May 1981), p.
54-57. English.

AN: Detailed article on the career of
Judy Baca, director of SPARC (Social and
Public Arts Resource Center) in Venice,
Calif., and of the Great Wall of Los
Angeles, a five year mural project at the
Tujunga Wash. Well illustrated in black and
white and color.

5319 Rodriguez, Alfred. A historical survey of
Chicano murals in the Southwest: an
interdisciplinary teaching unit. Unpublished
paper, 1980. English.

AN: Lists murals by title, artist and
date (when known), location and subject. Los
Angeles, San Francisco, San Diego, Fresno,
San Antonio, Austin, Corpus Christi, Santa
Fe, New Mexico murals are included.
Circulated by the Institute of Latin
American Studies, University of Austin,
Texas.

5320 Romero, Raul V. Chicanarte, a major
exposition of California arts. NEWORLD,
(Fall   1975). English.

AN: CHICANARTE at the Los Angeles
Municipal Gallery, Barnsdall Park from Sept.
14 -Oct. 12, 1975 remains the most
comprehensive statewide exposition of
Chicano arts in California. This article
details the production apparatus and history
of the exposition. In particular, the
contributions of Al Frente Communications,
Inc., the Chicano Arts Council of U.C.L.A.
and the Comite Chicanarte. Illustrated.

5321 Romotsky, Jerry and Romotsky, Sally R. Los
Angeles barrio calligraphy. Los Angeles, CA:
Dawson's Book Shop, 1976. English.

AN: Deals with visual quality, styles,
and meanings of Los Angeles "placas," or
graffiti. Well illustrated.

5322 Romotsky, Sally R. and Romotsky, Jerry.
Plaqueaso on the wall. HUMAN BEHAVIOR, Vol.
4, no. 5 (May 1975), p. 64-69. English.

AN: Detailed discussion of meaning of
Los Angeles Chicano graffiti. Many
illustrations, one in color.

5323 Street art explosion in Los Angeles. SUNSET,
(April 1973), p. 110-113. English.

AN: Illustrated article on Los Angeles
street murals including those by Roberto
Chavez, Willie Herron, Frank Romero, Richard
Jimenez, William Bejarano, Gilbert Lujan,
Armando Cabrera, Frank Martinez, Charles
Felix, and others.

5324 Street murals. Q-VO, Vol. 1, no. 11 (March
1980). English.

AN: 5 illustrations of Los Angeles
murals.

5325 Symposium on the politics of the arts:
minorities and the arts. ARTS IN SOCIETY,
Vol. 10, no. 3 (Fall , Winter, 1973), p.
66-73. English.

AN: One panel from the Colloquium
"Politics of the Arts" presented by the UCLA
Management in the Arts Program, Graduate
School of Management, 1972, included, among
others, Leonard Castellanos of Mechicano Art
Center, and James Woods of Studio Watts
Workshop, both in Los Angeles. A major topic
was how minorities dealing with the
corporate capitalist structure can keep
control of their art programs.

5326 Torres, Louis R. A Profile of an Hispano
Artist: Charlie "Clavos" Felix. LA LUZ, Vol.
4, no. 6-7 (September, October, 1975), p.
3-4. English.

AN: Biographical data on artist and his
unique nail relief sculpture.

5327 Trillin, Calvin and Koren, Edward. Low and
slow, mean and clean. NEW YORKER, Vol. 54,
no. 21 (July 10, 1978), p. 70-74. English.

AN: An important in-depth account of
Chicano lowriding culture in California.
Detailed analysis of how cars are lowered
and customized. Information on "cruising"
and "low rider happenings -- car shows at
which trophies are awarded for the best
interior and the finest paint job and the
highest hop off the ground." Distinctions
and variations between "cholos" and car
clubbers. Historical information on barrio
youth subcultures in Los Angeles.
Illustrated with cartoons.

5328 Valadez, Kathy L. and Valadez, Kathy L.
Living in the understanding of success/el
endendimiento [sic] del exito. CAMINOS, Vol.
1, no. 6 (October 1980), p. 12-14, 40.
Bilingual.

AN: Story about financially successful
Los Angeles illustrator Ignacio Gomez who
produced the illustration for the play ZOOT
SUIT and designs posters, catalogs, magazine
covers and layouts. Also see front cover and
inside of front cover for illustrations.

5329 Varda, Agnes. Mur murs/mural murals on the
wall ... Film, Cine Tamaris, Paris, 1980.
English.

AN: Full length documentary film
produced for French television; also
available with English subtitles. Deals
impressionistically with the murals and
muralists of Los Angeles. Included are Wayne
Alaniz Healy, David Botello, Willie Herron,
Manuel Cruz, Judy Baca, the murals in
Venice, CA, graffiti - among others. Color.

5330 Wilson, William. A blending of Hispanic
roots, visions. CALENDAR, (July 30, 1978),
p. 90. English.

AN: Review of ANCIENT ROOTS/NEW VISIONS
exhibit held at the Municipal Art Gallery in
Los Angeles.

5331 Wood carving art. EASTSIDE JRNL, (January
7, 1971), p. 2. English.

AN: Two photographs and commentary on
woodcarver Roberto H. Rodriguez on the
occasion of his one man show at the East Los
Angeles Library. Illustrated work shows
pre-Columbian motifs.

Los Angeles, CA (cont.)

5332 Zahn, Debbie. Citywide murals: outlook bleak
     for funding of art work by Chicanos.
     FORTY-NINER, (May 4, 1976). English.

     AN: The Los Angeles City Council decides
     to terminate the 1974 program, Citywide
     Murals, which provided funds for Chicano
     artists. Description of Joe Bravo's 2000 sq
     ft mural at the Wilmington Recreation
     Center, painted with a team, which makes a
     positive statement against gang warfare.
     Illustrated.

Los Angeles Citywide Mural Project

5333 Kim, Howard. Judithe Hernandez and a glimpse
     at the Chicana artist. SOMOS, (October,
     November, 1979), p. 6-11. English.

     AN: Biographical information on Chicana
     artist Judithe Hernandez. Commentary on her
     contributions to Plaza de la Raza, Los
     Angeles Citywide Mural Project and her work
     as designer consultant to AZTLAN:
     INTERNATIONAL JOURNAL OF CHICANO RESEARCH.
     The article focuses on her mural activity,
     particularly two murals: EL MUNDO DE BARRIO
     SOTEL and LA CHICANA DE AZTLAN. Her personal
     art philosophy is presented in relation to
     Third World Art.

5334 Miranda, Keta. Refunding battle for mural
     project. PEOPLE'S WORLD, Vol. 39, no. 20
     (May 15, 1976), p. 5+. English.

     AN: History of the Mural Arts and
     Resource Center (Los Angeles Citywide Mural
     Project) from 1974 to its imminent demise in
     1976. Joe Bravo mural illustrated.

5335 NATIONAL MURALS NETWORK COMMUNITY
     NEWSLETTER. (1978). English.

     AN: This issue features reports from
     muralists. Includes information about murals
     at: La Pena Cultural Center in Berkeley, CA;
     the Social and Public Art Resource Center's
     Tujunga Wash Mural in Venice, CA; the
     Citywide Mural Project in Los Angeles, CA;
     activities at Chicano Park, and of the
     Congress of American Cosmic Artists (CACA),
     both in San Diego, CA; murals in San Mateo
     County, CA; the Task Force on Hispanic
     American Arts headed by Jacinto Quirarte of
     San Antonio; the 1978 Canto Al Pueblo in
     Corpus Christi, TX; murals in Chicago; and
     other works by non-Chicano artists.

Los Angeles Contemporary Exhibitions (L.A.C.E.)

5336 Dreva & Gronk exhibit at L.A.C.E.: Gronkart
     live; Bonbon returns. Exhibition invitation,
     1978. English.

     AN: Illustrated invitation/poster to
     exhibit of Asco's Gronk, and Jerry Dreva, a
     collaborative show featuring ten years of
     work:photos, correspondence, documents,
     ephemera and other art.

5337 Lucas, Jerry. Testimonios de Latinoamerica.
     CHISMEARTE, no. 6 (February 1980), p. 6-9.
     English.

     AN: Review of the exhibits TESTIMONIOS
     DE LATINOAMERICA and AMERICA EN LA MIRA,
     brought to Los Angeles Contemporary
     Exhibitions Gallery by Chicano curator
     Roberto Gil de Montes, as part of a cultural
     exchange between the Mexican Cultural
     Workers Front and Felipe Ehrenberg of the
     Grupo Proceso Pentagono of Mexico, and

Chicano artists and photographers from the
Council of Latino Photography/USA in Los
Angeles. Well illustrated.

5338 Testimonios de Latinoamerica. LA PRENSA SAN
     DIEGO, (October 26, 1979), p. 3. Spanish.

     AN: Announcement of an exhibit at the
     Centro Cultural de la Raza, San Diego,
     "Testimonios de Latino America" and "America
     en la mira," political graphics organized by
     Mexican artist Felipe Ehrenberg and also
     shown at the Los Angeles Contemporary
     Exhibitions gallery (LACE).

Los Angeles County, CA

5339 Galeria, Santa Ana, CA. The last Chicano art
     show. Exhibition brochure, 1981. English.

     AN: Invitation-brochure for an exhibit
     of Los Angeles and Orange County artists in
     a gallery underwritten by the Friendly
     Center, Inc. with grants from local
     government and from businesses. Exhibiting
     are (Roberto) Gil de Montes, Gilbert Lujan,
     Judy Miranda, Patricia Murillo, Alonso
     Pardo, Teddy Sandoval, Mexican artist
     Artemio Sepulveda, Joey Terrill, Art
     Valenzuela, Ben Valenzuela, Linda Vallejo,
     Jack A. Vargas, Emigdio Vasquez, Richard
     Serrato, and J. William Hernandez, who is
     the gallery director.

Los Angeles County Museum of Art

5340 Canavier, Elena Karina. Los Four. ARTWEEK,
     Vol. 5, no. 10 (March 9, 1974), p. 1, 16.
     English.

     AN: Illustrated review, with detailed
     description of work of the Los Four exhibit
     at the Los Angeles County Museum of Art.

5341 Flaco, Eduardo. Chicanismo en el arte.
     ARTWEEK, Vol. 6, no. 20 (May 17, 1975), p.
     3. English.

     AN: Review of competitive exhibition
     composed of Chicano artists between
     seventeen and twenty-six from Los Angeles
     colleges, universities and art schools.
     Focuses on work of ASCO, the only noteworthy
     art in the show, according to the critic.

5342 Los Angeles County Museum of Art, Los
     Angeles, CA and D'Andrea, Jeanne. Chicanismo
     en el arte. Exhibit brochure, 1975. English.

     AN: An exhibit of Southern California
     Chicano student artists organized in
     cooperation with East Los Angeles College.
     Thirty-one artists displayed 73 works. The
     show was exhibited at the Vincent Price
     Gallery of East Los Angeles College prior to
     moving to the Los Angeles County Museum of
     Art. 70 illustrations.

5343 Moreno, Eduardo. Los Four. Half-hour 16mm
     film. English.

     AN: Film about the Los Angeles group of
     artists known as Los Four (originally Carlos
     Almaraz, Gilbert Sanchez Lujan, Roberto de
     la Rocha, Frank Romero), at the time of
     their exhibit at the Los Angeles County
     Museum of Art - the first time Chicano art
     was shown at the Museum.

Los Angeles County Museum of Art (cont.)

5344 Polack, Clark. A question of style - Los Four and the Los Angeles County Museum of Art. SOUTHWEST ART, (July, August, 1974). English.

AN: A double-edged assessment of the "Los Four" exhibit. The exhibition is at once lauded for being provocative and stimulating while at the same time failing artistically. Author feels that special treatment given Carlos Almaraz, Gilbert Lujan, Roberto de la Rocha and Frank Romero by the L.A. County Art Museum has not been extended to other young Los Angeles artists.

5345 Rand, Steve. Carlos David Almaraz. LOS ANGELES FREE PRESS, Vol. 11, no. 10 (March 8, 1974), p. 14. English.

AN: Brief biographical sketch on Mexican-born, Los Angeles artist Carlos Almaraz on the occasion of the Los Four exhibit at the Los Angeles County Museum of Art, artists who are, the author says inaccurately, largely self-taught. Almaraz studied at Garfield High School with David Ramirez, and at Otis Art Institute. One illustration.

5346 Wilson, William. A bit of the barrio at County Museum. LOS ANGELES TIMES, (February 27, 1974), p. IV, 1+. English.

AN: Review of the Los Four exhibit at the Los Angeles County Museum of Art. Quotes from artists, history of group's formation in 1973.

5347 Wilson, William. 'Los Four' a statement of Chicano spirit. CALENDAR, (March 10, 1974), p. 64+. English.

AN: Lengthy critical review of Los Four exhibit at Los Angeles County Museum of Art. Illustrated.

Los Angeles Institute of Contemporary Art

5348 Muchnic, Suzanne. LAICA looks at social works. CALENDAR, (October 7, 1979), p. 93. English.

AN: Review of the exhibit SOCIAL WORKS at the Los Angeles Institute of Contemporary Art. Illustration and discussion of Judith F. Baca's mural UPRISING OF THE MUJERES, a four-part portable canvas mural in the style of Siqueiros.

Los Angeles Municipal Art Gallery

5349 Wilson, William. A multicultural celebration of photos. CALENDAR, (February 8, 1981), p. 89-90. English.

AN: Review of multi-ethnic photography show at the Los Angeles Municipal Art Gallery. Wilson finds the photographs about equally divided between sociological reality and expression/art for its own sake.

Louie, Harry

5350 The Mexican Museum, San Francisco, CA and Quirarte, Jacinto. 17 artists: Hispano/Mexican-American/Chicano. Exhibition catalog, 1977. English.

AN: Catalog of an exhibit for artists Emilio Aguirre, Consuelo Gonzalez Amezcua, Al Barela, Pedro Cervantez, Edward Chavez, Antonio Garcia, Louis Gutierrez, Harry

Louie, Vincent Perez, Michael Ponce de Leon, Eugenio Quesada, Gustavo Rivera, Peter Rodriguez, Alex Sanchez, Darryl Sapien, Rudy Trevino, Manuel Villamor. Illustrated.

Low Riders

5351 Castillo, Rafael. Gonzo journalism goes for a low ride. SAN ANTONIO EXPRESS-NEWS, (December 6, 1981), p. 7-B. English.

AN: George Velasquez, editor and publisher of San Antonio's VAJITO magazine, views lowriders as a positive and evolving form of urban youth culture. Counters stereotypes about lowriders as drug-oriented high school drop-outs. There is a new and significant discourse being developed in literary and visual forms among Chicano lowriders.

5352 Galeria de la Raza/Studio 24, San Francisco, CA. "Low 'n slow": checking out low rider art. Exhibition invitation, 1979. English.

AN: Invitation to an exhibit of drawings, photographs, and graphics. Participation by LOWRIDER MAGAZINE and local car and bike clubs.

5353 Galeria de la Raza/Studio 24, San Francisco, CA and Jimenez, David "Sir Loco". Low rider art book. San Francisco, CA: Galeria de la Raza, 1979. English.

AN: A portfolio of ten low-rider car drawings suitable for coloring and framing.

5354 Gamboa, Harry, Jr. Fantasias moviles. COMUNIDAD, (August 30, 1981), p. 8-9. Spanish.

AN: An illustrated article by ASCO artist Harry Gamboa, Jr. on lowriders, and the magazines LOWRIDER, Q-VO and FIRME.

5355 Johnston, Tracy. La vida loca. NEW WEST MAGAZINE, (January 29, 1979), p. 38-46. English.

AN: A journalistic account of barrio lifestyles composed from conversations with young Cholos in Los Angeles. Amid poverty, unemployment, drug abuse and familial disintegration, codes of group solidarity and rituals of connection occur. Information on urban Chicano forms of self expression such as mascaras (chola make up), tattoos and graffiti. Well illustrated with photographs.

5356 Low n slow - lowrider art. PEOPLE'S WORLD, Vol. 42, no. 34 (August 25, 1979), p. 10. English.

AN: Announcement of the Galeria de la Raza's exhibit of lowrider art. The article mentions the history of the lowrider car from the 1940s Pachuco zootsuiters, to the 1950s car clubs. The lowrider exhibit was prepared by the Galeria in response to white neighbors' recent protests against Saturday night cruising in the Mission District.

5357 Low riders of the urban range. LIFE, Vol. 3, no. 5 (May 1980), p. 88-94. English.

AN: Visual documentation of lowrider culture in Los Angeles. Car murals, custom paint jobs, upholstery and clothing styles are featured. Well illustrated with color photography.

Low Riders (cont.)

5358 Lowrider: arte del varrio. A.T.M.
     Communications, Inc., 1979. English.

     AN: Issue of LOWRIDER Magazine dedicated
     to drawings and paintings by "cholos" sent
     in to the editor for publication. Good
     example of a popular art form by largely
     self-taught neighborhood youth, with a
     distinctive style and symbolism. Related to
     graffiti and tattoos. Most images are of
     lowrider cars, young women and men.

5359 Lowrider: arte del varrio. San Jose, CA:
     A.T.M. Communications, 1980. English.

     AN: Second issue of LOWRIDER Magazine
     dedicated to drawings and pantings by
     "cholos" sent in to the editor for
     publication.

5360 Ortega, Gil. The 50's and other assorted
     Chicano graffiti. La Habra, CA: s.n., 1981.
     English.

     AN: Album of caricatures of barrio
     types; black and white drawings in six
     categories: The Parties and Dances,
     Schooldays, Oldtime Lowriders, Refine, Los
     Veteranos, Los Vatos. Some drawings
     accompanied by commentary.

5361 Temko, Allan. Teen Angel's low riders -
     Chicano art on the rise. THIS WORLD,
     (August 26, 1979), p. 42-43. English.

     AN: Important and insightful analysis of
     the lowrider phenomenon among Chicano youth
     in California. Analysis of publications like
     LOW RIDER Magazine of San Jose, information
     on graphic artists like "Teen Angel" and
     Ramon Cisneros and thematic relationship of
     recognized Chicano artists like Gilbert
     Lujan, John Valadez, and Luis Jimenez to the
     lowrider movement. The lowrider is
     provocatively related to world wide cultural
     manifestations from diverse epochs.

5362 Trillin, Calvin and Koren, Edward. Low and
     slow, mean and clean. NEW YORKER, Vol. 54,
     no. 21 (July 10, 1978), p. 70-74. English.

     AN: An important in-depth account of
     Chicano lowriding culture in California.
     Detailed analysis of how cars are lowered
     and customized. Information on "cruising"
     and "low rider happenings -- car shows at
     which trophies are awarded for the best
     interior and the finest paint job and the
     highest hop off the ground." Distinctions
     and variations between "cholos" and car
     clubbers. Historical information on barrio
     youth subcultures in Los Angeles.
     Illustrated with cartoons.

LOWRIDER MAGAZINE

5363 Galeria de la Raza/Studio 24, San Francisco,
     CA. "Low 'n slow": checking out low rider
     art. Exhibition invitation, 1979. English.

     AN: Invitation to an exhibit of
     drawings, photographs, and graphics.
     Participation by LOWRIDER MAGAZINE and local
     car and bike clubs.

5364 Gamboa, Harry, Jr. Fantasias moviles.
     COMUNIDAD, (August 30, 1981), p. 8-9.
     Spanish.

     AN: An illustrated article by ASCO
     artist Harry Gamboa, Jr. on lowriders, and
     the magazines LOWRIDER, Q-VO and FIRME.

5365 Temko, Allan. Teen Angel's low riders -
     Chicano art on the rise. THIS WORLD,
     (August 26, 1979), p. 42-43. English.

     AN: Important and insightful analysis of
     the lowrider phenomenon among Chicano youth
     in California. Analysis of publications like
     LOW RIDER Magazine of San Jose, information
     on graphic artists like "Teen Angel" and
     Ramon Cisneros and thematic relationship of
     recognized Chicano artists like Gilbert
     Lujan, John Valadez, and Luis Jimenez to the
     lowrider movement. The lowrider is
     provocatively related to world wide cultural
     manifestations from diverse epochs.

Lucas, Costa Ben

5366 Lucas, Costa Ben. Chato [comic strip].
     ABRAZO, Vol. 1, no. 2 (Summer 1979), p.
     16-17. English.

     AN: One installment of CHATO, the
     cartoon strip created by Costa Ben Lucas.
     Also provides a brief explanation of how the
     character was created and his principal
     characteristics.

Lucas, Jerry

5367 Diaz, Jean; Dominguez, Edward; and Torres,
     Kay. Bi-Lingual blues [fotonovela]. SOMOS,
     Vol. 1, no. 1 (April, May, 1978), p. 33-36.
     English.

     AN: Reproduction of a "fotonovela",
     BI-LINGUAL BLUES by Ojo Productions, a group
     of students connected with the Latin
     American Studies Department of California
     State University, Los Angeles.

5368 Lucas, Jerry and Gil de Montes, Roberto, et
     al. CHOQUE DE AMOR: fotonovela by Lamp. Los
     Angeles, CA: Colectivo El Ojo, Latin
     American Studies Dept., CSULA, 1979.
     English.

     AN: "Fotonovela" featuring Elsa Flores,
     Rosa Marin, and Jerry Lucas produced by the
     collective work of Lucas, Roberto Gil de
     Montes, Mario Massinelli, Luis Soto, and Kay
     Torres.

Lucero, Felix

5369 Negri, Sam. Garden grows as shrine to
     sculptor. ARIZONA REPUBLIC, (April 5,
     1980), p. C-1. English.

     AN: Felix Lucero, a self-taught
     Colorado-born sculptor who came to Tucson in
     1938, spent 20 years sculpting religious
     statues. He started the Garden of Gethsemane
     in 1945 on the Congress Street bridge.

Lucero, Juan

5370 Sanchez, Arley. Santeros. ALBUQUERQUE JRNL, (August 21, 1977), p. C, 1. English.

AN: Review of THE SANTERO EXPERIENCE, an exhibition of contemporary folk art by eleven New Mexican santeros, most in their 30s, at the Albuquerque Museum. The carvers include Juan Lucero, Ben Lopez, Luisito Lujan, Horacio Valdez, C. Garcia, George Lopez. A revival of the art has been taking place within last several years due to cultural awareness being experienced by Hispanos. Contemporary santeros still donate some pieces to the church, but most are marketed to private collectors, displayed in museums, or kept.

Lucero, Leo

5371 Chicano muralists maintain traditions. LA CUCARACHA, (November 20, 1979), p. 7. English.

AN: Introduction to Chicano muralism in Pueblo and comparison to the Mexican mural movement from which it draws inspiration. 20 murals painted from 1977 to 1979. The muralists include Bernardo Duran, Juan Espinoza, Miguel "Freeloader" Garcia, Lola Gutierrez, Leo Lucero, Juan Pacheco, Dolores Pena, Pedro Romero, Stan Salazar, David Sandoval. Diego Rivera murals illustrated.

5372 En nuestra opinion. LA CUCARACHA, (July 4, 1980), Spanish.

AN: An editorial commending the mural efforts by Chicano artists in Pueblo, Colorado. Community artists should be supported and encouraged, not threatened with jail for their efforts. Illustrated with photograph of a mural by Puebloan Leo Lucero at Plaza Verde Park in Pueblo, Colorado.

Lucero, Linda

5373 Corcoran Gallery of Art, Washington, D.C. Images of an era: the American poster 1945-75. Washington, D.C.: Corcoran Gallery of Art, 1976. English.

AN: Uncredited poster [La Raza Silkscreen Center, San Francisco], (centerfold). Posters by Rupert Garcia, Linda Lucero, and Ralph Maradiaga, all of San Francisco, CA. Introduction by John Garriga. Essays by Margaret Cogswell, Milton Glaser, Dore Ashton, Alan Gowens.

5374 Lucero, Linda. Compositions from my kitchen/composiciones de mi cocina: an international cookbook. San Francisco, CA: La Raza Graphic Center, 1981. English.

AN: International recipes illustrated with drawings and a poster by Linda Lucero, as well as other artists.

Lucero, Roberto

5375 Denver. NATIONAL MURALS NETWORK COMMUNITY NEWSLETTER, (Spring 1980), p. 10. English.

AN: Denver, Colorado murals by Manuel Martinez, the Chilean Orlando Letelier Brigade, Roberto Lucero, Al Sanchez, Jerry Jaramillo. Illustrated.

5376 Denver muralist here for workshop. TEMPE DAILY NEWS, (March 28, 1975). English.

AN: Denver muralist Roberto Lucero is invited to give a weekend mural workshop for the Quetzalcoatl Youth Organization of Escalante Community Center in Tempe, Arizona.

5377 Incorporated Artes Monumentales/Inc., Denver, CO. IAM: art exhibit. Exhibition brochure, n.d. English.

AN: Large format, well illustrated brochure with information on muralists Roberto Lucero, Al Sanchez, Andrew Manning, Ricardo Barrera and Bob Reyes. Includes some biographical information situating these artists within the dynamic artistic traditions of the Mexican and the Chicano mural movements.

5378 NATIONAL MURALS NETWORK COMMUNITY NEWSLETTER. (Spring 1980). English.

AN: Reports on the Sept. 1979 conference of Chicano visual arts held at UT Austin, organized by the Mujeres Artistas del Suroeste, and the Liga Unida de Chicanos Artistas, which brought together participants from the U.S. and Mexico City; on Manuel Martinez's five murals (1976-78); murals by Roberto Lucero, Al Sanchez, and Jerry Jaramillo; as well as by the Chilean group Orlando Letelier Brigade, all in Denver, Colorado; murals by Leo Tanguma in Houston; the story about the "forbidden" Chicano mural in Blue Island, Illinois. Illustrated.

Lucero, Stephen Pascual

5379 Meta studio I. Denver, CO: s.n., [1980]. English.

AN: Portfolio of colored prints by Colorado artists Ernie Gallegos, Jerry Jaramillo, Steve Lucero and Carlos M. Sandoval. Biographical information and photograph of each artist. Presentation of the group under the rubric of "metarealism" by Stephen Pascual Lucero.

Lucero, Steve

5380 Meta studio I. Denver, CO: s.n., [1980]. English.

AN: Portfolio of colored prints by Colorado artists Ernie Gallegos, Jerry Jaramillo, Steve Lucero and Carlos M. Sandoval. Biographical information and photograph of each artist. Presentation of the group under the rubric of "metarealism" by Stephen Pascual Lucero.

5381 Metro Denver Urban Coalition, Denver, CO. City walls. Brochure, 1979. English.

AN: Brochure/poster giving history of City Walls Project and biographies of seven artists: Jon Howe, Jerry Jaramillo, Steve Lucero, Jowinnie Moore, Al Sanchez, Fred Sanchez, Carlos M. Sandoval. Illustrated.

Lucero, Steve (cont.)

5382 Tully, Robert. City walls. LA VOZ (Denver,
CO), (August 3, 1979), p. 7. English.

AN: In a project managed by Metro Denver
Urban Coalition, several Chicano artists
were hired to work consistently in creating
murals for the inner city. Article focuses
on the goals, procedures, and activities of
the muralists. Grouped as Incorporated Artes
Monumentales, the group included Jerry
Jaramillo, Steve Lucero, Al Sanchez, Fred
Sanchez, and Carlos Sandoval. Illustrated by
a group photograph of artists and a
photograph of a wall painting by the
Chilean-led Brigada Orlando Letelier in
Denver.

LUIS JIMENEZ: PROGRESS I [exhibit]

5383 Contemporary Arts Museum, Houston, TX and
Harithas, James. Luis Jimenez: Progress I.
Exhibition catalog, 1974-75. English.

AN: Catalog for a major exhibit of
Jimenez sculptures, drawings and studies for
sculptural works from 1967 to 1974. The
latest project, PROGRESS, involves a series
of monumental sculptures depicting the
history of the West. Jimenez combines social
comment with advanced plastic values. Well
illustrated.

Lujan, Gilbert Sanchez "Magu"

5384 Art Gallery, California State University,
Long Beach and Lujan, Gilbert Sanchez
"Magu". El arte del pocho. Exhibit brochure,
October 1968. English.

AN: Information about Southern
California artists John Deheras, Marcus
Villagran, Roberto de la Rocha, Santos
Zuniga, Crispin Gonzales, Richard Martinez,
Jesus Gutierrez, Ed Oropeza, Pete Mendez,
David Ramirez, Gilbert Sanchez Lujan, Willie
Hernandez, Art Ponce, Carmen Tostado, Al
Almeida, David Ceja, Robert E. Chavez,
Thomas A. Ferriera. All art students,
graduates, or faculty.

5385 Art Gallery, University of California,
Irvine and Los Angeles County Museum of Art,
Los Angeles, CA. Los Four: Almaraz, de la
Rocha, Lujan, Romero. Exhibition brochure,
1973-74. English.

AN: Photographs and biographies of
Carlos Almaraz, Roberto de la Rocha, Gilbert
S. Lujan, Frank Romero.

5386 California. State College. Los Angeles. Art
Department. Fifth California small images
exhibition. Exhibition catalog, [1972].
English.

AN: Catalog for an exhibit including the
work of Charles D. Almaraz, Mary Lynn
Dominguez, Gilbert Sanchez Lujan (who won
Purchase Awards), Stephen Anaya, Martha
Villegas. Illustrated.

5387 California. State College. Los Angeles. Art
Gallery. Twelve Chicano artists. Exhibition
invitation, n.d. English.

AN: Invitation to an exhibit: Jose
Montoya, Gilbert Sanchez Lujan, Esteban
Villa, Rene Yanez, Joe Moran, Armando Cid,
Leonard Castellas, Juanishi Orozco, Rudy
Cuellar, Beltran, Lopez and Cabrera.

5388 Chicano art. ARTES VISUALES, no. 29 (1981).
English.

AN: Issue on Chicano art, introduced by
Los Angeles artist Roberto Gil de Montes.
Includes works and statements by: Pedro
Lujan (Texas); Raul M. Guerrero (Calif.);
Sylvia Salazar Simpson (New Mexico/Calif.);
Carlos Almaraz (Calif.); Rene Yanez
(Calif.); Jack Vargas (Calif.); Ray Bravo
(Calif.); John Valadez (Calif.); Gloria Maya
(Calif.); Elsa Flores (Calif.); Willie
Herron (Calif.); Gilbert "Magu" Lujan
(Calif.); Kay Torres, Jerry Lucas, and Louis
Perez (Calif.).

5389 Concilio de arte popular. CHISMEARTE, Vol.
1, no. 2 (Winter, Spring, 1977), p. 54.
English.

AN: Report of a meeting February 12,
1977 by the Concilio de Arte Popular (CAP)
which published CHISMEARTE. Introduces
members of the Board and summarizes
discussions of problems of the organization
and their publication.

5390 Los Four exhibit in Union Gallery.
UNIVERSITY TIMES, (November 6, 1975), p. 4.
English.

AN: "Los Four," a group of four Chicano
artists - Frank Romero, Roberto "Beto" de la
Rocha, Gilbert Lujan, and Carlos Almaraz,
with newcomer Judithe Hernandez - work with
political cartoons, Catholic symbols, works
of sardonic humor. They also paint street
murals: several have been done recently in
Los Angeles, La Puente, and Long Beach.
Illustrated.

5391 Galeria, Santa Ana, CA. The last Chicano art
show. Exhibition brochure, 1981. English.

AN: Invitation-brochure for an exhibit
of Los Angeles and Orange County artists in
a gallery underwritten by the Friendly
Center, Inc. with grants from local
government and from businesses. Exhibiting
are (Roberto) Gil de Montes, Gilbert Lujan,
Judy Miranda, Patricia Murillo, Alonso
Pardo, Teddy Sandoval, Mexican artist
Artemio Sepulveda, Joey Terrill, Art
Valenzuela, Ben Valenzuela, Linda Vallejo,
Jack A. Vargas, Emigdio Vasquez, Richard
Serrato, and J. William Hernandez, who is
the gallery director.

5392 Knapp, Dan. KCET's show for Chicano viewers.
LOS ANGELES TIMES, (April 3, 1970), p. IV,
18. English.

AN: Story on the television series
AHORA! started September 1969 on KCET, Los
Angeles' National Educational Television.
Edward Moreno is program director and host;
Victor Millan is producer-director; Claudio
Fenner-Lopez, senior producer, has staff
including set-designer David Villasenor,
production manager James Val, and alternate
host-narrator Jesus Trevino. The program has
shown exhibits of artists Gilberto Lujan and
Daniel Ramirez.

Lujan, Gilbert Sanchez "Magu" (cont.)

5393 Lujan, Gilbert Sanchez "Magu". El arte del
Chicano - "The Spirit of the Experience".
CON SAFOS, no. 7 (Winter 1971), p. 11-13.
English.

AN: Definition of Chicano Art by artist
Lujan as the expression of an unique
experience that is neither Mexican nor U.S.
Anglo, that has its own vitality and
dynamics. Chicanos can draw upon common
cultural elements and transform them into
images and art forms such as sculptured
menudo bones, tortilla drawings, vato loco
portraits, etc. Four woodcuts by Roberto de
la Rocha are shown as examples.

5394 Moreno, Eduardo. Los Four. Half-hour 16mm
film. English.

AN: Film about the Los Angeles group of
artists known as Los Four (originally Carlos
Almaraz, Gilbert Sanchez Lujan, Roberto de
la Rocha, Frank Romero), at the time of
their exhibit at the Los Angeles County
Museum of Art - the first time Chicano art
was shown at the Museum.

5395 Oakland Museum, Oakland, CA and Laney
College, Oakland, CA. In search of Aztlan.
Exhibition brochure, 1974. English.

AN: Brochure for exhibit featuring Los
Four: Carlos Almaraz, Gilbert Lujan, Roberto
de la Rocha, Frank Romero, Judithe
Hernandez.

5396 Oakland Museum, Oakland, CA. In search of
Aztlan. Exhibition invitation, 1974.
English.

AN: Invitation to an exhibit by Los
Four, a Chicano art group started about 1973
in Los Angeles. On exhibit are the original
members, Carlos Almaraz, Gilbert Lujan,
Roberto de la Rocha, Frank Romero, and new
member Judithe Hernandez.

5397 Oakland Museum presents 5 L.A. Chicano
artists. EL MUNDO (Hayward, CA), (August
1974). English.

AN: Report on the exhibit THE SEARCH FOR
AZTLAN, featuring paintings, murals,
tortilla art, folk and religious symbols and
totems by Carlos Almaraz, Roberto de la
Rocha, Gilbert Lujan, Frank Romero and
Judithe Hernandez. Included in the more than
100 works are a wall mural, a folk art
pyramid, and part of a primed '51 Chevy
lowrider. Illustrated.

5398 Plagens, Peter. Los Four (Roberto de la
Rocha, Carlos Almaraz, Gilbert Lujan and
Frank Romero) at LACMA. ARTFORUM,
(September 1974), p. 87-88. English.

AN: Review of Los Four exhibit at Los
Angeles County Museum of Art which calls it
a "sociological bazaar" in which Chicanos
have been "corrupted" by art schools and
"museumized".

5399 The Point Gallery, Santa Monica, CA. ASCO
(Gronk, Patssi, Gamboa, Herron), Los Four
(Almaraz, de la Rocha, Judithe Hernandez,
Gloriamalia Flores, Mauricio Ramirez, John
Valadez. Exhibition invitation, [1975].
English.

AN: Illustrated invitation to an exhibit
of Los Angeles artists.

5400 Polack, Clark. A question of style - Los
Four and the Los Angeles County Museum of
Art. SOUTHWEST ART, (July, August, 1974).
English.

AN: A double-edged assessment of the
"Los Four" exhibit. The exhibition is at
once lauded for being provocative and
stimulating while at the same time failing
artistically. Author feels that special
treatment given Carlos Almaraz, Gilbert
Lujan, Roberto de la Rocha and Frank Romero
by the L.A. County Art Museum has not been
extended to other young Los Angeles artists.

5401 San Francisco Museum of Modern Art, San
Francisco, CA and Pearlstein, Howard.
Aesthetics of graffiti. Exhibition catalog,
1978. English.

AN: Graffiti are defined as any
coherently-intended presence written,
scratched, painted, engraved, printed,
pasted or otherwise impressed in a public
place. Graffiti have been incorporated into
works by artists. In this catalog, works by
Chicano artists Carlos Almaraz, Wilfred
Castano, Judithe Hernandez, Gilbert Lujan,
Gustavo Rivera, Frank Romero, John M.
Valadez, Victor M. Valle, Xavier Viramontes
- as well as many Latino and non-Latino
artist, appear.

5402 Santa Ana College, Santa Ana, CA and
Goldman, Shifra M. Chicano art. Exhibition
catalog, 1974. English.

AN: Thirteen California artists are
presented in a short essay defining Chicano
as a double mestizaje of Mexican mestizo and
U.S. influences that exists in a state of
"reconciled conflict." Its aim is
communication. Artists included are
Malaquias Montoya, Rupert Garcia, Manuel
Hernandez, Esteban Villa, Robert Gomez,
Harvey Tarango, Mary Helen Castro, Eduardo
Carrillo, Graciela Carrillo, and "Los Four":
Carlos Almaraz, Robert de la Rocha, Judithe
Hernandez, Gilbert Lujan and Frank Romero.

5403 Santa Ana College, Santa Ana, CA. MECHA
presents la semana de la Raza. Exhibition
brochure, 1970. English.

AN: Program for the week's activities,
including EL ARTE DE LA RAZA exhibition,
Gilbert Sanchez Lujan speaking on "Chicano
Art in the Barrio," art demonstrations by
Gilbert Vasquez, Emigdio Vasquez, Esau
Quiroz, and Richard Garcia.

5404 Semana de la Raza: international panel of
the arts, Mexico and the United States.
Santa Ana, CA: MEChA, Santa Ana College,
1972. English.

AN: An International Panel of the Arts,
organized by art historian Shifra Goldman,
featured Mexicans Hector Garcia,
prize-winning photographer; Jaime Mejia,
painter, restorer, filmmaker; Alejandro
Vichir, director of Teatro Trashumante; and
Chicanos Gilbert Sanchez Lujan, sculptor and
painter; Gloria Osuna, painter and artist
for Teatro Campesino; and Jesus Salvador
Trevino, filmmaker.

Lujan, Gilbert Sanchez "Magu" (cont.)

5405 Street art explosion in Los Angeles. SUNSET,
(April 1973), p. 110-113. English.

AN: Illustrated article on Los Angeles
street murals including those by Roberto
Chavez, Willie Herron, Frank Romero, Richard
Jimenez, William Bejarano, Gilbert Lujan,
Armando Cabrera, Frank Martinez, Charles
Felix, and others.

5406 Temko, Allan. Teen Angel's low riders -
Chicano art on the rise. THIS WORLD,
(August 26, 1979), p. 42-43. English.

AN: Important and insightful analysis of
the lowrider phenomenon among Chicano youth
in California. Analysis of publications like
LOW RIDER Magazine of San Jose, information
on graphic artists like "Teen Angel" and
Ramon Cisneros and thematic relationship of
recognized Chicano artists like Gilbert
Lujan, John Valadez, and Luis Jimenez to the
lowrider movement. The lowrider is
provocatively related to world wide cultural
manifestations from diverse epochs.

Lujan, Luisito

5407 Sanchez, Arley. Santeros. ALBUQUERQUE JRNL,
(August 21, 1977), p. C, 1. English.

AN: Review of THE SANTERO EXPERIENCE, an
exhibition of contemporary folk art by
eleven New Mexican santeros, most in their
30s, at the Albuquerque Museum. The carvers
include Juan Lucero, Ben Lopez, Luisito
Lujan, Horacio Valdez, C. Garcia, George
Lopez. A revival of the art has been taking
place within last several years due to
cultural awareness being experienced by
Hispanos. Contemporary santeros still donate
some pieces to the church, but most are
marketed to private collectors, displayed in
museums, or kept.

Lujan, Maria Theofila

5408 Benson, Nancy C. Preserving an early
Hispanic art. EMPIRE MAGAZINE, (June 8,
1980), p. 50. English.

AN: 84-year-old colcha-stitchery artist
Maria Theofila Lujan is a founding member of
a stitchery group of the 1930s, now called
Artes Antigua Society. Her work is in museum
collections.

Lujan, Pedro

5409 Chicano art. ARTES VISUALES, no. 29 (1981).
English.

AN: Issue on Chicano art, introduced by
Los Angeles artist Roberto Gil de Montes.
Includes works and statements by: Pedro
Lujan (Texas); Raul M. Guerrero (Calif.);
Sylvia Salazar Simpson (New Mexico/Calif.);
Carlos Almaraz (Calif.); Rene Yanez
(Calif.); Jack Vargas (Calif.); Ray Bravo
(Calif.); John Valadez (Calif.); Gloria Maya
(Calif.); Elsa Flores (Calif.); Willie
Herron (Calif.); Gilbert "Magu" Lujan
(Calif.); Kay Torres, Jerry Lucas, and Louis
Perez (Calif.).

5410 Lujan, Pedro and Morton, Carlos. Una platica
entre Carlos Morton y Pedro Lujan. CARACOL,
Vol. 3, no. 4 (December 1976), p. 10-12.
Bilingual.

AN: Carlos Morton interviews Pedro
Lujan, a Chicano sculptor who spends six

months a year in New York and six
months traveling throughout the Southwest. Lujan
discusses his preference for creating works
from available materials such as scraps of
wood, wire, and rope.

5411 Moisan, Jim. Ancient roots, new visions.
ARTWEEK, Vol. 9, no. 26 (July 29, 1978), p.
8. English.

AN: Review of the show held at the
Municipal Arts Gallery of Los Angeles, the
first national touring show of Latino
artists in the United States. Includes
commentary on work of Larry Fuente, Luis
Jimenez, Frank Romero, Harry Gamboa, Gronk,
Rudy Martinez, Benjamin Serrano, Ricardo
Diaz, Patssi Valdez, Mel Casas, Luis Leroy,
Pedro Lujan. A related show, NEW VISIONS,
L.A., includes Robert Delgado, Ray Bravo,
Joe Moran, Rosalyn Mesquita, Patricia
Murillo and others.

5412 Morton, Carlos. Pedro Lujan: sculptor. LA
LUZ, Vol. 6, no. 5 (May 1977), p. 22-26.
Bilingual.

AN: Biographical and artistic trajectory
of Pedro Lujan. As a sculptor, he is
identified with the Levi-Straussian idea of
the "bricoleur" (a person who solves
artistic problems with the materials on
hand). Basically working with wood and
simple tools, Pedro Lujan feels related to
santero and Penitente art of his native
Southwest.

5413 Raza sculptors coast to coast - Lujan y
Rodriguez. EL TECOLOTE LITERARY MAGAZINE,
Vol. 10, no. 9 (June 1980), p. 7. English.

AN: Pedro Lujan, originally from the
Southwest, now lives in SOHO in New York.
Lujan defines himself as a bricoleur who
works primarily with wood and simple tools
like hatchets and chisels. Ismael Rodriguez,
self-taught sculptor from Berkeley,
California, works in stone or wood. Includes
photo of Lujan's wood sculpture "Man
Running" and photo of Rodriguez at work.

Machado, Anthony

5414 San Francisco Museum of Modern Art, San
Francisco, CA and Castellon, Rolando.
People's murals: some events in American
history. Exhibition catalog, 1976. English.

AN: Eight portable murals by San
Francisco Bay Area artists including
Graciela Carrillo, Anthony Machado, Robert
Mendoza, Irene Perez, Mike Rios. Well
Illustrated.

Maciel, David

5415 California. University. Los Angeles. Cine
sin fronteras. Festival brochure, 1981.
English.

AN: Brochure program for a cinema
festival and series of seminars and
discussions featuring films and discussants
from Mexico and Chicanos of the United
States. Participating were Chicano directors
Moctezuma Esparza, Richard Soto, David
Sandoval, and Robert Young, and film
historian David Maciel.

Maciel, Leonel

5416 MEXICAN MUSEUM NEWSLETTER. Vol. 6, no. 1
(Winter 1980, 1981). English.

AN: Regular report on the activities,
finances, membership, and other information
about the Museum. Announces several upcoming
shows: Rupert Garcia, six Mexican geometric
artists, paintings and prints by Mexican
American and Mexican women artists, Mexican
Leonel Maciel and Chicano Carlos Almaraz,
Mexican folk art, Manuel Neri sculpture, and
Mexican Luis Jaso.

5417 The Mexican Museum, San Francisco, CA.
Recent works of Leonel Maciel and Carlos
Almaraz. Exhibition invitation, 1981.
English.

AN: Invitation to an exhibit of works by
Mexican artist Maciel and Chicano painter
Almaraz.

MADRE TIERRA [mural]

5418 Montoya, Emmanuel; Rodriguez, Patricia; and
Acevedo, Mario (Torero). Canto al pueblo
'78. NATIONAL MURALS NETWORK COMMUNITY
NEWSLETTER, (1978). English.

AN: The second annual Canto al Pueblo
took place in Corpus Christi, Texas, where
more than six murals were painted: "Wall of
Cultural Education" by 13 artists headed by
Roel Montealva, with Carlota Espinoza, with
children; Gilberto Romero, Jose Antonio
Burciaga and Patricia Rodriguez,
"Incomprehension al arte"; "Madre Tierra" by
Manuel Martinez of Denver with Amador
Hinojosa (Corpus Christi) and Enriquette
Vasquez (New Mexico); Mario Torero; Salvador
Vega of Chicago whose mural some Canto
participants considered "insulting".

Maes, Bob

5419 Chicano art show. EL DIARIO DE LA GENTE,
Vol. 1, no. 7 (February 6, 1973), p. 4.
English.

AN: Fine arts students at the University
of Colorado led by Rudy Fernandez hope to
educate high school students about Chicano
art. This article documents an exhibit held
at Lafayette, CO. Members of the group are
Bob Maez, Jerry Jaramillo, Anthony Mendoza,
and Rudy Fernandez. Illustrated by four
exhibition photographs by John L. Espinosa.

Maestas, Jose Alfredo

5420 Corazon del norte: Jose Alfredo Maestas.
GRITO DEL NORTE, Vol. 2, no. 7 (May 19,
1969), p. 13. English.

AN: Jose Alfredo Maestas, born in San
Juan Pueblo is a folk carver imbued with the
mythical and spiritual Indo-Hispano
tradition. His carved figurines made from
cotton wood roots, balsam and driftwood are
in many museums and private collections.
Illustrated with photographs of artist at
work and two photographs of his sculpture.

MAGIA BLANCA [exhibit]

5421 De Marroquin, Moron. Denver Harbor artists.
LA PRENSA, (June 2, 1978). Spanish.

AN: Commentary on two exhibitions. THE
DENVER HARBOR ARTISTS includes information
on paintings by Lupe Aguirre, Josie Mendoza
and Abel Gonzalez--all from Houston. The

solo show MAGIC BLANCA featured the work of
Brownsville, Texas artist Jorge Truan.
Truan's work is mystical and visionary.

MAIZE [journal], San Diego, CA

5422 Yarbro-Bejarano, Yvonne. Resena de revistas
chicanas: problemas y tendencias, Part I. LA
PALABRA, Vol. 2, no. 1 (Spring 1980), p.
76-85. Spanish.

AN: Review of five Chicano magazines of
California discussing their contents, both
literary and artistic, taking a critical
attitude toward both. The five are FUEGO DE
AZTLAN, VORTICE, PRISMA, MAIZE, and MANGO.

Make up
      USE: Fashion

Maldonado, Adal

5423 Opton, Suzanne. Short strokes. SAN FRANCISCO
FAULT, (December 29, 1971), p. 9-10.
English.

AN: The currently homeless Galeria de la
Raza has begun a series of wall painting
projects. Artist "Spain" did a Horizons
mural; Puerto Rican photographer Adal
Maldonado did photographic murals; Jerry
Concha, Tom Rios, did rooms in the Center
for Change drug program building, Chuy
Campusano, working with cartoonist R. Crumb,
and the Mission Rebel Kids did a cartoon
mural. Model Cities day care centers are
next to be painted.

Maldonado, Alexander

5424 Albright, Thomas. 'Unspoiled' Bay Area art.
SAN FRANCISCO CHRONICLE, (August 29, 1974),
p. 40. English.

AN: Review of an exhibit titled ART NAIF
curated by Rolando Castellon. The show
featured 15 Bay Area painters who are
basically self-taught and share a personal
expression unhampered by prevailing art
conventions and trends. Includes material on
Alexander Maldonado, 72-year-old "primitive"
painter from San Francisco. Some of
Maldonado's work includes references to his
childhood and youth in Mexico.

5425 Alex Maldonado, primitive painter. SAN
FRANCISCO FOCUS MAGAZINE, (1973). English.

AN: Biographical information on 72 year
old Alexander Maldonado who started painting
upon his retirement. His "naif" work has
gained wide critical acclaim and he has had
more than 200 exhibitions throughout the
United States. Illustrated with reproduction
of one of Maldonado's paintings.

5426 Edwards, Jim. The folk art tradition.
ARTWEEK, Vol. 6, no. 18 (May 3, 1975), p. 7.
English.

AN: Includes commentary on painter
Alexander Maldonado who is placed within the
surrealist mode. His imagination sees a dual
world of earthly landscapes filled with
strange architecture and celestial visions
in which the moon, stars and comets prevail.

Maldonado, Alexander (cont.)

5427 The Mexican Museum, San Francisco, CA.
Alexander Maldonado. Exhibition brochure,
1979. English.

AN: One page autobiographical statement
by Alexander Maldonado. Includes sources of
his imagery.

5428 Morch, Albert. Mexican art through a
cartoonist's eyes. SAN FRANCISCO EXAMINER,
(September 24, 1979), p. 28. English.

AN: Review of "GORDO'S WORLD" and the
paintings of Alexander Maldonado, an
exhibition at the Mexican Museum.
Biographical information on Gustavo Montano
Arriola, creator of the Gordo cartoon in
1941. The exhibit conceived and designed by
the San Diego Museum of Art, had
representative blow-ups of the strip along
with artifacts. Maldonado, a self-taught
artist started painting at age 60. His
canvases embrace a fascination with towers,
unique buildings, underground cities and
skylines from an imagined urban environment.

Male and Female Roles
USE: Sex Roles

Malinche

5429 Reyes, Felipe. Malinche complex [drawing].
REVISTA CHICANO-RIQUENA, Vol. 2, no. 3
(Summer 1974), p. 26. English.

5430 Reyes, Felipe. La Malinche [drawing].
REVISTA CHICANO-RIQUENA, Vol. 2, no. 3
(Summer 1974), p. 12. Spanish.

MAN RUNNING [sculpture]

5431 Raza sculptors coast to coast - Lujan y
Rodriguez. EL TECOLOTE LITERARY MAGAZINE,
Vol. 10, no. 9 (June 1980), p. 7. English.

AN: Pedro Lujan, originally from the
Southwest, now lives in SOHO in New York.
Lujan defines himself as a bricoleur who
works primarily with wood and simple tools
like hatchets and chisels. Ismael Rodriguez,
self-taught sculptor from Berkeley,
California, works in stone or wood. Includes
photo of Lujan's wood sculpture "Man
Running" and photo of Rodriguez at work.

Mandela, Nelson

5432 De Lappe, Pele. Saga of Rupert Garcia's
poster: from pen to UN. PEOPLE'S WORLD, Vol.
44, no. 28 (July 11, 1981), p. 10. English.

AN: Desiring to produce a poster on
Nelson Mandela and South African political
prisoners, San Francisco artist Rupert
Garcia, appealed for support to the African
National Congress, and the Liberation
Support Movement. The United Nations Center
Against Apartheid provided a grant for
production, indicating it should be
distributed free. Illustrated.

Mandeville Art Gallery, UC San Diego, La Jolla, CA

5433 Five views on Mexican culture. LA JOLLA
LIGHT, (September 10, 1981), p. B-6.
English.

AN: Review of a show at the University
of California, San Diego's Mandeville Art
Gallery called FIVE PHOTOGRAPHERS:
CONTEMPORARY VIEWS OF MEXICAN AND
MEXICAN-AMERICAN CULTURE and featuring
Arizona photographers Louis Carlos Bernal,
Robert C. Buitron, and three others.

5434 Mandeville Art Gallery, University of
California, San Diego. Five photographers:
contemporary views of Mexican and
Mexican-American culture. Exhibition
catalog, 1981. English.

AN: Catalog of exhibit including Louis
Carlos Bernal, Robert C. Buitron, Alberto
Lau, Richard Tichich, and Meridel
Rubenstein. Illustrated.

Mandeville Center, UC San Diego, La Jolla, CA

5435 Exhibit at UCSD: Chicana artist to show
works. LOS ANGELES TIMES [San Diego County
edition], (December 6, 1978), p. II, 8.
English.

AN: Artist and activist from San Diego,
Yolanda Lopez, will be showing sketches and
paintings at the Mandeville Center,
University of California, San Diego, from
which she was the first Chicana to graduate
with a Master's degree in visual arts. Her
show is based on her family, and the icon of
the Virgin of Guadalupe. Illustrated.

MANGO [journal], San Jose, CA

5436 Yarbro-Bejarano, Yvonne. Resena de revistas
chicanas: problemas y tendencias, Part I. LA
PALABRA, Vol. 2, no. 1 (Spring 1980), p.
76-85. Spanish.

AN: Review of five Chicano magazines of
California discussing their contents, both
literary and artistic, taking a critical
attitude toward both. The five are FUEGO DE
AZTLAN, VORTICE, PRISMA, MAIZE, and MANGO.

Manilla, Manuel

5437 Camacho, Eduardo. Por los cien anos de la
fundacion de su editorial: inauguraran hoy
en San Diego la exposicion 'Homenaje a
Posada, Manilla y Vanegas Arroyo'.
EXCELSIOR, (February 14, 1980). Spanish.

AN: Announcing the exhibit of 19th
Century Mexican engravers Jose Guadalupe
Posada and Manuel Manilla, with publisher
Antonio Vanegas Arroyo, at the Centro
Cultural de la Raza and Southwestern
College, of San Diego, CA.

5438 El Centro Cultural de La Raza, San Diego,
CA. One hundred year anniversary: Jose
Guadalupe Posada, Antonio Vanegas Arroyo.
Exhibition invitation, 1980. English.

AN: Invitation to an exhibition of
Mexican engravers Posada and Manuel Manilla
and an homage to their publisher. Also, a
"Chicano Tribute to Jose Guadalupe Posada,"
with contemporary works influenced by
Posada. At the Centro, and at Southwestern
College in Chula Vista.

Manning, Andrew

5439 Incorporated Artes Monumentales/Inc.,
Denver, CO. IAM: art exhibit. Exhibition
brochure, n.d. English.

AN: Large format, well illustrated
brochure with information on muralists
Roberto Lucero, Al Sanchez, Andrew Manning,
Ricardo Barrera and Bob Reyes. Includes some
biographical information situating these
artists within the dynamic artistic
traditions of the Mexican and the Chicano
mural movements.

Maps

5440 Mission community mural map. San Francisco,
CA: Galeria de la Raza, n.d.. English.

AN: Map showing ten sites for murals in
the San Franciso Mission District. Published
as a guide to a community mural tour.

Maradiaga, Ralph

5441 An.i.ma.tion: the arts, techniques, and
processes involved in giving apparent life
and movement to inanimate objects by means
of cinematography. San Francisco, CA:
Galeria de la Raza, n.d. English.

AN: Illustrated booklet on animation.
Reproductions and sequences illustrated by
Leslie Cabarga, Xavier Viramontes and Ralph
Maradiaga.

5442 Burkhardt, Dorothy. Chicano pride and anger
mix at 'Califas'. THE TAB, (April 12,
1981), p. 34. English.

AN: CALIFAS: AN EXHIBITION OF CHICANO
ARTISTS IN CALIFORNIA represents a
cross-section of artists exhibiting work for
at least ten years: Rupert Garcia, Ernie
Palomino, Eduardo Carrillo, Judy Baca, Rene
Yanez, Carmen Lomas Garza, Salvador Roberto
Torres, Roberto Chavez, Willie Herron, Ralph
Maradiaga, Sue Martinez, Jose Montoya,
Malaquias Montoya, Ramses Noriega and
Esteban Villa. Illustrated.

5443 Calendario de comida 1976. San Francisco,
CA: Galeria de la Raza, 1976. English.

AN: Handprinted silkscreen calendar
consisting of twelve sheets and a cover. The
work of the following artists is included:
Ralph Maradiaga, Juanishi Orozco, Francisco
Camplis, Ruben Guzman, Rodolfo Cuellar,
Xavier Viramontes, Jose Montoya, Esteban
Villa, Rene Yanez, Max Garcia and Louis "The
Foot" Gonzalez, Patricia Rodriguez, and
Ricardo Favela. All of the above are
associated with the Galeria de la Raza, or
the Royal Chicano Air Force of Sacramento,
CA.

5444 Corcoran Gallery of Art, Washington, D.C.
Images of an era: the American poster
1945-75. Washington, D.C.: Corcoran Gallery
of Art, 1976. English.

AN: Uncredited poster [La Raza
Silkscreen Center, San Francisco],
(centerfold). Posters by Rupert Garcia,
Linda Lucero, and Ralph Maradiaga, all of
San Francisco, CA. Introduction by John
Garriga. Essays by Margaret Cogswell, Milton
Glaser, Dore Ashton, Alan Gowens.

5445 Garcia, Rupert. 'Fifth Sun' Raza art show at
UC Berkeley Museum. EL TECOLOTE, Vol. 8, no.
3 (November 1977), p. 8+. English.

AN: Review of THE FIFTH SUN:
CONTEMPORARY TRADITIONAL CHICANO AND LATINO
ART, co-sponsored by University of
California, Berkeley Chicano Studies and
Arte Popular, and curated by artist Ralph
Maradiaga, co-director of Galeria de la
Raza, showing at the UC Berkeley Museum. It
will travel to the University of California,
Santa Barbara's Art Museum. Illustrated.

5446 Garcia, Rupert. Laminas de la Raza. San
Francisco: Garcia Litho and Printing
Service, 1975. English.

AN: Portfolio of drawings and prints by
Patricia Rodriguez, Ricardo Apodaca,
Xochitl, Domingo Rivera, Francisco Camplis,
Rafael Maradiaga, Tom Rios, Juan Fuentes,
Ricardo Diaz, Jose Romero, Consuelo Mendez,
Jose Antonio Burciaga, Irene Perez, Ricardo
Rios, Mike Rios, Graciela Carrillo, Rene
Yanez, Luis Talamantez, Guillermo Bermudez,
all from Northern California.

5447 Gonzales, Juan. Galeria de la Raza: "our
people deserve the best". EL TECOLOTE, Vol.
7, no. 11 (July 1977), p. 14. English.

AN: "We are not here to sell our art,
but to sell the idea of art." This could
well be the motto of Galeria de la Raza who
under co-directors Rene Yanez and Ralph
Maradiaga has become a key cultural
institution in the Mission District of San
Francisco. The two directors have a broad
definition of art that encompasses
everything from cartoons to craftwork. The
article details past exhibits and future
goals. A half-page photograph of the
exterior of Galeria de la Raza by Pilar
Mejia illustrates the article. Reprint of
article entitled "Our people deserve the
best" which appeared in NUESTRO, Vol. 1, no.
2 (May, 1977), p. 56-57.

5448 Gonzales, Juan. Regional report, The arts:
"Our people deserve the best". NUESTRO, Vol.
1, no. 2 (May 1977), p. 56-57. English.

AN: Activities of San Francisco's
Galeria de la Raza; interviews with its
directors, Rene Yanez and Ralph Maradiaga.
Reprinted as "Galeria de la Raza: our people
deserve the best" in EL TECOLOTE (San
Francisco, CA), Vol. 7, no. 11 (July, 1977),
p. 14.

5449 Gonzalez, Tobias and Gonzalez, Sandra.
Perspectives on Chicano education. Stanford,
CA: Stanford University, 1975. English.

AN: Reproductions of artworks by Ralph
Maradiaga, Patricia Rodriguez, Roberto
Bonilla, Francisco Camplis, Graciela
Carrillo-Lopez, Juan Fuentes, Irene Perez,
Roger Reyes, Carlos Loarca, Xavier
Viramontes, Ralph McNeill, Rupert Garcia,
Jose Romero.

Maradiaga, Ralph (cont.)

5450 La historia de California, 1977. San
Francisco, CA: Galeria de la Raza, 1977.
English.

AN: Handprinted silkscreen calendar of
history seen from a Mexican point of view.
Twelve sheets and a cover. Artists are:
Ralph Maradiaga, Irene Perez, Louie "The
Foot" Gonzalez, Max Garcia, Patricia
Rodriguez, Jose Romero, Esteban Villa,
Juanishi Orozco, Rodolfo Cuellar, Jose
Montoya, Xavier Viramontes, Rene Yanez,
Ricardo Favela, associated with the Galeria
de la Raza, or the Royal Chicano Air Force
of Sacramento.

5451 Martinez, Anita. Raza art. EL TECOLOTE, Vol.
1, no. 8 (November 30, 1970), p. 1. English.

AN: Jay Ojeda, newly selected director
of Galeria de la Raza, describes the
memorial exhibition dedicated to Ruben
Salazar installed at the Galeria on Dec. 12,
1970. Salazar symbolized and synthesized
many of the goals subscribed to by artist
members of La Galeria. The exhibit included
work by Chicano and Latino artists Francisco
Camplis, Jay Ojeda, Jose Romero, Rolando
Castellon, Rene Yanez, Luis Valsoto, Mike
Ruiz, Carlos Perez, Gustavo Rivera, Peter
Rodriguez, Carlos Loarca and Ralph
Maradiaga.

5452 San Francisco Museum of Art, San Francisco,
CA. M.I.X. graphics I: prints. Exhibition
invitation, 1974. English.

AN: Invitation to an exhibit of 15
multi-ethnic artists, including San
Francisco artists Ralph Maradiaga and Rupert
Garcia.

5453 Stofflet-Santiago, Mary. The fifth sun:
esthetic quality versus curatorial intent.
ARTWEEK, Vol. 8, no. 37 (November 5, 1977),
p. 6. English.

AN: Review of the exhibit THE FIFTH SUN
at the University Art Museum in Berkeley,
Calif., curated by Ralph Maradiaga of the
Galeria de la Raza. It contains folk art,
and posters by Chicano artists Maradiaga,
Rupert Garcia, Juan Fuentes, mural studies
by Graciela Carrillo and Mike Rios, ceramics
by Anna de Leon, an altar by Amalia
Mesa-Bains, and mural drawings by Mexican
muralists. The writer criticizes the uneven
quality of the show, but encourages better
ones in the future. Illustrated.

5454 Street, Sharon. Califas - a celebration of
Chicano culture and art. CITY ON A HILL,
(April 16, 1981). English.

AN: Review of an exhibit at College V's
Sesnon Gallery featuring 15 California
artists: Ramses Noriega, Judy Baca, Salvador
Roberto Torres, Malaquias Montoya, Rene
Yanez, Ralph Maradiaga, Jose Montoya,
Esteban Villa, Carmen Lomas Garza, Robert
Chavez, among others. Illustrated.

MARCH (Movimiento Artistico Chicano)
USE: Movimiento Artistico Chicano (MARCH),
Chicago, IL

MARCHA/PEREGRINACION DE LOS CAMPESINOS DE TEJAS

5455 Guerra, Luis. Hasta la gloria [drawing].
TEJIDOS, Vol. 4, no. 2 (Summer 1977), p.
COVER. Spanish.

5456 Guerra, Victor. Primavera: happy in Khaki.
TEJIDOS, Vol. 5, no. 2-4 (1978), p. 68.
English.

Marcos, Darlene

5457 Tucson Public Library; Sonoran Heritage; and
De la Cruz, Frank. Mexican American mural
art: the power of cultural identity.
Brochure, 1980. English.

AN: Brochure on Tucson murals painted by
Antonio Pazos, David Tineo, Danny Garza,
Cynthia Reyes, Darlene Marcos, Roberto
Borboa, and others.

Marfa, TX

5458 Thalacker, Donald W. The place of art in the
world of architecture. Chelsa House/R.R.
Bowker, n.d. English.

AN: Includes a chapter on Roberto Rios'
1978-79 mural for the Border Patrol Sector
Headquarters, Marfa, Texas.

Marijuana

5459 Galeria de la Raza/Studio 24, San Francisco,
CA. Photographs by Angel Del Valle. Los
sembradores: the marijuana growers.
Exhibition catalog, 1976. English.

AN: Illustrated catalog. Del Valle
documents the growing, customs, and
merchandising of marijuana in the Sierras of
Mexico.

Marin, Jose D.

5460 Galeria de arte de Aztlan. AZTLAN (U.S.
Penitentiary, Leavenworth, KA), Vol. 1, no.
2. English.

AN: Pictorial supplement with
reproductions of pinto art by Manuel
Aguilera, Jessie Hernandez, Ruben Estrella,
Tomas Torres and Jose D. Marin. Many of
these works were reproduced in other Chicano
newspapers demonstrating the solidarity that
existed in the Chicano movement inside and
outside the prison walls.

5461 Rodriguez, Pedro. Chicano art arising. PAPEL
CHICANO, Vol. 1, no. 9 (December 21, 1971),
p. 5. English.

AN: A concise formulation on the nature
of Chicano Art. It arises from a new
cultural formation influenced by Mexican and
Anglo American cultural forms yet distinct
from either. In visual terms, artists are
reflecting and affirming this new cultural
synthesis. Illustrated with reproductions of
three oil paintings: GRITO DE LIBERTAD by
Jose D. Marin, WOMAN IN BLUE by Manuel
Aguilera, and ALEGORIA MEXICANA by Tomas
Torres. All three are pinto artists from
Leavenworth Penitentiary.

Marin, Rosa

5462 Colectivo El Ojo. CHOQUE DE AMOR: fotonovela
     by Lamp. CHISMEARTE, Vol. 1, no. 4 (Fall ,
     Winter, 1977), p. 35-37. Bilingual.

     AN: Several students with the help of
     the Latin American Media Project (LAMP) and
     the Latin American Studies Department of
     California State University, Los Angeles
     produced the fotonovela CHOQUE DE AMOR, a
     variation on the typical "fotonovela"
     romance. This one encourages readers to
     reevaluate traditional female roles. The
     group also includes Kay Torres. Six frames
     of the fotonovela are reproduced.

5463 Lucas, Jerry and Gil de Montes, Roberto, et
     al. CHOQUE DE AMOR: fotonovela by Lamp. Los
     Angeles, CA: Colectivo El Ojo, Latin
     American Studies Dept., CSULA, 1979.
     English.

     AN: "Fotonovela" featuring Elsa Flores,
     Rosa Marin, and Jerry Lucas produced by the
     collective work of Lucas, Roberto Gil de
     Montes, Mario Massinelli, Luis Soto, and Kay
     Torres.

Martinez, Agueda

5464 Vasquez, Esperanza and Esparza, Moctezuma.
     Agueda Martinez. 16 mm. color film. English.

     AN: Sixteen-minute film directed by
     Esperanza Vasquez and produced by Moctezuma
     Esparza concerning the life and weaving of
     an elderly New Mexican woman. Martinez
     carries on the tradition of floor loom
     weaving, as well as farming.

Martinez, Andres

5465 Guadalupe Historic Foundation, Santa Fe, NM.
     Artes en la primavera. (1981). English.

     AN: Catalog of exhibit by four New
     Mexico artists: Manuel Lopez, sculptor from
     Chili; Andres Martinez, painter from Santa
     Cruz; Victoria Lopez, colcha embroiderer
     from San Pedro; Sam Quintana, jeweler from
     La Mesilla.

Martinez, Baltazar

5466 Sutherland-Martinez, Elizabeth. Corazon del
     norte: Baltasar Martinez. GRITO DEL NORTE,
     Vol. 2, no. 2 (January 29, 1968), p. 5.
     English.

     AN: Baltazar Martinez from Conjilon (one
     of the defendants in the Tierra Amarilla
     Courthouse "Raid" Case) is a noted naif
     painter. This article focuses on his
     methods, techniques and subject matter. His
     work is related to that current of cultural
     production outside mainstream channels.
     Illustrated with photograph of artist and
     several of his paintings.

Martinez, Cesar Augusto

5467 59th Street Gallery, St. Louis, MO. Midwest
     Mexican-American art exhibit: Mexico and its
     artists. Exhibition brochure, 1981. English.

     AN: Sponsored by the Sociedad Mexicana
     "Benito Juarez" and the international
     Institute of St. Louis, this three-part
     exhibit includes 1) MEXICO AS SEEN BY HER
     CHILDREN, a bilingual exhibit from Mexico
     traveling under Smithsonian Institution
     auspices, 2) MEXICAN CHILDREN IN THE U.S.A.,
     3) MEXICAN AMERICAN ARTISTS. In the latter

are included Stephen Capiz (Roseville,
Minn.), Jose Gonzalez (Chicago), Cesar A.
Martinez (San Antonio), Ada Medina (Des
Moines), Nora Chapa Mendoza (West
Bloomfield, Mich.), Rene David
Michel-Trapaga (St. Louis), David Munoz
(Kansas City, Mo.), Jose Luis Narezo (Grand
Rapids, Mich.), Benny Ordonez, Roman
Villarreal (Chicago), Alejandro Romero
(Chicago), Aurelio Diaz "Tekpankalli"
(Chicago), Simon Ybarra (St. Louis).

5468 Alurista. Timespace huracan: poems,
     1972-1975. Albuquerque, NM: Pajarito
     Publications, 1976. English.

     AN: Seven woodcuts by Cesar Augusto
     Martinez.

5469 Le Bistro Restaurant, San Antonio, TX.
     Contemporary paintings by Cesar Augusto
     Martinez. Exhibition catalog, 1980. English.

     AN: Catalog of an exhibit. Blurb about
     the artist.

5470 Cardenas de Dwyer, Carlota, ed. Chicano
     voices. Boston, MS: Houghton Mifflin, 1975.
     English.

     AN: Includes artwork by: Peter
     Rodriguez, Arturo Anselmo Roman, Carmen
     Lomas Garza, Santa Barraza, and Cesar
     Augusto Martinez.

5471 Cesar Martinez. ARTES VISUALES, no. 29 (June
     1981), p. 63. Bilingual.

     AN: Two illustrations by the San
     Antonio, Texas artist, a brief biography,
     and the reprint of a letter published in the
     catalog CUATRO CAMINOS, Southwest Texas
     State University, San Marcos.

5472 Chicano art of the Southwest. San Antonio,
     TX: Instituto Chicano de Artes y Artesanias
     of the Texas Institute for Educational
     Development, 1975. English.

     AN: Collection of 220 slides
     supplemented by slide annotation and
     artists' biographies researched and
     photographed by Texas artist Cesar A.
     Martinez over two years. Biographies cover
     20 Texas, 6 New Mexico, and 15 northern
     California artists. Slides include, in
     addition, murals from Los Angeles and San
     Diego.

5473 Con Safo. San Antonio, TX: Pintores Chicanos
     de San Antonio, [ca. 1975]. English.

     AN: Illustrated pamphlet issued by the
     San Antonio artists' group Con Safo.
     Includes a self-definition and a brief
     history of the group under the names El
     Grupo, Los Pintores de Aztlan, Los Pintores
     de la Nueva Raza, Con Safo (from 1967 on).
     Members include Jesse A. Almazan, Mel Casas,
     Jose Esquivel, Jose P. Garza, Cesar Augusto
     Martinez, Santos Martinez, Felipe Reyes,
     Roberto Rios, Jesus C. Trevino, and Vicente
     Velasquez.

Martinez, Cesar Augusto (cont.)

5474 Contemporary Arts Museum, Houston, TX. Dale gas: give it gas. The continued acceleration of Chicano art. Exhibition catalog, 1977. English.

AN: A comprehensive catalog including 28 works of art exhibited by 13 Texas artists: Melesio (Mel) Casas, Jose Esquivel, Francisco (Frank) Fajardo, Carmen Lomas Garza, Luis Jimenez, Cesar Augusto Martinez, Santos G. Martinez, Jr., Amado Pena, Roberto Rios, Jose Rivera, Joe B. Rodriguez, Jesus (Jesse) Trevino, and George Truan. Many illustrations, some in color. Introduction by James Harithas. Essay by Santos Martinez, Jr. Poetry, literature and essays by Chicano writers.

5475 Contemporary Arts Museum, Houston, TX. Fire! An exhibition of 100 Texas artists. Exhibition brochure, 1979. English.

AN: Includes eleven Chicano artists. Unfortunately, not illustrated, though a checklist of works is included. Mel Casas, Carmen Lomas Garza, Xavier Gorena, Luis Jimenez, Cesar Martinez, Guillermo Z. Pulido, Philip Renteria, Jose L. Rivera, Joe Rodriguez, George Truan, Juan B. Vela. Introduction by James Surls. Statements by the artists.

5476 Contemporary Arts Museum, Houston, TX and Martinez, Santos G., Jr. Mexican movie posters. Exhibition invitation, 1979. English.

AN: Invitation to an exhibit of posters primarily from the collecttion of Enrique Flores and Xavier Gorena of Xochil Art Center, Mission, Texas. Martinez considers the posters monumental, with expressive qualities that have influenced Chicano poster makers like the Royal Chicano Air Force, and Rupert Garcia, and Texas artists like Luis Jimenez, Jesse Trevino and Cesar Martinez. One illustration. Introduction by guest curator Santos G. Martinez, Jr. (See Rupert Garcia's essay in the exhibition catalog: POSTERS FROM THE GOLDEN AGE OF MEXICAN CINEMA, for another point of view).

5477 Corpus Christy State University for the Arts and Weil Gallery Center for the Arts, Corpus Christi State University. Southwest artists invitational: an exhibition of contemporary art by seven Texas artists of Hispanic American descent. Ehxibition brochure, 1980. English.

AN: Artists Jesse Almazan, Luis Jimenez, Cesar Martinez, Lydia Martinez, Manuel Mauricio, Guillermo Pulido, and Jesse Trevino show a variety of techniques and styles. Text by Roberto Tomas Esparza. Statements by and about the artists. Illustrated.

5478 Crossley, Mimi. Tejano artists. HOUSTON POST, (August 19, 1976). English.

AN: Exhibition of 19 Texas artists organized by Joe Rodriguez of the AAMA (Association for the Advancement of Mexican Americans) Art Center in Houston, Texas. Working within a wide range of styles and a great scope of subject matter. Includes brief commentary on the work of Amado Pena, Carmen Lomas Garza, Cesar Martinez, Enrique Campos, Carolina Flores, Jesus Trevino and a host of others.

5479 Estudios Rio: gallery of contemporary arts and crafts. Exhibition catalog, 1976. English.

AN: Catalog including identification, portraits and works of participating artists: Joe Bova, Enrique Flores, Carmen Lomas Garza, Xavier Gorena, Erik Gronborg, Lucas Hinojosa, Ben Holland, Kris Hotvedt, William Kaars-Sijpesteijn, Cesar Martinez, Chris Mende, Roberto Mungia, Steve Reynolds, Vicente Rodriguez, William Wilhelmi.

5480 First Federal Plaza Display Gallery, Austin, TX. Tejano artists: an exhibit of Mexican-American art. Exhibit brochure, 1976. English.

AN: Announcement of exhibit illustrated by Cesar A. Martinez's woodcut.

5481 Galeria de la Raza, San Antonio, TX. Celebration seventy-four. Exhibition catalog, [ca. 1974]. English.

AN: Catalog of extensive exhibition including European, Mexican, and the following Texan Chicano artists: Rolando Garces, Cesar Martinez, Ray Chavez, Vicente Rodriguez, Jorge Garza, Alfred Rodriguez, Luis Guerra, Carmen Lomas Garza, Bruno Andrade, Jr., Amado M. Pena Jr., Roberto Rios, Jose Trevino, Rudy Trevino, Luis Santoyo, Tati Rubio, Eduardo C. Garza, Arthur de la Fuente, and Jesus Campos Trevino.

5482 Galeria de la Raza/Studio 24, San Francisco, CA. Ajo, granadas y tres flores. Exhibition announcement, 1981.

AN: Announcement for an exhibition featuring Ruben Trejo, sculpture (Spokane, Washington), Cesar A. Martinez, paintings (San Antonio, Texas), Xavier Gorena, paper cut-outs (Mission, Texas).

5483 Galeria de la Raza/Studio 24, San Francisco, CA. Images of the Southwest. Exhibition catalog, 1977. English.

AN: Invitation/catalog for an exhibit including Rudy M. Fernandez(Utah), Enrique Flores(Texas), Xavier Gorena(Texas), C.A.[Cesar] Martinez(Texas), Santos Martinez, Jr.(Texas), Pedro Rodriguez(Texas), Arnold Trujillo(New Mexico). Block prints, paper cut-outs, drawings, photographs, copper enamels, and sculpture were shown. Five illustrations.

5484 Goldman, Shifra M. Chicano art alive and well in Texas: a 1981 update. REVISTA CHICANO-RIQUENA, Vol. 9, no. 1 (Winter 1981), p. 34-40. English.

AN: Reprint of article published as "Supervivencia y prosperidad del arte chicano en Texas: nueva revision" in COMUNIDAD (Los Angeles, CA) [Sunday Supplement to LA OPINION], September 21, 1980, p. 3, 15+.

Martinez, Cesar Augusto (cont.)

5485 Goldman, Shifra M. Supervivencia y
prosperidad del arte chicano en Texas: nueva
revision. COMUNIDAD, Vol. 55, no. 5
(September 21, 1980), p. 3,15+. Spanish.

AN: Focuses on six Chicano artists from
Austin, Houston, San Antonio, and
Kingsville: Mel Casas, Cesar Martinez, Amado
M. Pena, Leo Tanguma, Carmen Lomas Garza,
and Santa Barraza. Well illustrated. This
article was reprinted as "Chicano Art Alive
and Well in Texas: A 1981 Update," in
REVISTA CHICANO-RIQUENA (Houston), Vol. 9,
no. 1, Winter 1981, p. 34-40.

5486 Instituto Chicano de Artes y Artesanias
(Texas Instit. Educational Development) and
Instituto Cultural Mexicano (SER/UNAM), San
Antonio, TX. Artistas chicanos: Los
Quemados. San Antonio, TX: Instituto
Chicano, Texas Institute for Educational
Development, 1975. English.

AN: Invitation to an exhibit and
manifesto of 1975 Austin-San Antonio
artists' group, Los Quemados. Included Santa
Barraza, Carolina Flores, Carmen Lomas
Garza, Luis Guerra, Cesar Augusto Martinez,
Santos Martinez, Amado Maurilio Pena, Jr.,
Jose Rivera, Vicente Rodriguez, Jose
Trevino.

5487 Instituto Chicano de Artes y Artesanias
(Texas Instit. Educational Development).
Chicano art of the Southwest. San Antonio,
TX: Texas Institute for Educational
Development, [ca. 1975]. English.

AN: Illustrated brochure announcing a
color slide library on Chicano art
supplemented by slide annotation and artists
biographies available to institutions.
Statement of purpose by Executive Director
of program, Cesar Augusto Martinez.

5488 Martinez, Cesar Augusto; Garcia-Camarillo,
Mia; and Garcia-Camarillo, Cecilio. Don Juan
Volador, Platica con Cesar Augusto Martinez.
CARACOL, Vol. 2, no. 4 (December 1975), p.
3-5. Spanish.

AN: Interview with Cesar Martinez about
his acrylic painting DON JUAN VOLADOR. Based
on themes suggested by the writings of
Carlos Castaneda, the painting deals with
the spiritual nature of Chicanismo. This
issue of CARACOL is illustrated by the
painting in question.

5489 Mendiville, Miguel and Saavedra-Vela, Pilar.
A time for less talk and more action.
AGENDA, Vol. 7, no. 5 (September, October,
1977), p. 33-34. English.

AN: The exhibit RAICES Y VISIONES,
funded by the National Endowment for the
Arts, was composed of more than 100 artworks
by Chicano and Latino artists and toured the
United States in 1977. The exposition was
organized in four sections; artists whose
work is influenced or related to
Pre-Columbian art, art that explores social
and political realities, and works that are
more personal and introspective. Gives
itinerary and listing of participating
artists. Illustrated by photographs of the
work of Rudy Trevino, Cesar Martinez, Luis
Jimenez from Texas and Larry Fuente from
California.

5490 San Antonio Museum Association, San Antonio,
TX. Visiones nuevas en Tejas/new visions in
Texas. Exhibtion catalog, 1979. English.

AN: Supplementary regional catalog for
the exhibit RAICES ANTIGUAS/VISIONES NUEVAS;
ANCIENT ROOTS/NEW VISIONS. Illustrations for
works by George Cisneros, Francisco (Frank)
Fajardo, Robert Gonzalez, Cesar Augusto
Martinez, Roland Mazuca, Guillermo Pulido,
Felipe Reyes, Jesus (Jesse) Trevino.

5491 Smith, Roberta. Twelve days of Texas. ART IN
AMERICA, Vol. 64, no. 4 (July, August,
1976), p. 42-48. English.

AN: Overview of Texas art in Fort
Worth/Dallas, Houston, San Antonio, Tyler,
and Galveston. Includes reproductions of
works by Luis Jimenez (color, on cover),
Roberto Rios mural, Jesse Trevino, Mel
Casas. Also mentioned in text are Phil
Renteria and Cesar Martinez.

5492 Southwest Texas State University, San
Marcos, TX and Carlisle, Charles Richard.
Cuatro caminos: four perspectives on Chicano
art. Exhibition catalog, 1980. English.

AN: Exhibition pamphlet with photographs
of the artists. Alex Flores, Luis Jimenez,
Cesar Augusto Martinez and Amado Pena, Jr.
comment on their work and the Chicano art
movement.

5493 Valdez, Armando. El calendario chicano 1977.
Hayward, CA: Southwest Network, 1977.
English.

AN: Fifth in a series of historical
calendars produced in 1972, 1974, 1975, 1976
by La Causa Publications and Southwest
Network. Artists whose work is reproduced
are Malaquias Montoya, Amado Maurilio Pena,
Ramori Zamora, Glugio J.L. Nicandro [Gronk],
Etta Delgado, Ricardo Alaniz, Diane Gamboa,
Elisa Marina Coleman, Margarita Calderon,
Jose Antonio Burciaga, Cesar Augusto
Martinez, Maria Ochoa y Valtierra, Juan
Renteria Fuentes, from California, New
Mexico, and Texas.

5494 Woodcuts by Cesar Augusto Martinez.
Albuquerque, NM: Pajarito Publications,
1976, p. 13, 29, 43, 54, 74, 90, 96.
English.

AN: Seven woodcuts from 1975-1976 by the
San Antonio artist.

5495 Xochil Art and Culture Center, Mission, TX.
!Que te vaya pretty nice! Exhibition
brochure, 1979. English.

AN: Exhibition of Chicano art including
Carmen Lomas Garza, Luis Jimenez, Cesar
Martinez, Guillermo Pulido, Roberto Rios,
Jose Rivera and Jesse Trevino. [See also
Estudios Rio].

Martinez, Daniel

5496 Blanco, Gil. Art on the walls: a vehicle for
positive change. LATIN QUARTER, Vol. 1, no.
2 (October 1974), p. 26-30. English.

AN: East Los Angeles artists Ismael
"Smiley" Pereira and C.W. (Charles) Felix
started painting murals with young people at
the Estrada Courts Housing Project in May
1973. There are now more 30 murals, and the
residents are more receptive, noting the
changes that are taking place. Illustrated
with murals by Herron and Gronk, and Daniel
Martinez.

Martinez, Daniel (cont.)

5497 Los Angeles Municipal Art Gallery, Los
Angeles, CA. Multicultural focus: a
photography exhibition for the Los Angeles
Bicentennial. Exhibition catalog, 1981.
English.

AN: Catalog of an exhibit demonstrating
the multi-ethnic character of Los Angeles.
Chicano photographers include Don Anton, Ron
Bernal, Daniel Martinez, Rick Tejada-Flores.
Illustrated.

Martinez, Dennis

5498 Garcia-Camarillo, Cecilio and Martinez,
Dennis. Platicando con Dennis Martinez.
RAYAS, Vol. 1, no. 5 (September, October,
1978), p. 12, 11. Bilingual.

AN: Interview with Dennis Martinez,
illustrator of BLESS ME ULTIMA, NAMBE: YEAR
ONE, and MI ABUELA FUMABA PUROS. The books
share New Mexican setting and their
illustrator seeks to capture the essence of
the landscape in that region. In his
drawings Dennis Martinez hopes to evoke
history in relation to landscape and
culture. Illustrated.

5499 Romero, Orlando. Nambe - year one. Berkeley,
Ca: Tonatiuh International, 1976. English.

AN: Illustrations by Dennis Martinez.

Martinez, Eddie

5500 Nevarez, Joe R. Chicano art blooms in barrio
warehouse. LOS ANGELES TIMES, (December 26,
1974), p. I, 32. English.

AN: Former meat packing warehouse
transformed into Goez Art Studios by Joe and
John Gonzalez. Exhibiting David Negron,
Eddie Martinez, David Lopez (Hollywood
scenic artists) and Roberto Arenivar. Lists
activities of the gallery: exhibits, murals,
restoration.

Martinez, Efrain

5501 Calendario de March: 1977. Chicago, IL:
MARCH, Inc., 1976. English.

AN: Historical calendar with photos and
biographies of artists. Illustrations of
artwork by Ray Patlan, Jose Nario, Frank J.
Sanchez, Salvador Dominguez, Salvador Vega,
Marguerite Ortega, Aurelio Diaz, Carlos
Cortez, Mario E. Castillo, Francisco Blasco,
Rey Vasquez, and Efrain Martinez. History of
MARCH (Movimiento Artistico Chicano).

Martinez, Filomeno

5502 La Sociedad Historica de Nuestra Senora de
Guadalupe, Santa Fe, NM. Meditacion.
Exhibition invitation, 1980. English.

AN: Invitation to an exhibit by four
artists: Filomeno Martinez (graphic artist,
Albuquerque), Ruben Montoya (santero, Santa
Fe), Santiago Chavez (painter, Santa Rosa),
Jose Alberto Baros (sculptor, Espanola).

Martinez, Frank

5503 Mascorro, Julie. Mechicano Art Center
exhibit to grace Price gallery walls. CAMPUS
NEWS, (November 24, 1971). English.

AN: Brief history of Mechicano Art
Center activities from its establishment in

1969 to 1971. Exhibiting are Charles
Almaraz, Roberto Amaral, Raymond Atilano,
William Bejarano, Armando Cabrera, Edward
Carbajal, Leonard Castellanos, Henry de
Vega, Antonio Esparza, Bob Gomez, Lucila V.
Grijalva, Jesus Gutierrez, Santos Lira,
Frank Martinez, Ernest Palomino, Louis
Quijada, Richard Raya, Frank Romero.
Illustrated.

5504 Mechicano Art Center. Los Angeles, CA:
Mechicano Art Center, 1971. English.

AN: Announcement of an exhibit by
painters Ramon Atilano, Xavier Lopez Ortega,
and Frank A. Martinez. Martinez and Lopez
Ortega are also muralists. Brief profiles of
the artists. Illustrated.

5505 Musica hispana en nuestras vidas/Hispanic
music in our lives: almanaque 1982/calendar.
Milwaukee, WI: Miller Brewing Co., 1981.
English.

AN: Twelve Latino artists were
commissioned to illustrate a calendar with
paintings on Hispanic music. The Chicano
artists include Frederico Vigil (New
Mexico), Joe Bastida Rodriguez
(Texas/Washington, D.C.), Manuel Martinez
(Colorado), Jose Antonio Burciaga
(California), Ignacio Gomez (California),
Carolina Flores (Texas), Frank Martinez
(California). Color.

5506 Street art explosion in Los Angeles. SUNSET,
(April 1973), p. 110-113. English.

AN: Illustrated article on Los Angeles
street murals including those by Roberto
Chavez, Willie Herron, Frank Romero, Richard
Jimenez, William Bejarano, Gilbert Lujan,
Armando Cabrera, Frank Martinez, Charles
Felix, and others.

5507 [Untitled photograph]. LOS ANGELES TIMES,
(June 4, 1971), p. II, 2. English.

AN: Captioned illustration of Frank
Martinez's mural painting of slain LOS
ANGELES TIMES reporter Ruben Salazar.
Unveiling of the mural at the Doctor's
Hospital, East Los Angeles, during
groundbreaking ceremonies for a new wing.

Martinez, Gilberto

5508 Galeria de la Raza/Studio 24, San Francisco,
CA; Sorell, Victor A.; and Vaughan, Kay.
Images of the Mexican Revolution:
photographs by Agustin V. Casasola.
Exhibition catalog, 1980. English.

AN: Catalog of an exhibit of Mexican
photographer Agustin V. Casasola from prints
owned by the Martinezes of Lansing, MI. The
exhibit traveled to Raza galleries in many
parts of the United States. Illustrated.

Martinez, Guillermo

5509 Wilson, William. 30 works from the grass
     roots. LOS ANGELES TIMES, (June 4, 1973),
     p. IV,2. English.

     AN: Review of a show at the Junior Arts
     Center in Barnsdall Park by 15 members of
     the Mechicano Art Center. The critic feels
     contemporary groups that aim for change
     today (unlike past groups) are unable to
     articulate their spirit in a cohesive style.
     The top talent in this show is Charles
     Almaraz; also on exhibit are paintings by
     Jose Cervantes, Guillermo Martinez, Ray
     Atilano, sculpture by Manuel Cruz, and
     photography by (Oscar) R. Castillo.

Martinez, Larry

5510 DE COLORES. Vol. 2, no. 4 (1976), p. 1-68.
     English.

     AN: Photographs by Moises Medina, Jose
     Luis Sedano; drawings by Jerry Lujan,
     Gilbert "Sparky" Espinoza, Rebecca Polanco;
     paintings by John Herrera, Sonny Duran,
     Larry Martinez. Cover by Fernando Penalosa.

Martinez, Lydia

5511 Corpus Christy State University for the Arts
     and Weil Gallery Center for the Arts, Corpus
     Christi State University. Southwest artists
     invitational: an exhibition of contemporary
     art by seven Texas artists of Hispanic
     American descent. Ehxibition brochure, 1980.
     English.

     AN: Artists Jesse Almazan, Luis Jimenez,
     Cesar Martinez, Lydia Martinez, Manuel
     Mauricio, Guillermo Pulido, and Jesse
     Trevino show a variety of techniques and
     styles. Text by Roberto Tomas Esparza.
     Statements by and about the artists.
     Illustrated.

Martinez, Manuel

5512 Culver, Virginia. Church's secession
     depicted on canvas. DENVER POST: RELIGION
     NEWS WEEKLY, (June 24, 1977). English.

     AN: Article commenting on mural created
     by Manuel Martinez as part of a secession
     movement by St. Mary's Episcopal Church in
     Denver whose members voted to leave the
     Episcopal Diocese of Colorado and the
     national Episcopal Church. Details of the
     controversy and examination of the
     iconography in Martinez's mural. Illustrated
     with photograph of controversial mural.

5513 Denver. NATIONAL MURALS NETWORK COMMUNITY
     NEWSLETTER, (Spring 1980), p. 10. English.

     AN: Denver, Colorado murals by Manuel
     Martinez, the Chilean Orlando Letelier
     Brigade, Roberto Lucero, Al Sanchez, Jerry
     Jaramillo. Illustrated.

5514 Martinez, Manuel. The art of the Chicano
     movement, and the movement of Chicano art.
     In: Valdez, Luis and Steiner, Stan eds.
     AZTLAN: AN ANTHOLOGY OF MEXICAN AMERICAN
     LITERATURE. New York: Vintage, 1972,
     p.349-353. English.

     AN: "Like the modern art of Mexico, the
     new Chicano art is essentially an art of
     social protest," writes Denver, Colorado
     muralist and easel painter Martinez. He
     traces the roots of Chicano art back into
     Indian, colonial and modern Mexican art, and

defines two kinds of Chicano art.

5515 Martinez, Manuel. Promotional brochure.
     Brochure, n.d. English.

     AN: Biographical information on Chicano
     muralist who was a pupil of David Alfaro
     Siqueiros. Illustrated with photographs of
     two acrylic murals and a photo of the
     artist.

5516 Montoya, Emmanuel; Rodriguez, Patricia; and
     Acevedo, Mario (Torero). Canto al pueblo
     '78. NATIONAL MURALS NETWORK COMMUNITY
     NEWSLETTER, (1978). English.

     AN: The second annual Canto al Pueblo
     took place in Corpus Christi, Texas, where
     more than six murals were painted: "Wall of
     Cultural Education" by 13 artists headed by
     Roel Montealva; Carlota Espinoza, with
     children; Gilberto Romero, Jose Antonio
     Burciaga and Patricia Rodriguez,
     "Incomprehension al arte"; "Madre Tierra" by
     Manuel Martinez of Denver with Amador
     Hinojosa (Corpus Christi) and Enriquette
     Vasquez (New Mexico); Mario Torero; Salvador
     Vega of Chicago whose mural some Canto
     participants considered "insulting".

5517 Musica hispana en nuestras vidas/Hispanic
     music in our lives: almanaque 1982/calendar.
     Milwaukee, WI: Miller Brewing Co., 1981.
     English.

     AN: Twelve Latino artists were
     commissioned to illustrate a calendar with
     paintings on Hispanic music. The Chicano
     artists include Frederico Vigil (New
     Mexico), Joe Bastida Rodriguez
     (Texas/Washington, D.C.), Manuel Martinez
     (Colorado), Jose Antonio Burciaga
     (California), Ignacio Gomez (California),
     Carolina Flores (Texas), Frank Martinez
     (California). Color.

5518 NATIONAL MURALS NETWORK COMMUNITY
     NEWSLETTER. (Spring 1980). English.

     AN: Reports on the Sept. 1979 conference
     of Chicano visual arts held at UT Austin,
     organized by the Mujeres Artistas del
     Suroeste, and the Liga Unida de Chicanos
     Artistas, which brought together
     participants from the U.S. and Mexico City;
     on Manuel Martinez's five murals (1976-78);
     murals by Roberto Lucero, Al Sanchez, and
     Jerry Jaramillo; as well as by the Chilean
     group Orlando Letelier Brigade, all in
     Denver, Colorado; murals by Leo Tanguma in
     Houston; the story about the "forbidden"
     Chicano mural in Blue Island, Illinois.
     Illustrated.

5519 Pared da historia de la Raza. PAPEL CHICANO,
     Vol. 1, no. 4 (September 26, 1971). English.

     AN: Discussion of Manuel Martinez' wall
     painting at Parque Aztlan titled PASADO,
     PRESENTE Y FUTURO DE LA RAZA BRONCE. Among
     the images used to convey the theme are
     Emiliano Zapata, Quetzalcoatl, a mestizo
     three faceted head symbolizing the
     indigenous mother, the Spanish father and
     the mestizo child. Included also is a symbol
     formed by four clasped hands suggesting
     unity among world faces. Illustrated with
     photograph of wall painting.

Martinez, Manuel (cont.)

5520 Sinisi, J. Sebastian J. Following footsteps
     of Diego Rivera. CONTEMPORARY, (January 13,
     1980), p. 28-30. English.

     AN: Story on West Denver murals,
     particularly by Manuel Martinez and Carlos
     Sandoval at the La Alma Recreation Center,
     Summer 1979. Murals done through the Denver
     City Walls Project by artists belonging to
     Incorporated Artes Monumentales.
     Illustrated.

5521 Troelstrup, Glenn. Former delinquent paints
     his way out of corner. DENVER POST, (April
     23, 1977), p. 2. English.

     AN: Manuel Martinez started sketching at
     13; at 29, after studying with Siqueiros
     (1967-68), he painted a number of murals in
     Denver and Albuquerque. In 1977 he organized
     Incorporated Artists Monumentales. Color
     illustration.

Martinez, Minerva

5522 Galeria de la Raza/Studio 24, San Francisco,
     CA; Sorell, Victor A.; and Vaughan, Kay.
     Images of the Mexican Revolution:
     photographs by Agustin V. Casasola.
     Exhibition catalog, 1980. English.

     AN: Catalog of an exhibit of Mexican
     photographer Agustin V. Casasola from prints
     owned by the Martinezes of Lansing, MI. The
     exhibit traveled to Raza galleries in many
     parts of the United States. Illustrated.

Martinez, Pedro

5523 Vergara, Dora Maria. New artist del barrio
     Canta Ranas. REVISTA RIO BRAVO, Vol. 1, no.
     1 (Winter 1981), p. 2. English.

     AN: Biography of self-taught artist
     Pedro Martinez who lives in and records the
     life and people of the westside barrio
     "Cantaranas" in Laredo, Texas. Five drawings
     reproduced in this issue.

Martinez, Raul

5524 Notes on 2nd National Community Muralists'
     Network Conference, Chicago, Ill. April
     20-23, 1978. San Francisco, CA, 1978.
     English.

     AN: Rupert Garcia, Raul Martinez,
     Patricia Rodriguez, Ray Patlan (San
     Francisco Bay Area) and Jaime Valadez (San
     Jose), among others, attended the conference
     in Chicago. Reports were heard from many
     parts of the United States on mural
     activities, including that of Aurelio Diaz
     of Chicago, representing MARCH (Movimiento
     Artistico Chicano). A workshop presentation
     was made by Luis Arenal and others from the
     Taller Siqueiros of Cuernavaca, Mexico. An
     experimental mural to try Siqueiros'
     techniques was created. Illustrated.

Martinez, Richard

5525 Art Gallery, California State University,
     Long Beach and Lujan, Gilbert Sanchez
     "Magu". El arte del pocho. Exhibit brochure,
     October 1968. English.

     AN: Information about Southern
     California artists John Deheras, Marcus
     Villagran, Roberto de la Rocha, Santos
     Zuniga, Crispin Gonzales, Richard Martinez,
     Jesus Gutierrez, Ed Oropeza, Pete Mendez,

David Ramirez, Gilbert Sanchez Lujan, Willie
Hernandez, Art Ponce, Carmen Tostado, Al
Almeida, David Ceja, Robert E. Chavez,
Thomas A. Ferriera. All art students,
graduates, or faculty.

Martinez, Rick

5526 Guggenheim Gallery, Chapman College, Orange,
     CA. Hexagono: paintings, sculpture,
     drawings, prints. Exhibit invitation, 1977.
     English.

     AN: Invitation to an exhibit for artists
     Tito Aguirre, Isabel Castro, Rick Martinez,
     Esau Quiroz, Linda Vallejo, Emigdio Vasquez,
     Barrows, and Shanahan, sponsored by MEChA.
     Profiles and pictures of the artists.

Martinez, Rudy

5527 Moisan, Jim. Ancient roots, new visions.
     ARTWEEK, Vol. 9, no. 26 (July 29, 1978), p.
     8. English.

     AN: Review of the show held at the
     Municipal Arts Gallery of Los Angeles, the
     first national touring show of Latino
     artists in the United States. Includes
     commentary on work of Larry Fuente, Luis
     Jimenez, Frank Romero, Harry Gamboa, Gronk,
     Rudy Martinez, Benjamin Serrano, Ricardo
     Diaz, Patssi Valdez, Mel Casas, Luis Leroy,
     Pedro Lujan. A related show, NEW VISIONS,
     L.A., includes Robert Delgado, Ray Bravo,
     Joe Moran, Rosalyn Mesquita, Patricia
     Murillo and others.

5528 Orth, Maureen. The soaring spirit of Chicano
     arts. NEW WEST MAGAZINE, Vol. 3, no. 19
     (September 11, 1978), p. 41-46. English.

     AN: Overview of California Chicano
     culture. Color illustrations of works by
     Mexican muralist David Alfaro Siqueiros,
     Rupert Garcia, Mujeres Muralistas, Willie
     Herron, Rene Yanez, Rudy Martinez, San
     Diego's Chicano Park, ASCO, Jose Montoya.

Martinez, Santos G., Jr.

5529 Canto al pueblo: an anthology of
     experiences. San Antonio, TX: Penca Books,
     1978. English.

     AN: Includes works by: Mario E.
     Castillo, Carlos Rosas, Jose G. Gonzalez,
     Santos Martinez, Gilbert Munoz, Fred Loa,
     Armando Ibanez and others.

5530 Con Safo. San Antonio, TX: Pintores Chicanos
     de San Antonio, [ca. 1975]. English.

     AN: Illustrated pamphlet issued by the
     San Antonio artists' group Con Safo.
     Includes a self-definition and a brief
     history of the group under the names El
     Grupo, Los Pintores de Aztlan, Los Pintores
     de la Nueva Raza, Con Safo (from 1967 on).
     Members include Jesse A. Almazan, Mel Casas,
     Jose Esquivel, Jose P. Garza, Cesar Augusto
     Martinez, Santos Martinez, Felipe Reyes,
     Roberto Rios, Jesus C. Trevino, and Vicente
     Velasquez.

Martinez, Santos G., Jr (cont.)

5531 Contemporary Arts Museum, Houston, TX. Dale gas: give it gas. The continued acceleration of Chicano art. Exhibition catalog, 1977. English.

AN: A comprehensive catalog including 28 works of art exhibited by 13 Texas artists: Melesio (Mel) Casas, Jose Esquivel, Francisco (Frank) Fajardo, Carmen Lomas Garza, Luis Jimenez, Cesar Augusto Martinez, Santos G. Martinez, Jr., Amado Pena, Roberto Rios, Jose Rivera, Joe B. Rodriguez, Jesus (Jesse) Trevino, and George Truan. Many illustrations, some in color. Introduction by James Harithas. Essay by Santos Martinez, Jr. Poetry, literature and essays by Chicano writers.

5532 Galeria de la Raza/Studio 24, San Francisco, CA. Images of the Southwest. Exhibition catalog, 1977. English.

AN: Invitation/catalog for an exhibit including Rudy M. Fernandez(Utah), Enrique Flores(Texas), Xavier Gorena(Texas), C.A.[Cesar] Martinez(Texas), Santos Martinez, Jr.(Texas), Pedro Rodriguez(Texas), Arnold Trujillo(New Mexico). Block prints, paper cut-outs, drawings, photographs, copper enamels, and sculpture were shown. Five illustrations.

5533 Instituto Chicano de Artes y Artesanias (Texas Instit. Educational Development) and Instituto Cultural Mexicano (SER/UNAM), San Antonio, TX. Artistas chicanos: Los Quemados. San Antonio, TX: Instituto Chicano, Texas Institute for Educational Development, 1975. English.

AN: Invitation to an exhibit and manifesto of 1975 Austin-San Antonio artists' group, Los Quemados. Included Santa Barraza, Carolina Flores, Carmen Lomas Garza, Luis Guerra, Cesar Augusto Martinez, Santos Martinez, Amado Maurilio Pena, Jr., Jose Rivera, Vicente Rodriguez, Jose Trevino.

Martinez, Sue

5534 Burkhardt, Dorothy. Chicano pride and anger mix at 'Califas'. THE TAB, (April 12, 1981), p. 34. English.

AN: CALIFAS: AN EXHIBITION OF CHICANO ARTISTS IN CALIFORNIA represents a cross-section of artists exhibiting work for at least ten years: Rupert Garcia, Ernie Palomino, Eduardo Carrillo, Judy Baca, Rene Yanez, Carmen Lomas Garza, Salvador Roberto Torres, Roberto Chavez, Willie Herron, Ralph Maradiaga, Sue Martinez, Jose Montoya, Malaquias Montoya, Ramses Noriega and Esteban Villa. Illustrated.

Mass Media

5535 Gamboa, Harry, Jr. Film, television, and Trevino. LA LUZ, Vol. 6, no. 10 (October 1977), p. 7-8. English.

AN: Jesus Salvador Trevino has been an active proponent and participant in transforming cultural inaccuracy about Chicanos in the media to accurate mass media models. A biography of Trevino follows, including discussion of some of his films: THE SALAZAR INQUEST, CHICANO MORATORIUM AFTERMATH, SOLEDAD, AMERICA TROPICAL, YO SOY CHICANO, RAICES DE SANGRE, as well as television series like ACCION CHICANO, AHORA, and INFINITY FACTORY.

5536 Gamboa, Harry, Jr. Seis imaginaciones: artistas chicanos en Los Angeles. COMUNIDAD, (July 13, 1980), p. 10. Spanish.

AN: A limited flow of media information about Los Angeles Chicanos has produced a "ghost" culture. Only sensational events are published. Alternative magazines like LA RAZA, CON SAFOS, and REGENERACION have disseminated Chicano ideas of the 1970s. The Chicano imagination has appeared in murals by Willie Herron, Gronk, Carlos Almaraz, John Valadez; in pieces like "walking" and "instant" murals by the group ASCO; by the group Los Four; by group exhibits like "Chicanismo en el arte," and "Chicanarte." Patssi Valdez showed Photobooth Piece at the "Chicanismo" show. Gronk and Jerry Dreva exhibited their mail art at "Punk Meets Art." In Spanish.

5537 Garcia, Rupert. The politics of popular art. CHISMEARTE, Vol. 2, no. 1 (Summer 1978), p. 2-4. English.

AN: Defines and discusses the terms "Popular Art", "Mass Art", and "Folk Art" and gives examples of their correct and incorrect usages.

5538 Montoya, Jose E. Thoughts on la cultura, the media, con safos and survival. CARACOL, Vol. 5, no. 9 (May 1979), p. 6-8,19. English.

AN: Remarks by Sacramento, CA, artist and poet, Jose Montoya, presented at the First Annual Chicano Film Series, Stanford University, California, January 10, 11, and 12, 1979.

5539 Montoya, Jose E. Thoughts on la cultura, the media, con safos and survival. Sacramento, CA: Royal Chicano Air Force, 1979. English.

AN: Important theoretical article on the state of Chicano culture. Reprinted in METAMORFOSIS (Seattle, WA), vol. 3, no. 1(Spring/Summer 1980), p. 28-31.

Massinelli, Mario

5540 Lucas, Jerry and Gil de Montes, Roberto, et al. CHOQUE DE AMOR: fotonovela by Lamp. Los Angeles, CA: Colectivo El Ojo, Latin American Studies Dept., CSULA, 1979. English.

AN: "Fotonovela" featuring Elsa Flores, Rosa Marin, and Jerry Lucas produced by the collective work of Lucas, Roberto Gil de Montes, Mario Massinelli, Luis Soto, and Kay Torres.

MASTERWORKS OF MEXICAN ART [film]

5541 Films for the inner city. Los Angeles, CA:
Los Angeles Public Library Federal Project,
1971. English.

AN: Annotated catalog of 16mm films and
filmstrips, educational and documentary.
Those concerning Mexican heritage include
CHICANO FROM THE SOUTHWEST (1970),
HENRY...BOY OF THE BARRIO (1969); HOW'S
SCHOOL, ENRIQUE (1970), I AM JOAQUIN (1970),
THE MEXICAN AMERICAN: HERITAGE AND DESTINY
(1970), A MEXICAN AMERICAN FAMILY (1970),
MEXICAN AMERICANS: QUEST FOR EQUALITY
(1968), MEXICAN OR AMERICAN (1970),
SIQUEIROS: "EL MAESTRO" (THE MARCH OF
HUMANITY IN LATIN AMERICA) (1969).
Filmstrips include THE AWAKENING (LA RAZA) -
Part IV, CONFLICT OF CULTURES (LA RAZA) -
Part III, MASTERWORKS OF MEXICAN ART, OUT OF
THE MAINSTREAM, PILGRIMAGE (GRAPE STRIKERS).
Also listed are films and filmstrips for
children.

Mauricio, Manuel

5542 Corpus Christy State University for the Arts
and Weil Gallery Center for the Arts, Corpus
Christi State University. Southwest artists
invitational: an exhibition of contemporary
art by seven Texas artists of Hispanic
American descent. Ehxibition brochure, 1980.
English.

AN: Artists Jesse Almazan, Luis Jimenez,
Cesar Martinez, Lydia Martinez, Manuel
Mauricio, Guillermo Pulido, and Jesse
Trevino show a variety of techniques and
styles. Text by Roberto Tomas Esparza.
Statements by and about the artists.
Illustrated.

Maxims
USE: Dichos

Maya, Gloria

5543 Chicano art. ARTES VISUALES, no. 29 (1981).
English.

AN: Issue on Chicano art, introduced by
Los Angeles artist Roberto Gil de Montes.
Includes works and statements by: Pedro
Lujan (Texas); Raul M. Guerrero (Calif.);
Sylvia Salazar Simpson (New Mexico/Calif.);
Carlos Almaraz (Calif.); Rene Yanez
(Calif.); Jack Vargas (Calif.); Ray Bravo
(Calif.); John Valadez (Calif.); Gloria Maya
(Calif.); Elsa Flores (Calif.); Willie
Herron (Calif.); Gilbert "Magu" Lujan
(Calif.); Kay Torres, Jerry Lucas, and Louis
Perez (Calif.).

Maya Images

5544 Rodriguez, Vicente. Mayan gods [drawing].
TEJIDOS, Vol. 4, no. 2 (Summer 1977), p. 20.
Spanish.

5545 Rodriguez, Vicente. Mayan gods [drawing].
TEJIDOS, Vol. 4, no. 2 (Summer 1977), p. 21.
English.

5546 Rodriguez, Vicente. Mayan religious
ceremonies [drawing]. TEJIDOS, Vol. 4, no. 2
(Summer 1977), p. 18. English.

5547 Rodriguez, Vicente. Mayas cazando ganado
para comer=Mayas hunting game for food
[drawing]. TEJIDOS, Vol. 4, no. 2 (Summer
1977), p. 19. Bilingual.

5548 Rodriguez, Vicente. Mayas plantando

maiz=Mayas planting corn [drawing]. TEJIDOS,
Vol. 4, no. 2 (Summer 1977), p. 17.
Bilingual.

Mazuca, Roland

5549 San Antonio Museum Association, San Antonio,
TX. Visiones nuevas en Tejas/new visions in
Texas. Exhibtion catalog, 1979. English.

AN: Supplementary regional catalog for
the exhibit RAICES ANTIGUAS/VISIONES NUEVAS;
ANCIENT ROOTS/NEW VISIONS. Illustrations for
works by George Cisneros, Francisco (Frank)
Fajardo, Robert Gonzalez, Cesar Augusto
Martinez, Roland Mazuca, Guillermo Pulido,
Felipe Reyes, Jesus (Jesse) Trevino.

MEChA
USE: Movimiento Estudiantil Chicano de
Aztlan (MEChA)

Mechicano Art Center, Los Angeles, CA

5550 Blaine, John and Baker, Decia. Finding
community through the arts: spotlight on
cultural pluralism in Los Angeles. ARTS IN
SOCIETY, Vol. 10, no. 1 (Spring, Summer,
1973), p. 125-138. English.

AN: Community arts expression by ethnic
minorities is burgeoning everywhere,
especially in Los Angeles. Various Black,
Asian, and Chicano art administrators are
interviewed, including Frank Lopez of Plaza
de la Raza and Leonard Castellanos of
Mechicano Art Center. Illustrated.

5551 Bright, John; Bright, Mura; and Castellanos,
Leonard. L.A. Chicano street art. Venice,
CA: Environmental Communications, 1974.
English.

AN: Annotated slide catalog of Chicano
murals in East Los Angeles compiled by staff
of Mechicano Art Center. Also includes
article reprints on painted bus benches by
Mechicano artists (SUNSET Magazine, n.d.),
murals of East Los Angeles (LOS ANGELES
TIMES, 12/3/73, and SUNSET Magazine, April
1973). Well illustrated.

5552 Bright, John; Bright, Mura; and Castellanos,
Leonard. "Placas": graffiti and the
environment. Venice, CA: Environmental
Communications, 1974. English.

AN: Annotated slide catalog of Chicano
graffiti on walls, murals, and tattoos,
compiled by staff of Mechicano Art Center.

5553 Castellanos, Leonard. Chicano centros,
murals, and art. ARTS IN SOCIETY, Vol. 12,
no. 1 (Spring, Summer, 1975), p. 38-43.
English.

AN: One of the organizers of the
Mechicano Art Center in Los Angeles talks
about the history of the Center, the
artist's relationship to the mainstream; the
importance of the street mural movement; the
economic problems of the muralists and their
dedication to the community; the need for
alternative centers like the "centros." An
excerpt of this article appeared in
CHISMEARTE, no. 1 (Fall 1976), p. 26-27.

5554 Castillo, Oscar R.; Esparza, Antonio; and
Cabrera, Antonio. Writing on the walls
[photograph]. CON SAFOS, no. 8 (1972), p.
56-57.

Mechicano Art Center, Los Angeles, CA (cont.)

5555 Chavez, Jaime and Vallecillo, Ana Maria. A political, historical, philosophical perspective of muralist art in the Southwest. RAYAS, Vol. 1, no. 3 (May, June, 1978), p. 6. English.

AN: Relates Chicano mural art to main issues of the Chicano movement. The Mechicano Art Center in Los Angeles and Artes Guadalupanos de Aztlan in Santa Fe are seen as examples of groups creating a new people's art; art forms where esthetics are allied to politics.

5556 Chicano artists exhibit at USC. CALENDAR, (September 23, 1973), p. 61. English.

AN: Announcement of an exhibit of paintings, drawings, sculpture and graphics by artists from the Mechicano Art Center of Los Angeles at the University of Southern California Art Galleries. Slide presentations of murals and supergraphics.

5557 Gardiner, Henry G. Painted exterior walls of Southern California. CURRANT ART MAGAZINE, Vol. 1, no. 2 (June, July, 1975), p. 16-23+. English.

AN: Good survey of street muralism, primarily in Los Angeles and San Diego, which started in 1968. Divided into eight "schools," including Chicano and non-Chicano muralists. Most Chicano murals associated with Goez Brothers Art Gallery and Mechicano Art Center in Los Angeles, the Coronado Bay Bridge group [Chicano Park] and Balboa Park group [Centro Cultural de la Raza]. Mural discussed in detail. Well illustrated.

5558 La historia de Mechicano. LA GENTE DE AZTLAN, Vol. 8, no. 1 (November 2, 1977), p. 14. English.

AN: Excellent and complete account of the formation and development of Mechicano Art Center from 1968 to 1977. Explains goals, activities and participating artists.

5559 Images of Aztlan at Mechicano. CHISMEARTE, Vol. 1, no. 1 (Fall 1976), p. 3-4. English.

AN: History of Mechicano Art Center from its opening in West Los Angeles in 1969 through its 1976 location during which it decided to become a center serving its own community in East Los Angeles. Led by Leonard Castellanos, Victor Franco and Ray Atilano, the Center developed programs in supergraphics, silkscreen, and mural painting, as well as an "open-wall" art gallery for artists not allowed in establishment galleries.

5560 Mascorro, Julie. Mechicano Art Center exhibit to grace Price gallery walls. CAMPUS NEWS, (November 24, 1971). English.

AN: Brief history of Mechicano Art Center activities from its establishment in 1969 to 1971. Exhibiting are Charles Almaraz, Roberto Amaral, Raymond Atilano, William Bejarano, Armando Cabrera, Edward Carbajal, Leonard Castellanos, Henry de Vega, Antonio Esparza, Bob Gomez, Lucila V. Grijalva, Jesus Gutierrez, Santos Lira, Frank Martinez, Ernest Palomino, Louis Quijada, Richard Raya, Frank Romero. Illustrated.

5561 Mechicano Art Center. Brochure, [1975].

English.

AN: Illustrated brochure detailing the history, community programs (drawing, painting, silkscreen, sculpture and mural classes), gallery exhibits, travelling exhibits, murals and supergraphics, and financial status of the Whittier Blvd. Center.

5562 Mechicano Art Center attracts community artists. EL HISPANO, Vol. 5, no. 2 (June 10, 1972). English.

AN: Commentary by Leonard Castellanos, Director of Mechicano Art Center, who explains funding sources and programs of the Centro.

5563 Mechicano Art Center. Los Angeles, CA: Mechicano Art Center, 1971. English.

AN: Announcement of an exhibit by painters Ramon Atilano, Xavier Lopez Ortega, and Frank A. Martinez. Martinez and Lopez Ortega are also muralists. Brief profiles of the artists. Illustrated.

5564 Mechicano Art Center, Los Angeles, CA. Lucila [V. Grijalva] reception. Exhibition announcement [1976]. English.

AN: Flyer announcing an exhibit for the Los Angeles painter and muralist.

5565 Mechicano Art Center, Los Angeles, CA. Paper pieces by C.D.A. [Carlos D. Almaraz]. Exhibition invitation, [1973]. English.

AN: Invitation to a gallery exhibit by the artist, with his manifesto, "Notes on an Aesthetic Alternative".

5566 Mechicano Art Center, Los Angeles, CA. Recent works of Armando Cabrera, Ed Carbajal, Joe Cervantes. Exhibition invitation, 1971. English.

AN: Invitation to an exhibit.

5567 Sommer, Robert. Street art. New York: Quick Fox, 1975. English.

AN: Introductory essay covering the history of the new mural movement, forms of street art, politics, street sculpture, how to locate and photograph street art. Chicano murals include Charles Felix and others at Estrada Courts (L.A.), RCAF murals in Sacramento, Jose Montoya and others (Broderick, Ca.) Marcos Raya (Chicago), Mike Rios (Neighborhood Legal Aid, S.F.) Mechicano Art Center (L.A.) Johnny Alvarez (L.A.), New Mexico State Employment Bldg., Albuquerque mural, Lorena Street School (L.A.), two murals, Casa de la Raza Alternative School (Berkeley), Santa Fe, New Mexico mural, Francisco Hernandez (L.A.), Artes Guadalupanos de Aztlan (N. Mexico), Willie Herron (L.A.). Better documentation would have been welcome.

Mechicano Art Center, Los Angeles, CA (cont.)

5568 Symposium on the politics of the arts: minorities and the arts. ARTS IN SOCIETY, Vol. 10, no. 3 (Fall , Winter, 1973), p. 66-73. English.

AN: One panel from the Colloquium "Politics of the Arts" presented by the UCLA Management in the Arts Program, Graduate School of Management, 1972, included, among others, Leonard Castellanos of Mechicano Art Center, and James Woods of Studio Watts Workshop, both in Los Angeles. A major topic was how minorities dealing with the corporate capitalist structure can keep control of their art programs.

5569 Unique $1000 art competition beautifies East L.A.: community votes for favorite bus bench paintings. PACEMAKER, (February 1972). English.

AN: Mechicano Art Center contest to beautify the community by painting bus benches for maximum public exposure. Eight of 29 benches illustrated.

5570 Wilson, William. 30 works from the grass roots. LOS ANGELES TIMES, (June 4, 1973), p. IV,2. English.

AN: Review of a show at the Junior Arts Center in Barnsdall Park by 15 members of the Mechicano Art Center. The critic feels contemporary groups that aim for change today (unlike past groups) are unable to articulate their spirit in a cohesive style. The top talent in this show is Charles Almaraz; also on exhibit are paintings by Jose Cervantes, Guillermo Martinez, Ray Atilano, sculpture by Manuel Cruz, and photography by (Oscar) R. Castillo.

Medellin, Octavio

5571 The art of Mexican America. EMPIRE MAGAZINE, (November 1, 1970), p. 24-25. English.

AN: Visual portfolio with minimal text. Includes paintings by Amado Pena, Mel Casas, Porfirio Salinas, and sculpture by Octavio Medellin. On the same page, Dr. Jacinto Quirarte gives views on the nature of Mexican art, the Mexican American artist, and the connection between Mexican and Mexican American art.

5572 S.A. site for National Symposium on Mexican American Art. CHICANO TIMES, Vol. 4, no. 30 (November 9, 1973), p. 5. English.

AN: Held at Trinity University, the Symposium discussed such issues as, creative evolution, art education, artistic relationships to Mexico and the evolution of Mexican American art in the California barrios. Participating artists included Rudy Trevino, Mel Casas, Octavio Medellin, Antonio Garcia, Carmen Garza, Esteban Villa, Jose Montoya, Ernesto Palomino, Michael Ponce de Leon, Luis Jimenez and Eugenio Quesada.

Media
    USE: Mass Media

Medina, Ada

5573 59th Street Gallery, St. Louis, MO. Midwest Mexican-American art exhibit: Mexico and its artists. Exhibition brochure, 1981. English.

AN: Sponsored by the Sociedad Mexicana

"Benito Juarez" and the international Institute of St. Louis, this three-part exhibit includes 1) MEXICO AS SEEN BY HER CHILDREN, a bilingual exhibit from Mexico traveling under Smithsonian Institution auspices, 2) MEXICAN CHILDREN IN THE U.S.A., 3) MEXICAN AMERICAN ARTISTS. In the latter are included Stephen Capiz (Roseville, Minn.), Jose Gonzalez (Chicago), Cesar A. Martinez (San Antonio), Ada Medina (Des Moines), Nora Chapa Mendoza (West Bloomfield, Mich.), Rene David Michel-Trapaga (St. Louis), David Munoz (Kansas City, Mo.), Jose Luis Narezo (Grand Rapids, Mich.), Benny Ordonez, Roman Villarreal (Chicago), Alejandro Romero (Chicago), Aurelio Diaz "Tekpankalli" (Chicago), Simon Ybarra (St. Louis).

MEETING IN THE STREET [mural]

5574 Garcia, Rupert. Echos de la Mision - Alfaro Siqueiros (1896-1974). EL TECOLOTE, Vol. 4, no. 3 (February 22, 1974), p. 11. English.

AN: Biographical and artistic trajectory of Mexican artist David Alfaro Siqueiros. Artist painted three murals in Southern California in 1932 (MEETING IN THE STREET and TROPICAL AMERICA were done in Los Angeles on the walls of the Chouinard School of Art and the Plaza Art Center, Olvera Street area respectively. The third mural PORTRAIT OF MEXICO was privately commissioned in Santa Monica). The three California murals deal with themes of censorship, racism, colonialism, capitalism, and imperialism. Article suggests that Raza artists are much influenced by the ideas and work of Siqueiros. Illustrated with Rupert Garcia's silkscreen poster SIQUEIROS.

Melendez, Bill

5575 Champlin, Chuck, Jr. Working for more than peanuts. LOS ANGELES TIMES, (June 21, 1980), p. II, 8, 10. English.

AN: Bill Melendez has been an animator 21 years for Charles Schulz's Charlie Brown and Peanuts comic strips, TV specials, and feature films. Melendez began his career with Walt Disney Productions in 1938.

Mena, Luis Gustavo

5576 Salas, Joanne. Mural painting that comes from the heart; 'impact' is the word for muralist Luis Mena. TUCSON CITIZEN, OLD PUEBLO SECTION, (June 25, 1981), p. 4-5. English.

AN: Illustrated story on wall murals in Tucson. Color.

5577 Turner, Mark. Muralist uses walls to break barriers between people. ARIZONA DAILY STAR, (July 23, 1981). English.

AN: Luis Gustavo Mena works on his latest mural, an image of Benito Juarez with the Mexican and "Latin Empire" flags, and a scale of justice. Information about the artist, son of an artistic family, and recent high school graduate.

Mende, Chris

5578 Estudios Rio: gallery of contemporary arts
and crafts. Exhibition catalog, 1976.
English.

AN: Catalog including identification,
portraits and works of participating
artists: Joe Bova, Enrique Flores, Carmen
Lomas Garza, Xavier Gorena, Erik Gronborg,
Lucas Hinojosa, Ben Holland, Kris Hotvedt,
William Kaars-Sijpesteijn, Cesar Martinez,
Chris Mende, Roberto Mungia, Steve Reynolds,
Vicente Rodriguez, William Wilhelmi.

Mendez, Pete

5579 Art Gallery, California State University,
Long Beach and Lujan, Gilbert Sanchez
"Magu". El arte del pocho. Exhibit brochure,
October 1968. English.

AN: Information about Southern
California artists John Deheras, Marcus
Villagran, Roberto de la Rocha, Santos
Zuniga, Crispin Gonzales, Richard Martinez,
Jesus Gutierrez, Ed Oropeza, Pete Mendez,
David Ramirez, Gilbert Sanchez Lujan, Willie
Hernandez, Art Ponce, Carmen Tostado, Al
Almeida, David Ceja, Robert E. Chavez,
Thomas A. Ferriera. All art students,
graduates, or faculty.

Mendez, Raoul

5580 Teatro de la Tierra Morena, Santa Cruz, CA.
Fuego en Aztlan: a Chicano arts show.
Exhibition brochure, 1980. English.

AN: Folder of information on the
exhibition curated by Cruz Zamarron and
Eduardo Carrillo. Exhibiting artists were:
Justina Avila, Terry Benitez, Eduardo
Carrillo, Hernando Chavez, Bob Cruz, Juanita
Estrada, Juana Franklin, Sal Garcia, Leticia
Hernandez, David "Sir Loco" Jimenez, Raoul
Mendez, Vicente Mendez, Maria V. Pinedo,
Gonzalo Placencia, Ramon Rodriguez, Roberto
Salas, George Silva and Cruz Zamarron. A
special feature was a live tattoo
demonstration entitled "Walking Art".

Mendez, Xavier

5581 Los Angeles City College. Latinos de tres
mundos. Exhibition invitation, 1980.
English.

AN: Invitation to an exhibit featuring
the work of ASCO members Harry Gamboa, Jr.,
Gronk, Willie Herron; painters Xavier Mendez
and Olivia Sanchez; and photographer Ricardo
Valverde.

Mendoza, Anthony

5582 Chicano art show. EL DIARIO DE LA GENTE,
Vol. 1, no. 7 (February 6, 1973), p. 4.
English.

AN: Fine arts students at the University
of Colorado led by Rudy Fernandez hope to
educate high school students about Chicano
art. This article documents an exhibit held
at Lafayette, CO. Members of the group are
Bob Maez, Jerry Jaramillo, Anthony Mendoza,
and Rudy Fernandez. Illustrated by four
exhibition photographs by John L. Espinosa.

Mendoza, John L.

5583 Andrews, Rena. The fine arts. ROUNDUP,
(September 27, 1970), p. 18. English.

AN: Commentary on one-man exhibition by
John L. Mendoza at the International House
Gallery in Denver. Noted for his water-color
landscapes, the artists is a full time art
teacher at East High School in Pueblo
Colorado. Illustrated with photograph of the
artist and one of his paintings.

5584 Sharing a bit of magic with John Mendoza.
ARTISTS OF THE ROCKIES, Vol. 1, no. 2
(Spring 1974), p. 14-17. English.

AN: Growing up in the St. Charles Mesa
east of Pueblo Colorado, John Mendoza has
sought to capture the essence of nature in
that part of the country in his paintings.
Blending realism and abstraction, Mendoza
has evolved a distinctive personal idiom.
Illustrated with reproductions of two
watercolors and six drawings. Includes two
photos of the artist and his pupils.

Mendoza, Josie

5585 De Marroquin, Moron. Denver Harbor artists.
LA PRENSA, (June 2, 1978). Spanish.

AN: Commentary on two exhibitions. THE
DENVER HARBOR ARTISTS includes information
on paintings by Lupe Aguirre, Josie Mendoza
and Abel Gonzalez--all from Houston. The
solo show MAGIC BLANCA featured the work of
Brownsville, Texas artist Jorge Truan.
Truan's work is mystical and visionary.

5586 Houston Chicanismo. LA PRENSA, Vol. 1, no. 2
(March 31, 1978). English.

AN: In Houston, Texas, the AMA Gallery
(Association for the Advancement of Mexican
Americans) was opened in February 1976 to
showcase Chicano art. Noel Rodriguez,
gallery director, informs about the goals
and objectives of the gallery. A current
exhibit presents paintings by Josie Mendoza
and Atanacio Davila, ceramics by Jesse
Sifuentes and mixed-media works by Joe
Ramirez. Illustrated with two pieces from
exhibit, THANKSGIVING, an acrylic painting
by Josie Mendoza and BIRDS, a ceramic piece.

Mendoza, Nora Chapa

5587 59th Street Gallery, St. Louis, MO. Midwest
Mexican-American art exhibit: Mexico and its
artists. Exhibition brochure, 1981. English.

AN: Sponsored by the Sociedad Mexicana
"Benito Juarez" and the international
Institute of St. Louis, this three-part
exhibit includes 1) MEXICO AS SEEN BY HER
CHILDREN, a bilingual exhibit from Mexico
traveling under Smithsonian Institution
auspices, 2) MEXICAN CHILDREN IN THE U.S.A.,
3) MEXICAN AMERICAN ARTISTS. In the latter
are included Stephen Capiz (Roseville,
Minn.), Jose Gonzalez (Chicago), Cesar A.
Martinez (San Antonio), Ada Medina (Des
Moines), Nora Chapa Mendoza (West
Bloomfield, Mich.), Rene David
Michel-Trapaga (St. Louis), David Munoz
(Kansas City, Mo.), Jose Luis Narezo (Grand
Rapids, Mich.), Benny Ordonez, Roman
Villarreal (Chicago), Alejandro Romero
(Chicago), Aurelio Diaz "Tekpankalli"
(Chicago), Simon Ybarra (St. Louis).

Mendoza, Nora Chapa (cont.)

5588 Acosta, Dan. Paintings reflect life
experiences. THE ECCENTRIC, (June 26,
1980). English.

AN: Review of one-woman show by Nora
Chapa Mendoza at the Heritage Art Gallery,
Ypsilanti, MI. Mendoza works in abstract
impressionist style with wet streams of
colors that express energy. Her subjects are
landscapes, moods, nudes, and Hispanic
themes. She is active in the Detroit Latino
Artist Association, Nuestras Artes de
Michigan, and the New Detroit Art Council.

5589 Arts Council Center for the Arts of Greater
Lansing, Lansing, MI. Raza fine arts
festival. Festival program, 1978. English.

AN: This festival program mentions Jose
Narezo's mural at the Holland National Guard
Armory, Grand Rapids; includes a statement
of the Raza Art/Media Collective, Inc.; the
philosophy of artists Zaragosa Vargas and S.
Kaneta Kosiba-Vargas; and profiles of
exhibiting artists George Vargas, Martin
Moreno, Hector Perez, Michael L. Selley,
Jesse Gonzales, Nora Chapa Mendoza, Jesse
Soriano, Jose Luis Narezo.

5590 El calendario hispano de Michigan, 1981.
Stanton, MI: Montcalm Intermediate School
District and Nuestras Artes de Michigan,
1981. English.

AN: Months of historical calendar
illustrated with art works by George Vargas,
Nora Chapa Mendoza, Jesse Gonzalez, Julio
Perazza(Puerto Rican), Hector Valdez, Pamela
M. Gonzalez, Isabell Escojico (7-year-old
child), Jose Narezo, Martin Moreno, Laurie
Mendoza Psarianos, Rosa Maria Arenas.

5591 Capitol Art Gallery, Lansing, MI. Arte de
Nora Mendoza, Hector Perez, George Vargas,
Martin Moreno. Exhibition invitation [1979].
English.

AN: Invitation to an art exhibit
organized by Nuestras Artes de Michigan.

5592 Hispanic artists' [sic] mural unveiled.
SOUTHFIELD ECCENTRIC, Exhibition catalog,
1980. English.

AN: A mural titled SYNERGY by Michigan
artist Nora Mendoza is unveiled at the R.J.
Sullivan Funeral Home. Mendoza has exhibited
at numerous one-person shows.

5593 Lansing Community College, Lansing, MI.
Festival! Festival program, [1978]. English.

AN: Program of a festival which includes
an Hispanic Arts Exhibit, including Juan
Ortega, Nora Mendoza, Jose Luis Narezo, and
Brazilian-born Veronica Dalia de
Albuquerque.

5594 Nora Mendoza: pintora de ascendencia
mexicana triunfa en los EE. UU. BUENHOGAR,
(May 1979), p. 7. Spanish.

AN: Profile of Texas-born Nora Mendoza
of Michigan, a painter of abstractions in
acrylic. She is an active member of many
Detroit and Michigan organizations,
including Nuestras Artes de Michigan which
she co-founded with Jorge Vargas, Martin
Moreno and Jessie Gonzalez.

5595 Oakland County Cultural Affairs, MI. Nora
Mendoza: an exhibition of

abstract/impressionism. Exhibition brochure,
[1981]. English.

AN: Exhibit brochure for Texas-born Nora
Chapa Mendoza who studied
abstract-impressionism with Michigan artist
Ljubo Biro. She is a leader in the artistic
and Hispanic communities and runs galleries
in Clarkston and Detroit.

Mendoza Psarianos, Laurie

5596 El calendario hispano de Michigan, 1981.
Stanton, MI: Montcalm Intermediate School
District and Nuestras Artes de Michigan,
1981. English.

AN: Months of historical calendar
illustrated with art works by George Vargas,
Nora Chapa Mendoza, Jesse Gonzalez, Julio
Perazza(Puerto Rican), Hector Valdez, Pamela
M. Gonzalez, Isabell Escojico (7-year-old
child), Jose Narezo, Martin Moreno, Laurie
Mendoza Psarianos, Rosa Maria Arenas.

Mendoza, Robert

5597 San Francisco Museum of Modern Art, San
Francisco, CA and Castellon, Rolando.
People's murals: some events in American
history. Exhibition catalog, 1976. English.

AN: Eight portable murals by San
Francisco Bay Area artists including
Graciela Carrillo, Anthony Machado, Robert
Mendoza, Irene Perez, Mike Rios. Well
Illustrated.

Mendoza, Vicente

5598 Cockcroft, Eva; Weber, John; and Cockcroft,
James D. Towards a people's art: the
contemporary mural movement. New York: E.P.
Dutton, 1977. English.

AN: A survey of the street mural
movement in the United States, from about
1967 on. Several chapters are written by the
artists themselves: John Weber on the
Chicago mural group; Susan Shapiro-Kiok on
Cityarts Workshop of New York; Eva Cockcroft
on People's painters of New Jersey; Geronimo
Garduno on Artes Guadalupanos de Aztlan of
New Mexico. Chicano murals illustrated
include those of Mujeres Muralistas, Ray
Patlan, William F. Herron, Hoyo-Mara Gang,
Artes Guadalupanos de Aztlan, Vicente
Mendoza and Jose Nario (with Patlan) Mario
Castillo, Michael Rios, Toltecas en Aztlan,
Roberto Chavez, Ernie Palomino, Chuy
Campusano and Luis Cortazar (with Rios).

5599 MARCH: Movimiento artistico Chicano
(Mexican-American Art Movement). QUARTERLY,
(Spring 1976), p. 10. English.

AN: Brief history of MARCH.
Illustrations of murals by Ricarco Alonzo,
Jose Gonzalez, Vicente Mendoza. Ray Patlan.

Mendoza, Vicente (cont.)

5600 Teatro de la Tierra Morena, Santa Cruz, CA.
Fuego en Aztlan: a Chicano arts show.
Exhibition brochure, 1980. English.

AN: Folder of information on the
exhibition curated by Cruz Zamarron and
Eduardo Carrillo. Exhibiting artists were:
Justina Avila, Terry Benitez, Eduardo
Carrillo, Hernando Chavez, Bob Cruz, Juanita
Estrada, Juana Franklin, Sal Garcia, Leticia
Hernandez, David "Sir Loco" Jimenez, Raoul
Mendez, Vicente Mendez, Maria V. Pinedo,
Gonzalo Placencia, Ramon Rodriguez, Roberto
Salas, George Silva and Cruz Zamarron. A
special feature was a live tattoo
demonstration entitled "Walking Art".

Mesa, AZ

5601 Memorial Union Display Cases, Arizona State
University, Tempe, AZ. The material culture
of the Cabezas Redondas, reconstructed by
Liz Lerma Bowerman. Exhibition invitation,
1977. English.

AN: Invitation to an exhibit of pottery
helmets and other artifacts of an imaginary
Bronze Age people, conceived and created by
Liz Lerma Bowerman from Mesa, AZ.

Mesa-Baines, Amalia

5602 Rangel, Jesus. Heirs of Jose Posada:
revolution lives in Chicano art. SAN DIEGO
UNION, (February 24, 1980), p. D6. English.

AN: 19th century Mexican engraver Jose
Guadalupe Posada has been an inspiration to
Chicano artists. Along with two exhibits of
his work, the Centro Cultural de la Raza is
also showing calavera (skeleton) images by
Chicano artists: skull-masks from the Teatro
Campesino, a print by Amalia Mesa-Baines of
Frida Kahlo, and a collaged box by Jose
Antonio Burciaga. Illustration: Salvador
Roberto Torres work.

5603 San Francisco Museum of Modern Art, San
Francisco, CA and Marra, Patricia. Day of
the dead. Exhibition catalog, 1980. English.

AN: Broadside announcement in the manner
of Jose Gudalupe Posada for an exhibit of
prints by Posada and an altar by Amalia Mesa
-Baines and Friends. Text presents customs
and traditions for celebrating the Day of
the Dead in Mexico and among the Chicano
community.

5604 Stofflet-Santiago, Mary. The fifth sun:
esthetic quality versus curatorial intent.
ARTWEEK, Vol. 8, no. 37 (November 5, 1977),
p. 6. English.

AN: Review of the exhibit THE FIFTH SUN
at the University Art Museum in Berkeley,
Calif., curated by Ralph Maradiaga of the
Galeria de la Raza. It contains folk art,
and posters by Chicano artists Maradiaga,
Rupert Garcia, Juan Fuentes, mural studies
by Graciela Carrillo and Mike Rios, ceramics
by Anna de Leon, an altar by Amalia
Mesa-Baines, and mural drawings by Mexican
muralists. The writer criticizes the uneven
quality of the show, but encourages better
ones in the future. Illustrated.

Mestizaje

5605 Baca, Walter R. Mestizo [mural]. DE COLORES,
Vol. 1, no. 2 (Spring 1974), p. 60. Spanish.

5606 Mestiza [drawing]. LA LUZ, Vol. 8, no. 8
(October, November, 1980), p. 10. English.

5607 Santa Ana College, Santa Ana, CA and
Goldman, Shifra M. Chicano art. Exhibition
catalog, 1974. English.

AN: Thirteen California artists are
presented in a short essay defining Chicano
as a double mestizaje of Mexican mestizo and
U.S. influences that exists in a state of
"reconciled conflict." Its aim is
communication. Artists included are
Malaquias Montoya, Rupert Garcia, Manuel
Hernandez, Esteban Villa, Robert Gomez,
Harvey Tarango, Mary Helen Castro, Eduardo
Carrillo, Graciela Carrillo, and "Los Four":
Carlos Almaraz, Robert de la Rocha, Judithe
Hernandez, Gilbert Lujan and Frank Romero.

5608 Torres, Salvador Roberto. Teatro Mono meets
Teatro Mestizo. DE COLORES, Vol. 1, no. 1
(Winter 1973), p. 38.

EL MESTIZO CHICANO [mural]

5609 Los murales del pueblo. PAPEL CHICANO, Vol.
2, no. 12 (February 1973), p. 1+. Spanish.

AN: Analysis of Leo Tanguma's work as
"an expression not only of artistic creative
opinion but also of the suppressed and
accumulated feeling of La Raza in the United
States." Includes thematic and stylistic
information on four murals in the Houston
barrio: "The Rebirth of Our Nationality,"
"Towards a Humanitarian Technology for La
Raza," "Historia de la Raza," and "El
Mestizo Chicano".

MESTIZO [mural]

5610 Johnson, Richard. The mural at Zihuatanejo.
EMPIRE MAGAZINE, (October 12, 1980).
English.

AN: Denver artist Carlos M. Sandoval is
said to be the first Chicano commissioned by
the Mexican government to paint a mural in
Mexico. Sandoval's mural is on the facade of
the public library in Zihuatanejo. Its theme
is unity and synthesis and its title is
MESTIZO. Article contains much information
on mural act ivity in Denver, Colorado. Well
illustrated with color and black and white
photographs.

METAFISICA [mural]

5611 Sorell, Victor A. Barrio murals in Chicago:
painting the Hispanic-American experience on
"our community" walls. REVISTA
CHICANO-RIQUENA, Vol. 4, no. 4 (Fall
1976), p. 51-72. English.

AN: Important survey of Chicago's Latino
murals, with key works considered in detail.
Among the Chicano art organizations and
muralists mentioned are MARCH (Movimiento
Artistico Chicano), and Yolanda Galvan,
Juanita Jaramillo, Jose Nario, Raymond
Patlan, Vicente Mendoza, Marcos Raya,
Ricardo Alonzo, Jose G. Gonzalez and Mario
Castillo, author of the earliest Latino
mural in Chicago (1968). Puerto Rican and
non-Latino muralists and mural groups are
also discussed. Well illustrated.

METAMORFOSIS [journal], Seattle, WA

5612 Yarbro-Bejarano, Yvonne. Resena critica de
     revistas literarias chicanas: problemas y
     tendencias. LA PALABRA, Vol. 3, no. 1-2
     (Spring, Fall , 1981), p. 123-137. Spanish.

     AN: Continuation of review of Chicano
     magazines from Texas, California, and
     Washington. The article discusses content,
     literary and artistic format, and other
     aspects, taking a critical stance (See LA
     PALABRA, Spring 1980).

Metro Denver Urban Coalition: City Walls

5613 La Familia Recreation Center, Denver, CO.
     Mural unveiling and swim party. Exhibition
     invitation, 1980. English.

     AN: Invitation to the unveiling of La
     Familia Cosmica, a mural by Jerry Jaramillo
     assisted by Carlos Sandoval, Al Sanchez,
     Stephen Lucero. An art exhibit featured the
     muralists, Jon Howe, and Fred Sanchez, all
     of the Metro Denver Urban Coalition's City
     Walls artists. Illustrated.

MEXICAN AMERICAN ARTISTS

5614 A beautiful book just published...: book
     review of MEXICAN AMERICAN ARTISTS. LA LUZ,
     Vol. 2, no. 4 (August 1973), p. 26. English.

5615 Martinez, Santos G., Jr. Review of: MEXICAN
     AMERICAN ARTISTS. DE COLORES, Vol. 2, no. 2
     (1975), p. 47-51. English.

     AN: A review essay by a noted Chicano
     artist. The basic shortcoming of Quirarte's
     book is "the author's failure to recognize
     the distinction between the terms Mexican
     American and Chicano. Consequently, Dr.
     Quirarte has failed to establish what
     exactly a Chicano is and in turn has failed
     to fully recognize the existence of Chicano
     art; an art by Chicanos about Chicanos and
     their culture." Reprinted in CARACOL, vol.
     2, no. 3, 1975 and in TEJIDOS, vol. 3, no.
     3, 1976.

MEXICAN AMERICAN CULTURE, ITS HERITAGE [film]

5616 Films for the inner city. Los Angeles, CA:
     Los Angeles Public Library Federal Project,
     1971. English.

     AN: Annotated catalog of 16mm films and
     filmstrips, educational and documentary.
     Those concerning Mexican heritage include
     CHICANO FROM THE SOUTHWEST (1970),
     HENRY...BOY OF THE BARRIO (1969); HOW'S
     SCHOOL, ENRIQUE (1970), I AM JOAQUIN (1970),
     THE MEXICAN AMERICAN: HERITAGE AND DESTINY
     (1970), A MEXICAN AMERICAN FAMILY (1970),
     MEXICAN AMERICANS: QUEST FOR EQUALITY
     (1968), MEXICAN OR AMERICAN (1970),
     SIQUEIROS: "EL MAESTRO" (THE MARCH OF
     HUMANITY IN LATIN AMERICA) (1969).
     Filmstrips include THE AWAKENING (LA RAZA) -
     Part IV, CONFLICT OF CULTURES (LA RAZA) -
     Part III, MASTERWORKS OF MEXICAN ART, OUT OF
     THE MAINSTREAM, PILGRIMAGE (GRAPE STRIKERS).
     Also listed are films and filmstrips for
     children.

A MEXICAN AMERICAN FAMILY [film]

5617 Films for the inner city. Los Angeles, CA:
     Los Angeles Public Library Federal Project,
     1971. English.

     AN: Annotated catalog of 16mm films and
     filmstrips, educational and documentary.

Those concerning Mexican heritage include
CHICANO FROM THE SOUTHWEST (1970),
HENRY...BOY OF THE BARRIO (1969); HOW'S
SCHOOL, ENRIQUE (1970), I AM JOAQUIN (1970),
THE MEXICAN AMERICAN: HERITAGE AND DESTINY
(1970), A MEXICAN AMERICAN FAMILY (1970),
MEXICAN AMERICANS: QUEST FOR EQUALITY
(1968), MEXICAN OR AMERICAN (1970),
SIQUEIROS: "EL MAESTRO" (THE MARCH OF
HUMANITY IN LATIN AMERICA) (1969).
Filmstrips include THE AWAKENING (LA RAZA) -
Part IV, CONFLICT OF CULTURES (LA RAZA) -
Part III, MASTERWORKS OF MEXICAN ART, OUT OF
THE MAINSTREAM, PILGRIMAGE (GRAPE STRIKERS).
Also listed are films and filmstrips for
children.

THE MEXICAN AMERICAN: HERITAGE AND DESTINY [film]

5618 Films for the inner city. Los Angeles, CA:
     Los Angeles Public Library Federal Project,
     1971. English.

     AN: Annotated catalog of 16mm films and
     filmstrips, educational and documentary.
     Those concerning Mexican heritage include
     CHICANO FROM THE SOUTHWEST (1970),
     HENRY...BOY OF THE BARRIO (1969); HOW'S
     SCHOOL, ENRIQUE (1970), I AM JOAQUIN (1970),
     THE MEXICAN AMERICAN: HERITAGE AND DESTINY
     (1970), A MEXICAN AMERICAN FAMILY (1970),
     MEXICAN AMERICANS: QUEST FOR EQUALITY
     (1968), MEXICAN OR AMERICAN (1970),
     SIQUEIROS: "EL MAESTRO" (THE MARCH OF
     HUMANITY IN LATIN AMERICA) (1969).
     Filmstrips include THE AWAKENING (LA RAZA) -
     Part IV, CONFLICT OF CULTURES (LA RAZA) -
     Part III, MASTERWORKS OF MEXICAN ART, OUT OF
     THE MAINSTREAM, PILGRIMAGE (GRAPE STRIKERS).
     Also listed are films and filmstrips for
     children.

Mexican American Legal Defense and Educational Fund (MALDEF)

5619 Fischer, Hal. Espejo: reflections of the
     Mexican American: Louis Carlos Bernal,
     Morrie Camhi, Abigail Heyman, Roger Minick,
     Neal Slavin. PICTURE MAGAZINE, no. 9 (1978).
     English.

     AN: Oversize portfolio of photographs
     recording contemporary Mexican American life
     commissioned by the Mexican American Legal
     Defense and Education Fund. Three
     photographers, Louis Carlos Bernal (from
     Arizona), Morrie Camhi and Abagail Heyman
     focus on the family and the home; the
     fourth, Roger Minick, juxtaposes the Mexican
     American against "barrio" murals. Only
     Bernal is Chicano. 24 photographs, six of
     which (Bernal's) are in color.

5620 Oakland Museum, Oakland, CA. Espejo:
     reflections of the Mexican American: Louis
     Carlos Bernal, Morrie Camhi, Abigail Heyman,
     Roger Minick, Neal Slavin. Exhibit brochure,
     1978. English.

     AN: Twenty-five photographs from the
     documentary series commissioned by the
     Mexican American Legal Defense and Education
     Fund. Only Bernal is Chicano.

Mexican American Liberation Art Front (MALAF)

5621 La Causa Publications, Oakland, CA. New symbols for la Nueva Raza. Exhibition announcement, [ca. 1969]. English.

AN: Announcement for exhibition of the four founding artists of the Mexican American Liberation Art Front (MALAF): Esteban Villa, Rene Yanez, Manuel Hernandez, Malaquias Montoya. Collage of portraits by the artists.

5622 Mexican American liberation art front: la Raza Nueva, Rene Yanez, Esteban Villa, Malaquias Montoya, Manuel Hernandez. BRONCE, Vol. 1, no. 3 (March 1969), p. 6-7. English.

AN: Manifesto of MALAF, a germinal Chicano art group in northern California. Compares revolutionary Chicanos of 1968 with the Mexicans of 1910; equally Chicano artists reject European-influenced art. Announces the exhibit NEW SYMBOLS FOR LA RAZA NUEVA, at La Causa in Oakland, March 22 to April 5, 1969. Puts forth the group's philosophy and goals, particularly exhibits and art services to the "barrio". Illustrated.

5623 Tapia, Ludy. Montoya and the art of survival. LA VOZ DEL PUEBLO, Vol. 3, no. 5 (June 1972), p. 6. English.

AN: Profile of San Francisco Bay area poster maker and artist Malaquias Montoya, who first became involved in the Chicano movement in San Jose working with MASC and EL MACHETE paper. In Berkeley (1968), he met Esteban Villa and, with others, formed the Mexican American Liberation Art Front (MALAF). Montoya is against elitism influencing Chicano art, and is concerned with commercialization of Chicano art and artists. Illustrated.

MEXICAN AMERICANS: QUEST FOR EQUALITY [film]

5624 Films for the inner city. Los Angeles, CA: Los Angeles Public Library Federal Project, 1971. English.

AN: Annotated catalog of 16mm films and filmstrips, educational and documentary. Those concerning Mexican heritage include CHICANO FROM THE SOUTHWEST (1970), HENRY...BOY OF THE BARRIO (1969); HOW'S SCHOOL, ENRIQUE (1970), I AM JOAQUIN (1970), THE MEXICAN AMERICAN: HERITAGE AND DESTINY (1970), A MEXICAN AMERICAN FAMILY (1970), MEXICAN AMERICANS: QUEST FOR EQUALITY (1968), MEXICAN OR AMERICAN (1970), SIQUEIROS: "EL MAESTRO" (THE MARCH OF HUMANITY IN LATIN AMERICA) (1969). Filmstrips include THE AWAKENING (LA RAZA) - Part IV, CONFLICT OF CULTURES (LA RAZA) - Part III, MASTERWORKS OF MEXICAN ART, OUT OF THE MAINSTREAM, PILGRIMAGE (GRAPE STRIKERS). Also listed are films and filmstrips for children.

Mexican Art

5625 Barrera, Manuel. "Maestro" Siqueiros. LA RAZA, Vol. 2, no. 2 (1974), p. 40-41. English.

5626 Beltran, Alberto. [Untitled woodcut]. CARACOL, Vol. 1, no. 12 (August 1975), p. 13.

5627 Bonilla, Guillermo. [Untitled woodcut]. CARACOL, Vol. 1, no. 12 (August 1975), p. 10.

5628 Cattleth, Elizabeth. [Untitled woodcut]. CARACOL, Vol. 1, no. 12 (August 1975), p. 1.

5629 Danzas mexicanas. Flyer, 1978. English.

AN: Illustrated flyer about a mural designed and painted by Chicano artist and poet Jose Antonio Burciaga and Mexican muralist Gilberto Romero Rodriguez. Detail of the 147 x 22 feet mural in Redwood City, California is reproduced.

5630 Garcia, Rupert. Echos de la Mision - Alfaro Siqueiros (1896-1974). EL TECOLOTE, Vol. 4, no. 3 (February 22, 1974), p. 11. English.

AN: Biographical and artistic trajectory of Mexican artist David Alfaro Siqueiros. Artist painted three murals in Southern California in 1932 (MEETING IN THE STREET and TROPICAL AMERICA were done in Los Angeles on the walls of the Chouinard School of Art and the Plaza Art Center, Olvera Street area respectively. The third mural PORTRAIT OF MEXICO was privately commissioned in Santa Monica). The three California murals deal with themes of censorship, racism, colonialism, capitalism, and imperialism. Article suggests that Raza artists are much influenced by the ideas and work of Siqueiros. Illustrated with Rupert Garcia's silkscreen poster SIQUEIROS.

5631 Garcia, Rupert. Muralista mexicano habla sobre los murales y los muralistas en los E.U. EL TECOLOTE, Vol. 5, no. 9 (May 28, 1975), p. 5, 8. Spanish.

AN: Thirty-two-year-old Mexican muralist Gilberto Ramirez has painted 23 murals in Mexico and two murals in the United States (in San Diego and San Francisco, California). Ramirez states that in Mexico, mural painting is more personal and individualized, different from the collective ideal of Chicano muralists. In the U.S., the muralists enjoy more liberty because muralism is not yet controlled by one group of painters. Chicano muralists have much to learn in terms of technique but their best work is fresh and vital. Includes iconographic description of Ramirez mural at the LULAC office, 3000 Folsom St., San Francisco.

5632 Garcia's art. Gallery brochure, n.d.. English.

AN: Brochure of a non-profit center featuring an art gallery and other cultural activities to promote knowledge and education about Chicano and Mexican arts. [Headed by Ralph Garcia who in 1981 is director of PAN, Performance Artists Nucleus.].

5633 Huerta, Elena. [Untitled woodcut]. CARACOL, Vol. 1, no. 12 (August 1975), p. 11.

5634 Iniguez, Javier. [Untitled woodcut]. CARACOL, Vol. 1, no. 12 (August 1975), p. 14.

5635 Iniguez, Javier. [Untitled woodcut]. CARACOL, Vol. 1, no. 12 (August 1975), p. 13.

5636 Jimenez, Sarah. [Untitled woodcut]. CARACOL, Vol. 1, no. 12 (August 1975), p. 12.

Mexican Art (cont.)

5637 The legend of the five murals. [Los Angeles, CA]: Pan American Bank of East Los Angeles, [1966]. Spanish.

AN: Iconography of the five murals in Venetian mosaic created for the Bank by Mexican artist Jose Reyes Meza, information about mosaics, and a brief biography of the artist are included in a biligual brochure. The murals are 10x14-ft each and adorn thefacade of the building.

5638 Martin, Maria Luisa. [Untitled woodcut]. CARACOL, Vol. 1, no. 12 (August 1975), p. 12.

5639 Martinez, Sue. New mural unveiled in Redwood City. EL TECOLOTE, Vol. 8, no. 7 (April 1978), p. 7. English.

AN: Commentary on the 147x22-ft. mural, DANZAS MEXICANAS, painted by Chicano artist Jose Antonio Burciaga and Mexican artist Gilberto Romero at the Redwood City Civic Center. The mural depicts dance rituals from various Mexican regions and the flora and fauna of Mexico. The mural became a subject of controversy when its creators splattered paint on it during its unveiling as a form of protest against the San Mateo Arts Council for its exploitation of Third World artists. Detail of mural showing "La Danza De Los Viejitos".

5640 Mexiac, Adolfo. [Untitled woodcut]. CARACOL, Vol. 1, no. 12 (August 1975), p. 14.

5641 Meza to paint Pan American National Bank murals. MEXICAN AMERICAN SUN, (October 14, 1965). English.

AN: Mexican painter Jose Reyes Meza is commissioned to create a mosaic mural titled OUR PAST, OUR PRESENT, AND OUR FUTURE for the facade of the Pan American National Bank of East Los Angeles being erected on First Street.

5642 Montoya, Jose E. and Carrillo, John M. Posada: the man and his art. A comparative analysis of Jose Guadalupe Posada and the current Chicano art movement as they apply toward social and cultural change: a visual resource unit for Chicano education. Unpublished thesis, 1975. English.

AN: Includes a historical background of 19th century Mexican engraver Posada, the significance of his work, a background of Chicano art, and the influence of Posada and the "calavera" on Chicano art. The unit includes 227 slides of Posada and other Mexican artists; and slides of Chicano artists using the calavera theme.

5643 Notes on 2nd National Community Muralists' Network Conference, Chicago, Ill. April 20-23, 1978. San Francisco, CA, 1978. English.

AN: Rupert Garcia, Raul Martinez, Patricia Rodriguez, Ray Patlan (San Francisco Bay Area) and Jaime Valadez (San Jose), among others, attended the conference in Chicago. Reports were heard from many parts of the United States on mural activities, including that of Aurelio Diaz of Chicago, representing MARCH (Movimiento Artistico Chicano). A workshop presentation was made by Luis Arenal and others from the Taller Siqueiros of Cuernavaca, Mexico. An experimental mural to try Siqueiros'

techniques was created. Illustrated.

5644 Orozco, Jose Clemente. [Untitled painting]. CON SAFOS, no. 8 (1972), p. 35-36.

5645 Orth, Maureen. The soaring spirit of Chicano arts. NEW WEST MAGAZINE, Vol. 3, no. 19 (September 11, 1978), p. 41-46. English.

AN: Overview of California Chicano culture. Color illustrations of works by Mexican muralist David Alfaro Siqueiros, Rupert Garcia, Mujeres Muralistas, Willie Herron, Rene Yanez, Rudy Martinez, San Diego's Chicano Park, ASCO, Jose Montoya.

5646 Palacios, Procopio. Partido Liberal Mexicano [print]. AZTLAN, Vol. 4, no. 2 (Fall 1973), p. Cover. Spanish.

5647 Posada, Jose Guadalupe. [El jarabe en ultratumba (graphic)]. CARACOL, Vol. 1, no. 3 (November 1974), p. Cover.

5648 Rabel, Fanny. [Untitled woodcut]. CARACOL, Vol. 1, no. 12 (August 1975), p. 11.

5649 Rodriguez, Jose Luis. Nuestra voz, arte. LA VOZ CHICANA, Vol. 1, no. 1 (January 1978), p. 5. English.

AN: Brief resume of Diego Rivera as a central figure of Mexican muralism and contributor to a great tradition of realist art. Commentary on the Rockefeller Center Mural of 1933 and The New Workers School Mural of 1969. Intent is to relate the Chicano art movement to its Mexican antecedents. Illustrated with drawings of Diego Rivera and a reproduction of Rivera's mural SUNDAY DREAM AT ALAMEDA PARK.

5650 Rowe, Richard. On Olvera Street: one vision realized, another white washed. REVIEW (Society of Architectural Historians, Pasadena, CA), Vol. 1, no. 1 (Fall 1981), p. 7. English.

AN: Documentation about AMERICA TROPICAL, 1932 mural by David Alfaro Siqueiros. The mural, commissioned by F.K. Ferenz of the Plaza Art Center on Olvera Street in Los Angeles, was a 16' by 80' painting on the second-story wall of the old Italian Hall. From 1968 on, art historian Shifra M. Goldman, working with a small committee, has been actively involved in the attempt to restore the mural. Article details the travails of restoration and underscores the mural's importance. Illustrated.

5651 The stolen art: the O'Higgins mural. RECOBRANDO, Vol. 1, no. 2, p. 15, 16. English.

AN: Historical documentation on 60-foot long 8-foot high fresco mural painted for the Seattle Shipscalers Union in 1949 by Mexican artist Pablo O'Higgins. In 1974, John Caughlan, a people's lawyer documented the existence of the mural to Chicano community groups. M.E.C.H.A. students at the University of Washington lobbied for the murals restoration and permanent exhibition.

Mexican Art (cont.)

5652 Vasquez, Richard. Mojado power: a boost for illegal aliens. CALENDAR, (February 22, 1981), p. 41. English.

AN: An uncritical review of the commercial film made by Mexican film star and comedian Alfonso Arau in the United States primarily for the "American-Hispanic" market on a low-cost budget. Arau planned to distribute in Mexico, Latin America and Spain. The film is a light-weight comedy about a "wetback" who launches a campaign for "mojado power" but falls victim to dope smugglers and is sent to jail.

5653 Vasquez y Sanchez, Ramon. Documentacion del ejercito mexicano en la campana del Alamo [drawings]. CARACOL, Vol. 1, no. 9 (May 1975), p. 12-13.

Mexican Art, Fraternal Ties

5654 11 reproduccion - significacion politica: arte fotocopia. Exhibition invitation, 1979. English.

AN: Invitation to an international exhibit of photocopy artists from Europe, Latin America and the United States. Includes Rene Yanez of San Francisco.

5655 The art of Mexican America. EMPIRE MAGAZINE, (November 1, 1970), p. 24-25. English.

AN: Visual portfolio with minimal text. Includes paintings by Amado Pena, Mel Casas, Porfirio Salinas, and sculpture by Octavio Medellin. On the same page, Dr. Jacinto Quirarte gives views on the nature of Mexican art, the Mexican American artist, and the connection between Mexican and Mexican American art.

5656 Avalos, David. A pure Mexican accent: the popular engravings of Jose Guadalupe Posada. PROCEEDINGS OF THE PACIFIC COAST COUNCIL ON LATIN AMER STUDIES, Vol. 7, (1980, 1981), p. 123-138. English.

AN: As a documentor of injustice and oppression, Posada, 19th century Mexican engraver, is a master who inspires Chicano artists. Appreciation for his art has been expressed by Sacramento artist Jose E. Montoya. Arsacio Vanegas Arroyo, grandson of Posada's publisher, has made his private collection available to Chicano cultural centers, including El Centro Cultural de la Raza, San Diego. Illustrated.

5657 Baciu, Joyce A. and Diaz, Katherine A. Margo Albert: a woman who gets things done = una mujer que realiza lo que desea. CAMINOS, Vol. 2, no. 5 (September 1981), p. 44-46. Bilingual.

AN: Mexican-born Margo Albert is a well-known Los Angeles, CA artist, dancer, and actress who has been most active on behalf of the Plaza de la Raza in East Los Angeles. This article describes her activities as Co-chairperson of the Los Angeles Bicentennial Committee. For Margo, the highlights of the celebration marking the 200th anniversary of the founding of Los Angeles, included a day-long Fiesta del Bicentenario; groundbreaking ceremonies for the Ruben Salazar Bicentennial Building; and the reception for an official delegation of charros, sponsored as a gift to the people of Los Angeles by the Mexican government.

5658 Briseno, Rodolfo. Interview with a muralist. ARRIBA, Vol. 1, no. 1 (July 1980), p. 5+. English.

AN: Raul Valdez, muralist from Del Rio, Texas has been painting murals in Austin and was a founding member of LUCHA (League of United Chicano Artists) in 1976. Having studied with Siqueiros in Mexico, Valdez sees strong affinities in content and form between Chicano and Mexican muralism. Illustrated with two photographs of Valdez's Juarez-Lincoln mural.

5659 California. University. Los Angeles. Cine sin fronteras. Festival brochure, 1981. English.

AN: Brochure program for a cinema festival and series of seminars and discussions featuring films and discussants from Mexico and Chicanos of the United States. Participating were Chicano directors Moctezuma Esparza, Richard Soto, David Sandoval, and Robert Young, and film historian David Maciel.

5660 California. University. Santa Barbara. Coleccion Tloque Nahuaque. Mexican soldaderas and workers during the revolution. Exhibition catalog, 1979. English.

AN: Well illustrated catalog of an exhibition of original lithographs by artists associated with the Taller de Grafica Popular of Mexico. Biographical information and illustrations by Raul Anguiano, Luis Arenal, Alberto Beltran, Angel Bracho, photographer, Agustin V. Casasola, Fernando Castro Pacheco, Jesus Escobedo, Arturo Garcia Bustos, Leopolda Mendez, Francisco Mora, Isidoro Ocampo, Pablo O'Higgins, Mariana Yampolsky and Alfredo Zolca.

5661 Camacho, Eduardo. Por los cien anos de la fundacion de su editorial: inauguraran hoy en San Diego la exposicion 'Homenaje a Posada, Manilla y Vanegas Arroyo'. EXCELSIOR, (February 14, 1980). Spanish.

AN: Announcing the exhibit of 19th Century Mexican engravers Jose Guadalupe Posada and Manuel Manilla, with publisher Antonio Vanegas Arroyo, at the Centro Cultural de la Raza and Southwestern College, of San Diego, CA.

5662 Carlos Pineda shows art in Centennial Museum. EL PASO TIMES, (November 5, 1972). English.

AN: Themes from Mexican folk culture predominate in paintings by Carlos R. Pineda shown at the El Paso Centennial Museum. He has exhibited in Panama, Guadalajara, Phoenix, Tucson, and Dallas and is represented by the Jinx Gallery in El Paso.

5663 Carlos Sandoval to complete mural in Zihuatanejo, Mexico. TIERRA Y LIBERTAD, Vol. 2, no. 4 (July 1980), p. 3, 10. English.

AN: Biographical information on Colorado artist Carlos Sandoval. The Municipal Library in the city of Zihuatanejo in the state of Guerrero is the site of Sandoval's mural which visually and symbolically projects the cultural and historical unity between Mejicanos and Chicanos.

Mexican Art, Fraternal Ties (cont.)

5664 El Centro Cultural de La Raza, San Diego,
CA. One hundred year anniversary: Jose
Guadalupe Posada, Antonio Vanegas Arroyo.
Exhibition invitation, 1980. English.

AN: Invitation to an exhibition of
Mexican engravers Posada and Manuel Manilla
and an homage to their publisher. Also, a
"Chicano Tribute to Jose Guadalupe Posada,"
with contemporary works influenced by
Posada. At the Centro, and at Southwestern
College in Chula Vista.

5665 Chicago. Public Library Cultural Center,
Chicago, IL. La mujer: a visual dialogue.
Exhibition invitation, 1978. English.

AN: Invitation to an exhibit
spotlighting women artists from Mexico and
the United States. Organized by the
Movimiento Artistico Chicano (MARCH) of
Chicago. 40 paintings by women artists
included, and 50 works based on the theme of
women. Poetry readings, music, dance, film,
theatre, and panels of men and women artists
included. Illustrated by work by Linda
Vallejo.

5666 Chicano muralists maintain traditions. LA
CUCARACHA, (November 20, 1979), p. 7.
English.

AN: Introduction to Chicano muralism in
Pueblo and comparison to the Mexican mural
movement from which it draws inspiration. 20
murals painted from 1977 to 1979. The
muralists include Bernardo Duran, Juan
Espinoza, Miguel "Freeloader" Garcia, Lola
Gutierrez, Leo Lucero, Juan Pacheco, Dolores
Pena, Pedro Romero, Stan Salazar, David
Sandoval. Diego Rivera murals illustrated.

5667 Conferencia plastica chicana. Conference
brochure, 1979. English.

AN: Schedule of proceedings at
internationally attended conference on
Chicano and Mexican art and photography
sponsored by the Centro Cultural de LUCHA
(League of United Chicano Artistas) and MAS
(Mujeres Artistas del Suroeste). Brief
biographies of presentors. Illustrated.

5668 Congreso de Artistas Chicanos en Aztlan, San
Diego, CA. Diego Rivera, David Alfaro
Siqueiros, Jose Clemente Orozco: exhibit of
local artists, La Logan [San Diego].
Exhibition brochure, n.d. [c.1974]. English.

AN: Announcement of a traveling exhibit
organized by Galeria de la Raza, San
Francisco, from the collection of the San
Francisco Museum of Art. Illustrated with a
San Diego mural.

5669 Contemporary Arts Museum, Houston, TX and
Martinez, Santos G., Jr. Mexican movie
posters. Exhibition invitation, 1979.
English.

AN: Invitation to an exhibit of posters
primarily from the collecttion of Enrique
Flores and Xavier Gorena of Xochil Art
Center, Mission, Texas. Martinez considers
the posters monumental, with expressive
qualities that have influenced Chicano
poster makers like the Royal Chicano Air
Force, and Rupert Garcia, and Texas artists
like Luis Jimenez, Jesse Trevino and Cesar
Martinez. One illustration. Introduction by
guest curator Santos G. Martinez, Jr. (See
Rupert Garcia's essay in the exhibition

catalog: POSTERS FROM THE GOLDEN AGE OF
MEXICAN CINEMA, for another point of view).

5670 Dittmar Memorial Gallery, Northwestern
University, Evanston, IL and King, Elaine A.
Alejandro Romero: new works. Exhibit
catalog, 1981. English.

AN: Full color illustrated catalog of
paintings by the Mexican-born artist who has
been living in the United States since the
early 1970s. His images appear to be
grounded in the work of Bosch, Goya,
Brueghel, and Diego Rivera. There is a
synthesis of personal symbolism and
expressionism.

5671 Espinosa, Juan. Carlos Sandoval completing
mural in Mexico. LA CUCARACHA, (June 1980).
English.

AN: Details how Carlos Sandoval, Denver
Chicano artist was invited by the Mexican
government to paint mural in Zihuantanejo,
Mexico. The mayor of the Mexican town
states, "this work represents an expression
of two pueblos who want to expand their
relations, as a product of one common
people." Illustrated with photograph of
Carlos Sandoval and one preliminary drawing
of the mural.

5672 Four and four: Mexican and Latino
photography, April 25 through June 14 on the
balcony. CALENDAR: SANTA BARBARA MUSEUM OF
ART, (April 1981). English.

AN: Announcement of exhibit organized by
Lorenzo Hernandez of the Cityscape Foto
Gallery, Pasadena, Calif. Sought to present
"the observable differences between the
'classic' vision of the Mexican National and
the 'realistic' vision of the re-rooted
Mexican/American." The latter included Louis
Bernal (Tucson) and Ricardo Valverde (Los
Angeles) as well as two Spanish Sephardics
of Los Angeles, Camhi and Sisco.

5673 Fourth annual San Antonio film festival. San
Antonio, TX: Oblate College of the
Southwest, 1979. Bilingual.

AN: Symposium and film festival catalog
featuring motion pictures and videocassettes
made by and about Mexicans, Chicanos and
Latinos. The Symposium focused on Latina
women in film and television, Margarita
Galban, Carmen Tafolla, Leticia Ponce, Grace
Castro Nagata, Marcela Fernandez Violante of
Mexico, and Sylvia Morales.

5674 Frankenstein, Alfred. A senior senor's
approach. SAN FRANCISCO CHRONICLE, (May 27,
1976), p. 48. English.

AN: Review of an exhibit of Mexican
painter Jesus Reyes Ferreira at the Mexican
Museum of San Francisco, as well as that of
San Francisco artist Gustavo Rivera, an
abstract expressionist painter. Also
mentions the Museum's mural map, and Angel
del Valle's photography show at the Galeria
de la Raza.

Mexican Art, Fraternal Ties (cont.)

5675 Freedom of expression and the Chicano
Movement: an open letter to Dr. Philip
Ortego. LA LUZ, Vol. 2, no. 5 (September
1973), p. 28-29. English.

AN: An unattributed letter questioning
the imposition of norms on Chicano art. The
author criticizes the practice of
unquestioningly assigning rubrics like
"Mexican" or "Chicano" to certain styles
while excluding others produced by Mexican
American artists.

5676 Galeria de la Raza/Studio 24, San Francisco,
CA. Calacas huesudas. Exhibition brochure,
1980.

AN: Exhibition of Chicano artists for El
Dia de los Muertos with brochure using text
adapted from POSADA'S MEXICO, edited by Ron
Tyler, Library of Congress, Washington,
D.C., 1979. The Galeria exhibit was curated
by Kate Connell, Maria Pinedo and Galeria
staff.

5677 Galeria de la Raza/Studio 24, San Francisco,
CA. Homenaje a Frida Kahlo. Exhibition
brochure, 1978.

AN: 51 artists, Chicano and non-Chicano.

5678 Galeria de la Raza/Studio 24, San Francisco,
CA and Garcia, Rupert. Posters from the
golden age of Mexican cinema. Exhibition
catalog, 1979. English.

AN: The Galeria's second exhibit of
Mexican movie posters features those of the
1940s and early 1950s (in 1971, the exhibit
covered 1943-1971) from the collection of
Enrique Flores, owner of the Rio Theatre,
Mission, Texas, and the Xochil Art Center.
Garcia's essay includes a history of Mexican
cinema, and the mythologizing period of the
"Golden Age" reflected in the posters which
promoted movie-consumership. One
illustration. (See Santos G. Martinez, Jr.'s
essay in the exhibition catalog: MEXICAN
MOVIE POSTERS, for another point of view).

5679 Galeria Tonantzin, Centro Cultural de LUCHA,
Austin, TX. Mexican faces in San Antonio.
Exhibition brochure, [1980]. English.

AN: Photography show by 24 young
Chicanos from Texas sponsored by the
Secretaria de Relaciones Exteriores and the
Universidad Autonoma de Mexico, Cultural
Extension program (SRE-UNAM) in San Antonio.

5680 Garcia, Ralph. Misconceptions or
stereotyping the Chicano and Mexican arts in
San Antonio. CARACOL, Vol. 5, no. 10 (June
1979), p. 9, 10. English.

AN: Brief overview of the arts in San
Antonio, TX, and the desirability of
cultural interchange between Chicano and
Mexican artists.

5681 Garcia, Rupert. Echos de la Mision - Alfaro
Siqueiros (1896-1974). EL TECOLOTE, Vol. 4,
no. 3 (February 22, 1974), p. 11. English.

AN: Biographical and artistic trajectory
of Mexican artist David Alfaro Siqueiros.
Artist painted three murals in Southern
California in 1932 (MEETING IN THE STREET
and TROPICAL AMERICA were done in Los
Angeles on the walls of the Chouinard School
of Art and the Plaza Art Center, Olvera
Street area respectively. The third mural

PORTRAIT OF MEXICO was privately
commissioned in Santa Monica). The three
California murals deal with themes of
censorship, racism, colonialism, capitalism,
and imperialism. Article suggests that Raza
artists are much influenced by the ideas and
work of Siqueiros. Illustrated with Rupert
Garcia's silkscreen poster SIQUEIROS.

5682 Garcia, Rupert. Muralista mexicano habla
sobre los murales y los muralistas en los
E.U. EL TECOLOTE, Vol. 5, no. 9 (May 28,
1975), p. 5, 8. Spanish.

AN: Thirty-two-year-old Mexican muralist
Gilberto Ramirez has painted 23 murals in
Mexico and two murals in the United States
(in San Diego and San Francisco,
California). Ramirez states that in Mexico,
mural painting is more personal and
individualized, different from the
collective ideal of Chicano muralists. In
the U.S., the muralists enjoy more liberty
because muralism is not yet controlled by
one group of painters. Chicano muralists
have much to learn in terms of technique but
their best work is fresh and vital. Includes
iconographic description of Ramirez mural at
the LULAC office, 3000 Folsom St., San
Francisco.

5683 Garcia, Rupert. Raza murals & muralists: an
historical perspective. San Francisco, CA:
Rupert Garcia, n.d.. English.

AN: Basic assumptions are that
socio-economic, political and cultural
relationships exist between the Raza of
Mexico and those of Aztlan (the Southwest
United States) Half the text deals with
Mexican murals, the other half sets Raza
murals in social context, and focuses on
murals in San Francisco's Mission District,
in four locations. 19 illustrations; 9 of
Raza murals. Mural map of the Mission
district.

5684 Geyer, Anne; Hernandez, Lorenzo; and
Valverde, Ricardo. Latino photographers of
U.S. still seeking identity. THE NEWS,
(September 5, 1981), p. 17. English.

AN: Interview with Lorenzo Hernandez,
photo dealer and owner of Cityscape Foto
Gallery, Pasadena, Calif. in which he
compares Mexican with U.S. Latino
photography. Interview with Ricardo
Valverde, Chicano photographer and co-chair
of the Council of Latino Photography/USA,
discussing his work. Illustrated.

5685 Goldman, Shifra M. Las creaturas de la
America tropical: Siqueiros y los murales
chicanos en Los Angeles. REVISTA DE BELLAS
ARTES, no. 25 (January, February, 1976), p.
38-46. Spanish.

AN: Treats the influence of Siqueiros'
1932 outdoor mural in Los Angeles on the
Chicano street mural movement of the 1970s.

5686 Goldman, Shifra M. The intense realism of
Frida Kahlo. CHISMEARTE, Vol. 1, no. 4 (Fall,
Winter, 1977), p. 8-11. English.

AN: A brief, one-page biographical
sketch of Frida Kahlo's life and work. This
is accompanied by black and white
reproductions of her paintings: AUTORRETRATO
COMO TEHUANA (1943), AUTORRETRATO (1946),
RAICES (1943), LA VENADITA (1946), and LA
NOVIA QUE SE ESPANTA DE VER LA VIDA ABIERTA
(n.d.).

Mexican Art, Fraternal Ties (cont.)

5687 Goldman, Shifra M. Resistance and identity: street murals of occupied Aztlan. LATIN AMERICAN LITERARY REVIEW, Vol. 5, no. 10 (Spring, Summer, 1977), p. 124-128. English.

AN: Two periods of Mexican muralism's influence in the U.S.: 1930s and 1960s. Differences between Mexican and Chicano murals nationally. Comparison of the respective iconographies and funding sources. This article was reprinted as "Resistencia e Identidad: Los Murales Callejeros de Aztlan, La Ciudad (sic) Ocupada," in ARTES VISUALES (Mexico, D.F.), no. 16, Fall-Winter, 1977, p. 22-25.

5688 Goldman, Shifra M. Resistencia e identidad: los murales callejeros de Aztlan, la ciudad (sic) ocupada. ARTES VISUALES, no. 16 (Fall, Winter, 1977), p. 22-25. Spanish.

AN: Reprint of article published as "Resistance and identity: street murals of occupied Aztlan" in LATIN AMERICAN LITERARY REVIEW, Vol. 5, no. 10, Spring-Summer 1977, p. 124-128.

5689 Highfill, Holly. MARCH (Movimiento Artistico Chicano). NEW ART EXAMINER, (June 1975), p. 4. English.

AN: Brief history of MARCH (started 1972; chartered 1975). Resume of its activities, including report on most ambitious show of 25 Mexican artists, MEXPOSICION.

5690 Institute, Plaza Mexico unique cultural gift. SAN ANTONIO EXPRESS-NEWS, (June 19, 1972), p. 6-B. English.

AN: Pres. Luis Echeverria of Mexico dedicates the Mexican Cultural Institute and Plaza Mexico, which will house an extension campus of National University of Mexico, in San Antonio. Mexican artists will be brought in and the Institute has a permanent art gallery.

5691 Intar, International Art Relations, Inc., New York, NY and Ferez Kuri, F. Jose. Alejandro E. Romero. Exhibition catalog, 1977. English.

AN: Exhibit catalog of drawings and paintings by Mexican-born painter and muralist living in Chicago. Illustrated in color.

5692 Invitational art exhibition/exposicion artistas invitados. Exhibition invitation, [ca. 1976]. English.

AN: A benefit night for the Chicano Health Clinic included an exhibit of San Diego, as well as Ensenada, Mexicali and Tijuana (Mexico) artists. San Diego Latino artists include Peruvians Guillermo Acevedo and Mario Acevedo Torero, Chicano Salvador Roberto Torres, and Mexican-born Raul Trejo.

5693 Johnson, Richard. The mural at Zihuatanejo. EMPIRE MAGAZINE, (October 12, 1980). English.

AN: Denver artist Carlos M. Sandoval is said to be the first Chicano commissioned by the Mexican government to paint a mural in Mexico. Sandoval's mural is on the facade of the public library in Zihuatanejo. Its theme is unity and synthesis and its title is MESTIZO. Article contains much information on mural activity in Denver, Colorado. Well illustrated with color and black and white photographs.

5694 Kahlo, Frida and Del Solar, Daniel. Frida Kahlo's THE BIRTH OF MOSES. TIN TAN, Vol. 1, no. 2 (September 1975), p. 2-6. Bilingual.

AN: Mexican painter Frida Kahlo's explanation of her painting THE BIRTH OF MOSES in Spanish, with an error-ridden translation to English. Source of the original text not given. Illustrated.

5695 Kamin, Ira. Memories of Frida Kahlo. CALIFORNIA LIVING, (May 6, 1979), p. 44-50. English.

AN: Chatty review of the sixth annual Dia de los Muertos, celebrated by the Galeria de la Raza this year with an homage to Mexican painter Frida Kahlo. Local artists filled the gallery with their homages; the Galeria's outdoor billboard was painted with her image; guests brought gifts and dressed in Kahlo style, including older women who wore jewelry given them by Kahlo. Biographical material on Kahlo and Diego Rivera should be read with caution. Well illustrated.

5696 Lefebre, Francisco. El mural chicano en Nuevo Mexico. RAYAS, Vol. 1, no. 2 (March, April, 1978), p. 7. Spanish.

AN: Albuquerque muralist writes about Chicano murals which derive from pre-Columbian and modern Mexican murals. New Mexican muralism started in 1970 with the Muralistas Guadalupanos de Aztlan in Santa Fe. In 1971 and 1972 students at the Highlands University of Las Vegas, New Mexico also painted murals. In addition, murals have appeared in Albuquerque. Brief biography of Lefebre. Illustrated.

5697 Lucas, Jerry. Testimonios de Latinoamerica. CHISMEARTE, no. 6 (February 1980), p. 6-9. English.

AN: Review of the exhibits TESTIMONIOS DE LATINOAMERICA and AMERICA EN LA MIRA, brought to Los Angeles Contemporary Exhibitions Gallery by Chicano curator Roberto Gil de Montes, as part of a cultural exchange between the Mexican Cultural Workers Front and Felipe Ehrenberg of the Grupo Proceso Pentagono of Mexico, and Chicano artists and photographers from the Council of Latino Photography/USA in Los Angeles. Well illustrated.

5698 Martinez, Manuel. The art of the Chicano movement, and the movement of Chicano art. In: Valdez, Luis and Steiner, Stan eds. AZTLAN: AN ANTHOLOGY OF MEXICAN AMERICAN LITERATURE. New York: Vintage, 1972, p.349-353. English.

AN: "Like the modern art of Mexico, the new Chicano art is essentially an art of social protest," writes Denver, Colorado muralist and easel painter Martinez. He traces the roots of Chicano art back into Indian, colonial and modern Mexican art, and defines two kinds of Chicano art.

Mexican Art, Fraternal Ties (cont.)

5699 M.E.C.H.A. cultura y evolucion mexicana. EL
CLARIN, (May 2, 1974), p. 3. Spanish.

AN: Report on the mural designed and
painted under the direction of Mexican-born
designer Sergio O'Cadiz at Santa Ana
College, Santa Ana, Calif. Collaborators
were instructor Shifra Goldman and gallery
director Mike Davis, with members of the
MEChA Club and other students. The mural
concerns the history of Mexico and of the
Chicano and includes a tribute to David
Alfaro Siqueiros' Los Angeles mural AMERICA
TROPICAL, painted and white-washed in the
1930s. Illustrated.

5700 Mesa-Bains, Amalia. Homage to Frida Kahlo
opens Nov. 2, at Galeria de la Raza. EL
TECOLOTE, Vol. 9, no. 1 (September 1978), p.
7. English.

AN: Announcement and call for artwork to
Galeria de la Raza's exhibition honoring
Frida Kahlo on Nov. 2, 1978. The proposed
"Homage to Frida Kahlo" will encompass four
major areas; artists' work,
documentation/publication, related art
productions, and educational activities. The
Galeria educated participating artists to
the life and art of Frida Kahlo through
slide presentations and written material.
The exhibition became a milestone in the
Galeria de la Raza history.

5701 MEXICAN MUSEUM NEWSLETTER. Vol. 6, no. 1
(Winter 1980, 1981). English.

AN: Regular report on the activities,
finances, membership, and other information
about the Museum. Announces several upcoming
shows: Rupert Garcia, six Mexican geometric
artists, paintings and prints by Mexican
American and Mexican women artists, Mexican
Leonel Maciel and Chicano Carlos Almaraz,
Mexican folk art, Manuel Neri sculpture, and
Mexican Luis Jaso.

5702 The Mexican Museum, San Francisco, CA. Bruno
Andrade (from Missouri) and Antonio Lopez
Saenz (from Mexico). Exhibition
announcement, 1978. English.

AN: Flyer announcing an exhibit at the
Mexican Museum of Texas-born Andrade who is
exhibiting large abstract landscapes.
Andrade teaches in Columbia, Missouri; this
is his first California exhibit.

5703 The Mexican Museum, San Francisco, CA. Los
primeros cinco anos: fifth anniversary
exhibit. Exhibition brochure, 1980-81.
English.

AN: 65 Mexican, Chicano, and Latino
artists exhibited for the fifth anniversary
of the Mexican Museum, directed by artist
Peter Rodriguez. Cover is drawing by Carmen
Lomas Garza.

5704 The Mexican Museum, San Francisco, CA.
Recent works of Leonel Maciel and Carlos
Almaraz. Exhibition invitation, 1981.
English.

AN: Invitation to an exhibit of works by
Mexican artist Maciel and Chicano painter
Almaraz.

5705 The Mexican Museum, San Francisco, CA.
Recent works of Luis Jaso from Mexico City
and Carlos Chavez Cordova from Los Angeles.
Exhibition invitation, 1981. English.

AN: Invitation to an exhibit.

5706 Mexican-American Advisory Committee of the
Museum of Science and Industry.. Second
annual Mexican-American art fiesta.
Exhibition brochure, 1975. English.

AN: Exhibit of paintings, sculpture,
crafts, and photography by 49 artists from
Illinois, Indiana, and Mexico. Includes many
of the most important Chicano artists of the
Chicago area.

5707 Mexican-American Institute of Cultural
Exchange, San Antonio, TX and Alvarez
Acosta, Miguel. Mel Casas paintings.
Exhibition brochure, 1963. Bilingual.

AN: Exhibition brochure with
biographical and exhibition chronology for
El Paso born painter, Meliseo Casas. He is
the first non-Mexican born artist invited to
exhibit at the art gallery sponsored by the
International Organization of Cultural
Promotion for Foreign Relations in San
Antonio.

5708 Miguelez, Armando. La cultura chicana: los
murales. RAYAS, Vol. 1, no. 5 (September,
October, 1978), p. 9. Spanish.

AN: Miguelez, a writer from Tucson,
Arizona, divides muralistic production into
two categories: cultural muralism and
creative muralism. Both types of murals
function as alternatives to establishment
art, to mono-cultural education and to
ethnocentric history. Relates Chicano mural
movement to its antecedent in Mexico, but
most especially to the mural production of
other ethnic minorities in the United
States.

5709 Mills House Visual Arts Complex, Garden
Grove, CA. Menudo: artistas latinos de
Orange County. Exhibit invitation, 1980.
English.

AN: Invitation to an exhibit organized
for the first anniversary of Artistas
Latinos de Orange County including Delores
Grajeda, William Hernandez, Marylee Montano,
Patricia Murillo, Irene Ramos, Juan Ramos,
Ricardo Serrato, Miguel Shanahan, Arthur
Valenzuela, Benjamin Valenzuela, Jack
Vargas, Alonzo Whitney, Emigdio Vasquez,
Susana Zaccagnino, and Mexican artist
Artemio Sepulveda.

5710 Mission to honor Frida Kahlo: famous Mexican
artist. EL TECOLOTE, Vol. 9, no. 3 (November
1978), p. 1. Bilingual.

AN: Announcement of an homage to Mexican
painter Frida Kahlo at the Galeria de la
Raza's annual celebration of Dia de los
Muertos. Works reproduced with the article
include those of Emmanuel C. Montoya, Yreina
Cervantez, Jose Antonio Burciaga, Nina
Serrano and Lisa Kokin. Bilingual.

Mexican Art, Fraternal Ties (cont.)

5711 Montoya, Jose E. and Carrillo, John M.
Posada: the man and his art. A comparative
analysis of Jose Guadalupe Posada and the
current Chicano art movement as they apply
toward social and cultural change: a visual
resource unit for Chicano education.
Unpublished thesis, 1975. English.

AN: Includes a historical background of
19th century Mexican engraver Posada, the
significance of his work, a background of
Chicano art, and the influence of Posada and
the "calavera" on Chicano art. The unit
includes 227 slides of Posada and other
Mexican artists; and slides of Chicano
artists using the calavera theme.

5712 Moreno, Dorinda. La mujer y el arte.
TEJIDOS, Vol. 3, no. 1 (Spring 1976), p. 17.
Spanish.

AN: Brief introduction to the collection
of poems by Dorinda Moreno published in this
issue of TEJIDOS. She also dedicates the
collection by alluding to the significance
and influence of two artists: Frida Kahlo
and Rosaura Revueltas.

5713 Orange Co. Library. El Modena Branch.
Empanada: a tasty Mexican group art exhibit
filled with a variety of digestable treats.
Exhibition catalog, [1979]. English.

AN: Catalog of an exhibit by 15 artists:
Dolores Grajeda, William Hernandez-M.,
Marylee Montano, Patricia Murillo, Eduardo
Navarro, Susana A. Zaccagnino, Esau Quiroz,
Juan Elias Ramos, Ricardo M. Serrato,
Benjamin Valenzuela, Emigdio C. Vasquez,
Arthur Valenzuela, Jack Vargas, Alonso
Whitney, and Mexican artist Artemio
Sepulveda living in Orange County. Brief
profiles of the artists.

5714 Patterson, Ann. Exhibit at Unitarian: Smith,
Quesada art black, white contrast. TEMPE
DAILY NEWS, (March 16, 1976). English.

AN: Eugenio Quesada presented drawings
of female torsos along with Smith. Both are
industrial design faculty members at Arizona
State University. Article mentions other
Quesada shows, and his participation on the
Jean Charlot mural at the University.

5715 Quirarte, Jacinto. Mexican-American artists.
Austin, TX: University of Texas Press, 1973.
English.

AN: First comprehensive historical text
on artists of Mexican descent in the United
States. Sets up the antecedents from
settlement to the visits of Mexican
muralists Rivera, Siqueiros, Orozco and
Tamayo in the U.S., though only Orozco and
Tamayo are considered at length. Mexican
American artists are divided by decades of
birth, from 1901 to 1946. Twenty-seven
artists (two women) are discussed. The
epilogue is a discussion on the terms
"Mexican American" and "Chicano," the latter
articulated by Esteban Villa, who is not in
the text.

5716 Rangel, Jesus. Heirs of Jose Posada:
revolution lives in Chicano art. SAN DIEGO
UNION, (February 24, 1980), p. D6. English.

AN: 19th century Mexican engraver Jose
Guadalupe Posada has been an inspiration to
Chicano artists. Along with two exhibits of
his work, the Centro Cultural de la Raza is
also showing calavera (skeleton) images by
Chicano artists: skull-masks from the Teatro
Campesino, a print by Amalia Mesa-Baines of
Frida Kahlo, and a collaged box by Jose
Antonio Burciaga. Illustration: Salvador
Roberto Torres work.

5717 Rodriguez, Jose Luis. Nuestra voz, arte. LA
VOZ CHICANA, Vol. 1, no. 1 (January 1978),
p. 5. English.

AN: Brief resume of Diego Rivera as a
central figure of Mexican muralism and
contributor to a great tradition of realist
art. Commentary on the Rockefeller Center
Mural of 1933 and The New Workers School
Mural of 1969. Intent is to relate the
Chicano art movement to its Mexican
antecedents. Illustrated with drawings of
Diego Rivera and a reproduction of Rivera's
mural SUNDAY DREAM AT ALAMEDA PARK.

5718 S.A. site for National Symposium on Mexican
American Art. CHICANO TIMES, Vol. 4, no. 30
(November 9, 1973), p. 5. English.

AN: Held at Trinity University, the
Symposium discussed such issues as, creative
evolution, art education, artistic
relationships to Mexico and the evolution of
Mexican American art in the California
barrios. Participating artists included Rudy
Trevino, Mel Casas, Octavio Medellin,
Antonio Garcia, Carmen Garza, Esteban Villa,
Jose Montoya, Ernesto Palomino, Michael
Ponce de Leon, Luis Jimenez and Eugenio
Quesada.

5719 Stofflet-Santiago, Mary. The fifth sun:
esthetic quality versus curatorial intent.
ARTWEEK, Vol. 8, no. 37 (November 5, 1977),
p. 6. English.

AN: Review of the exhibit THE FIFTH SUN
at the University Art Museum in Berkeley,
Calif., curated by Ralph Maradiaga of the
Galeria de la Raza. It contains folk art,
and posters by Chicano artists Maradiaga,
Rupert Garcia, Juan Fuentes, mural studies
by Graciela Carrillo and Mike Rios, ceramics
by Anna de Leon, an altar by Amalia
Mesa-Bains, and mural drawings by Mexican
muralists. The writer criticizes the uneven
quality of the show, but encourages better
ones in the future. Illustrated.

5720 Testimonios de Latinoamerica. LA PRENSA SAN
DIEGO, (October 26, 1979), p. 3. Spanish.

AN: Announcement of an exhibit at the
Centro Cultural de la Raza, San Diego,
"Testimonios de Latino America" and "America
en la mira," political graphics organized by
Mexican artist Felipe Ehrenberg and also
shown at the Los Angeles Contemporary
Exhibitions gallery (LACE).

5721 Thwaites, Lynette. Art on the border.
COMMUNITY ARTS NEWSLETTER, Vol. 3, no. 3
(July 1981). English.

AN: The Centro Cultural de la Raza has
been a pioneer of intercultural activity
between Mexico and the United States in the
San Diego area. The Arizona Commission on
the Arts has promoted numerous exchanges and
publishes a bilingual quarterly bulletin. In
Mission, Texas, Xavier Gorena of the Xochil
Art Center is forging ties with Mexico City.

Mexican Art, Fraternal Ties (cont.)

5722 The Tortuga paints a new mural. CHISMEARTE, Vol. 2, no. 1 (Summer 1978), p. 12-13. English.

AN: Black and white details of new indoor mural painted at the Gilroy's Recreation Center.

5723 University Art Museum, Berkeley, CA. The Fifth Sun: Contemporary/Traditional Chicano & Latino Art. Exhibition catalog, 1977. English.

AN: Catalog of exhibit including 45 artists of northern California. Texts deal with Mexican muralists, Mujeres Muralistas & other muralists, posters, the Chicano art movement, altars, La Raza Silkscreen Center, Galeria de la Raza, the Mexican Museum, the Sacramento Centro de Artistas Chicanos/RCAF. Mural maps of S.F. Bay Area and Sacramento. Many illustrations.

5724 Vigil, Maria. Hello, walls: Tucson's murals. WEEKENDER MAGAZINE, (March 29, 1980), p. 14-16. English.

AN: Article on muralism, from the Mexican to those of Chicanos. Focuses on Tucson murals by Roberto Borboa, Antonio Pazos, David Tineo and Fred Monreal. Color illustrations.

5725 Viva Siqueiros. CON SAFOS, no. 7 (Winter 1971), p. 26-27. English.

AN: Brief recapitulation of the controversy surrounding David Alfaro Siqueiros' visit to Los Angeles, CA in 1932. It was during this visit that he painted the only public Siqueiros mural in the U.S. which still remains, albeit covered over with whitewash. The details of the visit are explained by Siqueiros in his book: MI RESPUESTA. The article is illustrated with two black and white details of the mural.

5726 Wasserman, Isabelle. Photos on exhibit capture Mexican revolution. SAN DIEGO UNION, (November 26, 1981), p. D10. English.

AN: Report on the photographic exhibition of Mexican revolutionary photographer Agustin V. Casasola at the Centro Cultural de la Raza in San Diego. Illustrated.

Mexican Cultural Institute, San Antonio, TX

5727 Institute, Plaza Mexico unique cultural gift. SAN ANTONIO EXPRESS-NEWS, (June 19, 1972), p. 6-B. English.

AN: Pres. Luis Echeverria of Mexico dedicates the Mexican Cultural Institute and Plaza Mexico, which will house an extension campus of National University of Mexico, in San Antonio. Mexican artists will be brought in and the Institute has a permanent art gallery.

Mexican Cultural Workers Front

5728 Lucas, Jerry. Testimonios de Latinoamerica. CHISMEARTE, no. 6 (February 1980), p. 6-9. English.

AN: Review of the exhibits TESTIMONIOS DE LATINOAMERICA and AMERICA EN LA MIRA, brought to Los Angeles Contemporary Exhibitions Gallery by Chicano curator Roberto Gil de Montes, as part of a cultural exchange between the Mexican Cultural Workers Front and Felipe Ehrenberg of the Grupo Proceso Pentagono of Mexico, and Chicano artists and photographers from the Council of Latino Photography/USA in Los Angeles. Well illustrated.

Mexican Museum, San Francisco, CA

5729 Alarcon, Francisco X. El Museo Mexicano, quinto aniversario. EL TECOLOTE LITERARY MAGAZINE, (December 10, 1981). Spanish.

AN: Goals of the Mexican Museum in San Francisco are contextualized within the social nexus of the Chicano Art Movement of the 1960s. Explains functional difference between Mexican Museum and community art galleries.

5730 Alarcon, Francisco X. and Herrera, Juan Felipe. Portraits plus struggles plus consciousness: nine pastels by Rupert Garcia. METAMORFOSIS, Vol. 3, no. 2 (1980), p. 104-106. English.

AN: Reprint of article published as "Rupert Garcia: portraits/retratos" in EL TECOLOTE LITERARY MAGAZINE (San Francisco, CA), Vol. 2, no. 1, March 1981, p. 6.

5731 Alarcon, Francisco X. Rupert Garcia: portraits/retratos. EL TECOLOTE LITERARY MAGAZINE, Vol. 2, no. 1 (March 1981), p. 6+. Bilingual.

AN: Review of Garcia exhibit at the Mexican Museum (S.F.) in 1981. Includes portraits of Frida Kahlo and the Flores Magon brothers, Goya, Van Gogh, Ethel and Julius Rosenberg, etc. Illustrated. This article has been reprinted in METAMORFOSIS under a different title: "Portraits Plus Struggles Plus Consciousness: Nine Pastels by Rupert Garcia," Vol. 3-4, no. 1-2, (1980-81), p. 104-106.

5732 Around the Bay. METAMORFOSIS, Vol. 3, no. 2 (1980), p. 101-108. English.

AN: Cultural review of activities in the Bay Area, northern California, and Sacramento. Includes history of the Galeria de la Raza/Studio 24 (San Francisco), the Centro de Artistas Chicanos/RCAF, Royal Chicano Air Force (Sacramento), and a review of Rupert Garcia's pastel portraits exhibit at the Mexican Museum (S.F.) in 1981. Illustrated. Continued in Vol. 4, no. 1, 1981.

5733 Bloomfield, Arthur. Zesty show at Mexican museum. SAN FRANCISCO EXAMINER, (February 1, 1977), p. 24. English.

AN: Review of an exhibit of Mexican and Mexican American artists from the Southwest and the San Francisco area. Commentary and analysis on artists Vincent Perez and Gustavo Rivera, Rudy Trevino and Al Barela. The work selected focused on aesthetic quality rather than the ethnic identification of the artist.

--   --

Mexican Museum, San Francisco, CA (cont.)

5734 Cardona, Patricia. Gana adeptos de Museo
     Mexicano de San Francisco: Pedro Rodriguez.
     UNO MAS UNO, (February 6, 1978), p. 18.
     Spanish.

     AN: Report and brief history of the
     Mexican Museum which opened in 1975 with a
     collection of colonial santos. The museum
     offers a vista of Mexican culture to people
     in the United States. Director Peter
     Rodriguez says that Chicano artists Roberto
     Gonzalez, Felipe Reyes, Alfredo Arreguin,
     Gustavo Rivera, and Carmen Lomas Garza are
     some of the best. Illustrated.

5735 Cardona, Patricia. El museo mexicano de San
     Francisco. EL DIA, (July 6, 1977), p. 10.
     Spanish.

     AN: Report on the Mexican Museum giving
     a brief overview of its programs. The
     Mexican Museum opened Nov. 20, 1975 and has
     been a vital force in the cultural life of
     San Francisco, showing the work of one
     Mexican and one Chicano artist every two
     months.

5736 De Lappe, Pele. Gordo plus folk art.
     PEOPLE'S WORLD, Vol. 42, no. 41 (October 13,
     1979), p. 10. English.

     AN: Announcement of an exhibit at the
     Mexican Museum of Gus Arriola's syndicated
     comic strip "Gordo." Arizona-born Arriola
     was an animator for Columbia and MGM
     cartoons until he created "Gordo" in 1941.
     Illustrated.

5737 Editorial - Mexican Museum. SAN FRANCISCO
     CHRONICLE, (November 2, 1981), p. 38.
     English.

     AN: Editorial statement lauding the
     Mexican Museum as an important cultural
     asset for the city of San Francisco. As the
     Museum relocates to Ft. Mason from its old
     headquarters in The Mission District, it
     expands its exhibitions, cultural and
     educational programs.

5738 Frankenstein, Alfred. An artistic taste of
     Mexico in the city. SAN FRANCISCO CHRONICLE,
     (November 29, 1975), p. 29. English.

     AN: A very favorable review of the
     inaugural exhibit at the Mexican Museum. The
     opening show was a panoramic view of Mexican
     art including pre-Hispanic, colonial, folk
     art and fine art. Among the Mexican American
     artists presented were Roberto Gonzalez,
     Raul Mora and Gustavo Rivera.

5739 Frankenstein, Alfred. Just for the record.
     SAN FRANCISCO CHRONICLE, (May 27, 1976), p.
     48. English.

     AN: Positive review of exhibit at the
     Mexican Museum featuring the work of Jesus
     Reyes Ferreira from Mexico and Gustavo
     Rivera from San Francisco.
     Ninety-five-year-old Ferreira uses tempera
     on tissue paper to render brilliant
     paintings focusing on Mexican folk motifs.
     Rivera paints in the abstract expressionist
     mode with power and passion. Article also
     lauds the photographic work of Angel del
     Valle in his exhibition: SEMBRADORES at the
     Galeria de la Raza.

5740 Frankenstein, Alfred. A senior senor's
     approach. SAN FRANCISCO CHRONICLE, (May 27,
     1976), p. 48. English.

     AN: Review of an exhibit of Mexican
     painter Jesus Reyes Ferreira at the Mexican
     Museum of San Francisco, as well as that of
     San Francisco artist Gustavo Rivera, an
     abstract expressionist painter. Also
     mentions the Museum's mural map, and Angel
     del Valle's photography show at the Galeria
     de la Raza.

5741 MEXICAN MUSEUM NEWSLETTER. Vol. 6, no. 1
     (Winter 1980, 1981). English.

     AN: Regular report on the activities,
     finances, membership, and other information
     about the Museum. Announces several upcoming
     shows: Rupert Garcia, six Mexican geometric
     artists, paintings and prints by Mexican
     American and Mexican women artists, Mexican
     Leonel Maciel and Chicano Carlos Almaraz,
     Mexican folk art, Manuel Neri sculpture, and
     Mexican Luis Jaso.

5742 The Mexican Museum, San Francisco, CA and
     Quirarte, Jacinto. 17 artists:
     Hispano/Mexican-American/Chicano. Exhibition
     catalog, 1977. English.

     AN: Catalog of an exhibit for artists
     Emilio Aguirre, Consuelo Gonzalez Amezcua,
     Al Barela, Pedro Cervantez, Edward Chavez,
     Antonio Garcia, Louis Gutierrez, Harry
     Louie, Vincent Perez, Michael Ponce de Leon,
     Eugenio Quesada, Gustavo Rivera, Peter
     Rodriguez, Alex Sanchez, Darryl Sapien, Rudy
     Trevino, Manuel Villamor. Illustrated.

5743 The Mexican Museum, San Francisco, CA.
     Alexander Maldonado. Exhibition brochure,
     1979. English.

     AN: One page autobiographical statement
     by Alexander Maldonado. Includes sources of
     his imagery.

5744 The Mexican Museum, San Francisco, CA. Bruno
     Andrade (from Missouri) and Antonio Lopez
     Saenz (from Mexico). Exhibition
     announcement, 1978. English.

     AN: Flyer announcing an exhibit at the
     Mexican Museum of Texas-born Andrade who is
     exhibiting large abstract landscapes.
     Andrade teaches in Columbia, Missouri; this
     is his first California exhibit.

5745 The Mexican Museum, San Francisco, CA. Cinco
     de Mayo exhibit at the Cannery. Exhibition
     brochure, 1980. English.

     AN: Well-illustrated brochure with text
     by Nora Wagner and Bea Carrillo Hocker.
     Succinct statements on the history, purpose
     and programs of the Mexican Museum.

5746 The Mexican Museum, San Francisco, CA.
     Manuel Neri: sculpture and drawings.
     Exhibition invitation, 1981. English.

     AN: Illustrated invitation to an
     exhibit.

5747 The Mexican Museum, San Francisco, CA. Los
     primeros cinco anos: fifth anniversary
     exhibit. Exhibition brochure, 1980-81.
     English.

     AN: 65 Mexican, Chicano, and Latino
     artists exhibited for the fifth anniversary
     of the Mexican Museum, directed by artist
     Peter Rodriguez. Cover is drawing by Carmen
     Lomas Garza.

Mexican Museum, San Francisco, CA (cont.)

5748 The Mexican Museum, San Francisco, CA.
Rupert Garcia: portraits/retratos.
Exhibition brochure, 1981. English.

AN: Exhibition brochure with
biographical information and exhibition
chronology for Rupert Garcia.

5749 The Mexican Museum, San Francisco, CA.
Virginia Jaramillo. Exhibition brochure,
1980. English.

AN: Exhibition brochure with
biographical information, exhibition
chronology and an artist's statement.

5750 Morch, Albert. He put down his brushes for a
dream. SAN FRANCISCO SUNDAY EXAMINER AND
CHRONICLE, (October 2, 1977), p. Scene, 3.
English.

AN: Brief profile of painter Peter
Rodriguez, founder and director of the
Mexican Museum in San Francisco which opened
in 1975. On exhibit are the works of San
Francisco artist Jerry Concha. Illustrated.

5751 Morch, Albert. Mexican art through a
cartoonist's eyes. SAN FRANCISCO EXAMINER,
(September 24, 1979), p. 28. English.

AN: Review of "GORDO'S WORLD" and the
paintings of Alexander Maldonado, an
exhibition at the Mexican Museum.
Biographical information on Gustavo Montano
Arriola, creator of the Gordo cartoon in
1941. The exhibit conceived and designed by
the San Diego Museum of Art, had
representative blow-ups of the strip along
with artifacts. Maldonado, a self-taught
artist started painting at age 60. His
canvases embrace a fascination with towers,
unique buildings, underground cities and
skylines from an imagined urban environment.

5752 Neri, Manuel. Untitled standing figure no. 4
[sculpture]. PEOPLE'S WORLD, Vol. 44, no. 19
(May 9, 1981), p. 10. English.

AN: Illustration of a painted bronze
figure by San Francisco Bay artist Manuel
Neri. Drawings and sculpture by Neri to be
shown at the Mexican Museum.

5753 Penate, Luis Humberto. Crisis economica
limita accion de museo mexicano. TIEMPO
LATINO, Vol. 14, (October 21, 1981), p. 3.
Spanish.

AN: Article stresses the severe
financial limitations under which the
Mexican Museum operates. Gives reasons for
the Museum leaving the Mission district and
quotes its Director, Pedro Rodriguez, on
future goals and aspirations of the museum.

5754 Temko, Allan. Ole! It's already a triumph.
REVIEW [supplement to SAN FRANCISCO SUNDAY
EXAMINER], (December 28, 1980), p. 13-14.
English.

AN: A glowing report on the Mexican
Museum as it celebrates its fifth
anniversary. Provides details about
programs, financing and goals. Brief
analysis of the work of sculptor Manuel Neri
and painters Manuel Villamor, Gustavo
Rivera, Alfredo Arreguin and Miguel
Almaguer. Informative profile on Peter
Rodriguez, founder and Executive Director of
the Museum.

5755 Torres, Miguel. Mexican Museum - artifacts
and culture to open in S.F. EL TECOLOTE,
Vol. 6, no. 1 (October 1975), p. 4. English.

AN: On April 1972, the first
organizational meeting of a new Mexican
Museum was held. Later, a Board of Directors
was organized and fifteen months later, the
Museum was incorporated by the state of
California as a non-profit organization.
Pedro Rodriguez, founder-director of the
Museum tells his aspirations and goals for
this unique repository of Mexican culture in
the United States. Illustrated with
photograph of the Director and examples of
work from the Museum's collection.

5756 University Art Museum, Berkeley, CA. The
Fifth Sun: Contemporary/Traditional Chicano
& Latino Art. Exhibition catalog, 1977.
English.

AN: Catalog of exhibit including 45
artists of northern California. Texts deal
with Mexican muralists, Mujeres Muralistas &
other muralists, posters, the Chicano art
movement, altars, La Raza Silkscreen Center,
Galeria de la Raza, the Mexican Museum, the
Sacramento Centro de Artistas Chicanos/RCAF.
Mural maps of S.F. Bay Area and Sacramento.
Many illustrations.

5757 Vasquez Tagle, Jose Jorge. Museo Mexicano,
un rincon de nuestra cultura en San
Francisco, California. EL OCCIDENTAL,
(October 19, 1980). Spanish.

AN: Rotogravure with twelve colored
illustrations of works from the Mexican
Museum collections. Text is a mini catalog
of the museum's holdings and includes
information on funding sources.

MEXICAN OR AMERICAN [film]

5758 Films for the inner city. Los Angeles, CA:
Los Angeles Public Library Federal Project,
1971. English.

AN: Annotated catalog of 16mm films and
filmstrips, educational and documentary.
Those concerning Mexican heritage include
CHICANO FROM THE SOUTHWEST (1970),
HENRY...BOY OF THE BARRIO (1969); HOW'S
SCHOOL, ENRIQUE (1970), I AM JOAQUIN (1970),
THE MEXICAN AMERICAN: HERITAGE AND DESTINY
(1970), A MEXICAN AMERICAN FAMILY (1970),
MEXICAN AMERICANS: QUEST FOR EQUALITY
(1968), MEXICAN OR AMERICAN (1970),
SIQUEIROS: "EL MAESTRO" (THE MARCH OF
HUMANITY IN LATIN AMERICA) (1969).
Filmstrips include THE AWAKENING (LA RAZA) -
Part IV, CONFLICT OF CULTURES (LA RAZA) -
Part III, MASTERWORKS OF MEXICAN ART, OUT OF
THE MAINSTREAM, PILGRIMAGE (GRAPE STRIKERS).
Also listed are films and filmstrips for
children.

Mexican Revolution - 1910-1920

5759 Drescher, Tim and Garcia, Rupert. Recent Raza murals in the U.S. RADICAL AMERICA, Vol. 12, no. 2 (March, April, 1978), p. 14-31. English.

AN: Like the cultural revolution of Mexico in the 1920s, La Raza of Aztlan emphasizes the Native American and mestizo heritage as well as the Mexican revolutionary heritage. Withn a social context, the authors discuss Chicano and Latino murals nationally. Iconography and its relation to Chicano experience is explored, as well as images by and about women. Illustrations.

5760 Wasserman, Isabelle. Photos on exhibit capture Mexican revolution. SAN DIEGO UNION, (November 26, 1981), p. D10. English.

AN: Report on the photographic exhibition of Mexican revolutionary photographer Agustin V. Casasola at the Centro Cultural de la Raza in San Diego. Illustrated.

Mexico

5761 CODEX NEWSLETTER (Galeria de la Raza, San Francisco, CA). Vol. 1, no. 2 (September 1973). English.

AN: An in-house bulletin of upcoming events: EL SOL NUNCA MUERE, photography/poster exhibit, Rolando Garces, and Peruvian posters; Mujeres de Aztlan, women artists' collective exhibit; Filipino/Samoan art exhibit; Galeria Christmas art sale; Galeria pavilion at S.F. annual art festival; Rockefeller scholarship for Galeria curator Luis Santana; Galeria coloring book; Balmy Alley mural project; Diego Rivera exhibit; first installment of Rupert Garcia's RAZA MURALS AND MURALISTS: AN HISTORICAL VIEW.

5762 S.A. site for National Symposium on Mexican American Art. CHICANO TIMES, Vol. 4, no. 30 (November 9, 1973), p. 5. English.

AN: Held at Trinity University, the Symposium discussed such issues as, creative evolution, art education, artistic relationships to Mexico and the evolution of Mexican American art in the California barrios. Participating artists included Rudy Trevino, Mel Casas, Octavio Medellin, Antonio Garcia, Carmen Garza, Esteban Villa, Jose Montoya, Ernesto Palomino, Michael Ponce de Leon, Luis Jimenez and Eugenio Quesada.

5763 Torres, Louis R. RAICES DE SANGRE: first full length film directed by a Chicano. SOMOS, Vol. 1, no. 2 (July 1978), p. 16-19. English.

AN: Report on Jesus Salvador Trevino's RAICES DE SANGRE, the only film made by a Chicano at the Mexican film studio, CONACINE. Deals with the efforts of Chicanos and Mexicans living in border cities to organize an international labor union. Trevino's previous work is briefly mentioned. Illustrated.

Mexico City

5764 Goldman, Shifra M. Hecho en Latino America: first photography colloquium and exhibition. CHISMEARTE, no. 6 (February 1980), p. 16-25. English.

AN: Report on the first colloquium of Latin American photography, Mexico City, May 1978. Analysis and critique of U.S. Latino photographers' work presented in exhibition. Well illustrated.

5765 Mexican-American lawyers' club donates Kennedy mural to the people of Mexico. EASTSIDE SUN, (November 28, 1968). English.

AN: East Los Angeles artist Armando Campero commissioned to paint mural for "Unidad de Kennedy" housing development in Mexico City.

Mexico. Secretaria de Relaciones Exteriores/UNAM

5766 Extension Cultural SRE/UNAM, San Antonio, TX. Second non professional (black & white) photography contest: Mexican women in Texas. Competition announcement, [ca. 1980]. English.

AN: Announcement of photographic competition sponsored by the Extension arm of the Secretaria de Relaciones Exteriores/Universidad Nacional Autonoma de Mexico in San Antonio. The theme specified an homage to the Mexican woman in Texas.

5767 Galeria Tonantzin, Centro Cultural de LUCHA, Austin, TX. Mexican faces in San Antonio. Exhibition brochure, [1980]. English.

AN: Photography show by 24 young Chicanos from Texas sponsored by the Secretaria de Relaciones Exteriores and the Universidad Autonoma de Mexico, Cultural Extension program (SRE-UNAM) in San Antonio.

5768 Galeria Tonantzin, Centro Cultural de LUCHA, Austin, TX. Young Chicano photographers from throughout Texas. Exhibition brochure, n.d. English.

AN: This exhibition is the collection of the winners of the contest (by the same name) sponsored by the Extension Cultural SRE-UNAM in San Antonio. Photographers represented were: Grace Alvarez, David Cardenas, Hector Cardenas, Stephen Casanova, Ronald Cortez, Raul Espinosa, Felix Almanza, Carolina Flores, David Garza Perez, Xavier Garza, Conrad Guerra, Melinda Hasbrook, Juan Jose de Hoyes, Beverly Kennon, Art Moreno, David Perez, Isabelle Purden, Patricia Santell, Nancy de los Santos, Jose Soria, Richard Tichich, Kathy Vargas, Vivian Yaten, and Johnny Zamarria.

MEXICO Y EL GENERO HUMANO [mural]

5769 [Untitled photograph]. HISPANIC BUSINESS, (September 16, 1975). English.

AN: Captioned illustration of Raul Esparza's 24x60 foot ceramic mural on the wall of the Exposition Park Museum of Science and Industry. Esparza worked a year and a half on the mural, MEXICO Y EL GENERO HUMANO.

Mexposicion III [exhibit]

5770 Highfill, Holly. MARCH (Movimiento Artistico
     Chicano). NEW ART EXAMINER, (June 1975), p.
     4. English.

     AN: Brief history of MARCH (started
     1972; chartered 1975). Resume of its
     activities, including report on most
     ambitious show of 25 Mexican artists,
     MEXPOSICION.

5771 Movimiento Artistico Chicano (MARCH),
     Chicago, IL. Letter to CARACOL. CARACOL,
     Vol. 4, no. 10 (June 1978), p. 3. Spanish.

     AN: Press release announcing LA MUJER:
     UN DIALOGO VISUAL, an art exhibit focusing
     on women sponsored by MARCH of the Chicago
     Public Library.

Meza, Jose Reyes

5772 The legend of the five murals. [Los Angeles,
     CA]: Pan American Bank of East Los Angeles,
     [1966]. Spanish.

     AN: Iconography of the five murals in
     Venetian mosaic created for the Bank by
     Mexican artist Jose Reyes Meza, information
     about mosaics, and a brief biography of the
     artist are included in a biligual brochure.
     The murals are 10x14-ft each and adorn
     thefacade of the building.

5773 Meza to paint Pan American National Bank
     murals. MEXICAN AMERICAN SUN, (October 14,
     1965). English.

     AN: Mexican painter Jose Reyes Meza is
     commissioned to create a mosaic mural titled
     OUR PAST, OUR PRESENT, AND OUR FUTURE for
     the facade of the Pan American National Bank
     of East Los Angeles being erected on First
     Street.

MI RESPUESTA

5774 Viva Siqueiros. CON SAFOS, no. 7 (Winter
     1971), p. 26-27. English.

     AN: Brief recapitulation of the
     controversy surrounding David Alfaro
     Siqueiros' visit to Los Angeles, CA in 1932.
     It was during this visit that he painted the
     only public Siqueiros mural in the U.S.
     which still remains, albeit covered over
     with whitewash. The details of the visit are
     explained by Siqueiros in his book: MI
     RESPUESTA. The article is illustrated with
     two black and white details of the mural.

Michel-Trapaga, Rene David

5775 59th Street Gallery, St. Louis, MO. Midwest
     Mexican-American art exhibit: Mexico and its
     artists. Exhibition brochure, 1981. English.

     AN: Sponsored by the Sociedad Mexicana
     "Benito Juarez" and the international
     Institute of St. Louis, this three-part
     exhibit includes 1) MEXICO AS SEEN BY HER
     CHILDREN, a bilingual exhibit from Mexico
     traveling under Smithsonian Institution
     auspices, 2) MEXICAN CHILDREN IN THE U.S.A.,
     3) MEXICAN AMERICAN ARTISTS. In the latter
     are included Stephen Capiz (Roseville,
     Minn.), Jose Gonzalez (Chicago), Cesar A.
     Martinez (San Antonio), Ada Medina (Des
     Moines), Nora Chapa Mendoza (West
     Bloomfield, Mich.), Rene David
     Michel-Trapaga (St. Louis), David Munoz
     (Kansas City, Mo.), Jose Luis Narezo (Grand
     Rapids, Mich.), Benny Ordonez, Roman

Villarreal (Chicago), Alejandro Romero
(Chicago), Aurelio Diaz "Tekpankalli"
(Chicago), Simon Ybarra (St. Louis).

Michigan

5776 Arts Council Center for the Arts of Greater
     Lansing, Lansing, MI. Raza fine arts
     festival. Festival program, 1978. English.

     AN: This festival program mentions Jose
     Narezo's mural at the Holland National Guard
     Armory, Grand Rapids; includes a statement
     of the Raza Art/Media Collective, Inc.; the
     philosophy of artists Zaragosa Vargas and S.
     Kaneta Kosiba-Vargas; and profiles of
     exhibiting artists George Vargas, Martin
     Moreno, Hector Perez, Michael L. Selley,
     Jesse Gonzales, Nora Chapa Mendoza, Jesse
     Soriano, Jose Luis Narezo.

5777 El calendario hispano de Michigan, 1981.
     Stanton, MI: Montcalm Intermediate School
     District and Nuestras Artes de Michigan,
     1981. English.

     AN: Months of historical calendar
     illustrated with art works by George Vargas,
     Nora Chapa Mendoza, Jesse Gonzalez, Julio
     Perazza(Puerto Rican), Hector Valdez, Pamela
     M. Gonzalez, Isabell Escojico (7-year-old
     child), Jose Narezo, Martin Moreno, Laurie
     Mendoza Psarianos, Rosa Maria Arenas.

5778 Hispanic artists' [sic] mural unveiled.
     SOUTHFIELD ECCENTRIC, Exhibition catalog,
     1980. English.

     AN: A mural titled SYNERGY by Michigan
     artist Nora Mendoza is unveiled at the R.J.
     Sullivan Funeral Home. Mendoza has exhibited
     at numerous one-person shows.

5779 Latin American council bicentennial mural.
     Exhibition brochure, [1976]. English.

     AN: Brochure giving history and
     iconography of a 8 x 16 foot portable mural
     by Grand Rapids, Mich. artist Jose Narezo
     with a team of students. The mural honors
     North and South American revolutionaries
     with portraits of George Washington, Jose
     Marti, Eugenio Maria de Hostos, and Benito
     Juarez.

5780 Michigan State University, East Lansing, MI.
     Voces del norte. Brochure, 1978. English.

     AN: Photos and graphics by 11 Chicanos
     residing in Michigan.

5781 Nora Mendoza: pintora de ascendencia
     mexicana triunfa en los EE. UU. BUENHOGAR,
     (May 1979), p. 7. Spanish.

     AN: Profile of Texas-born Nora Mendoza
     of Michigan, a painter of abstractions in
     acrylic. She is an active member of many
     Detroit and Michigan organizations,
     including Nuestras Artes de Michigan which
     she co-founded with Jorge Vargas, Martin
     Moreno and Jessie Gonzalez.

5782 Valade, Carole. Mural depicts artist's
     heritage. ADRIAN DAILY TELEGRAM, (September
     15, 1978). English.

     AN: Detailed description of Vibrations
     of a New Awakening, mural at Community
     Action Art Center by Martin Moreno with
     assistants Hector Perez and Walter Burrow.

Midwest Canto al Pueblo, Milwaukee, WI April 29-May 8, 1977

5783 Guernica, Antonio Jose and Saavedra-Vela, Pilar. El Midwest Canto al pueblo: "Otra Vez, C/S". AGENDA, Vol. 7, no. 3 (May, June, 1977), p. 4-13. Bilingual.

> **AN:** A thorough report on the various phases and events of the Midwest Canto al Pueblo in Milwaukee, Wisconsin on April 28 to May 8, 1977. The festival brought together artists, poets, musicians, and cultural workers to reaffirm, share, and celebrate the identity of La Raza with El Pueblo. Includes a thematic and iconographic overview of Chicano murals in California by Jose Montoya, and an analysis of his sculpture by Zarco Guerrero from Meza, Arizona. Well illustrated. Includes a photograph of the collective mural painted at 5th St. and National Avenue in Milwaukee, Wisconsin during the course of the conference.

Midwestern States

5784 59th Street Gallery, St. Louis, MO. Midwest Mexican-American art exhibit: Mexico and its artists. Exhibition brochure, 1981. English.

> **AN:** Sponsored by the Sociedad Mexicana "Benito Juarez" and the international Institute of St. Louis, this three-part exhibit includes 1) MEXICO AS SEEN BY HER CHILDREN, a bilingual exhibit from Mexico traveling under Smithsonian Institution auspices, 2) MEXICAN CHILDREN IN THE U.S.A., 3) MEXICAN AMERICAN ARTISTS. In the latter are included Stephen Capiz (Roseville, Minn.), Jose Gonzalez (Chicago), Cesar A. Martinez (San Antonio), Ada Medina (Des Moines), Nora Chapa Mendoza (West Bloomfield, Mich.), Rene David Michel-Trapaga (St. Louis), David Munoz (Kansas City, Mo.), Jose Luis Narezo (Grand Rapids, Mich.), Benny Ordonez, Roman Villarreal (Chicago), Alejandro Romero (Chicago), Aurelio Diaz "Tekpankalli" (Chicago), Simon Ybarra (St. Louis).

5785 Sorell, Victor A. Barrio murals in Chicago: painting the Hispanic-American experience on "our community" walls. REVISTA CHICANO-RIQUENA, Vol. 4, no. 4 (Fall 1976), p. 51-72. English.

> **AN:** Important survey of Chicago's Latino murals, with key works considered in detail. Among the Chicano art organizations and muralists mentioned are MARCH (Movimiento Artistico Chicano), and Yolanda Galvan, Juanita Jaramillo, Jose Nario, Raymond Patlan, Vicente Mendoza, Marcos Raya, Ricardo Alonzo, Jose G. Gonzalez and Mario Castillo, author of the earliest Latino mural in Chicago (1968). Puerto Rican and non-Latino muralists and mural groups are also discussed. Well illustrated.

Millan, Victor

5786 Knapp, Dan. KCET's show for Chicano viewers. LOS ANGELES TIMES, (April 3, 1970), p. IV, 18. English.

> **AN:** Story on the television series AHORA! started September 1969 on KCET, Los Angeles' National Educational Television. Edward Moreno is program director and host; Victor Millan is producer-director; Claudio Fenner-Lopez, senior producer, has staff including set-designer David Villasenor, production manager James Val, and alternate host-narrator Jesus Trevino. The program has shown exhibits of artists Gilberto Lujan and Daniel Ramirez.

Miller, Monticello

5787 Los Angeles City College. Contemporary times 2. Exhibition announcement, 1980. English.

> **AN:** Illustrated announcement for photography show of Monticello Miller and William Ortiz.

Milwaukee, WI

5788 Forest Home Library, Milwaukee, WI. Arte chicano de Carlos Rosas, Chicano muralist. Exhibition invitation, 1978. English.

> **AN:** Invitation to an exhibit by Carlos Rosas [originally from El Paso, TX] who has created murals with Chicano themes in many parts of the United States. Sponsored by El Taller Obrero Cultural de Milwaukee.

5789 Garcia-Camarillo, Cecilio and Rosas, Carlos. Platicando con Carlos Rosas. RAYAS, Vol. 1, no. 6 (November, December, 1978), p. 12, 11. Spanish.

> **AN:** Muralist Carlos Rosas painted murals in Boulder and Denver, Colorado; Milwaukee, Wisconsin, and El Paso, Texas. Commentary on cross ethnic murals, views on art in socialist countries, influence of Mexican murals and information on his personal preocupation as a politically engaged artist.

5790 Guernica, Antonio Jose and Saavedra-Vela, Pilar. El Midwest Canto al pueblo: "Otra Vez, C/S". AGENDA, Vol. 7, no. 3 (May, June, 1977), p. 4-13. Bilingual.

> **AN:** A thorough report on the various phases and events of the Midwest Canto al Pueblo in Milwaukee, Wisconsin on April 28 to May 8, 1977. The festival brought together artists, poets, musicians, and cultural workers to reaffirm, share, and celebrate the identity of La Raza with El Pueblo. Includes a thematic and iconographic overview of Chicano murals in California by Jose Montoya, and an analysis of his sculpture by Zarco Guerrero from Meza, Arizona. Well illustrated. Includes a photograph of the collective mural painted at 5th St. and National Avenue in Milwaukee, Wisconsin during the course of the conference.

Minick, Roger

5791 Blum, Walter. The vision behind the mirror. CALIFORNIA LIVING, (November 26, 1978), p. 40-44. English.

> **AN:** Illustrated article with background information on the non-Chicano photographers (Roger Minick, Morrie Camhi, and Abigail Heyman) who spent a year documenting the Chicano community. Their work was issued as a portfolio, "Espejo: Reflections of the Mexican American," by the Mexican-American Legal Defense and Educational Fund (MALDEF). It is one of the most extensive photographic records made of the Chicano experience.

Minick, Roger (cont.)

5792 Espejo: reflections of the Mexican American: Louis Carlos Bernal, Morrie Camhi, Abigail Heyman, Roger Minick, Neal Slavin. SOMOS, Vol. 2, no. 1 (February 1978), p. 26-35. English.

AN: Announcement of the ESPEJO photographic exhibit to be held at Goez Gallery in East Los Angeles. Statements by the four artists and a portfolio of their works: Abigail Heyman, Roger Minick, Morrie Camhi, and Arizona Chicano photographer Louis Carlos Bernal. Includes color photographs by Bernal on cover. This 1979 issue is erroneously dated 1978.

5793 Fischer, Hal. Espejo: reflections of the Mexican American: Louis Carlos Bernal, Morrie Camhi, Abigail Heyman, Roger Minick, Neal Slavin. PICTURE MAGAZINE, no. 9 (1978). English.

AN: Oversize portfolio of photographs recording contemporary Mexican American life commissioned by the Mexican American Legal Defense and Education Fund. Three photographers, Louis Carlos Bernal (from Arizona), Morrie Camhi and Abagail Heyman focus on the family and the home; the fourth, Roger Minick, juxtaposes the Mexican American against "barrio" murals. Only Bernal is Chicano. 24 photographs, six of which (Bernal's) are in color.

Minnesota

5794 Community Programs in the Arts and Sciences (COMPAS). Flor y Canto in Minnesota. St. Paul, MN: Northwestern Press, 1978. English.

AN: Survey of community arts projects. Includes commentary on Chicano mural activity in Minnesota. Cover design by Chicano artist Armando Estrella.

5795 Knapp, Martha. West side is part of mural art renaissance. WEST SAINT PAUL VOICE, Vol. 5, no. 19 (November 21, 1977). English.

AN: Pre-Columbian symbology in the mural program painted by Paul Basquez and Armando Estrella in the Chicano barrio; information and data on the mural renaissance in Minnesota.

Miranda, Judith

5796 Galeria, Santa Ana, CA. The last Chicano art show. Exhibition brochure, 1981. English.

AN: Invitation-brochure for an exhibit of Los Angeles and Orange County artists in a gallery underwritten by the Friendly Center, Inc. with grants from local government and from businesses. Exhibiting are (Roberto) Gil de Montes, Gilbert Lujan, Judy Miranda, Patricia Murillo, Alonso Pardo, Teddy Sandoval, Mexican artist Artemio Sepulveda, Joey Terrill, Art Valenzuela, Ben Valenzuela, Linda Vallejo, Jack A. Vargas, Emigdio Vasquez, Richard Serrato, and J. William Hernandez, who is the gallery director.

5797 William Grant Still Community Arts Center, Los Angeles, CA. Latin American artists exhibition. Exhibition brochure, 1978. English.

AN: Exhibit curated by Linda Vallejo including Carlos Almaraz, Michael M. Amescua, Ray Bravo, Isabel Castro, Yreina Cervantez, Luis Serrano-Cordero, Cynthia Honesto, Judith Miranda, Teddy Sandoval, John Taboada, Emigdio Vasquez. Illustrated.

Mission Cultural Center, San Francisco, CA

5798 Rodriguez, Patricia. Portfolio: Patricia Rodriguez; the visual interview. METAMORFOSIS, Vol. 3, no. 1-2 (1980, 1981), p. 38-45. English.

AN: Statement by the artist reprinted from her exhibit "The Visual Interview" at the Mission Cultural Center, San Francisco. Discusses her fifteen mask-box-sculptures of Chicano artists from northern California. Illustrated with photographs of the artist at work and five of her sculptures. This issue of METAMORFOSIS combines volumes 3 and 4.

Mission District, San Francisco, CA
SEE ALSO: San Francisco, CA, Mission District

5799 Albright, Thomas. Three remarkable Latin murals. SAN FRANCISCO CHRONICLE, (June 7, 1974), p. 48. English.

AN: The myth of the melting pot is vanishing: we recognize a variety of "publics" today. This is shown in three remarkable murals in the San Francisco Mission District. The Mission branch of the Bank of America has a 90 foot mural designed by Jesus Campusano, assisted by Luis Cortazar and Michael Rios, with technical advice from Emmy Lou Packard. Another mural is by the Mujeres Muralistas (Graciela Carrillo, Consuelo Mendez, Irene Perez, Patricia Rodriguez); the third by Michael Rios on the 24th St. mini-park.

5800 Barnes, Peter. Fringe benefits of a depression: bringing back the WPA. NEW REPUBLIC, Vol. 172, no. 11 (March 15, 1975), p. 19-21. English.

AN: A well-researched and comprehensive analysis of the CETA (Comprehensive Employment and Training Act) impact on public art in San Francisco. Material on Chicano-Latino murals in the Mission district. Includes viewpoints by artist-activists Patricia Rodriguez, Mike Rios, and writer Roberto Vargas. Important compendium on funding sources of various neighborhood art programs stressing their value as community assets.

5801 Echos de la Mision: the newest in Mission murals. EL TECOLOTE, Vol. 6, no. 4 (January 1976), p. 11. English.

AN: Panoramic view of new murals in the Mission District of San Francisco. Contains brief descriptions and photographs of mural art at Valencia Gardens, Garfield Park, Folsom Project and The Bart mural at 24th and Mission streets. Includes five photos by Francisco Garcia.

5802 Galeria de la Raza/Studio 24, San Francisco, CA. Otra onda (the other wave): an exhibition of the Mission scene. Exhibition invitation, [1981]. English.

AN: Invitation to an exhibit.

Mission District, San Francisco, CA (cont.)

5803 Garcia, Rupert. Pulqueria art--defiant art
of the barrios [Part II]. EL TECOLOTE, Vol.
8, no. 5 (February 1978), p. 8. Bilingual.

AN: In the Mission District of San
Francisco, various artists like Irene Perez,
Esther Fernandez, Chuy Campusano, Graciela
Carrillo de Lopez, Consuelo Mendez Castillo,
and Mike Rios have embellished business
sites with wall decorations similar in
spirit to the "Pulqueria" art of Mexico.
Illustrated with three "Pulqueria"-type wall
paintings: ATARDECER DE UN IMPERIO by Oscar
Carveo at the Azteca Restaurant (Mission and
20th Sts.), El Buen Boricano Restaurant
facade (24th and Harrison Sts.) and
Fruitlandia facade (24th and Treat Sts.).

5804 Garcia, Rupert. Raza murals & muralists: an
historical perspective. San Francisco, CA:
Rupert Garcia, n.d.. English.

AN: Basic assumptions are that
socio-economic, political and cultural
relationships exist between the Raza of
Mexico and those of Aztlan (the Southwest
United States) Half the text deals with
Mexican murals, the other half sets Raza
murals in social context, and focuses on
murals in San Francisco's Mission District,
in four locations. 19 illustrations; 9 of
Raza murals. Mural map of the Mission
district.

5805 Garcia, Rupert. "This mural is not for the
bankers. It's for the people". EL TECOLOTE,
Vol. 4, no. 6 (June 10, 1974), p. 11+.
English.

AN: On June 4, 1974, a mural by eight
Mission District artists was unveiled inside
the Bank of America on 23rd and Mission Sts.
in San Francisco. Roberto Vargas, Bay Area
poet was prevented from reading his poetry
during the mural inauguration. Finally
allowed to read, Vargas compared this event
to one in the 1930s when Diego Rivera
painted a mural for the Pacific Stock
Exchange Building in San Francisco. Includes
commentary by community activists about
incident. Illustrated by photograph of
Roberto Vargas reading in front of the
controversial mural.

5806 Hagen, Carol. Mission murals. ARTWEEK, Vol.
5, no. 30 (September 14, 1974), p. 6.
English.

AN: Report on two recently completed
murals in San Francisco's Mission District:
Jesus Campusano's 90x10-ft mural in the Bank
of America branch, and the Mujeres
Muralistas' mural adjacent to the Mission
Model Cities building. Illustrated.

5807 Kagawa, Paul and Rilkin, Scott. La Raza
Silkscreen Center, in step with the Mission.
ARTS BIWEEKLY, no. 44 (March 15, 1977).
English.

AN: Concise history and goals of the
Silkscreen Center: the Center's values are
reflected in the collective process that
produces the posters, as well as in the
collective style of the art; in the emphasis
upon education. The Center trains
apprentices, educates the student community
about the silkscreen process and Raza
history and produces posters that have an
information impact. The Silkscreen Center is
part of a coalition of La Raza Information
Center, Tutorial Center, and Centro Legal

which evolved from La Raza En Accion Social
founded in 1970.

5808 Kamin, Ira. Come on in, bring your paint.
PACIFIC SUN, (May 30, 1974), p. 11-12.
English.

AN: Chatty report on murals and art
exhibit in San Francisco's Mission District:
murals by Chuy Campusano, Michael Rios,
Richard Montez, Trish (Patricia) Rodriguez,
Graciela Carrillo, Consuelo Mendez and Irene
Perez. Illustrated.

5809 Martinez, Anita. Raza! Arte! Raza! Arte!
EL TECOLOTE, Vol. 1, no. 2 (September 7,
1970), p. 3. Bilingual.

AN: Galeria de la Raza opened on July,
1970 at 425 14th St. San Francisco. It was
an outgrowth of the Arte Seis organization
(an art effort established in the Mission
District in 1967 by Francisco Camplis,
Rupert Garcia, Ralph McNeil, Jay Ojeda and
Jack Ruiz). These and other artists brought
together by the Neighborhood Arts Program
have coalesced in the new Galeria de la
Raza. Article gives goals, organizational
scheme and plans for the Galeria. It's first
exhibit was a one man show by Esteban Villa
together with a photo and sketch exhibit on
Cuba by Jay Ojeda, Roberto Diaz Perez and
Gloria Ozuna. Illustrated with installation
view of new Galeria.

5810 Mission community mural map. San Francisco,
CA: Galeria de la Raza, n.d.. English.

AN: Map showing ten sites for murals in
the San Franciso Mission District. Published
as a guide to a community mural tour.

5811 Las mujeres muralistas. Exhibition
invitation, 1974. English.

AN: Invitation to the inauguration of
the mural PARA EL MERCADO at Paco's Tacos in
San Francisco's Mission District by the
Mujeres Muralistas, Sept. 15, 1974.
Illustrated by Venezuelan artist Consuelo
Mendez.

5812 Las muralistas: Patricia Rodriguez, Consuelo
Mendez, Graciela Carrillo, Irene Perez.
Exhibition invitation, 1974. English.

AN: Invitation to the inauguration of
the mural LATINO AMERICA by the Mujeres
Muralistas at the Mission Neighborhood Model
Cities in San Francisco's Mission District,
May 31, 1974.

5813 New mural on Mission Street. EL HISPANO,
Vol. 7, no. 13 (September 19, 1974), p. 5.
English.

AN: Description of mural at the corner
of 24th Street and South Van Ness in San
Francisco. Painted by Mujeres
Muralistas--Consuelo Mendez, Graciela
Carrillo, Susan Cervantes and Miriam Olivo,
the 30-foot mural depicts people in a
tropical, Latin American setting.

Mission District, San Francisco, CA (cont.)

5814   Portraying Latino women in the Mission. SAN FRANCISCO EXAMINER, (September 10, 1974), p. 26. English.

> **AN:** Three muralists of the Mission District, Irene Perez, Patricia Rodriguez, and Venezuelan Consuelo Mendez, are preparing a six-paneled painting-construction, the RHOMBOIDAL PARALLELOGRAM, for the 28th annual San Francisco Art Festival. It will illustrate the life of women in the Mission. Illustrated.

5815   Preuss, Karen. The new Mission murals. SAN FRANCISCO BAY GUARDIAN, (June 28, 1975), p. 14-15. English.

> **AN:** Mural art in San Francisco's Mission District has covered nearly every wall and alley on lower 24th Street. Murals by Mike Rios, the Mujeres Muralistas (Patricia Rodriguez, Graciela Carrillo, Consuelo Mendez, Miriam Olivo, Irene Perez, Susan Cervantes) appear in the area. Others have been painted by artists associated with the Galeria de la Raza. Illustrations.

La Mission Media Arts, San Francisco, CA

5816   Soberon, Mercedes. La revolucion se trata de amor: Mercedes Soberon. CHISMEARTE, Vol. 1, no. 1 (Fall 1976), p. 14-18. Spanish.

> **AN:** Short interview with Mercedes Soberon, San Francisco artist involved with the art group Mission Media Arts. Mercedes talks about the role of women as organizers and artists, the sacrifices associated with this role, and the politics of San Francisco museums.

Mission, TX

5817   Estudios Rio: gallery of contemporary arts and crafts. Exhibition catalog, 1976. English.

> **AN:** Catalog including identification, portraits and works of participating artists: Joe Bova, Enrique Flores, Carmen Lomas Garza, Xavier Gorena, Erik Gronborg, Lucas Hinojosa, Ben Holland, Kris Hotvedt, William Kaars-Sijpesteijn, Cesar Martinez, Chris Mende, Roberto Mungia, Steve Reynolds, Vicente Rodriguez, William Wilhelmi.

Missouri

5818   The Mexican Museum, San Francisco, CA. Bruno Andrade (from Missouri) and Antonio Lopez Saenz (from Mexico). Exhibition announcement, 1978. English.

> **AN:** Flyer announcing an exhibit at the Mexican Museum of Texas-born Andrade who is exhibiting large abstract landscapes. Andrade teaches in Columbia, Missouri; this is his first California exhibit.

Mixed media

5819   Coe, Kathryn. Heritage plus science yields art. SCOTTSDALE DAILY PROGRESS, (August 28, 1981), p. 27. English.

> **AN:** Biography of Colorado-born Rudy Fernandez who bases many of his paintings and mixed media boxes on the religious imagery of Colorado. He studied geology; travelled to Spain and Mexico to know his heritage. All these factors influence his

art, in which he uses symbols personally.

5820   Donnell-Kotrozo, Carol. Rudy Fernandez. SOUTHWESTERN CONTEMPORARY ARTS QUARTERLY, (Fall 1981). English.

> **AN:** Well-illustrated article on the mixed media creations of Rudy Fernandez who lives in Scottsdale, AZ.

Models

USE: Fashion

MOJADO POWER [film]

5821   Vasquez, Richard. Mojado power: a boost for illegal aliens. CALENDAR, (February 22, 1981), p. 41. English.

> **AN:** An uncritical review of the commercial film made by Mexican film star and comedian Alfonso Arau in the United States primarily for the "American-Hispanic" market on a low-cost budget. Arau planned to distribute in Mexico, Latin America and Spain. The film is a light-weight comedy about a "wetback" who launches a campaign for "mojado power" but falls victim to dope smugglers and is sent to jail.

Mojados

USE: Undocumented Workers

Mojica, Adolfo

5822   Mural en Quinto Sol. SOL DE AZTLAN, Vol. 2, no. 3 (July 1971). English.

> **AN:** Full-page illustrated article describing mural by Jose Mojica at the Edificio Quinto Sol in Lansing. Mural traces the history of La Raza and was painted by the self-taught artist with the assistance of his brother Adolfo.

Mojica, Jose

5823   Mural en Quinto Sol. SOL DE AZTLAN, Vol. 2, no. 3 (July 1971). English.

> **AN:** Full-page illustrated article describing mural by Jose Mojica at the Edificio Quinto Sol in Lansing. Mural traces the history of La Raza and was painted by the self-taught artist with the assistance of his brother Adolfo.

Monreal, Fred

5824   Vigil, Maria. Hello, walls: Tucson's murals. WEEKENDER MAGAZINE, (March 29, 1980), p. 14-16. English.

> **AN:** Article on muralism, from the Mexican to those of Chicanos. Focuses on Tucson murals by Roberto Borboa, Antonio Pazos, David Tineo and Fred Monreal. Color illustrations.

Montage

5825   Arriaga, Sergio. [Untitled montage]. CARACOL, Vol. 5, no. 1 (September 1978), p. 11. Spanish.

5826   [Asco (montage)]. REGENERACION, Vol. 2, no. 4 (1975), p. 27.

5827   De la Rocha, Roberto. [Untitled woodcuts]. CON SAFOS, no. 7 (Winter 1971), p. 12-13.

--   --
Montage (cont.)

5828 Gronk; Herron, Willie; and Gamboa, Harry,
     Jr. [Untitled montage]. REGENERACION, Vol.
     2, no. 4 (1975), p. 30.

5829 Hernandez, Sergio. [Untitled photo collage].
     CON SAFOS, Vol. 2, no. 5 (1970), p. 28.
     Bilingual.

5830 Lopez, Yolanda M. [Untitled montage from the
     SERIE GUADALUPE]. MAIZE, Vol. 1, no. 4
     (Summer 1978), p. Ft cover. English.

5831 Lopez, Yolanda M. [Untitled montage from the
     SERIE GUADALUPE]. MAIZE, Vol. 1, no. 4
     (Summer 1978), p. 55-59. English.

5832 Luna, Benjamin R. Zoot [montage]. CON SAFOS,
     Vol. 1, no. 3 (March 1969), p. 24-25.
     Bilingual.

5833 Patssi. [Untitled montage]. REGENERACION,
     Vol. 2, no. 4 (1975), p. 56.

5834 Quiroz, Martin, III. [Untitled photo collage
     of Chicanas]. REGENERACION, Vol. 1, no. 10
     (1971), p. COVER.

5835 La razon [montage]. CON SAFOS, no. 8 (1972),
     p. 52.

5836 Valdez, Patssi. [Untitled montage].
     REGENERACION, Vol. 2, no. 4 (1975), p. 28.

5837 Valdez, Patssi. [Untitled montage].
     REGENERACION, Vol. 2, no. 4 (1975), p. 29.

Montano, Marylee

5838 Mills House Visual Arts Complex, Garden
     Grove, CA. Menudo: artistas latinos de
     Orange County. Exhibit invitation, 1980.
     English.

     AN: Invitation to an exhibit organized
     for the first anniversary of Artistas
     Latinos de Orange County including Delores
     Grajeda, William Hernandez, Marylee Montano,
     Patricia Murillo, Irene Ramos, Juan Ramos,
     Ricardo Serrato, Miguel Shanahan, Arthur
     Valenzuela, Benjamin Valenzuela, Jack
     Vargas, Alonzo Whitney, Emigdio Vasquez,
     Susana Zaccagnino, and Mexican artist
     Artemio Sepulveda.

5839 Orange Co. Library. El Modena Branch.
     Empanada: a tasty Mexican group art exhibit
     filled with a variety of digestable treats.
     Exhibition catalog, [1979]. English.

     AN: Catalog of an exhibit by 15 artists:
     Dolores Grajeda, William Hernandez-M.,
     Marylee Montano, Patricia Murillo, Eduardo
     Navarro, Susana A. Zaccagnino, Esau Quiroz,
     Juan Elias Ramos, Ricardo M. Serrato,
     Benjamin Valenzuela, Emigdio C. Vasquez,
     Arthur Valenzuela, Jack Vargas, Alonso
     Whitney, and Mexican artist Artemio
     Sepulveda living in Orange County. Brief
     profiles of the artists.

Montealva, Roel

5840 Montoya, Emmanuel; Rodriguez, Patricia; and
     Acevedo, Mario (Torero). Canto al pueblo
     '78. NATIONAL MURALS NETWORK COMMUNITY
     NEWSLETTER, (1978). English.

     AN: The second annual Canto al Pueblo
     took place in Corpus Christi, Texas, where
     more than six murals were painted: "Wall of
     Cultural Education" by 13 artists headed by
     Roel Montealva; Carlota Espinoza, with

children; Gilberto Romero, Jose Antonio
Burciaga and Patricia Rodriguez,
"Incomprehension al arte"; "Madre Tierra" by
Manuel Martinez of Denver with Amador
Hinojosa (Corpus Christi) and Enriquette
Vasquez (New Mexico); Mario Torero; Salvador
Vega of Chicago whose mural some Canto
participants considered "insulting".

Montemayor, Alice Dickerson "Admonty"

5841 Mexico. Secretaria de Relaciones Exteriores.
     Direccion General de Asuntos.. Exposicion:
     estampas y remembranzas; Admonty y Geomonte.
     Exhibition catalog, 1979. Bilingual.

     AN: Catalog of an exhibit by Alice
     Dickerson Montemayor (Admonty). Born in
     Laredo, Texas in 1902, she began painting in
     1976. Her nephew, George A. Montemayor, who
     resides in Houston, is the Coordinator for
     the La Porte Independent School District.

5842 Painting changes woman's life at age when
     most ready to retire. LAREDO NEWS,
     (November 4, 1979), p. 1-C. English.

     AN: Interview with 77 year old Alice D.
     Montemayor "Admonty" on the occasion of her
     San Antonio exhibit with her nephew George
     "Geomonte" Montemayor.

5843 Salazar, Veronica. Aspiration comes true.
     SAN ANTONIO EXPRESS-NEWS, (October 28,
     1979), p. 8-H. English.

     AN: History of Alice Dickerson
     Montemayor of Laredo, Texas (known as
     "Admonty") who started to paint at 74 on the
     occasion of her second exhibit at the
     Mexican government's Instituto Cultural.

5844 Vincent, Kathy Ariana. Monty Montemayor:
     portrait of an artist. ARRIBA, Vol. 1, no. 7
     (1980). English.

     AN: Born in Laredo, TX, in 1902, "Monty"
     Montemayor paints in the naif tradition. As
     an older artist, she has been a role model
     for younger Chicana artists. Brief profile
     of the self-taught artist. Illustrated.

5845 Woman who began at 73 is shaping Chicano
     art. SAN ANTONIO EXPRESS-NEWS, (August 18,
     1978), p. 6-W. English.

     AN: 76-year-old Laredoan Alicia
     Dickerson Montemayor who began painting on
     guajes (gourds) from her garden three years
     ago, now paints on canvas stories from her
     life in the Valley, nature, and people. An
     exhibit of her work, referred to by Chicano
     art critics as "el arte de la inocencia"
     opens at Gallery of El Centro Cultural de
     LUCHA, in Austin, TX.

Montemayor, George A. "Geomonte"

5846 Mexico. Secretaria de Relaciones Exteriores.
     Direccion General de Asuntos.. Exposicion:
     estampas y remembranzas; Admonty y Geomonte.
     Exhibition catalog, 1979. Bilingual.

     AN: Catalog of an exhibit by Alice
     Dickerson Montemayor (Admonty). Born in
     Laredo, Texas in 1902, she began painting in
     1976. Her nephew, George A. Montemayor, who
     resides in Houston, is the Coordinator for
     the La Porte Independent School District.

--- ---

Montemayor, George A. "Geomonte" (cont.)

5847 Painting changes woman's life at age when
     most ready to retire. LAREDO NEWS,
     (November 4, 1979), p. 1-C. English.

     AN: Interview with 77 year old Alice D.
     Montemayor "Admonty" on the occasion of her
     San Antonio exhibit with her nephew George
     "Geomonte" Montemayor.

Montez, Richard

5848 Kamin, Ira. Come on in, bring your paint.
     PACIFIC SUN, (May 30, 1974), p. 11-12.
     English.

     AN: Chatty report on murals and art
     exhibit in San Francisco's Mission District:
     murals by Chuy Campusano, Michael Rios,
     Richard Montez, Trish (Patricia) Rodriguez,
     Graciela Carrillo, Consuelo Mendez and Irene
     Perez. Illustrated.

Montoya, Emmanuel

5849 Aguila, Pancho. 11 poems. MANGO, (1977).
     English.

     AN: Art works by Northern California
     artists Emmanuel Montoya and Jose Antonio
     Burciaga.

5850 Goll, Dave. More than handball on this
     court. MENLO-ATHERTON RECORDER, (May 23,
     1978), p. 15. English.

     AN: Emmanuel Montoya is painting a mural
     on African and Chicano unity at the handball
     court of Fair Oaks Community Center in
     Redwood City, CA. Montoya is working because
     of CETA (Comprehensive Employment Training
     Act) funds. Illustrated.

5851 In the middle of something good.
     MENLO-ATHERTON RECORDER, (September 19,
     1978), p. 16. English.

     AN: Illustration of Emmanuel Montoya's
     African-Mexican unity mural at the Redwood
     City Fair Oaks Community Center handball
     courts.

5852 Mission to honor Frida Kahlo: famous Mexican
     artist. EL TECOLOTE, Vol. 9, no. 3 (November
     1978), p. 1. Bilingual.

     AN: Announcement of an homage to Mexican
     painter Frida Kahlo at the Galeria de la
     Raza's annual celebration of Dia de los
     Muertos. Works reproduced with the article
     include those of Emmanuel C. Montoya, Yreina
     Cervantez, Jose Antonio Burciaga, Nina
     Serrano and Lisa Kokin. Bilingual.

5853 Seniors mural to be dedicated at RC Center.
     REDWOOD CITY TRIBUNE, (December 31, 1977),
     p. 3. English.

     AN: A portable mural depicting the birth
     of the senior citizen hot meal program in
     San Mateo County will be dedicated at the
     Senior Citizens Drop-In Center. The 12x18-ft
     mural was painted by Emmanuel Montoya of
     Menlo Park, CA. Illustrated.

Montoya, Jose E.

5854 Art Space - Open Ring Gallery, Sacramento,
     CA. El Pachuco art de Jose Montoya: a
     historical update. Exhibition invitation,
     1977. English.

     AN: Invitation to an exhibit.

Illustrated with a reproduction of a 1977
silkscreen calendar page in color by
Montoya.

5855 Avalos, David. A pure Mexican accent: the
     popular engravings of Jose Guadalupe Posada.
     PROCEEDINGS OF THE PACIFIC COAST COUNCIL ON
     LATIN AMER STUDIES, Vol. 7, (1980, 1981),
     p. 123-138. English.

     AN: As a documentor of injustice and
     oppression, Posada, 19th century Mexican
     engraver, is a master who inspires Chicano
     artists. Appreciation for his art has been
     expressed by Sacramento artist Jose E.
     Montoya. Arsacio Vanegas Arroyo, grandson of
     Posada's publisher, has made his private
     collection available to Chicano cultural
     centers, including El Centro Cultural de la
     Raza, San Diego. Illustrated.

5856 Bruce Novoa, Juan. [Interview with Jose
     Montoya]. IN CHICANO AUTHORS: INQUIRY BY
     INTERVIEW. Austin, TX: University of Texas
     Press, 1980, p. 115-136. English.

     AN: Biography of Sacramento, CA artist
     and poet Jose Montoya. Emphasizes the close
     relationship between art and poetry in his
     life and in that of the Royal Chicano Air
     Force, which he co-founded.

5857 Burkhardt, Dorothy. Chicano pride and anger
     mix at 'Califas'. THE TAB, (April 12,
     1981), p. 34. English.

     AN: CALIFAS: AN EXHIBITION OF CHICANO
     ARTISTS IN CALIFORNIA represents a
     cross-section of artists exhibiting work for
     at least ten years: Rupert Garcia, Ernie
     Palomino, Eduardo Carrillo, Judy Baca, Rene
     Yanez, Carmen Lomas Garza, Salvador Roberto
     Torres, Roberto Chavez, Willie Herron, Ralph
     Maradiaga, Sue Martinez, Jose Montoya,
     Malaquias Montoya, Ramses Noriega and
     Esteban Villa. Illustrated.

5858 Calendario de comida 1976. San Francisco,
     CA: Galeria de la Raza, 1976. English.

     AN: Handprinted silkscreen calendar
     consisting of twelve sheets and a cover. The
     work of the following artists is included:
     Ralph Maradiaga, Juanishi Orozco, Francisco
     Camplis, Ruben Guzman, Rodolfo Cuellar,
     Xavier Viramontes, Jose Montoya, Esteban
     Villa, Rene Yanez, Max Garcia and Louis "The
     Foot" Gonzalez, Patricia Rodriguez, and
     Ricardo Favela. All of the above are
     associated with the Galeria de la Raza, or
     the Royal Chicano Air Force of Sacramento,
     CA.

5859 California. State College. Los Angeles. Art
     Gallery. Twelve Chicano artists. Exhibition
     invitation, n.d. English.

     AN: Invitation to an exhibit: Jose
     Montoya, Gilbert Sanchez Lujan, Esteban
     Villa, Rene Yanez, Joe Moran, Armando Cid,
     Leonard Castellas, Juanishi Orozco, Rudy
     Cuellar, Beltran, Lopez and Cabrera.

5860 California. University. Santa Cruz. College
     Eight Gallery. Four artists: Edward
     Carrillo, Consuelo Mendez Castillo, Louis
     Gutierrez, Jose Montoya. Exhibition catalog,
     n.d. English.

     AN: Exhibit of three Chicano artists and
     Venezuelan-born artist Consuelo Mendez de
     Castillo.

Montoya, Jose E.(cont.)

5861 Chicano art show at Contra Costa College. EL HISPANO, Vol. 8, no. 25 (December 11, 1973). English.

AN: Information on exhibition organized by Ramses Noriega that included the work of Jose Montoya, Esteban Villa, Mario Sinape, Ricardo Rios, Malaquias Montoya, Fuchi Queso, and Joe Palomino.

5862 Fong, Katheryn M. Pachuco art records era of zootsuits and anti-Mexican riots. SAN FRANCISCO JRNL, Vol. 2, no. 32 (March 1, 1978), p. 6. English.

AN: Review of Galeria de la Raza exhibit of Jose Montoya's Pachuco Art. Installation included historical photographs and documents. Montoya work (drawings and paintings) were contextualized by written commentary aiming to re-interpret an important aspect of Chicano cultural history.

5863 Frankenstein, Alfred. Montoya's artistic update on Chicano zoot suiters. SAN FRANCISCO CHRONICLE, (February 18, 1978), p. 36. English.

AN: Review of Pachuco show at San Francisco's Galeria de la Raza, especially Jose Montoya's sketches and paintings.

5864 Guernica, Antonio Jose and Saavedra-Vela, Pilar. El Midwest Canto al pueblo: "Otra Vez, C/S". AGENDA, Vol. 7, no. 3 (May, June, 1977), p. 4-13. Bilingual.

AN: A thorough report on the various phases and events of the Midwest Canto al Pueblo in Milwaukee, Wisconsin on April 28 to May 8, 1977. The festival brought together artists, poets, musicians, and cultural workers to reaffirm, share, and celebrate the identity of La Raza with El Pueblo. Includes a thematic and iconographic overview of Chicano murals in California by Jose Montoya, and an analysis of his sculpture by Zarco Guerrero from Meza, Arizona. Well illustrated. Includes a photograph of the collective mural painted at 5th St. and National Avenue in Milwaukee, Wisconsin during the course of the conference.

5865 La historia de California, 1977. San Francisco, CA: Galeria de la Raza, 1977. English.

AN: Handprinted silkscreen calendar of history seen from a Mexican point of view. Twelve sheets and a cover. Artists are: Ralph Maradiaga, Irene Perez, Louie "The Foot" Gonzalez, Max Garcia, Patricia Rodriguez, Jose Romero, Esteban Villa, Juanishi Orozco, Rodolfo Cuellar, Jose Montoya, Xavier Viramontes, Rene Yanez, Ricardo Favela, associated with the Galeria de la Raza, or the Royal Chicano Air Force of Sacramento.

5866 Hurtado, Debbie. A historical update: Montoya's vindication of fabricated biases. THE STATE HORNET, (December 13, 1977), p. 6. English.

AN: Review of Jose Montoya's show "Pachuco Art - A Historical Update; "a rekindling of pachuquismo from the 1940s prevalent in Montoya's paintings and pen-and-ink drawings. The show featured historical photographs, and an animated hologram. Visitors wore zoot suit outfits to the opening. Illustrated.

5867 Johnson, Charles. J street galleries: politics flavor alternative art shows. SACRAMENTO BEE, (December 20, 1977), p. A13. English.

AN: Review of a Pachuco show by Jose Montoya that is half drawings and paintings, and half politics - photographs of Pachucos of the 1940s. Montoya's essay that accompanies the exhibit attempts to dispel the image of Pachucos as gangsters, and declares that Pachucos were the first "freedom Fighters." The reviewer feels this is one-sided. Illustrated.

5868 Jose Montoya: poeta, pintor, profesor, humanista, padre, abuelo. EL HISPANO, Vol. 8, no. 27 (December 23, 1975), p. 5. Spanish.

AN: Biographical data on the Sacramento artist, his contributions to the Chicano Movement and his life as an artist-activist. Photographs of his family and reproduction of one drawing.

5869 Joseph Chowning Gallery; Laguna Beach Museum of Art; and Fitzgibbon, John. California connections: Sacramento State College, the early 1970s. Exhibit brochure, 1982. English.

AN: Works by 35 artists, teachers and students at Sacramento State College. Color plate by Eduardo Carrillo and anecdotal material about Carrillo in text. Time frame is important for Jose Montoya and Esteban Villa, co-founders of the Royal Chicano Air Force in Sacramento.

5870 MacLatchie, Sharon. Art in the barrios: one man's commitment. LA LUZ, Vol. 3, no. 9 (December 1974), p. 17-18. English.

AN: Describes the Centro de Artistas Chicanos in Sacramento, California. Highlights the program for art in the Barrio and focuses on the work and personality of Jose Montoya.

5871 Montoya, Jose E. Pachuco art: a historical update. Sacramento, CA: Royal Chicano Air Force, 1977. English.

AN: Booklet outlining the history of the Zoot Suit Riots of 1943 and the making of the Pachuco myth, written by Montoya and illustrated with his pen-and-ink drawings of Pachucos and Pachucas.

5872 Oakes College, University of California, Santa Cruz, CA and Carrillo, Eduardo. Corazon de Aztlan: a Chicano arts show. Exhibition catalog, 1981. English.

AN: Catalog of exhibit including works by Eduardo Carrillo, Juana Franklin, Cruz Zamarron, Jerry Astorga, Jaime Valadez, Ernesto Palomino, Sal Garcia, Roger Sierra, Jose Montoya, Esteban Villa, Juanishi Orozco, from Santa Cruz, San Jose, Fresno and Sacramento. Presentations of films and by the Teatro de la Tierra Morena of Santa Cruz County.

Montoya, Jose E.(cont.)

5873 Orth, Maureen. The soaring spirit of Chicano
     arts. NEW WEST MAGAZINE, Vol. 3, no. 19
     (September 11, 1978), p. 41-46. English.

   AN: Overview of California Chicano
   culture. Color illustrations of works by
   Mexican muralist David Alfaro Siqueiros,
   Rupert Garcia, Mujeres Muralistas, Willie
   Herron, Rene Yanez, Rudy Martinez, San
   Diego's Chicano Park, ASCO, Jose Montoya.

5874 Photo-graphics/foto-grafica. MAIZE, Vol. 4,
     no. 1-2 (Fall , Winter, 1980, 1981).
     Bilingual.

   AN: 9 drawings and prints by Royal
   Chicano Air Force (Sacramento, Calif.)
   artists Jose Montoya, Juanishi Orozco,
   Esteban Villa.

5875 R.C.A.F. artistas precursores del arte
     chicano. EL HISPANO, Vol. 8, no. 35
     (February 17, 1976), p. 1. English.

   AN: Information on the R.C.A.F.
   organization. Includes group photograph of
   R.C.A.F. members, Jose Montoya, Esteban
   Villa, John Carrillo, Ricardo Fabela, Rudy
   Cuellar, Juanishi Orozco and Frank Godena.

5876 Rios, Sam. Chicano muralist: Toltecotl in
     Aztlan. Unpublished paper, 1980. English.

   AN: History of pre-Columbian, Mexican,
   and Chicano wall paintings. Describes in
   detail murals by Jose Montoya, Juanishi
   Orozco, Esteban Villa, Stan Padilla, Juan
   Cervantes, Lorraine Garcia of the Centro de
   Artistas Chicanos, Royal Chicano Air Force,
   painted in 1977 at Southside Park,
   Sacramento, Calif. Symbolism is explained.

5877 S.A. site for National Symposium on Mexican
     American Art. CHICANO TIMES, Vol. 4, no. 30
     (November 9, 1973), p. 5. English.

   AN: Held at Trinity University, the
   Symposium discussed such issues as, creative
   evolution, art education, artistic
   relationships to Mexico and the evolution of
   Mexican American art in the California
   barrios. Participating artists included Rudy
   Trevino, Mel Casas, Octavio Medellin,
   Antonio Garcia, Carmen Garza, Esteban Villa,
   Jose Montoya, Ernesto Palomino, Michael
   Ponce de Leon, Luis Jimenez and Eugenio
   Quesada.

5878 Sommer, Robert. Street art. New York: Quick
     Fox, 1975. English.

   AN: Introductory essay covering the
   history of the new mural movement, forms of
   street art, politics, street sculpture, how
   to locate and photograph street art. Chicano
   murals include Charles Felix and others at
   Estrada Courts (L.A.), RCAF murals in
   Sacramento, Jose Montoya and others
   (Broderick, Ca.) Marcos Raya (Chicago), Mike
   Rios (Neighborhood Legal Aid, S.F.)
   Mechicano Art Center (L.A.) Johnny Alvarez
   (L.A.), New Mexico State Employment Bldg.,
   Albuquerque mural, Lorena Street School
   (L.A.), two murals, Casa de la Raza
   Alternative School (Berkeley), Santa Fe, New
   Mexico mural, Francisco Hernandez (L.A.),
   Artes Guadalupanos de Aztlan (N. Mexico),
   Willie Herron (L.A.). Better documentation
   would have been welcome.

5879 Street, Sharon. Califas - a celebration of
     Chicano culture and art. CITY ON A HILL,

(April 16, 1981). English.

   AN: Review of an exhibit at College V's
   Sesnon Gallery featuring 15 California
   artists: Ramses Noriega, Judy Baca, Salvador
   Roberto Torres, Malaquias Montoya, Rene
   Yanez, Ralph Maradiaga, Jose Montoya,
   Esteban Villa, Carmen Lomas Garza, Robert
   Chavez, among others. Illustrated.

5880 Valadez, Kathy L. Zoot suit, by Luis Valdez.
     SOMOS, Vol. 1, no. 2 (July 1978), p. 20-29.
     English.

   AN: Two reviews of Valdez's new play
   ZOOT SUIT, both enthusiastic. Historical
   material and photographs with an essay by
   Jose Montoya and his Pachuco drawing, as
   well as views of the play are included.

5881 Valencia, Manuel. Store front academy for
     Chicano artists. SACRAMENTO UNION, (January
     17, 1973). English.

   AN: Article includes comments by Armando
   Cid, Ricardo Fabela and Jose Montoya in a
   free-wheeling discussion of the goals and
   underlying philosophy of the Centro de
   Artistas Chicanos in Sacramento. More than
   simply exposing the people to art, the
   artists explain that they are looking for an
   alternative art expression and method of
   instruction never offered in traditional art
   schools or university departments of art.

Montoya, Malaquias

5882 Burkhardt, Dorothy. Chicano pride and anger
     mix at 'Califas'. THE TAB, (April 12,
     1981), p. 34. English.

   AN: CALIFAS: AN EXHIBITION OF CHICANO
   ARTISTS IN CALIFORNIA represents a
   cross-section of artists exhibiting work for
   at least ten years: Rupert Garcia, Ernie
   Palomino, Eduardo Carrillo, Judy Baca, Rene
   Yanez, Carmen Lomas Garza, Salvador Roberto
   Torres, Roberto Chavez, Willie Herron, Ralph
   Maradiaga, Sue Martinez, Jose Montoya,
   Malaquias Montoya, Ramses Noriega and
   Esteban Villa. Illustrated.

5883 La Causa Publications, Oakland, CA. New
     symbols for la Nueva Raza. Exhibition
     announcement, [ca. 1969]. English.

   AN: Announcement for exhibition of the
   four founding artists of the Mexican
   American Liberation Art Front (MALAF):
   Esteban Villa, Rene Yanez, Manuel Hernandez,
   Malaquias Montoya. Collage of portraits by
   the artists.

5884 Chicano art show at Contra Costa College. EL
     HISPANO, Vol. 8, no. 25 (December 11, 1973).
     English.

   AN: Information on exhibition organized
   by Ramses Noriega that included the work of
   Jose Montoya, Esteban Villa, Mario Sinape,
   Ricardo Rios, Malaquias Montoya, Fuchi
   Queso, and Joe Palomino.

5885 Gomez, Linda. Malaquias Montoya exhibit
     opens at La Pena. EL MUNDO (San Francisco,
     CA), (October 29, 1975), p. 3. English.

   AN: Over 50 paintings, silkscreens, and
   drawings by Montoya at La Pena Cultural
   Center, Berkeley, CA. Statement by the
   artist who refuses to exhibit in museums and
   is opposed to murals that are "pretty
   decorations.".

Montoya, Malaquias (cont.)

5886 Karam, Bruce G. Stanford mural. NUESTRO, Vol. 5, no. 8 (November 1981), p. 61.

5887 Malaquias Montoya. ARTE, (Fall 1977). English.

AN: Interview with northern California printmaker, painter and muralist, Malaquias Montoya. He discusses his life, his dedication to Chicano art, his resistance to the institutionalization of the Chicano struggle and its art, their cooptation by the establishment. He says he transcended nationalism at one period and became a Third World internationalist. Four drawings and two posters reproduced.

5888 Mexican American liberation art front: la Raza Nueva, Rene Yanez, Esteban Villa, Malaquias Montoya, Manuel Hernandez. BRONCE, Vol. 1, no. 3 (March 1969), p. 6-7. English.

AN: Manifesto of MALAF, a germinal Chicano art group in northern California. Compares revolutionary Chicanos of 1968 with the Mexicans of 1910; equally Chicano artists reject European-influenced art. Announces the exhibit NEW SYMBOLS FOR LA RAZA NUEVA, at La Causa in Oakland, March 22 to April 5, 1969. Puts forth the group's philosophy and goals, particularly exhibits and art services to the "barrio". Illustrated.

5889 Pro Arts Gallery, Oakland, CA. Si se puede! We can do it!: an exhibition of silkscreen prints and posters by Malaquias Montoya. Exhibition announcement, [1981]. English.

AN: Announcement of a traveling exhibit of prints and posters in Oakland, California. Illustrated.

5890 Santa Ana College, Santa Ana, CA and Goldman, Shifra M. Chicano art. Exhibition catalog, 1974. English.

AN: Thirteen California artists are presented in a short essay defining Chicano as a double mestizaje of Mexican mestizo and U.S. influences that exists in a state of "reconciled conflict." Its aim is communication. Artists included are Malaquias Montoya, Rupert Garcia, Manuel Hernandez, Esteban Villa, Robert Gomez, Harvey Tarango, Mary Helen Castro, Eduardo Carrillo, Graciela Carrillo, and "Los Four": Carlos Almaraz, Robert de la Rocha, Judithe Hernandez, Gilbert Lujan and Frank Romero.

5891 Street, Sharon. Califas - a celebration of Chicano culture and art. CITY ON A HILL, (April 16, 1981). English.

AN: Review of an exhibit at College V's Sesnon Gallery featuring 15 California artists: Ramses Noriega, Judy Baca, Salvador Roberto Torres, Malaquias Montoya, Rene Yanez, Ralph Maradiaga, Jose Montoya, Esteban Villa, Carmen Lomas Garza, Robert Chavez, among others. Illustrated.

5892 Tapia, Ludy. Montoya and the art of survival. LA VOZ DEL PUEBLO, Vol. 3, no. 5 (June 1972), p. 6. English.

AN: Profile of San Francisco Bay area poster maker and artist Malaquias Montoya, who first became involved in the Chicano movement in San Jose working with MASC and EL MACHETE paper. In Berkeley (1968), he met Esteban Villa and, with others, formed the Mexican American Liberation Art Front (MALAF). Montoya is against elitism influencing Chicano art, and is concerned with commercialization of Chicano art and artists. Illustrated.

5893 Valdez, Armando. El calendario chicano 1975. Hayward, CA: Southwest Network, 1975. English.

AN: Third in a series of historical calendars produced in 1972 and 1974 by La Causa Publications and Southwest Network. Artists included for each month are Carmen Lomas Garza, Sergio Hernandez, Malaquias Montoya, Mujeres Muralistas (Graciela Carrillo, Venezuelan Consuelo Mendez, Irene Perez, Patricia Rodriguez), Ramses Noriega, Ernie Palomino, Amado Maurilio Pena, Martin Perez. All but Texan Pena are California artists.

5894 Valdez, Armando. El calendario chicano 1977. Hayward, CA: Southwest Network, 1977. English.

AN: Fifth in a series of historical calendars produced in 1972, 1974, 1975, 1976 by La Causa Publications and Southwest Network. Artists whose work is reproduced are Malaquias Montoya, Amado Maurilio Pena, Ramori Zamora, Glugio J.L. Nicandro [Gronk], Etta Delgado, Ricardo Alaniz, Diane Gamboa, Elisa Marina Coleman, Margarita Calderon, Jose Antonio Burciaga, Cesar Augusto Martinez, Maria Ochoa y Valtierra, Juan Renteria Fuentes, from California, New Mexico, and Texas.

Montoya, Ruben

5895 Fabricant, Don. Show reveals Hispanic art. NEW MEXICAN WEEKEND, (June 1, 1979). English.

AN: Review of two exhibits in Santa Fe: EL FESTIVAL HISPANICO, mounted by La Cofradia de Artes y Artesanos Hispanicos and Gilberto Guzman at the Black Kachina Gallery. The reviewer feels the traditional-style woodcarving done by contemporaries is the strongest part of the show; works that break with these forms seem weaker, less skillful and cliche-ridden. Crafts are excellent. Muralist Guzman has blossomed in murals and easel paintings since he was employed by the 1978 Art in Public Places project. His work is intense and expressive, sometimes erotic. Illustration of work by sculptor Ruben Montoya.

5896 La Sociedad Historica de Nuestra Senora de Guadalupe, Santa Fe, NM. Meditacion. Exhibition invitation, 1980. English.

AN: Invitation to an exhibit by four artists: Filomeno Martinez (graphic artist, Albuquerque), Ruben Montoya (santero, Santa Fe), Santiago Chavez (painter, Santa Rosa), Jose Alberto Baros (sculptor, Espanola).

Mora, Raul

5897 Frankenstein, Alfred. An artistic taste of
     Mexico in the city. SAN FRANCISCO CHRONICLE,
     (November 29, 1975), p. 29. English.

     AN: A very favorable review of the
     inaugural exhibit at the Mexican Museum. The
     opening show was a panoramic view of Mexican
     art including pre-Hispanic, colonial, folk
     art and fine art. Among the Mexican American
     artists presented were Roberto Gonzalez,
     Raul Mora and Gustavo Rivera.

5898 Los Medanos College Gallery, [CA].
     Cinco/five: an exhibit of five Bay Area
     artists. Exhibition brochure, n.d. English.

     AN: Artists Gerry Concha, Gustavo
     Rivera, Raoul Mora, Manuel Villamor and
     Peter Rodriguez included in the show.
     Illustrated by Peter Rodriguez's portraits
     of the five.

5899 Raoul Mora. ESENCIA, Vol. 1, no. 3 (March,
     April, 1982).

     AN: Brief article on Stockton-born
     landscape painter and lithographer who
     records the beauties of Northern California
     in flat patterns and strong color.
     Illustrated.

Morales, Sylvia

5900 Cine chicano: primer acercamiento.
     COMUNIDAD, no. 20 (November 16, 1980), p.
     1-15. Spanish.

     AN: The entire cultural supplement of LA
     OPINION is dedicated to Chicano film.
     Includes articles by Jason Johansen, Jeff
     Penichet, Harry Gamboa, Jr., Jesus Salvador
     Trevino, Carlos Penichet, Sylvia Morales,
     Julio Moran, and Jose Luis Borau. Also
     includes a declaration of purpose by the
     Asociacion Chicana de Cineastas, and a
     filmography of Chicano cinema compiled by
     Trevino.

5901 Fourth annual San Antonio film festival. San
     Antonio, TX: Oblate College of the
     Southwest, 1979. Bilingual.

     AN: Symposium and film festival catalog
     featuring motion pictures and videocassettes
     made by and about Mexicans, Chicanos and
     Latinos. The Symposium focused on Latina
     women in film and television, Margarita
     Galban, Carmen Tafolla, Leticia Ponce, Grace
     Castro Nagata, Marcela Fernandez Violante of
     Mexico, and Sylvia Morales.

5902 Kleinhaus, Chuck; Seiter, Ellen; and Steven,
     Peter. Conference report: struggling for
     unity. JUMP CUT, no. 21 (November 1979), p.
     35-37. English.

     AN: Report and critique of the U.S.
     Conference for an Alternative Cinema held in
     mid-June 1979 at Bard College in New York
     state to chart a course for independent
     filmmakers. Chicano, Black, Asian and Puerto
     Rican film people attended, including Jesus
     Salvador Trevino and Sylvia Morales from the
     Chicano Cinema Coalition of Los Angeles.

5903 Morales, Sylvia. Chicana. 20 min., 16 mm,
     color, 1979. English.

     AN: Color film tracing the history of
     the Chicana back to pre-Columbian women's
     history. Utilizes images of pre-Columbian
     and modern Mexican murals, as well as

filming of contemporary Chicanas and their
activities. Based on a slide show by Anna
Nieto-Gomez, adapted for the screen by
Morales.

5904 Peyton, Patricia, ed. Reel change: a guide
     to social issue films. San Francisco, CA:
     Film Fund, 1979. English.

     AN: Includes a section on Hispanic film
     with descriptions, sources, and rentals.
     Listed are Esperanza Vasquez's AGUEDA
     MARTINEZ, Sylvia Morales' CHICANA, Adolfo
     Vargas' CONSUELO: QUIENES SOMOS?/WHO ARE
     WE?, El Teatro Campesino's I AM JOAQUIN,
     Jose Luis Ruiz's THE UNWANTED, Jesus
     Salvador Trevino's YO SOY CHICANO, and
     others. Listings are international in scope.

5905 Wilson, William. Chicana artists still
     seeking identification. LOS ANGELES TIMES,
     (June 23, 1975), p. VI, 5. English.

     AN: Ten Chicana artists are exhibiting
     their work in the Boathouse Gallery of Plaza
     de la Raza in Lincoln Park: Judithe
     Hernandez, Patssi Valdez, Judy Baca,
     Josefina Quesada, Victoria del
     Castillo-Leon, Olga Muniz, Gloria Flores,
     Sylvia Morales, Isabel Castro and Celia
     Tejadak. The work is still tentative and may
     develop.

Moran, Joe

5906 California. State College. Los Angeles. Art
     Gallery. Twelve Chicano artists. Exhibition
     invitation, n.d. English.

     AN: Invitation to an exhibit: Jose
     Montoya, Gilbert Sanchez Lujan, Esteban
     Villa, Rene Yanez, Joe Moran, Armando Cid,
     Leonard Castellas, Juanishi Orozco, Rudy
     Cuellar, Beltran, Lopez and Cabrera.

Moreno, Edward

5907 Knapp, Dan. KCET's show for Chicano viewers.
     LOS ANGELES TIMES, (April 3, 1970), p. IV,
     18. English.

     AN: Story on the television series
     AHORA! started September 1969 on KCET, Los
     Angeles' National Educational Television.
     Edward Moreno is program director and host;
     Victor Millan is producer-director; Claudio
     Fenner-Lopez, senior producer, has staff
     including set-designer David Villasenor,
     production manager James Val, and alternate
     host-narrator Jesus Trevino. The program has
     shown exhibits of artists Gilberto Lujan and
     Daniel Ramirez.

Moreno, Martin

5908 Arts Council Center for the Arts of Greater
     Lansing, Lansing, MI. Raza fine arts
     festival. Festival program, 1978. English.

     AN: This festival program mentions Jose
     Narezo's mural at the Holland National Guard
     Armory, Grand Rapids; includes a statement
     of the Raza Art/Media Collective, Inc.; the
     philosophy of artists Zaragosa Vargas and S.
     Kaneta Kosiba-Vargas; and profiles of
     exhibiting artists George Vargas, Martin
     Moreno, Hector Perez, Michael L. Selley,
     Jesse Gonzales, Nora Chapa Mendoza, Jesse
     Soriano, Jose Luis Narezo.

Moreno, Martin (cont.)

5909 El calendario hispano de Michigan, 1981.
Stanton, MI: Montcalm Intermediate School
District and Nuestras Artes de Michigan,
1981. English.

> **AN:** Months of historical calendar
> illustrated with art works by George Vargas,
> Nora Chapa Mendoza, Jesse Gonzalez, Julio
> Perazza(Puerto Rican), Hector Valdez, Pamela
> M. Gonzalez, Isabell Escojico (7-year-old
> child), Jose Narezo, Martin Moreno, Laurie
> Mendoza Psarianos, Rosa Maria Arenas.

5910 Capitol Art Gallery, Lansing, MI. Arte de
Nora Mendoza, Hector Perez, George Vargas,
Martin Moreno. Exhibition invitation [1979].
English.

> **AN:** Invitation to an art exhibit
> organized by Nuestras Artes de Michigan.

5911 Nora Mendoza: pintora de ascendencia
mexicana triunfa en los EE. UU. BUENHOGAR,
(May 1979), p. 7. Spanish.

> **AN:** Profile of Texas-born Nora Mendoza
> of Michigan, a painter of abstractions in
> acrylic. She is an active member of many
> Detroit and Michigan organizations,
> including Nuestras Artes de Michigan which
> she co-founded with Jorge Vargas, Martin
> Moreno and Jessie Gonzalez.

5912 Raices y visiones [portfolio]. REVISTA
CHICANO-RIQUENA, Vol. 7, no. 2 (Spring
1979), p. 29-44.

> **AN:** Portfolio of works from the exhibit
> RAICES ANTIGUAS/VISIONES NUEVAS: ANCIENT
> ROOTS/NEW VISIONS. Artists included are
> Patssi Valdez (Los Angeles), Eloisa
> Castellanos-Sanchez (New York), Benjamin
> Serrano, Jr. (Tijuana, Mexico), Alex Garza
> (Chicago), Martin Y. Moreno (Michigan), Luis
> A. Jimenez (New Mexico), Rene Castro
> (Oakland, CA), Sita Gomez de Kanelba (New
> York), Susana Lasta (Tucson, AZ), Domingo
> Garcia (New York), Consuelo Mendez Castillo
> (Caracas, Venezuela), Naomi Castillo
> Simonetti (New Jersey), Louis Carlos Bernal,
> and Eddie Comptis.

5913 Valade, Carole. Mural depicts artist's
heritage. ADRIAN DAILY TELEGRAM, (September
15, 1978). English.

> **AN:** Detailed description of Vibrations
> of a New Awakening, mural at Community
> Action Art Center by Martin Moreno with
> assistants Hector Perez and Walter Burrow.

Moron, Jesus G.

5914 De Marroquin, Moron. Arte negativo en
exposicion. LA PRENSA, Vol. 1, no. 18
(September 18, 1978). Spanish.

> **AN:** Florida-born Jesus G. Moron produces
> art within the canons of surrealism and
> mystical art. Strongly influenced by ancient
> cultures like those of the Mayas, Olmecs and
> "Lemurians". Illustrated with an ink on
> paper drawing titled CAIDA DEL CONSCIENTE.

Motion Pictures
USE: Films

Mount San Antonio College, CA

5915 [Untitled photograph]. CHISMEARTE, no. 2
(Winter, Spring, 1977), p. 34.

> **AN:** Reproduction of the invitation to a
> Los Four exhibit at Mount San Antonio
> College Art Gallery, BANNERS AND PAPER,
> April 12 - May 6, 1977.

Movimiento Artistico del Rio Salado (MARS)

5916 Adams Hotel, Phoenix, AZ. Chicano and Indian
art exhibit. Exhibit invitation, 1979.
English.

> **AN:** Invitation to an exhibit of 16
> artists. Brief history of the organization
> MARS (Moviemiento Artistico del Rio Salado)
> of Phoenix, AZ, formed in Summer 1978 after
> a Floricanto Culture Week. 98% of MARS
> members are Chicano or Indian. Their purpose
> is to build the Salt River Valley as a
> cultural center of the Southwest.

5917 Armas, Jose and Buitron, Robert. Issues.
ARIZTLAN NEWSLETTER, (August 1981).
English.

> **AN:** Thoughts and definitions of Chicano
> art by Dr. Jose Armas, founder of Pajarito
> Publications, and by photographer and MARS
> member Robert Buitron.

5918 Donaghy, Kathleen. Two Arizona firsts:
Chicano gallery and Spanish theatre. ARIZONA
ARTS AND LIFESTYLE, (1981). English.

> **AN:** The MARS (Movimiento Artistico del
> Rio Salado) Gallery has opened in downtown
> Phoenix, run by MARS founder Jim
> Covarrubias. Louis Leroy, expansion arts
> coordinator for the Arizona Commission on
> the Arts, says it is the only arts-oriented
> space that caters to Chicanos in Arizona.

5919 Encanto Pavilion, Encanto Park, Phoenix, AZ.
Exposicion de arte para la raza: Arizona
Chicano art show. Exhibition catalog, [ca.
1978]. English.

> **AN:** Catalog for an exhibit organized by
> MARS (Movimiento Artistico del Rio Salado).
> Colombian-born Antonio L. Tocora, Jim
> Covarrubias, Ed Dias, Robert C. Buitron,
> Armando Leon Hernandez, Guillermo Galindo,
> Richard Luna Cisneros, Jose Andres Giron,
> Robert L. Matta included.

5920 MARS: Movimiento Artistico del Rio Salado.
Phoenix, AZ: Mars Studio/Gallery, 1978.
English.

> **AN:** History and manifesto of MARS, 13
> member group of Arizona painters, sculptors,
> designers, and photographers: Jose Andres
> Giron, Jose Jimenez Rodriguez, Antonio
> Tocora (Colombian-born), Ramon Delgadillo,
> Francisco Zuniga, Jim Covarrubias, Ed Diaz,
> David Martinez, Roberto Buitron, Juan
> Rodriguez, Eddie Lopez, Zarco Guerrero, Joe
> Sanchez.

5921 MARS: Movimiento Artistico del Rio Salado.
Exhibition brochure, [1981]. English.

> **AN:** Illustrated brochure for the MARS
> organization and its studio-gallery.
> Includes a brief history, list of
> exhibitions from 1978 to 1981, news about
> its studio-workshop for the community, and
> its goals.

Movimiento Artistico del Rio Salado (MARS) (cont.)

5922 MARS: Movimiento Artistico del Rio Salado. Phoenix, AZ: [MARS], n.d. English.

AN: Illustrated brochure for the MARS organization and its studio-gallery. Includes a brief history, list of exhibitions from 1978 to 1981, news about its studio-workshop for the community, and its goals.

Movimiento Artistico Chicano (MARCH), Chicago, IL

5923 Allen, Jane and Guthrie, Derek. La mujer: a visual dialogue. NEW ART EXAMINER, Vol. 5, no. 10 (July 1978), p. 14. English.

AN: Review of international show by MARCH of Chicago on women's themes. Criticizes male Chicano artistic stereotypes of women compared to women's art on women from California.

5924 Calendario de March: 1977. Chicago, IL: MARCH, Inc., 1976. English.

AN: Historical calendar with photos and biographies of artists. Illustrations of artwork by Ray Patlan, Jose Nario, Frank J. Sanchez, Salvador Dominguez, Salvador Vega, Marguerite Ortega, Aurelio Diaz, Carlos Cortez, Mario E. Castillo, Francisco Blasco, Rey Vasquez, and Efrain Martinez. History of MARCH (Movimiento Artistico Chicano).

5925 Chicago. Public Library Cultural Center, Chicago, IL. La mujer: a visual dialogue. Exhibition invitation, 1978. English.

AN: Invitation to an exhibit spotlighting women artists from Mexico and the United States. Organized by the Movimiento Artistico Chicano (MARCH) of Chicago. 40 paintings by women artists included, and 50 works based on the theme of women. Poetry readings, music, dance, film, theatre, and panels of men and women artists included. Illustrated by work by Linda Vallejo.

5926 Highfill, Holly. MARCH (Movimiento Artistico Chicano). NEW ART EXAMINER, (June 1975), p. 4. English.

AN: Brief history of MARCH (started 1972; chartered 1975). Resume of its activities, including report on most ambitious show of 25 Mexican artists, MEXPOSICION.

5927 MARCH: Movimiento artistico Chicano (Mexican-American Art Movement). QUARTERLY, (Spring 1976), p. 10. English.

AN: Brief history of MARCH. Illustrations of murals by Ricarco Alonzo, Jose Gonzalez, Vicente Mendoza. Ray Patlan.

5928 Mitchell, Raye Bemis. March to an aesthetic of revolution. NEW ART EXAMINER, (February 1977). English.

AN: Interesting article that defines Chicano social-realism as a compelling aesthetic in opposition to avant-garde formalism. Exhibit by members of Chicago's MARCH group. Illustrated.

5929 Movimiento Artistico Chicano (MARCH), Chicago, IL. Letter to CARACOL. CARACOL, Vol. 4, no. 10 (June 1978), p. 3. Spanish.

AN: Press release announcing LA MUJER:

UN DIALOGO VISUAL, an art exhibit focusing on women sponsored by MARCH of the Chicago Public Library.

5930 Notes on 2nd National Community Muralists' Network Conference, Chicago, Ill. April 20-23, 1978. San Francisco, CA, 1978. English.

AN: Rupert Garcia, Raul Martinez, Patricia Rodriguez, Ray Patlan (San Francisco Bay Area) and Jaime Valadez (San Jose), among others, attended the conference in Chicago. Reports were heard from many parts of the United States on mural activities, including that of Aurelio Diaz of Chicago, representing MARCH (Movimiento Artistico Chicano). A workshop presentation was made by Luis Arenal and others from the Taller Siqueiros of Cuernavaca, Mexico. An experimental mural to try Siqueiros' techniques was created. Illustrated.

5931 Sorell, Victor A. Barrio murals in Chicago: painting the Hispanic-American experience on "our community" walls. REVISTA CHICANO-RIQUENA, Vol. 4, no. 4 (Fall 1976), p. 51-72. English.

AN: Important survey of Chicago's Latino murals, with key works considered in detail. Among the Chicano art organizations and muralists mentioned are MARCH (Movimiento Artistico Chicano), and Yolanda Galvan, Juanita Jaramillo, Jose Nario, Raymond Patlan, Vicente Mendoza, Marcos Raya, Ricardo Alonzo, Jose G. Gonzalez and Mario Castillo, author of the earliest Latino mural in Chicago (1968). Puerto Rican and non-Latino muralists and mural groups are also discussed. Well illustrated.

5932 El Taller, Inc., Chicago, IL and Movimiento Artistico Chicano (MARCH), Chicago, IL. Skyjacked: screenprinted posters from California by the Royal Chicano Air Force (R.C.A.F.), 1980. Exhibition invitation, 1980. English.

AN: Invitation to an exhibit at the El Taller Gallery, co-sponsored by MARCH. Illustrated with a print by San Francisco artist Xavier Viramontes.

5933 Woodblock and linoleum prints by Carlos Cortez, member of the Chicago mural group. TIN TAN, Vol. 2, no. 6 (December 1, 1977). English.

AN: Seven works reproduced from prints by Cortez, also an active member of the Movimiento Artistico Chicano of Chicago, dating from 1971 to 1976.

Movimiento Estudiantil Chicano de Aztlan (MEChA)

5934 Ackerman Student Union, University of California, Los Angeles. Raza women in the arts: brotando del silencio. Exhibit invitation, 1979. English.

AN: Invitation to a MEChA-sponsored exhibit of women's art. Illustrated.

Movimiento Estudiantil Chicano de Aztlan (MEChA)
(cont.)

5935 Kennedy, Bailey. The American pageant: a
history of the republic, 6th ed. 6th ed.,
Lexington, MA: D.C. Heath, 1979, p. 674.
English.

AN: Reproduction of two sections of the
MEChA mural painted in 1974 by students
directed by Sergio O'Cadiz at Santa Ana
College,Santa Ana, Calif. The mural includes
Mexican and Mexican American themes.

5936 M.E.C.H.A. cultura y evolucion mexicana. EL
CLARIN, (May 2, 1974), p. 3. Spanish.

AN: Report on the mural designed and
painted under the direction of Mexican-born
designer Sergio O'Cadiz at Santa Ana
College, Santa Ana, Calif. Collaborators
were instructor Shifra Goldman and gallery
director Mike Davis, with members of the
MEChA Club and other students. The mural
concerns the history of Mexico and of the
Chicano and includes a tribute to David
Alfaro Siqueiros' Los Angeles mural AMERICA
TROPICAL, painted and white-washed in the
1930s. Illustrated.

Moya, Jose Oscar

5937 Chicago-Raza murals. NATIONAL MURALS NETWORK
COMMUNITY NEWSLETTER, (Fall 1979), p. 22.
English.

AN: Murals by Ray Patlan, Aurelio Diaz,
Marcos Raya, Salvador Vega, Jaime Longoria,
Malu Ortega y Alberro, Oscar Moya in
Chicago's Pilsen district.

LA MUJER [mural]

5938 Rogelio Cardenas--making murals. EL MUNDO
(San Francisco, CA), (September 14, 1978).
English.

AN: Rogelio Cardenas' fourth mural, LA
MUJER, on the La Mexicana Tortilleria in
Hayward, California. Interview with the
artist who explains the mural's symbolism
and his future plans. Illustrated.

LA MUJER: UN DIALOGO VISUAL [exhibit], Chicago, IL, June 15-July 19, 1978

5939 Chicago. Public Library Cultural Center,
Chicago, IL. La mujer: a visual dialogue.
Exhibition invitation, 1978. English.

AN: Invitation to an exhibit
spotlighting women artists from Mexico and
the United States. Organized by the
Movimiento Artistico Chicano (MARCH) of
Chicago. 40 paintings by women artists
included, and 50 works based on the theme of
women. Poetry readings, music, dance, film,
theatre, and panels of men and women artists
included. Illustrated by work by Linda
Vallejo.

Mujeres Artistas del Suroeste (MAS), Austin, TX

5940 Conferencia plastica chicana. Conference
brochure, 1979. English.

AN: Schedule of proceedings at
internationally attended conference on
Chicano and Mexican art and photography
sponsored by the Centro Cultural de LUCHA
(League of United Chicano Artistas) and MAS
(Mujeres Artistas del Suroeste). Brief
biographies of presenters. Illustrated.

5941 Documentary to include work by Cuate Santos.
LAREDO NEWS, (July 17, 1980). English.

AN: Photography by Laredo News
photographer Cuate Santos included in
exhibit "Un encuentro sin palabras," a
documentary show on Mexican American life in
Texas sponsored by Mujeres Artistas del
Suroeste (MAS). The state-wide show was
juried by Los Angeles photographer Isabel
Castro. Illustrated.

5942 Galeria Tonantzin, Centro Cultural de LUCHA,
Austin, TX. Visiones Chicanas: images and
demonstrations by Chicana and Latina visual
artists. Exhibition invitation, 1979.
English.

AN: Invitational poster for an exhibit
and a series of workshops organized by
Mujeres Artistas del Suroeste (MAS),
affiliated with LUCHA, League of United
Chicano Artists of Austin, TX.

5943 Garcia, Ruperto. Las companeras art exhibit.
ARRIBA, Vol. 1, no. 4 (October 1980), p. 9.
English.

AN: Illustrated story on an art show
featuring Texas Latinas organized by MAS
(Mujeres Artistas del Suroeste) in Austin.
More than 18 women were represented.

5944 Goldman, Shifra M. Chicana artists at work.
ARRIBA, [n.d.], p. 3+. English.

AN: Excerpt of a longer article on the
Texas women's group Mujeres Artistas del
Suroeste (MAS). Integral to the group are
artists Santa Barraza, Nora Gonzalez-Dodson,
Alicia Arredondo, Maria Flores, Sylvia
Orozco, and Modesta Trevino.

5945 Goldman, Shifra M. Women artists of Texas:
MAS = More + Artists + Women = MAS.
CHISMEARTE, no. 7 (January 1981), p. 21-22.
English.

AN: History of Texas Chicana women
artists' organization, Mujeres Artistas del
Suroeste (MAS), co-founded in 1977 by Santa
Barraza and Nora Gonzalez-Dodson in the
framework of the burgeoning feminist art
movement, particularly Women and Their Work
of Texas. Brief history of Chicano politics
and the corresponding art movement of
southern and central Texas. In addition to
Barraza and Gonzalez-Dodson, Alicia
Arredondo, Modesta Trevino, and Maria Flores
are considered. Illustrated.

5946 Moody Hall, St. Edwards University, Austin,
TX. Las companeras. Exhibition invitation,
1980. English.

AN: Invitation to an exhibition of
Chicana/Latina artists sponsored by Mujeres
Muralistas del Suroeste (MAS). Illustrated.

Mujeres Artistas del Suroeste (MAS), Austin, TX (cont.)

5947 NATIONAL MURALS NETWORK COMMUNITY
      NEWSLETTER. (Spring 1980). English.

      AN: Reports on the Sept. 1979 conference
      of Chicano visual arts held at UT Austin,
      organized by the Mujeres Artistas del
      Suroeste, and the Liga Unida de Chicanos
      Artistas, which brought together
      participants from the U.S. and Mexico City;
      on Manuel Martinez's five murals (1976-78);
      murals by Roberto Lucero, Al Sanchez, and
      Jerry Jaramillo; as well as by the Chilean
      group Orlando Letelier Brigade, all in
      Denver, Colorado; murals by Leo Tanguma in
      Houston; the story about the "forbidden"
      Chicano mural in Blue Island, Illinois.
      Illustrated.

5948 Orozco, Sylvia. Las mujeres - Chicana
      artists come into their own. MOVING ON, Vol.
      2, no. 3 (May 1978), p. 14-16. English.

      AN: Illustrated feature prepared by
      artist Sylvia Orozco on the founding of
      Mujeres Artistas del Suroeste in Austin,
      September 1977. Artworks and statements by
      Nora Gonzalez Dodson, Maria Flores, Modesta
      Trevino, Santa Barraza, as well as musicians
      and singers.

5949 Palma Castroman, Janis. ENCUENTRO ARTISTICO
      FEMENIL [exhibit], Austin, TX, November 28,
      1977. TEJIDOS, Vol. 5, no. 1 (1978), p.
      1-47. Bilingual.

      AN: A multimedia, multicultural
      exposition by 26 Chicana artists held at
      Juarez-Lincoln University. The exhibit was
      sponsored by Chicanos Artistas Sirviendo a
      Aztlan (CASA) and Mujeres Artistas del
      Suroeste (MAS).

5950 Palma Castroman, Janis. Introduccion.
      TEJIDOS, Vol. 5, no. 1 (1978), p. i.
      Spanish.

      AN: One-page introduction to theme issue
      featuring the work of Chicana artists
      exhibited at the ENCUENTRO ARTISTICO FEMENIL
      exposition held on November 28, 1977 in
      Austin, TX.

5951 Women artists: forming a Texas network.
      Brochure, 1979. English.

      AN: Biographic and bibliographic
      information on women artists groups from
      Austin, Dallas, Houston and San Antonio.
      Includes brief history of MAS (Mujeres
      Artistas del Suroeste), a list of members,
      and biographies of Alicia Arredondo, Santa
      Barraza, Mary Ann Ambray Gonzalez, and
      Sylvia Orozco.

5952 Xochil Art and Culture Center, Mission, TX.
      Besame mucho. Exhibition invitation, 1979.
      English.

      AN: Invitation to exhibit of Texas
      artists from Mujeres Artistas del Suroeste
      (MAS): Mary Ann Anguiano, Alicia Arredondo,
      Santa Barraza, Nora Gonzales-Dodson, Maria
      Flores, Carolina Flores, Mary Ann Ambray
      Gonzales, Sylvia Orozco, Nancy de los
      Santos, Modesta Barbina Trevino.
      Illustrated.

Mujeres de Aztlan

5953 CODEX NEWSLETTER (Galeria de la Raza, San
      Francisco, CA). Vol. 1, no. 2 (September

1973). English.

      AN: An in-house bulletin of upcoming
      events: EL SOL NUNCA MUERE,
      photography/poster exhibit, Rolando Garces,
      and Peruvian posters; Mujeres de Aztlan,
      women artists' collective exhibit;
      Filipino/Samoan art exhibit; Galeria
      Christmas art sale; Galeria pavilion at S.F.
      annual art festival; Rockefeller scholarship
      for Galeria curator Luis Santana; Galeria
      coloring book; Balmy Alley mural project;
      Diego Rivera exhibit; first installment of
      Rupert Garcia's RAZA MURALS AND MURALISTS:
      AN HISTORICAL VIEW.

5954 Mujeres de Aztlan. EL TECOLOTE, Vol. 4, no.
      1 (October 10, 1973), p. 3. English.

      AN: A collective of Third World women
      artists plan an art show at Galeria de la
      Raza in San Francisco. Stressing the need
      for art forms that bring awareness and
      present the true nature of women's living
      conditions, this call for submission of art
      work reflects some feminist concerns of the
      period.

Mujeres Muralistas del Valle, Fresno, CA

5955 Ruiz, Elvia. Whitewashed mural.
      SENTIMIENTOS, Vol. 1, no. 2 (May 1978), p.
      7-10. English.

      AN: Illustrated article about Las
      Mujeres Muralistas del Valle. Their mural
      titled, "History of the Chicanos From a
      Woman's Perspective" was vandalized. Members
      of the mural group recall its creation and
      comment on its destruction.

Las Mujeres Muralistas, San Francisco, CA

5956 Albright, Thomas. Three remarkable Latin
      murals. SAN FRANCISCO CHRONICLE, (June 7,
      1974), p. 48. English.

      AN: The myth of the melting pot is
      vanishing: we recognize a variety of
      "publics" today. This is shown in three
      remarkable murals in the San Francisco
      Mission District. The Mission branch of the
      Bank of America has a 90 foot mural designed
      by Jesus Campusano, assisted by Luis
      Cortazar and Michael Rios, with technical
      advice from Emmy Lou Packard. Another mural
      is by the Mujeres Muralistas (Graciela
      Carrillo, Consuelo Mendez, Irene Perez,
      Patricia Rodriguez); the third by Michael
      Rios on the 24th St. mini-park.

5957 Clark, Yoko and Hama, Chizu. California
      murals. Berkeley, CA: Lancaster-Miller,
      1979. English.

      AN: Picture book of Bay Area and Los
      Angeles murals with brief descriptions.
      Chicano artists included: Daniel Galvez,
      Irene Perez, Patricia Rodriguez, Graciela
      Carrillo (Mujeres Muralistas), Ray Patlan.

5958 Cockcroft, Eva. Women in the community mural
      movement. HERESIES, no. 1 (January 1977), p.
      14-22. English.

      AN: Women's role in the community mural
      movement is much greater than generally
      recognized. Among the many women muralists
      discussed are included the Mujeres
      Muralistas (Patricia Rodriguez, Irene Perez,
      Graciela Carrillo de Lopez, and Venezuelan
      Consuelo Mendez Castillo) of San Francisoc,
      and Judy Baca of Los Angeles. Illustrated.

Las Mujeres Muralistas, San Francisco, CA (cont.)

5959 Galeria Museo, Mission Cultural Center, San Francisco, CA and Rodriguez, Patricia. Patricia Rodriguez: simbolos y fantasias culturales. Exhibition catalog, 1981. English.

AN: Catalog of an exhibition of sculpture and painting. Autobiographical information about the Texas-born artist who lives in San Francisco and was a co-founder of Mujeres Muralistas. She explains her techniques in making portrait masks of Chicano/a artists in plaster and mixed media. Well illustrated.

5960 Greenberg, David; Smith, Kathryn; and Teacher, Stuart. Megamurals & supergraphics: big art. Philadelphia, PN: Running Press, 1977. English.

AN: A full-color picture book of murals throughout the United States. Chicano murals include Michael Rios (San Francisco), Mujeres Muralistas (San Francisco), Leonard Castellanos and Tomas Gonzales with others (Los Angeles), Los Artes Guadalupanos de Aztlan (New Mexico), Willie Herron (Los Angeles), Toltecas en Aztlan (San Diego), David Botello (Los Angeles), David Lopez and Arizona Mara Gang (Los Angeles), Vatos de Maravilla (Los Angeles), Carlito Gaegos (Los Angeles), Gil Hernandez (Los Angeles), Wayne [Alaniz] Healy (Los Angeles).

5961 Hagen, Carol. Mission murals. ARTWEEK, Vol. 5, no. 30 (September 14, 1974), p. 6. English.

AN: Report on two recently completed murals in San Francisco's Mission District: Jesus Campusano's 90x10-ft mural in the Bank of America branch, and the Mujeres Muralistas' mural adjacent to the Mission Model Cities building. Illustrated.

5962 Las mujeres muralistas. Exhibition invitation, 1974. English.

AN: Invitation to the inauguration of the mural PARA EL MERCADO at Paco's Tacos in San Francisco's Mission District by the Mujeres Muralistas, Sept. 15, 1974. Illustrated by Venezuelan artist Consuelo Mendez.

5963 Las muralistas: Patricia Rodriguez, Consuelo Mendez, Graciela Carrillo, Irene Perez. Exhibition invitation, 1974. English.

AN: Invitation to the inauguration of the mural LATINO AMERICA by the Mujeres Muralistas at the Mission Neighborhood Model Cities in San Francisco's Mission District, May 31, 1974.

5964 New mural on Mission Street. EL HISPANO, Vol. 7, no. 13 (September 19, 1974), p. 5. English.

AN: Description of mural at the corner of 24th Street and South Van Ness in San Francisco. Painted by Mujeres Muralistas--Consuelo Mendez, Graciela Carrillo, Susan Cervantes and Miriam Olivo, the 30-foot mural depicts people in a tropical, Latin American setting.

5965 Orth, Maureen. The soaring spirit of Chicano arts. NEW WEST MAGAZINE, Vol. 3, no. 19 (September 11, 1978), p. 41-46. English.

AN: Overview of California Chicano

culture. Color illustrations of works by Mexican muralist David Alfaro Siqueiros, Rupert Garcia, Mujeres Muralistas, Willie Herron, Rene Yanez, Rudy Martinez, San Diego's Chicano Park, ASCO, Jose Montoya.

5966 Petersen, Karen and Wilson, J.J. Women artists: Third World. New York, NY: Harper & Row, 1975. English.

AN: Catalog of slides with accompanying notes. Slides of Chicana artists available: Margaret Herrera (Chavez), Consuelo (Chelo) Gonzalez Amezcua, Santa Barraza, Mujeres Muralistas, El Grupo de Santa Ana, Carmen Lomas Garza, Carolina Flores.

5967 Preuss, Karen. The new Mission murals. SAN FRANCISCO BAY GUARDIAN, (June 28, 1975), p. 14-15. English.

AN: Mural art in San Francisco's Mission District has covered nearly every wall and alley on lower 24th Street. Murals by Mike Rios, the Mujeres Muralistas (Patricia Rodriguez, Graciela Carrillo, Consuelo Mendez, Miriam Olivo, Irene Perez, Susan Cervantes) appear in the area. Others have been painted by artists associated with the Galeria de la Raza. Illustrations.

5968 Quintero, Victoria. Mujeres muralistas. LA RAZON MESTIZA, Vol. 11, (Summer 1975).

AN: Goals and artistic procedures of the Mujeres Muralistas Collective. Article emphasizes the solidarity of Latin American women and Chicanas and how their joint artistic production reflects a woman's viewpoint in aesthetic terms.

5969 Quintero, Victoria. A mural is a painting on a wall done by human hands. EL TECOLOTE, Vol. 5, no. 1 (September 13, 1974), p. 6+. English.

AN: The women's collective, Mujeres Muralistas, exists within the strong San Francisco mural movement. Originally the group included Graciela Carrillo, Consuelo Mendez, Irene Perez, and Patricia Rodriguez. The group has expanded to include Susan Cervantes, Ester Hernandez, and Miriam Olivo. The two murals completed have been criticized for not being political; the women answer that they want the atmosphere to be surrounded with life, with colors. Illustrated.

5970 University Art Museum, Berkeley, CA. The Fifth Sun: Contemporary/Traditional Chicano & Latino Art. Exhibition catalog, 1977. English.

AN: Catalog of exhibit including 45 artists of northern California. Texts deal with Mexican muralists, Mujeres Muralistas & other muralists, posters, the Chicano art movement, altars, La Raza Silkscreen Center, Galeria de la Raza, the Mexican Museum, the Sacramento Centro de Artistas Chicanos/RCAF. Mural maps of S.F. Bay Area and Sacramento. Many illustrations.

Las Mujeres Muralistas, San Francisco, CA (cont.)

5971 Valdez, Armando. El calendario chicano 1975. Hayward, CA: Southwest Network, 1975. English.

AN: Third in a series of historical calendars produced in 1972 and 1974 by La Causa Publications and Southwest Network. Artists included for each month are Carmen Lomas Garza, Sergio Hernandez, Malaquias Montoya, Mujeres Muralistas (Graciela Carrillo, Venezuelan Consuelo Mendez, Irene Perez, Patricia Rodriguez), Ramses Noriega, Ernie Palomino, Amado Maurilio Pena, Martin Perez. All but Texan Pena are California artists.

5972 Venegas, Sybil. The artists and their work--the role of the Chicana artist. CHISMEARTE, Vol. 1, no. 4 (Fall , Winter, 1977), p. 3, 5. English.

5973 Venegas, Sybil. Conditions for producing Chicana art. CHISMEARTE, Vol. 1, no. 4 (Fall, Winter, 1977, 1978), p. 2, 4. English.

AN: Chicana artists face more obstacles than white women or Chicano counterparts in the arts. Mexican life style has portrayed the ideal of a submissive woman, but the values have changed. Chicana artists are concerned with women and their struggles. Muralists include Patricia Rodriguez, Irene Perez, Consuelo Mendez de Castillo, Susan Cervantes, Ester Hernandez, Miriam Olivo, Ruth Rodriguez, of the Mujeres Muralistas (San Francisco). Other artists are Etta Delgado and Barbara Carrasco.

Multicultural Arts Council of San Mateo County, CA

5974 Burciaga, Jose Antonio. Mural protest. CHISMEARTE, Vol. 2, no. 1 (Summer 1978), p. 27-28. English.

AN: Mexican muralist Gilberto Romero Rodriguez and Chicano poet and artist Burciaga splatter their own mural at dedication ceremonies to protest their exploitation as artists and the opportunism and insensitivity of the commissioning organization, The Multicultural Arts Council of San Mateo County, CA. The mural was painted in Redwood City, CA. Illustrated.

5975 Largest mural in San Mateo County becomes official Saturday. REDWOOD CITY TRIBUNE, (February 23, 1978), p. 12. English.

AN: Mural DANZAS MEXICANAS by Chicano artist and poet Jose Antonio Burciaga and Mexican muralist Gilberto Romero Rodriguez was commissioned by the Multi-cultural Arts Council of San Mateo County. Color illustration.

EL MUNDO DE BARRIO SOTEL [mural]

5976 Kim, Howard. Judithe Hernandez and a glimpse at the Chicana artist. SOMOS, (October, November, 1979), p. 6-11. English.

AN: Biographical information on Chicana artist Judithe Hernandez. Commentary on her contributions to Plaza de la Raza, Los Angeles Citywide Mural Project and her work as designer consultant to AZTLAN: INTERNATIONAL JOURNAL OF CHICANO RESEARCH. The article focuses on her mural activity, particularly two murals: EL MUNDO DE BARRIO SOTEL and LA CHICANA DE AZTLAN. Her personal art philosophy is presented in relation to Third World Art.

MUNDOS PERDIDOS [exhibit]

5977 Frankenstein, Alfred. Prison's artist in residence. SAN FRANCISCO CHRONICLE, (May 5, 1978), p. 60. English.

AN: Review of the exhibition MUNDOS PERDIDOS, curated at the Galeria de la Raza by Leonard Castellanos. Show consisted of work by Castellanos and inmates at Lompoc Federal Correctional Institution near Santa Barbara. Documents a prison mural, tattoos and silkscreen prints with socially critical themes.

Munguia, Roberto

5978 Estudios Rio: gallery of contemporary arts and crafts. Exhibition catalog, 1976. English.

AN: Catalog including identification, portraits and works of participating artists: Joe Bova, Enrique Flores, Carmen Lomas Garza, Xavier Gorena, Erik Gronborg, Lucas Hinojosa, Ben Holland, Kris Hotvedt, William Kaars-Sijpesteijn, Cesar Martinez, Chris Mende, Roberto Mungia, Steve Reynolds, Vicente Rodriguez, William Wilhelmi.

5979 San Antonio Museum of Modern Art. Paperwork: an exhibition of Texas artists. San Antonio, TX: San Antonio Museum of Modern Art, 1979. English.

AN: Includes Roberto Munguia, Mexican American artist from Kingsville, Texas. Working with shaped paper, the artist describes his material and methods of creation. Includes biography of artist together with an exhibition list. Illustrated with photographs of five paper constructions by Roberto Munguia.

Municipal Arts Gallery of Los Angeles

5980 Moisan, Jim. Ancient roots, new visions. ARTWEEK, Vol. 9, no. 26 (July 29, 1978), p. 8. English.

AN: Review of the show held at the Municipal Arts Gallery of Los Angeles, the first national touring show of Latino artists in the United States. Includes commentary on work of Larry Fuente, Luis Jimenez, Frank Romero, Harry Gamboa, Gronk, Rudy Martinez, Benjamin Serrano, Ricardo Diaz, Patssi Valdez, Mel Casas, Luis Leroy, Pedro Lujan. A related show, NEW VISIONS, L.A., includes Robert Delgado, Ray Bravo, Joe Moran, Rosalyn Mesquita, Patricia Murillo and others.

5981 Wilson, William. A blending of Hispanic roots, visions. CALENDAR, (July 30, 1978), p. 90. English.

AN: Review of ANCIENT ROOTS/NEW VISIONS exhibit held at the Municipal Art Gallery in Los Angeles.

Muniz, Olga

5982 Wilson, William. Chicana artists still
     seeking identification. LOS ANGELES TIMES,
     (June 23, 1975), p. VI, 5. English.

     AN: Ten Chicana artists are exhibiting
     their work in the Boathouse Gallery of Plaza
     de la Raza in Lincoln Park: Judithe
     Hernandez, Patssi Valdez, Judy Baca,
     Josefina Quesada, Victoria del
     Castillo-Leon, Olga Muniz, Gloria Flores,
     Sylvia Morales, Isabel Castro and Celia
     Tejadak. The work is still tentative and may
     develop.

Munoz, David

5983 59th Street Gallery, St. Louis, MO. Midwest
     Mexican-American art exhibit: Mexico and its
     artists. Exhibition brochure, 1981. English.

     AN: Sponsored by the Sociedad Mexicana
     "Benito Juarez" and the international
     Institute of St. Louis, this three-part
     exhibit includes 1) MEXICO AS SEEN BY HER
     CHILDREN, a bilingual exhibit from Mexico
     traveling under Smithsonian Institution
     auspices, 2) MEXICAN CHILDREN IN THE U.S.A.,
     3) MEXICAN AMERICAN ARTISTS. In the latter
     are included Stephen Capiz (Roseville,
     Minn.), Jose Gonzalez (Chicago), Cesar A.
     Martinez (San Antonio), Ada Medina (Des
     Moines), Nora Chapa Mendoza (West
     Bloomfield, Mich.), Rene David
     Michel-Trapaga (St. Louis), David Munoz
     (Kansas City, Mo.), Jose Luis Narezo (Grand
     Rapids, Mich.), Benny Ordonez, Roman
     Villarreal (Chicago), Alejandro Romero
     (Chicago), Aurelio Diaz "Tekpankalli"
     (Chicago), Simon Ybarra (St. Louis).

Munoz, Gilbert

5984 Canto al pueblo: an anthology of
     experiences. San Antonio, TX: Penca Books,
     1978. English.

     AN: Includes works by: Mario E.
     Castillo, Carlos Rosas, Jose G. Gonzalez,
     Santos Martinez, Gilbert Munoz, Fred Loa,
     Armando Ibanez and others.

Mural Art

5985 450 anos del pueblo chicano/450 years of
     Chicano history in pictures. Albuquerque,
     NM: Chicano Communications Center, 1976.
     English.

     AN: A pictorial history of Mexico,
     Mexican Americans and Chicanos through
     photographs and art works. P. 138 is
     dedicated to murals, graphics, cartoons and
     photographs from Chicago and the Southwest,
     but other murals, graphics, cartoons and
     photographs by Chicanos and non-Chicanos are
     scattered throughout. In addition, 450 ANOS
     has been a rich source book of imagery for
     Chicano artists, especially historical works
     of art.

5986 The affectionate realism of Jesse Trevino.
     SA: THE MAGAZINE OF SAN ANTONIO, Vol. 3, no.
     10 (December 1979), p. 70-73. English.

     AN: Brief story about, and personal
     statement by San Antonio photorealist
     painter and muralist. Trevino focuses on
     portraits of people and sites in the
     Westside barrio. Color illustrations.

5987 Albright, Thomas. Three remarkable Latin
     murals. SAN FRANCISCO CHRONICLE, (June 7,

1974), p. 48. English.

     AN: The myth of the melting pot is
     vanishing: we recognize a variety of
     "publics" today. This is shown in three
     remarkable murals in the San Francisco
     Mission District. The Mission branch of the
     Bank of America has a 90 foot mural designed
     by Jesus Campusano, assisted by Luis
     Cortazar and Michael Rios, with technical
     advice from Emmy Lou Packard. Another mural
     is by the Mujeres Muralistas (Graciela
     Carrillo, Consuelo Mendez, Irene Perez,
     Patricia Rodriguez); the third by Michael
     Rios on the 24th St. mini-park.

5988 Almaraz, Carlos. The artist as a
     revolutionary. CHISMEARTE, no. 1 (Fall
     1976), p. 47-55. English.

     AN: Los Angeles painter Carlos D.
     Almaraz gives a detailed history of a
     cartoon-banner he made for the first
     constitutional convention of the United Farm
     Workers of America while he was an
     illustrator for EL MALCRIADO, and a mural he
     did for the UFWA administration building in
     La Paz. He also elucidates his philosophy
     about politics, the role of the
     revolutionary artist in our time, and the
     artist's relation to the bourgeois art
     market.

5989 Almaraz, Carlos. Introduccion: vida urbana y
     artistas chicanos. COMUNIDAD, Vol. 55, no.
     22 (May 3, 1981), p. 2. Spanish.

     AN: In the controversial period of the
     early 1980s, Chicano advances are being
     attacked. In this political climate, some
     Los Angeles artists are interested in beauty
     and artistic creation: Carlos Almaraz,
     best-known of the Los Four group; Yreina
     Cervantez; Elsa Flores; John Valadez,
     presently working on a mural; and musicians
     Louie Perez and Tito Rodriguez Larriva.

5990 Amalgamated Meat Cutters and Butcher Workmen
     of North America. Cry for justice. 1972.
     English.

     AN: Well-illustrated catalog of Chicago
     street murals by Black, Chicano, White and
     Puerto Rican artists.

5991 Art in public places. Program statement,
     1977-78. English.

     AN: Documents an eleven-month program
     funded by CETA for 21 artists to produce
     murals, prints and weavings as public art.
     Includes murals by Gilberto Guzman and
     Graciela Carrillo-Lopez in Santa Fe.
     Statements by the artists. Illustrated.

5992 Art outdoors. CONCEPT, (September 1980).
     English.

     AN: Illustrated article on outdoor
     murals in Tucson by Antonio Pazos and David
     Tineo.

5993 Arte del varrio. San Jose: A.T.M
     Communications, Inc., Nos. 1-3, 1979-81..
     English.

     AN: Large format color illustrated
     albums of "Varrio art." Includes examples of
     tattoo art, placasos (graffiti) and barrio
     murals.

Mural Art (cont.)

5994 Artist views murals as dialogue with
oppressed. HOUSTON POST, (June 13, 1979),
p. 3A. English.

AN: There are doubts that Houston
muralist Leo Tanguma's latest structural
mural about police brutality will ever see
the light of day. Painted on three pointed
plywood panels, it was originally destined
for Moody Park. Other Tanguma murals have
been painted over. Illustrated.

5995 Artist's vow: delay-plagued state building
mural will be finished. FRESNO BEE,
(November 10, 1980), p. B4. English.

AN: Five-story-high mural "PLANTING OF
CULTURES" by John Sierra. Illustrated.

5996 Baca, Elfego and Martinez, Manuel. [Untitled
mural]. LA LUZ, Vol. 3, no. 12 (March,
April, 1975), p. 18.

5997 Baca, Judith F. Judith F. Baca. In: SOCIAL
WORKS: AN EXHIBITION OF ART CONCERNED WITH
SOCIAL CHANGE. Los Angeles, CA: Institute of
Contemporary Art, 1979, p. 44. English.

AN: Statement of purpose and history of
the Tujunga Wash Mural (San Fernando Valley,
CA) in process from 1976 on, by muralist and
founder of Social and Public Art Resource
Center (SPARC), Judith Baca. Illustrated.

5998 Baca, Walter R. Aguila y maiz [mural]. DE
COLORES, Vol. 1, no. 2 (Spring 1974), p. 61.
Spanish.

5999 Baca, Walter R. Campesino [mural]. DE
COLORES, Vol. 1, no. 2 (Spring 1974), p. 64.
Spanish.

6000 Baca, Walter R. Cosecha [mural]. DE COLORES,
Vol. 1, no. 2 (Spring 1974), p. 63. Spanish.

6001 Baca, Walter R. En el principio [mural]. DE
COLORES, Vol. 1, no. 2 (Spring 1974), p. 62.
Spanish.

6002 Baca, Walter R. Mestizo [mural]. DE COLORES,
Vol. 1, no. 2 (Spring 1974), p. 60. Spanish.

6003 Baca, Walter R. Mural historico [mural]. DE
COLORES, Vol. 1, no. 2 (Spring 1974), p. 57.
Spanish.

6004 Baca, Walter R. Vicios [mural]. DE COLORES,
Vol. 1, no. 2 (Spring 1974), p. 62. Spanish.

6005 Baca, Walter R. Vida y muerte. DE COLORES,
Vol. 1, no. 2 (Spring 1974), p. 56. Spanish.

6006 Baca, Walter R. La Virgen. DE COLORES, Vol.
1, no. 2 (Spring 1974), p. 58-59. Spanish.

6007 Bank of America, Mission-23rd St. Branch,
San Francisco, CA. A community mural
dedicated by the artists to Mexican muralist
David Alfaro Siqueiros. 1974. English.

AN: Brochure about the Bank of America
mural in the Mission District of San
Francisco designed by Jesus Campusano and
Luis J. Cortazar, assisted by Michael Rios,
Jaime Carrillo, Candice Ho, Julio Lopez,
Anthony Machado, Jack Nevarez. Technical
advisor, Emmy Lou Packard. Well illustrated.

6008 Barnes, Peter. Fringe benefits of a
depression: bringing back the WPA. NEW
REPUBLIC, Vol. 172, no. 11 (March 15, 1975),
p. 19-21. English.

AN: A well-researched and comprehensive
analysis of the CETA (Comprehensive
Employment and Training Act) impact on
public art in San Francisco. Material on
Chicano-Latino murals in the Mission
district. Includes viewpoints by
artist-activists Patricia Rodriguez, Mike
Rios, and writer Roberto Vargas. Important
compendium on funding sources of various
neighborhood art programs stressing their
value as community assets.

6009 Barnett, Alan. Southern journey. NATIONAL
MURALS NETWORK COMMUNITY NEWSLETTER, (Fall
1980), p. 22-32. English.

AN: Rather gossipy account of murals
seen in a swing of the southern United
States. Includes the work of dozens of
artists and arts groups from California,
Arizona, New Mexico, Texas, and Colorado.

6010 Barnstone, Gertrude and Tanguma, Leo. The
big picture: 'I want to indict the system
that has condemned us!'. HOUSTON
BREAKTHROUGH, (March 1980), p. 16-19.
English.

AN: Houston muralist Leo Tanguma studied
with John Biggers at Texas Southern
University who encouraged him and other
Chicanos to study Mexican murals. The
article is an interview with Tanguma which
details his strong political orientation and
ideals, and the problems he has encountered
as a result. Three illustrations.

6011 Barrera, Manuel. "Maestro" Siqueiros. LA
RAZA, Vol. 2, no. 2 (1974), p. 40-41.
English.

6012 Barrera, Manuel. Wall murals. LA RAZA, Vol.
1, no. 10 (February 1973), p. 24-25.
Bilingual.

6013 Barrio heritage reflected in bank mural. EL
CHICANO, Vol. 8, no. 50 (May 30, 1974), p.
8-9. English.

AN: Jesus Campusano and Luis J. Cortazar
were artist-designers of a monumental mural
painted inside the Mission Branch of the
Bank of America. Michael Rios was color
coordinator and five young artists worked
collectively on the project for four months.
Realistic scenes of everyday life in the
Mission barrio are contrasted to heroic
personalities from Latin America. Folk art
imagery, Indian and Spanish cultural symbols
and historical personages form a pageant of
Latin American history. Mural was
inaugurated on June 4, 1974.

6014 Barrio, Raymond. Art for our sake. NUESTRO,
Vol. 1, no. 6 (September 1977), p. 30-34.
English.

AN: Brief text with three color
reproductions of murals by Mike Rios (Bart
Mural, San Francisco), Gilberto Guzman (West
Las Vegas High School, NM), Willie Herron
(Farmacia Hidalgo, East Los Angeles, CA).

6015 Barrios, Greg. Big art comes of age. RIVER
CITY SUN, (July 21, 1978), p. 9. English.

AN: Report on the meeting of Mexican and
Chicano muralists at a mural conference in
Austin. Includes a "Guide to Mural Art in
East Austin," most of whose murals were done
by Raul Valdez. Illustrated.

Mural Art (cont.)

6016 Barrios, Lex. The barrio as a work of art:
Chicano muralism in Laredo, Texas? REVISTA
RIO BRAVO, Vol. 1, no. 3 (Fall   1981), p.
5, 15-16. English.

AN: Report by Laredo sociologist on
local conservative attitudes toward the
Chicano movement and muralism, and a meeting
held to plan a mural project in Laredo so it
could finally enter the mural movement.
Illustrated.

6017 Bartak, Bonnie. Murals make walls political
forum. ARIZONA REPUBLIC, (April 21, 1975),
p. A-12. English.

AN: Tempe, AZ murals located at the
Valle del Sol Institute (South 1st St.), the
Tempe Escalante Center (East Orange), and
the Barrio Youth Project (South 1st St.).
Illustrated.

6018 Basta con la migra [mural]. CARACOL, Vol. 3,
no. 11 (July 1977), p. 13.

6019 Bauer, Bernard. Angry artists deface own
mural. BERKELEY BARB, (March 1978), p. 7.
English.

AN: Chicano artists Jose Antonio
Burciaga and Gilberto Romero Rodriguez
recall a few struggles to sensitize local
arts organizations to Raza art. Financial
and political aspects of their painting a
patriotic mural, "Danzas mexicanas" in
Redwood City. Artists explain why they
defaced their own mural as an act of
protest.

6020 Beronius, George. The murals of East Los
Angeles. HOME MAGAZINE, (April 11, 1976),
p. 10-11+. English.

AN: Well-illustrated historical article
focusing on murals at Estrada Courts and
those produced through Goez Gallery and
Judith Baca in East Los Angeles.

6021 Blanco, Gil. Art on the walls: a vehicle for
positive change. LATIN QUARTER, Vol. 1, no.
2 (October 1974), p. 26-30. English.

AN: East Los Angeles artists Ismael
"Smiley" Pereira and C.W. (Charles) Felix
started painting murals with young people at
the Estrada Courts Housing Project in May
1973. There are now 30 murals, and the
residents are more receptive, noting the
changes that are taking place. Illustrated
with murals by Herron and Gronk, and Daniel
Martinez.

6022 Boettner, Jack. Youths help in fight against
graffiti: muralist fights spray cans with
brushes. LOS ANGELES TIMES [Orange County
edition], (May 26, 1979), p. II, 12-13.
English.

AN: Illustrated and descriptive story
about Orange County painter Emigdio Vasquez
working on a series of murals with youth.
Locations of murals by the group,
biographical information about Vasquez, and
his statement about art are given.
Illustrated.

6023 Botello, David Rivas and Healy, Wayne
Alaniz. Los Dos Streetscapers. SOMOS, Vol.
1, no. 3 (August 1978), p. 12-17. English.

AN: Autobiographical material by Los
Angeles street muralists Botello and Healy.

Illustrated.

6024 Bright, John; Bright, Mura; and Castellanos,
Leonard. L.A. Chicano street art. Venice,
CA: Environmental Communications, 1974.
English.

AN: Annotated slide catalog of Chicano
murals in East Los Angeles compiled by staff
of Mechicano Art Center. Also includes
article reprints on painted bus benches by
Mechicano artists (SUNSET Magazine, n.d.),
murals of East Los Angeles (LOS ANGELES
TIMES, 12/3/73, and SUNSET Magazine, April
1973). Well illustrated.

6025 Bright, John; Bright, Mura; and Castellanos,
Leonard. "Placas": graffiti and the
environment. Venice, CA: Environmental
Communications, 1974. English.

AN: Annotated slide catalog of Chicano
graffiti on walls, murals, and tattoos,
compiled by staff of Mechicano Art Center.

6026 Briseno, Rodolfo. Interview with a muralist.
ARRIBA, Vol. 1, no. 1 (July 1980), p. 5+.
English.

AN: Raul Valdez, muralist from Del Rio,
Texas has been painting murals in Austin and
was a founding member of LUCHA (League of
United Chicano Artists) in 1976. Having
studied with Siqueiros in Mexico, Valdez
sees strong affinities in content and form
between Chicano and Mexican muralism.
Illustrated with two photographs of Valdez's
Juarez-Lincoln mural.

6027 The Broadway mural, 1981, by John Manuel
Valadez. Los Angeles, CA: Victor Clothing
Co., n.d. English.

AN: Postcard/brochure about Valadez's
8x48-ft mural, oil on canvas, displayed at
the Victor Clothing Co. in downtown Los
Angeles. Brief profile of the photographer
and muralist. Full color reproduction of a
section of the complete mural.

6028 Brunazzi, Ceci. Writing on the walls: murals
in the mission. COMMON SENSE, (May 1975),
p. 1, 8. English.

AN: History of the early murals in the
Mission District of San Francisco, CA.
Illustrated.

6029 Burciaga, Jose Antonio. Mural protest.
CHISMEARTE, Vol. 2, no. 1 (Summer 1978), p.
27-28. English.

AN: Mexican muralist Gilberto Romero
Rodriguez and Chicano poet and artist
Burciaga splatter their own mural at
dedication ceremonies to protest their
exploitation as artists and the opportunism
and insensitivity of the commissioning
organization, The Multicultural Arts Council
of San Mateo County, CA. The mural was
painted in Redwood City, CA. Illustrated.

Mural Art (cont.)

6030 Cabaniss, Joe H. Mural painters believes vandalism political act. CHULA VISTA STAR NEWS, (March 16, 1980), p. 40-41. English.

AN: Recent vandalism on Chicano Park's twenty outdoor murals left seven splattered with paint. It was the second such incident in five months. Michael Schnorr, Southwestern College art instructor and painter of two murals, believes the attack was politically motivated. Illustrated. Reprinted in COMMUNITY MURALISTS NEWSLETTER, Spring 1981.

6031 Callum, Diane. Regional report, The arts: walls of passion. NUESTRO, Vol. 3, no. 11 (December 1979), p. 16, 51. English.

AN: Focusing on muralist Gilberto Guzman, one of the founders of Artes Guadalupanos in Santa Fe, the article details his efforts in the promotion and preservation of Chicano murals in New Mexico.

6032 Canto al pueblo: an anthology of experiences. San Antonio, TX: Penca Books, 1978. English.

AN: Includes works by: Mario E. Castillo, Carlos Rosas, Jose G. Gonzalez, Santos Martinez, Gilbert Munoz, Fred Loa, Armando Ibanez and others.

6033 Cantu, Jesus "Chista". Entrevista con "Chista" Cantu. SIN FRONTERAS, Vol. 1, no. 12 (November 15, 1974), p. 16. Spanish.

AN: Conversation in which Cantu speaks about his art which is based on the essential duality of all things. Includes photograph of design for an album cover CANTOS SIN FRONTERAS and a photograph of one of his murals representing the "cosmic unity of things as seen by people of the corn culture".

6034 Cantu, Jesus "Chista". Entrevista: Jesus Maria Cantu, 'El Chista'. MAGAZIN, Vol. 1, no. 4 (April 1972), p. 52-65. Spanish.

AN: Discusses his life in San Antonio; his apprenticeship since childhood to his uncle Miguel Angel Tellez who taught him to paint billboards, wall signs and church decorations; his membership in the group Artistas de la Nueva Raza; his artistic and political philosophy. In Spanish.

6035 Carlos Sandoval to complete mural in Zihuatanejo, Mexico. TIERRA Y LIBERTAD, Vol. 2, no. 4 (July 1980), p. 3, 10. English.

AN: Biographical information on Colorado artist Carlos Sandoval. The Municipal Library in the city of Zihuatanejo in the state of Guerrero is the site of Sandoval's mural which visually and symbolically projects the cultural and historical unity between Mejicanos and Chicanos.

6036 Carlson, Scott. Artist's mural puts a little beauty in prison cellblock. ST. PAUL DISPATCH, (December 5, 1978), p. East,1,3. English.

AN: Biographical information on Chicano artist Paul Basquez and his eleven mural projects at Stillwater State Prison.

6037 Carrillo, Eduardo; Hernandez, Sergio; and Noriega, Ramses. Mural, Chicano Research Library, UCLA [photograph]. AZTLAN, Vol. 3, no. 1 (Spring 1972), p. [VIII-IX].

6038 La Casa de la Raza Gallery, Santa Barbara, CA. Judithe Hernandez: virgen, madre, mujer; imagenes de la mujer chicana. Exhibition invitation [1979]. English.

AN: Invitation to an exhibit with a list of projects, murals, and exhibitions. Illustrated.

6039 Castellanos, Leonard. Chicano centros, murals, and art. CHISMEARTE, Vol. 1, no. 1 (Fall 1976), p. 26-27. English.

AN: Excerpt of an article originally published under the same title in ARTS IN SOCIETY (Spring-Summer 1975).

6040 Castellanos, Leonard. Chicano centros, murals, and art. ARTS IN SOCIETY, Vol. 12, no. 1 (Spring, Summer, 1975), p. 38-43. English.

AN: One of the organizers of the Mechicano Art Center in Los Angeles talks about the history of the Center, the artist's relationship to the mainstream; the importance of the street mural movement; the economic problems of the muralists and their dedication to the community; the need for alternative centers like the "centros." An excerpt of this article appeared in CHISMEARTE, no. 1 (Fall 1976), p. 26-27.

6041 Castillo, Oscar R.; Esparza, Antonio; and Cabrera, Antonio. Writing on the walls [photograph]. CON SAFOS, no. 8 (1972), p. 56-57.

6042 Centro Cultural de La Raza [mural]. MAIZE, Vol. 5, no. 1-2 (Fall , Winter, 1981, 1982), p. Bk cover. Spanish.

6043 El Centro Cultural de La Raza, San Diego, CA. Espejo del barrio-art exposition. Exhibition brochure, June 1975. English.

AN: Illustrated brochure announcement for a cultural exposition of Chicano music, art and drama. Includes some biographical information and one reproduction of painter Manuel Unzueta, woodworker Ambriz, muralist Victor Orozco Ochoa and designer/illustrator J. Armando Nunez.

6044 El Centro Cultural de La Raza, San Diego, CA and Enrique, Veronica. Tenth anniversary celebration, July 11, 1981. San Diego, CA: El Centro Cultural de la Raza, 1981. English.

AN: Anniversary brochure of the Centro, founded in 1970 by the Toltecas en Aztlan artistic collective and established at its Balboa Park location in 1971. Briefly reviews the history and activities of the Centro, including the establishment of Chicano Park in 1970 and the painting of murals at the Park and at the Centro. Well illustrated.

Mural Art (cont.)

6045 Centro de artistas, Sacra: recuerdo ...
descubrimiento ... voluntad. CHISMEARTE,
Vol. 1, no. 1 (Fall 1976), p. 6-7.
English.

AN: Summary of activities of the Centro
de Artistas Chicanos, made up of artists
from the Royal Chicano Air Force and other
groups. The Centro makes posters, T-shirts,
decals, murals and puts on a number of
cultural and social events. Report on a
"mass migration" July 1976 to the Academia
de la Nueva Raza in Dixon, NM for two weeks
of communion.

6046 Centro mural recipient of orchid award. LA
PRENSA SAN DIEGO, (November 20, 1981), p.
5. English.

AN: The American Institute of
Architects, the American Society of Interior
Designers, the American Planning Association
and the American Society of Landscape
Architects award the Centro Cultural de la
Raza of Balboa Park, San Diego, CA for
Victor Ochoa's mural on its walls.
Illustrated.

6047 Cesaretti, Gusmano and Hirtz, Jacqueline.
Uplifting the city: the mural-painter's
goal. HOME MAGAZINE, (May 8, 1977), p.
50-51. English.

AN: Illustrated report on murals in Los
Angeles and Pasadena by Anthony Padilla.

6048 Chapple, Paul. FV [Fountain Valley] wall
mural stirs contention. THE REGISTER,
(December 29, 1974), p. A3. English.

AN: Artist Sergio O'Cadiz has included a
panel showing gas-masked police dragging off
a Chicano youth. The panel has caused
controversy in Fountain Valley, CA; police
object to the image.

6049 Chapple, Paul. Mural, graffiti painters wage
endurance contest in F.V. [Fountain Valley].
THE REGISTER, (December 4, 1975), p. B5.
English.

AN: Mexican-born architect and designer
Sergio O'Cadiz, with a team, paints a 600
foot mural in Colonia Juarez, an older
section of Fountain Valley in Orange County,
CA. Local police objected to a scene showing
police brutality. White paint was hurled at
this panel one night, and the mural was
constantly attacked by vandals. Illustrated.

6050 Chavez, Jaime and Vallecillo, Ana Maria. A
political, historical, philosophical
perspective of muralist art in the
Southwest. RAYAS, Vol. 1, no. 3 (May, June,
1978), p. 6. English.

AN: Relates Chicano mural art to main
issues of the Chicano movement. The
Mechicano Art Center in Los Angeles and
Artes Guadalupanos de Aztlan in Santa Fe are
seen as examples of groups creating a new
people's art; art forms where esthetics are
allied to politics.

6051 Chavez, Jaime. Rayaprofiles: Manuel Unzueta.
RAYAS, Vol. 2, no. 3 (May, June, 1979), p.
5. Spanish.

AN: Brief biography of Mexican-born
Chicano artist and muralist from Santa
Barbara, California. Manuel Unzueta is
active with La Casa de la Raza and its

publication XALMAN. Unzueta is invited to
paint a mural in Albuquerque. A Santa
Barbara mural is illustrated.

6052 Chavez, Lucy. A Chicano muralist. REVISTA
MARYKNOLL, (July 1981). English.

AN: Denver artist Carlotta Espinosa
decided early in life that she was going to
be an artist. Espinosa has painted murals in
Arizona, Texas and the San Luis Valley in
Colorado. Illustrated with photographs of
artist and details from her murals.

6053 Chicago-Raza murals. NATIONAL MURALS NETWORK
COMMUNITY NEWSLETTER, (Fall 1979), p. 22.
English.

AN: Murals by Ray Patlan, Aurelio Diaz,
Marcos Raya, Salvador Vega, Jaime Longoria,
Malu Ortega y Alberro, Oscar Moya in
Chicago's Pilsen district.

6054 Chicano art of the Southwest. San Antonio,
TX: Instituto Chicano de Artes y Artesanias
of the Texas Institute for Educational
Development, 1975. English.

AN: Collection of 220 slides
supplemented by slide annotation and
artists' biographies researched and
photographed by Texas artist Cesar A.
Martinez over two years. Biographies cover
20 Texas, 6 New Mexico, and 15 northern
California artists. Slides include, in
addition, murals from Los Angeles and San
Diego.

6055 Chicano muralists maintain traditions. LA
CUCARACHA, (November 20, 1979), p. 7.
English.

AN: Introduction to Chicano muralism in
Pueblo and comparison to the Mexican mural
movement from which it draws inspiration. 20
murals painted from 1977 to 1979. The
muralists include Bernardo Duran, Juan
Espinoza, Miguel "Freeloader" Garcia, Lola
Gutierrez, Leo Lucero, Juan Pacheco, Dolores
Pena, Pedro Romero, Stan Salazar, David
Sandoval. Diego Rivera murals illustrated.

6056 Chicano pride theme of mural. EL DIARIO DE
LA GENTE, Vol. 2, no. 11 (January 25, 1974).
English.

AN: Commentary on the 11x15 ft. mural
painted by Carlos Rosas outside the entrance
to the Tabor Inn in University Memorial
Center. Mural composed of Indio-Chicano
symbols.

6057 Citywide mural project. Los Angeles, CA:
Citywide Mural Project, n.d. [c. 1975].
English.

AN: Brochure giving history, resources
and procedures for doing a mural by the Los
Angeles Citywide Mural Project/Mural
Resource Mural Program of 1973-1974.
Illustrated. Available in Social and Public
Art Resource Center (Venice, CA) archives.

6058 Clark, Yoko and Hama, Chizu. California
murals. Berkeley, CA: Lancaster-Miller,
1979. English.

AN: Picture book of Bay Area and Los
Angeles murals with brief descriptions.
Chicano artists included: Daniel Galvez,
Irene Perez, Patricia Rodriguez, Graciela
Carrillo (Mujeres Muralistas), Ray Patlan.

Mural Art (cont.)

6059 Cockcroft, Eva; Weber, John; and Cockcroft, James D. Towards a people's art: the contemporary mural movement. New York: E.P. Dutton, 1977. English.

AN: A survey of the street mural movement in the United States, from about 1967 on. Several chapters are written by the artists themselves: John Weber on the Chicago mural group; Susan Shapiro-Kiok on Cityarts Workshop of New York; Eva Cockcroft on People's painters of New Jersey; Geronimo Garduno on Artes Guadalupanos de Aztlan of New Mexico. Chicano murals illustrated include those of Mujeres Muralistas, Ray Patlan, William F. Herron, Hoyo-Mara Gang, Artes Guadalupanos de Aztlan, Vicente Mendoza and Jose Nario (with Patlan) Mario Castillo, Michael Rios, Toltecas en Aztlan, Roberto Chavez, Ernie Palomino, Chuy Campusano and Luis Cortazar (with Rios).

6060 Cockcroft, Eva. Women in the community mural movement. HERESIES, no. 1 (January 1977), p. 14-22. English.

AN: Women's role in the community mural movement is much greater than generally recognized. Among the many women muralists discussed are included the Mujeres Muralistas (Patricia Rodriguez, Irene Perez, Graciela Carrillo de Lopez, and Venezuelan Consuelo Mendez Castillo) of San Francisoc, and Judy Baca of Los Angeles. Illustrated.

6061 CODEX NEWSLETTER (Galeria de la Raza, San Francisco, CA). Vol. 1, no. 2 (September 1973). English.

AN: An in-house bulletin of upcoming events: EL SOL NUNCA MUERE, photography/poster exhibit, Rolando Garces, and Peruvian posters; Mujeres de Aztlan, women artists' collective exhibit; Filipino/Samoan art exhibit; Galeria Christmas art sale; Galeria pavilion at S.F. annual art festival; Rockefeller scholarship for Galeria curator Luis Santana; Galeria coloring book; Balmy Alley mural project; Diego Rivera exhibit; first installment of Rupert Garcia's RAZA MURALS AND MURALISTS: AN HISTORICAL VIEW.

6062 COMMUNITY MURALS (San Francisco, CA). (Fall 1981). English.

AN: Citywide Murals Group of Denver, Colorado assisted the Chilean-oriented Brigada Orlando Letelier with a mural in their city; Carlos Sandoval of Denver doing mural in Guerrero, Mexico; Ray Patlan of Berkeley, California assisting with mural in Mexico painted by Arnold Belkin's class at the Academy of San Carlos; report on the exhibit MURALS OF AZTLAN: THE STREET PAINTERS OF EAST LOS with a reprint of debate on the event by Shifra M. Goldman, Judithe Elena Hernandez de Neikrug, and comments by John Pitman Weber and Tim Drescher; report on DAR LUZ mural directed by Santa Barraza in Austin, Texas, and a new mural in Hayward, California directed by Enrique Romero; a mural sponsored by the Chicano Youth Center of Fresno, California showing the influence of Mexican calendars; a new mural, OAKLAND'S PORTRAIT by Daniel Galvez in Oakland, California; pro-and-con discussion of social function of graffiti in response to letter from Belgian source; reprint of story on spray paint crime bill (anti-graffiti) sponsored by California Assemblyman Richard Alatorre. Entire issue illustrated.

6063 Community Programs in the Arts and Sciences (COMPAS). Artists in the city: a report on C.E.T.A. artists in St. Paul. St. Paul, MN: COMPAS, 1978. English.

AN: Includes data on Chicano muralists John Acosta, Thomas Acosta, Paul Basquez, Armando Estrella, and photographer Raphael Romo.

6064 Community Programs in the Arts and Sciences (COMPAS). Flor y Canto in Minnesota. St. Paul, MN: Northwestern Press, 1978. English.

AN: Survey of community arts projects. Includes commentary on Chicano mural activity in Minnesota. Cover design by Chicano artist Armando Estrella.

6065 Congreso de Artistas Chicanos en Aztlan, San Diego, CA. Diego Rivera, David Alfaro Siqueiros, Jose Clemente Orozco: exhibit of local artists, La Logan [San Diego]. Exhibition brochure, n.d. [c.1974]. English.

AN: Announcement of a traveling exhibit organized by Galeria de la Raza, San Francisco, from the collection of the San Francisco Museum of Art. Illustrated with a San Diego mural.

6066 Contreras, Carlos. Nuestra cultura. LA VOZ: Concilio for the Spanish Speaking of King Co., Seattle, no. 7 (August 1979).

AN: Information of Washington state murals painted by members of La Extension Cultural; Armando Lara's autobiographical mural titled "El Rio" is installed at the Concilio offices, 107 Cherry St. Suite 210. Arturo Artorez completed a wall painting using the image of Quetzalcoatl at El Centro de la Raza with funding from the Seattle Arts Commission. Francisco Siqueiros used the themes of ecology and Mexican mythology for two murals at Seattle Community College. Commentary on Alfredo Arreguin's painting exhibition at the Kiku Gallery and his wall painting at the Childrens Orthopedic Hospital in Seattle.

6067 Corneil, Paul. Militant barrio murals of Santa Fe. Venice, CA: Environmental Communications, n.d. English.

AN: Annotated slide catalog with introductory text about the mural group Los Artes Guadalupanos de Aztlan of Santa Fe. Gilberto Guzman is mentioned as one of the group.

6068 Culver, Virginia. Church's secession depicted on canvas. DENVER POST: RELIGION NEWS WEEKLY, (June 24, 1977). English.

AN: Article commenting on mural created by Manuel Martinez as part of a secession movement by St. Mary's Episcopal Church in Denver whose members voted to leave the Episcopal Diocese of Colorado and the national Episcopal Church. Details of the controversy and examination of the iconography in Martinez's mural. Illustrated with photograph of controversial mural.

Mural Art (cont.)

6069 Danzantes. LA GENTE DE AZTLAN, Vol. 8, no. 5 (May 31, 1978), p. 12. English.

AN: Ernie de la Torre, muralist from El Sereno, Los Angeles, CA, describes style and meaning of his mural DANZANTES. Painted on the wall of the Alameda Theatre (Woods and Whittier Blvd.), the mural portrays cultural and historic aspects of Chicano culture. Illustrated with photographs.

6070 Danzas mexicanas. Flyer, 1978. English.

AN: Illustrated flyer about a mural designed and painted by Chicano artist and poet Jose Antonio Burciaga and Mexican muralist Gilberto Romero Rodriguez. Detail of the 147 x 22 feet mural in Redwood City, California is reproduced.

6071 Davis, Alonzo, ed. Los Angeles street graphics. Los Angeles, CA: Brockman Gallery Productions, [ca. 1975]. English.

AN: Portfolio of art in public places. Includes Charles Felix (murals), Leo Limon (mural), Charles Almaraz (billboard mural), Johnny Alvarez (mural), Mexican artist Gonzalo Duran, and graffiti.

6072 De colores mural team. Brochure, [ca. 1975]. English.

AN: Brochure giving brief history of the De Colores Mural Team established in 1972 as part of the Horizons Unlimited program with Chuy Campusano as coordinator. The team participated in murals at the Jamestown Center, Balmy Alley, Redding Elementary School, Mission Childcare Center, Mission Branch Bank of America and Horizons Unlimited from 1972 to 1975.

6073 De la Torre, Alfredo. Editorial. CARACOL, Vol. 4, no. 6 (February 1978), p. 3. Bilingual.

AN: An editorial seeking support for a proposal by El Centro Inc., a Chicano art center in San Antonio, TX to commission murals and decorations in the downtown San Antonio area.

6074 De Leon, Hector. Barrio art--the community's reflection of itself. AGENDA, Vol. 9, no. 4 (July, August, 1979), p. 7, 38. English.

AN: Barrio art is communal, its forms such as posters, pamphlets, graffiti, and murals have an educative function. Its style is eclectic and its content is stark and direct. Through various forms of graphic representation, people in the barrio have reappropriated art forms to give meaning to their daily experiences. Includes nine illustrations of barrio art.

6075 Deitch, Donna. The great wall of Los Angeles. Film, 1976. Bilingual.

AN: Eight minute 16 mm film produced by SPARC (Social and Public Art Resource Center) on the GREAT WALL OF LOS ANGELES mural. In English with Spanish subtitles.

6076 Del Olmo, Frank. Chicano gang turns to art. LOS ANGELES TIMES, (September 11, 1973), p. II, 3. English.

AN: Residents of the East Los Angeles barrio "Lil' Valley" dedicate a mural memorializing Chicano gang members who have died violently. The mural was painted by 40 gang members guided by professional artist Bill Butler.

6077 Del Olmo, Frank. Gang-inspired mural now a shrine. LOS ANGELES TIMES, (March 27, 1975), p. II, 1, 6. English.

AN: Two 1973 murals by David Lopez in the old Maravilla Housing Project which received a papal blessing and continue to be shrines at new housing location.

6078 Del Olmo, Frank. Murals changing face of East L.A. LOS ANGELES TIMES, (December 3, 1973), p. II, 1+. English.

AN: First Los Angeles Times report on burgeoning Los Angeles mural movement with a map of 15 mural sites. Mentioned are C.W. Felix (originator of Estrada Courts project), Willie Herron, David Botello, Armando Campero, Edward Carbajal. (Chicano Art Committee).

6079 Denver. NATIONAL MURALS NETWORK COMMUNITY NEWSLETTER, (Spring 1980), p. 10. English.

AN: Denver, Colorado murals by Manuel Martinez, the Chilean Orlando Letelier Brigade, Roberto Lucero, Al Sanchez, Jerry Jaramillo. Illustrated.

6080 Denver muralist here for workshop. TEMPE DAILY NEWS, (March 28, 1975). English.

AN: Denver muralist Roberto Lucero is invited to give a weekend mural workshop for the Quetzalcoatl Youth Organization of Escalante Community Center in Tempe, Arizona.

6081 Depicts Chicano attitudes: library receives new mural. DAILY BRUIN, (September 29, 1970), p. 6. English.

AN: Illustrated story of mural painted in UCLA's Mexican American Library by Eduardo Carrillo, Ramses Noriega, Sergio Hernandez, Saul Solache.

6082 Desiga, Daniel. Days historical dawn in the Northwest. Olympia, WA: Legislative Artworks Project, n.d. English.

AN: Personal statement submitted by Daniel Design with drawings for mural project to reflect the natural and human elements thathave forged Northwest reality. The artist states: "The key elements as envisaged are land and water integrated with racial groupings, diverse technologies and invested labor. Incorporating Northwest symbols, the mural will be seen as a manifestation of the physical and natural energies which have combined to give expression to an unique force in the Northwest.".

6083 Diaz, Katherine A. Murals of New Mexico. CAMINOS, Vol. 2, no. 5 (October 1981), p. 9-10. English.

AN: Illustrations of murals in Santa Fe and Albuquerque by Gilberto Guzman, Francisco Le Fevere[sic; Lefebre], Manuel Unzueta, and Fernando Penalosa.

Mural Art (cont.)

6084 Los Dos Streetscapers. Los Dos
Streetscapers, mural detail. NATIONAL
GEOGRAPHIC, Vol. 155, no. 1 (January 1979),
p. 38-39. English.

AN: One panel of Los Angeles mural by
Wayne Alaniz Healey and David Botello,
CHICANO TIME TRIP.

6085 Drescher, Tim and Garcia, Rupert. Recent
Raza murals in the U.S. RADICAL AMERICA,
Vol. 12, no. 2 (March, April, 1978), p.
14-31. English.

AN: Like the cultural revolution of
Mexico in the 1920s, La Raza of Aztlan
emphasizes the Native American and mestizo
heritage as well as the Mexican
revolutionary heritage. Witnn a social
context, the authors discuss Chicano and
Latino murals nationally. Iconography and
its relation to Chicano experience is
explored, as well as images by and about
women. Illustrations.

6086 Drescher, Tim and Goldman, Ruth. A survey of
East Bay murals of the 1970s. San Francisco,
CA: Murals, 1980. English.

AN: Compendium of murals including
title, location, size, artists,dates,
funding, materials, content, and comments on
each mural.

6087 Dunsmore de Carrillo, Patricia. On Rene
Yanez of the Galeria de la Raza. CHISMEARTE,
Vol. 1, no. 1 (Fall   1976), p. 8-9.
English.

AN: Report on Yanez's negotiations with
the Foster Kleiser Company to take over a
billboard located outside the Galeria in San
Fancisco which has been painted by Michael
Rios, the Centro de Cambio and TIN TAN
magazine, Zaiver (Xavier) Viramontes, and
others.

6088 [East L.A. mural (detail)]. REVISTA RIO
BRAVO, Vol. 1, no. 3 (Fall   1981), p. 14,
15.

6089 Echos de la Mision: the newest in Mission
murals. EL TECOLOTE, Vol. 6, no. 4 (January
1976), p. 11. English.

AN: Panoramic view of new murals in the
Mission District of San Francisco. Contains
brief descriptions and photographs of mural
art at Valencia Gardens, Garfield Park,
Folsom Project and The Bart mural at 24th
and Mission streets. Includes five photos by
Francisco Garcia.

6090 Edward Chavez: sculptor-painter. LA LUZ,
Vol. 2, no. 2 (May 1973), p. 28-31. English.

AN: Lavishly illustrated biographical
account of Edward Chavez. Born in Ocate, New
Mexico in 1917, Chavez has a distinguished
career as a painter and sculptor. During the
1940's he executed a number of murals under
sponsorship of various government art
projects. These murals were placed in public
buildings in Nebraska, Colorado and Wyoming.
Although living and working in New York most
of his adult life, the work of Edward Chavez
has always been influenced by the Southwest.

6091 Edy. A true barrio art. EL CHICANO,
(December 7, 1972), p. 9. English.

AN: Interview with East Los Angeles

artists Harry Gamboa, Robert Gronk and
Willie Herron (also included in the
conversation are Patsy Valdez and Eddie
Ytuarte). Suffering, fatalism, existential
reality and the awareness of cultural
colonialism are cited as sources of
inspiration for urban barrio art.
Illustrated with a photograph of Willie
Herron's Quetzalcoatl mural in City Terrace
barrio and two drawings by Robert Gronk and
Harry Gamboa.

6092 Elitzik, Paul. Mural magic. AMERICAS,
(June, July, 1981). English.

AN: Brief illustrated account of murals
in the Pilsen barrio of Chicago. Mentions
work by Aurelio Diaz, Marcos Raya, and
Salvador Vega. Focuses on the controversial
mural at Benito Juarez High School painted
by Jaime Longoria and Malu Ortega.

6093 En nuestra opinion. LA CUCARACHA, (July 4,1980)
Spanish.

AN: An editorial commending the mural
efforts by Chicano artists in Pueblo,
Colorado. Community artists should be
supported and encouraged, not threatened
with jail for their efforts. Illustrated
with photograph of a mural by Puebloan Leo
Lucero at Plaza Verde Park in Pueblo,
Colorado.

6094 Environmental Communications, Venice, CA.
Street paintings of Los Angeles: a study of
environmental reactionism. Slide catalog,
n.d. English.

AN: Well illustrated annotated slide
catalog of greater Los Angeles murals.
Includes 7 Chicano murals. Articles
reprinted from NEWSWEEK, LOS ANGELES TIMES,
EARTH (Mar. 1972), ARTWORKERS NEWS (Oct.
1973), ARTFORUM (Feb. 1971), LOS ANGELES
FREE PRESS (9/4/70), EVENING OUTLOOK
(5/4/72), SUNSET (April 1973).

6095 Erickson, Barbara. La Pena's new face. NORTH
EAST BAY INDEPENDENT, no. 4 (September 5,
1978), p. 11. English.

AN: Illustrated story on the relief
mural SONG OF UNITY by Ray Patlan, O'Brien
Thiele, Osha Neumann, and Anna de Leon on
the facade of La Pena cultural center in
Berkeley, California. Chilean songwriter
Victor Jara and the music of North and South
America are the motifs.

6096 Espinosa, Juan. Carlos Sandoval completing
mural in Mexico. LA CUCARACHA, (June 1980).
English.

AN: Details how Carlos Sandoval, Denver
Chicano artist was invited by the Mexican
government to paint mural in Zihuantanejo,
Mexico. The mayor of the Mexican town
states, "this work represents an expression
of two pueblos who want to expand their
relations, as a product of one common
people." Illustrated with photograph of
Carlos Sandoval and one preliminary drawing
of the mural.

Mural Art (cont.)

6097 Exxon Company, Houston, TX and Quirarte, Jacinto. Chicano art of the barrio. Exhibition brochure, n.d. [c.1976]. English.

AN: Brochure for a traveling exhibit of photographically-reproduced Chicano murals: Leo Limon, Lucila Villasenor Grijalva, Antonio Esparza, Susan Saenz, Charles Felix, Hoyo-Mara gang, David A. Lopez and team, Roberto Chavez and team (Los Angeles); Jerry Concha, Ruben Guzman, Chuy Campusano (San Francisco); Manuel Unzueta (Santa Barbara). Ernie Palomino and Leo Esequiel Ozona (Fresno). Leo Tanguma (Houston), Roberto Lucero, Manuel Martinez and Al Sanchez (Denver).

6098 Fabricant, Don. Show reveals Hispanic art. NEW MEXICAN WEEKEND, (June 1, 1979). English.

AN: Review of two exhibits in Santa Fe: EL FESTIVAL HISPANICO, mounted by La Cofradia de Artes y Artesanos Hispanicos and Gilberto Guzman at the Black Kachina Gallery. The reviewer feels the traditional-style woodcarving done by contemporaries is the strongest part of the show; works that break with these forms seem weaker, less skillful and cliche-ridden. Crafts are excellent. Muralist Guzman has blossomed in murals and easel paintings since he was employed by the 1978 Art in Public Places project. His work is intense and expressive, sometimes erotic. Illustration of work by sculptor Ruben Montoya.

6099 La Familia Recreation Center, Denver, CO. Mural unveiling and swim party. Exhibition invitation, 1980. English.

AN: Invitation to the unveiling of La Familia Cosmica, a mural by Jerry Jaramillo assisted by Carlos Sandoval, Al Sanchez, Stephen Lucero. An art exhibit featured the muralists, Jon Howe, and Fred Sanchez, all of the Metro Denver Urban Coalition's City Walls artists. Illustrated.

6100 Fenwick, Red. Why gifted artist's works won't sell. DENVER POST, (October 28, 1979), p. F, 75. English.

AN: Profile of Denver artist Carlota Espinoza--a painter, sculptor and creator of historic dioramas. Espinoza is mainly self-taught. A mural she created for the Byers branch library in Denver portraying "Hispanic" history in America was selected from more than 2,000 entries for national honors. She was chosen to do a stained glass window in the Colorado State House portraying the state's Spanish heritage, and has done art work for the Denver Museum of Natural History and other institutions. The article laments that such a talented artist has been unable to penetrate the mainstream art market.

6101 Fischer, Hal. Espejo: reflections of the Mexican American: Louis Carlos Bernal, Morrie Camhi, Abigail Heyman, Roger Minick, Neal Slavin. PICTURE MAGAZINE, no. 9 (1978). English.

AN: Oversize portfolio of photographs recording contemporary Mexican American life commissioned by the Mexican American Legal Defense and Education Fund. Three photographers, Louis Carlos Bernal (from Arizona), Morrie Camhi and Abagail Heyman

focus on the family and the home; the fourth, Roger Minick, juxtaposes the Mexican American against "barrio" murals. Only Bernal is Chicano. 24 photographs, six of which (Bernal's) are in color.

6102 Fitch, Bob. Los artes: a story the people live as well as paint. YOUTH MAGAZINE, Vol. 26, no. 3 (March 1975), p. 2-11. English.

AN: Illustrated story on the formation and early murals of Los Artes Guadalupanos de Aztlan of Santa Fe.

6103 Flanagan, Barbara. Murals warm up west St. Paul. MINNEAPOLIS STAR, (December 20, 1977). English.

AN: Discussion of mural activity in West St. Paul, Minnesota by Armando Estrella, Paul Basquez and John Acosta. The subject of most murals in Minnesota is either political, religious or historic. Of the three artists involved, Paul Basquez grew up in the barrio of West St. Paul. He tells how mural activity in the region is related to the Chicano art movement. About a half-dozen murals have been painted in St. Paul.

6104 Forest Home Library, Milwaukee, WI. Arte chicano de Carlos Rosas, Chicano muralist. Exhibition invitation, 1978. English.

AN: Invitation to an exhibit by Carlos Rosas [originally from El Paso, TX] who has created murals with Chicano themes in many parts of the United States. Sponsored by El Taller Obrero Cultural de Milwaukee.

6105 Fortune, Thomas. Mural will mirror barrio pride. LOS ANGELES TIMES, (December 27, 1974), p. II, 1, 8. English.

AN: Artist Sergio O'Cadiz has been painting a 625-foot concrete wall constructed to separate old Colonia Juarez and a new Anglo housing complex in Fountain Valley (Orange County), Calif., to eliminate graffiti. The mural depicts the barrio's history: Mexican Americans try on white masks for Anglo acceptance. Other scenes will show the arrival of the surrounding city, and resident's awareness of their Chicano identity. O'Cadiz is assisted by 40 students from surrounding colleges and universities. Illustrated.

6106 Los Four exhibit in Union Gallery. UNIVERSITY TIMES, (November 6, 1975), p. 4. English.

AN: "Los Four," a group of four Chicano artists - Frank Romero, Roberto "Beto" de la Rocha, Gilbert Lujan, and Carlos Almaraz, with newcomer Judithe Hernandez - work with political cartoons, Catholic symbols, works of sardonic humor. They also paint street murals: several have been done recently in Los Angeles, La Puente, and Long Beach. Illustrated.

6107 Frankenstein, Alfred. One artist's self-defense. SAN FRANCISCO CHRONICLE, (March 9, 1978), p. 44. English.

AN: Art critic Frankenstein opens his columns to Jose Antonio Burciaga to explain why he, and fellow muralist Gilberto Romero Rodriguez, splattered red, white and blue paint on their completed mural at the dedication ceremony. They were protesting the exploitation, use and abuse of artists, particularly by arts councils.

Mural Art (cont.)

6108 Frankenstein, Alfred. Prison's artist in
     residence. SAN FRANCISCO CHRONICLE, (May 5,
     1978), p. 60. English.

     AN: Review of the exhibition MUNDOS
     PERDIDOS, curated at the Galeria de la Raza
     by Leonard Castellanos. Show consisted of
     work by Castellanos and inmates at Lompoc
     Federal Correctional Institution near Santa
     Barbara. Documents a prison mural, tattoos
     and silkscreen prints with socially critical
     themes.

6109 Frankenstein, Alfred. A senior senor's
     approach. SAN FRANCISCO CHRONICLE, (May 27,
     1976), p. 48. English.

     AN: Review of an exhibit of Mexican
     painter Jesus Reyes Ferreira at the Mexican
     Museum of San Francisco, as well as that of
     San Francisco artist Gustavo Rivera, an
     abstract expressionist painter. Also
     mentions the Museum's mural map, and Angel
     del Valle's photography show at the Galeria
     de la Raza.

6110 Future Mural at Alberca Tlaloc, Rude Park
     Pool. LA LUZ, Vol. 3, no. 12 (March, April,
     1975), p. 18.

6111 Una galeria de artistas = A gallery of
     artists. CAMINOS, Vol. 1, no. 6 (October
     1980), p. 20-26. Bilingual.

     AN: Features California artists Domingo
     O. Ulloa (Imperial Valley images), Gloria
     Chacon, photographer Maria Pinedo (San
     Francisco), Willie Herron (Los Angeles),
     Joaquin Patino (Delano), Pedro Pelayo (Long
     Beach), sculptor Rudi Sigala (San Diego),
     Mario Torero (San Diego), sculptor Michael
     M. Amescua (Los Angeles), and the East Los
     Streetscapers. Illustrated.

6112 Galeria de la Raza/Studio 24, San Francisco,
     CA and Garcia, Rupert. Community art-murals:
     an exhibition of original drawings,
     sketches, and designs. Exhibition brochure,
     1978. English.

     AN: The current crisis of contemporary
     art is relatively resolved by
     community-based muralists who engage
     themselves against repressive forces as
     artists, organizers, propagandists. However,
     art and politics are not identical, though
     they may overlap. Color xerox illustrations
     of murals.

6113 Galeria de la Raza/Studio 24, San Francisco,
     CA. Mundos perdidos/lost worlds. Exhibition
     invitation, 1978. English.

     AN: Invitatiion to a multi-media exhibit
     from a cultural workshop inside Lompoc
     Federal Correctional Institution by Leonard
     Castellanos, National Endowment for the Arts
     Artist in Residence. Included are murals and
     tattoo documentation, and silkscreen
     posters.

6114 Gamboa, Harry, Jr. Los murales de Aztlan.
     COMUNIDAD, (June 28, 1981), p. 8-9+.
     Spanish.

     AN: Review of the exhibit at the Craft
     and Folk Art Museum of Los Angeles of MURALS
     OF AZTLAN: THE STREET PAINTERS OF EAST LOS
     in which Carlos Almaraz, Gronk, Judithe
     Hernandez, Willie Herron, Frank Romero, John
     Valadez and the East Los Streetscapers
     (David Botello, Wayne Healy, George Yepes)

painted portable murals in the gallery. The
murals are described and illustrated.

6115 Gamboa, Harry, Jr. Seis imaginaciones:
     artistas chicanos en Los Angeles. COMUNIDAD,
     (July 13, 1980), p. 10. Spanish.

     AN: A limited flow of media information
     about Los Angeles Chicanos has produced a
     "ghost" culture. Only sensational events are
     published. Alternative magazines like LA
     RAZA, CON SAFOS, and REGENERACION have
     disseminated Chicano ideas of the 1970s. The
     Chicano imagination has appeared in murals
     by Willie Herron, Gronk, Carlos Almaraz,
     John Valadez; in pieces like "walking" and
     "instant" murals by the group ASCO; by the
     group Los Four; by group exhibits like
     "Chicanismo en el arte," and "Chicanarte."
     Patssi Valdez showed Photobooth Piece at the
     "Chicanismo" show. Gronk and Jerry Dreva
     exhibited their mail art at "Punk Meets
     Art." In Spanish.

6116 Garcia, Guillermo. Wall-to-wall art for the
     people. AUSTIN AMERICAN STATESMAN, (January
     22, 1978), p. E-1. English.

     AN: Illustrated story on Raul Valdez's
     mural (in progress) The Oral Tradition.
     Valdez discusses his methods and art
     philosophy when creating community murals.

6117 Garcia, Rupert. Echos de la Mision - Alfaro
     Siqueiros (1896-1974). EL TECOLOTE, Vol. 4,
     no. 3 (February 22, 1974), p. 11. English.

     AN: Biographical and artistic trajectory
     of Mexican artist David Alfaro Siqueiros.
     Artist painted three murals in Southern
     California in 1932 (MEETING IN THE STREET
     and TROPICAL AMERICA were done in Los
     Angeles on the walls of the Chouinard School
     of Art and the Plaza Art Center, Olvera
     Street area respectively. The third mural
     PORTRAIT OF MEXICO was privately
     commissioned in Santa Monica). The three
     California murals deal with themes of
     censorship, racism, colonialism, capitalism,
     and imperialism. Article suggests that Raza
     artists are much influenced by the ideas and
     work of Siqueiros. Illustrated with Rupert
     Garcia's silkscreen poster SIQUEIROS.

6118 Garcia, Rupert. Muralista mexicano habla
     sobre los murales y los muralistas en los
     E.U. EL TECOLOTE, Vol. 5, no. 9 (May 28,
     1975), p. 5, 8. Spanish.

     AN: Thirty-two-year-old Mexican muralist
     Gilberto Ramirez has painted 23 murals in
     Mexico and two murals in the United States
     (in San Diego and San Francisco,
     California). Ramirez states that in Mexico,
     mural painting is more personal and
     individualized, different from the
     collective ideal of Chicano muralists. In
     the U.S., the muralists enjoy more liberty
     because muralism is not yet controlled by
     one group of painters. Chicano muralists
     have much to learn in terms of technique but
     their best work is fresh and vital. Includes
     iconographic description of Ramirez mural at
     the LULAC office, 3000 Folsom St., San
     Francisco.

Mural Art (cont.)

6119 Garcia, Rupert. Pulqueria art--defiant art of the barrios [Part I]. EL TECOLOTE, Vol. 8, no. 4 (December 1977), p. 7. Bilingual.

AN: In contrast to billboards that function as calculated visual corporate advertisements, Chicano-Latino communities have evolved a form of colorful wall paintings that draw attention to goods available in the neighborhood. Related to the "Pulqueria" paintings of Mexico, these wall paintings are validated as a true people's art. In the best examples, pulqueria art functions to provide images of a positive and innovative nature.

6120 Garcia, Rupert. Pulqueria art--defiant art of the barrios [Part II]. EL TECOLOTE, Vol. 8, no. 5 (February 1978), p. 8. Bilingual.

AN: In the Mission District of San Francisco, various artists like Irene Perez, Esther Fernandez, Chuy Campusano, Graciela Carrillo de Lopez, Consuelo Mendez Castillo, and Mike Rios have embellished business sites with wall decorations similar in spirit to the "Pulqueria" art of Mexico. Illustrated with three "Pulqueria"-type wall paintings: ATARDECER DE UN IMPERIO by Oscar Carveo at the Azteca Restaurant (Mission and 20th Sts.), El Buen Boricano Restaurant facade (24th and Harrison Sts.) and Fruitlandia facade (24th and Treat Sts.).

6121 Garcia, Rupert. Raza murals & muralists: an historical perspective. San Francisco, CA: Rupert Garcia, n.d.. English.

AN: Basic assumptions are that socio-economic, political and cultural relationships exist between the Raza of Mexico and those of Aztlan (the Southwest United States) Half the text deals with Mexican murals, the other half sets Raza murals in social context, and focuses on murals in San Francisco's Mission District, in four locations. 19 illustrations; 9 of Raza murals. Mural map of the Mission district.

6122 Garcia, Rupert. La Raza murals of California, 1963 to 1970: a period of social change and protest. Master's thesis, UC Berkeley, 1981. English.

AN: Important introduction to a selected group of murals from Northern and Southern California. Garcia deals with murals of "accommodation" from 1960 to 1965; the Chicano protest movement, 1965 and 1970; and Chicano protest murals from 1968 to 1970. Murals are discussed within historical, political and cultural contexts. Illustrated.

6123 Garcia, Rupert. A source for mural art education: an annotated bibliography of three Chicano newspapers. Unpublished paper, 1974 (Chicano Studies Library, Univ. of California, Berkeley). English.

AN: A research project showing how Chicano newspapers reported and educated their readers to mural activity by Raza artists during the period 1968-1978. The newspapers analized are EL GALLO (Denver, CO), EL CHICANO (San Bernardino, CA), and EL TECOLOTE (San Francisco, CA). Author draws eight conclusions about the form, meaning and significance of mural activity in Chicano barrios and the importance of community newspapers as a fruitful and meaningful source for art education.

6124 Garcia, Rupert. "This mural is not for the bankers. It's for the people". EL TECOLOTE, Vol. 4, no. 6 (June 10, 1974), p. 11+. English.

AN: On June 4, 1974, a mural by eight Mission District artists was unveiled inside the Bank of America on 23rd and Mission Sts. in San Francisco. Roberto Vargas, Bay Area poet was prevented from reading his poetry during the mural inauguration. Finally allowed to read, Vargas compared this event to one in the 1930s when Diego Rivera painted a mural for the Pacific Stock Exchange Building in San Francisco. Includes commentary by community activists about incident. Illustrated by photograph of Roberto Vargas reading in front of the controversial mural.

6125 Garcia-Camarillo, Cecilio and Rosas, Carlos. Platicando con Carlos Rosas. RAYAS, Vol. 1, no. 6 (November, December, 1978), p. 12, 11. Spanish.

AN: Muralist Carlos Rosas painted murals in Boulder and Denver, Colorado; Milwaukee, Wisconsin, and El Paso, Texas. Commentary on cross ethnic murals, views on art in socialist countries, influence of Mexican murals and information on his personal preocupation as a politically engaged artist.

6126 Gardiner, Henry G. Painted exterior walls of Southern California. CURRANT ART MAGAZINE, Vol. 1, no. 2 (June, July, 1975), p. 16-23+. English.

AN: Good survey of street muralism, primarily in Los Angeles and San Diego, which started in 1968. Divided into eight "schools," including Chicano and non-Chicano muralists. Most Chicano murals associated with Goez Brothers Art Gallery and Mechicano Art Center in Los Angeles, the Coronado Bay Bridge group [Chicano Park] and Balboa Park group [Centro Cultural de la Raza]. Mural discussed in detail. Well illustrated.

6127 Geyer, Anne and Gamboa, Harry, Jr. Artists' exhibits are street performances. THE NEWS, (September 11, 1981), p. 18. English.

AN: Illustrated interview with photographer/writer Harry Gamboa, Jr., member and documenter of the performance art group ASCO. Description of the NO MOVIE, NO PHANTOM, walking and instant murals of the group, and other performance street art which Gamboa considers as Chicano self-documentation and expression.

6128 Geyer, Anne. Muralist works to dispel negative Latino images. THE NEWS, (September 2, 1981), p. 22. English.

AN: John Valadez is painting a mural on canvas depicting the Latino people of downtown Los Angeles. It will be housed in Victor Clothing Co. Valadez is one of an increasing number of artists and dealers who have moved to the downtown area. Valadez discusses the images he makes and his attempt to correct media stereotypes about Latinos. Illustrated.

Mural Art (cont.)

6129 Gilroy's public art form. THE VALLEY WORLD,
     (July 19, 1978). English.

     AN: Article cites activities of "The
     Tortuga Patrol" a Chicano muralist group
     from the Watsonville California area.

6130 Goez Imports & Fine Arts, Los Angeles, CA.
     We invite you to see the birth of our art.
     Gallery brochure, 1971. English.

     AN: Brochure with history of gallery,
     mural map, iconography of Goez mural.

6131 The Goez map guide to the murals of East Los
     Angeles. Los Angeles, CA: Goez, 1975.
     English.

     AN: Street map indicating location of
     murals in the vicinity of East Los Angeles,
     CA.

6132 Goldman, Jane. Art against the wall.
     SACRAMENTO MAGAZINE, (August 1980).
     English.

     AN: Muralists Esteban Villa, Stan
     Padilla and Juanishi Orozco from the Centro
     de Artistas Chicanos are planning a symbolic
     65 foot, four-story mural on the parking
     structure opposite Macy's. The mural is
     described in detail. Illustrated.

6133 Goldman, Shifra M. Affirmations of
     existence, barrio murals of Los Angeles.
     REVISTA CHICANO-RIQUENA, Vol. 4, no. 4 (Fall
     1976), p. 73-76. Bibliography. English.

     AN: Brief history, communicative thrust,
     community orientation, and special
     iconography of Chicano murals in Los
     Angeles.

6134 Goldman, Shifra M. Canto de unidad: nuevo
     mural de Berkeley. PLURAL, Vol. 8, no. 96
     (September 1979), p. 33-44. Spanish.

     AN: Report on significance,
     inconography, and new technical
     experimentation in street mural on facade of
     La Pena Cultural Center, Berkeley, CA. Deals
     with Latin American "nueva cancion." Ray
     Patlan and Anna de Leon on team of four
     muralists. Illustrated. This article was
     reprinted as "Song of Unity: Berkeley's New
     Raza Mural," in ARTWORKERS NEWS (New York),
     Vol. 11, no. 30, September 20, 1980, p. 1.

6135 Goldman, Shifra M. Chicano art - looking
     backward. ARTWEEK, Vol. 12, no. 22 (June 20,
     1981), p. 3-4. English.

     AN: Review of Chicano art shows in Santa
     Cruz (CALIFAS) and Los Angeles (MURALS OF
     AZTLAN: THE STREET PAINTERS OF EAST LOS)
     featuring a total of 24 artists and how the
     shows reflect the critical crossroad at
     which Chicano artists presently find
     themselves.

6136 Goldman, Shifra M. Las creaturas de la
     America tropical: Siqueiros y los murales
     chicanos en Los Angeles. REVISTA DE BELLAS
     ARTES, no. 25 (January, February, 1976), p.
     38-46. Spanish.

     AN: Treats the influence of Siqueiros'
     1932 outdoor mural in Los Angeles on the
     Chicano street mural movement of the 1970s.

6137 Goldman, Shifra M. Les muraux chicanos aux
     Etats-Unis: un double language. In L'ART

PUBLIC. Paris: Jacques Damase Editeur, 1981,
p. 20-32. Other.

     AN: Updating of new artistic and social
     developments surrounding Chicano mural
     production. Illustrated.

6138 Goldman, Shifra M. Resistance and identity:
     street murals of occupied Aztlan. LATIN
     AMERICAN LITERARY REVIEW, Vol. 5, no. 10
     (Spring, Summer, 1977), p. 124-128. English.

     AN: Two periods of Mexican muralism's
     influence in the U.S.: 1930s and 1960s.
     Differences between Mexican and Chicano
     murals nationally. Comparison of the
     respective iconographies and funding
     sources. This article was reprinted as
     "Resistencia e Identidad: Los Murales
     Callejeros de Aztlan, La Ciudad (sic)
     Ocupada," in ARTES VISUALES (Mexico, D.F.),
     no. 16, Fall-Winter, 1977, p. 22-25.

6139 Goldman, Shifra M. Resistencia e identidad:
     los murales callejeros de Aztlan, la ciudad
     (sic) ocupada. ARTES VISUALES, no. 16 (Fall,
     Winter, 1977), p. 22-25. Spanish.

     AN: Reprint of article published as
     "Resistance and identity: street murals of
     occupied Aztlan" in LATIN AMERICAN LITERARY
     REVIEW, Vol. 5, no. 10, Spring-Summer 1977,
     p. 124-128.

6140 Goldman, Shifra M. Song of unity: Berkeley's
     new raza mural. ARTWORKERS NEWS, Vol. 11,
     no. 30 (September 20, 1980), p. 1. English.

     AN: Reprint of article published as
     "Canto de unidad: nuevo mural de Berkeley"
     in PLURAL (Mexico, D.F.), Vol. 8, no. 96,
     September 1979, p. 33-44.

6141 Goll, Dave. More than handball on this
     court. MENLO-ATHERTON RECORDER, (May 23,
     1978), p. 15. English.

     AN: Emmanuel Montoya is painting a mural
     on African and Chicano unity at the handball
     court of Fair Oaks Community Center in
     Redwood City, CA. Montoya is working because
     of CETA (Comprehensive Employment Training
     Act) funds. Illustrated.

6142 Gonzales, Jose G. [Untitled collage].
     REVISTA CHICANO-RIQUENA, Vol. 4, no. 4 (Fall
     1976), p. Cover. English.

6143 Gonzalez, Ellen. U.S. art project: Chicanas
     painting 'future history'. LOS ANGELES
     TIMES, (March 16, 1978), p. II, 4. English.

     AN: Women muralists from the murals
     workshop of the Chicana Service Action
     Center working on murals at City Terrace and
     Humphrey Avenue elementary schools in East
     Los Angeles. Illustrated.

6144 Gonzalez, Hector. Rivera paints Boalt Hall
     mural. EL HISPANO, Vol. 5, no. 29 (January
     2, 1973). English.

     AN: Brief commentary on Sacramento
     artist Edward Rivera and his design for a
     mural to be installed in Boalt Hall at the
     University of California's Berkeley campus.

Mural Art (cont.)

6145 Gonzalez, Victoria. Chair in the sky:
Ernesto Palomino. HERE AND NOW, Vol. 2, no.
2 (Fall 1981). English.

AN: An important article tracing the
artistic career of Ernie Palomino, professor
of art at California State University,
Fresno. Includes biographical information,
formation of La Brocha Del Valle (Chicano
Arts Organization), information about
Palomino's film MY TRIP IN A '52 FORD and
commentary on Palomino's music and artistic
philosophy. Well illustrated.

6146 Graffiti gone: murals in full bloom. PHOENIX
GAZETTE, (April 13, 1974). English.

AN: Mural explosion at Estrada Courts
Housing Project in Los Angeles led by C.W.
Felix. Estimates 60 murals in East Los
Angeles. Illustrated.

6147 Grand Rapids Jr. College, MI. Dedication "El
Centro de Vida". Brochure, 1977. English.

AN: Brochure announcing unveiling of a
mural by painter Jose Narezo working with a
team of young people.

6148 Greenberg, David; Smith, Kathryn; and
Teacher, Stuart. Megamurals & supergraphics:
big art. Philadelphia, PN: Running Press,
1977. English.

AN: A full-color picture book of murals
throughout the United States. Chicano murals
include Michael Rios (San Francisco),
Mujeres Muralistas (San Francisco), Leonard
Castellanos and Tomas Gonzales with others
(Los Angeles), Los Artes Guadalupanos de
Aztlan (New Mexico), Willie Herron (Los
Angeles), Toltecas en Aztlan (San Diego),
David Botello (Los Angeles), David Lopez and
Arizona Mara Gang (Los Angeles), Vatos de
Maravilla (Los Angeles), Carlito Gaegos (Los
Angeles), Gil Hernandez (Los Angeles), Wayne
[Alaniz] Healy (Los Angeles).

6149 Guernica, Antonio Jose and Saavedra-Vela,
Pilar. El Midwest Canto al pueblo: "Otra
Vez, C/S". AGENDA, Vol. 7, no. 3 (May, June,
1977), p. 4-13. Bilingual.

AN: A thorough report on the various
phases and events of the Midwest Canto al
Pueblo in Milwaukee, Wisconsin on April 28
to May 8, 1977. The festival brought
together artists, poets, musicians, and
cultural workers to reaffirm, share, and
celebrate the identity of La Raza with El
Pueblo. Includes a thematic and iconographic
overview of Chicano murals in California by
Jose Montoya, and an analysis of his
sculpture by Zarco Guerrero from Meza,
Arizona. Well illustrated. Includes a
photograph of the collective mural painted
at 5th St. and National Avenue in Milwaukee,
Wisconsin during the course of the
conference.

6150 Gustaitis, Rasa. Arts imperiled. PEOPLE'S
WORLD, Vol. 44, no. 26 (June 27, 1981), p.
10. English.

AN: A decade ago the San Francisco
Neighborhood Arts Program received new
commitments from the National Endowment for
the Arts to fund local, unknown and
chronically poor neighborhood artists. With
these funds, murals were painted on the
walls and other art events were created with
young people, minorities, old people. This

program piloted the Expansion Arts Program
of NEA. These funds are now being cut,
especially with the Reagan administration's
proposed cuts for 1981 and 1982.

6151 Gutierrez, Helga. The walls of Estrada
Courts. LA GENTE DE AZTLAN, Vol. 7, no. 3
(February 1977), p. 19. English.

AN: Photographic essay of Estrada murals
by Helga Gutierrez.

6152 Hagen, Carol. Mission murals. ARTWEEK, Vol.
5, no. 30 (September 14, 1974), p. 6.
English.

AN: Report on two recently completed
murals in San Francisco's Mission District:
Jesus Campusano's 90x10-ft mural in the Bank
of America branch, and the Mujeres
Muralistas' mural adjacent to the Mission
Model Cities building. Illustrated.

6153 Hale, David. Fresnan gets grant to create
five story high mural. FRESNO BEE, (April
16, 1978), p. Forum, C4. English.

AN: Details on the awarding of a grant
to John Sierra, Fresno artist, for the
creation of what will be the largest piece
of public art in that city. The artwork is a
6000 square foot mural titled THE PLANTING
OF THE CULTURES. Article contains
biographical information on the artist and
presents goals of his mural project.

6154 Hamm, Madeline McDermott. Artist envisions a
'Sistine' ceiling. HOUSTON CHRONICLE,
(September 19, 1978), p. III, 1-3. English.

AN: Illustrated article on mural that
Ernesto Pedregon Martinez (who was active in
El Paso in the 1950s) was doing for St.
Joseph Catholic Church in Houston. The mural
depicts the crucifixion.

6155 Hand me down. AUSTIN AMERICAN STATESMAN,
(August 17, 1978), p. B-1. English.

AN: Illustration of Raul Valdez's mural
La Raza Cosmica on the outdoor stage of the
Pan American Center, East Austin.

6156 Hanson, Matt. Barren walls toned into bold
works of art. ARIZONA DAILY STAR, (May 24,
1979). English.

AN: Tucson high school students under
direction of Antonio Pazos paint murals with
a $10,000 grant from the Law Enforcement
Assistance Administration. Color
illustrations.

6157 Harper, Hilliard. Native Americans stand
tall again as Balboa Park mural takes shape.
LOS ANGELES TIMES [San Diego County
edition], (March 2, 1981), p. II, 5.
English.

AN: Victor Ochoa paints the figure of
Geronimo on the wall of San Diego's Balboa
Park Centro Cultural de la Raza to replace a
skeletal calavera figure disturbing patients
at a hospital across the street. The central
figure is part of a planned 70 x 18 foot
mural promoting Mexican, Chicano and Indian
art. Activities at the Centro are described.
Illustrated.

Mural Art (cont.)

6158 Hernandez, Judithe Elena and Goldman, Shifra
M. Readers' forum. ARTWEEK, Vol. 12, no. 25
(August 1, 1981), p. 16. English.

AN: Critical interchange between artist
Judithe Elena Hernandez de Neikrug and
critic Shifra M. Goldman concerning the
latter's review of MURALS OF AZTLAN exhibit.

6159 Hernandez, Manuel de Jesus. Zapata murals
depict Chicano struggle. LA HONDA, Vol. 5,
no. 3 (March, April, 1979). English.

AN: Critical vignettes on the content of
Chicano murals at Casa Zapata, a Chicano
theme dorm at Stanford University. The
muralists include Zarco Guerrero, Esteban
Chavez, Hector Chacon, and Tina Alvarez.

6160 Herrera, Barbara. Bisected barrio seeks new
unity: Chicano part bridges past and future.
EVENING TRIBUNE, (August 7, 1974), p. E-1.
English.

AN: Bisected by the Coronado bridge,
remains of the Logan barrio are unified by
Chicano Park and its murals recording
Chicano culture. Inspired by Salvador
Torres, who returned to Logan in 1967,
barrio activists are working to restore
community spirit and dignity. Illustrated.

6161 Herrera, Barbara. Chicano park expansion
sought: barrio idealists face strong
barriers. EVENING TRIBUNE, (August 10,
1974), p. A-10. English.

AN: Last of a three part series on
Chicano Park. Barrio activists of the
Chicano Park Steering Committee plan to
extend the Chicano Park under the Coronado
bridge from 5.8 acres to the bay, painting
all the pillars with murals, and ending with
a small marina. They are facing opposition
from government officials, but are hopeful
of success.

6162 Herrera, Barbara. The pillars are our trees:
Chicano park needs planning, power. EVENING
TRIBUNE, (August 8, 1974), p. D-1. English.

AN: In the face of government and
business opposition, activists obtained the
land under the Coronado bridge to establish
Chicano Park. They want to extend the park
to the waterfront. Illustrated.

6163 Herrera, Estela. La mujer en el mundo: una
chicana en las artes. LA OPINION, (March
25, 1982), p. III,6. Spanish.

AN: Illustrated interview with Judith
Elena Hernandez de Niekrug including
biographical information and discussion of
her attitudes toward her murals, paintings,
and graphics.

6164 Herron, Willie. [Chicanitas (painting)].
REGENERACION, Vol. 2, no. 1 (1971), p. 24.

6165 Herron, Willie and Gronk. [Detail of mural].
CHISMEARTE, Vol. 2, no. 1 (1978), p. 4.

6166 Herron, Willie. [Faces (painting)].
REGENERACION, Vol. 2, no. 1 (1971), p. 23.

6167 Herron, Willie. [Indigenista graphic
design]. REGENERACION, Vol. 2, no. 1 (1971),
p. COVER.

6168 Herron, Willie. [Two murals]. REGENERACION,
Vol. 2, no. 2 (1972), p. 12-13.

6169 Hispanic artists' [sic] mural unveiled.
SOUTHFIELD ECCENTRIC, Exhibition catalog,
1980. English.

AN: A mural titled SYNERGY by Michigan
artist Nora Mendoza is unveiled at the R.J.
Sullivan Funeral Home. Mendoza has exhibited
at numerous one-person shows.

6170 History and Traditions Museum. San Antonio,
TX: Lackland Air Force Base, n.d. English.

AN: Brochure of the Museum with
reproduction of two murals (unattributed) by
Roberto Rios of San Antonio.

6171 History traced in mural. THE REGISTER, (May
1, 1974), p. C-1. English.

AN: Illustrated story of History of the
Chicano mural painted by Sergio O'Cadiz and
fifty students from MEChA at Santa Ana
College.

6172 Huge mural displayed at El Con Shopping
Center. ARIZONA DAILY STAR, (January 31,
1979). English.

AN: A 15 x 50 foot mural called The
Creation of Cultures, a latex-enamel on
panels, was painted by Tucson muralist
Roberto Borboa. Its final site has not been
determined. Illustrated.

6173 Images of Aztlan at Mechicano. CHISMEARTE,
Vol. 1, no. 1 (Fall 1976), p. 3-4.
English.

AN: History of Mechicano Art Center from
its opening in West Los Angeles in 1969
through its 1976 location during which it
decided to become a center serving its own
community in East Los Angeles. Led by
Leonard Castellanos, Victor Franco and Ray
Atilano, the Center developed programs in
supergraphics, silkscreen, and mural
painting, as well as an "open-wall" art
gallery for artists not allowed in
establishment galleries.

6174 In the middle of something good.
MENLO-ATHERTON RECORDER, (September 19,
1978), p. 16. English.

AN: Illustration of Emmanuel Montoya's
African-Mexican unity mural at the Redwood
City Fair Oaks Community Center handball
courts.

6175 Incorporated Artes Monumentales/Inc.,
Denver, CO. IAM: art exhibit. Exhibition
brochure, n.d. English.

AN: Large format, well illustrated
brochure with information on muralists
Roberto Lucero, Al Sanchez, Andrew Manning,
Ricardo Barrera and Bob Reyes. Includes some
biographical information situating these
artists within the dynamic artistic
traditions of the Mexican and the Chicano
mural movements.

Mural Art (cont.)

6176 Inner City Mural Program. Glendale, CA: Los
     Angeles County Dept. of Parks and
     Recreation, [ca. 1974]. English.

     AN: Brief history and philosophy of the
     Inner City Mural Program from June 1, 1973
     to May 31, 1974, when it was sponsored by
     the Cultural Arts Section of the Los Angeles
     County Department of Parks and Recreation,
     and coordinated by Lukman Glasgow. Artists
     Judithe Hernandez and Frank Romero included.
     20 illustrations, some in color.

6177 Intar, International Art Relations, Inc.,
     New York, NY and Ferez Kuri, F. Jose.
     Alejandro E. Romero. Exhibition catalog,
     1977. English.

     AN: Exhibit catalog of drawings and
     paintings by Mexican-born painter and
     muralist living in Chicago. Illustrated in
     color.

6178 Johnson, Richard. The mural at Zihuatanejo.
     EMPIRE MAGAZINE, (October 12, 1980).
     English.

     AN: Denver artist Carlos M. Sandoval is
     said to be the first Chicano commissioned by
     the Mexican government to paint a mural in
     Mexico. Sandoval's mural is on the facade of
     the public library in Zihuatanejo. Its theme
     is unity and synthesis and its title is
     MESTIZO. Article contains much information
     on mural act ivity in Denver, Colorado. Well
     illustrated with color and black and white
     photographs.

6179 Johnston, Beatriz. Valadez: exponente de la
     vida urbana en mural contemporaneo. LA
     OPINION, Vol. 56, no. 68 (November 22,
     1981), p. II, 1. Spanish.

     AN: Report on the mural in preparation
     by John Valadez for Victor Clothing Co. in
     downtown Los Angeles. It deals with people
     walking in the streets of the downtown area.
     Illustrated with the sketch for the mural
     which Valadez has been painting in the
     basement of the building for nine months.

6180 Kahn, David. Chicano street murals: people's
     art in the East Los Angeles barrio. AZTLAN,
     Vol. 6, no. 1 (Spring 1975), p. 117-121.
     Bibliography. English.

     AN: A study of Chicano mural painting
     starting with the 1970 mural at UCLA by
     Eduardo Carrillo, Ramses Noriega, Sergio
     Hernandez, and Saul Solache. Deals with
     mural symbols, graffiti, and works by John
     Alverer [sic] and Willie Herron's murals in
     the Ramona Gardens Housing Project.

6181 Kalil, Susie. Provocative painting: muralist
     Leo Tanguma advances the tradition of
     Mexico's masters. HOUSTON CITY MAGAZINE,
     (March 1980), p. 88+. English.

     AN: 38 year old Leo Tanguma from
     Beeville, Texas joined the Mexican-American
     Youth Organization in Houston in 1968, which
     provided a stimulus to say what he felt in
     large paintings. His firsHouston mural was
     in 1970, followed by meeting Mexican
     muralisDavid Alfaro Siqueiros in 1972. A
     monumental mural for Continental Can Co.
     followed in 1973. Many of Tanguma's murals
     have been controversial and destroyed, or
     the commissions withdrawn.Color illustration
     of maquette for an ecology mural.

6182 Kamin, Ira. Come on in, bring your paint.
     PACIFIC SUN, (May 30, 1974), p. 11-12.
     English.

     AN: Chatty report on murals and art
     exhibit in San Francisco's Mission District:
     murals by Chuy Campusano, Michael Rios,
     Richard Montez, Trish (Patricia) Rodriguez,
     Graciela Carrillo, Consuelo Mendez and Irene
     Perez. Illustrated.

6183 Karam, Bruce G. The murals of Tucson.
     NUESTRO, Vol. 5, no. 8 (November 1981), p.
     58-60. English.

     AN: Themes of ethnic pride, cultural
     unity and cooperation define the murals of
     Tucson. Brief commentary on the relationship
     of artists and the community. Illustrated
     with color photographs.

6184 Karam, Bruce G. Stanford mural. NUESTRO,
     Vol. 5, no. 8 (November 1981), p. 61.

6185 Karkabi, Barbara. For artist Atanacio P.
     Davila, mural is way to express love for
     children. HOUSTON CHRONICLE, (May 14,
     1980), p. IV-I. English.

     AN: Color-illustrated story on
     mural-in-progress at the Ripley House
     medical clinic by 70 year old Davila titled
     THE HEALTHY FAMILY. Son of an artist,
     Mexican-born Davila was raised in Texas and
     did commercial art and painting until 1938.
     After retirement, he has resumed his art.

6186 Kennedy, Bailey. The American pageant: a
     history of the republic, 6th ed. 6th ed.,
     Lexington, MA: D.C. Heath, 1979, p. 674.
     English.

     AN: Reproduction of two sections of the
     MEChA mural painted in 1974 by students
     directed by Sergio O'Cadiz at Santa Ana
     College,Santa Ana, Calif. The mural includes
     Mexican and Mexican American themes.

6187 Kerschen, Karen. Where politics and music
     mix: La Pena. BERKELEY BARB, (August 18,
     1978), p. 12. English.

     AN: A new three-dimensional mural has
     been completed on the outside of Berkeley's
     La Pena Community Center. It incorporates
     ceramic and papier mache relief in a painted
     mural. One side of the painting is dominated
     by a relief sculpture of Victor Jara, the
     Chilean musician and poet killed by the
     junta. Illustrated.

6188 Kim, Howard. Judithe Hernandez and a glimpse
     at the Chicana artist. SOMOS, (October,
     November, 1979), p. 6-11. English.

     AN: Biographical information on Chicana
     artist Judithe Hernandez. Commentary on her
     contributions to Plaza de la Raza, Los
     Angeles Citywide Mural Project and her work
     as designer consultant to AZTLAN:
     INTERNATIONAL JOURNAL OF CHICANO RESEARCH.
     The article focuses on her mural activity,
     particularly two murals: EL MUNDO DE BARRIO
     SOTEL and LA CHICANA DE AZTLAN. Her personal
     art philosophy is presented in relation to
     Third World Art.

Mural Art (cont.)

6189 Knapp, Martha. West side is part of mural
     art renaissance. WEST SAINT PAUL VOICE, Vol.
     5, no. 19 (November 21, 1977). English.

     AN: Pre-Columbian symbology in the mural
     program painted by Paul Basquez and Armando
     Estrella in the Chicano barrio; information
     and data on the mural renaissance in
     Minnesota.

6190 Knight, Christopher. Urban eye sites up
     against the wall. HERALD EXAMINER, (May 31,
     1981). English.

     AN: Review of the exhibit MURALS OF
     AZTLAN: THE STREET PAINTERS OF EAST LOS at
     the Craft and Folk Art Museum of Los
     Angeles. Illustration.

6191 Knilli, Monika and Knilli, Friedrich. Linke
     allegorien & lebende bilder der ghettos: das
     Americanische mural-movement. TENDENZEN,
     (November, December, 1977), p. 27-32. Other.

     AN: Illustrated story on U.S. murals
     including those of East Los Angeles and
     Chicano Park, San Diego. The
     November-December issue of 1977 is numbered
     116.

6192 Kroll, Eric. Folk art in the barrios.
     NATURAL HISTORY, Vol. 82, no. 5 (May 1973),
     p. 56-65. English.

     AN: Well-illustrated informative report
     on Santa Fe, New Mexico murals by Los Artes
     Guadalupanos de Aztlan. Author's somewhat
     condescending attitude rectified in the
     ARTFORUM reprint which drops the term "folk
     art". [See Murals in New Mexico].

6193 Kutner, Janet. Total freedom in Chicano art.
     DALLAS MORNING STAR, (December 18, 1977),
     p. 10C. English.

     AN: Review of traveling photo-exhibition
     of Chicano murals organized by Jacinto
     Quirarte for Exxon USA.

6194 Largest mural in San Mateo County becomes
     official Saturday. REDWOOD CITY TRIBUNE,
     (February 23, 1978), p. 12. English.

     AN: Mural DANZAS MEXICANAS by Chicano
     artist and poet Jose Antonio Burciaga and
     Mexican muralist Gilberto Romero Rodriguez
     was commissioned by the Multi-cultural Arts
     Council of San Mateo County. Color
     illustration.

6195 Latin American council bicentennial mural.
     Exhibition brochure, [1976]. English.

     AN: Brochure giving history and
     iconography of a 8 x 16 foot portable mural
     by Grand Rapids, Mich. artist Jose Narezo
     with a team of students. The mural honors
     North and South American revolutionaries
     with portraits of George Washington, Jose
     Marti, Eugenio Maria de Hostos, and Benito
     Juarez.

6196 Lefebre, Francisco. El mural chicano en
     Nuevo Mexico. RAYAS, Vol. 1, no. 2 (March,
     April, 1978). p. 7. Spanish.

     AN: Albuquerque muralist writes about
     Chicano murals which derive from
     pre-Columbian and modern Mexican murals. New
     Mexican muralism started in 1970 with the
     Muralistas Guadalupanos de Aztlan in Santa
     Fe. In 1971 and 1972 students at the

Highlands University of Las Vegas, New
Mexico also painted murals. In addition,
murals have appeared in Albuquerque. Brief
biography of Lefebre. Illustrated.

6197 The legend of the five murals. [Los Angeles,
     CA]: Pan American Bank of East Los Angeles,
     [1966]. Spanish.

     AN: Iconography of the five murals in
     Venetian mosaic created for the Bank by
     Mexican artist Jose Reyes Meza, information
     about mosaics, and a brief biography of the
     artist are included in a biligual brochure.
     The murals are 10x14-ft each and adorn
     thefacade of the building.

6198 Leo Tanguma and Houston murals. NATIONAL
     MURALS NETWORK COMMUNITY NEWSLETTER,
     (Spring 1980), p. 11. English.

     AN: Report on environmental and police
     brutality murals in Houston, Texas.
     Illustrated.

6199 Lopez, Armando. 'Chicano' art gains
     cross-culture recognition: 'the street mural
     has flourished in the barrio'. LAREDO NEWS,
     (July 20, 1980), p. 6-A. English.

     AN: Report on a lecture "The First
     Decade of the Chicano Renaissance: Mexican
     American Art in the United States" given by
     Dr. Shifra M. Goldman under the sponsorship
     of the Laredo Philosophical Society.
     Mentions the "delicate Issue" of using the
     word "Chicano" in conservative Laredo.
     Illustrated with works of Laredo-born Amado
     M. Pena.

6200 Lopez, Gerard. Estrada murals. LA LUZ, Vol.
     4, no. 3 (June 1975), p. 21. English.

     AN: Describes goals and procedures of a
     barrio mural project under the guidance of
     "Los Ninos del Mundo", a group of Chicano
     artists, musicians and social workers.

6201 Lopez, Gerard. Estrada murals. LA GENTE DE
     AZTLAN, Vol. 4, no. 6 (May, June, 1974), p.
     4. English.

     AN: Article explains how the community
     at Estrada Courts was mobilized to support a
     mural project uniting artists with
     residents. Includes interview with artist
     C.W. Felix who comments on the goals of the
     mural program and cites the themes and
     symbolism of the murals.

6202 Lugavere, Joel P. Artists to add '40s to
     Great Wall mural. LOS ANGELES TIMES
     [Glendale/Burbank edition], (September 20,
     1981), p. 1. English.

     AN: Brief illustrated story on 1981
     extension of the Tujunga Wash mural, THE
     GREAT WALL OF LOS ANGELES, directed by Judy
     Baca of SPARC, (Social and Public Arts
     Resource Center in Venice California).

6203 Lyle, Cindy. Chicano mural art: a mixture of
     the barrio's rage and pride. NEW YORK TIMES,
     (August 17, 1975), p. Sec.2, 21. English.

     AN: Brief history of San Diego's Chicano
     Park, why and how it was established, and
     the establishment of the Centro Cultural de
     la Raza in Balboa Park. Iconography of
     several murals is examined, and the
     longevity of outdoor murals discussed.
     Illustrated.

Mural Art (cont.)

6204 Malaquias Montoya. ARTE, (Fall 1977).
English.

AN: Interview with northern California
printmaker, painter and muralist, Malaquias
Montoya. He discusses his life, his
dedication to Chicano art, his resistance to
the institutionalization of the Chicano
struggle and its art, their cooptation by
the establishment. He says he transcended
nationalism at one period and became a Third
World internationalist. Four drawings and
two posters reproduced.

6205 Manley, Paula. If walls could speak, a
festival of murals. DAILY TEXAN, (August 4,
1980). English.

AN: Commentary on community murals in
Austin, including murals painted by LUCHA
(The League of United Chicano Artists).

6206 Manning, Andrew. Damaged mural inspires
community restoration project. CHISMEARTE,
Vol. 2, no. 1 (Summer 1978), p. 28. English.

AN: Describes the damage caused to a
Willie Herron mural by inclement weather
conditions and the community drive to fund a
restoration project. The project is being
directed by Ricardo Barrera.

6207 MARCH: Movimiento artistico Chicano
(Mexican-American Art Movement). QUARTERLY,
(Spring 1976), p. 10. English.

AN: Brief history of MARCH.
Illustrations of murals by Ricarco Alonzo,
Jose Gonzalez, Vicente Mendoza. Ray Patlan.

6208 Mario Falcon. CHISMEARTE, Vol. 2, no. 1
(Summer 1978), p. 29. Spanish.

AN: Mexican muralist Mario Falcon, who
has painted murals in Long Beach and
Wilmington (Los Angeles, County), is a
political exile in the U. S. Support is
asked to prevent his return to Mexico.
Illustrated.

6209 Marquez, Rosa Maria. Artistas chicanas
together at C.S.A.C., an interview by Rosa
Maria Marquez. CHISMEARTE, Vol. 1, no. 4
(Fall , Winter, 1977), p. 39. English.

AN: An interview with several women
doing murals as part of the East Los Angeles
Senior Citizens Housing and Mural
Beautification Program under the sponsorship
of the Chicana Service Action Center.
Funding for the project through CETA
(Comprehensive Employment Training Act).

6210 Martinez, Manuel. The art of the Chicano
movement, and the movement of Chicano art.
In: Valdez, Luis and Steiner, Stan eds.
AZTLAN: AN ANTHOLOGY OF MEXICAN AMERICAN
LITERATURE. New York: Vintage, 1972,
p.349-353. English.

AN: "Like the modern art of Mexico, the
new Chicano art is essentially an art of
social protest," writes Denver, Colorado
muralist and easel painter Martinez. He
traces the roots of Chicano art back into
Indian, colonial and modern Mexican art, and
defines two kinds of Chicano art.

6211 Martinez, Manuel. Promotional brochure.
Brochure, n.d. English.

AN: Biographical information on Chicano

muralist who was a pupil of David Alfaro
Siqueiros. Illustrated with photographs of
two acrylic murals and a photo of the
artist.

6212 Martinez, Sue. New mural unveiled in Redwood
City. EL TECOLOTE, Vol. 8, no. 7 (April
1978), p. 7. English.

AN: Commentary on the 147x22-ft. mural,
DANZAS MEXICANAS, painted by Chicano artist
Jose Antonio Burciaga and Mexican artist
Gilberto Romero at the Redwood City Civic
Center. The mural depicts dance rituals from
various Mexican regions and the flora and
fauna of Mexico. The mural became a subject
of controversy when its creators splattered
paint on it during its unveiling as a form
of protest against the San Mateo Arts
Council for its exploitation of Third World
artists. Detail of mural showing "La Danza
De Los Viejitos".

6213 McClellan, Bill. Army of volunteers paints a
little history in Phoenix. PHOENIX GAZETTE,
(April 20, 1977). English.

AN: Adolfo "El Zarco" Guerrero with 100
residents from the Duppa Villa Housing
Project completes a mural funded by the
Arizona Commission on Arts and Humanities.
Guerrero completed six murals, but prefers
sculpture.

6214 M.E.C.H.A. cultura y evolucion mexicana. EL
CLARIN, (May 2, 1974), p. 3. Spanish.

AN: Report on the mural designed and
painted under the direction of Mexican-born
designer Sergio O'Cadiz at Santa Ana
College, Santa Ana, Calif. Collaborators
were instructor Shifra Goldman and gallery
director Mike Davis, with members of the
MEChA Club and other students. The mural
concerns the history of Mexico and of the
Chicano and includes a tribute to David
Alfaro Siqueiros' Los Angeles mural AMERICA
TROPICAL, painted and white-washed in the
1930s. Illustrated.

6215 Mechicano Art Center. Los Angeles, CA:
Mechicano Art Center, 1971. English.

AN: Announcement of an exhibit by
painters Ramon Atilano, Xavier Lopez Ortega,
and Frank A. Martinez. Martinez and Lopez
Ortega are also muralists. Brief profiles of
the artists. Illustrated.

6216 Mencion Don Quijote: Atanasio P. Davila. LA
VOZ DE HOUSTON, (June 5, 1980). English.

AN: Illustrated biography of 70-year-old
Mexican-born Texas painter who returned to
art after his retirement and had just
completed a mural for Houston's Ripley House
medical clinic.

6217 Mendoza, Vicente; Nario, Jose; and Patlan,
Ray. The history of the Mexican-American
worker (1974-75) [detail of mural]. REVISTA
CHICANO-RIQUENA, Vol. 4, no. 4 (Fall
1976), p. 50,54. English.

6218 Metro Denver Urban Coalition, Denver, CO.
City walls. Brochure, 1979. English.

AN: Brochure/poster giving history of
City Walls Project and biographies of seven
artists: Jon Howe, Jerry Jaramillo, Steve
Lucero, Jowinnie Moore, Al Sanchez, Fred
Sanchez, Carlos M. Sandoval. Illustrated.

Mural Art (cont.)

6219 Mexican artists paint mural for Bank of
America. EL HISPANO, Vol. 6, no. 49.
English.

AN: Commentary by Jesus Campusano and
Michael Rios about the 90-ft. mural they
painted inside the Bank of America on
Mission and 23rd Streets in San Francisco.
They describe the mural as "...a montage of
symbols and images depicting the heritage,
day-to-day experiences and hopes of the
people in the area.

6220 Mexican-American lawyers' club donates
Kennedy mural to the people of Mexico.
EASTSIDE SUN, (November 28, 1968). English.

AN: East Los Angeles artist Armando
Campero commissioned to paint mural for
"Unidad de Kennedy" housing development in
Mexico City.

6221 Meza to paint Pan American National Bank
murals. MEXICAN AMERICAN SUN, (October 14,
1965). English.

AN: Mexican painter Jose Reyes Meza is
commissioned to create a mosaic mural titled
OUR PAST, OUR PRESENT, AND OUR FUTURE for
the facade of the Pan American National Bank
of East Los Angeles being erected on First
Street.

6222 Miguelez, Armando. La cultura chicana: los
murales. RAYAS, Vol. 1, no. 5 (September,
October, 1978), p. 9. Spanish.

AN: Miguelez, a writer from Tucson,
Arizona, divides muralistic production into
two categories: cultural muralism and
creative muralism. Both types of murals
function as alternatives to establishment
art, to mono-cultural education and to
ethnocentric history. Relates Chicano mural
movement to its antecedent in Mexico, but
most especially to the mural production of
other ethnic minorities in the United
States.

6223 Miguelez, Armando. La cultura chicana: los
murales. AZTEC CAMPUS NEWS, Vol. 5, no. 24
(April 4, 1978), p. 7. English.

AN: Article arguing for two classes of
murals: the cultural (or traditional,
political, historical) and the creative
(symbolic, mythical, with contemporary
forms), both of which are found among
Chicano art. Illustrated with, presumably,
examples of each. Translated into Spanish in
RAYAS, (Sept.-Oct., 1978).

6224 Mills, James. Hispano history mural ready.
DENVER POST, (October 17, 1975), p. 27+.
English.

AN: PASADO, PRESENTE Y FUTURO, a 20-ft.
mural by Denver artist Carlota Espinoza was
commissioned by the Friends of the Denver
Public Library for the Byers Branch (W. 7th
Ave. and Santa Fe Drive). Blending myth and
reality, the mural progresses from Aztec
empires through the Spanish conquest, from
alienation to the struggle for a collective
identity and heritage by the Mexican
American. Brief commentary by the artist on
the mural's significance. Ms. Espinoza's
mural was designated as an official
Centennial-Bicentennial creation.
Illustrated with photograph of artist.

6225 Mills, Kay. The great wall of Los Angeles.

MS.MAGAZINE, (October 1981), p. 66-69+.
English.

AN: THE GREAT WALL OF LOS ANGELES in the
Tujunga flood control channel in the San
Fernando Valley, was started as a
Bicentennial project in 1976. Artistic
director Judy Baca of the Social and Public
Art Resource Center, works with crews of
young people painting aspects of Los Angeles
history that is not generally found in
textbooks. Well illustrated.

6226 Minutaglio, Bill. Chicano take the art to
the street of S.A. SAN ANTONIO EXPRESS-NEWS,
(January 11, 1981), p. M, 1-2. English.

AN: Survey of Chicano murals in San
Antonio including 30 two-story murals at
Westside Cassiano Homes by students from the
commercial art program of Lanier High
directed by Anastacio "Tache" Torres and
Rudy Trevino; 8 murals at Lanier High
School; one at the City Hall offices; and
others throughout the city. Illustrated.

6227 Minutaglio, Bill. S.A. aims at becoming
Hispanic art center. SAN ANTONIO
EXPRESS-NEWS, (January 18, 1981), p. 3-M+.
English.

AN: Rick Reyna is director of the
fledging San Antonio Consortium for Hispanic
Arts (SACHA), a city-funded umbrella
organization covering seven art groups,
three of which - Centro Cultural del Pueblo
(instruction for young people), Community
Cultural Arts Program (murals), and
Performance Artists Nucleus (displays and
exhibits) - concern the visual arts. Rudy
Garcia, Anastacio "Tache" Torres, and Ralph
Garcia (formerly of Garcia's Art Gallery)
head the three groups respectively.

6228 Miranda, Keta. Refunding battle for mural
project. PEOPLE'S WORLD, Vol. 39, no. 20
(May 15, 1976), p. 5+. English.

AN: History of the Mural Arts and
Resource Center (Los Angeles Citywide Mural
Project) from 1974 to its imminent demise in
1976. Joe Bravo mural illustrated.

6229 Mission community mural map. San Francisco,
CA: Galeria de la Raza, n.d.. English.

AN: Map showing ten sites for murals in
the San Franciso Mission District. Published
as a guide to a community mural tour.

6230 Mitchell, John L. History restarted with
mural grant. LOS ANGELES TIMES [Valley
edition], (February 3, 1980), p. XI,1,4.
English.

AN: Interview with Judith Baca on the
goals and purposes of the "Great Wall of Los
Angeles" mural project. The central aim is
to provide work, educational experience and
skills for 40 ethnically-mixed unemployed
youngsters between the ages of 14-21.
Article details evolution of the project and
funding sources. Illustrated.

6231 Monroe mural brightens school. THE REGISTER,
(December 13, 1973), p. G3. English.

AN: James Monroe School in Santa Ana, CA
has a huge mural painted by Costa Mesa
artist Sergio O'Cadiz. The mural cost $4250,
but the artist donated much time and talent.
Illustrated.

Mural Art (cont.)

6232 Montoya, Emmanuel; Rodriguez, Patricia; and Acevedo, Mario (Torero). Canto al pueblo '78. NATIONAL MURALS NETWORK COMMUNITY NEWSLETTER, (1978). English.

AN: The second annual Canto al Pueblo took place in Corpus Christi, Texas, where more than six murals were painted: "Wall of Cultural Education" by 13 artists headed by Roel Montealva; Carlota Espinoza, with children; Gilberto Romero, Jose Antonio Burciaga and Patricia Rodriguez, "Incomprehension al arte"; "Madre Tierra" by Manuel Martinez of Denver with Amador Hinojosa (Corpus Christi) and Enriquette Vasquez (New Mexico); Mario Torero; Salvador Vega of Chicago whose mural some Canto participants considered "insulting".

6233 Muchnic, Suzanne. LAICA looks at social works. CALENDAR, (October 7, 1979), p. 93. English.

AN: Review of the exhibit SOCIAL WORKS at the Los Angeles Institute of Contemporary Art. Illustration and discussion of Judith F. Baca's mural UPRISING OF THE MUJERES, a four-part portable canvas mural in the style of Siqueiros.

6234 Muchnic, Suzanne. Mural: a lullaby of another Broadway. LOS ANGELES TIMES, (December 18, 1981), p. VI, 1+. English.

AN: Commentary on the panoramic mural painted by John Valadez inside the Victor Clothing Company at 242 S. Broadway. Mural depicts Broadway street life. Photograph of the artist and the mural.

6235 Muchnic, Suzanne. Passion, paint splatter folk art museum show. LOS ANGELES TIMES, (June 25, 1981), p. VI, 1. English.

AN: Review of the MURALS OF AZTLAN: STREET PAINTERS OF EAST LOS exhibit at the Craft and Folk Art Museum in Los Angeles. The critic considered the show "revved-up, highly emotional art descended from Mexico's political muralists" that made up what it lacked in subtlety with passion, and one of the most visually exciting shows of the Museum. Illustrations.

6236 Las mujeres muralistas. Exhibition invitation, 1974. English.

AN: Invitation to the inauguration of the mural PARA EL MERCADO at Paco's Tacos in San Francisco's Mission District by the Mujeres Muralistas, Sept. 15, 1974. Illustrated by Venezuelan artist Consuelo Mendez.

6237 Mujeres muralistas de San Diego. CITYBENDER, Vol. 2, no. 7 (1978). English.

AN: Photographic essay on four women working on their mural at Chicano Park, San Diego.

6238 Mural. ARTE, no. 1 (1977). English.

AN: Describes a section of the mural A PEOPLE'S HISTORY OF TELEGRAPH AVENUE painted by Daniel Galvez and Brian Thiele. The mural represents the work of dozens of additional artists.

6239 Mural at U.C.L.A.'s Chicano Library: detail. LA GENTE DE AZTLAN, Vol. 1, no. 6 (May 31, 1971), p. 1. English.

AN: Reproduction of detail, Chicano Library mural painted in 1971.

6240 Mural at U.C.L.A.'s Chicano Library: detail. LA GENTE DE AZTLAN, Vol. 1, no. 6 (May 31, 1971), p. Ft cover,4. English.

AN: UCLA's Chicano Library mural: details of the mural on the front page and p. 4.

6241 Mural celebration. GRASSROOTS, (September 6, 1978), p. 8. English.

AN: Illustrated story on the new mural of plywood, papier mache and ceramic painted and modeled by artists from Commonarts for la Pena Cultural Center. The mural depicts peoples of the Americas coming together, singing and playing musical instruments, with Chilean musician Victor Jara as the major symbol.

6242 Mural depicts history of Mexican Americans. EASTSIDE JRNL, (December 16, 1971), p. 1. English.

AN: Richard Jimenez of the Goez Gallery depicts the past and present of Mexican American culture on an interior mural at the First Street Store (3640 E. First St.) The 6 ft. by 15 ft. mural has central image of a clock with a faceless figure (The Mexican American of the future). Artist comments on another of his murals titled EDUCATION OF LIFE.

6243 Mural depicts la lucha campesina del mexicano. EL HISPANO, Vol. 8, no. 12 (September 9, 1975). English.

AN: Photograph and commentary on the mural by J. Orozco for the Sacramento Farmworker's Migrant Program on F. Street. Centered by the Virgin of Guadalupe, the mural is divided into four sections: The Farmworker in the Fields, The Tree of Life, Violence Against the Farmworkers, and the Racist System.

6244 Mural en Quinto Sol. SOL DE AZTLAN, Vol. 2, no. 3 (July 1971). English.

AN: Full-page illustrated article describing mural by Jose Mojica at the Edificio Quinto Sol in Lansing. Mural traces the history of La Raza and was painted by the self-taught artist with the assistance of his brother Adolfo.

6245 The mural message. TIME, Vol. 105, no. 14 (April 7, 1975), p. 79. English.

AN: Brief illustrated story of murals painted in East Los Angeles during the 1970s. Spotlights activities of Goez Gallery.

6246 Mural Resource Center, Los Angeles, CA. Citywide murals: mural manual. Mimeographed booklet, n.d. English.

AN: Condensed from the Mark Rogovin and Marie Burton MURAL MANUAL published in 1973 by Chicago's Public Art Workshop. See citation under Rogovin.

Mural Art (cont.)

6247 Mural Resource Center, Los Angeles, CA.
Woman's manual: how to assemble scaffolding.
Mimeographed booklet, n.d. English.

AN: Publication to service increasing
number of women participating in muralism.

6248 A mural tour of San Francisco. SUNSET, Vol.
15, (July 1975). English.

AN: Illustrations and map of seven
Latino murals in the Mission district of San
Francisco.

6249 Murales - 'expresan nuestra realidad'.
AYUDA, Vol. 1, no. 6 (September 1977).
English.

AN: Brief illustrated article on Raul
Valdez's 1977 mural LOS ELEMENTOS on the
outside wall of Antioch's Juarez-Lincoln
College (Centro Cultural de LUCHA). Explains
the iconography of the mural. Includes brief
biography of the artist.

6250 Los murales del pueblo. PAPEL CHICANO, Vol.
2, no. 12 (February 1973), p. 1+. Spanish.

AN: Analysis of Leo Tanguma's work as
"an expression not only of artistic creative
opinion but also of the suppressed and
accumulated feeling of La Raza in the United
States." Includes thematic and stylistic
information on four murals in the Houston
barrio: "The Rebirth of Our Nationality,"
"Towards a Humanitarian Technology for La
Raza," "Historia de la Raza," and "El
Mestizo Chicano".

6251 Muralist Campero shows works. EASTSIDE JRNL,
(June 3, 1971), p. 6. English.

AN: Photograph of artist Armando Campero
with samples of his graphic work. The artist
was completing a 3,000 square foot mural,
JOHN KENNEDY SAGA NUMBER 2 for installation
at the City Terrace Social Hall.

6252 Muralist helps youth paint better world.
YUMA DAILY SUN, (November 14, 1980).
English.

AN: Adolfo "Zarco" Guerrero meeting with
students, educators, officials, and the
community in Yuma.

6253 Las muralistas del barrio. CHISMEARTE, no. 2
(Winter, Spring, 1977), p. 48-49. English.

AN: Brief announcement about a Chicana
artists' organization formed in Fresno,
California which started work on a
billboard-like mural, 60x8 feet on the theme
of women. The mural received funding through
Fresno's La Brocha del Valle. About fifteen
women are involved, including Helen Gonzalez
and Cecelia Risco.

6254 Las muralistas: Patricia Rodriguez, Consuelo
Mendez, Graciela Carrillo, Irene Perez.
Exhibition invitation, 1974. English.

AN: Invitation to the inauguration of
the mural LATINO AMERICA by the Mujeres
Muralistas at the Mission Neighborhood Model
Cities in San Francisco's Mission District,
May 31, 1974.

6255 Murals around the U.S.A. TEJANO ARTISTS INC.
NEWSLETTER, Vol. 2, no. 2 (January,
February, 1981). English.

AN: Mimeographed newsletter published by
Tejano Artists, Inc. of Houston. Survey of
U.S. mural events and publications; report
on murals in Texas: El Paso, San Antonio,
Austin, Crystal City, San Juan, Corpus
Christi, Houston.

6256 NATIONAL MURALS NETWORK COMMUNITY
NEWSLETTER. (Spring 1981). English.

AN: Reports, or illustrations, of murals
by Guillermo Aranda (Calif.), Francisco
Lefebre (New Mexico); Marcos Raya's section
of Chicago's anti-war mural; Gilberto
Guzman's mural (New Mexico); vandalism on a
Michael Schnorr mural at Chicano Park, San
Diego, Calif.

6257 NATIONAL MURALS NETWORK COMMUNITY
NEWSLETTER. (Spring 1980). English.

AN: Reports on the Sept. 1979 conference
of Chicano visual arts held at UT Austin,
organized by the Mujeres Artistas del
Suroeste, and the Liga Unida de Chicanos
Artistas, which brought together
participants from the U.S. and Mexico City;
on Manuel Martinez's five murals (1976-78);
murals by Roberto Lucero, Al Sanchez, and
Jerry Jaramillo; as well as by the Chilean
group Orlando Letelier Brigade, all in
Denver, Colorado; murals by Leo Tanguma in
Houston; the story about the "forbidden"
Chicano mural in Blue Island, Illinois.
Illustrated.

6258 NATIONAL MURALS NETWORK COMMUNITY
NEWSLETTER. (Fall 1979). English.

AN: Reports on mural projects by Fermin
Coronado working with students in Houston;
Galeria de la Raza's billboard used as a
mural surface for changing images; murals
under the Flor en la Comunidad program of El
Centro Cultural de la Gente in San Jose,
California and led by artist Jaime Valadez;
murals in Grand Rapids and other cities of
western Michigan; murals by Jose Guerrero
and others from the Chicago Mural Group; a
survey of Chicano murals in the Pilsen area
of Chicago guided by Jose Gonzalez.

6259 NATIONAL MURALS NETWORK COMMUNITY
NEWSLETTER. (Fall 1980). English.

AN: Reports on murals in San Francisco,
CA, by the Chicano Moratorium Coalition; in
Chicago about the Anti-War Preparations
mural; in Houston by a student at the
Association for Advancement of Mexican
Americans; on Michael Schorr's mural in
Chicanok, San Diego, CA; on a segment being
painted at the Tujunga Wash mural in Los
Angeles under Judy Baca; on south San Diego
murals being painted out; Alan Barnett's
survey of Southwest murals. Illustrated.

Mural Art (cont.)

6260 NATIONAL MURALS NETWORK COMMUNITY
     NEWSLETTER. (1978). English.

     AN: This issue features reports from
     muralists. Includes information about murals
     at: La Pena Cultural Center in Berkeley, CA;
     the Social and Public Art Resource Center's
     Tujunga Wash Mural in Venice, CA; the
     Citywide Mural Project in Los Angeles, CA;
     activities at Chicano Park, and of the
     Congress of American Cosmic Artists (CACA),
     both in San Diego, CA; murals in San Mateo
     County, CA; the Task Force on Hispanic
     American Arts headed by Jacinto Quirarte of
     San Antonio; the 1978 Canto Al Pueblo in
     Corpus Christi, TX; murals in Chicago; and
     other works by non-Chicano artists.

6261 Nevarez, Joe R. Chicano art blooms in barrio
     warehouse. LOS ANGELES TIMES, (December 26,
     1974), p. I, 32. English.

     AN: Former meat packing warehouse
     transformed into Goez Art Studios by Joe and
     John Gonzalez. Exhibiting David Negron,
     Eddie Martinez, David Lopez (Hollywood
     scenic artists) and Roberto Arenivar. Lists
     activities of the gallery: exhibits, murals,
     restoration.

6262 A new gallery of art on city streets. U.S.
     NEWS & WORLD REPORT, Vol. 50, no. 18 (May 8,
     1978), p. 86-87. English.

     AN: Brief illustrated story on street
     murals across the U.S. including Chicano
     murals in East Los Angeles and Santa Ana
     College, Calif.

6263 New Mexico Arts Division, Santa Fe, NM. Art
     in public places. Catalog, 1977-78, p. 9,
     11. English.

     AN: Catalog of CETA-funded project.
     Illustrated murals by Graciela Carrillo of
     San Francisco, and Gilbert Guzman of Santa
     Fe.

6264 New mural on Mission Street. EL HISPANO,
     Vol. 7, no. 13 (September 19, 1974), p. 5.
     English.

     AN: Description of mural at the corner
     of 24th Street and South Van Ness in San
     Francisco. Painted by Mujeres
     Muralistas--Consuelo Mendez, Graciela
     Carrillo, Susan Cervantes and Miriam Olivo,
     the 30-foot mural depicts people in a
     tropical, Latin American setting.

6265 New name, new face. TUCSON CITIZEN, OLD
     PUEBLO SECTION, (December 6, 1979), p. 6.
     English.

     AN: Tucson muralist Roberto Borboa works
     on a mural EDUCATION at the Edward L.
     Lindsay Adult learning Center. Illustrated.

6266 New radical wall art. PEOPLE'S WORLD, Vol.
     41, no. 37 (September 16, 1978), p. 10.
     English.

     AN: Illustrated story and explanation of
     the imagery on the new mural resulting from
     a collaboration of Commonarts and La Pena
     Cultural Center. The artists are Ray Patlan,
     O'Brien Thiele, Osha Neumann, and Anna de
     Leon.

6267 Notes on 2nd National Community Muralists'
     Network Conference, Chicago, Ill. April
     20-23, 1978. San Francisco, CA, 1978.

English.

     AN: Rupert Garcia, Raul Martinez,
     Patricia Rodriguez, Ray Patlan (San
     Francisco Bay Area) and Jaime Valadez (San
     Jose), among others, attended the conference
     in Chicago. Reports were heard from many
     parts of the United States on mural
     activities, including that of Aurelio Diaz
     of Chicago, representing MARCH (Movimiento
     Artistico Chicano). A workshop presentation
     was made by Luis Arenal and others from the
     Taller Siqueiros of Cuernavaca, Mexico. An
     experimental mural to try Siqueiros'
     techniques was created. Illustrated.

6268 Oakland Museum, Oakland, CA and Laney
     College, Oakland, CA. In search of Aztlan.
     Exhibition brochure, 1974. English.

     AN: Brochure for exhibit featuring Los
     Four: Carlos Almaraz, Gilbert Lujan, Roberto
     de la Rocha, Frank Romero, Judithe
     Hernandez.

6269 Oakland Museum presents 5 L.A. Chicano
     artists. EL MUNDO (Hayward, CA), (August
     1974). English.

     AN: Report on the exhibit THE SEARCH FOR
     AZTLAN, featuring paintings, murals,
     tortilla art, folk and religious symbols and
     totems by Carlos Almaraz, Roberto de la
     Rocha, Gilbert Lujan, Frank Romero and
     Judithe Hernandez. Included in the more than
     100 works are a wall mural, a folk art
     pyramid, and part of a primed '51 Chevy
     lowrider. Illustrated.

6270 OMICA Housing Corp., Inc., Homestead
     (Miami), FL. Dedication of heritage village.
     Brochure, 1977. English.

     AN: Brochure of non-profit housing
     corporation which built, with Housing and
     Urban Development (HUD) funds, public
     homeownership housing for farmworkers and
     low-income rural residents of South Dade
     County. Illustrated with a mural by Roberto
     Rios of San Antonio, one of three done in
     Florida.

6271 Opton, Suzanne. Short strokes. SAN FRANCISCO
     FAULT, (December 29, 1971), p. 9-10.
     English.

     AN: The currently homeless Galeria de la
     Raza has begun a series of wall painting
     projects. Artist "Spain" did a Horizons
     mural; Puerto Rican photographer Adal
     Maldonado did photographic murals; Jerry
     Concha, Tom Rios, did rooms in the Center
     for Change drug program building, Chuy
     Campusano, working with cartoonist R. Crumb,
     and the Mission Rebel Kids did a cartoon
     mural. Model Cities day care centers are
     next to be painted.

6272 Ordorica, Leticia. Community expression in
     muralism. VOZ FRONTERIZA, Vol. 3, no. 5
     (March 1978). English.

     AN: Brief history of Chicano Park in San
     Diego. Announcement of the "Mural Marathon"
     from April 1 to April 20, two days before
     the Eighth Annual Chicano Park Celebration.
     Five pillars and the kiosk will be painted.
     Illustration.

Mural Art (cont.)

6273 Painted walls - a New Mexico folk art. NEW MEXICO, (January 1977), p. 34-35. English.

AN: Five color illustrations of murals from New Mexico including those done by Gilberto Guzman, Geronimo Garduno, and Sam Leyba. The murals are located in Santa Fe, Chimayo, Embudo and Albuquerque.

6274 Painting pride for everyone to see - a Chicano artist and his giant murals. TEXAS MAGAZINE, (April 22, 1973), p. 4-6+. English.

AN: Brief story and photographs of 31-year-old Leo Tanguma's murals at Continental Can Co., Lamons Metal Gasket Co., McAshan Community Center, and Casa de Amigos Clinic, in Houston. His large murals deal with Chicano history and oppression. Tanguma is unpaid for his labor.

6275 Parachini, Allan. Tujunga wash mural stands up to storm. LOS ANGELES TIMES, (March 13, 1980), p. V, 1. English.

AN: Information about the mural project near Los Angeles Valley College in Van Nuys, Calif. sponsored by SPARC (Social and Public Art Resource Center) of Venice, Calif. and coordinated by Judy Baca. Illustrated.

6276 Pared da historia de la Raza. PAPEL CHICANO, Vol. 1, no. 4 (September 26, 1971). English.

AN: Discussion of Manuel Martinez' wall painting at Parque Aztlan titled PASADO, PRESENTE Y FUTURO DE LA RAZA BRONCE. Among the images used to convey the theme are Emiliano Zapata, Quetzalcoatl, a mestizo three faceted head symbolizing the indigenous mother, the Spanish father and the mestizo child. Included also is a symbol formed by four clasped hands suggesting unity among world faces. Illustrated with photograph of wall painting.

6277 Park murals to be censored. EL DIARIO DE LA GENTE, Vol. 1, no. 1 (October 20, 1972), p. 3. English.

AN: Controversy over Chicano murals at La Raza Park in North Denver caused the Denver City Council to pass an ordinance which requires all artists wishing to paint a mural on a public building to secure a permit and obtain approval from the department in question. The disputed mural is one of Aztec symbols that express the elements of an eternal struggle. Illustrated with photograph of controversial mural.

6278 Patterson, Ann. Exhibit at Unitarian: Smith, Quesada art black, white contrast. TEMPE DAILY NEWS, (March 16, 1976). English.

AN: Eugenio Quesada presented drawings of female torsos along with Smith. Both are industrial design faculty members at Arizona State University. Article mentions other Quesada shows, and his participation on the Jean Charlot mural at the University.

6279 Pepe and Pepito. SANTA FE NEW MEXICAN, (October 11, 1972), p. A7. English.

AN: The unveiling of a mural entitled "Rebirth of the Chicano" will take places on the eve (Oct., 19) of the First Chicano National Congress for Land and Cultural Reform held in Albuquerque Oct., 20-22.

6280 Perales Leven, Humberto. Marcos Raya - Mexican painter. IMAGENES, Vol. 1, no. 1 (July 1976). Bilingual.

AN: Mexican born Chicago muralist Marcos Raya painted a mural titled HOMAGE TO RIVERA in the Pilsen barrio of Chicago at the corner of 18th Street and May. Raya articulates the role of the muralist and his function within the working class community. Also in this issue is an article on the formation of MARCH (Movimiento Artistico Chicano) in 1972 in East Chicago Indiana. Portfolio of drawings by Marcos Raya and photographs by Mario Castillo. Bilingual text.

6281 Petraitis, Louise. Student union murals: walls with tongues. PHOENIX MAGAZINE, (April 21, 1977), p. 12. English.

AN: San Francisco State University instructor Ray Patlan and his La Raza Mural Workshop are painting murals in the Student Union basement. The relationship of a mural to architecture, the process of transferring a sketch to the wall, the underpainting, and the finishing painting processes are explained. A videotape of the mural is being made. Illustrated.

6282 Pimentel, Ricardo. Graffiti: expression or scourge? FRESNO BEE, (February 23, 1981), p. Metro, B1+. English.

AN: A rapid review of graffiti symbols, their meaning and social context. Commentary by various young people explaining the value, style and meanings of plaqueasos (spray painted graffiti). Some Chicano artists like Bob Cruz, director of La Brocha del Valle, see mural painting as a positive alternative to graffiti art forms. Article also provides views of local businessmen to the graffiti phenomenon.

6283 Plous, F.K. Street scenes. MIDWEST MAGAZINE, (September 1, 1974), p. 10. English.

AN: Article focusing on the mural production of Ray Patlan in the Pilsen barrio of Chicago. Description of the community and how Patlan functions as a community worker and muralist. Includes a directory of Chicago's murals. Well illustrated with photographs, some in color.

6284 Portraying Latino women in the Mission. SAN FRANCISCO EXAMINER, (September 10, 1974), p. 26. English.

AN: Three muralists of the Mission District, Irene Perez, Patricia Rodriguez, and Venezuelan Consuelo Mendez, are preparing a six-paneled painting-construction, the RHOMBOIDAL PARALLELOGRAM, for the 28th annual San Francisco Art Festival. It will illustrate the life of women in the Mission. Illustrated.

6285 President's Gallery, Chicago State University and Sorell, Victor A. Alejandro Romero. Exhibition catalog, 1979. English.

AN: Catalog of an exhibit by Mexican-born painter and muralist who has been working in the United States since about 1973. He has lived in Chicago since 1976. Illustrated.

Mural Art (cont.)

6286 Preuss, Karen. The new Mission murals. SAN FRANCISCO BAY GUARDIAN, (June 28, 1975), p. 14-15. English.

AN: Mural art in San Francisco's Mission District has covered nearly every wall and alley on lower 24th Street. Murals by Mike Rios, the Mujeres Muralistas (Patricia Rodriguez, Graciela Carrillo, Consuelo Mendez, Miriam Olivo, Irene Perez, Susan Cervantes) appear in the area. Others have been painted by artists associated with the Galeria de la Raza. Illustrations.

6287 Quintero, Victoria. Mujeres muralistas. LA RAZON MESTIZA, Vol. 11, (Summer 1975).

AN: Goals and artistic procedures of the Mujeres Muralistas Collective. Article emphasizes the solidarity of Latin American women and Chicanas and how their joint artistic production reflects a woman's viewpoint in aesthetic terms.

6288 Quintero, Victoria. A mural is a painting on a wall done by human hands. EL TECOLOTE, Vol. 5, no. 1 (September 13, 1974), p. 6+. English.

AN: The women's collective, Mujeres Muralistas, exists within the strong San Francisco mural movement. Originally the group included Graciela Carrillo, Consuelo Mendez, Irene Perez, and Patricia Rodriguez. The group has expanded to include Susan Cervantes, Ester Hernandez, and Miriam Olivo. The two murals completed have been criticized for not being political; the women answer that they want the atmosphere to be surrounded with life, with colors. Illustrated.

6289 Quirarte, Jacinto. The murals of el barrio. EXXON USA, (February 1974), p. 2-9. English.

AN: Well illustrated article on California murals from Santa Barbara, San Diego, Los Angeles, Fresno, and San Francisco.

6290 Reaves, John. Santa Barbara. NEWORLD, Vol. 6, no. 2 (March, April, 1980), p. 7+. English.

AN: Report on the activities of Casa de la Raza in Santa Barbara within social context. Erroneous attribution of murals, not all of which are by Vallejo.

6291 Renacimiento del arte chicano en Texas. EL HISPANO, Vol. 6, no. 3 (July 10, 1973). English.

AN: Remigio Garcia and Mariana Escalante, young muralists, describe their work and the collective goals of a mural workshop begun by Leo Tanguma in Houston, TX.

6292 Renteria, Ramon. Struggle of barrio life reflected in mural. EL PASO TIMES, (November 21, 1976). English.

AN: Carlos Rosas paints a 100x35-foot mural on the El Paso Boys Club building, as an homage to a child. It also reflects the artist's roots in El Paso. Iconography of the mural is discussed. Illustrated.

6293 Rickey, Carrie. The passion of Ana. VILLAGE VOICE, Vol. 25, no. 37 (September 10, 1980), p. 75. English.

AN: Review of the exhibition DIALECTICS OF ISOLATION, AN EXHIBITION OF THIRD WORLD WOMEN ARTISTS OF THE UNITED STATES at the A.I.R Gallery in New York, September 1980. Includes a capsule analysis of Judith Baca's colossal mural in Tujunga Wash in Los Angeles. The mural "proposes to restore to public consciousness the ethnic and cultural history of the city's minorities." Details work procedures, content and political aims of the project. Eleven blue prints of mural cartoons detailing highlights of the mural's visual narrative were displayed in the exhibit.

6294 Rios, Sam. Chicano muralist: Toltecotl in Aztlan. Unpublished paper, 1980. English.

AN: History of pre-Columbian, Mexican, and Chicano wall paintings. Describes in detail murals by Jose Montoya, Juanishi Orozco, Esteban Villa, Stan Padilla, Juan Cervantes, Lorraine Garcia of the Centro de Artistas Chicanos, Royal Chicano Air Force, painted in 1977 at Southside Park, Sacramento, Calif. Symbolism is explained.

6295 Rivas, Maggie. Art of the barrio: Exxon's traveling art show comes to headquarters. HQ HOUSTON, (August 1976), p. 6-7. English.

AN: Report on traveling photo-exhibition of 29 Chicano murals organized by Jacinto Quirarte for Exxon USA.

6296 Rivera, Humberto R. and Howell, Heather R. The murals of East Los Angeles. Film. English.

AN: Puerto Rican filmmaker Rivera deals with Chicano murals and their makers. Views of the murals and interviews with the artists make up the bulk of the film. Unfortunately Rivera focuses the camera on the artists and the streets and seldom gives the viewer a detailed look at the mural under discussion.

6297 Roberts, Tim. For art's sake, for the community, for the working class. ORANGE CITY NEWS, Vol. 10, (March 14, 1979), p. 1,8-9. English.

AN: Illustrated article on Orange County, Calif. realist painter Emigdio Vasquez. Focuses on his community murals, and his attitudes toward his art. Also announces the first exhibit, "Empanada" of the newly formed Hispanic Artists Association of Orange County. 13 participants including Vasquez.

6298 Rodebaugh, Dale. Graffiti replaces popular mural in Santa Cruz arcade. SAN JOSE MERCURY, (April 13, 1979), p. B, [1]. English.

AN: The efforts of Eduardo Carrillo to restore his mural, "Birth Death and Resurrection in a downtown arcade. The artist comments on the intention and significance of the mural and the political reasons for its obliteration.

Mural Art (cont.)

6299 Rodriguez, Alfred. A historical survey of
     Chicano murals in the Southwest: an
     interdisciplinary teaching unit. Unpublished
     paper, 1980. English.

     AN: Lists murals by title, artist and
     date (when known), location and subject. Los
     Angeles, San Francisco, San Diego, Fresno,
     San Antonio, Austin, Corpus Christi, Santa
     Fe, New Mexico murals are included.
     Circulated by the Institute of Latin
     American Studies, University of Austin,
     Texas.

6300 Rodriguez, Jose Luis. Nuestra voz, arte. LA
     VOZ CHICANA, Vol. 1, no. 1 (January 1978),
     p. 5. English.

     AN: Brief resume of Diego Rivera as a
     central figure of Mexican muralism and
     contributor to a great tradition of realist
     art. Commentary on the Rockefeller Center
     Mural of 1933 and The New Workers School
     Mural of 1969. Intent is to relate the
     Chicano art movement to its Mexican
     antecedents. Illustrated with drawings of
     Diego Rivera and a reproduction of Rivera's
     mural SUNDAY DREAM AT ALAMEDA PARK.

6301 Rodriguez, Patricia, ed. Selected readings
     on Chicano art. Berkeley, CA: Chicano
     Studies Department, University of
     California, 1977. English.

     AN: Compendium of mechanically
     reproduced articles on Chicano and Latin
     American art prepared for Chicano Studies
     130--Introduction to Chicano Art. Includes
     sections on Mexican Muralists in the U.S:
     Contemporary Chicano Art; Views on Chicano
     Art; Chicano Artists; Pinto Art: Raza Murals
     and Muralists; Plaqueasos (Graffiti);
     Chicana Artists: Art, Politics and the
     Community, Two Historical Examples: Cuba and
     Chile; Chicano Art Reproductions, 557 pp.

6302 Rogelio Cardenas--making murals. EL MUNDO
     (San Francisco, CA), (September 14, 1978).
     English.

     AN: Rogelio Cardenas' fourth mural, LA
     MUJER, on the La Mexicana Tortilleria in
     Hayward, California. Interview with the
     artist who explains the mural's symbolism
     and his future plans. Illustrated.

6303 Rogovin, Mark and Burton, Marie. Mural
     manual: how to paint murals for the
     classroom, community center and street
     corner. Boston, MA: Beacon Press, 1975.
     English.

     AN: The aesthetics, methodology,
     techniques, materials and equipment for
     producing popular murals, indoors and out.
     Also deals with documentation, finances,
     copyright laws and the history of modern
     murals. Source book for muralists throughout
     U.S. Well illustrated with murals and work
     diagrams.

6304 Romotsky, Jerry and Romotsky, Sally R.
     Placas and murals. ARTS IN SOCIETY, Vol. 2,
     no. 1 (Summer, Fall , 1974), p. 286-299.
     English.

     AN: Details how Chicano muralists have
     recognized the aesthetics of graffiti and
     incorporated them into their murals. Among
     the earliest to do so were Lucille Grijalva
     and Willie Herron. Illustrated.

6305 Rosas, Carlos. Entelequia [detail of mural].
     REVISTA CHICANO-RIQUENA, Vol. 6, no. 1
     (Winter 1977), p. 21. Spanish.

6306 Rosenthal art slides. Chicago, IL: Rosenthal
     Art Slides, 1978. English.

     AN: Includes a selection on murals from
     Canada, Chile, Cuba, Mexico, and murals from
     the United States including the cities of
     Los Angeles, Chicago, and New York, and the
     states of Massachusetts, New Jersey, New
     York, and New Mexico. Many slides of Chicano
     murals from Los Angeles, Chicago and New
     Mexico are available, fully documented.

6307 Ross, Bob and Lyndon, George. The case of
     three California muralists: Roberto Chavez,
     Eduardo Carrillo, John Chamberlin. ARTS AND
     ENTERTAINMENT, (July 1981). English.

     AN: Well documented reports on the
     destruction of the Carrillo, Chavez and
     Chamberlin murals. Focus is on the legal
     implications of mural effacement in relation
     to present California law.

6308 Rowe, Richard. On Olvera Street: one vision
     realized, another white washed. REVIEW
     (Society of Architectural Historians,
     Pasadena, CA), Vol. 1, no. 1 (Fall 1981),
     p. 7. English.

     AN: Documentation about AMERICA
     TROPICAL, 1932 mural by David Alfaro
     Siqueiros. The mural, commissioned by F.K.
     Ferenz of the Plaza Art Center on Olvera
     Street in Los Angeles, was a 16' by 80'
     painting on the second-story wall of the old
     Italian Hall. From 1968 on, art historian
     Shifra M. Goldman, working with a small
     committee, has been actively involved in the
     attempt to restore the mural. Article
     details the travails of restoration and
     underscores the mural's importance.
     Illustrated.

6309 Ruiz, Elvia. Whitewashed mural.
     SENTIMIENTOS, Vol. 1, no. 2 (May 1978), p.
     7-10. English.

     AN: Illustrated article about Las
     Mujeres Muralistas del Valle. Their mural
     titled, "History of the Chicanos From a
     Woman's Perspective" was vandalized. Members
     of the mural group recall its creation and
     comment on its destruction.

6310 Saenz, John. Felix completes art project:
     artist's murals mask East LA graffiti
     [sic]. EAST LOS ANGELES TRIBUNE, (November
     30, 1972), p. A-4. English.

     AN: Charles Felix is doing murals as
     part of a community beautification "Wall
     Project" to cover graffiti. His present
     project is a series of murals intended to
     make Whittier Blvd. into a street gallery.
     Illustrated.

6311 Salas, Joanne. Mural painting that comes
     from the heart; 'impact' is the word for
     muralist Luis Mena. TUCSON CITIZEN, OLD
     PUEBLO SECTION, (June 25, 1981), p. 4-5.
     English.

     AN: Illustrated story on wall murals in
     Tucson. Color.

Mural Art (cont.)

6312 San Antonio Museum Association, San Antonio, TX. Real, really real, super real. Exhibition brochure, 1981. English.

AN: Exhibit surveying modern and contemporary realism in the U.S. Includes a brief biography, personal statement, and color illustration of work by Jesse C. Trevino, San Antonio, Texas photorealist painter and muralist, (pp. 146-147).

6313 San Francisco Museum of Modern Art, San Francisco, CA and Castellon, Rolando. People's murals: some events in American history. Exhibition catalog, 1976. English.

AN: Eight portable murals by San Francisco Bay Area artists including Graciela Carrillo, Anthony Machado, Robert Mendoza, Irene Perez, Mike Rios. Well Illustrated.

6314 Sanchez, Al. Murals destroyed. EL DIARIO DE LA GENTE, Vol. 4, no. 14 (August 13, 1976), p. 7. English.

AN: Open letter from Al Sanchez, originator of the cartoon "The Tortilla Kid" and graphics contributor to EL DIARIO. Letter details events which led to painting over of six "cultural" paintings at the Denver Community Development Corporation Building (4142 Tejon, Denver, CO). Artist wants due compensation, specifically monies for "the replacement of artwork to be done by a community artist on portable murals".

6315 Sanchez, Jesus. Auditorium mural "wipe out" during recent renovation move. EAST LOS ANGELES COLLEGE NEWS, (September 26, 1979). English.

AN: "The Path to Knowledge and the False University," a mural by Roberto Chavez on the facade of ELAC's Ingalls Auditorium was painted over on Sept. 11, 1979. Contrasting views on the mural's fate are offered by the Chicano Faculty Association President and the Dean of Educational Services.

6316 Sanchez, Jesus. Resolution passed to support artist's paintings of new mural. EAST LOS ANGELES COLLEGE NEWS, (October 3, 1979). English.

AN: Statements and counter-statements between Arthur Avila, president of East Los Angeles College, Roberto Chavez, artist, and the Chicano Faculty Association about the controversial painting over of a Chavez mural on the exterior of the college auditorium.

6317 Santuario de N.S. [Nuestra Senora] de Guadalupe, Santa Fe, NM. Artes Guadalupanos de Aztlan: Samuel Leyba, Gilberto Guzman, Geronimo Garduno, Carlos Leyba, Pancho Hunter. Exhibition invitation, 1979. English.

6318 Schmidt-Brummer, Horst and Lee, Feelie. Die bemalte stadt: initiativen zur veranderung der strassen in USA. Biespiele in Europa. Cologne, Germany: Verlag M. Dumont Schauberg, 1973. Other.

AN: A picture book of painted walls (murals) in the United States and their influnce in Europe. Locations, cities and names of artists (when known) are included. Essays by the authors: on supergraphics as street decoration, fantasy murals, school

murals, mural collectives in minority neighborhoods. Los Angeles, Detroit, San Francisco, Berkeley, New York, Chicago are covered, including Chicano murals. Color. In German.

6319 Seniors mural to be dedicated at RC Center. REDWOOD CITY TRIBUNE, (December 31, 1977), p. 3. English.

AN: A portable mural depicting the birth of the senior citizen hot meal program in San Mateo County will be dedicated at the Senior Citizens Drop-In Center. The 12x18-ft mural was painted by Emmanuel Montoya of Menlo Park, CA. Illustrated.

6320 SF muralists display paintings. VIVA, (October 8, 1972), p. 19. English.

AN: Paintings, and photos of murals taken by Gilberto Romero, on display at the New Mexico Arts Commission. Artists Sammy, Carlos and Albert Leyba (the original members), Gilberto Guzman and Geronimo Garduno, part of the Artes Guadalupanos de Aztlan, finished a mural at Tot Lot in 1971 and are team-painting La Clinica de la Gente. They have also painted a mural for West Las Vegas High School.

6321 Silent protest. ARIZONA DAILY STAR, (May 18, 1978), p. 6-H. English.

AN: Outdoor murals in Tucson by Ausberto Sandoval, Antonio Pazos and Sylvia de la Huerta on a house in community being displaced by urban renewal. Illustrated.

6322 Simpson, Eve. Chicano street murals: a sociological perspective. JRNL OF POPULAR CULTURE, Vol. 13, no. 3 (Spring 1980), p. 516-525. English.

AN: Condescending article by mid-western academic based on inadequate or spurious source and filled with factual and conceptual inaccuracies.

6323 Sinisi, J. Sebastian J. Following footsteps of Diego Rivera. CONTEMPORARY, (January 13, 1980), p. 28-30. English.

AN: Story on West Denver murals, particularly by Manuel Martinez and Carlos Sandoval at the La Alma Recreation Center, Summer 1979. Murals done through the Denver City Walls Project by artists belonging to Incorporated Artes Monumentales. Illustrated.

6324 Smith, Arva. CEU unveils Chicano mural. DESERET NEWS, (May 13, 1978), p. 12A. English.

AN: On Cinco de Mayo 1978, a 14x5-ft. mural was unveiled in the library of the College of Eastern Utah. Painted by Salt Lake City artist Alfred de Avila, the mural focuses on incidents from Mexican and Chicano history including a panel on Carbon County's coal mining industry. Mural was a bicentennial community art project. Illustrated with photograph of artist and section of mural.

Mural Art (cont.)

6325 Smith, Roberta. Twelve days of Texas. ART IN
AMERICA, Vol. 64, no. 4 (July, August,
1976), p. 42-48. English.

AN: Overview of Texas art in Fort
Worth/Dallas, Houston, San Antonio, Tyler,
and Galveston. Includes reproductions of
works by Luis Jimenez (color, on cover),
Roberto Rios mural, Jesse Trevino, Mel
Casas. Also mentioned in text are Phil
Renteria and Cesar Martinez.

6326 Social and public art resource center.
Brochure, [1977]. English.

AN: Brochure including the history,
philosophy, and resources of SPARC, an
outgrowth of the Los Angeles Citywide Mural
Project/Mural Resource Center headed by Judy
Baca. Illustrated.

6327 Solache, Saul. Chicano murals. CHISMEARTE,
Vol. 1, no. 1 (Fall 1976), p. 24-25.
English.

AN: Brief statement by a Chicano artist
about the significance of Chicano murals as
the "legitimate voice of the spirit of La
Raza." Also includes an outline of concepts
used by the author to analyze Chicano murals
for a book in progress at the time (May,
1975).

6328 Sommer, Robert. Street art. New York: Quick
Fox, 1975. English.

AN: Introductory essay covering the
history of the new mural movement, forms of
street art, politics, street sculpture, how
to locate and photograph street art. Chicano
murals include Charles Felix and others at
Estrada Courts (L.A.), RCAF murals in
Sacramento, Jose Montoya and others
(Broderick, Ca.) Marcos Raya (Chicago), Mike
Rios (Neighborhood Legal Aid, S.F.)
Mechicano Art Center (L.A.) Johnny Alvarez
(L.A.), New Mexico State Employment Bldg.,
Albuquerque mural, Lorena Street School
(L.A.), two murals, Casa de la Raza
Alternative School (Berkeley), Santa Fe, New
Mexico mural, Francisco Hernandez (L.A.),
Artes Guadalupanos de Aztlan (N. Mexico),
Willie Herron (L.A.). Better documentation
would have been welcome.

6329 Sorell, Victor A. Barrio murals in Chicago:
painting the Hispanic-American experience on
"our community" walls. REVISTA
CHICANO-RIQUENA, Vol. 4, no. 4 (Fall
1976), p. 51-72. English.

AN: Important survey of Chicago's Latino
murals, with key works considered in detail.
Among the Chicano art organizations and
muralists mentioned are MARCH (Movimiento
Artistico Chicano), and Yolanda Galvan,
Juanita Jaramillo, Jose Nario, Raymond
Patlan, Vicente Mendoza, Marcos Raya,
Ricardo Alonzo, Jose G. Gonzalez and Mario
Castillo, author of the earliest Latino
mural in Chicago (1968). Puerto Rican and
non-Latino muralists and mural groups are
also discussed. Well illustrated.

6330 Sorell, Victor A. and Bernstein, Barbara.
Guide to Chicago murals: yesterday and
today. Chicago, IL: Chicago Council on the
Fine Arts, 1978. English.

AN: Valuable compendium of New Deal and
contemporary murals in Chicago giving
titles, artists' names, dates and locations.

Well illustrated.

6331 SPARC (Social and Public Arts Resource
Center), Venice, CA. The great wall of Los
Angeles. Brochure, n.d. English.

AN: Publicity brochure for the rental or
purchase of the film The Great Wall of Los
Angeles. Reproduces photographs of the
mural, statements of youth participants, and
names of the mural director and supervisors.

6332 Stephens, Martha. Murals introduce Carlos
Castaneda to Neil Armstrong. SAN ANTONIO
EXPRESS-NEWS, (January 11, 1981), p. M, 1,
3. English.

AN: Survey of commissioned murals in San
Antonio including Mexican artist Juan
O'Gorman's mosaic at the Theatre for
Performing Arts; Carlos Merida's and Fred
Samuelson's at the Convention Center; Howard
Cook's New Deal mural in the downtown
post-office; Peter Hurd's, and James
Sicner's (in progress) mural at Trinity
University; Jesse "Chista" Cantu's at
Mario's Restaurant; and Jesse Trevino's
mural at Our Lady of the Lake University.
Illustrated.

6333 Stofflet-Santiago, Mary. The fifth sun:
esthetic quality versus curatorial intent.
ARTWEEK, Vol. 8, no. 37 (November 5, 1977),
p. 6. English.

AN: Review of the exhibit THE FIFTH SUN
at the University Art Museum in Berkeley,
Calif., curated by Ralph Maradiaga of the
Galeria de la Raza. It contains folk art,
and posters by Chicano artists Maradiaga,
Rupert Garcia, Juan Fuentes, mural studies
by Graciela Carrillo and Mike Rios, ceramics
by Anna de Leon, an altar by Amalia
Mesa-Bains, and mural drawings by Mexican
muralists. The writer criticizes the uneven
quality of the show, but encourages better
ones in the future. Illustrated.

6334 The stolen art: the O'Higgins mural.
RECOBRANDO, Vol. 1, no. 2, p. 15, 16.
English.

AN: Historical documentation on 60-foot
long 8-foot high fresco mural painted for
the Seattle Shipscalers Union by Mexican
artist Pablo O'Higgins in 1949. In 1974,
John Caughlan, a people's lawyer documented
the existence of the mural to Chicano
community groups. M.E.C.H.A. students at the
University of Washington lobbied for the
murals restoration and permanent exhibition.

6335 Street art explosion in Los Angeles. SUNSET,
(April 1973), p. 110-113. English.

AN: Illustrated article on Los Angeles
street murals including those by Roberto
Chavez, Willie Herron, Frank Romero, Richard
Jimenez, William Bejarano, Gilbert Lujan,
Armando Cabrera, Frank Martinez, Charles
Felix, and others.

6336 Street murals. Q-VO, Vol. 1, no. 11 (March
1980). English.

AN: 5 illustrations of Los Angeles
murals.

Mural Art (cont.)

6337 Takahashi, Keith. Art replaces writing on wall. LOS ANGELES TIMES, (January 13, 1974), p. XI-H, 1. English.

AN: Junior high school student's mural in Pico Rivera, Los Angeles County, with aid of teacher and a commercial sign painter. Some censorship by officials mentioned.

6338 Tang, Paul. Artist sustains proud Hispanic mural tradition. ARIZONA DAILY WILDCAT-ENCORE, (March 29, 1979), p. 1. English.

AN: Born and educated in Hermosillo, Sonora, Mexico, Antonio Pazos is painting murals around Tucson. Pazos got his first mural experience helping paint the Centro Cultural de la Raza building in San Diego, CA in the early 1970s. He also spent a summer at Paolo Soleri's city north of Phoenix, Arcosanti. Illustrated.

6339 Thalacker, Donald W. The place of art in the world of architecture. Chelsa House/R.R. Bowker, n.d. English.

AN: Includes a chapter on Roberto Rios' 1978-79 mural for the Border Patrol Sector Headquarters, Marfa, Texas.

6340 The Third World in art. LA LUZ, Vol. 3, no. 12 (March, April, 1975), p. 18, 27. English.

6341 Tijerina lauds Chicano Congress results. SANTA FE NEW MEXICAN, (October 24, 1972), p. A3. English.

AN: At the First National Chicano Congress for Land and Cultural Reform in Albuquerque, it was pointed out that younger delegates are just coming to the realization of being Chicano but are behind in knowledge about the relationships between Spaniards, Mexicans and Indians. This was the reason for unveiling the mural BIRTH OF THE INDO-HISPANO [called elsewhere REBIRTH OF THE CHICANO] at the Alianza headquarters October 19, 1972.

6342 Torres, Louis R. An innovation in children's t.v.: THE INFINITY FACTORY. LA LUZ, Vol. 6, no. 2 (February 1977), p. 10-11. English.

AN: Illustrated report on a new television series for children aimed at teaching mathematics fundamentals in a crisply-paced series of half-hour programs. The executive producer, Jesus Salvador Trevino, filmed the segments in a New York Black community, and in the East Los Angeles Chicano barrio. In one segment, muralist Willie Herron works with youngsters to design and paint an outdoor mural.

6343 Torres, Louis R. A Profile of an Hispano Artist: Charlie "Clavos" Felix. LA LUZ, Vol. 4, no. 6-7 (September, October, 1975), p. 3-4. English.

AN: Biographical data on artist and his unique nail relief sculpture.

6344 The Tortuga paints a new mural. CHISMEARTE, Vol. 2, no. 1 (Summer 1978), p. 12-13. English.

AN: Black and white details of new indoor mural painted at the Gilroy's Recreation Center.

6345 Tovar, Carlos. Chicano muralist interviewed.

NUESTRA COSA, Vol. 8, no. 1 (November, December, 1979), p. 7. English.

AN: Interview with artist Roberto Chavez concerning the white-washing of a mural he painted on the outside front wall of the campus auditorium at East Los Angeles College.

6346 Trafford, Al. The giant painted photo album: Jesse Trevino. SOUTHWEST ART, (April 1979). English.

AN: Well illustrated story on San Antonio photorealist painter Jesse Trevino. Includes biographical material, description of his working methods for murals and easel paintings, and self-characterization of his work as "cultural documentary painting".

6347 Transcendente y majestuoso mural de las tres aguilas. EL HISPANO, Vol. 8, no. 4 (July 15, 1975), p. 6. Spanish.

AN: Biographical data on Juan Ishi Orozco and commentary on his mural "Las Tres Aguilas." One eagle represents mother earth, another the dominant racist system and the third is symbolic of the United Farmworkers and their struggle.

6348 Trevino, Jesus Salvador. America tropical. (1971). English.

AN: Half-hour 16mm color film produced and written by Jesus Salvador Trevino and directed by Barry Nye about the painting and whitewashing in 1932-34 of Mexican muralist David Alfaro Siqueiros' mural AMERICA TROPICAL in Olvera Street, Los Angeles. Traces the attempts at restoration of the mural starting in the late 1960s and continuing in the 1970s. History of the mural set within social/political context of Mexican Americans in the 1930s, and counterpart struggles of Chicanos in the 1970s.

6349 Trevino, Rudy. San Antonio murals a self portrait. PICANTE, Vol. 1, no. 3, p. 60-61. English.

AN: Commentary on the San Antonio Mural Project assisted by the CETA program and the Barrio Betterment and Development Corporation (BBDC). Goals and information on the light murals in progress in the Casiano Housing Project. Participating artists: Juan Hernandez, Esteban Adame, Andrew Gutierrez, Bob Tate, and Roberto de La Fuente.

6350 Tribute to El Rio organizers: Mexican-American mural to be unveiled. ARIZONA DAILY STAR, (September 13, 1975). English.

AN: $1100, 1775-square-foot mural on two outdoor walls by Antonio Pazos, 22 year old art student from Hermosillo, Sonora. Completed on the third anniversary of El Rio Neighborhood Center in Tucson. Color illustration.

6351 Troelstrup, Glenn. Former delinquent paints his way out of corner. DENVER POST, (April 23, 1977), p. 2. English.

AN: Manuel Martinez started sketching at 13; at 29, after studying with Siqueiros (1967-68), he painted a number of murals in Denver and Albuquerque. In 1977 he organized Incorporated Artists Monumentales. Color illustration.

Mural Art (cont.)

6352 Tsutakaua, Mayumi. Artist paints from heritage. SEATTLE TIMES, (September 15, 1980). English.

AN: Biographical information on Armond Lara, Northwest Chicano-Navajo artist. He is coordinating the restoration of a mural done in Seattle by Mexican artist Pablo O'Higgins. In his own work Lara is experimenting with paper making and the use of natural pigments.

6353 Tucson Public Library; Sonoran Heritage; and De la Cruz, Frank. Mexican American mural art: the power of cultural identity. Brochure, 1980. English.

AN: Brochure on Tucson murals painted by Antonio Pazos, David Tineo, Danny Garza, Cynthia Reyes, Darlene Marcos, Roberto Borboa, and others.

6354 Tully, Robert. City walls. LA VOZ (Denver, CO), (August 3, 1979), p. 7. English.

AN: In a project managed by Metro Denver Urban Coalition, several Chicano artists were hired to work consistently in creating murals for the inner city. Article focuses on the goals, procedures, and activities of the muralists. Grouped as Incorporated Artes Monumentales, the group included Jerry Jaramillo, Steve Lucero, Al Sanchez, Fred Sanchez, and Carlos Sandoval. Illustrated by a group photograph of artists and a photograph of a wall painting by the Chilean-led Brigada Orlando Letelier in Denver.

6355 Turner, Mark. Muralist uses walls to break barriers between people. ARIZONA DAILY STAR, (July 23, 1981). English.

AN: Luis Gustavo Mena works on his latest mural, an image of Benito Juarez with the Mexican and "Latin Empire" flags, and a scale of justice. Information about the artist, son of an artistic family, and recent high school graduate.

6356 University Art Museum, Berkeley, CA. The Fifth Sun: Contemporary/Traditional Chicano & Latino Art. Exhibition catalog, 1977. English.

AN: Catalog of exhibit including 45 artists of northern California. Texts deal with Mexican muralists, Mujeres Muralistas & other muralists, posters, the Chicano art movement, altars, La Raza Silkscreen Center, Galeria de la Raza, the Mexican Museum, the Sacramento Centro de Artistas Chicanos/RCAF. Mural maps of S.F. Bay Area and Sacramento. Many illustrations.

6357 [Untitled photograph]. CALENDAR, (April 30, 1978), p. 102. English.

AN: Illustration of Joe Bravo mural in progress, Venice, California.

6358 [Untitled photograph]. LOS ANGELES TIMES, (May 5, 1972), p. II, 1. English.

AN: Captioned illustration of Chicano high school students' 25x5 foot mural at Compton's Thomas Jefferson Elementary School. The mural, which took a year to paint, is based on Mexican history.

6359 [Untitled photograph]. LOS ANGELES TIMES, (June 4, 1971), p. II, 2. English.

AN: Captioned illustration of Frank Martinez's mural painting of slain LOS ANGELES TIMES reporter Ruben Salazar. Unveiling of the mural at the Doctor's Hospital, East Los Angeles, during groundbreaking ceremonies for a new wing.

6360 [Untitled photograph]. HISPANIC BUSINESS, (September 16, 1975). English.

AN: Captioned illustration of Raul Esparza's 24x60 foot ceramic mural on the wall of the Exposition Park Museum of Science and Industry. Esparza worked a year and a half on the mural, MEXICO Y EL GENERO HUMANO.

6361 [Untitled photograph]. NUESTRO, Vol. 1, no. 4 (July 1977), p. 31. English.

AN: Color reproduction of mural (now destroyed) in Santa Fe, New Mexico by Gilberto Guzman.

6362 Unzueta, Manuel and La Casa de la Raza Gallery, Santa Barbara, CA. Murals art murals art: featuring the murals of la Casa de la Raza, Santa Barbara, California. Exhibition brochure, n.d. English.

AN: Illustrated booklet of Unzueta's murals and easel paintings.

6363 Unzueta, Manuel. Social commentary on Chicano art: a painter's critical brush. XALMAN, Vol. 1, no. 5 (Fall 1977), p. 63-68. English.

AN: Personal manifesto of painter Unzueta. Description of popular Chicano iconography and esthetics.

6364 Valade, Carole. Mural depicts artist's heritage. ADRIAN DAILY TELEGRAM, (September 15, 1978). English.

AN: Detailed description of Vibrations of a New Awakening, mural at Community Action Art Center by Martin Moreno with assistants Hector Perez and Walter Burrow.

6365 Valadez, Kathy L. Chicano murals tell of Mexican heritage. EL CHICANO, Vol. 7, no. 34 (January 25, 1973), p. 10-11. English.

AN: Focus on Roy Duarte's murals in the Casa Blanca area of Riverside, California.

6366 Valadez, Kathy L. Colton history told in mural. EL CHICANO, Vol. 8, no. 7 (July 19, 1973), p. 3, 9. English.

AN: Esau Quiroz was commissioned by the Mexican American Political Association to paint mural for their 1973 Convention. Mural portrays arrival of Mexican workers after the Revolution of 1910, the railroad industry in Colton, and the labor struggles organized by "La Cruz Azul".

6367 Valadez, Kathy L. What is Chicano art? A Chicano artist's concept. EL CHICANO, Vol. 7, no. 47 (April 26, 1973), p. 12-13. English.

AN: Esau Quiroz is a Chicano artist who states that Chicano art is that art by which a Chicano can be identified. He further defines Chicano art as that which contains a Chicano consciousness and portrays Chicanismo in terms of the exploitation of Chicanos.

Mural Art (cont.)

6368 Valdez, Raul. Hombre de bronce [mural].
     VILLAGER, no. 48 (April 9, 1976), p. 9.
     English.

     AN: Illustration and description of Raul
     Valdez's indoor mural HOMBRE DE BRONCE at
     Antioch Juarez-Lincoln College (Centro
     Cultural de LUCHA).

6369 Valenzuela-Crocker, Elvira. Tanguma: a man
     and his murals. AGENDA, no. 5 (Summer 1974),
     p. 14-17. English.

     AN: Illustrated report on Houston
     muralist Leo Tanguma's 1973 work REBIRTH OF
     OUR NATIONALITY as well as other murals in
     progress. Tanguma's social views and his
     debt to Mexican muralist David Alfaro
     Siqueiros are detailed.

6370 Vallejo, Armando. Murales en progreso.
     XALMAN, Vol. 3, no. 1 (Spring 1980), p.
     24-37. English.

     AN: Description of Santa Barbara,
     California's Ortega "Salazar" Park and its
     murals. Illustrated.

6371 Varda, Agnes. Mur murs/mural murals on the
     wall ... Film, Cine Tamaris, Paris, 1980.
     English.

     AN: Full length documentary film
     produced for French television; also
     available with English subtitles. Deals
     impressionistically with the murals and
     muralists of Los Angeles. Included are Wayne
     Alaniz Healy, David Botello, Willie Herron,
     Manuel Cruz, Judy Baca, the murals in
     Venice, CA, graffiti - among others. Color.

6372 Venegas, Sybil. The artists and their
     work--the role of the Chicana artist.
     CHISMEARTE, Vol. 1, no. 4 (Fall , Winter,
     1977), p. 3, 5. English.

6373 Vigil, Maria. Art bridging culture gap.
     TUCSON CITIZEN, OLD PUEBLO SECTION, (March
     22, 1979). English.

     AN: Students under tutelage of Antonio
     Pazos paint a mural at the Perfection
     Plumbing Co. in Tucson. Illustrated.

6374 Vigil, Maria. Hello, walls: Tucson's murals.
     WEEKENDER MAGAZINE, (March 29, 1980), p.
     14-16. English.

     AN: Article on muralism, from the
     Mexican to those of Chicanos. Focuses on
     Tucson murals by Roberto Borboa, Antonio
     Pazos, David Tineo and Fred Monreal. Color
     illustrations.

6375 "Viva la causa", a documentary film on the
     Mexican mural movement in Chicago. Chicago,
     IL: Kartemquin Films, [1974]. English.

     AN: Advertising brochure for a film made
     of Chicano muralist Ray Patlan working with
     young people in Chicago. The film shows
     murals in Mexico and Chicago, and follows
     one mural from its sketch to its completion.

6376 Viva Siqueiros. CON SAFOS, no. 7 (Winter
     1971), p. 26-27. English.

     AN: Brief recapitulation of the
     controversy surrounding David Alfaro
     Siqueiros' visit to Los Angeles, CA in 1932.
     It was during this visit that he painted the
     only public Siqueiros mural in the U.S.

which still remains, albeit covered over
with whitewash. The details of the visit are
explained by Siqueiros in his book: MI
RESPUESTA. The article is illustrated with
two black and white details of the mural.

6377 Wagner, Kathie and Lujan, Lori. Public
     works: beyond the city. CALIFORNIA LIVING,
     (September 28, 1975), p. 26-35. English.

     AN: Illustrative descriptive survey of
     murals in a number of northern California
     cities, excluding San Francisco. Helpful
     inclusion of mural locations and artist's
     names. Second of two-part article.

6378 Wagner, Kathie and Lujan, Lori. Public
     works: San Francisco. CALIFORNIA LIVING,
     (September 21, 1975), p. 26, 33. English.

     AN: Illustrative descriptive survey of
     San Francisco murals. Helpful inclusion of
     mural locations and artists' names. First of
     a two-part article.

6379 Walking tour and guide to the Great Wall at
     Tujunga Wash. Venice, CA: Social and Public
     Art Resource Center, [1981]. English.

     AN: History and symbolism of the GREAT
     WALL, directed by Judy Baca, and created by
     teams of young people working on the mural
     since 1976. Illustrated.

6380 Weber, John. A wall mural belongs to
     everyone. YOUTH MAGAZINE, Vol. 23, no. 9
     (September 1972), p. 58-66. English.

     AN: Illustrated article by muralist
     about Chicago street murals.

6381 Weiss, Margaret R. and Sommer, Robert.
     Camera assignment: documenting street art.
     SATURDAY REVIEW, (May 17, 1975), p. 41-43.
     English.

     AN: Interview with Robert Sommer.
     Illustrations of six murals: in Santa Fe,
     NM; Estrada Courts in Los Angeles; a John
     Weber mural in Chicago; and Cityarts mural
     in New York.

6382 Werley, Lenora. Murals give young artists
     community pride, sculptor says. YUMA DAILY
     SUN, (February 4, 1981). English.

     AN: Mesa, Arizona sculptor Adolfo
     "Zarco" Guerrero feels murals give young
     people pride in their community. Guerrero is
     part of the Xicanindio Artist Coalition that
     is CETA-contracted to run summer art
     programs for high school students.
     Illustrated.

6383 Wilson, Anne. Chicanos show off talents in
     Magna SOCIO projects. SALT LAKE CITY
     TRIBUNE, (July 9, 1979), p. C-1. English.

     AN: In the rural Utah community of
     Magna, SOCIO (Spanish Speaking Organization
     for Community Integrity and Opportunity)
     established various art projects. Three
     murals were painted by community youth under
     the guidance of Robert Archuleta and Becky
     Berru. One of the murals depicts "man and
     labor." Illustrated with photographs of
     project directors, maquette of the mural and
     a mural painting "brigade".

Mural Art (cont.)

6384 Wu, Ying Ying. Mural, mural on the Great
Wall. LOS ANGELES TIMES, (September 16,
1980), p. VI,4. English.

AN: Information on a video project
directed by John Rier to document work on
the 1700-ft. mural THE GREAT WALL OF LOS
ANGELES which depicts California history
with an emphasis on the role that minorities
had in forging that history. Three
teen-agers were trained in video production
while assisting with taping the mural
project. Simultaneously, 40 other youngsters
hired from the Summer Program for the
Employment of Disadvantaged Youth painted a
400-ft. section of the mural in 1980.
Article describes the various skills
mathematical, social and artistic developed
by youth involved in the project. The mural
was started as a Bicentennial Project in
1976 by Judy Baca for the Social and Public
Art Resources Center in Venice, California.
Illustrated with 3 photographs of various
aspects of the Project.

6385 Xap, Pablo. The wall of art. Q-VO, (August
1981). English.

AN: 1980 competition for East Los
Angeles College Library mural awarded to
East Los Streetscapers who did the three
walls totaling 51x24 feet, THE EDUCATION
SUITE - ARTE, CIENCIA Y FILOSOFIA on canvas
bonded to wall. Illustrated.

6386 Xochitiotzin, Antonia. Que viva el arte de
la Raza! GRITO DEL NORTE, Vol. 5, no. 4
(June 27, 1972), p. 1. English.

AN: Front page article on "Los Artes
Guadalupanos de Aztlan," a mural group in
Santa Fe, NM. Focus on aims and function of
organization. Illustrated with photographs
of four murals painted by group.

6387 Zahn, Debbie. Citywide murals: outlook bleak
for funding of art work by Chicanos.
FORTY-NINER, (May 4, 1976). English.

AN: The Los Angeles City Council decides
to terminate the 1974 program, Citywide
Murals, which provided funds for Chicano
artists. Description of Joe Bravo's 2000 sq
ft mural at the Wilmington Recreation
Center, painted with a team, which makes a
positive statement against gang warfare.
Illustrated.

6388 Zucker, Martin. Walls of barrio are brought
to life by street gang art. SMITHSONIAN,
Vol. 9, no. 7 (October 1978), p. 105-111.
English.

AN: Illustrated survey of East Los
Angeles murals.

6389 Zuniga, R. and Gonzalez, M. Entrevista con
los muralistas de East Austin. TEJIDOS, Vol.
5, no. 2-4 (1978), p. 128-130. Spanish.

AN: Extremely brief interview with two
Austin, TX, muralists. Includes 5 black and
white photographs of different murals.

Mural Arts and Resource Center, Los Angeles, CA

6390 Miranda, Keta. Refunding battle for mural
project. PEOPLE'S WORLD, Vol. 39, no. 20
(May 15, 1976), p. 5+. English.

AN: History of the Mural Arts and
Resource Center (Los Angeles Citywide Mural

Project) from 1974 to its imminent demise in
1976. Joe Bravo mural illustrated.

Mural Resource Center (MRC), Los Angeles, CA

6391 Citywide mural project. Los Angeles, CA:
Citywide Mural Project, n.d. [c. 1975].
English.

AN: Brochure giving history, resources
and procedures for doing a mural by the Los
Angeles Citywide Mural Project/Mural
Resource Mural Program of 1973-1974.
Illustrated. Available in Social and Public
Art Resource Center (Venice, CA) archives.

Las Muralistas del Barrio, Fresno, CA

6392 Las muralistas del barrio. CHISMEARTE, no. 2
(Winter, Spring, 1977), p. 48-49. English.

AN: Brief announcement about a Chicana
artists' organization formed in Fresno,
California which started work on a
billboard-like mural, 60x8 feet on the theme
of women. The mural received funding through
Fresno's La Brocha del Valle. About fifteen
women are involved, including Helen Gonzalez
and Cecelia Risco.

Los Muralistas Guadalupanos de Aztlan

6393 Lefebre, Francisco. El mural chicano en
Nuevo Mexico. RAYAS, Vol. 1, no. 2 (March,
April, 1978), p. 7. Spanish.

AN: Albuquerque muralist writes about
Chicano murals which derive from
pre-Columbian and modern Mexican murals. New
Mexican muralism started in 1970 with the
Muralistas Guadalupanos de Aztlan in Santa
Fe. In 1971 and 1972 students at the
Highlands University of Las Vegas, New
Mexico also painted murals. In addition,
murals have appeared in Albuquerque. Brief
biography of Lefebre. Illustrated.

MURALS OF AZTLAN: THE STREET PAINTERS OF EAST LOS [exhibit], Los Angeles, CA

6394 COMMUNITY MURALS (San Francisco, CA). (Fall
1981). English.

AN: Citywide Murals Group of Denver,
Colorado assisted the Chilean-oriented
Brigada Orlando Letelier with a mural in
their city; Carlos Sandoval of Denver doing
mural in Guerrero, Mexico; Ray Patlan of
Berkeley, California assisting with mural in
Mexico painted by Arnold Belkin's class at
the Academy of San Carlos; report on the
exhibit MURALS OF AZTLAN: THE STREET
PAINTERS OF EAST LOS with a reprint of
debate on the event by Shifra M. Goldman,
Judithe Elena Hernandez de Neikrug, and
comments by John Pitman Weber and Tim
Drescher; report on DAR LUZ mural directed
by Santa Barraza in Austin, Texas, and a new
mural in Hayward, California directed by
Enrique Romero; a mural sponsored by the
Chicano Youth Center of Fresno, California
showing the influence of Mexican calendars;
a new mural, OAKLAND'S PORTRAIT by Daniel
Galvez in Oakland, California; pro-and-con
discussion of social function of graffiti in
response to letter from Belgian source;
reprint of story on spray paint crime bill
(anti-graffiti) sponsored by California
Assemblyman Richard Alatorre. Entire issue
illustrated.

MURALS OF AZTLAN: THE STREET PAINTERS OF EAST LOS [exhibit], Los Angeles, CA (cont.)

6395 Gamboa, Harry, Jr. Los murales de Aztlan. COMUNIDAD, (June 28, 1981), p. 8-9+. Spanish.

AN: Review of the exhibit at the Craft and Folk Art Museum of Los Angeles of MURALS OF AZTLAN: THE STREET PAINTERS OF EAST LOS in which Carlos Almaraz, Gronk, Judithe Hernandez, Willie Herron, Frank Romero, John Valadez and the East Los Streetscapers (David Botello, Wayne Healy, George Yepes) painted portable murals in the gallery. The murals are described and illustrated.

6396 Goldman, Shifra M. Chicano art - looking backward. ARTWEEK, Vol. 12, no. 22 (June 20, 1981), p. 3-4. English.

AN: Review of Chicano art shows in Santa Cruz (CALIFAS) and Los Angeles (MURALS OF AZTLAN: THE STREET PAINTERS OF EAST LOS) featuring a total of 24 artists and how the shows reflect the critical crossroad at which Chicano artists presently find themselves.

6397 Hernandez, Judithe Elena and Goldman, Shifra M. Readers' forum. ARTWEEK, Vol. 12, no. 25 (August 1, 1981), p. 16. English.

AN: Critical interchange between artist Judithe Elena Hernandez de Neikrug and critic Shifra M. Goldman concerning the latter's review of MURALS OF AZTLAN exhibit.

6398 Knight, Christopher. Urban eye sites up against the wall. HERALD EXAMINER, (May 31, 1981). English.

AN: Review of the exhibit MURALS OF AZTLAN: THE STREET PAINTERS OF EAST LOS at the Craft and Folk Art Museum of Los Angeles. Illustration.

6399 Muchnic, Suzanne. Passion, paint splatter folk art museum show. LOS ANGELES TIMES, (June 25, 1981), p. VI, 1. English.

AN: Review of the MURALS OF AZTLAN: STREET PAINTERS OF EAST LOS exhibit at the Craft and Folk Art Museum in Los Angeles. The critic considered the show "revved-up, highly emotional art descended from Mexico's political muralists" that made up what it lacked in subtlety with passion, and one of the most visually exciting shows of the Museum. Illustrations.

MURALS OF EAST LOS ANGELES [film]

6400 Rivera, Humberto R. Film notes. CHISMEARTE, Vol. 1, no. 2 (Winter, Spring, 1977), p. 20-24. English.

AN: Summary of films produced by and/or about Chicanos for cinema and television. Includes REALIDADES (TV) by David Sandoval, Rudy Vargas, Luis Torres, Jose Luis Ruiz, Antonio Reyes; A POLITICAL RENAISSANCE from the LA RAZA series (TV) by Moctezuma Esparza; CHILDREN OF THE STATE by Andres Markovits, Richard Trubo, Frank Christopher (film); LA RAZA UNIDA (released as RAICES DE SANGRE) by Jesus Salvador Trevino (Mexican film by a Chicano); CHULAS FRONTERAS (film) by Les Blank; THE MURALS OF EAST LOS ANGELES, A MUSEUM WITHOUT WALLS by Humberto R. Rivera and Heather R. Howell. Announcement for the National Latino Media Coalition.

Murillo, Jesus

6401 Kreneck, Tom. With the eye of an artist: Jesus Murillo's Houston, 1927-1933. REVISTA CHICANO-RIQUENA, Vol. 8, no. 3 (Summer 1980), p. 104-105. English.

AN: Biographical sketch of Mexican-born commercial and portrait photographer who worked professionally in Texas from 1916 until his death in 1971. The illustrations concern his Houston stay.

Murillo, Patricia

6402 Galeria, Santa Ana, CA. The last Chicano art show. Exhibition brochure, 1981. English.

AN: Invitation-brochure for an exhibit of Los Angeles and Orange County artists in a gallery underwritten by the Friendly Center, Inc. with grants from local government and from businesses. Exhibiting are (Roberto) Gil de Montes, Gilbert Lujan, Judy Miranda, Patricia Murillo, Alonso Pardo, Teddy Sandoval, Mexican artist Artemio Sepulveda, Joey Terrill, Art Valenzuela, Ben Valenzuela, Linda Vallejo, Jack A. Vargas, Emigdio Vasquez, Richard Serrato, and J. William Hernandez, who is the gallery director.

6403 Mills House Visual Arts Complex, Garden Grove, CA. Menudo: artistas latinos de Orange County. Exhibit invitation, 1980. English.

AN: Invitation to an exhibit organized for the first anniversary of Artistas Latinos de Orange County including Delores Grajeda, William Hernandez, Marylee Montano, Patricia Murillo, Irene Ramos, Juan Ramos, Ricardo Serrato, Miguel Shanahan, Arthur Valenzuela, Benjamin Valenzuela, Jack Vargas, Alonzo Whitney, Emigdio Vasquez, Susana Zaccagnino, and Mexican artist Artemio Sepulveda.

6404 Newport Harbor Art Museum, Newport Beach, CA. Our own artists: art in Orange County. Exhibition catalog, 1979. English.

AN: Includes Patricia Murillo and Emigdio Vasquez with illustrations of one work each. Biographies of the artists.

6405 Orange Co. Library. El Modena Branch. Empanada: a tasty Mexican group art exhibit filled with a variety of digestable treats. Exhibition catalog, [1979]. English.

AN: Catalog of an exhibit by 15 artists: Dolores Grajeda, William Hernandez-M., Marylee Montano, Patricia Murillo, Eduardo Navarro, Susana A. Zaccagnino, Esau Quiroz, Juan Elias Ramos, Ricardo M. Serrato, Benjamin Valenzuela, Emigdio C. Vasquez, Arthur Valenzuela, Jack Vargas, Alonso Whitney, and Mexican artist Artemio Sepulveda living in Orange County. Brief profiles of the artists.

6406 Wilson, William. Artistic get-together in Orange County exhibit. CALENDAR, (November 4, 1979), p. 99. English.

AN: Review of exhibit OUR OWN ARTISTS: ART IN ORANGE COUNTY at the Newport Harbor Art Museum. Mention of Patricia Murillo and Emigdio Vasquez.

Murillo, Patricia (cont.)

6407 Woman's Building, Los Angeles, CA.
Crosspollination: a blending of traditional
and contemporary art by Asian, Black and
Chicana women. Los Angeles, CA: Woman's
Building, 1979. English.

AN: Invitation to an exhibit in which
are included Patricia Murillo and Linda
Vallejo.

Museum of International Folk Art, NM

6408 Celebrate!: the story of the Museum of
International Folk Art. Santa Fe, NM: Museum
of New Mexico Press, 1979. English.

AN: History of the Museum; its founding
in 1953 by Chicago philanthropist Florence
Dibell Bartlett; its patronage of New Mexico
Hispanic crafts as well as international
crafts.

6409 Frankenstein, Alfred. Report from New
Mexico. Needlework narrative of parish
life. ART IN AMERICA, Vol. 66, no. 5
(September, October, 1978), p. 52-55.
English.

AN: Illustrated report on the Villanueva
Tapestry: an embroidered history of a New
Mexico town by women residents, coached
through and documented by the Museum of
International Folk Art of Santa Fe.

MUSEUM WITHOUT WALLS [film]

6410 Rivera, Humberto R. Film notes. CHISMEARTE,
Vol. 1, no. 2 (Winter, Spring, 1977), p.
20-24. English.

AN: Summary of films produced by and/or
about Chicanos for cinema and television.
Includes REALIDADES (TV) by David Sandoval,
Rudy Vargas, Luis Torres, Jose Luis Ruiz,
Antonio Reyes; A POLITICAL RENAISSANCE from
the LA RAZA series (TV) by Moctezuma
Esparza; CHILDREN OF THE STATE by Andres
Markovits, Richard Trubo, Frank Christopher
(film); LA RAZA UNIDA (released as RAICES DE
SANGRE) by Jesus Salvador Trevino (Mexican
film by a Chicano); CHULAS FRONTERAS (film)
by Les Blank; THE MURALS OF EAST LOS
ANGELES, A MUSEUM WITHOUT WALLS by Humberto
R. Rivera and Heather R. Howell.
Announcement for the National Latino Media
Coalition.

Museums

6411 Alarcon, Francisco X. and Herrera, Juan
Felipe. Portraits plus struggles plus
consciousness: nine pastels by Rupert
Garcia. METAMORFOSIS, Vol. 3, no. 2 (1980),
p. 104-106. English.

AN: Reprint of article published as
"Rupert Garcia: portraits/retratos" in EL
TECOLOTE LITERARY MAGAZINE (San Francisco,
CA), Vol. 2, no. 1, March 1981, p. 6.

6412 Alarcon, Francisco X. Rupert Garcia:
portraits/retratos. EL TECOLOTE LITERARY
MAGAZINE, Vol. 2, no. 1 (March 1981), p. 6+.
Bilingual.

AN: Review of Garcia exhibit at the
Mexican Museum (S.F.) in 1981. Includes
portraits of Frida Kahlo and the Flores
Magon brothers, Goya, Van Gogh, Ethel and
Julius Rosenberg, etc. Illustrated. This
article has been reprinted in METAMORFOSIS
under a different title: "Portraits Plus

Struggles Plus Consciousness: Nine Pastels
by Rupert Garcia," Vol. 3-4, no. 1-2,
(1980-81), p. 104-106.

6413 Bellevue Art Museum, Bellevue, WA. Alfredo
Arreguin. s.n.:s.l., n.d. English.

AN: Profusely illustrated exhibition
catalog for a one-man retrospective of
paintings by Alfredo Arreguin. Exploring the
possibilities of pattern painting, the
intent of his art is to be visionary. His
paintings have affinity with Pre-Columbian
and Colonial Mexican designs and is related
to decorative emotional images of various
cultures. Includes photograph of artist and
a selected bibliography.

6414 Canavier, Elena Karina. Los Four. ARTWEEK,
Vol. 5, no. 10 (March 9, 1974), p. 1, 16.
English.

AN: Illustrated review, with detailed
description of work of the Los Four exhibit
at the Los Angeles County Museum of Art.

6415 Figoten, Sheldon. Building and painting the
figure. ARTWEEK, Vol. 12, no. 22 (June 20,
1981), p. 5-6. English.

AN: Review of eight sculptures and 25
drawings by Manuel Neri at the Redding Art
Museum. Neri was influenced as a student in
the San Francisco Bay Area in the 1950s by
abstract expressionist philosophy and
methodology, which he transferred to
sculpture. Plaster, bronze, and marble
figures are freely and loosely painted in
areas. Illustration.

6416 Frankenstein, Alfred. An artistic taste of
Mexico in the city. SAN FRANCISCO CHRONICLE,
(November 29, 1975), p. 29. English.

AN: A very favorable review of the
inaugural exhibit at the Mexican Museum. The
opening show was a panoramic view of Mexican
art including pre-Hispanic, colonial, folk
art and fine art. Among the Mexican American
artists presented were Roberto Gonzalez,
Raul Mora and Gustavo Rivera.

6417 Gamboa, Harry, Jr. Los murales de Aztlan.
COMUNIDAD, (June 28, 1981), p. 8-9+.
Spanish.

AN: Review of the exhibit at the Craft
and Folk Art Museum of Los Angeles of MURALS
OF AZTLAN: THE STREET PAINTERS OF EAST LOS
in which Carlos Almaraz, Gronk, Judithe
Hernandez, Willie Herron, Frank Romero, John
Valadez and the East Los Streetscapers
(David Botello, Wayne Healy, George Yepes)
painted portable murals in the gallery. The
murals are described and illustrated.

6418 MEXICAN MUSEUM NEWSLETTER. Vol. 6, no. 1
(Winter 1980, 1981). English.

AN: Regular report on the activities,
finances, membership, and other information
about the Museum. Announces several upcoming
shows: Rupert Garcia, six Mexican geometric
artists, paintings and prints by Mexican
American and Mexican women artists, Mexican
Leonel Maciel and Chicano Carlos Almaraz,
Mexican folk art, Manuel Neri sculpture, and
Mexican Luis Jaso.

Museums (cont.)

6419 Montoya, Jose E. Rupert Garcia and the SF
Museum of Modern Art. RAYAS, Vol. 2, no. 2
(March, April, 1979), p. 5,11. English.

AN: Commentary apropos an exhibit of
pastel drawings by Rupert Garcia at the San
Francisco Museum of Modern Art. Author
gives a capsule history of the relationship
between Raza artists and mainstream cultural
institutions. Rupert Garcia is seen as
belonging to a stalwart group of Chicano
artists.

6420 Morch, Albert. He put down his brushes for a
dream. SAN FRANCISCO SUNDAY EXAMINER AND
CHRONICLE, (October 2, 1977), p. Scene, 3.
English.

AN: Brief profile of painter Peter
Rodriguez, founder and director of the
Mexican Museum in San Francisco which opened
in 1975. On exhibit are the works of San
Francisco artist Jerry Concha. Illustrated.

6421 Penate, Luis Humberto. Crisis economica
limita accion de museo mexicano. TIEMPO
LATINO, Vol. 14, (October 21, 1981), p. 3.
Spanish.

AN: Article stresses the severe
financial limitations under which the
Mexican Museum operates. Gives reasons for
the Museum leaving the Mission district and
quotes its Director, Pedro Rodriguez, on
future goals and aspirations of the museum.

6422 Temko, Allan. Ole! It's already a triumph.
REVIEW [supplement to SAN FRANCISCO SUNDAY
EXAMINER], (December 28, 1980), p. 13-14.
English.

AN: A glowing report on the Mexican
Museum as it celebrates its fifth
anniversary. Provides details about
programs, financing and goals. Brief
analysis of the work of sculptor Manuel Neri
and painters Manuel Villamor, Gustavo
Rivera, Alfredo Arreguin and Miguel
Almaguer. Informative profile on Peter
Rodriguez, founder and Executive Director of
the Museum.

6423 Torres, Miguel. Mexican Museum - artifacts
and culture to open in S.F. EL TECOLOTE,
Vol. 6, no. 1 (October 1975), p. 4. English.

AN: On April 1972, the first
organizational meeting of a new Mexican
Museum was held. Later, a Board of Directors
was organized and fifteen months later, the
Museum was incorporated by the state of
California as a non-profit organization.
Pedro Rodriguez, founder-director of the
Museum tells his aspirations and goals for
this unique repository of Mexican culture in
the United States. Illustrated with
photograph of the Director and examples of
work from the Museum's collection.

6424 Vasquez Tagle, Jose Jorge. Museo Mexicano,
un rincon de nuestra cultura en San
Francisco, California. EL OCCIDENTAL,
(October 19, 1980). Spanish.

AN: Rotogravure with twelve colored
illustrations of works from the Mexican
Museum collections. Text is a mini catalog
of the museum's holdings and includes
information on funding sources.

Museums, Chicano

6425 Alarcon, Francisco X. El Museo Mexicano,
quinto aniversario. EL TECOLOTE LITERARY
MAGAZINE, (December 10, 1981). Spanish.

AN: Goals of the Mexican Museum in San
Francisco are contextualized within the
social nexus of the Chicano Art Movement of
the 1960s. Explains functional difference
between Mexican Museum and community art
galleries.

6426 Alarcon, Francisco X. and Herrera, Juan
Felipe. Portraits plus struggles plus
consciousness: nine pastels by Rupert
Garcia. METAMORFOSIS, Vol. 3, no. 2 (1980),
p. 104-106. English.

AN: Reprint of article published as
"Rupert Garcia: portraits/retratos" in EL
TECOLOTE LITERARY MAGAZINE (San Francisco,
CA), Vol. 2, no. 1, March 1981, p. 6.

6427 Alarcon, Francisco X. Rupert Garcia:
portraits/retratos. EL TECOLOTE LITERARY
MAGAZINE, Vol. 2, no. 1 (March 1981), p. 6+.
Bilingual.

AN: Review of Garcia exhibit at the
Mexican Museum (S.F.) in 1981. Includes
portraits of Frida Kahlo and the Flores
Magon brothers, Goya, Van Gogh, Ethel and
Julius Rosenberg, etc. Illustrated. This
article has been reprinted in METAMORFOSIS
under a different title: "Portraits Plus
Struggles Plus Consciousness: Nine Pastels
by Rupert Garcia," Vol. 3-4, no. 1-2,
(1980-81), p. 104-106.

6428 Baciu, Joyce A. and Diaz, Katherine A. Margo
Albert: a woman who gets things done = una
mujer que realiza lo que desea. CAMINOS,
Vol. 2, no. 5 (September 1981), p. 44-46.
Bilingual.

AN: Mexican-born Margo Albert is a
well-known Los Angeles, CA artist, dancer,
and actress who has been most active on
behalf of the Plaza de la Raza in East Los
Angeles. This article describes her
activities as Co-chairperson of the Los
Angeles Bicentennial Committee. For Margo,
the highlights of the celebration marking
the 200th anniversary of the founding of Los
Angeles, included a day-long Fiesta del
Bicentenario; groundbreaking ceremonies for
the Ruben Salazar Bicentennial Building; and
the reception for an official delegation of
charros, sponsored as a gift to the people
of Los Angeles by the Mexican government.

6429 Cardona, Patricia. Gana adeptos de Museo
Mexicano de San Francisco: Pedro Rodriguez.
UNO MAS UNO, (February 6, 1978), p. 18.
Spanish.

AN: Report and brief history of the
Mexican Museum which opened in 1975 with a
collection of colonial santos. The museum
offers a vista of Mexican culture to people
in the United States. Director Peter
Rodriguez says that Chicano artists Roberto
Gonzalez, Felipe Reyes, Alfredo Arreguin,
Gustavo Rivera, and Carmen Lomas Garza are
some of the best. Illustrated.

Music

6430 Arte chicano y el pueblo. COMUNIDAD, no. 41 (May 3, 1981), p. 1-15. Spanish.

AN: The whole issue of the Sunday Supplement deals with Los Angeles Chicano art and music. Works by painter Carlos Almaraz, photographer Elsa Flores, painter Yreina Cervantez, muralist and draftsman John Valadez, and a performance piece by Elsa Flores and Louie Perez are featured. Biographical information, and statements by the artists.

6431 El Centro Cultural de La Raza, San Diego, CA. Espejo del barrio-art exposition. Exhibition brochure, June 1975. English.

AN: Illustrated brochure announcement for a cultural exposition of Chicano music, art and drama. Includes some biographical information and one reproduction of painter Manuel Unzueta, woodworker Ambriz, muralist Victor Orozco Ochoa and designer/illustrator J. Armando Nunez.

6432 Cultura chicana: Los Angeles. COMUNIDAD, no. 11 (July 13, 1980), p. 1-15. Spanish.

AN: The whole issue of the Cultural Supplement concerns Chicano art and music. Captioned photographs deal with visual artists Carlos Almaraz, Jerry Dreva [not Chicano], Glugio Gronk, Willie Herron, John Valadez, Patssi Valdez, with examples of their work. With the exception of Dreva, all the artists are members of Los Four or Asco. Asco member Harry Gamboa, Jr. sums up the 1960s and 1970s and activities of artists in his essay "Seis imaginaciones: Artistas chicanos en Los Angeles." Well illustrated.

6433 Cultural department. RECOBRANDO, Vol. 1, no. 15. Spanish.

AN: The development of "Raza" culture in the Northwest and the role played by the Centro de la Raza. Mentions the "talleres de arte" set up by Carlos Contreras and Arturo Artorez, artists from Mexico who moved to Seattle in 1978. Details cultural events sponsored by the Centro in the fields of art, music, dance, and theater.

6434 Gonzalez, Victoria. Chair in the sky: Ernesto Palomino. HERE AND NOW, Vol. 2, no. 2 (Fall 1981). English.

AN: An important article tracing the artistic career of Ernie Palomino, professor of art at California State University, Fresno. Includes biographical information, formation of La Brocha Del Valle (Chicano Arts Organization), information about Palomino's film MY TRIP IN A '52 FORD and commentary on Palomino's music and artistic philosophy. Well illustrated.

6435 Guernica, Antonio Jose and Saavedra-Vela, Pilar. El Midwest Canto al pueblo: "Otra Vez, C/S". AGENDA, Vol. 7, no. 3 (May, June, 1977), p. 4-13. Bilingual.

AN: A thorough report on the various phases and events of the Midwest Canto al Pueblo in Milwaukee, Wisconsin on April 28 to May 8, 1977. The festival brought together artists, poets, musicians, and cultural workers to reaffirm, share, and celebrate the identity of La Raza with El Pueblo. Includes a thematic and iconographic overview of Chicano murals in California by Jose Montoya, and an analysis of his

sculpture by Zarco Guerrero from Meza, Arizona. Well illustrated. Includes a photograph of the collective mural painted at 5th St. and National Avenue in Milwaukee, Wisconsin during the course of the conference.

6436 Musica hispana en nuestras vidas/Hispanic music in our lives: almanaque 1982/calendar. Milwaukee, WI: Miller Brewing Co., 1981. English.

AN: Twelve Latino artists were commissioned to illustrate a calendar with paintings on Hispanic music. The Chicano artists include Frederico Vigil (New Mexico), Joe Bastida Rodriguez (Texas/Washington, D.C.), Manuel Martinez (Colorado), Jose Antonio Burciaga (California), Ignacio Gomez (California), Carolina Flores (Texas), Frank Martinez (California). Color.

6437 Public invited to weekend fiesta at Lincoln High. LOS ANGELES TIMES, (April 29, 1969), p. II. English.

AN: Fiesta of art, music, dance and literature organized by the committee formed after the East Los Angeles high school "blowouts" to press for better and more relevant education. Hundreds of works of art were collected for display at the "Fiesta de los Barrios".

Narezo, Jose Luis

6438 59th Street Gallery, St. Louis, MO. Midwest Mexican-American art exhibit: Mexico and its artists. Exhibition brochure, 1981. English.

AN: Sponsored by the Sociedad Mexicana "Benito Juarez" and the international Institute of St. Louis, this three-part exhibit includes 1) MEXICO AS SEEN BY HER CHILDREN, a bilingual exhibit from Mexico traveling under Smithsonian Institution auspices, 2) MEXICAN CHILDREN IN THE U.S.A., 3) MEXICAN AMERICAN ARTISTS. In the latter are included Stephen Capiz (Roseville, Minn.), Jose Gonzalez (Chicago), Cesar A. Martinez (San Antonio), Ada Medina (Des Moines), Nora Chapa Mendoza (West Bloomfield, Mich.), Rene David Michel-Trapaga (St. Louis), David Munoz (Kansas City, Mo.), Jose Luis Narezo (Grand Rapids, Mich.), Benny Ordonez, Roman Villarreal (Chicago), Alejandro Romero (Chicago), Aurelio Diaz "Tekpankalli" (Chicago), Simon Ybarra (St. Louis).

6439 Arts Council Center for the Arts of Greater Lansing, Lansing, MI. Raza fine arts festival. Festival program, 1978. English.

AN: This festival program mentions Jose Narezo's mural at the Holland National Guard Armory, Grand Rapids; includes a statement of the Raza Art/Media Collective, Inc.; the philosophy of artists Zaragosa Vargas and S. Kaneta Kosiba-Vargas; and profiles of exhibiting artists George Vargas, Martin Moreno, Hector Perez, Michael L. Selley, Jesse Gonzales, Nora Chapa Mendoza, Jesse Soriano, Jose Luis Narezo.

Narezo, Jose Luis (cont.)

6440 El calendario hispano de Michigan, 1981.
Stanton, MI: Montcalm Intermediate School
District and Nuestras Artes de Michigan,
1981. English.

AN: Months of historical calendar
illustrated with art works by George Vargas,
Nora Chapa Mendoza, Jesse Gonzalez, Julio
Perazza(Puerto Rican), Hector Valdez, Pamela
M. Gonzalez, Isabell Escojico (7-year-old
child), Jose Narezo, Martin Moreno, Laurie
Mendoza Psarianos, Rosa Maria Arenas.

6441 Grand Rapids Art Museum, Grand Rapids, MI.
Jose Narezo: paintings on paper. Exhibition
announcement, 1979. English.

AN: Announcement of an exhibit of
paintings by Michigan abstractionist Jose
Narezo. Illustrated.

6442 Grand Rapids Jr. College, MI. Dedication "El
Centro de Vida". Brochure, 1977. English.

AN: Brochure announcing unveiling of a
mural by painter Jose Narezo working with a
team of young people.

6443 Lansing Community College, Lansing, MI.
Festival! Festival program, [1978]. English.

AN: Program of a festival which includes
an Hispanic Arts Exhibit, including Juan
Ortega, Nora Mendoza, Jose Luis Narezo, and
Brazilian-born Veronica Dalia de
Albuquerque.

6444 Latin American council bicentennial mural.
Exhibition brochure, [1976]. English.

AN: Brochure giving history and
iconography of a 8 x 16 foot portable mural
by Grand Rapids, Mich. artist Jose Narezo
with a team of students. The mural honors
North and South American revolutionaries
with portraits of George Washington, Jose
Marti, Eugenio Maria de Hostos, and Benito
Juarez.

Nario, Jose

6445 Calendario de March: 1977. Chicago, IL:
MARCH, Inc., 1976. English.

AN: Historical calendar with photos and
biographies of artists. Illustrations of
artwork by Ray Patlan, Jose Nario, Frank J.
Sanchez, Salvador Dominguez, Salvador Vega,
Marguerite Ortega, Aurelio Diaz, Carlos
Cortez, Mario E. Castillo, Francisco Blasco,
Rey Vasquez, and Efrain Martinez. History of
MARCH (Movimiento Artistico Chicano).

6446 Cockcroft, Eva; Weber, John; and Cockcroft,
James D. Towards a people's art: the
contemporary mural movement. New York: E.P.
Dutton, 1977. English.

AN: A survey of the street mural
movement in the United States, from about
1967 on. Several chapters are written by the
artists themselves: John Weber on the
Chicago mural group; Susan Shapiro-Kiok on
Cityarts Workshop of New York; Eva Cockcroft
on People's painters of New Jersey; Geronimo
Garduno on Artes Guadalupanos de Aztlan of
New Mexico. Chicano murals illustrated
include those of Mujeres Muralistas, Ray
Patlan, William F. Herron, Hoyo-Mara Gang,
Artes Guadalupanos de Aztlan, Vicente
Mendoza and Jose Nario (with Patlan) Mario
Castillo, Michael Rios, Toltecas en Aztlan,

Roberto Chavez, Ernie Palomino, Chuy
Campusano and Luis Cortazar (with Rios).

National Endowment for the Arts

6447 CHICANO CINEMA NEWSLETTER. Vol. 1, no. 1
(December 1978). English.

AN: Reports on activities of Chicano
filmmakers in producing films, meeting with
organizations like the American Film
Institute, the Hispanic Task Force of the
National Endowment for the Arts, the WNET
Independent Documentary Film Fund.
International film news also included.

6448 Gonzales, Juan. Regional report, The arts:
"Our people deserve the best". NUESTRO, Vol.
1, no. 2 (May 1977), p. 56-57. English.

AN: Activities of San Francisco's
Galeria de la Raza; interviews with its
directors, Rene Yanez and Ralph Maradiaga.
Reprinted as "Galeria de la Raza: our people
deserve the best" in EL TECOLOTE (San
Francisco, CA), Vol. 7, no. 11 (July, 1977),
p. 14.

6449 Gustaitis, Rasa. Arts imperiled. PEOPLE'S
WORLD, Vol. 44, no. 26 (June 27, 1981), p.
10. English.

AN: A decade ago the San Francisco
Neighborhood Arts Program received new
commitments from the National Endowment for
the Arts to fund local, unknown and
chronically poor neighborhood artists. With
these funds, murals were painted on the
walls and other art events were created with
young people, minorities, old people. This
program piloted the Expansion Arts Program
of NEA. These funds are now being cut,
especially with the Reagan administration's
proposed cuts for 1981 and 1982.

6450 Holliday-Abbott, Anne. Suitcase is 2nd home
for arts liaison. ARIZONA DAILY STAR, (June
18, 1981), p. H-3. English.

AN: Arizona artist Louis LeRoy who
paints, makes prints, and does assemblage is
also a regional representative for the
National Endowment for the Arts in Arizona,
New Mexico, Colorado, Utah, and Wyoming.
LeRoy has always been an "advocate of people
being proud of their ethnic backgrounds." He
feels artists can be self-supporting without
commercializing.

National Hispanic Heritage Week

6451 Gala evening at OAS. NUESTRO, Vol. 5, no. 7
(October 1981), p. 21. English.

AN: Brief description of "Salute to
Hispanic Arts" held as part of Hispanic
Heritage Week festivities in Washington,
D.C. Special guest at the affair was Amado
Pena who was there to be recognized and to
unveil his work LA FAMILIA which was used on
the posters announcing Hispanic Heritage
Week nationwide.

National Hispanic Heritage Week (cont.)

6452 Work of Southwest artist sings to soul,
heart. NUESTRO, Vol. 5, no. 7 (October
1981), p. 57-61. English.

AN: Brief profile of Laredo-born Texas
artist Amado Pena who designed the first
commemorative poster for the Congressional
Hispanic Caucus' observance of National
Hispanic Heritage Week. The poster is
reproduced on the cover. The article
includes full-color illustrations.

National Latino Media Coalition (NLMC)

6453 Rivera, Humberto R. Film notes. CHISMEARTE,
Vol. 1, no. 2 (Winter, Spring, 1977), p.
20-24. English.

AN: Summary of films produced by and/or
about Chicanos for cinema and television.
Includes REALIDADES (TV) by David Sandoval,
Rudy Vargas, Luis Torres, Jose Luis Ruiz,
Antonio Reyes; A POLITICAL RENAISSANCE from
the LA RAZA series (TV) by Moctezuma
Esparza; CHILDREN OF THE STATE by Andres
Markovits, Richard Trubo, Frank Christopher
(film); LA RAZA UNIDA (released as RAICES DE
SANGRE) by Jesus Salvador Trevino (Mexican
film by a Chicano); CHULAS FRONTERAS (film)
by Les Blank; THE MURALS OF EAST LOS
ANGELES, A MUSEUM WITHOUT WALLS by Humberto
R. Rivera and Heather R. Howell.
Announcement for the National Latino Media
Coalition.

National Task Force of Hispanic American Art

6454 Ariav, Al. Hispanics' work ignored, artist
says. ARIZONA DAILY STAR, (June 3, 1978).
English.

AN: Hispanic-Americans in Tucson have no
gallery, little access to museums, and no
recognition for their work, says Roberto
Borboa, artist and cultural organizer. He
welcomes the National Task Force of Hispanic
American art which visited Tucson.

National Women's Conference, Houston, TX, November, 1977

6455 Quesada-Weiner, Rosemary. Las mujeres: 1977
National Women's Conference. Los Angeles,
CA: Rosemary Quesada-Weiner, 1978. English.

AN: Portfolio (with captions) of
photographs taken by Quesada-Weiner.

Native Americans

6456 Amado Maurilio Pena, Jr. PAPEL CHICANO, Vol.
1, no. 13 (July 21, 1978). Spanish.

AN: Includes the artist's resume, an
exhibition list, and a gallery statement
situating the work of Pena within both
Native American and Chicano art traditions.
Includes reproduction of four works.

6457 Anaya, Rudolfo A. and Ortiz, Simon J.
1680-1980: a ceremony of brotherhood.
Albuquerque, NM: Academic, 1981. English.

AN: A cooperative publication by members
of the former La Academia de la Nueva Raza
(1969-1976) formed of writers and artists,
and the Tri-Centennial Commission of the
All-Indian Pueblo Council. Includes writings
and artworks by Chicanos and Indians from
New Mexico, California, Texas, and Arizona.
Chicano artists works included are by Ellen
Arellano, Juan Estevan Arellano, Alberto
Baros, Jose Antonio Burciaga, Juan Reyes
Cervantes, Rudy Cuellar, Ricardo Favela, El
Zarco Guerrero, Luis Jimenez, Jr., Carlos
Quinto Kemm, Alejandro Lopez, Floyd Lujan,
Jose Montoya, Juanishi Orozco, Leo Romero,
Secundino Sandoval, Jaime Valdez, Maria
Varela, Esteban Villa.

6458 Chicano pride theme of mural. EL DIARIO DE
LA GENTE, Vol. 2, no. 11 (January 25, 1974).
English.

AN: Commentary on the 11x15 ft. mural
painted by Carlos Rosas outside the entrance
to the Tabor Inn in University Memorial
Center. Mural composed of Indio-Chicano
symbols.

6459 CJL. Artist profile-Amado Pena. FOUR WINDS,
Vol. 1, no. 4 (1980), p. 10. English.

AN: Amado Pena works within the
expectations of an American Indian artist,
but also within the context of the Mexican
American culture. The article treats Pena's
artistic trajectory and provides
biographical information. Illustrated with
photograph of the artist and reproductions
of one lithograph and one mixed-media
drawing.

6460 Drescher, Tim and Garcia, Rupert. Recent
Raza murals in the U.S. RADICAL AMERICA,
Vol. 12, no. 2 (March, April, 1978), p.
14-31. English.

AN: Like the cultural revolution of
Mexico in the 1920s, La Raza of Aztlan
emphasizes the Native American and mestizo
heritage as well as the Mexican
revolutionary heritage. Witha a social
context, the authors discuss Chicano and
Latino murals nationally. Iconography and
its relation to Chicano experience is
explored, as well as images by and about
women. Illustrations.

6461 Guerrero, Adolfo "El Zarco". The new vision
of Xicanindio art. RAYAS, Vol. 2, no. 1
(January, February, 1979), p. 3. Bilingual.

AN: Zarco Guerrero explains his personal
artistic philosophy that unites Amerindian
concepts of art to contemporary art forms,
especially in sculpture. For Guerrero, "the
Chicano artist is making a monumental effort
to arrive at a new universal language and to
create a new meaning of community through
art.

6462 Harper, Hilliard. Native Americans stand
tall again as Balboa Park mural takes shape.
LOS ANGELES TIMES [San Diego County
edition], (March 2, 1981), p. II, 5.
English.

AN: Victor Ochoa paints the figure of
Geronimo on the wall of San Diego's Balboa
Park Centro Cultural de la Raza to replace a
skeletal calavera figure disturbing patients
at a hospital across the street. The central
figure is part of a planned 70 x 18 foot
mural promoting Mexican, Chicano and Indian
art. Activities at the Centro are described.
Illustrated.

Native Americans (cont.)

6463 Hennessey, Kathy. Amado Pena, Chicano
     artist. REVISTA RIO BRAVO, no. 1 (Fall
     1980), p. 2+. English.

     AN: Review of the life and art of
     Laredo-born artist Pena whose early work in
     the 1960s was abstracted figures in bright
     colors; in the 1970s his work became
     political commentary for the Chicano
     movement; most recently he is doing
     paintings and silkscreens about New Mexican
     Indian life. As a teacher he influenced many
     students, especially in Anderson High School
     (Austin). Illustrations throughout the
     issue.

6464 Institute of American Indian Arts Museum,
     Santa Fe, NM. Native American/Hispanic
     festival, contemporary & historic visions.
     Santa Fe, NM: Institute of American Indian
     Arts Museum, 1981. English.

     AN: Catalog for exhibit co-sponsored by
     La Cofradia de Artes y Artesanos Hispanicos,
     the Institute of American Indian Arts, and
     the Santa Fe Council for the Arts. Exhibit
     stresses the inter-relationship between the
     Indian and Hispano peoples of New Mexico. 31
     contemporary Hispano artists included.
     Illustrated.

6465 Le Page, David. He was pioneer in permanent
     Indian sand paintings: artist found his
     niche by returning to his roots. LOS ANGELES
     TIMES [San Gabriel Valley edition], (April
     26, 1981), p. IX,1,11. English.

     AN: David Villasenor learned crafts from
     Indian students at school he attended in
     Sonora, after his family moved to the U.S.
     in 1929. He was brought to Santa Fe, New
     Mexico at 16 to teach boyscouts
     wood-carving. He perfected a method for
     gluing Indian-influenced sand paintings to a
     surface, and has made many for museums. Well
     illustrated.

6466 Parr, June. Amado Maurilio Pena, Jr.: a
     talented and dedicated artist. ARRIBA,
     (October 1980), p. 1. English.

     AN: Pena is represented in forty-two
     galleries internationally. Recently, Pena
     opened his studio and gallery, El Taller, in
     Austin. His latest works focus on the Indian
     heritage and are based on trips to New
     Mexico. Illustrated.

6467 Pena, Amado Maurilio, Jr. Amado Maurilio
     Pena, Jr. Brochure [1980]. English.

     AN: Promotional brochure including a
     biographical profile of the artist, a list
     of representing galleries throughout the
     United States, and eight good quality
     reproductions of serigraphs and mixed media
     drawings, six in color, on the theme of New
     Mexican Pueblo Indians.

6468 Villasenor, David and Villasenor, Jean. How
     to do permanent sand painting. Glendora, CA:
     David and Jean Villasenor, 1972. English.

     AN: A how-to book with techniques,
     examples, and explanations of Indian motifs
     by David Villasenor who has made a career of
     producing sand paintings for museums and
     other clients. Color and black and white
     illustrations.

6469 Weegar, Sally. Native Mexican images. DAILY
     TEXAN, (October 23, 1978), p. 16. English.

     AN: Review of an exhibit of watercolors,
     tiles, and silkscreen prints by Amado Pena
     at the Wagner Gallery in Austin. Earlier
     work of Laredo-born Pena were politically
     oriented toward La Raza. Recent work
     concentrates on New Mexican landscape and
     Indian peoples. Illustrated.

Native Americans, Images of

6470 Carraro, Francine. Refined rhythmic
     references: Amado Pena, Jr. SOUTHWEST ART,
     Vol. 9, no. 6 (November 1979), p. 70-75.
     English.

     AN: Well-illustrated (including 4 color)
     story on Austin silkscreen artist Amado M.
     Pena. Features his recent stylized work
     based on New Mexican indian motifs.

Nava, Julian

6471 Chairez, Bob. Bob's Chicano chronicles:
     putting the pieces back together=pegando las
     piezas otra vez [drawing]. CAMINOS, Vol. 1,
     no. 2 (April 1980), p. 46. Bilingual.

Navarrete, Juan

6472 El centro cultural y museo del barrio,
     history and activities. Taos, NM: El Centro
     Cultural y Museo del Barrio, n.d.. English.

     AN: Photo-copied history of the New
     Mexico organization which is a centro and
     museo "without walls" begun in 1973. Founded
     by Juan and Patricia Navarrete, it
     collaborates with established museums for
     community art events.

Navarrete, Patricia

6473 El centro cultural y museo del barrio,
     history and activities. Taos, NM: El Centro
     Cultural y Museo del Barrio, n.d.. English.

     AN: Photo-copied history of the New
     Mexico organization which is a centro and
     museo "without walls" begun in 1973. Founded
     by Juan and Patricia Navarrete, it
     collaborates with established museums for
     community art events.

Navarro, Eduardo

6474 Orange Co. Library. El Modena Branch.
     Empanada: a tasty Mexican group art exhibit
     filled with a variety of digestable treats.
     Exhibition catalog, [1979]. English.

     AN: Catalog of an exhibit by 15 artists:
     Dolores Grajeda, William Hernandez-M.,
     Marylee Montano, Patricia Murillo, Eduardo
     Navarro, Susana A. Zaccagnino, Esau Quiroz,
     Juan Elias Ramos, Ricardo M. Serrato,
     Benjamin Valenzuela, Emigdio C. Vasquez,
     Arthur Valenzuela, Jack Vargas, Alonso
     Whitney, and Mexican artist Artemio
     Sepulveda living in Orange County. Brief
     profiles of the artists.

6475 Santa Ana Public Library, Newhope Branch,
     Santa Ana, CA. Artistas latinos de Orange
     County. Exhibition brochure, 1979. English.

     AN: Exhibit of six artists: Dolores
     Grajeda, Eduardo Navarro, Arthur Valenzuela,
     Benjamin Valenzuela, Emigdio Vasquez, Susana
     A. Zaccagnino.

Navarro, Fernando

6476 The First Unitarian Universalist Church, Paradise Valley, AZ. Five Chicano artists. Exhibition brochure, 1971. English.

AN: Exhibit organized by L. Eugene Grigsby, Jr., Art Department of Arizona State University, Tempe, AZ. 21 works by Eugene Quesada, David Nunez, Fernando Navarro, Luis Baiz (of Arizona) and Saul Solache (of Los Angeles). Brief biographies of the artists.

Nebraska

6477 Edward Chavez: sculptor-painter. LA LUZ, Vol. 2, no. 2 (May 1973), p. 28-31. English.

AN: Lavishly illustrated biographical account of Edward Chavez. Born in Ocate, New Mexico in 1917, Chavez has a distinguished career as a painter and sculptor. During the 1940's he executed a number of murals under sponsorship of various government art projects. These murals were placed in public buildings in Nebraska, Colorado and Wyoming. Although living and working in New York most of his adult life, the work of Edward Chavez has always been influenced by the Southwest.

Negron, David

6478 Nevarez, Joe R. Chicano art blooms in barrio warehouse. LOS ANGELES TIMES, (December 26, 1974), p. I, 32. English.

AN: Former meat packing warehouse transformed into Goez Art Studios by Joe and John Gonzalez. Exhibiting David Negron, Eddie Martinez, David Lopez (Hollywood scenic artists) and Roberto Arenivar. Lists activities of the gallery: exhibits, murals, restoration.

Neri, Manuel

6479 Albright, Thomas. Forceful masterpieces from Manuel Neri. SAN FRANCISCO CHRONICLE, (May 17, 1979), p. 47. English.

AN: A rave review of Neri's one-person sculpture show at the Paula Anglum Gallery.

6480 Albright, Thomas. Manuel Neri's survivors: sculpture for the age of anxiety. ART NEWS MAGAZINE, Vol. 80, no. 1 (January 1981), p. 54-59. English.

AN: Critical evaluation of Neri's development as a sculptor in the figurative tradition. Biographical information and placement of artist within California art and international tendencies.

6481 Albright, Thomas. San Francisco: sleepers and spectacles [Manuel Neri exhibit review]. ART NEWS MAGAZINE, Vol. 78, no. 7 (September 1979), p. 118. English.

AN: Review of an exhibit at the Paula Anglum Gallery of San Francisco by Manuel Neri who has been developing over the last twenty years into one of the country's most profound and compelling sculptors. These pieces are life-sized plaster figures of nude female models.

6482 Charles Cowles Gallery. Manuel Neri. New York: Charles Cowles Gallery, 1981. English.

AN: Brochure for one-person show with two color photographs of Neri's sculpture.

Exhibition chronology and bibliography.

6483 Dickson, Joanne. Manuel Neri. El Cajon, CA: Grossmont College Gallery, 1980. English.

AN: Essay documents Neri's career and situates him within the Bay Area figurative style. As a sculptor, the artist has worked in plaster or bronze, cast paper, fiberglass and more recently in marble.

6484 Dunham, Judith L. Manuel Neri: life with the figure. ARTWEEK, Vol. 7, no. 39 (November 13, 1976), p. 1+. English.

AN: Favorable review of Neri's exhibition of more than 80 figures or fragments of figures at the Oakland Museum. Explores relationship of Neri's sculpture with developments in Bay Area figurative painting and expressionism. Inventories Neri's thematic and material concerns. Analysis of his work in plaster, bronze and fiberglass. An important assessment of Neri's contribution to Bay Area art.

6485 Figoten, Sheldon. Building and painting the figure. ARTWEEK, Vol. 12, no. 22 (June 20, 1981), p. 5-6. English.

AN: Review of eight sculptures and 25 drawings by Manuel Neri at the Redding Art Museum. Neri was influenced as a student in the San Francisco Bay Area in the 1950s by abstract expressionist philosophy and methodology, which he transferred to sculpture. Plaster, bronze, and marble figures are freely and loosely painted in areas. Illustration.

6486 MEXICAN MUSEUM NEWSLETTER. Vol. 6, no. 1 (Winter 1980, 1981). English.

AN: Regular report on the activities, finances, membership, and other information about the Museum. Announces several upcoming shows: Rupert Garcia, six Mexican geometric artists, paintings and prints by Mexican American and Mexican women artists, Mexican Leonel Maciel and Chicano Carlos Almaraz, Mexican folk art, Manuel Neri sculpture, and Mexican Luis Jaso.

6487 The Mexican Museum, San Francisco, CA. Manuel Neri: sculpture and drawings. Exhibition invitation, 1981. English.

AN: Illustrated invitation to an exhibit.

6488 Neri, Manuel. Untitled standing figure no. 4 [sculpture]. PEOPLE'S WORLD, Vol. 44, no. 19 (May 9, 1981), p. 10. English.

AN: Illustration of a painted bronze figure by San Francisco Bay artist Manuel Neri. Drawings and sculpture by Neri to be shown at the Mexican Museum.

Neri, Manuel (cont.)

6489 Plagens, Peter. Sunshine muse: contemporary art on the West Coast. New York: Praeger, 1974. English.

AN: Despite his rather "chic" art critical prose and mainstream orientation, Plagen's book is an important compendium of arts and cultural activities on the West Coast, primarily California. Gives the history of important artists, movements, and art schools. These set the institutional framework for the education of Chicano artists from the 1950s on. Manuel Neri discussed (p. 89, 94, 99) and illustrated (p. 92).

6490 Seattle Art Museum, Seattle, WA and Dickson, Joanne. Manuel Neri, sculpture and drawings. Exhibition catalog, 1981. English.

AN: Beautifully illustrated catalog. Text by Joanne Dickson from Oakland California, biography and very complete chronology of Neri exhibitions.

6491 Temko, Allan. Ole! It's already a triumph. REVIEW [supplement to SAN FRANCISCO SUNDAY EXAMINER], (December 28, 1980), p. 13-14. English.

AN: A glowing report on the Mexican Museum as it celebrates its fifth anniversary. Provides details about programs, financing and goals. Brief analysis of the work of sculptor Manuel Neri and painters Manuel Villamor, Gustavo Rivera, Alfredo Arreguin and Miguel Almaguer. Informative profile on Peter Rodriguez, founder and Executive Director of the Museum.

Neuman, Osha

6492 Erickson, Barbara. La Pena's new face. NORTH EAST BAY INDEPENDENT, no. 4 (September 5, 1978), p. 11. English.

AN: Illustrated story on the relief mural SONG OF UNITY by Ray Patlan, O'Brien Thiele, Osha Neumann, and Anna de Leon on the facade of La Pena cultural center in Berkeley, California. Chilean songwriter Victor Jara and the music of North and South America are the motifs.

6493 New radical wall art. PEOPLE'S WORLD, Vol. 41, no. 37 (September 16, 1978), p. 10. English.

AN: Illustrated story and explanation of the imagery on the new mural resulting from a collaboration of Commonarts and La Pena Cultural Center. The artists are Ray Patlan, O'Brien Thiele, Osha Neumann, and Anna de Leon.

New Detroit Art Council

6494 Acosta, Dan. Paintings reflect life experiences. THE ECCENTRIC, (June 26, 1980). English.

AN: Review of one-woman show by Nora Chapa Mendoza at the Heritage Art Gallery, Ypsilanti, MI. Mendoza works in abstract impressionist style with wet streams of colors that express energy. Her subjects are landscapes, moods, nudes, and Hispanic themes. She is active in the Detroit Latino Artist Association, Nuestras Artes de Michigan, and the New Detroit Art Council.

NEW FACADE [mural]

6495 Sorell, Victor A. Barrio murals in Chicago: painting the Hispanic-American experience on "our community" walls. REVISTA CHICANO-RIQUENA, Vol. 4, no. 4 (Fall 1976), p. 51-72. English.

AN: Important survey of Chicago's Latino murals, with key works considered in detail. Among the Chicano art organizations and muralists mentioned are MARCH (Movimiento Artistico Chicano), and Yolanda Galvan, Juanita Jaramillo, Jose Nario, Raymond Patlan, Vicente Mendoza, Marcos Raya, Ricardo Alonzo, Jose G. Gonzalez and Mario Castillo, author of the earliest Latino mural in Chicago (1968). Puerto Rican and non-Latino muralists and mural groups are also discussed. Well illustrated.

New Mexico

6496 Ahlborn, Richard E. The Penitente Moradas of Abiquiu. Washington, D.C.: Smithsonian Institution Press, 1968 (Contributions from the Museum of History and Technology, Paper 63). English.

AN: The history and organization of the Penitente Brotherhood. Detailed analysis of the architecture of Penitente moradas and the artifacts within them. Illustrated with many ethnographic photographs.

6497 Artist registry financed. RIO GRANDE SUN, (January 17, 1980). English.

AN: A $15,000 grant received from the National Endowment for the Arts to begin a New Mexico Hispanic Arts Community Outreach project, which will include a central registry of New Mexico Hispanic artists with current resume, documentation of work, and other information. In charge will be artists Estevan Arellano, Albert Baros, and Susan Jamison of the Santa Fe Council for the Arts.

6498 Barnett, Alan. Southern journey. NATIONAL MURALS NETWORK COMMUNITY NEWSLETTER, (Fall 1980), p. 22-32. English.

AN: Rather gossipy account of murals seen in a swing of the southern United States. Includes the work of dozens of artists and arts groups from California, Arizona, New Mexico, Texas, and Colorado.

6499 Bendau, Clifford P. Preserving an ancient craft. MS.MAGAZINE, Vol. 9, no. 11 (May 1981), p. 26. English.

AN: 40-year-old native Taos, NM resident Anita Otilia Rodriguez travels the Southwest as a professional enjarradora building homes and fireplaces from earth and straw. Article discusses the history of adobe construction, Rodriguez's innovations with the ancient technique. Illustrated.

6500 Blue Sky Productions. Los santeros. Color film, 29 min., 1979. English.

AN: A 29 minute color film produced with funding assistance from New Mexico Highlands University and the National Endowment for the Arts. Features santeros Luis Tapia, Orlando Romero, Horacio Valdez.

New Mexico (cont.)

6501 Briggs, Charles L. The wood carvers of
     Cordova, New Mexico: social dimensions of an
     artistic "revival". Knoxville, TN:
     University of Tennessee Press, 1980.
     English.

     AN: One of the few books that deals with
     the traditional and contemporary-traditional
     religious art of New Mexico within social
     context. The author explores the influence
     of Anglo patronage and tourism on the
     meaning, aesthetics and distribution of the
     santos, and non-religious carving of the
     town of Cordoba.

6502 Callum, Diane. Regional report, The arts:
     walls of passion. NUESTRO, Vol. 3, no. 11
     (December 1979), p. 16, 51. English.

     AN: Focusing on muralist Gilberto
     Guzman, one of the founders of Artes
     Guadalupanos in Santa Fe, the article
     details his efforts in the promotion and
     preservation of Chicano murals in New
     Mexico.

6503 Celebrate!: the story of the Museum of
     International Folk Art. Santa Fe, NM: Museum
     of New Mexico Press, 1979. English.

     AN: History of the Museum; its founding
     in 1953 by Chicago philanthropist Florence
     Dibell Bartlett; its patronage of New Mexico
     Hispanic crafts as well as international
     crafts.

6504 Chicano exhibit set. SANTA FE NEW MEXICAN,
     (September 22, 1972), p. A4. English.

     AN: A Chicano art show organized by El
     Instituto Chicano de Artes y Artesanias of
     San Antonio, TX is scheduled for Highlands
     University Gallery, Las Vegas, NM.

6505 La Cofradia de Artes y Artesanos Hispanicos
     and Santa Fe Council for the Arts. El
     festival hispanico. Festival program, [ca.
     1979]. English.

     AN: Program for the festival which
     included over 70 visual artists from
     northern New Mexico selected and hung by the
     Cofradia at the Armory for the Arts gallery
     in Santa Fe. The poster for the festival,
     reproduced on the program cover, is taken
     from a painting by Gilberto Guzman. The
     festival also featured music, cuentos,
     dance, slide show, poetry, films.

6506 Corazon del norte: wood carving. GRITO DEL
     NORTE, Vol. 2, no. 5 (March 28, 1969), p.
     11. English.

     AN: Focus on the Aguilar family, folk
     artists from Los Ojos (Parkview), northern
     New Mexico. Sr. Cruz Aguilar is a sculptor
     and furniture maker, his 80-year-old mother
     Dona Cresanta Cruz is a quilter. Illustrated
     with photographs of the Aguilars and
     examples of their work.

6507 De Cordova, Lorenzo. Echoes of the flute.
     Santa Fe, NM: Ancient City Press, 1972.
     English.

     AN: First person reminiscences on
     Penitente traditions in northern New Mexico
     at the turn of the century. Reprints two
     Works progress Administration (WPA)
     manuscripts: "Lent in Cordoba" (n.d.) and
     "The Wake" (1937). Illustrated with drawings
     by Eliseo Rodriguez. Notes by Marta Weigle.

6508 Diaz, Katherine A. Murals of New Mexico.
     CAMINOS, Vol. 2, no. 5 (October 1981), p.
     9-10. English.

     AN: Illustrations of murals in Santa Fe
     and Albuquerque by Gilberto Guzman,
     Francisco Le Fevere[sic; Lefebre], Manuel
     Unzueta, and Fernando Penalosa.

6509 Fabricant, Don. Show reveals Hispanic art.
     NEW MEXICAN WEEKEND, (June 1, 1979).
     English.

     AN: Review of two exhibits in Santa Fe:
     EL FESTIVAL HISPANICO, mounted by La
     Cofradia de Artes y Artesanos Hispanicos and
     Gilberto Guzman at the Black Kachina
     Gallery. The reviewer feels the
     traditional-style woodcarving done by
     contemporaries is the strongest part of the
     show; works that break with these forms seem
     weaker, less skillful and cliche-ridden.
     Crafts are excellent. Muralist Guzman has
     blossomed in murals and easel paintings
     since he was employed by the 1978 Art in
     Public Places project. His work is intense
     and expressive, sometimes erotic.
     Illustration of work by sculptor Ruben
     Montoya.

6510 'Festival of arts' planned by Arthritis
     Foundation. SANTA FE NEW MEXICAN, (October
     11, 1972), p. B6. English.

     AN: The Albuquerque Arthritis Foundation
     has invited professional artists and
     craftsmen from New Mexico to display their
     paintings, watercolors, sculpture, prints,
     lithographs, jewelry. Joel Ramirez's
     painting THE WEAVERS is selected for full
     color art prints. Illustrated.

6511 Frankenstein, Alfred. Report from New
     Mexico. Needlework narrative of parish
     life. ART IN AMERICA, Vol. 66, no. 5
     (September, October, 1978), p. 52-55.
     English.

     AN: Illustrated report on the Villanueva
     Tapestry: an embroidered history of a New
     Mexico town by women residents, coached
     through and documented by the Museum of
     International Folk Art of Santa Fe.

6512 From the barrios. OBSERVER, (September 23,
     1979), p. 16+. English.

     AN: Short story on Gilberto Guzman from
     Santa Fe, New Mexico, announcing an exhibit
     of his work in the October Gallery, London.
     Two color reproductions of his paintings.

6513 Garcia-Camarillo, Cecilio and Martinez,
     Dennis. Platicando con Dennis Martinez.
     RAYAS, Vol. 1, no. 5 (September, October,
     1978), p. 12, 11. Bilingual.

     AN: Interview with Dennis Martinez,
     illustrator of BLESS ME ULTIMA, NAMBE: YEAR
     ONE, and MI ABUELA FUMABA PUROS. The books
     share New Mexican setting and their
     illustrator seeks to capture the essence of
     the landscape in that region. In his
     drawings Dennis Martinez hopes to evoke
     history in relation to landscape and
     culture. Illustrated.

New Mexico (cont.)

6514 Guadalupe Historic Foundation, Santa Fe, NM.
Artes en la primavera. (1981). English.

AN: Catalog of exhibit by four New
Mexico artists: Manuel Lopez, sculptor from
Chili; Andres Martinez, painter from Santa
Cruz; Victoria Lopez, colcha embroiderer
from San Pedro; Sam Quintana, jeweler from
La Mesilla.

6515 Hennessey, Kathy. Amado Pena, Chicano
artist. REVISTA RIO BRAVO, no. 1 (Fall
1980), p. 2+. English.

AN: Review of the life and art of
Laredo-born artist Pena whose early work in
the 1960s was abstracted figures in bright
colors; in the 1970s his work became
political commentary for the Chicano
movement; most recently he is doing
paintings and silkscreens about New Mexican
Indian life. As a teacher he influenced many
students, especially in Anderson High School
(Austin). Illustrations throughout the
issue.

6516 Lefebre, Francisco. El mural chicano en
Nuevo Mexico. RAYAS, Vol. 1, no. 2 (March,
April, 1978), p. 7. Spanish.

AN: Albuquerque muralist writes about
Chicano murals which derive from
pre-Columbian and modern Mexican murals. New
Mexican muralism started in 1970 with the
Muralistas Guadalupanos de Aztlan in Santa
Fe. In 1971 and 1972 students at the
Highlands University of Las Vegas, New
Mexico also painted murals. In addition,
murals have appeared in Albuquerque. Brief
biography of Lefebre. Illustrated.

6517 Martinez, Eluid Levi. What is a New Mexico
santo? Santa Fe, NM: Sunstone Press, 1978.
Bilingual.

AN: Martinez is a carver of saints from
the well-known Lopez family of santeros of
Cordova, New Mexico, who have carved for
seven generations. An oversimplified history
of the settlement of New Mexico and the rise
of religious imagery production. Of interest
are the illustrated steps of the carving
process. Many reproductions.

6518 Museum of Fine Arts, Santa Fe, NM. John
Hernandez, Douglas Johnson. Exhibition
invitation, 1979. English.

AN: Invitation to an exhibit including
the jeweled sculpture of John Hernandez from
New Mexico.

6519 Museum of Fine Arts, Santa Fe, NM. Luis
Jimenez, sculpture, drawings and prints: La
Cofradia de Artes y Artesanos Hispanicos,
selected works. Exhibition invitation, 1979.
English.

AN: Invitation to an exhibit of Texas
sculptor and printmaker Luis Jimenez, and
New Mexican artists and artisans.

6520 Painted walls - a New Mexico folk art. NEW
MEXICO, (January 1977), p. 34-35. English.

AN: Five color illustrations of murals
from New Mexico including those done by
Gilberto Guzman, Geronimo Garduno, and Sam
Leyba. The murals are located in Santa Fe,
Chimayo, Embudo and Albuquerque.

6521 Pepe and Pepito. SANTA FE NEW MEXICAN,
(August 16, 1972), p. A2. English.

AN: Among the barrio groups receiving
funding from the COPAS Cultural Awareness
Program of the Model Cities program are Los
Artesanos and Los Artes Guadalupanos.

6522 Rodriguez, Alfred. A historical survey of
Chicano murals in the Southwest: an
interdisciplinary teaching unit. Unpublished
paper, 1980. English.

AN: Lists murals by title, artist and
date (when known), location and subject. Los
Angeles, San Francisco, San Diego, Fresno,
San Antonio, Austin, Corpus Christi, Santa
Fe, New Mexico murals are included.
Circulated by the Institute of Latin
American Studies, University of Austin,
Texas.

6523 Rodriguez, Anita. Las enjarradoras: women of
the earth. NEW MEXICO, (February 1980), p.
46-47+. English.

AN: History of adobe construction in New
Mexico, its decline and its present revival
in Arizona and New Mexico. Written by a
professional adobe architect and feminist
who defines the traditional terms and
techniques of this woman's craft.
Illustrated.

6524 Rodriguez, Anita. Tradiciones de adobe en
Nuevo Mejico norteno = adobe traditions in
Northern New Mexico. ADOBE NEWS, no. 15
(1977). Bilingual.

AN: History of adobe construction in New
Mexico, from primarily Indian sources with
Spanish input. For 400 years, women were
builders and architects of the Southwest;
today they are "enjarradoras" (plasterers).
Written by a professional enjarradora from
New Mexico. Illustrated.

6525 Romero, Leo. Celso: poetry by Leo Romero,
New Mexico. Berkeley, CA: Tonatiuh
International, 1980. English.

AN: Book illustrated by poet-artist Leo
Romero from New Mexico. Drawings.

6526 Sagel, Jaime. Art of brothers taps New
Mexico heritage. JOURNAL NORTH, (December
16, 1981). English.

AN: Three brothers, graphics artist,
painter, photographer, potter and poet
Alejandro Lopez and his older self-taught
brothers Felix and Manuel, are working with
traditional New Mexican art forms (bultos,
straw inlay crosses) and with newer
innovative forms - reflecting the fusion of
traditional-experimental art developing in
New Mexico among young artists.

6527 Sanchez, Arley. Santeros. ALBUQUERQUE JRNL,
(August 21, 1977), p. C, 1. English.

AN: Review of THE SANTERO EXPERIENCE, an
exhibition of contemporary folk art by
eleven New Mexican santeros, most in their
30s, at the Albuquerque Museum. The carvers
include Juan Lucero, Ben Lopez, Luisito
Lujan, Horacio Valdez, C. Garcia, George
Lopez. A revival of the art has been taking
place within last several years due to
cultural awareness being experienced by
Hispanos. Contemporary santeros still donate
some pieces to the church, but most are
marketed to private collectors, displayed in
museums, or kept.

New Mexico (cont.)

6528 Santos of New Mexico, art of our people. GRITO DEL NORTE, Vol. 3, no. 1 (January 17, 1970), p. 8-9. English.

AN: Historical trajectory of santero tradition in New Mexico. Distinguished santeros like Rafael Aragon of Cordova, Miguel Herrera of Arroyo Hondo, Juan Ramon Velasquez of Conjilon, Jose Benito Ortega of La Cueva all created art wedded to the environment of the Southwest. Illustrated with a portfolio of santos and retablos from the Folk Art Museum of Santa Fe, NM.

6529 Simon, Joan. Report from New Mexico. ART IN AMERICA, Vol. 68, no. 6 (Summer 1980), p. 33-41. English.

AN: Luis Jimenez worked four years as artist-in-residence at the Roswell Museum and Art Center, Roswell, NM, which enabled him to produce his PROGRESS series and other monumental sculpture.

6530 Simpson, Claudette. An adobe fireplace: Anita Rodriguez has built many - each one different. PRESCOTT COURIER-WEEKLY FEATURE, (December 1, 1978). English.

AN: Anita Rodriguez is an enjarradora--a professional specializing in adobe architecture--in New Mexico. She builds fireplaces, lays mud floors, builds hornos (outdoor ovens) and does interior and exterior plastering. Well illustrated.

6531 La Sociedad Historica de Nuestra Senora de Guadalupe, Santa Fe, NM. Meditacion. Exhibition invitation, 1980. English.

AN: Invitation to an exhibit by four artists: Filomeno Martinez (graphic artist, Albuquerque), Ruben Montoya (santero, Santa Fe), Santiago Chavez (painter, Santa Rosa), Jose Alberto Baros (sculptor, Espanola).

6532 Sutherland-Martinez, Elizabeth. Corazon del norte: Baltasar Martinez. GRITO DEL NORTE, Vol. 2, no. 2 (January 29, 1968), p. 5. English.

AN: Baltazar Martinez from Conjilon (one of the defendants in the Tierra Amarilla Courthouse "Raid" Case) is a noted naif painter. This article focuses on his methods, techniques and subject matter. His work is related to that current of cultural production outside mainstream channels. Illustrated with photograph of artist and several of his paintings.

6533 Valdez, Armando. El calendario chicano 1977. Hayward, CA: Southwest Network, 1977. English.

AN: Fifth in a series of historical calendars produced in 1972, 1974, 1975, 1976 by La Causa Publications and Southwest Network. Artists whose work is reproduced are Malaquias Montoya, Amado Maurilio Pena, Ramori Zamora, Glugio J.L. Nicandro [Gronk], Etta Delgado, Ricardo Alaniz, Diane Gamboa, Elisa Marina Coleman, Margarita Calderon, Jose Antonio Burciaga, Cesar Augusto Martinez, Maria Ochoa y Valtierra, Juan Renteria Fuentes, from California, New Mexico, and Texas.

6534 Weegar, Sally. Native Mexican images. DAILY TEXAN, (October 23, 1978), p. 16. English.

AN: Review of an exhibit of watercolors, tiles, and silkscreen prints by Amado Pena at the Wagner Gallery in Austin. Earlier work of Laredo-born Pena were politically oriented toward La Raza. Recent work concentrates on New Mexican landscape and Indian peoples. Illustrated.

6535 Wilson, Michael and Biberman, Herbert. Salt of the earth [film]. 16mm, 94 min., b&w. English.

AN: The first feature film made in the U.S. of, by and for labor, it deals with a real strike of Mexican American miners in New Mexico in which women played a key role in the men's victory and their own demands. Mexican actress Rosaura Revueltas starred with labor leader Juan Chacon. One of the best films on the subject.

NEW SYMBOLS FOR LA RAZA NUEVA [exhibit]

6536 Mexican American liberation art front: la Raza Nueva, Rene Yanez, Esteban Villa, Malaquias Montoya, Manuel Hernandez. BRONCE, Vol. 1, no. 3 (March 1969), p. 6-7. English.

AN: Manifesto of MALAF, a germinal Chicano art group in northern California. Compares revolutionary Chicanos of 1968 with the Mexicans of 1910; equally Chicano artists reject European-influenced art. Announces the exhibit NEW SYMBOLS FOR LA RAZA NUEVA, at La Causa in Oakland, March 22 to April 5, 1969. Puts forth the group's philosophy and goals, particularly exhibits and art services to the "barrio". Illustrated.

NEW VISIONS, L.A. [exhibit]

6537 Moisan, Jim. Ancient roots, new visions. ARTWEEK, Vol. 9, no. 26 (July 29, 1978), p. 8. English.

AN: Review of the show held at the Municipal Arts Gallery of Los Angeles, the first national touring show of Latino artists in the United States. Includes commentary on work of Larry Fuente, Luis Jimenez, Frank Romero, Harry Gamboa, Gronk, Rudy Martinez, Benjamin Serrano, Ricardo Diaz, Patssi Valdez, Mel Casas, Luis Leroy, Pedro Lujan. A related show, NEW VISIONS, L.A., includes Robert Delgado, Ray Bravo, Joe Moran, Rosalyn Mesquita, Patricia Murillo and others.

New York

6538 Edward Chavez: sculptor-painter. LA LUZ, Vol. 2, no. 2 (May 1973), p. 28-31. English.

AN: Lavishly illustrated biographical account of Edward Chavez. Born in Ocate, New Mexico in 1917, Chavez has a distinguished career as a painter and sculptor. During the 1940's he executed a number of murals under sponsorship of various government art projects. These murals were placed in public buildings in Nebraska, Colorado and Wyoming. Although living and working in New York most of his adult life, the work of Edward Chavez has always been influenced by the Southwest.

--   --

New York (cont.)

6539 Weiss, Margaret R. and Sommer, Robert.
     Camera assignment: documenting street art.
     SATURDAY REVIEW, (May 17, 1975), p. 41-43.
     English.

     AN: Interview with Robert Sommer.
     Illustrations of six murals: in Santa Fe,
     NM; Estrada Courts in Los Angeles; a John
     Weber mural in Chicago; and Cityarts mural
     in New York.

Newport Harbor Art Museum

6540 Wilson, William. Artistic get-together in
     Orange County exhibit. CALENDAR, (November
     4, 1979), p. 99. English.

     AN: Review of exhibit OUR OWN ARTISTS:
     ART IN ORANGE COUNTY at the Newport Harbor
     Art Museum. Mention of Patricia Murillo and
     Emigdio Vasquez.

Newspapers

6541 Garcia, Rupert. A source for mural art
     education: an annotated bibliography of
     three Chicano newspapers. Unpublished paper,
     1974 (Chicano Studies Library, Univ. of
     California, Berkeley). English.

     AN: A research project showing how
     Chicano newspapers reported and educated
     their readers to mural activity by Raza
     artists during the period 1968-1978. The
     newspapers analized are EL GALLO (Denver,
     CO), EL CHICANO (San Bernardino, CA), and EL
     TECOLOTE (San Francisco, CA). Author draws
     eight conclusions about the form, meaning
     and significance of mural activity in
     Chicano barrios and the importance of
     community newspapers as a fruitful and
     meaningful source for art education.

Nicandro, Glugio J.L. (Gronk)
     USE: Gronk (Pseud.)

Nieto Gomez, Ana

6542 Morales, Sylvia. Chicana. 20 min., 16 mm,
     color, 1979. English.

     AN: Color film tracing the history of
     the Chicana back to pre-Columbian women's
     history. Utilizes images of pre-Columbian
     and modern Mexican murals, as well as
     filming of contemporary Chicanas and their
     activities. Based on a slide show by Anna
     Nieto-Gomez, adapted for the screen by
     Morales.

Los Ninos del Mundo

6543 Lopez, Gerard. Estrada murals. LA LUZ, Vol.
     4, no. 3 (June 1975), p. 21. English.

     AN: Describes goals and procedures of a
     barrio mural project under the guidance of
     "Los Ninos del Mundo", a group of Chicano
     artists, musicians and social workers.

Nixon, Richard

6544 Gonzalez, Jose Gamaliel. Boycott [drawing].
     REVISTA CHICANO-RIQUENA, Vol. 5, no. 1
     (Winter 1977), p. 9. English.

NO MOVIE [exhibit]

6545 Exploratorium, Student Union, California
     State University, Los Angeles. Herron/Gronk
     in ILLEGAL LANDSCAPE. Exhibition catalog,
     1980. English.

     AN: Invitation to a "performance" piece
     NO MOVIE by Willie Herron and Gronk, two
     members of ASCO. Illustrated.

6546 Gamboa, Harry, Jr. ASCO: no phantoms. HIGH
     PERFORMANCE, Vol. 4, no. 2 (Summer 1981), p.
     15. English.

     AN: "The media's hit and run attitude
     has generally relegated the influence by
     Chicanos on Los Angeles to that of a phantom
     culture," says Gamboa's introduction to an
     ASCO No Movie event, NO PHANTOMS: "various
     overt acts of communal alienation."
     Illustrated.

6547 Geyer, Anne and Gamboa, Harry, Jr. Artists'
     exhibits are street performances. THE NEWS,
     (September 11, 1981), p. 18. English.

     AN: Illustrated interview with
     photographer/writer Harry Gamboa, Jr.,
     member and documenter of the performance art
     group ASCO. Description of the NO MOVIE, NO
     PHANTOM, walking and instant murals of the
     group, and other performance street art
     which Gamboa considers as Chicano
     self-documentation and expression.

6548 L.A.C.E. (Los Angeles Contemporary
     Exhibitions), Los Angeles, CA. No Movie: Gil
     de Montes, Teddy, Glugio [Gronk], Patssi,
     Gamboa. Exhibition invitation, 1978.
     English.

     AN: Invitation to "performance" piece by
     Roberto Gil de Montes, Teddy Sandoval,
     Gronk, Patssi Valdez and Harry Gamboa, Jr.,
     the latter three of the ASCO group.
     Illustrated.

NO PHANTOMS [exhibit]

6549 Gamboa, Harry, Jr. ASCO: no phantoms. HIGH
     PERFORMANCE, Vol. 4, no. 2 (Summer 1981), p.
     15. English.

     AN: "The media's hit and run attitude
     has generally relegated the influence by
     Chicanos on Los Angeles to that of a phantom
     culture," says Gamboa's introduction to an
     ASCO No Movie event, NO PHANTOMS: "various
     overt acts of communal alienation."
     Illustrated.

6550 Geyer, Anne and Gamboa, Harry, Jr. Artists'
     exhibits are street performances. THE NEWS,
     (September 11, 1981), p. 18. English.

     AN: Illustrated interview with
     photographer/writer Harry Gamboa, Jr.,
     member and documenter of the performance art
     group ASCO. Description of the NO MOVIE, NO
     PHANTOM, walking and instant murals of the
     group, and other performance street art
     which Gamboa considers as Chicano
     self-documentation and expression.

Nochebuena
     USE: Christmas

Noriega, Ramses

6551 Baciu, Joyce A. Hispanic artists: combining
     energy and emotion. CAMINOS, Vol. 2, no. 5
     (October 1981), p. 14-17. English.

     AN: Brief profiles of Mario Uribe,
     Ernest De Soto, Peter Rodriguez, Margarita
     Jauregui Weiner, Virginia Jaramillo, Luis
     Urrea, Ramses Noriega, Jose Lopez, Olivia
     Sanchez.

Noriega, Ramses (cont.)

6552 Burkhardt, Dorothy. Chicano pride and anger
     mix at 'Califas'. THE TAB, (April 12,
     1981), p. 34. English.

     AN: CALIFAS: AN EXHIBITION OF CHICANO
     ARTISTS IN CALIFORNIA represents a
     cross-section of artists exhibiting work for
     at least ten years: Rupert Garcia, Ernie
     Palomino, Eduardo Carrillo, Judy Baca, Rene
     Yanez, Carmen Lomas Garza, Salvador Roberto
     Torres, Roberto Chavez, Willie Herron, Ralph
     Maradiaga, Sue Martinez, Jose Montoya,
     Malaquias Montoya, Ramses Noriega and
     Esteban Villa. Illustrated.

6553 Chicano art show at Contra Costa College. EL
     HISPANO, Vol. 8, no. 25 (December 11, 1973).
     English.

     AN: Information on exhibition organized
     by Ramses Noriega that included the work of
     Jose Montoya, Esteban Villa, Mario Sinape,
     Ricardo Rios, Malaquias Montoya, Fuchi
     Queso, and Joe Palomino.

6554 Depicts Chicano attitudes: library receives
     new mural. DAILY BRUIN, (September 29,
     1970), p. 6. English.

     AN: Illustrated story of mural painted
     in UCLA's Mexican American Library by
     Eduardo Carrillo, Ramses Noriega, Sergio
     Hernandez, Saul Solache.

6555 Street, Sharon. Califas - a celebration of
     Chicano culture and art. CITY ON A HILL,
     (April 16, 1981). English.

     AN: Review of an exhibit at College V's
     Sesnon Gallery featuring 15 California
     artists: Ramses Noriega, Judy Baca, Salvador
     Roberto Torres, Malaquias Montoya, Rene
     Yanez, Ralph Maradiaga, Jose Montoya,
     Esteban Villa, Carmen Lomas Garza, Robert
     Chavez, among others. Illustrated.

6556 Valdez, Armando. El calendario chicano 1975.
     Hayward, CA: Southwest Network, 1975.
     English.

     AN: Third in a series of historical
     calendars produced in 1972 and 1974 by La
     Causa Publications and Southwest Network.
     Artists included for each month are Carmen
     Lomas Garza, Sergio Hernandez, Malaquias
     Montoya, Mujeres Muralistas (Graciela
     Carrillo, Venezuelan Consuelo Mendez, Irene
     Perez, Patricia Rodriguez), Ramses Noriega,
     Ernie Palomino, Amado Maurilio Pena, Martin
     Perez. All but Texan Pena are California
     artists.

Northern California

6557 University Art Museum, Berkeley, CA. The
     Fifth Sun: Contemporary/Traditional Chicano
     & Latino Art. Exhibition catalog, 1977.
     English.

     AN: Catalog of exhibit including 45
     artists of northern California. Texts deal
     with Mexican muralists, Mujeres Muralistas &
     other muralists, posters, the Chicano art
     movement, altars, La Raza Silkscreen Center,
     Galeria de la Raza, the Mexican Museum, the
     Sacramento Centro de Artistas Chicanos/RCAF.
     Mural maps of S.F. Bay Area and Sacramento.
     Many illustrations.

6558 Wagner, Kathie and Lujan, Lori. Public
     works: beyond the city. CALIFORNIA LIVING,
     (September 28, 1975), p. 26-35. English.

     AN: Illustrative descriptive survey of
     murals in a number of northern California
     cities, excluding San Francisco. Helpful
     inclusion of mural locations and artist's
     names. Second of two-part article.

Northwest U.S

6559 And/Or Gallery, Seattle, WA. Artistas de
     Aztlan. Exhibition announcement, 1975.
     English.

     AN: Exhibition announcement for an
     important exhibit of Northwest Chicano art.
     Co-sponsored by MEChA and the Chicano
     Studies Program at the University of
     Washington, the exhibit presented works by
     Emilio Aguayo, Danny Desiga, Ricardo
     Aguirre, Ramiro Benavidez, Elma Herada,
     Pedro Rodriguez and others. A selection of
     posters by Armando Cid of the R.C.A.F. group
     from Sacramento, California was also
     presented. Concurrently, at the Heny Gallery
     of the University of Washington, Esteban
     Villa presented a one-man show.

6560 Cultural department. RECOBRANDO, Vol. 1, no.
     15. Spanish.

     AN: The development of "Raza" culture in
     the Northwest and the role played by the
     Centro de la Raza. Mentions the "talleres de
     arte" set up by Carlos Contreras and Arturo
     Artorez, artists from Mexico who moved to
     Seattle in 1978. Details cultural events
     sponsored by the Centro in the fields of
     art, music, dance, and theater.

6561 Desiga, Daniel. Days historical dawn in the
     Northwest. Olympia, WA: Legislative Artworks
     Project, n.d. English.

     AN: Personal statement submitted by
     Daniel Design with drawings for mural
     project to reflect the natural and human
     elements thathave forged Northwest reality.
     The artist states: "The key elements as
     envisaged are land and water integrated with
     racial groupings, diverse technologies and
     invested labor. Incorporating Northwest
     symbols, the mural will be seen as a
     manifestation of the physical and natural
     energies which have combined to give
     expression to an unique force in the
     Northwest.".

NOSOTROS [art group], Los Angeles, CA

6562 CHICANO CINEMA NEWSLETTER. Vol. 1, no. 3
     (May 1979). English.

     AN: Announcements for the U.S.
     Conference for an Alternative Cinema (N.Y.),
     a "Nosotros" banquet, application dates for
     the Film Fund, deadlines for the National
     Endowment for the Humanities, and criticism
     of the Hollywood feature film BOULEVARD
     NIGHTS.

Novelists
     USE: Authors

Nuestras Artes de Michigan

6563 Acosta, Dan. Paintings reflect life experiences. THE ECCENTRIC, (June 26, 1980). English.

AN: Review of one-woman show by Nora Chapa Mendoza at the Heritage Art Gallery, Ypsilanti, MI. Mendoza works in abstract impressionist style with wet streams of colors that express energy. Her subjects are landscapes, moods, nudes, and Hispanic themes. She is active in the Detroit Latino Artist Association, Nuestras Artes de Michigan, and the New Detroit Art Council.

6564 Capitol Art Gallery, Lansing, MI. Arte de Nora Mendoza, Hector Perez, George Vargas, Martin Moreno. Exhibition invitation [1979]. English.

AN: Invitation to an art exhibit organized by Nuestras Artes de Michigan.

6565 Nora Mendoza: pintora de ascendencia mexicana triunfa en los EE. UU. BUENHOGAR, (May 1979), p. 7. Spanish.

AN: Profile of Texas-born Nora Mendoza of Michigan, a painter of abstractions in acrylic. She is an active member of many Detroit and Michigan organizations, including Nuestras Artes de Michigan which she co-founded with Jorge Vargas, Martin Moreno and Jessie Gonzalez.

Nunez, David

6566 The First Unitarian Universalist Church, Paradise Valley, AZ. Five Chicano artists. Exhibition brochure, 1971. English.

AN: Exhibit organized by L. Eugene Grigsby, Jr., Art Department of Arizona State University, Tempe, AZ. 21 works by Eugene Quesada, David Nunez, Fernando Navarro, Luis Baiz (of Arizona) and Saul Solache (of Los Angeles). Brief biographies of the artists.

6567 Grigsby, J. Eugene, Jr. Art & ethnics: background for teaching youth in a pluralistic society. Dubuque, IO: Wm.C. Brown Co. Publishers, 1977. English.

AN: Grigsby teaches in the Art Department of Arizona State University, Tempe. His book contains illustrations of Arizona artists Eugenio Quedada, David Nunez, and Luis Baiz, and a chapter called "The Spanish-Speaking Ethnics: Chicano/Mexican-American/Puerto Rican/Cuban/South American artists".

Nunez, J. Armando

6568 Alurista. Nationchild plumaroja: 1969-1972. San Diego, CA: Toltecas en Aztlan, Centro Cultural de La Raza, 1972. English.

AN: Drawings by Esteban Villa and Armando Nunez.

6569 El Centro Cultural de La Raza, San Diego, CA. Espejo del barrio-art exposition. Exhibition brochure, June 1975. English.

AN: Illustrated brochure announcement for a cultural exposition of Chicano music, art and drama. Includes some biographical information and one reproduction of painter Manuel Unzueta, woodworker Ambriz, muralist Victor Orozco Ochoa and designer/illustrator J. Armando Nunez.

Oakes College, UC Santa Cruz

6570 Fuegos en Aztlan (fires in Aztlan): a Chicano arts show. Unpublished program, 1980. English.

AN: Program for a Chicano arts event, including an art show of 23 artists working in all media. Unpublished program.

Oakland, CA

6571 Albright, Thomas. Oakland Museum: a wide range in Latin art. SAN FRANCISCO CHRONICLE, (September 12, 1970), p. 33. English.

AN: A large show called ARTES DE LA RAZA at the Oakland Museum includes Mercedes Gutierrez-McDermid, Louis Gutierrez, Luis Cervantez, Calvin Tondre, Manuel Villamor, Rene Yanez, Jose Ramirez, Jorge Lerma, Rolando Castellon, Esteban Villa, Rupert Garcia, and Gustavo Rivera who is also having an exhibit at the Galeria de la Raza.

Oakland Museum, Oakland, CA

6572 Calendar 1977. CHISMEARTE, no. 2 (Winter, Spring, 1977), p. 26-27. English.

AN: Reproduction of one month of the 1977 silkscreen calendar produced in limited edition by the Galeria de la Raza of San Francisco and the Royal Chicano Air Force of Sacramento, California. Displayed is Rene Yanez's screen HISTORICAL PHOTO-SILKSCREENMOVIE.

6573 Oakland Museum presents 5 L.A. Chicano artists. EL MUNDO (Hayward, CA), (August 1974). English.

AN: Report on the exhibit THE SEARCH FOR AZTLAN, featuring paintings, murals, tortilla art, folk and religious symbols and totems by Carlos Almaraz, Roberto de la Rocha, Gilbert Lujan, Frank Romero and Judithe Hernandez. Included in the more than 100 works are a wall mural, a folk art pyramid, and part of a primed '51 Chevy lowrider. Illustrated.

O'Cadiz, Sergio

6574 Chapple, Paul. FV [Fountain Valley] wall mural stirs contention. THE REGISTER, (December 29, 1974), p. A3. English.

AN: Artist Sergio O'Cadiz has included a panel showing gas-masked police dragging off a Chicano youth. The panel has caused controversy in Fountain Valley, CA; police object to the image.

6575 Chapple, Paul. Mural, graffiti painters wage endurance contest in F.V. [Fountain Valley]. THE REGISTER, (December 4, 1975), p. B5. English.

AN: Mexican-born architect and designer Sergio O'Cadiz, with a team, paints a 600 foot mural in Colonia Juarez, an older section of Fountain Valley in Orange County, CA. Local police objected to a scene showing police brutality. White paint was hurled at this panel one night, and the mural was constantly attacked by vandals. Illustrated.

O'Cadiz, Sergio (cont.)

6576 Fortune, Thomas. Mural will mirror barrio pride. LOS ANGELES TIMES, (December 27, 1974), p. II, 1, 8. English.

AN: Artist Sergio O'Cadiz has been painting a 625-foot concrete wall constructed to separate old Colonia Juarez and a new Anglo housing complex in Fountain Valley (Orange County), Calif., to eliminate graffiti. The mural depicts the barrio's history: Mexican Americans try on white masks for Anglo acceptance. Other scenes will show the arrival of the surrounding city, and resident's awareness of their Chicano identity. O'Cadiz is assisted by 40 students from surrounding colleges and universities. Illustrated.

6577 History traced in mural. THE REGISTER, (May 1, 1974), p. C-1. English.

AN: Illustrated story of History of the Chicano mural painted by Sergio O'Cadiz and fifty students from MEChA at Santa Ana College.

6578 Kennedy, Bailey. The American pageant: a history of the republic, 6th ed. 6th ed., Lexington, MA: D.C. Heath, 1979, p. 674. English.

AN: Reproduction of two sections of the MEChA mural painted in 1974 by students directed by Sergio O'Cadiz at Santa Ana College, Santa Ana, Calif. The mural includes Mexican and Mexican American themes.

6579 M.E.C.H.A. cultura y evolucion mexicana. EL CLARIN, (May 2, 1974), p. 3. Spanish.

AN: Report on the mural designed and painted under the direction of Mexican-born designer Sergio O'Cadiz at Santa Ana College, Santa Ana, Calif. Collaborators were instructor Shifra Goldman and gallery director Mike Davis, with members of the MEChA Club and other students. The mural concerns the history of Mexico and of the Chicano and includes a tribute to David Alfaro Siqueiros' Los Angeles mural AMERICA TROPICAL, painted and white-washed in the 1930s. Illustrated.

6580 Monroe mural brightens school. THE REGISTER, (December 13, 1973), p. G3. English.

AN: James Monroe School in Santa Ana, CA has a huge mural painted by Costa Mesa artist Sergio O'Cadiz. The mural cost $4250, but the artist donated much time and talent. Illustrated.

Ochoa, Victor Orozco

6581 El Centro Cultural de La Raza, San Diego, CA. Espejo del barrio-art exposition. Exhibition brochure, June 1975. English.

AN: Illustrated brochure announcement for a cultural exposition of Chicano music, art and drama. Includes some biographical information and one reproduction of painter Manuel Unzueta, woodworker Ambriz, muralist Victor Orozco Ochoa and designer/illustrator J. Armando Nunez.

6582 Centro mural recipient of orchid award. LA PRENSA SAN DIEGO, (November 20, 1981), p. 5. English.

AN: The American Institute of Architects, the American Society of Interior Designers, the American Planning Association and the American Society of Landscape Architects award the Centro Cultural de la Raza of Balboa Park, San Diego, CA for Victor Ochoa's mural on its walls. Illustrated.

6583 Harper, Hilliard. Native Americans stand tall again as Balboa Park mural takes shape. LOS ANGELES TIMES [San Diego County edition], (March 2, 1981), p. II, 5. English.

AN: Victor Ochoa paints the figure of Geronimo on the wall of San Diego's Balboa Park Centro Cultural de la Raza to replace a skeletal calavera figure disturbing patients at a hospital across the street. The central figure is part of a planned 70 x 18 foot mural promoting Mexican, Chicano and Indian art. Activities at the Centro are described. Illustrated.

6584 Murphy, Patricia Lee. Artists renew Toltecas crafts heritage. LOS ANGELES TIMES, (May 23, 1971), p. E, 10. English.

AN: The Toltecas en Aztlan, creative arm of the Chicano Federation of San Diego County, Inc., will shortly move into their new Centro Cultural de la Raza in Balboa Park, San Diego. The group includes Mario Acevedo (Peruvian), Guillermo Aranda, Tomas Castaneda, Victor Ochoa and Salvador Torres (visual artists) and poet Alurista.

Ochoa y Valtierra, Maria

6585 Valdez, Armando. El calendario chicano 1977. Hayward, CA: Southwest Network, 1977. English.

AN: Fifth in a series of historical calendars produced in 1972, 1974, 1975, 1976 by La Causa Publications and Southwest Network. Artists whose work is reproduced are Malaquias Montoya, Amado Maurilio Pena, Ramori Zamora, Glugio J.L. Nicandro [Gronk], Etta Delgado, Ricardo Alaniz, Diane Gamboa, Elisa Marina Coleman, Margarita Calderon, Jose Antonio Burciaga, Cesar Augusto Martinez, Maria Ochoa y Valtierra, Juan Renteria Fuentes, from California, New Mexico, and Texas.

October Gallery, London, England

6586 From the barrios. OBSERVER, (September 23, 1979), p. 16+. English.

AN: Short story on Gilberto Guzman from Santa Fe, New Mexico, announcing an exhibit of his work in the October Gallery, London. Two color reproductions of his paintings.

O'Gorman, Juan

6587 Stephens, Martha. Murals introduce Carlos
     Castaneda to Neil Armstrong. SAN ANTONIO
     EXPRESS-NEWS, (January 11, 1981), p. M, 1,
     3. English.

     AN: Survey of commissioned murals in San
     Antonio including Mexican artist Juan
     O'Gorman's mosaic at the Theatre for
     Performing Arts; Carlos Merida's and Fred
     Samuelson's at the Convention Center; Howard
     Cook's New Deal mural in the downtown
     post-office; Peter Hurd's, and James
     Sicner's (in progress) mural at Trinity
     University; Jesse "Chista" Cantu's at
     Mario's Restaurant; and Jesse Trevino's
     mural at Our Lady of the Lake University.
     Illustrated.

O'Higgins, Pablo

6588 The stolen art: the O'Higgins mural.
     RECOBRANDO, Vol. 1, no. 2, p. 15, 16.
     English.

     AN: Historical documentation on 60-foot
     long 8-foot high fresco mural painted for
     the Seattle Shipscalers Union by Mexican
     artist Pablo O'Higgins in 1949. In 1974,
     John Caughlan, a people's lawyer documented
     the existence of the mural to Chicano
     community groups. M.E.C.H.A. students at the
     University of Washington lobbied for the
     murals restoration and permanent exhibition.

6589 Tsutakaua, Mayumi. Artist paints from
     heritage. SEATTLE TIMES, (September 15,
     1980). English.

     AN: Biographical information on Armond
     Lara, Northwest Chicano-Navajo artist. He is
     coordinating the restoration of a mural done
     in Seattle by Mexican artist Pablo
     O'Higgins. In his own work Lara is
     experimenting with paper making and the use
     of natural pigments.

Ojeda, Jay

6590 Grimke, Angelina. Chicano art finds home in
     Mission galeria. PEOPLE'S WORLD, Vol. 33,
     no. 32 (August 8, 1970), p. 11. English.

     AN: Commentary on the exhibition
     CHICANOS, CUBA Y LOS 10 MILLONES held at the
     original Galeria de la Raza at 425 14th
     Street in San Francisco. The show presented
     photographs by Jay Ojeda and Roberto
     Perez-Diaz, drawings by Gloria Ozuna
     together with paintings and photographs by
     Cuban artist Mederos. Provides information
     about the goals of the Galeria as the visual
     arts department of Casa Hispana de Bellas
     Artes. Exhibition curator was Rolando
     Castellon.

6591 Martinez, Anita. Raza! Arte! Raza! Arte!
     EL TECOLOTE, Vol. 1, no. 2 (September 7,
     1970), p. 3. Bilingual.

     AN: Galeria de la Raza opened on July,
     1970 at 425 14th St. San Francisco. It was
     an outgrowth of the Arte Seis organization
     (an art effort established in the Mission
     District in 1967 by Francisco Camplis,
     Rupert Garcia, Ralph McNeil, Jay Ojeda and
     Jack Ruiz). These and other artists brought
     together by the Neighborhood Arts Program
     have coalesced in the new Galeria de la
     Raza. Article gives goals, organizational
     scheme and plans for the Galeria. It's first
     exhibit was a one man show by Esteban Villa
     together with a photo and sketch exhibit on

Cuba by Jay Ojeda, Roberto Diaz Perez and
Gloria Ozuna. Illustrated with installation
view of new Galeria.

6592 Martinez, Anita. Raza art. EL TECOLOTE, Vol.
     1, no. 8 (November 30, 1970), p. 1. English.

     AN: Jay Ojeda, newly selected director
     of Galeria de la Raza, describes the
     memorial exhibition dedicated to Ruben
     Salazar installed at the Galeria on Dec. 12,
     1970. Salazar symbolized and synthesized
     many of the goals subscribed to by artist
     members of La Galeria. The exhibit included
     work by Chicano and Latino artists Francisco
     Camplis, Jay Ojeda, Jose Romero, Rolando
     Castellon, Rene Yanez, Luis Valsoto, Mike
     Ruiz, Carlos Perez, Gustavo Rivera, Peter
     Rodriguez, Carlos Loarca and Ralph
     Maradiaga.

Old Age
     USE: Ancianos

Olguin, Muriel

6593 Jesus Gutierrez Gallery, San Pedro, CA. "Two
     of a kind" prints by Linda Vallejo, Muriel
     Olguin. Exhibition invitation [1978].
     English.

     AN: Invitation to an exhibit.

6594 Joslyn Art Center. Multi-media art exhibit:
     Muriel Olguin (printmaking), Myrna Shiras
     (mixed media), Linda Vallejo (painting).
     Exhibition invitation, 1979. English.

     AN: Invitation to an exhibit.

6595 San Pedro Municipal Art Gallery, San Pedro,
     CA. Celebration: Muriel Olguin and Linda
     Vallejo. San Pedro, CA: San Pedro Municipal
     Art Gallery, [1978]. English.

     AN: Invitation to an exhibit.
     Illustrated.

Olivares, Virginia

6596 Union Gallery, University of Arizona Student
     Union, Tucson, AZ. Chicanarte: Cynthia Reyes
     Aponte, Zarco Guerrero, Virginia Federico
     Olivares, Antonio Pazos. Exhibition catalog,
     1981. English.

     AN: Illustrated catalog of exhibit
     featuring four artists.

Olivo, Miriam

6597 New mural on Mission Street. EL HISPANO,
     Vol. 7, no. 13 (September 19, 1974), p. 5.
     English.

     AN: Description of mural at the corner
     of 24th Street and South Van Ness in San
     Francisco. Painted by Mujeres
     Muralistas--Consuelo Mendez, Graciela
     Carrillo, Susan Cervantes and Miriam Olivo,
     the 30-foot mural depicts people in a
     tropical, Latin American setting.

Olivo, Miriam (cont.)

6598 Preuss, Karen. The new Mission murals. SAN
      FRANCISCO BAY GUARDIAN, (June 28, 1975), p.
      14-15. English.

      AN: Mural art in San Francisco's Mission
      District has covered nearly every wall and
      alley on lower 24th Street. Murals by Mike
      Rios, the Mujeres Muralistas (Patricia
      Rodriguez, Graciela Carrillo, Consuelo
      Mendez, Miriam Olivo, Irene Perez, Susan
      Cervantes) appear in the area. Others have
      been painted by artists associated with the
      Galeria de la Raza. Illustrations.

6599 Quintero, Victoria. A mural is a painting on
      a wall done by human hands. EL TECOLOTE,
      Vol. 5, no. 1 (September 13, 1974), p. 6+.
      English.

      AN: The women's collective, Mujeres
      Muralistas, exists within the strong San
      Francisco mural movement. Originally the
      group included Graciela Carrillo, Consuelo
      Mendez, Irene Perez, and Patricia Rodriguez.
      The group has expanded to include Susan
      Cervantes, Ester Hernandez, and Miriam
      Olivo. The two murals completed have been
      criticized for not being political; the
      women answer that they want the atmosphere
      to be surrounded with life, with colors.
      Illustrated.

6600 Venegas, Sybil. Conditions for producing
      Chicana art. CHISMEARTE, Vol. 1, no. 4 (Fall,
      Winter, 1977, 1978), p. 2, 4. English.

      AN: Chicana artists face more obstacles
      than white women or Chicano counterparts in
      the arts. Mexican life style has portrayed
      the ideal of a submissive woman, but the
      values have changed. Chicana artists are
      concerned with women and their struggles.
      Muralists include Patricia Rodriguez, Irene
      Perez, Consuelo Mendez de Castillo, Susan
      Cervantes, Ester Hernandez, Miriam Olivo,
      Ruth Rodriguez, of the Mujeres Muralistas
      (San Francisco). Other artists are Etta
      Delgado and Barbara Carrasco.

Olympia, WA

6601 Desiga, Daniel. Days historical dawn in the
      Northwest. Olympia, WA: Legislative Artworks
      Project, n.d. English.

      AN: Personal statement submitted by
      Daniel Design with drawings for mural
      project to reflect the natural and human
      elements thathave forged Northwest reality.
      The artist states: "The key elements as
      envisaged are land and water integrated with
      racial groupings, diverse technologies and
      invested labor. Incorporating Northwest
      symbols, the mural will be seen as a
      manifestation of the physical and natural
      energies which have combined to give
      expression to an unique force in the
      Northwest.".

OMICA Housing Corp. Inc., Miami, FL

6602 OMICA Housing Corp., Inc., Homestead
      (Miami), FL. Dedication of heritage village.
      Brochure, 1977. English.

      AN: Brochure of non-profit housing
      corporation which built, with Housing and
      Urban Development (HUD) funds, public
      homeownership housing for farmworkers and
      low-income rural residents of South Dade
      County. Illustrated with a mural by Roberto
      Rios of San Antonio, one of three done in

Florida.

ONLY ONCE IN A LIFETIME [film]

6603 CHICANO CINEMA NEWSLETTER. Vol. 1, no. 4
      (June 1979). English.

      AN: Report and cautionary note on the
      upcoming Alternative Cinema Conference;
      announcement of ONLY ONCE IN A LIFETIME and
      CHICANA film releases; other new films and
      TV programs; a Chicano cinema bibliography;
      a list of Chicano production companies and
      distributors; a theoretical article on the
      nature (proposed) of Chicano cinema as an
      alternative cinema; statement of purpose of
      the Los Angeles Chicano Cinema Coalition.

6604 Gloria, Juan J. En San Antonio: se celebrara
      el tercer festival de cine, 'La vida chicana
      a traves del celuloide'. EL VISITANTE
      DOMINICAL, (August 20, 1978), p. 6-8, 12.
      Spanish.

      AN: The Third Chicano Film Festival
      honors the only two feature-length films
      made by Chicanos: Moctezuma Esparza's ONLY
      ONCE IN A LIFETIME (made in Hollywood) and
      Jesus Salvador Trevino's RAICES DE SANGRE
      (Blood Roots), (made with CONACINE in
      Mexico). Illustrated.

THE ORAL TRADITION [mural]

6605 Garcia, Guillermo. Wall-to-wall art for the
      people. AUSTIN AMERICAN STATESMAN, (January
      22, 1978), p. E-1. English.

      AN: Illustrated story on Raul Valdez's
      mural (in progress) The Oral Tradition.
      Valdez discusses his methods and art
      philosophy when creating community murals.

Orange County, CA

6606 Boettner, Jack. Youths help in fight against
      graffiti: muralist fights spray cans with
      brushes. LOS ANGELES TIMES [Orange County
      edition], (May 26, 1979), p. II, 12-13.
      English.

      AN: Illustrated and descriptive story
      about Orange County painter Emigdio Vasquez
      working on a series of murals with youth.
      Locations of murals by the group,
      biographical information about Vasquez, and
      his statement about art are given.
      Illustrated.

6607 Galeria, Santa Ana, CA. The last Chicano art
      show. Exhibition brochure, 1981. English.

      AN: Invitation-brochure for an exhibit
      of Los Angeles and Orange County artists in
      a gallery underwritten by the Friendly
      Center, Inc. with grants from local
      government and from businesses. Exhibiting
      are (Roberto) Gil de Montes, Gilbert Lujan,
      Judy Miranda, Patricia Murillo, Alonso
      Pardo, Teddy Sandoval, Mexican artist
      Artemio Sepulveda, Joey Terrill, Art
      Valenzuela, Ben Valenzuela, Linda Vallejo,
      Jack A. Vargas, Emigdio Vasquez, Richard
      Serrato, and J. William Hernandez, who is
      the gallery director.

Orange County, CA (cont.)

6608 Mills House Visual Arts Complex, Garden
Grove, CA. Menudo: artistas latinos de
Orange County. Exhibit invitation, 1980.
English.

AN: Invitation to an exhibit organized
for the first anniversary of Artistas
Latinos de Orange County including Delores
Grajeda, William Hernandez, Marylee Montano,
Patricia Murillo, Irene Ramos, Juan Ramos,
Ricardo Serrato, Miguel Shanahan, Arthur
Valenzuela, Benjamin Valenzuela, Jack
Vargas, Alonzo Whitney, Emigdio Vasquez,
Susana Zaccagnino, and Mexican artist
Artemio Sepulveda.

6609 Newport Harbor Art Museum, Newport Beach,
CA. Our own artists: art in Orange County.
Exhibition catalog, 1979. English.

AN: Includes Patricia Murillo and
Emigdio Vasquez with illustrations of one
work each. Biographies of the artists.

6610 Santa Ana Public Library, Newhope Branch,
Santa Ana, CA. Artistas latinos de Orange
County. Exhibition brochure, 1979.

AN: Exhibit of six artists: Dolores
Grajeda, Eduardo Navarro, Arthur Valenzuela,
Benjamin Valenzuela, Emigdio Vasquez, Susana
A. Zaccagnino.

Ordonez, Benny

6611 59th Street Gallery, St. Louis, MO. Midwest
Mexican-American art exhibit: Mexico and its
artists. Exhibition brochure, 1981. English.

AN: Sponsored by the Sociedad Mexicana
"Benito Juarez" and the international
Institute of St. Louis, this three-part
exhibit includes 1) MEXICO AS SEEN BY HER
CHILDREN, a bilingual exhibit from Mexico
traveling under Smithsonian Institution
auspices, 2) MEXICAN CHILDREN IN THE U.S.A.,
3) MEXICAN AMERICAN ARTISTS. In the latter
are included Stephen Capiz (Roseville,
Minn.), Jose Gonzalez (Chicago), Cesar A.
Martinez (San Antonio), Ada Medina (Des
Moines), Nora Chapa Mendoza (West
Bloomfield, Mich.), Rene David
Michel-Trapaga (St. Louis), David Munoz
(Kansas City, Mo.), Jose Luis Narezo (Grand
Rapids, Mich.), Benny Ordonez, Roman
Villarreal (Chicago), Alejandro Romero
(Chicago), Aurelio Diaz "Tekpankalli"
(Chicago), Simon Ybarra (St. Louis).

Orendain, Antonio

6612 Guerra, Luis. Hasta la gloria [drawing].
TEJIDOS, Vol. 4, no. 2 (Summer 1977), p.
COVER. Spanish.

6613 Guerra, Victor. Primavera: happy in Khaki.
TEJIDOS, Vol. 5, no. 2-4 (1978), p. 68.
English.

Orlando Letelier Brigade

6614 Denver. NATIONAL MURALS NETWORK COMMUNITY
NEWSLETTER, (Spring 1980), p. 10. English.

AN: Denver, Colorado murals by Manuel
Martinez, the Chilean Orlando Letelier
Brigade, Roberto Lucero, Al Sanchez, Jerry
Jaramillo. Illustrated.

6615 NATIONAL MURALS NETWORK COMMUNITY
NEWSLETTER. (Spring 1980). English.

AN: Reports on the Sept. 1979 conference
of Chicano visual arts held at UT Austin,
organized by the Mujeres Artistas del
Suroeste, and the Liga Unida de Chicanos
Artistas, which brought together
participants from the U.S. and Mexico City;
on Manuel Martinez's five murals (1976-78);
murals by Roberto Lucero, Al Sanchez, and
Jerry Jaramillo; as well as by the Chilean
group Orlando Letelier Brigade, all in
Denver, Colorado; murals by Leo Tanguma in
Houston; the story about the "forbidden"
Chicano mural in Blue Island, Illinois.
Illustrated.

Orona, Lee

6616 Campesino Business and Joint Enterprise
Building, Fresno, CA. Sabor a Fresno. Arte
chicano: los Four and la Brocha. Exhibition
invitation [1976]. English.

AN: Invitation to an exhibit of works by
Los Four of Los Angeles and members of La
Brocha del Valle of Fresno: Arturo Roman,
Sal Garcia, John Sierra, Juan Truner, Sapo
de Aztlan, Fernando Hernandez, Alberto
Reyes, Ernesto Palomino, Lee Orona,
Francisco Barrios, Juan Ybarra, Bobby Reyes,
Alberto Hernandez. Brocha was started by
Palomino (California State University,
Fresno professor) to pool talents of Central
Valley artists.

Oropeza, Eduardo

6617 Art Gallery, California State University,
Long Beach and Lujan, Gilbert Sanchez
"Magu". El arte del pocho. Exhibit brochure,
October 1968. English.

AN: Information about Southern
California artists John Deheras, Marcus
Villagran, Roberto de la Rocha, Santos
Zuniga, Crispin Gonzales, Richard Martinez,
Jesus Gutierrez, Ed Oropeza, Pete Mendez,
David Ramirez, Gilbert Sanchez Lujan, Willie
Hernandez, Art Ponce, Carmen Tostado, Al
Almeida, David Ceja, Robert E. Chavez,
Thomas A. Ferriera. All art students,
graduates, or faculty.

6618 Galeria: a place you should visit. CAMINOS,
Vol. 2, no. 5 (October 1981), p. 24-25.
English.

AN: Announcement of the opening of
Galeria, specializing in Hispanic art, in
Orange County, California. Illustrations of
sculpture by Richard G. Villa and Eduardo
Oropeza.

Orozco, Jose Clemente

6619 Congreso de Artistas Chicanos en Aztlan, San
Diego, CA. Diego Rivera, David Alfaro
Siqueiros, Jose Clemente Orozco: exhibit of
local artists, La Logan [San Diego].
Exhibition brochure, n.d. [c.1974]. English.

AN: Announcement of a traveling exhibit
organized by Galeria de la Raza, San
Francisco, from the collection of the San
Francisco Museum of Art. Illustrated with a
San Diego mural.

--   --

Orozco, Jose Clemente (cont.)

6620 Salvador R. Torres Chicano Underground
     Studio-Gallery, San Diego, CA. Diego Rivera,
     David Alfaro Siqueiros, Jose Clemente
     Orozco, from the collection of the S.F.
     Museum of Art. Exhibition invitation,
     [1974]. English.

     AN: Illustrated invitation of an exhibit
     organized by the Galeria de la Raza of San
     Francisco loaned to the Congreso de Artistas
     Chicanos en Aztlan, and held in artist
     Torres' studio.

Orozco, Juan Ishi

6621 Anaya, Rudolfo A. and Ortiz, Simon J.
     1680-1980: a ceremony of brotherhood.
     Albuquerque, NM: Academic, 1981. English.

     AN: A cooperative publication by members
     of the former La Academia de la Nueva Raza
     (1969-1976) formed of writers and artists,
     and the Tri-Centennial Commission of the
     All-Indian Pueblo Council. Includes writings
     and artworks by Chicanos and Indians from
     New Mexico, California, Texas, and Arizona.
     Chicano artists works included are by Ellen
     Arellano, Juan Estevan Arellano, Alberto
     Baros, Jose Antonio Burciaga, Juan Reyes
     Cervantes, Rudy Cuellar, Ricardo Favela, El
     Zarco Guerrero, Luis Jimenez, Jr., Carlos
     Quinto Kemm, Alejandro Lopez, Floyd Lujan,
     Jose Montoya, Juanishi Orozco, Leo Romero,
     Secundino Sandoval, Jaime Valdez, Maria
     Varela, Esteban Villa.

6622 Calendario de comida 1976. San Francisco,
     CA: Galeria de la Raza, 1976. English.

     AN: Handprinted silkscreen calendar
     consisting of twelve sheets and a cover. The
     work of the following artists is included:
     Ralph Maradiaga, Juanishi Orozco, Francisco
     Camplis, Ruben Guzman, Rodolfo Cuellar,
     Xavier Viramontes, Jose Montoya, Esteban
     Villa, Rene Yanez, Max Garcia and Louis "The
     Foot" Gonzalez, Patricia Rodriguez, and
     Ricardo Favela. All of the above are
     associated with the Galeria de la Raza, or
     the Royal Chicano Air Force of Sacramento,
     CA.

6623 California. State College. Los Angeles. Art
     Gallery. Twelve Chicano artists. Exhibition
     invitation, n.d. English.

     AN: Invitation to an exhibit: Jose
     Montoya, Gilbert Sanchez Lujan, Esteban
     Villa, Rene Yanez, Joe Moran, Armando Cid,
     Leonard Castellas, Juanishi Orozco, Rudy
     Cuellar, Beltran, Lopez and Cabrera.

6624 Goldman, Jane. Art against the wall.
     SACRAMENTO MAGAZINE, (August 1980).
     English.

     AN: Muralists Esteban Villa, Stan
     Padilla and Juanishi Orozco from the Centro
     de Artistas Chicanos are planning a symbolic
     65 foot, four-story mural on the parking
     structure opposite Macy's. The mural is
     described in detail. Illustrated.

6625 La historia de California, 1977. San
     Francisco, CA: Galeria de la Raza, 1977.
     English.

     AN: Handprinted silkscreen calendar of
     history seen from a Mexican point of view.
     Twelve sheets and a cover. Artists are:
     Ralph Maradiaga, Irene Perez, Louie "The
     Foot" Gonzalez, Max Garcia, Patricia

Rodriguez, Jose Romero, Esteban Villa,
Juanishi Orozco, Rodolfo Cuellar, Jose
Montoya, Xavier Viramontes, Rene Yanez,
Ricardo Favela, associated with the Galeria
de la Raza, or the Royal Chicano Air Force
of Sacramento.

6626 Mural depicts la lucha campesina del
     mexicano. EL HISPANO, Vol. 8, no. 12
     (September 9, 1975). English.

     AN: Photograph and commentary on the
     mural by J. Orozco for the Sacramento
     Farmworker's Migrant Program on F. Street.
     Centered by the Virgin of Guadalupe, the
     mural is divided into four sections: The
     Farmworker in the Fields, The Tree of Life,
     Violence Against the Farmworkers, and the
     Racist System.

6627 Oakes College, University of California,
     Santa Cruz, CA and Carrillo, Eduardo.
     Corazon de Aztlan: a Chicano arts show.
     Exhibition catalog, 1981. English.

     AN: Catalog of exhibit including works
     by Eduardo Carrillo, Juana Franklin, Cruz
     Zamarron, Jerry Astorga, Jaime Valadez,
     Ernesto Palomino, Sal Garcia, Roger Sierra,
     Jose Montoya, Esteban Villa, Juanishi
     Orozco, from Santa Cruz, San Jose, Fresno
     and Sacramento. Presentations of films and
     by the Teatro de la Tierra Morena of Santa
     Cruz County.

6628 Photo-graphics/foto-grafica. MAIZE, Vol. 4,
     no. 1-2 (Fall , Winter, 1980, 1981).
     Bilingual.

     AN: 9 drawings and prints by Royal
     Chicano Air Force (Sacramento, Calif.)
     artists Jose Montoya, Juanishi Orozco,
     Esteban Villa.

6629 R.C.A.F. artistas precursores del arte
     chicano. EL HISPANO, Vol. 8, no. 35
     (February 17, 1976), p. 1. English.

     AN: Information on the R.C.A.F.
     organization. Includes group photograph of
     R.C.A.F. members, Jose Montoya, Esteban
     Villa, John Carrillo, Ricardo Fabela, Rudy
     Cuellar, Juanishi Orozco and Frank Godena.

6630 Rios, Sam. Chicano muralist: Toltecotl in
     Aztlan. Unpublished paper, 1980. English.

     AN: History of pre-Columbian, Mexican,
     and Chicano wall paintings. Describes in
     detail murals by Jose Montoya, Juanishi
     Orozco, Esteban Villa, Stan Padilla, Juan
     Cervantes, Lorraine Garcia of the Centro de
     Artistas Chicanos, Royal Chicano Air Force,
     painted in 1977 at Southside Park,
     Sacramento, Calif. Symbolism is explained.

6631 Transcendente y majestuoso mural de las tres
     aguilas. EL HISPANO, Vol. 8, no. 4 (July 15,
     1975), p. 6. Spanish.

     AN: Biographical data on Juan Ishi
     Orozco and commentary on his mural "Las Tres
     Aguilas." One eagle represents mother earth,
     another the dominant racist system and the
     third is symbolic of the United Farmworkers
     and their struggle.

Orozco, Sylvia

6632 Orozco, Irma. Women & their work. PARA LA
     GENTE, Vol. 1, no. 4 (October 1977), p. 12.
     English.

     AN: Illustrated story about "Women &
     Their Work" festival in Austin, Texas,
     Oct-Dec 1977. Photographers Maria Flores and
     Teresina Guerra, Santa Barraza, Nora
     Gonzalez Dodson, Sylvia Orozco, and Modesta
     Trevino exhibited.

6633 Women artists: forming a Texas network.
     Brochure, 1979. English.

     AN: Biographic and bibliographic
     information on women artists groups from
     Austin, Dallas, Houston and San Antonio.
     Includes brief history of MAS (Mujeres
     Artistas del Suroeste), a list of members,
     and biographies of Alicia Arredondo, Santa
     Barraza, Mary Ann Ambray Gonzalez, and
     Sylvia Orozco.

6634 Xochil Art and Culture Center, Mission, TX.
     Besame mucho. Exhibition invitation, 1979.
     English.

     AN: Invitation to exhibit of Texas
     artists from Mujeres Artistas del Suroeste
     (MAS): Mary Ann Anguiano, Alicia Arredondo,
     Santa Barraza, Nora Gonzales-Dodson, Maria
     Flores, Carolina Flores, Mary Ann Ambray
     Gonzales, Sylvia Orozco, Nancy de los
     Santos, Modesta Barbina Trevino.
     Illustrated.

Ortega, Gil

6635 Ortega, Gil. The 50's and other assorted
     Chicano graffiti. La Habra, CA: s.n., 1981.
     English.

     AN: Album of caricatures of barrio
     types; black and white drawings in six
     categories: The Parties and Dances,
     Schooldays, Oldtime Lowriders, Refine, Los
     Veteranos, Los Vatos. Some drawings
     accompanied by commentary.

Ortega, Jose Benito

6636 Santos of New Mexico, art of our people.
     GRITO DEL NORTE, Vol. 3, no. 1 (January 17,
     1970), p. 8-9. English.

     AN: Historical trajectory of santero
     tradition in New Mexico. Distinguished
     santeros like Rafael Aragon of Cordova,
     Miguel Herrera of Arroyo Hondo, Juan Ramon
     Velasquez of Conjilon, Jose Benito Ortega of
     La Cueva all created art wedded to the
     environment of the Southwest. Illustrated
     with a portfolio of santos and retablos from
     the Folk Art Museum of Santa Fe, NM.

Ortega, Juan

6637 Lansing Community College, Lansing, MI.
     Festival! Festival program, [1978]. English.

     AN: Program of a festival which includes
     an Hispanic Arts Exhibit, including Juan
     Ortega, Nora Mendoza, Jose Luis Narezo, and
     Brazilian-born Veronica Dalia de
     Albuquerque.

Ortega, Malu

6638 Chicago-Raza murals. NATIONAL MURALS NETWORK
     COMMUNITY NEWSLETTER, (Fall 1979), p. 22.
     English.

     AN: Murals by Ray Patlan, Aurelio Diaz,
     Marcos Raya, Salvador Vega, Jaime Longoria,
     Malu Ortega y Alberro, Oscar Moya in
     Chicago's Pilsen district.

6639 Elitzik, Paul. Mural magic. AMERICAS,
     (June, July, 1981). English.

     AN: Brief illustrated account of murals
     in the Pilsen barrio of Chicago. Mentions
     work by Aurelio Diaz, Marcos Raya, and
     Salvador Vega. Focuses on the controversial
     mural at Benito Juarez High School painted
     by Jaime Longoria and Malu Ortega.

Ortega, Marguerite

6640 Calendario de March: 1977. Chicago, IL:
     MARCH, Inc., 1976. English.

     AN: Historical calendar with photos and
     biographies of artists. Illustrations of
     artwork by Ray Patlan, Jose Nario, Frank J.
     Sanchez, Salvador Dominguez, Salvador Vega,
     Marguerite Ortega, Aurelio Diaz, Carlos
     Cortez, Mario E. Castillo, Francisco Blasco,
     Rey Vasquez, and Efrain Martinez. History of
     MARCH (Movimiento Artistico Chicano).

Ortega "Salazar" Park, Santa Barbara, CA

6641 Vallejo, Armando. Murales en progreso.
     XALMAN, Vol. 3, no. 1 (Spring 1980), p.
     24-37. English.

     AN: Description of Santa Barbara,
     California's Ortega "Salazar" Park and its
     murals. Illustrated.

Ortiz, William

6642 Los Angeles City College. Contemporary times
     2. Exhibition announcement, 1980. English.

     AN: Illustrated announcement for
     photography show of Monticello Miller and
     William Ortiz.

Osorio, Gilberto

6643 Galeria Museo - new art gallery opens in the
     Mission. EL TECOLOTE, Vol. 8, no. 1
     (September 1977), p. 8. Bilingual.

     AN: Brief article on the inauguration of
     the Art Gallery at the Mission Cultural
     Center. The opening Exhibit (August 13,
     1977) was entitled SIXTY-THREE SHOW and
     included work in various media by Sixty
     three Bay Area Latino artists. Gilberto
     Osorio was designated as the first
     artist-in-residence. Information on future
     plans for the Galeria-Museo.

OTHER SOURCES: AN AMERICAN ESSAY [exhibit]

6644 Gonzalez, Lila. Ideas on a Third World art
     exhibit. SAN FRANCISCO ODALISQUE, (October,
     November, 1976), p. 5-6. English.

     AN: Review essay on the exhibition
     "Other Sources: An American Essay" sponsored
     by the San Francisco Art Institute.

Otis Art Institute of Parsons School of Design, Los Angeles

6645 Muchnic, Suzanne. Damaged goods in the big city. LOS ANGELES TIMES, (July 23, 1979), p. IV-11. English.

AN: Review of the exhibit at Otis Art Institute of Parsons School of Design of L.A. PARKS AND WRECKS, featuring Carlos Almaraz, John Valadez, and Black artist John Woods. Almaraz paints auto wrecks, and landscapes of Echo Park. Valadez does pencil portraits of young Chicanos. Illustrated.

OUR PAST, OUR PRESENT, AND OUR FUTURE [MURAL]

6646 Meza to paint Pan American National Bank murals. MEXICAN AMERICAN SUN, (October 14, 1965). English.

AN: Mexican painter Jose Reyes Meza is commissioned to create a mosaic mural titled OUR PAST, OUR PRESENT, AND OUR FUTURE for the facade of the Pan American National Bank of East Los Angeles being erected on First Street.

OUT OF THE MAINSTREAM [film]

6647 Films for the inner city. Los Angeles, CA: Los Angeles Public Library Federal Project, 1971. English.

AN: Annotated catalog of 16mm films and filmstrips, educational and documentary. Those concerning Mexican heritage include CHICANO FROM THE SOUTHWEST (1970), HENRY...BOY OF THE BARRIO (1969); HOW'S SCHOOL, ENRIQUE (1970), I AM JOAQUIN (1970), THE MEXICAN AMERICAN: HERITAGE AND DESTINY (1970), A MEXICAN AMERICAN FAMILY (1970), MEXICAN AMERICANS: QUEST FOR EQUALITY (1968), MEXICAN OR AMERICAN (1970), SIQUEIROS: "EL MAESTRO" (THE MARCH OF HUMANITY IN LATIN AMERICA) (1969). Filmstrips include THE AWAKENING (LA RAZA) - Part IV, CONFLICT OF CULTURES (LA RAZA) - Part III, MASTERWORKS OF MEXICAN ART, OUT OF THE MAINSTREAM, PILGRIMAGE (GRAPE STRIKERS). Also listed are films and filmstrips for children.

Ozona, Leo Esequiel

6648 Exxon Company, Houston, TX and Quirarte, Jacinto. Chicano art of the barrio. Exhibition brochure, n.d. [c.1976]. English.

AN: Brochure for a traveling exhibit of photographically-reproduced Chicano murals: Leo Limon, Lucila Villasenor Grijalva, Antonio Esparza, Susan Saenz, Charles Felix, Hoyo-Mara gang, David A. Lopez and team, Roberto Chavez and team (Los Angeles); Jerry Concha, Ruben Guzman, Chuy Campusano (San Francisco); Manuel Unzueta (Santa Barbara). Ernie Palomino and Leo Esequiel Ozona (Fresno). Leo Tanguma (Houston), Roberto Lucero, Manuel Martinez and Al Sanchez (Denver).

Ozuna, Gloria

6649 Grimke, Angelina. Chicano art finds home in Mission galeria. PEOPLE'S WORLD, Vol. 33, no. 32 (August 8, 1970), p. 11. English.

AN: Commentary on the exhibition CHICANOS, CUBA Y LOS 10 MILLONES held at the original Galeria de la Raza at 425 14th Street in San Francisco. The show presented photographs by Jay Ojeda and Roberto Perez-Diaz, drawings by Gloria Ozuna

together with paintings and photographs by Cuban artist Mederos. Provides information about the goals of the Galeria as the visual arts department of Casa Hispana de Bellas Artes. Exhibition curator was Rolando Castellon.

6650 Martinez, Anita. Raza! Arte! Raza! Arte! EL TECOLOTE, Vol. 1, no. 2 (September 7, 1970), p. 3. Bilingual.

AN: Galeria de la Raza opened on July, 1970 at 425 14th St. San Francisco. It was an outgrowth of the Arte Seis organization (an art effort established in the Mission District in 1967 by Francisco Camplis, Rupert Garcia, Ralph McNeil, Jay Ojeda and Jack Ruiz). These and other artists brought together by the Neighborhood Arts Program have coalesced in the new Galeria de la Raza. Article gives goals, organizational scheme and plans for the Galeria. It's first exhibit was a one man show by Esteban Villa together with a photo and sketch exhibit on Cuba by Jay Ojeda, Roberto Diaz Perez and Gloria Ozuna. Illustrated with installation view of new Galeria.

6651 Semana de la Raza: international panel of the arts, Mexico and the United States. Santa Ana, CA: MEChA, Santa Ana College, 1972. English.

AN: An International Panel of the Arts, organized by art historian Shifra Goldman, featured Mexicans Hector Garcia, prize-winning photographer; Jaime Mejia, painter, restorer, filmmaker; Alejandro Vichir, director of Teatro Trashumante; and Chicanos Gilbert Sanchez Lujan, sculptor and painter; Gloria Osuna, painter and artist for Teatro Campesino; and Jesus Salvador Trevino, filmmaker.

Pacheco, Juan

6652 Chicano muralists maintain traditions. LA CUCARACHA, (November 20, 1979), p. 7. English.

AN: Introduction to Chicano muralism in Pueblo and comparison to the Mexican mural movement from which it draws inspiration. 20 murals painted from 1977 to 1979. The muralists include Bernardo Duran, Juan Espinoza, Miguel "Freeloader" Garcia, Lola Gutierrez, Leo Lucero, Juan Pacheco, Dolores Pena, Pedro Romero, Stan Salazar, David Sandoval. Diego Rivera murals illustrated.

PACHUCO ART - A HISTORICAL UPDATE [exhibit]

6653 Hurtado, Debbie. A historical update: Montoya's vindication of fabricated biases. THE STATE HORNET, (December 13, 1977), p. 6. English.

AN: Review of Jose Montoya's show "Pachuco Art - A Historical Update; "a rekindling of pachuquismo from the 1940s prevalent in Montoya's paintings and pen-and-ink drawings. The show featured historical photographs, and an animated hologram. Visitors wore zoot suit outfits to the opening. Illustrated.

Pachuco Images

6654 Art Space - Open Ring Gallery, Sacramento, CA. El Pachuco art de Jose Montoya: a historical update. Exhibition invitation, 1977. English.

AN: Invitation to an exhibit. Illustrated with a reproduction of a 1977 silkscreen calendar page in color by Montoya.

6655 Fong, Katheryn M. Pachuco art records era of zootsuits and anti-Mexican riots. SAN FRANCISCO JRNL, Vol. 2, no. 32 (March 1, 1978), p. 6. English.

AN: Review of Galeria de la Raza exhibit of Jose Montoya's Pachuco Art. Installation included historical photographs and documents. Montoya work (drawings and paintings) were contextualized by written commentary aiming to re-interpret an important aspect of Chicano cultural history.

6656 Hernandez, Sergio. [Untitled drawing]. CON SAFOS, Vol. 1, no. 3 (March 1969), p. 28.

6657 Herron, Willie. [Anglo meets three Chicano youths (drawing)]. REGENERACION, Vol. 2, no. 1 (1971), p. 21. English.

6658 Hurtado, Debbie. A historical update: Montoya's vindication of fabricated biases. THE STATE HORNET, (December 13, 1977), p. 6. English.

AN: Review of Jose Montoya's show "Pachuco Art - A Historical Update; "a rekindling of pachuquismo from the 1940s prevalent in Montoya's paintings and pen-and-ink drawings. The show featured historical photographs, and an animated hologram. Visitors wore zoot suit outfits to the opening. Illustrated.

6659 Lowrider: arte del varrio. A.T.M. Communications, Inc., 1979. English.

AN: Issue of LOWRIDER Magazine dedicated to drawings and paintings by "cholos" sent in to the editor for publication. Good example of a popular art form by largely self-taught neighborhood youth, with a distinctive style and symbolism. Related to graffiti and tattoos. Most images are of lowrider cars, young women and men.

6660 Lowrider: arte del varrio. San Jose, CA: A.T.M. Communications, 1980. English.

AN: Second issue of LOWRIDER Magazine dedicated to drawings and pantings by "cholos" sent in to the editor for publication.

6661 Martinez, Cesar Augusto. Manito [drawing]. CARACOL, Vol. 4, no. 10 (June 1978), p. 19. Bilingual.

6662 Martinez, Cesar Augusto. La papa [drawing]. CARACOL, Vol. 4, no. 10 (June 1978), p. BACK COVER. Spanish.

6663 Martinez, Cesar Augusto. El Sonny [drawing]. CARACOL, Vol. 4, no. 10 (June 1978), p. 7. Bilingual.

6664 Montoya, Jose E. Chuco series [drawings]. MAIZE, Vol. 2, no. 1 (Fall   1978), p. Bk cover. English.

6665 Montoya, Jose E. Pachuco art: a historical update. Sacramento, CA: Royal Chicano Air Force, 1977. English.

AN: Booklet outlining the history of the Zoot Suit Riots of 1943 and the making of the Pachuco myth, written by Montoya and illustrated with his pen-and-ink drawings of Pachucos and Pachucas.

6666 Montoya, Jose E. [Untitled drawing]. MAIZE, Vol. 4, no. 1-2 (Fall , Winter, 1980, 1981), p. Ft cover. Bilingual.

6667 Montoya, Jose E. [Untitled drawing]. MAIZE, Vol. 4, no. 1-2 (Fall , Winter, 1980, 1981), p. 13. Bilingual.

6668 Montoya, Jose E. [Untitled drawings from the CHUCO SERIES]. MAIZE, Vol. 2, no. 1 (Fall 1978), p. 32-35. English.

6669 Montoya, Jose E. [Untitled drawings from the CHUCO SERIES]. MAIZE, Vol. 2, no. 1 (Fall 1978), p. Ft cover. English.

6670 Montoya, Jose E. [Untitled paintings]. CHISMEARTE, Vol. 2, no. 1 (1978), p. 10.

6671 Rafas. Social comment in barrio pop [drawing]. CON SAFOS, no. 8 (1972), p. 34.

6672 Rafas. A social comment in Chicano pop [drawing]. CON SAFOS, Vol. 1, no. 4 (1969), p. 10.

6673 Valadez, John. [Untitled drawing]. CHISMEARTE, Vol. 2, no. 1 (Summer 1978), p. 5. English.

Pachucos

6674 Barrio graffiti. In Castaneda-Shular, Ybarra-Frausto, and Sommers, eds. LITERATURA CHICANA. Englewood Cliffs, NJ: Prentice-Hall, 1972. Spanish.

AN: Drawings and explanations of Chicano graffiti that originated in the Pachuco era.

6675 Creations by Cruz. Color brochure, n.d. English.

AN: Color brochure of genre-like figures produced for sale by Los Angeles sculptor Manuel Cruz in hydro-stone. The figures, which run from 3" to 12" high depict images from Aztec legends to Pachucos, Brown Berets, and hippies.

6676 Frankenstein, Alfred. Montoya's artistic update on Chicano zoot suiters. SAN FRANCISCO CHRONICLE, (February 18, 1978), p. 36. English.

AN: Review of Pachuco show at San Francisco's Galeria de la Raza, especially Jose Montoya's sketches and paintings.

6677 Garcia, Rupert. The politics of popular art. CHISMEARTE, Vol. 2, no. 1 (Summer 1978), p. 2-4. English.

AN: Defines and discusses the terms "Popular Art", "Mass Art", and "Folk Art" and gives examples of their correct and incorrect usages.

Pachucos (cont.)

6678 Johnson, Charles. J street galleries: politics flavor alternative art shows. SACRAMENTO BEE, (December 20, 1977), p. A13. English.

AN: Review of a Pachuco show by Jose Montoya that is half drawings and paintings, and half politics - photographs of Pachucos of the 1940s. Montoya's essay that accompanies the exhibit attempts to dispel the image of Pachucos as gangsters, and declares that Pachucos were the first "freedom fighters." The reviewer feels this is one-sided. Illustrated.

6679 Montoya, Jose E. Pachuco art: a historical update. Sacramento, CA: Royal Chicano Air Force, 1977. English.

AN: Booklet outlining the history of the Zoot Suit Riots of 1943 and the making of the Pachuco myth, written by Montoya and illustrated with his pen-and-ink drawings of Pachucos and Pachucas.

6680 Neumeier, Marty. Ignacio Gomez. COMMUNICATION ARTS MAGAZINE, Vol. 21, no. 6 (January, February, 1980), p. 78-87. English.

AN: Story on commercial designer and illustrator Ignacio Gomez of Los Angeles which describes his background, education and life style. 17 full-color illustrations of his art work, including the ZOOT SUIT poster for the Mark Taper Forum play.

6681 Posters by Ignacio Gomez: in full color suitable for framing. CAMINOS, (May 1981), p. 49. English.

AN: Six full-color posters on Latino subjects by illustrator Gomez advertised for sale. The best-known is Gomez's poster for ZOOT SUIT, a play by Luis Valdez.

6682 Valadez, Kathy L. Zoot suit, by Luis Valdez. SOMOS, Vol. 1, no. 2 (July 1978), p. 20-29. English.

AN: Two reviews of Valdez's new play ZOOT SUIT, both enthusiastic. Historical material and photographs with an essay by Jose Montoya and his Pachuco drawing, as well as views of the play are included.

Packard, Emmy Lou

6683 Albright, Thomas. Three remarkable Latin murals. SAN FRANCISCO CHRONICLE, (June 7, 1974), p. 48. English.

AN: The myth of the melting pot is vanishing: we recognize a variety of "publics" today. This is shown in three remarkable murals in the San Francisco Mission District. The Mission branch of the Bank of America has a 90 foot mural designed by Jesus Campusano, assisted by Luis Cortazar and Michael Rios, with technical advice from Emmy Lou Packard. Another mural is by the Mujeres Muralistas (Graciela Carrillo, Consuelo Mendez, Irene Perez, Patricia Rodriguez); the third by Michael Rios on the 24th St. mini-park.

Padilla, Anthony

6684 Cesaretti, Gusmano and Hirtz, Jacqueline. Uplifting the city: the mural-painter's goal. HOME MAGAZINE, (May 8, 1977), p. 50-51. English.

AN: Illustrated report on murals in Los Angeles and Pasadena by Anthony Padilla.

Padilla, Stan

6685 Goldman, Jane. Art against the wall. SACRAMENTO MAGAZINE, (August 1980). English.

AN: Muralists Esteban Villa, Stan Padilla and Juanishi Orozco from the Centro de Artistas Chicanos are planning a symbolic 65 foot, four-story mural on the parking structure opposite Macy's. The mural is described in detail. Illustrated.

6686 Rios, Sam. Chicano muralist: Toltecotl in Aztlan. Unpublished paper, 1980. English.

AN: History of pre-Columbian, Mexican, and Chicano wall paintings. Describes in detail murals by Jose Montoya, Juanishi Orozco, Esteban Villa, Stan Padilla, Juan Cervantes, Lorraine Garcia of the Centro de Artistas Chicanos, Royal Chicano Air Force, painted in 1977 at Southside Park, Sacramento, Calif. Symbolism is explained.

Painters
   USE: Artists

Paintings

6687 Acosta, Dan. Paintings reflect life experiences. THE ECCENTRIC, (June 26, 1980). English.

AN: Review of one-woman show by Nora Chapa Mendoza at the Heritage Art Gallery, Ypsilanti, MI. Mendoza works in abstract impressionist style with wet streams of colors that express energy. Her subjects are landscapes, moods, nudes, and Hispanic themes. She is active in the Detroit Latino Artist Association, Nuestras Artes de Michigan, and the New Detroit Art Council.

6688 Adrienne Simard Gallery, Los Angeles, CA. Presenting Carlos Almaraz: pastel drawings, 1969-1981. Exhibition invitation, 1981. English.

AN: Invitation to exhibit of Los Angeles painter Carlos Almaraz. includes color illustration.

6689 The affectionate realism of Jesse Trevino. SA: THE MAGAZINE OF SAN ANTONIO, Vol. 3, no. 10 (December 1979), p. 70-73. English.

AN: Brief story about, and personal statement by San Antonio photorealist painter and muralist. Trevino focuses on portraits of people and sites in the Westside barrio. Color illustrations.

6690 Alarcon, Carlos. [Untitled painting]. TIN TAN, no. 4 (Fall 1976), p. Cover.

Paintings (cont.)

6691 Alarcon, Francisco X. Rupert Garcia: portraits/retratos. EL TECOLOTE LITERARY MAGAZINE, Vol. 2, no. 1 (March 1981), p. 6+. Bilingual.

AN: Review of Garcia exhibit at the Mexican Museum (S.F.) in 1981. Includes portraits of Frida Kahlo and the Flores Magon brothers, Goya, Van Gogh, Ethel and Julius Rosenberg, etc. Illustrated. This article has been reprinted in METAMORFOSIS under a different title: "Portraits Plus Struggles Plus Consciousness: Nine Pastels by Rupert Garcia," Vol. 3-4, no. 1-2, (1980-81), p. 104-106.

6692 Albright, Thomas. San Francisco: the force of universals. ART NEWS MAGAZINE, Vol. 77, no. 6 (Summer 1978), p. 174. English.

AN: Review of Rupert Garcia pastel show at the San Francisco Museum of Modern Art. Reviewer suggests he is one of the very few real artists to emerge from the "unfortunate genre" of poster art. His images are highly charged: political prisoners, corpses, revolutionary martyrs.

6693 Albright, Thomas. The sensual moods of nature. SAN FRANCISCO CHRONICLE, (January 23, 1971), p. 34. English.

AN: Review of an exhibition of paintings by Pedro Rodriguez of San Francisco at the Galeria de La Raza. Work classified as lyrical abstractions "in the vein of introspective lyric poetry".

6694 Albright, Thomas. 'Unspoiled' Bay Area art. SAN FRANCISCO CHRONICLE, (August 29, 1974), p. 40. English.

AN: Review of an exhibit titled ART NAIF curated by Rolando Castellon. The show featured 15 Bay Area painters who are basically self-taught and share a personal expression unhampered by prevailing art conventions and trends. Includes material on Alexander Maldonado, 72-year-old "primitive" painter from San Francisco. Some of Maldonado's work includes references to his childhood and youth in Mexico.

6695 Alex Maldonado, primitive painter. SAN FRANCISCO FOCUS MAGAZINE, (1973). English.

AN: Biographical information on 72 year old Alexander Maldonado who started painting upon his retirement. His "naif" work has gained wide critical acclaim and he has had more than 200 exhibitions throughout the United States. Illustrated with reproduction of one of Maldonado's paintings.

6696 Anderson, Howard J.; Young, Robert S.; and Kilgore, Andrew. Amado Maurilio Pena, Jr. Albuquerque, NM: Robert Stephan Young Publishing Co., 1981. English.

AN: Coffee-table type of art book about the Laredo-born painter and printmaker. The text includes impressionistic writing about Pena's life, interlaced with statements by the artist about his life and work. Though including a few plates from his early (1974-1978) political and family silkscreens, over 50 color plates reproduce his "Santa Fe Indian" works from 1978 to the present.

6697 Andrews, Colman. Art of the state: California. NEW WEST MAGAZINE, (January 1981), p. 54-59. English.

AN: Short text on California artists who are presumably influenced by the state's light, color, space, etc. Works of 16 artists reproduced in full color, including one by Carlos Almaraz of Los Angeles. Statements by each artist.

6698 Andrews, Rena. The fine arts. ROUNDUP, (March 15, 1970), p. 16+. English.

AN: Biographical information on Chicano artist Ramon Kelley. Described as an impressionist, his work has affinity with Monet and Manet.

6699 Andrews, Rena. The fine arts. ROUNDUP, (September 27, 1970), p. 18. English.

AN: Commentary on one-man exhibition by John L. Mendoza at the International House Gallery in Denver. Noted for his water-color landscapes, the artists is a full time art teacher at East High School in Pueblo Colorado. Illustrated with photograph of the artist and one of his paintings.

6700 Andrews, Rena. The fine arts. ROUNDUP, (November 25, 1973), p. 22. English.

AN: Article places work of Ramon Kelley within the impressionist mode. At the De Colores Gallery in his hometown of Denver, Kelley's exhibit titled, "Faces of the Southwest" included drawings, water color and pastel painting, oils and acrylics.

6701 Andrews, Rena. The fine arts. EMPIRE MAGAZINE, (December 19, 1971), p. 32. English.

AN: Review of first one person show by John Flores at the Nathan Galleries in Denver. Born in El Paso, Texas but reared in Denver, Flores depicts his Indo-Hispanic heritage in his creations. Concentrating on portraits, still-lifes, and landscapes, Flores paints within the Impressionistic mode. Critic feels Flores is not fully realized, yet has some impressive work and is a promising younger artist.

6702 Arenas, Eva. Sabino Canyon [painting]. LA PALABRA, Vol. 2, no. 2 (Fall 1980), p. 11.

6703 Arenas, Eva. Sonoran Desert [painting]. LA PALABRA, Vol. 2, no. 2 (Fall 1980), p. 11.

6704 Armando Cid art works on display at Barrio Gallery. EL HISPANO, Vol. 5, no. 44 (April 24, 1973). English.

AN: Description of Armando Cid's M.A. thesis exhibition. The dominant impulse in the paintings is an attempt to define and reflect a Chicano style.

6705 Armendarez, Linda. Tiger [painting]. TEJIDOS, Vol. 4, no. 3 (Fall 1977), p. 28. English.

6706 The art of Mexican America. EMPIRE MAGAZINE, (November 1, 1970), p. 24-25. English.

AN: Visual portfolio with minimal text. Includes paintings by Amado Pena, Mel Casas, Porfirio Salinas, and sculpture by Octavio Medellin. On the same page, Dr. Jacinto Quirarte gives views on the nature of Mexican art, the Mexican American artist, and the connection between Mexican and Mexican American art.

Paintings (cont.)

6707 Arts review. ARTS REVIEW, Vol. 31, no. 20
(October 12, 1979), p. 558. English.

AN: Review of show in October Gallery
London by Gilberto Guzman of Santa Fe, New
Mexico. Guzman is characterized as a
"figurative expressionist.".

6708 Barajas, Salvador. A mi amor [painting].
MAIZE, Vol. 1, no. 3 (Spring 1978), p. Bk
cover. Spanish.

6709 Barajas, Salvador. Primavera [painting].
MAIZE, Vol. 1, no. 3 (Spring 1978), p.
32-33. English.

6710 Barrett, Marjorie. Experimental art of a
realist. ROCKY MOUNTAIN NEWS, (August 2,
1970), p. 74. English.

AN: Recognized as one of the area's top
realist painters, Ramon Kelley is a
diligent, hard-working artist. Current work
includes experiments with abstraction,
strong facial studies and landscapes.
Includes photograph of artist and three
examples of his work.

6711 Barrett, Marjorie and Flores, John. Flores:
artist's gamble paid off. ROCKY MOUNTAIN
NEWS, (May 18, 1980), p. 27. English.

AN: In less than a decade, John Flores
has gone from being a part-time painter
working in a meat packing plant to a
prolific fulltime artist. This interview on
the occasion of Flores' one person show at
the De Colores Gallery reviews his artistic
trajectory. The 30 odd paintings in the
exhibit include still lifes, pastel
portraits, street scenes and landscapes in
oil. Experimenting with vivid color, Flores
is turning to his own cultural roots.

6712 Bayview Federal Savings, San Francisco, CA.
Peter Rodriguez. [S.n.: s.l.], 1974.
English.

AN: Well-illustrated brochure includes
photograph of San Francisco artist Peter
Rodriguez and four of his paintings. Also
provides biographical information,
exhibition chronology and critical excerpts
from reviews of several shows. Artist's
basic style is lyrical abstractionism
centered on organic forms derived from
nature.

6713 Bejarano, William. [Untitled painting]. CON
SAFOS, Vol. 2, no. 5 (1970), p. 13.

6714 Bellevue Art Museum, Bellevue, WA. Alfredo
Arreguin. s.n.:s.l., n.d. English.

AN: Profusely illustrated exhibition
catalog for a one-man retrospective of
paintings by Alfredo Arreguin. Exploring the
possibilities of pattern painting, the
intent of his art is to be visionary. His
paintings have affinity with Pre-Columbian
and Colonial Mexican designs and is related
to decorative emotional images of various
cultures. Includes photograph of artist and
a selected bibliography.

6715 Le Bistro Restaurant, San Antonio, TX.
Contemporary paintings by Cesar Augusto
Martinez. Exhibition catalog, 1980. English.

AN: Catalog of an exhibit. Blurb about
the artist.

6716 Bloomfield, Arthur. Zesty show at Mexican
museum. SAN FRANCISCO EXAMINER, (February
1, 1977), p. 24. English.

AN: Review of an exhibit of Mexican and
Mexican American artists from the Southwest
and the San Francisco area. Commentary and
analysis on artists Vincent Perez and
Gustavo Rivera, Rudy Trevino and Al Barela.
The work selected focused on aesthetic
quality rather than the ethnic
identification of the artist.

6717 Bolger, Kathryn McKenna. Amado Pena's art.
AUSTIN AMERICAN STATESMAN, (March 29,
1980), p. 10-11. English.

AN: A review of Pena's show of
silkscreens, watercolors, and drawings at
the Laguna Gloria Art Museum in Austin,
Texas, March-May, 1980. Suggests that the
artist has turned from a confrontational to
an assimilationist stance. At present he
visually documents the peaceful amalgamation
of the cultural heritage on both sides of
the Rio Grande.

6718 Brand Library Art Center, Glendale, CA. Los
hermanos: Jesus, Jacob & Frank Gutierrez,
sculpture, paintings, drawings, &
photographs. Exhibition catalog, 1974.
English.

AN: Exhibit of the work of three
brothers living in the Los Angeles area.

6719 Cantu, Jesus "Chista". [Emiliano Zapata
(painting)]. CARACOL, Vol. 1, no. 7 (March
1975), p. 1.

6720 Cantu, Jesus "Chista". Entrevista: Jesus
Maria Cantu, 'El Chista'. MAGAZIN, Vol. 1,
no. 4 (April 1972), p. 52-65. Spanish.

AN: Discusses his life in San Antonio;
his apprenticeship since childhood to his
uncle Miguel Angel Tellez who taught him to
paint billboards, wall signs and church
decorations; his membership in the group
Artistas de la Nueva Raza; his artistic and
political philosophy. In Spanish.

6721 Cantu, Jesus "Chista". No tengo que ir a la
luna... [painting]. EL CUADERNO, Vol. 2, no.
1 (1972), p. 49.

6722 Cantu, Jesus "Chista". No todos los que
estan son... [painting]. EL CUADERNO, Vol.
2, no. 1 (1972), p. 47.

6723 Cantu, Jesus "Chista". Santa Rosita, santo
remedio... [painting]. EL CUADERNO, Vol. 2,
no. 1 (1972), p. 48.

6724 Cantu, Jesus "Chista". Yo-soy-el-sol...
[painting]. EL CUADERNO, Vol. 2, no. 1
(1972), p. 46.

6725 Carlos Pineda shows art in Centennial
Museum. EL PASO TIMES, (November 5, 1972).
English.

AN: Themes from Mexican folk culture
predominate in paintings by Carlos R. Pineda
shown at the El Paso Centennial Museum. He
has exhibited in Panama, Guadalajara,
Phoenix, Tucson, and Dallas and is
represented by the Jinx Gallery in El Paso.

6726 Carrillo, Graciela. [Untitled painting]. TIN
TAN, Vol. 1, no. 2 (September 1975), p.
Cover.

Paintings (cont.)

6727 Castellanos-Sanchez, Eloisa.
Meditacion/Meditation [painting]. REVISTA
CHICANO-RIQUENA, Vol. 7, no. 2 (Spring
1979), p. 32.

6728 Castro, Rene. A minute of light, etc.
[painting]. REVISTA CHICANO-RIQUENA, Vol. 7,
no. 2 (Spring 1979), p. 37.

6729 La Causa Publications, Oakland, CA. Rene
Yanez: paintings. Exhibition invitation,
[ca. 1968]. English.

AN: Invitation to an exhibit of
paintings by San Francisco artist Rene
Yanez. Illustrated.

6730 Center for the Visual Arts, Oakland, CA.
Fujioka, Herman, Rivera and Rodriguez.
ARTSLETTER, Vol. 6, no. 3 (May, June, 1980).
English.

AN: Article unites Gustavo Rivera and
Peter Rodriguez as artists who share a
commitment to expressionist techniques.
Illustrated with one black and white
photograph of each artist's work.

6731 El Centro Cultural de La Raza, San Diego,
CA. Espejo del barrio-art exposition.
Exhibition brochure, June 1975. English.

AN: Illustrated brochure announcement
for a cultural exposition of Chicano music,
art and drama. Includes some biographical
information and one reproduction of painter
Manuel Unzueta, woodworker Ambriz, muralist
Victor Orozco Ochoa and designer/illustrator
J. Armando Nunez.

6732 Centro Cultural Rafael Cintron Ortiz,
University of Illinois, Chicago. Alejandro
Romero. Exhibition catalog, 1978. English.

AN: Full color catalog of drawings and
paintings by Mexican-born artist living in
Chicago.

6733 Chicano artists exhibit at USC. CALENDAR,
(September 23, 1973), p. 61. English.

AN: Announcement of an exhibit of
paintings, drawings, sculpture and graphics
by artists from the Mechicano Art Center of
Los Angeles at the University of Southern
California Art Galleries. Slide
presentations of murals and supergraphics.

6734 Coe, Kathryn. Heritage plus science yields
art. SCOTTSDALE DAILY PROGRESS, (August 28,
1981), p. 27. English.

AN: Biography of Colorado-born Rudy
Fernandez who bases many of his paintings
and mixed media boxes on the religious
imagery of Colorado. He studied geology;
travelled to Spain and Mexico to know his
heritage. All these factors influence his
art, in which he uses symbols personally.

6735 La Cofradia de Artes y Artesanos Hispanicos
and Santa Fe Council for the Arts. El
festival hispanico. Festival program, [ca.
1979]. English.

AN: Program for the festival which
included over 70 visual artists from
northern New Mexico selected and hung by the
Cofradia at the Armory for the Arts gallery
in Santa Fe. The poster for the festival,
reproduced on the program cover, is taken
from a painting by Gilberto Guzman. The
festival also featured music, cuentos,
dance, slide show, poetry, films.

6736 Comptis, Eddy. Diptico no. 1 U.S.A.
[painting]. REVISTA CHICANO-RIQUENA, Vol. 7,
no. 2 (Spring 1979), p. [44].

6737 Coronado, Sam. 'Buelito [painting]. TEJIDOS,
Vol. 2, no. 6 (Summer 1975), p. iv. Spanish.

6738 Coronado, Sam. Denise [painting]. TEJIDOS,
Vol. 4, no. 1 (Spring 1977), p. 22. English.

6739 Coronado, Sam. Mi mundo [painting]. TEJIDOS,
Vol. 4, no. 1 (Spring 1977), p. 26. Spanish.

6740 Coronado, Sam. The mourners [painting].
TEJIDOS, Vol. 4, no. 1 (Spring 1977), p. 47.
English.

6741 Coronado, Sam. Recuerdos [painting].
TEJIDOS, Vol. 4, no. 1 (Spring 1977), p. 23.
Spanish.

6742 Coronado, Sam. Secretos [painting]. TEJIDOS,
Vol. 4, no. 1 (Spring 1977), p. 25. Spanish.

6743 Coronado, Sam. Sonia [painting]. TEJIDOS,
Vol. 4, no. 1 (Spring 1977), p. 24. English.

6744 Coronado, Sam. [Untitled painting]. TEJIDOS,
Vol. 4, no. 1 (Spring 1977), p. Cover.

6745 Coronado, Sam. [Untitled painting]. TEJIDOS,
Vol. 4, no. 1 (Spring 1977), p. 45.

6746 Curtis, Cathy. Six aspiring watercolorists.
SUNDAY MAGAZINE [Supplement to CONTRA COSTA
COUNTY TIMES, CA], (October 14, 1979), p.
19. English.

AN: In a recent show at the Richmond Art
Center (Calif.), David Gallegos was one of
the watercolorists. Working in a traditional
modernist style, Gallegos deals with light
and air in his views of the waterfront.

6747 DE COLORES. Vol. 2, no. 4 (1976), p. 1-68.
English.

AN: Photographs by Moises Medina, Jose
Luis Sedano; drawings by Jerry Lujan,
Gilbert "Sparky" Espinoza, Rebecca Polanco;
paintings by John Herrera, Sonny Duran,
Larry Martinez. Cover by Fernando Penalosa.

6748 De La Zerda, Nancy and De Leon, Nephtali.
Entrevista con Nephtali de Leon. CARACOL,
Vol. 5, no. 9 (May 1979), p. 12-13, 19.
Spanish.

AN: Discusses the iconography of his
painting EL DESTINO DE LAS AMERICAS.

6749 De Leon, Nephtali. El destino de las
americas [painting]. CARACOL, Vol. 5, no. 9
(May 1979), p. 1. Spanish.

6750 De Leon, Nephtali. [Untitled paintings].
CARACOL, Vol. 1, no. 10 (June 1975), p.
12-13.

6751 De Marroquin, Moron. Denver Harbor artists.
LA PRENSA, (June 2, 1978). Spanish.

AN: Commentary on two exhibitions. THE
DENVER HARBOR ARTISTS includes information
on paintings by Lupe Aguirre, Josie Mendoza
and Abel Gonzalez--all from Houston. The
solo show MAGIC BLANCA featured the work of
Brownsville, Texas artist Jorge Truan.
Truan's work is mystical and visionary.

Paintings (cont.)

6752 Dean, Nancy. Denver artist dues are paid in full. ROCKY MOUNTAIN NEWS, (April 5, 1981), p. 6. English.

AN: Profile of artist Ramon Kelley focusing on his successful career and detailing his rise on the art market. Includes photograph of the artist.

6753 Diaz, Aurelio. El aguila cae [painting]. REVISTA CHICANO-RIQUENA, Vol. 8, no. 4 (Fall 1980), p. 44. Bilingual.

6754 Diaz, Aurelio. Labrar la esperanza para poderla cosechar [painting]. REVISTA CHICANO-RIQUENA, Vol. 8, no. 4 (Fall 1980), p. 38. Bilingual.

6755 Diaz, Aurelio. Nuestra leyenda [painting]. REVISTA CHICANO-RIQUENA, Vol. 8, no. 4 (Fall 1980), p. 24. Bilingual.

6756 Dietmeier, R. C. City artist finds his inspiration where he lives. ORANGE CITY NEWS, (December 23, 1981), p. 2. English.

AN: Illustrated story on Emigdio Vasquez's ten year retrospective of realistic paintings taken from photographs, held at the Galeria in Santa Ana, Calif. Vasquez records his environment and events from the 1940s and 1950s as an artistic and documentary statement.

6757 Dittmar Memorial Gallery, Northwestern University, Evanston, IL and King, Elaine A. Alejandro Romero: new works. Exhibit catalog, 1981. English.

AN: Full color illustrated catalog of paintings by the Mexican-born artist who has been living in the United States since the early 1970s. His images appear to be grounded in the work of Bosch, Goya, Brueghel, and Diego Rivera. There is a synthesis of personal symbolism and expressionism.

6758 Donnell-Kotrozo, Carol. Rudy Fernandez. ARTSPACE, Vol. 5, no. 4 (Fall 1981), p. 18-23. English.

AN: Scottsdale, Arizona resident Rudy Fernandez converts cultural symbols into a private system language that revolves around love, family, manhood and self-identity. His mixed media altar-like forms are based on interest in Southwest santos, their format and presentation. Fernandez does paintings, and assembled wood pieces. Handsomely illustrated, with color.

6759 Edward Chavez: sculptor-painter. LA LUZ, Vol. 2, no. 2 (May 1973), p. 28-31. English.

AN: Lavishly illustrated biographical account of Edward Chavez. Born in Ocate, New Mexico in 1917, Chavez has a distinguished career as a painter and sculptor. During the 1940's he executed a number of murals under sponsorship of various government art projects. These murals were placed in public buildings in Nebraska, Colorado and Wyoming. Although living and working in New York most of his adult life, the work of Edward Chavez has always been influenced by the Southwest.

6760 Edwards, Jim. The folk art tradition. ARTWEEK, Vol. 6, no. 18 (May 3, 1975), p. 7. English.

AN: Includes commentary on painter

Alexander Maldonado who is placed within the surrealist mode. His imagination sees a dual world of earthly landscapes filled with strange architecture and celestial visions in which the moon, stars and comets prevail.

6761 Erban, Lehann. Ancient times [painting]. TEJIDOS, Vol. 4, no. 3 (Fall 1977), p. 27. English.

6762 Fabricant, Don. Show reveals Hispanic art. NEW MEXICAN WEEKEND, (June 1, 1979). English.

AN: Review of two exhibits in Santa Fe: EL FESTIVAL HISPANICO, mounted by La Cofradia de Artes y Artesanos Hispanicos and Gilberto Guzman at the Black Kachina Gallery. The reviewer feels the traditional-style woodcarving done by contemporaries is the strongest part of the show; works that break with these forms seem weaker, less skillful and cliche-ridden. Crafts are excellent. Muralist Guzman has blossomed in murals and easel paintings since he was employed by the 1978 Art in Public Places project. His work is intense and expressive, sometimes erotic. Illustration of work by sculptor Ruben Montoya.

6763 'Festival of arts' planned by Arthritis Foundation. SANTA FE NEW MEXICAN, (October 11, 1972), p. B6. English.

AN: The Albuquerque Arthritis Foundation has invited professional artists and craftsmen from New Mexico to display their paintings, watercolors, sculpture, prints, lithographs, jewelry. Joel Ramirez's painting THE WEAVERS is selected for full color art prints. Illustrated.

6764 Fine Arts Gallery, California State University, Los Angeles and Goldberg, Aron. Edward Carrillo: selected works, 1960-1975. Exhibition catalog, 1975. English.

AN: Catalog of exhibit covering fifteen years of this California figurative painter's work. Eight illustrations, including one in color. (A printing error reproduced the same illustrations twice.).

6765 Flores, Carolina. Benito Juarez [painting]. TEJIDOS, Vol. 1, no. 3 (Summer 1974), p. 35. Spanish.

6766 Flores, Carolina. Two women [painting]. TEJIDOS, Vol. 1, no. 3 (Summer 1974), p. 29. English.

6767 Fong, Katheryn M. Pachuco art records era of zootsuits and anti-Mexican riots. SAN FRANCISCO JRNL, Vol. 2, no. 32 (March 1, 1978), p. 6. English.

AN: Review of Galeria de la Raza exhibit of Jose Montoya's Pachuco Art. Installation included historical photographs and documents. Montoya work (drawings and paintings) were contextualized by written commentary aiming to re-interpret an important aspect of Chicano cultural history.

Paintings (cont.)

6768 Frankenstein, Alfred. At the museum: when politics and art do mix. SAN FRANCISCO CHRONICLE, (March 15, 1978), p. 54. English.

AN: Glowing review of exhibit at the San Francisco Museum of Modern Art by Rupert Garcia who, the critic says, has a genius for saying the essential thing without a line, a gesture or a touch of color more than necessary. Illustrated.

6769 Frankenstein, Alfred. Just for the record. SAN FRANCISCO CHRONICLE, (May 27, 1976), p. 48. English.

AN: Positive review of exhibit at the Mexican Museum featuring the work of Jesus Reyes Ferreira from Mexico and Gustavo Rivera from San Francisco. Ninety-five-year-old Ferreira uses tempera on tissue paper to render brilliant paintings focusing on Mexican folk motifs. Rivera paints in the abstract expressionist mode with power and passion. Article also lauds the photographic work of Angel del Valle in his exhibition: SEMBRADORES at the Galeria de la Raza.

6770 Frankenstein, Alfred. Montoya's artistic update on Chicano zoot suiters. SAN FRANCISCO CHRONICLE, (February 18, 1978), p. 36. English.

AN: Review of Pachuco show at San Francisco's Galeria de la Raza, especially Jose Montoya's sketches and paintings.

6771 Frankenstein, Alfred. A senior senor's approach. SAN FRANCISCO CHRONICLE, (May 27, 1976), p. 48. English.

AN: Review of an exhibit of Mexican painter Jesus Reyes Ferreira at the Mexican Museum of San Francisco, as well as that of San Francisco artist Gustavo Rivera, an abstract expressionist painter. Also mentions the Museum's mural map, and Angel del Valle's photography show at the Galeria de la Raza.

6772 Freedom of expression and the Chicano Movement: an open letter to Dr. Philip Ortego. LA LUZ, Vol. 2, no. 5 (September 1973), p. 28-29. English.

AN: An unattributed letter questioning the imposition of norms on Chicano art. The author criticizes the practice of unquestioningly assigning rubrics like "Mexican" or "Chicano" to certain styles while excluding others produced by Mexican American artists.

6773 From the barrios. OBSERVER, (September 23, 1979), p. 16+. English.

AN: Short story on Gilberto Guzman from Santa Fe, New Mexico, announcing an exhibit of his work in the October Gallery, London. Two color reproductions of his paintings.

6774 Galbraith Guerrero, Antonia. [Untitled painting]. CARACOL, Vol. 3, no. 11 (July 1977), p. Ft cover.

6775 Galeria de arte de Aztlan. AZTLAN (U.S. Penitentiary, Leavenworth, KA), Vol. 1, no. 2. English.

AN: Pictorial supplement with reproductions of pinto art by Manuel

Aguilera, Jessie Hernandez, Ruben Estrella, Tomas Torres and Jose D. Marin. Many of these works were reproduced in other Chicano newspapers demonstrating the solidarity that existed in the Chicano movement inside and outside the prison walls.

6776 Una galeria de artistas = A gallery of artists. CAMINOS, Vol. 1, no. 6 (October 1980), p. 20-26. Bilingual.

AN: Features California artists Domingo O. Ulloa (Imperial Valley images), Gloria Chacon, photographer Maria Pinedo (San Francisco), Willie Herron (Los Angeles), Joaquin Patino (Delano), Pedro Pelayo (Long Beach), sculptor Rudi Sigala (San Diego), Mario Torero (San Diego), sculptor Michael M. Amescua (Los Angeles), and the East Los Streetscapers. Illustrated.

6777 La Galeria de Colores, Las Vegas, NM. La galeria de colores. Gallery brochure, [1980]. English.

AN: Brochure for a gallery/studio run by painter Pola Lopez de Jaramillo since 1980.

6778 Galeria de la Raza/Studio 24, San Francisco, CA. Ajo, granadas y tres flores. Exhibition announcement, 1981.

AN: Announcement for an exhibition featuring Ruben Trejo, sculpture (Spokane, Washington), Cesar A. Martinez, paintings (San Antonio, Texas), Xavier Gorena, paper cut-outs (Mission, Texas).

6779 Galeria de la Raza/Studio 24, San Francisco, CA. Blanca Flor Gutierrez - oil pastels. Exhibition announcement, 1981.

AN: Color xeroxed announcement for a window display of oil pastels by Gutierrez.

6780 Galeria de la Raza/Studio 24, San Francisco, CA. Images of the Southwest. Exhibition catalog, 1977. English.

AN: Invitation/catalog for an exhibit including Rudy M. Fernandez(Utah), Enrique Flores(Texas), Xavier Gorena(Texas), C.A.[Cesar] Martinez(Texas), Santos Martinez, Jr.(Texas), Pedro Rodriguez(Texas), Arnold Trujillo(New Mexico). Block prints, paper cut-outs, drawings, photographs, copper enamels, and sculpture were shown. Five illustrations.

6781 Galeria de la Raza/Studio 24, San Francisco, CA. Licita Fernandez (watercolor paintings), Pete Davalos (ceramic pots). Exhibition invitation, 1981. English.

AN: Invitation to an exhibit.

6782 Gamaliel, A.E. [Untitled painting]. REVISTA CHICANO-RIQUENA, Vol. 2, no. 4 (Fall 1974), p. Cover. Spanish.

6783 Gamaliel, A.E. [Untitled painting]. REVISTA CHICANO-RIQUENA, Vol. 2, no. 4 (Fall 1974), p. [32]. English.

6784 Garcia, Domingo. El galan etc. [painting]. REVISTA CHICANO-RIQUENA, Vol. 7, no. 2 (Spring 1979), p. 40.

6785 Garcia Perez, Linda Mary. Cactus prisoner [painting]. MAIZE, Vol. 2, no. 3 (Spring 1979), p. Bk cover. English.

Paintings (cont.)

6786 Garcia Perez, Linda Mary. Chicano nights [painting]. MAIZE, Vol. 2, no. 3 (Spring 1979), p. 17. English.

6787 Garcia Perez, Linda Mary. El otro mundo [painting]. MAIZE, Vol. 2, no. 3 (Spring 1979), p. 3. English.

6788 Garcia Perez, Linda Mary. Tortilla bits [painting]. MAIZE, Vol. 2, no. 3 (Spring 1979), p. 9. English.

6789 Garcia, Rupert. Assassination of a striking Mexican worker [painting]. PEOPLE'S WORLD, (January 31, 1981), p. 10.

    AN: Reproduction of a Rupert Garcia pastel being exhibited at the Mexican Museum in San Francisco, CA.

6790 Gaytan, Ray. The center of the universe [painting]. TEJIDOS, Vol. 3, no. 1 (Spring 1976), p. 22. English.

6791 Gaytan, Ray. Desnudo [painting]. TEJIDOS, Vol. 3, no. 1 (Spring 1976), p. 31. Spanish.

6792 Gaytan, Ray. A drop of blood [painting]. TEJIDOS, Vol. 3, no. 1 (Spring 1976), p. 27. English.

6793 Gaytan, Ray. Flower vendor [painting]. TEJIDOS, Vol. 3, no. 1 (Spring 1976), p. 36. English.

6794 Gaytan, Ray. Head [painting]. TEJIDOS, Vol. 3, no. 1 (Spring 1976), p. 12. English.

6795 Gaytan, Ray. Passion belongs to the world of flesh & blood [painting]. TEJIDOS, Vol. 3, no. 1 (Spring 1976), p. 45. English.

6796 Gaytan, Ray. Sunglass portrait [painting]. TEJIDOS, Vol. 3, no. 1 (Spring 1976), p. 1. Spanish.

6797 Gaytan, Ray. [Untitled painting]. TEJIDOS, Vol. 3, no. 1 (Spring 1976), p. 16. English.

6798 Gaytan, Ray. [Untitled painting]. TEJIDOS, Vol. 2, no. 6 (Summer 1975), p. 21.

6799 Gaytan, Ray. Wings [painting]. TEJIDOS, Vol. 3, no. 1 (Spring 1976), p. 8. English.

6800 Gerardo, Rocky. Albert Einstein [painting]. MAIZE, Vol. 2, no. 3 (Spring 1979), p. INSIDE FR. English.

6801 Gerardo, Rocky. Children of the sun [painting]. MAIZE, Vol. 2, no. 3 (Spring 1979), p. 51. English.

6802 Gerardo, Rocky. El Sandinista [painting]. MAIZE, Vol. 2, no. 3 (Spring 1979), p. In BkCover. English.

6803 Gerardo, Rocky. Twilight cat [painting]. MAIZE, Vol. 2, no. 3 (Spring 1979), p. 61. English.

6804 Goddarth, Ruth. Porfirio Salinas. Austin, TX: Rock House Press, 1975. English.

    AN: Born on Nov. 6, 1910 on a farm near Bastrop, Texas, Porfirio Salinas studied art with Spanish artist Jose Arpa in San Antonio and gradually became a regional landscapist of wide renown. Salinas died April 18, 1973 at the age of 62. The book is lavishly illustrated.

6805 Goldman, Shifra M. The intense realism of Frida Kahlo. CHISMEARTE, Vol. 1, no. 4 (Fall, Winter, 1977), p. 8-11. English.

    AN: A brief, one-page biographical sketch of Frida Kahlo's life and work. This is accompanied by black and white reproductions of her paintings: AUTORRETRATO COMO TEHUANA (1943), AUTORRETRATO (1946), RAICES (1943), LA VENADITA (1946), and LA NOVIA QUE SE ESPANTA DE VER LA VIDA ABIERTA (n.d.).

6806 Gomez, Ignacio. [Untitled painting]. SOMOS, Vol. 1, no. 2 (July 1978), p. Cover.

6807 Gomez, Linda. Malaquias Montoya exhibit opens at La Pena. EL MUNDO (San Francisco, CA), (October 29, 1975), p. 3. English.

    AN: Over 50 paintings, silkscreens, and drawings by Montoya at La Pena Cultural Center, Berkeley, CA. Statement by the artist who refuses to exhibit in museums and is opposed to murals that are "pretty decorations.".

6808 Gonzalez Dodson, Nora. Cerulean depth [painting]. TEJIDOS, Vol. 2, no. 8 (Winter 1975), p. 7. English.

6809 Grand Rapids Art Museum, Grand Rapids, MI. Jose Narezo: paintings on paper. Exhibition announcement, 1979. English.

    AN: Announcement of an exhibit of paintings by Michigan abstractionist Jose Narezo. Illustrated.

6810 Guadalupe Historic Foundation, Santa Fe, NM. Artes en la primavera. (1981). English.

    AN: Catalog of exhibit by four New Mexico artists: Manuel Lopez, sculptor from Chili; Andres Martinez, painter from Santa Cruz; Victoria Lopez, colcha embroiderer from San Pedro; Sam Quintana, jeweler from La Mesilla.

6811 Guerra, Victor, ed. El camino de la cruz. Austin, TX: Tejidos Publications, 1981. Spanish.

    AN: Carlos Andres Guerra, portfolio; painting (in color), sculpture, drawing, jewelry. Luis Guerra drawing on cover.

6812 Guerrero, Xochitl Nevel. Peruvian wind songs [painting]. LA PALABRA, Vol. 2, no. 2 (Fall 1980), p. 29.

6813 Guerrero, Xochitl Nevel. Self-portrait [painting]. LA PALABRA, Vol. 2, no. 2 (Fall 1980), p. 28.

6814 Guerrero, Xochitl Nevel. [Untitled painting]. LA PALABRA, Vol. 2, no. 2 (Fall 1980), p. 30. Bilingual.

6815 Guggenheim Gallery, Chapman College, Orange, CA. Hexagono: paintings, sculpture, drawings, prints. Exhibit invitation, 1977. English.

    AN: Invitation to an exhibit for artists Tito Aguirre, Isabel Castro, Rick Martinez, Esau Quiroz, Linda Vallejo, Emigdio Vasquez, Barrows, and Shanahan, sponsored by MEChA. Profiles and pictures of the artists.

Paintings (cont.)

6816 Haddad, Barbara. The fine arts. ROUNDUP, (January 25, 1970), p. 12. English.

AN: Mixed review of Ray Espinoza's one-person show at the International House Gallery in Denver. The exhibition included drawings, paintings, prints, assemblages and sculptures. Selecting work from each medium, the critic comments on pieces that are successful and those not fully realized. Illustrated with a wood and metal relief of a guitar and a graphic of "Che" Guevara.

6817 Haines, Bruce J. Gonzales' works are controlled and full of detail. ANCHORAGE DAILY NEWS, (May 23, 1980). English.

AN: Positive review of an exhibit titled THE HEAD TASTES BEST by Mariano Gonzales. Born in El Paso, Texas but reared in Alaska, Gonzales' works in various media from drawings and paintings to metals, ivory, enamel and plastics. The critic praises the artist for his "volatile intricacy" and his fusion of materials "always with craft and finesse". Includes reproductions of two paintings.

6818 HEMBRA: HERMANAS EN MOVIMIENTO BROTANDO RAICES DE AZTLAN (University of Texas, Austin). (Spring 1976).

AN: Raul Valdez, drawing, p. 3; Carolina Flores, drawing, p. 5; Maria Flores, photograph, pp. 7, 11, 30; M.E. Secrest-Ramirez, drawing, p. 12; Amacio Zarate, drawing, p. 15; Santa Barraza, drawings, pp. 16, 17, 18, 26, 32; Nora Gonzales-Dodson, painting, p. 19; Gilberto Cardenas, photograph, pp. 22, 28; Nanci de los Santos, photograph, p. 23, 29; Amado Maurilio Pena, Jr. p. 31.

6819 Hennessey, Kathy. Amado Pena, Chicano artist. REVISTA RIO BRAVO, no. 1 (Fall 1980), p. 2+. English.

AN: Review of the life and art of Laredo-born artist Pena whose early work in the 1960s was abstracted figures in bright colors; in the 1970s his work became political commentary for the Chicano movement; most recently he is doing paintings and silkscreens about New Mexican Indian life. As a teacher he influenced many students, especially in Anderson High School (Austin). Illustrations throughout the issue.

6820 Hernandez, Greg. Bilingual education [painting]. SOMOS, Vol. 1, no. 3 (August 1978), p. 21. English.

6821 Hernandez-Trujillo, Manuel. Ejecutado [painting]. EL GRITO, Vol. 2, no. 3 (Spring 1969), p. [27]. Spanish.

6822 Herrera, Estela. La mujer en el mundo: una chicana en las artes. LA OPINION, (March 25, 1982), p. III,6. Spanish.

AN: Illustrated interview with Judith Elena Hernandez de Niekrug including biographical information and discussion of her attitudes toward her murals, paintings, and graphics.

6823 Herrera, Philip. The Latino eye. NUESTRO, Vol. 2, no. 4 (April 1978), p. 46-48. English.

AN: Commentary on the traveling

exhibition ANTIGUAS RAICES/NUEVAS VISIONES. Illustrated with selections from the exhibition that included several Chicano artists.

6824 Herrera, Yvonne. Me on my bike [painting]. TEJIDOS, Vol. 4, no. 3 (Fall 1977), p. 23. English.

6825 Herron, Willie. Partir la alma [painting]. EL TECOLOTE LITERARY MAGAZINE, Vol. 2, no. 2 (July 1981), p. 4.

6826 Heymann, Ann W. Robert Gonzalez. ART VOICES SOUTH, Vol. 3, no. 1 (January, February, 1980), p. 68. English.

AN: Brief resume on art and life of San Francisco painter. Illustrated.

6827 Hispanic American artist - Secundino Sandoval. LA LUZ, Vol. 7, no. 9 (September 1978), p. 51. English.

AN: Biographical data and analysis of "Sec", Sandoval's technique as a realist watercolorist.

6828 Holliday-Abbott, Anne. Suitcase is 2nd home for arts liaison. ARIZONA DAILY STAR, (June 18, 1981), p. H-3. English.

AN: Arizona artist Louis LeRoy who paints, makes prints, and does assemblage is also a regional representative for the National Endowment for the Arts in Arizona, New Mexico, Colorado, Utah, and Wyoming. LeRoy has always been an "advocate of people being proud of their ethnic backgrounds." He feels artists can be self-supporting without commercializing.

6829 Intar, International Art Relations, Inc., New York, NY and Ferez Kuri, F. Jose. Alejandro E. Romero. Exhibition catalog, 1977. English.

AN: Exhibit catalog of drawings and paintings by Mexican-born painter and muralist living in Chicago. Illustrated in color.

6830 Jaramillo, Juanita. Hunger [painting]. REVISTA CHICANO-RIQUENA, Vol. 5, no. 1 (Winter 1977), p. 98. English.

6831 Joe B. Rodriguez. LA PRENSA, Vol. 1, no. 13 (July 21, 1978). Spanish.

AN: Commentary on an exhibition by Joe B. Rodriguez at the George I. Sanchez Center in Houston, Texas. Rodriguez's work is seen as having affinity with the art of Diego Rivera and Raul Anguiano. Illustrated with a reproduction of a watercolor, THE LANDING OF THE SALSA PEOPLE.

6832 Johnson, Charles. J street galleries: politics flavor alternative art shows. SACRAMENTO BEE, (December 20, 1977), p. A13. English.

AN: Review of a Pachuco show by Jose Montoya that is half drawings and paintings, and half politics - photographs of Pachucos of the 1940s. Montoya's essay that accompanies the exhibit attempts to dispel the image of Pachucos as gangsters, and declares that Pachucos were the first "freedom fighters." The reviewer feels this is one-sided. Illustrated.

Paintings (cont.)

6833 Johnston, Jerry. A man with a message: let's build strength, pride. DESERET NEWS, (June 28, 1980), p. S3. English.

AN: Story on Nephtali De Leon, playwright, poet, and illustrator of children's literature. In addition to I WILL CATCH THE SUN and I COLOR MY GARDEN children's books, he works with oil painting, stained glass and woodcuts.

6834 Joslyn Art Center. Multi-media art exhibit: Muriel Olguin (printmaking), Myrna Shiras (mixed media), Linda Vallejo (painting). Exhibition invitation, 1979. English.

AN: Invitation to an exhibit.

6835 Kahlo, Frida. Autorretrato como tehuana [painting]. CHISMEARTE, Vol. 1, no. 4 (Fall, Winter, 1977), p. 9. Spanish.

6836 Kahlo, Frida. Autorretrato [painting]. CHISMEARTE, Vol. 1, no. 4 (Fall , Winter, 1977), p. 10. Spanish.

6837 Kahlo, Frida. Unos cuantos piquetitos [paintings]. DE COLORES, Vol. 3, no. 3 (1977), p. 54. Spanish.

6838 Kahlo, Frida. Las dos Fridas [painting]. DE COLORES, Vol. 3, no. 3 (1977), p. 51. Spanish.

6839 Kahlo, Frida. Henry Ford Hospital [painting]. DE COLORES, Vol. 3, no. 3 (1977), p. 57. English.

6840 Kahlo, Frida. Mi nana y yo [painting]. DE COLORES, Vol. 3, no. 3 (1977), p. 60. Spanish.

6841 Kahlo, Frida. La novia que se espanta de ver la vida abierta [painting]. CHISMEARTE, Vol. 1, no. 4 (Fall , Winter, 1977), p. 11. Spanish.

6842 Kahlo, Frida. Pensando en la muerte [painting]. DE COLORES, Vol. 3, no. 3 (1977), p. 63. Spanish.

6843 Kahlo, Frida. Raices [painting]. CHISMEARTE, Vol. 1, no. 4 (Fall , Winter, 1977), p. 10. Spanish.

6844 Kahlo, Frida. Retrato de la familia de Frida [painting]. DE COLORES, Vol. 3, no. 3 (1977), p. 65. Spanish.

6845 Kahlo, Frida. La venadita [painting]. CHISMEARTE, Vol. 1, no. 4 (Fall , Winter, 1977), p. 11. Spanish.

6846 Kantar, Chris and Villa, Esteban. An interview with Esteban Villa. Unpublished paper, 1978. English.

AN: A detailed and informative interview with Esteban Villa, prominent Chicano artist. Focus on Villa's philosophy of art, life, and the Chicano art movement. A good primary source. (The unpublished manuscript is deposited in the archives of the R.C.A.F. in Scaramento).

6847 Karkabi, Barbara. For artist Atanacio P. Davila, mural is way to express love for children. HOUSTON CHRONICLE, (May 14, 1980), p. IV-I. English.

AN: Color-illustrated story on mural-in-progress at the Ripley House

medical clinic by 70 year old Davila titled THE HEALTHY FAMILY. Son of an artist, Mexican-born Davila was raised in Texas and did commercial art and painting until 1938. After retirement, he has resumed his art.

6848 Kelley sparks Chicano growth. ROCKY MOUNTAIN NEWS, (February 18, 1973), p. Festival,7. English.

AN: Denver artist John Flores speaks about his work and provides details about the small but strong Chicano art colony in Denver. Flores credits Ramon Kelley, an established Chicano artist, with providing much leadership and encouragement in the development of Chicano art in Colorado.

6849 Lasta, Susana. Self portrait/Autorretrato [painting]. REVISTA CHICANO-RIQUENA, Vol. 7, no. 2 (Spring 1979), p. 39.

6850 Loniak, Walter. The true New Mexico contemporary style. SANTA FE REPORTER, (May 31, 1979). English.

AN: Review of three exhibits in Santa Fe, EL FESTIVAL HISPANICO co-sponsored by the Cofradia de Artes y Artesanos Hispanicos and the Santa Fe Council for the Arts; a wood carving exhibit at Elaine Horwitch Gallery, and easel paintings by muralist Gilberto Guzman at the Black Kachina Gallery. Concerning the Festival exhibit, the critic states that the sculptural pieces are the strongest; two dimensional work is inconsistent or unimpressive, weaving is not well represented (though usually the strongest medium), and there are few photographs or prints. Illustration.

6851 Lopez, Israel. My church [painting]. TEJIDOS, Vol. 4, no. 3 (Fall 1977), p. 20. English.

6852 Lopez, Yolanda M. [Untitled paintings from the SERIE GUADALUPE]. MAIZE, Vol. 1, no. 4 (Summer 1978), p. Bk cover. English.

6853 Los Angeles City College. Latinos de tres mundos. Exhibition invitation, 1980. English.

AN: Invitation to an exhibit featuring the work of ASCO members Harry Gamboa, Jr., Gronk, Willie Herron; painters Xavier Mendez and Olivia Sanchez; and photographer Ricardo Valverde.

6854 Lujan, Pedro. Ruby I [sculpture]. REVISTA CHICANO-RIQUENA, Vol. 8, no. 3 (Summer 1980), p. 71. Bilingual.

6855 Malaquias Montoya. ARTE, (Fall 1977). English.

AN: Interview with northern California printmaker, painter and muralist, Malaquias Montoya. He discusses his life, his dedication to Chicano art, his resistance to the institutionalization of the Chicano struggle and its art, their cooptation by the establishment. He says he transcended nationalism at one period and became a Third World internationalist. Four drawings and two posters reproduced.

6856 Martinez, Cesar Augusto. Bato con cruz [painting]. REVISTA CHICANO-RIQUENA, Vol. 9, no. 4 (Fall 1981), p. [23].

Paintings (cont.)

6857 Martinez, Cesar Augusto. Bato con sunglasses [painting]. REVISTA CHICANO-RIQUENA, Vol. 9, no. 4 (Fall 1981), p. [44].

6858 Martinez, Cesar Augusto. Don Juan Volador [Painting]. CARACOL, Vol. 2, no. 4 (December 1975), p. FRNT COVER.

6859 Martinez, Cesar Augusto; Garcia-Camarillo, Mia; and Garcia-Camarillo, Cecilio. Don Juan Volador, Platica con Cesar Augusto Martinez. CARACOL, Vol. 2, no. 4 (December 1975), p. 3-5. Spanish.

AN: Interview with Cesar Martinez about his acrylic painting DON JUAN VOLADOR. Based on themes suggested by the writings of Carlos Castaneda, the painting deals with the spiritual nature of Chicanismo. This issue of CARACOL is illustrated by the painting in question.

6860 Martinez, Cesar Augusto. Pareja [painting]. REVISTA CHICANO-RIQUENA, Vol. 9, no. 4 (Fall 1981), p. [32].

6861 Martinez, Cesar Augusto. La parot [painting]. REVISTA CHICANO-RIQUENA, Vol. 9, no. 4 (Fall 1981), p. [51].

6862 Martinez, Larry. Hey lady [painting]. DE COLORES, Vol. 2, no. 4 (1976), p. 56.

6863 Martinez, Larry. Mestizo [painting]. DE COLORES, Vol. 2, no. 4 (1976), p. 57.

6864 Martinez, Larry. Pinturas/Paintings [portfolio]. DE COLORES, Vol. 2, no. 4 (1976), p. [55]-57.

6865 Martinez, Manuel. The art of the Chicano movement, and the movement of Chicano art. In: Valdez, Luis and Steiner, Stan eds. AZTLAN: AN ANTHOLOGY OF MEXICAN AMERICAN LITERATURE. New York: Vintage, 1972, p.349-353. English.

AN: "Like the modern art of Mexico, the new Chicano art is essentially an art of social protest," writes Denver, Colorado muralist and easel painter Martinez. He traces the roots of Chicano art back into Indian, colonial and modern Mexican art, and defines two kinds of Chicano art.

6866 Martinez, O.W. "Bill". Here comes la gente fragmented and fused [paintings]. LA LUZ, Vol. 1, no. 1 (April 1972), p. 56-57. English.

6867 Martinez, Ruben. [Untitled painting]. TEJIDOS, Vol. 2, no. 6 (Summer 1975), p. Cover. English.

6868 McAlister, John. Carrillo paintings on view in art gallery. UNIVERSITY TIMES, (April 2, 1975), p. 7. English.

AN: Review of 25 works by California painter Eduardo Carrillo. Illustrated.

6869 McCullom, Pat. Gonzales: his paintings are like hieroglyphs. ANCHORAGE TIMES, (June 25, 1978), p. I, 3. English.

AN: Mariano Gonzales born in El Paso Texas, reared in Anchorage and trained at the Rhode Island School of Design has a developing reputation as an artist from the far north. This positive review is for an exhibit of paintings, jewelry and metal work pieces. Gonzales' paintings are heavily saturated with subconscious symbolism and his sculptures generally feature mechanical, movable parts.

6870 Medina, Melissa. La primavera [painting]. TEJIDOS, Vol. 4, no. 3 (Fall 1977), p. 18. Spanish.

6871 The Mexican Museum, San Francisco, CA. Recent works of Leonel Maciel and Carlos Almaraz. Exhibition invitation, 1981. English.

AN: Invitation to an exhibit of works by Mexican artist Maciel and Chicano painter Almaraz.

6872 Mexican-American Advisory Committee of the Museum of Science and Industry.. Second annual Mexican-American art fiesta. Exhibition brochure, 1975. English.

AN: Exhibit of paintings, sculpture, crafts, and photography by 49 artists from Illinois, Indiana, and Mexico. Includes many of the most important Chicano artists of the Chicago area.

6873 Mexico. Secretaria de Relaciones Exteriores. Direccion General de Asuntos.. Exposicion: estampas y remembranzas; Admonty y Geomonte. Exhibition catalog, 1979. Bilingual.

AN: Catalog of an exhibit by Alice Dickerson Montemayor (Admonty). Born in Laredo, Texas in 1902, she began painting in 1976. Her nephew, George A. Montemayor, who resides in Houston, is the Coordinator for the La Porte Independent School District.

6874 Miller, Marlan. Vigil paintings examine Indian life. PHOENIX GAZETTE, (November 29, 1975), p. 20. English.

AN: Review of an exhibit by Denver-born Veloy Vigil at the Sue Brown Galley in Scottsdale, Arizona. The artist works in watercolor, gouache and acrylic. Several works are discussed in detail.

6875 Montoya, Delilah Merriman. [Untitled painting]. MAIZE, Vol. 3, no. 1-2 (Fall , Winter, 1979, 1980), p. 38. English.

6876 Montoya, Delilah Merriman. [Untitled painting]. MAIZE, Vol. 3, no. 1-2 (Fall , Winter, 1979), p. 45. English.

6877 Montoya, Jose E. Campesinos [painting]. EL GRITO, Vol. 2, no. 3 (Spring 1969), p. [49]. English.

6878 Montoya, Jose E. The general [painting]. EL GRITO, Vol. 2, no. 3 (Spring 1969), p. [53]. English.

6879 Montoya, Jose E. Girl leaning [painting]. EL GRITO, Vol. 2, no. 3 (Spring 1969), p. [56]. English.

6880 Montoya, Jose E. The journey [painting]. EL GRITO, Vol. 2, no. 3 (Spring 1969), p. [50]. English.

6881 Montoya, Jose E. Portfolio 5: Campesinos; The Journey; Untitled; The Year of the Pigs; The General; The Priest; Visting Day; Girl Learning 0. EL GRITO, Vol. 2, no. 3 (Spring 1969), p. 48-57. English.

Paintings (cont.)

6882 Montoya, Jose E. The priest [painting]. EL GRITO, Vol. 2, no. 3 (Spring 1969), p. [54]. English.

6883 Montoya, Jose E. [Untitled paintings]. CHISMEARTE, Vol. 2, no. 1 (1978), p. 10.

6884 Montoya, Jose E. Visiting day [painting]. EL GRITO, Vol. 2, no. 3 (Spring 1969), p. [55]. English.

6885 Montoya, Malaquias. Cantina [painting]. EL GRITO, Vol. 2, no. 3 (Spring 1969), p. [7]. English.

6886 Montoya, Malaquias. Cristo [painting]. EL GRITO, Vol. 2, no. 3 (Spring 1969), p. [11]. English.

6887 Montoya, Malaquias. Democracy in action [painting]. EL GRITO, Vol. 2, no. 3 (Spring 1969), p. [8]. English.

6888 Montoya, Malaquias. El domingo [painting]. EL GRITO, Vol. 2, no. 3 (Spring 1969), p. [5]. English.

6889 Montoya, Malaquias. Images [painting]. EL GRITO, Vol. 2, no. 3 (Spring 1969), p. [10]. English.

6890 Montoya, Malaquias. Jefe y la jefita [painting]. EL GRITO, Vol. 2, no. 3 (Spring 1969), p. [12]. English.

6891 Montoya, Malaquias. JoAnna [painting]. EL GRITO, Vol. 2, no. 3 (Spring 1969), p. [6]. English.

6892 Montoya, Malaquias. Lady [painting]. EL GRITO, Vol. 2, no. 3 (Spring 1969), p. [12]. English.

6893 Montoya, Malaquias. Man and woman, number 1 [painting]. EL GRITO, Vol. 2, no. 3 (Spring 1969), p. [3]. English.

6894 Montoya, Malaquias. Man and woman, number 2 [painting]. EL GRITO, Vol. 2, no. 3 (Spring 1969), p. [6]. English.

6895 Montoya, Malaquias. Man and woman, number 3 [painting]. EL GRITO, Vol. 2, no. 3 (Spring 1969), p. [7]. English.

6896 Montoya, Malaquias. Muerte [painting]. EL GRITO, Vol. 2, no. 3 (Spring 1969), p. [10]. English.

6897 Montoya, Malaquias. Patron [painting]. EL GRITO, Vol. 2, no. 3 (Spring 1969), p. 9. Spanish.

6898 Montoya, Malaquias. Portfolio 1. EL GRITO, Vol. 2, no. 3 (Spring 1969), p. 3-14. English.

6899 Montoya, Malaquias. Portfolio: Malaquias Montoya [paintings]. EL GRITO, Vol. 2, no. 2 (Winter 1969), p. 81-84. English.

6900 Montoya, Malaquias. [Untitled painting]. EL GRITO, Vol. 2, no. 2 (Winter 1969), p. 81. Bilingual.

6901 Montoya, Malaquias. [Untitled painting]. EL GRITO, Vol. 2, no. 2 (Winter 1969), p. 82. Bilingual.

6902 Montoya, Malaquias. [Untitled painting]. EL GRITO, Vol. 2, no. 2 (Winter 1969), p. 83. Bilingual.

6903 Montoya, Malaquias. [Untitled painting]. EL GRITO, Vol. 2, no. 2 (Winter 1969), p. 84. Bilingual.

6904 Montoya, Malaquias. [Untitled painting]. EL GRITO, Vol. 2, no. 3 (Spring 1969), p. Ft cover. Bilingual.

6905 Montoya, Malaquias. [Untitled painting]. EL POCHO CHE, Vol. 1, no. 2 (1970), p. 21.

6906 Morch, Albert. Mexican art through a cartoonist's eyes. SAN FRANCISCO EXAMINER, (September 24, 1979), p. 28. English.

AN: Review of "GORDO'S WORLD" and the paintings of Alexander Maldonado, an exhibition at the Mexican Museum. Biographical information on Gustavo Montano Arriola, creator of the Gordo cartoon in 1941. The exhibit conceived and designed by the San Diego Museum of Art, had representative blow-ups of the strip along with artifacts. Maldonado, a self-taught artist started painting at age 60. His canvases embrace a fascination with towers, unique buildings, underground cities and skylines from an imagined urban environment.

6907 Moreno, Martin. Mujer [painting]. REVISTA CHICANO-RIQUENA, Vol. 8, no. 4 (Fall 1980), p. 34. Bilingual.

6908 Moser, Charlotte; Renteria, Phil; and Wray, Dick. Phil Renteria and Dick Wray. ART IN AMERICA, Vol. 64, no. 4 (July, August, 1976), p. 82-83. English.

AN: Interview with Laredo-born Houston artist Renteria, and Wray, both of whom teach at the Museum of Fine Arts. Renteria gives much biographical information and his philosophy of art. Illustrated in color.

6909 Muchnic, Suzanne. Damaged goods in the big city. LOS ANGELES TIMES, (July 23, 1979), p. IV-11. English.

AN: Review of the exhibit at Otis Art Institute of Parsons School of Design of L.A. PARKS AND WRECKS, featuring Carlos Almaraz, John Valadez, and Black artist John Woods. Almaraz paints auto wrecks, and landscapes of Echo Park. Valadez does pencil portraits of young Chicanos. Illustrated.

6910 Munguia, Roberto. [Untitled painting]. TEJIDOS, Vol. 2, no. 6 (Summer 1975), p. 14.

6911 Murillo, Jesus. Depression [painting]. REVISTA CHICANO-RIQUENA, Vol. 8, no. 3 (Summer 1980), p. 80. Bilingual.

6912 Murillo, Jesus. Our Hercules [painting]. REVISTA CHICANO-RIQUENA, Vol. 8, no. 3 (Summer 1980), p. 79. Bilingual.

6913 Musica hispana en nuestras vidas/Hispanic music in our lives: almanaque 1982/calendar. Milwaukee, WI: Miller Brewing Co., 1981. English.

AN: Twelve Latino artists were commissioned to illustrate a calendar with paintings on Hispanic music. The Chicano artists include Frederico Vigil (New Mexico), Joe Bastida Rodriguez (Texas/Washington, D.C.), Manuel Martinez (Colorado), Jose Antonio Burciaga (California), Ignacio Gomez (California), Carolina Flores (Texas), Frank Martinez (California). Color.

Paintings (cont.)

6914 Nora Mendoza: pintora de ascendencia
mexicana triunfa en los EE. UU. BUENHOGAR,
(May 1979), p. 7. Spanish.

AN: Profile of Texas-born Nora Mendoza
of Michigan, a painter of abstractions in
acrylic. She is an active member of many
Detroit and Michigan organizations,
including Nuestras Artes de Michigan which
she co-founded with Jorge Vargas, Martin
Moreno and Jessie Gonzalez.

6915 Oakland County Cultural Affairs, MI. Nora
Mendoza: an exhibition of
abstract/impressionism. Exhibition brochure,
[1981]. English.

AN: Exhibit brochure for Texas-born Nora
Chapa Mendoza who studied
abstract-impressionism with Michigan artist
Ljubo Biro. She is a leader in the artistic
and Hispanic communities and runs galleries
in Clarkston and Detroit.

6916 Oakland Museum, Oakland, CA and Laney
College, Oakland, CA. In search of Aztlan.
Exhibition brochure, 1974. English.

AN: Brochure for exhibit featuring Los
Four: Carlos Almaraz, Gilbert Lujan, Roberto
de la Rocha, Frank Romero, Judithe
Hernandez.

6917 Oakland Museum presents 5 L.A. Chicano
artists. EL MUNDO (Hayward, CA), (August
1974). English.

AN: Report on the exhibit THE SEARCH FOR
AZTLAN, featuring paintings, murals,
tortilla art, folk and religious symbols and
totems by Carlos Almaraz, Roberto de la
Rocha, Gilbert Lujan, Frank Romero and
Judithe Hernandez. Included in the more than
100 works are a wall mural, a folk art
pyramid, and part of a primed '51 Chevy
lowrider. Illustrated.

6918 Ojeda, Jay. Galeria de la Raza--art for the
community. SAN FRANCISCO PROGRESS, (March
24, 1972). English.

AN: Analysis of group exhibition by
thirty-four Raza artists. Commentary on the
work of Latin American artists Consuelo
Mendez, Rolando Castellon, and Chicano
artists Rupert Garcia, Chuy Campusano and
Peter Rodriguez.

6919 Orozco, Jose Clemente. The slave [painting].
CON SAFOS, Vol. 1, no. 3 (March 1969), p. 3.

6920 Orozco, Jose Clemente. [Untitled painting].
CON SAFOS, no. 8 (1972), p. 35-36.

6921 Orozco, Juan Ishi. Tu eres mi otro yo
[painting]. MAIZE, Vol. 4, no. 1-2 (Fall ,
Winter, 1980, 1981), p. 53. Spanish.

6922 Orozco, Juan Ishi. [Untitled painting].
MAIZE, Vol. 4, no. 1-2 (Fall , Winter,
1980, 1981), p. 37. English.

6923 Ortega, Francisco. Piramide [painting].
TEJIDOS, Vol. 2, no. 6 (Summer 1975), p. 27.
Spanish.

6924 Painting changes woman's life at age when
most ready to retire. LAREDO NEWS,
(November 4, 1979), p. 1-C. English.

AN: Interview with 77 year old Alice D.
Montemayor "Admonty" on the occasion of her

San Antonio exhibit with her nephew George
"Geomonte" Montemayor.

6925 Palma Castroman, Janis. Dancer [painting].
TEJIDOS, Vol. 3, no. 2 (Summer 1976), p. 9.
English.

6926 Palma Castroman, Janis. Desintegracion
[painting]. TEJIDOS, Vol. 3, no. 2 (Summer
1976), p. 36. Spanish.

6927 Palma Castroman, Janis. Gigolo (#2)
[painting]. TEJIDOS, Vol. 3, no. 2 (Summer
1976), p. 4. English.

6928 Palma Castroman, Janis. Girl in the forest
[painting]. TEJIDOS, Vol. 3, no. 2 (Summer
1976), p. 28. English.

6929 Palma Castroman, Janis. Girl [painting].
TEJIDOS, Vol. 3, no. 2 (Summer 1976), p. 1.
English.

6930 Palma Castroman, Janis. Landscape
[painting]. TEJIDOS, Vol. 3, no. 2 (Summer
1976), p. 33. English.

6931 Palma Castroman, Janis. Male nude
[painting]. TEJIDOS, Vol. 3, no. 2 (Summer
1976), p. 41. English.

6932 Palma Castroman, Janis. Las meninas no son
solo de Velazquez [painting]. TEJIDOS, Vol.
3, no. 2 (Summer 1976), p. 45. Spanish.

6933 Palma Castroman, Janis. La puta [painting].
TEJIDOS, Vol. 3, no. 2 (Summer 1976), p. 17.
Spanish.

6934 Palma Castroman, Janis. El te de las cuatro
[painting]. TEJIDOS, Vol. 3, no. 2 (Summer
1976), p. 23. Spanish.

6935 Palma Castroman, Janis. Tinieblas
[painting]. TEJIDOS, Vol. 3, no. 2 (Summer
1976), p. 12. English.

6936 Palma Castroman, Janis. [Untitled painting].
TEJIDOS, Vol. 5, no. 1 (1978), p. 1.
English.

6937 Palma Castroman, Janis. The yawn [painting].
TEJIDOS, Vol. 3, no. 2 (Summer 1976), p.
COVER. English.

6938 Patlan, Ray. La raza cosmica [painting].
REVISTA CHICANO-RIQUENA, Vol. 8, no. 4 (Fall
1980), p. Cover. Bilingual.

6939 Patssi. Take one/Toma una [painting].
REVISTA CHICANO-RIQUENA, Vol. 7, no. 2
(Spring 1979), p. [30-31].

6940 Pazos, Antonio. [Untitled painting]. LLUEVE
TLALOC, no. 4 (1977), p. [97].

6941 Pazos, Antonio. [Untitled painting]. LLUEVE
TLALOC, no. 8 (1981), p. 40.

6942 Pena, Amado Maurilio, Jr. Pareja con pared
[painting]. REVISTA CHICANO-RIQUENA, Vol. 8,
no. 3 (Summer 1980), p. 75. Bilingual.

6943 Pena, Amado Maurilio, Jr. El vestido
[painting]. REVISTA CHICANO-RIQUENA, Vol. 8,
no. 3 (Summer 1980), p. 74. Bilingual.

6944 Pena, Gerardo. Sidro [drawing]. MAIZE, Vol.
3, no. 1-2 (Fall , Winter, 1979, 1980), p.
Ft cover. Spanish.

Paintings (cont.)

6945 Pena, Gerardo. [Untitled painting]. MAIZE,
Vol. 3, no. 1-2 (Fall , Winter, 1979,
1980), p. Bk cover. English.

6946 Pena, Ruben R. Mel Casas - people in the
arts. BUSINESS AND THE ARTS, (September,
October, 1979), p. 15. English.

AN: Probing analysis of the work and
life of San Antonio artist Mel Casas.
Article is divided into five sections in
which the artist gives his views on culture,
art, society, the Southwest and himself.
Contains biographical information and
artistic trajectory.

6947 Penalosa, Fernando. Los pintos de America
[painting]. DE COLORES, Vol. 3, no. 1
(1976), p. Cover.

6948 Perez, Demetrio. Mel Casas - humanscapes.
Houston, TX: Contemporary Arts Museum, 1976.
English.

AN: Catalog for Mel Casas exhibition
Oct. 22-Nov. 23, 1976. Artist calls his
paintings "visual conundrums which play with
our cultural concepts, with our cultural
vision." Includes biographical information
and exhibition chronology. Well illustrated
with nine reproductions of artists work and
two photos of the artist.

6949 Perez, Irene. La huichola [painting]. LA
PALABRA, Vol. 2, no. 2 (Fall 1980), p. 34.

6950 Perez, Irene. Tata Tanis [painting]. LA
PALABRA, Vol. 2, no. 2 (Fall 1980), p. 35.

6951 Perez, Trinidad. [Untitled painting].
TEJIDOS, Vol. 2, no. 6 (Summer 1975), p. 33.

6952 Phelon, Craig. Sculptor survives on the edge
of a concrete canyon. EL PASO TIMES, (July
11, 1980). English.

AN: 84 year old Jesus Barrera sculpted
and painted hundreds of religious plaster
statues until forced to abandon sculpture in
1962 because lead-based paint ruined his
health.

6953 Pollock, Duncan. Recognition arrives for
Martin Saldana. ROCKY MOUNTAIN NEWS,
(January 13, 1972), p. 55. English.

AN: After a long career as a vegetable
cook at the venerable Brown Palace Hotel in
Denver, Martin Saldana started art classes
at the Denver Art Museum. His work was
fresh, imaginative and totally naive. After
the artist's death in 1965 at age 90, his
paintings started to receive critical
acclaim. Article details Saldana's rise to
prominence and compares his artwork to that
of Henry Rousseau. Illustrated with
photograph of Martin Saldana.

6954 Powers, Willie. Bleach vase [painting].
TEJIDOS, Vol. 4, no. 3 (Fall 1977), p. 30.
English.

6955 President's Gallery, Chicago State
University and Sorell, Victor A. Alejandro
Romero. Exhibition catalog, 1979. English.

AN: Catalog of an exhibit by
Mexican-born painter and muralist who has
been working in the United States since
about 1973. He has lived in Chicago since
1976. Illustrated.

6956 Pulido, Guillermo. La lucha continental
[painting]. REVISTA CHICANO-RIQUENA, Vol. 8,
no. 3 (Summer 1980), p. 81. Spanish.

6957 Ramon Kelley. ARTISTS OF THE ROCKIES, Vol.
1, no. 1 (Spring 1974), p. 6-11. English.

AN: Biographical information on Ramon
Kelley and a listing of his invitational
shows. Illustrated with a photograph of the
artist and a portfolio of ten works (three
in color).

6958 Raoul Mora. ESENCIA, Vol. 1, no. 3 (March,
April, 1982).

AN: Brief article on Stockton-born
landscape painter and lithographer who
records the beauties of Northern California
in flat patterns and strong color.
Illustrated.

6959 Raya, Marcos. Made in the U.S.A. [painting].
REVISTA CHICANO-RIQUENA, Vol. 6, no. 4 (Fall
1978), p. 63. English.

6960 Raya, Marcos. Mechanics of the imagination
[painting]. REVISTA CHICANO-RIQUENA, Vol. 6,
no. 4 (Fall 1978), p. 74. English.

6961 Raya, Marcos. New York-New York - self
portrait [painting]. REVISTA
CHICANO-RIQUENA, Vol. 6, no. 4 (Fall
1978), p. 41. English.

6962 Richard Henkin, Inc., Beverly Hills, CA.
Veloy Vigil. Exhibition Catalog, n.d..
English.

AN: Full color catalog of graphics by
Denver-born painter who lives in Taos and
Southern California. Biographical
information, but lacks dates.

6963 Richard Henkin, Inc., Beverly Hills, CA.
Veloy Vigil. Exhibition brochure, n.d.
English.

AN: Full color brochure about the
Denver-born artist who has exhibited in many
galleries and museums in the United States.
His paintings deal with western subjects.

6964 Roberts, Tim. For art's sake, for the
community, for the working class. ORANGE
CITY NEWS, Vol. 10, (March 14, 1979), p.
1,8-9. English.

AN: Illustrated article on Orange
County, Calif. realist painter Emigdio
Vasquez. Focuses on his community murals,
and his attitudes toward his art. Also
announces the first exhibit, "Empanada" of
the newly formed Hispanic Artists
Association of Orange County. 13
participants including Vasquez.

6965 Rodriguez, Joe. Arte tejana [painting].
REVISTA CHICANO-RIQUENA, Vol. 8, no. 3
(Summer 1980), p. [83]. Bilingual.

6966 Rodriguez, Joe. Corazon sangriento de Tejas
[painting]. REVISTA CHICANO-RIQUENA, Vol. 8,
no. 3 (Summer 1980), p. [84]. Bilingual.

6967 Rodriguez, Joe B. Kahlo pains/Dolor de Kahlo
[painting]. REVISTA CHICANO-RIQUENA, Vol. 7,
no. 2 (Spring 1979), p. [29].

Paintings (cont.)

6968 Rodriguez, Pedro and Walla Walla Community
College, Walla Walla, WA. Chicano art
exhibition. Exhibition invitation, 1981.
English.

AN: Poster invitation to exhibition by
Pedro Rodriguez, Associate professor of
Chicano Studies at Washington State
University, Pullman, Washington. Rodriguez
presented a lecture in English, "Chicano Art
and Its Mexican Antecedents," and one in
Spanish, "El Muralismo en Mexico y
Mexico-America." Illustrated with painting
of woman shrouded in a rebozo.

6969 Rodriguez, Pedro. Fronteras falsas
[painting]. REVISTA CHICANO-RIQUENA, Vol. 8,
no. 3 (Summer 1980), p. 73. Bilingual.

6970 Rodriguez, Pedro. La mazonista [painting].
REVISTA CHICANO-RIQUENA, Vol. 8, no. 3
(Summer 1980), p. 72. Bilingual.

6971 Rosas, Carlos. Aztlan [painting]. REVISTA
CHICANO-RIQUENA, Vol. 6, no. 1 (Winter
1977), p. 28. Spanish.

6972 Ruiz, Elizabeth. Fiesta artist. THE RANGER,
(April 23, 1981). English.

AN: Biographical information on San
Antonio painter Jesus Trevino. Artist
describes his work as "realism" with "a
focus on Mexican American and Chicano
culture, the people and their lives".

6973 Sagel, Jaime. Art of brothers taps New
Mexico heritage. JOURNAL NORTH, (December
16, 1981). English.

AN: Three brothers, graphics artist,
painter, photographer, potter and poet
Alejandro Lopez and his older self-taught
brothers Felix and Manuel, are working with
traditional New Mexican art forms (bultos,
straw inlay crosses) and with newer
innovative forms - reflecting the fusion of
traditional-experimental art developing in
New Mexico among young artists.

6974 Saks Galleries, Denver, CO. Ramon K.
Exhibition brochure, 1971. English.

AN: Promotional brochure for major
one-man exhibition. Ramon Kelley is a
Chicano artist of international stature
whose artistic roots are firmly planted in
the American west. The Gallery director
states, "His impressionistic paintings
reveal a strong affinity to the land and
people of the southwest and they are the
major subject of his work. Lavishly
illustrated with full color reproductions of
several pastel and oil paintings.

6975 Salazar, Veronica. Artist doesn't starve
now. SAN ANTONIO EXPRESS-NEWS, (June 13,
1976), p. 18-A. English.

AN: Raul Gutierrez, water colorist from
Laredo, Texas, has emerged as a nationally
recognized master painter of western and
wildlife themes. His work is avidly
collected and exhibited. Article details his
artistic trajectory and provides
biographical information.

6976 Salazar, Veronica. Aspiration comes true.
SAN ANTONIO EXPRESS-NEWS, (October 28,
1979), p. 8-H. English.

AN: History of Alice Dickerson

Montemayor of Laredo, Texas (known as
"Admonty") who started to paint at 74 on the
occasion of her second exhibit at the
Mexican government's Instituto Cultural.

6977 Salazar, Veronica. Mel Casas sees things
brown. SAN ANTONIO EXPRESS-NEWS, (December
23, 1973). English.

AN: Searching for "visual congruity,"
Mel Casas has slowly moved toward figurative
art. Article traces aspects of his artistic
trajectory and the philosophic basis of his
aesthetic vision. Includes photograph of
artist.

6978 Salinas, Porfirio. Bluebonnets and cactus:
an album of southwestern paintings. Austin,
TX: Pemberton Press, 1967. English.

AN: Portfolio of Salinas landscape
paintings and five short stories. Lavishly
illustrated as a special edition.

6979 Salinas, Porfirio. Porfirio Salinas: blue
bonnets and cactus; an album of Southwestern
paintings. Austin, TX: Pemberton Press,
1967. English.

AN: A lavishly illustrated edition of
five short stories interspersed with
reproductions of Porfirio Salinas
landscapes. Salinas is considered an
important Southwestern landscapist.

6980 Salinas, Rael. The city [painting]. REVISTA
CHICANO-RIQUENA, Vol. 3, no. 1 (Winter
1974), p. 2. English.

6981 Salinas, Rael. Illusions of reality [detail
of painting]. REVISTA CHICANO-RIQUENA, Vol.
3, no. 1 (Winter 1975), p. COVER. English.

6982 Salinas, Rael. Illusions of reality. REVISTA
CHICANO-RIQUENA, Vol. 3, no. 1 (Winter
1974), p. 10. English.

6983 Salinas, Rael. Outcry [detail of painting].
REVISTA CHICANO-RIQUENA, Vol. 3, no. 1
(Winter 1974), p. 25. English.

6984 Salinas, Rael. Outcry [painting]. REVISTA
CHICANO-RIQUENA, Vol. 3, no. 1 (Winter
1974), p. 24. English.

6985 Salinas, Raul. Nueva estrella en el
horizonte. AZTLAN (U.S. Penitentiary,
Leavenworth, KA), Vol. 1, no. 1 (May 5,
1970). English.

AN: Brief article on San Antonio artist
Ruben Estrella who perfected his art within
the walls of Leavenworth. Especially noted
for his portraits, Estrella was illustrator
of NEW ERA, the prison's literary journal.
Illustrated with photograph of artist and
four of his oil paintings.

6986 Samuels, Peggy and Samuels, Harold. Salinas,
Porfirio. In THE ILLUSTRATED BIBLIOGRAPHICAL
ENCYCLOPEDIA OF THE AMERICAN WEST. Garden
City, NY: Doubleday, 1976, p. 415. English.

AN: Brief biography of Texas "bluebonnet
painter" (b. 1910). Only teachers were Jose
Arpa and Robert Wood of San Antonio. (See
also Jacinto Quirarte's book: MEXICAN
AMERICAN ARTISTS).

Paintings (cont.)

6987 San Antonio Museum Association, San Antonio, TX. Real, really real, super real. Exhibition brochure, 1981. English.

AN: Exhibit surveying modern and contemporary realism in the U.S. Includes a brief biography, personal statement, and color illustration of work by Jesse C. Trevino, San Antonio, Texas photorealist painter and muralist, (pp. 146-147).

6988 San Antonio Public Library. Art in the little world. News release, n.d. English.

AN: This news release includes a statement by the San Antonio born artist Edmon H. Benavides. Expressing himself through the medium of water color, Benavides paints Texas wildlife and nature scenes in a realistic style.

6989 San Francisco Museum of Modern Art, San Francisco, CA and Castellon, Rolando. Rupert Garcia/pastel drawings. Exhibition catalog, 1978. English.

AN: Exhibit by San Francisco artist Rupert Garcia.

6990 Sanchez, Ricardo. Hechizo/spells. Los Angeles, CA: Chicano Studies Publications, UCLA, 1976. English.

AN: Willie Herron, drawings and paintings on pp. 68, 70, 75, 89, 93, 97, 99, 123, 129, 135, 137, 151, 165, 167, 170, 181, 195, 229, 231, 235, 236, 238, 256, 258, 261, 268, 279, 284, 288, 312 and inside front and back covers.

6991 Sandoval, Carlos. [[Untitled art work]. TEJIDOS, Vol. 2, no. 6 (Summer 1975), p. 7. English.

6992 Sandoval, Moises "Sandy". [Untitled painting]. CARACOL, Vol. 5, no. 2 (October 1978), p. 21. Bilingual.

6993 Segade, Gustavo V. Alfredo Arreguin. CITYBENDER, Vol. 2, no. 9 (1978). English.

AN: Brief profile of Mexican-born painter Arreguin who lives in the state of Washington. Three illustrations.

6994 Sharing a bit of magic with John Mendoza. ARTISTS OF THE ROCKIES, Vol. 1, no. 2 (Spring 1974), p. 14-17. English.

AN: Growing up in the St. Charles Mesa east of Pueblo Colorado, John Mendoza has sought to capture the essence of nature in that part of the country in his paintings. Blending realism and abstraction, Mendoza has evolved a distinctive personal idiom. Illustrated with reproductions of two watercolors and six drawings. Includes two photos of the artist and his pupils.

6995 Silva, Rufino. Fragmentos horizontales con cuatro cabezas [painting]. REVISTA CHICANO-RIQUENA, Vol. 2, no. 2 (Spring 1974), p. 2. Spanish.

6996 Silva, Rufino. Fragmentos y formas femeninas con tres profiles [painting]. REVISTA CHICANO-RIQUENA, Vol. 2, no. 2 (Spring 1974), p. 23. Spanish.

6997 Silva, Rufino. Hombre vestido de negro, camisa blanca y mujer que sonrie [painting]. REVISTA CHICANO-RIQUENA, Vol. 2, no. 2

(Spring 1974), p. COVER. Spanish.

6998 Silva, Rufino. Ocultandose con panos blancos, sonrisa [painting]. REVISTA CHICANO-RIQUENA, Vol. 2, no. 2 (Spring 1974), p. 40. Spanish.

6999 Smith, Roberta. Twelve days of Texas. ART IN AMERICA, Vol. 64, no. 4 (July, August, 1976), p. 42-48. English.

AN: Overview of Texas art in Fort Worth/Dallas, Houston, San Antonio, Tyler, and Galveston. Includes reproductions of works by Luis Jimenez (color, on cover), Roberto Rios mural, Jesse Trevino, Mel Casas. Also mentioned in text are Phil Renteria and Cesar Martinez.

7000 La Sociedad Historica de Nuestra Senora de Guadalupe, Santa Fe, NM. Meditacion. Exhibition invitation, 1980. English.

AN: Invitation to an exhibit by four artists: Filomeno Martinez (graphic artist, Albuquerque), Ruben Montoya (santero, Santa Fe), Santiago Chavez (painter, Santa Rosa), Jose Alberto Baros (sculptor, Espanola).

7001 Southwest Chicano Arts Center, Houston, TX. The oil and acrylic paintings of Jose Perez. Exhibition invitation, 1977. English.

AN: Illustrated invitation to exhibit.

7002 Southwest Texas State University, San Marcos, TX and Carlisle, Charles Richard. El mundo de Luis Santiago. Exhibition brochure, n.d. English.

AN: Illustrated exhibition brochure with biographical data and exhibition chronology on Luis Santiago. Both as a sculptor and painter, Santiago works in various techniques and styles to project the dynamic and multi-faceted aspects of Chicano life.

7003 Stamper, Frances. Fluid washes of ink and acrylic. TEXAS HOMES MAGAZINE, Vol. 4, no. 1 (January, February, 1980), p. 104-112. English.

AN: Well illustrated article with color reproductions of the work of Philip Renteria. Provides biographical information and focuses on the consumate craftsmanship of his drawings and paintings.

7004 Terronez, Irene R. [Untitled painting]. HERESIES, Vol. 3, no. 1 (1980), p. 44.

7005 Terronez, Irene R. [Untitled painting]. MAIZE, Vol. 2, no. 4 (Summer 1979), p. 31.

7006 Terronez, Irene R. [Untitled painting]. MAIZE, Vol. 2, no. 4 (Summer 1979), p. 32-33. English.

7007 Terronez, Irene R. [Untitled painting]. MAIZE, Vol. 2, no. 4 (Summer 1979), p. 35. English.

7008 Terronez, Irene R. [Untitled painting]. MAIZE, Vol. 2, no. 4 (Summer 1979), p. Bk cover. English.

7009 Terronez, Irene R. [Untitled paintings]. MAIZE, Vol. 2, no. 4 (Summer 1979), p. Ft cover. English.

Paintings (cont.)

7010 Thorne, Judy. Alfredo Arreguin - painting in patterns. SEATTLE TIMES, (June 15, 1980), p. 18-19. English.

AN: Biographical information on Mexican-born Seattle painter Alfredo Arreguin. Includes mention of his selection as a city art commissioner in Seattle. Discussion of artist's distinctive style based on use of intricate patterns. Well illustrated with four color reproductions of artist's work.

7011 Torres, Pablo, Jr. [Untitled painting]. TEJIDOS, Vol. 2, no. 6 (Summer 1975), p. 40.

7012 Torres, Salvador Roberto. Creative aspects of la Raza inspired by Chicano experiences. Unpublished thesis, 1973. Bilingual.

AN: Project presents six paintings and six drawings by San Diego artist Torres based on the feeling and impact of United Farm Workers Huelga banner, used on a personal level. Torres wants to make an "imaginary theatre" of the ideas drawn from the Chicano movement. Bilingual. Illustrated.

7013 Trafford, Al. The giant painted photo album: Jesse Trevino. SOUTHWEST ART, (April 1979). English.

AN: Well illustrated story on San Antonio photorealist painter Jesse Trevino. Includes biographical material, description of his working methods for murals and easel paintings, and self-characterization of his work as "cultural documentary painting".

7014 Trevino, Rudy. Lettuce garden for Alamo [painting]. REVISTA CHICANO-RIQUENA, Vol. 8, no. 3 (Summer 1980), p. 70. Bilingual.

7015 Trevino, Rudy. Lettuce on ice [painting]. REVISTA CHICANO-RIQUENA, Vol. 8, no. 3 (Summer 1980), p. 69. Bilingual.

7016 Tsutakaua, Mayumi. Despite hostilities, Arreguin is transcending. SEATTLE TIMES, (September 2, 1979). English.

AN: Biographical sketch of Northwest Chicano painter and ceramicist Alfredo Arreguin. Artistic chronology and negative relationship with local mainstream art institutions.

7017 University of Texas. El Paso. Chicano Studies Program. "Chicanotations": paintings and drawings by Manuel Unzueta. Exhibition brochure, 1979. English.

AN: Exhibition handout includes biographical data and a listing of the 20 works exhibited by Unzueta.

7018 [Untitled]. Exhibition invitation. Santa Fe, NM: Santuario de Nuestra Senora de Guadalupe, 1980. English.

AN: Invitation to an exhibit by three northern New Mexico artists: Claudio Salazar (sculptor from Espanola), Eliud Salazar (painter from Canones)--both members of the Escuela Artesana--and Donald Romero (painter from Santa Fe).

7019 Unzueta, Manuel. En la catedral [painting]. XALMAN, Vol. 1, no. 4 (Spring 1977), p. 56.

7020 Unzueta, Manuel. Iconography: strictly Chicano. XALMAN, Vol. 1, no. 4 (Spring 1977), p. 17-18. English.

AN: Only a Chicano artist can portray the unique experience of being Chicano through visual images of despair and self pride: opinion of painter Unzueta.

7021 Unzueta, Manuel. Liberation call [painting]. XALMAN, Vol. 1, no. 4 (Spring 1977), p. Cover.

7022 Unzueta, Manuel. Mystic night [painting]. XALMAN, Vol. 1, no. 4 (Spring 1977), p. 3.

7023 Unzueta, Manuel. [Teatro (painting)]. XALMAN, Vol. 2, no. 2 (Spring 1979), p. Cover.

7024 Unzueta, Manuel. [Untitled painting]. XALMAN, Vol. 1, no. 5 (Fall 1977), p. Cover.

7025 Valadez, John. [Untitled painting]. COMUNIDAD, (May 24, 1981), p. Cover.

7026 Valdez, Salvador. A forgotten artist's work lives on. NOSOTROS, Vol. 2, no. 6. English.

AN: Narrative of the life and times of Jose Aceves, a self taught El Paso artist (1909-1968), noted for his desert landscapes.

7027 Valle, Victor Manuel and Vasquez, Emigdio. Emigdio Vasquez Interview. SOMOS, (December, January, 1978, 1979), p. 42-43. English.

AN: Article on Arizona-born painter, son of a miner, living in Orange County, California. Discusses his realistic style (from photographs), technique, humanism, interest in murals, and loan of work for Alejandro Grattan's film ONLY ONCE IN A LIFETIME. Illustrated.

7028 Vargas, Ben. [Untitled painting]. TEJIDOS, Vol. 2, no. 6 (Summer 1975), p. 28.

7029 Vasquez, Emigdio. The Cypress Street Barrio and my art: a statement of intent. Unpublished manuscript, 1978. English.

AN: The Arizona-born artist whose family moved to Orange, Calif. in 1941 describes his working class barrio and the perspective it gave him of "life, people and society." He turned to this subject matter as a young artist and has continued to paint the barrio. Description of sources and methods of work.

7030 Vasquez, Emigdio and Goldman, Shifra M. Painter: Emigdio Vasquez. Brochure, [1981]. English.

AN: Brochure including a brief biography and illustrations of eight paintings.

7031 Vasquez, Emigdio. La vida through the eyes of Emigdio Vasquez. Q-VO, (April 1979), p. 36. English.

AN: Interview with Orange County, California, realist and documentary painter Emigdio Vasquez who focuses on barrio life he knew in the 1940s and 1950s. Vasquez works from his own photographs and those of others. Includes biographical information and illustrations.

Paintings (cont.)

7032 Vasquez, Ricardo. Night dance [painting].
      TEJIDOS, Vol. 4, no. 3 (Fall 1977), p. 33.
      English.

7033 Villa, Esteban. The bride [painting]. EL
      GRITO, Vol. 2, no. 3 (Spring 1969), p. [21].
      English.

7034 Villa, Esteban. Durmiente [painting]. EL
      GRITO, Vol. 2, no. 3 (Spring 1969), p. [17].
      Spanish.

7035 Wagner Gallery presents paintings by Manuel
      Garza. SOUTHWEST ART COLLECTOR, Vol. 1, no.
      3 (March, April, 1980), p. 3. English.

      AN: Story on Texas landscape and
      blue-bonnet painter influenced by Porfirio
      Salinas.

7036 Weegar, Sally. Native Mexican images. DAILY
      TEXAN, (October 23, 1978), p. 16. English.

      AN: Review of an exhibit of watercolors,
      tiles, and silkscreen prints by Amado Pena
      at the Wagner Gallery in Austin. Earlier
      work of Laredo-born Pena were politically
      oriented toward La Raza. Recent work
      concentrates on New Mexican landscape and
      Indian peoples. Illustrated.

7037 White, Ron. Bluebonnet the flower of South
      Texas painting. SAN ANTONIO EXPRESS-NEWS,
      (December 14, 1975), p. 7-H. English.

      AN: The South Texas landscape paintings
      by Porfirio Salinas are immensely popular
      and command high prices. This analysis of
      the career and the production of the late
      artist (died April 18, 1973), concludes that
      Salinas was "a mediocre artist with mediocre
      skills and a poor sense of imagination".

7038 Wilson, William. 30 works from the grass
      roots. LOS ANGELES TIMES, (June 4, 1973),
      p. IV,2. English.

      AN: Review of a show at the Junior Arts
      Center in Barnsdall Park by 15 members of
      the Mechicano Art Center. The critic feels
      contemporary groups that aim for change
      today (unlike past groups) are unable to
      articulate their spirit in a cohesive style.
      The top talent in this show is Charles
      Almaraz; also on exhibit are paintings by
      Jose Cervantes, Guillermo Martinez, Ray
      Atilano, sculpture by Manuel Cruz, and
      photography by (Oscar) R. Castillo.

7039 Winn Galleries, Seattle, WA. Alfredo
      Arreguin. Exhibition catalog, 1981. English.

      AN: Catalog of an exhibit by
      Mexican-born Washington painter. Many
      reproductions, some in color.

7040 Yanez, Rene. 1 [painting]. EL GRITO, Vol. 2,
      no. 3 (Spring 1969), p. [39]. Bilingual.

7041 Yanez, Rene. 2 [painting]. EL GRITO, Vol. 2,
      no. 3 (Spring 1969), p. 40. Bilingual.

7042 Yanez, Rene. 3 [painting]. EL GRITO, Vol. 2,
      no. 3 (Spring 1969), p. [41]. Bilingual.

7043 Yanez, Rene. 4 [painting]. EL GRITO, Vol. 2,
      no. 3 (Spring 1969), p. [42]. Bilingual.

7044 Yanez, Rene. 5 [painting]. EL GRITO, Vol. 2,
      no. 3 (Spring 1969), p. [43]. Bilingual.

7045 Yanez, Rene. 6 [painting]. EL GRITO, Vol. 2,

no. 3 (Spring 1969), p. [43]. Bilingual.

7046 Yanez, Rene. 7 [painting]. EL GRITO, Vol. 2,
      no. 3 (Spring 1969), p. [44]. Bilingual.

7047 Yanez, Rene. Portfolio [mixed media]. EL
      GRITO, Vol. 1, no. 4 (Summer 1968), p.
      21-28. English.

7048 Yanez, Rene. [Untitled painting]. EL GRITO,
      Vol. 1, no. 4 (Summer 1968), p. 22.
      Bilingual.

7049 Yanez, Rene. [Untitled painting]. EL GRITO,
      Vol. 1, no. 3 (Summer 1968), p. 23.
      Bilingual.

7050 Yanez, Rene. [Untitled painting]. EL GRITO,
      Vol. 1, no. 4 (Summer 1968), p. 24-25.

7051 Yanez, Rene. [Untitled painting]. EL GRITO,
      Vol. 1, no. 4 (Summer 1968), p. 26.

7052 Yanez, Rene. [Untitled painting]. EL GRITO,
      Vol. 1, no. 3 (Summer 1968), p. 27.

7053 Yarbro-Bejarano, Yvonne. La forma del sueno:
      arte y pensamiento de Alfredo Arreguin.
      METAMORFOSIS, Vol. 3, no. 2 (1980, 1981), p.
      10-24. Spanish.

      AN: Interview and portfolio of
      Mexican-born painter who has been living in
      Seattle for more than 20 years. Contains
      biographical data and the artist's view on
      the role of the Chicano artist. Ten
      illustrations.

Palomino, Ernesto

7054 Burkhardt, Dorothy. Chicano pride and anger
      mix at 'Califas'. THE TAB, (April 12,
      1981), p. 34. English.

      AN: CALIFAS: AN EXHIBITION OF CHICANO
      ARTISTS IN CALIFORNIA represents a
      cross-section of artists exhibiting work for
      at least ten years: Rupert Garcia, Ernie
      Palomino, Eduardo Carrillo, Judy Baca, Rene
      Yanez, Carmen Lomas Garza, Salvador Roberto
      Torres, Roberto Chavez, Willie Herron, Ralph
      Maradiaga, Sue Martinez, Jose Montoya,
      Malaquias Montoya, Ramses Noriega and
      Esteban Villa. Illustrated.

7055 Campesino Business and Joint Enterprise
      Building, Fresno, CA. Sabor a Fresno. Arte
      chicano: los Four and la Brocha. Exhibition
      invitation [1976]. English.

      AN: Invitation to an exhibit of works by
      Los Four of Los Angeles and members of La
      Brocha del Valle of Fresno: Arturo Roman,
      Sal Garcia, John Sierra, Juan Truner, Sapo
      de Aztlan, Fernando Hernandez, Alberto
      Reyes, Ernesto Palomino, Lee Orona,
      Francisco Barrios, Juan Ybarra, Bobby Reyes,
      Alberto Hernandez. Brocha was started by
      Palomino (California State University,
      Fresno professor) to pool talents of Central
      Valley artists.

Palomino, Ernesto (cont.)

7056 Cockcroft, Eva; Weber, John; and Cockcroft, James D. Towards a people's art: the contemporary mural movement. New York: E.P. Dutton, 1977. English.

AN: A survey of the street mural movement in the United States, from about 1967 on. Several chapters are written by the artists themselves: John Weber on the Chicago mural group; Susan Shapiro-Kiok on Cityarts Workshop of New York; Eva Cockcroft on People's painters of New Jersey; Geronimo Garduno on Artes Guadalupanos de Aztlan of New Mexico. Chicano murals illustrated include those of Mujeres Muralistas, Ray Patlan, William F. Herron, Hoyo-Mara Gang, Artes Guadalupanos de Aztlan, Vicente Mendoza and Jose Nario (with Patlan) Mario Castillo, Michael Rios, Toltecas en Aztlan, Roberto Chavez, Ernie Palomino, Chuy Campusano and Luis Cortazar (with Rios).

7057 Delgado, Abelardo "Lalo". Chicano: 25 pieces of a Chicano mind. El Paso, TX: Barrio Publications, 1972. English.

AN: Three drawings by Ernesto Palomino.

7058 Exxon Company, Houston, TX and Quirarte, Jacinto. Chicano art of the barrio. Exhibition brochure, n.d. [c.1976]. English.

AN: Brochure for a traveling exhibit of photographically-reproduced Chicano murals: Leo Limon, Lucila Villasenor Grijalva, Antonio Esparza, Susan Saenz, Charles Felix, Hoyo-Mara gang, David A. Lopez and team, Roberto Chavez and team (Los Angeles); Jerry Concha, Ruben Guzman, Chuy Campusano (San Francisco); Manuel Unzueta (Santa Barbara). Ernie Palomino and Leo Esequiel Ozona (Fresno). Leo Tanguma (Houston), Roberto Lucero, Manuel Martinez and Al Sanchez (Denver).

7059 Gonzalez, Victoria. Chair in the sky: Ernesto Palomino. HERE AND NOW, Vol. 2, no. 2 (Fall   1981). English.

AN: An important article tracing the artistic career of Ernie Palomino, professor of art at California State University, Fresno. Includes biographical information, formation of La Brocha Del Valle (Chicano Arts Organization), information about Palomino's film MY TRIP IN A '52 FORD and commentary on Palomino's music and artistic philosophy. Well illustrated.

7060 Hale, David. Exhibit backers hope for Chicano cultural center plan. FRESNO BEE, (July 14, 1974), p. K5. English.

AN: Review of a Chicano art exhibition in the Sarah McCardle Room of the downtown Fresno County Public Library. According to artist-organizer Ernie Palomino, the exhibit is a trial balloon to see if enough Chicano artists can surface and cooperate in the establishment of a Chicano Cultural Center in Southeast Fresno. Illustrated with reproduction of a portrait by Romero Arroyo of Mendota, California and a painting by Victor Hernandez from Visalia, California.

7061 Mascorro, Julie. Mechicano Art Center exhibit to grace Price gallery walls. CAMPUS NEWS, (November 24, 1971). English.

AN: Brief history of Mechicano Art Center activities from its establishment in 1969 to 1971. Exhibiting are Charles Almaraz, Roberto Amaral, Raymond Atilano, William Bejarano, Armando Cabrera, Edward Carbajal, Leonard Castellanos, Henry de Vega, Antonio Esparza, Bob Gomez, Lucila V. Grijalva, Jesus Gutierrez, Santos Lira, Frank Martinez, Ernest Palomino, Louis Quijada, Richard Raya, Frank Romero. Illustrated.

7062 Oakes College, University of California, Santa Cruz, CA and Carrillo, Eduardo. Corazon de Aztlan: a Chicano arts show. Exhibition catalog, 1981. English.

AN: Catalog of exhibit including works by Eduardo Carrillo, Juana Franklin, Cruz Zamarron, Jerry Astorga, Jaime Valadez, Ernesto Palomino, Sal Garcia, Roger Sierra, Jose Montoya, Esteban Villa, Juanishi Orozco, from Santa Cruz, San Jose, Fresno and Sacramento. Presentations of films and by the Teatro de la Tierra Morena of Santa Cruz County.

7063 Palomino, Ernesto ("Ernie"). In black and white: evolution of an artist. Fresno, CA: Academy Library Guild, 1956. English.

AN: Illustrations of Palomino's work between 1945 and 1955 when he was a student in Fresno's Edison High and Adult Schools with art teacher Elizabeth Daniels Baldwin, who promoted the publication of the book. Drawings show extraordinary power and the social commentary of a young, essentially self-taught artist.

7064 Palomino, Ernesto ("Ernie"). My trip in a '52 Ford. San Francisco State College: Unpublished typescript for film, 1966. English.

AN: Script for film of the same name by Fresno artist Ernesto Palomino. Master's project.

7065 Palomino, Ernesto ("Ernie"). My trip in a '52 Ford. 16 mm. film, 1966. English.

AN: Animated film based on works of junk sculpture produced by Fresno-based artist. Features "Mary '52 Ford, an immortal mother having children after death," George Go, Dorothy Dresser, Carol Chair, Steve Stove, and other characters.

7066 S.A. site for National Symposium on Mexican American Art. CHICANO TIMES, Vol. 4, no. 30 (November 9, 1973), p. 5. English.

AN: Held at Trinity University, the Symposium discussed such issues as, creative evolution, art education, artistic relationships to Mexico and the evolution of Mexican American art in the California barrios. Participating artists included Rudy Trevino, Mel Casas, Octavio Medellin, Antonio Garcia, Carmen Garza, Esteban Villa, Jose Montoya, Ernesto Palomino, Michael Ponce de Leon, Luis Jimenez and Eugenio Quesada.

Palomino, Ernesto (cont.)

7067 Valdez, Armando. El calendario chicano 1975.
Hayward, CA: Southwest Network, 1975.
English.

AN: Third in a series of historical
calendars produced in 1972 and 1974 by La
Causa Publications and Southwest Network.
Artists included for each month are Carmen
Lomas Garza, Sergio Hernandez, Malaquias
Montoya, Mujeres Muralistas (Graciela
Carrillo, Venezuelan Consuelo Mendez, Irene
Perez, Patricia Rodriguez), Ramses Noriega,
Ernie Palomino, Amado Maurilio Pena, Martin
Perez. All but Texan Pena are California
artists.

Palomino, Joe

7068 Chicano art show at Contra Costa College. EL
HISPANO, Vol. 8, no. 25 (December 11, 1973).
English.

AN: Information on exhibition organized
by Ramses Noriega that included the work of
Jose Montoya, Esteban Villa, Mario Sinape,
Ricardo Rios, Malaquias Montoya, Fuchi
Queso, and Joe Palomino.

Pan American Center, Austin, TX

7069 Hand me down. AUSTIN AMERICAN STATESMAN,
(August 17, 1978), p. B-1. English.

AN: Illustration of Raul Valdez's mural
La Raza Cosmica on the outdoor stage of the
Pan American Center, East Austin.

Pando, Alonso

7070 Galeria, Santa Ana, CA. The last Chicano art
show. Exhibition brochure, 1981. English.

AN: Invitation-brochure for an exhibit
of Los Angeles and Orange County artists in
a gallery underwritten by the Friendly
Center, Inc. with grants from local
government and from businesses. Exhibiting
are (Roberto) Gil de Montes, Gilbert Lujan,
Judy Miranda, Patricia Murillo, Alonso
Pardo, Teddy Sandoval, Mexican artist
Artemio Sepulveda, Joey Terrill, Art
Valenzuela, Ben Valenzuela, Linda Vallejo,
Jack A. Vargas, Emigdio Vasquez, Richard
Serrato, and J. William Hernandez, who is
the gallery director.

PARA EL MERCADO [mural]

7071 Las mujeres muralistas. Exhibition
invitation, 1974. English.

AN: Invitation to the inauguration of
the mural PARA EL MERCADO at Paco's Tacos in
San Francisco's Mission District by the
Mujeres Muralistas, Sept. 15, 1974.
Illustrated by Venezuelan artist Consuelo
Mendez.

Paramo, Bobby

7072 Herrera, Juan Felipe and Paramo, Bobby.
Cerco Blanco, the balloon man and fighting
City Hall: on being a Chicano filmmaker.
METAMORFOSIS, Vol. 3, no. 2 (1980, 1981), p.
77-82. English.

AN: Autobiographical article about his
life and his introduction and immersion in
filmmaking by Bobby Paramo. His experiences
with documentary films, television, the Los
Angeles Chicano film movement, are recorded.

Pasadena, CA

7073 Cesaretti, Gusmano and Hirtz, Jacqueline.
Uplifting the city: the mural-painter's
goal. HOME MAGAZINE, (May 8, 1977), p.
50-51. English.

AN: Illustrated report on murals in Los
Angeles and Pasadena by Anthony Padilla.

PATH TO KNOWLEDGE AND THE FALSE UNIVERSITY [mural]

7074 Sanchez, Jesus. Auditorium mural "wipe out"
during recent renovation move. EAST LOS
ANGELES COLLEGE NEWS, (September 26, 1979).
English.

AN: "The Path to Knowledge and the False
University," a mural by Roberto Chavez on
the facade of ELAC's Ingalls Auditorium was
painted over on Sept. 11, 1979. Contrasting
views on the mural's fate are offered by the
Chicano Faculty Association President and
the Dean of Educational Services.

Patino, Joaquin

7075 Una galeria de artistas = A gallery of
artists. CAMINOS, Vol. 1, no. 6 (October
1980), p. 20-26. Bilingual.

AN: Features California artists Domingo
O. Ulloa (Imperial Valley images), Gloria
Chacon, photographer Maria Pinedo (San
Francisco), Willie Herron (Los Angeles),
Joaquin Patino (Delano), Pedro Pelayo (Long
Beach), sculptor Rudi Sigala (San Diego),
Mario Torero (San Diego), sculptor Michael
M. Amescua (Los Angeles), and the East Los
Streetscapers. Illustrated.

Patlan, Ray

7076 Calendario de March: 1977. Chicago, IL:
MARCH, Inc., 1976. English.

AN: Historical calendar with photos and
biographies of artists. Illustrations of
artwork by Ray Patlan, Jose Nario, Frank J.
Sanchez, Salvador Dominguez, Salvador Vega,
Marguerite Ortega, Aurelio Diaz, Carlos
Cortez, Mario E. Castillo, Francisco Blasco,
Rey Vasquez, and Efrain Martinez. History of
MARCH (Movimiento Artistico Chicano).

7077 Chicago-Raza murals. NATIONAL MURALS NETWORK
COMMUNITY NEWSLETTER, (Fall 1979), p. 22.
English.

AN: Murals by Ray Patlan, Aurelio Diaz,
Marcos Raya, Salvador Vega, Jaime Longoria,
Malu Ortega y Alberro, Oscar Moya in
Chicago's Pilsen district.

7078 Clark, Yoko and Hama, Chizu. California
murals. Berkeley, CA: Lancaster-Miller,
1979. English.

AN: Picture book of Bay Area and Los
Angeles murals with brief descriptions.
Chicano artists included: Daniel Galvez,
Irene Perez, Patricia Rodriguez, Graciela
Carrillo (Mujeres Muralistas), Ray Patlan.

Patlan, Ray (cont.)

7079 Cockcroft, Eva; Weber, John; and Cockcroft, James D. Towards a people's art: the contemporary mural movement. New York: E.P. Dutton, 1977. English.

AN: A survey of the street mural movement in the United States, from about 1967 on. Several chapters are written by the artists themselves: John Weber on the Chicago mural group; Susan Shapiro-Kiok on Cityarts Workshop of New York; Eva Cockcroft on People's painters of New Jersey; Geronimo Garduno on Artes Guadalupanos de Aztlan of New Mexico. Chicano murals illustrated include those of Mujeres Muralistas, Ray Patlan, William F. Herron, Hoyo-Mara Gang, Artes Guadalupanos de Aztlan, Vicente Mendoza and Jose Nario (with Patlan) Mario Castillo, Michael Rios, Toltecas en Aztlan, Roberto Chavez, Ernie Palomino, Chuy Campusano and Luis Cortazar (with Rios).

7080 COMMUNITY MURALS (San Francisco, CA). (Fall 1981). English.

AN: Citywide Murals Group of Denver, Colorado assisted the Chilean-oriented Brigada Orlando Letelier with a mural in their city; Carlos Sandoval of Denver doing mural in Guerrero, Mexico; Ray Patlan of Berkeley, California assisting with mural in Mexico painted by Arnold Belkin's class at the Academy of San Carlos; report on the exhibit MURALS OF AZTLAN: THE STREET PAINTERS OF EAST LOS with a reprint of debate on the event by Shifra M. Goldman, Judithe Elena Hernandez de Neikrug, and comments by John Pitman Weber and Tim Drescher; report on DAR LUZ mural directed by Santa Barraza in Austin, Texas, and a new mural in Hayward, California directed by Enrique Romero; a mural sponsored by the Chicano Youth Center of Fresno, California showing the influence of Mexican calendars; a new mural, OAKLAND'S PORTRAIT by Daniel Galvez in Oakland, California; pro-and-con discussion of social function of graffiti in response to letter from Belgian source; reprint of story on spray paint crime bill (anti-graffiti) sponsored by California Assemblyman Richard Alatorre. Entire issue illustrated.

7081 Erickson, Barbara. La Pena's new face. NORTH EAST BAY INDEPENDENT, no. 4 (September 5, 1978), p. 11. English.

AN: Illustrated story on the relief mural SONG OF UNITY by Ray Patlan, O'Brien Thiele, Osha Neumann, and Anna de Leon on the facade of La Pena cultural center in Berkeley, California. Chilean songwriter Victor Jara and the music of North and South America are the motifs.

7082 Goldman, Shifra M. Canto de unidad: nuevo mural de Berkeley. PLURAL, Vol. 8, no. 96 (September 1979), p. 33-44. Spanish.

AN: Report on significance, inconography, and new technical experimentation in street mural on facade of La Pena Cultural Center, Berkeley, CA. Deals with Latin American "nueva cancion." Ray Patlan and Anna de Leon on team of four muralists. Illustrated. This article was reprinted as "Song of Unity: Berkeley's New Raza Mural," in ARTWORKERS NEWS (New York), Vol. 11, no. 30, September 20, 1980, p. 1.

7083 Goldman, Shifra M. Song of unity: Berkeley's new raza mural. ARTWORKERS NEWS, Vol. 11,

no. 30 (September 20, 1980), p. 1. English.

AN: Reprint of article published as "Canto de unidad: nuevo mural de Berkeley" in PLURAL (Mexico, D.F.), Vol. 8, no. 96, September 1979, p. 33-44.

7084 MARCH: Movimiento artistico Chicano (Mexican-American Art Movement). QUARTERLY, (Spring 1976), p. 10. English.

AN: Brief history of MARCH. Illustrations of murals by Ricarco Alonzo, Jose Gonzalez, Vicente Mendoza. Ray Patlan.

7085 New radical wall art. PEOPLE'S WORLD, Vol. 41, no. 37 (September 16, 1978), p. 10. English.

AN: Illustrated story and explanation of the imagery on the new mural resulting from a collaboration of Commonarts and La Pena Cultural Center. The artists are Ray Patlan, O'Brien Thiele, Osha Neumann, and Anna de Leon.

7086 Notes on 2nd National Community Muralists' Network Conference, Chicago, Ill. April 20-23, 1978. San Francisco, CA, 1978. English.

AN: Rupert Garcia, Raul Martinez, Patricia Rodriguez, Ray Patlan (San Francisco Bay Area) and Jaime Valadez (San Jose), among others, attended the conference in Chicago. Reports were heard from many parts of the United States on mural activities, including that of Aurelio Diaz of Chicago, representing MARCH (Movimiento Artistico Chicano). A workshop presentation was made by Luis Arenal and others from the Taller Siqueiros of Cuernavaca, Mexico. An experimental mural to try Siqueiros' techniques was created. Illustrated.

7087 Petraitis, Louise. Student union murals: walls with tongues. PHOENIX MAGAZINE, (April 21, 1977), p. 12. English.

AN: San Francisco State University instructor Ray Patlan and his La Raza Mural Workshop are painting murals in the Student Union basement. The relationship of a mural to architecture, the process of transferring a sketch to the wall, the underpainting, and the finishing painting processes are explained. A videotape of the mural is being made. Illustrated.

7088 Plous, F.K. Street scenes. MIDWEST MAGAZINE, (September 1, 1974), p. 10. English.

AN: Article focusing on the mural production of Ray Patlan in the Pilsen barrio of Chicago. Description of the community and how Patlan functions as a community worker and muralist. Includes a directory of Chicago's murals. Well illustrated with photographs, some in color.

7089 "Viva la causa", a documentary film on the Mexican mural movement in Chicago. Chicago, IL: Kartemquin Films, [1974]. English.

AN: Advertising brochure for a film made of Chicano muralist Ray Patlan working with young people in Chicago. The film shows murals in Mexico and Chicago, and follows one mural from its sketch to its completion.

Patssi

USE: Valdez, Patssi

Paula Anglum Gallery, San Francisco, CA

7090 Albright, Thomas. Forceful masterpieces from Manuel Neri. SAN FRANCISCO CHRONICLE, (May 17, 1979), p. 47. English.

AN: A rave review of Neri's one-person sculpture show at the Paula Anglum Gallery.

7091 Albright, Thomas. San Francisco: sleepers and spectacles [Manuel Neri exhibit review]. ART NEWS MAGAZINE, Vol. 78, no. 7 (September 1979), p. 118. English.

AN: Review of an exhibit at the Paula Anglum Gallery of San Francisco by Manuel Neri who has been developing over the last twenty years into one of the country's most profound and compelling sculptors. These pieces are life-sized plaster figures of nude female models.

Pazos, Antonio

7092 Art outdoors. CONCEPT, (September 1980). English.

AN: Illustrated article on outdoor murals in Tucson by Antonio Pazos and David Tineo.

7093 Hanson, Matt. Barren walls toned into bold works of art. ARIZONA DAILY STAR, (May 24, 1979). English.

AN: Tucson high school students under direction of Antonio Pazos paint murals with a $10,000 grant from the Law Enforcement Assistance Administration. Color illustrations.

7094 Heard Museum, Phoenix, AZ. Second Southwest Chicano Art Invitational. Exhibit catalog, 1978. English.

AN: Exhibit by eight artists: Antonio Pazos (Tucson), Rudy Fernandez (Salt Lake City), Harry Gamboa (Los Angeles), Rupert Garcia and Xavier Viramontes (San Francisco), Roberto Rios (San Antonio), Roberto Espinoza (Yuma), and Roberto Borboa (Tucson). Brief biographies of all but Rios. 29 illustrations.

7095 Miller, Marlan. Heard speaks Spanish through art. PHOENIX GAZETTE, (September 23, 1978). English.

AN: Four new exhibits at the Heard Museum of Phoenix include "Hispanic crafts of the Southwest", and "Southwest Chicano Art Invitational". The former focuses on New Mexico and Colorado crafts, organized by the Taylor Museum if the Colorado Springs Fine Arts Center; the latter includes Rupert Garcia and Xavier Miramontes of San Francisco, Rudy Fernandez of Salt Lake City (now in Scottsdale, AZ), and Antonio Pazos of Tucson.

7096 Silent protest. ARIZONA DAILY STAR, (May 18, 1978), p. 6-H. English.

AN: Outdoor murals in Tucson by Ausberto Sandoval, Antonio Pazos and Sylvia de la Huerta on a house in community being displaced by urban renewal. Illustrated.

7097 Tang, Paul. Artist sustains proud Hispanic mural tradition. ARIZONA DAILY

WILDCAT-ENCORE, (March 29, 1979), p. 1. English.

AN: Born and educated in Hermosillo, Sonora, Mexico, Antonio Pazos is painting murals around Tucson. Pazos got his first mural experience helping paint the Centro Cultural de la Raza building in San Diego, CA in the early 1970s. He also spent a summer at Paolo Soleri's city north of Phoenix, Arcosanti. Illustrated.

7098 Tribute to El Rio organizers: Mexican-American mural to be unveiled. ARIZONA DAILY STAR, (September 13, 1975). English.

AN: $1100, 1775-square-foot mural on two outdoor walls by Antonio Pazos, 22 year old art student from Hermosillo, Sonora. Completed on the third anniversary of El Rio Neighborhood Center in Tucson. Color illustration.

7099 Tucson Public Library; Sonoran Heritage; and De la Cruz, Frank. Mexican American mural art: the power of cultural identity. Brochure, 1980. English.

AN: Brochure on Tucson murals painted by Antonio Pazos, David Tineo, Danny Garza, Cynthia Reyes, Darlene Marcos, Roberto Borboa, and others.

7100 Union Gallery, University of Arizona Student Union, Tucson, AZ. Chicanarte: Cynthia Reyes Aponte, Zarco Guerrero, Virginia Federico Olivares, Antonio Pazos. Exhibition catalog, 1981. English.

AN: Illustrated catalog of exhibit featuring four artists.

7101 Vigil, Maria. Art bridging culture gap. TUCSON CITIZEN, OLD PUEBLO SECTION, (March 22, 1979). English.

AN: Students under tutelage of Antonio Pazos paint a mural at the Perfection Plumbing Co. in Tucson. Illustrated.

7102 Vigil, Maria. Hello, walls: Tucson's murals. WEEKENDER MAGAZINE, (March 29, 1980), p. 14-16. English.

AN: Article on muralism, from the Mexican to those of Chicanos. Focuses on Tucson murals by Roberto Borboa, Antonio Pazos, David Tineo and Fred Monreal. Color illustrations.

Pedregon Martinez, Ernesto

7103 Hamm, Madeline McDermott. Artist envisions a 'Sistine' ceiling. HOUSTON CHRONICLE, (September 19, 1978), p. III, 1-3. English.

AN: Illustrated article on mural that Ernesto Pedregon Martinez (who was active in El Paso in the 1950s) was doing for St. Joseph Catholic Church in Houston. The mural depicts the crucifixion.

Pelayo, Pedro

7104 Una galeria de artistas = A gallery of artists. CAMINOS, Vol. 1, no. 6 (October 1980), p. 20-26. Bilingual.

AN: Features California artists Domingo O. Ulloa (Imperial Valley images), Gloria Chacon, photographer Maria Pinedo (San Francisco), Willie Herron (Los Angeles), Joaquin Patino (Delano), Pedro Pelayo (Long Beach), sculptor Rudi Sigala (San Diego), Mario Torero (San Diego), sculptor Michael M. Amescua (Los Angeles), and the East Los Streetscapers. Illustrated.

Pena, Amado Maurilio, Jr

7105 Amado Maurilio Pena, Jr. PAPEL CHICANO, Vol. 1, no. 13 (July 21, 1978). Spanish.

AN: Includes the artist's resume, an exhibition list, and a gallery statement situating the work of Pena within both Native American and Chicano art traditions. Includes reproduction of four works.

7106 Anderson, Howard J.; Young, Robert S.; and Kilgore, Andrew. Amado Maurilio Pena, Jr. Albuquerque, NM: Robert Stephan Young Publishing Co., 1981. English.

AN: Coffee-table type of art book about the Laredo-born painter and printmaker. The text includes impressionistic writing about Pena's life, interlaced with statements by the artist about his life and work. Though including a few plates from his early (1974-1978) political and family silkscreens, over 50 color plates reproduce his "Santa Fe Indian" works from 1978 to the present.

7107 The art of Mexican America. EMPIRE MAGAZINE, (November 1, 1970), p. 24-25. English.

AN: Visual portfolio with minimal text. Includes paintings by Amado Pena, Mel Casas, Porfirio Salinas, and sculpture by Octavio Medellin. On the same page, Dr. Jacinto Quirarte gives views on the nature of Mexican art, the Mexican American artist, and the connection between Mexican and Mexican American art.

7108 Bolger, Kathryn McKenna. Amado Pena's art. AUSTIN AMERICAN STATESMAN, (March 29, 1980), p. 10-11. English.

AN: A review of Pena's show of silkscreens, watercolors, and drawings at the Laguna Gloria Art Museum in Austin, Texas, March-May, 1980. Suggests that the artist has turned from a confrontational to an assimilationist stance. At present he visually documents the peaceful amalgamation of the cultural heritage on both sides of the Rio Grande.

7109 Carraro, Francine. Refined rhythmic references: Amado Pena, Jr. SOUTHWEST ART, Vol. 9, no. 6 (November 1979), p. 70-75. English.

AN: Well-illustrated (including 4 color) story on Austin silkscreen artist Amado M. Pena. Features his recent stylized work based on New Mexican indian motifs.

7110 CJL. Artist profile-Amado Pena. FOUR WINDS, Vol. 1, no. 4 (1980), p. 10. English.

AN: Amado Pena works within the expectations of an American Indian artist, but also within the context of the Mexican American culture. The article treats Pena's artistic trajectory and provides biographical information. Illustrated with photograph of the artist and reproductions of one lithograph and one mixed-media drawing.

7111 Contemporary Arts Museum, Houston, TX. Dale gas: give it gas. The continued acceleration of Chicano art. Exhibition catalog, 1977. English.

AN: A comprehensive catalog including 28 works of art exhibited by 13 Texas artists: Melesio (Mel) Casas, Jose Esquivel, Francisco (Frank) Fajardo, Carmen Lomas Garza, Luis Jimenez, Cesar Augusto Martinez, Santos G. Martinez, Jr., Amado Pena, Roberto Rios, Jose Rivera, Joe B. Rodriguez, Jesus (Jesse) Trevino, and George Truan. Many illustrations, some in color. Introduction by James Harithas. Essay by Santos Martinez, Jr. Poetry, literature and essays by Chicano writers.

7112 Crossley, Mimi. Tejano artists. HOUSTON POST, (August 19, 1976). English.

AN: Exhibition of 19 Texas artists organized by Joe Rodriguez of the AAMA (Association for the Advancement of Mexican Americans) Art Center in Houston, Texas. Working within a wide range of styles and a great scope of subject matter. Includes brief commentary on the work of Amado Pena, Carmen Lomas Garza, Cesar Martinez, Enrique Campos, Carolina Flores, Jesus Trevino and a host of others.

7113 Galeria de la Raza, San Antonio, TX. Celebration seventy-four. Exhibition catalog, [ca. 1974]. English.

AN: Catalog of extensive exhibition including European, Mexican, and the following Texan Chicano artists: Rolando Garces, Cesar Martinez, Ray Chavez, Vicente Rodriguez, Jorge Garza, Alfred Rodriguez, Luis Guerra, Carmen Lomas Garza, Bruno Andrade, Jr., Amado M. Pena Jr., Roberto Rios, Jose Trevino, Rudy Trevino, Luis Santoyo, Tati Rubio, Eduardo C. Garza, Arthur de la Fuente, and Jesus Campos Trevino.

7114 Goldman, Shifra M. Chicano art alive and well in Texas: a 1981 update. REVISTA CHICANO-RIQUENA, Vol. 9, no. 1 (Winter 1981), p. 34-40. English.

AN: Reprint of article published as "Supervivencia y prosperidad del arte chicano en Texas: nueva revision" in COMUNIDAD (Los Angeles, CA) [Sunday Supplement to LA OPINION], September 21, 1980, p. 3, 15+.

7115 Goldman, Shifra M. Supervivencia y prosperidad del arte chicano en Texas: nueva revision. COMUNIDAD, Vol. 55, no. 5 (September 21, 1980), p. 3,15+. Spanish.

AN: Focuses on six Chicano artists from Austin, Houston, San Antonio, and Kingsville: Mel Casas, Cesar Martinez, Amado M. Pena, Leo Tanguma, Carmen Lomas Garza, and Santa Barraza. Well illustrated. This article was reprinted as "Chicano Art Alive and Well in Texas: A 1981 Update," in REVISTA CHICANO-RIQUENA (Houston), Vol. 9, no. 1, Winter 1981, p. 34-40.

Pena, Amado Maurilio, Jr (cont.)

7116 HEMBRA: HERMANAS EN MOVIMIENTO BROTANDO RAICES DE AZTLAN (University of Texas, Austin). (Spring 1976).

AN: Raul Valdez, drawing, p. 3; Carolina Flores, drawing, p. 5; Maria Flores, photograph, pp. 7, 11, 30; M.E. Secrest-Ramirez, drawing, p. 12; Amacio Zarate, drawing, p. 15; Santa Barraza, drawings, pp. 16, 17, 18, 26, 32; Nora Gonzales-Dodson, painting, p. 19; Gilberto Cardenas, photograph, pp. 22, 28; Nanci de los Santos, photograph, p. 23, 29; Amado Maurilio Pena, Jr. p. 31.

7117 Hennessey, Kathy. Amado Pena, Chicano artist. REVISTA RIO BRAVO, no. 1 (Fall 1980), p. 2+. English.

AN: Review of the life and art of Laredo-born artist Pena whose early work in the 1960s was abstracted figures in bright colors; in the 1970s his work became political commentary for the Chicano movement; most recently he is doing paintings and silkscreens about New Mexican Indian life. As a teacher he influenced many students, especially in Anderson High School (Austin). Illustrations throughout the issue.

7118 Instituto Chicano de Artes y Artesanias (Texas Instit. Educational Development) and Instituto Cultural Mexicano (SER/UNAM), San Antonio, TX. Artistas chicanos: Los Quemados. San Antonio, TX: Instituto Chicano, Texas Institute for Educational Development, 1975. English.

AN: Invitation to an exhibit and manifesto of 1975 Austin-San Antonio artists' group, Los Quemados. Included Santa Barraza, Carolina Flores, Carmen Lomas Garza, Luis Guerra, Cesar Augusto Martinez, Santos Martinez, Amado Maurilio Pena, Jr., Jose Rivera, Vicente Rodriguez, Jose Trevino.

7119 Laguna Gloria Art Museum, Austin, TX. Tierra, familia sociedad, Amado Pena's themes. Exhibition catalog, 1980. Bilingual.

AN: Illustrated exhibition catalog with artist's biography and chronology of exhibitions. The bi-lingual text by Santos G. Martinez, Jr. situates the artist's work within a dual phased trajectory. First a period (1971-1975) in which the artist creates images armed with a social-political focus and (1975-present), a period starting with the PEOPLESCAPE series in which the artist enters a more lyrical introspective phase.

7120 Lopez, Armando. 'Chicano' art gains cross-culture recognition: 'the street mural has flourished in the barrio'. LAREDO NEWS, (July 20, 1980), p. 6-A. English.

AN: Report on a lecture "The First Decade of the Chicano Renaissance: Mexican American Art in the United States" given by Dr. Shifra M. Goldman under the sponsorship of the Laredo Philosophical Society. Mentions the "delicate Issue" of using the word "Chicano" in conservative Laredo. Illustrated with works of Laredo-born Amado M. Pena.

7121 Martinez, Cesar Augusto. Arte chicano. CARACOL, Vol. 1, no. 6 (February 1975), p. 3. English.

AN: Thoughts on the form, function and meaning of Chicano Art. Stylistically, it is seen as a fusion. It is dynamic, expressing multiple political sentiments and has an irreverent attitude towards dominant culture. Front cover of issue is a black and white reproduction of a silkscreen print by Amado Maurilio Pena, Jr.

7122 Parr, June. Amado Maurilio Pena, Jr.: a talented and dedicated artist. ARRIBA, (October 1980), p. 1. English.

AN: Pena is represented in forty-two galleries internationally. Recently, Pena opened his studio and gallery, El Taller, in Austin. His latest works focus on the Indian heritage and are based on trips to New Mexico. Illustrated.

7123 Pena, Amado Maurilio, Jr. Amado Maurilio Pena, Jr. Brochure [1980]. English.

AN: Promotional brochure including a biographical profile of the artist, a list of representing galleries throughout the United States, and eight good quality reproductions of serigraphs and mixed media drawings, six in color, on the theme of New Mexican Pueblo Indians.

7124 Southwest Texas State University, San Marcos, TX and Carlisle, Charles Richard. Cuatro caminos: four perspectives on Chicano art. Exhibition catalog, 1980. English.

AN: Exhibition pamphlet with photographs of the artists. Alex Flores, Luis Jimenez, Cesar Augusto Martinez and Amado Pena, Jr. comment on their work and the Chicano art movement.

7125 Spurgin, Judy. Amado Maurilio Pena, Jr. ULTRA MAGAZINE, Vol. 1, no. 1 (September 1981). English.

AN: Succinct treatment of Pena's artistic trajectory and a superficial analysis of his work. Information on his patrons and supporters.

7126 Tannous, David. Problems of the artist as a hyphenated commodity. THE WASHINGTON STAR, (August 28, 1977), p. G-20. English.

AN: Review of ANCIENT ROOTS, NEW VISIONS show in Washington, D.C. describing Mel Casas' painting (San Antonio), Louis LeRoy's assemblage (Coolidge, Arizona), Amado Pena's silkscreen, Rogelio Ruiz Valdovin's costume (Tucson).

7127 Valdez, Armando. El calendario chicano 1975. Hayward, CA: Southwest Network, 1975. English.

AN: Third in a series of historical calendars produced in 1972 and 1974 by La Causa Publications and Southwest Network. Artists included for each month are Carmen Lomas Garza, Sergio Hernandez, Malaquias Montoya, Mujeres Muralistas (Graciela Carrillo, Venezuelan Consuelo Mendez, Irene Perez, Patricia Rodriguez), Ramses Noriega, Ernie Palomino, Amado Maurilio Pena, Martin Perez. All but Texan Pena are California artists.

Pena, Amado Maurilio, Jr (cont.)

7128 Valdez, Armando. El calendario chicano 1977.
Hayward, CA: Southwest Network, 1977.
English.

AN: Fifth in a series of historical
calendars produced in 1972, 1974, 1975, 1976
by La Causa Publications and Southwest
Network. Artists whose work is reproduced
are Malaquias Montoya, Amado Maurilio Pena,
Ramori Zamora, Glugio J.L. Nicandro [Gronk],
Etta Delgado, Ricardo Alaniz, Diane Gamboa,
Elisa Marina Coleman, Margarita Calderon,
Jose Antonio Burciaga, Cesar Augusto
Martinez, Maria Ochoa y Valtierra, Juan
Renteria Fuentes, from California, New
Mexico, and Texas.

7129 Weegar, Sally. Native Mexican images. DAILY
TEXAN, (October 23, 1978), p. 16. English.

AN: Review of an exhibit of watercolors,
tiles, and silkscreen prints by Amado Pena
at the Wagner Gallery in Austin. Earlier
work of Laredo-born Pena were politically
oriented toward La Raza. Recent work
concentrates on New Mexican landscape and
Indian peoples. Illustrated.

7130 Work of Southwest artist sings to soul,
heart. NUESTRO, Vol. 5, no. 7 (October
1981), p. 57-61. English.

AN: Brief profile of Laredo-born Texas
artist Amado Pena who designed the first
conmemorative poster for the Congressional
Hispanic Caucus' observance of National
Hispanic Heritage Week. The poster is
reproduced on the cover. The article
includes full-color illustrations.

La Pena Cultural Center, Berkeley, CA

7131 Erickson, Barbara. La Pena's new face. NORTH
EAST BAY INDEPENDENT, no. 4 (September 5,
1978), p. 11. English.

AN: Illustrated story on the relief
mural SONG OF UNITY by Ray Patlan, O'Brien
Thiele, Osha Neumann, and Anna de Leon on
the facade of La Pena cultural center in
Berkeley, California. Chilean songwriter
Victor Jara and the music of North and South
America are the motifs.

7132 Goldman, Shifra M. Canto de unidad: nuevo
mural de Berkeley. PLURAL, Vol. 8, no. 96
(September 1979), p. 33-44. Spanish.

AN: Report on significance,
inconography, and new technical
experimentation in street mural on facade of
La Pena Cultural Center, Berkeley, CA. Deals
with Latin American "nueva cancion." Ray
Patlan and Anna de Leon on team of four
muralists. Illustrated. This article was
reprinted as "Song of Unity: Berkeley's New
Raza Mural," in ARTWORKERS NEWS (New York),
Vol. 11, no. 30, September 20, 1980, p. 1.

7133 Goldman, Shifra M. Song of unity: Berkeley's
new raza mural. ARTWORKERS NEWS, Vol. 11,
no. 30 (September 20, 1980), p. 1. English.

AN: Reprint of article published as
"Canto de unidad: nuevo mural de Berkeley"
in PLURAL (Mexico, D.F.), Vol. 8, no. 96,
September 1979, p. 33-44.

7134 Gomez, Linda. Malaquias Montoya exhibit
opens at La Pena. EL MUNDO (San Francisco,
CA), (October 29, 1975), p. 3. English.

AN: Over 50 paintings, silkscreens, and
drawings by Montoya at La Pena Cultural
Center, Berkeley, CA. Statement by the
artist who refuses to exhibit in museums and
is opposed to murals that are "pretty
decorations.".

7135 Kerschen, Karen. Where politics and music
mix: La Pena. BERKELEY BARB, (August 18,
1978), p. 12. English.

AN: A new three-dimensional mural has
been completed on the outside of Berkeley's
La Pena Community Center. It incorporates
ceramic and papier mache relief in a painted
mural. One side of the painting is dominated
by a relief sculpture of Victor Jara, the
Chilean musician and poet killed by the
junta. Illustrated.

7136 Mural celebration. GRASSROOTS, (September
6, 1978), p. 8. English.

AN: Illustrated story on the new mural
of plywood, papier mache and ceramic painted
and modeled by artists from Commonarts for
la Pena Cultural Center. The mural depicts
peoples of the Americas coming together,
singing and playing musical instruments,
with Chilean musician Victor Jara as the
major symbol.

7137 NATIONAL MURALS NETWORK COMMUNITY
NEWSLETTER. (1978). English.

AN: This issue features reports from
muralists. Includes information about murals
at: La Pena Cultural Center in Berkeley, CA;
the Social and Public Art Resource Center's
Tujunga Wash Mural in Venice, CA; the
Citywide Mural Project in Los Angeles, CA;
activities at Chicano Park, and of the
Congress of American Cosmic Artists (CACA),
both in San Diego, CA; murals in San Mateo
County, CA; the Task Force on Hispanic
American Arts headed by Jacinto Quirarte of
San Antonio; the 1978 Canto Al Pueblo in
Corpus Christi, TX; murals in Chicago; and
other works by non-Chicano artists.

7138 New radical wall art. PEOPLE'S WORLD, Vol.
41, no. 37 (September 16, 1978), p. 10.
English.

AN: Illustrated story and explanation of
the imagery on the new mural resulting from
a collaboration of Commonarts and La Pena
Cultural Center. The artists are Ray Patlan,
O'Brien Thiele, Osha Neumann, and Anna de
Leon.

Pena, Dolores

7139 Chicano muralists maintain traditions. LA
CUCARACHA, (November 20, 1979), p. 7.
English.

AN: Introduction to Chicano muralism in
Pueblo and comparison to the Mexican mural
movement from which it draws inspiration. 20
murals painted from 1977 to 1979. The
muralists include Bernardo Duran, Juan
Espinoza, Miguel "Freeloader" Garcia, Lola
Gutierrez, Leo Lucero, Juan Pacheco, Dolores
Pena, Pedro Romero, Stan Salazar, David
Sandoval. Diego Rivera murals illustrated.

Penalosa, Fernando

7140 DE COLORES. Vol. 2, no. 4 (1976), p. 1-68.
English.

AN: Photographs by Moises Medina, Jose
Luis Sedano; drawings by Jerry Lujan,
Gilbert "Sparky" Espinoza, Rebecca Polanco;
paintings by John Herrera, Sonny Duran,
Larry Martinez. Cover by Fernando Penalosa.

7141 Diaz, Katherine A. Murals of New Mexico.
CAMINOS, Vol. 2, no. 5 (October 1981), p.
9-10. English.

AN: Illustrations of murals in Santa Fe
and Albuquerque by Gilberto Guzman,
Francisco Le Fevere[sic; Lefebre], Manuel
Unzueta, and Fernando Penalosa.

Penichet, Jeff

7142 Cine chicano: primer acercamiento.
COMUNIDAD, no. 20 (November 16, 1980), p.
1-15. Spanish.

AN: The entire cultural supplement of LA
OPINION is dedicated to Chicano film.
Includes articles by Jason Johansen, Jeff
Penichet, Harry Gamboa, Jr., Jesus Salvador
Trevino, Carlos Penichet, Sylvia Morales,
Julio Moran, and Jose Luis Borau. Also
includes a declaration of purpose by the
Asociacion Chicana de Cineastas, and a
filmography of Chicano cinema compiled by
Trevino.

Penitentes
USE: Hermanos Penitentes

PEOPLE'S HISTORY OF TELEGRAPH AVENUE [mural]

7143 Mural. ARTE, no. 1 (1977). English.

AN: Describes a section of the mural A
PEOPLE'S HISTORY OF TELEGRAPH AVENUE painted
by Daniel Galvez and Brian Thiele. The mural
represents the work of dozens of additional
artists.

Pereira, Ismael "Smiley"

7144 Blanco, Gil. Art on the walls: a vehicle for
positive change. LATIN QUARTER, Vol. 1, no.
2 (October 1974), p. 26-30. English.

AN: East Los Angeles artists Ismael
"Smiley" Pereira and C.W. (Charles) Felix
started painting murals with young people at
the Estrada Courts Housing Project in May
1973. There are now 30 murals, and the
residents are more receptive, noting the
changes that are taking place. Illustrated
with murals by Herron and Gronk, and Daniel
Martinez.

Perez, Carlos

7145 Martinez, Anita. Raza art. EL TECOLOTE, Vol.
1, no. 8 (November 30, 1970), p. 1. English.

AN: Jay Ojeda, newly selected director
of Galeria de la Raza, describes the
memorial exhibition dedicated to Ruben
Salazar installed at the Galeria on Dec. 12,
1970. Salazar symbolized and synthesized
many of the goals subscribed to by artist
members of La Galeria. The exhibit included
work by Chicano and Latino artists Francisco
Camplis, Jay Ojeda, Jose Romero, Rolando
Castellon, Rene Yanez, Luis Valsoto, Mike
Ruiz, Carlos Perez, Gustavo Rivera, Peter
Rodriguez, Carlos Loarca and Ralph
Maradiaga.

Perez, Hector

7146 Arts Council Center for the Arts of Greater
Lansing, Lansing, MI. Raza fine arts
festival. Festival program, 1978. English.

AN: This festival program mentions Jose
Narezo's mural at the Holland National Guard
Armory, Grand Rapids; includes a statement
of the Raza Art/Media Collective, Inc.; the
philosophy of artists Zaragosa Vargas and S.
Kaneta Kosiba-Vargas; and profiles of
exhibiting artists George Vargas, Martin
Moreno, Hector Perez, Michael L. Selley,
Jesse Gonzales, Nora Chapa Mendoza, Jesse
Soriano, Jose Luis Narezo.

7147 Capitol Art Gallery, Lansing, MI. Arte de
Nora Mendoza, Hector Perez, George Vargas,
Martin Moreno. Exhibition invitation [1979].
English.

AN: Invitation to an art exhibit
organized by Nuestras Artes de Michigan.

7148 Valade, Carole. Mural depicts artist's
heritage. ADRIAN DAILY TELEGRAM, (September
15, 1978). English.

AN: Detailed description of Vibrations
of a New Awakening, mural at Community
Action Art Center by Martin Moreno with
assistants Hector Perez and Walter Burrow.

Perez, Irene

7149 Albright, Thomas. Three remarkable Latin
murals. SAN FRANCISCO CHRONICLE, (June 7,
1974), p. 48. English.

AN: The myth of the melting pot is
vanishing: we recognize a variety of
"publics" today. This is shown in three
remarkable murals in the San Francisco
Mission District. The Mission branch of the
Bank of America has a 90 foot mural designed
by Jesus Campusano, assisted by Luis
Cortazar and Michael Rios, with technical
advice from Emmy Lou Packard. Another mural
is by the Mujeres Muralistas (Graciela
Carrillo, Consuelo Mendez, Irene Perez,
Patricia Rodriguez); the third by Michael
Rios on the 24th St. mini-park.

7150 Clark, Yoko and Hama, Chizu. California
murals. Berkeley, CA: Lancaster-Miller,
1979. English.

AN: Picture book of Bay Area and Los
Angeles murals with brief descriptions.
Chicano artists included: Daniel Galvez,
Irene Perez, Patricia Rodriguez, Graciela
Carrillo (Mujeres Muralistas), Ray Patlan.

7151 Cockcroft, Eva. Women in the community mural
movement. HERESIES, no. 1 (January 1977), p.
14-22. English.

AN: Women's role in the community mural
movement is much greater than generally
recognized. Among the many women muralists
discussed are included the Mujeres
Muralistas (Patricia Rodriguez, Irene Perez,
Graciela Carrillo de Lopez, and Venezuelan
Consuelo Mendez Castillo) of San Franfisoc,
and Judy Baca of Los Angeles. Illustrated.

Perez, Irene (cont.)

7152 Garcia, Rupert. Laminas de la Raza. San Francisco: Garcia Litho and Printing Service, 1975. English.

AN: Portfolio of drawings and prints by Patricia Rodriguez, Ricardo Apodaca, Xochitl, Domingo Rivera, Francisco Camplis, Rafael Maradiaga, Tom Rios, Juan Fuentes, Ricardo Diaz, Jose Romero, Consuelo Mendez, Jose Antonio Burciaga, Irene Perez, Ricardo Rios, Mike Rios, Graciela Carrillo, Rene Yanez, Luis Talamantez, Guillermo Bermudez, all from Northern California.

7153 Garcia, Rupert. Pulqueria art--defiant art of the barrios [Part II]. EL TECOLOTE, Vol. 8, no. 5 (February 1978), p. 8. Bilingual.

AN: In the Mission District of San Francisco, various artists like Irene Perez, Esther Fernandez, Chuy Campusano, Graciela Carrillo de Lopez, Consuelo Mendez Castillo, and Mike Rios have embellished business sites with wall decorations similar in spirit to the "Pulqueria" art of Mexico. Illustrated with three "Pulqueria"-type wall paintings: ATARDECER DE UN IMPERIO by Oscar Carveo at the Azteca Restaurant (Mission and 20th Sts.), El Buen Boricano Restaurant facade (24th and Harrison Sts.) and Fruitlandia facade (24th and Treat Sts.).

7154 Gonzalez, Tobias and Gonzalez, Sandra. Perspectives on Chicano education. Stanford, CA: Stanford University, 1975. English.

AN: Reproductions of artworks by Ralph Maradiaga, Patricia Rodriguez, Roberto Bonilla, Francisco Camplis, Graciela Carrillo-Lopez, Juan Fuentes, Irene Perez, Roger Reyes, Carlos Loarca, Xavier Viramontes, Ralph McNeill, Rupert Garcia, Jose Romero.

7155 Hartnell College Studio Gallery, Salinas, CA. Paintings, drawings, prints by San Francisco Bay Area Chicano artists. Exhibit brochure, 1971. English.

AN: Brochure for exhibit featuring Francisco Camplis, Graciela Carrillo, Sal Castaneda, Priscilla Dominguez, J. Duarte, Rupert Garcia, Carlos Loarca, Irene Perez, Vincent Rascon, Michael Rios, Peter Rodriguez, Luis Valsoto, Esteban Villa, Rene Yanez, Zala. Illustrated by Rupert Carcia print.

7156 La historia de California, 1977. San Francisco, CA: Galeria de la Raza, 1977. English.

AN: Handprinted silkscreen calendar of history seen from a Mexican point of view. Twelve sheets and a cover. Artists are: Ralph Maradiaga, Irene Perez, Louie "The Foot" Gonzalez, Max Garcia, Patricia Rodriguez, Jose Romero, Esteban Villa, Juanishi Orozco, Rodolfo Cuellar, Jose Montoya, Xavier Viramontes, Rene Yanez, Ricardo Favela, associated with the Galeria de la Raza, or the Royal Chicano Air Force of Sacramento.

7157 Kamin, Ira. Come on in, bring your paint. PACIFIC SUN, (May 30, 1974), p. 11-12. English.

AN: Chatty report on murals and art exhibit in San Francisco's Mission District: murals by Chuy Campusano, Michael Rios, Richard Montez, Trish (Patricia) Rodriguez, Graciela Carrillo, Consuelo Mendez and Irene Perez. Illustrated.

7158 Las muralistas: Patricia Rodriguez, Consuelo Mendez, Graciela Carrillo, Irene Perez. Exhibition invitation, 1974. English.

AN: Invitation to the inauguration of the mural LATINO AMERICA by the Mujeres Muralistas at the Mission Neighborhood Model Cities in San Francisco's Mission District, May 31, 1974.

7159 Portraying Latino women in the Mission. SAN FRANCISCO EXAMINER, (September 10, 1974), p. 26. English.

AN: Three muralists of the Mission District, Irene Perez, Patricia Rodriguez, and Venezuelan Consuelo Mendez, are preparing a six-paneled painting-construction, the RHOMBOIDAL PARALLELOGRAM, for the 28th annual San Francisco Art Festival. It will illustrate the life of women in the Mission. Illustrated.

7160 Preuss, Karen. The new Mission murals. SAN FRANCISCO BAY GUARDIAN, (June 28, 1975), p. 14-15. English.

AN: Mural art in San Francisco's Mission District has covered nearly every wall and alley on lower 24th Street. Murals by Mike Rios, the Mujeres Muralistas (Patricia Rodriguez, Graciela Carrillo, Consuelo Mendez, Miriam Olivo, Irene Perez, Susan Cervantes) appear in the area. Others have been painted by artists associated with the Galeria de la Raza. Illustrations.

7161 Quintero, Victoria. A mural is a painting on a wall done by human hands. EL TECOLOTE, Vol. 5, no. 1 (September 13, 1974), p. 6+. English.

AN: The women's collective, Mujeres Muralistas, exists within the strong San Francisco mural movement. Originally the group included Graciela Carrillo, Consuelo Mendez, Irene Perez, and Patricia Rodriguez. The group has expanded to include Susan Cervantes, Ester Hernandez, and Miriam Olivo. The two murals completed have been criticized for not being political; the women answer that they want the atmosphere to be surrounded with life, with colors. Illustrated.

7162 San Francisco Museum of Modern Art, San Francisco, CA and Castellon, Rolando. People's murals: some events in American history. Exhibition catalog, 1976. English.

AN: Eight portable murals by San Francisco Bay Area artists including Graciela Carrillo, Anthony Machado, Robert Mendoza, Irene Perez, Mike Rios. Well Illustrated.

Perez, Irene (cont.)

7163 Valdez, Armando. El calendario chicano 1975.
Hayward, CA: Southwest Network, 1975.
English.

AN: Third in a series of historical
calendars produced in 1972 and 1974 by La
Causa Publications and Southwest Network.
Artists included for each month are Carmen
Lomas Garza, Sergio Hernandez, Malaquias
Montoya, Mujeres Muralistas (Graciela
Carrillo, Venezuelan Consuelo Mendez, Irene
Perez, Patricia Rodriguez), Ramses Noriega,
Ernie Palomino, Amado Maurilio Pena, Martin
Perez. All but Texan Pena are California
artists.

7164 Venegas, Sybil. Conditions for producing
Chicana art. CHISMEARTE, Vol. 1, no. 4 (Fall,
Winter, 1977, 1978), p. 2, 4. English.

AN: Chicana artists face more obstacles
than white women or Chicano counterparts in
the arts. Mexican life style has portrayed
the ideal of a submissive woman, but the
values have changed. Chicana artists are
concerned with women and their struggles.
Muralists include Patricia Rodriguez, Irene
Perez, Consuelo Mendez de Castillo, Susan
Cervantes, Ester Hernandez, Miriam Olivo,
Ruth Rodriguez, of the Mujeres Muralistas
(San Francisco). Other artists are Etta
Delgado and Barbara Carrasco.

Perez, Jose

7165 Southwest Chicano Arts Center, Houston, TX.
The oil and acrylic paintings of Jose Perez.
Exhibition invitation, 1977. English.

AN: Illustrated invitation to exhibit.

Perez, Louie

7166 Almaraz, Carlos. Introduccion: vida urbana y
artistas chicanos. COMUNIDAD, Vol. 55, no.
22 (May 3, 1981), p. 2. Spanish.

AN: In the controversial period of the
early 1980s, Chicano advances are being
attacked. In this political climate, some
Los Angeles artists are interested in beauty
and artistic creation: Carlos Almaraz,
best-known of the Los Four group; Yreina
Cervantez; Elsa Flores; John Valadez,
presently working on a mural; and musicians
Louie Perez and Tito Rodriguez Larriva.

7167 Arte chicano y el pueblo. COMUNIDAD, no. 41
(May 3, 1981), p. 1-15. Spanish.

AN: The whole issue of the Sunday
Supplement deals with Los Angeles Chicano
art and music. Works by painter Carlos
Almaraz, photographer Elsa Flores, painter
Yreina Cervantez, muralist and draftsman
John Valadez, and a performance piece by
Elsa Flores and Louie Perez are featured.
Biographical information, and statements by
the artists.

7168 Chicano art. ARTES VISUALES, no. 29 (1981).
English.

AN: Issue on Chicano art, introduced by
Los Angeles artist Roberto Gil de Montes.
Includes works and statements by: Pedro
Lujan (Texas); Raul M. Guerrero (Calif.);
Sylvia Salazar Simpson (New Mexico/Calif.);
Carlos Almaraz (Calif.); Rene Yanez
(Calif.); Jack Vargas (Calif.); Ray Bravo
(Calif.); John Valadez (Calif.); Gloria Maya
(Calif.); Elsa Flores (Calif.); Willie

Herron (Calif.); Gilbert "Magu" Lujan
(Calif.); Kay Torres, Jerry Lucas, and Louis
Perez (Calif.).

7169 L.A.C.E. (Los Angeles Contemporary
Exhibitions), Los Angeles, CA. Espina
(Thorn): Carlos Almaraz, Elsa Flores, Louie
Perez, Teddy Sandoval, John Valadez, Linda
Vallejo. Exhibition announcement, 1980.
English.

AN: Announcement of an exhibition and a
performance piece by six Los Angeles
artists.

Perez, Martin

7170 Valdez, Armando. El calendario chicano 1975.
Hayward, CA: Southwest Network, 1975.
English.

AN: Third in a series of historical
calendars produced in 1972 and 1974 by La
Causa Publications and Southwest Network.
Artists included for each month are Carmen
Lomas Garza, Sergio Hernandez, Malaquias
Montoya, Mujeres Muralistas (Graciela
Carrillo, Venezuelan Consuelo Mendez, Irene
Perez, Patricia Rodriguez), Ramses Noriega,
Ernie Palomino, Amado Maurilio Pena, Martin
Perez. All but Texan Pena are California
artists.

Perez, Trini

7171 Gaytan, Ray; Leone, Betty; and Cisneros,
Rene. An interview. TEJIDOS, Vol. 2, no. 6
(Summer 1975), p. 29-38. English.

AN: Interview with Texas artists Ray
Gaytan, Trini Perez, and Sam Coronado on the
topic "What Is Chicano Art?".

Perez, Vincent

7172 Bloomfield, Arthur. Zesty show at Mexican
museum. SAN FRANCISCO EXAMINER, (February
1, 1977), p. 24. English.

AN: Review of an exhibit of Mexican and
Mexican American artists from the Southwest
and the San Francisco area. Commentary and
analysis on artists Vincent Perez and
Gustavo Rivera, Rudy Trevino and Al Barela.
The work selected focused on aesthetic
quality rather than the ethnic
identification of the artist.

7173 The Mexican Museum, San Francisco, CA and
Quirarte, Jacinto. 17 artists:
Hispano/Mexican-American/Chicano. Exhibition
catalog, 1977. English.

AN: Catalog of an exhibit for artists
Emilio Aguirre, Consuelo Gonzalez Amezcua,
Al Barela, Pedro Cervantez, Edward Chavez,
Antonio Garcia, Louis Gutierrez, Harry
Louie, Vincent Perez, Michael Ponce de Leon,
Eugenio Quesada, Gustavo Rivera, Peter
Rodriguez, Alex Sanchez, Darryl Sapien, Rudy
Trevino, Manuel Villamor. Illustrated.

Perez-Diaz, Roberto

7174 Grimke, Angelina. Chicano art finds home in
     Mission galeria. PEOPLE'S WORLD, Vol. 33,
     no. 32 (August 8, 1970), p. 11. English.

     AN: Commentary on the exhibition
     CHICANOS, CUBA Y LOS 10 MILLONES held at the
     original Galeria de la Raza at 425 14th
     Street in San Francisco. The show presented
     photographs by Jay Ojeda and Roberto
     Perez-Diaz, drawings by Gloria Ozuna
     together with paintings and photographs by
     Cuban artist Mederos. Provides information
     about the goals of the Galeria as the visual
     arts department of Casa Hispana de Bellas
     Artes. Exhibition curator was Rolando
     Castellon.

Performance Artists Nucleus (PAN)

7175 Garcia's art. Gallery brochure, n.d..
     English.

     AN: Brochure of a non-profit center
     featuring an art gallery and other cultural
     activities to promote knowledge and
     education about Chicano and Mexican arts.
     [Headed by Ralph Garcia who in 1981 is
     director of PAN, Performance Artists
     Nucleus.].

Performing Arts

7176 Exploratorium, Student Union, California
     State University, Los Angeles. Herron/Gronk
     in ILLEGAL LANDSCAPE. Exhibition catalog,
     1980. English.

     AN: Invitation to a "performance" piece
     NO MOVIE by Willie Herron and Gronk, two
     members of ASCO. Illustrated.

7177 Gamboa, Harry, Jr. ASCO: no phantoms. HIGH
     PERFORMANCE, Vol. 4, no. 2 (Summer 1981), p.
     15. English.

     AN: "The media's hit and run attitude
     has generally relegated the influence by
     Chicanos on Los Angeles to that of a phantom
     culture," says Gamboa's introduction to an
     ASCO No Movie event, NO PHANTOMS: "various
     overt acts of communal alienation."
     Illustrated.

7178 Gamboa, Harry, Jr.; Gronk; and Herron,
     Willie. Gronk and Herron. NEWORLD, Vol. 2,
     no. 3 (Spring 1976), p. 28-30. English.

     AN: An interview with ASCO members Gronk
     and Willie Herron by a third member, Gamboa.
     Brief historical introduction (1970 on). The
     witty tongue-in-cheek interview can be
     considered an artwork by this performance
     art group. Illustrated.

7179 Gamboa, Harry, Jr. and Gronk. Gronk:
     off-the-wall artist. NEWORLD, Vol. 6, no. 4
     (1980), p. 33-43. English.

     AN: Interview with Gronk about his No
     Movies, by Harry Gamboa, Jr., both members
     (with Willie Herron and Patssi Valdez) of
     ASCO. The interview itself can be seen as an
     "art piece" with photographs by Gamboa; it
     contains valuable information about the
     ideas and activities of the group.

7180 Gamboa, Harry, Jr. Phobia friend. TIN TAN,
     Vol. 2, no. 6 (December 1, 1977), p. 13-14.
     English.

     AN: Short story written and illustrated
     as a conceptual art piece by ASCO member,

Gamboa, as a "Cinema Chicano" work.

7181 Gamboa, Harry, Jr. Seis imaginaciones:
     artistas chicanos en Los Angeles. COMUNIDAD,
     (July 13, 1980), p. 10. Spanish.

     AN: A limited flow of media information
     about Los Angeles Chicanos has produced a
     "ghost" culture. Only sensational events are
     published. Alternative magazines like LA
     RAZA, CON SAFOS, and REGENERACION have
     disseminated Chicano ideas of the 1970s. The
     Chicano imagination has appeared in murals
     by Willie Herron, Gronk, Carlos Almaraz,
     John Valadez; in pieces like "walking" and
     "instant" murals by the group ASCO; by the
     group Los Four; by group exhibits like
     "Chicanismo en el arte," and "Chicanarte."
     Patssi Valdez showed Photobooth Piece at the
     "Chicanismo" show. Gronk and Jerry Dreva
     exhibited their mail art at "Punk Meets
     Art." In Spanish.

7182 Geyer, Anne and Gamboa, Harry, Jr. Artists'
     exhibits are street performances. THE NEWS,
     (September 11, 1981), p. 18. English.

     AN: Illustrated interview with
     photographer/writer Harry Gamboa, Jr.,
     member and documenter of the performance art
     group ASCO. Description of the NO MOVIE, NO
     PHANTOM, walking and instant murals of the
     group, and other performance street art
     which Gamboa considers as Chicano
     self-documentation and expression.

7183 L.A.C.E. (Los Angeles Contemporary
     Exhibitions), Los Angeles, CA. Espina
     (Thorn): Carlos Almaraz, Elsa Flores, Louie
     Perez, Teddy Sandoval, John Valadez, Linda
     Vallejo. Exhibition announcement, 1980.
     English.

     AN: Announcement of an exhibition and a
     performance piece by six Los Angeles
     artists.

7184 L.A.C.E. (Los Angeles Contemporary
     Exhibitions), Los Angeles, CA. No Movie: Gil
     de Montes, Teddy, Glugio [Gronk], Patssi,
     Gamboa. Exhibition invitation, 1978.
     English.

     AN: Invitation to "performance" piece by
     Roberto Gil de Montes, Teddy Sandoval,
     Gronk, Patssi Valdez and Harry Gamboa, Jr.,
     the latter three of the ASCO group.
     Illustrated.

7185 Literally live movie at NO MOVIE exhibit.
     CIVIC CENTER NEWS, Vol. 7, no. 17 (April 25,
     1978), p. 1. English.

     AN: Story on the ASCO "performance" NO
     MOVIE, described by "Glugio" Gronk as
     "movies without celluloid" to be held at
     LACE Gallery. Illustrated.

7186 Mechicano Art Center, Los Angeles, CA.
     Schizophrenibeneficial. Exhibition
     invitation, 1977. English.

     AN: Invitation to an ASCO "performance"
     work: "Projecting of Visual and/or Verbal
     Personality Disorders Onto Person or Persons
     Unknown." Glugio (Gronk), Teddy (Sandoval),
     (Roberto) Gil de Montes, Patssi (Valdez),
     (Harry) Gamboa.

Performing Arts (cont.)

7187 Vincent, Stephen. Omens from the flight of the birds: the first 101 days of Jimmy Carter: a collective journal of writers & artists. San Francisco, CA: Momos Press, 1977. English.

AN: Rene Yanez, performance piece on El Santero, and two comic strips.

Periodicals

7188 Concilio de arte popular. CHISMEARTE, Vol. 1, no. 2 (Winter, Spring, 1977), p. 54. English.

AN: Report of a meeting February 12, 1977 by the Concilio de Arte Popular (CAP) which published CHISMEARTE. Introduces members of the Board and summarizes discussions of problems of the organization and their publication.

7189 Gamboa, Harry, Jr. Fantasias moviles. COMUNIDAD, (August 30, 1981), p. 8-9. Spanish.

AN: An illustrated article by ASCO artist Harry Gamboa, Jr. on lowriders, and the magazines LOWRIDER, Q-VO and FIRME.

7190 Temko, Allan. Teen Angel's low riders - Chicano art on the rise. THIS WORLD, (August 26, 1979), p. 42-43. English.

AN: Important and insightful analysis of the lowrider phenomenon among Chicano youth in California. Analysis of publications like LOW RIDER Magazine of San Jose, information on graphic artists like "Teen Angel" and Ramon Cisneros and thematic relationship of recognized Chicano artists like Gilbert Lujan, John Valadez, and Luis Jimenez to the lowrider movement. The lowrider is provocatively related to world wide cultural manifestations from diverse epochs.

7191 Yarbro-Bejarano, Yvonne. Resena critica de revistas literarias chicanas: problemas y tendencias. LA PALABRA, Vol. 3, no. 1-2 (Spring, Fall , 1981), p. 123-137. Spanish.

AN: Continuation of review of Chicano magazines from Texas, California, and Washington. The article discusses content, literary and artistic format, and other aspects, taking a critical stance (See LA PALABRA, Spring 1980).

7192 Yarbro-Bejarano, Yvonne. Resena de revistas chicanas: problemas y tendencias, Part I. LA PALABRA, Vol. 2, no. 1 (Spring 1980), p. 76-85. Spanish.

AN: Review of five Chicano magazines of California discussing their contents, both literary and artistic, taking a critical attitude toward both. The five are FUEGO DE AZTLAN, VORTICE, PRISMA, MAIZE, and MANGO.

Perraza, Julio

7193 El calendario hispano de Michigan, 1981. Stanton, MI: Montcalm Intermediate School District and Nuestras Artes de Michigan, 1981. English.

AN: Months of historical calendar illustrated with art works by George Vargas, Nora Chapa Mendoza, Jesse Gonzalez, Julio Perazza(Puerto Rican), Hector Valdez, Pamela M. Gonzalez, Isabell Escojico (7-year-old child), Jose Narezo, Martin Moreno, Laurie

Mendoza Psarianos, Rosa Maria Arenas.

Philosophy of Art

7194 Almaraz, Carlos. The artist as a revolutionary. CHISMEARTE, no. 1 (Fall 1976), p. 47-55. English.

AN: Los Angeles painter Carlos D. Almaraz gives a detailed history of a cartoon-banner he made for the first constitutional convention of the United Farm Workers of America while he was an illustrator for EL MALCRIADO, and a mural he did for the UFWA administration building in La Paz. He also elucidates his philosophy about politics, the role of the revolutionary artist in our time, and the artist's relation to the bourgeois art market.

7195 Almaraz, Carlos. Introduccion: vida urbana y artistas chicanos. COMUNIDAD, Vol. 55, no. 22 (May 3, 1981), p. 2. Spanish.

AN: In the controversial period of the early 1980s, Chicano advances are being attacked. In this political climate, some Los Angeles artists are interested in beauty and artistic creation: Carlos Almaraz, best-known of the Los Four group; Yreina Cervantez; Elsa Flores; John Valadez, presently working on a mural; and musicians Louie Perez and Tito Rodriguez Larriva.

7196 Amado Maurilio Pena, Jr. PAPEL CHICANO, Vol. 1, no. 13 (July 21, 1978). Spanish.

AN: Includes the artist's resume, an exhibition list, and a gallery statement situating the work of Pena within both Native American and Chicano art traditions. Includes reproduction of four works.

7197 Armando Cid art works on display at Barrio Gallery. EL HISPANO, Vol. 5, no. 44 (April 24, 1973). English.

AN: Description of Armando Cid's M.A. thesis exhibition. The dominant impulse in the paintings is an attempt to define and reflect a Chicano style.

7198 Armas, Jose and Buitron, Robert. Issues. ARIZTLAN NEWSLETTER, (August 1981). English.

AN: Thoughts and definitions of Chicano art by Dr. Jose Armas, founder of Pajarito Publications, and by photographer and MARS member Robert Buitron.

7199 The art of Mexican America. EMPIRE MAGAZINE, (November 1, 1970), p. 24-25. English.

AN: Visual portfolio with minimal text. Includes paintings by Amado Pena, Mel Casas, Porfirio Salinas, and sculpture by Octavio Medellin. On the same page, Dr. Jacinto Quirarte gives views on the nature of Mexican art, the Mexican American artist, and the connection between Mexican and Mexican American art.

Philosophy of Art (cont.)

7200 Arte chicano y el pueblo. COMUNIDAD, no. 41 (May 3, 1981), p. 1-15. Spanish.

AN: The whole issue of the Sunday Supplement deals with Los Angeles Chicano art and music. Works by painter Carlos Almaraz, photographer Elsa Flores, painter Yreina Cervantez, muralist and draftsman John Valadez, and a performance piece by Elsa Flores and Louie Perez are featured. Biographical information, and statements by the artists.

7201 Arts Council Center for the Arts of Greater Lansing, Lansing, MI. Raza fine arts festival. Festival program, 1978. English.

AN: This festival program mentions Jose Narezo's mural at the Holland National Guard Armory, Grand Rapids; includes a statement of the Raza Art/Media Collective, Inc.; the philosophy of artists Zaragosa Vargas and S. Kaneta Kosiba-Vargas; and profiles of exhibiting artists George Vargas, Martin Moreno, Hector Perez, Michael L. Selley, Jesse Gonzales, Nora Chapa Mendoza, Jesse Soriano, Jose Luis Narezo.

7202 Baca, Judith F. Judith F. Baca. In: SOCIAL WORKS: AN EXHIBITION OF ART CONCERNED WITH SOCIAL CHANGE. Los Angeles, CA: Institute of Contemporary Art, 1979, p. 44. English.

AN: Statement of purpose and history of the Tujunga Wash Mural (San Fernando Valley, CA) in process from 1976 on, by muralist and founder of Social and Public Art Resource Center (SPARC), Judith Baca. Illustrated.

7203 Baeza, Armando M. In disagreement. CON SAFOS, no. 7 (Winter 1971), p. 60-61. Bilingual.

AN: Reply to a CON SAFOS editorial (Vol.2, no.5) in which it is stated that Chicanos have no "...body of visual arts...no theatre...no music...", etc.

7204 Bauer, Bernard. Angry artists deface own mural. BERKELEY BARB, (March 1978), p. 7. English.

AN: Chicano artists Jose Antonio Burciaga and Gilberto Romero Rodriguez recall a few struggles to sensitize local arts organizations to Raza art. Financial and political aspects of their painting a patriotic mural, "Danzas mexicanas" in Redwood City. Artists explain why they defaced their own mural as an act of protest.

7205 Beardsley, John. Personal sensibilities in public places. ARTFORUM, Vol. 19, no. 10 (June 1981), p. 43-45. English.

AN: Distinction is made between art in public places and public art. The latter is assumed to have content and symbolism accessible to the majority of the population. Luis Jimenez, sculptor of VAQUERO intended for Houston's Moody Park, feels people should be able to identify with art. Color illustration.

7206 Bloomfield, Arthur. Zesty show at Mexican museum. SAN FRANCISCO EXAMINER, (February 1, 1977), p. 24. English.

AN: Review of an exhibit of Mexican and Mexican American artists from the Southwest and the San Francisco area. Commentary and analysis on artists Vincent Perez and Gustavo Rivera, Rudy Trevino and Al Barela. The work selected focused on aesthetic quality rather than the ethnic identification of the artist.

7207 Briggs, Charles L. The wood carvers of Cordova, New Mexico: social dimensions of an artistic "revival". Knoxville, TN: University of Tennessee Press, 1980. English.

AN: One of the few books that deals with the traditional and contemporary-traditional religious art of New Mexico within social context. The author explores the influence of Anglo patronage and tourism on the meaning, aesthetics and distribution of the santos, and non-religious carving of the town of Cordoba.

7208 Camplis, Francisco X. Towards the development of a Raza cinema. TIN TAN, Vol. 2, no. 5 (June 1, 1977), p. 5-7. English.

AN: Chicanos and other minorities remain invisible to white America, an expression of neo-colonialism. Camplis defines "Chicano" and "Raza" as terms, and states there are few, if any, full-length feature films available. Without role models, Chicano/Raza filmmakers can learn from contemporary revolutionary Latin American filmmakers, be familiar with European and Hollywood films, though the latter are alien models. Camplis suggests directions for Chicano films, and reviews films by Jesus Trevino, Jose Camacho, and Luis Valdez.

7209 Cantu, Jesus "Chista". Entrevista: Jesus Maria Cantu, 'El Chista'. MAGAZIN, Vol. 1, no. 4 (April 1972), p. 52-65. Spanish.

AN: Discusses his life in San Antonio; his apprenticeship since childhood to his uncle Miguel Angel Tellez who taught him to paint billboards, wall signs and church decorations; his membership in the group Artistas de la Nueva Raza; his artistic and political philosophy. In Spanish.

7210 Carrillo, Eduardo. Califas, is Chicano art safe in Santa Cruz? ARTS AT SANTA CRUZ, Vol. 1, no. 1 (1981). English.

AN: Illustrated essay surveying Chicano art in Santa Cruz with details about the planning and presentation of the CALIFAS exhibit at the Mary Porter Seanon Gallery. This exhibition presented the work of fifteen Chicano(a) artists united and defined by a shared vision: a conscious identification with Mexican/Chicano culture and an alliance with art circuits outside the mainstream.

7211 Castellanos, Leonard. Chicano centros, murals, and art. ARTS IN SOCIETY, Vol. 12, no. 1 (Spring, Summer, 1975), p. 38-43. English.

AN: One of the organizers of the Mechicano Art Center in Los Angeles talks about the history of the Center, the artist's relationship to the mainstream; the importance of the street mural movement; the economic problems of the muralists and their dedication to the community; the need for alternative centers like the "centros." An excerpt of this article appeared in CHISMEARTE, no. 1 (Fall 1976), p. 26-27.

Philosophy of Art (cont.)

7212 Castillo, Rafael. Gonzo journalism goes for a low ride. SAN ANTONIO EXPRESS-NEWS, (December 6, 1981), p. 7-B. English.

AN: George Velasquez, editor and publisher of San Antonio's VAJITO magazine, views lowriders as a positive and evolving form of urban youth culture. Counters stereotypes about lowriders as drug-oriented high school drop-outs. There is a new and significant discourse being developed in literary and visual forms among Chicano lowriders.

7213 Chavez, Jaime and Vallecillo, Ana Maria. A political, historical, philosophical perspective of muralist art in the Southwest. RAYAS, Vol. 1, no. 3 (May, June, 1978), p. 6. English.

AN: Relates Chicano mural art to main issues of the Chicano movement. The Mechicano Art Center in Los Angeles and Artes Guadalupanos de Aztlan in Santa Fe are seen as examples of groups creating a new people's art; art forms where esthetics are allied to politics.

7214 Chicano art. ARTES VISUALES, no. 29 (1981). English.

AN: Issue on Chicano art, introduced by Los Angeles artist Roberto Gil de Montes. Includes works and statements by: Pedro Lujan (Texas); Raul M. Guerrero (Calif.); Sylvia Salazar Simpson (New Mexico/Calif.); Carlos Almaraz (Calif.); Rene Yanez (Calif.); Jack Vargas (Calif.); Ray Bravo (Calif.); John Valadez (Calif.); Gloria Maya (Calif.); Elsa Flores (Calif.); Willie Herron (Calif.); Gilbert "Magu" Lujan (Calif.); Kay Torres, Jerry Lucas, and Louis Perez (Calif.).

7215 Chicano art show. EL DIARIO DE LA GENTE, Vol. 1, no. 7 (February 6, 1973), p. 4. English.

AN: Fine arts students at the University of Colorado led by Rudy Fernandez hope to educate high school students about Chicano art. This article documents an exhibit held at Lafayette, CO. Members of the group are Bob Maez, Jerry Jaramillo, Anthony Mendoza, and Rudy Fernandez. Illustrated by four exhibition photographs by John L. Espinosa.

7216 CHICANO CINEMA NEWSLETTER. Vol. 1, no. 4 (June 1979). English.

AN: Report and cautionary note on the upcoming Alternative Cinema Conference; announcement of ONLY ONCE IN A LIFETIME and CHICANA film releases; other new films and TV programs; a Chicano cinema bibliography; a list of Chicano production companies and distributors; a theoretical article on the nature (proposed) of Chicano cinema as an alternative cinema; statement of purpose of the Los Angeles Chicano Cinema Coalition.

7217 Cisneros, Rene. Ars poetica: editorial. TEJIDOS, Vol. 3, no. 3 (Fall 1976), p. 3-4. Spanish.

AN: A tongue-in-cheek exploration of artistic philosophy of TEJIDOS and its contributors. This philosophy is based on the recognition of the fact that Art is created by human beings who work diligently at their craft. As such, the efforts of even the most humble of artisans is as deserving

of recognition as is that produced by recognized "masters" of Western European civilization. Simply stated, "Beauty is in the eye of the beholder.".

7218 Con safo to hold Lutheran college exhibition at Texas. CHICANO TIMES, Vol. 7, no. 89 (March 26, 1976), p. [15]. English.

AN: Discusses the aims of "Con Safos" group: to interpret their environment and react to it; to act as spokespeople and give visual reality to the Chicano vision; to destroy stereotypes and demolish visual cliches. The participating artists include Rudy R. Trevino, Mel Casas, Lucas Hinojosa, Kathy Vargas, Joe Frank Acosta, Emilio Aguirre and Homero Ureste.

7219 Conversation on photography in the Los Angeles Latino community. OBSCURA, Vol. 2, no. 2 (December, February, 1981, 1982), p. 22-32. English.

AN: Interview on the nature and distinguishing characteristics of Chicano photography with Chicano photographers Isabel Castro (Council for Latino Photography), Lorenzo Hernandez (Director of Cityscape Gallery, publisher PHOTOSHOW magazine), Joseph G. Uribe (California State University, Los Angeles, Center for the Visual Arts, Director of West Colorado Gallery), Patssi Valdez, Becky Villasenor, and sculptor, curator, and Art Director for Academia Quinto Sol, Inc., Linda Vallejo, Portfolio of photography by Chicanos Don Anton, Louis Carlos Bernal, Sean Carrillo, Patssi Valdez, Ricardo Valverde, and by Morrie Camhi and Elizabeth Sisco on Chicano subjects.

7220 Crusade for Justice, Denver, CO. Los artistas de Aztlan. Mimeographed copy, 1969. English.

AN: Resolutions from the Chicano Youth Conference (March-April, 1969) on the role of art and artists within the Chicano movement. An important document.

7221 De Leon, Hector. Barrio art--the community's reflection of itself. AGENDA, Vol. 9, no. 4 (July, August, 1979), p. 7, 38. English.

AN: Barrio art is communal, its forms such as posters, pamphlets, graffiti, and murals have an educative function. Its style is eclectic and its content is stark and direct. Through various forms of graphic representation, people in the barrio have reappropriated art forms to give meaning to their daily experiences. Includes nine illustrations of barrio art.

7222 Desiga, Daniel. Days historical dawn in the Northwest. Olympia, WA: Legislative Artworks Project, n.d. English.

AN: Personal statement submitted by Daniel Design with drawings for mural project to reflect the natural and human elements thathave forged Northwest reality. The artist states: "The key elements as envisaged are land and water integrated with racial groupings, diverse technologies and invested labor. Incorporating Northwest symbols, the mural will be seen as a manifestation of the physical and natural energies which have combined to give expression to an unique force in the Northwest.".

Philosophy of Art (cont.)

7223 Dunham, Judith L. Manuel Neri: life with the figure. ARTWEEK, Vol. 7, no. 39 (November 13, 1976), p. 1+. English.

AN: Favorable review of Neri's exhibition of more than 80 figures or fragments of figures at the Oakland Museum. Explores relationship of Neri's sculpture with developments in Bay Area figurative painting and expressionism. Inventories Neri's thematic and material concerns. Analysis of his work in plaster, bronze and fiberglass. An important assessment of Neri's contribution to Bay Area art.

7224 Editorial. CON SAFOS, Vol. 2, no. 5 (1970), p. 45-46. English.

AN: Editorial calling attention to the greatest "weakness" of La Raza as the lack of clear and tangible art forms.

7225 Edy. A true barrio art. EL CHICANO, (December 7, 1972), p. 9. English.

AN: Interview with East Los Angeles artists Harry Gamboa, Robert Gronk and Willie Herron (also included in the conversation are Patsy Valdez and Eddie Ytuarte). Suffering, fatalism, existential reality and the awareness of cultural colonialism are cited as sources of inspiration for urban barrio art. Illustrated with a photograph of Willie Herron's Quetzalcoatl mural in City Terrace barrio and two drawings by Robert Gronk and Harry Gamboa.

7226 Figoten, Sheldon. Building and painting the figure. ARTWEEK, Vol. 12, no. 22 (June 20, 1981), p. 5-6. English.

AN: Review of eight sculptures and 25 drawings by Manuel Neri at the Redding Art Museum. Neri was influenced as a student in the San Francisco Bay Area in the 1950s by abstract expressionist philosophy and methodology, which he transferred to sculpture. Plaster, bronze, and marble figures are freely and loosely painted in areas. Illustration.

7227 Frankenstein, Alfred. One artist's self-defense. SAN FRANCISCO CHRONICLE, (March 9, 1978), p. 44. English.

AN: Art critic Frankenstein opens his columns to Jose Antonio Burciaga to explain why he, and fellow muralist Gilberto Romero Rodriguez, splattered red, white and blue paint on their completed mural at the dedication ceremony. They were protesting the exploitation, use and abuse of artists, particularly by arts councils.

7228 Freedom of expression and the Chicano Movement: an open letter to Dr. Philip Ortego. LA LUZ, Vol. 2, no. 5 (September 1973), p. 28-29. English.

AN: An unattributed letter questioning the imposition of norms on Chicano art. The author criticizes the practice of unquestioningly assigning rubrics like "Mexican" or "Chicano" to certain styles while excluding others produced by Mexican American artists.

7229 Galeria de la Raza/Studio 24, San Francisco, CA and Garcia, Rupert. Community art-murals: an exhibition of original drawings, sketches, and designs. Exhibition brochure, 1978. English.

AN: The current crisis of contemporary art is relatively resolved by community-based muralists who engage themselves against repressive forces as artists, organizers, propagandists. However, art and politics are not identical, though they may overlap. Color xerox illustrations of murals.

7230 Gamboa, Harry, Jr. Film, television, and Trevino. LA LUZ, Vol. 6, no. 10 (October 1977), p. 7-8. English.

AN: Jesus Salvador Trevino has been an active proponent and participant in transforming cultural inaccuracy about Chicanos in the media to accurate mass media models. A biography of Trevino follows, including discussion of some of his films: THE SALAZAR INQUEST, CHICANO MORATORIUM AFTERMATH, SOLEDAD, AMERICA TROPICAL, YO SOY CHICANO, RAICES DE SANGRE, as well as television series like ACCION CHICANO, AHORA, and INFINITY FACTORY.

7231 Garcia, Guillermo. Wall-to-wall art for the people. AUSTIN AMERICAN STATESMAN, (January 22, 1978), p. E-1. English.

AN: Illustrated story on Raul Valdez's mural (in progress) The Oral Tradition. Valdez discusses his methods and art philosophy when creating community murals.

7232 Garcia, Ignacio. Senior exhibit attempts to define Chicano art. SOUTH TEXAN, (August 1, 1975). English.

AN: DIRECTAMENTE DEL BARRIO, a senior art exhibit at Texas A & I University by art majors Raul Valdez and Jesus Reyes. Sets forth their ideas about Chicano arts and their future plans.

7233 Garcia, Rupert. The politics of popular art. CHISMEARTE, Vol. 2, no. 1 (Summer 1978), p. 2-4. English.

AN: Defines and discusses the terms "Popular Art", "Mass Art", and "Folk Art" and gives examples of their correct and incorrect usages.

7234 Garcia, Ruperto. Photography. ARRIBA, Vol. 1, no. 6 (1980). English.

AN: Statement of photographic credo and portfolio of photographs by Ruperto Garcia, photographer from the Rio Grande Valley.

7235 Garcia-Camarillo, Cecilio and Rosas, Carlos. Platicando con Carlos Rosas. RAYAS, Vol. 1, no. 6 (November, December, 1978), p. 12, 11. Spanish.

AN: Muralist Carlos Rosas painted murals in Boulder and Denver, Colorado; Milwaukee, Wisconsin, and El Paso, Texas. Commentary on cross ethnic murals, views on art in socialist countries, influence of Mexican murals and information on his personal preocupation as a politically engaged artist.

7236 Gaytan, Ray; Leone, Betty; and Cisneros, Rene. An interview. TEJIDOS, Vol. 2, no. 6 (Summer 1975), p. 29-38. English.

AN: Interview with Texas artists Ray Gaytan, Trini Perez, and Sam Coronado on the topic "What Is Chicano Art?".

Philosophy of Art (cont.)

7237 Goldman, Shifra M. Response: another opinion on the state of Chicano art. METAMORFOSIS, Vol. 3, no. 1 (1980, 1981), p. 2-7. English.

AN: Redefinition of the problems facing Chicano artists in the 1980s raised by Malaquias and Lezlie Salkowitz-Montoya article in the Spring-Summer 1980 issue of METAMORFOSIS.

7238 Gonzales, Juan. Chicano film festival earns pluses and minuses. EL TECOLOTE, Vol. 9, no. 3 (November 1978), p. 7. English.

AN: Critical review of the Third Annual Chicano Film Festival in San Antonio, TX. The writer criticizes lack of critical exchange and dialogue between filmmakers and audience; expresses disappointment at the exploitive nature of Cheech and Chong film; reports audience tribute to Jesus S. Trevino's RAICES DE SANGRE; feels ONLY ONCE IN A LIFETIME was technically excellent, but passive and without a significant message. Question is posed about the role and expected audience of Chicano filmmakers.

7239 Gonzales, Juan. Galeria de la Raza: "our people deserve the best". EL TECOLOTE, Vol. 7, no. 11 (July 1977), p. 14. English.

AN: "We are not here to sell our art, but to sell the idea of art." This could well be the motto of Galeria de la Raza who under co-directors Rene Yanez and Ralph Maradiaga has become a key cultural institution in the Mission District of San Francisco. The two directors have a broad definition of art that encompasses everything from cartoons to craftwork. The article details past exhibits and future goals. A half-page photograph of the exterior of Galeria de la Raza by Pilar Mejia illustrates the article. Reprint of article entitled "Our people deserve the best" which appeared in NUESTRO, Vol. 1, no. 2 (May, 1977), p. 56-57.

7240 Gonzalez, Hector. El arte de Esteban Villa. EL HISPANO, Vol. 6, no. 20 (November 6, 1973). Spanish.

AN: Commenting on Esteban Villa's one man show at the Centro de Artistas Chicanos that presented sixty-five pieces of art ranging from acrylics, watercolors, woodcuts, to pen and ink drawings. Villa fuses Indian symbols, mythology, folklore and customs to create a new "cosmic" dimension for the Chicano experience.

7241 Gonzalez, Victoria. Chair in the sky: Ernesto Palomino. HERE AND NOW, Vol. 2, no. 2 (Fall 1981). English.

AN: An important article tracing the artistic career of Ernie Palomino, professor of art at California State University, Fresno. Includes biographical information, formation of La Brocha Del Valle (Chicano Arts Organization), information about Palomino's film MY TRIP IN A '52 FORD and commentary on Palomino's music and artistic philosophy. Well illustrated.

7242 Guernica, Antonio Jose and Saavedra-Vela, Pilar. El Midwest Canto al pueblo: "Otra Vez, C/S". AGENDA, Vol. 7, no. 3 (May, June, 1977), p. 4-13. Bilingual.

AN: A thorough report on the various phases and events of the Midwest Canto al Pueblo in Milwaukee, Wisconsin on April 28 to May 8, 1977. The festival brought together artists, poets, musicians, and cultural workers to reaffirm, share, and celebrate the identity of La Raza with El Pueblo. Includes a thematic and iconographic overview of Chicano murals in California by Jose Montoya, and an analysis of his sculpture by Zarco Guerrero from Meza, Arizona. Well illustrated. Includes a photograph of the collective mural painted at 5th St. and National Avenue in Milwaukee, Wisconsin during the course of the conference.

7243 Guerrero, Adolfo "El Zarco". The new vision of Xicanindio art. RAYAS, Vol. 2, no. 1 (January, February, 1979), p. 3. Bilingual.

AN: Zarco Guerrero explains his personal artistic philosophy that unites Amerindian concepts of art to contemporary art forms, especially in sculpture. For Guerrero, "the Chicano artist is making a monumental effort to arrive at a new universal language and to create a new meaning of community through art.

7244 Hollister, Kelly. Linda Vallejo. CAMINOS, Vol. 1, no. 6 (October 1980), p. 19. Bilingual.

AN: Story on Long Beach, California artist Linda Vallejo who also works with Self-Help Graphics in Los Angeles and has curated a number of exhibits. Vallejo describes her work as containing "archetypal, mythological or dream-world imagery" combined with the "modern idea of self-knowledge." Illustrated on p. 17.

7245 Inner City Mural Program. Glendale, CA: Los Angeles County Dept. of Parks and Recreation, [ca. 1974]. English.

AN: Brief history and philosophy of the Inner City Mural Program from June 1, 1973 to May 31, 1974, when it was sponsored by the Cultural Arts Section of the Los Angeles County Department of Parks and Recreation, and coordinated by Lukman Glasgow. Artists Judithe Hernandez and Frank Romero included. 20 illustrations, some in color.

7246 Kantar, Chris and Villa, Esteban. An interview with Esteban Villa. Unpublished paper, 1978. English.

AN: A detailed and informative interview with Esteban Villa, prominent Chicano artist. Focus on Villa's philosophy of art, life, and the Chicano art movement. A good primary source. (The unpublished manuscript is deposited in the archives of the R.C.A.F. in Scaramento).

7247 Karam, Bruce G. The murals of Tucson. NUESTRO, Vol. 5, no. 8 (November 1981), p. 58-60. English.

AN: Themes of ethnic pride, cultural unity and cooperation define the murals of Tucson. Brief commentary on the relationship of artists and the community. Illustrated with color photographs.

Philosophy of Art (cont.)

two posters reproduced.

7248 Kelley sparks Chicano growth. ROCKY MOUNTAIN NEWS, (February 18, 1973), p. Festival,7. English.

AN: Denver artist John Flores speaks about his work and provides details about the small but strong Chicano art colony in Denver. Flores credits Ramon Kelley, an established Chicano artist, with providing much leadership and encouragement in the development of Chicano art in Colorado.

7249 Kim, Howard. Chicano art: is it an art form? Or simply art by Chicanos. NEWORLD, Vol. 6, no. 4 (1980), p. 26-30. English.

AN: An attempt to define Chicano art through interviews with Carlos Almaraz, John Valadez, (Los Four), Robert Delgado, Sister Karen Boccalero (Self-Help Graphics), Harry Gamboa, Jr. (ASCO), Ricardo Duardo, Ignacio Gomez, and others. Well illustrated.

7250 Kim, Howard. Judithe Hernandez and a glimpse at the Chicana artist. SOMOS, (October, November, 1979), p. 6-11. English.

AN: Biographical information on Chicana artist Judithe Hernandez. Commentary on her contributions to Plaza de la Raza, Los Angeles Citywide Mural Project and her work as designer consultant to AZTLAN: INTERNATIONAL JOURNAL OF CHICANO RESEARCH. The article focuses on her mural activity, particularly two murals: EL MUNDO DE BARRIO SOTEL and LA CHICANA DE AZTLAN. Her personal art philosophy is presented in relation to Third World Art.

7251 Lefebre, Francisco. El mural chicano en Nuevo Mexico. RAYAS, Vol. 1, no. 2 (March, April, 1978), p. 7. Spanish.

AN: Albuquerque muralist writes about Chicano murals which derive from pre-Columbian and modern Mexican murals. New Mexican muralism started in 1970 with the Muralistas Guadalupanos de Aztlan in Santa Fe. In 1971 and 1972 students at the Highlands University of Las Vegas, New Mexico also painted murals. In addition, murals have appeared in Albuquerque. Brief biography of Lefebre. Illustrated.

7252 Lujan, Gilbert Sanchez "Magu". El arte del Chicano - "The Spirit of the Experience". CON SAFOS, no. 7 (Winter 1971), p. 11-13. English.

AN: Definition of Chicano Art by artist Lujan as the expression of an unique experience that is neither Mexican nor U.S. Anglo, that has its own vitality and dynamics. Chicanos can draw upon common cultural elements and transform them into images and art forms such as sculptured menudo bones, tortilla drawings, vato loco portraits, etc. Four woodcuts by Roberto de la Rocha are shown as examples.

7253 Malaquias Montoya. ARTE, (Fall 1977). English.

AN: Interview with northern California printmaker, painter and muralist, Malaquias Montoya. He discusses his life, his dedication to Chicano art, his resistance to the institutionalization of the Chicano struggle and its art, their cooptation by the establishment. He says he transcended nationalism at one period and became a Third World internationalist. Four drawings and

7254 MARS: Movimiento Artistico del Rio Salado. Phoenix, AZ: Mars Studio/Gallery, 1978. English.

AN: History and manifesto of MARS, 13 member group of Arizona painters, sculptors, designers, and photographers: Jose Andres Giron, Jose Jimenez Rodriguez, Antonio Tocora (Colombian-born), Ramon Delgadillo, Francisco Zuniga, Jim Covarrubias, Ed Diaz, David Martinez, Roberto Buitron, Juan Rodriguez, Eddie Lopez, Zarco Guerrero, Joe Sanchez.

7255 Martinez, Anita. Villa - "arte por toda la Raza". EL TECOLOTE, Vol. 1, no. 5 (October 19, 1970), p. 2. English.

AN: Biographical information and artistic trajectory of Esteban Villa, artist from Sacramento. Villa says that to be a Chicano is to have developed a cultural independence. He posits his ideas on the nature of Chicano art, its forms, functions, and educative role. Villa describes the evolving Chicano Art Movement with its goals based on moral principles. Illustrated with one of Villa's works, "Chicano Rebirth".

7256 Martinez, Cesar Augusto. Arte chicano. CARACOL, Vol. 1, no. 4 (December 1974), p. 8. Bilingual.

AN: Initial installment of on-going column on Chicano art by the well-known artist and art director for CARACOL, Cesar Augusto Martinez.

7257 Martinez, Cesar Augusto. Arte chicano. CARACOL, Vol. 1, no. 6 (February 1975), p. 3. English.

AN: Thoughts on the form, function and meaning of Chicano Art. Stylistically, it is seen as a fusion. It is dynamic, expressing multiple political sentiments and has an irreverent attitude towards dominant culture. Front cover of issue is a black and white reproduction of a silkscreen print by Amado Maurilio Pena, Jr.

7258 Martinez, Manuel. The art of the Chicano movement, and the movement of Chicano art. In: Valdez, Luis and Steiner, Stan eds. AZTLAN: AN ANTHOLOGY OF MEXICAN AMERICAN LITERATURE. New York: Vintage, 1972, p.349-353. English.

AN: "Like the modern art of Mexico, the new Chicano art is essentially an art of social protest," writes Denver, Colorado muralist and easel painter Martinez. He traces the roots of Chicano art back into Indian, colonial and modern Mexican art, and defines two kinds of Chicano art.

7259 Mechicano Art Center attracts community artists. EL HISPANO, Vol. 5, no. 2 (June 10, 1972). English.

AN: Commentary by Leonard Castellanos, Director of Mechicano Art Center, who explains funding sources and programs of the Centro.

Philosophy of Art (cont.)

7260 Mechicano Art Center, Los Angeles, CA. Paper pieces by C.D.A. [Carlos D. Almaraz]. Exhibition invitation, [1973]. English.

AN: Invitation to a gallery exhibit by the artist, with his manifesto, "Notes on an Aesthetic Alternative".

7261 Merritt College, Oakland, CA. The role of the Chicano artist and the involvement of the barrio: integrity and tokenism. RASCA TRIPAS, Vol. 2, no. 1 (October 12, 1970). English.

AN: First of an important three-part statement on the form and content of Chicano art and the social role of the Chicano artist. Essential reading for understanding the evolving polemic in the early stages of the Chicano art movement. Part II, entitled "Chicano Art Style," was published in vol. 2, no. 2 (Dec. 1970); and part III, "The Chicano Artist and the Involvement of the Community: Point of View of the Chicano Artist," is in vol. 3, no. 1 (Jan. 1971).

7262 Mexican American liberation art front: la Raza Nueva, Rene Yanez, Esteban Villa, Malaquias Montoya, Manuel Hernandez. BRONCE, Vol. 1, no. 3 (March 1969), p. 6-7. English.

AN: Manifesto of MALAF, a germinal Chicano art group in northern California. Compares revolutionary Chicanos of 1968 with the Mexicans of 1910; equally Chicano artists reject European-influenced art. Announces the exhibit NEW SYMBOLS FOR LA RAZA NUEVA, at La Causa in Oakland, March 22 to April 5, 1969. Puts forth the group's philosophy and goals, particularly exhibits and art services to the "barrio". Illustrated.

7263 Miguelez, Armando. La cultura chicana: los murales. RAYAS, Vol. 1, no. 5 (September, October, 1978), p. 9. Spanish.

AN: Miguelez, a writer from Tucson, Arizona, divides muralistic production into two categories: cultural muralism and creative muralism. Both types of murals function as alternatives to establishment art, to mono-cultural education and to ethnocentric history. Relates Chicano mural movement to its antecedent in Mexico, but most especially to the mural production of other ethnic minorities in the United States.

7264 Miguelez, Armando. La cultura chicana: los murales. AZTEC CAMPUS NEWS, Vol. 5, no. 24 (April 4, 1978), p. 7. English.

AN: Article arguing for two classes of murals: the cultural (or traditional, political, historical) and the creative (symbolic, mythical, with contemporary forms), both of which are found among Chicano art. Illustrated with, presumably, examples of each. Translated into Spanish in RAYAS, (Sept.-Oct., 1978).

7265 Mitchell, Raye Bemis. March to an aesthetic of revolution. NEW ART EXAMINER, (February 1977). English.

AN: Interesting article that defines Chicano social-realism as a compelling aesthetic in opposition to avant-garde formalism. Exhibit by members of Chicago's MARCH group. Illustrated.

7266 Montoya, Jose E. Thoughts on la cultura, the media, con safos and survival. CARACOL, Vol. 5, no. 9 (May 1979), p. 6-8,19. English.

AN: Remarks by Sacramento, CA, artist and poet, Jose Montoya, presented at the First Annual Chicano Film Series, Stanford University, California, January 10, 11, and 12, 1979.

7267 Montoya, Jose E. Thoughts on la cultura, the media, con safos and survival. Sacramento, CA: Royal Chicano Air Force, 1979. English.

AN: Important theoretical article on the state of Chicano culture. Reprinted in METAMORFOSIS (Seattle, WA), vol. 3, no. 1(Spring/Summer 1980), p. 28-31.

7268 Montoya, Malaquias and Salkowitz-Montoya, Lezlie. A critical perspective on the state of Chicano art. METAMORFOSIS, Vol. 3, no. 1 (Spring, Summer, 1980), p. 3-7. English.

AN: Seminal article evaluating the position of Chicano artists today, the dangers of mainstream cooptation, and the loss of commitment that characterized the beginnings of the movement.

7269 Moser, Charlotte. Arte chicano de Texas/Texas Chicano art. ARTES VISUALES, no. 29 (June 1981), p. 57-63. Bilingual.

AN: History of Chicano art and art organizations in Texas. A younger generation of artists is complying with a mainstream European esthetic rather than a regional Chicano one. Statements and biographies of artists. Many illustrations.

7270 Moser, Charlotte; Renteria, Phil; and Wray, Dick. Phil Renteria and Dick Wray. ART IN AMERICA, Vol. 64, no. 4 (July, August, 1976), p. 82-83. English.

AN: Interview with Laredo-born Houston artist Renteria, and Wray, both of whom teach at the Museum of Fine Arts. Renteria gives much biographical information and his philosophy of art. Illustrated in color.

7271 Mujeres de Aztlan. EL TECOLOTE, Vol. 4, no. 1 (October 10, 1973), p. 3. English.

AN: A collective of Third World women artists plan an art show at Galeria de la Raza in San Francisco. Stressing the need for art forms that bring awareness and present the true nature of women's living conditions, this call for submission of art work reflects some feminist concerns of the period.

7272 Pena, Ruben R. Mel Casas - people in the arts. BUSINESS AND THE ARTS, (September, October, 1979), p. 15. English.

AN: Probing analysis of the work and life of San Antonio artist Mel Casas. Article is divided into five sections in which the artist gives his views on culture, art, society, the Southwest and himself. Contains biographical information and artistic trajectory.

Philosophy of Art (cont.)

7273 Pimentel, Ricardo. Graffiti: expression or scourge? FRESNO BEE, (February 23, 1981), p. Metro, B1+. English.

AN: A rapid review of graffiti symbols, their meaning and social context. Commentary by various young people explaining the value, style and meanings of plaqueasos (spray painted graffiti). Some Chicano artists like Bob Cruz, director of La Brocha del Valle, see mural painting as a positive alternative to graffiti art forms. Article also provides views of local businessmen to the graffiti phenomenon.

7274 Pino, Thomas E. Ramon Kelley: the business of art. LA LUZ, Vol. 7, no. 5 (May 1978), p. 24-26. English.

AN: Biographical information on Colorado artist Ramon Kelley. Business aspects of art: marketing, selling, art as investment.

7275 Plous, F.K. Street scenes. MIDWEST MAGAZINE, (September 1, 1974), p. 10. English.

AN: Article focusing on the mural production of Ray Patlan in the Pilsen barrio of Chicago. Description of the community and how Patlan functions as a community worker and muralist. Includes a directory of Chicago's murals. Well illustrated with photographs, some in color.

7276 Quintero, Victoria. A mural is a painting on a wall done by human hands. EL TECOLOTE, Vol. 5, no. 1 (September 13, 1974), p. 6+. English.

AN: The women's collective, Mujeres Muralistas, exists within the strong San Francisco mural movement. Originally the group included Graciela Carrillo, Consuelo Mendez, Irene Perez, and Patricia Rodriguez. The group has expanded to include Susan Cervantes, Ester Hernandez, and Miriam Olivo. The two murals completed have been criticized for not being political; the women answer that they want the atmosphere to be surrounded with life, with colors. Illustrated.

7277 Quiroz, Esau and Cuevas, Jose Luis. Chicano art: an identity crisis. NEWORLD, Vol. 1, no. 4 (Summer 1975). English.

AN: Interview between Chicano muralist Esau Quiroz and Mexican artist Jose Luis Cuevas. Chicano art is described as a search for pictorial roots in Mexico expressed through contemporary forms adopted from United States art movements. Cuevas suggests that Chicanos travel, exhibit and "project to the United States from Latin America." Illustrated with one drawing by Cuevas and photographs of Quiroz.

7278 Renacimiento del arte chicano en Texas. EL HISPANO, Vol. 6, no. 3 (July 10, 1973). English.

AN: Remigio Garcia and Mariana Escalante, young muralists, describe their work and the collective goals of a mural workshop begun by Leo Tanguma in Houston, TX.

7279 Roberts, Tim. For art's sake, for the community, for the working class. ORANGE CITY NEWS, Vol. 10, (March 14, 1979), p. 1,8-9. English.

AN: Illustrated article on Orange County, Calif. realist painter Emigdio Vasquez. Focuses on his community murals, and his attitudes toward his art. Also announces the first exhibit, "Empanada" of the newly formed Hispanic Artists Association of Orange County. 13 participants including Vasquez.

7280 Rodriguez, Patricia. Portfolio: Patricia Rodriguez; the visual interview. METAMORFOSIS, Vol. 3, no. 1-2 (1980, 1981), p. 38-45. English.

AN: Statement by the artist reprinted from her exhibit "The Visual Interview" at the Mission Cultural Center, San Francisco. Discusses her fifteen mask-box-sculptures of Chicano artists from northern California. Illustrated with photographs of the artist at work and five of her sculptures. This issue of METAMORFOSIS combines volumes 3 and 4.

7281 Rodriguez, Pedro. Arte como expresion del pueblo. METAMORFOSIS, Vol. 3, no. 2 (1980, 1981), p. 59-62. English.

AN: Texas-born artist and teacher traces the history of the Chicano art movement from early struggles to limited recognition, takes a critical position toward artistic cooptation and the anti-political stance of many artists, and suggests a direction for the future.

7282 Rodriguez, Pedro and Walla Walla Community College, Walla Walla, WA. Chicano art exhibition. Exhibition invitation, 1981. English.

AN: Poster invitation to exhibition by Pedro Rodriguez, Associate professor of Chicano Studies at Washington State University, Pullman, Washington. Rodriguez presented a lecture in English, "Chicano Art and Its Mexican Antecedents," and one in Spanish, "El Muralismo en Mexico y Mexico-America." Illustrated with painting of woman shrouded in a rebozo.

7283 Rodriguez, Pedro. Chicano artist's paintings on display at WWC. UNION BULLETIN, (February 19, 1981). English.

AN: Commentary by artist Pedro Rodriguez stressing the social context of Chicano art and the role and function of the Chicano artist. Illustrated with a photograph of the artist and reproductions of two oil paintings: EL OBRERO and CIUDAD LIBERTAD.

7284 Ruiz, Elizabeth. Fiesta artist. THE RANGER, (April 23, 1981). English.

AN: Biographical information on San Antonio painter Jesus Trevino. Artist describes his work as "realism" with "a focus on Mexican American and Chicano culture, the people and their lives".

7285 Rupert Garcia. SAN FRANCISCO BAY GUARDIAN, (October 3, 1975), p. 22-23. English.

AN: Informative piece focusing on the artist's work procedures; his techniques of image selection, transformation and manipulation. Presents Garcia's political and aesthetic credo and situates him as a community activist and artist. Illustrated with reproduction of Garcia's BICENTENNIAL POSTER.

Philosophy of Art (cont.)

7286 Salazar, Veronica. Mel Casas sees things brown. SAN ANTONIO EXPRESS-NEWS, (December 23, 1973). English.

AN: Searching for "visual congruity," Mel Casas has slowly moved toward figurative art. Article traces aspects of his artistic trajectory and the philosophic basis of his aesthetic vision. Includes photograph of artist.

7287 Santa Ana College, Santa Ana, CA and Goldman, Shifra M. Chicano art. Exhibition catalog, 1974. English.

AN: Thirteen California artists are presented in a short essay defining Chicano as a double mestizaje of Mexican mestizo and U.S. influences that exists in a state of "reconciled conflict." Its aim is communication. Artists included are Malaquias Montoya, Rupert Garcia, Manuel Hernandez, Esteban Villa, Robert Gomez, Harvey Tarango, Mary Helen Castro, Eduardo Carrillo, Graciela Carrillo, and "Los Four": Carlos Almaraz, Robert de la Rocha, Judithe Hernandez, Gilbert Lujan and Frank Romero.

7288 Santa Ana College, Santa Ana, CA. MECHA presents la semana de la Raza. Exhibition brochure, 1970. English.

AN: Program for the week's activities, including EL ARTE DE LA RAZA exhibition, Gilbert Sanchez Lujan speaking on "Chicano Art in the Barrio," art demonstrations by Gilbert Vasquez, Emigdio Vasquez, Esau Quiroz, and Richard Garcia.

7289 Schwartz, Barry. The new humanism: art in a time of change. New York, Praeger, 1974. English.

AN: Schwartz compiled an international roster of over 100 artists whom he believed formed a "movement" away from abstraction and toward an art expressing a belief in human values and human dignity. He divides humanism into categories like metaphysical, existential, absurd, etc. Included are Luis Jimenez's BARFLY and OLD WOMAN WITH CAT (illustrated p. 121), and a brief biography (p. 171).

7290 Semana de la Raza: international panel of the arts, Mexico and the United States. Santa Ana, CA: MEChA, Santa Ana College, 1972. English.

AN: An International Panel of the Arts, organized by art historian Shifra Goldman, featured Mexicans Hector Garcia, prize-winning photographer; Jaime Mejia, painter, restorer, filmmaker; Alejandro Vichir, director of Teatro Trashumante; and Chicanos Gilbert Sanchez Lujan, sculptor and painter; Gloria Osuna, painter and artist for Teatro Campesino; and Jesus Salvador Trevino, filmmaker.

7291 Soberon, Mercedes. La revolucion se trata de amor: Mercedes Soberon. CHISMEARTE, Vol. 1, no. 1 (Fall 1976), p. 14-18. Spanish.

AN: Short interview with Mercedes Soberon, San Francisco artist involved with the art group Mission Media Arts. Mercedes talks about the role of women as organizers and artists, the sacrifices associated with this role, and the politics of San Francisco museums.

7292 Southwest Texas State University, San Marcos, TX and Carlisle, Charles Richard. Cuatro caminos: four perspectives on Chicano art. Exhibition catalog, 1980. English.

AN: Exhibition pamphlet with photographs of the artists. Alex Flores, Luis Jimenez, Cesar Augusto Martinez and Amado Pena, Jr. comment on their work and the Chicano art movement.

7293 Stellweg, Carla. De como el arte chicano es tan indocumentado como los indocumentados/the way in which Chicano art is as undocumented as the 'undocumented'. ARTES VISUALES, no. 29 (June 1981), p. 23-32. Bilingual.

AN: An overview of Chicano art from its beginnings to the present. Suggestion that present art is improved by abandoning the nationalist, derivative and folkloric phase. Statements and biographies of artists. Some non-Chicanos included as Chicanos. Many illustrations. Bilingual.

7294 Symposium on the politics of the arts: minorities and the arts. ARTS IN SOCIETY, Vol. 10, no. 3 (Fall , Winter, 1973), p. 66-73. English.

AN: One panel from the Colloquium "Politics of the Arts" presented by the UCLA Management in the Arts Program, Graduate School of Management, 1972, included, among others, Leonard Castellanos of Mechicano Art Center, and James Woods of Studio Watts Workshop, both in Los Angeles. A major topic was how minorities dealing with the corporate capitalist structure can keep control of their art programs.

7295 Tibol, Raquel. Primera conferencia de plastica chicana. PROCESO, (September 24, 1979), p. 57-58. Spanish.

AN: Report on the internationally attended CONFERENCIA PLASTICA CHICANA held in Austin, Texas September 13th to 16th, 1979.

7296 Tonitines: Chicano architecture por Chicanos in architecture. Unpublished manuscript, Spring 1972. English.

AN: Manuscript deposited at Chicano Library, University of California, Berkeley. Aspirations for service; esthetics; interface between architecture and economics politics for group of students in Department of Architecture, University of California, Berkeley.

7297 Torres, Salvador Roberto. Creative aspects of la Raza inspired by Chicano experiences. Unpublished thesis, 1973. Bilingual.

AN: Project presents six paintings and six drawings by San Diego artist Torres based on the feeling and impact of United Farm Workers Huelga banner, used on a personal level. Torres wants to make an "imaginary theatre" of the ideas drawn from the Chicano movement. Bilingual. Illustrated.

Philosophy of Art (cont.)

7298 Unzueta, Manuel. Social commentary on
Chicano art: a painter's critical brush.
XALMAN, Vol. 1, no. 5 (Fall   1977), p.
63-68. English.

AN: Personal manifesto of painter
Unzueta. Description of popular Chicano
iconography and esthetics.

7299 Valdez, James. Analysis of Chicano
aesthetics in visual art. Symposium paper,
1973 [unpublished]. English.

AN: The basic premise of this paper,
presented at the Third Annual El Alma
Symposium at California State University,
San Jose, is that Chicano artists (as a
group) are imitators and only by a process
that develops self-knowledge can they
transcend their situation. Of the six
potential positions for the Chicano analyzed
in this paper, only one articulates how
Chicanos could create art reflective of
their experience as truth. Only when
Chicanos have an awareness of their identity
can they function creatively in their
environment.

7300 Valle, Victor Manuel and Vasquez, Emigdio.
Emigdio Vasquez Interview. SOMOS,
(December, January, 1978, 1979), p. 42-43.
English.

AN: Article on Arizona-born painter, son
of a miner, living in Orange County,
California. Discusses his realistic style
(from photographs), technique, humanism,
interest in murals, and loan of work for
Alejandro Grattan's film ONLY ONCE IN A
LIFETIME. Illustrated.

7301 Vasquez, Pedro. One definition of Chicano
art. PAPEL CHICANO, Vol. 1, no. 9 (December
12, 1971). English.

AN: A workshop discussion on Chicano
fine arts provokes various ideas towards a
definition of Chicano Art: first, the artist
is not to be separated from the masses nor
is he/she seen as a special breed of person;
second, everyday life and customs of the
barrio are to be closely examined as
nutrient sources of creative expression; and
third, Chicanos themselves will determine
the standards for judging and validating
Chicano Art.

7302 Yarbro-Bejarano, Yvonne. La forma del sueno:
arte y pensamiento de Alfredo Arreguin.
METAMORFOSIS, Vol. 3, no. 2 (1980, 1981), p.
10-24. Spanish.

AN: Interview and portfolio of
Mexican-born painter who has been living in
Seattle for more than 20 years. Contains
biographical data and the artist's view on
the role of the Chicano artist. Ten
illustrations.

Phoenix, AZ

7303 MARS: Movimiento Artistico del Rio Salado.
Phoenix, AZ: [MARS], n.d. English.

AN: Illustrated brochure for the MARS
organization and its studio-gallery.
Includes a brief history, list of
exhibitions from 1978 to 1981, news about
its studio-workshop for the community, and
its goals.

7304 McClellan, Bill. Army of volunteers paints a
little history in Phoenix. PHOENIX GAZETTE,
(April 20, 1977). English.

AN: Adolfo "El Zarco" Guerrero with 100
residents from the Duppa Villa Housing
Project completes a mural funded by the
Arizona Commission on Arts and Humanities.
Guerrero completed six murals, but prefers
sculpture.

Photography

7305 450 anos del pueblo chicano/450 years of
Chicano history in pictures. Albuquerque,
NM: Chicano Communications Center, 1976.
English.

AN: A pictorial history of Mexico,
Mexican Americans and Chicanos through
photographs and art works. P. 138 is
dedicated to murals, graphics, cartoons and
photographs from Chicago and the Southwest,
but other murals, graphics, cartoons and
photographs by Chicanos and non-Chicanos are
scattered throughout. In addition, 450 ANOS
has been a rich source book of imagery for
Chicano artists, especially historical works
of art.

7306 Adal. Sitio de debate [photograph]. TIN TAN,
Vol. 1, no. 2 (September 1975), p. [23].

7307 Adams, Robert. The architecture and art of
early Hispanic Colorado. Boulder, CO:
Colorado Associated University Press in
cooperation with the State Historical
Society of Colorado, 1974. English.

AN: Robert Adams is a photographer and
writer from Longmont, CO who has evocatively
captured scenes in the San Luis and
Purgatory Valleys of Southern Colorado. The
text and photographs focus on "Hispano"
village life, customs and traditions.

7308 Alarcon, Carlos. Untitled [photograph]. TIN
TAN, Vol. 1, no. 2 (September 1975), p.
[18].

7309 Almaraz, Carlos and Estrada, Jose (Pepe).
[Untitled photograph]. CHISMEARTE, Vol. 2,
no. 1 (1978), p. Ft Cover.

7310 Arizona. ARIZONA REPUBLIC, (September 11,
1977), p. 50. English.

AN: Exhibit of photographs by Louis
Carlos Bernal from Tucson in the Heard
Museum in Phoenix, Arizona. Includes 6
illustrations.

7311 Armas, Jose and Buitron, Robert. Issues.
ARIZTLAN NEWSLETTER, (August 1981).
English.

AN: Thoughts and definitions of Chicano
art by Dr. Jose Armas, founder of Pajarito
Publications, and by photographer and MARS
member Robert Buitron.

7312 Barrera, Manuel. Wall murals. LA RAZA, Vol.
1, no. 10 (February 1973), p. 24-25.
Bilingual.

7313 Bernal, Luis Carlos. Alma Rosa [photograph].
LLUEVE TLALOC, no. 8 (1981), p. 30.

7314 Bernal, Luis Carlos. Dia de los muertos
[photograph]. LLUEVE TLALOC, no. 8 (1981),
p. [7].

Photography (cont.)

7315 Bernal, Luis Carlos. La fotografia como reflejo de las estructuras sociales. In HECHO EN LATINOAMERICA: SEGUNDO COLOQUIO LATINOAMERICANO DE FOTOGRAFIA, MEXICO CITY, 1982, p. 92-94. Spanish.

AN: Presentation made by Tucson, AZ photographer Louis Carlos Bernal at the Second Latin American Colloquium of Photography and exhibit in 1981.

7316 Bernal, Luis Carlos. A luminous view of a simple lifestyle. NUESTRO, Vol. 2, no. 7 (July 1978), p. 26-27. English.

AN: Color photographic essay with notes by the photographer Luis Carlos Bernal. Documenting Arizona Chicanos, Bernal focuses on the objects and environments that help define their lifestyle.

7317 Bernal, Luis Carlos. Marines [photograph]. LLUEVE TLALOC, no. 8 (1981), p. 37.

7318 Bernal, Luis Carlos. Panadero [photograph]. LLUEVE TLALOC, no. 8 (1981), p. 2.

7319 Bernal, Luis Carlos. La Raza [photograph]. LLUEVE TLALOC, no. 8 (1981), p. 21.

7320 Bernal, Luis Carlos. Sin documentados [photograph]. LLUEVE TLALOC, no. 8 (1981), p. 14.

7321 Bernal, Luis Carlos. Sr. Ricardo Gallegos, etc. [photograph]. REVISTA CHICANO-RIQUENA, Vol. 7, no. 2 (Spring 1979), p. 43.

7322 Blum, Walter. The vision behind the mirror. CALIFORNIA LIVING, (November 26, 1978), p. 40-44. English.

AN: Illustrated article with background information on the non-Chicano photographers (Roger Minick, Morrie Camhi, and Abigail Heyman) who spent a year documenting the Chicano community. Their work was issued as a portfolio, "Espejo: Reflections of the Mexican American," by the Mexican-American Legal Defense and Educational Fund (MALDEF). It is one of the most extensive photographic records made of the Chicano experience.

7323 Bolger, Kathryn McKenna. Photo exhibit direct, human. AUSTIN AMERICAN STATESMAN, (July 25, 1980), p. E-4. English.

AN: Review of photo-documentary group exhibit "Un Encuentro Sin Palabras." The reviewer felt that there was nothing "unique" about the Chicano experience, as claimed by the show's organizers.

7324 Brand Library Art Center, Glendale, CA. Los hermanos: Jesus, Jacob & Frank Gutierrez, sculpture, paintings, drawings, & photographs. Exhibition catalog, 1974. English.

AN: Exhibit of the work of three brothers living in the Los Angeles area.

7325 Bravo, Antonio. Manuel Alvarez Bravo at the San Francisco Art Institute. CHISMEARTE, Vol. 2, no. 1 (Summer 1978), p. 37. English.

AN: Presentation of the Mexican photographer's work in relation to a visiting exhibit in the United States. Illustrated.

7326 The Broadway mural, 1981, by John Manuel

Valadez. Los Angeles, CA: Victor Clothing Co., n.d. English.

AN: Postcard/brochure about Valadez's 8x48-ft mural, oil on canvas, displayed at the Victor Clothing Co. in downtown Los Angeles. Brief profile of the photographer and muralist. Full color reproduction of a section of the complete mural.

7327 Buitron, Robert. [Untitled photograph]. COMMUNITY ARTS NEWSLETTER, Vol. 3, no. 5 (September 1981).

7328 Canto al pueblo: an anthology of experiences. San Antonio, TX: Penca Books, 1978. English.

AN: Includes works by: Mario E. Castillo, Carlos Rosas, Jose G. Gonzalez, Santos Martinez, Gilbert Munoz, Fred Loa, Armando Ibanez and others.

7329 Castano, Wilfredo. El santero [photograph]. TIN TAN, Vol. 2, no. 5 (June 1, 1977), p. 10-12.

7330 Castillo Simonetti, Naomi. Untitled/Sin titulo [photograph]. REVISTA CHICANO-RIQUENA, Vol. 7, no. 2 (Spring 1979), p. 42.

7331 Chu, Amy. Focus on cultural heritage. READER: SAN DIEGO WEEKLY, (September 17, 1981). English.

AN: Review of exhibit FIVE PHOTOGRAPHERS: CONTEMPORARY VIEWS OF MEXICAN AND MEXICAN-AMERICAN CULTURE which includes two Chicano photographers from Arizona: Louis Carlos Bernal (Tucson), and Robert C. Buitron (Tempe). Details some of Bernal's work between 1973 and 1980; Buitron's more personal work (1978-1981) is from his FAMILY AND PHOTOGRAPHY book-in-progress.

7332 The class of '79. SA: THE MAGAZINE OF SAN ANTONIO, Vol. 3, no. 4 (June 1979). English.

AN: Well-illustrated article on students of James Newberry, photography teacher at the University of Texas, San Antonio. Includes photos of top prizewinners and members of Ladrones de la Luz, David Cardenas and Kathy Vargas.

7333 Colectivo El Ojo. CHOQUE DE AMOR: fotonovela by Lamp. CHISMEARTE, Vol. 1, no. 4 (Fall , Winter, 1977), p. 35-37. Bilingual.

AN: Several students with the help of the Latin American Media Project (LAMP) and the Latin American Studies Department of California State University, Los Angeles produced the fotonovela CHOQUE DE AMOR, a variation on the typical "fotonovela" romance. This one encourages readers to reevaluate traditional female roles. The group also includes Kay Torres. Six frames of the fotonovela are reproduced.

7334 Community Programs in the Arts and Sciences (COMPAS). Artists in the city: a report on C.E.T.A. artists in St. Paul. St. Paul, MN: COMPAS, 1978. English.

AN: Includes data on Chicano muralists John Acosta, Thomas Acosta, Paul Basquez, Armando Estrella, and photographer Raphael Romo.

Photography (cont.)

7335 Conferencia plastica chicana. Conference
brochure, 1979. English.

AN: Schedule of proceedings at
internationally attended conference on
Chicano and Mexican art and photography
sponsored by the Centro Cultural de LUCHA
(League of United Chicano Artistas) and MAS
(Mujeres Artistas del Suroeste). Brief
biographies of presentors. Illustrated.

7336 Consejo Mexicano de Fotografia, A.C., Mexico
City and Tibol, Raquel. Hecho en
Latinoamerica: primera muestra de la
fotografia latinoamericana contemporanea.
Exhibition catalog, 1978. Spanish.

AN: Catalog/book of the first colloquium
and exhibit of Latin American photography.
Among the Chicano artists in the exhibit
were Francisco X. Camplis, Louis Carlos
Bernal, Harry Gamboa, Jose P. Romero, Harvey
J. Tarango, Isabel Castro. Statements by
some of the artists. Great number of
illustrations.

7337 Consejo Mexicano de Fotografia, A.C., Mexico
City. Hecho en latinoamerica: segundo
coloquio latinoamericano de fotografia.
Exhibition catalog, 1982. Spanish.

AN: Catalog/book of the second
colloquium and exhibit of Latin American
photography. Among the Chicano artists whose
work is reproduced are Louis Carlos Bernal,
Robert C. Buitron, David Cardenas, Isabel
Castro, Harry Gamboa, Jr., Luis Garza,
Roberto Gil de Montes, John M. Valadez,
Kathy Vargas. In the exhibit were also
Porfirio Aguilar, Elsa Marie Flores, Ricardo
Valverde. Great number of illustrations. In
Spanish.

7338 Conversation on photography in the Los
Angeles Latino community. OBSCURA, Vol. 2,
no. 2 (December, February, 1981, 1982), p.
22-32. English.

AN: Interview on the nature and
distinguishing characteristics of Chicano
photography with Chicano photographers
Isabel Castro (Council for Latino
Photography), Lorenzo Hernandez (Director of
Cityscape Gallery, publisher PHOTOSHOW
magazine), Joseph G. Uribe (California State
University, Los Angeles, Center for the
Visual Arts, Director of West Colorado
Gallery), Patssi Valdez, Becky Villasenor,
and sculptor, curator, and Art Director for
Academia Quinto Sol, Inc., Linda Vallejo,
Portfolio of photography by Chicanos Don
Anton, Louis Carlos Bernal, Sean Carrillo,
Patssi Valdez, Ricardo Valverde, and by
Morrie Camhi and Elizabeth Sisco on Chicano
subjects.

7339 COUNCIL OF LATINO PHOTOGRAPHY/USA
NEWSLETTER. no. 1 (January 1979). English.

AN: First number of photocopied
newsletter produced by the Council of Latino
Photography/USA announcing the formation of
the organization and its affiliation with
the Consejo Latinoamericano de Fotografia
established in Mexico City in May 1978.
Organizers of CLP/USA were photographers
Isabel Castro, Harry Gamboa, Jr., Adam
Avila, Luis Garza, and art historian Shifra
Goldman.

7340 COUNCIL OF LATINO PHOTOGRAPHY/USA
NEWSLETTER. no. 2 (January 1980). English.

AN: Photocopied newsletter reporting on
the "First Communication" meeting of the
organization, the opening of a Council
gallery and darkroom in Pasadena, news from
San Francisco/Berkeley group, news of the
activities of the Consejo Mexicano de
Fotografia, Mexico, and an announcement of
the II COLLOQUIUM OF LATIN AMERICAN
PHOTOGRAPHY for 1981.

7341 DE COLORES. Vol. 2, no. 4 (1976), p. 1-68.
English.

AN: Photographs by Moises Medina, Jose
Luis Sedano; drawings by Jerry Lujan,
Gilbert "Sparky" Espinoza, Rebecca Polanco;
paintings by John Herrera, Sonny Duran,
Larry Martinez. Cover by Fernando Penalosa.

7342 Documentary to include work by Cuate Santos.
LAREDO NEWS, (July 17, 1980). English.

AN: Photography by Laredo News
photographer Cuate Santos included in
exhibit "Un encuentro sin palabras," a
documentary show on Mexican American life in
Texas sponsored by Mujeres Artistas del
Suroeste (MAS). The state-wide show was
juried by Los Angeles photographer Isabel
Castro. Illustrated.

7343 ENCUENTRO FEMENIL (San Fernando, CA). Vol.
1, no. 1 (Spring 1973), p. 1+. English.

AN: Publication sponsored by Hijas de
Cuauhtemoc, a Chicana femenist group. Black
and white drawings on cover by Pat Portera
Crary. Art work by Vicki Thrall, Adelaida
del Castillo, and Maria Hortencia Garcia.
Photography by Cindy Honesto and David
Lazarin.

7344 Espejo: reflections of the Mexican American:
Louis Carlos Bernal, Morrie Camhi, Abigail
Heyman, Roger Minick, Neal Slavin. SOMOS,
Vol. 2, no. 1 (February 1978), p. 26-35.
English.

AN: Announcement of the ESPEJO
photographic exhibit to be held at Goez
Gallery in East Los Angeles. Statements by
the four artists and a portfolio of their
works: Abigail Heyman, Roger Minick, Morrie
Camhi, and Arizona Chicano photographer
Louis Carlos Bernal. Includes color
photographs by Bernal on cover. This 1979
issue is erroneously dated 1978.

7345 Extension Cultural SRE/UNAM, San Antonio,
TX. Second non professional (black & white)
photography contest: Mexican women in Texas.
Competition announcement, [ca. 1980].
English.

AN: Announcement of photographic
competition sponsored by the Extension arm
of the Secretaria de Relaciones
Exteriores/Universidad Nacional Autonoma de
Mexico in San Antonio. The theme specified
an homage to the Mexican woman in Texas.

Photography (cont.)

7346 Fischer, Hal. Espejo: reflections of the Mexican American: Louis Carlos Bernal, Morrie Camhi, Abigail Heyman, Roger Minick, Neal Slavin. PICTURE MAGAZINE, no. 9 (1978). English.

AN: Oversize portfolio of photographs recording contemporary Mexican American life commissioned by the Mexican American Legal Defense and Education Fund. Three photographers, Louis Carlos Bernal (from Arizona), Morrie Camhi and Abagail Heyman focus on the family and the home; the fourth, Roger Minick, juxtaposes the Mexican American against "barrio" murals. Only Bernal is Chicano. 24 photographs, six of which (Bernal's) are in color.

7347 Five views on Mexican culture. LA JOLLA LIGHT, (September 10, 1981), p. B-6. English.

AN: Review of a show at the University of California, San Diego's Mandeville Art Gallery called FIVE PHOTOGRAPHERS: CONTEMPORARY VIEWS OF MEXICAN AND MEXICAN-AMERICAN CULTURE and featuring Arizona photographers Louis Carlos Bernal, Robert C. Buitron, and three others.

7348 Four and four: Mexican and Latino photography, April 25 through June 14 on the balcony. CALENDAR: SANTA BARBARA MUSEUM OF ART, (April 1981). English.

AN: Announcement of exhibit organized by Lorenzo Hernandez of the Cityscape Foto Gallery, Pasadena, Calif. Sought to present "the observable differences between the 'classic' vision of the Mexican National and the 'realistic' vision of the re-rooted Mexican/American." The latter included Louis Bernal (Tucson) and Ricardo Valverde (Los Angeles) as well as two Spanish Sephardics of Los Angeles, Camhi and Sisco.

7349 Frankenstein, Alfred. Just for the record. SAN FRANCISCO CHRONICLE, (May 27, 1976), p. 48. English.

AN: Positive review of exhibit at the Mexican Museum featuring the work of Jesus Reyes Ferreira from Mexico and Gustavo Rivera from San Francisco. Ninety-five-year-old Ferreira uses tempera on tissue paper to render brilliant paintings focusing on Mexican folk motifs. Rivera paints in the abstract expressionist mode with power and passion. Article also lauds the photographic work of Angel del Valle in his exhibition: SEMBRADORES at the Galeria de la Raza.

7350 Frankenstein, Alfred. A senior senor's approach. SAN FRANCISCO CHRONICLE, (May 27, 1976), p. 48. English.

AN: Review of an exhibit of Mexican painter Jesus Reyes Ferreira at the Mexican Museum of San Francisco, as well as that of San Francisco artist Gustavo Rivera, an abstract expressionist painter. Also mentions the Museum's mural map, and Angel del Valle's photography show at the Galeria de la Raza.

7351 Galeria: a place you should visit. CAMINOS, Vol. 2, no. 5 (October 1981), p. 24-25. English.

AN: Announcement of the opening of Galeria, specializing in Hispanic art, in Orange County, California. Illustrations of sculpture by Richard G. Villa and Eduardo Oropeza.

7352 Una galeria de artistas = A gallery of artists. CAMINOS, Vol. 1, no. 6 (October 1980), p. 20-26. Bilingual.

AN: Features California artists Domingo O. Ulloa (Imperial Valley images), Gloria Chacon, photographer Maria Pinedo (San Francisco), Willie Herron (Los Angeles), Joaquin Patino (Delano), Pedro Pelayo (Long Beach), sculptor Rudi Sigala (San Diego), Mario Torero (San Diego), sculptor Michael M. Amescua (Los Angeles), and the East Los Streetscapers. Illustrated.

7353 Galeria de la Raza/Studio 24, San Francisco, CA and Milkie, Anne. Carnaval '80. Exhibition catalog, 1980. English.

AN: Catalog of an exhibit of photographs and other media recording San Francisco's multi-ethnic CARNAVAL, organized in 1978 by Panamanian-born dancer. Included in the exhibit were the photographs of Chicana Maria V. Pinedo, who also designed the catalog.

7354 Galeria de la Raza/Studio 24, San Francisco, CA; Sorell, Victor A.; and Vaughan, Kay. Images of the Mexican Revolution: photographs by Agustin V. Casasola. Exhibition catalog, 1980. English.

AN: Catalog of an exhibit of Mexican photographer Agustin V. Casasola from prints owned by the Martinezes of Lansing, MI. The exhibit traveled to Raza galleries in many parts of the United States. Illustrated.

7355 Galeria de la Raza/Studio 24, San Francisco, CA. Images of the Southwest. Exhibition catalog, 1977. English.

AN: Invitation/catalog for an exhibit including Rudy M. Fernandez(Utah), Enrique Flores(Texas), Xavier Gorena(Texas), C.A.[Cesar] Martinez(Texas), Santos Martinez, Jr.(Texas), Pedro Rodriguez(Texas), Arnold Trujillo(New Mexico). Block prints, paper cut-outs, drawings, photographs, copper enamels, and sculpture were shown. Five illustrations.

7356 Galeria de la Raza/Studio 24, San Francisco, CA. "Low 'n slow": checking out low rider art. Exhibition invitation, 1979. English.

AN: Invitation to an exhibit of drawings, photographs, and graphics. Participation by LOWRIDER MAGAZINE and local car and bike clubs.

7357 Galeria de la Raza/Studio 24, San Francisco, CA. Photographs by Angel Del Valle. Los sembradores: the marijuana growers. Exhibition catalog, 1976. English.

AN: Illustrated catalog. Del Valle documents the growing, customs, and merchandising of marijuana in the Sierras of Mexico.

7358 Galeria Otra Vez, Los Angeles, CA. Inner/urban landscapes: Ricardo Valverde, Suda House, David Feldman. Exhibition invitation, 1979. English.

AN: Invitation to a photography exhibition held at Self-Help Graphic's gallery.

Photography (cont.)

7359 Galeria Otra Vez, Los Angeles, CA. Rosemary Quesada-Weiner, Mary McNally: a photographic exhibition. Exhibition invitation, [1981]. English.

AN: Invitation to an exhibition including Chicana photographer Quesada-Weiner. Illustrated.

7360 Galeria Tonantzin, Centro Cultural de LUCHA, Austin, TX. Mexican faces in San Antonio. Exhibition brochure, [1980]. English.

AN: Photography show by 24 young Chicanos from Texas sponsored by the Secretaria de Relaciones Exteriores and the Universidad Autonoma de Mexico, Cultural Extension program (SRE-UNAM) in San Antonio.

7361 Galeria Tonantzin, Centro Cultural de LUCHA, Austin, TX. Young Chicano photographers from throughout Texas. Exhibition brochure, n.d. English.

AN: This exhibition is the collection of the winners of the contest (by the same name) sponsored by the Extension Cultural SRE-UNAM in San Antonio. Photographers represented were: Grace Alvarez, David Cardenas, Hector Cardenas, Stephen Casanova, Ronald Cortez, Raul Espinosa, Felix Almanza, Carolina Flores, David Garza Perez, Xavier Garza, Conrad Guerra, Melinda Hasbrook, Juan Jose de Hoyes, Beverly Kennon, Art Moreno, David Perez, Isabelle Purden, Patricia Santell, Nancy de los Santos, Jose Soria, Richard Tichich, Kathy Vargas, Vivian Yaten, and Johnny Zamarria.

7362 Gamboa, Harry, Jr. Cafe en blanco y negro. COMUNIDAD, (April 26, 1981), p. 3-5. Spanish.

AN: An essay on how to take black and white photographs in the barrio as works of art, as visual propaganda, and as visual history by ASCO photographer Harry Gamboa. Illustrated with five of his photographs.

7363 Gamboa, Harry, Jr. Pistol whippersnapper. R.A.M. COLLECTIVE, Vol. 2, no. 1 (June 1, 1977), p. 10-11. English.

AN: Photography and poetry by Harry Gamboa, Jr., member of ASCO, Los Angeles.

7364 Gamboa, Harry, Jr. [Untitled photography]. REGENERACION, Vol. 2, no. 4 (1975), p. COVER.

7365 Garcia, Ruperto. Photography. ARRIBA, Vol. 1, no. 6 (1980). English.

AN: Statement of photographic credo and portfolio of photographs by Ruperto Garcia, photographer from the Rio Grande Valley.

7366 Garza, Alex. Earth abyss [sculpture]. REVISTA CHICANO-RIQUENA, Vol. 8, no. 3 (Summer 1980), p. 82.

7367 Geyer, Anne and Gamboa, Harry, Jr. Artists' exhibits are street performances. THE NEWS, (September 11, 1981), p. 18. English.

AN: Illustrated interview with photographer/writer Harry Gamboa, Jr., member and documenter of the performance art group ASCO. Description of the NO MOVIE, NO PHANTOM, walking and instant murals of the group, and other performance street art which Gamboa considers as Chicano self-documentation and expression.

7368 Geyer, Anne; Hernandez, Lorenzo; and Valverde, Ricardo. Latino photographers of U.S. still seeking identity. THE NEWS, (September 5, 1981), p. 17. English.

AN: Interview with Lorenzo Hernandez, photo dealer and owner of Cityscape Foto Gallery, Pasadena, Calif. in which he compares Mexican with U.S. Latino photography. Interview with Ricardo Valverde, Chicano photographer and co-chair of the Council of Latino Photography/USA, discussing his work. Illustrated.

7369 Gil de Montes, Roberto. [Untitled photograph]. CHISMEARTE, Vol. 2, no. 1 (1978), p. 40.

7370 Goldman, Shifra M. Hecho en Latino America: first photography colloquium and exhibition. CHISMEARTE, no. 6 (February 1980), p. 16-25. English.

AN: Report on the first colloquium of Latin American photography, Mexico City, May 1978. Analysis and critique of U.S. Latino photographers' work presented in exhibition. Well illustrated.

7371 Goldman, Shifra M. Women artists of Texas: MAS = More + Artists + Women = MAS. CHISMEARTE, no. 7 (January 1981), p. 21-22. English.

AN: History of Texas Chicana women artists' organization, Mujeres Artistas del Suroeste (MAS), co-founded in 1977 by Santa Barraza and Nora Gonzalez-Dodson in the framework of the burgeoning feminist art movement, particularly Women and Their Work of Texas. Brief history of Chicano politics and the corresponding art movement of southern and central Texas. In addition to Barraza and Gonzalez-Dodson, Alicia Arredondo, Modesta Trevino, and Maria Flores are considered. Illustrated.

7372 Gonzales, Jose G. [Untitled collage]. REVISTA CHICANO-RIQUENA, Vol. 4, no. 4 (Fall 1976), p. Cover. English.

7373 Gonzalez, Hector. [Untitled photo collage]. TIN TAN, Vol. 1, no. 2 (September 1975), p. [24-25].

7374 Gonzalez, Jose Carlos. Consejo mexicano de fotografia: foto latino en el suroeste de los Estado Unidos. ARTES VISUALES, Vol. 29, no. 29 (June 1981), p. 55-56. Spanish.

AN: Review of a photography show in Mexico City organized by Lorenzo Hernandez, Cityscape Photo Gallery of Pasadena, and the Council of Latino Photography/USA. The show featured Latinos of the Southwest and Latino themes by non-Latino photographers.

Photography (cont.)

7375 Grimke, Angelina. Chicano art finds home in Mission galeria. PEOPLE'S WORLD, Vol. 33, no. 32 (August 8, 1970), p. 11. English.

AN: Commentary on the exhibition CHICANOS, CUBA Y LOS 10 MILLONES held at the original Galeria de la Raza at 425 14th Street in San Francisco. The show presented photographs by Jay Ojeda and Roberto Perez-Diaz, drawings by Gloria Ozuna together with paintings and photographs by Cuban artist Mederos. Provides information about the goals of the Galeria as the visual arts department of Casa Hispana de Bellas Artes. Exhibition curator was Rolando Castellon.

7376 Gutierrez, Helga. The walls of Estrada Courts. LA GENTE DE AZTLAN, Vol. 7, no. 3 (February 1977), p. 19. English.

AN: Photographic essay of Estrada murals by Helga Gutierrez.

7377 HEMBRA: HERMANAS EN MOVIMIENTO BROTANDO RAICES DE AZTLAN (University of Texas, Austin). (Spring 1976).

AN: Raul Valdez, drawing, p. 3; Carolina Flores, drawing, p. 5; Maria Flores, photograph, pp. 7, 11, 30; M.E. Secrest-Ramirez, drawing, p. 12; Amacio Zarate, drawing, p. 15; Santa Barraza, drawings, pp. 16, 17, 18, 26, 32; Nora Gonzales-Dodson, painting, p. 19; Gilberto Cardenas, photograph, pp. 22, 28; Nanci de los Santos, photograph, p. 23, 29; Amado Maurilio Pena, Jr. p. 31.

7378 Herrera, Juan Felipe. The four quarters of the heart: a photographic portfolio by Maria Pinedo. METAMORFOSIS, Vol. 3, no. 2 (1980, 1981), p. 66-74. English.

AN: Statement by San Francisco photographer Maria Pineda and review of her photography by Herrera. Fourteen illustrations.

7379 Hurtado, Debbie. A historical update: Montoya's vindication of fabricated biases. THE STATE HORNET, (December 13, 1977), p. 6. English.

AN: Review of Jose Montoya's show "Pachuco Art - A Historical Update; "a rekindling of pachuquismo from the 1940s prevalent in Montoya's paintings and pen-and-ink drawings. The show featured historical photographs, and an animated hologram. Visitors wore zoot suit outfits to the opening. Illustrated.

7380 Imagenes de la Chicana. Menlo Park, CA: Nowels Publications (Stanford University Chicano Press), [ca 1975]. English.

AN: Collections of writings by Chicanas; illustrated by unsigned drawings, and photographs by Lena Bugarin, Martina Puente, Francisco Camplis, Mario Anzaldua.

7381 Jimenez, Luis. Vaquero [sculpture]. REVISTA CHICANO-RIQUENA, Vol. 8, no. 3 (Summer 1980), p. 76-77. Bilingual.

7382 Kreneck, Tom. With the eye of an artist: Jesus Murillo's Houston, 1927-1933. REVISTA CHICANO-RIQUENA, Vol. 8, no. 3 (Summer 1980), p. 104-105. English.

AN: Biographical sketch of Mexican-born

commercial and portrait photographer who worked professionally in Texas from 1916 until his death in 1971. The illustrations concern his Houston stay.

7383 L.A.C.E. (Los Angeles Contemporary Exhibitions), Los Angeles, CA. First communication. Exhibition invitation, 1979. English.

AN: Invitation to a showing of photographic slides and prints organized by the Council of Latino Photography/USA.

7384 Lopez, Yolanda M. [Untitled photograph]. METRO MAGAZINE, Vol. 1, no. 7 (Summer 1981), p. 28.

7385 Los Angeles City College. Contemporary times 2. Exhibition announcement, 1980. English.

AN: Illustrated announcement for photography show of Monticello Miller and William Ortiz.

7386 Los Angeles City College. Latinos de tres mundos. Exhibition invitation, 1980. English.

AN: Invitation to an exhibit featuring the work of ASCO members Harry Gamboa, Jr., Gronk, Willie Herron; painters Xavier Mendez and Olivia Sanchez; and photographer Ricardo Valverde.

7387 Los Angeles Municipal Art Gallery, Los Angeles, CA. Multicultural focus: a photography exhibition for the Los Angeles Bicentennial. Exhibition catalog, 1981. English.

AN: Catalog of an exhibit demonstrating the multi-ethnic character of Los Angeles. Chicano photographers include Don Anton, Ron Bernal, Daniel Martinez, Rick Tejada-Flores. Illustrated.

7388 Mandeville Art Gallery, University of California, San Diego. Five photographers: contemporary views of Mexican and Mexican-American culture. Exhibition catalog, 1981. English.

AN: Catalog of exhibit including Louis Carlos Bernal, Robert C. Buitron, Alberto Lau, Richard Tichich, and Meridel Rubenstein. Illustrated.

7389 Mendoza, Vicente; Nario, Jose; and Patlan, Ray. The history of the Mexican-American worker (1974-75) [detail of mural]. REVISTA CHICANO-RIQUENA, Vol. 4, no. 4 (Fall 1976), p. 50,54. English.

7390 Mexican-American Advisory Committee of the Museum of Science and Industry.. Second annual Mexican-American art fiesta. Exhibition brochure, 1975. English.

AN: Exhibit of paintings, sculpture, crafts, and photography by 49 artists from Illinois, Indiana, and Mexico. Includes many of the most important Chicano artists of the Chicago area.

7391 Michigan State University, East Lansing, MI. Voces del norte. Brochure, 1978. English.

AN: Photos and graphics by 11 Chicanos residing in Michigan.

Photography (cont.)

7392 Montoya, Delilah Merriman. [Untitled photograph]. MAIZE, Vol. 2, no. 4 (Summer 1979), p. 24. English.

7393 Montoya, Delilah Merriman. [Untitled photograph]. MAIZE, Vol. 2, no. 4 (Summer 1979), p. 59. English.

7394 Oakland Museum, Oakland, CA. Espejo: reflections of the Mexican American: Louis Carlos Bernal, Morrie Camhi, Abigail Heyman, Roger Minick, Neal Slavin. Exhibit brochure, 1978. English.

AN: Twenty-five photographs from the documentary series commissioned by the Mexican American Legal Defense and Education Fund. Only Bernal is Chicano.

7395 Ochoa, Victor Orozco. [Untitled photographs]. MAIZE, Vol. 1, no. 3 (Spring 1978), p. 45-47,50+. English.

7396 Orozco, Irma. Women & their work. PARA LA GENTE, Vol. 1, no. 4 (October 1977), p. 12. English.

AN: Illustrated story about "Women & Their Work" festival in Austin, Texas, Oct-Dec 1977. Photographers Maria Flores and Teresina Guerra, Santa Barraza, Nora Gonzalez Dodson, Sylvia Orozco, and Modesta Trevino exhibited.

7397 Ortegon, Veronica. [Photographs and drawings]. REVISTA RIO BRAVO, Vol. 1, no. 3 (Fall 1981), p. Passim.

7398 Perales Leven, Humberto. Marcos Raya - Mexican painter. IMAGENES, Vol. 1, no. 1 (July 1976). Bilingual.

AN: Mexican born Chicago muralist Marcos Raya painted a mural titled HOMAGE TO RIVERA in the Pilsen barrio of Chicago at the corner of 18th Street and May. Raya articulates the role of the muralist and his function within the working class community. Also in this issue is an article on the formation of MARCH (Movimiento Artistico Chicano) in 1972 in East Chicago Indiana. Portfolio of drawings by Marcos Raya and photographs by Mario Castillo. Bilingual text.

7399 Quesada-Weiner, Rosemary. Las mujeres: 1977 National Women's Conference. Los Angeles, CA: Rosemary Quesada-Weiner, 1978. English.

AN: Portfolio (with captions) of photographs taken by Quesada-Weiner.

7400 Quesada-Weiner, Rosemary. [Untitled collection of photographs]. COMUNIDAD, (August 24, 1980), p. 15.

AN: Photographs of the CONFERENCIA DE LAS MUJERES CHICANAS taken by Rosemary Quesada-Weiner.

7401 Ramos, Joe. [Untitled photograph]. EL TECOLOTE LITERARY MAGAZINE, Vol. 2, no. 2 (July 1981), p. Cover.

7402 La Raza art festival. PAPEL CHICANO, Vol. 1, no. 6 (May 21, 1971), p. 8-9. English.

AN: Two-page centerfold of photographs by Johnny Almendarez of the LA RAZA ART FESTIVAL held at Ripley House in Segundo Barrio of Houston, Texas, May 5-9, 1971. Includes installation view of the exhibit,

two photos of artists in action and a cover photograph of artist Pedro Rodriguez conducting a silkscreen workshop.

7403 Riches of the barrios. ARIZONA [supplement to ARIZONA REPUBLIC], (September 11, 1977), p. 50. English.

AN: Louis Carlos Bernal of Tucson shows his collection of photographic portratis of the barrios at the Heard Museum in Phoenix. Well illustrated.

7404 Rivera, Gato. Officer Bradley interrogates Chuy Chicano [photograph]. EL TECOLOTE LITERARY MAGAZINE, Vol. 1, no. 1 (April 1980), p. 3.

7405 Sagel, Jaime. Art of brothers taps New Mexico heritage. JOURNAL NORTH, (December 16, 1981). English.

AN: Three brothers, graphics artist, painter, photographer, potter and poet Alejandro Lopez and his older self-taught brothers Felix and Manuel, are working with traditional New Mexican art forms (bultos, straw inlay crosses) and with newer innovative forms - reflecting the fusion of traditional-experimental art developing in New Mexico among young artists.

7406 San Antonio Museum of Modern Art. Zarzamora: inaugural exhibition of Ladrones de la Luz. Exhibition invitation, 1979. English.

AN: Illustrated invitation to photographic exhibition including Norman Avila, David Cardenas, Franco Cernero, Enrique Hernandez, Robert Maxham, James Newberry, Isaac Rodriguez, Daryl Studebaker, Richard Tichich, Beverly Ulmer, Kathy Vargas.

7407 Sanchez, Marisabel. America morena [photograph]. LA PALABRA, Vol. 2, no. 2 (Fall 1980), p. 68.

7408 Sanchez, Marisabel. Sone que... [photograph]. LA PALABRA, Vol. 2, no. 2 (Fall 1980), p. 67.

7409 Taboada, John. Impresiones. SOMOS, Vol. 1, no. 4 (September 1978), p. 34-35.

7410 Through the eyes of Joe Giron. NUESTRO, Vol. 5, no. 9 (December 1981), p. 34-40. English.

AN: A 9-photo collection of the work of Las Cruces, NM photographer, Joe Giron. Typical scenes in Texas, NM, and Ohio.

7411 Tolin Fine Art Gallery, Lancaster, CA. Presentation of photographic works by David Feldman, Richard Valverde. Exhibition invitation, 1979. English.

AN: Invitation to an exhibit.

7412 Trevino, Jose. Los monitos de Jose Trevino: esculturas de barro. TEJIDOS, Vol. 5, no. 2-4 (1978), p. 134-144. English.

7413 Tucker, Glen. Art scene. TODAY MAGAZINE, (April 16, 1978), p. 3. English.

AN: Commentary on photographic exhibit by Robert Tapias and the gift to the Witte Museum from the American Academy and Institute of Arts and Letters of a colored pencil drawing titled "El Filos Lowrider" by Luis Jimenez.

Photography (cont.)

7414 University of Houston/Lawndale Annex and
     Xochil Art and Culture Center, Mission, TX.
     The instant image: an exhibition of polaroid
     photography. Exhibition catalog, 1980.
     English.

     AN: Exhibit of 14 artists including
     Tejanos Frank Fajardo, Guillermo Pulido,
     Gregorio Salazar and Armando Rodriguez.

7415 Valle, Victor Manuel. Rosemary
     Quesada-Weiner. SOMOS, Vol. 1, no. 3 (August
     1978), p. 36-39. English.

     AN: Profile of photographer, feminist,
     community activist Rosemary Quesada-Weiner
     who was a school "drop-out" at 13, but
     received her journalism degree and
     discovered photography at La Verne College.
     She is a freelance photo-journalist who
     specializes in Chicana/Latina women's
     images, but is not limited to that theme.
     Well illustrated.

7416 Vasquez, Emigdio. La vida through the eyes
     of Emigdio Vasquez. Q-VO, (April 1979), p.
     36. English.

     AN: Interview with Orange County,
     California, realist and documentary painter
     Emigdio Vasquez who focuses on barrio life
     he knew in the 1940s and 1950s. Vasquez
     works from his own photographs and those of
     others. Includes biographical information
     and illustrations.

7417 Venegas, Sybil. Dia de los muertos. SOMOS,
     Vol. 1, no. 5 (October 1978), p. 42-47.
     English.

     AN: Brief history of Dia de los muertos
     ceremonies. While the custom is dying in
     Mexico (except for tourists), Chicano
     organizations like Galeria de la Raza
     (S.F.), El Centro de Artistas Chicanos
     (Sacramento, Ca.) celebrate the event
     annually, as does [Self-Help Graphics and
     Art, Inc.] in East Los Angeles. Well
     illustrated with photographs by Guillermo
     Bejarano and Daniel Duran.

7418 Wasserman, Isabelle. Photos on exhibit
     capture Mexican revolution. SAN DIEGO UNION,
     (November 26, 1981), p. D10. English.

     AN: Report on the photographic
     exhibition of Mexican revolutionary
     photographer Agustin V. Casasola at the
     Centro Cultural de la Raza in San Diego.
     Illustrated.

7419 Wilson, William. 30 works from the grass
     roots. LOS ANGELES TIMES, (June 4, 1973),
     p. IV,2. English.

     AN: Review of a show at the Junior Arts
     Center in Barnsdall Park by 15 members of
     the Mechicano Art Center. The critic feels
     contemporary groups that aim for change
     today (unlike past groups) are unable to
     articulate their spirit in a cohesive style.
     The top talent in this show is Charles
     Almaraz; also on exhibit are paintings by
     Jose Cervantes, Guillermo Martinez, Ray
     Atilano, sculpture by Manuel Cruz, and
     photography by (Oscar) R. Castillo.

7420 Wilson, William. A multicultural celebration
     of photos. CALENDAR, (February 8, 1981), p.
     89-90. English.

     AN: Review of multi-ethnic photography

show at the Los Angeles Municipal Art
Gallery. Wilson finds the photographs about
equally divided between sociological reality
and expression/art for its own sake.

7421 Wilson, William. Photography - the state of
     the art. CALENDAR, (January 28, 1979), p.
     87. English.

     AN: Includes review of ESPEJO:
     REFLECTIONS OF THE MEXICAN-AMERICAN exhibit:
     four photographers--Louis Carlos Bernal,
     Abigail Heyman, Morrie Camhi, and Roger
     Minick--who worked independently for a year
     to record facets of Chicano life.

7422 Wine and cheese: foto fun. Berkeley, CA:
     Exhibition invitation, 1979. English.

     AN: Invitation to an evening of
     photographic slides and prints and
     discussion by photographers Jose Romero and
     Maria Pinedo.

7423 Zuniga, R. and Gonzalez, M. Entrevista con
     los muralistas de East Austin. TEJIDOS, Vol.
     5, no. 2-4 (1978), p. 128-130. Spanish.

     AN: Extremely brief interview with two
     Austin, TX, muralists. Includes 5 black and
     white photographs of different murals.

Pico Rivera, CA

7424 Takahashi, Keith. Art replaces writing on
     wall. LOS ANGELES TIMES, (January 13,
     1974), p. XI-H, 1. English.

     AN: Junior high school student's mural
     in Pico Rivera, Los Angeles County, with aid
     of teacher and a commercial sign painter.
     Some censorship by officials mentioned.

PILGRIMAGE (GRAPE STRIKERS) [film]

7425 Films for the inner city. Los Angeles, CA:
     Los Angeles Public Library Federal Project,
     1971. English.

     AN: Annotated catalog of 16mm films and
     filmstrips, educational and documentary.
     Those concerning Mexican heritage include
     CHICANO FROM THE SOUTHWEST (1970),
     HENRY...BOY OF THE BARRIO (1969); HOW'S
     SCHOOL, ENRIQUE (1970), I AM JOAQUIN (1970),
     THE MEXICAN AMERICAN: HERITAGE AND DESTINY
     (1970), A MEXICAN AMERICAN FAMILY (1970),
     MEXICAN AMERICANS: QUEST FOR EQUALITY
     (1968), MEXICAN OR AMERICAN (1970),
     SIQUEIROS: "EL MAESTRO" (THE MARCH OF
     HUMANITY IN LATIN AMERICA) (1969).
     Filmstrips include THE AWAKENING (LA RAZA) -
     Part IV, CONFLICT OF CULTURES (LA RAZA) -
     Part III, MASTERWORKS OF MEXICAN ART, OUT OF
     THE MAINSTREAM, PILGRIMAGE (GRAPE STRIKERS).
     Also listed are films and filmstrips for
     children.

Pilsen, IL

7426 NATIONAL MURALS NETWORK COMMUNITY
     NEWSLETTER. (Fall 1979). English.

     AN: Reports on mural projects by Fermin
     Coronado working with students in Houston;
     Galeria de la Raza's billboard used as a
     mural surface for changing images; murals
     under the Flor en la Comunidad program of El
     Centro Cultural de la Gente in San Jose,
     California and led by artist Jaime Valadez;
     murals in Grand Rapids and other cities of
     western Michigan; murals by Jose Guerrero
     and others from the Chicago Mural Group; a
     survey of Chicano murals in the Pilsen area
     of Chicago guided by Jose Gonzalez.

Pineda, Carlos R.

7427 Carlos Pineda shows art in Centennial
     Museum. EL PASO TIMES, (November 5, 1972).
     English.

     AN: Themes from Mexican folk culture
     predominate in paintings by Carlos R. Pineda
     shown at the El Paso Centennial Museum. He
     has exhibited in Panama, Guadalajara,
     Phoenix, Tucson, and Dallas and is
     represented by the Jinx Gallery in El Paso.

Pineda, Maria Vita

7428 Una galeria de artistas = A gallery of
     artists. CAMINOS, Vol. 1, no. 6 (October
     1980), p. 20-26. Bilingual.

     AN: Features California artists Domingo
     O. Ulloa (Imperial Valley images), Gloria
     Chacon, photographer Maria Pinedo (San
     Francisco), Willie Herron (Los Angeles),
     Joaquin Patino (Delano), Pedro Pelayo (Long
     Beach), sculptor Rudi Sigala (San Diego),
     Mario Torero (San Diego), sculptor Michael
     M. Amescua (Los Angeles), and the East Los
     Streetscapers. Illustrated.

7429 Galeria de la Raza/Studio 24, San Francisco,
     CA and Milkie, Anne. Carnaval '80.
     Exhibition catalog, 1980. English.

     AN: Catalog of an exhibit of photographs
     and other media recording San Francisco's
     multi-ethnic CARNAVAL, organized in 1978 by
     Panamanian-born dancer. Included in the
     exhibit were the photographs of Chicana
     Maria V. Pinedo, who also designed the
     catalog.

7430 Herrera, Juan Felipe. The four quarters of
     the heart: a photographic portfolio by Maria
     Pinedo. METAMORFOSIS, Vol. 3, no. 2 (1980,
     1981), p. 66-74. English.

     AN: Statement by San Francisco
     photographer Maria Pineda and review of her
     photography by Herrera. Fourteen
     illustrations.

7431 Teatro de la Tierra Morena, Santa Cruz, CA.
     Fuego en Aztlan: a Chicano arts show.
     Exhibition brochure, 1980. English.

     AN: Folder of information on the
     exhibition curated by Cruz Zamarron and
     Eduardo Carrillo. Exhibiting artists were:
     Justina Avila, Terry Benitez, Eduardo
     Carrillo, Hernando Chavez, Bob Cruz, Juanita
     Estrada, Juana Franklin, Sal Garcia, Leticia
     Hernandez, David "Sir Loco" Jimenez, Raoul
     Mendez, Vicente Mendez, Maria V. Pinedo,
     Gonzalo Placencia, Ramon Rodriguez, Roberto
     Salas, George Silva and Cruz Zamarron. A
     special feature was a live tattoo

demonstration entitled "Walking Art".

7432 Wine and cheese: foto fun. Berkeley, CA:
     Exhibition invitation, 1979. English.

     AN: Invitation to an evening of
     photographic slides and prints and
     discussion by photographers Jose Romero and
     Maria Pinedo.

Pinto Art

7433 Angulo, Hector "H". [Untitled drawing].
     CARACOL, Vol. 4, no. 3 (November 1977), p.
     7.

7434 Carlson, Scott. Artist's mural puts a little
     beauty in prison cellblock. ST. PAUL
     DISPATCH, (December 5, 1978), p. East,1,3.
     English.

     AN: Biographical information on Chicano
     artist Paul Basquez and his eleven mural
     projects at Stillwater State Prison.

7435 DE COLORES. Vol. 2, no. 4 (1976), p. 1-68.
     English.

     AN: Photographs by Moises Medina, Jose
     Luis Sedano; drawings by Jerry Lujan,
     Gilbert "Sparky" Espinoza, Rebecca Polanco;
     paintings by John Herrera, Sonny Duran,
     Larry Martinez. Cover by Fernando Penalosa.

7436 Espinoza, Gilbert "Sparky". [Untitled
     drawing]. DE COLORES, Vol. 2, no. 4 (1976),
     p. 13.

7437 Espinoza, Gilbert "Sparky". [Untitled
     drawing]. DE COLORES, Vol. 2, no. 4 (1976),
     p. 14.

7438 Espinoza, Gilbert "Sparky". [Untitled
     drawing]. DE COLORES, Vol. 2, no. 4 (1976),
     p. 15.

7439 Espinoza, Gilbert "Sparky". [Untitled
     drawing]. DE COLORES, Vol. 2, no. 4 (1976),
     p. 16.

7440 Espinoza, Gilbert "Sparky". [Untitled
     drawing]. DE COLORES, Vol. 2, no. 4 (1976),
     p. 17.

7441 Espinoza, Gilbert "Sparky". [Untitled
     drawing]. DE COLORES, Vol. 2, no. 4 (1976),
     p. 18.

7442 Espinoza, Gilbert "Sparky". [Untitled
     drawing]. DE COLORES, Vol. 2, no. 4 (1976),
     p. 19.

7443 Espinoza, Gilbert "Sparky". [Untitled
     drawing]. DE COLORES, Vol. 2, no. 4 (1976),
     p. 20.

7444 Espinoza, Gilbert "Sparky". [Untitled
     drawing]. DE COLORES, Vol. 2, no. 4 (1976),
     p. 21.

7445 Espinoza, Gilbert "Sparky". [Untitled
     drawing]. DE COLORES, Vol. 2, no. 4 (1976),
     p. 22.

7446 Espinoza, Gilbert "Sparky". [Untitled
     drawing]. DE COLORES, Vol. 2, no. 4 (1976),
     p. 23.

7447 Espinoza, Gilbert "Sparky". [Untitled
     drawing]. DE COLORES, Vol. 2, no. 4 (1976),
     p. 25.

Pinto Art (cont.)

7448 Espinoza, Gilbert "Sparky". Untitled pen and ink drawings from la pinta [portfolio]. DE COLORES, Vol. 2, no. 4 (1976), p. [12]-25. English.

7449 Espinoza, Gilbert "Sparky". [Untitled pen and ink drawing from la pinta]. DE COLORES, Vol. 2, no. 4 (1976), p. 24.

7450 Frankenstein, Alfred. Prison's artist in residence. SAN FRANCISCO CHRONICLE, (May 5, 1978), p. 60. English.

AN: Review of the exhibition MUNDOS PERDIDOS, curated at the Galeria de la Raza by Leonard Castellanos. Show consisted of work by Castellanos and inmates at Lompoc Federal Correctional Institution near Santa Barbara. Documents a prison mural, tattoos and silkscreen prints with socially critical themes.

7451 Galeria de arte de Aztlan. AZTLAN (U.S. Penitentiary, Leavenworth, KA), Vol. 1, no. 2. English.

AN: Pictorial supplement with reproductions of pinto art by Manuel Aguilera, Jessie Hernandez, Ruben Estrella, Tomas Torres and Jose D. Marin. Many of these works were reproduced in other Chicano newspapers demonstrating the solidarity that existed in the Chicano movement inside and outside the prison walls.

7452 Galeria de la Raza/Studio 24, San Francisco, CA. Mundos perdidos/lost worlds. Exhibition invitation, 1978. English.

AN: Invitatiion to a multi-media exhibit from a cultural workshop inside Lompoc Federal Correctional Institution by Leonard Castellanos, National Endowment for the Arts Artist in Residence. Included are murals and tattoo documentation, and silkscreen posters.

7453 Lujan, Jerry. Vida y muerte [drawing]. DE COLORES, Vol. 2, no. 4 (1976), p. 54.

7454 Martinez, Larry. Hey lady [painting]. DE COLORES, Vol. 2, no. 4 (1976), p. 56.

7455 Martinez, Larry. Mestizo [painting]. DE COLORES, Vol. 2, no. 4 (1976), p. 57.

7456 Martinez, Larry. Pinturas/Paintings [portfolio]. DE COLORES, Vol. 2, no. 4 (1976), p. [55]-57.

7457 NEW ERA (U.S. Penitentiary, Leavenworth, KA). (Fall , Winter, 1970). English.

AN: Under the art direction of Ruben Estrella from San Antonio, Texas, NEW ERA, a prison cultural magazine also featured the caricatures and cartoons of Tone Briones from Laredo, Texas. Raul Salinas, poet from Austin, Texas was Associate Editor for both issues.

7458 Penalosa, Fernando. Los pintos de America [painting]. DE COLORES, Vol. 3, no. 1 (1976), p. Cover.

7459 Rodriguez, Patricia, ed. Selected readings on Chicano art. Berkeley, CA: Chicano Studies Department, University of California, 1977. English.

AN: Compendium of mechanically reproduced articles on Chicano and Latin American art prepared for Chicano Studies 130--Introduction to Chicano Art. Includes sections on Mexican Muralists in the U.S: Contemporary Chicano Art; Views on Chicano Art; Chicano Artists; Pinto Art: Raza Murals and Muralists; Plaqueasos (Graffiti); Chicana Artists: Art, Politics and the Community, Two Historical Examples: Cuba and Chile; Chicano Art Reproductions, 557 pp.

7460 Rodriguez, Pedro. Chicano art arising. PAPEL CHICANO, Vol. 1, no. 9 (December 21, 1971), p. 5. English.

AN: A concise formulation on the nature of Chicano Art. It arises from a new cultural formation influenced by Mexican and Anglo American cultural forms yet distinct from either. In visual terms, artists are reflecting and affirming this new cultural synthesis. Illustrated with reproductions of three oil paintings: GRITO DE LIBERTAD by Jose D. Marin, WOMAN IN BLUE by Manuel Aguilera, and ALEGORIA MEXICANA by Tomas Torres. All three are pinto artists from Leavenworth Penitentiary.

7461 Salinas, Raul. Nueva estrella en el horizonte. LA RAZA, Vol. 1, no. 2 (1970), p. 79. Spanish.

AN: Brief introduction to the work of painter Ruben Estrella, a native of San Antonio, who at the time was serving out his penalty at Leavenworth State Prison.

7462 Salinas, Raul. Nueva estrella en el horizonte. AZTLAN (U.S. Penitentiary, Leavenworth, KA), Vol. 1, no. 1 (May 5, 1970). English.

AN: Brief article on San Antonio artist Ruben Estrella who perfected his art within the walls of Leavenworth. Especially noted for his portraits, Estrella was illustrator of NEW ERA, the prison's literary journal. Illustrated with photograph of artist and four of his oil paintings.

7463 Salinas, Raul. Portrait of an artist. ENTRELINEAS, Vol. 1, no. 5-6 (October, December, 1971), p. 3-5. English.

AN: Biographical and artistic information on Ruben Estrella who developed as a "pinto" artist within Leavenworth Penitentiary.

7464 Tijerina, Jose A. Drawings by Jose A. Tijerina. CARACOL, Vol. 3, no. 2 (October 1976), p. 5.

7465 Tijerina, Jose A. [Untitled drawings]. CARACOL, Vol. 2, no. 12 (August 1976), p. 12.

Los Pintores de Aztlan [art group]

7466 Con Safo. San Antonio, TX: Pintores Chicanos de San Antonio, [ca. 1975]. English.

AN: Illustrated pamphlet issued by the San Antonio artists' group Con Safo. Includes a self-definition and a brief history of the group under the names El Grupo, Los Pintores de Aztlan, Los Pintores de la Nueva Raza, Con Safo (from 1967 on). Members include Jesse A. Almazan, Mel Casas, Jose Esquivel, Jose P. Garza, Cesar Augusto Martinez, Santos Martinez, Felipe Reyes, Roberto Rios, Jesus C. Trevino, and Vicente Velasquez.

Los Pintores de la Raza Nueva [art group]

7467 Con Safo. San Antonio, TX: Pintores Chicanos de San Antonio, [ca. 1975]. English.

AN: Illustrated pamphlet issued by the San Antonio artists' group Con Safo. Includes a self-definition and a brief history of the group under the names El Grupo, Los Pintores de Aztlan, Los Pintores de la Nueva Raza, Con Safo (from 1967 on). Members include Jesse A. Almazan, Mel Casas, Jose Esquivel, Jose P. Garza, Cesar Augusto Martinez, Santos Martinez, Felipe Reyes, Roberto Rios, Jesus C. Trevino, and Vicente Velasquez.

Placa
USE: Graffiti

PLANTING OF CULTURES [mural]

7468 Hale, David. Fresnan gets grant to create five story high mural. FRESNO BEE, (April 16, 1978), p. Forum, C4. English.

AN: Details on the awarding of a grant to John Sierra, Fresno artist, for the creation of what will be the largest piece of public art in that city. The artwork is a 6000 square foot mural titled THE PLANTING OF THE CULTURES. Article contains biographical information on the artist and presents goals of his mural project.

Plays
USE: Teatro

Plaza de La Raza, Los Angeles, CA

7469 Art wall for Plaza de la Raza March 28. EASTSIDE JRNL, (March 11, 1971), p. 1. English.

AN: On March 28, 1971, the art dealers of Los Angeles sponsored an"art walk" on "Gallery Row" on Melrose Place and La Cienega Blvds as a benefit for Plaza de la Raza, Mexican American cultural Center at Lincoln Park. Art dealers financed a limited edition lithograph by Mexican muralist David Alfaro Siqueiros. The print shows Ruben Salazar, slain Mexican American journalist and community leader with the famous figure from Siqueiros' mural "New Democracy" below it. Illustrated.

7470 Baciu, Joyce A. and Diaz, Katherine A. Margo Albert: a woman who gets things done = una mujer que realiza lo que desea. CAMINOS, Vol. 2, no. 5 (September 1981), p. 44-46. Bilingual.

AN: Mexican-born Margo Albert is a well-known Los Angeles, CA artist, dancer, and actress who has been most active on behalf of the Plaza de la Raza in East Los Angeles. This article describes her activities as Co-chairperson of the Los Angeles Bicentennial Committee. For Margo, the highlights of the celebration marking the 200th anniversary of the founding of Los Angeles, included a day-long Fiesta del Bicentenario; groundbreaking ceremonies for the Ruben Salazar Bicentennial Building; and the reception for an official delegation of charros, sponsored as a gift to the people of Los Angeles by the Mexican government.

7471 Blaine, John and Baker, Decia. Finding community through the arts: spotlight on cultural pluralism in Los Angeles. ARTS IN SOCIETY, Vol. 10, no. 1 (Spring, Summer, 1973), p. 125-138. English.

AN: Community arts expression by ethnic minorities is burgeoning everywhere, especially in Los Angeles. Various Black, Asian, and Chicano art administrators are interviewed, including Frank Lopez of Plaza de la Raza and Leonard Castellanos of Mechicano Art Center. Illustrated.

7472 Hebert, Ray. $10 million Latin cultural center: Lincoln Park to get new life. LOS ANGELES TIMES, (March 19, 1972), p. B-7. English.

AN: Report on the start of East Los Angeles cultural center Plaza de la Raza, intended as a showcase for Model Cities agency funding.

7473 Kim, Howard. Judithe Hernandez and a glimpse at the Chicana artist. SOMOS, (October, November, 1979), p. 6-11. English.

AN: Biographical information on Chicana artist Judithe Hernandez. Commentary on her contributions to Plaza de la Raza, Los Angeles Citywide Mural Project and her work as designer consultant to AZTLAN: INTERNATIONAL JOURNAL OF CHICANO RESEARCH. The article focuses on her mural activity, particularly two murals: EL MUNDO DE BARRIO SOTEL and LA CHICANA DE AZTLAN. Her personal art philosophy is presented in relation to Third World Art.

7474 Plaza de la Raza: place of the people. Brochure, n.d. English.

AN: Glossy promotional brochure for Plaza de la Raza, a cultural center in East Los Angeles. Brief history of the Plaza and photographs of its activities with children.

Plaza Mexico, San Antonio, TX

7475 Institute, Plaza Mexico unique cultural gift. SAN ANTONIO EXPRESS-NEWS, (June 19, 1972), p. 6-B. English.

AN: Pres. Luis Echeverria of Mexico dedicates the Mexican Cultural Institute and Plaza Mexico, which will house an extension campus of National University of Mexico, in San Antonio. Mexican artists will be brought in and the Institute has a permanent art gallery.

Poetry

7476 Burciaga, Jose Antonio and Zamora, Bernice. Restless serpents. Menlo Park, CA: Disenos Literarios, 1976. English.

AN: Includes numerous drawings by northern California artist and poet Jose Antonio Burciaga.

7477 De Leon, Nephtali. Coca cola dreams. Lubbock, TX: Trucha Publications, 1976. English.

AN: Poems and illustrations by Nephtali de Leon.

7478 Delgado, Abelardo "Lalo". Reflexiones. TEJIDOS, Vol. 2, no. 8 (Winter 1975), p. 26. Spanish.

Poetry (cont.)

7479 Galerias Paco, New York, NY. Consuelo
Gonzalez Amezcua - filigree art. Exhibition
announcement, n.d. English.

AN: Two-page exhibition announcement
illustrated with two examples of the Texas
artist's "filigree art" and a sample of her
poetry.

7480 Gamboa, Harry, Jr. Pistol whippersnapper.
R.A.M. COLLECTIVE, Vol. 2, no. 1 (June 1,
1977), p. 10-11. English.

AN: Photography and poetry by Harry
Gamboa, Jr., member of ASCO, Los Angeles.

7481 Garcia-Camarillo, Cecilio. Aire triste
[poetry in graphic design]. EL GRITO, Vol.
7, no. 3 (Spring 1974), p. 44. Spanish.

7482 Garcia-Camarillo, Cecilio. Frio [poetry in
graphic design]. EL GRITO, Vol. 7, no. 3
(Spring 1974), p. 41. English.

7483 Garcia-Camarillo, Cecilio. Hormiguero
[poetry in graphic design]. EL GRITO, Vol.
7, no. 3 (Spring 1974), p. 43. English.

7484 Garcia-Camarillo, Cecilio. Lluvia Marxista
[poetry in graphic design]. EL GRITO, Vol.
7, no. 3 (Spring 1974), p. 40. English.

7485 Garcia-Camarillo, Cecilio. Naturaleza es
cadaver [poetry in graphic design]. EL
GRITO, Vol. 7, no. 3 (Spring 1974), p. 45.
Spanish.

7486 Garcia-Camarillo, Cecilio. [Untitled poetry
in graphic design]. EL GRITO, Vol. 7, no. 3
(Spring 1974), p. 42. English.

7487 Montoya, Jose E. and Murguia, Alejandro. El
sol y los de abajo and other R.C.A.F. poems
/ oracion a la mano poderosa. San Francisco,
CA: Ediciones Pocho-Che, 1972. English.

AN: 10 illustrations by Sacramento, CA
artist Armando Cid.

7488 Moreno, Dorinda. La mujer y el arte.
TEJIDOS, Vol. 3, no. 1 (Spring 1976), p. 17.
Spanish.

AN: Brief introduction to the collection
of poems by Dorinda Moreno published in this
issue of TEJIDOS. She also dedicates the
collection by alluding to the significance
and influence of two artists: Frida Kahlo
and Rosaura Revueltas.

7489 Romero, Leo. Celso: poetry by Leo Romero,
New Mexico. Berkeley, CA: Tonatiuh
International, 1980. English.

AN: Book illustrated by poet-artist Leo
Romero from New Mexico. Drawings.

7490 Vallejo, Armando. Luna llena: ocho anos de
poesia chicana, 1971-1979. Santa Barbara,
CA: Ediciones Aztlan, 1979. English.

AN: Cover and illustrations Manuel
Unzueta of Santa Barbara, Calif.

Poets
    USE: Authors

Police Brutality

7491 Artist views murals as dialogue with
oppressed. HOUSTON POST, (June 13, 1979),
p. 3A. English.

AN: There are doubts that Houston
muralist Leo Tanguma's latest structural
mural about police brutality will ever see
the light of day. Painted on three pointed
plywood panels, it was originally destined
for Moody Park. Other Tanguma murals have
been painted over. Illustrated.

7492 Chapple, Paul. FV [Fountain Valley] wall
mural stirs contention. THE REGISTER,
(December 29, 1974), p. A3. English.

AN: Artist Sergio O'Cadiz has included a
panel showing gas-masked police dragging off
a Chicano youth. The panel has caused
controversy in Fountain Valley, CA; police
object to the image.

7493 Chapple, Paul. Mural, graffiti painters wage
endurance contest in F.V. [Fountain Valley].
THE REGISTER, (December 4, 1975), p. B5.
English.

AN: Mexican-born architect and designer
Sergio O'Cadiz, with a team, paints a 600
foot mural in Colonia Juarez, an older
section of Fountain Valley in Orange County,
CA. Local police objected to a scene showing
police brutality. White paint was hurled at
this panel one night, and the mural was
constantly attacked by vandals. Illustrated.

7494 Gamboa, Harry, Jr. He threw a rock at me
[drawing]. REGENERACION, Vol. 1, no. 9
(1970), p. 12-13.

7495 Gamboa, Harry, Jr. Mexican Murder Comix
presents Genocide Patrol [drawing].
REGENERACION, Vol. 2, no. 1 (1971), p.
12-13. English.

7496 Leo Tanguma and Houston murals. NATIONAL
MURALS NETWORK COMMUNITY NEWSLETTER,
(Spring 1980), p. 11. English.

AN: Report on environmental and police
brutality murals in Houston, Texas.
Illustrated.

7497 Luna, Benjamin R. [Chicanos and police clash
- a drawing]. REGENERACION, Vol. 1, no. 6
(1970), p. 10-11. English.

7498 Ramirez de Robe, Jose "Controll". Police
scoreboard [drawing]. CARACOL, Vol. 4, no. 2
(October 1977), p. 20.

Political Ideology

7499 Bejarano, William. Utah Chicano forum.
CHISMEARTE, Vol. 1, no. 1 (Fall 1976), p.
9-10. English.

AN: Report on the CULTURE, ARTE Y MEDIOS
DE COMUNICACION workshop at the Third
National Chicano Forum at the University of
Utah, Salt Lake City. The panel, moderated
by artist Carmen Lomas Garza, set up a plan
of action for the visual, literary,
performing arts and the mass media which
included planning a national conference to
discuss cultural work, financial support,
recognition and moral support, among other
issues.

Political Ideology (cont.)

7500 Garcia, Rupert. The politics of popular art.
CHISMEARTE, Vol. 2, no. 1 (Summer 1978), p.
2-4. English.

AN: Defines and discusses the terms
"Popular Art", "Mass Art", and "Folk Art"
and gives examples of their correct and
incorrect usages.

Political Participation
USE: Voter Turnout

Political Prisoners

7501 De Lappe, Pele. Saga of Rupert Garcia's
poster: from pen to UN. PEOPLE'S WORLD, Vol.
44, no. 28 (July 11, 1981), p. 10. English.

AN: Desiring to produce a poster on
Nelson Mandela and South African political
prisoners, San Francisco artist Rupert
Garcia, appealed for support to the African
National Congress, and the Liberation
Support Movement. The United Nations Center
Against Apartheid provided a grant for
production, indicating it should be
distributed free. Illustrated.

Political Refugees

7502 Mario Falcon. CHISMEARTE, Vol. 2, no. 1
(Summer 1978), p. 29. Spanish.

AN: Mexican muralist Mario Falcon, who
has painted murals in Long Beach and
Wilmington (Los Angeles, County), is a
political exile in the U. S. Support is
asked to prevent his return to Mexico.
Illustrated.

A POLITICAL RENAISSANCE [film]

7503 Rivera, Humberto R. Film notes. CHISMEARTE,
Vol. 1, no. 2 (Winter, Spring, 1977), p.
20-24. English.

AN: Summary of films produced by and/or
about Chicanos for cinema and television.
Includes REALIDADES (TV) by David Sandoval,
Rudy Vargas, Luis Torres, Jose Luis Ruiz,
Antonio Reyes; A POLITICAL RENAISSANCE from
the LA RAZA series (TV) by Moctezuma
Esparza; CHILDREN OF THE STATE by Andres
Markovits, Richard Trubo, Frank Christopher
(film); LA RAZA UNIDA (released as RAICES DE
SANGRE) by Jesus Salvador Trevino (Mexican
film by a Chicano); CHULAS FRONTERAS (film)
by Les Blank; THE MURALS OF EAST LOS
ANGELES, A MUSEUM WITHOUT WALLS by Humberto
R. Rivera and Heather R. Howell.
Announcement for the National Latino Media
Coalition.

Politics

7504 Garcia, Rupert. "This mural is not for the
bankers. It's for the people". EL TECOLOTE,
Vol. 4, no. 6 (June 10, 1974), p. 11+.
English.

AN: On June 4, 1974, a mural by eight
Mission District artists was unveiled inside
the Bank of America on 23rd and Mission Sts.
in San Francisco. Roberto Vargas, Bay Area
poet was prevented from reading his poetry
during the mural inauguration. Finally
allowed to read, Vargas compared this event
to one in the 1930s when Diego Rivera
painted a mural for the Pacific Stock
Exchange Building in San Francisco. Includes
commentary by community activists about
incident. Illustrated by photograph of

Roberto Vargas reading in front of the
controversial mural.

7505 Garcia-Camarillo, Cecilio and Rosas, Carlos.
Platicando con Carlos Rosas. RAYAS, Vol. 1,
no. 6 (November, December, 1978), p. 12, 11.
Spanish.

AN: Muralist Carlos Rosas painted murals
in Boulder and Denver, Colorado; Milwaukee,
Wisconsin, and El Paso, Texas. Commentary on
cross ethnic murals, views on art in
socialist countries, influence of Mexican
murals and information on his personal
preocupation as a politically engaged
artist.

7506 Lopez Oliva, Manuel. Proyeccion chicana en
RAICES DE SANGRE. CINE CUBANO, (1981), p.
75-80. Spanish.

AN: A Latin American view of Jesus
Salvador Trevino's 1976 film RAICES DE
SANGRE, particularly its concern with the
exploitation by U.S. multinationals of
Mexicans and Chicanos on both sides of the
border. The author notes Trevino's tendency
to relate Chicano culture and problems to
continental and world problems of workers.
Illustrated.

7507 Martinez, Cesar Augusto. Arte chicano.
CARACOL, Vol. 1, no. 6 (February 1975), p.
3. English.

AN: Thoughts on the form, function and
meaning of Chicano Art. Stylistically, it is
seen as a fusion. It is dynamic, expressing
multiple political sentiments and has an
irreverent attitude towards dominant
culture. Front cover of issue is a black and
white reproduction of a silkscreen print by
Amado Maurilio Pena, Jr.

7508 Rodriguez, Patricia, ed. Selected readings
on Chicano art. Berkeley, CA: Chicano
Studies Department, University of
California, 1977. English.

AN: Compendium of mechanically
reproduced articles on Chicano and Latin
American art prepared for Chicano Studies
130--Introduction to Chicano Art. Includes
sections on Mexican Muralists in the U.S:
Contemporary Chicano Art; Views on Chicano
Art; Chicano Artists; Pinto Art: Raza Murals
and Muralists; Plaqueasos (Graffiti);
Chicana Artists: Art, Politics and the
Community, Two Historical Examples: Cuba and
Chile; Chicano Art Reproductions, 557 pp.

7509 Symposium on the politics of the arts:
minorities and the arts. ARTS IN SOCIETY,
Vol. 10, no. 3 (Fall , Winter, 1973), p.
66-73. English.

AN: One panel from the Colloquium
"Politics of the Arts" presented by the UCLA
Management in the Arts Program, Graduate
School of Management, 1972, included, among
others, Leonard Castellanos of Mechicano Art
Center, and James Woods of Studio Watts
Workshop, both in Los Angeles. A major topic
was how minorities dealing with the
corporate capitalist structure can keep
control of their art programs.

Politics (cont.)

7510 Testimonios de Latinoamerica. LA PRENSA SAN DIEGO, (October 26, 1979), p. 3. Spanish.

AN: Announcement of an exhibit at the Centro Cultural de la Raza, San Diego, "Testimonios de Latino America" and "America en la mira," political graphics organized by Mexican artist Felipe Ehrenberg and also shown at the Los Angeles Contemporary Exhibitions gallery (LACE).

Pollution

7511 Cross, Miriam Dungan. A satirical brutal view of pollution. THE TRIBUNE (Oakland, CA), (January 25, 1970), p. 26-EN. English.

AN: (Includes reproduction of Rupert Garcia's silkscreen print "D.D.T." dated 1969).

Ponce, Art

7512 Art Gallery, California State University, Long Beach and Lujan, Gilbert Sanchez "Magu". El arte del pocho. Exhibit brochure, October 1968. English.

AN: Information about Southern California artists John Deheras, Marcus Villagran, Roberto de la Rocha, Santos Zuniga, Crispin Gonzales, Richard Martinez, Jesus Gutierrez, Ed Oropeza, Pete Mendez, David Ramirez, Gilbert Sanchez Lujan, Willie Hernandez, Art Ponce, Carmen Tostado, Al Almeida, David Ceja, Robert E. Chavez, Thomas A. Ferriera. All art students, graduates, or faculty.

Ponce de Leon, Michael

7513 The Mexican Museum, San Francisco, CA and Quirarte, Jacinto. 17 artists: Hispano/Mexican-American/Chicano. Exhibition catalog, 1977. English.

AN: Catalog of an exhibit for artists Emilio Aguirre, Consuelo Gonzalez Amezcua, Al Barela, Pedro Cervantez, Edward Chavez, Antonio Garcia, Louis Gutierrez, Harry Louie, Vincent Perez, Michael Ponce de Leon, Eugenio Quesada, Gustavo Rivera, Peter Rodriguez, Alex Sanchez, Darryl Sapien, Rudy Trevino, Manuel Villamor. Illustrated.

7514 S.A. site for National Symposium on Mexican American Art. CHICANO TIMES, Vol. 4, no. 30 (November 9, 1973), p. 5. English.

AN: Held at Trinity University, the Symposium discussed such issues as, creative evolution, art education, artistic relationships to Mexico and the evolution of Mexican American art in the California barrios. Participating artists included Rudy Trevino, Mel Casas, Octavio Medellin, Antonio Garcia, Carmen Garza, Esteban Villa, Jose Montoya, Ernesto Palomino, Michael Ponce de Leon, Luis Jimenez and Eugenio Quesada.

PORTRAIT OF MEXICO [mural]

7515 Garcia, Rupert. Echos de la Mision - Alfaro Siqueiros (1896-1974). EL TECOLOTE, Vol. 4, no. 3 (February 22, 1974), p. 11. English.

AN: Biographical and artistic trajectory of Mexican artist David Alfaro Siqueiros. Artist painted three murals in Southern California in 1932 (MEETING IN THE STREET and TROPICAL AMERICA were done in Los Angeles on the walls of the Chouinard School of Art and the Plaza Art Center, Olvera Street area respectively. The third mural PORTRAIT OF MEXICO was privately commissioned in Santa Monica). The three California murals deal with themes of censorship, racism, colonialism, capitalism, and imperialism. Article suggests that Raza artists are much influenced by the ideas and work of Siqueiros. Illustrated with Rupert Garcia's silkscreen poster SIQUEIROS.

Posada, Jose Guadalupe

7516 Avalos, David. A pure Mexican accent: the popular engravings of Jose Guadalupe Posada. PROCEEDINGS OF THE PACIFIC COAST COUNCIL ON LATIN AMER STUDIES, Vol. 7, (1980, 1981), p. 123-138. English.

AN: As a documentor of injustice and oppression, Posada, 19th century Mexican engraver, is a master who inspires Chicano artists. Appreciation for his art has been expressed by Sacramento artist Jose E. Montoya. Arsacio Vanegas Arroyo, grandson of Posada's publisher, has made his private collection available to Chicano cultural centers, including El Centro Cultural de la Raza, San Diego. Illustrated.

7517 Camacho, Eduardo. Por los cien anos de la fundacion de su editorial: inauguraran hoy en San Diego la exposicion 'Homenaje a Posada, Manilla y Vanegas Arroyo'. EXCELSIOR, (February 14, 1980). Spanish.

AN: Announcing the exhibit of 19th Century Mexican engravers Jose Guadalupe Posada and Manuel Manilla, with publisher Antonio Vanegas Arroyo, at the Centro Cultural de la Raza and Southwestern College, of San Diego, CA.

7518 El Centro Cultural de La Raza, San Diego, CA. One hundred year anniversary: Jose Guadalupe Posada, Antonio Vanegas Arroyo. Exhibition invitation, 1980. English.

AN: Invitation to an exhibition of Mexican engravers Posada and Manuel Manilla and an homage to their publisher. Also, a "Chicano Tribute to Jose Guadalupe Posada," with contemporary works influenced by Posada. At the Centro, and at Southwestern College in Chula Vista.

7519 Galeria de la Raza/Studio 24, San Francisco, CA. Calacas huesudas. Exhibition brochure, 1980.

AN: Exhibition of Chicano artists for El Dia de los Muertos with brochure using text adapted from POSADA'S MEXICO, edited by Ron Tyler, Library of Congress, Washington, D.C., 1979. The Galeria exhibit was curated by Kate Connell, Maria Pinedo and Galeria staff.

Posada, Jose Guadalupe (cont.)

7520 Montoya, Jose E. and Carrillo, John M.
Posada: the man and his art. A comparative
analysis of Jose Guadalupe Posada and the
current Chicano art movement as they apply
toward social and cultural change: a visual
resource unit for Chicano education.
Unpublished thesis, 1975. English.

AN: Includes a historical background of
19th century Mexican engraver Posada, the
significance of his work, a background of
Chicano art, and the influence of Posada and
the "calavera" on Chicano art. The unit
includes 227 slides of Posada and other
Mexican artists; and slides of Chicano
artists using the calavera theme.

7521 Rangel, Jesus. Heirs of Jose Posada:
revolution lives in Chicano art. SAN DIEGO
UNION, (February 24, 1980), p. D6. English.

AN: 19th century Mexican engraver Jose
Guadalupe Posada has been an inspiration to
Chicano artists. Along with two exhibits of
his work, the Centro Cultural de la Raza is
also showing calavera (skeleton) images by
Chicano artists: skull-masks from the Teatro
Campesino, a print by Amalia Mesa-Baines of
Frida Kahlo, and a collaged box by Jose
Antonio Burciaga. Illustration: Salvador
Roberto Torres work.

7522 San Francisco Museum of Modern Art, San
Francisco, CA and Marra, Patricia. Day of
the dead. Exhibition catalog, 1980. English.

AN: Broadside announcement in the manner
of Jose Gudalupe Posada for an exhibit of
prints by Posada and an altar by Amalia Mesa
-Baines and Friends. Text presents customs
and traditions for celebrating the Day of
the Dead in Mexico and among the Chicano
community.

7523 The Tortuga paints a new mural. CHISMEARTE,
Vol. 2, no. 1 (Summer 1978), p. 12-13.
English.

AN: Black and white details of new
indoor mural painted at the Gilroy's
Recreation Center.

Posters

7524 Albright, Thomas. San Francisco: the force
of universals. ART NEWS MAGAZINE, Vol. 77,
no. 6 (Summer 1978), p. 174. English.

AN: Review of Rupert Garcia pastel show
at the San Francisco Museum of Modern Art.
Reviewer suggests he is one of the very few
real artists to emerge from the "unfortunate
genre" of poster art. His images are highly
charged: political prisoners, corpses,
revolutionary martyrs.

7525 And/Or Gallery, Seattle, WA. Artistas de
Aztlan. Exhibition announcement, 1975.
English.

AN: Exhibition announcement for an
important exhibit of Northwest Chicano art.
Co-sponsored by MEChA and the Chicano
Studies Program at the University of
Washington, the exhibit presented works by
Emilio Aguayo, Danny Desiga, Ricardo
Aguirre, Ramiro Benavidez, Elma Herada,
Pedro Rodriguez and others. A selection of
posters by Armando Cid of the R.C.A.F. group
from Sacramento, California was also
presented. Concurrently, at the Heny Gallery
of the University of Washington, Esteban

Villa presented a one-man show.

7526 Arnold, Frank. Posters and society. PEOPLE'S
WORLD, Vol. 23, no. 2. English.

AN: An exhibit at the San Francisco
Museum of Art curated by Rolando Castellon.
The article focuses on the posters of Xavier
Viramontes and Rupert Garcia of San
Francisco.

7527 Canto al Pueblo Steering Committee. Canto al
Pueblo [poster]. CARACOL, Vol. 4, no. 9 (May
1978), p. 23.

7528 Contemporary Arts Museum, Houston, TX and
Martinez, Santos G., Jr. Mexican movie
posters. Exhibition invitation, 1979.
English.

AN: Invitation to an exhibit of posters
primarily from the collecttion of Enrique
Flores and Xavier Gorena of Xochil Art
Center, Mission, Texas. Martinez considers
the posters monumental, with expressive
qualities that have influenced Chicano
poster makers like the Royal Chicano Air
Force, and Rupert Garcia, and Texas artists
like Luis Jimenez, Jesse Trevino and Cesar
Martinez. One illustration. Introduction by
guest curator Santos G. Martinez, Jr. (See
Rupert Garcia's essay in the exhibition
catalog: POSTERS FROM THE GOLDEN AGE OF
MEXICAN CINEMA, for another point of view).

7529 Corcoran Gallery of Art, Washington, D.C.
Images of an era: the American poster
1945-75. Washington, D.C.: Corcoran Gallery
of Art, 1976. English.

AN: Uncredited poster [La Raza
Silkscreen Center, San Francisco],
(centerfold). Posters by Rupert Garcia,
Linda Lucero, and Ralph Maradiaga, all of
San Francisco, CA. Introduction by John
Garriga. Essays by Margaret Cogswell, Milton
Glaser, Dore Ashton, Alan Gowens.

7530 Cortez, Carlos. Ricardo Flores-Magon
[graphic]. CARACOL, Vol. 5, no. 2 (October
1978), p. BACK COVER. Spanish.

7531 De Lappe, Pele. Saga of Rupert Garcia's
poster: from pen to UN. PEOPLE'S WORLD, Vol.
44, no. 28 (July 11, 1981), p. 10. English.

AN: Desiring to produce a poster on
Nelson Mandela and South African political
prisoners, San Francisco artist Rupert
Garcia, appealed for support to the African
National Congress, and the Liberation
Support Movement. The United Nations Center
Against Apartheid provided a grant for
production, indicating it should be
distributed free. Illustrated.

7532 El dia de los muertos [poster]. CARACOL,
Vol. 4, no. 7 (March 1978), p. BACK COVER.
Bilingual.

7533 Feliz Navidad y prospero ano nuevo [poster].
CARACOL, Vol. 3, no. 4 (December 1976), p.
FRNT COVER.

Posters (cont.)

7534 Gala evening at OAS. NUESTRO, Vol. 5, no. 7 (October 1981), p. 21. English.

AN: Brief description of "Salute to Hispanic Arts" held as part of Hispanic Heritage Week festivities in Washington, D.C. Special guest at the affair was Amado Pena who was there to be recognized and to unveil his work LA FAMILIA which was used on the posters announcing Hispanic Heritage Week nationwide.

7535 Galeria de la Raza/Studio 24, San Francisco, CA and Franco, Jean. Juan Fuentes y Rupert Garcia: posters, drawings, prints. Exhibition catalog, 1975. English.

AN: Catalog of an exhibit. Illustrated with drawings and posters.

7536 Galeria de la Raza/Studio 24, San Francisco, CA. Mexican film poster (1943-71): an exhibition/exhibicion de fotos/cartelones del cine mexicano. Exhibition invitation, 1971. English.

AN: Invitation to an exhibit.

7537 Galeria de la Raza/Studio 24, San Francisco, CA. Mundos perdidos/lost worlds. Exhibition invitation, 1978. English.

AN: Invitatiion to a multi-media exhibit from a cultural workshop inside Lompoc Federal Correctional Institution by Leonard Castellanos, National Endowment for the Arts Artist in Residence. Included are murals and tattoo documentation, and silkscreen posters.

7538 Galeria de la Raza/Studio 24, San Francisco, CA. Por Chile: silkscreens from President Allende cultural campaign. Exhibition invitation, [1973]. English.

AN: Invitation to an exhibit: the first U.S. showing of Chilean posters.

7539 Galeria de la Raza/Studio 24, San Francisco, CA and Garcia, Rupert. Posters from the golden age of Mexican cinema. Exhibition catalog, 1979. English.

AN: The Galeria's second exhibit of Mexican movie posters features those of the 1940s and early 1950s (in 1971, the exhibit covered 1943-1971) from the collection of Enrique Flores, owner of the Rio Theatre, Mission, Texas, and the Xochil Art Center. Garcia's essay includes a history of Mexican cinema, and the mythologizing period of the "Golden Age" reflected in the posters which promoted movie-consumership. One illustration. (See Santos G. Martinez, Jr.'s essay in the exhibition catalog: MEXICAN MOVIE POSTERS, for another point of view).

7540 Galeria de la Raza/Studio 24, San Francisco, CA and Garcia, Rupert. La Raza Silkscreen Center: "Images of a community", an exhibit of silkscreen posters and graphic works from 1971 to 1979. Exhibition catalog, 1979. English.

AN: First large scale retrospective exhibit of the La Raza Silkscreen Center's eight years of postermaking. Includes list of 90 artists.

7541 Garcia, Rupert. Rupert Garcia. TRA, Vol. 2, no. 6 (1975), p. 20-27. English.

AN: Statement by the artist and portfolio of nine silkscreen posters, five in color.

7542 Kagawa, Paul and Rilkin, Scott. La Raza Silkscreen Center, in step with the Mission. ARTS BIWEEKLY, no. 44 (March 15, 1977). English.

AN: Concise history and goals of the Silkscreen Center: the Center's values are reflected in the collective process that produces the posters, as well as in the collective style of the art; in the emphasis upon education. The Center trains apprentices, educates the student community about the silkscreen process and Raza history and produces posters that have an information impact. The Silkscreen Center is part of a coalition of La Raza Information Center, Tutorial Center, and Centro Legal which evolved from La Raza En Accion Social founded in 1970.

7543 Lucero, Linda. Compositions from my kitchen/composiciones de mi cocina: an international cookbook. San Francisco, CA: La Raza Graphic Center, 1981. English.

AN: International recipes illustrated with drawings and a poster by Linda Lucero, as well as other artists.

7544 Malaquias Montoya. ARTE, (Fall 1977). English.

AN: Interview with northern California printmaker, painter and muralist, Malaquias Montoya. He discusses his life, his dedication to Chicano art, his resistance to the institutionalization of the Chicano struggle and its art, their cooptation by the establishment. He says he transcended nationalism at one period and became a Third World internationalist. Four drawings and two posters reproduced.

7545 Marta. National Chicano/Latino Conference on Immigration and Public Policy [poster]. CARACOL, Vol. 4, no. 2 (October 1977), p. BACK COVER. Bilingual.

7546 Martinez, Cesar Augusto. Don Pedrito Jaramillo [woodcut]. CARACOL, Vol. 3, no. 4 (December 1976), p. Bk Cover.

7547 Martinez, Cesar Augusto. Texas farm workers [poster]. CARACOL, Vol. 3, no. 9 (May 1977), p. 24.

7548 Martinez, Oscar. Cartel [poster]. REVISTA CHICANO-RIQUENA, Vol. 9, no. 4 (Fall 1981), p. Cover, 4. Bilingual.

7549 Mechicano art posters. CON SAFOS, no. 8 (1972), p. 38. Bilingual.

7550 Montoya, Malaquias. [Bakke (poster)]. EL TECOLOTE LITERARY MAGAZINE, Vol. 2, no. 2 (July 1981), p. 4.

7551 Neumeier, Marty. Ignacio Gomez. COMMUNICATION ARTS MAGAZINE, Vol. 21, no. 6 (January, February, 1980), p. 78-87. English.

AN: Story on commercial designer and illustrator Ignacio Gomez of Los Angeles which describes his background, education and life style. 17 full-color illustrations of his art work, including the ZOOT SUIT poster for the Mark Taper Forum play.

Posters (cont.)

7552 New co-op in San Cristobal. GRITO DEL NORTE, Vol. 3, no. 8 (July 5, 1970), p. 13. English.

AN: Details formation of the San Cristobal Valley Arts Inc., a community corporation formed to train people in a silkscreen business venture. Aiming to use expressive forms as a source of economic development, the corporation published and distributed a line of Chicano silkscreen posters. Illustrated by three posters, WE SHALL ENDURE, SOMOS AZTLAN, and TAOS PUEBLO.

7553 Ohlone College Art Department Gallery, Fremont, CA. Impressions: a California print invitational. Exhibition catalog, 1976. English.

AN: Exhibition catalog includes commentary on the artist and reproduction of two silkscreen posters "El Grito Rebelde" and "The Bicentennial Art Poster" by Rupert Garcia.

7554 Ojeda, Jay. Galeria de la Raza--art for the community. SAN FRANCISCO PROGRESS, (March 24, 1972). English.

AN: Analysis of group exhibition by thirty-four Raza artists. Commentary on the work of Latin American artists Consuelo Mendez, Rolando Castellon, and Chicano artists Rupert Garcia, Chuy Campusano and Peter Rodriguez.

7555 Orozco, Sylvia and Trevino, Jose. Trevino's arte interprets el mundo Chicano. PARA LA GENTE, Vol. 1, no. 10 (May 1978), p. 7-9. English.

AN: Interview with Jose Trevino of Austin and his artist wife, Modesta. Reproduction and discussion of four works. Centerspread reproduction of a Trevino poster, part of a set of 10 designed for bilingual classrooms.

7556 Pena, Amado Maurilio, Jr. Chicano gothic [poster]. TEJIDOS, Vol. 1, no. 2 (Spring 1974), p. 38. English.

7557 Pena, Amado Maurilio, Jr. Hembra chicana [poster]. TEJIDOS, Vol. 1, no. 2 (Spring 1974), p. 30. Spanish.

7558 Pena, Amado Maurilio, Jr. Migrante, hermano de la tierra hijo de la desesperacion [poster]. TEJIDOS, Vol. 1, no. 2 (Spring 1974), p. 16. Spanish.

7559 Pena, Amado Maurilio, Jr. Wanted, el rinche [poster]. TEJIDOS, Vol. 1, no. 2 (Spring 1974), p. 7. Bilingual.

7560 Posters by Ignacio Gomez: in full color suitable for framing. CAMINOS, (May 1981), p. 49. English.

AN: Six full-color posters on Latino subjects by illustrator Gomez advertised for sale. The best-known is Gomez's poster for ZOOT SUIT, a play by Luis Valdez.

7561 Pro Arts Gallery, Oakland, CA. Si se puede! We can do it!: an exhibition of silkscreen prints and posters by Malaquias Montoya. Exhibition announcement, [1981]. English.

AN: Announcement of a traveling exhibit of prints and posters in Oakland, California. Illustrated.

7562 La Raza Silk Screen Center. TRA, no. 4 (1973), p. 18-25. English.

AN: Manifesto and portfolio of four posters by the San Francisco Center.

7563 Royal Chicano Air Force (RCAF), Sacramento, CA. [RCAF posters]. CHISMEARTE, no. 1 (Fall 1976), p. 42-44.

7564 San Francisco Museum of Modern Art, San Francisco, CA and Castellon, Rolando. Posters and society. Exhibition catalog, 1975. English.

AN: 26 artists exhibiting public announcement and social political commentary posters. Includes 14 Bay Area and Sacramento, Calif. Latino artists.

7565 Stofflet-Santiago, Mary. The fifth sun: esthetic quality versus curatorial intent. ARTWEEK, Vol. 8, no. 37 (November 5, 1977), p. 6. English.

AN: Review of the exhibit THE FIFTH SUN at the University Art Museum in Berkeley, Calif., curated by Ralph Maradiaga of the Galeria de la Raza. It contains folk art, and posters by Chicano artists Maradiaga, Rupert Garcia, Juan Fuentes, mural studies by Graciela Carrillo and Mike Rios, ceramics by Anna de Leon, an altar by Amalia Mesa-Bains, and mural drawings by Mexican muralists. The writer criticizes the uneven quality of the show, but encourages better ones in the future. Illustrated.

7566 El Taller, Inc., Chicago, IL and Movimiento Artistico Chicano (MARCH), Chicago, IL. Skyjacked: screenprinted posters from California by the Royal Chicano Air Force (R.C.A.F.), 1980. Exhibition invitation, 1980. English.

AN: Invitation to an exhibit at the El Taller Gallery, co-sponsored by MARCH. Illustrated with a print by San Francisco artist Xavier Viramontes.

7567 Tapia, Ludy. Montoya and the art of survival. LA VOZ DEL PUEBLO, Vol. 3, no. 5 (June 1972), p. 6. English.

AN: Profile of San Francisco Bay area poster maker and artist Malaquias Montoya, who first became involved in the Chicano movement in San Jose working with MASC and EL MACHETE paper. In Berkeley (1968), he met Esteban Villa and, with others, formed the Mexican American Liberation Art Front (MALAF). Montoya is against elitism influencing Chicano art, and is concerned with commercialization of Chicano art and artists. Illustrated.

7568 University Art Museum, Berkeley, CA. The Fifth Sun: Contemporary/Traditional Chicano & Latino Art. Exhibition catalog, 1977. English.

AN: Catalog of exhibit including 45 artists of northern California. Texts deal with Mexican muralists, Mujeres Muralistas & other muralists, posters, the Chicano art movement, altars, La Raza Silkscreen Center, Galeria de la Raza, the Mexican Museum, the Sacramento Centro de Artistas Chicanos/RCAF. Mural maps of S.F. Bay Area and Sacramento. Many illustrations.

Posters (cont.)

7569 Valley artist is basking in rosy glory.
     ARIZONA REPUBLIC, (October 14, 1981), p.
     Extra,11. English.

     AN: Rudy M. Fernandez has been invited
     to the White House, selected to create a
     Festival poster, included in a group show of
     emerging artists. He is presently working on
     a series called TROPHIES featuring roses,
     and sometimes trout--both trophies of sorts.
     Illustrated.

7570 Work of Southwest artist sings to soul,
     heart. NUESTRO, Vol. 5, no. 7 (October
     1981), p. 57-61. English.

     AN: Brief profile of Laredo-born Texas
     artist Amado Pena who designed the first
     conmemorative poster for the Congressional
     Hispanic Caucus' observance of National
     Hispanic Heritage Week. The poster is
     reproduced on the cover. The article
     includes full-color illustrations.

POSTERS AND SOCIETY [exhibit]

7571 Arnold, Frank. Posters and society. PEOPLE'S
     WORLD, Vol. 23, no. 2. English.

     AN: An exhibit at the San Francisco
     Museum of Art curated by Rolando Castellon.
     The article focuses on the posters of Xavier
     Viramontes and Rupert Garcia of San
     Francisco.

Precolumbian Art

7572 Henry Gallery, University of Washington,
     Seattle, WA and Ybarra-Frausto, Tomas. Arte
     prehispanico, arte popular. Exhibit Catalog,
     19. English.

     AN: Exhibition catalog for an exhibit
     prepared almost entirely by students from
     the School of Art with assistance from MEChA
     and members of the faculty of the School of
     Art. The pre-Columbian sections presented
     objects from sites in Mexico and Peru from
     pre-classic, classic and post-classic
     periods. The arte popular sections exhibited
     wares from craft centers in Mexico, Peru,
     Ecuador and Guatemala. Includes statement by
     Tomas Ybarra-Frausto on the relevance of
     this exhibition to the cultural identity of
     Chicanos in the Pacific Northwest.

7573 Ochoa, Victor Orozco. [Untitled
     photographs]. MAIZE, Vol. 1, no. 3 (Spring
     1978), p. 45-47,50+. English.

7574 Xochipilli Macuilxochitl [graphic].
     REGENERACION, Vol. 1, no. 9 (1970), p. 22.

Precolumbian Images

7575 Creations by Cruz. Color brochure, n.d.
     English.

     AN: Color brochure of genre-like figures
     produced for sale by Los Angeles sculptor
     Manuel Cruz in hydro-stone. The figures,
     which run from 3" to 12" high depict images
     from Aztec legends to Pachucos, Brown
     Berets, and hippies.

7576 Evans, Marylin. Tucson barrio janitor
     designs authentic Aztec costumes. LA PRENSA,
     Vol. 1, no. 6 (October 11, 1978). English.

     AN: Rogelio Valdovin, self-taught artist
     from Tucson, Arizona feels he has received a
     spiritual call to create authentic

Pre-Columbian costumes and regalia.
Specializing in Aztec costumes, the artist
works with metal, beads, feathers, leather
and many fabrics and fibers in designing and
making his creations. He exhibits them as a
form of body art.

7577 Ochoa, Victor Orozco. [Resistencia!
     (drawing)]. MAIZE, Vol. 2, no. 2 (Winter
     1979), p. 61. Spanish.

7578 Pazos, Antonio. [Untitled drawing]. LLUEVE
     TLALOC, no. 5 (1978), p. Cover.

7579 Pazos, Antonio. [Untitled graphic]. LLUEVE
     TLALOC, no. 6 (1979), p. Cover.

7580 Penalosa, Fernando. [Untitled graphic]. DE
     COLORES, Vol. 2, no. 4 (1976), p. Cover.

7581 Trevino, Jose. Devocion al sol [drawing].
     TEJIDOS, Vol. 4, no. 2 (Summer 1977), p. 25.
     Bilingual.

7582 Wood carving art. EASTSIDE JRNL, (January
     7, 1971), p. 2. English.

     AN: Two photographs and commentary on
     woodcarver Roberto H. Rodriguez on the
     occasion of his one man show at the East Los
     Angeles Library. Illustrated work shows
     pre-Columbian motifs.

PRISMA

7583 Yarbro-Bejarano, Yvonne. Resena de revistas
     chicanas: problemas y tendencias, Part I. LA
     PALABRA, Vol. 2, no. 1 (Spring 1980), p.
     76-85. Spanish.

     AN: Review of five Chicano magazines of
     California discussing their contents, both
     literary and artistic, taking a critical
     attitude toward both. The five are FUEGO DE
     AZTLAN, VORTICE, PRISMA, MAIZE, and MANGO.

Prisoners of War
     USE: Political Prisoners

Prisons

7584 Frankenstein, Alfred. Prison's artist in
     residence. SAN FRANCISCO CHRONICLE, (May 5,
     1978), p. 60. English.

     AN: Review of the exhibition MUNDOS
     PERDIDOS, curated at the Galeria de la Raza
     by Leonard Castellanos. Show consisted of
     work by Castellanos and inmates at Lompoc
     Federal Correctional Institution near Santa
     Barbara. Documents a prison mural, tattoos
     and silkscreen prints with socially critical
     themes.

Proverbios
     USE: Dichos

Proverbs
     USE: Dichos

Publicize
     USE: Advertising

Pueblo
     USE: Barrios

Pueblo, CO

7585 Chicano muralists maintain traditions. LA
     CUCARACHA, (November 20, 1979), p. 7.
     English.

     AN: Introduction to Chicano muralism in
     Pueblo and comparison to the Mexican mural
     movement from which it draws inspiration. 20
     murals painted from 1977 to 1979. The
     muralists include Bernardo Duran, Juan
     Espinoza, Miguel "Freeloader" Garcia, Lola
     Gutierrez, Leo Lucero, Juan Pacheco, Dolores
     Pena, Pedro Romero, Stan Salazar, David
     Sandoval. Diego Rivera murals illustrated.

7586 En nuestra opinion. LA CUCARACHA, (July 4, 1980).
     Spanish.

     AN: An editorial commending the mural
     efforts by Chicano artists in Pueblo,
     Colorado. Community artists should be
     supported and encouraged, not threatened
     with jail for their efforts. Illustrated
     with photograph of a mural by Puebloan Leo
     Lucero at Plaza Verde Park in Pueblo,
     Colorado.

Puente, Martina

7587 Imagenes de la Chicana. Menlo Park, CA:
     Nowels Publications (Stanford University
     Chicano Press), [ca 1975]. English.

     AN: Collections of writings by Chicanas;
     illustrated by unsigned drawings, and
     photographs by Lena Bugarin, Martina Puente,
     Francisco Camplis, Mario Anzaldua.

Pulido, Guillermo

7588 Contemporary Arts Museum, Houston, TX. Fire!
     An exhibition of 100 Texas artists.
     Exhibition brochure, 1979. English.

     AN: Includes eleven Chicano artists.
     Unfortunately, not illustrated, though a
     checklist of works is included. Mel Casas,
     Carmen Lomas Garza, Xavier Gorena, Luis
     Jimenez, Cesar Martinez, Guillermo Z.
     Pulido, Philip Renteria, Jose L. Rivera, Joe
     Rodriguez, George Truan, Juan B. Vela.
     Introduction by James Surls. Statements by
     the artists.

7589 Corpus Christy State University for the Arts
     and Weil Gallery Center for the Arts, Corpus
     Christi State University. Southwest artists
     invitational: an exhibition of contemporary
     art by seven Texas artists of Hispanic
     American descent. Ehxibition brochure, 1980.
     English.

     AN: Artists Jesse Almazan, Luis Jimenez,
     Cesar Martinez, Lydia Martinez, Manuel
     Mauricio, Guillermo Pulido, and Jesse
     Trevino show a variety of techniques and
     styles. Text by Roberto Tomas Esparza.
     Statements by and about the artists.
     Illustrated.

7590 Out in the open/Allen Parkway: Frank
     Fajardo, Jesse Lott, Guillermo Pulido, Jana
     Vander Lee. Exhibit invitation, 1979.
     English.

     AN: Invitation to the installation of
     conceptual pieces in public areas of
     Houston. Includes Chicano artist Frank
     Fajardo and Bolivian-born Pulido.

7591 San Antonio Museum Association, San Antonio,
     TX. Visiones nuevas en Tejas/new visions in
     Texas. Exhibtion catalog, 1979. English.

     AN: Supplementary regional catalog for
     the exhibit RAICES ANTIGUAS/VISIONES NUEVAS;
     ANCIENT ROOTS/NEW VISIONS. Illustrations for
     works by George Cisneros, Francisco (Frank)
     Fajardo, Robert Gonzalez, Cesar Augusto
     Martinez, Roland Mazuca, Guillermo Pulido,
     Felipe Reyes, Jesus (Jesse) Trevino.

7592 Tennant, Donna. Conceptual art dots city
     landscape. HOUSTON CHRONICLE, (October 27,
     1979), p. II, 7. English.

     AN: Frank Fajardo and Bolivian-born
     Guillermo Pulido are two of several artists
     creating conceptual art pieces in various
     parts of Houston. Fajardo marked out space
     with 25 stakes tipped with day-glo orange
     paint. Pulido constructed two large
     triangles on opposite hillsides, like giant
     markers.

7593 University of Houston/Lawndale Annex and
     Xochil Art and Culture Center, Mission, TX.
     The instant image: an exhibition of polaroid
     photography. Exhibition catalog, 1980.
     English.

     AN: Exhibit of 14 artists including
     Tejanos Frank Fajardo, Guillermo Pulido,
     Gregorio Salazar and Armando Rodriguez.

7594 Xochil Art and Culture Center, Mission, TX.
     !Que te vaya pretty nice! Exhibition
     brochure, 1979. English.

     AN: Exhibition of Chicano art including
     Carmen Lomas Garza, Luis Jimenez, Cesar
     Martinez, Guillermo Pulido, Roberto Rios,
     Jose Rivera and Jesse Trevino. [See also
     Estudios Rio].

Los Quemados

7595 Instituto Chicano de Artes y Artesanias
     (Texas Instit. Educational Development) and
     Instituto Cultural Mexicano (SER/UNAM), San
     Antonio, TX. Artistas chicanos: Los
     Quemados. San Antonio, TX: Instituto
     Chicano, Texas Institute for Educational
     Development, 1975. English.

     AN: Invitation to an exhibit and
     manifesto of 1975 Austin-San Antonio
     artists' group, Los Quemados. Included Santa
     Barraza, Carolina Flores, Carmen Lomas
     Garza, Luis Guerra, Cesar Augusto Martinez,
     Santos Martinez, Amado Maurilio Pena, Jr.,
     Jose Rivera, Vicente Rodriguez, Jose
     Trevino.

Quesada, Eugenio

7596 The First Unitarian Universalist Church,
     Paradise Valley, AZ. Five Chicano artists.
     Exhibition brochure, 1971. English.

     AN: Exhibit organized by L. Eugene
     Grigsby, Jr., Art Department of Arizona
     State University, Tempe, AZ. 21 works by
     Eugene Quesada, David Nunez, Fernando
     Navarro, Luis Baiz (of Arizona) and Saul
     Solache (of Los Angeles). Brief biographies
     of the artists.

Quesada, Eugenio (cont.)

7597 Grigsby, J. Eugene, Jr. Art & ethnics: background for teaching youth in a pluralistic society. Dubuque, IO: Wm.C. Brown Co. Publishers, 1977. English.

AN: Grigsby teaches in the Art Department of Arizona State University, Tempe. His book contains illustrations of Arizona artists Eugenio Quedada, David Nunez, and Luis Baiz, and a chapter called "The Spanish-Speaking Ethnics: Chicano/Mexican-American/Puerto Rican/Cuban/South American artists".

7598 Heard Museum, Phoenix, AZ. First Annual Southwest Chicano Art Invitational Exposition. Invitation for reception, 1976. English.

AN: Invitation to a reception for artists Luis Jimenez (Roswell, New Mexico), Eugenio Quesada (Phoenix), Felipe Reyes (San Antonio), Pedro Rodriguez (San Francisco), Pedro Romero (Cannon City, Colo.) One illustration.

7599 The Mexican Museum, San Francisco, CA and Quirarte, Jacinto. 17 artists: Hispano/Mexican-American/Chicano. Exhibition catalog, 1977. English.

AN: Catalog of an exhibit for artists Emilio Aguirre, Consuelo Gonzalez Amezcua, Al Barela, Pedro Cervantez, Edward Chavez, Antonio Garcia, Louis Gutierrez, Harry Louie, Vincent Perez, Michael Ponce de Leon, Eugenio Quesada, Gustavo Rivera, Peter Rodriguez, Alex Sanchez, Darryl Sapien, Rudy Trevino, Manuel Villamor. Illustrated.

7600 Patterson, Ann. Exhibit at Unitarian: Smith, Quesada art black, white contrast. TEMPE DAILY NEWS, (March 16, 1976). English.

AN: Eugenio Quesada presented drawings of female torsos along with Smith. Both are industrial design faculty members at Arizona State University. Article mentions other Quesada shows, and his participation on the Jean Charlot mural at the University.

7601 S.A. site for National Symposium on Mexican American Art. CHICANO TIMES, Vol. 4, no. 30 (November 9, 1973), p. 5. English.

AN: Held at Trinity University, the Symposium discussed such issues as, creative evolution, art education, artistic relationships to Mexico and the evolution of Mexican American art in the California barrios. Participating artists included Rudy Trevino, Mel Casas, Octavio Medellin, Antonio Garcia, Carmen Garza, Esteban Villa, Jose Montoya, Ernesto Palomino, Michael Ponce de Leon, Luis Jimenez and Eugenio Quesada.

Quesada-Weiner, Rosemary

7602 Galeria Otra Vez, Los Angeles, CA. Rosemary Quesada-Weiner, Mary McNally: a photographic exhibition. Exhibition invitation, [1981]. English.

AN: Invitation to an exhibition including Chicana photographer Quesada-Weiner. Illustrated.

7603 Quesada-Weiner, Rosemary. Las mujeres: 1977 National Women's Conference. Los Angeles, CA: Rosemary Quesada-Weiner, 1978. English.

AN: Portfolio (with captions) of photographs taken by Quesada-Weiner.

7604 Quesada-Weiner, Rosemary. [Untitled collection of photographs]. COMUNIDAD, (August 24, 1980), p. 15.

AN: Photographs of the CONFERENCIA DE LAS MUJERES CHICANAS taken by Rosemary Quesada-Weiner.

7605 Valle, Victor Manuel. Rosemary Quesada-Weiner. SOMOS, Vol. 1, no. 3 (August 1978), p. 36-39. English.

AN: Profile of photographer, feminist, community activist Rosemary Quesada-Weiner who was a school "drop-out" at 13, but received her journalism degree and discovered photography at La Verne College. She is a freelance photo-journalist who specializes in Chicana/Latina women's images, but is not limited to that theme. Well illustrated.

Queso, Fuchi

7606 Chicano art show at Contra Costa College. EL HISPANO, Vol. 8, no. 25 (December 11, 1973). English.

AN: Information on exhibition organized by Ramses Noriega that included the work of Jose Montoya, Esteban Villa, Mario Sinape, Ricardo Rios, Malaquias Montoya, Fuchi Queso, and Joe Palomino.

Quetzalcoatl Youth Organization, Tempe, AZ

7607 Denver muralist here for workshop. TEMPE DAILY NEWS, (March 28, 1975). English.

AN: Denver muralist Roberto Lucero is invited to give a weekend mural workshop for the Quetzalcoatl Youth Organization of Escalante Community Center in Tempe, Arizona.

Quintana, Sam

7608 Guadalupe Historic Foundation, Santa Fe, NM. Artes en la primavera. (1981). English.

AN: Catalog of exhibit by four New Mexico artists: Manuel Lopez, sculptor from Chili; Andres Martinez, painter from Santa Cruz; Victoria Lopez, colcha embroiderer from San Pedro; Sam Quintana, jeweler from La Mesilla.

Quirarte, Jacinto

7609 A beautiful book just published...: book review of MEXICAN AMERICAN ARTISTS. LA LUZ, Vol. 2, no. 4 (August 1973), p. 26. English.

7610 Hancock de Sandoval, Judith. Regional report, The arts: the workaholic. NUESTRO, Vol. 2, no. 10 (October 1978), p. 14. English.

AN: Biographical sketch of Jacinto Quirarte, author and educator, currently Dean of the College of Fine and Applied Arts at the University of Texas, San Antonio.

7611 Kutner, Janet. Total freedom in Chicano art. DALLAS MORNING STAR, (December 18, 1977), p. 10C. English.

AN: Review of traveling photo-exhibition of Chicano murals organized by Jacinto Quirarte for Exxon USA.

Quirarte, Jacinto (cont.)

7612 Martinez, Santos G., Jr. Review of: MEXICAN AMERICAN ARTISTS. DE COLORES, Vol. 2, no. 2 (1975), p. 47-51. English.

AN: A review essay by a noted Chicano artist. The basic shortcoming of Quirarte's book is "the author's failure to recognize the distinction between the terms Mexican American and Chicano. Consequently, Dr. Quirarte has failed to establish what exactly a Chicano is and in turn has failed to fully recognize the existence of Chicano art; an art by Chicanos about Chicanos and their culture." Reprinted in CARACOL, vol. 2, no. 3, 1975 and in TEJIDOS, vol. 3, no. 3, 1976.

7613 NATIONAL MURALS NETWORK COMMUNITY NEWSLETTER. (1978). English.

AN: This issue features reports from muralists. Includes information about murals at: La Pena Cultural Center in Berkeley, CA; the Social and Public Art Resource Center's Tujunga Wash Mural in Venice, CA; the Citywide Mural Project in Los Angeles, CA; activities at Chicano Park, and of the Congress of American Cosmic Artists (CACA), both in San Diego, CA; murals in San Mateo County, CA; the Task Force on Hispanic American Arts headed by Jacinto Quirarte of San Antonio; the 1978 Canto Al Pueblo in Corpus Christi, TX; murals in Chicago; and other works by non-Chicano artists.

7614 Rivas, Maggie. Art of the barrio: Exxon's traveling art show comes to headquarters. HQ HOUSTON, (August 1976), p. 6-7. English.

AN: Report on traveling photo-exhibition of 29 Chicano murals organized by Jacinto Quirarte for Exxon USA.

Quiroz, Esau

7615 Guggenheim Gallery, Chapman College, Orange, CA. Hexagono: paintings, sculpture, drawings, prints. Exhibit invitation, 1977. English.

AN: Invitation to an exhibit for artists Tito Aguirre, Isabel Castro, Rick Martinez, Esau Quiroz, Linda Vallejo, Emigdio Vasquez, Barrows, and Shanahan, sponsored by MEChA. Profiles and pictures of the artists.

7616 Orange Co. Library. El Modena Branch. Empanada: a tasty Mexican group art exhibit filled with a variety of digestable treats. Exhibition catalog, [1979]. English.

AN: Catalog of an exhibit by 15 artists: Dolores Grajeda, William Hernandez-M., Marylee Montano, Patricia Murillo, Eduardo Navarro, Susana A. Zaccagnino, Esau Quiroz, Juan Elias Ramos, Ricardo M. Serrato, Benjamin Valenzuela, Emigdio C. Vasquez, Arthur Valenzuela, Jack Vargas, Alonso Whitney, and Mexican artist Artemio Sepulveda living in Orange County. Brief profiles of the artists.

7617 Quiroz, Esau and Cuevas, Jose Luis. Chicano art: an identity crisis. NEWORLD, Vol. 1, no. 4 (Summer 1975). English.

AN: Interview between Chicano muralist Esau Quiroz and Mexican artist Jose Luis Cuevas. Chicano art is described as a search for pictorial roots in Mexico expressed through contemporary forms adopted from United States art movements. Cuevas suggests

that Chicanos travel, exhibit and "project to the United States from Latin America." Illustrated with one drawing by Cuevas and photographs of Quiroz.

7618 Santa Ana College, Santa Ana, CA. MECHA presents la semana de la Raza. Exhibition brochure, 1970. English.

AN: Program for the week's activities, including EL ARTE DE LA RAZA exhibition, Gilbert Sanchez Lujan speaking on "Chicano Art in the Barrio," art demonstrations by Gilbert Vasquez, Emigdio Vasquez, Esau Quiroz, and Richard Garcia.

7619 Valadez, Kathy L. Colton history told in mural. EL CHICANO, Vol. 8, no. 7 (July 19, 1973), p. 3, 9. English.

AN: Esau Quiroz was commissioned by the Mexican American Political Association to paint mural for their 1973 Convention. Mural portrays arrival of Mexican workers after the Revolution of 1910, the railroad industry in Colton, and the labor struggles organized by "La Cruz Azul".

7620 Valadez, Kathy L. What is Chicano art? A Chicano artist's concept. EL CHICANO, Vol. 7, no. 47 (April 26, 1973), p. 12-13. English.

AN: Esau Quiroz is a Chicano artist who states that Chicano art is that art by which a Chicano can be identified. He further defines Chicano art as that which contains a Chicano consciousness and portrays Chicanismo in terms of the exploitation of Chicanos.

Q-VO MAGAZINE

7621 Gamboa, Harry, Jr. Fantasias moviles. COMUNIDAD, (August 30, 1981), p. 8-9. Spanish.

AN: An illustrated article by ASCO artist Harry Gamboa, Jr. on lowriders, and the magazines LOWRIDER, Q-VO and FIRME.

Race Awareness
    USE: Identity

Race Identity
    USE: Identity

Racism

7622 Camplis, Francisco X. Towards the development of a Raza cinema. TIN TAN, Vol. 2, no. 5 (June 1, 1977), p. 5-7. English.

AN: Chicanos and other minorities remain invisible to white America, an expression of neo-colonialism. Camplis defines "Chicano" and "Raza" as terms, and states there are few, if any, full-length feature films available. Without role models, Chicano/Raza filmmakers can learn from contemporary revolutionary Latin American filmmakers, be familiar with European and Hollywood films, though the latter are alien models. Camplis suggests directions for Chicano films, and reviews films by Jesus Trevino, Jose Camacho, and Luis Valdez.

Racism (cont.)

7623 Pettit, Arthur G. Images of the Mexican American in fiction and film. College Station, TX: Texas A & M Univ. Press, 1980. English.

AN: A study on Anglo-American attitudes toward Mexican people in the Southwest as reflected in the sterotypes of popular literature and film. Most of the book is historical. The afterword (by Dennis Showalter) argues that these patterns have not improved, citing television series such as CHICO AND THE MAN and CHIPS.

7624 Ramirez de Robe, Jose "Controll". Human rights defender [drawing]. CARACOL, Vol. 4, no. 4 (December 1977), p. FRNT COVER. Bilingual.

RAICES ANTIGUAS/VISIONES NUEVAS [exhibit]

7625 Fondo del Sol, Washington, D.C. Raices antiguas/visiones nuevas; ancient roots/new visions. Exhibition catalog, 1977. English.

AN: Well illustrated catalog of traveling exhibition featuring Latin American and Latino artists living in the United States. Supplemental regional catalogs of local artists.

7626 Herrera, Philip. The Latino eye. NUESTRO, Vol. 2, no. 4 (April 1978), p. 46-48. English.

AN: Commentary on the traveling exhibition ANTIGUAS RAICES/NUEVAS VISIONES. Illustrated with selections from the exhibition that included several Chicano artists.

7627 Mendiville, Miguel and Saavedra-Vela, Pilar. A time for less talk and more action. AGENDA, Vol. 7, no. 5 (September, October, 1977), p. 33-34. English.

AN: The exhibit RAICES Y VISIONES, funded by the National Endowment for the Arts, was composed of more than 100 artworks by Chicano and Latino artists and toured the United States in 1977. The exposition was organized in four sections; artists whose work is influenced or related to Pre-Columbian art, art that explores social and political realities, and works that are more personal and introspective. Gives itinerary and listing of participating artists. Illustrated by photographs of the work of Rudy Trevino, Cesar Martinez, Luis Jimenez from Texas and Larry Fuente from California.

7628 Moisan, Jim. Ancient roots, new visions. ARTWEEK, Vol. 9, no. 26 (July 29, 1978), p. 8. English.

AN: Review of the show held at the Municipal Arts Gallery of Los Angeles, the first national touring show of Latino artists in the United States. Includes commentary on work of Larry Fuente, Luis Jimenez, Frank Romero, Harry Gamboa, Gronk, Rudy Martinez, Benjamin Serrano, Ricardo Diaz, Patssi Valdez, Mel Casas, Luis Leroy, Pedro Lujan. A related show, NEW VISIONS, L.A., includes Robert Delgado, Ray Bravo, Joe Moran, Rosalyn Mesquita, Patricia Murillo and others.

7629 Museum of Contemporary Art, Chicago, IL. Raices antiguas/visiones nuevas; ancient roots/new visions. Exhibition catalog, 1979. English.

AN: Catalog produced for the mid-West exhibit of RAICES ANTIGUAS. Includes 12 illustrations.

7630 Palacio de Mineria, Mexico, D.F. Raices antiguas/visiones nuevas: arte chicano y latinoamericano en los estados unidos. Exhibition catalog, 1980. Spanish.

AN: Catalog of an exhibit circulated by the Fondo del Sol in the United States, and in Mexico. Included are Chicanos and Latin Americans living in the United States. Well illustrated.

7631 Raices y visiones [portfolio]. REVISTA CHICANO-RIQUENA, Vol. 7, no. 2 (Spring 1979), p. 29-44.

AN: Portfolio of works from the exhibit RAICES ANTIGUAS/VISIONES NUEVAS: ANCIENT ROOTS/NEW VISIONS. Artists included are Patssi Valdez (Los Angeles), Eloisa Castellanos-Sanchez (New York), Benjamin Serrano, Jr. (Tijuana, Mexico), Alex Garza (Chicago), Martin Y. Moreno (Michigan), Luis A. Jimenez (New Mexico), Rene Castro (Oakland, CA), Sita Gomez de Kanelba (New York), Susana Lasta (Tucson, AZ), Domingo Garcia (New York), Consuelo Mendez Castillo (Caracas, Venezuela), Naomi Castillo Simonetti (New Jersey), Louis Carlos Bernal, and Eddie Comptis.

7632 Saavedra-Vela, Pilar. Exposicion nacional de raices hispanicas. AGENDA, Vol. 7, no. 5 (September, October, 1977), p. 33-34. Spanish.

AN: Announcement of the national tour of the exhibition entitled: RAICES Y VISIONES organized by the group Fondo del Sol, from Washington, D.C.

7633 San Antonio Museum Association, San Antonio, TX. Visiones nuevas en Tejas/new visions in Texas. Exhibtion catalog, 1979. English.

AN: Supplementary regional catalog for the exhibit RAICES ANTIGUAS/VISIONES NUEVAS; ANCIENT ROOTS/NEW VISIONS. Illustrations for works by George Cisneros, Francisco (Frank) Fajardo, Robert Gonzalez, Cesar Augusto Martinez, Roland Mazuca, Guillermo Pulido, Felipe Reyes, Jesus (Jesse) Trevino.

7634 Tannous, David. Problems of the artist as a hyphenated commodity. THE WASHINGTON STAR, (August 28, 1977), p. G-20. English.

AN: Review of ANCIENT ROOTS, NEW VISIONS show in Washington, D.C. describing Mel Casas' painting (San Antonio), Louis LeRoy's assemblage (Coolidge, Arizona), Amado Pena's silkscreen, Rogelio Ruiz Valdovin's costume (Tucson).

7635 Tucson Museum of Art and Pima Community College, Tucson, AZ. Raices antiguas/visiones nuevas; ancient roots/new visions. Exhibition invitation, 1977. English.

AN: Invitation to "Raices" exhibit of Chicano and Latino artists living in the United States originated by the Washington D.C.-based Fondo del Sol and the concurrent exhibit at Pima, "Art of the Barrio and Political Art." Illustrated.

RAICES ANTIGUAS/VISIONES NUEVAS [exhibit] (cont.)

7636 Tucson Museum of Art. Raices antiguas/visiones nuevas; ancient roots/new visions. Exhibition catalog, 1977-78. English.

AN: An exhibit of Chicano and Latino artists living in the United States. The exhibit traveled continuously for several years and was supplemented by local artists. Statements by the artists. 59 illustrations, some in color.

7637 Wilson, William. A blending of Hispanic roots, visions. CALENDAR, (July 30, 1978), p. 90. English.

AN: Review of ANCIENT ROOTS/NEW VISIONS exhibit held at the Municipal Art Gallery in Los Angeles.

RAICES DE SANGRE [film]

7638 Gamboa, Harry, Jr. Film, television, and Trevino. LA LUZ, Vol. 6, no. 10 (October 1977), p. 7-8. English.

AN: Jesus Salvador Trevino has been an active proponent and participant in transforming cultural inaccuracy about Chicanos in the media to accurate mass media models. A biography of Trevino follows, including discussion of some of his films: THE SALAZAR INQUEST, CHICANO MORATORIUM AFTERMATH, SOLEDAD, AMERICA TROPICAL, YO SOY CHICANO, RAICES DE SANGRE, as well as television series like ACCION CHICANO, AHORA, and INFINITY FACTORY.

7639 Gloria, Juan J. En San Antonio: se celebrara el tercer festival de cine, 'La vida chicana a traves del celuloide'. EL VISITANTE DOMINICAL, (August 20, 1978), p. 6-8, 12. Spanish.

AN: The Third Chicano Film Festival honors the only two feature-length films made by Chicanos: Moctezuma Esparza's ONLY ONCE IN A LIFETIME (made in Hollywood) and Jesus Salvador Trevino's RAICES DE SANGRE (Blood Roots), (made with CONACINE in Mexico). Illustrated.

7640 Lopez Oliva, Manuel. Proyeccion chicana en RAICES DE SANGRE. CINE CUBANO, (1981), p. 75-80. Spanish.

AN: A Latin American view of Jesus Salvador Trevino's 1976 film RAICES DE SANGRE, particularly its concern with the exploitation by U.S. multinationals of Mexicans and Chicanos on both sides of the border. The author notes Trevino's tendency to relate Chicano culture and problems to continental and world problems of workers. Illustrated.

7641 Poster, Corky. Cuba welcomes Latin film festival. GUARDIAN, (January 16, 1980), p. 21. English.

AN: Report on the First International Festival of New Latin American Cinema held in Havana December 3-10, 1979. The Festival focused on emerging cinema of Latin America, especially of Nicaraguans and Chicanos. Festival organizers hoped to "internationalize" the Chicano struggle by encouraging it toward a Latin American political perspective and moving it from a limited "la raza" view to one of class analysis and solidarity. Jesus Trevino's film RAICES DE SANGRE was shown.

7642 Rivera, Humberto R. Film notes. CHISMEARTE, Vol. 1, no. 2 (Winter, Spring, 1977), p. 20-24. English.

AN: Summary of films produced by and/or about Chicanos for cinema and television. Includes REALIDADES (TV) by David Sandoval, Rudy Vargas, Luis Torres, Jose Luis Ruiz, Antonio Reyes; A POLITICAL RENAISSANCE from the LA RAZA series (TV) by Moctezuma Esparza; CHILDREN OF THE STATE by Andres Markovits, Richard Trubo, Frank Christopher (film); LA RAZA UNIDA (released as RAICES DE SANGRE) by Jesus Salvador Trevino (Mexican film by a Chicano); CHULAS FRONTERAS (film) by Les Blank; THE MURALS OF EAST LOS ANGELES, A MUSEUM WITHOUT WALLS by Humberto R. Rivera and Heather R. Howell. Announcement for the National Latino Media Coalition.

7643 Torres, Louis R. RAICES DE SANGRE: first full length film directed by a Chicano. SOMOS, Vol. 1, no. 2 (July 1978), p. 16-19. English.

AN: Report on Jesus Salvador Trevino's RAICES DE SANGRE, the only film made by a Chicano at the Mexican film studio, CONACINE. Deals with the efforts of Chicanos and Mexicans living in border cities to organize an international labor union. Trevino's previous work is briefly mentioned. Illustrated.

7644 Zheutlin, Barbara and Talbot, David. Jesus Salvador Trevino. In: CREATIVE DIFFERENCES: PROFILES OF HOLLYWOOD DISSIDENTS. Boston, MS: South End Press, 1978, p. 345-352. English.

AN: Within the context of New Left alternative filmmakers who chose to work within Hollywood, Trevino sets forth his standards and goals. His films and TV productions include SOLEDAD (1971), AMERICA TROPICAL (1971), YO SOY CHICANO (1972), RAICES DE SANGRE (1977) and INFINITY FACTORY (1975-1976).

Ramirez, Daniel

7645 Knapp, Dan. KCET's show for Chicano viewers. LOS ANGELES TIMES, (April 3, 1970), p. IV, 18. English.

AN: Story on the television series AHORA! started September 1969 on KCET, Los Angeles' National Educational Television. Edward Moreno is program director and host; Victor Millan is producer-director; Claudio Fenner-Lopez, senior producer, has staff including set-designer David Villasenor, production manager James Val, and alternate host-narrator Jesus Trevino. The program has shown exhibits of artists Gilberto Lujan and Daniel Ramirez.

Ramirez, David

7646 Finalists in $540 E.L.A. art contest provide dazzling show at local hospital. EASTSIDE SUN, (November 21, 1968). English.

AN: First East Los Angeles art festival. Juried by artists Donald Manion, John Bene, Rubin Holguin. Show hung at Doctors' Hospital by Garfield High School art teacher David Ramirez.

Ramirez, Gilberto

7647 Garcia, Rupert. Muralista mexicano habla
     sobre los murales y los muralistas en los
     E.U. EL TECOLOTE, Vol. 5, no. 9 (May 28,
     1975), p. 5, 8. Spanish.

     AN: Thirty-two-year-old Mexican muralist
     Gilberto Ramirez has painted 23 murals in
     Mexico and two murals in the United States
     (in San Diego and San Francisco,
     California). Ramirez states that in Mexico,
     mural painting is more personal and
     individualized, different from the
     collective ideal of Chicano muralists. In
     the U.S., the muralists enjoy more liberty
     because muralism is not yet controlled by
     one group of painters. Chicano muralists
     have much to learn in terms of technique but
     their best work is fresh and vital. Includes
     iconographic description of Ramirez mural at
     the LULAC office, 3000 Folsom St., San
     Francisco.

Ramirez, Joe

7648 Houston Chicanismo. LA PRENSA, Vol. 1, no. 2
     (March 31, 1978). English.

     AN: In Houston, Texas, the AMA Gallery
     (Association for the Advancement of Mexican
     Americans) was opened in February 1976 to
     showcase Chicano art. Noel Rodriguez,
     gallery director, informs about the goals
     and objectives of the gallery. A current
     exhibit presents paintings by Josie Mendoza
     and Atanacio Davila, ceramics by Jesse
     Sifuentes and mixed-media works by Joe
     Ramirez. Illustrated with two pieces from
     exhibit, THANKSGIVING, an acrylic painting
     by Josie Mendoza and BIRDS, a ceramic piece.

Ramirez, Joel

7649 'Festival of arts' planned by Arthritis
     Foundation. SANTA FE NEW MEXICAN, (October
     11, 1972), p. B6. English.

     AN: The Albuquerque Arthritis Foundation
     has invited professional artists and
     craftsmen from New Mexico to display their
     paintings, watercolors, sculpture, prints,
     lithographs, jewelry. Joel Ramirez's
     painting THE WEAVERS is selected for full
     color art prints. Illustrated.

Ramirez, Jose

7650 Albright, Thomas. Oakland Museum: a wide
     range in Latin art. SAN FRANCISCO CHRONICLE,
     (September 12, 1970), p. 33. English.

     AN: A large show called ARTES DE LA RAZA
     at the Oakland Museum includes Mercedes
     Gutierrez-McDermid, Louis Gutierrez, Luis
     Cervantez, Calvin Tondre, Manuel Villamor,
     Rene Yanez, Jose Ramirez, Jorge Lerma,
     Rolando Castellon, Esteban Villa, Rupert
     Garcia, and Gustavo Rivera who is also
     having an exhibit at the Galeria de la Raza.

Ramirez, Mauricio

7651 The Point Gallery, Santa Monica, CA. ASCO
     (Gronk, Patssi, Gamboa, Herron), Los Four
     (Almaraz, de la Rocha, Judithe Hernandez,
     Gloriamalia Flores, Mauricio Ramirez, John
     Valadez. Exhibition invitation, [1975].
     English.

     AN: Illustrated invitation to an exhibit
     of Los Angeles artists.

Ramos, Juan Elias

7652 Mills House Visual Arts Complex, Garden
     Grove, CA. Menudo: artistas latinos de
     Orange County. Exhibit invitation, 1980.
     English.

     AN: Invitation to an exhibit organized
     for the first anniversary of Artistas
     Latinos de Orange County including Delores
     Grajeda, William Hernandez, Marylee Montano,
     Patricia Murillo, Irene Ramos, Juan Ramos,
     Ricardo Serrato, Miguel Shanahan, Arthur
     Valenzuela, Benjamin Valenzuela, Jack
     Vargas, Alonzo Whitney, Emigdio Vasquez,
     Susana Zaccagnino, and Mexican artist
     Artemio Sepulveda.

7653 Orange Co. Library. El Modena Branch.
     Empanada: a tasty Mexican group art exhibit
     filled with a variety of digestable treats.
     Exhibition catalog, [1979]. English.

     AN: Catalog of an exhibit by 15 artists:
     Dolores Grajeda, William Hernandez-M.,
     Marylee Montano, Patricia Murillo, Eduardo
     Navarro, Susana A. Zaccagnino, Esau Quiroz,
     Juan Elias Ramos, Ricardo M. Serrato,
     Benjamin Valenzuela, Emigdio C. Vasquez,
     Arthur Valenzuela, Jack Vargas, Alonso
     Whitney, and Mexican artist Artemio
     Sepulveda living in Orange County. Brief
     profiles of the artists.

Rascon, Vincent P.

7654 Artes 6 Gallery, San Francisco, CA. Mixed
     media. Exhibition announcement, [ca.
     1969-70]. English.

     AN: Announcement of exhibit including
     Jim Cortez, Luis Cervantez, Vicente Rascon,
     Rene Yanes, Graciela Carrillo, Lorenza
     Camplis. The Artes 6 artists eventually
     formed the Galeria de la Raza of San
     Francisco.

7655 Hartnell College Studio Gallery, Salinas,
     CA. Paintings, drawings, prints by San
     Francisco Bay Area Chicano artists. Exhibit
     brochure, 1971. English.

     AN: Brochure for exhibit featuring
     Francisco Camplis, Graciela Carrillo, Sal
     Castaneda, Priscilla Dominguez, J. Duarte,
     Rupert Garcia, Carlos Loarca, Irene Perez,
     Vincent Rascon, Michael Rios, Peter
     Rodriguez, Luis Valsoto, Esteban Villa, Rene
     Yanez, Zala. Illustrated by Rupert Carcia
     print.

7656 Mexican American Community Service
     Organization, San Jose, CA. Exhibition of
     contemporary art. Exhibition brochure, 1968.
     English.

     AN: Biographical and exhibition data for
     Al Barela, Bert Hermosillo, Octavio Romano,
     Luis Valdez, Vincent P. Rascon, John Soares
     and Al Espinoza.

Raya, Marcos

7657 Chicago-Raza murals. NATIONAL MURALS NETWORK
     COMMUNITY NEWSLETTER, (Fall 1979), p. 22.
     English.

     AN: Murals by Ray Patlan, Aurelio Diaz,
     Marcos Raya, Salvador Vega, Jaime Longoria,
     Malu Ortega y Alberro, Oscar Moya in
     Chicago's Pilsen district.

Raya, Marcos (cont.)

7658 Elitzik, Paul. Mural magic. AMERICAS,
      (June, July, 1981). English.

      AN: Brief illustrated account of murals
      in the Pilsen barrio of Chicago. Mentions
      work by Aurelio Diaz, Marcos Raya, and
      Salvador Vega. Focuses on the controversial
      mural at Benito Juarez High School painted
      by Jaime Longoria and Malu Ortega.

7659 NATIONAL MURALS NETWORK COMMUNITY
      NEWSLETTER. (Spring 1981). English.

      AN: Reports, or illustrations, of murals
      by Guillermo Aranda (Calif.), Francisco
      Lefebre (New Mexico); Marcos Raya's section
      of Chicago's anti-war mural; Gilberto
      Guzman's mural (New Mexico); vandalism on a
      Michael Schnorr mural at Chicano Park, San
      Diego, Calif.

7660 Perales Leven, Humberto. Marcos Raya -
      Mexican painter. IMAGENES, Vol. 1, no. 1
      (July 1976). Bilingual.

      AN: Mexican born Chicago muralist Marcos
      Raya painted a mural titled HOMAGE TO RIVERA
      in the Pilsen barrio of Chicago at the
      corner of 18th Street and May. Raya
      articulates the role of the muralist and his
      function within the working class community.
      Also in this issue is an article on the
      formation of MARCH (Movimiento Artistico
      Chicano) in 1972 in East Chicago Indiana.
      Portfolio of drawings by Marcos Raya and
      photographs by Mario Castillo. Bilingual
      text.

7661 Sommer, Robert. Street art. New York: Quick
      Fox, 1975. English.

      AN: Introductory essay covering the
      history of the new mural movement, forms of
      street art, politics, street sculpture, how
      to locate and photograph street art. Chicano
      murals include Charles Felix and others at
      Estrada Courts (L.A.), RCAF murals in
      Sacramento, Jose Montoya and others
      (Broderick, Ca.) Marcos Raya (Chicago), Mike
      Rios (Neighborhood Legal Aid, S.F.)
      Mechicano Art Center (L.A.) Johnny Alvarez
      (L.A.), New Mexico State Employment Bldg.,
      Albuquerque mural, Lorena Street School
      (L.A.), two murals, Casa de la Raza
      Alternative School (Berkeley), Santa Fe, New
      Mexico mural, Francisco Hernandez (L.A.),
      Artes Guadalupanos de Aztlan (N. Mexico),
      Willie Herron (L.A.). Better documentation
      would have been welcome.

La Raza Art Festival, Houston, TX, May 5-9, 1971

7662 La Raza art festival. PAPEL CHICANO, Vol. 1,
      no. 6 (May 21, 1971), p. 8-9. English.

      AN: Two-page centerfold of photographs
      by Johnny Almendarez of the LA RAZA ART
      FESTIVAL held at Ripley House in Segundo
      Barrio of Houston, Texas, May 5-9, 1971.
      Includes installation view of the exhibit,
      two photos of artists in action and a cover
      photograph of artist Pedro Rodriguez
      conducting a silkscreen workshop.

Raza Art/Media Collective, Inc.

7663 Arts Council Center for the Arts of Greater
      Lansing, Lansing, MI. Raza fine arts
      festival. Festival program, 1978. English.

      AN: This festival program mentions Jose
      Narezo's mural at the Holland National Guard

Armory, Grand Rapids; includes a statement
of the Raza Art/Media Collective, Inc.; the
philosophy of artists Zaragosa Vargas and S.
Kaneta Kosiba-Vargas; and profiles of
exhibiting artists George Vargas, Martin
Moreno, Hector Perez, Michael L. Selley,
Jesse Gonzales, Nora Chapa Mendoza, Jesse
Soriano, Jose Luis Narezo.

LA RAZA COSMICA [mural]

7664 Hand me down. AUSTIN AMERICAN STATESMAN,
      (August 17, 1978), p. B-1. English.

      AN: Illustration of Raul Valdez's mural
      La Raza Cosmica on the outdoor stage of the
      Pan American Center, East Austin.

LA RAZA (film series): A POLITICAL RENAISSANCE

7665 Rivera, Humberto R. Film notes. CHISMEARTE,
      Vol. 1, no. 2 (Winter, Spring, 1977), p.
      20-24. English.

      AN: Summary of films produced by and/or
      about Chicanos for cinema and television.
      Includes REALIDADES (TV) by David Sandoval,
      Rudy Vargas, Luis Torres, Jose Luis Ruiz,
      Antonio Reyes; A POLITICAL RENAISSANCE from
      the LA RAZA series (TV) by Moctezuma
      Esparza; CHILDREN OF THE STATE by Andres
      Markovits, Richard Trubo, Frank Christopher
      (film); LA RAZA UNIDA (released as RAICES DE
      SANGRE) by Jesus Salvador Trevino (Mexican
      film by a Chicano); CHULAS FRONTERAS (film)
      by Les Blank; THE MURALS OF EAST LOS
      ANGELES, A MUSEUM WITHOUT WALLS by Humberto
      R. Rivera and Heather R. Howell.
      Announcement for the National Latino Media
      Coalition.

LA RAZA MAGAZINE

7666 Gamboa, Harry, Jr. Seis imaginaciones:
      artistas chicanos en Los Angeles. COMUNIDAD,
      (July 13, 1980), p. 10. Spanish.

      AN: A limited flow of media information
      about Los Angeles Chicanos has produced a
      "ghost" culture. Only sensational events are
      published. Alternative magazines like LA
      RAZA, CON SAFOS, and REGENERACION have
      disseminated Chicano ideas of the 1970s. The
      Chicano imagination has appeared in murals
      by Willie Herron, Gronk, Carlos Almaraz,
      John Valadez; in pieces like "walking" and
      "instant" murals by the group ASCO; by the
      group Los Four; by group exhibits like
      "Chicanismo en el arte," and "Chicanarte."
      Patssi Valdez showed Photobooth Piece at the
      "Chicanismo" show. Gronk and Jerry Dreva
      exhibited their mail art at "Punk Meets
      Art." In Spanish.

La Raza Silkscreen Center, San Francisco, CA

7667 Corcoran Gallery of Art, Washington, D.C.
      Images of an era: the American poster
      1945-75. Washington, D.C.: Corcoran Gallery
      of Art, 1976. English.

      AN: Uncredited poster [La Raza
      Silkscreen Center, San Francisco],
      (centerfold). Posters by Rupert Garcia,
      Linda Lucero, and Ralph Maradiaga, all of
      San Francisco, CA. Introduction by John
      Garriga. Essays by Margaret Cogswell, Milton
      Glaser, Dore Ashton, Alan Gowens.

La Raza Silkscreen Center, San Francisco, CA
(cont.)

7668 Galeria de la Raza/Studio 24, San Francisco, CA and Garcia, Rupert. La Raza Silkscreen Center: "Images of a community", an exhibit of silkscreen posters and graphic works from 1971 to 1979. Exhibition catalog, 1979. English.

AN: First large scale retrospective exhibit of the La Raza Silkscreen Center's eight years of postermaking. Includes list of 90 artists.

7669 Kagawa, Paul and Rilkin, Scott. La Raza Silkscreen Center, in step with the Mission. ARTS BIWEEKLY, no. 44 (March 15, 1977). English.

AN: Concise history and goals of the Silkscreen Center: the Center's values are reflected in the collective process that produces the posters, as well as in the collective style of the art; in the emphasis upon education. The Center trains apprentices, educates the student community about the silkscreen process and Raza history and produces posters that have an information impact. The Silkscreen Center is part of a coalition of La Raza Information Center, Tutorial Center, and Centro Legal which evolved from La Raza En Accion Social founded in 1970.

7670 La Raza Silk Screen Center. TRA, no. 4 (1973), p. 18-25. English.

AN: Manifesto and portfolio of four posters by the San Francisco Center.

7671 University Art Museum, Berkeley, CA. The Fifth Sun: Contemporary/Traditional Chicano & Latino Art. Exhibition catalog, 1977. English.

AN: Catalog of exhibit including 45 artists of northern California. Texts deal with Mexican muralists, Mujeres Muralistas & other muralists, posters, the Chicano art movement, altars, La Raza Silkscreen Center, Galeria de la Raza, the Mexican Museum, the Sacramento Centro de Artistas Chicanos/RCAF. Mural maps of S.F. Bay Area and Sacramento. Many illustrations.

LA RAZA UNIDA [film]

7672 Rivera, Humberto R. Film notes. CHISMEARTE, Vol. 1, no. 2 (Winter, Spring, 1977), p. 20-24. English.

AN: Summary of films produced by and/or about Chicanos for cinema and television. Includes REALIDADES (TV) by David Sandoval, Rudy Vargas, Luis Torres, Jose Luis Ruiz, Antonio Reyes; A POLITICAL RENAISSANCE from the LA RAZA series (TV) by Moctezuma Esparza; CHILDREN OF THE STATE by Andres Markovits, Richard Trubo, Frank Christopher (film); LA RAZA UNIDA (released as RAICES DE SANGRE) by Jesus Salvador Trevino (Mexican film by a Chicano); CHULAS FRONTERAS (film) by Les Blank; THE MURALS OF EAST LOS ANGELES, A MUSEUM WITHOUT WALLS by Humberto R. Rivera and Heather R. Howell. Announcement for the National Latino Media Coalition.

La Raza Unida Party, Crystal City, TX

7673 Raza Unida Party [graphic]. CARACOL, Vol. 4, no. 5 (January 1978), p. 5. Bilingual.

REALIDADES [film]

7674 Rivera, Humberto R. Film notes. CHISMEARTE, Vol. 1, no. 2 (Winter, Spring, 1977), p. 20-24. English.

AN: Summary of films produced by and/or about Chicanos for cinema and television. Includes REALIDADES (TV) by David Sandoval, Rudy Vargas, Luis Torres, Jose Luis Ruiz, Antonio Reyes; A POLITICAL RENAISSANCE from the LA RAZA series (TV) by Moctezuma Esparza; CHILDREN OF THE STATE by Andres Markovits, Richard Trubo, Frank Christopher (film); LA RAZA UNIDA (released as RAICES DE SANGRE) by Jesus Salvador Trevino (Mexican film by a Chicano); CHULAS FRONTERAS (film) by Les Blank; THE MURALS OF EAST LOS ANGELES, A MUSEUM WITHOUT WALLS by Humberto R. Rivera and Heather R. Howell. Announcement for the National Latino Media Coalition.

REBIRTH OF OUR NATIONALITY [mural]

7675 Los murales del pueblo. PAPEL CHICANO, Vol. 2, no. 12 (February 1973), p. 1+. Spanish.

AN: Analysis of Leo Tanguma's work as "an expression not only of artistic creative opinion but also of the suppressed and accumulated feeling of La Raza in the United States." Includes thematic and stylistic information on four murals in the Houston barrio: "The Rebirth of Our Nationality," "Towards a Humanitarian Technology for La Raza," "Historia de la Raza," and "El Mestizo Chicano".

7676 Valenzuela-Crocker, Elvira. Tanguma: a man and his murals. AGENDA, no. 5 (Summer 1974), p. 14-17. English.

AN: Illustrated report on Houston muralist Leo Tanguma's 1973 work REBIRTH OF OUR NATIONALITY as well as other murals in progress. Tanguma's social views and his debt to Mexican muralist David Alfaro Siqueiros are detailed.

REBIRTH OF THE CHICANO [mural]
USE: BIRTH OF THE INDO-HISPANO [mural]

Redwood City, CA

7677 Bauer, Bernard. Angry artists deface own mural. BERKELEY BARB, (March 1978), p. 7. English.

AN: Chicano artists Jose Antonio Burciaga and Gilberto Romero Rodriguez recall a few struggles to sensitize local arts organizations to Raza art. Financial and political aspects of their painting a patriotic mural, "Danzas mexicanas" in Redwood City. Artists explain why they defaced their own mural as an act of protest.

7678 Calendario 1973. San Francisco, CA: Galeria de la Raza, 1973. English.

AN: Handprinted silkscreen calendar by artists of the Galeria de la Raza.

Redwood City, CA (cont.)

7679 Danzas mexicanas. Flyer, 1978. English.

> **AN:** Illustrated flyer about a mural
> designed and painted by Chicano artist and
> poet Jose Antonio Burciaga and Mexican
> muralist Gilberto Romero Rodriguez. Detail
> of the 147 x 22 feet mural in Redwood City,
> California is reproduced.

7680 Goll, Dave. More than handball on this
court. MENLO-ATHERTON RECORDER, (May 23,
1978), p. 15. English.

> **AN:** Emmanuel Montoya is painting a mural
> on African and Chicano unity at the handball
> court of Fair Oaks Community Center in
> Redwood City, CA. Montoya is working because
> of CETA (Comprehensive Employment Training
> Act) funds. Illustrated.

7681 In the middle of something good.
MENLO-ATHERTON RECORDER, (September 19,
1978), p. 16. English.

> **AN:** Illustration of Emmanuel Montoya's
> African-Mexican unity mural at the Redwood
> City Fair Oaks Community Center handball
> courts.

7682 Martinez, Sue. New mural unveiled in Redwood
City. EL TECOLOTE, Vol. 8, no. 7 (April
1978), p. 7. English.

> **AN:** Commentary on the 147x22-ft. mural,
> DANZAS MEXICANAS, painted by Chicano artist
> Jose Antonio Burciaga and Mexican artist
> Gilberto Romero at the Redwood City Civic
> Center. The mural depicts dance rituals from
> various Mexican regions and the flora and
> fauna of Mexico. The mural became a subject
> of controversy when its creators splattered
> paint on it during its unveiling as a form
> of protest against the San Mateo Arts
> Council for its exploitation of Third World
> artists. Detail of mural showing "La Danza
> De Los Viejitos".

Refranes
USE: Dichos

REGENERACION [magazine]

7683 Gamboa, Harry, Jr. Seis imaginaciones:
artistas chicanos en Los Angeles. COMUNIDAD,
(July 13, 1980), p. 10. Spanish.

> **AN:** A limited flow of media information
> about Los Angeles Chicanos has produced a
> "ghost" culture. Only sensational events are
> published. Alternative magazines like LA
> RAZA, CON SAFOS, and REGENERACION have
> disseminated Chicano ideas of the 1970s. The
> Chicano imagination has appeared in murals
> by Willie Herron, Gronk, Carlos Almaraz,
> John Valadez; in pieces like "walking" and
> "instant" murals by the group ASCO; by the
> group Los Four; by group exhibits like
> "Chicanismo en el arte," and "Chicanarte."
> Patssi Valdez showed Photobooth Piece at the
> "Chicanismo" show. Gronk and Jerry Dreva
> exhibited their mail art at "Punk Meets
> Art." In Spanish.

Regional Planning
USE: Urban Planning

Religious Art

7684 Adams, Robert. The architecture and art of
early Hispanic Colorado. Boulder, CO:
Colorado Associated University Press in
cooperation with the State Historical

Society of Colorado, 1974. English.

> **AN:** Robert Adams is a photographer and
> writer from Longmont, CO who has evocatively
> captured scenes in the San Luis and
> Purgatory Valleys of Southern Colorado. The
> text and photographs focus on "Hispano"
> village life, customs and traditions.

7685 Ahlborn, Richard E. The Penitente Moradas of
Abiquiu. Washington, D.C.: Smithsonian
Institution Press, 1968 (Contributions from
the Museum of History and Technology, Paper
63). English.

> **AN:** The history and organization of the
> Penitente Brotherhood. Detailed analysis of
> the architecture of Penitente moradas and
> the artifacts within them. Illustrated with
> many ethnographic photographs.

7686 Almaraz, Carlos and Estrada, Jose (Pepe).
[Untitled photograph]. CHISMEARTE, Vol. 2,
no. 1 (1978), p. Ft Cover.

7687 Altars as folk art. ARRIBA, Vol. 1, no. 1
(July 1980, 194), p. 4. English.

> **AN:** Focusing on the home altar of
> Josefina De Leon from Cuero, Texas, the
> article describes this folk expression on
> two levels: first as a subjective religious
> intermediator and secondly as a masterpiece
> of collected objects. Contains interesting
> information on the form, function and
> meaning of altars. Illustrated with
> photographs.

7688 Blue Sky Productions. Los santeros. Color
film, 29 min., 1979. English.

> **AN:** A 29 minute color film produced with
> funding assistance from New Mexico Highlands
> University and the National Endowment for
> the Arts. Features santeros Luis Tapia,
> Orlando Romero, Horacio Valdez.

7689 Briggs, Charles L. The wood carvers of
Cordova, New Mexico: social dimensions of an
artistic "revival". Knoxville, TN:
University of Tennessee Press, 1980.
English.

> **AN:** One of the few books that deals with
> the traditional and contemporary-traditional
> religious art of New Mexico within social
> context. The author explores the influence
> of Anglo patronage and tourism on the
> meaning, aesthetics and distribution of the
> santos, and non-religious carving of the
> town of Cordoba.

7690 Coe, Kathryn. Heritage plus science yields
art. SCOTTSDALE DAILY PROGRESS, (August 28,
1981), p. 27. English.

> **AN:** Biography of Colorado-born Rudy
> Fernandez who bases many of his paintings
> and mixed media boxes on the religious
> imagery of Colorado. He studied geology;
> travelled to Spain and Mexico to know his
> heritage. All these factors influence his
> art, in which he uses symbols personally.

Religious Art (cont.)

7691 Crews, Mildred T. Saint-maker from Taos. AMERICAS, Vol. 21, no. 3 (March 1969). English.

AN: An in-depth study of woodcarver Patrocino Barela (died 1964). Barela's work is an evolvement of the "santero" tradition filtered through an intensely personal style. His work was widely collected by institutions like The Museum of Modern Art, New York, The San Francisco Museum of Art and The New Mexico Fine Arts Museum. Well-illustrated with photographs of the artist and example of his work.

7692 Donnell-Kotrozo, Carol and Perlman, Barbara. Male passages: a secular santero of the '80s interprets machismo. ARIZONA ARTS AND LIFESTYLE, Vol. 4, no. 1 (1982), p. 32-39. English.

AN: Rudy Fernandez moves freely between two- and three-dimensional forms using personal symbols such as cacti, roosters, flying hearts, trout, in paintings or lead-covered shelves of boxes reminiscent of retablos. Colorado-born Fernandez has lived in Arizona, Utah, New Mexico, and Washington. His art is not religious, but is influenced by a strong Catholic background. Many color illustrations, including the cover.

7693 Donnell-Kotrozo, Carol. Rudy Fernandez. ARTSPACE, Vol. 5, no. 4 (Fall 1981), p. 18-23. English.

AN: Scottsdale, Arizona resident Rudy Fernandez converts cultural symbols into a private system language that revolves around love, family, manhood and self-identity. His mixed media altar-like forms are based on interest in Southwest santos, their format and presentation. Fernandez does paintings, and assembled wood pieces. Handsomely illustrated, with color.

7694 Fine Arts Society of San Diego, CA. The cross and the sword. Exhibition catalog, 1976. Bilingual.

AN: Bi-lingual exhibition catalog of Southwestern art forms; santero art, vernacular architecture and traditional folk art. Important essays by experts in each field. Contains an iconographical summary of santos and a good bibliography. Profusely illustrated.

7695 Hamm, Madeline McDermott. Artist envisions a 'Sistine' ceiling. HOUSTON CHRONICLE, (September 19, 1978), p. III, 1-3. English.

AN: Illustrated article on mural that Ernesto Pedregon Martinez (who was active in El Paso in the 1950s) was doing for St. Joseph Catholic Church in Houston. The mural depicts the crucifixion.

7696 Lomas Garza, Carmen. Altares: arte espiritual del hogar. HOJAS, (1976). English.

AN: Commentary and five photographs from the author's visual documentation of home altars in Kingsville, Texas. Brief analysis of the form, meaning and function of home altars in Chicano daily life.

7697 Martinez, Eluid Levi. What is a New Mexico santo? Santa Fe, NM: Sunstone Press, 1978. Bilingual.

AN: Martinez is a carver of saints from the well-known Lopez family of santeros of Cordova, New Mexico, who have carved for seven generations. An oversimplified history of the settlement of New Mexico and the rise of religious imagery production. Of interest are the illustrated steps of the carving process. Many reproductions.

7698 Navar, M. Margarita. La vela prendida: home altars. ARRIBA, Vol. 1, no. 5 (February 1980), p. 12. English.

AN: Brief commentary on the exhibit LA VELA PRENDIDA: MEXICAN AMERICAN WOMEN'S HOME ALTARS at the Texas Memorial Museum during December 1980. Aside from altars, the exhibit focused on nichos, grutas and lapidas.

7699 Negri, Sam. Garden grows as shrine to sculptor. ARIZONA REPUBLIC, (April 5, 1980), p. C-1. English.

AN: Felix Lucero, a self-taught Colorado-born sculptor who came to Tucson in 1938, spent 20 years sculpting religious statues. He started the Garden of Gethsemane in 1945 on the Congress Street bridge.

7700 Sagel, Jaime. Art of brothers taps New Mexico heritage. JOURNAL NORTH, (December 16, 1981). English.

AN: Three brothers, graphics artist, painter, photographer, potter and poet Alejandro Lopez and his older self-taught brothers Felix and Manuel, are working with traditional New Mexican art forms (bultos, straw inlay crosses) and with newer innovative forms - reflecting the fusion of traditional-experimental art developing in New Mexico among young artists.

7701 Sanchez, Arley. Santeros. ALBUQUERQUE JRNL, (August 21, 1977), p. C, 1. English.

AN: Review of THE SANTERO EXPERIENCE, an exhibition of contemporary folk art by eleven New Mexican santeros, most in their 30s, at the Albuquerque Museum. The carvers include Juan Lucero, Ben Lopez, Luisito Lujan, Horacio Valdez, C. Garcia, George Lopez. A revival of the art has been taking place within last several years due to cultural awareness being experienced by Hispanos. Contemporary santeros still donate some pieces to the church, but most are marketed to private collectors, displayed in museums, or kept.

7702 La Sociedad Historica de Nuestra Senora de Guadalupe, Santa Fe, NM. Meditacion. Exhibition invitation, 1980. English.

AN: Invitation to an exhibit by four artists: Filomeno Martinez (graphic artist, Albuquerque), Ruben Montoya (santero, Santa Fe), Santiago Chavez (painter, Santa Rosa), Jose Alberto Baros (sculptor, Espanola).

7703 [Tapia exhibit invitation]. Exhibition invitation. Santa Fe, NM: Santuario de Nuestra Senora de Guadalupe, 1979. English.

AN: Invitation to an exhibit of works by Luis and Star Tapia.

Renteria Fuentes, Juan

7704 Valdez, Armando. El calendario chicano 1977.
Hayward, CA: Southwest Network, 1977.
English.

AN: Fifth in a series of historical
calendars produced in 1972, 1974, 1975, 1976
by La Causa Publications and Southwest
Network. Artists whose work is reproduced
are Malaquias Montoya, Amado Maurilio Pena,
Ramori Zamora, Glugio J.L. Nicandro [Gronk],
Etta Delgado, Ricardo Alaniz, Diane Gamboa,
Elisa Marina Coleman, Margarita Calderon,
Jose Antonio Burciaga, Cesar Augusto
Martinez, Maria Ochoa y Valtierra, Juan
Renteria Fuentes, from California, New
Mexico, and Texas.

Renteria, Philip

7705 Contemporary Arts Museum, Houston, TX. Fire!
An exhibition of 100 Texas artists.
Exhibition brochure, 1979. English.

AN: Includes eleven Chicano artists.
Unfortunately, not illustrated, though a
checklist of works is included. Mel Casas,
Carmen Lomas Garza, Xavier Gorena, Luis
Jimenez, Cesar Martinez, Guillermo Z.
Pulido, Philip Renteria, Jose L. Rivera, Joe
Rodriguez, George Truan, Juan B. Vela.
Introduction by James Surls. Statements by
the artists.

7706 Moser, Charlotte; Renteria, Phil; and Wray,
Dick. Phil Renteria and Dick Wray. ART IN
AMERICA, Vol. 64, no. 4 (July, August,
1976), p. 82-83. English.

AN: Interview with Laredo-born Houston
artist Renteria, and Wray, both of whom
teach at the Museum of Fine Arts. Renteria
gives much biographical information and his
philosophy of art. Illustrated in color.

7707 Philip Renteria drawings, 1974-77. In YOUNG
TEXAS ARTISTS SERIES. Amarillo, TX: Amarillo
Art Center, 1977. English.

AN: Catalog of series of exhibits
co-sponsored by the Texas commission of the
Arts and Humanities and the Amarillo Art
Center. Illustrated with a biography of the
artist.

7708 Smith, Roberta. Twelve days of Texas. ART IN
AMERICA, Vol. 64, no. 4 (July, August,
1976), p. 42-48. English.

AN: Overview of Texas art in Fort
Worth/Dallas, Houston, San Antonio, Tyler,
and Galveston. Includes reproductions of
works by Luis Jimenez (color, on cover),
Roberto Rios mural, Jesse Trevino, Mel
Casas. Also mentioned in text are Phil
Renteria and Cesar Martinez.

7709 Stamper, Frances. Fluid washes of ink and
acrylic. TEXAS HOMES MAGAZINE, Vol. 4, no. 1
(January, February, 1980), p. 104-112.
English.

AN: Well illustrated article with color
reproductions of the work of Philip
Renteria. Provides biographical information
and focuses on the consumate craftsmanship
of his drawings and paintings.

**Resource Coalition for Minority Artists, Denver,
CO**

7710 Minority artists exhibit works at Auraria.
ROUNDUP, (January 13, 1980), p. 27.
English.

AN: Gala art exhibit organized by the
Resource Coalition for Minority Artists of
Denver. Included Black, Chicano and Native
American visual artists as well as film
makers and musicians.

REVISTA CHICANO-RIQUENA

7711 Yarbro-Bejarano, Yvonne. Resena critica de
revistas literarias chicanas: problemas y
tendencias. LA PALABRA, Vol. 3, no. 1-2
(Spring, Fall , 1981), p. 123-137. Spanish.

AN: Continuation of review of Chicano
magazines from Texas, California, and
Washington. The article discusses content,
literary and artistic format, and other
aspects, taking a critical stance (See LA
PALABRA, Spring 1980).

REVISTA LITERARIA EL TECOLOTE

7712 Yarbro-Bejarano, Yvonne. Resena critica de
revistas literarias chicanas: problemas y
tendencias. LA PALABRA, Vol. 3, no. 1-2
(Spring, Fall , 1981), p. 123-137. Spanish.

AN: Continuation of review of Chicano
magazines from Texas, California, and
Washington. The article discusses content,
literary and artistic format, and other
aspects, taking a critical stance (See LA
PALABRA, Spring 1980).

Revueltas, Rosaura

7713 Moreno, Dorinda. La mujer y el arte.
TEJIDOS, Vol. 3, no. 1 (Spring 1976), p. 17.
Spanish.

AN: Brief introduction to the collection
of poems by Dorinda Moreno published in this
issue of TEJIDOS. She also dedicates the
collection by alluding to the significance
and influence of two artists: Frida Kahlo
and Rosaura Revueltas.

Reyes, Alberto

7714 Campesino Business and Joint Enterprise
Building, Fresno, CA. Sabor a Fresno. Arte
chicano: los Four and la Brocha. Exhibition
invitation [1976]. English.

AN: Invitation to an exhibit of works by
Los Four of Los Angeles and members of La
Brocha del Valle of Fresno: Arturo Roman,
Sal Garcia, John Sierra, Juan Truner, Sapo
de Aztlan, Fernando Hernandez, Alberto
Reyes, Ernesto Palomino, Lee Orona,
Francisco Barrios, Juan Ybarra, Bobby Reyes,
Alberto Hernandez. Brocha was started by
Palomino (California State University,
Fresno professor) to pool talents of Central
Valley artists.

Reyes Aponte, Cynthia

7715 Tucson Public Library; Sonoran Heritage; and
De la Cruz, Frank. Mexican American mural
art: the power of cultural identity.
Brochure, 1980. English.

AN: Brochure on Tucson murals painted by
Antonio Pazos, David Tineo, Danny Garza,
Cynthia Reyes, Darlene Marcos, Roberto
Borboa, and others.

Reyes Aponte, Cynthia (cont.)

7716 Union Gallery, University of Arizona Student
Union, Tucson, AZ. Chicanarte: Cynthia Reyes
Aponte, Zarco Guerrero, Virginia Federico
Olivares, Antonio Pazos. Exhibition catalog,
1981. English.

AN: Illustrated catalog of exhibit
featuring four artists.

Reyes, Bob

7717 Campesino Business and Joint Enterprise
Building, Fresno, CA. Sabor a Fresno. Arte
chicano: los Four and la Brocha. Exhibition
invitation [1976]. English.

AN: Invitation to an exhibit of works by
Los Four of Los Angeles and members of La
Brocha del Valle of Fresno: Arturo Roman,
Sal Garcia, John Sierra, Juan Truner, Sapo
de Aztlan, Fernando Hernandez, Alberto
Reyes, Ernesto Palomino, Lee Orona,
Francisco Barrios, Juan Ybarra, Bobby Reyes,
Alberto Hernandez. Brocha was started by
Palomino (California State University,
Fresno professor) to pool talents of Central
Valley artists.

7718 Incorporated Artes Monumentales/Inc.,
Denver, CO. IAM: art exhibit. Exhibition
brochure, n.d. English.

AN: Large format, well illustrated
brochure with information on muralists
Roberto Lucero, Al Sanchez, Andrew Manning,
Ricardo Barrera and Bob Reyes. Includes some
biographical information situating these
artists within the dynamic artistic
traditions of the Mexican and the Chicano
mural movements.

Reyes, Felipe

7719 Cardona, Patricia. Gana adeptos de Museo
Mexicano de San Francisco: Pedro Rodriguez.
UNO MAS UNO, (February 6, 1978), p. 18.
Spanish.

AN: Report and brief history of the
Mexican Museum which opened in 1975 with a
collection of colonial santos. The museum
offers a vista of Mexican culture to people
in the United States. Director Peter
Rodriguez says that Chicano artists Roberto
Gonzalez, Felipe Reyes, Alfredo Arreguin,
Gustavo Rivera, and Carmen Lomas Garza are
some of the best. Illustrated.

7720 Con Safo. San Antonio, TX: Pintores Chicanos
de San Antonio, [ca. 1975]. English.

AN: Illustrated pamphlet issued by the
San Antonio artists' group Con Safo.
Includes a self-definition and a brief
history of the group under the names El
Grupo, Los Pintores de Aztlan, Los Pintores
de la Nueva Raza, Con Safo (from 1967 on).
Members include Jesse A. Almazan, Mel Casas,
Jose Esquivel, Jose P. Garza, Cesar Augusto
Martinez, Santos Martinez, Felipe Reyes,
Roberto Rios, Jesus C. Trevino, and Vicente
Velasquez.

7721 Heard Museum, Phoenix, AZ. First Annual
Southwest Chicano Art Invitational
Exposition. Invitation for reception, 1976.
English.

AN: Invitation to a reception for
artists Luis Jimenez (Roswell, New Mexico),
Eugenio Quesada (Phoenix), Felipe Reyes (San
Antonio), Pedro Rodriguez (San Francisco),

Pedro Romero (Cannon City, Colo.) One
illustration.

7722 San Antonio Museum Association, San Antonio,
TX. Visiones nuevas en Tejas/new visions in
Texas. Exhibtion catalog, 1979. English.

AN: Supplementary regional catalog for
the exhibit RAICES ANTIGUAS/VISIONES NUEVAS;
ANCIENT ROOTS/NEW VISIONS. Illustrations for
works by George Cisneros, Francisco (Frank)
Fajardo, Robert Gonzalez, Cesar Augusto
Martinez, Roland Mazuca, Guillermo Pulido,
Felipe Reyes, Jesus (Jesse) Trevino.

Reyes Ferreira, Jesus

7723 Frankenstein, Alfred. Just for the record.
SAN FRANCISCO CHRONICLE, (May 27, 1976), p.
48. English.

AN: Positive review of exhibit at the
Mexican Museum featuring the work of Jesus
Reyes Ferreira from Mexico and Gustavo
Rivera from San Francisco.
Ninety-five-year-old Ferreira uses tempera
on tissue paper to render brilliant
paintings focusing on Mexican folk motifs.
Rivera paints in the abstract expressionist
mode with power and passion. Article also
lauds the photographic work of Angel del
Valle in his exhibition: SEMBRADORES at the
Galeria de la Raza.

7724 Frankenstein, Alfred. A senior senor's
approach. SAN FRANCISCO CHRONICLE, (May 27,
1976), p. 48. English.

AN: Review of an exhibit of Mexican
painter Jesus Reyes Ferreira at the Mexican
Museum of San Francisco, as well as that of
San Francisco artist Gustavo Rivera, an
abstract expressionist painter. Also
mentions the Museum's mural map, and Angel
del Valle's photography show at the Galeria
de la Raza.

Reyes, Jesus

7725 Garcia, Ignacio. Senior exhibit attempts to
define Chicano art. SOUTH TEXAN, (August 1,
1975). English.

AN: DIRECTAMENTE DEL BARRIO, a senior
art exhibit at Texas A & I University by art
majors Raul Valdez and Jesus Reyes. Sets
forth their ideas about Chicano arts and
their future plans.

Reyes, Roger

7726 Gonzalez, Tobias and Gonzalez, Sandra.
Perspectives on Chicano education. Stanford,
CA: Stanford University, 1975. English.

AN: Reproductions of artworks by Ralph
Maradiaga, Patricia Rodriguez, Roberto
Bonilla, Francisco Camplis, Graciela
Carrillo-Lopez, Juan Fuentes, Irene Perez,
Roger Reyes, Carlos Loarca, Xavier
Viramontes, Ralph McNeill, Rupert Garcia,
Jose Romero.

RHOMBOIDAL PARALLELOGRAM [painting]

7727 Portraying Latino women in the Mission. SAN
FRANCISCO EXAMINER, (September 10, 1974),
p. 26. English.

AN: Three muralists of the Mission
District, Irene Perez, Patricia Rodriguez,
and Venezuelan Consuelo Mendez, are
preparing a six-paneled
painting-construction, the RHOMBOIDAL
PARALLELOGRAM, for the 28th annual San
Francisco Art Festival. It will illustrate
the life of women in the Mission.
Illustrated.

Richmond Art Center, Richmond, CA

7728 Curtis, Cathy. Six aspiring watercolorists.
SUNDAY MAGAZINE [Supplement to CONTRA COSTA
COUNTY TIMES, CA], (October 14, 1979), p.
19. English.

AN: In a recent show at the Richmond Art
Center (Calif.), David Gallegos was one of
the watercolorists. Working in a traditional
modernist style, Gallegos deals with light
and air in his views of the waterfront.

El Rio Neighborhood Center, Tucson, AZ

7729 Tribute to El Rio organizers:
Mexican-American mural to be unveiled.
ARIZONA DAILY STAR, (September 13, 1975).
English.

AN: $1100, 1775-square-foot mural on two
outdoor walls by Antonio Pazos, 22 year old
art student from Hermosillo, Sonora.
Completed on the third anniversary of El Rio
Neighborhood Center in Tucson. Color
illustration.

Rio Theatre, Mission, TX

7730 Galeria de la Raza/Studio 24, San Francisco,
CA and Garcia, Rupert. Posters from the
golden age of Mexican cinema. Exhibition
catalog, 1979. English.

AN: The Galeria's second exhibit of
Mexican movie posters features those of the
1940s and early 1950s (in 1971, the exhibit
covered 1943-1971) from the collection of
Enrique Flores, owner of the Rio Theatre,
Mission, Texas, and the Xochil Art Center.
Garcia's essay includes a history of Mexican
cinema, and the mythologizing period of the
"Golden Age" reflected in the posters which
promoted movie-consumership. One
illustration. (See Santos G. Martinez, Jr.'s
essay in the exhibition catalog: MEXICAN
MOVIE POSTERS, for another point of view).

Rios, Michael

7731 Albright, Thomas. Three remarkable Latin
murals. SAN FRANCISCO CHRONICLE, (June 7,
1974), p. 48. English.

AN: The myth of the melting pot is
vanishing: we recognize a variety of
"publics" today. This is shown in three
remarkable murals in the San Francisco
Mission District. The Mission branch of the
Bank of America has a 90 foot mural designed
by Jesus Campusano, assisted by Luis
Cortazar and Michael Rios, with technical
advice from Emmy Lou Packard. Another mural
is by the Mujeres Muralistas (Graciela
Carrillo, Consuelo Mendez, Irene Perez,
Patricia Rodriguez); the third by Michael
Rios on the 24th St. mini-park.

7732 Barnes, Peter. Fringe benefits of a
depression: bringing back the WPA. NEW
REPUBLIC, Vol. 172, no. 11 (March 15, 1975),
p. 19-21. English.

AN: A well-researched and comprehensive
analysis of the CETA (Comprehensive
Employment and Training Act) impact on
public art in San Francisco. Material on
Chicano-Latino murals in the Mission
district. Includes viewpoints by
artist-activists Patricia Rodriguez, Mike
Rios, and writer Roberto Vargas. Important
compendium on funding sources of various
neighborhood art programs stressing their
value as community assets.

7733 Barrio, Raymond. Art for our sake. NUESTRO,
Vol. 1, no. 6 (September 1977), p. 30-34.
English.

AN: Brief text with three color
reproductions of murals by Mike Rios (Bart
Mural, San Francisco), Gilberto Guzman (West
Las Vegas High School, NM), Willie Herron
(Farmacia Hidalgo, East Los Angeles, CA).

7734 Cockcroft, Eva; Weber, John; and Cockcroft,
James D. Towards a people's art: the
contemporary mural movement. New York: E.P.
Dutton, 1977. English.

AN: A survey of the street mural
movement in the United States, from about
1967 on. Several chapters are written by the
artists themselves: John Weber on the
Chicago mural group; Susan Shapiro-Kiok on
Cityarts Workshop of New York; Eva Cockcroft
on People's painters of New Jersey; Geronimo
Garduno on Artes Guadalupanos de Aztlan of
New Mexico. Chicano murals illustrated
include those of Mujeres Muralistas, Ray
Patlan, William F. Herron, Hoyo-Mara Gang,
Artes Guadalupanos de Aztlan, Vicente
Mendoza and Jose Nario (with Patlan) Mario
Castillo, Michael Rios, Toltecas en Aztlan,
Roberto Chavez, Ernie Palomino, Chuy
Campusano and Luis Cortazar (with Rios).

7735 Dunsmore de Carrillo, Patricia. On Rene
Yanez of the Galeria de la Raza. CHISMEARTE,
Vol. 1, no. 1 (Fall 1976), p. 8-9.
English.

AN: Report on Yanez's negotiations with
the Foster Kleiser Company to take over a
billboard located outside the Galeria in San
Fancisco which has been painted by Michael
Rios, the Centro de Cambio and TIN TAN
magazine, Zaiver (Xavier) Viramontes, and
others.

7736 Garcia, Rupert. Laminas de la Raza. San
Francisco: Garcia Litho and Printing
Service, 1975. English.

AN: Portfolio of drawings and prints by
Patricia Rodriguez, Ricardo Apodaca,
Xochitl, Domingo Rivera, Francisco Camplis,
Rafael Maradiaga, Tom Rios, Juan Fuentes,
Ricardo Diaz, Jose Romero, Consuelo Mendez,
Jose Antonio Burciaga, Irene Perez, Ricardo
Rios, Mike Rios, Graciela Carrillo, Rene
Yanez, Luis Talamantez, Guillermo Bermudez,
all from Northern California.

Rios, Michael (cont.)

7737 Garcia, Rupert. Pulqueria art--defiant art
     of the barrios [Part II]. EL TECOLOTE, Vol.
     8, no. 5 (February 1978), p. 8. Bilingual.

AN: In the Mission District of San
Francisco, various artists like Irene Perez,
Esther Fernandez, Chuy Campusano, Graciela
Carrillo de Lopez, Consuelo Mendez Castillo,
and Mike Rios have embellished business
sites with wall decorations similar in
spirit to the "Pulqueria" art of Mexico.
Illustrated with three "Pulqueria"-type wall
paintings: ATARDECER DE UN IMPERIO by Oscar
Carveo at the Azteca Restaurant (Mission and
20th Sts.), El Buen Boricano Restaurant
facade (24th and Harrison Sts.) and
Fruitlandia facade (24th and Treat Sts.).

7738 Greenberg, David; Smith, Kathryn; and
     Teacher, Stuart. Megamurals & supergraphics:
     big art. Philadelphia, PN: Running Press,
     1977. English.

AN: A full-color picture book of murals
throughout the United States. Chicano murals
include Michael Rios (San Francisco),
Mujeres Muralistas (San Francisco), Leonard
Castellanos and Tomas Gonzales with others
(Los Angeles), Los Artes Guadalupanos de
Aztlan (New Mexico), Willie Herron (Los
Angeles), Toltecas en Aztlan (San Diego),
David Botello (Los Angeles), David Lopez and
Arizona Mara Gang (Los Angeles), Vatos de
Maravilla (Los Angeles), Carlito Gaegos (Los
Angeles), Gil Hernandez (Los Angeles), Wayne
[Alaniz] Healy (Los Angeles).

7739 Hartnell College Studio Gallery, Salinas,
     CA. Paintings, drawings, prints by San
     Francisco Bay Area Chicano artists. Exhibit
     brochure, 1971. English.

AN: Brochure for exhibit featuring
Francisco Camplis, Graciela Carrillo, Sal
Castaneda, Priscilla Dominguez, J. Duarte,
Rupert Garcia, Carlos Loarca, Irene Perez,
Vincent Rascon, Michael Rios, Peter
Rodriguez, Luis Valsoto, Esteban Villa, Rene
Yanez, Zala. Illustrated by Rupert Carcia
print.

7740 Kamin, Ira. Come on in, bring your paint.
     PACIFIC SUN, (May 30, 1974), p. 11-12.
     English.

AN: Chatty report on murals and art
exhibit in San Francisco's Mission District:
murals by Chuy Campusano, Michael Rios,
Richard Montez, Trish (Patricia) Rodriguez,
Graciela Carrillo, Consuelo Mendez and Irene
Perez. Illustrated.

7741 Mexican artists paint mural for Bank of
     America. EL HISPANO, Vol. 6, no. 49.
     English.

AN: Commentary by Jesus Campusano and
Michael Rios about the 90-ft. mural they
painted inside the Bank of America on
Mission and 23rd Streets in San Francisco.
They describe the mural as "...a montage of
symbols and images depicting the heritage,
day-to-day experiences and hopes of the
people in the area.

7742 Preuss, Karen. The new Mission murals. SAN
     FRANCISCO BAY GUARDIAN, (June 28, 1975), p.
     14-15. English.

AN: Mural art in San Francisco's Mission
District has covered nearly every wall and
alley on lower 24th Street. Murals by Mike

Rios, the Mujeres Muralistas (Patricia
Rodriguez, Graciela Carrillo, Consuelo
Mendez, Miriam Olivo, Irene Perez, Susan
Cervantes) appear in the area. Others have
been painted by artists associated with the
Galeria de la Raza. Illustrations.

7743 San Francisco Museum of Modern Art, San
     Francisco, CA and Castellon, Rolando.
     People's murals: some events in American
     history. Exhibition catalog, 1976. English.

AN: Eight portable murals by San
Francisco Bay Area artists including
Graciela Carrillo, Anthony Machado, Robert
Mendoza, Irene Perez, Mike Rios. Well
Illustrated.

7744 Sommer, Robert. Street art. New York: Quick
     Fox, 1975. English.

AN: Introductory essay covering the
history of the new mural movement, forms of
street art, politics, street sculpture, how
to locate and photograph street art. Chicano
murals include Charles Felix and others at
Estrada Courts (L.A.), RCAF murals in
Sacramento, Jose Montoya and others
(Broderick, Ca.) Marcos Raya (Chicago), Mike
Rios (Neighborhood Legal Aid, S.F.)
Mechicano Art Center (L.A.) Johnny Alvarez
(L.A.), New Mexico State Employment Bldg.,
Albuquerque mural, Lorena Street School
(L.A.), two murals, Casa de la Raza
Alternative School (Berkeley), Santa Fe, New
Mexico mural, Francisco Hernandez (L.A.),
Artes Guadalupanos de Aztlan (N. Mexico),
Willie Herron (L.A.). Better documentation
would have been welcome.

7745 Stofflet-Santiago, Mary. The fifth sun:
     esthetic quality versus curatorial intent.
     ARTWEEK, Vol. 8, no. 37 (November 5, 1977),
     p. 6. English.

AN: Review of the exhibit THE FIFTH SUN
at the University Art Museum in Berkeley,
Calif., curated by Ralph Maradiaga of the
Galeria de la Raza. It contains folk art,
and posters by Chicano artists Maradiaga,
Rupert Garcia, Juan Fuentes, mural studies
by Graciela Carrillo and Mike Rios, ceramics
by Anna de Leon, an altar by Amalia
Mesa-Bains, and mural drawings by Mexican
muralists. The writer criticizes the uneven
quality of the show, but encourages better
ones in the future. Illustrated.

Rios, Ricardo

7746 Chicano art show at Contra Costa College. EL
     HISPANO, Vol. 8, no. 25 (December 11, 1973).
     English.

AN: Information on exhibition organized
by Ramses Noriega that included the work of
Jose Montoya, Esteban Villa, Mario Sinape,
Ricardo Rios, Malaquias Montoya, Fuchi
Queso, and Joe Palomino.

7747 Garcia, Rupert. Laminas de la Raza. San
     Francisco: Garcia Litho and Printing
     Service, 1975. English.

AN: Portfolio of drawings and prints by
Patricia Rodriguez, Ricardo Apodaca,
Xochitl, Domingo Rivera, Francisco Camplis,
Rafael Maradiaga, Tom Rios, Juan Fuentes,
Ricardo Diaz, Jose Romero, Consuelo Mendez,
Jose Antonio Burciaga, Irene Perez, Ricardo
Rios, Mike Rios, Graciela Carrillo, Rene
Yanez, Luis Talamantez, Guillermo Bermudez,
all from Northern California.

Rios, Roberto

7748 Con Safo. San Antonio, TX: Pintores Chicanos de San Antonio, [ca. 1975]. English.

AN: Illustrated pamphlet issued by the San Antonio artists' group Con Safo. Includes a self-definition and a brief history of the group under the names El Grupo, Los Pintores de Aztlan, Los Pintores de la Nueva Raza, Con Safo (from 1967 on). Members include Jesse A. Almazan, Mel Casas, Jose Esquivel, Jose P. Garza, Cesar Augusto Martinez, Santos Martinez, Felipe Reyes, Roberto Rios, Jesus C. Trevino, and Vicente Velasquez.

7749 Contemporary Arts Museum, Houston, TX. Dale gas: give it gas. The continued acceleration of Chicano art. Exhibition catalog, 1977. English.

AN: A comprehensive catalog including 28 works of art exhibited by 13 Texas artists: Melesio (Mel) Casas, Jose Esquivel, Francisco (Frank) Fajardo, Carmen Lomas Garza, Luis Jimenez, Cesar Augusto Martinez, Santos G. Martinez, Jr., Amado Pena, Roberto Rios, Jose Rivera, Joe B. Rodriguez, Jesus (Jesse) Trevino, and George Truan. Many illustrations, some in color. Introduction by James Harithas. Essay by Santos Martinez, Jr. Poetry, literature and essays by Chicano writers.

7750 Galeria de la Raza, San Antonio, TX. Celebration seventy-four. Exhibition catalog, [ca. 1974]. English.

AN: Catalog of extensive exhibition including European, Mexican, and the following Texan Chicano artists: Rolando Garces, Cesar Martinez, Ray Chavez, Vicente Rodriguez, Jorge Garza, Alfred Rodriguez, Luis Guerra, Carmen Lomas Garza, Bruno Andrade, Jr., Amado M. Pena Jr., Roberto Rios, Jose Trevino, Rudy Trevino, Luis Santoyo, Tati Rubio, Eduardo C. Garza, Arthur de la Fuente, and Jesus Campos Trevino.

7751 Heard Museum, Phoenix, AZ. Second Southwest Chicano Art Invitational. Exhibit catalog, 1978. English.

AN: Exhibit by eight artists: Antonio Pazos (Tucson), Rudy Fernandez (Salt Lake City), Harry Gamboa (Los Angeles), Rupert Garcia and Xavier Viramontes (San Francisco), Roberto Rios (San Antonio), Roberto Espinoza (Yuma), and Roberto Borboa (Tucson). Brief biographies of all but Rios. 29 illustrations.

7752 History and Traditions Museum. San Antonio, TX: Lackland Air Force Base, n.d. English.

AN: Brochure of the Museum with reproduction of two murals (unattributed) by Roberto Rios of San Antonio.

7753 OMICA Housing Corp., Inc., Homestead (Miami), FL. Dedication of heritage village. Brochure, 1977. English.

AN: Brochure of non-profit housing corporation which built, with Housing and Urban Development (HUD) funds, public homeownership housing for farmworkers and low-income rural residents of South Dade County. Illustrated with a mural by Roberto Rios of San Antonio, one of three done in Florida.

7754 Smith, Roberta. Twelve days of Texas. ART IN AMERICA, Vol. 64, no. 4 (July, August, 1976), p. 42-48. English.

AN: Overview of Texas art in Fort Worth/Dallas, Houston, San Antonio, Tyler, and Galveston. Includes reproductions of works by Luis Jimenez (color, on cover), Roberto Rios mural, Jesse Trevino, Mel Casas. Also mentioned in text are Phil Renteria and Cesar Martinez.

7755 Thalacker, Donald W. The place of art in the world of architecture. Chelsa House/R.R. Bowker, n.d. English.

AN: Includes a chapter on Roberto Rios' 1978-79 mural for the Border Patrol Sector Headquarters, Marfa, Texas.

7756 Xochil Art and Culture Center, Mission, TX. !Que te vaya pretty nice! Exhibition brochure, 1979. English.

AN: Exhibition of Chicano art including Carmen Lomas Garza, Luis Jimenez, Cesar Martinez, Guillermo Pulido, Roberto Rios, Jose Rivera and Jesse Trevino. [See also Estudios Rio].

Risco, Cecilia

7757 Las muralistas del barrio. CHISMEARTE, no. 2 (Winter, Spring, 1977), p. 48-49. English.

AN: Brief announcement about a Chicana artists' organization formed in Fresno, California which started work on a billboard-like mural, 60x8 feet on the theme of women. The mural received funding through Fresno's La Brocha del Valle. About fifteen women are involved, including Helen Gonzalez and Cecelia Risco.

Rivera, Diego

7758 Chicano muralists maintain traditions. LA CUCARACHA, (November 20, 1979), p. 7. English.

AN: Introduction to Chicano muralism in Pueblo and comparison to the Mexican mural movement from which it draws inspiration. 20 murals painted from 1977 to 1979. The muralists include Bernardo Duran, Juan Espinoza, Miguel "Freeloader" Garcia, Lola Gutierrez, Leo Lucero, Juan Pacheco, Dolores Pena, Pedro Romero, Stan Salazar, David Sandoval. Diego Rivera murals illustrated.

7759 CODEX NEWSLETTER (Galeria de la Raza, San Francisco, CA). Vol. 1, no. 2 (September 1973). English.

AN: An in-house bulletin of upcoming events: EL SOL NUNCA MUERE, photography/poster exhibit, Rolando Garces, and Peruvian posters; Mujeres de Aztlan, women artists' collective exhibit; Filipino/Samoan art exhibit; Galeria Christmas art sale; Galeria pavilion at S.F. annual art festival; Rockefeller scholarship for Galeria curator Luis Santana; Galeria coloring book; Balmy Alley mural project; Diego Rivera exhibit; first installment of Rupert Garcia's RAZA MURALS AND MURALISTS: AN HISTORICAL VIEW.

Rivera, Diego (cont.)

7760 Congreso de Artistas Chicanos en Aztlan, San
     Diego, CA. Diego Rivera, David Alfaro
     Siqueiros, Jose Clemente Orozco: exhibit of
     local artists, La Logan [San Diego].
     Exhibition brochure, n.d. [c.1974]. English.

     AN: Announcement of a traveling exhibit
     organized by Galeria de la Raza, San
     Francisco, from the collection of the San
     Francisco Museum of Art. Illustrated with a
     San Diego mural.

7761 Martinez, O.W. "Bill". Here comes la gente
     fragmented and fused [paintings]. LA LUZ,
     Vol. 1, no. 1 (April 1972), p. 56-57.
     English.

7762 Rodriguez, Jose Luis. Nuestra voz, arte. LA
     VOZ CHICANA, Vol. 1, no. 1 (January 1978),
     p. 5. English.

     AN: Brief resume of Diego Rivera as a
     central figure of Mexican muralism and
     contributor to a great tradition of realist
     art. Commentary on the Rockefeller Center
     Mural of 1933 and The New Workers School
     Mural of 1969. Intent is to relate the
     Chicano art movement to its Mexican
     antecedents. Illustrated with drawings of
     Diego Rivera and a reproduction of Rivera's
     mural SUNDAY DREAM AT ALAMEDA PARK.

7763 Salvador R. Torres Chicano Underground
     Studio-Gallery, San Diego, CA. Diego Rivera,
     David Alfaro Siqueiros, Jose Clemente
     Orozco, from the collection of the S.F.
     Museum of Art. Exhibition invitation,
     [1974]. English.

     AN: Illustrated invitation of an exhibit
     organized by the Galeria de la Raza of San
     Francisco loaned to the Congreso de Artistas
     Chicanos en Aztlan, and held in artist
     Torres' studio.

Rivera, Domingo

7764 Garcia, Rupert. Laminas de la Raza. San
     Francisco: Garcia Litho and Printing
     Service, 1975. English.

     AN: Portfolio of drawings and prints by
     Patricia Rodriguez, Ricardo Apodaca,
     Xochitl, Domingo Rivera, Francisco Camplis,
     Rafael Maradiaga, Tom Rios, Juan Fuentes,
     Ricardo Diaz, Jose Romero, Consuelo Mendez,
     Jose Antonio Burciaga, Irene Perez, Ricardo
     Rios, Mike Rios, Graciela Carrillo, Rene
     Yanez, Luis Talamantez, Guillermo Bermudez,
     all from Northern California.

Rivera, Edward

7765 Gonzalez, Hector. Rivera paints Boalt Hall
     mural. EL HISPANO, Vol. 5, no. 29 (January
     2, 1973). English.

     AN: Brief commentary on Sacramento
     artist Edward Rivera and his design for a
     mural to be installed in Boalt Hall at the
     University of California's Berkeley campus.

Rivera, Gustavo

7766 Albright, Thomas. Oakland Museum: a wide
     range in Latin art. SAN FRANCISCO CHRONICLE,
     (September 12, 1970), p. 33. English.

     AN: A large show called ARTES DE LA RAZA
     at the Oakland Museum includes Mercedes
     Gutierrez-McDermid, Louis Gutierrez, Luis
     Cervantez, Calvin Tondre, Manuel Villamor,

Rene Yanez, Jose Ramirez, Jorge Lerma,
Rolando Castellon, Esteban Villa, Rupert
Garcia, and Gustavo Rivera who is also
having an exhibit at the Galeria de la Raza.

7767 Bloomfield, Arthur. Zesty show at Mexican
     museum. SAN FRANCISCO EXAMINER, (February
     1, 1977), p. 24. English.

     AN: Review of an exhibit of Mexican and
     Mexican American artists from the Southwest
     and the San Francisco area. Commentary and
     analysis on artists Vincent Perez and
     Gustavo Rivera, Rudy Trevino and Al Barela.
     The work selected focused on aesthetic
     quality rather than the ethnic
     identification of the artist.

7768 Cardona, Patricia. Gana adeptos de Museo
     Mexicano de San Francisco: Pedro Rodriguez.
     UNO MAS UNO, (February 6, 1978), p. 18.
     Spanish.

     AN: Report and brief history of the
     Mexican Museum which opened in 1975 with a
     collection of colonial santos. The museum
     offers a vista of Mexican culture to people
     in the United States. Director Peter
     Rodriguez says that Chicano artists Roberto
     Gonzalez, Felipe Reyes, Alfredo Arreguin,
     Gustavo Rivera, and Carmen Lomas Garza are
     some of the best. Illustrated.

7769 Center for the Visual Arts, Oakland, CA.
     Fujioka, Herman, Rivera and Rodriguez.
     ARTSLETTER, Vol. 6, no. 3 (May, June, 1980).
     English.

     AN: Article unites Gustavo Rivera and
     Peter Rodriguez as artists who share a
     commitment to expressionist techniques.
     Illustrated with one black and white
     photograph of each artist's work.

7770 Frankenstein, Alfred. An artistic taste of
     Mexico in the city. SAN FRANCISCO CHRONICLE,
     (November 29, 1975), p. 29. English.

     AN: A very favorable review of the
     inaugural exhibit at the Mexican Museum. The
     opening show was a panoramic view of Mexican
     art including pre-Hispanic, colonial, folk
     art and fine art. Among the Mexican American
     artists presented were Roberto Gonzalez,
     Raul Mora and Gustavo Rivera.

7771 Frankenstein, Alfred. Just for the record.
     SAN FRANCISCO CHRONICLE, (May 27, 1976), p.
     48. English.

     AN: Positive review of exhibit at the
     Mexican Museum featuring the work of Jesus
     Reyes Ferreira from Mexico and Gustavo
     Rivera from San Francisco.
     Ninety-five-year-old Ferreira uses tempera
     on tissue paper to render brilliant
     paintings focusing on Mexican folk motifs.
     Rivera paints in the abstract expressionist
     mode with power and passion. Article also
     lauds the photographic work of Angel del
     Valle in his exhibition: SEMBRADORES at the
     Galeria de la Raza.

Rivera, Gustavo (cont.)

7772 Frankenstein, Alfred. A senior senor's approach. SAN FRANCISCO CHRONICLE, (May 27, 1976), p. 48. English.

AN: Review of an exhibit of Mexican painter Jesus Reyes Ferreira at the Mexican Museum of San Francisco, as well as that of San Francisco artist Gustavo Rivera, an abstract expressionist painter. Also mentions the Museum's mural map, and Angel del Valle's photography show at the Galeria de la Raza.

7773 Martinez, Anita. Raza art. EL TECOLOTE, Vol. 1, no. 8 (November 30, 1970), p. 1. English.

AN: Jay Ojeda, newly selected director of Galeria de la Raza, describes the memorial exhibition dedicated to Ruben Salazar installed at the Galeria on Dec. 12, 1970. Salazar symbolized and synthesized many of the goals subscribed to by artist members of La Galeria. The exhibit included work by Chicano and Latino artists Francisco Camplis, Jay Ojeda, Jose Romero, Rolando Castellon, Rene Yanez, Luis Valsoto, Mike Ruiz, Carlos Perez, Gustavo Rivera, Peter Rodriguez, Carlos Loarca and Ralph Maradiaga.

7774 Los Medanos College Gallery, [CA]. Cinco/five: an exhibit of five Bay Area artists. Exhibition brochure, n.d. English.

AN: Artists Gerry Concha, Gustavo Rivera, Raoul Mora, Manuel Villamor and Peter Rodriguez included in the show. Illustrated by Peter Rodriguez's portraits of the five.

7775 The Mexican Museum, San Francisco, CA and Quirarte, Jacinto. 17 artists: Hispano/Mexican-American/Chicano. Exhibition catalog, 1977. English.

AN: Catalog of an exhibit for artists Emilio Aguirre, Consuelo Gonzalez Amezcua, Al Barela, Pedro Cervantez, Edward Chavez, Antonio Garcia, Louis Gutierrez, Harry Louie, Vincent Perez, Michael Ponce de Leon, Eugenio Quesada, Gustavo Rivera, Peter Rodriguez, Alex Sanchez, Darryl Sapien, Rudy Trevino, Manuel Villamor. Illustrated.

7776 San Francisco Art Commission Gallery. Rolando Castellon, Gustavo Rivera, Jerry Concha. Exhibition brochure, 1971. English.

AN: Brochure for exhibit by Sacramento-born Jerry Concha, Mexican-born Gustavo Rivera, and Nicaraguan-born Rolando Castellon titled CAPRICORN ASUNDER. Brief biographies of the artists.

7777 San Francisco Museum of Modern Art, San Francisco, CA and Pearlstein, Howard. Aesthetics of graffiti. Exhibition catalog, 1978. English.

AN: Graffiti are defined as any coherently-intended presence written, scratched, painted, engraved, printed, pasted or otherwise impressed in a public place. Graffiti have been incorporated into works by artists. In this catalog, works by Chicano artists Carlos Almaraz, Wilfred Castano, Judithe Hernandez, Gilbert Lujan, Gustavo Rivera, Frank Romero, John M. Valadez, Victor M. Valle, Xavier Viramontes - as well as many Latino and non-Latino artist, appear.

7778 Temko, Allan. Ole! It's already a triumph. REVIEW [supplement to SAN FRANCISCO SUNDAY EXAMINER], (December 28, 1980), p. 13-14. English.

AN: A glowing report on the Mexican Museum as it celebrates its fifth anniversary. Provides details about programs, financing and goals. Brief analysis of the work of sculptor Manuel Neri and painters Manuel Villamor, Gustavo Rivera, Alfredo Arreguin and Miguel Almaguer. Informative profile on Peter Rodriguez, founder and Executive Director of the Museum.

Rivera, Jose

7779 Contemporary Arts Museum, Houston, TX. Dale gas: give it gas. The continued acceleration of Chicano art. Exhibition catalog, 1977. English.

AN: A comprehensive catalog including 28 works of art exhibited by 13 Texas artists: Melesio (Mel) Casas, Jose Esquivel, Francisco (Frank) Fajardo, Carmen Lomas Garza, Luis Jimenez, Cesar Augusto Martinez, Santos G. Martinez, Jr., Amado Pena, Roberto Rios, Jose Rivera, Joe B. Rodriguez, Jesus (Jesse) Trevino, and George Truan. Many illustrations, some in color. Introduction by James Harithas. Essay by Santos Martinez, Jr. Poetry, literature and essays by Chicano writers.

7780 Contemporary Arts Museum, Houston, TX. Fire! An exhibition of 100 Texas artists. Exhibition brochure, 1979. English.

AN: Includes eleven Chicano artists. Unfortunately, not illustrated, though a checklist of works is included. Mel Casas, Carmen Lomas Garza, Xavier Gorena, Luis Jimenez, Cesar Martinez, Guillermo Z. Pulido, Philip Renteria, Jose L. Rivera, Joe Rodriguez, George Truan, Juan B. Vela. Introduction by James Surls. Statements by the artists.

7781 Instituto Chicano de Artes y Artesanias (Texas Instit. Educational Development) and Instituto Cultural Mexicano (SER/UNAM), San Antonio, TX. Artistas chicanos: Los Quemados. San Antonio, TX: Instituto Chicano, Texas Institute for Educational Development, 1975. English.

AN: Invitation to an exhibit and manifesto of 1975 Austin-San Antonio artists' group, Los Quemados. Included Santa Barraza, Carolina Flores, Carmen Lomas Garza, Luis Guerra, Cesar Augusto Martinez, Santos Martinez, Amado Maurilio Pena, Jr., Jose Rivera, Vicente Rodriguez, Jose Trevino.

7782 Xochil Art and Culture Center, Mission, TX. !Que te vaya pretty nice! Exhibition brochure, 1979. English.

AN: Exhibition of Chicano art including Carmen Lomas Garza, Luis Jimenez, Cesar Martinez, Guillermo Pulido, Roberto Rios, Jose Rivera and Jesse Trevino. [See also Estudios Rio].

Riverside, CA

7783 Valadez, Kathy L. Chicano murals tell of
     Mexican heritage. EL CHICANO, Vol. 7, no. 34
     (January 25, 1973), p. 10-11. English.

     AN: Focus on Roy Duarte's murals in the
     Casa Blanca area of Riverside, California.

Rodriguez, Alfred

7784 Galeria de la Raza, San Antonio, TX.
     Celebration seventy-four. Exhibition
     catalog, [ca. 1974]. English.

     AN: Catalog of extensive exhibition
     including European, Mexican, and the
     following Texan Chicano artists: Rolando
     Garces, Cesar Martinez, Ray Chavez, Vicente
     Rodriguez, Jorge Garza, Alfred Rodriguez,
     Luis Guerra, Carmen Lomas Garza, Bruno
     Andrade, Jr., Amado M. Pena Jr., Roberto
     Rios, Jose Trevino, Rudy Trevino, Luis
     Santoyo, Tati Rubio, Eduardo C. Garza,
     Arthur de la Fuente, and Jesus Campos
     Trevino.

Rodriguez, Anita Otilia

7785 Bendau, Clifford P. Preserving an ancient
     craft. MS.MAGAZINE, Vol. 9, no. 11 (May
     1981), p. 26. English.

     AN: 40-year-old native Taos, NM resident
     Anita Otilia Rodriguez travels the Southwest
     as a professional enjarradora building homes
     and fireplaces from earth and straw. Article
     discusses the history of adobe construction,
     Rodriguez's innovations with the ancient
     technique. Illustrated.

7786 Rodriguez, Anita. Las enjarradoras: women of
     the earth. NEW MEXICO, (February 1980), p.
     46-47+. English.

     AN: History of adobe construction in New
     Mexico, its decline and its present revival
     in Arizona and New Mexico. Written by a
     professional adobe architect and feminist
     who defines the traditional terms and
     techniques of this woman's craft.
     Illustrated.

7787 Rodriguez, Anita. Tradiciones de adobe en
     Nuevo Mejico norteno = adobe traditions in
     Northern New Mexico. ADOBE NEWS, no. 15
     (1977). Bilingual.

     AN: History of adobe construction in New
     Mexico, from primarily Indian sources with
     Spanish input. For 400 years, women were
     builders and architects of the Southwest;
     today they are "enjarradoras" (plasterers).
     Written by a professional enjarradora from
     New Mexico. Illustrated.

7788 Simpson, Claudette. An adobe fireplace:
     Anita Rodriguez has built many - each one
     different. PRESCOTT COURIER-WEEKLY FEATURE,
     (December 1, 1978). English.

     AN: Anita Rodriguez is an enjarradora--a
     professional specializing in adobe
     architecture--in New Mexico. She builds
     fireplaces, lays mud floors, builds hornos
     (outdoor ovens) and does interior and
     exterior plastering. Well illustrated.

Rodriguez, Armando

7789 University of Houston/Lawndale Annex and
     Xochil Art and Culture Center, Mission, TX.
     The instant image: an exhibition of polaroid
     photography. Exhibition catalog, 1980.
     English.

     AN: Exhibit of 14 artists including
     Tejanos Frank Fajardo, Guillermo Pulido,
     Gregorio Salazar and Armando Rodriguez.

Rodriguez, Celia

7790 Lomas Garza, Carmen; Montoya, Jose E.; and
     Pinedo, Maria Vita. What we are...now.
     Exhibition catalog, n.d. English.

     AN: Drawings by Sacramento women
     artists: Lorraine Garcia, Eva C. Garcia,
     Kathryn E. Garcia, Celia Rodriguez, Patricia
     Carrillo.

Rodriguez, Eliseo

7791 De Cordova, Lorenzo. Echoes of the flute.
     Santa Fe, NM: Ancient City Press, 1972.
     English.

     AN: First person reminiscences on
     Penitente traditions in northern New Mexico
     at the turn of the century. Reprints two
     Works progress Administration (WPA)
     manuscripts: "Lent in Cordoba" (n.d.) and
     "The Wake" (1937). Illustrated with drawings
     by Eliseo Rodriguez. Notes by Marta Weigle.

Rodriguez, Isaac

7792 San Antonio Museum of Modern Art. Zarzamora:
     inaugural exhibition of Ladrones de la Luz.
     Exhibition invitation, 1979. English.

     AN: Illustrated invitation to
     photographic exhibition including Norman
     Avila, David Cardenas, Franco Cernero,
     Enrique Hernandez, Robert Maxham, James
     Newberry, Isaac Rodriguez, Daryl Studebaker,
     Richard Tichich, Beverly Ulmer, Kathy
     Vargas.

Rodriguez, Ismael

7793 Raza sculptors coast to coast - Lujan y
     Rodriguez. EL TECOLOTE LITERARY MAGAZINE,
     Vol. 10, no. 9 (June 1980), p. 7. English.

     AN: Pedro Lujan, originally from the
     Southwest, now lives in SOHO in New York.
     Lujan defines himself as a bricoleur who
     works primarily with wood and simple tools
     like hatchets and chisels. Ismael Rodriguez,
     self-taught sculptor from Berkeley,
     California, works in stone or wood. Includes
     photo of Lujan's wood sculpture "Man
     Running" and photo of Rodriguez at work.

Rodriguez, Joe

7794 Contemporary Arts Museum, Houston, TX. Fire!
     An exhibition of 100 Texas artists.
     Exhibition brochure, 1979. English.

     AN: Includes eleven Chicano artists.
     Unfortunately, not illustrated, though a
     checklist of works is included. Mel Casas,
     Carmen Lomas Garza, Xavier Gorena, Luis
     Jimenez, Cesar Martinez, Guillermo Z.
     Pulido, Philip Renteria, Jose L. Rivera, Joe
     Rodriguez, George Truan, Juan B. Vela.
     Introduction by James Surls. Statements by
     the artists.

Rodriguez, Joe (cont.)

7795 Crossley, Mimi. Tejano artists. HOUSTON
     POST, (August 19, 1976). English.

     AN: Exhibition of 19 Texas artists
     organized by Joe Rodriguez of the AAMA
     (Association for the Advancement of Mexican
     Americans) Art Center in Houston, Texas.
     Working within a wide range of styles and a
     great scope of subject matter. Includes
     brief commentary on the work of Amado Pena,
     Carmen Lomas Garza, Cesar Martinez, Enrique
     Campos, Carolina Flores, Jesus Trevino and a
     host of others.

Rodriguez, Joe Bastida

7796 Contemporary Arts Museum, Houston, TX. Dale
     gas: give it gas. The continued
     acceleration of Chicano art. Exhibition
     catalog, 1977. English.

     AN: A comprehensive catalog including 28
     works of art exhibited by 13 Texas artists:
     Melesio (Mel) Casas, Jose Esquivel,
     Francisco (Frank) Fajardo, Carmen Lomas
     Garza, Luis Jimenez, Cesar Augusto Martinez,
     Santos G. Martinez, Jr., Amado Pena, Roberto
     Rios, Jose Rivera, Joe B. Rodriguez, Jesus
     (Jesse) Trevino, and George Truan. Many
     illustrations, some in color. Introduction
     by James Harithas. Essay by Santos Martinez,
     Jr. Poetry, literature and essays by Chicano
     writers.

7797 Joe B. Rodriguez. LA PRENSA, Vol. 1, no. 13
     (July 21, 1978). Spanish.

     AN: Commentary on an exhibition by Joe
     B. Rodriguez at the George I. Sanchez Center
     in Houston, Texas. Rodriguez's work is seen
     as having affinity with the art of Diego
     Rivera and Raul Anguiano. Illustrated with a
     reproduction of a watercolor, THE LANDING OF
     THE SALSA PEOPLE.

7798 Musica hispana en nuestras vidas/Hispanic
     music in our lives: almanaque 1982/calendar.
     Milwaukee, WI: Miller Brewing Co., 1981.
     English.

     AN: Twelve Latino artists were
     commissioned to illustrate a calendar with
     paintings on Hispanic music. The Chicano
     artists include Frederico Vigil (New
     Mexico), Joe Bastida Rodriguez
     (Texas/Washington, D.C.), Manuel Martinez
     (Colorado), Jose Antonio Burciaga
     (California), Ignacio Gomez (California),
     Carolina Flores (Texas), Frank Martinez
     (California). Color.

Rodriguez, Jose

7799 Concilio de arte popular. CHISMEARTE, Vol.
     1, no. 2 (Winter, Spring, 1977), p. 54.
     English.

     AN: Report of a meeting February 12,
     1977 by the Concilio de Arte Popular (CAP)
     which published CHISMEARTE. Introduces
     members of the Board and summarizes
     discussions of problems of the organization
     and their publication.

7800 Monroe, Julie T. A splash of art from
     Idaho's Mexican-Americans. IDAHO STATESMAN,
     (March 11, 1977), p. 4D. English.

     AN: As a Bicentennial tribute to all
     people of Latin American heritage, Illinois
     Bell Telephone Company organized a national
     exhiibit of 17 Mexican-American/Chicano

artists. In Idaho, the touring exhibition
was augmented by a local presentation,
MEXICAN-AMERICAN: IDAHO, shown at the Boise
Gallery of Art under sponsorship of Boise
Cascade. Jose Rodriguez, local artist
presents his views on the meanings of the
word "Chicano" and "Chicano Art."
Illustrated with a photograph of Jose
Rodriguez and a reproduction of one of his
oil paintings entitled THE HOE.

Rodriguez, Jose Jimenez

7801 MARS: Movimiento Artistico del Rio Salado.
     Phoenix, AZ: Mars Studio/Gallery, 1978.
     English.

     AN: History and manifesto of MARS, 13
     member group of Arizona painters, sculptors,
     designers, and photographers: Jose Andres
     Giron, Jose Jimenez Rodriguez, Antonio
     Tocora (Colombian-born), Ramon Delgadillo,
     Francisco Zuniga, Jim Covarrubias, Ed Diaz,
     David Martinez, Roberto Buitron, Juan
     Rodriguez, Eddie Lopez, Zarco Guerrero, Joe
     Sanchez.

Rodriguez Larriva, Tito

7802 Almaraz, Carlos. Introduccion: vida urbana y
     artistas chicanos. COMUNIDAD, Vol. 55, no.
     22 (May 3, 1981), p. 2. Spanish.

     AN: In the controversial period of the
     early 1980s, Chicano advances are being
     attacked. In this political climate, some
     Los Angeles artists are interested in beauty
     and artistic creation: Carlos Almaraz,
     best-known of the Los Four group; Yreina
     Cervantez; Elsa Flores; John Valadez,
     presently working on a mural; and musicians
     Louie Perez and Tito Rodriguez Larriva.

Rodriguez, Noel

7803 Houston Chicanismo. LA PRENSA, Vol. 1, no. 2
     (March 31, 1978). English.

     AN: In Houston, Texas, the AMA Gallery
     (Association for the Advancement of Mexican
     Americans) was opened in February 1976 to
     showcase Chicano art. Noel Rodriguez,
     gallery director, informs about the goals
     and objectives of the gallery. A current
     exhibit presents paintings by Josie Mendoza
     and Atanacio Davila, ceramics by Jesse
     Sifuentes and mixed-media works by Joe
     Ramirez. Illustrated with two pieces from
     exhibit, THANKSGIVING, an acrylic painting
     by Josie Mendoza and BIRDS, a ceramic piece.

Rodriguez, Patricia

7804 Albright, Thomas. Three remarkable Latin
     murals. SAN FRANCISCO CHRONICLE, (June 7,
     1974), p. 48. English.

     AN: The myth of the melting pot is
     vanishing: we recognize a variety of
     "publics" today. This is shown in three
     remarkable murals in the San Francisco
     Mission District. The Mission branch of the
     Bank of America has a 90 foot mural designed
     by Jesus Campusano, assisted by Luis
     Cortazar and Michael Rios, with technical
     advice from Emmy Lou Packard. Another mural
     is by the Mujeres Muralistas (Graciela
     Carrillo, Consuelo Mendez, Irene Perez,
     Patricia Rodriguez); the third by Michael
     Rios on the 24th St. mini-park.

Rodriguez, Patricia (cont.)

7805 Barnes, Peter. Fringe benefits of a
     depression: bringing back the WPA. NEW
     REPUBLIC, Vol. 172, no. 11 (March 15, 1975),
     p. 19-21. English.

     AN: A well-researched and comprehensive
     analysis of the CETA (Comprehensive
     Employment and Training Act) impact on
     public art in San Francisco. Material on
     Chicano-Latino murals in the Mission
     district. Includes viewpoints by
     artist-activists Patricia Rodriguez, Mike
     Rios, and writer Roberto Vargas. Important
     compendium on funding sources of various
     neighborhood art programs stressing their
     value as community assets.

7806 Calendario de comida 1976. San Francisco,
     CA: Galeria de la Raza, 1976. English.

     AN: Handprinted silkscreen calendar
     consisting of twelve sheets and a cover. The
     work of the following artists is included:
     Ralph Maradiaga, Juanishi Orozco, Francisco
     Camplis, Ruben Guzman, Rodolfo Cuellar,
     Xavier Viramontes, Jose Montoya, Esteban
     Villa, Rene Yanez, Max Garcia and Louis "The
     Foot" Gonzalez, Patricia Rodriguez, and
     Ricardo Favela. All of the above are
     associated with the Galeria de la Raza, or
     the Royal Chicano Air Force of Sacramento,
     CA.

7807 Clark, Yoko and Hama, Chizu. California
     murals. Berkeley, CA: Lancaster-Miller,
     1979. English.

     AN: Picture book of Bay Area and Los
     Angeles murals with brief descriptions.
     Chicano artists included: Daniel Galvez,
     Irene Perez, Patricia Rodriguez, Graciela
     Carrillo (Mujeres Muralistas), Ray Patlan.

7808 Cockcroft, Eva. Women in the community mural
     movement. HERESIES, no. 1 (January 1977), p.
     14-22. English.

     AN: Women's role in the community mural
     movement is much greater than generally
     recognized. Among the many women muralists
     discussed are included the Mujeres
     Muralistas (Patricia Rodriguez, Irene Perez,
     Graciela Carrillo de Lopez, and Venezuelan
     Consuelo Mendez Castillo) of San Francisoc,
     and Judy Baca of Los Angeles. Illustrated.

7809 Galeria Museo, Mission Cultural Center, San
     Francisco, CA and Rodriguez, Patricia.
     Patricia Rodriguez: simbolos y fantasias
     culturales. Exhibition catalog, 1981.
     English.

     AN: Catalog of an exhibition of
     sculpture and painting. Autobiographical
     information about the Texas-born artist who
     lives in San Francisco and was a co-founder
     of Mujeres Muralistas. She explains her
     techniques in making portrait masks of
     Chicano/a artists in plaster and mixed
     media. Well illustrated.

7810 Garcia, Rupert. Laminas de la Raza. San
     Francisco: Garcia Litho and Printing
     Service, 1975. English.

     AN: Portfolio of drawings and prints by
     Patricia Rodriguez, Ricardo Apodaca,
     Xochitl, Domingo Rivera, Francisco Camplis,
     Rafael Maradiaga, Tom Rios, Juan Fuentes,
     Ricardo Diaz, Jose Romero, Consuelo Mendez,
     Jose Antonio Burciaga, Irene Perez, Ricardo
     Rios, Mike Rios, Graciela Carrillo, Rene

Yanez, Luis Talamantez, Guillermo Bermudez,
all from Northern California.

7811 Gonzalez, Tobias and Gonzalez, Sandra.
     Perspectives on Chicano education. Stanford,
     CA: Stanford University, 1975. English.

     AN: Reproductions of artworks by Ralph
     Maradiaga, Patricia Rodriguez, Roberto
     Bonilla, Francisco Camplis, Graciela
     Carrillo-Lopez, Juan Fuentes, Irene Perez,
     Roger Reyes, Carlos Loarca, Xavier
     Viramontes, Ralph McNeill, Rupert Garcia,
     Jose Romero.

7812 Helen Euphrat Gallery, De Anza College,
     Cupertino, CA. Staying visible: the
     importance of archives. Art and "saved
     stuff" of eleven 20th century California
     artists. Cupertino, CA: Helen Euphrat
     Gallery, De Anza College, 1981. English.

     AN: Catalog issued in conjunction with
     an exhibit held in the gallery Sept. 22 to
     October 23, 1981 which included
     documentation on Chicana artists Patricia
     Rodriguez and Carmen Lomas Garza. Each
     artist explains her method of saving,
     storing and using cultural material in her
     creations. Includes biographical sketch,
     photograph of the artist and reproduction of
     artwork.

7813 La historia de California, 1977. San
     Francisco, CA: Galeria de la Raza, 1977.
     English.

     AN: Handprinted silkscreen calendar of
     history seen from a Mexican point of view.
     Twelve sheets and a cover. Artists are:
     Ralph Maradiaga, Irene Perez, Louie "The
     Foot" Gonzalez, Max Garcia, Patricia
     Rodriguez, Jose Romero, Esteban Villa,
     Juanishi Orozco, Rodolfo Cuellar, Jose
     Montoya, Xavier Viramontes, Rene Yanez,
     Ricardo Favela, associated with the Galeria
     de la Raza, or the Royal Chicano Air Force
     of Sacramento.

7814 Kamin, Ira. Come on in, bring your paint.
     PACIFIC SUN, (May 30, 1974), p. 11-12.
     English.

     AN: Chatty report on murals and art
     exhibit in San Francisco's Mission District:
     murals by Chuy Campusano, Michael Rios,
     Richard Montez, Trish (Patricia) Rodriguez,
     Graciela Carrillo, Consuelo Mendez and Irene
     Perez. Illustrated.

7815 Montoya, Emmanuel; Rodriguez, Patricia; and
     Acevedo, Mario (Torero). Canto al pueblo
     '78. NATIONAL MURALS NETWORK COMMUNITY
     NEWSLETTER, (1978). English.

     AN: The second annual Canto al Pueblo
     took place in Corpus Christi, Texas, where
     more than six murals were painted: "Wall of
     Cultural Education" by 13 artists headed by
     Roel Montealva; Carlota Espinoza, with
     children; Gilberto Romero, Jose Antonio
     Burciaga and Patricia Rodriguez,
     "Incomprehension al arte"; "Madre Tierra" by
     Manuel Martinez of Denver with Amador
     Hinojosa (Corpus Christi) and Enriquette
     Vasquez (New Mexico); Mario Torero; Salvador
     Vega of Chicago whose mural some Canto
     participants considered "insulting".

Rodriguez, Patricia (cont.)

7816 Las muralistas: Patricia Rodriguez, Consuelo
     Mendez, Graciela Carrillo, Irene Perez.
     Exhibition invitation, 1974. English.

     AN: Invitation to the inauguration of
     the mural LATINO AMERICA by the Mujeres
     Muralistas at the Mission Neighborhood Model
     Cities in San Francisco's Mission District,
     May 31, 1974.

7817 Notes on 2nd National Community Muralists'
     Network Conference, Chicago, Ill. April
     20-23, 1978. San Francisco, CA, 1978.
     English.

     AN: Rupert Garcia, Raul Martinez,
     Patricia Rodriguez, Ray Patlan (San
     Francisco Bay Area) and Jaime Valadez (San
     Jose), among others, attended the conference
     in Chicago. Reports were heard from many
     parts of the United States on mural
     activities, including that of Aurelio Diaz
     of Chicago, representing MARCH (Movimiento
     Artistico Chicano). A workshop presentation
     was made by Luis Arenal and others from the
     Taller Siqueiros of Cuernavaca, Mexico. An
     experimental mural to try Siqueiros'
     techniques was created. Illustrated.

7818 Portraying Latino women in the Mission. SAN
     FRANCISCO EXAMINER, (September 10, 1974),
     p. 26. English.

     AN: Three muralists of the Mission
     District, Irene Perez, Patricia Rodriguez,
     and Venezuelan Consuelo Mendez, are
     preparing a six-paneled
     painting-construction, the RHOMBOIDAL
     PARALLELOGRAM, for the 28th annual San
     Francisco Art Festival. It will illustrate
     the life of women in the Mission.
     Illustrated.

7819 Preuss, Karen. The new Mission murals. SAN
     FRANCISCO BAY GUARDIAN, (June 28, 1975), p.
     14-15. English.

     AN: Mural art in San Francisco's Mission
     District has covered nearly every wall and
     alley on lower 24th Street. Murals by Mike
     Rios, the Mujeres Muralistas (Patricia
     Rodriguez, Graciela Carrillo, Consuelo
     Mendez, Miriam Olivo, Irene Perez, Susan
     Cervantes) appear in the area. Others have
     been painted by artists associated with the
     Galeria de la Raza. Illustrations.

7820 Quintero, Victoria. A mural is a painting on
     a wall done by human hands. EL TECOLOTE,
     Vol. 5, no. 1 (September 13, 1974), p. 6+.
     English.

     AN: The women's collective, Mujeres
     Muralistas, exists within the strong San
     Francisco mural movement. Originally the
     group included Graciela Carrillo, Consuelo
     Mendez, Irene Perez, and Patricia Rodriguez.
     The group has expanded to include Susan
     Cervantes, Ester Hernandez, and Miriam
     Olivo. The two murals completed have been
     criticized for not being political; the
     women answer that they want the atmosphere
     to be surrounded with life, with colors.
     Illustrated.

7821 Rodriguez, Patricia. Portfolio: Patricia
     Rodriguez; the visual interview.
     METAMORFOSIS, Vol. 3, no. 1-2 (1980, 1981),
     p. 38-45. English.

     AN: Statement by the artist reprinted
     from her exhibit "The Visual Interview" at

the Mission Cultural Center, San Francisco.
Discusses her fifteen mask-box-sculptures of
Chicano artists from northern California.
Illustrated with photographs of the artist
at work and five of her sculptures. This
issue of METAMORFOSIS combines volumes 3 and
4.

7822 Ruben Salazar Library, Sonoma State
     University, Sonoma, CA. Patricia Rodriguez:
     Chicano sculpture and masks. Exhibition
     invitation, 1981. English.

     AN: Invitation to an exhibit.

7823 Valdez, Armando. El calendario chicano 1975.
     Hayward, CA: Southwest Network, 1975.
     English.

     AN: Third in a series of historical
     calendars produced in 1972 and 1974 by La
     Causa Publications and Southwest Network.
     Artists included for each month are Carmen
     Lomas Garza, Sergio Hernandez, Malaquias
     Montoya, Mujeres Muralistas (Graciela
     Carrillo, Venezuelan Consuelo Mendez, Irene
     Perez, Patricia Rodriguez), Ramses Noriega,
     Ernie Palomino, Amado Maurilio Pena, Martin
     Perez. All but Texan Pena are California
     artists.

7824 Venegas, Sybil. Conditions for producing
     Chicana art. CHISMEARTE, Vol. 1, no. 4 (Fall,
     Winter, 1977, 1978), p. 2, 4. English.

     AN: Chicana artists face more obstacles
     than white women or Chicano counterparts in
     the arts. Mexican life style has portrayed
     the ideal of a submissive woman, but the
     values have changed. Chicana artists are
     concerned with women and their struggles.
     Muralists include Patricia Rodriguez, Irene
     Perez, Consuelo Mendez de Castillo, Susan
     Cervantes, Ester Hernandez, Miriam Olivo,
     Ruth Rodriguez, of the Mujeres Muralistas
     (San Francisco). Other artists are Etta
     Delgado and Barbara Carrasco.

Rodriguez, Pedro

7825 Galeria de la Raza/Studio 24, San Francisco,
     CA. Images of the Southwest. Exhibition
     catalog, 1977. English.

     AN: Invitation/catalog for an exhibit
     including Rudy M. Fernandez(Utah), Enrique
     Flores(Texas), Xavier Gorena(Texas),
     C.A.[Cesar] Martinez(Texas), Santos
     Martinez, Jr.(Texas), Pedro
     Rodriguez(Texas), Arnold Trujillo(New
     Mexico). Block prints, paper cut-outs,
     drawings, photographs, copper enamels, and
     sculpture were shown. Five illustrations.

7826 La Raza art festival. PAPEL CHICANO, Vol. 1,
     no. 6 (May 21, 1971), p. 8-9. English.

     AN: Two-page centerfold of photographs
     by Johnny Almendarez of the LA RAZA ART
     FESTIVAL held at Ripley House in Segundo
     Barrio of Houston, Texas, May 5-9, 1971.
     Includes installation view of the exhibit,
     two photos of artists in action and a cover
     photograph of artist Pedro Rodriguez
     conducting a silkscreen workshop.

Rodriguez, Pedro (cont.)

7827 Rodriguez, Pedro. Chicano artist's paintings on display at WWC. UNION BULLETIN, (February 19, 1981). English.

AN: Commentary by artist Pedro Rodriguez stressing the social context of Chicano art and the role and function of the Chicano artist. Illustrated with a photograph of the artist and reproductions of two oil paintings: EL OBRERO and CIUDAD LIBERTAD.

7828 Romero, Ernestina. Chicano culture to be explored at conference. DAILY TEXAN, (September 10, 1979). English.

AN: Announcement of the internationally attended CONFERENCIA PLASTICA CHICANA. Statements by organizers Santa Barraza and Pedro Rodriguez.

Rodriguez, Peter

7829 Albright, Thomas. The sensual moods of nature. SAN FRANCISCO CHRONICLE, (January 23, 1971), p. 34. English.

AN: Review of an exhibition of paintings by Pedro Rodriguez of San Francisco at the Galeria de La Raza. Work classified as lyrical abstractions "in the vein of introspective lyric poetry".

7830 And/Or Gallery, Seattle, WA. Artistas de Aztlan. Exhibition announcement, 1975. English.

AN: Exhibition announcement for an important exhibit of Northwest Chicano art. Co-sponsored by MEChA and the Chicano Studies Program at the University of Washington, the exhibit presented works by Emilio Aguayo, Danny Desiga, Ricardo Aguirre, Ramiro Benavidez, Elma Herada, Pedro Rodriguez and others. A selection of posters by Armando Cid of the R.C.A.F. group from Sacramento, California was also presented. Concurrently, at the Heny Gallery of the University of Washington, Esteban Villa presented a one-man show.

7831 Baciu, Joyce A. Hispanic artists: combining energy and emotion. CAMINOS, Vol. 2, no. 5 (October 1981), p. 14-17. English.

AN: Brief profiles of Mario Uribe, Ernest De Soto, Peter Rodriguez, Margarita Jauregui Weiner, Virginia Jaramillo, Luis Urrea, Ramses Noriega, Jose Lopez, Olivia Sanchez.

7832 Bayview Federal Savings, San Francisco, CA. Peter Rodriguez. [S.n.: s.l.], 1974. English.

AN: Well-illustrated brochure includes photograph of San Francisco artist Peter Rodriguez and four of his paintings. Also provides biographical information, exhibition chronology and critical excerpts from reviews of several shows. Artist's basic style is lyrical abstractionism centered on organic forms derived from nature.

7833 Cardenas de Dwyer, Carlota, ed. Chicano voices. Boston, MS: Houghton Mifflin, 1975. English.

AN: Includes artwork by: Peter Rodriguez, Arturo Anselmo Roman, Carmen Lomas Garza, Santa Barraza, and Cesar Augusto Martinez.

7834 Cardona, Patricia. Gana adeptos de Museo Mexicano de San Francisco: Pedro Rodriguez. UNO MAS UNO, (February 6, 1978), p. 18. Spanish.

AN: Report and brief history of the Mexican Museum which opened in 1975 with a collection of colonial santos. The museum offers a vista of Mexican culture to people in the United States. Director Peter Rodriguez says that Chicano artists Roberto Gonzalez, Felipe Reyes, Alfredo Arreguin, Gustavo Rivera, and Carmen Lomas Garza are some of the best. Illustrated.

7835 Center for the Visual Arts, Oakland, CA. Fujioka, Herman, Rivera and Rodriguez. ARTSLETTER, Vol. 6, no. 3 (May, June, 1980). English.

AN: Article unites Gustavo Rivera and Peter Rodriguez as artists who share a commitment to expressionist techniques. Illustrated with one black and white photograph of each artist's work.

7836 Hartnell College Studio Gallery, Salinas, CA. Paintings, drawings, prints by San Francisco Bay Area Chicano artists. Exhibit brochure, 1971. English.

AN: Brochure for exhibit featuring Francisco Camplis, Graciela Carrillo, Sal Castaneda, Priscilla Dominguez, J. Duarte, Rupert Garcia, Carlos Loarca, Irene Perez, Vincent Rascon, Michael Rios, Peter Rodriguez, Luis Valsoto, Esteban Villa, Rene Yanez, Zala. Illustrated by Rupert Carcia print.

7837 Heard Museum, Phoenix, AZ. First Annual Southwest Chicano Art Invitational Exposition. Invitation for reception, 1976. English.

AN: Invitation to a reception for artists Luis Jimenez (Roswell, New Mexico), Eugenio Quesada (Phoenix), Felipe Reyes (San Antonio), Pedro Rodriguez (San Francisco), Pedro Romero (Cannon City, Colo.) One illustration.

7838 Martinez, Anita. Raza art. EL TECOLOTE, Vol. 1, no. 8 (November 30, 1970), p. 1. English.

AN: Jay Ojeda, newly selected director of Galeria de la Raza, describes the memorial exhibition dedicated to Ruben Salazar installed at the Galeria on Dec. 12, 1970. Salazar symbolized and synthesized many of the goals subscribed to by artist members of La Galeria. The exhibit included work by Chicano and Latino artists Francisco Camplis, Jay Ojeda, Jose Romero, Rolando Castellon, Rene Yanez, Luis Valsoto, Mike Ruiz, Carlos Perez, Gustavo Rivera, Peter Rodriguez, Carlos Loarca and Ralph Maradiaga.

7839 Los Medanos College Gallery, [CA]. Cinco/five: an exhibit of five Bay Area artists. Exhibition brochure, n.d. English.

AN: Artists Gerry Concha, Gustavo Rivera, Raoul Mora, Manuel Villamor and Peter Rodriguez included in the show. Illustrated by Peter Rodriguez's portraits of the five.

Rodriguez, Peter (cont.)

7840 The Mexican Museum, San Francisco, CA. Los primeros cinco anos: fifth anniversary exhibit. Exhibition brochure, 1980-81. English.

AN: 65 Mexican, Chicano, and Latino artists exhibited for the fifth anniversary of the Mexican Museum, directed by artist Peter Rodriguez. Cover is drawing by Carmen Lomas Garza.

7841 Morch, Albert. He put down his brushes for a dream. SAN FRANCISCO SUNDAY EXAMINER AND CHRONICLE, (October 2, 1977), p. Scene, 3. English.

AN: Brief profile of painter Peter Rodriguez, founder and director of the Mexican Museum in San Francisco which opened in 1975. On exhibit are the works of San Francisco artist Jerry Concha. Illustrated.

7842 Ojeda, Jay. Galeria de la Raza--art for the community. SAN FRANCISCO PROGRESS, (March 24, 1972). English.

AN: Analysis of group exhibition by thirty-four Raza artists. Commentary on the work of Latin American artists Consuelo Mendez, Rolando Castellon, and Chicano artists Rupert Garcia, Chuy Campusano and Peter Rodriguez.

7843 Rodriguez, Pedro and Walla Walla Community College, Walla Walla, WA. Chicano art exhibition. Exhibition invitation, 1981. English.

AN: Poster invitation to exhibition by Pedro Rodriguez, Associate professor of Chicano Studies at Washington State University, Pullman, Washington. Rodriguez presented a lecture in English, "Chicano Art and Its Mexican Antecedents," and one in Spanish, "El Muralismo en Mexico y Mexico-America." Illustrated with painting of woman shrouded in a rebozo.

7844 Temko, Allan. Ole! It's already a triumph. REVIEW [supplement to SAN FRANCISCO SUNDAY EXAMINER], (December 28, 1980), p. 13-14. English.

AN: A glowing report on the Mexican Museum as it celebrates its fifth anniversary. Provides details about programs, financing and goals. Brief analysis of the work of sculptor Manuel Neri and painters Manuel Villamor, Gustavo Rivera, Alfredo Arreguin and Miguel Almaguer. Informative profile on Peter Rodriguez, founder and Executive Director of the Museum.

7845 Torres, Miguel. Mexican Museum - artifacts and culture to open in S.F. EL TECOLOTE, Vol. 6, no. 1 (October 1975), p. 4. English.

AN: On April 1972, the first organizational meeting of a new Mexican Museum was held. Later, a Board of Directors was organized and fifteen months later, the Museum was incorporated by the state of California as a non-profit organization. Pedro Rodriguez, founder-director of the Museum tells his aspirations and goals for this unique repository of Mexican culture in the United States. Illustrated with photograph of the Director and examples of work from the Museum's collection.

Rodriguez, Raul

7846 Aguilar, George. Raul Rodriguez, parade artist extraordinaire. NUESTRO, Vol. 6, no. 10 (December 1982), p. 11-14. English.

AN: Raul Rodriguez, a Mexican American float designer is considered a top artist in his field and one of the most successful in the country. Many of his floats have won prizes in the Tournament of Roses. In addition, Rodriguez designs facades for hotels on the Las Vegas Strip, most notably the facades of the Flamingo Hotel, the Dunes, and the Oasis.

Rodriguez, Roberto

7847 Wood carving art. EASTSIDE JRNL, (January 7, 1971), p. 2. English.

AN: Two photographs and commentary on woodcarver Roberto H. Rodriguez on the occasion of his one man show at the East Los Angeles Library. Illustrated work shows pre-Columbian motifs.

Rodriguez, Ruth

7848 Venegas, Sybil. Conditions for producing Chicana art. CHISMEARTE, Vol. 1, no. 4 (Fall, Winter, 1977, 1978), p. 2, 4. English.

AN: Chicana artists face more obstacles than white women or Chicano counterparts in the arts. Mexican life style has portrayed the ideal of a submissive woman, but the values have changed. Chicana artists are concerned with women and their struggles. Muralists include Patricia Rodriguez, Irene Perez, Consuelo Mendez de Castillo, Susan Cervantes, Ester Hernandez, Miriam Olivo, Ruth Rodriguez, of the Mujeres Muralistas (San Francisco). Other artists are Etta Delgado and Barbara Carrasco.

Rodriguez, Santos

7849 Salazar, Juan Albert. Entelequia. 16 MM Film, 1978. Bilingual.

AN: This production is Salazar's MFA thesis from the Department of Art, University of Utah. Its purpose is to explore the Chicano mentality. Based on the shooting of Santos Rodriguez in Texas, the historical fact is abstracted and the emotional impact transformed to an analytical examination of the whys and hows raised by such a situation.

Rodriguez, Vicente

7850 Galeria de la Raza, San Antonio, TX. Celebration seventy-four. Exhibition catalog, [ca. 1974]. English.

AN: Catalog of extensive exhibition including European, Mexican, and the following Texan Chicano artists: Rolando Garces, Cesar Martinez, Ray Chavez, Vicente Rodriguez, Jorge Garza, Alfred Rodriguez, Luis Guerra, Carmen Lomas Garza, Bruno Andrade, Jr., Amado M. Pena Jr., Roberto Rios, Jose Trevino, Rudy Trevino, Luis Santoyo, Tati Rubio, Eduardo C. Garza, Arthur de la Fuente, and Jesus Campos Trevino.

Rodriguez, Vicente (cont.)

7851 Instituto Chicano de Artes y Artesanias
(Texas Instit. Educational Development) and
Instituto Cultural Mexicano (SER/UNAM), San
Antonio, TX. Artistas chicanos: Los
Quemados. San Antonio, TX: Instituto
Chicano, Texas Institute for Educational
Development, 1975. English.

AN: Invitation to an exhibit and
manifesto of 1975 Austin-San Antonio
artists' group, Los Quemados. Included Santa
Barraza, Carolina Flores, Carmen Lomas
Garza, Luis Guerra, Cesar Augusto Martinez,
Santos Martinez, Amado Maurilio Pena, Jr.,
Jose Rivera, Vicente Rodriguez, Jose
Trevino.

Roman, Arturo

7852 Art directors, take note. INTERRACIAL BOOKS
FOR CHILDREN, Vol. 5, no. 7-8 (1975), p. 19.
English.

AN: Focus on the work of three Chicano
illustrators: Salvador Barajas V., Arturo
Roman, and Guillermo Aranda. Includes
representative examples of their work.

7853 Campesino Business and Joint Enterprise
Building, Fresno, CA. Sabor a Fresno. Arte
chicano: los Four and la Brocha. Exhibition
invitation [1976]. English.

AN: Invitation to an exhibit of works by
Los Four of Los Angeles and members of La
Brocha del Valle of Fresno: Arturo Roman,
Sal Garcia, John Sierra, Juan Truner, Sapo
de Aztlan, Fernando Hernandez, Alberto
Reyes, Ernesto Palomino, Lee Orona,
Francisco Barrios, Juan Ybarra, Bobby Reyes,
Alberto Hernandez. Brocha was started by
Palomino (California State University,
Fresno professor) to pool talents of Central
Valley artists.

7854 Cardenas de Dwyer, Carlota, ed. Chicano
voices. Boston, MS: Houghton Mifflin, 1975.
English.

AN: Includes artwork by: Peter
Rodriguez, Arturo Anselmo Roman, Carmen
Lomas Garza, Santa Barraza, and Cesar
Augusto Martinez.

Romano-V., Octavio Ignacio

7855 Mexican American Community Service
Organization, San Jose, CA. Exhibition of
contemporary art. Exhibition brochure, 1968.
English.

AN: Biographical and exhibition data for
Al Barela, Bert Hermosillo, Octavio Romano,
Luis Valdez, Vincent P. Rascon, John Soares
and Al Espinoza.

Romero, Alejandro E.

7856 59th Street Gallery, St. Louis, MO. Midwest
Mexican-American art exhibit: Mexico and its
artists. Exhibition brochure, 1981. English.

AN: Sponsored by the Sociedad Mexicana
"Benito Juarez" and the international
Institute of St. Louis, this three-part
exhibit includes 1) MEXICO AS SEEN BY HER
CHILDREN, a bilingual exhibit from Mexico
traveling under Smithsonian Institution
auspices, 2) MEXICAN CHILDREN IN THE U.S.A.,
3) MEXICAN AMERICAN ARTISTS. In the latter
are included Stephen Capiz (Roseville,
Minn.), Jose Gonzalez (Chicago), Cesar A.

Martinez (San Antonio), Ada Medina (Des
Moines), Nora Chapa Mendoza (West
Bloomfield, Mich.), Rene David
Michel-Trapaga (St. Louis), David Munoz
(Kansas City, Mo.), Jose Luis Narezo (Grand
Rapids, Mich.), Benny Ordonez, Roman
Villarreal (Chicago), Alejandro Romero
(Chicago), Aurelio Diaz "Tekpankalli"
(Chicago), Simon Ybarra (St. Louis).

7857 Centro Cultural Rafael Cintron Ortiz,
University of Illinois, Chicago. Alejandro
Romero. Exhibition catalog, 1978. English.

AN: Full color catalog of drawings and
paintings by Mexican-born artist living in
Chicago.

7858 Dittmar Memorial Gallery, Northwestern
University, Evanston, IL and King, Elaine A.
Alejandro Romero: new works. Exhibit
catalog, 1981. English.

AN: Full color illustrated catalog of
paintings by the Mexican-born artist who has
been living in the United States since the
early 1970s. His images appear to be
grounded in the work of Bosch, Goya,
Brueghel, and Diego Rivera. There is a
synthesis of personal symbolism and
expressionism.

7859 Intar, International Art Relations, Inc.,
New York, NY and Ferez Kuri, F. Jose.
Alejandro E. Romero. Exhibition catalog,
1977. English.

AN: Exhibit catalog of drawings and
paintings by Mexican-born painter and
muralist living in Chicago. Illustrated in
color.

7860 President's Gallery, Chicago State
University and Sorell, Victor A. Alejandro
Romero. Exhibition catalog, 1979. English.

AN: Catalog of an exhibit by
Mexican-born painter and muralist who has
been working in the United States since
about 1973. He has lived in Chicago since
1976. Illustrated.

Romero, Donald

7861 [Untitled]. Exhibition invitation. Santa Fe,
NM: Santuario de Nuestra Senora de
Guadalupe, 1980. English.

AN: Invitation to an exhibit by three
northern New Mexico artists: Claudio Salazar
(sculptor from Espanola), Eliud Salazar
(painter from Canones)--both members of the
Escuela Artesana--and Donald Romero (painter
from Santa Fe).

Romero, Enrique

7862 COMMUNITY MURALS (San Francisco, CA). (Fall 1981). English.

AN: Citywide Murals Group of Denver, Colorado assisted the Chilean-oriented Brigada Orlando Letelier with a mural in their city; Carlos Sandoval of Denver doing mural in Guerrero, Mexico; Ray Patlan of Berkeley, California assisting with mural in Mexico painted by Arnold Belkin's class at the Academy of San Carlos; report on the exhibit MURALS OF AZTLAN: THE STREET PAINTERS OF EAST LOS with a reprint of debate on the event by Shifra M. Goldman, Judithe Elena Hernandez de Neikrug, and comments by John Pitman Weber and Tim Drescher; report on DAR LUZ mural directed by Santa Barraza in Austin, Texas, and a new mural in Hayward, California directed by Enrique Romero; a mural sponsored by the Chicano Youth Center of Fresno, California showing the influence of Mexican calendars; a new mural, OAKLAND'S PORTRAIT by Daniel Galvez in Oakland, California; pro-and-con discussion of social function of graffiti in response to letter from Belgian source; reprint of story on spray paint crime bill (anti-graffiti) sponsored by California Assemblyman Richard Alatorre. Entire issue illustrated.

Romero, Frank

7863 Art Gallery, University of California, Irvine and Los Angeles County Museum of Art, Los Angeles, CA. Los Four: Almaraz, de la Rocha, Lujan, Romero. Exhibition brochure, 1973-74. English.

AN: Photographs and biographies of Carlos Almaraz, Roberto de la Rocha, Gilbert S. Lujan, Frank Romero.

7864 Los Four [art group]. Tales from the barrio by Los Four and friends. Los Angeles, CA: Los Four, Liberty Hill Foundation, United Steel Workers, [1977]. English.

AN: Comic book designed with drawings, comic strips, and calligraphy by Frank Romero, George Yepes, Carlos D. Almaraz, Leo Limon, Judithe Hernandez.

7865 Los Four exhibit in Union Gallery. UNIVERSITY TIMES, (November 6, 1975), p. 4. English.

AN: "Los Four," a group of four Chicano artists - Frank Romero, Roberto "Beto" de la Rocha, Gilbert Lujan, and Carlos Almaraz, with newcomer Judithe Hernandez - work with political cartoons, Catholic symbols, works of sardonic humor. They also paint street murals: several have been done recently in Los Angeles, La Puente, and Long Beach. Illustrated.

7866 Gamboa, Harry, Jr. Los murales de Aztlan. COMUNIDAD, (June 28, 1981), p. 8-9+. Spanish.

AN: Review of the exhibit at the Craft and Folk Art Museum of Los Angeles of MURALS OF AZTLAN: THE STREET PAINTERS OF EAST LOS in which Carlos Almaraz, Gronk, Judithe Hernandez, Willie Herron, Frank Romero, John Valadez and the East Los Streetscapers (David Botello, Wayne Healy, George Yepes) painted portable murals in the gallery. The murals are described and illustrated.

7867 Inner City Mural Program. Glendale, CA: Los Angeles County Dept. of Parks and Recreation, [ca. 1974]. English.

AN: Brief history and philosophy of the Inner City Mural Program from June 1, 1973 to May 31, 1974, when it was sponsored by the Cultural Arts Section of the Los Angeles County Department of Parks and Recreation, and coordinated by Lukman Glasgow. Artists Judithe Hernandez and Frank Romero included. 20 illustrations, some in color.

7868 Moisan, Jim. Ancient roots, new visions. ARTWEEK, Vol. 9, no. 26 (July 29, 1978), p. 8. English.

AN: Review of the show held at the Municipal Arts Gallery of Los Angeles, the first national touring show of Latino artists in the United States. Includes commentary on work of Larry Fuente, Luis Jimenez, Frank Romero, Harry Gamboa, Gronk, Rudy Martinez, Benjamin Serrano, Ricardo Diaz, Patssi Valdez, Mel Casas, Luis Leroy, Pedro Lujan. A related show, NEW VISIONS, L.A., includes Robert Delgado, Ray Bravo, Joe Moran, Rosalyn Mesquita, Patricia Murillo and others.

7869 Moreno, Eduardo. Los Four. Half-hour 16mm film. English.

AN: Film about the Los Angeles group of artists known as Los Four (originally Carlos Almaraz, Gilbert Sanchez Lujan, Roberto de la Rocha, Frank Romero), at the time of their exhibit at the Los Angeles County Museum of Art - the first time Chicano art was shown at the Museum.

7870 Oakland Museum, Oakland, CA and Laney College, Oakland, CA. In search of Aztlan. Exhibition brochure, 1974. English.

AN: Brochure for exhibit featuring Los Four: Carlos Almaraz, Gilbert Lujan, Roberto de la Rocha, Frank Romero, Judithe Hernandez.

7871 Oakland Museum, Oakland, CA. In search of Aztlan. Exhibition invitation, 1974. English.

AN: Invitation to an exhibit by Los Four, a Chicano art group started about 1973 in Los Angeles. On exhibit are the original members, Carlos Almaraz, Gilbert Lujan, Roberto de la Rocha, Frank Romero, and new member Judithe Hernandez.

7872 Oakland Museum presents 5 L.A. Chicano artists. EL MUNDO (Hayward, CA), (August 1974). English.

AN: Report on the exhibit THE SEARCH FOR AZTLAN, featuring paintings, murals, tortilla art, folk and religious symbols and totems by Carlos Almaraz, Roberto de la Rocha, Gilbert Lujan, Frank Romero and Judithe Hernandez. Included in the more than 100 works are a wall mural, a folk art pyramid, and part of a primed '51 Chevy lowrider. Illustrated.

Romero, Frank (cont.)

7873 Plagens, Peter. Los Four (Roberto de la
     Rocha, Carlos Almaraz, Gilbert Lujan and
     Frank Romero) at LACMA. ARTFORUM,
     (September 1974), p. 87-88. English.

     AN: Review of Los Four exhibit at Los
     Angeles County Museum of Art which calls it
     a "sociological bazaar" in which Chicanos
     have been "corrupted" by art schools and
     "museumized".

7874 The Point Gallery, Santa Monica, CA. ASCO
     (Gronk, Patssi, Gamboa, Herron), Los Four
     (Almaraz, de la Rocha, Judithe Hernandez,
     Gloriamalia Flores, Mauricio Ramirez, John
     Valadez. Exhibition invitation, [1975].
     English.

     AN: Illustrated invitation to an exhibit
     of Los Angeles artists.

7875 Polack, Clark. A question of style - Los
     Four and the Los Angeles County Museum of
     Art. SOUTHWEST ART, (July, August, 1974).
     English.

     AN: A double-edged assessment of the
     "Los Four" exhibit. The exhibition is at
     once lauded for being provocative and
     stimulating while at the same time failing
     artistically. Author feels that special
     treatment given Carlos Almaraz, Gilbert
     Lujan, Roberto de la Rocha and Frank Romero
     by the L.A. County Art Museum has not been
     extended to other young Los Angeles artists.

7876 San Francisco Museum of Modern Art, San
     Francisco, CA and Pearlstein, Howard.
     Aesthetics of graffiti. Exhibition catalog,
     1978. English.

     AN: Graffiti are defined as any
     coherently-intended presence written,
     scratched, painted, engraved, printed,
     pasted or otherwise impressed in a public
     place. Graffiti have been incorporated into
     works by artists. In this catalog, works by
     Chicano artists Carlos Almaraz, Wilfred
     Castano, Judithe Hernandez, Gilbert Lujan,
     Gustavo Rivera, Frank Romero, John M.
     Valadez, Victor M. Valle, Xavier Viramontes
     - as well as many Latino and non-Latino
     artist, appear.

7877 Santa Ana College, Santa Ana, CA and
     Goldman, Shifra M. Chicano art. Exhibition
     catalog, 1974. English.

     AN: Thirteen California artists are
     presented in a short essay defining Chicano
     as a double mestizaje of Mexican mestizo and
     U.S. influences that exists in a state of
     "reconciled conflict." Its aim is
     communication. Artists included are
     Malaquias Montoya, Rupert Garcia, Manuel
     Hernandez, Esteban Villa, Robert Gomez,
     Harvey Tarango, Mary Helen Castro, Eduardo
     Carrillo, Graciela Carrillo, and "Los Four":
     Carlos Almaraz, Robert de la Rocha, Judithe
     Hernandez, Gilbert Lujan and Frank Romero.

7878 Street art explosion in Los Angeles. SUNSET,
     (April 1973), p. 110-113. English.

     AN: Illustrated article on Los Angeles
     street murals including those by Roberto
     Chavez, Willie Herron, Frank Romero, Richard
     Jimenez, William Bejarano, Gilbert Lujan,
     Armando Cabrera, Frank Martinez, Charles
     Felix, and others.

Romero, Gilberto

7879 Martinez, Sue. New mural unveiled in Redwood
     City. EL TECOLOTE, Vol. 8, no. 7 (April
     1978), p. 7. English.

     AN: Commentary on the 147x22-ft. mural,
     DANZAS MEXICANAS, painted by Chicano artist
     Jose Antonio Burciaga and Mexican artist
     Gilberto Romero at the Redwood City Civic
     Center. The mural depicts dance rituals from
     various Mexican regions and the flora and
     fauna of Mexico. The mural became a subject
     of controversy when its creators splattered
     paint on it during its unveiling as a form
     of protest against the San Mateo Arts
     Council for its exploitation of Third World
     artists. Detail of mural showing "La Danza
     De Los Viejitos".

7880 Montoya, Emmanuel; Rodriguez, Patricia; and
     Acevedo, Mario (Torero). Canto al pueblo
     '78. NATIONAL MURALS NETWORK COMMUNITY
     NEWSLETTER, (1978). English.

     AN: The second annual Canto al Pueblo
     took place in Corpus Christi, Texas, where
     more than six murals were painted: "Wall of
     Cultural Education" by 13 artists headed by
     Roel Montealva; Carlota Espinoza, with
     children; Gilberto Romero, Jose Antonio
     Burciaga and Patricia Rodriguez,
     "Incomprehension al arte"; "Madre Tierra" by
     Manuel Martinez of Denver with Amador
     Hinojosa (Corpus Christi) and Enriquette
     Vasquez (New Mexico); Mario Torero; Salvador
     Vega of Chicago whose mural some Canto
     participants considered "insulting".

7881 SF muralists display paintings. VIVA,
     (October 8, 1972), p. 19. English.

     AN: Paintings, and photos of murals
     taken by Gilberto Romero, on display at the
     New Mexico Arts Commission. Artists Sammy,
     Carlos and Albert Leyba (the original
     members), Gilberto Guzman and Geronimo
     Garduno, part of the Artes Guadalupanos de
     Aztlan, finished a mural at Tot Lot in 1971
     and are team-painting La Clinica de la
     Gente. They have also painted a mural for
     West Las Vegas High School.

Romero, Jose

7882 Consejo Mexicano de Fotografia, A.C., Mexico
     City and Tibol, Raquel. Hecho en
     Latinoamerica: primera muestra de la
     fotografia latinoamericana contemporanea.
     Exhibition catalog, 1978. Spanish.

     AN: Catalog/book of the first colloquium
     and exhibit of Latin American photography.
     Among the Chicano artists in the exhibit
     were Francisco X. Camplis, Louis Carlos
     Bernal, Harry Gamboa, Jose P. Romero, Harvey
     J. Tarango, Isabel Castro. Statements by
     some of the artists. Great number of
     illustrations.

Romero, Jose (cont.)

7883 Garcia, Rupert. Laminas de la Raza. San
     Francisco: Garcia Litho and Printing
     Service, 1975. English.

     AN: Portfolio of drawings and prints by
     Patricia Rodriguez, Ricardo Apodaca,
     Xochitl, Domingo Rivera, Francisco Camplis,
     Rafael Maradiaga, Tom Rios, Juan Fuentes,
     Ricardo Diaz, Jose Romero, Consuelo Mendez,
     Jose Antonio Burciaga, Irene Perez, Ricardo
     Rios, Mike Rios, Graciela Carrillo, Rene
     Yanez, Luis Talamantez, Guillermo Bermudez,
     all from Northern California.

7884 Gonzalez, Tobias and Gonzalez, Sandra.
     Perspectives on Chicano education. Stanford,
     CA: Stanford University, 1975. English.

     AN: Reproductions of artworks by Ralph
     Maradiaga, Patricia Rodriguez, Roberto
     Bonilla, Francisco Camplis, Graciela
     Carrillo-Lopez, Juan Fuentes, Irene Perez,
     Roger Reyes, Carlos Loarca, Xavier
     Viramontes, Ralph McNeill, Rupert Garcia,
     Jose Romero.

7885 La historia de California, 1977. San
     Francisco, CA: Galeria de la Raza, 1977.
     English.

     AN: Handprinted silkscreen calendar of
     history seen from a Mexican point of view.
     Twelve sheets and a cover. Artists are:
     Ralph Maradiaga, Irene Perez, Louie "The
     Foot" Gonzalez, Max Garcia, Patricia
     Rodriguez, Jose Romero, Esteban Villa,
     Juanishi Orozco, Rodolfo Cuellar, Jose
     Montoya, Xavier Viramontes, Rene Yanez,
     Ricardo Favela, associated with the Galeria
     de la Raza, or the Royal Chicano Air Force
     of Sacramento.

7886 Martinez, Anita. Raza art. EL TECOLOTE, Vol.
     1, no. 8 (November 30, 1970), p. 1. English.

     AN: Jay Ojeda, newly selected director
     of Galeria de la Raza, describes the
     memorial exhibition dedicated to Ruben
     Salazar installed at the Galeria on Dec. 12,
     1970. Salazar symbolized and synthesized
     many of the goals subscribed to by artist
     members of La Galeria. The exhibit included
     work by Chicano and Latino artists Francisco
     Camplis, Jay Ojeda, Jose Romero, Rolando
     Castellon, Rene Yanez, Luis Valsoto, Mike
     Ruiz, Carlos Perez, Gustavo Rivera, Peter
     Rodriguez, Carlos Loarca and Ralph
     Maradiaga.

7887 Wine and cheese: foto fun. Berkeley, CA:
     Exhibition invitation, 1979. English.

     AN: Invitation to an evening of
     photographic slides and prints and
     discussion by photographers Jose Romero and
     Maria Pinedo.

Romero, Leo

7888 Anaya, Rudolfo A. and Ortiz, Simon J.
     1680-1980: a ceremony of brotherhood.
     Albuquerque, NM: Academic, 1981. English.

     AN: A cooperative publication by members
     of the former La Academia de la Nueva Raza
     (1969-1976) formed of writers and artists,
     and the Tri-Centennial Commission of the
     All-Indian Pueblo Council. Includes writings
     and artworks by Chicanos and Indians from
     New Mexico, California, Texas, and Arizona.
     Chicano artists works included are by Ellen
     Arellano, Juan Estevan Arellano, Alberto

Baros, Jose Antonio Burciaga, Juan Reyes
Cervantes, Rudy Cuellar, Ricardo Favela, El
Zarco Guerrero, Luis Jimenez, Jr., Carlos
Quinto Kemm, Alejandro Lopez, Floyd Lujan,
Jose Montoya, Juanishi Orozco, Leo Romero,
Secundino Sandoval, Jaime Valdez, Maria
Varela, Esteban Villa.

7889 Romero, Leo. Celso: poetry by Leo Romero,
     New Mexico. Berkeley, CA: Tonatiuh
     International, 1980. English.

     AN: Book illustrated by poet-artist Leo
     Romero from New Mexico. Drawings.

Romero, Orlando

7890 Blue Sky Productions. Los santeros. Color
     film, 29 min., 1979. English.

     AN: A 29 minute color film produced with
     funding assistance from New Mexico Highlands
     University and the National Endowment for
     the Arts. Features santeros Luis Tapia,
     Orlando Romero, Horacio Valdez.

Romero, Pedro

7891 Chicano muralists maintain traditions. LA
     CUCARACHA, (November 20, 1979), p. 7.
     English.

     AN: Introduction to Chicano muralism in
     Pueblo and comparison to the Mexican mural
     movement from which it draws inspiration. 20
     murals painted from 1977 to 1979. The
     muralists include Bernardo Duran, Juan
     Espinoza, Miguel "Freeloader" Garcia, Lola
     Gutierrez, Leo Lucero, Juan Pacheco, Dolores
     Pena, Pedro Romero, Stan Salazar, David
     Sandoval. Diego Rivera murals illustrated.

7892 Heard Museum, Phoenix, AZ. First Annual
     Southwest Chicano Art Invitational
     Exposition. Invitation for reception, 1976.
     English.

     AN: Invitation to a reception for
     artists Luis Jimenez (Roswell, New Mexico),
     Eugenio Quesada (Phoenix), Felipe Reyes (San
     Antonio), Pedro Rodriguez (San Francisco),
     Pedro Romero (Cannon City, Colo.) One
     illustration.

Romero Rodriguez, Gilberto

7893 Bauer, Bernard. Angry artists deface own
     mural. BERKELEY BARB, (March 1978), p. 7.
     English.

     AN: Chicano artists Jose Antonio
     Burciaga and Gilberto Romero Rodriguez
     recall a few struggles to sensitize local
     arts organizations to Raza art. Financial
     and political aspects of their painting a
     patriotic mural, "Danzas mexicanas" in
     Redwood City. Artists explain why they
     defaced their own mural as an act of
     protest.

7894 Burciaga, Jose Antonio. Mural protest.
     CHISMEARTE, Vol. 2, no. 1 (Summer 1978), p.
     27-28. English.

     AN: Mexican muralist Gilberto Romero
     Rodriguez and Chicano poet and artist
     Burciaga splatter their own mural at
     dedication ceremonies to protest their
     exploitation as artists and the opportunism
     and insensitivity of the commissioning
     organization, The Multicultural Arts Council
     of San Mateo County, CA. The mural was
     painted in Redwood City, CA. Illustrated.

Romero Rodriguez, Gilberto (cont.)

7895 Danzas mexicanas. Flyer, 1978. English.

AN: Illustrated flyer about a mural
designed and painted by Chicano artist and
poet Jose Antonio Burciaga and Mexican
muralist Gilberto Romero Rodriguez. Detail
of the 147 x 22 feet mural in Redwood City,
California is reproduced.

7896 Frankenstein, Alfred. One artist's
self-defense. SAN FRANCISCO CHRONICLE,
(March 9, 1978), p. 44. English.

AN: Art critic Frankenstein opens his
columns to Jose Antonio Burciaga to explain
why he, and fellow muralist Gilberto Romero
Rodriguez, splattered red, white and blue
paint on their completed mural at the
dedication ceremony. They were protesting
the exploitation, use and abuse of artists,
particularly by arts councils.

7897 Largest mural in San Mateo County becomes
official Saturday. REDWOOD CITY TRIBUNE,
(February 23, 1978), p. 12. English.

AN: Mural DANZAS MEXICANAS by Chicano
artist and poet Jose Antonio Burciaga and
Mexican muralist Gilberto Romero Rodriguez
was commissioned by the Multi-cultural Arts
Council of San Mateo County. Color
illustration.

Romo, Rafael

7898 Community Programs in the Arts and Sciences
(COMPAS). Artists in the city: a report on
C.E.T.A. artists in St. Paul. St. Paul, MN:
COMPAS, 1978. English.

AN: Includes data on Chicano muralists
John Acosta, Thomas Acosta, Paul Basquez,
Armando Estrella, and photographer Raphael
Romo.

Rosas, Carlos

7899 Canto al pueblo: an anthology of
experiences. San Antonio, TX: Penca Books,
1978. English.

AN: Includes works by: Mario E.
Castillo, Carlos Rosas, Jose G. Gonzalez,
Santos Martinez, Gilbert Munoz, Fred Loa,
Armando Ibanez and others.

7900 Chicano pride theme of mural. EL DIARIO DE
LA GENTE, Vol. 2, no. 11 (January 25, 1974).
English.

AN: Commentary on the 11x15 ft. mural
painted by Carlos Rosas outside the entrance
to the Tabor Inn in University Memorial
Center. Mural composed of Indio-Chicano
symbols.

7901 Forest Home Library, Milwaukee, WI. Arte
chicano de Carlos Rosas, Chicano muralist.
Exhibition invitation, 1978. English.

AN: Invitation to an exhibit by Carlos
Rosas [originally from El Paso, TX] who has
created murals with Chicano themes in many
parts of the United States. Sponsored by El
Taller Obrero Cultural de Milwaukee.

7902 Garcia-Camarillo, Cecilio and Rosas, Carlos.
Platicando con Carlos Rosas. RAYAS, Vol. 1,
no. 6 (November, December, 1978), p. 12, 11.
Spanish.

AN: Muralist Carlos Rosas painted murals

in Boulder and Denver, Colorado; Milwaukee,
Wisconsin, and El Paso, Texas. Commentary on
cross ethnic murals, views on art in
socialist countries, influence of Mexican
murals and information on his personal
preoccupation as a politically engaged
artist.

7903 Renteria, Ramon. Struggle of barrio life
reflected in mural. EL PASO TIMES,
(November 21, 1976). English.

AN: Carlos Rosas paints a 100x35-foot
mural on the El Paso Boys Club building, as
an homage to a child. It also reflects the
artist's roots in El Paso. Iconography of
the mural is discussed. Illustrated.

Royal Chicano Air Force (RCAF), Sacramento, CA

7904 And/Or Gallery, Seattle, WA. Artistas de
Aztlan. Exhibition announcement, 1975.
English.

AN: Exhibition announcement for an
important exhibit of Northwest Chicano art.
Co-sponsored by MEChA and the Chicano
Studies Program at the University of
Washington, the exhibit presented works by
Emilio Aguayo, Danny Desiga, Ricardo
Aguirre, Ramiro Benavidez, Elma Herada,
Pedro Rodriguez and others. A selection of
posters by Armando Cid of the R.C.A.F. group
from Sacramento, California was also
presented. Concurrently, at the Heny Gallery
of the University of Washington, Esteban
Villa presented a one-man show.

7905 Around the Bay. METAMORFOSIS, Vol. 3, no. 2
(1980), p. 101-108. English.

AN: Cultural review of activities in the
Bay Area, northern California, and
Sacramento. Includes history of the Galeria
de la Raza/Studio 24 (San Francisco), the
Centro de Artistas Chicanos/RCAF, Royal
Chicano Air Force (Sacramento), and a review
of Rupert Garcia's pastel portraits exhibit
at the Mexican Museum (S.F.) in 1981.
Illustrated. Continued in Vol. 4, no. 1,
1981.

7906 Bruce Novoa, Juan. [Interview with Jose
Montoya]. In CHICANO AUTHORS: INQUIRY BY
INTERVIEW. Austin, TX: University of Texas
Press, 1980, p. 115-136. English.

AN: Biography of Sacramento, CA artist
and poet Jose Montoya. Emphasizes the close
relationship between art and poetry in his
life and in that of the Royal Chicano Air
Force, which he co-founded.

7907 Calendar 1977. CHISMEARTE, no. 2 (Winter,
Spring, 1977), p. 26-27. English.

AN: Reproduction of one month of the
1977 silkscreen calendar produced in limited
edition by the Galeria de la Raza of San
Francisco and the Royal Chicano Air Force of
Sacramento, California. Displayed is Rene
Yanez's screen HISTORICAL
PHOTO-SILKSCREENMOVIE.

Royal Chicano Air Force (RCAF), Sacramento, CA
(cont.)

7908 Calendario de comida 1976. San Francisco,
     CA: Galeria de la Raza, 1976. English.

     AN: Handprinted silkscreen calendar
     consisting of twelve sheets and a cover. The
     work of the following artists is included:
     Ralph Maradiaga, Juanishi Orozco, Francisco
     Camplis, Ruben Guzman, Rodolfo Cuellar,
     Xavier Viramontes, Jose Montoya, Esteban
     Villa, Rene Yanez and Louis "The
     Foot" Gonzalez, Patricia Rodriguez, and
     Ricardo Favela. All of the above are
     associated with the Galeria de la Raza, or
     the Royal Chicano Air Force of Sacramento,
     CA.

7909 Case study: Centro de Artistas Chicanos,
     Sacramento, California. Washington, D.C.:
     Neighborhood Art Program National Organizing
     Committee, n.d. English.

     AN: In various regions of the Southwest,
     local artists have started Centros
     Culturales "whose primary purpose is the
     proliferation and safeguarding of Chicano
     art and culture." This case study presents
     pertinent information on the Centro de
     Artistas Chicanos founded in 1972 in
     Sacramento, California. It spells out the
     philosophy, goals, programs, components and
     management structure of the R.C.A.F. (Royal
     Chicano Air Force) and Centro de Artistas. A
     useful and important document. Illustrated.

7910 Centro de artistas chicanos. EL HISPANO,
     Vol. 6, no. 39 (March 19, 1974). English.

     AN: Description of goals and community
     oriented programs of the Centro. Illustrated
     with an R.C.A.F. poster announcing Teatro
     Campesino production of "LA CARPA DE LOS
     RASQUACHIS".

7911 Centro de Artistas Chicanos, Sacramento, CA.
     La arte cosmica [sic] de Esteban Villa:
     Chicano art exposition. Sacramento, CA:
     Centro de Artistas Chicanos, 1973. English.

     AN: Invitation to an exhibition of works
     by Esteban Villa at the RCAF's center.

7912 Centro de artistas, Sacra: recuerdo ...
     descubrimiento ... voluntad. CHISMEARTE,
     Vol. 1, no. 1 (Fall   1976), p. 6-7.
     English.

     AN: Summary of activities of the Centro
     de Artistas Chicanos, made up of artists
     from the Royal Chicano Air Force and other
     groups. The Centro makes posters, T-shirts,
     decals, murals and puts on a number of
     cultural and social events. Report on a
     "mass migration" July 1976 to the Academia
     de la Nueva Raza in Dixon, NM for two weeks
     of communion.

7913 Contemporary Arts Museum, Houston, TX and
     Martinez, Santos G., Jr. Mexican movie
     posters. Exhibition invitation, 1979.
     English.

     AN: Invitation to an exhibit of posters
     primarily from the collecttion of Enrique
     Flores and Xavier Gorena of Xochil Art
     Center, Mission, Texas. Martinez considers
     the posters monumental, with expressive
     qualities that have influenced Chicano
     poster makers like the Royal Chicano Air
     Force, and Rupert Garcia, and Texas artists
     like Luis Jimenez, Jesse Trevino and Cesar
     Martinez. One illustration. Introduction by

guest curator Santos G. Martinez, Jr. (See
Rupert Garcia's essay in the exhibition
catalog: POSTERS FROM THE GOLDEN AGE OF
MEXICAN CINEMA, for another point of view).

7914 Cuellar, Rodolfo. Esteban Villa-maximo
     exponente del arte indigena mexicano. EL
     HISPANO, Vol. 8, no. 23 (January 27, 1976),
     p. 3. Spanish.

     AN: Biographical data on the artist
     focusing on his activism in the formation of
     the Centro de Artistas Chicanos in
     Sacramento and the coalition of Centros
     Chicanos in California. Illustrated with
     photographs of the artist, one of his murals
     and a special emblem for the "Esteban Villa
     Fan Club" designed by the R.C.A.F.

7915 Galeria de la Raza/Studio 24, San Francisco,
     CA. Royal Chicano Air Force presents
     "Chicanos del Valle Tortilla Opening".
     Exhibition invitation, 1971. English.

7916 Hillinger, Charles. 'Chicano Air Force'
     flies high. LOS ANGELES TIMES, (July 22,
     1979), p. I, 3+. English.

     AN: Illustrated review of the personnel
     and purpose of the Royal Chicano Air Force.

7917 La historia de California, 1977. San
     Francisco, CA: Galeria de la Raza, 1977.
     English.

     AN: Handprinted silkscreen calendar of
     history seen from a Mexican point of view.
     Twelve sheets and a cover. Artists are:
     Ralph Maradiaga, Irene Perez, Louie "The
     Foot" Gonzalez, Max Garcia, Patricia
     Rodriguez, Jose Romero, Esteban Villa,
     Juanishi Orozco, Rodolfo Cuellar, Jose
     Montoya, Xavier Viramontes, Rene Yanez,
     Ricardo Favela, associated with the Galeria
     de la Raza, or the Royal Chicano Air Force
     of Sacramento.

7918 Montoya, Jose E. Pachuco art: a historical
     update. Sacramento, CA: Royal Chicano Air
     Force, 1977. English.

     AN: Booklet outlining the history of the
     Zoot Suit Riots of 1943 and the making of
     the Pachuco myth, written by Montoya and
     illustrated with his pen-and-ink drawings of
     Pachucos and Pachucas.

7919 Montoya, Jose E. and Murguia, Alejandro. El
     sol y los de abajo and other R.C.A.F. poems
     / oracion a la mano poderosa. San Francisco,
     CA: Ediciones Pocho-Che, 1972. English.

     AN: 10 illustrations by Sacramento, CA
     artist Armando Cid.

7920 Photo-graphics/foto-grafica. MAIZE, Vol. 4,
     no. 1-2 (Fall   , Winter, 1980, 1981).
     Bilingual.

     AN: 9 drawings and prints by Royal
     Chicano Air Force (Sacramento, Calif.)
     artists Jose Montoya, Juanishi Orozco,
     Esteban Villa.

7921 R.C.A.F. artistas precursores del arte
     chicano. EL HISPANO, Vol. 8, no. 35
     (February 17, 1976), p. 1. English.

     AN: Information on the R.C.A.F.
     organization. Includes group photograph of
     R.C.A.F. members, Jose Montoya, Esteban
     Villa, John Carrillo, Ricardo Fabela, Rudy
     Cuellar, Juanishi Orozco and Frank Godena.

Royal Chicano Air Force (RCAF), Sacramento, CA
(cont.)

7922 Rios, Sam. Chicano muralist: Toltecotl in
Aztlan. Unpublished paper, 1980. English.

AN: History of pre-Columbian, Mexican,
and Chicano wall paintings. Describes in
detail murals by Jose Montoya, Juanishi
Orozco, Esteban Villa, Stan Padilla, Juan
Cervantes, Lorraine Garcia of the Centro de
Artistas Chicanos, Royal Chicano Air Force,
painted in 1977 at Southside Park,
Sacramento, Calif. Symbolism is explained.

7923 Royal Chicano Air Force (RCAF), Sacramento,
CA. [RCAF posters]. CHISMEARTE, no. 1 (Fall
1976), p. 42-44.

7924 San Jose Museum of Art. Cinco de Mayo: el
arte chicano de hoy, the works of Mexican
American artists. Exhibition catalog, 1974.
English.

AN: Bilingual, illustrated, small
exhibition catalogue. Includes collective
work by Centro de la Gente of San Jose and
the Royal Chicano Air Force (R.C.A.F.) of
Sacramento, California. Also lists more than
twenty other exhibiting artists.

7925 Sommer, Robert. Street art. New York: Quick
Fox, 1975. English.

AN: Introductory essay covering the
history of the new mural movement, forms of
street art, politics, street sculpture, how
to locate and photograph street art. Chicano
murals include Charles Felix and others at
Estrada Courts (L.A.), RCAF murals in
Sacramento, Jose Montoya and others
(Broderick, Ca.) Marcos Raya (Chicago), Mike
Rios (Neighborhood Legal Aid, S.F.)
Mechicano Art Center (L.A.) Johnny Alvarez
(L.A.), New Mexico State Employment Bldg.,
Albuquerque mural, Lorena Street School
(L.A.), two murals, Casa de la Raza
Alternative School (Berkeley), Santa Fe, New
Mexico mural, Francisco Hernandez (L.A.),
Artes Guadalupanos de Aztlan (N. Mexico),
Willie Herron (L.A.). Better documentation
would have been welcome.

7926 El Taller, Inc., Chicago, IL and Movimiento
Artistico Chicano (MARCH), Chicago, IL.
Skyjacked: screenprinted posters from
California by the Royal Chicano Air Force
(R.C.A.F.), 1980. Exhibition invitation,
1980. English.

AN: Invitation to an exhibit at the El
Taller Gallery, co-sponsored by MARCH.
Illustrated with a print by San Francisco
artist Xavier Viramontes.

7927 University Art Museum, Berkeley, CA. The
Fifth Sun: Contemporary/Traditional Chicano
& Latino Art. Exhibition catalog, 1977.
English.

AN: Catalog of exhibit including 45
artists of northern California. Texts deal
with Mexican muralists, Mujeres Muralistas &
other muralists, posters, the Chicano art
movement, altars, La Raza Silkscreen Center,
Galeria de la Raza, the Mexican Museum, the
Sacramento Centro de Artistas Chicanos/RCAF.
Mural maps of S.F. Bay Area and Sacramento.
Many illustrations.

**Ruben E. Salazar Bicentennial Building, Plaza de
la Raza, Los Angeles, CA**

7928 Townsend, Dorothy and Driscoll, John. Fiesta

honors expansion of Latino center. LOS
ANGELES TIMES, (June 28, 1981), p. I, 3.
English.

AN: Ground is broken for the Ruben
Salazar Bicentennial Building in Plaza de la
Raza's Lincoln Park location.

**[RUBEN SALAZAR MEMORIAL EXHIBIT], Galeria de la
Raza, San Francisco, CA**

7929 Martinez, Anita. Raza art. EL TECOLOTE, Vol.
1, no. 8 (November 30, 1970), p. 1. English.

AN: Jay Ojeda, newly selected director
of Galeria de la Raza, describes the
memorial exhibition dedicated to Ruben
Salazar installed at the Galeria on Dec. 12,
1970. Salazar symbolized and synthesized
many of the goals subscribed to by artist
members of La Galeria. The exhibit included
work by Chicano and Latino artists Francisco
Camplis, Jay Ojeda, Jose Romero, Rolando
Castellon, Rene Yanez, Luis Valsoto, Mike
Ruiz, Carlos Perez, Gustavo Rivera, Peter
Rodriguez, Carlos Loarca and Ralph
Maradiaga.

Rubin, Pilar C.

7930 Southwest Chicano Arts Center, Houston, TX.
Pilar C. Rubin. Exhibition invitation, 1977.
English.

AN: Illustrated invitation to exhibit of
sculpture.

Ruiz, Jack

7931 Martinez, Anita. Raza! Arte! Raza! Arte!
EL TECOLOTE, Vol. 1, no. 2 (September 7,
1970), p. 3. Bilingual.

AN: Galeria de la Raza opened on July,
1970 at 425 14th St. San Francisco. It was
an outgrowth of the Arte Seis organization
(an art effort established in the Mission
District in 1967 by Francisco Camplis,
Rupert Garcia, Ralph McNeil, Jay Ojeda and
Jack Ruiz). These and other artists brought
together by the Neighborhood Arts Program
have coalesced in the new Galeria de la
Raza. Article gives goals, organizational
scheme and plans for the Galeria. It's first
exhibit was a one man show by Esteban Villa
together with a photo and sketch exhibit on
Cuba by Jay Ojeda, Roberto Diaz Perez and
Gloria Ozuna. Illustrated with installation
view of new Galeria.

Ruiz, Jose Luis

7932 Peyton, Patricia, ed. Reel change: a guide
to social issue films. San Francisco, CA:
Film Fund, 1979. English.

AN: Includes a section on Hispanic film
with descriptions, sources, and rentals.
Listed are Esperanza Vasquez's AGUEDA
MARTINEZ, Sylvia Morales' CHICANA, Adolfo
Vargas' CONSUELO: QUIENES SOMOS?/WHO ARE
WE?, El Teatro Campesino's I AM JOAQUIN,
Jose Luis Ruiz's THE UNWANTED, Jesus
Salvador Trevino's YO SOY CHICANO, and
others. Listings are international in scope.

Ruiz, Mike

7933 Martinez, Anita. Raza art. EL TECOLOTE, Vol. 1, no. 8 (November 30, 1970), p. 1. English.

AN: Jay Ojeda, newly selected director of Galeria de la Raza, describes the memorial exhibition dedicated to Ruben Salazar installed at the Galeria on Dec. 12, 1970. Salazar symbolized and synthesized many of the goals subscribed to by artist members of La Galeria. The exhibit included work by Chicano and Latino artists Francisco Camplis, Jay Ojeda, Jose Romero, Rolando Castellon, Rene Yanez, Luis Valsoto, Mike Ruiz, Carlos Perez, Gustavo Rivera, Peter Rodriguez, Carlos Loarca and Ralph Maradiaga.

Ruiz Productions, Inc,. Los Angeles, CA

7934 Ruiz Productions. Los Angeles, CA: Ruiz Productions [ca. 1977]. English.

AN: Illustrated catalog of films produced by or about Chicanos and Mexicans, including LOS FOUR (artists group) by Jim Tartan; MESSAGES IN CLAY (pre-Columbian) by Ed Moreno and Barry Nye; LOS CARROS (cars) part I: EL CARRO NUEVO and part II: LOW RIDER by Frank Lisciandro and Alejandro Nogales.

Sacramento, CA

7935 Armando Cid art works on display at Barrio Gallery. EL HISPANO, Vol. 5, no. 44 (April 24, 1973). English.

AN: Description of Armando Cid's M.A. thesis exhibition. The dominant impulse in the paintings is an attempt to define and reflect a Chicano style.

7936 Around the Bay. METAMORFOSIS, Vol. 3, no. 2 (1980), p. 101-108. English.

AN: Cultural review of activities in the Bay Area, northern California, and Sacramento. Includes history of the Galeria de la Raza/Studio 24 (San Francisco), the Centro de Artistas Chicanos/RCAF, Royal Chicano Air Force (Sacramento), and a review of Rupert Garcia's pastel portraits exhibit at the Mexican Museum (S.F.) in 1981. Illustrated. Continued in Vol. 4, no. 1, 1981.

7937 Art Space - Open Ring Gallery, Sacramento, CA. El Pachuco art de Jose Montoya: a historical update. Exhibition invitation, 1977. English.

AN: Invitation to an exhibit. Illustrated with a reproduction of a 1977 silkscreen calendar page in color by Montoya.

7938 Centro de artistas, Sacra: recuerdo ... descubrimiento ... voluntad. CHISMEARTE, Vol. 1, no. 1 (Fall 1976), p. 6-7. English.

AN: Summary of activities of the Centro de Artistas Chicanos, made up of artists from the Royal Chicano Air Force and other groups. The Centro makes posters, T-shirts, decals, murals and puts on a number of cultural and social events. Report on a "mass migration" July 1976 to the Academia de la Nueva Raza in Dixon, NM for two weeks of communion.

7939 Goldman, Jane. Art against the wall.

SACRAMENTO MAGAZINE, (August 1980). English.

AN: Muralists Esteban Villa, Stan Padilla and Juanishi Orozco from the Centro de Artistas Chicanos are planning a symbolic 65 foot, four-story mural on the parking structure opposite Macy's. The mural is described in detail. Illustrated.

7940 Gonzalez, Hector. Aztlandia. EL HISPANO, Vol. 5, no. 2 (June 20, 1972).

AN: Story and photographs of a childrens sculptural park created by Pedro Ximenez.

7941 Gonzalez, Hector and Cid, Armando. An interview with Armando Cid. EL HISPANO, Vol. 5, no. 32 (January 23, 1973). English.

AN: Biographical information and commentary on Cid's career and his art style which is described as containing pre-Columbian motifs and mannerisms of the people in the barrio.

7942 Gonzalez, Hector. Rivera paints Boalt Hall mural. EL HISPANO, Vol. 5, no. 29 (January 2, 1973). English.

AN: Brief commentary on Sacramento artist Edward Rivera and his design for a mural to be installed in Boalt Hall at the University of California's Berkeley campus.

7943 Hillinger, Charles. 'Chicano Air Force' flies high. LOS ANGELES TIMES, (July 22, 1979), p. I, 3+. English.

AN: Illustrated review of the personnel and purpose of the Royal Chicano Air Force.

7944 Lomas Garza, Carmen; Montoya, Jose E.; and Pinedo, Maria Vita. What we are...now. Exhibition catalog, n.d. English.

AN: Drawings by Sacramento women artists: Lorraine Garcia, Eva C. Garcia, Kathryn E. Garcia, Celia Rodriguez, Patricia Carrillo.

7945 MacLatchie, Sharon. Art in the barrios: one man's commitment. LA LUZ, Vol. 3, no. 9 (December 1974), p. 17-18. English.

AN: Describes the Centro de Artistas Chicanos in Sacramento, California. Highlights the program for art in the Barrio and focuses on the work and personality of Jose Montoya.

7946 Photo-graphics/foto-grafica. MAIZE, Vol. 4, no. 1-2 (Fall , Winter, 1980, 1981). Bilingual.

AN: 9 drawings and prints by Royal Chicano Air Force (Sacramento, Calif.) artists Jose Montoya, Juanishi Orozco, Esteban Villa.

7947 San Francisco Museum of Modern Art, San Francisco, CA and Castellon, Rolando. Posters and society. Exhibition catalog, 1975. English.

AN: 26 artists exhibiting public announcement and social political commentary posters. Includes 14 Bay Area and Sacramento, Calif. Latino artists.

Sacramento, CA (cont.)

7948 Transcendente y majestuoso mural de las tres
     aguilas. EL HISPANO, Vol. 8, no. 4 (July 15,
     1975), p. 6. Spanish.

     AN: Biographical data on Juan Ishi
     Orozco and commentary on his mural "Las Tres
     Aguilas." One eagle represents mother earth,
     another the dominant racist system and the
     third is symbolic of the United Farmworkers
     and their struggle.

Sacramento Farmworkers Migrant Program

7949 Mural depicts la lucha campesina del
     mexicano. EL HISPANO, Vol. 8, no. 12
     (September 9, 1975). English.

     AN: Photograph and commentary on the
     mural by J. Orozco for the Sacramento
     Farmworker's Migrant Program on F. Street.
     Centered by the Virgin of Guadalupe, the
     mural is divided into four sections: The
     Farmworker in the Fields, The Tree of Life,
     Violence Against the Farmworkers, and the
     Racist System.

Sacramento State University
USE: California State University, Sacramento

Saenz, Susan

7950 Exxon Company, Houston, TX and Quirarte,
     Jacinto. Chicano art of the barrio.
     Exhibition brochure, n.d. [c.1976]. English.

     AN: Brochure for a traveling exhibit of
     photographically-reproduced Chicano murals:
     Leo Limon, Lucila Villasenor Grijalva,
     Antonio Esparza, Susan Saenz, Charles Felix,
     Hoyo-Mara gang, David A. Lopez and team,
     Roberto Chavez and team (Los Angeles); Jerry
     Concha, Ruben Guzman, Chuy Campusano (San
     Francisco); Manuel Unzueta (Santa Barbara).
     Ernie Palomino and Leo Esequiel Ozona
     (Fresno). Leo Tanguma (Houston), Roberto
     Lucero, Manuel Martinez and Al Sanchez
     (Denver).

Saints
USE: Santos

Salazar, Claudio

7951 [Untitled]. Exhibition invitation. Santa Fe,
     NM: Santuario de Nuestra Senora de
     Guadalupe, 1980. English.

     AN: Invitation to an exhibit by three
     northern New Mexico artists: Claudio Salazar
     (sculptor from Espanola), Eliud Salazar
     (painter from Canones)--both members of the
     Escuela Artesana--and Donald Romero (painter
     from Santa Fe).

Salazar, Eliud

7952 [Untitled]. Exhibition invitation. Santa Fe,
     NM: Santuario de Nuestra Senora de
     Guadalupe, 1980. English.

     AN: Invitation to an exhibit by three
     northern New Mexico artists: Claudio Salazar
     (sculptor from Espanola), Eliud Salazar
     (painter from Canones)--both members of the
     Escuela Artesana--and Donald Romero (painter
     from Santa Fe).

Salazar, Gregorio

7953 University of Houston/Lawndale Annex and
     Xochil Art and Culture Center, Mission, TX.

The instant image: an exhibition of polaroid
photography. Exhibition catalog, 1980.
English.

     AN: Exhibit of 14 artists including
     Tejanos Frank Fajardo, Guillermo Pulido,
     Gregorio Salazar and Armando Rodriguez.

THE SALAZAR INQUEST [film]

7954 Gamboa, Harry, Jr. Film, television, and
     Trevino. LA LUZ, Vol. 6, no. 10 (October
     1977), p. 7-8. English.

     AN: Jesus Salvador Trevino has been an
     active proponent and participant in
     transforming cultural inaccuracy about
     Chicanos in the media to accurate mass media
     models. A biography of Trevino follows,
     including discussion of some of his films:
     THE SALAZAR INQUEST, CHICANO MORATORIUM
     AFTERMATH, SOLEDAD, AMERICA TROPICAL, YO SOY
     CHICANO, RAICES DE SANGRE, as well as
     television series like ACCION CHICANO,
     AHORA, and INFINITY FACTORY.

Salazar, Ruben

7955 Baciu, Joyce A. and Diaz, Katherine A. Margo
     Albert: a woman who gets things done = una
     mujer que realiza lo que desea. CAMINOS,
     Vol. 2, no. 5 (September 1981), p. 44-46.
     Bilingual.

     AN: Mexican-born Margo Albert is a
     well-known Los Angeles, CA artist, dancer,
     and actress who has been most active on
     behalf of the Plaza de la Raza in East Los
     Angeles. This article describes her
     activities as Co-chairperson of the Los
     Angeles Bicentennial Committee. For Margo,
     the highlights of the celebration marking
     the 200th anniversary of the founding of Los
     Angeles, included a day-long Fiesta del
     Bicentenario; groundbreaking ceremonies for
     the Ruben Salazar Bicentennial Building; and
     the reception for an official delegation of
     charros, sponsored as a gift to the people
     of Los Angeles by the Mexican government.

7956 De la Rocha, Roberto. [Untitled woodcuts].
     CON SAFOS, no. 7 (Winter 1971), p. 12-13.

7957 Martinez, Anita. Raza art. EL TECOLOTE, Vol.
     1, no. 8 (November 30, 1970), p. 1. English.

     AN: Jay Ojeda, newly selected director
     of Galeria de la Raza, describes the
     memorial exhibition dedicated to Ruben
     Salazar installed at the Galeria on Dec. 12,
     1970. Salazar symbolized and synthesized
     many of the goals subscribed to by artist
     members of La Galeria. The exhibit included
     work by Chicano and Latino artists Francisco
     Camplis, Jay Ojeda, Jose Romero, Rolando
     Castellon, Rene Yanez, Luis Valsoto, Mike
     Ruiz, Carlos Perez, Gustavo Rivera, Peter
     Rodriguez, Carlos Loarca and Ralph
     Maradiaga.

7958 Martinez, O.W. "Bill". Here comes la gente
     fragmented and fused [paintings]. LA LUZ,
     Vol. 1, no. 1 (April 1972), p. 56-57.
     English.

Salazar, Ruben (cont.)

7959 [Untitled photograph]. LOS ANGELES TIMES,
(June 4, 1971), p. II, 2. English.

AN: Captioned illustration of Frank
Martinez's mural painting of slain LOS
ANGELES TIMES reporter Ruben Salazar.
Unveiling of the mural at the Doctor's
Hospital, East Los Angeles, during
groundbreaking ceremonies for a new wing.

Salazar Simpson, Sylvia

7960 Chicano art. ARTES VISUALES, no. 29 (1981).
English.

AN: Issue on Chicano art, introduced by
Los Angeles artist Roberto Gil de Montes.
Includes works and statements by: Pedro
Lujan (Texas); Raul M. Guerrero (Calif.);
Sylvia Salazar Simpson (New Mexico/Calif.);
Carlos Almaraz (Calif.); Rene Yanez
(Calif.); Jack Vargas (Calif.); Ray Bravo
(Calif.); John Valadez (Calif.); Gloria Maya
(Calif.); Elsa Flores (Calif.); Willie
Herron (Calif.); Gilbert "Magu" Lujan
(Calif.); Kay Torres, Jerry Lucas, and Louis
Perez (Calif.).

Salazar, Stan

7961 Chicano muralists maintain traditions. LA
CUCARACHA, (November 20, 1979), p. 7.
English.

AN: Introduction to Chicano muralism in
Pueblo and comparison to the Mexican mural
movement from which it draws inspiration. 20
murals painted from 1977 to 1979. The
muralists include Bernardo Duran, Juan
Espinoza, Miguel "Freeloader" Garcia, Lola
Gutierrez, Leo Lucero, Juan Pacheco, Dolores
Pena, Pedro Romero, Stan Salazar, David
Sandoval. Diego Rivera murals illustrated.

Saldana, Martin

7962 Pollock, Duncan. He sallied forth to paint.
ROCKY MOUNTAIN NEWS, (February 7, 1971), p.
1. English.

AN: Biographical information about
Martin Saldana, an eccentric personality
labeled as Denver's answer to Grandma Moses.
Saldana died in 1965 leaving behind a cache
of "primitive" paintings that soon became
much sought after by collectors. His work
portrayed the rural pageant of Mexican life.
Illustrated with self-portrait.

7963 Pollock, Duncan. Recognition arrives for
Martin Saldana. ROCKY MOUNTAIN NEWS,
(January 13, 1972), p. 55. English.

AN: After a long career as a vegetable
cook at the venerable Brown Palace Hotel in
Denver, Martin Saldana started art classes
at the Denver Art Museum. His work was
fresh, imaginative and totally naive. After
the artist's death in 1965 at age 90, his
paintings started to receive critical
acclaim. Article details Saldana's rise to
prominence and compares his artwork to that
of Henry Rousseau. Illustrated with
photograph of Martin Saldana.

Saldivar, Armandina

7964 Garcia-Camarillo, Mia. [Untitled drawing].
CARACOL, Vol. 2, no. 12 (August 1976), p. 3.
Spanish.

Salinas, Porfirio

7965 The art of Mexican America. EMPIRE MAGAZINE,
(November 1, 1970), p. 24-25. English.

AN: Visual portfolio with minimal text.
Includes paintings by Amado Pena, Mel Casas,
Porfirio Salinas, and sculpture by Octavio
Medellin. On the same page, Dr. Jacinto
Quirarte gives views on the nature of
Mexican art, the Mexican American artist,
and the connection between Mexican and
Mexican American art.

7966 Ashford, Gerald. Artistic styles have no
ethnic bonds. SUNDAY ONE, (October 18,
1970), p. [18]. English.

AN: Biographical information on
Spanish-surnamed artists living and working
in San Antonio. Includes commentary on
Porfirio Salinas Jr. and Mel Casas.

7967 Goddarth, Ruth. Porfirio Salinas. Austin,
TX: Rock House Press, 1975. English.

AN: Born on Nov. 6, 1910 on a farm near
Bastrop, Texas, Porfirio Salinas studied art
with Spanish artist Jose Arpa in San Antonio
and gradually became a regional landscapist
of wide renown. Salinas died April 18, 1973
at the age of 62. The book is lavishly
illustrated.

7968 Salazar, Veronica. Prominent
Mexican-Americans-Porfirio Salinas. SAN
ANTONIO EXPRESS-NEWS, (April 1, 1973), p.
I-4. English.

AN: Biographical information and
artistic chronology of Porfirio Salinas.
This self-taught artist is the most
prominent painter of Texas landscapes,
especially with bluebonnets. Former
president Lyndon B. Johnson was an ardent
fan and patron.

7969 Salinas, Porfirio. Bluebonnets and cactus:
an album of southwestern paintings. Austin,
TX: Pemberton Press, 1967. English.

AN: Portfolio of Salinas landscape
paintings and five short stories. Lavishly
illustrated as a special edition.

7970 Salinas, Porfirio. Porfirio Salinas: blue
bonnets and cactus; an album of Southwestern
paintings. Austin, TX: Pemberton Press,
1967. English.

AN: A lavishly illustrated edition of
five short stories interspersed with
reproductions of Porfirio Salinas
landscapes. Salinas is considered an
important Southwestern landscapist.

7971 Samuels, Peggy and Samuels, Harold. Salinas,
Porfirio. In THE ILLUSTRATED BIBLIOGRAPHICAL
ENCYCLOPEDIA OF THE AMERICAN WEST. Garden
City, NY: Doubleday, 1976, p. 415. English.

AN: Brief biography of Texas "bluebonnet
painter" (b. 1910). Only teachers were Jose
Arpa and Robert Wood of San Antonio. (See
also Jacinto Quirarte's book: MEXICAN
AMERICAN ARTISTS).

Salinas, Porfirio (cont.)

7972 White, Ron. Bluebonnet the flower of South
Texas painting. SAN ANTONIO EXPRESS-NEWS,
(December 14, 1975), p. 7-H. English.

AN: The South Texas landscape paintings
by Porfirio Salinas are immensely popular
and command high prices. This analysis of
the career and the production of the late
artist (died April 18, 1973), concludes that
Salinas was "a mediocre artist with mediocre
skills and a poor sense of imagination".

Salinas, Raul

7973 NEW ERA (U.S. Penitentiary, Leavenworth,
KA). (Fall , Winter, 1970). English.

AN: Under the art direction of Ruben
Estrella from San Antonio, Texas, NEW ERA, a
prison cultural magazine also featured the
caricatures and cartoons of Tone Briones
from Laredo, Texas. Raul Salinas, poet from
Austin, Texas was Associate Editor for both
issues.

SALT OF THE EARTH

7974 Wilson, Michael and Biberman, Herbert. Salt
of the earth [film]. 16mm, 94 min., b&w.
English.

AN: The first feature film made in the
U.S. of, by and for labor, it deals with a
real strike of Mexican American miners in
New Mexico in which women played a key role
in the men's victory and their own demands.
Mexican actress Rosaura Revueltas starred
with labor leader Juan Chacon. One of the
best films on the subject.

Salt River Valley, AZ

7975 Adams Hotel, Phoenix, AZ. Chicano and Indian
art exhibit. Exhibit invitation, 1979.
English.

AN: Invitation to an exhibit of 16
artists. Brief history of the organization
MARS (Moviemiento Artistico del Rio Salado)
of Phoenix, AZ, formed in Summer 1978 after
a Floricanto Culture Week. 98% of MARS
members are Chicano or Indian. Their purpose
is to build the Salt River Valley as a
cultural center of the Southwest.

**San Antonio Chicano Film Festival, Aug. 24-25,
1979**

7976 CHICANO CINEMA NEWSLETTER. Vol. 1, no. 6
(August 1979). English.

AN: Announcements of the San Antonio
Chicano Film Festival, a seminar on the
business of art, the receipt of a report of
the Task Force on Minorities in Public
Broadcasting, a critical report on the
Alternative Cinema Conference in New York,
which was attended by eleven members of the
Chicano Cinema Coalition, and a report and
critique of the report by the Task Force.

7977 Fourth annual San Antonio film festival. San
Antonio, TX: Oblate College of the
Southwest, 1979. Bilingual.

AN: Symposium and film festival catalog
featuring motion pictures and videocassettes
made by and about Mexicans, Chicanos and
Latinos. The Symposium focused on Latina
women in film and television, Margarita
Galban, Carmen Tafolla, Leticia Ponce, Grace
Castro Nagata, Marcela Fernandez Violante of

Mexico, and Sylvia Morales.

San Antonio Consortium for Hispanic Arts (SACHA)

7978 Minutaglio, Bill. S.A. aims at becoming
Hispanic art center. SAN ANTONIO
EXPRESS-NEWS, (January 18, 1981), p. 3-M+.
English.

AN: Rick Reyna is director of the
fledging San Antonio Consortium for Hispanic
Arts (SACHA), a city-funded umbrella
organization covering seven art groups,
three of which - Centro Cultural del Pueblo
(instruction for young people), Community
Cultural Arts Program (murals), and
Performance Artists Nucleus (displays and
exhibits) - concern the visual arts. Rudy
Garcia, Anastacio "Tache" Torres, and Ralph
Garcia (formerly of Garcia's Art Gallery)
head the three groups respectively.

San Antonio Mural Project

7979 Trevino, Rudy. San Antonio murals a self
portrait. PICANTE, Vol. 1, no. 3, p. 60-61.
English.

AN: Commentary on the San Antonio Mural
Project assisted by the CETA program and the
Barrio Betterment and Development
Corporation (BBDC). Goals and information on
the light murals in progress in the Casiano
Housing Project. Participating artists: Juan
Hernandez, Esteban Adame, Andrew Gutierrez,
Bob Tate, and Roberto de La Fuente.

San Antonio, TX

7980 Ashford, Gerald. Artistic styles have no
ethnic bonds. SUNDAY ONE, (October 18,
1970), p. [18]. English.

AN: Biographical information on
Spanish-surnamed artists living and working
in San Antonio. Includes commentary on
Porfirio Salinas Jr. and Mel Casas.

7981 Association for Resources and Technical
Services, Inc. (ARTS); Tejano Artists, Inc.;
and Performing Artists Nucleus, Inc. (PAN).
Tejano arts workshop. Brochure, 1981.
English.

AN: Call to a two-day arts workshop in
San Antonio designed to inform participants
on organizational development, networking,
fundraising, touring, marketing, public
relations, and audience development.
Southwest in scope, with input and
organization from Washington, D.C. and New
York.

7982 Le Bistro Restaurant, San Antonio, TX.
Contemporary paintings by Cesar Augusto
Martinez. Exhibition catalog, 1980. English.

AN: Catalog of an exhibit. Blurb about
the artist.

7983 Cesar Martinez. ARTES VISUALES, no. 29 (June
1981), p. 63. Bilingual.

AN: Two illustrations by the San
Antonio, Texas artist, a brief biography,
and the reprint of a letter published in the
catalog CUATRO CAMINOS, Southwest Texas
State University, San Marcos.

San Antonio, TX (cont.)

7984 Con Safo. San Antonio, TX: Pintores Chicanos de San Antonio, [ca. 1975]. English.

AN: Illustrated pamphlet issued by the San Antonio artists' group Con Safo. Includes a self-definition and a brief history of the group under the names El Grupo, Los Pintores de Aztlan, Los Pintores de la Nueva Raza, Con Safo (from 1967 on). Members include Jesse A. Almazan, Mel Casas, Jose Esquivel, Jose P. Garza, Cesar Augusto Martinez, Santos Martinez, Felipe Reyes, Roberto Rios, Jesus C. Trevino, and Vicente Velasquez.

7985 De la Torre, Alfredo. Editorial. CARACOL, Vol. 4, no. 6 (February 1978), p. 3. Bilingual.

AN: An editorial seeking support for a proposal by El Centro Inc., a Chicano art center in San Antonio, TX to commission murals and decorations in the downtown San Antonio area.

7986 De la Torre, Alfredo and Tellez, Miguel Angel. Entrevista con Don Miguel Angel Tellez=Interview with Don Miguel Angel Tellez. CARACOL, Vol. 5, no. 11-12 (July, August, 1979), p. 16-22. Bilingual.

AN: Tellez, born in San Antonio about 1915, son and grandson of painters who taught him the trade, tells about his life as commercial artist and his more symbolic work started in 1962. Illustrated.

7987 Extension Cultural SRE/UNAM, San Antonio, TX. Second non professional (black & white) photography contest: Mexican women in Texas. Competition announcement, [ca. 1980]. English.

AN: Announcement of photographic competition sponsored by the Extension arm of the Secretaria de Relaciones Exteriores/Universidad Nacional Autonoma de Mexico in San Antonio. The theme specified an homage to the Mexican woman in Texas.

7988 Galeria Tonantzin, Centro Cultural de LUCHA, Austin, TX. Mexican faces in San Antonio. Exhibition brochure, [1980]. English.

AN: Photography show by 24 young Chicanos from Texas sponsored by the Secretaria de Relaciones Exteriores and the Universidad Autonoma de Mexico, Cultural Extension program (SRE-UNAM) in San Antonio.

7989 Garcia, Ralph. Misconceptions or stereotyping the Chicano and Mexican arts in San Antonio. CARACOL, Vol. 5, no. 10 (June 1979), p. 9, 10. English.

AN: Brief overview of the arts in San Antonio, TX, and the desirability of cultural interchange between Chicano and Mexican artists.

7990 Institute, Plaza Mexico unique cultural gift. SAN ANTONIO EXPRESS-NEWS, (June 19, 1972), p. 6-B. English.

AN: Pres. Luis Echeverria of Mexico dedicates the Mexican Cultural Institute and Plaza Mexico, which will house an extension campus of National University of Mexico, in San Antonio. Mexican artists will be brought in and the Institute has a permanent art gallery.

7991 Mexican-American Institute of Cultural Exchange, San Antonio, TX and Alvarez Acosta, Miguel. Mel Casas paintings. Exhibition brochure, 1963. Bilingual.

AN: Exhibition brochure with biographical and exhibition chronology for El Paso born painter, Meliseo Casas. He is the first non-Mexican born artist invited to exhibit at the art gallery sponsored by the International Organization of Cultural Promotion for Foreign Relations in San Antonio.

7992 Minutaglio, Bill. Chicano take the art to the street of S.A. SAN ANTONIO EXPRESS-NEWS, (January 11, 1981), p. M, 1-2. English.

AN: Survey of Chicano murals in San Antonio including 30 two-story murals at Westside Cassiano Homes by students from the commercial art program of Lanier High directed by Anastacio "Tache" Torres and Rudy Trevino; 8 murals at Lanier High School; one at the City Hall offices; and others throughout the city. Illustrated.

7993 Minutaglio, Bill. S.A. aims at becoming Hispanic art center. SAN ANTONIO EXPRESS-NEWS, (January 18, 1981), p. 3-M+. English.

AN: Rick Reyna is director of the fledging San Antonio Consortium for Hispanic Arts (SACHA), a city-funded umbrella organization covering seven art groups, three of which - Centro Cultural del Pueblo (instruction for young people), Community Cultural Arts Program (murals), and Performance Artists Nucleus (displays and exhibits) - concern the visual arts. Rudy Garcia, Anastacio "Tache" Torres, and Ralph Garcia (formerly of Garcia's Art Gallery) head the three groups respectively.

7994 LA MOVIDA CON SAFO. no. 2 (February 1976). English.

AN: Mimeographed newsletter issued by Mel Casas about the San Antonio artists' group Con Safo. Reports on the exhibits, symposium, festival, TV appearance, film, and other activities of the group or its individual members. Illustrated.

7995 LA MOVIDA CON SAFO. no. 1 (Fall 1975). English.

AN: Mimeographed newletter issued by Mel Casas about the San Antonio artists' group Con Safo. Includes history of the group and its activities.

7996 OMICA Housing Corp., Inc., Homestead (Miami), FL. Dedication of heritage village. Brochure, 1977. English.

AN: Brochure of non-profit housing corporation which built, with Housing and Urban Development (HUD) funds, public homeownership housing for farmworkers and low-income rural residents of South Dade County. Illustrated with a mural by Roberto Rios of San Antonio, one of three done in Florida.

San Antonio, TX (cont.)

7997 Pena, Ruben R. Mel Casas - people in the arts. BUSINESS AND THE ARTS, (September, October, 1979), p. 15. English.

AN: Probing analysis of the work and life of San Antonio artist Mel Casas. Article is divided into five sections in which the artist gives his views on culture, art, society, the Southwest and himself. Contains biographical information and artistic trajectory.

7998 Rodriguez, Alfred. A historical survey of Chicano murals in the Southwest: an interdisciplinary teaching unit. Unpublished paper, 1980. English.

AN: Lists murals by title, artist and date (when known), location and subject. Los Angeles, San Francisco, San Diego, Fresno, San Antonio, Austin, Corpus Christi, Santa Fe, New Mexico murals are included. Circulated by the Institute of Latin American Studies, University of Austin, Texas.

7999 Rodriguez, Roland V. Urban design primer: comparative analyses of San Antonio urbanscapes. [s.l.: s.n., ca. 1979]. English.

AN: Proposal for a study to compare six sites in San Antonio with models of European townscapes. The purpose is to educate the public to enjoy its city and make future city planners sensitive to urban design. Also useful for architectural students.

8000 San Antonio Museum of Modern Art. Zarzamora: inaugural exhibition of Ladrones de la Luz. Exhibition invitation, 1979. English.

AN: Illustrated invitation to photographic exhibition including Norman Avila, David Cardenas, Franco Cernero, Enrique Hernandez, Robert Maxham, James Newberry, Isaac Rodriguez, Daryl Studebaker, Richard Tichich, Beverly Ulmer, Kathy Vargas.

8001 Stephens, Martha. Murals introduce Carlos Castaneda to Neil Armstrong. SAN ANTONIO EXPRESS-NEWS, (January 11, 1981), p. M, 1, 3. English.

AN: Survey of commissioned murals in San Antonio including Mexican artist Juan O'Gorman's mosaic at the Theatre for Performing Arts; Carlos Merida's and Fred Samuelson's at the Convention Center; Howard Cook's New Deal mural in the downtown post-office; Peter Hurd's, and James Sicner's (in progress) mural at Trinity University; Jesse "Chista" Cantu's at Mario's Restaurant; and Jesse Trevino's mural at Our Lady of the Lake University. Illustrated.

8002 Trafford, Al. The giant painted photo album: Jesse Trevino. SOUTHWEST ART, (April 1979). English.

AN: Well illustrated story on San Antonio photorealist painter Jesse Trevino. Includes biographical material, description of his working methods for murals and easel paintings, and self-characterization of his work as "cultural documentary painting".

8003 Trejo, Frank. S.A. mission doors inspired wood carver. SAN ANTONIO LIGHT, (January 10, 1971), p. 18. English.

AN: Biographical and exhibition information on San Antonio woodcarver Jesse V. Garcia. Illustrated by photograph of artist.

San Cristobal Valley Arts, Inc., NM

8004 New co-op in San Cristobal. GRITO DEL NORTE, Vol. 3, no. 8 (July 5, 1970), p. 13. English.

AN: Details formation of the San Cristobal Valley Arts Inc., a community corporation formed to train people in a silkscreen business venture. Aiming to use expressive forms as a source of economic development, the corporation published and distributed a line of Chicano silkscreen posters. Illustrated by three posters, WE SHALL ENDURE, SOMOS AZTLAN, and TAOS PUEBLO.

San Diego, CA

8005 Centro mural recipient of orchid award. LA PRENSA SAN DIEGO, (November 20, 1981), p. 5. English.

AN: The American Institute of Architects, the American Society of Interior Designers, the American Planning Association and the American Society of Landscape Architects award the Centro Cultural de la Raza of Balboa Park, San Diego, CA for Victor Ochoa's mural on its walls. Illustrated.

8006 Chicano art of the Southwest. San Antonio, TX: Instituto Chicano de Artes y Artesanias of the Texas Institute for Educational Development, 1975. English.

AN: Collection of 220 slides supplemented by slide annotation and artists' biographies researched and photographed by Texas artist Cesar A. Martinez over two years. Biographies cover 20 Texas, 6 New Mexico, and 15 northern California artists. Slides include, in addition, murals from Los Angeles and San Diego.

8007 Congreso de Artistas Chicanos en Aztlan, San Diego, CA. Diego Rivera, David Alfaro Siqueiros, Jose Clemente Orozco: exhibit of local artists, La Logan [San Diego]. Exhibition brochure, n.d. [c.1974]. English.

AN: Announcement of a traveling exhibit organized by Galeria de la Raza, San Francisco, from the collection of the San Francisco Museum of Art. Illustrated with a San Diego mural.

8008 Gardiner, Henry G. Painted exterior walls of Southern California. CURRANT ART MAGAZINE, Vol. 1, no. 2 (June, July, 1975), p. 16-23+. English.

AN: Good survey of street muralism, primarily in Los Angeles and San Diego, which started in 1968. Divided into eight "schools," including Chicano and non-Chicano muralists. Most Chicano murals associated with Goez Brothers Art Gallery and Mechicano Art Center in Los Angeles, the Coronado Bay Bridge group [Chicano Park] and Balboa Park group [Centro Cultural de la Raza]. Mural discussed in detail. Well illustrated.

San Diego, CA (cont.)

8009 Herrera, Barbara. Bisected barrio seeks new
     unity: Chicano part bridges past and future.
     EVENING TRIBUNE, (August 7, 1974), p. E-1.
     English.

> **AN:** Bisected by the Coronado bridge,
> remains of the Logan barrio are unified by
> Chicano Park and its murals recording
> Chicano culture. Inspired by Salvador
> Torres, who returned to Logan in 1967,
> barrio activists are working to restore
> community spirit and dignity. Illustrated.

8010 Herrera, Barbara. Chicano park expansion
     sought: barrio idealists face strong
     barriers. EVENING TRIBUNE, (August 10,
     1974), p. A-10. English.

> **AN:** Last of a three part series on
> Chicano Park. Barrio activists of the
> Chicano Park Steering Committee plan to
> extend the Chicano Park under the Coronado
> bridge from 5.8 acres to the bay, painting
> all the pillars with murals, and ending with
> a small marina. They are facing opposition
> from government officials, but are hopeful
> of success.

8011 Herrera, Barbara. The pillars are our trees:
     Chicano park needs planning, power. EVENING
     TRIBUNE, (August 8, 1974), p. D-1. English.

> **AN:** In the face of government and
> business opposition, activists obtained the
> land under the Coronado bridge to establish
> Chicano Park. They want to extend the park
> to the waterfront. Illustrated.

8012 Invitational art exhibition/exposicion
     artistas invitados. Exhibition invitation,
     [ca. 1976]. English.

> **AN:** A benefit night for the Chicano
> Health Clinic included an exhibit of San
> Diego, as well as Ensenada, Mexicali and
> Tijuana (Mexico) artists. San Diego Latino
> artists include Peruvians Guillermo Acevedo
> and Mario Acevedo Torero, Chicano Salvador
> Roberto Torres, and Mexican-born Raul Trejo.

8013 NATIONAL MURALS NETWORK COMMUNITY
     NEWSLETTER. (Fall 1980). English.

> **AN:** Reports on murals in San Francisco,
> CA, by the Chicano Moratorium Coalition; in
> Chicago about the Anti-War Preparations
> mural; in Houston by a student at the
> Association for Advancement of Mexican
> Americans; on Michael Schorr's mural in
> Chicanok, San Diego, CA; on a segment being
> painted at the Tujunga Wash mural in Los
> Angeles under Judy Baca; on south San Diego
> murals being painted out; Alan Barnett's
> survey of Southwest murals. Illustrated.

8014 Ordorica, Leticia. Community expression in
     muralism. VOZ FRONTERIZA, Vol. 3, no. 5
     (March 1978). English.

> **AN:** Brief history of Chicano Park in San
> Diego. Announcement of the "Mural Marathon"
> from April 1 to April 20, two days before
> the Eighth Annual Chicano Park Celebration.
> Five pillars and the kiosk will be painted.
> Illustration.

8015 Rodriguez, Alfred. A historical survey of
     Chicano murals in the Southwest: an
     interdisciplinary teaching unit. Unpublished
     paper, 1980. English.

> **AN:** Lists murals by title, artist and

date (when known), location and subject. Los
Angeles, San Francisco, San Diego, Fresno,
San Antonio, Austin, Corpus Christi, Santa
Fe, New Mexico murals are included.
Circulated by the Institute of Latin
American Studies, University of Austin,
Texas.

8016 Torres, Salvador Roberto. Creative aspects
     of la Raza inspired by Chicano experiences.
     Unpublished thesis, 1973. Bilingual.

> **AN:** Project presents six paintings and
> six drawings by San Diego artist Torres
> based on the feeling and impact of United
> Farm Workers Huelga banner, used on a
> personal level. Torres wants to make an
> "imaginary theatre" of the ideas drawn from
> the Chicano movement. Bilingual.
> Illustrated.

San Francisco Art Institute

8017 Bravo, Antonio. Manuel Alvarez Bravo at the
     San Francisco Art Institute. CHISMEARTE,
     Vol. 2, no. 1 (Summer 1978), p. 37. English.

> **AN:** Presentation of the Mexican
> photographer's work in relation to a
> visiting exhibit in the United States.
> Illustrated.

8018 Gonzalez, Lila. Ideas on a Third World art
     exhibit. SAN FRANCISCO ODALISQUE, (October,
     November, 1976), p. 5-6. English.

> **AN:** Review essay on the exhibition
> "Other Sources: An American Essay" sponsored
> by the San Francisco Art Institute.

San Francisco, CA

8019 Alarcon, Francisco X. El Museo Mexicano,
     quinto aniversario. EL TECOLOTE LITERARY
     MAGAZINE, (December 10, 1981). Spanish.

> **AN:** Goals of the Mexican Museum in San
> Francisco are contextualized within the
> social nexus of the Chicano Art Movement of
> the 1960s. Explains functional difference
> between Mexican Museum and community art
> galleries.

8020 Albright, Thomas. The sensual moods of
     nature. SAN FRANCISCO CHRONICLE, (January
     23, 1971), p. 34. English.

> **AN:** Review of an exhibition of paintings
> by Pedro Rodriguez of San Francisco at the
> Galeria de La Raza. Work classified as
> lyrical abstractions "in the vein of
> introspective lyric poetry".

8021 Albright, Thomas. 'Unspoiled' Bay Area art.
     SAN FRANCISCO CHRONICLE, (August 29, 1974),
     p. 40. English.

> **AN:** Review of an exhibit titled ART NAIF
> curated by Rolando Castellon. The show
> featured 15 Bay Area painters who are
> basically self-taught and share a personal
> expression unhampered by prevailing art
> conventions and trends. Includes material on
> Alexander Maldonado, 72-year-old "primitive"
> painter from San Francisco. Some of
> Maldonado's work includes references to his
> childhood and youth in Mexico.

San Francisco, CA (cont.)

8022 Arnold, Frank. Posters and society. PEOPLE'S
WORLD, Vol. 23, no. 2. English.

AN: An exhibit at the San Francisco
Museum of Art curated by Rolando Castellon.
The article focuses on the posters of Xavier
Viramontes and Rupert Garcia of San
Francisco.

8023 Around the Bay. METAMORFOSIS, Vol. 3, no. 2
(1980), p. 101-108. English.

AN: Cultural review of activities in the
Bay Area, northern California, and
Sacramento. Includes history of the Galeria
de la Raza/Studio 24 (San Francisco), the
Centro de Artistas Chicanos/RCAF, Royal
Chicano Air Force (Sacramento), and a review
of Rupert Garcia's pastel portraits exhibit
at the Mexican Museum (S.F.) in 1981.
Illustrated. Continued in Vol. 4, no. 1,
1981.

8024 The art of Rodolfo Leal. TIN TAN, Vol. 2,
no. 6 (December 1, 1977), p. 15-18. English.

AN: Two calligraphic ink drawings and a
serigraph by Texas-born Leal who lives in
San Francisco.

8025 Barnes, Peter. Fringe benefits of a
depression: bringing back the WPA. NEW
REPUBLIC, Vol. 172, no. 11 (March 15, 1975),
p. 19-21. English.

AN: A well-researched and comprehensive
analysis of the CETA (Comprehensive
Employment and Training Act) impact on
public art in San Francisco. Material on
Chicano-Latino murals in the Mission
district. Includes viewpoints by
artist-activists Patricia Rodriguez, Mike
Rios, and writer Roberto Vargas. Important
compendium on funding sources of various
neighborhood art programs stressing their
value as community assets.

8026 Barrio, Raymond. Art for our sake. NUESTRO,
Vol. 1, no. 6 (September 1977), p. 30-34.
English.

AN: Brief text with three color
reproductions of murals by Mike Rios (Bart
Mural, San Francisco), Gilberto Guzman (West
Las Vegas High School, NM), Willie Herron
(Farmacia Hidalgo, East Los Angeles, CA).

8027 Bloomfield, Arthur. Zesty show at Mexican
museum. SAN FRANCISCO EXAMINER, (February
1, 1977), p. 24. English.

AN: Review of an exhibit of Mexican and
Mexican American artists from the Southwest
and the San Francisco area. Commentary and
analysis on artists Vincent Perez and
Gustavo Rivera, Rudy Trevino and Al Barela.
The work selected focused on aesthetic
quality rather than the ethnic
identification of the artist.

8028 Cardona, Patricia. El museo mexicano de San
Francisco. EL DIA, (July 6, 1977), p. 10.
Spanish.

AN: Report on the Mexican Museum giving
a brief overview of its programs. The
Mexican Museum opened Nov. 20, 1975 and has
been a vital force in the cultural life of
San Francisco, showing the work of one
Mexican and one Chicano artist every two
months.

8029 Corcoran Gallery of Art, Washington, D.C.
Images of an era: the American poster
1945-75. Washington, D.C.: Corcoran Gallery
of Art, 1976. English.

AN: Uncredited poster [La Raza
Silkscreen Center, San Francisco],
(centerfold). Posters by Rupert Garcia,
Linda Lucero, and Ralph Maradiaga, all of
San Francisco, CA. Introduction by John
Garriga. Essays by Margaret Cogswell, Milton
Glaser, Dore Ashton, Alan Gowens.

8030 De colores mural team. Brochure, [ca. 1975].
English.

AN: Brochure giving brief history of the
De Colores Mural Team established in 1972 as
part of the Horizons Unlimited program with
Chuy Campusano as coordinator. The team
participated in murals at the Jamestown
Center, Balmy Alley, Redding Elementary
School, Mission Childcare Center, Mission
Branch Bank of America and Horizons
Unlimited from 1972 to 1975.

8031 Dunham, Judith L. Manuel Neri: life with the
figure. ARTWEEK, Vol. 7, no. 39 (November
13, 1976), p. 1+. English.

AN: Favorable review of Neri's
exhibition of more than 80 figures or
fragments of figures at the Oakland Museum.
Explores relationship of Neri's sculpture
with developments in Bay Area figurative
painting and expressionism. Inventories
Neri's thematic and material concerns.
Analysis of his work in plaster, bronze and
fiberglass. An important assessment of
Neri's contribution to Bay Area art.

8032 Galeria de la Raza/Studio 24, San Francisco,
CA and Milkie, Anne. Carnaval '80.
Exhibition catalog, 1980. English.

AN: Catalog of an exhibit of photographs
and other media recording San Francisco's
multi-ethnic CARNAVAL, organized in 1978 by
Panamanian-born dancer. Included in the
exhibit were the photographs of Chicana
Maria V. Pinedo, who also designed the
catalog.

8033 Garcia, Rupert. Raza murals & muralists: an
historical perspective. San Francisco, CA:
Rupert Garcia, n.d.. English.

AN: Basic assumptions are that
socio-economic, political and cultural
relationships exist between the Raza of
Mexico and those of Aztlan (the Southwest
United States) Half the text deals with
Mexican murals, the other half sets Raza
murals in social context, and focuses on
murals in San Francisco's Mission District,
in four locations. 19 illustrations; 9 of
Raza murals. Mural map of the Mission
district.

8034 Heymann, Ann W. Robert Gonzalez. ART VOICES
SOUTH, Vol. 3, no. 1 (January, February,
1980), p. 68. English.

AN: Brief resume on art and life of San
Francisco painter. Illustrated.

San Francisco, CA (cont.)

8035 Mexican artists paint mural for Bank of
America. EL HISPANO, Vol. 6, no. 49.
English.

AN: Commentary by Jesus Campusano and
Michael Rios about the 90-ft. mural they
painted inside the Bank of America on
Mission and 23rd Streets in San Francisco.
They describe the mural as "...a montage of
symbols and images depicting the heritage,
day-to-day experiences and hopes of the
people in the area.

8036 NATIONAL MURALS NETWORK COMMUNITY
NEWSLETTER. (Fall   1980). English.

AN: Reports on murals in San Francisco,
CA, by the Chicano Moratorium Coalition; in
Chicago about the Anti-War Preparations
mural; in Houston by a student at the
Association for Advancement of Mexican
Americans; on Michael Schorr's mural in
Chicanok, San Diego, CA; on a segment being
painted at the Tujunga Wash mural in Los
Angeles under Judy Baca; on south San Diego
murals being painted out; Alan Barnett's
survey of Southwest murals. Illustrated.

8037 Quintero, Victoria. A mural is a painting on
a wall done by human hands. EL TECOLOTE,
Vol. 5, no. 1 (September 13, 1974), p. 6+.
English.

AN: The women's collective, Mujeres
Muralistas, exists within the strong San
Francisco mural movement. Originally the
group included Graciela Carrillo, Consuelo
Mendez, Irene Perez, and Patricia Rodriguez.
The group has expanded to include Susan
Cervantes, Ester Hernandez, and Miriam
Olivo. The two murals completed have been
criticized for not being political; the
women answer that they want the atmosphere
to be surrounded with life, with colors.
Illustrated.

8038 Rodriguez, Alfred. A historical survey of
Chicano murals in the Southwest: an
interdisciplinary teaching unit. Unpublished
paper, 1980. English.

AN: Lists murals by title, artist and
date (when known), location and subject. Los
Angeles, San Francisco, San Diego, Fresno,
San Antonio, Austin, Corpus Christi, Santa
Fe, New Mexico murals are included.
Circulated by the Institute of Latin
American Studies, University of Austin,
Texas.

8039 San Francisco's neighborhood arts program.
San Francisco, CA: San Francisco Art
Commission, [1971]. English.

AN: Booklet in pictures describing the
activities underwritten by the city and
county of San Francisco, the National
Endowment for the Arts, the San Francisco
Foundation, and the Zellerbach Family Fund.
The interracial, interethnic staff includes
Rene Yanez. Organizations listed are Galeria
de la Raza, Galeria de la Comunidad, Galeria
de las Bellas Artes, Galeria de las
Pinturas, Galeria de la Musica, Galeria de
la Poesia, Galeria de la Instruccion.

8040 Soberon, Mercedes. La revolucion se trata de
amor: Mercedes Soberon. CHISMEARTE, Vol. 1,
no. 1 (Fall   1976), p. 14-18. Spanish.

AN: Short interview with Mercedes
Soberon, San Francisco artist involved with

the art group Mission Media Arts. Mercedes
talks about the role of women as organizers
and artists, the sacrifices associated with
this role, and the politics of San Francisco
museums.

8041 Wagner, Kathie and Lujan, Lori. Public
works: San Francisco. CALIFORNIA LIVING,
(September 21, 1975), p. 26, 33. English.

AN: Illustrative descriptive survey of
San Francisco murals. Helpful inclusion of
mural locations and artists' names. First of
a two-part article.

8042 Xerox Reproductions Center, San Francisco,
CA. Fine arts exhibitions of color xerox.
Exhibition invitation, 1978-79. English.

AN: Invitation to an exhibit featuring
Rene Yanez and 11 other artists working in
color Xerox.

San Francisco, CA, Mission District
SEE ALSO: Mission District, San Francisco, CA
8043 Bank of America, Mission-23rd St. Branch,
San Francisco, CA. A community mural
dedicated by the artists to Mexican muralist
David Alfaro Siqueiros. 1974. English.

AN: Brochure about the Bank of America
mural in the Mission District of San
Francisco designed by Jesus Campusano and
Luis J. Cortazar, assisted by Michael Rios,
Jaime Carrillo, Candice Ho, Julio Lopez,
Anthony Machado, Jack Nevarez. Technical
advisor, Emmy Lou Packard. Well illustrated.

8044 Barrio heritage reflected in bank mural. EL
CHICANO, Vol. 8, no. 50 (May 30, 1974), p.
8-9. English.

AN: Jesus Campusano and Luis J. Cortazar
were artist-designers of a monumental mural
painted inside the Mission Branch of the
Bank of America. Michael Rios was color
coordinator and five young artists worked
collectively on the project for four months.
Realistic scenes of everyday life in the
Mission barrio are contrasted to heroic
personalities from Latin America. Folk art
imagery, Indian and Spanish cultural symbols
and historical personages form a pageant of
Latin American history. Mural was
inaugurated on June 4, 1974.

8045 Brunazzi, Ceci. Writing on the walls: murals
in the mission. COMMON SENSE, (May 1975),
p. 1, 8. English.

AN: History of the early murals in the
Mission District of San Francisco, CA.
Illustrated.

8046 Gonzales, Juan. Regional report, The arts:
"Our people deserve the best". NUESTRO, Vol.
1, no. 2 (May 1977), p. 56-57. English.

AN: Activities of San Francisco's
Galeria de la Raza; interviews with its
directors, Rene Yanez and Ralph Maradiaga.
Reprinted as "Galeria de la Raza: our people
deserve the best" in EL TECOLOTE (San
Francisco, CA), Vol. 7, no. 11 (July, 1977),
p. 14.

8047 A mural tour of San Francisco. SUNSET, Vol.
15, (July 1975). English.

AN: Illustrations and map of seven
Latino murals in the Mission district of San
Francisco.

San Francisco Museum of Art, San Francisco, CA

8048 Albright, Thomas. San Francisco: the force of universals. ART NEWS MAGAZINE, Vol. 77, no. 6 (Summer 1978), p. 174. English.

AN: Review of Rupert Garcia pastel show at the San Francisco Museum of Modern Art. Reviewer suggests he is one of the very few real artists to emerge from the "unfortunate genre" of poster art. His images are highly charged: political prisoners, corpses, revolutionary martyrs.

8049 Arnold, Frank. Posters and society. PEOPLE'S WORLD, Vol. 23, no. 2. English.

AN: An exhibit at the San Francisco Museum of Art curated by Rolando Castellon. The article focuses on the posters of Xavier Viramontes and Rupert Garcia of San Francisco.

8050 Congreso de Artistas Chicanos en Aztlan, San Diego, CA. Diego Rivera, David Alfaro Siqueiros, Jose Clemente Orozco: exhibit of local artists, La Logan [San Diego]. Exhibition brochure, n.d. [c.1974]. English.

AN: Announcement of a traveling exhibit organized by Galeria de la Raza, San Francisco, from the collection of the San Francisco Museum of Art. Illustrated with a San Diego mural.

8051 Frankenstein, Alfred. At the museum: when politics and art do mix. SAN FRANCISCO CHRONICLE, (March 15, 1978), p. 54. English.

AN: Glowing review of exhibit at the San Francisco Museum of Modern Art by Rupert Garcia who, the critic says, has a genius for saying the essential thing without a line, a gesture or a touch of color more than necessary. Illustrated.

San Francisco Neighborhood Arts Program

8052 Gustaitis, Rasa. Arts imperiled. PEOPLE'S WORLD, Vol. 44, no. 26 (June 27, 1981), p. 10. English.

AN: A decade ago the San Francisco Neighborhood Arts Program received new commitments from the National Endowment for the Arts to fund local, unknown and chronically poor neighborhood artists. With these funds, murals were painted on the walls and other art events were created with young people, minorities, old people. This program piloted the Expansion Arts Program of NEA. These funds are now being cut, especially with the Reagan administration's proposed cuts for 1981 and 1982.

San Luis Valley, CO

8053 Adams, Robert. The architecture and art of early Hispanic Colorado. Boulder, CO: Colorado Associated University Press in cooperation with the State Historical Society of Colorado, 1974. English.

AN: Robert Adams is a photographer and writer from Longmont, CO who has evocatively captured scenes in the San Luis and Purgatory Valleys of Southern Colorado. The text and photographs focus on "Hispano" village life, customs and traditions.

8054 Ditmar, Joanne. A new industry, done the old way. EMPIRE MAGAZINE, (September 26, 1976), p. 22-25. English.

AN: The Virginia Blue Resource Center for Colorado Women is embarked on a project to revive handicrafts and skills among Hispano women in the San Luis Valley. Igniting interest in traditional crafts like embroideries, tin work, straw mosaic and filigree jewelry, the Center hopes to revive or maintain these traditions. Detailed information on a project to create a group of embroidered wall hangings depicting San Luis Valley life past and present. Illustrated with examples of the completed wall hangings.

8055 Nelson, Kathryn J. Excerpts from los testamentos: Hispanic women folk artists of the San Luis Valley, Colorado. FRONTIERS, Vol. 5, no. 3 (Fall 1980), p. 34-43. English.

AN: Eppie Archuleta, weaver from the San Luis Valley in Southern Colorado talks about her life philosophy, Hispanic cultural traditions and her role as a community artist. First person account amply illustrated with photographs.

San Mateo County, CA

8056 NATIONAL MURALS NETWORK COMMUNITY NEWSLETTER. (1978). English.

AN: This issue features reports from muralists. Includes information about murals at: La Pena Cultural Center in Berkeley, CA; the Social and Public Art Resource Center's Tujunga Wash Mural in Venice, CA; the Citywide Mural Project in Los Angeles, CA; activities at Chicano Park, and of the Congress of American Cosmic Artists (CACA), both in San Diego, CA; murals in San Mateo County, CA; the Task Force on Hispanic American Arts headed by Jacinto Quirarte of San Antonio; the 1978 Canto Al Pueblo in Corpus Christi, TX; murals in Chicago; and other works by non-Chicano artists.

8057 Seniors mural to be dedicated at RC Center. REDWOOD CITY TRIBUNE, (December 31, 1977), p. 3. English.

AN: A portable mural depicting the birth of the senior citizen hot meal program in San Mateo County will be dedicated at the Senior Citizens Drop-In Center. The 12x18-ft mural was painted by Emmanuel Montoya of Menlo Park, CA. Illustrated.

Sanchez, Al

8058 Denver. NATIONAL MURALS NETWORK COMMUNITY NEWSLETTER, (Spring 1980), p. 10. English.

AN: Denver, Colorado murals by Manuel Martinez, the Chilean Orlando Letelier Brigade, Roberto Lucero, Al Sanchez, Jerry Jaramillo. Illustrated.

8059 La Familia Recreation Center, Denver, CO. Mural unveiling and swim party. Exhibition invitation, 1980. English.

AN: Invitation to the unveiling of La Familia Cosmica, a mural by Jerry Jaramillo assisted by Carlos Sandoval, Al Sanchez, Stephen Lucero. An art exhibit featured the muralists, Jon Howe, and Fred Sanchez, all of the Metro Denver Urban Coalition's City Walls artists. Illustrated.

Sanchez, Al (cont.)

8060 Incorporated Artes Monumentales/Inc.,
Denver, CO. IAM: art exhibit. Exhibition
brochure, n.d. English.

AN: Large format, well illustrated
brochure with information on muralists
Roberto Lucero, Al Sanchez, Andrew Manning,
Ricardo Barrera and Bob Reyes. Includes some
biographical information situating these
artists within the dynamic artistic
traditions of the Mexican and the Chicano
mural movements.

8061 Metro Denver Urban Coalition, Denver, CO.
City walls. Brochure, 1979. English.

AN: Brochure/poster giving history of
City Walls Project and biographies of seven
artists: Jon Howe, Jerry Jaramillo, Steve
Lucero, Jowinnie Moore, Al Sanchez, Fred
Sanchez, Carlos M. Sandoval. Illustrated.

8062 NATIONAL MURALS NETWORK COMMUNITY
NEWSLETTER. (Spring 1980). English.

AN: Reports on the Sept. 1979 conference
of Chicano visual arts held at UT Austin,
organized by the Mujeres Artistas del
Suroeste, and the Liga Unida de Chicanos
Artistas, which brought together
participants from the U.S. and Mexico City;
on Manuel Martinez's five murals (1976-78);
murals by Roberto Lucero, Al Sanchez, and
Jerry Jaramillo; as well as by the Chilean
group Orlando Letelier Brigade, all in
Denver, Colorado; murals by Leo Tanguma in
Houston; the story about the "forbidden"
Chicano mural in Blue Island, Illinois.
Illustrated.

8063 Tully, Robert. City walls. LA VOZ (Denver,
CO), (August 3, 1979), p. 7. English.

AN: In a project managed by Metro Denver
Urban Coalition, several Chicano artists
were hired to work consistently in creating
murals for the inner city. Article focuses
on the goals, procedures, and activities of
the muralists. Grouped as Incorporated Artes
Monumentales, the group included Jerry
Jaramillo, Steve Lucero, Al Sanchez, Fred
Sanchez, and Carlos Sandoval. Illustrated by
a group photograph of artists and a
photograph of a wall painting by the
Chilean-led Brigada Orlando Letelier in
Denver.

Sanchez Brown, Olivia

8064 Baciu, Joyce A. Hispanic artists: combining
energy and emotion. CAMINOS, Vol. 2, no. 5
(October 1981), p. 14-17. English.

AN: Brief profiles of Mario Uribe,
Ernest De Soto, Peter Rodriguez, Margarita
Jauregui Weiner, Virginia Jaramillo, Luis
Urrea, Ramses Noriega, Jose Lopez, Olivia
Sanchez.

8065 Los Angeles City College. Latinos de tres
mundos. Exhibition invitation, 1980.
English.

AN: Invitation to an exhibit featuring
the work of ASCO members Harry Gamboa, Jr.,
Gronk, Willie Herron; painters Xavier Mendez
and Olivia Sanchez; and photographer Ricardo
Valverde.

Sanchez, Frank J.

8066 Calendario de March: 1977. Chicago, IL:

MARCH, Inc., 1976. English.

AN: Historical calendar with photos and
biographies of artists. Illustrations of
artwork by Ray Patlan, Jose Nario, Frank J.
Sanchez, Salvador Dominguez, Salvador Vega,
Marguerite Ortega, Aurelio Diaz, Carlos
Cortez, Mario E. Castillo, Francisco Blasco,
Rey Vasquez, and Efrain Martinez. History of
MARCH (Movimiento Artistico Chicano).

Sanchez, Fred

8067 La Familia Recreation Center, Denver, CO.
Mural unveiling and swim party. Exhibition
invitation, 1980. English.

AN: Invitation to the unveiling of La
Familia Cosmica, a mural by Jerry Jaramillo
assisted by Carlos Sandoval, Al Sanchez,
Stephen Lucero. An art exhibit featured the
muralists, Jon Howe, and Fred Sanchez, all
of the Metro Denver Urban Coalition's City
Walls artists. Illustrated.

8068 Metro Denver Urban Coalition, Denver, CO.
City walls. Brochure, 1979. English.

AN: Brochure/poster giving history of
City Walls Project and biographies of seven
artists: Jon Howe, Jerry Jaramillo, Steve
Lucero, Jowinnie Moore, Al Sanchez, Fred
Sanchez, Carlos M. Sandoval. Illustrated.

8069 Tully, Robert. City walls. LA VOZ (Denver,
CO), (August 3, 1979), p. 7. English.

AN: In a project managed by Metro Denver
Urban Coalition, several Chicano artists
were hired to work consistently in creating
murals for the inner city. Article focuses
on the goals, procedures, and activities of
the muralists. Grouped as Incorporated Artes
Monumentales, the group included Jerry
Jaramillo, Steve Lucero, Al Sanchez, Fred
Sanchez, and Carlos Sandoval. Illustrated by
a group photograph of artists and a
photograph of a wall painting by the
Chilean-led Brigada Orlando Letelier in
Denver.

Sanchez Lujan, Gilbert
USE: Lujan, Gilbert Sanchez "Magu"

Sanchez, Ricardo

8070 De la Torre, Susana. [Untitled portrait].
CARACOL, Vol. 5, no. 1 (September 1978), p.
18. Bilingual.

Sandoval, Ausberto

8071 Silent protest. ARIZONA DAILY STAR, (May
18, 1978), p. 6-H. English.

AN: Outdoor murals in Tucson by Ausberto
Sandoval, Antonio Pazos and Sylvia de la
Huerta on a house in community being
displaced by urban renewal. Illustrated.

Sandoval, Carlos M.

8072 Carlos Sandoval to complete mural in
Zihuatanejo, Mexico. TIERRA Y LIBERTAD, Vol.
2, no. 4 (July 1980), p. 3, 10. English.

AN: Biographical information on Colorado
artist Carlos Sandoval. The Municipal
Library in the city of Zihuatanejo in the
state of Guerrero is the site of Sandoval's
mural which visually and symbolically
projects the cultural and historical unity
between Mejicanos and Chicanos.

Sandoval, Carlos M.(cont.)

8073 COMMUNITY MURALS (San Francisco, CA). (Fall 1981). English.

AN: Citywide Murals Group of Denver, Colorado assisted the Chilean-oriented Brigada Orlando Letelier with a mural in their city; Carlos Sandoval of Denver doing mural in Guerrero, Mexico; Ray Patlan of Berkeley, California assisting with mural in Mexico painted by Arnold Belkin's class at the Academy of San Carlos; report on the exhibit MURALS OF AZTLAN: THE STREET PAINTERS OF EAST LOS with a reprint of debate on the event by Shifra M. Goldman, Judithe Elena Hernandez de Neikrug, and comments by John Pitman Weber and Tim Drescher; report on DAR LUZ mural directed by Santa Barraza in Austin, Texas, and a new mural in Hayward, California directed by Enrique Romero; a mural sponsored by the Chicano Youth Center of Fresno, California showing the influence of Mexican calendars; a new mural, OAKLAND'S PORTRAIT by Daniel Galvez in Oakland, California; pro-and-con discussion of social function of graffiti in response to letter from Belgian source; reprint of story on spray paint crime bill (anti-graffiti) sponsored by California Assemblyman Richard Alatorre. Entire issue illustrated.

8074 Espinosa, Juan. Carlos Sandoval completing mural in Mexico. LA CUCARACHA, (June 1980). English.

AN: Details how Carlos Sandoval, Denver Chicano artist was invited by the Mexican government to paint mural in Zihuantanejo, Mexico. The mayor of the Mexican town states, "this work represents an expression of two pueblos who want to expand their relations, as a product of one common people." Illustrated with photograph of Carlos Sandoval and one preliminary drawing of the mural.

8075 La Familia Recreation Center, Denver, CO. Mural unveiling and swim party. Exhibition invitation, 1980. English.

AN: Invitation to the unveiling of La Familia Cosmica, a mural by Jerry Jaramillo assisted by Carlos Sandoval, Al Sanchez, Stephen Lucero. An art exhibit featured the muralists, Jon Howe, and Fred Sanchez, all of the Metro Denver Urban Coalition's City Walls artists. Illustrated.

8076 Johnson, Richard. The mural at Zihuatanejo. EMPIRE MAGAZINE, (October 12, 1980). English.

AN: Denver artist Carlos M. Sandoval is said to be the first Chicano commissioned by the Mexican government to paint a mural in Mexico. Sandoval's mural is on the facade of the public library in Zihuatanejo. Its theme is unity and synthesis and its title is MESTIZO. Article contains much information on mural act ivity in Denver, Colorado. Well illustrated with color and black and white photographs.

8077 Meta studio I. Denver, CO: s.n., [1980]. English.

AN: Portfolio of colored prints by Colorado artists Ernie Gallegos, Jerry Jaramillo, Steve Lucero and Carlos M. Sandoval. Biographical information and photograph of each artist. Presentation of the group under the rubric of "metarealism"

by Stephen Pascual Lucero.

8078 Metro Denver Urban Coalition, Denver, CO. City walls. Brochure, 1979. English.

AN: Brochure/poster giving history of City Walls Project and biographies of seven artists: Jon Howe, Jerry Jaramillo, Steve Lucero, Jowinnie Moore, Al Sanchez, Fred Sanchez, Carlos M. Sandoval. Illustrated.

8079 Sinisi, J. Sebastian J. Following footsteps of Diego Rivera. CONTEMPORARY, (January 13, 1980), p. 28-30. English.

AN: Story on West Denver murals, particularly by Manuel Martinez and Carlos Sandoval at the La Alma Recreation Center, Summer 1979. Murals done through the Denver City Walls Project by artists belonging to Incorporated Artes Monumentales. Illustrated.

8080 Tully, Robert. City walls. LA VOZ (Denver, CO), (August 3, 1979), p. 7. English.

AN: In a project managed by Metro Denver Urban Coalition, several Chicano artists were hired to work consistently in creating murals for the inner city. Article focuses on the goals, procedures, and activities of the muralists. Grouped as Incorporated Artes Monumentales, the group included Jerry Jaramillo, Steve Lucero, Al Sanchez, Fred Sanchez, and Carlos Sandoval. Illustrated by a group photograph of artists and a photograph of a wall painting by the Chilean-led Brigada Orlando Letelier in Denver.

Sandoval, David [filmmaker]

8081 California. University. Los Angeles. Cine sin fronteras. Festival brochure, 1981. English.

AN: Brochure program for a cinema festival and series of seminars and discussions featuring films and discussants from Mexico and Chicanos of the United States. Participating were Chicano directors Moctezuma Esparza, Richard Soto, David Sandoval, and Robert Young, and film historian David Maciel.

8082 Rivera, Humberto R. Film notes. CHISMEARTE, Vol. 1, no. 2 (Winter, Spring, 1977), p. 20-24. English.

AN: Summary of films produced by and/or about Chicanos for cinema and television. Includes REALIDADES (TV) by David Sandoval, Rudy Vargas, Luis Torres, Jose Luis Ruiz, Antonio Reyes; A POLITICAL RENAISSANCE from the LA RAZA series (TV) by Moctezuma Esparza; CHILDREN OF THE STATE by Andres Markovits, Richard Trubo, Frank Christopher (film); LA RAZA UNIDA (released as RAICES DE SANGRE) by Jesus Salvador Trevino (Mexican film by a Chicano); CHULAS FRONTERAS (film) by Les Blank; THE MURALS OF EAST LOS ANGELES, A MUSEUM WITHOUT WALLS by Humberto R. Rivera and Heather R. Howell. Announcement for the National Latino Media Coalition.

Sandoval, David [muralist]

8083 Chicano muralists maintain traditions. LA
     CUCARACHA, (November 20, 1979), p. 7.
     English.

     AN: Introduction to Chicano muralism in
     Pueblo and comparison to the Mexican mural
     movement from which it draws inspiration. 20
     murals painted from 1977 to 1979. The
     muralists include Bernardo Duran, Juan
     Espinoza, Miguel "Freeloader" Garcia, Lola
     Gutierrez, Leo Lucero, Juan Pacheco, Dolores
     Pena, Pedro Romero, Stan Salazar, David
     Sandoval. Diego Rivera murals illustrated.

Sandoval, Secundino

8084 Anaya, Rudolfo A. and Ortiz, Simon J.
     1680-1980: a ceremony of brotherhood.
     Albuquerque, NM: Academic, 1981. English.

     AN: A cooperative publication by members
     of the former La Academia de la Nueva Raza
     (1969-1976) formed of writers and artists,
     and the Tri-Centennial Commission of the
     All-Indian Pueblo Council. Includes writings
     and artworks by Chicanos and Indians from
     New Mexico, California, Texas, and Arizona.
     Chicano artists works included are by Ellen
     Arellano, Juan Estevan Arellano, Alberto
     Baros, Jose Antonio Burciaga, Juan Reyes
     Cervantes, Rudy Cuellar, Ricardo Favela, El
     Zarco Guerrero, Luis Jimenez, Jr., Carlos
     Quinto Kemm, Alejandro Lopez, Floyd Lujan,
     Jose Montoya, Juanishi Orozco, Leo Romero,
     Secundino Sandoval, Jaime Valdez, Maria
     Varela, Esteban Villa.

8085 Hispanic American artist - Secundino
     Sandoval. LA LUZ, Vol. 7, no. 9 (September
     1978), p. 51. English.

     AN: Biographical data and analysis of
     "Sec", Sandoval's technique as a realist
     watercolorist.

Sandoval, Teddy

8086 Galeria, Santa Ana, CA. The last Chicano art
     show. Exhibition brochure, 1981. English.

     AN: Invitation-brochure for an exhibit
     of Los Angeles and Orange County artists in
     a gallery underwritten by the Friendly
     Center, Inc. with grants from local
     government and from businesses. Exhibiting
     are (Roberto) Gil de Montes, Gilbert Lujan,
     Judy Miranda, Patricia Murillo, Alonso
     Pardo, Teddy Sandoval, Mexican artist
     Artemio Sepulveda, Joey Terrill, Art
     Valenzuela, Ben Valenzuela, Linda Vallejo,
     Jack A. Vargas, Emigdio Vasquez, Richard
     Serrato, and J. William Hernandez, who is
     the gallery director.

8087 Goldman, Shifra M. Thorns and roses.
     ARTWEEK, Vol. 11, no. 30 (September 20,
     1980), p. 1. English.

     AN: Report on four Chicano artists
     exhibiting at L.A.C.E. Gallery, Los Angeles:
     Carlos Almaraz, Teddy Sandoval, John
     Valadez, and Linda Vallejo. Illustrated.

8088 L.A.C.E. (Los Angeles Contemporary
     Exhibitions), Los Angeles, CA. Espina
     (Thorn): Carlos Almaraz, Elsa Flores, Louie
     Perez, Teddy Sandoval, John Valadez, Linda
     Vallejo. Exhibition announcement, 1980.
     English.

     AN: Announcement of an exhibition and a
     performance piece by six Los Angeles

artists.

8089 L.A.C.E. (Los Angeles Contemporary
     Exhibitions), Los Angeles, CA. No Movie: Gil
     de Montes, Teddy, Glugio [Gronk], Patssi,
     Gamboa. Exhibition invitation, 1978.
     English.

     AN: Invitation to "performance" piece by
     Roberto Gil de Montes, Teddy Sandoval,
     Gronk, Patssi Valdez and Harry Gamboa, Jr.,
     the latter three of the ASCO group.
     Illustrated.

8090 Mechicano Art Center, Los Angeles, CA.
     Schizophrenibeneficial. Exhibition
     invitation, 1977. English.

     AN: Invitation to an ASCO "performance"
     work: "Projecting of Visual and/or Verbal
     Personality Disorders Onto Person or Persons
     Unknown." Glugio (Gronk), Teddy (Sandoval),
     (Roberto) Gil de Montes, Patssi (Valdez),
     (Harry) Gamboa.

8091 William Grant Still Community Arts Center,
     Los Angeles, CA. Latin American artists
     exhibition. Exhibition brochure, 1978.
     English.

     AN: Exhibit curated by Linda Vallejo
     including Carlos Almaraz, Michael M.
     Amescua, Ray Bravo, Isabel Castro, Yreina
     Cervantez, Luis Serrano-Cordero, Cynthia
     Honesto, Judith Miranda, Teddy Sandoval,
     John Taboada, Emigdio Vasquez. Illustrated.

Santa Ana, CA

8092 Day, Orman. Hispanic life mirrored by ethnic
     artists. THE REGISTER, (July 5, 1981), p.
     B1+. English.

     AN: Story on artists Manuel Hernandez
     Trujillo and Emigdio Vasquez whose work
     opened the new Galeria in Santa Ana, and
     poet Manuel Gomez. Color illustrations.

8093 History traced in mural. THE REGISTER, (May
     1, 1974), p. C-1. English.

     AN: Illustrated story of History of the
     Chicano mural painted by Sergio O'Cadiz and
     fifty students from MEChA at Santa Ana
     College.

Santa Ana College, Santa Ana, CA

8094 History traced in mural. THE REGISTER, (May
     1, 1974), p. C-1. English.

     AN: Illustrated story of History of the
     Chicano mural painted by Sergio O'Cadiz and
     fifty students from MEChA at Santa Ana
     College.

8095 Kennedy, Bailey. The American pageant: a
     history of the republic, 6th ed. 6th ed.,
     Lexington, MA: D.C. Heath, 1979, p. 674.
     English.

     AN: Reproduction of two sections of the
     MEChA mural painted in 1974 by students
     directed by Sergio O'Cadiz at Santa Ana
     College, Santa Ana, Calif. The mural includes
     Mexican and Mexican American themes.

Santa Ana College, Santa Ana, CA (cont.)

8096 M.E.C.H.A. cultura y evolucion mexicana. EL
     CLARIN, (May 2, 1974), p. 3. Spanish.

     AN: Report on the mural designed and
     painted under the direction of Mexican-born
     designer Sergio O'Cadiz at Santa Ana
     College, Santa Ana, Calif. Collaborators
     were instructor Shifra Goldman and gallery
     director Mike Davis, with members of the
     MEChA Club and other students. The mural
     concerns the history of Mexico and of the
     Chicano and includes a tribute to David
     Alfaro Siqueiros' Los Angeles mural AMERICA
     TROPICAL, painted and white-washed in the
     1930s. Illustrated.

8097 A new gallery of art on city streets. U.S.
     NEWS & WORLD REPORT, Vol. 50, no. 18 (May 8,
     1978), p. 86-87. English.

     AN: Brief illustrated story on street
     murals across the U.S. including Chicano
     murals in East Los Angeles and Santa Ana
     College, Calif.

Santa Barbara, CA

8098 Chavez, Jaime. Rayaprofiles: Manuel Unzueta.
     RAYAS, Vol. 2, no. 3 (May, June, 1979), p.
     5. Spanish.

     AN: Brief biography of Mexican-born
     Chicano artist and muralist from Santa
     Barbara, California. Manuel Unzueta is
     active with La Casa de la Raza and its
     publication XALMAN. Unzueta is invited to
     paint a mural in Albuquerque. A Santa
     Barbara mural is illustrated.

8099 Reaves, John. Santa Barbara. NEWORLD, Vol.
     6, no. 2 (March, April, 1980), p. 7+.
     English.

     AN: Report on the activities of Casa de
     la Raza in Santa Barbara within social
     context. Erroneous attribution of murals,
     not all of which are by Vallejo.

8100 Rodriguez, Luis. A Center for Cultural
     Preservation and Human Resources. SOMOS,
     Vol. 1, no. 4 (September 1978), p. 26-29.
     English.

     AN: Report on the founding, purposes,
     and continuing social and cultural
     activities of the Casa de La Raza.
     Illustrated.

Santa Cruz, CA

8101 California. University. Santa Cruz. College
     Eight Gallery. Four artists: Edward
     Carrillo, Consuelo Mendez Castillo, Louis
     Gutierrez, Jose Montoya. Exhibition catalog,
     n.d. English.

     AN: Exhibit of three Chicano artists and
     Venezuelan-born artist Consuelo Mendez de
     Castillo.

8102 Carrillo, Eduardo. Califas, is Chicano art
     safe in Santa Cruz? ARTS AT SANTA CRUZ, Vol.
     1, no. 1 (1981). English.

     AN: Illustrated essay surveying Chicano
     art in Santa Cruz with details about the
     planning and presentation of the CALIFAS
     exhibit at the Mary Porter Seanon Gallery.
     This exhibition presented the work of
     fifteen Chicano(a) artists united and
     defined by a shared vision: a conscious
     identification with Mexican/Chicano culture

and an alliance with art circuits outside
the mainstream.

8103 Goldman, Shifra M. Chicano art - looking
     backward. ARTWEEK, Vol. 12, no. 22 (June 20,
     1981), p. 3-4. English.

     AN: Review of Chicano art shows in Santa
     Cruz (CALIFAS) and Los Angeles (MURALS OF
     AZTLAN: THE STREET PAINTERS OF EAST LOS)
     featuring a total of 24 artists and how the
     shows reflect the critical crossroad at
     which Chicano artists presently find
     themselves.

8104 Rodebaugh, Dale. Graffiti replaces popular
     mural in Santa Cruz arcade. SAN JOSE
     MERCURY, (April 13, 1979), p. B, [1].
     English.

     AN: The efforts of Eduardo Carrillo to
     restore his mural, "Birth Death and
     Resurrection in a downtown arcade. The
     artist comments on the intention and
     significance of the mural and the political
     reasons for its obliteration.

Santa Fe Council for the Arts

8105 Artist registry financed. RIO GRANDE SUN,
     (January 17, 1980). English.

     AN: A $15,000 grant received from the
     National Endowment for the Arts to begin a
     New Mexico Hispanic Arts Community Outreach
     project, which will include a central
     registry of New Mexico Hispanic artists with
     current resume, documentation of work, and
     other information. In charge will be
     artists Estevan Arellano, Albert Baros, and
     Susan Jamison of the Santa Fe Council for
     the Arts.

8106 Eichstaedt, Peter. Hispanic festival
     cultural showcase. NEW MEXICAN WEEKEND,
     (May 25, 1979), p. 3. English.

     AN: Announcement of the week-long
     HISPANIC HERITAGE FESTIVAL/EL FESTIVAL
     HISPANICO co-sponsored by La Cofradia de
     Artes y Artesanos Hispanicos and the Santa
     Fe Council fo the Arts at the Armory for the
     Arts in Santa Fe. Outlines the cultural
     activities, including a visual arts exhibit.
     La Cofradia is a recently formed
     organization which has assembled regional
     shows at the Santuario de Guadalupe which
     gave opportunities to local artists to show
     their work. Festival artists are primarily
     from the upper Rio Grande but also include
     artists from the State Penitentiary, as well
     as Albuquerque and Las Cruces. Illustration
     of painting by Sam Leyba.

8107 Institute of American Indian Arts Museum,
     Santa Fe, NM. Native American/Hispanic
     festival, contemporary & historic visions.
     Santa Fe, NM: Institute of American Indian
     Arts Museum, 1981. English.

     AN: Catalog for exhibit co-sponsored by
     La Cofradia de Artes y Artesanos Hispanicos,
     the Institute of American Indian Arts, and
     the Santa Fe Council for the Arts. Exhibit
     stresses the inter-relationship between the
     Indian and Hispano peoples of New Mexico. 31
     contemporary Hispano artists included.
     Illustrated.

Santa Fe Council for the Arts (cont.)

8108 Loniak, Walter. The true New Mexico
     contemporary style. SANTA FE REPORTER, (May
     31, 1979). English.

     AN: Review of three exhibits in Santa
     Fe, EL FESTIVAL HISPANICO co-sponsored by
     the Cofradia de Artes y Artesanos Hispanicos
     and the Santa Fe Council for the Arts; a
     wood carving exhibit at Elaine Horwitch
     Gallery, and easel paintings by muralist
     Gilberto Guzman at the Black Kachina
     Gallery. Concerning the Festival exhibit,
     the critic states that the sculptural pieces
     are the strongest; two dimensional work is
     inconsistent or unimpressive, weaving is not
     well represented (though usually the
     strongest medium), and there are few
     photographs or prints. Illustration.

Santa Fe, NM

8109 Art in public places. Program statement,
     1977-78. English.

     AN: Documents an eleven-month program
     funded by CETA for 21 artists to produce
     murals, prints and weavings as public art.
     Includes murals by Gilberto Guzman and
     Graciela Carrillo-Lopez in Santa Fe.
     Statements by the artists. Illustrated.

8110 Barrett, Marjorie. Carving out a living - a
     primitive process. ROCKY MOUNTAIN NEWS,
     (December 15, 1979), p. 90. English.

     AN: In the village of Teseque outside
     Santa Fe, NM, Felipe Archuleta, a
     69-year-old folk carver has emerged as an
     international art celebrity, famous for his
     naive animal carvings. His work expecially
     life-sized renditions of animals, is
     represented in many distinguished
     collections and is prized for its wit and
     lack of predictability. Illustrated with
     photograph of carver and one of his
     creations.

8111 Callum, Diane. Regional report, The arts:
     walls of passion. NUESTRO, Vol. 3, no. 11
     (December 1979), p. 16, 51. English.

     AN: Focusing on muralist Gilberto
     Guzman, one of the founders of Artes
     Guadalupanos in Santa Fe, the article
     details his efforts in the promotion and
     preservation of Chicano murals in New
     Mexico.

8112 Corneil, Paul. Militant barrio murals of
     Santa Fe. Venice, CA: Environmental
     Communications, n.d. English.

     AN: Annotated slide catalog with
     introductory text about the mural group Los
     Artes Guadalupanos de Aztlan of Santa Fe.
     Gilberto Guzman is mentioned as one of the
     group.

8113 Diaz, Katherine A. Murals of New Mexico.
     CAMINOS, Vol. 2, no. 5 (October 1981), p.
     9-10. English.

     AN: Illustrations of murals in Santa Fe
     and Albuquerque by Gilberto Guzman,
     Francisco Le Fevere[sic; Lefebre], Manuel
     Unzueta, and Fernando Penalosa.

8114 Fitch, Bob. Los artes: a story the people
     live as well as paint. YOUTH MAGAZINE, Vol.
     26, no. 3 (March 1975), p. 2-11. English.

     AN: Illustrated story on the formation

and early murals of Los Artes Guadalupanos
de Aztlan of Santa Fe.

8115 Kroll, Eric. Folk art in the barrios.
     NATURAL HISTORY, Vol. 82, no. 5 (May 1973),
     p. 56-65. English.

     AN: Well-illustrated informative report
     on Santa Fe, New Mexico murals by Los Artes
     Guadalupanos de Aztlan. Author's somewhat
     condescending attitude rectified in the
     ARTFORUM reprint which drops the term "folk
     art". [See Murals in New Mexico].

8116 Loniak, Walter. The true New Mexico
     contemporary style. SANTA FE REPORTER, (May
     31, 1979). English.

     AN: Review of three exhibits in Santa
     Fe, EL FESTIVAL HISPANICO co-sponsored by
     the Cofradia de Artes y Artesanos Hispanicos
     and the Santa Fe Council for the Arts; a
     wood carving exhibit at Elaine Horwitch
     Gallery, and easel paintings by muralist
     Gilberto Guzman at the Black Kachina
     Gallery. Concerning the Festival exhibit,
     the critic states that the sculptural pieces
     are the strongest; two dimensional work is
     inconsistent or unimpressive, weaving is not
     well represented (though usually the
     strongest medium), and there are few
     photographs or prints. Illustration.

8117 Rodriguez, Alfred. A historical survey of
     Chicano murals in the Southwest: an
     interdisciplinary teaching unit. Unpublished
     paper, 1980. English.

     AN: Lists murals by title, artist and
     date (when known), location and subject. Los
     Angeles, San Francisco, San Diego, Fresno,
     San Antonio, Austin, Corpus Christi, Santa
     Fe, New Mexico murals are included.
     Circulated by the Institute of Latin
     American Studies, University of Austin,
     Texas.

8118 Santuario de N.S. [Nuestra Senora] de
     Guadalupe, Santa Fe, NM. Artes Guadalupanos
     de Aztlan: Samuel Leyba, Gilberto Guzman,
     Geronimo Garduno, Carlos Leyba, Pancho
     Hunter. Exhibition invitation, 1979.
     English.

8119 SF muralists display paintings. VIVA,
     (October 8, 1972), p. 19. English.

     AN: Paintings, and photos of murals
     taken by Gilberto Romero, on display at the
     New Mexico Arts Commission. Artists Sammy,
     Carlos and Albert Leyba (the original
     members), Gilberto Guzman and Geronimo
     Garduno, part of the Artes Guadalupanos de
     Aztlan, finished a mural at Tot Lot in 1971
     and are team-painting La Clinica de la
     Gente. They have also painted a mural for
     West Las Vegas High School.

8120 [Untitled photograph]. NUESTRO, Vol. 1, no.
     4 (July 1977), p. 31. English.

     AN: Color reproduction of mural (now
     destroyed) in Santa Fe, New Mexico by
     Gilberto Guzman.

Santa Fe, NM (cont.)

8121 Weiss, Margaret R. and Sommer, Robert. Camera assignment: documenting street art. SATURDAY REVIEW, (May 17, 1975), p. 41-43. English.

AN: Interview with Robert Sommer. Illustrations of six murals: in Santa Fe, NM; Estrada Courts in Los Angeles; a John Weber mural in Chicago; and Cityarts mural in New York.

Santana, Luis

8122 CODEX NEWSLETTER (Galeria de la Raza, San Francisco, CA). Vol. 1, no. 2 (September 1973). English.

AN: An in-house bulletin of upcoming events: EL SOL NUNCA MUERE, photography/poster exhibit, Rolando Garces, and Peruvian posters; Mujeres de Aztlan, women artists' collective exhibit; Filipino/Samoan art exhibit; Galeria Christmas art sale; Galeria pavilion at S.F. annual art festival; Rockefeller scholarship for Galeria curator Luis Santana; Galeria coloring book; Balmy Alley mural project; Diego Rivera exhibit; first installment of Rupert Garcia's RAZA MURALS AND MURALISTS: AN HISTORICAL VIEW.

Santeros

8123 Crews, Mildred T. Saint-maker from Taos. AMERICAS, Vol. 21, no. 3 (March 1969). English.

AN: An in-depth study of woodcarver Patrocino Barela (died 1964). Barela's work is an evolvement of the "santero" tradition filtered through an intensely personal style. His work was widely collected by institutions like The Museum of Modern Art, New York, The San Francisco Museum of Art and The New Mexico Fine Arts Museum. Well-illustrated with photographs of the artist and example of his work.

8124 Donnell-Kotrozo, Carol and Perlman, Barbara. Male passages: a secular santero of the '80s interprets machismo. ARIZONA ARTS AND LIFESTYLE, Vol. 4, no. 1 (1982), p. 32-39. English.

AN: Rudy Fernandez moves freely between two- and three-dimensional forms using personal symbols such as cacti, roosters, flying hearts, trout, in paintings or lead-covered shelves of boxes reminiscent of retablos. Colorado-born Fernandez has lived in Arizona, Utah, New Mexico, and Washington. His art is not religious, but is influenced by a strong Catholic background. Many color illustrations, including the cover.

8125 Donnell-Kotrozo, Carol. Rudy Fernandez. ARTSPACE, Vol. 5, no. 4 (Fall 1981), p. 18-23. English.

AN: Scottsdale, Arizona resident Rudy Fernandez converts cultural symbols into a private system language that revolves around love, family, manhood and self-identity. His mixed media altar-like forms are based on interest in Southwest santos, their format and presentation. Fernandez does paintings, and assembled wood pieces. Handsomely illustrated, with color.

8126 Sanchez, Arley. Santeros. ALBUQUERQUE JRNL, (August 21, 1977), p. C, 1. English.

AN: Review of THE SANTERO EXPERIENCE, an exhibition of contemporary folk art by eleven New Mexican santeros, most in their 30s, at the Albuquerque Museum. The carvers include Juan Lucero, Ben Lopez, Luisito Lujan, Horacio Valdez, C. Garcia, George Lopez. A revival of the art has been taking place within last several years due to cultural awareness being experienced by Hispanos. Contemporary santeros still donate some pieces to the church, but most are marketed to private collectors, displayed in museums, or kept.

8127 Santos of New Mexico, art of our people. GRITO DEL NORTE, Vol. 3, no. 1 (January 17, 1970), p. 8-9. English.

AN: Historical trajectory of santero tradition in New Mexico. Distinguished santeros like Rafael Aragon of Cordova, Miguel Herrera of Arroyo Hondo, Juan Ramon Velasquez of Conjilon, Jose Benito Ortega of La Cueva all created art wedded to the environment of the Southwest. Illustrated with a portfolio of santos and retablos from the Folk Art Museum of Santa Fe, NM.

Santiago, Luis

8128 Southwest Texas State University, San Marcos, TX and Carlisle, Charles Richard. El mundo de Luis Santiago. Exhibition brochure, n.d. English.

AN: Illustrated exhibition brochure with biographical data and exhibition chronology on Luis Santiago. Both as a sculptor and painter, Santiago works in various techniques and styles to project the dynamic and multi-faceted aspects of Chicano life.

Santos

8129 Adams, Robert. The architecture and art of early Hispanic Colorado. Boulder, CO: Colorado Associated University Press in cooperation with the State Historical Society of Colorado, 1974. English.

AN: Robert Adams is a photographer and writer from Longmont, CO who has evocatively captured scenes in the San Luis and Purgatory Valleys of Southern Colorado. The text and photographs focus on "Hispano" village life, customs and traditions.

8130 Ahlborn, Richard E. The Penitente Moradas of Abiquiu. Washington, D.C.: Smithsonian Institution Press, 1968 (Contributions from the Museum of History and Technology, Paper 63). English.

AN: The history and organization of the Penitente Brotherhood. Detailed analysis of the architecture of Penitente moradas and the artifacts within them. Illustrated with many ethnographic photographs.

8131 Blue Sky Productions. Los santeros. Color film, 29 min., 1979. English.

AN: A 29 minute color film produced with funding assistance from New Mexico Highlands University and the National Endowment for the Arts. Features santeros Luis Tapia, Orlando Romero, Horacio Valdez.

Santos (cont.)

8132 Briggs, Charles L. The wood carvers of
     Cordova, New Mexico: social dimensions of an
     artistic "revival". Knoxville, TN:
     University of Tennessee Press, 1980.
     English.

> **AN:** One of the few books that deals with
> the traditional and contemporary-traditional
> religious art of New Mexico within social
> context. The author explores the influence
> of Anglo patronage and tourism on the
> meaning, aesthetics and distribution of the
> santos, and non-religious carving of the
> town of Cordoba.

8133 Cardona, Patricia. Gana adeptos de Museo
     Mexicano de San Francisco: Pedro Rodriguez.
     UNO MAS UNO, (February 6, 1978), p. 18.
     Spanish.

> **AN:** Report and brief history of the
> Mexican Museum which opened in 1975 with a
> collection of colonial santos. The museum
> offers a vista of Mexican culture to people
> in the United States. Director Peter
> Rodriguez says that Chicano artists Roberto
> Gonzalez, Felipe Reyes, Alfredo Arreguin,
> Gustavo Rivera, and Carmen Lomas Garza are
> some of the best. Illustrated.

8134 Crews, Mildred T. Saint-maker from Taos.
     AMERICAS, Vol. 21, no. 3 (March 1969).
     English.

> **AN:** An in-depth study of woodcarver
> Patrocino Barela (died 1964). Barela's work
> is an evolvement of the "santero" tradition
> filtered through an intensely personal
> style. His work was widely collected by
> institutions like The Museum of Modern Art,
> New York, The San Francisco Museum of Art
> and The New Mexico Fine Arts Museum.
> Well-illustrated with photographs of the
> artist and example of his work.

8135 Donnell-Kotrozo, Carol and Perlman, Barbara.
     Male passages: a secular santero of the '80s
     interprets machismo. ARIZONA ARTS AND
     LIFESTYLE, Vol. 4, no. 1 (1982), p. 32-39.
     English.

> **AN:** Rudy Fernandez moves freely between
> two- and three-dimensional forms using
> personal symbols such as cacti, roosters,
> flying hearts, trout, in paintings or
> lead-covered shelves of boxes reminiscent of
> retablos. Colorado-born Fernandez has lived
> in Arizona, Utah, New Mexico, and
> Washington. His art is not religious, but is
> influenced by a strong Catholic background.
> Many color illustrations, including the
> cover.

8136 Donnell-Kotrozo, Carol. Rudy Fernandez.
     ARTSPACE, Vol. 5, no. 4 (Fall 1981), p.
     18-23. English.

> **AN:** Scottsdale, Arizona resident Rudy
> Fernandez converts cultural symbols into a
> private system language that revolves around
> love, family, manhood and self-identity. His
> mixed media altar-like forms are based on
> interest in Southwest santos, their format
> and presentation. Fernandez does paintings,
> and assembled wood pieces. Handsomely
> illustrated, with color.

8137 Fine Arts Society of San Diego, CA. The
     cross and the sword. Exhibition catalog,
     1976. Bilingual.

> **AN:** Bi-lingual exhibition catalog of

Southwestern art forms; santero art,
vernacular architecture and traditional folk
art. Important essays by experts in each
field. Contains an iconographical summary of
santos and a good bibliography. Profusely
illustrated.

8138 Martinez, Eluid Levi. What is a New Mexico
     santo? Santa Fe, NM: Sunstone Press, 1978.
     Bilingual.

> **AN:** Martinez is a carver of saints from
> the well-known Lopez family of santeros of
> Cordova, New Mexico, who have carved for
> seven generations. An oversimplified history
> of the settlement of New Mexico and the rise
> of religious imagery production. Of interest
> are the illustrated steps of the carving
> process. Many reproductions.

8139 Santos of New Mexico, art of our people.
     GRITO DEL NORTE, Vol. 3, no. 1 (January 17,
     1970), p. 8-9. English.

> **AN:** Historical trajectory of santero
> tradition in New Mexico. Distinguished
> santeros like Rafael Aragon of Cordova,
> Miguel Herrera of Arroyo Hondo, Juan Ramon
> Velasquez of Conjilon, Jose Benito Ortega of
> La Cueva all created art wedded to the
> environment of the Southwest. Illustrated
> with a portfolio of santos and retablos from
> the Folk Art Museum of Santa Fe, NM.

Santos, Cuate

8140 Documentary to include work by Cuate Santos.
     LAREDO NEWS, (July 17, 1980). English.

> **AN:** Photography by Laredo News
> photographer Cuate Santos included in
> exhibit "Un encuentro sin palabras," a
> documentary show on Mexican American life in
> Texas sponsored by Mujeres Artistas del
> Suroeste (MAS). The state-wide show was
> juried by Los Angeles photographer Isabel
> Castro. Illustrated.

Santuario de Guadalupe, Santa Fe, NM

8141 Eichstaedt, Peter. Hispanic festival
     cultural showcase. NEW MEXICAN WEEKEND,
     (May 25, 1979), p. 3. English.

> **AN:** Announcement of the week-long
> HISPANIC HERITAGE FESTIVAL/EL FESTIVAL
> HISPANICO co-sponsored by La Cofradia de
> Artes y Artesanos Hispanicos and the Santa
> Fe Council fo the Arts at the Armory for the
> Arts in Santa Fe. Outlines the cultural
> activities, including a visual arts exhibit.
> La Cofradia is a recently formed
> organization which has assembled regional
> shows at the Santuario de Guadalupe which
> gave opportunities to local artists to show
> their work. Festival artists are primarily
> from the upper Rio Grande but also include
> artists from the State Penitentiary, as well
> as Albuquerque and Las Cruces. Illustration
> of painting by Sam Leyba.

8142 [Tapia exhibit invitation]. Exhibition
     invitation. Santa Fe, NM: Santuario de
     Nuestra Senora de Guadalupe, 1979. English.

> **AN:** Invitation to an exhibit of works by
> Luis and Star Tapia.

Santuario de Guadalupe, Santa Fe, NM (cont.)

8143 [Untitled]. Exhibition invitation. Santa Fe, NM: Santuario de Nuestra Senora de Guadalupe, 1980. English.

AN: Invitation to an exhibit by three northern New Mexico artists: Claudio Salazar (sculptor from Espanola), Eliud Salazar (painter from Canones)--both members of the Escuela Artesana--and Donald Romero (painter from Santa Fe).

Sapo de Aztlan
USE: Avilez, Tomas "Sapo"

Satire
USE: Caricature

Scholarship
USE: Financial Aid

Schorr, Michael

8144 NATIONAL MURALS NETWORK COMMUNITY NEWSLETTER. (Fall 1980). English.

AN: Reports on murals in San Francisco, CA, by the Chicano Moratorium Coalition; in Chicago about the Anti-War Preparations mural; in Houston by a student at the Association for Advancement of Mexican Americans; on Michael Schorr's mural in Chicanok, San Diego, CA; on a segment being painted at the Tujunga Wash mural in Los Angeles under Judy Baca; on south San Diego murals being painted out; Alan Barnett's survey of Southwest murals. Illustrated.

Scottsdale, AZ

8145 Donnell-Kotrozo, Carol. Rudy Fernandez. SOUTHWESTERN CONTEMPORARY ARTS QUARTERLY, (Fall 1981). English.

AN: Well-illustrated article on the mixed media creations of Rudy Fernandez who lives in Scottsdale, AZ.

Sculptors
USE: Artists

Sculpture

8146 Albright, Thomas. Forceful masterpieces from Manuel Neri. SAN FRANCISCO CHRONICLE, (May 17, 1979), p. 47. English.

AN: A rave review of Neri's one-person sculpture show at the Paula Anglum Gallery.

8147 Albright, Thomas. Manuel Neri's survivors: sculpture for the age of anxiety. ART NEWS MAGAZINE, Vol. 80, no. 1 (January 1981), p. 54-59. English.

AN: Critical evaluation of Neri's development as a sculptor in the figurative tradition. Biographical information and placement of artist within California art and international tendencies.

8148 Albright, Thomas. San Francisco: sleepers and spectacles [Manuel Neri exhibit review]. ART NEWS MAGAZINE, Vol. 78, no. 7 (September 1979), p. 118. English.

AN: Review of an exhibit at the Paula Anglum Gallery of San Francisco by Manuel Neri who has been developing over the last twenty years into one of the country's most profound and compelling sculptors. These pieces are life-sized plaster figures of nude female models.

8149 Arizona Commission on the Arts and Humanities. Humanizarte: the art of Zarco Guerrero. Exhibition brochure, 1978. English.

AN: Illustrated brochure of ceramic masks and bronze sculptures by Zarco Guerrero. The exhibit traveled throughout Arizona.

8150 Arizona Commission on the Arts and Humanities. Humanizarte: the art of Zarco Guerrero. Announcement, n.d. English.

AN: Poster announcement for an exhibition of bronze sculptures and ceramic masks by Zarco Guerrero.

8151 The art of Mexican America. EMPIRE MAGAZINE, (November 1, 1970), p. 24-25. English.

AN: Visual portfolio with minimal text. Includes paintings by Amado Pena, Mel Casas, Porfirio Salinas, and sculpture by Octavio Medellin. On the same page, Dr. Jacinto Quirarte gives views on the nature of Mexican art, the Mexican American artist, and the connection between Mexican and Mexican American art.

8152 Barrett, Marjorie. Carving out a living - a primitive process. ROCKY MOUNTAIN NEWS, (December 15, 1979), p. 90. English.

AN: In the village of Teseque outside Santa Fe, NM, Felipe Archuleta, a 69-year-old folk carver has emerged as an international art celebrity, famous for his naive animal carvings. His work expecially life-sized renditions of animals, is represented in many distinguished collections and is prized for its wit and lack of predictability. Illustrated with photograph of carver and one of his creations.

8153 Barrett, Marjorie. Ray Espinoza: versatile artist. ROCKY MOUNTAIN NEWS, (February 12, 1973), p. 44. English.

AN: Ray Espinoza whose family spans six generations in the San Luis Valley of Colorado is steeped in Southwestern art traditions. Drawing from his ancestral heritage, he has become a prominent sculptor working in wax. Illustrated with photograph of artist and two of his sculptures.

8154 Beardsley, John. Personal sensibilities in public places. ARTFORUM, Vol. 19, no. 10 (June 1981), p. 43-45. English.

AN: Distinction is made between art in public places and public art. The latter is assumed to have content and symbolism accessible to the majority of the population. Luis Jimenez, sculptor of VAQUERO intended for Houston's Moody Park, feels people should be able to identify with art. Color illustration.

8155 Bowerman, Liz Lerma. Jarro de chiles flamante [sculpture]. LA PALABRA, Vol. 2, no. 2 (Fall 1980), p. 23.

8156 Bowerman, Liz Lerma. Ladies helmet [sculpture]. LA PALABRA, Vol. 2, no. 2 (Fall 1980), p. 24.

Sculpture (cont.)

8157 Bowerman, Liz Lerma. Planting helmet
     [sculpture]. LA PALABRA, Vol. 2, no. 2 (Fall
     1980), p. 22.

8158 Brand Library Art Center, Glendale, CA. Los
     hermanos: Jesus, Jacob & Frank Gutierrez,
     sculpture, paintings, drawings, &
     photographs. Exhibition catalog, 1974.
     English.

     AN: Exhibit of the work of three
     brothers living in the Los Angeles area.

8159 Briggs, Charles L. The wood carvers of
     Cordova, New Mexico: social dimensions of an
     artistic "revival". Knoxville, TN:
     University of Tennessee Press, 1980.
     English.

     AN: One of the few books that deals with
     the traditional and contemporary-traditional
     religious art of New Mexico within social
     context. The author explores the influence
     of Anglo patronage and tourism on the
     meaning, aesthetics and distribution of the
     santos, and non-religious carving of the
     town of Cordoba.

8160 Canto al pueblo: an anthology of
     experiences. San Antonio, TX: Penca Books,
     1978. English.

     AN: Includes works by: Mario E.
     Castillo, Carlos Rosas, Jose G. Gonzalez,
     Santos Martinez, Gilbert Munoz, Fred Loa,
     Armando Ibanez and others.

8161 El Centro Cultural de La Raza, San Diego,
     CA. Espejo del barrio-art exposition.
     Exhibition brochure, June 1975. English.

     AN: Illustrated brochure announcement
     for a cultural exposition of Chicano music,
     art and drama. Includes some biographical
     information and one reproduction of painter
     Manuel Unzueta, woodworker Ambriz, muralist
     Victor Orozco Ochoa and designer/illustrator
     J. Armando Nunez.

8162 Charles Cowles Gallery. Manuel Neri. New
     York: Charles Cowles Gallery, 1981. English.

     AN: Brochure for one-person show with
     two color photographs of Neri's sculpture.
     Exhibition chronology and bibliography.

8163 Chicano artists exhibit at USC. CALENDAR,
     (September 23, 1973), p. 61. English.

     AN: Announcement of an exhibit of
     paintings, drawings, sculpture and graphics
     by artists from the Mechicano Art Center of
     Los Angeles at the University of Southern
     California Art Galleries. Slide
     presentations of murals and supergraphics.

8164 Coe, Kathryn. Heritage plus science yields
     art. SCOTTSDALE DAILY PROGRESS, (August 28,
     1981), p. 27. English.

     AN: Biography of Colorado-born Rudy
     Fernandez who bases many of his paintings
     and mixed media boxes on the religious
     imagery of Colorado. He studied geology;
     travelled to Spain and Mexico to know his
     heritage. All these factors influence his
     art, in which he uses symbols personally.

8165 Coffman Gallery I, The University of
     Minnesota, Minneapolis, MN. Ruben Trejo:
     visiting Chicano artist. Exhibition
     brochure, 1981. English.

     AN: Exhibition brochure of a sculpture
     show by Ruben Trejo presented from April 25
     to May 6. Trejo's sculptures are created
     from laminated wood, metal and plastic.
     Dominant motifs in this exhibit were the
     skull, the pepper and the heart. Brochure
     includes biographical information, checklist
     of the 28 works exhibited and one black and
     white photograph.

8166 Collection by Mexican American artist:
     Manuel Cruz. EL CHICANO, Vol. 3, no. 15
     (December 5, 1969), p. [3]. English.

     AN: Manuel Cruz creates ceramic
     figurines of Chicano types. The small,
     painted and glazed figures depict aspects of
     the daily life of the Mexican people from
     pre-Colombian times to the present.
     Illustrated with photographs of more than
     two dozen of the figurines.

8167 Contemporary Arts Museum, Houston, TX and
     Harithas, James. Luis Jimenez: Progress I.
     Exhibition catalog, 1974-75. English.

     AN: Catalog for a major exhibit of
     Jimenez sculptures, drawings and studies for
     sculptural works from 1967 to 1974. The
     latest project, PROGRESS, involves a series
     of monumental sculptures depicting the
     history of the West. Jimenez combines social
     comment with advanced plastic values. Well
     illustrated.

8168 Conversation on photography in the Los
     Angeles Latino community. OBSCURA, Vol. 2,
     no. 2 (December, February, 1981, 1982), p.
     22-32. English.

     AN: Interview on the nature and
     distinguishing characteristics of Chicano
     photography with Chicano photographers
     Isabel Castro (Council for Latino
     Photography), Lorenzo Hernandez (Director of
     Cityscape Gallery, publisher PHOTOSHOW
     magazine), Joseph G. Uribe (California State
     University, Los Angeles, Center for the
     Visual Arts, Director of West Colorado
     Gallery), Patssi Valdez, Becky Villasenor,
     and sculptor, curator, and Art Director for
     Academia Quinto Sol, Inc., Linda Vallejo,
     Portfolio of photography by Chicanos Don
     Anton, Louis Carlos Bernal, Sean Carrillo,
     Patssi Valdez, Ricardo Valverde, and by
     Morrie Camhi and Elizabeth Sisco on Chicano
     subjects.

8169 Corazon del norte: Jose Alfredo Maestas.
     GRITO DEL NORTE, Vol. 2, no. 7 (May 19,
     1969), p. 13. English.

     AN: Jose Alfredo Maestas, born in San
     Juan Pueblo is a folk carver imbued with the
     mythical and spiritual Indo-Hispano
     tradition. His carved figurines made from
     cotton wood roots, balsam and driftwood are
     in many museums and private collections.
     Illustrated with photographs of artist at
     work and two photographs of his sculpture.

8170 Corazon del norte: wood carving. GRITO DEL
     NORTE, Vol. 2, no. 5 (March 28, 1969), p.
     11. English.

     AN: Focus on the Aguilar family, folk
     artists from Los Ojos (Parkview), northern
     New Mexico. Sr. Cruz Aguilar is a sculptor
     and furniture maker, his 80-year-old mother
     Dona Cresanta Cruz is a quilter. Illustrated
     with photographs of the Aguilars and
     examples of their work.

Sculpture (cont.)

8171 Craft and Folk Art Museum, Los Angeles, CA
and Shapira, Nathan. From flat to form: Ben
Gurule and Carlo Cattaneo. Exhibition
catalog, 1978. English.

AN: Catalog for an exhibit by Los
Angeles Chicano artist Ben Gurule and
Italian artist Cattaneo, both involved with
three-dimensional expression in paper.
Gurule's works examine the interwoven
families of waves, polygons, and circles,
exploring relationships between geometry,
wave mechanics and quantum mechanics. Well
illustrated.

8172 Creations by Cruz. Color brochure, n.d.
English.

AN: Color brochure of genre-like figures
produced for sale by Los Angeles sculptor
Manuel Cruz in hydro-stone. The figures,
which run from 3" to 12" high depict images
from Aztec legends to Pachucos, Brown
Berets, and hippies.

8173 Dickson, Joanne. Manuel Neri. El Cajon, CA:
Grossmont College Gallery, 1980. English.

AN: Essay documents Neri's career and
situates him within the Bay Area figurative
style. As a sculptor, the artist has worked
in plaster or bronze, cast paper, fiberglass
and more recently in marble.

8174 Donnell-Kotrozo, Carol. Containment and
discovery. ARTWEEK, Vol. 11, no. 41
(December 6, 1980), p. 12. English.

AN: Review of an exhibit at Scottsdale,
Arizona gallery, C.G. Rein by Rudy
Fernandez. Discussed in detail is one of his
altar-like boxes of mixed media which
contain personal symbolisms. Illustrated.

8175 Donnell-Kotrozo, Carol and Perlman, Barbara.
Male passages: a secular santero of the '80s
interprets machismo. ARIZONA ARTS AND
LIFESTYLE, Vol. 4, no. 1 (1982), p. 32-39.
English.

AN: Rudy Fernandez moves freely between
two- and three-dimensional forms using
personal symbols such as cacti, roosters,
flying hearts, trout, in paintings or
lead-covered shelves of boxes reminiscent of
retablos. Colorado-born Fernandez has lived
in Arizona, Utah, New Mexico, and
Washington. His art is not religious, but is
influenced by a strong Catholic background.
Many color illustrations, including the
cover.

8176 Donnell-Kotrozo, Carol. Rudy Fernandez.
ARTSPACE, Vol. 5, no. 4 (Fall 1981), p.
18-23. English.

AN: Scottsdale, Arizona resident Rudy
Fernandez converts cultural symbols into a
private system language that revolves around
love, family, manhood and self-identity. His
mixed media altar-like forms are based on
interest in Southwest santos, their format
and presentation. Fernandez does paintings,
and assembled wood pieces. Handsomely
illustrated, with color.

8177 Doty, Robert. Human concern/personal
torment: the grotesque in American art. New
York: Praeger, 1969. English.

AN: Acknowledging the revival of realism
after fifty years of abstraction, the
Whitney Museum of American Art in New York
mounted a controversial show of modern and
contemporary painters and sculptors. Two
sculptures and a drawing by Luis Jimenez
were included, one of which, THE AMERICAN
DREAM, (1968) is illustrated.

8178 Dunham, Judith L. Manuel Neri: life with the
figure. ARTWEEK, Vol. 7, no. 39 (November
13, 1976), p. 1+. English.

AN: Favorable review of Neri's
exhibition of more than 80 figures or
fragments of figures at the Oakland Museum.
Explores relationship of Neri's sculpture
with developments in Bay Area figurative
painting and expressionism. Inventories
Neri's thematic and material concerns.
Analysis of his work in plaster, bronze and
fiberglass. An important assessment of
Neri's contribution to Bay Area art.

8179 Edward Chavez: sculptor-painter. LA LUZ,
Vol. 2, no. 2 (May 1973), p. 28-31. English.

AN: Lavishly illustrated biographical
account of Edward Chavez. Born in Ocate, New
Mexico in 1917, Chavez has a distinguished
career as a painter and sculptor. During the
1940's he executed a number of murals under
sponsorship of various government art
projects. These murals were placed in public
buildings in Nebraska, Colorado and Wyoming.
Although living and working in New York most
of his adult life, the work of Edward Chavez
has always been influenced by the Southwest.

8180 Espinoza. EMPIRE MAGAZINE, (October 22,
1972), p. 28. English.

AN: Biographical information and
artistic trajectory of Ray Espinoza from
Colorado's San Luis Valley. Focus on
Espinoza as a community artist who expresses
aspects of Southwestern culture. Illustrated
with photographs of three wax sculptures by
Ray Espinoza.

8181 Fabricant, Don. Show reveals Hispanic art.
NEW MEXICAN WEEKEND, (June 1, 1979).
English.

AN: Review of two exhibits in Santa Fe:
EL FESTIVAL HISPANICO, mounted by La
Cofradia de Artes y Artesanos Hispanicos and
Gilberto Guzman at the Black Kachina
Gallery. The reviewer feels the
traditional-style woodcarving done by
contemporaries is the strongest part of the
show; works that break with these forms seem
weaker, less skillful and cliche-ridden.
Crafts are excellent. Muralist Guzman has
blossomed in murals and easel paintings
since he was employed by the 1978 Art in
Public Places project. His work is intense
and expressive, sometimes erotic.
Illustration of work by sculptor Ruben
Montoya.

8182 'Festival of arts' planned by Arthritis
Foundation. SANTA FE NEW MEXICAN, (October
11, 1972), p. B6. English.

AN: The Albuquerque Arthritis Foundation
has invited professional artists and
craftsmen from New Mexico to display their
paintings, watercolors, sculpture, prints,
lithographs, jewelry. Joel Ramirez's
painting THE WEAVERS is selected for full
color art prints. Illustrated.

--   --

Sculpture (cont.)

8183 Figoten, Sheldon. Building and painting the figure. ARTWEEK, Vol. 12, no. 22 (June 20, 1981), p. 5-6. English.

AN: Review of eight sculptures and 25 drawings by Manuel Neri at the Redding Art Museum. Neri was influenced as a student in the San Francisco Bay Area in the 1950s by abstract expressionist philosophy and methodology, which he transferred to sculpture. Plaster, bronze, and marble figures are freely and loosely painted in areas. Illustration.

8184 Galeria: a place you should visit. CAMINOS, Vol. 2, no. 5 (October 1981), p. 24-25. English.

AN: Announcement of the opening of Galeria, specializing in Hispanic art, in Orange County, California. Illustrations of sculpture by Richard G. Villa and Eduardo Oropeza.

8185 Una galeria de artistas = A gallery of artists. CAMINOS, Vol. 1, no. 6 (October 1980), p. 20-26. Bilingual.

AN: Features California artists Domingo O. Ulloa (Imperial Valley images), Gloria Chacon, photographer Maria Pinedo (San Francisco), Willie Herron (Los Angeles), Joaquin Patino (Delano), Pedro Pelayo (Long Beach), sculptor Rudi Sigala (San Diego), Mario Torero (San Diego), sculptor Michael M. Amescua (Los Angeles), and the East Los Streetscapers. Illustrated.

8186 Galeria de la Raza/Studio 24, San Francisco, CA. Ajo, granadas y tres flores. Exhibition announcement, 1981.

AN: Announcement for an exhibition featuring Ruben Trejo, sculpture (Spokane, Washington), Cesar A. Martinez, paintings (San Antonio, Texas), Xavier Gorena, paper cut-outs (Mission, Texas).

8187 Galeria de la Raza/Studio 24, San Francisco, CA. Images of the Southwest. Exhibition catalog, 1977. English.

AN: Invitation/catalog for an exhibit including Rudy M. Fernandez(Utah), Enrique Flores(Texas), Xavier Gorena(Texas), C.A.[Cesar] Martinez(Texas), Santos Martinez, Jr.(Texas), Pedro Rodriguez(Texas), Arnold Trujillo(New Mexico). Block prints, paper cut-outs, drawings, photographs, copper enamels, and sculpture were shown. Five illustrations.

8188 Galeria Museo, Mission Cultural Center, San Francisco, CA and Rodriguez, Patricia. Patricia Rodriguez: simbolos y fantasias culturales. Exhibition catalog, 1981. English.

AN: Catalog of an exhibition of sculpture and painting. Autobiographical information about the Texas-born artist who lives in San Francisco and was a co-founder of Mujeres Muralistas. She explains her techniques in making portrait masks of Chicano/a artists in plaster and mixed media. Well illustrated.

8189 Garza, Alex. Earth abyss [sculpture]. REVISTA CHICANO-RIQUENA, Vol. 8, no. 3 (Summer 1980), p. 82.

8190 Garza, Alex. Emerging [sculpture]. REVISTA CHICANO-RIQUENA, Vol. 7, no. 2 (Spring 1979), p. 34.

8191 Garza, Alex. Entrevista con Alex Garza. ABRAZO, Vol. 1, no. 2 (Summer 1979), p. 27-29. English.

AN: Brief article exploring Alex Garza's technique, philosophy, and setting for his sculptural work. The artist expresses his desire to see artists break with tradition and not allow the political rhetoric of the early Chicano Movement to promote stagnation. His connection to the art organization ALBA is also briefly mentioned.

8192 Gonzalez, Hector. Aztlandia. EL HISPANO, Vol. 5, no. 2 (June 20, 1972).

AN: Story and photographs of a childrens sculptural park created by Pedro Ximenez.

8193 Graham Gallery, New York, NY and Amaya, Mario. Luis Jimenez. Exhibition catalog, 1969. English.

AN: Well-illustrated catalog of an exhibit by El Paso-born sculptor. Some biographical material.

8194 Graham Gallery, New York, NY and Perreault, John. Luis Jimenez. Exhibition catalog, 1970. English.

AN: Well-illustrated catalog of an exhibit by El Paso-born sculptor. Some biographical material.

8195 Guadalupe Historic Foundation, Santa Fe, NM. Artes en la primavera. (1981). English.

AN: Catalog of exhibit by four New Mexico artists: Manuel Lopez, sculptor from Chili; Andres Martinez, painter from Santa Cruz; Victoria Lopez, colcha embroiderer from San Pedro; Sam Quintana, jeweler from La Mesilla.

8196 Guernica, Antonio Jose and Saavedra-Vela, Pilar. El Midwest Canto al pueblo: "Otra Vez, C/S". AGENDA, Vol. 7, no. 3 (May, June, 1977), p. 4-13. Bilingual.

AN: A thorough report on the various phases and events of the Midwest Canto al Pueblo in Milwaukee, Wisconsin on April 28 to May 8, 1977. The festival brought together artists, poets, musicians, and cultural workers to reaffirm, share, and celebrate the identity of La Raza with El Pueblo. Includes a thematic and iconographic overview of Chicano murals in California by Jose Montoya, and an analysis of his sculpture by Zarco Guerrero from Meza, Arizona. Well illustrated. Includes a photograph of the collective mural painted at 5th St. and National Avenue in Milwaukee, Wisconsin during the course of the conference.

8197 Guerra, Victor, ed. El camino de la cruz. Austin, TX: Tejidos Publications, 1981. Spanish.

AN: Carlos Andres Guerra, portfolio; painting (in color), sculpture, drawing, jewelry. Luis Guerra drawing on cover.

8198 Guerrero, Adolfo "El Zarco". Aztlan [sculpture]. EL GRITO DEL SOL, Vol. 2, no. 4 (Fall 1977), p. 118. Spanish.

Sculpture (cont.)

8199 Guerrero, Adolfo "El Zarco". Canto al pueblo
     [sculpture]. EL GRITO DEL SOL, Vol. 2, no. 4
     (Fall 1977), p. 21. Spanish.

8200 Guerrero, Adolfo "El Zarco". El grito de
     guerra [sculpture]. EL GRITO DEL SOL, Vol.
     2, no. 4 (Fall 1977), p. 65. Spanish.

8201 Guerrero, Adolfo "El Zarco". Homenaje a
     Wounded Knee [sculpture]. TIN TAN, Vol. 1,
     no. 2 (September 1975), p. 40.

8202 Guerrero, Adolfo "El Zarco". Huehueteotl
     [sculpture]. EL GRITO DEL SOL, Vol. 2, no. 4
     (Fall 1977), p. 109. Spanish.

8203 Guerrero, Adolfo "El Zarco". La Llorona
     [sculpture]. EL GRITO DEL SOL, Vol. 2, no. 4
     (Fall 1977), p. 47. Spanish.

8204 Guerrero, Adolfo "El Zarco". El mestizo
     [sculpture]. EL GRITO DEL SOL, Vol. 2, no. 4
     (Fall 1977), p. 11. Spanish.

8205 Guerrero, Adolfo "El Zarco". Mictlan
     [sculpture]. EL GRITO DEL SOL, Vol. 2, no. 4
     (Fall 1977), p. 35. Spanish.

8206 Guerrero, Adolfo "El Zarco". La miseria
     [sculpture]. EL GRITO DEL SOL, Vol. 2, no. 4
     (Fall 1977), p. 29. Spanish.

8207 Guerrero, Adolfo "El Zarco". La mulatta
     [sculpture]. EL GRITO DEL SOL, Vol. 2, no. 4
     (Fall 1977), p. 115. Spanish.

8208 Guerrero, Adolfo "El Zarco". The new vision
     of Xicanindio art. RAYAS, Vol. 2, no. 1
     (January, February, 1979), p. 3. Bilingual.

     AN: Zarco Guerrero explains his personal
     artistic philosophy that unites Amerindian
     concepts of art to contemporary art forms,
     especially in sculpture. For Guerrero, "the
     Chicano artist is making a monumental effort
     to arrive at a new universal language and to
     create a new meaning of community through
     art.

8209 Guerrero, Adolfo "El Zarco". La olvidada
     [sculpture]. EL GRITO DEL SOL, Vol. 2, no. 4
     (Fall 1977), p. 55. Spanish.

8210 Guerrero, Adolfo "El Zarco". La pesadumbre
     [sculpture]. EL GRITO DEL SOL, Vol. 2, no. 4
     (Fall 1977), p. 15. Spanish.

8211 Guerrero, Adolfo "El Zarco". La Raza
     embarazada [sculpture]. EL GRITO DEL SOL,
     Vol. 2, no. 4 (Fall 1977), p. 93. Spanish.

8212 Guerrero, Adolfo "El Zarco". La Raza
     embarazada [sculpture]. AGENDA, Vol. 7, no.
     3 (May, June, 1977), p. 12. Spanish.

8213 Guerrero, Adolfo "El Zarco". Self-portrait
     [plaster mask]. TIN TAN, Vol. 1, no. 2
     (September 1975), p. [20].

8214 Guerrero, Adolfo "El Zarco".
     Tescatlipocamadre [sculpture]. EL GRITO DEL
     SOL, Vol. 2, no. 4 (Fall 1977), p. 87.
     Spanish.

8215 Guerrero, Adolfo "El Zarco".
     Tescatlipocamadre [sculpture]. AGENDA, Vol.
     7, no. 3 (May, June, 1977), p. 13. Spanish.

8216 Guerrero, Adolfo "El Zarco". La tradicion
     [sculpture]. EL GRITO DEL SOL, Vol. 2, no. 4
     (Fall 1977), p. 41. Spanish.

8217 Guerrero, Adolfo "El Zarco". Untitled
     [plaster mask]. TIN TAN, Vol. 1, no. 2
     (September 1975), p. [21].

8218 Guerrero, Adolfo "El Zarco". Xipe-totec
     [sculpture]. EL GRITO DEL SOL, Vol. 2, no. 4
     (Fall 1977), p. 75. Spanish.

8219 Guggenheim Gallery, Chapman College, Orange,
     CA. Hexagono: paintings, sculpture,
     drawings, prints. Exhibit invitation, 1977.
     English.

     AN: Invitation to an exhibit for artists
     Tito Aguirre, Isabel Castro, Rick Martinez,
     Esau Quiroz, Linda Vallejo, Emigdio Vasquez,
     Barrows, and Shanahan, sponsored by MEChA.
     Profiles and pictures of the artists.

8220 Haddad, Barbara. The fine arts. ROUNDUP,
     (January 25, 1970), p. 12. English.

     AN: Mixed review of Ray Espinoza's
     one-person show at the International House
     Gallery in Denver. The exhibition included
     drawings, paintings, prints, assemblages and
     sculptures. Selecting work from each medium,
     the critic comments on pieces that are
     successful and those not fully realized.
     Illustrated with a wood and metal relief of
     a guitar and a graphic of "Che" Guevara.

8221 Haines, Bruce J. Gonzales' works are
     controlled and full of detail. ANCHORAGE
     DAILY NEWS, (May 23, 1980). English.

     AN: Positive review of an exhibit titled
     THE HEAD TASTES BEST by Mariano Gonzales.
     Born in El Paso, Texas but reared in Alaska,
     Gonzales' works in various media from
     drawings and paintings to metals, ivory,
     enamel and plastics. The critic praises the
     artist for his "volatile intricacy" and his
     fusion of materials "always with craft and
     finesse". Includes reproductions of two
     paintings.

8222 Helen Euphrat Gallery, De Anza College,
     Cupertino, CA. Staying visible: the
     importance of archives. Art and "saved
     stuff" of eleven 20th century California
     artists. Cupertino, CA: Helen Euphrat
     Gallery, De Anza College, 1981. English.

     AN: Catalog issued in conjunction with
     an exhibit held in the gallery Sept. 22 to
     October 23, 1981 which included
     documentation on Chicana artists Patricia
     Rodriguez and Carmen Lomas Garza. Each
     artist explains her method of saving,
     storing and using cultural material in her
     creations. Includes biographical sketch,
     photograph of the artist and reproduction of
     artwork.

8223 Holliday-Abbott, Anne. Suitcase is 2nd home
     for arts liaison. ARIZONA DAILY STAR, (June
     18, 1981), p. H-3. English.

     AN: Arizona artist Louis LeRoy who
     paints, makes prints, and does assemblage is
     also a regional representative for the
     National Endowment for the Arts in Arizona,
     New Mexico, Colorado, Utah, and Wyoming.
     LeRoy has always been an "advocate of people
     being proud of their ethnic backgrounds." He
     feels artists can be self-supporting without
     commercializing.

8224 Jimenez, Luis. Grandmother with a cat
     [sculpture]. REVISTA CHICANO-RIQUENA, Vol.
     7, no. 2 (Spring 1979), p. 36.

Sculpture (cont.)

8225 Jimenez, Luis. Vaquero [sculpture]. REVISTA
     CHICANO-RIQUENA, Vol. 8, no. 3 (Summer
     1980), p. Cover. Bilingual.

8226 Jimenez, Luis. Vaquero [sculpture]. REVISTA
     CHICANO-RIQUENA, Vol. 8, no. 3 (Summer
     1980), p. 76-77. Bilingual.

8227 Loniak, Walter. The true New Mexico
     contemporary style. SANTA FE REPORTER, (May
     31, 1979). English.

     AN: Review of three exhibits in Santa
     Fe, EL FESTIVAL HISPANICO co-sponsored by
     the Cofradia de Artes y Artesanos Hispanicos
     and the Santa Fe Council for the Arts; a
     wood carving exhibit at Elaine Horwitch
     Gallery, and easel paintings by muralist
     Gilberto Guzman at the Black Kachina
     Gallery. Concerning the Festival exhibit,
     the critic states that the sculptural pieces
     are the strongest; two dimensional work is
     inconsistent or unimpressive, weaving is not
     well represented (though usually the
     strongest medium), and there are few
     photographs or prints. Illustration.

8228 Lujan, Gilbert Sanchez "Magu". El arte del
     Chicano - "The Spirit of the Experience".
     CON SAFOS, no. 7 (Winter 1971), p. 11-13.
     English.

     AN: Definition of Chicano Art by artist
     Lujan as the expression of an unique
     experience that is neither Mexican nor U.S.
     Anglo, that has its own vitality and
     dynamics. Chicanos can draw upon common
     cultural elements and transform them into
     images and art forms such as sculptured
     menudo bones, tortilla drawings, vato loco
     portraits, etc. Four woodcuts by Roberto de
     la Rocha are shown as examples.

8229 Lujan, Pedro. Grandes problemas [sculpture].
     CARACOL, Vol. 3, no. 4 (December 1976), p.
     10.

8230 Lujan, Pedro and Morton, Carlos. Una platica
     entre Carlos Morton y Pedro Lujan. CARACOL,
     Vol. 3, no. 4 (December 1976), p. 10-12.
     Bilingual.

     AN: Carlos Morton interviews Pedro
     Lujan, a Chicano sculptor who spends six
     months a year in New York and six months
     traveling throughout the Southwest. Lujan
     discusses his preference for creating works
     from available materials such as scraps of
     wood, wire, and rope.

8231 Lujan, Pedro. Ruby I [sculpture]. REVISTA
     CHICANO-RIQUENA, Vol. 8, no. 3 (Summer
     1980), p. 71. Bilingual.

8232 McClellan, Bill. Army of volunteers paints a
     little history in Phoenix. PHOENIX GAZETTE,
     (April 20, 1977). English.

     AN: Adolfo "El Zarco" Guerrero with 100
     residents from the Duppa Villa Housing
     Project completes a mural funded by the
     Arizona Commission on Arts and Humanities.
     Guerrero completed six murals, but prefers
     sculpture.

8233 McCullom, Pat. Gonzales: his paintings are
     like hieroglyphs. ANCHORAGE TIMES, (June
     25, 1978), p. I, 3. English.

     AN: Mariano Gonzales born in El Paso
     Texas, reared in Anchorage and trained at
     the Rhode Island School of Design has a

developing reputation as an artist from the
far north. This positive review is for an
exhibit of paintings, jewelry and metal work
pieces. Gonzales' paintings are heavily
saturated with subconscious symbolism and
his sculptures generally feature mechanical,
movable parts.

8234 The Mexican Museum, San Francisco, CA.
     Manuel Neri: sculpture and drawings.
     Exhibition invitation, 1981. English.

     AN: Illustrated invitation to an
     exhibit.

8235 Mexican-American Advisory Committee of the
     Museum of Science and Industry.. Second
     annual Mexican-American art fiesta.
     Exhibition brochure, 1975. English.

     AN: Exhibit of paintings, sculpture,
     crafts, and photography by 49 artists from
     Illinois, Indiana, and Mexico. Includes many
     of the most important Chicano artists of the
     Chicago area.

8236 Montini, Ed. Masks reflect the spirit of an
     artist. ARIZONA REPUBLIC, (May 31, 1981),
     p. G-1,G-3. English.

     AN: The paper and ceramic masks of Zarco
     Guerrero reflect many different emotions.
     Masking has long been a tradition in Mexico,
     where Guerrero got his inspiration. Guerrero
     uses his masks for theatre and as an
     educational tool. Illustrated.

8237 Moreno, Martin. M'Chicana [sculpture].
     REVISTA CHICANO-RIQUENA, Vol. 7, no. 2
     (Spring 1979), p. 35.

8238 Morton, Carlos. Pedro Lujan: sculptor. LA
     LUZ, Vol. 6, no. 5 (May 1977), p. 22-26.
     Bilingual.

     AN: Biographical and artistic trajectory
     of Pedro Lujan. As a sculptor, he is
     identified with the Levi-Straussian idea of
     the "bricoleur" (a person who solves
     artistic problems with the materials on
     hand). Basically working with wood and
     simple tools, Pedro Lujan feels related to
     santero and Penitente art of his native
     Southwest.

8239 Museum of Fine Arts, Santa Fe, NM. John
     Hernandez, Douglas Johnson. Exhibition
     invitation, 1979. English.

     AN: Invitation to an exhibit including
     the jeweled sculpture of John Hernandez from
     New Mexico.

8240 Museum of Fine Arts, Santa Fe, NM. Luis
     Jimenez, sculpture, drawings and prints: La
     Cofradia de Artes y Artesanos Hispanicos,
     selected works. Exhibition invitation, 1979.
     English.

     AN: Invitation to an exhibit of Texas
     sculptor and printmaker Luis Jimenez, and
     New Mexican artists and artisans.

8241 Negri, Sam. Garden grows as shrine to
     sculptor. ARIZONA REPUBLIC, (April 5,
     1980), p. C-1. English.

     AN: Felix Lucero, a self-taught
     Colorado-born sculptor who came to Tucson in
     1938, spent 20 years sculpting religious
     statues. He started the Garden of Gethsemane
     in 1945 on the Congress Street bridge.

Sculpture (cont.)

8242 Neri, Manuel. Untitled standing figure no. 4 [sculpture]. PEOPLE'S WORLD, Vol. 44, no. 19 (May 9, 1981), p. 10. English.

AN: Illustration of a painted bronze figure by San Francisco Bay artist Manuel Neri. Drawings and sculpture by Neri to be shown at the Mexican Museum.

8243 New Mexico State University, University Art Gallery, Las Cruces, NM. Luis Jimenez: sculpture, drawings and prints. Exhibition catalog, 1977. English.

AN: Well illustrated catalog, some illustrations in color. Text is interview tracing Jimenez's artistic development. Artists identifies Mexican American connections in his work.

8244 Oakland Museum presents 5 L.A. Chicano artists. EL MUNDO (Hayward, CA), (August 1974). English.

AN: Report on the exhibit THE SEARCH FOR AZTLAN, featuring paintings, murals, tortilla art, folk and religious symbols and totems by Carlos Almaraz, Roberto de la Rocha, Gilbert Lujan, Frank Romero and Judithe Hernandez. Included in the more than 100 works are a wall mural, a folk art pyramid, and part of a primed '51 Chevy lowrider. Illustrated.

8245 Out in the open/Allen Parkway: Frank Fajardo, Jesse Lott, Guillermo Pulido, Jana Vander Lee. Exhibit invitation, 1979. English.

AN: Invitation to the installation of conceptual pieces in public areas of Houston. Includes Chicano artist Frank Fajardo and Bolivian-born Pulido.

8246 Paez, Carlos. [Untitled sculpture]. XALMAN, Vol. 1, no. 5 (Fall 1977), p. 6.

8247 Phelon, Craig. Sculptor survives on the edge of a concrete canyon. EL PASO TIMES, (July 11, 1980). English.

AN: 84 year old Jesus Barrera sculpted and painted hundreds of religious plaster statues until forced to abandon sculpture in 1962 because lead-based paint ruined his health.

8248 Rabyor, Jozanne. Luis Jimenez at Contemporary Arts Museum. ART IN AMERICA, Vol. 63, no. 1 (January, February, 1975), p. 88. English.

AN: Texas-born Luis Jimenez's first major museum show of 77 pieces spanning eight years of production is dazzling. Superbly crafted fiberglass sculptures comment on indigenous mythologies often with macabre humor. His work, according to the critic, is too moralistic to be Pop, and too passionate to be dumped into the California-plastic bag.

8249 Rangel, Jesus. Heirs of Jose Posada: revolution lives in Chicano art. SAN DIEGO UNION, (February 24, 1980), p. D6. English.

AN: 19th century Mexican engraver Jose Guadalupe Posada has been an inspiration to Chicano artists. Along with two exhibits of his work, the Centro Cultural de la Raza is also showing calavera (skeleton) images by Chicano artists: skull-masks from the Teatro Campesino, a print by Amalia Mesa-Baines of Frida Kahlo, and a collaged box by Jose Antonio Burciaga. Illustration: Salvador Roberto Torres work.

8250 Raza sculptors coast to coast - Lujan y Rodriguez. EL TECOLOTE LITERARY MAGAZINE, Vol. 10, no. 9 (June 1980), p. 7. English.

AN: Pedro Lujan, originally from the Southwest, now lives in SOHO in New York. Lujan defines himself as a bricoleur who works primarily with wood and simple tools like hatchets and chisels. Ismael Rodriguez, self-taught sculptor from Berkeley, California, works in stone or wood. Includes photo of Lujan's wood sculpture "Man Running" and photo of Rodriguez at work.

8251 Rios, Esther. Spotted leopard [sculpture]. TEJIDOS, Vol. 4, no. 3 (Fall 1977), p. 26. English.

8252 Ripley, Deborah. A sticky business. NEW WEST MAGAZINE, (July 28, 1980). English.

AN: Essay on California artists who take discarded objects and upgrade them into art works. Includes photographs of Larry Fuentes and three of his creations.

8253 Rodriguez, Patricia. Portfolio: Patricia Rodriguez; the visual interview. METAMORFOSIS, Vol. 3, no. 1-2 (1980, 1981), p. 38-45. English.

AN: Statement by the artist reprinted from her exhibit "The Visual Interview" at the Mission Cultural Center, San Francisco. Discusses her fifteen mask-box-sculptures of Chicano artists from northern California. Illustrated with photographs of the artist at work and five of her sculptures. This issue of METAMORFOSIS combines volumes 3 and 4.

8254 Ruben Salazar Library, Sonoma State University, Sonoma, CA. Patricia Rodriguez: Chicano sculpture and masks. Exhibition invitation, 1981. English.

AN: Invitation to an exhibit.

8255 San Antonio Museum of Modern Art. Paperwork: an exhibition of Texas artists. San Antonio, TX: San Antonio Museum of Modern Art, 1979. English.

AN: Includes Roberto Munguia, Mexican American artist from Kingsville, Texas. Working with shaped paper, the artist describes his material and methods of creation. Includes biography of artist together with an exhibition list. Illustrated with photographs of five paper constructions by Roberto Munguia.

8256 San Francisco Museum of Modern Art, San Francisco, CA and Marra, Patricia. Day of the dead. Exhibition catalog, 1980. English.

AN: Broadside announcement in the manner of Jose Gudalupe Posada for an exhibit of prints by Posada and an altar by Amalia Mesa-Baines and Friends. Text presents customs and traditions for celebrating the Day of the Dead in Mexico and among the Chicano community.

Sculpture (cont.)

8257 Sanchez, Arley. Santeros. ALBUQUERQUE JRNL,
(August 21, 1977), p. C, 1. English.

AN: Review of THE SANTERO EXPERIENCE, an
exhibition of contemporary folk art by
eleven New Mexican santeros, most in their
30s, at the Albuquerque Museum. The carvers
include Juan Lucero, Ben Lopez, Luisito
Lujan, Horacio Valdez, C. Garcia, George
Lopez. A revival of the art has been taking
place within last several years due to
cultural awareness being experienced by
Hispanos. Contemporary santeros still donate
some pieces to the church, but most are
marketed to private collectors, displayed in
museums, or kept.

8258 Schwartz, Barry. The new humanism: art in a
time of change. New York, Praeger, 1974.
English.

AN: Schwartz compiled an international
roster of over 100 artists whom he believed
formed a "movement" away from abstraction
and toward an art expressing a belief in
human values and human dignity. He divides
humanism into categories like metaphysical,
existential, absurd, etc. Included are Luis
Jimenez's BARFLY and OLD WOMAN WITH CAT
(illustrated p. 121), and a brief biography
(p. 171).

8259 Seattle Art Museum, Seattle, WA and Dickson,
Joanne. Manuel Neri, sculpture and drawings.
Exhibition catalog, 1981. English.

AN: Beautifully illustrated catalog.
Text by Joanne Dickson from Oakland
California, biography and very complete
chronology of Neri exhibitions.

8260 Serrano, Benjamin, Jr. Judge's
feast/Banquete de juez [sculpture]. REVISTA
CHICANO-RIQUENA, Vol. 7, no. 2 (Spring
1979), p. 33.

8261 Shakti Gallery, Long Beach, CA. "Fire in the
lodge," paper sculptures by Linda Vallejo.
Exhibit invitation, 1981. English.

AN: Invitation to an exhibit by Long
Beach, CA artist Linda Vallejo. Illustrated.

8262 Simon, Joan. Report from New Mexico. ART IN
AMERICA, Vol. 68, no. 6 (Summer 1980), p.
33-41. English.

AN: Luis Jimenez worked four years as
artist-in-residence at the Roswell Museum
and Art Center, Roswell, NM, which enabled
him to produce his PROGRESS series and other
monumental sculpture.

8263 Smith, Roberta. Twelve days of Texas. ART IN
AMERICA, Vol. 64, no. 4 (July, August,
1976), p. 42-48. English.

AN: Overview of Texas art in Fort
Worth/Dallas, Houston, San Antonio, Tyler,
and Galveston. Includes reproductions of
works by Luis Jimenez (color, on cover),
Roberto Rios mural, Jesse Trevino, Mel
Casas. Also mentioned in text are Phil
Renteria and Cesar Martinez.

8264 La Sociedad Historica de Nuestra Senora de
Guadalupe, Santa Fe, NM. Meditacion.
Exhibition invitation, 1980. English.

AN: Invitation to an exhibit by four
artists: Filomeno Martinez (graphic artist,
Albuquerque), Ruben Montoya (santero, Santa

Fe), Santiago Chavez (painter, Santa Rosa),
Jose Alberto Baros (sculptor, Espanola).

8265 Southwest Chicano Arts Center, Houston, TX.
Pilar C. Rubin. Exhibition invitation, 1977.
English.

AN: Illustrated invitation to exhibit of
sculpture.

8266 Southwest Texas State University, San
Marcos, TX and Carlisle, Charles Richard. El
mundo de Luis Santiago. Exhibition brochure,
n.d. English.

AN: Illustrated exhibition brochure with
biographical data and exhibition chronology
on Luis Santiago. Both as a sculptor and
painter, Santiago works in various
techniques and styles to project the dynamic
and multi-faceted aspects of Chicano life.

8267 Tannous, David. Report from Washington
'directions' and the 'First Western
Biennial'. ART IN AMERICA, Vol. 67, no. 8
(December 1979), p. 29, 31. English.

AN: Among the best and most eye-catching
works at the First Western Biennial are
three large fiberglass-and-epoxy sculptures
by Luis A. Jimenez, Jr. from the series
PROGRESS, PART II.

8268 Tennant, Donna. Conceptual art dots city
landscape. HOUSTON CHRONICLE, (October 27,
1979), p. II, 7. English.

AN: Frank Fajardo and Bolivian-born
Guillermo Pulido are two of several artists
creating conceptual art pieces in various
parts of Houston. Fajardo marked out space
with 25 stakes tipped with day-glo orange
paint. Pulido constructed two large
triangles on opposite hillsides, like giant
markers.

8269 Torres, Louis R. A Profile of an Hispano
Artist: Charlie "Clavos" Felix. LA LUZ, Vol.
4, no. 6-7 (September, October, 1975), p.
3-4. English.

AN: Biographical data on artist and his
unique nail relief sculpture.

8270 Trejo, Frank. S.A. mission doors inspired
wood carver. SAN ANTONIO LIGHT, (January
10, 1971), p. 18. English.

AN: Biographical and exhibition
information on San Antonio woodcarver Jesse
V. Garcia. Illustrated by photograph of
artist.

8271 Trevino, Jose. Los monitos de Jose Trevino:
esculturas de barro. TEJIDOS, Vol. 5, no.
2-4 (1978), p. 134-144. English.

8272 University Art Museum, Berkeley, CA. The
Fifth Sun: Contemporary/Traditional Chicano
& Latino Art. Exhibition catalog, 1977.
English.

AN: Catalog of exhibit including 45
artists of northern California. Texts deal
with Mexican muralists, Mujeres Muralistas &
other muralists, posters, the Chicano art
movement, altars, La Raza Silkscreen Center,
Galeria de la Raza, the Mexican Museum, the
Sacramento Centro de Artistas Chicanos/RCAF.
Mural maps of S.F. Bay Area and Sacramento.
Many illustrations.

Sculpture (cont.)

8273 [Untitled]. Exhibition invitation. Santa Fe,
NM: Santuario de Nuestra Senora de
Guadalupe, 1980. English.

AN: Invitation to an exhibit by three
northern New Mexico artists: Claudio Salazar
(sculptor from Espanola), Eliud Salazar
(painter from Canones)--both members of the
Escuela Artesana--and Donald Romero (painter
from Santa Fe).

8274 Washington State University, Pullman. Fine
Arts Center Gallery II. Ruben M. Trejo-mi
ultimo fracaso. Exhibition announcement,
1976. English.

AN: Exhibit announcement for Trejo's
show of sculpture and drawings. Illustrated
with a Trejo "jalapeno" sculpture.

8275 Weil Gallery Center for the Arts, Corpus
Christi State University. Caras y mascaras:
the art of El Zarco Guerrero. Exhibition
invitation, 1981. English.

AN: Invitation to exhibit of Arizona
artist. Color illustration.

8276 Werley, Lenora. Murals give young artists
community pride, sculptor says. YUMA DAILY
SUN, (February 4, 1981). English.

AN: Mesa, Arizona sculptor Adolfo
"Zarco" Guerrero feels murals give young
people pride in their community. Guerrero is
part of the Xicanindio Artist Coalition that
is CETA-contracted to run summer art
programs for high school students.
Illustrated.

8277 Wilks, Flo. Joseph A. Chavez. ART VOICES
SOUTH, Vol. 3, no. 1 (January, February,
1980), p. 30. English.

AN: Brief resume on art and life of
Albuquerque sculptor. Illustrated.

8278 Wilson, William. 30 works from the grass
roots. LOS ANGELES TIMES, (June 4, 1973),
p. IV,2. English.

AN: Review of a show at the Junior Arts
Center in Barnsdall Park by 15 members of
the Mechicano Art Center. The critic feels
contemporary groups that aim for change
today (unlike past groups) are unable to
articulate their spirit in a cohesive style.
The top talent in this show is Charles
Almaraz; also on exhibit are paintings by
Jose Cervantes, Guillermo Martinez, Ray
Atilano, sculpture by Manuel Cruz, and
photography by (Oscar) R. Castillo.

8279 Wood carving art. EASTSIDE JRNL, (January
7, 1971), p. 2. English.

AN: Two photographs and commentary on
woodcarver Roberto H. Rodriguez on the
occasion of his one man show at the East Los
Angeles Library. Illustrated work shows
pre-Columbian motifs.

SEARCH FOR AZTLAN [exhibit]

8280 Oakland Museum presents 5 L.A. Chicano
artists. EL MUNDO (Hayward, CA), (August
1974). English.

AN: Report on the exhibit THE SEARCH FOR
AZTLAN, featuring paintings, murals,
tortilla art, folk and religious symbols and
totems by Carlos Almaraz, Roberto de la
Rocha, Gilbert Lujan, Frank Romero and
Judithe Hernandez. Included in the more than
100 works are a wall mural, a folk art
pyramid, and part of a primed '51 Chevy
lowrider. Illustrated.

Seattle Shipscalers Union

8281 The stolen art: the O'Higgins mural.
RECOBRANDO, Vol. 1, no. 2, p. 15, 16.
English.

AN: Historical documentation on 60-foot
long 8-foot high fresco mural painted for
the Seattle Shipscalers Union by Mexican
artist Pablo O'Higgins in 1949. In 1974,
John Caughlan, a people's lawyer documented
the existence of the mural to Chicano
community groups. M.E.C.H.A. students at the
University of Washington lobbied for the
murals restoration and permanent exhibition.

Seattle, WA

8282 Aguayo, Emilio. Chicano art: a new art-style
of the future. (Unpublished Study Project
for Prof. Brauman, Art Dept., Univ. of
Washington, Seattle), June 6, 1972. English.

AN: Autobiographical account and
self-analysis of artist's work. Beginning in
1965 the artist has created 40,000 small ink
drawings in a contour line technique.
Situating himself within the Chicano Arts
Movement, Aguayo describes his dominant
themes, symbols, and stylistic
preoccupations.

8283 Bellevue Art Museum, Bellevue, WA. Alfredo
Arreguin. s.n.:s.l., n.d. English.

AN: Profusely illustrated exhibition
catalog for a one-man retrospective of
paintings by Alfredo Arreguin. Exploring the
possibilities of pattern painting, the
intent of his art is to be visionary. His
paintings have affinity with Pre-Columbian
and Colonial Mexican designs and is related
to decorative emotional images of various
cultures. Includes photograph of artist and
a selected bibliography.

8284 Contreras, Carlos. Nuestra cultura. LA VOZ:
Concilio for the Spanish Speaking of King
Co., Seattle, no. 7 (August 1979).

AN: Information of Washington state
murals painted by members of La Extension
Cultural; Armando Lara's autobiographical
mural titled "El Rio" is installed at the
Concilio offices, 107 Cherry St. Suite 210.
Arturo Artorez completed a wall painting
using the image of Quetzalcoatl at El Centro
de la Raza with funding from the Seattle
Arts Commission. Francisco Siqueiros used
the themes of ecology and Mexican mythology
for two murals at Seattle Community College.
Commentary on Alfredo Arreguin's painting
exhibition at the Kiku Gallery and his wall
painting at the Childrens Orthopedic
Hospital in Seattle.

Seattle, WA (cont.)

8285 Cultural department. RECOBRANDO, Vol. 1, no. 15. Spanish.

AN: The development of "Raza" culture in the Northwest and the role played by the Centro de la Raza. Mentions the "talleres de arte" set up by Carlos Contreras and Arturo Artorez, artists from Mexico who moved to Seattle in 1978. Details cultural events sponsored by the Centro in the fields of art, music, dance, and theater.

8286 Henry Gallery, University of Washington, Seattle, WA and Ybarra-Frausto, Tomas. Arte prehispanico, arte popular. Exhibit Catalog, 19. English.

AN: Exhibition catalog for an exhibit prepared almost entirely by students from the School of Art with assistance from MEChA and members of the faculty of the School of Art. The pre-Columbian sections presented objects from sites in Mexico and Peru from pre-classic, classic and post-classic periods. The arte popular sections exhibited wares from craft centers in Mexico, Peru, Ecuador and Guatemala. Includes statement by Tomas Ybarra-Frausto on the relevance of this exhibition to the cultural identity of Chicanos in the Pacific Northwest.

8287 The stolen art: the O'Higgins mural. RECOBRANDO, Vol. 1, no. 2, p. 15, 16. English.

AN: Historical documentation on 60-foot long 8-foot high fresco mural painted for the Seattle Shipscalers Union by Mexican artist Pablo O'Higgins in 1949. In 1974, John Caughlan, a people's lawyer documented the existence of the mural to Chicano community groups. M.E.C.H.A. students at the University of Washington lobbied for the murals restoration and permanent exhibition.

8288 Thorne, Judy. Alfredo Arreguin - painting in patterns. SEATTLE TIMES, (June 15, 1980), p. 18-19. English.

AN: Biographical information on Mexican-born Seattle painter Alfredo Arreguin. Includes mention of his selection as a city art commissioner in Seattle. Discussion of artist's distinctive style based on use of intricate patterns. Well illustrated with four color reproductions of artist's work.

8289 Tsutakaua, Mayumi. Artist paints from heritage. SEATTLE TIMES, (September 15, 1980). English.

AN: Biographical information on Armond Lara, Northwest Chicano-Navajo artist. He is coordinating the restoration of a mural done in Seattle by Mexican artist Pablo O'Higgins. In his own work Lara is experimenting with paper making and the use of natural pigments.

8290 Tsutakaua, Mayumi. Despite hostilities, Arreguin is transcending. SEATTLE TIMES, (September 2, 1979). English.

AN: Biographical sketch of Northwest Chicano painter and ceramicist Alfredo Arreguin. Artistic chronology and negative relationship with local mainstream art institutions.

Second Latin American Colloquium of Photography, 1981

8291 Bernal, Luis Carlos. La fotografia como reflejo de las estructuras sociales. In HECHO EN LATINOAMERICA: SEGUNDO COLOQUIO LATINOAMERICANO DE FOTOGRAFIA, MEXICO CITY, 1982, p. 92-94. Spanish.

AN: Presentation made by Tucson, AZ photographer Louis Carlos Bernal at the Second Latin American Colloquium of Photography and exhibit in 1981.

Second National Community Muralists' Network Conference, Chicago, IL, April 20-23, 1978

8292 Notes on 2nd National Community Muralists' Network Conference, Chicago, Ill. April 20-23, 1978. San Francisco, CA, 1978. English.

AN: Rupert Garcia, Raul Martinez, Patricia Rodriguez, Ray Patlan (San Francisco Bay Area) and Jaime Valadez (San Jose), among others, attended the conference in Chicago. Reports were heard from many parts of the United States on mural activities, including that of Aurelio Diaz of Chicago, representing MARCH (Movimiento Artistico Chicano). A workshop presentation was made by Luis Arenal and others from the Taller Siqueiros of Cuernavaca, Mexico. An experimental mural to try Siqueiros' techniques was created. Illustrated.

Secondary School Education

8293 Chicano art show. EL DIARIO DE LA GENTE, Vol. 1, no. 7 (February 6, 1973), p. 4. English.

AN: Fine arts students at the University of Colorado led by Rudy Fernandez hope to educate high school students about Chicano art. This article documents an exhibit held at Lafayette, CO. Members of the group are Bob Maez, Jerry Jaramillo, Anthony Mendoza, and Rudy Fernandez. Illustrated by four exhibition photographs by John L. Espinosa.

8294 Fiesta de los barrios observes Cinco de Mayo. EASTSIDE SUN, (May 1, 1969). English.

AN: The Fiesta de los Barrios is a cultural festival organized by the committee pressuring the Los Angeles Board of Education for better and more relevant education after the East Los Angeles high school "blowouts." The Fiesta features art, music, dance and literature.

8295 Public invited to weekend fiesta at Lincoln High. LOS ANGELES TIMES, (April 29, 1969), p. II. English.

AN: Fiesta of art, music, dance and literature organized by the committee formed after the East Los Angeles high school "blowouts" to press for better and more relevant education. Hundreds of works of art were collected for display at the "Fiesta de los Barrios".

Secrest-Ramirez, M.E.

8296 HEMBRA: HERMANAS EN MOVIMIENTO BROTANDO
RAICES DE AZTLAN (University of Texas,
Austin). (Spring 1976).

AN: Raul Valdez, drawing, p. 3; Carolina
Flores, drawing, p. 5; Maria Flores,
photograph, pp. 7, 11, 30; M.E.
Secrest-Ramirez, drawing, p. 12; Amacio
Zarate, drawing, p. 15; Santa Barraza,
drawings, pp. 16, 17, 18, 26, 32; Nora
Gonzales-Dodson, painting, p. 19; Gilberto
Cardenas, photograph, pp. 22, 28; Nanci de
los Santos, photograph, p. 23, 29; Amado
Maurilio Pena, Jr. p. 31.

Seguin, Juan

8297 Reyes, Luis. Seguin: traidor o heroe.
COMUNIDAD, (April 12, 1981), p. 8-9.
Spanish.

AN: Report on the pilot film for an
eight-part series called LA HISTORIA made by
Jesus Trevino for the Public Broadcasting
Service. The pilot treats the life of an
"anti-hero," Juan Seguin, during the Texas
war for independence from Mexico, and
relates the little-known history of the
Mexican defenders of the Alamo. Trevino
chose this controversial subject because it
exemplified an early case of the dual nature
of bilingualism and biculturalism.
Description of the research and filming of
the pilot. Illustrated.

SEGUIN [movie]

8298 Cinefestival. ARRIBA, [n.d.], p. 5. English.

AN: Announcement of the 6th Annual
International Hispanic Film Festival in San
Antonio, TX. Willie Varela will conduct a
workshop, and Jesus Trevino will premiere
his hour-long production, SEGUIN.

8299 Reyes, Luis. Seguin: traidor o heroe.
COMUNIDAD, (April 12, 1981), p. 8-9.
Spanish.

AN: Report on the pilot film for an
eight-part series called LA HISTORIA made by
Jesus Trevino for the Public Broadcasting
Service. The pilot treats the life of an
"anti-hero," Juan Seguin, during the Texas
war for independence from Mexico, and
relates the little-known history of the
Mexican defenders of the Alamo. Trevino
chose this controversial subject because it
exemplified an early case of the dual nature
of bilingualism and biculturalism.
Description of the research and filming of
the pilot. Illustrated.

**Segundo Festival Estudiantial Chicano de Arte y
Literatura, Austin, TX, 1977**

8300 SEGUNDO FESTIVAL ESTUDIANTIL CHICANO DE ARTE
Y LITERATURA, Austin, TX, 1977. TEJIDOS,
Vol. 4, no. 3 (Fall 1977), p. 1-2.
Bilingual.

AN: Introduction to this theme issue
which presents selected works of art and
literature submitted at the 2nd Annual
Festival Estudiantil.

Self Concept
USE: Identity

Self Perception
USE: Identity

Self-Help Graphics, Los Angeles, CA

8301 Amescua, Michael M. Dia de los muertos.
SOMOS, Vol. 1, no. 6 (November 1978), p.
39-40. English.

AN: Report on Self-Help Graphics'
project involving fifteen humanists who
explored history, literature, philosophy and
religion as they relate to the Dia de los
Muertos, an annual program of Self-Help.
Illustrated.

8302 Berges, Marshall. Sister Karen Boccalero:
dedicated to the community, she helps others
find strength in art. HOME MAGAZINE,
(December 17, 1978), p. 42-45. English.

AN: History of the Franciscan nun who
studied with Sister Mary Corita at
Immaculate Heart College. Details the
founding and concepts of Self-Help Graphics
in East Los Angeles, a year-round program to
"help Chicanos rediscover their cultural
heritage".

8303 Galeria Otra Vez, Los Angeles, CA.
Inner/urban landscapes: Ricardo Valverde,
Suda House, David Feldman. Exhibition
invitation, 1979. English.

AN: Invitation to a photography
exhibition held at Self-Help Graphic's
gallery.

8304 Hansen, Barbara. Food for the soul: an
earthly delight. HOME MAGAZINE, (October
22, 1978), p. 53-54. English.

AN: Story on El Dia de los Muertos.
Color illustrations of annual celebration by
Self-Help Graphics and Art, Inc. with
costumes, masks, floats.

8305 Hollister, Kelly. Linda Vallejo. CAMINOS,
Vol. 1, no. 6 (October 1980), p. 19.
Bilingual.

AN: Story on Long Beach, California
artist Linda Vallejo who also works with
Self-Help Graphics in Los Angeles and has
curated a number of exhibits. Vallejo
describes her work as containing
"archetypal, mythological or dream-world
imagery" combined with the "modern idea of
self-knowledge." Illustrated on p. 17.

8306 Hunt, Annette and McNally, Mary. Community
art centers in Los Angeles. SPINNING OFF,
Vol. 2, no. 19 (January 1980), p. 1.
English.

AN: Article includes an interview with
Linda Vallejo on the community artistic work
of Self-Help Graphics and Art, Inc.

8307 Kim, Howard. Chicano art: is it an art form?
Or simply art by Chicanos. NEWORLD, Vol. 6,
no. 4 (1980), p. 26-30. English.

AN: An attempt to define Chicano art
through interviews with Carlos Almaraz, John
Valadez, (Los Four), Robert Delgado, Sister
Karen Boccalero (Self-Help Graphics), Harry
Gamboa, Jr. (ASCO), Ricardo Duardo, Ignacio
Gomez, and others. Well illustrated.

Self-Help Graphics, Los Angeles, CA (cont.)

8308 Venegas, Sybil. Dia de los muertos. SOMOS, Vol. 1, no. 5 (October 1978), p. 42-47. English.

AN: Brief history of Dia de los muertos ceremonies. While the custom is dying in Mexico (except for tourists), Chicano organizations like Galeria de la Raza (S.F.), El Centro de Artistas Chicanos (Sacramento, Ca.) celebrate the event annually, as does [Self-Help Graphics and Art, Inc.] in East Los Angeles. Well illustrated with photographs by Guillermo Bejarano and Daniel Duran.

8309 Venegas, Sybil. Towards a Chicano cultural renaissance. LA GENTE DE AZTLAN, Vol. 8, no. 1 (November 2, 1977), p. 12. English.

AN: The revival of celebrations like El Dia de Los Muertos are seen as catalysts for barrio unification. Detailed information on how Self Help Graphics in East Los Angeles mobilizes artists and community for a communal celebration.

Selley, Michael L.

8310 Arts Council Center for the Arts of Greater Lansing, Lansing, MI. Raza fine arts festival. Festival program, 1978. English.

AN: This festival program mentions Jose Narezo's mural at the Holland National Guard Armory, Grand Rapids; includes a statement of the Raza Art/Media Collective, Inc.; the philosophy of artists Zaragosa Vargas and S. Kaneta Kosiba-Vargas; and profiles of exhibiting artists George Vargas, Martin Moreno, Hector Perez, Michael L. Selley, Jesse Gonzales, Nora Chapa Mendoza, Jesse Soriano, Jose Luis Narezo.

Seriography
USE: Silkscreen

Serrano, Benjamin

8311 Moisan, Jim. Ancient roots, new visions. ARTWEEK, Vol. 9, no. 26 (July 29, 1978), p. 8. English.

AN: Review of the show held at the Municipal Arts Gallery of Los Angeles, the first national touring show of Latino artists in the United States. Includes commentary on work of Larry Fuente, Luis Jimenez, Frank Romero, Harry Gamboa, Gronk, Rudy Martinez, Benjamin Serrano, Ricardo Diaz, Patssi Valdez, Mel Casas, Luis Leroy, Pedro Lujan. A related show, NEW VISIONS, L.A., includes Robert Delgado, Ray Bravo, Joe Moran, Rosalyn Mesquita, Patricia Murillo and others.

8312 Raices y visiones [portfolio]. REVISTA CHICANO-RIQUENA, Vol. 7, no. 2 (Spring 1979), p. 29-44.

AN: Portfolio of works from the exhibit RAICES ANTIGUAS/VISIONES NUEVAS: ANCIENT ROOTS/NEW VISIONS. Artists included are Patssi Valdez (Los Angeles), Eloisa Castellanos-Sanchez (New York), Benjamin Serrano, Jr. (Tijuana, Mexico), Alex Garza (Chicago), Martin Y. Moreno (Michigan), Luis A. Jimenez (New Mexico), Rene Castro (Oakland, CA), Sita Gomez de Kanelba (New York), Susana Lasta (Tucson, AZ), Domingo Garcia (New York), Consuelo Mendez Castillo (Caracas, Venezuela), Naomi Castillo Simonetti (New Jersey), Louis Carlos Bernal,

and Eddie Comptis.

Serrano, Nina

8313 Mission to honor Frida Kahlo: famous Mexican artist. EL TECOLOTE, Vol. 9, no. 3 (November 1978), p. 1. Bilingual.

AN: Announcement of an homage to Mexican painter Frida Kahlo at the Galeria de la Raza's annual celebration of Dia de los Muertos. Works reproduced with the article include those of Emmanuel C. Montoya, Yreina Cervantez, Jose Antonio Burciaga, Nina Serrano and Lisa Kokin. Bilingual.

Serrano-Cordero, Luis

8314 William Grant Still Community Arts Center, Los Angeles, CA. Latin American artists exhibition. Exhibition brochure, 1978. English.

AN: Exhibit curated by Linda Vallejo including Carlos Almaraz, Michael M. Amescua, Ray Bravo, Isabel Castro, Yreina Cervantez, Luis Serrano-Cordero, Cynthia Honesto, Judith Miranda, Teddy Sandoval, John Taboada, Emigdio Vasquez. Illustrated.

Serrato, Ricardo M.

8315 Mills House Visual Arts Complex, Garden Grove, CA. Menudo: artistas latinos de Orange County. Exhibit invitation, 1980. English.

AN: Invitation to an exhibit organized for the first anniversary of Artistas Latinos de Orange County including Delores Grajeda, William Hernandez, Marylee Montano, Patricia Murillo, Irene Ramos, Juan Ramos, Ricardo Serrato, Miguel Shanahan, Arthur Valenzuela, Benjamin Valenzuela, Jack Vargas, Alonzo Whitney, Emigdio Vasquez, Susana Zaccagnino, and Mexican artist Artemio Sepulveda.

8316 Orange Co. Library. El Modena Branch. Empanada: a tasty Mexican group art exhibit filled with a variety of digestable treats. Exhibition catalog, [1979]. English.

AN: Catalog of an exhibit by 15 artists: Dolores Grajeda, William Hernandez-M., Marylee Montano, Patricia Murillo, Eduardo Navarro, Susana A. Zaccagnino, Esau Quiroz, Juan Elias Ramos, Ricardo M. Serrato, Benjamin Valenzuela, Emigdio C. Vasquez, Arthur Valenzuela, Jack Vargas, Alonso Whitney, and Mexican artist Artemio Sepulveda living in Orange County. Brief profiles of the artists.

Sex Roles

8317 Donnell-Kotrozo, Carol and Perlman, Barbara. Male passages: a secular santero of the '80s interprets machismo. ARIZONA ARTS AND LIFESTYLE, Vol. 4, no. 1 (1982), p. 32-39. English.

AN: Rudy Fernandez moves freely between two- and three-dimensional forms using personal symbols such as cacti, roosters, flying hearts, trout, in paintings or lead-covered shelves of boxes reminiscent of retablos. Colorado-born Fernandez has lived in Arizona, Utah, New Mexico, and Washington. His art is not religious, but is influenced by a strong Catholic background. Many color illustrations, including the cover.

Sex Roles (cont.)

8318 Donnell-Kotrozo, Carol. Rudy Fernandez.
ARTSPACE, Vol. 5, no. 4 (Fall 1981), p.
18-23. English.

AN: Scottsdale, Arizona resident Rudy
Fernandez converts cultural symbols into a
private system language that revolves around
love, family, manhood and self-identity. His
mixed media altar-like forms are based on
interest in Southwest santos, their format
and presentation. Fernandez does paintings,
and assembled wood pieces. Handsomely
illustrated, with color.

8319 Johansen, Jason. Preliminaries toward an
Hispanic media: a cultural imperative.
Unpublished manuscript, 1980. English.

AN: Presentation made at the Hispanic
Southwest Conference on Media and the
Humanities. Johansen outlines the
culturally-leveling and stereotypical roles
for men and women of mass media in our
century which is dominated by communication
means owned by industries interested in
profits from products. Within this context,
Hispanic media producers must find new ways
of relaying values, judgements and ideas
that combat the dominant culture and
strengthen humanity and social change.

8320 Soberon, Mercedes. La revolucion se trata de
amor: Mercedes Soberon. CHISMEARTE, Vol. 1,
no. 1 (Fall 1976), p. 14-18. Spanish.

AN: Short interview with Mercedes
Soberon, San Francisco artist involved with
the art group Mission Media Arts. Mercedes
talks about the role of women as organizers
and artists, the sacrifices associated with
this role, and the politics of San Francisco
museums.

Sex Stereotypes

8321 Venegas, Sybil. Conditions for producing
Chicana art. CHISMEARTE, Vol. 1, no. 4 (Fall,
Winter, 1977, 1978), p. 2, 4. English.

AN: Chicana artists face more obstacles
than white women or Chicano counterparts in
the arts. Mexican life style has portrayed
the ideal of a submissive woman, but the
values have changed. Chicana artists are
concerned with women and their struggles.
Muralists include Patricia Rodriguez, Irene
Perez, Consuelo Mendez de Castillo, Susan
Cervantes, Ester Hernandez, Miriam Olivo,
Ruth Rodriguez, of the Mujeres Muralistas
(San Francisco). Other artists are Etta
Delgado and Barbara Carrasco.

Shiras, Myrna

8322 Joslyn Art Center. Multi-media art exhibit:
Muriel Olguin (printmaking), Myrna Shiras
(mixed media), Linda Vallejo (painting).
Exhibition invitation, 1979. English.

AN: Invitation to an exhibit.

Sierra, John

8323 Artist's vow: delay-plagued state building
mural will be finished. FRESNO BEE,
(November 10, 1980), p. B4. English.

AN: Five-story-high mural "PLANTING OF
CULTURES" by John Sierra. Illustrated.

8324 Campesino Business and Joint Enterprise
Building, Fresno, CA. Sabor a Fresno. Arte

chicano: los Four and la Brocha. Exhibition
invitation [1976]. English.

AN: Invitation to an exhibit of works by
Los Four of Los Angeles and members of La
Brocha del Valle of Fresno: Arturo Roman,
Sal Garcia, John Sierra, Juan Truner, Sapo
de Aztlan, Fernando Hernandez, Alberto
Reyes, Ernesto Palomino, Lee Orona,
Francisco Barrios, Juan Ybarra, Bobby Reyes,
Alberto Hernandez. Brocha was started by
Palomino (California State University,
Fresno professor) to pool talents of Central
Valley artists.

8325 Hale, David. Fresnan gets grant to create
five story high mural. FRESNO BEE, (April
16, 1978), p. Forum, C4. English.

AN: Details on the awarding of a grant
to John Sierra, Fresno artist, for the
creation of what will be the largest piece
of public art in that city. The artwork is a
6000 square foot mural titled THE PLANTING
OF THE CULTURES. Article contains
biographical information on the artist and
presents goals of his mural project.

Sierra, Roger

8326 Oakes College, University of California,
Santa Cruz, CA and Carrillo, Eduardo.
Corazon de Aztlan: a Chicano arts show.
Exhibition catalog, 1981. English.

AN: Catalog of exhibit including works
by Eduardo Carrillo, Juana Franklin, Cruz
Zamarron, Jerry Astorga, Jaime Valadez,
Ernesto Palomino, Sal Garcia, Roger Sierra,
Jose Montoya, Esteban Villa, Juanishi
Orozco, from Santa Cruz, San Jose, Fresno
and Sacramento. Presentations of films and
by the Teatro de la Tierra Morena of Santa
Cruz County.

Sifuentes, Jesse

8327 Houston Chicanismo. LA PRENSA, Vol. 1, no. 2
(March 31, 1978). English.

AN: In Houston, Texas, the AMA Gallery
(Association for the Advancement of Mexican
Americans) was opened in February 1976 to
showcase Chicano art. Noel Rodriguez,
gallery director, informs about the goals
and objectives of the gallery. A current
exhibit presents paintings by Josie Mendoza
and Atanacio Davila, ceramics by Jesse
Sifuentes and mixed-media works by Joe
Ramirez. Illustrated with two pieces from
exhibit, THANKSGIVING, an acrylic painting
by Josie Mendoza and BIRDS, a ceramic piece.

Sigala, Rudy

8328 Una galeria de artistas = A gallery of
artists. CAMINOS, Vol. 1, no. 6 (October
1980), p. 20-26. Bilingual.

AN: Features California artists Domingo
O. Ulloa (Imperial Valley images), Gloria
Chacon, photographer Maria Pinedo (San
Francisco), Willie Herron (Los Angeles),
Joaquin Patino (Delano), Pedro Pelayo (Long
Beach), sculptor Rudi Sigala (San Diego),
Mario Torero (San Diego), sculptor Michael
M. Amescua (Los Angeles), and the East Los
Streetscapers. Illustrated.

Silkscreen

8329 Galeria de la Raza/Studio 24, San Francisco,
     CA. Mundos perdidos/lost worlds. Exhibition
     invitation, 1978. English.

     AN: Invitatiion to a multi-media exhibit
     from a cultural workshop inside Lompoc
     Federal Correctional Institution by Leonard
     Castellanos, National Endowment for the Arts
     Artist in Residence. Included are murals and
     tattoo documentation, and silkscreen
     posters.

8330 Galeria de la Raza/Studio 24, San Francisco,
     CA and Garcia, Rupert. La Raza Silkscreen
     Center: "Images of a community", an exhibit
     of silkscreen posters and graphic works from
     1971 to 1979. Exhibition catalog, 1979.
     English.

     AN: First large scale retrospective
     exhibit of the La Raza Silkscreen Center's
     eight years of postermaking. Includes list
     of 90 artists.

8331 Garcia, Rupert. Rupert Garcia. TRA, Vol. 2,
     no. 6 (1975), p. 20-27. English.

     AN: Statement by the artist and
     portfolio of nine silkscreen posters, five
     in color.

8332 Gomez, Linda. Malaquias Montoya exhibit
     opens at La Pena. EL MUNDO (San Francisco,
     CA), (October 29, 1975), p. 3. English.

     AN: Over 50 paintings, silkscreens, and
     drawings by Montoya at La Pena Cultural
     Center, Berkeley, CA. Statement by the
     artist who refuses to exhibit in museums and
     is opposed to murals that are "pretty
     decorations.".

8333 Maradiaga, Ralph. Untitled [serigraph]. TIN
     TAN, Vol. 2, no. 5 (June 1, 1977), p.
     [16-17].

8334 New co-op in San Cristobal. GRITO DEL NORTE,
     Vol. 3, no. 8 (July 5, 1970), p. 13.
     English.

     AN: Details formation of the San
     Cristobal Valley Arts Inc., a community
     corporation formed to train people in a
     silkscreen business venture. Aiming to use
     expressive forms as a source of economic
     development, the corporation published and
     distributed a line of Chicano silkscreen
     posters. Illustrated by three posters, WE
     SHALL ENDURE, SOMOS AZTLAN, and TAOS PUEBLO.

8335 Pena, Amado Maurilio, Jr. [Untitled
     silkscreen]. CARACOL, Vol. 1, no. 6
     (February 1975), p. COVER.

8336 Rodriguez, Patricia. [Untitled silkscreen].
     CHISMEARTE, Vol. 1, no. 4 (Fall , Winter,
     1977, 1978), p. 5.

8337 El Taller, Inc., Chicago, IL and Movimiento
     Artistico Chicano (MARCH), Chicago, IL.
     Skyjacked: screenprinted posters from
     California by the Royal Chicano Air Force
     (R.C.A.F.), 1980. Exhibition invitation,
     1980. English.

     AN: Invitation to an exhibit at the El
     Taller Gallery, co-sponsored by MARCH.
     Illustrated with a print by San Francisco
     artist Xavier Viramontes.

8338 Torres, Pablo, Jr. La Cena [silkscreen].
     CARACOL, Vol. 3, no. 4 (December 1976), p.
     13.

8339 Torres, Pablo, Jr. Ella [silkscreen].
     CARACOL, Vol. 3, no. 4 (December 1976), p.
     13.

SIMBOLOS [mural]

8340 Sorell, Victor A. Barrio murals in Chicago:
     painting the Hispanic-American experience on
     "our community" walls. REVISTA
     CHICANO-RIQUENA, Vol. 4, no. 4 (Fall
     1976), p. 51-72. English.

     AN: Important survey of Chicago's Latino
     murals, with key works considered in detail.
     Among the Chicano art organizations and
     muralists mentioned are MARCH (Movimiento
     Artistico Chicano), and Yolanda Galvan,
     Juanita Jaramillo, Jose Nario, Raymond
     Patlan, Vicente Mendoza, Marcos Raya,
     Ricardo Alonzo, Jose G. Gonzalez and Mario
     Castillo, author of the earliest Latino
     mural in Chicago (1968). Puerto Rican and
     non-Latino muralists and mural groups are
     also discussed. Well illustrated.

Sinape, Mario

8341 Chicano art show at Contra Costa College. EL
     HISPANO, Vol. 8, no. 25 (December 11, 1973).
     English.

     AN: Information on exhibition organized
     by Ramses Noriega that included the work of
     Jose Montoya, Esteban Villa, Mario Sinape,
     Ricardo Rios, Malaquias Montoya, Fuchi
     Queso, and Joe Palomino.

Siqueiros, David Alfaro

8342 Art wall for Plaza de la Raza March 28.
     EASTSIDE JRNL, (March 11, 1971), p. 1.
     English.

     AN: On March 28, 1971, the art dealers
     of Los Angeles sponsored an"art walk" on
     "Gallery Row" on Melrose Place and La
     Cienega Blvds as a benefit for Plaza de la
     Raza, Mexican American cultural Center at
     Lincoln Park. Art dealers financed a limited
     edition lithograph by Mexican muralist David
     Alfaro Siqueiros. The print shows Ruben
     Salazar, slain Mexican American journalist
     and community leader with the famous figure
     from Siqueiros' mural "New Democracy" below
     it. Illustrated.

8343 Barrera, Manuel. "Maestro" Siqueiros. LA
     RAZA, Vol. 2, no. 2 (1974), p. 40-41.
     English.

8344 Congreso de Artistas Chicanos en Aztlan, San
     Diego, CA. Diego Rivera, David Alfaro
     Siqueiros, Jose Clemente Orozco: exhibit of
     local artists, La Logan [San Diego].
     Exhibition brochure, n.d. [c.1974]. English.

     AN: Announcement of a traveling exhibit
     organized by Galeria de la Raza, San
     Francisco, from the collection of the San
     Francisco Museum of Art. Illustrated with a
     San Diego mural.

Siqueiros, David Alfaro (cont.)

8345 Garcia, Rupert. Echos de la Mision - Alfaro Siqueiros (1896-1974). EL TECOLOTE, Vol. 4, no. 3 (February 22, 1974), p. 11. English.

AN: Biographical and artistic trajectory of Mexican artist David Alfaro Siqueiros. Artist painted three murals in Southern California in 1932 (MEETING IN THE STREET and TROPICAL AMERICA were done in Los Angeles on the walls of the Chouinard School of Art and the Plaza Art Center, Olvera Street area respectively. The third mural PORTRAIT OF MEXICO was privately commissioned in Santa Monica). The three California murals deal with themes of censorship, racism, colonialism, capitalism, and imperialism. Article suggests that Raza artists are much influenced by the ideas and work of Siqueiros. Illustrated with Rupert Garcia's silkscreen poster SIQUEIROS.

8346 Goldman, Shifra M. Las creaturas de la America tropical: Siqueiros y los murales chicanos en Los Angeles. REVISTA DE BELLAS ARTES, no. 25 (January, February, 1976), p. 38-46. Spanish.

AN: Treats the influence of Siqueiros' 1932 outdoor mural in Los Angeles on the Chicano street mural movement of the 1970s.

8347 Kalil, Susie. Provocative painting: muralist Leo Tanguma advances the tradition of Mexico's masters. HOUSTON CITY MAGAZINE, (March 1980), p. 88+. English.

AN: 38 year old Leo Tanguma from Beeville, Texas joined the Mexican-American Youth Organization in Houston in 1968, which provided a stimulus to say what he felt in large paintings. His firsHouston mural was in 1970, followed by meeting Mexican muralisDavid Alfaro Siqueiros in 1972. A monumental mural for Continental Can Co. followed in 1973. Many of Tanguma's murals have been controversial and destroyed, or the commissions withdrawn. Color illustration of maquette for an ecology mural.

8348 M.E.C.H.A. cultura y evolucion mexicana. EL CLARIN, (May 2, 1974), p. 3. Spanish.

AN: Report on the mural designed and painted under the direction of Mexican-born designer Sergio O'Cadiz at Santa Ana College, Santa Ana, Calif. Collaborators were instructor Shifra Goldman and gallery director Mike Davis, with members of the MEChA Club and other students. The mural concerns the history of Mexico and of the Chicano and includes a tribute to David Alfaro Siqueiros' Los Angeles mural AMERICA TROPICAL, painted and white-washed in the 1930s. Illustrated.

8349 Orth, Maureen. The soaring spirit of Chicano arts. NEW WEST MAGAZINE, Vol. 3, no. 19 (September 11, 1978), p. 41-46. English.

AN: Overview of California Chicano culture. Color illustrations of works by Mexican muralist David Alfaro Siqueiros, Rupert Garcia, Mujeres Muralistas, Willie Herron, Rene Yanez, Rudy Martinez, San Diego's Chicano Park, ASCO, Jose Montoya.

8350 Rowe, Richard. On Olvera Street: one vision realized, another white washed. REVIEW (Society of Architectural Historians, Pasadena, CA), Vol. 1, no. 1 (Fall 1981), p. 7. English.

AN: Documentation about AMERICA TROPICAL, 1932 mural by David Alfaro Siqueiros. The mural, commissioned by F.K. Ferenz of the Plaza Art Center on Olvera Street in Los Angeles, was a 16' by 80' painting on the second-story wall of the old Italian Hall. From 1968 on, art historian Shifra M. Goldman, working with a small committee, has been actively involved in the attempt to restore the mural. Article details the travails of restoration and underscores the mural's importance. Illustrated.

8351 Salvador R. Torres Chicano Underground Studio-Gallery, San Diego, CA. Diego Rivera, David Alfaro Siqueiros, Jose Clemente Orozco, from the collection of the S.F. Museum of Art. Exhibition invitation, [1974]. English.

AN: Illustrated invitation of an exhibit organized by the Galeria de la Raza of San Francisco loaned to the Congreso de Artistas Chicanos en Aztlan, and held in artist Torres' studio.

8352 Trevino, Jesus Salvador. America tropical. (1971). English.

AN: Half-hour 16mm color film produced and written by Jesus Salvador Trevino and directed by Barry Nye about the painting and whitewashing in 1932-34 of Mexican muralist David Alfaro Siqueiros' mural AMERICA TROPICAL in Olvera Street, Los Angeles. Traces the attempts at restoration of the mural starting in the late 1960s and continuing in the 1970s. History of the mural set within social/political context of Mexican Americans in the 1930s, and counterpart struggles of Chicanos in the 1970s.

8353 Viva Siqueiros. CON SAFOS, no. 7 (Winter 1971), p. 26-27. English.

AN: Brief recapitulation of the controversy surrounding David Alfaro Siqueiros' visit to Los Angeles, CA in 1932. It was during this visit that he painted the only public Siqueiros mural in the U.S. which still remains, albeit covered over with whitewash. The details of the visit are explained by Siqueiros in his book: MI RESPUESTA. The article is illustrated with two black and white details of the mural.

SIQUEIROS: "EL MAESTRO" (THE MARCH OF HUMANITY IN LATIN AMERICA) [film]

8354 Films for the inner city. Los Angeles, CA: Los Angeles Public Library Federal Project, 1971. English.

AN: Annotated catalog of 16mm films and filmstrips, educational and documentary. Those concerning Mexican heritage include CHICANO FROM THE SOUTHWEST (1970), HENRY...BOY OF THE BARRIO (1969); HOW'S SCHOOL, ENRIQUE (1970), I AM JOAQUIN (1970), THE MEXICAN AMERICAN: HERITAGE AND DESTINY (1970), A MEXICAN AMERICAN FAMILY (1970), MEXICAN AMERICANS: QUEST FOR EQUALITY (1968), MEXICAN OR AMERICAN (1970), SIQUEIROS: "EL MAESTRO" (THE MARCH OF HUMANITY IN LATIN AMERICA) (1969). Filmstrips include THE AWAKENING (LA RAZA) - Part IV, CONFLICT OF CULTURES (LA RAZA) - Part III, MASTERWORKS OF MEXICAN ART, OUT OF THE MAINSTREAM, PILGRIMAGE (GRAPE STRIKERS). Also listed are films and filmstrips for children.

Siqueiros, Francisco

8355 Contreras, Carlos. Nuestra cultura. LA VOZ:
Concilio for the Spanish Speaking of King
Co., Seattle, no. 7 (August 1979).

AN: Information of Washington state
murals painted by members of La Extension
Cultural; Armando Lara's autobiographical
mural titled "El Rio" is installed at the
Concilio offices, 107 Cherry St. Suite 210.
Arturo Artorez completed a wall painting
using the image of Quetzalcoatl at El Centro
de la Raza with funding from the Seattle
Arts Commission. Francisco Siqueiros used
the themes of ecology and Mexican mythology
for two murals at Seattle Community College.
Commentary on Alfredo Arreguin's painting
exhibition at the Kiku Gallery and his wall
painting at the Childrens Orthopedic
Hospital in Seattle.

**Sixth Annual International Hispanic Film Festival,
San Antonio, TX**

8356 Cinefestival. ARRIBA, [n.d.], p. 5. English.

AN: Announcement of the 6th Annual
International Hispanic Film Festival in San
Antonio, TX. Willie Varela will conduct a
workshop, and Jesus Trevino will premiere
his hour-long production, SEGUIN.

Soares, John

8357 Mexican American Community Service
Organization, San Jose, CA. Exhibition of
contemporary art. Exhibition brochure, 1968.
English.

AN: Biographical and exhibition data for
Al Barela, Bert Hermosillo, Octavio Romano,
Luis Valdez, Vincent P. Rascon, John Soares
and Al Espinoza.

Soberon, Mercedes

8358 Soberon, Mercedes. La revolucion se trata de
amor: Mercedes Soberon. CHISMEARTE, Vol. 1,
no. 1 (Fall 1976), p. 14-18. Spanish.

AN: Short interview with Mercedes
Soberon, San Francisco artist involved with
the art group Mission Media Arts. Mercedes
talks about the role of women as organizers
and artists, the sacrifices associated with
this role, and the politics of San Francisco
museums.

**Social and Public Art Resource Center, Venice, CA
(SPARC)**

8359 Baca, Judith F. Judith F. Baca. In: SOCIAL
WORKS: AN EXHIBITION OF ART CONCERNED WITH
SOCIAL CHANGE. Los Angeles, CA: Institute of
Contemporary Art, 1979, p. 44. English.

AN: Statement of purpose and history of
the Tujunga Wash Mural (San Fernando Valley,
CA) in process from 1976 on, by muralist and
founder of Social and Public Art Resource
Center (SPARC), Judith Baca. Illustrated.

8360 Deitch, Donna. The great wall of Los
Angeles. Film, 1976. Bilingual.

AN: Eight minute 16 mm film produced by
SPARC (Social and Public Art Resource
Center) on the GREAT WALL OF LOS ANGELES
mural. In English with Spanish subtitles.

8361 Lugavere, Joel P. Artists to add '40s to
Great Wall mural. LOS ANGELES TIMES
[Glendale/Burbank edition], (September 20,
1981), p. 1. English.

AN: Brief illustrated story on 1981
extension of the Tujunga Wash mural, THE
GREAT WALL OF LOS ANGELES, directed by Judy
Baca of SPARC, (Social and Public Arts
Resource Center in Venice California).

8362 Parachini, Allan. Tujunga wash mural stands
up to storm. LOS ANGELES TIMES, (March 13,
1980), p. V, 1. English.

AN: Information about the mural project
near Los Angeles Valley College in Van Nuys,
Calif. sponsored by SPARC (Social and Public
Art Resource Center) of Venice, Calif. and
coordinated by Judy Baca. Illustrated.

8363 Rickey, Carrie. The writing on the wall. ART
IN AMERICA, Vol. 69, no. 5 (May 1981), p.
54-57. English.

AN: Detailed article on the career of
Judy Baca, director of SPARC (Social and
Public Arts Resource Center) in Venice,
Calif., and of the Great Wall of Los
Angeles, a five year mural project at the
Tujunga Wash. Well illustrated in black and
white and color.

8364 Social and public art resource center.
Brochure, [1977]. English.

AN: Brochure including the history,
philosophy, and resources of SPARC, an
outgrowth of the Los Angeles Citywide Mural
Project/Mural Resource Center headed by Judy
Baca. Illustrated.

8365 SPARC (Social and Public Arts Resource
Center), Venice, CA and Los Angeles. Ceta
VI, Venice, CA. Hecho en Aztlan multiples:
screen printed works. Exhibition invitation,
1980. English.

AN: Invitation to an exhibit of
silkscreen prints by Hecho en Aztlan
Multiples, a small business run by Richard
Duardo. At the Social and Public Art
Resource Center, Venice, Calif.

Social Organizations
USE: Cultural Organizations

Sociedad Mexicana "Benito Juarez"

8366 59th Street Gallery, St. Louis, MO. Midwest
Mexican-American art exhibit: Mexico and its
artists. Exhibition brochure, 1981. English.

AN: Sponsored by the Sociedad Mexicana
"Benito Juarez" and the international
Institute of St. Louis, this three-part
exhibit includes 1) MEXICO AS SEEN BY HER
CHILDREN, a bilingual exhibit from Mexico
traveling under Smithsonian Institution
auspices, 2) MEXICAN CHILDREN IN THE U.S.A.,
3) MEXICAN AMERICAN ARTISTS. In the latter
are included Stephen Capiz (Roseville,
Minn.), Jose Gonzalez (Chicago), Cesar A.
Martinez (San Antonio), Ada Medina (Des
Moines), Nora Chapa Mendoza (West
Bloomfield, Mich.), Rene David
Michel-Trapaga (St. Louis), David Munoz
(Kansas City, Mo.), Jose Luis Narezo (Grand
Rapids, Mich.), Benny Ordonez, Roman
Villarreal (Chicago), Alejandro Romero
(Chicago), Aurelio Diaz "Tekpankalli"
(Chicago), Simon Ybarra (St. Louis).

Solache, Saul

8367 Depicts Chicano attitudes: library receives new mural. DAILY BRUIN, (September 29, 1970), p. 6. English.

AN: Illustrated story of mural painted in UCLA's Mexican American Library by Eduardo Carrillo, Ramses Noriega, Sergio Hernandez, Saul Solache.

8368 The First Unitarian Universalist Church, Paradise Valley, AZ. Five Chicano artists. Exhibition brochure, 1971. English.

AN: Exhibit organized by L. Eugene Grigsby, Jr., Art Department of Arizona State University, Tempe, AZ. 21 works by Eugene Quesada, David Nunez, Fernando Navarro, Luis Baiz (of Arizona) and Saul Solache (of Los Angeles). Brief biographies of the artists.

SOLEDAD [film]

8369 Gamboa, Harry, Jr. Film, television, and Trevino. LA LUZ, Vol. 6, no. 10 (October 1977), p. 7-8. English.

AN: Jesus Salvador Trevino has been an active proponent and participant in transforming cultural inaccuracy about Chicanos in the media to accurate mass media models. A biography of Trevino follows, including discussion of some of his films: THE SALAZAR INQUEST, CHICANO MORATORIUM AFTERMATH, SOLEDAD, AMERICA TROPICAL, YO SOY CHICANO, RAICES DE SANGRE, as well as television series like ACCION CHICANO, AHORA, and INFINITY FACTORY.

8370 Zheutlin, Barbara and Talbot, David. Jesus Salvador Trevino. In: CREATIVE DIFFERENCES: PROFILES OF HOLLYWOOD DISSIDENTS. Boston, MS: South End Press, 1978, p. 345-352. English.

AN: Within the context of New Left alternative filmmakers who chose to work within Hollywood, Trevino sets forth his standards and goals. His films and TV productions include SOLEDAD (1971), AMERICA TROPICAL (1971), YO SOY CHICANO (1972), RAICES DE SANGRE (1977) and INFINITY FACTORY (1975-1976).

Sommer, Robert

8371 Weiss, Margaret R. and Sommer, Robert. Camera assignment: documenting street art. SATURDAY REVIEW, (May 17, 1975), p. 41-43. English.

AN: Interview with Robert Sommer. Illustrations of six murals: in Santa Fe, NM; Estrada Courts in Los Angeles; a John Weber mural in Chicago; and Cityarts mural in New York.

SONG OF UNITY [mural]

8372 Erickson, Barbara. La Pena's new face. NORTH EAST BAY INDEPENDENT, no. 4 (September 5, 1978), p. 11. English.

AN: Illustrated story on the relief mural SONG OF UNITY by Ray Patlan, O'Brien Thiele, Osha Neumann, and Anna de Leon on the facade of La Pena cultural center in Berkeley, California. Chilean songwriter Victor Jara and the music of North and South America are the motifs.

Soriano, Jesse

8373 Arts Council Center for the Arts of Greater Lansing, Lansing, MI. Raza fine arts festival. Festival program, 1978. English.

AN: This festival program mentions Jose Narezo's mural at the Holland National Guard Armory, Grand Rapids; includes a statement of the Raza Art/Media Collective, Inc.; the philosophy of artists Zaragosa Vargas and S. Kaneta Kosiba-Vargas; and profiles of exhibiting artists George Vargas, Martin Moreno, Hector Perez, Michael L. Selley, Jesse Gonzales, Nora Chapa Mendoza, Jesse Soriano, Jose Luis Narezo.

Soto, Luis

8374 Colectivo El Ojo. CHOQUE DE AMOR: fotonovela by Lamp. CHISMEARTE, Vol. 1, no. 4 (Fall , Winter, 1977), p. 35-37. Bilingual.

AN: Several students with the help of the Latin American Media Project (LAMP) and the Latin American Studies Department of California State University, Los Angeles produced the fotonovela CHOQUE DE AMOR, a variation on the typical "fotonovela" romance. This one encourages readers to reevaluate traditional female roles. The group also includes Kay Torres. Six frames of the fotonovela are reproduced.

8375 Lucas, Jerry and Gil de Montes, Roberto, et al. CHOQUE DE AMOR: fotonovela by Lamp. Los Angeles, CA: Colectivo El Ojo, Latin American Studies Dept., CSULA, 1979. English.

AN: "Fotonovela" featuring Elsa Flores, Rosa Marin, and Jerry Lucas produced by the collective work of Lucas, Roberto Gil de Montes, Mario Massinelli, Luis Soto, and Kay Torres.

Soto, Richard

8376 California. University. Los Angeles. Cine sin fronteras. Festival brochure, 1981. English.

AN: Brochure program for a cinema festival and series of seminars and discussions featuring films and discussants from Mexico and Chicanos of the United States. Participating were Chicano directors Moctezuma Esparza, Richard Soto, David Sandoval, and Robert Young, and film historian David Maciel.

South Africa

8377 De Lappe, Pele. Saga of Rupert Garcia's poster: from pen to UN. PEOPLE'S WORLD, Vol. 44, no. 28 (July 11, 1981), p. 10. English.

AN: Desiring to produce a poster on Nelson Mandela and South African political prisoners, San Francisco artist Rupert Garcia, appealed for support to the African National Congress, and the Liberation Support Movement. The United Nations Center Against Apartheid provided a grant for production, indicating it should be distributed free. Illustrated.

Southern California

8378 Sol Art Gallery, San Diego, CA. Group
     showing of Southern California artists.
     Exhibition brochure, 1980. English.

     AN: First exhibit of new Chicano art
     gallery showing Los Angeles artists Carlos
     Almaraz, Judithe Hernandez, John Valadez,
     Linda Vallejo, Ricardo Duardo, Barbara
     Carrasco.

SOUTHWEST ARTISTS INVITATIONAL: AN EXHIBITION OF CONTEMPORARY ART BY SEVEN TEXAS ARTISTS OF HISPANIC AMERICAN DESCENT [exhibit]

8379 Corpus Christy State University for the Arts
     and Weil Gallery Center for the Arts, Corpus
     Christi State University. Southwest artists
     invitational: an exhibition of contemporary
     art by seven Texas artists of Hispanic
     American descent. Ehxibition brochure, 1980.
     English.

     AN: Artists Jesse Almazan, Luis Jimenez,
     Cesar Martinez, Lydia Martinez, Manuel
     Mauricio, Guillermo Pulido, and Jesse
     Trevino show a variety of techniques and
     styles. Text by Roberto Tomas Esparza.
     Statements by and about the artists.
     Illustrated.

Southwest Network of Hayward, CA

8380 Chicano pride reflected in '75 calendar. LOS
     ANGELES TIMES, (December 2, 1974), p. I,
     34. English.

     AN: The 1975 edition of EL CALENDARIO
     CHICANO, developed for the Southwest Network
     of Hayward, focuses on Chicano history and
     dates that are significant to Mexican
     Americans.

Southwest United States

8381 Afro American, Mexican American, Native
     American art slide catalog, 1973-74. Mobile,
     AL: Ethnic American Art Slide Library, The
     College of Arts & Sciences, Univ. of South
     Alabama, 1973-74. English.

     AN: Preceded by the 1971-72 Ethnic
     American Art Catalog which dealt with
     Afro-American artists only, the Slide
     Library issues the present catalog of slides
     for sale. Slides are available for eighteen
     Chicano artists from the Southwest.

8382 Afro American, Mexican American, Native
     American art slide catalog, 1974-75. Mobile,
     AL: Ethnic American Art Slide Library, The
     College of Arts & Sciences, Univ. of South
     Alabama, 1974-75. English.

     AN: Preceded by the 1971-72 Ethnic
     American Art Catalog which dealt with Afro
     American artists only, the Slide Library has
     issued a 1973-74 catalog including Mexican
     American and Native American slides for
     sale, followed by the present catalog.
     Slides are available for twenty-three
     Chicano artists from the Southwest.

8383 Anaya, Rudolfo A. and Ortiz, Simon J.
     1680-1980: a ceremony of brotherhood.
     Albuquerque, NM: Academic, 1981. English.

     AN: A cooperative publication by members
     of the former La Academia de la Nueva Raza
     (1969-1976) formed of writers and artists,
     and the Tri-Centennial Commission of the
     All-Indian Pueblo Council. Includes writings
     and artworks by Chicanos and Indians from

New Mexico, California, Texas, and Arizona.
Chicano artists works included are by Ellen
Arellano, Juan Estevan Arellano, Alberto
Baros, Jose Antonio Burciaga, Juan Reyes
Cervantes, Rudy Cuellar, Ricardo Favela, El
Zarco Guerrero, Luis Jimenez, Jr., Carlos
Quinto Kemm, Alejandro Lopez, Floyd Lujan,
Jose Montoya, Juanishi Orozco, Leo Romero,
Secundino Sandoval, Jaime Valdez, Maria
Varela, Esteban Villa.

8384 Bloomfield, Arthur. Zesty show at Mexican
     museum. SAN FRANCISCO EXAMINER, (February
     1, 1977), p. 24. English.

     AN: Review of an exhibit of Mexican and
     Mexican American artists from the Southwest
     and the San Francisco area. Commentary and
     analysis on artists Vincent Perez and
     Gustavo Rivera, Rudy Trevino and Al Barela.
     The work selected focused on aesthetic
     quality rather than the ethnic
     identification of the artist.

8385 Cisneros, Jose. Riders of the border. El
     Paso, TX: Texas Western Press, 1971.
     English.

     AN: Jose Cisneros, El Paso artist has
     illustrated (in total or in part) over forty
     books, most of which deal with the
     Southwest. This collection ia a picture book
     rendering the picturesqueness and pagentry
     of the various riders along the border.
     Illustrated with 30 black and white drawings
     and text by the artist.

8386 Fine Arts Society of San Diego, CA. The
     cross and the sword. Exhibition catalog,
     1976. Bilingual.

     AN: Bi-lingual exhibition catalog of
     Southwestern art forms; santero art,
     vernacular architecture and traditional folk
     art. Important essays by experts in each
     field. Contains an iconographical summary of
     santos and a good bibliography. Profusely
     illustrated.

8387 Galeria de la Raza/Studio 24, San Francisco,
     CA. Images of the Southwest. Exhibition
     catalog, 1977. English.

     AN: Invitation/catalog for an exhibit
     including Rudy M. Fernandez(Utah), Enrique
     Flores(Texas), Xavier Gorena(Texas),
     C.A.[Cesar] Martinez(Texas), Santos
     Martinez, Jr.(Texas), Pedro
     Rodriguez(Texas), Arnold Trujillo(New
     Mexico). Block prints, paper cut-outs,
     drawings, photographs, copper enamels, and
     sculpture were shown. Five illustrations.

8388 Gonzalez, Jose Carlos. Consejo mexicano de
     fotografia: foto latino en el suroeste de
     los Estado Unidos. ARTES VISUALES, Vol. 29,
     no. 29 (June 1981), p. 55-56. Spanish.

     AN: Review of a photography show in
     Mexico City organized by Lorenzo Hernandez,
     Cityscape Photo Gallery of Pasadena, and the
     Council of Latino Photography/USA. The show
     featured Latinos of the Southwest and Latino
     themes by non-Latino photographers.

Southwest United States (cont.)

8389 Heard Museum, Phoenix, AZ. First Annual
Southwest Chicano Art Invitational
Exposition. Invitation for reception, 1976.
English.

AN: Invitation to a reception for
artists Luis Jimenez (Roswell, New Mexico),
Eugenio Quesada (Phoenix), Felipe Reyes (San
Antonio), Pedro Rodriguez (San Francisco),
Pedro Romero (Cannon City, Colo.) One
illustration.

8390 Heard Museum, Phoenix, AZ. Second Southwest
Chicano Art Invitational. Exhibit catalog,
1978. English.

AN: Exhibit by eight artists: Antonio
Pazos (Tucson), Rudy Fernandez (Salt Lake
City), Harry Gamboa (Los Angeles), Rupert
Garcia and Xavier Viramontes (San
Francisco), Roberto Rios (San Antonio),
Roberto Espinoza (Yuma), and Roberto Borboa
(Tucson). Brief biographies of all but Rios.
29 illustrations.

8391 Holliday-Abbott, Anne. Suitcase is 2nd home
for arts liaison. ARIZONA DAILY STAR, (June
18, 1981), p. H-3. English.

AN: Arizona artist Louis LeRoy who
paints, makes prints, and does assemblage is
also a regional representative for the
National Endowment for the Arts in Arizona,
New Mexico, Colorado, Utah, and Wyoming.
LeRoy has always been an "advocate of people
being proud of their ethnic backgrounds." He
feels artists can be self-supporting without
commercializing.

8392 Saks Galleries, Denver, CO. Ramon K.
Exhibition brochure, 1971. English.

AN: Promotional brochure for major
one-man exhibition. Ramon Kelley is a
Chicano artist of international stature
whose artistic roots are firmly planted in
the American west. The Gallery director
states, "His impressionistic paintings
reveal a strong affinity to the land and
people of the southwest and they are the
major subject of his work. Lavishly
illustrated with full color reproductions of
several pastel and oil paintings.

8393 Stedman, Myrtle and Stedman, Wilfred. Adobe
architecture. Santa Fe, NM: Sunstone Press,
1973. English.

AN: The technology and aesthetics of
adobe homes. An illustrated manual of house
plans and building techniques. Includes
drawings of Southwestern "colonial"
furniture.

Southwestern College, San Diego, CA

8394 Camacho, Eduardo. Por los cien anos de la
fundacion de su editorial: inauguraran hoy
en San Diego la exposicion 'Homenaje a
Posada, Manilla y Vanegas Arroyo'.
EXCELSIOR, (February 14, 1980). Spanish.

AN: Announcing the exhibit of 19th
Century Mexican engravers Jose Guadalupe
Posada and Manuel Manilla, with publisher
Antonio Vanegas Arroyo, at the Centro
Cultural de la Raza and Southwestern
College, of San Diego, CA.

8395 El Centro Cultural de La Raza, San Diego,
CA. One hundred year anniversary: Jose
Guadalupe Posada, Antonio Vanegas Arroyo.

Exhibition invitation, 1980. English.

AN: Invitation to an exhibition of
Mexican engravers Posada and Manuel Manilla
and an homage to their publisher. Also, a
"Chicano Tribute to Jose Guadalupe Posada,"
with contemporary works influenced by
Posada. At the Centro, and at Southwestern
College in Chula Vista.

Spanish Education Development (SED) Center

8396 Contemporary Arts Museum, Houston, TX and
Martinez, Santos G., Jr. Mexican movie
posters. Exhibition invitation, 1979.
English.

AN: Invitation to an exhibit of posters
primarily from the collecttion of Enrique
Flores and Xavier Gorena of Xochil Art
Center, Mission, Texas. Martinez considers
the posters monumental, with expressive
qualities that have influenced Chicano
poster makers like the Royal Chicano Air
Force, and Rupert Garcia, and Texas artists
like Luis Jimenez, Jesse Trevino and Cesar
Martinez. One illustration. Introduction by
guest curator Santos G. Martinez, Jr. (See
Rupert Garcia's essay in the exhibition
catalog: POSTERS FROM THE GOLDEN AGE OF
MEXICAN CINEMA, for another point of view).

Spanish-Speaking Organization for Community, Integrity and Opportunity(SOCIO)

8397 Wilson, Anne. Chicanos show off talents in
Magna SOCIO projects. SALT LAKE CITY
TRIBUNE, (July 9, 1979), p. C-1. English.

AN: In the rural Utah community of
Magna, SOCIO (Spanish Speaking Organization
for Community Integrity and Opportunity)
established various art projects. Three
murals were painted by community youth under
the guidance of Robert Archuleta and Becky
Berru. One of the murals depicts "man and
labor." Illustrated with photographs of
project directors, maquette of the mural and
a mural painting "brigade".

St. Joseph Catholic Church, Houston, TX

8398 Hamm, Madeline McDermott. Artist envisions a
'Sistine' ceiling. HOUSTON CHRONICLE,
(September 19, 1978), p. III, 1-3. English.

AN: Illustrated article on mural that
Ernesto Pedregon Martinez (who was active in
El Paso in the 1950s) was doing for St.
Joseph Catholic Church in Houston. The mural
depicts the crucifixion.

St. Paul, MN

8399 Carlson, Scott. Artist's mural puts a little
beauty in prison cellblock. ST. PAUL
DISPATCH, (December 5, 1978), p. East,1,3.
English.

AN: Biographical information on Chicano
artist Paul Basquez and his eleven mural
projects at Stillwater State Prison.

8400 Community Programs in the Arts and Sciences
(COMPAS). Artists in the city: a report on
C.E.T.A. artists in St. Paul. St. Paul, MN:
COMPAS, 1978. English.

AN: Includes data on Chicano muralists
John Acosta, Thomas Acosta, Paul Basquez,
Armando Estrella, and photographer Raphael
Romo.

St. Paul, MN (cont.)

8401 Flanagan, Barbara. Murals warm up west St.
Paul. MINNEAPOLIS STAR, (December 20,
1977). English.

   AN: Discussion of mural activity in West
   St. Paul, Minnesota by Armando Estrella,
   Paul Basquez and John Acosta. The subject of
   most murals in Minnesota is either
   political, religious or historic. Of the
   three artists involved, Paul Basquez grew up
   in the barrio of West St. Paul. He tells how
   mural activity in the region is related to
   the Chicano art movement. About a half-dozen
   murals have been painted in St. Paul.

8402 Knapp, Martha. West side is part of mural
art renaissance. WEST SAINT PAUL VOICE, Vol.
5, no. 19 (November 21, 1977). English.

   AN: Pre-Columbian symbology in the mural
   program painted by Paul Basquez and Armando
   Estrella in the Chicano barrio; information
   and data on the mural renaissance in
   Minnesota.

Stanford University, Stanford, CA

8403 Karam, Bruce G. Stanford mural. NUESTRO,
Vol. 5, no. 8 (November 1981), p. 61.

Stereotypes

8404 Allen, Jane and Guthrie, Derek. La mujer: a
visual dialogue. NEW ART EXAMINER, Vol. 5,
no. 10 (July 1978), p. 14. English.

   AN: Review of international show by
   MARCH of Chicago on women's themes.
   Criticizes male Chicano artistic stereotypes
   of women compared to women's art on women
   from California.

8405 Castillo, Rafael. Gonzo journalism goes for
a low ride. SAN ANTONIO EXPRESS-NEWS,
(December 6, 1981), p. 7-B. English.

   AN: George Velasquez, editor and
   publisher of San Antonio's VAJITO magazine,
   views lowriders as a positive and evolving
   form of urban youth culture. Counters
   stereotypes about lowriders as drug-oriented
   high school drop-outs. There is a new and
   significant discourse being developed in
   literary and visual forms among Chicano
   lowriders.

8406 Geyer, Anne. Muralist works to dispel
negative Latino images. THE NEWS,
(September 2, 1981), p. 22. English.

   AN: John Valadez is painting a mural on
   canvas depicting the Latino people of
   downtown Los Angeles. It will be housed in
   Victor Clothing Co. Valadez is one of an
   increasing number of artists and dealers who
   have moved to the downtown area. Valadez
   discusses the images he makes and his
   attempt to correct media stereotypes about
   Latinos. Illustrated.

8407 Johansen, Jason. Preliminaries toward an
Hispanic media: a cultural imperative.
Unpublished manuscript, 1980. English.

   AN: Presentation made at the Hispanic
   Southwest Conference on Media and the
   Humanities. Johansen outlines the
   culturally-leveling and stereotypical roles
   for men and women of mass media in our
   century which is dominated by communication
   means owned by industries interested in
   profits from products. Within this context,

Hispanic media producers must find new ways
of relaying values, judgements and ideas
that combat the dominant culture and
strengthen humanity and social change.

8408 Pettit, Arthur G. Images of the Mexican
American in fiction and film. College
Station, TX: Texas A & M Univ. Press, 1980.
English.

   AN: A study on Anglo-American attitudes
   toward Mexican people in the Southwest as
   reflected in the sterotypes of popular
   literature and film. Most of the book is
   historical. The afterword (by Dennis
   Showalter) argues that these patterns have
   not improved, citing television series such
   as CHICO AND THE MAN and CHIPS.

8409 Ramirez de Robe, Jose "Controll".
[Pensamientos de... (drawing)]. CARACOL,
Vol. 1, no. 3 (November 1974), p. 3.
Bilingual.

Stockton, CA

8410 Raoul Mora. ESENCIA, Vol. 1, no. 3 (March,
April, 1982).

   AN: Brief article on Stockton-born
   landscape painter and lithographer who
   records the beauties of Northern California
   in flat patterns and strong color.
   Illustrated.

Street Theater
   USE: Teatro

Strikes and Lockouts

8411 Beltran, Alberto. [Untitled woodcut].
CARACOL, Vol. 1, no. 12 (August 1975), p.
13.

8412 Bonilla, Guillermo. [Untitled woodcut].
CARACOL, Vol. 1, no. 12 (August 1975), p.
10.

8413 Gonzalez, Jose Gamaliel. Boycott [drawing].
REVISTA CHICANO-RIQUENA, Vol. 5, no. 1
(Winter 1977), p. 9. English.

8414 Huerta, Elena. [Untitled woodcut]. CARACOL,
Vol. 1, no. 12 (August 1975), p. 11.

8415 Iniguez, Javier. [Untitled woodcut].
CARACOL, Vol. 1, no. 12 (August 1975), p.
14.

8416 Iniguez, Javier. [Untitled woodcut].
CARACOL, Vol. 1, no. 12 (August 1975), p.
13.

8417 Jimenez, Sarah. [Untitled woodcut]. CARACOL,
Vol. 1, no. 12 (August 1975), p. 12.

8418 Martin, Maria Luisa. [Untitled woodcut].
CARACOL, Vol. 1, no. 12 (August 1975), p.
12.

8419 Mexiac, Adolfo. [Untitled woodcut]. CARACOL,
Vol. 1, no. 12 (August 1975), p. 14.

Strikes and Lockouts (cont.)

8420 Public invited to weekend fiesta at Lincoln High. LOS ANGELES TIMES, (April 29, 1969), p. II. English.

AN: Fiesta of art, music, dance and literature organized by the committee formed after the East Los Angeles high school "blowouts" to press for better and more relevant education. Hundreds of works of art were collected for display at the "Fiesta de los Barrios".

8421 Rabel, Fanny. [Untitled woodcut]. CARACOL, Vol. 1, no. 12 (August 1975), p. 11.

8422 Wilson, Michael and Biberman, Herbert. Salt of the earth [film]. 16mm, 94 min., b&w. English.

AN: The first feature film made in the U.S. of, by and for labor, it deals with a real strike of Mexican American miners in New Mexico in which women played a key role in the men's victory and their own demands. Mexican actress Rosaura Revueltas starred with labor leader Juan Chacon. One of the best films on the subject.

Students

8423 Fiesta de los barrios observes Cinco de Mayo. EASTSIDE SUN, (May 1, 1969). English.

AN: The Fiesta de los Barrios is a cultural festival organized by the committee pressuring the Los Angeles Board of Education for better and more relevant education after the East Los Angeles high school "blowouts." The Fiesta features art, music, dance and literature.

Symbolism

8424 Coe, Kathryn. Heritage plus science yields art. SCOTTSDALE DAILY PROGRESS, (August 28, 1981), p. 27. English.

AN: Biography of Colorado-born Rudy Fernandez who bases many of his paintings and mixed media boxes on the religious imagery of Colorado. He studied geology; travelled to Spain and Mexico to know his heritage. All these factors influence his art, in which he uses symbols personally.

8425 Culver, Virginia. Church's secession depicted on canvas. DENVER POST: RELIGION NEWS WEEKLY, (June 24, 1977). English.

AN: Article commenting on mural created by Manuel Martinez as part of a secession movement by St. Mary's Episcopal Church in Denver whose members voted to leave the Episcopal Diocese of Colorado and the national Episcopal Church. Details of the controversy and examination of the iconography in Martinez's mural. Illustrated with photograph of controversial mural.

8426 Dittmar Memorial Gallery, Northwestern University, Evanston, IL and King, Elaine A. Alejandro Romero: new works. Exhibit catalog, 1981. English.

AN: Full color illustrated catalog of paintings by the Mexican-born artist who has been living in the United States since the early 1970s. His images appear to be grounded in the work of Bosch, Goya, Brueghel, and Diego Rivera. There is a synthesis of personal symbolism and expressionism.

8427 Donnell-Kotrozo, Carol. Containment and discovery. ARTWEEK, Vol. 11, no. 41 (December 6, 1980), p. 12. English.

AN: Review of an exhibit at Scottsdale, Arizona gallery, C.G. Rein by Rudy Fernandez. Discussed in detail is one of his altar-like boxes of mixed media which contain personal symbolisms. Illustrated.

8428 Donnell-Kotrozo, Carol and Perlman, Barbara. Male passages: a secular santero of the '80s interprets machismo. ARIZONA ARTS AND LIFESTYLE, Vol. 4, no. 1 (1982), p. 32-39. English.

AN: Rudy Fernandez moves freely between two- and three-dimensional forms using personal symbols such as cacti, roosters, flying hearts, trout, in paintings or lead-covered shelves of boxes reminiscent of retablos. Colorado-born Fernandez has lived in Arizona, Utah, New Mexico, and Washington. His art is not religious, but is influenced by a strong Catholic background. Many color illustrations, including the cover.

8429 Donnell-Kotrozo, Carol. Rudy Fernandez. ARTSPACE, Vol. 5, no. 4 (Fall 1981), p. 18-23. English.

AN: Scottsdale, Arizona resident Rudy Fernandez converts cultural symbols into a private system language that revolves around love, family, manhood and self-identity. His mixed media altar-like forms are based on interest in Southwest santos, their format and presentation. Fernandez does paintings, and assembled wood pieces. Handsomely illustrated, with color.

8430 Evans, Marylin. Tucson barrio janitor designs authentic Aztec costumes. LA PRENSA, Vol. 1, no. 6 (October 11, 1978). English.

AN: Rogelio Valdovin, self-taught artist from Tucson, Arizona feels he has received a spiritual call to create authentic Pre-Columbian costumes and regalia. Specializing in Aztec costumes, the artist works with metal, beads, feathers, leather and many fabrics and fibers in designing and making his creations. He exhibits them as a form of body art.

8431 Guernica, Antonio Jose and Saavedra-Vela, Pilar. El Midwest Canto al pueblo: "Otra Vez, C/S". AGENDA, Vol. 7, no. 3 (May, June, 1977), p. 4-13. Bilingual.

AN: A thorough report on the various phases and events of the Midwest Canto al Pueblo in Milwaukee, Wisconsin on April 28 to May 8, 1977. The festival brought together artists, poets, musicians, and cultural workers to reaffirm, share, and celebrate the identity of La Raza with El Pueblo. Includes a thematic and iconographic overview of Chicano murals in California by Jose Montoya, and an analysis of his sculpture by Zarco Guerrero from Meza, Arizona. Well illustrated. Includes a photograph of the collective mural painted at 5th St. and National Avenue in Milwaukee, Wisconsin during the course of the conference.

Symbolism (cont.)

8432 Guerrero, Adolfo "El Zarco". The new vision
of Xicanindio art. RAYAS, Vol. 2, no. 1
(January, February, 1979), p. 3. Bilingual.

AN: Zarco Guerrero explains his personal
artistic philosophy that unites Amerindian
concepts of art to contemporary art forms,
especially in sculpture. For Guerrero, "the
Chicano artist is making a monumental effort
to arrive at a new universal language and to
create a new meaning of community through
art.

8433 Jaramillo, Juanita. Tierra madre [drawing].
REVISTA CHICANO-RIQUENA, Vol. 5, no. 1
(Winter 1977), p. 60. Spanish.

8434 Knapp, Martha. West side is part of mural
art renaissance. WEST SAINT PAUL VOICE, Vol.
5, no. 19 (November 21, 1977). English.

AN: Pre-Columbian symbology in the mural
program painted by Paul Basquez and Armando
Estrella in the Chicano barrio; information
and data on the mural renaissance in
Minnesota.

8435 Murales - 'expresan nuestra realidad'.
AYUDA, Vol. 1, no. 6 (September 1977).
English.

AN: Brief illustrated article on Raul
Valdez's 1977 mural LOS ELEMENTOS on the
outside wall of Antioch's Juarez-Lincoln
College (Centro Cultural de LUCHA). Explains
the iconography of the mural. Includes brief
biography of the artist.

8436 The new logo. LA VOZ: Concilio for the
Spanish Speaking of King Co., Seattle, no. 5
(June 1979). English.

AN: Biographical information on artist
Alfredo Arreguin. Born in Uruapan, Michoacan
Mexico and residing in Seattle for eighteen
years, Arrequin is active in La Extension
Cultural, an agency formed to meet the
cultural needs of "Hispanics" in the Pacific
Northwest. In his logo for the "Concilio,"
Arreguin employs symbols representing
history, beauty, unity, ethnicity and
communication.

8437 Pared da historia de la Raza. PAPEL CHICANO,
Vol. 1, no. 4 (September 26, 1971). English.

AN: Discussion of Manuel Martinez' wall
painting at Parque Aztlan titled PASADO,
PRESENTE Y FUTURO DE LA RAZA BRONCE. Among
the images used to convey the theme are
Emiliano Zapata, Quetzalcoatl, a mestizo
three faceted head symbolizing the
indigenous mother, the Spanish father and
the mestizo child. Included also is a symbol
formed by four clasped hands suggesting
unity among world faces. Illustrated with
photograph of wall painting.

8438 Pimentel, Ricardo. Graffiti: expression or
scourge? FRESNO BEE, (February 23, 1981),
p. Metro, B1+. English.

AN: A rapid review of graffiti symbols,
their meaning and social context. Commentary
by various young people explaining the
value, style and meanings of plaqueasos
(spray painted graffiti). Some Chicano
artists like Bob Cruz, director of La Brocha
del Valle, see mural painting as a positive
alternative to graffiti art forms. Article
also provides views of local businessmen to
the graffiti phenomenon.

8439 Rabyor, Jozanne. Luis Jimenez at
Contemporary Arts Museum. ART IN AMERICA,
Vol. 63, no. 1 (January, February, 1975), p.
88. English.

AN: Texas-born Luis Jimenez's first
major museum show of 77 pieces spanning
eight years of production is dazzling.
Superbly crafted fiberglass sculptures
comment on indigenous mythologies often with
macabre humor. His work, according to the
critic, is too moralistic to be Pop, and
too passionate to be dumped into the
California-plastic bag.

8440 Trujillo, Marcella. The dilemma of the
modern Chicana artist and critic. HERESIES,
Vol. 2, no. 4 (1979), p. 5-10. English.

AN: Recommended for its application to
the visual arts in its discussion of
iconography common to literature and art,
and symbols popular with Chicana artists: La
Malinche, the Virgin of Guadalupe,
Tonantzin, Mother Earth, etc.

8441 Vasquez, Emigdio. The Cypress Street Barrio
and my art: a statement of intent.
Unpublished manuscript, 1978. English.

AN: The Arizona-born artist whose family
moved to Orange, Calif. in 1941 describes
his working class barrio and the perspective
it gave him of "life, people and society."
He turned to this subject matter as a young
artist and has continued to paint the
barrio. Description of sources and methods
of work.

8442 Walking tour and guide to the Great Wall at
Tujunga Wash. Venice, CA: Social and Public
Art Resource Center, [1981]. English.

AN: History and symbolism of the GREAT
WALL, directed by Judy Baca, and created by
teams of young people working on the mural
since 1976. Illustrated.

SYNERGY [mural]

8443 Hispanic artists' [sic] mural unveiled.
SOUTHFIELD ECCENTRIC, Exhibition catalog,
1980. English.

AN: A mural titled SYNERGY by Michigan
artist Nora Mendoza is unveiled at the R.J.
Sullivan Funeral Home. Mendoza has exhibited
at numerous one-person shows.

Taboada, John

8444 William Grant Still Community Arts Center,
Los Angeles, CA. Latin American artists
exhibition. Exhibition brochure, 1978.
English.

AN: Exhibit curated by Linda Vallejo
including Carlos Almaraz, Michael M.
Amescua, Ray Bravo, Isabel Castro, Yreina
Cervantez, Luis Serrano-Cordero, Cynthia
Honesto, Judith Miranda, Teddy Sandoval,
John Taboada, Emigdio Vasquez. Illustrated.

Tafolla, Carmen

8445 Fourth annual San Antonio film festival. San
Antonio, TX: Oblate College of the
Southwest, 1979. Bilingual.

AN: Symposium and film festival catalog
featuring motion pictures and videocassettes
made by and about Mexicans, Chicanos and
Latinos. The Symposium focused on Latina
women in film and television, Margarita
Galban, Carmen Tafolla, Leticia Ponce, Grace
Castro Nagata, Marcela Fernandez Violante of
Mexico, and Sylvia Morales.

El Taller, Austin, TX

8446 Parr, June. Amado Maurilio Pena, Jr.: a
talented and dedicated artist. ARRIBA,
(October 1980), p. 1. English.

AN: Pena is represented in forty-two
galleries internationally. Recently, Pena
opened his studio and gallery, El Taller, in
Austin. His latest works focus on the Indian
heritage and are based on trips to New
Mexico. Illustrated.

Taller de Arte, San Antonio, TX

8447 Taller de Arte, San Antonio, TX. Felipe
Varelas Reyes. Exhibition announcement, n.d.
English.

AN: Artist statement and reproduction of
one drawing in an announcement for a one man
show at the Taller.

Taller de Grafica Popular

8448 California. University. Santa Barbara.
Coleccion Tloque Nahuaque. Mexican
soldaderas and workers during the
revolution. Exhibition catalog, 1979.
English.

AN: Well illustrated catalog of an
exhibition of original lithographs by artists
associated with the Taller de
Grafica Popular of Mexico. Biographical
information and illustrations by Raul
Anguiano, Luis Arenal, Alberto Beltran,
Angel Bracho, photographer, Agustin V.
Casasola, Fernando Castro Pacheco, Jesus
Escobedo, Arturo Garcia Bustos, Leopolda
Mendez, Francisco Mora, Isidoro Ocampo,
Pablo O'Higgins, Mariana Yampolsky and
Alfredo Zolca.

Taller Obrero Cultural de Milwaukee

8449 Forest Home Library, Milwaukee, WI. Arte
chicano de Carlos Rosas, Chicano muralist.
Exhibition invitation, 1978. English.

AN: Invitation to an exhibit by Carlos
Rosas [originally from El Paso, TX] who has
created murals with Chicano themes in many
parts of the United States. Sponsored by El
Taller Obrero Cultural de Milwaukee.

Tanguma, Leo

8450 Artist views murals as dialogue with
oppressed. HOUSTON POST, (June 13, 1979),
p. 3A. English.

AN: There are doubts that Houston
muralist Leo Tanguma's latest structural
mural about police brutality will ever see
the light of day. Painted on three pointed
plywood panels, it was originally destined
for Moody Park. Other Tanguma murals have
been painted over. Illustrated.

8451 Barnstone, Gertrude and Tanguma, Leo. The
big picture: 'I want to indict the system
that has condemned us!'. HOUSTON
BREAKTHROUGH, (March 1980), p. 16-19.
English.

AN: Houston muralist Leo Tanguma studied
with John Biggers at Texas Southern
University who encouraged him and other
Chicanos to study Mexican murals. The
article is an interview with Tanguma which
details his strong political orientation and
ideals, and the problems he has encountered
as a result. Three illustrations.

8452 Goldman, Shifra M. Chicano art alive and
well in Texas: a 1981 update. REVISTA
CHICANO-RIQUENA, Vol. 9, no. 1 (Winter
1981), p. 34-40. English.

AN: Reprint of article published as
"Supervivencia y prosperidad del arte
chicano en Texas: nueva revision" in
COMUNIDAD (Los Angeles, CA) [Sunday
Supplement to LA OPINION], September 21,
1980, p. 3, 15+.

8453 Goldman, Shifra M. Supervivencia y
prosperidad del arte chicano en Texas: nueva
revision. COMUNIDAD, Vol. 55, no. 5
(September 21, 1980), p. 3,15+. Spanish.

AN: Focuses on six Chicano artists from
Austin, Houston, San Antonio, and
Kingsville: Mel Casas, Cesar Martinez, Amado
M. Pena, Leo Tanguma, Carmen Lomas Garza,
and Santa Barraza. Well illustrated. This
article was reprinted as "Chicano Art Alive
and Well in Texas: A 1981 Update," in
REVISTA CHICANO-RIQUENA (Houston), Vol. 9,
no. 1, Winter 1981, p. 34-40.

8454 Kalil, Susie. Provocative painting: muralist
Leo Tanguma advances the tradition of
Mexico's masters. HOUSTON CITY MAGAZINE,
(March 1980), p. 88+. English.

AN: 38 year old Leo Tanguma from
Beeville, Texas joined the Mexican-American
Youth Organization in Houston in 1968, which
provided a stimulus to say what he felt in
large paintings. His firsHouston mural was
in 1970, followed by meeting Mexican
muralisDavid Alfaro Siqueiros in 1972. A
monumental mural for Continental Can Co.
followed in 1973. Many of Tanguma's murals
have been controversial and destroyed, or
the commissions withdrawn.Color illustration
of maquette for an ecology mural.

8455 Leo Tanguma and Houston murals. NATIONAL
MURALS NETWORK COMMUNITY NEWSLETTER,
(Spring 1980), p. 11. English.

AN: Report on environmental and police
brutality murals in Houston, Texas.
Illustrated.

8456 Los murales del pueblo. PAPEL CHICANO, Vol.
2, no. 12 (February 1973), p. 1+. Spanish.

AN: Analysis of Leo Tanguma's work as
"an expression not only of artistic creative
opinion but also of the suppressed and
accumulated feeling of La Raza in the United
States." Includes thematic and stylistic
information on four murals in the Houston
barrio: "The Rebirth of Our Nationality,"
"Towards a Humanitarian Technology for La
Raza," "Historia de la Raza," and "El
Mestizo Chicano".

Tanguma, Leo (cont.)

8457 NATIONAL MURALS NETWORK COMMUNITY
NEWSLETTER. (Spring 1980). English.

AN: Reports on the Sept. 1979 conference
of Chicano visual arts held at UT Austin,
organized by the Mujeres Artistas del
Suroeste, and the Liga Unida de Chicanos
Artistas, which brought together
participants from the U.S. and Mexico City;
on Manuel Martinez's five murals (1976-78);
murals by Roberto Lucero, Al Sanchez, and
Jerry Jaramillo; as well as by the Chilean
group Orlando Letelier Brigade, all in
Denver, Colorado; murals by Leo Tanguma in
Houston; the story about the "forbidden"
Chicano mural in Blue Island, Illinois.
Illustrated.

8458 Painting pride for everyone to see - a
Chicano artist and his giant murals. TEXAS
MAGAZINE, (April 22, 1973), p. 4-6+.
English.

AN: Brief story and photographs of
31-year-old Leo Tanguma's murals at
Continental Can Co., Lamons Metal Gasket
Co., McAshan Community Center, and Casa de
Amigos Clinic, in Houston. His large murals
deal with Chicano history and oppression.
Tanguma is unpaid for his labor.

8459 Renacimiento del arte chicano en Texas. EL
HISPANO, Vol. 6, no. 3 (July 10, 1973).
English.

AN: Remigio Garcia and Mariana
Escalante, young muralists, describe their
work and the collective goals of a mural
workshop begun by Leo Tanguma in Houston,
TX.

8460 Tanguma, Leo. Raza art festival. PAPEL
CHICANO, Vol. 1, no. 6 (May 21, 1971), p.
10. English.

AN: Purpose of festival was to bring
Chicano artists together to exhibit their
work. Contingents of artists from throughout
Texas participated. Barrio people were
invited to present their arts and crafts and
show their creativity. Artist Leo Tanguma
affirms festival goal as "the idea of
Chicano artists getting together to use art
as a tool for mass education of our heritage
and culture or in whatever way La Raza's
needs direct us".

8461 Valenzuela-Crocker, Elvira. Tanguma: a man
and his murals. AGENDA, no. 5 (Summer 1974),
p. 14-17. English.

AN: Illustrated report on Houston
muralist Leo Tanguma's 1973 work REBIRTH OF
OUR NATIONALITY as well as other murals in
progress. Tanguma's social views and his
debt to Mexican muralist David Alfaro
Siqueiros are detailed.

Tapestry

8462 Benson, Nancy C. Preserving an early
Hispanic art. EMPIRE MAGAZINE, (June 8,
1980), p. 50. English.

AN: 84-year-old colcha-stitchery artist
Maria Theofila Lujan is a founding member of
a stitchery group of the 1930s, now called
Artes Antigua Society. Her work is in museum
collections.

8463 Frankenstein, Alfred. Report from New
Mexico. Needlework narrative of parish
life. ART IN AMERICA, Vol. 66, no. 5
(September, October, 1978), p. 52-55.
English.

AN: Illustrated report on the Villanueva
Tapestry: an embroidered history of a New
Mexico town by women residents, coached
through and documented by the Museum of
International Folk Art of Santa Fe.

Tapia, Luis

8464 Blue Sky Productions. Los santeros. Color
film, 29 min., 1979. English.

AN: A 29 minute color film produced with
funding assistance from New Mexico Highlands
University and the National Endowment for
the Arts. Features santeros Luis Tapia,
Orlando Romero, Horacio Valdez.

8465 [Tapia exhibit invitation]. Exhibition
invitation. Santa Fe, NM: Santuario de
Nuestra Senora de Guadalupe, 1979. English.

AN: Invitation to an exhibit of works by
Luis and Star Tapia.

Tapia, Star

8466 [Tapia exhibit invitation]. Exhibition
invitation. Santa Fe, NM: Santuario de
Nuestra Senora de Guadalupe, 1979. English.

AN: Invitation to an exhibit of works by
Luis and Star Tapia.

Tapias, Robert

8467 Tucker, Glen. Art scene. TODAY MAGAZINE,
(April 16, 1978), p. 3. English.

AN: Commentary on photographic exhibit
by Robert Tapias and the gift to the Witte
Museum from the American Academy and
Institute of Arts and Letters of a colored
pencil drawing titled "El Filos Lowrider" by
Luis Jimenez.

Tarango, Harvey J.

8468 Consejo Mexicano de Fotografia, A.C., Mexico
City and Tibol, Raquel. Hecho en
Latinoamerica: primera muestra de la
fotografia latinoamericana contemporanea.
Exhibition catalog, 1978. Spanish.

AN: Catalog/book of the first colloquium
and exhibit of Latin American photography.
Among the Chicano artists in the exhibit
were Francisco X. Camplis, Louis Carlos
Bernal, Harry Gamboa, Jose P. Romero, Harvey
J. Tarango, Isabel Castro. Statements by
some of the artists. Great number of
illustrations.

8469 Santa Ana College, Santa Ana, CA and
Goldman, Shifra M. Chicano art. Exhibition
catalog, 1974. English.

AN: Thirteen California artists are
presented in a short essay defining Chicano
as a double mestizaje of Mexican mestizo and
U.S. influences that exists in a state of
"reconciled conflict." Its aim is
communication. Artists included are
Malaquias Montoya, Rupert Garcia, Manuel
Hernandez, Esteban Villa, Robert Gomez,
Harvey Tarango, Mary Helen Castro, Eduardo
Carrillo, Graciela Carrillo, and "Los Four":
Carlos Almaraz, Robert de la Rocha, Judithe
Hernandez, Gilbert Lujan and Frank Romero.

Task Force on Hispanic American Arts, National Endowment for the Arts

8470 NATIONAL MURALS NETWORK COMMUNITY NEWSLETTER. (1978). English.

AN: This issue features reports from muralists. Includes information about murals at: La Pena Cultural Center in Berkeley, CA; the Social and Public Art Resource Center's Tujunga Wash Mural in Venice, CA; the Citywide Mural Project in Los Angeles, CA; activities at Chicano Park, and of the Congress of American Cosmic Artists (CACA), both in San Diego, CA; murals in San Mateo County, CA; the Task Force on Hispanic American Arts headed by Jacinto Quirarte of San Antonio; the 1978 Canto Al Pueblo in Corpus Christi, TX; murals in Chicago; and other works by non-Chicano artists.

Task Force on Minorities in Public Broadcasting

8471 CHICANO CINEMA NEWSLETTER. Vol. 1, no. 6 (August 1979). English.

AN: Announcements of the San Antonio Chicano Film Festival, a seminar on the business of art, the receipt of a report of the Task Force on Minorities in Public Broadcasting, a critical report on the Alternative Cinema Conference in New York, which was attended by eleven members of the Chicano Cinema Coalition, and a report and critique of the report by the Task Force.

Tattoos

8472 Almaraz, Carlos and Estrada, Jose (Pepe). [Untitled photograph]. CHISMEARTE, Vol. 2, no. 1 (1978), p. Ft Cover.

8473 Arte del varrio. San Jose: A.T.M Communications, Inc., Nos. 1-3, 1979-81. English.

AN: Large format color illustrated albums of "Varrio art." Includes examples of tattoo art, placasos (graffiti) and barrio murals.

8474 Bright, John; Bright, Mura; and Castellanos, Leonard. "Placas": graffiti and the environment. Venice, CA: Environmental Communications, 1974. English.

AN: Annotated slide catalog of Chicano graffiti on walls, murals, and tattoos, compiled by staff of Mechicano Art Center.

8475 Frankenstein, Alfred. Prison's artist in residence. SAN FRANCISCO CHRONICLE, (May 5, 1978), p. 60. English.

AN: Review of the exhibition MUNDOS PERDIDOS, curated at the Galeria de la Raza by Leonard Castellanos. Show consisted of work by Castellanos and inmates at Lompoc Federal Correctional Institution near Santa Barbara. Documents a prison mural, tattoos and silkscreen prints with socially critical themes.

8476 Galeria de la Raza/Studio 24, San Francisco, CA. Mundos perdidos/lost worlds. Exhibition invitation, 1978. English.

AN: Invitatiion to a multi-media exhibit from a cultural workshop inside Lompoc Federal Correctional Institution by Leonard Castellanos, National Endowment for the Arts Artist in Residence. Included are murals and tattoo documentation, and silkscreen posters.

8477 Johnston, Tracy. La vida loca. NEW WEST MAGAZINE, (January 29, 1979), p. 38-46. English.

AN: A journalistic account of barrio lifestyles composed from conversations with young Cholos in Los Angeles. Amid poverty, unemployment, drug abuse and familial disintegration, codes of group solidarity and rituals of connection occur. Information on urban Chicano forms of self expression such as mascaras (chola make up), tattoos and graffiti. Well illustrated with photographs.

8478 Lowrider: arte del varrio. A.T.M. Communications, Inc., 1979. English.

AN: Issue of LOWRIDER Magazine dedicated to drawings and paintings by "cholos" sent in to the editor for publication. Good example of a popular art form by largely self-taught neighborhood youth, with a distinctive style and symbolism. Related to graffiti and tattoos. Most images are of lowrider cars, young women and men.

8479 Lowrider: arte del varrio. San Jose, CA: A.T.M. Communications, 1980. English.

AN: Second issue of LOWRIDER Magazine dedicated to drawings and pantings by "cholos" sent in to the editor for publication.

8480 Orozco, Sylvia. Chicano tattoos, dibujos de mano - an expression of Chicano life. ARRIBA, Vol. 1, no. 2 (August 1980), p. 9. English.

AN: Detailing the barrio tradition of handmade tatoos, the article describes techniques of application, subject matter and tatoo art traditions. Illustrated with one photograph by author.

8481 Orozco, Sylvia. Chicanos and tattoos: dibujos de mano - an expression of Chicano life. PARA LA GENTE, Vol. 1, no. 12 (July, August, 1978), p. 13. English.

AN: Illustrated description of Chicano tattooing with ink or pencil and sewing needles.

8482 Teatro de la Tierra Morena, Santa Cruz, CA. Fuego en Aztlan: a Chicano arts show. Exhibition brochure, 1980. English.

AN: Folder of information on the exhibition curated by Cruz Zamarron and Eduardo Carrillo. Exhibiting artists were: Justina Avila, Terry Benitez, Eduardo Carrillo, Hernando Chavez, Bob Cruz, Juanita Estrada, Juana Franklin, Sal Garcia, Leticia Hernandez, David "Sir Loco" Jimenez, Raoul Mendez, Vicente Mendez, Maria V. Pinedo, Gonzalo Placencia, Ramon Rodriguez, Roberto Salas, George Silva and Cruz Zamarron. A special feature was a live tattoo demonstration entitled "Walking Art".

Teatro

8483 El Centro Cultural de La Raza, San Diego,
CA. Espejo del barrio-art exposition.
Exhibition brochure, June 1975. English.

AN: Illustrated brochure announcement
for a cultural exposition of Chicano music,
art and drama. Includes some biographical
information and one reproduction of painter
Manuel Unzueta, woodworker Ambriz, muralist
Victor Orozco Ochoa and designer/illustrator
J. Armando Nunez.

8484 El dia de los muertos [poster]. CARACOL,
Vol. 4, no. 7 (March 1978), p. BACK COVER.
Bilingual.

8485 Torres, Salvador Roberto. Arte de la Raza
[portfolio]. DE COLORES, Vol. 1, no. 1
(Winter 1973), p. 34-43. Bilingual.

AN: A portfolio consisting of four
drawings representing the "progression" of
the symbol of the banner adopted by the
United Farm Workers (UFW). Included are four
out of six drawings, each with its own
explication in English and Spanish, and
brief biographical data about the artist.

8486 Torres, Salvador Roberto. Oso State
[drawing]. DE COLORES, Vol. 1, no. 1 (Winter
1973), p. 40.

8487 Torres, Salvador Roberto. Teatro Mono meets
Teatro Mascarones [drawing]. DE COLORES,
Vol. 1, no. 1 (Winter 1973), p. 36.

8488 Torres, Salvador Roberto. Teatro Mono meets
Teatro Mestizo. DE COLORES, Vol. 1, no. 1
(Winter 1973), p. 38.

8489 Valadez, Kathy L. Zoot suit, by Luis Valdez.
SOMOS, Vol. 1, no. 2 (July 1978), p. 20-29.
English.

AN: Two reviews of Valdez's new play
ZOOT SUIT, both enthusiastic. Historical
material and photographs with an essay by
Jose Montoya and his Pachuco drawing, as
well as views of the play are included.

El Teatro Campesino

8490 El dia de los muertos [poster]. CARACOL,
Vol. 4, no. 7 (March 1978), p. BACK COVER.
Bilingual.

8491 Peyton, Patricia, ed. Reel change: a guide
to social issue films. San Francisco, CA:
Film Fund, 1979. English.

AN: Includes a section on Hispanic film
with descriptions, sources, and rentals.
Listed are Esperanza Vasquez's AGUEDA
MARTINEZ, Sylvia Morales' CHICANA, Adolfo
Vargas' CONSUELO: QUIENES SOMOS?/WHO ARE
WE?, El Teatro Campesino's I AM JOAQUIN,
Jose Luis Ruiz's THE UNWANTED, Jesus
Salvador Trevino's YO SOY CHICANO, and
others. Listings are international in scope.

Teatro Mascarones

8492 Torres, Salvador Roberto. Arte de la Raza
[portfolio]. DE COLORES, Vol. 1, no. 1
(Winter 1973), p. 34-43. Bilingual.

AN: A portfolio consisting of four
drawings representing the "progression" of
the symbol of the banner adopted by the
United Farm Workers (UFW). Included are four
out of six drawings, each with its own

explication in English and Spanish, and
brief biographical data about the artist.

8493 Torres, Salvador Roberto. Teatro Mono meets
Teatro Mascarones [drawing]. DE COLORES,
Vol. 1, no. 1 (Winter 1973), p. 36.

Teatro Mestizo

8494 Torres, Salvador Roberto. Arte de la Raza
[portfolio]. DE COLORES, Vol. 1, no. 1
(Winter 1973), p. 34-43. Bilingual.

AN: A portfolio consisting of four
drawings representing the "progression" of
the symbol of the banner adopted by the
United Farm Workers (UFW). Included are four
out of six drawings, each with its own
explication in English and Spanish, and
brief biographical data about the artist.

8495 Torres, Salvador Roberto. Teatro Mono meets
Teatro Mestizo. DE COLORES, Vol. 1, no. 1
(Winter 1973), p. 38.

Teatro Mono

8496 Torres, Salvador Roberto. Arte de la Raza
[portfolio]. DE COLORES, Vol. 1, no. 1
(Winter 1973), p. 34-43. Bilingual.

AN: A portfolio consisting of four
drawings representing the "progression" of
the symbol of the banner adopted by the
United Farm Workers (UFW). Included are four
out of six drawings, each with its own
explication in English and Spanish, and
brief biographical data about the artist.

8497 Torres, Salvador Roberto. Teatro Mono meets
Teatro Mascarones [drawing]. DE COLORES,
Vol. 1, no. 1 (Winter 1973), p. 36.

8498 Torres, Salvador Roberto. Teatro Mono meets
Teatro Mestizo. DE COLORES, Vol. 1, no. 1
(Winter 1973), p. 38.

EL TECOLOTE (San Francisco, CA)

8499 Garcia, Rupert. A source for mural art
education: an annotated bibliography of
three Chicano newspapers. Unpublished paper,
1974 (Chicano Studies Library, Univ. of
California, Berkeley). English.

AN: A research project showing how
Chicano newspapers reported and educated
their readers to mural activity by Raza
artists during the period 1968-1978. The
newspapers analized are EL GALLO (Denver,
CO), EL CHICANO (San Bernardino, CA), and EL
TECOLOTE (San Francisco, CA). Author draws
eight conclusions about the form, meaning
and significance of mural activity in
Chicano barrios and the importance of
community newspapers as a fruitful and
meaningful source for art education.

Teen Angel

8500 Temko, Allan. Teen Angel's low riders - Chicano art on the rise. THIS WORLD, (August 26, 1979), p. 42-43. English.

AN: Important and insightful analysis of the lowrider phenomenon among Chicano youth in California. Analysis of publications like LOW RIDER Magazine of San Jose, information on graphic artists like "Teen Angel" and Ramon Cisneros and thematic relationship of recognized Chicano artists like Gilbert Lujan, John Valadez, and Luis Jimenez to the lowrider movement. The lowrider is provocatively related to world wide cultural manifestations from diverse epochs.

Tejada-Flores, Rick

8501 Los Angeles Municipal Art Gallery, Los Angeles, CA. Multicultural focus: a photography exhibition for the Los Angeles Bicentennial. Exhibition catalog, 1981. English.

AN: Catalog of an exhibit demonstrating the multi-ethnic character of Los Angeles. Chicano photographers include Don Anton, Ron Bernal, Daniel Martinez, Rick Tejada-Flores. Illustrated.

Tejano Artists, Inc., Houston, TX

8502 Murals around the U.S.A. TEJANO ARTISTS INC. NEWSLETTER, Vol. 2, no. 2 (January, February, 1981). English.

AN: Mimeographed newsletter published by Tejano Artists, Inc. of Houston. Survey of U.S. mural events and publications; report on murals in Texas: El Paso, San Antonio, Austin, Crystal City, San Juan, Corpus Christi, Houston.

Tejeda, Celia

8503 Wilson, William. Chicana artists still seeking identification. LOS ANGELES TIMES, (June 23, 1975), p. VI, 5. English.

AN: Ten Chicana artists are exhibiting their work in the Boathouse Gallery of Plaza de la Raza in Lincoln Park: Judithe Hernandez, Patssi Valdez, Judy Baca, Josefina Quesada, Victoria del Castillo-Leon, Olga Muniz, Gloria Flores, Sylvia Morales, Isabel Castro and Celia Tejadak. The work is still tentative and may develop.

Television

8504 Gamboa, Harry, Jr. Film, television, and Trevino. LA LUZ, Vol. 6, no. 10 (October 1977), p. 7-8. English.

AN: Jesus Salvador Trevino has been an active proponent and participant in transforming cultural inaccuracy about Chicanos in the media to accurate mass media models. A biography of Trevino follows, including discussion of some of his films: THE SALAZAR INQUEST, CHICANO MORATORIUM AFTERMATH, SOLEDAD, AMERICA TROPICAL, YO SOY CHICANO, RAICES DE SANGRE, as well as television series like ACCION CHICANO, AHORA, and INFINITY FACTORY.

8505 Knapp, Dan. KCET's show for Chicano viewers. LOS ANGELES TIMES, (April 3, 1970), p. IV, 18. English.

AN: Story on the television series

AHORA! started September 1969 on KCET, Los Angeles' National Educational Television. Edward Moreno is program director and host; Victor Millan is producer-director; Claudio Fenner-Lopez, senior producer, has staff including set-designer David Villasenor, production manager James Val, and alternate host-narrator Jesus Trevino. The program has shown exhibits of artists Gilberto Lujan and Daniel Ramirez.

8506 Torres, Louis R. An innovation in children's t.v.: THE INFINITY FACTORY. LA LUZ, Vol. 6, no. 2 (February 1977), p. 10-11. English.

AN: Illustrated report on a new television series for children aimed at teaching mathematics fundamentals in a crisply-paced series of half-hour programs. The executive producer, Jesus Salvador Trevino, filmed the segments in a New York Black community, and in the East Los Angeles Chicano barrio. In one segment, muralist Willie Herron works with youngsters to design and paint an outdoor mural.

Tellez, Miguel Angel

8507 Cantu, Jesus "Chista". Entrevista: Jesus Maria Cantu, 'El Chista'. MAGAZIN, Vol. 1, no. 4 (April 1972), p. 52-65. Spanish.

AN: Discusses his life in San Antonio; his apprenticeship since childhood to his uncle Miguel Angel Tellez who taught him to paint billboards, wall signs and church decorations; his membership in the group Artistas de la Nueva Raza; his artistic and political philosophy. In Spanish.

8508 De la Torre, Alfredo and Tellez, Miguel Angel. Entrevista con Don Miguel Angel Tellez=Interview with Don Miguel Angel Tellez. CARACOL, Vol. 5, no. 11-12 (July, August, 1979), p. 16-22. Bilingual.

AN: Tellez, born in San Antonio about 1915, son and grandson of painters who taught him the trade, tells about his life as commercial artist and his more symbolic work started in 1962. Illustrated.

Tempe, AZ

8509 Bartak, Bonnie. Murals make walls political forum. ARIZONA REPUBLIC, (April 21, 1975), p. A-12. English.

AN: Tempe, AZ murals located at the Valle del Sol Institute (South 1st St.), the Tempe Escalante Center (East Orange), and the Barrio Youth Project (South 1st St.). Illustrated.

Terrill, Joey

8510 Galeria, Santa Ana, CA. The last Chicano art show. Exhibition brochure, 1981. English.

AN: Invitation-brochure for an exhibit of Los Angeles and Orange County artists in a gallery underwritten by the Friendly Center, Inc. with grants from local government and from businesses. Exhibiting are (Roberto) Gil de Montes, Gilbert Lujan, Judy Miranda, Patricia Murillo, Alonso Pardo, Teddy Sandoval, Mexican artist Artemio Sepulveda, Joey Terrill, Art Valenzuela, Ben Valenzuela, Linda Vallejo, Jack A. Vargas, Emigdio Vasquez, Richard Serrato, and J. William Hernandez, who is the gallery director.

Testimonios de Latinoamerica [exhibit]

8511 Lucas, Jerry. Testimonios de Latinoamerica.
CHISMEARTE, no. 6 (February 1980), p. 6-9.
English.

AN: Review of the exhibits TESTIMONIOS
DE LATINOAMERICA and AMERICA EN LA MIRA,
brought to Los Angeles Contemporary
Exhibitions Gallery by Chicano curator
Roberto Gil de Montes, as part of a cultural
exchange between the Mexican Cultural
Workers Front and Felipe Ehrenberg of the
Grupo Proceso Pentagono of Mexico, and
Chicano artists and photographers from the
Council of Latino Photography/USA in Los
Angeles. Well illustrated.

Texas

8512 Amado Maurilio Pena, Jr. PAPEL CHICANO, Vol.
1, no. 13 (July 21, 1978). Spanish.

AN: Includes the artist's resume, an
exhibition list, and a gallery statement
situating the work of Pena within both
Native American and Chicano art traditions.
Includes reproduction of four works.

8513 The art of Rodolfo Leal. TIN TAN, Vol. 2,
no. 6 (December 1, 1977), p. 15-18. English.

AN: Two calligraphic ink drawings and a
serigraph by Texas-born Leal who lives in
San Francisco.

8514 Barnett, Alan. Southern journey. NATIONAL
MURALS NETWORK COMMUNITY NEWSLETTER, (Fall
1980), p. 22-32. English.

AN: Rather gossipy account of murals
seen in a swing of the southern United
States. Includes the work of dozens of
artists and arts groups from California,
Arizona, New Mexico, Texas, and Colorado.

8515 Contemporary Arts Museum, Houston, TX. Dale
gas: give it gas. The continued
acceleration of Chicano art. Exhibition
catalog, 1977. English.

AN: A comprehensive catalog including 28
works of art exhibited by 13 Texas artists:
Melesio (Mel) Casas, Jose Esquivel,
Francisco (Frank) Fajardo, Carmen Lomas
Garza, Luis Jimenez, Cesar Augusto Martinez,
Santos G. Martinez, Jr., Amado Pena, Roberto
Rios, Jose Rivera, Joe B. Rodriguez, Jesus
(Jesse) Trevino, and George Truan. Many
illustrations, some in color. Introduction
by James Harithas. Essay by Santos Martinez,
Jr. Poetry, literature and essays by Chicano
writers.

8516 Contemporary Arts Museum, Houston, TX. Fire!
An exhibition of 100 Texas artists.
Exhibition brochure, 1979. English.

AN: Includes eleven Chicano artists.
Unfortunately, not illustrated, though a
checklist of works is included. Mel Casas,
Carmen Lomas Garza, Xavier Gorena, Luis
Jimenez, Cesar Martinez, Guillermo Z.
Pulido, Philip Renteria, Jose L. Rivera, Joe
Rodriguez, George Truan, Juan B. Vela.
Introduction by James Surls. Statements by
the artists.

8517 Corpus Christy State University for the Arts
and Weil Gallery Center for the Arts, Corpus
Christi State University. Southwest artists
invitational: an exhibition of contemporary
art by seven Texas artists of Hispanic
American descent. Ehxibition brochure, 1980.

English.

AN: Artists Jesse Almazan, Luis Jimenez,
Cesar Martinez, Lydia Martinez, Manuel
Mauricio, Guillermo Pulido, and Jesse
Trevino show a variety of techniques and
styles. Text by Roberto Tomas Esparza.
Statements by and about the artists.
Illustrated.

8518 Crossley, Mimi. Tejano artists. HOUSTON
POST, (August 19, 1976). English.

AN: Exhibition of 19 Texas artists
organized by Joe Rodriguez of the AAMA
(Association for the Advancement of Mexican
Americans) Art Center in Houston, Texas.
Working within a wide range of styles and a
great scope of subject matter. Includes
brief commentary on the work of Amado Pena,
Carmen Lomas Garza, Cesar Martinez, Enrique
Campos, Carolina Flores, Jesus Trevino and a
host of others.

8519 De Marroquin, Moron. Denver Harbor artists.
LA PRENSA, (June 2, 1978). Spanish.

AN: Commentary on two exhibitions. THE
DENVER HARBOR ARTISTS includes information
on paintings by Lupe Aguirre, Josie Mendoza
and Abel Gonzalez--all from Houston. The
solo show MAGIC BLANCA featured the work of
Brownsville, Texas artist Jorge Truan.
Truan's work is mystical and visionary.

8520 Documentary to include work by Cuate Santos.
LAREDO NEWS, (July 17, 1980). English.

AN: Photography by Laredo News
photographer Cuate Santos included in
exhibit "Un encuentro sin palabras," a
documentary show on Mexican American life in
Texas sponsored by Mujeres Artistas del
Suroeste (MAS). The state-wide show was
juried by Los Angeles photographer Isabel
Castro. Illustrated.

8521 Extension Cultural SRE/UNAM, San Antonio,
TX. Second non professional (black & white)
photography contest: Mexican women in Texas.
Competition announcement, [ca. 1980].
English.

AN: Announcement of photographic
competition sponsored by the Extension arm
of the Secretaria de Relaciones
Exteriores/Universidad Nacional Autonoma de
Mexico in San Antonio. The theme specified
an homage to the Mexican woman in Texas.

8522 First Federal Plaza Display Gallery, Austin,
TX. Tejano artists: an exhibit of
Mexican-American art. Exhibit brochure,
1976. English.

AN: Announcement of exhibit illustrated
by Cesar A. Martinez's woodcut.

Texas (cont.)

8523 Galeria Tonantzin, Centro Cultural de LUCHA, Austin, TX. Young Chicano photographers from throughout Texas. Exhibition brochure, n.d. English.

AN: This exhibition is the collection of the winners of the contest (by the same name) sponsored by the Extension Cultural SRE-UNAM in San Antonio. Photographers represented were: Grace Alvarez, David Cardenas, Hector Cardenas, Stephen Casanova, Ronald Cortez, Raul Espinosa, Felix Almanza, Carolina Flores, David Garza Perez, Xavier Garza, Conrad Guerra, Melinda Hasbrook, Juan Jose de Hoyes, Beverly Kennon, Art Moreno, David Perez, Isabelle Purden, Patricia Santell, Nancy de los Santos, Jose Soria, Richard Tichich, Kathy Vargas, Vivian Yaten, and Johnny Zamarria.

8524 Garcia, Ignacio. Senior exhibit attempts to define Chicano art. SOUTH TEXAN, (August 1, 1975). English.

AN: DIRECTAMENTE DEL BARRIO, a senior art exhibit at Texas A & I University by art majors Raul Valdez and Jesus Reyes. Sets forth their ideas about Chicano arts and their future plans.

8525 Garcia, Ruperto. Las companeras art exhibit. ARRIBA, Vol. 1, no. 4 (October 1980), p. 9. English.

AN: Illustrated story on an art show featuring Texas Latinas organized by MAS (Mujeres Artistas del Suroeste) in Austin. More than 18 women were represented.

8526 Goldman, Shifra M. Chicano art alive and well in Texas: a 1981 update. REVISTA CHICANO-RIQUENA, Vol. 9, no. 1 (Winter 1981), p. 34-40. English.

AN: Reprint of article published as "Supervivencia y prosperidad del arte chicano en Texas: nueva revision" in COMUNIDAD (Los Angeles, CA) [Sunday Supplement to LA OPINION], September 21, 1980, p. 3, 15+.

8527 Goldman, Shifra M. Supervivencia y prosperidad del arte chicano en Texas: nueva revision. COMUNIDAD, Vol. 55, no. 5 (September 21, 1980), p. 3,15+. Spanish.

AN: Focuses on six Chicano artists from Austin, Houston, San Antonio, and Kingsville: Mel Casas, Cesar Martinez, Amado M. Pena, Leo Tanguma, Carmen Lomas Garza, and Santa Barraza. Well illustrated. This article was reprinted as "Chicano Art Alive and Well in Texas: A 1981 Update," in REVISTA CHICANO-RIQUENA (Houston), Vol. 9, no. 1, Winter 1981, p. 34-40.

8528 Goldman, Shifra M. Women artists of Texas: MAS = More + Artists + Women = MAS. CHISMEARTE, no. 7 (January 1981), p. 21-22. English.

AN: History of Texas Chicana women artists' organization, Mujeres Artistas del Suroeste (MAS), co-founded in 1977 by Santa Barraza and Nora Gonzalez-Dodson in the framework of the burgeoning feminist art movement, particularly Women and Their Work of Texas. Brief history of Chicano politics and the corresponding art movement of southern and central Texas. In addition to Barraza and Gonzalez-Dodson, Alicia Arredondo, Modesta Trevino, and Maria Flores

are considered. Illustrated.

8529 Guerra, Victor, ed. El camino de la cruz. Austin, TX: Tejidos Publications, 1981. Spanish.

AN: Carlos Andres Guerra, portfolio; painting (in color), sculpture, drawing, jewelry. Luis Guerra drawing on cover.

8530 Instituto Chicano de Artes y Artesanias (Texas Instit. Educational Development) and Instituto Cultural Mexicano (SER/UNAM), San Antonio, TX. Artistas chicanos: Los Quemados. San Antonio, TX: Instituto Chicano, Texas Institute for Educational Development, 1975. English.

AN: Invitation to an exhibit and manifesto of 1975 Austin-San Antonio artists' group, Los Quemados. Included Santa Barraza, Carolina Flores, Carmen Lomas Garza, Luis Guerra, Cesar Augusto Martinez, Santos Martinez, Amado Maurilio Pena, Jr., Jose Rivera, Vicente Rodriguez, Jose Trevino.

8531 Instituto Cultural Mexicano (SER/UNAM), San Antonio, TX. Jesse Trevino's one man exhibit. San Antonio, TX: Instituto Cultural Mexicano, 1981. Bilingual.

AN: Bilingual statement on the work of Jesse Trevino; biography and list of selected exhibitions; quotations from several publications about his work.

8532 Laguna Gloria Art Museum, Austin, TX. Tierra, familia sociedad, Amado Pena's themes. Exhibition catalog, 1980. Bilingual.

AN: Illustrated exhibition catalog with artist's biography and chronology of exhibitions. The bi-lingual text by Santos G. Martinez, Jr. situates the artist's work within a dual phased trajectory. First a period (1971-1975) in which the artist creates images armed with a social-political focus and (1975-present), a period starting with the PEOPLESCAPE series in which the artist enters a more lyrical introspective phase.

8533 Marion Koogler McNay Art Institute, San Antonio, TX and Lee, Amy Freeman. Filigree drawings by Consuelo Gonzalez Amezcua. Exhibition catalog, 1968. English.

AN: Illustrated catalog for an exhibition of 42 filigree drawings by Texas artist "Chelo" Amezcua. Apart from biographical and historical information, the text evokes the ambiance of magic and mysticism surrounding the artist.

8534 The Mexican Museum, San Francisco, CA. Bruno Andrade (from Missouri) and Antonio Lopez Saenz (from Mexico). Exhibition announcement, 1978. English.

AN: Flyer announcing an exhibit at the Mexican Museum of Texas-born Andrade who is exhibiting large abstract landscapes. Andrade teaches in Columbia, Missouri; this is his first California exhibit.

Texas (cont.)

8535 Moser, Charlotte. Arte chicano de Texas/Texas Chicano art. ARTES VISUALES, no. 29 (June 1981), p. 57-63. Bilingual.

AN: History of Chicano art and art organizations in Texas. A younger generation of artists is complying with a mainstream European esthetic rather than a regional Chicano one. Statements and biographies of artists. Many illustrations.

8536 Moser, Charlotte; Renteria, Phil; and Wray, Dick. Phil Renteria and Dick Wray. ART IN AMERICA, Vol. 64, no. 4 (July, August, 1976), p. 82-83. English.

AN: Interview with Laredo-born Houston artist Renteria, and Wray, both of whom teach at the Museum of Fine Arts. Renteria gives much biographical information and his philosophy of art. Illustrated in color.

8537 Murals around the U.S.A. TEJANO ARTISTS INC. NEWSLETTER, Vol. 2, no. 2 (January, February, 1981). English.

AN: Mimeographed newsletter published by Tejano Artists, Inc. of Houston. Survey of U.S. mural events and publications; report on murals in Texas: El Paso, San Antonio, Austin, Crystal City, San Juan, Corpus Christi, Houston.

8538 Philip Renteria drawings, 1974-77. In YOUNG TEXAS ARTISTS SERIES. Amarillo, TX: Amarillo Art Center, 1977. English.

AN: Catalog of series of exhibits co-sponsored by the Texas commission of the Arts and Humanities and the Amarillo Art Center. Illustrated with a biography of the artist.

8539 Quirarte, Jacinto. Chelo Gonzalez Amezcua. QUETZAL, Vol. 1, no. 2 (Winter 1970, 1971), p. 33-36.

AN: Biographical information based on a taped interview with the Del Rio, Texas artist. As a self-taught artist, Chelo Gonzalez Amezcua developed a drawing style using colored ball point pens which she calls "Filigree Art", a new Texas culture. Poorly illustrated.

8540 S.A. site for National Symposium on Mexican American Art. CHICANO TIMES, Vol. 4, no. 30 (November 9, 1973), p. 5. English.

AN: Held at Trinity University, the Symposium discussed such issues as, creative evolution, art education, artistic relationships to Mexico and the evolution of Mexican American art in the California barrios. Participating artists included Rudy Trevino, Mel Casas, Octavio Medellin, Antonio Garcia, Carmen Garza, Esteban Villa, Jose Montoya, Ernesto Palomino, Michael Ponce de Leon, Luis Jimenez and Eugenio Quesada.

8541 Salazar, Veronica. Prominent Mexican-Americans-Porfirio Salinas. SAN ANTONIO EXPRESS-NEWS, (April 1, 1973), p. I-4. English.

AN: Biographical information and artistic chronology of Porfirio Salinas. This self-taught artist is the most prominent painter of Texas landscapes, especially with bluebonnets. Former president Lyndon B. Johnson was an ardent fan and patron.

8542 San Antonio Museum of Modern Art. Paperwork: an exhibition of Texas artists. San Antonio, TX: San Antonio Museum of Modern Art, 1979. English.

AN: Includes Roberto Munguia, Mexican American artist from Kingsville, Texas. Working with shaped paper, the artist describes his material and methods of creation. Includes biography of artist together with an exhibition list. Illustrated with photographs of five paper constructions by Roberto Munguia.

8543 Smith, Roberta. Twelve days of Texas. ART IN AMERICA, Vol. 64, no. 4 (July, August, 1976), p. 42-48. English.

AN: Overview of Texas art in Fort Worth/Dallas, Houston, San Antonio, Tyler, and Galveston. Includes reproductions of works by Luis Jimenez (color, on cover), Roberto Rios mural, Jesse Trevino, Mel Casas. Also mentioned in text are Phil Renteria and Cesar Martinez.

8544 Stamper, Frances. Fluid washes of ink and acrylic. TEXAS HOMES MAGAZINE, Vol. 4, no. 1 (January, February, 1980), p. 104-112. English.

AN: Well illustrated article with color reproductions of the work of Philip Renteria. Provides biographical information and focuses on the consumate craftsmanship of his drawings and paintings.

8545 Tanguma, Leo. Raza art festival. PAPEL CHICANO, Vol. 1, no. 6 (May 21, 1971), p. 10. English.

AN: Purpose of festival was to bring Chicano artists together to exhibit their work. Contingents of artists from throughout Texas participated. Barrio people were invited to present their arts and crafts and show their creativity. Artist Leo Tanguma affirms festival goal as "the idea of Chicano artists getting together to use art as a tool for mass education of our heritage and culture or in whatever way La Raza's needs direct us".

8546 Valdez, Armando. El calendario chicano 1975. Hayward, CA: Southwest Network, 1975. English.

AN: Third in a series of historical calendars produced in 1972 and 1974 by La Causa Publications and Southwest Network. Artists included for each month are Carmen Lomas Garza, Sergio Hernandez, Malaquias Montoya, Mujeres Muralistas (Graciela Carrillo, Venezuelan Consuelo Mendez, Irene Perez, Patricia Rodriguez), Ramses Noriega, Ernie Palomino, Amado Maurilio Pena, Martin Perez. All but Texan Pena are California artists.

8547 Xochil Art and Culture Center, Mission, TX. Besame mucho. Exhibition invitation, 1979. English.

AN: Invitation to exhibit of Texas artists from Mujeres Artistas del Suroeste (MAS): Mary Ann Anguiano, Alicia Arredondo, Santa Barraza, Nora Gonzales-Dodson, Maria Flores, Carolina Flores, Mary Ann Ambray Gonzales, Sylvia Orozco, Nancy de los Santos, Modesta Barbina Trevino. Illustrated.

Texas A & I University

8548 Garcia, Ignacio. Senior exhibit attempts to define Chicano art. SOUTH TEXAN, (August 1, 1975). English.

AN: DIRECTAMENTE DEL BARRIO, a senior art exhibit at Texas A & I University by art majors Raul Valdez and Jesus Reyes. Sets forth their ideas about Chicano arts and their future plans.

Texas Farmworkers' Union

8549 Guerra, Luis. Hasta la gloria [drawing]. TEJIDOS, Vol. 4, no. 2 (Summer 1977), p. COVER. Spanish.

8550 Guerra, Victor. Primavera: happy in Khaki. TEJIDOS, Vol. 5, no. 2-4 (1978), p. 68. English.

Texas Rangers

8551 Burciaga, Jose Antonio. Which way did they go, slim? [drawing]. CARACOL, Vol. 5, no. 2 (October 1978), p. 9. English.

THE MURALS OF EAST OF LOS ANGELES (film)

8552 Rivera, Humberto R. Film notes. CHISMEARTE, Vol. 1, no. 2 (Winter, Spring, 1977), p. 20-24. English.

AN: Summary of films produced by and/or about Chicanos for cinema and television. Includes REALIDADES (TV) by David Sandoval, Rudy Vargas, Luis Torres, Jose Luis Ruiz, Antonio Reyes; A POLITICAL RENAISSANCE from the LA RAZA series (TV) by Moctezuma Esparza; CHILDREN OF THE STATE by Andres Markovits, Richard Trubo, Frank Christopher (film); LA RAZA UNIDA (released as RAICES DE SANGRE) by Jesus Salvador Trevino (Mexican film by a Chicano); CHULAS FRONTERAS (film) by Les Blank; THE MURALS OF EAST LOS ANGELES, A MUSEUM WITHOUT WALLS by Humberto R. Rivera and Heather R. Howell. Announcement for the National Latino Media Coalition.

Theater
USE: Teatro

Thiele, O'Brien

8553 Erickson, Barbara. La Pena's new face. NORTH EAST BAY INDEPENDENT, no. 4 (September 5, 1978), p. 11. English.

AN: Illustrated story on the relief mural SONG OF UNITY by Ray Patlan, O'Brien Thiele, Osha Neumann, and Anna de Leon on the facade of La Pena cultural center in Berkeley, California. Chilean songwriter Victor Jara and the music of North and South America are the motifs.

8554 New radical wall art. PEOPLE'S WORLD, Vol. 41, no. 37 (September 16, 1978), p. 10. English.

AN: Illustrated story and explanation of the imagery on the new mural resulting from a collaboration of Commonarts and La Pena Cultural Center. The artists are Ray Patlan, O'Brien Thiele, Osha Neumann, and Anna de Leon.

Third Annual Chicano Film Festival, San Antonio, TX

8555 Gonzales, Juan. Chicano film festival earns pluses and minuses. EL TECOLOTE, Vol. 9, no.

3 (November 1978), p. 7. English.

AN: Critical review of the Third Annual Chicano Film Festival in San Antonio, TX. The writer criticizes lack of critical exchange and dialogue between filmmakers and audience; expresses disappointment at the exploitive nature of Cheech and Chong film; reports audience tribute to Jesus S. Trevino's RAICES DE SANGRE; feels ONLY ONCE IN A LIFETIME was technically excellent, but passive and without a significant message. Question is posed about the role and expected audience of Chicano filmmakers.

Third National Chicano Forum, Salt Lake City, May 27-30, 1976

8556 Bejarano, William. Utah Chicano forum. CHISMEARTE, Vol. 1, no. 1 (Fall 1976), p. 9-10. English.

AN: Report on the CULTURE, ARTE Y MEDIOS DE COMUNICACION workshop at the Third National Chicano Forum at the University of Utah, Salt Lake City. The panel, moderated by artist Carmen Lomas Garza, set up a plan of action for the visual, literary, performing arts and the mass media which included planning a national conference to discuss cultural work, financial support, recognition and moral support, among other issues.

Thomas Jefferson Elementary School, Compton, CA

8557 [Untitled photograph]. LOS ANGELES TIMES, (May 5, 1972), p. II, 1. English.

AN: Captioned illustration of Chicano high school students' 25x5 foot mural at Compton's Thomas Jefferson Elementary School. The mural, which took a year to paint, is based on Mexican history.

Thrall, Vicki

8558 ENCUENTRO FEMENIL (San Fernando, CA). Vol. 1, no. 1 (Spring 1973), p. 1+. English.

AN: Publication sponsored by Hijas de Cuauhtemoc, a Chicana femenist group. Black and white drawings on cover by Pat Portera Crary. Art work by Vicki Thrall, Adelaida del Castillo, and Maria Hortencia Garcia. Photography by Cindy Honesto and David Lazarin.

Tijerina, Reies Lopez

8559 De la Rocha, Roberto. [Untitled woodcuts]. CON SAFOS, no. 7 (Winter 1971), p. 12-13.

TIN TAN [magazine], San Francisco, CA

8560 Dunsmore de Carrillo, Patricia. On Rene Yanez of the Galeria de la Raza. CHISMEARTE, Vol. 1, no. 1 (Fall 1976), p. 8-9. English.

AN: Report on Yanez's negotiations with the Foster Kleiser Company to take over a billboard located outside the Galeria in San Fancisco which has been painted by Michael Rios, the Centro de Cambio and TIN TAN magazine, Zaiver (Xavier) Viramontes, and others.

Tineo, David

8561 Art outdoors. CONCEPT, (September 1980). English.

  AN: Illustrated article on outdoor murals in Tucson by Antonio Pazos and David Tineo.

8562 Tucson Public Library; Sonoran Heritage; and De la Cruz, Frank. Mexican American mural art: the power of cultural identity. Brochure, 1980. English.

  AN: Brochure on Tucson murals painted by Antonio Pazos, David Tineo, Danny Garza, Cynthia Reyes, Darlene Marcos, Roberto Borboa, and others.

8563 Vigil, Maria. Hello, walls: Tucson's murals. WEEKENDER MAGAZINE, (March 29, 1980), p. 14-16. English.

  AN: Article on muralism, from the Mexican to those of Chicanos. Focuses on Tucson murals by Roberto Borboa, Antonio Pazos, David Tineo and Fred Monreal. Color illustrations.

Tocora, Antonio L.

8564 Encanto Pavilion, Encanto Park, Phoenix, AZ. Exposicion de arte para la raza: Arizona Chicano art show. Exhibition catalog, [ca. 1978]. English.

  AN: Catalog for an exhibit organized by MARS (Movimiento Artistico del Rio Salado). Colombian-born Antonio L. Tocora, Jim Covarrubias, Ed Dias, Robert C. Buitron, Armando Leon Hernandez, Guillermo Galindo, Richard Luna Cisneros, Jose Andres Giron, Robert L. Matta included.

Toltecas en Aztlan, San Diego, CA

8565 El Centro Cultural de La Raza, San Diego, CA and Enrique, Veronica. Tenth anniversary celebration, July 11, 1981. San Diego, CA: El Centro Cultural de la Raza, 1981. English.

  AN: Anniversary brochure of the Centro, founded in 1970 by the Toltecas en Aztlan artistic collective and established at its Balboa Park location in 1971. Briefly reviews the history and activities of the Centro, including the establishment of Chicano Park in 1970 and the painting of murals at the Park and at the Centro. Well illustrated.

8566 Cockcroft, Eva; Weber, John; and Cockcroft, James D. Towards a people's art: the contemporary mural movement. New York: E.P. Dutton, 1977. English.

  AN: A survey of the street mural movement in the United States, from about 1967 on. Several chapters are written by the artists themselves: John Weber on the Chicago mural group; Susan Shapiro-Kiok on Cityarts Workshop of New York; Eva Cockcroft on People's painters of New Jersey; Geronimo Garduno on Artes Guadalupanos de Aztlan of New Mexico. Chicano murals illustrated include those of Mujeres Muralistas, Ray Patlan, William F. Herron, Hoyo-Mara Gang, Artes Guadalupanos de Aztlan, Vicente Mendoza and Jose Nario (with Patlan) Mario Castillo, Michael Rios, Toltecas en Aztlan, Roberto Chavez, Ernie Palomino, Chuy Campusano and Luis Cortazar (with Rios).

8567 Greenberg, David; Smith, Kathryn; and Teacher, Stuart. Megamurals & supergraphics: big art. Philadelphia, PN: Running Press, 1977. English.

  AN: A full-color picture book of murals throughout the United States. Chicano murals include Michael Rios (San Francisco), Mujeres Muralistas (San Francisco), Leonard Castellanos and Tomas Gonzales with others (Los Angeles), Los Artes Guadalupanos de Aztlan (New Mexico), Willie Herron (Los Angeles), Toltecas en Aztlan (San Diego), David Botello (Los Angeles), David Lopez and Arizona Mara Gang (Los Angeles), Vatos de Maravilla (Los Angeles), Carlito Gaegos (Los Angeles), Gil Hernandez (Los Angeles), Wayne [Alaniz] Healy (Los Angeles).

8568 Monteverde, Mildred. Contemporary Chicano art. AZTLAN, Vol. 2, no. 2 (Fall 1971), p. 51-61. Bibliography. English.

  AN: An historical survey of trends and influences on contemporary Chicano art. Discusses San Diego's Toltecas en Aztlan and the projected Centro Cultural de la Raza; Los Angeles' Mechicano Art Center, Goez Gallery and Plaza de la Raza; pinto (prison) art; New Mexican art. Many artists are mentioned.

8569 Murphy, Patricia Lee. Artists renew Toltecas crafts heritage. LOS ANGELES TIMES, (May 23, 1971), p. E, 10. English.

  AN: The Toltecas en Aztlan, creative arm of the Chicano Federation of San Diego County, Inc., will shortly move into their new Centro Cultural de la Raza in Balboa Park, San Diego. The group includes Mario Acevedo (Peruvian), Guillermo Aranda, Tomas Castaneda, Victor Ochoa and Salvador Torres (visual artists) and poet Alurista.

Tondre, Calvin

8570 Albright, Thomas. Oakland Museum: a wide range in Latin art. SAN FRANCISCO CHRONICLE, (September 12, 1970), p. 33. English.

  AN: A large show called ARTES DE LA RAZA at the Oakland Museum includes Mercedes Gutierrez-McDermid, Louis Gutierrez, Luis Cervantez, Calvin Tondre, Manuel Villamor, Rene Yanez, Jose Ramirez, Jorge Lerma, Rolando Castellon, Esteban Villa, Rupert Garcia, and Gustavo Rivera who is also having an exhibit at the Galeria de la Raza.

Torres, Anastacio "Tache"

8571 Minutaglio, Bill. Chicano take the art to the street of S.A. SAN ANTONIO EXPRESS-NEWS, (January 11, 1981), p. M, 1-2. English.

  AN: Survey of Chicano murals in San Antonio including 30 two-story murals at Westside Cassiano Homes by students from the commercial art program of Lanier High directed by Anastacio "Tache" Torres and Rudy Trevino; 8 murals at Lanier High School; one at the City Hall offices; and others throughout the city. Illustrated.

Torres, Anastacio "Tache" (cont.)

8572 Minutaglio, Bill. S.A. aims at becoming
     Hispanic art center. SAN ANTONIO
     EXPRESS-NEWS, (January 18, 1981), p. 3-M+.
     English.

     AN: Rick Reyna is director of the
     fledging San Antonio Consortium for Hispanic
     Arts (SACHA), a city-funded umbrella
     organization covering seven art groups,
     three of which - Centro Cultural del Pueblo
     (instruction for young people), Community
     Cultural Arts Program (murals), and
     Performance Artists Nucleus (displays and
     exhibits) - concern the visual arts. Rudy
     Garcia, Anastacio "Tache" Torres, and Ralph
     Garcia (formerly of Garcia's Art Gallery)
     head the three groups respectively.

Torres, Kay

8573 Chicano art. ARTES VISUALES, no. 29 (1981).
     English.

     AN: Issue on Chicano art, introduced by
     Los Angeles artist Roberto Gil de Montes.
     Includes works and statements by: Pedro
     Lujan (Texas); Raul M. Guerrero (Calif.);
     Sylvia Salazar Simpson (New Mexico/Calif.);
     Carlos Almaraz (Calif.); Rene Yanez
     (Calif.); Jack Vargas (Calif.); Ray Bravo
     (Calif.); John Valadez (Calif.); Gloria Maya
     (Calif.); Elsa Flores (Calif.); Willie
     Herron (Calif.); Gilbert "Magu" Lujan
     (Calif.); Kay Torres, Jerry Lucas, and Louis
     Perez (Calif.).

8574 Colectivo El Ojo. CHOQUE DE AMOR: fotonovela
     by Lamp. CHISMEARTE, Vol. 1, no. 4 (Fall ,
     Winter, 1977), p. 35-37. Bilingual.

     AN: Several students with the help of
     the Latin American Media Project (LAMP) and
     the Latin American Studies Department of
     California State University, Los Angeles
     produced the fotonovela CHOQUE DE AMOR, a
     variation on the typical "fotonovela"
     romance. This one encourages readers to
     reevaluate traditional female roles. The
     group also includes Kay Torres. Six frames
     of the fotonovela are reproduced.

8575 Diaz, Jean; Dominguez, Edward; and Torres,
     Kay. Bi-Lingual blues [fotonovela]. SOMOS,
     Vol. 1, no. 1 (April, May, 1978), p. 33-36.
     English.

     AN: Reproduction of a "fotonovela",
     BI-LINGUAL BLUES by Ojo Productions, a group
     of students connected with the Latin
     American Studies Department of California
     State University, Los Angeles.

8576 Lucas, Jerry and Gil de Montes, Roberto, et
     al. CHOQUE DE AMOR: fotonovela by Lamp. Los
     Angeles, CA: Colectivo El Ojo, Latin
     American Studies Dept., CSULA, 1979.
     English.

     AN: "Fotonovela" featuring Elsa Flores,
     Rosa Marin, and Jerry Lucas produced by the
     collective work of Lucas, Roberto Gil de
     Montes, Mario Massinelli, Luis Soto, and Kay
     Torres.

Torres, Luis

8577 Rivera, Humberto R. Film notes. CHISMEARTE,
     Vol. 1, no. 2 (Winter, Spring, 1977), p.
     20-24. English.

     AN: Summary of films produced by and/or
     about Chicanos for cinema and television.

Includes REALIDADES (TV) by David Sandoval,
Rudy Vargas, Luis Torres, Jose Luis Ruiz,
Antonio Reyes; A POLITICAL RENAISSANCE from
the LA RAZA series (TV) by Moctezuma
Esparza; CHILDREN OF THE STATE by Andres
Markovits, Richard Trubo, Frank Christopher
(film); LA RAZA UNIDA (released as RAICES DE
SANGRE) by Jesus Salvador Trevino (Mexican
film by a Chicano); CHULAS FRONTERAS (film)
by Les Blank; THE MURALS OF EAST LOS
ANGELES, A MUSEUM WITHOUT WALLS by Humberto
R. Rivera and Heather R. Howell.
Announcement for the National Latino Media
Coalition.

Torres, Salvador Roberto

8578 Burkhardt, Dorothy. Chicano pride and anger
     mix at 'Califas'. THE TAB, (April 12,
     1981), p. 34. English.

     AN: CALIFAS: AN EXHIBITION OF CHICANO
     ARTISTS IN CALIFORNIA represents a
     cross-section of artists exhibiting work for
     at least ten years: Rupert Garcia, Ernie
     Palomino, Eduardo Carrillo, Judy Baca, Rene
     Yanez, Carmen Lomas Garza, Salvador Roberto
     Torres, Roberto Chavez, Willie Herron, Ralph
     Maradiaga, Sue Martinez, Jose Montoya,
     Malaquias Montoya, Ramses Noriega and
     Esteban Villa. Illustrated.

8579 Herrera, Barbara. Bisected barrio seeks new
     unity: Chicano part bridges past and future.
     EVENING TRIBUNE, (August 7, 1974), p. E-1.
     English.

     AN: Bisected by the Coronado bridge,
     remains of the Logan barrio are unified by
     Chicano Park and its murals recording
     Chicano culture. Inspired by Salvador
     Torres, who returned to Logan in 1967,
     barrio activists are working to restore
     community spirit and dignity. Illustrated.

8580 Invitational art exhibition/exposicion
     artistas invitados. Exhibition invitation,
     [ca. 1976]. English.

     AN: A benefit night for the Chicano
     Health Clinic included an exhibit of San
     Diego, as well as Ensenada, Mexicali and
     Tijuana (Mexico) artists. San Diego Latino
     artists include Peruvians Guillermo Acevedo
     and Mario Acevedo Torero, Chicano Salvador
     Roberto Torres, and Mexican-born Raul Trejo.

8581 Murphy, Patricia Lee. Artists renew Toltecas
     crafts heritage. LOS ANGELES TIMES, (May
     23, 1971), p. E, 10. English.

     AN: The Toltecas en Aztlan, creative arm
     of the Chicano Federation of San Diego
     County, Inc., will shortly move into their
     new Centro Cultural de la Raza in Balboa
     Park, San Diego. The group includes Mario
     Acevedo (Peruvian), Guillermo Aranda, Tomas
     Castaneda, Victor Ochoa and Salvador Torres
     (visual artists) and poet Alurista.

Torres, Salvador Roberto (cont.)

8582 Rangel, Jesus. Heirs of Jose Posada: revolution lives in Chicano art. SAN DIEGO UNION, (February 24, 1980), p. D6. English.

AN: 19th century Mexican engraver Jose Guadalupe Posada has been an inspiration to Chicano artists. Along with two exhibits of his work, the Centro Cultural de la Raza is also showing calavera (skeleton) images by Chicano artists: skull-masks from the Teatro Campesino, a print by Amalia Mesa-Baines of Frida Kahlo, and a collaged box by Jose Antonio Burciaga. Illustration: Salvador Roberto Torres work.

8583 Street, Sharon. Califas - a celebration of Chicano culture and art. CITY ON A HILL, (April 16, 1981). English.

AN: Review of an exhibit at College V's Sesnon Gallery featuring 15 California artists: Ramses Noriega, Judy Baca, Salvador Roberto Torres, Malaquias Montoya, Rene Yanez, Ralph Maradiaga, Jose Montoya, Esteban Villa, Carmen Lomas Garza, Robert Chavez, among others. Illustrated.

8584 Torres, Salvador Roberto. Arte de la Raza [portfolio]. DE COLORES, Vol. 1, no. 1 (Winter 1973), p. 34-43. Bilingual.

AN: A portfolio consisting of four drawings representing the "progression" of the symbol of the banner adopted by the United Farm Workers (UFW). Included are four out of six drawings, each with its own explication in English and Spanish, and brief biographical data about the artist.

8585 Torres, Salvador Roberto. Creative aspects of la Raza inspired by Chicano experiences. Unpublished thesis, 1973. Bilingual.

AN: Project presents six paintings and six drawings by San Diego artist Torres based on the feeling and impact of United Farm Workers Huelga banner, used on a personal level. Torres wants to make an "imaginary theatre" of the ideas drawn from the Chicano movement. Bilingual. Illustrated.

Torres, Tomas

8586 Galeria de arte de Aztlan. AZTLAN (U.S. Penitentiary, Leavenworth, KA), Vol. 1, no. 2. English.

AN: Pictorial supplement with reproductions of pinto art by Manuel Aguilera, Jessie Hernandez, Ruben Estrella, Tomas Torres and Jose D. Marin. Many of these works were reproduced in other Chicano newspapers demonstrating the solidarity that existed in the Chicano movement inside and outside the prison walls.

8587 Rodriguez, Pedro. Chicano art arising. PAPEL CHICANO, Vol. 1, no. 9 (December 21, 1971), p. 5. English.

AN: A concise formulation on the nature of Chicano Art. It arises from a new cultural formation influenced by Mexican and Anglo American cultural forms yet distinct from either. In visual terms, artists are reflecting and affirming this new cultural synthesis. Illustrated with reproductions of three oil paintings: GRITO DE LIBERTAD by Jose D. Marin, WOMAN IN BLUE by Manuel Aguilera, and ALEGORIA MEXICANA by Tomas Torres. All three are pinto artists from Leavenworth Penitentiary.

Tortuga Patrol [art group], Watsonville, CA

8588 Gilroy's public art form. THE VALLEY WORLD, (July 19, 1978). English.

AN: Article cites activities of "The Tortuga Patrol" a Chicano muralist group from the Watsonville California area.

Tostado, Carmen

8589 Art Gallery, California State University, Long Beach and Lujan, Gilbert Sanchez "Magu". El arte del pocho. Exhibit brochure, October 1968. English.

AN: Information about Southern California artists John Deheras, Marcus Villagran, Roberto de la Rocha, Santos Zuniga, Crispin Gonzales, Richard Martinez, Jesus Gutierrez, Ed Oropeza, Pete Mendez, David Ramirez, Gilbert Sanchez Lujan, Willie Hernandez, Art Ponce, Carmen Tostado, Al Almeida, David Ceja, Robert E. Chavez, Thomas A. Ferriera. All art students, graduates, or faculty.

TOWARDS A HUMANITARIAN TECHNOLOGY FOR LA RAZA [mural]

8590 Los murales del pueblo. PAPEL CHICANO, Vol. 2, no. 12 (February 1973), p. 1+. Spanish.

AN: Analysis of Leo Tanguma's work as "an expression not only of artistic creative opinion but also of the suppressed and accumulated feeling of La Raza in the United States." Includes thematic and stylistic information on four murals in the Houston barrio: "The Rebirth of Our Nationality," "Towards a Humanitarian Technology for La Raza," "Historia de la Raza," and "El Mestizo Chicano".

TRABAJO COLECTIVO DE EDUARDO DOMINGUEZ

8591 Diaz, Jean; Dominguez, Edward; and Torres, Kay. Bi-Lingual blues [fotonovela]. SOMOS, Vol. 1, no. 1 (April, May, 1978), p. 33-36. English.

AN: Reproduction of a "fotonovela", BI-LINGUAL BLUES by Ojo Productions, a group of students connected with the Latin American Studies Department of California State University, Los Angeles.

Trejo, Raul

8592 Invitational art exhibition/exposicion artistas invitados. Exhibition invitation, [ca. 1976]. English.

AN: A benefit night for the Chicano Health Clinic included an exhibit of San Diego, as well as Ensenada, Mexicali and Tijuana (Mexico) artists. San Diego Latino artists include Peruvians Guillermo Acevedo and Mario Acevedo Torero, Chicano Salvador Roberto Torres, and Mexican-born Raul Trejo.

Trejo, Ruben

8593 Coffman Gallery I, The University of
Minnesota, Minneapolis, MN. Ruben Trejo:
visiting Chicano artist. Exhibition
brochure, 1981. English.

AN: Exhibition brochure of a sculpture
show by Ruben Trejo presented from April 25
to May 6. Trejo's sculptures are created
from laminated wood, metal and plastic.
Dominant motifs in this exhibit were the
skull, the pepper and the heart. Brochure
includes biographical information, checklist
of the 28 works exhibited and one black and
white photograph.

8594 Galeria de la Raza/Studio 24, San Francisco,
CA. Ajo, granadas y tres flores. Exhibition
announcement, 1981.

AN: Announcement for an exhibition
featuring Ruben Trejo, sculpture (Spokane,
Washington), Cesar A. Martinez, paintings
(San Antonio, Texas), Xavier Gorena, paper
cut-outs (Mission, Texas).

8595 Washington State University, Pullman. Fine
Arts Center Gallery II. Ruben M. Trejo-mi
ultimo fracaso. Exhibition announcement,
1976. English.

AN: Exhibit announcement for Trejo's
show of sculpture and drawings. Illustrated
with a Trejo "jalapeno" sculpture.

LAS TRES AGUILAS [mural]

8596 Transcendente y majestuoso mural de las tres
aguilas. EL HISPANO, Vol. 8, no. 4 (July 15,
1975), p. 6. Spanish.

AN: Biographical data on Juan Ishi
Orozco and commentary on his mural "Las Tres
Aguilas." One eagle represents mother earth,
another the dominant racist system and the
third is symbolic of the United Farmworkers
and their struggle.

Trevino, Jesse

8597 Instituto Cultural Mexicano (SER/UNAM), San
Antonio, TX. Jesse Trevino's one man
exhibit. San Antonio, TX: Instituto Cultural
Mexicano, 1981. Bilingual.

AN: Bilingual statement on the work of
Jesse Trevino; biography and list of
selected exhibitions; quotations from
several publications about his work.

Trevino, Jesus C. (Jesse)

8598 The affectionate realism of Jesse Trevino.
SA: THE MAGAZINE OF SAN ANTONIO, Vol. 3, no.
10 (December 1979), p. 70-73. English.

AN: Brief story about, and personal
statement by San Antonio photorealist
painter and muralist. Trevino focuses on
portraits of people and sites in the
Westside barrio. Color illustrations.

8599 Con Safo. San Antonio, TX: Pintores Chicanos
de San Antonio, [ca. 1975]. English.

AN: Illustrated pamphlet issued by the
San Antonio artists' group Con Safo.
Includes a self-definition and a brief
history of the group under the names El
Grupo, Los Pintores de Aztlan, Los Pintores
de la Nueva Raza, Con Safo (from 1967 on).
Members include Jesse A. Almazan, Mel Casas,
Jose Esquivel, Jose P. Garza, Cesar Augusto

Martinez, Santos Martinez, Felipe Reyes,
Roberto Rios, Jesus C. Trevino, and Vicente
Velasquez.

8600 Contemporary Arts Museum, Houston, TX. Dale
gas: give it gas. The continued
acceleration of Chicano art. Exhibition
catalog, 1977. English.

AN: A comprehensive catalog including 28
works of art exhibited by 13 Texas artists:
Melesio (Mel) Casas, Jose Esquivel,
Francisco (Frank) Fajardo, Carmen Lomas
Garza, Luis Jimenez, Cesar Augusto Martinez,
Santos G. Martinez, Jr., Amado Pena, Roberto
Rios, Jose Rivera, Joe B. Rodriguez, Jesus
(Jesse) Trevino, and George Truan. Many
illustrations, some in color. Introduction
by James Harithas. Essay by Santos Martinez,
Jr. Poetry, literature and essays by Chicano
writers.

8601 Contemporary Arts Museum, Houston, TX and
Martinez, Santos G., Jr. Mexican movie
posters. Exhibition invitation, 1979.
English.

AN: Invitation to an exhibit of posters
primarily from the collecttion of Enrique
Flores and Xavier Gorena of Xochil Art
Center, Mission, Texas. Martinez considers
the posters monumental, with expressive
qualities that have influenced Chicano
poster makers like the Royal Chicano Air
Force, and Rupert Garcia, and Texas artists
like Luis Jimenez, Jesse Trevino and Cesar
Martinez. One illustration. Introduction by
guest curator Santos G. Martinez, Jr. (See
Rupert Garcia's essay in the exhibition
catalog: POSTERS FROM THE GOLDEN AGE OF
MEXICAN CINEMA, for another point of view).

8602 Corpus Christy State University for the Arts
and Weil Gallery Center for the Arts, Corpus
Christi State University. Southwest artists
invitational: an exhibition of contemporary
art by seven Texas artists of Hispanic
American descent. Ehxibition brochure, 1980.
English.

AN: Artists Jesse Almazan, Luis Jimenez,
Cesar Martinez, Lydia Martinez, Manuel
Mauricio, Guillermo Pulido, and Jesse
Trevino show a variety of techniques and
styles. Text by Roberto Tomas Esparza.
Statements by and about the artists.
Illustrated.

8603 Crossley, Mimi. Tejano artists. HOUSTON
POST, (August 19, 1976). English.

AN: Exhibition of 19 Texas artists
organized by Joe Rodriguez of the AAMA
(Association for the Advancement of Mexican
Americans) Art Center in Houston, Texas.
Working within a wide range of styles and a
great scope of subject matter. Includes
brief commentary on the work of Amado Pena,
Carmen Lomas Garza, Cesar Martinez, Enrique
Campos, Carolina Flores, Jesus Trevino and a
host of others.

8604 Instituto Cultural Mexicano (SER/UNAM), San
Antonio, TX. Jesse Trevino's one man
exhibit. San Antonio, TX: Instituto Cultural
Mexicano, 1981. Bilingual.

AN: Bilingual statement on the work of
Jesse Trevino; biography and list of
selected exhibitions; quotations from
several publications about his work.

Trevino, Jesus C. (Jesse) (cont.)

8605 Ruiz, Elizabeth. Fiesta artist. THE RANGER, (April 23, 1981). English.

> **AN:** Biographical information on San Antonio painter Jesus Trevino. Artist describes his work as "realism" with "a focus on Mexican American and Chicano culture, the people and their lives".

8606 San Antonio Museum Association, San Antonio, TX. Real, really real, super real. Exhibition brochure, 1981. English.

> **AN:** Exhibit surveying modern and contemporary realism in the U.S. Includes a brief biography, personal statement, and color illustration of work by Jesse C. Trevino, San Antonio, Texas photorealist painter and muralist, (pp. 146-147).

8607 San Antonio Museum Association, San Antonio, TX. Visiones nuevas en Tejas/new visions in Texas. Exhibtion catalog, 1979. English.

> **AN:** Supplementary regional catalog for the exhibit RAICES ANTIGUAS/VISIONES NUEVAS; ANCIENT ROOTS/NEW VISIONS. Illustrations for works by George Cisneros, Francisco (Frank) Fajardo, Robert Gonzalez, Cesar Augusto Martinez, Roland Mazuca, Guillermo Pulido, Felipe Reyes, Jesus (Jesse) Trevino.

8608 Smith, Roberta. Twelve days of Texas. ART IN AMERICA, Vol. 64, no. 4 (July, August, 1976), p. 42-48. English.

> **AN:** Overview of Texas art in Fort Worth/Dallas, Houston, San Antonio, Tyler, and Galveston. Includes reproductions of works by Luis Jimenez (color, on cover), Roberto Rios mural, Jesse Trevino, Mel Casas. Also mentioned in text are Phil Renteria and Cesar Martinez.

8609 Stephens, Martha. Murals introduce Carlos Castaneda to Neil Armstrong. SAN ANTONIO EXPRESS-NEWS, (January 11, 1981), p. M, 1, 3. English.

> **AN:** Survey of commissioned murals in San Antonio including Mexican artist Juan O'Gorman's mosaic at the Theatre for Performing Arts; Carlos Merida's and Fred Samuelson's at the Convention Center; Howard Cook's New Deal mural in the downtown post-office; Peter Hurd's, and James Sicner's (in progress) mural at Trinity University; Jesse "Chista" Cantu's at Mario's Restaurant; and Jesse Trevino's mural at Our Lady of the Lake University. Illustrated.

8610 Trafford, Al. The giant painted photo album: Jesse Trevino. SOUTHWEST ART, (April 1979). English.

> **AN:** Well illustrated story on San Antonio photorealist painter Jesse Trevino. Includes biographical material, description of his working methods for murals and easel paintings, and self-characterization of his work as "cultural documentary painting".

8611 Xochil Art and Culture Center, Mission, TX. ¡Que te vaya pretty nice! Exhibition brochure, 1979. English.

> **AN:** Exhibition of Chicano art including Carmen Lomas Garza, Luis Jimenez, Cesar Martinez, Guillermo Pulido, Roberto Rios, Jose Rivera and Jesse Trevino. [See also Estudios Rio].

Trevino, Jesus Salvador

8612 Camplis, Francisco X. Towards the development of a Raza cinema. TIN TAN, Vol. 2, no. 5 (June 1, 1977), p. 5-7. English.

> **AN:** Chicanos and other minorities remain invisible to white America, an expression of neo-colonialism. Camplis defines "Chicano" and "Raza" as terms, and states there are few, if any, full-length feature films available. Without role models, Chicano/Raza filmmakers can learn from contemporary revolutionary Latin American filmmakers, be familiar with European and Hollywood films, though the latter are alien models. Camplis suggests directions for Chicano films, and reviews films by Jesus Trevino, Jose Camacho, and Luis Valdez.

8613 Cine chicano: primer acercamiento. COMUNIDAD, no. 20 (November 16, 1980), p. 1-15. Spanish.

> **AN:** The entire cultural supplement of LA OPINION is dedicated to Chicano film. Includes articles by Jason Johansen, Jeff Penichet, Harry Gamboa, Jr., Jesus Salvador Trevino, Carlos Penichet, Sylvia Morales, Julio Moran, and Jose Luis Borau. Also includes a declaration of purpose by the Asociacion Chicana de Cineastas, and a filmography of Chicano cinema compiled by Trevino.

8614 Cinefestival. ARRIBA, [n.d.], p. 5. English.

> **AN:** Announcement of the 6th Annual International Hispanic Film Festival in San Antonio, TX. Willie Varela will conduct a workshop, and Jesus Trevino will premiere his hour-long production, SEGUIN.

8615 Gamboa, Harry, Jr. Film, television, and Trevino. LA LUZ, Vol. 6, no. 10 (October 1977), p. 7-8. English.

> **AN:** Jesus Salvador Trevino has been an active proponent and participant in transforming cultural inaccuracy about Chicanos in the media to accurate mass media models. A biography of Trevino follows, including discussion of some of his films: THE SALAZAR INQUEST, CHICANO MORATORIUM AFTERMATH, SOLEDAD, AMERICA TROPICAL, YO SOY CHICANO, RAICES DE SANGRE, as well as television series like ACCION CHICANO, AHORA, and INFINITY FACTORY.

8616 Gloria, Juan J. En San Antonio: se celebrara el tercer festival de cine, 'La vida chicana a traves del celuloide'. EL VISITANTE DOMINICAL, (August 20, 1978), p. 6-8, 12. Spanish.

> **AN:** The Third Chicano Film Festival honors the only two feature-length films made by Chicanos: Moctezuma Esparza's ONLY ONCE IN A LIFETIME (made in Hollywood) and Jesus Salvador Trevino's RAICES DE SANGRE (Blood Roots), (made with CONACINE in Mexico). Illustrated.

Trevino, Jesus Salvador (cont.)

8617 Kleinhaus, Chuck; Seiter, Ellen; and Steven, Peter. Conference report: struggling for unity. JUMP CUT, no. 21 (November 1979), p. 35-37. English.

AN: Report and critique of the U.S. Conference for an Alternative Cinema held in mid-June 1979 at Bard College in New York state to chart a course for independent filmmakers. Chicano, Black, Asian and Puerto Rican film people attended, including Jesus Salvador Trevino and Sylvia Morales from the Chicano Cinema Coalition of Los Angeles.

8618 Knapp, Dan. KCET's show for Chicano viewers. LOS ANGELES TIMES, (April 3, 1970), p. IV, 18. English.

AN: Story on the television series AHORA! started September 1969 on KCET, Los Angeles' National Educational Television. Edward Moreno is program director and host; Victor Millan is producer-director; Claudio Fenner-Lopez, senior producer, has staff including set-designer David Villasenor, production manager James Val, and alternate host-narrator Jesus Trevino. The program has shown exhibits of artists Gilberto Lujan and Daniel Ramirez.

8619 Lopez Oliva, Manuel. Proyeccion chicana en RAICES DE SANGRE. CINE CUBANO, (1981), p. 75-80. Spanish.

AN: A Latin American view of Jesus Salvador Trevino's 1976 film RAICES DE SANGRE, particularly its concern with the exploitation by U.S. multinationals of Mexicans and Chicanos on both sides of the border. The author notes Trevino's tendency to relate Chicano culture and problems to continental and world problems of workers. Illustrated.

8620 Peyton, Patricia, ed. Reel change: a guide to social issue films. San Francisco, CA: Film Fund, 1979. English.

AN: Includes a section on Hispanic film with descriptions, sources, and rentals. Listed are Esperanza Vasquez's AGUEDA MARTINEZ, Sylvia Morales' CHICANA, Adolfo Vargas' CONSUELO: QUIENES SOMOS?/WHO ARE WE?, El Teatro Campesino's I AM JOAQUIN, Jose Luis Ruiz's THE UNWANTED, Jesus Salvador Trevino's YO SOY CHICANO, and others. Listings are international in scope.

8621 Poster, Corky. Cuba welcomes Latin film festival. GUARDIAN, (January 16, 1980), p. 21. English.

AN: Report on the First International Festival of New Latin American Cinema held in Havana December 3-10, 1979. The Festival focused on emerging cinema of Latin America, especially of Nicaraguans and Chicanos. Festival organizers hoped to "internationalize" the Chicano struggle by encouraging it toward a Latin American political perspective and moving it from a limited "la raza" view to one of class analysis and solidarity. Jesus Trevino's film RAICES DE SANGRE was shown.

8622 Reyes, Luis. Seguin: traidor o heroe. COMUNIDAD, (April 12, 1981), p. 8-9. Spanish.

AN: Report on the pilot film for an eight-part series called LA HISTORIA made by Jesus Trevino for the Public Broadcasting Service. The pilot treats the life of an "anti-hero," Juan Seguin, during the Texas war for independence from Mexico, and relates the little-known history of the Mexican defenders of the Alamo. Trevino chose this controversial subject because it exemplified an early case of the dual nature of bilingualism and biculturalism. Description of the research and filming of the pilot. Illustrated.

8623 Semana de la Raza: international panel of the arts, Mexico and the United States. Santa Ana, CA: MEChA, Santa Ana College, 1972. English.

AN: An International Panel of the Arts, organized by art historian Shifra Goldman, featured Mexicans Hector Garcia, prize-winning photographer; Jaime Mejia, painter, restorer, filmmaker; Alejandro Vichir, director of Teatro Trashumante; and Chicanos Gilbert Sanchez Lujan, sculptor and painter; Gloria Osuna, painter and artist for Teatro Campesino; and Jesus Salvador Trevino, filmmaker.

8624 Smith, Cecil. YO SOY captures the Chicano soul. LOS ANGELES TIMES, (August 17, 1972), p. IV, 20. English.

AN: Trevino's films YO SOY CHICANO and AMERICA TROPICAL shown on KCET.

8625 Torres, Louis R. An innovation in children's t.v.: THE INFINITY FACTORY. LA LUZ, Vol. 6, no. 2 (February 1977), p. 10-11. English.

AN: Illustrated report on a new television series for children aimed at teaching mathematics fundamentals in a crisply-paced series of half-hour programs. The executive producer, Jesus Salvador Trevino, filmed the segments in a New York Black community, and in the East Los Angeles Chicano barrio. In one segment, muralist Willie Herron works with youngsters to design and paint an outdoor mural.

8626 Torres, Louis R. RAICES DE SANGRE: first full length film directed by a Chicano. SOMOS, Vol. 1, no. 2 (July 1978), p. 16-19. English.

AN: Report on Jesus Salvador Trevino's RAICES DE SANGRE, the only film made by a Chicano at the Mexican film studio, CONACINE. Deals with the efforts of Chicanos and Mexicans living in border cities to organize an international labor union. Trevino's previous work is briefly mentioned. Illustrated.

8627 Trevino, Jesus Salvador. America tropical. (1971). English.

AN: Half-hour 16mm color film produced and written by Jesus Salvador Trevino and directed by Barry Nye about the painting and whitewashing in 1932-34 of Mexican muralist David Alfaro Siqueiros' mural AMERICA TROPICAL in Olvera Street, Los Angeles. Traces the attempts at restoration of the mural starting in the late 1960s and continuing in the 1970s. History of the mural set within social/political context of Mexican Americans in the 1930s, and counterpart struggles of Chicanos in the 1970s.

Trevino, Jesus Salvador (cont.)

8628 Zheutlin, Barbara and Talbot, David. Jesus
     Salvador Trevino. In: CREATIVE DIFFERENCES:
     PROFILES OF HOLLYWOOD DISSIDENTS. Boston,
     MS: South End Press, 1978, p. 345-352.
     English.

     AN: Within the context of New Left
     alternative filmmakers who chose to work
     within Hollywood, Trevino sets forth his
     standards and goals. His films and TV
     productions include SOLEDAD (1971), AMERICA
     TROPICAL (1971), YO SOY CHICANO (1972),
     RAICES DE SANGRE (1977) and INFINITY FACTORY
     (1975-1976).

Trevino, Jose

8629 Aguirre, Tito. Interview with artist Jose
     Trevino. ARRIBA, Vol. 2, no. 2 (1981).
     English.

     AN: Biographical information and
     artistic trajectory of Austin artist Jose
     Trevino. Illustrated with photo of artist
     and three of his portraits.

8630 Flores, Jose. Peregrino [drawing]. In MESQUI
     + TIERRA. Albuquerque, NM: Pajarito
     Publications, 1977. English.

     AN: Drawings by Jose F. Trevino of
     Austin, Texas.

8631 Galeria de la Raza, San Antonio, TX.
     Celebration seventy-four. Exhibition
     catalog, [ca. 1974]. English.

     AN: Catalog of extensive exhibition
     including European, Mexican, and the
     following Texan Chicano artists: Rolando
     Garces, Cesar Martinez, Ray Chavez, Vicente
     Rodriguez, Jorge Garza, Alfred Rodriguez,
     Luis Guerra, Carmen Lomas Garza, Bruno
     Andrade, Jr., Amado M. Pena Jr., Roberto
     Rios, Jose Trevino, Rudy Trevino, Luis
     Santoyo, Tati Rubio, Eduardo C. Garza,
     Arthur de la Fuente, and Jesus Campos
     Trevino.

8632 Instituto Chicano de Artes y Artesanias
     (Texas Instit. Educational Development) and
     Instituto Cultural Mexicano (SER/UNAM), San
     Antonio, TX. Artistas chicanos: Los
     Quemados. San Antonio, TX: Instituto
     Chicano, Texas Institute for Educational
     Development, 1975. English.

     AN: Invitation to an exhibit and
     manifesto of 1975 Austin-San Antonio
     artists' group, Los Quemados. Included Santa
     Barraza, Carolina Flores, Carmen Lomas
     Garza, Luis Guerra, Cesar Augusto Martinez,
     Santos Martinez, Amado Maurilio Pena, Jr.,
     Jose Rivera, Vicente Rodriguez, Jose
     Trevino.

8633 Orozco, Sylvia and Trevino, Jose. Trevino's
     arte interprets el mundo Chicano. PARA LA
     GENTE, Vol. 1, no. 10 (May 1978), p. 7-9.
     English.

     AN: Interview with Jose Trevino of
     Austin and his artist wife, Modesta.
     Reproduction and discussion of four works.
     Centerspread reproduction of a Trevino
     poster, part of a set of 10 designed for
     bilingual classrooms.

Trevino, Modesta Barbina

8634 Goldman, Shifra M. Women artists of Texas:
     MAS = More + Artists + Women = MAS.

CHISMEARTE, no. 7 (January 1981), p. 21-22.
English.

     AN: History of Texas Chicana women
     artists' organization, Mujeres Artistas del
     Suroeste (MAS), co-founded in 1977 by Santa
     Barraza and Nora Gonzalez-Dodson in the
     framework of the burgeoning feminist art
     movement, particularly Women and Their Work
     of Texas. Brief history of Chicano politics
     and the corresponding art movement of
     southern and central Texas. In addition to
     Barraza and Gonzalez-Dodson, Alicia
     Arredondo, Modesta Trevino, and Maria Flores
     are considered. Illustrated.

8635 Orozco, Irma. Women & their work. PARA LA
     GENTE, Vol. 1, no. 4 (October 1977), p. 12.
     English.

     AN: Illustrated story about "Women &
     Their Work" festival in Austin, Texas,
     Oct-Dec 1977. Photographers Maria Flores and
     Teresina Guerra, Santa Barraza, Nora
     Gonzalez Dodson, Sylvia Orozco, and Modesta
     Trevino exhibited.

8636 Orozco, Sylvia. Las mujeres - Chicana
     artists come into their own. MOVING ON, Vol.
     2, no. 3 (May 1978), p. 14-16. English.

     AN: Illustrated feature prepared by
     artist Sylvia Orozco on the founding of
     Mujeres Artistas del Suroeste in Austin,
     September 1977. Artworks and statements by
     Nora Gonzalez Dodson, Maria Flores, Modesta
     Trevino, Santa Barraza, as well as musicians
     and singers.

8637 Orozco, Sylvia and Trevino, Jose. Trevino's
     arte interprets el mundo Chicano. PARA LA
     GENTE, Vol. 1, no. 10 (May 1978), p. 7-9.
     English.

     AN: Interview with Jose Trevino of
     Austin and his artist wife, Modesta.
     Reproduction and discussion of four works.
     Centerspread reproduction of a Trevino
     poster, part of a set of 10 designed for
     bilingual classrooms.

8638 Xochil Art and Culture Center, Mission, TX.
     Besame mucho. Exhibition invitation, 1979.
     English.

     AN: Invitation to exhibit of Texas
     artists from Mujeres Artistas del Suroeste
     (MAS): Mary Ann Anguiano, Alicia Arredondo,
     Santa Barraza, Nora Gonzales-Dodson, Maria
     Flores, Carolina Flores, Mary Ann Ambray
     Gonzales, Sylvia Orozco, Nancy de los
     Santos, Modesta Barbina Trevino.
     Illustrated.

Trevino, Rudy R.

8639 Bloomfield, Arthur. Zesty show at Mexican
     museum. SAN FRANCISCO EXAMINER, (February
     1, 1977), p. 24. English.

     AN: Review of an exhibit of Mexican and
     Mexican American artists from the Southwest
     and the San Francisco area. Commentary and
     analysis on artists Vincent Perez and
     Gustavo Rivera, Rudy Trevino and Al Barela.
     The work selected focused on aesthetic
     quality rather than the ethnic
     identification of the artist.

Trevino, Rudy R (cont.)

8640 Con safo to hold Lutheran college exhibition
at Texas. CHICANO TIMES, Vol. 7, no. 89
(March 26, 1976), p. [15]. English.

AN: Discusses the aims of "Con Safos"
group: to interpret their environment and
react to it; to act as spokespeople and give
visual reality to the Chicano vision; to
destroy stereotypes and demolish visual
cliches. The participating artists include
Rudy R. Trevino, Mel Casas, Lucas Hinojosa,
Kathy Vargas, Joe Frank Acosta, Emilio
Aguirre and Homero Ureste.

8641 Galeria de la Raza, San Antonio, TX.
Celebration seventy-four. Exhibition
catalog, [ca. 1974]. English.

AN: Catalog of extensive exhibition
including European, Mexican, and the
following Texan Chicano artists: Rolando
Garces, Cesar Martinez, Ray Chavez, Vicente
Rodriguez, Jorge Garza, Alfred Rodriguez,
Luis Guerra, Carmen Lomas Garza, Bruno
Andrade, Jr., Amado M. Pena Jr., Roberto
Rios, Jose Trevino, Rudy Trevino, Luis
Santoyo, Tati Rubio, Eduardo C. Garza,
Arthur de la Fuente, and Jesus Campos
Trevino.

8642 Mendiville, Miguel and Saavedra-Vela, Pilar.
A time for less talk and more action.
AGENDA, Vol. 7, no. 5 (September, October,
1977), p. 33-34. English.

AN: The exhibit RAICES Y VISIONES,
funded by the National Endowment for the
Arts, was composed of more than 100 artworks
by Chicano and Latino artists and toured the
United States in 1977. The exposition was
organized in four sections; artists whose
work is influenced or related to
Pre-Columbian art, art that explores social
and political realities, and works that are
more personal and introspective. Gives
itinerary and listing of participating
artists. Illustrated by photographs of the
work of Rudy Trevino, Cesar Martinez, Luis
Jimenez from Texas and Larry Fuente from
California.

8643 Minutaglio, Bill. Chicano take the art to
the street of S.A. SAN ANTONIO EXPRESS-NEWS,
(January 11, 1981), p. M, 1-2. English.

AN: Survey of Chicano murals in San
Antonio including 30 two-story murals at
Westside Cassiano Homes by students from the
commercial art program of Lanier High
directed by Anastacio "Tache" Torres and
Rudy Trevino; 8 murals at Lanier High
School; one at the City Hall offices; and
others throughout the city. Illustrated.

8644 S.A. site for National Symposium on Mexican
American Art. CHICANO TIMES, Vol. 4, no. 30
(November 9, 1973), p. 5. English.

AN: Held at Trinity University, the
Symposium discussed such issues as, creative
evolution, art education, artistic
relationships to Mexico and the evolution of
Mexican American art in the California
barrios. Participating artists included Rudy
Trevino, Mel Casas, Octavio Medellin,
Antonio Garcia, Carmen Garza, Esteban Villa,
Jose Montoya, Ernesto Palomino, Michael
Ponce de Leon, Luis Jimenez and Eugenio
Quesada.

**Tri-Centennial Commission of the All-Indian Pueblo
Council**

8645 Anaya, Rudolfo A. and Ortiz, Simon J.
1680-1980: a ceremony of brotherhood.
Albuquerque, NM: Academic, 1981. English.

AN: A cooperative publication by members
of the former La Academia de la Nueva Raza
(1969-1976) formed of writers and artists,
and the Tri-Centennial Commission of the
All-Indian Pueblo Council. Includes writings
and artworks by Chicanos and Indians from
New Mexico, California, Texas, and Arizona.
Chicano artists works included are by Ellen
Arellano, Juan Estevan Arellano, Alberto
Baros, Jose Antonio Burciaga, Juan Reyes
Cervantes, Rudy Cuellar, Ricardo Favela, El
Zarco Guerrero, Luis Jimenez, Jr., Carlos
Quinto Kemm, Alejandro Lopez, Floyd Lujan,
Jose Montoya, Juanishi Orozco, Leo Romero,
Secundino Sandoval, Jaime Valdez, Maria
Varela, Esteban Villa.

TRILOGY [sculpture]

8646 Garza, Alex. Entrevista con Alex Garza.
ABRAZO, Vol. 1, no. 2 (Summer 1979), p.
27-29. English.

AN: Brief article exploring Alex Garza's
technique, philosophy, and setting for his
sculptural work. The artist expresses his
desire to see artists break with tradition
and not allow the political rhetoric of the
early Chicano Movement to promote
stagnation. His connection to the art
organization ALBA is also briefly mentioned.

Truan, George

8647 Contemporary Arts Museum, Houston, TX. Dale
gas: give it gas. The continued
acceleration of Chicano art. Exhibition
catalog, 1977. English.

AN: A comprehensive catalog including 28
works of art exhibited by 13 Texas artists:
Melesio (Mel) Casas, Jose Esquivel,
Francisco (Frank) Fajardo, Carmen Lomas
Garza, Luis Jimenez, Cesar Augusto Martinez,
Santos G. Martinez, Jr., Amado Pena, Roberto
Rios, Jose Rivera, Joe B. Rodriguez, Jesus
(Jesse) Trevino, and George Truan. Many
illustrations, some in color. Introduction
by James Harithas. Essay by Santos Martinez,
Jr. Poetry, literature and essays by Chicano
writers.

8648 Contemporary Arts Museum, Houston, TX. Fire!
An exhibition of 100 Texas artists.
Exhibition brochure, 1979. English.

AN: Includes eleven Chicano artists.
Unfortunately, not illustrated, though a
checklist of works is included. Mel Casas,
Carmen Lomas Garza, Xavier Gorena, Luis
Jimenez, Cesar Martinez, Guillermo Z.
Pulido, Philip Renteria, Jose L. Rivera, Joe
Rodriguez, George Truan, Juan B. Vela.
Introduction by James Surls. Statements by
the artists.

Truan, George (cont.)

8649 De Marroquin, Moron. Denver Harbor artists.
LA PRENSA, (June 2, 1978). Spanish.

AN: Commentary on two exhibitions. THE
DENVER HARBOR ARTISTS includes information
on paintings by Lupe Aguirre, Josie Mendoza
and Abel Gonzalez--all from Houston. The
solo show MAGIC BLANCA featured the work of
Brownsville, Texas artist Jorge Truan.
Truan's work is mystical and visionary.

Trujillo, Arnold

8650 Galeria de la Raza/Studio 24, San Francisco,
CA. Images of the Southwest. Exhibition
catalog, 1977. English.

AN: Invitation/catalog for an exhibit
including Rudy M. Fernandez(Utah), Enrique
Flores(Texas), Xavier Gorena(Texas),
C.A.[Cesar] Martinez(Texas), Santos
Martinez, Jr.(Texas), Pedro
Rodriguez(Texas), Arnold Trujillo(New
Mexico). Block prints, paper cut-outs,
drawings, photographs, copper enamels, and
sculpture were shown. Five illustrations.

Tucson, AZ

8651 Ariav, Al. Hispanics' work ignored, artist
says. ARIZONA DAILY STAR, (June 3, 1978).
English.

AN: Hispanic-Americans in Tucson have no
gallery, little access to museums, and no
recognition for their work, says Roberto
Borboa, artist and cultural organizer. He
welcomes the National Task Force of Hispanic
American art which visited Tucson.

8652 Art outdoors. CONCEPT, (September 1980).
English.

AN: Illustrated article on outdoor
murals in Tucson by Antonio Pazos and David
Tineo.

8653 Hanson, Matt. Barren walls toned into bold
works of art. ARIZONA DAILY STAR, (May 24,
1979). English.

AN: Tucson high school students under
direction of Antonio Pazos paint murals with
a $10,000 grant from the Law Enforcement
Assistance Administration. Color
illustrations.

8654 Huge mural displayed at El Con Shopping
Center. ARIZONA DAILY STAR, (January 31,
1979). English.

AN: A 15 x 50 foot mural called The
Creation of Cultures, a latex-enamel on
panels, was painted by Tucson muralist
Roberto Borboa. Its final site has not been
determined. Illustrated.

8655 Karam, Bruce G. The murals of Tucson.
NUESTRO, Vol. 5, no. 8 (November 1981), p.
58-60. English.

AN: Themes of ethnic pride, cultural
unity and cooperation define the murals of
Tucson. Brief commentary on the relationship
of artists and the community. Illustrated
with color photographs.

8656 Negri, Sam. Garden grows as shrine to
sculptor. ARIZONA REPUBLIC, (April 5,
1980), p. C-1. English.

AN: Felix Lucero, a self-taught

Colorado-born sculptor who came to Tucson in
1938, spent 20 years sculpting religious
statues. He started the Garden of Gethsemane
in 1945 on the Congress Street bridge.

8657 New name, new face. TUCSON CITIZEN, OLD
PUEBLO SECTION, (December 6, 1979), p. 6.
English.

AN: Tucson muralist Roberto Borboa works
on a mural EDUCATION at the Edward L.
Lindsay Adult learning Center. Illustrated.

8658 Salas, Joanne. Mural painting that comes
from the heart; 'impact' is the word for
muralist Luis Mena. TUCSON CITIZEN, OLD
PUEBLO SECTION, (June 25, 1981), p. 4-5.
English.

AN: Illustrated story on wall murals in
Tucson. Color.

8659 Silent protest. ARIZONA DAILY STAR, (May
18, 1978), p. 6-H. English.

AN: Outdoor murals in Tucson by Ausberto
Sandoval, Antonio Pazos and Sylvia de la
Huerta on a house in community being
displaced by urban renewal. Illustrated.

8660 Tang, Paul. Artist sustains proud Hispanic
mural tradition. ARIZONA DAILY
WILDCAT-ENCORE, (March 29, 1979), p. 1.
English.

AN: Born and educated in Hermosillo,
Sonora, Mexico, Antonio Pazos is painting
murals around Tucson. Pazos got his first
mural experience helping paint the Centro
Cultural de la Raza building in San Diego,
CA in the early 1970s. He also spent a
summer at Paolo Soleri's city north of
Phoenix, Arcosanti. Illustrated.

8661 Tucson Museum of Art and Pima Community
College, Tucson, AZ. Raices
antiguas/visiones nuevas; ancient roots/new
visions. Exhibition invitation, 1977.
English.

AN: Invitation to "Raices" exhibit of
Chicano and Latino artists living in the
United States originated by the Washington
D.C.-based Fondo del Sol and the concurrent
exhibit at Pima, "Art of the Barrio and
Political Art." Illustrated.

8662 Tucson Public Library; Sonoran Heritage; and
De la Cruz, Frank. Mexican American mural
art: the power of cultural identity.
Brochure, 1980. English.

AN: Brochure on Tucson murals painted by
Antonio Pazos, David Tineo, Danny Garza,
Cynthia Reyes, Darlene Marcos, Roberto
Borboa, and others.

8663 Turner, Mark. Muralist uses walls to break
barriers between people. ARIZONA DAILY STAR,
(July 23, 1981). English.

AN: Luis Gustavo Mena works on his
latest mural, an image of Benito Juarez with
the Mexican and "Latin Empire" flags, and a
scale of justice. Information about the
artist, son of an artistic family, and
recent high school graduate.

Tucson, AZ (cont.)

8664 Vigil, Maria. Art bridging culture gap.
TUCSON CITIZEN, OLD PUEBLO SECTION, (March
22, 1979). English.

AN: Students under tutelage of Antonio
Pazos paint a mural at the Perfection
Plumbing Co. in Tucson. Illustrated.

8665 Vigil, Maria. Hello, walls: Tucson's murals.
WEEKENDER MAGAZINE, (March 29, 1980), p.
14-16. English.

AN: Article on muralism, from the
Mexican to those of Chicanos. Focuses on
Tucson murals by Roberto Borboa, Antonio
Pazos, David Tineo and Fred Monreal. Color
illustrations.

Tujunga Wash Mural, Los Angeles, CA
USE: GREAT WALL OF LOS ANGELES [mural]

Turner, Juan

8666 Campesino Business and Joint Enterprise
Building, Fresno, CA. Sabor a Fresno. Arte
chicano: los Four and la Brocha. Exhibition
invitation [1976]. English.

AN: Invitation to an exhibit of works by
Los Four of Los Angeles and members of La
Brocha del Valle of Fresno: Arturo Roman,
Sal Garcia, John Sierra, Juan Turner, Sapo
de Aztlan, Fernando Hernandez, Alberto
Reyes, Ernesto Palomino, Lee Orona,
Francisco Barrios, Juan Ybarra, Bobby Reyes,
Alberto Hernandez. Brocha was started by
Palomino (California State University,
Fresno professor) to pool talents of Central
Valley artists.

TWENTY-EIGHTH SAN FRANCISCO ART FESTIVAL

8667 Portraying Latino women in the Mission. SAN
FRANCISCO EXAMINER, (September 10, 1974),
p. 26. English.

AN: Three muralists of the Mission
District, Irene Perez, Patricia Rodriguez,
and Venezuelan Consuelo Mendez, are
preparing a six-paneled
painting-construction, the RHOMBOIDAL
PARALLELOGRAM, for the 28th annual San
Francisco Art Festival. It will illustrate
the life of women in the Mission.
Illustrated.

Ulloa, Domingo

8668 Celebracion Chican-india. CAMINOS, Vol. 1,
no. 3 (May 1980), p. 38-39+. English.

AN: Portfolio of works exhibited at the
Galeria Capistrano in southern California:
Zarco Guerrero, Domingo Ulloa, Mario Torero,
Guillermo Acevedo. Judithe Hernandez, who
also exhibited, is not included in the
portfolio.

8669 Galeria Capistrano, San Juan Capistrano, CA.
Celebracion Chican-india 1980: Acevedo,
Hernandez, Torero, Ulloa, Zarco. Exhibition
brochure, 1980. English.

AN: Exhibition of Chicano artists
Judithe Hernandez, Domingo Ulloa, El Zarco
Guerrero, and Peruvian-born artists
Guillermo Acevedo and Mario Acevedo Torero.
Color illustration by Torero.

8670 Una galeria de artistas = A gallery of
artists. CAMINOS, Vol. 1, no. 6 (October
1980), p. 20-26. Bilingual.

AN: Features California artists Domingo
O. Ulloa (Imperial Valley images), Gloria
Chacon, photographer Maria Pinedo (San
Francisco), Willie Herron (Los Angeles),
Joaquin Patino (Delano), Pedro Pelayo (Long
Beach), sculptor Rudi Sigala (San Diego),
Mario Torero (San Diego), sculptor Michael
M. Amescua (Los Angeles), and the East Los
Streetscapers. Illustrated.

Undocumented Workers

8671 Nelson, Eugene. Pablo Cruz and the American
dream. Salt Lake City, UT: Peregrine Smith,
1975. English.

AN: A first-person account of a typical
"alambrista" (a wire jumper or undocumented
Mexican worker in the U.S.) compiled from
several accounts by the author. Illustrated
with 14 prints by Carlos Cortez, Chicago
artist, then the editor of THE INDUSTRIAL
WORKER.

8672 Ojo Production. Migra migraine. SOMOS, Vol.
1, no. 3 (August 1978), p. 40-1,49-50.
Bilingual.

AN: Reproduction of a fotonovela MIGRA
MIGRAINE produced by Ojo Productions, a
group of students with the Latin American
Studies Department at California State
University, Los Angeles.

8673 Rodriguez, Pedro. Fronteras falsas
[painting]. REVISTA CHICANO-RIQUENA, Vol. 8,
no. 3 (Summer 1980), p. 73. Bilingual.

8674 Vasquez, Richard. Mojado power: a boost for
illegal aliens. CALENDAR, (February 22,
1981), p. 41. English.

AN: An uncritical review of the
commercial film made by Mexican film star
and comedian Alfonso Arau in the United
States primarily for the "American-Hispanic"
market on a low-cost budget. Arau planned to
distribute in Mexico, Latin America and
Spain. The film is a light-weight comedy
about a "wetback" who launches a campaign
for "mojado power" but falls victim to dope
smugglers and is sent to jail.

Unidad de Kennedy, Mexico City [housing project]

8675 Mexican-American lawyers' club donates
Kennedy mural to the people of Mexico.
EASTSIDE SUN, (November 28, 1968). English.

AN: East Los Angeles artist Armando
Campero commissioned to paint mural for
"Unidad de Kennedy" housing development in
Mexico City.

UNIDOS PARA TRIUNFAR [mural]

8676 Sorell, Victor A. Barrio murals in Chicago:
painting the Hispanic-American experience on
"our community" walls. REVISTA
CHICANO-RIQUENA, Vol. 4, no. 4 (Fall
1976), p. 51-72. English.

AN: Important survey of Chicago's Latino
murals, with key works considered in detail.
Among the Chicano art organizations and
muralists mentioned are MARCH (Movimiento
Artistico Chicano), and Yolanda Galvan,
Juanita Jaramillo, Jose Nario, Raymond
Patlan, Vicente Mendoza, Marcos Raya,
Ricardo Alonzo, Jose G. Gonzalez and Mario
Castillo, author of the earliest Latino
mural in Chicago (1968). Puerto Rican and
non-Latino muralists and mural groups are
also discussed. Well illustrated.

United Farmworkers of America

8677 Almaraz, Carlos. The artist as a
revolutionary. CHISMEARTE, no. 1 (Fall
1976), p. 47-55. English.

AN: Los Angeles painter Carlos D.
Almaraz gives a detailed history of a
cartoon-banner he made for the first
constitutional convention of the United Farm
Workers of America while he was an
illustrator for EL MALCRIADO, and a mural he
did for the UFWA administration building in
La Paz. He also elucidates his philosophy
about politics, the role of the
revolutionary artist in our time, and the
artist's relation to the bourgeois art
market.

8678 Torres, Salvador Roberto. Arte de la Raza
[portfolio]. DE COLORES, Vol. 1, no. 1
(Winter 1973), p. 34-43. Bilingual.

AN: A portfolio consisting of four
drawings representing the "progression" of
the symbol of the banner adopted by the
United Farm Workers (UFW). Included are four
out of six drawings, each with its own
explication in English and Spanish, and
brief biographical data about the artist.

8679 Torres, Salvador Roberto. Creative aspects
of la Raza inspired by Chicano experiences.
Unpublished thesis, 1973. Bilingual.

AN: Project presents six paintings and
six drawings by San Diego artist Torres
based on the feeling and impact of United
Farm Workers Huelga banner, used on a
personal level. Torres wants to make an
"imaginary theatre" of the ideas drawn from
the Chicano movement. Bilingual.
Illustrated.

United States-Mexico Relations

8680 Lopez Oliva, Manuel. Proyeccion chicana en
RAICES DE SANGRE. CINE CUBANO, (1981), p.
75-80. Spanish.

AN: A Latin American view of Jesus
Salvador Trevino's 1976 film RAICES DE
SANGRE, particularly its concern with the
exploitation by U.S. multinationals of
Mexicans and Chicanos on both sides of the
border. The author notes Trevino's tendency
to relate Chicano culture and problems to
continental and world problems of workers.
Illustrated.

Universidad Nacional Autonoma de Mexico

8681 Institute, Plaza Mexico unique cultural

gift. SAN ANTONIO EXPRESS-NEWS, (June 19,
1972), p. 6-B. English.

AN: Pres. Luis Echeverria of Mexico
dedicates the Mexican Cultural Institute and
Plaza Mexico, which will house an extension
campus of National University of Mexico, in
San Antonio. Mexican artists will be brought
in and the Institute has a permanent art
gallery.

University Memorial Center, Boulder, CO

8682 Chicano pride theme of mural. EL DIARIO DE
LA GENTE, Vol. 2, no. 11 (January 25, 1974).
English.

AN: Commentary on the 11x15 ft. mural
painted by Carlos Rosas outside the entrance
to the Tabor Inn in University Memorial
Center. Mural composed of Indio-Chicano
symbols.

University of California, Irvine. Department of Spanish and Portuguese

8683 Canto al pueblo: an anthology of
experiences. San Antonio, TX: Penca Books,
1978. English.

AN: Includes works by: Mario E.
Castillo, Carlos Rosas, Jose G. Gonzalez,
Santos Martinez, Gilbert Munoz, Fred Loa,
Armando Ibanez and others.

University of California, Berkeley, Museum

8684 Garcia, Rupert. 'Fifth Sun' Raza art show at
UC Berkeley Museum. EL TECOLOTE, Vol. 8, no.
3 (November 1977), p. 8+. English.

AN: Review of THE FIFTH SUN:
CONTEMPORARY TRADITIONAL CHICANO AND LATINO
ART, co-sponsored by University of
California, Berkeley Chicano Studies and
Arte Popular, and curated by artist Ralph
Maradiaga, co-director of Galeria de la
Raza, showing at the UC Berkeley Museum. It
will travel to the University of California,
Santa Barbara's Art Museum. Illustrated.

University of California, Santa Barbara, Art Museum

8685 Garcia, Rupert. 'Fifth Sun' Raza art show at
UC Berkeley Museum. EL TECOLOTE, Vol. 8, no.
3 (November 1977), p. 8+. English.

AN: Review of THE FIFTH SUN:
CONTEMPORARY TRADITIONAL CHICANO AND LATINO
ART, co-sponsored by University of
California, Berkeley Chicano Studies and
Arte Popular, and curated by artist Ralph
Maradiaga, co-director of Galeria de la
Raza, showing at the UC Berkeley Museum. It
will travel to the University of California,
Santa Barbara's Art Museum. Illustrated.

University of Colorado, Boulder

8686 Chicano art show. EL DIARIO DE LA GENTE,
Vol. 1, no. 7 (February 6, 1973), p. 4.
English.

AN: Fine arts students at the University
of Colorado led by Rudy Fernandez hope to
educate high school students about Chicano
art. This article documents an exhibit held
at Lafayette, CO. Members of the group are
Bob Maez, Jerry Jaramillo, Anthony Mendoza,
and Rudy Fernandez. Illustrated by four
exhibition photographs by John L. Espinosa.

University of Texas, San Antonio, TX

8687 The class of '79. SA: THE MAGAZINE OF SAN
ANTONIO, Vol. 3, no. 4 (June 1979). English.

AN: Well-illustrated article on students
of James Newberry, photography teacher at
the University of Texas, San Antonio.
Includes photos of top prizewinners and
members of Ladrones de la Luz, David
Cardenas and Kathy Vargas.

Unzueta, Manuel

8688 El Centro Cultural de La Raza, San Diego,
CA. Espejo del barrio-art exposition.
Exhibition brochure, June 1975. English.

AN: Illustrated brochure announcement
for a cultural exposition of Chicano music,
art and drama. Includes some biographical
information and one reproduction of painter
Manuel Unzueta, woodworker Ambriz, muralist
Victor Orozco Ochoa and designer/illustrator
J. Armando Nunez.

8689 Chavez, Jaime. Rayaprofiles: Manuel Unzueta.
RAYAS, Vol. 2, no. 3 (May, June, 1979), p.
5. Spanish.

AN: Brief biography of Mexican-born
Chicano artist and muralist from Santa
Barbara, California. Manuel Unzueta is
active with La Casa de la Raza and its
publication XALMAN. Unzueta is invited to
paint a mural in Albuquerque. A Santa
Barbara mural is illustrated.

8690 Concilio de arte popular. CHISMEARTE, Vol.
1, no. 2 (Winter, Spring, 1977), p. 54.
English.

AN: Report of a meeting February 12,
1977 by the Concilio de Arte Popular (CAP)
which published CHISMEARTE. Introduces
members of the Board and summarizes
discussions of problems of the organization
and their publication.

8691 Diaz, Katherine A. Murals of New Mexico.
CAMINOS, Vol. 2, no. 5 (October 1981), p.
9-10. English.

AN: Illustrations of murals in Santa Fe
and Albuquerque by Gilberto Guzman,
Francisco Le Fevere[sic; Lefebre], Manuel
Unzueta, and Fernando Penalosa.

8692 Exxon Company, Houston, TX and Quirarte,
Jacinto. Chicano art of the barrio.
Exhibition brochure, n.d. [c.1976]. English.

AN: Brochure for a traveling exhibit of
photographically-reproduced Chicano murals:
Leo Limon, Lucila Villasenor Grijalva,
Antonio Esparza, Susan Saenz, Charles Felix,
Hoyo-Mara gang, David A. Lopez and team,
Roberto Chavez and team (Los Angeles); Jerry
Concha, Ruben Guzman, Chuy Campusano (San
Francisco); Manuel Unzueta (Santa Barbara).
Ernie Palomino and Leo Esequiel Ozona
(Fresno). Leo Tanguma (Houston), Roberto
Lucero, Manuel Martinez and Al Sanchez
(Denver).

8693 University of Texas. El Paso. Chicano
Studies Program. "Chicanotations": paintings
and drawings by Manuel Unzueta. Exhibition
brochure, 1979. English.

AN: Exhibition handout includes
biographical data and a listing of the 20
works exhibited by Unzueta.

8694 Unzueta, Manuel. Iconography: strictly
Chicano. XALMAN, Vol. 1, no. 4 (Spring
1977), p. 17-18. English.

AN: Only a Chicano artist can portray
the unique experience of being Chicano
through visual images of despair and self
pride: opinion of painter Unzueta.

8695 Unzueta, Manuel and La Casa de la Raza
Gallery, Santa Barbara, CA. Murals art
murals art: featuring the murals of la Casa
de la Raza, Santa Barbara, California.
Exhibition brochure, n.d. English.

AN: Illustrated booklet of Unzueta's
murals and easel paintings.

8696 Vallejo, Armando. Luna llena: ocho anos de
poesia chicana, 1971-1979. Santa Barbara,
CA: Ediciones Aztlan, 1979. English.

AN: Cover and illustrations Manuel
Unzueta of Santa Barbara, Calif.

UPRISING OF THE MUJERES [mural]

8697 Muchnic, Suzanne. LAICA looks at social
works. CALENDAR, (October 7, 1979), p. 93.
English.

AN: Review of the exhibit SOCIAL WORKS
at the Los Angeles Institute of Contemporary
Art. Illustration and discussion of Judith
F. Baca's mural UPRISING OF THE MUJERES, a
four-part portable canvas mural in the style
of Siqueiros.

Urban Communities

8698 Castellanos, Leonard. Chicano centros,
murals, and art. CHISMEARTE, Vol. 1, no. 1
(Fall   1976), p. 26-27. English.

AN: Excerpt of an article originally
published under the same title in ARTS IN
SOCIETY (Spring-Summer 1975).

8699 A new cultural center for Houston. AGENDA,
Vol. 7, no. 2 (March, April, 1977), p.
17-18. English.

AN: Goals and programs of a proposed
Mexican American cultural center for
Houston, Texas. Since August of 1976, the
center has been operating from a temporary
location and has sponsored various art
exhibits. Expected to be in full operation
by 1980, the Houston Bellas Artes will
sponsor workshops, symposia, performances
and exhibits related to Mexican American
culture. Illustrated with two photographs of
the cultural activities of the Houston
Bellas Artes Center.

Urban Planning

8700 Rodriguez, Roland V. Urban design primer:
comparative analyses of San Antonio
urbanscapes. [s.l.: s.n., ca. 1979].
English.

AN: Proposal for a study to compare six
sites in San Antonio with models of European
townscapes. The purpose is to educate the
public to enjoy its city and make future
city planners sensitive to urban design.
Also useful for architectural students.

Urbanization
   USE: Urban Communities

Ureste, Homero

8701 Con safo to hold Lutheran college exhibition at Texas. CHICANO TIMES, Vol. 7, no. 89 (March 26, 1976), p. [15]. English.

AN: Discusses the aims of "Con Safos" group: to interpret their environment and react to it; to act as spokespeople and give visual reality to the Chicano vision; to destroy stereotypes and demolish visual cliches. The participating artists include Rudy R. Trevino, Mel Casas, Lucas Hinojosa, Kathy Vargas, Joe Frank Acosta, Emilio Aguirre and Homero Ureste.

Uribe, Joseph G.

8702 Conversation on photography in the Los Angeles Latino community. OBSCURA, Vol. 2, no. 2 (December, February, 1981, 1982), p. 22-32. English.

AN: Interview on the nature and distinguishing characteristics of Chicano photography with Chicano photographers Isabel Castro (Council for Latino Photography), Lorenzo Hernandez (Director of Cityscape Gallery, publisher PHOTOSHOW magazine), Joseph G. Uribe (California State University, Los Angeles, Center for the Visual Arts, Director of West Colorado Gallery), Patssi Valdez, Becky Villasenor, and sculptor, curator, and Art Director for Academia Quinto Sol, Inc., Linda Vallejo, Portfolio of photography by Chicanos Don Anton, Louis Carlos Bernal, Sean Carrillo, Patssi Valdez, Ricardo Valverde, and by Morrie Camhi and Elizabeth Sisco on Chicano subjects.

Uribe, Mario

8703 Baciu, Joyce A. Hispanic artists: combining energy and emotion. CAMINOS, Vol. 2, no. 5 (October 1981), p. 14-17. English.

AN: Brief profiles of Mario Uribe, Ernest De Soto, Peter Rodriguez, Margarita Jauregui Weiner, Virginia Jaramillo, Luis Urrea, Ramses Noriega, Jose Lopez, Olivia Sanchez.

Urrea, Luis

8704 Baciu, Joyce A. Hispanic artists: combining energy and emotion. CAMINOS, Vol. 2, no. 5 (October 1981), p. 14-17. English.

AN: Brief profiles of Mario Uribe, Ernest De Soto, Peter Rodriguez, Margarita Jauregui Weiner, Virginia Jaramillo, Luis Urrea, Ramses Noriega, Jose Lopez, Olivia Sanchez.

U.S. Conference for an Alternative Cinema, Bard College, New York, June 1979

8705 Kleinhaus, Chuck; Seiter, Ellen; and Steven, Peter. Conference report: struggling for unity. JUMP CUT, no. 21 (November 1979), p. 35-37. English.

AN: Report and critique of the U.S. Conference for an Alternative Cinema held in mid-June 1979 at Bard College in New York state to chart a course for independent filmmakers. Chicano, Black, Asian and Puerto Rican film people attended, including Jesus Salvador Trevino and Sylvia Morales from the Chicano Cinema Coalition of Los Angeles.

U.S.A. Bicentennial

8706 Latin American council bicentennial mural. Exhibition brochure, [1976]. English.

AN: Brochure giving history and iconography of a 8 x 16 foot portable mural by Grand Rapids, Mich. artist Jose Narezo with a team of students. The mural honors North and South American revolutionaries with portraits of George Washington, Jose Marti, Eugenio Maria de Hostos, and Benito Juarez.

8707 Mills, James. Hispano history mural ready. DENVER POST, (October 17, 1975), p. 27+. English.

AN: PASADO, PRESENTE Y FUTURO, a 20-ft. mural by Denver artist Carlota Espinoza was commissioned by the Friends of the Denver Public Library for the Byers Branch (W. 7th Ave. and Santa Fe Drive). Blending myth and reality, the mural progresses from Aztec empires through the Spanish conquest, from alienation to the struggle for a collective identity and heritage by the Mexican American. Brief commentary by the artist on the mural's significance. Ms. Espinoza's mural was designated as an official Centennial-Bicentennial creation. Illustrated with photograph of artist.

8708 Mills, Kay. The great wall of Los Angeles. MS.MAGAZINE, (October 1981), p. 66-69+. English.

AN: THE GREAT WALL OF LOS ANGELES in the Tujunga flood control channel in the San Fernando Valley, was started as a Bicentennial project in 1976. Artistic director Judy Baca of the Social and Public Art Resource Center, works with crews of young people painting aspects of Los Angeles history that is not generally found in textbooks. Well illustrated.

8709 Monroe, Julie T. A splash of art from Idaho's Mexican-Americans. IDAHO STATESMAN, (March 11, 1977), p. 4D. English.

AN: As a Bicentennial tribute to all people of Latin American heritage, Illinois Bell Telephone Company organized a national exhiibit of 17 Mexican-American/Chicano artists. In Idaho, the touring exhibition was augmented by a local presentation, MEXICAN-AMERICAN: IDAHO, shown at the Boise Gallery of Art under sponsorship of Boise Cascade. Jose Rodriguez, local artist presents his views on the meanings of the word "Chicano" and "Chicano Art." Illustrated with a photograph of Jose Rodriguez and a reproduction of one of his oil paintings entitled THE HOE.

U.S.A. Bicentennial (cont.)

8710 Wu, Ying Ying. Mural, mural on the Great
     Wall. LOS ANGELES TIMES, (September 16,
     1980), p. VI,4. English.

     AN: Information on a video project
     directed by John Rier to document work on
     the 1700-ft. mural THE GREAT WALL OF LOS
     ANGELES which depicts California history
     with an emphasis on the role that minorities
     had in forging that history. Three
     teen-agers were trained in video production
     while assisting with taping the mural
     project. Simultaneously, 40 other youngsters
     hired from the Summer Program for the
     Employment of Disadvantaged Youth painted a
     400-ft. section of the mural in 1980.
     Article describes the various skills
     mathematical, social and artistic developed
     by youth involved in the project. The mural
     was started as a Bicentennial Project in
     1976 by Judy Baca for the Social and Public
     Art Resources Center in Venice, California.
     Illustrated with 3 photographs of various
     aspects of the Project.

Utah

8711 Miller, Marlan. Heard speaks Spanish through
     art. PHOENIX GAZETTE, (September 23, 1978).
     English.

     AN: Four new exhibits at the Heard
     Museum of Phoenix include "Hispanic crafts
     of the Southwest", and "Southwest Chicano
     Art Invitational". The former focuses on New
     Mexico and Colorado crafts, organized by the
     Taylor Museum if the Colorado Springs Fine
     Arts Center; the latter includes Rupert
     Garcia and Xavier Miramontes of San
     Francisco, Rudy Fernandez of Salt Lake City
     (now in Scottsdale, AZ), and Antonio Pazos
     of Tucson.

8712 Wilson, Anne. Chicanos show off talents in
     Magna SOCIO projects. SALT LAKE CITY
     TRIBUNE, (July 9, 1979), p. C-1. English.

     AN: In the rural Utah community of
     Magna, SOCIO (Spanish Speaking Organization
     for Community Integrity and Opportunity)
     established various art projects. Three
     murals were painted by community youth under
     the guidance of Robert Archuleta and Becky
     Berru. One of the murals depicts "man and
     labor." Illustrated with photographs of
     project directors, maquette of the mural and
     a mural painting "brigade".

VAJITO MAGAZINE

8713 Castillo, Rafael. Gonzo journalism goes for
     a low ride. SAN ANTONIO EXPRESS-NEWS,
     (December 6, 1981), p. 7-B. English.

     AN: George Velasquez, editor and
     publisher of San Antonio's VAJITO magazine,
     views lowriders as a positive and evolving
     form of urban youth culture. Counters
     stereotypes about lowriders as drug-oriented
     high school drop-outs. There is a new and
     significant discourse being developed in
     literary and visual forms among Chicano
     lowriders.

Val, James

8714 Knapp, Dan. KCET's show for Chicano viewers.
     LOS ANGELES TIMES, (April 3, 1970), p. IV,
     18. English.

     AN: Story on the television series
     AHORA! started September 1969 on KCET, Los

Angeles' National Educational Television.
Edward Moreno is program director and host;
Victor Millan is producer-director; Claudio
Fenner-Lopez, senior producer, has staff
including set-designer David Villasenor,
production manager James Val, and alternate
host-narrator Jesus Trevino. The program has
shown exhibits of artists Gilberto Lujan and
Daniel Ramirez.

Valadez, Jaime

8715 Anaya, Rudolfo A. and Ortiz, Simon J.
     1680-1980: a ceremony of brotherhood.
     Albuquerque, NM: Academic, 1981. English.

     AN: A cooperative publication by members
     of the former La Academia de la Nueva Raza
     (1969-1976) formed of writers and artists,
     and the Tri-Centennial Commission of the
     All-Indian Pueblo Council. Includes writings
     and artworks by Chicanos and Indians from
     New Mexico, California, Texas, and Arizona.
     Chicano artists works included are by Ellen
     Arellano, Juan Estevan Arellano, Alberto
     Baros, Jose Antonio Burciaga, Juan Reyes
     Cervantes, Rudy Cuellar, Ricardo Favela, El
     Zarco Guerrero, Luis Jimenez, Jr., Carlos
     Quinto Kemm, Alejandro Lopez, Floyd Lujan,
     Jose Montoya, Juanishi Orozco, Leo Romero,
     Secundino Sandoval, Jaime Valdez, Maria
     Varela, Esteban Villa.

8716 NATIONAL MURALS NETWORK COMMUNITY
     NEWSLETTER. (Fall 1979). English.

     AN: Reports on mural projects by Fermin
     Coronado working with students in Houston;
     Galeria de la Raza's billboard used as a
     mural surface for changing images; murals
     under the Flor en la Comunidad program of El
     Centro Cultural de la Gente in San Jose,
     California and led by artist Jaime Valadez;
     murals in Grand Rapids and other cities of
     western Michigan; murals by Jose Guerrero
     and others from the Chicago Mural Group; a
     survey of Chicano murals in the Pilsen area
     of Chicago guided by Jose Gonzalez.

8717 Notes on 2nd National Community Muralists'
     Network Conference, Chicago, Ill. April
     20-23, 1978. San Francisco, CA, 1978.
     English.

     AN: Rupert Garcia, Raul Martinez,
     Patricia Rodriguez, Ray Patlan (San
     Francisco Bay Area) and Jaime Valadez (San
     Jose), among others, attended the conference
     in Chicago. Reports were heard from many
     parts of the United States on mural
     activities, including that of Aurelio Diaz
     of Chicago, representing MARCH (Movimiento
     Artistico Chicano). A workshop presentation
     was made by Luis Arenal and others from the
     Taller Siqueiros of Cuernavaca, Mexico. An
     experimental mural to try Siqueiros'
     techniques was created. Illustrated.

8718 Oakes College, University of California,
     Santa Cruz, CA and Carrillo, Eduardo.
     Corazon de Aztlan: a Chicano arts show.
     Exhibition catalog, 1981. English.

     AN: Catalog of exhibit including works
     by Eduardo Carrillo, Juana Franklin, Cruz
     Zamarron, Jerry Astorga, Jaime Valadez,
     Ernesto Palomino, Sal Garcia, Roger Sierra,
     Jose Montoya, Esteban Villa, Juanishi
     Orozco, from Santa Cruz, San Jose, Fresno
     and Sacramento. Presentations of films and
     by the Teatro de la Tierra Morena of Santa
     Cruz County.

Valadez, John

8719 Almaraz, Carlos. Introduccion: vida urbana y artistas chicanos. COMUNIDAD, Vol. 55, no. 22 (May 3, 1981), p. 2. Spanish.

AN: In the controversial period of the early 1980s, Chicano advances are being attacked. In this political climate, some Los Angeles artists are interested in beauty and artistic creation: Carlos Almaraz, best-known of the Los Four group; Yreina Cervantez; Elsa Flores; John Valadez, presently working on a mural; and musicians Louie Perez and Tito Rodriguez Larriva.

8720 Arte chicano y el pueblo. COMUNIDAD, no. 41 (May 3, 1981), p. 1-15. Spanish.

AN: The whole issue of the Sunday Supplement deals with Los Angeles Chicano art and music. Works by painter Carlos Almaraz, photographer Elsa Flores, painter Yreina Cervantez, muralist and draftsman John Valadez, and a performance piece by Elsa Flores and Louie Perez are featured. Biographical information, and statements by the artists.

8721 The Broadway mural, 1981, by John Manuel Valadez. Los Angeles, CA: Victor Clothing Co., n.d. English.

AN: Postcard/brochure about Valadez's 8x48-ft mural, oil on canvas, displayed at the Victor Clothing Co. in downtown Los Angeles. Brief profile of the photographer and muralist. Full color reproduction of a section of the complete mural.

8722 Consejo Mexicano de Fotografia, A.C., Mexico City. Hecho en latinoamerica: segundo coloquio latinoamericano de fotografia. Exhibition catalog, 1982. Spanish.

AN: Catalog/book of the second colloquium and exhibit of Latin American photography. Among the Chicano artists whose work is reproduced are Louis Carlos Bernal, Robert C. Buitron, David Cardenas, Isabel Castro, Harry Gamboa, Jr., Luis Garza, Roberto Gil de Montes, John M. Valadez, Kathy Vargas. In the exhibit were also Porfirio Aguilar, Elsa Marie Flores, Ricardo Valverde. Great number of illustrations. In Spanish.

8723 Cultura chicana: Los Angeles. COMUNIDAD, no. 11 (July 13, 1980), p. 1-15. Spanish.

AN: The whole issue of the Cultural Supplement concerns Chicano art and music. Captioned photographs deal with visual artists Carlos Almaraz, Jerry Dreva [not Chicano], Glugio Gronk, Willie Herron, John Valadez, Patssi Valdez, with examples of their work. With the exception of Dreva, all the artists are members of Los Four or Asco. Asco member Harry Gamboa, Jr. sums up the 1960s and 1970s and activities of artists in his essay "Seis imaginaciones: Artistas chicanos en Los Angeles." Well illustrated.

8724 Exploratorium, Student Union, California State University, Los Angeles. An exhibit of published prints of Aztlan Multiples. Exhibition catalog, 1981. English.

AN: The published silkscreen prints of Aztlan Multiples, a small business run by Richard Duardo of Los Angeles, features works by Duardo, John Valadez, and Carlos Almaraz, among others. Illustrations.

8725 Gamboa, Harry, Jr. Los murales de Aztlan. COMUNIDAD, (June 28, 1981), p. 8-9+. Spanish.

AN: Review of the exhibit at the Craft and Folk Art Museum of Los Angeles of MURALS OF AZTLAN: THE STREET PAINTERS OF EAST LOS in which Carlos Almaraz, Gronk, Judithe Hernandez, Willie Herron, Frank Romero, John Valadez and the East Los Streetscapers (David Botello, Wayne Healy, George Yepes) painted portable murals in the gallery. The murals are described and illustrated.

8726 Gamboa, Harry, Jr. Seis imaginaciones: artistas chicanos en Los Angeles. COMUNIDAD, (July 13, 1980), p. 10. Spanish.

AN: A limited flow of media information about Los Angeles Chicanos has produced a "ghost" culture. Only sensational events are published. Alternative magazines like LA RAZA, CON SAFOS, and REGENERACION have disseminated Chicano ideas of the 1970s. The Chicano imagination has appeared in murals by Willie Herron, Gronk, Carlos Almaraz, John Valadez; in pieces like "walking" and "instant" murals by the group ASCO; by the group Los Four; by group exhibits like "Chicanismo en el arte," and "Chicanarte." Patssi Valdez showed Photobooth Piece at the "Chicanismo" show. Gronk and Jerry Dreva exhibited their mail art at "Punk Meets Art." In Spanish.

8727 Geyer, Anne. Muralist works to dispel negative Latino images. THE NEWS, (September 2, 1981), p. 22. English.

AN: John Valadez is painting a mural on canvas depicting the Latino people of downtown Los Angeles. It will be housed in Victor Clothing Co. Valadez is one of an increasing number of artists and dealers who have moved to the downtown area. Valadez discusses the images he makes and his attempt to correct media stereotypes about Latinos. Illustrated.

8728 Goldman, Shifra M. Thorns and roses. ARTWEEK, Vol. 11, no. 30 (September 20, 1980), p. 1. English.

AN: Report on four Chicano artists exhibiting at L.A.C.E. Gallery, Los Angeles: Carlos Almaraz, Teddy Sandoval, John Valadez, and Linda Vallejo. Illustrated.

8729 Johnston, Beatriz. Valadez: exponente de la vida urbana en mural contemporaneo. LA OPINION, Vol. 56, no. 68 (November 22, 1981), p. II, 1. Spanish.

AN: Report on the mural in preparation by John Valadez for Victor Clothing Co. in downtown Los Angeles. It deals with people walking in the streets of the downtown area. Illustrated with the sketch for the mural which Valadez has been painting in the basement of the building for nine months.

8730 Kim, Howard. Chicano art: is it an art form? Or simply art by Chicanos. NEWORLD, Vol. 6, no. 4 (1980), p. 26-30. English.

AN: An attempt to define Chicano art through interviews with Carlos Almaraz, John Valadez, (Los Four), Robert Delgado, Sister Karen Boccalero (Self-Help Graphics), Harry Gamboa, Jr. (ASCO), Ricardo Duardo, Ignacio Gomez, and others. Well illustrated.

Valadez, John (cont.)

8731 L.A.C.E. (Los Angeles Contemporary
     Exhibitions), Los Angeles, CA. Espina
     (Thorn): Carlos Almaraz, Elsa Flores, Louie
     Perez, Teddy Sandoval, John Valadez, Linda
     Vallejo. Exhibition announcement, 1980.
     English.

     AN: Announcement of an exhibition and a
     performance piece by six Los Angeles
     artists.

8732 Muchnic, Suzanne. Damaged goods in the big
     city. LOS ANGELES TIMES, (July 23, 1979),
     p. IV-11. English.

     AN: Review of the exhibit at Otis Art
     Institute of Parsons School of Design of
     L.A. PARKS AND WRECKS, featuring Carlos
     Almaraz, John Valadez, and Black artist John
     Woods. Almaraz paints auto wrecks, and
     landscapes of Echo Park. Valadez does pencil
     portraits of young Chicanos. Illustrated.

8733 Muchnic, Suzanne. Mural: a lullaby of
     another Broadway. LOS ANGELES TIMES,
     (December 18, 1981), p. VI, 1+. English.

     AN: Commentary on the panoramic mural
     painted by John Valadez inside the Victor
     Clothing Company at 242 S. Broadway. Mural
     depicts Broadway street life. Photograph of
     the artist and the mural.

8734 Otis/Parsons Gallery, Los Angeles, CA;
     Nieto, Margarita; and Price, Aimee Brown.
     L.A. parks & wrecks: a reflection of urban
     life/parques y choques: un reflejo de la
     vida urbana. Exhibition catalog, [1979].
     Bilingual.

     AN: Catalog poster discussing the works
     of the three artists on exhibit: Carlos
     Almaraz, John Valadez and John Woods who
     concentrate on urban images. Detailed
     descriptions of each artist's work accompany
     the many illustrations. Essays in English
     and Spanish.

8735 The Point Gallery, Santa Monica, CA. ASCO
     (Gronk, Patssi, Gamboa, Herron), Los Four
     (Almaraz, de la Rocha, Judithe Hernandez,
     Gloriamalia Flores, Mauricio Ramirez, John
     Valadez. Exhibition invitation, [1975].
     English.

     AN: Illustrated invitation to an exhibit
     of Los Angeles artists.

8736 San Francisco Museum of Modern Art, San
     Francisco, CA and Pearlstein, Howard.
     Aesthetics of graffiti. Exhibition catalog,
     1978. English.

     AN: Graffiti are defined as any
     coherently-intended presence written,
     scratched, painted, engraved, printed,
     pasted or otherwise impressed in a public
     place. Graffiti have been incorporated into
     works by artists. In this catalog, works by
     Chicano artists Carlos Almaraz, Wilfred
     Castano, Judithe Hernandez, Gilbert Lujan,
     Gustavo Rivera, Frank Romero, John M.
     Valadez, Victor M. Valle, Xavier Viramontes
     - as well as many Latino and non-Latino
     artist, appear.

8737 Sol Art Gallery, San Diego, CA. Group
     showing of Southern California artists.
     Exhibition brochure, 1980. English.

     AN: First exhibit of new Chicano art
     gallery showing Los Angeles artists Carlos

Almaraz, Judithe Hernandez, John Valadez,
Linda Vallejo, Ricardo Duardo, Barbara
Carrasco.

8738 Temko, Allan. Teen Angel's low riders -
     Chicano art on the rise. THIS WORLD,
     (August 26, 1979), p. 42-43. English.

     AN: Important and insightful analysis of
     the lowrider phenomenon among Chicano youth
     in California. Analysis of publications like
     LOW RIDER Magazine of San Jose, information
     on graphic artists like "Teen Angel" and
     Ramon Cisneros and thematic relationship of
     recognized Chicano artists like Gilbert
     Lujan, John Valadez, and Luis Jimenez to the
     lowrider movement. The lowrider is
     provocatively related to world wide cultural
     manifestations from diverse epochs.

Valadez, Hector

8739 El calendario hispano de Michigan, 1981.
     Stanton, MI: Montcalm Intermediate School
     District and Nuestras Artes de Michigan,
     1981. English.

     AN: Months of historical calendar
     illustrated with art works by George Vargas,
     Nora Chapa Mendoza, Jesse Gonzalez, Julio
     Perazza(Puerto Rican), Hector Valdez, Pamela
     M. Gonzalez, Isabell Escojico (7-year-old
     child), Jose Narezo, Martin Moreno, Laurie
     Mendoza Psarianos, Rosa Maria Arenas.

Valdez, Horacio

8740 Blue Sky Productions. Los santeros. Color
     film, 29 min., 1979. English.

     AN: A 29 minute color film produced with
     funding assistance from New Mexico Highlands
     University and the National Endowment for
     the Arts. Features santeros Luis Tapia,
     Orlando Romero, Horacio Valdez.

8741 Elaine Horwitch Galleries, Santa Fe, NM. New
     Mexico woodcarving. Exhibition catalog,
     1980. English.

     AN: Invitation to an exhibit at the
     Horwitch galleries of Scottsdale, Arizona,
     and Santa Fe, NM of sculptors Felipe
     Archuleta, Leroy Archuleta, Frank Brito,
     Alonso Jimenez, Horatio Valdez, and others.
     Illustration.

8742 Sanchez, Arley. Santeros. ALBUQUERQUE JRNL,
     (August 21, 1977), p. C, 1. English.

     AN: Review of THE SANTERO EXPERIENCE, an
     exhibition of contemporary folk art by
     eleven New Mexican santeros, most in their
     30s, at the Albuquerque Museum. The carvers
     include Juan Lucero, Ben Lopez, Luisito
     Lujan, Horacio Valdez, C. Garcia, George
     Lopez. A revival of the art has been taking
     place within last several years due to
     cultural awareness being experienced by
     Hispanos. Contemporary santeros still donate
     some pieces to the church, but most are
     marketed to private collectors, displayed in
     museums, or kept.

Valdez, Luis

8743 Camplis, Francisco X. Towards the development of a Raza cinema. TIN TAN, Vol. 2, no. 5 (June 1, 1977), p. 5-7. English.

AN: Chicanos and other minorities remain invisible to white America, an expression of neo-colonialism. Camplis defines "Chicano" and "Raza" as terms, and states there are few, if any, full-length feature films available. Without role models, Chicano/Raza filmmakers can learn from contemporary revolutionary Latin American filmmakers, be familiar with European and Hollywood films, though the latter are alien models. Camplis suggests directions for Chicano films, and reviews films by Jesus Trevino, Jose Camacho, and Luis Valdez.

8744 Mexican American Community Service Organization, San Jose, CA. Exhibition of contemporary art. Exhibition brochure, 1968. English.

AN: Biographical and exhibition data for Al Barela, Bert Hermosillo, Octavio Romano, Luis Valdez, Vincent P. Rascon, John Soares and Al Espinoza.

8745 Valadez, Kathy L. Zoot suit, by Luis Valdez. SOMOS, Vol. 1, no. 2 (July 1978), p. 20-29. English.

AN: Two reviews of Valdez's new play ZOOT SUIT, both enthusiastic. Historical material and photographs with an essay by Jose Montoya and his Pachuco drawing, as well as views of the play are included.

Valdez, Patssi

8746 Conversation on photography in the Los Angeles Latino community. OBSCURA, Vol. 2, no. 2 (December, February, 1981, 1982), p. 22-32. English.

AN: Interview on the nature and distinguishing characteristics of Chicano photography with Chicano photographers Isabel Castro (Council for Latino Photography), Lorenzo Hernandez (Director of Cityscape Gallery, publisher PHOTOSHOW magazine), Joseph G. Uribe (California State University, Los Angeles, Center for the Visual Arts, Director of West Colorado Gallery), Patssi Valdez, Becky Villasenor, and sculptor, curator, and Art Director for Academia Quinto Sol, Inc., Linda Vallejo, Portfolio of photography by Chicanos Don Anton, Louis Carlos Bernal, Sean Carrillo, Patssi Valdez, Ricardo Valverde, and by Morrie Camhi and Elizabeth Sisco on Chicano subjects.

8747 Cultura chicana: Los Angeles. COMUNIDAD, no. 11 (July 13, 1980), p. 1-15. Spanish.

AN: The whole issue of the Cultural Supplement concerns Chicano art and music. Captioned photographs deal with visual artists Carlos Almaraz, Jerry Dreva [not Chicano], Glugio Gronk, Willie Herron, John Valadez, Patssi Valdez, with examples of their work. With the exception of Dreva, all the artists are members of Los Four or Asco. Asco member Harry Gamboa, Jr. sums up the 1960s and 1970s activities of artists in his essay "Seis imaginaciones: Artistas chicanos en Los Angeles." Well illustrated.

8748 Edy. A true barrio art. EL CHICANO, (December 7, 1972), p. 9. English.

AN: Interview with East Los Angeles artists Harry Gamboa, Robert Gronk and Willie Herron (also included in the conversation are Patsy Valdez and Eddie Ytuarte). Suffering, fatalism, existential reality and the awareness of cultural colonialism are cited as sources of inspiration for urban barrio art. Illustrated with a photograph of Willie Herron's Quetzalcoatl mural in City Terrace barrio and two drawings by Robert Gronk and Harry Gamboa.

8749 Gamboa, Harry, Jr. and Gronk. Gronk: off-the-wall artist. NEWORLD, Vol. 6, no. 4 (1980), p. 33-43. English.

AN: Interview with Gronk about his No Movies, by Harry Gamboa, Jr., both members (with Willie Herron and Patssi Valdez) of ASCO. The interview itself can be seen as an "art piece" with photographs by Gamboa; it contains valuable information about the ideas and activities of the group.

8750 Gamboa, Harry, Jr. Seis imaginaciones: artistas chicanos en Los Angeles. COMUNIDAD, (July 13, 1980), p. 10. Spanish.

AN: A limited flow of media information about Los Angeles Chicanos has produced a "ghost" culture. Only sensational events are published. Alternative magazines like LA RAZA, CON SAFOS, and REGENERACION have disseminated Chicano ideas of the 1970s. The Chicano imagination has appeared in murals by Willie Herron, Gronk, Carlos Almaraz, John Valadez; in pieces like "walking" and "instant" murals by the group ASCO; by the group Los Four; by group exhibits like "Chicanismo en el arte," and "Chicanarte." Patssi Valdez showed Photobooth Piece at the "Chicanismo" show. Gronk and Jerry Dreva exhibited their mail art at "Punk Meets Art." In Spanish.

8751 L.A.C.E. (Los Angeles Contemporary Exhibitions), Los Angeles, CA. No Movie: Gil de Montes, Teddy, Glugio [Gronk], Patssi, Gamboa. Exhibition invitation, 1978. English.

AN: Invitation to "performance" piece by Roberto Gil de Montes, Teddy Sandoval, Gronk, Patssi Valdez and Harry Gamboa, Jr., the latter three of the ASCO group. Illustrated.

8752 Mechicano Art Center, Los Angeles, CA. Schizophrenibeneficial. Exhibition invitation, 1977. English.

AN: Invitation to an ASCO "performance" work: "Projecting of Visual and/or Verbal Personality Disorders Onto Person or Persons Unknown." Glugio (Gronk), Teddy (Sandoval), (Roberto) Gil de Montes, Patssi (Valdez), (Harry) Gamboa.

Valdez, Patssi (cont.)

8753 Moisan, Jim. Ancient roots, new visions.
ARTWEEK, Vol. 9, no. 26 (July 29, 1978), p.
8. English.

AN: Review of the show held at the
Municipal Arts Gallery of Los Angeles, the
first national touring show of Latino
artists in the United States. Includes
commentary on work of Larry Fuente, Luis
Jimenez, Frank Romero, Harry Gamboa, Gronk,
Rudy Martinez, Benjamin Serrano, Ricardo
Diaz, Patssi Valdez, Mel Casas, Luis Leroy,
Pedro Lujan. A related show, NEW VISIONS,
L.A., includes Robert Delgado, Ray Bravo,
Joe Moran, Rosalyn Mesquita, Patricia
Murillo and others.

8754 EL PLAYANO (Loyola University, Los Angeles).
(Spring 1973).

AN: Illustrations by Simon Gonzales,
Gronk, Harry Gamboa, Jr., Willie Herron,
Charles Almaraz, Sister Teresa Munoz, Patsy
Valdez, Diane Gamboa.

8755 The Point Gallery, Santa Monica, CA. ASCO
(Gronk, Patssi, Gamboa, Herron), Los Four
(Almaraz, de la Rocha, Judithe Hernandez,
Gloriamalia Flores, Mauricio Ramirez, John
Valadez. Exhibition invitation, [1975].
English.

AN: Illustrated invitation to an exhibit
of Los Angeles artists.

8756 Raices y visiones [portfolio]. REVISTA
CHICANO-RIQUENA, Vol. 7, no. 2 (Spring
1979), p. 29-44.

AN: Portfolio of works from the exhibit
RAICES ANTIGUAS/VISIONES NUEVAS: ANCIENT
ROOTS/NEW VISIONS. Artists included are
Patssi Valdez (Los Angeles), Eloisa
Castellanos-Sanchez (New York), Benjamin
Serrano, Jr. (Tijuana, Mexico), Alex Garza
(Chicago), Martin Y. Moreno (Michigan), Luis
A. Jimenez (New Mexico), Rene Castro
(Oakland, CA), Sita Gomez de Kanelba (New
York), Susana Lasta (Tucson, AZ), Domingo
Garcia (New York), Consuelo Mendez Castillo
(Caracas, Venezuela), Naomi Castillo
Simonetti (New Jersey), Louis Carlos Bernal,
and Eddie Comptis.

8757 West Colorado Gallery, Pasadena, CA.
Gronk/Patssi. Exhibition brochure, 1979.
English.

AN: Works on exhibit by ASCO members
Gronk and Patssi Valdez. Photo of artists.

8758 Wilson, William. Chicana artists still
seeking identification. LOS ANGELES TIMES,
(June 23, 1975), p. VI, 5. English.

AN: Ten Chicana artists are exhibiting
their work in the Boathouse Gallery of Plaza
de la Raza in Lincoln Park: Judithe
Hernandez, Patssi Valdez, Judy Baca,
Josefina Quesada, Victoria del
Castillo-Leon, Olga Muniz, Gloria Flores,
Sylvia Morales, Isabel Castro and Celia
Tejadak. The work is still tentative and may
develop.

Valdez, Raul

8759 Barrios, Greg. Big art comes of age. RIVER
CITY SUN, (July 21, 1978), p. 9. English.

AN: Report on the meeting of Mexican and
Chicano muralists at a mural conference in

Austin. Includes a "Guide to Mural Art in
East Austin," most of whose murals were done
by Raul Valdez. Illustrated.

8760 Briseno, Rodolfo. Interview with a muralist.
ARRIBA, Vol. 1, no. 1 (July 1980), p. 5+.
English.

AN: Raul Valdez, muralist from Del Rio,
Texas has been painting murals in Austin and
was a founding member of LUCHA (League of
United Chicano Artists) in 1976. Having
studied with Siqueiros in Mexico, Valdez
sees strong affinities in content and form
between Chicano and Mexican muralism.
Illustrated with two photographs of Valdez's
Juarez-Lincoln mural.

8761 Garcia, Guillermo. Wall-to-wall art for the
people. AUSTIN AMERICAN STATESMAN, (January
22, 1978), p. E-1. English.

AN: Illustrated story on Raul Valdez's
mural (in progress) The Oral Tradition.
Valdez discusses his methods and art
philosophy when creating community murals.

8762 Garcia, Ignacio. Senior exhibit attempts to
define Chicano art. SOUTH TEXAN, (August 1,
1975). English.

AN: DIRECTAMENTE DEL BARRIO, a senior
art exhibit at Texas A & I University by art
majors Raul Valdez and Jesus Reyes. Sets
forth their ideas about Chicano arts and
their future plans.

8763 Hand me down. AUSTIN AMERICAN STATESMAN,
(August 17, 1978), p. B-1. English.

AN: Illustration of Raul Valdez's mural
La Raza Cosmica on the outdoor stage of the
Pan American Center, East Austin.

8764 HEMBRA: HERMANAS EN MOVIMIENTO BROTANDO
RAICES DE AZTLAN (University of Texas,
Austin). (Spring 1976).

AN: Raul Valdez, drawing, p. 3; Carolina
Flores, drawing, p. 5; Maria Flores,
photograph, pp. 7, 11, 30; M.E.
Secrest-Ramirez, drawing, p. 12; Amacio
Zarate, drawing, p. 15; Santa Barraza,
drawings, pp. 16, 17, 18, 26, 32; Nora
Gonzales-Dodson, painting, p. 19; Gilberto
Cardenas, photograph, pp. 22, 28; Nanci de
los Santos, photograph, p. 23, 29; Amado
Maurilio Pena, Jr. p. 31.

8765 Murales - 'expresan nuestra realidad'.
AYUDA, Vol. 1, no. 6 (September 1977).
English.

AN: Brief illustrated article on Raul
Valdez's 1977 mural LOS ELEMENTOS on the
outside wall of Antioch's Juarez-Lincoln
College (Centro Cultural de LUCHA). Explains
the iconography of the mural. Includes brief
biography of the artist.

Valdovin, Rogelio Ruiz

8766 Evans, Marylin. Tucson barrio janitor
designs authentic Aztec costumes. LA PRENSA,
Vol. 1, no. 6 (October 11, 1978). English.

AN: Rogelio Valdovin, self-taught artist
from Tucson, Arizona feels he has received a
spiritual call to create authentic
Pre-Columbian costumes and regalia.
Specializing in Aztec costumes, the artist
works with metal, beads, feathers, leather
and many fabrics and fibers in designing and
making his creations. He exhibits them as a
form of body art.

8767 Tannous, David. Problems of the artist as a
hyphenated commodity. THE WASHINGTON STAR,
(August 28, 1977), p. G-20. English.

AN: Review of ANCIENT ROOTS, NEW VISIONS
show in Washington, D.C. describing Mel
Casas' painting (San Antonio), Louis LeRoy's
assemblage (Coolidge, Arizona), Amado Pena's
silkscreen (Coolidge, Arizona), Rogelio Ruiz
Valdovin's costume (Tucson).

Valenzuela, Arthur

8768 Galeria, Santa Ana, CA. Egg-sploration: a
comprehensive exhibit by Art & Ben
Valenzuela. Exhibition invitation, 1981.
English.

AN: Invitation to an exhibit of two
Orange County, CA artists in a new
Chicano-run gallery. Illustrated with work
of art by Art Valenzuela.

8769 Galeria, Santa Ana, CA. The last Chicano art
show. Exhibition brochure, 1981. English.

AN: Invitation-brochure for an exhibit
of Los Angeles and Orange County artists in
a gallery underwritten by the Friendly
Center, Inc. with grants from local
government and from businesses. Exhibiting
are (Roberto) Gil de Montes, Gilbert Lujan,
Judy Miranda, Patricia Murillo, Alonso
Pardo, Teddy Sandoval, Mexican artist
Artemio Sepulveda, Joey Terrill, Art
Valenzuela, Ben Valenzuela, Linda Vallejo,
Jack A. Vargas, Emigdio Vasquez, Richard
Serrato, and J. William Hernandez, who is
the gallery director.

8770 Mills House Visual Arts Complex, Garden
Grove, CA. Menudo: artistas latinos de
Orange County. Exhibit invitation, 1980.
English.

AN: Invitation to an exhibit organized
for the first anniversary of Artistas
Latinos de Orange County including Delores
Grajeda, William Hernandez, Marylee Montano,
Patricia Murillo, Irene Ramos, Juan Ramos,
Ricardo Serrato, Miguel Shanahan, Arthur
Valenzuela, Benjamin Valenzuela, Jack
Vargas, Alonzo Whitney, Emigdio Vasquez,
Susana Zaccagnino, and Mexican artist
Artemio Sepulveda.

8771 Orange Co. Library. El Modena Branch.
Empanada: a tasty Mexican group art exhibit
filled with a variety of digestable treats.
Exhibition catalog, [1979]. English.

AN: Catalog of an exhibit by 15 artists:
Dolores Grajeda, William Hernandez-M.,
Marylee Montano, Patricia Murillo, Eduardo
Navarro, Susana A. Zaccagnino, Esau Quiroz,
Juan Elias Ramos, Ricardo M. Serrato,
Benjamin Valenzuela, Emigdio C. Vasquez,
Arthur Valenzuela, Jack Vargas, Alonso

Whitney, and Mexican artist Artemio
Sepulveda living in Orange County. Brief
profiles of the artists.

8772 Santa Ana Public Library, Newhope Branch,
Santa Ana, CA. Artistas latinos de Orange
County. Exhibition brochure, 1979. English.

AN: Exhibit of six artists: Dolores
Grajeda, Eduardo Navarro, Arthur Valenzuela,
Benjamin Valenzuela, Emigdio Vasquez, Susana
A. Zaccagnino.

Valenzuela, Ben

8773 Galeria, Santa Ana, CA. Egg-sploration: a
comprehensive exhibit by Art & Ben
Valenzuela. Exhibition invitation, 1981.
English.

AN: Invitation to an exhibit of two
Orange County, CA artists in a new
Chicano-run gallery. Illustrated with work
of art by Art Valenzuela.

8774 Galeria, Santa Ana, CA. The last Chicano art
show. Exhibition brochure, 1981. English.

AN: Invitation-brochure for an exhibit
of Los Angeles and Orange County artists in
a gallery underwritten by the Friendly
Center, Inc. with grants from local
government and from businesses. Exhibiting
are (Roberto) Gil de Montes, Gilbert Lujan,
Judy Miranda, Patricia Murillo, Alonso
Pardo, Teddy Sandoval, Mexican artist
Artemio Sepulveda, Joey Terrill, Art
Valenzuela, Ben Valenzuela, Linda Vallejo,
Jack A. Vargas, Emigdio Vasquez, Richard
Serrato, and J. William Hernandez, who is
the gallery director.

8775 Mills House Visual Arts Complex, Garden
Grove, CA. Menudo: artistas latinos de
Orange County. Exhibit invitation, 1980.
English.

AN: Invitation to an exhibit organized
for the first anniversary of Artistas
Latinos de Orange County including Delores
Grajeda, William Hernandez, Marylee Montano,
Patricia Murillo, Irene Ramos, Juan Ramos,
Ricardo Serrato, Miguel Shanahan, Arthur
Valenzuela, Benjamin Valenzuela, Jack
Vargas, Alonzo Whitney, Emigdio Vasquez,
Susana Zaccagnino, and Mexican artist
Artemio Sepulveda.

8776 Orange Co. Library. El Modena Branch.
Empanada: a tasty Mexican group art exhibit
filled with a variety of digestable treats.
Exhibition catalog, [1979]. English.

AN: Catalog of an exhibit by 15 artists:
Dolores Grajeda, William Hernandez-M.,
Marylee Montano, Patricia Murillo, Eduardo
Navarro, Susana A. Zaccagnino, Esau Quiroz,
Juan Elias Ramos, Ricardo M. Serrato,
Benjamin Valenzuela, Emigdio C. Vasquez,
Arthur Valenzuela, Jack Vargas, Alonso
Whitney, and Mexican artist Artemio
Sepulveda living in Orange County. Brief
profiles of the artists.

8777 Santa Ana Public Library, Newhope Branch,
Santa Ana, CA. Artistas latinos de Orange
County. Exhibition brochure, 1979. English.

AN: Exhibit of six artists: Dolores
Grajeda, Eduardo Navarro, Arthur Valenzuela,
Benjamin Valenzuela, Emigdio Vasquez, Susana
A. Zaccagnino.

Valle, Victor M.

8778 San Francisco Museum of Modern Art, San Francisco, CA and Pearlstein, Howard. Aesthetics of graffiti. Exhibition catalog, 1978. English.

AN: Graffiti are defined as any coherently-intended presence written, scratched, painted, engraved, printed, pasted or otherwise impressed in a public place. Graffiti have been incorporated into works by artists. In this catalog, works by Chicano artists Carlos Almaraz, Wilfred Castano, Judithe Hernandez, Gilbert Lujan, Gustavo Rivera, Frank Romero, John M. Valadez, Victor M. Valle, Xavier Viramontes - as well as many Latino and non-Latino artist, appear.

Vallejo, Linda

8779 Chicago. Public Library Cultural Center, Chicago, IL. La mujer: a visual dialogue. Exhibition invitation, 1978. English.

AN: Invitation to an exhibit spotlighting women artists from Mexico and the United States. Organized by the Movimiento Artistico Chicano (MARCH) of Chicago. 40 paintings by women artists included, and 50 works based on the theme of women. Poetry readings, music, dance, film, theatre, and panels of men and women artists included. Illustrated by work by Linda Vallejo.

8780 Conversation on photography in the Los Angeles Latino community. OBSCURA, Vol. 2, no. 2 (December, February, 1981, 1982), p. 22-32. English.

AN: Interview on the nature and distinguishing characteristics of Chicano photography with Chicano photographers Isabel Castro (Council for Latino Photography), Lorenzo Hernandez (Director of Cityscape Gallery, publisher PHOTOSHOW magazine), Joseph G. Uribe (California State University, Los Angeles, Center for the Visual Arts, Director of West Colorado Gallery), Patssi Valdez, Becky Villasenor, and sculptor, curator, and Art Director for Academia Quinto Sol, Inc., Linda Vallejo, Portfolio of photography by Chicanos Don Anton, Louis Carlos Bernal, Sean Carrillo, Patssi Valdez, Ricardo Valverde, and by Morrie Camhi and Elizabeth Sisco on Chicano subjects.

8781 Galeria, Santa Ana, CA. The last Chicano art show. Exhibition brochure, 1981. English.

AN: Invitation-brochure for an exhibit of Los Angeles and Orange County artists in a gallery underwritten by the Friendly Center, Inc. with grants from local government and from businesses. Exhibiting are (Roberto) Gil de Montes, Gilbert Lujan, Judy Miranda, Patricia Murillo, Alonso Pardo, Teddy Sandoval, Mexican artist Artemio Sepulveda, Joey Terrill, Art Valenzuela, Ben Valenzuela, Linda Vallejo, Jack A. Vargas, Emigdio Vasquez, Richard Serrato, and J. William Hernandez, who is the gallery director.

8782 Goldman, Shifra M. Thorns and roses. ARTWEEK, Vol. 11, no. 30 (September 20, 1980), p. 1. English.

AN: Report on four Chicano artists exhibiting at L.A.C.E. Gallery, Los Angeles: Carlos Almaraz, Teddy Sandoval, John

Valadez, and Linda Vallejo. Illustrated.

8783 Guggenheim Gallery, Chapman College, Orange, CA. Hexagono: paintings, sculpture, drawings, prints. Exhibit invitation, 1977. English.

AN: Invitation to an exhibit for artists Tito Aguirre, Isabel Castro, Rick Martinez, Esau Quiroz, Linda Vallejo, Emigdio Vasquez, Barrows, and Shanahan, sponsored by MEChA. Profiles and pictures of the artists.

8784 Hollister, Kelly. Linda Vallejo. CAMINOS, Vol. 1, no. 6 (October 1980), p. 19. Bilingual.

AN: Story on Long Beach, California artist Linda Vallejo who also works with Self-Help Graphics in Los Angeles and has curated a number of exhibits. Vallejo describes her work as containing "archetypal, mythological or dream-world imagery" combined with the "modern idea of self-knowledge." Illustrated on p. 17.

8785 Hunt, Annette and McNally, Mary. Community art centers in Los Angeles. SPINNING OFF, Vol. 2, no. 19 (January 1980), p. 1. English.

AN: Article includes an interview with Linda Vallejo on the community artistic work of Self-Help Graphics and Art, Inc.

8786 Jesus Gutierrez Gallery, San Pedro, CA. "Two of a kind" prints by Linda Vallejo, Muriel Olguin. Exhibition invitation [1978]. English.

AN: Invitation to an exhibit.

8787 Joslyn Art Center. Multi-media art exhibit: Muriel Olguin (printmaking), Myrna Shiras (mixed media), Linda Vallejo (painting). Exhibition invitation, 1979. English.

AN: Invitation to an exhibit.

8788 L.A.C.E. (Los Angeles Contemporary Exhibitions), Los Angeles, CA. Espina (Thorn): Carlos Almaraz, Elsa Flores, Louie Perez, Teddy Sandoval, John Valadez, Linda Vallejo. Exhibition announcement, 1980. English.

AN: Announcement of an exhibition and a performance piece by six Los Angeles artists.

8789 San Pedro Municipal Art Gallery, San Pedro, CA. Celebration: Muriel Olguin and Linda Vallejo. San Pedro, CA: San Pedro Municipal Art Gallery, [1978]. English.

AN: Invitation to an exhibit. Illustrated.

8790 Shakti Gallery, Long Beach, CA. "Fire in the lodge," paper sculptures by Linda Vallejo. Exhibit invitation, 1981. English.

AN: Invitation to an exhibit by Long Beach, CA artist Linda Vallejo. Illustrated.

Vallejo, Linda (cont.)

8791 Sol Art Gallery, San Diego, CA. Group
     showing of Southern California artists.
     Exhibition brochure, 1980. English.

     AN: First exhibit of new Chicano art
     gallery showing Los Angeles artists Carlos
     Almaraz, Judithe Hernandez, John Valadez,
     Linda Vallejo, Ricardo Duardo, Barbara
     Carrasco.

8792 Vallejo, Linda. I am...Linda Vallejo.
     CHISMEARTE, Vol. 1, no. 4 (Fall , Winter,
     1977, 1978), p. 27-30.

     AN: Brief autobiographical sketch
     illustrated with three drawings.

8793 William Grant Still Community Arts Center,
     Los Angeles, CA. Latin American artists
     exhibition. Exhibition brochure, 1978.
     English.

     AN: Exhibit curated by Linda Vallejo
     including Carlos Almaraz, Michael M.
     Amescua, Ray Bravo, Isabel Castro, Yreina
     Cervantez, Luis Serrano-Cordero, Cynthia
     Honesto, Judith Miranda, Teddy Sandoval,
     John Taboada, Emigdio Vasquez. Illustrated.

8794 Woman's Building, Los Angeles, CA.
     Crosspollination: a blending of traditional
     and contemporary art by Asian, Black and
     Chicana women. Los Angeles, CA: Woman's
     Building, 1979. English.

     AN: Invitation to an exhibit in which
     are included Patricia Murillo and Linda
     Vallejo.

Valsoto, Luis

8795 Hartnell College Studio Gallery, Salinas,
     CA. Paintings, drawings, prints by San
     Francisco Bay Area Chicano artists. Exhibit
     brochure, 1971. English.

     AN: Brochure for exhibit featuring
     Francisco Camplis, Graciela Carrillo, Sal
     Castaneda, Priscilla Dominguez, J. Duarte,
     Rupert Garcia, Carlos Loarca, Irene Perez,
     Vincent Rascon, Michael Rios, Peter
     Rodriguez, Luis Valsoto, Esteban Villa, Rene
     Yanez, Zala. Illustrated by Rupert Carcia
     print.

8796 Martinez, Anita. Raza art. EL TECOLOTE, Vol.
     1, no. 8 (November 30, 1970), p. 1. English.

     AN: Jay Ojeda, newly selected director
     of Galeria de la Raza, describes the
     memorial exhibition dedicated to Ruben
     Salazar installed at the Galeria on Dec. 12,
     1970. Salazar symbolized and synthesized
     many of the goals subscribed to by artist
     members of La Galeria. The exhibit included
     work by Chicano and Latino artists Francisco
     Camplis, Jay Ojeda, Jose Romero, Rolando
     Castellon, Rene Yanez, Luis Valsoto, Mike
     Ruiz, Carlos Perez, Gustavo Rivera, Peter
     Rodriguez, Carlos Loarca and Ralph
     Maradiaga.

Valverde, Ricardo

8797 Consejo Mexicano de Fotografia, A.C., Mexico
     City. Hecho en latinoamerica: segundo
     coloquio latinoamericano de fotografia.
     Exhibition catalog, 1982. Spanish.

     AN: Catalog/book of the second
     colloquium and exhibit of Latin American
     photography. Among the Chicano artists whose

work is reproduced are Louis Carlos Bernal,
Robert C. Buitron, David Cardenas, Isabel
Castro, Harry Gamboa, Jr., Luis Garza,
Roberto Gil de Montes, John M. Valadez,
Kathy Vargas. In the exhibit were also
Porfirio Aguilar, Elsa Marie Flores, Ricardo
Valverde. Great number of illustrations. In
Spanish.

8798 Conversation on photography in the Los
     Angeles Latino community. OBSCURA, Vol. 2,
     no. 2 (December, February, 1981, 1982), p.
     22-32. English.

     AN: Interview on the nature and
     distinguishing characteristics of Chicano
     photography with Chicano photographers
     Isabel Castro (Council for Latino
     Photography), Lorenzo Hernandez (Director of
     Cityscape Gallery, publisher PHOTOSHOW
     magazine), Joseph G. Uribe (California State
     University, Los Angeles, Center for the
     Visual Arts, Director of West Colorado
     Gallery), Patssi Valdez, Becky Villasenor,
     and sculptor, curator, and Art Director for
     Academia Quinto Sol, Inc., Linda Vallejo,
     Portfolio of photography by Chicanos Don
     Anton, Louis Carlos Bernal, Sean Carrillo,
     Patssi Valdez, Ricardo Valverde, and by
     Morrie Camhi and Elizabeth Sisco on Chicano
     subjects.

8799 Four and four: Mexican and Latino
     photography, April 25 through June 14 on the
     balcony. CALENDAR: SANTA BARBARA MUSEUM OF
     ART, (April 1981). English.

     AN: Announcement of exhibit organized by
     Lorenzo Hernandez of the Cityscape Foto
     Gallery, Pasadena, Calif. Sought to present
     "the observable differences between the
     'classic' vision of the Mexican National and
     the 'realistic' vision of the re-rooted
     Mexican/American." The latter included Louis
     Bernal (Tucson) and Ricardo Valverde (Los
     Angeles) as well as two Spanish Sephardics
     of Los Angeles, Camhi and Sisco.

8800 Galeria Otra Vez, Los Angeles, CA.
     Inner/urban landscapes: Ricardo Valverde,
     Suda House, David Feldman. Exhibition
     invitation, 1979. English.

     AN: Invitation to a photography
     exhibition held at Self-Help Graphic's
     gallery.

8801 Geyer, Anne; Hernandez, Lorenzo; and
     Valverde, Ricardo. Latino photographers of
     U.S. still seeking identity. THE NEWS,
     (September 5, 1981), p. 17. English.

     AN: Interview with Lorenzo Hernandez,
     photo dealer and owner of Cityscape Foto
     Gallery, Pasadena, Calif. in which he
     compares Mexican with U.S. Latino
     photography. Interview with Ricardo
     Valverde, Chicano photographer and co-chair
     of the Council of Latino Photography/USA,
     discussing his work. Illustrated.

8802 Los Angeles City College. Latinos de tres
     mundos. Exhibition invitation, 1980.
     English.

     AN: Invitation to an exhibit featuring
     the work of ASCO members Harry Gamboa, Jr.,
     Gronk, Willie Herron; painters Xavier Mendez
     and Olivia Sanchez; and photographer Ricardo
     Valverde.

Valverde, Ricardo (cont.)

8803 Tolin Fine Art Gallery, Lancaster, CA.
Presentation of photographic works by David
Feldman, Richard Valverde. Exhibition
invitation, 1979. English.

AN: Invitation to an exhibit.

Vandalism

8804 Cabaniss, Joe H. Mural painters believes
vandalism political act. CHULA VISTA STAR
NEWS, (March 16, 1980), p. 40-41. English.

AN: Recent vandalism on Chicano Park's
twenty outdoor murals left seven splattered
with paint. It was the second such incident
in five months. Michael Schnorr,
Southwestern College art instructor and
painter of two murals, believes the attack
was politically motivated. Illustrated.
Reprinted in COMMUNITY MURALISTS NEWSLETTER,
Spring 1981.

8805 Chapple, Paul. FV [Fountain Valley] wall
mural stirs contention. THE REGISTER,
(December 29, 1974), p. A3. English.

AN: Artist Sergio O'Cadiz has included a
panel showing gas-masked police dragging off
a Chicano youth. The panel has caused
controversy in Fountain Valley, CA; police
object to the image.

8806 Chapple, Paul. Mural, graffiti painters wage
endurance contest in F.V. [Fountain Valley].
THE REGISTER, (December 4, 1975), p. B5.
English.

AN: Mexican-born architect and designer
Sergio O'Cadiz, with a team, paints a 600
foot mural in Colonia Juarez, an older
section of Fountain Valley in Orange County,
CA. Local police objected to a scene showing
police brutality. White paint was hurled at
this panel one night, and the mural was
constantly attacked by vandals. Illustrated.

8807 Ross, Bob and Lyndon, George. The case of
three California muralists: Roberto Chavez,
Eduardo Carrillo, John Chamberlin. ARTS AND
ENTERTAINMENT, (July 1981). English.

AN: Well documented reports on the
destruction of the Carrillo, Chavez and
Chamberlin murals. Focus is on the legal
implications of mural effacement in relation
to present California law.

8808 Ruiz, Elvia. Whitewashed mural.
SENTIMIENTOS, Vol. 1, no. 2 (May 1978), p.
7-10. English.

AN: Illustrated article about Las
Mujeres Muralistas del Valle. Their mural
titled, "History of the Chicanos From a
Woman's Perspective" was vandalized. Members
of the mural group recall its creation and
comment on its destruction.

8809 Sanchez, Al. Murals destroyed. EL DIARIO DE
LA GENTE, Vol. 4, no. 14 (August 13, 1976),
p. 7. English.

AN: Open letter from Al Sanchez,
originator of the cartoon "The Tortilla Kid"
and graphics contributor to EL DIARIO.
Letter details events which led to painting
over of six "cultural" paintings at the
Denver Community Development Corporation
Building (4142 Tejon, Denver, CO). Artist
wants due compensation, specifically monies
for "the replacement of artwork to be done

by a community artist on portable murals".

8810 Sanchez, Jesus. Auditorium mural "wipe out"
during recent renovation move. EAST LOS
ANGELES COLLEGE NEWS, (September 26, 1979).
English.

AN: "The Path to Knowledge and the False
University," a mural by Roberto Chavez on
the facade of ELAC's Ingalls Auditorium was
painted over on Sept. 11, 1979. Contrasting
views on the mural's fate are offered by the
Chicano Faculty Association President and
the Dean of Educational Services.

8811 Tovar, Carlos. Chicano muralist interviewed.
NUESTRA COSA, Vol. 8, no. 1 (November,
December, 1979), p. 7. English.

AN: Interview with artist Roberto Chavez
concerning the white-washing of a mural he
painted on the outside front wall of the
campus auditorium at East Los Angeles
College.

Vanegas Arroyo, Antonio

8812 Camacho, Eduardo. Por los cien anos de la
fundacion de su editorial: inauguraran hoy
en San Diego la exposicion 'Homenaje a
Posada, Manilla y Vanegas Arroyo'.
EXCELSIOR, (February 14, 1980). Spanish.

AN: Announcing the exhibit of 19th
Century Mexican engravers Jose Guadalupe
Posada and Manuel Manilla, with publisher
Antonio Vanegas Arroyo, at the Centro
Cultural de la Raza and Southwestern
College, of San Diego, CA.

VAQUERO [sculpture]

8813 Beardsley, John. Personal sensibilities in
public places. ARTFORUM, Vol. 19, no. 10
(June 1981), p. 43-45. English.

AN: Distinction is made between art in
public places and public art. The latter is
assumed to have content and symbolism
accessible to the majority of the
population. Luis Jimenez, sculptor of
VAQUERO intended for Houston's Moody Park,
feels people should be able to identify with
art. Color illustration.

Vaqueros

8814 Cisneros, Jose. Riders of the border. El
Paso, TX: Texas Western Press, 1971.
English.

AN: Jose Cisneros, El Paso artist has
illustrated (in total or in part) over forty
books, most of which deal with the
Southwest. This collection ia a picture book
rendering the picturesqueness and pagentry
of the various riders along the border.
Illustrated with 30 black and white drawings
and text by the artist.

Varela, Maria

8815 Anaya, Rudolfo A. and Ortiz, Simon J.
1680-1980: a ceremony of brotherhood.
Albuquerque, NM: Academic, 1981. English.

AN: A cooperative publication by members
of the former La Academia de la Nueva Raza
(1969-1976) formed of writers and artists,
and the Tri-Centennial Commission of the
All-Indian Pueblo Council. Includes writings
and artworks by Chicanos and Indians from
New Mexico, California, Texas, and Arizona.
Chicano artists works included are by Ellen
Arellano, Juan Estevan Arellano, Alberto
Baros, Jose Antonio Burciaga, Juan Reyes
Cervantes, Rudy Cuellar, Ricardo Favela, El
Zarco Guerrero, Luis Jimenez, Jr., Carlos
Quinto Kemm, Alejandro Lopez, Floyd Lujan,
Jose Montoya, Juanishi Orozco, Leo Romero,
Secundino Sandoval, Jaime Valdez, Maria
Varela, Esteban Villa.

Varela, Willie

8816 Cinefestival. [n.d.], p. 5. English.

AN: Announcement of the 6th Annual
International Hispanic Film Festival in San
Antonio, TX. Willie Varela will conduct a
workshop, and Jesus Trevino will premiere
his hour-long production, SEGUIN.

Varelas Reyes, Felipe

8817 Taller de Arte, San Antonio, TX. Felipe
Varelas Reyes. Exhibition announcement, n.d.
English.

AN: Artist statement and reproduction of
one drawing in an announcement for a one man
show at the Taller.

Vargas, Adolfo

8818 Peyton, Patricia, ed. Reel change: a guide
to social issue films. San Francisco, CA:
Film Fund, 1979. English.

AN: Includes a section on Hispanic film
with descriptions, sources, and rentals.
Listed are Esperanza Vasquez's AGUEDA
MARTINEZ, Sylvia Morales' CHICANA, Adolfo
Vargas' CONSUELO: QUIENES SOMOS?/WHO ARE
WE?, El Teatro Campesino's I AM JOAQUIN,
Jose Luis Ruiz's THE UNWANTED, Jesus
Salvador Trevino's YO SOY CHICANO, and
others. Listings are international in scope.

Vargas, George

8819 Arts Council Center for the Arts of Greater
Lansing, Lansing, MI. Raza fine arts
festival. Festival program, 1978. English.

AN: This festival program mentions Jose
Narezo's mural at the Holland National Guard
Armory, Grand Rapids; includes a statement
of the Raza Art/Media Collective, Inc.; the
philosophy of artists Zaragosa Vargas and S.
Kaneta Kosiba-Vargas; and profiles of
exhibiting artists George Vargas, Martin
Moreno, Hector Perez, Michael L. Selley,
Jesse Gonzales, Nora Chapa Mendoza, Jesse
Soriano, Jose Luis Narezo.

8820 El calendario hispano de Michigan, 1981.
Stanton, MI: Montcalm Intermediate School
District and Nuestras Artes de Michigan,
1981. English.

AN: Months of historical calendar
illustrated with art works by George Vargas,
Nora Chapa Mendoza, Jesse Gonzalez, Julio
Perazza(Puerto Rican), Hector Valdez, Pamela
M. Gonzalez, Isabell Escojico (7-year-old
child), Jose Narezo, Martin Moreno, Laurie
Mendoza Psarianos, Rosa Maria Arenas.

8821 Capitol Art Gallery, Lansing, MI. Arte de
Nora Mendoza, Hector Perez, George Vargas,
Martin Moreno. Exhibition invitation [1979].
English.

AN: Invitation to an art exhibit
organized by Nuestras Artes de Michigan.

8822 Nora Mendoza: pintora de ascendencia
mexicana triunfa en los EE. UU. BUENHOGAR,
(May 1979), p. 7. Spanish.

AN: Profile of Texas-born Nora Mendoza
of Michigan, a painter of abstractions in
acrylic. She is an active member of many
Detroit and Michigan organizations,
including Nuestras Artes de Michigan which
she co-founded with Jorge Vargas, Martin
Moreno and Jessie Gonzalez.

Vargas, Jack

8823 Chicano art. ARTES VISUALES, no. 29 (1981).
English.

AN: Issue on Chicano art, introduced by
Los Angeles artist Roberto Gil de Montes.
Includes works and statements by: Pedro
Lujan (Texas); Raul M. Guerrero (Calif.);
Sylvia Salazar Simpson (New Mexico/Calif.);
Carlos Almaraz (Calif.); Rene Yanez
(Calif.); Jack Vargas (Calif.); Ray Bravo
(Calif.); John Valadez (Calif.); Gloria Maya
(Calif.); Elsa Flores (Calif.); Willie
Herron (Calif.); Gilbert "Magu" Lujan
(Calif.); Kay Torres, Jerry Lucas, and Louis
Perez (Calif.).

8824 Galeria, Santa Ana, CA. The last Chicano art
show. Exhibition brochure, 1981. English.

AN: Invitation-brochure for an exhibit
of Los Angeles and Orange County artists in
a gallery underwritten by the Friendly
Center, Inc. with grants from local
government and from businesses. Exhibiting
are (Roberto) Gil de Montes, Gilbert Lujan,
Judy Miranda, Patricia Murillo, Alonso
Pardo, Teddy Sandoval, Mexican artist
Artemio Sepulveda, Joey Terrill, Art
Valenzuela, Ben Valenzuela, Linda Vallejo,
Jack A. Vargas, Emigdio Vasquez, Richard
Serrato, and J. William Hernandez, who is
the gallery director.

8825 Mills House Visual Arts Complex, Garden
Grove, CA. Menudo: artistas latinos de
Orange County. Exhibit invitation, 1980.
English.

AN: Invitation to an exhibit organized
for the first anniversary of Artistas
Latinos de Orange County including Delores
Grajeda, William Hernandez, Marylee Montano,
Patricia Murillo, Irene Ramos, Juan Ramos,
Ricardo Serrato, Miguel Shanahan, Arthur
Valenzuela, Benjamin Valenzuela, Jack
Vargas, Alonzo Whitney, Emigdio Vasquez,
Susana Zaccagnino, and Mexican artist
Artemio Sepulveda.

Vargas, Jack (cont.)

8826 Orange Co. Library. El Modena Branch.
     Empanada: a tasty Mexican group art exhibit
     filled with a variety of digestable treats.
     Exhibition catalog, [1979]. English.

     AN: Catalog of an exhibit by 15 artists:
     Dolores Grajeda, William Hernandez-M.,
     Marylee Montano, Patricia Murillo, Eduardo
     Navarro, Susana A. Zaccagnino, Esau Quiroz,
     Juan Elias Ramos, Ricardo M. Serrato,
     Benjamin Valenzuela, Emigdio C. Vasquez,
     Arthur Valenzuela, Jack Vargas, Alonso
     Whitney, and Mexican artist Artemio
     Sepulveda living in Orange County. Brief
     profiles of the artists.

Vargas, Kathy

8827 The class of '79. SA: THE MAGAZINE OF SAN
     ANTONIO, Vol. 3, no. 4 (June 1979). English.

     AN: Well-illustrated article on students
     of James Newberry, photography teacher at
     the University of Texas, San Antonio.
     Includes photos of top prizewinners and
     members of Ladrones de la Luz, David
     Cardenas and Kathy Vargas.

8828 Con safo to hold Lutheran college exhibition
     at Texas. CHICANO TIMES, Vol. 7, no. 89
     (March 26, 1976), p. [15]. English.

     AN: Discusses the aims of "Con Safos"
     group: to interpret their environment and
     react to it; to act as spokespeople and give
     visual reality to the Chicano vision; to
     destroy stereotypes and demolish visual
     cliches. The participating artists include
     Rudy R. Trevino, Mel Casas, Lucas Hinojosa,
     Kathy Vargas, Joe Frank Acosta, Emilio
     Aguirre and Homero Ureste.

8829 Consejo Mexicano de Fotografia, A.C., Mexico
     City. Hecho en latinoamerica: segundo
     coloquio latinoamericano de fotografia.
     Exhibition catalog, 1982. Spanish.

     AN: Catalog/book of the second
     colloquium and exhibit of Latin American
     photography. Among the Chicano artists whose
     work is reproduced are Louis Carlos Bernal,
     Robert C. Buitron, David Cardenas, Isabel
     Castro, Harry Gamboa, Jr., Luis Garza,
     Roberto Gil de Montes, John M. Valadez,
     Kathy Vargas. In the exhibit were also
     Porfirio Aguilar, Elsa Marie Flores, Ricardo
     Valverde. Great number of illustrations. In
     Spanish.

8830 San Antonio Museum of Modern Art. Zarzamora:
     inaugural exhibition of Ladrones de la Luz.
     Exhibition invitation, 1979. English.

     AN: Illustrated invitation to
     photographic exhibition including Norman
     Avila, David Cardenas, Franco Cernero,
     Enrique Hernandez, Robert Maxham, James
     Newberry, Isaac Rodriguez, Daryl Studebaker,
     Richard Tichich, Beverly Ulmer, Kathy
     Vargas.

Vasquez, Emigdio

8831 Boettner, Jack. Youths help in fight against
     graffiti: muralist fights spray cans with
     brushes. LOS ANGELES TIMES [Orange County
     edition], (May 26, 1979), p. II, 12-13.
     English.

     AN: Illustrated and descriptive story
     about Orange County painter Emigdio Vasquez
     working on a series of murals with youth.

Locations of murals by the group,
biographical information about Vasquez, and
his statement about art are given.
Illustrated.

8832 Day, Orman. Hispanic life mirrored by ethnic
     artists. THE REGISTER, (July 5, 1981), p.
     B1+. English.

     AN: Story on artists Manuel Hernandez
     Trujillo and Emigdio Vasquez whose work
     opened the new Galeria in Santa Ana, and
     poet Manuel Gomez. Color illustrations.

8833 Dietmeier, R. C. City artist finds his
     inspiration where he lives. ORANGE CITY
     NEWS, (December 23, 1981), p. 2. English.

     AN: Illustrated story on Emigdio
     Vasquez's ten year retrospective of
     realistic paintings taken from photographs,
     held at the Galeria in Santa Ana, Calif.
     Vasquez records his environment and events
     from the 1940s and 1950s as an artistic and
     documentary statement.

8834 Galeria, Santa Ana, CA. Diez anos con
     Emigdio (ten years with Emigdio), works by
     Emigdio Vasquez: 1971-1981. Exhibition
     invitation, 1982.

     AN: Invitation to exhibit by Emigdio
     Vasquez. Illustrated.

8835 Guggenheim Gallery, Chapman College, Orange,
     CA. Hexagono: paintings, sculpture,
     drawings, prints. Exhibit invitation, 1977.
     English.

     AN: Invitation to an exhibit for artists
     Tito Aguirre, Isabel Castro, Rick Martinez,
     Esau Quiroz, Linda Vallejo, Emigdio Vasquez,
     Barrows, and Shanahan, sponsored by MEChA.
     Profiles and pictures of the artists.

8836 Mills House Visual Arts Complex, Garden
     Grove, CA. Menudo: artistas latinos de
     Orange County. Exhibit invitation, 1980.
     English.

     AN: Invitation to an exhibit organized
     for the first anniversary of Artistas
     Latinos de Orange County including Delores
     Grajeda, William Hernandez, Marylee Montano,
     Patricia Murillo, Irene Ramos, Juan Ramos,
     Ricardo Serrato, Miguel Shanahan, Arthur
     Valenzuela, Benjamin Valenzuela, Jack
     Vargas, Alonzo Whitney, Emigdio Vasquez,
     Susana Zaccagnino, and Mexican artist
     Artemio Sepulveda.

8837 Newport Harbor Art Museum, Newport Beach,
     CA. Our own artists: art in Orange County.
     Exhibition catalog, 1979. English.

     AN: Includes Patricia Murillo and
     Emigdio Vasquez with illustrations of one
     work each. Biographies of the artists.

Vasquez, Emigdio (cont.)

8838 Orange Co. Library. El Modena Branch.
Empanada: a tasty Mexican group art exhibit
filled with a variety of digestable treats.
Exhibition catalog, [1979]. English.

AN: Catalog of an exhibit by 15 artists:
Dolores Grajeda, William Hernandez-M.,
Marylee Montano, Patricia Murillo, Eduardo
Navarro, Susana A. Zaccagnino, Esau Quiroz,
Juan Elias Ramos, Ricardo M. Serrato,
Benjamin Valenzuela, Emigdio C. Vasquez,
Arthur Valenzuela, Jack Vargas, Alonso
Whitney, and Mexican artist Artemio
Sepulveda living in Orange County. Brief
profiles of the artists.

8839 Roberts, Tim. For art's sake, for the
community, for the working class. ORANGE
CITY NEWS, Vol. 10, (March 14, 1979), p.
1,8-9. English.

AN: Illustrated article on Orange
County, Calif. realist painter Emigdio
Vasquez. Focuses on his community murals,
and his attitudes toward his art. Also
announces the first exhibit, "Empanada" of
the newly formed Hispanic Artists
Association of Orange County. 13
participants including Vasquez.

8840 Santa Ana College, Santa Ana, CA. MECHA
presents la semana de la Raza. Exhibition
brochure, 1970. English.

AN: Program for the week's activities,
including EL ARTE DE LA RAZA exhibition,
Gilbert Sanchez Lujan speaking on "Chicano
Art in the Barrio," art demonstrations by
Gilbert Vasquez, Emigdio Vasquez, Esau
Quiroz, and Richard Garcia.

8841 Santa Ana Public Library, Newhope Branch,
Santa Ana, CA. Artistas latinos de Orange
County. Exhibition brochure, 1979. English.

AN: Exhibit of six artists: Dolores
Grajeda, Eduardo Navarro, Arthur Valenzuela,
Benjamin Valenzuela, Emigdio Vasquez, Susana
A. Zaccagnino.

8842 Valle, Victor Manuel and Vasquez, Emigdio.
Emigdio Vasquez Interview. SOMOS,
(December, January, 1978, 1979), p. 42-43.
English.

AN: Article on Arizona-born painter, son
of a miner, living in Orange County,
California. Discusses his realistic style
(from photographs), technique, humanism,
interest in murals, and loan of work for
Alejandro Grattan's film ONLY ONCE IN A
LIFETIME. Illustrated.

8843 Vasquez, Emigdio. The Cypress Street Barrio
and my art: a statement of intent.
Unpublished manuscript, 1978. English.

AN: The Arizona-born artist whose family
moved to Orange, Calif. in 1941 describes
his working class barrio and the perspective
it gave him of "life, people and society."
He turned to this subject matter as a young
artist and has continued to paint the
barrio. Description of sources and methods
of work.

8844 Vasquez, Emigdio and Goldman, Shifra M.
Painter: Emigdio Vasquez. Brochure, [1981].
English.

AN: Brochure including a brief biography
and illustrations of eight paintings.

8845 Vasquez, Emigdio. La vida through the eyes
of Emigdio Vasquez. Q-VO, (April 1979), p.
36. English.

AN: Interview with Orange County,
California, realist and documentary painter
Emigdio Vasquez who focuses on barrio life
he knew in the 1940s and 1950s. Vasquez
works from his own photographs and those of
others. Includes biographical information
and illustrations.

8846 William Grant Still Community Arts Center,
Los Angeles, CA. Latin American artists
exhibition. Exhibition brochure, 1978.
English.

AN: Exhibit curated by Linda Vallejo
including Carlos Almaraz, Michael M.
Amescua, Ray Bravo, Isabel Castro, Yreina
Cervantez, Luis Serrano-Cordero, Cynthia
Honesto, Judith Miranda, Teddy Sandoval,
John Taboada, Emigdio Vasquez. Illustrated.

8847 Wilson, William. Artistic get-together in
Orange County exhibit. CALENDAR, (November
4, 1979), p. 99. English.

AN: Review of exhibit OUR OWN ARTISTS:
ART IN ORANGE COUNTY at the Newport Harbor
Art Museum. Mention of Patricia Murillo and
Emigdio Vasquez.

Vasquez, Enriquetta

8848 Montoya, Emmanuel; Rodriguez, Patricia; and
Acevedo, Mario (Torero). Canto al pueblo
'78. NATIONAL MURALS NETWORK COMMUNITY
NEWSLETTER, (1978). English.

AN: The second annual Canto al Pueblo
took place in Corpus Christi, Texas, where
more than six murals were painted: "Wall of
Cultural Education" by 13 artists headed by
Roel Montealva; Carlota Espinoza, with
children; Gilberto Romero, Jose Antonio
Burciaga and Patricia Rodriguez,
"Incomprehension al arte"; "Madre Tierra" by
Manuel Martinez of Denver with Amador
Hinojosa (Corpus Christi) and Enriquette
Vasquez (New Mexico); Mario Torero; Salvador
Vega of Chicago whose mural some Canto
participants considered "insulting".

Vasquez, Esperanza

8849 Vasquez, Esperanza and Esparza, Moctezuma.
Agueda Martinez. 16 mm. color film. English.

AN: Sixteen-minute film directed by
Esperanza Vasquez and produced by Moctezuma
Esparza concerning the life and weaving of
an elderly New Mexican woman. Martinez
carries on the tradition of floor loom
weaving, as well as farming.

Vasquez, Gilbert

8850 Santa Ana College, Santa Ana, CA. MECHA
presents la semana de la Raza. Exhibition
brochure, 1970. English.

AN: Program for the week's activities,
including EL ARTE DE LA RAZA exhibition,
Gilbert Sanchez Lujan speaking on "Chicano
Art in the Barrio," art demonstrations by
Gilbert Vasquez, Emigdio Vasquez, Esau
Quiroz, and Richard Garcia.

Vasquez, Rey

8851 Calendario de March: 1977. Chicago, IL:
     MARCH, Inc., 1976. English.

     AN: Historical calendar with photos and
     biographies of artists. Illustrations of
     artwork by Ray Patlan, Jose Nario, Frank J.
     Sanchez, Salvador Dominguez, Salvador Vega,
     Marguerite Ortega, Aurelio Diaz, Carlos
     Cortez, Mario E. Castillo, Francisco Blasco,
     Rey Vasquez, and Efrain Martinez. History of
     MARCH (Movimiento Artistico Chicano).

Vatos

8852 Ortega, Gil. The 50's and other assorted
     Chicano graffiti. La Habra, CA: s.n., 1981.
     English.

     AN: Album of caricatures of barrio
     types; black and white drawings in six
     categories: The Parties and Dances,
     Schooldays, Oldtime Lowriders, Refine, Los
     Veteranos, Los Vatos. Some drawings
     accompanied by commentary.

Vatos de Maravilla, Los Angeles, CA

8853 Greenberg, David; Smith, Kathryn; and
     Teacher, Stuart. Megamurals & supergraphics:
     big art. Philadelphia, PN: Running Press,
     1977. English.

     AN: A full-color picture book of murals
     throughout the United States. Chicano murals
     include Michael Rios (San Francisco),
     Mujeres Muralistas (San Francisco), Leonard
     Castellanos and Tomas Gonzales with others
     (Los Angeles), Los Artes Guadalupanos de
     Aztlan (New Mexico), Willie Herron (Los
     Angeles), Toltecas en Aztlan (San Diego),
     David Botello (Los Angeles), David Lopez and
     Arizona Mara Gang (Los Angeles), Vatos de
     Maravilla (Los Angeles), Carlito Gaegos (Los
     Angeles), Gil Hernandez (Los Angeles), Wayne
     [Alaniz] Healy (Los Angeles).

8854 Nevarez, Joe R. Chicano art blooms in barrio
     warehouse. LOS ANGELES TIMES, (December 26,
     1974), p. I, 32. English.

     AN: Former meat packing warehouse
     transformed into Goez Art Studios by Joe and
     John Gonzalez. Exhibiting David Negron,
     Eddie Martinez, David Lopez (Hollywood
     scenic artists) and Roberto Arenivar. Lists
     activities of the gallery: exhibits, murals,
     restoration.

Vega, Salvador

8855 Calendario de March: 1977. Chicago, IL:
     MARCH, Inc., 1976. English.

     AN: Historical calendar with photos and
     biographies of artists. Illustrations of
     artwork by Ray Patlan, Jose Nario, Frank J.
     Sanchez, Salvador Dominguez, Salvador Vega,
     Marguerite Ortega, Aurelio Diaz, Carlos
     Cortez, Mario E. Castillo, Francisco Blasco,
     Rey Vasquez, and Efrain Martinez. History of
     MARCH (Movimiento Artistico Chicano).

8856 Chicago-Raza murals. NATIONAL MURALS NETWORK
     COMMUNITY NEWSLETTER, (Fall 1979), p. 22.
     English.

     AN: Murals by Ray Patlan, Aurelio Diaz,
     Marcos Raya, Salvador Vega, Jaime Longoria,
     Malu Ortega y Alberro, Oscar Moya in
     Chicago's Pilsen district.

8857 Elitzik, Paul. Mural magic. AMERICAS,

(June, July, 1981). English.

     AN: Brief illustrated account of murals
     in the Pilsen barrio of Chicago. Mentions
     work by Aurelio Diaz, Marcos Raya, and
     Salvador Vega. Focuses on the controversial
     mural at Benito Juarez High School painted
     by Jaime Longoria and Malu Ortega.

8858 Montoya, Emmanuel; Rodriguez, Patricia; and
     Acevedo, Mario (Torero). Canto al pueblo
     '78. NATIONAL MURALS NETWORK COMMUNITY
     NEWSLETTER, (1978). English.

     AN: The second annual Canto al Pueblo
     took place in Corpus Christi, Texas, where
     more than six murals were painted: "Wall of
     Cultural Education" by 13 artists headed by
     Roel Montealva; Carlota Espinoza, with
     children; Gilberto Romero, Jose Antonio
     Burciaga and Patricia Rodriguez,
     "Incomprehension al arte"; "Madre Tierra" by
     Manuel Martinez of Denver with Amador
     Hinojosa (Corpus Christi) and Enriquette
     Vasquez (New Mexico); Mario Torero; Salvador
     Vega of Chicago whose mural some Canto
     participants considered "insulting".

Vela, Juan B.

8859 Contemporary Arts Museum, Houston, TX. Fire!
     An exhibition of 100 Texas artists.
     Exhibition brochure, 1979. English.

     AN: Includes eleven Chicano artists.
     Unfortunately, not illustrated, though a
     checklist of works is included. Mel Casas,
     Carmen Lomas Garza, Xavier Gorena, Luis
     Jimenez, Cesar Martinez, Guillermo Z.
     Pulido, Philip Renteria, Jose L. Rivera, Joe
     Rodriguez, George Truan, Juan B. Vela.
     Introduction by James Surls. Statements by
     the artists.

Velasquez, George

8860 Castillo, Rafael. Gonzo journalism goes for
     a low ride. SAN ANTONIO EXPRESS-NEWS,
     (December 6, 1981), p. 7-B. English.

     AN: George Velasquez, editor and
     publisher of San Antonio's VAJITO magazine,
     views lowriders as a positive and evolving
     form of urban youth culture. Counters
     stereotypes about lowriders as drug-oriented
     high school drop-outs. There is a new and
     significant discourse being developed in
     literary and visual forms among Chicano
     lowriders.

Velasquez, Juan Ramon

8861 Santos of New Mexico, art of our people.
     GRITO DEL NORTE, Vol. 3, no. 1 (January 17,
     1970), p. 8-9. English.

     AN: Historical trajectory of santero
     tradition in New Mexico. Distinguished
     santeros like Rafael Aragon of Cordova,
     Miguel Herrera of Arroyo Hondo, Juan Ramon
     Velasquez of Conjilon, Jose Benito Ortega of
     La Cueva all created art wedded to the
     environment of the Southwest. Illustrated
     with a portfolio of santos and retablos from
     the Folk Art Museum of Santa Fe, NM.

Velasquez, Vicente

8862 Con Safo. San Antonio, TX: Pintores Chicanos de San Antonio, [ca. 1975]. English.

AN: Illustrated pamphlet issued by the San Antonio artists' group Con Safo. Includes a self-definition and a brief history of the group under the names El Grupo, Los Pintores de Aztlan, Los Pintores de la Nueva Raza, Con Safo (from 1967 on). Members include Jesse A. Almazan, Mel Casas, Jose Esquivel, Jose P. Garza, Cesar Augusto Martinez, Santos Martinez, Felipe Reyes, Roberto Rios, Jesus C. Trevino, and Vicente Velasquez.

Venice, CA

8863 [Untitled photograph]. CALENDAR, (April 30, 1978), p. 102. English.

AN: Illustration of Joe Bravo mural in progress, Venice, California.

8864 Varda, Agnes. Mur murs/mural murals on the wall ... Film, Cine Tamaris, Paris, 1980. English.

AN: Full length documentary film produced for French television; also available with English subtitles. Deals impressionistically with the murals and muralists of Los Angeles. Included are Wayne Alaniz Healy, David Botello, Willie Herron, Manuel Cruz, Judy Baca, the murals in Venice, CA, graffiti - among others. Color.

VIBRATIONS OF A NEW AWAKENING [mural]

8865 Valade, Carole. Mural depicts artist's heritage. ADRIAN DAILY TELEGRAM, (September 15, 1978). English.

AN: Detailed description of Vibrations of a New Awakening, mural at Community Action Art Center by Martin Moreno with assistants Hector Perez and Walter Burrow.

Vichir, Alejandro

8866 Semana de la Raza: international panel of the arts, Mexico and the United States. Santa Ana, CA: MEChA, Santa Ana College, 1972. English.

AN: An International Panel of the Arts, organized by art historian Shifra Goldman, featured Mexicans Hector Garcia, prize-winning photographer; Jaime Mejia, painter, restorer, filmmaker; Alejandro Vichir, director of Teatro Trashumante; and Chicanos Gilbert Sanchez Lujan, sculptor and painter; Gloria Osuna, painter and artist for Teatro Campesino; and Jesus Salvador Trevino, filmmaker.

Victor Clothing Co., Los Angeles, CA

8867 The Broadway mural, 1981, by John Manuel Valadez. Los Angeles, CA: Victor Clothing Co., n.d. English.

AN: Postcard/brochure about Valadez's 8x48-ft mural, oil on canvas, displayed at the Victor Clothing Co. in downtown Los Angeles. Brief profile of the photographer and muralist. Full color reproduction of a section of the complete mural.

8868 Geyer, Anne. Muralist works to dispel negative Latino images. THE NEWS, (September 2, 1981), p. 22. English.

AN: John Valadez is painting a mural on canvas depicting the Latino people of downtown Los Angeles. It will be housed in Victor Clothing Co. Valadez is one of an increasing number of artists and dealers who have moved to the downtown area. Valadez discusses the images he makes and his attempt to correct media stereotypes about Latinos. Illustrated.

8869 Johnston, Beatriz. Valadez: exponente de la vida urbana en mural contemporaneo. LA OPINION, Vol. 56, no. 68 (November 22, 1981), p. II, 1. Spanish.

AN: Report on the mural in preparation by John Valadez for Victor Clothing Co. in downtown Los Angeles. It deals with people walking in the streets of the downtown area. Illustrated with the sketch for the mural which Valadez has been painting in the basement of the building for nine months.

8870 Muchnic, Suzanne. Mural: a lullaby of another Broadway. LOS ANGELES TIMES, (December 18, 1981), p. VI, 1+. English.

AN: Commentary on the panoramic mural painted by John Valadez inside the Victor Clothing Company at 242 S. Broadway. Mural depicts Broadway street life. Photograph of the artist and the mural.

Vigil, Frederico

8871 Musica hispana en nuestras vidas/Hispanic music in our lives: almanaque 1982/calendar. Milwaukee, WI: Miller Brewing Co., 1981. English.

AN: Twelve Latino artists were commissioned to illustrate a calendar with paintings on Hispanic music. The Chicano artists include Frederico Vigil (New Mexico), Joe Bastida Rodriguez (Texas/Washington, D.C.), Manuel Martinez (Colorado), Jose Antonio Burciaga (California), Ignacio Gomez (California), Carolina Flores (Texas), Frank Martinez (California). Color.

Vigil, Veloy

8872 Miller, Marlan. Vigil paintings examine Indian life. PHOENIX GAZETTE, (November 29, 1975), p. 20. English.

AN: Review of an exhibit by Denver-born Veloy Vigil at the Sue Brown Galley in Scottsdale, Arizona. The artist works in watercolor, gouache and acrylic. Several works are discussed in detail.

8873 Richard Henkin, Inc., Beverly Hills, CA. Veloy Vigil. Exhibition Catalog, n.d.. English.

AN: Full color catalog of graphics by Denver-born painter who lives in Taos and Southern California. Biographical information, but lacks dates.

8874 Richard Henkin, Inc., Beverly Hills, CA. Veloy Vigil. Exhibition brochure, n.d. English.

AN: Full color brochure about the Denver-born artist who has exhibited in many galleries and museums in the United States. His paintings deal with western subjects.

Vigil, Veloy (cont.)

8875 Vigil, Rita. Veloy Vigil: artist capturing
ethereal horizons and the Indian spirit.
SOUTHWEST ART COLLECTOR, Vol. 1, no. 3
(March, April, 1980), p. 2. English.

AN: Denver-born artist who changed from
commercial to fine art in 1972 when he was
40 years old, though he "sidelined" in fine
art from the early 1960s. Resides in Taos
and Southern California.

Villa, Esteban

8876 Albright, Thomas. Oakland Museum: a wide
range in Latin art. SAN FRANCISCO CHRONICLE,
(September 12, 1970), p. 33. English.

AN: A large show called ARTES DE LA RAZA
at the Oakland Museum includes Mercedes
Gutierrez-McDermid, Louis Gutierrez, Luis
Cervantez, Calvin Tondre, Manuel Villamor,
Rene Yanez, Jose Ramirez, Jorge Lerma,
Rolando Castellon, Esteban Villa, Rupert
Garcia, and Gustavo Rivera who is also
having an exhibit at the Galeria de la Raza.

8877 Albright, Thomas. Pre-Columbian art: New
Galeria de la Raza. SAN FRANCISCO CHRONICLE,
(July 15, 1970), p. 49. English.

AN: A new gallery is launched at 425
14th St. in San Francisco with an exhibit by
Sacramento State College teacher Esteban
Villa, with bold angular abstractions of
roosters, comments on the Frito Bandito, and
expressionist pen and pencil drawings. Other
exhibits are also on display. The Galeria is
sponsored by Casa Hispana de Bellas Artes.

8878 Alurista. Nationchild plumaroja: 1969-1972.
San Diego, CA: Toltecas en Aztlan, Centro
Cultural de La Raza, 1972. English.

AN: Drawings by Esteban Villa and
Armando Nunez.

8879 Anaya, Rudolfo A. and Ortiz, Simon J.
1680-1980: a ceremony of brotherhood.
Albuquerque, NM: Academic, 1981. English.

AN: A cooperative publication by members
of the former La Academia de la Nueva Raza
(1969-1976) formed of writers and artists,
and the Tri-Centennial Commission of the
All-Indian Pueblo Council. Includes writings
and artworks by Chicanos and Indians from
New Mexico, California, Texas, and Arizona.
Chicano artists works included are by Ellen
Arellano, Juan Estevan Arellano, Alberto
Baros, Jose Antonio Burciaga, Juan Reyes
Cervantes, Rudy Cuellar, Ricardo Favela, El
Zarco Guerrero, Luis Jimenez, Jr., Carlos
Quinto Kemm, Alejandro Lopez, Floyd Lujan,
Jose Montoya, Juanishi Orozco, Leo Romero,
Secundino Sandoval, Jaime Valdez, Maria
Varela, Esteban Villa.

8880 And/Or Gallery, Seattle, WA. Artistas de
Aztlan. Exhibition announcement, 1975.
English.

AN: Exhibition announcement for an
important exhibit of Northwest Chicano art.
Co-sponsored by MEChA and the Chicano
Studies Program at the University of
Washington, the exhibit presented works by
Emilio Aguayo, Danny Desiga, Ricardo
Aguirre, Ramiro Benavidez, Elma Herada,
Pedro Rodriguez and others. A selection of
posters by Armando Cid of the R.C.A.F. group
from Sacramento, California was also
presented. Concurrently, at the Heny Gallery

of the University of Washington, Esteban
Villa presented a one-man show.

8881 Burkhardt, Dorothy. Chicano pride and anger
mix at 'Califas'. THE TAB, (April 12,
1981), p. 34. English.

AN: CALIFAS: AN EXHIBITION OF CHICANO
ARTISTS IN CALIFORNIA represents a
cross-section of artists exhibiting work for
at least ten years: Rupert Garcia, Ernie
Palomino, Eduardo Carrillo, Judy Baca, Rene
Yanez, Carmen Lomas Garza, Salvador Roberto
Torres, Roberto Chavez, Willie Herron, Ralph
Maradiaga, Sue Martinez, Jose Montoya,
Malaquias Montoya, Ramses Noriega and
Esteban Villa. Illustrated.

8882 Calendario de comida 1976. San Francisco,
CA: Galeria de la Raza, 1976. English.

AN: Handprinted silkscreen calendar
consisting of twelve sheets and a cover. The
work of the following artists is included:
Ralph Maradiaga, Juanishi Orozco, Francisco
Camplis, Ruben Guzman, Rodolfo Cuellar,
Xavier Viramontes, Jose Montoya, Esteban
Villa, Rene Yanez, Max Garcia and Louis "The
Foot" Gonzalez, Patricia Rodriguez, and
Ricardo Favela. All of the above are
associated with the Galeria de la Raza, or
the Royal Chicano Air Force of Sacramento,
CA.

8883 California. State College. Los Angeles. Art
Gallery. Twelve Chicano artists. Exhibition
invitation, n.d. English.

AN: Invitation to an exhibit: Jose
Montoya, Gilbert Sanchez Lujan, Esteban
Villa, Rene Yanez, Joe Moran, Armando Cid,
Leonard Castellas, Juanishi Orozco, Rudy
Cuellar, Beltran, Lopez and Cabrera.

8884 La Causa Publications, Oakland, CA. New
symbols for la Nueva Raza. Exhibition
announcement, [ca. 1969]. English.

AN: Announcement for exhibition of the
four founding artists of the Mexican
American Liberation Art Front (MALAF):
Esteban Villa, Rene Yanez, Manuel Hernandez,
Malaquias Montoya. Collage of portraits by
the artists.

8885 Centro de Artistas Chicanos, Sacramento, CA.
La arte cosmica [sic] de Esteban Villa:
Chicano art exposition. Sacramento, CA:
Centro de Artistas Chicanos, 1973. English.

AN: Invitation to an exhibition of works
by Esteban Villa at the RCAF's center.

8886 Chicano art show at Contra Costa College. EL
HISPANO, Vol. 8, no. 25 (December 11, 1973).
English.

AN: Information on exhibition organized
by Ramses Noriega that included the work of
Jose Montoya, Esteban Villa, Mario Sinape,
Ricardo Rios, Malaquias Montoya, Fuchi
Queso, and Joe Palomino.

Villa, Esteban (cont.)

8887 A Chicano artist: Emigdio Vasquez. CANNERY
WORKER, Vol. 1, no. 4 (February 1977), p. 5.
Bilingual.

AN: Story on an exhibit by Esteban Villa
in the Galeria Barrios of Sacramento,
California, which is dedicated to the
Cannery Workers Committee on its eighth
anniversary. Five works by Villa are
illustrated, and a group photograph of the
Centro de Artistas Chicanos is included.

8888 Cuellar, Rodolfo. Esteban Villa-maximo
exponente del arte indigena mexicano. EL
HISPANO, Vol. 8, no. 23 (January 27, 1976),
p. 3. Spanish.

AN: Biographical data on the artist
focusing on his activism in the formation of
the Centro de Artistas Chicanos in
Sacramento and the coalition of Centros
Chicanos in California. Illustrated with
photographs of the artist, one of his murals
and a special emblem for the "Esteban Villa
Fan Club" designed by the R.C.A.F.

8889 Goldman, Jane. Art against the wall.
SACRAMENTO MAGAZINE, (August 1980).
English.

AN: Muralists Esteban Villa, Stan
Padilla and Juanishi Orozco from the Centro
de Artistas Chicanos are planning a symbolic
65 foot, four-story mural on the parking
structure opposite Macy's. The mural is
described in detail. Illustrated.

8890 Gonzalez, Hector. El arte de Esteban Villa.
EL HISPANO, Vol. 6, no. 20 (November 6,
1973). Spanish.

AN: Commenting on Esteban Villa's one
man show at the Centro de Artistas Chicanos
that presented sixty-five pieces of art
ranging from acrylics, watercolors,
woodcuts, to pen and ink drawings. Villa
fuses Indian symbols, mythology, folklore
and customs to create a new "cosmic"
dimension for the Chicano experience.

8891 Hartnell College Studio Gallery, Salinas,
CA. Paintings, drawings, prints by San
Francisco Bay Area Chicano artists. Exhibit
brochure, 1971. English.

AN: Brochure for exhibit featuring
Francisco Camplis, Graciela Carrillo, Sal
Castaneda, Priscilla Dominguez, J. Duarte,
Rupert Garcia, Carlos Loarca, Irene Perez,
Vincent Rascon, Michael Rios, Peter
Rodriguez, Luis Valsoto, Esteban Villa, Rene
Yanez, Zala. Illustrated by Rupert Carcia
print.

8892 La historia de California, 1977. San
Francisco, CA: Galeria de la Raza, 1977.
English.

AN: Handprinted silkscreen calendar of
history seen from a Mexican point of view.
Twelve sheets and a cover. Artists are:
Ralph Maradiaga, Irene Perez, Louie "The
Foot" Gonzalez, Max Garcia, Patricia
Rodriguez, Jose Romero, Esteban Villa,
Juanishi Orozco, Rodolfo Cuellar, Jose
Montoya, Xavier Viramontes, Rene Yanez,
Ricardo Favela, associated with the Galeria
de la Raza, or the Royal Chicano Air Force
of Sacramento.

8893 Joseph Chowning Gallery; Laguna Beach Museum
of Art; and Fitzgibbon, John. California

connections: Sacramento State College, the
early 1970s. Exhibit brochure, 1982.
English.

AN: Works by 35 artists, teachers and
students at Sacramento State College. Color
plate by Eduardo Carrillo and anecdotal
material about Carrillo in text. Time frame
is important for Jose Montoya and Esteban
Villa, co-founders of the Royal Chicano Air
Force in Sacramento.

8894 Kantar, Chris and Villa, Esteban. An
interview with Esteban Villa. Unpublished
paper, 1978. English.

AN: A detailed and informative interview
with Esteban Villa, prominent Chicano
artist. Focus on Villa's philosophy of art,
life, and the Chicano art movement. A good
primary source. (The unpublished manuscript
is deposited in the archives of the R.C.A.F.
in Scaramento).

8895 Martinez, Anita. Raza! Arte! Raza! Arte!
EL TECOLOTE, Vol. 1, no. 2 (September 7,
1970), p. 3. Bilingual.

AN: Galeria de la Raza opened on July,
1970 at 425 14th St. San Francisco. It was
an outgrowth of the Arte Seis organization
(an art effort established in the Mission
District in 1967 by Francisco Camplis,
Rupert Garcia, Ralph McNeil, Jay Ojeda and
Jack Ruiz). These and other artists brought
together by the Neighborhood Arts Program
have coalesced in the new Galeria de la
Raza. Article gives goals, organizational
scheme and plans for the Galeria. It's first
exhibit was a one man show by Esteban Villa
together with a photo and sketch exhibit on
Cuba by Jay Ojeda, Roberto Diaz Perez and
Gloria Ozuna. Illustrated with installation
view of new Galeria.

8896 Martinez, Anita. Villa - "arte por toda la
Raza". EL TECOLOTE, Vol. 1, no. 5 (October
19, 1970), p. 2. English.

AN: Biographical information and
artistic trajectory of Esteban Villa, artist
from Sacramento. Villa says that to be a
Chicano is to have developed a cultural
independence. He posits his ideas on the
nature of Chicano art, its forms, functions,
and educative role. Villa describes the
evolving Chicano Art Movement with its goals
based on moral principles. Illustrated with
one of Villa's works, "Chicano Rebirth".

8897 Mexican American liberation art front: la
Raza Nueva, Rene Yanez, Esteban Villa,
Malaquias Montoya, Manuel Hernandez. BRONCE,
Vol. 1, no. 3 (March 1969), p. 6-7. English.

AN: Manifesto of MALAF, a germinal
Chicano art group in northern California.
Compares revolutionary Chicanos of 1968 with
the Mexicans of 1910; equally Chicano
artists reject European-influenced art.
Announces the exhibit NEW SYMBOLS FOR LA
RAZA NUEVA, at La Causa in Oakland, March 22
to April 5, 1969. Puts forth the group's
philosophy and goals, particularly exhibits
and art services to the "barrio".
Illustrated.

Villa, Esteban (cont.)

8898 New Galeria de la Raza. EL HISPANO, (July
     28, 1970), p. 9. English.

     AN: Review of the first exhibit at the
     Galeria de la Raza at 425 14th St. in San
     Francisco. The inaugural exhibition featured
     Esteban Villa, Luis Gutierrez and Luis
     Cervantes. The new Galeria is sponsored by
     Casa Hispana de Bellas Artes assisted by San
     Francisco Art Commission through its
     Neighborhood Arts Program.

8899 Oakes College, University of California,
     Santa Cruz, CA and Carrillo, Eduardo.
     Corazon de Aztlan: a Chicano arts show.
     Exhibition catalog, 1981. English.

     AN: Catalog of exhibit including works
     by Eduardo Carrillo, Juana Franklin, Cruz
     Zamarron, Jerry Astorga, Jaime Valadez,
     Ernesto Palomino, Sal Garcia, Roger Sierra,
     Jose Montoya, Esteban Villa, Juanishi
     Orozco, from Santa Cruz, San Jose, Fresno
     and Sacramento. Presentations of films and
     by the Teatro de la Tierra Morena of Santa
     Cruz County.

8900 Photo-graphics/foto-grafica. MAIZE, Vol. 4,
     no. 1-2 (Fall , Winter, 1980, 1981).
     Bilingual.

     AN: 9 drawings and prints by Royal
     Chicano Air Force (Sacramento, Calif.)
     artists Jose Montoya, Juanishi Orozco,
     Esteban Villa.

8901 Quirarte, Jacinto. Mexican-American artists.
     Austin, TX: University of Texas Press, 1973.
     English.

     AN: First comprehensive historical text
     on artists of Mexican descent in the United
     States. Sets up the antecedents from
     settlement to the visits of Mexican
     muralists Rivera, Siqueiros, Orozco and
     Tamayo in the U.S., though only Orozco and
     Tamayo are considered at length. Mexican
     American artists are divided by decades of
     birth, from 1901 to 1946. Twenty-seven
     artists (two women) are discussed. The
     epilogue is a discussion on the terms
     "Mexican American" and "Chicano," the latter
     articulated by Esteban Villa, who is not in
     the text.

8902 R.C.A.F. artistas precursores del arte
     chicano. EL HISPANO, Vol. 8, no. 35
     (February 17, 1976), p. 1. English.

     AN: Information on the R.C.A.F.
     organization. Includes group photograph of
     R.C.A.F. members, Jose Montoya, Esteban
     Villa, John Carrillo, Ricardo Fabela, Rudy
     Cuellar, Juanishi Orozco and Frank Godena.

8903 Rios, Sam. Chicano muralist: Toltecotl in
     Aztlan. Unpublished paper, 1980. English.

     AN: History of pre-Columbian, Mexican,
     and Chicano wall paintings. Describes in
     detail murals by Jose Montoya, Juanishi
     Orozco, Esteban Villa, Stan Padilla, Juan
     Cervantes, Lorraine Garcia of the Centro de
     Artistas Chicanos, Royal Chicano Air Force,
     painted in 1977 at Southside Park,
     Sacramento, Calif. Symbolism is explained.

8904 S.A. site for National Symposium on Mexican
     American Art. CHICANO TIMES, Vol. 4, no. 30
     (November 9, 1973), p. 5. English.

     AN: Held at Trinity University, the

Symposium discussed such issues as, creative
evolution, art education, artistic
relationships to Mexico and the evolution of
Mexican American art in the California
barrios. Participating artists included Rudy
Trevino, Mel Casas, Octavio Medellin,
Antonio Garcia, Carmen Garza, Esteban Villa,
Jose Montoya, Ernesto Palomino, Michael
Ponce de Leon, Luis Jimenez and Eugenio
Quesada.

8905 San Francisco. ART NEWS MAGAZINE, Vol. 69,
     no. 6 (October 1970), p. 83. English.

     AN: Review of Esteban Villa's show, the
     first held by the newly constituted Galeria
     de la Raza in San Francisco. Illustrated.

8906 Santa Ana College, Santa Ana, CA and
     Goldman, Shifra M. Chicano art. Exhibition
     catalog, 1974. English.

     AN: Thirteen California artists are
     presented in a short essay defining Chicano
     as a double mestizaje of Mexican mestizo and
     U.S. influences that exists in a state of
     "reconciled conflict." Its aim is
     communication. Artists included are
     Malaquias Montoya, Rupert Garcia, Manuel
     Hernandez, Esteban Villa, Robert Gomez,
     Harvey Tarango, Mary Helen Castro, Eduardo
     Carrillo, Graciela Carrillo, and "Los Four":
     Carlos Almaraz, Robert de la Rocha, Judithe
     Hernandez, Gilbert Lujan and Frank Romero.

8907 Schlesinger, Ellen. At the Galeria Posada
     there is sophistication, machismo and humor:
     Villa has varied impact. SACRAMENTO BEE,
     (August 23, 1981), p. Scene, 3. English.

     AN: Favorable review of exhibit by
     Esteban Villa showing etchings, xerox
     prints, lithographs and other graphics.
     Villa's world view is broad, critical,
     political and romantic and encompasses
     comments of computerized society to stylized
     landscapes. Illustrated.

8908 Street, Sharon. Califas - a celebration of
     Chicano culture and art. CITY ON A HILL,
     (April 16, 1981). English.

     AN: Review of an exhibit at College V's
     Sesnon Gallery featuring 15 California
     artists: Ramses Noriega, Judy Baca, Salvador
     Roberto Torres, Malaquias Montoya, Rene
     Yanez, Ralph Maradiaga, Jose Montoya,
     Esteban Villa, Carmen Lomas Garza, Robert
     Chavez, among others. Illustrated.

8909 Tapia, Ludy. Montoya and the art of
     survival. LA VOZ DEL PUEBLO, Vol. 3, no. 5
     (June 1972), p. 6. English.

     AN: Profile of San Francisco Bay area
     poster maker and artist Malaquias Montoya,
     who first became involved in the Chicano
     movement in San Jose working with MASC and
     EL MACHETE paper. In Berkeley (1968), he met
     Esteban Villa and, with others, formed the
     Mexican American Liberation Art Front
     (MALAF). Montoya is against elitism
     influencing Chicano art, and is concerned
     with commercialization of Chicano art and
     artists. Illustrated.

Villa, Pancho

8910 Hernandez, Sergio. Hero worship poster pop
     [drawing]. CON SAFOS, Vol. 2, no. 5 (1970),
     p. 24-25.

Villa, Richard G

8911 Galeria: a place you should visit. CAMINOS, Vol. 2, no. 5 (October 1981), p. 24-25. English.

AN: Announcement of the opening of Galeria, specializing in Hispanic art, in Orange County, California. Illustrations of sculpture by Richard G. Villa and Eduardo Oropeza.

Villagran, Marcus

8912 Art Gallery, California State University, Long Beach and Lujan, Gilbert Sanchez "Magu". El arte del pocho. Exhibit brochure, October 1968. English.

AN: Information about Southern California artists John Deheras, Marcus Villagran, Roberto de la Rocha, Santos Zuniga, Crispin Gonzales, Richard Martinez, Jesus Gutierrez, Ed Oropeza, Pete Mendez, David Ramirez, Gilbert Sanchez Lujan, Willie Hernandez, Art Ponce, Carmen Tostado, Al Almeida, David Ceja, Robert E. Chavez, Thomas A. Ferriera. All art students, graduates, or faculty.

Villalvazo, Adolph

8913 Help the Delano farm workers. Flyer, 1966. English.

AN: Adolph Villalvazo, drawing reproduced.

8914 The plan of Delano. Brochure, n.d. English.

AN: Los Angeles artist Adolph Villavazo, Charcoal drawing, 1966.

Villamor, Manuel

8915 Albright, Thomas. Oakland Museum: a wide range in Latin art. SAN FRANCISCO CHRONICLE, (September 12, 1970), p. 33. English.

AN: A large show called ARTES DE LA RAZA at the Oakland Museum includes Mercedes Gutierrez-McDermid, Louis Gutierrez, Luis Cervantez, Calvin Tondre, Manuel Villamor, Rene Yanez, Jose Ramirez, Jorge Lerma, Rolando Castellon, Esteban Villa, Rupert Garcia, and Gustavo Rivera who is also having an exhibit at the Galeria de la Raza.

8916 Los Medanos College Gallery, [CA]. Cinco/five: an exhibit of five Bay Area artists. Exhibition brochure, n.d. English.

AN: Artists Gerry Concha, Gustavo Rivera, Raoul Mora, Manuel Villamor and Peter Rodriguez included in the show. Illustrated by Peter Rodriguez's portraits of the five.

8917 Temko, Allan. Ole! It's already a triumph. REVIEW [supplement to SAN FRANCISCO SUNDAY EXAMINER], (December 28, 1980), p. 13-14. English.

AN: A glowing report on the Mexican Museum as it celebrates its fifth anniversary. Provides details about programs, financing and goals. Brief analysis of the work of sculptor Manuel Neri and painters Manuel Villamor, Gustavo Rivera, Alfredo Arreguin and Miguel Almaguer. Informative profile on Peter Rodriguez, founder and Executive Director of the Museum.

Villanueva, NM

8918 Frankenstein, Alfred. Report from New Mexico. Needlework narrative of parish life. ART IN AMERICA, Vol. 66, no. 5 (September, October, 1978), p. 52-55. English.

AN: Illustrated report on the Villanueva Tapestry: an embroidered history of a New Mexico town by women residents, coached through and documented by the Museum of International Folk Art of Santa Fe.

Villarreal, Roman

8919 59th Street Gallery, St. Louis, MO. Midwest Mexican-American art exhibit: Mexico and its artists. Exhibition brochure, 1981. English.

AN: Sponsored by the Sociedad Mexicana "Benito Juarez" and the international Institute of St. Louis, this three-part exhibit includes 1) MEXICO AS SEEN BY HER CHILDREN, a bilingual exhibit from Mexico traveling under Smithsonian Institution auspices, 2) MEXICAN CHILDREN IN THE U.S.A., 3) MEXICAN AMERICAN ARTISTS. In the latter are included Stephen Capiz (Roseville, Minn.), Jose Gonzalez (Chicago), Cesar A. Martinez (San Antonio), Ada Medina (Des Moines), Nora Chapa Mendoza (West Bloomfield, Mich.), Rene David Michel-Trapaga (St. Louis), David Munoz (Kansas City, Mo.), Jose Luis Narezo (Grand Rapids, Mich.), Benny Ordonez, Roman Villarreal (Chicago), Alejandro Romero (Chicago), Aurelio Diaz "Tekpankalli" (Chicago), Simon Ybarra (St. Louis).

Villasenor, Becky

8920 Conversation on photography in the Los Angeles Latino community. OBSCURA, Vol. 2, no. 2 (December, February, 1981, 1982), p. 22-32. English.

AN: Interview on the nature and distinguishing characteristics of Chicano photography with Chicano photographers Isabel Castro (Council for Latino Photography), Lorenzo Hernandez (Director of Cityscape Gallery, publisher PHOTOSHOW magazine), Joseph G. Uribe (California State University, Los Angeles, Center for the Visual Arts, Director of West Colorado Gallery), Patssi Valdez, Becky Villasenor, and sculptor, curator, and Art Director for Academia Quinto Sol, Inc., Linda Vallejo, Portfolio of photography by Chicanos Don Anton, Louis Carlos Bernal, Sean Carrillo, Patssi Valdez, Ricardo Valverde, and by Morrie Camhi and Elizabeth Sisco on Chicano subjects.

Villasenor, David

8921 Knapp, Dan. KCET's show for Chicano viewers. LOS ANGELES TIMES, (April 3, 1970), p. IV, 18. English.

AN: Story on the television series AHORA! started September 1969 on KCET, Los Angeles' National Educational Television. Edward Moreno is program director and host; Victor Millan is producer-director; Claudio Fenner-Lopez, senior producer, has staff including set-designer David Villasenor, production manager James Val, and alternate host-narrator Jesus Trevino. The program has shown exhibits of artists Gilberto Lujan and Daniel Ramirez.

Villasenor, David (cont.)

8922 Le Page, David. He was pioneer in permanent
     Indian sand paintings: artist found his
     niche by returning to his roots. LOS ANGELES
     TIMES [San Gabriel Valley edition], (April
     26, 1981), p. IX,1,11. English.

     AN: David Villasenor learned crafts from
     Indian students at school he attended in
     Sonora, after his family moved to the U.S.
     in 1929. He was brought to Santa Fe, New
     Mexico at 16 to teach boyscouts
     wood-carving. He perfected a method for
     gluing Indian-influenced sand paintings to a
     surface, and has made many for museums. Well
     illustrated.

8923 Villasenor, David and Villasenor, Jean. How
     to do permanent sand painting. Glendora, CA:
     David and Jean Villasenor, 1972. English.

     AN: A how-to book with techniques,
     examples, and explanations of Indian motifs
     by David Villasenor who has made a career of
     producing sand paintings for museums and
     other clients. Color and black and white
     illustrations.

Villasenor Grijalva, Lucila
     USE: Grijalva, Lucila V.

Villegas, Martha

8924 California. State College. Los Angeles. Art
     Department. Fifth California small images
     exhibition. Exhibition catalog, [1972].
     English.

     AN: Catalog for an exhibit including the
     work of Charles D. Almaraz, Mary Lynn
     Dominguez, Gilbert Sanchez Lujan (who won
     Purchase Awards), Stephen Anaya, Martha
     Villegas. Illustrated.

Viramontes, Xavier

8925 An.i.ma.tion: the arts, techniques, and
     processes involved in giving apparent life
     and movement to inanimate objects by means
     of cinematography. San Francisco, CA:
     Galeria de la Raza, n.d. English.

     AN: Illustrated booklet on animation.
     Reproductions and sequences illustrated by
     Leslie Cabarga, Xavier Viramontes and Ralph
     Maradiaga.

8926 Arnold, Frank. Posters and society. PEOPLE'S
     WORLD, Vol. 23, no. 2. English.

     AN: An exhibit at the San Francisco
     Museum of Art curated by Rolando Castellon.
     The article focuses on the posters of Xavier
     Viramontes and Rupert Garcia of San
     Francisco.

8927 Calendario de comida 1976. San Francisco,
     CA: Galeria de la Raza, 1976. English.

     AN: Handprinted silkscreen calendar
     consisting of twelve sheets and a cover. The
     work of the following artists is included:
     Ralph Maradiaga, Juanishi Orozco, Francisco
     Camplis, Ruben Guzman, Rodolfo Cuellar,
     Xavier Viramontes, Jose Montoya, Esteban
     Villa, Rene Yanez, Max Garcia and Louis "The
     Foot" Gonzalez, Patricia Rodriguez, and
     Ricardo Favela. All of the above are
     associated with the Galeria de la Raza, or
     the Royal Chicano Air Force of Sacramento,
     CA.

8928 Dunsmore de Carrillo, Patricia. On Rene

Yanez of the Galeria de la Raza. CHISMEARTE,
Vol. 1, no. 1 (Fall   1976), p. 8-9.
English.

     AN: Report on Yanez's negotiations with
     the Foster Kleiser Company to take over a
     billboard located outside the Galeria in San
     Fancisco which has been painted by Michael
     Rios, the Centro de Cambio and TIN TAN
     magazine, Zaiver (Xavier) Viramontes, and
     others.

8929 Gonzalez, Tobias and Gonzalez, Sandra.
     Perspectives on Chicano education. Stanford,
     CA: Stanford University, 1975. English.

     AN: Reproductions of artworks by Ralph
     Maradiaga, Patricia Rodriguez, Roberto
     Bonilla, Francisco Camplis, Graciela
     Carrillo-Lopez, Juan Fuentes, Irene Perez,
     Roger Reyes, Carlos Loarca, Xavier
     Viramontes, Ralph McNeill, Rupert Garcia,
     Jose Romero.

8930 Heard Museum, Phoenix, AZ. Second Southwest
     Chicano Art Invitational. Exhibit catalog,
     1978. English.

     AN: Exhibit by eight artists: Antonio
     Pazos (Tucson), Rudy Fernandez (Salt Lake
     City), Harry Gamboa (Los Angeles), Rupert
     Garcia and Xavier Viramontes (San
     Francisco), Roberto Rios (San Antonio),
     Roberto Espinoza (Yuma), and Roberto Borboa
     (Tucson). Brief biographies of all but Rios.
     29 illustrations.

8931 La historia de California, 1977. San
     Francisco, CA: Galeria de la Raza, 1977.
     English.

     AN: Handprinted silkscreen calendar of
     history seen from a Mexican point of view.
     Twelve sheets and a cover. Artists are:
     Ralph Maradiaga, Irene Perez, Louie "The
     Foot" Gonzalez, Max Garcia, Patricia
     Rodriguez, Jose Romero, Esteban Villa,
     Juanishi Orozco, Rodolfo Cuellar, Jose
     Montoya, Xavier Viramontes, Rene Yanez,
     Ricardo Favela, associated with the Galeria
     de la Raza, or the Royal Chicano Air Force
     of Sacramento.

8932 Miller, Marlan. Heard speaks Spanish through
     art. PHOENIX GAZETTE, (September 23, 1978).
     English.

     AN: Four new exhibits at the Heard
     Museum of Phoenix include "Hispanic crafts
     of the Southwest", and "Southwest Chicano
     Art Invitational". The former focuses on New
     Mexico and Colorado crafts, organized by the
     Taylor Museum if the Colorado Springs Fine
     Arts Center; the latter includes Rupert
     Garcia and Xavier Miramontes of San
     Francisco, Rudy Fernandez of Salt Lake City
     (now in Scottsdale, AZ), and Antonio Pazos
     of Tucson.

Viramontes, Xavier (cont.)

8933 San Francisco Museum of Modern Art, San
     Francisco, CA and Pearlstein, Howard.
     Aesthetics of graffiti. Exhibition catalog,
     1978. English.

     AN: Graffiti are defined as any
     coherently-intended presence written,
     scratched, painted, engraved, printed,
     pasted or otherwise impressed in a public
     place. Graffiti have been incorporated into
     works by artists. In this catalog, works by
     Chicano artists Carlos Almaraz, Wilfred
     Castano, Judithe Hernandez, Gilbert Lujan,
     Gustavo Rivera, Frank Romero, John M.
     Valadez, Victor M. Valle, Xavier Viramontes
     - as well as many Latino and non-Latino
     artist, appear.

8934 El Taller, Inc., Chicago, IL and Movimiento
     Artistico Chicano (MARCH), Chicago, IL.
     Skyjacked: screenprinted posters from
     California by the Royal Chicano Air Force
     (R.C.A.F.), 1980. Exhibition invitation,
     1980. English.

     AN: Invitation to an exhibit at the El
     Taller Gallery, co-sponsored by MARCH.
     Illustrated with a print by San Francisco
     artist Xavier Viramontes.

8935 Time to greez: incantations from the Third
     World. San Francisco, CA: Glide
     Publications/Third World Communications,
     1975. English.

     AN: Rupert Garcia, drawing, p. 158;
     Xavier Viramontes, silkscreen, p. 181; Juan
     Fuentes, drawing, p. 188; Graciela Carrillo,
     drawing, p. 196.

Virgin of Guadalupe

8936 Baca, Walter R. La Virgen. DE COLORES, Vol.
     1, no. 2 (Spring 1974), p. 58-59. Spanish.

8937 Lopez, Yolanda M. [Untitled montage from the
     SERIE GUADALUPE]. MAIZE, Vol. 1, no. 4
     (Summer 1978), p. Ft cover. English.

8938 Lopez, Yolanda M. [Untitled montage from the
     SERIE GUADALUPE]. MAIZE, Vol. 1, no. 4
     (Summer 1978), p. 55-59. English.

8939 Lopez, Yolanda M. [Untitled paintings from
     the SERIE GUADALUPE]. MAIZE, Vol. 1, no. 4
     (Summer 1978), p. Bk cover. English.

8940 Mandeville Center for the Arts, La Jolla, CA
     and Lopez, Yolanda M. Yolanda M. Lopez
     works: 1975-1978. Exhibition catalog, 1978.
     English.

     AN: Catalog of an exhibit dedicated to
     Lopez's female family members, expecially
     her grandmother and mother, to the artist
     herself as a track runner, and to the
     Guadalupe series, icons of the Virgin
     transformed to reflect the life of
     contemporary women. Well illustrated.

8941 Rodriguez, Vicente. Nuestra Senora de
     Guadalupe=Our Lady of Guadalupe [drawing].
     TEJIDOS, Vol. 4, no. 2 (Summer 1977), p. 23.
     Bilingual.

Virginia Blue Resource Center, Denver, CO

8942 Ditmar, Joanne. A new industry, done the old
     way. EMPIRE MAGAZINE, (September 26, 1976),
     p. 22-25. English.

     AN: The Virginia Blue Resource Center

for Colorado Women is embarked on a project
to revive handicrafts and skills among
Hispano women in the San Luis Valley.
Igniting interest in traditional crafts like
embroideries, tin work, straw mosaic and
filigree jewelry, the Center hopes to revive
or maintain these traditions. Detailed
information on a project to create a group
of embroidered wall hangings depicting San
Luis Valley life past and present.
Illustrated with examples of the completed
wall hangings.

VORTICE (Stanford University)

8943 Yarbro-Bejarano, Yvonne. Resena de revistas
     chicanas: problemas y tendencias, Part I. LA
     PALABRA, Vol. 2, no. 1 (Spring 1980), p.
     76-85. Spanish.

     AN: Review of five Chicano magazines of
     California discussing their contents, both
     literary and artistic, taking a critical
     attitude toward both. The five are FUEGO DE
     AZTLAN, VORTICE, PRISMA, MAIZE, and MANGO.

Voter Turnout

8944 Ramirez de Robe, Jose "Controll".
     [Pensamientos de... (drawing)]. CARACOL,
     Vol. 1, no. 3 (November 1974), p. 3.
     Bilingual.

WALL OF BROTHERHOOD [mural]

8945 Sorell, Victor A. Barrio murals in Chicago:
     painting the Hispanic-American experience on
     "our community" walls. REVISTA
     CHICANO-RIQUENA, Vol. 4, no. 4 (Fall
     1976), p. 51-72. English.

     AN: Important survey of Chicago's Latino
     murals, with key works considered in detail.
     Among the Chicano art organizations and
     muralists mentioned are MARCH (Movimiento
     Artistico Chicano), and Yolanda Galvan,
     Juanita Jaramillo, Jose Nario, Raymond
     Patlan, Vicente Mendoza, Marcos Raya,
     Ricardo Alonzo, Jose G. Gonzalez and Mario
     Castillo, author of the earliest Latino
     mural in Chicago (1968). Puerto Rican and
     non-Latino muralists and mural groups are
     also discussed. Well illustrated.

WALL OF CULTURAL EDUCATION [mural]

8946 Montoya, Emmanuel; Rodriguez, Patricia; and
     Acevedo, Mario (Torero). Canto al pueblo
     '78. NATIONAL MURALS NETWORK COMMUNITY
     NEWSLETTER, (1978). English.

     AN: The second annual Canto al Pueblo
     took place in Corpus Christi, Texas, where
     more than six murals were painted: "Wall of
     Cultural Education" by 13 artists headed by
     Roel Montealva; Carlota Espinoza, with
     children; Gilberto Romero, Jose Antonio
     Burciaga and Patricia Rodriguez,
     "Incomprehension al arte"; "Madre Tierra" by
     Manuel Martinez of Denver with Amador
     Hinojosa (Corpus Christi) and Enriquette
     Vasquez (New Mexico); Mario Torero; Salvador
     Vega of Chicago whose mural some Canto
     participants considered "insulting".

Washington (state)

8947 Segade, Gustavo V. Alfredo Arreguin.
     CITYBENDER, Vol. 2, no. 9 (1978). English.

     AN: Brief profile of Mexican-born
     painter Arreguin who lives in the state of
     Washington. Three illustrations.

Watsonville, CA

8948 Gilroy's public art form. THE VALLEY WORLD,
     (July 19, 1978). English.

     AN: Article cites activities of "The
     Tortuga Patrol" a Chicano muralist group
     from the Watsonville California area.

Weaving

8949 Arredondo, Alicia. Bolsillo [weaving].
     TEJIDOS, Vol. 5, no. 1 (1978), p. 23.
     Spanish.

8950 Guerrero, Yolanda Eligia. Weaving [artwork].
     TEJIDOS, Vol. 5, no. 1 (1978), p. 24.
     Bilingual.

Whitney Museum of American Art, New York

8951 Doty, Robert. Human concern/personal
     torment: the grotesque in American art. New
     York: Praeger, 1969. English.

     AN: Acknowledging the revival of realism
     after fifty years of abstraction, the
     Whitney Museum of American Art in New York
     mounted a controversial show of modern and
     contemporary painters and sculptors. Two
     sculptures and a drawing by Luis Jimenez
     were included, one of which, THE AMERICAN
     DREAM, (1968) is illustrated.

Whittier Blvd., Los Angeles, CA

8952 Saenz, John. Felix completes art project:
     artist's murals mask East LA graffitti
     [sic]. EAST LOS ANGELES TRIBUNE, (November
     30, 1972), p. A-4. English.

     AN: Charles Felix is doing murals as
     part of a community beautification "Wall
     Project" to cover graffiti. His present
     project is a series of murals intended to
     make Whittier Blvd. into a street gallery.
     Illustrated.

WNET Independent Documentary Film Fund

8953 CHICANO CINEMA NEWSLETTER. Vol. 1, no. 1
     (December 1978). English.

     AN: Reports on activities of Chicano
     filmmakers in producing films, meeting with
     organizations like the American Film
     Institute, the Hispanic Task Force of the
     National Endowment for the Arts, the WNET
     Independent Documentary Film Fund.
     International film news also included.

Women

     USE: Chicanas

WOMEN & THEIR WORK [festival], Austin, TX

8954 Encuentro artistico femenil. Austin, TX:
     Juarez-Lincoln Institute, Centro Cultural de
     LUCHA, 1977. English.

     AN: Program of music, literature and
     visual art. Lists works by 12 Latina artists
     and brief biographies. Part of "Women &
     Their Work" festival.

8955 Goldman, Shifra M. Women artists of Texas:
     MAS = More + Artists + Women = MAS.
     CHISMEARTE, no. 7 (January 1981), p. 21-22.
     English.

     AN: History of Texas Chicana women
     artists' organization, Mujeres Artistas del
     Suroeste (MAS), co-founded in 1977 by Santa
     Barraza and Nora Gonzalez-Dodson in the
     framework of the burgeoning feminist art
     movement, particularly Women and Their Work
     of Texas. Brief history of Chicano politics
     and the corresponding art movement of
     southern and central Texas. In addition to
     Barraza and Gonzalez-Dodson, Alicia
     Arredondo, Modesta Trevino, and Maria Flores
     are considered. Illustrated.

Women's Rights

8956 Allen, Jane and Guthrie, Derek. La mujer: a
     visual dialogue. NEW ART EXAMINER, Vol. 5,
     no. 10 (July 1978), p. 14. English.

     AN: Review of international show by
     MARCH of Chicago on women's themes.
     Criticizes male Chicano artistic stereotypes
     of women compared to women's art on women
     from California.

8957 ENCUENTRO FEMENIL (San Fernando, CA). Vol.
     1, no. 1 (Spring 1973), p. 1+. English.

     AN: Publication sponsored by Hijas de
     Cuauhtemoc, a Chicana femenist group. Black
     and white drawings on cover by Pat Portera
     Crary. Art work by Vicki Thrall, Adelaida
     del Castillo, and Maria Hortencia Garcia.
     Photography by Cindy Honesto and David
     Lazarin.

8958 Goldman, Shifra M. Women artists of Texas:
     MAS = More + Artists + Women = MAS.
     CHISMEARTE, no. 7 (January 1981), p. 21-22.
     English.

     AN: History of Texas Chicana women
     artists' organization, Mujeres Artistas del
     Suroeste (MAS), co-founded in 1977 by Santa
     Barraza and Nora Gonzalez-Dodson in the
     framework of the burgeoning feminist art
     movement, particularly Women and Their Work
     of Texas. Brief history of Chicano politics
     and the corresponding art movement of
     southern and central Texas. In addition to
     Barraza and Gonzalez-Dodson, Alicia
     Arredondo, Modesta Trevino, and Maria Flores
     are considered. Illustrated.

8959 Mujeres de Aztlan. EL TECOLOTE, Vol. 4, no.
     1 (October 10, 1973), p. 3. English.

     AN: A collective of Third World women
     artists plan an art show at Galeria de la
     Raza in San Francisco. Stressing the need
     for art forms that bring awareness and
     present the true nature of women's living
     conditions, this call for submission of art
     work reflects some feminist concerns of the
     period.

8960 Venegas, Sybil. Conditions for producing
     Chicana art. CHISMEARTE, Vol. 1, no. 4 (Fall,
     Winter, 1977, 1978), p. 2, 4. English.

     AN: Chicana artists face more obstacles
     than white women or Chicano counterparts in
     the arts. Mexican life style has portrayed
     the ideal of a submissive woman, but the
     values have changed. Chicana artists are
     concerned with women and their struggles.
     Muralists include Patricia Rodriguez, Irene
     Perez, Consuelo Mendez de Castillo, Susan
     Cervantes, Ester Hernandez, Miriam Olivo,
     Ruth Rodriguez, of the Mujeres Muralistas
     (San Francisco). Other artists are Etta
     Delgado and Barbara Carrasco.

Wood Carving

8961 Hernandez-Trujillo, Manuel. Girl leaning [painting]. EL GRITO, Vol. 2, no. 3 (Spring 1969), p. [33]. Spanish.

Woodcuts

8962 Aguirre, Ignacio. [Untitled woodcut]. REGENERACION, Vol. 1, no. 7 (1970), p. 7.

8963 Beltran, Alberto. [Untitled woodcut]. CARACOL, Vol. 1, no. 12 (August 1975), p. 13.

8964 Bonilla, Guillermo. [Untitled woodcut]. CARACOL, Vol. 1, no. 12 (August 1975), p. 10.

8965 Huerta, Elena. [Untitled woodcut]. CARACOL, Vol. 1, no. 12 (August 1975), p. 11.

8966 Iniguez, Javier. [Untitled woodcut]. CARACOL, Vol. 1, no. 12 (August 1975), p. 14.

8967 Iniguez, Javier. [Untitled woodcut]. CARACOL, Vol. 1, no. 12 (August 1975), p. 13.

8968 Jimenez, Sarah. [Untitled woodcut]. CARACOL, Vol. 1, no. 12 (August 1975), p. 12.

8969 Maradiaga, Ralph. La gente [woodcut]. TIN TAN, Vol. 2, no. 5 (June 1, 1977), p. [18].

8970 Maradiaga, Ralph. Old woman [woodcut]. TIN TAN, Vol. 2, no. 5 (June 1, 1977), p. [15].

8971 Maradiaga, Ralph. Serpent [woodcut]. TIN TAN, Vol. 2, no. 5 (June 1, 1977), p. [15].

8972 Martin, Maria Luisa. [Untitled woodcut]. CARACOL, Vol. 1, no. 12 (August 1975), p. 12.

8973 Martinez, Cesar Augusto. Don Pedrito Jaramillo [woodcut]. CARACOL, Vol. 3, no. 4 (December 1976), p. Bk Cover.

8974 Mexiac, Adolfo. [Untitled woodcut]. CARACOL, Vol. 1, no. 12 (August 1975), p. 14.

8975 Mora, Francisco. [Woodcut of Emiliano Zapata]. REGENERACION, Vol. 1, no. 7 (1970), p. 5.

8976 Rabel, Fanny. [Untitled woodcut]. CARACOL, Vol. 1, no. 12 (August 1975), p. 11.

Writers
USE: Authors

Wyoming

8977 Edward Chavez: sculptor-painter. LA LUZ, Vol. 2, no. 2 (May 1973), p. 28-31. English.

AN: Lavishly illustrated biographical account of Edward Chavez. Born in Ocate, New Mexico in 1917, Chavez has a distinguished career as a painter and sculptor. During the 1940's he executed a number of murals under sponsorship of various government art projects. These murals were placed in public buildings in Nebraska, Colorado and Wyoming. Although living and working in New York most of his adult life, the work of Edward Chavez has always been influenced by the Southwest.

XALMAN [journal]

8978 Chavez, Jaime. Rayaprofiles: Manuel Unzueta.

RAYAS, Vol. 2, no. 3 (May, June, 1979), p. 5. Spanish.

AN: Brief biography of Mexican-born Chicano artist and muralist from Santa Barbara, California. Manuel Unzueta is active with La Casa de la Raza and its publication XALMAN. Unzueta is invited to paint a mural in Albuquerque. A Santa Barbara mural is illustrated.

Xicanindio Art

8979 Acevedo, Esperanza "Inky". [Untitled drawing]. REVISTA CHICANO-RIQUENA, Vol. 5, no. 1 (Winter 1977), p. 44. English.

8980 Acevedo, Esperanza "Inky". [Untitled drawing]. REVISTA CHICANO-RIQUENA, Vol. 5, no. 1 (Winter 1977), p. 93. English.

8981 Celebracion Chican-india. CAMINOS, Vol. 1, no. 3 (May 1980), p. 38-39+. English.

AN: Portfolio of works exhibited at the Galeria Capistrano in southern California: Zarco Guerrero, Domingo Ulloa, Mario Torero, Guillermo Acevedo. Judithe Hernandez, who also exhibited, is not included in the portfolio.

8982 Chicano pride theme of mural. EL DIARIO DE LA GENTE, Vol. 2, no. 11 (January 25, 1974). English.

AN: Commentary on the 11x15 ft. mural painted by Carlos Rosas outside the entrance to the Tabor Inn in University Memorial Center. Mural composed of Indio-Chicano symbols.

8983 De la Rocha, Roberto. [Untitled drawings]. CON SAFOS, no. 8 (1972), p. 21-24.

8984 Eloy. [Untitled drawing]. TEJIDOS, Vol. 1, no. 2 (Spring 1974), p. 19-20. English.

8985 Garza, Efrain and Tijerina, Ramon. Caracol azteca - el tiempo limitado del hombre de la ciencia [drawing]. CARACOL, Vol. 4, no. 12 (August 1978), p. 8. Spanish.

8986 Guernica, Antonio Jose and Saavedra-Vela, Pilar. El Midwest Canto al pueblo: "Otra Vez, C/S". AGENDA, Vol. 7, no. 3 (May, June, 1977), p. 4-13. Bilingual.

AN: A thorough report on the various phases and events of the Midwest Canto al Pueblo in Milwaukee, Wisconsin on April 28 to May 8, 1977. The festival brought together artists, poets, musicians, and cultural workers to reaffirm, share, and celebrate the identity of La Raza with El Pueblo. Includes a thematic and iconographic overview of Chicano murals in California by Jose Montoya, and an analysis of his sculpture by Zarco Guerrero from Meza, Arizona. Well illustrated. Includes a photograph of the collective mural painted at 5th St. and National Avenue in Milwaukee, Wisconsin during the course of the conference.

Xicanindio Art (cont.)

8987 Guerrero, Adolfo "El Zarco". The new vision
of Xicanindio art. RAYAS, Vol. 2, no. 1
(January, February, 1979), p. 3. Bilingual.

AN: Zarco Guerrero explains his personal
artistic philosophy that unites Amerindian
concepts of art to contemporary art forms
especially in sculpture. For Guerrero, "the
Chicano artist is making a monumental effort
to arrive at a new universal language and to
create a new meaning of community through
art."

8988 Guerrero, Xochitl Nevel. Avatar de la paloma
de la paz: las naciones la van a convertir
en monstruo [drawing]. CARACOL, Vol. 4, no.
12 (August 1978), p. 18. Spanish.

8989 Jaramillo, Juanita. Tierra madre [drawing].
REVISTA CHICANO-RIQUENA, Vol. 5, no. 1
(Winter 1977), p. 60. Spanish.

8990 Moreno, Martin. Mujer [painting]. REVISTA
CHICANO-RIQUENA, Vol. 8, no. 4 (Fall
1980), p. 34. Bilingual.

8991 Pena, Amado Maurilio, Jr. Pareja con pared
[painting]. REVISTA CHICANO-RIQUENA, Vol. 8,
no. 3 (Summer 1980), p. 75. Bilingual.

8992 Pena, Amado Maurilio, Jr. El vestido
[painting]. REVISTA CHICANO-RIQUENA, Vol. 8,
no. 3 (Summer 1980), p. 74. Bilingual.

8993 Penalosa, Fernando. [Untitled graphic]. DE
COLORES, Vol. 2, no. 4 (1976), p. Cover.

8994 Rosas, Carlos. Aztlan [painting]. REVISTA
CHICANO-RIQUENA, Vol. 6, no. 1 (Winter
1977), p. 28. Spanish.

Xicanindio Artist Coalition

8995 Werley, Lenora. Murals give young artists
community pride, sculptor says. YUMA DAILY
SUN, (February 4, 1981). English.

AN: Mesa, Arizona sculptor Adolfo
"Zarco" Guerrero feels murals give young
people pride in their community. Guerrero is
part of the Xicanindio Artist Coalition that
is CETA-contracted to run summer art
programs for high school students.
Illustrated.

**XIe Festival International de la Peinture,
Cagnes-Sur-Mer, France, 1980**

8996 XIe festival international de la peinture.
Exhibition catalog, 1980. English.

AN: Catalog of an international
exposition in Cagnes-Sur-Mer, France. The
United States exhibit included the work of
Seattle artist Alfredo Mendoza Arreguin.
Biographical information and reproduction of
Arreguin's oil painting URUAPAN.

Ximenez, Pedro

8997 Gonzalez, Hector. Aztlandia. EL HISPANO,
Vol. 5, no. 2 (June 20, 1972).

AN: Story and photographs of a childrens
sculptural park created by Pedro Ximenez.

Xochil Art Center, Mission, TX

8998 Contemporary Arts Museum, Houston, TX and
Martinez, Santos G., Jr. Mexican movie
posters. Exhibition invitation, 1979.
English.

AN: Invitation to an exhibit of posters
primarily from the collecttion of Enrique
Flores and Xavier Gorena of Xochil Art
Center, Mission, Texas. Martinez considers
the posters monumental, with expressive
qualities that have influenced Chicano
poster makers like the Royal Chicano Air
Force, and Rupert Garcia, and Texas artists
like Luis Jimenez, Jesse Trevino and Cesar
Martinez. One illustration. Introduction by
guest curator Santos G. Martinez, Jr. (See
Rupert Garcia's essay in the exhibition
catalog: POSTERS FROM THE GOLDEN AGE OF
MEXICAN CINEMA, for another point of view).

8999 Galeria de la Raza/Studio 24, San Francisco,
CA and Garcia, Rupert. Posters from the
golden age of Mexican cinema. Exhibition
catalog, 1979. English.

AN: The Galeria's second exhibit of
Mexican movie posters features those of the
1940s and early 1950s (in 1971, the exhibit
covered 1943-1971) from the collection of
Enrique Flores, owner of the Rio Theatre,
Mission, Texas, and the Xochil Art Center.
Garcia's essay includes a history of Mexican
cinema, and the mythologizing period of the
"Golden Age" reflected in the posters which
promoted movie-consumership. One
illustration. (See Santos G. Martinez, Jr.'s
essay in the exhibition catalog: MEXICAN
MOVIE POSTERS, for another point of view).

9000 Giepen, Hubert. Xochil Art Center taking big
steps. PROGRESS, Vol. 10, no. 1 (August 12,
1981). English.

AN: Brief history of the founding and
expansion plans of the Xochil Art Institute
in Mission which includes an old theatre,
workshop. studio, and gallery. Artists
Xavier Gorena and Enrique Flores are
responsible for the development.

9001 Thwaites, Lynette. Art on the border.
COMMUNITY ARTS NEWSLETTER, Vol. 3, no. 3
(July 1981). English.

AN: The Centro Cultural de la Raza has
been a pioneer of intercultural activity
between Mexico and the United States in the
San Diego area. The Arizona Commission on
the Arts has promoted numerous exchanges and
publishes a bilingual quarterly bulletin. In
Mission, Texas, Xavier Gorena of the Xochil
Art Center is forging ties with Mexico City.

Xochitl
USE: Guerrero, Xochitl Nevel

Yanez, Rene

9002 11 reproduccion - significacion politica:
arte fotocopia. Exhibition invitation, 1979.
English.

AN: Invitation to an international
exhibit of photocopy artists from Europe,
Latin America and the United States.
Includes Rene Yanez of San Francisco.

Yanez, Rene (cont.)

9003 Albright, Thomas. Oakland Museum: a wide range in Latin art. SAN FRANCISCO CHRONICLE, (September 12, 1970), p. 33. English.

AN: A large show called ARTES DE LA RAZA at the Oakland Museum includes Mercedes Gutierrez-McDermid, Louis Gutierrez, Luis Cervantez, Calvin Tondre, Manuel Villamor, Rene Yanez, Jose Ramirez, Jorge Lerma, Rolando Castellon, Esteban Villa, Rupert Garcia, and Gustavo Rivera who is also having an exhibit at the Galeria de la Raza.

9004 Artes 6 Gallery, San Francisco, CA. Mixed media. Exhibition announcement, [ca. 1969-70]. English.

AN: Announcement of exhibit including Jim Cortez, Luis Cervantez, Vicente Rascon, Rene Yanes, Graciela Carrillo, Lorenza Camplis. The Artes 6 artists eventually formed the Galeria de la Raza of San Francisco.

9005 Burkhardt, Dorothy. Chicano pride and anger mix at 'Califas'. THE TAB, (April 12, 1981), p. 34. English.

AN: CALIFAS: AN EXHIBITION OF CHICANO ARTISTS IN CALIFORNIA represents a cross-section of artists exhibiting work for at least ten years: Rupert Garcia, Ernie Palomino, Eduardo Carrillo, Judy Baca, Rene Yanez, Carmen Lomas Garza, Salvador Roberto Torres, Roberto Chavez, Willie Herron, Ralph Maradiaga, Sue Martinez, Jose Montoya, Malaquias Montoya, Ramses Noriega and Esteban Villa. Illustrated.

9006 Calendar 1977. CHISMEARTE, no. 2 (Winter, Spring, 1977), p. 26-27. English.

AN: Reproduction of one month of the 1977 silkscreen calendar produced in limited edition by the Galeria de la Raza of San Francisco and the Royal Chicano Air Force of Sacramento, California. Displayed is Rene Yanez's screen HISTORICAL PHOTO-SILKSCREENMOVIE.

9007 Calendario de comida 1976. San Francisco, CA: Galeria de la Raza, 1976. English.

AN: Handprinted silkscreen calendar consisting of twelve sheets and a cover. The work of the following artists is included: Ralph Maradiaga, Juanishi Orozco, Francisco Camplis, Ruben Guzman, Rodolfo Cuellar, Xavier Viramontes, Jose Montoya, Esteban Villa, Rene Yanez, Max Garcia and Louis "The Foot" Gonzalez, Patricia Rodriguez, and Ricardo Favela. All of the above are associated with the Galeria de la Raza, or the Royal Chicano Air Force of Sacramento, CA.

9008 California. State College. Los Angeles. Art Gallery. Twelve Chicano artists. Exhibition invitation, n.d. English.

AN: Invitation to an exhibit: Jose Montoya, Gilbert Sanchez Lujan, Esteban Villa, Rene Yanez, Joe Moran, Armando Cid, Leonard Castellas, Juanishi Orozco, Rudy Cuellar, Beltran, Lopez and Cabrera.

9009 La Causa Publications, Oakland, CA. New symbols for la Nueva Raza. Exhibition announcement, [ca. 1969]. English.

AN: Announcement for exhibition of the four founding artists of the Mexican American Liberation Art Front (MALAF): Esteban Villa, Rene Yanez, Manuel Hernandez, Malaquias Montoya. Collage of portraits by the artists.

9010 La Causa Publications, Oakland, CA. Rene Yanez: paintings. Exhibition invitation, [ca. 1968]. English.

AN: Invitation to an exhibit of paintings by San Francisco artist Rene Yanez. Illustrated.

9011 Chicano art. ARTES VISUALES, no. 29 (1981). English.

AN: Issue on Chicano art, introduced by Los Angeles artist Roberto Gil de Montes. Includes works and statements by: Pedro Lujan (Texas); Raul M. Guerrero (Calif.); Sylvia Salazar Simpson (New Mexico/Calif.); Carlos Almaraz (Calif.); Rene Yanez (Calif.); Jack Vargas (Calif.); Ray Bravo (Calif.); John Valadez (Calif.); Gloria Maya (Calif.); Elsa Flores (Calif.); Willie Herron (Calif.); Gilbert "Magu" Lujan (Calif.); Kay Torres, Jerry Lucas, and Louis Perez (Calif.).

9012 Dunsmore de Carrillo, Patricia. On Rene Yanez of the Galeria de la Raza. CHISMEARTE, Vol. 1, no. 1 (Fall 1976), p. 8-9. English.

AN: Report on Yanez's negotiations with the Foster Kleiser Company to take over a billboard located outside the Galeria in San Fancisco which has been painted by Michael Rios, the Centro de Cambio and TIN TAN magazine, Zaiver (Xavier) Viramontes, and others.

9013 Electro Arts Gallery, San Francisco, CA. Electric realizations: an exhibition by Rene Yanez & Carl Heyward. Exhibition invitation, 1981. English.

AN: Invitation to an exhibit of color Xerox prints by Rene Yanez, Co-director of the Galeria de la Raza of San Francisco. Yanez feels that Xerox has opened new frontiers in presenting graphic work at a different scale and size.

9014 Gallery Sanchez, San Francisco, CA. Xerox art: an exhibit of local color xerox artists. Exhibition invitation, 1981. English.

AN: Invitation to an exhibit featuring Rene Yanez and eight other artists working in color Xerox.

9015 Gonzales, Juan. Galeria de la Raza: "our people deserve the best". EL TECOLOTE, Vol. 7, no. 11 (July 1977), p. 14. English.

AN: "We are not here to sell our art, but to sell the idea of art." This could well be the motto of Galeria de la Raza who under co-directors Rene Yanez and Ralph Maradiaga has become a key cultural institution in the Mission District of San Francisco. The two directors have a broad definition of art that encompasses everything from cartoons to craftwork. The article details past exhibits and future goals. A half-page photograph of the exterior of Galeria de la Raza by Pilar Mejia illustrates the article. Reprint of article entitled "Our people deserve the best" which appeared in NUESTRO, Vol. 1, no. 2 (May, 1977), p. 56-57.

Yanez, Rene (cont.)

9016 Gonzales, Juan. Regional report, The arts: "Our people deserve the best". NUESTRO, Vol. 1, no. 2 (May 1977), p. 56-57. English.

AN: Activities of San Francisco's Galeria de la Raza; interviews with its directors, Rene Yanez and Ralph Maradiaga. Reprinted as "Galeria de la Raza: our people deserve the best" in EL TECOLOTE (San Francisco, CA), Vol. 7, no. 11 (July, 1977), p. 14.

9017 Hartnell College Studio Gallery, Salinas, CA. Paintings, drawings, prints by San Francisco Bay Area Chicano artists. Exhibit brochure, 1971. English.

AN: Brochure for exhibit featuring Francisco Camplis, Graciela Carrillo, Sal Castaneda, Priscilla Dominguez, J. Duarte, Rupert Garcia, Carlos Loarca, Irene Perez, Vincent Rascon, Michael Rios, Peter Rodriguez, Luis Valsoto, Esteban Villa, Rene Yanez, Zala. Illustrated by Rupert Carcia print.

9018 La historia de California, 1977. San Francisco, CA: Galeria de la Raza, 1977. English.

AN: Handprinted silkscreen calendar of history seen from a Mexican point of view. Twelve sheets and a cover. Artists are: Ralph Maradiaga, Irene Perez, Louie "The Foot" Gonzalez, Max Garcia, Patricia Rodriguez, Jose Romero, Esteban Villa, Juanishi Orozco, Rodolfo Cuellar, Jose Montoya, Xavier Viramontes, Rene Yanez, Ricardo Favela, associated with the Galeria de la Raza, or the Royal Chicano Air Force of Sacramento.

9019 Martinez, Anita. Raza art. EL TECOLOTE, Vol. 1, no. 8 (November 30, 1970), p. 1. English.

AN: Jay Ojeda, newly selected director of Galeria de la Raza, describes the memorial exhibition dedicated to Ruben Salazar installed at the Galeria on Dec. 12, 1970. Salazar symbolized and synthesized many of the goals subscribed to by artist members of La Galeria. The exhibit included work by Chicano and Latino artists Francisco Camplis, Jay Ojeda, Jose Romero, Rolando Castellon, Rene Yanez, Luis Valsoto, Mike Ruiz, Carlos Perez, Gustavo Rivera, Peter Rodriguez, Carlos Loarca and Ralph Maradiaga.

9020 Mexican American liberation art front: la Raza Nueva, Rene Yanez, Esteban Villa, Malaquias Montoya, Manuel Hernandez. BRONCE, Vol. 1, no. 3 (March 1969), p. 6-7. English.

AN: Manifesto of MALAF, a germinal Chicano art group in northern California. Compares revolutionary Chicanos of 1968 with the Mexicans of 1910; equally Chicano artists reject European-influenced art. Announces the exhibit NEW SYMBOLS FOR LA RAZA NUEVA, at La Causa in Oakland, March 22 to April 5, 1969. Puts forth the group's philosophy and goals, particularly exhibits and art services to the "barrio". Illustrated.

9021 Orth, Maureen. The soaring spirit of Chicano arts. NEW WEST MAGAZINE, Vol. 3, no. 19 (September 11, 1978), p. 41-46. English.

AN: Overview of California Chicano culture. Color illustrations of works by

Mexican muralist David Alfaro Siqueiros, Rupert Garcia, Mujeres Muralistas, Willie Herron, Rene Yanez, Rudy Martinez, San Diego's Chicano Park, ASCO, Jose Montoya.

9022 Reser, Phil. Rene Yanez: state-of-the-xerox art. CITY ARTS, Vol. 3, no. 8 (August 1981). English.

AN: Five years ago when Xerox came out with a color copier, Yanez started experimenting with the machine's color buttons, which he uses like a musical instrument or a paint brush. Yanez's work is showing at the Electro-Arts Gallery in San Francisco. Brief profile of the artist, whose father and grandfather were both artists.

9023 San Francisco's neighborhood arts program. San Francisco, CA: San Francisco Art Commission, [1971]. English.

AN: Booklet in pictures describing the activities underwritten by the city and county of San Francisco, the National Endowment for the Arts, the San Francisco Foundation, and the Zellerbach Family Fund. The interracial, interethnic staff includes Rene Yanez. Organizations listed are Galeria de la Raza, Galeria de la Comunidad, Galeria de las Bellas Artes, Galeria de las Pinturas, Galeria de la Musica, Galeria de la Poesia, Galeria de la Instruccion.

9024 Street, Sharon. Califas - a celebration of Chicano culture and art. CITY ON A HILL, (April 16, 1981). English.

AN: Review of an exhibit at College V's Sesnon Gallery featuring 15 California artists: Ramses Noriega, Judy Baca, Salvador Roberto Torres, Malaquias Montoya, Rene Yanez, Ralph Maradiaga, Jose Montoya, Esteban Villa, Carmen Lomas Garza, Robert Chavez, among others. Illustrated.

9025 Vincent, Stephen. Omens from the flight of the birds: the first 101 days of Jimmy Carter: a collective journal of writers & artists. San Francisco, CA: Momos Press, 1977. English.

AN: Rene Yanez, performance piece on El Santero, and two comic strips.

9026 Xerox Reproductions Center, San Francisco, CA. Fine arts exhibitions of color xerox. Exhibition invitation, 1978-79. English.

AN: Invitation to an exhibit featuring Rene Yanez and 11 other artists working in color Xerox.

Ybarra, Juan

9027 Campesino Business and Joint Enterprise Building, Fresno, CA. Sabor a Fresno. Arte chicano: los Four and la Brocha. Exhibition invitation [1976]. English.

AN: Invitation to an exhibit of works by Los Four of Los Angeles and members of La Brocha del Valle of Fresno: Arturo Roman, Sal Garcia, John Sierra, Juan Truner, Sapo de Aztlan, Fernando Hernandez, Alberto Reyes, Ernesto Palomino, Lee Orona, Francisco Barrios, Juan Ybarra, Bobby Reyes, Alberto Hernandez. Brocha was started by Palomino (California State University, Fresno professor) to pool talents of Central Valley artists.

Ybarra, Juan (cont.)

9028 Hale, David. La Brocha del Valle artists
      deal with Chicano reality. FRESNO BEE,
      (October 1, 1978), p. G, 5. English.

      AN: Positive critique of a collective
      exhibition by members of La Brocha del Valle
      Group held at Fresno State University's
      Phebe Conley Art Building Gallery. With
      divergent attitudes, styles and ideas, the
      group is united by their focus on subject
      matter that deals with the diverse realities
      of being Chicano. Illustrated with
      photograph of Juan Ybarra's bronze
      sculpture, ONLY ONE TIME.

Yepes, George

9029 Los Four [art group]. Tales from the barrio
      by Los Four and friends. Los Angeles, CA:
      Los Four, Liberty Hill Foundation, United
      Steel Workers, [1977]. English.

      AN: Comic book designed with drawings,
      comic strips, and calligraphy by Frank
      Romero, George Yepes, Carlos D. Almaraz, Leo
      Limon, Judithe Hernandez.

9030 Una galeria de artistas = A gallery of
      artists. CAMINOS, Vol. 1, no. 6 (October
      1980), p. 20-26. Bilingual.

      AN: Features California artists Domingo
      O. Ulloa (Imperial Valley images), Gloria
      Chacon, photographer Maria Pinedo (San
      Francisco), Willie Herron (Los Angeles),
      Joaquin Patino (Delano), Pedro Pelayo (Long
      Beach), sculptor Rudi Sigala (San Diego),
      Mario Torero (San Diego), sculptor Michael
      M. Amescua (Los Angeles), and the East Los
      Streetscapers. Illustrated.

9031 Gamboa, Harry, Jr. Los murales de Aztlan.
      COMUNIDAD, (June 28, 1981), p. 8-9+.
      Spanish.

      AN: Review of the exhibit at the Craft
      and Folk Art Museum of Los Angeles of MURALS
      OF AZTLAN: THE STREET PAINTERS OF EAST LOS
      in which Carlos Almaraz, Gronk, Judithe
      Hernandez, Willie Herron, Frank Romero, John
      Valadez and the East Los Streetscapers
      (David Botello, Wayne Healy, George Yepes)
      painted portable murals in the gallery. The
      murals are described and illustrated.

YO SOY CHICANO [film]   **Austin, TX**

9032 Gamboa, Harry, Jr. Film, television, and
      Trevino. LA LUZ, Vol. 6, no. 10 (October
      1977), p. 7-8. English.

      AN: Jesus Salvador Trevino has been an
      active proponent and participant in
      transforming cultural inaccuracy about
      Chicanos in the media to accurate mass media
      models. A biography of Trevino follows,
      including discussion of some of his films:
      THE SALAZAR INQUEST, CHICANO MORATORIUM
      AFTERMATH, SOLEDAD, AMERICA TROPICAL, YO SOY
      CHICANO, RAICES DE SANGRE, as well as
      television series like ACCION CHICANO,
      AHORA, and INFINITY FACTORY.

9033 Smith, Cecil. YO SOY captures the Chicano
      soul. LOS ANGELES TIMES, (August 17, 1972),
      p. IV, 20. English.

      AN: Trevino's films YO SOY CHICANO and
      AMERICA TROPICAL shown on KCET.

9034 Zheutlin, Barbara and Talbot, David. Jesus
      Salvador Trevino. In: CREATIVE DIFFERENCES:

PROFILES OF HOLLYWOOD DISSIDENTS. Boston,
MS: South End Press, 1978, p. 345-352.
English.

      AN: Within the context of New Left
      alternative filmmakers who chose to work
      within Hollywood, Trevino sets forth his
      standards and goals. His films and TV
      productions include SOLEDAD (1971), AMERICA
      TROPICAL (1971), YO SOY CHICANO (1972),
      RAICES DE SANGRE (1977) and INFINITY FACTORY
      (1975-1976).

Young, Robert

9035 California. University. Los Angeles. Cine
      sin fronteras. Festival brochure, 1981.
      English.

      AN: Brochure program for a cinema
      festival and series of seminars and
      discussions featuring films and discussants
      from Mexico and Chicanos of the United
      States. Participating were Chicano directors
      Moctezuma Esparza, Richard Soto, David
      Sandoval, and Robert Young, and film
      historian David Maciel.

Youth

9036 Boettner, Jack. Youths help in fight against
      graffiti: muralist fights spray cans with
      brushes. LOS ANGELES TIMES [Orange County
      edition], (May 26, 1979), p. II, 12-13.
      English.

      AN: Illustrated and descriptive story
      about Orange County painter Emigdio Vasquez
      working on a series of murals with youth.
      Locations of murals by the group,
      biographical information about Vasquez, and
      his statement about art are given.
      Illustrated.

9037 Mitchell, John L. History restarted with
      mural grant. LOS ANGELES TIMES [Valley
      edition], (February 3, 1980), p. XI,1,4.
      English.

      AN: Interview with Judith Baca on the
      goals and purposes of the "Great Wall of Los
      Angeles" mural project. The central aim is
      to provide work, educational experience and
      skills for 40 ethnically-mixed unemployed
      youngsters between the ages of 14-21.
      Article details evolution of the project and
      funding sources. Illustrated.

9038 Southwest Chicano Arts Center, Houston, TX.
      Chicano youth in art. Exhibition invitation,
      1978. English.

      AN: Invitation to exhibit featuring
      works from Chicano youth in the Houston
      area.

Youth (cont.)

9039 Wu, Ying Ying. Mural, mural on the Great Wall. LOS ANGELES TIMES, (September 16, 1980), p. VI,4. English.

AN: Information on a video project directed by John Rier to document work on the 1700-ft. mural THE GREAT WALL OF LOS ANGELES which depicts California history with an emphasis on the role that minorities had in forging that history. Three teen-agers were trained in video production while assisting with taping the mural project. Simultaneously, 40 other youngsters hired from the Summer Program for the Employment of Disadvantaged Youth painted a 400-ft. section of the mural in 1980. Article describes the various skills mathematical, social and artistic developed by youth involved in the project. The mural was started as a Bicentennial Project in 1976 by Judy Baca for the Social and Public Art Resources Center in Venice, California. Illustrated with 3 photographs of various aspects of the Project.

Yuma, AZ

9040 Muralist helps youth paint better world. YUMA DAILY SUN, (November 14, 1980). English.

AN: Adolfo "Zarco" Guerrero meeting with students, educators, officials, and the community in Yuma.

Zaccagnino, Susana A.

9041 Mills House Visual Arts Complex, Garden Grove, CA. Menudo: artistas latinos de Orange County. Exhibit invitation, 1980. English.

AN: Invitation to an exhibit organized for the first anniversary of Artistas Latinos de Orange County including Delores Grajeda, William Hernandez, Marylee Montano, Patricia Murillo, Irene Ramos, Juan Ramos, Ricardo Serrato, Miguel Shanahan, Arthur Valenzuela, Benjamin Valenzuela, Jack Vargas, Alonzo Whitney, Emigdio Vasquez, Susana Zaccagnino, and Mexican artist Artemio Sepulveda.

9042 Orange Co. Library. El Modena Branch. Empanada: a tasty Mexican group art exhibit filled with a variety of digestable treats. Exhibition catalog, [1979]. English.

AN: Catalog of an exhibit by 15 artists: Dolores Grajeda, William Hernandez-M., Marylee Montano, Patricia Murillo, Eduardo Navarro, Susana A. Zaccagnino, Esau Quiroz, Juan Elias Ramos, Ricardo M. Serrato, Benjamin Valenzuela, Emigdio C. Vasquez, Arthur Valenzuela, Jack Vargas, Alonso Whitney, and Mexican artist Artemio Sepulveda living in Orange County. Brief profiles of the artists.

9043 Santa Ana Public Library, Newhope Branch, Santa Ana, CA. Artistas latinos de Orange County. Exhibition brochure, 1979. English.

AN: Exhibit of six artists: Dolores Grajeda, Eduardo Navarro, Arthur Valenzuela, Benjamin Valenzuela, Emigdio Vasquez, Susana A. Zaccagnino.

Zala

9044 Hartnell College Studio Gallery, Salinas, CA. Paintings, drawings, prints by San

Francisco Bay Area Chicano artists. Exhibit brochure, 1971. English.

AN: Brochure for exhibit featuring Francisco Camplis, Graciela Carrillo, Sal Castaneda, Priscilla Dominguez, J. Duarte, Rupert Garcia, Carlos Loarca, Irene Perez, Vincent Rascon, Michael Rios, Peter Rodriguez, Luis Valsoto, Esteban Villa, Rene Yanez, Zala. Illustrated by Rupert Carcia print.

Zamarron, Cruz

9045 Oakes College, University of California, Santa Cruz, CA and Carrillo, Eduardo. Corazon de Aztlan: a Chicano arts show. Exhibition catalog, 1981. English.

AN: Catalog of exhibit including works by Eduardo Carrillo, Juana Franklin, Cruz Zamarron, Jerry Astorga, Jaime Valadez, Ernesto Palomino, Sal Garcia, Roger Sierra, Jose Montoya, Esteban Villa, Juanishi Orozco, from Santa Cruz, San Jose, Fresno and Sacramento. Presentations of films and by the Teatro de la Tierra Morena of Santa Cruz County.

9046 Teatro de la Tierra Morena, Santa Cruz, CA. Fuego en Aztlan: a Chicano arts show. Exhibition brochure, 1980. English.

AN: Folder of information on the exhibition curated by Cruz Zamarron and Eduardo Carrillo. Exhibiting artists were: Justina Avila, Terry Benitez, Eduardo Carrillo, Hernando Chavez, Bob Cruz, Juanita Estrada, Juana Franklin, Sal Garcia, Leticia Hernandez, David "Sir Loco" Jimenez, Raoul Mendez, Vicente Mendez, Maria V. Pinedo, Gonzalo Placencia, Ramon Rodriguez, Roberto Salas, George Silva and Cruz Zamarron. A special feature was a live tattoo demonstration entitled "Walking Art".

Zamora, Ramori

9047 Valdez, Armando. El calendario chicano 1977. Hayward, CA: Southwest Network, 1977. English.

AN: Fifth in a series of historical calendars produced in 1972, 1974, 1975, 1976 by La Causa Publications and Southwest Network. Artists whose work is reproduced are Malaquias Montoya, Amado Maurilio Pena, Ramori Zamora, Glugio J.L. Nicandro [Gronk], Etta Delgado, Ricardo Alaniz, Diane Gamboa, Elisa Marina Coleman, Margarita Calderon, Jose Antonio Burciaga, Cesar Augusto Martinez, Maria Ochoa y Valtierra, Juan Renteria Fuentes, from California, New Mexico, and Texas.

Zapata, Emiliano

9048 Cantu, Jesus "Chista". [Emiliano Zapata (painting)]. CARACOL, Vol. 1, no. 7 (March 1975), p. 1.

9049 Feliz Navidad y prospero ano nuevo [poster]. CARACOL, Vol. 3, no. 4 (December 1976), p. FRNT COVER.

9050 Gonzalez, Jose Gamaliel. Zapata [print]. REVISTA CHICANO-RIQUENA, Vol. 5, no. 1 (Winter 1977), p. 36. English.

9051 Hernandez, Sergio. Hero worship poster pop [drawing]. CON SAFOS, Vol. 2, no. 5 (1970), p. 24-25.

Zapata, Emiliano (cont.)

9052 La Lomita. [Emiliano Zapata (graphic)].
CARACOL, Vol. 1, no. 4 (December 1974), p.
9.

9053 Mendez, Leopoldo. [Untitled woodcut].
CARACOL, Vol. 1, no. 7 (March 1975), p. 12.

9054 Pazos, Antonio. [Untitled drawing]. LLUEVE
TLALOC, no. 4 (1977), p. [61].

Zarate, Amancio

9055 HEMBRA: HERMANAS EN MOVIMIENTO BROTANDO
RAICES DE AZTLAN (University of Texas,
Austin). (Spring 1976).

AN: Raul Valdez, drawing, p. 3; Carolina
Flores, drawing, p. 5; Maria Flores,
photograph, pp. 7, 11, 30; M.E.
Secrest-Ramirez, drawing, p. 12; Amacio
Zarate, drawing, p. 15; Santa Barraza,
drawings, pp. 16, 17, 18, 26, 32; Nora
Gonzales-Dodson, painting, p. 19; Gilberto
Cardenas, photograph, pp. 22, 28; Nanci de
los Santos, photograph, p. 23, 29; Amado
Maurilio Pena, Jr. p. 31.

El Zarco
USE: Guerrero, Adolfo "El Zarco"

Zermeno, Andy

9056 Zermeno, Andy. Don Sotaco: caricaturas de la
huelga de Delano. Delano, CA: Farmworkers
Press, 1966. English.

AN: Short vignettes depicting the
farmworkers' struggle and how Don Sotaco
comes to understand his role in that social
movement. Illustrated with caricatures of
the various personages in the struggle;
patrones, coyotes, esquiroles, campesinos
and huelguistas. Centerfold and back cover
photographs by Jon Lewis.

Zihuatanejo, Ixtapa, Mexico

9057 Johnson, Richard. The mural at Zihuatanejo.
EMPIRE MAGAZINE, (October 12, 1980).
English.

AN: Denver artist Carlos M. Sandoval is
said to be the first Chicano commissioned by
the Mexican government to paint a mural in
Mexico. Sandoval's mural is on the facade of
the public library in Zihuatanejo. Its theme
is unity and synthesis and its title is
MESTIZO. Article contains much information
on mural act ivity in Denver, Colorado. Well
illustrated with color and black and white
photographs.

ZOOT SUIT [play]

9058 Neumeier, Marty. Ignacio Gomez.
COMMUNICATION ARTS MAGAZINE, Vol. 21, no. 6
(January, February, 1980), p. 78-87.
English.

AN: Story on commercial designer and
illustrator Ignacio Gomez of Los Angeles
which describes his background, education
and life style. 17 full-color illustrations
of his art work, including the ZOOT SUIT
poster for the Mark Taper Forum play.

9059 Posters by Ignacio Gomez: in full color
suitable for framing. CAMINOS, (May 1981),
p. 49. English.

AN: Six full-color posters on Latino
subjects by illustrator Gomez advertised for

sale. The best-known is Gomez's poster for
ZOOT SUIT, a play by Luis Valdez.

9060 Valadez, Kathy L. and Valadez, Kathy L.
Living in the understanding of success/el
endendimiento [sic] del exito. CAMINOS, Vol.
1, no. 6 (October 1980), p. 12-14, 40.
Bilingual.

AN: Story about financially successful
Los Angeles illustrator Ignacio Gomez who
produced the illustration for the play ZOOT
SUIT and designs posters, catalogs, magazine
covers and layouts. Also see front cover and
inside of front cover for illustrations.

9061 Valadez, Kathy L. Zoot suit, by Luis Valdez.
SOMOS, Vol. 1, no. 2 (July 1978), p. 20-29.
English.

AN: Two reviews of Valdez's new play
ZOOT SUIT, both enthusiastic. Historical
material and photographs with an essay by
Jose Montoya and his Pachuco drawing, as
well as views of the play are included.

Zoot Suit Riots, Los Angeles, CA, 1943

9062 Montoya, Jose E. Pachuco art: a historical
update. Sacramento, CA: Royal Chicano Air
Force, 1977. English.

AN: Booklet outlining the history of the
Zoot Suit Riots of 1943 and the making of
the Pachuco myth, written by Montoya and
illustrated with his pen-and-ink drawings of
Pachucos and Pachucas.

Zoot Suiter
USE: Pachucos

Zuniga, Francisco

9063 MARS: Movimiento Artistico del Rio Salado.
Phoenix, AZ: Mars Studio/Gallery, 1978.
English.

AN: History and manifesto of MARS, 13
member group of Arizona painters, sculptors,
designers, and photographers: Jose Andres
Giron, Jose Jimenez Rodriguez, Antonio
Tocora (Colombian-born), Ramon Delgadillo,
Francisco Zuniga, Jim Covarrubias, Ed Diaz,
David Martinez, Roberto Buitron, Juan
Rodriguez, Eddie Lopez, Zarco Guerrero, Joe
Sanchez.

Zuniga, Santos

9064 Art Gallery, California State University,
Long Beach and Lujan, Gilbert Sanchez
"Magu". El arte del pocho. Exhibit brochure,
October 1968. English.

AN: Information about Southern
California artists John Deheras, Marcus
Villagran, Roberto de la Rocha, Santos
Zuniga, Crispin Gonzales, Richard Martinez,
Jesus Gutierrez, Ed Oropeza, Pete Mendez,
David Ramirez, Gilbert Sanchez Lujan, Willie
Hernandez, Art Ponce, Carmen Tostado, Al
Almeida, David Ceja, Robert E. Chavez,
Thomas A. Ferriera. All art students,
graduates, or faculty.

Author/Artist Index

--   --

"Placas": graffiti and the environment, 899.
Briseno, Rodolfo
    Interview with a muralist, 290.
Bruce Novoa, Juan
    [Interview with Jose Montoya], 291.
Brunazzi, Ceci
    Writing on the walls: murals in the mission,
        4912.
Buitron, Robert
    Issues, 174.
    [Untitled photograph], 7327.
Burciaga, Jose Antonio
    Adoracion [drawing], 2035.
    Al frente [drawing], 2419.
    Aliens [drawing], 2420.
    Batos locos [graphic], 4439.
    [Inside the public school (drawing)], 2421.
    Mestizo [drawing], 2422.
    Mujeres [woodcut], 4440.
    Mural protest, 1280.
    Nacimiento [drawing], 2036.
    La posada [drawing], 2037.
    Restless serpents, 1281.
    Spirit of '76 [drawing], 2426.
    Los tres magos [drawing], 2038.
    [Untitled drawing], 2428.
    [Untitled drawing], 2429.
    [Untitled drawing], 2430.
    [Untitled drawing], 2431.
    [Untitled drawing], 2432.
    [Untitled drawing], 2433.
    [Untitled drawing], 2434.
    [Untitled drawing], 2435.
    [Untitled drawing], 2436.
    [Untitled drawing], 2437.
    [Untitled drawing], 2438.
    [Untitled drawing], 2439.
    [Untitled drawing], 2440.
    [Untitled drawing], 2441.
    [Untitled drawing], 2442.
    [Untitled drawing], 2443.
    [Untitled drawing], 2444.
    [Untitled drawing], 2445.
    [Untitled drawing], 2446.
    [Untitled drawing], 2447.
    [Untitled drawing], 2448.
    [Untitled drawing], 2449.
    [Untitled drawings], 2450.
    [Untitled drawings], 2451.
    [Untitled drawings], 2452.
    Which way did they go, slim? [drawing], 2453.
Burkhardt, Dorothy
    Chicano pride and anger mix at 'Califas', 571.
Burton, Marie
    Mural manual: how to paint murals for the
        classroom, community center and street
        corner, 2253.
Cabaniss, Joe H.
    Mural painters believes vandalism political
        act, 1996.
Cabrera, Antonio
    Writing on the walls [photograph], 5554.
California. State College. Los Angeles. Art
        Department
    Fifth California small images exhibition, 59.
California. State College. Los Angeles. Art
        Gallery
    Twelve Chicano artists, 573.
California. University. Los Angeles.
    Cine sin fronteras, 3264.
California. University. Santa Barbara. Coleccion
        Tloque Nahuaque
    Mexican soldaderas and workers during the
        revolution, 1543.
California. University. Santa Cruz. College Eight
        Gallery
    Four artists: Edward Carrillo, Consuelo Mendez
        Castillo, Louis Gutierrez, Jose Montoya,
        1432.
California. University. Los Angeles. Instructional
        Media Library
    1975-76 film catalog, 498.
Callum, Diane
    Regional report, The arts: walls of passion,

293.
Camacho, Eduardo
    Por los cien anos de la fundacion de su
        editorial: inauguraran hoy en San Diego la
        exposicion 'Homenaje a Posada, Manilla y
        Vanegas Arroyo', 1648.
Camacho, Jose
    [Untitled drawing], 2454.
Camargo, Arturo
    [Untitled drawing], 2455.
Campbell, Roberto Bruce
    [Untitled drawings], 2457.
Campesino Business and Joint Enterprise Building,
        Fresno, CA
    Sabor a Fresno. Arte chicano: los Four and la
        Brocha, 294.
Camplis, Francisco X.
    Towards the development of a Raza cinema,
        1342.
Canavier, Elena Karina
    Los Four, 295.
Canto al Pueblo Steering Committee
    Canto al Pueblo [poster], 1373.
Cantu, Jesus "Chista"
    [Emiliano Zapata (painting)], 6719.
    Entrevista con "Chista" Cantu, 1377.
    Entrevista: Jesus Maria Cantu, 'El Chista',
        296.
    [Una interpretacion de la Raza Cosmica en
        armonia con la tierra y el cosmos
        (drawing)], 2459.
    No tengo que ir a la luna... [painting], 6721.
    No todos los que estan son... [painting],
        6722.
    Santa Rosita, santo remedio... [painting],
        6723.
    Yo-soy-el-sol... [painting], 6724.
Capitol Art Gallery, Lansing, MI
    Arte de Nora Mendoza, Hector Perez, George
        Vargas, Martin Moreno, 297.
Cardenas de Dwyer, Carlota, ed.
    Chicano voices, 968.
Cardenas, Valentin
    Arte de Valentin Cardenas [drawing], 2461.
    [Untitled drawing], 2462.
    [Untitled drawing], 2463.
    [Untitled drawings], 2464.
Cardona, Patricia
    Gana adeptos de Museo Mexicano de San
        Francisco: Pedro Rodriguez, 194.
    El museo mexicano de San Francisco, 298.
Carlisle, Charles Richard
    Cuatro caminos: four perspectives on Chicano
        art, 1617.
    El mundo de Luis Santiago, 3668.
Carlson, Scott
    Artist's mural puts a little beauty in prison
        cellblock, 1004.
Carraro, Francine
    Refined rhythmic references: Amado Pena, Jr.,
        577.
Carrasco, Barbara
    Untitled [drawing], 2465.
    [Untitled drawing], 2466.
    [Untitled drawing], 2467.
    [Untitled drawings], 2468.
Carrillo, Eduardo
    Califas, is Chicano art safe in Santa Cruz?,
        1314.
    Corazon de Aztlan: a Chicano arts show, 890.
    Mural, Chicano Research Library, UCLA
        [photograph], 2015.
Carrillo, Graciela
    El frijol magico, 2029.
    [Untitled painting], 6726.
Carrillo, John M.
    Posada: the man and his art. A comparative
        analysis of Jose Guadalupe Posada and the
        current Chicano art movement as they apply
        toward social and cultural change: a visual
        resource unit for Chicano education, 233.
La Casa de la Raza Gallery, Santa Barbara, CA
    Judithe Hernandez: virgen, madre, mujer;
        imagenes de la mujer chicana, 578.

[Woman sitting with rabbit (drawing)], 2576.
[Women (drawing)], 2577.
Galvan, Yolanda
  Breathe [drawing], 2578.
  Coming out [print], 4486.
  Penetration [print], 4487.
Gamaliel, A.E.
  [Untitled painting], 6782.
  [Untitled painting], 6783.
Gamboa, Diane
  [Chicanas (drawing)], 1957.
  [Man (drawing)], 2579.
  [Mother and child (drawing)], 2580.
  [Untitled drawing], 2581.
Gamboa, Harry, Jr.
  Artists' exhibits are street performances,
    875.
  ASCO: no phantoms, 868.
  Cafe en blanco y negro, 869.
  [Chicana (drawing)], 2582.
  [Chicana in pen and ink (drawing)], 2583.
  [Chicana portrait (drawing)], 2584.
  [Chicano in shadow (drawing)], 2585.
  Chicano power [drawing], 2586.
  Chile [graphic], 4488.
  [Crying (drawing)], 2587.
  [Eagle, serpent and man (graphic)], 4530.
  Fadein ,870

  Fantasias moviles, 3868.
  Film, television, and Trevino, 3.
  Gronk and Herron, 871.
  Gronk: off-the-wall artist, 221.
  He threw a rock at me [drawing], 2588.
  Interview: Gronk and Gamboa, 876.
  [Man, woman and child (graphic)], 4532.
  Mexican Murder Comix presents Genocide Patrol
    [drawing], 1405.
  Los murales de Aztlan, 66.
  [Old man (drawing)], 2589.
  Phobia friend, 2123.
  Pistol whippersnapper, 873.
  Seis imaginaciones: artistas chicanos en Los
    Angeles, 67.
  [Split head (drawing)], 2590.
  [Untitled drawing], 2591.
  [Untitled drawing], 2592.
  [Untitled drawing], 2593.
  [Untitled drawing], 2594.
  [Untitled drawing], 2595.
  [Untitled drawing], 2596.
  [Untitled drawing], 2597.
  [Untitled drawing], 2598.
  [Untitled graphic], 4489.
  [Untitled graphic], 4490.
  [Untitled graphic], 4491.
  [Untitled montage], 5828.
  [Untitled photography], 7364.
  [Woman (drawing)], 1818.
  [Women (drawing)], 2680.
  [Women (drawing)], 2600.
Gamez, Eddie
  [Untitled drawing], 2601.
Garcia, Daniel C.
  Pan dulce [drawing], 2602.
Garcia, Domingo
  El galan etc. [painting], 6784.
Garcia, Edward E.
  Chicano art, 2603.
  [Untitled drawing], 2604.
Garcia, Guillermo
  Wall-to-wall art for the people, 910.
Garcia, Ignacio
  Senior exhibit attempts to define Chicano art,
    2367.
Garcia Perez, Linda Mary
  Cactus prisoner, 4492.
  Cactus prisoner [painting], 6785.
  Chicano nights [painting], 6786.
  Mejico [drawing], 2605.
  El otro mundo [painting], 6787.
  Tortilla bits [painting], 6788.
Garcia, Ralph
  Misconceptions or stereotyping the Chicano and

Mexican arts in San Antonio, 5680.
Garcia, Raul Roy
  La justicia, 2606.
Garcia, Ruben A.
  Chicano comics [comic strip], 1406.
Garcia, Rupert
  Assassination of a striking Mexican worker
    [painting], 4235.
  Community art-murals: an exhibition of
    original drawings, sketches, and designs,
    1566.
  Echos de la Mision - Alfaro Siqueiros
    (1896-1974), 119.
  'Fifth Sun' Raza art show at UC Berkeley
    Museum, 353.
  Laminas de la Raza, 146.
  Muralista mexicano habla sobre los murales y
    los muralistas en los E.U., 5631.
  Para Olga Talamante [drawing], 2608.
  The politics of popular art, 3928.
  Portfolio [drawings], 2609.
  Posters from the golden age of Mexican cinema,
    3462.
  Pulqueria art--defiant art of the barrios
    [Part I], 19.
  Pulqueria art--defiant art of the barrios
    [Part II], 20.
  Raza murals & muralists: an historical
    perspective, 222.
  La Raza murals of California, 1963 to 1970: a
    period of social change and protest, 223.
  La Raza Silkscreen Center: "Images of a
    community", an exhibit of silkscreen posters
    and graphic works from 1971 to 1979, 220.
  Realismo: Chicano drawings by Juan Fuentes,
    2487.
  Recent Raza murals in the U.S., 615.
  Rupert Garcia, 4238.
  A source for mural art education: an annotated
    bibliography of three Chicano newspapers,
    1046.
  "This mural is not for the bankers. It's for
    the people", 957.
  [Untitled drawing], 2610.
  [Untitled drawing], 2611.
  [Untitled drawing], 2612.
  [Untitled drawing], 2613.
  [Untitled drawing], 2614.
Garcia, Ruperto
  Las companeras art exhibit, 644.
  Photography, 4257.
Garcia, Sol
  Vato Loco y Chata La Gata [comic strip], 354.
Garcia-Camarillo, Cecilio
  Aire triste [poetry in graphic design], 4494.
  Don Juan Volador, Platica con Cesar Augusto
    Martinez, 1502.
  Frio [poetry in graphic design], 4495.
  Hormiguero [poetry in graphic design], 4496.
  Lluvia Marxista [poetry in graphic design],
    4497.
  Medianoche [graphic], 4498.
  Naturaleza es cadaver [poetry in graphic
    design], 4499.
  Nopal y piedras [graphic], 4500.
  Platicando con Carlos Rosas, 1112.
  Platicando con Dennis Martinez, 1113.
  Sol y nube, 4501.
  [Untitled poetry in graphic design], 4502.
  Viendo un lago [graphic], 4503.
  Zaz y Cuas, 1408.
Garcia-Camarillo, Mia
  Don Juan Volador, Platica con Cesar Augusto
    Martinez, 1502.
  Don Pedrito Jaramillo [drawing], 2616.
  [Five men (drawing)], 2617.
  [Jose Angel Gutierrez (drawing)], 2618.
  [Jose Angel Gutierrez (drawing)], 2619.
  [Jose Angel Gutierrez (drawing)], 2620.
  Oscarin y Lorina [drawing], 2621.
  Pen and Ink Drawings, 2622.
  [Untitled drawing], 2623.
  [Untitled drawing], 2624.
  [Untitled drawing], 2625.

[Untitled drawing], 2626.
[Untitled drawing], 2627.
[Untitled drawing], 2628.
[Untitled drawing], 2629.
[Untitled drawings], 2630.
[Untitled drawings], 2631.
[Untitled drawings], 2632.
[Untitled drawings], 2366.
Gardiner, Henry G.
    Painted exterior walls of Southern California,
        356.
Garza, Alex
    Earth abyss [sculpture], 7366.
    Emerging [sculpture], 8190.
    Entrevista con Alex Garza, 44.
Garza, Eduardo C.
    The awakening of la teqnica chit [drawing],
        2634.
    Chispas reales [drawing], 2635.
    [Untitled drawing], 2636.
Garza, Efrain
    Caracol azteca - el tiempo limitado del hombre
        de la ciencia [drawing], 2637.
Garza, Rose
    [Untitled drawing], 2638.
Garza, Sabino
    [Family (graphic)], 4504.
    [Untitled graphic], 1820.
Gaytan, Ray
    B.I.T.C.H. [drawing], 2639.
    The center of the universe [painting], 6790.
    Desnudo [painting], 6791.
    A drop of blood [painting], 6792.
    Fallen leaves [drawing], 2640.
    Flower vendor [painting], 6793.
    Head [painting], 6794.
    An interview, 2055.
    Passion belongs to the world of flesh & blood
        [painting], 6795.
    Sunglass portrait [painting], 6796.
    [[Untitled art work], 846.
    [Untitled painting], 6797.
    [Untitled painting], 6798.
    La vida [drawing], 2641.
    Wings [painting], 6799.
Gerardo, Rocky
    Albert Einstein [painting], 6800.
    Children of the sun [painting], 6801.
    El Sandinista [painting], 6802.
    Twilight cat [painting], 6803.
Geyer, Anne
    Artists' exhibits are street performances,
        875.
    Latino photographers of U.S. still seeking
        identity, 251.
    Muralist works to dispel negative Latino
        images, 5293.
Giepen, Hubert
    Xochil Art Center taking big steps, 3895.
Gil de Montes, Roberto
    [Untitled photograph], 7369.
Gil de Montes, Roberto, et al
    CHOQUE DE AMOR: fotonovela by Lamp, 505.
Glickman, Hal
    Chicano graffiti: the signatures and symbols
        of Mexican-American youth, 1604.
Gloria, Juan J.
    En San Antonio: se celebrara el tercer
        festival de cine, 'La vida chicana a traves
        del celuloide', 1982.
Goddarth, Ruth
    Porfirio Salinas, 188.
Goez Imports & Fine Arts, Los Angeles, CA
    We invite you to see the birth of our art,
        4126.
Goldberg, Aron
    Edward Carrillo: selected works, 1960-1975,
        1325.
Goldman, Jane
    Art against the wall, 1661.
Goldman, Ruth
    A survey of East Bay murals of the 1970s,
        1013.
Goldman, Shifra M.

Affirmations of existence, barrio murals of
    Los Angeles, 4882.
Artistas en accion: conferencia de las mujeres
    chicanas, 647.
Canto de unidad: nuevo mural de Berkeley,
    1822.
Chicana artists at work, 189.
Chicano art, 88.
Chicano art - looking backward, 1315.
Chicano art alive and well in Texas: a 1981
    update, 225.
Las creaturas de la America tropical:
    Siqueiros y los murales chicanos en Los
    Angeles, 120.
Hecho en Latino America: first photography
    colloquium and exhibition, 2163.
The intense realism of Frida Kahlo, 650.
Les muraux chicanos aux Etats-Unis: un double
    language, 227.
Painter: Emigdio Vasquez, 816.
Readers' forum, 667.
Resistance and identity: street murals of
    occupied Aztlan, 228.
Resistencia e identidad: los murales
    callejeros de Aztlan, la ciudad (sic)
    ocupada, 229.
Response: another opinion on the state of
    Chicano art, 7237.
Song of unity: Berkeley's new raza mural,
    1825.
Supervivencia y prosperidad del arte chicano
    en Texas: nueva revision, 230.
Thorns and roses, 68.
Women artists of Texas: MAS = More + Artists +
    Women = MAS, 190.
Goll, Dave
    More than handball on this court, 21.
Gomez, Gricelle
    Chicano soy [drawing], 2642.
Gomez, Ignacio
    [Untitled painting], 6806.
Gomez, Linda
    Malaquias Montoya exhibit opens at La Pena,
        2643.
Gomez-Quinones, Juan
    On culture, 4924.
    Toward a concept of culture, 4925.
Gonzales, Jose G.
    [Untitled collage], 6142.
Gonzales, Juan
    Chicano film festival earns pluses and
        minuses, 3792.
    Galeria de la Raza: "our people deserve the
        best", 361.
    Regional report, The arts: "Our people deserve
        the best", 652.
Gonzalez, David M.
    Al sol y la luna [drawing], 2644.
Gonzalez Dodson, Nora
    Cerulean depth [painting], 6808.
    Maternity [graphic], 4506.
    Terrestrial flight II [drawing], 2645.
    [Untitled drawing], 2646.
    [Untitled drawing], 2647.
    [Untitled drawing], 2648.
    [Untitled graphic], 4507.
    El vendedor [drawing], 2649.
Gonzalez, Ellen
    U.S. art project: Chicanas painting 'future
        history', 362.
Gonzalez, Gracie
    The Chicano singers [drawing], 2650.
Gonzalez, Hector
    Aztlandia, 2025.
    El arte de Esteban Villa, 363.
    An interview with Armando Cid, 654.
    Rivera paints Boalt Hall mural, 1225.
    [Untitled photo collage], 2084.
Gonzalez, Johnny
    Arte de ninos coloring book, 2657.
Gonzalez, Jose Carlos
    Consejo mexicano de fotografia: foto latino en
        el suroeste de los Estado Unidos, 364.
Gonzalez, Jose Gamaliel

Boycott [drawing], 1409.
Lenina of BRAVE NEW WORLD [drawing], 2652.
La LLorona [drawing], 2653.
Metamorphosis [drawing], 2654.
Three ages of man [drawing], 2655.
Yo soy chicana [drawing], 2656.
Zapata [print], 4508.
Gonzalez, Lila
Ideas on a Third World art exhibit, 3494.
Gonzalez, M.
Entrevista con los muralistas de East Austin,
919.
Gonzalez, Reveca
Arte de ninos coloring book, 2657.
Gonzalez, Sandra
Perspectives on Chicano education, 1229.
Gonzalez, Tobias
Perspectives on Chicano education, 1229.
Gonzalez, Victoria
Chair in the sky: Ernesto Palomino, 365.
Gordon, Allan M.
Carmen Lomas Garza/prints and gouaches: Margo
Humphrey/monotypes, 780.
Graham Gallery, New York, NY
Luis Jimenez, 1118.
Luis Jimenez, 656.
Grand Rapids Art Museum, Grand Rapids, MI
Jose Narezo: paintings on paper, 3497.
Grand Rapids Jr. College, MI
Dedication "El Centro de Vida", 4418.
The Green Line Gallery, San Pedro, CA
Lithographs and woodcuts by Muriel Olguin,
657.
Greenberg, David
Megamurals & supergraphics: big art, 186.
Grigsby, J. Eugene, Jr.
Art & ethnics: background for teaching youth
in a pluralistic society, 182.
Grimke, Angelina
Chicano art finds home in Mission galeria,
367.
Gronk
[Agony (drawing)], 2660.
[Chicana (drawing)], 2661.
[Detail of mural], 6165.
[Faces (drawing)], 2662.
[Faces (graphic)], 4510.
Gronk and Herron, 871.
Gronk: off-the-wall artist, 221.
Interview: Gronk and Gamboa, 876.
[Nude (drawing)], 2663.
The same cave down the street [graphic], 4511.
The Tortuga paints a new mural, 1831.
[Untitled drawing], 2665.
[Untitled drawing], 2666.
[Untitled drawing], 2667.
[Untitled drawing], 2668.
[Untitled drawing], 2733.
[Untitled drawing], 2669.
[Untitled drawing], 2670.
[Untitled drawing], 2671.
[Untitled drawing], 2672.
[Untitled drawing], 2673.
[Untitled drawing], 2674.
[Untitled drawing], 2675.
[Untitled drawing], 2676.
[Untitled montage], 5828.
[Woman (drawing)], 2677.
[Women (drawing)], 1832.
[Women (drawing)], 1833.
[Women (drawing)], 2680.
Guadalupe Historic Foundation, Santa Fe, NM
Artes en la primavera, 847.
Cofradia de artes y artesanos hispanicos, 368.
Guernica, Antonio Jose
El Midwest Canto al pueblo: "Otra Vez, C/S",
1372.
Guerra, Luis
Hasta la gloria [drawing], 2681.
Guerra, Victor
Primavera: happy in Khaki, 2682.
Guerra, Victor, ed.
El camino de la cruz, 849.
Guerrero, Adolfo "El Zarco"

Aztlan [sculpture], 8198.
Canto al pueblo [sculpture], 8199.
El grito de guerra [sculpture], 8200.
Homenaje a Wounded Knee [sculpture], 8201.
Huehueteotl [sculpture], 8202.
La Llorona [sculpture], 8203.
El mestizo [sculpture], 8204.
Mictlan [sculpture], 8205.
La miseria [sculpture], 8206.
La mulatta [sculpture], 8207.
The new vision of Xicanindio art, 659.
La olvidada [sculpture], 8209.
La pesadumbre [sculpture], 8210.
La Raza embarazada [sculpture], 8211.
La Raza embarazada [sculpture], 8212.
Self-portrait [plaster mask], 8213.
Tescatlipocamadre [sculpture], 8214.
Tescatlipocamadre [sculpture], 8215.
La tradicion [sculpture], 8216.
Untitled [plaster mask], 8217.
Xipe-totec [sculpture], 8218.
Guerrero, Jose
[Untitled drawing], 2684.
Guerrero, Lalo
No way Jose [comic strip], 1412.
Guerrero, Xochitl Nevel
Avatar de la paloma de la paz: las naciones la
van a convertir en monstruo [drawing], 2685.
Peruvian wind songs [painting], 6812.
Self-portrait [painting], 6813.
[Untitled painting], 6814.
Guerrero, Yolanda Eligia
Weaving [artwork], 850.
Guggenheim Gallery, Chapman College, Orange, CA
Hexagono: paintings, sculpture, drawings,
prints, 38.
Gustaitis, Rasa
Arts imperiled, 4374.
Guthrie, Derek
La mujer: a visual dialogue, 1318.
Gutierrez, Helga
The walls of Estrada Courts, 3289.
Gutierrez, Juan Pablo
Bird [yarn drawing], 2687.
H
USE: Angulo, Hector "H"
Haddad, Barbara
The fine arts, 3282.
Hagen, Carol
Mission murals, 660.
Haines, Bruce J.
Gonzales' works are controlled and full of
detail, 136.
Hale, David
La Brocha del Valle artists deal with Chicano
reality, 369.
Exhibit backers hope for Chicano cultural
center plan, 206.
Fresnan gets grant to create five story high
mural, 661.
Hama, Chizu
California murals, 317.
Hamm, Madeline McDermott
Artist envisions a 'Sistine' ceiling, 3244.
Hancock de Sandoval, Judith
Regional report, The arts: the workaholic,
1121.
Hansen, Barbara
Food for the soul: an earthly delight, 851.
Hanson, Matt
Barren walls toned into bold works of art,
3993.
Harbor Area Community Art Center, San Pedro, CA
Mi arte, mi raza: an exhibition of current
work by Judithe Hernandez, 662.
Harithas, James
Luis Jimenez: Progress I, 1550.
Harper, Hilliard
Native Americans stand tall again as Balboa
Park mural takes shape, 1652.
Hartnell College Studio Gallery, Salinas, CA
Paintings, drawings, prints by San Francisco
Bay Area Chicano artists, 1015.
Healy, Wayne Alaniz

Patron [painting], 6897.
[El Pocho Che (logo)], 2864.
Portfolio 1, 6898.
Portfolio: Malaquias Montoya [paintings], 6899.
El sabado en la tarde [drawing], 2865.
[Untitled drawing], 2866.
[Untitled drawing], 2867.
[Untitled drawing], 2868.
[Untitled drawing], 2869.
[Untitled painting], 6900.
[Untitled painting], 6901.
[Untitled painting], 6902.
[Untitled painting], 6903.
[Untitled painting], 6904.
[Untitled painting], 6905.
Moody Hall, St. Edwards University, Austin, TX
Las companeras, 409.
Mora, Francisco
[Woodcut of Emiliano Zapata], 4581.
Morales, Sylvia
Chicana, 714.
Morch, Albert
He put down his brushes for a dream, 410.
Mexican art through a cartoonist's eyes, 205.
Moreno, Dorinda
La mujer y el arte, 1881.
Moreno, Eduardo
Los Four, 76.
Moreno, Juan M.
[Untitled drawings], 2870.
Moreno, Martin
M'Chicana [sculpture], 8237.
Mujer [painting], 6907.
Morton, Carlos
Pedro Lujan: sculptor, 5412.
Una platica entre Carlos Morton y Pedro Lujan, 689.
Moser, Charlotte
Arte chicano de Texas/Texas Chicano art, 412.
Phil Renteria and Dick Wray, 715.
Movimiento Artistico Chicano (MARCH), Chicago, IL
Letter to CARACOL, 1725.
Skyjacked: screenprinted posters from California by the Royal Chicano Air Force (R.C.A.F.), 1980, 3673.
Muchnic, Suzanne
Damaged goods in the big city, 77.
LAICA looks at social works, 716.
Mural: a lullaby of another Broadway, 5311.
Passion, paint splatter folk art museum show, 2200.
Munguia, Roberto
[Untitled painting], 6910.
Munoz, Victor
One way [collage], 2085.
Mural Resource Center, Los Angeles, CA
Citywide murals: mural manual, 6246.
Woman's manual: how to assemble scaffolding, 719.
Murguia, Alejandro
El sol y los de abajo and other R.C.A.F. poems / oracion a la mano poderosa, 2044.
Murillo, Jesus
Depression [painting], 6911.
Our Hercules [painting], 6912.
Murphy, Patricia Lee
Artists renew Toltecas crafts heritage, 104.
Museum of Contemporary Art, Chicago, IL
Raices antiguas/visiones nuevas; ancient roots/new visions, 1593.
Museum of Fine Arts, Santa Fe, NM
John Hernandez, Douglas Johnson, 3592.
Luis Jimenez, sculpture, drawings and prints: La Cofradia de Artes y Artesanos Hispanicos, selected works, 419.
Narezo, Jose
[Drawing for CRONICA DE AZTLAN], 2873.
[Drawing for CRONICA DE AZTLAN], 2874.
[Drawing for CRONICA DE AZTLAN], 2875.
[Drawing for CRONICA DE AZTLAN], 2876.
Nario, Jose
The history of the Mexican-American worker (1974-75) [detail of mural], 1722.

Navar, M. Margarita
La vela prendida: home altars, 99.
Negri, Sam
Garden grows as shrine to sculptor, 5369.
Nelson, Eugene
Pablo Cruz and the American dream, 2184.
Nelson, Kathryn J.
Excerpts from los testamentos: Hispanic women folk artists of the San Luis Valley, Colorado, 162.
Neri, Manuel
Untitled standing figure no. 4 [sculpture], 5752.
Neumeier, Marty
Ignacio Gomez, 724.
Nevarez, Joe R.
Chicano art blooms in barrio warehouse, 171.
New Mexico Arts Division, Santa Fe, NM
Art in public places, 1455.
New Mexico State University, University Art Gallery, Las Cruces, NM
Luis Jimenez: sculpture, drawings and prints, 1594.
Newport Harbor Art Museum, Newport Beach, CA
Our own artists: art in Orange County, 727.
Nieto, Margarita
L.A. parks & wrecks: a reflection of urban life/parques y choques: un reflejo de la vida urbana, 81.
La Nopalera
Hace un chingo de anos ... (drawing)], 1417.
Noriega, Ramses
Mural, Chicano Research Library, UCLA [photograph], 2015.
[Untitled drawing], 2878.
[Untitled drawing], 2879.
[Untitled drawing], 2880.
[Untitled drawing], 2881.
[Untitled drawing], 2882.
[Untitled drawings], 2883.
Novoa, Juan Bruce
USE: Bruce Novoa, Juan
Oakes College, University of California, Santa Cruz, CA
Corazon de Aztlan: a Chicano arts show, 890.
Oakland County Cultural Affairs, MI
Nora Mendoza: an exhibition of abstract/impressionism, 729.
Oakland Museum, Oakland, CA
Espejo: reflections of the Mexican American: Louis Carlos Bernal, Morrie Camhi, Abigail Heyman, Roger Minick, Neal Slavin, 507.
In search of Aztlan, 78.
In search of Aztlan, 79.
Ochoa, Victor Orozco
Centerfold-arte [drawing], 2885.
Posadas [graphic], 4589.
[Resistencia! (drawing)], 2886.
[La tierra mia, all the way to the Bay (drawing)], 2887.
[Untitled drawing], 2888.
[Untitled photographs], 7395.
Ohlone College Art Department Gallery, Fremont, CA
Impressions: a California print invitational, 1598.
Ojeda, Jay
Galeria de la Raza--art for the community, 431.
Ojo Production
Migra migraine, 8672.
OMICA Housing Corp., Inc., Homestead (Miami), FL
Dedication of heritage village, 26.
Opton, Suzanne
Short strokes, 1369.
Orange Co. Library. El Modena Branch
Empanada: a tasty Mexican group art exhibit filled with a variety of digestable treats, 731.
The Hispanic Artist Association of Orange County presents "Empanada," a tasty Mexican group art exhibit filled with a variety of digestible treats, 432.
Ordorica, Leticia
Community expression in muralism, 2008.

Orozco, Irma
    Women & their work, 733.
Orozco, Jose Clemente
    The slave [painting], 6919.
    [Untitled painting], 4866.
Orozco, Juan Ishi
    Tu eres mi otro yo [painting], 6921.
    [Untitled drawing], 2891.
    [Untitled painting], 6922.
Orozco, Sylvia
    Chicano tattoos, dibujos de mano - an
        expression of Chicano life, 4397.
    Chicanos and tattoos: dibujos de mano - an
        expression of Chicano life, 8481.
    Las mujeres - Chicana artists come into their
        own, 433.
    Trevino's arte interprets el mundo Chicano,
        735.
    [Untitled painting], 2892.
Ortega, Francisco
    Piramide [painting], 6923.
Ortega, Gil
    The 50's and other assorted Chicano graffiti,
        998.
Ortegon, Veronica
    [Illustration of Orozco's mural HERNAN
        CORTEZ], 2893.
    [Low riders c/s (drawing)], 2894.
    [Photographs and drawings], 2895.
    [Untitled drawing], 2896.
    [Untitled drawing], 2897.
Orth, Maureen
    The soaring spirit of Chicano arts, 434.
Ortiz, Leo
    [Untitled drawing], 2898.
Ortiz, Simon J.
    1680-1980: a ceremony of brotherhood, 1.
Otis/Parsons Gallery, Los Angeles, CA
    L.A. parks & wrecks: a reflection of urban
        life/parques y choques: un reflejo de la
        vida urbana, 81.
Ozuna, Gloria
    Un companero de lejos [drawing], 2899.
    [Familia (drawing)], 2900.
    La Senora Soliz de la Calle "D" [drawing],
        2901.
    El tamal [drawing], 2026.
Paez, Carlos
    [Untitled sculpture], 8246.
Palacio de Mineria, Mexico, D.F.
    Raices antiguas/visiones nuevas: arte chicano
        y latinoamericano en los estados unidos,
        1601.
Palacios, Procopio
    Partido Liberal Mexicano [print], 4592.
Palma Castroman, Janis
    Dancer [painting], 6925.
    Desintegracion [painting], 6926.
    ENCUENTRO ARTISTICO FEMENIL [exhibit], Austin,
        TX, November 28, 1977, 1908.
    Gigolo (#2) [painting], 6927.
    Girl in the forest [painting], 6928.
    Girl [painting], 6929.
    Introduccion, 1909.
    Landscape [painting], 6930.
    Male nude [painting], 6931.
    Las meninas no son solo de Velazquez
        [painting], 6932.
    La puta [painting], 6933.
    El te de las cuatro [painting], 6934.
    Tinieblas [painting], 6935.
    [Untitled drawing], 2903.
    [Untitled drawing], 2904.
    [Untitled drawing], 2905.
    [Untitled drawing], 2906.
    [Untitled painting], 6936.
    The yawn [painting], 6937.
Palma, Janis
    USE: Palma Castroman, Janis
Palomino, Ernesto ("Ernie")
    In black and white: evolution of an artist,
        737.
    My trip in a '52 Ford, 3843.
    My trip in a '52 Ford, 3844.

Parachini, Allan
    Tujunga wash mural stands up to storm, 435.
Paramo, Bobby
    Cerco Blanco, the balloon man and fighting
        City Hall: on being a Chicano filmmaker,
        1125.
Parr, June
    Amado Maurilio Pena, Jr.: a talented and
        dedicated artist, 262.
Patlan, Ray
    The history of the Mexican-American worker
        (1974-75) [detail of mural], 1722.
    La raza cosmica [painting], 6938.
Patssi
    USE: Valdez, Patssi
Patterson, Ann
    Exhibit at Unitarian: Smith, Quesada art
        black, white contrast, 1692.
Pazos, Antonio
    [Con el poncho embravecido (drawing)], 2909.
    [Loui Romero (drawing)], 2910.
    El poeta suena... [drawing], 2911.
    [Untitled drawing], 2912.
    [Untitled drawing], 2913.
    [Untitled drawing], 2914.
    [Untitled drawing], 2915.
    [Untitled drawing], 2916.
    [Untitled drawing], 2917.
    [Untitled drawing], 2918.
    [Untitled drawing], 2919.
    [Untitled drawing], 2920.
    [Untitled drawing], 2921.
    [Untitled drawing], 2922.
    [Untitled drawing], 2923.
    [Untitled drawing], 2924.
    [Untitled drawing], 2925.
    [Untitled drawing], 2926.
    [Untitled drawing], 2927.
    [Untitled drawing], 2928.
    [Untitled drawing], 2929.
    [Untitled drawing], 2930.
    [Untitled drawing], 2931.
    [Untitled drawing], 2932.
    [Untitled drawing], 2933.
    [Untitled drawing], 2934.
    [Untitled drawing], 2935.
    [Untitled drawing], 2936.
    [Untitled drawing], 2937.
    [Untitled drawing], 2938.
    [Untitled drawing], 2939.
    [Untitled drawing], 2940.
    [Untitled drawing], 2941.
    [Untitled drawing], 2942.
    [Untitled drawing], 2943.
    [Untitled drawing], 2944.
    [Untitled drawing], 2945.
    [Untitled drawing], 2946.
    [Untitled drawing], 2947.
    [Untitled drawing], 2948.
    [Untitled drawing], 2949.
    [Untitled drawing], 2950.
    [Untitled drawing], 2951.
    [Untitled drawing], 2952.
    [Untitled drawing], 2953.
    [Untitled drawing], 2954.
    [Untitled drawing], 2955.
    [Untitled drawing], 2956.
    [Untitled drawing], 2957.
    [Untitled drawing], 2958.
    [Untitled drawing], 2959.
    [Untitled drawing], 2960.
    [Untitled drawing], 2961.
    [Untitled drawing], 2962.
    [Untitled graphic], 4593.
    [Untitled graphic], 4594.
    [Untitled graphic], 4595.
    [Untitled graphic], 4596.
    [Untitled graphic], 4597.
    [Untitled graphic], 4598.
    [Untitled graphic], 4599.
    [Untitled graphic], 4600.
    [Untitled graphic], 4601.
    [Untitled graphic], 4602.
    [Untitled graphic], 4603.

Quiroz, Esau
    Chicano art: an identity crisis, 2219.
Quiroz, Martin, III
    Cuauhtemoc [drawing], 2981.
    [Untitled photo collage of Chicanas], 5834.
Rabel, Fanny
    [Untitled woodcut], 4633.
Rabyor, Jozanne
    Luis Jimenez at Contemporary Arts Museum,
        3622.
Rafas
    Social comment in barrio pop [drawing], 2982.
    Social comment in barrio pop [drawing], 2983.
    A social comment in Chicano pop [drawing],
        2984.
    Social commentary in Chicano pop art
        [drawing], 2985.
    Social commentary in Chicano pop art
        [drawing], 2986.
    [Untitled drawing], 1628.
Raffel, Stefan
    [Portfolio (drawings)], 2988.
Ramirez de Robe, Jose "Controll"
    Carton de Jose "Controll" Ramirez, 2989.
    [Cartoon], 1420.
    Human rights defender [drawing], 1468.
    [Pensamientos de... (drawing)], 1421.
    Police scoreboard [drawing], 2991.
    [Which way to the revolution, ese?
        (caricature)], 1422.
Ramirez, Fern
    [Untitled drawings], 2993.
Ramirez, Mickey
    A letter in depth [drawing], 2994.
Ramos, Joe
    [Untitled photograph], 7401.
Rand, Steve
    Carlos David Almaraz, 86.
Rangel, Jesus
    Heirs of Jose Posada: revolution lives in
        Chicano art, 447.
Raya, Marcos
    Ladies and gentlemen, we got a new pope
        [drawing], 2995.
    Made in the U.S.A. [painting], 6959.
    Mechanics of the imagination [painting], 6960.
    New York-New York - self portrait [painting],
        6961.
    [Untitled drawing], 2996.
Reaves, John
    Santa Barbara, 451.
Renteria, Phil
    Phil Renteria and Dick Wray, 715.
Renteria, Ramon
    Struggle of barrio life reflected in mural,
        3248.
Resendez, Izabel
    Christ [drawing], 2997.
Reser, Phil
    Rene Yanez: state-of-the-xerox art, 757.
Reyes Aponte, Cynthia
    Untitled [drawing], 2998.
    Untitled [drawing], 2999.
Reyes, Felipe
    Malinche complex [drawing], 3000.
    La Malinche [drawing], 3001.
    [Untitled drawing], 3002.
    Untitled [drawing], 3003.
Reyes, Luis
    Seguin: traidor o heroe, 1051.
Rezendez, Mark
    Christian cross [drawing], 3004.
Richard Henkin, Inc., Beverly Hills, CA
    Veloy Vigil, 1172.
    Veloy Vigil, 758.
Rickey, Carrie
    The passion of Ana, 945.
    The writing on the wall, 452.
Rilkin, Scott
    La Raza Silkscreen Center, in step with the
        Mission, 380.
Rios, Esther
    Spotted leopard [sculpture], 857.
Rios, Roberto

La familia [silkscreen], 4638.
Rios, Sam
    Chicano muralist: Toltecotl in Aztlan, 453.
Ripley, Deborah
    A sticky business, 1333.
Rivas, Maggie
    Art of the barrio: Exxon's traveling art show
        comes to headquarters, 2176.
Rivera, Domingo
    [Untitled drawing], 3005.
    [Untitled drawing], 3006.
    [Untitled drawing], 3007.
Rivera, Gato
    Officer Bradley interrogates Chuy Chicano
        [photograph], 7404.
Rivera, Humberto R.
    Film notes, 509.
    The murals of East Los Angeles, 760.
Roberts, Tim
    For art's sake, for the community, for the
        working class, 454.
Rocha, Adrian
    [Untitled drawings], 3008.
Rodebaugh, Dale
    Graffiti replaces popular mural in Santa Cruz
        arcade, 1213.
Rodriguez, Alfred
    A historical survey of Chicano murals in the
        Southwest: an interdisciplinary teaching
        unit, 918.
Rodriguez, Anita
    Las enjarradoras: women of the earth, 14.
    Tradiciones de adobe en Nuevo Mejico norteno =
        adobe traditions in Northern New Mexico, 15.
Rodriguez, Joe
    Arte tejana [painting], 6965.
    Corazon sangriento de Tejas [painting], 6966.
Rodriguez, Joe B.
    Kahlo pains/Dolor de Kahlo [painting], 6967.
Rodriguez, Jose
    El hombre pequeno [drawing], 3009.
    Remigia, la mama de Manuel [drawing], 3010.
    Timoteo y su burro [drawing], 3011.
Rodriguez, Jose Luis
    Nuestra voz, arte, 5649.
Rodriguez, Julia
    El control humano [drawing], 3012.
Rodriguez, Luis
    A Center for Cultural Preservation and Human
        Resources, 455.
Rodriguez, Patricia
    Bibliografia sobre el arte chicano, 1047.
    Canto al pueblo '78, 1288.
    Chicano Studies 130, 2251.
    Patricia Rodriguez: simbolos y fantasias
        culturales, 351.
    Portfolio: Patricia Rodriguez; the visual
        interview, 763.
    Untitled [drawing], 3013.
    Untitled [drawing], 3014.
    Untitled [graphic], 4639.
    [Untitled silkscreen], 8336.
Rodriguez, Patricia, ed.
    Selected readings on Chicano art, 1932.
Rodriguez, Pedro
    Arte como expresion del pueblo, 238.
    Chicano art arising, 33.
    Chicano art exhibition, 3632.
    Chicano artist's paintings on display at WWC,
        765.
    Fronteras falsas [painting], 1238.
    La mazonista [painting], 6970.
Rodriguez, Roland V.
    Urban design primer: comparative analyses of
        San Antonio urbanscapes, 158.
Rodriguez, Vicente
    Dia de la coneja [drawing], 3015.
    Drawing commemorating the 16th of September,
        Mexico's Independence Day, 3016.
    La hormiga [drawing], 3017.
    Mayan gods [drawing], 2070.
    Mayan gods [drawing], 2071.
    Mayan religious ceremonies [drawing], 3020.
    Mayas cazando ganado para comer=Mayas hunting

game for food [drawing], 3021.
Mayas plantando maiz=Mayas planting corn
[drawing], 3022.
Nuestra Senora de Guadalupe=Our Lady of
Guadalupe [drawing], 3023.
El pajaro grande [drawing], 3024.
Por ahi en la luna [drawing], 3025.

Rogovin, Mark
Mural manual: how to paint murals for the
classroom, community center and street
corner, 2253.

Romero, Alejandro E.
[Untitled drawing], 3026.
[Untitled drawing], 3027.
[Untitled drawing], 3028.

Romero, Ernestina
Chicano art movement: conference celebrates
transformation, 2148.
Chicano culture to be explored at conference,
981.

Romero, Leo
Celso: poetry by Leo Romero, New Mexico, 3029.

Romero, Orlando
A Canto al Pueblo artist at the second "Canto"
en 1978, Corpus Christi, Tex Aztlan,
enjoying the fruits of the struggle on to
the third ... Canto al Pueblo!!!, 1376.
Nambe - year one, 3031.

Romero, Raul V.
Chicanarte, a major exposition of California
arts, 41.

Romotsky, Jerry
Chicano graffiti, 2254.
Los Angeles barrio calligraphy, 1000.
Placas and murals, 766.
Plaqueaso on the wall, 4410.

Romotsky, Sally R.
Chicano graffiti, 2254.
Los Angeles barrio calligraphy, 1000.
Placas and murals, 766.
Plaqueaso on the wall, 4410.

Rosas, Carlos
3er paisaje [drawing], 3032.
Aztlan [painting], 934.
Entelequia [detail of mural], 6305.
Miseria [drawing], 3033.
Platicando con Carlos Rosas, 1112.

Rosenstone, Robert A.
In search of...four women/four cultures, 564.

Ross, Bob
The case of three California muralists:
Roberto Chavez, Eduardo Carrillo, John
Chamberlin, 1334.

Rowe, Richard
On Olvera Street: one vision realized, another
white washed, 122.

Royal Chicano Air Force (RCAF), Sacramento, CA
[RCAF posters], 7563.
[Untitled collage], 2086.

Ruben Salazar Library, Sonoma State University,
Sonoma, CA
Patricia Rodriguez: Chicano sculpture and
masks, 767.

Ruiz, Elizabeth
Fiesta artist, 768.

Ruiz, Elvia
Whitewashed mural, 457.

Saavedra-Vela, Pilar
Exposicion nacional de raices hispanicas,
3635.
El Midwest Canto al pueblo: "Otra Vez, C/S",
1372.
A time for less talk and more action, 698.

Saenz, John
Felix completes art project: artist's murals
mask East LA graffitti [sic], 3225.

Sagel, Jaime
Art of brothers taps New Mexico heritage, 858.

Saks Galleries, Denver, CO
Ramon K., 3636.

Salas, Joanne
Mural painting that comes from the heart;
'impact' is the word for muralist Luis Mena,
5576.

Salazar, Juan Albert
Entelequia, 2234.

Salazar, Veronica
Artist doesn't starve now, 1175.
Aspiration comes true, 770.
Mel Casas sees things brown, 1176.
Prominent Mexican-Americans-Porfirio Salinas,
771.

Salinas, Paula
Easter egg breaktime [drawing], 3034.

Salinas, Porfirio
Bluebonnets and cactus: an album of
southwestern paintings, 2218.
Porfirio Salinas: blue bonnets and cactus; an
album of Southwestern paintings, 772.

Salinas, Rael
The city [painting], 6980.
Illusions of reality [detail of painting],
6981.
Illusions of reality, 6982.
Outcry [detail of painting], 6983.
Outcry [painting], 6984.

Salinas, Raul
Nueva estrella en el horizonte, 773.
Nueva estrella en el horizonte, 3301.
Portrait of an artist, 774.

Salkowitz-Montoya, Lezlie
A critical perspective on the state of Chicano
art, 7268.

Salvador R. Torres Chicano Underground
Studio-Gallery, San Diego, CA
Diego Rivera, David Alfaro Siqueiros, Jose
Clemente Orozco, from the collection of the
S.F. Museum of Art, 2161.

Samuels, Harold
Cisneros, Jose, 775.
Grandee, Joe Ruiz, 776.
Salinas, Porfirio, 777.

Samuels, Peggy
Cisneros, Jose, 775.
Grandee, Joe Ruiz, 776.
Salinas, Porfirio, 777.

San Antonio Museum Association, San Antonio, TX
Real, really real, super real, 778.
Visiones nuevas en Tejas/new visions in Texas,
1607.

San Antonio Museum of Modern Art
Paperwork: an exhibition of Texas artists,
1182.
Zarzamora: inaugural exhibition of Ladrones de
la Luz, 1390.

San Antonio Public Library
Art in the little world, 1022.

San Francisco Art Commission Gallery
Rolando Castellon, Gustavo Rivera, Jerry
Concha, 1183.

San Francisco Art Institute
Other sources: an American essay, 1609.

San Francisco Museum of Art, San Francisco, CA
M.I.X. graphics I: prints, 3647.

San Francisco Museum of Modern Art, San Francisco,
CA
Aesthetics of graffiti, 87.
Carmen Lomas Garza/prints and gouaches: Margo
Humphrey/monotypes, 780.
Day of the dead, 1939.
People's murals: some events in American
history, 1459.
Posters and society, 1017.
Rupert Garcia/pastel drawings, 1613.

San Jose Museum of Art
Cinco de Mayo: el arte chicano de hoy, the
works of Mexican American artists, 460.

San Pedro Municipal Art Gallery, San Pedro, CA
Celebration: Muriel Olguin and Linda Vallejo,
781.

Sanchez, Al
Murals destroyed, 1423.

Sanchez, Arley
Santeros, 47.

Sanchez, James
Fighters [drawing], 3035.

Sanchez, Jesus
Auditorium mural "wipe out" during recent

--   ---

--   --

        6 [painting], 7045.
        7 [painting], 7046.
        8 [print], 4664.
        9 [print], 4665.
        [Free Los 7 (drawing)], 3176.
        Portfolio 4: 1; 2; 3; 4; 5; 6; 7; 8; 9; 10,
          3177.
        Portfolio [mixed media], 3178.
        The Tin-Tan I know [comic strip], 1426.
        [Untitled drawing], 3179.
        [Untitled drawing], 3180.
        [Untitled drawing], 3181.
        [Untitled painting], 7048.
        [Untitled painting], 7049.
        [Untitled painting], 7050.
        [Untitled painting], 7051.
        [Untitled painting], 7052.
        [Untitled painting], 3182.
Yarbro-Bejarano, Yvonne
        La forma del sueno: arte y pensamiento de
          Alfredo Arreguin, 203.
        Resena critica de revistas literarias
          chicanas: problemas y tendencias, 2033.
        Resena de revistas chicanas: problemas y
          tendencias, Part I, 1339.
Ybarra-Frausto, Tomas
        Arte prehispanico, arte popular, 3511.
        A history of Chicano art, 246.
Young, Robert S.
        Amado Maurilio Pena, Jr., 550.
Zahn, Debbie
        Citywide murals: outlook bleak for funding of
          art work by Chicanos, 1257.
Zamora, Bernice
        Restless serpents, 1281.
Zapata, Eloy
        [Untitled drawing], 3183.
Zarco
        USE: Guerrero, Adolfo "El Zarco"
Zermeno, Andy
        Don Sotaco: caricaturas de la huelga de
          Delano, 27.
Zheutlin, Barbara
        Jesus Salvador Trevino, 117.
Zucker, Martin
        Walls of barrio are brought to life by street
          gang art, 3227.
Zufelt, Wilma
        Untitled [drawing], 3184.
        Untitled [drawing], 3185.
        Untitled [drawing], 3186.
Zuniga, R.
        Entrevista con los muralistas de East Austin,
          919.
Zuniga, Ramiro
        Calle [graphic], 4666.
        Losing hold [drawing], 3187.
        Red and blue [graphic], 4667.
        [Untitled drawing], 3188.
        [Untitled drawing], 3189.
        [Untitled graphic], 4668.

Title Index

1 [painting], 7040.

$10 million Latin cultural center: Lincoln Park to get new life, 371.

10 [print], 4663.

11 poems, 543.

11 reproduccion - significacion politica: arte fotocopia, 3304.

1680-1980: a ceremony of brotherhood, 1.

17 artists: Hispano/Mexican-American/Chicano, 35, 1228.

1975-76 film catalog, 498.

2 [painting], 7041.

2001: a group exhibit of mixed media, 630.

3 [painting], 7042.

30 works from the grass roots, 91.

3er paisaje [drawing], 3032.

4 [painting], 7043.

450 anos del pueblo chicano/450 years of Chicano history in pictures, 1394.

5 [painting], 7044.

The 50's and other assorted Chicano graffiti, 998.

6 [painting], 7045.

7 [painting], 7046.

8 [print], 4664.

9 [print], 4665.

A mi amor [painting], 6708.

La abuela [drawing], 2378.

Abuelita [etching], 4547.

Acosta, a man and his art, 8.

Additions to Ethnic Art Slide Catalog. Supplement to the Afro American, Mexican American, Native American Art Slide Catalog, 895.

La Adelita, 12.

Adobe architecture, 18.

An adobe fireplace: Anita Rodriguez has built many - each one different, 16.

Adoracion [drawing], 2035.

Aesthetics of graffiti, 87.

The affectionate realism of Jesse Trevino, 989.

Affirmations of existence, barrio murals of Los Angeles, 4882.

Afro American, Mexican American, Native American art slide catalog, 1973-74, 896.

Afro American, Mexican American, Native American art slide catalog, 1974-75, 897.

[Agony (drawing)], 2660.

Agueda Martinez, 817.

El aguila cae [painting], 6753.

Aguila y maiz [mural], 5998.

Aire triste [poetry in graphic design], 4494.

Ajo, granadas y tres flores, 844.

Al frente [drawing], 2419.

Al sol y la luna [drawing], 2644.

Albert Einstein [painting], 6800.

Alejandro E. Romero, 1582.

Alejandro Romero, 1545, 1605.

Alejandro Romero: new works, 1553.

Alex Maldonado, primitive painter, 546.

Alexander Maldonado, 703.

Alfredo Arreguin, 193, 197, 201.

Alfredo Arreguin - painting in patterns, 199.

Aliens [drawing], 2420.

Alma Rosa [photograph], 7313.

Altares: arte espiritual del hogar, 98.

Altars as folk art, 97.

Amado Maurilio Pena, Jr., 263, 267, 550, 3321.

Amado Maurilio Pena, Jr.: a talented and dedicated artist, 262.

Amado Pena, Chicano artist, 911.

Amado Pena's art, 905.

America morena [photograph], 7407.

America tropical, 116.

American Consul General, visa section [drawing], 2697.

The American pageant: a history of the republic, 6th ed., 5935.

The American way [drawing], 2493.

Amor sin fronteras, 152.

Analysis of Chicano aesthetics in visual art, 5009.

Ancient roots, new visions, 1490.

Ancient times [painting], 6761.

[Angel baby (drawing)], 3098.

[Anglo meets three Chicano youths (drawing)], 2729.

Angry artists deface own mural, 1279.

An.i.ma.tion: the arts, techniques, and processes involved in giving apparent life and movement to inanimate objects by means of cinematography, 1294.

The architecture and art of early Hispanic Colorado, 153.

Arizona, 1030.

Armando Cid art works on display at Barrio Gallery, 214.

Army of volunteers paints a little history in Phoenix, 3198.

Around the Bay, 279.

Ars poetica: editorial, 7217.

Art & ethnics: background for teaching youth in a pluralistic society, 182.

Art against the wall, 1661.

Art bridging culture gap, 6373.

Art directors, take note, 148.

Art for our sake, 4754.

Art in public places, 1443, 1455.

Art in the barrios: one man's commitment, 390.

Art in the little world, 1022.

Art is business: an interview with Joe L. Gonzalez, 260.

Art of barrios in East L.A., 489.

Art of brothers taps New Mexico heritage, 858.

The art of Mexican America, 235, 1481.

The art of Rodolfo Leal, 556.

Art of the barrio: Exxon's traveling art show comes to headquarters, 2176.

The art of the Chicano movement, and the movement of Chicano art, 1992.

Art of the state: California, 56.

Art on the border, 185.

Art on the walls: a vehicle for positive change, 3287.

Art outdoors, 5992.

Art replaces writing on wall, 6337.

Art scene, 3683.

Art wall for Plaza de la Raza March 28, 280.

Arte, 3051.

Arte chicano, 4567, 7256.

Arte chicano de Carlos Rosas, Chicano muralist, 346.

Arte chicano de Texas/Texas Chicano art, 412.

Arte chicano y el pueblo, 58.

Arte como expresion del pueblo, 238.

La arte cosmica [sic] de Esteban Villa: Chicano art exposition, 307.

Arte de Aurelio Diaz [drawings], 2521.

Arte de la Raza [portfolio], 1253.

Arte de ninos coloring book, 2657.

Arte de Nora Mendoza, Hector Perez, George Vargas, Martin Moreno, 297.

Arte de Santa Barraza, 2403.

Arte de Valentin Cardenas [drawing], 2461.

El arte del Chicano - "The Spirit of the Experience", 1009.

El arte del pocho, 94.

Arte del varrio, 990.

Arte negativo en exposicion, 3395.

Arte prehispanico, arte popular, 3511.

Arte tejana [painting], 6965.

Los artes: a story the people live as well as paint, 345.

Artes en la primavera, 847.

Artes Guadalupanos de Aztlan: Samuel Leyba, Gilberto Guzman, Geronimo Garduno, Carlos Leyba, Pancho Hunter, 462.

The artist as a revolutionary, 54.

Artist doesn't starve now, 1175.

Artist envisions a 'Sistine' ceiling, 3244.

Artist paints from heritage, 801.

Artist profile-Amado Pena, 591.

Artist registry financed, 168.

Artist sustains proud Hispanic mural tradition, 1637.

Artist views murals as dialogue with oppressed, 4950.

Artista de Aztlan, 558.

Artistas chicanas together at C.S.A.C., an

Appendices

APPENDIX A
ALPHABETICAL LIST OF CHICANO ARTISTS

Acevedo, Esperanza "Inky"
Aceves, José
Acosta, Joe Frank
Acosta, John
Acosta, Manuel
Acosta, Thomas
Adame, Esteban
"Admonty"
    USE Montemayor, Alice Dickerson
Aguayo, Emilio
Aguilar, Cruz
Aguilar, Porfirio
Aguilera, Manuel
Aguirre, Lupe
Aguirre, Ricardo
Alaníz, Ricardo
Alaníz Healy, Wayne
    USE Healy, Wayne Alaníz
Alberro, Malu
    USE Ortega, Malu
Albuquerque, Veronica Dalia de
    USE de Albuquerque, Veronica Dalia
Almaguér, Miguel
Almanza, Félix
Almaráz, Carlos D.
Almazán, Jesse
Almeida, Al
Almendarez, Johnny
Alonzo, Ricardo
Alvarez, Félix
Alvarez, Grace
Alvarez, Johnny
Alvarez, Tina
Amaral, Roberto
Ambriz
Amescua, Michael M.
Amezcua, Consuelo González "Chelo"
Anaya, Stephen
Andrade, Bruno, Jr.
Anguiano, Mary Ann
Angulo, Hector "H"
Anton, Don
Anzaldua, Mario
Apodaca, Ricardo
Aponte, Cynthia Reyes
    USE Reyes Aponte, Cynthia
Aragón, Rafael
Aranda, Guillermo
Arce, Josefina

Archuleta, Eppie
Archuleta, Felipe
Archuleta, Leroy
Archuleta, Robert
Arellano, Estevan

Arenas, Eva
Arenas, Rosa María
Arenivar, Roberto
Arredondo, Alicia
Arreguín, Alfredo
Arreola, Tomás
Arriola, Gustavo Montano
Arroyo, Romero
Artorez, Arturo
Astorga, Jerry
Atilano, Raymond
Avalos, David
Avila, Adam
Avila, Justina
Avila, Norman
Avilez, Tomás "Sapo"

Baca, Judith F.
Baíz, Luis
Barajas, Salvador
Barela, Al
Barela, Patrocinio
Baros, José Alberto
Barraza, Santa
Barrera, Jesús
Barrera, Ricardo
Barrios, Francisco
Básquez, Paul
Bejarano, William
Benavides, Edmon
Benavides, Ramiro
Bernal, Louis Carlos
Berru, Becky
Blasco, Francisco
Bonilla, Roberto
Borboa, Roberto
Botello, David
Bova, Joe
Bowerman, Liz Lerma
Bravo, Joe
Bravo, Ray
Briones, Tone
Bugarín, Lena

Buitrón, Robert C.
Burciaga, José Antonio

Cabrera, Armando
Calderón, Margarita
Camacho, José
Campero, Armando
Camplís, Francisco X.
Camplís, Lorenza
Campos, Enrique
Campusano, Jesús "Chuy"
Cantú, Jesús "Chista"
Capiz, Stephen
Carbajal, Edward
Cárdenas, David
Cárdenas, Gilberto
Cárdenas, Hector
Cárdenas, Rogelio
Carlos Borjas, Armando
Carrasco, Bárbara
Carrillo, Eduardo
Carrillo, Graciela
Carrillo, Juan
Carrillo, Patricia
Carrillo, Sean
Carveo, Oscar
Casanova, Stephen
Casas, Melesio
Castañeda, Sal
Castañeda, Tomás
Castaño, Wilfredo
Castellanos, Leonard
Castellanos-Sánchez, Eloísa
Castellas, Leonard
Castillo Simonetti, Naomi
Castillo, Mario E.
Castillo, Oscar R.
Castro, Isabel
Castro, René
Ceja, David
Cernero, Franco
Cervantes, Juan
Cervantes, José
Cervantez, Luis
Cervantez, Pedro
Cervantez, Yreina
Chacón, Hector
Chapa Mendoza, Nora
    USE Mendoza, Nora Chapa
Chávez, Edward
Chávez, Estéban
Chávez, Hernando
Chávez, Joseph A.

Chávez, Ray
Chávez, Roberto
Chávez, Santiago
"Chista"
    USE Cantú, Jesús "Chista"
Cid, Armando
Cisneros, George
Cisneros, José
Cisneros, Ramón
Cisneros, René
"Clavos"
    USE Félix, Charles "Clavos"
Coleman, Elisa Marina
Concha, Jerry
Contreras, Carlos
"Controll"
    USE Ramirez de Robe, José "Controll"
Cordova, Carlos Chávez
Coronado, Sam
Cortázar, Luis J.
Cortéz, Carlos
Cortéz, Jim
Cortéz, Ronald
Covarrubias, Jim
Crary, Pat Portera
Cruz, Bob
Cruz, Cresanta
Cruz, Manuel
Cuellar, Rodolfo

Dávalos, Pete
Dávila, Atanacio
De Albuquerque, Veronica Dalia
de Ávila, Alfred
de la Fuente, Roberto
de la Huerta, Sylvia
de la Riva, Lola
De la Rocha, Roberto
De la Torre, Ernie
de Leon, Anna
De Leon, Josefina
De los Santos, Nanci
Del Castillo-Leon, Victoria
del Valle, Angel
Delgadillo, Ramón
Delgado, Etta
Delgado, Roberto
Desiga, Daniel
Díaz, Aurelio
Díaz, Ed
Díaz, Ricardo
Díaz Pérez, Roberto
Domínguez, Mary Lynn

Domínguez, Priscilla
Domínguez, Salvador
Duardo, Richard
Duarte, J.
Duarte, Roy
Durán, Bernardo
Durán, Daniel

Escalante, Mariana
Escojico, Isabell
Esparza, Antonio
Esparza, Moctezuma
Esparza, Raúl S.
Espinoza, Al
Espinoza, Carlos
Espinoza, Carlota
Espinoza, Gilbert "Sparky"
Espinoza, Juan
Espinoza, Raúl
Espinoza, Ray
Espinoza, Roberto
Esquivel, José
Estrada, José "Pepe"
Estrada, Juanita
Estrella, Armando
Estrella, Rubén

Fajardo, Francisco "Frank"
Favela, Ricardo V.
Félix, Charles "Clavos"
Félix, Charles W.
Fernández, Esther
Fernández, Licita
Fernández, Rudy
Flores, Alex
Flores, Carolina
Flores, Elsa
Flores, Enrique
Flores, Gloria
Flores, Gloriamalia
Flores, John
Flores, María
"The Foot"
    USE González, Louie "The Foot"
Franklin, Juana
Fuentes, Juan
Fuentes, Larry

Gaégos, Carlito
Galbán, Margarita
Galindo, Guillermo
Gallegos, David
Gallegos, Ernie

Galván, Yolanda
Galvez, Daniel
Gamboa, Diane
Gamboa, Harry, Jr.
Garces, Roland
García, Antonio
García, C.
García, Domingo
García, Eva C.
García, Francisco
García, Jesse V.
García, Kathryn E.
García, Lorraine
García, María Hortencia
García, Max
García, Miguel "Freeloader"
García, Mike
García, Ralph
García, Rubén A.
García, Rupert
García, Ruperto
García, Sal
García-Camarillo, Cecilio
García-Camarillo, Mia
Garduno, Gerónimo
Garza, Alex
Garza, Danny
Garza, Jorge
Garza, José P.
Garza, Luis
Garza, Manuel
Garza Pérez, David
Gaytán, Ray
"Geomonte"
    USE Montemayor, George "Monty"
Gil de Montes, Roberto
Girón, José
Godena, Frank
Gómez, Ignacio
Gómez, Robert
Gonzales, Jesse
Gonzales, Mariano
Gonzales, Tomás
González, Abel
González, Crispín
González, Helen
González, Jesse
González, Joe L.
González, John
González, José
González, José G.
González, Louie "The Foot"
González, Mary Ann Ambray

González, Pamela M.
González, Robert
González Dodson, Nora
Gorena, Xavier
Grajeda, Dolores
Grandee, Joe Ruíz
Grijalva, Lucila V.
Gronk
Guerra, Carlos Andrés
Guerra, Luis
Guerra, Teresina
Guerrero, Adolfo "El Zarco"
Guerrero, José
Guerrero, Raúl M.
Guerrero, Xóchitl Nevel
Gurule, Ben
Gutiérrez, Andrew
Gutiérrez, Blanca Flor
Gutiérrez, Frank
Gutiérrez, Jacob
Gutiérrez, James
Gutiérrez, Jesús
Gutiérrez, Lola
Gutiérrez, Raúl
Gutiérrez-Mcdermid, Mercedes
Guzmán, Gilberto
Guzmán, Leo
Guzmán, Rubén

"H"
    USE Angulo, Hector "H"
Healy, Wayne Alaníz
Herada, Elma
Hermosillo, Bert
Hernández, Armando Leon
Hernández, Enrique
Hernández, Esther
Hernández, Fernando
Hernández, Francisco
Hernández, Gil
Hernández, Jessie
Hernández, John
Hernández, Juan
Hernández, Judithe E.
Hernández, Lorenzo
Hernández, Leticia
Hernández, Manuel
Hernández, Sergio
Hernández-M., William
Hernández-Trujillo, Manuel
Herrera (Chávez) Margaret
Herrera, Miguel
Herrón, Willie

Hinojosa, Amador
Hinojosa, Lucas
Holguín, Rubén
Honesto, Cynthia
Hunter, Pancho

Ibánez, Armando
"Inky"
    USE Acevedo, Esperanza "Inky"

Jaramillo, Jerry
Jaramillo, Juanita
Jaramillo, Virginia
Jaúregui, Mike
Jaúregui Weiner, Margarita
Jiménez, David "Sir Loco"

Jiménez, Luis
Jiménez, Richard

Kaneta Kosiba-Vargas, S.

Lara, Armando
Lasta, Susana
Lau, Alberto
Lazarín, David
Leal, Rodolfo
Lefebre, Francisco
LeRoy, Louis
Leyba, Albert
Leyba, Carlos
Leyba, Sam
Limón, Leo
Lira, Santos
Loa, Fred
Lomas Garza, Carmen
Lomelí, Filiberto
Longoria, Jaime
López Ortega, Xavier
López de Jaramillo, Pola
López, Alejandro
López, Ben
López, David
López, Félix
López, Frank
López, George
López, Manuel
López, Yolanda M.
Louie, Harry
Lucero, Félix
Lucero, Juan
Lucero, Leo
Lucero, Linda

Lucero, Roberto
Lucero, Steve
Luján, Gilbert Sánchez "Magu"
Luján, Jerry
Luján, Luisito
Luján, María Theofila
Luján, Pedro

Machado, Anthony
Madrid, Lydia Rede
Maestas, José Alfredo
Maes, Bob
"Magu"
    USE Luján, Gilbert Sánchez "Magu"
Maldonado, Alexander
Maradiaga, Ralph
Marcos, Darlene
Marín, José D.
Martínez, Agueda
Martínez, Andrés
Martínez, Baltazar
Martínez, César Augusto
Martínez, Daniel
Martínez, David
Martínez, Efrain
Martínez, Filomeno
Martínez, Frank
Martínez, Guillermo
Martínez, Lydia
Martínez, Manuel
Martínez, Pedro
Martínez, Raúl
Martínez, Richard
Martínez, Rudy
Martínez, Santos G., Jr.
Martínez, Sue
Mauricio, Manuel
Maya, Gloria
Mazuca, Roland
Medellín, Octavio
Medina, Ada
Meléndez, Bill
Mena, Luis Gustavo
Mende, Chris
Méndez, Pete
Méndez, Raoul
Méndez, Xavier
Mendoza Psarianos, Laurie
Mendoza, Anthony
Mendoza, Enrique
Mendoza, John L.
Mendoza, Josie
Mendoza, Nora Chapa

Mendoza, Robert
Mendoza, Vicente
Merriman Montoya, Delilah
Mesa-Baines, Amalia
Michel-Trapaga, Rene David
Miranda, Judith
Mojica, Adolfo
Mojica, José
Monreal, Fred
Montano, Marylee
Montealva, Roel
Montemayor, Alice Dickerson "Admonty"
Montemayor, George "Monty"
Montez, Richard
Montoya, Emmanuel
Montoya, José E.
Montoya, Malaquías
Montoya, Rubén
Mora, Raúl
Morán, Joe
Moreno, Martín
Morón, Jesús G.
Moya, José Oscar
Munguía, Roberto
Muñiz, Olga
Muñoz, David
Muñoz, Gilbert
Murillo, Patricia

Narezo, José Luis
Nario, José
Navarro, Eduardo
Navarro, Fernando
Negrón, David
Neri, Manuel
Noriega, Ramses
Nuñez, David
Nuñez, J. Armando

O'Cadiz, Sergio
Ochoa, Victor Orozco
Ochoa y Valtierra, María
Ojeda, Jay
Olguín, Muriel
Olivares, Virginia
Olivo, Miriam
Ordoñez, Benny
Orona, Lee
Oropeza, Eduardo
Orozco, Juan Ishi
Orozco, Sylvia
Ortega, José Benito
Ortega, Juan

Ortega, Malu
Ortega, Marguerite
Ortegón, Veronica
Ortíz, William
Osorio, Gilberto
Ozona, Leo Esequiel
Ozuna, Gloria

Pacheco, Juan
Padilla, Anthony
Padilla, Stan
Paez, Carlos
Palomino, Ernesto
Palomino, Joe
Páramo, Bobby
Pardo, Alonso
Patlán, Ray
Patssi
    USE Valdez, Patssi
Pazos, Antonio
Pedregón Martínez, Ernesto
Pelayo, Pedro
Peña, Amado Maurilio, Jr.
Peña, Dolores
Peñalosa, Fernando
Perales, Tony
Pereira, Ismael "Smiley"
Pérez, Carlos
Pérez, Hector
Pérez, Irene
Pérez, José
Pérez, Louie
Pérez, Martin
Pérez, Vincent
Pérez-Díaz, Roberto
Pineda, Carlos R.
Pinedo, María Vita
Ponce de Leon, Michael
Ponce, Art
Puente, Martina
Pulido, Guillermo

Quesada, Eugenio
Queso, Fuchi
Quintana, Sam
Quinto Kemm, Carlos
Quiróz, Esau

Rámirez, Daniel
Rámirez, David
Rámirez, Gilberto
Rámirez, Joe
Rámirez, Joel

Rámirez, José
Rámirez, Mauricio
Ramos, Joe Bernal
Ramos, Juan Elias
Rascón, Vincent P.
Raya, Marcos
Renteria Fuentes, Juan
Renteria, Philip
Reyes, Alberto
Reyes, Bob
Reyes, Bobby
Reyes Aponte, Cynthia
Reyes, Felipe
Reyes, Jesús
Reyes, Roger
Rios, Michael
Rios, Ricardo
Rios, Roberto
Risco, Cecilia
Rivera, Domingo
Rivera, Edward
Rivera, Gustavo
Rivera, José
Rocha, Adrian
Rocha, Julie
Rodríguez Larriva, Tito
Rodríguez, Alfred
Rodríguez, Anita Otilia
Rodríguez, Armando
Rodríguez, Celia
Rodríguez, Eliseo
Rodríguez, Isaac
Rodríguez, Ismael
Rodríguez, Joe
Rodríguez, Joe B.
Rodríguez, José
Rodríguez, José Jiménez
Rodríguez, José Luis
Rodríguez, Noel
Rodríguez, Patricia
Rodríguez, Pedro
Rodríguez, Peter
Rodríguez, Raúl
Rodríguez, Roberto
Rodríguez, Ruth
Rodríguez, Santos
Rodríguez, Vicente
Román, Arturo
Romero Rodríguez, Gilberto
Romero, Alejandro E.
Romero, Donald
Romero, Enrique
Romero, Frank

Romero, José
Romero, Orlando
Romero, Pedro
Romo, Rafael
Rosas, Carlos
Rubin, Pilar C.
Ruíz, Jack
Ruíz, Mike

Saenz, Susan
Salazar Simpson, Sylvia
Salazar, Claudio
Salazar, Eliud
Salazar, Gregorio
Salazar, Stan
Saldana, Martin
Salinas, Porfirio
Sánchez, Al
Sánchez, Frank J.
Sánchez, Fred
Sánchez, Marisabel
Sánchez Brown, Olivia
Sánchez, Rita
Sandoval, Ausberto
Sandoval, Carlos M.
Sandoval, David [filmmaker]
Sandoval, David [muralist]
Sandoval, Secundino
Sandoval, Teddy
Santiago, Luis
"Sapo de Aztlán"
    USE Ávilez, Tomás "Sapo"
Santos, Cuate
"Sec"
    USE Sandoval, Secundino
Secrest-Rámirez, M.E.
Serrano, Benjamín
Serrano, Nina
Serrano-Cordero, Luis
Serrato, Ricardo M.
Sierra, John
Sierra, Roger
Sifuentes, Jesse
Sigala, Rudy
Silvas, Jimmie E.
Sinape, Mario
"Sir Loco"
    USE Jiménez, David
Siqueiros, Francisco
"Smiley"
    USE Pereira, Ismael "Smiley"
Soberón, Mercedes
Solache, Saúl

Soriano, Jesse
Soto, Luis
Soto, Richard

Taboada, John
Tafolla, Carmen
Tanguma, Leo
Tapia, Luis
Tapia, Star
Tapias, Robert
Tarango, Harvey J.
Tejada-Flores, Rick
Tejeda, Celia
"Teen Angel"
Tellez, Miguel Angel
Terronez, Irene R.
Tineo, David
Tizoc
Tocora, Antonia L.
Torres, Anastacio "Tache"
Torres, Kay
Torres, Salvador Roberto
Torres, Tomás
Tostado, Carmen
Trejo, Raúl
Trejo, Rubén
Treviño, Jesús C. "Jesse"
Treviño, Jesús Salvador
Treviño, José
Treviño, Modesta
Treviño, Rudy R.
Truan, George
Trujillo, Arnold
Turner, Juan

Ullóa, Domingo
Unzueta, Manuel
Ureste, Homero
Uribe, Joséph G.
Urista, Tizoc
    USE Tizoc

Valadez, Jaime
Valadez, John
Valdez, Hector
Valdez, Horacio
Valdez, Patssi
Valdez, Raúl
Valdovin, Rogelio Ruíz
Valenzuela, Art
Valenzuela, Ben
Valle, Victor M.
Vallejo, Hilda Esqueda

Vallejo, Linda
Valsoto, Luis
Valverde, Ricardo
Varela, María
Varela, Willie
Varelas Reyes, Felipe
Vargas, George
Vargas, Jack
Vargas, Kathy
Vásquez, Emigdio
Vásquez, Enriqueta
Vásquez, Gilbert
Vásquez, Rey
Vega, Salvador
Vela, Juan B.
Velásquez, Juan Ramón
Velásquez, Vicente
Vigil, Frederico
Vigil, Veloy
Villa, Esteban
Villa, Richard G.
Villagómez, Edel
Villagrán, Marcus
Villalvazo, Adolph

Villamor, Manuel
Villarreal, Roman
Villaseñor Grijalva, Lucila
    USE Grijalva, Lucila V.
Villaseñor, Becky
Villaseñor, David
Villegas, Martha
Viramontes, Xavier

Xóchitl
    USE Guerrero, Xóchitl Nevel

Yánez, René
Ybarra, Juan
Yepes, George

Zamarrón, Cruz
Zamora, Ramori
Zuñiga, Ramiro
Zuñiga, Santos

ABRAZO (Chicago, IL)
ADOBE NEWS (Albuquerque, NM)
ADRIAN DAILY TELEGRAM (Michigan)
AGENDA (Washington, DC)
ALBUQUERQUE JOURNAL (Albuquerque, NM)
AMERICAS (Washington, DC)
ANCHORAGE DAILY NEWS (Anchorage, AK)
ANCHORAGE TIMES (Anchorage, AK)
ARIZONA (Phoenix, AZ) [supplement to ARIZONA REPUBLIC]
ARIZONA ARTS AND LIFESTYLE (Phoenix, AZ)
ARIZONA DAILY STAR (Tucson, AZ)
ARIZONA DAILY WILDCAT-ENCORE (Tucson, AZ)
ARIZONA REPUBLIC (Phoenix, AZ)
ARIZTLAN NEWSLETTER (Tempe, AZ)
ARRIBA (Austin, TX)
ART IN AMERICA (New York, NY)
ART NEWS MAGAZINE (New York, NY)
ART VOICES SOUTH
ARTE (Berkeley, CA)
ARTES VISUALES (Mexico, D.F.)
ARTFORUM (New York, NY)
ARTISTS OF THE ROCKIES (Colorado Springs, CO)
ARTS AND ENTERTAINMENT (Mendocino Art Center, CA)
ARTS AT SANTA CRUZ (Univ. of Calif., Santa Cruz, CA)
ARTS BIWEEKLY (San Francisco, CA)
ARTS IN SOCIETY
ARTS REVIEW (London)
ARTSLETTER
ARTSPACE (Albuquerque, NM)
ARTWEEK (Oakland, CA)
ARTWORKERS NEWS (New York, NY)
ATISBOS (Stanford, CA)
AUSTIN AMERICAN STATESMAN (Austin, TX)
AYUDA (Austin, TX)
AZTEC CAMPUS NEWS (Pima Community College, Tucson, AZ)
AZTLAN (Los Angeles, CA)
AZTLAN (U.S. Penitentiary, Leavenworth, KA)
BERKELEY BARB (Berkeley, CA)
BRONCE (Oakland, CA)
BUENHOGAR (Mexico)
BUSINESS AND THE ARTS
CALENDAR (Los Angeles, CA) [supplement to LOS ANGELES TIMES]
CALENDAR: SANTA BARBARA MUSEUM OF ART (Santa Barbara, CA)
CALIFORNIA LIVING [supplement to SAN FRANCISCO SUNDAY EXAMINER]
CAMINOS (Los Angeles, CA)
CAMPUS NEWS (East Los Angeles College, Los Angeles, CA)
CANNERY WORKER/EL TRABAJADOR DE CANERIA (Sacramento, CA)
CARACOL (San Antonio, TX)
EL CHICANO (San Bernardino, CA)
CHICANO CINEMA NEWSLETTER
CHICANO TIMES (San Antonio, TX)

CHISMEARTE (Los Angeles, CA)
CHULA VISTA STAR NEWS (Chula Vista, CA)
CINE CUBANO (Havana, Cuba)
CITY ARTS (San Francisco, CA)
CITY ON A HILL (UC SANTA CRUZ, CA)
CITYBENDER (San Diego, CA)
CIVIC CENTER NEWS (Los Angeles, CA)
EL CLARIN (Santa Ana, CA)
CODEX NEWSLETTER (Galeria de la Raza, San Francisco, CA)
COMMON SENSE (San Francisco, CA)
COMMUNICATION ARTS MAGAZINE (Palo Alto, CA)
COMMUNITY ARTS NEWSLETTER (San Diego, CA)
COMUNIDAD (Los Angeles, CA) [supplement to LA OPINION]
COMMUNITY MURALS (San Francisco, CA)
CON SAFOS (Los Angeles, CA)
CONCEPT (Tucson, AZ / Nogales, Sonora, Mexico)
CONNEXIONS: AN INTERNATIONAL WOMENS' QUARTERLY (Oakland, CA)
CONTEMPORARY (Denver, CO) [supplement to SUNDAY DENVER POST]
COUNCIL OF LATINO PHOTOGRAPHY/USA NEWSLETTER
EL CUADERNO (DE VEZ EN CUANDO) (DIXON, NM)
LA CUCARACHA (Pueblo, CO)
CURRANT ART MAGAZINE (San Francisco, CA)
DAILY BRUIN (UCLA, Los Angeles, CA)
DAILY TEXAN (University of Texas, Austin, TX)
DALLAS MORNING STAR (Dallas, TX)
DE COLORES (Albuquerque, NM)
DENVER POST (Denver, CO)
DENVER POST: RELIGION NEWS WEEKLY (Denver, CO)
DESERET NEWS (Salt Lake City, UT)
EL DIA (Mexico, D.F.)
EL DIARIO DE LA GENTE (Boulder, CO)
EAST LOS ANGELES COLLEGE NEWS (East Los Angeles, CA)
EAST LOS ANGELES TRIBUNE (Los Angeles, CA)
EASTSIDE JOURNAL (Los Angeles, CA)
EASTSIDE SUN (Los Angeles, CA)
THE ECCENTRIC (Birmingham-Bloomfield Ed., MI)
EL PASO TIMES (El Paso, TX)
EL SERENO STAR (Los Angeles, CA)
EMPIRE MAGAZINE (Denver, CO) [supplement to DENVER POST]
ENCUENTRO FEMENIL (San Fernando, CA)
ENTRELINEAS (Kansas City, MO)
ESENCIA MAGAZINE (San Francisco, CA)
EVENING TRIBUNE (San Diego, CA)
EXCELSIOR (Mexico, D.F.)
EXXON USA
FORTY-NINER (CSU Long Beach, CA)
FOUR WINDS: INTERNATIONAL FORUM FOR NATIVE AMERICAN ART, LITERATURE, AND
  HISTORY (Austin, TX)
FRESNO BEE (Fresno, CA)
FRONTIERS: A JOURNAL OF WOMEN STUDIES (University of CO, Boulder, CO)
LA GENTE DE AZTLAN (UCLA, Los Angeles, CA)
GRASSROOTS (Berkeley, CA)
EL GRITO (Berkeley, CA)
EL GRITO DEL SOL (Berkeley, CA)

GRITO DEL NORTE (Espanola, NM)
GUARDIAN (New York, NY)
HEMBRA: HERMANAS EN MOVIMIENTO BROTANDO RAICES DE AZTLAN
    (University of Texas, Austin)
HERALD EXAMINER (Los Angeles, CA)
HERE AND NOW (Fresno City College, Fresno, CA)
HERESIES: A FEMINIST PUBLICATION OF ART AND POLITICS (New York, NY)
HIGH PERFORMANCE: THE PERFORMANCE ART QUARTERLY (Los Angeles, CA)
HISPANIC BUSINESS (Santa Barbara, CA)
EL HISPANO (Sacramento, CA)
HOJAS (A CHICANO JOURNAL OF EDUCATION) (Austin, TX)
HOME MAGAZINE (Los Angeles, CA) [supplement to L.A. TIMES]
LA HONDA (Stanford, CA)
HOUSTON BREAKTHROUGH (Houston, TX)
HOUSTON CHRONICLE (Houston, TX)
HOUSTON CITY MAGAZINE (Houston, TX)
HOUSTON POST (Houston, TX)
HQ HOUSTON (Houston, TX)
HUMAN BEHAVIOR (Boulder, CO)
HUMBLE WAY (Houston Oil and Refining Co.)
IDAHO STATESMAN (Boise, ID)
IMAGENES (Chicago, IL)
INDUSTRIAL WORKER (Chicago, IL)
INTERRACIAL BOOKS FOR CHILDREN (New York, NY)
LA JOLLA LIGHT (La Jolla, CA)
JOURNAL NORTH (New Mexico)
JOURNAL OF POPULAR CULTURE (Bowling Green, OH)
JUMP CUT: A REVIEW OF CONTEMPORARY CINEMA (Berkeley, CA)
KPFA FOLIO (Berkeley, CA)
LAREDO NEWS (Laredo, TX)
LATIN AMERICAN LITERARY REVIEW (Carnegie - Mellon University)
LATIN QUARTER (Los Angeles, CA)
LIFE (New York, NY)
LLUEVE TLALOC (Pima Community College, Tucson, AZ)
LO SENCILLO (San Fernando, CA)
LOS ANGELES FREE PRESS (Los Angeles, CA)
LOS ANGELES TIMES (Los Angeles, CA)
LOS ANGELES TIMES (Los Angeles, CA) [Central section]
LOS ANGELES TIMES (Los Angeles, CA) [Glendale/Burbank edition]
LOS ANGELES TIMES (Los Angeles, CA) [Orange County edition]
LOS ANGELES TIMES (Los Angeles, CA) [San Diego County edition]
LOS ANGELES TIMES (Los Angeles, CA) [San Gabriel Valley edition]
LOS ANGELES TIMES (Los Angeles, CA) [Valley edition]
LA LUZ (Denver, CO)
MAGAZIN (San Antonio, TX)
MAIZE: XICANO ART AND LITERATURE NOTEBOOKS (San Diego, CA)
MANGO (San Jose, CA)
MENLO-ATHERTON RECORDER (Menlo Park, CA)
METAMORFOSIS (Seattle, WA)
METRO MAGAZINE (San Francisco, CA)
MEXICAN AMERICAN SUN (Los Angeles, CA)
MEXICAN MUSEUM NEWSLETTER (San Francisco, CA)
MIDWEST MAGAZINE (Chicago, IL) [supplement to CHICAGO SUN TIMES]

MINNEAPOLIS STAR (Minneapolis, MN)
LA MOVIDA CON SAFO
MOVING ON (New American Research Institute, Chicago, IL)
MS. MAGAZINE (New York, NY)
EL MUNDO (Hayward, CA)
EL MUNDO (San Francisco, CA)
NATIONAL GEOGRAPHIC (Washington, DC)
NATIONAL MURALS NETWORK COMMUNITY NEWSLETTER (San Francisco, CA)
NATURAL HISTORY (New York, NY)
NEW ART EXAMINER (Chicago, IL)
NEW ERA (U.S. Penitentiary, Leavenworth, KA)
NEW MEXICAN WEEKEND
NEW MEXICO (Santa Fe, NM)
NEW REPUBLIC (Washington, DC)
NEW WEST MAGAZINE (Beverly Hills, CA)
NEW YORK TIMES (New York, NY)
NEW YORKER (New York, NY)
NEWORLD: QUARTERLY OF THE INNER CITY CULTURAL CENTER (L.A., CA)
THE NEWS (Mexico, D.F.)
NORTH EAST BAY INDEPENDENT AND GAZETTE (Berkeley, CA)
NOSOTROS (UTEP, El Paso, TX)
NUESTRA COSA (UC Riverside, CA)
NUESTRO (New York, NY)
OBSCURA: PHOTOGRAPHY, THEORETICAL WRITING, AND CRITICISM
OBSERVER (London)
EL OCCIDENTAL (Guadalajara, Mexico)
LA OPINION (Los Angeles, CA)
ORANGE CITY NEWS (Orange, CA)
PACEMAKER (Journal of Century Medical, Inc., Los Angeles, CA)
PACIFIC SUN (Mill Valley, CA)
LA PALABRA (Tempe, AZ)
PAPEL CHICANO (Houston, TX)
PARA LA GENTE (Austin, TX)
THE PASSWORD (El Paso, TX)
PEOPLE'S WORLD (Berkeley, CA)
PHOENIX GAZETTE (Phoenix, AZ)
PHOENIX MAGAZINE (Phoenix, AZ)
PICANTE (San Antonio, TX)
PICTURE MAGAZINE (Los Angeles, CA)
EL PLAYANO (Loyola University, Los Angeles, CA)
PLURAL (Mexico, D.F.)
EL POCHO CHE
LA PRENSA (Houston, TX)
LA PRENSA SAN DIEGO (San Diego, CA)
PRESCOTT COURIER-WEEKLY FEATURE (Prescott, AZ)
PROCEEDINGS OF THE PACIFIC COAST COUNCIL ON LATIN AMERICAN STUDIES
PROCESO (Mexico, D.F.)
PROGRESS (Mission, TX)
QUARTERLY: THE SCHOOL OF THE ART INSTITUTE OF CHICAGO (Chicago, IL)
QUETZAL (Water Hole Swamp, NC)
Q-VO (Los Angeles, CA)
RADICAL AMERICA (Somerville, MA)
R.A.M. COLLECTIVE (Raza Art & Media Collective, Inc., Ann Arbor, MI)

THE RANGER (San Antonio, TX)
RASCA TRIPAS
RAYAS (Albuquerque, NM)
LA RAZA (Los Angeles, CA)
LA RAZON MESTIZA (Concilio Mujeres, San Francisco, CA)
READER: SAN DIEGO WEEKLY (San Diego, CA)
RECOBRANDO: CENTRO DE LA RAZA (Seattle, WA)
REDWOOD CITY TRIBUNE (Redwood City, CA)
REFLECTING IMAGE (Marion Co. Education Service District, Salem, OR)
REGENERACION (Los Angeles, CA)
THE REGISTER (Santa Ana, CA)
RESEARCH CENTER FOR THE ARTS REVIEW (Univ. of Texas, San Antonio, TX)
REVIEW (Society of Architectural Historians, Pasadena, CA)
REVIEW [supplement to SAN FRANCISCO SUNDAY EXAMINER]
REVISTA CHICANO-RIQUENA (Houston, TX)
REVISTA DE BELLAS ARTES (Mexico, D.F.)
REVISTA MARYKNOLL (Maryknoll, NY)
REVISTA RIO BRAVO (Laredo, TX)
RIO GRANDE SUN (Espanola, NM)
RIVER CITY SUN (Austin, TX)
ROCKY MOUNTAIN NEWS (Denver, CO)
ROUNDUP (Denver, CO) [supplement to SUNDAY DENVER POST]
SA: THE MAGAZINE OF SAN ANTONIO (San Antonio, TX)
SACRAMENTO BEE (Sacramento, CA)
SACRAMENTO MAGAZINE (Sacramento, CA)
SACRAMENTO UNION (Sacramento, CA)
SALT LAKE CITY TRIBUNE (Salt Lake City, UT)
SAN ANTONIO EXPRESS-NEWS (San Antonio, TX)
SAN ANTONIO LIGHT (San Antonio, TX)
SAN DIEGO UNION (San Diego, CA)
SAN FRANCISCO BAY GUARDIAN (San Francisco, CA)
SAN FRANCISCO CHRONICLE (San Francisco, CA)
SAN FRANCISCO EXAMINER (San Francisco, CA)
SAN FRANCISCO FAULT (San Francisco, CA)
SAN FRANCISCO FOCUS (San Francisco, CA)
SAN FRANCISCO JOURNAL (San Francisco, CA)
SAN FRANCISCO ODALISQUE (San Francisco, CA)
SAN FRANCISCO PROGRESS (San Francisco, CA)
SAN FRANCISCO SUNDAY EXAMINER AND CHRONICLE (San Francisco, CA)
SAN JOSE MERCURY (San Jose, CA)
SANTA FE NEW MEXICAN (Santa Fe, NM)
SANTA FE REPORTER (Santa Fe, NM)
SATURDAY REVIEW (Saint Louis, MO)
SCOTTSDALE DAILY PROGRESS (Scottsdale, AZ)
SEATTLE TIMES (Seattle, WA)
SENTIMIENTOS (Fresno, CA)
SIN FRONTERAS (Los Angeles, CA)
SMITHSONIAN MAGAZINE (Washington, DC)
SOL DE AZTLAN (Lansing, MI)
SOMOS (San Bernardino, CA)
SOUTH TEXAN (Texas A & I, Kingsville, TX)
SOUTHFIELD ECCENTRIC (MI)
SOUTHWEST ART (Houston, TX)

SOUTHWEST ART COLLECTOR (Wagner Gallery, Austin, TX)
SOUTHWESTERN CONTEMPORARY ARTS QUARTERLY
SPINNING OFF (Los Angeles, CA)
ST. PAUL DISPATCH (St. Paul, MN)
THE STATE HORNET (Sacramento, CA)
SUNDAY MAGAZINE [supplement to CONTRA COSTA COUNTY TIMES, CA]
SUNDAY ONE (San Antonio, TX) [supplement to SAN ANTONIO EXPRESS-NEWS]
SUNSET (Los Angeles, CA)
THE TAB (San Jose, CA) [supplement to SUNDAY MERCURY NEWS]
TAOS NEWS BULLETIN (Taos, NM)
EL TECOLOTE LITERARY MAGAZINE (San Francisco, CA)
EL TECOLOTE (San Francisco, CA)
TEJANO ARTISTS INC. NEWSLETTER (Houston, TX)
TEJIDOS (Austin, TX)
TEMPE DAILY NEWS (Tempe, AZ)
TENDENZEN (Munich, Germany)
TEXAS HOMES MAGAZINE (Dallas, TX)
TEXAS MAGAZINE (Houston, TX) [supplement to HOUSTON CHRONICLE]
THIS WORLD (San Francisco, CA) [supplement to SUNDAY EXAMINER &
  CHRONICLE]
TIEMPO LATINO (San Francisco, CA)
TIERRA Y LIBERTAD (El Valle de San Luis, CO)
TIME (New York, NY)
TIN TAN (San Francisco, CA)
TODAY MAGAZINE (San Antonio, TX) [supplement to SAN ANTONIO LIGHT]
TRA: TOWARD REVOLUTIONARY ART (San Francisco, CA)
THE TRIBUNE (Oakland, CA)
TUCSON CITIZEN, OLD PUEBLO SECTION (Tucson, AZ)
ULTRA MAGAZINE (Houston, TX)
UNION BULLETIN (Walla Walla Community College, WA)
UNIVERSITY TIMES (CSU Long Beach, CA)
UNO MAS UNO (Mexico, D.F.)
U.S. NEWS & WORLD REPORT (Washington, DC)
THE VALLEY WORLD
VILLAGE VOICE (New York, NY)
VILLAGER
EL VISITANTE DOMINICAL (Huntington, ID)
VIVA [supplement to SANTA FE NEW MEXICAN]
VORTICE: LITERATURA, ARTE Y CRITICA (Stanford University, CA)
LA VOZ: NEWSLETTER OF THE CONCILIO FOR THE SPANISH SPEAKING OF KING
  COUNTY (Seattle, WA)
LA VOZ (Denver, CO)
LA VOZ CHICANA (Idaho Migrant Council, Boise, ID)
LA VOZ DE HOUSTON (Houston, TX)
LA VOZ DEL PUEBLO (Hayward, CA)
VOZ FRONTERIZA (San Diego, CA)
THE WASHINGTON STAR (Washington, DC)
WEEKENDER MAGAZINE (Tucson, AZ) [supplement to THE TUCSON CITIZEN]
WEST SAINT PAUL VOICE (Saint Paul, MN)
WESTWAYS (Los Angeles, CA)
XALMAN (Santa Barbara, CA)
YOUTH MAGAZINE (United Church Press, Philadelphia, PA)
YUMA DAILY SUN (Yuma, AZ)